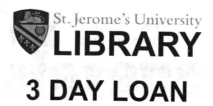

ENCYCLOPEDIC DICTIONARY OF
JUDAICA

ENCYCLOPEDIC DICTIONARY OF JUDAICA

Edited by Geoffrey Wigoder

LEON AMIEL PUBLISHER
New York–Paris

KETER PUBLISHING HOUSE JERUSALEM LTD.

First published in Israel by Keter Publishing House Jerusalem Ltd.

Published in the Western Hemisphere by
LEON AMIEL PUBLISHER
New York – Paris

ISBN 0-8148-0598-1
Library of Congress Catalog Card Number 74-12588

Distributed in the rest of the world by
KETER PUBLISHING HOUSE JERUSALEM LTD.
P.O.Box 7145, Jerusalem, Israel
ISBN 0-7065-1412-2
Cat. No. 51023

Set by Isratypeset Ltd., Jerusalem
Printed and bound by Keterpress Enterprises, Jerusalem

Printed in Israel

CONTENTS

INTRODUCTION

This one-volume **Encyclopedic Dictionary of Judaica** is designed as a handy reference work giving basic facts and figures. Its many entries, maps, lists, charts, etc., provide quick information covering all topics of Jewish interest from antiquity to the present day. It is a guide to the Bible, to Israel old and new, to Jewish communities throughout the world, to famous Jews – both within a Jewish context and as contributors to world culture – to Jewish concepts and customs, to Jewish history and literature – and to many more subjects. In addition, a further, vivid dimension is introduced by the wealth of illustrative material.

This work has been planned as complementary to the 16-volume *Encyclopaedia Judaica,* which was published in 1972 and is being updated regularly with Year Books. The *Encyclopaedia,* the first complete major Jewish encyclopedia to be published since before World War I, was designed to present in-depth information based on the latest scholarly research in all fields of Judaica. It has already taken its place as a standard and indispensable work of reference.

The need for a mini-encyclopedia on Jewish subjects has long been felt, especially in the English-speaking world, which today comprises the bulk of the Jewish people. Indeed, even in general encyclopedias such as the *Britannica* and the *Larousse* the tendency is to accompany the main encyclopedia with a much shorter work, making the basic data available for immediate retrieval.

The **Encyclopedic Dictionary of Judaica**, therefore, is meant for those who require reliable and up-to-date facts at their fingertips. It is intended for use in many ways and in many contexts – for example, for pupils and students in schools and colleges, for the office, and especially in the home. Those who require, or whose appetite is whetted for, further information on every subject mentioned in this Encyclopedic Dictionary will find a full and authoritative treatment in the *Encyclopaedia Judaica.*

Both these works have been produced under the same auspices in Jerusalem. Both were motivated by the same basic objective – the dissemination of the knowledge of the Jewish heritage.

HOW TO USE THIS DICTIONARY

To expand the scope as widely as possible, many lists and tables have been incorporated. A key to the major lists can be found above. The reader is asked to use this key as a guide to further information. For example, details on individual kibbutzim in Israel will be found not under the name of the kibbutz (with a few outstanding exceptions) but in the list under "Kibbutz."

The latest *reliable* statistics have been utilized. This accounts for the varying dates of certain population figures. For example, Israel figures are based on the 1971 census but in the areas administered by Israel since the Six-Day War the last reliable figures are the 1967 census. Some statistics on Russian Jewry are available from the 1970 census but in other places there is nothing later than the 1959 census.

Alphabetization

Entries are arranged in strict alphabetical order – disregarding spaces and hyphens. The criterion is the order of the letters up to the first punctuation sign (comma, period, etc).

The following elements are not considered in alphabetization: definite and indefinite articles, personal titles, material that appears in parentheses, the ordinal number of monarchs. Where persons have identical names, the earlier birth date takes precedence. Where the same name is used both as a first and family name, entries of the first name precede those of the family name.

Place Names

The basic guide for the form of place names has been the *Columbia Lippincott Gazetteer of the World*. Important alternative names are generally also given in their alphabetical place with a cross-reference to the place of the entry.

Place names occurring in the Bible are given according to the transliteration of the Jewish Publication Society of America's translation of the Holy Scriptures. However, names of places in Israel that are of post-Biblical origin are given according to the rules of transliteration listed below.

Proper Names

The title entry for an individual is given according to the name by which he was most commonly known. Other names follow in parentheses. Where the form is "A ben B" or "A ibn B," the entry is under A except in those cases where the "Ben" or "Ibn" has become a family name (e.g. Ibn Ezra, Ben Asher) in which case it appears under Ibn or Ben.

The tendency has been to anglicize first names. Thus the name Shlomo appears as Solomon. The exception is for names in modern Israel which have been left in their Hebrew form (Moshe – and not Moses – Dayan). Every effort has been made to give the spelling of surnames as the person himself spelt it, although doubts must arise concerning those who never signed their names in Latin characters (e.g., East European Jews who wrote only in Yiddish or Russian).

Special Terminology

Attention is drawn to the use of the word "Holocaust" referring to the fate of the Jews resulting from the Nazi persecutions, 1933–45.

The term "Ereẓ Israel" is used for the Land of Israel (which was known as Palestine in Roman and British mandate times).

Non-Jews

A number of non-Jews are the subject of entries by virtue of their impact on Jewish history. To prevent confusion, these have been identified by a small circle (°) placed before their name.

ABBREVIATIONS

Many standard abbreviations have been used which will all be clear to the ordinary reader. The following list gives those which may need explanation:

A.H.	*anno hegirae,* "in the year of Hegira," i.e., according to the Muslim calendar
Akk.	Akkadian
A.M.	*anno mundi*, "in the year (from the creation) of the world"
Ar.	Arabic
Ar.	*Arakhin* (talmudic tractate)
Aram.	Aramaic
Ass.	Assyrian
Avot	*Avot* (talmudic tractate)
Av.Zar.	*Avodah Zarah* (talmudic tractate)
b.	born; *ben, bar*
Bab.	Babylonian
BB	*Bava Batra* (talmudic tractate)
B.C.E.	Before Common Era (= B.C.)
Bek.	*Bekhorot* (talmudic tractate)
Ber.	*Berakhot* (talmudic tractate)
Beẓah	*Beẓah* (talmudic tractate)
Bik.	*Bikkurim* (talmudic tractate)
BK	*Bava Kamma* (talmudic tractate)
BM	*Bava Meẓia* (talmudic tractate)
C.	Central
C.E.	Common Era (= A.D.)
cf.	compare
ch. chs.	chapter, chapters
I (or II) Chron.	Chronicles, Book I or II (Bible)
Cz.	Czech
d.	died
Dan.	Daniel (Bible)
Dem.	*Demai* (talmudic tractate)
Deut.	Deuteronomy (Bible)
Deut.R.	*Deuteronomy Rabbah*
Eccles.	Ecclesiastes (Bible)
Eccles.R.	*Ecclesiastes Rabbah*
E.	East
ed.	editor, edited
Eduy.	*Eduyyot* (mishnaic tractate)
Eng.	English
Er.	*Eruvin* (talmudic tractate)
Esth.	Esther (Bible)
Est.R.	*Esther Rabbah*
Ex.	Exodus (Bible)
Ex.R.	*Exodus Rabbah*
Ezek.	Ezekiel (Bible)
Ezra	Ezra (Bible)
f., ff.	and following page(s)
fl.	flourished
Fr.	French
fr.	from
Gen.	Genesis (Bible)
Gen.R.	*Genesis Rabbah*
Ger.	German
Git.	*Gittin* (talmudic tractate)
Gr.	Greek
Hab.	Habakkuk (Bible)
Ḥag.	*Ḥagigah* (talmudic tractate)
Haggai	Haggai (Bible)
Ḥal.	*Ḥallah* (talmudic tractate)
Heb.	Hebrew
Hor.	*Horayot* (talmudic tractate)
Hos.	Hosea (Bible)
Ḥul.	*Ḥullin* (talmudic tractate)
Isa.	Isaiah (Bible)
It.	Italian
Jer.	Jeremiah (Bible)
Job	Job (Bible)
Joel	Joel (Bible)
Josh.	Joshua (Bible)
Judg.	Judges (Bible)
Kelim	*Kelim* (mishnaic tractate)
Ker.	*Keritot* (talmudic tractate)
Ket.	*Ketubbot* (talmudic tractate)
Kid.	*Kiddushin* (talmudic tractate)
Kil.	*Kilayim* (talmudic tractate (TJ))
Kin.	*Kinnim* (mishnaic tractate)
Lam.	Lamentations (Bible)
Lam.R.	*Lamentations Rabbah*
Lat.	Latin
Lev.	Leviticus (Bible)
Lev.R.	*Leviticus Rabbah*
lit.	literally
Ma'as.	*Ma'aserot* (talmudic tractate)
Ma'as.Sh.	*Ma'aser Sheni* (talmudic tractate)
Mak.	*Makkot* (talmudic tractate)
Makhsh.	*Makhshirin* (mishnaic tractate)
Mal.	Malachi (Bible)
Meg.	*Megillah* (talmudic tractate)
Me'il.	*Me'ilah* (mishnaic tractate)
Men.	*Menaḥot* (talmudic tractate)
Mid.	*Middot* (mishnaic tractate)
Mik.	*Mikva'ot* (mishnaic tractate)
Mish.	Mishnah
MK	*Mo'ed Katan* (talmudic tractate)
Ms., Mss.	manuscript(s)
N.	North
Nah.	Nahum (Bible)
Naz.	*Nazir* (talmudic tractate)
Ned.	*Nedarim* (talmudic tractate)
Neg.	*Nega'im* (mishnaic tractate)
Neh.	Nehemiah (Bible)
Nid.	*Niddah* (talmudic tractate)
no., nos.	number(s)
Num.	Numbers (Bible)
Num.R.	*Numbers Rabbah*
Obad.	Obadiah (Bible)

Oho.	*Oholot* (mishnaic tractate)
Or.	*Orlah* (talmudic tractate)
Par.	*Parah* (mishnaic tractate)
PdRE	*Pirkei de-R.Eliezer*
PdRK	*Pesikta de-Rav Kahana*
Pe'ah	*Pe'ah* (talmudic tractate)
Pes.	*Pesaḥim* (talmudic tractate)
Pol.	Polish
PR	*Pesikta Rabbati*
Prov.	Proverbs (Bible)
Ps.	Psalms (Bible)
R.	Rabbi or Rav (before names); River
RH	*Rosh Ha-Shanah* (talmudic tractate)
Rus(s).	Russian
Ruth	Ruth (Bible)
Ruth R.	*Ruth Rabbah*
S.	South
I and II Sam.	Samuel, Books I and II (Bible)
Sanh.	*Sanhedrin* (talmudic tractate)
Shab.	*Shabbat* (talmudic tractate)
Shek.	*Shekalim* (talmudic tractate)
Shev.	*Shevi'it* (talmudic tractate)
Shevu.	*Shevu'ot* (talmudic tractate)
Song	Song of Songs (Bible)
Song R.	*Song of Songs Rabbah*
Sot.	*Sotah* (talmudic tractate)
Sp.	Spanish
Suk.	*Sukkah* (talmudic tractate)
Ta'an.	*Ta'anit* (talmudic tractate)
Tam.	*Tamid* (mishnaic tractate)
Tanh.	*Tanḥuma*
TB	Babylonian Talmud or *Talmud Bavli*
Tem.	*Temurah* (mishnaic tractate)
Ter.	*Terumah* (talmudic tractate)
TJ	Jerusalem Talmud or *Talmud Yerushalmi*
Toh.	*Tohorot* (mishnaic tractate)
TY	*Tevul Yom* (mishnaic tractate)
Uk.	*Ukẓin* (mishnaic tractate)
W.	West
Yal.	*Yalkut Shimoni*
Yad.	*Yadayim* (mishnaic tractate)
Yev.	*Yevamot* (talmudic tractate)
Yid.	Yiddish
Yoma	*Yoma* (talmudic tractate)
Zav.	*Zavim* (mishnaic tractate)
Zech.	Zechariah (Bible)
Zeph.	Zephaniah (Bible)
Zev.	*Zevaḥim* (talmudic tractate)

TRANSLITERATION

HEBREW AND SEMITIC LANGUAGES:

	General	*Scientific*
א	not transliterated[1]	ʾ
בּ	b	b
ב	v	v, ḇ
גּ	g	g
ג		ḡ
דּ	d	d
ד		ḏ
ה	h	h
ו	v—when not a vowel	w
ז	z	z
ח	ḥ	ḥ
ט	t	ṭ, t
י	y—when vowel and at end of words—i	y
כּ	k	k
כ,ך	kh	kh, ḵ
ל	l	l
מ,ם	m	m
נ,ן	n	n
ס	s	s
ע	not transliterated[1]	ʿ
פּ	p	p
פ,ף	f	p, f, ph
צ,ץ	ẓ	ṣ, ẓ
ק	k	q, k
ר	r	r
שׁ	sh[2]	š
שׂ	s	ś, s
תּ	t	t
ת		ṯ
ג׳	dzh, J	ğ
ז׳	zh, J	ž
צ׳	ch	č
◌ָ		å, o, ō (short); â, ā (long)
◌ַ	a	a
◌ֲ		a, ᵃ
◌ֵ		e, ẹ, ē
◌ֶ	e	æ ä, ę
◌ֱ		œ, ě, ᵉ
◌ְ	only *sheva na* is transliterated	ə, ě, e; only *sheva na* transliterated
◌ִ, ◌ִי	i	i
◌ֹ, וֹ	o	o, ō, ô
◌ֻ	u	u, ŭ
וּ		û, ū
◌ֵי	ei; biblical e	
‡		reconstructed forms of words

YIDDISH

א	not transliterated
אַ	a
אָ	o
בּ	b
בֿ	v
ג	g
ד	d
ה	h
ו,וּ	u
וו	v
וי	oy
ז	z
זש	zh
ח	kh
ט	t
טש	tsh, ch
י	(consonant) y (vowel) i
יִ	i
יי	ey
ײַ	ay
כּ	k
כ,ך	kh
ל	l
מ,ם	m
נ,ן	n
ס	s
ע	e
פּ	p
פֿ,ף	f
צ,ץ	ts
ק	k
ר	r
ש	sh
שׂ	s
תּ	t
ת	s

1. Yiddish transliteration rendered according to U. Weinreich's *Modern English-Yiddish Yiddish-English Dictionary*.
2. Hebrew words in Yiddish are usually transliterated according to standard Yiddish pronunciation, e.g., חזנות = *khazones*.

---

1. The letters א and ע are not transliterated.
   An apostrophe (') between vowels indicates that they do not form a diphthong and are to be pronounced separately.
2. *Dagesh ḥazak* (forte) is indicated by doubling of the letter, except for the letter ש.
3. Names. Biblical names and biblical place names are rendered according to the Bible translation of the Jewish Publication Society of America. Post-biblical Hebrew names are transliterated: contemporary names are transliterated or rendered as used by the person. Place names are transliterated or rendered by the accepted spelling. Names and some words with an accepted English form are usually not transliterated.

Initial letter "A" from the Book of Amos in a 12th-cent. French Bible.

Aachen (Aix-la-Chapelle), city on German-Belgian border. One of oldest communities in Germany. Jews settled c. 820, expelled 1629, organized as community 1847. In 1939, 1,700 Jews in city and 3,500 in environs. Community ended in WWII. Refounded subsequently and numbered 163 in 1966.

Old Synagogue at Aachen.

Aargau, canton in N.Switzerland. A few Jewish families there in Middle Ages. Fr. 17th to mid-19th c. it remained sole area of permanent Jewish settlement in Switzerland. Jews obtained full citizenship rights 1878. 392 Jews in 1960s.

Aaron, brother of Moses and Miriam; first Israelite high priest and, according to Bible, progenitor of all priests. Died on Mt. Hor, aged 123. Rabbinic tradition stressed his love of peace.

Aaron ben Amram (9th–10th c.), court banker in Baghdad. Influential in Jewish community.

Aaron ben Batash (Harun al-Yahudīs,; d. 1465), vizier in Morocco. Assassinated along with sultan of Morocco.

Aaron ben David Cohen of Ragusa (d. 1656), rabbi, merchant in Ragusa (Dubrovnik). Victim of blood libel 1622.

Aaron ben Elijah (1328? –1369) Karaite philosopher, exegete in Nicomedia (Asia Minor). His *Eẓ Ḥayyim* written as Karaite counterpart to Maimonides' *Guide.*

Aaron ben Jacob ha-Kohen of Lunel (13th–14th c.), scholar in Provence. After expulsion fr. France 1306, emigrated to Majorca. Author of legal compendium *Orḥot Ḥayyim.*

Aaron ben Joseph ha-Kohen Sargado, *gaon,* head of Pumbedita academy 942–960; rival of Saadiah Gaon.

Aaron ben Joseph ha-Levi (HaRah; c. 1235–1300), Spanish talmudist. Influential halakhist, noted for originality. Wrote *Bedek ha-Bayit,* critique of Adret's *Torat ha-Bayit.*

Aaron ben Joseph ha-Rofe ("the Elder"; c. 1250–1320), Karaite philosopher, poet, lived in Crimea. Wrote commentary on Pentateuch.

Aaron ben Moses ha-Levi (Horwitz) of Starosielce (1766–1828), leader of group in Ḥabad Ḥasidism that favored emotional approach to prayer.

Aaron ben Samuel (c. 1620–1701), German rabbinical author. His *Beit Aharon* compiles all biblical references in Talmud, *midrashim,* etc.

Aaron Berechiah ben Moses of Modena (d. 1639), Italian kabbalistic writer. His *Ma'avar Yabbok* is compilation of laws and readings relating to the sickbed and mourning.

Aaronides, members of priesthood in Israel; traditionally descended fr. Aaron.

Aaron of Baghdad (9th c.). Babylonian scholar who brought mystical doctrines fr. East to S. Italy, subsequently important in Germany.

Aaron of Lincoln (c. 1123–1186), English financier. House in Lincoln still bearing his name has no connection in fact.

Aaron of Pesaro (d. 1563), Italian scholar, bibliophile. Author of *Toledot Aharon,* concordance of biblical passages cited in Babylonian Talmud.

Aaron of York (1190–1268), financier; *Presbyter Judaeorum* of English Jewry 1236–43. One of wealthiest and most active Jews in England under Henry III.

Aaron Selig ben Moses of Zolkiew (d. 1643), kabbalist. Wrote 5-vol. compendium of Zohar entitled *Ammudei Sheva.*

Aaronsohn, Aaron (1876–1919) agronomist, leader in Ereẓ Israel. Discovered wild Emmer wheat in Galilee. Established agricultural experimental station at Athlit 1910. During WWI organized underground group (Nili) against Turkish rule in Ereẓ Israel. Killed in airplane accident. His sister, **Sara** (1890–1917), also a member of Nili group, arrested and tortured by Turks. Died heroine's death.

The Aaronsohn family at Zikhron Ya'akov.

Abba (Aram. "father"). (1) Term used in Jewish and Christian sources in addressing God. (2) Honorific of *amoraim* and *tannaim.* (3) Personal name. (4) Ecclesiastical title (cf. Abbot).

Abba (Ba; 3rd–4th c.), *amora;* b. Babylonia, lived in Ereẓ Israel and transmitted Palestinian teachings to Babylonian academies.

Abba (Rava, Rabbah; 8th c.), rabbinical scholar. Author of *Halakhot Pesukot,* a juridical tract.

Abba Arikha, see Rav.

Abba bar Avina (3rd c.), Palestinian *amora;* of Babylonian origin. Quoted

mostly in Jerusalem Talmud and Midrash.

Abba bar Kahana (3rd c.), Palestinian *amora.* Leading exponent of *aggadah.*

Abba bar Zavda (3rd c.), Palestinian *amora.* Leading scholar at Tiberias academy.

Abba ben Abba ha-Kohen (3rd c.), Babylonian scholar; father of Samuel. Spent some time in Ereẓ Israel.

Abba Hilkiah (1st c.), sage. Like his grandfather Ḥoni ha-Me'aggel, had reputation for saintliness and rainmaking.

Abbahu (c. 300), Palestinian *amora,* aggadist. Head of rabbinical academy at Caesarea. Opposed Christians and other sects.

Abbas, Judah ben Samuel ibn (d. 1167), liturgical poet; b. Fez, lived in Aleppo. About 20 of his *piyyutim* are known.

Abbas (Abenabez), Moses ben Samuel (c. 1350–1420?), talmudist, poet, communal leader in Saragossa, Spain. Participated in disputation of Tortosa.

Abbas, Moses Judah ben Meir (c. 1601–1671), talmudist, halakhist, poet; b. Salonika, rabbi in Egypt. Encouraged young poets.

Abba Saul (2nd c.), *tanna.* His opinions are quoted as adjuncts to a Mishnah, and therefore suggested that there was a different "Mishnah of Abba Saul" used by Judah ha-Nasi.

Abbasi, Jacob ben Moses ibn (13th c.), translator in Huesca, Spain. Translated part of Maimonides' Mishnah commentary into Hebrew with important introduction.

Abba Sikra (Sakkara; 1st c.), Zealot leader in Jerusalem during war against Romans. Smuggled his uncle Johanan b. Zakkai out of city in coffin.

Abbaye (278–338), Babylonian *amora,* head of academy in Pumbedita. His discussions with his colleague Rava constitute a major element of Babylonian Talmud.

Abba Yose ben Ḥanin (1st c.), *tanna* who transmitted tradition concerning Temple service and Temple gates.

Abbell, Maxwell (1902–1957). U.S. communal worker, lawyer; lived in Chicago. Active in Conservative movement.

Abbreviations (Heb. *rashei tevot,* "initials of words"), use of parts or single letters of words to indicate whole. Found in Hebrew in 2nd c. B.C.E. on Maccabean coinage and frequent in talmudic period. System common in Middle Ages in Hebrew as well as European writing, because of limited writing material. Characteristic of Hebrew abbreviations was use of initials for groups of words.

'Abd al-Ḥaqq al-Islāmī (14th c.), convert to Islam, anti-Jewish pamphleteer in Morocco.

Abdallah, Yusuf (19th–20th c.), false messiah who achieved some following in Yemen.

Abdallah ibn Salam (7th c.), Jewish follower of Muhammad. After Muhammad's death, in entourage of Caliph 'Uthmān.

Abdon, minor judge mentioned in Book of Judges (12:13–15).

°**Abdullah ibn Hussein** (1882–1951), first king of Hashemite Kingdom of Jordan. Supported Britain in "Arab Revolt". Appointed emir of Transjordan 1923, and king 1946. In 1948, occupied greater part of Samaria and Judea, which was incorporated in his kingdom, henceforth called Jordan. Assassinated by Palestinian Arabs.

Abel, second son of Adam and Eve; a shepherd, he was murdered by his brother, Cain.

Cain killing Abel and burying him, fr. "Queen Mary Psalter," England, 14th cent.

Abel, Elie (1920–), U.S. journalist. With *N.Y. Times* 1949–59; dean of Graduate School of Journalism at Columbia 1969.

°**Abel, Louis Felix** (1878–1953), French archaeologist. Prof. at Ecole Biblique in Jerusalem 1903–53. Best-known work *Géographie de la Palestine.*

Abeles, Otto (1879–1945), author, Zionist worker in Austria and Holland; d. Bergen-Belsen.

Abelson, Joshua (1873–1940), Anglo-Jewish minister in Leeds. Wrote on Jewish mysticism.

Abelson, Paul (1878–1953), U.S. labor arbitrator. Edited *English-Yiddish Encyclopedic Dictionary.* Introduced arbitration into ladies' garment trade.

Abenaes (Heb. **Even Yaish**), **Solomon** (d. 1603), statesman of Marrano origin. Prominent at Turkish court and among architects of Anglo-Turkish alliance which stemmed advance of Spanish power.

Abenatar Melo, David (d. c. 1646), Marrano poet. Persecuted by Inquisition, escaped to Amsterdam and returned to Judaism.

Seal of the Abendana family.

Abendana, family of Marranos with branches in Amsterdam, Hamburg, London. **David** (d. 1625) fled Spanish Inquisition, became a leader of Sephardi community in Amsterdam. **Isaac** (c. 1640–c. 1710), scholar, taught Hebrew at Cambridge and Oxford. **Isaac Sardo** (c. 1662–1709), diamond merchant in India. **Jacob ben Joseph** (1630–1685), rabbi in Amsterdam, London.

Abendanan (Ibn Danan), family of rabbis and scholars. **Saadiah ben Maimon ibn Danan** (15th c.), physician, poet, halakhist in Granada and Oran, Algeria. **Samuel Abendanan** (d. c. 1566), rabbi of Constantine, author of responsa. **Solomon** (1848–1929), *av bet din* in Rabat, Morocco. His son **Saul** (1882–), *av bet din,* chief rabbi of Morocco 1949; settled in Israel 1965.

Abenmenasse, family of Spanish courtiers. **Samuel,** physician and Arabic secretary of Pedro III of Aragon 1276–85.

Abiathar, high priest appointed by David, whom he faithfully served. His support of Adonijah for succession led to banishment by Solomon.

Abiathar ben Elijah ha-Kohen (c. 1040–1110), last of Palestinian *geonim.*

Abib, see Nisan.

COMMON HEBREW ABBREVIATIONS

א׳ (אד׳)	adon	Mr., Sir
אאו״מ	adoni avi u-mori	my revered father and teacher
אב״ד	av bet din	president of Jewish court
אג׳	aguddah; agorah	society; agorah (Israel coin)
אַדְמוֹ״ר	adonenu morenu ve-rabbenu	our lord, master, and teacher (title of ḥasidic rabbi)
ארה״ב	arẓot ha-berit	U.S.A.
אה״ק	ereẓ ha-kodesh	the Holy Land
אוה״ע (או״ה, א״ה)	ummot ha-olam	nations of the world (gentile)
אוּ״ם	ummot me'uḥadot	U.N.
אחה״צ	aḥarei ha-ẓohoraim	afternoon
אח״כ (א״כ)	aḥar kakh	afterwards
א״י	Ereẓ Israel	Land of Israel
איה״ש (אי״ה)	im yirẓeh ha-shem	God willing
א.נ. (א״נ)	adon nikhbad	dear sir
אספה״נ	aharei sefirat ha-noẓrim	C.E., A.D.
אעפ״י (אע״פ)	af-al-pi	although
אעפי״כ (אעפ״כ)	af-al-pi-ken	nevertheless
א״ק	oniyyat kitor	S.S. (steamship)
אֲשֶׁ״ל	akhilah, shetiyyah, linah	board and lodging (traveling allowance)
בג״צ	bet din gavoha le-ẓedek	high court of justice
בד״צ (ביד״צ)	bet din ẓedek	court of justice
ב״ה	barukh ha-shem; be-ezrat ha-shem	thank God; God's help
בהמ״ק	bet ha-mikdash	the Temple
בהר״ר	ben ha-rav rabbi	son of rabbi
בחו״ק	be-ḥuppah ve-kiddushin	by marriage
בח״ז	be-ḥodesh zeh	this month
בח״י (בחת״י)	ba-ḥatimat yad	signature of
בי״ד	bet din	court of law
ביה״ח (ב״ח)	bet ha-ḥolim	hospital
ביה״כ (בהכ״נ)	bet ha-keneset	synagogue
ביהמ״ד (בהמ״ד)	bet ha-midrash	rabbinical school
ביהמ״ש (בימ״ש)	bet ha-mishpat	court of law
ביה״ס (בה״ס)	bet ha-sefer	school
ביה״ק	bet ha-kevarot	cemetery
ב״כ	ba ko'aḥ (baei koaḥ)	representative(s)
במז״ט	be-mazzal tov	with good luck
בס״ט	be-siman tov	with good luck
ב״ע	bet olam; bet almin	cemetery
בע״ה	be-ezrat ha-shem	with God's help
בעה״י (בעזהי״ת)	be-ezrat ha-shem yitbarakh	
בעה״ק	be-ir ha-kodesh	in the holy city (Jerusalem)
בע״מ	be-eravon mugbal	Ltd.
בע״פ	be'al peh	orally; by heart
בעש״ק	be-erev shabbat kodesh	on the eve of the holy Sabbath
ברה״מ	birkat ha-mazon; Berit ha-Moaẓot	grace after meal(s); U.S.S.R.
(ל)ברה״ע	(le-) beriat ha-olam	anno mundi
בשטו״מ	be-sha'ah tovah u-muẓlaḥat	may the hour prove propitious
גב׳	geveret	Miss, Madam, Mrs.
גח״ט (גמח״ט)	gemar ḥatimah tovah	"a propitious sealing" (Day of Atonement greeting)
גְּמַ״ח (ג״ח)	gemilut ḥesed	charity
ג.נ. (ג״נ)	geveret nikhbadah	dear Madam
ד״א	davar aḥer; derekh ereẓ; dalet amot	another version, "swine"; courtesy; four cubits
דו״חַ	din ve-ḥeshbon	report, statement
ד״ש	derishat shalom	best regards
ד״ת	din Torah	religious ruling
הח״מ	ha-ḥatum matah	the undersigned
הי״ד	ha-shem yikkom damo	may God avenge his blood
הי״ו	ha-shem yishmerehu vi-yḥayehu	may the Lord preserve him and keep him alive
ה.מ.	hod ma'alato	His Excellency
הַנַּ״ל (כנ״ל)	ha-nizkar lema'alah (le'eil)	the aforementioned; ditto
הק׳	ha-kodesh	the Holy
הקב״ה	ha-kadosh barukh hu	God
הרה״ג	ha-rav ha-gaon	the Illustrious Rabbi
הרה״ח	ha-rav he-ḥakham; ha-rav he-ḥasid	the Wise Rabbi; the Pious Rabbi
הרה״צ	ha-rav ha-ẓadik	the Righteous Rabbi
הרה״ק	ha-rav ha-kadosh	the Holy Rabbi
הר״ר	ha-rav rabbi	the Rabbi
הש״י	ha-shem yeraḥem	God will have mercy
השי״ת	ha-shem yitbarakh	God, blessed be He
התוה״ק	ha-torah ha-kedoshah	the Holy Torah
וב״ב	u-venei veto	and family
וגו׳	ve-gomer	etc.
וְכוּ׳	ve-khuleh	etc.
וכיו״ב	ve-khayyoẓeh ba-zeh	etc.

ועב״כ	ve-ad bi-khlal	inclusive
ועה״פ	va'ad ha-poel	executive
ועי״ש	ve-ayyen sham	vide; cf.
ושות׳	ve-shutafo (shutafav)	and Co.
ז׳	zakhar	masculine
ז״א (ז.א.)	zot omeret	that is to say
זַבְּלָ״א	ze borer lo eḥad	one chosen by each party (in arbitration)
ז״ל	zikhrono li-verakhah	blessed be his memory
זצ״ל	zekher ẓaddik li-verakhah	blessed be his memory
זצק״ל	zekher ẓaddik kadosh li-verakhah	blessed be his memory
ח״ו	ḥas ve-shalom; ḥalilah ve-ḥas; ḥas ve-ḥalilah	Heaven forbid
חוה״מ	ḥol ha-mo'ed	the intermediate days of a feast
חו״ל	ḥuẓ la-areẓ	abroad
חו״ק	ḥuppah ve-kiddushin	marriage
ח״ז	ḥodesh zeh	this month
חז״ל	ḥakhamenu zikhronam li-verakhah	our sages of blessed memory
ח״כ	ḥaver keneset	Knesset member
חכ״א	ḥakhamim omrim	sages say
ח״ק	ḥevra kaddisha	burial society
ח.נ.	ḥaver nikhbad	dear friend
ט״ו	tu	fifteenth (of Av or Shevat)
טו״ת	tallit u-tefillin	prayer shawl and phylacteries
טל׳	telefon	telephone
ט.ל.ח. (טל״ח)	ta'ut le-olam ḥozer	E. and O.E.
ט״ס	ta'ut sofer(im)	scribal error
י״א	yesh omrim	some say
יבל״ח(א)	yibbadel le-ḥayyim (arukkim)	may he live (long)
יה״ב	yemei he-benayim	Middle Ages
יה״ר (י״ר)	yehi raẓon	may it be [God's] will
יוה״כ	yom ha-kippurim	Day of Atonement
יו״ט	yom tov	festival
יו״ל (י״ל)	yoẓeh le-or (yaẓah le-or)	published
יו״ר	yoshev rosh	chairman
יי״ש	yayin saruf	brandy
יצ״ו	yishmerehu ẓuro vi-yḥayehu	May God protect and preserve him
יר״ה	yarum hodo	His Majesty
ימ״ש	yimaḥ shemo	cursed be he (may his name be wiped out)
ירו׳	yerushalmi	Jerusalem Talmud
ית׳	yitbarakh	may He be blessed
כב׳	kevod	the Honorable
כה״ק	kitvei ha-kodesh	the Scriptures
כיו״ב	kayyoẓe bo; kayyoẓe ba-zeh	and so forth
כ״י (כה״י)	ketav (kitvei) yad	manuscript(s); mss.
כ״כ	kol kakh	so much
כ״כ (כמו״כ)	kemo khen	moreover
כ״ע (כה״ע)	ketav (kitvei) et (ketav [kitvei] ha-et)	magazine(s); periodical(s)
לַ״ג	lamed gimmel (33)	thirty third (day of the Omer)
לַהֲדַ״ם	lo hayu devarim me-olam	nothing of the kind
לה״ק	leshon ha-kodesh	Hebrew
לה״ר	leshon ha-ra	slander
ל״י	lira yisraelit	Israel pound(s)
לסה״נ	li-sefirat ha-noẓrim	C.E. (A.D.)
לע״ע	le-et atah	for the present
לפנה״צ	lifnei ha-ẓohorayim	a.m.
לפ״ק	li-fekkudat	(pay) to the order of
לפה״ס	lifnei ha-sefirah	B.C.E. (B.C.)
מוכָ״ז	moser ketav zeh	the bearer
מו״ל	moẓi le-or	publisher
מו״מ	massah u-mattan	negotiations
מו״ס	mokher sefarim	bookseller
מוצ״ש	moẓa'ei shabbat	termination of the Sabbath
מז״ט	mazzal tov	good luck; congratulations
מַטְכַּ״ל	matteh kelali	general staff
מ״מ	memalleh makom; mareh makom	acting; reference
מַנְכַּ״ל	menahel kelali	director general
נ׳ (נק׳)	nekevah	feminine
ן׳	ben	son
נ״א	nosaḥ Ashkenaz	Ashkenazi version (of prayers)
נדל״נ	nikhsei de-la naidei	immovable property
נו״ע	nuḥo eden	may he rest in peace
נ״י	nero yair	may his light shine
נ״ך	nevi'im ketuvim	the Prophets and the Writings
נלב״ע	niftar le-veit olamo	died
נ״ע	nishmato eden	may his soul rest in peace
ס׳	sefer; siman; sa'if	book; sign; article, paragraph
סה״י	seder ha-yom	agenda
סה״כ (ס״ה)	sakh ha-kol	total
סה״נ (ספה״נ)	sefirat ha-noẓrim	C.E. (A.D.)
סה״ק	sifrei ha-kodesh	holy books (Bible)

ס״ט	siman tov; sefaradi tahor; sant	good omen; pure Sephardi; St.
סי׳	siman	sign
סנה׳	sanhedrin	Sanhedrin
(סה״ת) ס״ת	sefer (ha-)torah	scroll of the Law
סְתָ״ם	sefarim, tefillin, mezuzot	scroll (of the Law), phylacteries, mezuzot
ע׳	ayyen; erekh	see, vide; entry
עב״ל; עב״ג	im ben gilah, im bat gilo; im beḥir libah, im beḥirat libo	with her fiancé; with his fiancée
עב״ה	avodat ha-bore	divine service
עבה״י	ever ha-yarden	Trans-Jordan
(עה״ש) ע״ה	alav ha-shalom	may he rest in peace
עה״ח	al he-ḥatum	signed
(עיה״ק) עה״ק	ir ha-kodesh	the Holy City (Jerusalem)
עו״ד	orekh din	lawyer
עוה״ב	olam ha-ba	the world to come
עוה״ז	olam ha-zeh	this world
עו״ש	over va-shav	current (account)
(ע״ש) עי״ש	ayyen sham	ibid
ע״כ	al ken	therefore
עַכּוּ״ם	ovdei kokhavim u-mazzalot	idolaters, pagans
(ע׳) עמ׳	ammud	page
ע״ס	al sakh	amounting to
ע״ע	ayyen erekh	see entry, q.v.
עפ״י	al pi	according to
פ׳	pasuk; perek	verse; chapter
פ״א	peh eḥad	unanimously
פי׳	perush	commentary
פ״נ	po nitman, po nikbar	here lies buried
פס״ד	pesak din	judgment
צַהַ״ל	ẓeva haganah le-yisrael	Israel Defense Forces (IDF)
קב״ה	kudsha berikh hu	God
(קו״ח) קופ״ח	kuppat ḥolim	sick fund
ק״ק	kehillah kedoshah	holy community
(קהק״ל) קק״ל	keren kayyemet le-yisrael	Jewish National Fund
ק״ש	keriat shema; kabbalat Shabbat	recitation of Shema; reception of the Sabbath
ר״ב	raẓuf be-zeh	enclosed herewith
רבש״ע	ribbono shel olam	God
(ר״ה) רה״ש	Rosh ha-Shanah	Rosh ha-Shanah (New Year)
רז״ל	rabbotenu zikhronam li-verakhah	our sages of blessed memory
ר״ח	Rosh Ḥodesh	beginning of the month
(ר׳) רח׳	reḥov	street
ר״ל	raḥamana li-ẓlan; roẓeh lomar	Lord save us; i.e.
רַמַ״ח	248	248 organs in the human body
רַמַטְכַּ״ל	rosh ha-matteh ha-kelali	Chief of Staff
ר״פ	raẓuf po	enclosed herewith
ר״ת	rashei tevot	initials, abbreviations
ש׳	shenat	the year
שד׳	sederot	avenue, boulevard
שַׁדָ״ר	sheluḥa de-rabbanan	emissary
שו״ב	shoḥet u-vodek	ritual slaughterer
שו״ע	Shulḥan Arukh	name of standard code of Jewish Law
שו״ת	she'elot u-teshuvot	responsa
ש״ז	shanah zo	this year
שי׳	she-yiḥyeh	long life to him
שכ׳	shekhunat	quarter (of a town)
שכ״ד	sekhar dirah	rent
(ש״ט) שכ״ט	sekhar tirḥah	wages
שלב״ע	shevaḥ le-el boreh olam	praise be to the Lord
שְׁלִיטָ״א	she-yiḥyeh le-orekh yamim tovim amen	may he live long and happily, Amen
שנא׳	she-ne'emar	as it is said
שַׁ״ס	shishah sedarim	Mishnah
שׂ״ס	sekhar sofrim	author's fee
שְׁסָ״ה	365	365 veins of the body
שַׁ״ץ	sheliaḥ ẓibbur	cantor
שֶׁקֶ״ם	sherut kantinot u-miznonim	canteen service (of the Israel army)
ת״ב	Talmud Bavli	Babylonian Talmud
(ת״ד) ת.ד.	tevat do'ar	POB
תח׳	tiḥyeh	long may she live
ת״ח	talmid ḥakham (talmidei ḥakhamim)	scholar(s)
ת״ל	todah la-el; tehillah la-el; talmud lomar	thank God; it says
תַּנַ״ךְ	torah, nevi'im, ketuvim	the Bible
תַּנְצְבָּ״ה	tehi nishmato ẓerurah bi-ẓeror ha-ḥayyim	R.I.P.
ת״ר	tanu rabbanan	the Rabbis have taught
תַּרְיַ״ג	613	613 (commandments)
ת״ת	Talmud Torah	religious elementary school

Abiezer. (1) Name of person and a tribal unit of tribe of Manasseh, and clan in story of Gideon. (2) Abiezer the Anathothite, one of "David's Mighty Men."

Abigail, name of two women in Bible. (1) Wife of Nabal, later of David. (2) David's niece.

Abi-Ḥasira, family of Moroccan kabbalists and rabbis. **Jacob ben Masoud** (1807–1880), codifier, kabbalist; renowned for his piety.

Abihu, second son of Aaron. Died together with his brother Nadab when they offered "alien fire before the Lord" (Lev. 10:1-3).

Abijah, second king of Judah c. 914–912 B.C.E.; son of Rehoboam. Bible describes him unfavorably.

Abimelech, Philistine king of Gerar, with whom Abraham concluded pact of friendship.

Abimelech (12th c. B.C.E.), illegitimate son of Gideon. Murdered his 70 brothers (except Jotham) and was ruler of Shechem for 3 years. Killed in revolt.

Abinadab, person mentioned in Bible who resided in Kiriath-Jearim. The ark was brought to his home after its wanderings in the Philistine cities and remained there for 20 years.

Abir, David (1922–), Israel aeronautical engineer. Wrote on aircraft design. Prof. at Haifa Technion.

Abishag the Shunammite, girl chosen as concubine for David in his old age. After David's death, Adonijah's request to marry her led Solomon to have him killed.

Abishai, David's devoted general; son of his sister, Zeruiah, and brother of Joab.

Abitbol, family of Moroccan rabbis, talmudists, jurists who led community of Sefrou. **Saul Jeshua ben Isaac** (c. 1740–1809), rabbi, *dayyan* in Sefrou. Responsa published as *Avnei Shayish.* **Amor ben Solomon** (1782–1854), scholar, *dayyan*; b. Sefrou, where he maintained a yeshivah.

Abkhaz Autonomous Soviet Socialist Republic (Rus. **Abkhaziya**), Soviet republic on E. shore of Black Sea. Barred to Jews fr. European Russia during czarist regime. 1970 census recorded 4,400 Jews, concentrated mainly in Sukhumi, most of them fr. Georgia.

Abner, relation of King Saul, commander of his army. After Saul's death, supported Ish-Bosheth's claim to throne. Killed by Joab.

Abner of Burgos (Alfonso of Valladolid) (c. 1270–c. 1340), Spanish apostate. One of first apostates to formulate ideological justification for conversion. His writings served as basis for later polemics.

Aboab, widespread family of Spanish origin. **Immanuel** (c. 1555–1628), Spanish-born Marrano scholar who escaped to Italy and returned to Judaism. Vigorously defended Judaism. **Isaac I** (14th c.), rabbi and author whose *Menorat ha-Ma'or* was one of most popular works of religious edification in Middle Ages. **Isaac II** (1433–1493), "the last *gaon* of Castile"; d. Portugal. **Isaac de Mattathias** (1631–1707), Dutch Sephardi scholar, b. Oporto. **Jacob ben Samuel** (d. c. 1725), Venetian rabbi. **Samuel ben Abraham** (1610–1694), Italian rabbi who opposed Shabbateans and settled in Ereẓ Israel. **Isaac Aboab da Fonseca** (1605–1693), Dutch Sephardi rabbi in Recife, Brazil (first rabbi in America) and *ḥakham* in Amsterdam. Sat on tribunal which excommunicated Spinoza and later supported Shabbetai Ẓevi.

Isaac Aboab da Fonseca

Abrabanel, Abravanel, distinguished family of Spanish origin. **Judah of Córdoba** (13th–14th c.), treasurer, tax collector. **Samuel of Seville,** royal treasurer in Andalusia 1388. His son **Judah** (d. 1471), financier in Portugal. Judah's son **Isaac ben Judah** (1437–1508), statesman, philosopher, Bible exegete. Treasurer to Alfonso V of Portugal, whence he fled to Spain (1483), where he entered service of Ferdinand and Isabella and unsuccessfully attempted to prevent expulsion of Jews fr. Spain. After 1492 expulsion sailed to Naples where he served at court, and after various tribulations finally settled in Venice 1503. Wrote several works including a famous commentary on the Bible. His son **Judah** (c. 1460–c. 1523), physician, poet, Renaissance philosopher, known as Leone Ebreo. His *Dialoghi d'Amore* translated into many languages. Another son, **Samuel** (1473–1547), financier, community leader in Naples.

Abraham (c. 18th c. B.C.E.), first patriarch of people of Israel and founder of monotheism; son of Terah and father of Isaac by his wife Sarah and of Ishmael by his concubine Hagar; b. Ur of the Chaldees, went to Canaan, the land which God promised to his descendants. This covenant was consecrated by rite of circumcision, which Abraham instituted among Jews. His willingness to sacrifice his son Isaac was regarded as supreme test of faith.

Abraham in Nimrod's fiery furnace (top) and about to sacrifice Ishmael, with genealogy of Ishmael's children (bottom), from "Zubdat al-Tawārikh," 16th cent.

Abraham, Abraham (1843–1911), U.S. merchant, philanthropist. Founder of Brooklyn department store Abraham and Straus.

Abraham, Apocalypse of, apocalyptic work dating fr. 2nd c. C.E., extant only in Slavonic version.

Abraham, David (1909–), Indian actor; of Bene Israel family. Appeared in many Hindustani films.

Abraham, Karl (1877–1925), psychoanalyst. Pioneer in psychoanalysis in Germany and president of International Psychoanalytic Association.

"Abraham and Straus" horse-drawn delivery wagons, late 1890s.

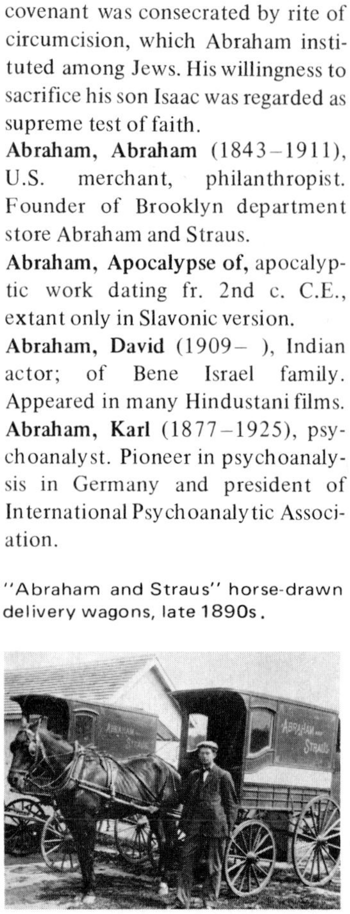

Abraham, Samuel (d. 1792), merchant in Cochin; first to establish contact between Jews of Cochin and those of the West.

Abraham Abusch ben Ẓevi Hirsch (1700–1769), rabbi, halakhist. Served in Lissa and Frankfort and was *parnas* of Council of the Lands.

°**Abraham a Sancta Clara** (c. 1644–1709), Augustinian friar in Vienna and anti-Jewish propagandist. Had influence in Viennese anti-Semitism.

Abraham bar Ḥiyya (d.c. 1136), philosopher, mathematician, astronomer, translator in Barcelona. One of earliest philosophical and scientific writers in Hebrew.

Abraham ben Alexander Katz of Kalisk (1741–1810), ḥasidic rabbi in Poland and Ereẓ Israel. Succeeded Menahem Mendel of Vitebsk as head of ḥasidic groups in Ereẓ Israel.

Abraham ben Alexander of Cologne (13th c.), kabbalist; disciple of R. Eleazar b. Judah of Worms. Emigrated to Spain.

Abraham ben Azriel (13th c.), liturgical commentator in Bohemia. Author of *Arugat ha-Bosem,* revealing comprehensive knowledge of Jewish sources.

Abraham ben Daniel (1511–1578), Italian rabbi, poet; officiated in Ferrara. Wrote over 5,000 poems.

Abraham ben David Maimuni (c. 1246–c. 1316), *nagid* of Egyptian Jewry; great-grandson of Maimonides.

Abraham ben David of Posquières (Rabad; c. 1125–1198), talmudist in Provence; b. Narbonne. Established yeshivah at Posquières. Published criticisms (*hassagot*) of Maimonides' *Mishneh Torah* as well as codification of rabbinic law, responsa, commentaries on talmudic literature, etc.

Abraham ben Dov of Mezhirech (known as *ha-Malakh*, "the Angel"; 1741–1776), ḥasidic sage. Author of commentary on Pentateuch.

Abraham ben Eliezer ha-Levi (c. 1460–c.1528), kabbalist; b. Spain, settled in Jerusalem c. 1514.

Abraham ben Eliezer ha-Levi Berukhim (c. 1515–1593), Safed kabbalist; b. Morocco. Disciple of Isaac Luria.

Abraham ben Elijah of Vilna (1750–1808), talmudic scholar; son of Vilna Gaon.

Abraham ben Garton ben Isaac (15th c.), first known Hebrew printer; probably fr. Spain. Produced Rashi's commentary on Pentateuch at Reggio Calabria in 1475.

Abraham ben Ḥalfon (15th or 16th c.), Hebrew poet in Yemen. Fifty of his poems published.

Abraham ben Ḥayyim (Heilprin; d. 1762), community leader in Lublin. *Parnas* of Council of Four Lands.

Abraham ben Ḥayyim, dei Tintori (the Dyer; 15th c.), early Hebrew printer in Italy. Worked with Soncinos on first printed Hebrew Bible (1488).

Abraham ben Hillel of Fostat (d. 1223), scholar, poet, physician in Egypt.

Abraham ben Isaac Gerondi (13th c.), kabbalist, *paytan* in Gerona, Spain. Composer of *Rosh ha-Shanah* eve hymn *Aḥot Ketannah.*

Abraham ben Isaac of Granada, kabbalist; putative author of *Berit Menuḥah,* one of main works of Kabbalah.

Abraham ben Isaac of Montpellier (d.c. 1315), talmudist in Provence. Known for his liberal outlook.

Abraham ben Isaac of Narbonne (c. 1110–1179), talmudist in Provence, known as Rabi Abad. His *Ha-Eshkol* was first work of Jewish codification in S. France and served as model for subsequent compilations.

Abraham ben Jacob (17th c.), convert to Judaism and *Haggadah* engraver in Amsterdam.

Abraham ben Jehiel Michal ha-Kohen (d.c. 1800), kabbalist, rabbinical emissary; of Lask, Poland. Before finally settling in Jerusalem, traveled widely in Europe on behalf of Jerusalem community.

Abraham ben Joseph of Lissa (d. 1777), communal leader in Poland. Represented Great Poland at Councils of the Lands, over which he presided.

Abraham ben Josiah Troki (1636–1687), Karaite poet, mystic in Lithuania; physician King Jan III Sobieski of Poland.

Abraham ben Josiah Yerushalmi (c. 1685–after 1734), Karaite scholar who lived in Crimea. Defended Karaite conception of Torah.

Abraham ben Moses ben Maimon (1186–1237), leader (*nagid*) of Jewish community in Egypt, court physician, halakhist; son of Moses Maimonides. Wrote encyclopedic work on Jewish religion *Kifāyat al-'Abidin,* in spirit of mystic piety.

Abraham ben Moses ha-Kohen ha-Sephardi (15th–16th c.), Italian rabbi; of Spanish birth. Lived in Ferrara, then Bologna, where he was appointed rabbi.

Abraham ben Nathan (c. 1125), first *nagid* of Jewish community of Kairouan, Tunisia.

Abraham ben Nathan ha-Yarḥi (i.e., "of Lunel"; c. 1155–c. 1215), Provençal talmudic scholar. Wrote *Sefer ha-Manhig* on prayer and synagogue usage.

Abraham ben Samuel he-Ḥasid (12th c.), rabbi, liturgical poet of Speyer, Germany; brother of Judah b. Samuel he-Ḥasid.

Abraham ben Shabbetai ha-Kohen (1670–1729), poet, physician, artist, b. Crete, lived in Zante.

Abraham b. Shabbetai ha-Kohen, engraved self-portrait.

Abraham ben Solomon of Torrutiel (b. 1482), chronicler; b. Spain, lived in Fez, Morocco.

Abraham Gershon of Kutow (d. c. 1760), ḥasid, talmudic scholar, kabbalist in Ukraine; fr. 1747 in Ereẓ Israel; brother-in-law of Ba'al Shem Tov.

Abraham ha-Bavli (11th c.?), grammarian. Author of work on Hebrew roots.

Abraham Ḥayyim ben Gedaliah (1750–1816), rabbi in Galicia. Author of works on Bible, *Avot,* etc.

Abrahamites, judaizing sect in Bohemia, 17th–18th c.

Abraham Joshua Heschel of Apta (Opatow; d. 1825), ḥasidic *ẓaddik* in Poland, known as "the Rabbi of Apta." Disciple of Elimelech of Lyzhansk. Exerted a wide influence and in his old age acknowledged as authority by many *ẓaddikim.* His son **Isaac Meir** (d. 1855) and grandson **Meshullam Zussia** (d. 1886), as well as his later descendants, were also revered as *ẓaddikim* in various places in Podolia.

Abraham Judaeus Bohemus (Abraham of Bohemia; d. 1533), banker, tax collector, *shtadlan* at royal court of Bohemia.

Abraham of Sarteano (15th c.), Italian Hebrew poet. Author of misogynist poem.

Abrahams, family of English athletes. **Sir Adolphe** (1883–1967),

physician, author, Cambridge sculling champion. His brother, **Sir Sidney** (1885–1957), colonial official, ran for Great Britain in 1908, 1912 Olympics. Another brother, **Harold Maurice** (1899–), lawyer, Olympic sprinter (winner of 100-yard dash 1924), captain of British Olympic team. Chairman of British amateur athletics board fr. 1969. Sports writer.

Abrahams, Abraham (d. 1792), English scholar who translated *Avot* into English.

Abrahams, Abraham (1897–1955), English journalist; editor of *Jewish Standard* 1940–48. Active Revisionist.

Abrahams, Israel (1858–1924), English scholar, Hebraist. Reader in rabbinics at Cambridge and a founder of Jewish Historical Society of England. Advanced cause of Liberal Judaism in England. Wrote *Jewish Life in the Middle Ages, Studies in Pharisaism and the Gospels,* and notes on prayer-book published by his father-in-law, S. Singer.

Abrahams, Israel (1903–1973), rabbi, scholar in England and S. Africa. Chief rabbi of Cape Province; settled in Israel 1967. Translated major works of M.D. Cassuto into English.

Abrahams, Sir Lionel (1869–1919), English civil servant, Anglo-Jewish historian.

Abrahams, Nicolai Christian Levin (1798–1870), Danish literary scholar. Prof. of French literature at Copenhagen Univ.

Abrahamsen, David (1903–), criminologist, psychiatrist; b. Norway, in U.S. fr. 1940.

Abrahão, Coje (16th c.), agent, diplomat in service of Portuguese in Goa, India

Abram, Morris Berthold (1918–), U.S. attorney, civic leader. Pres. of American Jewish Committee 1963–68, pres. of Brandeis Univ. 1968–70.

Abramovitz, Max (1908–), U.S. architect. Designed N.Y. Philharmonic Hall.

Abramovitz, Moses (1912–), U.S. economist. Main fields: economic history and development and business cycles.

Abramowitz, Bina (1865–1953), Yiddish actress; went from Russia to U.S. 1886.

Abramowitz, Emil (1864–1922), physician. One of first Social Democrats in Russia.

Abramowitz, Grigori (pseudonyms: **Zevi Abrahami, W. Farbman, Michael Farbman;** 1880? –1933), Zionist socialist, publisher in Russia; in England fr. 1915.

Yeḥezkel Abramsky

Abraham Abramson

Abramowitz, Herman (1880–1948), rabbi of Congregation Shaar Hashamayim, Montreal, 1903–48.

Abramowitz (Rein), Raphael (1880–1963), socialist leader, writer; b. Latvia. One of chief spokesmen of the Bund and played leading role as Menshevik in 1917 revolution. Went to Berlin 1920 and edited Menshevik organ. Moved to New York 1940.

Abrams, Charles (1901–1970), U.S. housing and urban planning expert. Laid groundwork of U.S. public housing laws.

Abramsky, Yeḥezkel (1886–), talmudic scholar, communal worker in Russia; b. Lithuania. Arrested 1930 as "counter-revolutionary," sentenced to hard labor in Siberia. Released after two years and went to London where he became *dayyan* of *bet din.* Moved to Jerusalem 1951. Wrote commentary on Tosefta. Israel Prize 1955.

Abramson (18th–19th c.), family of German medalists, engravers, **Jacob Abraham** (1723–1800), medalist at Berlin mint. His son **Abraham Abramson** (1754–1811), royal medalist fr. 1782.

Abramson, Shraga (1915–), rabbinic scholar; b. Poland, settled in Ereẓ Israel 1936. Prof. of Talmud at Heb. Univ. Wrote on Geonica, etc. Israel Prize 1974.

Abrass, Osias (Joshua; 1829–1883), *ḥazzan,* synagogue composer in Odessa; known as *Pitshe Odesser* ("The Mite from Odessa").

Absaban, Solomon (d. 1592), scholar of Safed and disciple of Isaac Luria. Headed Damascus yeshivah.

Absalom (b. c. 1007/06 B.C.E.), third son of David. Stirred up rebellion against David, but vanquished and killed when his long hair became entangled in a tree.

Absalom, younger son of John Hyrcanus I; prominent part in defense of Jerusalem against Pompey.

Absalom, Jewish partisan leader at beginning of Roman War (66 C.E.); assassinated by anti-Sicarii faction.

Abse, Dannie (1923–), English poet. His brother **Leo** (1917–), English parliamentarian who introduced liberalizing legislation governing homosexuality and divorce.

Abt, Isaac Arthur (1867–1955), U.S. pediatrician. First president of American Academy of Pediatrics.

Abtshuk, Avraham (1897–1937), Soviet Yiddish writer, critic. Ac-

Death of Absalom, "San Isidoro Bible," 12th cent., Spain.

A general view of Abu Ghosh.

cused of Trotskyist tendencies and reported to have been arrested and later killed.

Abu, Arabic word meaning "father of"; used in personal names of Jews living in Islamic countries.

Abu al-Faraj Harun ibn al-Faraj (Aaron b. Jeshua; 11th c.), Karaite grammarian, lexicographer; lived in Jerusalem. Pioneered investigation of biblical Aramaic grammar.

Abu al-Fat (14th c.), author of Samaritan chronicle in Arabic, *Kitāb al-Tarikh* ("Annals"); b. Damascus.

Abu al-Ḥasan of Tyre (11th c.), Samaritan halakhist, exegete, liturgical writer. His decisions still valid in Samaritan community.

Abu al-Munajja Solomon ben Shaya (12th c.), government official in Egypt; responsible for constructing irrigation canal which greatly benefited agriculture.

Abudarham, David ben Joseph (14th c.), liturgical commentator (*Sefer Abudarham*); of distinguished family in Spain.

Abu Ghosh, Israel Arab village W of Jerusalem. Site of crusader church. Pop. 1,910 (1971).

Abu 'Imrān al-Tiflīsī (9th c.), founder of Jewish religious sect; lived in Tiflis, Georgia. Developed his own *halakhah* and opposed Karaites. Sect of Tiflisites existed for several generations.

Abu 'Isā, Isaac ben Jacob al-Isfahīnī (8th c.), founder of Jewish sect in Persia. Led unsuccessful revolt against Muslims and was killed but his followers did not believe he had died and sect still existed in 10th c.

Abulafia, Abraham ben Samuel (1240–c.1291), kabbalist. Traveled to Ereẓ Israel, Greece, Italy fr. Spain and became convinced of his capacity for prophetic revelation. In 1280, called Pope Nicholas III to account for persecuting Jews; for this he was condemned to death by burning, but saved by Pope's death. Influenced 16th c. Safed kabbalists.

Abulafia, Ḥayyim ben David (c. 1700–1775), rabbi, codifier, *av bet din* in Salonika, rabbi of Smyrna.

Abulafia, Ḥayyim ben Jacob (1580–1668), Palestinian talmudist, *rosh yeshivah* in Hebron.

The Toledo synagogue built by Samuel ha-Levi Abulafia.

Abulafia, Ḥayyim ben Moses(?) (c.1660–1744), rabbi of Smyrna; b. Hebron. Fr. 1740 in Tiberias, which he and his family began rebuilding. Author of rabbinical works.

Abulafia, Ḥayyim Nissim ben Isaac (1775–1861), rabbi in Tiberias, Damascus, Jerusalem (*rishon le-Ẓion* fr. 1854).

Abulafia, Isaac (d. 1764), talmudist, emissary. Active with his father in rebuilding Tiberias, where he was rabbi fr. 1744.

Abulafia, Isaac ben Moses (1824–1910), rabbi, halakhist; b. Tiberias. Rabbi of Damascus fr. 1877.

Abulafia, Jacob ben Solomon (1550?–1622?), Damascus rabbi. Received ordination from Jacob (II) Berab.

Abulafia, Meir (1170?–1244), talmudic commentator (*Yad Ramah, Or Ẓaddikim,* etc.), poet, renowned rabbi in Toledo, Spain. Engaged in controversy with Maimonides over doctrine of resurrection.

Abulafia, Samuel ben Meir ha-Levi (c. 1320–1361), Spanish financier, philanthropist. Synagogue he built in Toledo as well as his own imposing residence still stand.

Abulafia, Todros ben Joseph ha-Levi (c. 1220–1298), Spanish rabbi, kabbalist; b. Burgos. Regarded as "Spanish exilarch" and spiritual leader of Jewish community in Castile.

Abulafia, Todros ben Judah ha-Levi (1247–c. 1298), poet in Toledo. His *Gan ha-Meshalim ve-ha-Ḥidot* contains over 1,000 poems.

Abulker, Henri-Samuel (1876–1957), professor of medicine, head of Algerian Zionist Federation. With his son, **José** (b. 1920), collaborated with the Allies to assist American landing in Algiers during WWII (Nov. 1942).

Abulrabi, Aaron (c. 1376–c. 1430), biblical scholar in Sicily. Author of supercommentary to Rashi's Bible commentary.

Abu Sa'd al-Tustari (Abraham b. Yashar; d. 1048), Egyptian financier, courtier. Dealer in precious objects and jewels. Assassinated on instigation of Jewish convert to Islam.

Abyaḍ, Yiḥya ben Shalom (1873–1935), Yemenite rabbi, biblical scholar. Among heads of Dor De'ah movement.

Abyssinia, see Ethiopia.

Academy (Heb. *yeshivah,* Aram. *metivta*), higher schools of Jewish learning in Ereẓ Israel and Babylonia. After destruction of Temple in 70 C.E., schools in Ereẓ Israel

became central authority of Jewish people. First academy established at Jabneh by Johanan b. Zakkai, succeeded to authority of Great Sanhedrin. After Bar Kokhba rebellion, center of Jewish learning moved to Galilee, first to Shepharam, then to

Heads of the academies of Ereẓ Israel and Babylon.

EREẒ ISRAEL	BABYLON
First Generation	**220 C.E.–250 C.E.**
R. Ḥanina b. Ḥama: head of the Council of Sepphoris Oshaya Rabbah: head of the Academy at Caesarea R. Yannai R. Joshua b. Levi: head of the Academy at Lydda	Rav (Abba b. Aivu): founder and head of the Academy of Sura Samuel: head of the Academy of Nehardea Karna: "Dayyan of the Golah" Mar Ukva: the Exilarch
Second Generation	**250 C.E.–290 C.E.**
R. Johanan: head of the Academy at Tiberias R. Simeon b. Lakish (Resh Lakish) R. Eleazar b. Pedat: head of the Academy at Tiberias	R. Huna: head of the Academy of Sura R. Judah b. Ezekiel: head of the Academy of Pumbedita R. Hamnuna
Third Generation	**290 C.E.–320 C.E.**
R. Ammi b. Nathan: head of the Academy at Tiberias R. Assi: head of the Academy at Tiberias R. Abbahu: head of the Academy at Caesarea R. Zeira	R. Ḥisda: head of the Academy of Sura Rabbah b. Huna: head of the Academy of Sura Rabbah b. Naḥmani: head of the Academy of Pumbedita R. Joseph b. Ḥiyya: head of the Academy of Pumbedita
Fourth Generation	**320 C.E.–350 C.E.**
R. Jonah: head of the Academy at Tiberias R. Yose: head of the Academy at Tiberias R. Jeremiah R. Haggai	Abbaye: head of the Academy of Pumbedita Rava b. Joseph: founder and head of the Academy of Maḥoza Rami b. Ḥami R. Zeira
Fifth Generation	**350 C.E.–375 C.E.**
R. Mana b. Jonah: head of the Academy at Tiberias R. Yose b. Avin R. Tanḥuma b. Abba	R. Pappa: founder and head of the Academy at Naresh R. Huna b. Joshua R. Zevid: head of the Academy of Pumbedita
Sixth Generation	**375 C.E.–425 C.E.**
	Rav Ashi: head of the Academy of Sura in Matah Mehasya Ravina Mar Zutra Ameimar
Seventh Generation	**425 C.E.–460 C.E.**
	Mar b. Rav Ashi (Tabyomi): head of the Academy of Sura R. Yeimar: head of the Academy of Sura R. Geviha of Bei-Katil: head of the Academy of Pumbedita
Eighth Generation	**460 C.E.–500 C.E.**
	Ravina II b. Huna: head of the Academy of Sura R. Yose: head of the Academy of Pumbedita Aḥai b. Huna

View of present-day Achzib.

Bet She'arim, finally to Sepphoris, where Judah ha-Nasi compiled Mishnah. After him, Jewish learning focused at Tiberias for centuries. Jerusalem Talmud and Masorah compiled there. In Babylonia Jewish learning flourished fr. 3rd c., with Samuel heading academy at Nehardea and Rav at Sura. After destruction of Nehardea (259), new academy opened at Pumbedita. Babylonian Talmud edited at Sura by Ashi and Ravina (late 5th c.). Supremacy of Sura and Pumbedita recognized by all Jewry until rise of new centers in N. Africa and Europe in 10th–11th c.

Academy of the Hebrew Language, Israel institution, supreme authority on Heb. language; established 1953 by Knesset. Succeeded Hebrew Language Committee (*Va'ad ha-Lashon ha-Ivrit*) founded in Jerusalem 1890.

Açan, Moses de Zaragua (c. 1300), Catalan poet. Author of verse treatise on chess.

Acco, see Acre.

Achan, member of tribe of Judah. Executed after capture of Jericho by Joshua for taking some of consecrated spoil.

Aerial view of Acre.

Acher, Mathias, see Birnbaum, Nathan.

°**Achish,** Philistine king of Gath at end of Saul's reign; gave refuge to David.

Joseph Achron

Achron, Joseph (1886–1943), composer, violinist; b. Poland, went to U.S. 1925. His brother **Isidor** (1892–1948), pianist, composer.

Achsah, daughter of Caleb, wife of Othniel.

Achzib, ancient Canaanite harbor N. of Acre. Occupied important position in ancient times. Nearby is kibbutz Gesher ha-Ziv.

Acosta, family name. See Costa.

Acosta, Cristobal (1515–1580), Marrano physician, botanist. Spent many years in India, later settling in Burgos, Spain.

Acra, Jerusalem fortress overlooking Temple; established 168 B.C.E. Exact location uncertain.

Acre (Heb. *Akko*), coastal city in N. Israel. Mentioned fr. 19th c. B.C.E.; became center of glass manufacture. Later, hellenistic city. In crusade period held by knights of St. John (as St. Jean d'Acre) and fr. 1191 was crusader capital of Erez Israel. Reconquered by Saracens 1291, captured by Turks 1517, resisted Napoleon's siege 1799. Stormed by Haganah forces and included in State of Israel, May 1948. Pop. 34,200 (1971), incl. 8,950 non-Jews.

Acsády, Ignác (1845–1906), Hungarian historian, writer. Fought for emancipation of Hungarian Jews.

Action Française, French royalist anti-Semitic movement formed after Dreyfus affair; active 1896–1939.

Adadi, Abraham Ḥayyim ben Masoud Hai (1801–1874), halakhic authority, kabbalist; *dayyan* in Tripoli, also lived in Safed.

Adah, (1) Wife of Lamech. (2) Wife of Esau.

Adalberg, Samuel (1868–1939), Polish historian, educator. Compiled compendium of 40,000 Polish proverbs. Committed suicide when Nazis occupied Warsaw.

Adam, first man and progenitor of human race. Expelled fr. Garden of Eden with wife Eve after disobeying Divine command.

Adam, Lajos (1879–1946), Hungarian physician. Contributed to technique of local anesthesia.

Adam and Eve, Book of the Life of, apocryphal work dealing with Adam's life and death. Composed probably bet. 100 B.C.E. and 200 C.E.; extant in Greek, Latin, Slavonic versions.

Adam ha-Kohen, see Lebensohn, Abraham Dov.

Adam Kadmon (Primordial Man), kabbalistic concept of spiritual man in whose image physical Adam was created.

Adams, Franklin Pierce (F.P.A.; 1881–1960), U.S. newspaper columnist, noted for wit. Wrote weekly *Diary of Our Own Samuel Pepys;* appeared on "Information Please" program.

°**Adams, Hannah** (1755–1831), U.S. authoress who wrote a history of the Jews.

Adani, David ben Amram (13th–14th c.), Yemenite scribe; compiler of *Midrash ha-Gadol.*

Adani, Saadiah ben David (15th c.), talmudist; lived in Damascus, Aleppo, Safed. Wrote commentary on Maimonides' *Mishneh Torah.*

Adar, post-Exilic name for 12th month of Jewish year. 30 days. Zodiac sign Pisces. Feast of Purim (Adar 14) gave period joyful character, hence dictum "When Adar comes in, gladness is increased" (Ta'an. 29a). Adar 7 is traditional date of birth and death of Moses. In leap years there is a second month of Adar (29 days); on such occasions festivals and anniversaries are observed in Second Adar.

Adar, Ẓvi (1917–), Israel educator. Headed Heb. Univ. School of Education 1958–65, prof. 1966, dean of faculty of humanities 1969–72. Wrote *Humanistic Values in the Bible, Ha-Ḥinnukh ha-Yehudi be-Yisrael u-ve-Arẓot ha-Berit* on Jewish education in Israel and U.S.

Adarbi, Isaac ben Samuel (c. 1510–c. 1584), rabbi of Lisbon Jews in Salonika, halakhist. Strove to unite Salonikan communities through his sermons (*Divrei Shalom*), wrote responsa.

Adass Jisroel, breakaway minority of Orthodox congregations in Germany founded in mid-19th c. Similar congregations (some called Adass Jeshurun) later established elsewhere.

Adda bar Ahavah (3rd c.), Babylonian *amora*; pupil of Rav. Main interest *halakhah.*

Addir bi-Melukhah (Heb. "Mighty in Kingship"), hymn recited toward end of Passover *seder* in Ashkenazi and some other rites; probably composed in 13th c. Germany.

Addir Hu (Heb. "Mighty is He"), alphabetic acrostic hymn recited toward end of Passover *seder* in Ashkenazi rite; composed in Middle Ages.

Additional Service, see Musaf.

Adel (Hodel), only daughter of Israel b. Eliezer Ba'al Shem Tov; her two sons, Moses Ḥayyim of Sodilkow and Baruch of Medzibezh, were *ẓaddikim.*

Adelaide, city in Australia. Established 1836. Jews among first settlers. First congregation organized 1848. Jewish pop. declined after WWI, increased in recent years, numbering 1,600 in 1972. HQ of S. Australian Board of Deputies.

Adelkind, Israel Cornelius (16th c.), Italian printer. Worked with Daniel Bomberg in Venice, supervised publication of first editions of Talmud.

Adelson, Howard Lawrence (1925–), U.S. medieval historian (*Medieval Commerce,* etc.). Taught at Princeton, N.Y. City College.

Aden, port in S. Arabia. Important Jewish community in medieval times and under Turkish rule. Under British rule pop. increased fr. 400 (1839) to 8,550 (1947). Following UN 1947 Palestine decision, Jewish quarter set upon by Arab rioters and number of persons killed or wounded. Yemenite Jews flown to Israel fr. Aden 1948–1950 ("Operation Magic Carpet"); followed by Adeni Jews, of whom last 150 left after 1967 Six-Day War.

Adeni, Solomon bar Joshua (1567–1625?), Mishnah commentator; went fr. Yemen to Safed with his family. His Mishnah commentary, *Melekhet Shelomo,* also valuable for philologists.

Aderca, Felix (1891–1962), Rumanian novelist, journalist. His *Moartea unei republici roșii,* about WW1, is outstanding war book.

Adiabene, ancient kingdom in upper Mesopotamia. Its queen, Helena, was converted to Judaism c. 30 C.E. Her sons, Monobaz and Izates, supported Jews during their war against Romans (66–70).

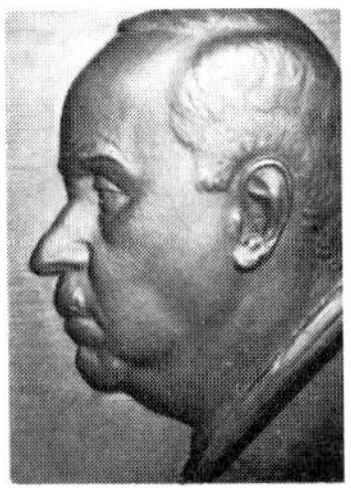

Alfred Adler, bronze plaque by Slavko Bril.

Cyrus Adler

Adler, Alfred (1870–1937), Austrian psychiatrist; originally disciple of Sigmund Freud. Formulated his own theory of "Individual Psychology," stressing "inferiority complex." Settled in U.S. 1934.

Adler, Cyrus (1863–1940), U.S. scholar, public worker. Librarian of Smithsonian Institution, president of Jewish Theological Seminary, a founder of American Jewish Committee, and president of Dropsie College. An editor of *American Jewish Year Book, Jewish Quarterly Review,* and member of editorial board of *Jewish Encyclopedia.* Influential in forming pattern of American Jewish cultural, communal life.

Adler, Dankmar (1844–1900), U.S. architect, engineer. With Louis Sulli-

van, credited with introducing new steel-framed structure for office buildings.

Adler, David Baruch (1826–1878), Danish banker, politician, philanthropist; promoted establishment of modern credit system in Denmark.

Adler, Elkan Nathan (1861–1946), English bibliophile, collector. Visited Egypt 1888, 1895–6, brought back 25,000 fragments fr. *Genizah.* Collected library of 4,500 manuscripts, 30,000 books. Wrote *History of the Jews of London, Jewish Travellers,* etc.

Adler, Elmer (1884–1962), U.S. publisher; cofounder of Random House. Published and edited bibliophile journal *The New Colophon.*

Adler, Felix (1851–1933), U.S. philosopher, educator; son of Samuel Adler. Founded Society for Ethical Culture.

Adler, Friedrich (1879–1960), Austrian socialist. In protest against WWI assassinated Austrian premier, Count Sturgkh. Sentenced to death but amnestied 1918. Secretary of Labor and Socialist International 1923–39. Baptized in childhood.

Adler, Georg (1863–1908), German economist, economic historian. Advocate of social insurance and labor legislation.

Adler, Guido (1855–1941), Austrian musicologist. Made Vienna center of musicological research.

Adler, Harry Clay (1865–1940), U.S. newspaper executive. Managed *Chattanooga Times.*

Adler, Hermann (1839–1911), British chief rabbi, succeeding his father Nathan Marcus Adler. Principal of Jews' College 1862, minister of Bayswater synagogue, London, 1864. Opposed Herzl's political Zionism.

Adler, Hugo Chaim (1894–1955), cantor, composer; escaped to U.S. fr. Germany 1938. Used contemporary idiom in synagogal music.

Adler, Jacob (1855–1926), actor-manager of Yiddish theater; b. Odessa. Left Russia 1883, settled in London, then U.S., where he was idol of Yiddish stage. His wife **Sarah** (c. 1858–1953), noted actress. His children **Celia** (1889–), **Stella** (1902–), **Luther** (1903–), appeared on both Yiddish and English stage.

Adler, Jankel (1895–1949), painter; b. Poland, lived in England fr. 1945 and exerted considerable influence on younger artists.

Adler, Julius Ochs (1892–1955), U.S. newspaperman, soldier (major-general). Vice-president and mana-

Hermann Adler

Jacob Adler

Jankel Adler, colored ink "Self Portrait"

Julius Ochs Adler

Nathan Marcus Adler

ger of *New York Times* and publisher of *Chattanooga Times.*

Adler, Larry (1914–), U.S. harmonica virtuoso. Appeared with symphony orchestras and gave recitals.

Adler, Lazarus Levi (1810–1886), German rabbi, pedagogue. Represented more conservative branch of German Reform movement.

Adler, Max (1866–1952), U.S. merchant-executive, musician, philanthropist. Financed first U.S. planetarium at Chicago.

Adler, Max (1873–1937), Austrian socialist and theoretician (*Politische oder soziale Demokratie,* etc.) and politician (deputy in Austrian parliament).

Adler, Michael (1868–1944), English minister, chaplain, historian (*Jews of Medieval England*).

Adler, Morris (1906–1966), U.S. Conservative rabbi, author (*Great Passages from the Torah, World of the Talmud,* etc.). Shot in his Detroit synagogue during Sabbath service by deranged youth.

Adler, Mortimer Jerome (1902–), U.S. philosopher, educator. Member of board of editors of *Encyclopaedia Britannica.*

Adler, Nathan ben Simeon ha-Kohen (1741–1800), rabbi, kabbalist in Frankfort, Germany, where he established famous yeshivah and was involved in bitter controversy with other rabbis in community (who at various times excommunicated him).

Adler, Nathan Marcus (1803–1890), German-born chief rabbi of Great Britain fr. 1844. Played important role in developing modern features of British Jewry. Established Jews' College in 1855 and helped found United Synagogue.

Adler, Paul (1878–1946), German author (*Elohim, Naemlich, Die Zauber-floete,* etc.); b. Prague, lived in France, Italy, Germany, and in hiding in Czechoslovakia in WWII.

Adler, Samuel (1809–1891), rabbi, pioneer of Reform movement in Germany; went to U.S. 1857. Served as rabbi of Congregation Emanuel, N.Y.

Adler, Samuel M. (1898–), U.S. painter. Prof. at New York Univ.

Adler, Saul Aaron (1895–1966), Israel parasitologist; brought up in Leeds, England. Organized scientific expeditions, settled in Ereẓ Israel 1924 and was one of first professors at Heb. Univ. Fellow of Royal Society.

Adler, Selig (1909–), U.S. historian. Prof. at Buffalo. Author of *Isolationist Impulse* and a history of Jews of Buffalo.

Adler, Victor (1852–1918), pioneer of Austrian Social-Democratic party and international labor movement. Austrian foreign minister 1918. Opposed Zionism.

Adler-Rudel, Salomon (1894–), social worker; b. Czernowitz, settled in Ereẓ Israel 1946. Prominent in rescuing Jews fr. Europe during WWII. Director of Leo Baeck Institute in Jerusalem. Wrote *Ostjuden in Deutschland 1880–1940.*

Adloyada, Purim carnival in Tel Aviv and elsewhere in Israel. Name derived fr. rabbinic saying that one should revel on Purim until one no longer knows (*ad de-lo yada*) the difference between the blessed Mordecai and the cursed Haman.

Admon (Gorochov), Yedidyah (1897–), Israel composer; b. Russia, settled in Ereẓ Israel 1906, in U.S. 1955–68. One of the creators of popular song in Israel (*Gamal Gamali,* etc.). Israel Prize in 1974.

Admon ben Gaddai, one of civil law judges in Jerusalem at close of Second Temple period.

Admoni, Vladimir Grigoryevich (1909–), Soviet Russian literary, linguistic scholar. Prof. at Pedagogical Institute of Leningrad.

Admor, title given to ḥasidic rabbis; abbreviation of Heb. words *Adonenu, Morenu ve-Rabbenu* ("our lord, teacher, and master").

Adonai, Adoshem, see God, Names of.

Adonai, Adonai, El Raḥum Ve-Ḥannun (Heb. "The Lord, the Lord, God, merciful and gracious" – Ex.34:6–7), initial words of Thirteen Attributes of God, recited on several occasions in prayers.

°**Adoni-Bezek,** Canaanite ruler, probably leader of anti-Israelite coalition defeated by Joshua (Jud. 1:1–7).

Adonijah, fourth son of King David by his wife Haggith of Hebron. When David was on his deathbed he attempted to seize the throne. When he wished to marry Abishag, his father's concubine, Solomon took this as a bid for the throne and had him executed.

Adoniram, official of David and Solomon in charge of forced labor. Stoned to death by discontented populace during Rehoboam's reign.

°**Adoni-Zedek,** king of Jerusalem at time of Israelite conquest of Canaan; led coalition in unsuccessful war with Joshua.

Adon Olam (Heb. "Lord of the World"), rhymed liturgical hymn in 12 verses incorporated in Ashkenazi morning service; of medieval origin.

Adorno, Theodor W. (1903–1969), German sociologist; lived in U.S. 1938–56. Wrote *The Authoritarian Personality,* with Nevitt R. Sanford. Combines influences of esthetics, philosophy, sociology.

Adret, Solomon ben Abraham (Rashba; c. 1235–c. 1310), rabbi, *posek* in Barcelona; one of leading figures in Spanish Jewry. Author of novellae and over 1,000 responsa and decisions regarded as authoritative by later codifiers. Wrote legal manual *Torat ha-Bayit.*

Adrianople (Edirne), town in Turkey. Jews fr. Byzantine period. Expanded in Ottoman era through influx of immigrants expelled fr. Hungary, France, and Spain, who established their own communities. 12,000 Jews in 1873, 28,000 before 1914, and only 2,000 in 1943, through wars, impoverishment, and emigration. 250 remained in 1971, with one synagogue.

Adullam, city of Judah. In vicinity were caves where David hid after fleeing fr. Saul. In modern Israel name given to settlement region NW and W. of Hebron Hills.

Aelia Capitolina, name given in 135 C.E. to rebuilt city of Jerusalem after Emperor Hadrian (Aelius Hadrianus) and the god Jupiter Capitolinus.

Aescoly, Aaron Ze'ev (1901–1948), Hebrew writer, historian, ethnologist; settled in Ereẓ Israel 1925. Wrote on David Reuveni and messianic movements and studies on Falashas.

Afam, see Apam.

Afendopolo, Caleb ben Elijah (c. 1464–1525), Karaite scholar, poet; lived nr. Constantinople and later in Belgrade. Wrote on various subjects, incl. philosophy, mathematics, astronomy.

Afghanistan, Muslim state in C. Asia. Medieval sources mention several Jewish centers, with most important at Balkh. Modern community developed in 19th c. as extension of Persian community. 5,000 Jews lived there in 1948; 4,000 emigrated to Israel fr. 1951. Jewish pop. 800 (1971).

Afia, Aaron (16th c.), Sephardi physician, philosopher in Salonika. Wrote treatise on nature of soul.

Afike Jehuda, society for "advancement of study of Judaism and of religious consciousness," founded in Prague 1869. Existed until 1939.

Afikim, kibbutz in C. Jordan Valley, Israel. Founded 1932 by pioneer youth fr. Soviet Russia. Engaged in extensive agriculture, production of plywood, etc. Affiliated to *Iḥud ha-Kevuẓot ve-ha-Kibbutzim.* Pop. 1,350 (1971).

Afikoman (Heb.; etymology uncertain), name of middle of three portions of *mazzah* (unleavened bread) on Passover *seder* plate. Customary for children present to attempt to "steal" it fr. person leading *seder* and receive "ransom" for its return.

"Adloyada" carnival, Tel Aviv 1968

Adrianople Jewish woman in local 16th-cent. costume

Map of Afghanistan showing places of Jewish settlement

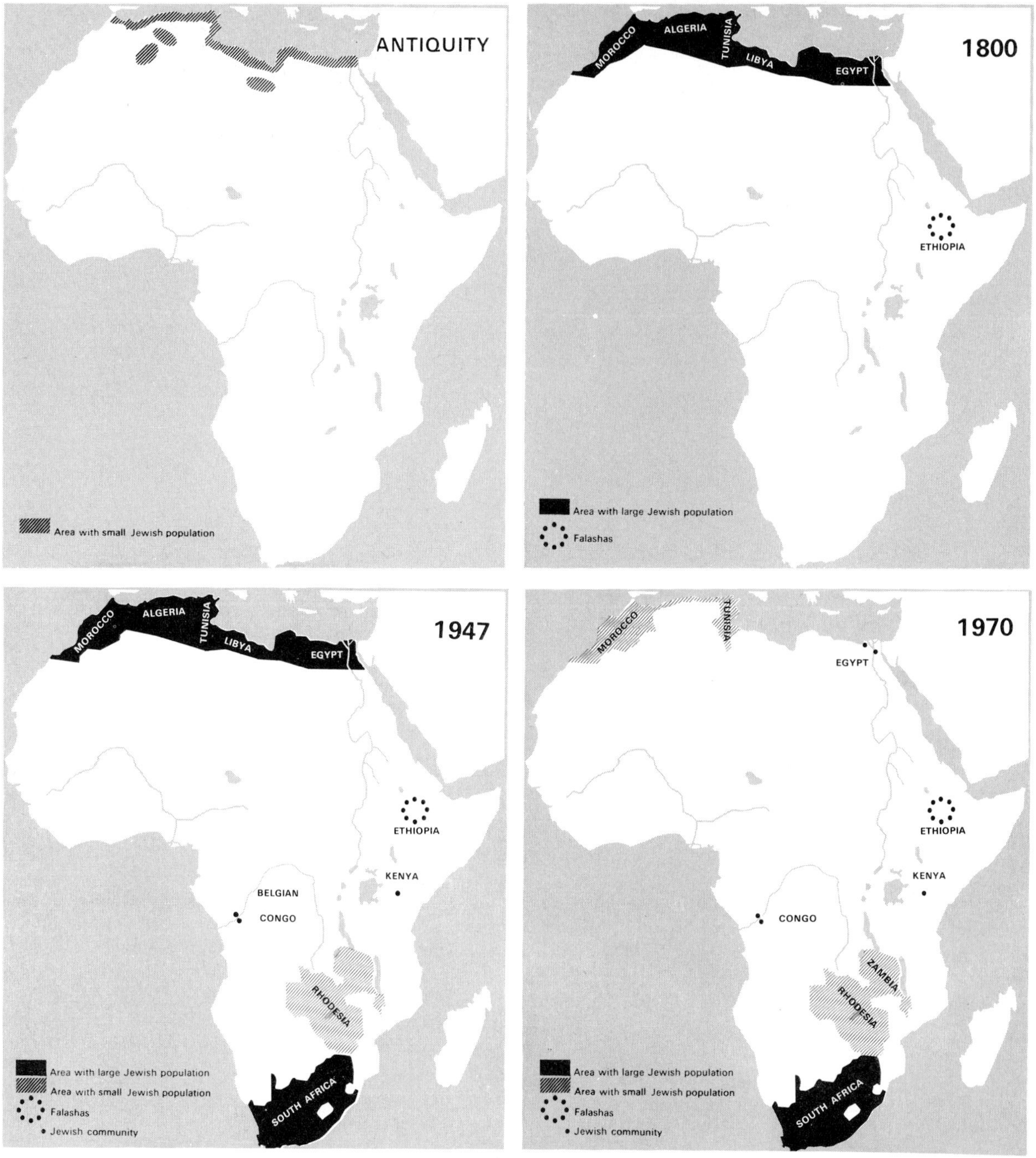

Main concentration of Jewish population on the African continent at different periods.

Africa, see specific countries.

Afternoon Service, see Minḥah.

Afulah, town on crossroads in Jezreel Valley, Israel. Founded 1925 by American Zionist Commonwealth. Developed slowly until 1948; main growth from new immigrants (in Afulah Illit). Site of regional hospital. Pop. 17,200 (1971).

Aga, Benjamin ben Samuel (d. 1824), Karaite communal leader, scholar in Crimea. Minter and treasury agent to last Tatar khan.

Agadir, town in Morocco. Jews settled 16th c., forced to leave 1773. Jewish settlements renewed 1913, community reestablished 1936. Half the Jewish pop. killed in 1960 earthquake. Numbered 1,600 in 1952, 100 in 1969.

°**Agag,** name of Amalekite king captured by Saul, who spared his life, disobeying Samuel's order to annihilate the Amalekites. Agag was thereupon beheaded by Samuel

Agai, Adolf (1836–1916), Hungarian novelist, editor, physician. Edited Hungary's first children's newspaper.

Agam, Yaacov (1928–), Israel painter; pioneer of optic and kinetic art.

Aggadah (Haggadah), those sections of Talmud and Midrash containing homiletic expositions of Bible, stories, legends, folklore, anecdotes, or maxims (in contradistinction to *halakhah,* which deals with legal aspects). Historical *aggadah* includes homiletic additions to stories of Bible as well as old legends preserved among the people. *Aggadah* is found throughout Talmud, intermingling with *halakhah.* It is rich in literary forms, in harmony with its colorful content. No aggadic work edited before 4th c. exists. Midrashim, consisting almost entirely of *aggadah,* were completed about the end of the 10th c. *Aggadah* is primarily creation of Ereẓ Israel Jewry. Modern popular collections in *Sefer Aggadah* by Bialik and Rawnitzki and *Legends of the Jews* by Louis Ginsberg.

Aggadat Bereshit, aggadic Midrash to Book of Genesis; edited c. 10th c.

Aghmati, Zechariah ben Judah (12th–13th c.), talmudist fr. Agmat, S. Morocco. Wrote *Sefer ha-Ner,* on *halakhot* of Alfasi.

Agmon (Bistritski), Nathan (1896–), dramatist, publicist; b. Russia, settled in Ereẓ Israel 1920. Worked in Jewish National Fund. Wrote plays on messianic themes, translated Cervantes.

Agnon (Czaczkes), Shmuel Yosef (1888–1970), Hebrew writer; Nobel Prize for Literature 1966, one of central figures in modern Heb. fiction; b. Buczacz, Galicia, settled in Jerusalem 1909, lived in Germany 1912–23. Works incl. *Agunot, Hakhnasat Kallah (The Bridal Canopy), Temol Shilshom, Ore'aḥ Natah Lalun (A Guest for the Night,), Yamim Nora'im (Days of Awe), Shirah.* His works, mostly set in Galicia or Ereẓ Israel, deal with contemporary spiritual problems. Unique Hebrew style influenced by rabbinic literature.

°**Agobard** (779–840), archbishop of Lyons; known as father of medieval anti-Semitism. Attacked various aspects of Jewish life.

Agorah, ancient coin, now smallest unit in Israel currency, 1/100 of Israel pound.

Agranat, Shimon (1906–), third president of Supreme Court of Israel (appointed 1965); b. Louisville, Kentucky, settled in Ereẓ Israel 1930.

Agrat bat Mahalath, Queen of the Demons in talmudic legend. Some scholars identify her with Lilith.

Agrippa I (10 B.C.E.–44 C.E.), king of Judea; son of Aristobulus, grandson of Herod. Educated at Roman emperor Tiberius' court, and befriended by latter's son Drusus. Appointed by Caligula ruler of some of his ancestral territories, incl. Transjordan (39 C.E.). Rule subsequently extended over Galilee, S. Transjordan, then Judea and Samaria (41 C.E.). Loved by his Jewish subjects for his respect of Jewish religion. Died suddenly while in Caesarea, possibly poisoned by Romans, who feared his popularity.

Agrippa II (28–92 C.E.), last king of Herodian line; son of Agrippa I. Received principality of Chalcis in 50 C.E. Entrusted with supervision of Temple in Jerusalem by Emperor Claudius. Domain extended under Nero at Galilee. Promoted Hellenistic culture and accompanied Titus at siege of Jerusalem. His domains were further extended.

Agro-Joint (American Jewish Joint Agriculture Corporation), organization founded 1924 with full Soviet support to serve as American Jewish Joint Distribution Committee's agent in settling Russian Jews on soil. Operated until 1938, esp. in Crimea and Ukraine.

Agron (Agronsky), Gershon (1894–1959), Israel journalist, Founder (1932) and editor of *Palestine Post* (later *Jerusalem Post*). Mayor of Jerusalem 1955–59.

Agudath Harabbonim, see Union of Orthodox Rabbis of the United States and Canada.

Agudat Israel, world organization of Orthodox Jews; founded 1912 at Kattowitz (Poland) to counter Reform trends and Zionism. Opposed secular use of Hebrew. Revised position after Holocaust, now aiming at "uniting all the people of Israel under the Torah . . . in the Land of Israel." Became political party in Israel 1948, participated in coalition governments 1949–55. Its workers' organization is Po'alei Agudat Israel. See also Knesset.

Aguddat Aḥim (Heb. "The Brotherhood"), assimilationist organization formed in Galicia 1880. Dissolved 1884.

Aguddat ha-Soferim, see Writers' Association in Israel.

Aguddat ha-Sozyalistim ha-Ivrim, first Jewish socialist workers' organization; founded 1876 in London by A.S. Liebermann.

Aguilar, Diego d' (Moses Lopez Pereira; c. 1699–1759), Marrano financier; b. Portugal. Reorganized state tobacco monopoly in Austria, where he settled 1722, reverting to Judaism. Moved to London 1757. His descendants include General **Sir George Charles** (1784–1855), General **Sir Charles Lawrence** (1821–1912), etc.

Aguilar, Grace (1816–1847), English author; of Marrano ancestry. Wrote popular books mostly on Jewish themes, best known being *The Vale of Cedars,* an idealized picture of Marranos in Spain.

Aguilar, Moses Raphael D' (d. 1679), Dutch rabbi, scholar, bibliophile. Rabbi in Brazil for a time fr. 1641.

Agunah (Heb.), woman unable to remarry according to Jewish law because of desertion by her husband or because his death cannot be certified.

Agursky, Samuel (1884–c. 1948), Russian Communist author. Among founders of Yevsektsiya. Disappeared during anti-Jewish purges.

Agur son of Jakeh, compiler of proverbs (Prov. 30); identity otherwise unknown.

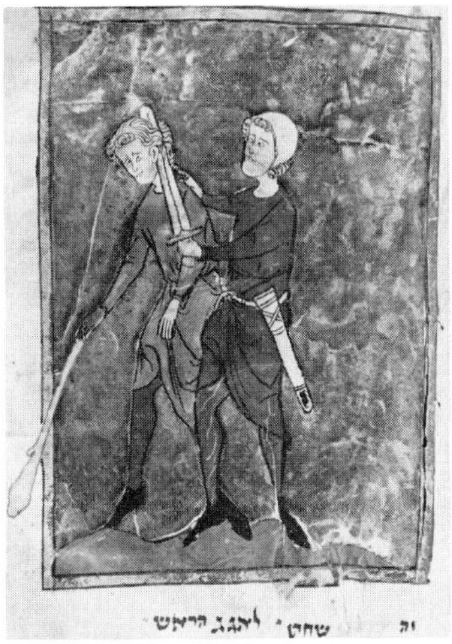

Samuel beheading Agag, fr. 13th-cent. Hebrew ms., France.

Yaacov Agam

Shmuel Yosef Agnon

Gershon Agron

Agus, Irving Abraham (1910–), U.S. educator, scholar (*Rabbi Meir of Rothenburg,* etc.). Prof. of Jewish history at Yeshiva Univ. His brother **Jacob Bernard** (1911–), U.S. rabbi, philosopher *(Modern Philosophies of Judaism, Meaning of Jewish History).*

Aḥa, (4th c.), Palestinian *amora;* b. Lydda. Studied under Joseph b. Ḥanina and Tanḥum b. Ḥiyya. Extensively quoted in Jerusalem Talmud.

Ahab, son of Omri and king of Israel c. 874–852 B.C.E. Baal worship introduced by his wife Jezebel led to fierce struggle between royal house and prophets headed by Elijah. Ambitious foreign policy helped bring economic prosperity at home. Killed while fighting Damascus in alliance with Jehoshaphat of Judah.

Aḥa bar Ḥanina (4th c.), Palestinian teacher. Quoted in Babylonian Talmud.

Aḥa ben Jacob (5th c.), Babylonian *amora;* disciple of Huna. Miracles attributed to him and story told of his exorcising a demon.

Aḥad ha-Am (Asher Ginsberg; 1856–1927), Hebrew essayist, thinker, leader of Ḥibbat Zion movement; b. Ukraine, in Odessa fr. 1884 and led Benei Moshe society. Published *Lo Zeh ha-Derekh* (1889), vigorous critique of Ḥovevei Zion policy. Fr. 1896 edited *Ha-Shiloaḥ.* Lived in London fr. 1907 and settled in Tel Aviv 1922. One of most influential of modern Jewish thinkers, he expounded his views, in favor of "cultural" rather than "political" Zionism, in his collected essays, *Al Parashat Derakhim,* etc. Wrote many works on Judaism, its thought and philosophy.

Aḥad ha-Am

Aḥai ben Josiah (2nd c.), Babylonian halakhist. Established academy at Ḥuzal (Babylonia), "the School of Aḥai."

Aḥa (Aḥai) of Shabḥa (680–752), Babylonian scholar of Pumbedita academy; settled in Ereẓ Israel c. 750. Author of *Sheiltot* ("Questions"), compilation of halakhic and aggadic material and first post-talmudic work to be attributed to its author.

Aharoni, Israel (1882–1946), Ereẓ Israel naturalist, zoologist; b. Lithuania, settled in Jerusalem 1904. Pioneer in study of Israel fauna.

Aharoni, Yohanan (1919–), Israel archaeologist, author (*The Land of the Bible, The Macmillan Bible Atlas,* etc.). Excavated at Arad, Ramat Raḥel, Beersheba, etc. Prof. of archaeology at Tel Aviv Univ.

Aḥaronim (Heb.), later rabbinic

Esther before Ahasuerus, fr. 13th-cent. Hebrew ms., France.

authorities (in contrast to early authorities, *rishonim*).

Aharonovitch, Yosef (1877–1937), writer, Ereẓ Israel labor leader; b. Ukraine. Editor of *Ha-Po'el ha-Ẓair* and a leader of labor party of that name.

Ahasuerus, king of Persia who married Esther. Figures in Book of Esther.

Ahasuerus, see Wandering Jew.

Ahavah Rabbah (Heb. "Great love"), initial words of ancient prayer preceding *Shema* in morning service. Corresponding prayer in evening service begins *Ahavat Olam* ("Everlasting love").

Ahaz, king of Judah 743–727 B.C.E. Under him Judah became Assyrian vassal, subjected by Ahaz to Canaanite idolatry.

Ahaziah. (1) King of Israel c. 853–852 B.C.E.; son of Ahab and Jezebel. Permitted his mother to maintain her Baal worship. (2) King of Judah 842–841 B.C.E. Followed his mother Athaliah in cult matters. Killed by Jehu.

Aḥdut ha-Avodah, Zionist Socialist Labor Party in Ereẓ Israel; founded 1919. Merged with Ha-Po'el ha-Ẓa'ir 1930 to form Mifleget Po'alei Ereẓ Israel (Mapai).

Aḥdut ha-Avodah-Po'alei Zion, Zionist Socialist Party. Originated as "Faction B" (Si'ah Bet) which seceded fr. Mapai 1944, adopting historical name of original Aḥdut ha-Avodah. United 1945 with left-wing Po'alei Zion. Merged 1948 with Ha-Shomer ha-Ẓa'ir to form Mapam. Resumed independence 1954. Membership 42,000 (1967). Merged 1968 with Mapai and Rafi to form Israel Labor Party. See also Knesset.

Aḥer, see Elisha ben Avuyah.

Ahijah, son of Ahitub, priest of house of Eli. Apparently chief priest in Shiloh during reign of Saul.

Ahijah the Shilonite, Israelite prophet under Solomon and his successors. Foretold split in kingdom (I Kings 11:29–39).

Ahikam, son of Shaphan and father of Gedaliah; one of men sent by King Josiah to prophetess Huldah (II Kings 22:12, 14).

Ahikar, Book of, folk work incorporating wisdom aphorisms, widespread in Aramaic-speaking lands during Assyrian rule. Ahikar the Wise, the hero of the work, mentioned in apocryphal book of Tobit as one of exiles of Ten Tribes.

Ahimaaz. (1) Father-in-law of King Saul. (2) Son of priest Zadok, who informed David of defeat of Absalom. (3) Son-in-law of Solomon.

Ahimaaz ben Paltiel (b. 1017), chronicler, poet of Capua, Italy. Composed *Megillat Aḥima'aẓ,* chronicle describing in rhymed prose genealogy of poet's family fr. 9th c. on. Important Jewish historical source.

Aḥimeir, Abba (A.S. Heisinovitch; 1898–1962), Belorussian-born journalist, writer; Revisionist leader in Ereẓ Israel. In 1933 accused of plotting murder of Chaim Arlosoroff but cleared.

Ahimelech. (1) Son of Ahitub, high priest in Nob; put to death by Saul for assisting David. (2) Son of Abiathar; probably grandson of (1). Priest in time of David. (3) Ahimelech the Hittite, one of David's warriors.

Ahithophel the Gilonite, adviser of King David; committed suicide when his advice to Absalom was overruled (II Sam. 15–17).

Ahitub, son of Phinehas, the son of Eli; priest during reign of Saul. Father of Ahimelech and Ahijah.

Ahitub ben Isaac (late 13th c.), rabbi, physician in Palermo. Author of allegorical poem *Maḥberet ha-Tene.* Translated Maimonides' *Treatise on Logic* into Heb.

Ahlem, village nr. Hanover, Germany. Site of first Jewish horticultural school in Germany (founded 1893).

Aḥot Ketannah (Heb. "Little Sister"), name of hymn for Rosh ha–Shanah composed by Abraham Ḥazzan Gerondi (13th c.) in S. France.

Ai, ancient town N. of Jerusalem, near Beth-El. Destroyed by Joshua (Josh. 7ff.). Often identified with present et-Tell, near Deir Dibwan (excavated 1933–35, 1964).

Aijalon, valley and ancient town situated in valley at foot of Judean

Hills. Scene of miracle when sun stood still to enable Joshua to complete his victory over Amorites (Josh. 10). Fort built there by Crusaders, at Latrun. Scene of fighting in 1917, 1948 War of Independence. Area occupied by Israel 1967.

Aikhenvald, Yuli Isayevich (1872–1928), Russian literary critic, essayist (*Pushkin, Studies of Western Writers,* etc.). Expelled fr. Russia 1922.

Aimée, Anouk (Françoise Dreyfus; 1932–), French movie actress (*La Dolce Vita, A Man and A Woman,* etc.).

Ai T'ien (b. c. 1545), Chinese Jew fr. Kaifeng. Through him West came to know existence of China's Kaifeng Jews.

Aix-en-Provence, town in S. France. Jews there fr. 5th c. Formed large community in 13th c., destroyed in 1501 riots. Reformed in 18th c. Almost all Jews (over 2,000, incl. refugees) arrested and deported to Germany May 1943. Jewish pop. 1,000 (1967), mostly recent arrivals fr. N. Africa.

Aix-la-Chapelle, see Aachen.

Aizman, David Yakolevich (1869–1922), Russian writer. Popular in his day. Wrote much about Jewish poor.

Akademie fuer die Wissenschaft des Judentums, academy founded 1919 in Berlin for furtherance of Jewish scholarship, under guidance of Franz Rosenzweig and Hermann Cohen. Closed 1934.

Akavya, Avraham Aryeh Leib (1882–1964), Hebrew, Yiddish writer, editor; b. Poland, settled in Ereẓ Israel 1935.

Akavyah ben Mahalalel (1st c.), *tanna,* member of Sanhedrin. Saying: "Reflect upon three things and you will not come within the power of sin; know whence you came, whither you are going, and before whom you are destined to give account" (*Avot* 3:1).

Akdamut Millin, opening words of Aramaic poem by Meir b. Isaac Nehorai generally recited before reading of Torah on first day of Shavuot.

Akedah (Heb. "binding," i.e., of Isaac), biblical account describing God's command to Abraham to offer Isaac, the son of his old age, as a sacrifice. Divine intervention prevented consummation at last minute. Abraham's willingness to make this sacrifice was regarded in Jewish tradition as supreme example of readiness to submit to will of God.

Akiva (c. 50–135), outstanding *tanna,* patriot, martyr. Had decisive influence on development of *halakhah.* Began education at age 40, with aid of his wife Rachel, who left her wealthy father and went with him. Developed original method of biblical exegesis. Arranged Oral Law according to subjects, which was basis for Mishnah. Enthusiastic supporter of Bar Kokhba, whom he hailed as king-messiah. Arrested as rebel by Romans (for teaching the Law), tortured and executed at Caesarea.

"Abraham's Sacrifice," etching by Rembrandt van Rijn (see Akedah).

Akiva Baer ben Joseph (17th c.), talmudist, kabbalist in Bohemia and Bavaria. Wrote kabbalistic commentary on daily prayers. His books of legends in Yiddish were popular.

Akkad, city and country in N. Babylonia. City flourished c. 3380–3200 B.C.E. but exact location unknown. Even after destruction of city, name of country survived into later periods, designating central axis of Sumero-Akkadian political hegemony. Fr. 1500–1000 B.C.E., used as virtual synonym for Babylonia. In Bible, one of capital cities of Nimrod (Gen. 10:8–12).

Akkadian, originally Semitic speech of Mesopotamia as distinguished fr. Sumerian; in modern terminology a collective term for all East Semitic dialects of Mesopotamia. Various forms of Akkadian in 2nd millennium B.C.E. for purposes of official correspondence in Syria and Palestine (e.g., Tell el-Amarna letters). Hundreds of Akkadian words entered Hebrew language. It closely resembles Hebrew (and Aramaic) in morphology and phonology.

Akko, see Acre.

Akkum (Heb. abbr. for "worship of stars and planets"), idolators.

Aklar, Mordecai ben Raphael (1856–1936), rabbi; b. Meshed, member of Persian *anusim* community, emigrated to Ereẓ Israel 1927. Translated liturgical works into Judeo-Persian.

Aknin, Joseph ben Judah ben Jacob ibn (c. 1150–1220), philosopher, poet; b. Barcelona, Spain, later lived in Fez. Works include introduction to Talmud, an ethical compilation, commentaries on *Avot* and Song of Songs.

Akrish, Isaac ben Abraham (b. 1530), talmudic scholar, traveler, publisher; of Spanish origin, lived in Naples, Constantinople, Egypt.

Akron, city in Ohio, U.S. Jews settled 1842. Reform congregation established 1864, Orthodox 1885. Jewish pop. 6,500 (1971).

Aktion (Ger.), expulsion fr. ghettos and other concentration points by Nazis during Holocaust.

Akzin, Benjamin (1904–), constitutional lawyer, political scientist; b. Riga, lived in U.S. (active in Revisionist movement), went to Israel 1949. Israel Prize 1967. Academic Head, Haifa Univ. College 1969–72.

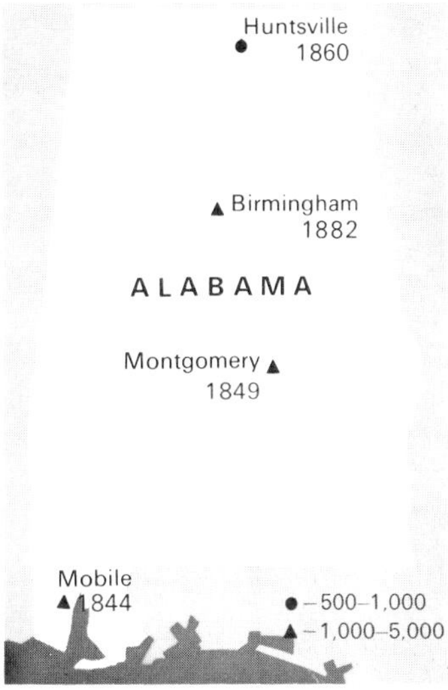

Jewish communities in Alabama and dates of establishment.

Alabama, U.S. state. Jewish traders active fr. 1757. First congregation in Mobile in 1820s. Jewish pop. 9,140 (1971), mostly in Birmingham, Mobile, Montgomery.

Alalakh (Tell-el Atchana), ancient city in Turkey, S. of Lake Antiochia. Archaeological finds by Woolley 1937–39, 1946–49, illuminate development bet. 18th–15th c. B.C.E. Finds include 450 clay tablets written in Akkadian throwing light on pre-Israelite Ereẓ Israel and on Ancient Near Eastern origin of Israel's institutions, spiritual culture.

Alamani, Aaron he-Ḥaver ben Yeshu'ah (12th c.), poet, rabbinical judge, physician; lived in Alexandria, Egypt. Judah Halevi stayed at his house.

Alami, Solomon (c. 1370–1420), Spanish moralist; in Portugal fr. 1391. Wrote *Iggeret ha-Musar* criticizing various classes of Spanish Jewry.

Alashkar, Moses ben Isaac (1466–1542), talmudist, liturgical poet; b. Spain, lived in Tunisia, Greece, Egypt, Jerusalem. Wrote "*Be-Mah Akaddem,*" poem on experiences as refugee fr. Spain.

Alaska, U.S. state. First permanent Jewish settler c. 1885. E. Gruening governor 1939–53, senator 1958–68. Jewish pop. 300 (1971), mostly in Fairbanks and Anchorage.

Alatino, Moses Amram (d. 1605), physician, translator; lived in Spoleto, Ferrara, Venice. His son **Azriel Pethahiah (Bonaiuto),** physician, defender of Judaism in public disputations.

Alatri, Samuel (1805–1889), Italian politician, communal leader. President of Rome Jewish community, director of papal bank, member of Italian parliament.

Alba Iulia (Karlsburg), city in Transylvania. First Jews there were Sephardim. Community 100 in 1700, 1,558 in 1930. Relatively unharmed in WWII. 2,070 in 1947. Most emigrated later.

Albalag, Isaac (13th c.), philosopher; probably lived in Catalonia. Translated into Heb. al-Ghazālī's *Maqāsid al-Falāsifa* ("Intentions of the Philosophers"), to which he added original notes.

Albalia, Baruch ben Isaac (1077–1126), judge; succeeded Isaac Alfasi as yeshivah head in Cordoba, Spain. His father, **Isaac** (1035–1094), astronomer, talmudist.

Albania, Balkan state. Jewish exiles fr. Spain settled in 16th c. in seaports (Durazzo, Valona, etc.). 204 Jews in 1930; refugees arrived 1939; 400 sent to Bergen-Belsen 1944. 300 Jews in 1973.

Albany, city in N.Y., U.S. First Jews recorded 17th c. First congregation (Bavarian Jews) 1830s. Isaac Mayer Wise first rabbi 1846. Jewish pop. 13,500 (1971).

Al-Bargeloni, Isaac ben Reuben (b. 1043), Spanish talmudist, liturgical poet. His *azharot* incorporated in N. African rites.

Al-Bargeloni, Judah, see Judah ben Barzilai al-Bargeloni.

Al-Bazak, Maẓli'aḥ ben Elijah ibn (11th c.), *dayyan* in Sicily. Pupil of Hai Gaon and teacher of Nathan b. Jehiel.

Albeck, Ḥanokh (1890–1972), talmudic scholar; b. Poland, settled in Ereẓ Israel 1936. Prof. at Heb. Univ. Author of commentary on Mishnah, critical editions of rabbinic works, midrashic studies. His father, **Shalom** (1858–1920), Polish talmudic, rabbinic scholar.

Albelda, Moses ben Jacob (1500–bef. 1583), rabbi, philosopher; lived in Greece, Albania. His commentaries and biblical expositions are mainly philosophical.

Albert, Calvin (1918–), U.S. sculptor, draftsman; known for his metal figures. Decorated several synagogues.

Alberta, province in Canada. Prospector Silverman came 1869 in search of gold. Diamond brothers first permanent Jewish settlers 1888–91 and founded communal institutions. Jewish pop. 6,500 (1971), mostly in Edmonton, Calgary.

"House of Jacob" synagogue, Calgary, Alberta

Albo, Joseph (15th c.), philosopher in Castile, Spain. His *Sefer ha-Ikkarim* ("Book of Principles") is one of main works of medieval Jewish philosophy, basing Judaism on three primary principles – divine existence, divine revelation, and reward and punishment. Took prominent part in Disputation of Tortosa.

Albotini, Judah ben Moses (d. 1519), kabbalist, commentator on Maimonides (*Yesod Mishneh Torah*). Headed Jerusalem yeshivah.

°**Albright, William Foxwell** (1891–1971), U.S. biblical archaeologist, scholar. Directed American School of Oriental Research, Jerusalem, 1920–29, 1933–36, fr. 1929 prof. of Semitic languages at Johns Hopkins Univ. Main excavations at Tell Beit Mirsim, Gibeath-Shaul, Beth-El, Petra, etc. Wrote *From the Stone Age to Christianity, The Archaeology of Palestine,* etc.

Albu, Sir George (1857–1935), S. African mining magnate, financier. Prominent in Kimberley and in Johannesburg goldfields.

Albu, Isidor (1837–1903), German physician, public health specialist. Wrote *Leçons d'Hygiene,* widely used handbook.

Alcalay, Isaac (1882–), rabbi. Chief rabbi of Serbia 1909, Yugoslavia 1924. Senator in Yugoslav parliament 1930–38. Settled in U.S. 1942. Chief rabbi of Central Sephardic Jewish Community of America.

Alcimus (Heb. **Eliakim**), high priest during Maccabean revolt (162–160 or 159 B.C.E.); opposed Judah Maccabee and ruled with Syrian help.

Aldabi, Meir ben Isaac (c. 1310–c. 1360), religious philosopher, with leanings toward Kabbalah; lived in Toledo, Jerusalem; grandson of Asher b. Jehiel.

Aldanov (Landau), Mark (1889–1957), Russian novelist; in France fr. 1919. Wrote biographies, historical novels (*The Tenth Symphony, The Fifth Seal,* etc.).

Aldrophe, Alfred-Philibert (1824–1895), French architect. Designed synagogues at Rue de la Victoire (Paris) and Versailles.

Alechinsky, Pierre (1927–), Belgian painter. Leader of Cobra group which fostered spontaneity and opposed social realism.

Alef, (**א**), 1st letter of Hebrew alphabet; numerical value 1.

Aleinu le-Shabbe'aḥ (Heb. "It is our duty to praise"), ancient prayer recited at the conclusion of synagogue service; proclaiming unity and sovereignty of God. In Middle Ages, censored by Christians as containing implied insult to Christianity.

Aleksandrow (Danziger), influential dynasty of ḥasidic rabbis living nr. Lodz, Poland, active fr. c. 1750. After WWII in Bene-Berak, Israel.

Alemán, Mateo (1547–c. 1615), novelist of "New Christian" descent; lived in Salamanca, Alcala; d. Mexico.

Decorative initial letter "alef," fr. German "Haggadah," c. 1450.

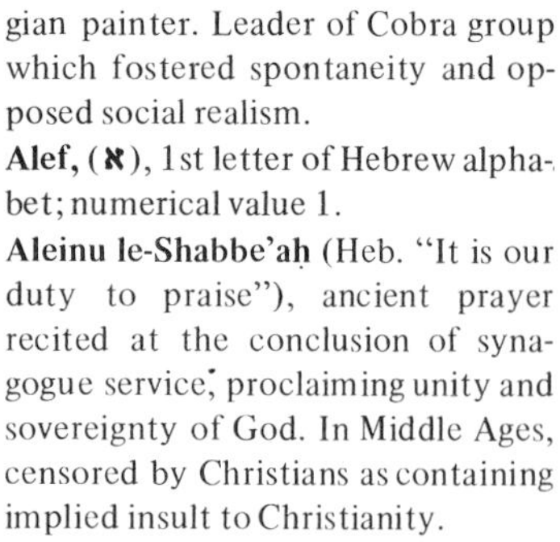

Aleppo (Heb. Aram-Zoba, Arab. Ḥalab), city in N. Syria. Jews there fr. Roman times. Community closely connected with Ereẓ Israel. 5,000 Jews in 1170. Jews fr. Spain settled after 1492 expulsion. 10,000 Jews before 1947 anti-Jewish riots; 1,000 in 1971 after emigration to Turkey. Israel, Europe, America. In 1960s lived under constant duress. Of many synagogues, oldest Mustaribah destroyed 1947; contained famous 10th c. Aleppo Bible codex, now in Israel.

Alexander (d. 49 B.C.E.), son of Aristobulus II, one of last Hasmoneans. Executed in Antiochia by order of Pompey.

Alexander (c. 36–7 B.C.E.), son of Herod and Mariamne. Executed at Sebaste (Samaria), with his brother Aristobulus, on his father's orders on charges of treachery.

Alexander, Abraham (Senior; 1743–1816), American Revolutionary War officer; *ḥazzan* of Charleston's Beth Elohim Congregation.

Alexander, Alexander (d.c. 1807), pioneer of Hebrew press in London. His son **Levy** (d. 1834?), also a printer.

Alexander, Bernard (1872–1935), S. African lawyer, communal worker. President of S. African Board of Deputies 1916–27.

Alexander, Franz (1891–1964), psychoanalyst, criminologist, author (*The Criminal, The Judge and the Public, Psychosomatic Specificity,* etc.); b. Budapest, in U.S. fr. 1931.

Alexander, Haim (1915–), Berlin-born Israel composer (*Six Israeli Dances, Lema'an Ẓiyyon, Jerusalem Eternal,* etc.).

Alexander, Michael Solomon (1799–1845), first Anglican bishop in Jerusalem. Brought up as orthodox Jew; *ḥazzan-shoḥet* in English communities. Converted to Christianity 1825. Engaged in missionary activities.

Alexander, Morris (1877–1946), S. African lawyer, politician, active Zionist. Member of S. African parliament fr. 1908; championed Indian and Colored communities against discriminatory laws.

Alexander, Moses (1853–1932), Idaho Democratic governor 1915–19; first Jewish governor of U.S. state. Town of Alexander, Idaho, named for him.

Alexander, Muriel (1885–), S. African actress, producer. Founded Johannesburg Repertory Players, later renamed The Alexander.

Alexander, Samuel (1859–1938), British philosopher (*Space, Time and Deity, Spinoza and Time,* etc.); b. Australia. Taught at Manchester Univ. Order of Merit 1930.

Alexander Lysimachus, leader of Jewish community in Alexandria, Egypt, 1st c. C.E.; brother of Philo.

Alexander Suslin ha-Kohen of Frankfort (d. 1349), talmudic scholar; b. Erfurt, Germany, where he died a martyr's death. Especially famed for his *Aguddah,* collection of halakhic decisions.

Alexander Susskind ben Moses of Grodno (d. 1793), kabbalist in Lithuania. Wrote *Yesod ve-Shoresh ha-Avodah,* a book of ethics.

Alexander the Great paying homage to the High Priest, 13th cent. illuminated Latin Bible

°**Alexander the Great** (356–323 B.C.E.), king of Macedonia. Extensively mentioned in talmudic, midrashic, medieval Jewish legends; passed through Ereẓ Israel but his visit to Jerusalem, although described by Josephus, never took place.

Alexander Yannai, see Yannai, Alexander.

Alexandra (d. 28 B.C.E.), daughter of Hyrcanus II; wife of Alexander, the son of Aristobulus II; mother of Herod's wife, Mariamne. Thinking that Herod was dying, she attempted to seize power, but Herod had her executed.

Alexandra Salome, see Salome Alexandra.

Alexandretta, see Iskenderun.

Alexandria, Egyptian port; the great center of the Jewish diaspora in classical times. Jews present fr. 3rd c. B.C.E. Under Roman rule autonomous community's quest for citizenship opposed by Alexandrians. Anti-Jewish riots broke out 38 C.E., Jewish disturbances 66, following Jewish revolt in Judea crushed by Tiberius Julius Alexander. In 115–117 C.E., with widespread Jewish uprising in Roman Empire, community further undermined, great synagogue burnt down. Jews expelled 414, owing to Christian preaching; reformed with Arab conquest fr. 642. In ancient Alexandria, Greek-speaking Jews created their version of Hellenistic culture, which found expression in the Septuagint, Philo, Ezekiel the playwright, etc. They also played important economic role. Jewish pop. 24,690 in 1937, 2,760 in 1960. Jews persecuted, abused after Israel 1948 War of Independence and Nasser's accession to power. Very few remained by 1970s.

Alfandari, Ḥayyim ben Isaac Raphael (c. 1660–1733), kabbalist, rabbi, Shabbatean; lived in Turkey and Jerusalem, where he headed the community; d. Constantinople.

Alfandari, Solomon Eliezer ben Jacob (1826–1930), rabbinic authority; b. Constantinople. Chief rabbi of Damascus and then of Safed 1904–18; d. Jerusalem.

Alfasi, David ben Abraham (10th c.), Karaite grammarian, commentator fr. Fez, Morocco. Composed Hebrew-Arabic Bible lexicon, one of earliest and most important in Heb. philology.

Alfasi, Isaac ben Jacob (Rif; 1013–1103), major talmudic scholar; b. nr. Constantine, Algeria, lived, taught at Fez, Morocco, until 1088 when he went to Spain and founded a yeshivah at Lucena which pioneered talmudic studies in Spain. His *Sefer Halakhot,* dealing with 24 tractates of the Talmud, the most important code prior to Maimonides' *Mishneh Torah.* Had many disciples and his responsa were authoritative.

Al-Fataḥ, see Fataḥ, al-.

Alfes (Alfas), Benzion (1850–1940), Yiddish, Hebrew writer; b. Vilna, settled in Ereẓ Israel 1924. His popular *Ma'aseh Alfes* consisted of moralistic love stories.

°**Alfonso de Espina** (15th c.), Franciscan friar, principal initiator and ideologist of Spanish Inquisition. Wrote *Fortalitium Fidei,* venomous anti-Jewish pamphlet. Possibly of Jewish descent.

Algazi, Isaac ben Solomon (1882–1964), Sephardi *ḥazzan,* composer; b. Izmir, settled in Uruguay c. 1935.

Algazi, Israel Jacob ben Yom Tov (1680–1756), halakhic scholar, kabbalist (*Emet le-Ya'akov,* etc.); probably b. Smyrna, lived in Safed.

Algazi, Leon (Yehudah; 1890–1971), Rumanian-born conductor, composer; collector of Jewish music, especially Sephardi folkmusic, in Paris.

Algazi, (Nissim) Solomon ben Abraham (c. 1610–c. 1683), rabbi; b. Turkey, settled in Jerusalem 1635, in Smyrna fr. 1646. Opposed and excommunicated Shabbetai Ẓevi.

Algazi, Solomon ben Abraham (1673–1762), rabbi, halakhist; half brother of Ḥayyim b. Moses Abulafia. Chief rabbi of Egypt c. 1740.

Algazi, Yom Tov ben Israel Jacob (1727–1802), kabbalist, halakhist, *rishon le-Zion* in Jerusalem. Traveled extensively in Europe as emissary.

Algeria, country in N. Africa. Presence of Jews attested under the Romans. Judeo-Berber tribe under a queen (al-Kahina) resisted 7th c. Arab invasions. Oriental Jews settled in urban centers. Jewish pop. diminished 12th–14th c. except for merchants connected with Spain and S. France. Few Spanish exiles came after 1492; descendants of Marranos and Jews came fr. Leghorn, Italy, in 17th–18th c. Under Turkish domination, deys chose counselors and financiers fr. upper-class Jews; otherwise Jews fared badly. French conquest 1830 found 30,000 Jews in Algeria. Grant of French citizenship to Algerian Jews by 1870 Crémieux Decree followed by anti-Semitic campaigns, worsened by Dreyfus affair. Agitation subsided until 1934 massacre in Constantine. During WWII Crémieux Decree abrogated and 117,000 Algerian Jews discriminated against by Vichy regime. Jewish underground movement assisted Allied liberation forces in 1942. Full equality reinstated after WWII. Jewish community caught between Algerian nationalist (F.L.N.) postwar independence struggle and French settlers counter-terror through O.A.S. With independence 130,000 Jews emigrated, great majority to France, others to Israel. By 1971, 1,500 remained.

Places of Jewish settlement in Algeria

Algiers, capital of Algeria. Jews settled in Middle Ages, number increased in 12th–15th c. In 16th c. town came under Turkish rule, many prominent Jewish families lived there. In 1870 they became French citizens, but were deeply affected by nationalist struggle for independence. Jewish pop. declined and increased according to economic and political situation; 95% of 34,000 Jews left after independence in 1962. By 1971 their number was reduced to a few hundred.

Alguades, Meir (d. 1410), court physician, chief rabbi and chief justice in Castile. Patron of Jewish learning.

Al-Ḥamma, see Hammat Gader.

Al ha-Nissim (Heb. "For the miracles"), opening words of thanksgiving prayer inserted in penultimate benediction of *Amidah* and in Grace after Meals on Ḥanukkah and Purim.

Al-Ḥarizi, Judah ben Solomon (1170–1235), Hebrew medieval poet, translator; b. Spain, traveled widely through Mediterranean. Translated fr. Arabic into Heb. the rhymed-prose maqamat of the Arabic poet al-Ḥariri, which also inspired al-Ḥarizi's *Taḥkemoni*, consisting of 50 rhymed prose narratives incl. fables, proverbs, satires, etc.

"Al ha-Nissim," fr. Italian manuscript, c. 1470.

Alḥayk, Uzziel ben Mordecai (c. 1740–c. 1820), rabbi in Tunis. Responsa important source of Tunisian Jewish history.

Al Ḥet (Heb. "'For the sin"), opening words of alphabetic confession of sins recited by congregation on Day of Atonement.

Aliger, Margarita Yosifovna (1915–), Soviet Russian poet. Early poetry dealt with conventional Soviet themes; later were more personal. Credited with poem bitterly condemning Soviet persecution of Jews.

Ali ibn Sahl ibn Rabbān al-Tabarī (9th c.), physician in Iraq, Iran. His medical writings introduced Indian medical lore to Arab readers. Became Muslim.

Aliturus (Alityros) (1st c.), Roman actor, a favorite of Nero.

Aliyah (Heb. "ascent"). (1) A "calling up" (*Aliyah le-Torah*) to read Scroll of Law in synagogue during worship. (2) Immigration of Jews to Israel. Five main immigration waves took place in modern period of Zionist resettlement. Independent Israel removed all restrictions on *aliyah.* Law of Return (1950) guaranteed every Jew the right to come as *oleh,* (immigrant) unless he constituted a danger to public health or security, and to become a citizen immediately on arrival. Mass immigration (*kibbuẓ galuyyot*) brought in over a million and a quarter in Israel's first two

Three 19th-cent. etchings of Jews of Algiers

"The Market in the Shtetl" by Joseph Budko, 1930.

"Russian Village" by Marc Chagall, c. 1957.

"Arab with Flower" by Pinḥas Litvinovsky, 1925—30.

"The High Commissioner" by Arieh Aroch.

Painting by Lea Nikel, 1965.

decades, mainly fr. E. and C. Europe, N. Africa, and Middle East.

Aliyah Bet, see "Illegal" immigration.

Aljama (fr. Arab. **al-Jamā'a**), self-governing Jewish or Moorish community in medieval Spain; also, a quarter inhabited by Jews or Moors.

Alkabez, Solomon ben Moses ha-Levi (c. 1505–1584), Hebrew poet, kabbalist; lived in Adrianople and Safed. Composer of Sabbath hymn *"Lekhah Dodi."*

Alkalai, Abraham ben Samuel (c. 1750–1811), Bulgarian rabbi, codifier; later settled in Safed. Wrote alphabetical arrangement of laws of *Shulḥan Arukh.*

Alkalai, David (1862–1933), founder and leader of Zionist movement in Serbia and Yugoslavia; delegate to First Zionist Congress.

Alkalai, Judah ben Solomon Ḥai (1798–1878), Sephardi rabbi and proto-Zionist; settled in Jerusalem 1874. In his writings preached return to Zion within framework of religious thought (*Darkhei No'am, Shelom Yerushalayim,* etc.).

Alkan, Charles Henri-Valentin (1813–1888), French pianist, composer. Wrote almost exclusively for piano. Killed when reaching for volume of Talmud and bookcase fell on him.

Allemanno, Johanan ben Isaac (c. 1435–c. 1504), philosopher, biblical exegete; lived in Florence and other Italian cities. Main work *Ḥai ha-Olamim* deals with how man may attain eternal life and rise to communion with God.

Allen, Woody (1936–), U.S. comedian, actor, playwright, film writer (*What's New Pussycat?*).

°**Allenby, Edmund Henry Hynman, Viscount** (1861–1936), British soldier. Headed forces which defeated Turks in Ereẓ Israel in WWI 1917–8. Captured Jerusalem Dec. 9, 1917, and entered city on foot. Attended opening of Heb. Univ. 1925.

Allgemeine Zeitung des Judentums, German-Jewish journal; founded by Ludwig Philippson, published in Leipzig and Berlin 1837–1922. One of first modern Jewish periodicals in C. Europe; fought for Jewish emancipation, moderate religious reform, and closer relations with non-Jews. With rise of Zionism, it declined in influence.

Alliance Israélite Universelle, first modern international Jewish organization; founded 1860 in Paris to defend Jewish civil and religious liberties. Established a French-inspired educational network in

MODERN ALIYYOT TO EREẒ ISRAEL

ALIYAH	PERIOD	NUMBER OF IMMIGRANTS
First Aliyah	1882–1903	25,000
Second Aliyah	1904–1914	40,000
Third Aliyah	1919–1923	35,000
Fourth Aliyah	1924–1928	90,000
Fifth Aliyah	1929–1939	225,000
	1939–1948	130,000
	1948–1972	1,433,719

Judah Alkalai

Allenby in Jerusalem, 1918

Yigal Allon

various lands of Balkans, Asia, N. Africa, and Middle East (pioneer agricultural school in Ereẓ Israel at Mikveh Israel). In 1968, 21,000 pupils in 64 schools and major impact on educational level of Jews in Arab lands. Its influence declined after WWII. Among its presidents: A. Crémieux, N. Leven, René Cassin.

Allianz, Israelitische, zu Wien, Jewish society in Vienna; originally founded 1873 to operate as branch of Alliance Israélite Universelle in Paris, with similar aims. Liquidated 1938 after Nazi *Anschluss.*

Allon, Gedalya (1901–1950), Russian-born Jewish historian; settled in Ereẓ Israel 1924. Taught Talmud, Jewish history at Heb. Univ. Wrote standard works on Ereẓ Israel in mishnaic-talmudic period.

Allon, Yigal (1918–), Israel statesman, military commander; b. Kefar Tavor, Lower Galilee. Palmaḥ commander 1945–48. As commander of S. front in War of Independence, drove Arab armies from Negev, Eilat, and part of Sinai. A leader of Aḥdut ha-Avodah; elected to Knesset 1954. Minister of labor 1961–68. Fr. 1968 deputy prime minister and also minister of education and culture; foreign minister fr. 1974.

Allonei Yiẓḥak, youth village in C. Israel, nr. Binyaminah. Founded 1948 within framework of Youth Aliyah; also courses for American high school students.

Allouche, Felix Nissim S'Aidou (1910–), Tunisian editor, Zionist. Founded Jewish weekly *Le Reveil Juif* 1924 and Zionist weekly *La Vie Juive.* Editor *Tunis Soir* 1934, which took militant Zionist line. In Israel fr. 1956.

Al-Madari, Judah ha-Kohen ben Eleazar he-Ḥasid (13th–14th c.), talmudic scholar in Aleppo who wrote commentary on code of Isaac Alfasi.

Almagià, Roberto (1884–1962), Italian geographer, historian of cartography (*Il mondo attuale, L'Italia,* etc.). Prof. in Rome.

Alman, Samuel (1877–1947), Russian-born composer of synagogue and secular music; settled in England 1903. Choirmaster at Hampstead synagogue.

Al-Mansur al-Yahūdī (9th c.), court musician of Umayyad caliph al-Ḥakam I in Córdoba, Spain.

Almanzi Joseph (1801–1860), Hebrew author, poet in Padua, Italy. His mss. collection bought by British Museum for £1,000 is basis of its Hebrew mss. department.

Almemar, see Bimah.

Almog (Kopeliovitz), Yehuda (1896–1972), leading figure of Third Aliyah and a founder of Gedud ha-Avodah; b. nr. Vilna, settled in Ereẓ Israel 1919. A founder of Kibbutz Ramat Raḥel, nr. Jerusalem, and a pioneer of settlement in Dead Sea region.

Almogi, Yosef Aharon (1910–), Israel labor leader; b. Poland, settled in Ereẓ Israel 1930. Secretary of Haifa Labor Council for many years. General secretary of Mapai 1960–2, minister of housing and development 1963–5, minister of labor fr. 1968–74. Mayor of Haifa fr. 1974.

Almoli Solomon ben Jacob (15th–16th c.), grammarian, physician,

THE HEBREW ALPHABET

1. Aḥiram sarcophagus, c. 1000 B.C.E., Phoenician;
2. Gezer Calendar, late tenth century B.C.E., Hebrew;
3. Mesha stele, mid-ninth century B.C.E., Moabite;
4. Samaria ostraca, eighth century B.C.E., Hebrew;
5. Bar-Rekub stele, late eighth century B.C.E., Aramaic;
6. Siloam inscription, c. 700 B.C.E., Hebrew;
7. Meẓad Ḥashavyahu ostracon, late seventh century B.C.E., Hebrew;
8. Saqqara papyrus, c. 600 B.C.E., Aramaic;
9. Hebrew seals, late seventh–early sixth century B.C.E.;
10. Lachish ostraca, early sixth century B.C.E., Hebrew;
11. Elephantine papyrus, late fifth century B.C.E., Aramaic;
12. Eshmun'azor inscription, fifth century B.C.E., Phoenician;
13. Exodus scroll fragment, second century B.C.E., Paleo-Hebrew.

Jewish relics in Musee Alsacien, Strasbourg.

philosopher, kabbalist; probably b. Spain, lived in Constantinople, serving as *dayyan*. Conceived idea of compiling general encyclopedia, producing 24-page prospectus.

Almond, Gabriel Abraham (1911–), U.S. political scientist. Prof. of political science at Princeton, Yale, Stanford. Stressed cultural dimensions in politics.

Almosnino, Joseph ben Isaac (1642–1689), rabbi, halakhic authority, kabbalist; probably b. Salonika, lived in Jerusalem and Belgrade, d. Nikolsburg. Supported Shabbetai Ẓevi.

Almosnino, Moses ben Baruch (c. 1515–c. 1580), Salonika rabbi, scholar, preacher. Wrote on ethics, astronomy, philosophy. Obtained from sultan confirmation of privileges of Salonika community.

Al-Mukammis (al-Mukammas), David ibn Marwān (c. 900), one of first Jewish philosophers of Islamic period; b. Mesopotamia. First to introduce method of Arab religious philosophy into Jewish thought.

Alnakar, Abraham ben Joseph (c. 1740–c. 1803), Sephardi liturgical scholar and publisher of prayer-books; b. Fez, Morocco, d. Leghorn.

Al-Nakawa, Israel ben Joseph (d. 1391), ethical writer, poet; martyred in Toledo, Spain. His *Menorat ha-Ma'or* was a compilation of aggadic and halakhic material, which includes many important citations fr. works otherwise lost. Isaac Aboab's *Menorat ha-Ma'or* probably largely adapted from this work.

Aloni, Nissim (1926–), Israel writer, playwright; influenced by Theater of the Absurd. Plays include *The King is Cruelest of All, The American Princess.*

Alphabet. Hebrews adopted the alphabetic script used by the Canaanites. In post-exilic times, Paleo-Hebrew script gradually replaced by square script, a Palestinian descendant of the Aramaic alphabet. Heb. alphabet developed fr. the square script, which evolved into the modern Heb. printing type. A cursive script was employed by medieval Jewish scholars. The Polish-German form became the present Heb. script. There are 22 letters in the Heb. alphabet. Originally no vowels were printed; later four letters י,ו,ה,א, were used as vowel-letters, and eventually vocalization was introduced. Five letters ף,ץ,ן,ם,ך, have different forms at the end of a word. There are no capitals. The Greek, Latin, and Cyrillic alphabets developed from the Hebrew.

Alphabet of Ben Sira, see Ben Sira, Alphabet of.

Alroy, David (Menahem 12th c.), leader of messianic movement in Kurdistan. Murdered when about to lead his followers into Amadiya, a fortified town. His followers, who continued to believe in him after his death, known as Menahemites.

Alsace, French province. Jews fr. mid-12th c. Communities organized in several towns fr. 13th c. Widespread persecutions fr. 14th c. Jews allowed to remain when Alsace came under French rule in 17th c., paid body-tax, numbered about 20,000 by 1785. Legal emancipation came in 1791. Annexed to Germany

1871–1918 when many Jews went elsewhere. Nazi Germany again appropriated Alsace-Lorraine in 1940, made it *judenrein,* expelling Jews to interior of France where most of them were saved. Jewish pop. 50,000 by 1970, incl. newcomers fr. Algeria. Main community Strasbourg.

Alschuler, Samuel (1859–1939), U.S. lawyer judge. Sat on U.S. Federal Court of Appeals.

Alsheikh, Shalom ben Joseph (1859–1944), rabbi of Yemenite community of Jerusalem. Went from San'a to Jerusalem 1891.

Alshekh, Moses (16th c.), biblical commentator; b. Adrianople. A pupil of Joseph Caro, he settled and taught in Safed. His biblical commentaries, permeated with talmudic and midrashic quotations, were very popular.

Alshvang, Arnold Aleksandrovich (1898–1960), Russian musicologist. Prof. at Moscow Conservatory fr. 1930. Wrote on Debussy, Tchaikovsky, Beethoven.

°**Alt, Albrecht** (1883–1956), German Bible scholar. Fr. 1913 a director of Deutsches Evangelisches Institut in Jerusalem. "The Alt School" or the "Alt-Noth Trend" refers to his (and M. Noth's) views on the nature of the traditions in Joshua 2–9 and on the period of the documents in Joshua 15–19.

Altalena, literary pseudonym of Vladimir Jabotinsky. Also name of ship in which Irgun Ẓeva'i Le'ummi attempted to bring arms to Israel in June 1948. Ship reached shores of Tel Aviv, but unloading was forbidden by Israel government. Order was resisted and vessel was shelled and sank.

Altar (Heb. *mizbe'aḥ*), originally the place for sacrificial slaughter and offerings. Eventually the place for offering all oblations, including grain, wine, and incense offerings. In biblical times it was built with protuberances ("horns of the altar") and a person grasping these was granted asylum. The Temple had one central altar and an incense altar. After the destruction of the Second Temple, there was no altar in Judaism.

Altaras, Jacques Isaac (1786–1873), French merchant, shipbuilder, philanthropist; lived in Marseilles. Visited Russia 1846 to negotiate resettlement of Russian Jews in Algeria. Project failed because Russians demanded 60-ruble payment for each Jew.

Altenberg, Peter (Richard Englaender; 1859–1919), Austrian author. Wrote short stories and vignettes depicting Vienna life.

Alter, Victor (1890–1941), leader of Bund in Poland. Member of Warsaw city committee for 20 years. Executed in Russian-occupied zone.

Alterman, Nathan (1910–1970), Israel poet, playwright; b. Poland, settled in Tel Aviv 1925. Fr. 1934, regular contributor of political verse to daily *Haaretz*; fr. 1943 to *Davar.* His popular weekly feature *Ha-Tur ha-Shevi'i* ("The Seventh Column") dealt with topical subjects. Also pioneered in writing libretti for Hebrew satirical theater. In his serious poetry, the leading "imagist" poet of his generation. Plays incl. *Kinneret, Kinneret* and *Pundak ha-Ruḥot.* Also translated plays by Molière, Shakespeare, etc. into Heb.

Al Tikrei (Heb. "Do not read"), term used to denote a change in the Masoretic reading of Scripture in order to give a meaning other than the literal one.

Altman, Benjamin (1840–1913), U.S. merchant, art collector, philanthropist; founder of Altman and Co. department store in New York.

Altman, Moishe (1890–), Yiddish poet, novelist; b. Bessarabia, lived in Rumania and Soviet Union; in forced labor camp 1949–52.

Altman, Nathan (1889–), Russian painter, sculptor, scenic designer. Constructionist style with cubist influence. Fr. 1930s conformed to artistic demands of Soviet regime.

Altman, Oscar Louis (1909–1968), U.S. economist, Treasurer of International Monetary Fund. Main interest: international liquidity problems.

Altmann, Alexander (1906–), rabbi, scholar. Communal rabbi in Manchester, prof. of Jewish philosophy at Brandeis Univ. fr. 1959. Wrote on Saadiah, Moses Mendelssohn, etc. His father **Adolf** (1879–1944), Hungarian-born rabbi; d. Auschwitz.

Altneuland, utopian Zionist novel by Theodor Herzl (1902) describing life in the future Jewish state. Its motto "If you will it, it is no fairytale."

Altneuschul, synagogue in Prague built at end of 14th c.; oldest surviving synagogue in Europe.

Altona, port in W. Germany, suburb of Hamburg. Portuguese Jewish community founded beginning of 17th c., later joined by Ashkenazi, amalgamated with communities of Hamburg and Wandsbeck into single community (AHW) until 1811. Was center of Jewish scholarship, im-

Anti-Jewish riots in Dürmenach, Alsace, 1848

Shalom b. Joseph Alsheikh

Stone horned altar found at Megiddo.

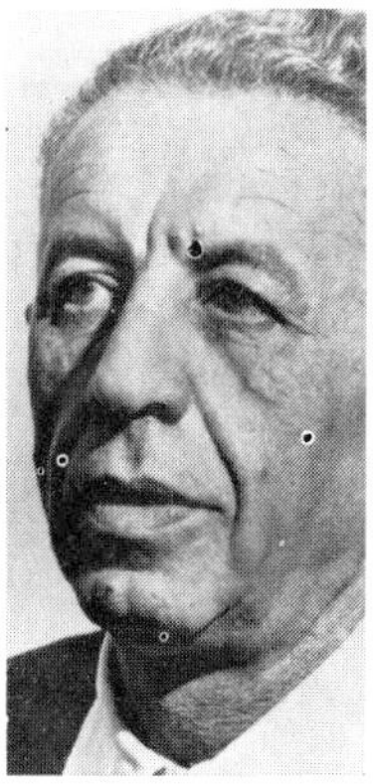

Nathan Alterman

Nathan Altman's "Head of a Young Jew."

Alexander Altmann

portant Hebrew printing. Jews engaged in commerce, shipbuilding, whaling. Numbered 5,000 in 1925. (See also Hamburg.)

Altschul, Aaron Meyer (1914–), U.S. nutrition chemist. Member of President's Science Advisory Committee. Prof. at Tulane.

Altschul, Emil (1797–1865), physician, homeopath in Prague. His criticism of Jewish burial customs led to modifications in rites in Europe.

Altschul, Moses ben Ḥanokh (c. 1546–1633), early Yiddish writer. Author of *Brant Shpigl*, first original comprehensive work of ethics in Yiddish.

Altschuler, David, (18th c.), Bible exegete; lived in Galicia. His Bible commentary was completed by his son **Jehiel Hillel** (18th c.) in *Binyan ha-Bayit*, consisting of *Meẓudat Ẓiyyon* (explaining individual words) and *Meẓudat David* (explaining the text). Reprinted in many editions of Bible.

Altschuler, Modest (1873–1963), conductor; b. Russia, emigrated to U.S. 1896. Founded Russian Symphony Society.

Alva, Solomon Siegfried (1901–1973), painter; b. Berlin, settled in England before WWII. Some of his work is symbolist and abstract.

Alvares, Duarte Henriques (17th c.), Marrano who escaped 1653 fr. Canary Islands to England. Burned in effigy by Inquisition 1658.

Alvarez Gato, Juan (c. 1445–c. 1510), Converso poet in Spain; keeper of royal household for Queen Isabella.

°**Amador des los Rios, Jose** (1818–1878), Spanish literary critic, historian. Wrote important study of Spanish Jewish history.

Amalekites, nomadic people of Negev, hereditary enemy of Israel, fr. Exodus time to early monarchy. Treacherously attacking Israelites after Exodus, they were defeated and Israel undertook holy war of extermination against them. Name remained in rabbinic literature as symbol of everlasting enmity to Israel.

"Western Wall" by Alva

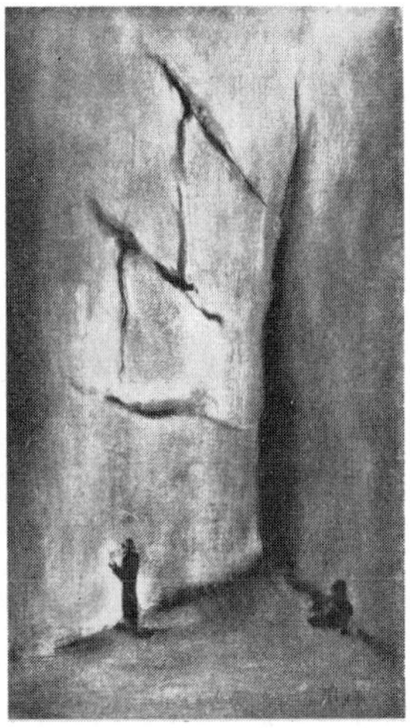

Amar, Licco (1891–1959), violinist; b. Budapest. Founded Amar Quartet 1922, incl. Paul Hindemith. Taught at Ankara Conservatory, Freiburg Musikhochschule.

Amarillo, Solomon ben Joseph (1645–1721), Salonikan halakhic authority, preacher. His sons: **Aaron** (1700–1772), halakhic authority, kabbalist; **Ḥayyim Moses** (1695–1748), halakhist, preacher.

Amasa, military commander of Absalom's army in his rebellion against his father David (II Sam. 17). Then went over to David but was treacherously slain by Joab.

Amatus Lusitanus (1511–1568), physician, medical author (*Centuriae curationum*); b. Portugal to Marrano parents as Joao Rodrigues. Went to Antwerp c. 1533, then lived in various places in Italy, in Ragusa, and Salonika, where he openly practiced Judaism. First to discover veins in valves which direct blood circulation.

Amatus Lusitanus

Amaziah, king of Judah, son of Joash. Reigned 798–c. 769 B.C.E. Won great victory over Edom but was defeated by Joash of Israel. Murdered in palace revolution.

Amaziah (8th c. B.C.E.), priest of king's sanctuary at Beth-El in time of Jeroboam II; an opponent of the prophet Amos.

Ambron, Shabbetai Isaac (17th–18th c.), scholar in Rome. Wrote treatise on universe in Latin.

Ameimar (c. 400), Babylonian *amora*; a leading sage of Nehardea.

Amelander, Menahem Mann ben Solomon ha-Levi (d.c. 1767), Hebrew grammarian, publisher, translator in Amsterdam. Wrote *She'erit Yisrael*, a history of the Jews, part fact, part legend.

Amen (Heb. "So be it"), word of endorsement or hope, on hearing a blessing, prayer, curse, or oath. Found 30 times in Bible, it became standard response in both Jewish and Christian liturgies.

America, see separate entries for specific countries.

America-Israel Cultural Foundation, fund-raising agency on behalf of educational and cultural institutions in Israel. Originally American Palestine Fund, Inc., founded 1939 by Edward A. Norman.

American, Sadie (1862–1944), U.S. social worker, civic leader; prominent in National Council of Jewish Women.

American Academy for Jewish Research, organization of scholars, rabbis, interested laymen, established 1920 by L. Ginzberg, G. Deutsch, H. Malter, J.Z. Lauterbach, for scholarly purposes.

American Association for Jewish Education, organization founded 1939 to promote Jewish education. Helped found 32 bureaus of Jewish education throughout U.S.

American Council for Judaism, anti-Zionist organization. Founded 1942 by group of Reform rabbis. Opposed establishment of Israel. Influence declined after 1967 Six-Day War.

American Federation of Jews from Central Europe, central representative agency of over 30 local and national organizations from C. Europe in U.S. Incorporated in New York 1941. By 1968 distributed over $4,000,000 for welfare and rehabilitation in U.S.

American Hebrew, The, New York Jewish weekly begun 1879, published by Philip Cowen. Appeared until 1956.

American Israelite, U.S. Anglo-Jewish weekly, founded 1854 in Cincinnati by I.M. Wise as a platform for his ideas. From 1855 contained German supplement *Die Deborah* later published as separate journal. Still exists as local community bulletin.

American Jewish Archives, archives established 1947 on Cincinnati campus of Hebrew Union College–Jewish Institute of Religion. Collects research materials on history of Jews in W. Hemisphere, primarily U.S.

American Jewish Committee, organization founded in U.S. 1906 "to prevent the infraction of the civil and religious rights of the Jews, in any part of the world." On outbreak of WWI extended emergency aid for Jewish war victims. During the 1920s and 30s fought anti-Semitic propaganda in U.S., intensified by the rise of Nazism, and turned to plans of rescue and emigration for

German Jews. Although non-Zionist, supported creation of Jewish state and interests of Israel. In postwar era, concentrated on combating anti-Semitism within Soviet orbit, Muslim countries, and S. America. Also labored successfully for revision of prejudiced Christian teachings about Jews. 40,000 members in 1973. Sponsors the monthly *Commentary,* the quarterly *Present Tense,* and co-sponsors *American Jewish Year Book.*

American Jewish Conference, representative American organization, established 1943 to deal with problems of Ereẓ Israel and European Holocaust. Composed of representatives of all major Jewish groups and delegates from local Jewish communities. Adopted pro-Zionist resolution in August 1943 causing American Jewish Committee to secede. Dissolved 1949.

American Jewish Congress, one of central agencies in American Jewish community relations. Outgrowth of first American Jewish Congress which met in Philadelphia 1918. Fully organized 1928. Leading force in anti-Nazi movement, fought anti-Semitism in U.S. Active on behalf of Negro civil rights. 300 chapters in General and Women's Divisions based on individual membership. Publications include *Congress Bi-Weekly* and *Judaism,* a quarterly devoted to theological issues.

Seal of the American Jewish Historical Society

American Jewish Historical Society, organization founded 1892 to promote study of American Jewish history. Proceedings published as quarterly, *Publications of the American Jewish Historical Society.* Headquarters moved 1968 fr. New York to campus of Brandeis Univ.

American Jewish Joint Agriculture Corporation, see Agro-Joint.

Population figures of the Americas, 1968. Black numerals: Jewish population. White numerals: total population.

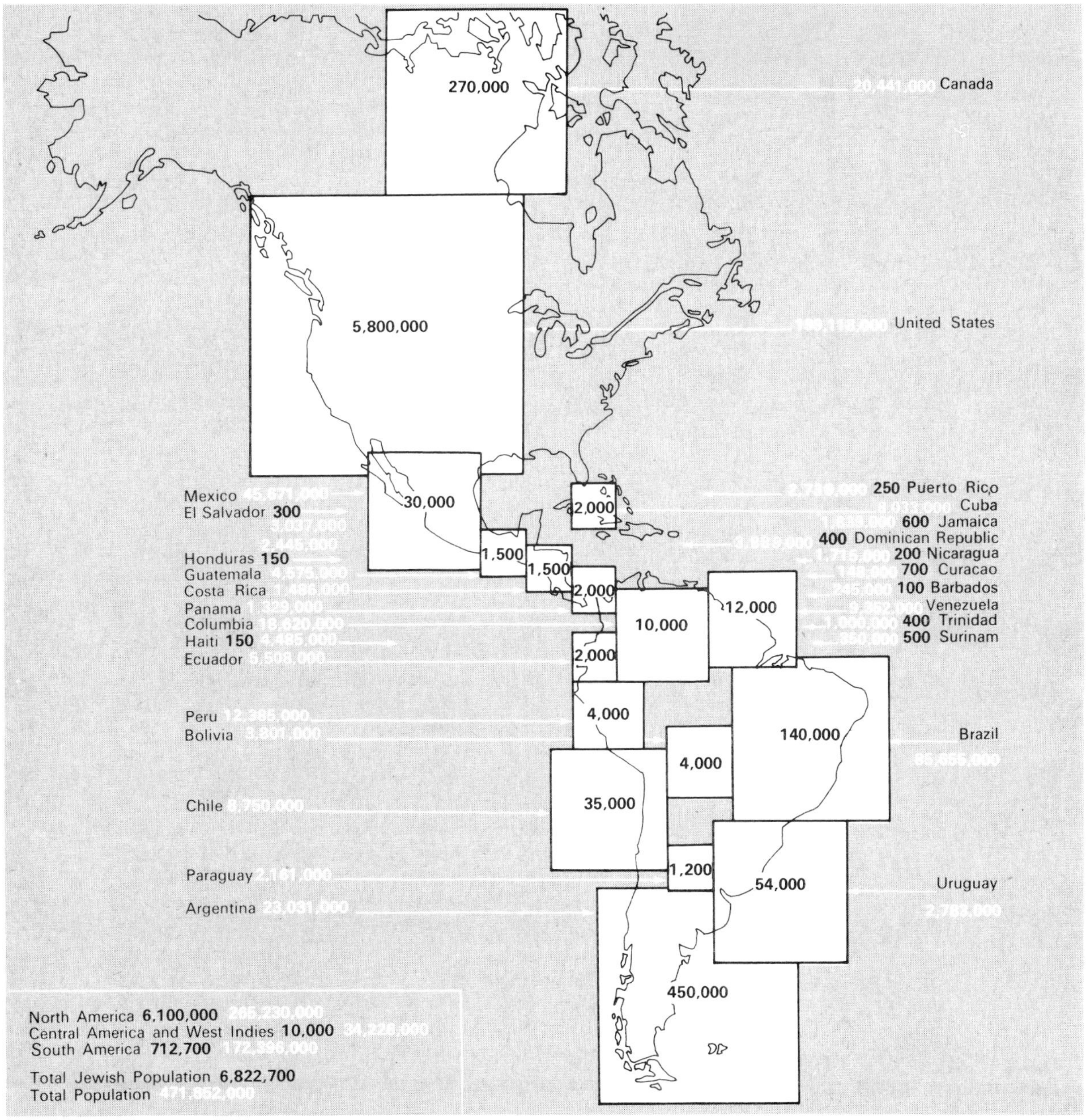

American Jewish Joint Distribution Committee ("Joint" or J.D.C.), American Jewry's overseas relief and rehabilitation agency, created 1914, with Felix M. Warburg as first chairman. Rescue and relief work carried out during both world wars and after, especially for Jews of E. and C. Europe afflicted by persecution, uprooting and wholesale massacres. During WW II worked to rescue and help Jews in Nazi Europe. After war, major tasks were assistance to Displaced Persons (DPs), emigration to Israel, reconstruction of Jewish life in Europe, care of ill, aged, and disabled in Israel (through Malben), and relief and communal help to Jews in Muslim countries.

Founders of the Joint Distribution Committee, photographed in 1918

American Zionist Council, coordinating body of American Zionist organizations, formed 1949.

Ames (Añes), Gonsalvo (16th c.), Marrano merchant, financial agent, purveyor and intelligence agent to Elizabeth I.

Am ha-Arez (Heb. "people of the land"), term used in Bible in sense of citizens or some particular class of citizens; later, social concept with pejorative connotation, applied to those who were not particular to govern their lives by religious faith and observance. In Temple times denoted those not particular about strict separation of tithes and ritual purity in contrast to *haverim;* later, and still today, applied to those ignorant of, or not careful in proper observance of precepts and study of Torah, as well as ignorant in Jewish learning.

A.M.I.A. (Asociación Mutual Israelita Argentina), organization of Buenos Aires Ashkenazi community, formed 1893, originally as burial society (Chevra Keduscha Aschkenazi) with 51,798 families registered (1968), the body engaged in a variety of educational, cultural, welfare, and research activities.

Amichai, Yehuda (1924–), Israel poet, novelist; b. Germany, settled in Erez Israel 1936. One of first to introduce modern technological idioms into Hebrew poetry. His novel *Lo me-Akhshav, Lo mi-Kan* is story of post-war Jewish-German relations.

Amidah (Heb. "standing"), main prayer at all services; must be recited standing as name indicates. Originally comprised 18 benedictions (hence alternative name *Shemoneh-Esreh,* i.e., eighteen), but 19th benediction introduced in Babylonian times. On Sabbath and festivals there are fewer benedictions and these are appropriate to the occasion. In talmudic sources *amidah* is known as *ha-Tefillah* i.e., "The Prayer" (*par excellence*).

Amidar, Israel national immigrant housing company. Established 1949 by Israel government as nonprofit institution.

Amiel, Moshe Avigdor (1883–1946), rabbi, scholar, preacher, Mizrachi leader. Fr. 1920 rabbi of Antwerp, fr. 1936 chief rabbi of Tel Aviv.

Amigo, Abraham (c. 1610–c. 1683), rabbi, author; probably b. Constantinople, settled in Jerusalem c. 1655 and was leading halakhic authority.

Amigo, Meir (18th c.), Sephardi merchant; b. Constantinople, settled in Temesvár, Hungary, and became head of community.

Amir, Aharon (1923–), Israel writer, translator, editor; b. Lithuania, settled in Erez Israel 1935. Edited literary periodical *Keshet.*

Amir (née Pinkerfeld), Anda (1902–), Israel poet; b. Galicia, settled in Erez Israel 1923. Wrote much verse for children.

Amira, Binyamin (1896–1968), Israel mathematician; b. Russia. Founded Institute of Math. at Heb. Univ., also *Journal d'analyse mathématique.*

Amiran, David (1910–), Israel geographer; b. Berlin, settled in Erez Israel 1935. Directed completion of *Atlas of Israel.* His wife, **Ruth** (1914 –), archaeologist, expert on ancient pottery of Erez Israel.

Amiran (Pougatchov), Emanuel (1909–), composer, teacher; b. Warsaw, settled in Erez Israel 1924. Wrote choral, orchestral music, popular songs (*Emek Emek Avodah, Mayim Mayim, Ki mi-Ziyyon,* etc.).

Amittai (c. 800), Hebrew liturgical poet in S. Italy; father of Shephatiah of Oria.

Amittai ben Shephatiah (9th c.), liturgical poet in S. Italy; son of Shephatiah of Oria. Several of his poems were incorporated in Italian and Ashkenazi liturgies.

Amman, see Rabbath-Ammon.

Ammi bar Nathan (3rd c.), Palestinian *amora.* Head of Tiberias academy. Together with his colleague R. Assi, the outstanding authority of his time.

Ammon, Ammonites, ancient Semitic people mentioned in Bible. Emerged fr. Syrio-Arabian desert c. 15th c. B.C.E., settling along upper and central Jabbok River. Rabbath-Ammon (now Amman) most important Ammonite settlement and royal city. Frequent wars with Israel, who were ordered not to let them enter "the congregation of the Lord" (Deut. 23:4). Their god was Moloch.

Amnon, eldest son of king David; killed by Absalom avenging Amnon's rape of his half-sister, Tamar.

Amnon of Mainz (10th c.), martyr and legendary figure. According to the legend the bishop of Mainz ordered Amnon's limbs to be amputated when he failed to appear for his conversion. As he was dying, on Rosh Ha-Shanah, he was carried into the synagogue where he recited the hymn *U-Netanneh Tokef* he had composed. In fact, *U-Netanneh Tokef* dates from an earlier period.

Am Olam, Russian Jewish society founded 1881 in Odessa to establish agricultural colonies in U.S. The first of these settled on Sicily Island, Louisiana, 1882. After a disastrous flood, many left for S. Dakota to found two colonies, "Crimea" and "Bethlehem of Judea." Both lasted until 1885. The longest-lived Am Olam communistic colony, "New Odessa," set up 1882 in Oregon, lasted until 1887. Am Olam was involved in intense ideological dispute with Bilu, which advocated settlement in Erez Israel.

Amon, king of Judah 642–640 B.C.E.; assassinated by members of his court.

Amon, Egyptian deity mentioned in Bible. Portrayed as ram or human with ram's head.

Amora, pl. **Amoraim** (Aram. "spokesmen"), title used originally for "interpreter" who communicated lessons of rabbi to pupils. Later used for Jewish scholars who taught in Erez Israel and especially Babylonia 3rd–6th c. in period after conclusion of Mishnah, their work being comprised in the *Gemara.* (3,000 *amoraim* are known by name.) Influence of Erez Israel *amoraim* declined after 4th c. (see table).

Amorites, subgroup of pre-Israelite inhabitants of Land of Israel or pre-Israelite inhabitants in general. In Sumero-Akkadian texts it occurs as

geographical term meaning literally "the west." the area extended westward from the Euphrates as far as the Mediterranean Sea.

Amos (8th c. B.C.E.), prophet in N. Kingdom of Israel. Book of Amos, 3rd book of 12 Minor Prophets. Considered earliest of Latter Prophets. Social morality is central theme. Foretells catastrophe to befall Israel as consequence of moral corruption.

Ampal (American Palestine), associated company of Bank ha-Poalim. Established 1942 in U.S. by the bank, the Histadrut, etc., to channel investments fr. U.S. to Israel (esp. to economic institutions of Histadrut), and to develop commercial ties between the two countries.

Amram, father of Aaron, Moses, and Miriam.

Amram, David Werner (1866–1939), U.S. jurist, community leader, scholar; lived in Philadelphia. Wrote books on Jewish law and also *Makers of Hebrew Books in Italy.*

Amram, Nathan ben Ḥayyim (1805–1870), Safed-born emissary of Ereẓ Israel in Egypt and Europe. Rabbi in Alexandria fr. 1863.

Page of "Seder R. Amram," fr. 15th-cent. ms., Spain.

Amram ben Sheshna (9th c.), *gaon* of Sura noted for his responsa, one of which, sent to community of Barcelona, contained oldest surviving order of prayers for entire year *("Maḥzor de-Rav Amram").*

Amram Darah (4th c.), Samaritan poet who wrote in Aramaic and whose poems are a central feature of the Samaritan prayer-book, the *Defter.*

Amraphel, king of Shinar, mentioned in Genesis 14:1–9. The identification with Hammurapi now thought unlikely.

Amshewitz, John Henry (1882–1942), British artist; known for his historical murals. In S. Africa fr. 1916; influenced S. African art.

Amsterdam, capital of The Netherlands. Sephardi congregation of Marranos fr. Spain, Portugal, established c. 1608. Toward end of 17th c., Ashkenazim outnumbered Sephardim, the latter remaining preeminent for wealth, culture and majestic 1675 synagogue. Important printing press established by Manasseh b. Israel 1626. Jews influential in all economic spheres, including diamond-polishing. Adass Jeshurun, first reformed congregation, established 1797. Community among most important throughout 19th c. for its institutions, libraries, staunch Jewish loyalties. Numbered c. 80,000 in 1941, Jews suffered terribly during Nazi occupation. Many deportations to death camps 1942–44. Jewish pop. c. 12,000 (1971).

Amsterdam, Abraham Meir (c. 1871–1899), pioneer of Jewish labor movement in Russia; lived in Moscow and Vitebsk. Introduced greater national consciousness in labor movement. After serving two-year prison sentence for underground activities, drowned in river.

Amter, Israel (1881–1954), U.S. communist leader. A founder of American Communist Party 1919. Imprisoned 1930 for leading demonstration of unemployed. Drew 100,000 votes in New York State senatorial campaign 1938.

Amulet, object worn to protect its wearer from evil or cure him from disease, or even as aid to greater wisdom. Belief in efficacy widespread among Jews. Frequently contain combinations of Divine Name, angel's name and biblical verses, and were very popular in kabbalistic circles and still have a wide folk usage (e.g. during childbirth).

A German amulet for a child named Kalonymus Kalman, 17th-18th cent.

Amzalak, Ḥayyim (1824–1916), Jewish communal leader in Ereẓ Israel. b. Gibraltar. British vice-consul in Jaffa. Land of Rishon le-Zion registered in his name because Jews of Russian origin forbidden to purchase land.

18th-cent. etching of Amsterdam's two adjoining Ashkenazi synagogues

Dedication of Sephardi Synagogue in Amsterdam, 1675

Moses Bensabat Amzalak

Amzalak, Moses Bensabat (1892–), Portuguese scholar, economist. President of Portuguese Academy of Sciences and chancellor of Lisbon Technical Univ. Headed Lisbon Jewish community.

Anak, Anakim, according to Bible, giant people who live in S. Ereẓ Israel.

Anan, son of Anan, high priest. Appointed by Agrippa II in 62 C.E. Officiated for only 3 months; deposed by public demand. Favored a conciliatory policy toward Romans. Fell while fighting Zealots.

Anan ben David (8th c.), ascetic sage in Babylonia; regarded by Karaites as their founder. Leader of separate Jewish sect, at first called Ananites, whose main feature was return to Bible as sole source of Divine Law and opposition to later rabbinic tradition.

Principal Amoraim of the Babylonian Academies

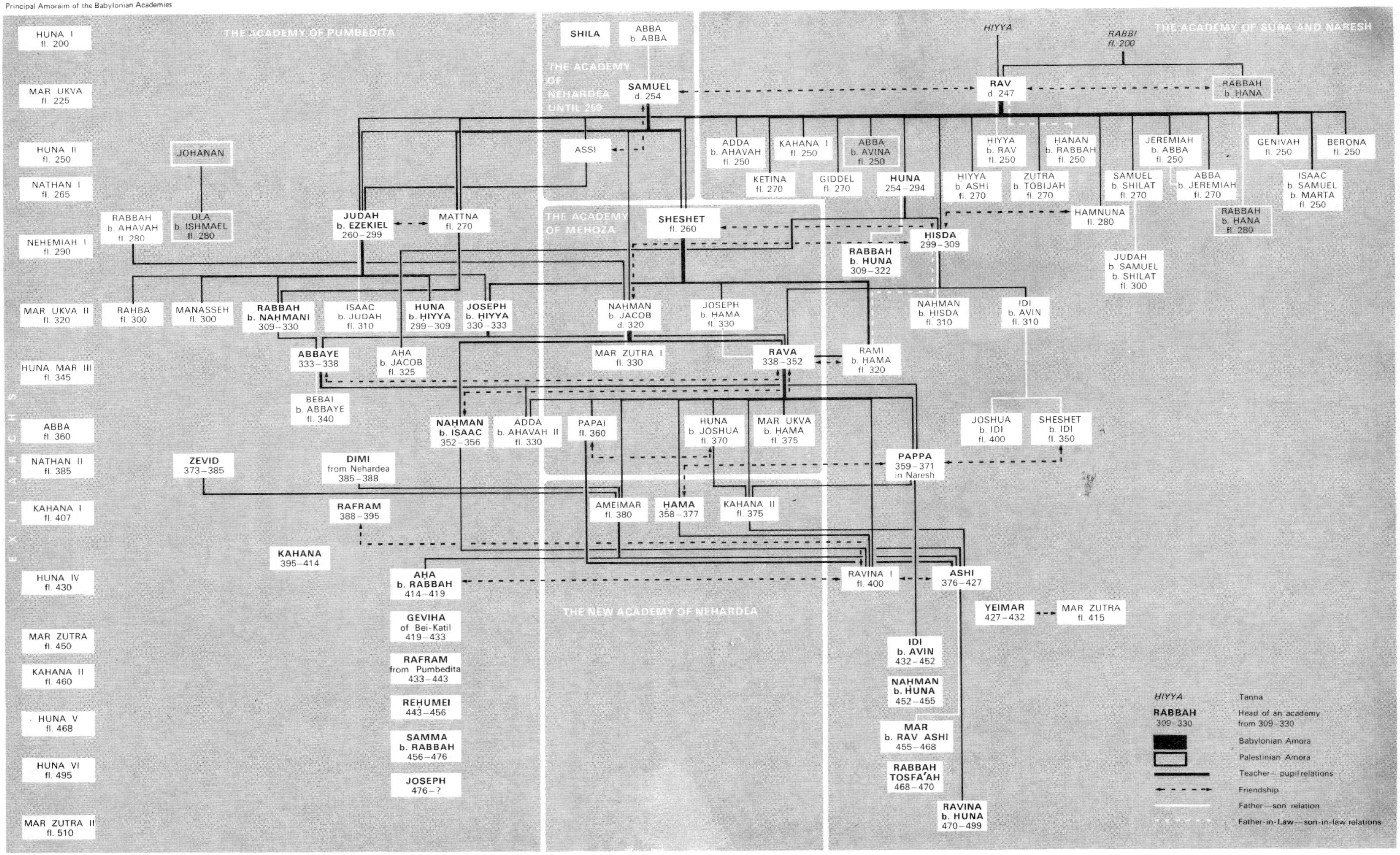
THE ACADEMY OF PUMBEDITA
THE ACADEMY OF NEHARDEA UNTIL 259
THE ACADEMY OF MEHOZA
THE ACADEMY OF SURA AND NARESH
THE NEW ACADEMY OF NEHARDEA
EXILARCHS
HUNA I fl. 200
MAR UKVA fl. 225
HUNA II fl. 250
NATHAN I fl. 265
NEHEMIAH I fl. 290
MAR UKVA II fl. 320
HUNA MAR III fl. 345
ABBA fl. 360
NATHAN II fl. 385
KAHANA I fl. 407
HUNA IV fl. 430
MAR ZUTRA fl. 450
KAHANA II fl. 460
HUNA V fl. 468
HUNA VI fl. 495
MAR ZUTRA II fl. 510
JOHANAN
ULA b. ISHMAEL fl. 280
RABBAH b. AHAVAH fl. 280
JUDAH b. EZEKIEL 260–299
MATTNA fl. 270
RAHBA fl. 300
MANASSEH fl. 300
RABBAH b. NAHMANI 309–330
ISAAC b. JUDAH fl. 310
HUNA b. ḤIYYA 299–309
JOSEPH b. ḤIYYA 330–333
ABBAYE 333–338
AHA b. JACOB fl. 325
BEBAI b. ABBAYE fl. 340
ZEVID 373–385
DIMI from Nehardea 385–388
RAFRAM 388–395
KAHANA 395–414
AḤA b. RABBAH 414–419
GEVIHA of Bei-Katil 419–433
RAFRAM from Pumbedita 433–443
REḤUMEI 443–456
SAMMA b. RABBAH 456–476
JOSEPH 476–?
SHILA
ABBA b. ABBA
SAMUEL d. 254
ASSI
SHESHET fl. 260
NAHMAN b. JACOB d. 320
JOSEPH b. ḤAMA fl. 330
MAR ZUTRA I fl. 330
RAVA 338–352
RAMI b. ḤAMA fl. 320
NAḤMAN b. ISAAC 352–356
ADDA b. AHAVAH II fl. 330
PAPAI fl. 360
HUNA b. JOSHUA fl. 370
MAR UKVA b. ḤAMA fl. 375
AMEIMAR fl. 380
ḤAMA 358–377
KAHANA II fl. 375
ḤIYYA
RABBI fl. 200
RAV d. 247
RABBAH b. ḤANA
ADDA b. AHAVAH fl. 250
KAHANA I fl. 250
ABBA b. AVINA fl. 250
ḤIYYA b. RAV fl. 250
ḤANAN b. RABBAH fl. 250
JEREMIAH b. ABBA fl. 250
GENIVAH fl. 250
BERONA fl. 250
KETINA fl. 270
GIDDEL fl. 270
HUNA 254–294
ḤIYYA b. ASHI fl. 270
ZUTRA b. TOBIJAH fl. 270
SAMUEL b. SHILAT fl. 270
ABBA b. JEREMIAH fl. 270
ISAAC b. SAMUEL b. MARTA fl. 250
HAMNUNA fl. 280
RABBAH b. ḤANA fl. 280
HISDA 299–309
RABBAH b. HUNA 309–322
JUDAH b. SAMUEL b. SHILAT fl. 300
NAHMAN b. HISDA fl. 310
IDI b. AVIN fl. 310
JOSHUA b. IDI fl. 400
SHESHET b. IDI fl. 350
PAPPA 359–371 in Naresh
RAVINA I fl. 400
ASHI 376–427
YEIMAR 427–432
MAR ZUTRA fl. 415
IDI b. AVIN 432–452
NAḤMAN b. ḤUNA 452–455
MAR b. RAV ASHI 455–468
RABBAH TOSFA'AH 468–470
RAVINA b. HUNA 470–499
ḤIYYA Tanna
RABBAH 309–330 Head of an academy from 309–330
Babylonian Amora
Palestinian Amora
Teacher—pupil relations
Friendship
Father—son relation
Father-in-Law—son-in-law relations

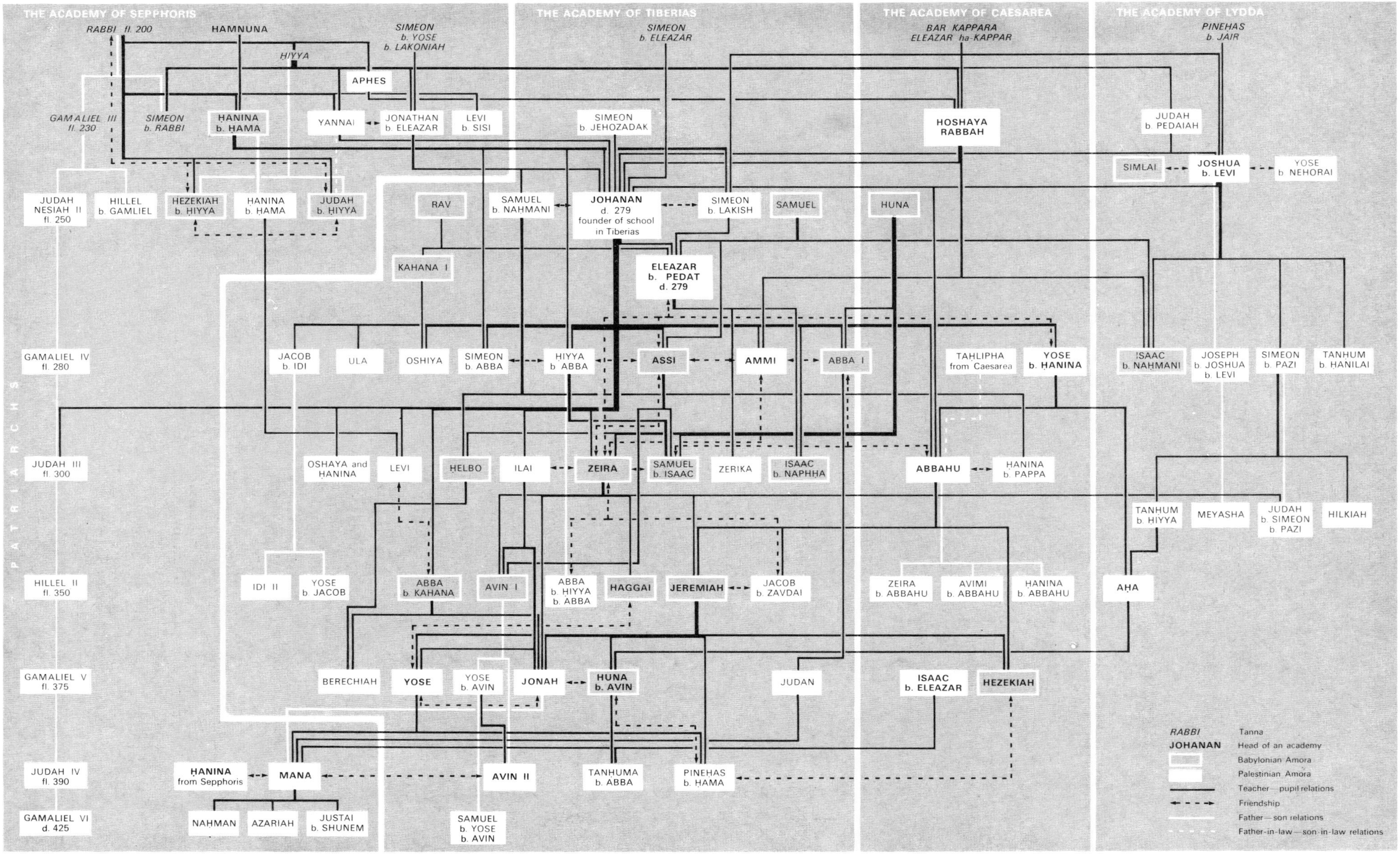

Principal Amoraim of the Palestinian Academies

Ananias and Helkias, two brothers, sons of Onias IV, generals in army of Cleopatra III, queen of Egypt (116–110 B.C.E.).

Ananias ben Nedebeus, high priest 47–59 C.E.; considered by Sicarii as one of major Roman collaborators and subsequently put to death by extreme elements.

Ananias of Adiabene (1st c. C.E.), Jewish merchant who was instrumental in conversion to Judaism of royal family of Adiabene.

Anaschehon (Anaschichun), Spanish family which settled in Ereẓ Israel and Turkey after expulsion fr. Spain in 1492. **Joseph** (d. 1632), referred to as "the perfect scholar"; **Meir,** lived in Ereẓ Israel and Egypt, younger contemporary of Ḥayyim Vital; **Joseph** (2nd half of 17th c.), rabbi in Turkey and kabbalist.

Anath, a major goddess of W. Semites (Amorites, Canaanites, Arameans); consort of Baal.

Anathoth, levitical city in territory of Benjamin; home of Jeremiah.

Anatoli, Jacob ben Abba Mari ben Samson (13th c.), physician, preacher, translator; b. Provence, lived in Naples under patronage of emperor Frederick II. Collected his homilies in his widely read *Malmad ha-Talmidim,* which contributed to knowledge of philosophy among Jews of Italy.

Anatolia, see Asia Minor.

Anatoli ben Joseph (12th–13th c.), European scholar who settled in Alexandria, where he became *dayyan.* Noted halakhist and poet.

Anau, ancient Italian family. Most of its members lived in Rome. Traditionally descended from one of few aristocratic families of Jerusalem taken by Titus to Rome.

Anav, Benjamin ben Abraham (c. 1215–c. 1295), Italian scholar, poet. Wrote *seliḥot* and *kinot* as well as satire, *Massa Gei Ḥizzayon,* on arrogance of affluent Jewish families in Rome.

Anav, Jehiel ben Jekuthiel ben Benjamin ha-Rofe (13th c.), author, copyist, *paytan.* Author of *Beit Middot,* popular ethical work.

Anav, Zedekiah ben Abraham (13th c.), Italian talmudist. Author of *Shibbolei ha-Leket,* major halakhic compendium on the liturgy.

Anchel, Robert (1880–1951), French archivist and historian (*Napoléon et les Juifs, Les Juifs de France,* etc.).

Ancona, Adriatic port in Italy. Center for Jewish moneylending fr. 14th c. Martyrdom of 25 Marranos burned there at the stake by Papal Inquisition 1555 moved Gracia Mendes to organize boycott of Ancona. On expulsion fr. Papal States 1569, Jews allowed to remain in Rome and Ancona. Ghetto removed 1797–98 under Napoleon. Jews finally emancipated 1861 in Italian kingdom. Jewish pop. 1,600 in 19th c.; 300 in 1969.

Ancona (D'Ancona), Alessandro (1835–1914), Italian statesman, philologist, literary critic. Prof. of Italian literature at Pisa; member of senate fr. 1904. His son **Paolo** (1878–1964), art historian. His brother, **Sansone** (1814–1894), politician; member of senate fr. 1882.

Ancona, Cesare D' (1832–1901), Italian geologist. Prof. of paleontology at Florence fr. 1874.

Ancona, Vito D' (1825–1884), Italian painter; b. Pesaro. Noted for landscape paintings.

Andrade, Edward Neville Da Costa (1887–1971), British physicist, author, science historian. Established Andrade's Laws concerning flow of metals.

Andrade, Velosino Jacob De (1639–1712), Marrano physician, philosophical author; b. Brazil, lived in The Hague and Antwerp. Wrote 6-vol. work presenting Jewish view on Messiah.

Andreas, see Lucuas.

Andronicus son of Meshullam (2nd c. B.C.E.), Alexandrian sage. Spokesman of Jews in dispute with Samaritans in Alexandria.

Angel, Baruch (c. 1595–1670), talmudist, preacher, kabbalist in Salonika. One of outstanding scholars of his day.

Angel, Meir ben Abraham (c. 1564–c. 1647), rabbi, preacher in Sofia and other communities. Sermons based on biblical *Masorah.*

Memorial to Mordecai Anielewicz in Yad Mordekhai

Angel of Death. Though in Bible God is unquestioned master of life and death, death is sometimes personified as His messenger. In later times Angel of Death became an independent agent, a well-known folk figure. Many Jewish death and mourning customs are derived from folk beliefs in Angel of Death.

Angels (Heb. *malakh,* lit. "messenger"). Angels are seen as agents to execute the will of God. They are a category of beings superior to men in knowledge and power, usually not visible, but can manifest themselves to suitable human beings (such as Moses, Isaiah, Ezekiel). Angelology received added significance in the Second Temple period as a result of foreign influences. The concept occurs frequently in the liturgy. There are angels of deliverance and those with destructive powers. In normative Judaism there is no cult of angels, save perhaps in kabbalistic literature, but this does occur in sectarian literature that sprang from Judaism. The rabbis stress that man needs no intermediary in his relation with God and that prayer is to be addressed to God alone. "True penitence does not need saints; feigned penitence will not be helped by the dead or the saints, by man or angel."

Anglo-Jewish Association (AJA), British organization founded 1871 to protect Jewish rights in backward countries by diplomatic means. Undertook educational work in various communities. Patterned after Alliance Israélite Universelle.

Anglo-Palestine Bank, see Bank Leumi le-Israel.

Angoff, Charles (1902–), U.S. novelist, editor. Edited *American Mercury.* Author of series of autobiographical novels centered around the character of his alter ego David Polonsky.

Angrist, Alfred Alvin (1902–), U.S. pathologist. Contributed to knowledge of endocarditis.

Anielewicz, Mordecai (1919–1943), commander of Warsaw ghetto uprising. Member of left-wing Ha-Shomer ha-Ẓa'ir movement and advocate of Jewish armed resistance. Fell in the command bunker in revolt. Kibbutz Yad Mordekhai named after him.

Anilaeus and Asinaeus two Babylonian Jewish brothers who founded outlaw state, ruling it c. 20–35 C.E. Their downfall unleashed wave of terror against Jews of Babylonia.

ANIMALS OF THE BIBLE AND TALMUD

English Name	Scientific Name	Order or Family	Hebrew Name	Reference
Addax	Addax nasomaculatus	Artiodactyla Ruminantia	יַחְמוּר	Deut. 14:5; I Kings 5:3
Ant	Messor semirufus	Formicidae	נְמָלָה	Prov. 6:6–8; 30:25
Ass	Equus asinus	Equidae	חֲמוֹר	Gen. 12:16; 24:35; etc.
			עַיִר	Gen. 32:16; 49:11; etc.
			אָתוֹן	Gen. 32:16; Judg. 5:10; etc.
Bat	Chiroptera	Chiroptera	עֲטַלֵּף	Lev. 11:19; Isa. 2:20
Bear, Syrian	Ursus arctus syriacus	Ursidae	דֹּב	I Sam. 17: 34–7; Hos. 13:8 etc.
Bee	Apis mellifica	Hymenoptera	דְּבוֹרָה	Deut. 1:44; Judg. 14:8; etc.
Beetle	Cerambyx; Capnodis	Coleoptera	תּוֹלַעַת	Deut. 28:39; Jonah 4:7
			חִפּוּשִׁית	Par. 9.2
Bison, European	Bison bonasus	Artiodactyla Ruminantia	תְּאוֹ	Deut. 14:5
			תּוֹא	Isa. 51:20
Boar, Wild	Sus scrofa	Artiodactyla non Ruminantia	חֲזִיר מִיַּעַר	Ps. 80:14
Buffalo, Water	Bos bubalus	Artiodactyla Ruminantia	מְרִיא	II Sam. 6:13; Isa. 1:11
Bug	Cimex lactularis	Rhynchota	פִּשְׁפֵּשׁ	Ter. 8, 2
Buzzard	Buteo sp.	Falconiformes	אַיָּה	Lev. 11:14; Deut. 14:13; Job. [28:7
			רָאָה	Deut. 14:13
			גַּס	Hul. 3.1
Camel	Camelus dromedarius	Tylopoda	גָּמָל	Gen. 12:16; Lev. 11:4; etc.
			בֵּכֶר, בִּכְרָה	Isa. 60:6; Jer. 2:23
			נַאֲקָה	Shab. 5.1; Kelim 23.2
Cattle	Bos taurus	Artiodactyla Ruminantia	בָּקָר	Gen. 13:5; 18:7; etc.
			שׁוֹר	Gen. 32:6; Ex. 20:17; etc.
			אֲלָפִים	Deut. 7:13; 28:4; etc.
			אַבִּירִים	Isa. 34:7; Jer. 46:15; etc.
			פַּר, פָּרָה	Gen. 32:16; Judg. 6:25; etc.
			עֵגֶל, עֶגְלָה	Gen. 15:9; Lev. 9:2; etc.
Centipedes	Scolopendra; Eraphidostrephus	Myriapoda	מַרְבֵּה רַגְלַיִם	Lev. 11:42
			נָדָל	Mik. 5, 3
Chameleon	Chamaeleon vulgaris	Chamaelonidae	תִּנְשֶׁמֶת (שֶׁרֶץ)	Lev. 11: 30
Cheetah	Acinonyx jubatus	Felidae	בַּרְדְּלָס	B.K. 1.4; Sanh. 1, 4
Cobra	Naja haje	Elapinae	פֶּתֶן	Deut. 32:33; Isa. 11:8
			שָׂרָף	Num. 21:6; Isa. 14:29; etc.
Cock	Gallus gallus domesticus	Galliformes	שֶׂכְוִי?	Job. 38:36
			זַרְזִיר מָתְנַיִם(?)	Prov. 30:31
Corals	Corallium rubrum	Coralliacae	פְּנִינִים	Lam. 4:7; Prov. 8:11; etc.
Crane	Grus grus	Gruidae	עָגוּר	Isa. 38:14; Jer. 8:7
Cricket, Mole	Gryllotalpa gryllotalpa	Orthoptera	צְלָצַל	Deut. 28:42
Crimson Worm	Kermes biblicus	Ryncotidae	תּוֹלַעַת שָׁנִי	Ex. 25:4; Num. 4:8; etc.
			כַּרְמִיל	II Chron. 2:6; 3:14
Crocodile	Crocodilus vulgaris	Crocodilia	תַּנִּין	Ex. 7:9; Jer. 51:34; etc.
			לִוְיָתָן	Job. 40:25–41:26
Deer, Fallow	Cervus dama dama	Artiodactyla Ruminantia	יַחְמוּר	Deut. 14:5; I Kings 5:3
Deer, Roe	Cervus capreolus	Artiodactyla Ruminantia	אַיָּל, אַיָּלָה	Deut. 14:5; Jer. 14:5; etc.
Dog	Canis familiaris	Canidae	כֶּלֶב	Ex. 22:30; Judg. 7:5; etc.
Dove	Columba sp.	Columbiformes	יוֹנָה	Gen. 8:8; 8:12; Isa. 38:14; etc.
Eagle	Aquila sp.	Falconiformes	עַיִט	Gen. 15:1.1; Isa. 18:6; etc.
Earthworm	Lumbricus sp.	Vermes	תּוֹלַעַת	Isa. 14:11; 41:14; etc.
Elephant Ivory	Elephas africanus	Proboscidae	פִּיל	Kil. 8, 6
			שֶׁנְהַבִּים	I Kings 10:22; II Chron. 9:21
			שֵׁן	I Kings 10:18; 22:39; etc.
Fish	Pisces	Pisces	דָּג דָּגִים	Gen. 9:2; Jonah 2:1; etc.
			דָּגָה	Gen. 1:26; Ex. 7:18; etc.
Flea	Pulex irritans	Aphaniptera	פַּרְעֹשׁ	I Sam. 24:14; 26:20; etc.
Fly	Musca domestica	Dyptera	זְבוּב	Isa. 7:18; Eccles. 10:1
Fly, Drosophila	Drosophila	Dyptera	יַבְחוּשׁ	Nid. 3, 2
Fox	Vulpes vulpes	Canidae	שׁוּעָל	Lam. 5:18; Ps. 63:11; etc.
Frog	Rana esculenta	Amphibia	צְפַרְדֵּעַ	Ex. 7:27; Ps. 78:45; etc.
Gazelle	Gazella sp.	Artiodactyla Ruminantia	צְבִי	Deut. 12:15; Song 4:5; etc.
Gecko	Hemidactylus; Ptyodoctylus	Geckoidae	אֲנָקָה	Lev. 11:30
			שְׂמָמִית	Prov. 30:28
Gnat	Culex; Anopheles	Dyptera	עָרוֹב	Ex. 8:17; Ps. 78:45; etc.
Goat	Capra hircus	Artiodactyla Ruminantia	עֵז	Lev. 7:23; Song 4:1; etc.
			שָׂעִיר	Gen. 37:31; Lev. 4:28; etc.
			תַּיִשׁ	Gen. 30:35; Prov. 30:31; etc.
			עַתּוּדִים	Gen. 31:10; Jer. 50:8; etc.
Goat, Wild	Capra aegagrus	Artiodactyla Ruminantia	אַקּוֹ	Deut. 14:5
Goose	Anser anser domesticus	Anseriformes	בַּרְבּוּר	I Kings 5:3
			אַוָּז	Bek. 7, 4; Shab. 24.3; etc.
Grasshopper, longhorned	Tettigonidae	Orthoptera	חַרְגּוֹל	Lev. 11:22
Grasshopper, shorthorned	Acrididae	Orthoptera	חָגָב	Num. 13:33; Isa. 40:22; etc.
		Orthoptera	סָלְעָם	Lev. 11:22
Gull	Larus sp.	Laridae	שַׁחַף	Lev. 11:16; Deut. 14:15
Hare	Lepus sp.	Leporidae	אַרְנֶבֶת	Lev. 11:6; Deut. 14:7
Hawk	Accipiter nissus	Falconiformes	נֵץ	Lev. 11:16; Job. 39:26; etc.
Heron	Egretta sp. Ardea sp.	Ardeidae	אֲנָפָה	Lev. 11:19; Deut. 14:18; etc.
Hippopotamus	Hippopotamus amphibius	Artiodactyla non Ruminantia	בְּהֵמוֹת	Job. 40:15–23
Horse	Equus caballus orientalis	Equidae	סוּס	Gen. 47:17; Ex. 9:3; etc.
			פָּרָשׁ	Isa. 28:28; Ezek. 27:14; etc.
Hyena	Hyaena hyaena	Hyaenidae	צָבוּעַ	I Sam. 13:18
Hyrax, Syrian	Procavia syriaca	Hyracoidea	שָׁפָן	Lev. 11:5; Ps. 104:18; etc.
Ibex	Capra nubiana	Artiodactyla Ruminantia	יָעֵל, יַעֲלָה	Ps. 104:18; Job 39:1; etc.
Jackal	Canis aureus	Canidae	שׁוּעָל	Judg. 15:4; Ps. 63:11; etc.
			אִיִּים(?)	Isa. 13:22;
Kestrel	Falco tinnunculus	Falconiformes	תַּחְמָס	Lev. 11:16; Deut. 14:15
Kite	Milvus sp.	Falconiformes	דָּאָה	Lev. 11:14
			דַּיָּה	Deut. 14:13; Isa. 34:15
Leech	Hirudo; Limnatis	Hirudinae	עֲלוּקָה	Prov. 30:15
Leopard	Felis pardus tullianus	Felidae	נָמֵר	Isa. 11:6; Jer. 13:23; etc.
Lion	Felis leo	Felidae	אֲרִי	Isa. 38:13; Amos 3:12; etc.
			אַרְיֵה	Gen. 49:9; Job. 4:10; etc.
			כְּפִיר	Ezek. 19:3; Job. 4:10; etc.
			לָבִיא	Gen. 49:9; Isa. 5:29; etc.
			לַיִשׁ	Job. 4:11; Prov. 30:30; etc.
			שַׁחַל	Hos. 5:14; Job 4:10; etc.
Lizard	Lacerta sp.	Lacertidae	לְטָאָה	Lev. 11:30
Lizard, Dab	Uromastix aegyptius	Agamida	צָב	Lev. 11:29
Lizard, Monitor	Varanus griseus niloticus	Varanidae	כֹּחַ	Lev. 11:30
Locust	Schistocerca gregaria	Orthoptera	אַרְבֶּה	Ex. 10:11–19; Deut. 28:38; etc.
			גָּזָם	Amos 4:9; Joel 1:4; 2; 25
			גּוֹבַי	Amos 7:1; Nahum 3:17
			חָסִיל	I Kings 8:37; Joel 1:4; etc.
			יֶלֶק	Jer. 51:14; Joel 1:4; etc.
Louse	Anoptura	Rhynchoidae	כֵּן, כִּנִּים	Isa. 51:6; Ex. 8:12
			כִּנָּם	Ex. 8:13–14; etc.
Mackerel	Scomber scomber	Scombridae	קוֹלְיָאס הָאִסְפָּנִין	Shab. 22.2
Maggot	Lucilia sp.; Drosophila sp.	Dyptera	רִמָּה	Ex. 16:24; Job 7:5; etc.
Mole Rat	Spalax ehrenbergi	Rodentia	חֲפַרְפָּרוֹת	Isa. 2:20;
			אשות	Kelim, 21, 3; M.K. 1.4
Mongoose	Herpestes ichneumon	Viverridae	נְמִיָּה	B.B. 2, 5
Monkey	Simia	Anthropoidea	קוֹף	I Kings, 10:22; II Chron. 9:21
Moth, Carpenter	Cossidae	Lepidoptera	נסס	Isa. 10:18
Moth, Clothes	Microlepidoptera	Lepidoptera	סָס	Isa. 51:8
			עָשׁ	Isa. 50:9; 51:8; etc.
Mouse	Microtus guenthri Mus musculus	Rodentia	עַכְבָּר	Lev. 11:29; Isa. 66:17; etc.
Mule	Equus asinus mulus	Equidae	פֶּרֶד, פִּרְדָּה	Isa. 66:20; I King 1:38; etc.
			רֶכֶשׁ(?)	Mic. 1:13; Esth. 8:10; etc.
Nightingale	Luscinia megarhynchos; Passeres	Passeres	זָמִיר	Song 2:12
Onager, Arabian Wild	Equus hemionus onager	Equidae	עָרוֹד	Job. 39:5
Onager, Syrian Wild	Equus hemionus hemihippus	Equidae	פֶּרֶא	Jer. 14:6; Job 6:5; etc.
Oryx	Oryx leucoryx	Artiodactyla Ruminantia	זֶמֶר(?)	Deut. 14:5
Ostrich	Struthio camelus	Struthionidae	יָעֵן	Lam. 4:3
			כְּנַף רְנָנִים	Job. 39:13–18
Owl, Barn	Tyto alba	Striges	תִּנְשֶׁמֶת (עוֹף)	Lev. 11:18; Deut. 14:16
Owl, Eagle	Bubo bubo aharonii	Striges	אֹחַ	Isa. 13:21
Owl, Eagle Desert Dark	Bubo bubo ascalaphus	Striges	בַּת־יַעֲנָה	Lev. 11:16; Isa. 34:13; etc.
Owl, Eagle Desert Pale	Bubo bubo desertorum	Striges	תַּנִּים(?)	Isa. 34:13; Mal. 1:3; etc.
Owl, Fish	Ketupa zeylonensis	Striges	שָׁלָךְ	Lev. 11:17; Deut. 14:17
Owl, Little Dark	Athene noctua glaux	Striges	כּוֹס	Lev. 11:17; Ps. 102:7; etc.
Owl, Little Desert	Athene noctua saharae	Striges	קָאַת	Lev. 11:18; Isa. 34:11; etc.
Owl, Longeared	Asio otus	Striges	יַנְשׁוּף	Lev. 11:17; Isa. 34:11; etc.
Owl, Scops Screech	Otus scopus	Striges	שָׂעִיר	Isa. 13:21; 34:14
Owl, Shorteared	Asio flammeus	Striges	קִפּוֹד	Isa. 14:23; Zeph. 2:14; etc.
			קִפּוֹז (?)	Isa. 34:15
Owl, Tawny	Strix aluco	Striges	לִילִית	Isa. 34:14
Ox, Wild	Bos primigenius	Artiodactyla Ruminantia	רְאֵם; רֵים	Num. 23:22; Job 39:9–10; etc.
Partridge, Chuckar	Alectoris graeca	Galliformes	חָגְלָה	Num. 26:33; 27:1; etc.
Partridge, See-see	Ammoperdix heyi	Galliformes	קֹרֵא	I Sam. 26:20; Jer. 17:11
Peacock	Pavo cristatus	Galliformes	תֻּכִּי	I Kings 10:22; II Chron. 9:21
Porcupine	Erinaceus; Hemiechinus	Erinaceidae	קוּפָד	Kil. 8, 5; Shab. 5, 4
Quail	Coturnix coturnix	Galliformes	שְׂלָו	Ex. 16:13; Num. 11:31; etc.
Rat	Rattus rattus	Rodentia	חֹלֶד	Lev. 11:29
			חוּלְדָּה	Kelim 15. 6; Par. 9.3
Raven	Corvus sp.	Corvidae	עוֹרֵב	Gen. 8:7; Lev. 11:15; etc.
Sardine	Sardinella maderensis	Clupeidae	טָרִית	Ned. 6, 4; Av. Zar. 2.6
	Sardinella aurita	Clupeidae	חִילָק	Av. Zar. 2.6
Scorpion	Scorpio sp. Buthus sp.	Scorpionidae	עַקְרָב	Deut. 8:15
Sheep	Ovis vignei platyura	Artiodactyla Ruminantia	צֹאן	Gen. 4:2; I Sam. 25:2; etc.
			אַיִל	Gen. 22:13; 31:38; etc.
			רָחֵל	Gen. 32:15; Isa. 53:7; etc.
			כֶּבֶשׂ, כִּבְשָׂה	Ex. 12:5; Lev. 14:10; etc.
			כֶּשֶׂב, כִּשְׂבָּה	Lev. 3:7; 5:6; etc.
			טָלֶה	I Sam. 7:9; Isa. 65:25; etc.
Sheep, Wild	Ovis musimon	Artiodactyla Ruminantia	כּוֹי (?)	Bik. 2.8; Bek. 1.5; etc.
Skink	Eumeces sp. Chalcides sp.	Skincidae	חֹמֶט	Lev. 11:30
Snake	Ophidia	Serpentes	נָחָשׁ	Gen. 3:1; Amos 5:19; etc.
Sparrow	Passer domesticus biblicus	Ploceidae	צִפּוֹר דְּרוֹר	Lev. 14:4; Ps. 84:4; etc.
Spider	Araneida; Solifugae	Arachnoidae	עַכָּבִישׁ	Isa. 59:5; Job 8:14
			עַכְשׁוּב	Ps. 140:4
Stork	Ciconia ciconia	Ciconidae	חֲסִידָה	Lev. 11:19; Jer. 8:7; etc.
Swift	Apus sp.	Apodidae	סִיס	Isa. 38:14; Jer. 8:7; etc.
Swine	Sus domestica	Artiodactyla non Ruminantia	חֲזִיר	Lev. 11:7; Prov. 11:22; etc.
Tahash	Dugong; Giraffa?		תַּחַשׁ	Ex. 36:19; Num. 4:6; etc.
Turtle dove	Streptopelia turtur	Columbiformes	תּוֹר	Gen. 15:9; Jer. 8:7; etc.
Viper, Carpet	Echis sp.	Viperidae	אֶפְעֶה	Isa. 30:6; Job 20:16; etc.
Viper, Horned	Cerastes sp.	Viperidae	שְׁפִיפֹן	Gen. 49:17
Viper, Palestinian	Vipera palaestina	Viperidae	צֶפַע	Isa. 14:29
			צִפְעוֹנִי	Isa. 11:8; Jer. 8:17; etc.
Vulture, Bearded	Gypaetus barbatus	Vultures	פֶּרֶס	Lev. 11:13; Deut. 14:12
Vulture, Black	Aegypius monachus	Vultures	עָזְנִיָּה	Lev. 11:13; Deut. 14:12
			עוֹז	Kelim 17, 4
Vulture, Egyptian	Neophron percnopterus	Vultures	רָחָם; רָחָמָה	Lev. 11:18; Deut. 14:17; etc.
Vulture, Griffon	Gyps fulvus	Vultures	נֶשֶׁר	Lev. 11:13; Deut. 32:11; etc.
Wasp	Vespa orientalis	Hymenoptera	צִרְעָה	Ex. 23:28; Deut. 7:20; etc.
Whale	Balenoptera; Physeter	Cetacea	לִוְיָתָן	Ps. 104:26; Isa. 27:1; etc.
Wolf	Canis lupus	Canidae	זְאֵב	Isa. 11:6; Jer. 5:6; etc.

אֲנִי מַאֲמִין בֶּאֱמוּנָה שְׁלֵמָה שֶׁהַבּוֹרֵא יִתְבָּרַךְ שְׁמוֹ הוּא בּוֹרֵא וּמַנְהִיג לְכָל־הַבְּרוּאִים. וְהוּא לְבַדּוֹ עָשָׂה וְעוֹשֶׂה וְיַעֲשֶׂה לְכָל־הַמַּעֲשִׂים:

I believe with perfect faith that the Creator, blessed be his name, is the Author and Guide of everything that has been created, and that he alone has made, does make, and will make all things.

2

אֲנִי מַאֲמִין בֶּאֱמוּנָה שְׁלֵמָה שֶׁהַבּוֹרֵא יִתְבָּרַךְ שְׁמוֹ הוּא יָחִיד. וְאֵין יְחִידוּת כָּמוֹהוּ בְּשׁוּם פָּנִים. וְהוּא לְבַדּוֹ אֱלֹהֵינוּ הָיָה הֹוֶה וְיִהְיֶה:

I believe with perfect faith that the Creator, blessed be his name, is a Unity, and that there is no unity in any manner like unto his, and that he alone is our God, who was, is, and will be.

3

אֲנִי מַאֲמִין בֶּאֱמוּנָה שְׁלֵמָה שֶׁהַבּוֹרֵא יִתְבָּרַךְ שְׁמוֹ אֵינוֹ גוּף. וְלֹא יַשִּׂיגוּהוּ מַשִּׂיגֵי הַגּוּף. וְאֵין לוֹ שׁוּם דִּמְיוֹן כְּלָל:

I believe with perfect faith that the Creator, blessed be his name, is not a body, and that he is free from all the accidents of matter, and that he has not any form whatsoever.

4

אֲנִי מַאֲמִין בֶּאֱמוּנָה שְׁלֵמָה שֶׁהַבּוֹרֵא יִתְבָּרַךְ שְׁמוֹ הוּא רִאשׁוֹן וְהוּא אַחֲרוֹן:

I believe with perfect faith that the Creator, blessed be his name, is the first and the last.

5

אֲנִי מַאֲמִין בֶּאֱמוּנָה שְׁלֵמָה שֶׁהַבּוֹרֵא יִתְבָּרַךְ שְׁמוֹ לוֹ לְבַדּוֹ רָאוּי לְהִתְפַּלֵּל. וְאֵין רָאוּי לְהִתְפַּלֵּל לְזוּלָתוֹ:

I believe with perfect faith that to the Creator, blessed be his name, and to him alone it is right to pray, and that it is not right to pray to any being besides him.

6

אֲנִי מַאֲמִין בֶּאֱמוּנָה שְׁלֵמָה שֶׁכָּל־דִּבְרֵי הַנְּבִיאִים אֱמֶת:

I believe with perfect faith that all the words of the prophets are true.

7

אֲנִי מַאֲמִין בֶּאֱמוּנָה שְׁלֵמָה שֶׁנְּבוּאַת מֹשֶׁה רַבֵּינוּ עָלָיו הַשָּׁלוֹם הָיְתָה אֲמִתִּית. וְשֶׁהוּא הָיָה אָב לַנְּבִיאִים לַקּוֹדְמִים לְפָנָיו וְלַבָּאִים אַחֲרָיו:

I believe with perfect faith that the prophecy of Moses our teacher, peace be unto him, was true, and that he was the chief of the prophets, both of those that preceded and of those that followed him.

8

אֲנִי מַאֲמִין בֶּאֱמוּנָה שְׁלֵמָה שֶׁכָּל־הַתּוֹרָה הַמְּצוּיָה עַתָּה בְּיָדֵינוּ הִיא הַנְּתוּנָה לְמֹשֶׁה רַבֵּינוּ עָלָיו הַשָּׁלוֹם:

I believe with perfect faith that the whole Law, now in our possession, is the same that was given to Moses our teacher peace be unto him.

9

אֲנִי מַאֲמִין בֶּאֱמוּנָה שְׁלֵמָה שֶׁזֹּאת הַתּוֹרָה לֹא תְהֵי מֻחְלֶפֶת. וְלֹא תְהֵי תוֹרָה אַחֶרֶת מֵאֵת הַבּוֹרֵא יִתְבָּרַךְ שְׁמוֹ:

I believe with perfect faith that this Law will not be changed, and that there will never be any other law from the Creator, blessed be his name.

10

אֲנִי מַאֲמִין בֶּאֱמוּנָה שְׁלֵמָה שֶׁהַבּוֹרֵא יִתְבָּרַךְ שְׁמוֹ יוֹדֵעַ כָּל־מַעֲשֵׂה בְנֵי אָדָם וְכָל־מַחְשְׁבֹתָם. שֶׁנֶּאֱמַר. הַיֹּצֵר יַחַד לִבָּם הַמֵּבִין אֶל־כָּל־מַעֲשֵׂיהֶם:

I believe with perfect faith that the Creator, blessed be his name, knows every deed of the children of men, and all their thoughts, as it is said, It is he that fashioneth the hearts of them all, that giveth heed to all their deeds.

11

אֲנִי מַאֲמִין בֶּאֱמוּנָה שְׁלֵמָה שֶׁהַבּוֹרֵא יִתְבָּרַךְ שְׁמוֹ גּוֹמֵל טוֹב לְשׁוֹמְרֵי מִצְוֹתָיו וּמַעֲנִישׁ לְעוֹבְרֵי מִצְוֹתָיו:

I believe with perfect faith that the Creator, blessed be his name, rewards those that keep his commandments, and punishes those that transgress them.

12

אֲנִי מַאֲמִין בֶּאֱמוּנָה שְׁלֵמָה בְּבִיאַת הַמָּשִׁיחַ. וְאַף עַל פִּי שֶׁיִּתְמַהְמֵהַּ עִם כָּל־זֶה אֲחַכֶּה־לּוֹ בְּכָל־יוֹם שֶׁיָּבֹא:

I believe with perfect faith in the coming of the Messiah, and, though he tarry, I will wait daily for his coming.

13

אֲנִי מַאֲמִין בֶּאֱמוּנָה שְׁלֵמָה שֶׁתִּהְיֶה תְּחִיַּת הַמֵּתִים בְּעֵת שֶׁיַּעֲלֶה רָצוֹן מֵאֵת הַבּוֹרֵא יִתְבָּרַךְ שְׁמוֹ וְיִתְעַלֶּה זִכְרוֹ לָעַד וּלְנֵצַח נְצָחִים:

I believe with perfect faith that there will be a resurrection of the dead at the time when it shall please the Creator, blessed be his name, and exalted be the remembrance of him for ever and ever.

Walter H. Annenberg

David anointed by Samuel, wall painting, Dura Europos synagogue

Ani Ma'amin (Heb. "I believe"), short creed by unknown author (c. 15th c.) based on Thirteen Articles of Faith formulated by Maimonides. Article expressing belief in advent of Messiah became martyrs' hymn during Nazi Holocaust.

An'im Zemirot, synagogue hymn ascribed to Judah he-Ḥasid of Regensburg. Also called *Shir ha-Kavod.* ("Song of Glory"). Alphabetic acrostic containing fervent paean to God's greatness and might.

Aninut (Heb.), status of bereaved person in period between death and burial of close relative. Bereaved person is known as *onen.*

Anisimov, Ilya Sherbatovich (b. 1862), ethnographer of Caucasian Jewry; b. Dagestan.

Anjou, former duchy in W. France. Jews lived in many towns of province; expelled 1289, returned after 1359, in particular to Anjou, but had to leave in general expulsion fr. France 1394.

Ankara, city in Turkey. Jews settled after 1492 expulsion fr. Spain. Organized community dwindled in 17th c. Revived but again reduced after WWII. Jewish pop. 1,200 (1971).

Ankawa, Abraham ben Mordecai (b. 1810), rabbi, kabbalist in Morocco. Published works include a prayerbook, responsa, rules of *terefah* in verse, etc.

Ankawa, Raphael ben Mordecai (1848–1935), rabbi, Jewish leader in Morocco. President of supreme court of Moroccan Jewry fr. 1918.

Ankori, Zvi (1920–), Jewish historian; b. Poland. Taught in Israel and U.S. At Ben-Gurion Univ. Beersheba fr. 1974. Author of *Karaites in Byzantium.*

Anna be-Kho'aḥ, 13th c. hymn recited in some rites in daily morning prayer and on Sabbath. In E. European rites, recited in counting of Omer.

Anna be-Korenu, *seliḥah* in Sephardi rite recited on eve of Day of Atonement; written by David b. Eleazar ibn Paquda (12th c.).

Annenberg, Walter H. (1908–), U.S. editor, diplomat, philanthropist. Publisher of oldest U.S. daily newspaper, the *Philadelphia Inquirer,* and other journals. Appointed U.S. ambassador to United Kingdom 1969.

Anointing. Use of oil as unguent common in ancient Israel. Used in religious rites to consecrate kings, priests, and sacred vessels of Tabernacle. David, anointed by Samuel, was called *mashi'aḥ* ("anointed"), the word that passed into English as "messiah."

Anokhi, Zalman Yizḥak (Z.I. Aronsohn; 1878–1947), Russianborn Hebrew author of romantic vignettes of Jewish life in E. Europe. Settled in Ereẓ Israel 1924.

Ansbach, city in W. Germany. Jewish community fr. early 14th c., synagogue built 1745, oldest to survive in Germany. Small community destroyed by Nazis.

Ansell, David Abraham (1834–1914), communal leader in Montreal, Canada. Consul-general for Mexico in Canada.

Anselm ha-Levi (15th c.), rabbi, communal leader in Germany. Appointed supreme rabbi of Holy Roman Empire on authority of Emperor.

Anshel of Cracow (16th c.), reputed author of *Mirkevet ha-Mishneh*, concordance of Bible.

An-Ski, S. (Solomon Zainwil Rapaport; 1863–1920), Yiddish, Russian author, folklorist, dramatist. Active in Russian socialist movement. Left Yiddish works in 15 vol., composed Bund hymn *Di Shvue*, and famous play *The Dybbuk*, first produced in Yiddish, then by Habimah company in Heb. transl. by Bialik.

S. An-Ski

Antebi, Albert (1869–1918), leader of Jewish community in Ereẓ Israel. Representative of ICA, Palestine Office of World Zionist Organization, and Alliance Israélite Universelle. Intervened with Turkish authorities on behalf of Jews of Ereẓ Israel in WWI.

Antheil, George (1900–1959), U.S. composer, pianist. Also published works on glandular criminology.

Antibi, Abraham ben Isaac (1765–1858), Syrian talmudist, leader of Aleppo community. Writings are important source of knowledge of Syrian Jewish life.

Antibi, Jacob (d. 1846), rabbi of Damascus, halakhic authority. Drew world attention to Damascus Affair (1840), during which he suffered detention and torture. Moved to Jerusalem 1841. His son **Ḥayyim Judah Shabbetai Raphael** (1808–1888), wealthy philanthropist, Cairo rabbi; grandson **Elijah Raḥamim** (1852–1920), Safed rabbi.

Anti-Defamation League, U.S. organization founded by B'nai B'rith 1913 to fight anti-Semitism, protect Jews fr. discrimination, and assure equal rights for them (see also B'nai B'rith).

Anti-Fascist Committee, Jewish, group of Jewish Soviet intellectuals and public figures organized in WWII (1941) by Soviet government to mobilize world Jewish support. Headed by Solomon Mikhoels. Published *Eynikeyt*. A memorandum on

Jewish Anti-Fascist Committee

renewed anti-Semitism in Russia, sent by the Committee to Stalin after the war, led to its dissolution and arrest of its members (1948). Its leading members were executed in 1952.

Antigonus (c. 135–104 B.C.E.), Hasmonean prince; son of John Hyrcanus. Met violent death after antagonizing his elder brother, Judah Aristobulus.

Antigonus II (Mattathias), last Hasmonean king, ruled 40–37 B.C.E.; son of Aristobulus II. Taken as hostage to Rome on Pompey's capture of Jerusalem (63). Allowed to return to Judea in 49, found refuge at Chalcis. Captured Jerusalem in 40, putting Herod's brother Phasael to death. Defeated in battle by Herod reinforced by the Romans, and executed on orders of Mark Antony.

Antigonus of Sokho (c. 200 B.C.E.), early mishnaic sage. Saying: "Be not like servants who minister to their master in order to receive a reward, but be like servants who minister to their master not in order to receive a reward; and let the fear of Heaven be upon you" (*Avot* 1:3).

Antin, Mary (1881–1949), U.S. author. Wrote *The Promised Land* expounding "melting pot" theory of Americanization.

Antioch, ancient Syrian city now in S. Turkey. Had large Jewish pop. 1st c. C.E. Conditions deteriorated during revolt against Rome (66–70). Center of Christian learning 3rd–4th c., with ecclesiastic intolerance increasing toward Jews. Jewish rebellion suppressed and many killed or exiled 608 C.E. Community prospered under Ottoman rule. About 400 Jews by 1894, most left by 1950s.

°**Antiochus,** name of Seleucid rulers of Syria. (1) Antiochus III, The Great, reigned 223–187 B.C.E. Involved in wars in Judea. Captured Jerusalem from Ptolemids 198, was magnanimous to Jews for their support. (2) Antiochus IV Epiphanes, reigned 175–163 B.C.E. Occupied Jerusalem 168 B.C.E., killed and enslaved many Jews, plundered Temple treasures. Decreed policy of enforced Hellenization forbidding Jews to observe their religion. His brutal rule caused the Hasmonean revolt. (3) Antiochus VII Sidetes, reigned 138–128 B.C.E., again invaded Judea, besieged Jerusalem 135–4, forced John Hyrcanus to surrender.

Antipas, Herod (b. 20 B.C.E.), son of Herod and Malthace of Samaria. Became tetrarch of Galilee and Perea on his father's death. Founded city of Tiberias in honor of emperor Tiberius. Violated Mosaic law by marrying Herodias, his brother Herod's wife, and according to the New Testament, had John the Baptist put to death for criticizing him. Accused of plotting against Rome in Caligula's reign, died an exile in Gaul.

Antipater II (or **Antipas;** d. 43 B.C.E.), ruler of Edom in time of Alexander Yannai and Salome Alexandra; son of Antipater I and father of Herod. Sided with Caesar after latter defeated Pompey, and was appointed regent of Judea. Poisoned.

Antipater (1st c. C.E.), eldest son of Herod by Doris, his first wife. Executed five days before Herod's death for plotting to murder his aged father.

Mamluk fort and caravanserai of Antipatris

Antipatris, ancient city in Ereẓ Israel near Kefar Sava. Built by Herod in memory of his father, Antipater. Identified with present biblical Aphek and Rosh ha-Ayin (Ras al-'Ayn).

Anti-Semitism, term coined 1879 by the German agitator Wilhelm Marr, soon applied to all forms of hostility toward Jews throughout history. Anti-Jewish prejudice appeared in antiquity mainly in countries which later became part of the Roman Empire. Refusal by the Jews to accept the imperial cult in any form was regarded by Rome as a refusal to recognize the authority of the state, and the rejection of rules then univ-

Dayan to Hitler: Move on!
Kazakhstanskaya Pravda, June 21, 1967.

Russian cartoon after the Six-Day War, 1967

ersally held sacred. However, Jews were unrestricted in their choice of residence and even received favored treatment in deference to their religious needs. This sometimes caused envy by other groups, and anti-Jewish riots ensued, as those organized by the Greeks against the Jews of Alexandria in the 1st c. B.C.E. Pagan anti-Semitism, though, did not hold such fateful consequences for Jews as those inherent in Christianity. These were based on gospel teaching: 1) Jews made to admit their collective responsibility for the crucifixion of the "son of God" (Matt. 27:25). 2) Jews identified with the powers of evil (John 8:44). With the political triumph of Christianity, the emperors began to translate its concepts into practice. From the theological standpoint, the Koran also contained attacks against the Jews, as they refused to recognize Muhammad as the prophet sent by God. But since Islam spread by force of arms rather than by spiritual propaganda, it generally displayed greater tolerance than Christians toward other creeds. In the Middle Ages, anti-Jewish prejudice in Catholic lands was a direct outgrowth of ecclesiastical propaganda sustained by continuous legislation by the Church Councils. In general, popular susceptibility to anti-Semitism developed in the Middle Ages, and was thenceforth perpetuated by linguistic usage and religious instruction. Modern anti-Semitism spread rapidly in grounds made propitious and receptive in socio-political, cultural and psychological terms by Christian prejudices. It was based on the unsound theory of Aryan and Semitic "races" formulated by the French Gobineau, and first became popular in Germany, the classical land of medieval Jew-baiting, with resentment and jealousy growing parallel to Jewish progress in all walks of life. In 1887 an anti-Semitic party was formed in Austria and a "ritual murder" charge brought in Tisza-Eszlar, Hungary. In France anti-Jewish agitation culminated in the Dreyfus case which convulsed French life bet. 1894–99. After WWI, the reactionary identification of Judaism with Bolshevism and the publication of the Protocols of the Elders of Zion, purporting to prove an international Jewish conspiracy to control the world, caused an upsurge of anti-Semitism in the new style in many countries. In the U.S., automobile manufacturer Henry Ford for a time lent his name and financial support to the movement. Exploiting old prejudices, widespread economic distress, and reactionary resentment against liberal ideas and defeat in the field, Adolf Hitler made racial anti-Semitism one of the mainstays of his National Socialist (Nazi) Party. From his advent to power in 1933, he used anti-Semitic currents in other lands to weaken resistance to German penetration. The passage from theory to practice of the anti-Semitic tenets is to be traced in the successive stages of increasing barbarity and tragedy which marked European history in WWII, with Nazi Germany providing the theorists, the organizers, and the executioners – with collaboration from anti-Semites in other countries. This resulted in the murder of 6 million European Jews. After WWII, anti-Semitism was advocated by marginal rightist groups and, from 1967, in certain leftist circles. Also manifestations among U.S. black extremists. Arab nationalism also made efforts to exploit potential anti-Semitism, e.g., in S. America, Africa. Soviet anti-Semitism reached climax during last years of Stalin but continued to appear under various forms thereafter.

Antoine, Nicolas (1603–1632), French Catholic who became a Protestant, then converted to Judaism, for which he was executed in Geneva.

Antokolski, Mark (1843–1902), Russian sculptor. At first used many Jewish themes but later concentrated on subjects from Russian history. Achieved great popularity but in 1880s was attacked as Jew and spent last years in Paris.

Mark Antokolski

Antonia, fortress N. of Temple Mount in Jerusalem, known as "The Citadel." During siege of Titus the breach through which Romans penetrated into Temple area passed through Antonia. Its remains are in vicinity of the Via Dolorosa.

°**Antoninus Pius,** Roman emperor, ruled 138–161. Repealed his predecessor Hadrian's harsh policies in Judea, allowed Jews freely to engage in their traditional worship. A Roman emperor called Antoninus is featured in a number of legends in the Talmud and Midrash as engaging in discussions with distinguished rabbis.

Antwerp, Belgian port. Important center for Marranos fr. Portugal in 16th c. Jews fr. C. and E. Europe came in late 18th and 19th c. Following Russian pogroms, many embarked for America via Antwerp. Jewish enterprise made Antwerp capital of diamond industry in Europe. Jewish pop. 8,000 in 1900, 55,000 in 1939. Nazi persecution during WWII. Most Jewish families arrested Aug. 1942 and deported to death camps. 800 survived. Jewish pop. 13,000 (1971), many engaged in diamond industry. Most of Polish origin, Orthodox or ultra-Orthodox, with 90% of children receiving Jewish education, the highest percentage in Europe.

Anusim (Heb. "forced ones"), persons compelled by pressure to abjure Judaism and adopt different faith (to be distinguished fr. *meshummadim,* or voluntary apostates; see Apostasy). Pressure by church fr. 4th c. led to many forced conversions, as in Clermont-Ferrand (476). This led to creation of Jewish "underground" within Christian society, formed by *anusim* who secretly maintained Jewish observances. Compulsory conversions in Rhineland in 10th c. and during Crusades amid anti-Jewish attacks after 1096. In 12th c. Spain and N. Africa, Muslim Almohads forced both their Jewish and Christian subjects to convert to Islam, the Jewish converts thereafter leading a

crypto-Jewish existence. Late in 13th c. Jews in S. Italy given choice of baptism or death. Following wave of forced conversion, Jewish population in Apulia completely disappeared. The best known and most numerous group of *anusim* found in Kingdoms of Christian Spain. These converts continued to live underground existence fr. 1391 to the 18th c. or later. Becoming known as Marranos, New Christians, or Conversos, they found themselves from the outset in a difficult social and moral position. The expulsion of the Jews fr. Spain in 1492 was officially justified on the ground that it was essential to separate the converts fr. Jewish influence.

Apam (Afam), initial letters of Asti, Fossano, Moncalvo, three Italian towns. Denotes special rite of prayers used in these communities by Jews originally fr. France.

Apel, Willi (1893–), musicologist (*Harvard Dictionary of Music,* etc). Emigrated fr. Germany to U.S. 1935.

Aphek, name of three places mentioned in the Bible. (1) Canaanite royal city E. of Jaffa. (2) Place where Aram defeated Israelites. (3) Canaanite city allotted to tribe of Asher. Nearby is plain of Acre, site of modern kibbutz (founded 1939).

Apikoros, one who negates the rabbinic tradition, an unbeliever or skeptic. Term derived fr. Epicurus, the Greek philosopher.

°**Apion** (1st c. C.E.), Greek rhetorician and anti-Jewish propagandist in Alexandria, against whom Josephus wrote his *Contra Apionem.*

Apocalypse, Jewish literature of revelations, and Christian writings derived fr. it. Arose after cessation of prophecy and flourished fr. 2nd c. B.C.E. to 2nd c. C.E. Deals with revelations of eschatology and secrets beyond human knowledge.

Apocrypha and Pseudepigrapha, two separate groups of works dating fr. Second Temple. Apocryphal books are those not included in canon of Bible, although incorporated in Roman Catholic and Greek Orthodox canon. Pseudepigraphical books, on the other hand, are not accepted in their entirety by any church, only individual books being considered sacred by the Eastern churches, particularly the Ethiopian. The most important are the Books of Enoch, Jubilees, the Ascension of Isaiah, the Assumption of Moses, the Book of Adam and Eve, the Testament of the Twelve Patriarchs. In addition to these there once existed another large series of books, whose authorship was attributed to biblical figures. The Talmud calls both Apocrypha and Pseudepigrapha *Sefarim Hizonim* ("extraneous books").

BOOKS OF THE APOCRYPHA AND ESTIMATED DATES OF COMPOSITION

Tobit	2nd-1st cent. B.C.E.
Judith	1st cent. B.C.E.
Ben-Sira	2nd cent. C.E.
Wisdom of Solomon	1st cent. C.E.
I Maccabees	2nd-1st cent. B.C.E.
II Maccabees	2nd cent. B.C.E.
III Esdras	1st cent. B.C.E-1st cent. C.E.
Additions to Esther	2nd cent. B.C.E.
Book of Baruch	2nd-1st cent. B.C.E.
Epistle of Jeremiah	4th cent. B.C.E.
Additions to Daniel	5th-1st cent. B.C.E.
III Maccabees	1st cent. B.C.E.
IV Maccabees	1st cent. C.E.
Prayer of Manasseh	1st cent. B.C.E.
Psalm 151	2nd-1st cent. B.C.E.
IV Esdras	1st cent. C.E.

Apollonia, ancient city on coast of Ereẓ Israel. Probably founded by Seleucus IV (186–174 B.C.E.). Conquered by Alexander Yannai, then by Pompey (63 B.C.E.). Known as Arsuf in Arab period, held by Crusaders 1101–87 and 1191–1265, captured by sultan Baybars. Today ruined site of Tel Arshaf, N. of Herzliyyah.

Apostasy, abandonment of one's faith. In Hellenistic period, Jewish apostates adopted Hellenistic ways of life, culture. Pressure of Christian or Islamic society caused waves of conversions fr. Judaism in early Middle Ages. Jewish law distinguished bet. forced converts (*anusim*) and voluntary ones (*meshummadim, mumarim*). In Middle Ages the latter often became zealous propagators of their new faith and active persecutors of their former coreligionists.

Appelfeld, Aharon (1932–), Hebrew writer; b. Czernowitz, settled in Ereẓ Israel 1947. Central theme of short stories is Holocaust.

Aptowitzer, Victor (Avigdor; 1871–1942), rabbinic scholar (*Das Schriftwort in der Rabbinischen Literatur,* etc.). Taught at Vienna Hebrew Teachers' College. Settled in Jerusalem 1938.

Apulia, region in S. Italy. Traditionally established by Jewish captives from Judea. Communities in Bari, Oria, Otranto, Taranto important centers of Jewish scholarship under Byzantine rule and in Dark Ages, although often subjected to persecutions and forced baptism. Came to an end in late 13th c. Jewish exiles fr. Spain and Portugal contributed to short-lived renascence in 15th c. Jews finally expelled 1540–41.

Aquila, see Onkelos and Aquila.

Ara, Muslim-Arab village near W. entrance of Iron Valley, on Ḥaderah-Afulah highway, Israel.

Arabah, The (Heb. *Aravah,* "arid steppe," "desert"), two stretches of depressed ground extending N. and S. of Dead Sea. Mainly a sandy desert with average yearly rainfall of up to 1 in. (25 mm.) Traces of ancient agriculture especially abundant in N. portion, where Nabateans irrigated and cultivated large areas. The Arabah is now divided between Israel and Jordan; the Sodom–Eilat road passes through its W. side. A number of settlements (e.g., Ein Yahav, Yotvata) have been established there in recent years.

Arab Refugees, Palestinian Arabs who fled during 1948–49 War of Independence to neighboring Arab countries and parts of Ereẓ Israel later occupied by Jordan and Egypt. Their flight was encouraged by Arab leaders who foretold that they would shortly return in the wake of the victorious Arab armies. There was never a reliable figure for *bona fide* Arab refugees as the numbers were inflated for various reasons. Initial efforts to give them emergency relief made by voluntary organizations but in 1950 United Nations Relief and Works Agency (UNRWA) took full responsibility. During and after Six-Day War there was another largescale population movement, mainly from West Bank of Jordan River into Jordan and from Golan Heights to Syria.

Arabia, The Arabian peninsula. Jews possibly present fr. biblical times. First definite information fr. 1st c. C.E. Arabs in S. Arabia converted to Judaism. Jew. pop. reached peak before advent of Islam (esp. in Hejaz, in town of Medina); Mohammed expelled or forcibly converted most; subsequently remnant only in South, Yemen, and Aden. Almost all Arabian Jews emigrated to Israel.

Arad, biblical and modern city in E. Negev, Israel. Excavations at Tell Arad under Y. Aharoni uncovered large city, destroyed not later than 2700 B.C.E. Site deserted until 11th c. B.C.E. when small settlement rose. Strong citadel built in 10th c. B.C.E. lasted until beginning 6th c. B.C.E. Followed by succession of Persian, Hellenistic, Roman fortresses. Outstanding discovery was temple, first Israelite sanctuary to be uncovered.

New town of Arad.

Remains of the ancient synagogue in the Arbel Valley.

Modern Arad 6 mi. (9 km.) E. of ancient Arad, 610 m. above sea level. Founded 1961. Economy based on region's chemical deposits. Pop. 5,450 (1971).

Arad, city in Transylvania, W. Rumania. Jews fr. early 18th c.; after 1789 center of Reform movement with Aaron Chorin as rabbi. Survived WWII; Jewish pop. 13,200 in 1947, decreased due to emigration mainly to Israel; 4,000 in 1969.

Aragon, former state in NE Spain. Densest Jewish population in Europe in 12th–13th c. and communities flourished under James the Conqueror (1213–76) but conditions deteriorated as Dominicans gained influence at end of 13th c.; massacres of 1391 and forced conversions of 15th c. led to depletion of community, culminating in expulsion of 1492.

Arakhin, 5th tractate in Mishnah order *Kodashim,* with *gemara* in both Talmuds. Deals with valuation of various objects dedicated to sanctuary.

Aram, Arameans, group of Semitic tribes who spread over Fertile Crescent in last quarter of 2nd millennium B.C.E. According to Gen. 10:22, Aram and Israel had common ancestry and Israelite patriarchs were of Aramean origin. Apart fr. Bible, earliest light shed by Akkadian sources of 12th c. B.C.E. Achieved considerable political importance with formation of independent Aramean states (Aram-Damascus, Aram-Naharaim, Aram-Zoba in Syria and Mesopotamia). In 743–2, Aramean states in Syria were overthrown and turned into Assyrian dependencies.

Arama, Isaac ben Moses (c. 1420–1494), rabbi, philosopher, preacher in Spain. Settled in Naples after 1492 expulsion. Wrote *Akedat Yiẓḥak,* commentaries on Pentateuch, a classic work in Jewish homiletics. His son **Meir b. Isaac** (c. 1460–c. 1545), rabbi in Salonika fr. 1495. Biblical commentator, philosopher.

Aramaic, ancient NW Semitic language. Historically there were 5 main groups: (a) Ancient A. found in Syria up to 700 B.C.E.; (b) Official A. (700–300 B.C.E.) includes inscriptions from Syria-Iraq area, biblical A. (notably in Daniel and Ezra), and the Elephantine documents. It was the lingua franca of the Near East; (c) Middle A. (300 B.C.E. ff.) found in documents from W. Asia and in the Onkelos translation (Targum) of the Bible and most of the Dead Sea Scrolls written in A.; (d) Late A. divided into two dialectal groups: (1) W. Aramaic, including Palestinian-Christian Aramaic and Galilean Aramaic (the A. of the Jerusalem Talmud, aggadic Midrashim, the Cairo Genizah, the Palestinian Targum, and Targum Pseudo-Jonathan of the Pentateuch). (2) E. Aramaic, consisting of Syriac, the language of the Babylonian Talmud, and Mandaic; (e) Neo-A. still spoken in a few places in Syria, Turkey, and Kurdistan.

Aram-Damascus (Aram-Dammesek), principal Aramean state 9th–8th c. B.C.E.; centered in Damascus, its capital.

Aram-Zoba, see Aleppo.

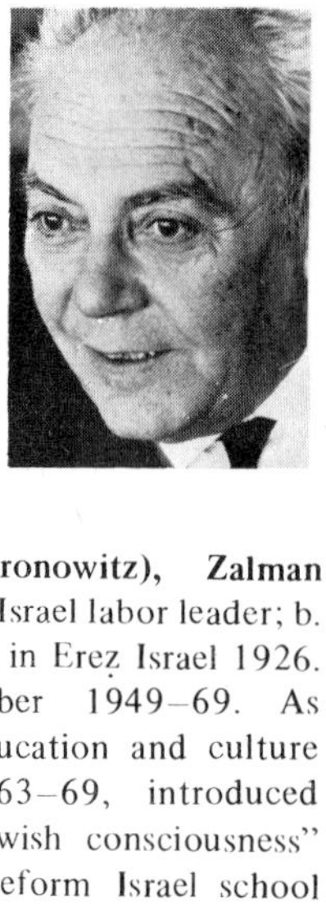

Zalman Aranne

Aranne (Aharonowitz), Zalman (1899–1970), Israel labor leader; b. Russia, settled in Ereẓ Israel 1926. Knesset member 1949–69. As minister of education and culture 1955–60, 1963–69, introduced course in "Jewish consciousness" and plan to reform Israel school system.

Ararat, name of land and mountains mentioned in Bible as place where Noah's ark came to rest. Identified by some as Mt. Massis, highest peak of Armenia.

Ararat, see Noah, Mordecai Manuel.

Araunah, last Jebusite ruler of Jerusalem from whom David purchased site on which Temple was later built.

Aravah, the willow; one of "four species" used on Sukkot together with *etrog, hadas, lulav.*

Arazi, Yehuda (1907–1959), Haganah leader, organizer of "illegal" immigration to Ereẓ Israel; b. Poland, settled in Ereẓ Israel 1923. Active after WWII, especially in Italy, for the immigration to Ereẓ Israel of survivors of the Holocaust.

Arba'ah Minim, see Four Species.

Arba Kanfot, see Tallit Katan.

Arba Kosot (Heb. "four cups"), four cups of wine drunk by each participant at Passover *seder* service.

Arbeiter Ring, see Workmen's Circle.

Arbel, name of three sites in Ereẓ Israel. (1) In Galilee, NW of Tiberias, contains remains of ancient synagogue, caves fortified by Josephus in Jewish War. Moshav established there 1949. (2) In Jezreel Valley. (3) In Transjordan.

Arbib, Edoardo (1840–1906), Italian soldier (with Garibaldi) and journalist (founded daily *La Libertà*). Senator fr. 1870.

Archa (Lat. "chest"), chest or coffer for deposit of records of Jewish financial transactions, officially set up in England fr. 1194. There were more than 20 archae, coordinated by Exchequer of the Jews.

Archaeology, in Ereẓ Israel. Surveys of Edward Robinson (in 1838 and 1852), Victor Guérin (in 1852), and that of the Palestine Exploration Fund (carried out from 1874 to 1882 by C.R. Conder, C. Warren, H.H. Kitchener and C.W. Wilson) started the modern phase in the research of the Holy Land. Excavations in the early 20th c. marked the beginning of modern methods of excavations. Under the British Mandate large-scale excavations were undertaken under various auspices. After 1948 Israel scholars and foreign expeditions (French,

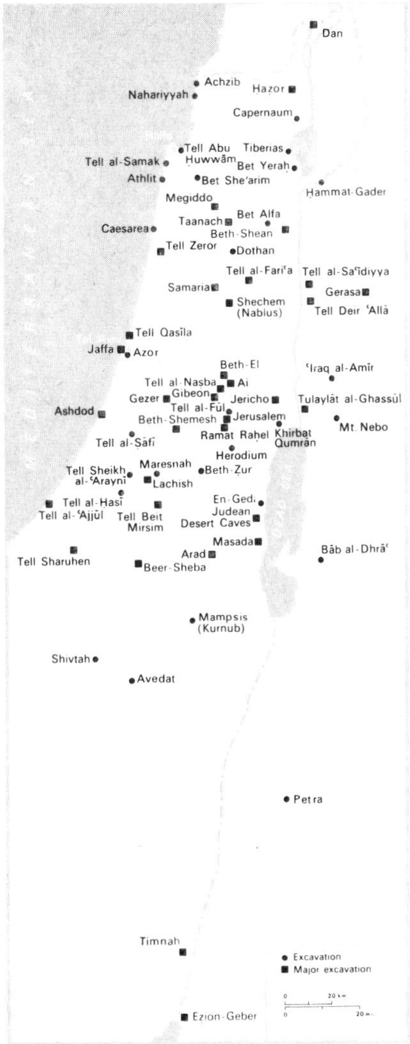

Archaeological sites in Ereẓ Israel.

Tell el-Milḥ near Arad.

Philistine clay jug, 12th cent. B.C.E., found at Tel Itun, south of Hebron.

Reconstructing a jar from pottery shards.

Ossuary from a Jerusalem tomb.

ARCHAEOLOGICAL PERIODS

DATE	ARCHAEOLOGICAL PERIOD	HISTORICAL PERIOD	
12,000–7500 B.C.E.	Mesolithic	Pre-History	Natufian Culture
7500–4000 B.C.E.	Neolithic	Pre-History	Yarmukian Culture
4000–3150 B.C.E.	Chalcolithic	Pre-History	Ghassulian Culture
3150–2850 B.C.E.	Early Bronze I	Early Canaanite	Bet Yeraḥ Culture
2850–2650 B.C.E.	Early Bronze II		
2650–2350 B.C.E.	Early Bronze III		
2350–2200 B.C.E.	Early Bronze IV (III A)		
2200–2000 B.C.E.	Middle Bronze I	Middle Canaanite	
2000–1750 B.C.E.	Middle Bronze II A		
1750–1550 B.C.E.	Middle Bronze II B		Hyksos Period
1550–1400 B.C.E.	Late Bronze I	Late Canaanite	Egyptian Rule
1400–1300 B.C.E.	Late Bronze II A		El Amarna Period
1300–1200 B.C.E.	Late Bronze II B		
1200–1150 B.C.E.	Iron Age I A	Israelite I	Israelite Invasion
1150–1000 B.C.E.	Iron Age I B	Israelite II	Philistine Invasion
1000– 900 B.C.E.	Iron Age II A		
900– 800 B.C.E.	Iron Age II B	Israelite III	
800– 586 B.C.E.	Iron Age II C		
586– 332 B.C.E.	Persian		
332– 152 B.C.E.	Hellenistic I		
152– 37 B.C.E.	Hellenistic (Hasmonean) II		
37 B.C.E.– 70 C.E.	Roman (Herodian) I		
70– 324 C.E.	Roman II, III		
324– 640 C.E.	Byzantine		
640–1099 C.E.	Early Arab		
1099–1291 C.E.	Crusader		
1291–1516 C.E.	Mamluk		

Ivory plaque in Phoenician style found at Nimrud.

Italian, Japanese) carried out numerous excavations in Israel, and after the Six-Day War (1967), Israel archaeologists commenced excavations in the Old City of Jerusalem. The Institutions that functioned in Ereẓ Israel were:

1. Palestine Exploration Fund, founded in Britain 1865.
2. British School of Archaeology, founded 1919.
3. Institutum Pontificum Biblicum, founded 1927.
4. Custodia di Terra Santa, a Franciscan archaeological center.
5. American School of Oriental Studies (fr. 1970 W.F. Albright Institute) founded 1900.
6. Ecole Biblique et Archéologique Française, founded 1892.
7. Department of Antiquities of the Mandate Government, functioned 1920–1948.
8. Israel Exploration Society (until 1948 Jewish Palestine Exploration Society).
9. Israel Department of Antiquities, founded 1948, succeeded the Mandate Department of Antiquities.
10. Archaeological departments of Hebrew Univ. and Tel Aviv Univ.

Archelaus, ethnarch of Judea 4 B.C.E.–c. 6 C.E.; son of Herod by his Samaritan wife, Malthace. His severity caused popular discontent and he was exiled by Augustus to Gaul; d.c. 16 C.E.

Archisynagogos, title used in classical times referring to head of the synagogue, who served as the leader of the Jewish community.

Archivolti, Samuel (1515–1611), Italian author, grammarian, poet. Wrote Hebrew grammar (*Arugat ha-Bosem*).

Archon, communal officer for independent Jewish community (*kehillah*) in Greek and Roman period.

Archpresbyter, title of official representative of medieval English Jewry, designated in Latin as *Presbyter Judaeorum.*

Arditi, Albert Judah (1891–1942), Greek socialist leader, deputy mayor of Salonika. Killed at Auschwitz.

Ardon (Bronstein), Mordecai (1896–), Israel painter; b. Poland, settled in Ereẓ Israel 1933. Taught at Bezalel School, became director 1940. Exhibited at Venice Biennale 1954. Israel Prize 1964. Evolved fr. impressionistic brush technique to symbolic abstract style.

Arenda, Polish term of late Middle Ages designating lease of fixed assets (land, mills, breweries, etc.) or special rights, such as collection of customs duties and taxes. Adopted with same meaning in Hebrew and Yiddish fr. 16th c., it referred to both the system and the lessees, who were often Jewish, especially in eastern districts of Poland-Lithuania.

Arendt, Hannah (1906–), German-born political, social philosopher; in U.S. fr. 1941. Author of *The Origins of Totalitarianism, On Revolution.* Her *Eichmann in Jerusalem* aroused violent controversy through its attacks on European Jewish leadership and its suggestion that European Jewry was partly to blame for Holocaust because it lacked the will to resist.

Arendt, Otto (1854–1936), German economist, politician. Advocate of bimetallism and protective tariffs. Converted to Protestantism.

Argentina, S. American republic. There are reports that a few Jews lived as "New Christians" in 16th and 17th c. Organized Jewish life began in 1860s, but major influx began only after Russian pogroms in 1880s, becoming large-scale from end of decade. Fear of communism led to some anti-Semitism after WWI, and there was a pogrom in 1919. 79,000 Jews arrived in 1920s. Despite varying degrees of government condemnation anti-Semitism continued; a contributing factor was presence of ex-Nazis and representatives of the Arab League. Representative bodies included D.A.I.A. and Va'ad ha-Kehillot. Argentina was site of various Jewish agricultural settlements promoted by Jewish Colonization Association financed by Baron de Hirsch. At the peak (1925) some 25,000 Jews lived in such settlements. 782 families remained in 1964. Jewish pop.

Jewish settlement in Argentina.

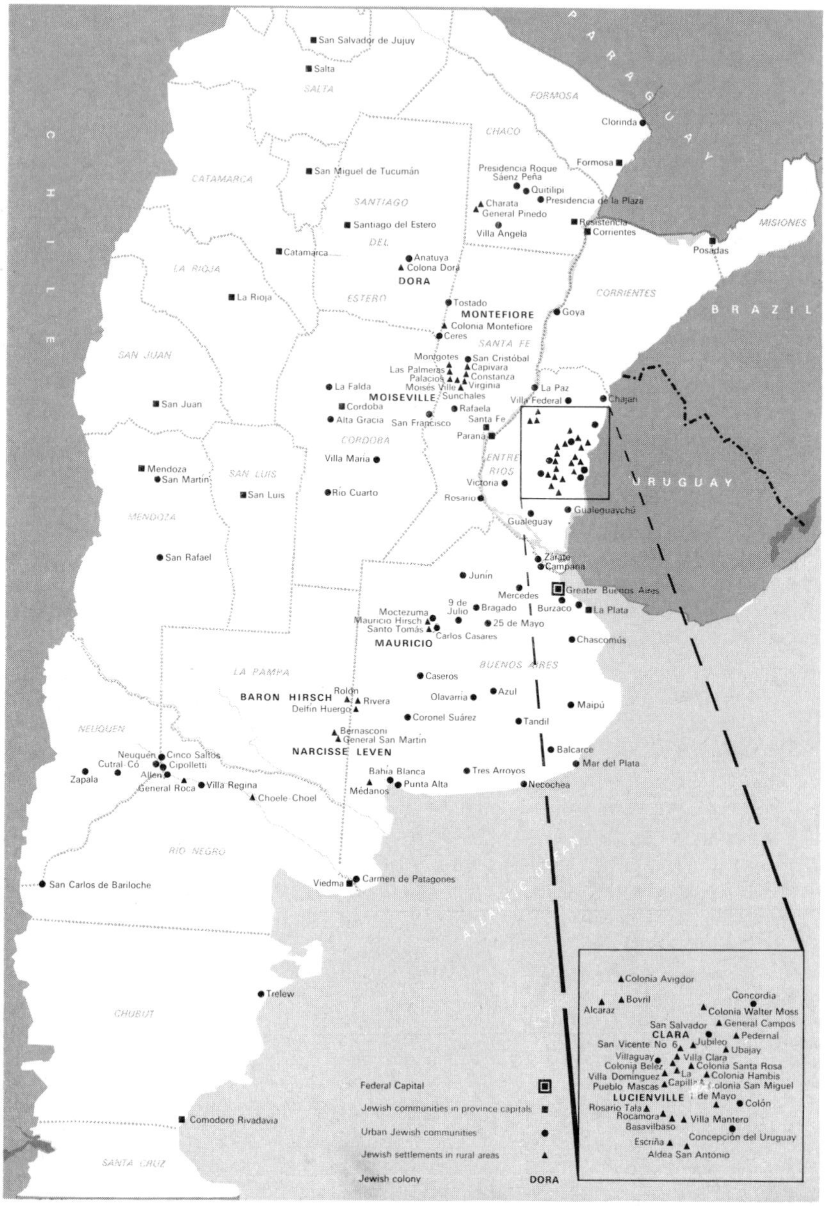

JEWISH ARCHIVES

POLAND

Jewish Historical Institute, Warsaw, established after W.W.II, closed 1968, archives transferred to Polish government and municipal archives	documents on Jewish communities and the fate of Jews in Poland including Emanuel Ringelblum archive

CZECHOSLOVAKIA

Jewish State Museum, Prague, founded after World War II	archives of Jewish communities in Czechoslovakia

ENGLAND

Jewish Historical Society of England, founded 1893	documents on British Jewry, including archives of Anglo-Jewish Association
Wiener Library, London, founded 1934	contemporary Jewish history, anti-Semitism, Nazi persecution

FRANCE

Central Jewish Consistoire, Paris, established 1808	history of the central consistory
Paris Jewish Consistoire, established 1808	history of Jews in Paris since 1808
Alliance Israélite Universelle, established 1860	correspondence with its offices and educational institutes in the Middle East and history of Jews in Muslim and East European countries
Centre de Documentation Juive Contemporaine, Paris founded 1942	Holocaust, including archives of Alfred Rosenberg, the German embassy in Paris and the Gestapo in France

U.S.A.

American Jewish Archives – Hebrew Union College, Cincinnati, established 1947	Archives of American Jewry
American Jewish Historical Society, founded 1892, since 1968 at Brandeis University	historical records of American Jewry including archives of Cyrus Adler and Stephen Wise
Yivo, founded 1925 in Vilna, moved to New York, 1940	documents of Jewish history (political, economical, sociological, cultural and folklore), including archives of Simon Dubnow, Elias Tcherikower, Friedman-Szajkowski (Jewish communities in Southern France) and Chaim Zhitlowsky
Bund, founded 1897 in Geneva moved 1920 to Berlin and after 1945 to New York	Bund's records (from 1897 on), material on the history of Jewish labor movement
Zionist Archives and Library, New York, founded 1939	history of Zionism in the U.S. including archives of L.D. Brandeis
Leo Baeck Institute, New York, founded 1955	history of Central European Jewry since Emancipation
The Institute of Jewish Affairs of the World Jewish Congress, New York, founded 1940	documents concerning the Holocaust and related issues

ISRAEL

Central Zionist Archives, founded in Berlin in 1919, moved to Jerusalem 1933	Zionist Movement, Zionist Organization, the *Yishuv*, and their affiliated institutions, including the political and literary archives of Theodor Herzl
Labor Archives and Museum Tel Aviv, founded 1932	Histadrut and its affiliated institutions
Central Archives for the History of the Jewish People, Jerusalem, founded 1939, taken over (1944) by the Historical Society of Israel, since 1970 an Israel Government Corporation	comprehensive archives on the history of Jewish communities
Israel Defense Forces, Givatayim, established 1948	documentary material of the IDF, also including the Haganah Archives (1920–1948)
Yad Vashem, Jerusalem, founded 1945	comprehensive Jewish archives devoted to the Holocaust era
The State (of Israel) Archives, Jerusalem, founded 1949	history of the State of Israel including archival records of Turkish and Mandatory government which remained in the country
Weizmann archives, Reḥovot, established 1951 (part of Yad Chaim Weizmann)	the correspondence and papers of Chaim Weizmann as well as documents relating to his activities
Jabotinsky Institute, Tel Aviv, founded 1933 as Betar Museum, took its present name 1947	material on the life and work of Jabotinsky and also youth movements and underground organizations founded or inspired by him.
Bet Aaronsohn, Zikhron Ya'akov	private and public archives, of Aaron, Alexander, and Sara Aaronsohn
Archives of Religious Zionism, Jerusalem, established 1953 as a part of Mosad ha-Rav Kook	it includes archives of Mizrachi World Organization (1919–48), Ha-Poel ha-Mizrachi Jerusalem branch (1930–48) and private archive of Rabbi J.L. Maimon
Archives of Ha-Kibbutz ha-Arẓi of Ha-Shomer ha-Ẓair, Merḥavyah, established 1937	Archives of Ha-Shomer ha-Ẓair kibbutzim and of the Ha-Shomer ha-Ẓair world movement (from 1911)
Archives of Ha-Kibbutz ha-Me'uḥad, En-Harod, established 1957	Archives of Ha-Kibbutz ha-Me'uḥad
The Isaac Katznelson Ghetto Fighters Museum, founded in 1950, kibbutz Loḥamei ha-Gettaot	Holocaust and the Resistance
Genazim, Tel Aviv, founded 1953	private papers, manuscripts, and correspondence of Hebrew writers
Bet Bialik, Tel Aviv	archives of Ḥ.N. Bialik
Bet Shalom Aleichem, Tel Aviv	archives of Shalom Aleichem and Y.D. Berkowitz
Archives of the Teachers' Association, Tel Aviv, founded 1959	Hebrew education abroad and education in Israel; records of Hebrew Teachers' Association
National and University Library in Jerusalem	*pinkasim* of communities, private papers of outstanding personalities; Abraham Schwadron-Sharon collection of autographs, portraits, letters and documents of prominent Jews
Bet Trumpeldor, Tel-Ḥai, founded 1947	documents concerning the life of Joseph Trumpeldor

400,000–500,000 (1972), incl. 80,000 Sephardim.

Argob, region in N. Transjordan which was part of Bashan. Allotted by Moses to the half-tribe of Manasseh.

Ari, see Luria, Isaac.

Aricha, Yosef (1907–1972), Hebrew writer; b. Ukraine, settled in Ereẓ Israel 1925. Wrote short stories, historical novels, stories for young people.

Arie, Rafael (1922–), Sofia-born Israel basso singer. Sang leading roles at La Scala, Milan, etc.

Ariel, poetic name for Jerusalem.

Arieli, Yehoshua (1916–), historian. Taught American and general history at Heb. Univ. Author of *Individualism and Nationalism in American Ideology.*

Avigdor Arikha, self-portrait

Arikha, Avigdor (1929–), painter; escaped fr. Rumania to Ereẓ Israel 1944, later settled in Paris. At first greatly influenced by Paris school, subsequently became more abstract.

Aripul, Samuel ben Isaac (c. 1540–c. 1586), rabbinical scholar, preacher in Salonika, Constantinople, Safed. Wrote rabbinical and philosophical commentaries on Bible emphasizing its ethical message.

Arish, see El-Arish.

Aristeas (2nd–1st c. B.C.E.), author of history *On the Jews,* of which only one fragment survives, summarizing part of Book of Job.

Aristeas, Letter of, Jewish-Alexandrian literary composition by anonymous Jew, in form of letter allegedly written by Aristeas, a Greek at court of Ptolemy II Philadelphus (285–246 B.C.E.). Meant for Hellenistic public, the work extols merits of Judaism, describes legendary origin of Septuagint, and includes stories of Jerusalem.

Aristobulus I (Judah), king of Judea 104–103 B.C.E.; eldest son of John Hyrcanus I, whose policies he continued.

Aristobulus II (d. 49 B.C.E.), last independent Hasmonean king, reigning 67–63 B.C.E.; younger son of Alexander Yannai and Salome Alexandra. Usurped throne of Judea fr. Hyrcanus II, but was ordered to surrender his possessions by Pompey. When he refused, Pompey laid siege to Temple hill, captured Temple 63 B.C.E., putting end to Judea's political independence. Taken prisoner to Rome, he later sided with Caesar against Pompey, was poisoned on latter's order.

Aristobulus III (Jonathan; d. 35 B.C.E.), last Hasmonean high priest. His popularity aroused Herod's jealousy, who had him drowned in baths at Jericho.

Aristobulus (c. 35 B.C.E.–7 B.C.E.), son of Herod and Mariamne. Eventually convinced of his treachery, Herod had him strangled at Sebaste (Samaria), together with his elder son, Alexander.

Aristobulus of Paneas (2nd c. B.C.E.), Jewish Hellenistic philosopher; one of earliest allegorical interpreters of Bible.

Arizona, U.S. state. Jewish businessmen settled in early 1860s. First Jewish community organized 1881 at Tombstone, coinciding with the mining boom. Jewish pop. 21,000 (1971).

Ark, receptacle in synagogue in which Torah scrolls are kept; among Sephardim known as *heikhal* (sanctuary); in Mishnah called *tevah* (box). It is the holiest part of the synagogue after the scrolls themselves. Originally the ark was a movable receptacle but eventually became a permanent feature. The ark is covered by a curtain (*parokhet*) but is opened during important prayers.

Baroque ark in the Great German synagogue, Venice

Philistines returning the captured ark, Dura Europos synagogue

Ark of the Law in 14th-cent. Spanish "Haggadah."

Priests carrying the ark across the Jordan, 12th cent. Spanish Bible

Ark in the Touro Synagogue, Newport, R.I.

Arkansas, U.S. state. First Jewish settlers arrived 1830, with large influx after 1865. 15 towns in Arkansas named for Jews. Jewish pop. 3,030 (1971).

Ark of Moses, box in which infant Moses was hidden by his mother and placed on Nile (Ex. 2:2–6) to save him from Pharaoh's decree that every Hebrew child should be killed.

Ark of Noah, vessel built by Noah at divine command (Gen. 6:14–16) to preserve his family and representatives of each species of living creatures during Flood. Came to rest on Mt. Ararat.

Ark of the Covenant, chest which stood in Holy of Holies and in which "the tables of the covenant" were kept (Exod. 25:10–22; 37:1–9). So sacred that seen solely by High Priest and then only on Day of Atonement. Not mentioned after destruction of First Temple.

Arkin, Alan W. (1934–), U.S. movie actor (*Wait until Dark, Catch-22,* etc.).

Arlen, Harold (1905–), U.S. composer of songs, musicals (*Stormy Weather, Wizard of Oz, Saratoga,* etc.).

Arles, town in S. France. Jews living there in 6th c. Augmented by exiles in 14th c. Frequently persecuted and attacked in 15th c. Last Jews expelled 1494. Center of Jewish scholarship, noted for Jewish translators fr. Arabic, incl. Samuel ibn Tibbon, Kalonymos b. Kalonymos.

Chaim Arlosoroff

Arlosoroff, Chaim (1899–1933), Zionist labor leader; b. Ukraine. Joined Ha-Po'el ha-Ẓa'ir in Germany and soon became one of its leaders. Advocated synthesis of Marxism and practical Jewish settlement in Ereẓ Israel. Also believed in cooperation bet. Arab and Jewish national movements. Settled in Ereẓ Israel 1924. Staunch supporter of Chaim Weizmann's policies; became head of Jewish Agency's Political Dept. 1931. In 1933 organized Jewish emigration fr. Nazi Germany to Ereẓ Israel. Assassinated by unknown assailants on Tel Aviv seashore.

Armageddon, name of traditional site of final battle between forces of good and evil in Christian eschatology. Possibly a corrupt spelling of Har Megiddo.

Armenia, republic of USSR. Jewish captives settled 1st c. B.C.E. Three of vassal kings appointed by Romans were of Herodian family. 80,000 Jews deported to Iran in 4th c. C.E. Armenian Jews disappeared as distinct entity in Middle Ages.

Armilus, legendary name of Messiah's antagonist, or anti-Messiah. Frequently mentioned in later Apocalyptic Midrashim. Name possibly derived fr. Romulus, founder of Rome.

Armleder, medieval German bands of peasant outlaws. Distinguished by their leather armpiece. Became identified with gang of Jew-killers (*Judenschlaeger*) who scourged Franconia and Alsace 1336–1339, ravaging 120 communities and killing hundreds of Jews.

Arnheim, Heymann (1796–1869), German translator. Translated books of Bible into German and also wrote Hebrew grammar.

Arnhem, town in Holland. Jews fr. 13th c. but community destroyed in Black Death (1348–49); returned, expelled in 16th c., returned in 18th c. In 1943 community liquidated by Germans. Jewish pop. 350 (1969).

Arnon, river in Transjordan, flowing into Dead Sea on E. shore. In biblical times, frontier of Moab.

Arnstein, family of 18th–19th c. Viennese court purveyors, financiers. Firm founded by **Isaac Aaron** (c. 1682–1744). His son **Adam Isaac** (1721–1785) helped prevent expulsion of Jews from Prague; grandsons **Joseph Michael von** (d. 1811), became a Catholic 1778 and was ennobled 1783, and **Nathan Adam** (1748–1838).

Arnstein, Fanny von (1757–1818), wife of N. A. von Arnstein; daughter of Daniel Itzig. Famed for charm and culture. Many leading personalities of day met at her salon. Metternich and Talleyrand attended her receptions during Congress of Vienna.

Fanny von Arnstein

Aroch, Arie (1908–), Israel painter, diplomat; b. Russia, settled in Ereẓ Israel 1924. Early work expressionist but later influenced by folk art. Israel Prize 1971.

Aron, Raymond (1905–), French sociologist, writer (*Introduction to the Philosophy of History, Progress and Disillusion,* etc.). Prof. of sociology at Sorbonne. His *De Gaulle, Israel and the Jews* analyzed De Gaulle's attitudes during and after Six-Day War.

Aron, Robert (1898–), French writer. Escaped Algiers after arrest by Nazis 1940. Worked with generals Giraud, De Gaulle. Wrote books on Liberation of France, Vichy, Algerian War. Traced talmudic and Jewish liturgical elements in Jesus' teachings *(Jesus of Nazareth, The Hidden Years).*

Aronius, Julius (1861–1893), German historian. His *Regesten zur Geschichte der Juden im fraenkischen und deutschen Reiche bis zum Jahre 1273* was first scholarly source book on German Jewish history.

Aronovich, Yuri Mikhaylovich (1932–), Leningrad-born conductor, active in USSR until 1972, when he immigrated to Israel.

Arons, Leo (1860–1919), German physicist, Social Democrat. Discovered mercury vapor lamp.

Aronson, Boris (1898–), U.S. stage designer, artist; son of Solomon Aronson. Designed sets for many leading Broadway productions.

Aronson, Grigori (1887–1968), Russian-born journalist, author, public figure. Left USSR 1922; settled in U.S. after 1940. Wrote on USSR and Soviet Jewry.

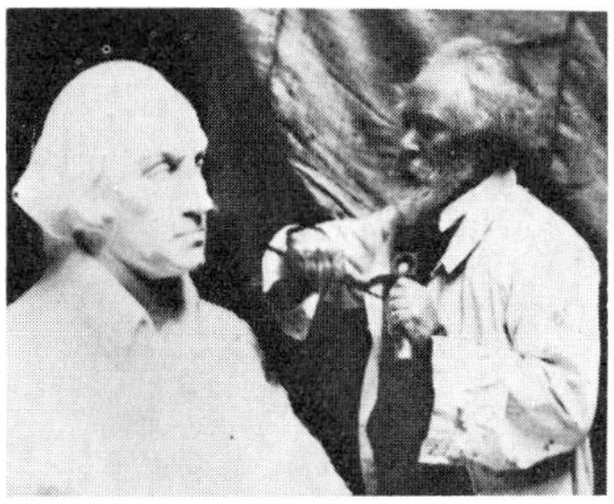

Naum Aronson working on a bust of George Washington

Aronson, Naum Lvovich (1872–1943), Latvian-born sculptor in Paris; many Jewish themes.

Aronson, Solomon (1862–1935), rabbi, Zionist leader. Chief rabbi of Kiev 1906–21. Settled in Ereẓ Israel 1923 and became chief rabbi of Tel Aviv.

Arpa, Abramo Dall' (c. 1542–c. 1577), Italian harpist; member of Mantuan family of musicians.

Arraby Moor (Rabbí Mór), official title of chief rabbi of Portugal fr. 13th c.

Moses Arragel presents his work to Don Luis de Guzman, "Alba Bible"

Benjamin Artom

Part of "Arvit" prayer from N. Italian siddur, Bertinoro, 1390.

Arragel, Moses (15th c.), scholar in Guadalajara, Spain. Translated Bible into Spanish.

Arta, Greek town. Jews in 11th c. and exiles from S. Italy settled 16th c. Fr. 1944 Jews were sent to Auschwitz. 20 Jews in 1958.

Artapanus (2nd c. B.C.E.), Hellenistic Jewish writer who tried to prove that Abraham and his descendants were true creators of Egyptian culture.

Artemion, leader of Jewish uprising in Cyprus 115–17 C.E. With suppression of revolt all Jews were prohibited on penalty of death to set foot on the island.

Articles of Faith, see Ani Ma'amin.

Artom, Benjamin (1835–1879), rabbi in Italy, haham of Sephardi community in London.

Artom, Elia Samuele (1887–1965), Italian rabbi; served in Florence, Turin, Tripoli. Author of well-known commentary to Bible, Hebrew translation of Apocrypha, etc. Settled in Ereẓ Israel 1939.

Artom, Isaac (1829–1900), Italian diplomat, writer, private secretary to Cavour. First Jewish member of Italian senate.

Arvey, Jacob M. (1893–), U.S. attorney; key figure in Chicago Democratic machine and in Adlai Stevenson's 1952 presidential bid.

Arvit, evening prayer, one of three regular daily services, popularly called *Ma'ariv.* Consists of *Shema* with two blessings preceding and following, together with *Amidah* (which is not repeated in congregational prayer as evening *Amidah* was originally optional). Friday night *Arvit* is preceded by *Kabbalat Shabbat.* According to rabbinical tradition, prayer was instituted by the patriarch Jacob.

Aryeh Judah Harari (13th–14th c.), *paytan,* probably in Montpellier.

Aryeh Judah Leib ben Ephraim ha-Kohen (1658–1720), Moravian rabbi. Published collected responsa on *Shulḥan Arukh* by his father, Ephraim b. Jacob ha-Kohen, rabbi of Ofen. D. in Safed.

Aryeh Judah Leib (*The Mokhi'aḥ*) of Polonnoye (d. 1770), popular ḥasidic preacher in Poland. An early follower of the Ba'al Shem Tov. Stressed the primacy of prayer.

Aryeh Leib of Ożarów (d. 1833), ḥasidic *ẓaddik* in Poland. Ożarów dynasty continued until WWII, when most of its members perished in the Holocaust.

Aryeh Leib of Shpola (1725–1812), ḥasidic *ẓaddik,* popular miracle-worker and faith-healer.

Aryeh Leib Sarahs (1730–1791), semilegendary ḥasidic *ẓaddik* in Ukraine. Said to have come, while invisible, to Imperial Court of Vienna, to obtain abrogation of Toleranzpatent.

Arzin, Joseph ben Jacob (16th c.), kabbalist; pupil of Isaac Luria in Safed. Author of commentary on *Idra Rabba.*

Arzt, Max (1897–), U.S. Conservative rabbi. Vice-chancellor of Jewish Theological Seminary. Author of *Justice and Mercy: A Commentary on the New Year and the Day of Atonement,* etc.

Asa, king of Judah 906–867 B.C.E.; son of Abijah. Won decisive victory over Zerah the Ethiopian, who invaded Judah. Endeavored to remove pagan influences and restore worship of the Lord in Jerusalem.

Asahel, son of Zeruiah, sister of David. Pursued Abner but was killed by him (II Sam. 3:27–30).

Asaph, ancestor of one of principal families of singers in Temple. Descended fr. Gershon son of Levi.

Asaph ha-Rofe (Asaph the Physician), physician, yet unidentified, who gave his name to a Hebrew book on medicine, *Sefer Asaf ha-Rofe,* written somewhere in Middle East. Constitutes source of information on ancient customs and Jewish medical ethics. Government hospital at Zerifin (Sarafand), Israel, named after him.

Asarah be-Tevet, fast on 10th of Tevet commemorating commencement of siege of Jerusalem by Nebuchadnezzar.

Asarah Harugei Malkhut, see Ten Martyrs, The.

Ascalon, see Ashkelon.

Ascama ("agreement"), Sephardi term for regulations governing a community. Corresponding to Ashkenazi *takkanot.*

Asch, Sholem (1880–1957), Polish-born Yiddish novelist, playwright. Early works about the *shtetl;* he connected Jewish world to mainstream of European and American culture through his novels, chiefly *Salvation, Three Cities, Moses, The Prophet, East River,* etc. Lived in U.S. during WWI and after 1938. Spent last years in Bat Yam, Israel. His trilogy on founders of Christianity (*The Nazarene, Mary, The Apostle*) was fiercely attacked in certain Jewish circles. Works translated into many languages. First Yiddish writer to enjoy international vogue.

Aschaffenburg, city in Bavaria, W. Germany. Jews in 12th c. expelled 1348, returned 1359. A leading community in 18th c. Jews deported and killed in WWII.

Aschaffenburg, Gustav (1866–1944), German criminologist, psychiatrist. Founded and edited *Monatsschrift fuer Kriminalpsychologie.* Emigrated to U.S. 1938.

Ascher, Saul (1767–1822), German author, philosopher, pioneer of religious reform.

Ascherson, Paul Friedrich August (1834–1913), German botanist. Wrote on flora of Brandenburg and N. Sinai.

Aschheim, Isidor (1891–1968), Israel painter, printmaker. Taught at Bezalel School of Art fr. 1943.

Ascoli, Aldo (1882–), naval officer; commander of Italian fleet in Aegean in 1930s.

Ascoli, Ettore (1873–1943), Italian general. Compelled to leave army 1938, following enactment of Fascist racial laws. Killed fighting with partisans against Germans.

Ascoli, Graziadio Isaia (1829–1907), Italian philologist; specialist in Romance linguistics (prof. in Milan). Senator 1889.

Ascoli, Max (1898–), jurist, author. Prof. of law in Genoa. Emigrated to U.S. 1938. Editor of *The Reporter* 1949–68.

Asefat ha-Nivḥarim, representative assembly elected by Jews in Erez Israel during period of British Mandate (1920–48).

Sholem Asch

Isidor Aschheim, self-portrait

Graziadio Isaia Ascoli

Asenath, wife of Joseph, daughter of Poti-Phera, the high priest of On (Heliopolis). Mother of Manasseh and Ephraim.

Aseret Yemei Teshuvah see Ten Days of Penitence.

Ash, Abraham Joseph (1813–1888), rabbi, halakhic authority; b. Grodno district, in New York fr. 1852. Among founders of Bet ha-Midrash ha-Gadol.

Ashamnu (Heb. "We have trespassed"), opening word in confession of sins forming part of Day of Atonement service.

Ashbel, Dov (1895–), Israel meteorologist, author (*Climate of Israel, Snow and Rain in the Middle East,* etc.). At Heb. Univ. fr. 1930.

Ashdod, port in S. Israel. One of five chief Philistine cities in ancient Ereẓ Israel and Philistine capital in post-Exilic period. Important Jewish center under Romans. Ancient city excavated in recent years. An Arab village (Isdūd) in British Mandate period, it was overrun in War of Independence (1948–9) by Egyptians, who withdrew Oct. 1948. Modern Ashdod founded 1956, pop. 39,700 (1971). Now Israel's second largest port and a manufacturing center.

Ashdot Ya'akov, two kibbutzim in Jordan Valley in Israel. After split in Ha-Kibbutz ha-Me'uḥad 1953, the original settlement divided into two, one of them joining Iḥud ha-Kevuẓot ve-ha-Kibbutzim. Combined pop. 1,200 (1968).

Ashendorf, Israel (1909–1956), Yiddish poet, writer, dramatist; b. in Galicia, settled in Argentina 1953.

Ashenheim, Louis (1816–1858), physician in Jamaica; b. Edinburgh. Editor, proprietor of *Daily Gleaner.*

Ashenheim, Sir Neville Noel (1900–), Jamaican lawyer, politician. Minister without portfolio 1962, ambassador of Jamaica to U.S. 1962–67, minister of state finance 1967.

Asher. (1) Jacob's second son by Zilpah, Leah's handmaid. (2) Tribe of Israel. Its territory included the whole of W. Galilee, as well as hinterland of Phoenician Tyre and Sidon, and W. Jezreel. (Map on next page.)

Asher, Abraham ben Gedaliah ibn ("Aba" 16th c.), talmudist, rabbi in Aleppo. Wrote commentary to *Midrash Rabbah.*

Asher, Joseph Michael (1872–1909), English-born rabbi, educator. Became rabbi of B'nai Jeshurun congregation in New York 1900, taught

Philistine figurine found at Ashdod

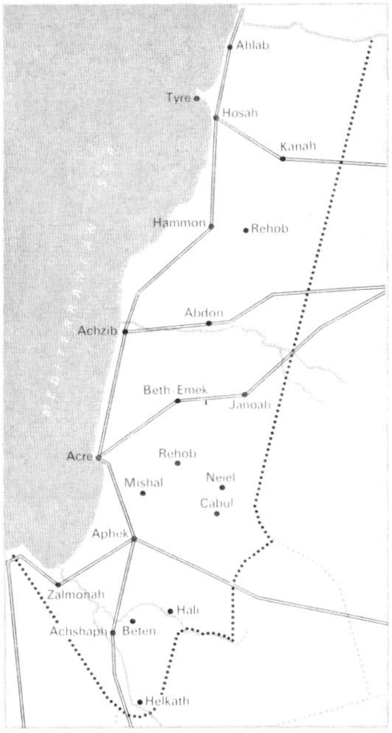

Territory of the tribe of Asher.

homiletics at Jewish Theological Seminary fr. 1902, rabbi of Orach Chaim Synagogue fr. 1906.

Asherah, wooden cult object mentioned in Bible. It is not known whether it was an image of the goddess Asherah placed near the altar, a sacred pole representing her, or an object of some other sort.

Antiquities Park, Ashkelon

Asherah, Canaanite fertility and mother goddess, popular throughout Ancient Near East. It was brought into court worship of Israel by Jezebel. Manasseh placed an idol of Asherah in the Temple (II K. 21:7), from where it was removed by Josiah (II K. 23:6).

Asher ben David (13th c.), kabbalist in Provence; grandson of Abraham b. David of Posquières, pupil of his uncle, Isaac the Blind. His kabbalistic treatises widely circulated and studied, collected in *Sefer ha-Yiḥud.*

Asher ben Jehiel (Rosh; c. 1250–1327), talmudist, codifier; b. Germany. A pupil of R. Meir of Rothenburg, regarded after him as spiritual leader of German Jewry. Left for Spain 1303, appointed rabbi in Toledo, and chief rabbinic authority in peninsula. His responsa a primary source for history of Jews in Spain. His decisions, *Piskei ha-Rosh,* still standard. His son was Jacob ben Asher (q.v.).

Asher ben Meshullam ha-Kohen of Lunel (late 12th c.), Provençal talmudist; son of Meshullam b. Jacob of Lunel, brother of Aaron b. Meshullam of Lunel. Author of *Sefer ha-Mattanot.*

Asher ben Saul (12th–13th c.), one of "sages of Lunel." Author of *Sefer ha-Minhagot* ("Book of Customs"), used extensively by codifiers.

Asheri (Bonaventura), David (1925–), scholar of ancient history, historian; b. Florence, son of Enzo Bonaventura. Taught at Heb. Univ., Jerusalem.

Ashi (Rabbana; c. 335–427/8), most celebrated Babylonian *amora* of his day. Head of academy of Sura for nearly 60 years, he gathered around him "the rabbis of the school of Rav Ashi." With their cooperation, began monumental task of editing Babylonian Talmud.

Ashinsky, Aaron Mordecai Halevi (1866–1954), rabbi, religious Zionist leader; b. Poland, in U.S. fr. 1895. Rabbi in Montreal, Pittsburgh. Among founders of Mizrachi Organization of America.

Ashkanasy, Maurice (1901–1971), Australian lawyer; president of Executive Council of Australian Jewry and lay leader of Australian Jewry.

Ashkavah (Heb. "laying to rest"), memorial prayer in Sephardi ritual. Also recited at graveside as part of funeral service.

Ashkelon, ancient port in S. Israel; one of five Philistine city-states. Retained its independence throughout Hasmonean period. Adorned by Herod with gardens and fine buildings. Crusader city destroyed by sultan Baybars 1270. Town of Majdal, NE of ancient site, scene of fighting in Israel 1948 War of Independence. Became modern Jewish Migdal-Ashkelon, replanned by S. African Zionist Federation, granted city status 1955. Area of ancient Ashkelon converted into National Park. Pop. 41,700 (1971).

Ashkenaz, (Heb.), people and country bordering on Armenia mentioned in Genesis 10:3, I Chronicles 1:6, Jeremiah 51:27.

Ashkenaz, designation of first compact area of Jewish settlement in NW Europe. Term specifically denotes Germany, German Jewry ("Ashke-

Asherah as sea goddess, casting figure (left) and bronze cast (right)

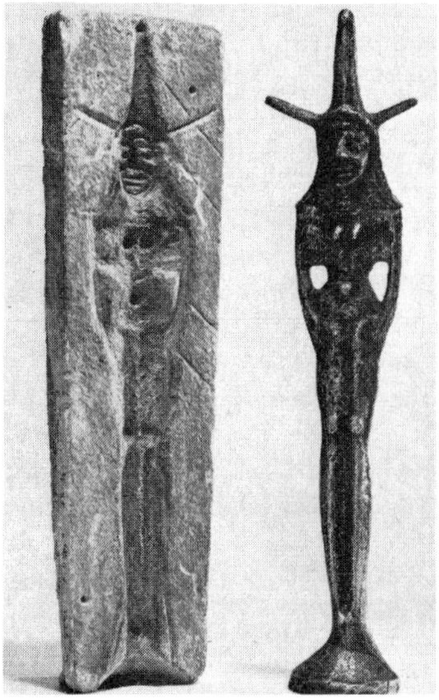

Members of burial society recite "Ashkavah", painted glass goblet, Turnau

nazim"), their descendants in other countries. More broadly, the entire Ashkenazi cultural complex, with its ideas, way of life, and institutions, in contradistinction to Sepharad, the Jewish cultural complex originating in Spain. In 15th–16th c. center of gravity of Ashkenazi Jewry shifted to Bohemia, Poland, and Lithuania. In Slavonic territories their use of Judeo-German (Yiddish) became prominent. After Chmielnicki massacres 1648, Ashkenazi Jews spread through W. Europe. Toward end of 19th c., as result of persecutions in Russia, Ashkenazi Jewry massively emigrated fr. E. Europe, gaining ascendancy in communities of Europe, the United States, Australia, S. Africa, and Ereẓ Israel. Before WWII Ashkenazi Jewry comprised 90% of global total. The destruction of European Jewry drastically reduced their number and to some extent their proportionate preponderance.

Ashkenazi, Abraham ben Jacob (1811–1880), rabbi in Jerusalem, Sephardi chief rabbi of Ereẓ Israel fr. 1869. Wrote many responsa and rabbinical works.

Ashkenazi, Beḥor (1840–1909), Turkish government official. Represented Jewish community in Ottoman parliament. Nominated to Senate 1908, the only Jew in Ottoman upper chamber.

Ashkenazi, Bezalel ben Abraham (c. 1520–c. 1592), talmudist, halakhic authority; b. Ereẓ Israel. Founded yeshivah in Cairo, became head of Egyptian rabbis c. 1553, of Jerusalem rabbis 1587 and put new life into Jerusalem community. His main work a compendium of commentaries on Talmud, known as *Shitah Mekubbeẓet*.

Ashkenazi, Dan (13th–14th c.), talmudist; left Germany c. 1300 following Rindfleisch persecutions, settling in Toledo, Spain. His responsa preserved in works of Solomon b. Abraham Adret and Yom Tov b. Abraham Ishbili. Wrote commentaries on Pentateuch.

Ashkenazi, Eliezer ben Elijah the Physician (1513–1586), rabbi, exegete; lived and officiated in Egypt, Cyprus, Italy, Poland, d. Cracow. Main work *Ma'aseh Adonai*, commentary on Torah.

Ashkenazi (Ulif), Gershon (d. 1693), rabbi in Prossnitz, *landesrabbiner* in Moravia, chief rabbi of Austria, where he bitterly opposed the Shabbateans, *av bet din* in Metz fr. 1671. Wrote responsa and novellae on *Shulḥan Arukh*.

Ashkenazi, Jonah ben Jacob (d. 1745), Hebrew printer in Constantinople and Smyrna. Printed more than 125 books, including Bible in Ladino. His press passed to his sons Reuben, Nissim, and Moses, and later to his grandsons.

Ashkenazi, Joseph (1525–1577), Mishnah annotator and commentator; known as "*ha-Tanna*" of Safed. Fiercely opposed philosophy, philosophical Kabbalah, and denounced Maimonides as heretic. Originally fr. Germany, went to Verona c. 1560, then Egypt. Settled in Safed 1569–70, devoting himself to his widely used textual criticism of entire Mishnah.

Ashkenazi, Judah ben Joseph (c. 1730–1791), rabbi, *rosh yeshivah* of Smyrna. Wrote commentaries on talmudic tractates.

Ashkenazi, Judah ben Simeon (18th c.), codifier, *dayyan* in Germany, Poland. Wrote *Be'er Heitev*, commentary on Joseph Caro's *Shulḥan Arukh*, etc.

Ashkenazi, Judah Samuel (c. 1780–1849), scholar in Ereẓ Israel. Went on missions to N. Africa, visited Gibraltar, Italy. Wrote halakhic clarification of marriage laws and other works connected with Sephardi liturgy.

Ashkenazi, Meir ben Benjamin Wolf (17th c.), first rabbi of united communities of Altona, Hamburg, and Wandsbeck (1664).

Ashkenazi, Nissim Abraham ben Raphael (c. 1790–1860), *dayyan* in Smyrna. Compiled commentary on Jerusalem Talmud, etc.

Ashkenazi, Saul ben Moses ha-Kohen (c. 1470–1523), philosopher in Crete. Wrote questions to Isaac Abarbanel concerning Maimonides, glosses of Averroes' *Physics*, etc.

Ashkenazi, Solomon (c. 1520–1602), physician, diplomat; b. Italy. Studied at Padua, was court physician in Poland. Settled in Turkey 1564, entering service of grand vizier Mehemet Sokolli. Went to Venice 1574 as Turkish ambassador, and thereafter continued to wield great influence in Constantinople.

Ashkenazi, Ẓevi Hirsch ben Jacob (Ḥakham Ẓevi; 1660–1718), Moravian rabbi, halakhist. Studied in Salonika, adopted Sephardi customs, assuming title "*ḥakham*" used by Sephardi rabbis. Appointed rabbi of Altona, then Amsterdam, where he was at center of bitter polemics between Portuguese and Ashkenazi communities. Resigned 1714 and eventually settled in Lemberg (Lwov). Chief work *Ḥakham Ẓevi*, collection of responsa reflecting his stormy life and wanderings. Father of Jacob Emden.

Ashkenazy, Vladimir Davidovich (1937–), Russian-born pianist. First public appearance at six. Shared first prize in Tchaikovsky competition 1962. Settled in England (later Iceland) after a tour in 1962.

Ashlag, Yehudah (1886–1955), Warsaw-born kabbalist, rabbi. Settled in Old City of Jerusalem 1920, establishing yeshivah, Beth Ulpena le-Rabbanim. Moved to Tel Aviv 1946.

Ashman, Aharon (1896–), Israel playwright, poet, editor; b. Russia. Plays include *Mikhal Bat Sha'ul, Ha-Adamah ha-Zot*, etc.

Ashmedai, see Asmodeus.

Ashrei (Heb. "Happy are they"), first word and name of a reading fr. Book of Psalms (Ps. 84:5, 144:15, 145, 115:18) recited in morning and afternoon prayers.

Ashriki, Mordecai (18th c.), adviser to ruler of Morocco, Muhammad ibn Abd'allah (1754–90). Died at stake.

Ashtor (Strauss), Eliahu (1914–), historian; b. Vienna, settled in Ereẓ Israel 1938. Prof. of Islamic civilization at Heb. Univ. Author of histories of Jews in Mamluk Egypt and Syria, Muslim Spain.

Ashtoreth (Astarte), Canaanite goddess of love and war.

Asia, see entries under individual countries.

Asia Minor (Anatolia), SW peninsula in Asia. Jews arrived probably not later than 6th c. B.C.E. In 3rd c. B.C.E. Antiochus III transferred 2,000 Jewish families from Babylonia to A.M. Under Roman rule important communities existed there incl. Pergamum, Caria, Pamphylia, and synagogues were built at that time (cf. Josephus, New Testament.)

Asimov, Isaac (1920–), U.S. biochemist, author of scientific books and science fiction.

Askenazy, Ludvík (1921–), Czech communist author, journalist.

JEWISH POPULATION OF ASIA, 1971

Country	Total Population	Jewish Population
Afghanistan	15,480,000	800
Burma	27,580,000	200
China	787,180,000	20
Hong Kong	4,050,000	200
India	550,370,000	14,500
Indonesia	124,890,000	100
Japan	104,660,000	1,000
Pakistan	116,600,000	250
Philippines	37,960,000	500
Singapore	2,110,000	600
Total Far East	1,770,880,000	18,170
Cyprus	630,000	30
Iran	29,780,000	80,000
Iraq	9,750,000	2,500
Lebanon	2,870,000	2,500
Syria	6,450,000	3,500
Turkey	36,160,000	37,000
Total Near East	85,640,000	125,530
Israel	3,090,000	2,632,000
Total	1,859,610,000	2,745,000

Books, stories, plays reflect socialist realism.

Askenazy, Simon (1867–1937), Polish historian. Wrote on Russia and Poland in *Cambridge Modern History,* besides several monographs and works on Napoleon. Mod. hist. prof. at Lemberg, Warsaw.

Asknazi, Isaac Lvovich (1856–1902), Russian painter. Painstakingly academic. Chose many Jewish subjects.

Asmakhta (Aram.), term used in Talmud to mean: (1) the use of a biblical text as the supposed source of a *halakhah* when it is not actually derived from it; (2) a penalty in a contract which presumes that the party to it did not expect to become liable and so entered into it without a binding intention. Such a penalty is normally not enforceable in court.

Asmodeus (Ashmedai), "the king of the demons" according to talmudic *aggadah.* Appears in Apocrypha (Book of Tobit) as malefactor, but in talmudic literature as mischievous creature. In Jewish folklore, the butt of popular irony and humor.

Assaf, Michael (1896–), Israel author, specialist in Arab affairs. Edited Arabic newspapers, wrote on history of Arabs in Ereẓ Israel.

Simḥa Assaf

Assaf (Osofsky), Simḥa (1889–1953), Israel rabbinical scholar, Jewish historian. Head of Odessa Yeshivah 1914–19, settled in Ereẓ Israel 1921. Prof. of rab. lit. at Heb. Univ. fr. 1936, rector 1948–50. Wrote on history of Jewish law, medieval Jewish culture, Jewish education, geonic literature, etc. Justice of Israel Supreme Court.

Asscher, Abraham (1880–1955), Dutch Jewish leader. President of Amsterdam Chamber of Commerce. Headed Jewish Council during WWII but eventually sent to concentration camps. After war his relations with Germany subject of controversy.

Assembly of Jewish Notables, see Sanhedrin, French.

Asseo, David (1914–), chief rabbi of Turkey fr. 1961.

Asser, Moses Solomon (1754–1826), Dutch jurist; protagonist of Jewish emancipation in Holland, a founder of Felix Libertate. His son **Carel** (1780–1836) drew up constitution of Jewish Consistory at request of Louis Napoleon. His grandson **Carel** (1843–1898), jurist, author of textbooks on civil law.

Tobias Asser

Asser, Tobias Michaël Carel (1838–1913), statesman, international law expert. Participated in Hague Peace Conferences 1899, 1907. Shared Nobel Peace Prize 1911.

Assi (3rd–4th c.), Palestinian *amora;* b. Babylonia. Frequently mentioned in Jerusalem and Babylonian Talmud, often with his colleague Ammi, and they are called the most important judges of the law of Israel. D. Tiberias.

Assi, Rav (3d c.), Babylonian *amora;* a contemporary of Rav and Samuel. Lived in Nehardea and was respected halakhist.

Assimilation, term describing process of Jewish absorption into environmental culture, generally involving denial of those aspects of Judaism that stressed special Jewish identity of "separateness," but stopping short of formal adoption of another religion. It has taken many forms, from the Hellenism of late antiquity to the social trends prevalent in C. Europe until 1933. Modern assimilation is particularly strong in the affluent West and the USSR. As a trend it is opposed by those factors that strengthen Jewish group allegiance, i.e., strong religious feelings, Jewish nationalism (either Zionist or "ethnic"), and anti-Semitism.

Assumption of Moses, see Moses, Assumption of.

Assumpçao, Diogo da (1579–1603), Portuguese Marrano martyr. Brought up devout Christian, embraced Judaism. Burned alive at auto-da-fé.

Assyria, designation of civilization which flourished in Mesopotamia from mid–3rd millennium B.C.E. up to 7th c. B.C.E.; named for its capital Ashur. Assyrian kings of 9th–7th c. B.C.E. came into direct contact with Israelites.

Astarte, see Ashtoreth.

Astrology, study and prediction of supposed influence of stars on human events. There is no explicit mention of astrology in the Bible, although its call for the extirpation of diviners and soothsayers probably refer to astrologers. In the Talmud astrologers are called "Chaldeans"; there are several references to the notion that every man has a celestial body (*mazzal*) as his patron. Certain important sages held that the Jews were not influenced by the stars. Study of astrology widespread among rabbis and philosophers in Middle Ages. Some were skeptical, but only Maimonides utterly rejected it dismissing it as superstition and mere foolishness, a negation of the Bible. However, many later rabbis believed in astrology. Kabbalah takes it for granted, but limits its significance. A few vestiges still remain of early Jewish astrological belief, e.g., the greeting *mazzal tov* ("congratulations!" – lit. "happy omen").

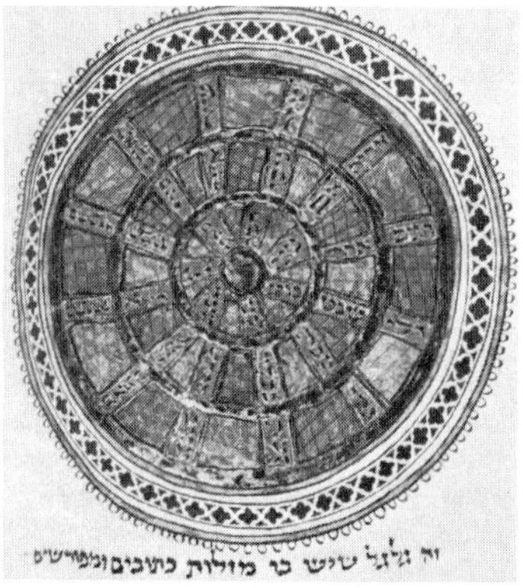

Diagram of a sphere, relating the names of the signs of the Zodiac to the months and the seven planets, from "British Museum Miscellany," N. France, c. 1280.

Astruc, Abba Mari ben Moses ben Joseph of Lunel (c. 1300), Provençal writer; opponent of Maimonides and leader of traditionalists. A leading advocate of 50-year ban pronounced in Barcelona 1305 against those engaging in study of science and metaphysics. This led to controversy ended by expulsion of Jews fr. France 1306. Letters and pamphlets of controversy collected by Astruc in his *Minḥat Kena'ot.*

Astruc, Elie-Aristide (1831–1905), French rabbi. Chief rabbi of Belgium

1866–79, a founder of Alliance Israélite Universelle. Wrote *Histoire abrégée des juifs*, etc.

Astruc, Zacharie (1839–1907), French sculptor, painter, writer. His book of art criticism had preface by George Sand.

Astruc ha-Levi (14th-15th c.), rabbi of Alcañiz, Spain. Took part in Tortosa Disputation (1413–14).

Aszod, Judah ben Israel (1794–1866), rabbi, *dayyan* in Dunaszerdahely, Hungary, where he was succeeded by his son, **Aaron Samuel** (1830–1905). Author of responsa and novellae.

Atar (Aptheker), Ḥaim (1902–1953), painter; b. Russia, settled in Ereẓ Israel 1922. A founder of En-Harod, established and directed its Art Center.

Atar, Moses (d.c. 1725), Moroccan statesman, leader of Jewish community, philanthropist. Treasurer to King Mulay Ishmael; negotiated peace settlement with England, securing privileges for Moroccan Jews.

Atarot, moshav N. of Jerusalem. First settled 1914, abandoned and resettled 1922, evacuated and destroyed during War of Independence. Its settlers founded Benei Atarot near Lydda 1949. After Six-Day War name given to nearby Jerusalem airport.

Athaliah, queen of Judah 842–836 B.C.E.; daughter of Ahab and Jezebel. Married Jehoram, crown prince (later king) of Judah. Seized power on her son Ahaziah's death, after murdering all possible rivals, except grandson Joash, who was saved. Introduced Baal worship in Jerusalem. Met violent end following revolt in favor of Joash.

Athens, capital of Greece. Jewish community attested fr. 1st c. C.E. In synagogue in Athens, Paul found both Jews and gentiles observing Jewish religion. A number of Spanish exiles found refuge there after 1492. Community developed after 1834 when Athens became capital of new Greece. Jews numbered 250 in 1887, 3,000 in 1939. From Sept. 1943 the Germans took over. 1,500 Jews were captured and sent to Auschwitz. 1,500 emigrated to Israel after the war. Jewish pop. 2,800 (1971).

Athias, David ben Moses (18th c.), merchant, traveler fr. Leghorn, Italy. Mastered many languages, wrote in Ladino *La Guerta de Oro* "The Golden Garden"), mixed fables, proverbs, remedies.

Athias, Joseph (d. 1700), publisher, printer in Amsterdam. Printed his first book, a Sephardi prayer-book, in 1658, and a famous Bible in 1661. Succeeded by his son, **Immanuel**, also successful printer.

Athias, Moses Israel (d. 1665), first minister of Sephardi community of London. Died in Great Plague.

Athlit, ancient port, S. of Cape Carmel, Israel. Site of Crusader castle (Castrum Peregrinorum), of which remains still stand. Village (moshavah) of Athlit founded 1903. Agricultural experimental station founded by Aaron Aaronsohn 1911. Detention camp for "illegal" immigrants set up there 1940 by British. Pop. 2,410 (1971).

Athronges, shepherd, rebel pretender to Judean throne on death of Herod (4 B.C.E.).

Atil, capital of Khazar kingdom on Volga river.

Atlan, Jean (1913–1960), French abstract painter; b. Constantine, Algeria. Influenced by primitive, magical, and erotic.

Atlanta, city in Ga., U.S. First Jewish settlers 1846. Hebrew Benevolent Society founded 1860, became Hebrew Benevolent Congregation 1867. Scene of Leo Frank case 1913–15. Sam Massell mayor 1970–73. Jewish pop. 16,500 (1971).

Atlantic City, vacation resort in N.J., U.S. First Jewish settlers 1880. First congregation Beth Israel (Reform) founded 1890. Jewish pop. 10,000 (1971). Popular resort for Jews.

Atlas, mountain range in Morocco and Algeria. Almohads did not succeed in conquering Atlas tribes and many Jews found shelter there. In Middle Atlas and Sous Valley they were converted to Islam in 16th c., and communities of Atlantic Atlas disappeared. In 1948 10,000 Jews in Moroccan Atlas. All of them emigrated to Israel.

Atlas, Eleazar (1851–1904), Hebrew scholar, critic; b. Lithuania, lived in Bialystok fr. 1895. Wrote on Jewish history and literature. Opposed Zionism.

Atlas, Jechezkiel (1913–1942), physician, partisan leader; died fighting Nazis in Poland in WWII.

Atlas, Samuel (1899–), philosopher, talmudist; b. Lithuania. Taught in Poland and England, settled in U.S. 1942, taught at New York school of Hebrew Union College fr. 1951. Follower of Hermann Cohen's critical idealism.

Atonement, Day of, see Day of Atonement.

Atran, Frank Z. (1885–1952), U.S. businessman, philanthropist; b. Russia. Established Yiddish chair at Columbia Univ.

Attah Eḥad (Heb. "Thou art One"), central section of Sabbath afternoon *Amidah* prayer, emphasizing oneness of God.

Attah Horeta Lada'at (Heb. "Unto thee [Israel] it was shown"), verses recited on *Simḥat Torah* before Scrolls of Law are taken out of the Ark to be carried in a procession in the synagogue.

Attah Zokher (Heb. "Thou rememberest"), opening words of middle section (*Zikhronot*) of Rosh Ha-Shanah Additional Service, emphasizing God's remembrance of His creations, especially Israel.

Attar, Ḥayyim ben Moses (1696–1743), rabbi, kabbalist; b. Morocco. Went to Ereẓ Israel with group of 30

"Tanit" by Jean Atlan

Blowing the "shofar" following "Attah Zokher", 14th-cent. Rheims maḥzor.

Princes St. Synagogue, Auckland

Berthold Auerbach

Jews and rabbis fr. Morocco and Italy. Finally settled in Jerusalem, establishing the Midrash Keneset Israel Yeshivah. Wrote *Or ha-Ḥayyim,* a commentary on the Pentateuch.

Attar, Judah ben Jacob ibn (1655–1733), Moroccan talmudist, known as "Rabbi al-Kabbir" (the great teacher). Wrote *Minḥat Yehudah* on the Pentateuch. Many of his responsa published. His grandson, **Judah b. Obed** (1725–1812), *dayyan* in Fez, wrote on persecution of Jews in Morocco during 1790–92.

Attia, Shem Tov (c. 1530–c. 1601), rabbi, kabbalist; lived in Salonika, settled in Safed c. 1570. Disciple of Isaac Luria.

Aub, Joseph (1805–1880), German Reform rabbi in Bayreuth, Mainz, Berlin; among first to preach in German.

Aub, Max (1903–), Spanish poet, novelist, playwright. A staunch anti-Fascist, fled to France after Spanish Civil War, to Mexico 1942. Wrote works of social-political character.

Auckland, city in New Zealand. Jews settled early 19th c., community organized early 1840s. There have been 5 Jewish mayors. Jewish pop. 2,000 (1967).

Auer, Leopold (1845–1930), Hungarian violinist, teacher. Soloist of Russian Imperial Orchestra and prof. at conservatoire in St. Petersburg. Pupils included Mischa Elman, Jascha Heifetz, Nathan Milstein. Left Russia 1918, lived in U.S.

Auerbach, Arnold Jacob ("Red"; 1917–), U.S. basketball coach. Fr. 1950 with Boston Celtics.

Auerbach, Berthold (1812–1882), German author, leader of fight for Jewish emancipation. Wrote historical novels and *Schwarzwaelder Dorfgeschichten* (English edition, *Village Stories* with foreword by Gladstone).

Auerbach, Elias (1882–1971), Israel Bible scholar, historical writer; b. Berlin, lived in Haifa fr. 1909. Main work: *Wueste und Gelobtes Land,* a history of Israel in biblical times.

Auerbach, Ephraim (1892–1973), Yiddish poet, essayist (*Di Vayse Shtot, Vakh iz der Step*); b. Bessarabia. Pioneer in Ereẓ Israel 1912, fought at Gallipoli, immigrated to U.S. 1915. Settled in Israel 1971.

Auerbach, Isaac Eisig ben Isaiah (Reis; 17th–18th c.), German Hebrew grammarian. Wrote supercommentary to Rashi's commentary on Bible.

Auerbach, Isaac Levin (1791–1853), German preacher, pioneer of Reform movement. His brother **Baruch** (1793–1864) founded the Berlin Jewish Orphanage 1833.

Auerbach, Israel (1878–1956), German Zionist, writer. Keren Hayesod director in France 1933–36, Jerusalem fr. 1936. Contributed articles to Zionist and Jewish press.

Auerbach, Leopold (1828–1897), German physician, biologist, pioneer of modern embryology (*Organologische Studien*). Taught at Breslau Univ. fr. 1863; being a Jew, never became professor.

Auerbach, Meir ben Isaac (1815–1878), Polish-born rabbi of Ashkenazi congregation of Jerusalem, where he arrived 1860. One of founders of Me'ah She'arim quarter, opponent of secular education. Wrote *Imrei Binah,* novellae on *Shulḥan Arukh,* responsa, etc.

Auerbach, Ẓevi Benjamin (Hirsch; 1808–1872), rabbi, rabbinical scholar. Preached in High German as rabbi of Darmstadt and Halberstadt. Published 12th c. halakhic composition *Sefer ha-Eshkol,* but accused of forgery by Shalom Albeck.

Augsburg, city in W. Germany. Jews settled 13th c. expelled 1439. Hebrew press established 1532, organized community 1803, numbering 800 in 1938. Ceased to exist in WWII.

S.S. officers making "selections" at Auschwitz

One of the crematoria at Auschwitz

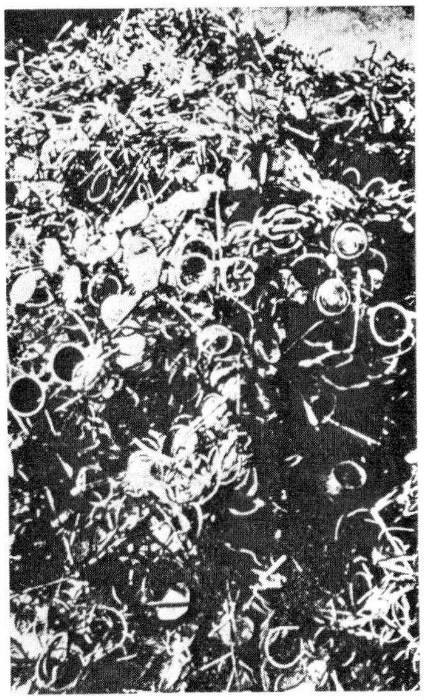

A storeroom of eyeglasses at Auschwitz

A storeroom of shoes at Auschwitz

Some of the accused in the Frankfort Auschwitz trial

Auschwitz (Oświecim), concentration and death camp in Poland, the largest of its kind, established 1940. In June 1941 S.S. Chief Himmler ordered the camp commandant, Rudolf Hoess, to make preparation for systematic mass murder. Estimates of Jewish dead in Auschwitz vary between 1,000,000 and 2,500,000. Thousands of gypsies and other prisoners were also killed. Four crematoria functioned in 1943 to burn corpses of gassed victims. Sterilization experiments were made on the living. "Selections" and gassing of Jews continued until Nov. 1944. In spite of the situation, a resistance movement was organized and a break-out attempt made in Oct. 1944. Some escaped but few survived. The camp survivors (7,650) were freed Jan. 1945 by the Soviet Army. A museum with official Polish archives was established in Auschwitz and a memorial opened 1967.

Auschwitz Trials, series of trials held after WWII of those responsible for the murders in Auschwitz. In 1947, Rudolf Hoess, the first commandant of the camp, was sentenced to death in Warsaw and executed on the site overlooking the camp. At a following trial in Cracow, 23 S.S. men condemned to death, 21 of the sentences carried out. Series of minor trials connected with Auschwitz later held in Poland. Similar trials also held by British, American, Soviet, French, Czech courts. Auschwitz trial in Germany began in Frankfort Dec. 1963, ending Aug. 1965, with six sentenced for life, three acquitted, two released for ill health, and prison terms for the rest. A second and third Auschwitz trial followed in 1966 and 1967. In East Germany, camp doctor Horst Fischer sentenced to death.

Auslaender, Nahum (1893–1962), Soviet Yiddish critic, literary historian, poet. Taught Yiddish at Moscow Western Univ. Headed department of Yiddish literature at Belorussian Academy of Sciences in Minsk 1926–28. Became an editor of Yiddish monthly *Sovetish Heymland* 1961.

Auslander, Joseph (1897–1965), U.S. poet. Writings incl. *Sunrise Trumpets.* Editor, *North American Review,* 1936.

Auster, Daniel (1893–1962), Israel lawyer; b. Galicia, settled in Ereẓ Israel 1914. Acting mayor of Jerusalem 1936–38, 1944–45. First mayor of Jerusalem in independent Israel 1948–51.

Australia, island continent in British Commonwealth. Jews arrived in significant numbers in 1830s. The goldrushes of 1850s and E. European persecutions at end of 19th c. led to considerable immigration with further influxes during Nazi period and after WWII. Pop. 72,000 (1971), mostly in major cities with representative bodies. Jews in Australian public life have included Sir Isaac Isaacs, chief justice and governor-general, and Sir John Monash, army general. Executive Council of Australian Jewry, working through Boards of Deputies in the states, represents the community.

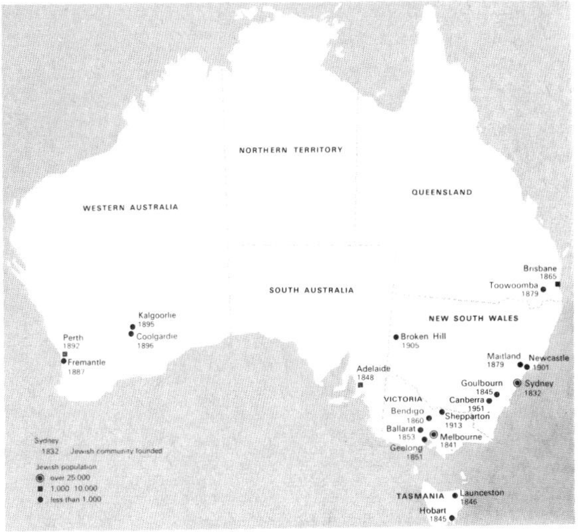

Distribution of Australian Jewry, giving date when the communities were organized.

Austria, C. European republic. Jews present fr. 10th c.; fr. late Middle Ages mainly in Vienna and environs. "Fredericianum" charter granted by Frederick II 1244. 13th–15th c. marked by persecutions culminating 1420 in host desecration libel, with 270 Jews burnt at stake (*Wiener geserah*) and the rest expelled. Community reformed to become center of Jewish learning, subject to intermittent restrictions and expulsions until general expulsion of 1669–70 when all (c. 1,700) had to leave, with exception of a number of Court Jews and their households. The restrictive Familiants laws, introduced 1727, in force until 1848. The "tolerated" Jews in Vienna and those influenced by the Haskalah movement welcomed Joseph II's 1782 *Toleranzpatent,* designed to enforce emancipation and turn Jews into "useful citizens." Full civil rights granted Jews in Austria-Hungary only in 1867. Toward end of 19th c., anti-

AUTOGRAPHS OF WELL-KNOWN PERSONALITIES

Abraham b. Moses b. Maimon
Cyrus Adler
Shmuel Yosef Agnon
Ahad Ha-Am
Hayyim Joseph David Azulai
Israel b. Eliezer Ba'al Shem Tov
David Ben-Gurion
Izhak Ben-Zvi
Sarah Bernhardt
Hayyim Nahman Bialik
Louis D. Brandeis
Joseph b. Ephraim Caro
Marc Chagall
Uriel da Costa

Adolphe Crémieux
Benjamin Disraeli
Simon Dubnow
Albert Einstein
Levi Eshkol
Jonathan Eybeschuetz
Sigmund Freud
Judah Leib Gordon
Heinrich Graetz
Heinrich Heine
Theodor Herzl
Baron Maurice de Hirsch
Moses Isserles
Franz Kafka

Levi Isaac of Berdichev
Samuel David Luzzatto
Maimonides
Manasseh ben Israel
Abraham Mapu
Golda Meir
Moses Mendelssohn
Solomon Molcho
Sir John Monash
Moses Montefiore
Mayer Amschel Rothschild
Shalom Aleichem

Sir Herbert Samuel
Moshe Sharett
Zalman Shazar
Baruch Spinoza
Henrietta Szold
Chaim Weizmann
Isaac M. Wise
Stephen S. Wise
Abraham Zacuto
Ludwig Lazar Zamenhof
Israel Zangwill
Leopold Zunz

Jewish population of Austria.

Semitism spread rapidly, causing a strengthening of national Jewish elements. Vienna was city of Theodor Herzl and Jews played major role in country's cultural and literary life. There were about 200,000 Jews in Austria on its annexation (*Anschluss*) to Nazi Germany in 1938; 70,000 died in concentration camps (Dachau, Mauthausen, etc.), many others having emigrated. Jewish pop. 9,000 (1971), almost all in Vienna.

Ausubel, David Paul (1918–), U.S. educator, psychiatrist; specialized in psychology of ethnic culture.

Ausubel, Nathan (1899–), U.S. author, folklorist (*A Treasury of Jewish Folklore, A Treasury of Jewish Humor,* etc.).

Auto-da-Fé ("Act of Faith"), ceremony first held in Portugal, at which Inquisition pronounced sentences on its victims. An estimated 2,000 autos took place in Spain, Portugal and other Roman Catholic countries bet. 1481–1826. More than 30,000 suffered death penalty, mostly Marranos and Crypto-Jews, but also Protestants, Crypto-Muslims, etc.

Autonomism, termed coined by Simon Dubnow in 1901 to designate his conception of Jewish nationalism in the Diaspora, giving rise to a program for the future of the Jews, who were to be politically and territorially members of the states in which they were dispersed but at the same time exist as a national-cultural entity. The policy of the Autonomists was accepted by the Folkspartei, the Sejmists, and the Bund. After WWI, their hopes seemed fulfilled by minority rights but the infringement of these rights and then the Holocaust ended the practical impact of the movement.

Av, 5th month of Jewish religious year. Lasts 30 days and falls in July-Aug. Zodiac sign: Leo.

Av, the Fifteenth of (Heb. *Tu be-Av*), minor holiday in Second Temple times; last day for bringing wood offering for Temple. On this day young girls danced in vineyards and young men selected prospective brides.

Av, the Ninth of (Heb. *Tishah be-Av*), traditional day of mourning and fasting for destruction of Temples in Jerusalem. *Kinot* and Book of Lamentations read in synagogue services. Became a symbol for all the persecutions and misfortunes of Jewish people, for loss of national independence and sufferings in exile.

Avadim, minor tractate appended to order *Nezikin* of Talmud. It deals with laws of slaves.

Av Bet Din (Heb. "father of law court"). (1) One who presides over a Jewish ecclesiastical court (*bet din*). (2) Vice-president of *Bet Din ha-Gadol* in Second Temple period. (3) From 14th c., used by communities to designate local rabbi.

Avdan (c. 200), pupil and *amora* ("interpreter") of Judah ha-Nasi.

Avdimi of Haifa (c. 400), Palestinian *amora.* Saying: "From the day the Temple was destroyed prophecy was taken from the prophets and given to the wise."

Avedat (Ovdat; Ar. "Abde"), former Nabatean road station in C. Negev. Conquered by Romans 106 C.E., abandoned in 3rd c. Resettled in Byzantine period (6th c.), with economy based on agriculture and wine production. Partially razed 614 in Persian invasion and deserted in Arab period. Ancient city reconstructed in recent years. Agricultural and experimental station established nearby.

Avelei Zion (Heb. "Mourners of Zion"), groups of Jews in many countries in early centuries C.E. devoted to mourning destruction of

Auto-da-Fé, painting by Alonso Berrugnete

Aerial view of Avedat.

Temple and praying for redemption of Zion. Customs arose after destruction of Second Temple. Most Karaites who settled in Jerusalem in first half of 9th c. lived acc. to precepts of Avelei Zion.

Avelut (Heb. "mourning"). In Jewish law the nearest relatives are bound to observe periods of mourning for their dead. These vary from seven to thirty days to a year and subject the persons to restrictions.

Avenary, Hanoch (H. Loewenstein; 1908–), musicologist; b. Danzig, settled in Ereẓ Israel 1935. Taught at Jerusalem and Tel Aviv Univ.

Avendauth, translator active in Toledo, Spain 1150–60. Probably identical with Abraham ibn Daud, philosopher and historian.

Avenger, Blood, near relative duty-bound to kill murderer of his relative acc. to biblical law (see Lev. 35). This was usually the next of kin.

Averah (Heb.), transgression; opposite of *mitzvah.*

Averbakh, Leopold Leonidovich (1903–1938?), Russian Soviet critic, a leader of *Rapp* – Russian Association of Proletarian Writers (1929–1932). Disappeared during 1930s purges.

Av ha-Raḥamim (Heb. "Merciful Father"), memorial prayer for Jewish martyrs and martyred communities. Composed by unknown author in memory of martyrs massacred in Germany during First Crusade. Became part of Ashkenazi Sabbath morning service.

Aviad, Yeshayahu (Oscar Wolfsberg; 1893–1957), author, leader of religious Zionism. Physician by profession. Lived in Germany until 1933 when he settled in Ereẓ Israel. Israel envoy in Scandinavia 1948–49, Switzerland 1956. Wrote on Jewish thought.

Avi Avi (Heb. "My father, my father"), refrain of lament *"Bore ad anna"* sung on Ninth of Av in Sephardi rite.

Avida (Zlotnick), Yehuda Leib (1887–1962), rabbi, folklorist. Founder, secretary of Mizrachi in Poland. Went to Canada 1920, to South Africa as director of Jewish education 1938. Settled in Jerusalem 1949. Wrote on Yiddish philology, Jewish folklore, etc.

Avidom (Mahler-Kalkstein), Menahem (1908–), Israel composer; b. Poland, settled in Ereẓ Israel 1925. Wrote operas, symphonies, chamber music. Israel Prize 1961. Fr. 1955 director-general of Israel Performing Rights Society.

Avidov, Zvi (Henry Klein; 1896–), Israel entomologist; b. Germany, settled in Ereẓ Israel 1921. With F.S. Bodenheimer laid the foundation of agricultural entomology in Israel. Appointed prof. at Heb. Univ., Reḥovot Fac. of Agr. 1955.

Avigad, Naḥman (1905–), Israel archaeologist. Heb. Univ. prof. 1963. Directed excavations at Bet She'arim and in Jewish quarter of Old City of Jerusalem (1969 ff.), etc. Specialist in Hebrew epigraphy.

Avigdor, Abraham (14th c.), Provençal physician, translator fr. Latin to Hebrew, author of philosophical works and translator of medical works.

Avigdor ben Elijah ha-Kohen (c. 1200–1275), talmudist in Italy and Vienna. A teacher of Meir b. Baruch of Rothenburg.

Avigdor ben Joseph Ḥayyim (18th–19th c.), rabbi and opponent of Ḥasidism in Poland-Lithuania. Complained to Czar's administration, charging Ḥasidism with being "heretical sect."

Avignon, city in S. France. Under Papal rule 1309–1791 and in consequence Jews permitted to reside there, even after 14th c. exclusion fr. France. Center of Jewish scholarship. Had its own prayer rite. Jews confined fr. 16th c. to ghetto known as *"carrière des Juifs."* Number of Jews dwindled to 149 in 1892. In WWII, Jewish refugees settled there. Many arrested and deported 1943. N. African Jews brought Jewish pop. to 2,000 (1968).

Avigur, Shaul (1899–), key figure in Haganah; b. Russia, settled in Ereẓ Israel 1912. Participated in 1920 defense of Tel-Ḥai. In Haganah's national committee fr. 1922. Active in "illegal" *aliyah.* Fr. 1948 served in special capacities in government offices.

Aviḥayil, moshav in C. Israel, NE of Netanyah; founded 1932 by veterans of Jewish Legion. Established museum of Jewish Legion. Pop. 590 (1971).

Avila, Eliezer ben Samuel ben Moses de ("Rav Adda' ; 1714–1761), rabbinical scholar in Morocco; son of **Samuel** (b. 1688), talmudic scholar. His responsa a source of information on Moroccan Jews in 18th c.

Avila, Prophet of, name given to seer who experienced visions at Avila, Spain, 1295. His forecast of advent of Messiah influenced community but failure led some to adopt Christianity.

Avimi (3rd c.), Babylonian *amora;* teacher of R. Ḥisda, who transmitted many of his *halakhot* and also the *aggadah* that the Tent of Meeting was the crypt of the First Temple.

Avinoam (Grossman), Reuben (1905–), poet, translator; b. Chicago, settled in Ereẓ Israel 1929. Published several volumes of poetry, stories, translations, Hebrew-English dictionary.

Avinu Malkenu (Heb. "Our Father, our King"), litany recited during Ten Days of Penitence.

Avinu she-ba-Shamayim (Heb. "Our Father in Heaven"), form of adoration frequently found at beginning of prayers of petition.

Avira (3rd–4th c.), Palestinian *amora.* Saying: "A man should always eat and drink for less than his means allow, clothe himself according to his means, and honor his wife and children beyond his means."

Avi-Shaul, Mordekhai (1898–), writer, translator; b. Hungary, settled in Ereẓ Israel 1921. Active in Berit Shalom and pacifist organizations. Wrote poems, plays, stories.

Avi-Yonah, Michael (1904–1974), Israel archaeologist; b. Lemberg, settled in Ereẓ Israel 1921. Prof. of classical archaeology, art history at Heb. Univ. fr. 1953. Wrote extensively on Ereẓ Israel and Jews in classical and Byzantine period, historical geography, archaeology, etc.

Avneri (Ostermann), Uri (1923–), Israel journalist, politician. Editor of sensationalist weekly *Ha-Olam ha-Zeh.* Member of Knesset representing Ha-Olam ha-Zeh–Koaḥ Ḥadash 1965–73.

Avni, Aharon (1906–1951), Israel painter; b. Ukraine, settled in Ereẓ Israel 1925. Headed Histadrut Seminary for Painting and Sculpture.

Avodah (Heb. "Service"), name for Temple ritual; applied to central part of *Musaf* liturgy on Day of Atonement which incorporates poetic description of Temple cult.

Avodah Zarah (Heb. "Idolatrous Worship"), tractate in Mishnah, order *Nezikin,* with *gemara* in both Talmuds. Deals with prohibitions concerning dealings with gentiles, idolatrous objects (images, shrines, etc.), etc. Early copies suffered greatly from Christian censorship.

Avot, or **Pirkei Avot** (Heb. "The Chapters of the Fathers"), tractate in Mishnah order *Nezikin,* a chapter of which is recited every Sabbath afternoon during summer months after Passover. Contains chain of tradition from Moses to *tannaim* and gives salient moral and doctrinal sayings of sages in each generation. Its pithy wisdom made it one of the most popular works in Judaism.

BAR-MITZVAH
A Bar-Mitzvah ceremony in the synagogue of the Hadassah Medical Center in Jerusalem. In the background above can be seen some of the stained glass windows by Marc Chagall symbolizing the Twelve Tribes of Israel.

BIBLE Illustration (fragment) from an illuminated Bible manuscript written in 929, probably in Egypt (now in the Leningrad Public Library). It depicts the Tabernacle and its implements, including the candelabrum and the Ark of the Covenant.

BIBLE Page from illuminated Bible manuscript made in Portugal in the late 15th cent. (now in New York at the Hispanic Society of America). It shows the beginning of the Book of Isaiah.

Avot de-Rabbi Nathan (Heb. "The Fathers according to Rabbi Nathan"), one of extra-canonical minor tractates of Talmud. Generally printed at end of *Nezikin*. Consists of commentary on *Avot*.

Avot Nezikin (Heb. "Fathers of Damage"), classification of torts. The Talmud distinguishes 3 main sources of tort-feasors or damage: animals, pits, fire.

Avrunin, Abraham (1869–1957), Russian-born Hebrew philologist, grammarian. Joined Ḥibbat Zion, settled in Ereẓ Israel 1910.

Avtalyon (1st c. B.C.E.), colleague of Shemaiah, with whom he constituted the fourth of the *Zugot* ("pairs"). Shemaiah was *nasi*, Avtalyon *av bet din*. Descendant of proselytes.

Avtinas, family in charge of mixing incense in Temple. Kept the formula secret lest it be used for idol worship.

Axelrod, George (1922–), U.S. comedy writer, director, producer (*Seven Year Itch, Bus Stop, Once More With Feeling*, etc.).

Axelrod, Julius (1912–), U.S. physiologist, pharmacologist. Shared 1970 Nobel Prize for physiology and medicine. Identified mechanisms that regulate formation of noradrenalin in nerve cells.

Axelrod, Pavel Borisovich (1850–1928), Russian revolutionary, a founder of Russian Social Democratic Party. Escaped abroad from Czarist repression, lived in Berlin and Geneva. A Menshevik, he was an uncompromising opponent of Bolshevik regime.

Axelrod, Selik (1904–1941), Soviet Yiddish poet. Deeply attached to Jewish values. Executed during Stalinist purge of Jewish writers.

Axenfeld, Israel (1787–1866), pioneering Yiddish novelist, dramatist. At first a follower of ḥasidic rabbi Naḥman of Bratslav; later violently anti-ḥasidic. Portrayed Jewish life realistically but satirized ḥasidic beliefs and customs.

Ayalon, David (1914–), Israel Arabist specializing in Islamic social and military history. Prof. at Heb. Univ. Israel Prize 1972.

Ayanot, agricultural school in C. Israel nr. Nes Ẓiyyonah. Founded 1930 by WIZO.

Ayash (Ayyāsh), family of rabbis and scholars. **Judah** (d. 1760), one of most famous rabbis of Algiers; went to Ereẓ Israel 1756. His son **Jacob Moses** (c. 1750–1817), chief rabbi of Ferrara.

Aydan, David (1873–1954), Tunisian printer; b. Djerba, where he founded its first Hebrew printing press. Printed works of rabbis from Djerba and North Africa.

Ayin (ע), 16th letter of Hebrew alphabet; numerical value 70. Original guttural pronunciation retained in oriental communities, not pronounced by Ashkenazim etc.

Ayllon, Solomon ben Jacob (c. 1655–1728), rabbi, kabbalist; b. Salonika. Went to Safed 1680. Served as *haham* in London 1689–1700 and Amsterdam 1700–28. Moderate Shabbatean and became involved in fierce controversies, especially with Ẓevi Ashkenazi.

David Ayalon

Scapegoat being cast over a cliff with the devil waiting below, 15th-cent. German "maḥzor" (see Azazel).

Ayrton, Hertha (1854–1923), British physicist; of Jewish parentage. Established laws governing behavior of electric arc. One daughter, **Barbara Ayrton Gould** (d. 1950), chairman of Labor Party 1939–40. Her other daughter married Israel Zangwill.

Ayyelet ha-Shaḥar, kibbutz in N. Israel. Founded 1918, affiliated with Iḥud ha-Kevuẓot ve-ha-Kibbutzim. Has museum of finds from nearby Hazor and popular guest house. Pop. 750 (1971).

Azancot, Moroccan family, several of whose members were leaders of Marrakesh community. They later settled in Tangiers and played diplomatic role. **Moses** (19th c.), kidnapped by Franciscan mission, converted in Madrid; his daughter was lady of honor to Isabella II. His brother **David** (19th c.), diplomat, antiquarian. Delacroix painted many portraits of his family.

Azariah, see Ahaziah; Uzziah.

Azazel, name of place or "power" to which one of two goats in Temple service on Day of Atonement was sent. The high priest cast lots upon two goats, one designated "for the Lord" and the other "for Azazel" (Lev. 16:8–10). The goat was not slaughtered but carried the sins of Israel into the wilderness. In modern Hebrew the word is used as an imprecation.

Azeff, Yevno Fishelevich (1869–1918), double agent of Czarist secret police and Russian social revolutionary movement. Betrayed many revolutionaries and at same time acquired reputation as courageous leader of Social Revolutionary Party and organizer of terrorist acts. Activities revealed 1908; sentenced to death *in absentia* by party court. Died in German prison.

Azekah, city of Judah where armies were drawn up during battle between David and Goliath. Generally identified with Tell Zakariyeh, excavated 1899–1900.

Azerbaijan, region divided between Iran (Persia) and Russia. Jews settled there 342 B.C.E. 1. Persian. Presence of Jews attested only fr. 12th c. Among Jews were adherents of David Alroy as well as Karaites. Dialect of Jews has been object of investigation by western scholars. 2. Russian. Soviet Socialist Republic. Jews generally engaged in agriculture, petty trade, manual labor. Suffered from persecution from local Muslims. Under Czars, region closed to Jews from European Russia. After 1917 became important Jewish center. Jewish pop. 41,300 (1970).

Aẓeret (Heb.), a general assembly; concluding celebration. In Second Temple period, used exclusively for festival of Shavuot.

Azevedo (D'Azevedo), Portuguese Sephardi family whose members were found in N. Africa, Amsterdam, London. **Melchior (Belchior) Vaz** (16th c.), Marrano diplomat and sea captain. Concluded peace treaty 1559 with ruler of Morocco on behalf of king of Navarre. **Henrico** (c. 1661) and **Louis** (c. 1675), ambassadors of Holland to dey of Algiers. **David Salom** (d. 1699), minister-resident of dey of Algiers in Amsterdam.

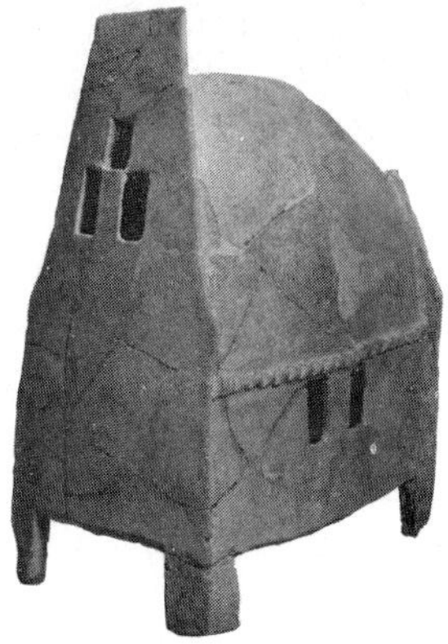

Clay ossuary from collective tomb at Azor, 4th cent. B.C.E.

Initial word panel for "Az Rov Nissim," "Darmstadt Haggadah"

Azharot (Heb. "warnings"), category of liturgical poems for Feast of Weeks (Shavuot) in which the 613 Commandments are enumerated (numerical value of word 613).

Azikri, Eleazar ben Moses (1533–1600), kabbalist. Studied in Safed. His mystical diaries contain meditations, revelations, and dreams jotted down in course of mystical experience.

Azilut, short treatise schematizing theories of older Kabbalah; of disputed date and authorship.

Azmon, mountain near Sepphoris to which Jewish rebels fled during Jewish War 66 C.E. Alt. 1,798 ft. (548 m.).

Azor, place SE of Tel Aviv with remains from Canaanite and Israelite period. Small fort built in Crusader period by Richard Coeur-de-Lion. Before 1948 an Arab village but Arabs fled and in 1949 settled by immigrants. Pop. 5,200 (1971).

Azriel of Gerona (13th c.), Spanish kabbalist; one of most profound speculative thinkers in kabbalistic mysticism. His work reflects process whereby neoplatonic thought penetrated into original kabbalistic tradition.

Az Rov Nissim (Heb. "Then many miracles"), alphabetical acrostic by Yannai (6th c. *paytan*) included in final section of the Passover *Haggadah.* Describes events that took place on night of first Passover.

Azulai, family of Italian majolica makers; active from early 16th to early 18th c.

Azulai, Abraham ben Israel (c. 1660–c. 1741), Moroccan kabbalist. Wrote commentary on Zohar and many responsa. Subject of many legends.

Azulai, Abraham ben Mordecai (c. 1570–1643), kabbalist; b. Fez. Preoccupied with question of relation between kabbalah and philosophy. Settled in Hebron. Wrote treatises on Zohar, reedited one of Luria's books.

Azulai, Ḥayyim Joseph David (acronym **Ḥida;** 1724–1806), halakhist, kabbalist, emissary, bibliographer; b. Jerusalem, traveled widely, eventually settled in Leghorn. His diary *Ma'agal Tov* is of historical importance. Visited many libraries, copied ancient works and mss.; one of first Jewish bibliographers, compiling *Shem ha-Gedolim,* a bibliographical lexicon.

Illuminated letter "B" in "Extracts from Gregory the Great" shows King David playing lyre and young David killing Goliath, N. France, 12th c.

Baal, designation of great weather-god of W. Semites. Plural designates minor local gods, singular in combination with other terms (e.g., Baal-Gad) designates minor or local gods. Most active deity in fertility cult of Canaan. Allure of its worship attracted Israelites during early centuries of their settlement in Canaan.

The "Baal of the lightning," a stele from Ras Shamra (Ugarit).

Initial letter "bet" showing the "ba'al ha-bayit" presiding at the "seder", from Amsterdam "Haggadah," 1712.

Baal-Berith (Heb. "Lord of Covenant"), name of deity worshiped in early Israelite period at the temple of Shechem; destroyed in 12th c. B.C.E. by Abimelech.

Ba'al Ha-Bayit, head of household; in Yid. "*Balebos*" (also "respected citizen"). Also, landlord.

Ba'al Ha-Turim, see Jacob ben Asher.

Ba'al Keri'ah, one who reads the Torah in synagogue.

Baal-Makhshoves (Israel Isidor Elyashev; 1873–1924), Yiddish literary critic; b. Kovno, journalist in Russia, Poland, Germany. Introduced European aesthetic standards and norms into his interpretation of Yiddish literature.

Ba'al Shem (Heb. "Master of the Divine Name"), title given fr. Middle Ages on to men to whom was ascribed power to work miracles by utilizing Divine Name. First to be so known was 11th c. poet Benjamin b. Zerah.

Ba'al Shem of London, see Falk, Samuel Jacob Ḥayyim.

Ba'al Shem Ṭov, see Israel ben Eliezer Ba'al Shem Tov.

Baars, Jacob (1886–1956), Dutch architect. Designed synagogues on Linnaeus Straat, Amsterdam-Oost (1927/8), Bentincklaan, Rotterdam (1955), etc.

Baasha (or **Baasa),** king of Israel c. 906–883 B.C.E. Assassinated his predecessor, Nadab. Constant war with Judah throughout his reign.

Baazov, Herzl (1904–1945), Georgian poet, playwright. Wrote mostly on Georgian Jewish life. Died in exile in Soviet north.

Bab, Julius (1880–1955), German drama critic, literary historian *(Die Chronik des deutschen Dramas).* Fled to U.S. 1940.

Babad, Joseph ben Moses (1800–1874), Polish rabbi. Author of *Minḥat Ḥinnukh,* an exposition of Aaron ha-Levi's *Sefer ha-Ḥinnukh.*

Babad, Joshua Heschel ben Isaac (1754–1838), halakhist in Lublin and Tarnopol. Author of responsa on *Shulḥan Arukh.*

Babad, Menahem Munish ben Joshua Heschel (1865–1938), halakhic authority; b. Brody. *Av bet din* in Strzyzow, rabbi of Jaworow.

Babai ibn Luṭf (17th c.), Persian poet, chronicler. Author of *Kitāb Anusi,* describing forced conversions and martyrdom of Persian Jews under Abbas I (1588–1629).

Baba Rabbah (4th c. C.E.), Samaritan high priest, outstanding Samaritan political leader, reformer. Led Samaritans for 40 years, achieving many victories over Romans and neighboring states. Invited to Constantinople by Byzantine emperor and held prisoner until his death.

Babel, Isaac Emmanuilovich (1894–1941?), Russian writer. Served in Cossack cavalry during Russian Civil War. Arrested and disappeared 1939. Most of his manuscripts destroyed by Soviet secret police (NKVD).

Isaac Babel

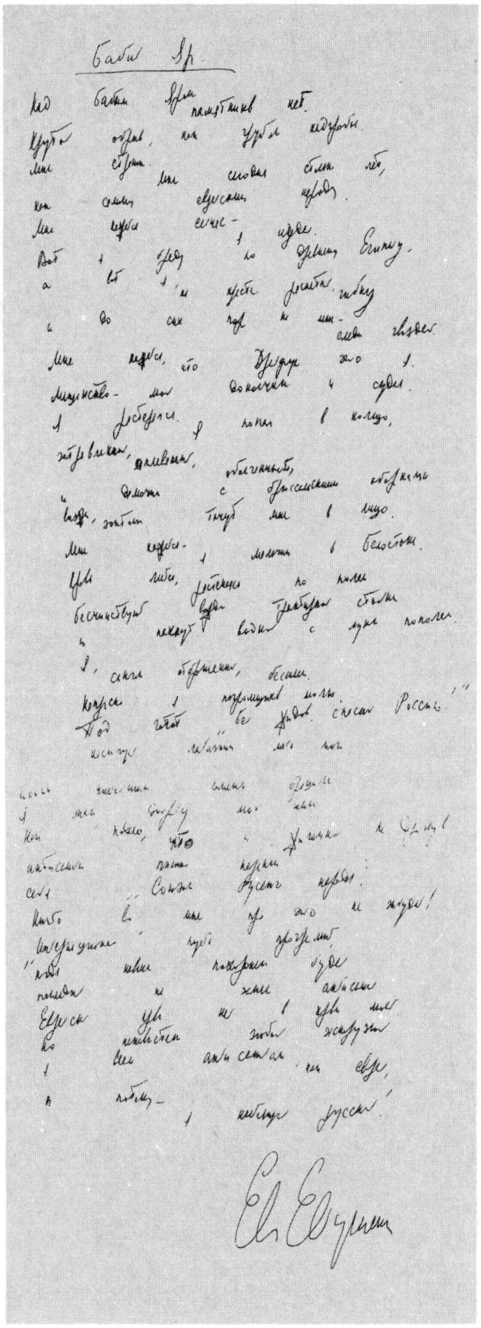

Beginning and end of ms. of poem "Babi Yar" by Yevgeni Yevtushenko.

Impression of walled city of Babylon in 7th-6th cent. B.C.E.

Small in quantity, his literary work includes stories and plays, chiefly on two themes: the civil war and life in his native Odessa, esp. among assimilated Jews, incl. underworld *(Red Cavalry, Odessa Tales)*.

Babel, Tower of, edifice whose building is described in Gen. 11:1–9 as direct cause of diversity of languages in the world and dispersion of mankind over all the earth. Story may have been inspired by ancient Babylonian *ziqqurat* towers.

Babilée (Gutmann), Jean (1923–), French dancer, choreographer. Formed Ballets Babilée 1956.

Babi Yar, ravine on outskirts of Kiev where over 10,000 persons, most of them Jews, were murdered by Germans 1941. Nazis tried unsuccessfully to erase all traces of mass burial. After 1949 Soviet authorities tried to eliminate all references to Babi Yar and intended to transform ravine into sport stadium. Opposition was expressed with poem *Babi Yar* by the non-Jewish poet Y. Yevtushenko (1961) and novel *Babi Yar* by Anatoli Kuznetsov. Failure to erect suitable memorial became symbol of Soviet anti-Semitism.

Babovich (Bobovitch), Simḥah ben Solomon (1790–1855), Karaite *ḥakham* in the Crimea. Mainly devoted himself to securing rights for Karaites in Russia.

Babylon, ancient city on Euphrates River. Capital fr. time of Hammurapi (1792–1749 B.C.E.). Figures on various occasions in Bible from tower built there (Babel) to end of Babylonian Empire and incident at Belshazzar's feast.

Babylonia, ancient country in W. Asia, between Tigris and Euphrates, corresponding approximately to modern Iraq. Known in Bible as the land of Shinar or Kasdim (Chaldees). Described in Book of Genesis as cradle of humanity. Many Jews exiled to Babylonia after Nebuchadnezzar II conquered Judah (597, 586 B.C.E.). Jews formed large settlement, many remaining there even after return to Ereẓ Israel permitted by Cyrus. (See Exile, Babylonian.) During Roman occupation, Jews rose against Trajan (116). Enjoyed extensive internal autonomy and were headed by Exilarch in Persian and Parthian period. Outstanding academies produced Babylonian Talmud, which reflects society preponderantly based on agriculture and crafts. In 3rd c. main center of rabbinic studies, with academies at Nehardea, Pumbedita, and Sura. With abolition of Palestinian patriarchate, became spiritual center for all Jewry. Persecutions in 5th c. led to 7 years' Jewish revolt under Mar Zutra II. Babylonian Talmud compiled and completed in Babylonian academies. Position of Jews precarious until Arab conquest in 7th c. (See also Iraq.)

Babylonian Talmud, see Talmud.

°**Bacchides** (2nd c. B.C.E.), Syrian general who in 161 B.C.E. fought Judah Maccabee in fierce battle in which Judah was killed. Later defeated by Jonathan the Hasmonean. Returned in 158 B.C.E., made peace with Jonathan, and returned to Syria.

Bacharach (Bacherach), town in Rhine Valley, W. Germany. Jews fr. 12th c. Suffered during Crusader, blood libel, Armleder, and Black Death persecutions. Community ended in Nazi period.

Bacharach, family of U.S. business and communal leaders in Atlantic City, New Jersey. **Isaac** (1870–1956), Republican congressman 1915–36. Wrote 1931 act providing for emergency loans based on value of insurance policies. Another brother, **Harry** (1873–1947), elected mayor of Atlantic City 1911, 1916, 1932.

Bacharach, Jair Ḥayyim ben Moses Samson (1638–1702), talmudic scholar, rabbi at Coblenz, Worms; son of Moses Samson Bacharach. Best known for collected responsa, *Ḥavvat Yair,* demonstrating wide knowledge of secular subjects.

Bacharach, Moses Samson ben Abraham Samuel (1607–1670), Moravian rabbi, author. Rabbi of Worms fr. 1650.

Bacharach, Naphtali ben Jacob Elhanan (17th c.), kabbalist; b. Frankfort. Author of *Emek ha-Melekh,* a systematic presentation of theology according to Lurianic Kabbalah.

Bache, family of U.S. investment bankers, art collectors. **Jules Semon** (1862–1944) headed J.S. Bache and Co. which became prominent in investment banking and securities trading. Gave outstanding collection of art to N.Y. State for Metropolitan Museum of Art.

Bacher, Eduard (1846–1908), Austrian journalist. Editor-in-chief (fr. 1879) and publisher (fr. 1888) of Vienna *Neue Freie Presse.* Opposed Zionism of Theodor Herzl, then on newspaper's staff.

Bacher, Robert Fox (1905–), U.S. physicist. Worked on A-bomb project in Los Alamos during WWII. Member Atomic Energy Commission 1946–49. Prof. of physics at

Cal. Institute of Technology fr. 1949.

Bacher, Simon (1823–1891), Hebrew poet, translator in Hungary. Wrote poetry in flowery style of Haskalah.

Bacher, Wilhelm (1850–1913), Hungarian Semitic scholar; son of Simon Bacher. Prof. at Budapest Rabbinical Seminary fr. 1877, director fr. 1907. Published standard works on talmudic *aggadah* and Midrash, medieval Jewish Bible exegesis, development of Hebrew in Middle Ages, etc.

Bachi, Armando (1883–1943), Italian soldier. Forced to resign commission as lieutenant-general by 1938 Fascist racial laws. D. in Auschwitz.

Bachi, Raphael (1717–1767), French miniature painter. Employed by French court to paint miniature portraits on snuffboxes presented to foreign notables. Clients included Duke of Modena and Prince de Condé.

Bachi, Riccardo (1875–1951), Italian economist, statistician (*Principi di scienza economica,* etc.). Went to Ereẓ Israel 1938 after enactment of racial laws in Italy; taught 1940–46 at Heb. Univ. Tel Aviv branch. Returned to Rome Univ. 1946.

Bachi, Roberto (1909–), statistician, b. Rome, settled in Ereẓ Israel 1938; son of Riccardo Bachi. Organized dept. of statistics at Heb. Univ.; appointed prof. of statistics and demography 1947. Directed Israel Central Bureau of Statistics fr. 1949.

Bachmann, Jacob (1846–1905), Russian *ḥazzan,* composer of synagogue music (*Schirath Jacob, Attah Zokher, Cantata,* etc.).

Bachrach, Jacob ben Moses (Ba'al ha-Ma'amarim; 1824–1896), rabbi, grammarian, b. Poland, lived in Koenigsberg, Bialystok. Played important role in founding Ḥovevei Zion. Attempted to prove antiquity of Hebrew calendar and Hebrew vowels and accents.

Bachrach, Judah ben Joshua Ezekiel (1775–1846), rabbi, author in Lithuania. Wrote novellae and glosses to Talmud and Alfasi.

Bachrach, Moses ben Isaiah Menahem (Moses Mendels; 1574–1641), talmudic scholar, *av bet din* in various Polish communities. Participated in sessions of Councils of Four Lands 1614, 1639.

Back, Samuel (1841–1899), rabbi, scholar. Served in Prague-Smichov fr. 1872. Wrote on philosophical, historical, talmudic subjects.

Backer, George (1902–1974), U.S. publisher, politician, communal leader. Active in Democratic politics. Publisher of *New York Post* 1939–42.

Bacri, David Coen (1770–1811), financier, communal leader in Algiers; son of Joseph Coen Bacri. Under his direction, the influential Bacri Busnach firm guaranteed 5-million franc loan to French Directory, authorized by dey. Dispute over settlement of loan was one of the factors leading to French conquest of Algeria. Executed for alleged treason.

Bacri, Joseph Coen (c. 1740–1817), banker, trader, communal leader; b. Algiers into family active in local politics. Founded Bacri Frères firm, important wheat supplier to France in Napoleonic period. Banished fr. Algiers 1816 by dey.

Baden former German grand duchy. Jews in region fr. 13th c. Various expulsions. Judaism recognized as tolerated religion in 1807. Full civic equality in 1862. Grand Duke Frederick I interested German Emperor in Zionism. Over 20,000 Jews in 1933, 8,725 in 1939. Killed in Holocaust. In 1969, 6 communities numbering 1,094 Jews.

Bader, Gershom (1868–1953), Hebrew, Yiddish journalist, writer; b. Cracow. Founded *Togblat,* first Yiddish daily in Galicia. Transl. Genesis into Polish, published Hebrew language textbooks. Settled in New York 1912.

Badge, Jewish, distinctive sign compulsorily worn by Jews. Originated in Islam c. 720 when non-Muslims were ordered to wear specific marks. Formally introduced in Christendom 1215 by 4th Lateran Council to "prevent intercourse" between Christians and non-Christians, esp. Jews. Consisting generally of circular, mostly yellow badge, or *rota* ("wheel"), sometimes of pointed hat or tablets *(tabula),* badge was introduced throughout Europe, sometimes remaining in force until end of 18th c., but its wearing only sporadically imposed. In Nazi era, Jews again compelled to wear distinguishing badge (with Yellow Shield of David).

Badḥan (Heb.), merrymaker, jester, particularly at traditional Jewish weddings in E. Europe.

Badhav, Isaac ben Michael (1859–1947), Jerusalem rabbi, scholar. His collection of manuscripts and old books a valuable source for research into Ereẓ Israel, particularly Jerusalem.

Red and white circular badge worn by French Jews in 13th-14th cent.

Replica of the Dutch Jewish badge printed and distributed by Dutch underground in 1942. The text reads: "Jews and non-Jews stand united in their struggle."

A "badḥan" dancing at a Galician wedding, postcard from Cracow, 1902.

Badiḥi, Yaḥya ben Judah (c. 1810–1887), Yemenite author of works on Pentateuch and *halakhah.*

Badt, Hermann (1887–1946), German civil servant, constitutional lawyer; active in Zionist movement. Settled in Ereẓ Israel 1933.

Baeck, Leo (1873–1956), German rabbi, theologian; son of Samuel Baeck. Rabbi in Berlin fr. 1912. Became spiritual leader of German Reform Jewry. On Hitler's advent in 1933, remained at his post with his

Leo Baeck

congregation. Sent to Theresienstadt 1943; survived until liberation. Settled in London, becoming chairman of the World Union for Progressive Judaism. Wrote on Jewish philosophy and theology *(The Essence of Judaism, The People Israel, Judaism and Christianity).*

Baeck, Samuel (1834–1912), German rabbi, scholar *(Geschichte des juedischen Volkes und seiner Literatur . . .).* Successfully advocated teaching of Jewish religion in Prussian high schools.

Baena, Juan Alfonso de (c. 1445), poet, scribe to Juan II of Castile. His *Cancionero de Baena,* an anthology of 14th–15th c. poetry, an important source for part played by Jews in Spanish cultural life.

Baer, Abraham (1834–1894), cantor in W. Prussia, Posen, Goteborg (Sweden). His *Baal T'fillah,* collection of 1,500 melodies, was basic manual for European cantors.

Baer, Max (1909–1959), U.S. prizefighter. World heavyweight champion 1934–5 after knocking out Germany's Max Schmeling. His claim of Jewish origin has been questioned.

Baer, Seligman Isaac (1825–1897), Hebrew grammarian, masorah scholar, and liturgist; b. Germany. Together with Franz Delitzsch published Psalms and most other Bible books with masorah texts. Edited popular prayer book, *Avodat Yisrael,* and other liturgical handbooks.

Baer, Yitzhak (Fritz; 1888–), Jewish historian; b. Germany. Prof. at Heb. Univ. fr. 1930. A founder and editor of historical journal *Zion.* Wrote authoritative *History of the Jews in Christian Spain, Galut, Yisrael ba-Ammim,* etc.

Baerwald, Alex (1878–1930), architect; b. Germany, settled in Ereẓ Israel 1925. Planned Technion, Reali school buildings in Haifa, Central Jezreel Valley Hospital, etc. Founded Technion Faculty of Architecture. Tried to create Jewish style, based on Muslim architecture.

Baerwald, Paul (1871–1961), banker, philanthropist, communal leader; b. Frankfort, in U.S. fr. 1896. Partner in N.Y. Lazard Frères. Treasurer, then chairman (fr. 1932) of American Jewish Joint Distribution Committee. Joined President Roosevelt's Advisory Committee on political refugees 1938.

Baeyer, Adolf von (1835–1917), German organic chemist; son of Jewish mother. Awarded Nobel Prize 1905, for "advancement of organic chemistry and the chemical industry, through his work on organic dyes and hydroaromatic compounds." Made first chemical discovery at 12. Ennobled 1885.

Baghdad, capital of Iraq. Jewish community, known fr. 8th c., became seat of Exilarchate, gaonate, and academies of Sura and Pumbedita. 40,000 Jews c. 1170. Jews not persecuted after coming of Mongols 1258, but most fled on conquest by Tamerlane 1393. Community reformed; suffered under Persians. Fared well under Ottomans (fr. 1514). 6,000 Jews in 1828, 50,000 in early 20th c., 100,000 in 1930s. Fr. British conquest 1917 until independence of Iraq 1929, Jews enjoyed complete freedom. Fr. 1929, Zionist activity prohibited, anti-Semitism increased, inspired by Nazi propaganda, reaching climax in WWII under Rashīd Ali, with 1941 pogrom. After 1950/1 exodus of Iraqi Jewry to Israel, 5,000 left out of 77,000 and a few hundred in 1972. Nine Jews hanged publicly 1969 for allegedly spying for Israel. Jews fr. Baghdad formed communities in India and Far East.

Baginsky, Adolf Aron (1843–1918), German physician. Founder of modern pediatrics, on which he wrote standard works.

Bagohi, governor of Persian satrapy Yehud (Judea) in time of Darius and Artaxerxes II. Jews of Elephantine sent him letter appealing for assistance in reconstructing their temple.

Bagrit, Sir Leon (1902–), British industrialist, automation pioneer. Developed automated control for nuclear, aeronautical, and industrial purposes.

Bagritski, Eduard Georgiyevich (pseudonym of **E.G. Dzyuba;** 1895–1934) Soviet Russian poet. Treated revolutionary themes. Most important work *Duma pro Opanasa* ("The Lay of Opanas"). Also known for Russian translations of English, French, Yiddish, Ukrainian verse.

Baḥ, see Sirkes, Joel.

Baḥad (initials of Heb. *Berit Ḥalutzim Datiyyim,* "League of Religious Pioneers"), religious youth organization founded in Germany 1928 and later spread to Britain and other countries. Among religious pioneer groups that established Ha-Kibbutz ha-Dati in Ereẓ Israel 1935.

Bahai, world religion whose center is in Israel. Adherents exiled 1868 to Acre and imposing mausoleum situated in beautiful gardens erected on Mt. Carmel in Haifa over body of its founder.

Bahia, Brazilian port. Marranos fr. Portugal among early 16th c. settlers and played leading and affluent role in community until 18th c. Jewish pop. 1,300 (1971).

Bahir, Sefer Ha- (Heb. "Book of Bahir"), earliest work of kabbalistic literature, known in S. France by end of 12th c.

Bahrein, territory on Persian Gulf. Jews fr. Talmudic period, Jewish merchants in 19th c. In 1968 c. 100 Jews in Manama (the capital).

Baḥur (Heb.), in the Bible a young man "selected for military fitness." Talmud used term in sense of unmarried (or innocent young) man, especially for yeshivah student.

Baḥur, Elijah, see Levita, Elijah.

Baḥuẓim (Heb. "outsiders"), name given by Jews to apparently Jewish tribes ("Judaized Berbers") living in 15th–16th c. along Algerian-Tunisian border. Observed Sabbath, circumcision, etc. Last remnants disappeared after WWI.

Baḥya (Pseudo), name given to otherwise unknown author of "On the Essence of the Soul," a neoplatonic work in Arabic, probably written in the 11th–12th c. (and at one time attributed to Baḥya ibn Paquda).

Baḥya ben Asher ben Ḥlava (13th c.), Saragossa exegete, preacher, kabbalist. Author of popular commentary on Pentateuch based on fourfold *pardes* (q.v.) system of interpretation.

Baḥya ben Joseph ibn Paquda (11th c.), moral philosopher in Spain. His major work, written in Arabic *(Kitāb al-Hidāya ilā Farā'iḍ al-Qulūb),* transl. into Heb. by Judah ibn Tibbon under the title *Ḥovot ha-Levavot* ("Duties of the Heart"). One of best-known Jewish ethical works. Influenced by Muslim mysticism and aimed at leading reader toward spiritual perfection and communion with God. It advocated ascetic way of life.

Bailyn, Bernard (1922–), U.S.

historian. Prof. at Harvard Univ. 1961. Specialized in American colonial and revolutionary history. Won Pulitzer Prize.

Baizerman, Saul (1899–1957), U.S. artist; b. Russia. Worked in hammered copper ("Crescendo," "Eroica", etc.). His wife **Eugenie** (1899–1949), neo-impressionist painter.

Bak (Pak), family of Jewish printers in Italy and Prague. **Jacob** (d. 1618), printed Midrash *Tanḥuma* in Verona 1595 and *Tanna de-Vei Eliyahu* in Venice 1598. Fr. 1605 printed numerous Hebrew, Judeo-German books in Prague. His sons **Joseph** (d. 1696) and **Judah** (1630–1688) set up new printing house 1673.

Bak, family of printers and pioneers in Ereẓ Israel. **Israel** (1797–1874), owned press in native Berdichev, settled in Safed 1831, becoming first Jewish farmer in Ereẓ Israel in mod. times. Established first Jewish press in Jerusalem 1841. His son **Nisan** (1815–1889) continued his father's business and was active in ḥasidic community in Jerusalem. Executed several building projects in Jerusalem, incl. Nisan Bak Synagogue, destroyed in 1948 War of Independence.

Printer's mark of Israel Bak, woodcut of Jerusalem

Costume design by Leon Bakst for ballet "Scheherazade," 1921

Baki (Heb. "expert"), person possessing expertise in particular field of ritual law; also a person well-versed in Talmud and rabbinic literature *("Baki be-Shas u-Fosekim").*

Bakkashah (Heb. "Supplication"), petitionary liturgical composition similar to *seliḥot.* Recited before dawn and during regular morning service.

Bakker-Nort, Betsy (1874–1946), Dutch parliamentarian, feminist. One of first women lawyers in Holland. Sat in parliament 1922–40. Survived deportation to Theresienstadt 1944.

Bakst, Leon (1867–1924), Russian artist; designer of theater decors. Associated with Diaghilev's Ballets Russes. Influenced theater design; teacher of Chagall.

Bakst, Nicolai Ignatyevich (1834–1904), Russian physiologist, writer, public figure. An initiator of ORT.

Baku, port on Caspian Sea, USSR. Persian Jews lived there in 18th c., but Muslims of town harassed Jews, who left. Returned in 1870s with development of oil industry in which Jews played major part. Jewish pop. was 29,716 in 1970 census but unofficially was put much higher. It was mostly of European origin.

Balaam, son of Beor, soothsayer fr. Aram invited by Balak, king of Moab to curse Israel (Num. 22, 24) but instead pronounced blessing "How fair are your tents, O Jacob, your dwelling places, O Israel." Slain in a battle bet. Israel and Midianites.

Balaban, Barney (1887–1971), U.S. motion picture executive. President of Paramount Pictures fr. 1936.

Balaban, Meir (1877–1942), historian of Polish Jewry. Directed Taḥkemoni rabbinical seminary and Institute of Jewish Studies in Warsaw; prof. at Warsaw Univ. Considered founder of Polish Jewish historiography, esp. of communal life. Based studies on archival material. D. Warsaw ghetto.

Balak, king of Moab who invited Balaam to curse Israel.

Balázs, Béla (1884–1949), Hungarian author, motion picture critic *(Aesthetics of Death, Dialogue about the Dialogue,* etc.). Between world wars taught at Moscow Film Academy.

Balbo, Michael ben Shabbetai Cohen (1411–c. 1484), rabbi, poet in Candia (Crete). Letters and poems valuable historical source.

Balcon, Sir Michael (1896–), British film producer whose films opened new avenues in realism and humor. Many of them from Ealing

Lord Balfour with Chaim Weizmann, Palestine, 1925.

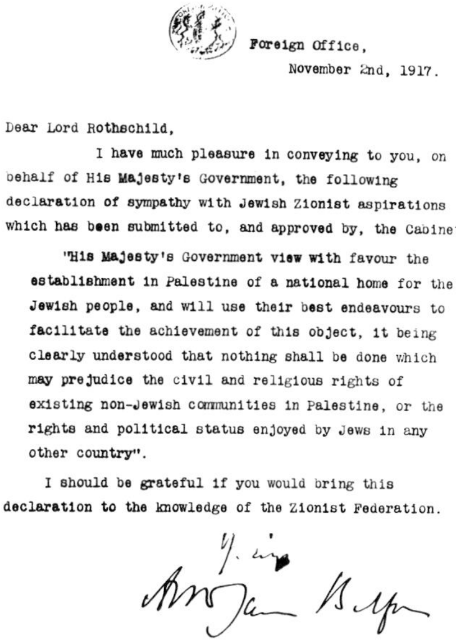

Foreign Office,
November 2nd, 1917.

Dear Lord Rothschild,

I have much pleasure in conveying to you, on behalf of His Majesty's Government, the following declaration of sympathy with Jewish Zionist aspirations which has been submitted to, and approved by, the Cabinet.

"His Majesty's Government view with favour the establishment in Palestine of a national home for the Jewish people, and will use their best endeavours to facilitate the achievement of this object, it being clearly understood that nothing shall be done which may prejudice the civil and religious rights of existing non-Jewish communities in Palestine, or the rights and political status enjoyed by Jews in any other country".

I should be grateful if you would bring this declaration to the knowledge of the Zionist Federation.

The Balfour Declaration, now in the British Museum, London.

Studios, which he headed *(Passport to Pimlico, Kind Hearts and Coronets,* etc).

Bal-Dimyen, see Shtif, Nahum.

°**Balfour, Arthur James, Earl of** (1848–1930), British statesman, philosopher. Began to take interest in Jewish question in 1902–03 when Herzl conducted negotiations with British government which he headed on settlement in Uganda. Later, strongly impressed by Weizmann and as foreign secretary signed Balfour Declaration on Nov. 2, 1917. Opened Hebrew University 1925.

Balfour Declaration, British declaration of sympathy with Zionist aspirations. Official statement took form of letter to Lord Rothschild on Nov. 2, 1917, by British foreign secretary Arthur James Balfour declaring that British government favors "the establishment in Palestine of a national home for the Jewish people, and will use their best endeavors to facilitate the achievement of this object." Statement was result of long negotiations initiated

by Chaim Weizmann, Nahum Sokolow, and others at end of 1914 and supported within government by Herbert Samuel, etc. There was much discussion of the formula of the Declaration and its timing, but in 1917 President Wilson, influenced by the representations of Louis Brandeis, agreed to the proposed declaration. This expedited the final decision of the British government and the document was approved. Later incorporated into terms of British Mandate over Palestine within framework of League of Nations.

Balideh (al-Balideh), Moses (15th c.), Yemenite scholar. Wrote commentary on *Midrash Yelammedenu* bearing strong resemblance to *Midrash ha-Gadol.*

Balint, Michael (1896–), Hungarian psychoanalyst. Researched mechanisms of human sexuality, esp. perversions.

Ballagi (Bloch), Mór (1815–1891), Hungarian linguist, theologian. Translated Pentateuch, prayer book etc. into Hungarian and compiled Hungarian dictionary. Became Protestant.

West German postage stamp commemorating centenary of Albert Ballin's birth.

Ballin, Albert (1857–1918), German shipping magnate, politician. Established International Mercantile Marine Company 1901. Advisor to Kaiser William II; organized food supplies for blockaded Reich in WWI. Committed suicide.

Ballin, Joel (1822–1885), Danish engraver, painter; in Paris and London 1846–83. Executed many reproductions.

Ballin, Samuel Jacob (1802–1866), Danish physician. Specialized in combating Asiatic cholera.

Bally, Davicion (1809–1884), merchant, banker, leader of Bucharest Sephardi community. Fought anti-Semitism. Went to Ereẓ Israel 1882.

Balmes, Abraham ben Meir de (c. 1440–1523), physician, philosopher, translator, grammarian. Studied at Univ. of Naples by special permission of Pope Innocent VIII. Composed famous grammar *Mikneh Avram.*

Balogh, Thomas, Baron (1905–), British economist; b. Budapest. Author of *Dollar Crisis, Economics of Poverty,* etc. Economic advisor to British Labor government under Harold Wilson.

Baltazar, Camil (pseud. of **Leopold Goldstein;** 1902–), Rumanian poet. Innovator in themes and modes of expression.

Balti, see Beltsy.

Baltimore's Lloyd Street Synagogue, oldest synagogue building in Maryland, built 1845.

Baltimore, city in Md., U.S. First synagogue established 1830, first Hebrew school 1842. Jewish Community Center one of largest in the country. Funds collected for Ereẓ Israel as early as 1847, Ḥibbat Zion group organized 1884. Home of only American delegate (R. Shepsel Schaffer) to 1st Zionist Congress and early Zionist leaders Harry Friedenwald and Henrietta Szold. Jewish pop. 100,000 (1971).

Bamberg, Samuel ben Baruch (13th c.), rabbi, *paytan;* b. Metz, lived in Bamberg. Teacher of Meir b. Baruch of Rothenberg.

Bamberger, Bernard Jacob (1904–), U.S. Reform rabbi, scholar (*Story of Judaism, Fallen Angels, Proselytism in the Talmudic Period,* etc.). Pres. of Synagogue Council of America 1950–51 and Central Conference of American Rabbis 1959–61.

Bamberger, Edouard-Adrien (1825–1910), French Republican politician, physician. Deputy in National Assembly 1870–81.

Bamberger, Eugen (1857–1932), German chemist; pioneer in semimicrotechniques. Prof. in Munich, Zurich.

Bamberger, Fritz (1902–), philosophical scholar, author; b. Frankfort, in U.S. fr. 1938. Editor-in-chief *Coronet* magazine 1942–61. Prof. at Chicago College for Jewish Studies, N.Y. Hebrew Union College. Wrote on modern Jewish philosophy esp. Moses Mendelssohn.

Bamberger, Heinrich von (1822–1888), physician; b. Prague. Prof. at Wuerzburg and Vienna (fr. 1872). Famous for brilliant lectures, diagnostic technique, textbook on cardiac disease. Name given to Bamberger's disease, B.'s bulbar pulse, B.'s sign for pericardial effusion.

Bamberger, Louis (1855–1944), U.S. merchant, philanthropist. Built Newark WOR radio station in 1920s. Contributed generously to Jewish causes, institutions. With his sister Mrs. Felix Fuld gave $5 million to establish Princeton Institute for Advanced Study.

Bamberger, Ludwig (1823–1899), German banker, politican, economist. Joined 1848 revolutionary movement, sat in Reichstag 1871–93 as liberal. Advocate of gold standard; influenced economic, financial legislation.

Bamberger, Seligmann Baer (Isaac Dov ha-Levi; 1807–1878), rabbinical scholar in Wuerzburg; leader of German Orthodoxy, fierce opponent of Reform movement. One of last great German-style talmudists; literary work devoted to subjects of practical *halakhah.* Founder of widespread family of rabbis. **Seckel Isaac** (1839–1885), *dayyan* at Frankfort; **Nathan** (1842–1919), succeeded his father at Wuerzburg, published *Likkutei ha-Levi.*

Simon Bamberger

Bamberger, Simon (1846–1926), U.S. mining industrialist, railroad builder, governor of Utah; b. Germany, in U.S. fr. 1860, Salt Lake City fr. 1869. First Democrat and non-Mormon to be governor of Utah (1916–20). A founder and president of Utah's first Jewish congregation.

Bambus, Willy (1863–1904), early member of Ḥibbat Zion in Germany.

Promoted Jewish settlement in Ereẓ Israel and Syria but disagreed with Herzl's political Zionism although participating in 1st Zionist Congress. First general secretary of the Hilfsverein.

Ba-Meh Madlikin (Heb. "With what may one kindle? "), opening words of 2nd chapter of Mishnah tractate *Shabbat* dealing with oils and wicks to be used in kindling Sabbath lights. Recited during Friday evening service.

Ban, see Ḥerem.

Bana'im, Essene-like Jewish sect in Ereẓ Israel in 2nd c.

Band, Max (1900–), Lithuanian-born U.S. painter, known for his portraits of Holocaust survivors, particularly children. In Paris fr. 1925; settled in California 1940.

Drawing by Max Band

Bandes, Louis E., see Miller, Louis E.

Banet, Mordecai ben Abraham (1753–1829), Moravian rabbi; one of leading talmudists of his time. Headed important yeshivah. Fought Reform movement.

Baneth, Eduard Ezekiel (1855–1930), talmudic scholar; b. Slovakia. Rabbi at Krotoszyn, lectured on Talmud in Berlin. Wrote on talmudic and rabbinic literature, development of *halakhah,* Jewish calendar.

Baneth, David Hartwig (1893–1973), Arabist; son of E.E. Baneth. Went to Ereẓ Israel 1924/5. Prof. of Arabic language, literature at Heb. Univ. fr. 1946. Studied Jewish thought as expressed in Arabic.

Banias, ruined city at foot of Mount Hermon at one of sources of River Jordan. Stood over grotto dedicated to Greek god Pan (hence Paneas). Situated on main road fr. Ereẓ Israel to Damascus. Mentioned in New Testament in connection with Jesus' visit to area. Served Syrians fr. 1948 as a base for attacks on Kibbutz Dan. Occupied June 1967 by Israel Defense Forces.

Bank Leumi Le-Israel, Israel's leading commercial bank, incorporated 1951 to take over and continue business of Anglo-Palestine Bank Ltd., which was registered in London 1902 under name of Anglo-Palestine Company as subsidiary of Jewish Colonial Trust Ltd., and opened its first office in Jaffa 1903.

Bank of Israel, Israel's central bank, established 1954 with sole right to issue currency and direct currency system. Bank presided over by government-appointed governor *(nagid)* who also serves as chief economic advisor to government.

Bánóczi, József (1849–1926), Hungarian literary historian, philologist, Jewish educator. Prof. at Budapest Univ. Studied history of Hungarian language, literature. His son **László** (1884–1945), playwright, author, translator.

Banu Nadīr, see Nadir.

Banu Qaynuqā, see Qaynuqā.

Banu Qurayẓa, see Qurayẓa.

Banus, Maria (1914–), Rumanian poet. Outstanding on feminine themes. After WWII, ardent communist.

Bāqā al-Gharbiyya and **Bāqā al-Sharqiyya,** two Muslim-Arab villages, E. of Ḥaderah. The first became part of Israel after 1949 armistice agreement with Jordan. Administrative center and seat of Muslim religious court for C. Israel. Pop. 7,600 (1971). The second occupied during Six-Day War (1967), and in contrast to the first remained largely traditional.

Bar, town in Ukrainian SSR. Jews fr. 1542; received rights of other residents 1556. During Chmielnicki uprising (1648), many Jews massacred; many slaughtered 1651 by Cossacks and Tatars. 5,270 Jews in 1926. Many Jews from Rumania expelled there in WWII and 12,000 Jews murdered in 1942.

Bara, Theda (Theodosia Goodman; 1890–1955), U.S. actress; noted for *femme fatale* roles. Films include *Carmen, Romeo and Juliet, Salome.*

Baraita (pl. **Beraitot;** Aram. "outside"), statement of *tanna* not found in Mishnah. Term covers every *halakhah,* halakhic Midrash, and historical or aggadic tractate not included in Mishnah as compiled by Judah ha-Nasi.

Baraita de-Melekhet ha-Mishkan, ancient collection describing building of Tabernacle. Written in mishnaic Hebrew; compiled after close of Mishnah but before that of Babylonian Talmud.

Baraita de-Niddah, ancient work on ritual purity, known fr. 13th c. Deals with laws of menstruant woman.

Baraita of 32 Rules, *baraita* giving 32 hermeneutic rules for aggadic interpretation of Scripture. Frequently used by Rashi.

Barak, Israelite military commander during period of Judges. Encouraged by prophetess Deborah, he routed Sisera, military commander of king Jabin of Hazor.

Baranga, Aurel (1913–), Rumanian playwright, poet. Twice winner of Rumania's state prize for literature.

Baranowicz, David Eliezer (1859–1915), Vilna Hebraist, grammarian. Wrote and edited works on Hebrew grammar.

Bárány, Robert (1876–1936), Austrian otologist; awarded Nobel Prize 1914. Prof. at Uppsala, Sweden, fr. 1917. Research into physiology and pathology of inner ear.

Barasch, Julius (1815–1863), physician, author, communal leader in Walachia. Settled in Bucharest 1841. Initiated first secular Jewish school there 1851, played important role in spreading Haskalah, and fought to obtain civil rights for Bucharest Jewry.

Barash, Asher (1889–1952), Hebrew writer; b. Galicia, settled in Tel Aviv 1914. Author of fiction, short stories, poetry, criticism. Also wrote *Torat ha-Sifrut,* first attempt in mod. Heb. literature to formulate systematic theory of literature.

Asher Barash

Barash, Ephraim (1892–1943), head of Judenrat in Bialystok. Organized ghetto life in Bialystok under Germans fr. 1941. Killed in Majdanek after liquidation of Bialystok ghetto.

Baratz, Hermann (1835–1922), jurist, historian; b. Volhynia. Contributed to Russian Jewish press fr. 1860. Wrote on history of Jews in

Kiev and influence of Bible on ancient Russian literature.

Baratz, Joseph (1890–1968), Zionist labor leader; b. Ukraine. Among founders of collective settlement movement in Ereẓ Israel, where he settled 1906. Among founders of Deganyah 1910. A leading figure in Ha-Po'el ha-Ẓa'ir, Mapai, Histadrut.

Barazani, Asenath bat Samuel (c. 1590–c. 1670), Kurdish woman poet; head of yeshivah. Taught by her father Samuel Barazani. Expert in Jewish literature and reputed to have studied Kabbalah. Headed Mosul yeshivah. Called *"tanna'it"* (lady *tanna*).

Barbados, island in W. Indies. First Jews Marrano refugees fr. Brazil. Community established in Bridgetown 1656. Prospered in 18th c.; all political disabilities repealed 1802. Community crumbled in 19th c. Jewish pop. c. 30 (1972).

Barbash, Samuel (c. 1850–1921), banker, leader of Ḥovevei Zion, political Zionism in Russia; in Odessa fr. early 1880s. Treasurer of Odessa Committee, center of Ḥovevei Zion movement.

Barby, Meir ben Saul (c. 1729–1789), rabbi of Pressburg, where he established a large yeshivah.

Stone on a house in Barcelona with Hebrew inscription (14th cent.).

Barcelona, port in NE Spain; seat of one of oldest Jewish communities in the country. Jews in special quarter fr. 11th c. Guided by Solomon b. Abraham Adret, community became foremost in Spain in wealth, scholarship. Suffered severely in 14th c. (Black Death 1348; Host desecration 1367). Gradually recovered, led by Ḥasdai Crescas, until 1391 persecutions when c. 400 killed. Resettlement finally prohibited 1401 by Martin I. Renewed prosperity during 15th c. credited in part to Conversos. Inquisition introduced in 1486. Modern settlement in 20th c. 5,000 by 1935. Served as refugee center during WWII. Jewish pop. 3,000 (1970).

Barcelona, Disputation of, religious disputation between Jews and Christians in 1263 before King James of Aragon and his court. The apostate Pablo Christiani and prominent Dominicans and Franciscans presented Christian case, Naḥmanides was sole Jewish representative. His answers were so convincing that the disputation was interrupted. Naḥmanides had to leave Spain.

Bard, Basil Joseph Asher (1914–), English lawyer, chemist. Chief executive of National Research Development Corporation.

Bardaki, Isaiah ben Issachar Ber (1790–1862), rabbi; b. Pinsk, settled in Jerusalem 1810 and became head of its community and *ḥakham bashi* ("chief rabbi"). Austrian vice-consul in Jerusalem.

Barekhi Nafshi (Heb. "Bless [the Lord,] O my soul"), initial words of Ps. 104. Recited among Ashkenazim in private on Sabbath afternoons between Sukkot and Passover and on New Moon after morning service.

Barekhu (Heb.), opening word of call to worship by reader at formal beginning of daily services. Full invocation is *Barekhu et Adonai ha-mevorakh* ("Bless ye the Lord who is [to be] blessed").

Barenboim, Daniel (1942–), pianist, conductor; b. Buenos Aires, settled in Israel 1952. Appeared with leading orchestras of world. Married cellist Jacqueline du Pré.

Bar-Giora, secret society founded in Ereẓ Israel 1907 on initiative of Israel Shoḥat. Aimed at guarding and developing Jewish settlements in new areas. Served as nucleus of Ha-Shomer and in effect merged with that body.

Bar Giora, Simeon, military leader in war against Rome (66–70 C.E.). Formed band of patriot partisans and waged open war against party in control in Jerusalem and John of Giscala. Private war ended when all joined forces to resist Titus' onslaught on Jerusalem. Led as prisoner in Titus' triumphal procession in Rome, then scourged and executed.

°**Bar Hebraeus, Johanan** (later **Gregorius** or **Abu al Faraj**; 1226–1286), the last important writer in Syriac; son of an apostate Jew. His commentary on the Bible reveals influence of traditional Jewish exegesis. Also wrote on Syriac grammar and a history of the world.

Bar-Hillel, Yehoshua (1915–), Israel theoretical linguist; b. Vienna. Taught at Heb. Univ. (prof. 1961). Wrote on philosophy of mathematics, language, and science, inductive logic, etc.

Bari, port in S. Italy. Center of talmudic learning in 10th c. Vicissitudes in later Middle Ages and community came to an end with expulsion of 1540–41. Many Jews fr. Italy and Yugoslavia took refuge there in 1943. Post-war "illegal" immigration to Ereẓ Israel initially centered in surrounding area.

Bar-Ilan (Berlin), Meir (1880–1949), leader of religious Zionism; b. Russia. Appointed secretary of World Mizrachi 1911. In U.S. fr. 1915; Pres. of U.S. Mizrachi. Settled in Jerusalem 1926; pres. of World Mizrachi Center and member of Zionist Executive 1929–31. Editor-in-chief *Ha-Ẓofeh* 1938–42. Son of Naphtali Ẓevi Judah Berlin.

Bar-Ilan University, Orthodox university near Ramat Gan in Israel, founded 1955 by Pinkhos Churgin, its first president. Headed by Joseph Lookstein fr. 1957. c. 5,000 students and 800 lecturers in 1972.

Barit, Jacob (1797–1883), Russian talmudist, communal leader in Vilna. Eloquent defender of Jewish rights.

Bar Kamẓa, see Kamẓa and Bar Kamẓa.

Bar Kappara (3rd c.), Palestinian scholar in transition period bet. *tannaim* and *amoraim.* Disciple of

Meir Bar-Ilan

Bar-Ilan University, 1969.

Coin of the Bar Kokhba revolt.

Haim Bar-Lev

Judah ha-Nasi; author of *halakhot* compilation "the Mishnah of Bar Kappara." Also renowned as poet and author of fables. His academy in Caesarea or Lydda.

Bar Kochba Association, organization of Jewish univ. students, founded in Prague 1893. Became forum of Zionist intellectual activities. Active until WWI.

Bar Kokhba (Heb. "son of a star"; real name **Bar Koseva;** d. 135 C.E.), leader of revolt in Judea against Rome during rule of Hadrian (132–135 C.E.). Referred to as "*nasi* of Israel." R. Akiva regarded him as "king messiah." Sparse information exists on his revolt. Forces captured Jerusalem and established revolutionary regime, minting coins inscribed "for the freedom of Jerusalem." Romans counterattacked in 133, retaking Galilee, Jezreel, Ephraim, and Jerusalem. Killed when last stronghold, Betar, fell by storm. 580,000 Jews reportedly fell in 3-years revolt. Excavations in 1952–61 in Judean Desert caves discovered remains and documents fr. period of revolt, incl. letters written in his name.

Bar-Lev, Haim (1924–), Israel military leader; 8th chief of staff of Israel army; b. Yugoslavia, settled in Ereẓ Israel 1939. C.O. Armored

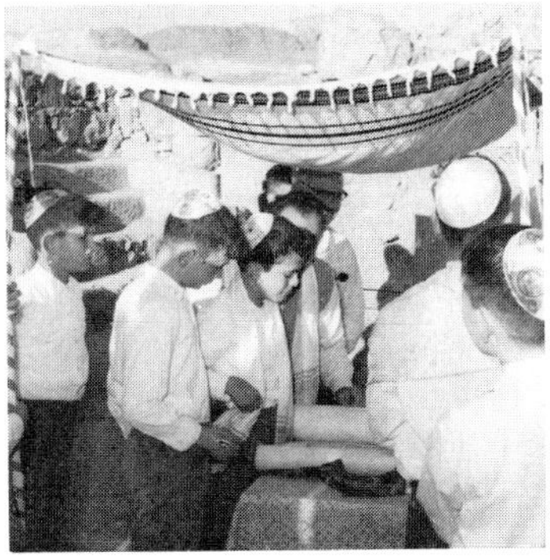

A bar mitzvah at Masada, 1968.

Corps 1957–61, deputy chief of staff in 1967 Six-Day War, chief of staff 1968–71. Became minister of commerce and industry 1972.

Bar Mitzvah, term denoting liability to observe precepts *(mitzvot)* of Judaism, occurring when boy passes 13th birthday; hence also applied to the boy himself. He then ranks as an adult, is included in the *minyan* for public services, and wears the phylacteries at morning services. The bar mitzvah boy reads a portion from the Torah himself and, if able, speaks on a biblical or rabbinic topic at the public or family celebration. The custom of bar mitzvah is of late origin. Reform Jews have a confirmation service held at age 16–17 when the youth declares his attachment to Judaism.

Barna, Gyozo Viktor (1911–1972), table tennis star; b. Hungary, settled in England. Won 22 world titles, incl. 5 singles championships.

Barnato, Barney (1852–1897), S. African financier. Went to Kimberley fr. London 1873. Leading diamond and gold magnate. A key and colorful figure in S. African business and politics.

Ludwig Barnay

Barnay, Ludwig (1842–1924), German actor. Distinguished himself in Schiller and Shakespeare. Founded German union of professional actors.

Barnert, Nathan (1838–1927), U.S. businessman, public figure, philanthropist. Mayor of Paterson, N.J., 1883, 1889.

Barnet, Will (1911–), U.S. painter, graphic artist, teacher. Technical adviser on lithography for Federal Art Project of WPA in 1930s. Deeply influenced by design of American Indian handicraft.

Barnett, John (1802–1890), English composer. Prolific composer for London stage. Reintroduced composed recitative in English opera in place of spoken word in his opera *The Mountain Sylph.*

Barnett, John Francis (1837–1916), English composer; nephew of John Barnett. Prof. at Royal College of Music 1883. Set Coleridge's *Ancient Mariner* and Keats' *Eve of St. Agnes* to music.

Barnett, Lionel David (1871–1960), British orientalist (*Antiquities of India, Hindu Gods and Heroes,* etc.). Keeper of dept. of oriental books and manuscripts at British Museum.

Barnett, Sir Louis Edward (1865–1946), New Zealand surgeon. Prof. of surgery at Otago Univ. Did research on cancer and hydatids.

Barnett, Richard David (1909–), Assyriologist, biblical archaeologist; son of L.D. Barnett. Headed Dept. of W. Asiatic Antiquities in British Museum. Wrote on Assyriology and also on Anglo-Jewish history.

Barnett, Zerah (1843–1935), pioneer of modern Ereẓ Israel settlement; a founder of Petaḥ Tikvah; b. Lithuania, settled in London 1864. Commuted bet. England and Ereẓ Israel 15 times before finally settling in Jaffa in 1890s.

Barnowsky, Viktor (1875–1952), German actor, theater director. Important figure in privately owned theaters in pre-Hitler Germany. Subsequently wrote film scripts and taught theater history at Fordham Univ. and Hunter College.

Baron, Bernhard (1850–1929), industrialist, philanthropist. Pioneer in cigarette manufacturing in U.S. and England.

Baron, Devorah (1887–1956), Hebrew author; b. Belorussia, settled in Ereẓ Israel 1911; married Yosef Aharonowitch. Wrote short stories, often dealing with Jewish life in E. Europe.

Devorah Baron

Salo W. Baron

Arturo Barros Basto

Hanoch Bartov

Bernard Baruch

Baron, Salo Wittmayer (1895–), Jewish historian; b. Galicia, in U.S. fr. 1927. Prof. at Columbia Univ.; first member of American faculty to teach Jewish studies. Pres. of American Academy for Jewish Research, Conference on Jewish Social Studies, etc. Undertook major Jewish history, *A Social and Religious History of the Jews* (14 vols. by 1969). Other works: *The Jewish Community, Modern Nationalism and Religion, History and Jewish Historians,* etc. Also editor of *Jewish Social Studies* quarterly fr. 1939.

Baron de Hirsch Fund, fund established 1889 by Baron Maurice de Hirsch for agricultural and vocational training of E. European Jewish immigrants in U.S.

Barondess, Joseph (1867–1928), U.S. labor, communal leader; b. Ukraine, in U.S. fr. 1888. Worked as cloakmaker; became labor organizer. Active in Socialist Labor Party and also early Zionist movement.

Barou, Noah (1889–1955), economist; authority on cooperative finance; b. Russia, in England fr. 1922. Sec. of Po'alei Zion World Federation 1923–36. A founder of World Jewish Congress. After WWII made first contacts with Germans which led to Reparations Agreement.

Barrett, David (1930–), Canadian politician. Social worker in Vancouver, leader of New Democratic Party in British Columbia, where he was prime minister fr. 1972. First Jewish provincial premier in Canada.

Barrios, Daniel Levi (Miguel) de (1635–1701), Spanish Marrano poet. Up to 1674 (when he was in Brussels), emphasized classical and pagan allusions. Afterward in Amsterdam, where he returned to Judaism, stressed his Jewishness. His works are source of information on history of Amsterdam Sephardi community.

Barron, Jennie Loitman (1891–1969), U.S. jurist. First woman appointed to a Superior Court in Massachusetts.

Barros Basto, Arturo Carlos de (1887–1961), soldier; of New Christian family, formally converted to Judaism after WWI. Strove to revive traditional Judaism among Portuguese Marranos, establishing synagogue at Oporto, etc.

Barsimson, Jacob, earliest Jewish resident of New Amsterdam (later New York), arriving there fr. Holland July 8, 1654, aboard the *Peartree.*

Bart, Lionel (1930–), British playwright, composer. Wrote musicals, incl. *Oliver!*

Barth, Jacob (1851–1914), German Semitic scholar. Prof. at Orthodox Rabbinical Seminary and Berlin Univ. His Semitic studies still standard works. His son, **Aharon** (1890–1957), Zionist, Mizrachi leader; settled in Ereẓ Israel 1933. Director-general of Anglo-Palestine Bank (Bank Leumi) fr. 1947. Wrote on Zionist and religious topics.

Bartholdy, Jacob (1779–1825), Prussian diplomat, art connoisseur. Prussian consul-general in Rome. Uncle of Felix Mendelssohn.

°**Bartolocci, Giulio** (1613–1687), Italian Christian Hebraist, bibliographer. Prepared *Bibliotheca Magna Rabbinica,* a comprehensive bibliography of Jewish books and first systematic, all-inclusive bibliography of Jewish literature.

Bartov, Hanoch (1926–), Israel novelist. Wrote stories, accounts of travels, etc. His novel *Shesh Kenafayim le-Eḥad,* dealing with problems of new immigrants, adapted for stage. Cultural attaché, Israel Embassy, London, 1966–68.

Baruch, scribe and companion of prophet Jeremiah. Taken to Egypt with Jeremiah after assassination of Gedaliah. Of considerable importance in apocryphal literature.

Baruch, Apocalypse of, apocalyptic work ascribed to Jeremiah's scribe Baruch. Preserved in Greek, partly in Syriac.

Baruch, Bernard (1870–1965), U.S. financier, public official. Instrumental in organizing American economy during WWI; chairman of War Industries Board 1918–9, economic adviser to American Peace Commission. Helped plan New Deal legislation as confidential adviser to President Roosevelt and mobilization of U.S. resources in WWII. Author of first U.S. plan on control of atomic energy (1946).

Baruch, Book of, apocryphal book. Associated in Septuagint with writings attributed to prophet Jeremiah. Regarded as canonical in both Eastern and Latin churches.

Baruch, Greek Apocalypse of, apocalypse describing journey of Baruch through heavens. Written in Koine-Greek. Present form (which is not original) is by Christian author.

Baruch, Jacob ben Moses Ḥayyim (18th c.), author, editor; b. Leghorn. Known for anthology *Shivḥei Yerushalayim* ("The Praises of Jerusalem").

Baruch, Joseph Marcou (1872–1899), early Zionist propagandist in Bulgaria and Mediterranean countries. Opposed small-scale settlement in Ereẓ Israel, proposing foundation of internationally recognized Jewish state. Some of his ideas influenced Herzl.

Baruch, Rest of the Words of, apocryphal book, also called *Paralipomena Jeremiae* (Chronicles of Jeremiah). Relates redemption fr. Babylon. Probably composed after destruction of Second Temple; in its present form, a Christian reworking of a Jewish source.

Baruch, Simon (1840–1921), U.S. physician; father of Bernard Baruch. Surgeon in Confederate Army; prof. at Columbia Univ., pioneered in surgery of appendix, treatment of malaria. His son **Herman** (1872–1953) practiced medicine until 1903; member of New York Stock Exchange, U.S. ambassador to Portugal 1945–47, Netherlands 1947–49.

Baruch ben David Yavan (18th c.), Court Jew to Polish king Augustus III, *shtadlan* for the Council of Four Lands.

Baruch ben Isaac of Aleppo (c. 1050–c. 1125), yeshivah head in Aleppo; b. Spain. Wrote commentaries on several tractates of Babylonian Talmud.

Baruch ben Isaac of Worms (12th–13th c.), tosafist in Worms; probably came fr. France. Traveled to Ereẓ Israel c. 1237. Wrote *Sefer ha-Terumah,* summary of established *halakhot,* incl. laws on Ereẓ Israel.

Baruch ben Jehiel of Medzibezh (1757–1810), ḥasidic *ẓaddik,* author; grandson of Baal Shem Tov. Regarded himself the leader of Ḥasidism by hereditary right. His luxurious mode of life aroused opposition of other ḥasidic leaders. His "court jester" was Hershele Ostropoler.

Baruch ben Samuel (d. 1834), adventurer, physician; b. Pinsk, settled in Safed 1819. Went to Yemen 1831 in search of Ten Tribes. Became court physician of imam al-Mahdi, who put him to death.

Baruch ben Samuel of Aleppo (Baruch of Greece; c. 1075–c. 1135), talmudic commentator. Emigrated to Ereẓ Israel, then to Aleppo.

Baruch ben Samuel of Mainz (c. 1150–1221), scholar, *paytan,* Served in *bet din* of Mainz. Best known for *Sefer ha-Ḥokhmah* (now lost) on *Nashim, Nezikin,* and laws of *Issur ve-Hetter.*

Baruch (ben Abraham) of Kosov (c. 1727–1795), kabbalist; *maggid* in Kosov. Saw in Isaac Luria and Ḥayyim Vital the highest authorities on Kabbalah. Fiercely opposed followers of Shabbetai Ẓevi and Jacob Frank.

Baruch Sheli'aḥ-Ẓibbur Togarmi, kabbalist, cantor, assumedly lived in Spain in 13th–14th c. Wrote commentary on *Sefer Yeẓirah* which probably influenced Abraham Abulafia.

Baruh, Bora (1901–1941), Yugoslav painter. Painted landscapes, portraits, Spanish Civil War scenes, mainly oils. Captured, executed while with partisans in Serbia in WWII.

Baruk, Henri (1897–), French psychiatrist. Prof. at Sorbonne 1946. Studied connections between psychiatric disorders and defective moral awareness in human beings. Active in Jewish affairs.

Barukh (Heb.), initial word of *berakhah* pattern of prayer. Conventional transl. "blessed." Original meaning possibly "bend (or fall) upon the knees" (*berekh* ="knee") in prayerful obeisance.

Barukh She-Amar (Heb. "Blessed be He who spoke"), benediction opening morning psalms of *Shaḥarit (Pesukei de-Zimra).*

Barukh Shem Kevod Malkhuto Le-Olam Va-Ed (Heb. "Blessed be His Name, whose glorious kingdom is for ever and ever"), doxology of ancient origin; customary response in Temple. In liturgy pronounced after first verse of *Shema.* In Ashkenazi rite also pronounced 3 times at close of *Ne'ilah* service.

Barukh She-Petarani (Heb. "Blessed be He who has relieved me," i.e., from responsibility for son's conduct), benediction pronounced by father at his son's bar mitzvah. In Reform congregations replaced by *She-Heḥeyanu* blessing.

Bar-Yehudah, Israel (1896–1965), Israel labor leader; b. Ukraine, settled in Ereẓ Israel 1926. Joined Kibbutz Yagur 1930. Sided with Aḥdut ha-Avodah in 1944 Mapai split; became member of its Knesset faction. Minister of transport 1962–65.

Bar-Yosef, Yehoshua (1911–), Israel novelist, playwright. Graphically realistic in early work, later showing tendency to symbolism. Wrote about life in Safed. His son **Yosef** (1933–), author of short stories and a play *(Tura).*

Barzilai, Israel (1913–1970), Israel socialist; b. Poland, settled in Ereẓ Israel 1934. A leader of Ha-Shomer ha-Ẓa'ir and later of Mapam. Israel minister to Poland 1948–51, minister of health 1955–61, deputy speaker of Knesset 1963–65.

Barzilai, Salvatore (1860–1939), Italian politician. Ardent Italian nationalist, interventionist in WWI, senator 1920. Authority on criminal law.

Barzilai (Eisenstadt), Yehoshua (1855–1918), Ḥibbat Zion leader, writer; b. Belorussia. A founder of Benei Moshe, secretary of Ḥovevei Zion in Jaffa fr. 1890. Worked in Anglo-Palestine Bank in Jerusalem fr. 1904.

Barzillai the Gileadite, wealthy man who with Machir and Shobi welcomed David and his men when they fled to Mahanaim because of Absalom's rebellion.

Basch, Victor Guillaume (1863–1944), French philosopher. Prof. of aesthetics at Sorbonne fr. 1918. Championed Alfred Dreyfus, founded League for Rights of Man, member of central committee of French underground in WWII. Executed with wife by Vichy government.

Baschko, Ẓevi Hirsch ben Benjamin (1740–1807), rabbi, halakhist; b. Zamosc, Poland. Last rabbi (fr. 1802) of joint communities of Altona, Hamburg, Wandsbek. Wrote responsa on *Shulḥan Arukh,* etc.

Basevi, Italian family of German origin. **Gioacchino** (1780–1867), one of first Jewish lawyers in Italy. **Abramo** (1818–1885), physician, musician. **Nathan** (1738–1808); of Verona, settled in London 1762, early pres. of Board of Deputies of British Jews. His daughter Maria the mother of Benjamin Disraeli.

Bashan, region N. of Yarmuk River, E. of the Jordan.

Isaac Bashevis Singer (right) in Jerusalem, 1969.

Bashevis Singer, Isaac (1904–), Yiddish novelist, writer; brother of I.J. Singer; b. Poland, in U.S. fr. 1935. Many of his works translated into English and achieved wide popularity, incl. *The Family Moskat, Gimpel the Fool, the Magician of Lublin, The Manor.* Reconstructed something of lost world of pre-WWII Poland with mystical and erotic elements.

Bashyazi, Elijah ben Moses (c. 1420–1490), Karaite ideologist and authority. Began compilation of Karaite code *Adderet Eliyahu;* completed by his pupil and son-in-law Caleb Afendopolo. Wrote polemical works to refute Karaite opponents.

Basilea, Solomon Aviad Sar-Shalom (c. 1680–1749), rabbi, kabbalist in Mantua. His *Emunat Ḥakhamim* emphasized mystic significance of Torah in Jewish tradition.

Baṣīr, Joseph ben Abraham Ha-Kohen Ha-Ro'eh al- (11th c.), blind Karaite author, philosopher; lived in Iraq or Persia. One of most important Karaite philosophers. Encouraged reform of Karaite law of consanguinity.

Basle, city in Switzerland. Jewish community fr. early 13th c. until Black Death persecution 1349. After 16th c. Jewish settlement intermittent. Community reestablished 1866. Zionist congresses held there. Jewish pop. 2,300 (1972).

Theodor Herzl leaving Basle synagogue, 1903.

BASLE PROGRAM

Zionism strives to create for the Jewish people a home in Palestine secured by public law. For the attainment of this aim the Congress envisages the following means:

1. The promotion, on suitable lines, of the settlement of Palestine by Jewish agriculturists, artisans, and tradesmen.

2. The organization and unification of the whole of Jewry by means of appropriate local and general institutions in accordance with the laws of each country.

3. The strengthening of Jewish national sentiment and national consciousness.

4. Preparatory steps toward securing the consent of governments, which is necessary to attain the aim of Zionism.

The Basle Program (translated from the German original)

Title page of first volume of "La république des hébreux" by Jacques Christian Basnage, 1713.

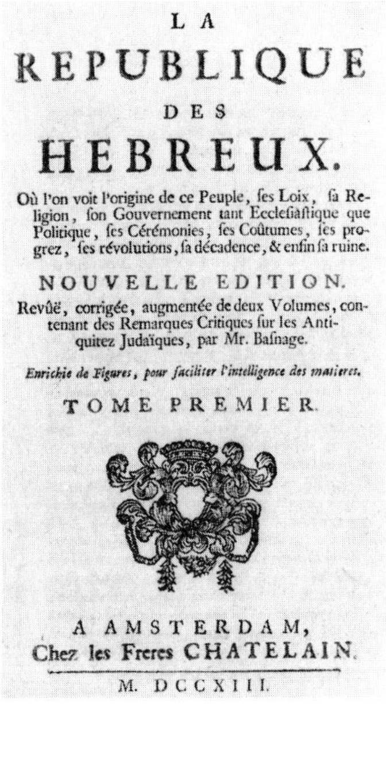

LA
REPUBLIQUE
DES
HEBREUX.
Où l'on voit l'origine de ce Peuple, ſes Loix, ſa Religion, ſon Gouvernement tant Eccleſiaſtique que Politique, ſes Cérémonies, ſes Coûtumes, ſes progrez, ſes révolutions, ſa décadence, & enfin ſa ruine.
NOUVELLE EDITION.
Revûë, corrigée, augmentée de deux Volumes, contenant des Remarques Critiques ſur les Antiquitez Judaïques, par Mr. Baſnage.
Enrichie de Figures, pour faciliter l'intelligence des matieres.
TOME PREMIER.
A AMSTERDAM,
Chez les Freres CHATELAIN.
M. DCCXIII.

Basle Program, original official program of Zionist Organization, adopted at 1st Zionist Congress in Basle 1897. Defines objective of Zionist movement as establishing home for Jewish people in Ereẓ Israel.

°**Basnage, Jacques Christian** (1653–1725), Protestant divine, historian; b. France, lived in Holland fr. 1686. His *L'Histoire et la religion des Juifs depuis Jésus Christ jusqu'à present* first comprehensive history of Jews in Christian era.

Basola, Moses ben Mordecai (1480–1560), Italian rabbi, traveler. Made pilgrimage to Ereẓ Israel 1521 and wrote lucid, detailed account of conditions there. As rabbi of Ancona opposed boycott of town organized by Gracia Nasi.

Basra, port in S. Iraq. Jews first settled under Umayyads. Close ties with academy of Sura and subsequently with Baghdad community. 10,000 Jews in 12th c. Community suffered during Tamerlane's conquest (14th c.), but regained importance in 18th c. Most Jews departed in 1949–50. Jewish pop. less than 500 (1970).

Bass (or **Bassista), Shabbetai ben Joseph** (1641–1718), first Jewish bibliographer. His *Siftei Yeshenim* listed in Hebrew 2,200 Hebraica and Judaica items, fruit of his researches in Poland, Germany, and Holland. Set up Hebrew printing press at Auras 1688, subsequently transferring it to Dyhernfurth.

Bassani, Giorgio (1916–), Italian author. Best known for his psychological novels, many set in Ferrara. Novels of Jewish interest include *The Garden of the Finzi Contini.* Edited literary review *Botteghe Oscure* 1948–61.

Bassevi of Truenberg (Treuenburg), Jacob (1570–1634), court Jew, head of Prague Jewry. First European Jew outside Italy to be ennobled. During the 30 Years' War formed consortium which leased imperial mint. Ultimately hounded by authorities, all his privileges declared illegal and abrogated after his death.

Bas-Tovim, Sarah (c. 17th c.), Ukrainian author of *tkhines* ("Yiddish prayers for women"). Her prayer pamphlet *Shloyshe Sheorim,* dealing with 3 main *mitzvot* prescribed for women (*ḥallah, mikveh,* kindling festival candles), became popular.

Bat Dor Dance Company, see Batsheva.

Bath-Sheba, wife of Uriah the Hittite, then of David; mother of Solomon. David had Uriah killed in order to take her as his wife. For this he was rebuked by Nathan and divinely punished. She and Nathan persuaded David to proclaim Solomon as his successor.

Bathyra, place in toparchy of Batanea (Bashan), founded by Jewish military settlers fr. Babylon. They received the patronage of Herod and defended not only the local pop. from brigandage but also Jewish pilgrims fr. Babylonia en route to Jerusalem.

Bathyra, Sons of, members of famous Jewish family, 1st c. B.C.E.–2nd c. C.E. Held patriarchate before resigning it to Hillel.

Bat Kol (Heb.), a heavenly divine voice which revealed God's judgment to man. According to rabbinic tradition, it was heard at several instances in the biblical period, and with the cessation of prophesy remained the sole means of communication between God and man. Thus a *bat kol* determined the ruling in the Bet Shammai and Bet Hillel controversies.

Batlanim (Heb.), originally an honorable title conferred on those who abstained from work to free themselves for community service. Communities possessed the institution of *asarah batlanim* – men who were either scholars supported by the community or who were engaged in communal affairs. In later Yiddish usage the term became pejorative, meaning a loafer.

Bat-Miriam, Yokheved (1901–), Hebrew poet; b. Belorussia, settled in Ereẓ Israel 1928. Influenced by Russian symbolist poetry, against background of Jewish tragedy. Israel Prize 1972.

Yokheved Bat-Miriam, bronze by Batya Lishansky.

Bat Mitzvah, age at which girl attains religious maturity, viz. 12 years and a day. In modern times, occasion for celebration. Forms of ceremony vary from calling girls to reading of Law (in non-Orthodox congregations) to holding collective ceremonies or calling male relatives to reading of the Law.

Batsheva and Bat-Dor Dance Companies, two ensembles founded in Tel Aviv by Baroness Bathsheva (Bethsabée) de Rothschild. Batsheva founded 1964, Bat-Dor 1968.

Battat, Reuben (1882–1962), Iraqi jurist. Served as judge, member of Iraqi parliament, and supported Zionist Organization in Baghdad (imprisoned 1949).

Bat Yam, town in C. Israel, S. of Tel Aviv, founded 1926. Received city status 1958; part of Tel Aviv conurbation. Pop. 90,700 (1971).

Batzir, Joseph Al-, see Baṣir, Joseph Al-.

Bauer, Hans (1878–1937), German Semitic scholar. Succeeded in deciphering most of Ugaritic alphabet.

Bauer, Otto (1881–1938), Austrian socialist leader. Prominent in Socialist International as spokesman for Marxist left wing of Social Democrats. Foreign Minister of Austria 1918–19. Helped organize workers' uprising in Vienna 1934. After its suppression fled and died in France.

Baum, Oscar (1883–1941), German-language Czech author. Blind musician and writer; belonged to Prague circle of Max Brod and Franz Kafka. His demand for equality of opportunity rather than compassion influenced modern education of the handicapped.

Baum, Vicki (1888–1960), novelist; b. Austria, in U.S. fr. 1931. Best known of her 25 novels *Grand Hotel* which became international best seller and popular movie.

Baumgardt, David (1890–1963), philosopher. Prof. in Berlin 1932–35; consultant on philosophy to Library of Congress in Washington 1941–54. Wrote penetrating critique of Kant, whose ethical system he judged negatively.

Baumgarten, Emanuel Mendel (1828–1908), economist, communal leader, German and Hebrew author in Vienna. Assisted Russian and Rumanian pogrom victims seeking refuge in Austria. Translated Baḥya's *Ḥovot ha-Levavot* into German.

Bava Batra (Aram. "last gate"), tractate of Mishnah, with *gemara* in Jerusalem and Babylonian Talmuds; last of three sections of original large tractate *Nezikin.* Deals largely with laws relating to ownership of real estate and moveables, and their acquisition by purchase or inheritance.

Bava Kamma (Aram. "first gate"), tractate of Mishnah, with *gemara* in Jerusalem and Babylonian Talmuds; first of three sections of original large tractate *Nezikin.* Discusses damages caused by property or agents, or by a man himself.

Bava Mezia (Aram. "middle gate"), tractate of Mishnah, with *gemara* in Jerusalem and Babylonian Talmuds; second of three sections of original large tractate *Nezikin.* Deals with laws of chattels, lost and found property, the four types of caretakers, embezzlement, fraud, interest, rights of hired labor and partnership.

Bavaria, S. German state. Jewish settlement fr. 10th c. with important connections in Nuremberg, Augsburg, and Regensburg. Excluded from Upper Bavaria in 13th c.; massacred in 14th c. All Jews expelled between 1551 and 18th c. Court Jews then returned, but adverse conditions in 19th c. led to large Jewish emigration to U.S. 41,939 Jews in 1933. Among first victims of Nazis. Jewish pop. 4,700 (1969).

Bavli, Hillel (1893–1961), Hebrew poet, educator; b. Lithuania, in U.S. fr. 1912. Prof. of modern Hebrew literature at Jewish Theological Seminary in N.Y. Wrote poems, critical essays, and translated English literature into Hebrew.

Bayefsky, Aba (1923–), Canadian painter. Specialist in human figure. Post-WWII canvasses depicted plight of German concentration camp victims.

Baylis, Lilian Mary (1874–1937), English theatrical manager; founder of London "Old Vic" theater. Took over derelict Sadler's Wells theater in 1931 and made it famous for opera and ballet.

Bayonne, town in SW France. Marranos settled in 16th–18th c. Recognized as French citizens 1790. Jews helped introduce chocolate industry into France. Declined after mid-18th c. Stopover for Jewish refugees in WWII. Jewish pop. 700 (1969), many fr. N. Africa.

Bayonne, see Hudson County.

Bayreuth, city in Germany and former principality. Jews fr. 13th c.; suffered several expulsions in 16th c. and 17th c. Over 2,000 Jews in 1805 but later number declined; 261 Jews in 1933. Postwar community numbered 550 in 1949, 40 in 1967.

Bazelon, David L. (1909–), U.S. judge. Assistant attorney general of U.S. 1946; chief judge of U.S. Court of Appeals for District of Columbia 1962. Authority on relationship between law and psychiatry.

Aerial view of Bat Yam.

Otto Bauer

Ark of the Law from synagogue in Westheim, Bavaria, c. 1725.

Cardinal Bea with Abraham J. Heschel, 1963.

°**Bea, Augustin** (1881–1968), Jesuit; b. Germany. Rector of Pontifical Biblical Institute in Rome. Charged by Pope John XXIII with preparing statement on relations of Catholic Church to other religions for Vatican council. Fought with some success attempts to weaken his original strong draft on Catholic attitude to Jews. Wrote *The Church and the Jewish People.*

Beaconsfield, Earl of, see Disraeli, Benjamin.

Beadle, see Shammash.

Bearsted, Marcus Samuel, First Viscount (1853–1927), founder of Shell Oil Co. Lord mayor of London 1902–3, created baron 1921, viscount 1925. Wide benefactions to Jewish and non-Jewish charities. His son **Walter Horace Samuel, Second Viscount** (1882–1948), succeeded his father as chairman of Shell 1920. Notable art collector; chairman of trustees of National Gallery in London.

Beame, Abraham David (1906–), U.S. politician; the first Jew to be elected mayor of New York. In 1952, budget director of New York and in 1961 comptroller. Elected mayor on Democratic ticket in 1973.

Beck, Karl Isidor (1817–1879), poet; b. Hungary. Wrote rhetorical German verse about Hungarian struggle for liberation against Austrian Empire. The refrain from one of his poems inspired Johann Strauss' "Blue Danube" waltz. Baptized 1843.

Beck, Moritz (Meir; 1845–1923), rabbi, leader of Rumanian Jewry. Rabbi of progressive elements in Bucharest community, promoted expansion of Jewish education in Rumania. Prominent in fight against anti-Semitism.

Beck, Willy (1844–1886), Hungarian painter, cartoonist. Published *Zeitgeist,* humorous periodical in German, and *Charivari* (in Vienna), political and satirical journal, until police suspended publication.

Beckelman, Moses W. (1906–1955), U.S. social worker. Worked for American Jewish Joint Distribution Committee (director-general in Europe 1951). Established Malben in Israel and extensive social work programs for Moroccan Jews.

Becker, family of U.S. bankers, philanthropists. **Abraham G.** (1857–1925), founded commercial paper house. Active in Chicago Jewish community. His son **James Herman** (1894–1970), banker; president of Chicago Jewish Welfare Fund for nearly 30 years.

Becker, Aharon (1906–), Israel labor leader; b. Belorussia, settled in Ereẓ Israel 1925. Secretary-general Histadrut 1961–69 and Mapai member of Knesset.

Becker, Julius (1882–1945), Zionist journalist; b. Germany. Edited *Die Welt* and other Zionist organs; worked for Zionist movement in Constantinople and at League of Nations fr. 1941 in U.S.

Becker, Lavy Mordecai (1905–), Canadian communal leader, rabbi, social worker. Worked for Joint Distribution Committee in Germany. Active in Canadian Jewish Congress, etc. Spiritual leader of Montreal Reconstructionist Synagogue.

Beda (Fritz Loehner; 1883–1942), Viennese journalist, satirist, operetta librettist. Best-known libretti (with co-authors) *Land of Smiles* and *Ball im Savoy.* Deported to Buchenwald 1938. Wrote camp song, "Buchenwaldlied." Died in Auschwitz.

Bedacht, Max (1885–), U.S. communist leader; b. Munich, in U.S. fr. 1908. Executive member of Communist Party until 1919. General Secretary of International Workers Order 1933, building its Jewish fraternal section into its largest auxiliary. Expelled from Party for factionalism 1946.

Bedersi, Abraham ben Isaac (c. 1230–c. 1300), Hebrew poet in S. France. Spent most of his life in Perpignan. Wrote poems and satires and composed first dictionary of Hebrew synonyms in the Bible.

Bedersi, Jedaiah ha-Penini, see Jedaiah b. Abraham Bedersi.

Bedikat Ḥameẓ (Heb. "search for leaven"), ceremony instituted to ensure that not even the smallest particle of leaven remains in the house during Passover. It takes place after nightfall on Nisan 13. The leaven collected is burned on the following morning in the ceremony of *bi'ur ḥameẓ.*

Bedzin (Bendin), town in Silesia, Poland. Jews fr. 17th c. Many Jewish industrial workers in community of over 10,000 at beginning of 20th c. Center of Jewish and Polish socialist activity during 1905 revolution. 21,625 Jews in 1931. Community liquidated by 1943.

"Bedikat ḥameẓ" in a Dutch household, drawing by Bernard Picart, 1725.

Aaron Beer

Beer, Aaron (1739–1821), German cantor, composer; known as *"der Bamberger ḥazzan."* Chief cantor of Heidereutergasse Synagogue in Berlin 1765–1821. Known for extensive repertory of liturgical melodies, incl. many of his own composition.

Beer, Bernhard (1801–1861), German scholar, community leader, bibliophile. Head of Dresden com-

munity. Fought for civic equality of Jews in Saxony. Wrote books on various aspects of Judaism.

Beer, George Louis (1872–1920), U.S. historian, publicist. Wrote on economic features of 17th–18th c. British colonial policy. At Paris Peace Conference, urged establishment of "mandates."

Beer, Israel (1912–1966), military commentator and Soviet agent in Israel; b. Vienna, settled in Ereẓ Israel 1938. Joined Haganah, served on general staff, became noted military commentator, and held chair of military history at Tel Aviv Univ. Arrested 1961, found guilty of treason, sentenced to 15 years' imprisonment. Died in prison.

Beer, Max (1864–1949), German socialist, historian, journalist. His *History of British Socialism* became standard work.

Beer, Michael (1800–1833), German poet, playwright; brother of Giacomo Meyerbeer and Wilhelm Beer. His poetic drama *Der Paria,* a plea for Jewish emancipation, was highly successful. *Struensee* is regarded his best play.

Beer, Peter (**Perez**; pen name: **Theophil Nikodem**; 1758 or 1764–1838), Austrian educator, author; representative of radical Haskalah in Hapsburg Empire. Probably first Jew to hold government appointment (1813). However, most Jews opposed his educational activities. Wrote several works on Jewish history and ethics.

Beer, Rachel (**Richa**; 1858–1927), owner, editor of London *Sunday Times* (1893–1904); daughter of Sasson David Sassoon. Married owner of *Observer,* became editor, and later bought and edited rival *Sunday Times.* Also a composer.

Beer, Wilhelm (1797–1850), German astronomer; brother of Giacomo Meyerbeer and Michael Beer. Published studies of Mars and drew map of moon's surface. Mountain on moon named for him.

Beer-Bing, Isaiah (1759–1805), leader in struggle for "regeneration" of Jews of France. Appointed to commission headed by Malesherbes to improve status of Jews 1788. Translated various Jewish works into French.

Beer-Hofmann, Richard (1866–1945), Austrian poet, playwright. Joined "Young Vienna" literary group and attracted attention with *Novellen* (1893) *Schlaflied fuer Miriam* (1898), and his biblical trilogy about Jacob and David (1918–36).

View of Beersheba

Beersheba, city in S. Israel. Excavations show settlement fr. Chalcolithic times. Patriarchs lived in its vicinity. After Israelite conquest, incorporated into territory of tribe of Judah (Josh. 15:28; 19:2). Regarded as extreme southern point of the country ("Dan to Beersheba"). Settled by Jews after the return fr. Babylon. Modern settlement dates fr. 1900. Early in 1949 Jews, mostly new immigrants, settled there. Became capital of Israel S. district and expanded rapidly with pop. over 80,000 in 1972. Includes communications center and industries, university, Institute for Arid Zone Research, market center for Negev bedouin.

Be'er Ya'akov, town in coastal plain of Israel, W. of Ramleh; founded 1907 by Jews fr. Russia. Pop. 4,120 (1971).

Beghi, Joseph ben Moses (15th–16th c.), Karaite scholar in Constantinople. His legal and philosophical works include valuable material on earlier Karaite history.

Bégin, Emile-Auguste (1802–1888), French physician, historian, librarian. Wrote laudatory biography of Napoleon I. As reward Napoleon III appointed him librarian at Louvre. Fr. 1874 librarian at Bibliothèque Nationale.

Begin, Menahem (1913–), Israel statesman, underground fighter; b. Poland. Head of Betar in Poland. In Ereẓ Israel fr. 1942. Commander of Irgun Ẓeva'i Le'ummi and conducted "armed warfare" against Mandatory government. Founded the Ḥerut party 1948 and became its leader and member of Knesset fr. its inception. Instrumental in establishing Gaḥal Knesset faction 1965. In government of national unity 1967–70 as minister without portfolio. Wrote *The Revolt* and *White Nights.*

Menahem Begin

Behar, Nissim (1848–1931), educator; b. Jerusalem. Founded Alliance school and was its headmaster; introduced direct method of teaching Hebrew *(Ivrit be-Ivrit).* Fr. 1901 in U.S. Founded and directed National Liberal Immigration League.

Behemoth, creature described in Job 40:15–24, identified with hippopotamus or some other mammoth living in marshes. In later Jewish literature, however, it appears as purely mythical creature, the male counterpart of Leviathan.

Fight of mythical Behemoth and Leviathan at end of the world, "Leipzig Maḥzor," c. 1320.

Behr (Baer), Issachar Falkensohn (1746–1817), Polish poet. Under patronage of Daniel Itzig, published *Gedichte von einem pohlnischen Juden* (1771), which attracted attention of Goethe.

Behrend, Jacob Friedrich (1833–1907), German jurist. Taught at Univ. of Berlin and Greifswald. Member of Supreme Court 1887. Expert on German and Roman law; wrote first comprehensive textbook on commercial law.

Behrends (Behrens), Leffmann (1634–1714), Hanover Court Jew who served as elector and money-lender, diplomatic mediator, and coin minister. Ardent talmudist and head of community of Hannover-Neustadt.

Behrman, Martin (1864–1926), U.S. public official. Four times mayor of New Orleans (1904–1920) and director of American Bank and Trust Co. Active in Democratic Party.

Behrman, Samuel Nathaniel (1893–1973), U.S. playwright. *The*

Second Man was first of long series of successful plays. Also wrote biographies *(Duveen)* and autobiography *(Worcester Account)*.

Bei Avidan, meeting place in talmudic times where scholars of various nations and faiths met for religious discussions and disputations. Institution enjoyed protection of authorities and was visited by Jewish sages.

Beilin, Asher (1881–1948), Hebrew, Yiddish writer; b. Russia. Worked intermittently as Shalom Aleichem's secretary. Moved to London 1906, collaborating with J.Ḥ. Brenner; settled in Ereẓ Israel 1933.

Beilinson (Belinson), Moses Eliezer (1835–1908), Hebrew, Yiddish writer, publisher; b. Russia. Established Hebrew printing press in 1860s and published many important books and newspapers in Hebrew and Yiddish.

Beilinson, Moshe (1889–1936), Hebrew writer, journalist, physician; a chief spokesman of labor movement in Ereẓ Israel; b. Russia, settled in Ereẓ Israel 1924. Joined editorial board of *Davar* and wrote most of its editorials.

Beilis, Menahem Mendel (1874–1934), victim of blood libel charge in Kiev in 1911. Owing to incitement by anti-Semitic "Black Hundred" gangs, accused of murder of 12-year-old boy and imprisoned for 2 years until brought to trial in 1913. Case attracted universal attention and protest. Acquitted by jury of simple Russian peasants. Left for Ereẓ Israel and settled in U.S. 1920.

The Beilis family, 1914

Beim, Solomon ben Abraham (1817–1867), Russian Karaite scholar. Attempted to raise educational level of Karaites. One of first Karaites to teach secular studies. Met strong opposition when attempting to ease severe Karaite laws.

Beimel, Jacob (c. 1875–1944), *ḥazzan;* b. Belorussia, in U.S. fr. 1915. Works and adaptations of synagogal music, folksongs, and ḥasidic melodies published in *Jewish Music Journal,* which he edited.

Bein, Alexander (1903–), archivist, historian of Zionism; b. Germany settled in Ereẓ Israel 1933. Director of General Zionist Archives and state archivist of Israel 1956–71. Writings include biography of Herzl and history of agricultural settlement in Ereẓ Israel.

Beirav, see Berab.

Bei-Rav (Aram.), term in talmudic literature designating academy of higher learning. Also applies to all sorts of halakhic Midrashim taught at Babylonian academies or to all those traditions *(Sifra, Sifrei)* upon which they are based.

Pupils of the Alliance Israélite Universelle girls' school, Beirut, early 1950s.

Beirut, capital of Lebanon. Jewish settlement fr. 2nd c. B.C.E. Community remained small despite some Spanish immigration fr. 15th c. to end of 19th c. Swelled by Syrian refugees after 1948, but declined after 1967. However, Jewish life continued almost normally. c. 2,000 Jews remained in 1972.

Beisan, see Bet(h) Shean.

Beit, Sir Alfred (1853–1906), S. African financier, cofounder of Rhodesia; b. Hamburg, emigrated to S. Africa and helped develop Kimberleydiamond fields and Witwatersrand gold reefs. Closely associated with Cecil Rhodes. Made numerous bequests to education, medical research, war relief.

Sir Alfred Beit

Beit . . . , see also Bet(h).

Beit Jann, Druze village in Upper Galilee, Israel. Alt. 3,082 ft. (940 m.) above sea level; one of Israel's highest inhabited places. A major Druze center in Israel. Pop. 4,590 (1971).

Beit Midrash, place of study, discussion, and prayer that lacked formality of *ḥeder* and yeshivah. Among ḥasidim it developed into the *shtibl.*

Bejerano, family of Israel industrialists; of Bulgarian origin. **Moshe** (1902–1951), and **Shimon** (1910–1971), settled in Ereẓ Israel in 1930s. Directed Assis factory (syrup and canning). Leaders of Israel Manufacturers' Association.

Bejerano, Bekhor Ḥayyim ben Moses (1850–1931), Bulgarian rabbi, scholar. *Dayyan* in Bucharest; chief rabbi of Adrianople 1908, Constantinople 1922.

Bekache, Shalom (1848–1927), printer, publisher in Leghorn and Algiers. Publications include miscellany on Ereẓ Israel and some 20 books in Judeo-Arabic on Jewish history which helped widen historical knowledge of Algerian Jewry.

Bekhor, see Firstborn.

Bekhorot (Heb. "firstborn"), 4th tractate in Mishnah in order *Kodashim,* with *gemara* in Babylonian Talmud. Deals with law relating to firstborn of both men and animals.

Bekhor Shor, Joseph ben Isaac (12th c.), N. French exegete, tosafist, poet. His commentary on Pentateuch is in spirit of literal rational interpretation.

Bekker (Baruch), Paul (1882–1937), German music critic, writer. As chief music critic for *Frankfurter Zeitung* (1911–25), promoted works of Mahler and Hindemith. Wrote on music history and aesthetics. In N.Y. fr. 1934.

Bel and the Dragon, two stories in Apocrypha, appearing as continuation of Book of Daniel. In "Bel" Daniel challenges the divinity of the idol Bel and in "The Dragon" Daniel causes the death of a dragon worshiped by the Babylonians. Apparently popular works composed in Babylon in 5th–4th c. B.C.E.

Belasco, David (1859–1931), U.S. theatrical producer, playwright. Pioneered in use of electricity for stage lighting. His 374 productions displayed a passion for flamboyant realism and sensational scenic effect.

Wrote *Madame Butterfly* and *Girl of the Golden West* (both turned into operas by Puccini).

Belaya Tserkov, town in Ukrainian S.S.R. Jews fr. late 16th c. Suffered from Chmielnicki massacres (1648), Gonta (1768), pogroms of 1905, 1919–20. Community numbered 15,624 in 1926. Liquidated by Nazis. Jewish pop. c. 15,000 (1970).

Belgium, W. European kingdom. Few Jews there in 13th c. massacred. Marrano community established in Antwerp in 16th c., open settlement permitted by Austria 1713 and fr. 1794 Ashkenazi Jews also began to settle, with religious equality in 19th c. Community organized on French pattern, but Antwerp, which became center for Ashkenazi Jews, retained distinctive character. Of 110,000 Jews in 1939, over 53,000 deported. Jewish pop. 40,500 (1971), with largest community in Brussels.

Belgrade, capital of Yugoslavia. Jewish settlement fr. 13th c. Community prospered until 17th c. but thereafter suffered fr. intermittent warfare in region. In 19th c. became capital of Serbia and Jews granted full rights. 12,000 Jews in 1941 when Germans entered; none remained in 1942. Community reestablished 1944, numbered 1,600 in 1971.

Belial (or **Beliar**), name of the Prince of Evil (Satan) in post-biblical literature; probably under influence of Iranian dualism.

Belinfante, Moses ben Ẓaddik (1761–1827), Dutch linguist, educationalist. Principal of Jewish school for poor at The Hague. Active in struggle for Jewish emancipation in Holland. Editor of official gazette of Kingdom of the Netherlands 1806. Collaborated in translation of prayer book.

Belkin, Samuel (1911–), U.S. rabbi, educator; b. Poland, in U.S. fr. 1929. Joined faculty of Yeshiva College (now Univ.) 1935, president 1943. Wrote on Jewish law and Hellenistic literature, esp. Philo.

Belkind, Ereẓ Israel family. Immigrated fr. Russia in early 1880s. **Meir** (1827–1898), one of first teachers of modern school system in Ereẓ Israel. **Israel** (1861–1929) teacher, writer. One of founders of Bilu. Founded Ben Shemen youth village and Shefeyah agricultural training school. **Na'aman** (1889–1917), member of Nili; executed by the Turks.

Belkowsky, Ẓevi Hirsch (Grigori; 1865–1948), Zionist leader, jurist; b. Russia. Prof. of law at Sofia Univ. Active in Zionist movement in Russia, helped organize first Zionist Congress. In Ereẓ Israel fr. 1924.

Bellow, Saul (1915–), U.S. novelist; one of the leading postwar writers; b. Quebec. Best known for *The Adventures of Augie March* and the international best seller *Herzog.*

Belmont, August (1816–1890), U.S. banker, diplomat, politician. Worked for Rothschilds; opened own banking house. Democratic National Committee chairman 1860–72. Introduced thoroughbred racing in U.S.

Belmonte, Isaac Nuñez (alias **Manuel;** d. 1705), Dutch merchant, diplomat. Spanish resident minister in Netherlands fr. 1674. Created count palatine by Emperor Leopold III 1693; the title of baron conferred on him by king of Spain. Founded poetic society in Amsterdam.

Beloff, Max (1913–), English historian, political scientist. Prof. of government and public administration at Oxford. Published numerous works on European history, American government, Soviet foreign policy.

Belorussia (White Russia), territory in U.S.S.R. Itinerant Jewish traders visited this area of Lithuania in 15th c. and communities were established in 16th c. Despite mass poverty, Jewish pop. increased (until mass emigration to U.S. in 1880s). Centers of learning established. Cradle of Ḥabad Ḥasidim, Labor Zionism. Religious and cultural life gradually stifled under Soviet rule, which in 1939 was extended to W. (previously Poland) Belorussia. In June 1941, most Jews in area killed by Nazis. Pop. (1970) 148,000.

°**Belshazzar,** son of Nebuchadnezzar and last king of Babylon, according to the Book of Daniel, which tells of the feast he made the night before Babylonia was captured by the Persians.

Belteshazzar, name given to Daniel in Babylonia (Dan. 1:7).

Beltsy (Balti), city in Bessarabia. Community established 1779 and grew throughout 19th c. Many emigrated at end of c. 14,259 Jews in 1930. In 1941 Rumanians hounded community and Germans deported survivors to concentration camps. Jews returned after the war. Jewish pop. 15,000 (1970).

Belvoir, see Agrippina.

Belz, major ḥasidic dynasty, resident in town of Belz in Galicia. Founder, **Shalom Roke'aḥ** (1779–1855), followed by **Joshua** (1825–1894), and **Issachar Dov** (1854–1927) and his

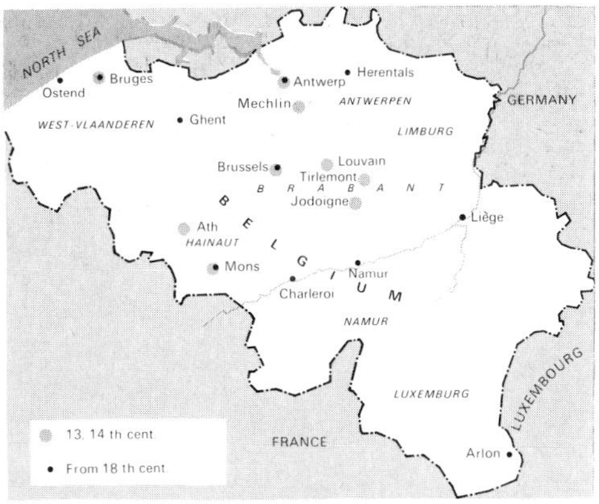

The Jewish communities of Belgium.

Samuel Belkin

Saul Bellow

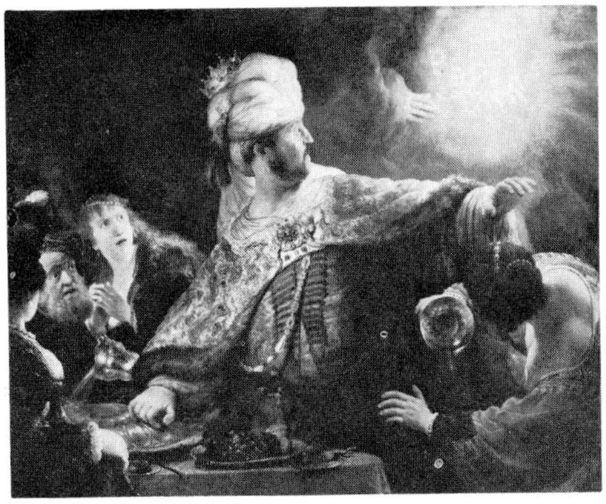

"Belshazzar's Feast" by Rembrandt, 1634.

The Belz "rebbe," Issachar Dov

son **Aaron** (1880–1957). Aaron first to deviate fr. extreme opposition to all new non-Orthodox ideas when he reached Ereẓ Israel 1944. **Issachar Dov** (1948–), established *bet midrash* in Jerusalem.

Belzec, site of German extermination camp in Poland. Functioned as labor camp May-Dec. 1940, extermination camp fr. 1942. More than 600,000 people killed (2,000 non-Jews). Camp liquidated 1943.

Belzer, Nissi, see Spivak, Nissan.

Be-Midbar, see Numbers, Book of.

Ben-Adir (pen name of **Abraham Rosin;** 1878–1942), writer, Jewish socialist leader in Russia. A founder and ideologist of the Vozrozhdeniye group and of its successor the Sejmists. Left Russia 1921. Later in Paris and New York, coedited a general encyclopedia in Yiddish.

Yiẓḥak Ben-Aharon

Ben Aharon (Nussenbaum), Yiẓḥak (1906–), Israel labor leader; b. Austrian Bukovina, settled in Ereẓ Israel 1928. Joined British Army 1940, prisoner of war 1941–45. Leader of Aḥdut ha-Avodah, member of Knesset, minister of communications and transport 1956–62, secretary-general of Histadrut 1969–73.

Benaiah, one of David's most honored warriors and Solomon's commander-in-chief. Together with Zadok and Nathan proclaimed Solomon king. Carried out liquidation of Shimei, Adonijah, and Joab.

Ben-Ami (Shieren), Jacob (1890–), actor, director. Traveled throughout E. Europe on Yiddish stage before going to U.S. 1912. Helped found Yiddish Art Theater in N.Y. 1918. Subsequently appeared in both English- and Yiddish-language plays and toured extensively.

Oved Ben-Ami, bronze by Duda (David Edelstein), 1965.

Ben-Ami, Oved (1905–), long-time mayor of Netanyah; b. Petaḥ Tikvah. Secretary of Benei Binyamin 1924–28, founder of Netanyah 1928–29 and Even Yehudah 1932. One of founders of Ashdod.

Ben-Amitai, Levi (1901–), Hebrew writer; b. Belorussia; settled in Ereẓ Israel 1920. Member of Kibbutz Deganyah. Much of his poetry has agricultural folk setting.

Ben-Ammi (Rabinowicz), Mordecai (1854–1932), author, journalist, writing in Russian, Yiddish; b. Russia, left for Geneva 1882, settled in Ereẓ Israel 1923. In articles criticized Jewish intelligentsia for renouncing Jewish values; stories portray traditional Jewish way of life.

Ben-Amotz, Dahn (1923–), Israel author, humorist; b. Poland, settled in Ereẓ Israel 1938. Witty conversationalist. Writings include semi-autobiographical novel and dictionary of modern Hebrew slang.

Benamozegh, Elijah ben Abraham (1822–1900), Italian rabbi, philosopher. Rabbi and prof. of theology in rabbinical school in Leghorn. Wrote on Judaism in Hebrew, French, Italian. Stressed possibility of non-Jews observing commandments even without conversion. Regarded Kabbalah as essential component of Judaism.

Ben-Aroya, Abraham (1887–), Greek socialist. Formed Salonika Workers' Organization with support of Jewish workers. Later helped found Greek Social Democratic Party. Emigrated to Israel 1953.

Ben-Asher, Aaron ben Moses (10th c.), masorete (probably Karaite) living in Tiberias. His tradition is the one accepted in the Jewish Bible; also one of first to lay foundations of Hebrew grammar.

Ben-Asher, Moses (9th c.), scribe and masorete living in Tiberias. A manuscript by him of the Former and Later Prophets has survived in Cairo, pointed and furnished with accents and masoretic notes.

Benatzky, Ralph (1884–1957), composer. Prolific writer of light music, composing 5,000 songs and 92 operettas, the best-known being *White Horse Inn.* Also wrote 250 film scores. D. in Zurich.

Ben-Avi, Ithamar (1882–1943), journalist, Hebrew writer; son of Eliezer Ben-Yehuda. Served on editorial board of father's newspaper; founder and editor of Hebrew daily *Do'ar ha-Yom* and editor of English-language *Palestine Weekly.*

Ithamar Ben-Avi

Ben-Avigdor, see Shalkovich, Abraham Leib.

Benayahu, Meir (1926–), Israel scholar; son of Chief Rabbi Isaac Nissim. Senior worker at the Ben-Zvi Institute fr. 1947 and director 1964–73. Prolific researcher, publishing numerous studies and documents on Jewish history in Middle East.

Ben Azzai, Simeon (2nd c. C.E.), *tanna* in Tiberias. Saintly, outstanding scholar. Never ordained; also never married. Reportedly one of four scholars who engaged in esoteric speculation and was led astray by mystical teaching. Numbered by some among Ten Martyrs.

Ben Baboi, see Pirkoi Ben Baboi.

Ben Bag Bag (1st c.), *tanna,* halakhic authority. Saying "Turn it and turn it [i.e., the Torah] for everything is in it, and contemplate it, and grow old and grey over it, and stir not from it, for you can have no better rule than this" (Avot 5:25).

Benda, Julian (1867–1956), French philosopher. Attacked most contemporary philosophers and defended reason and science against intuition, esp. in his famous work, *The Great Betrayal (Le trahison des clercs).*

Bendavid, Lazarus (Eleazar; 1762–1832), German mathematician, philosopher, educator. Authority on Kant. Also wrote extensively on

	Blessing before partaking of food. Each opens with the formula *Barukh Attah Adonai Eloheinu Melekh ha-Olam*
בָּרוּךְ אַתָּה ה׳ אֱלֹהֵינוּ מֶלֶךְ הָעוֹלָם	(**"Blessed art Thou, O Lord, Our God, King of the Universe"**)
	and then specifies the food for which thanksgiving is being made.
	Thus, before bread
הַמּוֹצִיא לֶחֶם מִן הָאָרֶץ	**"who bringest forth bread from the earth"**
	before wine
בּוֹרֵא פְּרִי הַגָּפֶן	**"who createst the fruit of the vine"**
	before partaking of food, other than bread, prepared from any of the "five species of grain" (wheat, barley, rye, oats, and spelt)
בּוֹרֵא מִינֵי מְזוֹנוֹת	**"who createst various kinds of food"**
	before fruit
בּוֹרֵא פְּרִי הָעֵץ	**"who createst the fruit of the tree"**
	before vegetables
בּוֹרֵא פְּרִי הָאֲדָמָה	**"who createst the fruit of the earth"**
	before meat, fish, eggs, cheese, or any drink other than wine
שֶׁהַכֹּל נִהְיֶה בִּדְבָרוֹ	**"by whose word all things exist."**
	Blessing before performance of specific *mitzvot*. In these cases, the opening formula ("Blessed . . . universe") is followed by
אֲשֶׁר קִדְּשָׁנוּ בְּמִצְוֹתָיו וְצִוָּנוּ...	**"who has sanctified us through his commandments, and has commanded us..."**
	This formula is also used before the performance of commandments of rabbinic origin. Where a *mitzvah* is performed for the first time in the year, an additional blessing (the *She-Heḥeyanu*) is added before the performance:
שֶׁהֶחֱיָנוּ וְקִיְּמָנוּ וְהִגִּיעָנוּ לַזְּמַן הַזֶּה	**"who has kept us alive and preserved us and enabled us to reach this season"**
	before washing the hands prior to a *mitzvah (netilat yadayim)*
עַל נְטִילַת יָדָיִם	**"concerning the washing of the hands"**
	before wearing a *tallit*
לְהִתְעַטֵּף בַּצִּיצִית	**"to enwrap ourselves in the fringed garment"**
	before wearing *tefillin* (on the arm)
לְהָנִיחַ תְּפִילִין	**"to put on the *tefillin*"**
	before study of the Torah
לַעֲסוֹק בְּדִבְרֵי תוֹרָה	**"to occupy ourselves with the words of the Torah"**
	this blessing must be distinguished from that recited before the Reading of the Law
בָּרוּךְ אַתָּה ה׳ אֱ־לֹהֵינוּ מֶלֶךְ הָעוֹלָם	**"Blessed art Thou, O Lord Our God, King of the Universe,**
אֲשֶׁר בָּחַר־בָּנוּ מִכָּל הָעַמִּים וְנָתַן לָנוּ אֶת־תּוֹרָתוֹ	**who has chosen us from all peoples and has given us the Torah.**
בָּרוּךְ אַתָּה ה׳ נוֹתֵן הַתּוֹרָה	**Blessed art thou, O Lord, who gives the Torah"**
	before taking the *lulav*
עַל נְטִילַת לוּלָב	**"concerning the taking of the *lulav*"**
	on fixing a *mezuzah*
לִקְבּוֹעַ מְזוּזָה	**"to affix the *mezuzah*"**
	before lighting candles: on eve of Sabbath
לְהַדְלִיק נֵר שֶׁל־שַׁבָּת	**"to kindle the Sabbath light"**
	on eve of festival
לְהַדְלִיק נֵר שֶׁל יוֹם טוֹב	**"to kindle the festival light"**
	on eve of Day of Atonement
לְהַדְלִיק נֵר שֶׁל יוֹם הַכִּפֻּרִים	**"to kindle the Day of Atonement light"**
	before reading the Book of Esther on Purim
עַל מִקְרָא מְגִלָּה	**"concerning the reading of the Megillah"**
	before the blowing of the *Shofar* on Rosh Ha-Shanah
לִשְׁמוֹעַ קוֹל שׁוֹפָר	**"concerning the hearing of the *shofar*"** (pronounced by the person about to blow the *shofar*)
	Blessings of praise for various occasions. Here the opening formula ("Blessed . . . universe") is followed by the benediction.
	Thus: on witnessing lightning, fallen stars, lofty mountains, or great deserts
עֹשֶׂה מַעֲשֵׂה בְרֵאשִׁית	**"who has made the creation"**
	on hearing thunder
שֶׁכֹּחוֹ וּגְבוּרָתוֹ מָלֵא עוֹלָם	**"whose strength and might fill the world"**
	at the sight of the sea
שֶׁעָשָׂה אֶת הַיָּם הַגָּדוֹל	**"who has made the great sea"**
	on seeing the rainbow
זוֹכֵר הַבְּרִית וְנֶאֱמָן בִּבְרִיתוֹ וְקַיָּם בְּמַאֲמָרוֹ	**"who remembers the covenant, is faithful to his covenant, and keeps his promise"**
	on hearing good tidings (the *hatov ve-ha-metiv* blessing)
הַטּוֹב וְהַמֵּטִיב	**"who is good and dispenses good"**
	on hearing bad tidings (the *dayyan emet* blessing)
דַּיַּן הָאֱמֶת	**"the true judge"**
	on seeing a king and his court
שֶׁנָּתַן מִכְּבוֹדוֹ לְבָשָׂר וָדָם	**"who has given his glory to flesh and blood"**
	after deliverance from peril, recovery from sickness or childbirth, and after a long journey (the *ha-gomel* blessing)
הַגּוֹמֵל לְחַיָּבִים טוֹבוֹת שֶׁגְּמָלַנִי כָּל טוֹב	**"who does good unto the undeserving, and who has also rendered all good unto me."**

Jewish problems and law. Advocated Reform Judaism.

Bendemann, Eduard Julius Friedrich (1811–1889), German painter. Best-known paintings "The Exiles of Babylon in Mourning" and "Jeremiah at the Destruction of Jerusalem." Also executed portraits, murals, illustrations for literary works. Converted to Christianity 1835. His elder son, **Felix** (1848–1915), admiral and chief of the German Naval Staff.

Bender, Alfred Philip (1863–1937), S. African minister. Minister of Cape Town congregation fr. 1897. Secular as well as religious leader of community.

Bender, Lauretta (1897–), U.S. research psychiatrist. Specialized in childhood schizophrenia, employing electroconvulsive shock therapy. Her research led to development of Bender Gestalt Test.

Bender, Morris Boris (1905–), U.S. neurologist. Wrote on physiology of visual and oculomotor systems. Held various chairs in clinical neurology in N.Y.

Benderly, Samson (1876–1944), U.S. educator; b. Ereẓ Israel, settled in U.S. 1898. Director of N.Y. Bureau of Jewish Education (first in U.S.) fr. 1910. Bureau initiated *Ivrit be-Ivrit* pedagogy, leadership training programs, and Jewish education for girls.

Bendin, see Bedzin.

Bendix, Reinhard (1916–), U.S. sociologist. Prof. at Berkeley. Approached sociological problems typologically, developing Max Weber's theories.

Bene-Berak, ancient city E. of Jaffa. After destruction of Second Temple, became center of Jewish learning when R. Akiva established his school there. Modern town forms part of Tel Aviv metropolitan area. Established 1924 by group of Orthodox families. Known for numerous yeshivahs and strict public observance of Jewish laws. Pop. 74,200 (1971).

Benedict, Sir Julius (Isaac; 1804–1885), composer, conductor; b. Germany, in London fr. 1835. Works include cantatas, symphonies, piano concertos, operas, his most successful being *The Lily of Killarney.* Converted to Protestantism.

Benedict ben Moses of Lincoln (d. 1278), English financier. One of the outstanding Anglo-Jewish halakhic scholars of his day.

Benedictions (Heb. *berakhot*). The Talmud enjoins every Jew to make 100 benedictions a day. Four classes were recognized – benedictions of daily prayers, before performance of religious duty, for enjoyments, and thanksgiving. All must contain formula *Barukh Attah Adonai* ("Blessed art Thou, O Lord") (see table p. 73).

Benedikt, Moritz (1835–1920), Austrian neurologist, anthropometrist, criminologist. A founder of criminal anthropology; engaged in anthropometric studies of criminals. Active in various reform movements, notably women's suffrage.

Benedikt, Moritz (1849–1920), Austrian journalist. Financial editor and later part owner of *Neue Freie Presse.* Violently opposed Zionism and would not permit Herzl, who worked for him, to publish pro-Zionist polemics in the paper. Active in Liberal Party; appointed to upper house of Austrian parliament 1917.

Benei Akiva (Heb. "Sons of Akiva'), youth movement of Ha-Po'el ha-Mizrachi, founded in Jerusalem 1929. Religion and pioneering major guidelines of movement. Established kibbutzim, moshavim, Naḥal settlements, etc., and sponsors variety of activities in Diaspora. 20,000 members in 1970.

Benei Binyamin (Heb. "Sons of Benjamin"), association of second-generation farmers in veteran moshavot of Ereẓ Israel, active 1921–39. Founded Netanyah, Even Yehudah, Kefar Aharon, and part of Herzliyyah.

Symbol of Benei Akiva used as postal cancellation during world conference, 1958.

Ezekiel Samuel, 19th-cent. Bene Israel officer.

Benei Moshe (Heb. "Sons of Moses"), secret order of Ḥovevei Zion founded in Russia 1889. Its aim, outlined by its leader Aḥad Ha'Am, was the return of the Jews to their historic homeland, but with prior spiritual preparation. Active in Russia and Ereẓ Israel until 1897.

Bene Israel, Jewish community in India. Legend shrouds origin. Maintain certain Jewish observances, but had no contact with Indian Jewry until 18th c. In 19th c. Cochin and Mesopotamian Jewry helped them establish educational institutions. Many then served in British military and civil services, others engaging as traders, artisans and agriculturists. Originally S. of Bombay, many moved to city. Language is Marathi. They numbered 24,000 in 1947; many emigrated to Israel; 10,000 left in 1972.

Ben Eliezer, Moshe (1882–1944), Hebrew editor, author, translator; b. Lithuania. Editor of general Hebrew journals for young people in Poland. Settled in Ereẓ Israel 1925 and joined editorial staff of newspaper *Haaretz.* Translated European literature into Hebrew.

Benfey, Theodor (1809–1881), German comparative philologist, Sanskritist. Converted to Christianity 1848. Prof. at Univ. of Goettingen fr. 1862. Recognized authority on Indian linguistics. His two Sanskrit grammars served as basic texts for many years.

Ben-Gavriel, Moshe Ya'akov (1891–1965), Israel author who wrote in German; b. Vienna, settled in Erez Israel 1927. Worked as journalist, foreign correspondent. After WWII wrote many books about Israel which became best sellers in W.Germany.

Benghazi, city in Libya. Jewish settlement fr. 1st c. B.C.E. Especially grew after Turkish occupation 1640. During 18th and 19th c. Jews enjoyed freedom and affluence. By 1935, under Italian occupation, they numbered 2,236. Suffered under Fascists and in WWII and fr. Arab nationalists in 1945 and 1948. Large numbers left for Israel after these persecutions, the last 200 emigrating after 1967.

Bengis, Selig Reuben (1864–1953), Lithuanian rabbi. Occupied rabbinic posts in E. Europe. *Av bet din* 1938 and rabbi 1949 of separatist Orthodox community Ha-Edah ha-Ḥaredit of Jerusalem. Directed its affairs into practical channels and curbed its most extreme wing, the Neturei Karta.

David Ben-Gurion in Jewish Legion uniform, 1918.

David Ben-Gurion in retirement.

Ben-Gurion, David (1886–1973), Israel statesman; b. Plonsk (then Russian Poland), settled in Ereẓ Israel 1906. Exiled by Turks 1915; went to U.S. and was active in formation of Jewish battalion, returning to Ereẓ Israel 1918 as soldier in Jewish Legion. Among founders of Aḥdut ha-Avodah 1919 (which merged with Ha-Po'el ha-Ẓa'ir 1930 into Mapai, which he headed). Secretary-general of Histadrut 1921–33; chairman of Jewish Agency Executive 1935–48. Headed group that drew up Biltmore Program 1942. In April 1948 headed People's Council, which proclaimed the rebirth of the independent Jewish nation – largely on his initiative – on May 14, 1948. Prime minister and minister of defense until Dec. 1953 when he joined kibbutz Sedeh Boker. Recalled as defense minister Feb. 1955, also resuming functions of prime minister Nov. 1955, leading country during Sinai campaign. Resigned again June 1963 and founded Rafi Party 1965. When it joined Israel Labor Party he sponsored in 1969 a new list, Reshimah Mamlakhtit ("State List"), but in 1970 resigned fr. Knesset. Stressed strengthening of Israel army, settlement of Negev, welding of diversified elements of population into one nation, and development of scientific research. Wrote memoirs and books on modern history of Zionism and Israel.

°**Ben-Hadad I,** king of Aram. Joined in invading territory of Baasha of Israel (I Kings 15:18–20).

°**Ben-Hadad II** (9th c. B.C.E.), king of Aram. On three occasions waged war against Ahab of Israel (I Kings 20–22).

°**Ben-Hadad III** (9th–8th c. B.C.E.), king of Aram. During the early years of his reign occupied greater part of kingdom of Israel.

Ben-Haim (orig. **Frankenburger**), **Paul** (1897–), Israel composer; b. Munich, settled in Tel Aviv 1933. Tried to achieve synthesis of western and eastern music. Most of his work is lyrical. His works include symphonies, concertos, cantatas. Israel Prize 1957.

Ben Ha-Melekh Ve-Ha-Nazir (Heb. "The Prince and the Hermit"), Hebrew version by Abraham ibn Ḥasdai of original Hindu tale about prince who eventually became ascetic. Popular in Middle Ages.

Ben Ḥayyim (Goldmann), Ze'ev (1907–), linguist; b. Galicia, settled in Ereẓ Israel 1935. Prof. of Hebrew at Heb. Univ. and pres. (1973) of Academy of Hebrew Language. Specialist in Samaritan Hebrew dialect and literature. Israel Prize 1964.

Ben He He (1st c.), *tanna.* Identified by some with Ben Bag Bag. Saying: "According to the labor is the reward" (Avot 5:22).

Ben-Horin, Meir (1918–), educator. Taught at Boston Hebrew Teachers College 1951–57 and at Dropsie Univ. (prof. fr. 1962). Publications include a work on Max Nordau.

Benisch, Abraham (1814–1878), scholar; precursor of Zionism. Advocated Jewish immigration to Ereẓ Israel as student in Prague and Vienna 1841. Went to England, where he edited *Hebrew Observer* (1853–4) and *Jewish Chronicle* (1854–67, 1875–78). One of founders and first directors of Anglo-Jewish Association. Wrote on Hebrew grammar, Jewish philosophy.

Paul Ben-Haim

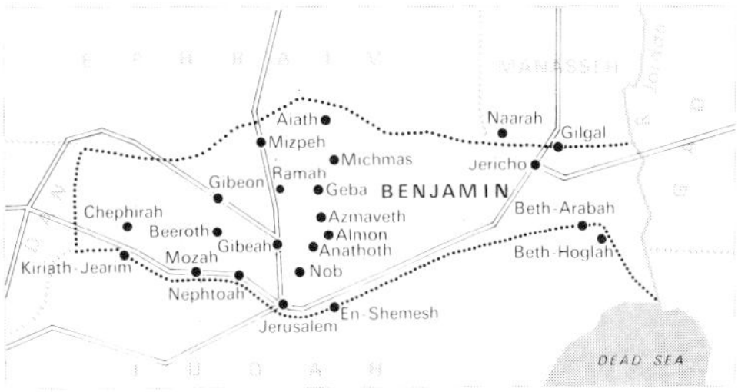

Territory of the tribe of Benjamin

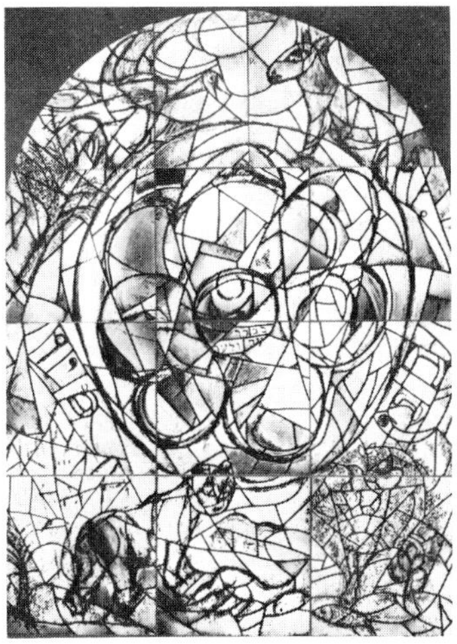

The tribe of Benjamin, one of 12 stained glass windows designed by Marc Chagall for Hadassah Medical Center synagogue, Jerusalem.

Benjacob, Isaac (1801–1863), first modern Hebrew bibliographer; lived in Vienna. His 17-vol. edition of Bible helped spread Haskalah among Russian Jewry (included Mendelssohn's German translation in Hebrew script). His *Ozar ha-Sefarim* lists 8,480 Hebrew manuscripts and 6,500 books.

Benjamin, youngest son of Jacob by Rachel; eponym of tribe of Benjamin. Tribal territory extended from hill country of Ephraim to hill country of Judah. Played important part in history of unification of tribes of Israel during period of Judges and beginning of monarchy (Judg. 3:15); first king to rule Israel was Saul the Benjamite.

Benjamin II (orig. **Israel Joseph Benjamin;** 1818–1864), Rumanian explorer, writer. Emulating Benjamin of Tudela, set out 1845 to search for remnants of Ten Lost Tribes, traveling to Near and Far East and N. Africa. Described journey and Jewish settlements in travelogue. Traveled through U.S. 1859–62.

Benjamin, Baruch ben Zion (1904–), Indian government official. Deputy chief controller imports and exports 1953. Undersecretary Ministry of Finance 1955–59.

Benjamin, Ernest Frank (1900–1969), British army officer; b. Toronto. Commanded Jewish Brigade 1944–46, seeing action in N. Italy. Rose to rank of brigadier.

Benjamin, Israel (c. 1570–1649), *posek,* kabbalist; among greatest Egyptian and Jerusalem scholars of his time. *Dayyan* in Jerusalem, becoming head of its rabbis 1646.

Benjamin, Judah Philip (1811–1884), U.S. statesman, lawyer; b. Virgin Islands. First professing Jew elected to U.S. Senate (1852). Supported secession from Union. Attorney-general of Confederate government 1861, then secretary of war and secretary of state. Escaped to England after Civil War and became distinguished barrister.

Benjamin, László (1915–), Hungarian poet. One of chief literary spokesmen of Hungarian Communists. After 1953 concerned himself more with self-criticism.

Benjamin, Walter (1892–1940), German philosopher, literary critic. Wrote philosophical commentaries on important literary events, stressing historical, philosophical, linguistic, and social motives. Considered the most important critic in the German language between the two wars. Committed suicide.

Benjamin ben Eliezer ha-Kohen Vitale of Reggio (1651–1730), Italian kabbalist, rabbi. One of major exponents of Isaac Luria's Kabbalah in Italy. Secret Shabbatean.

Benjamin ben Moses Alnahawendi, see Nah'āwendī, Benjamin ben Moses al-.

Benjamin of Tiberias (7th c.), leader of Ereẓ Israel Jewry. Negotiated on behalf of Jewish community with Persian conquerors in 614 and with Heraclius, the Byzantine emperor who recaptured the country in 628. Persuaded by emperor to convert to Christianity 629.

Benjamin (ben Jonah) of Tudela (12th c.), greatest medieval Jewish traveler, whose journeys through Europe and Middle East probably lasted 14 years (1159–72/3). His *Itinerary* describing conditions and governments of places he visited is unrivaled historical source.

Benjamin Ze'ev ben Mattathias of Arta (16th c.), *dayyan,* halakhist in Epirus. His legal decisions, sometimes lenient, reflect his independence in halakhic matters. They aroused opposition of German and Italian rabbis, some of whom questioned his authority.

Ben Kalba Savu'a (1st c. C.E.), wealthy man of Jerusalem. Zealots set fire to his stores from which he was supplying inhabitants of Jerusalem during Roman siege. Against his wishes, his daughter married R. Akiva, who had been his shepherd. Reconciled to son-in-law, and bequeathed him half his wealth when Akiva became great scholar.

Ben Meir, Aaron (10th c.), scholar, *rosh yeshivah* in Ereẓ Israel. Attempting to strengthen religious hegemony of Ereẓ Israel, in 921 announced changes in calendar adopted in Babylon. Jews of Ereẓ Israel thus celebrated Passover two days before Jews of Babylonia. Split caused considerable agitation and ended in his defeat.

Ben-Naphtali, Moses (or **Jacob**) **ben David** (9th or 10th c.), masorete; thought to have lived in Tiberias. Listed and probably collected c. 850 minor differences from reading of Ben-Asher in vowels and accents in Hebrew Bible.

Bennett, Salomon Yom Tov (1761–1838), engraver, author; b. Belorussia. Member of Royal Academy of Berlin. Settled in London 1799, writing theological and exegetical works attacking Jewish communal leaders.

Benny, Jack (Benny Kubelsky; 1894–), U.S. vaudeville, film, radio entertainer. Famed for roles as unyielding skinflint, atrocious fiddler, and demanding boss.

Benoit-Levy, Jean (1888–1959), French film producer-director, and writer on cinema. Directed *La Maternelle.*

Benrubi, Isaac (1876–1943), philosopher. Worked in Germany and France. Important authority on modern French philosophy, esp. Bergson.

Bensanchi, Mentesh (Mordecai; 1882–1943), Greek journalist, wrote in Ladino, French. Edited several Salonika newspapers. Represented Salonika Jewry in Greek parliament. Tortured to death by Nazis in Crete.

Ben-Sasson, Haim Hillel (1914–), Israel historian; b. Lithuania settled in Ereẓ Israel 1934. Prof. at Heb. Univ. Edited 3-vol. *Toledot Am Yisrael* and also editor of history division of *Encyclopaedia Judaica.*

List of masoretic differences between Ben-Asher and Ben-Naphtali in the "Lisbon Bible," 1482/3.

Bensaude, Joaquim (1859–1952), Portuguese historian; noted for research into history of Portuguese scientific navigation. Described important part played by Jewish astronomers and astrologers in Iberian peninsula during Middle Ages.

Benshalom, Benzion, see Katz, Benzion.

Ben Shemen, youth village and moshav in C. Israel established 1906. Agricultural school opened 1927; among first institutions included in framework of Youth Aliyah (1934). Pop. 1,045 (1971).

Ben Shemen, general view, 1966

Benshen, Ashkenazi term meaning "bless" or "pronounce a benediction." Mainly for grace after meals. Corresponds to the Sephardi *bençao.*

Ben Sira, Alphabet of, narrative satirical work probably written in geonic period in East. Contains 4 parts, consisting of epigrams, folklore, aphorisms alphabetically arranged and ascribed to Ben Sira.

Ben Sira, Simeon ben Jesus (2nd c. B.C.E.). Hebrew aphorist, sage, scribe; author of Wisdom of Ben Sira (Ecclesiasticus).

Ben Sira, Wisdom of (Ecclesiasticus), work of Apocrypha, written 2nd c. B.C.E. Consists mostly of maxims, poetic in form. Fragments of original Hebrew discovered in Qumran, Masada, and among Genizah fragments in Cairo. Previously known fr. Greek translation made by author's grandson 132 B.C.E.

Bensusan, Samuel Levy (1872–1958), English author, traveler. Edited *The Jewish World* 1897–8 and *The Theosophical Review* 1925–8.

Bentov (Gutgeld), Mordekhai (1900–), Israel politician; Mapam leader; b. Poland, settled in Ereẓ Israel 1920. Leader of Ha-Shomer ha-Ẓa'ir, editor of Mapam daily *Al ha-Mishmar* 1943–48. Member of Knesset 1949–65, minister of development 1955–61 and housing 1966–69.

Norman Bentwich

Bentwich, English Zionist family, many of whom settled in Ereẓ Israel. **Herbert** (1856–1932), lawyer, leader of Ḥovevei Zion and later of Zionist movement in England. Headed Order of Ancient Maccabeans. Edited *Law Journal.* Settled in Ereẓ Israel 1929. His son **Norman de Mattos** (1883–1971), first attorney-general in Ereẓ Israel under Mandate 1920–31, prof. of international relations at Heb. Univ. 1932–51, director of League of Nations Commission for Jewish Refugees from Germany 1933–36. Published books on legal, Palestinian, Hellenistic and Jewish subjects, as well as autobiographical volumes. His wife **Helen Caroline** (1892–1972), chairman of London County Council 1956–57 and alderman 1958–65. Another son, **Joseph Bentwich** (1902–), principal of Reali High School in Haifa 1948–55. Israel Prize 1962 for contribution to Israel education. A daughter, **Thelma** (1895–1959), cellist; married Eliezer Yellin, son of David Yellin. Active in musical life of Ereẓ Israel.

°**Bentzen, Aage** (1894–1953), Danish biblical scholar; expert in all phases of biblical exegisis. Emphasized historical narrative, historiography, strata of traditions.

Benveniste, Abraham (1406–1454), "court rabbi" in Castile. Tax farmer general of realm, chief justice and tax superintendent of Castilian Jewry. In this capacity framed ordinances to strengthen status of Spanish Jewry.

Benveniste (Benvenist), Ḥayyim ben Israel (1603–1673), rabbinic scholar in Smyrna and codifier. His *Keneset ha-Gedolah* amplified work of Joseph Caro and was accepted by Ashkenazim and Sephardim.

Benveniste, Isaac ben Joseph (d.c. 1224), physician to James I of Aragon, *nasi* of Aragonese Jewry. Leading figure at representative congresses of Jewish communities convened at Montpellier and Saint-Gilles 1214, 1215.

Benveniste, Joshua Raphael ben Israel (1590? –1665?), Turkish rabbi, physician, grammarian, poet. Halakhic authority who wrote responsa, sermons, and expositions, particularly devoting himself to Jerusalem Talmud, which was largely neglected in his day.

Benveniste, Manuel (Immanuel; 17th c.), Hebrew printer in Amsterdam. His outstanding production was a Talmud (1644–48), which restored some passages expunged by censor in previous editions.

Benveniste, Moses (16th c.), Turkish physician. Influential in Turkish politics; eventually one of three Turkish plenipotentiaries banished for exceeding instructions in peace negotiations with Spain. His attempt to escape this sentence by embracing Islam was unsuccessful. Died a political prisoner in Rhodes.

Benveniste, Sheshet ben Isaac ben Joseph (c. 1131–1209), Spanish financier, physician, poet; served king of Aragon. Wrote Hebrew poetry, was in touch with Muslim scholars, and wrote medical works.

Benwaish, Abraham (16th–17th c.), banker to sultan of Morocco. As superintendent of finances gained great influence at court. *Nagid* of Jews of kingdom of Marrakesh.

Ben-Yeḥezki'el, Mordekhai (1883–1971), Hebrew writer; b. Galicia, settled in Ereẓ Israel 1920. Adapted folktales (6 vols. 1957) and wrote on language, literature, Ḥasidism, etc.

Ben-Yehuda (Perelman), Eliezer (1858–1922), Hebrew writer, lexicographer; father of modern Hebrew; b. Lithuania. Went to Paris 1878 to study medicine. Published articles advocating Jewish settlement in Ereẓ Israel and in 1881 proposed that Hebrew become spoken

Eliezer Ben-Yehuda and his wife, Hemdah, 1912.

language. Settled in Erez Israel 1881, where he taught and edited. His household was first Hebrew-speaking home in Erez Israel. Founded Va'ad ha-Lashon 1890, which he headed until his death. Coined many Hebrew words based on roots in biblical and talmudic Hebrew and Aramaic. Largely responsible for revival of spoken Hebrew. His monumental dictionary includes all Hebrew words used in different periods of the language.

Ben-Yehuda, Ḥemdah (1873–1951), Hebrew author; second wife of Eliezer Ben-Yehuda; b. Lithuania, settled in Erez Israel 1892. Wrote stories and articles in her husband's newspapers, introducing sections for women, fashion, etc. Continued publication of his dictionary.

Ben-Yehudah, Barukh (1894–), Israel educator; b. Lithuania, settled in Erez Israel 1911. Member of Kibbutz Deganyah. Teacher in Herzlia Gymnasium fr. 1924 (principal 1952). First director-general of Israel ministry of education (until 1951). Wrote on Zionism, education, biblical cantillation, mathematics.

Ben Yizḥak, Avraham (1883–1950), Hebrew poet; b. Galicia, settled in Erez Israel 1938. Small output but considered distinguished figure in modern Hebrew poetry.

Ben-Yosef (Tabachnik), Shelomo (1913–1938), first Jew executed by British in Erez Israel. Emigrated there 1937 fr. Poland and joined Betar. Attacked Arab bus with two comrades to retaliate Arab terrorism; arrested, executed.

Ben Zaqen, Leon (1905–), Moroccan opthalmologist, politician. Minister of posts 1956–58.

Ben Ze'ev, Judah Leib (1764–1811), grammarian, lexicographer; the first Jewish scholar to apply Western research methods to study of Hebrew; b. Cracow. Literary work includes grammar and phonetics, lexicography, Bible exegesis, translation, poetry, parody, and editing of medieval texts. Best-known work Hebrew grammar. Also wrote Hebrew-German dictionary.

Monument in memory of Shelomo Ben-Yosef.

°**Benzinger, Immanuel** (1865–1935), German Protestant theologian, Orientalist. Taught in Jerusalem. Wrote comprehensive reference book of biblical archaeology.

Ben-Zion (Weinman; 1897–), U.S. painter; b. Ukraine, in U.S. fr. 1920, where he joined "The Group of Ten." Known for unconventional interpretation of biblical themes.

Ben-Zion, S. (Simḥah Alter Guttmann; 1870–1932), Hebrew writer, translator; b. Bessarabia, settled in Erez Israel 1905. Wrote short stories as realist, then visionary symbolist. Taught and wrote textbooks. Editor of many periodicals and translator of classical German poetry into Hebrew.

Ben Zoma, Simeon (2nd c.), *tanna.* Outstanding scholar and last of authoritative biblical expositors. Many of his sayings became proverbs. One of four sages who "entered paradise" (i.e., engaged in mystical studies) where it is said, "he cast a look and became demented."

Ben-Zvi, Izḥak (1884–1963), *yishuv* labor leader, scholar, second president of Israel (1952–63); b. Poltava, Ukraine. Founded with B. Borochov Po'alei Zion Party there; active in self-defense organization. Settled in Erez Israel 1907. Among founders of Ha-Shomer 1909. Exiled during WWI; went to U.S., returning 1918 as a soldier in Jewish Legion. Chairman of Va'ad Le'ummi 1931, president 1945–48. Mapai member of 1st and 2nd Knesset. Founded Institute for Study of Oriental Jewish Communities in the Middle East 1948, which became Ben-Zvi Institute 1952. Scholarly works devoted mainly to research on Jewish communities and sects, geography of Erez Israel, its ancient population, antiquities, and traditions.

Ben-Zvi, Raḥel Yanait (1886–), labor leader, writer; wife of Izḥak Ben-Zvi; b. Ukraine, settled in Erez Israel 1908. Pioneering role in Ha-Shomer, Women's Labor Movement, and Haganah. Expert in agronomy and founded first nursery in Jerusalem area. Founder and first principal of girls' agricultural high school near Jerusalem.

Ben-Zvi, Zeev (1904–1952), Israel sculptor; b. Poland, settled in Erez Israel 1924. Taught at Bezalel School fr. 1936. Specialized in portrait heads.

Beobachter an der Weichsel (Ger. "The Watcher by the Vistula"), first Polish Jewish newspaper, published 1823–24. Served ideals of Enlightenment. Received government support. Published in quasi-Yiddish with Polish translation. Never gained mass response.

Izḥak Ben-Zvi in 1918, as a soldier in the Jewish Legion, with his wife Raḥel.

Izḥak Ben-Zvi, bronze by Batya Lishansky, 1954.

Berab (Beirav), Jacob (c. 1474–1546), halakhic authority, leader of Jewish communities of Erez Israel, Egypt, Syria. Strongly advocated reinstitution of ordination *(semikhah)*, which he received fr. rabbis of Safed and gave to four others. Actions vigorously opposed by Levi b. Ḥabib in Jerusalem, and he was unable to implement his project of calling a "great *bet din.*" Wrote commentaries on Maimonides, novellae, responsa.

Berab (Beirav), Jacob ben Abraham (d. 1599), rabbi, halakhic authority in Safed. Gave *semikhah* to seven rabbis who agreed not to ordain others without his approval.

Berab (Beirav), Jacob ben Ḥayyim (17th–18th c.), poet, hymnologist. Helped found new Jewish settlement at Tiberias 1740, recording venture in account of travels and praising it in Hebrew and Ladino poems.

Beraita, see Baraita.

Berakhot (Heb. "Benedictions"), first tractate of Talmud, with *gemara* in Babylonian and Jerusalem Talmuds. Deals with recital and origin of various benedictions.

Bercovici, Konrad (1882–1961), U.S. novelist. Wrote *Crimes of Charity,* a controversial exposé, his autobiography *It's the Gypsy in Me,* and several books about gypsies.

Bercovitch, Peter (1871–1942), Canadian legislator; b. Montreal. K.C. 1911, first Jew in Quebec Assembly, elected to House of Commons of Dominion Parliament. Fought for Jewish rights in Quebec school system.

Berdichev, town in Ukrainian SSR. Jewish community fr. 18th c. Important center of Ḥasidism; seat of ḥasidic *ẓaddik* Levi Isaac of Berdichev. Noted for Jewish cloth trade. Second largest Jewish community in Russia in mid-19th c. (46,683 Jews in 1861). Economic problems and oppression contributed to decline in late 19th c. 30,000 Jews at outbreak of WWII. Nazis massacred community 1941. Jewish pop. 15,000 (1970).

Berdugo, Jekuthiel Ḥayyim ben Elisha (1858–1940), chief rabbi of Morocco. President of the supreme *bet din* fr. 1935.

Berdugo, Joshua ben Jacob (1878–1953), chief rabbi of Morocco 1941–53. A strong personality who occasionally came into conflict with leaders of the church and members of the French government, by whom he was respected.

Berdugo, Moses ben Abraham (Mashbir; c. 1679–1730), head of rabbinical court in Meknès (Morocco) and author of works on Talmud.

Berdyczewski (later **Bin-Gorion**), **Micha Josef** (1865–1921), Hebrew writer, thinker; b. Russia, went to Germany. Wrote in Hebrew, Yiddish, German, incl. essays, fiction, folklore, anthologies, scholarship. Embodied in writings painfully ambivalent attitudes toward traditional Judaism and European culture shared by many Jewish intellectuals. His son **Immanuel Bin-Gorion** (1903–), writer, settled in Ereẓ Israel 1936. Wrote essays, criticism, studies of folklore.

Berechiah ben Natronai ha-Nakdan (12th–13th c.), fabulist, translator,

Micha Josef Berdyczewski

grammarian; lived in France, England. Best-known work *Mishlei Shu'alim,* a collection of fables translated mostly fr. earlier French, Latin, and Oriental collections.

Berechiah Berakh ben Eliakim Getzel (c. 1670–1740), Polish rabbi, author. Outspoken criticism of moral standards of leaders of Polish Jewry earned him many opponents. Small part of his works on Bible and Talmud survives.

Beregowski, Moses (Moshe-Aaron), Yakovlevich (1892–1961), Soviet Russian musicologist. Head of ethnomusicological section of Institute for Jewish Proletarian Culture in the Ukraine 1930–48. Emphasized "proletarian" themes in E. European Jewish folksong.

Berenblum, Isaac (1903–), pathologist specializing in cancer research. At Oxford 1936–48 and Weizmann Institute 1950, where he developed a school of cell biologists and cancer workers. Israel Prize 1974.

Berendt, Gottlieb Michael (1836–1920), German geologist; one of first proponents of glacial theory. Prof. in Berlin 1875.

Berenice (1st c. B.C.E.), daughter of Salome (sister of Herod), wife of Aristobulus, mother of Agrippa I. Spent her last years in Rome, winning imperial favor.

Berenice (b. 28 C.E.), eldest daughter of Agrippa I. After unsuccessful attempts to prevent the Jerusalem riots of 66 C.E. went over to Roman camp. There Titus fell in love with her, but was prevented from marrying her by the ruling circles in Rome.

Title page of Berechiah ha-Nakdan's "Mishlei Shu'alim," 1756.

Berenson, Bernard (1865–1959), U.S. art historian, art connoisseur; lived most of his life in Italy. Authority on Renaissance and prolific writer. Best-known works *The Study and Criticism of Italian Art* and *Italian Pictures of the Renaissance.* His association with Joseph Duveen enabled him to amass a fortune. Converted to Christianity.

Berenson, Leon (1855–1943), Polish lawyer, diplomat. As defense counsel in political cases, became famous as courageous fighter for social justice. Entered Foreign Ministry, serving in Washington and the USSR. D. in Warsaw ghetto.

Berény, Róbert (1887–1953), Hungarian painter, graphic designer. Prof. at Academy of Creative Arts in Budapest 1948. Painted life studies, portraits, landscapes.

Bereshit see Genesis.

Berg, Gertrude (1900–1966), U.S. actress, scriptwriter. Creator of popular radio family "The Goldbergs," which played 17 years on radio and 5 on TV.

Berg, Leo (1862–1908), German essayist who popularized esthetic principles of German naturalism. Prophecied that national literatures would give way to common European literature.

Bergelson, David (1884–1952), Russian Yiddish writer; b. Ukraine. Early works in Russian and Hebrew, later Yiddish. Wrote novels, plays, stories, criticism. At first described slow decay of Jewish bourgeoisie in village and town, but in later works adapted himself to demands of socialist realism. Moved to Berlin 1920, traveled widely, returned to Moscow 1934. Imprisoned 1949, executed 1952, rehabilitated 1961.

Bergen-Belsen, Nazi concentration camp near Hanover, Germany. Established c. 1943 as a prisoner-of-war camp for Jews whom Nazis wished to exchange for Germans in allied territory. Functioned until 1945. 37,000 people died, mainly during March 1945 as result of epidemics Camp finally evacuated only in 1951, by which time a further 14,000 had died. Most survivors eventually left for Ereẓ Israel.

Bergen County, district in N.J., U.S. First Jews in 1880s, first congregation 1896. Huge migration fr. N.Y. started 1931; greatest increase in Jewish pop. after WWII. Jewish pop. c. 100,000 (1971).

Berger, Victor (1860–1929), U.S. journalist socialist leader; b. Aus-

tria, in U.S. fr. 1880. Editor of socialist newspapers, a founder of American Socialist Party, elected to Congress 1911. Opposition to America's entry into WWI led to 20-year prison sentence. Supreme Court reversed conviction and he sat in Congress again 1922–28.

Bergh, Herman van den (1897–), Dutch poet. A founder of the expressionist school in Holland.

Bergh, van den, family of Dutch industrialists. **Simon** (1818–1906) started production of "artificial butter" (oleomargarine) in Holland 1872. Firm became one of leading margarine manufacturers in Europe and giant international concern after merging with Lever Bros. as Unilever Ltd. His son **Sidney J.** (b. 1898) served as commissioner for UNICEF and Dutch minister of defense 1959.

Bergman, Samuel Hugo (1883–), philosopher. Librarian at Univ. Library in Prague 1907–19. Settled in Ereẓ Israel 1920 and became first director of National and Univ. Library (until 1935). Prof. at Heb. Univ. and its first rector 1935–38. Member of Ha-Po'el ha-Ẓa'ir and spokesman for Berit Shalom. Main interests science and religion. Wrote on Kant and Maimon. Israel Prize 1954, 1974.

Bergmann, Ernst David (1903–), Israel organic chemist, b. Germany. Director of the Daniel Sieff Research Institute in Reḥovot fr. 1934, working in close association with Chaim Weizmann. Head of science dept. of Israel Ministry of Defense for nearly 20 years and chairman of Israel's Atomic Energy Commission 1953–66. Prof. at Heb. Univ. Israel Prize 1968.

Bergmann, Felix Eliezer (1908–), Israel organic chemist, pharmacologist; brother of Ernst David Bergmann; b. Germany, settled in Ereẓ Israel 1934. Prof. of pharmacology at Heb. Univ.

Bergner, Elizabeth (1897–), actress. Under Max Reinhardt in Vienna and Berlin, gained international reputation in Shakespearean roles and as Shaw's Saint Joan. Appeared in English-speaking roles in New York 1930. Appeared in films, some directed by her husband, Paul Czinner. Appeared again in Germany and Austria after WWII.

Bergner, Herz (1907–1970), Yiddish novelist; brother of Yiddish poet Melech Ravitch; b. Galicia, in Australia fr. 1938. Wrote short stories and novels and described life of immigrants in Australia.

Bergner, Yossl (Yosef; 1920–), Israel painter; son of Yiddish poet

Students honoring Samuel Hugo Bergman on his 85th birthday, 1968.

Elizabeth Bergner

Ernst David Bergmann

Henri Bergson, medal by H. Kautsch, 1913.

Beriḥah: on foot to the frontier, through the forest and over the mountain.

Melech Ravitch; b. Vienna, grew up in Warsaw, emigrated to Australia 1937, and settled in Israel 1951. Early works expressionistic but later paintings tended to abstraction.

Bergson, Abram (1914–), U.S. economist and expert on Soviet Union. Prof. of economics at Harvard 1956, director of its Russian Research Center 1964.

Bergson, Henri Louis (1859–1941), French philosopher. Prof. at Collège de France 1908. Famous for his theory of creative evolution of vital, continuous, and generative impulse of the universe *(élan vital).* Member of French Academy. Awarded Nobel Prize for Literature 1928. Although attracted to Catholicism, insisted in 1940 on being identified as Jew.

Bergson, Michael (1820–1898), Polish pianist, composer; father of Henri Bergson. Works are in style of his teacher Chopin. Settled in London 1873, where he helped compile and edit synagogue music.

Bergson, Peter, see Kook, Hillel.

Bergstein, Fania (1908–1950), Hebrew poet; b. Poland, settled in Ereẓ Israel 1930. Wrote poems, stories, and plays for children.

Bergtheil, Jonas (1819–1902), pioneer in Natal S. Africa. Emigrated from Bavaria to Cape Colony 1934 and formed company to bring over European settlers and develop cotton growing. A founder of Cape Town Hebrew Congregation 1841 and member of Natal legislative council. Settled in England 1866.

Beriḥah (Heb. "Flight"), name of organized underground operation moving Jews out of E. Europe into C. and S. Europe between 1944 and 1948 as step towards their mostly "illegal" immigration to Ereẓ Israel; also name of spontaneous mass movement of Jewish survivors fr. Europe to Ereẓ Israel.

Berit Ivrit Olamit, see Brit Ivrit Olamit.

Berit Shalom (Heb., lit. "Covenant of Peace"; English name "The Peace Association"), society founded by A. Ruppin and group of Jewish in-

tellectuals in Jerusalem 1925 to foster amicable Jewish-Arab relations and seek a joint solution for future of Ereẓ Israel. Ceased to exist in 1930s. A similar society, Iḥud ("Unity"), was founded by J.L. Magnes in 1942 and existed until 1948.

Berk, Fred (1911–), exponent of Jewish and ethnic dance in U.S. Founded Jewish Dance Division, 92nd Street YMHA-YWHA, New York, 1950, and Hebraica Dancers 1958.

Berkman, Alexander (1870–1936), U.S. anarchist; b. Russia, in U.S. fr. 1888. Led anarchist movement in America with Emma Goldman. Deported to USSR 1919 after being imprisoned for shooting director of steel works. Unable to reconcile Bolshevik regime with his libertarian principles, he eventually settled in England, where he committed suicide.

Berkovits, Eliezer (1908–), Orthodox rabbi, theologian; b. Transylvania. Served in rabbinate in Berlin, Leeds, Sydney, Boston. Chairman of Jewish philosophy dept. at Hebrew Theological College in Chicago. Published books on Jewish theology.

Berkowicz, Joseph (Józef; 1789–1846), Polish army officer. Severely wounded and decorated during Napoleon's Russian campaign when he fought in Polish Legion. Exhorted Jews to support 1830–31 Polish uprising. Later settled in France and England.

Berkowitz, Henry (1857–1924), U.S. Reform rabbi. Served in Mobile, Alabama, Kansas City, and Rodeph Shalom, Philadelphia. Supported advanced Reform. First secretary of Central Conference of American Rabbis.

Berkowitz, Yitzḥak Dov (1885–1967), Hebrew and Yiddish novelist, editor, playwright, translator; b. Belorussia, went to U.S. 1913 and Ereẓ Israel 1928. Translated works of his father-in-law, Shalom Aleichem, into popular Hebrew. Wrote novels, stories and plays describing Jews in Russia, U.S., and Ereẓ Israel.

Yitzḥak Dov Berkowitz

Berkson, Isaac Baer (1891–), U.S. educator, philosopher. Superintendent of Jewish School System in Ereẓ Israel 1928–35. Taught philosophy of education at N.Y. City College (prof. 1955). Wrote on philosophy of education.

Berle, Milton (1908–), U.S. comedian. Appeared in nightclubs, films, Broadway shows, and starred in his own weekly TV variety show 1948–56.

Berlewi, Henryk (1894–1967), Polish painter. Developed abstract form of painting known as "Mechano-Faktura" ("mechanical painting"), characterized by geometric simplicity and total lack of representation. Lived in Paris fr. 1928.

Berligne, Eliyahu Meir (1866–1959), *yishuv* leader; b. Russia, settled in Ereẓ Israel 1907. Among founders of Tel Aviv, member of Va'ad Le'ummi 1920–48, signatory of Israel's Declaration of Independence.

Berlijn, Anton (Aron Wolf; 1817–1870), Dutch composer, conductor; director of Royal Theater. Founded choral groups, wrote liturgical works for synagogue, and composed much other music.

Burning of the Jews in the new market, Berlin, 1510.

Berlin, city in Germany. Jewish settlement fr. 13th c. Expelled 1571, and although some returned around 1670, synagogue only inaugurated 1714. Community prospered and became cradle of Enlightenment and Reform in 19th c. Jews recognized as citizens 1812. Community numbered 172,000 in 1933. Destroyed by Nazis. Some Jews returned after WWII. W. Berlin Jewish pop. 5,300, E. Berlin 700 (1971).

Berlin, Aryeh Loeb ben Abraham Meir (1738–1814), German rabbi. Rabbi of Bamberg fr. 1789; chief rabbi of kingdom of Westphalia fr. 1808. Works incl. Hebrew poem welcoming Jerome Bonaparte and annotations to Talmud.

Berlin, Irving (Israel Baline; 1888–), U.S. popular song writer; son of Russian cantor. Composed over 1,000 songs many of which have maintained their popularity. Wrote music for Broadway shows *(Annie Get Your Gun, Call Me Madam)*. Songs incl. *Alexander's Ragtime Band*, and *God Bless America*.

Sir Isaiah Berlin

Berlin, Sir Isaiah (1909–), English philosopher, political scientist; b. Latvia. First Jewish Fellow of All Souls College, Oxford, 1938; prof. of social and political theory at Oxford 1957 and pres. of Wolfson College 1966. Strongly liberal attitude to social and political questions. Wrote studies on Marx, Moses Hess, and Tolstoy. Friend and admirer of Weizmann; maintained close ties with Israel.

Berlin, Isaiah ben Judah Loeb (Isaiah Pick; 1725–1799), rabbi, author in Breslau. Renowned for conciliatory attitude. Extensive literary works included glosses and textual notes on talmudic literature. His *Masoret ha-Shas* is printed in every edition of Talmud. First scholar in Germany to study history of post-talmudic literature.

Berlin, Meir, see Bar-Ilan, Meir.

Berlin, Naphtali Ẓevi Judah (ha-Neẓiv; 1817–1893), rabbi and head of Volozhin yeshivah for 40 years. Method of enquiry followed *gaon* of Vilna and avoided *pilpul*. In communal matters opposed introduction of secular studies in yeshivah and was among first rabbis to support Zionism. Wrote responsa, exegetical works, commentary on Pentateuch. His son **Ḥayyim** (1832–1912), rabbi of Moscow 1865–69, chief rabbi of Ashkenazi community in Jerusalem 1909–12.

Berlin, Saul ben Ẓevi Hirsch Levin (Saul Hirschel; 1740–1794), German rabbi. Disenchanted with rabbinate, he joined *Me'assefim* Haskalah group and wrote several works which aroused much controversy for criticisms of earlier halakhic authorities. Branded by some as atheist, he left Germany.

Berliner, Abraham (1833–1915), German scholar. Lectured at the *bet ha-midrash* of Berlin Talmudic Society 1858–65. Works include editions and studies of Rashi, Italian and German Jewish history, and commentaries on liturgy and Talmud.

Berliner, Emile (1851–1929), inventor; b. Germany, in U.S. fr. 1870. Invented microphone, making possible long-distance telephone calls, and improvements to Edison's phonograph led to production of modern gramophone. Also pioneered helicopter, promoted pasteurization of milk, and helped fight spread of tuberculosis. His son, **Henry Adler** (1895–), aeronautical engineer. Worked with father on helicopter construction and became pres. of Berliner Aircraft in Washington.

Berman, Adolf Abraham (1906–), socialist Zionist; b. Poland. Active in Polish underground during WWII and member of Polish temporary parliament. In Israel fr. 1950. Mapam member of Knesset but joined Communist Party 1954.

Berman, Jacob (1901–), Polish Communist leader; brother of Adolf Berman. Joined Polish Communist Party 1928; in Soviet Union during WWII. Deputy premier of Poland 1952–56. Accused of Stalinism when Gomulka came to power; became editor in publishing house but forced to retire during 1968 anti-Semitic campaign.

Berman, Simeon (1818–1884), forerunner of agricultural settlement in Ereẓ Israel; b. Cracow, went to U.S. 1852, where he tried to found agricultural settlement societies. In Ereẓ Israel fr. 1870 engaged in buying land and establishing settlements.

Berman, Vasili (Ze'ev Wolf; 1862–1896), early member of Ḥovevei Zion in Russia. Secretary of ICA and head of emigration dept.

Bermant, Chaim Icyk (1929–), British humorist, journalist; b. Lithuania. Wrote novels satirizing English Jewish life and also *Troubled Eden* about British Jewry.

Bermuda Conference, Anglo-American government conference on refugees, April 19–30, 1943. Report inconclusive. Its only positive decision – to revive Evian Committee – came too late to save a single Jew from the Holocaust.

Bernard, Ḥayyim David (1782–1858), Polish physician, ḥasidic leader. Medical inspector for western regions of Grand Duchy of Warsaw 1807–15. Initially remained aloof from Polish Jewry, but ultimately became strictly Orthodox and was spiritual heir of Jacob Isaac ha-Levi Horowitz, the Seer of Lublin.

Bernard, Tristan (1866–1947), French playwright, novelist. Known for his bon mots and theatrical comedy *(L'Anglais tel qu'on le parle, Le sauvage).* His son, **Jean-Jacques** (1888–1972), also wrote popular plays. Convert to Catholicism; imprisoned by Nazis.

Bernardi, Herschel (1924–), U.S. actor. Performed in *The World Of Shalom Aleichem* and starred as Tevye in Broadway production of *Fiddler on the Roof.*

°**Bernardino da Feltre** (1439–1494), Franciscan friar, saint. Preached against Jews in N. Italy; mainly responsible for blood libel at Trent 1475. Had Jews expelled from several towns.

Bernays, Edward L. (1891–), U.S. public relations counselor whose methods revolutionized the field. Wrote first book on public relations 1929 and taught first college course on subject 1930.

Bernays, Isaac ben Jacob (1792–1849), rabbi of Hamburg, Germany. In his struggle against Reform in community, formulated "modern orthodoxy" which influenced views of disciple Samson Raphael Hirsch. Granddaughter married Sigmund Freud.

Bernays, Jacob (1824–1881), German philologist, classicist; son of Isaac Bernays. Taught at Bonn Univ. and Breslau Rabbinical Seminary, which he helped found 1853 after failing to secure promotion in Bonn because of his faith.

Bernays, Paul Isaac (1888–), mathematician. Taught at Goettingen 1917–34 and Zurich Polytechnicum. Co-author of classic work on mathematics.

Bernbach, William (1911–), U.S. advertising executive. Specialized in subtle copy and graphics. One of his most famous slogans was "You don't have to be Jewish to love Levy's" (rye bread).

Berne, capital of Switzerland. Jewish moneylenders in 13th c., community expelled 1392. Officially re-established 1848. Jewish pop. 800.

Bernfeld, Simon (1860–1940), rabbi, scholar. Chief rabbi of Belgrade Sephardi community 1886–94; then lived in Berlin. Wrote works on Bible, Jewish history, ethics; translated Bible into German. Best-known works *Da'at Elohim* (history of religious philosophy); *Sefer ha-Dema'ot* (anthology of sources on Jewish persecution).

Bernhard, Georg (1875–1944), German journalist. Represented Social Democrats in Reichstag and founded financial journal *Plutus* 1904. Active in German-Jewish communal organization. In France fr. 1933, U.S. 1941.

The Sarah Bernhardt stamp issued by the French Post Office, 1945.

Bernhardt, Sarah (Rosine Bernard; 1844–1923), French actress. Illegitimate daughter of Dutch Jewess; baptized 1854 but remained proud of Jewish heritage. One of the greatest interpreters of Racine. Played Edmond Rostand's *L'Aiglon* at 55. International appearances; first theater star to appear in movies. Although leg amputated 1914, continued acting until death.

Bernheim, Hippolyte (1840–1919), French neurologist. Prof. at Nancy Univ. Devoted himself to research on nervous and mental diseases and was among pioneers of hypnosis and suggestion as method of treatment.

Bernheim, Isaac Wolfe (1848–1945), U.S. distiller, philanthropist. Vehemently anti-Zionist. Treasurer of American Jewish Committee 1906–21.

Bernheimer, Carlo (1877–), Italian scholar. Taught Sanskrit at Univ. of Bologna 1906–38. Specialized in Hebrew paleography and bibliography.

Bernheimer, Charles Leopold (1864–1944), U.S. businessman, explorer. Known as "father of commercial arbitration"; helped write

New York State and Federal arbitration laws. Also made expeditions to N. Arizona, Utah, Guatemala, Yucatan, Mexico.

Bernheim Petition, petition against anti-Jewish Nazi legislation, signed by Franz Bernheim, submitted to League of Nations 1933. Successfully focused world attention on anti-Jewish legislation of Nazi Germany and was responsible for equal rights enjoyed by Jews of Upper Silesia until 1937.

Bernstein, Abraham Moshe (1866–1932), *ḥazzan,* composer; b. Minsk. Cantor of Taharas-Kodesh synagogue in Vilna. Compiled folksong, cantorial collections.

Bernstein, Aline (1881–1955), U.S. stage designer. Cofounder Museum of Costume Art, now housed in Metropolitan Museum of Art.

Bernstein, Arnold (1888–), German shipbuilder. His "Floating Garages" at one time carried more than half the uncrated automobiles exported to America. Established Palestine Shipping Co. in New York 1939.

Bernstein, Aron David (1812–1884), German political and scientific writer; a founder of Reform Judaism in Berlin. Wrote stories sentimentalizing small-town ghetto. Founded daily newspaper *Berliner Volkszeitung.*

Bernstein, Eduard (1850–1932), German socialist theoretician; spokesman for group which challenged orthodox Marxist doctrines and urged socialists to become party of reform. Lived in Switzerland and London 1878–1901. Sat in Reichstag before and after WWI.

Bernstein, Harold Joseph (1914–), Canadian physical chemist. On National Research Council of Canada fr. 1946.

Bernstein, Henri-Leon (1876–1953), French playwright. Early plays include *Samson* and *Israël,* which describe tragic results of assimilation. Later plays more concerned with psychological problems. In U.S. during WWII.

Bernstein, Herman (1876–1935), U.S. journalist. One of first to expose *The Protocols of the Elders of Zion.* Founded and edited Yiddish daily *Der Tog* 1914. Initiated legal proceedings against Henry Ford because of anti-Semitic articles appearing in his weekly. U.S. envoy to Albania 1931–33.

Bernstein, Ignatz (1836–1909), Yiddish folklorist, collector of proverbs; industrialist in Cracow. Published catalogue of books and manuscripts of folklore and book of proverbs current among E. European Jews.

Bernstein, Julius (1839–1917), German physiologist, medical educator; laid foundations of neurophysiology; son of Aron Bernstein. Prof. of physiology in Halle 1872.

Leonard Bernstein conducting the Israel Philharmonic Orchestra, 1970.

Bernstein, Leonard (1918–), U.S. composer, conductor. First American-born musician to become music director and conductor of New York Philharmonic (1958–69). Works include *Jeremiah Symphony,* oratorio *Kaddish,* and *Chichester Psalms.* Also wrote music for shows, *West Side Story* being most popular. Closely associated with Israel Philharmonic Orchestra.

Bernstein, Nathan Osipovitch (1836–1891), Russian physiologist, Odessa civic and communal leader. Wrote textbook on physiology. Edited *Zion.*

Bernstein, Peretz (Fritz; 1890–1971), Zionist leader, publicist, Israel politician; b. Germany. Lived in Holland and was president of Dutch Zionist Organization. In Ereẓ Israel fr. 1936. Leader of General Zionists and later of Liberal Party. Member of Jewish Agency Executive, member of Knesset until 1965, and minister of commerce and industry 1948–49, 1952–55.

Bernstein, Philip Sidney (1901–), U.S. rabbi in Rochester. Jewish adviser to U.S. Army commanders in Europe 1946–47; played significant role at time of *beriḥah.*

Bernstein, Sidney Lewis, Lord (1899–), British TV pioneer, publisher. Founded Granada chain of cinemas 1930 and Granada group of TV companies 1954.

Bernstein, Simon (1884–1962), journalist, Hebrew scholar; b. Latvia, settled in U.S., editing Z.O.A. organ *Dos Yiddishe Folk* until 1953. Published editions of Jewish medieval poetry and discovered *piyyutim* by Spanish, Italian, and Byzantine poets.

Bernstein, Zvi Hirsch (1846–1907), publisher; b. Russia, in U.S. fr. 1870. Founded first Yiddish newspaper *(Di Post)* and first Hebrew newspaper *(Ha-Zofeh ba-Arez ha-Ḥadashah)* in U.S.

Bernstein-Cohen, Miriam (1895–), actress; daughter of Jacob Bernstein-Kogan; settled in Ereẓ Israel 1921. Helped organize Teatron Ereẓ-Israeli, which later amalgamated with Habimah. Translated plays and stories.

Bernstein-Kogan (Cohen), Jacob (1859–1929), Russian Zionist leader, physician; b. Kishinev. Administered Zionist information service. Settled in Ereẓ Israel 1925. Founder of Ereẓ Israel Medical Association.

Ber of Bolechow, see Birkenthal, Dov Ber.

Berr (de Turique), Michel (1781–1843), French lawyer; son of Berr Isaac Berr. Advocated Mendelssohnian Enlightenment and fought for civic equalities for Jews. First Jewish lawyer to practice in France. Secretary of Napoleonic Sanhedrin 1807. Translated works fr. Hebrew.

Berr Isaac Berr de Turique (1744–1828), leader in the struggle for Jewish emancipation in France; member of Napoleonic Sanhedrin. Advocated institutional but not religious Reform.

Bershad, town in Ukrainian SSR. Ḥasidic center celebrated for *tallit*-weaving industry in 19th c. Most Jews died in WWII. Jewish pop. 8,000 (1970).

°**Bershadski, Sergey Alexandrovich** (1850–1896), historian of Lithuanian Jewry. Wrote history of Lithuanian Jewry 1388–1569 and Jewish community of Vilna 1593–1649.

Bershadsky (Domashevitzky), Isaiah (1871–1908), Hebrew novelist; b. Belorussia. Worked as teacher. Novels mark the entry of realism into Hebrew fiction, ending tradition of over-moralizing. Considered daring in their time, they were popular among youth.

Isaiah Bershadsky

Yehoshua Bertonoff in the title role of 1943 Habimah production "Tevye the Milkman."

Bersohn, Matthias (1823–1908), Polish art collector, historian. Donated collection of Jewish and Polish art to Warsaw Jewish community; plundered by Germans in WWII. Studied history of art in Poland.

Berson, Arthur Joseph Stanislav (1859–1942), Austrian meteorologist. His pioneering balloon flights at high altitudes were important contributions to study of troposphere and stratosphere.

Bertini, Gary (1927–), Israel composer, conductor; son of K. Aharon Bertini. Founded chamber music and opera ensembles and choirs. Conducted in Europe and Israel and composed in all fields of music.

Bertini, K. Aharon (1903–), poet, editor; b. Bessarabia, settled in Ereẓ Israel 1947. Fr. 1965 edited *Moznayim,* literary magazine of Hebrew Writers' Association.

Bertinoro, Obadiah ben Abraham Yare (c. 1450–before 1516), Italian rabbi, Mishnah commentator. Settled in Jerusalem 1488 and became spiritual leader of community. Wrote standard commentary on Mishnah.

Bertonoff, Yehoshua (1879–1971), Israel actor. Acted with Yiddish and Russian troupes in Russia. Emigrated to Ereẓ Israel 1927. Joined Habimah Theater and became one of its most popular actors. Israel Prize 1959.

Berurei Averah/Averot (Heb. "the elected [to control] sin"), institution found in Jewish communities in Spain fr. 13th c. and in Sephardi Diaspora in 16th–17th c. Officers mainly authorized to deal with religious and moral transgressions.

Beruryah (2nd c.), wife of Rabbi Meir, daughter of R. Hananiah b. Teradyon; only woman in talmudic literature whose views on halakhic matters were seriously considered by contemporary scholars. Also renowned for moral stature and incisiveness.

Besht, see Israel ben Eliezer Ba'al Shem Tov.

Besicovitch, Abram Samoilovitch (1891–), mathematician; of Karaite descent. Left Soviet Union and settled in Cambridge, England, 1926. Fellow of Royal Society 1934. Made important contributions to theories of measure, sets of points, real analysis, etc.

Besredka, Alexander (1870–1940), immunologist. Refusing to convert to Christianity, moved fr. Russia to France. Discovered method of eliminating hypersensitivity to foreign serum. Director of Pasteur Institute.

Bessarabia, province in Moldavian and Ukrainian SSR. Jews traded there in 15th c.; first communities established in 16th c. Included in Pale of Settlement in 19th c. Ḥasidism and Zionism gained many local adherents. Area was focus for anti-Semitism; large-scale emigration in early 20th c. Germans and Rumanians murdered or deported vast majority of 250,000 Jews there in 1941.

Bessis, Albert (1883–), Tunisian politician. Minister of housing and town planning 1954–55 and public works 1955–57. Active in Jewish community.

Bet (ב), second letter of Hebrew alphabet; pronounced *b* with *dagesh, v* without; numerical value 2.

Bet Alfa, place in Israel in E. Jezreel Valley (modern kibbutz); 6th c. synagogue uncovered there with impressive mosaics.

Plan of the Bet Alfa synagogue, showing the elaborate mosaic plan of the nave.

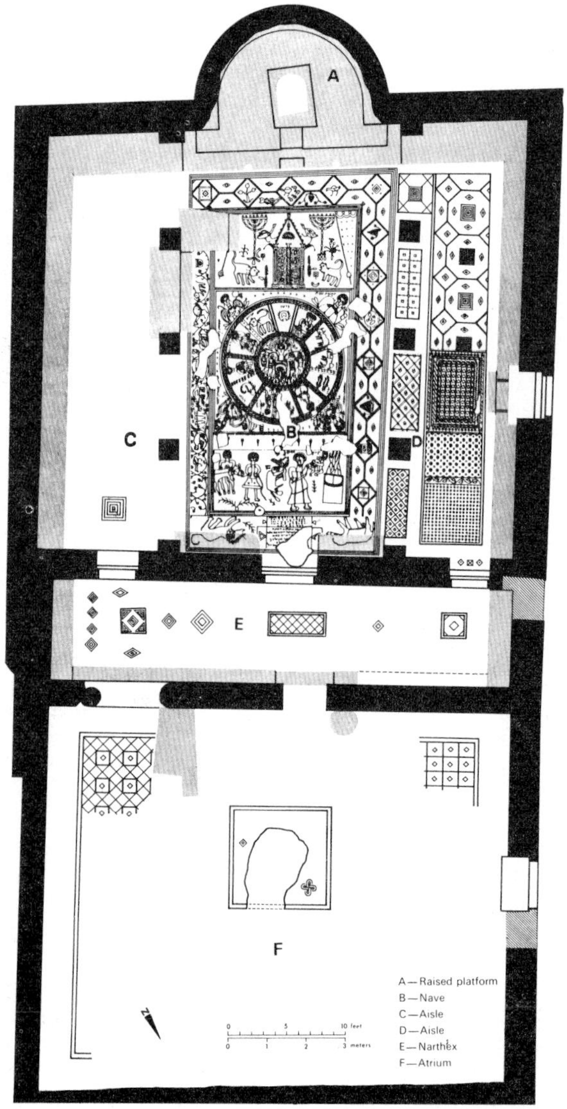

DAVID An illuminated panel of Psalm 144 from the *Rothschild Miscellany*, written and illuminated in Ferrara, c. 1470. It shows King David in a garden, playing his harp and surrounded by animals.

Polish ḥasidic couple, mid-19th cent.

Lithuanian family—father, mother, and (behind) daughter, early 19th cent.

DRESS The "Grand Costume" given to a Jewish bride by her father. Its origin can be traced to the dress worn in 15th-cent. Spain.

Typical filigree necklace worn by Jewish women in Yemen, 19th cent.

Betar, see Bethar.

Betar (abb. of **Berit Trumpeldor**), Zionist youth movement founded 1923 by Union of Zionist Revisionists (fr. 1935, New Zionist Organization). Ideology based on Revisionism. Established settlements in Erez Israel and engaged in "illegal" *aliyah.* Developed Betar Sports Organization. Most European branches destroyed during Holocaust, and Israel became its center with branches in 13 countries. In 1969, 8,000 members.

Bet(h)-Cherem, see Ramat Rachel.

Bet(h)-Dagon, semi-urban community in C. Israel, S. of Tel Aviv; founded 1948 as moshav in abandoned Arab village of Beit Dajan. Site of Israel Institute for Meteorology. Pop. 2,720 (1971).

Bet Din (Heb. "House of Judgment"), term, in rabbinic sources, for Jewish court of law. Minimum number of members three men. Courts of 23 judges generally exercised jurisdiction in criminal matters, while certain juridical and administrative functions were reserved to court of 71 judges. Stronghold of Jewish autonomy in Middle Ages; survived, with reduced powers, into modern times. In Israel it has exclusive jurisdiction over Jewish population in matters of personal status.

Bet Guvrin, prominent Israel city in Second Temple period, located in S. Shephelah. In 200 C.E. Septimus Severus conferred privileges of Roman city and called it Eleutheropolis. It had its own system of dating and coinage. Christian center in Byzantine times. Region abounds in large caves. Modern kibbutz.

Beth. For entries whose first word is 'Beth," see under "Bet."

Bet Ha-Aravah, former kibbutz nr. Dead Sea; founded 1939 and affiliated with Ha-Kibbutz ha-Me'uḥad. Saline soil made fertile by sweeping with fresh Jordan water. Settlement evacuated in 1948 war.

Bet Ha-Levi, see Levi.

Bet Ha-Mikdash, see Temple.

Bethany (Arab. **al-'Azariyya**), Arab village nr. Jerusalem, mentioned in Gospels as site of resurrection of Lazarus (John 11). Churches built there. Under Jordanian rule 1948–67.

Bethar (Betar), Bar Kokhba's last stronghold in his war against Rome (c. 135 C.E.). Identified with Khirbat al-Yahūd, NW of Arab village of Battīr, 7 mi. (11 km.) SW of Jerusalem.

Bethel, Canaanite and Israelite town, N. of Jerusalem. Settlement began in 3rd millennium B.C.E. Main fame derives fr. association with Jacob's dream (Gen. 28:10–22). Canaanite Bethel flourished in 15th–14th c. B.C.E. Destroyed in 13th c., probably by Israelites; with division of monarchy passed into Israel's hands and one of two principal shrines erected by Jeroboam I. Site excavated.

Bet Hillel and Bet Shammai, two schools of exposition of Oral Law, existing from 1st c. B.C.E. to 2nd c. C.E. Their numerous halakhic controversies comprise principal content of Oral Law in last two to three generations of Second Temple period. In most cases Bet Shammai took stricter view. Doctrines of Bet Hillel eventually became accepted in most cases in Jewish law.

Bethlehem, city 5 mi. (8 km.) S. of Jerusalem. Center of tribe of Judah and birthplace of David. On basis of Micah 5:1, early Christians identified it as Jesus' birthplace (e.g., Matt. 2:1, 5); first Church of the Nativity built in 4th c., and one in "Shepherds' Field" soon after. Under Jordanian rule 1948–67. Pop. 14,439 (1967). Focus of Christian pilgrimages.

Bet(h)-Horon, two adjacent biblical towns, Upper and Lower Beth-Horon, identified with sites strategically located on Gibeon-Aijalon road. Joshua pursued Canaanite kings there after battle of Gibeon and Judah Maccabee defeated Seron.

Bethuel, youngest son of Nahor and Milcah (Gen. 22:21–22); father of Laban and Rebekah (e.g. 22:23).

Bethulia, home of heroine of apocryphal Book of Judith. Described as Jewish city besieged by Assyrian general Holofernes. Probably imaginary place.

Bet Jacob Schools, network of religious schools for girls organized in Poland after WWI with the aid of Agudat Israel; later also in Lithuania, Latvia, and Austria. Activities discontinued during WWII. After war schools opened in Israel, Europe, Latin America, and U.S.

Bet Keneset, see Synagogue.

Bet Midrash, see Beit Midrash.

Betrothal (Heb. *shiddukhin*). Precedes marriage in Jewish law, but does not constitute matrimonial relationship and may be broken (in which case the other party may claim compensation).

Bet(h)-Shean (Beisan), historic city in valley of Beth-Shean, mentioned in Egyptian sources fr. 15th to 12th c. B.C.E. During the Hasmonean

A sitting of the Jerusalem "bet din," 1969.

Caves in the Bet Guvrin region

The Grotto of the Nativity, Bethlehem.

The Roman theater at Beth-Shean, c. 200 C.E.

Bas-relief of a "menorah" held by man dressed in Roman legionary's tunic. Wall carving in Bet Shearim catacombs.

Pottery bowl of Early Bronze Age III, typical specimen of red and black burnished "Bet Yeraḥ ware."

Students' show at Bezalel Academy

period important administrative center. In Roman times capital of Decapolis (Scythopolis) and during the mishnaic and talmudic periods had Jewish community. In 5th c. capital of province Palestina Secunda and seat of episcopate. In Mamluk period principal town of district of Damascus. During British Mandate Arab town hostile to Jewish settlement in region. Jewish resettlement began 1949. Pop. 12,100 (1971). Excavations include Roman theater.

Bet She'arim, ancient city in Lower Galilee. Important town in 2nd c. when Judah ha-Nasi took up residence there and made it seat of Sanhedrin. From 3rd c. a central burial place for Jews of Ereẓ Israel and the Diaspora. Excavations have uncovered rock-cut catacombs with decorations, epitaphs, etc.

Bet(h)-Shemesh, ancient Israel city in Shephelah. Samson narrative took place in vicinity. Excavations revealed that city first established 3rd millennium B.C.E., and site inhabited until end of First Temple period. Permanent urban settlement started 1951. Pop. 10,600 (1971), with industrial plants.

Bettan, Israel (1889–1957), Reform rabbi, scholar; b. Kovno, in U.S. fr. 1907. Rabbi in Charleston 1912–22, prof. at Hebrew Union College fr. 1922. Wrote studies on midrashic literature, liturgy, responsa, and Reform Judaism.

Bettelheim, Bruno (1903–), U.S. psychologist, educator; b. Vienna, sent to concentration camp, in U.S. fr. 1939. Known for pioneering techniques in treatment of emotionally disturbed children. Books include *Dynamics of Prejudice* and *The Children of the Dream,* an analysis of kibbutz childrearing.

Bettelheim, Samuel (1872–1942), early Zionist and Mizrachi leader in Hungary, then Czechoslovakia. Later joined Agudat Israel, taking extreme anti-Zionist stand.

Bet Yeraḥ, large Canaanite city on shore of Sea of Galilee. Earliest settlement fr. late Chalcolithic–early Bronze Age, reaching zenith in 26th–24th c. B.C.E. Now site of agricultural secondary school and Oholo study center.

Bet(h) Zur, ancient city in Israel, N. of Hebron. Fr. time of Nehemiah served as defense post against Idumeans. Played important role in Hasmonean wars.

Beur, see Biur.

Beyth, Hans (1901–1947), Youth Aliyah leader; b. Germany, settled in Ereẓ Israel 1935. Worked as Henrietta Szold's assistant in Youth Aliyah. Active in establishing Youth Aliyah institutions. Killed by Arabs.

Beẓah (Heb. "egg"), Mishnah tractate in order *Mo'ed,* with *gemara* in Babylonian and Jerusalem Talmuds. Deals with laws of festivals. Also called *Yom Tov* ("festival").

Bezalel, expert in metalwork, stonecutting, and woodcarving; head of artisans who constructed Tabernacle and its equipment (Ex. 31:1–11; 36–39).

Bezalel, academy of arts and design in Jerusalem, founded 1906 by Boris Schatz as school of arts and crafts with museum. Became "New Bezalel" 1935, separate fr. museum. Became Academy 1969, with museum now part of the Israel Museum.

Bezem, Naphtali (1924–), Israel painter, draftsman. Instructor of painting for immigrants in Cyprus detention camps 1947. Figurative artist strongly influenced by Italian neorealism.

Bezidul Nou, village in Transylvania. Important center of Sabbatarians fr. 17th c. During Holocaust some Sabbatarians granted exemption from racial laws, others deported to Auschwitz. Survivors began to emigrate to Israel 1960. Five families remained in village in 1969.

Béziers, city in France. Jewish settlement fr. 10th c.; by 12th c. community renowned for learning as "the little Jerusalem." Jews expelled 1394, did not return until 1943. Jewish pop. 400 (1968), mainly of N. African origin.

Bialeh, Ẓevi Hirsch ben Naphtali Herz (1670–1748). German rabbi, *rosh yeshivah* in Halberstadt. Renowned for acumen; a number of outstanding rabbis were his pupils. Wrote responsa, novellae, commentaries.

Bialik, Ḥayyim Naḥman (1873–1934), greatest modern Hebrew poet; essayist, storywriter, translator, editor; b. Volhynia, moved to Zhitomir. Engaged for a time in the

Ḥayyim Naḥman Bialik.

timber trade. First poem "To a Bird" expressed Zionist longings. Fr. 1900 lived in Odessa, working as teacher and/or literary editor of *Ha-Shilo'aḥ*. "City of Slaughter" expressed anger at Kishinev pogrom and helped inspire Jewish self-defense. Moved to Berlin 1921, Tel Aviv 1924. Literary editor of several periodicals, founder of two publishing houses, compiler of selection of aggadic lore, and editor of medieval Hebrew poetry. Wrote folk songs and children's songs. Many of his poems set to music. Translated *Don Quixote* and *Wilhelm Tell*. Regarded as poet of national renaissance and deeply influenced Hebrew literature and development of the language.

Bialoblocki, Samuel Sheraga (1888–1960), talmudic scholar; studied at Lithuanian yeshivot, taught in Germany, settled in Ereẓ Israel 1934. Taught at Mizrachi Teachers' College; prof. and head of Talmud dept. at Bar-Ilan Univ. fr. 1955.

Bialystok, city in Poland. Jewish community self-governing 1745, by 19th c. controlled local textile industry. Center of Zionism, Bund, Hebrew education. Severe pogrom 1906. 50,000 Jews herded into ghetto by Nazis 1941. Community liquidated by 1943, despite attempts at resistance.

Bibago, Abraham ben Shem Tov (15th c.), Spanish philosopher, preacher. Headed yeshivah at Saragossa and participated in religious disputation with Christian clergy. Wrote on principles of Judaism *(Derekh Emunah)* and on Creation, as well as commentary on Aristotle.

Bibas, Judah (1780–1852), rabbi in Corfu, precursor of Zionism. Influenced by Judah Alkalai; advocated return of Jews to Zion and proposed military means if necessary. Died in Hebron.

Bible. The Hebrew Bible is composed of 3 parts: 1) *Torah* or Pentateuch (q.v.); 2) *Nevi'im* or Prophets, subdivided into Former and Latter Prophets to differentiate between the narrative, historical works and the literary creations of the prophetic orators; 3) *Ketuvim* or Hagiographa, comprising liturgical poetry, secular poetry, wisdom and historical works. This division represents 3 distinct stages in the process of canonization. The work of finalizing the *Torah* text took place probably in the Babylonian Exile; the Prophets, during the Persian era; and the Hagiographa by 2nd c. C.E. The

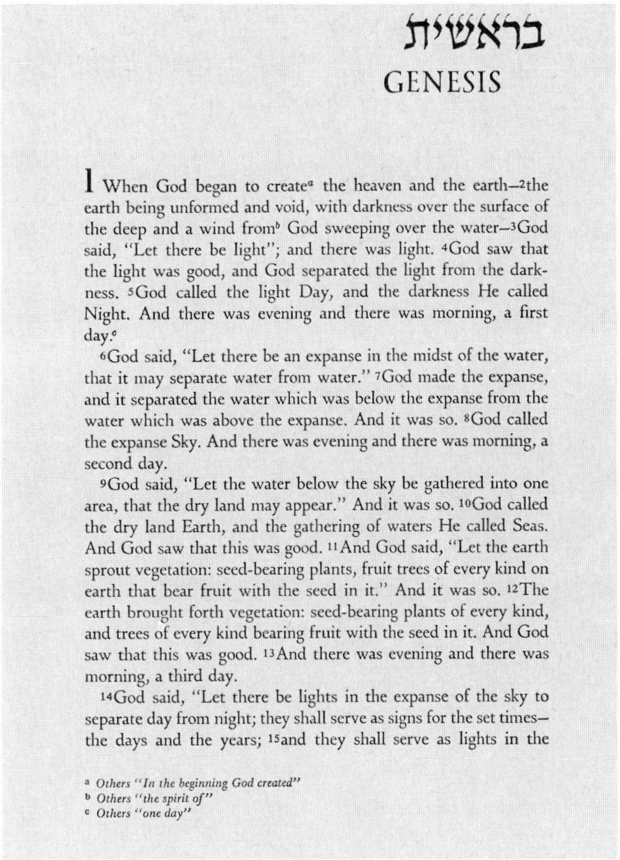

בראשית

GENESIS

1 When God began to create[a] the heaven and the earth—2the earth being unformed and void, with darkness over the surface of the deep and a wind from[b] God sweeping over the water—3God said, "Let there be light"; and there was light. 4God saw that the light was good, and God separated the light from the darkness. 5God called the light Day, and the darkness He called Night. And there was evening and there was morning, a first day.[c]

6God said, "Let there be an expanse in the midst of the water, that it may separate water from water." 7God made the expanse, and it separated the water which was below the expanse from the water which was above the expanse. And it was so. 8God called the expanse Sky. And there was evening and there was morning, a second day.

9God said, "Let the water below the sky be gathered into one area, that the dry land may appear." And it was so. 10God called the dry land Earth, and the gathering of waters He called Seas. And God saw that this was good. 11And God said, "Let the earth sprout vegetation: seed-bearing plants, fruit trees of every kind on earth that bear fruit with the seed in it." And it was so. 12The earth brought forth vegetation: seed-bearing plants of every kind, and trees of every kind bearing fruit with the seed in it. And God saw that this was good. 13And there was evening and there was morning, a third day.

14God said, "Let there be lights in the expanse of the sky to separate day from night; they shall serve as signs for the set times—the days and the years; 15and they shall serve as lights in the

[a] *Others "In the beginning God created"*
[b] *Others "the spirit of"*
[c] *Others "one day"*

First page of Genesis from "The Torah: The Five Books of Moses," new Bible translation by Jewish Publication Society of America, 1962.

Moses in the bullrushes, from a manuscript of Judeo-Persian paraphrase of stories from the Pentateuch, 1686.

BOOKS OF THE BIBLE – PERIODS AND MAIN CONTENTS

		BOOK	CONTENTS	PERIOD	CHAPTERS
THE LAW *TORAH* PENTATEUCH		Genesis	Creation, and patriarchal history until move to Egypt	c. 19th cent. B.C.E.	50
		Exodus	Bondage; Exodus; Revelation and various laws	until 13th cent. B.C.E.	40
		Leviticus	Mainly priestly legislation		27
		Numbers	History of the trek from Egypt to Canaan	13th cent. B.C.E.	36
		Deuteronomy	Legal recapitulation and Moses' ethical testament		34
THE PROPHETS *NEVI'IM*	FORMER PROPHETS	Joshua	Conquest and settlement of Canaan, until death of Joshua	13th cent. B.C.E.	24
		Judges	Invasions repulsed by tribal leaders until the monarchy	13th–11th cent. B.C.E.	21
		I Samuel	The prophet anoints Saul, the first king	11th cent. B.C.E.	31
		II Samuel	Internal and regional strife, and reign of David	10th cent. B.C.E.	24
		I Kings	Reign of Solomon; the Temple; division of the kingdom and early history of Israel and Judah	10th cent. B.C.E.	22
		II Kings	Later history and fall of Israel and Judah	10th–6th cent. B.C.E.	25
	LATTER PROPHETS	Isaiah	Ethics, admonition, and prophecy of ultimate Redemption	8th–6th cent. B.C.E.	66
		Jeremiah	Indictment of sin; fall of Jerusalem foretold and recounted	7th–6th cent. B.C.E.	52
		Ezekiel	Prophecies of Israel's doom; consolation to Babylonian exiles	6th cent. B.C.E.	48
	THE TWELVE PROPHETS	Hosea	Israel's infidelity and future repentance	8th cent. B.C.E.	14
		Joel	Retribution and Israel's restoration at the end of days	date uncertain	4
		Amos	Prophecies against the nations; reproof; visions	8th cent. B.C.E.	9
		Obadiah	Oracle of doom on Edom	date uncertain	1
		Jonah	Message of repentance to Nineveh	date uncertain	4
		Micah	Moral rebukes; vision of the universal reign of peace	8th cent. B.C.E.	7
		Nahum	Prophecy of the downfall of Nineveh	7th cent. B.C.E.	3
		Habakkuk	The problem of injustice; prayer for compassion	7th–6th cent. B.C.E.	3
		Zephaniah	Condemnation of idolatry; vision of restored Zion	7th cent. B.C.E.	3
		Haggai	Encouragement to build Second Temple; its role	6th cent. B.C.E.	2
		Zechariah	Visions of rebuilt Jerusalem and Divine rule of universe	6th cent. B.C.E.	14
		Malachi	Moral exhortations; condemnation of intermarriage	6th–5th cent. B.C.E.	3
THE WRITINGS *KETUVIM* HAGIOGRAPHA		Psalms	Poetic devotional literature		150
		Proverbs	Wisdom literature in the form of short maxims		31
		Job	The problem of evil discussed in narrative form		42
	FIVE SCROLLS *Megillot*	Song of Songs	Love poetry		8
		Ruth	Narrative of period of the Judges		4
		Lamentations	Descriptive dirge of the Babylonian destruction of Jeruslaem		5
		Ecclesiastes	Wisdom literature on worldly vanities		12
		Esther	The Purim story: the salvation of Jews in ancient Persia		10
		Daniel	Episode of martyrdom and eschatological prophecy in Babylonian exile		12
		Ezra	Return of Babylonian exiles and rebuilding of Jerusalem Temple	5th cent. B.C.E.	10
		Nehemiah	Rebuilding of walls of Jerusalem; religious and communal legislation	5th cent. B.C.E.	13
		I Chronicles	Genealogical lists and other historical information to period of David	c. 965 B.C.E.	29
		II Chronicles	History of the monarchy from David to decree of Cyrus	965–538 B.C.E.	36

books are in Hebrew, except for sections of Daniel and Ezra, which are in Aramaic. The modern text comprises 3 distinct components: consonants, vowel symbols, and the liturgical, diacritical notations. The latter 2 were invented by the masoretes (see Masorah). The earliest mss. are those found near the Dead Sea, dating fr. 1st c. B.C.E. The period c. 300 B.C.E. to 1st c. C.E. is characterized by diversity of text-types, though the number of recensions seems to have been limited. The activities of the *soferim* (q.v.) were toward textual unification and stabilization. The existence of a single official text from the period of the destruction of the Second Temple is reflected in halakhic discussion. Some of the early translations reflect textual variations. The main versions are: the Greek Septuagint (q.v.) and other Greek translations, the "Old Latin" and the Vulgate (q.v.), the Syriac Peshitta (q.v.), the Aramaic Targums (q.v.), a group of other Eastern versions (e.g., Coptic, Ethiopic, Aramaic), and the Samaritan Pentateuch. The Bible has been translated more than any other major literary work and appeared in almost all languages and dialects. Christianity spread its knowledge and the Reformation gave a further impetus to its translation. In the modern period, Jewish translators have directed their work to Jewish readers who are not familiar with Hebrew. The main Jewish approaches to biblical exegesis have been: 1) literal *(peshat)* based on the plain meaning of the text and context; 2) homiletical approach *(derash)*, which was also the basis of mystical interpretations. Modern scholarship has developed critical approaches consisting of 1) Literary (or Higher) Criticism, dealing with date, authorship, etc., and 2) Textual (or Lower) Criticism.

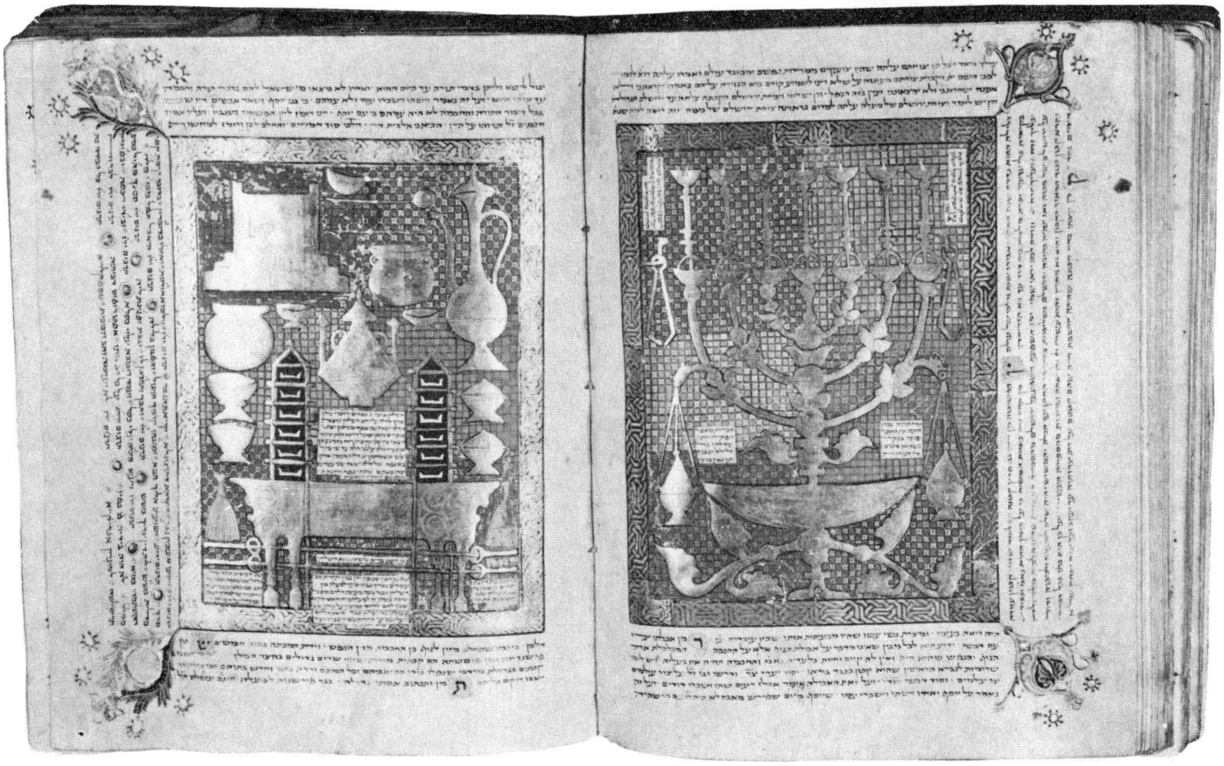

Implements of the Tabernacle, from "Farḥi Bible," 14th-cent. Hispano-Provençal manuscript.

International Bible Contest, Jerusalem, 1969.

Jonah and the whale in Ashkenazi Bible, Germany, c. 1300.

Bick, Jacob Samuel (1772–1831), Hebrew writer; b. Galicia. Pioneer of Haskalah in Galicia, but became devotee of Ḥasidism.

Bickel, Shlomo (1896–1969), Yiddish essayist, literary critic; b. Galicia, went to U.S. 1939, heading YIVO Commission of Research. One of foremost Yiddish literary critics.

Bickerman, Elias Joseph (1897–), historian; b. Russia, taught in Germany, France, and fr. 1946 in several universities in U.S. (prof. Columbia 1952–67). Specialized in Hellenistic period.

Bidney, David (1908–), U.S. anthropologist, philosopher. Prof. at Univ. of Indiana. Studied Descartes, Spinoza. Later turned to anthropology, writing on freedom in framework of diverse cultures.

Bieber, Hugo (1883–1950), German literary historian. Editor of Germany's most important book club. In U.S. fr. 1930s. Wrote history of intellectual and literary movements of 19th c. and works on Heine.

Bieber, Margarete (1879–), archaeological scholar, teacher. Lectured in Germany, Oxford, U.S., specializing in classical and Hellenistic art, notably sculpture.

Biedermann (Freistaedtl), Michael Lazar (1769–1843), Austrian financier, entrepreneur, communal leader. Pioneered modern production methods in Austrian wool industry. Leader in struggle for Jewish emancipation.

Biegeleisen, Henryk (1855–1934), Polish literary historian, ethnographer; grandson of Naḥman Krochmal. Assimilated Jew. Wrote on Polish romantic literature.

Bien, Julius (1826–1909), U.S. lithographer. Printed major geographical and geological publications for U.S. government. Pres. B'nai B'rith 1854–57, 1868–1900 and instrumental in forming its international order.

Bienenstock, Max (1881–1923), writer educator, Zionist leader of labor movement; b. Galicia. Progressive educator and gifted writer in many languages. As a socialist ideologist formed and led Hitaḥadut Party in E. Galicia. Elected to Polish Parliament 1922.

Bienstock, Judah Leib (Leon; 1836–1894), Russian writer, community leader. Secretary of St. Petersburg community. Ḥovevei Zion representative in Ereẓ Israel 1892; helped establish educational and cultural institutions in the country.

Bijur, Nathan (1862–1930), U.S. jurist, communal leader. For many years New York State Supreme Court justice.

Bikayam, Meir ben Ḥalifa (d. 1769), kabbalist, crypto-Shabbatean in Smyrna. Books concerned with Kabbalah and certain *piyyutim* on Redemption, which he expected by 1740.

Bikel, Theodore Meir (1924–), actor, folk singer; b. Vienna, went to Ereẓ Israel and then U.S., where he became popular on stage and screen as well as folk singer. National vice-president, American Jewish Congress.

Bikerman, Jacob Joseph (1898–), U.S. physical chemist; brother of Elias Bickerman. Held academic and industrial positions in USSR, Germany, Britain, before becoming head of Adhesives Laboratory of MIT 1956–64.

Bikkurei Ha-Ittim, Hebrew literary-scientific annual, published in Vienna 1827–32; a central forum for Haskalah literature.

Bikkur Ḥolim, see Sick, Visiting of.

Bikkurim, see First Fruits.

Bikkurim (Heb. "First Fruits"), last tractate of Mishnah in order *Zera'im,* with *gemara* only in Jerusalem Talmud. Deals mainly with laws relating to first-fruit offerings.

Bilbeis, capital of "Eastern Province" of Egypt during Middle Ages. Considered one of most important Jewish communities in Egypt until early 13th c.; had its own customs.

Bildersee, Adele (1883–), U.S. educator, author. Taught English at Hunter College for 20 years; acting dean 1926. Dean of women at Brooklyn College 1931–54. Wrote textbooks for Jewish children.

Biletzki, Israel Ḥayyim (1914–), Yiddish poet, Hebrew essayist; b. Poland, settled in Ereẓ Israel 1934. Critical essays discussed Yiddish masterpieces.

Bilhah, Rachel's servant girl whom she presented to Jacob as concubine. Bore him two children, Dan and Naphtali (Gen. 30:1–8). Reuben, eldest son of Jacob and Leah, cohabited with her while his father was still alive and as a consequence lost his birthright (49:3–4).

Bill-Belotserkovski, Vladimir Naumovich (1885–1966), Soviet-Russian playwright. Among founders of Communist propaganda theater. Also wrote anti-American works.

Billig, Levi (1897–1936), first lecturer in Arabic language and literature at Heb. Univ. 1926. Co-author of standard introduction to classical Arabic. Shot by Arab terrorist.

Billikopf, Jacob (1883–1950), U.S. social worker. Directed campaign to raise $25 million for Jewish war relief in WWI. Executive director of Federation of Jewish Charities in Philadelphia fr. 1919.

Bilqis, see Queen of Sheba.

Biltmore Program, declaration of Zionist policy adopted at conference held 1942 at New York Biltmore Hotel. Called for opening of Ereẓ Israel to Jewish immigration and settlement and establishment of Jewish Commonwealth. Program adopted at insistence of David Ben-Gurion and formed basis for subsequent political struggle that culminated in establishment of State of Israel.

BILTMORE PROGRAM – CONCLUSION

The Conference urges that the gates of Palestine be opened; that the Jewish Agency be vested with control of immigration into Palestine and with the necessary authority for upbuilding the country, including the development of its unoccupied and uncultivated lands; and that Palestine be established as a Jewish Commonwealth integrated in the structure of the new democratic world.

Then and only then will the age-old wrong to the Jewish people be righted.

Stamp of the Bilu organization

Bilu (Heb. initials of *Beit Ya'akov Lekhu ve-Nelkhah,* "House of Jacob, come ye and let us go," Isa. 2:5), group of young Russian Jews who pioneered modern return to Ereẓ Israel; organized 1882 at Kharkov and Moscow in reaction to 1881 pogroms in S. Russia. First group of 13 men and 1 girl reached Jaffa in summer 1882 and was nucleus of First Aliyah.

The "bimah" as a wooden platform on columns, from 14th-cent. Spanish "Sister to the Golden Haggadah."

Bimah (Heb. "elevated place"), platform in synagogue where desk from which Torah is read stands. Also place where *hazzan* conducts service in Sephardi and some Ashkenazi synagogues. Movement of *bimah* from center toward ark in Reform congregations led to heated dispute.

Bimko, Fishel (1890–1965), Yiddish dramatist, novelist; b. Poland, in New York fr. 1921. Wrote novels and plays produced in Yiddish theaters of Europe and America.

Binder, Abraham Wolf (1895–1966), U.S. composer. Taught Jewish music at Stephen Wise Free Synagogue and Hebrew Union College School of Sacred Music 1948. Prolific composer; works include synagogal music and Hebrew and Yiddish songs.

Binding of Isaac, see Akedah.

Bin-Gorion, Micha Josef, see Berdyczewski, Micha Josef.

Binyaminah, village in C. Israel, founded 1922 by Palestine Jewish Colonization Association. Pop. 2,560 (1971).

Biram, Arthur (Yizhak; 1878–1967), Hebrew educator; b. Germany, settled in Erez Israel 1914. Principal of Reali High School in Haifa 1920–48; initiator of paramilitary training program for high school pupils and military academy. Israel Prize 1954.

Biran, Avraham (1909–), Israel archaeologist. Israel consul-general in Los Angeles 1955–58. Director of Department of Antiquities and Museums fr. 1962. Directed excavations of Tell Dan 1966 ff.

Birds' Head Haggadah, manuscript of illustrated Haggadah produced in S. Germany in late 13th c. So named because most human figures are depicted with birds' heads to avoid transgressing biblical prohibition against making images.

Biriyyah, important Jewish town in talmudic period, located in Upper Galilee. At end of 1st c. C.E., regional center and place of learning. In 16th c. many Jews expelled from Spain settled there. Kibbutz founded on top of Mt. Biriyyah 1945. British attempt in 1946 to remove settlers failed in face of opposition of entire *yishuv*. Moshav founded 1949.

Birkat Ha-Hodesh, see New Moon, Announcement of.

Birkat Ha-Kohanim, see Priestly Blessing.

Birkat Ha-Levanah, see Moon, Blessing of the.

Birkat Ha-Mazon, see Grace After Meals.

Birkat Ha-Minim (Heb. "benediction concerning heretics"), 12th benediction of weekday *Amidah*. Invokes divine wrath on "slanderers," etc.; originally directed against Jewish collaborators with the Syrian-Hellenistic oppressors in Second Temple period. Later applied to Sadducees, heretics, apostates. Prayer modified or omitted in several Reform rites.

Birkat Ha-Torah (Heb.), blessing over Law, recited before liturgical readings of Torah and ordinary study. Three such blessings pronounced at beginning of daily morning prayer (see p. 93).

Birkenthal (Brezhover), Dov Ber (Ber of Bolechow; 1723–1805), Hebrew writer, memoirist; b. Austria. Wrote on false Messiah movements in Jewish history. Memoirs (translated into Yiddish and English) contain valuable information for study of 18th c. Jewish history in Galicia.

Birkhot Ha-Shahar, see Morning Benedictions.

Birmingham, city in Ala., U.S. Jewish communal life began 1882. Reform congregation founded 1882, Orthodox 1899, Conservative 1906. Jewish pop. 4,000 (1971).

Birmingham, city in England. Jewish community fr. c. 1730. Attracted relatively small immigration. Jewish pop. 6,300 (1971), lowest percentage of Jews of any great city in England.

Birnbaum, Abraham Baer (1864–1922), Polish cantor, composer. Published liturgical music, set Hebrew poems to music, and published textbooks on music in Hebrew and Yiddish. Organized conference in Warsaw to found the Aguddat ha-Hazzanim ("Cantorial Association").

Birnbaum, Eduard (Asher Anshel, 1855–1920), German cantor. Chief cantor at Koenigsberg. One of early research workers in Jewish music; prepared thematic collection of synagogal melodies.

Birnbaum, Menachem (1893–1944), Austrian portraitist, graphic artist; son of Nathan Birnbaum. Art editor Yiddish monthly *Der Ashmeday;* art editor *Der Schlemiel* 1919. Designed book covers and illustrations. Fled Nazis to Holland. D. Auschwitz.

Birnbaum, Nathan (pen name **Mathias Acher;** 1864–1937), writer, philosopher; b. Vienna. One of originators of Zionist ideology; coined term "Zionism." Close associate of Herzl, but broke with him after First Zionist Congress. Became spokesman of "diaspora nationalism." Later emphasized importance of Yiddish, which became his literary medium. Turned to Orthodoxy after 1912; general-secretary of Agudat Israel World Organization 1919.

Nathan Birnbaum

Birnbaum, Philip (1904–), U.S. author, translator; b. Poland, in U.S. fr. 1923, directing Hebrew schools. Published annotated editions of prayer books which he also translated.

Birnbaum, Solomon Asher (1891–), paleographer, Yiddish philologist; son of Nathan Birnbaum. Lecturer in Hamburg 1922–33, then London Univ., teaching Yiddish and Hebrew paleography. Major works on paleography and Dead Sea Scrolls.

Birnbaum, Uriel (1894–1956), Austrian poet, artist; son of Nathan Birnbaum. Published poems and portfolios of lithographs and paintings. In Netherlands fr. 1938.

Birnboim, Moses Joseph (1789–1831), secret agent of czarist police and blackmailer in Poland. Blackmailed Jews and earned hatred of both Jews and Poles. Eventually arrested by czarist regime and

hanged by Jews during Polish uprising.

Biró (Blau), Lajos (1880–1948), Hungarian author, playwright, settled in England after 1918. Wrote film scripts and founded London Film Co. with Alexander Korda.

Birobidzhan, autonomous region in E. Siberia, USSR. Allocated for Jewish settlement 1928 and Yiddish recognized as official language. Waves of Jewish immigration but most Jews returned to W. Russia. Purges in last years of Stalin aimed at stifling Jewish activity. Cultural activity in decline during 1950s; project to set up Jewish autonomous region abandoned. Jewish pop. c. 11,000 (1973).

Bischoffsheim, Louis (Ludwig) Raphael (1800–1873), banker, philanthropist in Holland, France. Bank with branches in Amsterdam, London, Paris cooperated with great French houses in national and international transactions. His brother **Raphael Jonathan** (1808–1883), a founder of National Bank of Belgium 1850. Advisor to Belgian royal house and senator 1862. Active member of Jewish consistory.

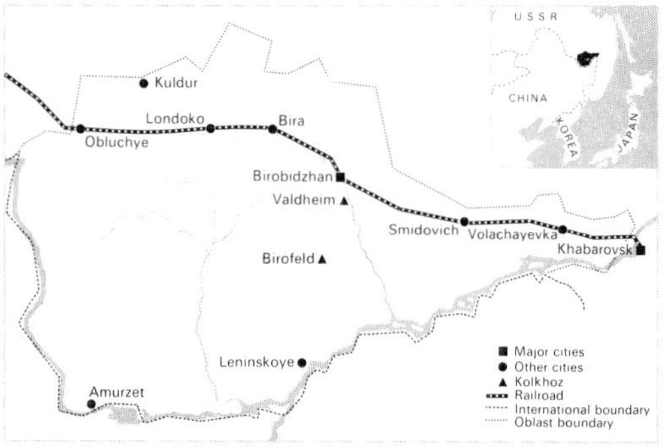

Map of the Birobidzhan region.

Bishop of the Jews, see Episcopus Judaeorum.

Bisliches (Bisseliches), Mordecai (Marcus) Leib (1786–1851), bibliophile, rabbinic scholar; b. Brody. Led unsettled life, traveling extensively in search of rare books and mss. Prepared several rabbinic works for publication.

Bistritski, Nathan, see Agmon, Nathan.

Bithiah, name given by rabbis to daughter of Pharaoh who found infant Moses. Subject of many legends.

Bittelman, Alexander (1890–), U.S. Communist; b. Russia, in U.S. fr. 1912. Became "Jewish specialist" of American Communist Party. Jailed 1955 for three-year term for conspiring to overthrow government. Expelled fr. party for "revisionism" 1958.

Bitter Herb, see Maror.

Bittul Ha-Tamid (Heb. lit. "abolition of the daily offering"), interruption of prayers and Torah reading in synagogue to seek redress of (mainly) judicial or moral wrong. Practice prevalent mainly in Middle Ages among Ashkenazi Jewry; also common in 19th c. Russia.

Black, Max (1909–), U.S. philosopher; b. Russia. Taught at Illinois and Cornell Univ. Works deal with contemporary analytical philosophy. Edited *The Philosophical Review.*

The Black Death. The map shows, in progressive shades of gray, the spread of the plague across Europe in six-month periods from Dec. 31, 1347 to June 30, 1350.

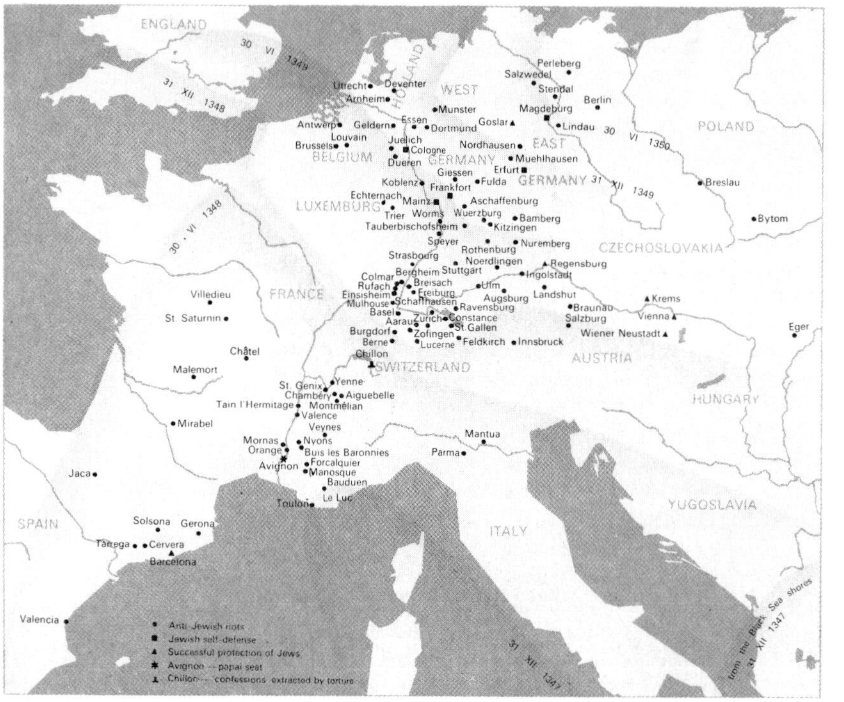

Black, Sir Misha (1910–), British architect, industrial designer. Co-founded Design Research Unit 1944; coordinating architect for 1951 Festival of Britain. Prof. of industrial engineering design at Royal College of Art 1959.

Black Death, epidemic which killed much of European population and led to murderous attacks on Jewish communities, esp. in Germany 1348–9. Jews accused of causing disease by poisoning wells. Although libel condemned by Pope Clement VI, attacks condoned by Emperor Charles. Jews less exposed to plague (because of enforced segregation and dietary laws), but attacks were greatest disaster which befell German Jewry in Middle Ages. Hundreds of communities wiped out.

Black Hundreds, armed bands recruited 1905 by right-wing political movement, Union of the Russian People, against Jews and members of the radical intelligentsia.

Blank, Maurice (1848–1921), Rumanian banker who developed many of country's industries. Marmoresh, Blank and Co. was second largest bank in country.

Blank, Samuel Leib (1893–1962), Hebrew novelist, short-story writer; b. Ukraine, lived in Bessarabia and fr. 1922 in U.S. Stories and novels describe Jewish farmers in Bessarabia, pogroms in Ukraine, and life of Jewish immigrants in America.

Blank, Sheldon Haas (1896–), U.S. rabbi, Bible scholar. Taught at Heb. Union College, Cincinnati. Wrote on many aspects of biblical scholarship.

Blankfort, Michael S. (1907–), U.S. novelist. Works include *The Juggler* with Israel setting and *Behold the Fire,* based on exploits of Nili.

Blankstein, Cecil N. (1908–), Canadian architect. Major projects include National Art Gallery building in Ottawa and Winnipeg City Hall.

Blaser, Isaac (1837–1907), Russian rabbi, educator. Leading exponent of Musar movement, opposition to which forced him to leave several communities. Wrote standard work on movement's teaching and several halakhic works. Settled in Jerusalem 1904.

Blau, Amram (1894–), rabbi; leader of ultra-Orthodox Neturei Karta sect. Native of Jerusalem;

refused to recognize "Zionist" State of Israel.

Blau, Bruno (1881–1954), German lawyer, sociologist. Confined to Berlin Jewish Hospital in WWII. Published works on German-Jewish history, Jewish statistics, and anti-Jewish Nazi legislation.

Blau, Herbert (1926–), U.S. theater director. Cofounded Actors' Workshop in San Francisco; directed Lincoln Center Repertory Theater in N.Y.

Blau, Joseph Leon (1909–), U.S. educator, historian of ideas. Prof. of religion at Columbia. In philosophy followed Dewey and in Jewish history emphasized interdisciplinary and cross-cultural influences. Wrote book on Jewish philosophy and religion.

Blau, Joshua (1919–), Israel Arabist; b. Rumania. Prof. at Heb. Univ. 1962. Authority on Judeo-Arabic and Christian-Arabic dialects.

Blau, Ludwig Lajos (1861–1936), Hungarian scholar. Directed Jewish Theological Seminary of Budapest fr. 1914. Wrote on many aspects of Jewish learning; among first to use Greek papyri for evaluation of talmudic law.

Blau, Moshe (1885–1946), Agudat Israel leader; brother of Amram Blau; b. Jerusalem. Directed Agudat Israel office there fr. 1924; cooperated with *yishuv* leaders in representing Jewish interests in dealing with Mandate government.

Jacob Blaustein

Blaustein, family of U.S. industrialists. **Louis** (1869–1937), b. Russia, in U.S. fr. 1888. Founded American Oil Company 1910 and introduced new methods of gasoline distribution. His son **Jacob** (1892–1970) succeeded his father in business, held executive positions in companies in fields of petroleum, insurance, and banking. Chairman 1944–49 and president 1949–54 of American Jewish Committee, and member of U.S. delegation to 10th UN General Assembly.

Blaustein, David (1866–1912), educator, communal worker; b. Russia, in U.S. fr. 1886. Rabbi of Providence Reform congregation 1892–96. Superintendent Educational Alliance of New York City fr. 1898.

Blau-Weiss ("Blue-White"), first Jewish youth movement in Germany, founded 1912. Initiated Zionist program, introduced new forms of celebrating Jewish holidays outdoors and interest in Hebrew language and songs and Yiddish folklore. 3,000 members in early 1920s. Also existed in Austria and Czechoslovakia.

Blazko, Martin (1920–), Argentine sculptor; b. Germany. Based work on relationship between plastic form and structure. A founder of Madi group.

Blech, Leo (1871–1958), German opera conductor, composer. Conducted Berlin State Opera 1926–37 and after 1949. Fled to Sweden 1941 and became conductor of Stockholm Royal Opera.

Blecher, Marcel (1909–1938), Rumanian author. His novel *Scarred Souls* is account of life in sanatorium. Early exponent of surrealism in Rumanian literature.

Bleichroeder, Samuel (1779–1855), German banker, founder of firm of same name which became member of Rothschild and the Preussen consortiums. His son **Gerson von** (1822–1893) developed it into one of leading German financial houses. Financial adviser and private banker to Bismarck. Ennobled 1872.

Blejer, David (1913–), Argentine lawyer, politician. Undersecretary in two ministries, ambassador to Mexico.

Blessing of the Torah, see Birkat ha-Torah.

Blessings, see Benedictions.

Blindman, Yeruḥam (c. 1798–1891), Russian cantor, composer. Cantor in Kishinev, Tarnopol, Berdichev. Attracted large crowds with choir and performed throughout Russia and Austria.

Bliokh (Bloch), Ivan Stanislavovich (1836–1901), Russian financier, pacifist. Played leading role in construction and management of Russian railroads. His 6-vol. work on futility of war influenced Nicholas II to convene 1899 Hague Peace Conference. Convert to Calvinism but wrote monumental defense of Jewish rights.

Blitzstein, Marc (1905–1964), U.S. composer. Developed genre of operas of "social significance." Composed *The Cradle Will Rock* and *The Airborne.*

Bloc, André (1896–1966), French sculptor, engineer. Helped to found "Espace" group 1951 and created "habitacles" and "constructions," forms between sculpture and architecture.

Bloch, family of U.S. book publishers. **Edward** (1816–1881) set up Bloch Publishing Co. in Cincinnati 1854. His son **Charles** (1861–1940) established branch in Chicago 1885 and moved company to New York 1901. Charles' son **Edward** (1885–) expanded activities.

Bloch, Camille (1865–1949), French historian, archivist, librarian. Prof. at Sorbonne and authority on French Revolution. After 1945 supervised for French government recovery of books looted by Germans.

BLESSINGS FOR THE READING OF THE TORAH

Before the Reading:
Those who are called to the Reading say the following Blessing:-

בָּרְכוּ אֶת־יְיָ הַמְבֹרָךְ׃	Bless ye the Lord who is to be blessed.

Congregation

בָּרוּךְ יְיָ הַמְבֹרָךְ לְעוֹלָם וָעֶד׃	Blessed be the Lord, who is to be blessed, for ever and ever.

The Response is repeated and the Blessing continued:-

בָּרוּךְ אַתָּה יְיָ אֱלֹהֵינוּ מֶלֶךְ הָעוֹלָם. אֲשֶׁר בָּחַר־בָּנוּ מִכָּל־הָעַמִּים וְנָתַן־לָנוּ אֶת־תּוֹרָתוֹ. בָּרוּךְ אַתָּה יְיָ, נוֹתֵן הַתּוֹרָה׃	Blessed art thou, O Lord our God, King of the universe, who hast chosen us from all peoples, and hast given us thy Torah. Blessed art thou, O Lord, Giver of the Torah.

After the Reading, the following Blessing is said:-

בָּרוּךְ אַתָּה יְיָ אֱלֹהֵינוּ מֶלֶךְ הָעוֹלָם, אֲשֶׁר נָתַן־לָנוּ תּוֹרַת אֱמֶת. וְחַיֵּי עוֹלָם נָטַע בְּתוֹכֵנוּ. בָּרוּךְ אַתָּה יְיָ, נוֹתֵן הַתּוֹרָה׃	Blessed art Thou, O Lord Our God, King of the universe, who hast given us the Torah of truth, and hast planted everlasting life in our midst. Blessed art thou, O Lord, Giver of the Torah.

Bloch, Claude (1878–1967), U.S. admiral. Commanded battleship *California* 1927. Commander in chief of U.S. Fleet 1938; retired 1942.

Bloch, Darius Paul, see Dassault, Darius Paul.

Bloch, Elijah Meyer (c. 1894–1955), Lithuanian rabbi. Taught at Telz Yeshivah, becoming dean when it moved to Cleveland 1941. Played leading role in Agudat Israel in America.

Bloch, Ernest (1880–1959), composer; b. Switzerland; won international acclaim in Europe and America, where he worked in 1920s and settled (in Oregon) in 1941. Consciousness of "Hebrew" heritage reflected in many works, incl. *Avodath Hakodesh* for Sabbath morning and *Schelomo* for cello and orchestra. Also wrote opera *Macbeth,* violin concerto, chamber music, etc.

Bloch, Ernst (1885–), German philosopher. Enlightened, active Marxist humanist; thought culminated in progressive-creative principle of hope. Prof. in Leipzig 1949–60. Fled to W. Germany and appointed prof. at Tuebingen.

Bloch, Felix (1905–), U.S. physicist; b. Zurich, in U.S. fr. 1934. Taught at Stanford Univ. First to determine magnetic moment of neutron. Nobel Prize for Physics 1952.

Felix Bloch

Bloch, Ḥayyim Isaac ben Ḥanokh Zundel Ha-Kohen (1864–1948), rabbi, scholar. Rabbi of Bausk, Lithuania. In U.S. fr. 1922. Rabbi in Jersey City. Hon. Pres. Union of Orthodox Rabbis of U.S.

Bloch, Hyman Morris (1905–1963), S. African Supreme Court judge. Also prominent Zionist.

Bloch, Ivan, see Bliokh, Ivan.

Bloch, Iwan (1872–1922), German dermatologist, medical historian. One of first to engage in scientific study of sex and leader in movement for sexual reform.

Bloch, Jean-Richard (1884–1947), French author, political journalist. Jewish themes played significant part in his writings. Active communist; in Moscow during WWII.

Bloch, Joseph Leib (1860–1930), Lithuanian rabbi. Under his leadership Telz Yeshivah became center of Musar movement. Also founded auxiliary teachers' seminary and preparatory school. A leader of Agudat Israel.

Bloch, Joseph Samuel (1850–1923), rabbi, publicist, politician in Austria. Gained distinction for defense of Judaism against blood libel 1883 and first parliamentarian to make Jewish affairs his main political concern. Founded weekly for combatting anti-Semitism 1884. His early support for Zionism did not last.

Bloch, Joshua (1890–1957), U.S. librarian, bibliographer, Reform rabbi; b. Lithuania, in U.S. fr. 1907. Head of Jewish Division of the N.Y. Public Library 1923–56. Published researches on Hebrew printing and other studies.

Konrad Bloch

Bloch, Konrad (1912–), U.S. biochemist; b. Germany, in U.S. fr. 1936. Prof. of biochemistry at Chicago and Harvard. Awarded Nobel Prize for Physiology and Medicine 1964 for discoveries of mechanism of cholesterol and fatty acid metabolism.

Bloch, Marc (1886–1944), French historian, Resistance leader. Specialist in French medieval agrarian history and feudalism. Executed by Gestapo.

Bloch, Marcel, see Dassault, Marcel.

Bloch, Marcus (Mordecai) Eliezer (1723–1799), German physician, zoologist. Main achievement morphological and systematic work on fish.

Bloch, Mattathias ben Benjamin Ze'ev (Wolf) Ashkenazi (1610/1620–after 1668), Polish preacher; a leader of Shabbatean movement in Egypt. As rabbi in Mosul, influence also spread to Kurdistan.

Bloch, Moses (1815–1909), Hungarian rabbi, author. Prof. of Talmud and Codes and rector at Budapest rabbinical seminary. Published 7-vol. work on development of *takkanot.*

Bloch, Philipp (1841–1923), German historian, Reform rabbi. Wrote on Jewish philosophy, history, Kabbalah.

Bloch, Pierre (1905–), French Socialist politician, writer, Resistance leader. Leading figure in French Socialist Party. Pres. International League Against Anti-Semitism.

Bloch, Rene (1923–), French naval officer, aeronautical engineer. Technical director of aviation in French navy 1952–61. Director of aeronautics for international affairs in French Ministry of Defense.

Bloch, Samson (Simson) Ha-Levi (1784–1845), early Hebrew Haskalah author in Galicia. His *Shevilei Olam* first general geography in Hebrew.

Block, Herbert Lawrence ("Herblock"; 1909–), U.S. newspaper cartoonist. Twice won Pulitzer Prize. Published collections in book form.

Bloemfontein, capital of Orange Free State, S. Africa. Jewish congregation formed 1876, synagogue built 1903. Jews active in municipal affairs. Jewish pop. 1,347 (1967).

Blois, town in France. Scene of first ritual murder accusation in France 1171, with entire community of 31 men burned at stake.

Blondes, David, Jewish barber, victim of blood libel in Vilna 1900. Eventually acquitted. Case deeply stirred Russian Jewry.

Blondheim, David Simon (1884–1934), U.S. Romance scholar. Prof. at Johns Hopkins Univ. fr. 1924. Published studies in Judeo-Romance dialects, incl. Rashi's French glosses.

Blood-Avenger, person in biblical times authorized or duty-bound to kill murderer. Rights progressively restricted in Jewish Law.

Herblock cartoon during the Six-Day War, June 1967. "Israel is winning—NOW we must DO something!"

15th-cent. German woodcut showing Jews extracting blood from Simon of Trent, subject of Italian blood libel, 1475.

Blood Libel, allegation that Jews murder non-Jews, esp. Christians, in order to obtain blood for Passover or other rituals. Led to many trials and massacres of Jews in Middle Ages and early Moslem times. Tiszaeszlar (1881) and Beilis trial (1911) among most notorious accusations. Revived by Nazis.

NOTED BLOOD LIBELS

Year	Place	Country	
1144	Norwich	England	Canonization of "martyr child": first recorded blood libel in Europe
1171	Blois	France	31 persons (the entire community) burned at the stake; first continental blood libel
1179	Boppard	Germany	13 Jews murdered
1233	Fulda	Germany	31 Jews burned
1255	Lincoln	England	Canonization of "martyr child"; 18 Jews executed
1285	Munich	Germany	180 Jews burned to death
1470	Endingen	Germany	2 Jews burned at the stake; Jews expelled
1475	Trent	Italy	Canonization of "martyr child"; 9 Jews died
1490–91	La-Guardia	Spain	Canonization of "martyr child"; 2 Jews and 2 conversos burned at the stake
1494	Trnava (Tyrnau)	Slovakia	16 Jews died
1747	Izyaslav (Zaslavl)	Volhynia	5 Jews put to death
1823	Velizh	Russia	Investigations and trial continued from 1826 to 1835
1840	Damascus	Ottoman Empire	Worldwide protests
1853	Saratov	Russia	Renewal of blood libel throughout Russia
1882	Tiszaeszlar	Hungary	Notorious trial
1891	Corfu (Island)	Greece	Led to large-scale emigration
1892	Xanten	Germany	Ruin of the Jewish community
1899	Polna	Bohemia	Hilsner case, notorious trial
1900	Konitz	Germany	Anti-Jewish riots
1900	Vilna	Russia	David Blondes case
1911–13	Kiev	Russia	Beilis case evoked worldwide reaction

Bloom, Claire (1931–), British actress. Active on both stage and screen, Britain and U.S. Appeared in Charlie Chaplin's *Limelight.*

Bloom, Sol (1870–1949), U.S. businessman, politician. Democratic congressman 1923–49, Chairman House Foreign Affairs Committee, and delegate 1945 San Francisco Conference.

Bloomfield, Leonard (1887–1949), U.S. linguist. Wrote on general philology and languages of N. American Indian tribes. His *Language* highly influential in development of American descriptive linguistics.

Bloomfield, Maurice (1855–1928), U.S. expert in Sanskrit. Prof. at Johns Hopkins Univ. Major works *A Vedic Concordance* and *Vedic Variants.*

Bloomgarden, Yehoash Solomon, see Yehoash.

Bloomingdale, U.S. family. **Lyman Gustavus** (1841–1905) and brother **Joseph Bernhardt** (1842–1904) founded Bloomingdale Bros. Department Store 1886. Other members of family active in general and Jewish philanthropy. **Alfred S.** (1916–), founder and chairman Diners Club credit organization.

Blowitz, Henri Georges Stephane Adolphe Opper de (1825–1903), French journalist. As chief Paris correspondent of London *Times,* originated technique of interviewing celebrities. Influential in European political circles. Converted to Christianity.

Léon Blum

Henri de Blowitz

Blum, Eliezer (1896–1963), Yiddish poet, short-story writer; b. Poland, in U.S. fr. 1914. Joined introspective movement of Yiddish literature and coedited its organ *In-Zikh.*

Blum, Jerome (1913–), U.S. historian. Prof. at Princeton 1961. Did research on agrarian structures and society in C. and E. Europe.

Blum, Julius (Blum Pasha; 1843–1919), Austro-Hungarian banker, Egyptian statesman. As undersecretary of finance 1877–90, helped rehabilitate Egyptian finances.

Blum, Léon (1872–1950), first Jewish premier of France, writer, literary critic, journalist. Among founders of modern French Socialist Party. Led Popular Front government 1936–37 and was architect of Socialist International between world wars. Interned during WWII. Member of the enlarged Jewish Agency in 1929. Led "caretaker" government 1946. Brilliant literary and dramatic critic.

Blum, Ludwig (1891–), Israel painter. Jerusalem portraits, landscapes, and still lifes executed in dry and naturalistic manner.

Blum, René (1878–1944), French ballet impressario; brother of Leon Blum. Director of Ballet de l'Opéra de Monte Carlo 1929–40. Refused to leave Paris in 1940 and d. in Auschwitz.

Blume, Peter (1906–), U.S. painter. In 1930s produced murals under auspices of WPA (Federal Arts Projects). Style was "magic realism" with fierce element of social criticism.

Blumenfeld, Hermann Faddeyevich (1861–1920), Russian civil lawyer. Banned from Bar under czarist government. Member of supreme court in Kerensky's regime (1917).

Blumenfeld, Kurt Yehuda (1884–1963), German Zionist leader. Pres. of German Zionist Federation 1923–33. Settled in Ereẓ Israel 1933. A founder and director of Keren Hayesod. Developed concept of "post-assimilation" Zionism, i.e. Zionist ideology designed to appeal to assimilated Jews.

Blumenfeld, Ralph David (1864–1948), British journalist. As editor of *Daily Express* 1904–32, raised paper's circulation to 2 million.

Blumenfeld, Walter (1882–1967), German psychologist. Prof. at Dresden, then Lima, Peru. Invented "Blumenfeld alloys," apparatus to measure perceptual relationship between size and distance.

Blumenfield, Samuel (1901–1972), U.S. educator. Superintendent of Chicago Board of Jewish Education until 1954; dean and later president of College of Jewish Studies there; director of Jewish Agency's (American Section) Dept. of Education 1954–68.

Blumenkranz, Bernhard (1913–), French historian. Wrote on Jewish-Christian relations in Middle Ages and history of medieval French Jewry.

Blumenthal, George (1858–1941), U.S. banker, philanthropist; in U.S. fr. 1882. After WWI, played important part in stabilizing franc. Donated large sums to Mount Sinai Hospital and Metropolitan Museum of Art; became president of both.

Blumenthal, Joseph (1834–1901), U.S. businessman. Commissioner of taxes and assessment in New York City. A founder of Jewish Theological Seminary and pres. of its Board of Trustees 1886–1901.

Blumenthal, Nissan (1805–1903), Russian cantor. Founded choir school in Odessa. His liturgical melodies effected synthesis of traditional tunes and new German classical influences.

Blumenthal, Oskar (1852–1917), German playwright. Plays attacked social foibles and some became internationally successful (the musical comedy *White Horse Inn)*.

Blumenthal, Werner Michael (1926–), U.S. economist; b. Germany, in U.S. fr. 1947. Chairman U.S. delegation to Kennedy Round of tariff negotiations 1963–67.

B'nai B'rith (Heb. "Sons of the Covenant"), world's oldest and largest Jewish service organization, with lodges and chapters in 45 countries; founded in New York 1843. Its objectives are moral, social, philanthropic, and educational. B'nai B'rith Women founded 1897; Anti-Defamation League (ADL), which protects status and rights of Jews and strengthens interreligious connections, 1913; B'nai B'rith Hillel Foundation, which serves on-campus requirements of Jewish students, 1923; B'nai B'rith Youth Organization (BBYO), incl. AZA for boys, BB girls, and BB young adults, 1924. B'nai B'rith in Jerusalem founded 1888. 500,000 members in 1970 throughout world.

Board of Delegates of American Israelites, first national organization of Jewish congregations in U.S.; founded 1859 in reaction to Mortara Case. Merged with Union of American Hebrew Congregations 1878.

Board of Deputies of British Jews, representative organization of British Jewry; founded 1760. Membership 400, representing synagogues and other communal organizations, elected triennially; plenary meetings held monthly. Board works through committees representing specific interests.

Boas, Franz (1858–1942), U.S. anthropologist; b. Germany, in U.S. fr. 1887. Prof. of anthropology at Columbia Univ. fr. 1899. Restructured anthropology into modern science. Stressed influence of environmental factors of human cultural life in modifying anatomy and physiology.

Boas, Frederick Samuel (1862–1957), English literary scholar. Specialized in Shakespearean and Elizabethan studies. His son, **Guy** (1896–1972), humorist; contributor to *Punch*.

Boas, George (1891–), U.S. philosopher; major figure in history of ideas movement in America. Prof. at Johns Hopkins Univ. 1924–57. Wrote on aesthetics, history of thought, French philosophy.

Boas, Isaac Herbert (1878–1955), Australian timber technologist. Perfected method for utilizing vast eucalyptus reserves for industry. Pres. Royal Australian Chemical Institute.

Boaz, great-grandfather of King David. Wealthy, land-owning Bethlehemite. Married Ruth (Ruth 2:4).

Boaz, see Jachin and Boaz.

Bobe-Mayse, Yiddish expression for fantastic or incredible tale.

B'nai B'rith national executive with President Taft (center) at the White House, 1910

Board of Deputies of British Jews, 1968

Bobrovy Kut, Jewish agricultural settlement in Ukrainian SSR. Established 1807 with private funds; numbered 2,000 settlers 1926. Underwent many changes under Soviet regime. Destroyed during Nazi occupation when almost all settlers perished.

Bobruisk, city in Belorussian SSR. Jewish settlement fr. 17th c. Community increased considerably with growth of lumbering trade in 19th c. Declined after WWI. In WWII Germans sent 20,000 Jews to death. Jewish pop. 30,000 (1970).

Bobtelsky, Mordekhai (Max; 1890–1965), Israel inorganic chemist, pioneer of heterometry; b. Vladislavov, Lithuania. Chief chemist of Palestine Potash Ltd. 1925. Prof. of inorganic and analytical chem. at Heb. Univ.

Bodansky, Oscar (1901–), U.S. biochemist. Director of medical research in U.S. Army Medical Corps in WWII. Prof. at Cornell Medical College, vice-president of Sloan-Kettering Institute for Cancer Research 1966.

Bodenheim, Maxwell (1893–1954), U.S. poet, novelist. His novels of New York's seamy side endeared him to radical circles. Last days in poverty and was murdered.

Bodenheimer, Frederick Simon (1897–1959), Israel zoologist; son of Max Bodenheimer; b. Cologne, settled in Ereẓ Israel 1922. Specialized in agricultural entomology.

Bodenheimer, Max Isidor (1865–1940), Zionist leader. Founded with David Wolffsohn Ḥibbat Zion society in Cologne and one of Herzl's first assistants. Helped formulate Basle Program. Accompanied Herzl to Ereẓ Israel 1898, put statutes of Jewish National Fund into final form and served as its director 1907–14. Settled in Jerusalem 1935.

°**Bodenschatz, Johann Christoph Georg** (1717–1797), German Protestant theologian. In his writings described contemporary Jewish customs in Germany and included many engravings of Jewish life in Germany.

Bodian, David (1910–), U.S. anatomist. Specialized in structure and function of microscopic neurology. Member of U.S. National Academy of Sciences.

Bodo (9th c.), French churchman (deacon) who became proselyte to Judaism. In Córdoba he attempted to persuade caliph to compel Christian subjects to convert to Judaism or Islam.

Max Bodenheimer

Frontispiece of Johann Bodenschatz' "Kirchliche Verfassung der heutigen Juden," 1748–49.

Ludwig Boerne, oil portrait by Moritz Oppenheim.

Bohemian glass "kiddush" cup, 19th cent.

Boehm, Adolf (1873–1941), Zionist historian; lived in Vienna. Wrote 2-vol. history of Zionist movement. Believed to have died in Nazi extermination center in Poland.

Boerne, Ludwig (1786–1837), German political essayist; champion of Jewish emancipation. Famed for satirical articles written in Frankfort and Paris; maintained that freedom of all mankind is bound up with freedom for Jews. Converted to Lutheranism 1818 to gain entry to wider public activity.

Boethusians, religious and political sect in century preceding destruction of Second Temple. In theological views closely resembled Sadducees, although they did not share their aristocratic background and supported Herodians rather than Hasmonean dynasty. Regarded by Talmud as cynical and materialistic priests.

Bogen, Boris David (1869–1929), U.S. social worker; b. Moscow, in U.S. fr. 1890s. Superintendent United Jewish Charities in Cincinnati 1904 and field secretary Conference of Jewish Charities fr. 1913. Directed international relief for Joint in WWI. Wrote *Jewish Philanthropy.*

Boger (Bograshov), Ḥayyim (1876–1963), educator, leader in Ereẓ Israel; b. Crimea, settled in Ereẓ Israel 1906. Headmaster of Herzlia Gymnasium in Tel Aviv fr. 1919. Leading figure in affairs of Tel Aviv and General Zionist member of 2nd Knesset.

Bogoraz, Vladimir Germanovich (1865–1936), Russian ethnographer, revolutionary, man of letters. Converted to Christianity 1885. Participated in N. Pacific exploration and became expert on Siberia. Imprisoned for part in 1905 revolution. Prof. at Leningrad Univ. after 1917.

Bogotá, capital of Colombia. Although Jews probably among first settlers, community did not grow until mid-20th c. Jewish pop. 7,500 (1971).

Bogrov (Beharav), Dmitri (1888–1911), Russian terrorist and revolutionary who was executed for shooting the czarist prime minister Stolypin.

Bohemia, former kingdom, now part of Czechoslovakia. Jews settled before recorded Bohemian history. Originally moneylenders, they suffered from various devastations in 11th, 12th, 15th c., from expulsion in 16th c. from all cities other than Prague, and from the Familiants Law regulating number of Jewish citizens

Niels Bohr

Memorial plaque to Jews of Bologna sent to extermination camps during WWII.

Magen David Synagogue in Byculla Bombay, founded 1861.

STATE OF ISRAEL BONDS

Name	Date of Issue	Date of Maturity after Purchase	Bonds Sold (millions of dollars)	Rate of Interest	Amount of Bonds Authorized (millions of dollars)
Independence Issue	1951–54	15 years	145	3½%	500
Development Bonds Issue No. 1	1954–59	15 years	234	a.b.[1]	350
Development Bonds Issue No. 2	1959–64	15 years	294	a.b.	300
Development Bonds Issue No. 3	1964–67	15 years	393	a.b.	400
Development Bonds Issue No. 4	1967–71	15 years	475	4%	500
Development Bonds Issue No. 5	1971–74	15 years	595	4%	750
Development Investment Bonds No. 1	1966–68	20 years	72	4¾%	100
Development Investment Bonds No. 2	1968–71	20 years	151	5½%	200
Development Investment Bonds No. 3	1971–73	20 years	224	5½%	250
Development Investment Bonds No. 4	1973	20 years	120	5½%	350

[1] a $100–$10,000 (capital appreciation bonds) at 160%
b $500–$100,000 (coupon bonds) at 4% in semi annual sums

in 18th c. Increasing toleration and rising Czech and German nationalism and economic opportunities in 19th c. gave rise to cultural assimilation and splits. In early 20th c. emigration, intermarriage and growing anti-Semitism led to decline. After 1918, see Czechoslovakia.

Bohr, Niels Henrik David (1885–1962), Danish physicist; son of Jewish mother. Revolutionized conceptions of structure of atom. Awarded Nobel Prize 1922. Escaped Nazis 1943 by fleeing to Sweden in fishing boat.

Bokanowski, Maurice (1879–1928), French politician. Minister of navy 1924, commerce and industry 1926–27. Killed in air accident.

Bokhara, see Bukhara.

Bokser, Ben Zion (1907–), U.S. Conservative rabbi, scholar. Rabbi Forest Hills Jewish Center fr. 1933. For many years editor of Jewish Theological Seminary's "Eternal Light" radio program. Wrote popular and scholarly books and translated prayer books.

Bolaffi, Michele (1768–1842), Italian musician, composer. Some of his religious music still sung in Florence synagogue. Also wrote secular music and worked in England, Germany, France.

Bolaffio, Leone (1848–1940), Italian jurist. Helped revive study of commercial law in Italy and wrote standard works in this field. Established Italian Society for the Study of Stenography.

Bolivia, S. American republic. Spanish Marranos settled in 16th c. and European Jews arrived 1905, but substantial immigration only took place in late 1930s, when many refugees arrived fr. Germany. Most established themselves in commerce and industry, chiefly in La Paz and Cochabamba. Comité Central Judío de Bolivia is representative roof organization. Jewish pop. 2,000 (1971).

Bologna, city in Italy. Jewish settlement before 12th c. Center for loan bankers in 14th c.; important in 15th, 16th c., maintaining two Hebrew printing presses. Jews expelled 1569, 1593; community reestablished in 17th c. Suffered during WWII. Jewish pop. 270 (1970).

Bombay, port in India. Marranos in 16th c. and English merchants in 17th c. first Jews to establish contact with city; succeeded by Bene Israel in 18th c. and Jewish merchants fr. Syria, Mesopotamia in 19th c. Jewish pop. 11,000 (1971), with strong emigration movement to Israel.

°**Bomberg, Daniel** (16th c.), one of first and most prominent of Christian printers of Hebrew books. Established printing house in Venice and published nearly 200 Hebrew books, incl. first complete editions of two Talmuds (1520–23), Tosefta, rabbinic Bible, etc. Pagination of his editions of Talmud has become standard.

Bomberg, David (1890–1957), British painter. Painted in several countries but died in poverty in Spain. Work included Jewish themes.

Bonafed (Bonfed), Solomon ben Reuben (14th–15th c.), Spanish poet, philosopher. His forte was satiric verse and he mocked several aspects of contemporary religious practice. Participated in Disputation of Tortosa 1413–14.

Bonaventura, Enzo Joseph (1891–1948), psychologist; b. Florence, Italy, settled in Jerusalem 1938. Prof. at Heb. Univ. Killed in Arab ambush 1948. His approach to psychology combined classical and modern schools of thought.

Bondi (Bondy), August (1833–1907), U.S. abolitionist, early Jewish settler in Kansas; b. Vienna; brought to U.S. after failure of 1848 revolution. Joined John Brown's forces 1855. Served in Union Army.

Bondi, Sir Hermann (1919–), British mathematician; b. Vienna, in England fr. 1937. Director-general of European Space Research Organization 1967, chief scientist to Ministry of Defense 1970. Wrote on cosmology.

Bondi, Jonas (1804–1874), editor; b. Germany, in U.S. fr. 1858. Established 1860 N.Y. Jewish periodical *The Hebrew Leader,* which he edited until his death.

Bonds, State of Israel, Israel government stock floated in various countries for purpose of raising capital for economic development of Israel. Israel Bond Organization inaugurated 1951 when Premier Ben-Gurion invited group of U.S. Jewish leaders to Jerusalem. Organization sold $2,100 million in bonds up to Dec. 1972, of which $900 million had been redeemed.

Bondy, Bohumil (Gottlieb; 1832–1907), Czech politician, industrialist. First Jew elected to any function on Czech nationalist ticket, serving as president of Prague Chamber of Commerce 1884. Published on history of Bohemian Jewry.

Bône (Bona), port in Algeria. Jewish community in Roman period. Jews taken into captivity 1153. Settlement in 13th c. Jewish nomads,

called *bahuzim* (q.v.), lived in mountains nr. city. 3,150 Jews in 1941; left in 1962 and none remained.

Bonfils (Tov Elem), Immanuel ben Jacob (14th c.), French mathematician, astronomer. Known for astronomical tables written in Hebrew. One of first to discuss decimal fractions.

Bonfils (Tov Elem), Joseph ben Samuel (11th c.), leading French rabbinic scholar, poet. Major decisions frequently quoted. Influential in establishing authoritative versions of texts. Wrote *piyyutim.*

Bonn, town in Germany. Community predates 11th c., early celebrated as center of Jewish learning. Jews engaged in moneylending and some were Court Jews. Gate of ghetto publicly torn down 1794 and Jews granted equal rights. In Nazi period community of c. 1,500 ended through emigration and destruction. Refounded community numbered 155 (1967).

The Bonn Synagogue, built 1878, destroyed 1938.

Bonn, Moritz Julius (1873–1965), German economist. Member of German delegation to Versailles peace negotiations and subsequently adviser to German chancellor on reparations. Taught in Austria, England and U.S. after 1933.

Bonné, Alfred Abraham (1899–1959), Israel economist; b. Germany, settled in Erez Israel 1925. Published studies on economy of Erez Israel, State of Israel, and Middle East. Prof. at the Heb. Univ.

Book of Creation, see Yezirah, Sefer.

Book of Jashar, lost source of early Israelite poetry from which were derived Joshua's command to sun and moon (Josh. 10:12–13) and David's lament for Saul and Jonathan (II Sam. 1:19–27).

Book of Life, heavenly book in which names of righteous are inscribed, mentioned once in Bible (Ps. 69:29). An aspect of High Holidays liturgy.

Book of the Covenant, designation for legal, moral, and cultic corpus of literature found in Exod. 20:22–23:33. Modern scholars give it very early date, fr. pre-monarchical period.

Book of the Wars of the Lord, lost book mentioned once in Bible (Num. 21:14) which contained anthology of poems describing victories of the Lord over Israel's enemies.

Books of the Chronicles of the Kings of Judah and Israel, two sets of royal annals, mentioned in I and II Kings, but subsequently lost. The historian of Kings refers to them as his source, where additional information on royal activities may be found.

Boorstin, Daniel J. (1914–), U.S. historian. Taught at Univ. of Chicago fr. 1944 (prof. fr. 1956). Joined Smithsonian Institution, Washington, 1969. Wrote on American history.

Booths, Feast of, see Sukkot.

Bor, Josef (1906–), Czech novelist. Wrote on experiences in concentration camps in *The Terezin Requiem.*

Boraisha, Menahem (1888–1949), Yiddish poet, essayist; b. Poland, in U.S. fr. 1914. Wrote for Yiddish newspaper. A prolific writer, his poems are emotional and his *Der Geyer* is a spiritual autobiography.

Borchardt, Georg, see Hermann, Georg.

Borchardt, Lucy (1878–1969), German shipping owner and operator. Helped Jews escape from Germany fr. 1933. Formed companies in England and Israel.

Borchardt, Ludwig (1863–1938), Egyptologist, archaeologist; b. Germany. Founder and director of German Institute for Ancient Egyptian History and Archaeology in Cairo 1906–14, 1923–29. Main interest ancient Egyptian architecture, also identification of Atlantis.

°**Borchsenius, Poul** (1897–), Danish pastor, author. In WWII in underground and escaped to Sweden. Became ardent Zionist and wrote history of Jews and books about Israel.

Bordeaux, port in France. Jewish settlement fr. 6th c. Under English rule 1154–1453, community enjoyed conditions superior to those of others in France. Large numbers of Marranos attracted by commercial opportunities settled in town in 16th–18th c. Freedom of worship granted 1706 and civil rights 1790. Community dwindled in 19th c. Final station for many Jewish refugees in 1940. Large-scale immigration from N. Africa after WWII. Jewish pop. 6,400 (1971).

Borge, Victor (**Borge Rosenbaum;** 1909–), Danish-U.S. pianist, comedian. Fled Denmark upon Nazi occupation 1940. Best known for one-man shows.

Borislav, city in Ukrainian SSR. Jews pioneered oil industry. Over 13,000 Jews in 1939, liquidated under Germans. Jewish pop. 3,000 (1970).

Born, Max (1882–1970), German physicist. Worked on quantum theory and use of matrix computations. Although dissociating himself fr. Jewish community, dismissed fr. Goettingen 1933 because of Jewish origin. Settled in U.K. Awarded Nobel Prize 1954.

Bornfriend, Jacob (**Jakub Bauernfreund;** 1904–). Slovak painter. Early work veered fr. impressionism and cubism to surrealism. Escaped to England 1939.

Bornstein, Eli (1922–), Canadian artist. Headed art dept. at Univ. of Saskatchewan. Headed structurist school which created pure geometric abstract form of art.

Bornstein, Hayyim Yehiel (1845–1928), Polish authority on Jewish calendar. Based theories on documents in Cairo Genizah. Translated several classics of world literature into Hebrew.

Borochov, Ber (**Dov;** 1881–1917), theoretician of Socialist Zionism; a founder and leader of Po'alei Zion; b. Ukraine. Joined Russian Social-Democratic Party and active in organizing Jewish self-defense in Po'alei Zion Party in Russia. Participated in founding World Union of Po'alei Zion 1907, went to U.S., returned to Russia 1917. Advanced theory of Jewish socialism, and provided Marxist basis for Zionism. Contributed to research into Yiddish language and literature.

Borodin (Gruzenberg), Michael Markovitsch (1884–1951), Russian communist politician. Adviser to Sun Yat-sen 1923–27 and later editor-in-chief of Soviet Information Bureau. Victim of Stalinist terror.

Borsook, Henry (1897–), U.S. biochemist. Prof. of biochemistry at California Institute of Technology fr. 1935. Research on nutrition, vitamins.

Boscovitch, Alexander Uriyah (1907–1964), Israel composer; b. Rumania, settled in Erez Israel 1938. Among pioneers of Israel music, attempting to achieve synthesis of Oriental and Western forms. Music critic of *Haaretz.*

Boskovice (Boskowitz), Czech town. Jewish settlement fr. 11th c. Jews segregated in special quarter 1727.

Center of Jewish learning. 395 Jews in 1930; community wiped out in WWII.

Boston, city in Mass., U.S. First congregation Ohabei Shalom, established 1842. In early 1940s anti-Semitism led to formation of Jewish Community Council of Metropolitan Boston. Boston's Federation of Jewish Charities was one of first of its kind in U.S. (1895). Early stronghold of Zionist movement. Jewish pop. 180,000 (1971), with 75 congregations. Site of Hebrew Teachers' College; Brandeis Univ.

Botarel, Moses ben Isaac (14th–15th c.), Spanish scholar, pseudo-Messiah. Wrote books and pamphlets in every branch of Torah, *halakhah,* Kabbalah, and philosophy, often containing spurious quotations and fabrications.

Boton, Abraham ben Moses di (1545? –1588), rabbi, halakhist in Salonika. Wrote commentary on Maimonides' *Mishneh Torah* and responsa.

Boton, Meir ben Abraham di (c. 1575–1649), Turkish rabbi, halakhist; son of Abraham b. Moses di Boton. His yeshivah at Gallipoli became center of study.

Botosani, town in Rumania. Community fr. 17th c. became second largest in Moldavia. Disrupted by internal disputes in late 14th c. and not reorganized until after WWI. 10,900 Jews in 1940. Most put on forced labor. Most of 19,550 Jews (1947) went to Israel. 500 families remained in 1969.

Botoshansky, Jacob (1892–1964), Yiddish novelist, journalist, critic; b. Bessarabia. Edited Yiddish periodical *Likht.* Settled in Buenos Aires 1926, playing dominant role in Jewish cultural life. Editor of daily *Di Presse.* Wrote dramas, travel sketches, essays.

Botvinnik, Mikhail (1911–), Soviet chess master. World champion 1947–57, 1958–60, 1961–63. Also achieved distinction as electrical engineer.

Bougie, town in Algeria. Jews settled in 13th and 14th c. After Spanish conquest (1510), Jewish property pillaged and many Jews sold as slaves. With arrival of French (1833) Jews left town. Thereafter never more than 800 Jews there; none remained by late 1960s.

Bove-Bukh, Yiddish adaptation of Anglo-French romance of 14th c. about Prince Bova. Composed in ottava rima by Elijah Baḥur Levita.

Bovshover, Joseph (1873–1915), Yiddish poet; b. Belorussia, in U.S. fr. 1891. Poetry influenced by radical Yiddish poets and Bible. Published essays on American poets and thinkers.

Ark of the Law in Mishkan Tefilla synagogue, Boston.

John Braham, drawing by Robert Dighton.

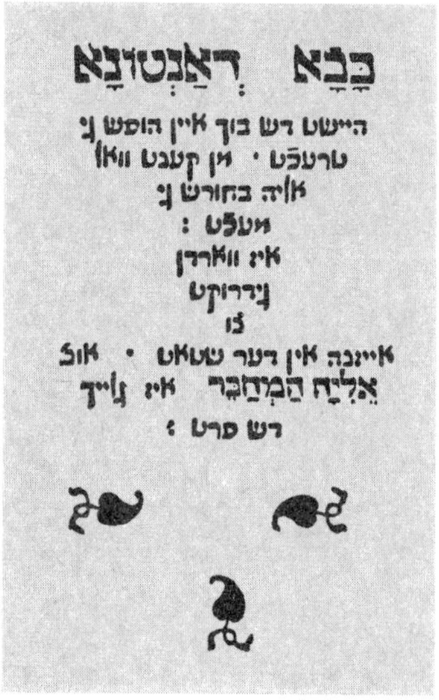

בבא דאנטונא
הייסט דש בוך אין הופש ג
טרעכט · מן קענט וואל
אויז בחורש ג
מעכט :
אין וואררן
גידרוקט
צו
אייזנה אין דער שטאט · אוב
אליה המחבר אויז גייד
דש פרט :

Title page of the Yiddish version of Buovo d'Antona (Bove-Bukh), 1541.

Reuben Brainin, etching by Hermann Struck.

Boyar, Louis H. (1898–), U.S. real estate developer, philanthropist in Los Angeles. Pioneer of large-scale home building and community planning after WWI. A leader of Israel Bonds Organization, Inc.

Bozecco (Bozecchi), Benjamin ben Judah (1290–1335), Italian grammarian, biblical exegete. Exegesis based on literal meaning; considered pioneer of this method among Italian Bible commentators.

Bozrah, city in Bashan. Capital of province of Arabia after 129 C.E. Jews there in Roman and Byzantine periods. In Arab times, capital of Hauran. Today a village in Jordan.

Brafman, Jacob (c. 1825–1879), Russian apostate, anti-Semitic author. Joined Greek Orthodox Church and taught Hebrew at government theological seminary at Minsk. Served as censor of Hebrew and Yiddish books in Vilna and St. Petersburg. Translated minutes of Minsk community into Russian with anti-Jewish objective.

°**Bragadini,** noble Venetian family, printers of Hebrew books 1550–1710.

Braham, John (1774 or 1777–1856), English singer. Tenor with wide vocal range. Composed and sang some of most popular songs of period.

Brahinsky, Mani-Leib, see Mani-Leib.

Brahm, Otto (1856–1912), German stage director, drama critic. Influential champion of Ibsen and new naturalist school.

Brainin, Reuben (1862–1939), Hebrew, Yiddish author, critic; b. Belorussia, lived in Vienna fr. 1892 and in U.S. fr. 1909. Wrote on Hebrew literature in context of world literature; introduced biography into Hebrew literature.

Brampton (Brandon, Brandão), Edward (c. 1440–1508), Anglo-Portugese adventurer. Baptized in England 1468. Rose to high office in England and Portugal (governor of Guernsey 1482).

Bramson, Leon (Leonty; 1869–1941), Russian communal worker, writer. Director of Jewish Colonization Assn. 1899–1906, elected to Duma 1906. Left Russia 1920 and worked for Ort in W. Europe.

Brand, Joel Jenö (1906–1964), Hungarian communal representative. As member of Budapest Jewish relief committee 1944, met Adolf Eichmann, who proposed exchange of Hungarian Jewry for various equipment, mainly trucks. Went to Turkey and Ereẓ Israel, but imprisoned by British. Later devoted himself to tracking down Nazi war criminals.

Brandâo, Ambrósio Fernandes (c. 1560–c. 1630), Portuguese author, soldier in Brazil. Distinguished officer; denounced to Inquisition but managed to retain freedom. Wrote history of Brazil claiming that Brazilian Indians descended fr. children of Israel.

Brandeis, Louis Dembitz (1856–1941), U.S. lawyer, jurist, Zionist leader; first Jew appointed to U.S. Supreme Court (1916). As lawyer, known in Boston as "People's Attorney." Voted to sustain such measures as minimum wage laws, price control laws, and legislation protecting trade unions against injunctions in labor disputes. As Zionist, served as chairman of Provisional Committee for General Zionist Affairs during WWI. His close relations with President Wilson secured support for Balfour Declaration and British Mandate in U.S. Resigned 1921 over controversy with Weizmann over methods concerning economic development of Jewish settlement in Ereẓ Israel. However, subsequently inspired organization of Palestine Cooperative Company, which became Palestine Economic Corporation.

Louis D. Brandeis, bust by Eleanor Pratt.

Brandeis University, first nonsectarian Jewish-sponsored liberal arts institution in America; in Waltham, Mass. Founded by group of Jewish communal leaders. 2,800 students in 1970.

Brandenburg, province in Germany. Jewish settlement in 13th c. Many communities annihilated in Black Death 1349–50. Favor later shown to Court Jews in 16th c. gave rise to riots. Immigrants from Poland increased Jewish pop. in 19th c.

Brandes (Cohen), Carl Edvard (1847–1931), Danish author, playwright, politician; brother of Georg Brandes. Finance minister 1909–10, 1913–20. Authority on Oriental languages and wrote on modern Danish and world drama.

Georg Brandes

Brandes, Georg (Morris Cohen; 1842–1927), Danish literary critic, writer. Influential in Scandinavian and European literature. First to recognize Nietzsche. Wrote books on great figures (Shakespeare, Goethe, Voltaire, Julius Caesar, Michelangelo).

Brandon, Oheb (Oeb) Isaac (c. 1830–1902), Dutch *ḥazzan* in Sephardi congregations, Amsterdam, 1861–1902. Guide to melodies used on various occasions.

Brandstaedter, Mordecai David (1844–1928), Galician Hebrew writer. In his stories ridiculed ḥasidim and their ẓaddikim and exposed foolishness of so-called "enlightened" Galician Jews and their materialism.

Brandstaetter, Roman (1906–), Polish poet, playwright; grandson of Mordecai David Brandstaedter. Edited Zionist periodicals and attacked anti-Semitism. In WWII in Ereẓ Israel. Returned to Poland 1948 and converted to Catholicism.

Brandt, Boris (Baruch; 1860–1907), Russian Zionist, economist. One of few Jewish senior officials in czarist government administration. Active Zionist and member of Benei Moshe.

Brandwein, Yehuda Ẓevi (1903–1969), kabbalistic author in Israel. Disciple of kabbalist Yehudah Ashlag, whose commentary on Zohar he completed. Published complete works of Isaac Luria (14 vols.). Active in Histadrut and known as "the rabbi of the Histadrut."

Brandys, Kazimierz (1916–), Polish author. After WWII a leading figure in Polish intellectual life. Wrote mainly novels.

Brann, Marcus (1849–1920), German-Jewish historian. Succeeded Graetz at Breslau Rabbinical Seminary. Published many historical works and was the first to use Jewish and general archives systematically.

Braslavi (Braslavski), Joseph (1896–1972), Israel geographer; b. Ukraine, settled in Ereẓ Israel 1906. Wrote extensively on geography of the country.

Bratislava (Pressburg), capital of Slovakia; one of most ancient and important Jewish centers in Danube region. Jewish contact probably fr. Roman times. Community grew and prospered between 13th c. and expulsion of 1526. Famed as center of learning and orthodoxy in 18th c. and center of Jewish national institutions and activities in Czech republic. Only fraction of community of 15,000 survived Holocaust. Community reestablished after war, Jewish pop. 1,500 (1969).

Braude, Markus (Mordekhai Ze'ev; 1869–1949), rabbi, educator, Zionist leader. Leader of Zionist Organization in Galicia, preacher in Lodz 1909–39, member of Polish senate 1920–26. Founded network of Jewish educational institutes. In Ereẓ Israel fr. 1940.

Braude, Max A. (1913–), U.S. rabbi, organization executive. Chaplain in WWII. Director-general international office of ORT in Geneva.

Braude, William Gordon (1907–), U.S. Reform rabbi, scholar. Rabbi in Providence, R.I. Translated (with critical notes) *Midrash on Psalms* and *Peskita Rabbati.*

Braudes, Reuben Asher (1851–1902), Hebrew novelist, advocate of social and religious reform; b. Vilna. Lived in various cities and in 1896 moved to Vienna and became editor of Yiddish edition of Zionist weekly *Die Welt.*

Braudo, Alexander Isayevich (1864–1924), Russian-Jewish historian, civic leader. Librarian of Im-

perial Public Library, St. Petersburg. Fought for social equality and freedom for Russian Jews.

Braun, Adolf (1862–1929), German socialist leader. Active in Social Democratic Party for over 40 years and sat in Reichstag. Wrote on economic, social, and trade union issues.

Brauner, Victor (1903–1966), Rumanian surrealist painter. Fr. 1930 in France, where he elaborated a complex private world of symbolism and mythology.

Braunschweig, see Brunswick.

Braunstein, Menahem Mendel (pen name **Mibashan;** 1858–1944), Hebrew writer; b. Rumania. Leading figure in Zionist movement there. Settled in Ereẓ Israel 1914. One of last modern Hebrew authors to use purely biblical style. Translated European literature into Hebrew.

Braunthal, Julius (1891–1972), Austrian journalist, historian, socialist leader. Fr. 1934 in London, where he wrote and edited socialist organs. Wrote on socialism and edited anthologies of socialist writings.

"Acolo" by Victor Brauner

Map showing the main areas of Jewish settlement in Brazil.

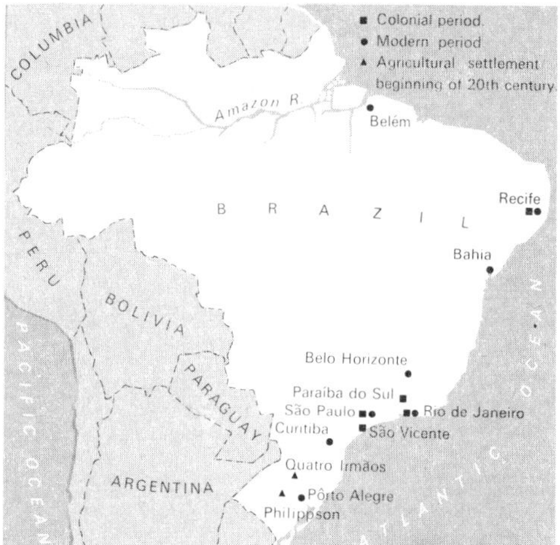

Brawer, Abraham Jacob (1884–), Israel geographer; b. Ukraine; settled in Ereẓ Israel 1911. Taught at teachers' seminaries in Jerusalem until 1949. Wrote first modern regional geography of Ereẓ Israel.

Brazen Serpent, see Copper Serpent.

Brazil, S. American Republic. Marranos among pioneers in 16th c. and fostered country's first industries. Jewish community flourished during Dutch rule (1631–54) in Recife (Pernambuco), but on Portuguese reconquest fled to W. Indies and back to Europe. Large-scale immigration only after WWI. Augmented by German refugees after 1933 and industrial magnates after WWII. Jewish pop. 150,000 (1971). Most merchants, manufacturers, professionals, concentrated mainly in Rio de Janeiro and São Paulo.

Breastplate, metal shield in front of mantle of Torah scroll in Ashkenazi communities.

Bregman, Sidney (1922–), Canadian architect. Executive architect for Toronto-Dominion Center and many public projects.

Breidenbach, Wolf (1751–1829), court agent of several German princes and champion of Jewish emancipation in Germany. Owing to his efforts "body tax" abolished in several towns.

Brenner, Joseph Ḥayyim (1881–1921), Hebrew writer; lived in Poland, went to London 1904. Edited *Ha-Meorer.* Fr. 1909 in Ereẓ Israel. Lived in Jaffa and was killed during Arab riots of 1921. Exercised great influence as novelist, short-story writer, critic, philosopher, translator, editor and publisher. Disciple of "psychology" approach to literature and writer of "uprooted" generation. Connected with Jewish labor movement.

Joseph Ḥayyim Brenner

Brenner, Victor (1871–1924), U.S. medalist; b. Lithuania, in U.S. fr. 1890. One of country's foremost medalists. Modeled Lincoln one-cent piece.

Brentano, family of U.S. booksellers. **August** (1831–1886), founded firm of Brentanos 1858, largest book-selling firm in the world, which was carried on by other members of the family.

Breslau (Wroclaw), city in Silesia. Jewish settlement fr. 12th c. After successive expulsion in 14th, 15th c., community reestablished in 17th c. and prospered after Silesia annexed to Prussia 1741. Held key position in modernist movement in 19th c. and was center of intellectual life in Germany until 1933. Its rabbinical seminary, founded 1854, perpetuated "historical" Judaism. Its pre-Nazi community of c. 20,000 destroyed during Holocaust. Polish Jews re-established the community after war, and in 1960 it numbered 1,200 families. Most emigrated to Israel after 1967.

Breslau, Aryeh Loeb ben Hayyim (1741–1809), rabbi, author; b. Breslau. Rabbi of Rotterdam 1781–1809. Famed as profound talmudist, his responsa, halakhic rulings, and expositions are distinguished for their pure Hebrew style and independence of thought.

Breslaw, Joseph (1887–1957), U.S. labor leader; b. Russia, in U.S. fr.

Breastplates for hanging on Torah scroll: (l.) silver and enamel, executed by Ludwig Wolpert, 20th cent.; (r.) Galician silver gilt set with semiprecious stones, c. 1780.

1907. Vice-president of International Ladies' Garment Workers' Union fr. 1922, leading Union's right wing in struggle against communists.

Bresselau, Meyer Israel (d. 1839), Hebrew writer, leader of Reform movement. Edited prayer book for Hamburg Reform Temple and published polemic works against Orthodox rabbis.

Bresslau, Harry (1848–1926), German historian. Member of editorial board of *Monumenta Germaniae Historica.* A founder and president of commission for history of Jews in Germany.

Bressler, David Maurice (1879–1942), U.S. social worker. Manager of Industrial Removal Office 1900–16, then joined American Jewish Joint Distribution Committee.

Brest-Litovsk (Brisk), capital of Belorussian SSR; a center of Lithuanian Jewry fr. 14th–17th c. Community played considerable role in Council of Four Lands. After Chmielnicki massacres 1648–9, communal life slowly reconstructed and town was home of important scholars in 18th and 19th c. Stronghold of *Mitnaggedim.* Community suffered expulsion and devastation during WWI. Pop. 60,000 in 1914, 30,000 in 1939. Vast majority destroyed in the Holocaust. 2,000 Jews in 1970.

Bretholz, Berthold (1862–1936), Moravian historian. Baptized when young. Official historian of Moravia. Ascribed descent of Bohemian and Moravian Germans to Teutonic tribes. Later turned to Jewish history in Moravia.

Breuer, Isaac (1883–1946), leader of German Orthodoxy. A spokesman for Agudat Israel. Settled in Jerusalem 1936 and became president of Po'alei Agudat Israel. Writings posited Agudism as preparation of Torah nation for renaissance in its ancestral home.

Breuer, Joseph (1842–1925), Austrian neurophysiologist and precursor of psychoanalysis. His early collaboration with Freud *(Studien ueber Hysterie)* was short-lived.

Breuer, Joseph (1882–), Orthodox rabbi; son of Solomon Breuer; b. Hungary. Headed yeshivah in Frankfort. In U.S. fr. 1939. Head of K'hal Adath Jeshurun and its yeshivah in Washington Heights, N.Y. Published biblical translations and commentaries.

Breuer, Raphael (1881–1932), German Orthodox rabbi; son of Solomon Breuer. Published German translations and commentaries of sections of Bible. Also wrote anti-Zionist polemics.

Breuer, Solomon (1850–1926), rabbi, author; leader of German Orthodoxy. Founded Association of Orthodox Rabbis in Germany 1888 and was cofounder of Agudat Israel movement. Writings include sermons and works in *halakhah* and *aggadah.* Married daughter of S.R. Hirsch.

Breyer, Julius (Gyula; 1893–1921), Hungarian chess master. Theorist of "Hyper-Modern" school.

Brice (Borach), Fanny (1891–1951), U.S. actress, singer; leading comedienne of stage, screen, radio. Appeared in annual productions of *Ziegfeld Follies* 1910–24. Broadway musical *Funny Girl* (1963) based on her life.

Brick, Daniel (1903–), Swedish journalist. General secretary of Zionist Organization in Sweden 1935–49.

Brickner, Barnett Robert (1892–1958), U.S. Reform rabbi. Fr. 1925 at Cleveland's Congregation Anshe Chesed. His son **Balfour** (1926–), also Reform rabbi. Officated at Temple Sinai, Washington, D.C., 1952–61 and fr. 1961 director of interfaith activities of Union of American Hebrew Congregations.

Bridegrooms of the Law, honorary titles bestowed on those called up to reading of last and first sections of Pentateuch during morning service of Simḥat Torah, when annual cycle is concluded and new one begun. Person called to conclude reading of Pentateuch is called Bridegroom of the Law *(ḥatan Torah);* person who commences new reading is Bridegroom of Genesis *(ḥatan Bereshit).*

Bridgeport, city in Conn., U.S. Jews fr. E. Europe, esp. Hungary, settled c. 1880. Jewish pop. 14,500 (1971), with 11 congregations.

Brie, Luis Hartwig (1834–1919), Argentinian communal leader; b. Germany, in S. America fr. 1847. Active in foundation and organization of Jewish institutions in Argentina and first president of ḥevrah kaddisha 1894–97.

Brill, Abraham Arden (1874–1948), psychoanalyst; b. Austria, studied with Freud, went to U.S. Instrumental in introducing Freudian writings to English-speaking world. Founded New York Psychoanalytical Society 1911.

Brill, Jehiel (1836–1886), pioneer of Hebrew press in Ereẓ Israel; b. Russia, settled in Jerusalem. Established with others Hebrew printing press and published first Hebrew monthly in Ereẓ Israel 1863; publication suspended 1864. Went to France, reviving paper as weekly. In 1880s led group of Jewish farmers who settled in Ekron, but left and settled in London.

Pair of carved and gilded chairs for the two Bridegrooms of the Law, Mantua, 1775.

Robert Briscoe receiving mayoral chain, 1961.

Brill, Joseph (Iyov of Minsk; 1839–1919), Hebrew writer, humorist; b. Russia. Wrote critical essays, satirical *feuilletons,* parodies.

Brinig, Myron (1900–), U.S. novelist. His novel *Singermann* painted grim picture of life of second-generation American Jews. Family chronicle continued in three later novels.

Brisbane, capital of Queensland, Australia. Community fr. 1865; congregation consisting principally of Russian immigrants fr. 1928. Jewish pop. 1,500 (1971).

Briscoe, Robert (1894–1969), Irish politician; first Jewish member of Irish Dail and the first Jewish lord mayor of Dublin 1956–57, 1961–62. Active in struggle for Irish independence 1917–24.

Brisk, see Brest-Litovsk.

Brisker, Ḥayyim, see Soloveichik, Ḥayyim.

Brisker Rov, see Diskin, Moses Joshua.

Bristol, city in England. Medieval Jewish community one of most important in England. Small modern community founded 1786. Jewish pop. 410 (1971).

Briszk, Mordecai ben Joshua (1884–1944), Hungarian rabbi, yeshivah head in Tasnad. Wrote responsa. D. in Auschwitz.

Britain, see England; Scotland; Wales.

Brith Abraham, fraternal order founded 1859 in New York by German and Hungarian Jews. Later joined by Russian, Polish, Rumanian Jews. Largest Jewish fraternal order in the world before its decline in mid-20s.

British Columbia, province of Canada. Jews arrived during 1858 gold rush and settled in Victoria. First synagogue 1863. Jews elected to many public offices. Jewish pop. 8,000 (1970), nearly all in Vancouver.

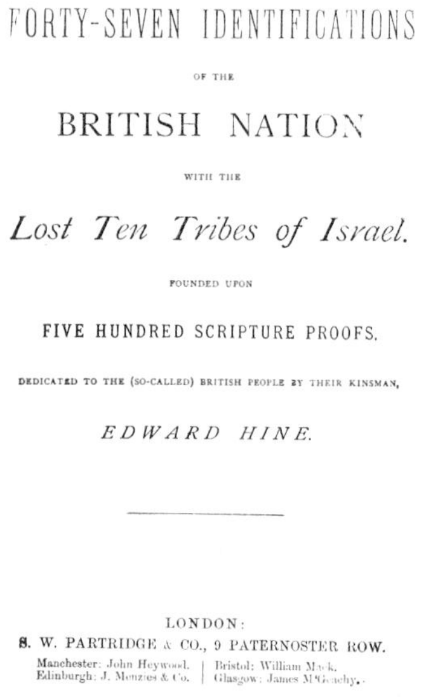

FORTY-SEVEN IDENTIFICATIONS

OF THE

BRITISH NATION

WITH THE

Lost Ten Tribes of Israel.

FOUNDED UPON

FIVE HUNDRED SCRIPTURE PROOFS.

DEDICATED TO THE (SO-CALLED) BRITISH PEOPLE BY THEIR KINSMAN,

EDWARD HINE.

LONDON:
S. W. PARTRIDGE & CO., 9 PATERNOSTER ROW.
Manchester: John Heywood. | Bristol: William Mack.
Edinburgh: J. Menzies & Co. | Glasgow: James M'Geachy.

Edward Hine's book identifying the British people with the lost ten tribes of Israel, 1871.

British Israelites, advocates of Anglo-Israel theory, which maintains that English and their ethnic kinfolk throughout the world are descended fr. Lost Ten Tribes of Israel. First manifesto issued 1649; movement gathered force in late 18th c.

Brit Ivrit Olamit (Heb. "World Association for Hebrew Language and Culture"), organization for promotion of Hebrew language and culture founded in Berlin 1931. Headquarters now in Jerusalem, with branches in 23 countries.

Brittany, region of France; former duchy. Jews fr. end of 12th c. Many massacred 1236; expelled 1240. Marranos settled in 17th c. After French Revolution Jews returned in small numbers. Three communities in 1970 (Nantes, Brest, Rennes).

Brno (Bruenn), city in Czechoslovakia. Jewish community fr. early 13th c. Jews formally expelled 1454, but individuals continued to live there. Community officially revived 1848. Important refugee center in WWI. In WWII, 11,000 Jews deported to death camps. Jewish pop. 700 (1969).

Broch, Hermann (1886–1951), Austrian novelist. Established reputation with *The Sleepwalkers.* In Nazi period settled in U.S., where he published *The Death of Vergil.*

Brociner, Joseph (1846–1918), publicist, communal leader in Rumania. Worked for civil rights for Rumanian Jewry and was instrumental in founding Union of Israelite Communities in Rumania (1901).

Max Brod reading a script to Habimah directors, c. 1939.

Brod, Max (1884–1968), Czech-born German author, composer; settled in Tel Aviv 1939. Wrote poetry, fiction (incl. novel on David Reuveni), plays, essays, and composed chamber music, Israel dances, etc. Friend of Franz Kafka, whose works he saved and published and whose biography he wrote.

Broda, see Uhersky Brod.

Broda, Abraham ben Saul (d. 1717), halakhic authority; b. Bohemia. Yeshivah head in Prague, Metz, and fr. 1713 Frankfort. Wrote *Eshel Avraham,* novellae on three talmudic tractates.

Broder (Margolis), Berl (c. 1815–1868), Yiddish balladist, *badhan* fr. Brody (Galicia). Organized first troupe of professional Yiddish folksingers (the Broder Singers).

Broderzon, Moshe (1890–1956), Yiddish poet, theater director; b. Moscow, lived in Lodz 1918–38, where he founded little theaters, headed literary group, etc. Returned to Moscow 1939; arrested and sent to Siberian work camp 1948–55 and then repatriated to Poland. His poetry combines Jewish folklore with European expressionism.

Brodetsky, Selig (1888–1954), mathematician, Zionist leader. Prof. of maths. at Leeds 1920–49. Member of Jewish Agency Executive and pres. of British Board of Deputies 1939–49. Pres. of Heb. Univ. 1949–52.

Selig Brodetsky

Sir Israel Brodie

Brodie, Sir Israel (1895–), chief rabbi of British Commonwealth 1948–65. Senior minister at Melbourne, Australia, 1923–37, senior Jewish chaplain of British Army in WWII.

Brodski, family of Russian industrialists, philanthropists. **Israel** (1823–1888), took leading part in development of Ukrainian sugar industry. Communal leader in Kiev. His sons **Eliezer (Lazar;** 1848–1904) and **Arieh Leibush (Lev;** 1852–1923), expanded business and contributed generously to Jewish and Russian cultural and welfare institutions.

Brodski, Aleksander Ilich (1895–), Russian physical chemist. Awarded Stalin Prize 1946. Wrote on electrochemistry, etc.

Brodski, Yosif (1940–), Soviet Russian poet, translator. His original verse not allowed to appear in USSR where he was known as translator and as poet published in "illegal" journal. Tried as a "social parasite" 1964 and sentenced to forced labor. Among best-known poems "The Jewish Cemetery near Leningrad." Left for U.S. 1972.

Brodsky, Adolf (1851–1929), Russian violinist. Tchaikovsky dedicated his *Violin Concerto* to him. Toured widely as soloist. Fr. 1895 director of Royal College of Music in Manchester, England.

Brodsky, Isaac Israelevich (1884–1930), Russian painter. Under Soviet regime, became Russia's most successful portrait painter, depicting various leaders.

Brody, city in Ukrainian SSR. Jewish settlement fr. 16th c., by 18th c. Jews controlled town's entire trade. Community prominent in opposition to Frankism and Ḥasidism and center of Galician Haskalah. Jewish pop. dwindled in late 19th c. and early 20th c. Despite some resistance, entire community of 10,000 annihilated during Holocaust.

17th-cent. fortress synagogue of Brody, destroyed 1943, drawing by Georges Leukomski.

Brody, Heinrich (Ḥayyim; 1868–1942), researcher of Hebrew poetry; b. Hungary. Edited bibliographical periodical 1896–1906. Chief rabbi of Prague fr. 1912. Settled in Jerusalem 1933 and headed Schocken institute for Hebrew poetry. Published Sephardi *piyyutim* and medieval Hebrew poetry.

Bródy, Sándor (1863–1924), Hungarian novelist, playwright. Portrayed typical citizen of Pest and prepared ground for flowering of Hungarian prose in 20th c.

Bródy, Zsigmond (1840–1906), Hungarian journalist, poet. Fought for equal rights for Jews and was founder of and contributor to several periodicals. Member of Hungarian Upper House fr. 1896.

Broida, Simḥah Zissel ben Israel (1824–1898), Russian rabbi, moralist; outstanding disciple and follower of Israel Lipkin (Salanter), founder of Musar movement. Founded centers of learning in Kelme and Grobin.

Broides, Abraham (1907–), Hebrew poet; b. Vilna, settled in Ereẓ Israel 1923. Secretary of Hebrew Writers Association 1928–64. Wrote proletarian poetry and later landscape verse.

Broido, Ephraim (1912–), Hebrew essayist, translator, editor; b. Poland, settled in Ereẓ Israel 1925. Founded and edited literary-political journal *Molad.* Translated Shakespeare, etc. into Hebrew.

Broido, Louis (1895–), U.S. business executive, communal leader. Pres. United Jewish Appeal 1951–52, chairman American Jewish Joint Distribution Committee fr. 1965.

Samuel Bronfman

Bronfman, family of Canadian businessmen, philanthropists. **Harry** (1886–1963), a founder and supporter of Canadian Jewish Congress fr. 1919. His son **Gerald** (1911–), pres. and director of various major Canadian businesses. Harry's brother **Samuel** (1891–1971), major figure in distillery industry as pres. of Distillers-Seagrams Ltd. Pres. of Canadian Jewish Congress for 23 years. His philanthropy extended to many aspects of Jewish social, cultural, and Zionist activities. Samuel's son **Edgar** (1929–), pres. of U.S. House of Seagram and active in Federation of Jewish Philanthropies. Another son, **Charles** (1931–), pres. of Joseph E. Seagram and Sons, Canada. Samuel's younger brother **Allan** (1895–), vice-pres. of Distillers Corporation-Seagrams Ltd. and associated with many Canadian and Israel communal enterprises.

Bronowski, Jacob (1908–), British mathematician, philosopher, writer. Participated in several government research projects. Settled in U.S. 1964. Authority on poet William Blake and advocate of need for scientist and humanist to understand each other's language.

Bronstein, David (1924–), Russian chess grand master. Defeated by Botvinnik for world championship 1950. His middlegames exceptionally original.

Bronstein, Mordecai, see Ardon, Mordecai.

Brook, Barry Shelley (1918–), U.S. musicologist. Prof. of musicology, Queens College, N.Y., fr. 1945. Specialized in 16th c. secular and 18th c. instrumental music, and application of computer technology to musicology.

Brooklyn, see New York.

Brooks, Richard (1912–), U.S. film director, writer. Directed *Elmer Gantry, Blackboard Jungle, Cat on a Hot Tin Roof, Brothers Karamazov.*

Brown, Benjamin (1885–1939), organizer of U.S. Jewish farm cooperatives; b. Russia, in U.S. fr. 1901. Pres. Jewish Agricultural and Colonial Association 1909–15. Active in cooperative movement in Utah, Idaho, Pacific Northwest, New Jersey.

Brown, Herbert Charles (1912–), U.S. chemist. Did research at Univ. of Chicago on new volatile compounds of uranium for Manhattan Project.

Brown, Saul Pardo (d. 1702), first known religious leader of New York. *Ḥazzan* by 1695, when recorded as ministering to Congregation Shearith Israel.

Browne, Lewis (1897–1949), U.S. author, rabbi. Occupied various pulpits before abandoning rabbinate. Works include popular history of Jews.

Bruce, Lenny (Leonard Alfred Schneider; 1926–1966), U.S. comedian. Noted for scatalogical commentary on current affairs and manners. Autobiography, *How to Talk Dirty and Influence People.*

Bruck, Grigori (Ẓevi Hirsch; 1869–1922), Russian Zionist, physician. Member of Ḥovevei Zion and Zionist movement. Opposed the Helsingfors Program (1906) and retired fr. Zionist leadership. Settled in Ereẓ Israel 1920.

Bruckner, Ferdinand (Theodor Tagger; 1891–1958), German poet, playwright. Founded and directed Renaissance Theater in Berlin 1923. Went to U.S. 1936. His plays about contemporary life much influenced by cinema.

Brudo, Abraham ben Elijah (Abraham Chelebi; 1625? –1717), Turkish rabbi, preacher. Initially adherent of Shabbetai Ẓevi and traveled widely to raise money for Jewish victims of the Turkish-Venetian war. Later became chief rabbi of Jerusalem.

Bruell, Adolf (Elhanan; 1846–1908), Austrian Jewish scholar; son of Jacob Bruell. Taught at Philanthropin Jewish High School in Frankfort 1871–1903. Special field of study Samaritan translation of Pentateuch.

Bruell, Ignaz (1846–1907), Austrian pianist, composer. Close friend of Brahms; often collaborated with him and gave first public performance of some of his works.

Bruell, Jacob (1812–1889), Moravian talmudic scholar. Rabbi in Kotejin 1843–1889. Developed his

own distinctive, scientific, critical approach. Major work *Mevo ha-Mishnah* ("Introduction to the Mishnah").

Bruell, Nehemiah (Nahum; 1843–1891), German Reform rabbi, scholar; son of Jacob Bruell. Opposed by S.R. Hirsch in Frankfort and eventually left rabbinate to devote himself to Jewish scholarship. Wrote on tannaitic literature and Babylonian Talmud.

Bruenn, see Brno.

Bruggen, Carry van (1881–1932), Dutch novelist, philosophical writer; sister of Jacob Israel de Haan. Her philosophical work *Promethus* influenced leading Dutch writers. Spent last years in mental hospital.

Bruna, Israel ben Ḥayyim (c. 1400–1480), German rabbi, communal leader. Established yeshivah in Regensburg. Twice imprisoned, once after blood libel. Recognized as halakhic authority of Germany.

Brunner, Arnold (1857–1925), U.S. architect. Specialized in public buildings. Earlier synagogues were Romanesque style and later ones (e.g., Shearith Israel, N.Y.) in classical style. Influenced by ancient synagogues in Galilee.

Brunner, Constantin (pen name of **Leopold Wertheimer;** 1862–1937), German philosopher; emigrated fr. Potsdam to Holland 1933. His philosophical system followed Plato and Spinoza. Advocated total assimilation of Jews.

Brunschvicg, Leon (1869–1944), French philosopher. Prof. at Sorbonne 1909. Spokesman of idealistic school of thought in France and attempted integration of Bergson's view of consciousness with Hegel's.

Brunschvig, Robert (1901–), French Orientalist. Director of Institute of Islamic Studies at Sorbonne 1955. Wrote on Islam and Islamic culture.

Brunswick (Ger. **Braunschweig),** city and former duchy in W. Germany. Jews settled in 12th c. Massacred during Black Death 1348–49, expelled 1590, 1571, 1590 returned in early 17th c. Center of Haskalah and Reform. 682 Jews in 1933; deported in WWII. 43 Jews in 1967.

Brusa, see Bursa.

Brussels, capital of Belgium. Jewish community fr. 13th c.; exterminated in 14th c. and not reestablished until 18th c. Administrative center of Belgian Jewry in 19th c. Since WWII largest community in Belgium (c. 24,500 in 1971).

Brutzkus, Boris Dov (1874–1938), Russian agrarian economist, communal leader. Worked for ICA, then ORT in Russia. Leading figure in Jewish People's Party. Prof. at Russian Scientific Institute in Berlin 1922–32, prof. of agrarian economy at Heb. Univ. fr. 1936.

Brutzkus, Julius (1870–1951), communal worker; brother of Boris Brutzkus. Minister for Jewish affairs in Lithuanian government 1921, member of parliament 1922. Settled in Berlin; among founders of Revisionist Party. Escaped to America in WWII and eventually settled in Ereẓ Israel. Wrote on Jews in Russia and Lithuania and on Khazars.

Martin Buber

Buber, Martin (1878–1965), philosopher, theologian, Zionist thinker and leader; b. Vienna, grandson of Solomon Buber. Worked in Germany until 1938 when he settled in Jerusalem and was prof. of social philosophy at Heb. Univ. Active in early Zionist movement, in faction emphasizing educational rather than political action; remained a Hebrew humanist, calling for peace and brotherhood with Arabs. Became interested in Ḥasidism, translating ḥasidic tales and later developing his own interpretation of the essence of ḥasidim ("neo-ḥasidim"). With Franz Rosenzweig translated Bible into German. His philosophical method, the dialogue theory in which all relationships can be classified as I-Thou or I-It; influential notably in Christian circles.

Buber, Solomon (1827–1906), Austrian scholar, authority on midrashic and medieval rabbinic literature. His editions revolutionized the production of reliable texts.

Bublick, Gedaliah (1875–1948), U.S. Yiddish journalist, religious Zionist leader; b. Russia, settled in New York 1904. Joined staff of *Yiddish News;* editor 1915–28. Pres. of Mizrachi Organization of America 1928–32.

Buchach, city in E. Galicia. Jewish settlement fr. 16th c.; large by 18th c. Jews engaged in distilling and commerce and controlled most large estates in region. S.Y. Agnon, who was born there, describes Jewish life in the town. In WWII, 10,000 Jews murdered or deported.

Buchalter, Louis ("Lepke"; 1897–1944), U.S. racketeer. At height of criminal career commanded 200 gangsters who extorted millions of dollars by "protecting" manufacturers from strikes and unionization. Executed for murder in New York.

Bucharest, capital of Rumania. Jews fr. 16th c., originally merchants and moneylenders fr. Turkey. Augmented by Ashkenazi Jews in 18th, 19th c. Suffered from local hostility, economic discrimination, and communal strife. Conditions improved after WWI (95,000 Jews in 1940). Conditions deteriorated during WWII but subsequently many survivors went there. 150,000 Jews in 1947. Many then left for Israel. Jewish pop. 50,200 (1971).

Buchbinder, Nahum (1895– ?), Soviet historian. First wrote on Russian-Jewish literature and later specialized in history of Jewish labor movement in Russia. Fate after 1930s unknown.

Buchenwald, German concentration camp. Operated 1937–45. Over 56,000 of total 238,380 prisoners perished.

The main gate to Buchenwald camp

Buchmil, Joshua Heshel (1869–1938), Zionist leader; b. Volhynia. Leading spokesman for Democratic Fraction. Zionist emissary in Russia and in many European countries. Sent by Ḥovevei Zion to Ereẓ Israel 1906 to study Jewish colonization. Settled in Ereẓ Israel 1923, working for Keren Hayesod.

Buchner, Abraham (1789–1869), Polish assimilationist, linguist. His early Hebrew works, incl. commentary on Maimonides, sympathetic toward Judaism. His later works on Talmud, however, inimical in tone.

Buchner, Ze'ev Wolf ben David Ha-Kohen (1750–1820), Hebrew grammarian, liturgical poet. Secretary of Jewish community of Brody.

Wrote several epistolary guides in poetic language, all dealing with Hebrew style.

Buchwald, Art (1925–), U.S. humorist. His witty columns have been syndicated and published in book form.

Buchwald, Theo (1920–), conductor; b. Vienna, in S. America fr. 1935. Created National Symphony Orchestra in Lima.

Bucky, Gustav (1880–1963), radiologist. Worked in Germany and U.S. Inventor of Bucky diaphragm for roentgenography.

Budapest, capital of Hungary. Jewish settlement in Buda fr. 12th c., Obuda and Pest fr. 15th. Communities and institutions flourished in late 19th and early 20th c. Economic and political conditions deteriorated after WWI. Large proportion of 184,000 Jews in 1941 deported; 20–25,000 left in 1956. 65,000 Jews in 1971.

°**Budde, Karl Ferdinand Reinhard** (1850–1933), German Protestant Bible scholar, Hebraist. Ardent supporter of Wellhausen theories. Wrote on biblical literature and its characteristics.

Budko, Joseph (1888–1940), painter, graphic artist; b. Russia; worked in Berlin until 1933, went to Ereẓ Israel 1935. Director of new Bezalel school of arts and crafts. Subject matter based on Jewish life.

Buechler, Adolf (1867–1939), theologian, historian; b. Hungary. Principal of Jews' College, London fr. 1907. Main research on latter part of Second Temple period.

Buechler, Alexander (1870–1944), Hungarian historian, rabbi. Wrote on Hungarian Jewish history. D. in Auschwitz.

Buedinger, Max (1828–1902), German historian. Prof. of general history at Vienna 1872–99 after converting to Christianity. Wrote on ancient, medieval, and modern Europe.

Bueno, Ephraim Hezekiah (Martin Alvarez; d. 1665), physician in Amsterdam. Translated liturgy into Spanish and cofounded Or Torah academy. Subject of Rembrandt's "The Jewish Doctor."

Buenos Aires. (1) Province in Argentinian republic. First colony of Jewish Colonization Association – Mauricio (1891) – established there, then Baron Hirsch colony (1904–05). Organized Jewish communities in 39 cities in 1964. (2) Capital of Argentina. A few Marranos settled in 16th, 17th c. First Jewish community organized 1862. In following decades Jews fr. N. Africa and esp. E. Europe arrived. Between two world wars immigration from E. Europe and Near East, and after 1933 fr. C. Europe. Community organized in AMIA. Seat of central Argentinian Jewish institutions (DAIA, Zionist Federation). Jewish pop. 350,000 (1971).

Buerger, Leo (1879–1943), U.S. physician. Contributed to knowledge of urology, pathology, bacteriology, and study of vascular diseases. Surgeon at Mt. Sinai Hospital, N.Y., later prof. in Los Angeles. Gave name to "Buerger's disease."

Buffalo, city in N.Y., U.S. First Jew 1812. Mordecai Manuel Noah launched utopian plan for Jewish homeland in nearby "city of Ararat" 1825. First congregation 1847. Most Jews descendants of E. Europeans who came after 1880. Jewish pop. 23,500 (1971), with 11 congregations.

°**Buhl, Franz Peder Willam Meyer** (1850–1932), Danish biblical, Semitic scholar. Studied canon and text of Bible and biblical poetry.

Bukhara, place in Uzbek SSR. Jews fr. 13th c. In 16th c. restricted to special quarter and many compelled to accept Islam. Emigration to Ereẓ Israel fr. 1868; founded quarter in Jerusalem 1892. Bukharan Jews speak Tajiki-Jewish dialect. 8,000 in 1970, living in various regions.

Buki ben Yogli, see Katzenelson, Judah Leib Benjamin.

Bukovina, region now divided between Rumania and USSR. Jewish settlement fr. 14th c. Ashkenazi element increased after 17th c. After emancipation (1848), took active part in industrial development. In June 1941, 3,800 Jews deported to Siberia; remainder subsequently massacred by Germans. After WWII Jews in N. Bukovina had to conform to Soviet rule. Those in S. allowed to emigrate by Rumanians.

Būlān, Khazar King who acc. to tradition instituted Judaism in Khazaria c. 730 C.E. after listening to religious disputation.

Bulawayo, town in Rhodesia. Jews among pioneers. Hebrew congregation formed 1894. First white child born there and first mayor Jewish. Jewish pop. 2,000 (1972), with one Orthodox and one Reform congregation.

Bulgaria, E. European republic. Jewish settlement fr. Roman times. Under Byzantine rule a haven for refugees from C. Europe and under Turkish rule new Sephardi com-

The Dohany Street Synagogue Budapest, consecrated 1859.

"Sitting Old Man" by Joseph Budko, lithograph, 1915.

Foundation stone of Ararat, the Jewish city founded 1825 near Buffalo.

Bukharan woman's ceremonial coat, a "kaltshak."

Jewish population of Bulgaria, 1878–1967.

munities established by refugees fr. Spain. In independent Bulgaria, religious equality (granted 1878) generally observed; Zionism gained numerous adherents. During WWII Bulgarian Jewry (48,565 in 1934) was the only occupied community to escape mass deportation. After 1948 most of community emigrated to Israel. 7,000 remained in 1971.

Buloff, Joseph (1899–), U.S. Yiddish actor. At age of 20 played in Vilna Troupe. Went to U.S. 1926. Also acted in English and appeared on Broadway and in S. America. Settled in Israel 1968.

Bund (Yid. abbr. "General Jewish Workers' Union in Lithuania, Poland, and Russia"), Jewish socialist party founded in Russia 1897. Particularly influential in Russia between 1905 and 1920 and in Poland until WWII. 40,000 members in Russia in 1917 and 99,000 in Poland in 1939. Committed to Yiddish, autonomism, and secular Jewish nationalism. Sharply opposed Zionism and other conceptions of a world-embracing Jewish national identity.

Bunin, Ḥayyim Isaac (1875–1943), author, teacher; b. Belorussia, in Warsaw fr. 1929. Noted for research on Ḥabad Ḥasidism. D. in Treblinka.

Bunshaft, Gordon (1909–), U.S. architect. Designed Lever Building in New York, which established his reputation as leading designer of large-scale commercial structures.

Bunzel, Ruth Leah (1898–), U.S. anthropologist. Prof. of anthropology at Columbia Univ. Did field research on American Indians in New Mexico, Arizona, Guatemala, and Mexico.

Burchardt, Hermann (1857–1909), German explorer. Journeyed to remote corners of Asia, N. Africa, Middle East, and Australia, and photographed and collected information on local inhabitants. Brought the almost-forgotten Jews of Yemen to attention of world Jewry.

Burg, Yosef (1909–), Israel politician; b. Germany, settled in Ereẓ Israel 1939. Member of central bodies of National Religious Party, member of Knesset fr. 1949. Minister of health 1951–2, min. of posts 1952–58, min. of social welfare 1959–70, min. of interior fr. 1970.

Burgenland, federal state in Austria. Jews fr. 14th c. In 17th c. famous as location of "seven communities" (Eisenstadt, Mattersburg, Deutschkreutz, Frauenkirchen, Kittsee, Kobersdorf, Lackenbach), noted for outstanding yeshivot and eminent rabbis. In late 19th c. mainstay of separatist Orthodoxy. Thereafter communities diminished in importance. 3,800 Jews in 1938, all driven out.

Burgos, city in Spain, formerly capital of Old Castile. Jews fr. 10th c; in 13th c. largest Jewish center in N. Castile and received help from civil authorities in enforcing Jewish observance. Declined in 14th c. when subject to persecutions. After further restrictions in 15th c. many Jews converted to Christianity in 1492.

Silver comb and other implements used in preparation of a corpse for burial, Hungary, mid-19th cent.

The restored Jason's Tomb, Jerusalem, first cent. B.C.E.

Yosef Burg

Yehuda Burla

Burgundy, former French duchy. Jews fr. 9th c, reaching maximum in 13th c. Numerous scholars. Community disappeared as result of successive expulsions in 14th c.

Burial. Basic duty to be performed for all, incl. suicides and enemies. Cremation and embalming are not Jewish customs, and expensive shrouds are forbidden. Burial is on day of death or next. Many communities have special customs. It was customary where possible in Diaspora to put some earth fr. the land of Israel in the grave. See also Ḥevra Kaddisha.

Burial Society, see Ḥevra Kaddisha.

Burla, Joseph Nissim ben Ḥayyim Jacob (1828–1903), rabbi, preacher in Jerusalem; among founders of Mishkenot Sha'ananim, first settlement outside walls of Jerusalem. Went as emissary to N. Africa and Europe. Wrote works on talmud, sermons, responsa.

Burla (Bourla), Yehuda (1886–1969), Hebrew novelist; b. Jerusalem. Taught for many years (incl. 5 years in Damascus after WWI). Head of Arab dept. of Histadrut. First modern Hebrew writer to deal extensively with life of Middle Eastern Sephardim; also wrote stories based on Jewish history.

Burle-Marx, Roberto (1909–), Brazilian landscape designer. Gardens include Flamingo scheme for reclaiming one million square yards of Rio de Janeiro's coastline, botanical and zoological garden for Brazilia, and six patios for UNESCO building, Paris.

The "burning bush" at St. Catherine's Monastery, Sinai Desert.

Arthur F. Burns

Burma, Asian republic. Small community fr. 1857. At one time a few hundred Jews in the country but community life disrupted in WWII and very few Jews remain.

Burnham, see Lawson.

Burning Bush, the flaming bush out of which God spoke to Moses at Mt. Horeb. It burned with fire but was not consumed (Ex. 3:1-4).

Burns, Arthur Frank (1904–), U.S. economist. Taught at Rutgers and Columbia Univ. Pres. of National Bureau of Economic Research fr. 1957. Economic adviser to President Eisenhower 1953–56, chairman of Board of Governors of U.S. Federal Reserve System fr. 1969.

Burns, George (1896–), U.S. comedian. Best known on radio, TV, and in films in partnership with his wife, Gracie Allen.

Bursa (Brusa), city in Turkey. Jews in Byzantine period. Spanish refugees fr. early 16th c; lived in special quarter. Blood libels 1592, 1865. 3,500 Jews before WWI. Many emigrated (S. America, etc.); 350–400 in 1969.

Burstein, family of actors. **Pesach** (1900–), b. Warsaw. Appeared on Yiddish stage in U.S., and in 1940 he and his wife Lilian formed their own theater. Fr. 1954 in Israel. Their son **Michael (Mordecai;** 1945–), popular singer in Israel.

Burstein, Israel (1891–1951), Hebraist; b. Galicia, settled in Ereẓ Israel 1939. Main work on Hebrew phonology. Elaborated new method of Hebrew shorthand.

Burton, Sir Montague (1885–1952), British industrialist, philanthropist. Pioneered inexpensive, well-made men's clothes and established large chain of stores. Endowed chairs of industrial and international relations at several British universities and Heb. Univ.

Busal, Ḥayyim ben Jacob Obadiah de (d.c. 1565), rabbi, kabbalist in Salonika. Tenure of office marked by dispute with community. Wrote responsa and kabbalistic works and began code of law.

Busel, Joseph (1891–1919), Zionist-Socialist pioneer; b. Belorussia, settled in Ereẓ Israel 1908. Among founders of Deganyah and an originator of idea of *kevuẓah.* Drowned in Lake Kinneret.

Bush, Isidor (1822–1898), journalist, political liberal, viticulturist; b. Prague. Engaged in Jewish publishing. Fled to U.S. after 1848 revolution; active in Jewish communal affairs and Republican politics.

Bush, Solomon (1753–1795), U.S. patriot, Revolutionary War soldier. Lieutenant-colonel in Continental Army 1779, highest rank held by Jewish officer in Revolutionary Army.

Busnach, family of Algerian shipowners, merchants. **Naphtali ben Moses** (d. 1805), influential in foreign policy and the treasury; nicknamed "viceroy of Algiers." Appointed "head of the Jewish nation" 1800. Assassinated by janissary.

Bustanai ben Ḥaninai (c. 618–670), first exilarch in Babylonia after Arab conquest. In addition to Jewish wives, married Persian princess.

"Universal Peace" by Leon Butensky, bronze.

Butensky, Jules Leon (1871–1947), U.S. sculptor; b. Russia, in U.S. fr. 1904. Most of his sculpture of biblical or Jewish inspiration. Works include "Universal Peace" in N.Y. Metropolitan Museum and "Exile" in White House.

Buttenwieser, Benjamin Joseph (1900–), banker, civic leader, philanthropist; son of Joseph Buttenwieser. Assistant high commissioner for Germany 1949–51, serving as adviser on economic matters and de-Nazification.

Buttenwieser, Joseph Leon (1865–1938), U.S. lawyer, realtor, community leader. Influenced N.Y. State real property legislation. Pres. of Federation for Support of Jewish Philanthropic Societies 1924–26 and played major role in Hebrew Sheltering Guardian Society and United Palestine Appeal.

Buttenwieser, Moses (1862–1939), U.S. Bible scholar; b. Germany. Prof. of biblical exegesis at Hebrew Union College, Cincinnati, fr. 1897. Wrote on biblical prophets, Job, Psalms, etc.

Buttons, Red (1919–), U.S. vaudeville, television comic. Won Oscar for role in *Sayonara.*

Butzel, U.S. family in Detroit. **Martin** (1828–1906), opened firm manufacturing ready-made clothing. Member of first Detroit Public Lighting Commission. His brother **Magnus** (1830–1900), member of Detroit Board of Education and a leader of Michigan Republican Party. **Henry M.** (1871–1963), son of Magnus, sat on Michigan Supreme Court and served as its chief justice. With brother **Fred** (1877–1948) founded Detroit Legal Aid Bureau. Both brothers served as pres. of United Jewish Charities. **Leo M.** (1874–1961), son of Martin, considered Detroit's outstanding lawyer and played important role in developing corporate structure of automobile industry.

Buxbaum, Nathan (1890–1943), Polish leader of Po'alei Zion movement and later of left-wing Po'alei Zion. Member of Warsaw city council fr. 1927. D. in Holocaust.

°**Buxtorf, Johannes (I)** (1564–1629), Hebraist. Prof. of Hebrew at Univ. of Basle. Compiled and edited Hebrew Bible with Aramaic Targum, Masoretic text, and Jewish commentaries. Also wrote Hebrew grammar, vocabularies, and lexicons.

°**Buxtorf, Johannes (II)** (1599–1664), Hebraist; son of Johannes Buxtorf I. Succeeded his father at Univ. of Basle and translated into

Latin Maimonides' *Guide,* Judah Halevi's *Kuzari,* etc.

Buzaglo, Abraham (1710–1782), inventor. Settled in England c. 1762. Patented "buzaglo" stove and introduced popular method for treating gout.

Buzaglo, Shalom ben Moses c. 1700–1780), Moroccan kabbalist. Settled in England after persecution by sultan. Wrote commentary on Zohar.

Byadulya-Yasakar, Zmitrok (1886–1941), Soviet Belorussian writer. Among founders of Belorussian literature.

Byk, Emil (1845–1906), lawyer, politician, assimilationist leader in Austrian Galicia. Member of Austrian parliament fr. 1891. Pres. of Lemberg community 1903–06. Opposed Zionism and establishment of special Jewish *curia.*

Caricature of Abraham Buzaglo's treatment for gout, aquatint engraved by Paul Sandby, 1783.

Byzantine Empire. Jews there throughout its history. 1) Fr. Constantine (330) to 720; Jews in Balkans, Greece, Asia Minor, Constantinople (q.v.), Syria, and Ereẓ Israel. As Christianity gained more influence and Roman laws guaranteeing Jews' legal status weakened, political, social, and religious conditions of Jews worsened. In 7th c. this culminated in violence against Jews. Study of Mishnah was forbidden, Bible had to be studied in Christian translation, etc. Anti-Semitic legislation reached peak under Justinian. Ereẓ Israel under Empire's rule was scene of cultural activity, esp. in liturgical verse (e.g., Eleazar Kallir) and midrash, but was dwarfed by Babylonian community. 2) Fr. 720 to Fourth Crusade (1204), security of Jews much improved and they worked in crafts and even agriculture. Active communities in S. Italy. Karaite community centered in Constantinople. 3) Fr. 1204 to 1453, period of general disruption in Empire, affecting also Jews. Borders changed and legislation of local rulers inconsistent. Little is known of period, but distinguished scholars were active (e.g., Moses b. Elijah Capsali). Ottoman successor empire welcomed by Jews.

Byzantine Empire, showing the major centers of Jewish settlement.

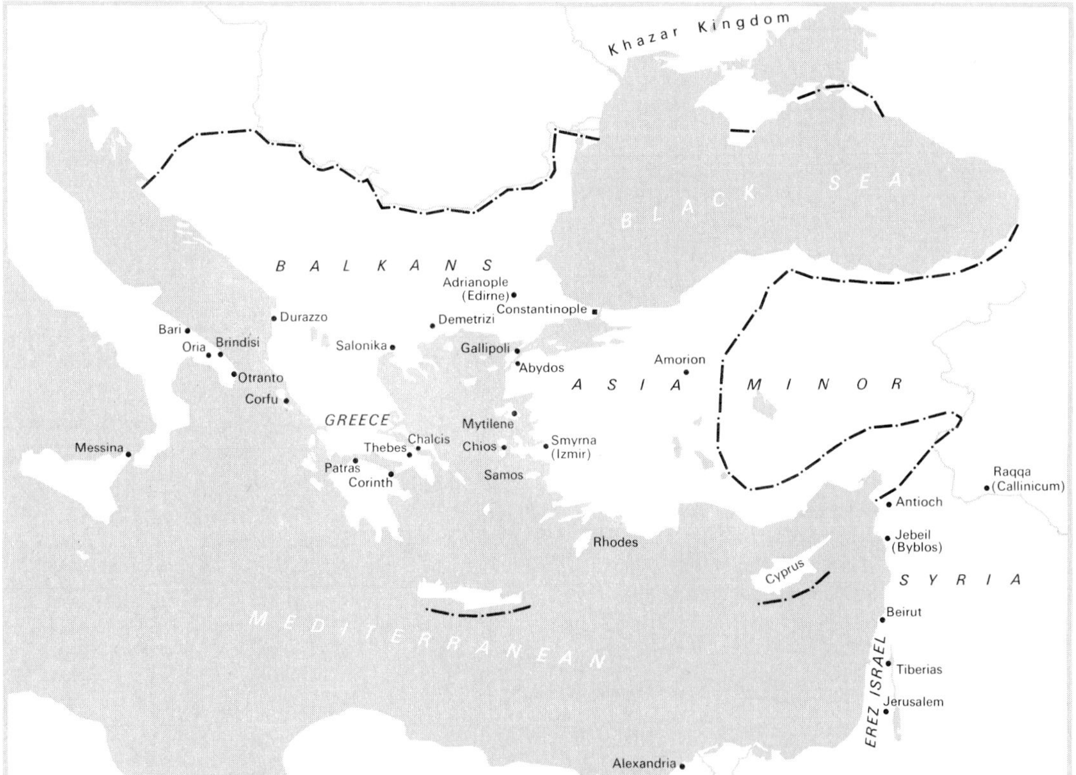

Initial "C" at opening of II Chronicles in the "Bible of Saint Martial of Limoge," Italy, 12th cent., depicting Solomon enthroned.

Caballeria, see Cavalleria.

Cabbalah, see Kabbalah.

Cabul, city in W. Galilee. Solomon built and settled Israelites there (II Chron. 8:2). Attacked by Cestius Gallus 66 C.E., served as Josephus' Galilee headquarters 67. After fall of Jerusalem, priests of Shecaniah family settled there.

Caceres (Casseres), Abraham (18th c.), Dutch composer. Wrote synagogue music, but little survived.

Caceres (Casseres), Francisco (Joseph) de (b.c. 1580), Marrano writer, translator, publisher; b. Spain, lived in France, Amsterdam.

Caceres, Simon (Jacob) de (d. 1704), English merchant; b. Amsterdam, settled in London before official readmission of Jews. Advised Cromwell during conquest of Jamaica.

Caecilius of Calacte (1st c. C.E.), literary critic, rhetorician, historian; b. Sicily; son of freed slave, Jew by religion, wrote Greek, active in Rome. First known European Jewish author who did not write on Jewish subjects, and pioneer in field of comparative literature.

Caesar, Sid (1922–), U.S. stage and television comedian. Became known with appearances in *Tars and Spars,* revue and film. His *Your Show of Shows* ran 11 years on TV.

Caesarea, ancient city on Israel coast between Tel Aviv and Haifa. Originally called Straton's Tower after its founder (4th c. B.C.E.). Captured by Alexander Yannai 104 B.C.E. and under Hasmonean rule until restoration as autonomous city by Pompey. Herod greatly enlarged the city and renamed it Caesarea for emperor Augustus. Fr. 6 C.E., seat of Roman procurators of Judea. Capital of Roman and Byzantine Palestine. Fr. 3rd c., seat of Christian learning but also important Jewish community. Important Crusader port; reconstructed by Louis IX (1251–52). In 1265 it fell to Baybars, and Mamluks systematically destroyed the city, which remained in ruins until 1884. Abandoned by its Arab inhabitants in War of Independence (1948). Excavations have uncovered ancient cities, Roman theater. Now tourist center with golf course, harbor for sailboats.

Headless porphyry statue on a granite throne at Caesarea, Herodian period.

Caesarea Philippi, see Banias.

Caffa, see Feodosiya.

Cagli, Corrado (1910–), Italian painter. In 1933 tried to establish School of Rome. In 1939 fled to France and then U.S. Painted pictures of release of prisoners from Buchenwald. Returned to Italy after war.

Cahan, Abraham (1860–1951), U.S. Yiddish journalist, editor, author, socialist leader. A founder (1897) and editor of *Jewish Daily Forward* for almost 50 years. Writings include classic novel of urban immigrant experience, *The Rise of David Levinsky.*

Cahan, Judah Loeb (1881–1937), U.S. Yiddish folklorist, born in Vilna; a founder of YIVO.

Cahan, Yaakov (1881–1960), Hebrew poet; b. Russia, lived in Poland, edited 23 volumes of the periodical *Ha-Tekufah,* settled in Ereẓ Israel 1934. Wrote lyrical poems, dramatic poems, ballads based on Jewish folklore, short stories, plays. Poetry revolves around messianism and nationalism.

Cahen, Isador (1826–1902), French scholar, journalist. For 40 years editor of *Archives Israélites,* official organ of French Jewish community, which he led into radical-liberal position. Published appeal culminating in Alliance Israélite Universelle, whose name he suggested.

Cahn, Edmond Nathaniel (1906–1964), U.S. lawyer, legal philosopher, author. Prof. at New York Univ. fr. 1950. Dealt mainly with ethical and moral insights found in the law.

Cahn, Marcelle (1895–), cubist painter; member School of Paris; Painted in rigorous and geometric style.

Cahnman, Werner J. (1902–), U.S. sociologist; b. Munich. Prof. of sociology at Rutgers (1961). Wrote *Sociology and History* (with Alvin Boskoff).

Caiaphas, Joseph, high priest, 18–36 C.E. Played minor role in crucifixion drama, but, according to New Testament, said to Jesus: "It is better for you that one man die for the nation than that the entire nation be lost" (John 11:49–51).

Caimis, Moises (1864–1929), Greek journalist, editor. One of first Jewish journalists to write in Greek. Headed Jewish community in Corfu.

Cain, firstborn son of Adam and Eve. Cain and his brother Abel brought offerings to God, who preferred Abel's gift. Cain killed Abel and was punished to wander. Later married and bore Enoch (Gen. 4).

Cain killing Abel with a club, "Harrison Miscellany," Italy, 18th cent.

12th-cent. carved wooden doors of Ben Ezra Synagogue, Cairo.

Cairo, capital of Egypt. Old town called Fostat. Active Jewish community almost from foundation in 641 to mid-20th c. Site of famous Genizah. Maimonides and his descendants lived there, as did strong Karaite community. Jewish pop. dropped steeply after establishment of State of Israel fr. 41,860 in 1947 to a few hundred in 1970.

Caiserman, Hanane Meier (1884–1950), Canadian communal leader, labor organizer; b. Rumania, emigrated to Montreal 1911. Union organizer for clothing workers and Jewish bakers in Montreal. A founder of Canadian Jewish Congress (1919), of which he was general secretary.

Jewish communities in California and dates of establishment.

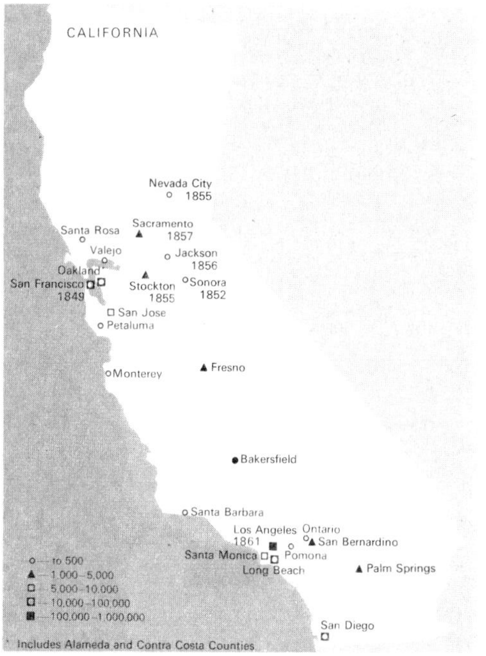

Caiserman-Roth, Ghita (1923–), Canadian representational painter. Taught at Sir George Williams Univ.

Calabria, region in S. Italy. Prosperous Jewish community fr. 4th c. In 13th c. Jews held silk monopoly. All Jews expelled 1510.

Calahora, Joseph ben Solomon (called **Joseph Darshan;** 1601–1696), rabbi, author of ethical and homiletical works; lived in Posen.

Calahor(r)a, Mattathias (d. 1663), Polish physician, apothecary, martyr. Accused of blaspheming the Virgin. Tortured and burnt at stake; ashes shot into the air.

Calahorra, Israel Samuel ben Solomon (? 1560–1640), Polish talmudist. Wrote *Yismaḥ Yisrael,* compendium of laws of *Shulḥan Arukh* arranged alphabetically.

Calcutta, city in India. Permanent Jewish settlement of immigrants fr. Syria and Iraq fr. early 19th c. prospered until economic decline and emigration after WWII. Pop. c. 700 (1971).

Caleb, one of 12 spies sent by Moses to reconnoiter Canaan. Only he and Joshua brought back favorable report. For this they were allowed to enter the Promised Land (Num. 13). Received inheritance in Hebron area and his descendants, the Calebites, were major family group in Judah.

Calendar. The Jewish calendar is lunisolar, months reckoned according to moon, years according to sun. To reconcile lunar year (354 days) with solar year (365 days) one month is added to lunar year 7 times in 19 solar years. Leap years occur in 3rd, 6th, 8th, 11th, 14th, 17th and 19th years of fixed cycle established in Temple times. There are 12 months in an ordinary year; 13 in a leap year. Months have 29 or 30 days. The religious year begins in the month of *Nisan;* the civil year in *Tishri.*

Calf, Golden, see Golden Calf.

Calgary, city in Alberta, Canada. First permanent Jewish settler 1888. First congregation, House of Jacob 1912. Jewish pop. 3,200 (1971).

California, U.S. state. First Jewish settlers arrived during gold rush of 1849, and Jewish communal life dates from those years. Rapid growth of Jewish community after WWII. Jews have achieved prominence in political and public life, business, motion picture industry, philanthropy. Jewish pop. 721,000 (1971), with 535,000 in Los Angeles.

°**Caligula, Caius Caesar Augustus,** Roman emperor 37–41 C.E. Granted Agrippa I territory in NE Ereẓ Israel along with royal title. His desire to impose his worship on all his subjects caused tension between Jews and gentiles. Assassination staved off calamity.

MONTHS OF THE JEWISH YEAR

MONTH	NON-LEAP YEAR	LEAP YEAR
Nisan	30 days	30 days
Iyyar	29 days	29 days
Sivan	30 days	30 days
Tammuz	29 days	29 days
Av	30 days	30 days
Elul	29 days	29 days
Tishri	30 days	30 days
Ḥeshvan	29(30) days	29(30) days
Kislev	30 days	29(30) days
Tevet	29 days	29 days
Shevat	30 days	30 days
Adar	29 days	30 days–Adar I 29 days–Adar II

GREGORIAN YEAR	HEBREW YEAR in letters	HEBREW YEAR in ciphers
1965	תשכ"ה	5725
1966	תשכ"ו	5726
1967	תשכ"ז	5727
1968	תשכ"ח	5728
1969	תשכ"ט	5729
1970	תש"ל	5730
1971	תשל"א	5731
1972	תשל"ב	5732
1973	תשל"ג	5733
1974	תשל"ד	5734
1975	תשל"ה	5735
1976	תשל"ו	5736
1977	תשל"ז	5737
1978	תשל"ח	5738
1979	תשל"ט	5739
1980	תש"מ	5740
1981	תשמ"א	5741
1982	תשמ"ב	5742
1983	תשמ"ג	5743
1984	תשמ"ד	5744
1985	תשמ"ה	5745

Calimani, Simon (Simḥah; 1699–1784), Italian grammarian, playwright, poet. Translated *Pirkei Avot* into Italian, wrote Hebrew grammar and (incomplete) Hebrew-Italian dictionary. Most important works are dramas.

Calin (Clejan), Vera (1921–), Rumanian literary historian. One of most original essayists of postwar generation. Works include biography of Lord Byron.

Calisch, Edward Nathan (1865–1946), U.S. Reform rabbi, author. Originator of rabbinical circuit work in U.S.

Calmanson, Jacob (Jacques; 18th c.), personal physician to Stanislas II Augustus, last king of Poland. Proponent of Emancipation.

Calmer, Antoine Louis Isaac (1764–1794), French Jacobin; son of Moses E.L. Calmer. President of Committee of Public Safety in Clichy quarter. Guillotined in Reign of Terror.

Calmer, Moses Eliezer Liefmann (1711–1784), first French Jewish noble. Rights as nobleman opposed by clergy.

Calugaru (originally **Croitoru), Ion** (1903–1956), Rumanian novelist, journalist. One of few Rumanian Jewish writers to portray Jewish life.

°**Calvin, John** (1509–1564), Church reformer; foremost Christian biblical exegete. Had little direct contact with Jews. Opposed Jews less than Christian heretics. Led Protestant movement back to Old Testament as source of enlightenment.

Calvin, Melvin (1912–), U.S. biochemist; Nobel Prize winner in chemistry in 1961 for elucidating reactions in process of photosynthesis. Worked with Manhattan Project 1944–45. Director of biodynamics laboratory at Univ. of California in Berkeley fr. 1960.

Camden, city in N.J., U.S. First permanent Jewish settlers arrived c. 1890. First congregation, Sons of Israel, founded 1894. Jewish pop. 18,230 (1971).

Cameri (The Chamber Theater), Tel Aviv repertory theater founded 1944 by Josef Millo.

Camerini, Eugenio Salomone (1811–1875), Italian literary critic. Active in cause of Jewish emancipation and establishment of schools for Jewish youth. Forced to leave Naples because of liberal ideas and patriotic activities. Moved to Turin.

Cammeo, Federico (1872–1939), Italian jurist; prof. at Bologna. First Italian to base study of administrative law on scientific principles. Drafted administrative rules of Vatican. Dismissed following anti-Semitic legislation.

Camondo, Abraham de (1785–1873), Turkish banker, philanthropist, Jewish community leader; referred to as "the Rothschild of the East." Influential in sultan's court.

Cameri Theater's 1948 production of "Hu Halakh ba-Sadot."

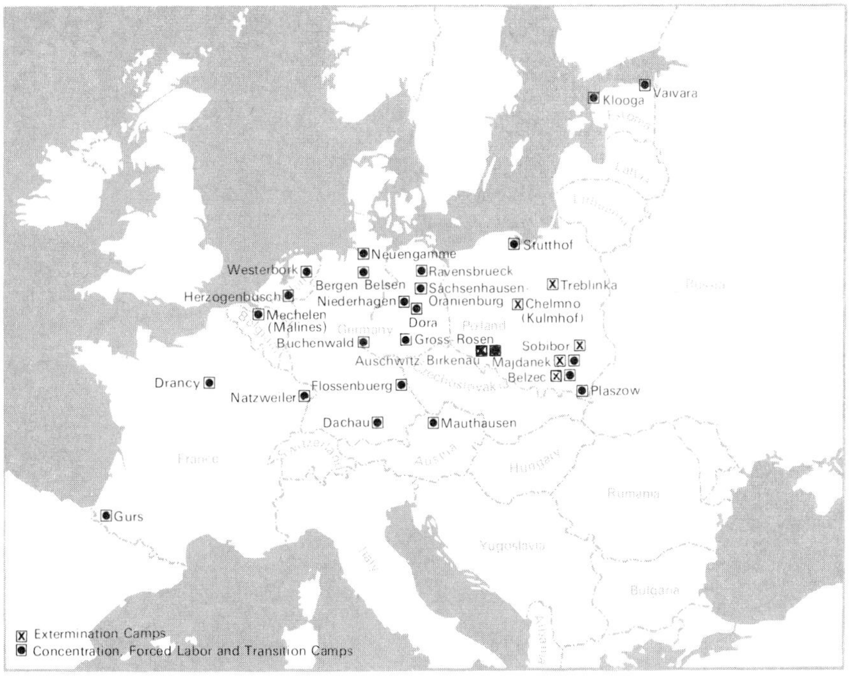

Major concentration, forced labor, transit, and extermination camps in Europe, WWII.

Campen, Michel Herman van (1874–1943), Dutch novelist; originally diamond worker. Religious Zionist. Writings include *Bikoerim* (1903). Died Nazi concentration camp.

Camps, Concentration and Extermination, Nazi mass detention and liquidation centers for civilians imprisoned for political, security, and racial reasons. After the Nazis came to power in Germany in 1933 they were established for detention of enemies of the new regime. By July 1933 they held c. 27,000 detainees, subject to torture. First general action directed against Jews in Nov. 1938 *(Kristallnacht)* when 35,000 Jews were arrested. Most were released if they could pay money to leave Germany. After outbreak of WWII, network of concentration camps broadened in all occupied countries. In these camps tens of thousands of Jews and others were tortured to death and died of hunger and disease. In Dec. 1941 the first extermination camp (Chelmno) with gas chambers was established. In 1941 Jewish masses were deported eastward from Germany, Austria, Czechoslovakia, and other Western countries, confined in ghettos, and then sent to extermination camps. Some sent via concentration, forced-labor, or transit camps. Jews sent directly to extermination camps from ghettos in 1942. C. 4,000,000 Jews exterminated in camps; greatest number in Auschwitz, reaching 20,000 victims per day, a total of 1,500,000. Jewish victims in the other extermination camps in Poland were: Treblinka, 750,000; Belzec, 600,000; Sobibor, 25,000; Chelmno, 360,000; Majdanek, 125,000. Jews died in other Nazi camps, the biggest being Mauthausen, Sachsenhausen, Ravensbrueck, Natzweiler-Struthog, Buchenwald, Dachau, Bergen-Belsen, Gross-Rosen, and Stutthof. In some camps the prisoners revolted against the Germans (Treblinka Aug. 2, 1943 , Sobibor Oct. 14, 1943, Auschwitz Oct. 4, 1944).

Cana, see Kanah.

Canaan, fourth son of Ham son of Noah and ancestor of Canaanites. Cursed by Noah to be slave of slaves to his brothers (Gen. 9:21–27).

Canaan, Land of, land promised to Israelites (e.g., Gen. 17:8; Ex. 6:4). No single geographical definition exists in Bible. Term occasionally indicates extensive area encompassing all of Erez Israel and Syria, at other times confined to strip of land along E. shore of Mediterranean. Its population was not homogeneous and various peoples lived there. The population was primarily Semitic. Its inhabitants were known as Canaanites. Israelite settlement c.1200 B.C.E. marks end of Canaanite period in Palestine.

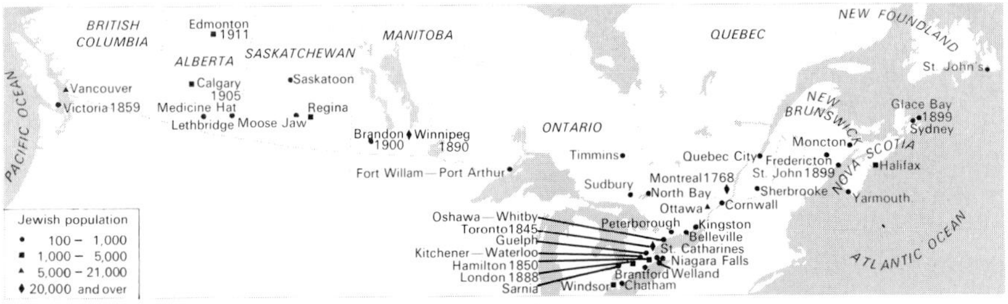

Jewish communities in Canada, 1969, and founding dates of communities.

Eddie Cantor

The earliest known notation of Pentateuch cantillation, Western Ashkenazi, in J. Reuchlin, "De accentibus et orthographia linguae hebraicae," Hagenau, 1518.

"Canaanites," group of Israel poets and artists active from c. 1942, whose ideology was creation of Hebrew nation that would also include Moslems, Christians, and all who wished to join, without connections with the Jewish people but on basis of Hebrew language and general integration into Middle East.

Canada, N. American country. Community dates fr. British conquest of New France (1759) and was mainly concentrated in Montreal. First congregation She'arith Israel (Sephardi), founded 1768. Most prominent Jewish families among early settlers were Hart, Joseph, and Judah families. Full civil rights granted 1832. Canada's present-day Jewish community dates from 1880s with large E. European influx. In 1930s anti-immigration and anti-Jewish sentiment kept Jewish immigration low. Twenty-two Conservative synagogues in Canada in 1960s, 13 Reform (by 1970), and 175 Orthodox. Cities with largest Jewish populations (1971) are: Montreal (113,000), Toronto (97,000), Winnipeg (21,000), and Vancouver (8,000). Representative organization: Canadian Jewish Congress. Active Zionist Federation. In post-WWII period, Jews prominent in distilling industries, textile, clothing and other light industries and academic fields. Jewish pop. 300,000 (1971).

Canadian Jewish Congress, national Canadian organization. Founded 1919 to assist E. European Jewry. Subsequently considered representative organ and official voice of Canadian Jewry.

Canadian Jewish Eagle, see Kanader Adler.

Canary Islands, islands belonging to Spain, off NW Africa. Jews sought refuge there fr. Spanish Inquisition. Scene of several autos-da-fé. In 1950s, some Moroccan Jews settled there.

Candelabrum, see Menorah.

Candia, see Crete.

Candle Tax, tax imposed on Jewish community in E. Europe in 18th and early 19th c. on Sabbath, festival and other candles connected with religious usage. It was heavy imposition on poor Jews.

Cannstadt, Karl (1807–1850), German physician. Established cholera hospital for Belgian government. Prof. of internal medicine at Erlangen Univ. (1844). His *Handbuch der medizinischen Klinik* (1841) substituted clinical observation for speculative natural philosophy.

Canpanton (Campanton), Isaac ben Jacob (1360–1463), Castilian rabbi; author of methodological study of Talmud. A student of Kabbalah whose doctrines were circulated by his many students.

°**Cantera Burgos, Francisco** (1901–), Spanish Hebraist; prof. at Madrid Univ. Co-edited scholarly journal *Sefarad* and wrote about Spanish Jewish history and culture.

Canticles, see Song of Songs.

Cantillation, term used to indicate musical rendition of Hebrew scriptures, talmudic texts, synagogue services.

Cantoni, Alberto (1841–1904), Italian humorous author. Wrote short stories, essays, and a novel.

Cantoni, Raffaele (1896–1971), Italian economist, communal leader. Pres. Union of Italian Jewish Communities.

Cantonists, Jewish children conscripted into Russian army for up to 25 years in conditions designed to force them to convert. Jewish communities had to supply annual quota. The system, in force fr. 1827 to 1856, left bitter memories in minds of Jewish masses in Russia.

Cantor, see Ḥazzan.

Cantor, Bernard (1892–1920), U.S. Reform rabbi, social worker. Member of first overseas unit of Joint Distribution Committee for relief service in Poland and Ukraine (1919). Murdered by bandits in Ukraine with Israel Friedlander.

Cantor, Eddie (1892–1964), U.S. comedian, vaudeville, radio, and film star. Starred in *Ziegfeld Follies* (1917 ff.) and other Broadway hits. Popularized many songs ("Whoopee", "If You Knew Susie"). Active in philanthropic causes, Jewish and non-Jewish. Founded and headed Screen Actors' Guild.

Cantor, Jacob Aaron (1854–1921), U.S. politician. Manhattan Borough president 1901, New York Democratic congressman 1913.

Cantor, Moritz Benedict (1829–1920), German mathematician; prof. at Heidelberg. Wrote extensively on history of mathematics.

Capa, Robert (1913–1954), U.S. combat photographer; b. Budapest. Covered Spanish Civil War, WWII, Israel War of Independence, and Indochina War, where he was killed by landmine. Brother **Cornell** (1918–), photographer for *Life*, etc.

Cape Province, province in S. Africa. Jewish immigration slow at beginning of 19th c., mostly fr. Germany, England; larger numbers came fr. E. Europe in 1880s. Various independent Jewish institutions, incl. Bet Din with chief rabbi. Jewish pop. 32,670 (1971), mainly in Capetown.

Capernaum (Kefar Naḥum), ancient village on NW shore of Sea of Galilee. In New Testament it appears as place of residence of Jesus and site of synagogue where he preached. At least five of the apostles were fisher-

men from Capernaum. A Judeo-Christian community continued there into talmudic times. Synagogue (fr. 2nd–3rd c. C.E.) was excavated and partly restored by the Franciscan fathers who own the site.

Capetown, city in S. Africa. Under British rule (1801) steady Jewish immigration, first from England and C. Europe, then E. Europe. Hebrew congregation, first in S.A., 1841; first synagogue 1849. Early center of Zionism. Jewish pop. 25,650 (1971).

Caphtor, place located either in Aegean Sea area or on S. coast of Asia Minor. Original home of Philistines (Amos 9:7, Jer. 47:4). Probably ancient name for Crete and surrounding islands.

°**Capistrano, John (Giovanni) of** (1386–1456), Franciscan friar and popular preacher, one of fiercest medieval opponents of Jews. Active in W. Europe, Poland.

Capital Punishment, penalty prescribed in Bible for certain offenses (e.g., murder, adultery, incest, idolatry, Sabbath desecration). In Talmud four methods are distinguished: stoning, burning, slaying, strangling. It is doubtful whether the detailed talmudic discussions reflect actual practice. Imposition was in fact almost impossible and discouraged. In Middle Ages it was applied in a few exceptional cases (for informing). In Israel, it can only be imposed in cases of genocide or wartime treason. Its only application has been in the case of Adolf Eichmann.

Capitolias, city E. of the Jordan founded 98/99 C.E.; later one of the cities of the Decapolis.

Caplan, Rupert (1896–), Canadian radio and TV executive. Pioneer in Canadian radio and TV drama. Produced plays in Montreal theaters.

Capon, Augusto (1872–1944), Italian admiral. Posts included frigate commander in WWI and chief of naval intelligence. Promoted admiral 1931. Italian racial laws forced him to resign commission (1938). Died in Auschwitz.

Capp, Al (Alfred Gerald Caplin; 1909–), U.S. cartoonist; creator of comic-strip character "Li'l Abner," satirizing U.S. political and social scene.

Capsali, Elijah (c. 1483–1555), rabbi, historian; lived in Candia, Crete. His *Seder Eliyahu Zuta* surveys Ottoman Empire history and Spanish and Portuguese expulsions with special reference to Jews.

Capsali, Moses ben Elijah (1420–1496 or 1497), Turkish rabbi, communal leader. *Dayyan* in Constantinople. Accused of misinstructing public on matters of family purity and excommunicated; decree later rescinded. Outstanding rabbi of Ottoman Empire.

Captives, Ransoming of (Heb. *pidyon shevuyim*), religious duty to ransom a fellow Jew who has been captured by slave traders or robbers or unjustly imprisoned. During Middle Ages, regarded as one of most important *mitzvot.* European communities organized special efforts to ransom captives of N. African pirates.

Capusi, Ḥayyim (c. 1540–1631), Egyptian rabbi; known as *"Ba'al Nes"* after his sight was restored after period of complete blindness. Cairo Jews went to visit his grave on annual anniversary of his death.

Carasso, Emmanuel (1862–1934), Turkish lawyer, politician. Prominent in Young Turk movement, parliamentary deputy fr. 1908.

Carben (Karben), Victor von (1422–1515), apostate, anti-Jewish writer. Participated in disputation with Jews. Taught at Cologne Univ.

Carcassonne, city in S. France. First evidence of Jews 839; community established later; expelled in 14th c. Center of Jewish scholarship in Middle Ages. 74 Jews in 1968.

Cardozo, Aaron Nuñez (1762–1834), Gibraltar merchant. Important local figure, consul for beys of Tunis and Algiers.

Cardozo, Abraham Miguel (1626–1706), physician, outstanding leader and propagandist of Shabbatean movement, especially after Shabbetai Ẓevi's apostasy. Became Marrano in Spain, reverted to Judaism in Italy. Killed by nephew in family quarrel in Cairo.

Cardozo, Albert Jacob (1828–1885), U.S. jurist. Elected to Court of Common Pleas on Tammany ticket 1863. Judge on New York State Supreme Court 1867; impeached following Tammany Hall exposé 1872 and resigned. Father of Benjamin Nathan Cardozo.

Cardozo, Benjamin Nathan (1870–1938), U.S. lawyer, Supreme Court justice. Justice of Supreme Court of New York 1913, Judge of Court of Appeals 1917 and its chief judge 1927. Appointed 1932 by President Hoover to Supreme Court. Staunch supporter of New Deal and outstanding writer on law.

Cardozo, David Nuñez (1752–1835), U.S. patriot in Revolutionary War. Fought in S. Carolina Grenadiers.

1st-cent. synagogue at Capernaum.

The "Old" Synagogue, Cape Town, built 1863.

Al Capp

Detail from 16th-cent. calvary in Carcassonne (showing Jews wearing pointed Jewish hat of the period).

Benjamin Cardozo

Cardozo, Isaac (Fernando; 1604–1681), Marrano physician, philosopher. Fled fr. Spain and returned to Judaism in Venice. Published medical and scientific works. Brother of Abraham Miguel Cardozo.

Cardozo, Jacob Newton (1786–1873), U.S. economist, journalist; lived in Charleston, S.C., 1796–1860. Noted early American economist in classical liberal tradition. Son of David Nuñez Cardozo.

Carigal (Carregal, Karigal), Raphael Ḥayyim Isaac (1729–1777), emissary of Hebron. In his travels he was engaged as visiting rabbi of Curaçao, teacher of Talmud in London, *ḥakham* in Surinam. Delivered sermon in Newport, Rhode Island, attended by governor and magistrates of the state. Friendly with Ezra Stiles, president of Yale.

Carlebach, Ezriel (1908–1956), writer, journalist in Hebrew, Yiddish, and German; b. Leipzig. Editor of Tel Aviv paper *Yedi'ot Aḥaronot* fr. 1939. Founded 1948 and edited *Ma'ariv*, Israel's largest newspaper.

Carlebach, Joseph (1882–1942), German rabbi, educator. Rabbi in Luebeck, Altona, Hamburg. D. in concentration camp.

Carlebach, Shlomo (1926–), rabbi, composer, singer; b. Berlin, in U.S. fr. 1939. Created neo-ḥasidic folk song style which became extremely popular.

Carmel, Moshe (1911–), Israel military commander, cabinet minister; b. Poland, settled in Ereẓ Israel 1924. Commanded Northern District in 1948 War of Independence. Edited Aḥdut-ha-Avodah daily, *La-Merḥav*. Minister of transport 1955–56, 1965–69.

Carmel, Mount, mountain range in N. Israel nr. Mediterranean coast. Highest pt. 1,742 ft. above sea-level. Scene of contest between Elijah and Baal priests (I Kings 18:19 ff.). In Crusader period monastery founded, but in 1921 destroyed by Muslims, who murdered the monks. With modern Jewish settlement the moshavah Zikhron Ya'akov was founded (1883) but no other Jewish settlement until suburbs of Haifa expanded to northern slope. Druse villages Isfiya, Dāliyat al-Karmil on its slopes. Much of it earmarked as nature reserve, national park, afforestation, and recreation areas. "Cave of Elijah" at the foot of the hill is sacred to Jews, Christians, and Muslims.

Carmi, T. (pseudonym of **Carmi Charney**; 1925–), Hebrew poet, editor; b. New York, settled in Ereẓ Israel 1947. Translated many works (mainly drama) into Hebrew.

Raphael Ḥayyim Isaac Carigal

The Mount Carmel caves

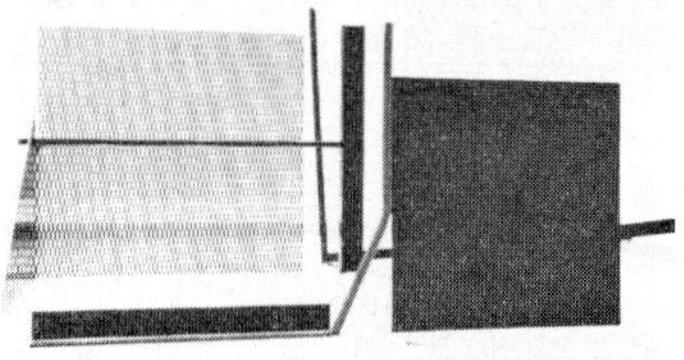

"The Window," sculpture by Anthony Caro.

Title page of early edition of Joseph Caro's "Shulḥan Arukh," Venice, 1594.

Carmoly, Eliakim (1802–1875), German rabbi, writer, editor. Pioneer in study of Jewish medical history; suspected of carelessness and even forgery in his work on ancient manuscripts.

Carmona, Bekhor Isaac David (1773–1826), Turkish financier who maintained a yeshivah. Accused by an Armenian rival of conspiracy and fraud, he was executed.

Carnovsky, Morris (1897–), U.S. stage, screen actor. Blacklisted for refusal to give names to House Committee on Un-American Activities. Fr. 1965 appeared in Shakespearean roles at Stratford, Conn.

Caro, Anthony (1924–), British sculptor. Assistant to Henry Moore. Fr. 1960 adopted uncompromising abstract style.

Caro, David (c. 1782–1839), Hebrew writer, educator; b. Poland, fr. 1800 in Posen, where he founded first Jewish school. Wrote *Berit Elohim* (1820), which supported Reform and was first open attack by Haskalah writer on rabbinate.

Caro, Georg Martin (1867–1912), German economist, social historian. Main field: medieval and modern C. Europe. Also wrote *Social and Economic History of the Jews in the Middle Ages and the Modern Age.*

Caro, Heinrich (1834–1910), German chemist. Worked in Germany and England; discovered many dyestuffs and industrial production techniques.

Caro, Isaac ben Joseph (late 15th c.), talmudist, rabbi in Spain and, after the expulsion, in Turkey. Adopted his nephew, Joseph Caro. Wrote commentary on Pentateuch.

Caro, Joseph ben Ephraim (1488–1575), codifier, mystic, author of *Shulḥan Arukh;* lived in Turkey, Safed. His *Beit Yosef,* a commentary on the legal code *Arba'ah Turim* of Jacob ben Asher, aimed at simplifying the law by investigating talmudic sources, discussing development and divergent views, and arriving at a decision. His *Shulḥan Arukh,* for which he is best known, is simplification of *Beit Yosef,* giving only the law and not the analysis. The *Shulḥan Arukh* (codifying Sephardi custom and to which was added Moses Isserles' *Mappah* codifying Ashkenazi custom) is the basis of Jewish law today. *Kesef Mishneh* is a commentary on Maimonides' *Mishneh Torah.* He also wrote many responsa. He was a kabbalist and

ETROG "Descendant of the High Priest" by Isidor Kaufmann, c. 1903. The young ḥasidic boy is holding the *etrog* ("citron") and *lulav*.

GLASS Jewish gold glass from Rome. 3rd–4th cent. Familiar Jewish artistic motifs are portrayed.

claimed that he received revelation from a heavenly mentor *(maggid)*. Parts of his mystical diary appeared as *Maggid Mesharim*.

Caro, Joseph Ḥayyim ben Isaac (1800–1895), Orthodox rabbi in Poland who quoted German sources and spoke Hebrew fluently, unusual for Orthodox rabbis in his day. Wrote book of sermons.

Caro, Nikodem (1871–1935), German chemist. Innovator in chemical and fertilizer industries. Developed method for assaying calcium carbide that is still standard.

Caro-Delvaille, Henri (1878–1928), French painter. Known for elegant and fashionable drawings of women. Published philosophical work *L'invitation à la vie intérieure*.

Carp, Horia (Jehoshua; 1869–1943), Rumanian journalist, writer. Member of Rumanian Senate; arrested 1941 and tortured by Rumanian Fascists. D. Ereẓ Israel.

Carpentras, town in S. France. Jews fr. 12th c. Papal possession 1274–1791 and hence Jews exempt fr. many expulsions that were lot of French Jews, though their economic activities were restricted. Had their own liturgical rites. Community declined fr. end of 18th c. Synagogue restored and declared historic site.

Carpi, Leone (1887–1964), Italian Zionist leader. Helped organize Betar naval school in Civitavecchia and illegal immigration from Italy. Settled in Jerusalem 1956.

Carregal, see Carigal.

Carter, Victor M. (1910–), businessman, philanthropist in Los Angeles; President of Republic Pictures. National chairman of American Israel Bonds Campaign 1962–65; Chairman of Board of Tel Aviv Univ.

Carthage, ancient city in N. Africa, nr. modern Tunis. Jews present fr. Roman times. Status declined sharply with advent of Christianity.

Carvajal, Abraham Israel (Antonio Fernandez; c. 1590–1659), founder of London Jewish community. Services were held in his house years before readmission of Jews to England.

Carvajal, Luis de, "El Mozo" (1566–1596), New Christian in Spanish Mexico, heir to his uncle the governor. Openly returned to Judaism and was burned at stake. Wrote autobiography, letters, religious poetry.

Carvajal Y de la Cueva, Luis de (1539–1591?), New Christian admiral of Spanish fleet, Spanish governor in Mexico. Imprisoned by Inquisition and sentenced to exile for not denouncing his niece Isabel as Judaizer.

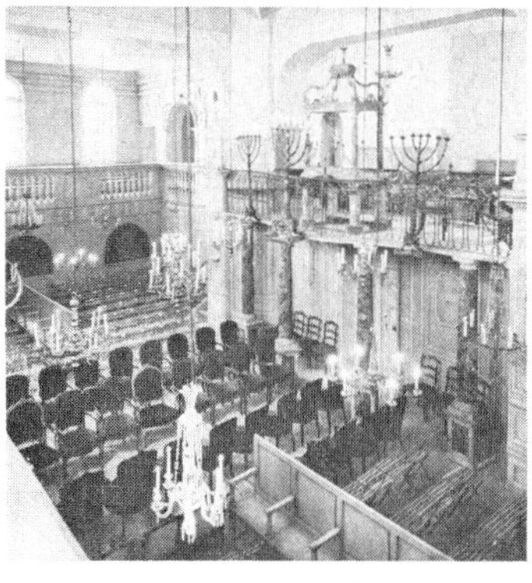

The synagogue of Carpentras, built 1367, reconstructed 1741–43.

A child from the Casablanca mellah learns to read Hebrew.

Caricature of Sir Ernest Cassel by Spy, "Vanity Fair," 1899.

René Cassin

Carvalho, Solomon Nunes (1815–1897), U.S. artist, photographer, inventor, and Jewish communal leader. First official photographer of exploratory expedition (mapping transcontinental railroad route 1853–4).

Casablanca, city in Morocco. Original Jewish community dispersed when city destroyed 1468; reestablished in 17–18th c. Fr. early 20th c. economic capital of Morocco, and its Jews prospered; also attracted Jews fr. interior of Morocco. Largest Jewish community of N. Africa. Emigration to France and Israel. Jewish pop. 70,000 (1948), 22,000 (1971).

Caspary, Eugen (1863–1931), German social welfare pioneer. Evolved new methods for meeting social problems and improving social services. Director of Central Welfare Bureau for German Jews 1917–28.

Casper, Bernard Moses (1917–), British rabbi. Served in London and Manchester as chaplain to Jewish Brigade in WWII and as dean of students at Heb. Univ. 1954–63. Chief rabbi of United Hebrew congregation of Johannesburg fr. 1963.

Caspi, Saul (c. 1600), Provençal Hebrew poet. Wrote religious and secular poems.

Cassab, Judy (1920–), Australian painter; b. Budapest, in Sydney fr. 1951. Painted portraits of British royalty, subsequently a leading nonrepresentational artist.

Cassel, David (1818–1893), German educator, scholar; member of group that founded Wissenschaft des Judentums. Ordained rabbi, devoted himself to scholarship, wrote and edited many books, and translated Apocrypha into German.

Cassel, Sir Ernest Joseph (1852–1921), British financier; b. Germany, in England fr. 1868. International banking figure. Close friend of Edward VII. Died a Roman Catholic. His granddaughter Edwina (1901–1960) married Earl Mountbatten.

Cassel, Paulus Stephanus (Selig; 1821–1892), German theologian, historian; convert to Christianity; brother of David Cassel. First to write Jewish history extensively using non-Jewish sources. Attacked anti-Semitism.

Cassin, René Samuel (1887–), French jurist, statesman; Nobel Prize laureate. Severely wounded in WWI and subsequently active on behalf of

war veterans and peace. Prof. of international law. Represented France at League of Nations and later United Nations. General de Gaulle's legal adviser in London and Algiers in WWII. President, Constitutional Council, 1959. Drafted Universal Declaration of Human Rights. Awarded Nobel Peace Prize in 1968. Headed Alliance Israélite Universelle fr. 1943.

Cassirer, Ernst (1874–1945), philosopher. Taught in Germany 1906–33, England and Sweden, and U.S. fr. 1941. Wrote on problem of knowledge. His *Essay on Man* contends that language, mythology, and sciences do not present different realms of real objects, but different symbolic expressions for understanding.

Cassirer, Paul (1871–1926), German art dealer, publisher. First to exhibit Manet, Monet, Van Gogh, Cézanne in Germany. Published works on modern artists.

Umberto Cassuto

Cassuto, Umberto (**Moses David**; 1883–1951), Italian historian, biblical and Semitic scholar. Fr. 1922–25 rabbi of Florence and director of rabbinical seminary there. Wrote history of Jews of Florence in Renaissance. Fr. 1939 prof. of Bible studies at Heb. Univ. While appreciating scholarly basis of Higher Criticism, he opposed the Graf-Wellhausen theories. Wrote important Ugaritic studies and was chief editor of *Enẓiklopedyah Mikra'it.*

Castel, Moshe Elazar (1909–), Israel painter. A founding member of New Horizons group which tried to introduce modernism to Israel art. Lived and painted in Safed.

Castelli, David (1836–1901), Italian scholar. For 25 years taught Heb. at Institute of Higher Studies in Florence. Translated fr. Bible and wrote on biblical and other Jewish topics.

Castelnuovo, Enrico (1839–1915), Italian author. Novels have social aim but describe Venetian scene romantically and affectionately in language of great elegance.

"Parchemin Rouge" by Moshe Castel.

Castelnuovo-Tedesco, Mario (1895–1968), composer. Forced by racial laws to leave Italy. In 1939 settled in Hollywood, where he also wrote film scores. His Jewish music included a violin concerto *The Prophets, Sacred Service,* and the opera *Saul.*

Castiglioni, Camillo (1879–1957), Austrian financier, art patron. Built economic empire that collapsed in mid-1920s. Became successful again after WWII. Converted to Christianity.

Castiglioni, Ḥayyim (**Vittorio**; 1840–1911), rabbi and author who taught mathematics in Trieste until appointment as chief rabbi of Rome 1903. Wrote book on Darwin's theories and collection of Hebrew sonnets.

Castile, former kingdom in Spain. Fr. late 11th c. major center of Spanish Jewry. Jews well treated in early Middle Ages, but status declined fr. 13th c. Until 15th c. Jews influential at court. Jews expelled in general expulsion fr. Spain 1492.

Castro, Abraham (16th c.), Egyptian mint-master, supervisor of economic affairs. Refused to mint new coin for a rebellious pasha and had to escape to Constantinople. The rebel was subsequently put to death after threatening Egyptian Jews and the anniversary of his death is celebrated annually by Cairo Jews as "Purim of Egypt."

Castro, Bendito de (alias **Baruch Nehemias**) (1597–1684), physician. Studied in Padua, worked in Hamburg; physician to Queen Christina of Sweden. Active in communal affairs. Supported Shabbetai Ẓevi.

Castro, David Henriques de (1832–1898), Dutch numismatist, bibliophile. Wrote on Jewish history. Sale catalog of his library and collection still studied.

Castro, Jacob ben Abraham (known as **Maharikas**; 1525?–1610), talmudic commentator, halakhic authority. Had regular correspondence with Joseph Caro, whose *Shulḥan Arukh* he annotated.

Castro, Rodrigo de (1550–1627), Marrano physician. Practiced in Lisbon and was of service to Spanish armada before it sailed (1588). Settled in Hamburg 1594 and returned to Judaism. Considered founder of scientific gynecology and one of fathers of medical jurisprudence.

Castro Sarmento, Jacob (Henrique) de (1691–1762), Marrano physician; b. Portugal, in London fr. 1721. Fellow of Royal Society 1730. Wrote on Jewish religious and medical subjects. Left Judaism.

Jacob de Castro Sarmento

Castro Tartas, David de (c. 1625–c. 1700), Amsterdam printer of Hebrew and other books. Printed *Gazeta de Amsterdam,* one of first Jewish newspapers.

Castro Tartas, Isaac de (c. 1625–1647), Marrano martyr. Settled in S. America, outwardly a Christian. Taken by Inquisition to Lisbon he declared his allegiance to Judaism and was burnt at stake. His dying cry of *Shema* made strong impression.

Catacombs, subterranean tunnels for burial of dead. Jewish catacombs have been found in Ereẓ Israel in Beth Shearim and elsewhere in Rome, Carthage, Malta, Sardinia.

Catechumens, House of, institution in Rome for converts to Christianity. Until 1810 Jews had to contribute to it.

Cattaui, Jacob (1801–1883), Egyptian merchant, community leader. Member of leading Egyptian Jewish family. First Jew in Egypt to receive title "bey"; director of treasury. In old age, president of Cairo community.

Cattaui, Joseph Aslan (1861–1942), Egyptian industrialist, politician,

community leader. Minister of finance 1924, minister of communications 1925, senator 1927–36. Leader of Jewish community.

Cattaui, René (1896–), Egyptian scholar, businessman. Employed by Royal Archives; directed many companies; member of parliament; president of Cairo Jewish community. Left Egypt 1957.

Caucasus, mountainous region in S. Soviet Union. Jews probably present since Second Temple period. Many Jews forced to convert at time of Muslim conquest (8th c.). Site of Khazar Jewish state. European Jews excluded at time of Pale of Settlement. 1959 Jewish pop. 125,000: 35,000 Georgians, 25,000 Mountain Jews (many speaking local Jewish dialects), rest Russian Jews. Strong Zionist and religious feelings were maintained and many emigrated to Israel fr. 1970.

Cavalleria, Alfonso (d.c. 1506), high church official of Jewish origin. Participated in establishing Inquisition in Barcelona, but remained friendly with Jews.

Cavalleria, Judah Benveniste (d. 1411), court official in Aragon. Banker and tax farmer; represented king in various matters. Jewish scholar and community leader; his home was refuge for many in 1391 persecutions.

Cavalleria, Judah de la (d. 1276), high official of King James I of Aragon. Bailiff of Saragossa and Valencia.

Cavalleria, Salomon de la (14th c.), Jewish communal leader, tax farmer, *dayyan* in Aragon. Active in culture, wrote poetry.

Cavalleria, Vidal de la (d. 1373), tax farmer, Jewish communal leader in Aragon.

Cavalleria, Vidal Joseph (c. 1370–c. 1456), Spanish scholar, communal leader. Represented community at Disputation of Saragossa. Baptized.

°**Cazalet, Edward** (1827–1883), British industrialist who worked for return of Jews to Ereẓ Israel. Wanted to build railroad fr. Syria to Mesopotamia and settle Jews on adjacent lands.

Cazès, David (1851–1913), Moroccan historian, educator. Worked for Alliance Israélite Universelle, established schools in Middle East and N. Africa. Wrote on Tunisian Jewish history.

Cechu-Zedu, Svaz ("League of Czech-Jews"), union established 1919 to embrace existing Czech-Jewish assimilationist associations. Suppressed by Nazis.

Emanuel Celler

Celler, Emanuel (1888–), U.S. congressman fr. Brooklyn, New York. Staunch New Deal supporter. Had consistent liberal record. Elected chairman of House Judiciary Committee 1948. Champion of political Zionism.

Centos, Polish organization for care of orphans. Established 1924 to centralize care for WWI orphans. In 1938, 15,000 children were in its care. Its best-known worker was Janusz Korczak. Activities ended with Holocaust, when children and teachers were killed.

Central British Fund (CBF), principal British refugee relief agency, founded 1933 as CBF for German Jewry. Assisted settlement of C. European Jews in U.K. Assisted refugees fr. Hungary, Egypt in 1956.

Central Conference of American Rabbis (CCAR), national association of Reform rabbis. Membership exceeds 900 (incl. rabbis from outside U.S.). Founded 1889 at initiative of I.M. Wise, who headed it until 1900.

Central-Verein Deutscher Staatsbuerger Juedischen Glaubens (C.V.), organization founded 1893 in Berlin to safeguard Jewish social and civil equality against German anti-Semitism. 70,000 members in 1927. Closed down by Gestapo and merged with Reichsvertretung on Nov. 10, 1938.

Centre de Documentation Juive Contemporaine (C.D.J.C.), French Jewish organization established 1943 by Isaac Schneersohn to collect material on Holocaust. Also concerned itself with racism, punishment of war criminals, and compensation of victims of Nazis.

Cerf, Bennett Alfred (1898–1971), U.S. publisher, editor, anthologist, humorous writer. Cofounder of Random House Publishing Company (1927). Popular radio-TV panelist ("What's My Line? ").

Cerfberr, Herz (1726–1794), French politician, philanthropist; b. Alsace. Established factories to draw Jews from petty trading to manual labor. Prominent in struggle for emancipation.

Cernauti, see Chernovtsy.

Cervetto, Jacob Basevi (1682–1783), violoncellist, composer. Settled in London 1728 and played in Theatre Royal orchestra, Drury Lane. Later manager. Introduced violoncello into England.

Ceylon, island state S. of India. Jews reported in 9th and 12th c. Small number of farmers in 19th c. No Jewish community today.

Chagall, Marc (1887–), artist; b. Vitebsk, Russia, in France fr. 1923 (in U.S. 1941–48). Work characterized by poetic cubism and sense of whimsicality and fantasy. Jewish themes prevalent. Worked in stained glass: cathedral in Metz, Hadassah synagogue in Jerusalem, UN Secretariat in New York, Vatican audience hall. Decorated New York, Paris opera houses.

Marc Chagall

Chagy, Berele (1892–1954), *ḥazzan,* composer. Served in Detroit, Boston, Johannesburg, S. Africa, and Temple Beth-El, Brooklyn. Concerts and recordings made him extremely popular. Published *Tefillot Chagy,* 87 recitatives for Sabbath services.

Chain, Sir Ernest Boris (1906–), British biochemist; received Nobel Prize for role in discovery of penicillin; b. Berlin, in Cambridge, England fr. 1933. Scientific director of International Research Center for Chemical Microbiology in Rome 1948–61; then prof. at Imperial College, London.

Chajes, Hirsch (Ẓevi) Perez (1876–1927), rabbi, scholar, Zionist leader. Taught religion in Lemberg and was librarian in Vienna, then taught Jewish history, Bible, Hebrew in Florence's Collegio Rabbinico Italiano. In 1918 returned to Vienna and became chief rabbi. Ardent Zionist and distinguished writer.

Chajes, Isaac ben Abraham (1538–c. 1615), rabbi of Prague and author of aggadic and halakhic works.

Chajes, Saul (1884–1935), E. European bibliographer. Worked in archives of Vienna Jewish community. Wrote *Oẓar Beduyei ha-Shem,* list of pseudonyms used in Hebrew literature.

Ẓevi Hirsch Chajes, cast bronze plaque by Ivan Sors.

Chajes, Ẓevi Hirsch (1805–1855), rabbinic scholar with broad secular knowledge. Rabbi in Zolkiew and Kalish. His annotations to Talmud incorporated in many editions. Also wrote *Student's Guide through the Talmud.*

Chajn, Leon (1910–), Polish lawyer, politician. Deputy minister of justice 1945–49, deputy chairman Polish Democratic Party after 1961.

Chaldea, Chaldeans, ethnic group related to Arameans. Penetrated S. Mesopotamia toward end of 2nd millenium B.C.E. Eventually became ruling class of Neo-Babylonian Empire and S. Mesopotamia became known in classical sources as Chaldea. Chaldean (Neo-Babylonian) Dynasty was founded by Nabopolassar (625–605 B.C.E.), who gained control of Babylon. Abraham came from "Ur of the Chaldees." Aramaic was often called "Chaldean" by scholars until recently. Chaldeans was also a technical term for "astrologers."

°**Chamberlain, Houston Stewart** (1855–1927), British-born German racist, anti-Semitic author. Friend of Richard Wagner, whose daughter he married, and Hitler. Regarded Jews as uncreative "mongrel race whose existence is crime against humanity."

Chamber Theater, see Cameri.

Chamecki, Samuel (1917–), Brazilian civil engineer. Posts include prof. of civil engineering at Univ. of Parana 1941 and director of construction at Polytechnic Center. Wrote *Course of Statistics of Construction.*

Channel Islands, English islands off coast of France. Converted Portuguese Jew, Edward Brampton, governor 1482. Jewish traders in 18th c. Few Jews in 19th, 20th c.

Chao Ch'eng (formerly **An San;** 15th c.), Chinese soldier; earliest known member of Chao, leading family of Jewish community of Kaifeng. Granted high military rank and post in Chekiang 1421–23.

Chao Ying-Ch'eng (d. 1657), Chinese administrator. Knew Hebrew; was responsible for rebuilding Kaifeng synagogue 1653. When in Fukien was regarded as Confucian mandarin. Remained religious Jew when in Honan, his home province.

Chapiro, Jacques (1887–), Russian painter; prominent member of School of Paris. Painted sets for Habimah production of *The Dybbuk.*

Charity, obligation to help the poor and needy; considered one of cardinal *mitzvot* of Judaism. Even recipient of charity is required to give charity. No stigma is placed on accepting charity for as Hebrew term implies *ẓedakah* ("righteousness"), rightfully belongs to the poor. Various methods of collecting and dispensing of charity have been used including: 1) charity wardens in each community; 2) begging; 3) charity box; 4) soup kitchens; 5) clothing funds; 6) burial groups known as *ḥevra kaddisha* and other charitable associations.

Charles, Gerda (**Edna Lipson;** c. 1915–), English novelist. Works reflect revolt against "insensitivity" of provincial life. Novels include *The Crossing Point, The Slanting Light.*

Charleston, city in S.C., U.S. One of oldest Jewish communities in America. First formal congregation Kahal Kadosh Beth Elohim organized 1749. Considered birthplace of Reform Judaism in America. Jewish pop. 2,800 (1971).

Charna, Shalom Yonah (1878–1932), educator in Lithuania. Wrote 3-vol. history of Jewish education.

A Jewish charity soup kitchen, London's East End, 1879.

Beth Elohim Synagogue, Charleston, built 1840.

Charney, Daniel (1888–1959), Yiddish poet, journalist; brother of S. Niger and B.C. Vladeck; b. Minsk, Russia, went to U.S. 1947. Wrote stories, fables, articles, incl. *Barg Aroyf,* and memoirs *A Yortsendlung Aza: 1914–24.*

Chasanowich, Joseph (1844–1919), Zionist; founder of Jewish National Library in Jerusalem. Worked in Bialystok most of his life as a doctor. Fervent supporter of Herzl. Collected 63,000 books, 20,000 in Hebrew, which became basis of National and University Library.

Chasanowich, Leon (pseudonym of **Katriel Shub;** 1882–1925), Labor Zionist leader; b. Vilna. Secretary of world Po'alei Zion movement 1913–19. Fr. 1920 worked for ORT in Carpatho-Russia.

Chasins, Abraham (1903–), pianist, writer on music. Composed character piano pieces that were very popular. Musical director of WQXR radio station, New York.

Chatzkels, Helene (1882–), pedagogue, writer, translator. A founder and leader of Yiddish school network in Lithuania. Wrote textbooks, children's stories, etc. Taught in Kovno until 1966.

Chavel, Charles (Dov) Ber (1906–), U.S. rabbi, scholar. Translated Maimonides' *Sefer ha-Mitzvot* and wrote extensively on Naḥmanides.

Chayefsky, Paddy (1923–), U.S. playwright. Wrote television and stage plays. Works include *The Tenth Man* based on the dybbuk legend and *Marty* (the movie version won an Academy Award).

Chebar, canal in Mesopotamia, most likely the modern silted-up Shatt el-Nil, on the banks of which, near the village of Tel Abib, the prophet Ezekiel experienced his initial vision.

Chedorlaomer, king of Elam who led a punitive expedition against Canaanite kings in the course of which Lot was taken prisoner. Abraham pursued the victors, rescued the captives, and retrieved the booty (Gen. 14).

Chein, Isidor (1912–), U.S. psychologist. Research worker in psychological aspects of social problems such as intergroup relations and narcotics addiction. Articles on adverse effects of segregation quoted by U.S. Supreme Court 1954 desegregation decision.

Chelm, town in Poland. One of earliest Jewish communities in Poland, possibly fr. 12th c. Many Jews killed in 1648 Chmielnicki massacres, but community revived in 18th c. Almost entire community murdered by Germans in WWII. In Jewish folklore, famous for alleged naïveté of its inhabitants, about whom many stories are told.

Chelm, Solomon ben Moses (1717–1781), Polish rabbi; one of the first *maskilim* in Poland. Rabbi in Zamosc; last years in Tiberias. Wrote *Mirkevet ha-Mishneh,* novellae on Talmud and Maimonides; also halakhic code based on *Shulḥan Arukh.*

Chelmno, Nazi extermination camp nr. Lodz for mass extermination of Jews. Estimates of number of Jews murdered vary fr. 152,000 to 360,000. Only 2 Jews survived the camp.

Chelouche, Avraham (1812–1858), early settler in modern Ereẓ Israel; b. Algeria. One of first Sephardim to settle in Jaffa. His nephew **Yosef Eliyahu** (1870–1934), a founder of Tel Aviv.

Chemosh, chief Moabite god. His cult was known to the Israelites and Solomon built a high place to him in Jerusalem which was only desecrated 400 years later in Josiah's time.

Cherethites, group of foreign mercenaries associated with Pelethites who formed royal bodyguard in time of King David. Name probably meant Cretan.

Cherith, brook in vicinity of the Jordan where Elijah hid (I Kings 17:3, 5). Various identifications have been suggested.

Cherkasky, Martin (1911–), U.S. medical administrator. Director Montefiore Hospital in N.Y. 1951 and prof. and chairman dept. of community health, Albert Einstein College of Medicine, Yeshiva Univ., 1967.

Cherniavski, family of Odessa musicians. **Jan** (1892–), pianist, **Leo** (1890–), violinist, and **Michael** (1893–), cellist, were a well-known trio. Made New York debut 1916. Performed individually after separating. Another brother, **Alexander** (1896–), sister **Marion,** and cousin **Boris** formed another trio. Alexander settled in S. Africa after WWI and became an impressario.

Chernigov, city and province in the Ukraine. Community fr. Middle Ages destroyed in 1648 massacres. Renewed after end 18th c. Centers of Ḥabad Ḥasidim. Over 10,000 Jews pre-WWII, killed during Nazi occupation. Estimated Jewish pop. (1970), 4,000.

Cherniss, Harold (1904–), U.S. scholar of classical philosophy; prof. at Institute of Advanced Studies at Princeton. Traced development of Aristotelian system.

Chernovtsy (Czernowitz; Cernăuţi), city in Ukrainian SSR. Jews present fr. 15th c. Early settlers Ashkenazim and Sephardim; late arrivals from Galicia and Poland, and community predominantly Ashkenazi. Intercommunal tensions (ḥasidim v. *maskilim;* Orthodox v. Reform) in 19th c. 50,000 Jews in 1941, many deported to their deaths in WWII. Jewish pop. 70,000 (1970) with single small synagogue.

Cherny, Sasha (Alexander Mikhailovich Glueckberg; 1880–1932), Russian poet; one of foremost humorists of early 20th c. Wrote rhymes for children. In 1920 left Russia for France and Germany; writings militantly anti-Soviet.

Cherub, winged celestial being. Cherubim were stationed at the entrance of the Garden of Eden to guard the way to the tree of life (Gen. 3:24). There were two facing cherubim in the Tabernacle and in Solomon's Temple. The Bible contains variant descriptions of the cherubim. Figures of winged creatures are well known from the art and religious symbolism of the Ancient Near East.

Chicago, city in Ill., U.S. Jews among Chicago's earliest settlers. First congregation Kehillath Anshe Ma'arav, founded 1846. Chicago Jewry participated in Chicago civic and political life very early in history of community. Recruited company of 100 volunteers to serve 82nd Regiment of Illinois Volunteers during Civil War. After 1880s Jewish immigrants from E. Europe mainly concentrated in clothing and tobacco industries. In 1961 Chicago had 43 Orthodox synagogues, 25 Conservative, 16 Reform, and 5 Traditional. Jewish institutions include College of Jewish Studies and Hebrew Theological College. Jewish pop. 269,000 (1971), 4th largest Jewish community in America.

Chief Rabbi, Chief Rabbinate, office representing continuation of ancient trend to confer on one or a few persons central religious authority for either the whole of Jewry or for a particular country or region. In medieval times the chief rabbi was often tax collector or liaison between royalty and the Jewish community. Titles included *rab de la corte* (Spain), *dienchelele* (Sicily), *ḥakham bashi* (Ottoman Empire), *grand rabbin* (France), *chief rabbi* (British Commonwealth; Israel).

Chile, S. American republic. Marranos were known from early Chilean history (16th c.) and occupied high positions in Spanish administration, but were extirpated by Inquisition. Presence of Jews forbidden until Independence in 1810. Jewish immigration slow until 1900. Persistent anti-Semitism inhibited communal activities. In 1919 first congress of Chilean Jewry convened. Settlers fr. E. Europe and also fr. Argentina as well as Sephardim fr. Mediterranean lands. Jewish pop. 32,000 (1971), 90% in Santiago.

The Great Synagogue of Chernovtsy

Sphinx-like cherub from King Ahab's ivory palace, Samaria, 9th cent. B.C.E.

Chinese clay figurine of Semitic appearance, probably a Jew, Tang dynasty (618–907 C.E.).

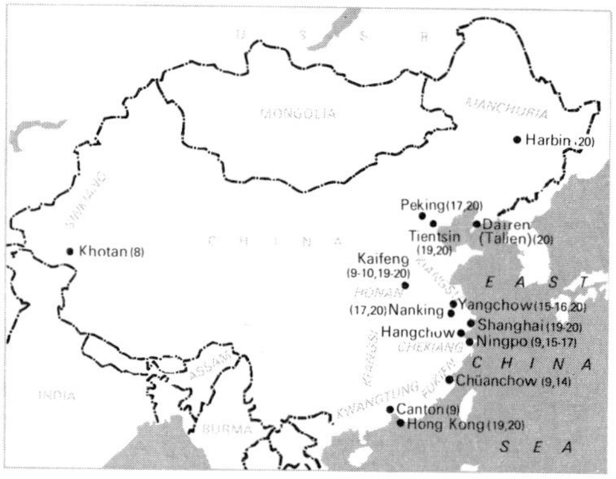

Main places of Jewish settlement in China from the 8th cent. to modern times. Number indicates cent.

Chilion, see Mahlon and Chilion.

Chim, see Seymour, David.

China, Asian republic. Jews lived in China fr. 9th c., probably coming by caravan fr. Persia. Subsequent communities existed at different periods, best-known at Kaifeng from 10th c. which disappeared fr. assimilation by 19th c. Jews from Russia settled fr. late 19th c. (Shanghai, Harbin, Tientsin). Community augmented by refugees fr. 1917 Russian Revolution, Hitler. Jewish pop. 25–30,000 during WWII. All left after the war. Communist China's attitude to Israel extremely hostile.

Chinnereth, Chinneroth, fortified city of tribe of Naphtali on shore of Sea of Galilee.

Chios, Greek island off Turkish coast. Jews there in antiquity. In Middle Ages in separate quarter. Blood libel 1892. Many Jews killed in WWII. No community after WWII.

Chipkin, Israel (1891–1955), U.S. Jewish educator. Director of Jewish Education Association of New York 1921–44 and American Association for Jewish Education 1944–49. Got Hebrew introduced into New York City high school system. Edited the journal *Jewish Education.*

Chiquatilla, see Gikatilla.

Chizhik, Barukh (1884–1955), Ereẓ Israel naturalist; b. Ukraine, settled in Ereẓ Israel 1906. Improved strains of fruit trees and other crops and wrote books on agriculture and Ereẓ Israel flora.

Chizhik, Efrayim (1899–1929), Haganah leader; b. Ukraine; brother of Barukh Chizhik. When kibbutz Ḥuldah was cut off in riots he led group of 23 defenders against thousands of Arabs. Killed in subsequent retreat.

Chizhik, Ḥannah (1899–1951), a founder of women's agricultural training in Israel; b. Ukraine, immigrated with brother Barukh in 1906.

Chizhik, Sarah (1897–1920), defender of Tel Ḥai; b. Ukraine; sister of Barukh Chizhik. Fell with Joseph Trumpeldor in Arab attack on Tel Ḥai.

Chmelnitzki, Melech (1885–1946), Yiddish poet, medical popularizer; b. Kiev, fr. 1939 in New York. Wrote on medical themes for *Jewish Daily Forward.*

Chmielnicki Massacres (1648–49), massacres of E. European Jewry by Cossacks led by Bogdan Chmielnicki (1595–1657). The Cossack uprising was directed against Polish rule in Ukraine; 100,000 Jews were killed and 300 communities destroyed.

Cholent, Sabbath dish; a stew generally prepared on Friday and kept in oven until Saturday lunch. Among the Sephardim, known as *Ḥamin.*

Chomsky, Dov (1913–), Hebrew poet, educator; b. Minsk, settled in Ereẓ Israel 1936. Fr. 1964 general secretary of Writers' Union.

Chomsky, Noam Avram (1928–), U.S. linguist; son of William Chomsky. Prof. at MIT. Outspoken critic of Vietnam war. Propounded revolutionary linguistic conceptions.

Chomsky, William (1896–), U.S. educator; b. Russia, in U.S. fr. 1913. Taught at Gratz College, Philadelphia, and Dropsie College. Advocated centrality of classical Hebrew language and literature in the curriculum of the Jewish school. Wrote on Hebrew language.

Cast bronze cholent pot, Frankfort, 1582.

Basalt chair found inside synagogue at Chorazin, believed to be a "seat of Moses" used by the elders of the congregation.

Chorazin, town in Galilee where Jesus preached. City in ruins by 4th c. Synagogues excavated in 1905, 1926, and 1962–63. Modern settlement, Almagor, founded 1961.

Chorin, Aaron (1766–1844), pioneer of Reform Judaism in Hungary. Began by abrogating minor customs, for which he was attacked and his books were burned. Later, extended his reforms to abolishment of the *Kol Nidrei* service, changing the text of other prayers, permitting prayer in the vernacular and with uncovered head, permitting the use of the organ, writing and riding on the Sabbath. Fought for secular education.

Chorny, Joseph Judah (1835–1880), traveler, ethnographer; settled in Caucasus as young man. Wrote about Mountain Jews and Jewish communities of Georgia, Bukhara, and Persia. Traveled in mountains and wrote memoirs.

Chosen People, common designation for the people of Israel, expressing the idea that the people of Israel stand in a special and unique relationship to God. Idea is central to history of Jewish thought. Modern thinkers have interpreted the aspect of chosenness by purpose of mission, i.e., the Jewish people have been chosen to relate the message of God to the world. Chosenness, then, in its modern sense, is quite distinct from "unique," "different," or "superior."

Chotzner, Joseph (1844–1914), scholar, writer. Studied in Breslau. Minister in Belfast and teacher at Harrow. Wrote on humor and satire in Jewish literature.

Chouraqui, André (1917–), Israel author, public figure; b. Algeria, moved to France, fought in Resistance in WWII, immigrated to Israel.

Deputy mayor of Jerusalem. Wrote many books, incl. history of Jews of N. Africa.

Christiani, Pablo (d. 1274), convert to Christianity and anti-Jewish polemist; b. S. France. In disputation at Barcelona with Naḥmanides, tried to prove validity of Christianity from Talmud.

Chroneck, Ludwig (1837–1891), German actor, stage director of Meiningen Court Theater, Weimar. Initially attacked for use of realism, his approach was ultimately adopted throughout German theater.

Chronicles, Book of, book of Hagiographa section of Bible. Now divided into I Chron. and II Chron., it was originally a single book. Division first found in the Septuagint, where it appears among historical books after Kings. Describes history of Israel until destruction of Kingdom of Judah. A lengthy introduction, mainly comprised of various lists, serves as background. Scholars hold it was composed during Persian period, in 4th c. B.C.E. Traditionally ascribed to Ezra and Nehemiah and modern scholars suggest Chronicles, Ezra, Nehemiah originally single work.

Chronology, Jewish Methods of. From beginning of Israelite Monarchy, years were counted according to the regnal years of the kings. In the Persian period (fr. 539 B.C.E.) the Jews, as Persian subjects, counted according to the regnal years of the contemporary Persian monarchs (cf. Zech. 1:1). From the Hellenistic period until the Middle Ages the Seleucid reckoning was used. The victory of Seleucus and Ptolemy over Demetrius Poliderates in 312 B.C.E. was taken to mark the beginning of a new era. Other eras which did not last were the Hasmonean era (from the accession of Simeon the Hasmonean, 143/2 B.C.E.), the "Era of the Redemption of Zion" (66–70 C.E.), and the era of "The Freedom of Israel" (131–135 C.E.). Dates have also been reckoned from the destruction of the Second Temple. The era at present in use among Jews is the "Era of the Creation," according to which the years are calculated from the creation of the world *(Anno Mundi),* placed at 3761 B.C.E. It came into popular use about the 9th c. C.E.

Chuetas, term of abuse given to Marranos of Majorca. Long after they converted to Christianity they were penalized and lived in special area.

Chufut-Kale, town in Crimea with Karaite community fr. 13th c. Center of Karaite Hebrew printing. Small Karaite community untouched during WWII.

Chujoy, Anatole (1894–1969), U.S. dance critic and historian. Founder-editor of *Dance News.* Compiled *Dance Encyclopedia* and *The New York City Ballet* and wrote books on ballet.

Churgin, Pinkhos (1894–1957), educator, religious Zionist leader; b. Belorussia, went to U.S. 1915. Helped develop Yeshiva Univ. President of Mizrachi Organization. Wrote studies on Targum and Second Temple period. Fr. 1955, first head of Bar-Ilan Univ., Ramat Gan.

Chwistek, Leon (1884–1944), Polish philosopher of science. Prof. of mathematical logic at Lvov fr. 1930. Best-known work: *The Limits of Science.*

Chwolson, Daniel (1819–1911), Russian orientalist. Converted to Christianity 1855. Leading Semitics scholar. Remained well disposed to Jews and Judaism, frequently intervening with government authorities on behalf of Orthodox Jews. Fought against blood libel. His rich Hebrew library given to Asiatic Museum of Russian Academy of Sciences.

Ciechanow (Tsekhanov), Abraham ben Raphael Landau of ("Czechanower"; 1789–1875), rabbi, author, ḥasidic *zaddik* in Poland. Extremely conservative talmudic scholar and ascetic.

Cilibi Moïse (pseudonym of **Ephraim Moses ben Sender;** 1812–1870), Rumanian popular philosopher. Originally peddler. Published 14 collections of his popular wisdom and anecdotes.

Cincinatti, city in Ohio, U.S. Home of oldest Jewish community west of Alleghenies and Hebrew Union College (founded 1875). First congregation Bene Israel founded 1824. Union of American Hebrew Congregations founded there 1873. Jewish pop. 28,000 (1971).

Circumcision, operation removing part or all of foreskin covering glans of penis; performed in Jewish tradition on 8th day after birth on healthy child or at earliest time thereafter on sickly child. Circumcision is the religious act of entering into the Jewish covenant with God. It is called the covenant of Abraham (cf. Gen. 17:11–12). The operation is performed by a *mohel.* The godfather who holds the child on his lap is the *sandak.* The chair on which the child is placed before the operation is called the Chair of Elijah.

BOOK OF CHRONICLES–CONTENTS

I Chron. 1:1–9:44		An introduction
	1:1–54	A collection of genealogical lists
	2:1–9:1	Various lists of the Israelite tribes.
	9:2–18	A list of the inhabitants of Jerusalem.
	9:19–34	Detailed list of the Levitical functionaries.
	9:19–44	A list of the inhabitants of Gibeon.
I Chron. 10:1–II Chron. 9:31		The monarchy under David and Solomon
	I Chron. 10:1–29:30	David
	II Chron. 1:1–9:31	Solomon.
II Chron. 10:1–36:23		History of the kings of Judah
	10:1–12:16	The reign of Rehoboam.
	13:1–23	The reign of Abijah.
	14:1–16:14	The reign of Asa.
	17:1–20:37	The reign of Jehoshaphat.
	21:1–20	The reign of Jehoram.
	22:1–9	The reign of Ahaziah.
	22:10–23:21	The reign of Athaliah.
	24:1–27	The reign of Joash.
	25:1–28	The reign of Amaziah.
	26:1–23	The reign of Uzziah.
	27:1–9	The reign of Jotham.
	28:1–27	The reign of Ahaz.
	29:1–32:33	The reign of Hezekiah.
	33:1–20	The reign of Manasseh.
	33:21–25	The reign of Amon.
	34:1–35:27	The reign of Josiah.
	36:1–4	The reign of Jehoahaz.
	36:5–8	The reign of Jehoiakim.
	36:9–10	The reign of Jehoiachin.
	36:11–21	The reign of Zedekiah.
	36:22–23	The decree of Cyrus.

The I.M. Wise Temple, Cincinnati, consecrated 1866.

Ritual circumcision implements. Silver and amber knife, Near East, 1819; silver bottle and foreskin bowl, Italy, 18th-19th cent.; silver protective shield, France, 19th cent. Set against manuscript book of rules and prayers for circumcision, Germany, 1729.

Citroën, André Gustave (1878–1935), French engineer, industrialist. In WWI increased production of ammunition. Developed the popular low-priced car.

Citroen, Paul (1896–), Dutch artist. Influenced by Sturm and Dada movements. Best known for pencil drawing portraits of famous personalities.

Citron, see Etrog.

City, Levitical, see Levitical Cities.

City of David, see David, City of.

City of Hope National Medical Center, medical center under Jewish auspices founded 1912 as Duarte Sanitorium, Duarte, California, nr. Los Angeles, for treatment of Jewish consumptives. Subsequently center for research in and treatment of catastrophic diseases.

City of Refuge, in the Bible 6 cities set aside for accidental killers as refuge from relatives of victim. Three cities were on each side of the Jordan and the accidental manslayer was immune. On the death of the high priest the manslayer could leave the city and if killed by the blood avenger the latter was liable to death.

Claims Conference, see Conference on Jewish Material Claims Against Germany.

Clermont-Ganneau, Charles (1846–1923), French orientalist. Discovered the Mesha Stele 1868 and an inscription from Herod's Temple.

Cleveland, city in Ohio, U.S. First Jewish settlers and congregation 1839. Stronghold of Reform (Rabbis Abba Hillel Silver, Barnett Brickner). After WWII, home of Telz Yeshivah. Jewish pop. of Greater Cleveland 80,000 (1971).

Clifton, see Passaic-Clifton.

Clore, Sir Charles (1904–), British financier. Started "takeover" method of company acquisition. Donated large sums to Israel.

Cluj (Hung. **Kolozsvár,** Ger. **Klausenberg**), city in Rumania, center of Transylvania. Jews lived there before prohibition on residence was abolished in 1848. Center of Jewish national movement. Most of the 15,000 Jews deported by Germans in WWII. 6,500 Jews in 1947 but steady decline; 1,100 remained in 1970.

Clurman, Harold (1901–), U.S. theater director. A founder and director of the Group Theater (1931). Drama critic for *The New Republic* (fr. 1948) and *The Nation* (fr. 1952).

CODIFICATION OF THE LAW

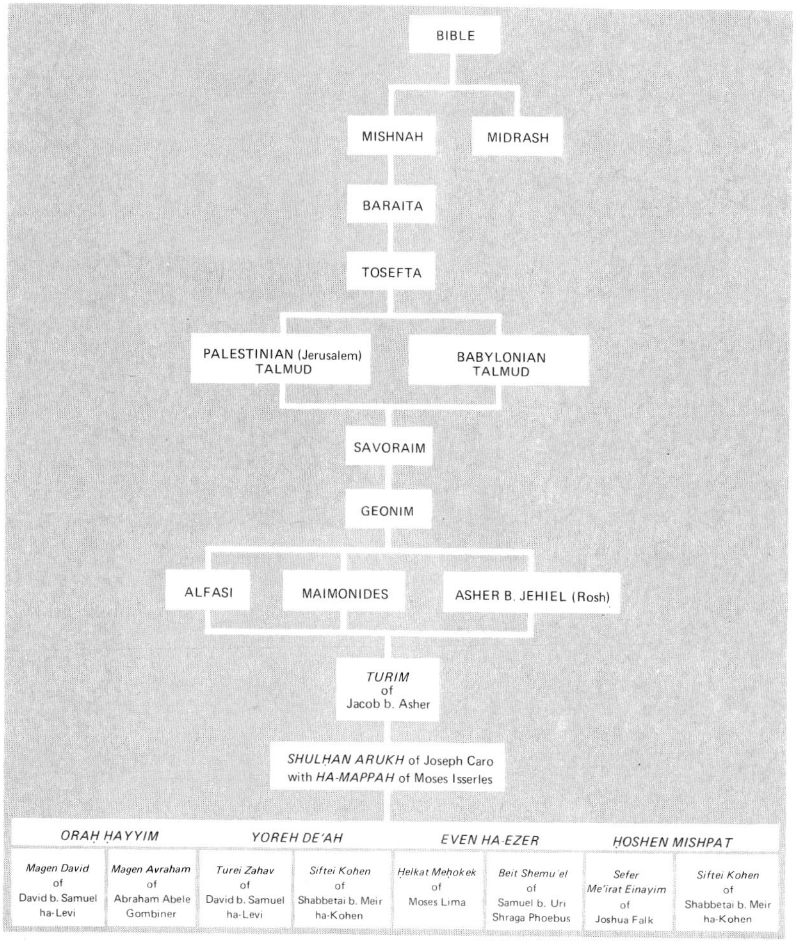

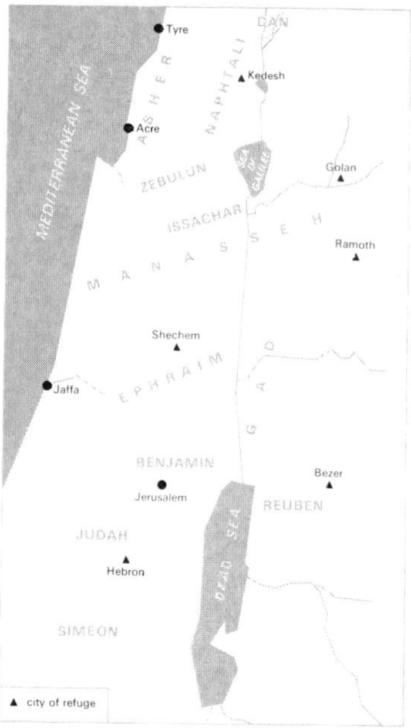

Cities of refuge in ancient Erez Israel.

The Great Synagogue of Cluj, opened 1887, partially destroyed 1944, restored 1970.

Cochin "White Jewish" bridal pair, 1932.

Cobb, Lee J. (1911–), U.S. actor. Worked in Group Theater 1930s. Portrayed Willy Loman in Arthur Miller's *Death of a Salesman* (1949). Appeared in numerous plays, films, TV series.

Cochin, city and former state in SW India. Jewish settlement in Cochin is ancient, earliest written records dating fr. c. 1000. There are 3 groups who did not intermarry: White Jews, Black Jews, and "Freedmen." The Cochin Jews were protected by the rajahs during Portugese rule (1502–1663), and obtained cultural autonomy and religious freedom under Dutch (1663–1795). Fr. c. 2,500 Jews in 1968, the community declined, mostly through emigration to Israel, to less than 100 in 1969.

Coele-Syria, official Seleucid designation for those portions of Erez Israel and S. Syria captured by Antiochus III from the **Ptolemies** (c. 200 B.C.E.). Geographical meaning of the term changed during last c. B.C.E.

Coen, Achille (1844–1921), Italian historian. Prof. of history at Univ. of Florence 1887–1911 and teacher of several noted Italian historians.

Coen, Giuseppi (1811–1856), Italian painter, pioneer art photographer. Landscape and architectural painter.

Coèn, Graziadio Vita Anania (1751–1834), Italian rabbi in Florence. Wrote early studies of Hebrew poetry.

Cohen, family of Italian majolica makers, active in Pesaro and Ancona fr. 1614 to 1673. Together with Azulai family they produced most of majolica seder dishes made in Renaissance Italy.

Cohen, Liverpool family. **Louis Samuel** (1846–1922), b. Australia, founder of Lewis' Ltd. chain stores, mayor of Liverpool 1899–1900; his son **Harold Leopold** (1873–1936), benefactor; another son, **Sir Jack Brunel** (1886–1956), lost both legs in WWI; treasurer of British Legion, member of parliament 1918–31; a grandson, **Sir Rex Arthur Louis** (1906–), chairman of Lewis' 1958–65.

Cohen, Abraham (1887–1957), English scholar, communal leader, and first minister to preside over Board of Deputies of British Jews. Minister in Birmingham fr. 1913. Wrote *Everyman's Talmud.*

Cohen, Albert (1895–), French novelist; b. Corfu. Active in international organizations. Wrote poems and novels with Jewish themes, often about Cephalonian Jewry, incl. *Solal of the Solals* and *Nail-cruncher. La Belle du Seigneur* won the Prix Goncourt.

Cohen, Alexander H. (1920–), U.S. producer; known on Broadway as "millionaire boy angel."

Cohen, Alfred Morton (1859–1949), U.S. lawyer, politician, Jewish civic leader. Served on Cincinatti City Council and state senate. A founder of national YMHA organization 1890 and international president of B'nai B'rith 1925–38.

Cohen, Sir Andrew (1909–1968), British colonial administrator. In WWII, organized food supply to Malta. Fr. 1947, as undersecretary of state at Colonial Office, prepared African colonies for independence; governor of Uganda 1952–57; at UN 1957–61; secretary of Ministry of Overseas Development 1961.

Cohen, Arthur (1830–1914), English lawyer. Member of parliament 1880–87; member of Privy Council; president of Board of Deputies 1874–94.

Cohen, Benjamin (1726–1800), Dutch financier. Financial adviser to Prince William of Orange. Made loans to governments, sponsored Hebrew publications.

Cohen, Benjamin I. (c. 1798–1845), U.S. banker; brother of Mendes I. and Jacob I. Cohen. He and another brother, **David I.** (1800–1847), helped establish the Baltimore Stock Exchange (1837).

Cohen, Benjamin Victor (1894–), U.S. lawyer, public official. One of Franklin Roosevelt's inner circle of advisers. Director of Office of Economic Stabilization 1942–43; legal adviser, International Monetary Conference, Bretton Woods, 1944.

Cohen, Bernard (1933–), British painter. Represented Britain at Venice Biennale 1966 with brother Harold. Abstract expressionist.

Cohen, Boaz (1899–1968), U.S. rabbinic scholar. Taught at Jewish Theological Seminary. Published bibliography of medieval rabbinic responsa, works on comparative law.

Cohen, Chapman (1868–1954), English philosopher. Editor of *Freethinker* and anti-religious activist.

Cohen, David (1883–1967), Dutch historian, Jewish leader. Prof. of ancient history at Leiden and Amsterdam. Co-chairman of Jewish council appointed by Germans 1941–43; Theresienstadt concentration camp 1943–45. In 1947 temporarily arrested on charges of collaboration with Nazis; Jewish court excluded him from participation in all Jewish functions.

Majolica Passover plate by Jacob Cohen, Ancona, 1654, and signed on the reverse.

Eli Cohen

Cohen, Eli (1924–1965), Israel intelligence officer executed in Damascus; b. Egypt, settled in Israel 1957, and joined intelligence service. Arrested in Damascus January 1965. Widely regarded as master spy, with high-level connections with Syrian government.

Cohen, Elliot Ettelson (1899–1959), U.S. journalist. Managing editor *The Menorah Journal* 1925–31 and later *Commentary* 1945–59.

Cohen, Emil Wilhelm (1842–1905), Danish prof. of minerology and geology; convert to Lutheranism. The mineral cohenite named after him.

Cohen, Ernst Julius (1869–1944), Dutch physical chemist; prof. at Utrecht. Explained phenomenon of "tin disease." In 1944 refused to flee country; d. Auschwitz.

Cohen, Felix (1907–1953), U.S. legal philosopher; son of Morris Raphael Cohen. Insisted that law cannot escape dealing with ethics. Writings include *Ethical Systems and Legal Ideals* and *The Legal Conscience.*

Cohen, Francis Lyon (1862–1934), British rabbi, writer on Jewish liturgical music. Chief minister in Sydney, Australia and senior chaplain, Australian Army, 1914–34.

Cohen Gustave (1879–1958), Belgian historian of medieval French theater and literature; convert to Catholicism. Prof. at Sorbonne and laureate of Académie Française.

Cohen, Harold, see Cohen, Bernard.

Cohen, Harriet (1901–1967), British concert pianist. Many composers wrote special pieces for her, notably Sir Arnold Bax.

Cohen, Harry (1885–1969), U.S. surgeon, inventor, author. Invented clamp tourniquet, ligature guide, and surgical forceps for intravesical use. Coedited *Jews in the World of Science.*

Cohen, Henry (1863–1952), U.S. Reform rabbi, humanitarian. As rabbi in Galveston, Texas, advocated penal reform. Headed Jewish Immigrants' Information Bureau, which helped settle over 10,000 Jews under the Galveston Plan.

Cohen, Henry Baron (1900–), British physician. Brilliant diagnostician and leading medical administrator; involved in establishment of National Health Service. Prof. of medicine at Liverpool 1934–65. Active in Jewish affairs.

Hermann Cohen, drawing by Max Liebermann, 1912.

Cohen, Hermann (1842–1918), German philosopher; founder of Marburg School of neo-Kantianism. His reinterpretation of Kant was extremely idealistic. Defended Judaism against critics, and when he left Marburg for Berlin (1912) he came closer to Judaism. Extremely influential on modern Jewish philosophers.

Cohen, I. Bernard (1914–), U.S. historian of science. Wrote on Benjamin Franklin and Isaac Newton. Prof. of history of science at Harvard.

Cohen, Irvin J. (1908–), U.S. medical administrator. Executive vice-president Maimonides Medical Center, Brooklyn, and chairman Health Care and Hospital Administration Program of State University of New York 1967.

Cohen, Isaac Kadmi (1892–1944), French Zionist writer, lawyer; father of Jean-François Steiner; b. Poland, lived in Ereẓ Israel, then went to France. Adherent of French left and Zionist extreme right; d. in Holocaust.

Cohen, Israel (1879–1961), British writer, Zionist. As Zionist official, toured world to investigate condition of Jews. Wrote many books and articles, incl. *A Short History of Zionism, Jewish Life in Modern Times.*

Cohen, Israel (1905–), Hebrew critic, editor. Spent childhood in Galicia and Czechoslovakia, settled in Ereẓ Israel 1925. Edited *Ha-Po'el ha-Ẓa'ir* 1948–70.

Cohen, Jacob I. (1744–1823), U.S. banker, merchant; b. Germany, in U.S. fr. 1773. Served in Revolutionary Army. Settled in Richmond, Va. 1780.

Cohen, Jacob I. (1789–1869), U.S. banker, public servant; nephew of Jacob I. Cohen. Participated with Solomon Etting in fight for Jewish equality in Maryland. In 1826 elected member of Baltimore City Council (president 1845–51).

Cohen, Sir John Edward (Jack; 1898–), British businessman. Founder and chairman of Tesco Stores, a chain of shops.

Cohen, John Michael (1903–), English critic, translator. Works include: translations of Cervantes' *Don Quixote* and Rabelais' *Gargantua and Pantagruel; History of Western Literature* and *Latin American Writing Today.*

Cohen, Joseph (1817–1899), French publicist, lawyer. Head of Algerian consistory 1845–48; edited first Jewish weekly in France, *La Vérité israélite,* 1860–62.

Cohen, Joshua I. (1801–1870), U.S. physician. One of first American otologists, prof. of minerology at Univ. of Maryland. His valuable collection of Judaica housed at Dropsie College. Brother of Benjamin I., David I., Jacob I., and Mendes I.

Cohen, Julius Berend (1859–1935), British organic chemist. Taught at Manchester until 1891, then Yorkshire (Leeds). Fellow of Royal Society.

Cohen, Leonard (1934–), Canadian poet, novelist, folksinger; b. Montreal, settled on Greek island of Hydra. Published books of verse. Famed for his ballads *(Songs of Leonard Cohen).*

Cohen, Levi-Abraham (1844–1888), Moroccan journalist. Founded *Le Réveil de Maroc* and was *Times* correspondent. Influential in political and diplomatic circles.

Cohen, Lionel Leonard, Baron (1888–1973), English judge, jurist. Appointed Lord Justice of Appeal and privy councillor 1946. Chaired Company Law Amendment Committee and Council on Prices, Productivity, and Incomes.

Cohen, Louis (1799–1882), British banker, broker. Manager of Stock Exchange and authority on Indian railroads and Turkish finance. Conservative M.P.

Cohen, Lyon (1868–1937), manufacturer, community leader in Montreal, Canada. Cofounder of *Jewish Times,* Canada's first Jewish periodical, and first president of Canadian Jewish Congress.

Cohen, Marcel (Samuel Raphael; 1884–), French linguist, philologist. Substantiated proofs for thesis that all Semitic idioms and all branches of Semitic-Hamitic languages are of same parentage. Founded research center for comparative Semitics and Hamitic called GLECS.

Cohen, Maxwell (1910–), Canadian lawyer. Member of Canadian delegation to UN 1959–60 and chairman of government commission on hate and propaganda 1965–66 which recommended legislation against dissemination of material causing racial or religious hatred. Prof. at McGill Univ., Montreal, fr. 1952 (dean of Law Faculty 1964).

Maxwell Cohen

Cohen, Mendes (1831–1915), U.S. engineer. Served as president of several railroad companies and American Society of Civil Engineers. A founder of American Jewish Historical Society. Son of David I. Cohen.

Cohen, Mendes I. (1796–1879), U.S. traveler, writer. Visited almost every country in Europe and Near East. His letters and diaries constitute rich source of information

about Jewish life in these countries. First American to explore the Nile. Brother of the banker Jacob I. Cohen.

Cohen, Morris Abraham ("Two-Gun Cohen"; 1887–1970), soldier of fortune; b. London. Made his fortune in Canada and went to China, where he was military adviser to Sun Yat-sen and Chiang Kai-shek, with rank of general. Captured by Japanese in WWII. Settled in England after war.

Cohen, Morris Raphael (1880–1947), U.S. naturalist philosopher, educator. Founded Conference on Jewish Relations 1933 and the quarterly *Jewish Social Studies* 1939. In *The Meaning of Human History* developed the theory that human history is expressed by a cyclical process of fruition and degeneration. *An Introduction to Logic and Scientific Method* (with Ernest Nagel) became a standard text in American universities.

Cohen, Mortimer Joseph (1894–1972), U.S. rabbi in Philadelphia. Editor of *Pathways Through the Bible.* Pres. of Jewish Book Council.

Cohen, Nathan Edward (1909–), U.S. social work educator. Dean of UCLA 1968. Writings include *Social Work in the American Tradition* and *Social Work and Social Problems.*

Cohen, Paul Joseph (1934–), U.S. mathematician. Prof. of mathematics at Stanford Univ. (1963). Wrote *Set Theory and the Continuum Hypothesis.*

Cohen, Philip Melvin (1808–1879), U.S. pharmacist. City apothecary of Charleston 1838, member of city board of health 1843–49.

Cohen, Sir Robert Waley (1877–1952), British industrialist, Jewish communal leader. One of directors of Shell Petroleum Co. Forceful president of United Synagogue; helped establish Jewish War Memorial and Council of Christians and Jews. His son **Sir Bernard Waley-Cohen** (1914–), lord mayor of London 1960–61; vice-president of United Synagogue.

Cohen, Ruth Louisa (1906–), British economist; sister of Sir Andrew Cohen. Specialized in agricultural economics; principal of Newnham College, Cambridge fr. 1954.

Cohen, Samuel Herbert (1918–1969), Australian Labor politician; lawyer in Melbourne. State senator fr. 1961, deputy leader of Labor opposition. Active in Jewish affairs.

Cohen, Shalom ben Jacob (1772–1845), Hebrew writer, poet, editor; b. Poland, lived in Germany and Vienna. Editor of *Ha-Me'assef* 1809–11. Founded and edited the periodical *Bikkurei ha-Ittim.* His poetic *Nir David* about King David is one of first romantic works in Hebrew.

Cohen, Simon (Sam; 1890–), SW African businessman; lived in Windhoek. Known as "uncrowned king of South-West Africa" for his extensive business interests there.

Cohen, Wilbur Joseph (1913–), U.S. social welfare authority. Participated in drafting of Social Security Act. Became assistant secretary (later undersecretary and in 1968 secretary) of Department of Health, Education and Welfare. Wrote on welfare problems.

Cohn, Swiss family. **Arthur** (1862–1926), rabbi, leader of Orthodox Jewry. **Marcus (Mordecai**; 1890–1953), jurist, Zionist leader. In Israel fr. 1950; assistant attorney-general in Israel government.

Cohn, Albert (1814–1877), French scholar, philanthropist. Worked closely with James de Rothschild in charge of his philanthropic works.

Cohn, Benedict (1913–), U.S. aerodynamicist. Worked on design and wind tunnel development of B-29, B-50 Superfortress, B-47 Stratojet, and other Boeing civil and military models. Member National Advisory Council on Aeronautics.

Cohn, Berthold (1870–1930), German astronomer, mathematician, historian. Astronomer at Strasbourg Observatory. Wrote on Jewish calendar.

Cohn, Edwin Joseph (1892–1953), U.S. biochemist, Head of the chemistry dept. at Harvard fr. 1938. Discovered method of fractioning blood plasma.

Cohn, Elkan (1820–1889), Reform rabbi first in Germany then U.S., where he succeeded I.M. Wise in Albany and later served in San Francisco.

Cohn, Emil Moses (pen name **Emil Bernhard**; 1881–1948), German rabbi (in Berlin, Kiel, Essen), writer, active Zionist; in U.S. fr. 1939. Wrote plays, poems, etc.

Cohn, Ferdinand Julius (1828–1898), German botanist, pioneer bacteriologist. Prof. at Breslau. Founded Institute of Plant Physiology. Regarded as founder of modern microbiology.

Cohn, Fritz (1866–1922), German astronomer. Prof. at Koeningsberg, Berlin. Specialized in celestial mechanics. Edited the basic bibliographical work in astronomy.

Cohn, Gustav (1840–1919), German economist. Prof. at Goettingen fr. 1885. Made contributions to transportation and public finance.

Cohn, Haim (1911–), Israel jurist; b. Germany, settled in Ereẓ Israel 1933. Attorney general 1950–52, 1953–60; minister of justice 1952–53; Supreme Court justice fr. 1960. Adopted liberal approach to religious problems. Wrote *The Trial of Jesus.*

Cohn, Harry (1891–1956), U.S. movie pioneer; president and executive producer of Columbia Pictures Corporation.

Cohn, Jonas (1869–1947), German neo-Kantian philosopher, educator. Prof. at Freiburg. During WWII in England. Major work in aesthetics.

Cohn, Lassar (later **Lassar-Cohn**; 1858–1922), German chemist. Prof. of chemistry at Univ. of Koenigsberg and head of Jewish community there.

Cohn, Leopold (1856–1915), German classical and Hellenistic scholar. Prof. at Breslau Univ. Produced an authoritative edition of Philo.

Cohn, Meshullam Zalman ben Solomon (1739–1811), rabbi in Poland, Germany (fr. 1789 in Fuerth). A halakhic authority, his responsa reflect great erudition, esp. in matrimonial law.

Cohn, Mildred (1913–), U.S. physical biochemist. Pioneered in use of oxygen-18 isotope to elucidate organic reactions. Prof. at Univ. of Pennsylvania.

Cohn, Morris Mandel (1898–), U.S. public health engineer. Taught at Univ. of California and City College of New York. Consultant Atomic Energy Commission.

Cohn, Oscar (1869–1936), German socialist politician. Socialist member of Reichstag 1912–18, 1921–24. Active Zionist.

Cohn, Tobias ben Moses (1652–1729), physician, Hebrew author. Studied medicine in Frankfort and Padua. Court physician in Turkey; last years in Jerusalem. Main work: *Ma'aseh Tuviyyah,* an encyclopedia of medicine and other topics.

Cohnheim, Julius (1839–1884), German pathologist. Prof. at Kiel, Breslau, Leipzig. Pioneer in study of inflammation and suppuration.

Cohn-Reiss, Ephraim (1863–1943), Ereẓ Israel educator. Representative of Hilfsverein 1904–17 and supported German as language of instruction for technical subjects. Contributed to development of Jewish school network in Ereẓ Israel,

COINS

Persian Period, 4th cent. B.C.E. Falcon. Inscription: "YHD."

Herodian Dynasty, Agrippa I, 37–44 C.E. Three ears of barley issuing from two leaves.

Hasmonean Dynasty, Alexander Yannai, 103–76 B.C.E. Anchor encircled by wheel, with Greek inscription, "King Alexander."

Judaea Capta, Vespasian, 69–79 C.E. Veiled Judean captive seated mourning on the foot of a trophy. Inscription below, "IUDAEA."

Hasmonean Dynasty, John Hyrcanus II, 67–40 B.C.E. Hebrew inscription within wreath, "Yehoḥanan / ha-kohen / ha-gadol / ve-ḥever ha- / yehudim."

Bar Kokhba War, First Year, 132/3 C.E. Amphora with two handles encircled by inscription, "shenat aḥat li-ge'ulat Yisrael" ("year one of redemption of Israel").

Herodian Dynasty, Herod the Great, 40 [37]–4 B.C.E. Greek inscription around crested helmet, "King Herod."

Bar Kokhba War, Second Year, 133/4 C.E. Facade of Temple of Jerusalem, with Ark in front, and inscription "Shim'on."

Herodian Dynasty, Herod Archelaus, 4 B.C.E. – 6 C.E. War galley to left, with oars, "aphlaston," and battering ram.

Bar Kokhba War, Second Year, 133/4 C.E. Palm tree, with seven branches and two clusters of dates. Hebrew inscription below, "Shim'[on]." Traces of coin on which this one was overstruck can be seen.

War against Rome, First Year, 66/67 C.E. Stem with three fruits (probably pomegranates) encircled by Hebrew inscription, "Jerusalem is holy."

Value 25 agorot.

Value 500 perutot. Value 100 perutot.

The Israel Perutah series, 1949–60.

Agorah series issued by Bank of Israel, 1960.

Value one lira.

Agorah series issues by Bank of Israel, 1960.

A one-pound bank note of the British Mandatory Government of Palestine.

Coins issued by British Mandatory Government of Palestine.

Value IL. 5.

Third banknote series issued by Bank of Israel, 1969–72.

Value IL. 100.

but became extremely anti-Zionist and left country in 1917, living in Germany and France.

Cohon, Samuel Solomon (1888–1959), U.S. Reform rabbi, theologian. Prof. of theology at Hebrew Union College, Cincinnati, fr. 1923. Principal draftsman of Reform position in "Columbus Platform."

COJO, see World Conference of Jewish Organizations.

Coleman, Edward Davidson (1891–1939), U.S. writer, bibliographer. Compiled the bibliographies *The Bible in English Drama* and *Plays of Jewish Interest on the American Stage, 1752–1821.*

College of Jewish Studies, Chicago institute organized 1924 for systematic Jewish studies and training teachers. 370 students in 1970.

Collegio Rabbinico Italiano, Italian rabbinical college; first modern institution of its kind, inaugurated 1829 at Padua. Later transferred to Rome and Florence, then back to Padua.

Collins, Lottie (1866–1910), British actress, music hall singer. Gained fame in London in 1891 with song "Ta-ra-ra-boom-de-ay." Her daughter **Jose Collins (Cooney:** 1887–1958), famous musical comedy star *(Maid of the Mountains).*

Colmar, city in Alsace. Jews lived there fr. 1278; community burnt at stake in Black Death persecutions (1349), readmitted 1385, expelled 1512. Modern settlement after 1789. Fr. 1808 seat of consistory and fr. 1823 of chief rabbinate of Alsace. 1,200 Jews before WWI, when they were expelled. New community after war numbered 1,000 in 1970.

Cologne (Köln), city in W. Germany. Settlement from Roman times; massacres at time of First Crusade (1096) and Black Death (1349). Jews protected by archbishop in Second Crusade. Expulsion 1424. Asher b. Jehiel (the *Rosh*) lived there until 1303. Civil equality 1856. Headquarters of World Zionist Organization 1904–11. Jewish pop. 20,000 in 1933. Destroyed in WWII. New community after war numbered 1,350 in 1971.

Exhibition of Jewish history and culture in the Rhineland, organized by Cologne Municipality, 1963–64.

Colombia, S. American republic. Early Spanish settlers included Marranos, who were ousted by Inquisition (esp. in Great Conspiracy in Lima 1636). Jews settled in 19th c. Modern community after WWI emanating fr. Mediterranean countries and E. Europe. Jewish pop. 10,000 (1971), more than half in Bogotá, others in Cali and Medellin.

Colombo, Samuel (1868–1923), Italian rabbi, scholar. Headed rabbinical seminary in Leghorn.

Colombo, Yoseph (1897–), Italian educator. Founded Hebrew high school in Milan (head 1938–45). Edited *Rassegna Mensile di Israel* fr. 1965.

Colon, Joseph ben Solomon (c. 1420–1480), halakhist; b. France, latter part of life in rabbinical positions in Italy. His decisions had great influence on later Italian *halakhah.*

Colonne, Jules Edouard (Judah; 1838–1910), conductor. Leading violinist Paris Opera and Lamoureux Quartet. Founded Concerts Colonne.

Colorado, U.S. state. Jewish pop. 26,925 (1971), all but 2,000 in Denver. Jews there from 2nd half of 19th c. Simon Guggenheim was U.S. senator.

Colorni, Vittore (1912–), Italian jurist. Prof. at Ferrara. His major work, *Legge ebraica e leggi locali,* dealt with special status of Jews and Jewish law in Italy from medieval times.

Columbus, city in Ohio, U.S. First permanent Jewish settler c. 1838. First congregation B'nai Jeshurun organized 1846. Jewish pop. 13,000 (1971).

Comden, Betty (1919–), U.S. theatrical writer. Performed in musical revues and wrote books for musicals (sometimes in collaboration), incl. *Two on the Aisle* and *Wonderful Town.*

Comité des Delegations Juives, body established at end of WWI with representatives fr. various countries to present Jewish case at Versailles Peace Conference. Worked for minority rights, etc., esp. in E. Europe. Headed by Leo Motzkin 1924–33. In existence until 1936, when succeeded by World Jewish Congress.

Commandments Ten, see Decalogue.

Commandments, The 613 (Heb. *taryag mitzvot*), the total number of commandments in Pentateuch, of which 365 are prohibitions and 248 positive precepts (see next pages).

Illuminated page from the "Lisbon Bible," 1483, listing 17 of the 613 commandments.

MANDATORY COMMANDMENTS

GOD

The Jew is required to [1]believe that God exists and to [2]acknowledge His unity; to [3]love, [4]fear, and [5]serve Him. He is also commanded to [6]cleave to Him (by associating with and imitating the wise) and to [7]swear only by His name. One must [8]imitate God and [9]sanctify His name.

TORAH

The Jew must [10]recite the *Shema* each morning and evening and [11]study the Torah and teach it to others. He should bind *tefillin* on his [12]head and [13]his arm. He should make [14] *zizit* for his garments and [15]fix a *mezuzah* on the door. The people are to be [16]assembled every seventh year to hear the Torah read and [17]the king must write a special copy of the Torah for himself. [18]Every Jew should have a Torah scroll. One should [19]praise God after eating.

TEMPLE AND THE PRIESTS

The Jews should [20]build a Temple and [21]respect it. It must be [22]guarded at all times and the [23] Levites should perform their special duties in it. Before entering the Temple or participating in its service the priests [24]must wash their hands and feet; they must also [25]light the candelabrum daily. The priests are required to [26]bless Israel and to [27]set the shewbread and frankincense before the Ark. Twice daily they must [28]burn the incense on the golden altar. Fire shall be kept burning on the altar [29]continually and the ashes should be [30]removed daily. Ritually unclean persons must be [31]kept out of the Temple. Israel [32]should honor its priests, who must be [33]dressed in special priestly raiment. The priests should [34]carry the Ark on their shoulders, and the holy anointing oil [35]must be prepared according to its special formula. The priestly families should officiate in [36]rotation. In honor of certain dead close relatives the priests should [37]make themselves ritually unclean. The high priest may marry [38]only a virgin.

SACRIFICES

The [39]*tamid* sacrifice must be offered twice daily and the [40]high priest must also offer a meal-offering twice daily. An additional sacrifice *(musaf)* should be offered [41]every Sabbath, [42]on the first of every month, and [43]on each of the seven days of Passover. On the second day of Passover [44]a meal offering of the first barley must also be brought. On Shavuot a [45]*musaf* must be offered and [46]two loaves of bread as a wave offering. The additional sacrifice must also be made on [47] Rosh Ha-Shanah and [48]on the Day of Atonement when the [49] Avodah must also be performed. On every day of the festival of [50] Sukkot a *musaf* must be brought as well as on the [51]eighth day thereof.

Every male Jew should make [52]pilgrimage to the Temple three times a year and [53]appear there during the three pilgrim Festivals. One should [54]rejoice on the Festivals.

On the 14th of Nisan one should [55]slaughter the paschal lamb and [56]eat of its roasted flesh on the night of the 15th. Those who were ritually impure in Nisan should slaughter the paschal lamb on [57]the 14th of Iyyar and eat it with [58] *mazzah* and bitter herbs.

Trumpets should be [59]sounded when the festive sacrifices are brought and also in times of tribulation.

Cattle to be sacrificed must be [60]at least eight days old and [61]with-

1. Ex. 20:2	2. Deut. 6:4
3. Deut. 6:5	5. Ex. 23:25;
4. Deut. 6:13	Deut. 11:13
6. Deut. 10:20	(Deut. 6:13 and
7. Deut. 10:20	also 13:5)
9. Lev. 22:32	8. Deut. 28:9
10. Deut. 6:7	
11. Deut. 6:7	
12. Deut. 6:8	
13. Deut. 6:8	14. Num. 15:38
	15. Deut. 6:9
16. Deut. 31:12	
17. Deut. 17:18	
18. Deut. 31:19	19. Deut. 8:10
20. Ex. 25:8	21. Lev. 19:30
22. Num. 18:4	23. Num. 18:23
24. Ex. 30:19	
25. Ex. 27:21	
26. Num. 6:23	27. Ex. 25:30
	28. Ex. 30:7
	29. Lev. 6:6
30. Lev. 6:3	
31. Num. 5:2	32. Lev. 21:8
33. Ex. 28:2	
34. Num. 7:9	
35. Ex. 30:31	
	36. Deut. 18:6–8
	37. Lev. 21:2–3
	38. Lev. 21:13
39. Num. 28:3	40. Lev. 6:13
	41. Num. 28:9
43. Lev. 23:36	42. Num. 28:11
44. Lev. 23:10	
46. Lev. 23:17	45. Num. 28:26–27
47. Num. 29:1–2	
49. Lev. 16	48. Num. 29:7–8
50. Num. 29:13	
51. Num. 29:36	
53. Ex. 34:23;	52. Ex. 23:14
Deut. 16:16	
54. Deut. 16:14	
56. Ex. 12:8	55. Ex. 12:6
57. Num. 9:11	
	58. Num. 9:11;
59. Num. 10:10;	Ex. 12:8
Num. 10:9	
60. Lev. 22:27	61. Lev. 22:21

63. Lev. 1:2	62. Lev. 2:13
66. Lev. 3:1	64. Lev. 6:18
67. Lev. 2:1; 6:7	65. Lev. 7:1

out blemish. All offerings must be [62]salted. It is a *mitzvah* to perform the ritual of [63]the burnt offering, [64]the sin offering, [65]the guilt offering, [66]the peace offering and [67]the meal offering.

Should the Sanhedrin err in a decision its members [68]must bring a sin offering which offering must also be brought [69]by a person who has unwittingly transgressed a *karet* prohibition (i.e., one which, if done deliberately, would incur *karet*). When in doubt as to whether one has transgressed such a prohibition a [70]"suspensive" guilt offering must be brought.

	68. Lev. 4:13
	69. Lev. 4:27
	70. Lev. 5:17–18

For [71]stealing or swearing falsely and for other sins of a like nature, a guilt offering must be brought. In special circumstances the sin offering [72]can be according to one's means.

One must [73]confess one's sins before God and repent for them.

A [74]man or [75]a woman who has a seminal issue must bring a sacrifice; a woman must also bring a sacrifice [76]after childbirth. A leper must [77]bring a sacrifice after he has been cleansed.

One must [78]tithe one's cattle. The [79]first born of clean (i.e., permitted) cattle are holy and must be sacrificed. The firstborn of man must be [80]redeemed. The firstling of the ass must be [81]redeemed; if not [82]its neck has to be broken.

Animals set aside as offerings [83]must be brought to Jerusalem without delay and [84]may be sacrificed only in the Temple. Offerings from outside the land of Israel [85]may also be brought to the Temple. Sanctified animals [86]which have become blemished must be redeemed. A beast exchanged for an offering [87]is also holy.

The priests should eat [88]the remainder of the meal offering and [89]the flesh of sin and guilt offerings; but consecrated flesh which has become [90]ritually unclean or [91]which was not eaten within its appointed time must be burned.

71. Lev. 5:15, 21–25; 19:20–21	
72. Lev. 5:1–11	
73. Num. 5:6–7	
74. Lev. 15:13–15	
75. Lev. 15:28–29	76. Lev. 12:6
77. Lev. 14:10	
78. Lev. 27:32	79. Ex. 13:2
80. Ex. 22:28; Num. 18:15	81. Ex. 34:20
82. Ex. 13:13	83. Deut. 12:5–5
84. Deut. 12:14	
85. Deut. 12:26	
86. Deut. 12:15	87. Lev. 27:33
88. Lev. 6:9	
89. Ex. 29:33	
90. Lev. 7:19	91. Lev. 7:17

VOWS

A Nazirite must [92]let his hair grow during the period of his separation. When that period is over he must [93]shave his head and bring his sacrifice.

A man must [94]honor his vows and his oaths which a judge can [95]annul only in accordance with the law.

92. Num. 6:5	93. Num. 6:18
94. Deut. 23:24	
95. Num. 30:3	

RITUAL PURITY

Anyone who touches [96]a carcass or [97]one of the eight species of reptiles becomes ritually unclean; food becomes unclean by [98]coming into contact with a ritually unclean object. Menstruous women [99]and those [100]lying-in after childbirth are ritually impure. A [101]leper, [102]a leprous garment, and [103]a leprous house are all ritually unclean. A man having [104]a running issue is unclean, as is [105]semen. A woman suffering from [106]running issue is also impure. A [107]human corpse is ritually unclean. The purification water *(mei niddah)* purifies [108]the unclean, but it makes the clean ritually impure. It is a *mitzvah* to become ritually clean [109]by ritual immersion. To become cleansed of leprosy one [110]must follow the specified procedure and also [111]shave off all of one's hair. Until cleansed the leper [112]must be bareheaded with clothing in disarray so as to be easily distinguishable.

The ashes of [113]the red heifer are to be used in the process of ritual purification.

96. Lev. 11:8, and 24	97. Lev. 11:29–31
98. Lev. 11:34	
99. Lev. 15:19	100. Lev. 12:2
101. Lev. 13:3	103. Lev. 14:44
102. Lev. 13:51	104. Lev. 15:2
105. Lev. 15:16	106. Lev. 15:19
107. Num. 19:14	
108. Num. 19:13, 21	
	109. Lev. 15:16
	110. Lev. 14:2
111. Lev. 14:9	
112. Lev. 13:45	
113. Num. 19:2–9	

DONATIONS TO THE TEMPLE

If a person [114]undertakes to give his own value to the Temple he must do so. Should a man declare [115]an unclean beast, [116]a house, or [117]a field as a donation to the Temple, he must give their value in money as fixed by the priest. If one unwittingly derives

114. Lev. 27:2–8	115. Lev. 27:11–12
117. Lev. 27:16, 22–23	116. Lev. 27:14

benefit from Temple property [118]full restitution plus a fifth must be made.

The fruit of [119]the fourth year's growth of trees is holy and may be eaten only in Jerusalem. When you reap your fields you must leave [120]the corners, [121]the gleanings, [122]the forgotten sheaves, [123]the misformed bunches of grapes and [124]the gleanings of the grapes for the poor.

The first fruits must be [125]separated and brought to the Temple and you must also [126]separate the great heave offering *(terumah)* and give it to the priests. You must give [127]one tithe of your produce to the Levites and separate [128]a second tithe which is to be eaten only in Jerusalem. The Levites [129]must give a tenth of their tithe to the priests.

In the third and sixth years of the seven year cycle you should [130]separate a tithe for the poor instead of the second tithe. A declaration [131]must be recited when separating the various tithes and [132]when bringing the first fruits to the Temple.

The first portion of the [133]dough must be given to the priest.

THE SABBATICAL YEAR

In the seventh year *(shemittah)* everything that grows is [134]ownerless and available to all; the fields [135]must lie fallow and you may not till the ground. You must [136]sanctify the Jubilee year (50th) and on the Day of Atonement in that year [137]you must sound the *shofar* and set all Hebrew slaves free. In the Jubilee year all land is to be [138]returned to its ancestral owners and, generally, in a walled city [139]the seller has the right to buy back a house within a year of the sale.

Starting from entry into the land of Israel, the years of the Jubilee must be [140]counted and announced yearly and septennially.

In the seventh year [141]all debts are annulled but [142]one may exact a debt owed by a foreigner.

CONCERNING ANIMALS FOR CONSUMPTION

When you slaughter an animal you must [143]give the priest his share as you must also give him [144]the first of the fleece. When a man makes a *ḥerem* (a special vow) you must [145]distinguish between that which belongs to the Temple (i.e., when God's name was mentioned in the vow) and between that which goes to the priests. To be fit for consumption, beast and fowl must be [146]slaughtered according to the law and if they are not of a domesticated species [147]their blood must be covered with earth after slaughter.

Set the parent bird [148]free when taking the nest. Examine [149]beast, [150]fowl, [151]locusts and [152]fish to determine whether they are permitted for consumption.

FESTIVALS

The Sanhedrin should [153]sanctify the first day of every month and reckon the years and the seasons.

You must [154]rest on the Sabbath day and [155]declare it holy at its onset and termination. On the 14th of Nisan [156]remove all leaven from your ownership and on the night of the 15th [157]relate the story of the exodus from Egypt; on that night [158]you must also eat *mazzah*. On the [159]first and [160]seventh days of Passover you must rest. Starting from the day of the first sheaf (16th of Nisan) you shall [161]count 49 days. You must rest on [162] Shavuot, and on [163] Rosh Ha-Shanah; on the Day of Atonement you must [164]fast and [165]rest. You must also rest on [166]the first and [167]the eighth day of Sukkot during which festival you shall [168]dwell in booths and [169]take the four species. On Rosh Ha-Shanah [170]you are to hear the sound of the *shofar*.

Ref	Citation
118.	Lev. 5:16
119.	Lev. 19:24
120.	Lev. 19:9
121.	Lev. 19:9
122.	Deut. 24:19
123.	Lev. 19:10
124.	Lev. 19:10
125.	Ex. 23:19
126.	Deut. 18:4
127.	Lev. 27:30; Num. 18:24
128.	Deut. 14:22
129.	Num. 18:26
130.	Deut. 14:28
131.	Deut. 26:13
132.	Deut. 26:5
133.	Num. 15:20
134.	Ex. 23:11
135.	Ex. 34:21
136.	Lev. 25:10
137.	Lev. 25:9
138.	Lev. 25:24
139.	Lev. 25:29–30
140.	Lev. 25:8
141.	Deut. 15:3
142.	Deut. 15:3
143.	Deut. 18:3
144.	Deut. 18:4
145.	Lev. 27:21, 28
146.	Deut. 12:21
147.	Lev. 17:13
148.	Deut. 22:7
149.	Lev. 11:2
150.	Deut. 14:11
151.	Lev. 11:21
152.	Lev. 11:9
153.	Ex. 12:2; Deut. 16:1
154.	Ex. 23:12
155.	Ex. 20:8
156.	Ex. 12:15
157.	Ex. 13:8
158.	Ex. 12:18
159.	Ex. 12:16
160.	Ex. 12:16
161.	Lev. 23:35
162.	Lev. 23
163.	Lev. 23:24
164.	Lev. 16:29
165.	Lev. 16:29, 31
166.	Lev. 23:35
167.	Lev. 23:36
168.	Lev. 23:42
169.	Lev. 23:40
170.	Num. 29:1

COMMUNITY

171. Ex. 30:12–13	
172. Deut. 18:15	
174. Deut. 17:11	173. Deut. 17:15
	175. Ex. 23:2
	176. Deut. 16:18
	177. Lev. 19:15
178. Lev. 5:1	
179. Deut. 13:15	
180. Deut. 19:19	
181. Deut. 21:4	
	182. Deut. 19:3
	183. Num. 35:2
184. Deut. 22:8	

Every male should [171]give half a shekel to the Temple annually. You must [172]obey a prophet and [173]appoint a king. You must also [174]obey the Sanhedrin; in the case of division, [175]yield to the majority. Judges and officials shall be [176]appointed in every town and they shall judge the people [177]impartially.

Whoever is aware of evidence [178]must come to court to testify. Witnesses shall be [179]examined thoroughly and, if found to be false, [180]shall have done to them what they intended to do to the accused.

When a person is found murdered and the murderer is unknown the ritual of [181]decapitating the heifer must be performed.

Six cities of refuge should be [182]established. The Levites, who have no ancestral share in the land, shall [183]be given cities to live in. You must [184]build a fence around your roof and remove potential hazards from your home.

IDOLATRY

	185. Deut. 12:2; 7:5
	186. Deut. 13:17
187. Deut. 20:17	
188. Deut. 25:19	
	189. Deut. 25:17

Idolatry and its appurtenances [185]must be destroyed, and a city which has become perverted must be [186]treated according to the law. You are commanded to [187]destroy the seven Canaanite nations, and [188]to blot out the memory of Amalek, and [189]to remember what they did to Israel.

WAR

190. Deut. 20:11–12	
	191. Deut. 20:2
	192. Deut. 23:14–15
	193. Deut. 23:14

The regulations for wars other than those commanded in the Torah [190]are to be observed and a priest should be [191]appointed for special duties in times of war. The military camp must be [192]kept in a sanitary condition. To this end, every soldier must be [193]equipped with the necessary implements.

SOCIAL

194. Lev. 5:23	
	195. Deut. 15:8; Lev. 25:35–36
197. Ex. 22:24	
198. Deut. 23:21	196. Deut. 15:14
	199. Deut. 24:13; Ex. 22:25
	200. Deut. 24:15
	201. Deut. 23:25–26
	202. Ex. 23:5
204. Deut. 22:1; Ex. 23:4	203. Deut. 22:4
205. Lev. 19:17	206. Lev. 19:18
207. Deut. 10:19	
208. Lev. 19:36	

Stolen property must be [194]restored to its owner. Give [195]charity to the poor. When a Hebrew slave goes free the owner must [196]give him gifts. Lend to [197]the poor without interest; to the foreigner you may [198]lend at interest. Restore [199]a pledge to its owner if he needs it. Pay the worker his wages [200]on time; [201]permit him to eat of the produce with which he is working. You must [202]help unload an animal when necessary, and also [203]help load man or beast. Lost property [204]must be restored to its owner. You are required [205]to reprove the sinner but you must [206]love your fellow as yourself. You are commanded [207]to love the proselyte. Your weights and measures [208]must be accurate.

FAMILY

	210. Ex. 20:12
209. Lev. 19:32	211. Lev. 19:3
212. Gen. 1:28	213. Deut. 24:1
	214. Deut. 24:5
215. Gen. 17:10; Lev. 12:3	
216. Deut. 25:5	217. Deut. 25:9
	218. Deut. 22:29
219. Deut. 22:18–19	
220. Ex. 22:15–23	
221. Deut. 21:11	
222. Deut. 24:1	
	223. Num. 5:15–27

Respect the [209]wise; [210]honor and [211]fear your parents. You should [212]perpetuate the human race by marrying [213]according to the law. A bridegroom is to [214]rejoice with his bride for one year. Male children must [215]be circumcised. Should a man die childless his brother must either [216]marry his widow or [217]release her (halizah). He who violates a virgin must [218]marry her and may never divorce her. If a man unjustly accuses his wife of premarital promiscuity [219]he shall be flogged, and may never divorce her. The seducer [220]must be punished according to the law. The female captive must be [221]treated in accordance with her special regulations. Divorce can be executed [222]only by means of a written document. A woman suspected of adultery [223]has to submit to the required test.

JUDICIAL

When required by the law [224]you must administer the punishment of flogging and you must [225]exile the unwitting homicide. Capital punishment shall be by [226]the sword, [227]strangulation, [228]fire, or [229]stoning, as specified. In some cases the body of the executed [230]shall be hanged, but it [231]must be brought to burial the same day.

Left		Right	
225.	Num. 35:25	224.	Deut. 25:2
226.	Ex. 21:20	227.	Ex. 21:16
229.	Deut. 22:24	228.	Lev. 20:14
230.	Deut. 21:22	231.	Deut. 21:23

SLAVES

Hebrew slaves [232]must be treated according to the special laws for them. The master should [233]marry his Hebrew maidservant or [234]redeem her. The alien slave [235]must be treated according to the regulations applying to him.

Left		Right	
232.	Ex. 21:2		
		233.	Ex. 21:8
234.	Ex. 21:8	235.	Lev. 25:46

TORTS

The applicable law must be administered in the case of injury caused by [236]a person, [237]an animal or [238]a pit. Thieves [239]must be punished. You must render judgment in cases of [240]trespass by cattle, [241]arson, [242]embezzlement by an unpaid guardian and in claims against [243]a paid guardian, a hirer, or [244]a borrower. Judgment must also be rendered in disputes arising out of [245]sales, [248]inheritance and [246]other matters generally. You are required to [247]rescue the persecuted even if it means killing his oppressor.

Left		Right	
236.	Ex. 21:18		
237.	Ex. 21:28	238.	Ex. 21:33–34
		239.	Ex. 21:37–22:3
241.	Ex. 22:5	240.	Ex. 22:4
242.	Ex. 22:6–8		
243.	Ex. 22:9–12	244.	Ex. 22:13
		245.	Lev. 25:14
246.	Ex. 22:8		
247.	Deut. 25:12		
248.	Num. 27:8		

PROHIBITIONS

IDOLATRY AND RELATED PRACTICES

It is [1]forbidden to believe in the existence of any but the One God. You may not make images [2]for yourself or [3]for others to worship or for [4]any other purpose.

You must not worship anything but God either in [5]the manner prescribed for His worship or [6]in its own manner of worship.

Do not [7]sacrifice children to Molech.

You may not [8]practice necromancy or [9]resort to "familiar spirits" neither should you take idolatry or its mythology [10]seriously.

It is forbidden to construct a [11]pillar or [12]dais even for the worship of God or to [13]plant trees in the Temple.

You may not [14]swear by idols or instigate an idolator to do so, nor may you encourage or persuade any [15]non-Jew or [16]Jew to worship idols.

You must not [17]listen to or love anyone who disseminates idolatry nor [18]should you withhold yourself from hating him. Do not [19]pity such a person. If somebody tries to convert you to idolatry [20]do not defend him or [21]conceal the fact.

It is forbidden to [22]derive any benefit from the ornaments of idols. You may not [23]rebuild that which has been destroyed as a punishment for idolatry nor may you [24]have any benefit from its wealth. Do not [25]use anything connected with idols or idolatry.

It is forbidden [26]to prophecy in the name of idols or prophecy [27]falsely in the name of God. Do not [28]listen to the one who prophesies for idols and do not [29]fear the false prophet or hinder his execution.

You must not [30]imitate the ways of idolators or practice their customs; [31]divination, [32]soothsaying, [33]enchanting, [34]sorcery, [35]charming, [36]consulting ghosts or [37]familiar spirits and [38]necromancy are forbidden. Women must not [39]wear male clothing nor men [40]that of women. Do not [41]tattoo yourself in the manner of the idolators.

You may not wear [42]garments made of both wool and linen nor may you shave (with a razor) the sides of [43]your head or [44]your beard. Do not [45]lacerate yourself over your dead.

Left		Right	
1.	Ex. 20:3		
		2.	Ex. 20:4
4.	Ex. 20:20	3.	Lev. 19:4
		5.	Ex. 20:5
		6.	Ex. 20:5
7.	Lev. 18:21		
8.	Lev. 19:31	9.	Lev. 19:31
		10.	Lev. 19:4
11.	Deut. 16:22	12.	Lev. 20:1
13.	Deut. 16:21		
14.	Ex. 23:13		
		15.	Ex. 23:13
		16.	Deut. 13:12
17.	Deut. 13:9	19.	Deut. 13:9
18.	Deut. 13:9	20.	Deut. 13:9
21.	Deut. 13:9		
22.	Deut. 7:25		
23.	Deut. 13:17		
		24.	Deut. 13:18
25.	Deut. 7:26		
26.	Deut. 18:20	28.	Deut. 13:3, 4
27.	Deut. 18:20		Deut. 13:4
		29.	Deut. 18:22
		32.	Deut. 18:10
30.	Lev. 20:23	33.	Deut. 18:10–11;
31.	Lev. 19:26;		Deut. 10–26
	Deut. 18:10	34.	Deut. 18:10–11
35.	Deut. 18:10–11	37.	Deut. 18:10–11
36.	Deut. 18:10–11	38.	Deut. 18:10–11
40.	Deut. 22:5	39.	Deut. 22:5
		41.	Lev. 19:28
42.	Deut. 22:11		
45.	Deut. 16:1;	43.	Lev. 19:27
	Deut. 14:1;	44.	Lev. 19:27
	also Lev. 19:28		

PROHIBITIONS RESULTING FROM HISTORICAL EVENTS

It is forbidden to return to Egypt to [46]dwell there permanently or to [47]indulge in impure thoughts or sights. You may not [48]make a pact with the seven Canaanite nations or [49]save the life of any member of them. Do not [50]show mercy to idolators, [51]permit them to dwell in the land of Israel or [52]intermarry with them. A Jewess may not [53]marry an Ammonite or Moabite even if he converts to Judaism but should not refuse (for reasons of genealogy alone) [54]a descendant of Esau or [55]an Egyptian who are proselytes. It is prohibited to [56]make peace with the Ammonite or Moabite nations.

The [57]destruction of fruit trees even in times of war is forbidden as is wanton waste at any time. Do not [58]fear the enemy and do not [59]forget the evil done by Amalek.

BLASPHEMY

You must not [60]blaspheme the Holy Name, [61]break an oath made by It, [62]take It in vain or [63]profane It. Do not [64]try the Lord God. You may not [65]erase God's name from the holy texts or destroy institutions devoted to His worship. Do not [66]allow the body of of one hanged to remain so overnight.

TEMPLE

Be not [67]lax in guarding the Temple.
The high priest must not enter the Temple [68]indiscriminately; a priest with a physical blemish may not [69]enter there at all or [70]serve in the sanctuary and even if the blemish is of a temporary nature he may not [71]participate in the service there until it has passed.
The Levites and the priests must not [72]interchange in their functions. Intoxicated persons may not [73]enter the sanctuary or teach the Law. It is forbidden for [74]non-priests, [75]unclean priests or [76]priests who have performed the necessary ablution but are still within the time limit of their uncleanness to serve in the Temple. No unclean person may enter [77]the Temple or [78]the Temple Mount.
The altar must not be made of [79]hewn stones nor may the ascent to it be by [80]steps. The fire on it may not be [81]extinguished nor may any other but the specified incense be [82]burned on the golden altar. You may not [83]manufacture oil with the same ingredients and in the same proportions as the anointing oil which itself [84]may not be misused. Neither may you [85]compound incense with the same ingredients and in the same proportions as that burnt on the altar. You must not [86]remove the staves from the Ark, [87]remove the breastplate from the ephod or [88]make any incision in the upper garment of the high priest.

SACRIFICES

It is forbidden to [89]offer sacrifices or [90]slaughter consecrated animals outside the Temple. You may not [91]sanctify, [92]slaughter, [93]sprinkle the blood of or [94]burn the inner parts of a blemished animal even if the blemish is [95]of a temporary nature and even if it is [96]offered by Gentiles. It is forbidden to [97]inflict a blemish on an animal consecrated for sacrifice.
Leaven or honey may not [98]be offered on the altar, neither may [99]anything unsalted. An animal received as the hire of a harlot or as the price of a dog [100]may not be offered.
Do not [101]kill an animal and its young on the same day.
It is forbidden to use [102]olive oil or [103]frankincense in the sin offering or [104], [105], in the jealousy offering (sotah). You may not [106]substitute sacrifices even [107]from one category to the other. You may not [108]redeem the firstborn of permitted animals.

47.	Num. 15:39
50.	Deut. 7:2
53.	Deut. 23:4
54.	Deut. 23:8
55.	Deut. 23:8
56.	Deut. 23:7
57.	Deut. 20:19
59.	Deut. 25:19
60.	Lev. 24:16; rather Ex. 22:27
62.	Ex. 20:7
65.	Deut. 12:4
67.	Num. 18:5
71.	Lev. 21:18
73.	Lev. 10:9–11
74.	Num. 18:4
75.	Lev. 22:2
77.	Num. 5:3
80.	Ex. 20:26
83.	Ex. 30:32
86.	Ex. 25:15
89.	Deut. 12:13
90.	Lev. 17:3–4
94.	Lev. 22:22
95.	Deut. 17:1
99.	Lev. 2:13
100.	Deut. 23:19
101.	Lev. 22:28
104.	Num. 5:15
105.	Num. 5:15
106.	Lev. 27:10

46.	Deut. 17:16
48.	Ex. 23:32; Deut. 7:2
49.	Deut. 20:16
51.	Ex. 23:33
52.	Deut. 7:3
58.	Deut. 7:21
61.	Lev. 19:12
63.	Lev. 22:32
64.	Deut. 6:16
66.	Deut. 21:23
68.	Lev. 16:2
69.	Lev. 21:23
70.	Lev. 21:17
72.	Num. 18:3
76.	Lev. 21:6
78.	Deut. 23:11
79.	Ex. 20:25
81.	Lev. 6:6
82.	Ex. 30:9
84.	Ex. 30:32
85.	Ex. 30:37
87.	Ex. 28:28
88.	Ex. 28:32
91.	Lev. 22:20
92.	Lev. 22:22
93.	Lev. 22:24
96.	Lev. 22:25
97.	Lev. 22:21
98.	Lev. 2:11
102.	Lev. 5:11
103.	Lev. 5:11
107.	Lev. 27:26
108.	Num. 18:17

109. Lev. 27:33 It is forbidden to [109]sell the tithe of the herd or [110]sell or [111]redeem 110. Lev. 27:28
a field consecrated by the *herem* vow. 111. Lev. 27:28
When you slaughter a bird for a sin offering you may not [112]split its 112. Lev. 5:8
head.
113. Deut. 15:19 It is forbidden to [113]work with or [114]to shear a consecrated animal. 114. Deut. 15:19
You must not slaughter the paschal lamb [115]while there is still 115. Ex. 34:25
leaven about; nor may you leave overnight [116]those parts that are 116. Ex. 23:10
117. Ex. 12:10 to be offered up or [117]to be eaten.
You may not leave any part of the festive offering [118]until the third 118. Deut. 16:4
119. Num. 9:13 day or any part of [119]the second paschal lamb or [120]the thanks- 120. Lev. 22:30
giving offering until the morning.
It is forbidden to break a bone of [121]the first or [122]the second 121. Ex. 12:46
123. Ex. 12:46 paschal lamb or [123]to carry their flesh out of the house where it 122. Num. 9:12
124. Lev. 6:10 is being eaten. You must not [124]allow the remains of the meal
offering to become leaven. It is also forbidden to eat the paschal
125. Ex. 12:9 lamb [125]raw or sodden or to allow [126]an alien resident, [127]an 126. Ex. 12:45
uncircumcised person or an [128]apostate to eat of it. 127. Ex. 12:48
A ritually unclean person [129]must not eat of holy things nor may 128. Ex. 12:43
130. Lev. 7:19 [130]holy things which have become unclean be eaten. Sacrificial 129. Lev. 12:4
131. Lev. 19:6–8 meat [131]which is left after the time-limit or [132]which was slaughtered 132. Lev. 7:18
with wrong intentions must not be eaten. The heave offering must
133. Lev. 22:10 not be eaten by [133]a non-priest, [134]a priest's sojourner or hired 134. Lev. 22:10
135. Lev. 22:10 worker, [135]an uncircumcised person, or [136]an unclean priest. 136. Lev. 22:4
The daughter of a priest who is married to a non-priest may not
137. Lev. 22:12 [137]eat of holy things.
The meal offering of the priest [138]must not be eaten, neither may 138. Lev. 6:16
139. Lev. 6:23 [139]the flesh of the sin offerings sacrificed within the sanctuary or
140. Deut. 14:3 [140]consecrated animals which have become blemished.
You may not eat the second tithe of [141]corn, [142]wine, or [143]oil 141. Deut. 12:17
144. Deut. 12:17 or [144]unblemished firstlings outside Jerusalem. The priests may not 142. Deut. 12:17
145. Deut. 12:17 eat the [145]sin-offerings or the trespass-offerings outside the Temple 143. Deut. 12:17
146. Deut. 12:17 courts or [146]the flesh of the burnt-offering at all. The lighter
147. Deut. 12:17 sacrifices [147]may not be eaten before the blood has been sprinkled.
A non-priest may not [148]eat of the holiest sacrifices and a priest 148. Deut. 12:17
149. Ex. 29:33 [149]may not eat the first-fruits outside the Temple courts.
150. Deut. 26:14 One may not eat [150]the second tithe while in a state of impurity or
151. Deut. 26:14 [151]in mourning; its redemption money [152]may not be used for 152. Deut. 26:14
anything other than food and drink.
153. Lev. 22:15 You must not [153]eat untithed produce or [154]change the order 154. Ex. 22:28
of separating the various tithes.
155. Deut. 23:22 Do not [155]delay payment of offerings—either freewill or obliga-
156. Ex. 23:15 tory—and do not [156]come to the Temple on the pilgrim festivals
without an offering.
157. Num. 30:3 Do not [157]break your word.

PRIESTS

158. Lev. 21:7 A priest may not marry [158]a harlot, [159]a woman who has been 159. Lev. 21:7
profaned from the priesthood, or [160]a divorcee; the high priest 160. Lev. 21:7
161. Lev. 21:14 must not [161]marry a widow or [162]take one as a concubine. Priests
162. Lev. 21:15 may not enter the sanctuary with [163]overgrown hair of the head 163. Lev. 10:6
164. Lev. 10:6 or [164]with torn clothing; they must not [165]leave the courtyard 165. Lev. 10:7
during the Temple service. An ordinary priest may not render
166. Lev. 21:1 himself [166]ritually impure except for those relatives specified, and
the high priest should not become impure [167]for anybody in [168]any 167. Lev. 21:11
way. 168. Lev. 21:11
The tribe of Levi shall have no part in [169]the division of the land of 169. Deut. 18:1
170. Deut. 18:1 Israel or [170]in the spoils of war.
171. Deut. 14:1 It is forbidden [171]to make oneself bald as a sign of mourning for
one's dead.

DIETARY LAWS

172. Deut. 14:7	
175. Deut. 14:19	
177. Lev. 11:44	
178. Lev. 11:42	

A Jew may not eat [172]unclean cattle, [173]unclean fish, [174]unclean fowl, [175]creeping things that fly, [176]creatures that creep on the ground, [177]reptiles, [178]worms found in fruit or produce or [179]any detestable creature.

173. Lev. 11:11
174. Lev. 11:13
176. Lev. 11:41
179. Lev. 11:43

An animal that has died naturally [180]is forbidden for consumption as is [181]a torn or mauled animal. One must not eat [182]any limb taken from a living animal. Also prohibited is [183]the sinew of the thigh (gid ha-nasheh) as is [184]blood and [185]certain types of fat (helev). It is forbidden [186]to cook meat together with milk or [187]eat of such a mixture. It is also forbidden to eat [188]of an ox condemned to stoning (even should it have been properly slaughtered).

One may not eat [189]bread made of new corn or the new corn itself, either [190]roasted or [191]green, before the omer offering has been brought on the 16th of Nisan. You may not eat [192]orlah or [193]the growth of mixed planting in the vineyard.

Any use of [194]wine libations to idols is prohibited, as is [195]gluttony and drunkenness. One may not eat anything on [196]the Day of Atonement. During Passover it is forbidden to eat [197]leaven (hamez) or [198]anything containing an admixture of such. This is also forbidden [199]after the middle of the 14th of Nisan (the day before Passover). During Passover no leaven may be [200]seen or [201]found in your possession.

181. Ex. 22:30

184. Lev. 7:26
186. Ex. 23:19

189. Lev. 23:14
190. Lev. 23:14
191. Lev. 23:14

194. Deut. 32:38

198. Ex. 13:20
199. Deut. 16:3

201. Ex. 12:19

180. Deut. 14:21
182. Deut. 12:23
183. Gen. 32:33
185. Lev. 7:23
187. Ex. 34:26
188. Ex. 21:28

192. Lev. 19:23
193. Deut. 22:9
195. Lev. 19:26; Deut. 21:20
196. Lev. 23:29
197. Ex. 13:3

200. Ex. 13:7

NAZIRITES

202. Num. 6:3
203. Num. 6:3

206. Num. 6:4

208. Lev. 21:11
209. Num. 6:5

A Nazirite may not drink [202]wine or any beverage made from grapes; he may not eat [203]fresh grapes, [204]dried grapes, [205]grape seeds or [206]grape peel. He may not render himself [207]ritually impure for his dead nor may he [208]enter a tent in which there is a corpse. He must not [209]shave his hair.

204. Num. 6:3
205. Num. 6:4
207. Num. 6:7

AGRICULTURE

210. Lev. 23:22

213. Lev. 19:10

215. Lev. 19:19

218. Deut. 22:10
219. Deut. 25:4
220. Lev. 25:4

224. Lev. 25:11

227. Lev. 25:23
228. Lev. 25:33

It is forbidden [210]to reap the whole of a field without leaving the corners for the poor; it is also forbidden to [211]gather up the ears of corn that fall during reaping or to harvest [212]the misformed clusters of grapes, or [213]the grapes that fall or to [214]return to take a forgotten sheaf.

You must not [215]sow different species of seed together or [216]corn in a vineyard; it is also forbidden to [217]crossbreed different species of animals or [218]work with two different species yoked together.

You must not [219]muzzle an animal working in a field to prevent it from eating.

It is forbidden to [220]till the earth, [221]to prune trees, [222]to reap (in the usual manner) produce or [223]fruit which has grown without cultivation in the seventh year (shemittah). One may also not [224]till the earth or prune trees in the Jubilee year, when it is also forbidden to harvest (in the usual manner) [225]produce or [226]fruit that has grown without cultivation.

One may not [227]sell one's landed inheritance in the land of Israel permanently or [228]change the lands of the Levites or [229]leave the Levites without support.

211. Lev. 19:9
212. Lev. 19:10
214. Deut. 24:19

216. Deut. 22:9
217. Lev. 19:19

221. Lev. 25:4
222. Lev. 25:5
223. Lev. 25:5

225. Lev. 25:11
226. Lev. 25:11

229. Deut. 12:19

LOANS, BUSINESS, AND THE TREATMENT OF SLAVES

230. Deut. 15:2

233. Deut. 15:13
234. Ex. 22:24

It is forbidden to [230]demand repayment of a loan after the seventh year; you may not, however, [231]refuse to lend to the poor because that year is approaching. Do not [232]deny charity to the poor or [233]send a Hebrew slave away empty-handed when he finishes his period of service. Do not [234]dun your debtor when you know that he cannot pay. It is forbidden to [235]lend to or [236]borrow from

231. Deut. 15:9
232. Deut. 15:7

235. Lev. 25:37
236. Deut. 23:20

another Jew at interest or [237]participate in an agreement involving interest either as a guarantor, witness, or writer of the contract. Do not [238]delay payment of wages.

You may not [239]take a pledge from a debtor by violence, [240]keep a poor man's pledge when he needs it, [241]take any pledge from a widow or [242]from any debtor if he earns his living with it.

Kidnaping [243]a Jew is forbidden.

Do not [244]steal or [245]rob by violence. Do not [246]remove a land-marker or [247]defraud.

It is forbidden [248]to deny receipt of a loan or a deposit or [249]to swear falsely regarding another man's property.

You must not [250]deceive anybody in business. You may not [251]mislead a man even verbally. It is forbidden to harm the stranger among you [252]verbally or [253]do him injury in trade.

You may not [254]return or [255]otherwise take advantage of, a slave who has fled to the land of Israel from his master, even if his master is a Jew.

Do not [256]afflict the widow or the orphan. You may not [257]misuse or [258]sell a Hebrew slave; do not [259]treat him cruelly or [260]allow a heathen to mistreat him. You must not [261]sell your Hebrew maidservant or, if you marry her, [262]withhold food, clothing, and conjugal rights from her. You must not [263]sell a female captive or [264]treat her as a slave.

Do not [265]covet another man's possessions even if you are willing to pay for them. Even [266]the desire alone is forbidden.

A worker must not [267]cut down standing corn during his work or [268]take more fruit than he can eat.

One must not [269]turn away from a lost article which is to be returned to its owner nor may you [270]refuse to help a man or an animal which is collapsing under its burden.

It is forbidden to [271]defraud with weights and measures or even [272]to possess inaccurate weights.

JUSTICE

A judge must not [273]perpetrate injustice, [274]accept bribes or be [275]partial or [276]afraid. He may [277]not favor the poor or [278]discriminate against the wicked; he should not [279]pity the condemned or [280]pervert the judgment of strangers or orphans.

It is forbidden to [281]hear one litigant without the other being present. A capital case cannot be decided by [282]a majority of one.

A judge should not [283]accept a colleague's opinion unless he is convinced of its correctness; it is forbidden to [284]appoint as a judge someone who is ignorant of the law.

Do not [285]give false testimony or accept [286]testimony from a wicked person or from [287]relatives of a person involved in the case. It is forbidden to pronounce judgment [288]on the basis of the testimony of one witness.

Do not [289]murder.

You must not convict on [290]circumstantial evidence alone.

A witness [291]must not sit as a judge in capital cases.

You must not [292]execute anybody without due proper trial and conviction.

Do not [293]pity or spare the pursuer.

Punishment is not to be inflicted for [294]an act committed under duress.

Do not accept ransom [295]for a murderer or [296]a manslayer.

Do not [297]hesitate to save another person from danger and do not [298]leave a stumbling block in the way or [299]mislead another person by giving wrong advice.

238. Lev. 19:13	237. Ex. 22:24
239. Deut. 24:10	240. Deut. 24:12
	241. Deut. 24:17
242. Deut. 24:6	
243. Ex. 20:13	
244. Lev. 19:11	
245. Lev. 19:13	246. Deut. 19:14
247. Lev. 19:13	
248. Lev. 19:11	249. Lev. 19:11
250. Lev. 25:14	251. Lev. 25:17
252. Ex. 22:20	
253. Ex. 22:20	
254. Deut. 23:16	
255. Deut. 23:17	
256. Ex. 22:21	257. Lev. 25:39
258. Lev. 25:42	259. Lev. 25:43
	260. Lev. 25:53
	261. Ex. 21:8
	262. Ex. 21:10
264. Deut. 21:14	263. Deut. 21:14
265. Ex. 20:17	
266. Deut. 5:18	
267. Deut. 23:26	
268. Deut. 23:25	
269. Deut. 22:3	
270. Ex. 23:5	
271. Lev. 19:35	
272. Deut. 25:13	
273. Lev. 19:15	274. Ex. 23:8
275. Lev. 19:15	277. Lev. 19:15, rather Ex. 23:3
276. Deut. 1:17	
280. Deut. 24:17	278. Ex. 23:6
281. Ex. 23:1	279. Deut. 19:13
	282. Ex. 23:2
283. Ex. 23:2	
	284. Deut. 1:17
285. Ex. 20:16	286. Ex. 23:1
287. Deut. 24:16	
	288. Deut. 19:15
289. Ex. 20:13	
290. Ex 23:7	
291. Num. 35:30	
292. Num. 35:12	
293. Deut. 25:12	
	294. Deut. 22:26
295. Num. 35:31	
297. Lev. 19:16	296. Num. 35:32
298. Deut. 22:8	299. Lev. 19:14

300.	Deut. 25:2-3
301.	Lev. 19:16
303.	Lev. 19:17
304.	Lev. 19:18
306.	Deut. 22:6
307.	Lev. 13:33
310.	Ex. 22:17
311.	Deut. 24:5
315.	Ex. 22:27
318.	Ex. 21:17
320.	Ex. 20:10
321.	Ex. 16:29
325.	Lev. 23:21
327.	Lev. 23:35
328.	Lev. 23:36
330.	Lev. 18:7
331.	Lev. 18:8
332.	Lev. 18:9
335.	Lev. 18:10
338.	Lev. 18:17
339.	Lev. 18:17
340.	Lev. 18:12
341.	Lev. 18:13
343.	Lev. 18:15
347.	Lev. 18:20
348.	Lev. 18:23
350.	Lev. 18:22
352.	Lev. 18:14
355.	Deut. 23:18
356.	Deut. 24:4
358.	Deut. 22:29
359.	Deut. 22:19
361.	Lev. 22:24
362.	Deut. 17:15
364.	Deut. 17:17
365.	Deut. 17:17

It is forbidden [300]to administer more than the assigned number of lashes to the guilty.

Do not [301]tell tales or [302]bear hatred in your heart. It is forbidden to [303]shame a Jew, [304]to bear a grudge or [305]to take revenge.

Do not [306]take the dam when you take the young birds.

It is forbidden to [307]shave a leprous scall or [308]remove other signs of that affliction. It is forbidden [309]to cultivate a valley in which a slain body was found and in which subsequently the ritual of breaking the heifer's neck (*eglah arufah*) was performed.

Do not [310]suffer a witch to live.

Do not [311]force a bridegroom to perform military service during the first year of his marriage. It is forbidden to [312]rebel against the transmitters of the tradition or to [313]add or [314]detract from the precepts of the law.

Do not curse [315]a judge, [316]a ruler or [317]any Jew.

Do not [318]curse or [319]strike a parent.

It is forbidden to [320]work on the Sabbath or [321]walk further than the permitted limits (*eruv*). You may not [322]inflict punishment on the Sabbath.

It is forbidden to work on [323]the first or [324]the seventh day of Passover, on [325]Shavuot, on [326]Rosh Ha-Shanah, on the [327]first and [328]eighth (*Shemini Azeret*) days of Sukkot and [329]on the Day of Atonement.

INCEST AND OTHER FORBIDDEN RELATIONSHIPS

It is forbidden to enter into an incestuous relationship with one's [330]mother, [331]step-mother, [332]sister, [333]step-sister, [334]son's daughter, [335]daughter's daughter, [336]daughter, [337]any woman and her daughter, [338]any woman and her son's daughter, [339]any woman and her daughter's daughter, [340]father's sister, [341]mother's sister, [342]paternal uncle's wife, [343]daughter-in-law, [344]brother's wife and [345]wife's sister.

It is also forbidden to [346]have sexual relations with a menstruous woman.

Do not [347]commit adultery.

It is forbidden for [348]a man or [349]a woman to have sexual intercourse with an animal.

Homosexuality [350]is forbidden, particularly with [351]one's father or [352]uncle.

It is forbidden to have [353]intimate physical contact (even without actual intercourse) with any of the women with whom intercourse is forbidden.

A *mamzer* may not [354]marry a Jewess.

Harlotry [355]is forbidden.

A divorcee may not be [356]remarried to her first husband if, in the meanwnile, she had married another.

A childless widow may not [357]marry anybody other than her late husband's brother.

A man may not [358]divorce a wife whom he married after having raped her or [359]after having slandered her.

A eunuch may not [360]marry a Jewess.

Castration [361]is forbidden.

THE MONARCHY

You may not [362]elect as king anybody who is not of the seed of Israel.

The king must not accumulate an excessive number of [363]horses, [364]wives, or [365]wealth.

302.	Lev. 19:17
305.	Lev. 19:18
308.	Deut. 24:8
309.	Deut. 21:4
312.	Deut. 17:11
313.	Deut. 13:1
314.	Deut. 13:1
316.	Ex. 22:27
317.	Lev. 19:14
319.	Ex. 21:15
322.	Ex. 35:3
323.	Ex. 12:16
324.	Ex. 12:16
326.	Lev. 23:25
329.	Lev. 23:28
333.	Lev. 18:11
334.	Lev. 18:10
336.	Lev. 18:10
337.	Lev. 18:17
342.	Lev. 18:14
344.	Lev. 18:16
345.	Lev. 18:18
346.	Lev. 18:19
349.	Lev. 18:23
351.	Lev. 18:7
353.	Lev. 18:6
354.	Deut. 23:3
357.	Deut. 25:5
360.	Deut. 23:2
363.	Deut. 17:16

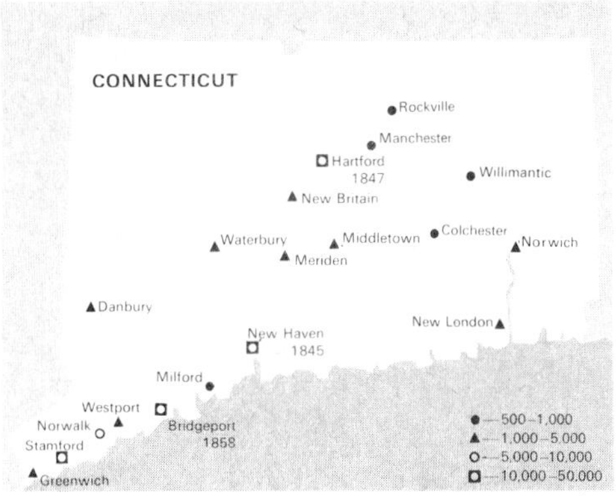

Jewish communities in Connecticut and dates of establishment.

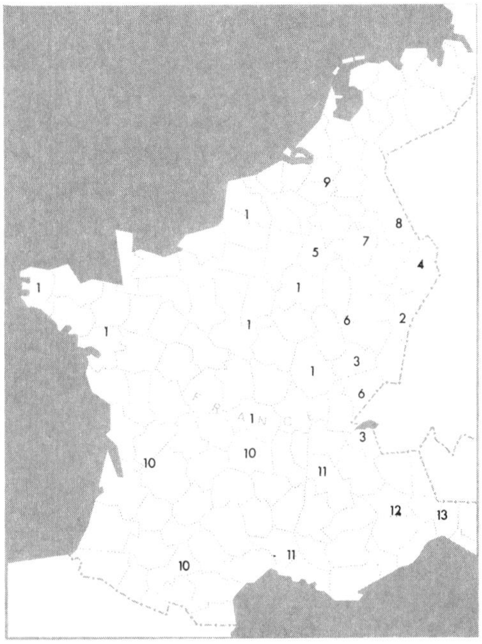

The consistories of France according to the Napoleonic decree of 1808

1. PARIS: (Allier, Côte-d'Or, Finistère, Ille-et-Vilaine, Loiret, Loiret-Cher, **Loire-Inférieure**, Marne, Nord, Pas-de-Calais, Seine, Seine-Inférieure, Seine-et-Marne, Seine-et-Oise, Somme, Yonne).
2. STRASBOURG: (Bas-Rhin).
3. WINTZENHEIM: (Léman, Haut-Rhin, Haute-Saûne).
4. MAINZ: (Mont-Tonnerre).
5. METZ: (Moselle Ardennes).
6. NANCY: (Doubs, Haute-Marne, Meurthe, Meuse, Vosges).
7. TREVES: (Forêts, Sambre-et-Meuse, Sarre).
8. COBLENZ: (Rhin-et-Moselle).
9. KREFELD: (Dyle, Escaut, Jemmapes, Lys, Meuse-Inférieure, Deux-Nèthes, Ourthe, Roër).
10. BORDEAUX: (Aude, Charente, Charente-Inférieure, Dordogne, Haute-Garonne, Gironde, Landes, Puy-de-Dôme, Basses-Pyrénées, Haute-Vienne).
11. MARSEILLES: (Alpes-Maritimes, Gard, Hérault, Isère, Rhône, Bouches-du-Rhône, Var, Vaucluse).
12. TURIN: (Pô, Stura).
13. CASAL: (Gênes, Doire, Marengo, **Montenotte, Sesia**).

Commentary, U.S. Jewish monthly. Founded 1945 by American Jewish Committee. Edited by Elliot Cohen until 1955 and by Norman Podhoretz fr. 1959. Circulation over 50,000 (1972). One of most influential journals of opinion in U.S.

Comtat Venaissin, district in SE France; papal territory until 1791. Jews allowed to remain there when expelled from other provinces of France. They spoke a Judeo-Provençal dialect and had their own synagogue rite. The four "holy communities" were Avignon, Carpentras, Cavaillon, L'Isle-sur-la-Sorgue. The communities were reconstructed in mid-20th c., mainly by Jews of N. African origin.

Comtino, Mordecai ben Eliezer (1420–before 1487), Bible commentator, philosopher, philologist, astronomer, mathematician; lived in Constantinople. Opposed study of Talmud without knowledge of the sciences.

Conat, Abraham ben Solomon (15th c.), Italian physician and one of earliest printers of Hebrew books; lived in Mantua.

Concentration Camps, see Camps.

Cone, U.S. commercial and philanthropic family. The brothers **Moses Herman** (1857–1908) and **Caesar** (1859–1917) founded the Cone Export and Commission Company (1891), which helped the southern textile industry to free itself from its dependence on northern finishers and distributors. Among the world's leading producers of flannels and denims. Their sister **Claribel** (1864–1929), prof. of pathology at Woman's Medical College in Baltimore. Collection of modern French paintings built up by her and her sister Etta is in Cone Wing of Baltimore Museum of Art.

Conference of Presidents of Major American Jewish Organizations, organization founded 1955 to unify action of major American Jewish organizations vis-à-vis Middle East policy. Later undertook action on behalf of Soviet Jewry, Jews in Arab countries, etc. Represented 24 national Jewish bodies in 1970s.

Conference on Jewish Material Claims Against Germany, organization established 1951 to obtain funds for relief, resettlement, and rehabilitation of victims of Nazism. German government provided $110,000,000 for its activities. Allocation ended in 1964 and the following year the Conference established the Memorial Foundation for Jewish Culture.

Conference on Jewish Social Studies, U.S. organization founded 1936 to sponsor social research. Publishes the quarterly *Jewish Social Studies* (1939 ff.).

Confession of Sins (Heb. *viddui*). In the Bible, confession of sins committed individually or collectively is an essential prerequisite for expiation and atonement. The various sin and guilt offerings had to be preceded by confession. Maimonides viewed confession as a positive commandment necessary when seeking atonement. A confession may be made by individuals during silent prayer or on other occasions. It is made directly to God and not through an intermediary.

Confirmation, see Bar Mitzvah; Bat Mitzvah.

Conforte, David (1617 or 1618–c. 1690), rabbi in Salonika, Jerusalem, Cairo. Author of *Kore ha-Dorot,* a chronicle of authors and works from post-talmudic times, of special importance for information on Sephardi scholars in 16th–17th c.

Congress for Jewish Culture, U.S. organization founded 1948 to promote secular Jewish culture and recognition of Yiddish as indispensable means of Jewish creative expression.

Coniah, see Jehoiachin.

Connecticut U.S. state. Earliest reference to Jews 1659. First congregations Mishkan Israel of New Haven (1840) and Beth Israel of Hartford (1843). Abraham A. Ribicoff governor 1955–61, senator 1962– . Jewish pop. 105,000 (1971).

Conrad, Victor (1876–1962), Austrian meteorologist. Escaped to U.S. 1938. Specialized in geophysical and bioclimatic problems.

Conreid, Heinrich (Cohn; 1848–1909), impressario. Arrived in U.S. 1878 fr. Germany. Achieved success as manager of Metropolitan Opera 1903–08, engaging Caruso, Chaliapin, and Scott. Returned to Europe 1908.

Conservative Judaism, trend in Judaism developed in U.S. in 20th c. While opposing extreme changes in traditional observances, it permits certain modifications in response to the changing life of the Jewish people. The first Conservative institutions in the U.S. were crystallized not in dissent from Orthodoxy but in reaction to the powerful Reform movement. Its rabbis are organized in the Rabbinical Assembly of America (incorporated 1924) and its congregations in the United Syna-

gogue of America (founded 1913). Its headquarters is the Jewish Theological Seminary (founded 1887). In 1970 some 350,000 families were in the formal structure of Conservative synagogues.

Consistory (Consistoire), official organization of Jewish congregations in France, established 1808 through French Sanhedrin. Includes both central and regional bodies, and still exists. The central consistory is in Paris.

Constance, city in W. Germany. Jews settled before 1241. During Black Death (1349) 350 Jews burned at stake. Expelled 1533; new community in 1863–66, numbering 386 in 1935 and destroyed in WWII. Jewish pop. 30 (1968).

Constantine, town in Algeria. Jews fr. classical times. After Arab conquest Jews maintained their identity and were important community until 1837, when captured by French. 12,000 Jews in 1934 and 15,000–20,000 in 1962, most of whom left for France and Israel at approach of Algerian independence. By 1970 only a few families left.

Constantinople, former capital of Byzantine Empire (now called Istanbul). Jews fr. 4th c. Lived in their own quarters. Their condition varied, the Byzantine authorities frequently being hostile. In 11th and 12th c. Jews had to serve as executioners. Important Karaite center. For later history, see Istanbul.

Contini, Gianfranco (1912–), Italian literary critic, philologist. Prof. at Fribourg, Florence. President Italian Dante Society fr. 1956.

Conversion from Judaism, see Apostasy.

Conversion to Judaism, see Proselytes.

Conversos, Spanish and Portuguese term for Moorish and Jewish converts to Christianity.

°**Cook, Stanley Arthur** (1873–1949), English Semitic scholar, historian of religion. Regius prof. of Hebrew at Cambridge 1932–38. Wrote archaeological, philological, and comparative religion studies.

°**Cooke, George Albert** (1865–1939), English Bible scholar, Semitist. Taught at Oxford. Collated and interpreted Hebrew, Moabite, Punic, Nabatean, Palmyrene, and Old Aramaic Semitic inscriptions.

Cooper, Alexander (1605–1660), English miniaturist; convert to Judaism. Fr. 1647 in Sweden.

Cooper (Kuper), Emil Albertovich (1877–1960), conductor. Conducted in Kiev, Moscow, St. Petersburg (Petrograd). After 1924 worked mainly in U.S. at Chicago Civic Opera (1929) and Metropolitan Opera (1944–50).

Copenhagen, capital of Denmark. First Jewish congregation founded 1684 by Ashkenazi Jews fr. Hamburg. First rabbi appointed 1687; synagogue built 1766. During WWI World Zionist Organization established central office there. Jews mostly rescued during Holocaust by transfer to Sweden. Home of most of Denmark's 6,000 Jews.

Pope Martin V blesses Jewish delegation at Constance, 1417, from "Chronicle of the Councils of Constance," 1414–18, by Ulrich von Richental.

Plan of Constantinople in 1420, showing sites of the Jewish quarter at different periods. (1) c. 10th cent.–c. 1050. (2) the gate of the quarter ("Porta indece"), whose correct position was at (3). (4) c. 1050–1203, when it was burned by the Crusaders. (5) 1280 onward. (The quarter was destroyed in 1453.) From "Liber insularum archipelagi" of Buondelmonte.

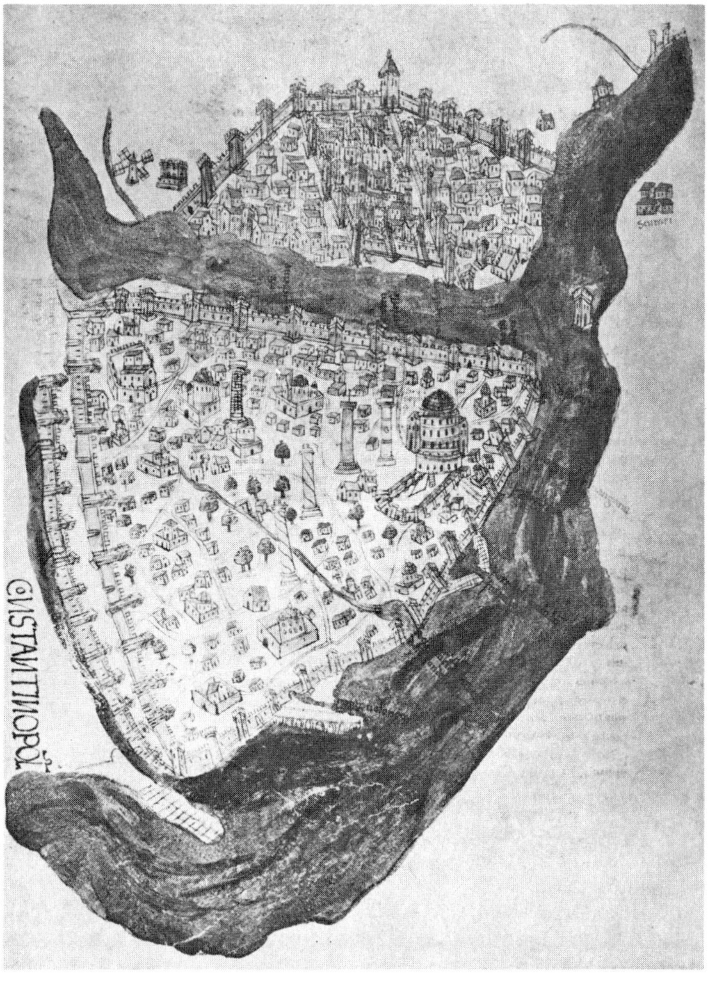

Copisarow, Maurice (1889–1959), British chemist. In WWI invented technique to prevent explosions in TNT factories. Went blind and continued to work as theoretician.

Copland, Aaron (1900–), U.S. composer, conductor, teacher. Many of his works based on distinctly American themes, such as the ballets *Billy the Kid, Rodeo, Appalachian Spring.* Wrote chamber music, piano concertos, film scores, etc.

Aaron Copland

Copper Scroll, one of Dead Sea Scrolls, made of copper; discovered in Qumran. Contains cryptic inventory of treasure deposited in various places.

Copper Serpent, see Neḥushtan.

Coralnik, Abraham (1883–1937), Yiddish essayist, literary critic; lived in various parts of Europe, later years in Russia. Wrote for *Der Tog.*

Corcos, Hezekiah Manoah Ḥayyim (Tranquillo Vita) The Younger (1660–1730), Italian rabbi, physician, preacher. Rabbi and secretary of Rome community fr. 1702. Outstanding personality of Rome ghetto.

Córdoba. (1) province in Argentina. In 1943 Jews lived in 98 communities in the province; pop. 8,639 (1960). In 1964 7 organized communities. (2) capital of above province. First Jews early 20th c. fr. agricultural settlements in Entre Ríos province, and at same time first Sephardi groups arrived. Ashkenazi community established 1915 and Sephardi 1917. Jewish pop. 7,409 (1960).

Córdoba (Cordova), city in Spain. Jewish settlement fr. 8th c. to expulsion in 1492. Forced conversion by Muslim Almohads in 12th c. Center of brilliant Jewish creative activity due largely to Ḥisdai ibn Shaprut. Birthplace of Maimonides (statue, 1964). Ancient Jewish quarter (Judéria) preserved.

Cordovero, Gedaliah ben Moses (1562–1625), rabbi, kabbalist; son of Moses Cordovero. Chief rabbi of Jerusalem fr. 1590.

Cordovero Moses ben Jacob (1522–1570), kabbalist in Safed; disciple of Joseph Caro and teacher of Isaac Luria. Wrote many kabbalistic works, incl. *Pardes Rimmonim* and *Elimah Rabbati.* Attempted to synthesize different kabbalistic trends into one speculative system.

Corfu, Greek island. Jewish presence known fr. 12th c. Under Venetian rule (fr. 1386) Jews enjoyed relatively good conditions, with occasional restrictions. Conditions declined in 19th c.; blood libel in 1891. Germans deported most Jews to their death in WWII. Jewish pop. 5,000 in 1891, 2,000 in 1940, 92 in 1968.

Corinth, Greek city. Jewish community 1st c., when apostle Paul visited the town. Community existed in Middle Ages but later disappeared. 400 Jews in 1923, but community ended in WWII.

Cornblat, Isidore Cyril (1914–), Canadian air force officer. Assistant chief of staff NATO headquarters in Europe 1953–58. Later comptroller of R.C.A.F. and member of Air Council with rank of air vice-marshal.

Coronel, Naḥman Nathan (1810–1890), talmudic scholar, author, bibliographer; lived in Jerusalem. Collected and published mss.

Corsica, Mediterranean island. Only major Mediterranean island without Jewish settlement either in ancient or medieval times. In late 19th c. Jews settled in Bastia, establishing community which in 1968 numbered 150.

Corwin, Norman Lewis (1910–), U.S. radio and film writer, director, producer. Achieved prominence with experimental radio programs, incl. *On a Note of Triumph,* written to celebrate Allied victory in WWII.

Cos, see Kos.

Coser, Lewis A. (1913–), U.S. sociologist; b. Germany, in U.S. fr. 1941. Prof. at Brandeis, State Univ. of N.Y. Leading proponent of conflict theory. Edited socialist magazine *Dissent.*

Detail of western wall of 14th-cent. Rambam synagogue in Córdoba.

"Cosmopolitan," derogatory term for Jewish intellectuals used in USSR 1949. Marked beginning of public anti-Jewish campaign of last years of Stalin's rule.

Costa, Emanuel Mendes da (1717–1791), English scientist. Lived in poverty all his life, but became eminent scientist, writing on conchology, mineralogy, etc.

Costa, Isaac da (1798–1860), Dutch poet, writer. Became a leader of Dutch Reformed Church. Wrote about Spanish and Portuguese Jewry and a Jewish history.

Costa (Acosta), Uriel da (1585–1640), free thinker; b. Portugal to Marrano family, fled to Amsterdam to profess Judaism, but discovered that his "biblical" Judaism differed from that of community. The conflict was life long, included 2 excommunications and a public penance. Committed suicide. Became symbol of fight of enlightenment against religious bigotry.

Costa Rica, C. American republic. First Jews Sephardim fr. W. Indies in 19th c. Present community founded after WWI by Jews fr. Turkey, E. Europe, later Germany. Jewish pop. 1,500 (1971).

Cota da Maguaque, Roderigo de (15th c.), Spanish Converso poet. Attacked Jews after converting to Christianity. His *Diálogo entre el amor y un viejo* highly regarded.

Council of Four Lands, see Councils of the Lands.

Council of Jewish Federations and Welfare Funds, association of U.S. Jewish community organizations, organized 1932 by Jewish federations in 15 cities. By end of 1960s operating in 200 cities, serving 800 communities, raising $140 million a year.

Council of Jews from Germany, organization dealing with restitution and compensation from Germany for survivors of the Holocaust, established 1945.

Councils of the Lands, central institutions of Jewish self-government in Poland and Lithuania fr. mid-16th c. until 1764. The councils, which were very powerful, dealt with taxation (distributing the tax burden among the provinces), settled disputes between provinces, controlled economic life, supervised schools and charities, and directed religious life (censorship, etc.), etc. Met during major fairs. Declined in 18th c. and

ended when Polish parliament instituted new form of tax collection, from each community separately. The "Lands" (= provinces) were Great Poland, Little Poland, Volhynia, and Lithuania, but the last also operated independently for part of the period.

Counting the Omer, see Omer.

Courant, Richard (1888–), German-U.S. mathematician, author; fr. 1936 at N.Y. Univ. His basic work later led to practical use of electronic computers.

Courland (Kurland), region on Baltic coast. In early Middle Ages settlement prohibited, but increased, with restrictions, after annexation by Poland (1561). In Czarist Russia fr. 1795, with Jews sharing fate of Jews of Russia. Jewish pop. 68,000 in 1914. During WWI, Jews suspected of treason and expelled to interior. Fr. 1918, part of Latvia (q.v.).

Cournos, John (1881–1966), U.S. novelist. Wrote trilogy based on own life. Converted to Christianity and urged other Jews to do same.

Court, see Bet Din.

Court Jews, Jews who served as commercial and banking agents for rulers of C. and E. European states in 17th–18th c. Advanced credit and engaged in tax farming, often intervening on behalf of fellow-Jews. Enjoyed special privileges; occasionally met a tragic end.

Covenant, a general obligation between two parties. The covenant par excellence in the Bible is between God and Israel, initially concluded by Abraham. Its external signs include circumcision, the Sabbath, and the tables of the covenant.

Doors of an Ark of the Law, Cracow, early 17th cent.

Covo, Isaac ben Joseph Hezekiah (1770–1854), Jerusalem rabbi, called *Morenu.* Went as emissary to Turkey and returned in old age to Jerusalem, becoming chief rabbi (*ḥakham bashi*) 1848.

Covo, Judah (d. 1636), Salonika rabbi. Put to death by Turkish authorities because clothes submitted in lieu of annual tax were of poor quality.

Cowen, Sir Frederic Hymen (1852–1935), British conductor, composer. Conducted London Philharmonic Society and numerous other orchestras. Works include 4 operas, 4 cantatas, 6 symphonies.

Cowen, Joseph (1868–1932), founder and leader of British Zionist movement. As assistant to Herzl, accompanied him to audience with Sultan. Appeared as major character in Herzl's novel, *Altneuland.*

Cowen, Philip (1853–1943), U.S. publisher, author; Immigration Service official (1905–27). A founder of *The American Hebrew* (1879) and its editor and publisher for 27 years.

Cowen, Zelman (1919–), Australian jurist, expert on constitutional law. Prof. of public law at Melbourne 1951, vice-chancellor Univ. of New England 1967, vice-chancellor Univ. of Brisbane 1970.

°**Cowley, Sir Arthur Ernest** (1861–1931), English orientalist. Published recovered Hebrew portions of Ecclesiasticus, Elephantine papyri, and catalogs of Hebrew mss and printed books. Main work on Samaritan liturgy.

Cracow (Kraków), city in Poland, one of most important Jewish communities in Europe. Community founded 14th c.; Jews expelled 1495 to twin city Kazimierz, after 100 years of deteriorating relations with townspeople. Pogroms late 17th c.;

Main Jewish communities in Poland and Lithuania under jurisdiction of Council of the Four Lands and Council of Lithuania.

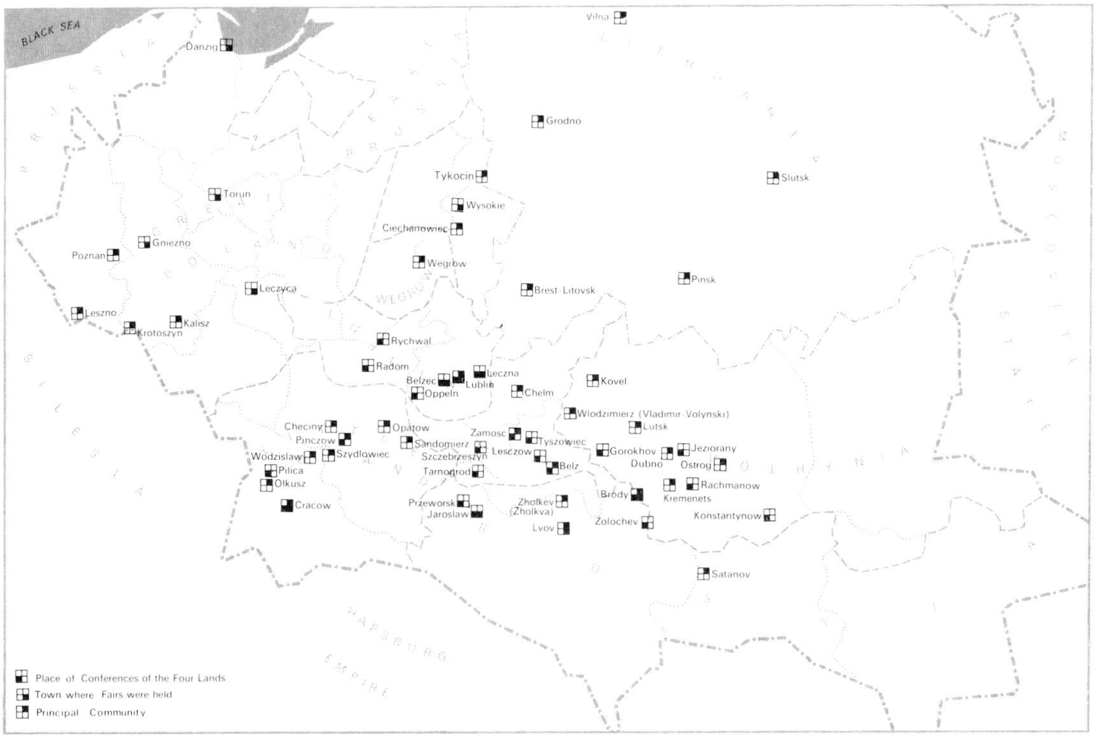

Kazimierz annexed 1772 by Austria, disrupting Jewish life. Many famous *yeshivot* and scholars in Cracow and Hebrew printing presses. Center of Zionism. 50,000 Jews in 1939; most perished. Jewish pop. 700 (1970).

Caricature of Isaac A. Crémieux by Daumier.

Warder Cresson

Karaite cemetery in Crimea. Lithograph by E. Walter, 1856, from painting by C. Bossoli.

David A. Croll

Cranganore, port and commercial center in medieval India, N. of Cochin. Traditionally first settlement of Jews on Malabar coast. Jewish settlement ended with Portuguese conquest 1523.

Créhange, Alexandre (1791–1872), French author, community leader; republican in politics and Orthodox in religion. A founder of Alliance Israélite Universelle and secretary of Paris Univ.

Creizenach, Michael (1789–1842), German mathematician, educator, proponent of Reform. Strong influence in Reform-inspired schools. Tried to show that talmudic Judaism was reform of biblical Judaism and that Reform was acceptable.

Crémieux, Benjamin (1888–1944), French author, literary historian. Joined French underground and was killed by Nazis.

Crémieux, Isaac Adolphe (1796–1880), French lawyer, statesman. Fought for persecuted Jews throughout the world, notably in Damascus Affair. Entered Chamber of Deputies 1842. President of Central Consistory 1843–45. Took part in 1848 revolution as minister of justice. Imprisoned 1851. Re-elected to parliament 1869, becoming minister of justice. Did much to help Algerian Jews (Crémieux Decree, 1870). Life senator fr. 1875. A founder of Alliance Israélite Universelle.

Cremin, Lawrence Arthur (1925–) U.S. educator, authority on progressive school system, author. Wrote history of progressive education movement in U.S.

Cremona, city in Lombardy, N. Italy. Jews first mentioned 1225 when expelled; appear again as loan bankers 1278. Center of Jewish scholarship and Hebrew printing 1556–67. 10,000 Hebrew books burned 1559 and Jews expelled 1592. Last Jew left 1614. No community established thereafter.

Crescas, Ḥasdai (d. 1412), Spanish philosopher, Jewish leader. Worked on rehabilitation of communities after 1391 massacres. Major philosophical opponent of Maimonides (q.v.), both on account of latter's Aristotelian ideas, which he attacked with acumen, and his theology, esp. his theory of negative attributes of God. Major work *Or Adonai.*

Cresques, Abraham (d. 1387), Majorcan cartographer. Made maps and compasses for kings of Aragon.

Cresques de Vivers (d. 1391), Spanish astrologer. Served kings of Aragon. Killed in anti-Jewish outbreaks.

Cresson, Warder (1798–1860), U.S. convert to Judaism, proto-Zionist. Assuming name Michael Boaz Israel undertook propaganda campaigns against Christian missionaries and on behalf of Jewish agricultural colonization in Ereẓ Israel.

Crestohl, Leon David (1900–1963), Canadian lawyer, politician. Elected 1950 to federal parliament as Liberal.

Crete (Candia), Greek island, biblical Caphtor. Jews fr. 2nd c. B.C.E. Oppressed by Byzantine rule; false messiah Moses in 440. Many refugees fr. Spain settled in island. Jewish pop. 400 in 1940, of whom only 7 survived Holocaust.

Crimea, Russian peninsula in Black Sea. Jewish settlement fr. 1st c. C.E. Controlled by Khazars, some of whom converted to Judaism, fr. 6th c. to 1016. Large Karaite community. Conversions to and from Judaism under Tatar rule. In modern times 3 communities: Russian Jews, Karaites, Krimchaks (native Jews). Jewish agricultural settlement under Soviet government; destroyed by Nazis. Nazis systematically destroyed Ashkenazi and Krimchak Jews, but probably spared Karaites. Jewish settlement renewed after WWII, in Simferopol and Sevastopol. 26,000 Jews in 1970.

Crohn, Burrill Bernard (1884–), U.S. gastroenterologist, author. Described the disease regional ileitis and granulomatous colitis (or Crohn's disease of the colon).

Croisset, Francis de (pen name **Frantz Wiener;** 1877–1937), French playwright. Wrote numerous "boulevard"-type plays.

Croll, David Arnold (1900–), Canadian lawyer, politician. Liberal member of Ontario Legislature 1934–45 and Canadian Parliament fr. 1945. Appointed first Canadian Jewish senator 1955.

°**Cromwell, Oliver,** Lord Protector of England 1653–58. Responsible for readmission of Jews into England c. 1656 after petition fr. **Manasseh b. Israel.**

Cronbach, Abraham (1882–1965), U.S. Reform rabbi, author, teacher. Prof. of Jewish Social Studies at Hebrew Union College, Cincinnati, fr. 1922. Anti-Zionist and, although a Hebrew scholar, anti-Hebraist.

°**Crowfoot, John Winter** (1873–1959), British orientalist. Director of British School of Archaeology in Jerusalem 1927–35. Excavated in Tyropoeon Valley, Jerusalem, 1927–29, Jarash in Transjordan 1928–30, Samaria 1931–33, 1935.

Crown, Henry (1896–), U.S. business executive. With his family owned Empire State Building.

Crusades, military expeditions of European Christians to recapture Holy Land from Muslims. Often accompanied by savage attacks on Jews, en route through Europe. First crusade (1096–99), massacres esp. in Rhineland and Jerusalem; established Latin Kingdom in Ereẓ Israel; second crusade (1147–49), in France and Rhineland, on lesser scale; third crusade (1189–92), in England; Shepherd's crusade (1320), southern France. Crusades marked beginning of period of deep insecurity for European Jewry.

Crypto-Jews, Jews who secretly remain faithful to Judaism while practicing religion they were forced to adopt, such as Marranos and Jadīd al-Islām.

Crystal Night, see Kristallnacht.

Csergo (Honig), Hugo (1877–1944), Hungarian author, journalist. Headed Budapest social welfare department. Died after deportation.

Csermely, Gyula (1869–1939), Hungarian author. Many of his works have Jewish settings and deal with conflict of generations and damaging effects of assimilation.

Cuba, island in West Indies. Earliest Spanish settlers included Marranos. Jewish refugees from Brazil arrived in 17th c. Modern community fr. early 20th c. Ashkenazim and Sephardim. After 1959 revolution most Jews left because of economic policy of new regime. 1,500 remained; assisted by government in their communal life.

Cukierman (Zuckerman), Itzhak (Antek; 1915–), Warsaw ghetto fighter. One of commanders of Jewish resistance. In Israel fr. 1946; a founder of kibbutz Loḥamei ha-Geta'ot. Married Ẓivia Lubetkin.

Cukor, George (1899–), U.S. movie director. Films include *Camille, Born Yesterday, My Fair Lady.*

Culi, Jacob (c. 1685–1732), rabbi, editor; b. Ereẓ Israel, *dayyan* in Constantinople. Initiator of important series of Ladino Bible commentaries *Me'am Lo'ez;* one of the founders of Ladino literature.

Cullman, Howard S. (1891–), U.S. business executive, public official. Chairman Port of New York Authority.

Cultural Zionism, trend in Zionism believing that Jewish cultural activity could only fully flower in its own homeland. Its outstanding exponent was Aḥad ha-Am.

Inner room at north gate of Crusader town at Caesarea, 1251.

Jewish Community House, Havana, Cuba.

Inscribed stone recording reconstruction of a 4th-cent. synagogue, Cyprus.

Cup of Elijah, see Elijah.

Curaçao, see Netherlands Antilles.

Curtis, Tony (Bernard Schwartz; 1925–), U.S. actor. Films include *Sweet Smell of Success, Some Like It Hot, The Boston Strangler.*

Cush. (1) Biblical designation of the land of the Kassites, in present-day Luristan, E. of the Tigris. (2) Ancient kingdom in NE Africa. The portion of the Nile Valley between First and Sixth Cataracts was called Cush by Egyptians (= Nubia). In modern Heb. *cushi* = Negro.

Cushan-Rishathaim, king of Aram-Naharaim, the first oppressor of Israel in the period of the Judges (Judg. 3:8–10).

Custom, see Minhag.

Cuth, Cuthah, Sumero-Akkadian and Babylonian cult city, NE of Babylon. One of cities from which king of Assyria brought colonists to province of Samaria (II Kings 17:24, 30). In rabbinic sources "Cuthean" is the fixed term for "Samaritan."

Cutler, Harry (1875–1920), U.S. industrialist, public official, communal leader. A founder of National Jewish Welfare Board and delegate to Versailles Conference in 1919 to represent Jewish interests.

C.Y.C.O., see Central Yiddish Culture Organization.

Cyon, Elie de (1842–1912), Russian physiologist. First Jewish professor in Russia 1870. Left for Paris 1875 following intrigues.

Cypros (1st c. B.C.E.), mother of Herod; descended from noble Nabatean family. Through her intrigues her daughter-in-law Mariamne was executed.

Cypros (1st c. B.C.E.), wife of Agrippa I. Saved her husband from suicide and was moderating influence on him.

Cyprus, E. Mediterranean island. Jewish settlement fr. 3rd c. B.C.E. In 116/7 C.E. Jews revolted and said to have killed 240,000 people, after which they were banned from the island. Returned in 3rd–4th c. Medieval community small. Unsuccessful attempts to settle Jews c. 1900. After WWII, British interned 50,000 "illegal" immigrants to Ereẓ Israel on island until 1948. 25 Jews 1970 (no community).

Cyrene, ancient capital of Cyrenaica (modern Libya). Jews there fr. 3rd c. B.C.E. Persecuted by local population but in 14 B.C.E. rights fully restored and close ties maintained with Jews in Ereẓ Israel. Played leading role in Jewish uprising during last years of Trajan (115–7) which spread across N. Africa.

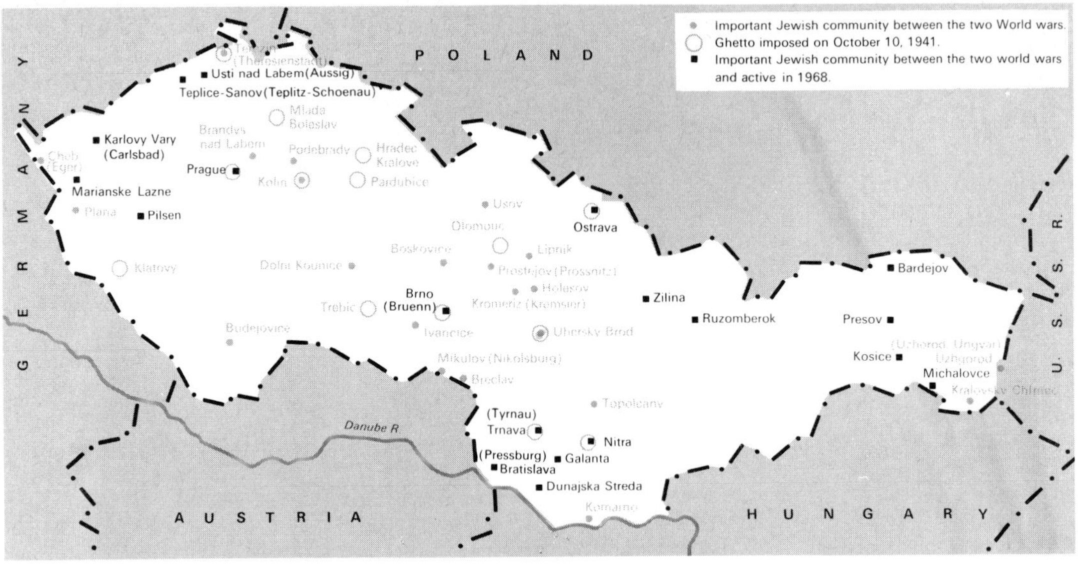

Major Jewish communities in Czechoslovakia from WWI to 1968 (including involuntary settlement-ghettos as of Oct. 1941).

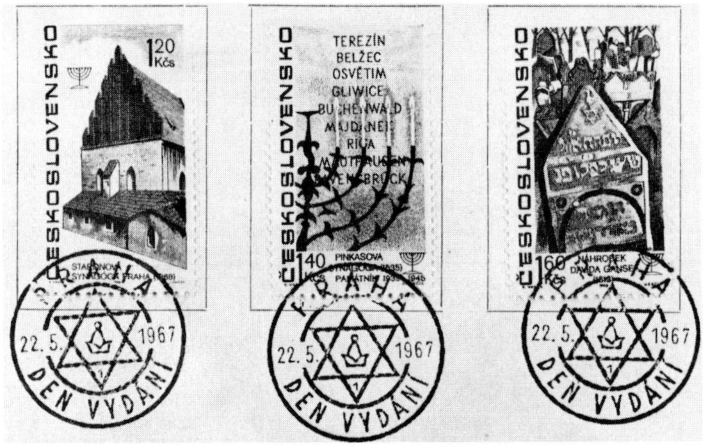

Stamps of the Prague commemorative issue, 1967. Left to right: the Altneuschul; WWII memorial in Pinkas Synagogue; tombstone of David Gans, historian and astronomer, d. 1613.

°**Cyrus,** king of Persia (559–529 B.C.E.). After his conquest of Babylonia, allowed conquered peoples to return to their lands, incl. Jews, whom he allowed to return to Zion and rebuild the destroyed Temple.

Czech, Ludwig (1870–1942), socialist politician in Czechoslovakia. Minister of social welfare 1929, minister of works 1934. D. in Theresienstadt.

Czechoslovakia, C. European republic. Founded 1915 from Bohemia, Moravia, and parts of Silesia. Jewish rights fully respected between world wars with great sympathy fr. Pres. Masaryk. Jews suffered severely under German occupation. Of c. 357,000 Jews before the war, all but 42,000 murdered during WWII. After war Jews prominent in administration but anti-Semitism reached climax in Slánský Trial of 1952. Situation improved after 1960. Jewish pop. c. 14,000 (1971).

Czerniak, Moshe (1910–), Israel chess master, writer; b. Warsaw, settled in Ereẓ Israel 1934. Three times Israel champion.

Czerniakow, Adam (1880–1942), engineer; head of Warsaw Judenrat while Warsaw community was enclosed in ghetto and during subsequent persecutions. Tried to fight in his many contacts with Germans, which he recorded in his diary. Committed suicide when he could not halt deportation of children.

Czernowitz, see Chernovtsy.

Czernowitz Yiddish Language Conference, Conference dealing with role of Yiddish in Jewish life; held Aug. 30–Sept. 4, 1908. Resulted with proclamation that Yiddish is "national language." Conference heightened prestige of Yiddish and laid ideological basis for later founding of YIVO.

Czestochowa, city in Poland. Jews settled 1765, community fr. 1808. 28,486 Jews in 1939. Ghetto established 1941. Jews later deported to extermination camps. Post-war attempts to reconstitute community unsuccessful.

Initial letter "D" from opening to prologue of Book of Daniel, Latin Bible, France, 12th cent., illustrating first beast in prophet's dream.

Dabbūriyya, Muslim-Arab village in C. Israel, W. of Mt. Tabor. Pop. 3,100 (1971), mainly engaged in farming. Legend associates village's name with the prophetess Deborah.

Dachau, concentration camp nr. town of Dachau, Germany. First concentration camp established by Nazis (1933). At least 40,000 killed there, 80–90% Jews.

Da Costa, see Costa, da.

Dagestan, see Mountain Jews.

Dagesh, in Hebrew punctuation, a dot in a letter to harden or change its pronunciation. Two types: *dagesh kal,* in letters *bet, gimel, dalet, kaph, pe,* or *tav* to harden its pronunciation; *dagesh ḥazak* shows that letter is to be pronounced double.

Dagon, Syrian and Canaanite god of seed, vegetation, and crops. Philistines accepted Dagon as their god and set up temples to him.

D'Aguilar, see Aguilar.

Dahiya al-Kāhina, see Kahina.

Dahlberg, Edward (1900–), U.S. novelist, critic. Outstanding prose stylist, with avant-garde reputation in 1930s.

Daia (Delegación de Asociaciones Israelitas Argentinas), umbrella organization and officially recognized representative body of Argentinian Jewry. Founded 1933 to fight anti-Semitism. Organized on basis of representative local, regional, and national bodies.

Daiches, British rabbinical family. **Israel Hayyim** (1850–1937), rabbi in Leeds; founded Union of Orthodox Rabbis in England. **Samuel** (1878–1949), rabbinic, oriental scholar, rabbi in Sunderland, England, and teacher at Jews' College fr. 1908. **Salis** (1880–1945), rabbi in Edinburgh fr. 1918.

Daiches, David (1912–), English scholar; son of Salis Daiches. Professor at Univ. of Sussex fr. 1961. Wrote on many literary topics. Autobiography *Two Worlds.*

Dainow, Ẕevi Hirsch ben Ze'ev Wolf (1832–1877), Russian preacher, known as "Maggid of Slutsk." In London fr. 1874. Active advocate of Haskalah.

Dalet (ד), 4th letter of Hebrew alphabet; numerical value 4. Pronounced *d* with *dagesh; dh* without *dagesh* (difference has generally disappeared).

Dāliyat al-Karmil, Druze village in Israel, on Mt. Carmel. Has existed at least since Middle Ages, but modern settlement dates fr. 17th c. Pop. 6,050 (1971).

Dallas, city in Tex., U.S. First permanent Jewish settlers 1870; first congregation Temple Emanu-el 1874. Jewish pop. 22,000 (1971).

Ark of the Law in synagogue of Congregation Shearith Israel, Dallas.

°**Dalman, Gustaf Hermann** (1855–1941), German Protestant theologian, philologist, Palestinologist. Director of German Evangelical Institute for Antiquity in Jerusalem 1902–17. Wrote on theology, Palestinian Aramaic, geography and topography of Ereẓ Israel, and Palestinian folklore.

Damascus, capital of Syria. In biblical times alternately friendly and hostile to Israel; capital of Aram-Damascus. Large Jewish population in Second Temple period. Under Moslem rule position of Jews generally good and seat of scholars until 1840 Damascus Affair, when decline began. Famous Jewish quarter (ghetto). Since 1948 Jewish pop. declined sharply owing to persecution and emigration; c. 1,500 Jews in 1971.

Damascus, Book of Covenant of (or **Damascus Document**), work presenting views of sect which is said to have left Judah and emigrated to land of Damascus. Sect probably to be identified with Qumran community. Two fragmentary manuscripts found by S. Schechter in Cairo Genizah; identification made after fragments found in Qumran caves.

Carpet page from Damascus Keter Bible, Burgos, Spain 1260.

Commemorative medal of Sir Moses Montefiore and Adolphe Crémieux on their mission to Middle East to secure release of Jews accused of Damascus ritual murder.

Damascus Affair, blood libel in Damascus in 1840 when disappearance of Franciscan and his assistant led to accusations that Jews were responsible. "Confessions" were extracted under torture. Outcry in West, incl. efforts by Sir Moses Montefiore and Adolphe Crémieux and intervention of Austrian emperor led to quashing of charges and reaffirmation of Jewish rights.

Damashek, William (1900–1969), U.S. hematologist, author. Founder and chief editor of *Blood,* the journal of hematology.

Leopold Damrosch and his son Walter.

Damrosch, family of musicians. **Leopold** (1832–1885), conductor, composer; b. Posen, in U.S. fr. 1871. Founder of Oratorio Society (1873) and New York Symphony Society (1878). His son **Frank Heino** (1859–1937), organist, Metropolitan Opera chorus master (1885–91), director of choral societies. His son **Walter Johannes** (1862–1950), conductor. Conducted Metropolitan Opera, Oratorio Society, New York Symphony Society (1885–1927). Played important role in development of American concert life.

Dan, 5th son of Jacob and first born of Bilhah, Rachel's maid (Gen. 30:1–6); the eponymous ancestor of tribe of Dan. Inheritance of tribe situated in S. maritime plain but limited by failure to conquer; therefore had to search for new area of settlement and moved as far north as sources of Jordan, capturing city of Laish (Dan).

Allotted territory of tribe of Dan.

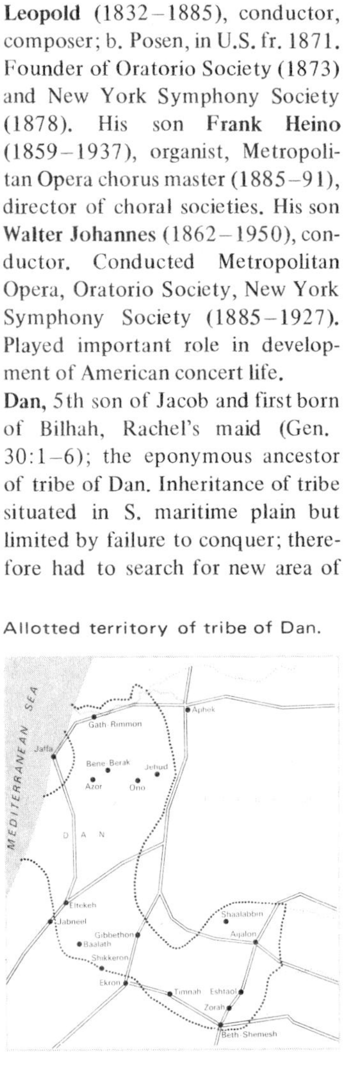

"Daniel in the Lion's Den" by Rubens, 1618.

Dan (originally **Laish**), biblical city in N. Israel nr. sources of Jordan. Danites established sanctuary there. Jeroboam erected temple with golden calf (I Kings 12:29 ff.). In Hellenistic period it marked N. point of Alexander Yannai's conquests. Excavations conducted at the site (1966 ff.) uncovered fortifications and building remains. Name given to nearby kibbutz founded 1939.

Dan, Fyodor Ilyich (1871–1947), Russian socialist, journalist; physician by profession. Belonged to Mensheviks and was imprisoned and exiled several times under Czars. Forced to leave Russia 1922. Leading member of Russian Social Democratic movement in exile. In New York fr. 1940.

Dan, Sergiu (1903–), Rumanian novelist, journalist. After WWII wrote novels on fate of Jewish families under Germans.

°**Danby, Herbert** (1889–1953), English Hebraist. Canon, St. George's Cathedral, Jerusalem. Prof. of Hebrew at Oxford. Translated Mishnah into English.

D'Ancona, see Ancona.

Danglow, Jacob (1880–1962), Australian rabbi; b. England. Minister of St. Kilda Hebrew Congregation, Victoria, fr. 1905 and chaplain of Australian forces in WWI.

Dangoor, Ezra Sasson ben Reuben (1848–1930), Iraqi rabbi; chief rabbi of Baghdad 1923–28. Established Hebrew press and published many books.

Daniel, pre-Mosaic righteous man (Ezek. 14:14, 20) and sage (28:3). Ugaritic documents also refer to a Daniel famed for piety and wisdom.

Daniel, hero of Book of Daniel. As young Jew of noble descent, carried captive to Babylon by Nebuchadnezzar and trained for king's service (Dan. 1:1–6). Gained reputation as interpreter of visions, incl. those of king and his own predictions of future triumph of messianic kingdom.

Daniel, Book of, book in Hagiographa section of Bible. Falls into two parts: Ch. 1–6 tell of trials and triumphs of Daniel and his companions; ch. 7–12 contain apocalyptic revelations. Part written in Hebrew (1:1–2:4a; 8–12), the rest in Aramaic. Authorship and date disputed.

Daniel, Books of (Apocryphal), additions to biblical Book of Daniel, found at Qumran. Extant Christian Daniel books include various forms of work called in Armenian *The Seventh Vision of Daniel.* A Persian work called *The History of Daniel* contains similar material.

Daniel, Ezra Menahem (d. 1952), member of Iraqi senate, succeeding his father, Menahem Saliḥ Daniel, in 1930s. Defended Jews but was anti-Zionist.

Daniel, M. (=Mark; 1897–1940), Soviet Yiddish writer, dramatist. Best known for novel *Yulis* (dramatized as *Fir Teg*), romantic treat-

BOOK OF DANIEL – CONTENTS

Chs. 1–6	Stories
1:1–21	Daniel and His Friends
2:1–49	Nebuchadnezzar's Dream
3:1–30	The Furnace
4:1–34	Nebuchadnezzar's Madness
5:1–30	The Writing on the Wall
6:1–29	Daniel in the Lion's Den
Chs. 7–12	Visions
7:1–28	The Four Beasts
8:1–27	The Ram and the He-Goat
9:1–27	The Seventy Weeks
10:1–12:13	The Revelation of the Angel

ment of episode in Bolshevik revolution.

Daniel, Menahem Saliḥ (1846–1940), leader of Baghdad community. Member of Ottoman and Iraqi parliaments and Iraqi senate as appointed representative of Jews. Opposed Zionism.

Daniel, Vision of, Hebrew apocalypse written in Byzantine Empire. Traces policies of Byzantine emperors toward Jews fr. 9th to mid-10th c.

Daniel, Yuli Markovich (1925–), Soviet-Russian writer, translator (from Yiddish and Slavic languages); son of M. Daniel. His trial (1966) together with Andrei Sinyavsky, on charges of slandering Soviet Union in works smuggled out of USSR and published in West, attracted world attention and protests. Released 1970.

Daniel ben Azariah (11th c.), Palestinian *gaon,* 1051–62. Honored in Egypt, where Fostat synagogue of Palestinian community called after him.

Daniel ben Ḥasdai (d. 1174), exilarch of Baghdad, with extensive authority. Noted for his personality and hospitality.

Daniel ben Moses al-Qūmisī (9th–10th c.), Karaite scholar; b. Persia, settled in Jerusalem. As leader of Avelei Zion, enjoined perpetual public mourning for destruction of Temple and constant supplication for redemption.

Daniel ben Peraḥyah ha-Kohen (d. 1575), head of yeshivah, author. Headed Italian community yeshivah in Salonika. Almost all his writings destroyed 1545 in fire.

Daniel ben Saadiah ha-Bavli (Daniel ibn al-Amshata; fl. c. 1200), Babylonian talmudist, head of yeshivah in Baghdad, preacher in Damascus.

Danin, Yeḥezkel (1867–1945), Ereẓ Israel pioneer; b. Bialystok, settled in Ereẓ Israel 1886. Promoted Heb. education; founded first kindergarten in Jaffa.

Danon, Abraham (1857–1925), Turkish scholar. Founded and headed rabbinical seminary in Adrianople. Wrote on Turkish Jewish history.

Danzig, see Gdansk.

Danzig (Danziger), Abraham ben Jehiel Michal (1748–1820), codifier; b. Danzig, lived in Vilna. Author of *Ḥayyei Adam* and *Hokhmat Adam,* both dealing with laws of *Shulḥan Arukh.*

Danziger, Yitshak (1916–). Israel sculptor. Taught at Haifa Technion. Won Israel Prize for Arts 1968.

Lorenzo da Ponte

Da Piera, Meshullam ben Solomon (13th c.), Hebrew poet in Spain. Initially attacked Maimonides, but relented. Member of Naḥmanides' group of mystics in Gerona.

Da Piera, Solomon ben Meshullam (c. 1342–c. 1418), Hebrew poet in Spain; converted to Christianity at Disputation of Tortosa. Major member of group which revived Hebrew poetry in Spain.

Da Ponte, Lorenzo (1749–1838), poet, librettist. Wrote libretti for Mozart's operas *Marriage of Figaro, Don Giovanni,* and *Cosi fan tutte.* Wandered in Europe and settled in New York, pioneering opera in U.S.

Dar'ī, Moses ben Abraham (12th–13th c.), Karaite Hebrew and Arabic poet; lived in Egypt.

°**Darius I,** king of Persia (522–486 B.C.E.). Forbade obstruction of rebuilding of Temple in Jerusalem, which was completed in his reign (Hag. 1:15).

Darmstadt Haggadah, 15th c. illuminated *Haggadah,* produced in Heidelberg. Many illustrations. Artist unknown.

Darmesteter, Arsène (1846–1888), French philologist, authority on Romance languages. Taught at Sorbonne. Studied French words used by medieval Bible and Talmud commentators, especially Rashi. His brother **James** (1849–1894), orientalist. Specialized in Indo-Iranian studies and translated *Zend-Avesta* into French and English.

Daroff, Samuel H. (1900–1967), U.S. clothing manufacturer in Philadelphia, philanthropist, Jewish and civic leader. Chaired governor's Industrial Race Relations Committee.

Darshan, professional or qualified expounder of Scripture. Originally the *darshan* expounded both halakhically and aggadically, but later the term was applied to the homiletical interpreter of the Torah. In medieval times it represented the professional preacher.

Dashewski, Pinḥas (1879–1934). Russian Zionist activist. Sentenced to 5 years' hard labor for assaulting Krushevan, instigator of Kishinev pogrom, but released. D. in Soviet prison.

Dassault (Bloch), Darius Paul (1882–), French army officer. Joined Resistance in WWII, and governor of Paris after Liberation. Brother of Marcel Dassault.

Dassault (Bloch), Marcel (1892–). French engineer. Deputy in National Assembly 1951–1955, senator 1957–58. Designed Mystère and Mirage aircraft. Converted to Catholicism 1947.

Dassin, Jules (1911–), U.S. film, stage director. Directed *Naked City, Topkapi, Rififi, Never On Sunday* (starring Melina Mercouri, whom he married).

Dathan and Abiram, leaders, with Korah, of revolt against leadership of Moses (Num. 16; 26:9–11), for which they were punished and swallowed up by the earth.

Dato, Mordecai ben Judah (1525–1591/1601), Italian kabbalist, author of *piyyutim.*

Daube, David (1909–), jurist, biblical scholar; b. Germany. Prof. of civil law at Oxford 1955–70, Univ. of California at Berkeley fr. 1970. Leading authority on Roman Law; contributed to understanding of history of biblical and talmudic law.

Daugavpils (until 1893 **Duenaburg;** until 1920 **Dvinsk**), city in Latvian SSR. In 1805 c. 800 Jews, majority of pop. Town developed from 1860s with Jews prominent in commerce and industry. Noted Torah center. 56,000 Jews in 1913 but most left in WWI. 11,000 before WWII. In 1970 c. 2,000.

Dauphiné, region and former province in SE France. Jews present fr. 9th c. Most emigrated by 15th c. Expelled 1717.

Davar, Hebrew daily newspaper of Histadrut founded 1925 under editorship of B. Katznelson, who was succeeded by Z. Shazar. Also publishes children's weekly *Davar li-Yladim; Ha-Meshek ha-Shittufi; Devar ha-Poelet; Omer,* a vocalized Hebrew daily, and *Ot.* Also maintains a publishing house.

Davenport, Marcia (1903–), U.S. novelist, daughter of Alma Gluck. Works incl. *Of Lena Geyer* and *Valley of Decision.*

Davičo, Oscar (1909–), Yugoslav poet, novelist. Partisan in WWII. Won Yugoslavia's highest literary award 3 times. Anti-Zionist.

Davičo, Hajim S. (1854–1918), Serbian author, diplomat. Pioneer of Jewish secular literature in Serbia; wrote short stories describing life among Belgrade Sephardim.

"King David's Entry into Jerusalem," part of Marc Chagall's Gobellin tapestry in the Knesset, Jerusalem.

David, king of Judah and Israel c. 1010–970 B.C.E. A shepherd boy of Beth-Lehem, he was anointed by Samuel as the future king. He began his career by killing Goliath the Philistine and became a captain in Saul's army. His popularity aroused Saul's jealousy. He fled the court and roamed the border region of Judah. Following death of Saul and his son Jonathan (David's close friend) on Mt. Gilboa fighting the Philistines, David was appointed king over the people of Judah and made his capital in Hebron. After the death of Ish-Bosheth son of Saul, David was anointed king over Israel. After decisively defeating the Philistines, he waged war E. of the Jordan and extended his kingdom from the Euphrates to the "River of Egypt." His most important task was to create a loose national union of tribes. He captured Jerusalem and made it his capital; later he put down a rebellion by his son Abshalom and by Sheba son of Bichri. Toward the end of his life, he enthroned Solomon as his successor. One of the most beloved figures in Jewish tradition. He was the founder of the dynasty of the kings of Judah and it was believed that the Messiah would come from his descendants. He was a skillful musician and the Book of Psalms was attributed to him. His traditional tomb is venerated on Mt. Zion in Jerusalem.

"Noah and the Ark" by Jean David.

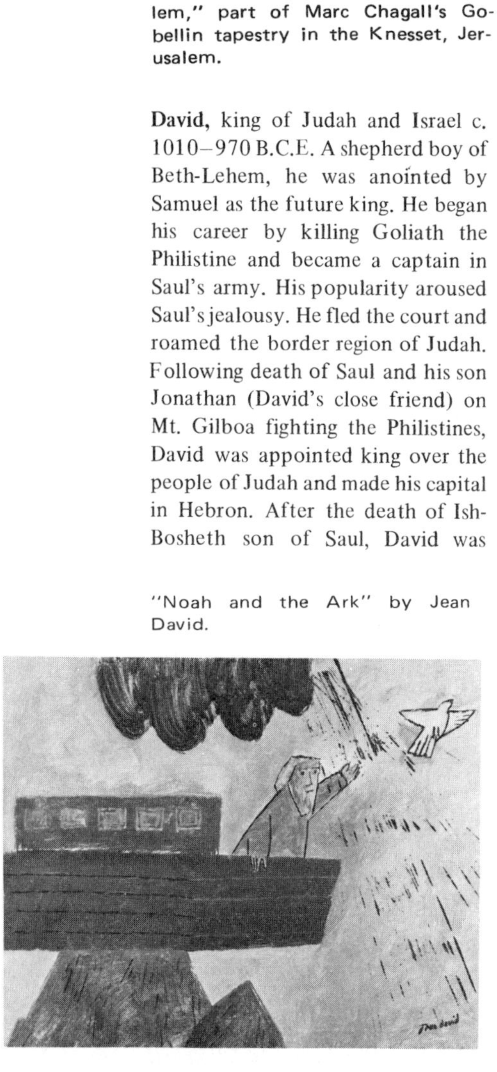

David, Aaron Hart (1812–1882), Canadian physician. Dean of faculty of medicine at Bishops College Univ. and general secretary of Canadian Medical Association.

David, City of, name given to fortified city of Jebusites (Jerusalem) after capture by David (II Sam. 5:7–8). David established his residence there.

David, Ferdinand (1810–1873). German violinist, composer, teacher. Gave first performance of Mendelssohn's violin concerto.

David, Jean (1908–), Israel painter. Worked on murals, posters, jewelry, enamels.

David, Joseph (Penker, 1876–1948), Indian playwright, director. Wrote more than 100 plays in 4 languages.

David, Martin (1898–), legal historian, papyrologist; b. Germany, fled to Holland in Nazi period. After WWII, prof. of comparative ancient legal history, director of Leiden Institute of Papyrology, member of Royal Dutch Academy.

David, Tower of, principal tower of Jerusalem citadel, adjacent to Jaffa Gate. Stands on foundation of Phasael tower built by Herod.

David ben Abraham Maimuni (1222–1300), *nagid* of Egyptian Jewry and grandson of Maimonides. Appointed *nagid* at age 15. In old age, forced to flee Egypt as result of slander. Eventually restored as *nagid.*

David ben Aryeh Leib of Lida (c. 1650–1696), rabbi, author of numerous homiletic and kabbalistic works. Accused of Shabbatean leanings but vindicated.

David ben Boaz (10th–11th c.). Karaite scholar. Head of Karaites in Jerusalem. Originated reform in laws of forbidden marriages.

David ben Daniel (11th c.), aspirant to Palestinian gaonate. Went to Egypt 1078 and plotted unsuccessfully to become Egyptian exilarch. Expelled from Cairo. Also failed in attempt to succeed his father as Palestinian *gaon.*

David ben Joshua (d. 1647), head and emissary of Karaite community in Jerusalem.

David ben Joshua Maimuni (14th–15th c.), *nagid* of Egyptian Jewry; last of Maimonides' descendants to hold position.

David ben Judah he-Ḥasid (14th c.), Spanish kabbalist. Writings reflect post-Zohar development of Kabbalah.

David ben Levi of Narbonne (13th c.), scholar of Provence. His halakhic rulings criticized by Joseph Caro and Moses Isserles.

David ben Manasseh Darshan (16th c.), preacher and author in Poland who prepared program to reform study in yeshivot.

David ben Meshullam of Speyer (12th c.), liturgical poet who described horrors of First Crusade.

David (Tevele) ben Nathan of Lissa (d. 1792), Galician rabbi who attacked N.H. Wessely's plan for educational reform.

David ben Samuel (d. after 1201), exilarch in Baghdad before 1195 whose learning was questioned but upheld by Maimonides.

David ben Samuel ha-Levi (Taz; 1586–1667), rabbi, halakhic commentator. Established *bet midrash* in Cracow; rabbi in Putalicze, Posen, Lemberg. His commentary *Turei Zahav* on *Shulḥan Arukh* greatly influenced practical halakhic rulings and is regarded as basic. Many supercommentaries written on his work.

David ben Solomon (1161–after 1236), Karaite physician, medical author in Cairo; personal physician to the sultan.

David ben Solomon ibn Abi (Avi, Ben Abi) Zimra (Radbaz; 1479–1573), talmudic scholar, halakhic authority, kabbalist; b. Spain, lived in Safed and Jerusalem before settling in Egypt and becoming head of Egyptian Jewry. Applied scientific method of talmudic study. Although a kabbalist, introduced Kabbalah in decisions only when not in contradiction to Talmud.

David ben Zakkai, exilarch in Iraq, 917–940. Career was stormy but strengthened authority of exilarchate and prevented rising wealthy class from seizing authority from the

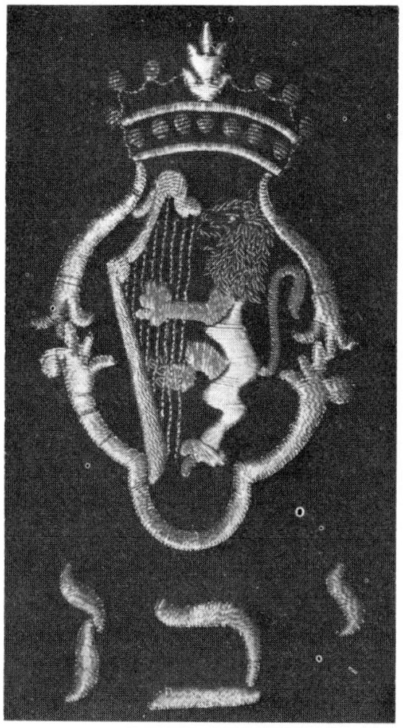

Family seal of David ibn Abi Zimra embroidered on a tallit bag.

learned.

David D'Beth Hillel (d. 1846), traveler, scholar; b. Vilna, settled Safed c. 1815. Wrote important accounts on Jewish communities in Asia.

Davíd-Gorodok, town in Belorussian SSR. Jews present fr. late 16th c. Main occupations innkeeping, sale of alcoholic liquor, timber trade. Ḥasidic dynasty founded by Ze'ev Wolf Ginsburg (early 19th c.) Almost entire community murdered in WWII.

Davidoff, Leo Max (1898–), U.S. neurosurgeon. Surgeon of Byrd-Macmillan Arctic expedition. Director of neurological surgery, Bronx Municipal Hospital Center (1954–66). Associate dean, Albert Einstein College of Medicine of Yeshiva University (1961–66).

David of Makow (d. 1814), *maggid, dayyan.* Originally ḥasid, later joined *mitnaggedim.* Wrote polemics against ḥasidism and commentaries on Bible and Mishnah.

David of Talna (David b. Mordecai Twersky; 1808–1882), *ẓaddik;* son of Menahem Nahum Twersky, the founder of the Chernobyl ḥasidic dynasty. Maintained luxurious "court."

David Reuveni, see Reuveni, David.

Davids, Aaron Issachar (Bernard) ben Naḥman (1895–1945), chief rabbi of Rotterdam and active Zionist; perished in Bergen-Belsen.

Davidsohn, Robert (1853–1937), historian of medieval Florence; the leading authority on the subject.

Davidson, Israel (1870–1939), U.S.

Statue of Walt Whitman by Jo Davidson.

scholar of medieval Hebrew Literature; b. Lithuania, in U.S. fr. 1888. Prof. at Jewish Theological Seminary. Best known for his 4-vol. *Ozar ha-Shirah ve-ha-Piyyut,* which records in alphabetical order initial words of more than 35,000 prayers and poems.

Davidson, Jo (1883–1952), U.S. sculptor. Works incl. busts of famous people; statue of Walt Whitman in Bear Mountain, N.Y.

Davidson, Lionel (1922–). English novelist. Wrote thrillers and romance, also adventure set in Israel *A Long Way to Shiloh (The Menorah Men).* Settled in Israel 1968.

°**Davidson, Samuel** (1806–1898), British Bible critic. Published commentary on Bible, pioneering new theories of Higher Criticism, denying Mosaic authorship of Pentateuch. Translated Fuerst's Bible lexicon.

D'Avigdor, Elim Henry (1841–1895), English engineer and author. Active in Ḥovevei Zion.

D'Avigdor-Goldsmid, Sir Osmond (1877–1940), English public figure. Active in Jewish community. President, Board of Deputies; president, Anglo-Jewish Association, chairman, Jewish Colonization Association. His son **Sir Henry Joseph** (1909–), Conservative MP 1955–74 and chairman of Jewish Colonization Association.

Davin (David) de Caderousse (15th c.), first Jew to attempt Hebrew printing (c. 1446). Worked in Avignon. No specimens have survived.

Davis, Alexander Barnard (1828–1913), Australian rabbi. Chief minister, Sydney, 1862–1904.

Davis, Sir Edmund (d. 1939), S. African mining magnate, art collector. Donated art collections to museums and bequests to hospitals and scholarship funds.

Davis, Edward ("Teddy the Jewboy"; 1816–1841), Australian convict and only known Jewish bushranger. Executed in Sydney.

Davis, Sir Ernest Hyam (1872–1962), New Zealand businessman, philanthropist. Mayor of Auckland 1935–41.

Davis, Moshe (1916–), historian, educator, rabbi. B. New York. Provost, Jewish Theological Seminary 1950–9. Head of Heb. Univ. Institute of Contemporary Jewry (1959). Wrote on contemporary Jewish life, esp. U.S. Jewry.

Da Volterra, Meshullam, see Volterra, Meshullam da.

Davydov, Karl Yulyevich (1838–1889), Russian cellist, composer, teacher. Established first cello school in Russia.

Dawidsohn, Ḥayyim (1760–1854), merchant, community leader, rabbi in Warsaw. Though a *mitnagged* and Orthodox, cooperated with ḥasidim and assimilationists in his position as community leader.

Dawidsohn, Joseph (1880–1947), physician, Zionist leader in Poland. Founded first Jewish newspaper in Polish and association to fight tuberculosis. In Polish Senate 1928–1931. Settled in Ereẓ Israel 1932.

Dawison, Bogumil (1818–1872), German actor. One of great character actors of his day. Toured Europe and U.S. fr. 1864.

Dayan, Moshe (1915–), Israel military commander, statesman; son of Shemuel Dayan. Participated in night squads commanded by Wingate. Sentenced 1940 to 10 years by British, but released after year. Lost eye in encounter with Vichy French in Syria 1941. Led troops that cap-

A meeting between Colonel Dayan and Colonels Himawy (l.) and Moita of the Arab Legion, November 1949.

tured Lydda and Ramleh in War of Independence. Appointed commander of Jerusalem Aug. 1948; negotiated cease-fire with Jordanians. Chief of Staff 1953–1958, commanded Sinai Campaign 1956. Mapai member of Knesset fr. 1959, minister of agriculture 1959–64. Joined Rafi party. Minister of defense 1967–74, incl. Six-Day and Yom Kippur Wars. Implemented policy of liberal military government. Daughter, **Yael** (1939–), novelist *(New Face in the Mirror; Death had Two Sons)*. His son **Assaf** (1945–), film actor, producer.

Dayan, Shemuel (1891–1968), Israel pioneer. Founding member of Kibbutz Deganyah and moshav Nahalal. Pioneer of moshav movement. Mapai member of 1st, 2nd, 3rd Knessets. Wrote about agricultural settlement and Second Aliyah.

Day-Morning Journal, see Jewish Morning Journal.

Day of Atonement (Heb. *Yom ha-Kippurim*), annual day of fasting and atonement, occurring on Tishri 10; the most important occasion of the religious year. All work is forbidden as are eating, drinking, washing, the wearing of leather shoes, and sexual intercourse. The day is spent in prayer in the synagogue as man's destiny is recorded by God for the coming year. There are five services: *Ma'ariv* (popularly known as Kol Nidrei, q.v.); *Shaḥarit; Musaf* (which includes the recitation of the solemn observance of the day in Temple times, the only occasion when the High Priest entered the Holy of Holies); *Minḥah;* and *Ne'ilah.*

Dayton, city in Ohio, U.S. First Jewish settler 1840s. First congregation Bnai Jeshuran founded 1850. Jewish pop. 7,200 (1971).

Dayyan, judge in cases of Jewish law; member of a rabbinic court.

Dayyeinu, refrain of a song of thanksgiving in Passover Haggadah service.

Silver belt buckle for a kitel, the robe worn on the Day of Atonement, Lublin 1821.

Dead Sea (Heb. *Yam ha-Melaḥ* = the Salt Sea), an inland lake in C. Israel; the lowest point on earth. 49 mi. long and 11 mi. wide. Waters rich in chemicals, which are extracted by Israel Potash Works at S. end (called Sedom according to tradition that biblical Sodom was in vicinity). Divided between Israel and Jordan after 1948, Israel only having access to SW section. After Six-Day War, entire W. bank under Israel control.

Dead Sea Scrolls, ancient mss. found in caves in vicinity of Dead Sea, esp. nr. Qumran. First scrolls discovered 1947. Linked to Dead Sea Sect (q.v.) living in Qumran. Finds include a number of complete scrolls and thousands of fragments. Among them: various sections of the Bible (the oldest known biblical mss.); books of the sect (e.g., *Manual of Discipline, War Scroll, Damascus Document, Thanksgiving Psalms*) and commentaries (*pesher*) on biblical books according to the outlook of the sect; fragments of Apocryphal works. Scrolls apparently written during 1st c. B.C.E. and 1st c. C.E. (but not later than 70 C.E.). Original find of seven well-kept scrolls now housed in Shrine of the Book at Israel Museum. Contents important for Bible study, for linguistic and paleographic studies of the period, for information on sectarianism in Second Temple times with implications for general history and for the origins of Christianity.

Scroll of the Thanksgiving Psalms before unrolling.

Complete Isaiah Scroll displayed in the Shrine of the Book, Israel Museum, Jerusalem.

Dead Sea Sect, ascetic Jewish community of late Second Temple period which became known through discovery of Dead Sea Scrolls and excavations at Qumrān. Sect was extremist offshoot of Jewish apocalyptic movement, living in expectation of imminent end of days. This demanded punctilious observance of *mitzvot,* separation from ordinary society, and maximum social unity. Many scholars identify sect with Essenes. Sect had basic differences with Temple cult. It came to an end during Roman war of 66–70 C.E.

Debenedetti, Giacomo (1901–1967), Italian author, critic. Taught at Univ. of Rome. Analyzed work of Croce, De Sanctis, Pirandello; described WWII sufferings of Rome Jews in 2 published diaries.

Debir (Kiriath-Sepher), Canaanite royal city in territory of Judah conquered by Othniel. Usually identified with Tell Beit Mirsim 15 mi. SW of Hebron, which was excavated by Albright (1926–32).

Deborah, judge and prophetess during period of Judges. Together with army commander Barak, led successful war of liberation from oppression of Jabin king of Canaan (Judg. 4). After victory she uttered

Dead Sea and surrounding areas.

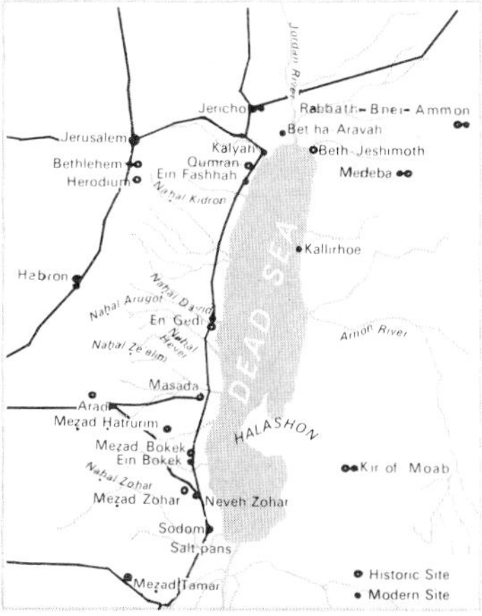

THE DECALOGUE

1. I am the Lord thy God, who brought thee out of the land of Egypt, out of the house of bondage.
2. Thou shalt have no other gods before Me.
   Thou shalt not make unto thee a graven image, nor any manner of likeness, of any thing that is in heaven above, or that is in the earth beneath, or that is in the water under the earth; thou shalt not bow down unto them, nor serve them; for I the Lord thy God am a jealous God, visiting the iniquity of the fathers upon the children unto the third and fourth generation of them that hate Me; and showing mercy unto the thousandth generation of them that love Me and keep My commandments.
3. Thou shalt not take the name of the Lord thy God in vain; for the Lord will not hold him guiltless that taketh His name in vain.
4. Remember the Sabbath day, to keep it holy. Six days shalt thou labor, and do all thy work; but the seventh day is a sabbath unto the Lord thy God, in it thou shalt not do any manner of work, thou, nor thy son, nor thy daughter, nor thy man-servant, nor thy maid-servant, nor thy cattle, nor thy stranger that is within thy gates; for in six days the Lord made heaven and earth, the sea, and all that in them is, and rested on the seventh day; wherefore the Lord blessed the Sabbath day, and hallowed it.
5. Honor thy father and thy mother, that thy days may be long upon the land which the Lord thy God giveth thee.
6. Thou shalt not murder.
7. Thou shalt not commit adultery.
8. Thou shalt not steal.
9. Thou shalt not bear false witness against thy neighbor.
10. Thou shalt not covet thy neighbor's house, thou shalt not covet thy neighbor's wife, nor his man-servant, nor his maid-servant, nor his ox, nor his ass, nor any thing that is thy neighbor's.

Decalogue from "menorah" at the Knesset, Jerusalem, by Benno Elkan.

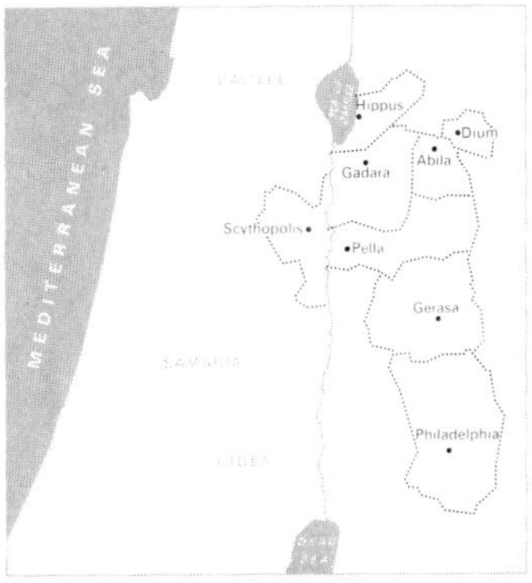

Map showing the eight cities constituting continuous bloc of Decapolis. Damascus and Kanatha lie north of this area.

"Dietary Laws" by Jacob Meijer de Haan, 1880.

"Song of Deborah" (Judg. 5), one of earliest of biblical heroic poems.

Deborin (Joffe), Abram Moiseyevich (1881–1963), Russian Marxist philosopher. Most influential Soviet academic philosopher by 1928 but did not adjust to Stalinism and played minor role subsequently.

Debrecen, city in E. Hungary. Jewish community fr. 1851; separate Orthodox community 1886. Jewish pop. 12,000 in 1940. Under Nazi regime many killed. In 1970, 1,200 Jews.

Decalogue, the 10 commandments given by God to Moses on Mt. Sinai. Engraved on two stone "tablets of the covenant" and regarded in Jewish tradition as the basis of all their legislation. Kept inside the ark of the covenant, housed first in the Tabernacle and ultimately in the Temple. The Decalogue is given twice in the Bible, with small variations (Exod. 20:2–14 and Deut. 5:6–18). Jewish tradition divides it into the first five dealing with man's relation to God and the latter with man's relation to man. Deeply embedded in Jewish consciousness, it played a major role in other monotheistic religions. It originally formed part of the daily service but this practice was dropped to refute sectarians who maintained that only the Decalogue was divinely given.

Decapolis, league of 10 Syrian-Greek cities in Ereẓ Israel in Roman and Byzantine periods, situated in N. Jordan Valley and Transjordan. Differing lists of these cities have survived. They possessed internal autonomy and were strongly Hellenized.

De Chaves, Aaron (d. 1705), Dutch painter, engraver. First Jewish artist in England after readmission of Jews.

De Cordova, Jacob (1808–1868), Texas pioneer, newspaper publisher. Founded Kingston *Daily Herald* 1834, Jamaica's first daily paper, then moved to Texas. Elected to Texas House of Representatives 1847, published with his brother the semi-monthly *Texas Herald.*

Decrees, see Takkanot.

Deed, see Shetar.

Deganyah, two kevuẓot, Deganyah Alef and Deganyah Bet, S. of Lake Kinneret, both affiliated to Iḥud ha-Kibbutzim. D. Alef founded 1909 but broke up after a year. New group 1911. Termed "Mother of the Kevuẓot." D. Bet founded 1920. During 1948 War of Independence Syrian army reached D. but was repulsed. In 1971 the two Deganyahs had a total of 987 inhabitants.

De Grunewald, Anatole (1910–1967), British film producer and writer. Films incl.: *Queen of Spades; The V.I.P.'s* and *The Yellow Rolls-Royce.*

De Haan, see also Haan.

De Haan, Jacob Meijer (1852–1895), Dutch painter. Closely associated with Gauguin, whom he helped financially and in whose paintings he appears. Also painted Jewish themes.

De Haas, Jacob (1872–1937), author, journalist, Zionist; b.

London. Closely associated with Herzl. In U.S. fr. 1902, edited *The Maccabean,* published the *Jewish Advocate* and was staunch supporter of Brandeis' Zionist policies. Headed Zionist Organization of America 1918–21. Wrote on Herzl and edited 1-vol. Jewish encyclopedia.

Deinard, Ephraim (1846–1930), bibliographer, Hebrew author; b. Latvia, in U.S. fr. 1916. Produced important catalogs (incl. listing of Hebrew books in U.S. 1735–1926) and wrote polemic and other books.

Deir (Dayr) al-Balaḥ, Arab town in Erez Israel, SW of Gaza. Existed since Byzantine times. Pop. 18,000 (1967), 7,000 in local refugee camp.

Dekker, Maurits (1896–1962). Dutch novelist, playwright. Wrote many books on Jewish themes.

De Klerk, Michel (1884–1923), Dutch architect; leader of "Amsterdam School." Noted for work on low-cost housing.

Delacrut, Mattathias ben Solomon (16th c.), kabbalist, astronomer; b. Poland, lived in Italy. Wrote on theoretical Kabbalah.

De La Motta, Jacob (1789–1845), U.S. physician; lived in Charleston, S.C. Secretary of Medical Society of South Carolina for 10 years and assistant commissioner of health.

Delaunay-Terk, Sonia (1885–), painter, fashion designer; b. Russia, in Paris fr. 1906. Cofounder of "Orphism," based on simultaneous color contrasts.

Delaware, U.S. state. Jewish traders arrived 1655 but Jewish settlement only fr. 1880s. Jewish pop. 9,000 (1971), nearly all in Wilmington.

Del Banco, Anselmo (16th c.), founder of Jewish community in Venice. Spokesman of community and owner of several loan banks.

De Lee, Joseph B. (1869–1942), U.S. obstetrician, gynecologist. Designed over 20 new obstetric instruments, incl. stethoscope to check heartbeat of fetus.

De Leon, Daniel (1852–1914), U.S. socialist leader; b. Curaçao, in N.Y. fr. 1872. Joined Socialist Labor Party in 1890 and soon became its most important figure, rejecting any compromise with the capitalist system. Edited the party's weekly *The People* (1892–1914) and the *Daily People* (1900–1914).

De Leon, David Camden (1816–1872), U.S. physician. Entered U.S. army 1838; served in Seminole and Mexican Wars. Resigned commission to enlist in Confederate Army, where he served as its first surgeon general and later in Florida, Alabama, Louisiana.

De Leon, Edwin (1828–1891), U.S. journalist, diplomat, Confederate agent; brother of David de Leon. Editor of several Southern newspapers, pro-slavery advocate, consul general in Egypt for 8 years, confidential agent for Confederate State Department.

De Leon, Thomas Cooper (1839–1914), U.S. author, editor; brother of David and Edwin de Leon. Versatile poet, novelist, essayist, and playwright.

Delfont, Bernard (1909–), British theatrical manager. Fr. 1941 managed many West End theaters and controlled companies with theater, film, TV, music, and other interests.

De Lieme, Nehemia (1882–1940), Dutch Zionist, economist. Actively involved in Zionist movement. Chairman J.N.F.; opposed purchase of Jezreel Valley. Headed World Zionist Office in London 1920 but resigned owing to differences with other Zionist leaders. Wrote on land settlement and on Aḥad Ha-Am.

Delilah, Samson's mistress who betrayed him to Philistines (Judg. 16:4 ff.). Induced Samson to disclose the secret of his strength, which lay in his long hair.

De Lima, Joseph Suasso (1791–1858), S. African writer, journalist; b. Holland, settled in S. Africa 1818. Ran first Dutch newspaper in S.A. Joined Dutch Reformed Church 1833.

°**Delitzsch, Franz (Julius;** 1813–1890), German-Protestant theologian, Bible and Judaica scholar. Established Institutum Judaicum (renamed "Delitzschianum" after his death) in Leipzig for training missionaries to Jews. Translated New Testament into Hebrew 1877. Wrote first comprehensive history of Hebrew poetry.

°**Delitzsch, Friedrich** (1850–1922), German orientalist, a founder of modern Assyriology; son of Franz Delitzsch. Investigated Hebrew in its relation to Akkadian. In lectures on 'Babel und Bibel" (1902), claimed absolute superiority of "Babylonia" over "Israel" and that Bible is devoid of religious and moral value. Contributed to slogans of anti-Semitic movements in Germany.

Della Seta, Alessandro (1897–1944), Italian architect, art historian. Prof. of Etruscology and Italian archaeology at Rome Univ. In charge of Italian Archaeological School in Athens 1919–38.

Della Seta, Ubo (1879–1958),

Colorprint by Sonia Delaunay-Terk.

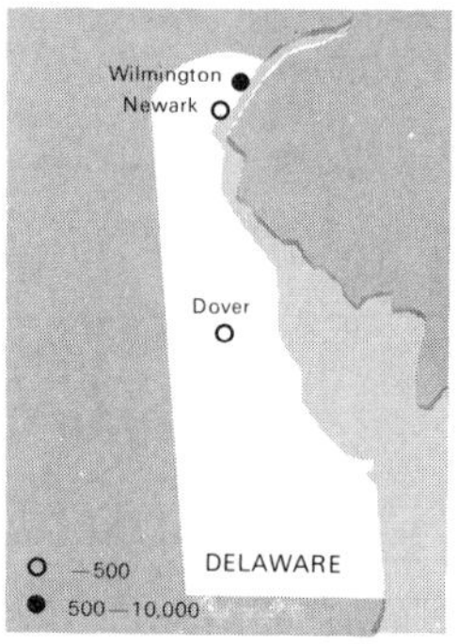

Jewish communities in Delaware.

"Samson and Delilah" by Andrea Mantegna.

Joseph Delmedigo, 1628.

Danish Jewish communities in the 18th century and after W.W. II.

Jewish refugees being rowed to safety from Denmark to Sweden, 1943.

National Jewish Hospital for Consumptives, Denver, opened 1899.

Italian politician, philosopher. Dismissed, persecuted by Fascist regime. Elected member of Constituent Assembly after WWII. Senator in first two Republican parliaments.

Della Torre, Lelio (Hillel; 1805–1871), Italian rabbi. Prof. of Talmud at Padua Rabbinical College. Wrote poems, sermons, Italian translation of liturgy.

Delmedigo, Elijah ben Moses Abba (c. 1460–1497), philosopher, talmudist; b. Crete, studied in Italy. Headed yeshivah in Padua and taught philosophy to general audiences. Last years in Crete. Main work on relationship of religion and philosophy.

Delmedigo, Joseph Solomon (Yashar; 1591–1655), rabbi, philosopher, mathematician, astronomer; b. Crete. Studied astronomy and mathematics with Galileo in Padua; practiced medicine in Crete. Traveled in Europe and Middle East popularizing scientific knowledge and practicing medicine. Wrote on wide variety of Jewish and secular subjects. First Jewish scholar to use logarithms.

Del Monte, Crescenzo (1868–1935), Italian poet. Wrote in old Jewish Italian and Roman dialects.

Delos, island in Aegean Sea. Jews present 2nd and 1st c. B.C.E. In 16th c. the island, now deserted, was part of Duchy of Naxos, ruled by Joseph Nasi.

Delougaz, Pierre Pinchas (1901–), educator, archaeologist. Conducted excavations in Iraq at Nuzi, Khorsabad, Khafaje and in Israel at Beth Yerah. Curator of Oriental Institute Museum at Chicago fr. 1944.

Delvalle, Max (1911–), Panamanian politican. President of state 1968 for short period following constitutional crisis.

Demai, agricultural produce grown in Ereẓ Israel about which there is doubt as to whether it has been truly tithed. Where such doubt exists, the produce may not be eaten.

Demai, tractate of Mishnah, Tosefta, Jerusalem Talmud in order *Zera'im,* dealing with law of doubtful produce (see previous entry).

Dember, Harry L. (1882–1943), physicist. Prof. in Germany, Turkey, U.S. Studied photoelectricity of crystals. Known for "Dember effect."

Dembitz, Lewis Naphtali (1833–1907), U.S. lawyer, Jewish leader; b. Prussia, in U.S. fr. 1849, settling in Louisville. Wrote books on American law. Uncle of Louis Brandeis. A founder of Jewish Theological Seminary.

Dembitzer, Ḥayyim Nathan (1820–1892), talmudist, historian, *dayyan* in Cracow. Pursued historical research and critical work in talmudic and rabbinic literature.

Demetrius (3rd c. B.C.E.), earliest known Greco-Jewish writer. Wrote on biblical chronology.

Democratic Fraction, faction in Zionist movement 1901–4, led by Leo Motzkin and Chaim Weizmann, which demanded democratization and secularization of movement.

Dénes (Springer), Béla (1904–1959), Hungarian physician, author, Zionist leader. Leading Zionist in Hungary 1945–48. Imprisoned 1949–54, reached Israel 1957.

°**Denikin, Anton Ivanovich** (1872–1947), general and organizer of "White Army" in Russian Civil War 1918–21. Regarded as responsible for savage pogroms against Jews.

Denis, Albertus (c. 1580–c. 1645), court agent, mintmaster; one of first members of Portuguese community in Hamburg. Operated Danish royal mint for a while.

Denmark, European kingdom. Jewish settlement fr. 17th c., originally mostly Sephardi financiers. Last restrictive anti-Jewish legislation abolished 1849. In 1943 almost entire community, helped by Danish population, escaped to Sweden, returning after WWII. Fr. 1969 settlement of Polish immigrants. Jewish pop. 6,000 (1971), nearly all in Copenhagen.

Denver, city in Col., U.S. First Jewish settlers 1859. Reform Congregation Emanuel established 1872. National Jewish Hospital for Consumptives opened 1899. Jewish pop. 25,000 (1971).

De Pass, Aaron (1815–1877), S. African shipowner, community leader; b. England. Developed coastal shipping and shipyards. Founder of Cape Town's first synagogue.

De Pass, Daniel (d. 1921), S. African industrialist; son of Aaron de Pass. Established first copper mine in SW Africa. Introduced new variety of sugar to Natal.

De Philippe (Phillips), Edis (1918–), operà singer, founder-director of Israel National Opera Company; b. New York, settled in Ereẓ Israel 1945.

Derash, method of exposition of scriptural verse, used fr. Middle Ages for homiletical exposition. *Derashah* is a sermon.

Derashot ha-Ran, collection of 12 homiletic works attributed to Nissim b. Reuben Gerondi, perhaps incorrectly.

Derekh Ereẓ, proper behavior of man toward his fellow man (incl. rules of etiquette). Stressed by rabbis, who however did not incorporate it as formal legislation, holding practice to be recommendation rather than commandment.

Derekh Ereẓ, minor tractate of Talmud, published at end of order *Nezikin;* deals with morals and customs.

Derenbourg, Hartwig (1844–1908), French orientalist; son of Joseph Derenbourg. Prof. of Arabic and Islam at Ecole des Hautes Etudes, Paris. Made contributions in Jewish and Islamic studies.

Derenbourg, Joseph Naphtali (1811–1895), French orientalist,

teacher. Prof. of Heb. language and literature at Ecole des Hautes Etudes. Catalogued Hebrew mss. at Bibliothèque Nationale. Active in Jewish community. Made major contribution in oriental languages and inscriptions.

Dernburg, Bernhard (1865–1937), German banker, expert on colonial affairs; nephew of Heinrich Dernburg. Cabinet minister 1919, member of Reichstag 1920–30.

Dernburg, Heinrich (1829–1907), German jurist. Prof. of Prussian and Roman law in Berlin. His works on Prussian private law influenced German jurisprudence.

Der Nister (pseudonym of **Pinkhes Kahanovich;** 1884–1950), Soviet Yiddish writer. One of greatest Yiddish writers. Famous for *Di Mishpokhe Mashber,* a family epic.

Temple Beth El, Detroit

BOOK OF DEUTERONOMY – CONTENTS

Chs. 1–32	**The Covenant before entering Canaan**
Chs. 1–11	Prologue and exhortation
1:1–5	Historical introduction
16–4:43	Moses' introductory discourse
4:44–11:32	The second discourse
Chs. 12–28	The Deuteronomic code of laws
12:1–31	Ceremonial laws
13:1–19	Injunction against idolatry
14:1–2	Pagan mourning rites
14:3–21	Clean and unclean food
14:22–29	Tithes
15:1–18	Year of release
15:19–23	Firstling offerings
16:1–17	Holy seasons
16:18–17:13	Appointment of judges and supreme tribunal
17:14–20	Election of a king
18:1–18	Rights and revenues of priests and levites
18:9–22	Prophets
19:1–13	Homicide
19:14	Encroachment on property
19:15–21	False testimony
20:1–26:15	Various laws
26:16–19	Epilogue
27:1–28:69	Ceremonial blessing and cursing
Chs. 29–32	Appendices
29:1–30:20	Moses' third discourse
31:1–50	The appointment of Joshua
32:1–52	The song of Moses
Chs. 33–34	**Moses' blessing and his death**
33:1–29	Moses' blessing
34:1–12	Moses' death

In exile 1921–26. Arrested 1949 and died in prison hospital.

De' Rossi, see Rossi.

Der Tunkeler, see Tunkel, Joseph.

Déry, Tibor (1894–), Hungarian author, poet. Communist for many years. Gained recognition after WWII; wrote works attacking "cult of personality." Imprisoned after Hungarian revolution 1956, released 1961.

°**Derzhavin, Gabriel Romanovich** (1743–1816), Russian administrator, poet. Sent by authorities in 1799/1800 to investigate conditions of Jews in Belorussia. His report, although generally unfriendly, contained certain positive proposals which influenced Czarist policy toward Jews.

Desart, Ellen Odette, Lady (1857–1933), woman senator of Irish Free State. Active in Irish economy and cultural welfare. Daughter of Louis Raphael Bischoffsheim.

De-Shalit, Amos (1926–1969), Israel scientist. Prof. at Weizmann Institute and its director-general 1966–68. Specialized in nuclear physics; outstanding lecturer and scientific educator. Received Israel Prize 1965.

De Sola, Canadian family. **Abraham** (1825–1882), Orthodox rabbi, orientalist; in Canada fr. 1847. Became rabbi of Shearith Israel, Montreal. Prof. in Hebrew at McGill Univ. Wrote many works on Jewish subjects. His son **Aaron David Meldola** (1853–1918), Zionist and first Canadian-born rabbi, succeeding his father in Shearith Israel. Another son, **Clarence Isaac** (1858–1920), industrialist and first head of Canadian Zionist Federation.

De Sola Pool, see Pool.

D'Espina, Alfonso, see Alfonso d'Espina.

Dessau, Bernardo (1863–1949), Italian experimental physicist, Zionist. Prof. at Univ. of Perugia 1904. *Shohet* for Perugia Jewish community. Founded *Il Vessillo Israelitico,* first Italian Zionist periodical. Wrote books on wireless telegraphy, etc.

Dessau, Hermann (1856–1931), German historian, philologist. Prof. of ancient history at Univ. of Berlin; scholar in Latin inscriptions, Roman administration.

Dessau, Paul (1894–), German composer; in New York 1939–48, then E. Germany. Influenced by Schoenberg's 12-tone music. Wrote oratorio *Haggadah,* opera *Einstein.*

Dessauer, Friedrich (1881–1963), German engineer, biophysicist, philosopher. Member of Reichstag 1924–1933. In Istanbul 1933–37, Switzerland 1937–50; prof. at Frankfort fr. 1950. Wrote extensively on philosophy of science.

Dessler, Elijah Eliezer (1891–1954), active in Musar movement; b. Russia, settled in England and became director of a *kolel* for advanced Talmud study at Gateshead. Settled in Israel 1947 and was spiritual supervisor of Ponevezh yeshivah.

Dessoir, Ludwig (1810–1874), German actor. A great character actor who excelled in Shakespearean roles.

Dessoir, Max (1867–1947), German philosopher, psychologist; part Jew, son of Ludwig Dessoir. Prof. of philosophy at Berlin Univ. In many ways anticipated Freud. Interested also in parapsychology (a term he coined) and aesthetics.

Detroit, city in Mich., U.S. German Jews arrived fr. 1840s. First congregation Beth El founded 1850. Massive influx of European Jews 1880–1914. Center of anti-Semitic activity (Henry Ford, Father Coughlin) in 1920s. Jewish pop. 80,000 (1971).

Deutero-Isaiah, see Isaiah.

Deuteronomy, 5th book of Pentateuch, containing farewell address by Moses, presented in autobiographical fashion. Includes his final blessing and an account of his death. Stressed cult centralization and fought heathen "high places." Scholars have suggested that it was originally an independent work (D) and that it was the book discovered in time of Josiah (II Kings 22–23).

Deuteronomy Rabbah, aggadic Midrash on the Book of Deuteronomy, part of *Midrash Rabbah.*

Deutsch, Babette (1895–), U.S. poet, critic; wife of Avrahm Yarmolinsky. Taught at Columbia Univ. Wrote poems, often touching on social problems, novels, children's books, and translations of German and Russian verse.

Deutsch, Bernard Seymour (1884–1935), U.S. lawyer, public official, communal leader. Elected president of Board of Aldermen on La Guardia's Fusion Party ticket. President American Jewish Congress 1929–35.

Deutsch, Eliezer Ḥayyim ben Abraham (1850–1916), Hungarian talmudist, author. Headed yeshivah at Bonyhad and was a leader of Hungarian Orthodoxy.

Deutsch, Emanuel Oskar (Menahem; 1829–1873), orientalist; b. Germany. Became assistant in oriental

dept. of British Museum 1855. His essays on Talmud implied that key to understanding Jesus was to be found in study of his Palestinian background.

Deutsch, Ernst (1890–1969), German actor. Exponent of expressionism on German stage. After Nazis came to power left for London and Hollywood.

Deutsch, Felix (1884–1964), U.S. psychiatrist, Zionist; b. Vienna, emigrated to U.S. 1935. A pioneer of psychosomatic medicine; established clinic for "organ-neuroses" 1919. Held various teaching positions in U.S.

Deutsch, Gotthard (1859–1921), historian, theologian. Studied, taught, and acted as rabbi in Germany and Bohemia before becoming prof. of Jewish history and philosophy at Hebrew Union College, Cincinnati, where he was a leading spokesman for Reform Judaism. Editor of monthly journal *Deborah.*

Deutsch, Helene (née **Rosenbach;** 1884–), psychoanalyst, psychiatrist; b. Poland, emigrated to U.S. 1935; wife of Felix Deutsch. Best known for exploration of particularities of female psyche on basis of psychoanalytical theory and exposition of Freud's findings.

Deutsch, Ignaz (1808–1881), extremist leader of Austrian Jewish Orthodoxy. Tried to further Orthodox aims even to point of giving in to Catholics on questions of Jewish rights.

Deutsch, Leo (Lev Grigoryevich; 1855–1941). Russian revolutionary. Active from 1870s; escaped from prison and wrote *Sixteen Years in Siberia.* After 1917 occupied himself with editing works of Plekhanov and other writings.

Deutsch, Moritz (1818–1892), cantor, teacher. Chief cantor at Reform synagogue in Breslau and taught cantorial music at Breslau Theological Seminary.

Deutsch, Otto Erich (1883–1967). Austrian musicologist, bibliographer; in England 1938–1956. Specialized in Schubert and Mozart.

Deutsch, Simon (c. 1822–1877). Austrian revolutionary. Condemned to death 1848 but escaped; participated in 1871 Paris Commune. Combined successful business with radicalism.

Deutsch De La Meurthe, Emile (1847–1924), French industrialist, philanthropist; brother of Henri. Pioneered petroleum industry and assisted war orphans and students.

Deutsch De La Meurthe, Henri (1846–1919), French industrialist, philanthropist. Pioneered commercial uses of petroleum. Founder of Aerotechnic Institute at St. Cyr and donor of chair in aeronautics.

Deutscher, Isaac (1907–1967), Marxist historian, political scientist; b. Poland, in London fr. 1939. Member of Communist Party fr. 1926, expelled 1932. Wrote biographies of Stalin, Trotsky. Became sharp opponent of Zionism.

Deutscher Palaestina-Verein, German Protestant society for study of Ereẓ Israel. Founded 1877, it did not engage in excavations but concentrated on publication of journal.

Deutsch-Israelitischer Gemeindebund (DIGB), union of German Jewish communities, founded 1869. Never became representative of all German communities. Widespread activities in culture, education, financial aid, etc.

Deutschlaender, Leo (1888–1935), educationalist, writer; b. Germany. Directed Jewish education in Lithuania during WWI, later helped develop Beth Jacob Orthodox girls' education in Poland.

Deutz, Simon (1802–1852), French politician; son of Emmanuel Deutz, chief rabbi of France 1822–42. Converted to Catholicism at age 23, but later returned to Judaism. Worked for rights of Jews of Rome. Involved in scandal in which anti-Semitic motives were apparent.

Devarim, see Deuteronomy.

Devekut, in kabbalistic thought, "communion with God" achieved at time of prayer. Usually highest step on spiritual ladder. Ḥasidim held it should be believer's constant state of mind.

Devir, see Dvir.

De Vries, André (1911–), Israel physician, medical scientist; b. Holland, settled in Ereẓ Israel 1940. A founder of faculty of medicine at Tel Aviv Univ., its dean 1964. Israel Prize 1970.

De Vries, Benjamin (1905–1966), Israel talmudic scholar; b. Holland, settled in Ereẓ Israel 1934. Prof. of Talmud at Tel Aviv Univ. Wrote on literary and legal study of Talmud.

De Vries, M. (19th c.), S. African lawyer and member of Transvaal parliament.

Dew, Prayer for, prayer recited because Ereẓ Israel depended on dew moisture during dry summers. Main prayer for dew is said in *Musaf* service on first day of Passover. A petition for dew is inserted in *amidah* during summer months.

Dhamārī, Mansur Suleiman (15th c.). Yemenite scholar and author of midrashic compilation and commentary on Maimonides' exposition of Mishnah.

Dhamārī, Sa'id ben David (15th c.), Yemenite scholar and author of commentary on Pentateuch.

Dhu Nūwās, see Yūsuf Dhu Nūwās.

Diamand, Herman (1860–1930), Polish socialist politician. A founder of the Social Democratic party in Galicia and Silesia. Deputy in Sejm 1919–30.

Diamond, David (1915–), U.S. composer of symphonies, concertos, chamber music.

Diamond, I.A.L. (1920–), U.S. screenwriter. Collaborated with Billy Wilder on *Some Like it Hot, The Apartment,* etc.

Diamond, John, Baron (1907–), British statesman. Minister in Labor Governments. His brother **Arthur Sigismund** (1897–), lawyer and Master of Supreme Court.

Diamond, Sigmund (1920–), U.S. sociologist. Taught at Columbia Univ.; specialized in entrepreneurial and economic history.

Dias, Luis (d. 1542), Marrano messianic pretender ("Messiah of Setúbal") in Portugal; burned by Inquisition with 83 of his followers.

Diaspora (Gk. "dispersion"), Jewish settlement outside Ereẓ Israel. In Heb. *Galut, Golah, Pezurah,* or *Tefuẓot.*

Scene from Habimah production of The Dibbuk with Hannah Rovina. Woodcut by Miron Sima.

Dibbuk (Heb. "adhesion"), in kabbalistic folklore the soul of a sinner which, after his death, transmigrates into the body of a living person. Title and subject of famous play by S. An-Ski.

Dibon, ancient town E. of Dead Sea. Capital city of Mesha, king of Moab (II Kings 3:4).

Dick, Isaac Meir (1814–1893), first Hebrew-Yiddish popular writer on

Note: This table is an academic summary only. It does not purport to lay down the *halakhah.*

CLEAN	UNCLEAN
MAMMALS	
RUMINANTS WITH WHOLLY CLOVEN HOOVES (Deut. 14:16), e.g. buffalo, cattle, goat, sheep, ibex, gazelle, deer, antelope, wild ox, wild goat, giraffe (?)	**a. CLOVEN-HOOFED BUT NON-RUMINANTS,** e.g. pig, bear, hippopotamus. **b. RUMINANTS BUT NO CLOVEN-HOOFED,** e.g. camel, llama. **c. SOLID-HOOFED,** e.g. horse, ass, mule, onager, zebra. **d. CARNIVEROUS,** e.g. cat, lion, leopard dog, wolf, jackal, fox, hyena, bear. **e. OTHER MAMMALS; NEITHER RUMINANTS NOR CLOVEN-HOOFED,** e.g. hare, mouse, hyrax, bat, rat, elephant, ape, whale.
BIRDS	
a. COLUMBIFORMES; pigeon, turtle dove, palm dove. **b. GALLIFORMES:** hen, quail, partridge, peacock, pheasant. **c. PASSERINAE:** house sparrow. **d. ANSERIFORMES:** domestic duck, domestic goose.	**a. DIURNAL BIRDS OF PREY** (i) Falconidae, e.g. kestrel, hawk, eagle, kite, buzzard. (ii) Vulturidae, e.g., griffon vulture, black vulture, Egyptian vulture, bearded vulture. **b. NOCTURNAL BIRDS OF PREY** (Strigiformes), e.g. owl. **c. WATER AND MARSH FOWLS.** With the exception of the goose and the duck, they are all regarded as unclean; e.g. stork, bittern, heron, crane, gull. **d. VARIOUS OTHER BIRDS** which either have no characteristics of a clean bird, or about which there is no tradition that they are permitted: e.g. warblers, crow, swift, hoopoe, ostrich.
REPTILES AND AMPHIBIANS	
All reptiles and amphibians are unclean (see Lev. 11:41–42). Regarding the crocodile, see Lev. 11:12.	
FISH	
According to the Bible those fish are permitted which have "fins and scales, in the waters, in the seas and in the rivers" (Lev. 11:9; Deut. 14:9). In this category only Bony-Skeletons are included, since they alone possess fins and scales. Those fish which have scales only early or late in life, are clean (Av. Zar. 39a). Examples: carp, trout, salmon, herring.	**a. CARTILAGINOUS** (Chondrichthytes). These fish either have no scales or have thick scales like teeth, which are not however true scales as they do not overlap: e.g. shark, ray. **b, CARTILAGINOUS-BONY** (Chondrostei). They also lack true scales. It is from these fish that much caviar (mainly black in color) is derived: e.g. sturgeon. **c. BONY SKELETONS** (Holostei). Fish which have no scales visible to the eye, or which have no fins, e.g. catfish, eel.
INVERTEBRATES	
Of all the invertebrates only a group of four species belonging to the order of locusts (Orthoptera) are permitted by the Bible. The Rabbis enumerate eight species of permitted Orthoptera (Ḥul. 65a–b, cf. Maim. Yad, Ma'akhalot Asurot 1:21–22). The Mishnah gives four signs whereby permitted insects may be recognized: four jointed legs, and four wings covering the greater part of the body (Ḥul. 3:7). If the wings develop only at a certain stage, the species is nonetheless permitted.	The invertebrates which live on land and in water are forbidden. The main group of forbidden invertebrates are: **LEECHES, MOLLUSKS** (snail, oyster, squid), **SEGMENTED WORMS, FLATWORMS, JELLYFISH, SPONGES, PROTOZOA.**

Jewish life in E. Europe; b. Vilna. Introduced sentimental and realistic story into Yiddish literature.

Dickstein, Samuel (1851–1939), mathematician, pedagogue in Warsaw. A leader of Polish assimilationism and its representative at Warsaw Communal Committee. Prof. of maths. at Warsaw Univ.

Dickstein, Samuel (1885–1954), U.S. Democratic congressman 1922–44; chairman of House of Representatives Immigration and Naturalization Committee.

Dickstein, Szymon (1858–1884), naturalist, socialist theoretician; b. Warsaw, lived in France. As popularizer and press columnist, influenced workers' ideology in Poland.

Dienchelele (Heb. *dayyan kelali,* "general judge"), crown office instituted in Sicily 1396. Held by Jewish official appointed to judge cases involving Jewish law.

Diesendruck, Zevi (1890–1940), philosopher. Taught at Heb. Univ 1928–30, Heb. Union College, Cincinnati, 1930–40.

Dietary Laws, Jewish laws pertaining to food and its preparation. Proscribed from Jewish diet are (1) meat from biblically "unclean" animals and birds or from "clean" ones not ritually slaughtered *(sheḥitah)* or found defective in one of their vital organs; and certain parts of the "clean" beasts; (2) meat and milk foods intermingled or eaten in proximity; (3) fish without fins or scales. These laws are not regarded as binding by Reform Jews.

Dimanstein, Simon (1886–1937), Russian revolutionary. Commissar for Jewish affairs after Bolshevik Revolution and a leader of Yevsektsiya. Executed during Stalin purges.

Dimi (Avdimi Naḥota) (4th c.), Babylonian *amora;* one of *Neḥutei,* scholars who traveled between Ereẓ Israel and Babylonia.

Dimi of Nehardea (4th c.), Babylonian *amora,* head of academy of Pumbedita 385–388 C.E.

Dimitrovsky, Chaim Zalman (1920–), talmudist, historian; b. Ereẓ Israel. Taught at Jewish Theological Seminary, New York, fr. 1951.

Dimonah, industrial town in S. Israel, SE of Beersheba; founded 1955. Pop. 23,200 (1971), mostly of N. African origin.

Dina de-Malkhuta Dina (Aram.), the halakhic rule that law of country of residence is binding with

Dimonah municipal garden.

Benzion Dinur

force of Jewish law.

Dinah, daughter of Jacob and Leah. Her rape by Shechem was avenged by her brothers (Gen. 34).

Dine, Jim (1935–), U.S. abstract painter; creator of "Happenings" in pop art.

Dineson, Jacob (1856–1919), Yiddish novelist (*Be-Oveyn Oves,* etc.). Pioneer of sentimental novel in Yiddish.

Dinin, Samuel (1902–), U.S. educator. Director of Los Angeles Bureau of Jewish Education 1945; dean of Univ. of Judaism 1957.

Dinur (Dinaburg), Benzion (1884–1973), historian, educator, b. Ukraine, settled in Ereẓ Israel 1921. Prof. of history at Heb. Univ. 1948. Israel minister of education and culture 1951–5; sponsored 1953 State Education Law. Author of history of Jewish people *(Yisrael be-Arẓo, Yisrael ba-Golah).* Israel Prize 1973.

°**Dio Cassius** (150–235), Roman historian; important source for Jewish uprisings against Trajan and Hadrian.

Diringer, David (1900–), epigraphist, orientalist; b. Galicia. Taught at Florence and Cambridge Univ. Founded Tel Aviv Alphabet Museum.

Discipline Scroll ("Manual of Discipline"), one of Dead Sea Scrolls, containing rules governing life in Dead Sea community.

Disegni, Dario (1878–1967), Italian rabbi, educator. Initiated new Italian translation of Bible 1960–67.

Diskin, Chaim (1923–), Russian army physician. Named Hero of Soviet Union for valor in WWII.

Diskin, Mordekhai (1844–1914), Ereẓ Israel pioneer; b. Russia, settled in Petaḥ Tikvah 1882.

Disputation between Jewish and Christian scholars. German woodcut, 1483.

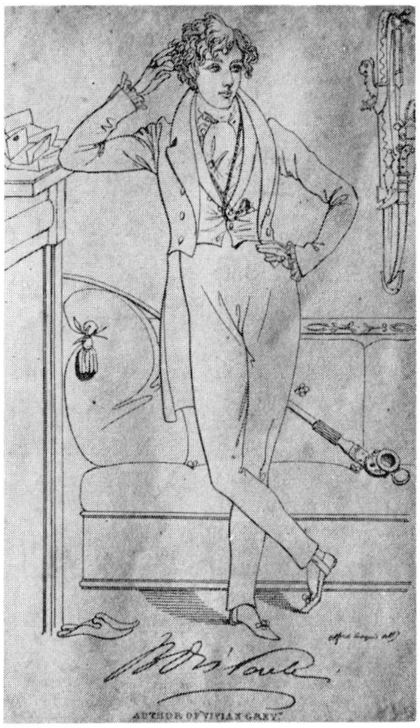

Disraeli by Daniel Maclise.

Diskin, Moses Joshua Judah Leib (1817–1898), rabbi, halakhist. Officiated in E. European communities (known as Brisker *rov*), went to Jerusalem 1877. Leader of old *Yishuv* and in vanguard of Orthodox activism.

Displaced Persons (DPs), people driven out of their homes as a result of Nazi decrees during WWII (1939–45). There were about 230,000 Jewish DPs in Germany, Austria, and Italy at end of war. Most settled in Israel 1948–9.

Disputations, organized debates bet. adherents of different religions. Of particular significance were those imposed by Church and held bet. Jewish and Christian scholars in Middle Ages (see Jehiel of Paris; Barcelona; Tortosa).

Meir Dizengoff

Disraeli, Benjamin, Earl of Beaconsfield (1804–1881), British statesman, novelist; prime minister 1868, 1874–80. Baptized at early age. Championed Jewish emancipation in Parliament, wrote admiringly of Jewish "race" *(Alroy, Coningsby, Tancred).* With financial assistance of Rothschilds, acquired control of Suez Canal for Britain.

D'Israeli, Isaac (1766–1848), English writer; father of Benjamin Disraeli. Author of *Curiosities of Literature.*

Dittenhoeffer, Abram Jesse (1836–1919), U.S. lawyer. Active in Republican politics.

Divekar, Samuel Ezekiel (d. 1797), soldier and benefactor of Bene Israel community in Bombay.

Divorce (Heb. *gerushin*), formal dissolution of marriage bond. Effected in Jewish law by a bill *(sefer keritut, get)* expressly written and given by husband to wife. Though the right of divorce was vested in the husband, in the course of time his power was in many cases considerably restricted. As Maimonides maintains, the wife "is not like a captive woman who is compelled to consort with a man against her will." In Israel, divorce among Jews is possible only under rabbinic auspices.

Diwan, Judah ben Amram (d.c. 1752), emissary of Ereẓ Israel communities to Iraq, Persia, Constantinople.

Dizengoff, Meir (1861–1937), Zionist leader, a founder and first mayor of Tel Aviv; b. Bessarabia, settled in Ereẓ Israel 1905.

Djerba (Jerba), island off Tunisian coast. Jewish community first evidenced in 10th c., consisting mainly of traders and craftsmen. In 19th–20th c., yeshivot, Hebrew printing press. Most of its members (4,900 in 1946) settled in Israel.

Dluzhnowsky, Moshe (1906–), Yiddish novelist (*Vint-Miln, Vi a Boym in Feld,* etc.); b. Poland, settled in U.S. 1941.

Dnepropetrovsk (formerly **Yekaterinoslav**), city in Ukrainian SSR. Jews fr. end of 18th c. Scene of several pogroms 1883–1905 and during Civil War 1918–20. Jewish population c. 100,000 in 1940. Severely reduced during Nazi invasion. 69,000 Jews in whole province in 1970.

Do'ar Ha-Yom, daily Hebrew newspaper established in Jerusalem 1919; under editorship of Ittamar Ben-Avi. Ceased publication 1936.

Dobkin, Eliyahu (1898–), Labor Zionist; b. Belorussia, settled in Ereẓ Israel 1932. Member of Jewish Agency Executive fr. 1946.

Dobrushin, Yekhezkel (1883–1953), Russian Yiddish literary critic, playwright; d. Siberian prison camp.

"Doctors' Plot," libel which alleged (1953) that 9 doctors (6 of them Jews) endeavored to poison Stalin and other Russian leaders. On death of Stalin his successor declared charges fraudulent.

Dóczy, Lajos (1845–1918), Hungarian author, poet, playwright. A founder of neo-Romantic school of Hungarian drama. Converted to Christianity; made a baron.

Doeblin, Alfred (1878–1957), German expressionistic poet, novelist. Embraced Catholicism 1940, escaping fr. France to U.S.

Doeg the Edomite, one of Saul's court officials and trusted advisers (I Sam. 21–22).

°**Dohm, Christian Wilhelm von** (1751–1820), German writer; friend of Moses Mendelssohn. Among first to champion Jewish emancipation *(Ueber die buergerliche Verbesserung der Juden).*

Piazza in Oria, S. Italy, honoring Shabbetai Donnolo.

(r.–l.) Ya'akov Dori, President Weizmann, and Prime Minister Ben-Gurion, 1949.

Dolitski, Menahem Mendel (1856–1931), Hebrew-Yiddish poet, author; lived in Russia, joined Ḥibbat Zion movement, emigrated to U.S. 1892.

Dombroveni, Jewish agricultural colony in Bessarabia; founded 1836. 1,198 Jews lived there in 1930. In WWII Jews exiled to Siberia or killed by Germans and Rumanians.

Domenico Gerosolimitano (c. 1552–1621), apostate, censor of Hebrew books; b. Jerusalem. Served the Inquisition in Italy.

Dominican Republic, country in West Indies. Jews, at first W. Indian Sephardim, later fr. European countries, settled fr. mid-19th c. One of few countries to offer to accept Jewish refugees on large scale in Nazi period. There were 40 in 1939, 1,000 in 1943 (refugees from occupied Europe), and 300 in 1971. There are two synagogues, one in Santo Domingo, one in Sosua. The Perroquia Israelita is the central Jewish body.

Dominicans, Catholic religious order. Deterioration of position of Jews in Europe fr. 13th c. on largely due to constant preaching and missionary activities of Dominicans, such as Vicente Ferrer (c. 1350–1419), in Spain.

Domninus of Larissa (c. 415–485), neoplatonic philosopher, mathematician in Laodicea, Syria.

Domus Conversorum (Lat. "House of Converts"), hostel for converted Jews established 1232 in London by Henry III.

Donath, Adolph (1876–1937), Austrian poet, art historian; b. Moravia.

Donath, Ludwig (1900–1967), Vienna-born stage and screen actor (*The Strange Death of Adolf Hitler*, etc.). Fled to U.S. 1940.

Donati, Angelo (1885–1960), member of Italian resistance, active in rescuing and assisting Jews in Holocaust period.

Donati, Enrico (1909–), Italian surrealist and abstract painter. Later works influenced by theme of fossilization.

Donetsk (until 1924 **Yuzovka,** until 1961 **Stalino**), industrial city in Ukrainian SSR. Prewar community destroyed by Germans in WWII. Jewish pop. 40,000 (1970).

Donin, Nicholas (13th c.), French apostate to Christianity and informer. Joined Franciscans and instigated disputations with R. Jehiel of Paris, which led to burning of Talmud.

Dönme, sect of adherents of Shabbetai Ẓevi in Balkans and Turkey. Like Shabbetai Ẓevi most of them embraced Islam, but continued sometimes secretly to practice Judaism.

Donnolo, Shabbetai (913–c. 982), Italian physician, writer on medicine (*Sefer ha-Mirkaḥot*). First person in Christian Europe to write on medicine in Hebrew.

Don-Yaḥia (Donchin), Yehudah Leib (1869–1941), rabbi, a founder of Mizrachi movement; b. Belorussia, settled in Tel Aviv 1936.

Dor, ancient harbor town on coast of Carmel, S. of Haifa, Israel.

Dorati, Antal (1906–), conductor and composer; b. Budapest. Conducted many orchestras in Europe and U.S. Recorded complete set of Haydn symphonies.

Dori (Dostrovsky), Ya'akov (1899–1973), Israel military leader; first chief of staff of Haganah and Israel Defense Forces (until 1949). President of Haifa Institute of Technology (Technion) 1951–65.

Doris (1st c. B.C.E.), first wife of Herod and mother of Antipater.

Dormido, David Abrabanel (d. 1667), pioneer of Jewish settlement in England. Born to Marrano family in Spain, escaped 1632 to Bordeaux, then to Amsterdam. Petitioned Cromwell in London 1654 to readmit Jews into England. His son **Solomon (Antonio)**, first Jew formally admitted to Royal Exchange in London.

Dorohoi, town in NE Rumania. Jews settled in 17th c., communal organization set up 1896. 5,384 Jews in 1941. Jews deported in WWII; only 2,000 returned, joined by other Jews fr. Transnistria. 7,600 Jews in 1947.

Dortmund, town in W. Germany. Jews known there fr. 11th c. Expelled in Black Death period (1350). Readmitted and expelled alternately until end of 16th c. New community prospered in 18th–19th c. Jews numbered 4,108 in 1933. Of 1,500 resident there on eve of WWII, majority perished in concentration camps. 351 Jews in 1970.

Dosa ben Harkinas (1st–2nd c.) Palestinian *tanna;* Active in Jerusalem. Saying: "Morning sleep, midday wine, children's talk, and sitting in the assembly of the ignorant put a man out of the world" (*Avot* 3:10).

Dosa ben Saadiah (930–1017), head of academy of Sura fr. 1013; son of Saadiah b. Joseph Gaon.
Dositheans, see Dustan.
Dostrovsky, Aryeh (1887–), Israel dermatologist, b. Russia, settled in Ereẓ Israel 1919. First dean Heb. Univ.–Hadassah Medical School 1948–53. Laid foundation for development of dermatology in Ereẓ Israel.
Dostrovsky, Israel (1918–), Israel chemist; b. Russia, settled in Israel 1919. Lecturer at Univ. College of N. Wales 1943–48, head of Isotope Research Dept. at Weizmann Inst. 1948–65, senior scientist at Brookhaven National Lab. in U.S. 1961–68, director-general of Israel Atomic Energy Commission 1965–71. Pres. of Weizmann Inst. fr. 1971.
Dothan, city in territory of Manasseh, mentioned in story of selling of Joseph (Gen. 37:13 ff.) and as residence of prophet Elisha (II Kings 6:13 ff.). Generally identified with Tell Dothan S. of Jenin.
Douglas, Kirk (1916–), U.S. film actor (*Cast a Giant Shadow,* etc.).
Dov Baer (The Maggid of Mezhirech; d. 1772), early leader of Ḥasidism; disciple and successor of Ba'al Shem Tov. His teachings provided Ḥasidism with speculative-mystical system.
Drabkin, Abraham (1844–1917), Russian rabbi. Editor of rabbinical section of first volumes of Russian Jewish encyclopedia (*Yevreyskaya Entsiklopediya*).
Drachman, Bernard (1861–1945), U.S. Orthodox rabbi, a founder of Jewish Theological Seminary where he taught until 1902; later taught at Yeshiva College. First Orthodox rabbi in U.S. to preach in English.
Drachsler, Julius (1889–1927), U.S. sociologist. Author of *Intermarriage in New York City.*
Dragunski, David Abramovich (1910–), Soviet Army officer. Commanded tank brigade on Ukrainian front in WWII. Promoted lieutenant general. Publicly declared allegiance to USSR and hostility to Israel and Zionism 1970.

Kirk Douglas in Cast a Giant Shadow, filmed in Jerusalem hills in 1965.

Drancy, town nr. Paris. Site of concentration camp established 1940 by the Germans, which became largest center of deportation of Jews fr. France in WWII.
Drapkin, Israel (1906–), Israel criminologist; b. Argentina. Established Institute of Criminology at Heb. Univ.
Dreben, Sam (1878–1925), U.S. soldier of fortune, known as "fighting Jew"; b. Russia, fought in China, Nicaragua, and France in WWI.
Dresden, capital of Saxony, E. Germany. Jews settled in 14th c., expelled 1430, returned in 18th c. In 1939 only 1,470 Jews remained; deported in WWII. Jewish pop. 100 (1970).
Dresden, Sem (1881–1957), Dutch composer. Director of Amsterdam Conservatory and Royal Conservatory at The Hague. Composed *Chorus Tragicus* for choir, wind, and percussion, an opera *Toto,* etc.
Dressler, William (1890–1969), U.S. cardiologist, electrocardiographer; lived in Austria until 1938. Wrote standard textbook on cardiological diagnoses.
Dreyfus, family of bankers in Alsace, Germany, Switzerland. Firm founded by **Isaac** (1786–1845). His son **Samuel** (1820–1905), president of Basle Jewish community. Another son, **Jacques** (1826–1890), established Dreyfus-Jeidels bank 1868, which became J. Dreyfus and Co. 1890; liquidated by Nazis 1937. **Jules** (1859–1941), president of Union of Jewish Communities in Switzerland.
Dreyfus Brothers, pioneers of cellulose acetate rayon industry. **Henry** (1876–1945), **Camille** (1878–1956).
Dreyfus, Alfred (1859–1935), French staff officer. Tried, sentenced, imprisoned 1894 on Devil's Island (Fr. Guyana) on framed charge of espionage; pardoned 1899 but finally cleared only in 1906, after fierce controversy which divided France and involved widespread anti-Semitism.
Dreyfuss, Barney (1865–1932), founder of baseball's World Series. Owned Pittsburgh Pirates fr. 1901.
°**Driver, Samuel Rolles** (1846–1914), Bible scholar, Hebraist. Prof. of Hebrew at Oxford fr. 1883. His son **Sir Godfrey Rolles** (1892–), Bible and Semitics scholar at Oxford.
Drobner, Boleslaw (1883–1968), Polish sociologist, politician; b. Cracow. Elected 1947 to Sejm (Parliament).
Drogobych (Pol. **Drohobycz**), city in Ukrainian SSR. Jews settled in 17th c. and entire trade was in Jewish hands. Jews controlled petroleum industry. 17,000 Jews in 1941; they were killed and deported, and only 400 survived.
Dropsie, Moses Aaron (1821–1905), U.S. lawyer, philanthropist; b. to Dutch-Jewish father and Christian mother; later embraced Judaism. Willed fortune to creation of Dropsie Univ. (College).
Dropsie University (formerly Dropsie College for Hebrew and Cognate Learning), non-theological graduate institution in Philadelphia, U.S., covering all branches of Jewish learning and Semitic studies. Establishment provided for in will of Moses Aaron Dropsie. Published *Jewish Quarterly Review* fr. 1910.
°**Drumont, Edouard-Adolphe** (1844–1917), French politician, journalist. Leader of anti-Semitic movement in France. Elected to Chamber of Deputies 1898.
Druyanow, Alter (1870–1938), Hebrew writer, Zionist leader in Russia; lived in Ereẓ Israel 1906–9, 1921–38. Compiled anthologies of Hibbat Ẓion writings and Jewish folk humor.

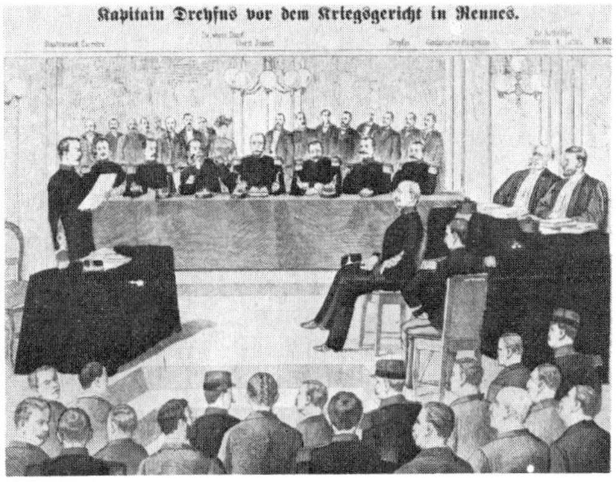

Dreyfus' second trial before a court-martial at Rennes, 1899.

Moses Aaron Dropsie

Alter Druyanow

Druze, religio-political community inhabiting parts of Syria, Lebanon, Israel. Religion based on Ismailism; includes belief in deity and prophet Shu'ayb (Jethro), whose putative grave near Ḥittim in Galilee is revered. Druze are not Muslims; they speak Arabic; in Israel they serve in army. Druze villages on Mt. Carmel and in Golan Heights. No. in Israel 38,000.

Duberman, Martin (1930–), U.S. historian, especially of Middle Period of American history. Also wrote plays (*In White America*).

Dubin, Mordecai (1889–1956), Agudat Israel leader in Latvia. Deported by Soviet authorities 1940, released 1942, arrested 1948; d. in concentration camp.

David Dubinsky

Dubinsky, David (1892–), U.S. labor leader; b. Poland, went to U.S. 1910. President of International Ladies Garment Workers' Union (ILGWU) fr. 1932, vice-president of AFL 1934–36 and 1945. A founder of American Labor Party and Jewish Labor Committee 1933.

Dublin, capital of Irish Republic. Marranos settled in mid-17th c. Modern community founded 19th c. by immigrants fr. C. Europe. Jewish pop. 3,900 (1971) with chief rabbinate. Robert Briscoe, lord mayor 1956–7, 1961–2.

Dubno, city in Ukrainian SSR. Jews there fr. 1532. Scholars lived there, among them Jacob Kranz. Hebrew printing. 12,000 Jews in June 1941. Massacred by Ukrainians and Germans; only 300 survived the war.

Dubno, Solomon ben Joel (1738–1813), Bible scholar, Hebrew poet; b. Dubno, Poland, lived in Amsterdam, Berlin.

Solomon Dubno

Simon Dubnow and wife in Berlin, 1920s.

Dubnow, Simon (1860–1941), historian, b. Mstislavl, Belorussia, moved to St. Petersburg 1908, Berlin 1922, Riga 1933. Founder of sociological method in Jewish history, in his 10-vol. history of Jewish people. Propounded doctrine of Jewish national autonomy (Autonomism) anchored on social and cultural rather than political or territorial independence. Murdered by Nazis in Riga. His brother **Ze'ev** (1858–1940?), Bilu member.

Dubrovnik (Ragusa), port in Yugoslavia. Jewish merchants known fr. 1368, handling most of trade with Turkey and Italy through 15th–16th c. Following restrictions imposed after 1622 blood libel most Jews left. Restrictions abolished by French 1808, full emancipation 1873. 250 Jews in 1939. During WWII, Jews persecuted; fought as partisans. 31 Jews in 1969.

Dubrovno, town in Belorussian SSR. Jews fr. 1685. Became center for weaving prayer shawls and also for scribes of Torah scrolls, phylacteries, *mezuzot.* Its 5,000 Jews were murdered by Germans in WWII.

Duckesz, Eduard (Yecheskel; 1868–1944), Hungarian-born scholar, rabbi in Hamburg. D. in Auschwitz concentration camp.

°**Duehring, Karl Eugen** (1833–1921), German economist, philosopher; an initial proponent of modern racial anti-Semitism. Paramount influence on German anti-Semitism.

Duenner, Joseph Ẓevi Hirsch (1833–1911), rabbi, talmudist; b. Cracow, settled in Amsterdam 1862. Became leader of Orthodox Jewry in Holland.

Dueren, Isaac ben Meir (13th c.), German rabbi, Major work, *Sha'arei Dura* deals with laws of forbidden food and menstruant women.

Duesseldorf, city in W. Germany. Jews first mentioned 1418, expelled 1438, returned 1582. In 19th c. important in trade and banking. Before Nazi era, numbered 5,130; after 1933 many left and remainder deported. Jewish pop. 1,535 (1971).

°**Dugdale, Blanche Elizabeth Campbell** (1880–1948), British Zionist; niece of Lord Balfour. Worked in political dept. of Jewish Agency.

°**Duhm, Bernhard** (1847–1928), German Protestant biblical scholar. Noted for work on Prophets.

Dujovne, Leon (1899–), Argentine lawyer, philosopher, community leader; settled in Israel 1966.

Dukas, Paul (1865–1935), French composer. Wrote *L'Apprenti sorcier,* the opera *Ariane et Barbe-Bleue,* the ballet *La Péri,* chamber music, and piano works.

Duker, Abraham Gordon (1907–), U.S. educator, historian. Pres. Chicago College of Jewish Studies 1956–62; fr. 1963 librarian and prof. at Yeshiva Univ.; at Brooklyn Coll. fr. 1972.

Dukes, Leopold (Judah Loeb; 1810–1891), historian of Jewish literature; b. Hungary. Translated Rashi's Bible commentary into German.

Dukhan (Heb. "platform"), priests' stand in Temple; hence "to recite the priestly blessing."

Dunash ben Labrat (10th c.), Baghdad linguist, Hebrew poet. Lived in Fez and probably in Córdoba and served as rabbi and *dayyan.* First to introduce Arabic meter into Hebrew poetry.

Dunash Ibn Tamim (c. 890–955/6), Kairouan scholar; wrote commentary on *Sefer Yeẓirah.*

Dunayevski, Isaac Osipovich (1900–1955), Soviet Russian popular composer (Stalin Prize 1941).

Dura-Europos, ancient city on Euphrates. 3rd c. C.E. synagogue discovered there 1932; its frescoes depicting biblical scenes provide focal point in ancient Jewish art.

Duran, Profiat ("Efod"; d. c. 1414), scholar, physician, polemicist of Spanish Jewry. Attacked Christianity in *Al Tehi ka-Avotekha, Kelimat ha-Goyim.* Wrote Hebrew grammar *Ma'aseh Efod.*

Synagogue in Duesseldorf, built 1958.

Dura-Europos, west wall panel: Priesthood of Aaron, temple, Ark of Covenant, menorah, and sacrificial animals.

Dura-Europos, part of north wall panel: Ezekiel's vision of the dry bones.

Duran Simeon ben Solomon (Rashbash "the Second"; 1438–1510?), rabbi, author; son of Solomon b. Simeon b. Duran; b. Algiers.

Duran, Simeon ben Ẓemaḥ (Rashbaẓ; 1361–1444), rabbinic codifier, philosopher, scientist; b. Majorca. Went to Algiers after 1391 Spanish persecution, joining Isaac b. Sheshet's *bet din*. Wrote important responsa, collected in *Tashbeẓ; Magen Avot,* which includes his philosophical views; many other works.

Duran, Solomon ben Simeon (Rashbash; c. 1400–1467), N. African rabbinical authority; son of Simeon b. Ẓemah Duran. Wrote *Milḥemet Mitzvah* to reject accusations against Talmud by apostate Joshua Lorki.

Duran, Ẓemaḥ ben Solomon (15th c.), rabbinical authority, *dayyan* in Algiers; son of Solomon b. Simeon Duran.

Durban, port in Natal, S. Africa. Congregation formed 1883. Has 3 synagogues (1 Reform). Jewish pop. 5,990 (1971).

Durkheim, Emile (1858–1917), French sociologist. One of founders of modern sociology (*The Rules of Sociological Method, Suicide,* etc.).

Duschak, Mordecai (1815–1890), Moravian rabbi, teacher, writer; lived in Cracow fr. 1877.

Duschinsky, Joseph Ẓevi ben Israel (1868–1948), rabbi, bibliophile; b. Hungary. Rabbi of Orthodox community in Jerusalem fr. 1933.

Dushkin, Alexander Mordechai (1890–), scholar, educator; b. Poland. Held important positions in education in U.S. and Israel. Prof. of education at Heb. Univ. fr. 1949. Awarded Israel Prize 1968.

Dustan (al-Dustân), Samaritan followers of Dusis or Dustis (Gr. Dositheos), probably a Jewish heretic or pseudo-messiah, c. 100 B.C.E. The Dositheans practiced circumcision, observed laws of Sabbath, refrained from eating meat, etc.

Duvdevani, Shmuel (1903–),

Emile Durkheim

Israel botanist, dew researcher; b. Ukraine, settled in Ereẓ Israel 1921. Established dew research station at Karkur.

Duveen, Joseph, Lord (1869–1939), English art dealer. Specialized in acquisition and sale of large collections, especially to American millionaires. Built new wing of London Tate Gallery and new gallery in British Museum.

Duvernois, Henri (pen name of **Henri Schwabacher**; 1875–1937), French popular author *(Crapotta, Faubourg Montmartre, Edgar, Maxime)*.

Dvir, Hebrew publishing house; founded 1922 in Berlin, by Ḥ.N. Bialik, S. Levin, Y.Ḥ. Rawnitzki; fr. 1924 in Tel Aviv.

Dvoretsky, Aryeh (1916–), Israel mathematician. Prof. of mathematics at Heb. Univ. 1951, vice-president of Univ. 1959–61. Chief scientist Israel army. Special fields include mathematical statistics and functional analysis. Israel Prize 1973.

Dyhernfurth (Pol. **Brzeg Dolny**), town in lower Silesia; fr. 1945 in Poland. Jewish community fr. 1688; famous center of Jewish printing up to 1834. Community dissolved 1916.

Joseph Duveen by Emil Fuchs, 1903.

Dykan (Dikstein), Paltiel (1885–1969), Israel jurist. Initiated Tel Aviv School for Law and Economics 1935; dean fr. 1948, rector 1958. Prof. at Heb. Univ. 1959.

Dykman, Shlomo (1917–1965), Warsaw-born translator, literary critic. Escaped to Bukhara in WWII. Sentenced to 15 years' hard labor in Soviet Union for "Zionist activities." Released 1957, emigrated to Israel. Translated Bialik's poems into Polish; Greek, Roman classics into Heb. Posthumously awarded Israel Prize 1965.

Dylan, Bob (Robert Zimmerman; (1941–), U.S. singer, composer of "folk-rock."

Dymov, Ossip (Perelman; 1878–1959), Yiddish-Russian author, playwright; b. **Bialystok**, in U.S. fr. 1913.

Dymshyts, Veniamin E. (1910–), Soviet economist. Became a deputy premier of Soviet Union 1959, only Jew in upper echelons of regime.

Dynow, Ẓevi Elimelech (1785–1841), ḥasidic *ẓaddik* in Dynow, Galicia; author of *Benei Yissakhar.*

Dzigan, Shimon (1905–), Yiddish satirical actor. Made reputation in Poland (in comic dialogs with Israel Schumacher). Settled in Israel 1952.

Initial letter "E" of "Ecclesia," from the "Sacramentary of Gellone," E. France, 8th cent.

Easter, Christian festival. At this season, during Middle Ages, customary to attack Jews physically throughout Christian world to avenge Passion of Jesus. Jews then confined to ghetto quarters fr. Holy Thursday onward.

East London, port in E. Cape Province, S. Africa. First Jewish resident settled 1873, became mayor 1889. First congregation established 1901; members prominent in civic affairs. Jewish pop. 800 (1971).

Shaar Hashomayim Synagogue, East London, S.A.

Easton, city in Penn., U.S. Jewish settlement fr. colonial times, mostly immigrants fr. Germany. Congregation of E. European Jews established 1890. Jewish pop. 1,675 (1971).

Ebal, see Gerizim.

Eban (Even), Abba (Aubrey; 1915–), Israel statesman; b. Cape Town, educated in England. In Jewish Agency political dept. fr. 1946, member of its delegation to U.N. 1947–8. Represented Israel at U.N. 1948–59, also Israel ambassador to U.S. 1950–9. Minister of education and culture 1960–3, foreign minister 1966–74. Noted for oratory in several languages. Wrote *My People, My Land.*

Abba Eban

Eber, great-grandson of Shem, son of Noah; eponymous ancestor of the Hebrews.

Ebionites, Judeo-Christian sect in Ereẓ Israel 2nd–4th c. Accepted Mosaic law (circumcision, Sabbath, etc.) but rejected sacrifices. Accepted Jesus as Messiah but not divine. Opposed Pauline doctrine.

Ebner, Meir (1872–1955), Jewish leader, Zionist in Bukovina and Rumania. Delegate to First Zionist Congress. Elected to Rumanian senate 1928, settled in Ereẓ Israel 1940.

Ecclesia et Synagoga, name given to representations symbolizing the victory of Church over Synagogue (latter usually depicted blindfold) in Christian art of Middle Ages.

King Solomon with Bible opened to Ecclesiastes. Drawing by Ben Shahn.

Ecclesiastes (Heb. *Kohelet*), one of five scrolls in Hagiographa section of Bible, traditionally ascribed to Solomon, probably of Second Temple period (3rd c. B.C.E.). Generally of pessimistic and skeptical nature, in line with opening verse "Vanity of vanities, all is vanity."

Ecclesiastes Rabbah (Heb. *Kohelet Rabbah*), Midrash written on Book of Ecclesiastes, c. 8th c. C.E. Part of *Midrash Rabbah.*

Ecclesiasticus, see Ben-Sira, Wisdom of.

Ecija, Joseph (Yuçaf) de (Joseph b. Ephraim ha-Levi ibn Shabbat; d. c. 1339), chief tax farmer of Alfonso XI of Castile. Built synagogue in Seville.

Eckman, Julius (1805–1877), U.S. rabbi in southern congregations until 1854, when he settled in San Francisco. Thereafter devoted himself to education of Jewish children and editing Jewish journals.

Ecole Rabbinique, see Séminaire Israélite de France.

Ecuador, S. American republic. Few Jews before 1933; 2,700 Jews entered 1933/43. 4,000 Jews in 1950, majority in Quito. Asociación de Beneficencia Israelita, founded 1938, is community's central body. Jewish pop. 1,800 (1971).

Edel, Yizḥak (1896–1974), composer, teacher; b. Poland, settled in Ereẓ Israel 1929. Works include orchestral and piano music, quartets for strings and wind instruments, songs and cantatas.

Edelman, Maurice (1911–), English author, politician. Labor MP fr. 1945, president of Anglo-Jewish Association 1963. Wrote novels, mostly on political themes.

Edelmann, Raphael (1902–1972), Danish scholar, librarian. Taught Jewish studies at Copenhagen Univ. and disseminated Jewish scholarship in Denmark. Settled in Israel 1971.

Edelmann, Ẓevi Hirsch (1805–1858), Hebrew scholar, printer, publisher; b. Belorussia, lived in various places in Europe, fr. 1852 in Berlin.

Edels, Samuel Eliezer (Maharsha; 1555–1631), Talmud commentator; lived in various Polish towns. Wrote *Ḥiddushei Halakhot*, explaining talmudic text, which became a standard work.

Edelstadt, David (1866–1892),

Yiddish-Russian socialist poet; b. Russia, went to U.S. 1882. Died of T.B. and became romantic legend to young Jewish labor movement.

Edelstein, Jacob (d. 1944), Czech Zionist leader, leading Jewish figure in Bohemia-Moravia during Nazi occupation. Murdered at Auschwitz.

Eden, see Garden of Eden.

Eder, Montague David (1865–1936), British psychoanalyst, Zionist leader. Member Zionist Executive in London and Jerusalem 1921–3, 1927–8.

Edessa (today **Urfa**), city in Asiatic Turkey. Jews may have lived there already in 2nd c. C.E. Sizable community in Middle Ages but dwindled steadily and in 1904 numbered 322. Many of the town's Jews settled in Jerusalem, where they formed a separate community, the "Urfalis." No Jews in 1960s.

Edinburgh, capital of Scotland. Jewish congregation established 1816, grew at close of 19th c., numbered 1,100 in 1972, with one synagogue.

Edinger, Ludwig (1855–1918), German neuro-anatomist, neurologist. Important researcher in brain anatomy.

Edirne, see Adrianople.

Edman, Irwin (1896–1954), U.S. philosopher. Taught at Columbia Univ. Wrote *Philosopher's Holiday.*

Edmonton, capital of Alberta, Canada. First Jewish settler 1891. First congregation 1906. Jewish pop. 2,700 (1971).

Edom (also called **Seir**), mountainous region in S. Transjordan. The Edomites (Idumeans), of Semitic origin and speaking a Semitic language, were traditional descendants of Esau and enemies of the Israelites. Conquered and forcibly converted to Judaism by John Hyrcanus (end 2nd c. B.C.E.). Herod was an Edomite by descent.

Edrehi, Moses ben Isaac (c. 1774–c. 1842), Moroccan scholar. Traveled to London, Amsterdam (where he published a preposterous book on the Ten Tribes with Yiddish translation), and Erez Israel.

Eduyyot • (Heb. "Testimonies"), tractate in Mishnah order *Nezikin,* with no *gemara.* Deals with laws on variety of subjects.

Efod, see Duran, Profiat.

Efron, Ilya (1847–1915), publisher in Russia (incl. Russian Jewish encyclopedia, *Yevreyskaya Entsiklopediya* published in association with Brockhaus).

Efros, Israel Isaac (1891–), Hebrew educator, poet, scholar; b. Poland, went to U.S. 1905. Rabbi, teacher of Hebrew in Baltimore, Buffalo, Dropsie College, and Hunter College. Settled in Israel 1955, rector, then honorary president, Tel Aviv Univ.

Eger, Akiva ben Moses Guens ("The Younger"; 1761–1837), rabbi; b. Eisenstadt, Germany. As rabbi of Posen fr. 1814 established famous yeshivah there. Wrote many rabbinic works and was widely recognized authority.

Eger, Akiva ben Simḥah Bunim (Akiva Eger the Elder; c. 1720–1758), rabbi, talmudic scholar; b. Halberstadt, Germany. Head of Pressburg Yeshivah 1756.

Eger, Judah Leib of Lublin (1816–1888), ḥasidic *ẓaddik* in Lublin; son of Solomon Eger. Disciple of Menahem Mendel of Kotsk (Kock).

Eger, Samuel ben Judah Loeb (1769–1842), talmudic scholar, author; b. Halberstadt, grandson of Akiva Eger the Elder. Rabbi of Brunswick fr. 1809. Opponent of Reform movement.

Eger, Solomon ben Akiva (1786–1852), rabbi, *rosh yeshivah*; son and disciple of R. Akiva Eger the Younger, whom he succeeded as rabbi of Posen 1839.

Egged, Israel public transport cooperative. Founded 1930, operated 3,100 buses 1973, with 38 branches and 8,740 workers.

Eglah Arufah (Heb. "broken-necked heifer"), ceremonial prescribed in Deuteronomy 21:1-9, involving the breaking of a heifer's neck in expiation for an untraceable murder.

°**Eglon,** king of Moab c. 12th c. B.C.E. Subdued Israel for 18 years. Assassinated by Ehud.

Egypt, country in NE Africa. History connected with Hebrews from earliest times. Egypt's involvement in the Land of Canaan in period of Semitic Hyksos dynasty (18th-16th c. B.C.E.) appears from Tel el-Amarna letters. The biblical bondage and Exodus probably took place in reign of Rameses II (c. 1290–c. 1223 B.C.E.). King Solomon married an Egyptian princess. Jewish military colonies existed in Egypt in pharaonic days (Elephantine). After conquest by Alexander the Great (333 B.C.E.), an influx of Jews followed focusing on Alexandria, seat of the great hellenistic Jewish civilization (Septuagint, Philo). The Jews then in Egypt possibly reached one million. Anti-Jewish feeling occasionally expressed itself in riots. Conditions of Jews deteriorated with the Christianization of the Roman Empire. Under Muslim rule, the community, now centered in Cairo (Fostat), became Arab in its culture (cf. documents in the Cairo Genizah). Important Karaite community survived to modern times. Despite an interlude of persecution under Caliph Ḥakim (996–1021), conditions generally favorable. Moses Maimonides settled in Egypt c. 1165. The record of Egyptian Jewry remained undistinguished under Turkish rule (fr. 1517) until 19th c., when penetration of western influences made for rapid occidentalization of the upper strata. After WWI Sephardi Jews from Salonika and other Turkish towns, as well as Jews from other countries, settled in E. 65,000 Jews

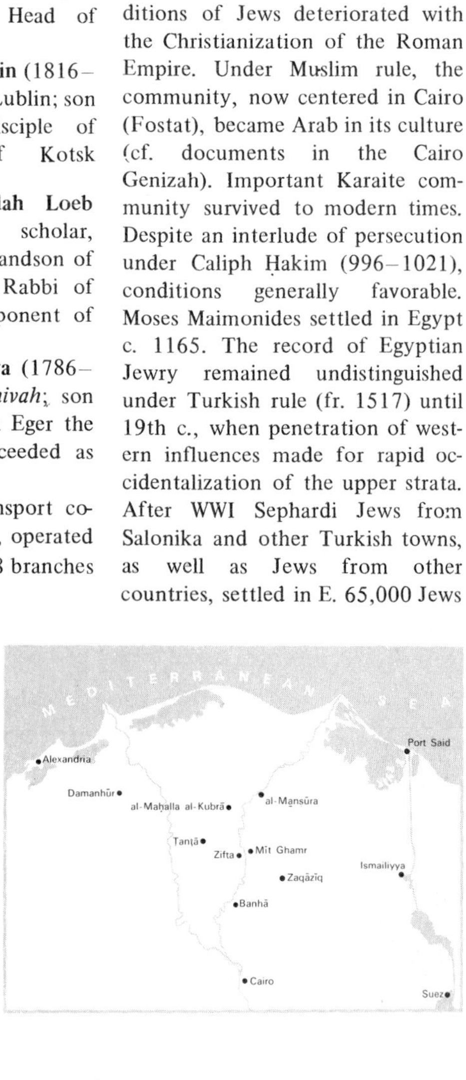

Main Jewish communities in Egypt at end of 19th century.

Arrival of Asiatic trade caravan as depicted in tomb of Egyptian Prince Khnumhotep III (c. 1890 B.C.E.).

in 1947 – 64% in Cairo, 32% in Alexandria. In Nov. 1945 attacks on Cairo Jewish quarter with many Jewish casualties. Many Jews left in the wake of the 1948, 1956, and 1967 wars between Egypt and Israel, some after internment or imprisonment. Less than 1,000 left in 1972. 35,000 former Egyptian Jews in Israel, 10,000 in France, 9,000 in U.S., 9,000 in Argentina, 4,000 in Great Britain.

Egypt, Brook of (Heb. *Naḥal Miẓrayim*), natural SW border of Canaan and Judah according to the Bible (e.g. Num. 34:5). Identified with Wadi el-Arish in N. Sinai.

Eḥad Mi Yode'a (Heb. "Who knows one?"), 13-stanza song "to keep children awake." Among concluding songs of Passover *Haggadah* in Ashkenazi rite.

Ehrenberg, Victor Leopold (1891–), historian; b. Altona, in England fr. 1939. Reader in ancient history at London Univ. Specialized in ancient Greek history.

Ehrenburg, Ilya Grigoryevich (1891–1967), Soviet Russian writer, journalist. Exiled 1908 for revolutionary activity, returned 1917-21. Lived in W. Europe fr. 1921. Settling in Russia in 1941, he adapted himself to the Soviet regime and became a chief spokesman during WWII, under Stalin, and after Stalin for liberal intellectuals. Received Stalin Prize 1952. Books include *The Fall of Paris, The Thaw,* and volumes of memoirs.

Ehrenfeld, Samuel ben David Ẓevi (1835–1883), rabbi, halakhist in Hungary. Known as "Ḥatan Sofer" ("son-in-law of Sofer") for his connection with Moses Sofer. Served in Szikszo and Mattersdorf. His son, **Simḥah Bunim** (1856–1926), succeeded his father as rabbi in Mattersdorf. His grandson **Samuel** founded Kiryat Mattersdorf in Jerusalem, Israel, 1958.

Ehrenkranz, Benjamin Zeev (Velvel Zbarazher; 1819–1883), popular Yiddish-Hebrew poet; b. Galicia. Traveled extensively, last years in Constantinople. Much of his work is witty satire.

Ehrenpreis, Marcus (Mordecai; 1869–1951), rabbi, author; b. Lemberg (Galicia). Chief rabbi of Bulgaria 1900–14, Sweden 1914–51. First a political Zionist and close supporter of Herzl, he became an advocate of a spiritual Jewish nationalism. Wrote in Swedish on Jewish themes.

Ehrenstein, Albert (1886–1950), poet, author; lived in Berlin, in New York fr. 1941. Published German adaptations of Chinese poetry.

Ehrentreu, Heinrich (1854–1927), Orthodox rabbi, author. Served in Munich. His son **Ernst (Jonah)** (1896–) rabbi in London.

Ehrlich, Abel (1919–), German-born Israel composer, teacher of theory and composition. Wrote chamber and choral music.

Ehrlich, Arnold Bogumil (1848–1919), biblical scholar; b. Russia. Helped F. Delitzsch translate New Testament into Heb. Wrote Heb. exegesis of Bible, *Mikra ki-Feshuto.* In U.S. fr. 1878.

Ehrlich, Georg (1897–1966), sculptor; b. Vienna, settled in England 1937.

Ehrlich, Jacob (1877–1938), Austrian Zionist leader. Member Vienna city council. Killed by Gestapo 1938.

Ehrlich, Paul (1854–1915), German biochemist, bacteriologist. Discovered (1909) arsenic compound "606" (Salvarsan), for treatment of syphilis. Awarded Nobel Prize for Medicine 1908.

Ehud, son of Gera the Benjaminite. In period of Judges, delivered Israel fr. Eglon, king of Moab (Judg. 3:15 ff.).

Eichenbaum, Jacob (1796–1861), Haskalah poet, educator, mathematician; b. Galicia. Fr. 1835 lived in Odessa, where he established a school. Wrote book in verse describing game of chess.

Eichmann Trial, trial held in Israel 1960–62 of Adolf Otto Eichmann (1906–62), Nazi official, SS officer who directed execution of Nazi scheme to annihilate European Jewry. Brought 1960 by Israel agents from Argentina to Israel. Trial attracted worldwide interest. Sentenced to death 1961 and executed after appeal was rejected.

Eichthal, Gustave D' (1804–1886), French publicist, Saint-Simonian, Hellenist. Baptized in youth. Active in support of civil rights for Jews and Negroes.

Eichthal-Seligmann, family of German court Jews, bankers, 18th–19th c.

Eidlitz, Leopold (1823–1908), U.S. architect. Designed churches, synagogues, banks.

Eidlitz, Zerah ben Meir (18th c.), rabbi, preacher in Prague. Published sermons, novellae, textbook on mathematics in Hebrew, Yiddish.

Eig, Alexander (1895–1938), botanist; b. Minsk, in Ereẓ Israel fr. 1909. Investigated geobotany in Middle East.

Paul Ehrlich

Adolf Eichmann (in glass booth) at his appeal before Israel Supreme Court, May 1962.

Statue of mother and child by Chana Orloff at Kibbutz Ein Gev.

Eighteen Benedictions, see Amidah.

Eikhah, see Lamentations.

Eilat, see Elath.

Eilshemius, Louis (1864–1941), U.S. landscape painter. Late representative of American romantic tradition. Became deranged.

Ein, see also En.

Einaeugler, Karol (1883–1952), lawyer, Bund leader in Galicia. Bet. 1939 and 1948 interned in Soviet prisons. Subsequently emigrated to U.S.

Ein Fashḥah, oasis on W. shore of Dead Sea, S. of Qumran, whose occupants had a secondary settlement at Ein Fashhah in late Second Temple times.

Ein Gev, kibbutz on E. shore of Lake Kinneret, Israel. Founded 1937. Under frequent attacks from Syrian-held heights 1948–67. Annual music festival held there during Passover. Economy based on

fishing, banana plantations, tourism.

Ein Hod, artists' village on Mt. Carmel, Israel.

Einhorn, David (1809–1879), Reform rabbi; b. Bavaria, emigrated to U.S. 1855. Minister in Baltimore, Philadelphia, New York. Led extreme Reform wing of U.S. Jewry, opposing moderate leadership of I.M. Wise. Opponent of slavery.

Einhorn, David (1886–), Yiddish poet; b. Belorussia, in U.S. fr. 1940. Socialist-oriented; regular contributor to *Forward.*

Einhorn, Ignaz (Eduard Horn; 1825–1875), Reform rabbi, economist. Had to flee his native Hungary as result of participation in 1848 revolt. Returned 1867 and became deputy undersecretary for commerce.

Einhorn, Max (1862–1953), U.S. internist, gastroenterologist. Prof. of medicine at N.Y. Postgraduate Medical School, Columbia Univ., 1896–1940. Specialist in gastric, digestive, intestinal disorders.

Einhorn, Moses (1896–1966), U.S. physician; founder and editor of Heb. medical journal *Harofe ha-Ivri.*

Ein Ke-Elohenu (Heb. "There is none like our God"), hymn recited at end of Additional Service, on Sabbaths and holidays in Ashkenazi ritual, on weekdays after Morning Service in Sephardi ritual. Known fr. 9th c.

Ein Kerem, village W. of Jerusalem; since 1949 part of Jerusalem municipality. In Christian tradition identified as birthplace of John the Baptist; site of various churches. Since 1949 settled by Jews.

Einsatzgruppen, in Nazi terminology a task force of mobile killing units *(Einsatzkommandos)* operating in German-occupied territories during WWII.

Ein-Sof (Heb. "The Infinite"), name given to God in Kabbalah.

Albert Einstein

Einstein, Albert (1879–1955), physicist, creator of theory of relativity which revolutionized modern physics with new concepts of space and time. Prepared ground for atomic physics, Nobel Prize winner 1921; b. Germany. Prof. at Univ. of Berlin and director of Kaiser Wilhelm Institute of Physics; in U.S. fr. 1933. Prof. at Institute of Advanced Study, Princeton. Active in humanitarian, Jewish, Zionist causes. One of greatest scientists of all time.

Einstein, Alfred (1880–1952), musicologist, specialist on Mozart; b. Germany, settled in U.S. 1939. Taught at Smith College.

Einstein, Lewis (1877–1967), U.S. diplomat, author. Wrote memoirs *A Diplomat Looks Back.*

Ein Yaakov, see Ibn Ḥabib, Jacob b. Solomon.

Einzig, Paul (1897–1973), economist; b. Rumania, settled in London after WWI. Main field monetary policy and foreign exchange. Political correspondent, *Financial Times.*

Eire, see Ireland.

Eis, Alexander von (1832–1921), Austro-Hungarian soldier (major-general). Supporter of Herzl; headed Vienna office, Jewish National Fund.

Eisenbaum, Anton (1791–1852), author, educator in Poland. Supporter of emancipation and advocate of assimilation.

Eisenberg, Aharon Eliyahu (1863–1931), pioneer of Jewish settlement in Ereẓ Israel, where he went from Russia in 1886. One of the founders of Reḥovot.

Eisendrath, Maurice Nathan (1902–1973), U.S. rabbi, leader of Reform Judaism. President of Union of American Hebrew Congregations 1943–72. Active in interfaith and civil rights issues.

Eisenmann, Louis (1869–1937), French historian. Specialized in Slavonic cultural history.

°Eisenmenger, Johann Andreas (1654–1704), German anti-Jewish author. His *Entdecktes Judenthum* ("Judaism Unmasked") became handbook for anti-Semites.

Eisenstadt, capital of Burgenland, E. Austria. Community dates from 14th c. and led "seven communities" of Burgenland. Known as "little Jerusalem." In 1938, Jews were expelled and community destroyed. After WWII only 5 survivors returned.

Eisenstadt, Abraham Seldin (1920–), U.S. historian. Prof. of history at Brooklyn College. Writings include 2-vol. *The Craft of American History.*

Eisenstadt, Abraham Ẓevi Hirsch ben Jacob (1813–1868), halakhic authority. Rabbi of Berestovitsa (Grodno district) and Utina (Kovno district). Collected and digested responsa related to *Shulḥan Arukh.*

Eisenstadt, Isaiah (1867–1937), pioneer of Jewish socialist labor movement in Russia, Bund leader; fr. 1922 in Berlin.

Eisenstadt, Meir ben Isaac (Maharam Esh; 1670–1744), rabbi, talmudist. fr. 1714 rabbi in Eisenstadt.

Eisenstadt, Moses Eleazar (1869–1943), rabbi, educator, author in Russia and France. Government-appointed rabbi of Rostov 1899–1910, St. Petersburg 1911–23. Reached U.S. 1942.

Eisenstadt, Samuel Noah (1923–), Israel sociologist. Head of sociology dept., Heb. Univ., fr. 1951. Wrote on political and historical sociology, especially analyzing social structure and bureaucracy. Several of his works deal with Israel society. Israel Prize 1973.

Eisenstadt, Yehoshua, see Barzillai, Yehoshua.

Eisenstadter, Meir ben Judah Leib (d. 1852), rabbinical authority, liturgical poet in Hungary. Rabbi and yeshivah head in Ungvar fr. 1835.

Eisenstaedt, Alfred (1898–), press photographer. Worked in Europe until 1935, when he went to U.S. Pioneered candid camera technique in news reporting.

Eisenstein, Ferdinand Gotthold (1823–1852), German mathematician. Lecturer at Berlin Univ. fr. 1847. Made important contributions to algebra and elliptic functions and their applications to number theory.

Eisenstein, Ira (1906–), U.S. rabbi, leader of Reconstructionist movement and editor of its magazine *Reconstructionist.* Coedited Reconstructionist prayer-books.

Eisenstein, Judah David (1854–1956), U.S. encyclopedist, anthologist, author. Published 10-vol. Jewish encyclopedia in Hebrew *Oẓar Yisrael.*

Eisenstein, Sergei Mikhailovich (1898–1948), major Soviet film director (*Battleship Potemkin, October, Alexander Nevsky, Ivan the Terrible*); son of Jewish father and non-Jewish mother.

Eisler, Edmund Menahem (1850–1942), writer who envisioned a Zionist utopia in his novel *Ein Zukunftsbild;* b. Slovakia.

Eisler, Gerhart (1897–1968), communist leader. In Germany until 1933, entered U.S. 1941 and became leading communist agitator.

Sentenced to prison 1949; escaped to E. Germany, where he became minister of information and chairman of radio authority.

Eisler, Hanns (1898–1962), German composer; brother of Gerhart Eisler, pupil of Schoenberg, Webern. Lived in U.S. 1937–48, composing choral music, film scores, an opera *Goliath*. Settled in E. Germany 1948.

Eisler, Mátyás (1865–1931), Hungarian rabbi, scholar. Chief rabbi of Kolozsvár fr. 1891. Wrote history of Jews in Transylvania.

Eisler, Rudolf (1873–1926), Austrian philosopher; father of Gerhart and Hanns Eisler. Wrote dictionaries of philosophy and biographies of philosophers.

Eisner, Kurt (1867–1919), German socialist leader, journalist. Founder, prime minister of Bavarian Republic 1918; assassinated.

Kurt Eisner

Eisner, Mark (1886–1953), U.S. lawyer, New York public official. President of American Association for Jewish Education 1939–47.

Eissler, Kurt R. (1908–), psychoanalyst; b. Vienna, in U.S. fr. 1938. First analyst to treat schizophrenics.

Eitinger, Leo S. (1912–), psychiatrist; b. Czechoslovakia, in Auschwitz, Buchenwald concentration camps during WWII. Prof. at Oslo Univ. Wrote on "concentration camp syndrome."

Eitingon, Max (1881–1943), psychoanalyst. Worked in Berlin and was central figure in psychoanalytical movement. In 1933 went to Jerusalem, founding Palestine Psychoanalytical Institute.

Ekron, one of five cities of Philistine confederation. Name was given to one of earliest modern settlements in Ereẓ Israel (near Reḥovot), now called Mazkeret Batyah.

El, name of God used relatively rarely in Bible and occurring chiefly in combinations such as El Elyon, "most high God." Its root meaning is power and the name appeared in Canaanite mythology.

Elah, king of Israel c. 883–882 B.C.E.; son of Baasha. Murdered by Zimri.

El Al poster designed by Dan Reisinger, 1970.

Road through the date-palm groves at El-Arish.

Hoisting the Israel flag at Umm Rashrash (Eilat), March 1949.

El Al (Heb. "Skyward"), Israel national airline, founded Nov. 1948, with service to Europe, America, Africa. Headquarters at Lod (Lydda) Airport. In 1971–72 carried 691,572 passengers.

Elam, region on edge of Iranian Plateau, modern Khuzistan, its capital was Susa (Shushan). Closely connected with Mesopotamia. Participated in coalition defeated by Abraham (Gen. 14). Part of pop. transferred to Samaria by Ashurbanipal of Assyria (Ezra 4:9-10).

El-Amarna, see Tell El-Amarna.

El-Arish, town on N. coast of Sinai Peninsula nr. wadi al-'Arish (Brook of Egypt). Border town bet. Egypt and Ereẓ Israel until 1895. Region proposed 1903 by D. Trietsch for Jewish settlement in Middle East. Opposed by Lord Cromer, "El-Arish Project" remained on paper. Temporarily occupied by Israel forces in and following 1956 Sinai campaign. Under Israel control fr. Six-Day War 1967.

Elath (in mod. Israel, **Eilat**), Israel harbor city at N. end of Red Sea nr. ancient Ezion-Geber. Key point in Roman-Byzantine times, then successively under Muslim, Crusader, Turkish rule. Mod. Eilat faces Jordanian Akaba across gulf. Included in future Jewish state in U.N. 1947 partition plan. Occupied by Israel forces March 1949. Pop. grew after opening of Tiran straits in 1956 Sinai campaign. New port developed trade with Asia and E. Africa; tourist center. Oil pipeline Eilat-Ashkelon finished 1970. Pop. 15,900 (1971).

Eliahu Elath

Elath (Epstein), Eliahu (1903–), Israel diplomat, Arabist. First Israel representative (then ambassador) to U.S. 1948–50; ambassador to Britain 1950–59; president Heb. Univ. 1962–68. Wrote books on modern history.

Elazar, David (1925–), Israel general; b. Yugoslavia. Headed Palmaḥ Harel forces in attempted breakthrough to Old City of Jerusalem 1948. Commanded brigade in 1956 Sinai campaign, Northern Sector in 1967 Six-Day War. Deputy chief of staff 1969. Israel chief of staff 1972–74.

Elazari-Volcani (Wilkansky), Yiẓḥak (1880–1955), agronomist and one of the planners of agricultural settlement in Ereẓ Israel; b. Lithuania, settled in Ereẓ Israel 1908.

Ismar Elbogen

Set up Ben-Shemen Agricultural Research Station (in Reḥovot fr. 1927). Prof. of agricultural economics at Heb. Univ. A prolific essayist and polemicist. His son, **Raanan Volcani** (1910–), prof. at Heb. Univ. agric. faculty, head of Husbandry Dept. at Reḥovot Institute.

Elbogen, Ismar (1874–1943), scholar, Jewish historian; b. Posen, emigrated fr. Germany to U.S. 1938. Wrote on Jewish history and liturgy. Main work *Der juedische Gottesdienst* on liturgy. Also wrote *A Century of Jewish Life* (a sequel to Graetz's *History*). Was an editor for *Germania Judaica* and various Jewish encyclopedias.

Eldad (Scheib), Israel (1910–), Israel author, publicist; b. Ukraine, went to Ereẓ Israel 1941. A leader of extremist underground group Loḥamei Ḥerut Israel (Leḥi) in Mandate period. Spokesman for "Greater Israel" group founded after Six-Day War.

Cover of French edition of the Protocols of the Elders of Zion, c. 1934.

Eldad and **Medad,** two of the 70 elders appointed by Moses to assist him in governing the Israelites (Num. 11:26–27).

Eldad ha-Dani (9th c.), traveler; of mysterious origin, claimed to originate fr. tribe of Dan, which with other lost tribes constituted independent kingdom nr. Ethiopia. His colorful description of Ten Tribes were embroidered legends but received widespread evidence.

Elder (Heb. *Zaken*), in ancient Israel a man of distinct social status and influence. Appointed to consulting body of city, nation, or throne.

Elders of Zion, Protocols of the Learned, anti-Semitic forgery purporting to reveal the existence of an international Jewish conspiracy aimed at world power. Concocted in Paris by an agent of the Russian secret police in the 1890s, who plagiarized Maurice Joby's satire on Napoleon III, the *Dialogue aux Enfers entre Machiavel et Montesquieu* (1864). Particularly widespread after WWI. Utilized by Nazis against Jews and by Arabs against Israel.

Eleazar, high priest after Aaron; Aaron's third son.

Eleazar (2nd c. B.C.E.), martyr during religious persecution instigated by Antiochus Epiphanes (167 B.C.E.). Gave his life rather than eat swine's flesh.

Eleazar ben Ananias, Zealot leader in Jerusalem during Jewish war with Rome 66–70 C.E.

Eleazar ben Arakh (1st c.), *tanna*, most outstanding pupil of Johanan ben Zakkai, Saying: "Be eager to study the Torah and know what you should answer an unbeliever" (*Avot* 2:14).

Eleazar ben Azariah (1st–2nd c.) *tanna*, halakhist, aggadist; one of Jabneh sages. A national leader and head of Sanhedrin, he went on a mission to Rome, with R. Gamaliel, R. Joshua, R. Akiva.

Eleazar ben Damma (2nd c.), *tanna.* Bitten by a snake, he died while debating with his uncle, Rabbi Ishmael, whether a heathen physician should be allowed to cure him.

Eleazar ben Dinai (1st c.), Zealot leader in Judea. Died a captive in Rome.

Eleazar ben Ḥarsom, high priest and scholar mentioned in Talmud. Said to have been rich but devoted his time to study.

Eleazar ben Jacob ha-Bavli (c. 1195–1250), Hebrew poet of Baghdad; a house poet for wealthy Jewish families in Iraq.

Eleazar ben Jair (1st c.), Sicarii leader, commander of besieged fortress of Masada in Roman war 66–73. The moving speech in which he persuaded the defenders to kill their families and themselves so as to avoid capture is recorded in Josephus.

Ostracon from Masada inscribed "Ben Jair" possibly referring to Eleazar ben Jair.

Eleazar ben Judah of Bartota (2nd c.), *tanna.* Noted for great generosity. Saying: "Render unto Him what is His, for thou and what thou hast are His . . . " (*Avot* 3:7).

Eleazar ben Judah of Worms (c. 1165–c. 1230), codifier, kabbalist, liturgical poet. His wife and daughters were killed by Crusaders 1196. Last major scholar of Ḥasidei Ashkenaz movement. Author of halakhic work *Sefer ha-Roke'aḥ*, which sets out principles of medieval Ḥasidism, and theological *Sodei Razayya.*

Eleazar ben Mattathias (2nd c. B.C.E.), Hasmonean; fourth of Mattathias' sons. Killed in battle with Syrians.

Eleazar ben Matya (2nd c.), *tanna* and leading student at Jabneh.

Eleazar ben Parta (2nd c.), *tanna* who was imprisoned by Romans for teaching Torah but was miraculously delivered.

Eleazar ben Pedat (d. 279), *amora* of Babylonia, successor of R. Johanan as head of council in Tiberias. One of great exponents of oral law and Mishnah.

Eleazar ben Shammua (c. 150), *tanna;* generally referred to as R. Eleazar. Student of Akiva and teacher of Judah ha-Nasi. Conducted *bet midrash* (but site unknown).

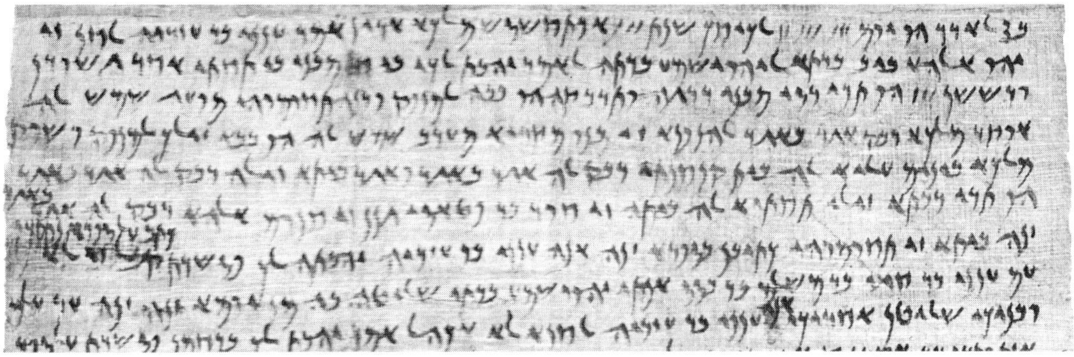

Part of Elephantine Aramaic papyrus, 5th century B.C.E.; a deed in which a father gives a house to his daughter.

Eleazar ben Simeon, Zealot leader during Roman war 66-70.

Eleazar ben Simeon (2nd c.), *tanna;* son and pupil of Simeon bar Yoḥai, with whom he hid in a cave to escape the Romans. Engaged in halakhic controversy with his colleague Judah ha-Nasi.

Eleazar ben Yose (2nd c.), *tanna;* son of Yose ben Ḥalafta. Went with Simeon bar Yoḥai to Rome on successful mission to try to reverse an edict against Jewish religious practices.

Eleazar (Eliezer) ben Zadok, name of at least two *tannaim* belonging to same family. (1) *Tanna* of 1st–2nd c. Priest who transmitted information concerning structures, procedures, and practices in Temple. (2) *Tanna* of late 2nd c., apparently grandson of (1). Engaged in halakhic discussions with Rabbi Judah and Rabbi Yose.

Eleazar of Modi'in (ha-Moda'i; 1st–2nd c.), *tanna;* uncle of Bar Kokhba. Noted aggadist. May be the "Eleazar the priest" mentioned on coins of Bar Kokhba. According to *aggadah,* Bar Kokhba suspected his loyalty and killed him, whereupon Bethar fell.

Elek (Fischer), Artur (1876–1944), Hungarian author, art historian. Translated French and Italian classics and wrote short stories. Convert to Christianity. Committed suicide during Nazi occupation.

Elephantine (Yeb), island with fortress town on Egyptian-Ethiopian frontier, on the Nile opposite Aswan. Under Persian rule of Egypt (525 B.C.E. ff.), Jewish mercenaries stationed there. Jewish temple erected by Jewish civilians; destroyed by local priests 411 B.C.E. Episode known from E. papyri written in Aramaic discovered early in 20th c.

Elfenbein, Israel (1890–1964), U.S. rabbi, talmudic scholar. Wrote on medieval rabbinic literature and published Rashi's responsa.

Elhanan ben Shemariah (d. 1026), head of academy in Fostat (Old Cairo), Egypt.

Elhanan ben Yakar (13th c.), Hasidei Ashkenaz theologian. Works based on *Sefer Yeẓirah.*

Elhanani (Elchanowicz), Aba (1918–), Israel architect, town planner. Prepared large commercial projects for Tel Aviv and designed President's residence in Jerusalem. Israel Prize 1973.

Eli (11th c. B.C.E.), chief priest at Shiloh shrine at end of period of Judges. Brought up Samuel.

Eliakim, see Jehoiakim.

Eliano, Giovanni Battista (1530–1589), Italian apostate, anti-Jewish propagandist; grandson of Elijah Levita.

Elias, Eduard (1900–1967), Dutch journalist, Zionist. Netherlands government information officer in Curacao, New York, 1940–45. Wrote light columns for several Dutch periodicals under own and pen names.

Elias, Joseph (d. 1927), Jewish community worker in Iraq. Represented Baghdad community in Iraqi parliament.

Elias, Ney (1844–1897), British explorer. Journeyed across Gobi desert by unexplored route.

Eliasberg, Mordecai (1817–1889), rabbi; b. Lithuania. One of the first Ḥovevei Zion in Russia. Rabbi of Bauska, Latvia, fr. 1862. Supported Haskalah movement and vocational training for Jews. Early supporter of settlement in Ereẓ Israel against ultra-Orthodox circles. His son **Jonathan** (1851–1898), rabbi, scholar, Zionist.

Eliash, Mordecai (1892–1950), lawyer; b. Ukraine, settled in Ereẓ Israel 1919. Israel's first minister in London 1949.

Eliashov, Solomon ben Ḥayyim (1841–1926), kabbalist in Lithuania; one of outstanding kabbalists in Russia at end of 19th c.

Elias Le Eveske (Elijah ben Berechiah ha-Kohen), archpresbyter of English Jewry 1243–57. Converted to Christianity 1259.

Eliel, Ernest Ludwig (1921–), U.S. organic chemist; b. Germany. Prof. of chemistry at Notre Dame Univ. 1960. Wrote *Stereochemistry of Carbon Compounds, Conformational Analysis.*

Eliezer, steward of Abraham's household (Gen. 15:2). Traditionally identified with messenger sent by Abraham to Laban (Gen. 24).

Eliezer ben Hyrcanus (1st–2nd c.), Palestinian *tanna;* pupil of R. Johanan b. Zakkai at Jabneh, teacher of R. Akiva. Set up Lydda academy. Accompanied R. Gamaliel on mission to Rome 95–6. Johanan b. Zakkai said: "If all the sages of Israel were balanced against Eliezer, he would outweigh them all" (*Avot* 2:8).

Eliezer ben Isaac (16th c.), Hebrew printer. Active in Lublin and Constantinople, established first press at Safed.

Eliezer ben Isaac of Worms (11th c.), talmudic scholar in Germany; pupil of Gershom Me'or ha-Golah. Headed Mainz yeshivah.

Eliezer ben Jacob, name of two *tannaim.* (1) Lived during period of destruction of Temple. Intimately acquainted with Temple, and tradition states that he is author of the Mishnah *Middot.* (2) *Tanna* of 2nd c., pupil of Akiva.

Eliezer ben Joel ha-Levi of Bonn (Ravyah, 1140–1225), rabbinic scholar in Germany. Spiritual leader of German Jewry. Rabbi of Cologne fr. 1200. Major works *Ravyah,* halakhot, and legal decisions.

Eliezer ben Meir ha-Levi of Pinsk (18th c.), rabbi, *darshan, rosh yeshivah* in Pinsk. Author of homiletic works.

Eliezer ben Nathan of Mainz (Raban; c. 1090–c. 1170), leading rabbinic authority in Germany in 12th c., one of "the elders of Mainz."

Eliezer ben Samuel ha-Levi (d.

1357), German Jew; son of Samuel ben Yakar. Known from his touching ethical will.
Eliezer ben Samuel of Metz (c. 1115–c. 1198), tosafist; pupil of Jacob Tam. Served as intermediary between rabbinic centers in France and Germany.
Eliezer (Eleazar) ben Yose ha-Gelili (2nd c.), *tanna;* pupil of R. Akiva, aggadist and author of *Baraita of Thirty-Two Rules* for expounding *aggadah.*
Eliezer Fischel ben Isaac of Strzyzow (18th c.), Galician kabbalist; opponent of Ḥasidism.
Eliezer of Beaugency (12th c.), biblical commentator fr. N. France. Gave literal exegesis of Bible.
Eliezer of Touques (d. c. 1291), one of last tosafists. Many of his *tosafot* are adaptations of those of his predecessors.
Elihu, character in Job (32:6–37) who justifies Divine action to Job and his friends.
Elijah, prophet in Israel in reigns of Ahab and Ahaziah (9th c. B.C.E.). A fiery ascetic, he fought to preserve Divine worship from the cult of Baal, defeating supporters of the latter on Mt. Carmel. Fiercely opposed the queen Jezebel and reproved the king Ahab, notably over the incident of Naboth's vineyard. Ascended to heaven in chariot of fire. A favorite figure of Jewish folklore, he is seen as the herald of the Messiah. A glass of wine is traditionally poured for him at the Passover *seder,* and a chair

Elijah's chair, England, 1809.

is prepared for him at the circumcision ceremony. Figures also in Christian and Moslem legend.
Elijah, Apocalypse of, apocryphal work known from references in early Christian sources and quotations in Latin documents describing torments in Hell. Christian sources date it to 6th c.
Elijah Baḥur, see Levita, Elijah.
Elijah ben Abraham (12th c.), Karaite scholar, possibly in Ereẓ Israel. Wrote polemical tract against Rabbanites.
Elijah ben Baruch the Elder (d. c. 1712), Karaite author in Constantinople and Crimea. Visited Ereẓ Israel. Works mainly polemical.
Elijah ben Benjamin ha-Levi (d. c. 1540), rabbi, *paytan* in Constantinople. Author of responsa.
Elijah ben Loeb of Fulda (c. 1650–c. 1720), rabbi, halakhic author fr. Poland. Made special study of Jerusalem Talmud.
Elijah ben Raphael Solomon ha-Levi (18th–19th c.), rabbi, author, kabbalist, liturgical poet in Mantua and Alessandria, Italy.
Elijah ben Shabbetai Be'er (also **Elia di Sabato of Fermo,** or **Elias Sabot;** 14th–15th c.), papal physician. First Jew to teach medicine at Pavia Univ.
Elijah ben Shemaiah (11th c.), liturgical poet in Bari, S. Italy. Some of his *seliḥot* included in Ashkenazi ritual.
Elijah ben Solomon Abraham ha-Kohen of Smyrna (d. 1729), rabbi, *dayyan,* outstanding preacher of his time; possibly a Shabbatean. Concerned with ethical behavior and social justice in his *Shevet Musar* and *Me'il Ẓedakah.*

Elijah ben Solomon Zalman, the Gaon of Vilna.

Elijah ben Solomon ha-Kohen, Palestinian *gaon* fr. 1062 to 1083. After conquest of Jerusalem by Seljuks 1071, moved to Tyre. Few of his responsa survived.
Elijah ben Solomon Zalman (the **"Vilna Gaon"**; 1720–1797), one of outstanding thinkers and spiritual leaders of Jewry in modern times. Led opponents *(mitnaggedim)* to Ḥasidism. Interested in secular sciences though far removed from Haskalah. Wrote over 70 works and commentaries to books of Scripture and Mishnah as well as other works on vast range of subjects. Basis of his outlook is eternity of Torah in actual practice.
Elijah Menahem ben Moses (c. 1220–1284), English rabbi, physician, financier; son of R. Moses b. Yom Tov of London.
Elijah of Ferrara (15th c.), Italian scholar. Emigrated to Ereẓ Israel 1434 and became *dayyan* in Jerusalem, describing its community in several letters.
Elijah Phinehas ben Meir (c. 1742–1821), Vilna-born scholar, kabbalist, *maskil.* Became known through his *Sefer ha-Berit,* a kind of encyclopedia in which he maintained that the earth is motionless.
Elimelech, husband of Naomi, in time of Judges (Book of Ruth); fr. Bethlehem.
Elimelech of Lyzhansk (1717–1787), popular *ẓaddik,* one of founders of Ḥasidism in Galicia. Disciple of Dov Baer, the *maggid* of Mezhirech. Formulated the mores of the *ẓaddik* in ḥasidic society.
Elionaeus, Son of Cantheras, high priest 43–44 C.E. Appointed by Agrippa I.
°**Eliot, George** (pseud. of **Mary Ann Evans;** 1819–1880), English novelist. Began to study Hebrew at early age and showed great interest in Jewish matters. Her celebrated novel, *Daniel Deronda,* has marked "Zionist" motif.
Eliphaz (1) oldest son of Esau and Adah; (2) Eliphaz the Temanite, one of three friends of Job.
Elisha (9th c. B.C.E.), prophet in kingdom of Israel; disciple and successor of Elijah. Biblical account (II Kings 1–13) relates many stories and miracles connected with his long period of activity. His relations with the kings were generally harmonious.

George Eliot, portrait by Sir F. Burton.

Elisha ben Abraham (d. 1749), rabbi, author; lived in Poland, Germany, Lithuania. Published commentary on Mishnah.
Elisha ben Avuyah (2nd c.), *tanna* and apostate; b. Jerusalem. One of great sages of his day; later renounced Judaism and was thereafter only referred to by his former colleagues as *Aḥer* ("another person"). Differing accounts attribute his apostasy to influence of sectarianism or Hellenism.
Elisha Ḥayyim ben Jacob Ashkenazi (d. 1673), emissary of Ashkenazi community of Jerusalem to N. Africa, Germany, Poland. Father of

Nathan of Gaza. His son, **Azariah Ḥayyim Ashkenazi,** also an emissary in Morocco.

Elisheba, wife of Aaron, mother of Nadab, Abihu, Eleazar, and Ithamar.

°**Elisheva Bikhowsky** (née **Elizaveta Zhirkova**; 1888–1949), Hebrew poet; b. Russia. Her admiration for Jewish people found expression first in Russian, then Hebrew. Settled in Ereẓ Israel 1925.

Eliyia, Joseph (1901–1931), neo-Greek poet, scholar. Translated Hebrew literature into Greek.

Eli Ẓiyyon ve-Areha (Heb. "Wail, Zion and its Cities"), initial words of anonymous dirge of Middle Ages written for fast day of Ninth of Av.

Eliẓur, sports organization of Ha-Po'el ha-Mizrachi. Founded 1939. Active in all sports but not a member of football league because its members do not play on Sabbath.

Elkan, Benno (1877–1960), sculptor, medalist, lived and worked in Germany, fr. 1933 in London. Produced among other works a historical candelabrum for Knesset in Jerusalem.

Elkan, Sophie (1853–1921), Swedish novelist. Wrote mostly on historical themes.

Elkanah, father of Samuel; husband of Hannah (I Sam. 1).

Elkes, Elhanan (1879–1944), physician, chairman of Kaunas (Kovno) *Aeltestenrat* (Council of Elders under the Nazis). His personality and dignity outstanding example. Died at Dachau concentration camp.

Elkin, Adolphus Peter (1891–), Australian anthropologist. Wrote on disappearing aborigines of Oceania.

Elkind, Arkadi Daniilovich (1869– ?), Russian physician, anthropometrist. Wrote on anthropology of Polish Jewry.

El-Kuds ("the sanctuary"), Arabic name for Jerusalem.

Elkus, Abram Isaac (1867–1947), U.S. lawyer, diplomat. Ambassador to Turkey 1916–19.

Ellenbogen, Wilhelm (1863–1951), Austrian socialist politician. Cabinet member early 1920s. Fled to France 1938, to U.S. 1940.

Ellenstein, Meyer C. (1886–1967), U.S. politician. Mayor of Newark 1933–41.

Ellinger, Moritz (1830–1907), U.S. public official; b. Germany, in U.S. fr. 1854. Active in B'nai B'rith.

Ellsberg, Edward (1891–), U.S. naval officer, engineer; authority on raising sunken vessels.

Ellstaetter, Moritz (1827–1905), German politician; first Jew to become minister in German state (Baden).

Menorah by Benno Elkan, presented to the Israel Knesset in Jerusalem by a group of members of the British Parliament, 1956.

Ellstein, Abraham (1907–1963), composer, conductor, pianist. Composed for films, Yiddish musicals; over 500 Yiddish songs and works (after 1957) for concert, stage, synagogue.

Elmaleh, family of rabbis and communal leaders in Turkey, Morocco, Italy; of Spanish origin. **Abraham b. Judah Elmalik,** 16th c. kabbalist in Pesaro. **Aaron b. Gershon Elmali,** 17th c. community leader in Salonika. **Joseph b. Ayyush Elmaleh** (1750–1823), kabbalist, halakhist, rabbi of Salé and Rabat, Morocco. **Joseph** (1788–1866), rabbi in Mogador, counsellor to sultan Abdul Raḥman. **Joseph b. Aaron** (1809–1886), *dayyan,* rabbi, in Rabat and Mogador, d. London. **Elijah b. Jacob** (1837–1908), b. Mogador, rabbi of Tangiers.

Elmaleh, Abraham (1885–1967), author, lexicologist, Sephardi leader in Ereẓ Israel. Elected 1949 to first Knesset on Sephardi list. Compiled Hebrew-French, French-Hebrew dictionary.

El Male Raḥamim (Heb. "God full of compassion"), prayer for departed recited at funeral services and memorial occasions.

Elman, Mischa (1891–1967), Russian-born violinist; in U.S. fr. 1908.

El Melekh Ne'eman (Heb. "God, King faithful King"), affirmation of faith pronounced before *Shema* when read privately.

El Melekh Yoshev (Heb. "God, King enthroned"), first words of petitional prayer in *Seliḥot* services that introduces invocation of Thirteen Attributes. Dates from 6th c. C.E.

El Nora Alilah (Heb. "God that doest wondrously"), solemn hymn for *Ne'ilah* service of Day of Atonement; written by Moses ibn Ezra (early 12th c.).

Eloesser, Arthur (1870–1938), German literary historian, critic. Wrote history of German literature.

Elohim, plural word for God, the singular being **Eloha.** One of most frequent words for Divinity in Bible. Also used for pagan gods.

El Paso city in Tex., U.S. Jews settled before Civil War; number increased after each of world wars by

Mount Sinai Temple, El Paso, designed by Sidney Eisenshtat.

Jacob Saul Elyashar.

Jews dancing around a statue of the English member of Parliament, Sir Robert Grant, who advocated granting political equality to Jews. From McLean's Monthly Sheet of Caricatures, London, May 1, 1833.

En-Gedi springs and waterfall.

Joel Engel

Jewish soldiers stationed in area who stayed on after discharge. Two congregations, Reform and Conservative. Jewish pop. 4,500 (1971).

El Salvador, Central American republic. Jewish pop. 300 (1971), mostly immigrants fr. Alsace, Germany, Poland, Rumania. Synagogue in the capital, San Salvador.

Elte, Harry (1880–1945), Dutch architect. Died at Theresienstadt concentration camp.

Elton, Geoffrey Rudolph (1921–), historian of Tudor period; b. Germany, in Britain fr. 1939. Prof. at Cambridge. Son of Victor Ehrenberg.

Elul, 6th month in Jewish year; 29 days. Zodiac sign Virgo. In anticipation of Ten Days of Penitence, regarded as month of repentance.

Elusa, Nabatean city in Negev, now the ruins of Ḥaluẓa, SW of Beersheba. Important road terminal. In Arab times seat of a district governor.

Elyan, Sir Isidore Victor (1909–), jurist; b. Dublin. Magistrate, British Colony of Gold Coast, 1946–55. Chief justice, Swaziland, 1965–70.

Elyashar, Jacob ben Ḥayyim Joseph (c. 1720–1788), rabbi, communal leader in Ereẓ Israel. Emissary of Hebron community to various countries in Europe and Middle East. Wrote *piyyutim* and poems. Later helped in redevelopment of Safed.

Elyashar, Jacob Saul ben Eliezer Jeroham (1817–1906), Sephardi chief rabbi (*rishon le-Ẓion)* of Ereẓ Israel; grandson of Jacob b. Ḥayyim Joseph Elyashar. Wrote thousands of responsa and many rabbinic works. His son **R. Ḥayyim Moshe** (1845–1924), merchant and businessman, *rishon le-Ẓion.* His son **Isaac** (1873–1933), first chairman of United Jewish Community Council of Jerusalem; grandson **Eliyahu** (1898–), member of 2nd Knesset and Sephardi leader.

Elyashev, Israel Isidor, see Baal Makhshoves.

Elzas, Barnett Abraham (1867–1939), U.S. reform rabbi. Fr. 1894 in Charleston. Wrote history of Jews of S. Carolina. Moved to New York 1910.

Emancipation, abolition of disabilities imposed on Jews and the formal granting of equal rights and duties of citizenship. Stemming from political and social thought in 18th c., it did not obliterate theological aversion toward Jews in the host nations. First to emancipate the Jews formally was the U.S. in 1787 federal constitution. J. Toland, Macaulay (England), Abbé Gregoire (France), C.W. Dohm (Germany), M. d'Azeglio (Italy), were among the foremost champions of Jewish emancipation. In France it was a corollary of the Declaration of the Rights of Man of 1789, reflecting the ideals of the Enlightenment. In 19th c., Jewish e. introduced by revolution and canceled by reaction in a seesaw process. Gradually introduced in united Italy (1848–1870), Germany (1833–1871), Austro-Hungary (1867), Denmark (1814–1848), followed by other Scandinavian countries. In Switzerland full religious liberty proclaimed in 1874 federal constitution. In England, Jews admitted to municipal offices 1830–55, to parliament 1858. Emancipation imposed on the Balkan states by the Berlin Congress of 1878, but obligations were evaded by Rumania. In Czarist Russia, discrimination ruthlessly continued throughout the 19th c.; full legal e. immediately followed the 1917 revolution. In central and E. Europe, Jewish equality was introduced constitutionally in the "succession states" formed after WWI, but carried out only in Czechoslovakia. In 1933, Nazi Germany reversed the process, taking as criterion race instead of religion. This reaction spread in the following years over most of Europe, caused by Nazi occupation or influence, and heralded the subsequent campaign of annihilation. With the overthrow of the Nazis in 1945, former conditions were reestablished.

Embden, Gustav (1874–1933), German biochemist. As prof. of physiology at Frankfort Univ. fr. 1914, made important contributions to biochemical research in field of metabolism.

Ember, Aaron (1878–1926), U.S. Orientalist, Egyptologist. Taught at Johns Hopkins Univ.

Emden, city in W. Germany. Reference to Jews fr. 16th c. Marranos from Portugal settled there and returned to Judaism. With advent of Nazi rule many Jews left. In 1939 they numbered 198, most of whom were deported.

Emden, Jacob (pen name **Yaveẓ;** 1697–1776), rabbi, halakhic authority, kabbalist, anti-Shabbatean polemicist; son and disciple of Ẓevi Hirsch Ashkenazi. Rabbi of Emden 1728–33. One of outstanding scholars of his generation. Conducted bitter controversy with Jonathan Eybeschuetz, whom he accused of being a secret Shab-

batean.

Emek, see Jezreel, Valley of.

Emes, Der Yiddish daily, official organ of Russian Communist Party relating to Jewish affairs (*Yevsektsiya*). Published fr. 1918 (originally as *Di Varhayt*) until 1938.

Emig-Direkt, emigration association organized 1921 in Berlin to assist emigrants fr. Europe, esp. Russia. Major financial support fr. Joint and ICA.

Emin Pasha (Eduard Schnitzer; 1840–1892), Austrian traveler, explorer. Succeeded General Gordon as governor of Sudan. Led expeditions in Central Africa. Murdered by slave traders. Southern Bay of Lake Victoria named Emin Pasha Gulf.

Emiot, Israel (Israel Goldwasser; 1909–), Yiddish poet fr. Poland. Deported to Siberia 1948. Repatriated to Poland in 1950s. Settled in U.S.

Emmanuel, Isaac Samuel (1899–), Greek-born rabbi. Jewish historian of Salonika and Curacao. Settled in U.S.

Emmaus, ancient town NW of Jerusalem. Site of camp of Seleucid army defeated by Judah Maccabee (166 B.C.E.). Traditional site where Jesus appeared to apostles after his death (Luke 24:13–16). In 221 C.E. received status of city and named Nicopolis. Became Arab village 'Imwās, destroyed in Six-Day War (1967).

Emsheimer, Ernst (1904–), musicologist. Main interests are music of N. Mongol peoples and study of musical instruments. Curator, Museum of Music History, Stockholm, 1949.

Endecja (also **Endeks**), Polish anti-Semitic right-wing party in the 1st half of 20th c.

Endingen, town in S. Germany. Jews mentioned 1331. Site of notorious blood libel 1470, after which Jews were expelled.

En-Dor, city in territory of Issachar. Site of Gideon's triumph over Midianites (Ps. 83:11). Saul visited there "the woman that divineth by a ghost" ("the witch of En Dor"; I Sam. 28:7).

Enelow, Hyman, (Hillel Gershom; 1877–1934), Lithuanian-born U.S. Reform rabbi, scholar, writer. Published 4-vol. edition of al-Nakawa's *Menorat ha-Ma'or.*

En-Gedi, oasis on the W. shore of Dead Sea; noted in biblical times for its vineyards. David found refuge there from Saul. Excavations have revealed various layers of settlement

Jewish settlement in Britain before the expulsion of 1290, and communities existing in 1971.

and Byzantine synagogue. Today site of kibbutz, with nature reserve around neighboring spring.

Engel, Joel (1868–1927), Russian-born composer, music editor. Wrote incidental music to An-ski's *Dybbuk.* Settled in Tel Aviv 1924 and pioneered in music life of Ereẓ Israel.

Engel, Joseph ben Judah (1859–1920), Polish rabbi, author. Fr. 1906 *av bet din* of Cracow. Wrote many works on *halakhah, aggadah,* Kabbalah.

Engel, József (1815–1901), Hungarian sculptor. Lived also in England, Italy.

England. First Jewish settlers, probably financiers, arrived after Norman Conquest. By mid-12th c. communities in many larger towns,

Sunday morning Jewish street market in London's Petticoat Lane, 1901.

especially London. At first tolerated, Jews later exploited by Crown. First known blood libel in Norwich 1144, while 3rd Crusade led to massacres. York community preferred suicide to surrender (1190). General expulsion 1290. Small Marrano community in 16th c. Jews had no official status in country until 1665, when Manasseh Ben Israel negotiated with Oliver Cromwell for their readmission. Charles II and his successors protected the newcomers; Sephardi synagogue (Bevis Marks) erected 1701. Ashkenazim came from Germany and Poland, and congregations established in provinces. Jewish Emancipation Bill passed in House of Commons 1833, first Jewish MP 1858, first peer 1885. Major communal organizations: Board of Deputies of British Jews (founded 1760), Jews' College (1855), Jewish Board of Guardians (1859), United Synagogue (1870), Anglo-Jewish Association (1871), Federation of Synagogues (1887). First Reform Synagogue in London 1840. British Zionist Federation (est. 1899). Massive immigration from E. Europe at end of 19th c., most newcomers settling in London and major industrial cities. 65,000

Jews in 1880, 300,000 in 1914. Aliens Immigration Act of 1905 restricted immigration. Chaim Weizmann and English Zionists did much to obtain 1917 Balfour Declaration. Jewish refugees from C. Europe arrived in 1930s. Jewish pop. (Great Britain) 410,000 (1973), with 280,000 in Greater London.

En-Harod, kibbutz founded 1921 in swamps of valley of Jezreel, nr. spring of Harod, where Gideon fought Midianites. In 1929 permanent settlement transferred to north. Affected by 1951 ideological split in Kibbutz Me'uḥad movement, it divided into two distinct though adjoining settlements, both with highly intensive farming and industrial enterprises. Pop. 785 (Me'uḥad) and 680 (Iḥud) (1971).

Mishkan le-Ommanut Museum at Kibbutz En-Harod, 1964.

High priest wearing ephod, an 18th century depiction.

Territory of tribe of Ephraim.

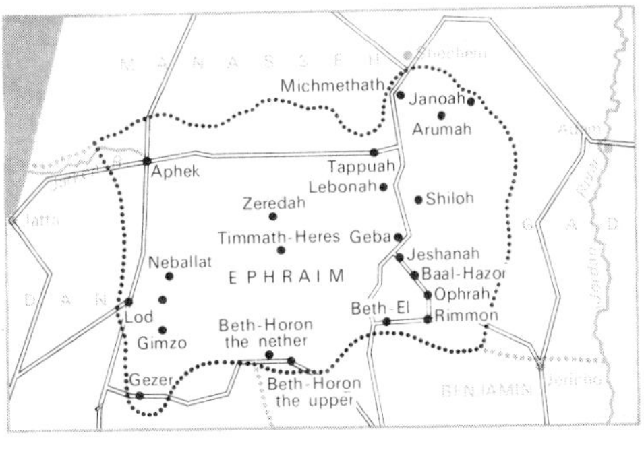

Enoch. (1) Son of Cain; (2) Son of Jared, father of Methuselah. Traditionally entered paradise without having died; seen by rabbis as model of righteousness. Various apocryphal works attributed to him.

Enoch, Books of. (1) Apocryphal work attributed to Enoch, son of Jared, probably composed during Hasmonean period (2nd–1st c. B.C.E.); original lost. Of apocalyphic, messianic nature. *Abyssinian version* found 1769. (2) *Slavonic version;* apocryphal work on Enoch, found 1886 in Belgrade; probably from Heb. original.

Enoch ben Moses (d. 1014), Spanish talmudist. Virtually chief rabbi of Muslim Spain; strove to establish independent Torah center there.

Enoch of Aleksandron (1798–1870), ḥasidic *ẓaddik,* successor of Isaac Meir Alter as leader of Gur Ḥasidism. Regarded *ẓaddik* as mere guide.

Enoch Zundel ben Joseph (d. 1867), Polish commentator on Midrash; known for his *En Yosef* and *Anaf Yosef.*

Enosh, eldest son of Seth. Lived 905 years.

Enríquez (Henríquez), Isabel (17th c.), poet; b. Spain. Fled c. 1636 to Amsterdam, where she openly professed Judaism.

Enríquez (Henriques) Basurto, Diego (b. 1621), Marrano poet. Lived in Rouen (France) and in Low Countries.

En-Rogel, spring SE of Jerusalem. Identified with well below walls of Old City of Jerusalem.

Ensheim, Moses (1750–1839), mathematician, Heb. versifier. Tutor in Moses Mendelssohn's home in Berlin.

Entin, Joel (1875–1959), Yiddish journalist, educator, translator. Emigrated fr. Russia to New York 1891.

Entre Ríos, province in Argentina. Jewish Colonization Association (ICA) purchased land there and first settlers arrived 1892. Became important center of Jewish agricultural settlement with area of 571,988 acres (1940) and Jewish pop. 8,000 (1968), of whom 3,000 live in the capital Paraná.

Ephesus, Greek city on the W. coast of Asia Minor. Paul's missionary activity there was opposed by local Jewish community (1st c.).

Ephod, upper garment worn during sacred rites in ancient Israel. Usually applied to ornamented vestment worn by high priest. To this was bound breastplate together with Urim and Thummim.

Ephraim, younger son of Joseph and Asenath. Also name of Israelite tribe in "Land of Ephraim," the hill country of central Ereẓ Israel. They were the dominant tribe in the northern kingdom of Israel.

Ephraim, Veitel Heine (1703–1775), court jeweler, head of Berlin community, financier of Frederick II during Seven Years' War. His son **Benjamin** (1742–1811) ran a lace factory in Potsdam and maintained important salon in Berlin, where he was first Jew to own an art collection.

Ephraim ben Isaac of Regensburg (1110–1175), tosafist, member of *bet din* of Regensburg; greatest of Jewish liturgical poets in Germany. His poems reflect sufferings of Jews in 1137 massacre at Regensburg and in Second Crusade (1146–47).

Ephraim ben Jacob ha-Kohen (1616–1678), rabbi, judge, in Vilna, Prague, Vienna. One of great legal authorities of his generation.

Ephraim ben Jacob of Bonn (b. 1132), liturgical poet, commentator. Also wrote *tosafot.*

Ephraim ben Shemariah (c. 980–c. 1060), leader of Palestinian community in Cairo.

Ephraim ibn Avi Alragan (11th–12th c.), halakhist in Algeria, referred to as "Rabbenu Ephraim"; disciple of Isaac Alfasi.

Ephraim Solomon ben Aaron of Luntshits (1550–1619), rabbi, preacher, *rosh yeshivah* in Lemberg, Prague. Noted for lucid and fascinating sermons which were collected in several volumes.

Ephrath, additional name for Bethlehem of Judah (Gen. 35:19; 48:7).

Ephrati, David Tevele ben Abraham (1849–1884), talmudic scholar; lived in Vitebsk, Berlin. Active in Ḥibbat Zion. Wrote halakhic works and *Toledot Anshei Shem,* biographies of Jewish scholars.

Ephron, son of Zohar; Hittite who sold Machpelah cave to Abraham (Gen. 23).

Ephros, Gershon (1890–), *ḥazzan.* Emigrated to U.S. fr. Ereẓ Israel. Main work 5-vol. *Cantorial Anthology,* practical collection of works for synagogues services of the year.

Ephrussi, Boris (1901–), French geneticist. Worked on cell heredity and differentiation. Also investigated heredity of yeasts.

Episcopus Judaeorum (Lat. "bishop of the Jews"), title given by Christian authorities in Middle Ages to head of Jewish community or its rabbi.

Eppenstein, Simon (1864–1920), German rabbi, scholar. Lecturer in Jewish history and Bible exegesis at Berlin Rabbinical Seminary. Main fields of study were geonic period and medieval Bible exegesis.

Eppstein, Paul (1901–1944), sociologist, community leader; one of heads of Germany community fr. 1933. Deported 1943 to Theresienstadt and made "Jewish elder" of camp. Shot there by Gestapo.

Epstein, Abraham (1841–1918), rabbinic scholar, outstanding in Midrash and Targum studies; b. Russia, lived in Vienna fr. 1876.

Epstein, Abraham (1880–1952), Russian-born literary critic. Settled in New York 1925. Wrote about modern Hebrew authors in U.S. and elsewhere.

Epstein, Abraham (1892–1942), economist, sociologist; b. Russia, in U.S. fr. 1910. Specialized in problems of aged.

Epstein, Abraham Meir ben Aryeh Leib (1726–1772), Polish talmudist. Wrote novellae, sermons, responsa. Son of Aryeh Leib Epstein.

Epstein, Aryeh Leib ben Mordecai (1705–1775), rabbi, kabbalist, educationalist in Grodno and Koenigsberg.

Epstein, Baruch ha-Levi (1860–1942), Russian talmudic scholar; son of Jehiel Michal Epstein. Worked in bank and devoted spare time to scholarship. Wrote *Torah Temimah,* annotated compilation of quotations from oral law arranged according to scriptural verse.

Epstein, Brian (1934–1967), British impresario. Managed Beatles to international fame. Autobiography, *A Cellarful of Noise.*

Epstein, Isaac ben Mordecai (c. 1780–1857), talmudist, kabbalist, rabbi of Gomel, Belorussia. Wrote on Ḥabad Ḥasidism.

Epstein, Isidore (1894–1962), English rabbi, scholar. Rabbi in Middlesborough 1921–28. Taught Semitics at Jews' College, and was its principal 1948–61. Supervised Engl. transl. of Babylonian Talmud (Soncino Talmud). Wrote on Judaism.

Epstein, Iẓhac (1863–1943), Hebrew writer, educationalist, philologist, in Salonika, Ereẓ Israel; brother of Zalman Epstein. A pioneer of modern Hebrew, he introduced *Ivrit be-Ivrit* (the teaching of Hebrew through the exclusive use of that language).

Epstein, Sir Jacob (1880–1959), sculptor; b. New York, lived in London fr. 1905. One of greatest sculptors of the 20th c. Monumental works (e.g., at Coventry Cathedral), sculptures ("Genesis," "Adam," "Lucifer"), busts of prominent personalities.

Epstein, Jacob Nahum (1878–1952), talmudist; b. Belorussia. Prof. of talmudic philology at Heb. Univ. fr. 1925. Formulated basis for new approach to talmudic studies and published many works, including most authoritative study of original text of Mishnah.

Epstein, Jean (1897–1953), French film director. Introduced use of slow motion into films (1928). Films include *La Chute de la Maison Usher* and *Les Feux de la Mer.*

Epstein, Jehiel Michal ben Aaron Isaac Halevi (1829–1908), rabbi, halakhic authority; b. Belorussia. Composed *Arukh ha-Shulḥan,* halakhic rulings on *Shulḥan Arukh.*

Epstein, Jehiel Michal ben Abraham ha-Levi (d. 1706), German rabbi, author. Published abridged version of Isaiah Horowitz' *Shenei Luḥot ha-Berit* and prayer-book in Yiddish translation.

Epstein, Judith (1895–), U.S. Hadassah leader. National president 1937–39, 1943–47.

Epstein, Kalonymus Kalman of Cracow (d. 1823), ḥasidic *ẓaddik* in Cracow. Noted for ecstatic mode of prayer.

Epstein, Louis M. (1887–1949), U.S. Conservative rabbi, authority on Jewish marriage and sex laws. Rabbi in Brookline, Mass. fr. 1925.

Epstein, Marie (1899–), French screenwriter and director; sister of Jean Epstein. Wrote screenplay for and co-directed *La Maternelle* with Benoit-Levy.

Epstein, Melech (1889–), Yiddish communist journalist, editor; b. Belorussia, emigrated to U.S. 1913.

Epstein, Moses Jehiel (of Ozarow; 1890–), rabbinical author. Settled in Israel 1953. Awarded Israel Prize 1967 for his 10-vol. series *Esh Dat* and *Be'er Moshe.*

Epstein, Moses Mordecai (1866–1933), talmudist, *rosh yeshivah* in Slobodka, Lithuania. In 1924 transferred yeshivah to Hebron and after 1929 riots to Jerusalem.

Epstein, Zalman (1860–1936), Hebrew essayist, critic, Zionist; b. Belorussia, settled in Ereẓ Israel 1925.

Erez, see Zederbaum, Alexander.

Ereẓ Israel, Heb. name of Land of Israel; see Israel.

Erfurt, city in E. Germany. Medieval settlement 12th c. to 1458, punctuated by expulsions and massacres, most notably at time of Black Death (1349); most famous resident Asher ben Jehiel (the Rosh). Jews readmitted 1820. 831 Jews in 1933. Community ended in WWII. 120 Jews in 1960.

Ergas, Joseph ben Emanuel (1685–1730), kabbalist, rabbi in Leghorn.

Erik, Max (1898–1937), Yiddish literary critic, author in Vilna, Minsk, Kiev. Arrested 1936 and died in prison camp in Siberia.

Abraham Epstein

Jacob Epstein in his studio with statues of "Lazarus" (l.) and "Ecce Homo" (r.), 1947.

Jacob Nahum Epstein

Erikson, Erik Homberger (1902–), U.S. psychoanalyst; prof. at Harvard.

Erlanger (D'Erlanger), family of bankers. **Raphael** (1806–1878) established firm in Frankfort. His sons: **Victor** (1840–1894) managed Vienna branch; **Frederic-Emile** (1832–1911) established London house; **Ludwig** (1836–1898) headed Frankfort bank.

Erlanger, Camille (1863–1919), French composer. Wrote operas and songs.

Erlanger, Joseph (1874–1965), U.S. physiologist. Nobel Prize winner 1944 for work on functional differentiation of nerves. Fr. 1910 prof. at Washington Univ. School of Medicine, St. Louis.

Erlanger, Michel (1828–1892), French communal worker, a founder of Alliance Israélite Universelle.

Erlanger, Philippe (1911–), historian, art critic. His *Louis XIV* rated as outstanding historical work.

Erlich, Henryk (1882–1941), journalist, leader of Bund in Poland. Leading figure in Petrograd's Workers' Soviet after 1917 revolution. Arrested 1941 with Victor Alter by Soviet authorities and shot. His wife **Sophia Dubnow-Erlich** (b. 1885), daughter of historian S. Dubnow, publicist and author, settled in U.S. 1942.

Erlich, Vera Stein (1897–), Yugoslav anthropologist, psychologist. Studied family relationships in rural areas.

Ernakulam, town in Kerala, India, nr. Cochin. "Black Jews" lived there since 15th c. In 1687, second largest community on Malabar Coast, after Cochin. In recent years community declined, mostly in emigration to Israel, and in 1970 c. 25 families and 2 large synagogues.

Errera, Jacques (1896–), Belgian physical chemist. Studied molecular structure, infrared spectroscopy, supersonics, and colloid chemistry.

Theckoobagam Synagogue congregation, Ernakulam (Cochin).

Isaac Erter

Errera, Léo (1858–1905), Belgian botanist, Jewish leader. Founded Brussels Botanical Institute. His brother **Paul Joseph Errera** (1860–1922), jurist.

Erter, Isaac (1791–1851), Hebrew satirist; born in Galicia and lived in Brody. Satires written in Biblical prose directed against Ḥasidism, which was to him an obstacle in expansion of Haskalah. Satirized hypocrisy. ignorance, superstition.

Erusin (Heb.), betrothal, first marriage stage, carrying with it most of the obligations but not all its privileges. It arises through *kiddushin.*

Eruv (Heb. "mixing"), term used for rabbinic provisions facilitating performance on Sabbath or festivals of otherwise forbidden acts, e.g., cooking on a festival immediately preceding the Sabbath becomes permitted if some food is prepared on the previous weekday and retained until the Sabbath (*eruv tavshilin*); carrying on the Sabbath becomes permitted by amalgamating individual holdings (*eruv ḥaẓerot*); and exceeding the Sabbath limit of 2,000 cubits outside a town becomes permitted by a nominal extension of boundaries (*eruv teḥumim*).

Eruvin, 2nd tractate in Mishnah order *Mo'ed* with *gemara* in both Talmuds. Deals with *eruv* (q.v.).

Esau, firstborn son of Isaac and Rebekah; twin brother of Jacob. Tried to kill Jacob after latter had obtained his birthright and firstborn's blessing by deception. Many years later they were reconciled. Traditional ancestor of the Edomites.

Escapa, Joseph ben Saul (1570–1662), Turkish rabbi, author; chief rabbi of Smyrna. Vehement opponent of Shabbetai Ẓevi, who had been his disciple.

Eschelbacher, Joseph (1848–1916), author, rabbi in Bruchsal, Baden, Berlin. Wrote *Das Judentum und das Wesen des Christentums* in answer to Harnack.

Escudero, Lorenzo (d. 1683), Capuchin friar, convert to Judaism, polemist. Lived in Córdoba, Amsterdam, London (1655–59).

Esdraelon, Plain of, see Jezreel, Valley of.

Eshet Ḥayil ("a woman of valor"), first words of Proverbs 31:10–31 describing the virtuous housewife, chanted in the home of Friday evenings.

Levi Eshkol

Eshkol (Shkolnik), Levi (1895–1969), labor leader, prime minister of Israel 1963–9; b. Oratova, Ukraine; settled in Ereẓ Israel 1914 as agricultural worker. Co-founded Deganyah Bet settlement. In charge of Mekorot Water Company 1937–51, and of Haganah finances. Secretary of Mapai Labor Party 1942–5, treasurer of Jewish Agency fr. 1949. Member of Knesset fr. 1951, minister of finance 1952–63. Succeeded Ben-Gurion in 1963 as prime minister and minister of defense. Noted as mediator and architect of 1965 alignment between Mapai and Aḥdut ha-Avodah, which won an impressive victory in 1965 Knesset elections. Subsequently extended to form the Israel Labor Party. In June 1967 he handed over defense portfolio to Moshe Dayan, establishing "National Unity" government. His efforts to strengthen and equip Israel army bore fruit in Six-Day War.

Eshtaol, biblical town in Judean Shephelah. Samson lived in neighborhood. Name given to moshav in Israel.

Remains of main entrance to synagogue at Eshtemoa.

Eshtemoa, levitical city in territory of Judah, S. of Hebron (Josh. 15:50; 21:14), that belonged to family of Caleb, and was still a large Jewish village in 4th c. C.E. Remains of ancient synagogue uncovered by excavations. Now Arab village al-Samū'.

Eskeles, Gabriel ben Judah Loew (d. 1718), Cracow-born rabbi of Olkusz, Metz, and chief rabbi of Moravia. His son **Issachar Berush** (1692–1753) succeeded his father as chief rabbi of Moravia. Chief rabbi of Hungary 1725. Established the Eskeles-Stiftung, a foundation for Torah teaching and providing dowries for poor brides. Issachar's son **Bernhard** (1753–1839), financier, founded 1816 Austrian National Bank. His wife **Cecily** (1759–1818) made their house a salon for high society, rivaling her sister, Fanny von Arnstein.

Espinosa, Edouard (1872–1950), British ballet master. Ballet master Covent Garden 1896–1939. Founded British Ballet Company 1928.

Espinoza, Enrique (the pseudonym of **Samuel Glusberg;** 1898–), Argentine author, journalist. Edited literary review *Babel* in Buenos Aires and Santiago de Chile. Best known work *La Levita gris* stories about Jews in Argentine capital.

Esra, organization supporting Jewish settlement in Ereẓ Israel and Syria. Founded in Berlin 1884, became superfluous with Zionist large-scale projects, winding up in early 1920s.

Esselin, Alter (Ore Serebrenik; 1889–), Ukraine-born U.S. Yiddish poet; lived in Milwaukee, Wisconsin.

Essen, city in W. Germany. Jews first mentioned in 13th c. Numbers rose in 19th c. Beautiful synagogue built 1913. Number of Jews 4,500 in 1933, 1,636 in 1939; those who remained were deported. 170 in 1970.

Essenes, Jewish ascetic religious sect, organized in monastic communities toward end of Second Temple period (2nd c. B.C.E.–end 1st c. C.E.). Located mainly NW of Dead Sea shore. Identified by many with the group responsible for the Dead Sea Scrolls.

Interior of synagogue of Essen.

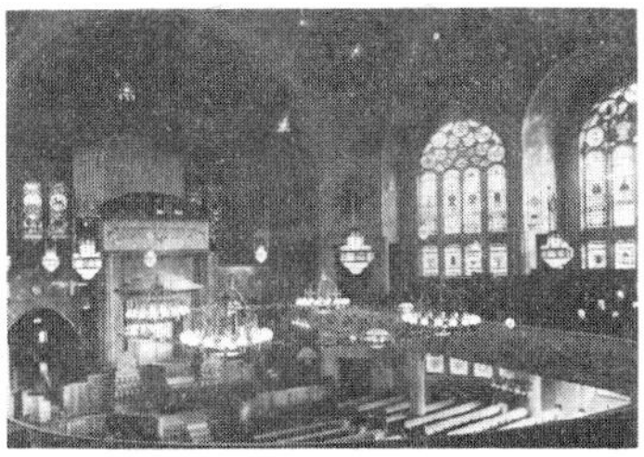

Essex County, county in N.J., U.S. Its principal city is Newark. First congregation established 1848 by German and Alsatian Jews, and later other congregations of Polish and East European Jews organized. Jewish pop. 100,000 (1971).

Esther, heroine of Book of Esther (*Megillat Ester,* read on Purim festival), which relates deliverance of Jews of Persia. Tentatively dated to Persian period (before 330 B.C.E.). Through her intervention with King Ahasuerus, who made her his queen, and with aid of her cousin Mordecai, she succeeded in averting annihilation of Persian Jewish community planned by king's adviser, Haman.

Esther (pseud. of **Malkah Lifschitz;** 1880–1943), communist, Yiddish author; b. Minsk. A leader of *Yevsektsiya* 1921–30. Edited Moscow Yiddish daily *Emes.* Arrested 1938; died in Soviet prison camp.

Esther, Fast of, fast on Adar 13, the day before Purim.

Esther Rabbah, Midrash to Book of Esther; part of *Midrash Rabbah.*

Estonia, Baltic Soviet Republic, independent 1918–40. Some 4,000 Jews lived there before WWII. Fascist anti-Semitic movement formed in 1930s. Jewish institutions disbanded 1940, following annexation of Estonia to Soviet Union. After 1941 German invasion, 3,000 Jews fled to Russia, the remainder massacred by Nazis. Jews again gathered in Estonia after war, numbering 5,436 in 1959.

Estori Ha-Parḥi (1280–1355), explorer and first topographer of Ereẓ Israel; b. in Provence, went to Ereẓ Israel c. 1313. Wrote *Sefer Kaftor va-Feraḥ,* with names, descriptions of towns, villages, ancient sites.

Eternal Lamp, see Ner Tamid.

Ethan, name of four individuals in Bible: (1) Ethan the Ezrahite, a sage; (2) a son of Zerah son of Judah; (3) a levite temple musician in the time of David; (4) an ancestor of Asaph.

Ethics of the Fathers, see Avot.

Ethiopia (Abyssinia; Heb. *Kush*), Christian Coptic kingdom in NE Africa. Its kings trace their origin to King Solomon and the Queen of Sheba. Full diplomatic relations established with Israel 1961–73, with subsequent cultural, economic, technical cooperation. For Jews in Ethiopia see Falashas.

Ethnarch (Gr. "head of the people"), title given to John Hyrcanus by decree of Julius Caesar 47 B.C.E. Also used for head of Jewish community at Alexandria.

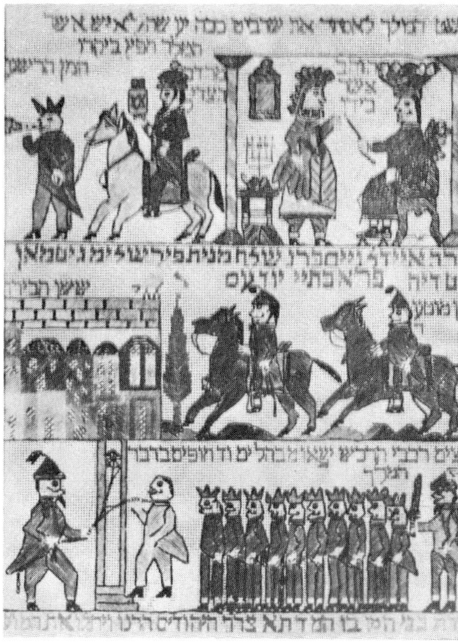

Embroidery depicting scenes from Book of Esther, Jerusalem c. 1900

Etrog, citrus fruit, one of Four Species used on Sukkot.

Etrog, Sorel (1933–), Canadian sculptor, painter. Used perpetually moving line and synthesis of geometric and organic form expressing natural growth.

Etting, pioneer Jewish family in Baltimore, Maryland. **Reuben** (1762–1848), Jeffersonian republican, U.S. marshal for Maryland 1801. **Solomon** (1764–1847), first American *shoḥet,* businessman, Jeffersonian republican. Prominent in struggle for Jewish civil rights.

Ettinger, Akiva Jacob (1872–1945), Vitebsk-born agronomist, founder and administrator of Jewish settlements in Ereẓ Israel. Prominent in Jewish National Fund purchases and

Etrog and lulav.

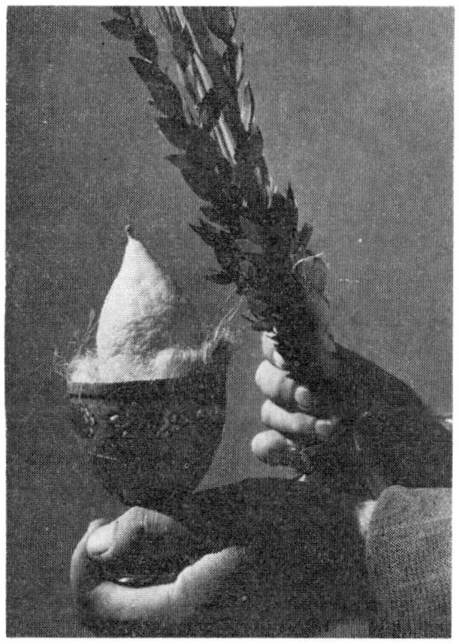

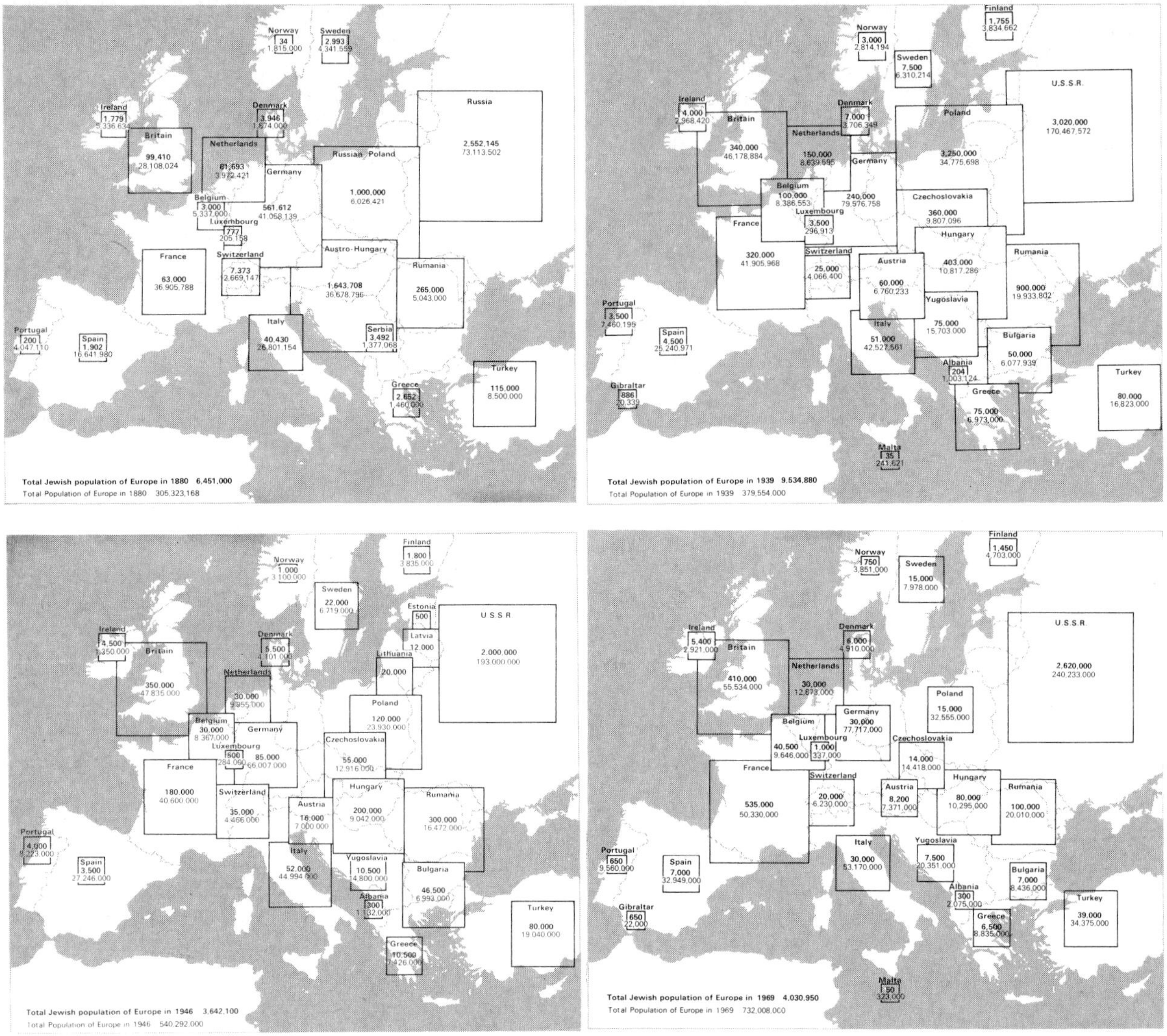

Jewish population of Europe.

settling of land (Kiryat Anavim, Jezreel Valley, etc.).

Ettinger, Mordecai Ze'ev ben Isaac Aaron Segal (1804–1863), rabbinical scholar in Poland. His son **Isaac Aaron** (1827–1891), rabbi in Przemysl and Lemberg.

Ettinger, Samuel (1919–), Kiev-born prof. of Jewish history at Heb. Univ.

Ettinger, Solomon (1803–1856), Warsaw poet, dramatist. Wrote satirical and witty plays, poems, epigrams, in Yiddish.

Ettlinger, Jacob (1798–1871), rabbi, halakhist, champion of neo-Orthodoxy in Germany. Chief rabbi of Altona.

Etzioni, Amitai Werner (1929–), sociologist; b. Germany, went to Ereẓ Israel and later U.S. Chairman sociology dept. of Columbia Univ. Wrote on political sociology and organizational analysis.

Euchel, Isaac Abraham (1756–1804), Hebrew author, Bible commentator; a leader of Haskalah in Germany; b. Copenhagen, in Koenigsberg fr. 1773, Berlin fr. 1787. Translated prayer-books into German.

Eulau, Heinz (1915–), U.S. political scientist; prof. at Stanford Univ. A leading exponent of behaviorist trend in political science.

Eulenburg, Ernst (1847–1926), music publisher. Founder Musikverlag Eulenberg, Leipzig (1874), subsequently publishers of scores, particularly miniature scores. His son, **Kurt** (1879–), transferred to London firm.

Eulogy, see Hesped.

Eupatoria, see Yevpatoriya.

Eupolemus (2nd c. B.C.E.), first significant Greco-Jewish historian. Wrote *On the Kings of Judah,* which described history to his time. Written in poor Greek, it was valuable chronicle that reflected situation in his time. An attached document, called Pseudo-Eupolemus, by someone else, is pro-Samaritan.

Europe, see entries under individual countries.

Europa, Madama (17th c.), Italian singer at Mantuan court; sister of composer Salomone de Rossi. Name came from singing part of "Europa" in musical interludes.

Eve, the first woman; wife of Adam from whose rib she was created. Cursed with pain in childbirth and subjection to her husband after tempting Adam to eat the fruit forbidden to them by divine interdict.

Even, Abba, see Eban, Abba.

Evenari, Michael (1904–), French-born Israel botanist. Prof. of plant physiology at Heb. Univ. 1934, vice-president of Univ. 1953–59. Set up experimental farms in Negev utilizing Nabatean irrigation methods.

Even ha-Ezer, see Shulḥan Arukh.

Evening Prayer, see Arvit.

Even Shemuel (Kaufmann), Judah (1886–), Israel educator, lexicographer, writer. Published vocalized

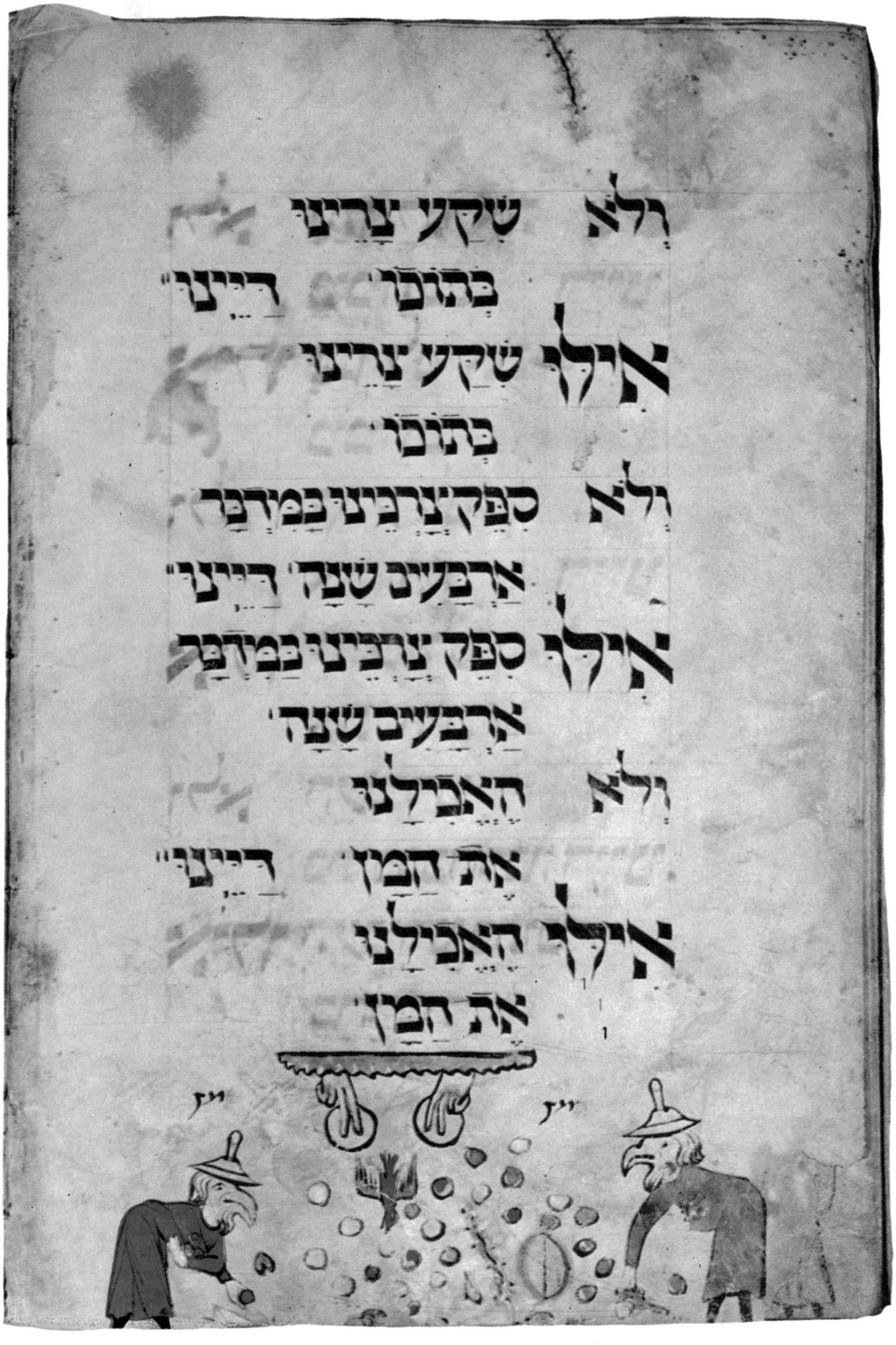
ולא שקע צרינו
בתוכו דיינו
אילו שקע צרינו
בתוכו
ולא ספק צרכינו במדבר
ארבעים שנה דיינו
אילו ספק צרכינו במדבר
ארבעים שנה
ולא האכילנו
את המן דיינו
אילו האכילנו
את המן

HAGADDAH A page from the "Birds' Head Haggadah," so called because birds' heads are substituted for the human head, which it was felt should not be depicted in accordance with the ban on graven images. The Haggadah was made in S. Germany, c. 1300. This page is part of the *Dayyeinu* hymn and shows at bottom the manna and quail falling from heaven.

HAGGADAH A page from a *Haggadah* written and illuminated in Altona-Hamburg, 1740, by a Jewish Moravian artist called Joseph Leipnick. It purports to show the labors of the Israelites in Egypt, although in fact it shows Jews in a contemporary German town.

edition of Hebrew translation of Maimonides' *Guide of the Perplexed* and Judah Halevi's *Kuzari*. Israel Prize 1973.

Even Shetiyyah, (Heb. "foundation stone"), a rock in the Holy of Holies of the Temple. In Jewish legend, the focal point of the world or the altar of the Temple. The Holy Ark was placed on it in the First Temple and in the Second Temple the censer rested on it. Identified with rock in the Dome of the Rock (Mosque of Omar).

Even-Shoshan, Avraham (1906–), Hebrew educator, writer, editor; b. Belorussia, settled in Ereẓ Israel 1925. Compiled well-known Heb. dictionary.

Ever Hadani (pseud. of **Aharon Feldman;** 1899–1972), Hebrew writer; b. Belorussia, went to Ereẓ Israel 1913. Wrote novels on and history of Jewish settlement in Galilee and Samaria.

Ever Min ha-Ḥai (Heb.), biblical injunction forbidding removal of limb or flesh from live animal and its consumption.

Evian Conference, conference of 32 nations on refugee problems called by President Roosevelt; held 1938 at Evian-les-Bains, France. Outcome of deliberations disappointed Jews who were most affected. The Great Powers refused to make any large-scale concessions to receive refugees. Only Dominican Republic announced willingness to accept many immigrants.

Evil Eye (Heb. *ayin ha-ra*), superstition that some persons may affect others malevolently by merely looking at them or at their property. It was fought by amulets, etc.

Persian amulet against evil eye, Silver, 17th century.

1 Bustanai d. 670
2 Hisdai I b. Bustanai
3 Bar Adai b. Bustanai
4 Ḥisdai II b. Bar Adai
5 Solomon b. Hisdai II c. 733–759
6 Isaac Iskoi b. Solomon
7 Judah (Zakkai b. Ahunai) d. before 771
8 Natronai b. Havivai 771
9 Moses
10 Isaac Iskoi b. Moses
11 David b. Judah c. 820–857
12 Judah I b. David c. 857
13 Natronai after 857
14 Hisdai III b. Natronai
15 Ukba c. 900–915
16 David b. Zakkai c. 918–940
17 Josiah (Hasan) b. Zakkai 930–933 (?)
18 Judah II b. David 940
19 Solomon b. Josiah c. 951–953
20 Azariah b. Solomon
21 Hezekiah I b. Judah ?
22 David I. b. Hezekiah I ?
23 Hezekiah II b. David I before 1021–1058
24 David II b. Hezekiah II 1058–d. c. 1090
25 Hezekiah III b. David II from c. 1090
26 David III b. Hezekiah III
27 Hisdai IV b. David III d. before 1135
28 Daniel b. Hisdai IV c. 1150–1174
29 Samuel of Mosul ? 1174 (?)–c.1195
30 David (b. Samuel ?) d. after 1201
31 Daniel
32 Samuel (b. Azariah ?) 1240(?)–1270(?)

1, 2, 6 H. Tykocinski, in: *Devir*, 1 (1923), 178–179.
7 *Iggeret Rav Sherira Gaon*, ed. by B.M. Lewin (1921), 104.
8 *ibid.*; L. Ginsberg, *Geonica*, 1 (1909), 16ff.
9, 10 A. Harkavy ed., *Teshuvot ha-Geonim* (1887), 378.
11–12 S. Abramson, *Ba-Merkazim u-va-Tefuẓot* (1965), 11–14.
13 Harkavy, loc. cit.
14 Abramson, op. cit., 10.
15, 16 J. Mann, in: *Tarbiz*, 5 (1934), 150 ff.
17 *ibid.*, 164; *Iggeret Rav Sherira Gaon*, 117.
18–22 Mann, in: *Sefer Zikkaron ... S. Poznański* (1927), 19, 20, 21.
23 *ibid.*, 21–22; S. Assaf, in: *Tarbiz*, 11 (1940), 152 ff.
24, 25 Mann, in: *Sefer ... Poznański*, 22–23.
26 Mann, Texts, 1 (1931), 208.
27 Abramson, in: KS, 26 (1950), 93.
28 *ibid.*, 93; idem, in: *Perakim*, 1 (1967/68), 14.
29–32 Mann, in: *Sefer ... Poznański*, 24–25; Abramson, in: *Perakim*, 1 (1967/68), 16.

Approximate list of Babylonian exilarchs during Middle Ages.

°**Ewald, Heinrich Georg August** (1803–1875), Protestant theologian; scholar of Bible, Israelite history, and Semitic languages. Studied personalities of biblical figures, particularly prophets. Considered father of theory of Hebrew syntax.

Excavations, see Archaeology.

Exchequer of the Jews, medieval English government department for Jewish affairs.

Exilarch (Aram. *resh galuta*, "head of the exile"), lay head of the Jewish community in Babylonia for the first 12 centuries C.E. An exilarch held a place in the king's council, acted as chief tax collector among the Jews, appointed judges and exercised criminal jurisdiction among his people.

Exile, Assyrian, deportation of Israelites from Northern kingdom by Assyrians. Tiglath-pileser III conquered Gilead and deported heads of Israelite clans from Transjordan (734–32 B.C.E.). When Shalmaneser V conquered Samaria (722), he exiled its people. In their place Sargon settled residents of other defeated countries. There is no certain information about the fate of the Israelite exiles (see Tribes, Lost Ten). They were settled mainly in Upper Mesopotamia first as land tenants of the king and were eventually absorbed into the foreign milieu. However, some apparently returned to Zion (Ezek. 16:53 ff.; 37:16 ff.; Ezra 2:2).

Exile, Babylonian, exiles of Judah deported to Babylonia in 6th c. B.C.E. As punishment for Jehoiakim's rebellion (598–597) Nebuchadnezzar sent 10,000 into exile, including the king and his family. Following Zedekiah's rebellion, Jerusalem was destroyed (587 or 586), and a further group sent into exile. Economically, the exiles did not fare badly, and socially they preserved their clan and family structure. Continuity in the cultural sphere is evidenced by the activity of the prophets Ezekiel, Deutero-Isaiah, Haggai, Zechariah. After Babylonia was conquered by Persians (538 B.C.E.), Cyrus permitted exiles to return.

Exodus, departure of Israelites fr. Egypt. Route and date subject of controversy but occurred sometime bet. 1450–1215 B.C.E.

Exodus, Book of (Heb. *Sefer Shemot*), second book of Pentateuch. Narrates oppression of Israelites in Egypt, Divine call to Moses, Ten Plagues, Exodus, revelation at Mt. Sinai.

BOOK OF EXODUS–CONTENTS

Chs. 1:1–18:27	The Liberation.
1:1–2:25	The enslavement of Israel and the advent of Moses.
3:1–7:13	The call and commissioning of Moses.
7:14–11:10	The plagues.
12:1–13:16	Firstborn plague and Passover rite.
13:17–15:21	The miracle at the sea.
15:22–17:16	Trouble and deliverance on the way to Sinai.
18:1–27	Jethro's visit and the organization of the people.
Chs. 19:1–24:18	The Covenant.
19:1–20:21	The theophany at Mt. Sinai and the Decalogue.
20:22–23:33	Rules and admonitions.
24:1–18	The Covenant ceremony.
Chs. 25:1–40:38	The Tabernacle and the Golden Calf.
25:1–27:19	Orders to build the Tabernacle.
27:20–31:18	Activities in the Sanctuary.
32:1–34:35	The Golden Calf.
35:1–40:38	Building the Tabernacle.

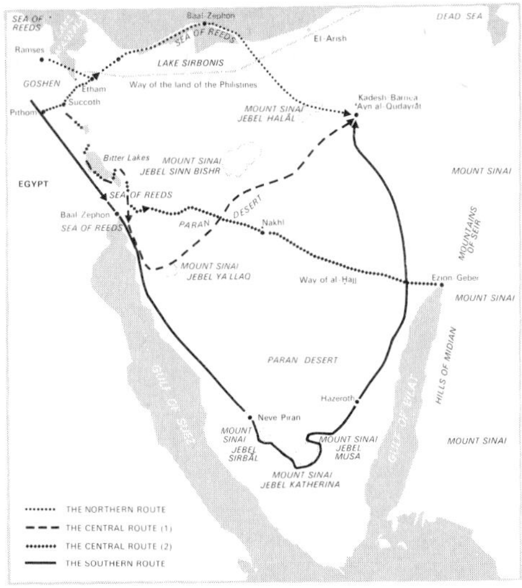

Map illustrating major theories on Israelites' Exodus route; major sites are given according to various theories.

Initial word panel depicting Exodus. Kaufmann Haggadah, Spain, 14th cent.

Exodus Rabbah, aggadic Midrash on Book of Exodus; part of *Midrash Rabbah.*

Eybeschuetz, Jonathan (c. 1690–1764), talmudist, kabbalist; b. Cracow, settled in Prague 1715, to become head of yeshivah and renowned preacher. Rabbi of Metz 1741, and of "Three Communities," Altona, Hamburg, Wandsbek, 1750. Controversy surrounded him for his suspected leanings toward Shabbateanism, with Jacob Emden as his main opponent.

Jonathan Eybeschuetz

Eydoux, Emmanuel (Roger Eisinger; 1913–), French author. Wrote poems and plays, many on Jewish themes.

Eylenburg, Issachar Baer ben Israel Leiser Parnas (1550–1623), talmudist; of Polish birth; rabbi in Gorizia, Italy.

Eynikeyt, official Yiddish organ of Jewish anti-Fascist Committee in the Soviet Union. About 700 issues appeared in 1943–48, when it was liquidated with all the other Jewish cultural institutions in the USSR.

Eytan (Ettinghausen), Walter (1910–), Israel diplomat. Director-general Foreign Ministry 1948–59. Ambassador to Paris 1959–70. Chairman, Israel Broadcasting Authority, fr. 1972.

BOOK OF EZEKIEL—CONTENTS

Chs. 1:1–3:21	The call of the prophet.
Chs. 3:22–24:27	The doom of Judah and Jerusalem.
3:22–5:17	House arrest and dramatic representation of siege and punishment.
6:1–7:27	Prophecies against the mountains of Israel and the populations of the land.
8:1–11:25	A visionary transportation to Jerusalem.
12:1–20	Dramatic representation of the exile of Judah and its king.
12:21–14:11	On false prophets and the popular attitude toward prophecy.
14:12–23	No salvation through vicarious merit.
15:1–8	Parable of the vine wood.
16:1–63	Parable of the nymphomaniacal adulteress.
17:1–24	Parable of the two eagles.
18:1–32	God's absolute justice.
19:1–14	A dirge over the monarchy.
20:1–44	The compulsory new exodus.
21:1–37	The punishing sword: three oracles.
22:1–31	Unclean Jerusalem: three oracles.
23:1–49	The dissolute sisters, Oholah and Oholibah.
24:1–14	The filthy pot: a parable of Jerusalem.
24:15–27	Death of the prophet's wife.
Chs. 25:1–32:32	Dooms against foreign nations.
25:1–17	Brief dooms against Ammon, Moab, Edom, and Philistia.
26:1–28:26	Doom against Phoenicia.
29:1–32:32	Seven oracles against Egypt.
Ch. 33:1–33	A miscellany from the time of the fall.
Chs. 34:1–39:29	Prophecies of Israel's restoration.
34:1–31	Renovation of the leadership of Israel.
35:1–36:15	Renovation of the mountains of Israel.
36:16–38	A new heart and spirit: the condition of lasting possession of the land.
37:1–28	The revival of the dead bones of Israel and the unification of its two scepters.
38:1–39:29	The invasion of Gog and his fall.
Chs. 40:1–48:35	A messianic priestly code.
40:1–43:12	A visionary transportation to the future temple.
43:13–46:24	Ordinances of the cult and its personnel.
47:1–12	The life-giving stream issuing from the temple.
47:13–48:35	Allocation of the land.

Ezekiel (6th c. B.C.E.) prophet, whose prophecies are recorded in biblical book that bears his name. A priest, he was deported to Babylonia almost certainly with King Jehoiachim in 597 B.C.E. Began prophesying in 605/4 B.C.E. and ended during reign of Nebuchadnezzar.

Ezekiel, Book of, third book of Major Prophets of Bible. Ezekiel's early prophecies rebuked the Jews who remained in Judah but after the destruction of Jerusalem, became consolatory. Then gave his vision of renewed state to be continued under theocratic guidance and including a vivid description of rebuilt Temple. Description of the Divine throne in Ch. 1 was major text for Jewish mysticism *(Ma'aseh Merkavah).*

Ezekiel, Mordecai Joseph Brill (1899–), U.S. agricultural economist. Worked in U.S. Department of Agriculture and UN Food and Agriculture Organization.

Ezekiel, Moses Jacob (1844–1917), U.S. sculptor; son of **Jacob Ezekiel** (1812–1899), communal leader in Richmond, Virginia, and Cincinnati. Sculpted many monuments in U.S. and Europe as well as portrait busts.

Ezekiel ben Reuben Manasseh (d. 1851), Baghdad philanthropist. Established Baghdad Rabbinical Seminary 1840 and several synagogues.

Ezekiel Feivel ben Ze'ev Wolf (1755–1833), "the *Maggid* of Deretschin," Lithuanian preacher; in Vilna fr. 1811.

Ezekiel the Poet, Hellenistic Jewish writer of tragedies. Author of play on the Exodus.

Ezel, see Irgun Ẓeva'i Le'ummi.

Ezion-Geber, a camping site of Israelites on their way to Canaan; port during reigns of Solomon and Jehoshaphat. N. Glueck excavated a site nr. Elath which he identified with it. Recently an alternative

Moses Jacob Ezekiel

identification with an island S. of Eilat has been suggested.

Ezobi, Jehoseph ben Hanan ben Nathan (13th c.), poet in Provence. Wrote *Ka'arat Kesef,* a well-known ethical hymn.

Ezofovich, see Jozefowicz.

Ezra (5th c. B.C.E.), priest and scribe who led group of settlers fr. Babylonian exile to Jerusalem and became key figure in reconstruction of religious life and rebuilding of Temple. Deeply involved in the proclamation of, instruction in, and observance of the Torah. His mission closely associated with that of Nehemiah. His dates are a matter of controversy. Rabbis said he established the Great Assembly and introduced square Hebrew alphabet, comparing him with Moses.

Ezra, Apocalypse of (IV Ezra), book of visions ascribed to Ezra the Scribe, written bet. 95–100 C.E. probably in Ereẓ Israel.

Ezra, David (1797–1882), president of Calcutta community, philanthropist; son of Joseph Ezra. Built synagogues.

Ezra, Sir David (1871–1947), president of Calcutta community, philanthropist.

Ezra, Elias David (1830–1886), Indian philanthropist; son of David Ezra. Built school for poor, synagogue, zoological garden in Calcutta.

Ezra, Greek Book of, Greek translation of last two chapters of II Chronicles, entire book of Ezra, and part of Nehemiah.

Ezra, Joseph ben Ezra ben Joseph Khlef (d. 1855), Baghdad notable who settled in Calcutta. Engaged in commerce, became very wealthy. D. Baghdad.

Ezra and Nehemiah, Book of, two biblical books in the Hagiographa. Originally one work written by a single hand in the 5th–4th c. B.C.E. The Book of Ezra contains 10 chapters relating events from the return from Babylon until after the return of Ezra in 458. The Book of Nehemiah contains 13 chapters describing Nehemiah's governorship of Judah. Parts of the Book of Ezra are in Aramaic.

Ezra ben Solomon (d.c. 1240), kabbalist in Gerona, Spain. His works, which greatly influenced subsequent kabbalists, bear the mark of his teacher Isaac the Blind.

BOOK OF EZRA – CONTENTS

Chs. 1–6	
The beginning of the return from Babylon and the reconstruction of the Temple.	
1:1–11	The decree of Cyrus and the response of the Exile.
2:1–70	A list of those who returned under Zerubbabel. (cf. Neh. 7:4–[73a])
3:1–13	Reestablishment of worship.
4:1–24	Building operations interrupted by Samaritan opposition.
5:1–6:22.	Reconstruction of the temple carried out after clearance with Persian authorities.
Chs. 7–10	
Character and Achievements of Ezra.	
7:1–10	Identification and journey to Jerusalem.
7:11–26	Ezra and Artaxerxes.
7:27–28	Ezra's praise of the Lord for his goodness.
8:1–14	List of the *golah* (repatriated exiles) who returned with Ezra.
8:15–20	Solicitation of Temple personnel.
8:21–23	Services of intercession before departure.
8:24–30	Selection of bearers for the sacred vessels and treasures.
8:31–36	Trip to and deliverance of vessels at Jerusalem.
9:1–10:44	The sin of the new community—marriage with outsiders.

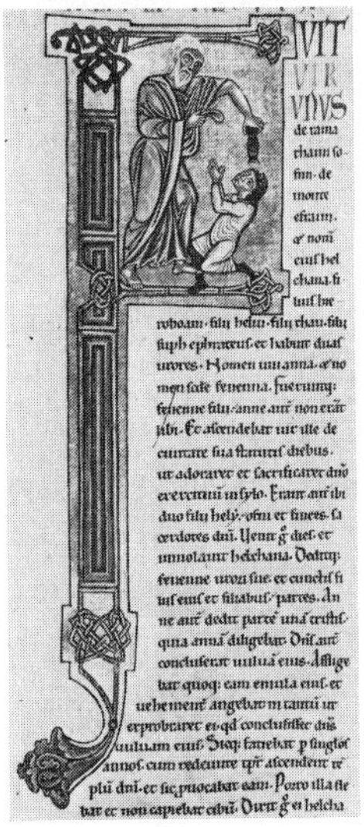

Initial letter "F" of "Fuit" from opening of I Sam. in a Latin Bible, France, 13th cent.

Fabricant, Solomon (1906–), U.S. economist. Director of research, National Bureau of Research, 1953–65. Prof. of economics, N.Y.U., 1948. Primary fields: developmental economics; business fluctuations; macroeconomic theory.

Fackenheim, Emil Ludwig (1916–), German-born rabbi, theologian, religious existentialist. Went to Canada 1940. Rabbi at Hamilton, Ontario, 1943–8. Taught philosophy at Toronto Univ. fr. 1948. Wrote on theological problems of the Nazi experience.

Factor, Max (1877–1938), U.S. cosmetics manufacturer; b. Poland, went to U.S. 1904. His firm became largest in international field by 1960s.

Fadenhecht, Yehoshua (1846–1910), religious Zionist, a founder of Mizrachi in Galicia.

Fadiman, Clifton (1904–), literary critic. Book editor, *New Yorker,* 1933–43. Widely known for radio program *Information Please* 1938–48.

Fahn, Reuben (1878–1939?), Hebrew writer, researcher on Karaism. Lived in Stanislav fr. 1918. After outbreak of WWII tried by Russians for Zionist activities, taken to Russia and disappeared.

Faïtlovitch, Jacques (1881–1955), Orientalist, researcher on Falashas. Visited Ethiopia several times before WWI and wrote about the Jews there. After WWI settled in New York and after WWII in Tel Aviv, at all times promoting interest in and obtaining assistance for the Falashas.

Faitusi, Jacob ben Abraham (d. 1812), talmudist; b. Tunis, went to Jerusalem c. 1800. Fr. 1806 emissary of Jerusalem community to N. Africa.

Faivovich Hitzcovich, Angel (1900–), Chilean lawyer, politician. Sat in deputies and senate; president of Radical Party.

Fajans, Kasimir (1887–), Warsaw-born physical chemist. Prof. at Munich Univ. 1923, Michigan Univ. fr. 1936. Discovered the element 91 (uranium x2 or brevium) with Goehring.

Falaquera (Ibn Falaguera, Palquera), Shem Tov ben Joseph (c. 1225–1295), philosopher, translator, Hebrew poet. Lived in Spain and France. Supporter of Maimonides in Maimonidean controversy. Wrote *Moreh ha-Moreh,* commentary on Maimonides' *Guide.*

Falashas, ethnic group in Ethiopia claiming to be of Jewish origin, living in the Gondar region N. of Lake Tana. The Falashas (meaning "wander," "emigrate" in their language, Old Ethiopic–Ge'ez) observe a form of Judaism based on an almost literal obedience to Bible. They are probably descended from converts to Judaism, possibly before the C.E. At one time a powerful group, they were defeated in battle and also lost many members to Christian missionaries. Falasha conditions somewhat improved at the beginning of 20th c. thanks to the activities of J. Faïtlovitch. Since 1948 the Jewish Agency assisted the Falashas and teachers were educated in Israel. Their number is estimated at 25,000–30,000.

Falasha high priest.

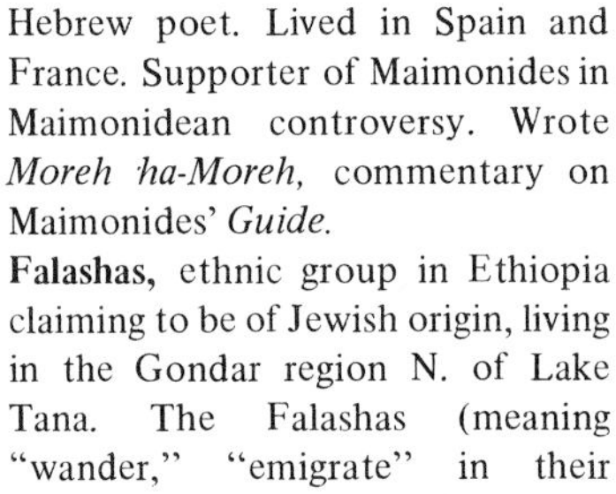

Falco, Mario (1884–1943), Italian jurist. Prof. of law at Milan until anti-Semitic laws of 1938. Wrote on canon law.

Falk, U.S. family of industrialists, philanthropists in Pittsburgh. **Maurice** (1866–1946) held extensive steel and refinery holdings. Founded Falk Foundation with his brother, **Leon** (1870–1928).

Falk, Bernard (1882–1960), British author. News editor of *Evening News,* editor of *Reynolds News* and *Sunday Dispatch.* Wrote books on Fleet Street life.

Falk, Jacob Joshua ben Ẓevi Hirsch (1680–1756), rabbi, halakhic authority; b. Cracow, lived in Lemberg, where his yeshivah was the main yeshivah of Poland. Later officiated in various German communities. Best known for his novellae on Talmud, *Penei Yehoshu'a.*

Falk, Joshua ben Alexander ha-Kohen (Sma; c. 1555–1614), Polish *rosh yeshivah* and halakhic authority. Wrote *Sefer Me'irat Einayim,* a commentary on part of Caro's *Shulḥan Arukh (Ḥoshen Mishpat).*

Falk, Kaufman George (1880–1953), U.S. physical chemist, biochemist. Taught at Columbia Univ. Wrote on ignition temperatures, refractive indexes, chemical equilibria, the electronic theory of valency.

Falk, Samuel Jacob Ḥayyim (c. 1710–1782), Galicia-born kabbalist, adventurer, Shabbatean and magician. Called the "Ba'al Shem of London," where he arrived 1742.

Fall, Leo (1873–1925), composer. Considered master of "second

Samuel Jacob Ḥayyim Falk, the "Ba'al Shem of London," by John Copley.

Faraj b. Solomon receiving a volume of medical encyclopedia from Charles I of Anjou for translation. Detail from 13th-cent. manuscript.

period of operetta." Most popular works *Die Rose von Stamboul* and *Madame Pompadour.*

Fall River, city in Mass., U.S. First Jewish settlers in 1860s and 1870s were German, but later Russian immigrants came. First congregation 1885. Jewish pop. 3,500 (1971).

Falticeni (Rum. Fălticeni), town in NE Rumania. First Jews settled c. 1772; first organized community 1780. 4,020 Jews in 1941; many sent for forced labor, returning 1944. Jewish pop. 4,700 in 1947 and 150 families in 1969.

Faludy, György (1913–), Hungarian poet, author. Served in U.S. Army in WWII. Returned to Hungary 1946, imprisoned 1951–53, fled to England 1956.

Familiants Laws (Familiantengesetze), 18th c. legislation limiting the number of Jews in Bohemia, Moravia, and Silesia entitled to found families. Introduced by Charles VI 1726–7; formally abolished 1859. The law forced many Jews to marry secretly and their offspring were not recognized as legitimate.

Fano, town in Italy. Jews there fr. 14th c. Soncino Press set up bet. 1502 and 1517. Community came to end 1593.

Fano, Guido Alberto (1875–1961), composer, writer on music. Director, conservatory, Parma (1905–11). Works include opera *Iturna.* Wrote 3-vol. *Le Studio de Pianoforte.*

Fano, Menahem Azariah da (1548–1620), rabbi, kabbalist in Italy. Expanded system of Moses Cordovero.

Faraj, Murad (1866–1956), Egyptian Karaite author, theologian. Wrote in Hebrew and Arabic. Member of Egyptian Academy for Arabic Language.

Faraj ben Solomon da Agrigento (13th c.), physician, translator, author. Attended Charles I of Anjou, king of Sicily.

Farband (Yiddish Natzionaler Arbeiter Forband – Jewish National Workers Alliance), N. American Jewish Labor Zionist fraternal order; established 1908. Merged 1971 with Po'ale Zion and American Habonim Association and name changed to Labor Zionist Alliance. 40,000 members (1972).

Farber, Marvin (1901–), U.S. philosopher; founder of International Phenomenological Society.

Farbstein, David Ẓevi (1868–1953), Warsaw-born lawyer, early political Zionist. Lived in Zurich and was member of Swiss parliament. Brother of Joshua Heschel Farbstein.

Farbstein, Joshua Heschel (1870–1948), a founder of Mizrachi in Poland. Settled in Jerusalem 1931. Member Zionist Executive 1931–33.

Farḥi, family of Damascus financiers in the 18th–19th c. **Ḥayyim,** treasurer and confidant of Aḥmad al-Jazzār Pasha (1790–1804), assisting him against Napoleon 1799. Executed 1820 by 'Abdallah Pasha. **Hillel b. Jacob** (1868–1940), physician, poet, translator *(Siddur Farḥi).* **Isaac Solomon** 19th c. author *(Tuv Yerushalayim, Zekhut ha-Rabbim).* **Joseph David** (1878–1945) headed Jewish community in Beirut.

Farrissol, Abraham ben Mordecai (c. 1451–c. 1525), Bible commentator, geographer, polemicist. Lived in Ferrara, where he represented Judaism before the duke in a religious dispute with two Dominican monks.

Farjeon, Benjamin Leopold (1838–1903), English novelist. Several of his 40 novels were on Jewish subjects.

Farkas, Ladislaus (1904–1948), Israel physical chemist; b. Slovakia. At Kaiser Wilhelm Institute in Berlin-Dahlem fr. 1928. Joined Sieff Institute in Reḥovot, Israel, and Heb. Univ. 1934. Killed in air crash.

Faro, city in Portugal. First Jewish community 15th c. Hebrew Pentateuch printed there 1487 was first book printed in Portugal. Jews expelled 1497, but settled again at beginning of 19th c. In 1970, 5 Jews in whole province.

Fast, (Heb. *ẓom, ta'anit*), voluntary abstention from food and drink.

Practiced in Judaism for spiritual ends, as a sign of repentance or mourning, or to request Divine assistance. Traditional Jewish fast days incl. the Day of Atonement (Yom Kippur) and Ninth of Av (*Tishah be-Av*), only these being observed from sundown to sundown; the 17th of Tammuz, commemorating the breaching of the walls of Jerusalem in the First Temple period and by Titus; the Tenth of Tevet, in memory of the siege of Jerusalem by Nebuchadnezzar; the Fast of Gedaliah, on the 3rd of Tishri, in memory of the slaying of Gedaliah and his associates; the Fast of Esther (*Ta'anit Ester*), on the 13th of Adar, the day before Purim; and Fast of Firstborn, the day before Passover. Private fasts incl. on yahrzeits, on wedding day until ceremony, after bad dreams, and after being present when a Torah scroll is dropped. These are observed fr. sunrise to sunset.

Howard Fast

Fast, Howard Melvin (1914–), U.S. author. His colorful historical novels include *Citizen Tom Paine* and *My Glorious Brothers,* inspired by the Maccabean revolt. Originally a strong leftist (awarded Stalin Peace Prize 1953), he described his disillusionment with communism in *The Naked God.*

Fataḥ (Ḥarakat Taḥrir Falistin – Palestine Liberation Movement), terrorist organization of Palestinian Arabs, whose aim is "liberation of the lost homeland" (i.e., Palestine) and destruction of State of Israel. Founded c. 1955 by Yassir Arafat. Initially supported by Syrian Ba'ath government and later by other Arab governments. Started with minor attacks on targets in Israel, but after Six-Day War concentrated along the cease-fire lines inside Jordan and Lebanon, and tried to infiltrate across frontier. Counteraction by Israel forces and later by Jordanian army forced them to withdraw from Jordan. Then concentrated in Lebanon and Syria while conducting terrorist activities against Israel and Zionist targets in other countries, esp. Europe.

Fearing, Kenneth (1902–1961), U.S. poet, novelist. Works largely satirical.

Feder, Ernst (1881–1964), German journalist, lawyer. Lived in Paris, Rio de Janeiro, 1933–57. Wrote *Politik und Humanitaet,* a biography of Paul Nathan.

Feder, Richard (1875–1970), Czech rabbi, author. In Theresienstadt concentration camp during WWII. Fr. 1953 chief rabbi of Moravia; fr. 1961 also of Bohemia. Wrote *Židovská tragedie* on Holocaust.

Feder, Tobias (pseud. of **Tobias Gutman;** c. 1760–1817), Haskalah writer, poet, grammarian; b. Cracow. Wrote anti-Yiddish polemic in Hebrew.

Federbusch, Simon (1892–1969), rabbi, scholar, Zionist leader; b. Galicia. Chief rabbi of Finland fr. 1931. Settled in New York 1940. President of Ha-Po'el ha-Mizrachi of America 1942–48.

Federman, Max (1902–), trade unionist, Zionist; b. Poland, in Canada fr. 1920. Leader in fur workers' union.

Federn, Paul (1871–1950), Austrian psychoanalyst; in U.S. fr. 1938. A member of Freud's inner circle. Wrote on ego psychology, psychosis, and psychology of revolution.

Fefer, Itzik (1900–1952), Soviet Yiddish poet. Faithful to party line and prominent representative of Jewish Anti-Fascist Committee during WWII. Arrested in 1948 Stalinist anti-Jewish purges and executed.

Feibush, Hans (1898–), English painter, sculptor, lithographer. Best known for his murals in churches (especially Chichester Cathedral), public buildings, and private houses.

Sculpture at Mizpeh Ramon by Dov Feigin.

Feierberg, Mordecai Ze'ev, see Feuerberg, Mordecai Ze'ev.

Feigenbaum, Aryeh (1885–), Israel ophthalmologist; b. Vienna, in Jerusalem fr. 1913. Head of Hadassah Hospital ophthalmological dept. 1922–54. Wrote first Hebrew textbook on ophthalmology.

Feigenbaum, Benjamin (1860–1932), Warsaw-born Yiddish journalist, socialist; settled in U.S. 1891. General secretary of Arbeiter-Ring.

Feigenbaum, Isaac ha-Kohen (1826–1911), Polish rabbi, *posek.* Founded first periodical devoted to rabbinic studies, the monthly *Sha'arei Torah* (1893).

Feigin, Dov (1907–), Israel sculptor; b. Russia, in Ereẓ Israel fr. 1927. A founder of the New Horizons Group.

Feigin, Samuel Isaac (1893–1950), orientalist, biblical scholar. Went fr. Russia to Ereẓ Israel and in 1920 to U.S. Taught at Univ. of Chicago. Main interest: ancient Babylonian civilization and relation to Bible.

Feigl, Bedrich (Friedrich 1884–1966), Czech painter. Best known for sketches of Prague ghetto life.

Feigl, Fritz (1891–1971), analytical chemist, leader of Brazilian Jewish community; b. Vienna, in Brazil fr. 1938. Prof. of chemistry at Univ. of Brazil; world authority on spot tests.

Feigl, Herbert (1902–), U.S. philosopher; one of founders of Vienna Circle discussion group, which espoused logical positivism. In U.S. fr. 1930; prof. at Univ. of Minnesota fr. 1940.

Feinberg, Abraham (1908–), U.S. communal leader, businessman. Headed board Kayser-Roth Corporation (until 1964). Supported Weizmann Institute and active in many organizations aiding Israel.

Feinberg, Abraham L. (1899–). Reform rabbi, b. U.S., in Toronto fr. 1943. Strong advocate of liberal social and political causes.

Feinberg, Avshalom (1889–1917), a founder of the Nili anti-Turkish underground group in Ereẓ Israel in WWI (1915). Killed by Bedouins near Rafah (N. Sinai); remains discovered 1967 and reburied on Mount Herzl, Jerusalem. Belonged to a family of pioneer settlers in Ereẓ Israel; of Russian origin.

Feinberg, David (1840–1916), Russian communal leader. Helped obtain permission to establish synagogue and cemetery in St. Petersburg. Secretary-general of Jewish

Avshalom Feinberg

Colonization Association, promoting its work in Argentina.
Feinberg, Leon (1897–1969), Russian Yiddish journalist, novelist, poet; settled in U.S. 1920. President of Yiddish PEN club.
Feinberg, Nathan (1895–), international jurist; b. Lithuania. Secretary of Comité des Délégations Juives at Paris 1922–24. Heb. Univ. fr. 1945 (prof. 1949). Published works on Jewish minority status in post-WWI Europe.
Feinberg, Samuel Yevgenyevich (1890–1962), composer. Director of piano faculty at Moscow Conservatory 1936–62. Compositions include 3 piano concertos (one awarded Stalin Prize).
Feinman, Dinah (1862–1946), Yiddish actress; wife of Sigmund Feinman. Best known for roles in *A Doll's House, Mirele Efros* and *La Dame aux Camelias.*
Feinman, Sigmund (1862–1909), Yiddish actor-manager. Best known for work in Jacob Gordin's plays.
Feinsinger, Joshua (Shaye; 1839–1872), Russian cantor. Famed as one of greatest *ḥazzanim* of mid-19th c. Chief *ḥazzan* Vilna 1868. Composed *Yoẓer* prayers for *Sefirah* Sabbaths.
Feinstein, Ḥayyim Jacob ha-Kohen (19th c.), emissary fr. Safed who visited Aden, Yemen, India. Championed the "Black Jews of Cochin" in their struggle for emancipation.
Feinstein, Moses (1895–), rabbi, leader of American Orthodoxy; b. Belorussia, went to U.S. 1937. Head of New York's Metivta Tiferet Jerusalem. A leading halakhic authority, he gave many decisions connected with modern science and technology. President of Union of Orthodox Rabbis.
Feinstein, Moses (1896–1964), Russian-born Hebrew poet, educator; went to U.S. 1912. Founded Herzliah – the Hebrew Academy and Teachers' Institute, 1921.
Feinstone, Morris (1878–1945), U.S. labor leader, secretary of United Hebrew Trades; b. Warsaw, in England until 1910. Supported labor Zionism.
Feis, Herbert (1893–), U.S. economic historian. Fr. 1948 member of Institute for Advanced Study, Princeton. Wrote, among others, *The Birth of Israel* (1969). Pulitzer Prize 1960.
Feitelson, Menahem Mendel (1870–1912), Hebrew writer, critic. Taught in Sebastopol, Yekaterinoslav. Committed suicide after Mendele Mokher Seforim had criticized him.
Feiwel, Berthold (1875–1937), Zionist leader; b. Moravia. Herzl's close associate, editor-in-chief of Zionist organ *Die Welt* 1901. One of Keren Hayesod's first directors. In London fr. 1919. Settled in Jerusalem 1933.
Fejér, Leopold (1880–1959), Hungarian mathematician. Prof. in Budapest. Author of Fejér's Theorem, which developed Fourier and divergent series.
Fekete, Michael (1886–1957), Israel mathematician. Prof. at Heb. Univ. 1929. Israel Prize 1955 for discovery of transfinite diameter.
Feld, Isaac (1862–1922), poet in Galicia, writing in German. Wrote *Dort wo die Zeder,* which was the Zionist anthem before *Ha-Tikvah.*
Feld, Jacob (1899–), U.S. civil engineer. Designs include N.Y. Coliseum, Guggenheim Museum, Yonkers Raceway. Chairman, engineering division, N.Y. Academy of Science.
Feldberg, Leon (1910–), S. African publisher, editor. Established *South African Jewish Times* 1936 and edited it until 1969.
Feldman, Grigory Petrovich (1910–1963), composer, pianist. Works include 10 Jewish songs for voice and piano, cello and piano concertos.
Feldman, Herman (1889–), U.S. army officer. Served in quartermaster corps in WWII, reaching rank of major general. Quartermaster, U.S. Army, 1949–51.
Feldman, Irving (1928–), U.S. poet. Taught at Kenyon College 1958–64 and N.Y. State Univ., Buffalo. Poetry, including *The Pripet Marshes,* frequently on Jewish themes.
Feldman, Miroslav (1899–), Yugoslav poet, playwright. Wrote mainly on war and love. President, Croatian Writers Association 1955.
Feldman, Wilhelm (1868–1919), Polish author, critic; of ḥasidic origin. Advocated assimilationism and converted to Christianity. Edited Cracow literary monthly *Krytyka* 1901–14.
Felix Libertate (Lat. "Happy through Freedom"), society for Jewish emancipation in The Netherlands. Founded in Amsterdam 1795.
Felix, Eliza Rachel, see Rachel.
Feller, Abraham Howard (1905–1952), U.S. lawyer, government official. General counsel, Office of War Information in WWII, and U.N. 1946–52, acting as Secretary-General's chief legal adviser. Committed suicide.
Feller, Shneyur Zalman (1913–), lawyer; b. Moldavia. Public prosecutor in Kishinev 1944–46. Prof. at Bucharest Univ. 1951 until 1963, when he settled in Israel; prof. of criminal law at Heb. Univ. fr. 1968.
Fellner, William John (1905–), U.S. economist; b. Budapest, emigrated to U.S. 1938. Taught at Univ. of California, Berkeley, Yale (fr. 1952). Consulting expert, U.S. Treasury Department and National Securities Board.

Berthold Feiwel, drawing by L.A. Rubitschek.

Felman, Aharon Leib (1867–1893), pioneer in citrus culture in Ereẓ Israel, author of first Heb. book on subject.
Fels, Joseph (1853–1914), U.S. manufacturer and philanthropist. Founded detergent giant Fels-Naphtha Company. Sought to spend fortune on ending unregulated free enterprise. Proselytized for Henry George's "single tax" movement and supported women's suffrage movements.
Fels, Mary (1863–1953), U.S. philanthropist; b. Bavaria; wife of Joseph Fels. Helped him with his causes. Active Zionist. Founded Joseph Fels Foundation 1925 to advance human welfare through education.
Fels, Samuel Simeon (1869–1950),

U.S. manufacturer, philanthropist; younger brother of Joseph Fels. Partner Fels-Naphtha Company. Founded Fels Planetarium, Philadelphia; established Samuel S. Fels Fund to promote research in natural and physical sciences.

Felsenthal, Bernhard (1822–1908), U.S. Reform rabbi in Chicago; b. Germany, in U.S. fr. 1854. Became enthusiastic Zionist. A founder of Jewish Publication Society and American Jewish Historical Society.

Fenichel, Otto (1897–1946), Austrian psychoanalyst. In U.S. fr. 1938. Wrote on neuroses.

Fenyes, Adolf (1867–1945), Hungarian painter. Painted scenes fr. nature, Bible, etc. Died of starvation shortly after WWII.

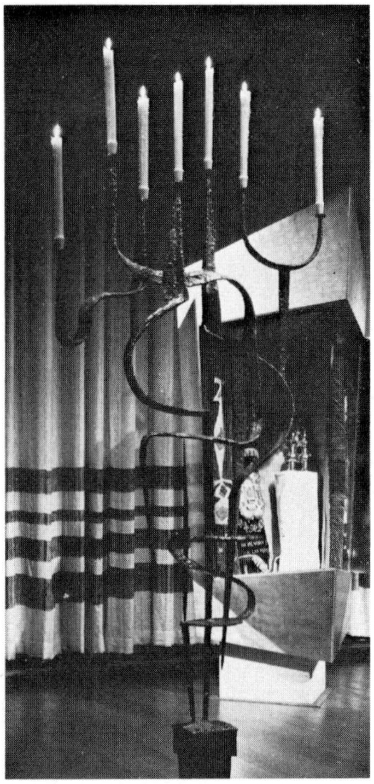

Wrought iron menorah by Herbert Ferber in Jewish chapel at Brandeis University.

Sephardi Synagogue in Ferrara, 17th century.

Fenyö, Laszlo (1902–1945), Hungarian poet. First collection pessimistic verse *Epites orgonaja* ("Organ of the Building") banned. Selected poems *Elitelt* ("The Judged") appeared 14 years after his murder by Nazis.

Fenyö (Fleischman), Miksa (1877–1972), Hungarian author, literary critic. Sec. Union of Industrialists in Hungary. Went to New York 1948. Founded and edited periodical *Nyugat.* Converted to Christianity.

Feraru, Leon (Otto Enselberg; 1887–1961), poet. Emigrated to U.S. 1913. Composed Rumanian verse about love and fate of working women. Writings include *The Development of Rumanian Poetry.*

Ferber, Edna (1887–1968), U.S. novelist, playwright. Wrote *So Big, Show Boat, Cimarron, Giant,* etc. In collaboration with George S. Kaufman wrote plays *Dinner at Eight, Stage Door.* Pulitzer Prize 1924.

Ferber (Silvers), Herbert (1906–), U.S. sculptor. Developed open calligraphic style in welded metals.

°**Ferdinand** (1452–1516), and °**Isabella** (1451–1504), Catholic monarchs of Castile and Aragon whose marriage created kingdom of Spain. Initially tolerant of Jews, employing and protecting them. Abolished Jewish communal rights 1476 and permitted establishment of Spanish Inquisition 1480. To prevent presumed large-scale influence on Conversos, Jews were expelled from Spain 1492, despite attempts at intervention. F. and I.'s motives were both political and religious.

Ferenczi (Fraenkel), Sándor (1873–1933), Hungarian pioneer psychoanalyst, psychiatrist. Wrote *Thalassa: A Theory of Genitality* (1938). Freud's closest friend, they exchanged over a thousand letters.

"Vicente Ferrer preaching" by Domenico Morone.

Ferkauf, Eugene (1921–), U.S. businessman, philanthropist. A founder of E.J. Korvette department store–supermarket chain. Endowed graduate school of social sciences at Yeshiva Univ., New York.

Fernandes Villareal, Manoel (1608–1652), Portuguese soldier, diplomat, author, of Marrano descent. Portuguese consul-general in Paris. Denounced for secret adherence to Judaism, condemned to death by Inquisition and garroted.

Fernberger, Samuel (1887–1956), U.S. psychologist. Prof. Univ. of Pennsylvania fr. 1920. Worked in psychophysics, sensation, perception, and history of psychology.

Ferrara, city in N. Italy. Jewish community fr. 1275. Important Italian Jewish center in the Renaissance. Printing press set up 1477. Refugees from Spain settled there after 1492, and Jews from Central Europe 1532. Talmud burned there 1553. In 1598, after passing under the rule of the Church, the condition of the Jews deteriorated; the Jewish badge was introduced. By 1624, Jews were confined to a ghetto, which was subject to mob attacks throughout the 17th and 18th c. Jews given civil rights 1796, finally obtaining freedom 1859–60. During Fascist period Jewish population dwindled – 822 in 1931. In WWII synagogues were devastated by the Fascists. About 100 Jews sent to extermination. There were 150 in 1970.

°**Ferrer, Vicente** (c. 1350–1419), Dominican friar, anti-Jewish preacher. His appearances frequently caused anti-Jewish outbursts. Proposed eviction of Jews fr. homes to prevent their influencing new converts. Jews forced to listen to his sermons.

Ferris, Iris (1910–1970), educator, social worker; b. Calcutta. Became gen. secr. World Girl Guide movement.

Ferrizuel, Joseph ha-Nasi (Cidellus; d.c. 1145), physician of Alfonso VI of Castile.

Festivals. Holy days enjoined by Pentateuch are divisible into two classes: (1) three pilgrimage festivals, Passover, Shavuot, and Sukkot which commemorate both historic events and agricultural cycle; and (2) Rosh Ha-Shanah and Day of Atonement in Penitential Season. Festivals are characterized by abstention from work in a lesser or greater degree and special services and customs. The post-Pentateuchal festivals are Purim and Ḥanukkah, when abstention from work is not compulsory.

FESTIVALS AND FASTS OF THE JEWISH YEAR

TISHRI
ROSH HA-SHANAH (New Year) 1
ROSH HA-SHANAH (New Year) 2
Fast of Gedaliah 3
Ten Days of Penitence
YOM KIPPUR (Day of Atonement) 10
SUKKOT (Tabernacles) 15
hol ha-mo'ed
Hoshanah Rabba
SHEMINI AZERET / SIMHAT TORAH
SIMHAT TORAH

HESHVAN

KISLEV
HANUKKAH 25 26 27 28 29 30

TEVET
1 2
Fast of Tenth of Tevet 10

SHEVAT
Tu bi-Shevat 15

ADAR
Fast of Esther 13
PURIM 14
Shushan Purim 15

NISAN
Fast of the Firstborn 14
PESAH (Passover) 15
hol ha-mo'ed 16 17 18 19 20
PESAH Last Day 21 22
Yom ha-Sho'ah (Day of Holocaust) 27

IYYAR
YOM HA-AZMA'UT (Independence Day) 5
Lag ba-Omer 18

SIVAN
SHAVUOT (Pentecost) 6 7

TAMMUZ
Fast of Seventeenth of Tammuz 17
Three Weeks of Mourning

AV
Fast of Tishah be-Av 9
Nine Days
Fifteenth of Av 15

ELUL

Counting of the Omer (Sefirah period) begins *

45 46 47 48 49

16 17 18 19 21 22 23 24 25 26 27 28 29 30 31 32 33 34 35 36 37 38 39 40 41 42 43 44

2 3 5 6 7 8 9 10 11 13 14 15

➤➤ Pilgrimage festivals

* Counting of the Omer (Sefirah period) begins

1 Simhat Torah in Israel only

MAJOR HOLIDAY | MINOR HOLIDAY | Second day holiday in Diaspora only

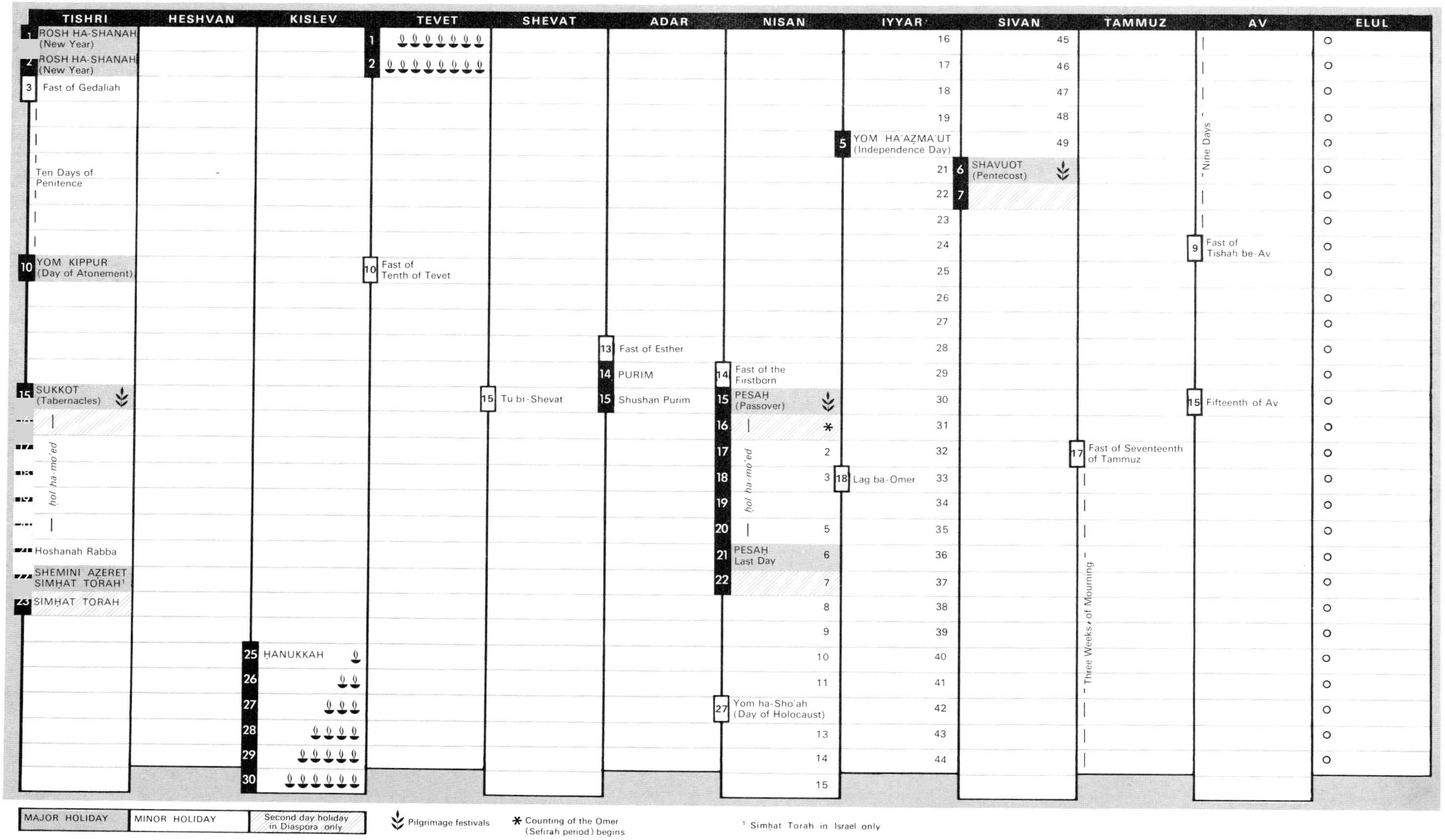

°**Fettmilch, Vincent** (d. 1616), anti-Jewish guild leader in Frankfort. Accused emperor of favoring Jews, led populace in anti-Jewish riots. Arrested and executed.

Feuchtwang, David (1864–1936), rabbi, scholar; chief rabbi of Vienna fr. 1927.

Feuchtwanger, Lion (1884–1958), German-born historical novelist. Works include *Jud Suess, The Ugly Duchess, The Oppermanns,* and a trilogy about life of Josephus. Escaped to U.S. 1940.

Feuer, Henry (1912–), U.S. organic chemist; b. Ukraine, in U.S. fr. 1941. Prof. of chemistry at Purdue Univ. fr. 1961. Wrote on organic nitrogen compounds, viscosity, absorption of gases, and rocket propellants.

Execution of Vincent Fettmilch and his followers.

Lion Feuchtwanger

Jewish family of Fez c. 1925.

Feuer, Leon I. (1903–), U.S. Reform rabbi and Zionist; officiated in Toledo, Ohio, fr. 1935.

Feuer, Lewis Samuel (1912–), U.S. educator. Prof. of sociology at Univ. of Toronto fr. 1966. Critic of theory that rise of Protestantism mainly responsible for scientific enquiry and development. Writings include *Spinoza and the Rise of Liberalism.*

Feuerberg, Mordecai Ze'ev (1874–1899), Hebrew writer; b. Russia. In his short life, he wrote essays and novels, of which *Le'an?* ("Whither? ") is regarded as one of the outstanding achievements in Hebrew fiction.

Feuerring, Maximilian (1896–), painter, art teacher, art critic. Prolific artist who twice represented Australia at Sao Paulo Biennial.

Feuermann, Emanuel (1902–1942), cellist. Emigrated to U.S. fr. Germany 1938. Considered one of great cellists of his time.

Feuerstein, Bedřich (1892–1934), Czech architect, stage designer. Introduced futurist and cubist elements into Czechoslovakia after WWI.

Feuerstein, Moses I. (1916–), U.S. lay leader of Orthodox Judaism. President of Union of Orthodox Jewish Congregations 1954–66.

Feygenberg (Imri), Rakhel (1885–1972), Yiddish and Hebrew author; b. Belorussia, settled in Ereẓ Israel 1933. Wrote about Russian Jewish life.

Feynman, Richard Phillips (1918–), U.S. physicist. Nobel Prize for Physics 1965 for modern theory of quantum electrodynamics. Prof. at California Institute of Technology.

Fez, city in Morocco. Jews settled there in 9th c. and were assigned a quarter (Funduk al-Yahudi), Persecutions occurred in the 11th and 12th c. under the Almoravides and Almohads. Conditions improved in 13th c. under the Merinides. From 1438 Jews lived in a special quarter, the mellah. Refugees fr. Spain arrived especially after 1492. Fez produced many outstanding scholars, including R. Isaac Alfasi. Hebrew presses functioned in 16th c. Several schools founded in latter 19th c. Anti-French rioters in 1912 ransacked mellah and killed 60 Jews. There were 22,484 Jews in Fez in 1947 and 12,648 in 1951, many having emigrated to Israel, France, or Canada. There were about 1,000 in 1969.

Fichman, Jacob (Ya'akov; 1881–1958), Hebrew poet, critic, editor; b. Bessarabia, settled in Ereẓ Israel 1925. Edited literary periodicals, anthologies. Works include prose poems, symbolic nature sketches, verse on nature and biblical themes.

Fiedler, Arthur (1894–), U.S. conductor. Led Boston Pops Orchestra fr. 1930.

Fiedler, Leslie Aaron (1917–), U.S. author, critic. Prof. at Montana State Univ. and fr. 1965 at New York State Univ. at Buffalo. Wrote short stories, novels, and especially literary studies and critical essays (*Love and Death in the American Novel, The Jew in the American Novel).*

Figo (Picho), Azariah (1579–1647), Venetian rabbi, preacher. Published *Binah le-Ittim,* collection of sermons.

Filderman, Wilhelm (1882–1963), Rumanian Jewish leader. Led Rumanian community before and after WWII. Escaped to Paris 1948.

Filene, family of U.S. entrepreneurs and social reformers in Boston, Mass. **William** (b. 1830), founded Boston dept. store Filene's. His son **Edward Albert** (1860–1937) promoted development of consumer cooperatives. Another son, **Albert Lincoln** (1865–1957), active in New Deal liberal economies.

Filipowski, Ẓevi Hirsch (1816–1872), Hebraist, editor, mathematician; b. Lithuania, settled in London 1839. Wrote *Mo'ed Mo'adim, Anti-Logarithms,* etc. Founded society for publishing medieval Heb. texts.

Filler, Louis (1912–), U.S. historian. Prof. of American civilization at Antioch College 1946. Major work on American reform movements and cultural history. Writings include *Crusaders for American Liberalism* and *Randolph Bourne.*

Fima (Effraim Roeytenberg; 1916–), painter; b. Harbin, emigrated to Israel 1949, in Paris fr. 1961.

Final Solution (Germ. *Endloesung),* the Nazi plan for the extermination of the Jews through mass murder by shooting, gassing, or starvation (1941–45). The order was given by Hitler in March 1941.

Finaly Case, the case of two Jewish orphans, Robert and Gerald Finaly, and the legal struggle for their return to Judaism in France, 1948–53. The two were baptized after WWII, their

parents having died in a German concentration camp, and were eventually smuggled out of France and handed over to Basque monks. Legal action was taken by the children's aunt, residing in Israel, and the two finally brought to Israel to be raised as Jews after a 5-year trial accompanied by violent controversy in France.

Finbert, Elian-J. (1899–), Jaffa-born French author; son of Israel Feinberg, Rishon le-Ẓion pioneer. Camel driver and Nile boatman before becoming writer. Writings include *Le Fou de Dieu* and *Le destin difficile,* both novels on Jewish problems.

Finci, Eli (1911–), Yugoslav editor, author. Department head, Geca Kon publishing organization; director, Yugoslav Dramatic Theater. Founder, publisher Brazda review (1935).

Fine, Louis (1894–), Canadian labor conciliator; b. England. International vice-president of United Hat and Millinery Workers Union of U.S. and Canada. Became conciliation officer, Ontario government, in 1934.

Fine, Reuben (1914–), U.S. chess master, psychoanalyst. Prof. of psychology at City College of New York. Wrote books on chess and psychology.

Fine, Sidney (1920–), U.S. historian. Prof. of history at Univ. of Michigan 1959. Main interests intellectual aspects of 20th c. American reform and automobile industry.

Fineman, Ḥayyim (1886–1959), U.S. educator, Zionist worker; b. Russia. Headed English dept., Temple Univ., Philadelphia, fr. 1911. A founder of American Organization of Po'alei Zion 1904 and *Jewish Frontier* magazine 1934, of which he was an editor. His son **Daniel** (1915–), settled in Israel 1953, headed English dept. of Tel Aviv Univ fr. 1964.

Fineman, Irving (1893–), U.S. novelist. Author of biography of Henrietta Szold.

Finer, Herman (1898–1969), U.S. political scientist. Wrote *Theory and Practice of Modern Government, Road to Reaction, Dulles over Suez.* Taught at London School of Economics 1920–42, Chicago Univ. 1946–63.

Fingerman, Gregorio (1890–), Argentinian psychologist. Head National Institute for Secondary Education, Buenos Aires. Director Institute of Professional Orientation.

"Self-Portrait" by Fima.

Louis Finkelstein

Finnish girls entering Jerusalem during 1965 Four-Day March (G.P.O.).

Fininberg, Ezra (1889–1946), Soviet Yiddish poet. Followed party line but with many Jewish themes. Died of wounds received in WWII.

Fink, Theodor (1855–1942), Australian press magnate, lawyer, politician. Member Legislative Assembly of Victoria 1894–1904, minister without portfolio. Controlled Herald Newspapers.

Finkel, Eliezer Judah (1879–1965), head of Mir yeshivah in Lithuania. Settled in Jerusalem c. 1940.

Finkel, Joshua (1904–), U.S. orientalist, scholar; b. Warsaw. Taught Semitic languages at Yeshiva Univ.

Finkel, Nathan Ẓevi ben Moses (1849–1927), head of Slobodka yeshivah in Lithuania, a leader of Musar movement. In Hebron fr. 1925.

Finkelman, Jacob (1907–), Canadian jurist, labor relations authority; b. Russia. Prof. at Univ. of Toronto 1944. Gave first labor law course in Canada 1932. Chairman, Ontario Labor Relations Board, 1934–37.

Finkelstein, Heinrich (1865–1942), German pediatrician. Headed Berlin hospital until Nazi regime, when he went to Chile. Wrote on his discoveries concerning infant diseases.

Finkelstein, Louis (1895–), U.S. rabbi, scholar, educator. Taught theology at Jewish Theological Seminary fr. 1924. Provost of the Seminary 1937, president 1940, chancellor 1951–72. Key figure in development of Conservative Judaism. Wrote on social and economic history of mishnaic period (*The Pharisees, Akiba).* Also *Jewish Self-Government in the Middle Ages.* Edited *The Jews: Their History, Culture, and Religion.*

Finkelstein, Noah (1871–1946), Zionist leader, Yiddish publisher. Founded influential Yiddish daily *Haynt* in Warsaw. Published Yiddish paper in Paris 1926–40.

Finland, republic in N. Europe. The first Jews there were Cantonists (first half 19th c.). There were about 1,000 Jews by 1889, when they were authorized to reside in Helsinki, Turku, and Vyborg. Full civil rights were granted in 1917, with Finland's independence. Jewish pop. increased to 2,000 between the two wars. In WWII, Finland resisted anti-Jewish legislation despite German pressure. Formal relations with Israel started 1948. Jewish pop. 1,450 (1971).

°**Finn, James** (1806–1872), English philo-Semite; British consul in Jerusalem 1845–62. Often protected Jews from Ottoman authorities. Active in resettlement of Jews in Ereẓ Israel.

Finzi, Italian family. **Mordecai (Angelo) ben Abraham** (d. 1476), scientist, physician, banker in Bologna and Mantua. **Isaac Raphael b. Elisha** (1728–1812), of Ferrara, preacher and vice-president of the French Sanhedrin 1806. **Joseph** (1815–1886), b. Mantua, patriot of the Risorgimento. **Gerald** (1901–1956), English musician, composer.

Fiorentino, Salomone (1743–1815), poet in Tuscany. Court poet to Grand Duke Ferdinand III.

Firkovich, Abraham (1786–1874), Karaite leader and scholar; b. Poland. Active mainly in Crimea, traveling and purchasing ancient mss., especially of Bible, which formed Firkovich collections in Leningrad Public Library. Wrote *Avnei Zikkaron.* His work was

Abraham Firkovich

"Redemption of the Firstborn" by Bernard Picart, 1722.

attacked as abounding in forgeries but his strict scientific contribution was also recognized.

Firstborn. The Bible gave the firstborn male special status and privileges. At one time they were devoted to cultic service. Later they were "redeemed" from this obligation from a *kohen* at a special ceremony, still customary in Orthodox circles. The firstborn was also entitled to receive a double portion of the parental heritage (but not in modern Israel law). On Nisan 14, the eve of Passover, all firstborn males are instructed to fast ("Fast of Firstborn"). Male firstlings of cattle were given to priest to be sacrificed.

First Fruits (Heb. *bikkurim*). The Bible (Deut. 26:1–11) obligated owner of land in Israel to take its first ripe fruits to the Temple. This duty was limited by the rabbis to the seven species (Deut. 8:8) peculiar to Israel. They were brought from Shavuot until Sukkot. In modern Israel kibbutzim celebrations evocative of the bringing of the first fruit are held on Shavuot.

Fischel, Harry (1865–1948), U.S. businessman, philanthropist; active in Jewish communal affairs. Established Foundation for Research in Talmud in Erez Israel 1933. D. in Jerusalem.

Fischel, Walter Joseph (1902–1973), scholar of Asian Jewry; b. Germany. Prof. at Univ. of California. Wrote on Jews in India, Persia, etc.

Fischer, Gyula (Julius; 1861–1944), Hungarian scholar, chief rabbi of Budapest 1921–43.

Fischer, Jean (1871–1929), Zionist leader in Belgium. A leader of Political Zionism after d. of Herzl. His son **Maurice** (1903–1965), Israel diplomat (ambassador to France, Italy, etc.).

Children at first-fruits festival in Tel Aviv.

Fischer, Josef (1871–1949), rabbi, historian of Danish Jewry; b. Hungary, *dayyan* and librarian in Copenhagen fr. 1893.

Fischer, Louis (1896–1970), U.S. writer, journalist; authority on Soviet Russia (*Stalin and Hitler, The Life and Death of Stalin, The Life of Lenin,* etc.). Described his disillusionment with Communism in *The God that Failed* (ed. Arthur Koestler).

Fischer, Otokar (1883–1938), Czech writer. Prof. of German literature in Prague. Wrote critical essays, poetry, plays.

Fischer, Robert (Bobby; 1943–), U.S. chess master. U.S. champion in his teens. Won world championship against Boris Spassky 1972. Joined Christian Sabbatarian Sect.

Fischer, Ruth (née **Eisler;** 1895–1961), leading figure in German Communist party; sister of Gerhardt and Hanns Eisler. Member of Reichstag 1924–33. Emigrated to U.S. 1941. Wrote on international communism.

Fischer, Samuel (1859–1934), German publisher. Fischer Verlag was leading literary publishing house in Germany until Nazi period. Then transferred to other countries but returned to Germany after WWII under son-in-law **Gottfried Bermann-Fischer** (1897–).

Fischhoff, Adolf (1816–1893), Austrian politician, a leader of 1848 revolution. Physician in Vienna.

Fiscus Judaicus (Lat. "Jewish Fund"), a fund of Roman Empire into which was paid special tax levied on Jews after destruction of Temple (70 C.E.).

Fishbein, Morris (1889–), U.S. physician, editor, medical author. Edited *Journal of the American Medical Association* 1924–49. Considered official spokesman for U.S. medicine. Edited *Medical World News* fr. 1960.

Bobby Fischer at tournament in Israel in 1968.

Adolf Fischhoff

Fishberg, Maurice (1872–1934), U.S. physician, physical anthropologist; b. Russia, in U.S. fr. 1889. Prof. of medicine at New York Univ. Authority on pulmonary tuberculosis. Wrote *The Jews: A Study of Race and Environment,* maintaining heterogeneity in racial composition of modern Jews.

Fishel, Ephraim (15th–16th c.), Polish banker, farmer, communal leader. Dealt with Polish aristocracy and became chief collector of Jewish taxes. Opposed by community leaders and failed to collect taxes.

Fishel, Moses (d. 1542), Polish physician, rabbi; martyr. Physician for state dignitaries; appointed leader of Jews without consent of community. D. in prison after false accusations.

Fishel, Rachel (fl. 1500), Polish moneylender; wife of Moses. Creditor of kings of Poland.

Fishel, Stephan (d. after 1532), Polish banker. Converted to Christianity c. 1495, but continued to be tax farmer. Ennobled, taking name of Powidzki.

Fisher, Eddie (1928–), U.S. singer. Became famous for such songs as "Oh My Papa." Appeared in films and on stage.

Fisher, Max M. (1908–), U.S. industrialist, community leader. Pioneer in Michigan's oil industry. Special adviser on urban and community affairs to President Nixon. A founder of the extended Jewish Agency and a leader of the UJA.

Fisher, Sir Woolf (1912–), New Zealand industrialist, philanthropist. Manufacturer of refrigerators and home appliances.

Fishman, Jacob (1878–1946), Yiddish editor, U.S. Zionist leader. Managing editor *Jewish Morning Journal.*

Fishman, Joshua Aaron (1926–), U.S. educator. Prof. of social sciences at Yeshiva Univ. fr. 1966. Pioneer in sociolinguistics. Active in Yiddish culture.

Fishman, Judah Leib, and **Ada,** see Maimon, Judah Leib.

Fishman, William Harold (1914–), U.S. biochemist. Joined Tufts–New England Center Hospital 1948; director, cancer research, 1957. Writings include *Physiopathology of Cancer.*

Fitelberg, Grzegorz (Gregor; 1879–1953), conductor, composer. Conducted Warsaw Philharmonic Orch. 1906–11, Vienna Opera 1912–13, Moscow Bolshoi Ballet. Formed Polish radio's symphony orchestra. Composed symphonies, overtures, rhapsodies.

Coin struck by Nerva to commemorate abolition of Fiscus Judaicus

Raising the flag at Gerofit, southern Aravah, Israel.

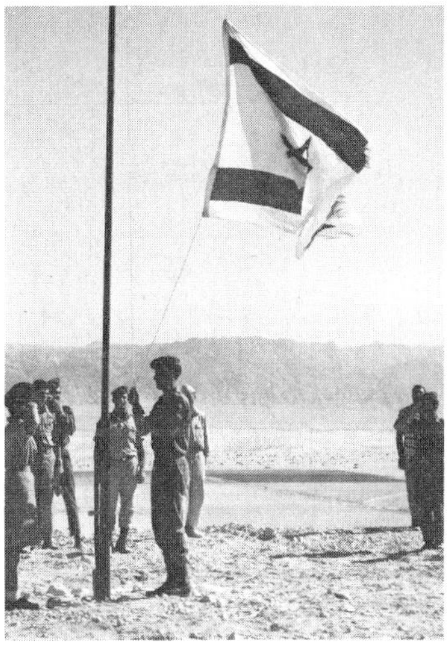

Five Books of Moses, see Pentateuch.

Flag. The Zionist flag, presently the flag of the State of Israel – two blue stripes on white background with a Shield of David in the center – was created by David Wolffsohn on the model of the *tallit.*

Flanagan, Bud (1896–1968), British comedian. Became prominent in 1930s with partner Chesney Allen. Part of "Crazy Gang" whose shows ran for many years at Victoria Palace.

Flavius, Josephus, see Josephus.

Fleckeles, Eleazar ben David (1754–1826), Prague-born rabbi, author. Headed opposition to Frankists. Sermons collected in *Olat Ḥodesh.*

Fleg, Edmond (Flegenheimer; 1874–1963), French poet, playwright. Many of works dealt with Jewish themes (*Le Mur des Pleurs, Pourquoi je suis Juif, Ecoute Israël).* Greatly influenced French Jewish youth. Wrote religious poetry, plays, biographical works, essays, translations.

Flegenheimer, Julien (1880–1938), Swiss architect; brother of Edmond Fleg. Designed League of Nations Palace, Geneva.

Fleischer, Judah Loeb (1886–1955), Hungarian scholar; expert on Abraham ibn Ezra. His son **Ezra** (1928–), Hebrew poet and scholar (*Massa Gog).* Emigrated to Israel 1960. Taught at Heb. Univ.

Edmond Fleg, bust by Chana Orloff, 1921.

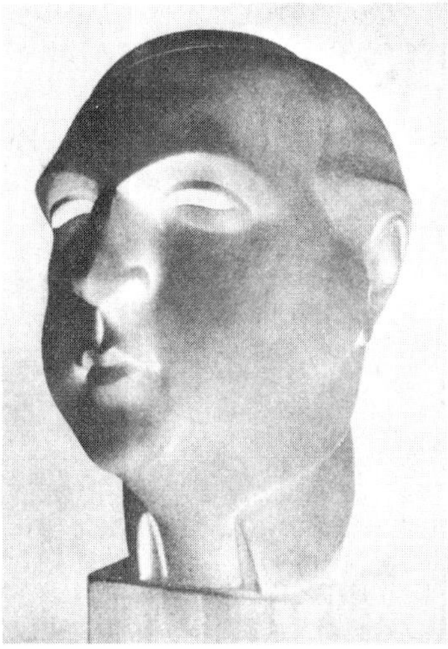

Fleischer, Max (1889–1972), cartoonist, producer. Creator of Popeye and other cartoon characters.

Fleischer, Nathaniel Stanley (Nat; 1887–1972), U.S. historian and writer on boxing (*The Ring Record Book and Boxing Encyclopedia).* Known as "Mr. Boxing."

Fleischmann, Gisi (1897–1944), Zionist women's leader in Slovakia. Played prominent part in rescue operations during Holocaust. Murdered at Auschwitz.

Flesch, Carl (1873–1944), violinist, teacher. Taught at Bucharest 1897–1902, Amsterdam 1903–08, Curtis Institute, Philadelphia 1924–28.

Flexner, Abraham (1866–1959), U.S. scholar, educator; b. Louisville. Founded and directed Institute for Advanced Study at Princeton 1930–39.

Flexner, Bernard (1865–1945), U.S. lawyer, Zionist leader; lived in Kentucky, Chicago, New York. First president of Palestine Economic Corporation.

Flohr, Salo (1908–), Russian chess master. A leading Soviet grand master and writer on chess.

Flood, The, deluge produced by God to destroy mankind for its sinfulness. Described in Book of Genesis, the central figure being the righteous Noah, who, alone of mankind, was to be saved. On God's instructions, he built an ark, taking aboard the members of his family, together with male and female representatives of all fauna specimen. The flood, which lasted 150 days, blotted out all existence on earth. Parallels to the story have been found in Mesopotamian literature.

Florence, city in Tuscany, C. Italy. Community established 1437, with the opening of loan banks by Jews. Despite occasional outbreaks of violence and expulsions, Jews generally fared well under the Medici,

Florence synagogue.

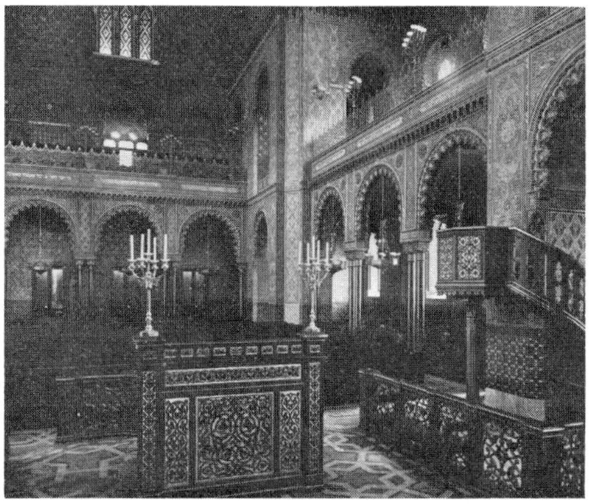

until the introduction of the Jewish badge and the ghetto by Cosimo (1567, 1571). They were emancipated bet. 1849–1860. Site of Collegio Rabbinico Italiano fr. 1899 when community became center of Jewish culture in Italy (due to influence of Chajes, Margulies, Pacifi, etc.). There were 2,730 Jews in 1931. In WWII (1943, 1944), 243 were deported to Germany. There were 1,400 Jews in 1971. The beautiful 1882 synagogue is a national monument.

Florida, U.S. state. First organized Jewish community in Jacksonville in early 1850s. First congregation, Congregation Ahavath Chesed, 1867. Jewish pop. increased rapidly after WWII with Jews playing important role in economic life and many spending winter months in southern area of state. Jewish pop. 260,000 (1971).

Flusser, David (1917–), scholar in comparative religion; of Czech origin. Prof. at Heb. Univ. fr. 1962. Authority on early Christianity.

Foa (Foà), Italian family, known fr. 15th c. **Eliezer Naḥman** (d.c. 1641), rabbi, kabbalist in Reggio Emilia. **Pio** (1848–1923), pathologist, Italian senator. Of the French branch, **Edouard** (1862–1897), African explorer. One branch of the family devoted itself to Hebrew printing.

Foa, Esther Eugenie Rebecca (1799–1853), French author. Wrote novels and stories on Jewish themes for juveniles. Subsequently abandoned Judaism.

Fodor, Andor (1884–1968), Israel biochemist, b. Budapest, in Ereẓ Israel fr. 1923. First prof. of biochemistry at Heb. Univ.

Foerder, Yeshayahu (Herbert; 1901–1970), Berlin-born Israel economist, banker. One of the founders of Haavarah for transferring Jewish assets fr. Germany to Palestine in 1930s. Fr. 1957 chairman of Bank Leumi.

Jewish communities in Florida, with dates of establishment.

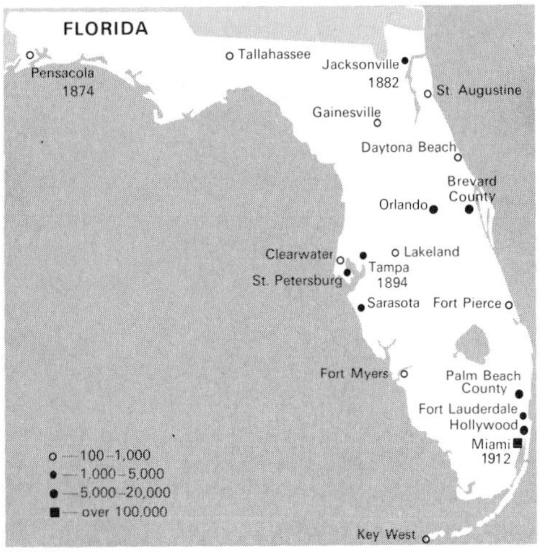

The Foa printers' mark.

Foldes, Jolan (1903–1963), Hungarian author. She wrote prizewinning novel *A halaszo macska utcaja* ("The Street of the Fishing Cat"), portraying emigré life in Paris.

Folkspartei. (1) In Poland, "Yidishe Folkspartei in Poilen" – Folkist Party, Jewish populist party founded 1918. Of secular character. Emphasized Yiddish as traditional language. (2) In Russia, Jewish populist party influential in E. Europe, active 1906–39. Founded by historian S. Dubnow, ideologist of Jewish autonomism. Disintegrated in 1930s.

Fomin, Yefim Moiseyevich (d. 1941), Soviet soldier. Conducted defense of Brest–Litovsk fortress against Germans. Captured with fall of fortress and executed. Made Hero of Soviet Union.

Fondane (Fundoianu), Benjamin (1898–1944), poet in French and Rumanian (*Ulysse, Titanic, L'Exode)*; b. Rumania, settled in France 1923. Murdered at Birkenau (Auschwitz).

Fondiller, William (1885–), U.S. electrical engineer. Vice-president and treasurer of Bell Telephone Laboratories. Research associate at Columbia Univ. school of engineering 1935–50. Patents on loading carts, transformers, cables, etc.

Fonseca, Alvaro de (c. 1652–1742), English merchant. Active in India 1683–1700. Alderman of Madras.

Fonseca, Daniel de (1672–c. 1740), Marrano physician, diplomat; fr. Portugal. Escaped to France and embraced Judaism. Attended Prince Mavrocordato at Bucharest and the Sultan at Constantinople.

Ford, Alexander (1908–), Polish film producer. Director, Film Polski, 1945. Films include *Border Street*, dealing with Warsaw Ghetto, *Five Boys of Barski Street*. Settled in Israel 1970.

Foreman, Carl (1914–), U.S. film writer, producer, director. Scenarios include *Champion, High Noon, and Bridge on the River Kwai.* Wrote and produced *Guns of Navaronne.*

Foreman, Milton J. (1862–1935), U.S. public official. Member Chicago City Council for 12 years after admission to bar 1899. Col. in field artillery during WWI. Retired Lieutenant General 1931. A founder of American Legion 1919.

Forman, Milos (1932–), Czech film director. Films include *Loves of a Blond, The Fireman's Ball,* wry treatment of Czech bureaucracy, and *Growing Up.*

Formiggini, Angelo Fortunato (1878–1938), Italian publisher, editor, writer. Committed suicide following introduction of anti-Semitic laws.

Formstecher, Solomon (1808–1889), German Reform rabbi, philosopher; editor of *Die Israelitische Wochenschrift,* author of *Die Religion des Geistes.* Believed that Emancipation was part of internal spiritual process in history of mankind for removal of barriers between nations.

Fortas, Abe (1910–), U.S. lawyer, Supreme Court justice. Public posts included undersecretary Dept. of Interior 1942–46, presidential aide to Pres. Johnson 1963, Supreme Court Justice fr. 1965. His nomination as chief justice, Supreme Court (1968), blocked by Senate opponents. Resigned post 1969 as result of disclosure of his having accepted fee while on the Court from doubtful sources.

Fortes, Meyer (1906–), British social anthropologist. Prof. at Cambridge. Developed modern theory of primitive political systems.

Forward, see Jewish Daily Forward.

Lukas Foss

Foss (Fuchs), Lukas (1922–), U.S. composer, conductor, pianist. Director of Buffalo Philharmonic Orchestra fr. 1963, Israel Radio Symphony Orchestra fr. 1972. Wrote cantatas, operas, and avant-garde orchestral works.

Fossoli, town in Emilia, N. Italy, used by Germans as Jewish concentration camp in WWII.

Fould, family of French bankers and politicians. Fould-Oppenheim banking house founded by **Ber Leon Fould** (1767–1855). His son **Benoît** (1792–1858), active in Jewish communal affairs, sat in the Chamber of Deputies. Minister of finance under Louis Napoleon.

Four Cups, see Arba Kosot.

Four Questions, see Mah Nishtannah.

Four Species (Heb. *arba'ah minim),* the *etrog,* palm branch, 2 willow and 3 myrtle twigs taken together on Sukkot in accordance with Lev. 23:40. They are popularly referred to as the *lulav* (=palm branch).

Fox, Bernard Joshua (1885–), N. Irish judge. Legal adviser to government of N. Ireland 1939–44. Chaired wartime Price Regulation Committee for N. Ireland. Given judgeship. Recorder of Belfast fr. 1944.

Fox (Fuchs), William (1879–1952), U.S. film producer. Founded Fox Films.

Fraenkel, Abraham Adolf (1891–1965), Israel mathematician. Prof. of mathematics at Heb. Univ. fr. 1933. Made important contributions to set theory.

Fraenkel, David ben Naphtali Hirsch (David Mirels; 1707–1762), German rabbi in Dessau (where Moses Mendelssohn was his pupil), chief rabbi of Berlin. His commentary to Jerusalem Talmud is one of two basic commentaries on that work.

Fraenkel, Eduard (1888–1970), classical scholar. Taught in Germany until 1933. Prof. of Latin at Oxford fr. 1935.

Fraenkel, Faiwel (Bar Tuviah; 1875–1933), Hebrew author, publicist; b. Russia, in W. Europe fr. 1901. First Hebrew author to discuss social sciences in depth. Wrote on history of asceticism among Jews.

Fraenkel, Isaac Seckel (1765–1835), German banker, Hebrew translator. Translated Apocrypha into Hebrew.

Fraenkel, Jonas (1879–1969), Swiss literary historian. Prof. at Berne. Specialized in German-Swiss literature.

Fraenkel, Liepmann (1774–1857), miniature painter. Painted members of Swedish nobility and Danish royal family.

Fraenkel-Teomim, Baruch ben Joshua Ezekiel Feiwel (1760–1828), rabbi in Poland and Moravia; founder of yeshivah in Leipnik. His glosses to Babylonian Talmud were published in most Lemberg editions.

Fram, David (1903–), Yiddish poet; b. Lithuania, in S. Africa fr. 1927. Much of his later poetry deals with S. African themes and landscapes.

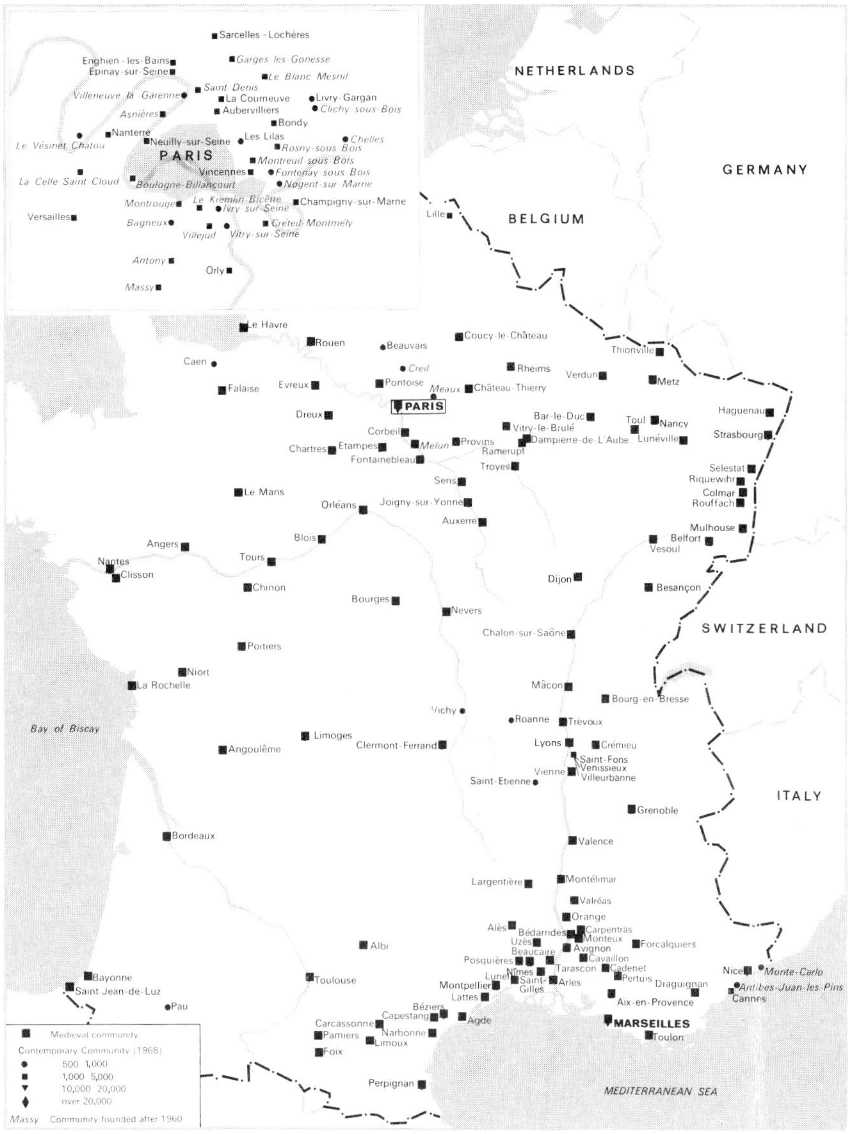

Main Jewish communities in France in the Middle Ages and in 1968.

France, republic in W. Europe. Individual Jews present from 1st c. (Roman period). Abundant evidence from 465 on. Despite some largely ineffective Church anti-Jewish legislation, conditions of Jews largely favorable until period before 1st Crusade. Jews well integrated into economy, incl. agriculture. Jewish scholarship developed only fr. 11th c., outstanding figure being Rashi. General reaction in 11th c. W. Europe. General persecutions throughout country, for 5 years following 1007, sparked by stories that Jews had helped in destroying Holy Sepulcher; Jews massacred, forced to convert, expelled. Similar events 1063. In 1st Crusade, Jews attacked in Rouen and Lorraine. In blood libel at Blois 1171, 31 Jews burnt at stake. Crusade against Albigenses 1209 ruined many Jewish communities in S. France that previously had prospered. Persecutions in W. provinces 1236. Talmud burned in Paris 1242. Series of local and general persecutions, worst being expulsion of 1306, Pastoureaux (1320) and Black Death (1348–49) massacres, culminated in almost total expulsion 1394. Several major medieval centers of Jewish scholarship, notably rabbis of N. France (Tosaphists and others) and Kabbalists and scholars of Provence. By 1550, "secret Jews" were arriving fr. Spain and Portugal, and Jews fr. E. Europe came fr. mid-17th c. On eve of French Revolution, c. 40,000

Charles de Gaulle at memorial to French Jewish soldiers who fell in WWI.

Jews, Ashkenazim in Alsace-Lorraine and Paris, Sephardim in S. Jews received French citizenship 1790–91. Napoleon convened Assembly of Jewish Notables 1806, Sanhedrin 1807, following which Consistorial system was established. Alongside progressive emancipation and improvement of conditions, manifestations of anti-Semitism continued throughout 19th c., notably Dreyfus Affair. Large immigration fr. E. Europe, esp. Russia, bet. 1880 and WWI, also fr. Balkans, and fr. Germany in 1930s. Jews actively involved in Resistance in WWII. 83,000 Jews murdered by Nazis in WWII. Jewish pop. 180,000 (1945). In 1950s and early 1960s community transformed by large immigrations fr. N. Africa, incl. almost all of 120,000 Algerian community. Jewish pop. 550,000 (1971).

Frances, Immanuel ben David (1618–c.1710), Italian Hebrew poet. Life filled with difficulties and misfortunes. Together with his brother **Jacob** (1615–1667), also a talented poet, fought against supporters of Kabbalah and Shabbetai Ẓevi. Introduced in his Hebrew poetry *terza rima* and *ottava rima* of Italian prosody.

Franche-Comté, region and former province in E. France. Jews there after expulsion fr. France 1182. Expelled at time of Black Death 1348, returned 1355, expelled again 1374. Last Jew to live there before French Revolution driven out 1409.

Franck, Adolphe (Jacob; 1809–1893), French philosopher. Prof. at Collège de France. Pres. Alliance Israélite Universelle. Wrote on general philosophy and Jewish topics, incl. first scientific work on Kabbalah.

Franck, Henri (1888–1912), French poet. Author of *La Danse devant l'Arche.* Model of hero of de Lacretelle's novel *Silbermann.*

Franck, James (1882–1964), physicist. Nobel Prize 1925 for discovery of laws governing impact of electron on atom. With rise of Hitler, settled in U.S.

Franco-Mendes, David (Ḥofshi-Mendes; 1713–1792), Dutch Hebrew poet, author of Haskalah period. Wrote prolifically, incl. *Gemul Atalyah,* biographies of famous Sephardi Jews, etc.

Francos (Franji), term used in Muslim countries of E. Mediterranean to designate all Europeans. Found in Sephardi rabbinic literature for European Jews. In E. Europe, used for Sephardi, Ladino-speaking Jew.

Frank, Albert Rudolph (1872–1965), German chemical engineer, industrial chemist. Developed industrial technique to produce calcium cyanamide, useful as fertilizer. In U.S. fr. 1938.

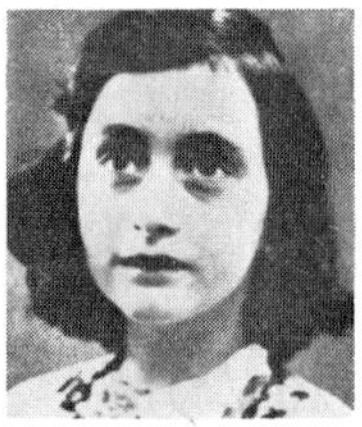

Anne Frank

Frank, Anne (1929–1945), Dutch girl famous for diary written while hiding fr. Nazis in Amsterdam; d. Bergen-Belsen. Became symbol of persecuted Jewish child.

Frank, Bruno (1887–1945), German author. One of most successful German playwrights after WWI; also noted novelist. In U.S. fr. 1933.

°**Frank, Hans Michael** (1900–1946), Nazi leader. As governor-general of Poland responsible for mass murder of Polish Jewry. Condemned to death at Nuremberg trials.

Frank, Jacob (1726–1791), founder of **Frankists,** Jewish sect emanating fr. Podolia, last stage of development of Shabbatean movement. Pseudo-messiah who led followers into external acceptance of Christianity while believing in him as reincarnation of Shabbetai Ẓevi. In fierce disputes with mainstream Judaism both sides sought support of Church, Frankists with greater success; after disputation at Kamieniec 1757, Talmud was burnt; in disputation at Lvov 1759, Frankists claimed that blood libel was based on Talmud. Transgressions of sexual prohibitions fr. Torah were part of their ritual. Movement declined after death of Frank and his daughter Eve (who was "high priestess"), though as social group it continued in Polish society into mid-19th c.

Jacob Frank

Frank, Jerome New (1889–1957), U.S. jurist, legal philosopher. Administrator of New Deal program. Appointed to U.S. Court of Appeals 1941.

Frank, Leo Max (1884–1915), only Jew ever lynched by mob in U.S. Accused of murdering 14-year-old girl. Trial and conviction due to anti-Semitism of prosecutor and jury in Atlanta.

Leo M. Frank

Frank, Philipp (1884–1966), Vienna-born philosopher, physicist; in U.S. fr. 1938. Taught mathematics and physics at Harvard. His writings are important source for history of logical positivism and empiricism.

Frank, Semyon Lyudvigovich (1877–1950), Russian philosophical theologian. Joined Orthodox Church. Banished fr. Russia, lived in Germany, England. Tried to give Christianity cosmic significance.

Frank, Waldo David (1889–1967), U.S. novelist, critic, philosopher who profoundly influenced American liberalism. Editor of *New Republic* 1925–40.

Frank, Ẓevi Pesaḥ (1873–1960), Jerusalem rabbi, halakhic authority; b. Lithuania, settled in Jerusalem 1893. Directed rabbinate affairs of city during WWI; initiator of Chief Rabbinate of Ereẓ Israel. Chief rabbi

of Jerusalem fr. 1936. His halakhic authority was respected by religious Jews the world over.

Frankau, English literary family. **Julia** (1859–1916), novelist, critic under pseud. Frank Danby. Her son **Gilbert** (1884–1952), novelist. Maintained no connection with Judaism. His daughter **Pamela** (1908–1967) writer; became Catholic.

Frankel, Lee Kaufer (1867–1931), social worker, insurance executive. Manager United Hebrew Charities fr. 1899. Pioneered development of social and health programs under private insurance auspices.

Frankel, Leo (1844–1896), Hungarian socialist. Minister of labor in Paris Commune. Engel's assistant in Socialist International.

Frankel, Naomi (1920–), Israel novelist; b. Berlin, settled in Ereẓ Israel 1933. Member of kibbutz Bet Alfa. Trilogy *Sha'ul ve-Yohannah* describes fate of German Jewry up to Nazi times.

Frankel, Sally Herbert (1903–), S. African economist. Wrote on economic affairs of underdeveloped countries on African continent. Prof. at Oxford fr. 1946. Member of East African Royal Commission 1953–55.

Frankel, Samuel Benjamin (1905–), U.S. naval officer. Intelligence officer after WWII. Chief of staff of Defense Intelligence Agency 1961–64.

Frankel, William (1917–), journalist. Editor of London *Jewish Chronicle* fr. 1958.

Frankel, Zacharias (1801–1875), rabbi, scholar; b. Prague. First director of Juedisch-Theologisches Seminar at Breslau and founder of "positivist-historical" school which later influenced Conservative Judaism in the U.S. Wrote on history of oral tradition, research on Mishnah, commentary to several tractates of Jerusalem Talmud, and study of Jewish oath which led to its repeal.

Frankenburger, Wolf (1827–1889), lawyer, politician in Hungary. Member of Bavarian diet and German Reichstag. Obtained abolition of Jewish taxes in Bavaria.

Frankenstein, Carl (1905–), psychologist, educator; b. Germany, settled in Ereẓ Israel 1935. Prof. at Heb. Univ. Wrote on depth psychology, juvenile delinquency, etc. Israel Prize 1968.

Frankenthaler, Helen (1928–), U.S. painter; daughter of N.Y. State Supreme Court Justice Frankenthaler, wife of Robert Motherwell, leading American abstract painter. Work is non-figurative.

Frankfort Jewish costume, etching by C. Weigel.

Frankfort, Henri (1897–1954), archaeologist; authority on culture and religion of Middle East. Participated in excavations in Egypt and Mesopotamia. Wrote on cultural-historical-archaeological interpretation of early civilizations. In Amsterdam until 1938, then prof. at Univ. of Chicago Oriental Institute.

Frankfort on the Main, city in W. Germany. Jews there 1074. Over 150 of community's 200 Jews massacred 1241; special Av 9 prayer written for martyrs. Community developed until wiped out by Black Death massacres 1349. Jews confined to special area 1462. 3,000 Jews in 1610. Community strong, center of learning, with many rich Jews. Vincent Fettmilch led anti-Jewish uprising 1614. Jewish printing developed in 17th c. In 18th c. communal solidarity began to wane, with tension between old patrician families (Rothschild, Kann, Schiff) and impoverished minority, accompanied by effects of Enlightenment. Incorporation into Napoleon's Confederation of the Rhine 1806 brought emancipation nearer, though reaction following Napoleon's downfall was sharp. In 19th c., Reform gained ground; congregation split 1876. Became focus of neo-Orthodoxy owing to influence of S.R. Hirsch. Franz Rosenzweig established institute for Jewish studies 1920. Many Jewish community institutions. 26,158 Jews in 1933. At end of large-scale deportations in 1943, only 602 remained. Jewish pop. 4,913 (1971).

Frankfort on the Oder, city in E. Germany. Jews fr. 13th c., expelled 1510, returned 1564. Famed Hebrew printing 1595–1826. 586 Jews in 1933; community ended under Holocaust. Refounded after WWII. 200 Jews in 1958.

Plundering of the Judengasse of Frankfort, August 22, 1614, engraving by G. Keller.

Frankfurter, David (1909–), medical student who shot Nazi leader in Switzerland and was sentenced to 18 years' imprisonment. After WWII banished fr. Switzerland and settled in Israel.

Frankfurter, Felix (1882–1965), U.S. jurist. Prof. at Harvard Law School 1914–39; Supreme Court justice 1939–62. Warm supporter of Roosevelt and New Deal legislation; founder of American Civil Liberties Union, legal adviser to NAACP, counsel for National Consumers' League. Through his close association with Louis D. Brandeis, brought into Zionist movement.

Felix Frankfurter

Went to Paris 1919 with Zionist delegation to peace conference. Received letter fr. Arab leader Emir Feisal welcoming Zionist proposals. Withdrew fr. formal participation in Zionist movement fr. 1921 but maintained active interest. Presidential Medal of Freedom 1963.

Frankfurter, Moses (1672–1762), author, *dayyan* printer in Amsterdam. Wrote commentary on Isaac Aboab's *Menorat ha-Ma'or* with Yiddish translation of text; also glosses to *Shulḥan Arukh* and commentary on parts of Bible.

Frankfurter, Solomon Friedrich (1856–1941), Austrian librarian, pedagogue, classical philologist; uncle of Felix Frankfurter, Director of Univ. of Vienna.

Frankl, Adolf (1859–1936), rabbi, banker, communal leader in Hungary. Pres. and chief rabbi of Orthodox community of Budapest, delegate in Hungarian Upper House.

Ludwig August Frankl

Frankl, Ludwig August (1810–1894), Austrian poet, author. His revolutionary lyric *Die Universitaet* circulated in half a million copies. Secretary and archivist of Vienna Jewish community. Founded Laemel secular-religious school in Jerusalem 1856. Ennobled.

Frankl, Pinkus (Pinḥas) Fritz (1848–1887), German rabbi, scholar. Rabbi of Berlin, lecturer in religious philosophy at Hochschule fuer die Wissenschaft des Judentums, coeditor (with Graetz) of *Monatsschrift fuer Geschichte und Wissenschaft des Judentums.*

Frankl, Victor E. (1905–), Austrian psychiatrist. From his internment in Auschwitz formulated theory of existential psychotherapy known as logotherapy. Wrote *From Death Camp to Existentialism (Man's Search for Meaning)* and *The Doctor and the Soul.*

Frankl-Gruen, Adolf Abraham (1847–1916), rabbi, historian in Moravia. Wrote 3-vol. *Geschichte der Juden in Kremsier* and *Geschichte der Juden in Ungarisch-Brod.*

Franklin, English family. **Jacob** (1809–1877), merchant, mathematician, advocate of Orthodoxy, founder of journal *Voice of Jacob.* His brother **Ellis Abraham** (1822–1909), noted banker whose daughter **Beatrice** married Herbert Samuel. His sons, **Sir Leonard** (1862–1944) and **Arthur Ellis** (1857–1938), bankers. The latter was chairman of Routledge publishing firm.

Franklin, Selim (1814–1883), Canadian politician; b. England, settled in Victoria, Canada, with his brother **Lumley** (1812–1873), where they played prominent part in political, social, and cultural life of general and Jewish communities.

Sidney Franklin

Franklin (Frumkin), Sidney (1903–), matador; b. U.S., lived mostly in Mexico. First non-Latin to gain fame in bullring. Dispatched over 5,000 bulls before retiring 1959.

Franks, David (1720–1794), Colonial American merchant who was exiled to England because of loyalty to Britain during American Revolution.

Franks, David Salisbury (c. 1743–1793), Colonial merchant who served in army against British during American Revolution.

Jacob Franks

Franks, Jacob (1688–1769), New York City merchant and founder of prominent mercantile family. Pres. of Shearith Israel congregation.

Franzblau, Abraham Norman (1901–), U.S. educator, psychiatrist. Pioneer of application of psychiatry to ministry. His wife, **Rose Nadler** (1905–), psychologist. Wrote human relations column for *New York Post* and ran daily radio program to discuss listeners' problems.

Franzos, Karl Emil (1848–1904), Austrian novelist, journalist. Published tales and sketches describing E. European Jewry; also novels. Helped spread reputation of new and established writers.

Fraternal Societies, organizations for mutual aid, fellowship, life insurance, relief of distress, and sick and death benefits. Jewish fraternal societies originated in 19th c., e.g., Order Achei Brith and Shield of Abraham in England; Independent Order B'nai B'rith in U.S. In S. and C. America organized as *Landsmannschaften,* e.g., Galician Farband. Many small organizations joined general orders formed along political lines, e.g., Workmen's Circle (socialism). Membership declined with growing popularity of commercial insurance, mortuary business, etc.

°**Frederick I** (1826–1907), grand duke of Baden; son-in-law of Kaiser William I. Sympathized with Herzl and arranged meetings for him with Kaiser.

Freed (orig. Grossman), Arthur (1894–1973), U.S. popular lyricist. Co-author of songs for first Hollywood musical *Broadway Melody of 1929.* Other productions incl. *Babes in Arms, American in Paris, Singing in the Rain.*

Freed, Isadore (1900–1960), composer. Chairman of music dept. at Hart College of Music, Hartford, Conn. 1944–60. Works of moderately modernistic idiom, incl. two symphonies, cello concertos, and opera.

Freedman, Barnett (1901–1958), British artist. Official war artist to British Army and Admiralty. Achieved fame as book illustrator.

Freedman, Samuel (1908–), Canadian jurist. Lecturer at Manitoba law school 1941–59, chancellor of Univ. of Manitoba 1959–68, judge in Manitoba Court of Appeal fr. 1960. Active in Jewish community.

Freehof, Solomon Bennett (1892–), U.S. Reform rabbi, scholar. Rabbi in Chicago 1924–34, Pittsburgh fr. 1934. Wrote on Jewish liturgy and Jewish law. Head of Responsa Committee of Central Conference of American Rabbis and author of books on responsa literature.

Freeman, Joseph (1897–1965), U.S. author, critic, journalist. Used his journalistic talents in support of socialism, helping to found monthly

Solomon B. Freehof

New Masses, which he edited in 1930s. Broke with Communists after Nazi-Soviet pact of 1939.

Free Sons of Israel, U.S. fraternal order; established 1849. Membership 10,000 (1970), with 46 lodges.

Freiburg im Breisgau, city in W. Germany. Jews there 1230, massacred during Black Death 1349, expelled 1424. First Jew to receive degree fr. Freiburg Univ. 1791. Small community in 19th–20th c.

Freidus, Abraham Solomon (1867–1923), U.S. librarian, bibliographer. First chief of Jewish Division of the N.Y. Public Library 1897. Developed classification scheme for Judaica.

Freier, Recha (1892–), founder of Youth Aliyah; b. Germany. Conceived idea of Youth Aliyah 1932; endorsed by Zionist Congress 1933. Settled in Ereẓ Israel 1941.

Freifield, Abraham (1921–), Chilean sculptor. Prof. of sculpture at Fine Arts School and director of Inst. for Extension of Fine Arts, Univ. of Chile.

Freiheit, see Morning Freiheit.

Freilich, Max Melech (1893–), Australian paper manufacturer, communal leader in Sydney. Pres. Australian Zionist Federation 1953–57.

Freiman, Canadian family. **Moses Bilsky** (1831–1923), pioneer, gold prospector; community leader and Zionist in Ottawa. **Lillian** (1885–1940), Zionist leader; first pres. Canadian Hadassah 1919–40; worked in both nonsectarian and Jewish charities. **Archibald Jacob** (1880–1944), merchant, Zionist leader; national pres. Zionist Organization of Canada 1920–44. **Lawrence** (1909–), merchant; pres. of Zionist Organization of Canada.

Freimann, Abraham Ḥayyim (Alfred; 1889–1948), jurist, rabbinical scholar. County judge in Germany until Nazi period, then went to Ereẓ Israel. Began lecturing in Jewish law at Heb. Univ. 1944. Killed in Heb. Univ. convoy by Arabs.

Freimann, Aron (1871–1948), German scholar, historian, bibliographer; b. Poznan, worked in Frankfort until Nazis came to power, in New York fr. 1938. Prepared mss. catalogues, books and incunabula in Judaica. His scholarship showed both industry and erudition.

Freimann, Jacob (1866–1937), German rabbi, scholar. Editor of rabbinics dept. of German *Encyclopaedia Judaica.* Lecturer on rabbinics and Jewish history at Berlin Rabbinical Seminary.

Freud, Anna (1895–), psychoanalyst; daughter of Sigmund Freud. Escaped with him fr. Austria to London 1938. Through direct observation wrote on reaction of young children separated fr. parents and deprived of emotional relationships, particularly in institutions. Influential in child analytic therapy.

Freud, Lucien (1922–), English painter; grandson of Sigmund Freud. Represented Britain at Venice Biennale 1954. Work closely resembled later German expressionists.

Freud, Sigmund (1856–1939), creator of psychoanalysis. A towering figure in modern thought. Worked with Viennese physician Josef Breuer on treatment of hysteria *(Studies in Hysteria),* setting out theory that damming-up emotions in unconscious could produce symptoms of hysterical illness. Developed theory of dreams, neurosis, infantile sexuality, ego, id, and superego, and process of psychoanalysis. Fled from Vienna to London 1938. His *Moses and Monotheism* suggested psychoanalytical origin for religion and charactistics of Jewish people.

Sigmund Freud

Freund, Ernst (1864–1932), U.S. jurist, legislative authority. Prof. of law at Univ. of Chicago fr. 1902. Made significant contributions in public law, particularly in administrative law and legislation.

Freund, Martin (1863–1920), German organic chemist. Prof. and rector at Akademie fuer Sozial- und Handelswissenschaften. Head of Chemical Inst. at Frankfort Univ. 1914. Some of his synthetic products became therapeutic pharmaceuticals.

Freund, Miriam Kottler (1906–), U.S. Hadassah leader. National pres. 1956–1960. Edited *Hadassah Magazine* fr. 1966.

Freund, Paul Abraham (1908–), U.S. constitutional lawyer, educator, author. Prof. at Harvard Law School fr. 1940. Authority on constitutional law.

Freundlich, Otto (1878–1943), German painter, sculptor; lived many years in France. Work close to pure abstraction or completely nonfigurative. D. in concentration camp.

"Ascension" by Otto Freundlich.

Fried, Alfred Hermann (1864–1921), Austrian publicist; Nobel Prize for Peace 1911. Worked for many pacifist organizations; accused of treason and spent WWI in Switzerland.

Friedberg, Abraham Shalom (1838–1902), Hebrew author, editor, translator; b. Grodno, lived in Russia, Poland. Editor of first Hebrew encyclopedia *Ha-Eshkol.* Wrote *Memoirs of the House of David,* popular series based on Jewish history.

Friedberg, Bernard (Bernhard, Ḥayyim Dov; 1876–1961), scholar, bibliographer; b. Cracow, lived in Frankfort, Antwerp, Tel Aviv. Worked most of his life in diamond trade, but wrote biographies, bibliographies, history. Best-known work *Beit Eked Sefarim,* bibliographical lexicon.

Friede, Shalom (1783–1854), Dutch *ḥazzan* whose collection of c. 200 melodies added considerably to knowledge of Polish cantorial and ḥasidic music.

Friedell, Egon (pseud. of **Egon Friedmann;** 1878–1938), Austrian playwright, cultural historian. Acted in his own plays. Wrote *A Cultural History of the Modern Age.*

Friedemann, Adolf (1871–1932), early Zionist. Faithful companion and supporter of Herzl. Wrote first biography of Herzl.

Friedenberg, Samuel (1886–1957), U.S. collector of medals. Built up most complete collection of Jewish medals in existence, which he left to N.Y. Jewish Museum, where his son **Daniel,** who wrote extensively on the subject, became honorary curator of Coins and Medals.

Friedenwald, family of U.S. ophthalmologists, community leaders in Baltimore. **Jonas** (1803–1893), Baltimore businessman, communal worker. **Aaron** (1836–1902), ophthalmologist; early Zionist and a founder of various Jewish organizations (e.g., Jewish Theological Seminary, Jewish Publication Society). **Harry** (1864–1950), ophthalmologist, Zionist. Taught at Baltimore College of Physicians and Surgeons; pres. American Association of Zionists; served as consultant for Jerusalem hospitals 1911, 1914. Wrote on medical history, esp. on medieval Jewish doctors. **Jonas** (1897–1955), prof. of ophthalmology at Johns Hopkins Univ.

Frieder, Armin (1911–1946), Slovakian rabbi, Zionist. Member of "Working Group" underground to save Slovakian Jewry 1942. After WWII, chief rabbi of Slovakia.

Friedlaender, David (1750–1834), communal leader, author in Berlin; pioneer of assimilation and forerunner of Reform. Successful silk manufacturer. Friend of Moses Mendelssohn. First Jew elected to Berlin City Council. Favored extreme religious reform; suggested replacing Talmud as object of study with national laws. Fought for emancipation of Jews.

Friedlaender, Israel (1876–1920), Semitics scholar, U.S. communal leader; b. Poland, in U.S. (at Jewish Theological Seminary, Dropsie College) fr. 1904. Arabist who wrote on Judeo-Arabic literature and Islamic sects; sought to reconcile American Zionists and non-Zionists. Murdered in Ukraine while on mission for Joint.

Friedlaender, Michael (1833–1910), scholar; b. Poland. Principal of Jews' College, London fr. 1865. His English translation of Maimonides' *Guide of the Perplexed* was for years standard.

Friedlaender, Saul (1932–), Israel historian; b. Prague, settled in Israel 1948. Prof. at Inst. of Higher International Studies, Geneva, 1964–67, then at Heb. Univ. Specialized in Nazi history.

Friedland, Abraham Hyman (1891–1939), U.S. Hebrew poet, short-story writer, educator; b. nr. Vilna, in U.S. fr. 1906. Directed Hebrew education in Cleveland.

Friedland, Moses Aryeh Leib (1826–1899), contractor for Russian army; wealthy Jewish philanthropist. Donated his collection of Hebrew books and mss. to Asiatic Museum, St. Petersburg.

Friedland, Natan (1808–1883), rabbi, precursor of Ḥibbat Zion movement. Presented petitions to Napoleon III and to Dutch government advocating restoration of Ereẓ Israel to Jews.

Friedlander, Max (1852–1934), musicologist. Prof. at Berlin Univ. Discovered more than 100 lost songs by Schubert. Writings incl. 3-vol. *Das deutsche Lied im 18. Jahrhundert.*

Friedman, Benjamin (Benny, 1905–), U.S. football player. All-America at Univ. of Michigan. Entered pro football 1927, revolutionizing game with liberal use of forward pass.

Friedman, Bruce Jay (1930–), U.S. novelist, playwright. Regarded as one of leaders of "black humor" school *(Stern, A Mother's Kisses).*

Friedman, Herbert A. (1918–), U.S. Reform rabbi. Executive vice-chairman (executive pres. fr. 1969) of United Jewish Appeal.

David Friedlaender

Friedman, Lee Max (1871–1957), U.S. lawyer, historian. Prof. of Law at Portia Law School, Boston; pres. American Jewish Historical Society. Wrote several books on American Jewish history.

Friedman, Milton (1912–), U.S. economist. Prof. at Univ. of Chicago; leader of "Chicago school" of economic thought. Adviser to Pres. Nixon. Proponent of "negative income tax" instead of social welfare.

Friedman, Nathan, see Yellin-Mor, Nathan.

Friedman, Philip (1901–1960), Polish Jewish historian; in U.S. fr. 1948. After WWII organized Jewish Historical Institute, Warsaw; directed Jewish Teachers Institute, N.Y. Laid foundations for historiography of Holocaust period.

Friedmann, Abraham (d. 1879), chief rabbi of Transylvania. One of first rabbis to preach in Hungarian.

Friedmann, Aron (1855–1936), German *ḥazzan.* Chief *ḥazzan* of old synagogue of Berlin community. Published collections of cantorial music.

Friedmann, David ben Samuel ("Dovidel" Karliner; 1828–1917), Lithuanian rabbi, *posek.* Wrote *Piskei Halakhot,* exposition and summary of matrimonial law. Active in Ḥibbat Zion movement and influenced many observant Jews to join.

Friedmann, Georges (1902–), French sociologist. In WWII organized resistance of Toulouse area. Concerned with sociology of labor. Wrote *The End of the Jewish People?*, sociological study that aroused wide controversy.

Friedmann, Israel, see Ruzhin, Israel of.

Friedmann, Meir (pen name **Ish-Shalom;** 1831–1908), rabbinic scholar; b. Slovakia, settled in Vienna 1858. Taught Talmud at rabbinical seminary. Specialized in *aggadah;* most important contributions in halakhic Midrashim. Published *Pesikta Rabbati* and *Tanna de-vei Eliyahu.*

Friedmann, Paul (1840– ?), philanthropist, author; Protestant of Jewish descent. Initiated settlement scheme in Midian (S. Sinai) which proved disastrous.

Friedsam, Michael (1858–1931), U.S. businessman, philanthropist. Pres. of Altman department store. Established Friedsam Foundation to assist young and aged and for educational purposes.

Friendly, Fred W. (Fred Wachenheimer; 1915–), U.S. television writer, director. Collaborated with Ed Murrow on *Hear It Now* series. TV adviser to Ford Foundation, prof. of journalism at Columbia Univ.

Frigeis, Lazaro De (16th c.), physician; b. Hungary or Holland. Friend of Vesalius, whom he furnished with Hebrew names of anatomic structures.

Frisch, Daniel (1897–1950), U.S. Zionist leader. Successful investment broker and businessman. Militant General Zionist; pres. ZOA, 1949.

Frisch, Otto Robert (1904–), British physicist; b. Vienna, worked in atomic research in Berlin until Nazi period, then Liverpool, Oxford, and Los Alamos. After WWII head of nuclear physics division, Harwell, England; prof. of natural philosophy, Cambridge. Fellow of Royal Society.

Frischmann, David (1859–1922), Hebrew writer; b. Poland. Wrote short stories, poetry, essays, satire, literary criticism, and biblical stories *Ba-Midbar.* Translated many classics (incl. Nietzsche, Tagore). Editor and publisher of many Hebrew and

David Frischmann

Erich Fromm

Shimon Shmuel Frug

Yiddish journals. Important influence on modern Hebrew literature and its broadening from artificiality of Haskalah period.

Frizzi, Benedetto (1756–1844), Italian physician, writer. Outstanding Jewish scholar of Enlightenment who wrote polemic and apologetic books attacking misconceptions on Jews' role in society.

Frohman, Charles (1860–1915), U.S. theater manager, director; also national booking agent. Organized syndicate that controlled U.S. theaters. Produced 125 plays in London. D. in *Lusitania.*

Frohman, Daniel (1851–1940), U.S. theater manager, producer. Business manager of Madison Square Theater, owner of Lyceum. Director of Paramount Company.

Fromm, Erich (1900–), U.S. psychoanalyst, social philosopher, writer; b. Germany, in U.S. fr. 1933. Many academic appointments. Neo-Freudian who applied psychoanalysis to problems of culture and society. Wrote *The Sane Society, Escape from Freedom, Art of Loving, You Shall Be As Gods,* etc.

Frug, Shimon Shmuel (1860–1916), poet; b. Russia. First wrote Russian poetry, but soon began writing in Yiddish, national songs, socialist and Zionist lyrics, and ballads based on Jewish folklore. Many of his lyrics became popular.

Frumkin, Aleksandr Naumovich (1895–), Russian physical chemist. Director of institutes of physical chemistry and electrochemistry of USSR Academy of Sciences.

Frumkin, Aryeh Leib (1845–1916), rabbinical scholar, writer; pioneer of Jewish settlement in Ereẓ Israel (in Petaḥ Tikvah); b. Lithuania. Works incl. history of rabbis and scholars of Jerusalem and edition of *Seder Rav Amram.*

Frumkin, Boris Markovich (1872–after 1939), Bund leader, publicist. Organized Bund activities and edited movement's journals. Not active politically after WWI.

Frumkin, Israel Dov (1850–1914), pioneer, journalist in Ereẓ Israel; b. Belorussia, settled in Jerusalem 1859. Published and edited *Havaẓẓelet*; initially favored agricultural settlement but became increasingly anti-secular.

Frumkin, Malkah, see Esther.

Frýd, Norbert (1913–), Czech novelist. Wrote several significant books about Holocaust; also anti-American novels. Received awards from Czech government.

Fuchs, Abraham Moshe (1890-1974), Yiddish short-story writer; b. E. Galicia, lived in Lemberg, New York, Vienna, London, Israel. Described poor Galician villagers. Many of his mss. lost in WWII.

Fuenn, Samuel Joseph (1818–1890), Hebrew writer. Member of Jewish Enlightenment in Russia. Copublished *Pirḥei Ẓafon,* first Hebrew literary periodical in Russia 1841–44. Active in Ḥibbat Zion. Compiled Hebrew dictionary *Ha-Oẓar.*

Fuerst, Julius (pseud. **Alsari**; 1805–1873), Polish Hebraist, bibliographer, historian; b. Poland, taught in Germany. Forerunner of scientific research in all branches of Judaic studies.

Fuerth, city in W. Germany. Jews fr. 1440; expelled, returned 1528. Community augmented 1670 by refugees fr. Vienna. Important in Hebrew publishing 1691–1867. Pre-WWII community of 2,000 ended with Holocaust.

Fuks, Alexander (1917–), Israel historian; b. Poland. Prof. of ancient history and classics at Heb. Univ. Authority on both ancient Jewish and classical history.

Fuks, Lajb (1908–), librarian, Yiddish scholar; b. Poland, in Holland fr. 1939. Librarian of Bibliotheca Rosenthaliana. Wrote on Old-Yiddish language and literature, and history of Dutch Jewry.

Fuld, Aaron ben Moses (1790–1847), defender of Orthodoxy and communal worker in Frankfort. Author of responsa and glosses to Talmud.

Jewish cemetery in Fuerth, 18th century etching.

Fuld, Stanley Howells (1903–), U.S. attorney. Chief judge of N.Y. State Court of Appeals fr. 1966.

Fulda, city in W. Germany. Jews first mentioned 1235, when 34 martyrs burnt to death following blood libel. Except for short periods of expulsion, Jewish presence almost continuous until WWII. Center of Orthodoxy. Destroyed in Holocaust.

Fulda, Ludwig (1862–1939), German playwright. Initially influenced by Ibsen and naturalism, turned to neo-romanticism. Translated many plays. Pres. of Prussian Academy until dismissed by Nazis.

Fulvia, (1st c. C.E.), Roman proselyte. Lady of rank; when gifts she sent to Temple in Jerusalem were not delivered, she told Emperor, who expelled all Jews from Rome.

Funeral, see Burial.

Funk, Casimir (1884–1967), U.S. biochemist; originator of word "vitamin"; b. Warsaw, worked in Berne, London, U.S., Warsaw, France. Pres. of Funk Foundation for Medical Research. Discovered that substance found in rice shavings prevents beriberi.

Furaydis, Al-, Arab village in Israel at foot of Mt. Carmel, nr. Zikhron Ya'akov. Pop. 3,230 (1971).

Furst, Moritz (1782–1840), U.S. medalist; b. Pressburg, in U.S. fr. 1807. Engraver for U.S. Mint in Philadelphia 1812–39. 33 of his patriotic commemoratives and portraits are still issued by Mint. Did first recorded American-Jewish medal on death of Gershom Mendes Seixas.

Furtado, Abraham (1756–1817), politician, communal leader in France; Bordeaux Jew of Marrano descent. Pres. of Assembly of Jewish Notables convened by Napoleon; Secretary of Paris Sanhedrin.

Abraham Furtado

Initial letter "G" of "Ge" ("I" in Old French) at opening of paraphrase of and commentary on I Sam. 19:11 in Old French and Latin, 13th cent.

Gaal, head of band that incited inhabitants of Shechem to revolt against Abimelech son of Gideon (Judg. 9:26ff.). Abimelech crushed revolt and Gaal was driven fr. city.

Gabbai, lay communal official; word is part of complete term *gabbai ẓedakah* ("charity warden").

Gabbai, family in Baghdad and India. **Isaac b. David b. Yeshu'ah** (d. 1773), head of Jewish community, chief banker for governor of Baghdad. **Ezekiel** (1825–1898), first Jew to hold office in Ottoman ministry of education, pres. of Supreme Criminal Court. **Ezekiel b. Joshua** (1824–1896), went to India, traded with China. **Ezekiel Ṣāliḥ** (1812–1887), went to India, directed charities for communities in Ereẓ Israel, possessed large personal fortune. **Solomon Ṣaliḥ** (1897–1961), poet, educator; lived in Baghdad, Persia, Israel.

Gabbai, Meir ben Ezekiel ibn (1480–after 1540), kabbalist, author; probably lived in Turkey. Wrote small, comprehensive, organized summary of Kabbalah doctrine prior to Safed period.

Gabel, Max (1877–1952), Yiddish actor, playwright. Wrote over 100 plays, mostly melodramas and adaptations of Broadway successes. Managed Gabel's Star Theater and other N.Y. theaters. Wrote and produced plays for wife Jennie Goldstein.

Gabès, maritime town in Tunisia. Community flourished materially and culturally until destroyed by Almohads 1159. After reconstitution, community lived in peace but did not reach previous heights. Under German occupation in WWII Jews suffered. In 1950s most Jews emigrated to France and Israel, and in 1970 only c. 200 rich landowning families remained.

Jewish women of Gabès.

Gabirol, Solomon ben Judah ibn (c. 1020–c. 1057), Spanish poet, philosopher; lived mostly in Saragossa. Began writing poetry by 16. Only 2 of his 20 books are extant. *Mekor Ḥayyim,* major work of medieval neo-Platonic philosophy, which was long known only in Latin translation as *Fons Vitae* by Avicebron (only identified as Ibn Gabirol in 19th c.), and his ethical code *Tikkun Middot ha-Nefesh.* Many of his secular and religious poems are known and are among outstanding products of medieval Hebrew literature, incl. elegy *Bi-Ymei Yekuti'el Asher Nigmaru,* considered one of greatest Jewish medieval secular poems, and *Keter Malkhut* a lofty poem about God. Gabirol's philosophy was slowly forgotten among Jews, although traces appear in Kabbalah.

Gabor, Dennis (1900–), British physicist, electrical engineer; b. Hungary, in England fr. 1933. Produced theory of holography 1947 which was implemented when laser beams were invented. Prof. at Imperial College, London. Nobel Prize 1971.

Gabriel, angel named in Daniel 8:16 and 9:21 whose function was to reveal messenger from God. In pseudepigraphical literature his title and position became more explicit. In New Testament he is both revealer and bringer of reassurance. Also prominent in Islamic folklore.

Gabrielovich, Osip Solomonovich (1878–1936), pianist, conductor. Conductor Detroit Symphony Orchestra fr. 1918, joint conductor Philadelphia Orchestra with Leopold Stokowski fr. 1928. Married Clara, daughter of Mark Twain.

Statue of Solomon ibn Gabirol in Malaga by Reed Armstrong.

Territory of the tribe of Gad.

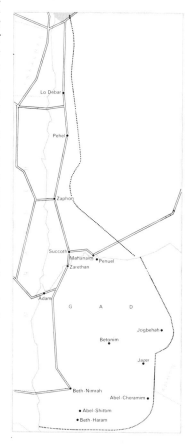

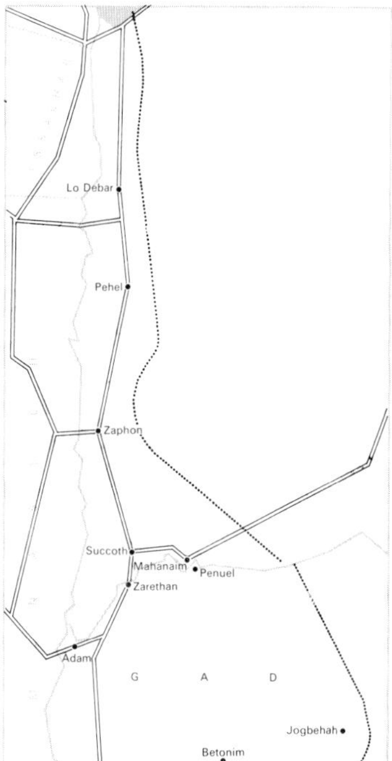

Gad, ancient Middle Eastern deity of fortune. In Bible generally mentioned as part of place and proper names, such as Baal-Gad, Gaddiel, Azgad.

Gad, son of Jacob; eponymous ancestor of tribe which settled in Gilead, E. of the Jordan. Its history consisted of succession of wars with Ammon and Moab in S., nomadic tribes in E., Aram in N.

Gad, one of three prophets during David's reign. Instructed David to purchase site where Solomon later built Temple (II Sam. 24) and was among organizers of levitical service in Temple (II Chron. 29:25).

Gadara, ancient city of Gilead. Important center of Hellenistic culture. On banks of Yarmuk are hot springs known as Ḥammat Gader.

Gadna, (Heb. abbr. for *Gedudei No'ar,* "Youth Corps"), Israel youth movement for training 13- to 18-year-olds in defense and national service, established 1948. Membership voluntary, functions in high schools and youth clubs. Its instructors have organized youth movements in African and Asian countries.

Gagin, Ḥayyim (b. 1450), Moroccan rabbi, poet; first known member of family which produced many talmudic scholars.

Gagin, Ḥayyim Abraham ben Moses (1787–1848), chief rabbi of Jerusalem; first to bear official title *ḥakham bashi.* His son **Shalom Moses ben Ḥayyim Abraham** (d. 1883), talmudist, emissary. Wrote responsa, homilies, additions to father's work.

Gaḥal, Israel party established 1965 by Ḥerut and Liberal Party. Largest opposition party, 1965, 1969 and 1973 elections. Leader, Menaḥem Begin. See Knesset.

Galai, Binyamin (1921–), Hebrew writer, poet. Published poems, plays, children's stories.

Galant, Eliahu Vladimirovich (1868–after 1929), historian of Ukrainian Jewry. Studied period of persecution in 16th and 17th c. Forced to discontinue work 1929 when politically suspect.

Galanté, Abraham (1873–1961), Turkish politician, scholar, historian. Campaigned for adoption of Turkish language by Jews. Prof. of Semitic languages and history of Ancient Orient at Istanbul Univ. Twice member of Turkish parliament. Wrote studies on Turkish-Jewish history.

Galante, Moses ben Jonathan (1620–1689), Jerusalem rabbi. For a time involved with Shabbatean movement and leading Shabbatean "prophet."

Galati (Galatz), port city in Rumania. Jews fr. 16th c. Suffered severe attacks bet. 1796 and 1859. Community not destroyed during Holocaust but diminished through emigration. 450 families in 1969.

Galicia, region in SE Poland and NW Ukraine. Under Austrian rule (after 1772) steps taken to "improve" situation of Jews with ultimate aim of their assimilation: communal autonomy abolished and Jews encouraged to take up agriculture. Attempts made to set up government schools for Jews. In 19th c. center of Jewish scholarship, both traditional and enlightened, and Ḥasidism also spread steadily. Jews finally given full rights 1867, and then participated in region's affairs, sitting in parliament, etc. Polish Catholics proclaimed economic boycott of Jews 1893 and applied other economic pressures. 236,000 Jews emigrated bet. 1881 and 1910. Jews suffered severely in WWI and Polish-Ukrainian wars. For subsequent history, see Poland; Ukraine.

Galilee, northernmost region of Erez Israel. Victories of Joshua at Merom and of Deborah ensured Israelite supremacy over region. In biblical times divided bet. Asher, Zebulun, Napthali, Isaachar. With division of monarchy, became part of kingdom of Israel. Assyrian province fr. 732 B.C.E. Incorporated into Hasmonean kingdom by Judah Aristobulus I (104 B.C.E.) and rapidly became completely Jewish. In mishnaic and talmudic periods, stronghold of Judaism in Ereẓ Israel. Scene of activities of Jesus and early Christian apostles. Center of Jewish revolt against Gallus Caesar 351 and Byzantines 614. In 16th c. Safed became center of Jewish kabbalism and Tiberias was temporarily settled by Joseph Nasi. In late 19th c. pop. increased and Jewish farming villages were established. Fr. 1948 part of state of Israel. In 1950s new moshavim founded to create continuous chain of Jewish settlements. Also considerable non-Jewish pop. with Arab villages esp. in C. Galilee.

Galili, Israel (1910–), labor, Haganah leader in Ereẓ Israel. A founder of Ha-No'ar ha-Oved (youth wing of Histadrut). A central figure in Haganah in critical pre-state period and during War of Independence. Leader of Aḥdut ha-Avodah, member of Knesset fr. foundation. Influential minister without portfolio fr. 1966.

Galipapa, Ḥayyim ben Abraham (1310–1380), Spanish talmudist. His leniency in *halakhah* aroused opposition.

Galut, (Heb.), exile; condition of Jewish people in dispersion.

Galveston Plan, project to divert European Jews immigrating to U.S. fr. large E. seaports to SW states. Plan initiated 1907, discontinued at beginning of WWI. Settled 10,000 immigrants.

Gama, Gaspar da (c. 1440–1510), Jewish traveler; probably b. E. Europe. Sold as slave to India, obtained freedom and employed by ruler of Goa, treacherously seized and forcibly baptized by Vasco da Gama. His linguistic abilities used by king of Portugal for fleet.

Gadna parade, Independence Day, 1970.

The Sea of Galilee, 1920s.

Israel Galili

Gamaliel, Rabban, name and title of six sages, descendants of Hillel, who filled office of *nasi* in Ereẓ Israel. (1) **Rabban Gamaliel ha-Zaken ("the Elder";** 1st c. C.E.), grandson of Hillel, pres. of Sanhedrin. Responsible for many *takkanot,* incl. decision to allow woman to remarry on basis of one witness (and not two) of husband's death. (2) **Rabban Gamaliel II of Jabneh,** grandson of (1), succeeded Johanan b. Zakkai as *nasi* c. 80. In effort to strengthen position of *nasi* and unify halakhic process, his firmness and use of power led to severe struggle with elders. For a time removed fr. office but reinstated. One of greatest scholars of his generation. (3) **Gamaliel** (3rd c.), son of Judah ha-Nasi. Appointed *nasi* in accordance with testament of his father. (4) **Rabban Gamaliel** (3rd c.), son of Judah Nesiah. (5) **Rabban Gamaliel** (4th c.), son of Hillel II. (6) **Rabban Gamaliel** (5th c.) last *nasi.*

Gamarnik, Yan Borisovich (1894–1938), Soviet army political officer. Headed political administration of Soviet army 1917–37. USSR Central Committee member and deputy people's commissar for defense. Committed suicide.

Games, Abram (1914–), English graphic designer. Official poster designer for British War Office in WWII. Designed 1951 Festival of Britain emblems and several English postage stamps.

Gamoran, Emanuel (1895–1962), U.S. educator. Educational director of Commission of Jewish Education of Union of American Hebrew Congregations 1923–62. Wrote books, textbooks, articles on Jewish education.

Gamzu, Ḥayyim (1910–), Israel drama, art critic. Director of Tel Aviv Museum. Wrote on painting, sculpture, theater in daily *Haaretz.*

Gandz, Solomon (1887–1954), Semitics scholar, historian of mathematics; b. Austria, in U.S. fr. 1924. Taught history of Semitic civilization at Dropsie College fr. 1942.

Gans, Bird Stein (1868–1944), U.S. educator. Director of first organization in U.S. in field of parent education 1896.

Gans, David ben Solomon (1541–1613), chronicler, astronomer, mathematician; b. Westphalia, lived in Prague, worked with Tycho Brahe. Main astronomical work rejects Copernican system in favor of Ptolemy's. Chronicle *Ẓemaḥ David*

Rabban Gamaliel teaching two pupils in 14th-cent. "Haggadah."

Tombstone of David Gans.

CHRONOLOGICAL LIST OF THE GEONIM IN SURA AND PUMBEDITA

SURA		PUMBEDITA
	589	Hanan of Iskiya
Mar bar Huna	591	(?) Mari b. Dimi (formerly of Firuz-Shapur and Nehardea)
Ḥanina	614	Ḥanina of Bei-Gihara (Firuz-Shapur)
	...	Ḥana (or Huna)
Huna	650	
Sheshna (called also Mesharsheya b. Taḥlifa)	...	
	651	Rabbah
	...	Bosai
Ḥanina of Nehar-Pekod	689	Huna Mari b. Joseph
	...	Ḥiyya of Meshan
	...	Ravya (or Mar Yanka)
Hilai ha-Levi of Naresh	694	
Jacob ha-Kohen of Nehar-Pekod	712	
	719	Natronai b. Nehemiah
	...	Judah
Samuel	730	
	739	Joseph
Mari Kohen of Nehar-Pekod	748	Samuel b. Mar
	752	(?) Natroi Kahana b. Mar Amunah
	...	Abraham Kahana
Aha	756	
Yehudai b. Naḥman	757	
Aḥunai Kahana b. Papa	761	Dodai b. Naḥman (brother of Yehudai the *gaon* of Sura)
	764	Hananiah b. Mesharsheya
Ḥaninai Kahana b. Huna	769	
	771	Malkha b. Aḥa
	773	Rabbah (Abba) b. Dodai
Mari ha-Levi b. Mesharsheya	774	
Bebai (Bivoi, Bivi) ha-Levi b. Abba of Nehar-Pekod	777	
	781	Shinoi
	782	Ḥaninai Kahana b. Abraham
	785	Huna ha-Levi b. Isaac
Hilai b. Mari	788	Manasseh b. Mar Joseph
	796	Isaiah ha-Levi b. Mar Abba
Jacob ha Kohen b. Mordecai	797	
	798	Joseph b. Shila
	804	Kahana b. Ḥaninai
	810	Ivomai (in both academies)
Ivomai, uncle of his predecessor	811	
	814	Joseph b. Abba
Zadok b. Jesse (or Ashi)	816	Abraham b. Sherira
Hilai b. Ḥanina	818	
Kimoi b. Ashi	822	
Moses (Mesharsheya) Kahana b. Jacob	825	
	828	Joseph b. Ḥiyya
	833	Isaac b. Hananiah
	836 [a]	
Kohen Ẓedek b. Ivomai	838	
	839	Joseph b. Ravi
	842	Paltoi b. Abbaye
Sar Shalom b. Boaz	848	
Natronai b. Hilai	853	
	857	Aḥa Kahana b. Rav
Amram b. Sheshna [b]	858	Menahem b. Joseph b. Ḥiyya
	860	Mattathias b. Mar Ravi
	869	Abba (Rabbah) b. Ammi
Nahshon b. Zadok	871	
	872	Ẓemah b. Paltoi
Ẓemaḥ b. Ḥayyim	879	
Malkha	885	
Hai b. Nahshon	885	
	890 [c]	Hai b. David
Hilai b. Natronai	896	
	898	Kimoi b. Aḥai
Shalom b. Mishael	904	
	906	Judah b. Samuel (grandfather of Sherira)
Jacob b. Natronai	911	
	917–926	Mevasser Kahana b. Kimoi
Yom Tov Kahana b. Jacob	924	
	926–936	Kohen Ẓedek b. Joseph (appointed during the life time of his predecessor)
Saadiah b. Joseph	928	
	936	Ẓemah b. Kafnai
	938	Hananiah b. Judah
Joseph b. Jacob	942–944 [d]	
	943	Aaron b. Joseph ha-Kohen Sargado
	960	Nehemiah b. Kohen Ẓedek
	968	Sherira b. Hananiah
Ẓemah b. Isaac (descendant of Paltoi)	988	
(?) Samuel b. Hophni ha-Kohen	997	
	998	Hai b. Sherira
Dosa b. Saadiah	1013	
Israel b. Samuel b. Hophni	1017	
Azariah ha-Kohen (son of Israel?)	1034	
(?) Isaac	1037	
	1038–(1058)	Hezekiah b. David (exilarch and head of the academy)

a. Until 838 position not filled in Sura.
b. Ruled with above, 853–858.
c. The first of the "geonim" who lived in Baghdad (R. Isaac ibn Ghayyat, "Sha'arei Simhah," pt. 1 no. 64).
d. The academy was closed for about 45 years, however, apparently several teachers and pupils remained.

written in two parts – one dealing with Jewish history to date of publication (1592), the other with general history.

Gans, Eduard (1798–1839), jurist, historian in Berlin. Founded, with Leopold Zunz and Moses Moser, Verein fuer Kultur und Wissenschaft der Juden, whose object was to bring general education to Jewish youth by expanding their cultural horizons and reform of traditional Jewish thinking. After baptism, prof. at Berlin Univ. Wrote on law and history, edited Hegel's lectures on philosophy of history.

Ganzfried, Solomon ben Joseph (1804–1886), Hungarian rabbi. Author of popular *Kiẓẓur Shulḥan Arukh,* abridgment of Joseph Caro's *Shulḥan Arukh.* Also wrote commentary to prayer book, novellae to Talmud, and homilies on Pentateuch.

Gaon (pl. **Geonim**), formal title of heads of academies of Sura and Pumbedita in Babylonia 6th–11th c. Title also used for a time in Ereẓ Israel.

Gaon, Moses David (1889–1958), Israel educator, journalist, writer; b. Yugoslavia, settled in Ereẓ Israel 1909. Taught in Jerusalem, Smyrna, Buenos Aires. Wrote on Oriental Jewry, active in Sephardi community. His son, **Yehoram,** popular singer, entertainer.

CHRONOLOGICAL LIST OF THE BAGHDAD GEONIM

1070	Isaac b. Moses
1140	Ali ha-Levi
1150	Solomon
1164	Samuel b. Ali ha-Levi
1194	Zechariah b. Barachel
1195	Eleazar b. Hillel
1209	Daniel b. Eleazar b. Ḥibbat Allah
1218	Isaac b. Israel ibn Shuwaykh
1240	Daniel b. Abi al-Rabīʿa ha-Kohen
1250	Eli II
1288	Samuel b. Daniel b. Abi al-Rabīʿa ha-Kohen

CHRONOLOGICAL LIST OF THE GEONIM OF EREẒ ISRAEL

...	Moses (head of the academy?)
...	Meir I (head of the academy?)
884–915	Ẓemah
915–932	Aaron b. Moses Ben Meir
932–934	Isaac (son of Aaron)
934–948	... Ben Meir (brother of Aaron)
948–955	Abraham b. Aaron
c.955	Aaron
...	Joseph ha-Kohen b. Ezron (ruled two years)
...	... (ruled thirty years)
988–?	Samuel b. Joseph ha-Kohen
...	Yose b. Samuel
...	Shemaiah
1015	Josiah b. Aaron ("member of the Great Synagogue") b. Abraham (lived in Ramleh)
1020–1027	Solomon b. Joseph ha-Kohen
1027–1051	Solomon b. Judah
1051–1062	Daniel b. Azariah (*nasi* and *gaon*)
1062–1083	Elijah b. Solomon b. Joseph ha-Kohen
1084–1109	Abiathar b. Elijah

Gaon, Solomon (1912–), English Sephardi rabbi; b. Yugoslavia. Haham of Sephardi communities of British Commonwealth fr. 1949.

Gaon of Vilna, see Elijah ben Solomon Zalman.

Garber, Michael (1892–), Canadian lawyer, communal leader. Pres. Zionist Organization of Canada 1956–58, national pres. Canadian Jewish Congress 1962–68.

Garden of Eden, garden planted by God which was first dwelling place of Adam and Eve (Gen 2–3). Exact location unknown. The phrase "Garden of Eden" became synonymous with paradise in Jewish tradition.

Cartoon by Kariel Gardosh (Dosh)

Gardosh, Kariel ("Dosh"; 1921–), Israel cartoonist; b. Budapest, settled in Israel 1948. Editorial cartoonist of *Ma'ariv.* His figure of young boy "Little Israel" became popular symbol. Published collections of cartoons.

Garfield, John (1913–1952), U.S. actor. Stage roles incl. lead in Clifford Odets' *Golden Boy.* Films incl. *Tortilla Flat* and *Body and Soul.*

°**Garstang, John** (1876–1956), British archaeologist. Director of British School of Archaeology in Jerusalem 1919–26, first director of Dept. of Antiquities during British Mandate. Excavated at Jericho. Author of *Joshua, Judges.*

Gary (Kacew), Romain (1914–), French novelist; of Jewish origin. Diplomat in French diplomatic service. Novels incl. *The Roots of Heaven, Lady L., The Dance of Genghis Cohen.* Some are of Jewish interest.

Gascony, duchy in France. Jews fr. 4th c. Expulsion orders fr. 1289 and after. Marrano refugees fr. Spain took refuge there fr. end of 15th c. and led to importance of Bordeaux community.

Gasser, Herbert Spencer (1888–1963), U.S. neurophysiologist. Nobel Prize for Medicine and Physiology 1944 for work toward understanding nerve impulse transmission.

Gassner, John (1903–1967), U.S. author, critic, anthropologist. Prof. of playwriting and dramatic literature at Yale Univ. fr. 1956.

Moses Gaster

Gaster, Moses (1856–1939), rabbi, scholar, Zionist leader. Went fr. Rumania to London, where he became haham of Sephardi community 1887. Active in Ḥibbat Zion and later in Zionist movement, playing role in negotiations leading to Balfour Declaration. His writings cover Rumanian literature, Jewish folklore, Samaritan history, etc. His library was bought by British Museum. His son **Theodor Herzl Gaster** (1906–), educator, scholar. Taught comparative religion at Dropsie College. Wrote on folklore, translated *Dead Sea Scriptures* into English.

Gaston-Marin (Grossman) Gheorghe (1919–), Rumanian politician, engineer. Active Zionist in youth. Member of French Resistance in WWII. Minister of electrical energy 1949, first vice-chairman of State Planning Commission fr. 1954, head of Rumanian industrialization program with rank of deputy premier 1962–69.

Gateshead on Tyne, town in NE England. Jews fr. 1890s. Site of yeshivah (opened 1929). 350 Jews in 1970.

Gath, one of five principal cities of Philistines; site uncertain. Originally inhabited by Anakim (Josh. 11:20). Philistines fled after defeat of Goliath (I Sam. 17:52). Persecuted by Saul, David took refuge there (21:11).

Gavsie, Charles (1906–1967), Canadian lawyer, public official. Twice deputy minister; vice pres., pres. St. Lawrence Seaway Authority.

Gaza, city in Israel's S. coastal plain. From early times base of Egyptian operations in Canaan. Fr. 12th c. B.C.E. one of Philistines' five cities. Some of Samson's exploits per-

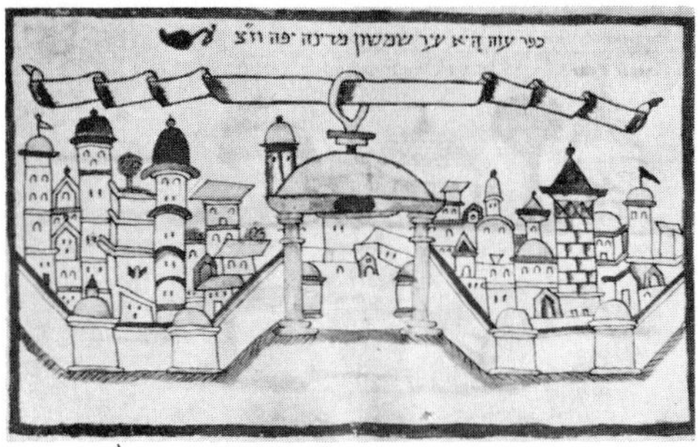

Miniature of Gaza, 16th cent.

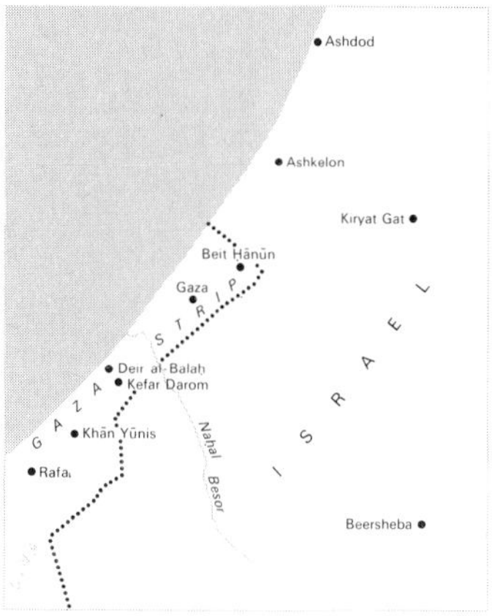

The Gaza Strip

formed there (cf. Judg. 16). Under Persians, royal fortress. Prospered under Romans and site of school of rhetoric. Jewish and Samaritan communities flourished under Arab rule. A center of Shabbatai Ẓevi's messianic movement 1665. Placed under Egyptian administration by armistice agreement 1949. In the Sinai campaign 1956 and after Six-Day War 1967, occupied by Israel army. Pop., 88,000 (1967), with another 30,000 refugees in camps within municipal boundaries.

Gaza Strip, area in Israel's S. coastal plain, covering 140 sq. mi. (362 sq. km.). Came into being as separate administrative unit during 1948 War of Independence. Armistice agreement placed it under Egyptian administration 1949 but never incorporated into Egypt. Fr. 1954, base of terrorists who infiltrated into Israel. Occupied by Israel army 1956 and again in 1967 Six-Day War, after which it was placed under Israel military administration.

Gdansk (Danzig), Polish port. Jews present fr. 15th c., when town became major trading center, but frictions led to restrictions throughout the centuries. Most Jews managed to leave before WWII; remainder killed.

Geba, ancient city N. of Jerusalem. Played central role in Saul's war with Philistines.

Gebirtig, Mordecai (1877–1942), Yiddish poet; b. Cracow. Carpenter by trade. Murdered by Nazis. Most famous song *"Undzer Shtetl Brent."*

Gedaliah, governor of Judah; appointed by Babylonians after capture of Jerusalem 586 B.C.E. Murdered by Ishmael together with Judahites and Babylonians stationed at Mizpah. Anniversary of his death (traditionally Tishri 3) observed as fast in Jewish calendar.

Gedaliah, (Don) Judah (d.c. 1526). Hebrew printer; b. Lisbon. Established first Hebrew printing press in Salonika.

Gederah, moshavah with municipal council status in Israel's coastal plain. Founded 1884 by members of Bilu movement. Pop. 5,200 (1971).

Gedud ha-Avodah (Heb. "Labor Legion"), first countrywide commune of Jewish workers in Ereẓ Israel. Founded 1920 by Third Aliyah pioneers to work land in disciplined group within general commune. Founded Ein Harod and Tel Yosef. Seriously weakened by ideological split. Its surviving groups joined Ha-Kibbutz ha-Me'uḥad 1929. Important pioneering role in settlement, defense, and labor.

Gehazi, servant of Elisha the prophet. Falsely represented master in requesting reward fr. Naaman and punished with leprosy.

Gehinnom, valley S. of Jerusalem. During monarchy, site of cult which involved burning of children. In Judaism, name is used metaphorically as appellation for place of torment reserved for wicked after death (cf. hell).

Abraham Geiger

Geiger, Abraham (1810–1874), German rabbi, Reform leader, scholar. As rabbi in Wiesbaden convened meeting of Reform rabbis 1837. Later rabbi in Breslau, Frankfort, Berlin. Helped establish Hochschule fuer die Wissenschaft and taught there. Regarded Judaism as religion with world mission and therefore endeavored to eliminate national element. Opposed Orthodoxy as too legalistic. Wrote on history of biblical translations, language of Mishnah, etc.

Geiger, Bernhard (1881–1964), Austrian philologist. Specialized in Iranian and Sanskrit. Taught at Univ. of Vienna until 1938, went to U.S. and taught at N.Y. Asia Institute and Columbia Univ.

Geiger, Lazarus (Eliezer Solomon; 1829–1870), German philosopher, philologist; nephew of Abraham Geiger. Taught at Jewish educational institute Philanthropin in Frankfort.

Geiger, Ludwig (1848–1919), German literary historian; son of Abraham Geiger. Prof. at Berlin Univ. fr. 1880. Wrote on Renaissance, Humanism, Reformation studies, German-Jewish history, and Goethe. Edited *Allgemeine Zeitung des Judentums* fr. 1909.

Geiger, Moritz (1860–1937), philosopher; nephew of Abraham Geiger. Prof. in Munich and Goettingen. Settled in U.S. 1933. Taught at Vassar College. His view of objectivity of aesthetics became basis for interpreting "aesthetic pleasure" in school of phenomenalism.

Gelb, Ignace Jay (1907–), U.S. Assyriologist; b. Poland, in U.S. fr. 1929. Prof. at Oriental Institute at Univ. of Chicago. Contributions to Assyriology centered around ethnolinguistic foundations of Ancient Near East.

Gelbard, José Ber (1917–), Argentinian politician. B. Poland, went to Argentina as a child. Prominent in economic life of country. Appointed minister of economy and finance in 1973, serving in Peronist cabinets.

Gelber, Canadian family. **Moses** (1876–1940), b. Galicia. A founder of Jewish education in Toronto. His son **Edward Elisha** (1903–1971), pres. of Zionist Organization of Canada 1950–52. Settled in Jerusalem, active in Yad Vashem and Heb. Univ. Edward's cousin, **Lionel Morris** (1907–), writer on international affairs. Special assistant to Canada's Prime Minister John Diefenbaker 1960–61. Lionel's sister **Sylva** (1910–), head of Women's Bureau of Canadian Department of Labor fr. 1969. Her brother **Marvin** (1912–), Liberal MP 1963–65, national pres. UN Association of Canada, member of Canadian UN delegation 1968. Another brother, **Arthur E.** (1915–), pres. United Jewish Welfare Fund of Toronto.

Gelber, Nathan Michael (1891–1966), Austrian historian, Zionist; b. Galicia, settled in Ereẓ Israel 1934. Worked in Keren Hayesod head office in Jerusalem. Prolific writer on Jewish life and history, esp. early Zionism and Galician Jewry.

Geldern, Simon von (1720–1788), German adventurer, traveler. Led life of adventure, gambling, philandering. Lived among royalty and in Christian society. Granduncle of Heinrich Heine.

Gelerter, Ludwig Litman (1873–1945), Rumanian socialist, physician; originally fr. Jassy, moved to Bucharest after WWI. Established Socialist Workers' Party of Rumania 1929.

Gelfand, Izrail Moisevich (1913–), Soviet mathematician. Prof. of mathematics at Academy of Sciences Inst. of Mathematics, Moscow 1943. A discoverer of general theory of normed algebras.

Gelfond, Aleksander Osipovich (1906–), Soviet mathematician. Prof. of mathematics at Moscow Univ. 1931. Important contributions to number theory, complex analysis, theory of transcendental numbers.

Gelilah (Heb. "rolling [of Torah scroll]"), rolling together of Torah scroll, its binding and dressing after reading of Law in synagogue. Immediately follows *hagbahah.*

Geller, Yefim Petrovich (1925–), Russian chess master. Won Soviet championship 1955.

Gellman, Leon (1887–1973), religious Zionist leader; b. Russia, in U.S. fr. 1910. An organizer and pres. 1935–39 of U.S. Mizrachi movement, editor of its publications. Settled in Israel 1949 and became chairman of World Mizrachi.

Gell-Mann, Murray (1929–), U.S. physicist. Nobel Prize 1969 for research into behavior of subatomic particles. Prof. at California Institute of Technology.

Gellner, František (1881–1914), Czech poet, cartoonist. Outstanding Czech satirist of his time. D. in WWI.

Gemara (Aram. "completion"), word popularly applied to Talmud as a whole, or more particularly to discussions and elaborations by *amoraim* on Mishnah.

Gemariah, high official in time of Jehoiakim (Jer. 36:10-12). Member of one of influential pro-Babylonian families in last days of Judah.

Gematria (Gr.), aggadic hermeneutical rules for interpreting Bible. Consists of explaining word or group of words according to numerical values of Hebrew letters, or of substituting other letters of alphabet for them in accordance with set system.

Gemilut Ḥasadim (Heb.), fundamental social virtue encompassing duties of sympathetic consideration toward one's fellowmen. Called one of three pillars of Judaism (Avot 1:2). During Middle Ages used for giving interest-free loans to those in need.

General Government, territory in Poland administered by German civilian governor with headquarters in Cracow after German occupation in WWII.

General Zionists, Zionist party; originally Zionists who were not members of existing Zionist political parties. In Ereẓ Israel party began to organize 1922. World union established 1929, advocating private enterprise, abolition of party control over national institutions. Various splits occurred in party fr. time to time. Participated in provisional government and government coalition 1952–55. Established Liberal Party 1961 but split occurred again 1965, with part of members joining Ḥerut to form Gaḥal and remainder forming Independent Liberal Party.

Genesis, Book of, (Heb. *Bereshit,* "In the beginning," from its first word), first book of Pentateuch. Account of history fr. creation of world to death of Joseph. Relates stories of Garden of Eden, Adam and his family, Noah, the Patriarchs, and Joseph. Although parallels to early chapters have been found in other Near Eastern literature, its monotheistic approach and interpretation are unparalleled.

Genesis Rabbah, aggadic Midrash on Genesis, product of Palestinian *amoraim.* Earliest, longest, and most important of extant amoraic aggadic Midrashim. Part of Midrash Rabbah.

Genesis Rabbati, Midrash on Book of Genesis usually ascribed to Moses ha-Darshan of Narbonne (11th c.). Quotes not only fr. classical sources of *halakhah* but also fr. Apocrypha and Pseudepigrapha (esp. fr. Testaments of Twelve Patriarchs).

Geneva, city in Switzerland. Jews there fr. 12th c. Expelled 1490. Residence permitted in nearby town 1783. Community officially recognized 1853. Synagogue inaugurated 1859. Jews went there fr. France, Alsace, and more recently, fr. Egypt and other Arab lands. A number of Jewish organizations established their European headquarters there. Jewish pop. 3,250 (1971).

Genizah (Heb.), place for storing books or ritual objects which have become unusable, usually room in synagogue. Best known found at synagogue in Fostat (Old Cairo); rediscovered by Solomon Schechter, who took 100,000 pages to Cam-

BOOK OF GENESIS – CONTENTS

1:1–11:32	**PART I: Universal History**
Chs. 1–6	Creation. From Adam to Noah.
1:1–2:4a	The story of Creation; the Sabbath.
2:4b–3:24	Adam and Eve in the Garden of Eden.
4:1–16	Cain and Abel.
4:17–26	The genealogy of Cain; the rise of civilization.
5:1–32	The line of Adam to Noah.
6:1–4	The "sons of God" and the daughters of men.
Chs. 6–11	From Noah to Abraham.
6:5–8:32	The Flood.
9:1–17	The blessing and the covenant with man.
9:18–29	Noah's drunkenness.
10:1–32	The table of nations.
11:1–9	The Tower of Babel.
11:10–32	The line of Shem to Abraham.
12:1–50:26	**PART 2: Patriarchal History.**
12–25	Abraham.
12:1–9	The call of Abraham; the migration to Canaan.
12:10–20	Abraham and Sarah in Egypt.
13:1–18	Abraham and Lot.
14:1–24	The battle of the kings; Abraham blessed by Melchizedek.
15:1–21	The covenant with Abraham.
16:1–16	Abraham, Sarah and Hagar; Divine promises regarding Ishmael.
17:1–27	The covenant concerning circumcision.
18:1–33	Abraham and the three messengers; the intercession for Sodom.
19:1–29	The destruction of Sodom and Gomorrah.
19:30–38	Lot and his daughters; the birth of Moab and Ammon.
20:1–18	Abraham and Sarah at Gerar.
21:1–8	The birth of Isaac.
21:9–21	The expulsion of Hagar and Ishmael
21:22–34	Abraham and Abimelech at Beer-Sheba.
22:1–19	The binding of Isaac *(Akedah).*
22:20–24	The line of Nahor.
23:1–20	The purchase of Machpelah and the burial of Sarah.
24:1–67	The marriage of Isaac to Rebekah.
25:1–6	The line of Keturah.
25:7–18	The death and burial of Abraham; the line of Ishmael.
Chs. 25–36	Isaac and Jacob.
25:19–34	The birth of Jacob and Esau; the sale of the birthright.
26:1–33	Isaac, Rebekah and Abimelech at Gerar.
26:34–35	Esau's Hittite wives.
27:1–28:5	Jacob's deception of Isaac.
28:6–9	Esau's Ishmaelite wife.
28:10–22	Jacob at Bethel.
29:1–30:43	Jacob with Laban.
31:1–54	Jacob's flight from Laban.
32:1–32	Jacob at Mahanaim and Penuel; Jacob wrestles with the angel.
33:1–20	Jacob meets Esau; his purchase of land at Shechem.
34:1–31	The rape of Dinah.
35:1–15	Jacob revisits Bethel.
35:16–29	Family affairs in Canaan.
36:1–43	The lines of Esau and Seir the Horite; early kings of Edom.
Chs. 37–50	Joseph and his brothers.
37:1–36	Joseph and his brothers.
38:1–30	Judah and Tamar
39:1–23	Joseph in Potiphar's house.
40:1–23	Joseph in prison.
41:1–57	Pharaoh's dreams; Joseph's rise to power; the years of abundance and the start of the famine.
42:1–44:34	Joseph encounters his brothers.
45:1–28	Joseph discloses his identity.
46:1–47:10	The migration of the Israelites to Egypt.
47:11–27	Joseph's agrarian policy.
48:1–50:21	Jacob's farewell blessings; his death and burial.
50:22–26	The death of Joseph.

bridge 1896. About another 100,000 pages were discovered. They contained literary treasures and historical documents, outstanding being most of Hebrew text of Ben Sira, Damascus Covenant (later found among Dead Sea documents), ancient Palestinian, Babylonian, and Spanish *piyyutim,* and many documents relating to history of Jews of Middle East.

Genoa, seaport in N. Italy. Jews there before 511. Expulsions and readmissions after 13th c. Ghetto 1660; equality 1848. 2,000 Jews before WWII; 1,000 Jews after war.

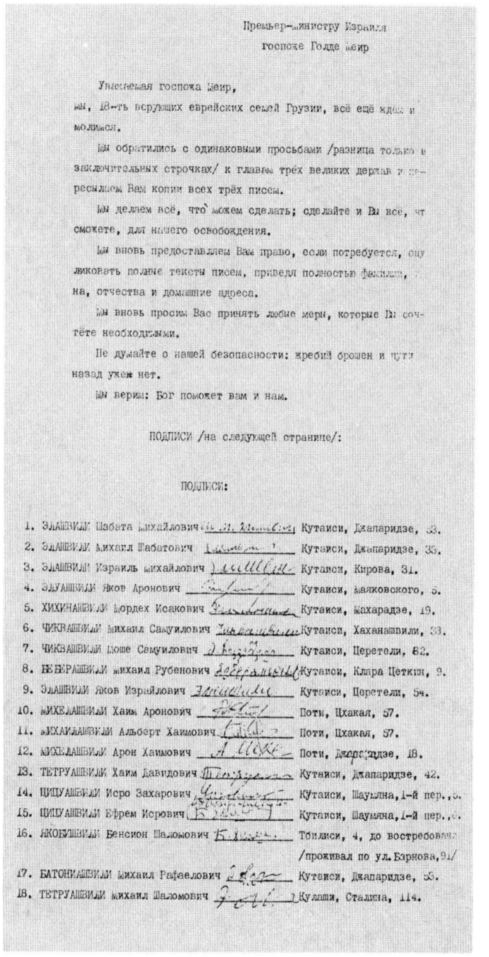

Премьер-министру Израиля
госпоже Голде Меир

Уважаемая госпожа Меир,

мы, 18-ть верующих еврейских семей Грузии, всё ещё ждём и молимся.

Мы обратились с одинаковыми просьбами /разница только в заключительных строчках/ к главам трёх великих держав и пересылаем Вам копии всех трёх писем.

Мы делаем всё, что можем сделать; сделайте и Вы всё, что сможете, для нашего освобождения.

Мы вновь предоставляем Вам право, если потребуется, опубликовать полные тексты писем, приведя полностью фамилии, имена, отчества и домашние адреса.

Мы вновь просим Вас принять любые меры, которые Вы сочтёте необходимыми.

Не думайте о нашей безопасности: жребий брошен и пути назад уже нет.

Мы верим: Бог поможет вам и нам.

ПОДПИСИ /на следующей странице/:

ПОДПИСИ:

1. ЭЛАШВИЛИ Шабата Михайлович ____ Кутаиси, Джапаридзе, 33.
2. ЭЛАШВИЛИ Михаил Шабатович ____ Кутаиси, Джапаридзе, 35.
3. ЭЛАШВИЛИ Израиль Михайлович ____ Кутаиси, Кирова, 31.
4. ЭЛУАШВИЛИ Яков Аронович ____ Кутаиси, Маяковского, 5.
5. ХИХИНАШВИЛИ Мордех Исакович ____ Кутаиси, Махарадзе, 19.
6. ЧИКВАШВИЛИ Михаил Самуилович ____ Кутаиси, Хаханашвили, 33.
7. ЧИКВАШВИЛИ Моше Самуилович ____ Кутаиси, Церетели, 82.
8. БЕБЕРАШВИЛИ Михаил Рубенович ____ Кутаиси, Клара Цеткин, 9.
9. ЭЛАШВИЛИ Яков Израйлович ____ Кутаиси, Церетели, 54.
10. МИХЕЛАШВИЛИ Хаим Аронович ____ Поти, Цхакая, 57.
11. МИХАИЛАШВИЛИ Альберт Хаимович ____ Поти, Цхакая, 57.
12. МИХЕЛАШВИЛИ Арон Хаимович ____ Поти, Джапаридзе, 18.
13. ТЕТРУАШВИЛИ Хаим Давидович ____ Кутаиси, Джапаридзе, 42.
14. ЦИЦУАШВИЛИ Исро Захарович ____ Кутаиси, Шаумяна, 1-й пер., 5.
15. ЦИЦУАШВИЛИ Ефрем Исрович ____ Кутаиси, Шаумяна, 1-й пер., 5.
16. ЯКОБАШВИЛИ Бенсион Шаломович ____ Тбилиси, 4, до востребования /проживал по ул. Бэрнова, 91/
17. БАТОНИАШВИЛИ Михаил Рафаелович ____ Кутаиси, Джапаридзе, 53.
18. ТЕТРУАШВИЛИ Михаил Шаломович ____ Кулаши, Сталина, 114.

Letter received by Israel Prime Minister from 18 Georgian families, 1969, appealing for help in emigrating to Israel.

Jewish communities in Georgian S.S.R.

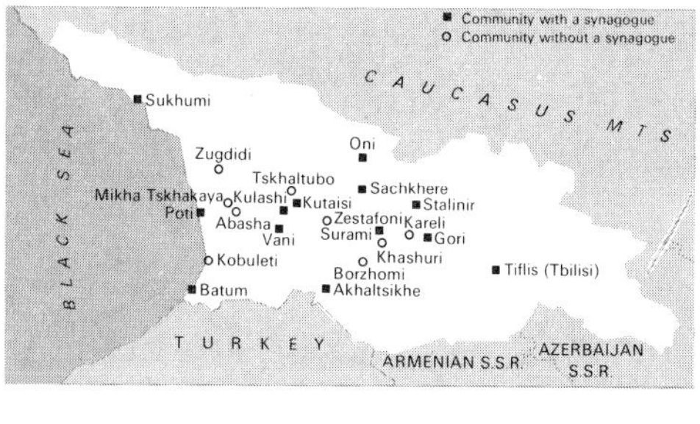

Moses Gentili

Genocide Convention, resolution adopted by UN 1948 declaring genocide to be crime against international law and describing responsibility of both actual perpetrators and rulers. Ratified by 67 countries by 1969.

Gentili (Ḥefez), family in N. Italy. **Moses ben Gershom** (1663–1711), rabbinical scholar in Venice who composed poems and wrote homiletical-philosophical commentary on Pentateuch. His son **Gershom ben Moses** (1683–1700), author of *Yad Ḥaruzim,* Hebrew rhyme-lexicon.

George (Cohn), Manfred (1893–1965), journalist; b. Berlin, in U.S. fr. 1938. Edited *Aufbau,* German-language weekly representing German-Jewish immigrant community.

Georgia (Gruziya), Soviet Socialist Republic. Origin of community hidden in legend. Persecuted 15th–early 19th c; some Jews degraded to status of slaves. Religious contacts with Babylonian academies and later with neighboring countries (e.g., Turkey). With Russian rule no differentiation fr. rest of population. European Jews arrived fr. 19th c. Zionism spread fr. late 19th c., initiated by Russian Jewish conscripts serving in Caucasus. Jews fr. Georgia started settling in Ereẓ Israel 1863. Despite anti-religious indoctrination by Soviet authorities and complete lack of Jewish educational facilities, many Georgian Jews succeeded in maintaining traditions among their families. Contact with Ḥabad Ḥasidim fr. 1920s. 1960s saw new upsurge of desire to go to Israel, culminating in considerable emigration. Acc. to 1970 census, Jewish pop. 55,000 with one-third in Tbilisi.

Georgia, U.S. state. Jews arrived 1733. Congregation Mikveh Israel founded in Savannah 1790. Rapid growth in 1840s with German Jews settling throughout state. E. European Jews arrived fr. 1880s. First Jewish governor of any U.S. state David Emmanuel 1801. Jews active in state and city governments. Jewish pop. 25,650 (1971), with 12 communities, largest in Atlanta.

Ger Dynasty, see Gur Dynasty.

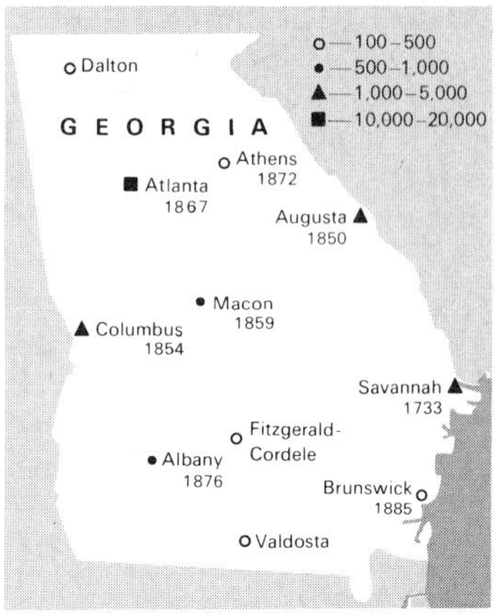

Jewish communities in Georgia, U.S., dates of establishment.

Temple of Artemis, Gerasa.

Alberto Gerchunoff

Gerar, ancient city NW of Beersheba. Abraham and Isaac dwelt there. Name survived as geographical term, even after destruction.

Gerasa (Jarash), ancient city in Transjordan. Inhabited by 7th millennium B.C.E. Important under Roman rule, esp. under Hadrian and his successors. Final decline precipitated by Muslim conquest 635. Excavations 1928ff. uncovered many remains, incl. mosaic pavement of synagogue.

Gerchunoff, Alberto (1884–1950), Argentine author, journalist. Wrote *Los Gauchos Judíos* describing life of Jewish colonists in Entre Ríos during early 20th c. Active Zionist fr. 1930s; helped secure S. American support for establishment of Israel 1947–8.

Gerhardt, Charles Frederic (1816–1856), French chemist. Revived radical theory of structure. Prof. at Strasbourg.

Gerim, (Heb.), minor tractate appended to Talmud. Deals with procedure and regulations for conversion to Judaism.

Gerizim, mountain facing Mt. Ebal, E. of Shechem (Nablus). Scene of ceremonial blessing connected with renewal of covenant in Joshua's time (Jos. 8:30ff.). Jotham uttered on its slope his fable against Abimelech (Jud. 9:7ff.). Acc. to Samaritan tradition, it is Mt. Moriah (Gen. 22:2) and Samaritans built temple there c. 330 B.C.E., destroyed by John Hyrcanus 129 B.C.E. Two churches constructed there in 5th–6th c. Samaritans still observe all their festivals and public holy ceremonies there, notably Paschal sacrifice.

Germany, country in N. Central Europe. First Jews were merchants who followed Roman legions. Earliest records of community at Cologne 321 C.E. Rhineland communities developed in 10th c.; beginnings of rich cultural life (e.g., Gershom b. Judah). First crusade 1096 accompanied by massacre of Jews, incl. development of ideology of martyrdom *(kiddush ha-Shem)* as

The burning of Jewish martyrs, 15th cent. Germany.

preferable to conversion. Jews became "crown property" *(servi camerae nostrae)* 1236, a unique status in tribal feudal society. 12th and 13th c. saw development of pietist movement Ḥasidei Ashkenaz. Moneylending into which Jews were pushed by restrictive legislation left no time for study. Community was strong. Persecution intensified in 13th–15th c. when expulsions began to be frequent, leading to gradual migration to east. Blood and host desecration libels became

JEWISH POPULATION IN GERMANY, 1871–1971.

1871	512,158
1880	562,612
1890	567,884
1900	586,833
1910	615,021
1925	564,379
1933	503,000[1]
1939	234,000[2]
1941	164,000
1942	51,000
1943	31,910
1944	14,574
1946	156,705[3]
1948	153,000[3]
1949	55,000[3]
1952	23,000
1957	30,000
1964	31,000
1971	30,000

[1] Jews defined by religion.
[2] Jews defined by Nuremberg law.
[3] Estimated number includes displaced persons.

Major Jewish communities in Germany, 1933 and 1970

common. Reformation brought no respite, though Jews began to break out of economic restrictions. 17th and 18th c. absolutist states saw increase in Jewish wealth and greater restrictions on their life; powers of community were reduced. Court Jews came to the fore. Emancipation process started in 18th c., its pioneer being Moses Mendelssohn. Napoleonic wars brought emancipation, then reaction. Emancipation completed 1820. Jews played increasingly large role in general culture and there was strong process of assimilation. Major 19th c. manifestations included Reform Judaism and development of modern Jewish scholarship *(Wissenschaft des Judentums)*. After WWI Jews attained great integration into German society. Anti-Semitism which had developed on racial basis fr. late 19th c. was whipped up by Nazi allegation of Jewish responsibility for WWI defeat. With coming of Nazis to power 1933, legislation excluded Jews fr. economic and social life, notably the Nuremberg Laws 1935. About 300,000 Jews emigrated 1933–39; those who remained perished in the Holocaust. After WWII temporary influx of Jews into Germany, mostly displaced persons, but after several years Jewish pop. became steady at 30,000. W. Germany accepted responsibility for Nazi crimes and made material compensation both to individuals and to Israel as successor of Jewish community. Diplomatic relations with Israel established 1965. E. Germany maintained consistently hostile attitude to Israel.

Gernsheim, Friedrich (1839–1916), German composer, conductor, teacher. Director of master class in composition at Prussian Academy of Fine Arts.

Gerona (Gerunda), city in Spain. Jewish community fr. 9th c. Jews active in city's life. Major force of Jewish culture (Naḥmanides) and first Spanish center of Kabbalah. Fr. end of 13th c. Jews forced out of administrative positions. Most Jews chose martyrdom in 1391 persecutions. Throughout 15th c. decline of community with many conversions.

Gerondi, Jacob ben Sheshet (13th c.), kabbalist in Gerona, Spain. Strong influence on subsequent kabbalistic literature.

Gerondi, Jonah ben Abraham, see Jonah ben Abraham Gerondi.

Gerondi, Nissim ben Reuben, see Nissim ben Reuben Gerondi.

Old Jewish quarter in Gerona

George Gershwin

Gerondi, Samuel ben Meshullam (c.1300), scholar in Gerona, Spain. Author of *Ohel Mo'ed,* comprehensive code dealing with Jewish laws of practical application.

Gerondi, Zerahiah ben Isaac ha-Levi (12th c.), rabbinical scholar, poet. Proficient in Arabic as well as philosophy and astronomy. His *halakhah* notes *Ha-Ma'or* and *Sefer ha-Ẓava* are highly critical of Alfasi.

Geronimo de Santa Fé, see Lorki, Joshua.

Gerovich, Eliezer Mordecai ben Isaac (1844–1913), Russian *ḥazzan,* composer. Chief *ḥazzan* at Rostov-on-Don fr. 1887, and famous for his own compositions, collected in *Schire Tefilla* and *Schire Simra.*

Gershenzon, Mikhail Osipovich (1869–1925), Russian literary historian, philosopher, essayist. An anti-Marxist liberal who hailed Russian Revolution as benefiting Russian culture. Enthusiastically advocated revival of Hebrew literature.

Gershom, elder son of Moses (Ex. 2:22; 18:3). Gershomites had no function in connection with Tabernacle and no levitical cities were apportioned to them. They were apparently priests of tribe of Dan (Judg. 18:30).

Gershom ben Judah Me'or ha-Golah (Rabbenu Gershom; c. 960–1028), one of first great German talmudic scholars and a spiritual molder of German Jewry. Head of yeshivah of Mainz. His name is connected with many *takkanot,* most famous of which is *ḥerem* ("ban") against bigamy. His responsa are scattered throughout works of French and German scholars. Rashi said of him that all Ashkenazi Jewry depends upon his teachings and all are his disciples.

Gershon, eldest son of Levi, from whom division of Levites (Gershonites) traced their descent.

Gershon, Karen (1923–), English poet and writer; b. Germany. Wrote of Holocaust and experiences of refugees.

Gershon ben Solomon of Arles (13th c.), Provençal scholar. Author of *Sha'ar ha-Shamayim,* popular summary of natural sciences, astronomy, theology of his day.

Gershuni, Grigori Andreyevich (1870–1908), Russian revolutionary; founder and leader of terrorist arm of Socialist-Revolutionary party. Ardent anti-czarist, responsible for assassinations of czarist officials and dignitaries.

Gershwin, George (1898–1937), U.S. composer. Pioneered in symphonic jazz (*Rhapsody in Blue*), other compositions for films and Broadway shows, and last work was folk opera *Porgy and Bess.* Many of his songs, some with lyrics by his brother **Ira** (1896–), have maintained lasting popularity.

Gersoni, Henry (Gershoni, Ẓevi Hirsch; 1844–1897), journalist, author; b. Vilna; converted to Christianity and later returned to Judaism. Emigrated to U.S., where he was pioneer of Hebrew literature and Yiddish periodicals.

Gersonides, see Levi ben Gershom.

Gerson-Kiwi, Edith (Esther; 1908–), Israel musicologist; b. Berlin, settled in Ereẓ Israel 1935. Writings deal with musical traditions of Jewish communities and mutual influences in Jewish, Christian, and Muslim music.

°**Gerstein, Kurt** (1905–1945), German anti-Nazi. As an S.S. officer heard about mass murders in camps and tried to stop them by informing Swedish and Swiss legations, the Holy See, etc., only to encounter disbelief and indifference. Arrested

by French at end of war as suspected war criminal. Found hanged in his cell.

Gertler, Mark (1891–1939), English artist. Early work influenced by his life in Whitechapel ghetto and later by post-impressionism. Depressed by poor health, Hitler's anti-Jewish campaign, and financial problems; committed suicide.

Gertz, Elmer (1906–), U.S. lawyer. Vigorously opposed capital punishment, defended freedom of expression, and prominent advocate in many cases involving civil rights and liberties.

Gerusia (Gr.), council of elders, common throughout Hellenistic world. Earliest Jewish *Gerusia* dates back to biblical times, functioning as high court together with high priest and prophets. In Hellenistic times it was representative of Jewish population of Judea.

Ger Ẓedek, see Proselytes.

Gesang, Nathan-Nachman (1886–1944), a founder and pres. of Zionist Organization of Argentina. Active in propagation of Hebrew language.

Gesellschaft zur Foerderung der Wissenschaft des Judentums (Ger. "Society for Advancement of Jewish Scholarship"), Jewish scholarly society in Berlin 1902–38.

°**Gesenius, Heinrich Friedrich Wilhelm** (1786–1842), German orientalist, lexicographer, Bible scholar. His biblical Hebrew lexicon and Hebrew grammar were long standard works. Also wrote history of Hebrew language and script.

Gesher Benot Ya'akov, bridge on the Jordan at S. end of Huleh valley. Original bridge built in 13th c. Because of strategic importance, scene of several famous battles.

Geshuri, Meir Shimon (1897–), writer on music. A founder of Ha-Po'el ha-Mizrachi and Israel Institute for Sacred Music 1958.

Gestapo (Abb. **Geheime Staatspolizei**), "Secret State Police" of Nazi Germany, persecuting Jews fr. beginning of regime and finally playing central role in carrying out "Final Solution." Became accepted synonym for terror.

Gestetner, David (1854–1939), British industrialist. Inventor of cyclostyle duplicating process and founder of modern stencil duplicating. His son, **Sigmund** (1897–1956), continued his father's business. Devoted Zionist; pres. Jewish National Fund fr. 1950.

Get, see Divorce.

Ge'ullah (Heb. "redemption"), title of several prayers, incl. section in

"The Artist's Mother" by Mark Gertler.

Gesher Benot Ya'akov

Gezer Calendar

morning and evening prayer recited bet. *Shema* and *Amidah,* and *piyyutim* recited on special Sabbaths and on pilgrim festival prior to *Amidah.*

Gewitsch, Aaron Wolf (c. 1700–c. 1770), Austrian scribe, illuminator of Jewish mss. Though following traditional lines, introduced new groupings and exceptional freshness of approach.

Gezer, ancient city in C. Ereẓ Israel. Mentioned in Egyptian documents fr. 15th c. B.C.E. Commanded approaches to Jerusalem and was fortified by Solomon. In Hasmonean times, major Greek base captured by Simeon, under whom it was military center. Declined after Hasmonean period. Modern excavations.

Gezer Calendar, 10th c. B.C.E. inscription of ancient Hebrew script found at Gezer. Cites annual cycle of agricultural activities. One of oldest known Hebrew inscriptions.

Gherea-Dobrogeanu, Constantin (orig. **Solomon Katz;** 1855–1920), Rumanian literary critic, socialist theoretician. His literary work reflected outlook of different social groups and classes. As political writer popularized Marxist socialism. Converted to Christianity.

Ghetto, compulsory urban residential quarter for Jews. Term fr. Venice quarter situated nr. foundry (*getto,* or *ghetto*) closed 1516 and declared only part of city open to Jewish settlement. Such ghettos were known until 19th c. in Christian Europe and until recent times in Moslem countries (see Mellah). Used also for voluntary concentration of Jews in specific neighborhood. Nazis revived concept when they segregated Jews into "ghettos" in many cities and then in E. Europe. They lived in conditions of terrible overcrowding and many died of hunger and diseases; the others were eventually shot or deported to death camps.

Ghetto Fighters' House, institution established in Kibbutz Loḥamei ha-Getta'ot 1950 as memorial and research and documentation center on Holocaust period and on Jewish resistance under Nazi rule in Europe.

Ghirondi, Mordecai Samuel ben Benzion Aryeh (1799–1852), Italian scholar, biographer. Chief rabbi of Padua 1831–52. Author of *Toledot Gedolei Yisrael,* biographical dictionary of Jewish scholars and rabbis.

Ghirshman, Roman (1895–), French archaeologist. Excavated in Iran and Afghanistan. Numerous publications on Iranian culture, art, and history.

Ghiyyat, see Ibn Ghayyat.

Gibeah (Gibeath-Benjamin, Gibeath-Shaul), center of territory of tribe of Benjamin, N. of Jerusalem. Site settled fr. early Iron Age. In 11th c. B.C.E. Saul's royal residence. Rebuilt in latter part of monarchy and destroyed by Chaldeans. New fortress built in 4th c. B.C.E.; survived until 2nd c. B.C.E.

Gibeon, ancient city, modern al-Jīb, NW of Jerusalem. Joshua's battle with Canaanite kings fought nearby; during event miracle commanded by Joshua took place; "Sun, stand thou still upon Gibeon; and thou, Moon, in the valley of Aijalon" (Josh. 10). Also figures in account of events during time of David. At beginning of monarchy "great high place" located there. Excavations conducted on site 1956–62.

Gibeonites and Nethinim, temple servants in Jerusalem. Joshua punished wily Gibeonites for their ruse by making them hewers of wood and water carriers (Josh. 9:29). Later tradition identified them with Nethinim mentioned in post-Exilic literature as Temple servants who maintained their identity down to amoraic times.

Gibraltar, British crown colony, S. of Spain. Jews there in 14th c. Legal right of Jewish settlement recognized 1749. Most Jews came fr. N. Africa. Sir Joshua A. Hassan first mayor and chief minister of colony. Jewish pop. 625 (1972), with 4 synagogues.

Giddal (3rd c.), Babylonian *amora;* pupil of Rav and contemporary of Huna, with whom he had many heated debates.

Ancient pool of Gibeon

Kibbutz Bet Alfa at the foot of Mount Gilboa.

Gideon (Jerubaal), Israelite judge. Delivered Israel from Midianites and their allies (Judg. 6:11–8:32). Offered kingship but refused.

Gideon, Samson (Gideon Abudiente; 1699–1762), English financier. Economic adviser to English government. His son, **Samson** (1745–1824), became Lord Eardley and had no contacts with Judaism.

Gihon, spring in Kidron Valley, E. of Jerusalem. King Hezekiah made tunnel which branched off fr. spring and led water to fortified perimeter of city (see Siloam).

Gikatilla (Chiquatilla), Isaac ibn (10th c.), Spanish Hebrew poet, grammarian. Student of Menahem ibn Saruq and defended him against Dunash b. Labrat. His pupil was Jonah ibn Janaḥ.

Gikatilla (Chiquatilla), Joseph ben Abraham (1248–c.1325), Spanish kabbalist whose works exerted profound influence on kabbalism. Pupil of Abraham Abulafia and friend of Moses b. Shem Tov de Leon. Works incl. *Ginnat Egoz,* introduction to mystic symbolism, and *Sha'arei Orah,* detailed explanation of kabbalistic symbolism.

Gikatilla (Chiquatilla), Moses ben Samuel ha-Kohen (11th c.), Spanish liturgical poet, grammarian. His works known fr. quotations.

Giladi (Butelbroit), Israel (1886–1918), Ereẓ Israel pioneer, leader of Ha-Shomer; b. Bessarabia, settled in Ereẓ Israel 1905. In charge of defense of settlements in Galilee, Samaria, and Judea.

Gilbert, Ina (1932–), Canadian painter. Pres. Society of Canadian Artists. Works executed in acrylic paint on canvas or sheets of plexiglas.

Gilboa, mountain ridge in Israel, NE of Samarian Hills. Scene of battle in which Saul and his sons were killed (I Sam. 31:1–6). In modern times site of afforestation and settlements founded on slopes and at its foot.

Gilboa, Amir (1917–), Israel poet; b. Russia, settled in Ereẓ Israel 1937. His verse blends personal and national motifs.

Gilead, region of Transjordan. First settlement c. 24th-21st c. B.C.E. Most of area was occupied by Og and Sihon, Amorite kings, from whom it was conquered by Israel tribes. S. part settled by Reuben. With division of kingdom it remained in hands of N. Israel, but scene of frequent conflict between Arameans and Israel. Conquered by Tiglath-Pileser III 733 and many of its inhabitants exiled.

Gilead, Zerubavel (1912–), Hebrew poet, writer, editor. Information officer of Palmaḥ and member of its general staff during Israel's War of Independence.

Gilels, Emil Grigoryevich (1916–), Russian pianist. Teacher at Moscow Conservatory. Winner of Stalin and Lenin Prize.

Gilgal, ancient city E. of Jericho. Israelites encamped there after crossing the Jordan and it served as base during Joshua's wars. Samuel judged Israel and Saul was crowned king there.

Gilgul (Heb.), transmigration of souls, metempsychosis. Kabbalistic doctrine (fr. 12th c.) that souls go through several bodies. Concept not found in Bible or Talmud. Originally considered severe punishment. Doctrine opposed by philosophers (e.g., Maimonides).

Gimbel, U.S. merchant family. **Adam** (1817–1896), b. Bavaria, settled in New Orleans 1835. Owned stores in Vincennes, Ind. His sons **Jacob** (1851–1922) and **Isaac** (1857–1931) founded Gimbel Brothers in Milwaukee and opened store in Philadelphia. Gimbels' opened in N.Y. 1910, bought Saks 1923, and extended chain to Pittsburgh, Chicago, Detroit, Beverly Hills, and San Francisco. Isaac's son **Bernard F.** (1885–1966), pres. of Gimbel Brothers 1927–53. Civic leader in N.Y. His son **Bruce A.** (1913–), pres. fr. 1953.

Gimmel (ג), 3rd letter of Hebrew alphabet; numerical value 3. Pronounced *g.*

Gingold, Pinchas M. (1893–1953), U.S. Labor Zionist, Yiddish educator. A founder of Jewish Legion in WWI. Director of Yiddish Teachers Seminary, N.Y.

Ginnosar, Plain of, narrow plain on the NW shore of Lake Kinneret.

Ginossar, Rosa (1890–), Zionist women's leader; daughter of Mordecai b. Hillel Hacohen and daughter-in-law of Aḥad Ha-Am; b. Russian, settled in Ereẓ Israel 1907. Practiced law. President of WIZO 1963–70.

Ginsberg, see also Guenzburg.

Ginsberg, Allen (1926–), U.S. poet, leader of mid-20th c. "Beat Generation." Works (*Kaddish, Howl*) known for jazz rhythms and hallucinatory imagery. Father **Louis** (1896–), teacher, poet.

Ginsberg, Edward (1917–), U.S. attorney, business executive. Active in American Jewish Joint Distribution Committee and United Jewish Appeal.

HANUKKAH

Ḥanukkah candelabra from Morocco, 17th–19th cent.

Pewter *Ḥanukkah* lamp from Germany, 18th cent.

Ḥanukkah lights being kindled near the Western Wall, Jerusalem, 1972.

HAVDALAH

Spice-box used in the *Havdalah* service, partly gilt. Germany, 17th cent.

ḤEDER "The *Ḥeder*" by Moritz Daniel Oppenheim, 19th cent. The pupils are studying the Hebrew alphabet.

HOLOCAUST Jewish badges decreed by the Nazis in World War II. 1. Bulgaria, Lithuania, Hungary, parts of Poland, and Greece. 2. Germany, Alsace, Bohemia-Moravia. 3. France. 4. Holland. 5. Greece, Serbia, Belgrade, Sofia. 6. Belgium. 7. Slovakia. 8. Bulgaria. 9. Slovakia. 10. Poland (part), East and Upper Silesia.

Ginsberg, Harold Louis (1903–), U.S. Bible scholar, Semitist; b. Canada, in U.S. fr. 1936. Prof. at Jewish Theological Seminary fr. 1941. Bulk of his studies in biblical field are philological – word studies, text restoration, and exegesis. Pioneered in interpretation of Ugaritic texts and their application to Bible. Bible editor, *Encyclopaedia Judaica.*

Ginsberg, Mitchell I. (1915–), U.S. social worker, educator. Prof. at Columbia Univ. School of Social Work fr. 1953. Commissioner of Public Welfare in N.Y. 1966; administrator of city's Human Resources Commission 1968.

Ginsberg, Morris (1889–1970), English sociologist. Prof. at London School of Economics 1929–54. Wrote on social structures, institutions, and groups, and custom and religion in various cultures.

Ginsberg, Norton Sidney (1921–), U.S. geographer. Prof. at Univ. of Chicago. Director of Association for Asian Studies fr. 1961.

Ginsburg, Christian David (1831–1914), Bible scholar; b. Warsaw, converted to Christianity 1846 and soon afterward moved to England. Devoted himself to research on Masoretic text of Bible. Also wrote on Karaites, Kabbalah, etc.

Ginsburg, David (1920–), organic chemist; b. New York, settled in Israel 1948. Prof. at Haifa Technion; acting pres. Technion 1961–62.

Ginsburg, Jekuthiel (1889–1957), mathematician, Hebrew writer; brother of Simon and Pesaḥ Ginzburg; b. Russia, in U.S. fr. 1912. Prof. at Yeshiva College. Founded quarterly *Scripta Mathematica* 1932.

Ginsburg, Saul (1866–1940), author, historian of Russian Jewry. Established *Der Fraynd* 1903, first Yiddish daily in Russia. Cofounder of Jewish Literary and Scientific Society. In N.Y. fr. 1933.

Ginzberg, Eli (1911–), U.S. economist, social planner; son of Louis Ginzberg. Prof. at Columbia Univ. Specialized in labor economics.

Ginzberg, Louis (1873–1953), scholar of Talmud and Midrash whose comprehensive work in Jewish law and lore made him doyen of Jewish scholars in U.S.; grandnephew of Vilna Gaon, whose life and work greatly influenced him; b. Lithuania, in U.S. fr. 1899. An editor of *Jewish Encyclopedia.* Fr. 1903 taught at Jewish Theological Seminary, where he became a principal architect of Conservative

Louis Ginzberg

movement. His towering scholarship included *The Legends of the Jews* (7 vols.), *Fragments of the Yerushalmi, Geonica, Genizah Studies,* and *Students, Scholars and Saints.*

Ginzburg, see also Guenzburg.

Ginzburg, Natalia (1917–), Italian novelist, playwright. Wrote *Family Sayings,* psychological novel based on author's family and events of her youth.

Ginzburg, Simon (1890–1944), Hebrew poet, critic; b. Volhynia, in N.Y. fr. 1912. Romantic poet, influenced by American rural landscape. Translated English lit. into Hebrew. His brother, **Pesaḥ** (1894–1947) wrote poems, short stories, articles; settled in Ereẓ Israel 1922.

Ginzburg, Vitalii Lazarevich (1916–), Soviet physicist. Published many papers and books on variety of subjects, from astrophysics to superconductivity. Received Lenin Prize for work on Cerenkov effect.

Girgashites, pre-Israelite nation in land of Canaan.

Girgenti, see Agrigento.

Giscala (Heb. **Gush Ḥalav**), ancient Jewish city in Upper Galilee, NW of Safed. Birthplace of Zealot leader John (Johanan) b. Levi. Last city in Galilee to fall to Romans. Jewish community continued at least until 13th c. Now Maronite village. Pop. 1,750 (1971).

Giszkalay (Gush Ḥalav), János (pseud. of **Dávid Widder;** 1888–1951), Hungarian poet, journalist, Zionist leader. Defended right of persecuted Jews' lack of patriotism to Hungarian government. Fled to Rumania, them settled in Ereẓ Israel 1941.

Gitlin, Jacob (1880–1953), S. African communal, Zionist leader. Helped found Cape Board of Jewish Education.

Gittelsohn, Roland Bertram (1910–), U.S. Reform rabbi. Fr. 1953 at Temple Israel, Boston. Wrote on aspects of Judaism.

Gittin (Heb. "divorces"), 6th tractate in Mishnah order *Nashim,* with *gemara* in both Talmuds. Deals with divorce.

Leib Glanz

Givatayim, city in C. Israel, founded 1922; situated within Tel Aviv conurbation. Pop. 47,600 (1971).

Givat Brenner, kibbutz in C. Israel; founded 1928, affiliated with Ha-Kibbutz ha-Me'uḥad. Largest collective settlement in Israel. Pop. 1,525 (1971).

Givens, Philip S. (1922–), Canadian politician. Mayor of Toronto 1963–66. Liberal MP fr. 1968. Active in Jewish communal and Zionist bodies.

Glanville, Brian Lester (1931–), English novelist, sports journalist. Books present critical portrayals of Jewish types.

Glanz, Leib (1898–1964), *ḥazzan,* composer; b. Kiev, in U.S. fr. 1926. *Ḥazzan* at Tiferet Ẓevi Synagogue of Tel Aviv fr. 1954. One of best-known cantors of his day.

Glanz-Leyeles, Aaron (1889–1966), Yiddish poet, essayist; b. Poland, in U.S. fr. 1909. Taught, lectured, edited Yiddish journals, and wrote for Yiddish daily *The Day.*

Glaser, Donald Arthur (1926–), U.S. physicist. Nobel Prize 1960 for invention of "bubble chamber," indispensable research tool in nuclear physics. Prof. of molecular biology at Univ. of California.

Glaser, Eduard (1855–1908), explorer; b. Bohemia. Traveled to Arabia, exploring and collecting mss., inscriptions, and specimens of diverse dialects.

Glaser, Julius Anton (Joshua; 1831–1885), Austrian jurist; convert to Christianity. Minister of justice 1871–79 and attorney-general. Introduced new penal code to protect the rights of accused.

Glasgow, city in Scotland. First Jews 1812; community started 1833. Most original settlers fr. E. Europe and after 1881 influx of immigrants. Pop. 13,400 (1971), with 10 Orthodox synagogues and 1 Reform.

Glasman, Baruch (1893–1945), Yiddish novelist; b. Belorussia, in U.S. fr. 1911. His short stories combined brooding psychoanalytic approach with exciting action.

Glasner, Moses Samuel (1856–1924), rabbi, early leader of

Mizrachi movement. Rabbi of Klausenburg 1878–1923, then settled in Jerusalem.

Glass, Montague Marsden (1877–1934), U.S. humorist. His short story collections *Potash and Perlmutter* and *Abe and Mawruss* became stage successes.

Glatstein (Gladstone), Jacob (1896–1971), Yiddish poet, novelist, critic; b. Lublin, in U.S. fr. 1914. Among founders of "Inzikhist" movement with aim of revitalizing Yiddish poetry and making it contemporary with use of free verse and individual experience. Wrote much about Holocaust.

Glatzer, Nahum Norbert (1903–), scholar, editor; b. Lemberg, taught at Frankfort Univ., in U.S. fr. 1938. Chief editor of Schocken Books 1945–51. Prof., dept. chairman Near Eastern and Judaic Studies at Brandeis Univ. fr. 1956. Wrote on talmudic history, history of Jews in 19th c., biography of his teacher *Franz Rosenzweig;* edited anthologies.

Glazer, Nathan (1923–), U.S. sociologist. Prof. at Univ. of California at Berkeley fr. 1963. Wrote on ethnic groups in U.S., incl. Jews.

Glazer, Simon (1878–1938), Orthodox rabbi, author; b. Lithuania, in U.S. fr. 1897. Chief rabbi of United Synagogues of Montreal 1907–18; founded 1907 and was first editor of Yiddish daily *Canadian Jewish Eagle (Kanader Adler).*

Gleanings, see Leket, Shikhhah, and Pe'ah.

Glicenstein, Enrico (Henoch; 1870–1942), sculptor, painter, print maker; b. Poland, settled in Italy 1897, U.S. in 1928. Predominantly carver, most of his works are in wood. Did portrait busts of famous people (e.g., Franklin D. Roosevelt). Glicenstein Museum containing his library in Safed,

"The Player" by Enrico Glicenstein

Nelson Glueck

Israel. His son, **Emanuel Romano** (1897–), painted portraits, murals.

Glick, Hirsh (1922–1944), Yiddish poet; b. Vilna, d. in Holocaust. His poem "*Mir Zaynen Do*" was battle song of Vilna partisans.

Glickson, Moshe, see Gluecksohn, Moshe.

°**Globocnik, Odilo** (1904–1945), Nazi executioner of Polish Jewry. Organized death camps of Belzec, Sobibor, Majdanek, Treblinka, but transferred fr. post because of irregularities concerning confiscated Jewish property. Probably committed suicide.

Glotz, Gustave (1862–1935), French historian. Prof. of Greek history at Sorbonne. Pres. Institut de France. Specialized in social and economic history of ancient Greece.

Gluck, Alma (Reba Fiersohn; 1884–1938), U.S. soprano. Sang at Metropolitan Opera, N.Y. Known fr. concerts and recordings. Married violinist Efrem Zimbalist.

Gluck, Sandor (1889–), U.S. dance teacher, director. Established (with wife) Dance Center, which introduced repertory dance theater to N.Y. in 1930s.

Gluckman, Henry (1893–), S. African physician, politician. Minister of health and housing in Smuts' government 1945–48, only Jew to hold cabinet post in S. Africa. Active in Jewish community.

Gluckman, Max (1911–), social anthropologist; b. S. Africa. Prof. at Univ. of Manchester fr. 1949. Expert on African societies (political anthropology).

Gluckstein, family of English caterers. **Isidore** (1851–1920), founder with brother-in-law Barnett of Salmon and Gluckstein (retail tobacconists). Founded catering firm J. Lyons & Co. with brother **Montague** (1853–1922), nephew Alfred Salmon, and Sir Joseph Lyons. **Isidore Montague** (1890–), chairman, then pres. of company 1956–68. **Sir Samuel** (1880–1958), mayor of Westminster 1920–21. **Sir Louis Halle** (1897–), Conservative MP 1931–45, chairman of Greater London Council 1968, pres. of Liberal Jewish Synagogue 1944.

Glueck, Nelson (1900–1971), U.S. archaeologist. Pres. of Hebrew Union College 1947–71, director of American School of Oriental Research in Jerusalem 1932–33, 1936–40, 1942–47. Undertook systematic excavations throughout Transjordan. Fr. 1952 onward surveyed ancient sites in Negev. Negotiated merger of Hebrew Union College and Jewish Institute of Religion, and established HUC branches in Los Angeles and Jerusalem. Writings incl. *Rivers in the Desert, The River Jordan,* and *Deities and Dolphins* (on the Nabateans).

Glueck, Sheldon (1896–), U.S. criminologist. Prof. of law at Harvard fr. 1931. Worked together with his wife, **Eleanor Glueck-Touroff** (1898–1972), on identification of potential juvenile delinquents.

Glueckel of Hameln (1645–1724), Yiddish memoirist; b. Hamburg. Memoirs are important source for C. European Jewish history and culture and for linguistic and literary studies of older aspects of Yiddish.

Gluecksohn (Glickson), Moshe (1878–1939), Hebrew journalist, Zionist leader. Sec. of Ḥovevei Ẓion Committee in Odessa. Settled in Ereẓ Israel 1919. Editor of daily *Haaretz* 1923–38. Ideological leader of Ha-No'ar ha-Ẓiyyoni.

Gluskin, Ze'ev (1859–1949), Zionist; b. Belorussia. Member of Ḥovevei Zion in Warsaw and among founders of Menuḥah ve-Naḥalah society, which established settlement of Reḥovot. Among founders of Geulah Company for private pur-

Glueckel of Hameln

chase of land in Ereẓ Israel. In Ereẓ Israel fr. 1905.

Gnesin, Mikhail Fabianovich (1883–1957), Russian composer, teacher, writer. Prof. of composition at Moscow Conservatory. Taught composition at Leningrad Conservatory. Published memoirs, books on composition, aesthetics, Jewish music, etc.

Gnessin, Menahem (1882–1952), actor, pioneer of Hebrew theater; brother of Uri Nissan Gnessin. Among founders of Habimah in Moscow. Fr. 1924 in Ereẓ Israel where he founded Israel theater company but when Habimah settled in Tel Aviv he rejoined it.

Gnessin, Uri Nissan (1881–1913), Hebrew author; b. Ukraine. Published poems, literary criticism, stories, translations. First to introduce psychologically orientated prose style in Hebrew. Introduced modern literary techniques (e.g., interior monologue) into Hebrew literature.

Goa, city and district on W. coast of India. First Jew mentioned Gaspar da Gama 1498. New Christians arrived in 16th c. Inquisition 1560–c. 1810.

°**Gobineau, Joseph Arthur, Comte de** (1816–1882). French diplomat, essayist. Essays on race were used by German philosophers to support their theories of race.

God, Supreme Being and Creator, unique, eternal, incorporeal, omnipresent, and omniscient. Also Lord of History and of fate of every individual. Both transcendent and immanent. Man can seek communion with Him. Despite God's prescience, man has free will. Kabbalah attempted to overcome tension between transcendent God of philosophy and vital God of religious experience. More recent Jewish speculation on God is indebted to problems posed and terminologies provided by various modern systems of philosophy.

Goddard, Paulette (Marian Levee; 1911–), U.S. film actress. Films incl. Chaplin's *Modern Times* and *The Great Dictator.* Husbands: Charlie Chaplin, Burgess Meredith, and Erich Maria Remarque.

Godefroi, Michael Henri (1813–1883), Dutch lawyer, statesman. First Jew to hold Dutch cabinet post (minister of justice 1860–62) and first Jewish member of Second Chamber. Active in Jewish affairs.

Godiner, Samuel Nissan (1893–1942), Soviet Yiddish poet, short story writer. Died fighting with partisans.

Godínez, Felipe (c. 1585–c. 1639), Spanish playwright; of New Christian family. Many of his plays influenced by Old Testament themes. Appeared at auto-da-fé, imprisoned for 2 years.

Godowsky, Leopold (1870–1938), pianist; b. Vilna. Composed études and pieces for both elementary and virtuoso level. His son **Leopold** (1900–), U.S. violinist and with Leopold Mannes co-inventor of Kodachrome color process.

°**Goebbels, Paul Josef** (1897–1945), Nazi leader, propaganda minister. Virtual dictator of Germany's communications media and artistic life. Among initiators of Final Solution. Committed suicide.

°**Goering, Hermann Wilhelm** (1893–1946), Nazi leader. Formed Gestapo and created German Air Force. Faithful to Hitler fr. beginning of his career. Involved in Final Solution; enlarged personal art collection fr. looted Jewish possessions. Condemned to death at Nuremberg trials but committed suicide.

Goetschel, Jules (1908–), Swiss politician, communal leader. Social Democratic member of Basle parliament 1949–68 (pres. 1967–68). Active in Basle Jewish community.

Gog and Magog. Gog of land of Magog is mentioned by Ezekiel (38–39) as leader of evil forces which rise up to war against the Lord in climactic battle. No certain historical identification has been made. In *aggadah* both names were reserved for enemy of Israel in end of days. This tradition passed to Church Fathers and Islam.

Goido, Isaac, see Gorin, Bernard.

Goitein, Shlomo Dov (Fritz; 1900–), orientalist; b. Burgkunstadt, settled in Ereẓ Israel 1923. Prof. at Hebrew Univ. and at Univ. of Pennsylvania 1957–70. Work on ancient Islam and Jews of Yemen; published documentary texts from Cairo *Genizah.*

Golah, see Diaspora.

Golan, see Ramat Ha-Golan.

Gold, Benjamin (1898–), U.S. labor leader. Left-wing unionist member of Socialist Party. Led fur workers strike 1926. Expelled from AFL and CIO for membership in Communist party. Headed fur union until 1954.

Gold, Herbert (1924–), U.S. novelist. Prof. at Univ. of California at Berkeley. His novels deal with search for love between men and women, parents and children.

Gold, Hugo (1895–), publisher, historian; b. Vienna, settled in Ereẓ Israel 1940. Head of publishing house Juedischer Buch- und Kunstverlag; publisher and editor of journal *Juedische Volksstimme.* Wrote on history of C. European Jewry.

Gold, Michael (Irwin Granich; 1893–1967), U.S. communist author, journalist. Editor of Communist papers *Liberator* and *New Masses.* His autobiographical novel *Jews Without Money* is noted account of N.Y. immigrant life.

Gold, Wolf (Ze'ev; 1889–1956), rabbi, leader of religious Zionism; b. Poland, in U.S. fr. 1907. Headed U.S. Mizrachi 1932–35. Settled in Ereẓ Israel 1935. Fr. 1945, member of Jewish Agency Executive and fr. 1951 headed Dept. for Torah Education and Culture. Outstanding orator and worked for religious education throughout Diaspora.

Goldberg, Alexander (1906–), Israel chemical engineer. Pioneer in development of techniques of crop preservation. Pres. of Haifa Technion 1965–73.

Wolf Gold

Arthur Goldberg

Goldberg, Arthur Joseph (1908–), U.S. statesman, jurist. Noted labor lawyer with reputation as arbitrator. Drafted major agreement between CIO and AFL. Appointed secretary of labor 1961, member of U.S. Supreme Court 1962–65, U.S. representative to UN 1965–68. Active in Zionist and Jewish affairs.

Goldberg, Baer (Dov) ben Alexander (Bag; 1800–1884), Polish scholar; in Paris fr. 1853. Published medieval Heb. and Arabic mss. and contributed many articles to Heb. journals.

Goldberg, Ben Zion (1895–1972), Yiddish journalist; married to daughter of Shalom Aleichem. Managing editor of N.Y. Yiddish daily *The Day* 1924–40. Wrote on psychology, politics, social problems, literature, Russian Jewry.

Goldberg, Bertrand (1913–), U.S. architect. Specialized in industrial design and city planning. Works incl. "Manna City," Chicago, featuring round 60-story residential towers.

Goldberg, Boris (1865–1922), economist, Zionist. Member of Central Office of Zionist Organization in Vilna. Left Russia 1919 as a representative of Russian Jews to the Comité des Délégations Juives. Settled in Ereẓ Israel.

Goldberg, Isaac Leib (1860–1935), Zionist leader, philanthropist in Russia, Ereẓ Israel; brother of Boris Goldberg. Founded Ohavei Zion society in Vilna. Helped establish Geulah Co. for purchase of private land in Ereẓ Israel. Purchased first plot of land on Mount Scopus in Jerusalem for future Hebrew Univ. 1908. Settled in Ereẓ Israel 1919. Among founders of *Haaretz* daily newspaper.

Goldberg, Isaiah-Nissan ha-Kohen, see Yaknehaz.

Goldberg, J.B. (1884–1946), Soviet Army commander. Within 2 years set up reserve corps of half a million men for Red Army fighting on front 1917–19. Deputy head of air force 1922.

Lea Goldberg

Goldberg, Lea (1911–1970), Hebrew poet, critic, b. E. Prussia, settled in Ereẓ Israel 1935. Organized and headed dept. of comparative literature at Heb. Univ. Prolific and versatile, wrote poetry in modern mode of younger poets of Mandate period, criticism (Russian, Italian literature), children's literature (stories and poems), novels, and a play (*Lady of the Manor*). Also outstanding translator of world literature into Hebrew.

Goldberg, Oscar (1885–1952), scholar, author; b. Berlin, settled in France, later U.S. Influenced by esoteric mysticism and Kabbalah. To him histories of religions constitute decline and not progress as they leave basic metaphysical reality.

Goldberg, Rube (Reuben Lucius; 1883–1970), U.S. cartoonist. Best known for sports cartoons, comic strips, humor panels, editorial cartoons, and sculpture. Pulitzer Prize 1947.

Goldberger, Joseph (1874–1929), U.S. physician, public health specialist. Discoverer of etiology and therapy of pellagra and introduced nicotinic acid as means of preventing the disease.

Goldbloom, Jacob Koppel (1872–1961), British Zionist leader; b. Poland, in London fr. 1892. Introduced "*Ivrit be-Ivrit*" method of Hebrew teaching in England; among architects of British Zionist Federation.

Golden, David Aaron (1920–), Canadian lawyer, government official. Deputy minister of defense production in federal government 1951–54; pres. Air Industries Association of Canada fr. 1962; founding pres. Telestat Canada Corp., responsible for development of Canadian communications satellite.

Golden, Harry Lewis (Herschel Goldhurst; 1902–), U.S. author, editor, publisher. Known for one-man newspaper *The Carolina Israelite;* humorous works *Only In America, For 2¢ Plain,* and *Enjoy.*

Goldenberg, H. Carl (1907–), Canadian lawyer, economist, government adviser. Special counsel for various Canadian provinces at Dominion-Provincial conferences; adviser to prime minister Pierre Trudeau on constitutional affairs.

Goldenberg, Lazar (1846–1916), Russian revolutionary. In Switzerland, secretary of Slavic dept. of International League of Socialist Revolutionaries. In London, established Agudat ha-Soẓialistim ha-Ivrim (first Jewish socialist organization in world) with Aaron Lieberman. Published English monthly *Free Russia* 1891–1900.

Golden Calf, golden image made by Aaron at demand of Israelites and venerated near Mt. Sinai (Ex. 32). Stern punishment was meted out to calf-worshippers, 3,000 of whom were killed by Levites, who had responded to Moses' call for volunteers. Henceforth Levites were consecrated to service of the Lord.

Goldene Keyt, Di, Israel Yiddish quarterly, founded 1949; leading literary organ of Yiddish interests.

Golden Haggadah, illuminated *Haggadah* produced in Spain, early 14th c. Full-page miniatures divided into 4 compartments, painted on burnished gold background.

Goldenthal, Jacob (1815–1868), Austrian orientalist. Taught at Univ. of Vienna fr. 1849. Published articles on medieval Jewish literature and edited many medieval texts.

Page from "Golden Haggadah."

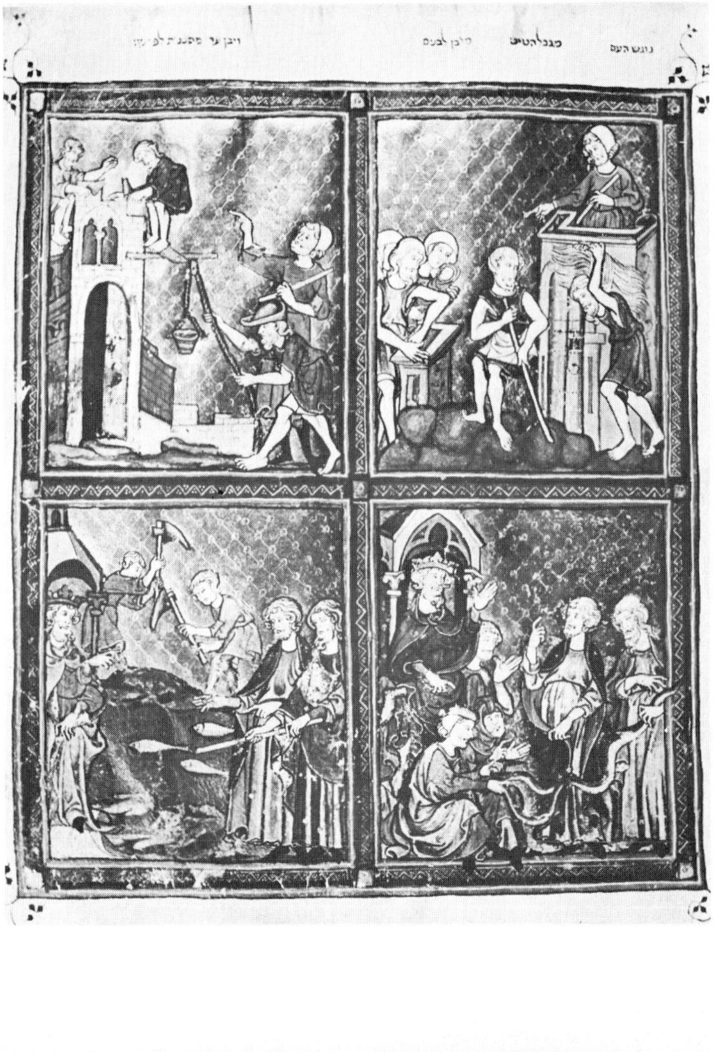

Poster for Goldfaden's operetta, "Shulamis".

Goldenweiser, Alexander Alexandrovich (1880–1936), U.S. anthropologist; b. Kiev. Taught at Columbia Univ., New School for Social Research, Univ. of Oregon. Regarded as most philosophical of American anthropologists.

Goldenweiser, Emanuel Alexandrovich (1883–1953), U.S. economist; b. Kiev, in U.S. fr. 1902. Director of research at Federal Reserve Board fr. 1927. One of main U.S. designers of International Monetary Fund and World Bank.

Goldfaden, Abraham (1840–1908), Yiddish poet, dramatist, composer; "the father of the Yiddish theater"; b. Ukraine. Under Haskalah influence began to compose Hebrew lyrics but later wrote only Yiddish. Went to Rumania where he composed scenarios for Broder Singers. Then engaged wandering minstrels, cantors' assistants, and actors and toured with his troupe throughout Rumania and Russia. Spent several years in U.S., where he died. Wrote about 60 plays (e.g., *Shmendrik, Tsvey Kuni Lemels, Shulamis*); many became very popular. Furnished tunes to his plays and many of them have also remained popular (e.g., "*Rozhinkes mit Mandlen*").

Goldhammer-Sahawi, Leo (1884–1949), Zionist leader in Austria, author, journalist; b. Rumania. Pres. Zionist Organization of Austria. A founder of World Union of Po'alei Zion. Settled in Haifa 1939.

Goldin, Ezra (1868–1915), Hebrew, Yiddish author; b. Grodno district. Wrote poetry, short stories, depicting traditional Jewish way of life.

Goldin, Judah (1914–), U.S. scholar, teacher. Taught Judaica at Yale. Published works on rabbinic Judaism.

Golding, Louis (1895–1958), English novelist. Made reputation with *Magnolia Street,* first of cycle of novels about Anglo-Jewish life. Also wrote travel books.

Goldman, Bernard (1841–1901), Polish patriot, assimilationist. Active in Polish revolutionary movements against czarist rule. Helped establish Agudat Aḥim, center of assimilationist activity in Poland. Member Galician Sejm.

Goldman, Edwin Franko (1878–1950), U.S. bandmaster. Founded Goldman Band. First pres. of American Bandmasters' Association.

Goldman, Emma (1869–1940), U.S. anarchist writer, lecturer. Believed in anarchism in theory and personal independence and radical political action in practice. Deported to her native Russia 1919 but fled USSR 1921.

Goldman, Eric Frederick (1915–), U.S. historian. Prof. at Princeton. Pres. of Society of American Historians 1962–69. Specialized in 20th c. U.S. history.

Goldman, Hetty (1881–), U.S. archaeologist. Excavations in Asia Minor, Tarsus, etc. Main interest in relationship bet. oriental cultures of E. Mediterranean and culture of Greek world.

Goldman, Moses ha-Kohen (1863–1918), Hebrew teacher, journalist; b. Pinsk, in U.S. fr. 1890. Edited first American Hebrew daily *Ha-Yom* 1909.

Goldman, Solomon (1893–1953), U.S. Conservative rabbi, author; in Chicago fr. 1929. Noted orator and Zionist leader. Works incl. series on Bible and its influence on world literature.

Goldmann, Nahum (1895–), statesman, Zionist leader; b. Lithuania. Worked for Jewish section of German Foreign Ministry during WWI. Founded Eshkol publishing house with Jacob Klatzkin, putting out 10 vols. in German and 2 in Hebrew of *Encyclopaedia Judaica* (1925–33). Represented Jewish Agency at League of Nations,Geneva, 1935–39. Active in diplomacy leading to establishment of Jewish state. Pres. World Zionist Organization 1955–68, World Jewish Congress, Conference of Jewish Organizations. Largely responsible for negotiating reparations and indemnifications for Nazi victims. Lived in U.S., Israel, Switzerland.

Nahum Goldmann

Goldmark, Viennese and U.S. family. **Joseph** (1819–1881), Austrian revolutionary leader, U.S. physician, chemist. Fled to N.Y. 1850 to escape death sentence (complicity in murder of minister of war Latour), later acquitted after returning voluntarily to stand trial in Austria. Manufactured percussion caps and cartridges. **Karl** (1830–1915), composer, conductor, teacher in Vienna. Operas incl. *Queen of Sheba.* His nephew **Rubin** (1872–1936), U.S. musician, teacher. Head of dept. of composition of Julliard Graduate School.

Goldscheid, Rudolf (1870–1932), Austrian sociologist, pacifist. Cofounder of German Sociological Society 1909. Edited *Friedenswarte.*

Goldschmidt, Ernst Daniel (1895–1972), librarian, scholar of Jewish liturgy. His various Passover *Haggadot* became very popular. Also published books of *Seliḥot, Kinot,* and a High Holiday *maḥzor,* which is a compendium of all Ashkenazi rites.

Goldschmidt, Guido (1850–1915), Austrian organic chemist. Prof. at Vienna Univ. and German Univ. of Prague. Among earliest organic chemists to elucidate structure of alkaloid.

Goldschmidt (née **Benas**), **Henriette** (1825–1920), German suffragette, educator; wife of Rabbi Abraham Meir Goldschmidt of Leipzig. Founder of German Women's League; Society for Family Education and Peoples' Welfare. Founded first institution of higher education for girls in Germany 1911.

Goldschmidt, Hermann (1802–1866), French astronomer, artist. Painter of historical events and portraits. Discovered 14 asteroids.

Goldschmidt, Lazarus (1871–1950), scholar, bibliophile, translator of Talmud into German. Also published edition of *Sefer Yeẓirah,* Hebrew translation of Koran, and wrote bibliographical works. In London fr. 1933. Collection of rare books acquired by Royal Library in Copenhagen.

Goldschmidt, Levin (1829–1897), German jurist, politician. Prof. of law at Heidelberg. Represented National Liberal Party in Reichstag.

Goldschmidt, Meir Aron (1819–1887), Danish novelist, political writer, journalist. Founded weeklies *Nestved Ugeblad* and *Corsaren;* latter attacked Denmark's conservative establishment. Published novels with worldly yet pious Jewish hero *(En Jøde).*

Goldschmidt, Richard Benedict (1878–1958), German geneticist. Head of genetics dept. at Kaiser Wilhelm Institute for Experimental Biology in Berlin. Settled in U.S. 1936. Prof. of zoology at Univ. of California in Berkeley. Research on sex determination.

Goldschmidt, Victor (1853–1933), crystallographer, inventor. Prof. at Heidelberg Univ. Chief work 9-vol. compilation of all published figures of crystals of minerals. Baptized.

Goldschmidt, Victor Moritz (1888–1947), Norwegian mineralogist, crystallographer, geochemist. Prof. at Oslo Univ. Worked with atomic energy in England during WWII. Founded new science of geochemistry.

Sir Isaac Lyon Goldsmid, caricature by R. Dighton.

Goldsmid, English family. **Benjamin** (1755–1808) and **Abraham** (1756–1810), financiers in London during French revolution. Active in affairs of Jewish community and general philanthropy. Both committed suicide. **Sir Isaac Lyon** (1778–1859), made baronet; first professing Jew to receive English hereditary title. A founder of non-sectarian Univ. College, London. **Sir Francis Henry** (1808–1878), first Jewish barrister in England, MP. **Sir Julian** (1838–1896), MP, chairman of Anglo-Jewish Association.

Goldsmid, Albert Edward Williamson (1846–1904), English soldier; of assimilated family, returned to Judaism in maturity. Founder of Maccabeans and Jewish Lads' Brigade. Active in English Ḥovevei Zion. Model for George Eliot's character Daniel Deronda.

Goldsmith, Raymond William (1904–), U.S. economist; b. Brussels, in U.S. fr. 1930. U.S. adviser on 1946 German currency reform. Prof. at New York Univ. and Yale.

Goldstein, Abraham Samuel (1925–), U.S. lawyer, educator. Dean of Yale Law School fr. 1970. Expert in U.S. criminal law and procedure.

Goldstein, Eugen (1850–1931), German physicist. Research devoted to radiant emissions. Discovered "Kanalstrahlen" ("canal rays").

Goldstein, Fanny (1888–1961), U.S. librarian. Curator of Judaica in Boston public library system. Pres. Jewish Book Council of America.

Goldstein, Herbert S. (1890–1970), U.S. rabbi. Pres. Synagogue Council of America and Union of Orthodox Jewish Congregations. Although graduate of Conservative Jewish Theological Seminary, belonged to right wing of English-speaking Orthodox rabbinate.

Goldstein, Israel (1896–), conservative rabbi, Zionist; b. U.S. Rabbi of Congregation B'nai Jeshurun in N.Y. 1918–61. Prominent public figure in many Jewish and Zionist organizations. Member of Jewish Agency Executive (treasurer 1948–49). Fr. 1961 in Jerusalem. World chairman of Keren Hayesod-United Israel Appeal.

Goldstein, Jennie (1896–1960), U.S. actress; wife of actor-playwright Max Gabel (divorced 1930). Star of Yiddish theater; also appeared on English-language stage.

Goldstein, Josef (1837–1899), *ḥazzan,* composer. *Ḥazzan* in Vienna, introducing Polish-Jewish style of singing.

Goldstein, Kurt (1878–1965), neurologist, psychiatrist; b. Poland, taught in U.S. fr. 1936. Cofounder of test measuring impairment of functions in brain injury in regard to abstract and concrete thinking. Considered brain as single unit ("holistic").

Goldstein, Sidney (1903–), mathematician, aerodynamicist. Prof. at Manchester. Chairman of British Aeronautical Research Council 1946–49, vice-pres. Haifa Technion 1950–55, then prof. of applied mathematics at Harvard.

Goldstein, Sidney Emanuel (1879–1955), U.S. Reform rabbi. Associate rabbi to Stephen S. Wise in Free Synagogue, directing social service dept. A founder of Jewish Institute of Religion.

Goldstuecker, Eduard (1913–), Czech literary historian, diplomat. First Czech minister to Israel. Figured in Slánský trial, sentenced to life imprisonment. Released after 8 years. Prof. of German literature at Prague Univ. Fought anti-liberal elements 1968, left Czechoslovakia for England.

Goldszmidt, Henryc, see Korczak, Janusz.

Goldwater (Goldwasser), family of early settlers in Arizona and American West. **Michael** founded town of Ehrenburg, Ariz. His grandson **Barry M.** (1905–), born Christian, U.S. senator and unsuccessful Republican candidate for presidency 1964.

Goldwater, Sigmund Schulz (1873–1942), U.S. hospital administrator, architect. N.Y. Commissioner of Hospitals under Mayor La Guardia. Pres. of Associated Hospital Services.

Samuel Goldwyn

Goldwyn (Goldfish), Samuel (1882–1974), U.S. motion picture producer. Formed Metro-Goldwyn-Mayer. One of best known and distinctive Hollywood producers. Established Samuel Goldwyn Foundation for assisting scholars and philanthropic causes.

Goldziher, Ignaz (Isaac Judah; 1850–1921), Hungarian scholar. Taught at Univ. of Budapest and Budapest Rabbinical Seminary. One of greatest modern scholars of Islam; also wrote on Jewish scholarly subjects.

Golem (Heb.), creature made in human form by magic, esp. use of holy names. Mentioned in Talmud, *Sefer Yeẓirah,* and later. Most famous exponent was R. Judah Loew b. Bezalel of Prague. Became object of folklore and literature for both Jews and non-Jews.

Miniature of David and Goliath

Goliath, Philistine champion killed by David in single combat (I Sam. 17).

Golinkin, Mordecai (1875–1963), conductor, pioneer of opera in Israel; b. Ukraine, settled in Ereẓ Israel 1923. Formed Palestine Opera. Conductor of Israel Opera 1948–53.

Goll, Yvan (1891–1950), Alsatian poet, author. Wrote in French and German. Established magazine *Surréalisme* in Paris. Published first German translation of Joyce's novel *Ulysses.* His poems abound in Jewish themes. In U.S. during WWII.

Gollancz, Sir Hermann (1852–1930), first English rabbi to be knighted. Taught Hebrew at Univ. College, London.

Gollancz, Sir Israel (1864–1930), English literary scholar; brother of Sir Hermann Gollancz. Prof. at King's College, London. Shakespearean scholar. Made important contribution to study of early English literature and philology.

Gollancz, Sir Victor (1893–1967), English publisher, author. Socialist and pacifist. Founded Gollancz publishing house 1928. Established Left Book Club 1936 to expose Nazism. Active in many humanitarian causes, incl. aid to refugees of WWII and Arab refugees after Israel's War of Independence.

Golomb, Abraham (1888–), Yiddish writer, educator. B. Lithuania; taught in Israel, Canada, Mexico. Propounded ideology of "integral Jewishness" incl. language, festivals, religious observances, family relationships.

Golomb, Eliyahu (1893–1945), leader of Jewish defense in Ereẓ Israel, main architect of Haganah; b. Belorussia, settled in Ereẓ Israel 1909. Insisted on formation of independent Jewish defense force in WWI. Leading figure in Haganah, which he brought under auspices of national institutions. A founder of Palmaḥ.

Gombiner, Abraham Abele ben Ḥayyim ha-Levi (c. 1637–1683), Polish rabbi. Author of *Magen Avraham,* commentary to *Shulḥan Arukh.* Also wrote commentary to *Yalkut Shimoni. Dayyan* and head of yeshivah in Kalisz.

Gomel (Homel), city in Belorussian SSR. Jews fr. 16th c. Massacres during Chmielnicki pogrom 1648. Center of Ḥabad Ḥasidism. Community flourished in 19th c. and had 30 synagogues. Jewish communal life came to standstill under Soviet rule. Pre-war community of 37,000 ended during WWII.

Gomel, Blessing of, thanksgiving benediction recited by those who have been saved from acute danger to life (those who have crossed sea or wilderness, recovered fr. serious illness, survived accident). Preferably recited in presence of *minyan,* often after being called to Reading of Law.

Gómez, Antonio Enríquez, or **Henríque** (pseud. of **Enrique Enriquez de Paz;** 17th c.), Spanish playwright, poet; son of Portuguese Marrano; left Spain, lived in France (published books), settled in Holland, where he reverted to Judaism. Lyric, dramatic, and epic poet and satirist. Returned to Spain and died in cells of Seville Inquisition.

Gompers, Samuel (1850–1924), U.S. trade unionist. Helped establish AFL (pres. 1886–1924). A formative influence on American labor movement and its spokesman. Strongly anti-socialist.

Gompertz, Lewis (1784–1861), British inventor, humanitarian. Founded Society for Prevention of Cruelty to Animals.

Gomperz, Theodor (1832–1912), Austrian classical philologist, historian of ancient philosophy. Prof. at Univ. Vienna. Wrote monumental work setting Greek philosophy within context of history of science and of general development of ancient civilization. His son **Heinrich** (1873–1942), historian of ancient philosophy. Taught in Vienna; in U.S. fr. 1938. Baptized.

°**Goodenough, Erwin Ramsdell** (1893–1965), U.S. scholar of Judaism in Hellenistic period. Taught at Yale. His 13-vol. *Jewish Symbols in the Greco-Roman Period* began new epoch in study of ancient Judaism.

Goodhart, Arthur Lehman (1891–), jurist; b. U.S. Prof. of jurisprudence at Oxford. Master of Univ. College, Oxford, 1951, first Jew and first American citizen to become master of an Oxford college. Chairman of International Law Association. Editor of *Law Quarterly Review.* His son, **Philip J.** (1925–), Conservative MP.

Goodman, Arnold Abraham, Lord (1913–), British lawyer, legal advisor. Successful as arbitrator in workers' strikes and industrial disputes. Sent by British govt. to find solution to constitutional dispute with Rhodesia. Chairman of British Arts Council 1965–72.

Goodman, Benny (Benjamin David; 1909–), U.S. clarinetist, band leader. Called "King of Swing." Had first jazz ensemble in which both white and Negro musicians played together. Appeared with symphony orchestras.

Goodman, Paul (1875–1949), British Zionist, public figure. Secretary of Spanish and Portuguese Congregation, London. Editor of *Zionist Review.* Works incl. a Jewish history.

Goodman, Paul (1911–1972), U.S. author, psychotherapist, educator; brother of Percival Goodman. Prof. at Univ. of Wisconsin and San Francisco State College's experimental college. Wrote poetry, novels, criticism (*Growing Up Absurd,* etc.). Described as "the father-figure of the New Left."

Sir Victor Gollancz

Eliyahu Golomb

Samuel Gompers

Benny Goodman

Synagogue designed by Percival Goodman, Albany, N.Y.

Goodman, Percival (1904–), U.S. architect. Expert on city planning. Prof. at Columbia Univ. Designed many synagogues which are brightly lit and tend to be small and intimate.

Goor (Grasovski), Yehudah (1862–1950), educator, lexicographer; b. Belorussia, settled in Ereẓ Israel 1887. Cofounder Teachers Association. Major work Hebrew dictionary, first in which words were traced to their period of origin. Also published small dictionaries and textbooks.

Gordimer, Nadine (1923–), S. African novelist. Novels deal with loss of innocence and development of self-awareness and maturity. Many of her works banned in S. Africa.

Gordin, Jacob (1853–1909), playwright, journalist; formative influence in modern Yiddish theater; b. Ukraine. Founded sect advocating ethical Judaism with agriculture as sole healthy and virtuous occupation. Disbanded by czarist police. Fled to U.S. 1891. Wrote melodramatic plays as vehicles for his social gospel. Among his plays *Mirele Efros, The Yiddish King Lear,* etc.

Gordis, Robert (1908–), U.S. Bible scholar, rabbi. Prof. at Jewish Theological Seminary. Editor of periodical *Judaism.* Wrote on biblical subjects and relationship of Judaism to contemporary problems.

Gordon, Aharon David (1856–1922), Hebrew political thinker, spiritual mentor of pioneering Zionism; b. Russia. Managed estate for his relative Baron Joseph Guenzburg. Settled in Ereẓ Israel 1904, working as laborer in Deganyah. Believed that Jews should themselves till fields, preached return to nature and doctrine of "Religion of Labor." Strong influence on Second Aliyah and Ereẓ Israel labor movement.

Gordon, Albert I. (1903–1968), U.S. Conservative rabbi, sociologist. His sociological studies are substantial contribution to study of American Jewry.

Gordon, Cyrus Herzl (1908–), U.S. Semitic scholar. Taught at Dropsie College 1946–56, Brandeis Univ. fr. 1956. His Ugaritic grammar and lexicon were pioneer works. His other major contribution was in "Helleno-Semitics," comparison of Eastern and Western civilizations, mainly through study of early Greece and Ancient Near East.

Gordon, David (1831–1886), Hebrew journalist, editor; b. Lithuania, settled in Lyck 1858. Editor of *Ha-Maggid,* first Hebrew weekly, which became monthly voice of Ḥibbat Zion movement.

Gordon, Eliezer (1840–1910), Lithuanian rabbinical scholar, head of Telz yeshivah. One of first to introduce study of *musar* (ethics) into yeshivah curriculum.

Gordon, Lord George (1757–1793), English proselyte. MP and pres. United Protestant League. Opposed measures to relieve Catholic disabilities. Became Orthodox proselyte 1787. Tried for libel, imprisoned in Newgate, London, where he died an Orthodox Jew.

Gordon, Jacob (1877–1934), Canadian Orthodox rabbi who established first *talmud torah* in Toronto to use Hebrew as language of instruction 1908.

Gordon, Judah Leib (Leon; abb. **Yalag;** 1831–1892), Hebrew poet, writer, critic; b. Vilna. Served as teacher in Kovno province (1853–72), moved to St. Petersburg, where he worked as communal official 1872–79; imprisoned by Czarist government following false accusation by Ḥasidim 1879. On returning fr. prison became editor of Hebrew daily *Ha-Meliẓ.* Wrote long epics on biblical themes imbued with Haskalah spirit (*Ahavat David u-Mikhal,* etc.). Many of his poems deal with ills of Jewish society and its leaders, position of poor and oppressed, esp. Jewish woman (e.g., *Koẓo shel Yod*). Urged Russian Jewry to leave its narrow existence and adapt itself to wider environment, stop speaking Yiddish, and engage in more productive occupations (*Hakiẓah Ammi*). Disillusioned by 1881 pogroms, advocated emigration to Western countries (*Aḥoti Ruḥama*). Also wrote fables and was gifted translator.

Aharon David Gordon

Judah Leib Gordon

Gordon, Mikhel (1823–1890), Hebrew, Yiddish poet; b. Vilna. Wrote Yiddish songs and composed melodies; published history of Russia in Yiddish.

Gordon, Samuel Leib (Shalag; 1865–1933), Hebrew writer, Bible scholar; b. Lithuania, lived in Jaffa and Warsaw, settled in Ereẓ Israel 1924. Wrote poems, translations, children's books, textbooks. Edited children's journals, etc. Wrote biblical commentary still used extensively in secondary schools in Israel.

Gordon, Willy (1918–), Swedish sculptor. Sculpted many monuments in Sweden, busts of leading Israelis, Jewish subjects.

Gordonia, pioneering Zionist youth movement founded 1923 in Galicia, headed by Pinḥas Lavon. Spread to Poland, Rumania, U.S., and by WWI had 40,000 members. Members founded settlements in Ereẓ Israel. Merged with similar movements (Maccabi ha-Ẓair, Maḥanot Olim).

Gorelik, Shemarya (1877–1942), Yiddish essayist, literary critic; b. Ukraine. Member of Zionist movement, wrote for Zionist publications. Settled in Ereẓ Israel 1933 and contributed for Hebrew press.

Goren, Charles Henry (1901–), U.S. bridge expert. Won national bridge championship of America 31 times. His widely read books explain his methods.

Goren (Gruenblatt), Natan (1887–1956), Hebrew author, journalist, critic; b. Lithuania. Active in Jewish revolutionary circles; imprisoned. Fr. 1935 in Tel Aviv.

Goren, Shlomo (1917–), Israel rabbi. Chief chaplain in Israel armed forces fr. 1948, introducing uniform ritual and service for Jewish soldiers of all communities. Chief Ashkenazi rabbi of Tel Aviv-Jaffa 1968–72; chief rabbi of Israel 1972. Wrote on

Maimonides' *Mishneh Torah* and Jerusalem Talmud. Israel Prize 1961.
Gorin, Bernard (pseud. of **Isaac Goido;** 1868–1925), Yiddish writer, playwright, drama critic; b. Lithuania, in New York fr. 1894. On staff of Yiddish daily *Jewish Morning Journal.* Major work *Di Geshikhte fun Yidishn Teater,* listing 2,000 plays produced on Yiddish stage.
Gorki, (until 1932 **Nizhni Novgorod**), city in Russia. Permanent Jewish community established by Cantonists; synagogue 1873. Community increased during WWI by refugees fr. war zone. Jewish pop. 30,000 (1970).
Gorni (pl. **Grana**), term used for Jewish immigrants fr. Leghorn who began to settle in N. Africa fr. 17th c. In Tunisia, community separate fr. older Jewish communities.
Gorochov, Yedidyah, see Admon, Yedidyah.
Goshen, grazing area in NE of Lower Egypt, E. of delta, assigned to Jacob and his family and where Israelites lived in Egypt (Gen. 45:10; Ex. 9:26).
Goslar, Hans (1889–1945), Mizrachi leader in Germany. Director of press section of Prussian government during Weimar Republic. Went to Amsterdam. D. in Holocaust.
Gotlieb, Allen (1928–), Canadian government official. Deputy minister of communications 1968.
Gotsfeld, Bessie Goldstein (1888–1962), U.S. social worker, Zionist. Instrumental in founding Mizrachi Women's Organization.
Gottesman, family of U.S. philanthropists. **Mendel** (1859–1942) founded investment trading company and established Gottesman Tree of Life Foundation. His son, **David Samuel** (1884–1956), established D.S. and R.H. Gottesman Foundation to further higher education, etc. Gave money for purchase of Dead Sea Scrolls for State of Israel and construction of Shrine of the Book in Jerusalem. His brother, **Benjamin** (1897–), a founder of Albert Einstein College of Medicine of Yeshiva Univ.
Gottheil, Gustav (1827–1903), Reform rabbi, liturgist, Zionist leader; lived in Germany and England before becoming co-rabbi of Temple Emanu-El in New York 1873. A founder of Federation of American Zionists.
Gottheil, Richard James Horatio (1862–1936), U.S. orientalist; son of Gustav Gottheil. Taught at Columbia Univ. Director of Oriental Dept. of N.Y. Public Library; pres. of American Oriental Society. Pres. of American Federation of Zionists. Published, wrote, edited, and translated works on Zionism, Syriac grammar, etc.
Gottlieb, Adolph (1903–1974), U.S. painter; exponent of abstract expressionism. Won first prize 1963 São Paulo Bienal. Designed ark curtains for synagogues.
Gottlieb, Hinko (1886–1948), Yugoslav author, translator, Zionist leader. Founded and edited Jewish monthly *Ommanut.* Fought with Tito against Nazis. Organized rescue of Croatian Jews; settled in Ereẓ Israel after war and wrote on Holocaust period.
Gottlieb, Maurycy (1856–1879), Polish painter. Painted Jewish themes, portraits. His brother **Leopold** (1883–1934), also painter. Taught at Bezalel School in Jerusalem.
Gottlieb, Yehoshua (1882–c. 1940/41), Zionist, journalist, leader in Poland. Member of Sejm. Chairman of Warsaw Journalists' Association 1907–34; member of Warsaw Jewish community council. Arrested by Soviets, his fate uncertain.
Gottlober, Abraham Baer (pseud. **Abag** and **Mahalalel;** 1810–1899), Hebrew, Yiddish writer, poet; b. Volhynia. Founded Hebrew monthly *Ha-Boker Or.* Member of Ḥibbat Zion. His poetry is imbued with longing for Ereẓ Israel. Published translations, literary criticism, research. In Yiddish wrote poems, plays, social satire, etc. Attacked obscurantism of the period.
Gottschalk, Alfred (1930–), U.S. Reform rabbi. Dean of California School of Hebrew Union College 1959, pres. Hebrew Union College Jewish Institute of Religion fr. 1971.
Gottschalk, Louis Reichenthal (1899–), U.S. historian. Editor of *Journal of Modern History;* pres. American Historical Association 1953. Fields of interest: era of French Revolution, modern European history, historiography. Pres. Chicago Board of Jewish Education.
Gottschalk, Max (1889–), Belgian social scientist, Jewish leader. Prof. at Institute of Sociology of Free University of Brussels. Specialized in problems of unemployment. President of Center of Regional Economy; Director of Centre National des Hauts Etudes Juives; founder of United Jewish Appeal in Brussels.
Goudchaux, Michel (1792–1862), French banker, politician. Founded

Shlomo Goren

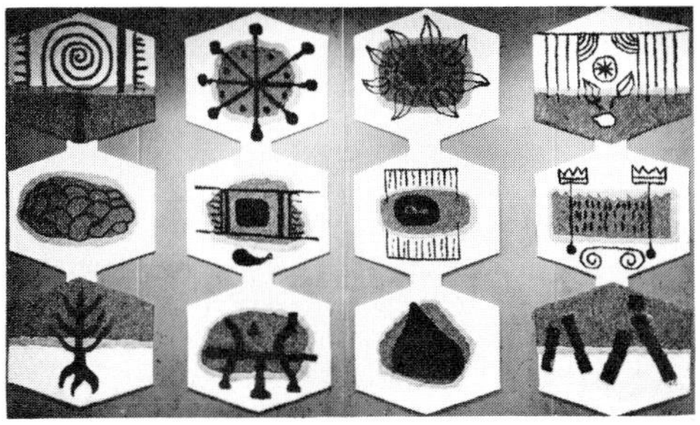

Tapestry designed by Adolph Gottlieb.

Maurycy Gottlieb, self-portrait

working-class newspaper *Le National.* Participated in Revolution of July 1830. Minister of finance in Second Republic; vice-pres. of National Assembly.
Goudsmit, Joel Emanuel (1813–1882), Dutch lawyer. First Jew to become university prof. in Holland (at Leyden) and member of Royal Netherlands Academy of Sciences.
Gould, Elliot (1938–), U.S. actor. After career on stage became one of leading young actors on screen (*M.A.S.H.* etc.).

Gould, Morton (1913–), U.S. composer, conductor, pianist. As composer, moved freely between light and serious music. Latter influenced folk and jazz.

Gould, Samuel Brookner (1910–), U.S. educator, university administrator. Pres. of Antioch College 1954–58; chancellor of Univ. of California, Santa Barbara, 1959–62; pres. State Univ. of New York 1964–70. Baptized.

Gouri, Haim (1923–), Israel author. Fought in Palmaḥ and Haganah. Wrote novel on Holocaust and book on Eichmann trial. After Six-Day War, wrote poems reflecting rediscovery of identification with collective experience of nation.

Prayer for Queen Anne, England, 1714.

Government, Prayer for the, prayer for welfare of government forming part of Sabbath and festival service. First mentioned in Mishnah.

Grace after Meals, blessing recited after meals. Recited only where bread has been eaten. If bread has not been eaten, shorter form is recited. Consists of 4 blessings. Special introduction is added when at least 3 adult males have eaten together (*mezumman*). Grace is introduced on weekdays by Ps. 177 and on Sabbath by Ps. 126.

Grace before Meals, blessing recited before partaking of food, each species having its own benediction.

Gracian (Ḥen), Zerahiah ben Isaac ben Shealtiel (13th c.), physician, philosopher, translator; b. Barcelona, emigrated to Italy. Expert on Maimonides' *Guide of the Perplexed*. Wrote commentaries on Proverbs, Job, Pentateuch, etc. Translated works fr. Arabic into Hebrew.

Grade, Chaim (1910–), Yiddish poet, novelist; b. Vilna. Member of

Chaim Grade

Heinrich Graetz

Young Vilna literary movement. In USSR during WWII, U.S. fr. 1948. Many of his poems depict loss and tragedy of Holocaust. Novels about Jewish life in Lithuania, incl. yeshivah milieu. Wrote for Yiddish daily *Jewish Morning Journal.*

Grade, Sir Lew (1906–), British television network director. Headed Associated Television Ltd. and Incorporated Television Company.

Gradenwitz, Peter Emanuel (1910–), Israel musicologist, publisher. Founded Israel Music Publications, first music publishing venture in Israel to achieve international standards.

Gradis, family of Bordeaux shipowners, community leaders of Marrano extraction. **David** (1665–1751), founder of import-export firm. His nephew **Abraham** (1699–1780) enlarged firm, was royal purveyor, and provisioned Quebec and French possessions in W. Africa.

Graetz, Heinrich (1817–1891), Jewish historian, Bible scholar. Taught at Jewish Theological Seminary of Breslau. His seminal *History of the Jews* became one of most widely read of Jewish scholarly books and was basis and source of other Jewish historiography; first comprehensive attempt to write history of Jews as history of living people and fr. Jewish point of view. Translated into various languages. Also wrote Bible studies and edited the *Monatsschrift fuer die Geschichte und Wissenschaft des Judentums.*

°**Graf, Karl Heinrich** (1815–1869), German Bible scholar. His hypothesis (1866) that Priestly Code, which had until then been considered earliest source of Pentateuch, was actually latest source, was later developed by J. Wellhausen.

Grajewski, Aryeh Leib (1896–1967), talmudic scholar, journalist; b. Poland, went to Ereẓ Israel 1913, in Paris 1921–35. Wrote many studies on Jewish law and Talmud, and also wrote for French Jewish press.

Grajewsky, Pinchas (1873–1941), Ereẓ Israel historian; official in Bikkur Holim Hospital in Jerusalem. Published documents, letters, memoirs, biographical sketches, relating to Jerusalem and Erez Israel.

Granach, Alexander (Isaiah Gronach; 1890–1945), German, Yiddish actor, Member of Reinhardt Theater. Specialized in modern plays. In U.S. fr. 1938.

Alexander Granach

Granada, city and province in S. Spain. Acc. to legend, founded by Jews. Earliest extant information 711 C.E. In 11th c. Jews held administrative posts. Samuel ha-Nagid vizier and military commander; most of pop. was Jewish. In mass revolt 1066, Joseph ha-Nagid and more than 1,500 householders killed. Community destroyed 1090; Ibn Ezra family among refugees. Community under Muslim rule fr. 1232. Surrender treaty between king of Granada and Ferdinand and Isabella 1491 paved way for expulsion of Jews.

Grandval (Hirsch-Ollendorf), Gilbert Yves Edmond (1904–), French statesman; of Jewish origin. A leader of French resistance in WWII. Military governor, Saar region, 1945; French High Commissioner for Saar 1948–52; resident-general of Morocco 1953. Secretary of state for foreign trade 1962; minister of labor 1962–66.

Granott (Granovsky), Abraham (1890–1962), Israel economist; pres. of Jewish National Fund; b. Bessarabia, settled in Jerusalem 1922. Cofounder and chairman of Progressive Party; member of first Knesset. Established principles for a progressive agrarian policy, on which he wrote books.

Granovsky, Alexander (pseud. of **Abraham Azarch**; 1890–1937), Soviet theatrical director, founder of post-Revolution Jewish State Theater.

Gratz, family of U.S. merchants, community leaders in Philadelphia. Brothers **Bernard** (1738–1801) and **Michael** (1740–1811) formed trading firm and helped found first Philadelphia synagogue. Michael's son **Hyman** (1776–1857) bequeathed money to found Gratz College. Michael's daughter **Richea** (1774–1858), first Jewish girl to attend college in U.S. Another daughter, **Rebecca** (1781–1869), reputedly model for Rebecca in Walter Scott's novel *Ivanhoe.* Active in social causes and founded first Jewish Sunday school.

Gratz College, first Jewish teacher-training institution in U.S. Formally opened 1897. Since 1952 accredited to award academic degrees. Enrollment 1,500 (1970).

Graubart, Judah Leib (1861–1937), rabbi, halakhic scholar; b. Russia, in Toronto fr. 1920, becoming recognized head of the city's Polish Jews.

Graumann, Sir Harry (1868–1938), S. African mining magnate, industrialist, financier. First Jewish mayor of Johannesburg.

Graur, Constantin (1877–1940), Rumanian journalist. Edited newspapers, incl. dailies *Dimineata* and *Adevârul.*

Gray, Herbert (1931–), Canadian legislator, cabinet minister. Minister of national revenue 1970; first Jew in federal cabinet.

Grayzel, Solomon (1896–), U.S. historian, Conservative rabbi. Taught at Gratz College and Dropsie College, Philadelphia. Editor in chief of Jewish Publication Society of America 1939–66. Wrote on relationship of Christians and Jews during Middle Ages and also a popular 1-vol. *History of the Jews.*

Graz, city in Austria. Jews fr. late 13th c., mostly moneylenders. Expelled 1439, returned by 1447; expelled again 1496. After 1848, could settle only with special permits. Special permits rescinded 1868. In late 1930s center of Austrian National Socialism. Most Jews perished in Holocaust.

Graziano, Abraham Joseph Solomon ben Mordecai (d. 1684), Italian rabbi. Member of Modena *bet din.* First collector of books and mss. among Italian Jews.

Great Assembly, see Synagogue, the Great.

Great Poland, historical administrative unit of Poland-Lithuania (see also Poland). Jewish communities founded 12th–14th c., expanded 16th–17th c. Organized within framework of Councils of Lands, which entered into enormous debts. Large-scale emigration to Germany and later to U.S. Emancipation movements were strong, and strongly opposed. Many Jews developed language and cultural ties with Germany, which further exacerbated relations with Poles. Community ceased to exist with Nazi occupation.

Greece, country in SE Europe (see also Byzantine Empire, Cyprus, Crete). Jews probably present fr. biblical period, definitely present in Second Temple period; communities in many towns. Greek Jews in late antiquity abandoned Hebrew and adopted Greek. Under Ottoman rule, largest community in Salonika. Jews of Crete important. Spanish refugees arrived in 15th, 16th c., creating two communities, original Greek (and Judeo-Greek)-speaking, called Romaniot, and Spanish-speaking. Culturally and religiously important center until late 17th c. Following population exchanges between Greece and Turkey after WWI, Jewish pop. grew. About 85% (65,000) of Greek Jewry murdered in WWII. Jewish pop. 6,500 (1971), mostly in Athens.

Green, Adolph (1915–), U.S. theatrical writer. Lyricist of many Broadway musicals, incl. *Two on the Aisle* and *Wonderful Town.* Often collaborated with Betty Comden and Jule Styne.

Green, Gerald (1922–), U.S. author. Wrote *The Last Angry Man* and *The Legion of Noble Christians.* Worked for NBC as writer, director, producer.

Greenacre, Phyllis (1894–), U.S. psychiatrist. Main interests anxiety and sexual anomaly of fetishism. On faculty of N.Y. Psychoanalytic Institute (pres. 1948–50).

Greenberg, Eliezer (1896–), Yiddish poet, literary critic; b. Bessarabia, in U.S. fr. 1913. Founded and edited *Getseltn,* periodical of verse and literary criticism; edited English anthologies of Yiddish literature.

Greenberg, Hayim (1889–1953), Zionist leader, thinker; b. Russia. Taught at Univ. of Kharkov and Kiev Academy. Edited *Haolam* in Berlin. In U.S. fr. 1924, editing labor Zionist journals, incl. *Der Yidisher Kempfer, The Jewish Frontier.* Fr. 1946 director of Jewish Agency dept. in America of education and culture. Influential writings expound philosophy of Zionism and its consistency with ideals of socialism, pacifism, and universalism.

Hayim Greenberg

Major Jewish settlements in Greece

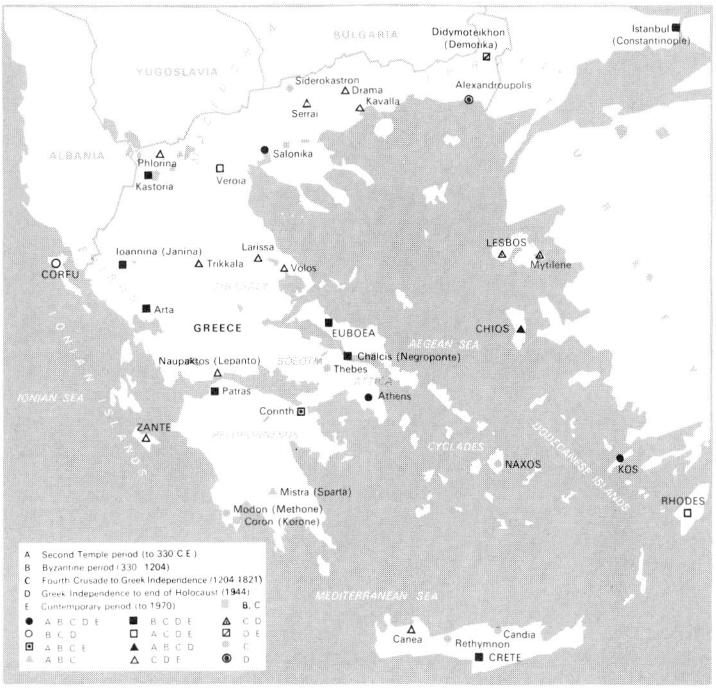

GREETINGS AND CONGRATULATIONS

			Hebrew	Literal meaning	Occasions when said	Origin and/or reference
GREETINGS AND CONGRATULATIONS – GENERAL FORMS OF						
1		Shalom or Shalom lekha	שָׁלוֹם שָׁלוֹם לְךָ	Peace Peace to you	As a common greeting equivalent to "hello," "goodbye," "good day."	Gen. 29:6, 43:27; Ex. 18:7; Judg. 6:24; I. Sam. 16:4
2		Shalom aleikhem	שָׁלוֹם עֲלֵיכֶם	Peace to you	As above	
3		Aleikhem shalom	עֲלֵיכֶם שָׁלוֹם	To you, peace	Response to greeting No. 2.	
4		Barukh ha-ba	בָּרוּךְ הַבָּא	Blessed be the one who comes.	A common greeting, equivalent to "welcome." A child brought to the circumcision ceremony and a bride and groom approaching the wedding canopy are also greeted thus. The response to the greeting is No. 5 or 6.	Ps. 118:26
5		Barukh ha-nimẓa	בָּרוּךְ הַנִּמְצָא	Blessed be the one (already) present.	Response to greeting No. 4.	
6		Barukh ha-yoshev	בָּרוּךְ הַיּוֹשֵׁב	Blessed be the one who is sitting.	Response to greeting No. 4. Used by a guest to the host sitting at the head of the table.	
7		Shalom berakhah ve-tovah	שָׁלוֹם בְּרָכָה וְטוֹבָה	Peace, blessing and (all) good (to you).	General blessing used by Sephardi Jews.	
8		Ḥazak u-varukh	חֲזַק וּבָרוּךְ	Be strong and blessed.	As above. Also used in Sephardi synagogues to a person who returns to his seat after having performed liturgical functions.	
9		Yishar koḥakha or Yasher ko'akh	יִישַׁר כֹּחֲךָ (Yiddish)	May your strength (increase) go straight	Congratulations for success and achievement. In traditional synagogues also extended to a person who has been called up to the Torah reading.	
10		Ḥazak ve-emaẓ	חֲזַק וֶאֱמָץ	Be strong and of good courage.	Congratulations for success and achievement. Also extended to a bar mitzvah boy after he has finished reading the *haftarah*.	e.g. Deut. 31:23
11		Biz hundert un tsvantsik	(Yiddish)	(May you live) until the age of 120.	A wish for long life.	
12		Tsu gezunt	(Yiddish)	Good health.	To a person who has sneezed; also to someone convalescing.	
13	*a.*	Li-veri'ut	לִבְרִיאוּת	Good health.	As above.	
	b.	Asuta	אָסוּתָא (Aramaic)	Good health.		
14		Refu'ah shelemah	רְפוּאָה שְׁלֵמָה	(May you have) a complete recovery.	Wish to a sick person.	
SABBATH AND HOLIDAY GREETINGS						
15	*a.*	Shabbat shalom Gut shabes	שַׁבָּת שָׁלוֹם (Yiddish)	Good Sabbath	The Sabbath greeting	
	b.	Shabbat hi mi-lizok u-refu'ah kerovah lavo	שַׁבָּת הִיא מִלִּזְעֹק וּרְפוּאָה קְרוֹבָה לָבוֹא	It is Sabbath and forbidden to make supplications but may you soon get well.	When visiting the sick on the Sabbath.	Shab. 12 a.
16	*a.*	Shavu'a tov	שָׁבוּעַ טוֹב	A good week.	A greeting on Saturday night at the end of the Sabbath.	
	b.	A gute vokh	(Yiddish)			
17		Gut khoydesh	(Yiddish)	A good new month.	On new moons.	
18		Gut Yontev	(Yiddish) (corrupted from the Hebrew Yom Tov	A good holiday (to you).	On holidays and festivals.	
19	*a.*	Mo'adim le-simḥah	מוֹעֲדִים לְשִׂמְחָה	Joyous holidays.	On festivals. The response to which is No. 20.	
	b.	Ḥag same'aḥ	חַג שָׂמֵחַ	Joyous holiday.		
20		Ḥaggim u-zemannim lesason	חַגִּים וּזְמַנִּים לְשָׂשׂוֹן	Holidays and festivals for joy and gladness.	Response to No. 19a, 19b.	This wording is from the prayer for the three festivals
21		Ve-hayita akh same'aḥ	וְהָיִיתָ אַךְ שָׂמֵחַ	You shall have nothing but joy.	On Sukkot, when visiting a person in his *sukkah*.	Deut. 16:15

NEW YEAR AND DAY OF ATONEMENT

22	*a.* Shanah tovah	שָׁנָה טוֹבָה	A good year (to you), or its more ample version:	During the Days of Penitence.	The wording is from prayers *Amidah* and *Avinu Malkenu*
	b. Le-shanah tovah tikkatevu (ve-teḥatemu)	לְשָׁנָה טוֹבָה תִּכָּתֵבוּ (וְתֵחָתֵמוּ)	May you be inscribed (and sealed) for a good year (i.e. in the Book of Life), or its shorter form:		
	c. Ketivah tovah	כתִיבָה טוֹבָה	A good inscription (in the Book of Life).		
23	Gam le-mar	גַּם לְמַר	To you too.	Response to one of the greetings in Nos. 22a, b, c. and 24 a, b.	
24	*a.* Ḥatimah tovah or	חֲתִימָה טוֹבָה	A sealing for good (to you), or its more ample version:	On the Day of Atonement, the day of "Sealing the book."	Wording from the prayerbook.
	b. Gemar ḥatimah tovah	גְּמַר חֲתִימָה טוֹבָה	A propitious final sealing (to you) (in the Book of Life).	As above. This form can be used until Hoshana Rabba.	

ON JOYOUS OCCASIONS AND FAMILY EVENTS

25	*a.* Mazzal tov	מַזָּל טוֹב	Good luck (i.e., may you enjoy a favorable zodiac constellation).	For joyous occasions, especially child-birth, betrothal, wedding, bar-mitzvah, etc. . .	Ashkenazi custom.
	b. Be-siman tov	בְּסִימָן טוֹב	As above	As above	Sephardi custom.
26	Barukh tihyeh	בָּרוּךְ תִּהְיֶה	Be you be blessed (too), (i.e., the same to you).	Response to Mazzal Tov wish.	
27	Le-ḥayyim or	לְחַיִּים	To life.	On taking a drink, usually alcoholic	Shab. 67 b.
28	Le-ḥayyim tovim u-le-shalom	לְחַיִּים טוֹבִים וּלְשָׁלוֹם	Good life and peace (to you).	More ample form of No. 27.	

DURING MOURNING

29	Ha-Makom yenaḥem etkhem be-tokh avelei Ziyyon vi-Yrushalayim	הַמָּקוֹם יְנַחֵם אֶתְכֶם בְּתוֹךְ אֲבֵלֵי צִיּוֹן וִירוּשָׁלַיִם	May the Lord comfort you among all mourners for Zion and Jerusalem.	To a mourner during the week of mourning.	See: Mourning

ON YAHRZEIT

30	Ad bi'at ha-go'el	עַד בִּיאַת הַגּוֹאֵל	(May you live) until the coming of the Messiah.	On the yearly anniversary of the death of a relative.	Among German Jews.

IN WRITTEN FORM ONLY (INITIALS)

31	Ad me'ah shanah	עַד מֵאָה שָׁנָה (עמ״ש)	Until a hundred years.	In the heading of a private letter, after the addressee's name.	
32	Zekhuto yagen aleinu	זְכוּתוֹ יָגֵן עָלֵינוּ (זי״ע)	May his merit protect us.	After name of distinguished deceased; usually ḥasidic.	
33	Zikhrono li-verakhah or Zekher zaddik li-verakhah	זִכְרוֹנוֹ לִבְרָכָה (ז״ל) זֵכֶר צַדִּיק לִבְרָכָה (זצ״ל)	May his memory be for a blessing. May the memory of the pious be for a blessing.	After name of deceased; also in speech.	
34	Alav ha-shalom	עָלָיו הַשָּׁלוֹם (ע״ה)	Peace be on him.	As above.	
35	Natreih Raḥamana u-varkhei	נַטְרֵיה רַחֲמָנָא וּבַרְכֵיה (נר״ו) (Aramaic)	May God guard and bless him (you).	Written form of address.	
36	She-yiḥyeh le-orekh yamim tovim amen	שֶׁיִּחְיֶה לְאֹרֶךְ יָמִים טוֹבִים אָמֵן (שליט״א)	May he (you) live for many good days, Amen.	As above.	

Hank Greenberg

Greenberg, Henry Benjamin (Hank; 1911–), U.S. baseball player for Detroit Tigers. Hit 58 home runs 1938. Lifetime batting average .313. Elected to Baseball Hall of Fame.

Greenberg, Irving (1933–), U.S. Orthodox rabbi. Prof. of history at Yeshiva Univ. Leading exponent of Musar movement and active in dialogue with Conservative and Reform movements.

Greenberg, Joanne (1932–), U.S. novelist. Best-known for *The King's Persons,* story of Jewish life in medieval England, and *I Never Promised You a Rose Garden,* written under pseud. Hannah Green.

Greenberg, Leopold (1885–1964), S. African judge. Sat in Appellate Division of Supreme Court fr. 1943. Active in Zionist Organization.

Uri Ẓevi Greenberg

Henri Grégoire

Synagogue in Grodno

Greenberg Leopold Jacob (1861–1931) English journalist, Zionist. Editor of *Jewish Chronicle* fr. 1907. Influenced by Herzl, one of first Zionists in Britain, and official representative vis-à-vis British government His son **Ivan Marion** (1896–1966), editor of *Jewish Chronicle* 1936–46; a leader of Revisionist Party in Britain.

Greenberg, Samuel Bernard (1893–1917), U.S. poet. Wrote mystical poetry filled with vivid and strange imagery. Unknown until Hart Crane discovered his mss.

Greenberg, Simon (1901–), U.S. Conservative rabbi, educator. Rabbi of Har Zion, Philadelphia, 1925–46, vice-chancellor of Jewish Theological Seminary fr. 1957. Settled in Jerusalem 1972. His son **Moshe** (1928–), Bible scholar. Taught at Univ. of Pennsylvania; prof. of Bible at Heb. Univ. 1970.

Greenberg, Uri Ẓevi (1894–), Hebrew poet; b. Galicia, settled in Ereẓ Israel 1924. First work in Yiddish, then exclusively in Hebrew. Fr. 1929 central figure in Revisionist movement; Ḥerut member of First Knesset. Israel Prize 1957. One of most influential poets in Israel, with religious mystical view of Zionism as fulfillment of Jewish historical destiny. His *Reḥovot ha-Nahar* is dirge about Nazi Holocaust.

Greene, Lorne (1915–), Canadian actor. Founder of Academy of Dramatic Arts in Toronto in late 1940s. Starred in TV series *Bonanza.*

Greenebaum, U.S. family in Chicago. Brothers **Elias** (1822–1919) and **Henry** (1833–1914) founded Greenebaum Brothers Banking House. Elias founded Congregation Sinai, first Reform Congregation in Chicago. First Jew to serve on Chicago City Council, founder and pres. United Hebrew Relief Association. Other members of family took leading roles in Jewish communal life.

Greenfield, Albert Monroe (1887–1967), U.S. financier, civic leader. Controlled many stores, hotels, etc. in Philadelphia and was power in Philadelphia politics.

Greenspoon, Henry (1919–), Canadian architect. Buildings designed incl. Place Victoria, Montreal.

Greenstone, Julius Hillel (1873–1955), U.S. educator, author. Taught Jewish education and religion at Gratz College. Wrote *The Messiah Idea in Jewish History.*

Greenwald, Jekuthiel Judah (Leopold; 1889–1955), Orthodox rabbi, scholar; b. Hungary, in U.S. fr. 1924. Rabbi in N.Y. and Columbus, Ohio. Wrote on Hungarian Jewish history.

Greetings, see pp. 224–5.

°**Grégoire, Henri Baptiste (Abbé Grégoire;** 1750–1831), Catholic clergyman; active in French Revolution. Led campaign in French National Assembly for civic emancipation of Jews, which started process of Emancipation for European Jewry.

Gregory, Sir Theodore (1890–1971), British economist. Prof. at Univ. of London. Main fields: general and monetary economics.

Grey, Joel (1932–), U.S. musical-comedy actor; son of bandleader Mickey Katz. Won critical approval in *Stop the World – I Want to Get Off* and in *Cabaret* (also in film).

Griliches, Avenir (1822–1905), Russian engraver. Employed by imperial mint in St. Petersburg. Engraved state seals of Alexander III and Nicholas II. His son **Abraham** (1852–c. 1916), engraver at imperial mint; medalist and gem engraver.

Grinberg, Aleksander Abramovich (1898–), Russian chemist. Prof. at Lensovet Leningrad Technological Institute. Stalin Prize 1946. Main field chemistry of complex compounds.

Grinker, Roy Richard Sr. (1900–), U.S. neuropsychiatrist, psychoanalyst. Director of institute for psychosomatic and psychiatric research and training at Michael Reese Hospital in Chicago; prof. at Univ. of Chicago. Chief editor of *Archives of General Psychiatry.*

Grock (Charles Adrien Wettach; 1880–1959), Swiss clown; son of Jewish father and non-Jewish mother. Built musical clown act into what was considered world's most famous comic display.

Grodno (Horodno), city in Belorussian SSR. Community granted charter 1389. Townsfolk and artisans hostile. Center of Jewish learning, early Hebrew printing press. When it passed to Russia 1795, Jewish pop. 85% of total; largest community in Lithuania. After return to Poland, Jews ousted from economic position. 20th c. Jewish labor movements led Jewish self-defense, fought for Jewish rights. Hebrew and Zionist movements strong. Almost all Jews murdered in WWII (22,000 fr. Grodno and 20,000 fr. vicinity).

Grodzinski, Ḥayyim Ozer (1863–1940), talmudic scholar, a spiritual leader of Lithuanian Orthodoxy. Leader of Vilna *bet din.* Vehement

opponent of Zionism and secular education for Jews. Author of responsa.

Gronemann, Samuel (Sammy; 1875–1952), German author, Zionist leader, lawyer, in Tel Aviv fr. 1936. Wrote novels and plays (*The King and the Cobbler*) adapted for Hebrew stage. Pres. Zionist Congress Court. Noted wit.

Groper, Jacob Ashel (1890–1968), pioneer of Yiddish poetry in Rumania; settled in Haifa 1960.

Gropper, William (1897–), U.S. cartoonist, painter. Worked for social justice. Painted Jewish subjects after 1948 visit to ruins of Warsaw ghetto.

Gross, Adolf (1862–1937), lawyer, communal worker; delegate in Austrian parliament. Founded Jewish Independent Party in Cracow. Opposed to Zionism.

Gross, Chaim (1904–), sculptor; b. Galicia, in U.S. fr. 1921. Worked in different media: wood, stone, bronze, pen and ink, water color.

Gross, Charles (1857–1909), U.S. historian. Prof. at Harvard. Main work *The Gild Merchant.*

Gross, Heinrich (Henri; 1835–1910), rabbi, scholar; b. Hungary, rabbi in Germany. Main work *Gallia Judaica,* geographic dictionary of France according to rabbinic sources.

Gross, John (1935–), British critic. After working as assistant editor of *Encounter* and literary editor of the *New Statesman,* he became editor of *The Times Literary Supplement* in 1974.

Gross, Naphtali (1896–1956), U.S. Yiddish poet, folklorist. On staff of N.Y. *Jewish Daily Forward.* Translations of Bible, Solomon ibn Gabirol.

Grosser, Bronislaw (pseud. **Slawek; Zelcer;** 1883–1912), lawyer; b. Poland. Bund leader and member of Fourth Duma.

Bronze menorah by Chaim Gross

Jennie Grossinger

Grossinger, Jennie (1892–1972), U.S. resort owner. Manager of famous Grossinger's hotel in Catskill Mountains, N.Y.

Grossman, Kurt Richard (1897–1972), German journalist; in U.S. fr. 1939. Spokesman on problems concerning Jewish refugees and restitution and compensation.

Grossman, Meir (1888–1964), journalist, Zionist leader; b. Russia. Edited Yiddish journals. Joined Jacob Landau in establishing Jewish Correspondence Bureau (later Jewish Telegraphic Agency) 1919. Member of Revisionist Party, left 1933 and founded Jewish State Party. In Ereẓ Israel fr. 1934. Later joined General Zionists and was member of Executive of Zionist Organization 1954–60.

Grossman, Reuven, see Avinoam, Reuven.

Grossman, Vasili Semyonovich (1905–1964), Soviet Russian writer. Early 3-vol. novel *Stepan Kolchugin* described Communist underground before Revolution. Fell out of favor by emphasizing Nazi atrocities to Jews in his novels.

Gruby, David (1810–1898), physician; pioneer of modern microbiology and parasitology. Denied appointment as prof. at Vienna Univ. medical school when he refused to convert. Settled in Paris 1839. Lectured at Museum of Nature. First to prove experimentally that fungus was likely to cause specific disease in man.

Gruenbaum, Henry (1911–), Danish economist, politician. In Danish Resistance during WWII. Minister of economics and Nordic affairs 1964, finance 1965–68.

Gruenbaum, Max (1817–1898), German researcher in Jewish folklore and popular languages of Jews; a founder of Yiddish philology. Published chrestomathy of Judeo-Spanish.

Gruenbaum, Yiẓhak (1879–1970), Polish Jewish leader, Zionist. Edited weekly *Ha-Olam.* Elected to Sejm. Fervent champion of minorities in Poland; formed "national minorities bloc." Leader Al ha-Mishmar Zionist faction. Settled in Ereẓ Israel 1933. Member of Zionist Executive, heading aliyah and labor dept. Minister of interior in provisional government 1948–9. Editor of *Encyclopaedia of the Jewish Diaspora.* Wrote 4-vol. History of Zionism. At first, General Zionist, later sympathized with Mapam. Spent last years in Kibbutz Gan Shemuel.

Yiẓhak Gruenbaum

Gruenberg, Louis (1884–1964), U.S. composer. Wrote opera *Emperor Jones.* One of first American composers to use elements of Negro spirituals and jazz in serious music. Organizer of League of Composers.

Gruenberg, Sidonie Matsner (1881–), U.S. educator. Director of Child Study Association of America 1923–50. Authority on child-parent relationships.

Gruening, Ernest Henry (1887–), U.S. journalist, administrator, politician. Crusading editor of *The Nation* 1920–23. Director of Division of Territories and Island Possessions of Dept. of Interior 1934–39, territorial governor of Alaska 1939–53, senator (Dem.) fr. Alaska 1958–68.

Grumbach, Salomon (1884–1952), French socialist. Editor of *L'Humanité.* Member of French Chamber of Deputies fr. 1928. Member of French resistance in WWII. Active in Jewish affiars.

Grunfeld, Isidor (1900–), rabbi, author; b. Germany , in England fr. 1933. *Dayyan* of London Beth Din fr. 1939. Translated and wrote on S.R. Hirsch.

Grünvald, Philip (Fülöp; 1887–1964), Hungarian historian. Taught at Jewish Theological Seminary in Budapest. Curator of Jewish Museum in Budapest. Wrote on history of Jews in Hungary.

Grunwald, Max (1871–1953), rabbi, historian, folklorist. Wrote histories of Jews of Hamburg and Vienna and served in both as rabbi. In Jerusalem fr. 1938. Main research in field of folklore; founded *Gesellschaft fuer juedische Volkskunde* 1897 and edited and largely wrote its publications.

Grusenberg, Oscar Osipovich (1866–1940), advocate in Russia. Made his name in political trials, defending revolutionaries, etc. Appeared in many *causes célèbres,* notably Beilis trial. During Russian civil war, headed Jewish Council for Self-Defense. Left Russia 1921, living in Berlin, Riga, Paris.

Grynszpan (Gruenspan), Herschel (1921– ?), assassin of German diplomat in Paris. Shot Ernst vom Rath to call attention of world to Nazi persecution of Jews. Served as pretext for *Kristallnacht.* Handed over to Germans in WWII; fate unknown.

Herschel Grynszpan

Guadalajara, city in C. Spain. Jews there in Visigoth times. Entrusted with defense of town after Arab conquest 714. After 1391 forced to live in special quarter. Birthplace of Kabbalah in Castile and important Jewish scholars lived there, with Hebrew printing press 1482 and important yeshivah. Jews expelled 1492 and established their own synagogue in Algiers in 16th c.

Guastalla, Enrico (1828–1903), Italian soldier. Joined Garibaldi in campaigns of 1860, 1866; elected to Italian parliament 1865.

Guatemala, C. America republic. Jews arrived fr. Germany in mid-19th c. and assimilated. Immigration restrictions limited community in 20th c. Main Jewish communities in Guatemala City, Quezaltenango, San Marcos, comprising German, Sephardi, E. European Jews. Jewish pop. 1,900 (1971). Country played important role in UN in establishment of State of Israel.

Guedalla, Haim (1815–1904), English philanthropist. Supporter of Jewish settlement in Erez Israel; instrumental in securing Spanish government's permission for Jews to return to Spain. Wrote on Jewish affairs.

Guedalla, Philip (1889–1944), English biographer, historian, essayist. Books on historical personalities and events of 19th–20th c. Pres. British Zionist Federation. Noted wit.

Guedemann, Moritz (1835–1918), Austrian rabbi, historian. Influential chief rabbi of Vienna fr. 1891; led rabbinical opponents of Herzl's Zionism ("protest rabbis"). Wrote important studies of trends and institutions of medieval Jewish life.

Guenzburg, family of Russian bankers, philanthropists, communal workers. Semi-official representatives before czarist authorities. **Horace** and father **Joseph Yozel** granted baronetcy in 1870s which was made hereditary by Czar Alexander II. **Baron Joseph Yozel (Yevsel)** (1812–1878) founded bank in St. Petersburg. Won rights for Jews in certain categories to reside outside Pale of Settlement. Helped build first synagogue in St. Petersburg. His son **Baron Horace (Naphtali Herz)** (1833–1909) helped his father in business and public activities. Patron of arts, scientific institutions, etc. His son **Baron David** (1857–1910) pursued scholarly works in Judaic and oriental studies. Published many works on medieval Jewish art, etc. Editor-in-chief of *Yevreyskaya Entsiklopediya.* Established Jewish Academy (Higher Courses in Oriental Studies) in St. Petersburg.

Baron Horace Guenzburg

Guenzburg, Ilya Yakovlevich (1860? –1939), Russian sculptor. Studied under Antokolski. Produced scenes of children; busts of contemporary writers, artists, scientists; abstract subjects.

Guenzburg, Mordecai Aaron (1795–1846), Hebrew author; founder of first modern Jewish school in Lithuania. His books on French and Russian history widely circulated and very popular; published anthologies, essays, short stories.

Guggenheim, U.S. family. **Meyer** (1829–1905), merchant, industrialist; b. Switzerland, in U.S. fr. 1848. Founded mining firm. Joined in business by seven sons. They incl. **Isaac** (1854–1922), active in Jewish affairs. **Daniel** (1856–1930), pres. American Smelting and Refining Company; established philanthropical foundation, founded free dental clinic in N.Y. **Solomon Robert** (1861–1949), formed Solomon R. Guggenheim Foundation. N.Y. Guggenheim Museum commemorates his interest in art. **Simon** (1867–1941), senator fr. Colorado 1907–13. Founded John Simon Guggenheim Foundation. Daniel's son, **Harry Frank** (1890–1971), established foundation. U.S. ambassador to Cuba 1929–33. Founded Long Island daily *Newsday.* **Marguerite (Peggy;** 1898–), patronized modern art, esp. American abstract expressionism.

Guggenheim, Paul (1899–), Swiss jurist, authority on international law. Member of Permanent Court of Arbitration at The Hague and judge ad hoc of International Court of Justice. Pres. Swiss Jewish community 1944–50.

Guggenheim-Gruenberg, Florence (1898–), Swiss pharmacist, historian. Pres. Juedische Vereinigung in Zurich fr. 1950. Wrote on Swiss Jewish history.

Guglielmo da Pesaro (known as **Guglielmo Ebreo;** 15th c.), Italian dancing master. Compiled "Treatise on the Art of Dancing."

Guiana, Dutch, see Surinam.

Guilt Offering, see Sacrifice.

Guinzburg, Harold Kleinert (1899–1961), U.S. publisher. Cofounder of Viking Press and Literary Guild Book Club.

Guiterman, Arthur (1871–1943), U.S. poet. Known for light verse. Collections incl. *Betel Nuts* and *Brave Laughter.*

Gulak, Asher (1881–1940), historian of Jewish law; b. Latvia, settled in Erez Israel 1925. Prof. at Hebrew Univ. fr. 1936. Wrote 4-vol. *Yesodei ha-Mishpat ha-Ivri,* first to present Jewish law systematically.

Gumpert, Martin (1897–1955), German author, physician; in U.S. fr. 1936. Dermatologist and geriatrician. Wrote lyrics, novels, biographies.

Gumplowicz, Ludwig (1838–1909), Austrian jurist, sociologist. Prof. of political science at Univ. of Graz. Convert; proponent of Jewish assim-

ilation. Pessimistic outlook on life.

Gundolf, Friedrich (pseud. of **Friedrich Gundelfinger;** 1880–1931), German literary historian. Taught at Heidelberg Univ. Wrote biographies of Goethe, Shakespeare, etc.

°**Gunkel, Hermann** (1862–1932), German Bible scholar. Stressed importance of determining oral prehistory of written sources and of classifying source material into appropriate categories of literary "forms."

Gunsberg, Isidor (1854–1930), British chess master, journalist. Lost world championship match against Steinitz. Wrote famous chess columns in *Morning Post.*

Gunzberg, Aryeh Leib (Loeb) ben Asher (1695–1785), talmudist who entered controversy with Jehiel Heilprin over method of instruction to be used in their respective Minsk yeshivot. Wrote halakhic work *Sha'agat Aryeh.*

Gunzberg, Niko (1882–), Belgian jurist, criminologist. Founded Institute of Criminology at Univ. of Ghent. Founded Central Committee for Jewish Welfare in Antwerp.

Gunzenhauser (Ashkenazi), Joseph ben Jacob (d. 1490) and his son **Azriel,** pioneers in Hebrew printing. Set up Hebrew press in Naples.

Gur Dynasty (Yid. *Ger*), ḥasidic dynasty in Poland, established by Meir Alter (1789–1866) and led by his descendants. In Poland until 1939, thereafter in Jerusalem. Gur Ḥasidim derived teaching mainly fr. Kotsk school but closer connection with masses.

Gurland, Ḥayyim Jonah (1843–1890), Russian rabbi, scholar who discovered that Firkovich mss. were forgeries. Main work on Islamic influence on Maimonides.

Gurs, one of France's largest concentration camps during WWII, nr. Pau, Basses-Pyrénées. Jews sent fr. Gurs to Drancy and then to death camps.

Gurvitch, Georges (1894–1966), sociologist. Taught at Petrograd, Strasbourg, Paris. Works dealt with sociology of law, nature of groups and social classes, and character of social time.

Gurwitsch, Aaron (1901–1973), philosopher, psychologist; b. Vilna. Taught at Sorbonne fr. 1933, U.S. univs. fr. 1940. Philosophical approach to problems of psychology.

Gurwitsch (Gurvich), Alexander Gavrilovich (1874–1954). Soviet Russian biologist. Prof. at Simferopol and Moscow Univ. Stalin prize 1941. Studies effects of certain types of drugs on development.

Gush Ḥalav, see Giscala.

Gutenberg, Beno (1889–1960), geophysicist. Prof. at Frankfort Univ., California Institute of Technology fr. 1936. Director of Seismological Laboratory. Originator of hypothesis of continental spreading (Fliess theory).

Gutfreund, Otto (1889–1927), Czech sculptor. Pioneer of cubism in sculpture. Later turned to simplified, stylized reality.

Gutheim, James Koppel (1817–1886), U.S. Reform rabbi. In New Orleans during Civil War; upon its capture by North, preferred exile to taking oath of allegiance to Union. Later returned to New Orleans and was acknowledged leader of community.

Gutman, Alexander B. (1902–), U.S. physician. Prof. at Mt. Sinai School of Medicine. Founder 1946 and editor-in-chief of *American Journal of Medicine.* Introduced acid phosphate test for prostate cancer; world authority on gout.

Gutman, Chaim (pseud. **"Der Lebediker";** 1887–1961), Yiddish humorist, satirist, theater critic. Edited comical weekly *Der Kundes.*

Gutman, Nahum (1898–), Israel painter, illustrator; son of Simḥah Ben Zion. Worked in oils and watercolors and illustrated children's stories. Wrote prose and children's stories.

Gutmann, Joseph (1923–), U.S. art historian. Taught at Hebrew Union College, Univ. of Cincinnati, Wayne State Univ. Wrote on Jewish art.

Gutmann, Joshua (1890–1963), scholar of Jewish Hellenism; b. Belorussia. Member of editorial board of German *Encyclopaedia Judaica.* In Ereẓ Israel fr. 1933. Taught Jewish-Hellenistic studies at Heb. Univ.

Gutmann, Simḥah Alter, see Ben-Zion, S.

Gutmann, Wilhelm, Ritter von (1825–1895). Austrian industrialist, philanthropist. His firm controlled bulk of Austro-Hungarian coal trade; established Witkowitz Steel Works. Member of Lower Austrian Diet. Pres. Vienna Jewish community.

Gutt, Camille (1884–1971), Belgian statesman. Minister of finance 1934–35, 1939–40. Managing director of International Monetary Fund 1946–51.

Guttmacher, Alan F. (1898–1974), U.S. prof. of obstetrics and proponent of world population control. Pres. Planned Parenthood Federation of America fr. 1962.

Guttmacher, Elijah (1795–1874), rabbi; forerunner of Ḥibbat Zion movement. Rabbi in province of Posen; his fame was widespread and many visitors made pilgrimages to him for cures and advice. Influenced by mystical thought; believed that Jews should not wait for Messiah passively but should engage in constructive work in Ereẓ Israel.

Meyer Guggenheim, center, with his seven sons.

"A Synagogue in Safed" by Nahum Gutman.

Elijah Guttmacher, lithograph by Hermann Struck.

Guttman, Louis (Eliahu; 1916–), sociologist; b. New York, settled in Ereẓ Israel 1947. Founded Israel Institute of Applied Social Research. Prof. at Heb. Univ. Important work on sociological methodology (the Guttman Scale).

Guttman, Robert (1880–1942), Czech primitive painter. Unusual personality who walked from Prague to each Zionist Congress held in his lifetime. D. in Lodz ghetto. Painting acclaimed only posthumously.

Guttmann, Jacob (1845–1919), German historian of Jewish philosophy. Rabbi in Hildesheim and Breslau. Wrote many important studies on medieval Jewish philosophy.

Guttmann, Julius (Yizhak; 1880–1950), philosopher, historian; son of Jacob Guttmann. Taught general philosophy at Univ. of Breslau, Jewish philosophy at Hochschule fuer die Wissenschaft des Judentums in Berlin. In Jerusalem fr. 1934. Prof. at Heb. Univ. Writings incl. *Philosophies of Judaism.*

Guttmann, Sir Ludwig (1899–), founder and director of National Spinal Injuries Center at Stoke Mandeville, England; b. Germany, in England fr. 1939. Famed for treatment and rehabilitation of paraplegics.

Guttmann, Michael (1872–1942), Hungarian talmudist. Prof. at Breslau Jewish Theological Seminary. Wrote on talmudic methodology, reasons for observance of commandments; planned vast talmudic encyclopedia but only 4 vols. appeared *(Mafte'aḥ ha-Talmud).*

Guyana (formerly **British Guiana**), state in S. America. Earliest Jews with Dutch rule 1581. Suggestion to settle Jewish refugees there 1939 dropped. 40 Jews in 1970.

"Sha'agat Aryeh," collection of responsa by Aryeh Leib Gunzberg.

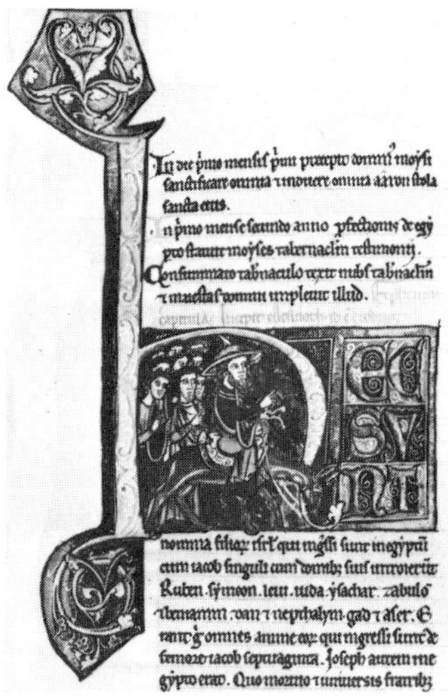

Initial letter "H" from beginning of Exodus in a Latin Bible, France, 12th cent. Illumination shows Jacob and his sons going to Egypt.

Haan, see also De Haan.

Haan, Jacob Israël de (1881–1924), Dutch poet, journalist; brother of Carry van Bruggen. Married non-Jew but returned to Orthodoxy. Became Zionist, left wife, children, settled in Jerusalem 1918, where he turned to extreme anti-Zionism, joined Agudat Israel, and was spokesman of Jerusalem Ashkenazi Council. Intrigued with Arabs and assassinated by two members of Haganah, the first political assassination committed by Jews in modern Israel. Wrote verse, travel sketches, etc.

Haaretz, Israel daily newspaper. Founded in Jerusalem (1919 as *Ḥadashot Haaretz*), moved to Tel Aviv 1923. From 1922 editor M. Gluecksohn. Acquired 1937 by S. Schocken and edited by his son Gershom Schocken. Independent, liberal orientation. Weekday circ. 53,000, weekend 75,000 (1973). Publishes children's weekly *Ha-Areẓ Shellanu.*

Ha-Ari, see Luria, Isaac.

Haas, Georg (1905–), Israel zoologist; b. Vienna, settled in Ereẓ Israel 1933. Prof. at Heb. Univ. Chief interest functional anatomy and evolution of reptiles.

Haas, Ludwig (1875–1930), German politician. Represented Progressive People's (later Democratic) Party in Reichstag and was its chairman 1929. Minister of interior in first republican government in Baden. Active in Jewish affairs.

Haase, Hugo (1863–1919), German socialist leader. Member of Reichstag. Worked for Franco-German friendship. Supported WWI initially but after 1915 opposed it and founded Independent Socialist Democratic Party. Assassinated by German nationalist.

Ha-Asif, six literary annuals published in Warsaw 1884–1894, edited by Nahum Sokolow. First attempt to bring Hebrew literature to masses at popular price.

Haavara, company for transfer of Jewish property fr. Nazi Germany to Ereẓ Israel, established 1933 to facilitate emigration of Jews to Ereẓ Israel by allowing transfer of their capital in form of German export goods. Fr. 1935 under Jewish Agency. Functioned until WWII.

Ḥabad, ḥasidic trend founded by Shneur Zalman of Lyady. Stresses intellectuality (hence its name: initials of *Ḥokhmah, Binah, Da'at,* "wisdom, understanding, knowledge") and thus emphasizes Torah study. Leadership of *ẓaddik* consists mainly in spiritual encounters bet. him and members of congregation devoted to study of Torah and ethics. Movement started in Belorussia; between world wars spread to Latvia, Poland, U.S. Headed by Lubavicher rabbi.

Sculpture by Shamai Haber at Naḥal Sorek, 1962.

Habakkuk (7th c. B.C.E.), prophet of Judah. His book is eighth of Minor Prophets. Contains three chapters and includes divine oracle prophesying that instrument of judgment, the Chaldeans, is at hand and description of Day of the Lord. Hebrew ms. of commentary *(pesher)* on book was found among Dead Sea Scrolls.

Habas, Bracha (1900–1968), Hebrew writer, editor; wife of David Hacohen. On editorial board of *Davar* and Am Oved publishing house. Wrote on history of modern Ereẓ Israel, D.P. camps, David Ben-Gurion.

Ḥabbān, see Hadramaut.

Habe, Hans (pseud. of **János Békessy;** 1911–), Budapest-born German novelist. His books show opposition to Nazism. They include work on assassination of John F. Kennedy and novel *The Mission* about Evian conference.

Haber, Fritz (1868–1934), German physical chemist. Prof. at Technische Hochschule at Karlsruhe. Nobel Prize 1918 for synthesizing ammonia fr. hydrogen and nitrogen, which assisted German effort in WWI. Director of Kaiser Wilhelm Research Institute in Berlin-Dahlem. Left Judaism. With Nazi accession, resigned his post and went to Switzerland.

Haber, Samuel L. (1903–), U.S. economist, organization executive. Director for Germany of Joint fr. 1947, executive vice-chairman of Joint fr. 1967.

Haber, Shamai (1922–), Israel sculptor. Created monumental compositions. Most of his works in stone.

Haberlandt, Gottlieb (1854–1945), German plant physiologist. Prof. at Univ. of Graz and Berlin. Described

important relationship between anatomy of plants and their physiological capacities.

Habermann, Abraham Meir (1901–), bibliographer, scholar of medieval Hebrew literature; b. Galicia. Worked at Schocken Library in Berlin, became its director in Jerusalem. Prof. at Tel Aviv Univ. Published many studies on medieval Hebrew literature, esp. poetry.

Ḥabib, see Ibn Ḥabib.

The renovated Habimah Theater, 1970.

Aerial view of Hadassah medical center complex at Ein Karem, 1970.

Woodcut illustrations for "Had Gadya" by Jacob Steinhardt, 1923.

Ḥabib, Moses ben Solomon ibn (c. 1654–1696), Turkish rabbi, author. Chief rabbi of Jerusalem fr. 1689. Wrote on various tractates of Talmud.

Ḥabiba, Joseph (15th c.), Spanish talmudic scholar. Wrote *Nimmukei Yosef* on work of Isaac Alfasi and was one of last *rishonim* to comment on Talmud.

Habimah, Hebrew repertory theater company, founded in Moscow 1918; initiated by N.D. Zemach, M. Gnessin, and H. Rovina. Adopted Stanislavsky method under direction of Yevgeni Vakhtangov. Greatest triumph was performance of An-Ski's *The Dybbuk* 1922. Left USSR 1927 and settled in Tel Aviv 1931. Awarded title National Theater of Israel 1958.

Ḥabiru (Ḥapiru), element of society in Fertile Crescent. First mentioned in documents of 18th c. B.C.E. Suggested identification with Hebrew people now held to be unlikely but there may be points of contact.

Ha-Boker. (1) Daily Hebrew newspaper in Warsaw Jan.–Aug. 1909. (2) Daily Hebrew newspaper in Tel Aviv 1935–65. Organ of General Zionists, Liberal Party. Merged with *Ḥerut* to become *Ha-Yom.*

Habonim, see Iḥud Habonim.

Habor, river flowing through Mesopotamia. Tiglath-Pileser III settled Israelite exiles fr. Transjordan in district and Sargon II settled exiles fr. Samaria there.

Ḥabshush, Ḥayyim (d. 1899), Yemenite writer. Guide to scholar Joseph Halévy when latter visited Yemen. Wrote *Travels in Yemen* about his travels with Halévy and *Halikhot Teiman,* episodes in history of Yemenite Jewry.

Hackett Buddy (Leonard Hacker; 1924–), U.S. comedian. Gained success as TV comedian and in roles in such films as *Its a Mad, Mad, Mad World* and *The Love Bug.*

Hacohen, David (1898–), Israel politician, diplomat; son of Mordecai ben Hillel Hacohen. Founder and director of Solel Boneh. Mapai member of Knesset and chairman of Foreign Affairs and Security Committee; Israel's first ambassador to Burma 1953–55.

Hacohen, Mordecai ben Hillel (1856–1936), Hebrew writer, Zionist; b. Belorussia. Wrote in Hebrew press in Europe *(Ha-Levanon, Ha-Ẓefirah, Ha-Kol).* Member of Ḥibbat Zion. Spoke in Hebrew at First Zionist Congress 1897. Settled in Ereẓ Israel 1907. A founder of Tel Aviv and active in its economic life. A founder of Association of Hebrew Writers.

Hadad, early Semitic god of elements and fertility, one of chief gods of Canaanites.

Hadamard, Jacques Salomon (1865–1963), French mathematician. Prof. at Ecole Polytechnique, member of Academy of Sciences; first to be awarded Feltrinelli Prize 1955. In England during WWII. Worked on analysis, differential geometry, hydrodynamics, etc.

Hadar Ramatayim, see Hod ha-Sharon.

Hadas, myrtle, one of four species used on Sukkot together with *etrog, lulav,* and *aravah.*

Hadas, Moses (1900–1966), U.S. classical scholar. Prof. of Greek at Columbia Univ. Produced popular translations, histories of Greek and Latin literature; also translations of medieval Jewish prose classics.

Hadassah, the Women's Zionist Organization of America, largest Zionist organization in world and one of largest women's organizations in U.S. Founded in 1912 by Henrietta Szold. Its program is carried out on two fronts: in Israel (fr. 1918), where it sponsors medical training, research, and care, along with special education, and in U.S., where members participate in fund raising and Jewish educational activities. Hebrew University–Hadassah Medical School established 1949 in conjunction with Hadassah Hospital. Also supports Youth Aliyah. Membership 325,000 (1973), with 1,440 chapters and groups.

Hadassi, Judah (ha-Avel) ben Elijah (12th c.), Karaite scholar of Constantinople. Main work *Eshkol ha-Kofer* (or *Sefer ha-Peles*), which explains commandments and *halakhot* and reasons for their observance in accordance with Karaite belief.

Ḥaderah, town in C. Israel, founded 1890 by Ḥovevei Zion fr. Lithuania. Settlers had to drain malarial swamps. Became regional center with several large industries. Pop. 31,500 (1971).

Ḥad Gadya (Aram. "An only kid"), initial phrase and name of popular Aramaic song chanted at conclusion of Passover *seder.* Its theme of retribution is developed in familiar nursery-song fashion.

Hadoar, Hebrew literary journal in U.S. Started as daily 1921; weekly fr. 1923 under auspices of Histadruth Ivrith of America. Editor

Menachem Ribalow 1925–1953, succeeded by Moses Maisels, Moshe Yinon

Hadramaut, region on S. coast of Saudi Arabia. Small distinctive Jewish community with own customs and dress lived in town of Ḥabbān and surrounding villages. Almost all went to Israel 1950, where they maintain close marriage and social ties.

Hadran (Aram. "We returned"), term indicating both the celebration held on completion of study of Talmud tractate and type of discourse delivered on that occasion.

°**Hadrian, Publius Aelius,** Roman emperor 117–138 C.E. His decision to erect city on ruins of Jerusalem led to Bar-Kokhba War. Revolt crushed by Julius Severus, after which harsh decrees enacted, and Aelia Capitolina built on ruins of Jerusalem.

Ha-Efrati (Tropplowitz), Joseph (c. 1770–1804), Hebrew poet, dramatist; b. Silesia. Principal work *Melukhat Sha'ul* portrayed pathos of suffering King Saul; first modern Hebrew drama of Haskalah period.

Ha-Emet, first Hebrew socialist periodical, published in Vienna 1877. Edited and published by Aaron Samuel Libermann.

Ḥafeẓ Ḥayyim, see Israel Meir ha-Kohen.

Haffkine, Waldemar Mordecai (1860–1930), bacteriologist; b. Odessa. Assistant to director of Pasteur Institute, Paris. Developed first vaccine against cholera and achieved remarkable results in fighting cholera in India. Active in Jewish organizations. Founded Haffkine Foundation to foster religious, scientific, and vocational education in yeshivot of E. Europe.

Haftarah, portion fr. prophets read in synagogue after reading fr. Torah on Sabbaths, festivals, and fast days. Usually portion has reference to Torah reading, but in some cases to calendar or historical circumstance. Possibly originated during time of persecutions by Antiochus Epiphanes when reading Torah was forbidden. See Torah, Reading of.

Haganah, underground military organization of Jewish community in Ereẓ Israel. Founded after Arab riots of 1920 when Jewish leaders realized that their defense could not depend on British authorities and they must create own, encompassing Jewish masses under authority of Jewish national institutions. Crisis in command led to secession of group that formed Irgun Ẓeva'i Le'ummi 1931. With outbreak of 1936 Arab riots, Haganah members formed Jewish Settlement Police and established field squads 1937 which later joined Special Night Squads under command of Orde Wingate. In WWII many members joined British army. Mobilized formation, Palmaḥ, established 1941. Fr. end of war to 1948 Haganah was very active in "illegal" immigration and anti-British activities. On May 31, 1948, Haganah became regular army of Israel.

Hagar, Egyptian maidservant of Sarah, given to Abraham as concubine. Expelled by Sarah when she conceived, but angel exhorted her to return and gave her favorable oracle concerning her future son, Ishmael. When Sarah had borne Isaac, she demanded expulsion of Hagar and Ishmael.

Hagbahah (Heb.), elevation of Scrolls of Law in synagogue, so that congregation may see writing therein.

First day cover and stamp in memory of Waldemar Haffkine, issued by Indian Post Office, 1964.

Haganah Special Night Squad on its way to guard Iraq Petroleum Company pipeline to Haifa, 1937.

Hagar expelled by Abraham, drawing by Rembrandt van Rijn.

"Hagbahah" in a synagogue, drawing by Bernard Picart, 1724.

Haggadah, see Aggadah.

Haggadah, Passover, set form of benedictions, prayers, midrashic comments, and psalms recited at *seder* ritual on first evening of Passover (two evenings outside Israel). It grew out of *seder* service prescribed in Temple times, which included eating of paschal sacrifice, unleavened bread, and bitter herbs; drinking of four cups of wine; and recital of Exodus story. *Haggadah* is account of Egyptian bondage and thanksgiving to God for redemption. It developed over a period of centuries and incorporates excerpts fr. Bible, Mishnah, and Midrash, interpolated with ritual performances. Stories, psalms, and songs were added. It formed a favorite book for artistic illustrations. Modern versions have been developed in Israel kibbutzim, etc.

Haggahot (Heb.), term used to mean both examination of mss. and printed works in order to correct errors and "glosses," i.e., notes and brief comments on text.

Haggahot Maimuniyyot, comprehensive halakhic work; important source for halakhic rulings of scholars of medieval Germany and France. Its author Meir ha-Kohen of Rothenburg compiled it as supplement to Maimonides' *Mishneh Torah* and it was printed in editions of *Mishneh Torah.*

Haggai, prophet fr. post-Exilic period whose book is 10th in Minor Prophets. His prophecies date fr. 520 B.C.E. and deal mainly with construction of Temple and great events which nation will experience in future as result.

Ḥaggai (or **Ḥagga;** c. 300), Palestinian *amora;* prominent member of Tiberias academy.

Ḥagigah, last tractate of Mishnah order *Mo'ed,* with *gemara* in both Talmuds. Deals with laws of peace-offering and rules connected with festivals, duty of pilgrimage, etc. *Gemara* contains much *aggadah,* esp. on cosmogony and Merkabah mysticism.

Hagiographa (Heb. *Ketuvim*), 3rd and last section of Hebrew Bible, after Pentateuch and Prophets, comprising Psalms, Proverbs, Job, Song of Songs, Ruth, Lamentations, Ecclesiastes, Esther, Daniel, Ezra and Nehemiah, I and II Chronicles.

Ḥagiz, Jacob (Israel; 1620–1674), Jerusalem scholar. Headed yeshivah where secular subjects and Spanish were also studied. In contrast to his father-in-law, Moses Galante, was vehement opponent of Shabbetai Ẓevi. Wrote commentary to Mishnah and other scholarly works.

Ḥagiz, Moses (1672–1751?), scholar, kabbalist, opponent of Shabbateanism; son of Jacob Ḥagiz; b. Jerusalem. Traveled as emissary in Europe. When in Amsterdam, joined Ẓevi Hirsch Ashkenazi in bitterly opposing Nehemiah Ḥayon and adherents of Shabbatean movement. Prolific writer on subjects of talmudic scholarship.

Hagozer, Jacob and Gershom (13th c.), father and son who were *mohalim* (practitioners of circumcision) in Germany. Jacob composed book on laws of circumcision which was basis for Gershom's more comprehensive work.

Hague, The, city in Netherlands. Jews there fr. late 17th c. First synagogue 1698. Sephardi and Ashkenzi communities flourished particularly in 18th c. 17,400 Jews in 1939; *judenrein* by 1943. 2,500 Jews in 1972.

Two pages from "Birds' Head Haggadah," S. Germany, c. 1300

Engraving of Sephardi synagogue in The Hague, constructed 1726.

Haham, see Ḥakham.

Ha-Ḥinnukh, anonymous work on 613 precepts. Compiled at end of 13th c. Many editions appeared, the best-known containing commentary *Minḥat Ḥinnukh* of Joseph Babad.

Hahn, Joseph ben Moses (c. 1730–1803), German talmudic scholar; *dayyan* of *bet din* of combined communities of Hamburg, Altona, and Wandsbeck.

Hahn (Nordlingen), Joseph Yuspa ben Phinehas Seligmann (1570–1637), German rabbi. Author of *Yosif Omeẓ,* dealing with laws and customs of Jewish calendar and liturgy. Valuable source for Frankfort Jewish history.

Hahn, Michael (1830–1886), U.S. politician. Union supporter during Civil War. Elected to Congress 1863, governor of Louisana 1864, senator 1865 but never took his seat. Elected to Congress as Republican 1884.

Hahn, Reynaldo (1875–1947), French composer, conductor. Noted for vocal music; wrote light operas, operas, and incidental music to plays, pantomimes, and ballets. Director Paris Opera fr. 1945.

Hai bar Rav David Gaon, head of Pumbedita academy 890–898; transferred Pumbedita academy to Baghdad.

Hai ben Sherira (939–1038), gaon of Pumbedita (fr. 998), molder of *halakhah,* and most prominent figure of his time. Students came to his academy fr. many countries and Jewish communities in all parts of the world addressed their queries to him. Later generations regarded him as supreme authority on halakhic matters. Of all extant geonic responsa, one third by him; also wrote treatises on talmudic subjects, poems.

Haidamacks, paramilitary bands that disrupted social order in Polish Ukraine in 18th c. Main victims were Jews. Outbreaks occurred in 1734, 1750, 1768; in latter year, wholesale massacres took place and neither women nor children were spared. Synagogues were razed and dese-

crated. Eventually suppressed by Russian and Polish troups.

Haifa, port in Israel and commercial and administrative center of N. of country. Small settlement in ancient times. First houses built outside walled city 1858. German Templers arrived (Shikmonah) 1868 and made important contribution to its development. Jewish community grew fr. 1880s. Port developed and town connected with Hejaz railroad 1905. Laying of cornerstone of Technion 1912 marked high point of intensified Jewish activities. After WWI it rapidly grew into large modern city with deepwater port, in which Jews played increasingly predominant role. Various industries developed. In 1948 War of Independence, Haganah took over city, which was second largest in country (until 1967), and built-up area continued to expand. Site of Technion, Haifa Univ., Haifa Municipal Theater. Also the religious center of Bahai. Pop. 219,200 (1971).

Haimowitz, Morris Jonah (1881–1958), U.S. Yiddish writer; b. Mir, in N.Y. fr. 1902. Wrote novels about Jewish life in America and historical novels about Jesus and Shabbetai Ẓevi.

Haiti, Caribbean republic. First Jews (fr. Brazil) in 17th c. but settlement disappeared. More arrived in 19th c. but few stayed. 10 families in Port-au-Prince in 1970.

Hajek, Markus (1861–1941), laryngologist. Prof. at Vienna. Developed systematic and scientific approach in diagnosis and therapy of sinus ailments. In London fr. 1938.

Ha-Karmel, Hebrew periodical published in Vilna under editorship of S.J. Fuenn; weekly 1860–70; monthly 1871–80. Advocate of Enlightenment.

Ḥakham (Heb. "sage"), title given to rabbinic scholars. Originally inferior to "rabbi" since a scholar who possessed *semikhah* was called "rabbi" while lesser savant was called *ḥakham.* Later utilized for ordained scholars. Sephardi Jews used title *ḥakham* for their local rabbis and reserved more honorable designation of rabbi for prominent scholars. Turkish Jewry designated its chief rabbi *ḥakham bashi;* British Sefardim call their chief rabbis haham.

Ḥakham, Simon (1843–1910), author, Bible translator; b. Bukhara, settled in Jerusalem 1890. Major achievement was translation of Bible into Judeo-Persian of Bukharan Jews.

Ḥakham Bashi, see Ḥakham.

Ḥakham Ẓevi, see Ashkenazi, Ẓevi Hirsch ben Jacob.

Hakhel (Heb.), assembly of whole Jewish people on first day of Tabernacles every seventh year in year following sabbatical year as enjoined in Deut. 31:10–13. At this ceremony king of Israel would read certain sections of Pentateuch. In recent years in Israel attempt made to revive it in symbolic form.

Hakhnasat Kallah (Heb. "bringing in the bride"), rabbinic commandment to provide for bride and rejoice at her wedding. Fulfillment of this precept is of utmost importance and communal societies are organized for the purpose.

Hakhnasat Orḥim, see Hospitality.

Hakhsharah (Heb. "preparation"), preparation of pioneers for settlement in Ereẓ Israel. Carried out by youth movements in Diaspora and supported by Jewish Agency.

Ha-Kibbutz ha-Arẓi ha-Shomer ha-Ẓa'ir, union of kibbutzim established 1927 by Ha-Shomer ha-Ẓa'ir pioneers. 77 kibbutzim, 31,945 members in 1973. Adheres strictly to principles of collective life of members and collective education.

Ha-Kibbutz ha-Dati, union of religious kibbutzim established 1935 by Ha-Po'el ha-Mizrachi. 15 kibbutzim, 5,200 members in 1973.

Ha-Kibbutz ha-Me'uḥad, union of kibbutzim established 1927 by pioneers of Third Aliyah. Mapai members seceded in 1951 split with left-wing Aḥdut ha-Avodah. 60 kibbutzim, 25,000–30,000 members in 1973.

Ḥakim, Samuel ben Moses ha-Levi ibn (1480? –after 1547), rabbi in Egypt, Turkey. Only small number of his responsa have survived.

Hakkafot (Heb.), ceremonial processional circuits both in synagogue and outside it on various occasions, such as carrying four species on Tabernacles, carrying Torah scrolls on Simḥat Torah or during dedication of synagogues and cemeteries.

Ha-Koaḥ, Jewish sports society founded in Vienna 1909. Became strong Austrian sports federation. Ceased to function in 1930s. Sport clubs with same name founded in Ereẓ Israel 1942.

Ha Laḥma Anya (Aram. "Behold the poor bread"), opening words of introductory paragraph of Passover *Haggadah.* Contains invitation to poor who lack means of providing themselves with *seder* necessities to join. Ends with prayer that "this year we are slaves, next year we shall be free men."

Halakhah (Heb.), legal part of talmudic and later Jewish literature, as distinct fr. *aggadah,* non-legal material. Refers especially to Oral Law, accepted traditional interpretation of Written Law as it was determined through the ages fr. Mishnah on and codified in *Shulḥan Arukh.*

Panorama of Haifa from Mount Carmel.

Engraving of "hakkafot" around a coffin by members of burial society of Amsterdam Portuguese Synagogue 18th cent.

Illuminated opening of "Ha Laḥma Anya" from "Sarajevo Haggadah," Spain, 14th cent.

Halakhah le-Moshe mi-Sinai (Heb. "A law given to Moses at Sinai"), laws regarded as possessing biblical authority, but neither stated in Scripture nor derived by hermeneutical principles.

Halakhot Gedolot, halakhic code fr. geonic period. Follows Babylonian Talmud for most part and groups together various *halakhot* in logical order, stating general principle before giving details.

Halakhot Keẓuvot, collection of *halakhot* fr. geonic period; attributed to Yehudai Gaon. A work of practical application without discussion or sources.

Halakhot Pesukot, first known halakhic work of *geonim;* written in 8th c., attributed to Yehudai Gaon or his pupils. Confined to laws of practical application, arranged acc. to subject matter.

Watercolor of Halberstadt synagogue, 19th cent.

Halberstadt, city in E. Germany. Jews fr. 1261, community 1364, expulsion 1493, 1595. Jews granted privileges 1650; became largest Jewish community in Prussia, renowned for Torah learning and philanthropy in 17th, 18th c. A center of Orthodox Jewry. 706 Jews in 1933; liquidated in Holocaust.

Halberstadt, Abraham ben Menahem Menke (d. 1782), German rabbi. Proponent of study of grammar for better understanding of Bible and Talmud.

Halberstam, ḥasidic dynasty originating in Galicia in mid-19th c. **Ḥayyim ben Leibush** (1793–1876), founder, rabbi of Zanz (Nowy Sacz). His descendant, **Jekuthiel Judah** (1904–) became Klausenburg Rebbe, settled in Israel, founded Kiryat Zanz nr. Netanyah.

Halberstam, Solomon (Zalman) Ḥayyim (**Shazḥah;** 1832–1900), Polish scholar, bibliophile. Collected rare books and mss. and published editions of some of them. Also published catalog of his library.

Ha-Levanon, first Hebrew newspaper in Ereẓ Israel, edited by Jehiel Brill. Appeared 1863 as organ of *ḥalukkah* trustees. Closed 1864, restarted in Paris 1865–71, Mainz 1872–82, London 1886. Supported Orthodoxy against Reform; later became ardent supporter of settlement in Ereẓ Israel (see also Israelit, Der).

Halevi, Joseph Ẓevi ben Abraham (1874–1960), Israel rabbi, halakhic authority; head of Jaffa *bet din.* His many writings deal with laws applying to Ereẓ Israel.

Halevi, Judah, see Judah Halevi.

Halévy (19th–20th c.), family of French authors. **Elie Halfon** (1760–1826), writer, poet in Hebrew, French. Cantor, secretary of Paris community and teacher. Edited and published weekly journal *L'Israélite Français.* Wrote poem "*Ha-Shalom*" commemorating cease-fire between France and England in 1802. His son **Léon** (1802–1883) taught French literature at Ecole Polytechnique; head of antiquities dept. in Ministry of Education. Wrote verse, translations, plays, etc. His son **Ludovic** (1834–1908) wrote comedies *(Frou-Frou),* novels, stories, and librettos for Offenbach, Bizet, etc. Elected to Academie Française 1884. His son **Daniel** (1872–1962), historian, essayist. Converted to Catholicism and showed anti-Semitic tendencies; defended Marshal Pétain and Charles Maurras. His other son, **Elie** (1870–1937), philosopher, historian; raised as Protestant. Taught English history and European socialism at Ecole libre des Sciences politiques. Wrote *History of the English People in the 19th Century.* Elie Halfon's son, **Jacques (François) Fromental Elie** (1799–1862), operatic composer at Paris Conservatory. Famous for grand opera *La Juive* and comic opera *L'Eclair.*

Jacques Halévy

Halevy (Rabinowitz), Isaac (1847–1914), Polish rabbinical scholar, historian. His idea of world Orthodox Jewry organization led to formation of Agudat Israel 1912. Major work 6-vol. *Dorot ha-Rishonim,* grandly conceived history of Oral Law.

Halévy, Joseph (1827–1917), French orientalist, Hebrew writer. Visited Ethiopia to study Falashas, his report leading to much interest in tribe. Commissioned by French Académie des Inscriptions et Belles Lettres to explore S. Arabia for Sabean inscriptions. (Expedition described by guide Ḥ. Ḥabshush in *Travels in Yemen.*) His Hebrew poems show love for Ereẓ Israel.

Halevy, Moshe (1895–), Israel theatrical director, actor. Assistant director of Habimah in Moscow, emigrated to Israel and founded Ohel Theater 1925 under auspices of Histadrut.

Halfan, Elijah Menahem (16th c.), Italian physician, rabbi, kabbalist; grandson of Joseph Colon. One of rabbis approached to express his view of Henry VIII's divorce from Catherine of Aragon (opinion affirmative). Supported Solomon Molcho.

Halicz, town in Ukrainian SSR. Jews fr. 1488. A center of Karaites, who formed majority of community until late 18th c. 1,000 Rabbanites and 100 Karaites in 1939. Annihilated under Nazis.

Halicz (16th c.), family of printers in Cracow. Brothers **Samuel, Asher,** and **Elyakim** established Poland's first Jewish press c. 1530. Baptized 1537 and boycotted by Jews. Obtained decree ordering Jews to buy entire stock.

Ha-Livni, David, see Weiss, David.

Ḥaliẓah, see Levirate Marriage.

Halkin, Abraham Solomon (1903–), orientalist, educator. Prof. at CCNY, taught at Jewish Theological Seminary. Settled in Jerusalem 1970. Edited many Jewish Arabic writings.

Halkin, Shmuel (1897–1960), Soviet Yiddish poet. Wrote plays, poems evincing love for his people and Ereẓ Israel. Sent to Siberia 1948–55. Rehabilitated 1958 and Russian translation of his poems appeared.

Halkin, Simon (1898–), Hebrew poet, novelist, educator; brother of Abraham Solomon Halkin. Prof. of Hebrew literature at Jewish Institute of Religion in N.Y. 1939–49; prof. of modern Hebrew literature at Heb. Univ. fr. 1949. Wrote poetry, novels (some with American setting), trans-

lations of American and English authors, literary criticism.

Ḥallah (Heb.), portion of dough set aside and given to priest (Num. 15:19–20). In post-Temple times rabbis ordained that part of dough used in baking should be set aside and burnt. This was one of commandments observed by women. Popularly applied to Sabbath loaf (white bread over which blessing is made in Jewish home on Sabbath and festivals).

Silver "ḥallah" platter

Ḥallah, tractate in Mishnah order *Zera'im* with *gemara* in Jerusalem Talmud. Deals with laws of separation of dough for priest.

Halle, Morris (1923–), U.S. linguist. Prof. of modern languages at MIT. Research in linguistic science, patterns of speech.

Hallel (Heb.), term for Psalms 113–118 when these form unit of liturgy. These psalms are expressions of thanksgiving and are read on festive occasions. "Full *Hallel*," consisting of Ps. 113–118, is recited on Sukkot, Ḥanukkah, first day(s) of Passover, at Passover *seder*, and in some synagogues on Israel Independence Day. "Half *Hallel*," omitting Ps. 115:1–11 and 116:1–11, is recited on last days of Passover and on New Moon.

The beginning of Hallel from Barcelona Haggadah, Spain, 14th cent.

Hallelujah (Heb. "Praise Ye the Lord"), liturgical expression occurring exclusively in Book of Psalms. In course of time became independent cultic exclamation (also in Christian Church).

Hallgarten, family of U.S. bankers, founded by **Lazarus** (d. 1875), who opened successful foreign exchange business and was member of New York Stock Exchange. Continued by his sons **Charles** (1838–1908) and **Julius** (d. 1884), who were active in Jewish community affairs.

Hallo, Rudolf (1896–1933), German art historian. Head of Freies Juedisches Lehrhaus in Frankfort. Wrote on biblical and archaeological subjects. Curator at state museum in Kassel, where he created dept. of Jewish art. His son **William W.** (1928–), Assyriologist. Taught at Yale Univ. and was curator of its Babylonian collection. Wrote on Ancient Near Eastern and biblical subjects and translated Rosenzweig's *Star of Redemption* into English.

Halper, Albert (1904–), U.S. novelist. Wrote on his experiences of working-class life, esp. in Chicago.

Halper, Benzion (1884–1924), Hebraist, Arabist, editor. Prof. of cognate languages at Dropsie College, editor of Jewish Publication Society of America 1916–24. Published studies on medieval Hebrew literature and translated into English.

Halperin, see also Helpern.

Halperin, Yeḥiel (1880–1942), Hebrew educator. Established first Hebrew kindergarten in Warsaw 1909 and Hebrew seminary for kindergarten teachers 1910. In Ereẓ Israel fr. 1920.

Halpern, Benjamin (Ben; 1912–), U.S. sociologist, Zionist. Edited *Jewish Frontier* magazine 1943–49. Prof. of Near Eastern studies at Brandeis Univ. Publications deal chiefly with problems of Zionism, Israel society, and role of Jews in U.S. society. Member of Jewish Agency Executive fr. 1968.

Halpern, Georg Gad (1878–1962), economist; leading figure in economic activities of Zionist organization; b. Pinsk. Director of Jewish Colonial Trust in London 1921–28. In Ereẓ Israel 1933. Founded Migdal Insurance Co.

Halpern (Halperin), Israel (1910–1971), Israel historian; b. Poland, settled in Ereẓ Israel 1934. Prof. at Heb. Univ. Wrote on history of E. European Jewry; edited historical-literary anthology of Jewish self-defense and martyrdom. His brother, **Lipman** (1902–1968), started neuropsychic outpatient clinic at Hadassah University Hospital; head of its dept. of neurology, dean of Heb. Univ.–Hadassah Medical School fr. 1965. Major work on posture and its relation to functions of organism. Israel Prize 1953.

Halpern, Moshe Leib (1886–1932), Yiddish poet; b. Galicia, in U.S. fr. 1908. Poetry represented immigrant Jewish youth of early 20th c. who saw freedom tainted by social injustice.

Halphen, Louis (1880–1950), French historian. Prof. of medieval history at Univ. of Paris. Emphasized importance of relating European history to Asian and Islamic history.

Halprin, Ann (1920–), U.S. dancer, choreographer; exponent of dance related to environment. Founded Dancers' Workshop 1950.

Rose Halprin

Halprin, Rose Luria (c. 1896–), U.S. Zionist leader. Pres. Hadassah 1932–34, 1947–51. Member of Executive of Jewish Agency and chairman of American Section.

Halsman, Philippe (1906–), U.S. photographer; b. Latvia, worked in Paris, fled to U.S. in WWII. Worked for *Life* magazine. First pres. American Society of Magazine Photographers.

Ḥalukkah (Heb.), distribution of money collected in Diaspora for support of poor in Ereẓ Israel. Origin of custom in talmudic times. At times (Middle Ages) sole means of support. Organized on community basis. Emissaries sent to many parts of world to collect funds. Continued into 20th c.; fiercely attacked by Zionists, who wanted Jewish society based on its own labor.

Ham, youngest of Noah's sons. Traditionally ancester of black (Hamitic) nations.

Hama (of Nehardea; 4th c.), Babylonian *amora,* head of Pumbedita academy 356–377 succeeding Naḥman b. Isaac.

Ha-Mabbit, see Trani, Moses ben Joseph.

Hamadan, city in W. Iran; biblical Ecbatana, where Cyrus issued his

decree permitting Jews to rebuild Temple in Jerusalem. Traditional site of tombs of Esther and Mordecai. Large community, cultural center, seat of celebrated yeshivah fr. 11th–12th c. Persecuted under Safavid shahs, subjected to forced conversion under the Qājār dynasty 1794–1925. 3,000–6,000 Jews in 1948; many emigrated to Israel and elsewhere and number diminished to 402 in 1966.

Ha-Maggid, first Hebrew newspaper, appeared as weekly in Lyck, E. Prussia, 1856, edited by Eliezer Lipmann Silbermann. Later appeared in Berlin and Cracow, edited by David Gordon. Jewish and general news. Advocated settlement in Ereẓ Israel. Closed 1903.

Haman, vizier of Ahasuerus who plotted to exterminate Jews. Hanged after intervention of Esther and Mordecai. Jewish victory commemorated by holiday of Purim. Story is told in Book of Esther. Became byword for enemy of Jews.

Haman leading Mordecai through the streets of Shushan. Legendarily, Haman's wife, mistaking him for Mordecai, dumps slops on him. Poland, 19th cent.

Front page of "Ha-Meliẓ," Oct. 12, 1861.

המליץ

№ 2.

Ha-Mavdil (Heb. "who distinguishes"), name of hymn sung in *Havdalah* ceremony at close of Sabbath.

Hambourg, Mark (1879–1960), pianist; b. Russia, in England fr. 1894. Dynamic player with superb finger technique. Gained world reputation.

Hambro, Joseph (1780–1848), Danish merchant, financier. Court banker to King of Denmark. His son **Carl Joachim** (1808–1877), baptized; established great banking firm of Hambros.

Hamburg, city in W. Germany. First Jews Marranos fr. Spain and Portugal in late 16th c. Shabbatean movement very strong 1666. Most rich Jews moved to Altona and Amsterdam 1697, when taxes raised. German Jews settled in Hamburg fr. 1627. Under Danish rule Jews worshiped in Altona. Three Ashkenazi congregations (Altona, Hamburg, Wandsbeck) united 1671. French authorities imposed single united congregation of Ashkenazim and Sephardim 1811. 19,900 Jews in 1933. Community ended in WWII. Jewish community reorganized after WWII. Jewish pop. 1,469 (1971).

Hamburg, Abraham Benjamin (Wolf; 1770–1850), German talmudic scholar; head of Fuerth Yeshivah. Reform majority in communal administration removed him fr. post and enlisted police to expel his students fr. city. Wrote sermons, responsa, talmudic novellae, memorial addresses.

Hamburger, Jacob (1826–1911), German rabbi, scholar. Author of *Real-Encyklopaedie fuer Bibel und Talmud,* first such work ever published in German.

Ha-Me'assef, see Me'assef.

Hameiri (Feuerstein), Avigdor (1890–1970), Hebrew author; b. Hungary, settled in Ereẓ Israel 1921. Edited several critical journals; founded satirical theater Ha-Kumkum; wrote novels, poetry, short stories, translated German classics into Hebrew. One of earliest exponents of expressionism in Hebrew poetry. Israel Prize 1968.

Ha-Meliẓ, first Hebrew paper in Russia; founded in Odessa 1860 by Alexander Zederbaum. Organ of moderate Haskalah; later became organ of Ḥibbat Zion movement in Russia. Originally weekly, became daily 1886; closed 1904.

Ha-Me'orer, Hebrew monthly published in London 1906–7, edited by J.Ḥ. Brenner. Influenced generation of Second Aliyah and Hebrew literature of the period.

Ḥameẓ (Heb. "fermented dough"). It is prohibited in Jewish religious usage in two instances: (1) on Passover, when it is forbidden to eat or be in possession of *ḥameẓ;* (2) as offering on altar as concomitant of sacrifices.

Ḥameẓ, Sale of, As leaven owned by Jew on Passover becomes forbidden forever (see above), method of removing it fr. Jew's ownership was devised in form of selling it to non-Jew. Gentile then becomes legal owner and Jew may buy it back after Passover.

Hamilton, city in Ont., Canada. Jews there fr. mid-19th c. Jewish pop. 4,000 (1971), with 5 congregations.

Ḥamishah Asar bi-Shevat, see Tu bi-Shevat.

Ḥammat Gader, ancient site SE of Sea of Galilee, with hot springs visited for healing purposes. In 1949 Armistice Agreement placed under Israel sovereignty. Occupied 1951 by Syrian forces and held until 1967 Six-Day War.

Hammath, ancient city in Israel in vicinity of Tiberias; famous for its hot baths in Second Temple period. Two synagogues excavated there.

Hammerstein, Oscar II (1895–1960), U.S. librettist. Played important role in developing "musical play" into integrated dramatic form. Famous partnership with Richard Rodgers. Wrote *Oklahoma, Carousel, South Pacific, The King and I,* and *The Sound of Music.* His grandfather, **Oscar I** (1847–1919), impresario; built 10 opera houses and theaters in N.Y.

Hamnuna, name of several Babylonian *amoraim:* (1) **Hamnuna Saba ("the Elder"**; 3rd c.), pupil of Rav and his successor as head of Sura academy; (2) **Hamnuna,** *amora* at beginning of 4th c.; pupil and colleague of Ḥisda; (3) **Hamnuna Zuta ("the Younger"**; 4th c.), author of part of confessional incorporated in liturgy of Day of Atonement.

The Bornplatz Synagogue in Hamburg, built 1906, destroyed 1938.

Hamon, family of Spanish and Portuguese origin which lived in Turkey. **Joseph ("the Elder"**; d.c. 1518), court physician to sultans Bayazid II and Selim I. His position enabled him to assist coreligionists in time of danger. His son, **Moses** (c. 1490–c. 1554), physician to Selim I and Suleiman the Magnificent. Also helped coreligionists in time of danger. Maintained yeshivah; wrote several works on medicine and dental care, etc. His son, **Joseph** (d. 1577), physician to Suleiman the Magnificent and Selim II. Obtained renewal of rights of Jews of Salonika.

Hamon, Leo (1908–), French lawyer, politician. Member of Resistance, French Provisional Assembly, Senate. Prof. of law at Institut des Hautes Etudes d'Outre-mer. Spokesman for French cabinet 1969–72, briefly cabinet minister 1972.

Hamor, leading citizen of town of Shechem in time of Jacob. Killed by Simon and Levi in revenge for his son's dishonoring of their sister Dinah (Gen. 34).

Hananel ben Ḥushi'el (d. 1055/56), N. African scholar, *posek*, commentator; b. Kairouan. Like his father, Ḥushi'el b. Elhanan, named *resh bei rabbanan* ("chief among the rabbis"). Wrote commentary to Talmud which served as main bridge between Babylonian–N. African scholars and those of Europe–Ereẓ Israel.

Hananiah (Hanina; 2nd c.), *tanna;* nephew and pupil of Joshua b. Hananiah. Even after his departure fr. Ereẓ Israel to Babylonia, continued to intercalate years and fix new moons, to the dissatisfaction of scholars in Ereẓ Israel.

Hananiah (Ḥanina) ben Ḥakhinai (2nd c.), *tanna* in Jabneh; pupil of Akiva. Acc. to later tradition, one of Ten Martyrs.

Hananiah (Ḥanina) ben Teradyon (2nd c.), *tanna* during Jabneh era and one of Ten Martyrs. Head of academy in Sikhnin. Sentenced to death for teaching Torah, burnt at stake wrapped in Torah Scroll. Father of Beruryah, who married R. Meir.

Hananiah (Ḥanina) of Sepphoris (4th c.), Palestinian *amora;* succeeded R. Jonah as head of Sepphoris academy.

Hananiah son of Azzur, "false prophet," contemporary of prophet Jeremiah (Jer. 28).

Hanau, city in W. Germany. Jews fr. 1313. Community destroyed in Black Death persecutions 1349. Re-

Burning of 17th-cent. Hanau synagogue by Nazis, November 1938.

turned 1429; permitted to build special quarter 1603. Important center of Hebrew printing in 17th, 18th c. 447 Jews before WWII; deported 1942.

Hanau, Solomon Zalman ben Judah Loeb ha-Kohen (1687–1746), German Hebrew grammarian. His *Binyan Shelomo* is Hebrew grammar written in form of criticism of earlier grammarians; also wrote explanation of grammatical passages in Rashi's commentary on Torah.

Hanbury, Lily (1875–1908), British actress; married to Herbert Guedalla. Debut at London's Savoy Theater 1888.

Handelsman, Marceli (1882–1945), Polish historiographer. Prof. at Warsaw Univ. Specialized in Polish history. Although a convert, perished in Holocaust.

Handler, Philip (1917–), U.S. biochemist. Prof. at Duke Univ. Pres. American Society of Biochemists, pres. National Academy of Sciences 1969.

Handlin, Oscar (1915–), U.S. historian. Prof. at Harvard. Wrote on general American history and American Jewish history, applying sociological insights to historical research. Pulitzer Prize for *The Uprooted.*

Hands, Washing of, see Netilat Yadayim.

Hanfmann, George Maxim Anossov (1911–), U.S. archaeologist; b. Russia, in U.S. fr. 1930s. Curator of classical art at Fogg Art Museum (prof. 1956). Excavated at Sardis in Asia Minor, incl. ancient synagogue.

Ḥanina (Hananiah; 3rd–4th c.), Palestinian *amora;* pupil of Johanan. Frequently mentioned with Oshaya.

Ḥanina bar Ḥama (early 3rd c.), Palestinian scholar of transitional generation fr. *tannaim* to *amoraim;* pupil of Judah ha-Nasi, who nominated him as his successor, but he refused because R. Afes was senior, though later succeeding the latter. Saying: "The disciples of the wise increase peace in the world."

Ḥanina ben Dosa (1st c.), *tanna,* disciple-colleague of Johanan b. Zakkai. Noted for great piety and humility. It was stated: "Every day a divine voice proclaims from Mt. Horeb: the whole world is sustained by the merit of my son Ḥanina and Ḥanina my son subsists on a few carobs from one week to the next" (Ber. 17b).

Ḥanina (Aḥonai) Kahana ben Huna (8th c.), *gaon* of Sura 769–774; his interpretations and rulings highly regarded by succeeding *geonim.*

Ḥanina Segan ha-Kohanim (1st c.), *tanna* in last years of Second Temple, deputy high priest. Transmitted details of Temple services.

Ḥanitah, kibbutz on Israel-Lebanese frontier, founded 1938 as tower and stockade outpost; first modern Jewish settlement in W. Galilee. Epitome of defense settlement at the time.

Hankin, Yehoshua (1864–1945), Ereẓ Israel pioneer; b. Ukraine, settled in Ereẓ Israel 1882. Director of Palestine Land Development Corporation. Purchased land on which Reḥovot and Ḥaderah were founded as well as tracts in Jezreel Valley (known as "the redeemer of the valley").

Hannah, mother of prophet Samuel. Expressed gratitude for his birth after years of barrenness by dedicating him to the Lord for service at Shiloh sanctuary (I Sam. 1).

Hannah and Her Seven Sons, story of 7 brothers seized along with their mother by Antiochus IV Epiphanes and put to death for refusing to eat swine's flesh (II Macc. 7). Venerated in the Catholic calendar of saints as "Seven Maccabee Brothers."

Yehoshua Hankin

Hannah lamenting her martyred sons, detail from "Hamburg Miscellany," Mainz (?) c. 1427.

Ḥanneles, Judah Leib ben Meir (Maharlaḥ; d. 1596), rabbi; probably fr. Posen. Author of commentary on *Arba'ah Turim* of Jacob b. Asher.

Hannover, Nathan Nata (d. 1683), preacher, kabbalist, chronicler. After leaving Volhynia because of Chmielnicki massacres, went to Italy 1653, publishing *Yeven Meẓulah,* account of Chmielnicki persecutions. Prolific writer on Kabbalah. Most of his works have been lost. His *Sha'arei Ẓiyyon,* collection of prayers for *tikkun ḥaẓot,* often reprinted. *Dayyan* in Ungarisch Brod, Moravia; killed by Turkish soldiers.

Ha-No'ar ha-Ivri–Akiba, pioneering, scouting Zionist youth movement with attachment to traditional values of Judaism; associated with General Zionists. Founded in Cracow, esp. active in E. Europe. Established settlements in Ereẓ Israel.

Ha-No'ar ha-Oved ve-ha-Lomed, Israel youth movement for boys and girls aged 9–18. Part of Histadrut. Founded 1926 as Ha-No'ar ha-Oved, which merged 1959 with Habonim –Ha-Tenu'ah ha-Me'uḥedet. Provided founding groups for 40 kibbutzim. Biggest youth movement in Israel with 106,000 members (1973).

Israel child lighting Ḥanukkah candles.

Tin Ḥanukkah lamp, Germany, 19th cent., in the form of little chairs.

Opening of Hapoel International Games, Ramat Gan, 1966.

Ḥanokh ben Moses (d. 1014), Spanish talmudist. As chief rabbi of Córdoba virtually chief rabbi of Muslim Spain. Teacher of Samuel ha-Nagid. Like his father, Moses b. Ḥanokh, worked to establish independent Torah center in Spain.

Ḥanokh of Aleksandrow (1798–1870), ḥasidic *ẓaddik* who succeeded Isaac Meir Alter as leader of Gur Ḥasidim. Emphasized value of Torah study, which he termed "internal worship."

Hanover, city in W. Germany. Jews fr. 1292. During Black Death persecutions, Jews driven out, returning after 1375; forced to wear badge 1451. Rabbinate founded for Duchy of Hanover in 17th c., synagogue built 1870, Hebrew printing in 18th–19th c. 4,839 Jews in 1933; community ended in Holocaust. 450 Jews in 1966.

Hantke, Arthur (Menahem; 1874–1955), Zionist leader. Director of office of Zionist Federation in Germany. Settled in Ereẓ Israel 1926. Head of Keren Hayesod in Jerusalem.

Ḥanukkah (Heb. "Dedication"), annual 8-day festival commencing Kislev 25 and commemorating victory of Judah Maccabee and his followers who recaptured Jerusalem after defeating Syrians and purified Temple on this day (miraculously one-day oil supply lasted 8 days). Festival ("Feast of Lights") is observed by kindling lights on each evening in special lamp (*ḥanukkiyah* or *menorah*). Children play game with *dreidel* or *sevivon* ("spinning top") and also receive gifts of money *(ḥanukkah gelt)*. In U.S., in particular, it has become popular family festival.

Haolam, central organ of World Zionist Organization, published weekly 1907–1950 (except for short intervals). Hebrew counterpart of *Die Welt.* Edited at Cologne, Vilna, Odessa, London, Berlin, Jerusalem.

Ha-Oved ha-Ẓiyyoni. Israel labor movement founded 1935 as Histadrut faction by pioneer immigrants of General Zionist Youth fr. E. Europe. Worked inside General Zionist Organization and Histadrut. Principle is Jewish labor as essential element in upbuilding of nation but not as matter for class conflict. Established settlements. Part of Independent Liberal Party.

Ha'palah, see "Illegal" Immigration.

Hapax Legomena (Gr. "once said"), words which occur only once in Bible. There are c. 1,300 instances.

Hapoel, Israel workers' sports organization affiliated with Histadrut. Organized 1926. Membership 90,000 (1973) with 500 branches.

Ha-Po'el ha-Mizrachi, Zionist religious pioneering and labor movement; founded 1922 in Jerusalem. Established settlements, sports organization (Eliẓur), and Benei Akiva youth movement. Merged with Mizrachi 1956 and founded National Religious Party. Membership 105,000 (1973). See also **Knesset.**

Ha-Po'el ha-Ẓa'ir, Ereẓ Israel labor party founded 1905 by pioneers of Second Aliyah. Merged 1929 into Aḥdut ha-Avodah to form Mapai.

Ha-Po'el ha-Ẓa'ir, first newspaper of labor movement in Ereẓ Israel; founded 1907, closed 1970. Editors: Yosef Aharonovitch (until 1923), Yizhak Laufbahn (1923–48), Israel Cohen (1948–70).

Haran, ancient city in Mesopotamia. Home of Terah, father of Abraham.

Harbin, city in N. Manchuria, China. Russian Jews settled there in early 20th c. as shopkeepers and constructors. 8,000 Jews in 1908. Active community and Zionist (esp. Revisionist) movement. Suffered during Japanese occupation. Jewish emigration began before WWII and completed in its wake. 3,500 Harbin Jews in Israel.

Harburg, E.Y. (Edgar "Yip"; 1898–), U.S. songwriter. Wrote lyrics for *Finian's Rainbow, The Wizard of Oz, Cabin in the Sky.*

Harby, Isaac (1788–1828), U.S. author, journalist, teacher, pioneer

Silhouette of Isaac Harby

of Reform Judaism. Important role in establishment of Reform Society of Israelites in Charleston which started U.S. Reform movement.

Harden, Maximilian (1861–1927), German journalist, polemist; convert. Political articles revealed talent for satire. Founded periodical *Die Zukunft,* mouthpiece of liberal opposition to Kaiser. In later years, interested in Jewish affairs. His brother **Georg Witkowski** (1863–1939), German literary historian; convert (but persecuted by Nazis).

Harendorf, Samuel Jacob (1900–1969), Yiddish playwright, journalist; b. Poland. Founded and edited Yiddish World News Agency 1940–69. Plays incl. London wartime hit *The King of Lampedusa* and *Hannah Senesh.*

Ha-Reubeni (Rubinowitz), Ephraim (1881–1953), botanist; b. Ukraine, settled in Ereẓ Israel 1906. Founded first museum of botany in Ereẓ Israel 1907. With his wife, **Hannah** (d. 1956), founded Museum of Flora of the Bible and Talmud in Rishon le-Zion 1912. Lecturer in botany of Bible and Talmud at Heb. Univ.

Har ha-Melekh, hilly district in Judah, probably to be identified with toparchy of Orine, district of Jerusalem in Hasmonean times.

Harkavy, Albert (Abraham Elijah; 1835–1919), Russian orientalist, scholar of Jewish history and literature. Head of dept. of Jewish literature and oriental manuscripts at Imperial Library in St. Petersburg. Wrote on origin of Russian Jews and history of Khazars. Published Jewish mss. of Middle Ages. Proved that Karaite scholar Abraham Firkovich had forged many mss. and tombstone epitaphs.

Harkavy, Alexander (1863–1939), lexicographer of Yiddish, author; b. Belorussia, in U.S. after 1881. Wrote for lectures and popular expositions of American history and culture. Published Yiddish dictionaries and translations of classics. Crowning work was his *Yiddish-English-Hebrew Dictionary.*

Ḥarlap, Jacob Moses ben Zebulun (1883–1951), Ereẓ Israel rabbi. Close to Rabbi A.I. Kook and headed Merkaz ha-Rav (Kook) yeshivah. His main work, *Bet Zevul* (6 parts), comprises his halakhic discourses, novellae on Talmud and on Maimonides' *Mishneh Torah.*

Harman (Herman), Avraham (1914–), Israel public figure; b. London, settled in Ereẓ Israel 1938. Israel Consul General in N.Y. 1953–55, member of Jewish Agency Executive 1955–59, Israel Ambassador to U.S. 1959–68, pres. Heb. Univ. fr. 1968. His wife, **Zena** (1914–), b. London. Chairman of UNICEF, member of Knesset for Israel Labor Party 1969–73.

Ḥaroset (Heb.), paste made of fruit, spices, wine, and *maẓẓah* meal which forms part of *seder* rite on Passover eve and is symbolic of mortar that Jews made while slaves in Egypt.

Silver "ḥaroset" container, Ereẓ Israel, 20th cent.

Harris, Sir David (1852–1942), S. African mining magnate, soldier, politician; b. London, in S. Africa fr. 1871. Conducted defense of Kimberley in Boer War. Sat in S. African parliament for 32 years. Authority on diamond industry.

Harris, Jed (Jacob Horowitz; 1900–), U.S. theatrical producer. Successes incl. *Our Town* and *The Crucible.*

Harris, Sam Henry (1872–1941), U.S. theatrical manager. Produced many successful plays and won several Pulitzer Prizes. Partner of George M. Cohan for 15 years. Successes incl. *Once in a Lifetime* and *You Can't Take It with You.*

Harris, Milton (1906–), U.S. polymer and textile chemist. Director of Textile Research Inst. 1938–44, chairman of American Inst. of Chemists 1961–62.

Harris, Sir Percy (1876–1952), English statesman. Member of London County Council 1907–34, 1946–52 (deputy chairman 1915–16); Liberal MP fr. 1916, 1922–45; deputy leader of Liberal Party in House of Commons 1940–45.

Harris, Zellig Sabbetai (1909–), U.S. linguist. Prof. at Univ. of Pennsylvania. Investigations resulted in development of computer programs for analysis of language structure.

Harrisburg, city in Penn., U.S. First Jews fr. Germany and England 1840s. Congregation established 1852; others later, incl. Lubavich ḥasidim. Jewish pop. 4,600 (1971).

Harrisse, Henry (1829–1910), U.S. historiographer; b. Paris, in U.S. fr. 1849. His *Bibliotheca Americana Vetustissima,* evaluating every book referring to America bet. 1493 and 1551, established his reputation.

Harry, Myriam (pen name of Mme. **Emile Perrault;** 1875–1958), French author; daughter of M.W. Shapira (see Shapira fragments) and Protestant deaconess; b. Jerusalem. Wrote accounts of her travels in Levant, showing sympathy for Zionism. Her *La petite fille de Jérusalem* contains memoirs of Jerusalem.

Hart, English family. **Aaron (Uri Phoebus;** 1670–1756), rabbi; b. Breslau, in England fr. 1704. Rabbi of Ashkenazi community in London. Published *Urim ve-Tummin,* first book printed entirely in Hebrew in London. Regarded as first chief rabbi of England. His brother **Moses** (1675–1756) made fortune as broker and was highly regarded in government circles.

Hart, Aaron (1724–1800), early settler in Canada; b. London, settled in Trois Rivières, Canada, where he played leading role. Postmaster of second post office established in British Canada. Reputed to be wealthiest man in British colonies. His son **Ezekiel** (1767–1843), twice elected to legislature of Lower Canada for Trois Rivières and both times prevented from taking seat, as Jew could not take oath "on the true faith of a Christian." Another son, **Benjamin** (1779–1855), officer, magistrate. Pres. Shearith Israel Synagogue in Montreal.

Hart, Abraham (1810–1885), first important U.S. Jewish publishing executive and leading Philadelphia Jew of his generation. Established publishing firm E.L. Carey & A. Hart. Pres. Mikveh Israel Congregation of Philadelphia, pres. Jewish Publication Society, pres. Maimonides College, etc.

Hart, Bernard (1763–1855), U.S. merchant, father of Emanuel B. Hart; b. London. *Parnas* of Shearith Israel Congregation in N.Y.; active in congregational affairs. Quartermaster in N.Y. State militia. Secretary of N.Y. Stock and Exchange Board.

Hart, Cecil M. (1883–1940), Canadian ice hockey pioneer. Organized, managed, and played for Star Hockey Club; organized first international amateur hockey series bet. Canada and U.S. Manager of Montreal Canadians.

Hart, Daniel (1800–1852), Jamaica lawyer, politician; first Jew granted civil and political privileges in Jamaica. Sat in House of Assembly; assistant judge of Court of Common Pleas.

Hart, Emanuel Bernard (1809–1897), U.S. Democratic politician in N.Y., Jewish leader. Pres. Mount Sinai Hospital, Hebrew Home for Aged and Infirm; N.Y. Excise commissioner. Member of Congress 1851–53.

Hart, Ephraim (1747–1825), U.S. communal leader, stockbroker; b. Bavaria, in N.Y. before Revolutionary War. Member of N.Y. State Senate.

Hart, Ernest Abraham (1836–1898), British physician, humanitarian. Ophthalmologic surgeon at St. Mary's Hospital in London. Editor of *British Medical Journal.* Campaigned for better treatment of sick among poor, against baby farming (responsible for Infant Protection Act 1872), and safeguarding health of workers.

Hart, Herbert Lionel Adolphus (1907–), British philosopher of law. Prof. at Univ. College, Oxford. His works oppose theory of philosophical determinism, notion that nobody can act differently from the way he does and therefore cannot be held responsible for what he does.

Hart, Jacob (1745–1814), kabbalist, grammarian; jeweler by profession. First native-born English scholar of kabbalism. Under his Hebrew name Eliakim b. Abraham published various Hebrew works on religion, Kabbalah, and grammar.

Hart, Moss (1904–1961), U.S. playwright. Wrote plays with George S. Kaufman, incl. *You Can't Take It With You* and *The Man Who Came to Dinner,* and by himself, incl. *George Washington Slept Here.*

Hart, Samuel (c. 1747–1810), Nova Scotia merchant. As member of Nova Scotia House of Assembly was first Jew to sit in legislative body in territory that was later to become Canada.

Hart, Solomon Alexander (1806–1881), English painter. Member, prof. of Royal Academy. Painted famous episodes of English history and Jewish themes.

Ha-Shomer group, 1910

Hartford, city in Conn., U.S. First congregation formed mid-19th c. by German immigrants. E. European immigration started 1880s. Jewish pop. 24,000 (1971), with Jews largely in professions and commerce.

Hartglas, Maximilian Meir Apolinary (1883–1953), Zionist leader in Poland. Lawyer, member of Sejm, instrumental in obtaining repeal of anti-Semitic czarist laws in Poland's former Russian provinces. Settled in Ereẓ Israel 1940. Director general and later legal adviser of minister of interior.

Hart Lyon, see Levin, Ẓevi Hirsch.

Hartmann, Heinz (1894–1970), psychoanalyst; b. Vienna. Leading theoretician in psychoanalysis and pioneer in field of psychoanalytic ego psychology. In U.S. fr. 1941. Pres. of International and N.Y. Psychoanalytic Association.

Hartmann, Moritz (1812–1872), German author, revolutionary; abandoned Judaism. Delegate to revolutionary German National Assembly in Frankfort 1848. His many novellae incl. stories with Jewish themes. An editor of *Neue Freie Presse* in Vienna fr. 1868. His son, **Ludo Moritz** (1865–1924), Social Democrat, Austrian ambassador in Berlin 1918–21.

Hartog, Sir Philip Joseph (1864–1947), British educator; authority on university education. Academic registrar of Univ. of London; a founder of School of Oriental and African Studies in London; first vice-chancellor of Univ. of Dacca, Bengal. Active in Jewish community.

Harvey, Laurence (1928–1973), British actor; b. S. Africa. Noted for cynical film roles in British realistic school, such as *Room at the Top* and *Darling.*

Harzfeld (Postrelko), Avraham (1888–1973), labor pioneer in Ereẓ Israel; b. Ukraine. Member of Russian Socialist Zionist Party. Sentenced to life imprisonment in Siberia; escaped to Ereẓ Israel 1914. A founder of Histadrut. Major role in planning agricultural settlement and personally participated in establishment of almost every new settlement. Mapai Knesset member 1949–1959.

Ḥasan, Abu Ali Jepheth ibn Bundār (11th c.), one of first Yemenite *negidim* who lived in Aden. Wealthy man who traded with India.

Ḥasdai ibn Shaprut, see Ḥisdai ibn Shaprut.

Hasenclever, Walter (1890–1940), German poet, playwright. Foreign correspondent in Paris, U.S. Committed suicide in detention camp. Expressed intergeneration conflict, pacifism, resistance to blind authority. Later plays comic or ironic.

Ha-Shachar, see Young Judaea.

Ha-Shaḥar, Hebrew journal published and edited in Vienna by Peretz Smolenskin 1868–84. Aim was diffusion of Haskalah. One of first journals to advocate Ḥibbat Zion program for Jewish settlement in Ereẓ Israel.

Ha-Shilo'aḥ, Hebrew literary monthly, founded 1896; first editor Aḥad Ha-Am, succeeded by Joseph Klausner. Edited in Odessa and Jerusalem fr. 1920. Devoted to Zionism, Jewish scholarship, and belles lettres. Model of Hebrew writing in form and content. Published works by outstanding modern Hebrew writers.

Hashkavah, see Ashkavah.

Hashkivenu (Heb. "Cause us to lie down"), initial word of second benediction after *Shema* of daily evening prayer. Mentioned in Talmud.

Ha-Shomer, association of Jewish watchmen in Ereẓ Israel 1909–1920. Founded on initiative of Israel Shoḥat by members of Second Aliyah Po'alei Zion Party. Originally secret society called Bar-Giora. Pioneered for Jewish self-defense; guarded and developed Jewish settlement in new areas. *Shomerim* wore mixture of Arab and Circassian dress, carried modern weapons, and many were expert horsemen. Nucleus of Haganah.

Ha-Shomer ha-Ẓa'ir, Zionist-socialist pioneering youth movement educating youth for kibbutz life in Israel. Founded in Poland before WWI as scouting movement; merged with Ẓe'irei Zion 1916 and later became worldwide Jewish youth movement. Members in Ereẓ Israel during Third Aliyah (1919–23), founded 1927 Kibbutz Arẓi ha-Shomer ha-Ẓa'ir with socialist ideology slanted toward orthodox Marxism and became political party. Merged 1948 with Aḥdut ha-Avodah–Po'alei Zion and founded Mapam.

Ḥasidei Ashkenaz, social and ideological circle, with particular religious outlook, in medieval Germany. Main literature composed in early 13 c.; most important work *Sefer Ḥasidim,* major ethical work. Outstanding leaders incl. Samuel b. Kalonymus he-Ḥasid ("the Pious"), Judah b. Samuel he-Ḥasid; Eleazar b. Judah b. Kalonymus of Worms (the Roke'aḥ). Ideology included mysticism and esoteric knowledge; highly

moral behavior, extending severity of law for themselves; asceticism, involving mortification of flesh as means of repentance; martyrdom where necessary. Even at height movement comprised only small group.

Ḥasidei Ummot ha-Olam (Heb. "The pious ones of the nations of the world"), rabbinic term denoting religious gentiles who also merit place in world to come.

Ḥasidim, Sefer (Heb. "Book of the Pious"), major work in field of ethics produced in medieval Germany. Comprises ethical teachings of Ḥasidei Ashkenaz movement. Traditionally ascribed to R. Judah he-Ḥasid, but part written by his father.

Ḥasidism, popular pietist religious and social movement founded by Israel b. Eliezer Ba'al Shem Tov in 18th c. In early stages egalitarianism (emphasis on importance of devotion and ecstatic prayer of masses rather than talmudic learning of few) and transfer of emphasis fr. messianic redemption to personal redemption were characteristic. Subsequently unique social structure developed, with charismatic leader (*ẓaddik*) who was ruler of highly cohesive group and transmitted authority to his descendants. Various streams developed within movement, e.g., Ḥabad, whose outlook was more rationalistic. In 19th c., movement entered decline with autocratic rule. From beginning it was fiercely attacked, opponents being called "*Mitnaggedim*"; chief opponent was Elijah, the Vilna Gaon. Ban and counterban were frequent. Ḥasidism developed its own rites and synagogues, but never separated from mainstream Judaism. Its doctrines incl. importance of devotion in prayer; "worship through corporeality," worshipping God while engaged in mundane matters (a doctrine with socially explosive consequences); importance of joy (incl. music); faith in *ẓaddik*. Movement's main center was in E.

Ḥasidim dancing in courtyard of tomb of Simeon b. Yoḥai, Meron, Lag ba-Omer, 1970.

A ḥasidic gathering with Lubavicher Rebbe, Brooklyn, N.Y., 1960s.

Main centers of Ḥasidism in Europe. Alternate names in Yiddish, Polish, Russian, and German are given in parentheses.

Europe which ended with Holocaust. Today main centers are in Israel and U.S. Enjoyed renewed popularity in recent years owing both to Ḥabad educational activity and popularization in writings by Buber, Wiesel, etc. (Neo-Ḥasidism).

Haskalah, Hebrew term for Enlightenment movement and ideology which began within Jewish society in 1770s and continued until early 1880s. Had its roots in general Enlightenment movement in 18th c. Europe. Started in Germany, Italy, and W. Europe, later spread to Galicia, Lithuania, and other provinces of Russian Pale of Settlement. Adopted secular culture, philosophy, and foreign languages, neglected Yiddish, developed Hebrew language and promoted Emancipation. In E. Europe it encountered resistance and after pogroms of 1881 in S. Russia Jews were disillusioned with it. Reaction led to creation of Zionism and modern Hebrew literature.

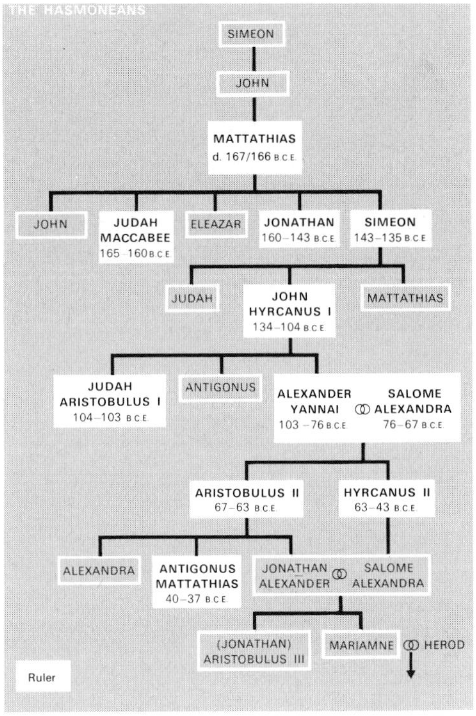

The melody and text of "Ha-Tikvah" as sung in Israel.

כָּל עוֹד בַּלֵּבָב פְּנִימָה
נֶפֶשׁ יְהוּדִי הוֹמִיָּה
וּלְפַאֲתֵי מִזְרָח קָדִימָה
עַיִן לְצִיּוֹן צוֹפִיָּה —

עוֹד לֹא אָבְדָה תִקְוָתֵנוּ,
הַתִּקְוָה בַּת שְׁנוֹת אַלְפַּיִם,
לִהְיוֹת עַם חָפְשִׁי בְּאַרְצֵנוּ,
אֶרֶץ צִיּוֹן וִירוּשָׁלַיִם!

Haskamah (Heb. "agreement," "approbation"). (1) Rabbinic approval of legal decisions of colleagues. (2) In Spanish, Italian, and Oriental communities, statutes and ordinances enacted by communities. (3) Recommendation of scholar or rabbi to book or treatise.

Haskell, Arnold Lionel (1903–), British ballet critic, author. Governor of Royal Ballet. Wrote books on ballet.

Haskil, Clara (1895–1960), pianist. Appeared with Ysaÿe, Enesco, Casals, and Grumiaux.

Hasmoneans, Maccabees. Led rebellion against Seleucid kingdom, established autonomous Jewish state, annexed most important regions of Ereẓ Israel, and absorbed neighboring Semitic peoples into Jewish people. Priestly family who lived in Modi'in. Banner of revolt raised by Mattathias b. Johanan and continued, upon his death (167 B.C.E.), by his sons Judah Maccabee, Jonathan, and Simeon. Great Assembly in Jerusalem 140 confirmed Simeon as high priest, ruler, and commander of Jewish people and made these offices hereditary. Rift during reign of John Hyrcanus between Hasmoneans and Pharisees developed against background of abrogation of royal and priestly authority by Hasmoneans. Hasmonean rule was brought to end by defeat of Antigonus Mattathias at hands of Romans 37 B.C.E.

Hassagat Gevul (Heb.), concept which originally had specific reference to unlawful taking of another's land; later extended to embrace encroachment on various economic, commercial, and incorporeal rights of others.

Hassagot (Heb.), rabbinic works wholly devoted to criticism, usually negative, of earlier books. First such works appeared in time of Saadiah Gaon, and genre reached its peak in 12th c. declining fr. 14th c.

Hassan, Sir Joshua (Abraham; 1915–), Gibraltar lawyer, politician. Mayor of Gibraltar, chief member of Legislative Council. When Gibraltar received independence became first chief minister 1964–69, fr. 1972. Pres. of Jewish community, active in Zionist affairs.

Hassid, William Zev (1897–), U.S. biochemist. Prof. at UCLA. Research fields: structural carbohydrate chemistry and carbohydrate metabolism in plants. Member of National Academy of Sciences.

Hassideans, religious group or sect originating c. 4th–3rd c. B.C.E. Revived and promoted Jewish rites, study of Law, and uprooting of paganism. Joined Maccabean revolt. When offered assurances of religious liberty by Syrians, ceased to cooperate with the Hasmoneans in their fight for political independence. Scholarly consensus places them as spiritual forerunners of Pharisees.

Ḥatan Bereshit, Ḥatan Torah, see Bridegroom of the Law.

Ha-Tekufah, Hebrew periodical devoted to literary, scientific, and social subjects which appeared intermittently bet. 1918 and 1950. First appeared in Moscow under editorship of David Frischmann, later moved to Warsaw, Berlin, Tel Aviv, U.S. Treasure trove of Hebrew literature of all genres.

Ha-Tikvah (Heb. "The Hope"), anthem of Zionist movement and national anthem of Israel. Poem written by Naphtali Herz Imber c. 1878. Set to music by Samuel Cohen in Rishon le-Zion. Melody based on Moldavian-Rumanian folk song.

Hatvany-Deutsch, 19th c. family of Hungarian industrialists, landowners, originally fr. province of Arad. **Ignac Deutsch** (1803–1873) founded Hungary's first sugar refinery. His sons **Bernát** and **József Deutsch** expanded business, aided Hungarian national economy, raised to nobility as "de Hatvan" (Hatvany). József's son **Sándor Hatvany-Deutsch** (1852–1913) founded Hungarian Manufacturers Association, established various charitable institutions. His son **Lajos Hatvany** (1880–1961), author, literary critic, journalist; founded literary periodical *Nyugat*. In England during WWII. Convert. Bernát's son, **Jozsef Hatvany Deutsch** (1858–1913), expanded business, active in Jewish communal affairs. Sat in upper house of Hungarian parliament.

Haubenstock-Ramati, Roman (1919–), composer. Radio conductor in Cracow. Headed Central Music Library in Tel Aviv. Settled in Vienna 1957. Compositions incl. opera *Amerika* based on Kafka's novel.

°**Haupt, Paul** (1858–1926), U.S. orientalist, Bible scholar. Taught at Johns Hopkins Univ. His biblical commentaries, etc., influenced American biblical and oriental studies. Wrote two learned articles on "Aryan" ancestry of Jesus, later used by Nazis as propaganda against Jews.

Hauran, region in NE Transjordan, today part of Syria. Mentioned by Ezekiel as falling within ideal boundaries of Ereẓ Israel. Augustus assigned it to Herod 23 B.C.E., who settled Jews in military colonies. Jewish settlement continued in talmudic times. Druze from Lebanon began settling there fr. 13th c. and it is called Jebel el-Druze.

Hausdorff, Felix (1868–1942), German mathematician. Prof. at Greifswald and Bonn. Committed suicide with his wife to avoid deportation order of Gestapo. His book *Mengenlehre* is one of great classics of set theory.

Hauser, Philip Morris (1909–), U.S. sociologist. Prof. at Univ. of Chicago. Pres. American Sociological Association 1967–8. Proponent of population control.

Hausner, Bernard (1874–1938), rabbi, Polish Zionist leader. Chaplain in Austrian army in WWI; a leader of Polish Mizrachi movement. Member of Polish Sejm 1922–27. Fr. 1927 in Tel Aviv, serving as Polish consul 1932–34. His son, **Gideon** (1915–), Israel's attorney general 1960–63, chief prosecutor in Eichmann trial, member of Knesset for Independent Liberal Party fr. 1965. Cabinet minister, 1974.

Ḥavaẓẓelet, Hebrew newspaper, first published in Jerusalem 1863–4; revived 1870 by Israel Bak. Organ of Ḥasidim under Bak's son-in-law I.D. Frumkin. Supported program for settlement in Ereẓ Israel; became mouthpiece of older generation, opposing political Zionism. Closed 1911.

Havdalah (Heb. "distinction"), blessing recited at termination of Sabbaths and festivals to emphasize distinction bet. sacred Sabbath and ordinary weekdays. Mention of *Havdalah* is also added in evening *Amidah* service following Sabbath (or festival). Consists of introductory verses, blessing over wine, spices, and light, and closing blessing of distinction. When Sabbath is followed by festival, *Havdalah* is shortened. Also recited without candles and spices. Spicebox (*hadas*) used in ceremony became favorite object of artistic decoration.

Ḥaver, pl. **Ḥaverim** (Heb. "member"), name given to member of group that undertook to observe meticulously laws of tithing and heave-offering and regulations of impurity and purity. Also title sometimes given to scholar.

Havilah, biblical name of territory watered by Pishon River (Gen. 2:11), noted for its gold, bdellium, and lapis lazuli. Identification unknown.

Ḥaviv, Ibn, see Habib, Ibn Habib.

Havvoth-Jair, area in N. Gilead, occupied by Jair, son of Manasseh (Num. 32:41). Later lost to Aram. Conquered and depopulated by Tiglath-Pileser III.

Hawaii, U.S. state. Organized Jewish community 1901. Honolulu Jewish community established 1938. Jewish pop. 1,500 (1971), almost all in Honolulu.

Ḥawaja Musa, see Smilansky, Moshe.

Hayden, Melissa (1928–), ballerina; b. Toronto, in U.S. fr. 1945. Soloist with N.Y.C. Ballet fr. 1950.

Hayes, Isaac Israel (1832–1881), U.S. explorer. Ship's surgeon on Kane's expedition to North Pole 1853; led own expedition 1860. Took first photographs of Arctic. Made valuable contribution to natural history, meteorology, glaciology, and hydrology. Member of N.Y. Assembly.

Hayes, Saul (1906–), Canadian lawyer, community executive. Executive director of Canadian Jewish Congress fr. 1942.

Haynt, leading Yiddish daily in Warsaw before WWII. Founded 1908. Circ. 70,000 in 1909. Supported Zionist ideology. Closed 1939.

Ha-Yom, first Hebrew daily newspaper. Published in St. Petersburg 1886–88; edited by Judah Leib Kantor. European-style daily; cool attitude toward Ḥibbat Zion.

Ḥayon, Nehemiah Ḥiyya ben Moses (c. 1655–c. 1730), kabbalist with Shabbatean tendencies; center of controversy that reverberated through Jewish world. Brought up in Ereẓ Israel, suspected of Shabbateanism, wandered throughout Europe. Wrote books originally accepted but subsequently denounced as heretical. In Amsterdam accepted by Sephardi but condemned by Ashkenazi community. Eventually excommunicated by most communities.

Hays, Arthur Garfield (1881–1954), U.S. lawyer, civil liberties advocate. General counsel of American Civil Liberties Union. Involved in Scopes Trial, defense of Sacco and Vanzetti, Scottsboro Negroes. Defended cause of liberty even for those he detested.

Hays, Isaac (1796–1879), U.S. physician. Oculist who pioneered study of astigmatism and color blindness and invented scalpel used in cataract surgery. A founder of American Medical Association; wrote U.S. code of medical ethics.

Ḥayyat, Judah ben Jacob (c. 1450–c. 1510), kabbalist; b. Spain, in Italy after expulsion. His *Minḥat Yehudah,* one of outstanding contributions to Kabbalah in period of Spanish expulsion.

Ḥayyim ben Abraham ha-Kohen (c. 1585–1655), kabbalist; pupil of Ḥayyim Vital; b. Aleppo. Rewrote his many writings after they were lost at sea when his ship was attacked by pirates. Wrote commentaries on *Shulḥan Arukh,* Five Scrolls, etc.

Ḥayyim ben Bezalel (c. 1520–1588), talmudic scholar; brother of Judah Loew b. Bezalel of Prague. Rabbi in Worms and Friedberg. Published polemic against Moses Isserles, objecting to all who published halakhic codes, because it leads to neglect of earlier authorities. Wrote supercommentary on Rashi's commentary to Pentateuch.

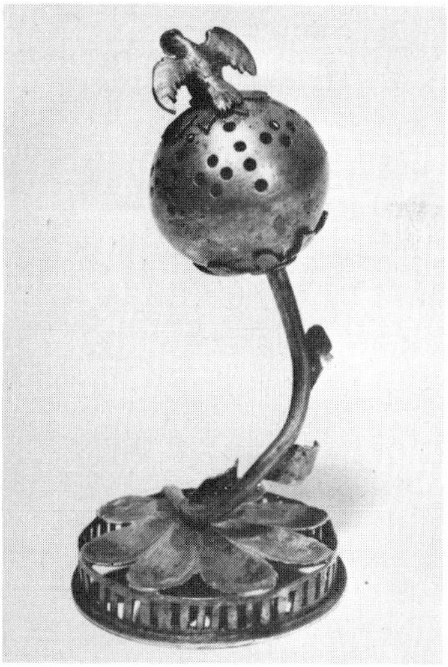

Silver "havdalah" spice box, Bohemia, 19th cent.

Front page of "Haynt," July 2, 1922.

№ 151

Hajnt

היינט

POLSKI BANK HANDLOWO-PRZEMYSŁOWY

Spółka Akcyjna w Krakowie

ODDZIAŁ WARSZAWSKI

Wierzbowa 9 (Plac Teatralny)

300.000.000

100.000.000

Ḥayyim ben Isaac of Volozhin, see Volozhiner, Ḥayyim ben Isaac.

Ḥayyim (Eliezer) ben Isaac "Or Zaru'a" (13th c.), German rabbi, halakhic authority; pupil of Meir b. Baruch of Rothenburg and Asher b. Jehiel. Most of his decisions based on his father's *Or Zaru'a,* which he abridged.

Ḥayyim Ḥaykl ben Samuel of Amdur (d. 1787), ḥasidic leader in Lithuania; pupil of Dov Baer of Mezhirech. Founded ḥasidic center in Amdur. Particularly hated by Lithuanian *Mitnaggedim.*

Ḥayyim Paltiel ben Jacob (13th–14th c.), German talmudic scholar. Author of *Sefer ha-Minhagim,* containing customs for whole year based on Ashkenazi rite.

Ḥayyuj, Judah ben David (c. 945–c. 1000), Hebrew grammarian; b. Fez, moved to Spain. Wrote on accentuation and vocalization and a philological commentary to certain books of Bible. His grammatical work pioneered concept of triliteral verb roots. All subsequent work in Hebrew language and biblical exegesis based on his ideas.

Ḥayyim Hazaz

Reconstruction of sanctuary found at Hazor.

A "ḥazzan," from "Birds' Head Haggadah," S. Germany, c. 1300.

Ḥayyun, Joseph ben Abraham (d. 1497), last rabbi of Lisbon Jewish community before expulsion. Wrote commentary on Psalms and on *Avot.*

°**Hazael,** king of Aram-Damascus c. 842–798 B.C.E. Murdered Ben-Hadad and founded new dynasty. Elisha played major role in his enthronement. Launched series of successful attacks on Israel and Judah.

Hazai, Samu (1851–1942), Hungarian army officer; convert to Christianity. Minister of defense 1910.

Ḥazak (Heb. "be strong"), salutation of well-wishing based on Moses' address to Joshua: "Be strong and of good courage." Fuller version is recited in synagogue when reading of each books of Pentateuch is completed.

Ḥazakah, Hebrew term expressing 3 concepts in Jewish law: (1) mode of acquiring property; (2) proof of ownership of rights regarding property; (3) factual-legal presumption as to existence of particular fact or state of affairs.

Hazan, Ya'akov (1899–), Israel political leader; b. Brest Litovsk. Among founders of Ha-Shomer ha-Ẓa'ir, He-Ḥalutz in Poland. Settled in Ereẓ Israel 1923. Among founders of Ha-Kibbutz ha-Arẓi. Member of Knesset 1949–73 and a leading ideologist of Mapam party.

Hazaz, Ḥayyim (1898–1973), Hebrew writer; b. Russia, traveled widely before settling in Jerusalem 1931. Outstanding stylist, wrote on wide variety of themes, fr. Revolutionary Russia to Yemen, and on different eras, fr. Second Temple period to Irgun struggle against British, exploring in depth many psychological types. Works incl. *Ya'ish,* 4-vol. story of young Yemenite who comes to Israel.

Ha-Ẓefirah, Hebrew paper appearing in Warsaw intermittently bet. 1862 and 1931. Founded by Ḥayyim Selig Slonimsky, with emphasis on science and technology. Under editorship of Nahum Sokolow, more current affairs. Supported Herzl and Zionism.

Ḥaẓer, pl. **Ḥaẓerim,** biblical term for seminomadic settlements on edge of Negev. Occupy intermediate position between nomadic encampments and settled towns, but in course of time some developed into towns.

Hazeroth, second station of Israelites on journey eastward fr. Mt. Sinai to Ezion-Geber.

Ḥaẓevah, moshav in C. Aravah valley, S. Israel. Under Roman rule, important road junction; under British Mandate, police station. Its occupation by Israel forces 1948 led to conquest of whole Negev.

Hazkarat Neshamot (Heb. "commemorating the souls [of the dead]"), memorial prayer. In Ashkenazi rite, said during morning service on last day of Passover, Shavuot, and Sukkot and on Day of Atonement; in Sephardi rite, recited also on Day of Atonement eve; in Reform congregations, on last day of Passover and Day of Atonement. Prayer begins with word *Yizkor,* and therefore rite has also become known as *Yizkor* or *Mazkir.*

Ha-Ẓofeh. (1) Daily Hebrew newspaper published in Warsaw 1903–5. Items of Jewish and general interest. Conducted first short-story contest in Hebrew literature. (2) Hebrew organ of National Religious Party, published in Israel fr. 1937. First editor-in-chief Rabbi Meir Bar-Ilan (Berlin). Covers all fields of modern daily.

Ḥazon Ish, see Karelitz, Avraham Yeshayahu.

Hazor, large Canaanite and Israelite city in Upper Galilee. Its king Jabin headed league of Canaanite cities against Joshua (Josh. 11:10–13). Rebuilt by Solomon. Conquered by Tiglath-Pileser III 732 B.C.E. Excavated under Y. Yadin 1955–58, 1963. Site is composed of two separate areas: the tell proper (upper city), covering c. 30 acres, and large rectangular plateau, c. 175 acres (lower city).

Ḥaẓor (ha-Gelilit), development town in E. Upper Galilee, founded 1953. Pop. 5,250 (1971).

Ḥazzan (Heb.), cantor officiating in synagogue. In talmudic sources word denotes various communal officials. In geonic time *ḥazzan* became permanent *sheli'aḥ ẓibbur* (cantor), owing to complexity of liturgy and decline of knowledge of Hebrew. In Middle Ages office became permanent synagogue position and great rabbis served in capacity. Fr. 19th c. Ashkenazi cantorial music influenced by European musical trends and techniques. Fr. 20th c. leading *ḥazzanim* reached wide audiences also through concerts,etc.

He (ה), 5th letter of Hebrew alphabet; numerical value 5. Pronounced *h.* Used as abbreviation for Divine Name.

Heave Offering (Heb. *Terumah*), offering for sanctuary or priests; generally fr. tithes.

Hebrew, NW Semitic language. Pre-biblical Hebrew was spoken in Canaan before Israelite conquest. Biblical (or Early) Hebrew is known mainly fr. the Bible and inscriptions. During last cents. B.C.E. ceased to be spoken and Aramaic became vernacular. Remained literary language. With destruction of Second Temple, standard literary language disappeared and place was taken by mishnaic Hebrew, which is not derived fr. biblical Hebrew but probably fr. some pre-Exilic colloquial dialect. After 200 C.E., became written language, based on biblical and mishnaic Hebrew. Through *piyyut* and Midrash, spread to Diaspora and became second language, read and often written by Jews wherever they were. The different languages with which Jews came in contact also had their influence on Hebrew. Haskalah (1750–1880) revised its use and applied it, e.g., to belles-lettres and scientific literature. Its growth as modern language, spoken by masses and gradually used in all areas of life and thought, may be divided into 3 stages: (1) 1881–1918, initiated by Eliezer Ben-Yehuda's arrival in Ereẓ Israel. He and his followers developed and propagated Hebrew in everyday life. (2) 1918–1948 (British Mandate), when Hebrew was first considered a language of Ereẓ Israel and in 1922 one of 3 official languages. (3) Since 1948, marked by foundation of the State of Israel. Hebrew became predominant and official language and was used in all branches of national life. Modern Hebrew is combination of all previous stages, although it took from each only the elements that suited it. Usage is controlled by Academy of Hebrew Language (q.v.).

CONJUGATION OF THE HEBREW (REGULAR) VERB

		Kal			Niphal	Piel	Pual	Hiphil	Hophal	Hitpael
Past (Perfect)		Active	Stative							
sg.	3. m.	קָטַל	כָּבֵד	קָטֹן	נִקְטַל	קִטֵּל [3]	קֻטַּל	הִקְטִיל	הָקְטַל	הִתְקַטֵּל [4]
	3. f.	קָטְלָה	כָּבְדָה	קָטְנָה	נִקְטְלָה	קִטְּלָה	קֻטְּלָה	הִקְטִילָה	הָקְטְלָה	הִתְקַטְּלָה
	2. m.	קָטַלְתָּ	כָּבַדְתָּ	קָטֹנְתָּ	נִקְטַלְתָּ	קִטַּלְתָּ	קֻטַּלְתָּ	הִקְטַלְתָּ	הָקְטַלְתָּ	הִתְקַטַּלְתָּ
	2. f.	קָטַלְתְּ	כָּבַדְתְּ	קָטֹנְתְּ	נִקְטַלְתְּ	קִטַּלְתְּ	קֻטַּלְתְּ	הִקְטַלְתְּ	הָקְטַלְתְּ	הִתְקַטַּלְתְּ
	1. c.	קָטַלְתִּי	כָּבַדְתִּי	קָטֹנְתִּי	נִקְטַלְתִּי	קִטַּלְתִּי	קֻטַּלְתִּי	הִקְטַלְתִּי	הָקְטַלְתִּי	הִתְקַטַּלְתִּי
pl.	3. c.	קָטְלוּ	כָּבְדוּ	קָטְנוּ	נִקְטְלוּ	קִטְּלוּ	קֻטְּלוּ	הִקְטִילוּ	הָקְטְלוּ	הִתְקַטְּלוּ
	2. m.	קְטַלְתֶּם	כְּבַדְתֶּם	קְטָנְתֶּם	נִקְטַלְתֶּם	קִטַּלְתֶּם	קֻטַּלְתֶּם	הִקְטַלְתֶּם	הָקְטַלְתֶּם	הִתְקַטַּלְתֶּם
	2. f.	קְטַלְתֶּן	כְּבַדְתֶּן	קְטָנְתֶּן	נִקְטַלְתֶּן	קִטַּלְתֶּן	קֻטַּלְתֶּן	הִקְטַלְתֶּן	הָקְטַלְתֶּן	הִתְקַטַּלְתֶּן
	1. c.	קָטַלְנוּ	כָּבַדְנוּ	קָטֹנּוּ [1]	נִקְטַלְנוּ	קִטַּלְנוּ	קֻטַּלְנוּ	הִקְטַלְנוּ	הָקְטַלְנוּ	הִתְקַטַּלְנוּ
Future (Imperfect)										
sg.	3. m.	יִקְטֹל	יִכְבַּד	יִקְטַן	יִקָּטֵל	יְקַטֵּל	יְקֻטַּל	יַקְטִיל	יָקְטַל	יִתְקַטֵּל
	3. f.	תִּקְטֹל	תִּכְבַּד		תִּקָּטֵל	תְּקַטֵּל	תְּקֻטַּל	תַּקְטִיל	תָּקְטַל	תִּתְקַטֵּל
	2. m.	תִּקְטֹל	תִּכְבַּד		תִּקָּטֵל	תְּקַטֵּל	תְּקֻטַּל	תַּקְטִיל	תָּקְטַל	תִּתְקַטֵּל
	2. f.	תִּקְטְלִי	תִּכְבְּדִי		תִּקָּטְלִי	תְּקַטְּלִי	תְּקֻטְּלִי	תַּקְטִילִי	תָּקְטְלִי	תִּתְקַטְּלִי
	1. c.	אֶקְטֹל	אֶכְבַּד		אֶקָּטֵל [2]	אֲקַטֵּל	אֲקֻטַּל	אַקְטִיל	אָקְטַל	אֶתְקַטֵּל
pl.	3. m.	יִקְטְלוּ	יִכְבְּדוּ		יִקָּטְלוּ	יְקַטְּלוּ	יְקֻטְּלוּ	יַקְטִילוּ	יָקְטְלוּ	יִתְקַטְּלוּ
	3. f.	תִּקְטֹלְנָה	תִּכְבַּדְנָה		תִּקָּטַלְנָה	תְּקַטֵּלְנָה	תְּקֻטַּלְנָה	תַּקְטֵלְנָה	תָּקְטַלְנָה	תִּתְקַטַּלְנָה
	2. m.	תִּקְטְלוּ	תִּכְבְּדוּ		תִּקָּטְלוּ	תְּקַטְּלוּ	תְּקֻטְּלוּ	תַּקְטִילוּ	תָּקְטְלוּ	תִּתְקַטְּלוּ
	2. f.	תִּקְטֹלְנָה	תִּכְבַּדְנָה		תִּקָּטַלְנָה	תְּקַטֵּלְנָה	תְּקֻטַּלְנָה	תַּקְטֵלְנָה	תָּקְטַלְנָה	תִּתְקַטַּלְנָה
	1. c.	נִקְטֹל	נִכְבַּד		נִקָּטֵל	נְקַטֵּל	נְקֻטַּל	נַקְטִיל	נָקְטַל	נִתְקַטֵּל
Cohortative										
sg.	1. c.	אֶקְטְלָה	אֶכְבְּדָה		אִקָּטְלָה	אֲקַטְּלָה		אַקְטִילָה		אֶתְקַטְּלָה
Jussive										
sg.	3. m.	יִקְטֹל	יִכְבַּד		יִקָּטֵל	יְקַטֵּל	יְקֻטַּל	יַקְטֵל	יָקְטַל	יִתְקַטֵּל
Imperative										
sg.	2. m.	קְטֹל (קָטְלָה)	כְּבַד		הִקָּטֵל	קַטֵּל	non-existent	הַקְטֵל	non-existent	הִתְקַטֵּל
	2. f.	קִטְלִי	כִּבְדִי		הִקָּטְלִי	קַטְּלִי		הַקְטִילִי		הִתְקַטְּלִי
pl.	2. m.	קִטְלוּ	כִּבְדוּ		הִקָּטְלוּ	קַטְּלוּ		הַקְטִילוּ		הִתְקַטְּלוּ
	2. f.	קְטֹלְנָה	כְּבַדְנָה		הִקָּטַלְנָה	קַטֵּלְנָה		הַקְטֵלְנָה		הִתְקַטַּלְנָה
Present (Participle) act.	sg. m.	קֹטֵל	כָּבֵד	קָטֹן		מְקַטֵּל		מַקְטִיל		מִתְקַטֵּל
Present (Participle) pass.	sg. m.	קָטוּל			נִקְטָל		מְקֻטָּל		מָקְטָל	
Infinitive absolute		קָטוֹל	כָּבוֹד		הִקָּטֹל, נִקְטֹל	קַטֹּל, קַטֵּל	קֻטֹּל	הַקְטֵל	(הָקְטֵל)	הִתְקַטֵּל
Infinitive construct		קְטֹל	כְּבַד		הִקָּטֵל	קַטֵּל		הַקְטִיל	(הָקְטַל)	

[1] For קָטֹנְנוּ [2] Also אִקָּטֵל [3] Also קִטַּל [4] Also הִתְקַטַּל

m.—masculine; f.—feminine; c.—common; sg.—singular; pl.—plural

Hebrew Sheltering and Immigrant Aid Society, see United Hias Service.

Hebrew Teachers College, college for Jewish studies in Boston; founded 1921. Enrollment 600 (1970).

Hebrew Theological College, Orthodox rabbinical school in Chicago: founded 1922. In addition to rabbinical ordination it offers degrees in Hebrew literature. Enrollment 466 (1968).

Cincinnati campus of Hebrew Union College

Official opening of Hebrew University by Lord Balfour, April 1, 1925.

19th-cent. etching of Hebron

William Hechler

Hebrews (Heb. *Ivrim*), descendants of Eber, grandson of Shem. In Bible used to distinguish Jews fr. non-Jews (e.g., Abraham, Jonah). Identification with Habiru disputable. Used as synonym for Jews in 19th c.

Hebrew Union College–Jewish Institute of Religion, Reform rabbinical seminary. HUC founded 1875 in Cincinnati by Isaac M. Wise, its pres. until 1900. In 1950 merged with JIR (New York) founded 1922 by Stephen S. Wise. Under presidency of Nelson Glueck branches opened in Los Angeles 1954 and Jerusalem 1963. College has trained over 1,000 Reform rabbis, publishes *Hebrew Union College Annual, American Jewish Archives, Studies in Bibliography and Booklore,* and has a 200,000 vol. library and American Jewish Archives. N.Y. school also trains cantors, teachers, and principals.

Hebrew University of Jerusalem, Israel institute for higher learning. First proposal made by Hermann Shapira. Foundation stone laid on Mt. Scopus July 24, 1918. First lecture given 1923 by Albert Einstein. Officially opened April 1, 1925 by Lord Balfour. Judah Leon Magnes first chancellor 1925–1935 and first president 1935–1948. Fr. 1948 to 1967 Mount Scopus campus remained inaccessible; university worked in scattered buildings until extensive new campus was dedicated at Givat Ram 1955. As result of Six-Day War Mt. Scopus was rebuilt. Also part of H.U. are Hadassah – H.U. Medical School at Ein Kerem and Agricultural Faculty at Reḥovot. Site of National and University Library with 1¾ million books. Enrollment 16,000 (1973), with staff of over 1,695.

Hebron (Kiryath Arba; Arab. **Al-Khalīl,** "beloved of God"), city in Ereẓ Israel S. of Jerusalem. Abraham purchased Cave of Machpelah (q.v.) there. David chose it initially as his royal city and was anointed there. After destruction of First Temple, taken by Edomites, with some Jews remaining. Recovered in 2nd c. B.C.E. Crusaders brought temporary end to Jewish community. Renewed under Mamluk rule. Jews prospered during Ottoman rule. Many of its Jews killed by Arab rioters 1929, but settlement renewed 1931, to be destroyed again 1936. Incorporated in Kingdom of Jordan 1948–67. Jewish settlement renewed 1968 (Kiryath Arba). Pop. 38,309 (1967).

°**Hechler, William Henry** (1845–1931), Christian Zionist, mystic. Attended first Zionist Congress 1897, accompanied Herzl on his journey to Ereẓ Israel 1898, and later attempted to arrange meeting bet. Herzl and the Czar.

Hecht, Ben (1893–1964), U.S. novelist, playwright. His initial portrayal of Jews was unsympathetic, but in 1941 publicly proclaimed his Jewish nationalism and became leading advocate of Irgun Ẓeva'i Le'ummi. Made his sympathies clear in *A Flag is Born,* and *Perfidy.* Works incl. play *Front Page* (with Charles MacArthur), *A Jew in Love,* and autobiography *A Child of the Century.*

Hecht, Jacob (1879–1963), shipping executive. Before WWII his Rhenania Rheinschiffahrts group (founded 1908) was prosperous in river shipping in Rhine states. His Neptun Transport and Navigation Co. later became the only private independent inland shipping combine in W. Europe.

Hecht, Reuben (Rudolf; 1909–), founder 1957 and chairman of Dagon Co., which built large Haifa silo; son of Jacob Hecht; b. Antwerp, settled in Ereẓ Israel 1936, organized "illegal" immigration in Europe and returned after war.

Heckscher, Eli Filip (1879–1952), Swedish economic historian. Main works dealt with mercantilism and Swedish economic history in 16th–19th c.

Ḥeder (Heb. "room"), old-fashioned elementary school for teaching of Judaism. Name first occurs in 13th c. In 19th c. attempts made to introduce an "improved *ḥeder*" *(ḥeder metukkan).*

Ḥefer (Feiner), Ḥayyim (1925–), Israel writer of light verse; b. Poland. Among founders of Chizbatron, army's popular entertainment troupe. Wrote verse and composed lyrics for various satirical works.

Ḥefer Plain, C. part of Sharon Plain, one of Israel's most thoroughly developed and densely settled rural districts.

Ḥefeẓ, see Gentili.

Ḥefeẓ ben Yaẓli'aḥ (ha-Ashuri, "the Assyrian"; 10th c.), Babylonian talmudic scholar. Renowned as grammarian and talmudic scholar. Most important work *Sefer ha-Mitzvot* ("Book of Commandments"), probably first comprehensive book of laws in Hebrew literature.

Hefker (Heb.), ownerless property and renunciation of ownership. This property can be legally acquired by person who first takes possession of

it; it is exempt from a number of commandments. In Israel ownerless property belongs to the State.

He-Ḥalutz, federation of Zionist Socialist pioneer youth movements. First such group founded in U.S. 1915 by D. Ben-Gurion and Y. Ben-Zvi; in E. Europe after WWI by Josef Trumpeldor. Later it grew strong in C. Europe. 100,000 members in 1939. Ceased to exist after WWII.

Heichelheim, Fritz Morris (1901–1968), ancient history scholar. Taught in Germany, England, Canada. Also wrote extensively on classical Judaism and active in Canadian Jewish communal and cultural life.

Heidelberg, city in W. Germany. Medieval Jewish community massacred during Black Death 1348; reconstituted and expelled 1391. Jews returned fr. mid-17th c., attracted by university. Community of 1,100 ended in WWII. 139 Jews in 1967.

Heidenhain, Rudolf (1834–1897), German physiologist. Prof. at Breslau. Laid foundations for recognition of secretory mechanism as system of intercellular physical and chemical processes. Converted to Christianity.

Heidenheim, Wolf (Benjamin Ze'ev; 1757–1832), German Hebrew grammarian, masoretic scholar, exegete, commentator on liturgy. Published 9-vol. edition of *maḥzor, Sefer Kerovot,* with commentary and German translation.

Heifetz, Jascha (1901–), U.S. violinist; b. Vilna. Child prodigy. Playing set new style in violin mastery. Left Russia after Revolution and settled in U.S. One of outstanding violinists of 20th c.

Heijermans, Herman (1864–1924), Dutch playwright, novelist; writer of naturalist school. His work reveals both socialist leanings and struggle with Jewish identity.

Heikhalot (Heb. "palaces"), early Jewish mystical and mystery traditions (talmudic times) centering on journeys through heavenly spheres and palaces. Such accounts appeared in special works *(Sefer Heikhalot).*

Heilbron, Sir Ian Morris (1886–1959), British organic chemist. Prof. at Imperial College, London. With H.M. Bunbury produced *Dictionary of Organic Compounds.* Fellow of Royal Society.

Heilbron, Rose (1914–), English lawyer. First woman appointed recorder in Britain 1956.

Heilbronn, city in W. Germany. Jews fr. 11th c. 143 Jews massacred in 1298 by Rindfleisch. Expelled in Black Death 1349; returned and expelled again 1490. Modern community established 1851. 790 Jews in 1933. Community ended in WWII.

Heilperin, Falk (1876–1945), educator, Yiddish writer; lived in E. Europe, settled in Ereẓ Israel 1938. Maintained that Yiddish should be language of Jewish instruction in E. Europe. Prepared Yiddish educational texts and readers; edited first Yiddish children's magazine.

Heilprin, Angelo (1853–1907), U.S. geologist, explorer, author. Went to Arctic on mission to bring relief to Peary 1892.

Heilprin, Jehiel ben Solomon (1660–1746), Lithuanian talmudic scholar, historian. Wrote historical-chronological *Seder ha-Dorot,* containing original research on lives of *tannaim* and *amoraim.*

Heilprin, Louis (1856–1912), U.S. encyclopedist. Author of *Historical Reference Book* and editor of *Nelson's Encyclopaedia.*

Heilprin, Michael (1823–1888), U.S. linguist, scholar, encyclopedist; b. Poland. Became known as revolutionary poet during 1848 Hungarian Revolution. In U.S. worked as encyclopedist and wrote on European literature and politics. Author of *Historical Poetry of the Ancient Hebrews.*

Heilprin, Samuel Helmann ben Israel (1675–1765), rabbi of Bohemia. Firm opponent of Shabbateanism; took leading part in controversy against Eybeschuetz.

Heimann, Moritz (1868–1925), German author, essayist. As chief literary adviser to Berlin publishing house of S. Fischer, influential in German literary circles.

Heine, Heinrich (orig. **Ḥayyim** or **Harry;** 1797–1856), German poet, essayist; one of great lyric poets in German and Germany's outstanding Jewish writer. Exile in Paris after 1831, virtually paralyzed after 1848. Works reveal sharp political insight and satire. Submitted to baptism 1825, but later said: "I make no secret of my Judaism to which I have not returned because I have never left it." Works of Jewish interest incl. *Der Rabbi von Bacharach, Hebraische Melodien, Prinzessin Sabbat.*

Heine, Solomon (1766–1844), German banker, philanthropist; uncle and supporter of Heinrich Heine. Despite his public service, refused citizenship and admission to Chamber of Commerce.

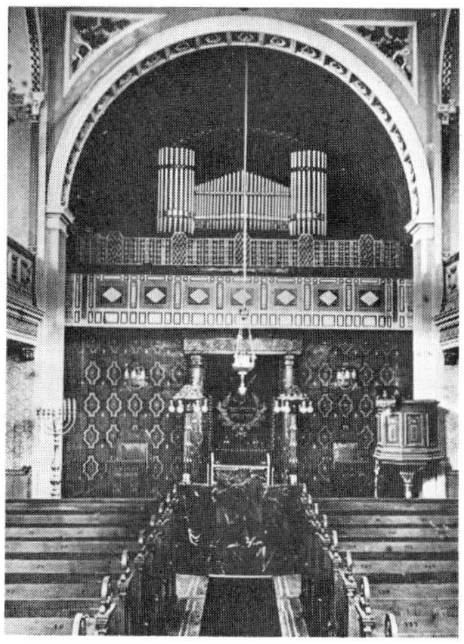

The old synagogue at Heidelberg, demolished 1938.

Wolf Heidenheim

Jascha Heifetz

Heinrich Heine

Heine, Thomas Theodor (1867–1947), German graphic artist, cartoonist. A founder of satirical review *Simplicissimus* 1895 and its best-known political cartoonist for 37 years.

Heinemann, Fritz (1889–), German philosopher. Taught at Frankfort and Oxford. Edited *Die Philosophie im 20. Jahrhundert,* encyclopedic survey of contemporary philosophy.

Heinemann, Jeremiah (1778–1855), German writer, educator, communal leader. Founded and edited *Jedidja,* periodical of Jewish studies, and wrote Hebrew commentary on Pentateuch.

Heinemann, Yiẓḥak (Isaac; 1876–1957), Israel philosopher. Prof. of Jewish theology at Jewish Theological Seminary in Breslau before settling in Jerusalem 1939. Works deal with Hellenism and medieval Jewish philosophy as well as *aggadah.*

Hejaz (al-Ḥijāz), region in NW Arabia. Jewish settlement fr. 6th c. B.C.E. Jewish nomadic tribes dominated area and settled in Medina, Tayma, and Khaybar in 5th–6th c. C.E. With rise of Islam they were subdued, oppressed, or expelled.

Hekdesh (Heb.), consecrated property, property dedicated to needs of Temple. In post-talmudic times the term without qualification came to mean property set aside for charitable purposes or for fulfillment of any other *mitzvah.* In small European towns, synagogues for poor; in popular parlance, deserted, neglected place.

Hekhsher (Heb. "approbation" or "attestation"), certificate issued by rabbinate or individual rabbis certifying that food product was prepared under their supervision. Product is thus declared *kasher* according to dietary laws or (in the case of Passover) free fr. all leaven.

Ḥelbo (3rd–4th c.), *amora;* apparently Babylonian who emigrated to Ereẓ Israel. His opposition to proselytization later influenced Jewish attitudes with regard to acceptance of converts.

Held, Adolph (1885–1969), U.S. communal and labor leader, Yiddish journalist. European director of Hebrew Immigrant Aid Society 1920, pres. Forward Association 1924, national chairman of Jewish Labor Committee 1938, general manager of *Jewish Daily Forward* 1962.

Held, Anna (1873–1918), French actress. Made debut at Folies Manguay in Paris 1895. Plays incl. Jean Richepin's *Mam'selle Napoleon* and *The Little Duchess.* Wife of Florenz Ziegfeld.

Helena (1st c. C.E.), proselyte; sister and wife of Monobaz I, king of Adiabene. Spent latter part of life in Jerusalem, where she built palace, made gifts to Temple and to poor, and was meticulous in observance of Judaism. Her burial place was discovered in 19th c. and originally thought to be "Tombs of the Kings."

Ḥeleẓ, site of Israel's first oilfield, discovered 1955. Located nr. moshav of same name in S. coastal plain of Israel.

Oil drilling at Ḥeleẓ

Helfman, Hessia Meyerovna (1855–1882), Russian revolutionary. One of six revolutionaries condemned to death for complicity in assassination of Czar Alexander II.

Heliopolis (Heb. **On**), ancient city of lower Egypt. Cult center for worship of sun god. Joseph's father-in-law, Poti-Phera, was priest there, and city is among those whose destruction by Nebuchadnezzar is foretold by Ezekiel.

Hellenism, Greek civilization as diffused through Roman Empire, incl. Middle East, bet. 4th c. B.C.E. and 1st c. C.E. Influenced Jews both in Judea and the Diaspora (notably Alexandria), where Greek names, language, and educational institutions were adopted in varying degrees. Septuagint translation of Bible in Egypt and writings of Philo and Josephus indicate penetration of Hellenistic forms, as do presence of Greek words in Midrash and Talmud. Contact also led to occasional deviations fr. Jewish observance and changes in some Jewish attitudes. Jewish spiritual resistance was evident during Maccabean and Roman periods.

Heller, Aryeh Leib ben Joseph ha-Kohen of Stry (1745? –1813), Galician rabbi. His commentaries on *Shulḥan Arukh* formed basis for method of Torah learning in yeshivot and are still regarded as classics.

Heller, Bernat (1871–1943), Hungarian scholar, Arabist, folklorist, literary historian. Main work on *aggadah,* Islam, Apocrypha. Superintendent of Jewish schools in Budapest fr. 1931.

Heller, Bunim (1908–), Yiddish poet; b. Warsaw. Played important role in Jewish cultural life of postwar Communist Poland. Became disillusioned with Communism and settled in Israel 1957.

Heller, Ḥayyim (1878–1960), rabbinical, biblical scholar; b. Bialystok. Founded new type of yeshivah for research in Bible and Talmud in Berlin 1922; taught at Isaac Elchanan Theological Seminary, New York, fr. 1929. Published novellae and rabbinic editions and commentaries.

Heller, Hermann (1891–1933), German political scientist. One of small group who revived political science in Germany in 1920s. Forced to leave Germany 1933; d. Madrid.

Heller, Joseph (1923–), U.S. author. Famed for his novel *Catch-22,* outstanding satire on military mind.

Heller, Maximilian (1860–1924), U.S. Reform rabbi; b. Prague. Rabbi of Temple Sinai, New Orleans; pres. Central Conference of American Rabbis 1909–11. Outstanding in Reform circles as early adherent of Zionism. His son, **James Gutheim** (1892–1971), Reform rabbi, musician. Served at Isaac M. Wise Temple in Cincinnati 1920–54, pres. Central Conference of American Rabbis 1942–43, pres. Labor Zionist Organization of America. Musical compositions incl. several pieces for synagogue.

Heller, Yom Tov Lipmann ben Nathan ha-Levi (1579–1654), Moravian rabbi. Author of *Tosefot Yom Tov,* commentary on Mishnah printed in many subsequent editions. Appointed *dayyan* in Prague when only 18, later served in Poland. Wrote also on secular subjects, autobiography.

Hellman, Isaias Wolf (1842–1920), U.S. banker, real estate owner in Los Angeles and San Francisco. Major philanthropist who contributed land for establishment of Univ. of Southern California.

Hellman, Jacob (1880–1950), labor Zionist leader, editor. Prominent leader of Latvian Jewry. Elected to Latvian parliament 1920. World Jewish Congress representative in S.

America. Later active in Zionist and general Jewish life in Argentina.
Hellman, Lillian Florence (1905–), U.S. playwright. Noted for dialogue and stage technique. Works incl. *The Children's Hour, The Little Foxes, Watch on the Rhine, Toys in the Attic.* Also vols. of autobiography.

Lillian Hellman

Helpern, Michael (1860–1919), socialist Zionist in Russia, pioneer in Ereẓ Israel. Bought land in Ereẓ Israel and supported Jewish labor movement. Advocated political redemption of Ereẓ Israel by military means. Colorful and romantic personality. His son **Yermiyahu** (1901–1962) organized and headed a Betar naval school at Civitavecchia, Italy. Founded the marine museum at Eilat.
Helpern, Milton (1902–), U.S. forensic pathologist. Chief medical examiner of N.Y.C. fr. 1954; pres. National Association of Medical Examiners fr. 1968.
Helsingfors Program, Zionist policy adopted at 3rd conference of Russian Zionists in Helsingfors (Helsinki) 1906, under chairmanship of Jehiel Tschlenow. Postulated principle that achievement of international recognition for Jewish Ereẓ Israel would be end and not precondition of systematic *aliyah* and settlement work. Emphasized that Zionists must "conquer" Jewish communities and also fight for Jewish rights and parliamentary representation.
Helsinki, see Finland.
Heltai, Jenö (orig. **Herzl;** 1871–1957), Hungarian poet, playwright, novelist; cousin of Theodor Herzl. A leading figure on Hungarian literary scene. His poetry synthesized French chanson and Hungarian folk poetry. Baptized.
Heman, orchestral leader in Israel in biblical times (e.g., I Chron. 15:2 ff.).
Ḥemdat Yamim (Heb. "The Best of Days"), 18th c. Hebrew work of homiletics and ethics. Product of ethical kabbalistic literature, probably written by Shabbatean, with considerable impact on Jewish life and letters (e.g., Agnon). Deals with halakhic observances and ethical behavior.
Hemerobaptists (Heb. *Tovelei Shaḥarit,* "Morning Bathers"), part of Jewish sect for whom baptismal rite of initiation is crucial. Repeated rite each day. Mentioned in Talmud; probably division of Essenes.
Ḥen, see Gracian.
Hendel, Ida (1924–), violinist; b. Poland, lived in England. Began international concert career after WWII. Regarded as one of leading soloists of her generation.
Hendricks, U.S. family in New York; owners of oldest Jewish business concern (copper) in America, established by **Uriah Hendricks** (1737–1798). His descendants enlarged firm, engaged in philanthropy, and were leaders of Congregation Shearith Israel.
Henle, Jacob (Friedrich Gustav; 1809–1885), German anatomist, pathologist; outstanding histologist and a founder of modern medicine. At least a dozen microscopic structures in anatomy were named after him. Baptized at age 11.
Henle, Moritz (1850–1925), German cantor, composer, choral conductor. Chief cantor in reformed Israelitischer Tempelverband of Hamburg fr. 1874, where he reintroduced biblical cantillation and Ashkenazi pronunciation.
Henochsberg, Edgar Samuel (1894–1966), S. African Supreme Court judge. Active in Jewish affairs in Durban.
Henriques (Quixano Henriques), English family established in London by Sephardi immigrants fr. Kingston, Jamaica, in 18th c. Many were leaders of Reform Judaism. **Henry Straus** (1864–1924), lawyer, pres. Board of Deputies of British Jews 1922–25, and author of *The Jews and the English Law* and *Jewish Marriages and the English Law.* **Sir Basil Lucas** (1890–1961), social worker, leading authority on juvenile delinquency. Established St. George's settlement in East End of London. Also spoke on behalf of progressive Judaism. His wife **Lady Rosa Louise** (1889–1972), sister of Herbert Loewe, chairman of British ORT and headed British-Jewish relief in postwar Germany. **Robert David** (1905–1967), soldier, author; wrote successful novels, *100 Hours to Suez* (about Sinai campaign), biographies of Herbert Samuel and Sir Robert Waley-Cohen.
Henry, Jacob (c. 1775–1847), representative in North Carolina's lower chamber who successfully challenged constitutional restrictions against non-Protestants in the legislature.
Henschel, family of four brothers. **August** (d. 1829), **Friedrich** (d. 1837), **Moritz** (d. 1862), and **Wilhelm** (d. 1865), German artists. Worked in Berlin as team fr. 1806 until August's suicide. Produced pastel portraits, miniatures, engravings. Subjects of engravings incl. theater scenes and "Scenes from the Life of Goethe."
Henschel, Sir George (Isador Georg; 1850–1934), conductor, singer, teacher. Baptized. First conductor of Boston Symphony Orchestra 1881–84, founded London Symphony Concerts 1886–97, conducted Scottish Symphony Orchestra 1893–95. Composed operas, requiem mass, songs.
Henshel, Harry D. (1890–1961), U.S. industrialist, sports administrator. Chairman of U.S. Olympic Basketball Committee 1952–56. Organized U.S. Committee for Sports for Israel.

Contemporary Frankfort print of scene from "Hep! Hep!" riots, 1819.

Hep! Hep! , derogatory rallying cry against Jews, common in Germany; also name given to series of anti-Jewish riots that broke out August 1819 in Germany and spread to several neighboring countries. Derived fr. initials of Lat. *Hierosolyma est perdita* ("Jerusalem is lost").
Herberg, Will (1909–), U.S. theologian, social critic. Broke fr. Communist Party, came under influence of Buber, Rosenzweig, S. Schechter. Wrote largely on Jewishness as convenantal existence. Also sociological study of U.S. religion *Protestant – Catholic – Jew.*
Herblock, see Block, Herbert.
Herbst, Karl (1865–1919), a founder of Bulgarian Zionism.

Senior Bulgarian government official, translated Herzl's *Judenstaat* into Bulgarian, attended 1st Zionist Congress, and established and edited organ of Bulgarian Zionism.

Herbstein, Joseph (1897–), S. African jurist; first Jew raised to bench in Cape Division. Outspoken Zionist; settled in Israel 1957.

Ḥerem (Heb.), excommunication imposed by rabbinical authorities for purposes of religious and/or communal discipline. Involved special ceremony. In biblical times term meant that which was separated fr. common use either because it was abomination or because it was consecrated to God. In Europe and Ereẓ Israel imposed for heretical views (cf. Uriel Acosta, Spinoza).

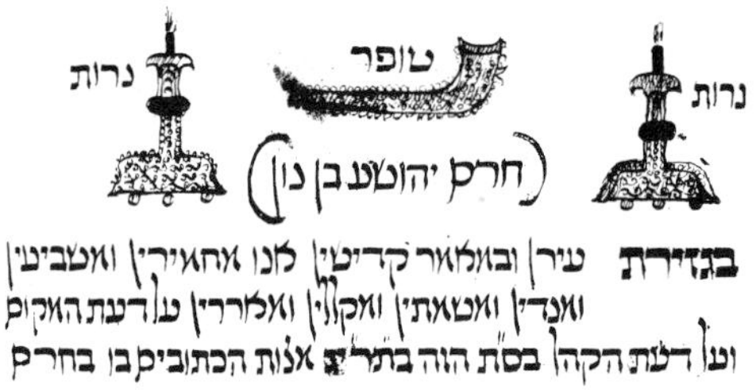

"Ḥerem" from memorial book, Konice, 1688–1878.

Ḥerem Bet Din (Heb. "ban of the court"), shortened and accepted form of *ḥerem bet din ha-gadol*; gave to court of local community rights and competences originally reserved for higher courts. One of earliest Jewish manifestations of spirit of commune-city, with its insistence on having justice dispensed within city walls.

Ḥerem ha-Yishuv (Heb. "ban on settlement"), refusal of community to allow newcomer to settle within it. Records of institution exist in European communities bet. 12th and 18th c., and in Russia probably lasted to 20th c. Designed to protect community fr. itinerant paupers or to protect trade.

°**Herford, Robert Travers** (1860–1950), English Unitarian theologian who studied Judaism of Second Temple period and Talmud, particularly Pharisees. Liberal scholar; attacked many Christian prejudices. Works incl. *The Pharisees* and an edition of *Pirkei Avot*.

Herlands, William Bernard (1905–1969), U.S. lawyer, judge. Held various legal posts in N.Y. Federal District Court judge fr. 1955. Active in Jewish life.

Herlitz, Georg (1885–1968), Zionist archivist, author. Headed Central Zionist Archives, first in Berlin, then Jerusalem. Editor of *Juedisches Lexikon*.

Herman, David (1876–1937), producer of Yiddish plays. Worked with Peretz Hirschbein troupe, ran dramatic school in Warsaw with Peretz and Michael Weichert, and directed Vilna Troupe.

Herman, Josef (1911–), painter; b. Poland, in Britain fr. 1940 (Glasgow, S. Wales, London). Found substitute for Polish *shtetl* among Welsh miners. Deeply involved in Jewish culture.

Hermann, Georg (pen name of **Georg Borchardt**; 1871–1943), German novelist, essayist, art historian; brother of Ludwig Borchardt; in Holland fr. 1933, d. Auschwitz. Wrote works with psychological insight; his *Jettchen Gebert* was called "the Jewish *Buddenbrooks.*"

Hermann, Leo (1888–1951), Zionist, journalist. Early Zionist in Bohemia. Helped organize Keren Hayesod in Berlin, became general-secretary when headquarters moved to Jerusalem 1926. Wrote on Jewish and Zionist topics. Pioneer producer of films about Israel.

Hermanus Quondam Judaeus (Herman of Scheda; c. 1107–1170 or 1198), apostate abbot of Scheda (Westphalia). Embraced Christianity and became priest. His autobiography describes Jewish life in 12th c. Germany.

Hermeneutics, science of biblical interpretation; formulated in 7 rules of Hillel, 13 rules of R. Ishmael, and 32 rules of R. Eliezer b. Yose ha-Gelili. R. Ishmael's rules are most famous: (1) *a fortiori* reference *(kal va-ḥomer);* (2) inference fr. analogy of words *(gezerah shavah);* (3) inference fr. single verse and inference from 2 verses, applied generally *(binyan av);* (4) general statement limited by particular which follows; (5) particular statement limited by general one which follows; (6) general, then particular, then general – how things similar to those specified may be derived; (7) general requires particular and particular general; (8) if particular instance of general rule is singled out for special treatment, whatever is postulated of this instance is to be applied to all instances embraced by general rule; (9) when particular instances of general rule are treated specifically in details included in general rule, then only relaxations of the general rule and not its restrictions are to be applied in those instances; (10) when particular instances of general rule are treated specifically in details dissimilar from those included in general rule, then both relaxations and restrictions are to be applied in those instances; (11) when particular instance of general rule is singled out for completely fresh treatment, details of general rule must not be applied to this instance unless Scripture does so specifically; (12) meaning of passage may be deduced (a) fr. its context, (b) fr. later reference in same passage; (13) two apparently contradictory verses may be reconciled by third.

Skiers on Mount Hermon, January, 1970.

Hermon, Mount, mountain range in Lebanon, Syria, and (after 1967) Israel on NW border of Transjordan. Highest peak 9,230 ft. above sea level. In Bible considered N. boundary of Transjordan and thought by local residents to be residence of god Baal-Hermon. In modern times, villages at foot inhabited by minority groups (e.g., Druze, Alaouites). Major part in Lebanon. Covered with snow most of year.

Herod I (73? –4 B.C.E.), king of Judea fr. 37 B.C.E.; son of Idumean Antipater. As governor of Galilee crushed revolt of Hezekiah the Zealot. Intimidated judges who found him guilty for this act by appearing before Sanhedrin with heavily armed guard. In 40 B.C.E. went to Rome and was proclaimed king of Judea. After war against Antigonus the Hasmonean, captured Jerusalem, killed members of Hasmonean house, and destroyed political power of Sanhedrin. Courageous soldier, energetic administrator, talented diplomat. Destroyed internal organization of Jewish community, abolished traditional institutions, and brought kingdom into Roman hellenistic cultural orbit. Great builder who rebuilt Temple in Jerusalem, cities of Sebaste and Caesarea, and palaces in

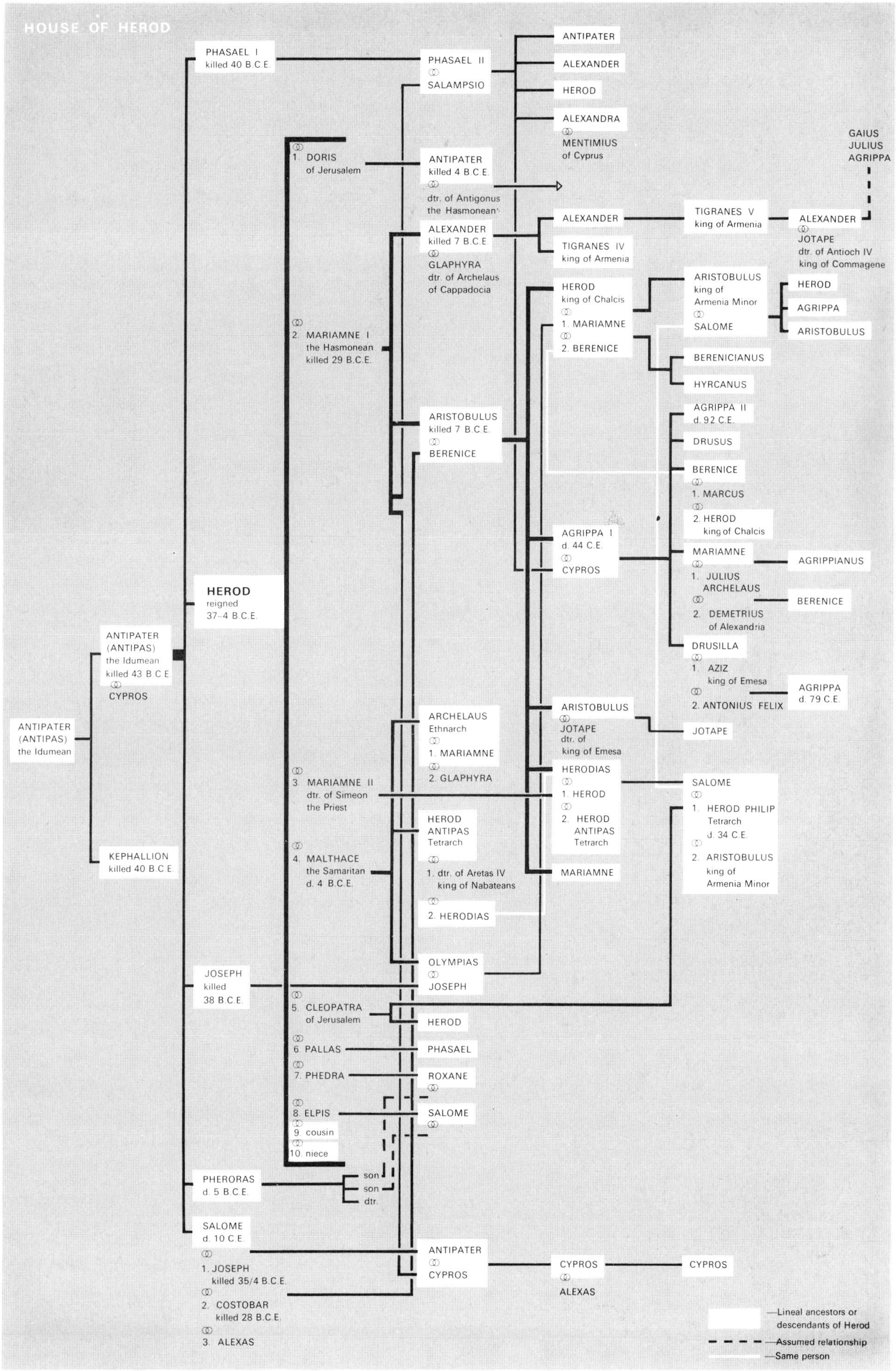
HOUSE OF HEROD
ANTIPATER (ANTIPAS) the Idumean
ANTIPATER (ANTIPAS) the Idumean killed 43 B.C.E. CYPROS
KEPHALLION killed 40 B.C.E.
PHASAEL I killed 40 B.C.E.
HEROD reigned 37–4 B.C.E.
JOSEPH killed 38 B.C.E.
PHERORAS d. 5 B.C.E.
son
son
dtr.
SALOME d. 10 C.E.
1. JOSEPH killed 35/4 B.C.E.
2. COSTOBAR killed 28 B.C.E.
3. ALEXAS
1. DORIS of Jerusalem
2. MARIAMNE I the Hasmonean killed 29 B.C.E.
3. MARIAMNE II dtr. of Simeon the Priest
4. MALTHACE the Samaritan d. 4 B.C.E.
5. CLEOPATRA of Jerusalem
6. PALLAS
7. PHEDRA
8. ELPIS
9. cousin
10. niece
PHASAEL II SALAMPSIO
ANTIPATER killed 4 B.C.E. dtr. of Antigonus the Hasmonean
ALEXANDER killed 7 B.C.E. GLAPHYRA dtr. of Archelaus of Cappadocia
ARISTOBULUS killed 7 B.C.E. BERENICE
ARCHELAUS Ethnarch 1. MARIAMNE 2. GLAPHYRA
HEROD ANTIPAS Tetrarch 1. dtr. of Aretas IV king of Nabateans 2. HERODIAS
OLYMPIAS JOSEPH
HEROD
PHASAEL
ROXANE
SALOME
ANTIPATER CYPROS
ANTIPATER
ALEXANDER
HEROD
ALEXANDRA MENTIMIUS of Cyprus
ALEXANDER
TIGRANES IV king of Armenia
HEROD king of Chalcis 1. MARIAMNE 2. BERENICE
AGRIPPA I d. 44 C.E. CYPROS
ARISTOBULUS JOTAPE dtr. of king of Emesa
HERODIAS 1. HEROD 2. HEROD ANTIPAS Tetrarch
MARIAMNE
CYPROS ALEXAS
CYPROS
TIGRANES V king of Armenia
ALEXANDER JOTAPE dtr. of Antioch IV king of Commagene
GAIUS JULIUS AGRIPPA
ARISTOBULUS king of Armenia Minor SALOME
HEROD
AGRIPPA
ARISTOBULUS
BERENICIANUS
HYRCANUS
AGRIPPA II d. 92 C.E.
DRUSUS
BERENICE 1. MARCUS 2. HEROD king of Chalcis
MARIAMNE 1. JULIUS ARCHELAUS 2. DEMETRIUS of Alexandria
AGRIPPIANUS
BERENICE
DRUSILLA 1. AZIZ king of Emesa 2. ANTONIUS FELIX
AGRIPPA d. 79 C.E.
JOTAPE
SALOME 1. HEROD PHILIP Tetrarch d. 34 C.E. 2. ARISTOBULUS king of Armenia Minor
—Lineal ancestors or descendants of Herod
—Assumed relationship
—Same person

Herodium and Masada. His private life was tragic and marked by brooding jealousies which led him to execute his wife Mariamne the Hasmonean and some of his sons.

Herod II (d. 48 C.E.), grandson of Herod I; king of Chalcis 41–48 C.E. In 45 C.E. he and his brother Agrippa I regained custody of vestments of high priest, and after death of Agrippa I (44 C.E.) he was given charge of Temple and right to appoint high priests.

Herodians, sect or party mentioned in New Testament as opponents of Jesus. Identity uncertain.

Herodias (1st c. C.E.), daughter of Aristobulus son of Herod. Her first husband was her uncle Herod, to whom she bore a daughter Salome. Left her husband and married his brother Herod Antipas, whom she accompanied when he was exiled to Gaul.

Herodium, Judean fortress during Second Temple period, SE of Bethlehem. Built by Herod and was his burial place. Excavated fortress consists of double circular curtain wall with 4 circular towers. Occupied during both Jewish wars against Romans and by monks in Byzantine times.

Reconstruction of Herod I's palace in a model of the ancient city of Jerusalem.

The fortress of Herodium

Herod Philip I, tetrarch 4 B.C.E.–34 C.E.; son of Herod the Great and Cleopatra of Jerusalem. Founded city of Caesarea Philippi (Banias) nr. source of Jordan and Julias N. of Sea of Galilee.

Herrera, Abraham Kohen de (Aloso Nunez de; Abraham Irira; c. 1570? –1635 or 1639), philosopher of religion, kabbalist; of Marrano origin. Studied Isaac Luria's Kabbalah at Ragusa and returned to Judaism in Holland. First to undertake systematic philosophical interpretation of kabbalistic doctrines.

Herrmann, Hugo (1887–1940), Zionist author, editor, propagandist. Editor of important Zionist organs, incl. *Selbstwehr, Juedische Rundschau, Juedisches Volksblatt.* An organizer of Keren Hayesod. Fr. 1934 in Jerusalem.

Hersch, Pesach Liebman (1882–1955), statistician, demographer; b. Lithuania. Prof. at Geneva Univ. A leader of Bund, but experience of Holocaust led him to advocate revision of Bund ideology. Active in Jewish and international welfare organizations.

Herschel, Solomon, see Hirschel, Solomon.

Herschberg, Abraham Samuel (1858–1943), Hebrew scholar, writer. Lived in Bialystok and wrote history of its community. Killed in Bialystok ghetto.

Herschman, Mordechai (1888–1940), *ḥazzan;* b. Ukraine, in U.S. fr. 1920. Made many concert tours in U.S., Europe, Ereẓ Israel. His cantorial and folksong records were popular.

Herskovits, Melville Jean (1895–1963), U.S. anthropologist. His studies of the New World Negro opened new field of research and contributed to new appreciation of Negro in American society.

Hertz, Gustav (1887–), German physicist; son of Jewish father. Remained in Germany throughout WWII; subsequently prof. at Univ. of Leipzig. Nobel Prize for Physics 1925 for role in discovering laws governing impact bet. electron and atom. Baptized.

Hertz, Henri (1875–1966), French poet, novelist, critic. Poet of revolt and distinguished journalist. Wrote much in press on Jewish problems. Secretary, Jewish Agency Political Office in Paris and WWII resistance fighter.

Hertz, Henrik (orig. **Heyman;** 1798–1870), Danish playwright, poet. Member of new school of Danish romantics.

Hertz, Joseph Herman (1872–1946), chief rabbi of British Commonwealth 1913–46. First graduate of Jewish Theological Seminary of America 1894. Fr. 1896 in S. Africa, where his outspoken opposition to Boer discrimination led to deportation. Ardent supporter of Zionism; played part in events leading to Balfour Declaration. His works on Jewish thought and literature incl. commentary on Pentateuch and prayerbook and *A Book of Jewish Thoughts.*

Joseph H. Hertz

Hertzberg, Arthur (1921–), U.S. Conservative rabbi, author. Rabbi of Temple Emanu-El, Englewood, N.J. Member of history faculty at Columbia Univ. Member of Jewish Agency Executive; pres. of American Jewish Congress fr. 1972. Works incl. *The Zionist Idea* and *French Enlightenment and the Jews.*

Hertzka, Theodor (1845–1924), Hungarian economist, journalist; editor of journals in Vienna, Budapest. In his novels proposed establishment in C. Africa of model state. Project abandoned after international mission failed to secure land for settlement 1893. His ideas influenced Franz Oppenheimer and were known to Herzl when he wrote *Der Judenstaat.*

Ḥerut Movement, political movement in Ereẓ Israel, established 1948 by Irgun Ẓeva'i Le'ummi. It was the second largest party in the Knesset fr. 1955; won 17 seats (13.8%) 1961. Party merged 1965 with General Zionist Party to form Gaḥal (Ḥerut–Liberal Bloc). Led fr. inauguration by Menahem Begin. Policies incl. Jewish state within whole of Ereẓ Israel and economy based on free enterprise. See also Knesset.

Ḥeruti, see Smilansky, Moshe.

Herxheimer, Salomon (1801–1884), German rabbi, Bible translator. Exponent of moderate Reform. Published translation of Bible into German with commentary.

Herz, Henri (Heinrich; 1802–1888), Austrian pianist, composer. Enjoyed fashionable popularity in France, where he taught and founded piano factory. Composed Mexican national anthem.

Herz, Henriette (1764–1847), society leader in Berlin; wife of Marcus Herz. Known for beauty, intelligence, and linguistic accomplishments. Her salon was a center of Berlin's intellectual life. Indifferent to Judaism; baptized 1817.

Henriette Herz

Herz, Leopold Edler von (1767–1828), Austrian financier, nobleman. Won Metternich's friendship by arranging subsidy promised by England to Austria 1813. Signatory of petition to Francis I for Jewish rights 1815. Baptized 1819.

Herz, Marcus (1747–1803), German physician, philosopher. Taught at Jewish Hospital, Berlin. Reputedly one of best doctors of his time. Close friend of Kant; his letters important source for understanding development of *Critique of Pure Reason.* Received title of "professor" 1787.

Herzberg, Abel Jacob (1893–), Dutch author, playwright. Enthusiastic Zionist in youth; later recorded experience in Bergen-Belsen and wrote study of Eichmann trial.

Herzberg-Fraenkel, Leo (1827–1915), Galician author, functionary. Secretary of Brody Chamber of Commerce; active in general and Jewish life. Published novels dealing with E. European Jewry. Skeptical of practicability of political Zionism but stressed need for speedy exodus of Jews from E. Europe.

Herzfeld, Ernst Emil (1879–1948), German archaeologist, orientalist. Taught at Berlin and Princeton and participated in several excavations in Middle East. Laid foundations for Arab archaeological research in Iraq and archaeology of Persia.

Herzfeld, Levi (1810–1884), German rabbi, historian. Spokesman of moderate Reform; took leading part in Rabbinical Conferences of 1844–46. First to pay attention to economic aspects of Jewish history; work marked by meticulous analysis of sources.

Theodor Herzl with his children, c. 1900

Herzl's tomb on Mount Herzl

Herzl, Theodor (Binyamin Ze'ev; 1860–1904), father of political Zionism, founder of World Zionist Organization; b. Budapest, in Vienna fr. 1878. Doctor of law 1884. Devoted himself to writing, publishing feuilletons, plays, etc. When Paris correspondent of Vienna *Neue Freie Presse* 1891–95 attention drawn to Jewish problems, reinforced by Dreyfus Case. Began Zionist activities 1895 and wrote *Der Judenstaat* 1896, containing his Zionist program, which he accompanied with intensive activity in meeting key people and preparing organization. Founded weekly *Die Welt* and convened first Zionist congress in Basle Aug. 29–31, 1897, where World Zionist Organization was established. Went to Ereẓ Israel 1898 to meet Kaiser William II but meeting and that with Turkish sultan were fruitless; therefore started negotiations with Great Britain. Established Jewish Colonial Trust 1899, and Jewish National Fund came into being 1901. Published utopian novel *Altneuland* 1902. British government proposed Uganda Scheme 1902; accepted by Herzl but opposed by many Zionists. Continued political negotiations, visiting Russia, Italy, Great Britain. Died while controversy over Uganda Scheme still raged. Buried in Vienna; reinterred on Mt. Herzl in Jerusalem 1949.

Herzliyyah, town in S. Sharon, Israel. Founded 1924 as city by American Zion Commonwealth but became moshavah; accorded city status 1960. Tel Aviv's proximity was among factors accelerating its growth. Section along coast (H.-Pittuaḥ) is location of several large hotels and is resort. Pop. 40,100 (1971).

Herzog, David (1869–1946), Austrian rabbi, scholar. Rabbi of Graz. Fr. 1938 in Oxford, England. Main scholarly interests medieval Jewish literature and history of Jews in Austria.

Herzog, Isaac (1888–1959), rabbinic scholar; first Ashkenazi chief rabbi of State of Israel; b. Poland. Rabbi in Belfast 1916–19, Dublin 1919–36 (chief rabbi of Irish Free State fr. 1921). Succeeded A.I. Kook as chief rabbi of Ereẓ Israel. Enjoyed widespread respect and wrote *The Main Institutions of Jewish Law.* His son **Chaim** (1918–), Israel military officer, commentator. Chief of intelligence 1949–51, 1959–62; fr. eve of Six-Day War was Israel's leading military commentator. His other son, **Jacob** (1921–1972), lawyer, diplomat. Minister in Washington, ambassador in Canada, served in senior posts in diplomatic service, director general of prime minister's office 1965–72.

Isaac Herzog

Abraham J. Heschel

Heschel, Abraham Joshua (1907–1972), U.S. scholar, philosopher. Taught in Berlin until 1938; fr. 1945 prof. of Jewish ethics and mysticism at Jewish Theological Seminary in N.Y. His writings (*Man Is Not Alone,* and *God In Search of Man*) bear stamp of neo-Ḥasidism. Played leading role in humanitarian causes, incl. civil rights campaigns and movement to support Soviet Jewry.

Heschel, Abraham Joshua ben Jacob (d. 1664), talmudic scholar; headed yeshivot in Lublin and Cracow. Wealthy and pious, renowned as teacher and legal authority. Particularly active on behalf of Polish Jewry after Chmielnicki massacres. Wrote responsa, talmudic novellae, homilies on Bible.

Heshbon, biblical city in Transjordan. Capital of Sihon, king of Amorites. Conquered by Israelites in their first victory on way to Promised Land (Num. 21:30). Remained Israelite until conquered by Mesha of Moab (c. 853 B.C.E.). Hasmoneans ceded it to Nabateans, but recovered by Herod.

Heshin, Shneur Zalman (1903–1959), Israel jurist, Supreme Court justice. Permanent deputy president of court fr. 1954.

Ḥeshvan, see Marḥeshvan.

Hesped (Heb.), eulogy in honor of departed and as comfort to bereaved. Pronounced in front of bier, either in public square or at cemetery.

Hess, Michael (1782–1860), German educator. Headmaster of Frankfort Philanthropin school 1806–55. Extreme advocate of Reform; gradually limited time allotted for Jewish studies.

Hess, Moses (1812–1875), Jewish socialist thinker; precursor of modern Zionism and particularly Zionist Socialism; b. Germany, lived mostly in France. In contrast to Marx and Engels, with whom he was on close terms, he advocated "philosophical Socialism." Published *Rome and Jerusalem* 1862, classic of Zionist literature which foresees all or parts of Zionist ideology, e.g. political, spiritual, Socialist. Forgotten for some time and only appreciated with birth of the Zionist movement.

Hess, Dame Myra (1890–1956), British pianist. During blitz in London in WWII, organized daily lunchtime concerts in National Gallery. One of Britain's best-known pianists.

Hesse, state in W. Germany. Jews fr. 12th c. Settlement interrupted only during Black Death and Nazi periods. Political conditions generally favorable and communities prospered, esp. in Hesse-Darmstadt (separated from Hesse-Kassel 1567). 17,888 Jews in 1933; communities reestablished after WWII. Jewish pop. 1,508 (1970).

Hessen, Joseph Vladimirovich (1866–1943), Russian lawyer, politician. Constitutional-Democrat, representative in Second Duma. Emigrated 1917, lived in Helsinki, Berlin. Wrote work on Russian history.

Hessen, Julius Isidorovich (1871–1939), historian of Russian Jewry. His studies of Russian Jewry are particularly valuable for 18th and 19th c. An editor of Russian Jewish encyclopedia. In last years of life, edited archives for Leningrad region and investigated Arctic expeditions.

Hestrin, Shlomo (1912–1962), Israel biochemist; b. Canada, settled in Ereẓ Israel 1933. Head of microbiological chemistry laboratory at Hadassah Medical School in Jerusalem fr. 1949; head of dept. of biochemistry at Heb. Univ. fr. 1959. Israel Prize 1957.

Ḥet (ח), 8th letter of Hebrew alphabet; numerical value 8. Pronounced as fricative pharyngeal (cf. *ch* in *loch*).

Ḥever ha-Yehudim (Heb.), name which appears on Hasmonean coins indicating some kind of ruling body. Some scholars associate this body with later Sanhedrin, others with Great Assembly of 142 B.C.E.

Hevesi (orig. Handler), Simon (1868–1943), rabbi, scholar in Hungary. Chief rabbi of Pest fr. 1927. Taught at rabbinical seminary. Leading role in public affairs of Hungarian Jewry.

Hevesy, George Charles de (1885–1966), Hungarian chemist, isotopes pioneer; Nobel Prize 1943. Worked in Hungary, Germany, Denmark, Sweden. Pioneered in isotope tracers.

Ḥevrah, Ḥavurah, formal membership association in framework of traditional Jewish community and distinguished fr. modern association by essentially religious nature. Each had specific religious, philanthropic, or vocational purpose. Best known is *ḥevra kaddisha.*

Copy of "Ḥevra kaddisha" jug fr. Moravia, 1776.

Ḥevra (Ḥavurah) Kaddisha (Aram. lit. "holy brotherhood"), term orig. applied to mutual benefit society; now (among Ashkenazi Jews) to volunteer charitable societies for reverential burial of the dead. Special brotherhoods perform this commandment, which was regarded as among the most meritorious, and membership in society was coveted honor. This mostly included washing corpse, accompanying it to grave, and burial. In some countries (e.g., Argentina) society was basis of communal organization.

Ḥevrat ha-Ovedim, roof organization for ramified enterprises run by Histadrut, incl. factories, cooperatives. Employs 25% of Israel's gainfully employed population.

Heyd, Uriel (1913–1968), Israel historian of Muslim institutions; b. Germany, settled in Ereẓ Israel 1934. Worked in Political Dept. of Jewish Agency 1943–48. Prof. at Heb. Univ. His scholarly interests centered on Ottoman Empire fr. 16th to 20th c.

°**Heydrich, Reinhard Tristan** (1904–1942), Nazi S.S. leader who was entrusted with execution of "Final Solution." Gauleiter of Bohemia. Killed by Czech resistance fighters.

Heym, Stefan (Helmut Flieg; 1913–), German novelist, biographer, and political writer. In U.S. during WWII. Wrote *The Crusaders* and *The King David Report.*

Heymann, Walter (1882–1915), German poet; pioneer of German expressionism. Killed on Western front. Most of his work published posthumously.

Heyse, Paul (1830–1914), first German author to win Nobel Prize for Literature 1910. Belonged to school of lyricists in Munich which devoted itself to perfection of form rather than innovation of subject matter.

Hezekiah, king of Judah 727–698 B.C.E. Purified cult fr. idolatrous elements to concentrate activity in Temple of Jerusalem. Reform gained widespread support, notably fr. prophet Isaiah. His penetration into Philistia connected with his rebellion against Sennacherib of Assyria, which was result of policy of expanding territory and ambition to achieve absolute political independence. In anticipation of this struggle, built Siloam tunnel in Jerusalem. Sennacherib's campaign to Ereẓ Israel ended with Assyrian withdrawal. In *aggadah* praised to extent of idealization.

Hezekiah (d.c. 46 B.C.E.), fighter against Roman rule in Judea. Led band of guerrillas and raided gentile towns on Syrian border. Captured and summararily executed by young Herod, then military governor of Galilee.

Hezekiah (Beribbi; 3rd c.), Palestinian *amora;* lived in Tiberias. Compiled collection of *beraitot* and added to extant halakhic Midrashim.

Hezekiah ben David da Silva (1659–1695), rabbi of Jerusalem. Wrote *Peri Ḥadash,* which contains trenchant criticism of rulings of Joseph Caro. Work aimed at nullifying authority of *Shulḥan Arukh* as representing final *halakhah.*

Hezekiah ben Jacob (of Magdeburg; Mahari'aḥ; 13th c.), one of last tosafists. Author of *tosafot* to tractate *Shabbat.*

Hezekiah ben Manoah (13th c.), biblical commentator of school of Rashi; apparently fr. France. His commentary *Ḥizzekuni* (or *Ḥazzekuni*) quotes many Midrashim no longer extant, for which he is the only source.

The "tomb of the sons of Hezir," Kidron Valley, Jerusalem, 1st cent. B.C.E.

Hezir, founder of 17th priestly watch (I Chron. 24:15). Catacomb with Hebrew inscription fr. 1st c. B.C.E. mentioning "sons of Hezir" discovered 1864 in Kidron Valley outside Jerusalem.

Hias, see United Hias Service.

Hibat Allah, Abu al-Barakāt (Nathanel) ben Ali (Eli) al-Baghdādī (11th–12th c.), philosopher, biblical commentator in Baghdad. Physician at court of Caliph al-Mustanjid. His *Kitāb al-Mu'tabar* criticizes certain Aristotelian physical, psychological, and metaphysical notions and had influence on Muslim philosophy. Converted to Islam at age 60.

Ḥibbat Zion (Heb. "Love of Zion"), movement and ideology whose aim was national renaissance of Jews and their return to Ereẓ Israel. Came into being in Russia 1882 as reaction to 1881 pogroms; flourished mainly in large communities of E. Europe (Russia, Poland, Rumania). Organization based on individual societies established at 1884 Kattowitz Conference and led by Leon Pinsker. Odessa Committee founded with government permission. Branches in Germany and W. Europe. Stimulated first modern *aliyah* movement (Bilu). Societies merged with Zionist Organization upon its establishment by Theodor Herzl, although some of them continued their formal existence until WWI. Members called Ḥovevei Zion.

Ḥibbut ha-Kever (Heb. "beating in the grave"), acc. to *aggadah,* punishment of deceased for his sins with fiery chain by Angel of Death immediately after burial. Only those who die in Ereẓ Israel or, if outside, who are buried Friday afternoon before sunset, are exempted.

Hicem (initials of HIAS, ICA, and EMIGDIREKT), emigration association set up 1927 by HIAS, ICA, and Emigdirekt to help refugees fr. E. Europe and later fr. Nazi Germany. Dissolved 1945 and offices and activities taken over by HIAS.

Ḥida, see Azulai, Ḥayyim Joseph David.

Ḥiddushim (Heb. "novellae"), results of method of study of rabbinical literature which derives new ideas fr. talmudic and also rabbinic texts in order to clarify *halakhah.* Scattered in responsa or collected in *tosafot* or separate works; became integral part of normal study of Talmud. Earliest date fr. geonic period.

Ḥidka (2nd c.), *tanna.* The fourth, optional Sabbath meal eaten by meticulous individuals is known as "R. Ḥidka's meal," a reference to his halakhic ruling in the matter.

Hiel, Bethelite who fortified Jericho in reign of King Ahab of Israel (I Kings 16:34). In course of work two of his sons perished. This was seen as fulfillment of curse of Joshua on anyone who fortified Jericho.

Higger, Michael (1898–1952), U.S. talmudic scholar; b. Lithuania, in U.S. fr. 1915. His major work *Oẓar ha-Beraitot* (10 vols.) incl. 10,000 *beraitot* annotated with variants and classified acc. to form and provenance.

High Commissioner for Palestine, head of British Mandatory administration called the government of Palestine. Ruled through council of senior British officials.

BRITISH HIGH COMMISSIONERS FOR PALESTINE

	Period of Office
Sir (later Viscount) Herbert Louis Samuel (1870–1963)	1920–1925
Field Marshal Herbert Charles Onslow, Lord Plumer (1857–1932)	1925–1928
Sir John Herbert Chancellor (1870–1952)	1928–1931
General Sir Arthur Grenfell Wauchope (1874–1947)	1931–1938
Sir Harold MacMichael (1882–1968)	1938–1944
Field Marshal John Standish Surtees Pendergast Verker (Viscount) Gort (1886–1946)	1944–1945
General Sir Alan Gordon Cunningham (1887–)	1945–1948

High Holidays, see Rosh Ha-Shanah; Day of Atonement.

High Place, cultic installation situated on high elevation, such as mountain top. Probably open-air installation intended to serve as site that deity would visit when invoked. They were essentially Canaanite, apparently fr. 2nd half of 3rd millennium B.C.E., and then Israelite. Partially removed by Asa, Hezekiah, and Josiah, but also built by Solomon, Rehoboam, and many kings of N. Israel.

High Priest, chief priest in Temple. Office conferred on Aaron and his descendants. During First Temple period responsible for certain functions within Temple, such as consul-

The high priest, detail from "Liber Chronicarum" by Hartmann Schedel, Nuremberg, 1493.

ting the divine oracle of Urim and Thummim. In Second Temple period, responsibilities greatly enhanced and regarded as chief administrator of internal secular policy as well as representative of Jewish community in all matters of external diplomacy. During last part of Second Temple period, office was held by Hasmoneans, and later was conferred by ruler.

Hildesheimer, Azriel (Israel; 1820–1889), German rabbi, scholar, educator, Orthodox leader. Strong opponent of Reform; aspired to combine traditional Judaism with European culture, for this purpose founding Berlin Rabbinical Seminary 1873, which he directed until his death. Enthusiastic supporter of building of *Yishuv*. Published many studies, notably critical edition of *Halakhot Gedolot*.

Azriel Hildesheimer

Hildesheimer, Meir (1864–1934), German rabbi. Executive director of rabbinical seminary founded in Berlin by his father, Azriel Hildesheimer. Represented Orthodox German Jewry on many national Jewish organizations.

Hilferding, Rudolf (1877–1941), Austrian socialist politician, theorist. Author of *Das Finanzkapital*, major work of Austrian Marxism. A leading member of German Social Democratic Party; minister of finance 1923, 1928–9. D. in Holocaust.

Hilfsverein der Deutschen Juden, German Jewish organization founded 1901 to improve social and political conditions of Jews in E. Europe and Orient. Before WWI its assimilationist policy provoked sharp conflicts with Zionists and other groups. Assisted Jews to emigrate fr. Russia before 1914 and fr. Germany and E. Europe bet. 1921 and 1941 (over 350,000 persons). Officially dissolved 1939; continued to exist until 1941.

Hilkiah, high priest at time of King Josiah of Judah. While arranging for Temple repair, found Scroll of Law and sent delegation to prophetess Huldah to inquire of Lord's will about it. On Josiah's orders, removed all appurtenances of pagan worship in Temple.

Ḥillazon, snail from which *tekhelet* (bluish or cerulean dye) was extracted to dye threads of fringes (*ẓiẓit*).

Hillel (the Elder; 1st c. B.C.E.–1st c. C.E.), greatest sage of Second Temple period; founder of school of Bet Hillel (q.v.), pres. of Sanhedrin, and ancestor of dynasty of patriarchs which held office until 5th c.; b. Babylonia, settled in Ereẓ Israel. Noted for wisdom, humility, and teaching of leniency (which contrasted with severity of his colleague Shammai). Instituted *prosbul;* laid down seven rules of Bible interpretation; author of several ethical religious teachings. Sayings: "What is hateful to you, do not do unto your neighbor" (Shab. 31a). "If I am not for myself, who is for me? And when I am for myself, what am I? And if not now, when?" (Avot 1:14).

Hillel (II; 4th c.), *nasi* of Palestinian Jewry 330–365; son of Judah Nesi'ah. Determined fixed calendar which is still accepted Jewish calendar and freed Babylonian community fr. dependence on Ereẓ Israel. Corresponded with Emperor Julian the Apostate.

Hillel ben Eliakim (c. 12th c.), talmudic scholar of Greece. Wrote commentaries on *Sifrei* and *Sifra*. Former is important in establishing original text.

Hillel ben Naphtali Ẓevi (Herz; 1615–1690), Lithuanian rabbi who also served in Altona, Hamburg, and Poland. Important halakhist; wrote novellae on *Shulḥan Arukh*.

Hillel ben Samuel (c. 1220–c. 1295), Italian physician, talmudist, philosopher. Defended Maimonides' philosophy in controversies of 1289–90. His *Tagmulei ha-Nefesh* deals systematically with question of universality of the soul. Translated medieval works fr. Latin into Hebrew.

Hillel Foundation, see B'nai B'rith.

Hillels, Shelomo (1873–1953), Russian Hebrew writer; settled in Ereẓ Israel 1925. Wrote stories of Jewish life during revolution and pogroms in Bessarabia and Ukraine.

Hiller, Ferdinand (1811–1885), German pianist, composer, conductor. Performed in Paris and held several positions in Germany and Italy. Founded 1850 and directed Conservatory of Cologne. Wrote biographies of contemporary Romantic composers. Baptized.

Hiller, Kurt (1885–), German socialist theoretician. Attracted many disciples when he organized them into activist groups. After living in London 1938–55, founded and became pres. of Neusozialistischer Bund of Hamburg 1956.

Hillesum, Jeremias (1863–1943), Dutch librarian, bibliographer, historian. Librarian Bibliotheca Rosenthaliana in Amsterdam. D. in concentration camp.

Hillman, Samuel Isaac (1868–1953), rabbi; b. Lithuania; went to Glasgow 1908, *dayyan* of London *bet din* fr. 1914. Prime mover in establishing influence of E. European rabbis in Anglo-Jewish community. Settled in Jerusalem 1934. Wrote on most tractates of Babylonian Talmud.

Hillman, Sidney (1887–1946), U.S. labor leader; b. Lithuania, in U.S. fr. 1907. Organized unions in Chicago, developing concept of "individual constitutionalism," his main contribution to American labor movement. Pres. Amalgamated Clothing Workers of America 1915–46. Held federal positions during New Deal and was a founder of CIO. In WWII, chief labor adviser to Pres. Roosevelt.

Sidney Hillman

Morris Hillquit

Hillquit, Morris (1869–1933), U.S. socialist, lawyer; b. Latvia, in New York fr. 1886. Active in radical intellectual life in New York's Lower East Side. Envisioned socialist control of trade unions. Played leading role in Socialist Party of America (formed 1900), representing moderate element.

Ḥillul ha-Shem, see Kiddush ha-Shem and Ḥillul ha-Shem.

Hillula (Aram.), festivity, esp. wedding celebration. Term used for anniversary of death of famous rabbis and scholars because such occasions were often celebrated by popular pilgrimages and rejoicings.

Hillula de-Rabbi Shimon bar Yoḥai, festivity of R. Simeon b. Yoḥai held in Meron on Lag ba-Omer, traditional date of his death. Originated in 16th–17th c. Characteristic of festivity are "kindling" of costly garments and money and of locks of hair of young boys given their first haircut on next day.

Hilsner Case, blood libel trial held in Bohemia at beginning of 20th c. As result of two trials, Leopold Hilsner, a young Jewish vagabond, was sentenced to life imprisonment for murdering two females. The affair, accompanied by anti-Semitic campaign throughout Europe, led to exodus of many small rural Jewish communities. T.G. Masaryk's demand for revision of trial attracted wide attention. Hilsner was pardoned 1916.

Him, George (1900–), English designer. Designer of publicity material. Designed Warsaw Ghetto Exhibition 1946 and Massada Exhibition 1966 in London. Coordinator, Israel Pavilion at Belgium's World Fair 1957 and Montreal's Expo '67.

Himmelstein, Lena (Lane Bryant Malsin; 1881–1951), U.S. chain store founder; b. Lithuania. Opened dressmaking shop in N.Y. during early 1900s which eventually became national chain of Lane Bryant.

°**Himmler, Heinrich** (1900–1945), Nazi leader and one of Hitler's principal lieutenants. Became chief of the S.S. 1929, chief of German police 1936, assumed overall responsibility for destruction of Europe's Jews when S.S. was placed in charge of Final Solution 1941. Committed suicide after war.

Ḥimyar, large tribe in S. Arabia. Under threat of Christian incursions in 4th–5th c. C.E., tribe drew closer to Judaism and Jewish ideas and some converted.

Hindus, Maurice Gerschon (1891–1969), U.S. author. Wrote many books on USSR, changing fr. sympathy to disenchantment with Soviet regime. Also wrote novels.

Hineni ha-Ani mi-Ma'as (Heb. "Behold, I the poor in deeds"), initial words of silent prayer recited by *ḥazzan* before additional service on Rosh Ha-Shanah and Day of Atonement, acc. to Ashkenazi ritual.

Hinnom, Valley of, see Gehinnom.

Hippos, see Susita.

°**Hiram,** king of Tyre c. 969–936 B.C.E. Under his rule Tyre became leading city on Phoenician coast. Had friendly relations with David and Solomon and helped in planning, building, and equipping Jerusalem Temple.

Ḥireq, Hebrew vowel sign indicating long or short *i*. Written form ִ or יִ.

Hirsch, Aron Siegmund (1858–1941?), German industrialist. His giant copper and brass foundry achieved leading role in German economic life. Communal figure and philanthropist.

Hirsch, August (Aron Simon; 1817–1894), German physician; founder of branch of historical and geographical pathology. Cofounder and pres. 1871–85 of German Public Health Association. Wrote on medical historical subjects.

Hirsch, Emil Gustave (1851–1923), U.S. rabbi, scholar, civic leader; son of Samuel Hirsch. Spokesman for radical wing of Reform in U.S. Led Chicago Sinai Congregation fr. 1880; taught at Univ. of Chicago, which he helped found. Propounded evolutionary concept of Judaism, in which disciplines of *halakhah* yielded to primacy of ethical idea.

Hirsch, Julius (1882–1961), economist; b. Germany. Taught at Berlin Univ. Secretary of state in Ministry of Economics 1919–23; participated in economic negotiations and plans in Germany. In U.S. fr. 1941. Writings deal with distribution and quantitative economic analysis.

Hirsch, Markus (Mordecai Amram; 1833–1909), Hungarian rabbi. Revitalized Obuda community and was conciliator at General Jewish Congress of Hungary 1868–69. Rabbi in Prague fr. 1880, chief rabbi of Hamburg fr. 1889.

Hirsch, Baron Maurice de (1831–1896), German financier, philanthropist. Acquired wealth fr. Turkish railway concession and enterprises in sugar and copper industries. Established Baron de Hirsch Foundation for educational work in Galicia and Bukovina 1888, Baron de Hirsch Fund in New York for settling immigrants to U.S. and later Canada, and Jewish Colonization Association (ICA) 1891. Attitude to Zionism negative, but convinced of future of Jews as farmers and ICA financed such settlement in S. America. His wife **Clara** (1833–1899), also donated large sums to charitable works.

Photomontage of Baron Maurice de Hirsch as "Tuerkenhirsch," c. 1875.

Hirsch, Mendel (1833–1900), German educator, writer. Principal of Frankfort high schools founded by his father (S.R. Hirsch) fr. 1877. Wrote on pedagogical subjects and Bible; opposed political Zionism.

Hirsch, Otto (1885–1941), leader of German Jewish community under Nazi rule and courageous spokesman on its behalf. Murdered at Mauthausen camp.

Hirsch, Rachel (1870–1953), German physician; granddaughter of S.R. Hirsch. First Jewish woman to receive title of prof. of medicine in Prussia 1913 and discoverer of "Rachel Hirsch Effect" in blood system. D. London.

Hirsch, Robert Paul (1925–), French actor, director. Distinguished comic actor and mime. Member Comédie Francaise fr. 1948. Appeared in films.

Samson Raphael Hirsch

Hirsch, Samson (ben) Raphael (1808–1888), rabbi, writer. Through him Frankfort became focus of German Orthodoxy. In his *Nineteen Letters of Ben Uzziel* and *Horeb,* opposed religious reform, expressing belief in need for unending loyalty to Torah, and conception that, until advent of Messiah, Jews are not a people but group of believers performing obligations of written and oral laws. Ideologist of neo-Orthodoxy, continuity of traditional Orthodoxy in European culture. Translated Pentateuch into German with commentary.

Hirsch, Samuel (1815–1889), rabbi, philosopher of Judaism, pioneer of Reform movement in Germany and U.S. A founder of *Wissenschaft des Judentums.* Chief rabbi of Luxembourg until 1866; then in Philadelphia. First rabbi to advocate transfer of the Sabbath to Sunday. Interpreted Judaism as dialectically evolving religious system. Leading role in formulating Pittsburgh Platform.

Hirsch, Solomon (1839–1902), U.S. politician, merchant; emigrated fr. Germany to U.S. 1854. Founded major mercantile firm in Portland, Oregon. State senator, and Republican state chairman; U.S. minister to Turkey 1889–92.

Peretz Hirschbein with his wife and child, 1938.

Hirschbein, Peretz (1880–1948), Yiddish dramatist, novelist; b. Poland. Began writing plays in Hebrew but later turned to Yiddish. In U.S. fr. 1930. His folk dramas were staged with great success by N.Y. Yiddish Art Theater, esp. his pastoral romance *Grine Felder* ("Green Fields").

Hirschberg, Ḥaim Z'ew (1903–), Israel historian; b. Galicia. Rabbi in Poland 1927–39. Settled in Ereẓ Israel 1943. Prof. at Bar Ilan Univ. Major works: *Yisrael ba-Arav* ("Jews in Arabia") and 2-vol. history of Jews in N. Africa.

Hirschberg, Julius (1843–1925), German ophthalmologist. Wrote 9-vol. encyclopedic study of history of ophthalmology.

Hirschel, Levie (Louis; 1894–1943), Dutch bibliographer, librarian. Chief librarian of Bibliotheca Rosenthaliana 1930; specialist in Dutch Jewish history. D. Auschwitz.

Hirschel (Hershel), Solomon (1762–1842), first chief rabbi of Great Britain; son of Ẓevi Hirsch Levin. Basically European rabbi of old type, with imperfect knowledge of English and out of touch with new currents beginning to permeate community.

Solomon Hirschel

Hirschensohn, family of rabbis active in revival of settlement in Ereẓ Israel in 19th c. **Jacob Mordecai** (1821–1888), rabbi; settled in Ereẓ Israel 1848. Administered yeshivot in Safed and Jerusalem. His sons **Isaac** (1845–1896) and **Ḥayyim** (1857–1935), rabbis, scholars. Both supported Eliezer ben-Yehuda's efforts to revive spoken Hebrew and were attacked by zealots for their views. Isaac moved to London and Ḥayyim became rabbi in Hoboken, N.J.

Hirschensohn-Lichtenstein, Jehiel Ẓevi Hermann (1827–1912), Russian apostate, missionary. After working for Protestant mission in Berlin, returned to Russia disguised as ḥasidic rabbi. Distributed his book on Judaism, but had to leave Russia when his identity was discovered.

Hirschfeld, Ephraim Joseph (c. 1755–1820), German author. Active Freemason at time when organization was generally inimical to Jewish membership. Student of mysticism; his aspiration toward religious fusion of Judaism and Christianity within kabbalistic framework was close to spirit of Frankism.

Hirschfeld, Gustav (1847–1895), German archaeologist, specialist in Greek and Roman epigraphy. Directed excavations at Olympia 1875–77. Baptized.

Hirschfeld, Hartwig (1854–1934), scholar of Judeo-Arabic literature; b. Germany. Prof. at Jews' College and Univ. College, London. Chief interest: interplay between Arab and Jewish culture. Published edition and English translation of Judah Halevi's *Kuzari.*

Hirschfeld, Heinrich Otto (1843–1922), German historian. Succeeded Mommsen at Berlin 1885. Chief interests: Roman imperial administration and Roman Gaul.

Hirschhorn, Samuel (1876–1942), author, journalist; a leader of Polish Jewry between world wars. A founder of Folkspartei 1916 and member of Polish Sejm 1919. Wrote history of Polish Jewry, poems, translations. D. Warsaw Ghetto.

Hirshenberg, Samuel (1865–1908), Polish painter. Painted large historical canvases and many Jewish subjects ("Diaspora"). Taught at Bezalel School of Art in Jerusalem fr. 1907.

Hirshhorn, Joseph Herman (1899–), U.S. financier, mining executive, art collector. Financed uranium discoveries in Canada. Donated vast modern art collection to U.S. Government.

Hirszfeld, Ludwik (1884–1954), Polish physician, immunologist, serologist, microbiologist. Before WWII worked in Heidelberg and Warsaw. Escaped fr. Warsaw Ghetto. After war, taught at Wroclaw and introduced study of seroanthropology in Poland.

Ḥisda (c. 217–309), Babylonian *amora;* together with R. Huna described as "the pious men of Babylon." Early years spent in poverty, but became wealthy brewer and rebuilt Sura academy with his own money. One of most frequently quoted scholars in Jerusalem and Babylonian Talmuds, both in *halakhah* and *aggadah.*

Ḥisdai ibn Ḥisdai, Abu al-Faḍl (b. 1050?), Hebrew poet in Spain. Appointed vizier by king of Saragossa.

Ḥisdai (Ḥasdai) Ibn Shaprut (c. 915–c. 970), Spanish statesman at Cordoba. Practicing physician who was entrusted with diplomatic missions and appointed leader of Jewish pop. in Muslim Spain. In this capacity supported Jewish poets and rabbinic scholarship. Conducted (alleged) correspondence with Joseph, king of Khazars.

Ḥisin, Ḥayyim (1865–1932), Bilu pioneer in Ereẓ Israel; b. Belorussia, first went to Ereẓ Israel 1882, later resettled 1905. One of first doctors in young settlements. Representative in Ereẓ Israel of Ḥovevei Zion. A founder of first workers' settlements and of city of Tel Aviv.

Histadrut (abb. of Heb. *Ha-Histadrut ha-Kelalit shel ha-Ovedim be-Ereẓ Yisrael,* "General Federation of Workers in Israel"), Israel labor federation, founded 1920. Four

Histadrut headquarters in Tel Aviv

main fields: trade unionism, economic and cooperative activities, mutual aid, and education. Economic activities controlled through General Cooperative Assoc., Ḥevrat Ovdim. Important agencies incl. Solel Boneh (building and public works company), Tnuva (agricultural industry company), and Hamashbir Hamerkazi (cooperative wholesale society). Moshavim and kibbutzim affiliated through Ha-Merkaz ha-Ḥakla'i. Social services incl. Kupat Ḥolim (health insurance services). Women's activities organized through Mo'eẓet ha-Po'alot. 100,000 young people under 18 in Ha-No'ar ha-Oved ve-ha-Lomed. Sports activity in Ha-Po'el. Membership 1,161,000 (1972). Since 1960, 73,000 Arab and Druze workers admitted with full membership rights.

Histadrut ha-Ovedim ha-Le'ummit (Heb. "National Labor Federation"), organization of Revisionist workers founded in Jerusalem 1934. Incl. workers' sick fund, housing company, two cooperative building companies, and youth wing. Membership 80,000 (1973).

Histadrut Ivrit of America, U.S. organization founded 1917 to encourage knowledge of Hebrew language, literature, and culture. Publishes Hebrew weekly *Hadoar* (since 1927).

Hitaḥadut, Socialist-Zionist party, formed 1920 by union of Ha-Po'el ha-Ẓa'ir with majority of Ẓe'irei Ẓion groups in Diaspora. Active in C. and E. Europe. Supported foundation of Gordonia. Amalgamated with Po'alei Ẓion and formed Iḥud Olami 1932.

°**Hitler, Adolf** (1889–1945), Austrian-born founder and leader of German National Socialist Party (NAZI) fr. 1920 and chancellor of Reich fr. 1933. Using concept of race struggle to justify his program, implemented most systematic, widespread, and destructive anti-Semitic policies ever known. Until his death by suicide, considered incessant struggle against Jews supreme task incumbent on German people and thus ordered destruction of Jewish people. (See Holocaust.)

Hitschmann, Edward (1871–1957), Austrian psychiatrist who wrote psychoanalytical studies of outstanding literary figures. Founded 1922 and headed Vienna Psychoanalytical Clinic. During later years lived in U.S.

Hittites, ancient Indo-European people of Anatolia. Their empire was centered in Asia Minor and extended to Syria. After empire declined, small Hittite kingdoms remained. Bible has references to Hittites in period of monarchy. In other contexts, term is used for part of pre-Israelite population of Canaan.

°**Hitzig, Ferdinand** (1807–1875), German Protestant theologian, Bible critic. In his day considered one of leading Bible exegetes, noted for ingenious, often bold, textual and exegetical hypotheses.

Hitzig, Julius Eduard (1780–1849), German author, publisher, criminologist. Founded Mittwochgesellschaft 1824, which became center for late Romantics. Best remembered for his many crime anthologies and detective stories. Baptized.

Hivites, one of seven pre-Israelite peoples in Canaan. In patriarchal period dwelt at Shechem; later mentioned elsewhere. Suggested as general Hebrew term for Hurrians.

Ḥiwi al-Balkhi (9th c.), freethinker, radical Bible critic in Persia. Wrote polemical work (no longer extant) with 200 criticisms of Bible. Vehemence with which he was rebuked by Rabbanite (e.g. Saadiah) and Karaite scholars alike testify to his great influence.

Ḥiyya (also called **Rabbah,** "the Great"; 2nd c.), *tanna* of Babylonian birth. Pupil of R. Judah ha-Nasi; leading halakhist, enjoying status of both *tanna* and *amora.* His special method of exposition by transposition of letters was known as "the *Atbaḥ* of R. Ḥiyya". Responsible for collection of *baraitot* contained in Tosefta.

Ḥiyya bar Abba (TJ: **Bar Ba** or **Va;** 3rd–4th c.), *amora,* b. Babylon, moved to Ereẓ Israel. Appointed by Judah ha-Nasi II as emissary to Diaspora; visited many localities, instituting communal reforms. Essentially halakhist, but aggadic statements found in his name.

Hobsbawm, Eric John Ernest (1911–), British historian. Taught at London Univ. Wrote on British labor history and pre-industrial types of social agitation.

Hobson, Laura (Zametkin; 1900–), U.S. author; daughter of Yiddish writer Michael Zametkin. Best-known work *Gentlemen's Agreement,* novel on anti-Semitism in America.

Hochman, Julius (1892–1970), U.S. labor leader; b. Bessarabia, in U.S. fr. 1907. Became leader in International Ladies Garment Workers Union. Formulated programs for stabilization of garment industry. Devoted to maintaining N.Y. as dressmaking center.

Hochschule fuer die Wissenschaft des Judentums, center for scientific study of Judaism and rabbinical seminary in Berlin 1872–1942, developing principally but not exclusively into seminary for training rabbis and religious school teachers to serve broad spectrum of German Jewry. Published series of scholarly studies and served as forum for adult education during Nazi period.

The Hochschule fuer die Wissenschaft des Judentums.

Hodel, see Adel.

Hod ha-Sharon, semi-urban community with municipal council status in C. Israel; created 1964 by amalgamation of four villages: Magdi'el, Ramatayim, Hadar, Ramat Hadar. Pop. 13,000 (1971).

Hoenigswald, Richard (1875–1947), German philosopher; of Jewish origin. Prof. at Breslau and Munich; emigrated to U.S. after Nazis came to power. Contributions to history of philosophy.

°**Hoess, Rudolf Franz Ferdinand** (1900–1947), Nazi commandant of Auschwitz extermination camp fr. 1940. Constructed extermination camp at Birkenau and personally dealt with annihilation of 400,000 Jews. Arrested 1946, extradited to Poland, hanged in Auschwitz.

Hoff, Hans (1897–1969), Austrian psychiatrist; in U.S. during WWII. Prof. of Neurology at Vienna 1949, director of Vienna neuropsychiatric hospital, pres. of World Federation for Mental Health 1958–9. Conducted studies of anti-depressant agents and of insulin and drug therapy for schizophrenia.

CHRONOLOGY OF JEWISH HISTORY

B.C.E.		
c. 20th–17th cents.	The Patriarchs	
c. 17th–13th cents.	Hebrews in Egypt	
c. 14th–13th cents.	Exodus	
c. 13th cent.	Conquest of Canaan under Joshua	
c. 1200–c. 1020	The Judges; Philistines settle in Ereẓ Israel	
c. 1020–1004	Saul	
1004–928	United Kingdom (David and Solomon)	
	Kingdom of Judah 928–586	Kingdom of Israel 928–722
c. 871–c. 851		Elijah
c. 775–c. 750		Amos
c. 740–c. 700	Prophecies of Isaiah	
c. 732–725		Hosea
722		Samaria captured by Shalmaneser V
720		Sargon makes Samaria an Assyrian province. Mass deportation of Israelites
701	Expedition of Sennacherib against Hezekiah	
c. 627–c. 585	Prophecies of Jeremiah	
597	First expeditions of Nebuchadnezzar against Judah	
593–571	Prophecies of Ezekiel	
586	Destruction of Jerusalem and Temple; Mass deportation to Babylonia	
585?	Murder of Gedaliah, son of Ahikam, governor of Judah	
538	Cyrus' edict; First return under Sheshbazzar	
c. 522	Zerubbabel governor	6th cent. Canonization of the Pentateuch (in Babylonian Exile)
520–15	Temple rebuilt	
458?	Second return under Ezra	
445	Walls of Jerusalem reconstructed under Nehemiah; Ezra reads the Torah	
411	Destruction of the temple of the Jewish colony at Elephantine	
4th cent.	Canonization of the Prophets Section of the Bible	
332	Alexander the Great conquers Ereẓ Israel	
301–198	Ereẓ Israel under Ptolemaic rule	
mid-3rd cent.	Pentateuch translated into Greek in Egypt (Septuagint)	
198–167	Ereẓ Israel under Seleucid rule	
167	The Hasmoneans' revolt begins	
164	Judah Maccabee captures Jerusalem and rededicates the Temple	
152–63	Hasmonean rule	
63	Jerusalem captured by Pompey; Judea becomes a Roman province	
37 B.C.E.–4 C.E.	Ereẓ Israel under Herod's rule	
19	Temple rebuilt	

C.E.	
6–41	Judea, Samaria, and Idumea formed into a Roman province (Iudaea)
beginning of Ist cent.	Hillel dies; Beginning of the Tannaitic era
30	Jesus crucified; d. of Shammai
38	Anti-Jewish riots in Alexandria
40	Legation of Jews of Egypt led by Philo to Rome
66	Massacre of the Jews at Alexandria
66	Beginning of the revolt against Rome in Ereẓ Israel
c. 70	Destruction of the Qumran community
70	Destruction of the Temple
70	Sanhedrin established at Jabneh by Johanan b. Zakkai
73	Fall of Masada
c. 79	Josephus completes "Jewish Wars"
115–117	Revolt of Jews in Cyprus and N. Africa
132–35	Bar Kokhba war
135	Fall of Bethar; Aelia Capitolina established; Akiva executed
c. 135–138	Persecutions of Hadrian
2nd cent.	Canonization of the "Ketuvim" (Hagiographa)
mid-2nd cent.	Beginning of Exilarchate in Babylonia
c. 140	Sanhedrin at Usha
c. 170	Sanhedrin at Bet She'arim
c. 200	Sanhedrin at Sepphoris
c. 210	Redaction of the Mishnah; end of the Tannaitic period and the beginning of the Amoraic period
219	Arrival of Rav at Babylonia; Academy of Sura established
c. 220	d. of Judah ha-Nasi
c. 235	Sanhedrin at Tiberias
259	Academy of Nehardea moves to Pumbedita
325	Christian Church formulates its policy toward Jews
c. 359	Permanent calendar committed to writing
361–363	Julian the Apostate permits Jews to start rebuilding of Temple
c. 390	Jerusalem Talmud completed
425	Patriarchate (office of "Nasi") abolished in Ereẓ Israel
c. 470	Persecutions by the authorities in Babylonia
5th cent.	Beginning of liturgical poetry
c. 499	Babylonian Talmud completed
c. 500	End of the Amoraic period and beginning of the Savoraic period in Babylonia
525	End of Jewish kingdom in southern Arabia
589	End of the Savoraic period and beginning of the Geonic period in Babylonia
614–617	Jewish rule established in Jerusalem under the Persians
624–628	Jewish tribes of Arabia destroyed by Muhammad
638	Jerusalem conquered by the Arabs

c. 740	Conversion of the Khazars
762–67	Anan b. David lays the foundation of Karaism
860	Amram b. Sheshna compiles order of prayers
942	Death of Saadiah Gaon
10th cent.	Jewish cultural revival in Muslim Spain
beginning of 11th cent.	End of Khazar Kingdom
c. 1066	Jews settle in England
1089	Beginning of the Golden Age in Christian Spain (ending at the beginning of 13th cent.)
11th cent.	Commentaries of Rashi
1096	Crusaders massacre the Jews of the Rhineland
1099	Jerusalem captured by Crusaders
1103	Death of Isaac Alfasi
1144	First blood libel (at Norwich, England)
1168–90	Maimonides completes commentary on the "Mishnah" (1168); "Mishneh Torah" (1180); "Guide of the Perplexed" (1190)
1180	Beginning of Maimonidean controversy
1187	Jerusalem captured by Saladin
12th–13th cent.	Tosafot (France and Germany); Ḥasidei Ashkenaz
1210–11	Settlement of 300 French and English rabbis in Ereẓ Israel
1215	Fourth Lateran Council introduces the Jewish Badge
1240	Disputation of Paris
1242	Burning of the Talmud at Paris
1263	Disputation of Barcelona (Spain)
1267–70	Naḥmanides in Ereẓ Israel
c. 1286	Zohar in final form completed by Moses b. Shem Tov de Leon in Spain
1290	Expulsion from England
1291	End of Latin Kingdom of Jerusalem
1293	Death of Meir of Rothenburg
1298–99	Rindfleisch persecutions (Germany)
1320–21	Persecutions in France (Pastoureaux 1320; Lepers 1321)
1322	Expulsion from the Kingdom of France
1336–37	Armleder massacres (Germany)
c. 1340	Jacob b. Asher completes "Arba'ah Turim"
1348–50	Black Death massacres throughout Europe
1391	Massacres of Jews in Spain
1394	Expulsion of Jews of France
1413–14	Disputation of Tortosa
1415	Benedict XIII orders censorship of Talmud
1421	Expulsion from Austria (Wiener Gesera)
1475	Beginning of Hebrew printing
1480	Inquisition established in Spain
1492	Expulsion from Castile and Aragon; Sultans open gates of Ottoman Empire for refugees from Spain
1496–97	Expulsion from Portugal; mass forced conversion
1510–20	Reuchlin – Pfefferkorn controversy
1516	Venice initiates the ghetto
1516	Ereẓ Israel conquered by the Turks
1520–23	First complete editions of the Talmuds printed
1531	Inquisition established in Portugal
1532	Pseudo-Messiah Solomon Molcho burned at Mantua (Italy)
1538	Jacob Berab attempts to renew semikhah in Safed (Ereẓ Israel)
1538	Pseudo-Messiah David Reuveni dies in Portugal
1544	Luther attacks the Jews (Germany)
1553	Talmud burned in Italy
1554	Censorship of Hebrew books introduced in Italy
1555	Pope Paul IV orders Jews to be confined to ghettos
1558–60	The "Zohar" printed
1564	Joseph Caro's "Shulḥan Arukh" published
mid-16th cent.	Council of the Lands in Poland and Lithuania established
1569–72	Isaac Luria in Safed
1569	Expulsion from Papal States
1579	Death of Joseph Nasi
c. 1590	Marranos settle in Amsterdam
1614	Fettmilch attacks in Frankfort
1619	Death of Maharal of Prague
1623	Separate council for Lithuania established
1624	Excommunication of Uriel da Costa in Amsterdam
1648–49	Chmielnicki massacres in Poland
1654	Jews arrive in New Amsterdam (New York) and found congregation
1655–56	Massacres during wars of Poland against Sweden and Russia
1656	Baruch Spinoza excommunicated in Amsterdam
1656	Readmission of Jews to England
1757	Disputations with Frankists in Poland
1665	Shabbetai Ẓevi claims to be Messiah (Smyrna); Fervor spreads throughout the Jewish world
1700	Judah Ḥasid and his group arrive in Jerusalem
1726	Familianten Laws
1747	Death of Moses Ḥayyim Luzzatto
1760	Board of Deputies of British Jews established
1760	Death of Ba'al Shem Tov
1764	Council of The Lands abrogated
1768	Haidamack massacres in E. Europe
1772	First "ḥerem" on the Ḥasidim (Poland)
1777	Menahem Mendel of Vitebsk and his group of Ḥasidim settle in Ereẓ Israel
1789	Jewish equality recognized under lines of U.S. Constitution
1780–83	Publication of Moses Mendelssohn's "Biur"
1782	Joseph II's Toleranzpatent (Austria-Hungary)
1791	Pale of Settlement established in Russia
1791	National Assembly grants full civil rights to all the Jews of France

1797	"Tanya" of Shneur Zalman of Lyady published
1806–07	Assembly of Jewish Notables in France
1807	French Sanhedrin
1818	Hamburg reform temple consecrated
1819	Verein fuer Kultur und Wissenschaft des Judentums founded in Germany
1819	"Hep! Hep! " riots in Germany
1827	Cantonist legislation introduced in Russia
1837	Disastrous earthquake in Safed and Tiberias
1839	Entire community of Meshed (Persia) forced to convert to Islam
1840	Damascus blood libel
1841	"Jewish Chronicle" founded in London
1842	Compulsory military service for the Jews of Russia
1844	Autonomy of the "Kahal" abolished in Russia
1848	Emancipation in Germany
1852	Confirmation of "Status Quo" in Holy Places in Ereẓ Israel
1856	Cantonist legislation in Russia abrogated
1856	"Ha-Maggid," first Hebrew weekly, founded in Lyck (East Prussia)
1858	Lionel de Rothschild takes his seat in Parliament in England after amendment of Parliament oath
1858	Mortara Case
1860	Alliance Israélite Universelle founded in France
1862	Moses Hess publishes "Rome and Jerusalem"
1863	Society for the Promotion of Culture among the Jews of Russia founded
1870	Mikveh Israel founded
1870	Jews of Algeria granted French citizenship
1870	End of Jewish disabilities in Italy
1872	Hochschule fuer die Wissenschaft des Judentums opened in Berlin
1873	Union of American Hebrew Congregations founded
1875	Hebrew Union College opened in Cincinnati
1876	Heinrich Graetz completes "Geschichte des Juden:" Goldfaden establishes Yiddish theater
1878	Beginning of political anti-Semitic movement in Berlin (A. Stoecker)
1878	Petaḥ Tikvah founded
1881–82	Pogroms sweep southern Russia; Beginning of mass emigration to West Europe and U.S.A.
1882	"May Laws" in Russia
1882	Leon Pinsker publishes "Autoemanzipation"
1882	Beginning of First Aliyah (Bilu)
1882	Tiszaeszlar (Hungary) blood libel
1883	Beginning of Baron Edmond de Rothschild's help to Jewish settlements in Ereẓ Israel
1884–90	Zionist Conferences in Russia (Kattowitz 1884; Druzgenik 1887; Vilna 1889; Odessa 1890)
1885	Death of Sir Moses Montefiore
1886	Jewish Theological Seminary opened in New York; Death of Leopold Zunz
1888	Jewish Publication Society of America established; Death of Samson Raphael Hirsch
1891	Anti-Semitic members enter Austrian Reichsrat
1891	Immigration to Argentina with help of Baron Maurice de Hirsch (Jewish Colonization Association)
1893	Anti-Semites elected to German Reichstag
1894	First Dreyfus Trial in France
1896	Cairo Genizah discovered
1896	Herzl publishes "Der Judenstaat"
1897	First Zionist Congress convenes in Basle
1897	Bund founded in Vilna
1898	Zola's "J'Accuse"
1901	Hilfsverein der deutschen Juden founded
1903	Sixth Zionist Congress in Basle—Uganda project
1903	Pogrom in Kishinev (Russia)
1904	Va'ad ha-Lashon founded in Jerusalem
1904	Theodor Herzl dies
1904	Beginning of 2nd Aliyah to Ereẓ Israel
1905	Pogroms in Russia
1909	First Kevuẓah (Deganyah) founded; Ha-Shomer organized; Tel Aviv founded
1911–13	Beilis case in Kiev, Russia
1915	Zion Mule Corps formed in Alexandria, Egypt
1916	L. Brandeis appointed to U.S. Supreme Court
1917	Anti-Jewish laws abrogated in Russia
1917	Balfour Declaration
1918	Zionist Commission appointed; Visits Palestine
1919	Comite des Délegations Juives formed in Paris
1919–23	Third Aliyah to Ereẓ Israel
1919	Pogroms in the Ukraine and Poland; Abolishment of community organization and Jewish institutions in Russia
1920	Britain granted Palestine Mandate; Histadrut founded; Haganah founded
1921	Arab riots in Jaffa
1922	Churchill White Paper separates Transjordan from area of Palestine Mandate
1924	Technion opened in Haifa
1924–32	Fourth Aliyah to Ereẓ Israel
1925	Hebrew University in Jerusalem opened
1925–27	Hitler's "Mein Kampf"
1925	YIVO founded in Vilna
1928	Yeshiva College opens in New York City
1929	Jewish Agency expanded
1929	Arab riots in Jerusalem; Massacres in Hebron and Safed

1930	Passfield White Paper
1933	Hitler German Chancellor; anti-Jewish economic boycott in Germany; First concentration camps in Germany camps in Germany
1933	DAIA established in Argentine
1933–39	Fifth Aliyah; Immigration from Germany to Ereẓ Israel
1934	Birobidzhan — Jewish Autonomous Oblast
1935	Nuremberg Laws come into effect in Germany
1936	World Jewish Congress founded
1936–39	Arab revolt in Ereẓ Israel
1937	Peel Commission proposes partition of Palestine
1938	Racial legislation in Italy
1938	"Kristallnacht" economic ruin of the Jews in Germany
1939	MacDonald White Paper on Ereẓ Israel; Beginning of World War II
1939	United Jewish Appeal founded in U.S.A.
1940	Formation of ghettos in Poland
1941	Massacres by Einsatzgruppen in occupied Russia
1941	Expulsions from the Reich to Poland; first death camp established (Chelmno)
1942	Wannsee Conference (Germany) decides on the "Final Solution"
1942	Death camps in Poland begin to function at full capacity
1942	Biltmore Program
1942–44	Mass transports to Auschwitz from Belgium and Holland; Transports from all over Europe to death camps in East Europe
1943	Warsaw ghetto revolt; Annihilation of most of the ghettos of East Europe
1943	Germany declared "Judenrein"
1944	Beriḥah; Displaced Persons camps in Europe
1945	Death of Hitler; end of World War II; struggle against the British in Ereẓ Israel intensified

1946	Pogrom at Kielce; Nuremberg Trial
1947	UNSCOP; U.N. General Assembly decides on partition of Palestine;
1947	Beginning of Arab attacks in Ereẓ Israel
1947	Discovery of Dead Sea Scrolls
1948	Jewish culture in U.S.S.R. suppressed and intellectuals shot
1948	Proclamation of the State of Israel (May 14, 1948); Seven Arab states invade; Israel takes offensive; Mass immigration to Israel begins
1949	First Knesset opens: Chaim Weizmann first president of Israel; David Ben-Gurion prime minister; Ceasefire agreement with Egypt, Lebanon, Transjordan, Syria; Israel member of U.N.
1949–50	Airborne transfer of c. 50,000 Jews from Yemen to Israel
1950–51	Airborne transfer of 123,000 Jews from Iraq to Israel
1952	Prague Trials
1952	Reparations agreement between W. Germany and Israel
1953	"Doctors' Plot" in U.S.S.R.; death of Stalin
1954	Emigration from N. Africa
1956	Sinai Campaign
1960	Eichmann taken to Israel
1961	Lavon Affair; Eichmann Trial
1966	Shmuel Yosef Agnon and Nelly Sachs awarded Nobel Prize for Literature
1967	Six-Day War; Jerusalem reunited
1968	Emigration of most Jews remaining in Poland
1970	Russian Jews agitate for right to emigrate
1971	Russian Jews begin to emigrate to Israel in considerable numbers
1973	Yom Kippur War

Hoffer, Willi (1897–1967), Austrian psychiatrist. Member of Vienna Psychoanalytic Society, director of Sigmund Freud archives and pres. of British Psychoanalytic Society. Writings deal mainly with children.

Hoffer, Yehiel (1906–1972), Yiddish story writer, essayist, poet; b. Poland, spent war years in Russia, settled in Israel 1951. His fiction concentrates on ḥasidic world of Warsaw.

Hoffman, Benzion, see Ẓivion.

Hoffman, Charles Isaiah (1864–1945), U.S. lawyer, Conservative rabbi, journalist. First editor and publisher of weekly *Jewish Exponent*. A founder of Rabbinical Assembly and United Synagogue.

Hoffman, Dustin (1937–), U.S. actor. Achieved fame in *The Graduate*. Other films incl. *Midnight Cowboy, Little Big Man, Straw Dogs.*

Hoffmann, Camill (1878–1944), Czech poet, anthropologist, translator who wrote in German. Counselor at Czech embassy in Berlin and head of its press bureau 1920–38. D. Auschwitz.

David Ẓevi Hoffmann, etching by Hermann Struck.

Hoffmann, David Ẓevi (1843–1921), rabbi, scholar; b. Hungary. Rector at Rabbinical Seminary of Berlin 1899. German halakhic authority. Prolific scholar who pioneered critical investigation of halakhic Midrashim. Wrote commentaries on parts of Pentateuch. Attacked theory of Wellhausen.

Hofjude, see Court Jews.

Hofmann, Isaac Loew (1759–1849), Austrian financier; leader of Vienna Jewish community. Established manufacture of silk in Austria and was instrumental in development of potash industry. Ennobled as Edler von Hofmannsthal. In communal affairs concerned with charitable institutions and school system. His son converted to Christianity and his great-grandson, poet and playwright **Hugo von Hofmannsthal** (1874–1929) was remote fr. Judaism.

Hofstadter, Richard (1916–1970), U.S. historian. Taught at Columbia Univ. Wrote on American politics and education. His *Age of Reform from Bryan to FDR* won Pulitzer Prize.

Hofstadter, Robert (1915–), U.S. physicist. Headed dept. of physics at Stanford Univ. fr. 1954. Nobel Prize 1961 for work on atomic nuclei.

Hofstein, David (1889–1952), Yiddish poet. Lived in Kiev. Many of his works praise Soviet achievements (incl. Jewish settlement in Birobidjan). Shot with other Yiddish writers.

Ludwig Hollaender

Holdheim, Samuel (1806–1860), leader of Reform Judaism in Germany. As rabbi of new Reform congregation in Berlin 1847–60, introduced radical reform in ritual. Advocated separation of religion and ethical content of Judaism fr. political-national context.

Ḥolem, Hebrew vowel sign indicating long or short *o*. Written form ˙– or וֹ –.

Ḥol ha-Mo'ed, intermediate days of Passover and Tabernacles. During these periods, only essential work may be pursued, marriages are not performed, mourning is forbidden. *Hallel* (or half-*Hallel*) and Additional Service are recited. In modern Israel, occasion for pilgrimages to holy sites (esp. Jerusalem) particularly by Oriental Jews.

Holidays, see Festivals.

Holiness, see Kedushah.

Holiness Code, name designating collection of laws in Leviticus 17–26 with its appendix in Ch. 27, which, acc. to documentary hypothesis, constitutes particular division within so-called priestly source.

Hollaender, Felix (1867–1931), German theater critic, director, novelist. Succeeded Reinhardt as director of Berlin's Deutsches Theater, and later turned to criticism. His brother **Gustav** (1855–1915), violinist, composer, music teacher; director of the Stern'sches Konservatorium in Berlin 1895–1915. Another brother, **Victor** (pseud. **Arricha de Tolvens;** 1866–1940), composer, conductor who wrote successful operas, revues, farces. D. Hollywood. His son **Friedrich** (1896–), composer; wrote music for films, notably *The Blue Angel.* In Hollywood fr. 1934.

Hollaender, Ludwig (1877–1936), lawyer; leader of Centralverein deutscher Staatsbuerger juedischen Glaubens 1921–33, largest Jewish organization in Germany. Promoter of German Jewish national consciousness and fighter against anti-Semitism; engaged in running debate with Zionists.

Holland, see Netherlands.

Hollander, John (1928–), U.S. poet, literary critic. Taught at Yale 1961–66, Hunter College fr. 1966. Verse volumes incl. *A Crackling of Thorns* and *Verses from the Ramble.*

Holliday, Judy (Judith Tuvim; 1923–1965), U.S. actress. Won Academy Award for role in *Born Yesterday.* Other films incl. *The Solid Gold Cadillac.* Also appeared in Broadway musicals.

Holman, Nat (1896–), U.S. basketball player, coach; known as "Mr. Basketball." With Original Celtics 1921–29, CCNY coach until 1960. Helped develop game in Israel. Elected to Basketball Hall of Fame 1964.

Holocaust (Heb. *Sho'ah*), mass persecution and destruction of European Jewry during period of Nazi rule 1933–45. National Socialists under Hitler came to power advocating extreme anti-Semitic legislation which they immediately proceeded to implement. First weeks of Nazi rule saw beginning of exclusion of Jews fr. social and business life, burning of books by Jewish authors, boycott of Jewish businesses, etc. Anti-Semitic decrees were applicable to any person having Jewish grandparent. Anti-Jewish legislation was

ESTIMATES OF JEWISH VICTIMS DURING THE HOLOCAUST[1]

Polish-Soviet area[2]	4,565,000
Germany[3]	125,000
Austria[4]	65,000
Czechoslovakia (in the pre-Munich boundaries)[5]	277,000
Hungary, including northern Transylvania[6]	402,000
France[7]	83,000
Belgium[8]	24,000
Luxembourg[9]	700
Italy[10]	7,500
The Netherlands[11]	106,000
Norway[12]	760
Rumania (Regat, southern Transylvania, southern Bukovina)[13]	40,000
Yugoslavia[14]	60,000
Greece[15]	65,000
Total loss	5,820,960

[1] With few exceptions, there are no mathematically exact Jewish statistics in accordance with generally accepted scientific standards. Not even official censuses qualify for this distinction. With the exception of the Polish-Soviet area, the figures here refer to factual losses, which are much less than the Nazi-caused demographic deficit.

coordinated in 1935 Nuremberg Laws and extended to countries occupied by Germans (Austria, Czechoslovakia). Killing of German diplomat in Paris was pretext for massive anti-Jewish outbreak of November 9–10, 1938 (*Kristallnacht*) in which Jewish synagogues were burnt down, Jewish businesses looted, and thousands of Jews sent to concentration camps. Considerable proportion of German Jewry fled before outbreak of war. Invasion of Poland marked new degree of terror. It was followed by herding of Jews into ghettos and by mass-shootings executed by *Einsatzkommandos* set up by S.S. In 1941 decision was taken by Hitler to implement total extermination of Jews in all countries under his control (for which code name was the Final Solution). Arrangements were finalized at Wannsee Conference called by Heydrich. Responsibility for its implementation was given to Adolf Eichmann. Extermination camps were established at various places in E. Europe (Auschwitz, Treblinka, Chelmno, Belzec, etc.) and Jews were transported to these places and killed, generally by gassing followed by cremation of their bodies in mass incinerators. Selection was made of able-bodied Jews who worked in labor camps and labor battalions under slave conditions before being sent to their death. In some ghettos and camps (notably the Warsaw ghetto) Jews organized desperate resistance. Others managed to escape to join partisan units. Attitudes of local population were ambivalent. There were cases of active cooperation in killing of Jews and cases of non-Jews risking their lives to save Jews. Estimated number of Jewish victims during the Holocaust is almost six million. Most survivors left Europe as soon as possible after the war, the majority to Israel. Many of those responsible for the Holocaust received punishment at hands of post-war tribunals. The Holocaust resulted in the destruction of the European center which had been the focus of world Jewry for a thousand years. (See also Camps, Concentration and Extermination.)

Holocaust Remembrance Day (Heb. *Yom ha-Sho'ah*), remembrance day for victims of Holocaust and Ghetto uprisings, observed in Israel Nisan 27 (outside Israel April 19). For victims of Holocaust whose day of death is unknown Tevet 10 was fixed by Israel rabbinate as *Yahrzeit* ("memorial anniversary").

---

2 This figure was arrived at by the following calculations:

The Jewish population of the Polish area on the eve of the German invasion (Sept. 1, 1939) was (Polish Ministry of Information, London, *Concise Statistical Yearbook of Poland, Sept. 1939 to June 1941*, p. 10).	3,351,000
In the U.S.S.R. (boundaries of Sept. 1, 1939) the census carried the round figure of 3,020,000 Jews plus an estimated natural increase in the period between the date of this census (Jan. 17, 1939) and that of the German invasion (June 22, 1941) of 80,000	3,100,000
in Lithuania	155,000
In Latvia	95,000
In Estonia	4,000
In Bessarabia and northern Bukovina, calculated on the basis of the 1930 Rumanian census of 278,000 plus minimal results of natural and mechanical population movement	300,000
Total Jewish population in the Polish-Soviet area, Sept. 1, 1939	7,005,000
Jewish population in the expanded U.S.S.R. in 1959: this figure also includes the former Carpatho-Ukraine, annexed to the U.S.S.R. after 1945, but with hardly any Jews left. The figure represents the number of Jews who declared themselves as such. The number of "hidden" Jews, a phenomenon as relevant to the 1939 as to the 1959 census, or the number of persons of mixed marriages (Jew-gentile) and how they registered in the census under the nationality category, is a matter of speculation	2,268,000
The growth of the Soviet population from the end of the war to the 1959 census was 25 percent; the growth of the Jewish population, estimated to be ¼ below the general percentage, should have been, by the end of the war (S.M. Schwarz, *Jews in the Soviet Union 1939–1965* (1966), 171–2, notes 36–39 [Russian]).	1,910,000
This figure must be amended by the "repatriates" to Poland from the U.S.S.R. and survivors of this area in Poland, in the various DP camps, and scattered all over the globe	300,000
Total Jewish population in the area by the end of the war	2,210,000
Subtracting this figure from 7,005,000 leaves	4,795,000
The last figure represents the total demographic deficit of Jewry in the Polish-Soviet area. To calculate the deficit due to the Holocaust, one must subtract Jewish military casualties in the Polish Army	30,000
and estimated Jewish losses in the Red Army	200,000
Jewish Holocaust deficit	4,565,000

3 According to Bruno Blau (in *Jewish Social Studies*, April 1950, 161–72) there were some 118,000 Jewish victims of deportation in Germany during the period beginning May 1, 1941. To this figure some 7,000 more victims must be added: deportations prior to May 1, 1941 (from Stettin), and all other cases of violent death in Germany, particularly in German concentration camps. The round figure of 125,000 may be accepted as a minimal figure. Not included are German Jews who fled to European countries and were caught by the Nazis there (e.g., in Belgium, France, the Netherlands), and are included in the statistics of victims of those areas. The additional demographic deficit was 72,000 (H. Hoehne, *Der Orden unter dem Totenkopf*, 1966, 306).

4 Moser, in: *Widerstand, Verfolgung und Emigration*. Forschungsinstitut der Friedrich-Ebert-Stiftung (1967), 21–22. The additional demographic deficit

5 Adler, in: *Algemeyne Entsiklopedye*, vol. 7, p. 90.

6 Roth, *ibid.*, p. 141 (297,000 in Trianon, Hungary). In northern Transylvania there were some 150,000 Jews (*ibid.*, p. 344), of whom 45,000 survived (*ibid.*, p. 141). Total loss, 105,000.

7 Calculated on the basis of the deportee lists (Lucien Steinberg, *Les autorités allemandes en France*, Paris. Census, 1966, p. 173).

8 Billig, in: *Algemeyne Entsiklopedye*, VII, p. 212.

9 Billig, *ibid.*, VII, p. 220.

10 Robinson, *And the Crooked Shall Be Made Straight*. New York (1965), p. 251.

11 Presser, in: *Algemeyne Entsiklopedye*, VII, p. 262.

12 Mendelson, *ibid.*, VII, p. 290.

13 Calculated on the basis of Matatias Carp, *Cartea Neagra*, vol. III, 41–42, and *Pinkas ha-Kehillot*, Rumania, vol. 1 (1969), pp. קצח—קצט. The figure of 40,000 does not include Rumanian and northern Bukovina Jews who perished either by the march of the *Einsatzgruppen* in the Ukraine or in Transnistria. Nor does it include the victims of northern Transylvania which are included in item Hungary.

14 Alcalay, in: *Algemeyne Entsiklopedye*, VII, p. 367.

15 M. Molho and J. Nehama, *Sho'at Yehudei Yavan* (1965), 222.

Areas of Nazi persecution and extermination in Europe, 1939–45.

1. "Greater Germany," on Sept. 1, 1939, embraced Germany, Sudetenland, Austria, and the Protectorate of Bohemia and Moravia
2. General Government, occupied Poland not incorporated into Germany
3. Eastern Galicia, attached to U.S.S.R. in Sept. 1939, occupied by Germany in June 1941, and attached to the General Government in Aug. 1941
4. Western Polish areas incorporated into Germany
5. Lithuania (including Vilna region), incorporated into U.S.S.R. in Aug. 1940, occupied by Germany June 1941
6. Latvia, see Lithuania
7. Estonia, see Lithuania
8. Parts of Polish Belorussia, first incorporated into the U.S.S.R. in Sept. 1939, occupied by Germany in June 1941
9. Bialystok and Ciechanow regions under the authority of Erich Koch as "Gauleiter" of East Prussia
10. "Reichskommisariat" Ukraine, embraced former Polish Volhynia, the Pinsk region, parts of Soviet Ukraine, and Crimea
11. The U.S.S.R. areas under German military administration
12. Rumania minus ceded territories: Bessarabia, northern Bukovina and Transylvania
13. Bessarabia and northern Bukovina, ceded by Rumania to U.S.S.R. in June 1940, occupied by Rumanian and German troops in June 1941
14. Transnistria, under Rumanian administration
15. Slovakia minus area ceded to Hungary
16. Hungary enlarged by annexations
17. Bulgaria proper and southern Dobruja, ceded by Rumania
18. Bulgarian-occupied southern Serbia (Macedonia), Skoplje, Bitolj, Greek Macedonia, and Greek western Thrace
19. Northern Greece with Salonica, under German occupation
20. Southern Greece and the Greek islands, under Italian occupation from April 1941 and German occupation from Sept. 1943
21. Serbia proper and Banat, under German military and/or civilian administration
22. Northern Slovenia, under German civilian administration from April 1941, incorporated

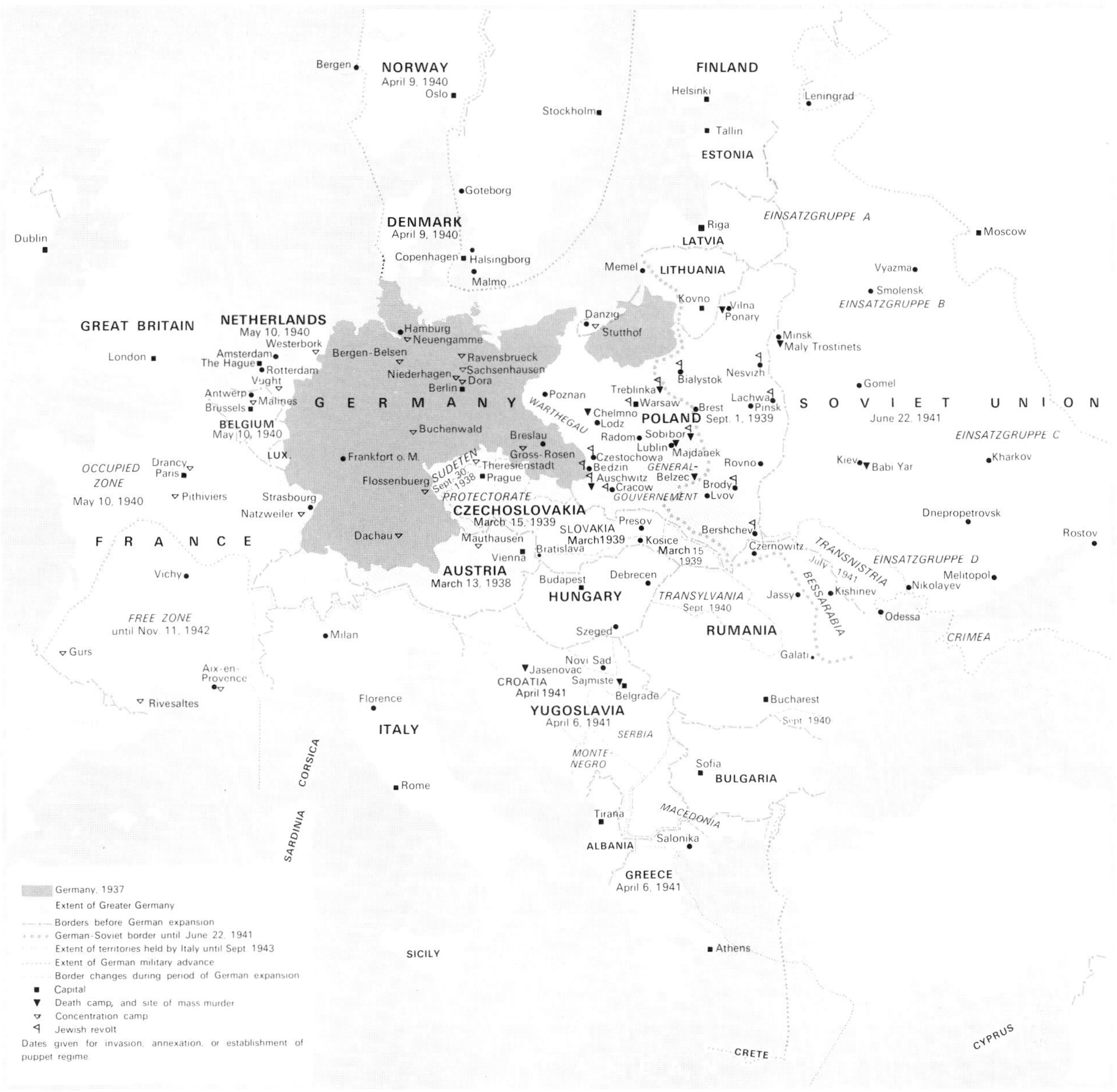

Europe during the Nazi period, showing political and military developments and main cities connected with the Holocaust.

---

into Germany on Oct. 1, 1942

23. "Independent" Croatia, including Bosnia and Herzegovina
24. Southern Slovenia, occupied and partly annexed by Italy
25. Dalmatia, part of Dalmatian Islands, and Montenegro, occupied by Italy
26. Italy
27. Belgium, under German occupation
28. The Netherlands, under German occupation
29. Luxembourg, occupied, later annexed, by Germany
30. Alsace-Lorraine, de facto annexed by Germany
31. France, occupied by Germany in June 1941
32. Vichy France, occupied by Germany in Nov. 1942
33. Southeastern France, occupied by Italy in Nov. 1942–Sept. 1943
34. Denmark, under German occupation
35. Norway, under German occupation

°**Holofernes,** army leader who besieged Jewish city and was beguiled and beheaded by Judith. Story is told in Book of Judith and is apparently fictitious.

Ḥolon, city in coastal plain of Israel nr. Tel Aviv; founded 1925. Expanded fr. 1949; major industrial center. Pop. 93,400 (1971).

Holy Places, places in Ereẓ Israel holy to three monotheistic religions (Judaism, Christianity, Islam). While veneration of these is ancient, historical authenticity of many is questionable. Struggle for possession of Christian holy places among various Christian groups assumed international importance and only "status quo" agreement of 1878 determined their de facto situation. After WWI, League of Nations empowered Mandatory authority to give access to members of three religions to their holy places, but Jewish rights were often disputed by authorities. After establishment of State of Israel most Christian and Muslim holy places remained in Jordan. After Six-Day War, Law for the Protection of Holy Places was passed in Knesset giving free access to these places, with management left entirely to spiritual heads concerned.

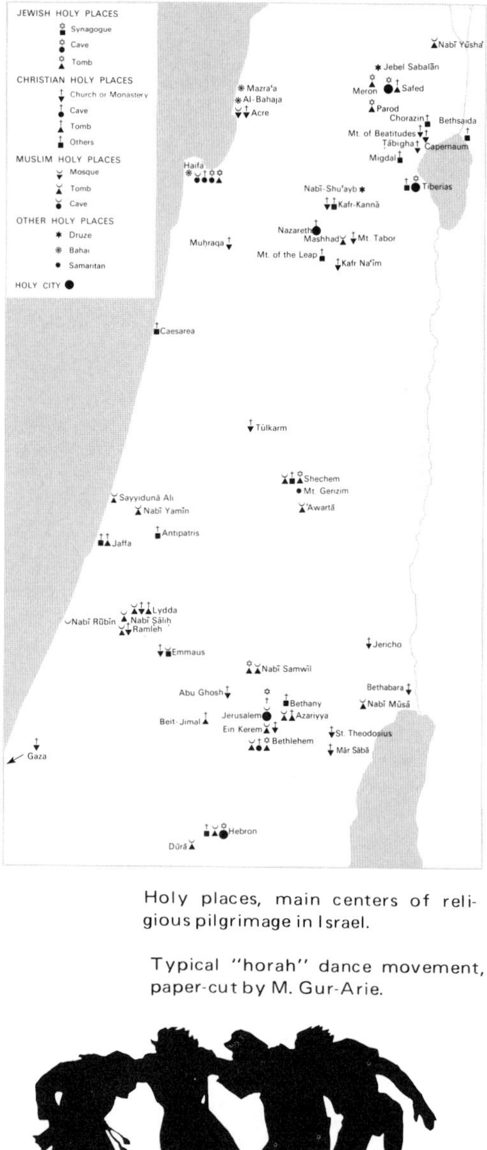

Holy places, main centers of religious pilgrimage in Israel.

Typical "horah" dance movement, paper-cut by M. Gur-Arie.

Ḥomah u-Migdal, see Stockade and Watchtower.

Homberg, Naphtali Herz (1749–1841), pioneer of Haskalah movement; b. Prague. Superintendent of German-language Jewish schools in Galicia and assistant censor of Jewish books. Advocated severe educational reform, forcing Jews to take up productive occupations, and prohibition or censorship of certain Jewish books. Incurred nearly universal hatred of Jewish contemporaries.

Homem, Antonio (1564–1624), Marrano martyr. Prof. of canon law at Univ. of Coimbra and leader of local secret Jewish community. Arrested by Inquisition 1619, perished in auto-da-fé in Lisbon.

Homolka, Oscar (1898–), actor. Played more than 400 parts in Austria and Germany by time Hitler came to power; then moved to England and appeared in plays and films.

Honduras, C. American republic. Some Jews there in colonial period. Modern community established by German Jewish refugees in 1930s. During WWII, Honduras consuls saved Jews by issuing passports and visas, often illegally. Emigration increased after 1947. 200 Jews in 1972.

Hong Kong, British crown colony in S. China. Jewish community established 1857, synagogue 1900. Jewish activities suspended during Japanese occupation in WWII. 200 Jews (mainly Sephardim) in 1972.

Ḥoni ha-Me'aggel, miracle worker in period of Second Temple; his name ha-Me'aggel ("circle drawer") is usually attributed to his refusal to move fr. circle until God answered his prayers for rain. Acc. to talmudic *aggadah,* once slept for 70 years. Grieved by subsequent inability to be recognized, prayed for death.

Honor, Leo L. (1894–1956), U.S. educator. Dean of Chicago College of Jewish Studies fr. 1929; director of Chicago Board of Jewish Education fr. 1934. Prof. of Jewish education at Dropsie College, Philadelphia. Organized National Council for Jewish Education.

Hoofien, Eliezer Sigfried (1881–1957), Israel banker; b. Holland. Deputy director of Anglo Palestine Bank in Ereẓ Israel (fr. 1949 Bank Leumi le-Israel) fr. 1912, director general 1924–47, chairman of board of directors fr. 1947. Directed financial affairs of *Yishuv* and prepared monetary system of Israel.

Hook, Sidney (1902–), U.S. philosopher. Prof. at NYU. Works deal with social and political thought and defend socialist form of political democracy. Books incl. *Reason, Social Myths, and Democracy* and *The Paradox of Freedom.*

Hophni and Phinehas, sons of Eli who served with him as priests in Shiloh. Abused their priestly privileges and corrupted sacred office. Killed on same day in battle between Philistines and Israel at Aphek.

Hor, mountain in Negev on border of Edom. During Exodus, first station of Israelites after Kadesh-Barnea. Burial place of Aaron.

Horah, best-known folk dance of pioneer Ereẓ Israel; derived fr. Rumania. Especially popular during Third Aliyah 1919–23.

Horayot (Heb. "Rulings"), short tractate attached to Mishnah order *Nezikin* with *gemara* in both Talmuds. Deals with problems resulting fr. erroneous rulings by high priest or Sanhedrin.

Horeb, see Sinai.

Hore-Belisha, Leslie, Lord (1898–1957), British politician. As minister of transport 1934, introduced illuminated beacons at pedestrian crossings ("Belisha beacons"). Secretary of state for war 1937–40, but resigned after attacked for democratization of army administration. Elder of Spanish and Portuguese congregation.

Horkheimer, Max (1895–1973), German sociologist. Taught in Frankfort (until 1933), Paris, U.S. Leading member of Deutsche Gesellschaft fuer Soziologie after war. Under his influence distinct school of sociological thought emerged.

Hormah, Canaanite royal city on border of Negev of Judah nr. Arad; identification disputed.

Hornbostel, Erich Moritz von (1877–1935), musicologist. Taught in Berlin (until 1933) and New York. A founder of ethnomusicology and major influence on formation of modern musicology. His regional researches incl. studies of music of Asian peoples.

Horner, Henry (1878–1940), Democratic governor of Illinois 1932–40; probate judge in Chicago 1914–32. Active in Jewish life.

Horodezky, Samuel Abba (1871–1957), scholar, historian of Jewish mysticism and Ḥasidism; b. Russia, lived in W. Europe 1908–38, then emigrated to Ereẓ Israel. Edited *Ha-Goren,* annual on Jewish scholarship; wrote monographs on great ḥasidim and famous kabbalists and their doctrines.

Horodno, see Grodno.

Horontchik, Simon (1889–1939), Yiddish novelist in Poland. His tales abound in strikes, riots, and pessimistic portraits of Jewish life in transition fr. stagnant villages to industrialized cities. Haunted by his fortuitous escape fr. Germans in 1914, committed suicide after Nazi invasion of 1939.

Horovitz, Josef (1874–1931), German orientalist. Taught in India and Germany and created dept. of oriental studies at Heb. Univ. Major work unfinished commentary on Koran.

Horovitz, Leopold (1838–1917), Hungarian painter. Subjects incl. Emperor Francis Joseph. Remembered chiefly for scenes fr. E. European Jewish life. *The Ninth of Av* is one of his notable works (see p. 51).

Horovitz, Marcus (1844–1910), Orthodox rabbi, historian, halakhist; b. Hungary. First Orthodox rabbi 1878 of Frankfort general community after Reform had eliminated all Orthodox institutions. Established Orthodox synagogues and institutions. Supported aid to *yishuv* but signed declaration of Protestrabbiner. Wrote on Jewish history and responsa.

Horovitz, Saul (1859–1921), Hungarian scholar of talmudic literature, medieval religious philosophy. Taught at Breslau rabbinical seminary. Contributed to Jewish and Islamic philosophical studies. Editor of midrashic texts.

Horovitz, Vladimir (1904–), pianist; b. Russia. Enjoyed great success in Europe and U.S., where he settled 1928. Married Toscanini's daughter. After 1953 appeared seldom but continued to record.

Horowitz, Abraham ben Shabbetai Sheftel (c. 1550–1615), Polish talmudist. *Dayyan* for province of Lvov. Initially favored teaching of Maimonides and general secular subjects. Later increasingly turned to mysticism. His ethical will, *Yesh Noḥalin* became popular ethical guide.

Vladimir Horovitz, drawing by Eugene Spiro, 1944

Horowitz, Aryeh Leib ben Eleazar ha-Levi (1758–1844), rabbi in Stanislav, Galicia, fr. 1784. Opposed Ḥasidism. Wrote responsa, homilies, novellae.

Horowitz, Aryeh Leib ben Isaac (1847–1909), Galician rabbi; known as "the Stryzer Rav." Main activities in yeshivah which he founded in Stanislav. One of few Galician rabbis to eulogize Herzl. Wrote responsa.

Horowitz, David (1899–), Israel economist; first governor of Bank of Israel 1954–71; b. Galicia. Active in Ha-Shomer ha-Ẓa'ir. In Ereẓ Israel fr. 1920. Directed Economic Dept. of Jewish Agency 1935–48. First director-general of Israel's Ministry of Finance. Wrote on international economic subjects.

Horowitz, Isaiah ben Abraham ha-Levi (Ha-Shelah ha-Kadosh; 1565? –1630), rabbi, kabbalist, communal leader. Officiated in various communities, incl. Frankfort and Prague. Of wealthy Moravian family; renowned for his charity. Fr. 1621 in Ereẓ Israel, active in strengthening Ashkenazi community. His *Shenei Luḥot ha-Berit* is work of kabbalistic tendencies in Jewish laws and customs. Buried next to Maimonides in Tiberias, where his grave is still visited.

Horowitz, Lazar (Eleazar) ben David Joshua Hoeschel (1803–1868), rabbi of Vienna. Advocate of communal harmony and Jewish political rights; campaigned against oath *more judaico,* took active part in 1848 revolution, and used his influence with archduchess Maria Dorothea to avert expulsion of several hundred Jewish families fr. Vienna 1851.

Horowitz, Phinehas (Pinḥas) ben Israel ha-Levi (1535–1618), talmudic scholar; leader of Cracow community. Headed Council of Four Lands fr. 1585. Wrote novellae on Talmud.

Horowitz, Phinehas (Pinḥas) ben Ẓevi Hirsch ha-Levi (1730–1805), German rabbi. Highly respected by scholars and community in Frankfort. Vigorous opponent of Haskalah and publicly denounced Mendelssohn's German translation of Pentateuch. Wrote *Sefer Hafla'ah* on Talmud, work of halakhic *pilpul.*

Horowitz, Samuel (Edler von) ben Isaiah Aryeh Leib ha-Levi (1836–1925), Galician financier, communal worker. Pres. chamber of commerce in Lemberg fr. 1906. *Maskil,* political representative of Jewish-Polish rapprochement, and a leading opponent of Zionism. Headed Lemberg "rescue committee" for refugees in WWI.

Horowitz, Shabbetai Sheftel ben Akiva (c. 1561–1619), author of kabbalistic works; physician in Prague. His writing based on ideas of Moses Cordovero. Main addition concerns his detailed exposition of the doctrine of *ẓimẓum* ("withdrawal").

Hort, Abraham (1790–1869), founder of Jewish community in New Zealand, where he hoped for extensive Jewish immigration. Although plans were not realized, and he returned to England 1859, he put Wellington community on firm foundation.

Horwitz, Phineas Jonathan (1822–1904), U.S. physician. Surgeon general during Civil War, later medical director of Bureau of Medicine and Surgery.

Hos, Dov (1894–1940), labor leader in Ereẓ Israel. A founder of Aḥdut ha-Avodah 1919, active in Histadrut and Haganah. Visited Britain to make contacts with Labor Party. Deputy mayor of Tel Aviv 1935–40. Brother-in-law of Eliyahu Golomb and Moshe Sharett. Killed with wife and daughter in road accident.

Hosea, Book of, 1st book of Minor Prophets in Bible; produced in Northern Kingdom of Israel shortly before death of king Jeroboam of Israel. Book falls into two parts: (a) Ch. 1–3 contains references to Hosea's personal experiences in marriage, relations with his unfaithful wife being interpreted as parable of God's relations with Israel; (b) Ch. 4–14 consists of brief oracles exposing corruption of nation and its leaders.

Hoshana Rabba (Heb. "The Great Hoshana"), seventh day of Sukkot. On this day seven processions are made around synagogue, after which five willow branches bound together are beaten. In post-talmudic times, day became supplement to Day of Atonement, special day of judgment on which God's decrees for coming year are finalized.

Hoshanot (Heb.), poetical prayers thus named because of recurrent expression "*Hoshana*" ("Save, I pray"). Recited on each day of Sukkot while circuit is made around synagogue. On seventh day seven circuits are made. *Hoshanot* is also name of special willow branches used on Hoshana Rabba.

Hoshea, last king of Israel 732–724 B.C.E. Initially Assyrian vassal; rebelled with aid of Pharaoh So. Shalmaneser V of Assyria imprisoned him.

Ḥoshen Mishpat, see Shulḥan Arukh.

Hospitality (Heb. *hakhnasat oreḥim*), virtue highly stressed in Judaism. Prototype seen in Abraham's reception of 3 "men" (Gen. 18). Medieval communities established associations to care for wayfarers.

Hoshana Rabba at the Amsterdam Portuguese Synagogue by Bernard Picart.

Harry Houdini.

Host, Desecration of, alleged profanation of wafer consecrated in Roman Catholic ceremony of Eucharist. Physical evidence for apparent "bleeding" of Host believed caused by fungus *Micrococcus prodigiosus.* Jews in many countries of Europe were accused of piercing Host to make it bleed and accusation served as pretext for persecution and massacres fr. 13th c.

Hostovský, Egon (1908–1973), Czech novelist, diplomat; in U.S. fr. 1948. Prominent Jewish assimilationist in youth, but novels preserved strong Jewish consciousness.

Houdini, Harry (Eric Weisz; 1874–1926), U.S. magician, escape artist. Began career at circus, later appeared in Europe and America. Became highest-paid and most popular performer of his time.

Hourwitz (Hurwitz), Zalkind (1740–1812), pioneer of Jewish emancipation; Jacobin during French Revolution. Wrote *Apologie des Juifs,* prize-winning essay containing self-deprecating description of Jews as debased by their own traditions.

Houseman, John (1902–), U.S. theatrical producer, director. Cofounded Mercury Theater with Orson Welles. Director of new drama division at Julliard School of Music, N.Y. 1965.

Houston, city in Tex., U.S. First known Jewish settler 1835. First synagogue (Orthodox) 1860. Community grew rapidly and by 1920 numbered 10,000. Ku Klux Klan activity during 1920s, 1930s discouraged Jews from entering civil and political life. Community grew after WWII. Jewish pop. 21,000 (1971).

Ḥovevei Zion, see Ḥibbat Zion.

Howard, Leslie (Leslie Stainer; 1893–1943), British actor. Famed for roles in *The Scarlet Pimpernel, Romeo and Juliet, Pimpernel Smith, Gone with the Wind.* Killed in plane shot down by Germans.

Howe, Irving (1920–), U.S. literary, social critic. Taught English literature at universities, wrote critical studies on writers in English language, and viewed literature in its social context. Coeditor of anthologies of Yiddish stories and poetry.

Huberman, Bronislaw (1882–1947), violinist; b. Poland. Child prodigy. Toured world. Founded Palestine Orchestra (later Israel Philharmonic Orchestra) 1936, assembling refugee musicians and raising financial backing.

H.U.C., see Hebrew Union College.

Bronislaw Huberman, lithograph by Eugene Spiro.

Hudson County, county in New Jersey, U.S. First Jewish congregation 1864 in Jersey City, second in Bayonne 1878. Immigrants fr. E. Europe in early 1900s. Jews first settled along Hudson River and gradually moved back into suburban setting of heights to west. Jewish pop. 12,000 in Jersey City, 8,500 in Bayonne (1971).

Huebsch, Adolph (1830–1884), rabbi, orientalist in Prague 1861–65, New York fr. 1865. His interest in liturgy led him to introduce moderate reformed ritual and to compose new prayer book, later adopted by many congregations. Edited Syriac Peshitta on Five Scrolls.

Huebsch, Ben W. (1875? –1964), U.S. publisher, editor-in-chief of Viking Press; son of Adolph Huebsch. Ardent anti-militarist during WWI and a founder of American Civil Liberties Union 1920. Later became U.S. representative to UNESCO.

Huesca (Osca), city in NE Spain. First information on Jews there after 1096. Community suffered during Black Death 1349; accused of stealing Host 1377 and some Jews burnt at stake. Oppressive measures increased in 15th c., culminating in 1492 expulsion.

°**Hugh of Lincoln** (d. 1255), alleged victim of ritual murder for which 18 Jews were executed. Regarded as saint, his alleged martyrdom is reverently mentioned by Chaucer in *The Prioress's Tale.*

Ḥukkat ha-Goi (Heb. "Law or custom of the gentiles"), term designating heathen customs of idolatrous (or superstitious) origin that Jews are forbidden to emulate. Proscription was long extended to gentile

The Ḥuleh Valley after swamp drainage, 1958

dress and fashion, although in most circles more lenient interpretation now prevails.

Huldah, prophetess in period of monarchy (II Kings 22:14 ff.). Consulted by Josiah concerning Book of Law discovered during restoration of Temple.

Ḥuleh, valley and former lake in NE Israel. Israelites under Joshua achieved control of valley except N. part, which remained unconquered until tribe of Dan settled there (Judg. 18). After division of monarchy, in kingdom of Israel. Under Persian rule held by Tyre. Conquered by Alexander Yannai. Augustus granted it to Herod in 20 B.C.E. and Jewish settlement was renewed. Belonged to Caesarea Philippi (Paneas) up to time of Arab conquest. Moslem Jewish settlements founded there fr. 1880s. After acquisition of Ḥuleh concession 1934, planned settlement was started. Drainage project of lake undertaken by Jewish National Fund 1951–58, with over 20,000 acres of highly fertile land reclaimed for intensive cultivation. Area of 750 acres set aside as nature reserve.

Ḥullin (Heb. "profane"), tractate of Mishnah order *Kodashim,* with *gemara* in Babylonian Talmud. Deals mainly with laws relating to ritual slaughter of animals for human consumption as distinct from sacrificial purposes.

Ḥummash (Heb. "Pentateuch"), Hebrew designation for first five books of Bible.

Ḥumra (Aram. "sternness"), legal term in talmudic and halakhic literature applied to stricter and more severe of two possible rulings in doubtful cases of ritual law and observance. (Its opposite is *kulla.*)

Huna (3rd c.), Babylonian *amora.* Numerous legal rulings are transmitted in Babylonian Talmud in his name, many details of his life and death are related, and descriptions given of his influence and piety. Presided over Sura Academy for more than 40 years. He and his colleague Ḥisda were called "the pious men of Babylon."

Huna ben (Bereih de-Rav) Joshua (4th c.), Babylonian *amora.* Frequently mentioned in Talmud together with Papa, with whom he studied and engaged in business. Founded yeshivah at Naresh, where he gave several decisions recorded in Talmud.

Hungary, C. European republic. Jews present fr. Roman times, but first written records fr. late 11th c. King Koloman protected Jews fr. crusaders. Jews expelled in Black Death 1349. Situation fluctuated thereafter bet. severe persecution and tolerance. Status of Jews under

Jewish communities in Hungary, 1910 and 1946.

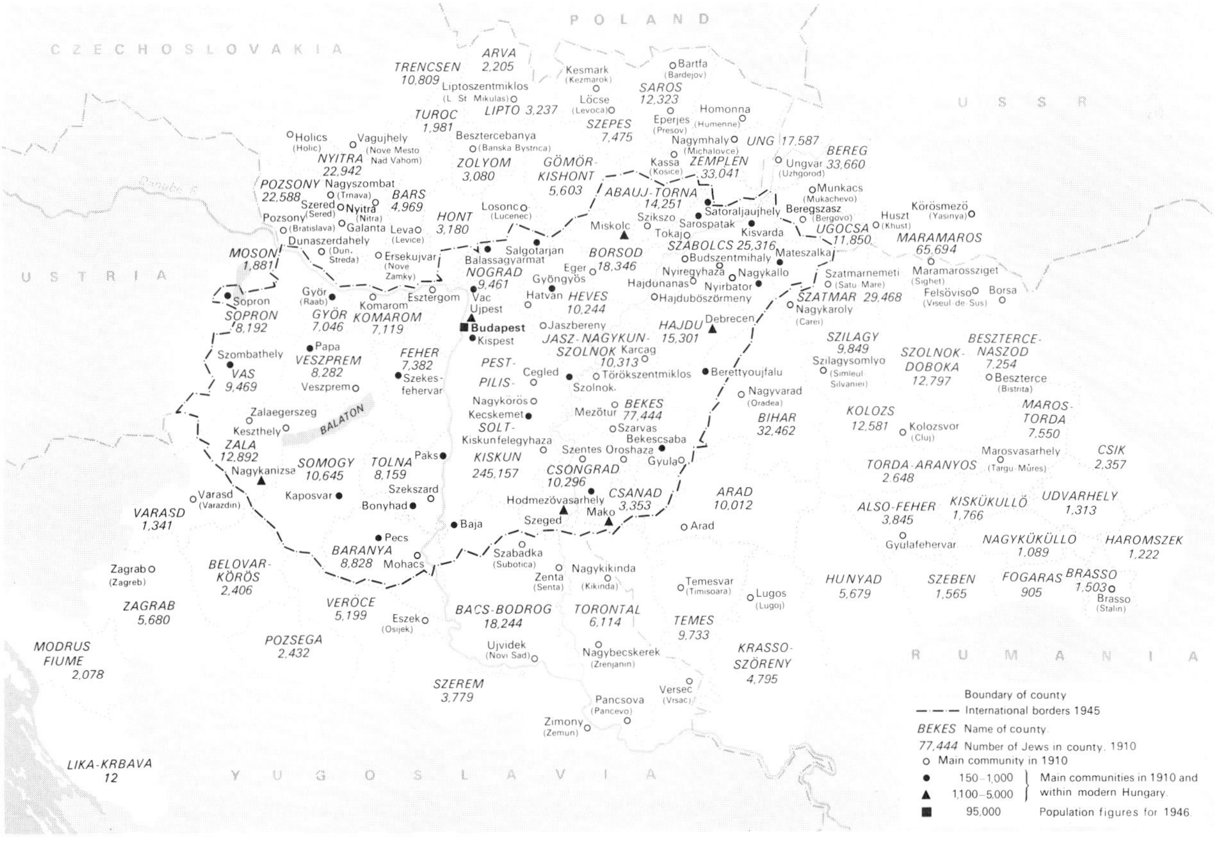

Drawing of the Jewish quarter of Mármores Sziget, Hungary.

Ottoman rule in C. Hungary satisfactory, but in Hapsburg areas hatred increased. Immigration started fr. late 17th c., mostly fr. Poland and Moravia. Jewish community paid annual "tolerance tax" fr. reign of Maria Theresa to end of 19th c. Community fined for participating in 1848–9 revolution. Jews finally emancipated 1867. Contributed greatly to both business (finance and industry) and intellectual development of country. Anti-Semitism emerged as political trend in 1870s; blood libel at Tiszaeszlar 1882. Internal life split by bitter polemics bet. Orthodox and Neologists (q.v.). Ḥasidism well established in NE regions. Many Jews participated in 1919 communist regime; suffered in subsequent "White Terror." Between WWI and WWII, anti-Semitic legislation restricted Jewish opportunities. 825,000 Jews in 1941; 565,000 killed in Holocaust. Jewish pop. 80,000 (1971).

Ḥuppah (Heb.), bridal canopy or bridal chamber; also wedding ceremony. In ancient times tent room of groom into which bride was brought at end of betrothal period. In talmudic times place of marital union. Fr. late Middle Ages, consisted of a cloth (or *tallit*) spread on four staves placed inside synagogue, but later it was moved to courtyard.

Hurok, Solomon (Sol; 1890–1974), U.S. impresario; b. Russia, in U.S. fr. 1906. Responsible for a brilliant array of musicians, dancers, etc.

Hurrians, Ancient Near Eastern ethnic group which spoke Hurrian, whose derivation and derivatives are uncertain. Kingdom was extensive, centered in Khabur Valley. Greatest influence in 15th–14th c. B.C.E. Called Horites and Hirites in Bible. Dwelt in Seir and C. Ereẓ Israel.

Hurst, Fannie (1889–1968), U.S. novelist. Wrote stories about New York's ordinary people. Several were made into plays and motion pictures. Best-known novel *Back Street.*

Hurwich, Louis (1886–1967), U.S. educator. Founded Boston Bureau of Jewish Education and Boston Hebrew Teachers College 1932.

Hurwitz, Henry (1886–1961), U.S. editor, Jewish educator. Founded Intercollegiate Menorah Association 1913 and *Menorah Journal,* which for many years was among the world's finest Jewish publications. Strongly opposed political Zionism.

Hurwitz, Stephan (1901–), Danish lawyer, criminologist. During WWII leader of Danish Refugee Organization in Sweden, and after war Dutch representative at War Crimes Commission. Elected ombudsman for civil and military administration 1955.

Hurwitz, Zalkind, see Hourwitz, Zalkind.

Hushai ha-Arkhi, see Levontin, Jehiel Joseph.

Hushai the Archite, court official under David. During rebellion of Absalom, remained faithful to David and frustrated counsel of Ahithophel (II Sam. 15 ff.).

Ḥushi'el ben Elhanan (10th–11th c.), talmudist; founder of talmudic studies in N. Africa. Under him, academy of Kairouan developed into center of Torah study. Introduced study of Jerusalem Talmud and stressed its importance (together with halakhic Midrashim) as source for establishing *halakhah.*

Husik, Isaac (1876–1939), historian of Jewish philosophy. Prof. at Univ. of Pennsylvania; editor of Jewish Publication Society. His *History of Medieval Jewish Philosophy* remained popular and useful.

°**Hussein (Hussayn bin Ṭalāl** (1935–), king of Hashemite Kingdom of Jordon fr. 1953; grandson of King Abdullah. His Arab Legion joined the Six-Day War 1967, as a result of which he lost E. Jerusalem and West Bank. Subsequently permitted terrorist activity fr. his territory but when it threatened to dominate his regime, he excluded them from his country by military action 1970.

°**Husseini, Hājj (Muḥammad) Amīn al-** (1893–), Palestinian Arab nationalist leader; b. Jerusalem. Sentenced to 10 years' imprisonment for role in 1920 riots, reprieved 1921 and appointed Mufti of Jerusalem; took active part in riots of 1929, directed riots of 1936, dismissed by Mandatory authorities fr. all duties 1937. Collaborated with Hitler in WWII. Continued anti-Israel activities after war but with diminished influence.

Hājj Amin al-Husseini with Hitler, WWII.

Husserl, Edmund Gustav Albrecht (1859–1938), German philosopher; founder of phenomenology. Taught at Halle, Goettingen, Freiburg. Converted to Protestantism 1886. An outstanding figure in 20th c. philosophy.

Hutner, Isaac (1907–), rabbinic scholar; b. Warsaw. Yeshivah head in Hebron (until 1929) and at Yeshiva Rabbi Chaim Berlin, New York, fr. 1939. Under his leadership, latter grew to prominence. Developed synthesis bet. Lithuanian *rosh yeshivah* and ḥasidic rabbi.

Ḥuẓpit ha-Meturgeman (2nd c.), *tanna;* "mouthpiece" (*meturgeman*) of Rabban Gamaliel of Jabneh. Acc. to midrashic tradition, one of Ten Martyrs.

Hyamson, Albert Montefiore (1875–1954), English civil servant, historian. Fr. 1921 Chief Immigration Officer in Ereẓ Israel, where his pedantic restrictions of Jewish immigration made him unpopular with Jews. Returned to England 1934. Published works on English Jewish history and edited *Dictionary of Universal Biography.*

Hyamson, Moses (1863–1949), rabbi, scholar; b. Lithuania. *Dayyan* in London 1902–11, acting chief rabbi of England 1911–13, taught at Jewish Theological Seminary 1915–40. Writings incl. commentaries on Jewish lore and English translation of Baḥya's *Ḥovot ha-Levavot.*

Hyatt, Abraham (1910–), U.S. space engineer. Chief scientist at U.S. Navy Bureau of Aeronautics 1956, director of program plans and evaluation at NASA 1960.

Hyksos, dynasty of Asiatics who exercised political control over Egypt c. 1635–1570 B.C.E. During their rule children of Israel entered Egypt. Their domination over Egypt must have been preceded by control over Ereẓ Israel, and their expulsion was toward S. Ereẓ Israel.

Hyman, Aaron (1862–1937), Russian-born London rabbi, scholar. Fr. 1933 in Tel Aviv. Published biographical dictionary of sages of Talmud and index of biblical references in Talmud, Midrash, and early rabbinic literature.

Hymans, Paul (1865–1941), Belgian statesman, son of Jewish father and Protestant mother. Four times foreign minister of Belgium and president of League of Nations Assembly.

Hypsistarians, semi-Jewish sect whose members lived on Bosphorus in 1st c. Observed Sabbath and some dietary laws but entertained pagan awe for fire and light, earth and sun.

Hyrcania, Judean fortress, probably built by Hasmonean ruler John Hyrcanus and named after him. A principal fortress of Herod.

Hyrcanus II (c. 103–30 B.C.E.), elder son of Alexander Yannai and Salome Alexandra. Appointed high priest during mother's lifetime, but lost both title and power to brother Aristobulus 67 B.C.E. Pompey appointed him high priest of truncated state 65 B.C.E. Ultimately lost all power to house of Antipater.

Hyrcanus, John (Johanan), ethnarch of Judea and high priest 135–104 B.C.E.; son of Simeon the Hasmonean. Most successful and energetic of rulers of Hasmonean dynasty fr. point of view of consolidation and territorial expansion of Judea. Achieved complete independence of Judea, undertook extensive conquests, and maintained ties of friendship with Rome. Defeated Samaritans, destroyed their temple, and compelled Idumeans to embrace Judaism. In domestic affairs, his early inclinations toward Pharisees were eventually replaced by friendship toward the Sadducees.

Hyrcanus son of Joseph (2nd c. B.C.E.), youngest and reputedly cleverest son of Joseph son of Tobiah. After obtaining contract for tax farming in place of his father, led the Ptolemaic faction and attempted to uphold Egyptian authority. His brothers, supported by high priest, supported Seleucids. After fratricidal battle, left Jerusalem for Transjordan, where he committed suicide c. 175 B.C.E.

Initial letter "I" for "In Anno" at beginning of Book of Ezra in the Latin "Bible of Citeaux," c. 1109. The letter is formed by figure of scribe holding scroll.

Ibn . . ., see also under proper names.

Ibn Abitur, Joseph ben Isaac (10th–11th c.), Spanish talmudic scholar, poet. Forced to leave Cordoba; visited Babylon, Ereẓ Israel, Egypt. Some 300 of his *piyyutim* are known. Also wrote responsa and commentaries.

Ibn Abi Zimra, David, see David ben Solomon ibn Abi Zimra.

Ibn 'Ādiyā, Al-Samaw'al, see Samuel ibn 'Adiya.

Ibn Adret, see Adret.

Ibn Aknin, see Aknin.

Ibn Bal'am, Judah ben Samuel (11th c.), biblical commentator, Hebrew grammarian. Came fr. Toledo and settled in Seville. Analyzed Bible text grammatically and made comparisons with Arabic. Greatly influenced later commmentators, esp. Abraham ibn Ezra.

Ibn Barun, Abu Ibrahim Isaac ben Joseph ben Benveniste (c. 1100), Hebrew grammarian, lexicographer. Lived in Saragossa and Málaga and associated with Moses ibn Ezra and Judah Halevi. His Hebrew and Arabic verse has not survived. Developed comparative linguistic studies.

Ibn Biklārish, Junas (Jonah) ben Isaac (11th c.), Spanish physician, authority on *materia medica.* His Arabic pharmacological treatise was used by Maimonides in his *Glossary of Medicines.*

Ibn Danan, see Abendanan.

Ibn Daud, Abraham, see Abraham ben David of Posquières.

Ibn Daud, Abraham ben David Halevi (Rabad; c. 1100–1180), Spanish historian, philosopher, physician, astronomer. Greatly influenced by Avicenna; first purely Aristotelian Jewish philosopher. Main philosophical work *Emunah Ramah.* Also wrote histories of Second Temple, Rome, and talmudic scholarship *(Sefer ha-Kabbalah),* which is of special importance for history of Spanish Jewry. Martyred at Toledo.

Ibn Ezra, Abraham (1089–1164), Spanish poet, grammarian, biblical commentator, philosopher, astronomer, physician. After 1140 lived life of wandering scholar, visiting Italy, France, England, and perhaps Ereẓ Israel. Almost all his extant writings, which are in Hebrew, date fr. period of his travels. Much of his penitential poetry has been incorporated into liturgy; and his Bible commentaries excel in depth and clarity of thought. Also tackled grammatical and philosophical problems, and wrote several studies on astrology.

Ibn Ezra, Isaac (12th c.), Hebrew poet in Near East; son of Abraham Ibn Ezra. Probably converted to Islam.

Ibn Ezra, Moses ben Jacob (c. 1055–after 1135), Spanish Hebrew poet, philosopher; best known for his impressive corpus of *seliḥot.* Early patron and firm friend of Judah Halevi. His later life was embittered by Almoravides' capture of Granada, disappointments caused by his own family, and his forced wandering through Christian Spain. Wrote secular as well as religious verse, treatise on rhetoric and poetry, one of earliest works on Hebrew poetics, and philosophical Neo-Platonic book written in Arabic.

Ibn Gabirol, see Gabirol.

Ibn Gaon, Shem Tov ben Abraham (13th–14th c.), kabbalist, halakhist in Safed; b. Spain. Wrote *Migdal Oz,* commentary on *Mishneh Torah* of Maimonides, first systematic attempt to determine latter's sources.

Ibn Ghayyat (Ghiyyat), Isaac ben Judah (1038–1089), halakhic authority, commentator, poet, yeshivah head in Lucena. His halakhic works are often only source for many quotations fr. works of *geonim.* His *piyyutim* incl. complete *ma'amad* (special prayer) for Day of Atonement.

Ibn Gikatilla, see Gikatilla.

Ibn Ḥabib, see also Ḥabib.

Ibn Ḥabib, Jacob ben Solomon (1445? –1515/16), rabbinic scholar in Spain, Portugal, and probably Salonika, where he constituted yeshivah, was active in communal affairs, and attempted to solve problems arising fr. expulsion fr. Spain. In his famous *Ein Ya'akov* assembled *aggadot* of Babylonian Talmud and some of Jerusalem Talmud and supplied a commentary.

Ibn Ḥabib, Levi (Ralbaḥ; c. 1483–1545), rabbi in Jerusalem, principal opponent of restoration of ordination; son of Jacob ibn Ḥabib. Forcibly baptized in his youth in Portugal, educated in Salonika, later settling in Ereẓ Israel. As rabbi of Jerusalem, refused to accept Jacob Berab's authority to restore ancient *semikhah.* Wrote responsa and halakhic commentaries, and completed his father's *Ein Ya'akov.*

Ibn Ḥasan, Jekuthiel ben Isaac (d. 1039), statesman, philanthropist. Filled important post in one of Muslim princedoms in Spain. Also held key position in Jewish community. Patron of Solomon ibn Gabirol. Deposed and executed on what was later revealed to be false charge.

Ibn Ḥasdai, Abraham ben Samuel ha-Levi (13th c.), translator, Hebrew poet in Barcelona. One of Mai-

HOSHANA The *Hoshana* prayer, recited on the Feast of Tabernacles, in the *Rothschild Miscellany*, Ferrara, c. 1470.

Landscape in Galilee.

ISRAEL

View of the Dead Sea and the Moab Plateau.

monides' staunchest adherents. His adaptation of Arabic text of *Barlaam and Josaphat* became popular in medieval times.

Ibn Ḥayyim, Aaron (ben Abraham; 1545–1632), rabbi, commentator; b. Fez, traveled extensively in Mediterranean lands, finally settled in Jerusalem. Wrote extensive expositions of *Sifra* which were largely responsible for text becoming subject of study.

Ibn Ḥayyim, Abraham ben Judah (mid-15th c.), author of treatise on art of ms. illumination, written in Portuguese with Hebrew characters. Most important extant document in medieval Judeo-Portuguese.

Ibn Hayyim, Joseph (15th c.), ms. illuminator. Illuminated Kennicott Bible.

Ibn Janāḥ, Jonah (11th c.), Spanish Hebrew grammarian, Hebrew lexicographer; lived in Córdoba and Saragossa. His most important work *Kitāb al-Tanqīs* (translated as *Sefer ha-Dikduk*) is first complete book on Hebrew philology to be preserved in its entirety. Incl. alphabetic list of Hebrew roots.

Ibn Jau, Jacob (d.c. 990), wealthy silk merchant and manufacturer, philanthropist, *nasi* (leader) of Jews in Muslim Spain.

Ibn Kammūna, Sa'd ibn Manṣūr (c. 1215–1285), philosopher, probably oculist; lived in Baghdad. Wrote compendium of interfaith polemics and tract on differences between Rabbanites and Karaites.

Ibn Killis, Abu al-Faraj Ya'qub ibn Yūsuf (930–991), businessman, administrator for various Egyptian rulers. In hope of becoming vizier converted to Islam and directed Fatimid invasion of Egypt. As vizier 977, reorganized entire administrative system of the Fatimid caliphate.

Ibn Labi, see Labi.

Ibn Latif, see Latif.

Ibn Migash, Joseph ben Meir ha-Levi (1077–1141), greatest Spanish talmudic scholar of third generation of Spanish rabbis; head of Lucena yeshivah for 38 years. Admired by Maimonides and Judah Halevi and his works (few of which are extant) decisively influenced study of Talmud in Spain and Provence. Wrote responsa and commentaries.

Ibn Motot, Samuel ben Saadiah (or **Matut, Matud;** fl. c. 1370), philosopher, kabbalist, translator in Spain. Works incl. numerous philosophical and kabbalistic speculations and reveal erudition in Jewish and Arabic philosophy, although little originality in ideas.

פירוש על פירוש החכם רבי

בויניציאה

Title page of "Megillat Setarim" by Samuel ibn Motot, Venice, 1553.

Ibn Paquda, Baḥya, see Baḥya ben Joseph ibn Paquda.

Ibn Paquda (Pakuda, Bakoda), David ben Eleazar (12th c.), Spanish Hebrew poet. Numerous liturgical poems by him have been preserved and printed in various *maḥzorim.*

Ibn Pollegar, see Pollegar.

Ibn Plat, Joseph (12th c.), rabbi in Spain and Provence. Best-known responsa deal with institution of blessings. Later headed yeshivah in Damascus.

Ibn Quraysh, Judah (9th c.), Hebrew grammarian, lexicographer; physician in Algeria. Among founders of comparative Semitic linguistics. Recognized similarity in vocabulary and grammatical structure of Hebrew, Aramaic, and Arabic.

Ibn Sahula, see Sahula.

Ibn Sa'īd (Sid), Isaac (13th c.), Spanish astronomer. Among compilers of "Alfonsine Tables" for Alfonso X. Extant records in his handwriting of his observations of lunar eclipses testify to his versatility.

Ibn Saqāwayh (10th c.), Karaite scholar in Babylonia or neighboring country. Collected legends fr. Talmud and *midrashim* which he considered curious. His allegations were answered by Saadiah Gaon.

Ibn Saruq, Menahem, see Menahem ben Jacob ibn Saruq.

Ibn Shaprut, Ḥisdai, see Ḥisdai ibn Shaprut.

Ibn Shem Tov, family of Spanish rabbis, philosophers. **Shem Tov** (c. 1380–c. 1441), rabbi, kabbalist, anti-Maimonidean polemicist. *Sefer ha-Emunot* held Maimonidean Aristotelianism responsible for facilitating apostasy. Despite his zeal, unsuccessful in winning many adherents to his fideism. Wrote on Kabbalah and commentary on *Avot.* His son **Ibn Shem Tov, Isaac ben Shem Tov** (15th c.), Spanish rabbi, philosopher. Taught philosophy in Castile and was erudite and prolific writer in Hebrew on Aristotelian themes. His other son **Joseph b. Shem Tov** (c. 1400–c. 1460), philosopher whose service in Castilian court enabled him to debate religious and philosophical questions with Christian scholars. Fell into disfavor c. 1456 and, increasingly blind, wandered around Spain. His philosophical system represents compromise between Aristotelian-Maimonidean rationalism and anti-philosophical tendency. His son, **Shem Tov b. Joseph b. Shem Tov** (15th c.), rabbi, philosopher, preacher. Vigorous defender of Aristotelian and Maimonidean philosophy. His commentary to *Guide of the Perplexed* printed in most Hebrew editions.

Ibn Shuaib, Joel (15th c.), rabbi, preacher in Spain. His sharp criticism of Marranos caused many of them to return to Jewish faith. Wrote sermons and commentary on Bible.

Ibn Shuaib, Joshua (14th c.), Spanish scholar. Known for his collection of weekly sermons on Pentateuch. Urged observance of precepts, attendance at synagogue, and recourse to Jewish law courts.

Ibn Susan, Issachar ben Mordecai (16th c.), Moroccan mathematician; eventually settled in Safed. Wrote on rituals to be followed acc. to yearly variations of Jewish calendar and apportioning of *haftarot* acc. to rites of different communities.

Ibn Tamim, Dunash, see Dunash ibn Tamim.

Ibn Tibbon, see Tibbon.

Ibn Verga, Solomon (15th–16th c.), historiographer; b. Spain, lived in Portugal, Rome. Wrote *Shevet Yehudah,* account of persecutions undergone by Jews; of special importance in annals of Jewish historical thought. His critical and empirical approach to phenomena of history made him herald of new era in Jewish historiography. His son **Joseph** (d.c. 1559), Turkish scholar, rabbi, *dayyan* in Adrianople. His writings incl. accounts of contemporary events and work on talmudic principles. Wrote addition to his father's *Shevet Yehudah.*

Ibn Waqar, Samuel (14th c.), physician, astronomer, director of mint in service of Alfonso XI of

Castile. Tortured to death after falling fr. power.

Ibn Waqar, Joseph ben Abraham (14th c.), Spanish philosopher, kabbalist. In his chief work attempted to reconcile philosophy and astrology with Kabbalah.

Ibn Yaḥya, David ben Solomon (c. 1440–1524), grammarian, Bible commentator in Portugal, Turkey. Wrote biblical commentaries, works on grammar and *halakhah,* and commentary on Maimonides' *Guide.*

Ibn Yaḥya (or **ibn Yiḥyah**), **Gedaliah ben Joseph** (1515–1587), historiographer, talmudist in Italy. His *Shalshelet ha-Kabbalah,* history fr. Creation to author's day, became one of most famous Hebrew chronicles and was used by later Hebrew historiographers. Also incorporates scientific tractates.

Ibn Yashush, Isaac Abu Ibrahim (d. 1056), Hebrew grammarian, Bible commentator; b. Toledo. Court physician of ruler of Denia. Wrote Bible commentary and was regarded in medieval times as one of greatest Hebrew grammarians.

Ibn Zabara, Joseph ben Meir (b.ca. 1140), physician, Hebrew writer in Barcelona. His *Sefer Sha'ashu'im* contains stories and proverbs within narrative framework. Reveals considerable knowledge of Talmud and shows Greek, Italian, and Arabic influence.

Ibn Ẓaddik, Joseph, see Ẓaddik, Joseph ben Jacob ibn.

Ibrahim ibn Sahl al-Andalusī al-Isra'ili (1208–1260?), poet, author of Judeo-Spanish origin; one of greatest Spanish Arabic poets. Most of his verse is dedicated to a Jewish youth Mūsā (Moses). Converted to Islam late in life.

Ibrahim ibn Ya'qūb of Tortosa (10th c.), traveler. Possibly slave merchant; visited France, Germany, E. Europe, and was first to speak of kingdom of Poland.

I.C.A., see Jewish Colonization Association.

Idaho, state in U.S. Jews settled during gold-rush days 1865. First Jewish congregation (Reform) organized in Boise 1895 by Moses Alexander, later mayor and governor. Jewish pop. 630 (1971).

Idelovitch, David (1863–1953), pioneer of settlement and education in Ereẓ Israel; b. Rumania, joined Bilu pioneers 1882. Became early Hebrew educator in Rishon le-Zion. Edited children's newspaper. Among founders of Carmel Wine-Growers' Cooperative, which he represented in Egypt 1906–24.

Abraham Zvi Idelsohn

Idelsohn, Abraham Zvi (1882–1938), musicologist; b. Russia, settled in Jerusalem 1906. Worked there as cantor, music teacher, bandmaster. In U.S. fr. 1922, teaching at Hebrew Union College, Cincinnati. Went to S. Africa 1937. Studied melodies of Jewish oriental communities, biblical cantillation, prayer melodies. Publications incl. 10-vol. *Thesaurus of Hebrew Oriental Melodies* and *Jewish Music.*

Idelson, Abraham (1865–1921), Zionist theoretician, publicist, editor; b. Lithuania. Wrote widely on aspects of Jewry and Zionism, edited Zionist weekly *Ha-Olam* 1919–20. Originated the 1906 Helsingfors Program. D. Berlin.

Idelson, Beba (neé **Trachtenberg;** 1895–), Israel labor leader. A founder and general-secretary of Mo'eẓet ha-Po'alot fr. 1930; member of Knesset fr. 1949; deputy speaker 1955–61.

I.D.F., see Israel Defense Forces.

Idi bar Avin (4th c.), Babylonian *amora.* Known as one of great scholars of Babylon of his time. Influenced establishment of talmudic *halakhah.*

Idumea, see Edom.

Iggeret ha-Kodesh (Heb. "Holy Epistle"), anonymous 13th c. kabbalistic work; first popular work in which kabbalistic teachings are applied to everyday behavior. Book's six chapters give particular emphasis to way in which pious Jew should conduct sexual intercourse with his wife.

Ignatoff, David (1885–1954), Yiddish novelist, dramatist; b. Ukraine, in U.S. fr. 1906. Alternated bet. colorful romanticism and radical realism. His *Dos Farborgene Likht* based on narrations of R. Naḥman of Bratslav; fiction trilogy *Oyf Vayte Vegen* describes rise of American Jewish labor movement.

Ignotus, Hugo (pen name of **Hugó Veigelsberg;** 1869–1949), Hungarian author, journalist, critic. Established modern Hungarian school of aesthetic criticism and was pioneer in literary exploitation of psychoanalysis. Left Hungary 1919, but returned shortly before his death.

Igra, Meshullam (Moses) ben Samson (c. 1752–1802), Galician, Hungarian rabbi. Preached in large synagogue of Brody when only 9 and was appointed rabbi of Tysmenitsa when 17. Opponent of Ḥasidism and renowned halakhist. His works are written in difficult, terse style.

Iḥud, see Berit Shalom.

Iḥud Habonim, largest youth movement of Labor Zionist movement, founded 1958 with headquarters in Israel. Amalgamation of various youth movements around the world. Founded organizations in Germany, Canada, U.S., Britain, Latin America, S. Africa, Australia. Movement graduates established over 20 kibbutzim in Israel with 20,000 members.

Iḥud ha-Kevutzot ve-ha-Kibbutzim, federation of kibbutzim founded 1951 by merger of Mapai-oriented kibbutzim which had seceded fr. Ha-Kibbutz ha-Meuḥad with union of settlements called Ḥever ha-Kevuẓot. 80 settlements with 30,000 members.

Iḥud Olami, see Po'alei Zion.

Ikor, Roger (1912–), French novelist. Best-known work *Les fils d'Avrom,* awarded Prix Goncourt, is story of Russian Jewish family in France glorifying their assimilation into French society in early 20th c.

Ikriti, see Shemariah ben Elijah ben Jacob.

Ilai (c. 100), *tanna;* sometimes referred to as Ilai the Elder. Talmud records various halakhic and aggadic statements in his name. Saying: "A person's character can be told by three things: by his cup, by his purse, and by his anger" *(be-khoso, be-hi be-khiso, u-ve-kha'aso).*

Ilaniyyah (Heb. for Arab. name **Sejera**), moshavah (since 1902) in Lower Galilee, founded 1899 by ICA as training farm. First settlers Kurdish Jews and Russian converts to Judaism. Ha-Shomer founded there as was Ha-Ḥoresh, first collective group of agricultural laborers. Pop. 190 (1971).

Ilf, Ilya (pseud. of **Ilya Arnoldovich Fainzilberg;** 1897–1937), Soviet Russian author. In most of his works (e.g., "The Twelve Chairs") collaborated with Yevgeni Petrov. They were among Soviet literature's most successful humorists. Denied existence of "Jewish problem" in USSR.

Ilfa (**Ḥilfai;** 3rd c.), Palestinian *amora;* pupil of Judah ha-Nasi. Exceptionally sharp-witted halakhist; several of his *aggadot* are quoted in Midrash. Renowned for exceptional piety.

The S.S. "Max Nordau," which left Constanza with 1,754 "illegal" immigrants on May 7, 1946, and was captured by the British six days later.

"Illegal" Immigration (Heb. **Aliyah Bet** or **Ha'palah**), clandestine immigration of Jews to Ereẓ Israel during Mandatory period when British administration sought to restrict Jewish immigration.

Illinois, U.S. state. Jews settled in Chicago in 1830s, Peoria 1847, Springfield 1850. By 1960s many suburbs of Chicago had substantial Jewish communities. Jewish governors Henry Horner 1932–40 and Samuel H. Shapiro 1968. Besides Chicago metropolitan area, 31 communities had one or more synagogues. Jewish pop. 284,285 (1971), all but 15,000 in Chicago.

Illowy, Bernard (1812–1871), Orthodox rabbi, scholar; b. Bohemia, in U.S. fr. 1848. Only Orthodox rabbi of his time in U.S. to hold doctorate. Polemicist against Reform Judaism.

Ilna'e (Schoenbaum), Eliezer Isaac (1885–1929), philosopher; b. Lithuania. Active in Zionist affairs. In Jerusalem after WWI. His theories help explain hypnotic and parapsychological phenomena.

Imber, Naphtali Herz (1856–1909), poet; author of *"Ha-Tikvah,"* Zionist and later Israel national anthem; b. Galicia. Traveled extensively, secretary to Laurence Oliphant in Ereẓ Israel 1882–88. Fr. 1892 in U.S., living in squalor, misery, and alcoholism. Also translated fr. English to Hebrew.

Imber, Samuel Jacob (1889–1942), pioneer and mentor of entire generation of Galician Yiddish poets; b. Ukraine; nephew of Naphtali Herz Imber. One of his innovations was poems of longing for Ereẓ Israel, which he visited 1912. Wrote poetic romance *Esterke.* Murdered by Ukrainians during Nazi occupation.

Jewish communities in Illinois, with dates of establishment of first synagogues.

The Inbal company in "The Wild Rose."

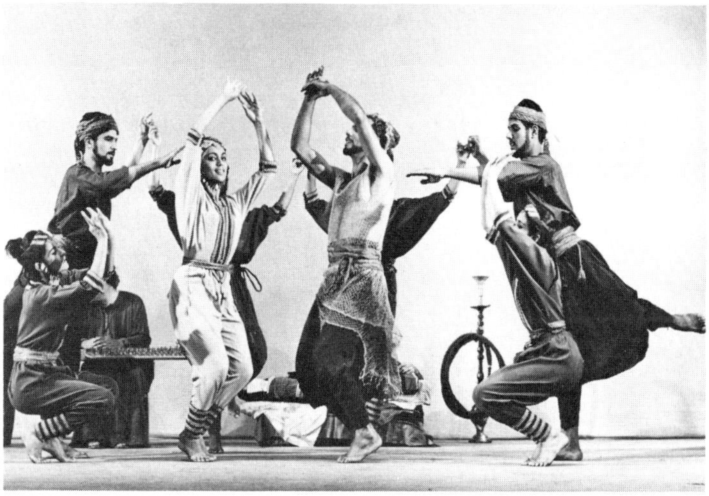

Naphtali Herz Imber

Immanuel, symbolic name (meaning "God is with us") of the child whose birth is foretold by Isaiah (7:14). Christian tradition identifies it with Jesus (Matt. 1:20 ff.).

Immanuel (ben Solomon) of Rome (c. 1261–after 1328), Italian poet. Wandered throughout Italy, teaching and writing. *Maḥbarot,* his best-known literary work, contains poems of both frivolous and serious nature. Introduced sonnet form into Hebrew. The *piyyut Yigdal,* included in daily prayer book, is abridged adaptation of one of his poems. Also wrote Italian verse under name Manoello Giudeo.

Imma Shalom (1st–2nd c. C.E.), wife of Eliezer b. Hyrcanus and sister of Rabban Gamaliel of Jabneh. Talmud praises her knowledge and devotion.

Immigration, see Aliyah; "Illegal" Immigration.

Impurity, Ritual, see Purity and Impurity, Ritual.

Imrānī (16th c.), Judeo-Persian poet. Used historical books of Bible as sources for his poetry. Also composed free poetical paraphrase and commentary on chaps. 1-4 of *Pirkei Avot.*

Imri, Rakhel, see Feygenberg, Rakhel.

Inbal Dance Theater, Israel dance company based mainly on Yemenite tradition, founded 1949 by Sara Levi-Tanai and Ovadia Tuvia.

TEXT OF THE DECLARATION OF INDEPENDENCE
(TRANSLATED FROM THE HEBREW ORIGINAL)

Eretz-Israel was the birthplace of the Jewish people. Here their spiritual, religious and political identity was shaped. Here they first attained to statehood, created cultural values of national and universal significance and gave to the world the eternal Book of Books.

After being forcibly exiled from their land, the people kept faith with it throughout their Dispersion and never ceased to pray and hope for their return to it and for the restoration in it of their political freedom.

Impelled by this historic and traditional attachment, Jews strove in every successive generation to re-establish themselves in their ancient homeland. In recent decades they returned in their masses. Pioneers, "ma'apilim" and defenders, they made deserts bloom, revived the Hebrew language, built villages and towns, and created a thriving community, controlling its own economy and culture, loving peace but knowing how to defend itself, bringing the blessings of progress to all the country's inhabitants, and aspiring towards independent nationhood.

In the year 5657 (1897), at the summons of the spiritual father of the Jewish State, Theodor Herzl, the First Zionist Congress convened and proclaimed the right of the Jewish people to national rebirth in its own country.

This right was recognized in the Balfour Declaration of the 2nd November, 1917, and re-affirmed in the Mandate of the League of Nations which, in particular, gave international sanction to the historic connection between the Jewish people and Eretz-Israel and to the right of the Jewish people to rebuild its National Home.

The catastrophe which recently befell the Jewish people — the massacre of millions of Jews in Europe — was another clear demonstration of the urgency of solving the problem of its homelessness by re-establishing in Eretz-Israel the Jewish State, which would open the gates of the homeland wide to every Jew and confer upon the Jewish people the status of a fully-privileged member of the comity of nations.

Survivors of the Nazi holocaust in Europe, as well as Jews from other parts of the world, continued to migrate to Eretz-Israel, undaunted by difficulties, restrictions and dangers, and never ceased to assert their right to a life of dignity, freedom and honest toil in their national homeland.

In the Second World War, the Jewish community of this country contributed its full share to the struggle of the freedom- and peace-loving nations against the force of Nazi wickedness and, by the blood of its soldiers and its war effort, gained the right to be reckoned among the peoples who founded the United Nations.

On the 29th November, 1947, the United Nations General Assembly passed a resolution calling for the establishment of a Jewish State in Eretz-Israel; the General Assembly required the inhabitants of Eretz-Israel to take such steps as were necessary on their part for the implementation of that resolution. This recognition by the United Nations of the right of the Jewish people to establish their State is irrevocable.

This right is the natural right of the Jewish people to be masters of their own fate, like all other nations, in their own sovereign State.

Accordingly we, members of the People's Council, representatives of the Jewish community of Eretz-Israel and of the Zionist movement, are here assembled on the day of the termination of the British Mandate over Eretz-Israel and, by virtue of our natural and historic right and on the strength of the resolution of the United Nations General Assembly, hereby declare the establishment of a Jewish State in Eretz-Israel, to be known as the State of Israel.

We declare that, with effect from the moment of the termination of the Mandate, being tonight, the eve of Sabbath, the 6th Iyar, 5708 (15th May, 1948), until the establishment of the elected, regular authorities of the State in accordance with the Constitution which shall be adopted by the Elected Constituent Assembly not later than the 1st October, 1948, the People's Council shall act as a Provisional Council of State, and its executive organ, the People's Administration, shall be the Provisional Government of the Jewish State, to be called "Israel."

The State of Israel will be open for Jewish immigration and for the Ingathering of the Exiles; it will foster the development of the country for the benefit of all inhabitants; it will be based on freedom, justice and peace as envisaged by the prophets of Israel; it will ensure complete equality of social and political rights to all its inhabitants irrespective of religion, race or sex; it will guarantee freedom of religion, conscience, language, education and culture; it will safeguard the Holy Places of all religions; and it will be faithful to the principles of the Charter of the United Nations.

The State of Israel is prepared to cooperate with the agencies and representatives of the United Nations in implementing the resolution of the General Assembly of the 29th November, 1947, and will take steps to bring about the economic union of the whole of Eretz-Israel.

We appeal to the United Nations to assist the Jewish people in the building-up of its State and to receive the State of Israel into the comity of nations.

We appeal — in the very midst of the onslaught launched against us now for months — to the Arab inhabitants of the State of Israel to preserve peace and participate in the upbuilding of the State on the basis of full and equal citizenship and due representation in all its provisional and permanent institutions.

We extend our hand to all neighbouring states and their peoples in an offer of peace and good neighbourliness, and appeal to them to establish bonds of cooperation and mutual help with the sovereign Jewish people settled in its own land. The State of Israel is prepared to do its share in common effort for the advancement of the entire Middle East.

We appeal to the Jewish people throughout the Diaspora to rally round the Jews of Eretz-Israel in the tasks of immigration and upbuilding and to stand by them in the great struggle for the realization of the age-old dream — the redemption of Israel.

Placing our trust in the Rock of Israel, we affix our signatures to this proclamation at this session of the Provisional Council of State, on the soil of the Homeland, in the city of Tel-Aviv, on this Sabbath eve, the 5th day of Iyar, 5708 (14th May, 1948).

David Ben-Gurion
Daniel Auster
Mordecai Bentov
Itzhak Ben Zvi
Eliahu Berligne
Fritz [Peretz] Bernstein
Rabbi Z'ev [Wolf] Gold
Meir Grabovsky [Argov]
Itzhak Gruenbaum
Dr. Abraham Granowsky [Granott]
Eliyahu Dobkin
Meir Wilner-Kovner
Zerah Wahrhaftig
Herzl Vardi

Rachel Cohen
Rabbi Kalman Kahana
Saadia Kobashi
Rabbi Yitzhak Meir Levin
Meir David Loevenstein
Zvi Luria
Golda Meyerson [Meir]
Nahum Y. Nir [Nahum Ya'akov Nir-Rafalkes]
Zvi Segal
Rabbi Yehuda Leib Hacohen-Fishman [Y'huda Leb HaKohen Maimon]
David Zvi Pinkas

Aharon Zisling
Moshe Kolodny [Kol]
Eliezer Kaplan
Avraham Katznelson [Nisan]
Felix Rosenblüth [Pinhas Rosen]
David Remez
Berl Repetur
Mordekhai Shattner
Ben Zion Sternberg
B'khor Shitrit
Moshe Shapira
Moshe Shertok [Sharett]

Inber, Vera Mikhailovna (1890–1972), Soviet Russian poet. Member of Constructivist Communist romantic group; her best-known work depicts siege of Leningrad, where she was war correspondent.

Inclination, Good and Evil, idea of existence in man's nature of inclination to evil is present in Bible. Doctrine of two inclinations is major feature of rabbinic psychology and anthropology. Evil inclination *(yezer ha-ra)* is present in man at birth and must be controlled rather than suppressed by good inclination *(yezer ha-tov).*

Independence Day, Israel (Heb. *Yom ha-Azma'ut*), Israel national holiday, celebrated Iyyar 5 as anniversary of May 14, 1948 Declaration of Independence. *Hallel* prayer is recited in many synagogues at special thanksgiving service.

Independent Jewish Workers Party, Jewish workers' party in Russia 1901–3. Aimed to raise economic and cultural level of Jewish proletariat by developing trade unions, funds, and clubs. Initiated and sponsored by Russian secret police, who wanted to estrange workers from Social-Democratic revolutionary intellegentsia; opposed by Bund.

Independent Liberal Party, Israel political party founded 1965 as result of split in Liberal Party; successor to Progressive Party. Affiliated with Liberal International. See also Knesset.

India, Asian republic. Earliest historical evidence of Jewish settlement dates fr. Cochin (q.v.) in 10th c. C.E. Portuguese Jews flocked to Goa in 16th c. and Cochin Jews, in particular, prospered under Dutch rule. Main communities in Bombay and Calcutta were augmented by movement of Bene Israel (q.v.) in 18th c. and by arrival of Iraqi Jews in19thc. Over 23,000 Jews emigrated to Israel after 1948, Jewish pop. 14,500 (1971), mostly in Bombay.

Indiana, U.S. state. First Jewish settlement in S. Indiana in first half of 19th c. First congregation in Fort Wayne 1848, others in Lafayette and Evansville. Jewish pop. 24,275 (1971), with largest communities in Indianapolis and Gary.

Indianapolis, city in Ind., U.S. First Jews 1850; first congregation 1856. Jewish pop. 8,800 (1971).

Indonesia, republic of Malay Archipelago. Dutch Jews contributed to development of "Spice Islands"; 2,000 Jews in 1920, many of Baghdadi origin. Community declined with independence and numbered 100 in 1972.

Industrial Removal, U.S. movement 1900–17 to disperse Jewish immigrants fr. congested immigrant districts to smaller places where Jewish communities existed and variety of jobs was available.

Infeld, Leopold (1898–1968), Polish physicist. Collaborated with Einstein for over 10 years in U.S. Returned to Poland 1950.

Ingathering of the Exiles (Heb. *Kibbutz Galuyyot*), phrase first found in rabbinic literature (although idea is prominent in Bible), referring to return of exiled communities to Erez Israel in messianic age. Theme figures largely in medieval Jewish apocalyptic literature and in liturgy. Since establish-

Jewish communities in Indiana, with dates of establishment of first synagogues.

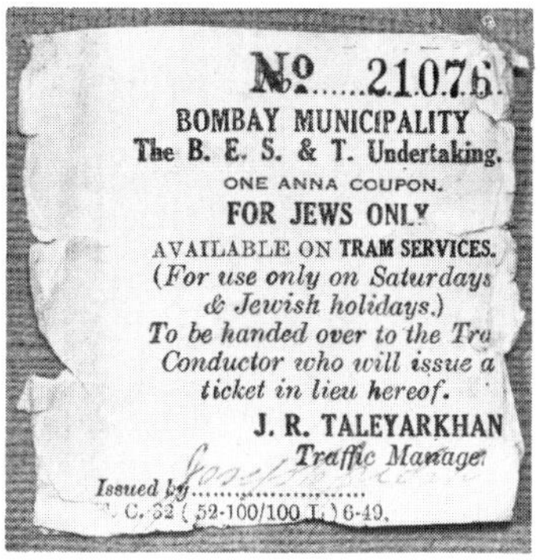
No. 21076
BOMBAY MUNICIPALITY
The B. E. S. & T. Undertaking.
ONE ANNA COUPON.
FOR JEWS ONLY
AVAILABLE ON TRAM SERVICES.
(For use only on Saturdays & Jewish holidays.)
To be handed over to the Tra[m] Conductor who will issue a ticket in lieu hereof.
J. R. TALEYARKHAN
Traffic Manager
Issued by ....
C. 62 (52-100/100 T.) 6-40.

Special tram coupon for Sabbath and festivals, used with rabbinic approval, Bombay, India, early 20th cent.

Major Jewish settlements in India in 19th and 20th centuries.

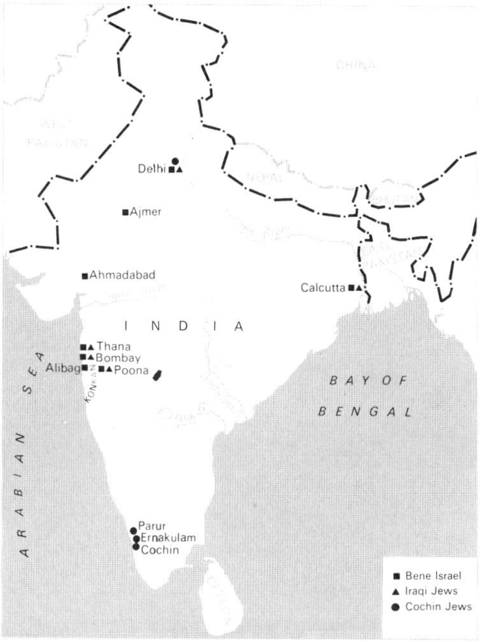

Parade celebrating Israel's 20th Independence Day, 1968, Jerusalem.

Detail from Rizi's "Auto da Fé," showing Judaizer, accused by Inquisition, with special robe and miter.

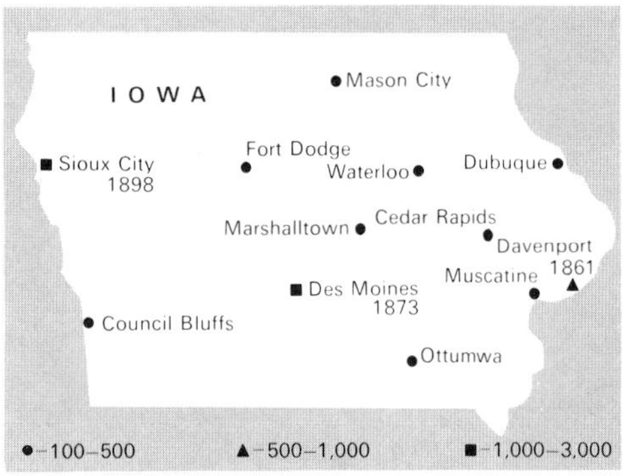

Jewish communities in Iowa, with dates of establishment of first synagogues.

The New Synagogue of Baghdad, Iraq, consecrated 1797.

Major Jewish settlements in Iraq in 1947 before mass exodus.

ment of State of Israel conception divested of messianic character and applied to phenomenon of mass immigration.

Innsbruck, city in W. Austria. Jews fr. 14th c. Suffered during Black Death 1348. Expelled 1674, 1714. Equal rights 1867. 300 Jews in 1930s, most leaving 1938. 50 Jews in 1969.

Inquisition, special permanent tribunal of medieval Catholic Church, established to investigate and combat heresy. Originally only incidentally concerned with Jews, it was revived in Spain 1478 for express purpose of dealing with Conversos. Particularly active in Spain and Portugal and in their overseas territories. Also existed in various Italian states and in Malta. Responsible for mass expropriations of property. 2,000 cases of auto-da-fé and at least 32,000 executions. Abolished in Portugal 1821, Spain 1834.

Institutum Judaicum Delitzschianum, institute for study of Judaism and (in original form) for missionary activity among Jews. First such institute opened in Halle 1728, and re-established by Franz Delitzsch (after whom it was subsequently renamed) in Leipzig 1886. Subsequently in Vienna 1936 and Munster 1948. Played important role in furthering Christian-Jewish dialogue.

In-Zikh, movement in American Yiddish poetry that espoused introspectivism as medium for expressing poet's personal experience. Movement centered around literary organ *In Zikh* (1920–40).

Ionesco, Eugène (1912–), French playwright; b. Rumania; mother Jewish. After WWII one of major exponents of "Theater of the Absurd". Plays incl. *Bald Soprano, Rhinoceros, Exit the King.* Elected to French Academy 1970; Jerusalem Prize 1973.

Iowa, U.S. state. Early Jewish settlers in 1830s–1840s were German and Polish peddlers. First organized Jewish community in Keokuk 1855. Des Moines' first congregation founded 1870. Jewish pop. 8,610 (1971), with 3,000 in Des Moines.

Iran, see Persia.

Iraq (for early history see Mesopotamia and Babylonia), Asian republic. Cultural center of Jewish life (c. 5th–11th c.) with authority of both Exilarch and Gaon recognized throughout Diaspora during first centuries of Arab rule. However, internal dissension, rise of Karaism, and closing of great academies altered situation. Information scanty for 14th c. ff. Community declined 16th–18th c. Jews prospered under early Moguls and occasionally under Turks; by 1917 controlled trade of Baghdad. Iraqi independence 1932 brought persecution; majority of community (150,000) emigrated to Israel 1948. Remaining 2,500 (1971) mostly live in fear. Government displayed hostile policy toward Israel, participating in 1948 invasion and 1973 war and refused to sign armistice agreement.

'Irāqī, Eleazar ben Aaron ha-Kohen (d. 1864), Yemenite-Indian scholar, printer; first Jewish printer in India. Made special efforts to print works of Yemenite authors and poets.

Irbil (or **Erbil;** formerly **Arbil**), town in Iraq. Jewish community fr. end of Second Temple persevered until 1950s. 4,800 Jews in 1919; number later dwindled. All Jews emigrated to Israel 1951.

Ireland, island W. of Britain. Individual Jews in 12th–13th c. Community started by ex-Marranos fr. Holland in late 17th c. and by C. European Ashkenazim in 18th c. No Jews by end of 18th c. Community reestablished by 19th c. (mainly petty traders); grew with E. European immigration fr. end of 19th c. Jewish pop. 5,400 (1971), mainly in Dublin.

Irgun Ẓeva'i Le'ummi (I.Ẓ.L., Eẓel, or **Irgun**), Jewish underground armed organization founded in Ereẓ Israel 1931. Linked with Betar and Revisionist movement 1937. Original aim was retaliation against Arab attacks, but with 1939 White Paper its target became British authority. Declared truce in WWII, which led to split of Loḥamei Ḥerut Israel. I.Ẓ.L. commander David Raziel killed in Iraq 1941 on British mission. Menahem Begin commander fr. 1943. Renewed anti-British activities 1944. After 1947 came out of hiding, joining Haganah in repulsing Arab attacks. Dismantled Sept. 1948 after period of tension with Israel government. Ḥerut became its political successor.

Iron Guard, right-wing, anti-Semitic movement and party in Rumania; responsible for anti-Jewish riots in 1930s and for anti-Jewish legislation and mass slaughters in early 1940s. Ceased to exist in Rumania 1944.

Irving, Jules (1925–), U.S. theatrical director. Founded Actors Workshop. Director of Lincoln Center Repertory Theater fr. 1965.

"Abraham and Isaac," etching by Rembrandt von Rijn, 1645.

Isaac, son of Abraham and Sarah, second patriarch; born after parents passed normal childbearing age. First to be circumcised at age of 8 days. Potential victim of sacrifice *(Akedah)* divinely ordered as test of Abraham's faith. Married his cousin Rebekah; father of Jacob and Esau. In his old age, when blind, deceived by Jacob into granting him birthright. Died aged 180 and buried in Cave of Machpelah.

Isaac, merchant of Aachen; first German Jew known by name. Envoy fr. Charlemagne to Harun al-Rashid 797.

Isaac, Aaron (Aron Izak, 1730–1816), German seal engraver; founder of Jewish community in Sweden 1774. Left Yiddish memoirs of historical and philological importance.

Isaac, Jules Marx (1877–1963), French historian. Chief inspector of history teaching at Ministry of Education; author of classical textbook of French history. Fr. 1943, dedicated himself to study of Christian anti-Semitism. Founded Amitié Judéo-Chrétienne. His work influenced Vatican Council decision to introduce statement on relations with Jews. Wrote *Jesus and Israel: The Teaching of Contempt.*

Isaac, Testament of, pseudepigraphical work. Relates story of how angel announced to Isaac his imminent death and commanded him to instruct his sons, and includes apocalyptic vision. In its present form probably late imitation of Testament of Abraham.

Isaac bar Dorbelo, (12th c.), pupil of Jacob Tam. Probable editor of *Mahzor Vitry,* which describes teachings and conduct of his teacher and of Rashi and his school. Traveled extensively in Europe.

Isaac ben Abba Mari of Marseilles (12th c.) rabbinical scholar in Provence and Spain. Wrote commentaries on Mishnah and on Isaac Alfasi. His encyclopedic *Sefer ha-Ittur* on practical *halakhah,* drawing on geonic literature, became authoritative.

Isaac ben Abraham ha-Gorni (13th c.), French Hebrew poet. Penniless wanderer who was persecuted because of love affairs and literary quarrels. One poem contemplates his fate after death with both sarcasm and anxiety.

Isaac ben Abraham of Posen (d. 1685), rabbi, author; known as R. Isaac the Great for expertise in Talmud and Kabbalah. Published novellae and responsa.

Isaac ben Abraham Troki, see Troki, Isaac ben Abraham.

Isaac ben Asher ha-Levi (Riba; 11th–12th c), talmudist of Speyer; first German tosafist. Pupil of Rashi, and known as *"ha-Kadosh"* ("the Saint"), possibly because of insistence on fasting on Day of Atonement when mortally ill. Published responsa and *tosafot,* and engaged in practical Kabbalah. His eponymous grandson, known as **Riba II** (d. 1195), halakhist; born on day his grandfather died. Martyred by rioters.

Isaac ben Eliakim of Posen (17th c.), Yiddish moralist. Wrote *Leftov* counseling men to honor wives on basis of equal rights.

Isaac ben Eliezer (known as **Segan Leviyyah,** "levite"; d. 1070), scholar of Worms. Pupil of Eliezer b. Isaac of Worms; headed yeshivah at Worms, his pupils including Rashi, who called him "guide of the generation." Some of his responsa and *piyyutim* are extant.

Isaac ben Jacob ha-Kohen (13th c.), spokesman of Gnostic circle in Spanish Kabbalah.

Isaac ben Jacob ha-Lavan of Prague (12th c.), tosafist of Bohemia; Also known as Isaac of Bohemia and Isaac of Regensburg; brother of Pethahiah of Regensburg. Wrote *tosafot,* responsa, *piyyutim.*

Isaac ben Jacob min ha-Leviyyim ("of the levites"; b. 1621), Italian rabbi, printer; grandson of Leone Modena. Wrote commentaries on talmudic *aggadot* and anthology of poems.

Isaac ben Joseph of Corbeil (Semak; d. 1280), French codifier; son-in law of Jehiel of Paris. His *Sefer Mitzvot Katan* is popular compendium of *halakhah,* interspersed with ethical homilies and parables. His enumeration of precepts became standard source for later codifiers. Also wrote responsa and *tosafot.*

Poster issued by Palestine Government offering rewards for information leading to capture of leaders responsible for I.Z.L. – Leḥi bombing, Tel Aviv, Jan. 20, 1942.

Isaac ben Judah of Mainz (11th c.), German scholar; pupil of Gershom b. Judah, whom he succeeded as head of Mainz Yeshivah. A teacher of Rashi. Author of responsa and novellae.

Isaac ben Meir (Ribam; 12th c.), early tosafist; brother of Samuel b. Meir (Rashbam) and Jacob Tam, grandson of Rashi. Wrote *tosafot* to *Yevamot* and *Nedarim* and was widely quoted.

Isaac ben Meir of Dueren, see Dueren, Isaac ben Meir.

Isaac ben Melchizedek of Siponto (c. 1090–1160), first Italian commentator on at least part of Mishnah. His eclectic commentary does not give halakhic decisions.

Isaac ben Menahem the Great (11th c.), French scholar. Studied in Mainz under Eliezer b. Isaac of Worms, who praised him. Rashi made extensive use of his teachings, esp. in determining correct text of Talmud.

Isaac ben Mordecai (Ribam; 12th c.), German tosafist. Headed *bet din* of Regensburg. Wrote *tosafot* on most of Talmud.

Isaac ben Moses of Vienna (c. 1180–1250), halakhic authority of Germany and France; known as

Isaac Or Zaru'a, after his monumental compilation of halakhic rulings. Provides valuable source material for medieval Jewish communal history. A number of abridgments of the work were made.

Isaac ben Samson ha-Kohen (d. 1624), talmudist of Bohemia; son-in-law of Judah Loew b. Bezalel of Prague. *Dayyan* and leader of Prague community, philanthropist, translator of Pentateuch into Yiddish. Wrote commentaries on Midrashim and edited halakhic works.

Sir Isaac Isaacs

Illustration by W. Bagg from Nathaniel Isaacs' "Travels and Adventures in Eastern Africa," 1836.

BOOK OF ISAIAH – CONTENTS

Chs. 1–12	Prophecies of reproof and consolation on Judah and Israel
Chs. 13–27	Oracles against the nations
13:1–23:18	Oracles on the neighbors of Judah, on Babylonia, and on Egypt
24:1–27:13	Universalistic prophecies and "apocalypses"
Chs. 28–35	Prophecies of consolation and reproof on Judah
Chs. 36–39	Miracle stories of the Prophet
Chs. 40–66	A collection of consolation prophecies assigned to an anonymous exilic prophet (40–48, 49–57, 58–66)

Isaac ben Samuel ha-Levi (1580–1646?), Polish talmudist, grammarian; elder brother and teacher of David b. Samuel ha-Levi, whose *Turei Zahav* shows his influence. Wrote responsa and works on grammar and biblical vocabulary.

Isaac ben Samuel of Acre (13th–14th c.), kabbalist; traveled fr. Ereẓ Israel to Italy and Spain and met Moses de Leon in search for origin of Zohar. Wrote commentary on Naḥmanides' mysticism and mystical diary of visions.

Isaac ben Samuel of Dampierre (Ri; d.c. 1185), leading Franco-German tosafist; pupil of Jacob Tam. His *tosafot* cover entire Talmud, but survive only in quotation. His responsa characterized by humility and rich historical information.

Isaac ben Sheshet Perfet (Ribash; 1326–1408), Spanish rabbi, halakhic authority. Frequently involved in communal controversies in Spain and Algiers. His responsa influenced *Shulḥan Arukh* and are valuable sources for contemporary history, incl. halakhic status of Marranos. His tomb was site of pilgrimage.

Isaac ben Solomon (d. after 1811), Karaite spiritual leader in Crimea. Attempted to regularize Karaite calendar by mathematical means.

Isaac Or Zaru'a, see Isaac b. Moses of Vienna.

Isaac the Blind ("Sagi Nahor"; c. 1160–1235), leading early kabbalist; son of Abraham b. David of Posquières. Known as "He-Ḥasid." Wrote on *Sefirot* and meditation in prayer, and commentary to *Sefer Yeẓirah*.

Isaac Nappaḥa ("The Smith"; 3rd c.), Palestinian *amora; dayyan* in Tiberias and Caesarea. Halakhist and aggadist whose parables reflect contemporary events and show deep insight into human nature.

Isaacs, U.S. family in N.Y. Founder **Samuel Myer** (1804–1878), b. Holland, immigrated to U.S. 1839 fr. London. Rabbi of congregation Shaarei Tefila; founder of weekly *Jewish Messenger.* A founder of Mt. Sinai Hospital 1852 and other Jewish institutions. His son **Myer Samuel** (1841–1904), lawyer, community leader. Lectured at NYU Law School. Another son, **Abram Samuel** (1852–1920), rabbi, writer, educator. Prof. of Semitic languages at NYU. **Stanley Myer** (1882–1962), son of Myer Samuel, lawyer who served as borough pres. of Manhattan and member of N.Y.C. Council.

Isaacs, see Reading.

Isaacs, Edith Juliet (1878–1956), editor of *Theater Arts* 1919–45. Printed early plays by O'Neill, Thornton Wilder, etc. Magazine encouraged growth of pioneer progressive theater groups.

Isaacs, Sir Isaac Alfred (1855–1948), Australian lawyer, politician. After serving as attorney-general and justice of federal high court, became chief justice 1930 and then first Australian-born governor-general 1931. Sought to strengthen power of federal government vis-à-vis states. Opposed political Zionism.

Isaacs, Jorge (1837–1895), Columbian novelist; son of converted English Jew and Columbian mother. Famous for classic novel *María.*

Isaacs, Nathaniel (1808–c.1860), S. African trader, explorer; regarded as a founder of Natal. His record of visits to kraal of two Zulu kings is important contemporary account of Zulu life.

Isaacs, Susan Sutherland (1885–1948), English educator. Wrote books on child development. Organized and directed Dept. of Child Development at Univ. of London.

Isabella of Castile, see Ferdinand and Isabella.

Isaiah, prophet whose prophecies are contained in Book of Isaiah, first of biblical Major Prophets. Critical opinion is that book is work of at least two distinct authors: first Isaiah (chs. 1–39), whose prophetic career in Jerusalem covers years c. 740–700 B.C.E., and an unknown prophet, so-called Deutero-Isaiah (chs. 40–66), whose prophecies reflect experience and events of Babylonian Exile. Some attribute chs. 56–66 to third author (Trito-Isaiah), living in Jerusalem close to time of Ezra and Nehemiah. First Isaiah was of noble family and close to royal court. Three features characterize his message: God's power extends beyond Israel to all other nations; God is given character of idealistic reality; righteous remnant will survive impending calamity of the people. Deutero-Isaiah teaches hope and consolation.

Isaiah, Ascension of, early Christian apocalypse, containing Jewish apocryphon of *Martyrdom of Isaiah.* Original book written in Greek as early as 1st c.

Isaiah ben Abraham (d. 1723), rabbi, kabbalist. Author of earlier of two commentaries on part of *Shulḥan Arukh,* both entitled *Ba'er Heitev.* Perished with family on way to Ereẓ Israel.

Isaiah ben Mali di Trani (the Elder; 13th c.), Italian halakhist. Author of commentaries and decisions on Talmud. His responsa are marked by clarity of reasoning and style. Wrote biblical commentaries and *piyyutim.*
Isaiah Ḥasid from Zbarazh (17th–18th c.), Shabbatean scholar; son-in-law of **Judah Ḥasid,** with whom he emigrated to Jerusalem 1700. In Germany fr. 1706; believed Prossnitz Loebele to be Messiah; propagated anti-talmudic beliefs. Excommunicated.
Isaiah Menahem ben Isaac (d. 1599), rabbi in Poland. Active in Council of Four Lands. Legal authority and author of supercommentary on Rashi.
Isak, Aron, see Isaac, Aaron.
Isenstein, Kurt Harald (1898–), Danish sculptor. Directed art school in Germany. Works incl. portraits of Einstein, Hindenburg, Pirandello, monument to Danish refugees in Sweden, and memorials to Norwegian Jews who died at Auschwitz.
Isfahan, city in Iran. Jews mentioned in 5th c. C.E.; increased under Arab rule. By 12th c. community of 15,000 known for Hebrew grammarians, exegetes, and prosperous merchants and artisans. 17th c. saw persecutions and forced conversions. When capital transferred to Teheran, community lost much of its vigor and prosperity. Many Jews moved to Israel or Teheran. Jewish pop. 2,500 (1968), most living in poverty.
Isfahanī Isaac ben Jacob al-, see Abu 'Isa, Isaac ben Jacob.
Isfiya, see 'Usifiyya.
Ishbili, Yom Tov ben Abraham, see Yom Tov ben Abraham Ishbili.
Ish-Bosheth (Eshbaal), son of Saul; reigned over Israel for two years at time David reigned over Judah in Hebron. Enthroned by Abner, Saul's uncle and general who concentrated full authority of government in his hands. Murdered by two officers (II Sam. 21:1).
Ish-Kishor (Blumenfeld), Ephraim (1863–1945), early follower of Ḥibbat Zion and political Zionism in England. Promoted Ḥibbat Zion as editor of Yiddish newspapers. Settled in Ereẓ Israel 1933.
Ishmael, first son of Abraham, born to him by Hagar, maidservant of Sarah (Gen. 16). After birth of Isaac, Abraham acceded to Sarah's demand and expelled Hagar and Ishmael (ch. 21). Traditional ancestor of Arabs.
Ishmael, military commander in period after destruction of First Temple. Descendant of Judean royal family. Assassinated Gedaliah, head of Judean puppet government, and attempted forcible transfer to Ammon of remnants of Judean population; plan frustrated and escaped to Ammon.
Ishmael ben Abraham Isaac ha-Kohen (1723–1811), last Italian rabbi accepted as worldwide halakhic authority. Responsa reflect liberal outlook. Wrote secular poetry.
Ishmael ben Elisha (2nd c.), *tanna;* generally mentioned as R. Ishmael. Ransomed fr. captivity in Rome by R. Joshua, who was later his teacher. Leading sage at Jabneh. Hermeneutics of Ishmael and his school postulated that "the Torah employed ordinary human idiom." Hence in halakhic Midrash sought literal meaning of biblical verse. Taught: "Receive all men joyfully"; and held that study of Torah should be combined with worldly occupation. Traditionally one of Ten Martyrs.
Ishmael ben Phiabi (Phabi), high priest for two years, appointed by Agrippa II 59 C.E. Member of delegation of intercession sent to Nero and held hostage there.
Ishmael ben Yose ben Ḥalafta (2nd c.), *tanna;* head of town of Sepphoris. As member of legal council of Judah ha-Nasi, influenced editing of Mishnah. As judge, exceptionally wary of partiality and presumptuousness.
Ishmaelites, group of nomadic tribes on borders of Ereẓ Israel, traditionally related to Ishmael son of Abraham.
Ishmael of 'Ukbara (9th c.), sectarian teacher who lived nr. Baghdad. Did not recognize Masoretic emendations in biblical text, legislated freely concerning Sabbath, and prohibited eating of meat. His few followers became Karaites.
Ish Shalom, Meir see Friedmann, Meir.
Isidor, Lazare (1814–1888), chief rabbi of Paris fr. 1847, France fr. 1867. His courageous stand (defended by Crémieux) over humiliating oath *more Judaico* led to its abolition in France 1846.
°**Isidore of Seville (Isidorus Hispalensis;** c. 560–636), archbishop of Seville; one of last Church Fathers. His exegetical writings were intended and used for anti-Jewish polemics and disputations. Up to 12th c. all anti-Jewish apologetic writers in W. Europe inspired by his writings.
Isidoros, see Lampon and Isidoros.
Iskowitz, Gershon (1921–), Canadian painter, b. Poland, survived concentration camp, in Canada fr. 1949. Paints Canadian landscape.
Israel, name of honor given to Jacob after struggle with angel (Gen. 32:22 f.). When descendants of Jacob grew into a people, they were called "the people of the children of Israel" (Ex. 1:9), and henceforth, until division of monarchy, it was name for what is now known as the Jewish people. With division, 10 defecting tribes united in kingdom of Israel. After kingdom of Israel fell 721 B.C.E., name continued to be used to denote the Jewish people as a whole. Term Ereẓ Israel (Land of Israel) is first used in Mishnah. In 19th c. name ("Israelites") was revived in some western countries to designate Jews, generally among assimilationist circles who regarded word "Jew" as degrading. Also used to designate Jew who is neither Kohen nor Levite. When Jewish state was established it was called State of Israel. Its inhabitants are Israelis (Fr. Israeliens; Sp. Israelianos) as compared with Israelites (Israélites, Israelitas) for Jews in general (archaic in Engl.).

Lazare Isidor

Hand-painted "ketubbah" from Isfahan, 1874.

Terracing in the Judean Mountains, mainly in a state of disrepair.

The meandering course of the Jordan, south of the embouchure of the Jabbok.

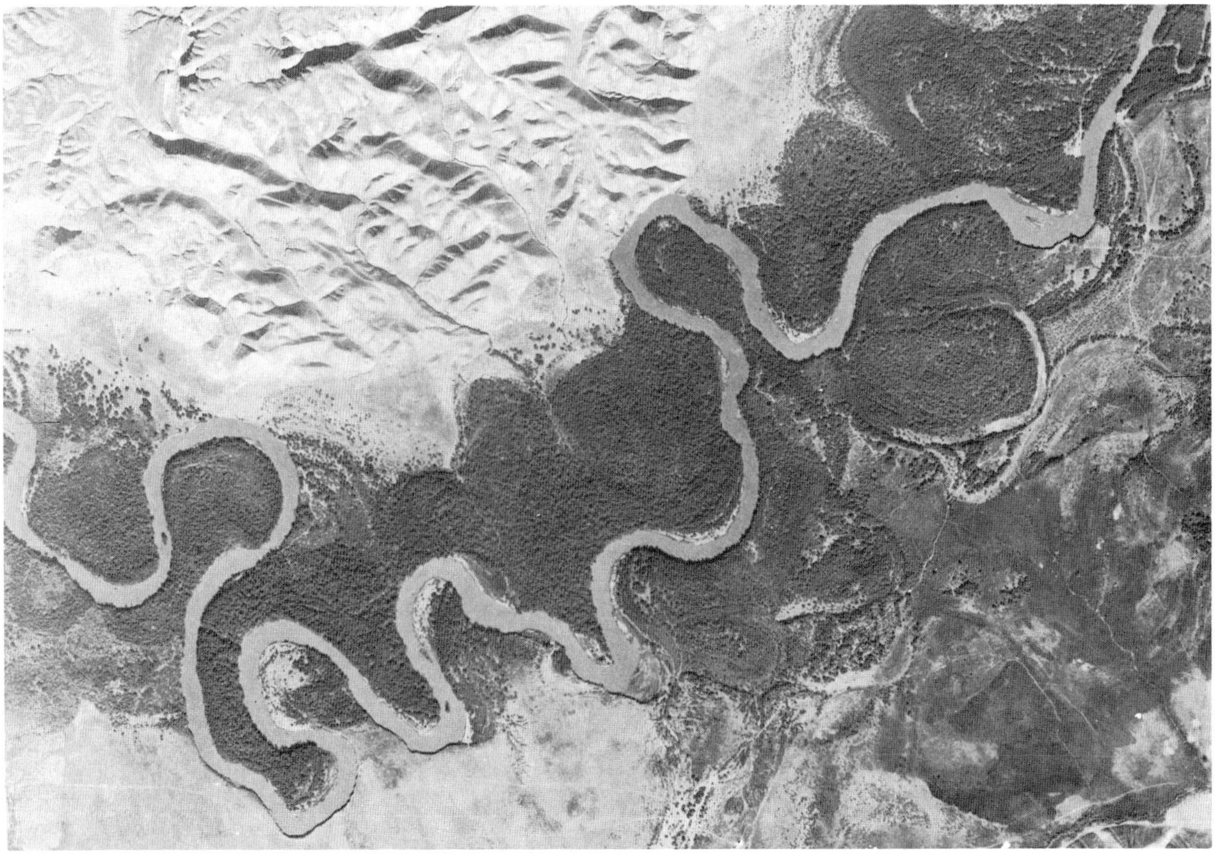

Israel (Name). Acc. to the Bible Land of Israel was promised as inheritance to Israelites and came to be regarded as national homeland of Jews and Holy Land. Prior to Second Temple period there was no name in general use. At different periods there were names that designated parts of country, alone or together with adjacent territory (e.g., Canaan). Second name Ereẓ (Land of) Israel became widespread by end of the Second Temple period. In post-Exilic period, Judea was official name of area of Jewish settlement. After Bar Kokhba War 132–35, Romans changed name to Palestine. Fr. Byzantine times Palestine became accepted name of Ereẓ Israel in non-Jewish languages. On May 14, 1948, Jewish-held part of W. Palestine was given name "State of Israel."

(Geography). Bet. Mediterranean and deserts, country exhibits complex climatic gradations and transitions ranging fr. conditions mainly influenced by sea to those which show all characteristics of fully desert region. Country can be subdivided into 4 major units: (1) Coastal Plains, extending fr. mouth of Wadi el-Arish to headland of Carmel, and fr. there to Rosh ha-Nikra promontory. Fr. earliest times plains were densely populated and intensively cultivated. They may be subdivided into: S. Plains (or Negev Plains); Judean Plain; Sharon; Carmel Coast Plain; Haifa (Zebulun) Plain; Galilean Plain (Acre Plain); Tyre Plain. (2) W. Mountain Zone, extending fr. Elath to valley of Qasimiye. It can be subdivided into: Negev Highlands, Central Mountain Massif, and Galilean Mountains. Each comprises several subregions. (3) Rift Valley. Fr. physiographical and morphotectonic points of view these may be subdivided into: Arabah, Dead Sea Region, Huleh Basin, and Jordan Sources Region. (4) Transjordan Plateau comprises region E. of Rift Valley fr. Gulf of Elath in S. into Hermon and Damascus Basin in N. Most of it gradually merges in E. with Syrian Desert. It may be subdivided physiographically into: Edom, Moab-Ammon, Gilead, and Bashan. Hermon Massif forms the terminal and transitional arch between two flanks of Rift Valley.

"Tannur" waterfall in Upper Galilee near Metullah.

The canyon of the Amaẓyahu River, cut into bedrock of the Lashon formation near the Dead Sea.

A canyon in the Eilat Mountains formed by tributary of Naḥal Timna.

Lake Kinneret, near Tiberias.

Mount Tabor.

Israel (History). Remains dating fr. prehistoric times have been found in Ereẓ Israel. First historically known settlers are Canaanites. Abraham emigrated to country and patriarchs traveled along hill country and Negev. After migration to Egypt, the Israelites returned and conquered Ereẓ Israel. Rise of Saul and establishment of monarchy was partly made possible by the growth of Philistine power in heart of land. David ruled over extensive area; captured Jerusalem fr. Jebusites and converted it into capital. Under David and Solomon kingdom was major political and economic factor in region. Solomon built royal palace and Temple in Jerusalem. With his death, monarchy split into two: southern small kingdom of Judah and northern kingdom of Israel with territory of ten tribes. S. remained loyal to dynasty of David. N. had frequent changes of dynasty and less stability. N. kingdom fell to Assyrians 721 B.C.E. and many of its inhabitants were deported. S. Kingdom survived until attack of Babylonians 586 B.C.E. and large numbers of its inhabitants were deported. After about 50 years, Cyrus of Persia permitted exiled Israelites to return and reestablish themselves around Jerusalem, which was consolidated under Ezra and Nehemiah, and Temple was rebuilt. Region fell to Alexander the Great 332 B.C.E. and in ensuing era was opened to influence of Greek culture, art, and religion (Hellenism). Attempt by Antiochus Epiphanes to hellenize country by force 168 B.C.E. led to Hasmonean revolt, which secured for Jews brief period of independence that lasted until Roman general Pompey captured Jerusalem 63 B.C.E.; henceforth Ereẓ Israel lay under Roman suzerainty. Herod became its ruler 40 B.C.E. With his death, his dominions were subdivided into tetrarchies, each under separate ruler, and Roman governor was real power. Jews became more and more embittered against Roman yoke, and violent rebellion broke out 66 C.E. which was quelled by Titus 70 C.E. when Jerusalem, incl. Temple, was destroyed. Pharisaic hierarchy reconstituted Jewish authority in Jabneh. Remnant remained, which attempted unsuccessful revolt under Bar Kokhba 132–35, leading to expulsion of Jews fr. Jerusalem and vicinity, persecution of spiritual leaders, and depopulation of Judea. Communal life recovered in Galilee, which was now center of Jewish life. Final redaction of Mishnah concluded there by Judah ha-Nasi. Christianity eventually gained commanding position, commencing with Constantine's recognition of Christian religion 313. In 4th c.

Fragment of carved ivory panel depicting Egyptian god Hah, from King Ahab's "ivory house," Samaria, 9th cent. B.C.E.

Ceramic lamp from Ereẓ Israel decorated with "menorah," 3rd/4th cent.

Looking out from cave near Dead Sea where excavations uncovered artifacts from Bar Kokhba rebellion.

Site of Battle of Hattin where Saladin defeated crusaders, 1187.

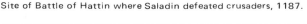

Mamluk tower of Ramleh, built c. 1318.

Tel Aviv, Herzl Street, 1915.

Jerusalem Talmud was redacted in Ereẓ Israel, mostly at Tiberias. During Byzantine rule economic position improved. Persians captured Jerusalem 614 with Jewish help and city was handed over to Jews. Persians defeated by Byzantine emperor 627. Jewish communities at first prospered under Arab rule fr. 634, but situation deteriorated under Omar II (717–720), who introduced numerous restrictions against non-Muslims in Omar Covenant. During Fatimid rule 969–1099 attitude of authorities generally favorable and Jews flourished economically and culturally. After wave of bloodshed perpetrated by crusaders at beginning of their rule in Ereẓ Israel 1099, there was period of respite and gradual recovery among Jewish communities. Large settlements had been destroyed and Jews were scattered in small towns and villages. During Mamluk period 1291–1516 Jewish community began to grow stronger and consolidate, esp. in Jerusalem. Jews fr. Spain settled in major cities. Fr. 1517 all Ereẓ Israel under Ottoman rule. Jewish community centered in Safed, which became a center of mysticism. Later communal focus moved to Jerusalem. Increased immigration of Jews started at beginning of 18th c. and economy was based mainly on charity received fr. abroad. After 1840 Jews began to enjoy protection of Western powers. Fr. 1880s, Jewish pioneers began to arrive and settle on land. First groups were under inspiration of Ḥibbat Zion and Bilu movement. Second Aliyah 1904–14 laid foundation for labor movement. Balfour Declaration 1917 affirmed establishment of Jewish National Home in country

Chaim Weizmann with Emir Faisal, Transjordan, 1918.

Protest against British White Paper by veterans of Jewish Legion, Jerusalem, 1939.

and after WWI, Mandate was conferred on Britain. Jews began coming in considerable numbers but opposition among Arab population led to riots 1921, 1929, 1936–39. Refugees fr. Nazi Germany arrived fr. 1933 but subsequently British drastically curtailed Jewish immigration. 1939 decision to leave permanent Arab majority in country led to strong opposition among Jews, who organized active resistance after WWII. British referred future of country to UN which on Nov. 29, 1947 decided to partition it into Arab and Jewish state. Although decision was violently opposed by Arabs, State of Israel was established on May 14, 1948 (see Israel, State of).

1

JEWISH POPULATION
OF EREZ ISRAEL, 1856–1972

1856	10,500
1882	24,000
1895	47,000
1914	85,000
1922	83,800
1931	174,600
1939	449,500
1948	758,700
1951	1,404,400
1961	1,981,700
1967	2,383,600
1972	2,723,600

2

3

4

1. Group of sabras.
2. Byway in Jerusalem's Me'ah She'arim quarter.
3. Nir David, the first tower and stockade kibbutz in the Beth-Shean Valley, 1936.
4. Israel Defense Forces artillery, 1948: three cannons manufactured in 1887 known as "Napoleonchiks."
5. Immigrants arriving in Haifa, Jan. 1949.
6. Yemenites arriving by "Magic Carpet" airlift, 1950.

5

6

Israel (State of). Middle East republic proclaimed May 14, 1948 when British left country. On next day armies of neighboring Arab countries invaded State, and were defeated in series of battles terminating Mar. 1949. First elections to Knesset held Jan. 25, 1949, with David Ben-Gurion chosen prime minister. Israel admitted to UN May 11, 1949. After armistice agreements, Arab states continued to regard themselves at war with Israel, and border violations became regular occurrences, with reprisals carried out from time to time by Israel army. W. Germany agreed 1952 to pay Israel considerable sums as reparation for material damage to European Jews in WWII. Close cooperation developed with France, esp. in arms. Egypt launched fedayeen squads to carry out murder and sabotage inside Israel 1955, Czechoslovak-Egyptian arms deal concluded, and Egypt blocked Straits of Tiran Oct. 24, 1956, leading to Sinai campaign (Oct. 29–Nov. 5, 1956), in which Israel occupied Sinai peninsula, but withdrew under pressure of U.S. and USSR with promises given that previous situation would not recur. For some time borders were quiet, but hostile activity developed along Syrian and Jordanian borders. Syrians shelled Israel settlements in Galilee, and together with Lebanon planned to deprive Israel of most of Jordan waters. In May 1967 Egypt moved large forces into Sinai, demanded withdrawal of UN Emergency Force stationed in Sinai since 1956, and declared Straits of Tiran closed. Jordan and other Arab countries placed their forces under Egyptian command. In Israel, government of national unity was established. Israel's swift victory in Six-Day War not only led to defeat of Arab countries but left Israel in possession of West Bank, Gaza Strip, Sinai Peninsula, and Golan Heights. France ceased to support Israel 1967 and most of country's arms needs were now filled by U.S., with whom very close relationship developed. Attempted war of attrition waged by Egypt along Suez Canal failed. Cease-fire with Egypt came into effect Aug. 1970.

On Day of Atonement 1973, Egypt and Syria attacked Israel. The Syrians after initial gains were driven back. The Egyptians maintained a hold along much of eastern bank of Suez Canal but Israel drove a wedge and crossed to the western bank

David Ben-Gurion reads Declaration of Independence, Tel Aviv, 1948.

reaching the suburbs of Suez and Ismayilla. Cease-fire at initiative of US and USSR called for peace talks which opened in Geneva with Egypt and Jordan toward end of 1973.

Israel is democracy headed by president. Its parliament (Knesset) is elected for four years and its government headed by prime minister. Suffrage is universal above age of 18 and election is by proportional representation based on nation-wide tally of votes. No party has received overall majority and all governments have been coalitions dominated by Mapai (later Israel Labor Party). Israel maintained diplomatic relations with 110 countries until 1973 War when most African countries broke off relations under Arab pressure. Fr. late 1950s, conducted extensive program of technical aid to underdeveloped countries. Establishment of state was signal for mass immigration fr. all parts of world and Jewish population tripled in 25 years. Its heterogeneous composition created problems but trend was toward overall integration. Early absorption processes included transit camps (*ma'barot*), but eventually ship-to-settlement method was achieved. Immigrants founded all types of settlement. One of country's first laws proclaimed right of all Jews to return to their own land as citizens. Funds from United Jewish Appeal (UJA) in many countries, U.S. grants-in-aid and long-term loans, and German Reparations helped state bear economic burdens. Israel Bond drive launched 1951. Despite political, religious, and other controversies, largely as result of heterogeneous nature of population,

"Ma'barah" in Tiberias.

IMMIGRATION OF JEWS TO EREZ ISRAEL (1919–1972)

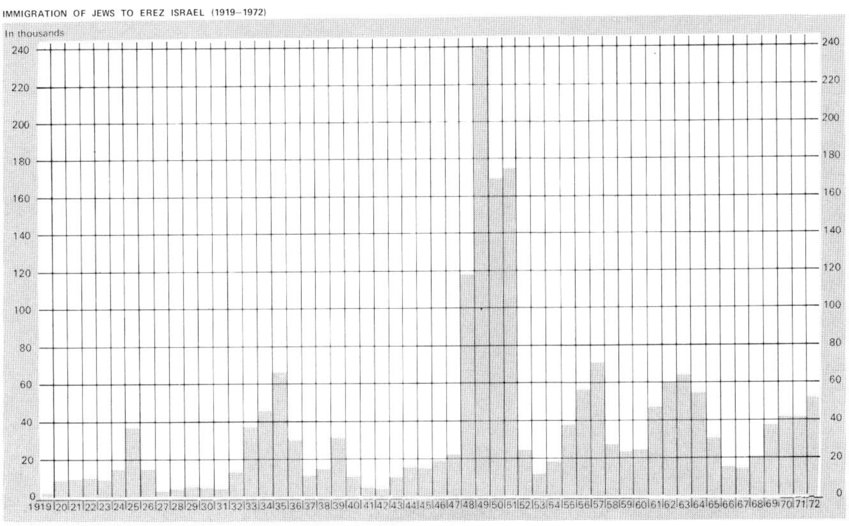

Israel armor during the Sinai Campaign, 1956.

ISRAEL POPULATION, BY POPULATION GROUP, CONTINENT OF BIRTH, PERIOD OF IMMIGRATION, AND RELIGION

Continent of birth, period of immigration and religion	8 XI 1948	1960	1972
		Thousands	
GRAND TOTAL	**872.7**	**2,150.4**	**3,200.5**
JEWS – TOTAL	716.7	1,911.2	2,723.6
ISRAEL-BORN	253.7	715.9	1,305.4
BORN ABROAD – TOTAL	463.0	1,195.3	1,418.2
ASIA–TOTAL	57.8	299.8	317.6
Immigrated up to 1947	55.4	48.1	41.2
1948–1945	2.4	228.9	206.1
1955–1960	–	22.8	20.1
1961–1964	–	–	17.7
1965–1971	–	–	29.9
1972	–	–	2.6
AFRICA–TOTAL	12.2	226.9	358.3
Immigrated up to 1947	7.4	6.5	5.4
1948–1954	4.9	108.7	99.3
1955–1960	–	111.7	101.7
1961–1964	–	–	106.5
1965–1971	–	–	41.8
1972	–	–	3.6
EUROPE -AMERICA–TOTAL	393.0	668.6	742.3
Immigrated up to 1947	318.3	267.5	215.8
1948–1954	74.7	309.5	256.4
1955–1960	–	91.6	74.8
1961–1964	–	–	77.4
1965–1971	–	–	77.0
1972	–	–	40.9
NON-JEWS – TOTAL	156.0	239.2	476.9
Moslems	..	166.3	358.6
Christians	..	49.6	79.6
Druze and Others	..	23.3	38.7
		Percentages	
TOTAL	100.0	100.0	100.0
Jews	82.1	88.9	85.1
Non-Jews	17.9	11.1	14.9
JEWS – TOTAL	100.0	100.0	100.0
Born in: Israel	35.4	37.4	47.9
Asia	8.1	15.7	11.7
Africa	1.7	11.9	13.2
Europe-America	54.8	35.0	27.2

Two moshavim of Taanach regional settlement area in Jezreel Valley.

Spinning division of textile factory at Kiryat Gat.
Atomic reactor at Naḥal Sorek.

most of second decade was period of rapid economic development. Industrialization rapidly increased and developments in agriculture included cultivation of N. Negev. Labor was largely organized in framework of Trade Union Federation (Histadrut). After 1965 elections government took steps to slow down economy, raising taxes and cutting expenditures. During 25 years, four devaluations of Israel pound were made; 1973 exchange rate was IL 4.20 to $1.00. Unified state education replaced "trends" which had prevailed in Mandatory period. Education was made compulsory up to age of 14 and number of institutes of higher learning grew. Agricultural settlement projects were extended and by 1973, 604 kibbutzim and moshavim had been founded. Minority citizens (Arabs, Druze, etc.) had full rights and several members in Knesset. After 1967, difficulties often arose with Arabs in administered areas, but Israel military government in these areas succeeded generally in surmounting them and helped Arabs develop economically. After Six-Day War Soviet Union and its satellites (except Rumania) severed diplomatic relations with Israel. Fr. 1970 a number of Russian Jews allowed to immigrate after prolonged struggle for right to leave USSR. Pop. (excl. administered areas) 3,164,000 (1972), incl. 2,636,600 Jews. 343,900 Muslims, 77,300 Christians, 37,300 Druze.

Israel postage stamp dedicated to export of diamonds, 1968.

Israel-Australia soccer match at the Ramat Gan Stadium, 1969.

ISRAEL GOVERNMENT INCOME, EXPENDITURE, AND BUDGETARY SURPLUSES OR DEFICITS (IL. millions)

Budget year	Income	Expenditure	Surplus (+) or deficit (–)	Cumulative surplus (+) or deficit (–)[1]
1948/49	28.9	[1] 27.5	+1.4	+1.4
1949/50	92.9	[1] 93.8	–0.9	+0.4
1950/51	150.1	[1] 149.1	+ 0.7	+1.1
1951/52	196.2	209.0	–12.8	–11.7
1952/53	295.5	287.6	+7.9	–3.8
1953/54	402.2	396.7	+5.5	+1.7
1954/55	661.4	[2] 653.5	+7.9	+9.5
1955/56	805.9	816.6	–10.7	–1.2
1956/57	978.0	1,049.8	–71.8	–73.0
1957/58	1,121.4	1,132.3	–10.9	–83.8
1958/59	1,377.2	1,298.8	+78.5	–5.4
1959/60	1,480.9	1,514.7	–33.3	–39.2
1960/61	1,708.2	1,728.8	–20.7	–59.8
1961/62	2,302.3	2,217.9	+30.4	–29.4
1962/63	2,594.6	2,476.5	+118.1	+88.7
1963/64	3,223.1	3,113.8	+109.3	+198.0
1964/65	3,655.0	3,676.0	–21.0	+177.0
1965/66	4,386.1	4,397.8	–11.8	+165.2
1966/67	4,471.5	4,855.5	–384.0	–218.8
1967/68	6,359.3	6,516.1	–156.8	–375.6
1968/69	7,427.1	7,862.4	–435.3	–810.9
1969/70	10,050.2	10,027.8	+22.4	–788.5
1970/71	12,537.3	12,341.4	+195.9	–592.6
1971/72	16,593.0	16,327.9	+265.1	–327.5

Source: Accountant General's Report
1. Does not include the entire defense budget
2. Including IL. 25.1 million of foreign exchange equalization fund.

Israel Museum, Jerusalem.

Israel, Kingdom of, the northerly of the two kingdoms with which Solomon's kingdom was divided after his death. Also called the Northern Kingdom and the Kingdom of Samaria. It consisted of Ten Tribes (i.e., all except Judah and Benjamin). Capital: Shechem and later, Samaria. Main sanctuaries: Shechem and Dan. In existence for 206 years, generally at war with Damascus and sometimes with Judah. Fell to Assyrians in 722 B.C.E. after which its inhabitants were deported.

KINGDOM OF ISRAEL – KINGS

928–907	Jeroboam I
907–906	Nadab
906–883	Baasha
883–882	Elah
882	Zimri
882–871	Omri
871–852	Ahab
852–851	Ahaziah
851–842	Jehoram
842–814	Jehu
814–800	Jehoahaz
800–784	Jehoash
784–748	Jeroboam II
748–747	Zechariah
748–747	Shallum
747–737	Menahem
737–735	Pekahiah
735–733	Pekah
733–724	Hoshea

French Mirages delivered to Israel Air Force, 1964.

Electronic computer at Bar Ilan University.

Kibbutz Gadot shelled from Syrian positions, 1966.

Jerusalem Arab voting in municipal election, Oct. 1969.

Soldiers at the Western Wall, Six-Day War, 1967.

Israel, Wilfrid (1899–1943), Jewish communal figure; member of prominent Berlin merchant family. Emigrated to England 1939. Helped rescue European refugees; died returning fr. mission in Portugal when plane shot down by Luftwaffe.

Israel Academy of Sciences and Humanities, institution to promote work in sciences and humanities, advise government, and represent Israel in international conferences; founded 1961, seat in Jerusalem.

Israel ben Eliezer Ba'al Shem Tov (Besht, c. 1700–1760), founder of Ḥasidism in E. Europe; b. Podolia, grew up in poverty, lived in remote Carpathian Mts. In mid-1730s revealed himself as healer, and leader of circle which grew rapidly. His aspiration to go to Ereẓ Israel never materialized. Folktales and his teachings show his personal charm and magnetism, and ecstatic personality. Advocated devotional joy. Typically described not as formal preacher but as holding conversations with individuals, incl. women and simple folk, which aroused criticism, as did his wonder-working and absence fr. his teachings of talmudic scholarship. Teachings known only fr. oral traditions recorded by disciples, such as Jacob Joseph of Polonnoye. Extensive later hagiography on him incl. both historical and legendary material.

The "bet ha-midrash" of Israel Ba'al Shem Tov, on stamp issued by Israel Post Office in 1960.

Israel ben Perez of Polotsk (d.c. 1785), ḥasidic rabbi; leading disciple of Dov Baer of Mezhirech. Helped Menahem Mendel of Vitebsk spread Ḥasidism in White Russia. Went to Ereẓ Israel with 300 ḥasidim 1777.

Israel ben Samuel of Shklov (d. 1839), Lithuanian talmudist. After settling in Ereẓ Israel with other disciples of Vilna Gaon 1809, became the broad-minded head of their community ("Kolel ha-Perushim") in Safed and Jerusalem. Prepared Vilna Gaon's commentaries for publication and printed laws on Ereẓ Israel. On Sabbath, spoke only Hebrew.

Israel Defense Forces (abbr. **IDF;** Heb. **Ẓeva Haganah le-Israel;** abbr. **Ẓahal**), Israel's army, established May 26, 1948 as successor to Haganah (with Irgun units disbanded and incorporated). Comprises three types of service: conscript, reserve, regular. Men aged 18–55 and women 18–38 are liable for service. Youths are conscripted at age 18, boys for 3 years, girls for 2. IDF is integrated organization controlling land, sea, and air forces. Regular forces limited mainly to officers and specialists. Headed by chief of staff subordinate to minister of defense. Army has achieved international reputation for efficiency, based largely on its victories against overwhelming material odds in War of Independence (1948), Sinai campaign (1956), Six-Day War (1967) and, after initial setback, in Yom Kippur War (1973). Also has major educational function and has played important role in integration of immigrants.

Israel Exploration Society, society founded 1914 on model of foreign societies engaged in exploration of Ereẓ Israel, its history and antiquities; originally called Jewish Palestine Exploration Society. Publications in Hebrew and English.

Israeli, Benzion (1887–1954), pioneer of Second Aliyah; b. Ukraine, settled in Ereẓ Israel 1906. A founder of Kinneret. Cultivation of bananas in Jordan Valley and date trees in Israel are to his credit. Important role in volunteer movement to British army in WWII.

Israeli, Isaac ben Joseph (14th c.), Spanish author of *Yesod Olam,* classic Hebrew work on astronomy.

Israeli, Isaac ben Solomon (c. 855–c. 955), physician, philosopher; b. Egypt, in Kairouan fr. c. 905. His philosophical works widely known. Also wrote various specialized medical treatises and is regarded as among great physicians of early Middle Ages.

Israeli, Israel (d. 1317), Spanish talmudist; brother of Isaac b. Solomon Israeli and pupil of Asher b. Jehiel, for whom he translated halakhic texts fr. Arabic and whose interpretation of *takkanot* he challenged. In his commentary on *Avot* defended study of "Greek wisdom."

Israel Independence Day, see Independence Day, Israel.

Israelit, Der, leading Orthodox weekly in Germany, founded 1860 by Marcus Lehmann in Mainz. Hebrew edition, *Ha-Levanon,* appeared 1872–82; also appeared in Yiddish 1873–79. Organ of Agudat Israel. Closed 1938.

Israelitisch-Theologische Lehranstalt, leading Jewish theological seminary in Vienna, founded 1893. First rector Adolf Schwarz. Closed by Nazis 1938; valuable library confiscated.

Israel Labor Party (Heb. **Mifleget ha-Avodah ha-Yisra'elit**), Israel political party founded 1968 by merger of Mapai, Aḥdut ha-Avodah, and Rafi. See Knesset.

Israel Meir ha-Kohen (Kagen; known as **Ḥafeẓ Ḥayyim;** 1838–1933), rabbi, ethical writer, talmudist; lived in Radun, Lithuania. Through his personality, humility, and integrity – all recounted in hundreds of anecdotes – rose to become towering influence. Known by name of his first book, *Ḥafeẓ Ḥayyim,* on laws of slander. Wrote *Mishnah Berurah,* commentary on *Shulḥan Arukh, Oraḥ Ḥayyim.* A founder of Agudat Israel and Va'ad ha-Yeshivot (central fund for yeshivot).

Israel Museum, museum completed 1966–67, situated in Jerusalem and consisting of four main divisions: Bezalel National Art Museum (Jewish ethnology and folk art), Samuel Bronfman Biblical and Archaeological Museum, Billy Rose Art Garden (19th and 20th c. sculpture displayed in open air), and Shrine of the Book (Dead Sea Scrolls and Bar Kokhba Letters).

Israel of Ruzhin, see Ruzhin, Israel of

Israel Philharmonic Orchestra, Israel orchestra; founded by Bronislaw

Israel Philharmonic Orchestra conducted by Zubin Mehta

Huberman 1936 as rescue operation for Jewish musicians persecuted by Nazis as well as contribution to cultural life in Ereẓ Israel. First concert directed by Arturo Toscanini. Orchestra toured many countries and has international reputation. Main hall in Tel Aviv; performs throughout Israel.

Israëls, Jozef (1824–1911), Dutch painter. Member of "Haagse School," which produced realistic Dutch landscapes. Also often depicted Jewish subjects. His son **Isaac** (1865–1934), painter of city life.

Israelsohn, Jacob Izrailevich (1856–1924), Russian Semitic scholar; in Brussels, fr. 1922. Defense researcher for Beilis trial. Published editions of Josephus and geonic literature.

Isru Ḥag (Heb.), day following each of three pilgrim festivals. Treated in liturgy as minor holiday.

Issachar, son of Jacob and Leah; eponymous ancestor of tribe bearing his name. His invariable association with Zebulun testifies to proximity of two, and close ties. Territory lay SW of Sea of Galilee to W. of Jordan R.

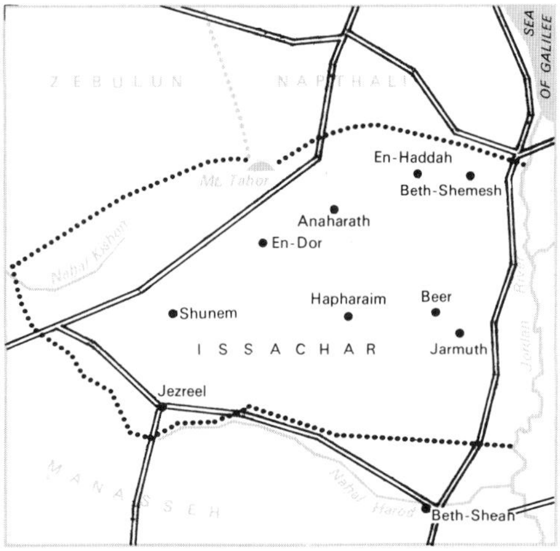

Territory of the tribe of Issachar

Issachar Baer ben Solomon Zalman (Klazki; d. 1807), Lithuanian talmudist; brother of Gaon of Vilna. Wrote commentary on Pentateuch and *Shulḥan Arukh.* Interested in secular learning.

Issachar Berman ben Naphtali ha-Kohen (Berman Ashkenazi; 16th c.), pupil of Moses Isserles and author of *Mattenot Kehunnah,* classic commentary on Midrash. Indexed subjects and biblical quotations in Zohar.

Isserlein, Israel ben Pethahiah (1390–1460), foremost German rabbi of his time. Made Wiener-Neustadt a Torah center, opposed excommunication, and quieted controversy. His responsa *(Terumat ha-Deshen),* which show erudition and respect for earlier rather than more recent legal authorities, are rich historical source.

Moses Isserles

Isserles, Moses ben Israel (Rema; 1525 or 1530–1572), Polish rabbi, *posek,* halakhic codifier. Left Cracow to study in Lublin under Shalom Shachna, whose daughter he married. Synagogue he built in her memory still stands. Also studied philosophy, astronomy, history. Until WWII his grave was site for widespread pilgrimage. Wrote on philosophy, Kabbalah, homiletics, science, but is best remembered for his *Mappah,* glosses on Caro's *Shulḥan Arukh,* which made it universally authoritative by adding Ashkenazi usage to Sephardi practice of codified law.

Issur ve-Hetter (Heb.), body of *halakhah* on forbidden foods and related topics. More specifically (fr. late 12th c.) literary genre dealing with this subject, reflecting local variations in religious practice, esp. in Germany.

Istanbul (before 1453 **Constantinople,** q.v.), city in Turkey. Jews left unscathed by 15th c. Ottoman conquerors. 40,000 Spanish and Portuguese refugees arrived following 1492 expulsion, raising local spiritual and cultural level. Congregations jealously kept local traditions. Jews prominent in scholarship, printing, commerce, medicine, and at court. One of world's great Jewish centers. In 17th c. community declined, esp. after failure of Shabbetai Ẓevi. Literacy in Hebrew declined; religious texts published in Spanish and Ladino. Refugees arrived after Russian revolution of 1905; 100,000 Jews before WWI. Under Kemal Ataturk Jews lost religious autonomy, and Zionist and religious activity was restricted. Jewish pop. 22,000 (1972), many having emigrated to Israel.

Istanbul Jewish woman, 17th cent., engraving by G. la Chapelle.

Italia, Shalom (c. 1619–c. 1655), engraver, etcher, draftsman. Active in Amsterdam, executing copper engravings, esp. of scrolls *(megillot)* of Esther, and portraits.

Italiener, Bruno (1881–1950), German army chaplain, later Reform rabbi in England, and historian of Jewish ms. illumination.

Italy, S. European republic. Jewish settlement continuous for 21 c. Expulsion already in 139 B.C.E. Most Roman conquerors followed liberal policies. Over 6,000 Judean captives brought there 70 C.E.; community numbered 50,000. Empire's acceptance of Christianity in 4th c. subjected Jews to limitations and persecutions incited by Church Fathers; Pope Gregory I (d. 604) preferred conversion without violence. Scholars and physicians in Rome in early Middle Ages. Church in 12th c. moved from attitude of protection to open hostility. Fr. 1230s Jews suffered under Inquisition, esp. in S. Became prominent in moneylending fr. 13th c. Scholarship and culture, religious and secular, produced rich array of devotees. Ritual murder charge in Trent 1475. Spain's attitude to Jews affected Italian possessions, so that they were expelled fr. region to region. Jews in C. and W. Italy fared better, though Venetians set up ghetto 1516. Pope Julius III ordered all copies of Talmud burned 1553, and for 2 c. Jews in papal states were oppressed, though scholarship still flourished. By late 16th c. ghetto was accepted all over country as was Jewish badge and compulsory attendance at conversionist sermons. Jews prominent in revolutionary activity of 19th c., which by stages brought emancipation; its academic

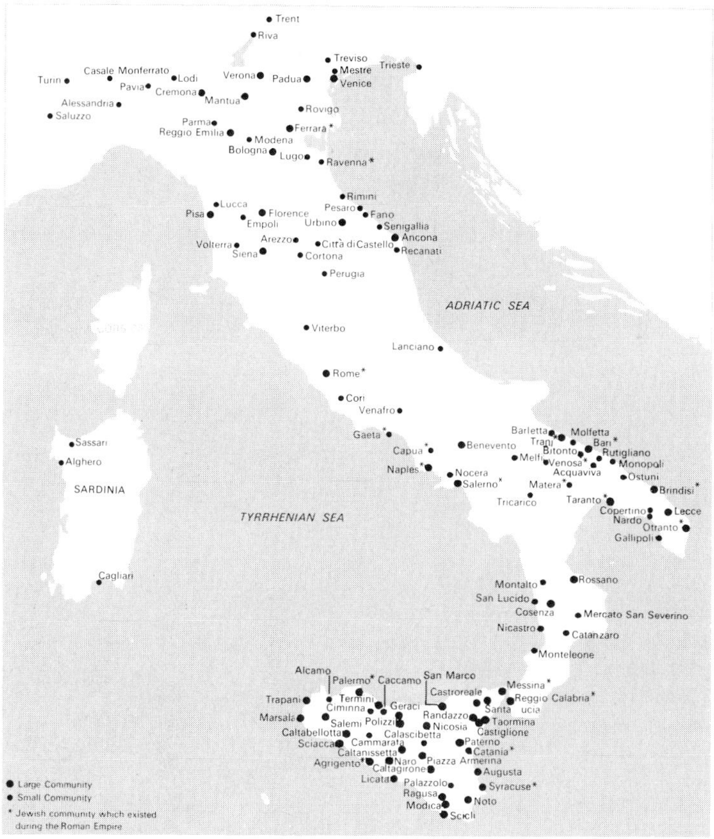

Major Jewish communities in Italy, 1450–1550

Engraving of a pageant display representing Mercury as bearer of peace, contributed by Jewish community of Leghorn, Italy, to festivities honoring arrival of Leopold I, 1766.

and political opportunities were immediately welcomed. Fascist movement became anti-Semitic only under German influence 1937–38. Introduced anti-Jewish legislation and many Jews emigrated. In WWII, 7,750 Jews became victims of Germans in "Final Solution." Jewish pop. 35,000 (1971), with main communities Rome and Milan.

Itelson, Gregor (1852–1926), philosopher; b. Russia, lived in Berlin. Interested in investigation of philosophical foundations of sciences; sought to reform principles of logic.

Jewish woman of Izmir, lithograph by E. Fulgenzi, 1838.

Ithamar, youngest son of Aaron. Assigned special duties as leader over all levites.

Itim, Israel's national news agency since its foundation 1950. Owned by all Israel daily newspapers. Its local news coverage is provided by its own network of correspondents all over Israel.

I.T.O. see Territorialism.

Itzig, Daniel (Daniel Jaffe, Daniel Berlin; 1723–1799), German banker, entrepreneur; leader of Berlin Jewish community. Confidential financier to Frederick William II of Prussia, who made him first Jew with full rights of citizenship 1791.

Iudex Judaeorum (Lat. "judge of the Jews"; Ger. **Judenrichter**), gentile official in medieval Austria who adjudicated conflicts and confirmed legal contracts bet. Christians and Jews.

Ivanov Frankovsk, see Stanislav.

Iyov of Minsk, see Brill, Joseph.

Iyyar, post-Exilic name of 2nd month of Jewish year; previously called Ziv. 29 days. Zodiac sign Taurus. 5th is Israel Independence Day; 18th is Lag ba-Omer.

Izates II, king of Adiabene c. 35–60 C.E. With his mother Helena, converted to Judaism. Buried in Jerusalem. Succeeded by none of 48 children, but by brother Monbaz II.

Izbica-Radzyn, ḥasidic dynasty; founded by **Mordecai Joseph Leiner of Izbica** (d. 1854). His atypical teachings center on moral determinism and eschatology. One of his descendants claimed to have discovered authentic *tekhelet* (blue coloring) which to this day distinguishes *ẓiẓit* of his followers. Last scion of dynasty, **Samuel Solomon,** perished in Holocaust.

I.Ẓ.L., see Irgun Ẓeva'i Le'ummi.

Izmir (Smyrna), city in Turkey. Jews there in early Christian era. During Middle Ages community decreased, possibly disappearing, though there was small Romaniot community in 16th c. In 17th c. center of commerce and culture, esp. Hebrew printing. Shabbetai Ẓevi born and had large following there. In following 2 c. community suffered fr. fires, epidemics, and blood libels; fell from 40,000 in 1868 to 25,000 in 1905 and 4,000 in 1971.

Izraelita, Polish-Jewish assimilationist weekly published 1866–1908. Under S.H. Peltin, opposed Orthodox camp and Zionism. Under Nahum Sokolow's editorship 1896, aired certain Zionist ideas. Had brief assimilationist revival 1915.

Initial "J" of "Jeremias," at beginning of prologue to Book of Haggai, 13th-cent. Bible, France.

Jabal, son of Lamech by Adah; originator of nomadism (Gen. 4:20).
Jabbok, one of principal E. tributaries of the Jordan. By cutting mountains of Gilead in two, forms natural boundary which served as political border through many historical periods. Jacob's struggle with angel took place on ford of Jabbok.
Jabesh-Gilead, Israelite city in Gilead in periods of Judges and monarchy. Inhabitants did not join Israelite expedition against Benjamin and in punishment city was destroyed (Judg. 21). Saul delivered it fr. Ammonites, and out of gratitude inhabitants saved bodies of Saul and his sons fr. indignity (I Sam. 31:11ff.).
Jabez, 16th c. family of scholars and Hebrew printers of Spanish origin. Produced scholarly works in Salonika, Adrianople, Constantinople, and partly reissued Talmud, which had been burned and banned in Italy 1553.
Jabez, Joseph ben Ḥayyim (d. 1507), Hebrew homilist, exegete; b. Spain, preached and wrote in Mantua. Blamed philosophical rationalism for some of his coreligionists' lapses of steadfastness under persecution.
Jabin, king of Hazor who headed Canaanite alliance and is mentioned in connection with battle of Merom (Josh. 11) and war of Deborah (Judg. 4-5).
Jabneh (Jamnia), ancient city on coastal plain of Israel, S. of Jaffa. Jabneh-Yam was harbor. By accession of Alexander Yannai already Hasmonean city and entire population was Jewish. After fall of Jerusalem, Sanhedrin reconstituted there under R. Johanan b. Zakkai and played key role in survival of Judaism in that crisis. Definitive canon of Bible concluded there. With outbreak of Bar Kokhba revolt ceased to be center of Jewish life, although strong Jewish element remained there. By 5th c. Christian. For modern period, see Yavneh.
Jabotinsky, Vladimir (Ze'ev; 1880–1940), Zionist leader, soldier, orator, and writer; b. Russia. Studied law in Rome and was correspondent of Odessa newspapers under the pen name "Altalena" 1898–1901. Back in Russia fr. 1903, leading force in Jewish self-defense, struggle for civic and minority rights. In WWI advocated Jewish Legion, which led to establishment of Zion Mule Corps which fought in Gallipoli, and in 1917 British government consented to formation of Jewish battalions, in one of which he served as lieutenant. Organized first self-defense in Ereẓ Israel (in riots of 1920). Sentenced to 15 years' imprisonment but reprieved. Joined Zionist Executive 1921 but resigned 1923, accusing it of acceptance of the Churchill White Paper. Formed and headed World Zionist Revisionists 1925. Seceded from Zionist movement 1935 and established New Zionist Organization. Fr. 1936 urged speedy evacuation of E. Europe and supported "illegal" immigration. Commander of I.Z.L. fr. 1937. Gifted writer in many languages. Translated Poe's *The Raven* and parts of Dante's *Divine Comedy* into Hebrew and wrote biblical novel *Samson the Nazirite* in Russian. His son **Eri** (1910–1969), engineer, mathematician, Prof. at Haifa Technion and headed Betar movement in Ereẓ Israel.
Jachin and Boaz, two pillars set up in front of Sanctuary in Solomon's Temple in Jerusalem. Probably free-standing pillars, one on each side of entrance. Function and meaning of names debated.

Jachin and Boaz, embroidered on velvet curtain for the Ark of the Law, Germany, 1716.

Vladimir Jabotinsky (right), as officer in Jewish Legion, with Jewish officer in French army, c. 1918.

Jackson, Solomon Henry (d. 1847), first Jewish printer in New York City. Translated Sephardi prayer book into English 1826; published first Jewish periodical in U.S. (*The Jew,* 1823–25).

Jacksonville, city in Fla., U.S. Jews there fr. early 19th c., but congregation (Reform) established only 1882. Orthodox congregation formed 1901. Jewish pop. 6,000 (1971).

Jacob, son of Isaac, younger twin brother of Esau, third of Patriarchs of people of Israel. Exploited Esau's hunger to purchase birthright (Gen. 25: 29–34) and deceived Isaac to obtain final blessing (ch. 27). Fled to his uncle Laban in Haran, en route having dream in which God confirmed to him his covenant with Abraham. Served Laban 14 years for his brides Leah and Rachel. Had 6 sons and daughter by Leah and 4 by concubines; Rachel gave birth to Joseph and Benjamin. By cheating Laban became prosperous and fled fr. Haran. Following encounter with angel at ford of Jabbok, name changed to Israel. His confrontation with Esau turned out to be cordial and Jacob settled in Shechem. In his old age grieved "loss" of Joseph, and when Joseph was discovered in Egypt took his family and settled there, dying at age 147. Body embalmed and eventually brought for burial in Cave of Machpelah.

Jacob welcoming his sons from Egypt "Sarajevo Haggadah," Spain, 14th cent.

Jacob, Benno (1862–1945), rabbi, Bible scholar; b. Breslau. Denied both claims of modern Bible criticism (as being tendentious) and dogma of Mosaic authorship and literal inspiration of Pentateuch. Opposed Zionism. Fr. 1939 in England.

Jacob, Berthold (pen name of **Berthold Salomon;** 1898–1944), German Jewish publicist. Radical pacifist who opposed German militarism and rearmament. Abducted by Nazis fr. Lisbon; d. in prison.

Jacob, François (1920–), French biologist. Nobel Prize 1965 for work on cellular genetic function and influence of viruses. Worked in Pasteur Inst.

Jacob, Max (1876–1944), French poet, novelist; converted to Catholicism 1915, lived in a monastery periodically; d. in concentration camp. His aesthetic principle centered on establishing "new harmony" to enable perception of reality.

Max Jacob, portrait by Picasso

Jacob, Naomi Ellington (1889–1964), English novelist. Wrote many books incl. *The Gollantz Saga.*

Jacob, Testament of, apocryphal work based on Genesis 49. Composed as supplement to extant testaments of Abraham and Isaac.

Jacob ben Asher (1270?–1340), halakhic authority; son and pupil of Asher b. Jehiel (the Rosh). Aimed at bringing uniformity into religious practices. His comprehensive compilation of private and public law, *Arba'ah Turim* (whence his name, "Ba'al ha-Turim") is milestone in halakhic codification. Chiefly followed legal decisions of his father and Maimonides. Universally accepted as authoritative, widely published and annotated, served as basis for Caro's monumental *Beit Yosef.* Also wrote commentary on Pentateuch.

Jacob ben Ḥayyim ben Isaac ibn Adonijah (c. 1470–c. 1538), masoretic scholar in Tunis and Italy; proofreader. Edited masorah for Rabbinic Bible 1524–25. Defended talmudic tradition. Late in life converted to Christianity.

Jacob ben Ḥayyim Talmid (d. after 1594), leader of Egyptian Jewry under Turkish authorities. After personal feud, excommunicated, and banished by Ottoman pasha.

Jacob ben Jacob ha-Kohen (13th c.), Spanish kabbalist. Prominent in Gnostic trend in Kabbalah. His records of his visions and writings on demonology and Divine names are veiled by numerical combinations of letters.

Jacob ben Judah of London (13th c.), English rabbinical scholar. Wrote *Eẓ Ḥayyim,* handbook on religious law and ritual. Throws light on medieval Anglo-Jewry.

Jacob ben Korshai (2nd c.), *tanna;* disciple of Meir, taught in school of R. Simeon b. Gamaliel. Judah ha-Nasi received Mishnah of Meir through Jacob. Saying: "This world is like a vestibule to the world to come."

Jacob ben Meir Tam, see Tam, Jacob ben Meir.

Jacob ben Nethanel ben (al-) Fayyūmī (12th c.), *nagid* of Yemenite Jewry during decrees against Judaism c. 1160. Recipient of Maimonides' celebrated "Epistle to Yemen" c. 1172 on steadfastness in faith.

Jacob ben Nissim ibn Shahin (d. 1106/7), scholar of Kairouan; father of Rav Nissim Gaon. N. African representative of Babylonian academies of Sura and Pumbedita on halakhic and financial matters. Recipient of historical responsum "The Letter of Sherira Gaon" 987 C.E. in reply to his question "How was the Mishnah written down?"

Jacob ben Yakar (d. 1064), German rabbi; principal teacher of Rashi. Studied under Gershom b. Judah in yeshivah of Mainz, which he evidently later headed together with Eliezer b. Isaac of Worms. Rashi commented on his humility.

Jacob ha-Kohen bar Mordecai, *gaon* of Sura 797–811. Possibly author of *Seder Tanna'im,* first methodological study of mishnaic and talmudic literature.

Jacobi, Abraham (1830–1919), pediatrician; founder of American pediatrics; b. Germany, lectured in pediatrics in New York for nearly 25 years. Established children's ward at Mt. Sinai Hospital. Published extensively.

Abraham Jacobi

Jacobi, Frederick (1891–1952), U.S. composer. Assistant conductor of Metropolitan Opera 1913–17; taught at Julliard School of Music. Composed quartet on American Indian themes and works on Jewish subjects for synagogue use.

Jacobi, Karl Gustav Jacob (1804–1851), German mathematician. His works on differential equations and calculus of variations serve as mathematical basis for modern physics. His brother, **Moritz (Moses) Hermann** (1801–1874), physicist, architect. Invented galvano-plastic process of electrotyping. Both brothers converted to Christianity.

Jacob Isaac ha-Ḥozeh mi-Lublin (1745–1815), ḥasidic *ẓaddik;* a founder of ḥasidic movement in Poland and Galicia; known posthumously as "the Seer of Lublin" for his psychological and spiritual insight. Studied under Elimelech of Lizhansk but broke away to lead his own group; did not found dynasty. Stressed "practical ẓaddikism" with material needs first, rather than purely spiritual aspirations.

Jacob Joseph ben Ẓevi Ha-Kohen Katz of Polonnoye (d.c. 1782), rabbi, preacher; first theoretician of Ḥasidism. Came under influence of Israel Ba'al Shem Tov, whom he expected (mistakenly) to succeed as leader of movement. His homiletical *Toledot Ya'akov Yosef* formulates basic teachings of Ba'al Shem Tov and is major source for his teachings. Wrote on joy in divine service and of responsibilities of *ẓaddik.*

Jacob Joseph of Ostrog (Yeivi; 1738–1791), pietist preacher (*maggid*); lived in poverty. In period of social upheaval in E. Europe, showed deep sense of social morality, demanding exemplary integrity of rabbis and communal leaders.

Jacob Koppel ben Moses of Mezhirech (d.c. 1740), Polish kabbalist, influenced by Shabbateanism, despite various disclaimers. His theosophy includes concepts introduced into Kabbalah by Nathan of Gaza.

Jacob Nazir (Jacob ben Saul of Lunel; 12th c.), scholar, kabbalist. One of group of Provençal hermits who wrote of their visions and meditations on *kavvanot* and *Sefirot.* Visited Ereẓ Israel, after 1187.

Jacob of Dubno, see Kranz, Jacob.

Jacob of Orleans (d. 1189), tosafist; pupil of Jacob Tam. Drew up controversial formula for Jewish moneylenders to circumvent prohibition of usury. Martyred in England.

Jacobowski, Ludwig (1868–1900), German poet, author. His works reflect attempt to find synthesis between Judaism and German culture.

Joseph Jacobs

Israel Jacobson

Jacobs, Aletta (1854–1929), Dutch physician, feminist, pacifist. First women to study at Dutch univ., first practicing Dutch woman doctor. Championed women's emancipation, neo-Malthusianism for working class. Sponsored Hague International Peace Conference 1915, which led to foundation of Women's International League for Peace and Freedom.

Jacobs, Joseph (1854–1916), historian, folklorist, scholar; b. Australia, settled in England. Editor of periodical *Folk-Lore;* founded and edited 1896–99 *Jewish Year Book;* wrote *Jews of Angevin England.* Fr. 1900 in U.S. as an editor of *Jewish Encyclopaedia;* also taught at Jewish Theological Seminary.

Jacobs, Louis (1920–), English rabbi, theological writer. Chief Rabbi I. Brodie's veto of his appointment to head Jews' College on grounds of heterodoxy led to violent controversy within British Jewry. In his *We Have Reason to Believe, Jewish Values,* and *Principles of the Jewish Faith,* accepted some of the methods and results of biblical Higher Criticism, denying literal inspiration of Pentateuch. Also wrote on Kabbalah and Ḥasidism.

Jacobs, Rose Gell (1888-), U.S. Zionist leader. Pres. Hadassah 1930–32, 1934–37, member of Executive of the Jewish Agency for Palestine 1937–46.

Jacobsen, Arne Emil (1902–1971), Danish architect. Influenced by Le Corbusier and Mies van der Rohe, Denmark's leading architect fr. 1930s. Gained international fame after WWII.

Jacobsohn, Siegfried (1881–1926), German critic, left-wing editor. His periodical *Weltbuehne* (fr. 1918) reflected outlook of independent-minded leftist intellectuals.

Jacobson, Dan (1929–), S. African novelist; in England fr. 1954. His novels and short stories center on moral implications of apartheid in S. Africa and problem of Jewish identity in modern world. Works incl. *The Beginners, The Rape of Tamar,* and *The Zulu and the Zeide* (also a musical).

Jacobson, Edward (Eddie; 1891–1955), U.S. businessman; active partner and longtime friend of President Truman in Independence, Mo. At critical moment in 1948 persuaded Truman to see Weizmann in what proved fateful meeting for nascent State of Israel.

Jacobson, Israel (1768–1828), German financier; pioneer of Reform Judaism through foundation of schools and temples. Founded school in Seesen which existed until 1930s. Helped Jews in civil rights. Fr. 1810 in Berlin where he had Reform services in his home. Most of his children were baptized.

Jacobson, Kurt (1904–), Portuguese biochemist. Prof. of organic chemistry and vice-rector at Univ. of Lisbon. Research in enzymology. Pres. Centro Israelita de Portugal.

Jacobson, Ludvig Levin (1783–1843), Danish physician, anatomist, naturalist. His anatomical discoveries and surgical inventions earned him great recognition.

Jacobson, Paul Henrich (1859–1923), German organic chemist. Wrote and edited major chemistry reference works. Research on azo-compounds.

Jacobson, Sydney (1908–), British editor. Edited *Daily Herald* 1962, *The Sun* 1964. Chairman of Odhams Newspapers 1968.

Jacobson, Victor (Avigdor; 1869–1935), Zionist leader, diplomat; b. Crimea. Unofficial representative of Zionist Organization in Turkey 1906. During WWI headed Copenhagen office of Zionist organization. Member of Zionist Executive and in his last years represented Zionist Organization and Jewish Agency in Paris and at League of Nations.

Jacobsthal, Paul Ferdinand (1880–1957), German classical archaeologist. Although baptized, forced by Nazi persecution to leave Germany; settled in England. Wrote standard work on floral ornaments in Greek vase paintings.

Jacoby, Hanokh (Heinrich; 1909–), composer; b. Germany. Taught at Conservatoire of Music, Jerusalem, 1934; director of Academy of Music, Jerusalem, 1954–58. Joined Israel Philharmonic Orchestra 1959. Composed symphonies, concertos, etc.

Jacoby, Johann (1805–1877), Prussian politician. Active in mid-19th c. struggle for liberalization. One of ideologists of German democracy. Member of Prussian National Assembly 1849, Chamber of Deputies 1858.

Jacoby, Oswald (1902–), U.S. bridge champion. Leading U.S. bridge player 1959, 1961, 1962. Author of books on card games.

Jadassohn, Josef (1863–1936), German dermatologist. Prof. at Breslau Univ. First identified scaling skin infection ("Jadassohn's disease").

Jaddua, high priest in Second Temple period fr. c. 400 B.C.E. Josephus' account, which makes him contemporary of Alexander the Great, is probably legendary.

Jadīd al-Islam (Arab. "new Muslims"), Jews converted by force to Islam, mainly crypto-Jewish victims of forced conversions in Persia in 17th–18th c. (especially in Meshed).

Jadlowker, Hermann (1878–1953), tenor. U.S. debut at Metropolitan Opera 1910. Settled in Tel Aviv as voice teacher after 1938.

Jael slaying Sisera, sepia drawing by Rembrandt.

Jael, wife of Heber the Kenite who killed the fleeing Canaanite commander Sisera. He had taken refuge in her tent after his defeat by Deborah and Barak (Judg. 4–5).

Jaffa (Joppa), ancient port in C. Israel. Oldest remains fr. 16th c. B.C.E. In 15th–13th c. B.C.E. ruled by Egypt. Probably remained outside Israelite settlement. Conquered by Sennacherib of Assyria in 8th c. Jonah's port of embarkation, and connected with Greek legend of

"Ḥalutzim" arriving in the port of Jaffa, c. 1935.

Andromeda. Fr. 301 B.C.E. Hellenistic city. Under Roman rule free city. Vespasian built port there for Tenth Legion. Jews lived there in 2nd–4th c. C.E. Fr. 7th c. important port for Muslims and later for Crusaders. Was almost deserted but developed quickly after opening of Suez Canal. Arabs settled there in 19th–20th c. Fell to Jewish forces 1948 and most Arab inhabitants left. Amalgamated with Tel Aviv 1949. Subsequently port was closed and Old Jaffa developed as artists' quarter and tourist center. (See also Tel Aviv).

Jaffa, German brothers who were early New Mexico settlers. **Henry N.** (1846–1901), first mayor of Albuquerque; organized first synagogue. **Nathan** (1863–1945), territorial secretary of New Mexico by presidential appointment; mayor of Santa Fe.

Jaffe, family of Hebrew printers in Lublin in 16th–17th c. Founded by **Kalonymus ben Mordecai Jaffe** (d.c. 1603). Produced biblical, liturgical, rabbinic works.

Jaffe, Abraham B. (1924–), Hebrew literary critic, editor; b. Bessarabia; settled in Ereẓ Israel 1940. Wrote on Shlonsky, French literature, Bessarabian Jewry. Literary editor of *Al ha-Mishmar* fr. 1951.

Jaffe, Bezalel (1868–1925), Zionist leader in Russia and Ereẓ Israel; brother of Leib Jaffe. Member of Benei Moshe, active in Zionist movement in Lithuania. Settled in Ereẓ Israel 1909, where he engaged in land purchases to extend area of Tel Aviv. A founder of Tel Aviv and pres. of Jaffa-Tel Aviv Jewish community.

Jaffe, Daniel, see Itzig, Daniel.

Jaffe, Israel ben Aaron (c. 1640–after 1703), kabbalist in Ukraine and Belorussia. His *Or Yisrael* on Zohar aroused charges of Shabbateanism.

Jaffe, Leib (1876–1948), Zionist leader; b. Lithuania. Leading Zionist propagandist. Participated in First Zionist Congress and later edited *Sefer ha-Congress* about it. Wrote poetry, mainly in Russian; translated Bialik into Russian. Edited Zionist periodicals in Russia, and when he arrived in Ereẓ Israel 1920 became editor of *Haaretz*. Joined Keren Hayesod 1923 and was its co-director. Killed in Arab bomb attack on Jewish Agency building.

Leib Jaffe

Jaffe, Leonard (1926–), U.S. space program engineer. Director of communication and navigation satellite programs of Office of Space Sciences and Applications Satellites fr. 1963.

Jaffe, Meir of Ulm (15th c.), German scribe, bookbinder. Wrote what came to be known as Cincinnati *Haggadah*.

Jaffe, Mordecai ben Abraham (c.1535–1612), talmudist, kabbalist, communal leader in Bohemia, Italy, Poland, Lithuania. Active in Council of Four Lands. His halakhic codification, *Levush Malkhut,* was based on Caro's *Beit Yosef* which Jaffe found too long; enjoyed widespread acceptance. Also wrote on philosophy and the calendar.

Jaffe, Mordecai-Gimpel (1820–1891), Russian rabbi, member of Ḥibbat Zion. Opposed religious reform. Encouraged *aliyah* of farmers. In Ereẓ Israel fr. 1888; demanded compliance with *shemittah* laws.

Jaffe, Sir Otto (1846–1929), Irish industrialist, communal leader; b. Germany. Head of linen firm that became major industrial concern in N. Ireland. Lord Mayor of Belfast 1899, 1904. Headed Belfast Jewish community. Hostility during WWI resulting fr. his German origin led him to move to England.

Jaffe, Sam (1897–), U.S. actor. Films incl. *Lost Horizon, Grand Hotel,* and *The Asphalt Jungle.*

Widely known in 1960s for role in U.S. TV series *Ben Casey*.

Jaffe, Samuel ben Isaac Ashkenazi (d. 16th c.), commentator on whole of *Midrash Rabbah,* author of legal and homiletical works. Rabbi of Ashkenazi community of Constantinople.

Jaffe-Margoliot, Israel David (c. 1802–1864), Hungarian rabbi. His clear expositions of Orthodox attitude against Reform made impression on moderate Reformers. Maintained that Reform innovations, although to be opposed, did not warrant schism in community.

Jagel, Abraham (16th c.), ethical writer; identified by some with Abraham b. Hananiah Jagel. Author of *Gei Ḥizzayon,* narrative and ethical work, partly autobiographical, partly moralistic Renaissance novellae on sojourns in heavenly regions, with quasi-kabbalistic accounts of visions.

Jagel, Abraham ben Hananiah Dei Galicchi (16th–17th c.), Italian philosopher. Author of *Lekaḥ Tov,* book of religious guidance modeled on contemporary Christian catechisms. Also wrote on law, astrology, astronomy.

Jahrzeit, see Yahrzeit.

Jair, family and head of ancestral house in tribe of Manasseh (Num. 32:41). After defeat of Og of Bashan, family took towns of Amorites in Argob (Deut. 3:14). See Havvoth-Jair.

Jair, Gileadite who judged Israel for 22 years in generation preceding Jephthah (Judg. 10: 3–5).

Immanuel Jakobovits

Jakobovits, Immanuel (1921–), British rabbi. Chief rabbi of Dublin fr. 1949, rabbi of Fifth Avenue Synagogue, New York, fr. 1958, chief rabbi of United Hebrew Congregations of British Commonwealth fr. 1966.

Jakobovits, Tobias (1887–1944), Prague librarian, historian of Czechoslovakian Jewry. When head of Jewish museum, deported with his staff to Auschwitz.

Jakobson, Max (1923–), Finnish journalist, diplomat. Press Attaché of Finnish embassy in Washington 1953–59, chief of press dept. at Finnish foreign ministry 1962–65, permanent representative of Finland in UN fr. 1965.

Synagogue of Kingston, Jamaica, built 1911.

Jewish Community Center, Tokyo, Japan.

Jakobson, Roman (1896–), philologist, literary historian. Cofounder of Prague linguistic group which pioneered major advances in modern linguistics. In U.S. fr. WWII. Taught at Columbia, Harvard, MIT. Made fundamental contributions in general linguistics and Slavic studies.

Jamaica, island in W. Indies. Sephardi Jews there before British conquest 1655; thereafter Jews fr. Brazil, England. Franchise granted 1831. Sephardim and Ashkenazim maintain joint congregation in Kingston, where most of 600 Jews live.

James, Harry (1916–), trumpet player, band leader. Started own group after two years with Benny Goodman's band which featured his brilliant trumpet solos. Popular swing arrangements in 1940s.

Jammer, Moshe (1915–), Israel physicist. Prof. of science, head of physics dept. at Bar Ilan Univ. fr. 1959, rector fr. 1962.

Jamnia, see Jabneh.

Jampel, Sigmund (1874–1934), rabbi, Bible scholar; b. Galicia. Rabbi at Schwedt, Brandenburg. Demonstrated value of archaeological and epigraphical finds in establishing antiquity of historical accounts of Bible and in questioning Wellhausen's hypotheses.

Janco, Marcel (1895–), Israel painter; b. Bucharest. Part of Dada movement in Paris. Settled in Ereẓ Israel 1941. A founder of New Horizon group 1947. Founded Ein Hod artists' village 1953 and headed its council for many years.

Jankélévitch, Vladimir (1903–), French philosopher. Prof. at Lille and Sorbonne. Influenced by Henri Bergson and exponent of his teachings. Writings reflect concern with overcoming consciousness directed to unchangeable past.

Janner, Barnett, Lord (1892–), British communal and Zionist leader, lawyer. Liberal MP 1931–35, Labour MP 1945–70 becoming leading Zionist spokesman. Pres. British Board of Deputies 1955–64. Pres. British Zionist Federation fr. 1950.

Janovsky, Saul Joseph (1864–1939), Yiddish journalist, editor; b. Russia. Editor in London and New York of anarchist Yiddish periodicals and workers' newspapers.

Janowitz, Morris (1919–), U.S. sociologist. Taught at Univ. of Chicago and Michigan. Books center on studies of prejudice, public opinion, military establishment.

Janowski, David Markelovich (1868–1927), French chess master. Attacked brilliantly but frequently failed to employ required defensive strategy. Lost world championship matches to Emanuel Lasker 1901, 1910.

Janowsky, Oscar Isaiah (1900–), U.S. historian. Prof. at CCNY fr. 1948. Principal interests recent European history and Jewish studies. His study for Jewish Welfare Board (Janowsky Report) affected orientation of Jewish community centers. Also wrote study of Jewish education in U.S.

Japan, Asian state. In 1860s 50 Jewish families fr. Poland, England, and U.S. set up community in Yokohama. Refugees fr. Russian revolution of 1905, 1917 settled, as did refugees fr. Nazism in early 1940s. Community increased temporarily through addition of military personnel during American Occupation 1945–52 and Korean War 1950–53. 500 Jews in 1972, mostly in Tokyo and Yokohama.

Japhet, Israel Meyer (1818–1892), German composer, teacher. Published liturgical melodies for cantor and choir in uncomplicated classical style.

Japheth, son of Noah. Eponymous ancestor of various ethnic groups to W. and N. of Israel, largely composed of Indo-European stock.

Japheth ben Ali ha-Levi (10th c.), Karaite scholar in Jerusalem. Published Arabic translation of Scriptures, with eclectic commentary which perpetuated Karaite traditions and grammatical notes. Wrote tracts against Saadiah Gaon and rabbinism.

Japhia, ancient city, identified with Yafa, Arab village SW of Nazareth. Largest village in Galilee; sacked by Romans. Remained Jewish town, and two synagogues were found on site.

Jarash, see Gerasa.

Jarblum, Marc (1887–1972), Zionist leader. A founder of Po'alei Zion in Poland. Moved to Paris 1907. Pres. French Zionist Organization. Won over Léon Blum and other French socialist leaders to Zionist cause. Fr. 1955 in Tel Aviv; active in Histadrut.

Jaroslaw, town in Poland. Great fairs in 16th–17th c. fostered growth of highly developed Jewish intercommunal institutions; Council of Lands frequently convened there. Jewish pop. of thousands deported and killed 1939.

Jasieński (Zyskind), Bruno (1901–1939), Polish author. Wrote Communist futurist novel in Paris. Moved to Russia 1929 and helped organize Union of Soviet Writers. His novel describing conflicts arising fr. Socialist reconstruction in Tadzhikistan resulted in his imprisonment, where he died.

Jasinowski, Israel Isidore (1842–1917), Russian Zionist leader. Headed Ḥibbat Zion movement in Warsaw, joined Zionist movement and supported Uganda Scheme. Later joined Jewish Territorial Organization.

Jasny, Naum (1883–1967), economist; b. Ukraine, devised food policies for Soviet government, worked in Germany, moved to U.S. 1933. Senior economist with Dept. of Agriculture; associated with Stanford Univ. fr. 1939.

Jason (2nd c. B.C.E.), high priest; son of Simeon II. Conspired through Antiochus Epiphanes to depose his brother Onias III and buy high priesthood for himself 175. Founded within Jerusalem city-state of Antiochia; its Hellenizing influence sparked Hasmonean revolt. Outbid and displaced fr. office by Menelaus. Died a vagabond 168.

Jason of Cyrene (2nd c. B.C.E.), Jewish historian who wrote on Maccabean revolt. His book is not extant and is known only from II Maccabees, which claims to be epitome (II Macc. 2:23).

Jassinowsky, Pinchas (1886–1954), *ḥazzan,* composer of liturgical music and Yiddish folksongs in Russia and U.S.

Jassy (Iasi), city in Rumania (in former Moldavia). Jewish merchants there in 15th c. Cossack massacres 1650, 1652, blood libel 1726, expulsion order 1867. Center of anti-Semitism in 1880s, 1890s. 40,000 Jews in 1899, incl. many merchants and bankers. Famed in 19th c. for Hebrew and Yiddish publishing and Yiddish theater. Violent anti-Semitism bet. wars. In mid-1941, German and Rumanian patrols slaughtered 12,000 Jews. 2,000 Jewish families in 1969.

Marcus M. Jastrow

Jastrow, family of scholars originating in Prussian Poland, later in U.S. **Marcus Mordecai** (1829–1903), progressive rabbi in Warsaw, among leaders of historical school, and opponent of radical Reform. Rabbi at Rodeph Shalom, Philadelphia, fr. 1886. Prominent in biblical scholarship. Wrote monumental *Dictionary of the Targumim, the Talmud Babli and Yerushalmi and the Midrashic Literature.* His son **Morris** (1861–1922), orientalist at Univ. of Pennsylvania; strongly anti-Zionist; another son, **Joseph** (1863–1944), wrote on psychology of perception and abnormality. Pres. American Psychological Association 1900.

Jastrun (Agatstein), Mieczyslaw (1903–), Polish poet, essayist, translator. Member of Skamander literary group. Independent-minded Communist who was among authors of 1964 manifesto protesting cultural policy of Polish Communist Party and government.

Jászi, Oszkár (1875–1957), Hungarian political scientist. Minister of national minorities 1918; recognized right of minorities' self-determination. In U.S. fr. 1921. Taught at Oberon College. Baptized.

Javal, French family. **Jacques** (1786–1858), Paris banker, established early printed-textile mill, pres. Paris Consistoire 1824–29. His son **Leopold** (1804–1872), cavalry officer, railway pioneer, member of Chamber of Deputies and National Assembly. Leopold's son **Emile** (1839–1907), renowned oculist, member of Academy of Medicine, Chamber of Deputies. Another son, **Ernest** (1843–1897), director of National Institute for the Deaf and Dumb.

Javan, son of Japheth son of Noah and father of Elishah, Tarshish, Kittim, Dodanim. Name reflects Hellenic tribal name of Ionia and designates W. coast of Asia Minor and Aegean archipelago. Continued to be Hebrew name for Greece.

Javid (Djavid) Bey (1875–1926), Turkish economist, statesman; born to Doenmeh family. Member of Young Turk movement and lecturer in Salonika. Minister of finance 1910, 1913–14, 1917–18. Arrested following assassination attempt on Kemal Ataturk, charged with trying to revive Young Turk movement, and executed.

Javitz, Jacob Koppel (1904–), U.S. lawyer, politician. Republican congressman 1946–54, senator fr. 1956. Favored by liberal and Jewish voters in N.Y. because of public-minded voting record. Active in Jewish and pro-Israel organizations.

Jawitz, Joseph, see Jabez, Joseph.

Ze'ev Jawitz

Jacob K. Javits

Jawitz, Ze'ev (1847–1924), writer, historian. His outlook had roots in Frankfort Orthodoxy and Ḥibbat Zion movement. Active in Va'ad ha-Lashon in Ereẓ Israel 1888–94. One of Hebrew writers to describe Jewish agricultural life in Ereẓ Israel. Wrote 14-vol. Jewish history in Hebrew. Last years in London.

J.D.C., see American Jewish Joint Distribution Committee.

J.D.L., see Jewish Defense League.

Jebusites, people of Canaan; of obscure origin. Early inhabitants of Jerusalem (Jebus) before conquest by David.

Jeconiah, see Jehoiachin.

Jedaiah, name of two priestly ancestral houses mentioned in list of heads of ancestral houses during term of office of Joiakim the high priest (Neh. 12). Relationship between the two unclear.

Jedaiah ben Abraham Bedersi (ha-Penini; c. 1270–1340), poet, philosopher. Wrote ascetic moralistic works in florid prose, notably *Sefer Beḥinat Olam* and notes on Avicenna and on Averroes' commentary on Aristotle's *Physics.* Defended Jews of Provence against Adret's charge of heresy 1305.

Jedīd al-Islam, see Jadīd al-Islam.

Jeduthun, head of family of singers whom David singled out fr. among levites.

Jehiel ben Joseph of Paris (d.c. 1265), French talmudist, tosafist. Main Jewish protagonist in Disputation of Paris 1240, which led to burning of Talmud. Founded academy in Acre 1260.

Jehiel Meir (Lifschits) of Gostynin (1816–1888), rabbi, ḥasidic *ẓaddik;* known as "Good Jew of Gostynin" or "Psalms Jew" (Yid. *Der Tilim Yid*) for his simple modesty and teachings on Psalms, advocating them as prayer texts. Sholem Asch's novel *Salvation* is based on his life.

Jehiel Michael ("Michel") of Zloczow (c. 1731–1786), early propagator of Ḥasidism in Galicia; disciple of Ba'al Shem Tov, then of Dov Baer of Mezhirech. Opened his sermons as follows: "I do not only command and admonish you but myself as well . . . " Founder of dynasty. His sons, **Joseph of Yampol, Mordecai of Kremenets, Isaac of Radzivilov, Moses of Vladimir-Volnyski,** and **Ze'ev Wolf of Zbarazh,** all founded dynasties.

Jehoahaz (Joahaz), king of Israel c. 814–800 B.C.E.; son of Jehu. Reigned during decline in Israel. Became vassal of Aram.

Jehoahaz (Shallum), king of Judah 609 B.C.E.; son of Josiah. After 3-month reign deposed by Pharaoh Neco, who put his elder brother Jehoiakim in his place. Exiled to Egypt, where he died.

Jehoash (Joash), king of Israel 801–785 B.C.E.; son of Jehoahaz. After Aramean power was broken by Adad-Nirari III of Assyria, freed Israel fr. Aramean control. Defeated Amaziah of Judah and entered Jerusalem, looting palace and Temple treasuries.

Jehoash, see Joash.

Jehoiachin (Coniah; Jeconiah), king of Judah 597 B.C.E.; son of Jehoiakim. Ascended throne at height of rebellion against Babylon and reigned 3 months. Nebuchadnezzar exiled him to Babylon with his family and officers and 10,000 captives. Mentioned in food-rationing lists found in Babylon.

Jehoiada (9th c. B.C.E.), chief priest in Jerusalem Temple during reigns of Athaliah and Joash. Married daughter of King Jehoram. Led popular resistance to Athaliah and new administrative procedures in Temple. Rescued Joash of house of David and enthroned him after Athaliah was killed. Acted as regent and restored Temple and its worship.

Jehoiakim (Eliakim), king of Judah 609–598 B.C.E.; son of Josiah. Made king by Pharaoh Neco in place of his brother Jehoahaz because of his pro-Egyptian policy. At first, vassal to Egypt fr. 605 B.C.E., under Babylonian yoke, but rebelled 602 and died while Jerusalem under siege.

Jehoiarib, one of 24 priestly divisions that served at First Temple. Jehoiarib family of Second Temple period was probably branch of high priestly family of Jedaiah-Jeshua. Hasmoneans and Josephus were descendants of this family.

Jehoram (Joram), king of Israel 850–842 B.C.E.; son of Ahab. Unsuccessfully fought against Mesha of Moab, who freed himself fr. Israel. Attacked Aram; wounded in battle, and while recovering, Jehu, his commander-in-chief, rebelled and killed him.

Jehoram (Joram), king of Judah 851–843 B.C.E.; son of Jehoshaphat, husband of Athaliah. During his reign close alliance existed between Judah and Israel. After unsuccessful war against Edom, Judah was ravaged by Philistines and others.

Jehoseph (Joseph) ha-Nagid (1035–1066), vizier of Granada at age 21; son of Samuel ha-Nagid. Taught Torah, composed Hebrew poems, and arranged his father's verse. Arrogant and indiscreet; became entangled in political intrigues which led to his assassination and to slaughter of Granada's Jews.

Jehoshaphat, king of Judah 870–846 B.C.E. Supported Israel in wars against Aram and Moab. Triple alliance Judah-Israel-Tyre brought commercial and economic vitality to three states. Made military and administrative reorganization.

Jehoshaphat, Valley of, place mentioned in Joel 4 where in fullness of time God will gather all nations to judge them. Popular tradition identified it with middle section of Kidron Valley, Jerusalem, site of "Absalom's tomb" and other sepulchers.

Jéhouda, Josué (1892–1966), Swiss author, journalist. Founded *Revue Juive de Genève.*

Jehu (9th c. B.C.E.), prophet during reign of Baasha of Israel and Jehoshaphat of Judah. Foretold destruction of house of Baasha, censured Jehoshaphat for joining Ahab of Israel in attack on Ramoth Gilead.

Jehu, king of Israel c. 842–814 B.C.E. While commander of garrison posted at Ramoth Gilead, seized throne fr. Jehoram and established line of kings who ruled Israel for nearly 100 years. Along with army and prophetic movement, poorer classes of people supported his coup. Destroyed Tyrian cult in Israel. During his reign Aram succeeded in penetrating deep into Israelite territory.

Jeiteles (Geidels), family of communal leaders and talmudic scholars, originating in Prague. **Baruch (Benedict;** 1762–1813), physician, talmudist polemized with both Enlightenment and traditional scholars. Died of tropical fever caring for wounded soldiers of all nationalities in Jewish quarter of Prague. His brother **Judah Loeb** (1773–1838), orientalist; coined term Haskalah. **Moses Wolf** (d. 1848), wrote history of Prague Jewry, utilizing gravestone inscriptions as sources. **Berthold (Issacher Baer;** 1875–1958) hid his monumental encyclopedic works on talmudic language and personalities before his deportation to Theresienstadt 1939 and returned fr. transport to Auschwitz to find his mss. intact. Some were published after war.

Jekuthiel ben Judah ha-Kohen (13th c.), Hebrew grammarian who lived in Prague or Rhineland. Wrote *Ein ha-Kore* with notes on vocalization and cantillation of Torah, etc., and grammatical study. Important source for pronunciation of Hebrew at that time. First Hebrew grammarian in Europe to formulate concept of open and closed syllables.

Jellinek, Adolf (Aaron, 1820/21–1893) preacher, scholar. Preacher in Leipzig synagogue fr. 1845, Vienna fr. 1857, where he founded Beit ha-Midrash Academy 1862. Considered greatest preacher of his day. 200 of his sermons were published. Personally lenient in ritual; strove for communal unity. Opposed expurgation of references to Zion from prayer book but hostile to rising Jewish nationalism. Wrote, edited, and translated works on Kabbalah and philosophy, published little known Midrashim (*Beit ha-Midrash* 6 vol.), various rabbinic commentaries, and wrote on historical and bibliographical subjects.

Jellinek, Hermann (1822–1848), writer, journalist, revolutionary; brother of Adolf Jellinek. Expelled fr. Leipzig Univ. and later fr. Berlin for revolutionary political activity. Wrote radical articles in Vienna; arrested upon failure of 1848 revolution in Vienna and executed.

Jellinek, Karl (1882–1955), German physical chemist. Joined Technische Hochschule of Danzig 1908; prof. of physical chemistry and director of institute 1922–37 until Nazis forced him out. Went to London. Did work in ammonia synthesis, electrochemistry, etc.

Jenin, Arab town in Samaria. Center of anti-Jewish forces during British Mandate. Fell to Israel 1967. Pop. 8,346 (1967), all Muslims, with another 4,480 in refugee camps.

Jephthah, judge of Israel and victor over Ammonites (Judg. 11–12); son of harlot who was driven out by his father's sons. Became leader of band of adventurers and was recalled by elders of Gilead to expel Ammonite invasion. Vowed to sacrifice to God whatever would come out of his house to meet him. To his immense grief, it was his only daughter, and he fulfilled his solemn vow.

Jerahmeel ben Solomon (c. 1150), chronicler; lived in S. Italy. His *Megillat Yeraḥme'el* is compilation of ancient Jewish and non-Jewish sources – historical, midrashic, and apocryphal. Also wrote poems, *piyyutim,* mathematical riddles.

Jerba, see Djerba.

Jeremiah (7th–6th c. B.C.E.), prophet; of priestly family. Began to prophesy in reign of Josiah. His gloomy prophecies aroused bitter resentment. Foretold that Nebuchadnezzar, king of Babylonia, would conquer Judah, and dictated his preaching to Baruch. Arrested 588 and remained in custody until fall of Jerusalem. Remained with new governor Gedaliah, but after latter was murdered had to flee to Egypt with his followers, finding asylum there. His prophecies are contained in Book of Jeremiah, second of biblical Major Prophets. Authorship of Book of Lamentations traditionally ascribed to him.

Jeremiah, Epistle of, apocryphal work written in form of copy of letter by prophet Jeremiah to Babylonian Exile. Consists of vehement polemic against idolatry. Author was Babylonian Jew, probably early 4th c. B.C.E.

Jeremiah ben Abba (4th c.), Babylonian *amora;* usually referred to as Jeremiah. After migrating to Ereẓ Israel and studying under Ḥiyya b. Abba, spoke disparagingly of Babylonian academies. His outlook stressed spiritual tension in divine worship. Precise and definitive as halakhist.

Jerez de la Frontera, city in Andalusia, SW Spain. Its Jews mostly engaged in commerce, crafts and viticulture. They suffered in persecutions of 1391. By 1485 community had ceased to exist. Autos-da-fé took place 1491–92.

Jericho, oldest town known in Ereẓ Israel, possibly in world; situated in oasis N. of Dead Sea. First settled in 8th millennium B.C.E.; urban culture developed, represented by building of defensive walls, the earliest thus far discovered. Fr. 15th–13th c. little remained of town, but inhabited during 13th c. Conquered by Joshua and destroyed by Babylonians 587 B.C.E. Destroyed again during Jewish war 66–70 and refounded under Byzantines. Arab caliph Hisham built winter palace 724. Conquered by Crusaders and reconquered by Saladin 1187. Modern town destroyed 1840 by Egyptians and 1871 by fire. Fell to Israel 1967. Pop. 6,837 (1967), with another 3,619 in vicinity.

Jeroboam I, first king of northern kingdom of Israel 928–907 B.C.E. Under Solomon, in charge of corvée, led unsuccessful rebellion, and fled to Egypt. Returned after Solomon died, and when ten tribes seceded, appointed king of Israel. Made two golden calves, placing one at Dan and the other at Beth-El. Suffered invasion fr. Shishak of Egypt and Abijah of Judah.

Tell al-Sultān, site of ancient Jericho.

BOOK OF JEREMIAH – CONTENTS

Chs. 1–6	Baruch's scroll.
1:1–19	The call of Jeremiah.
2:1–4:4	Indictment of the nation's sin.
4:5–6:30	The coming disaster "from the North."
Chs. 7–10	First editorial addition to Baruch's scroll.
7:1–8:3	Temple sermons and appended sayings.
8:4–9:21	An incorrigible people and their tragic ruin.
9:22–10:16	Miscellaneous sayings.
10:17–25	An incorrigible people and their tragic ruin.
Chs. 11–20	Second editorial addition to Baruch's scroll.
11:1–17	Preaching on the broken covenant.
11:18–12:6	Jeremiah's persecution by his relatives and fellow townsmen.
12:7–17	God expresses His sorrow for the dereliction of his people.
13:1–27	Parabolic vision of the linen waistcloth and attached sayings.
14:1–15:4	The time of drought and national emergency.
15:5–16:21	Oracles and confessions in poetry and prose.
17:1–27	Miscellany.
18:1–23	Jeremiah at the potter's house with attached sayings.
19:1–20:18	Prophetic symbolism and persecutions; further confessions.
Chs. 21–24	Oracles concerning the House of David and the prophets.
Chs. 25	Oracles against foreign nations.
Chs. 26–29	The biography of Jeremiah.
26:1–24	The "Temple sermon"; Jeremiah narrowly escapes death.
27:1–28:17	Events of 594 B.C.E.; The incident of the ox-yoke.
29:1–32	594 B.C.E.: Jeremiah and the exile in Babylon.
Chs. 30–31	The "Book of Consolation."
Chs. 32–44	The biography of Jeremiah.
32:1–33:26	Restoration of Judah and Jerusalem.
34:1–7	Words of Jeremiah as the Babylonian blockade tightens.
34:8–22	Incidents during lifting of siege.
35:1–19	Jeremiah and the Rechabites.
36:1–32	Incident of the scroll.
37:1–10	Incident during lifting of siege.
37:11–38:28	Jeremiah in prison.
39:1–40:6	Jeremiah's release from prison.
40:7–43:7	Assassination of Gedaliah and the flight to Egypt.
43:8–44:30	Jeremiah in Egypt.
Ch. 45	Baruch.
Chs. 46–51	Oracles against foreign nations.
Ch. 52	The fall of Jerusalem.

Cast of seal believed to have belonged to a minister of Jeroboam II.

Jeroboam II, king of Israel 789–748 B.C.E.; son of Joash; greatest ruler of dynasty of Jehu. Succeeded in elevating kingdom to final height before it fell. Recovered territories conquered by Aram and made Israel important political factor in S. and C. Syria.

Jeroham ben Meshullam (c. 1290–1350), Spanish talmudist. Classified civil law acc. to subject and talmudic source, then did the same (in *Toledot Adam ve-Ḥavvah*) with positive and negative commandments. Achievement was soon eclipsed by Jacob b. Asher's *Arba'ah Turim,* but Caro and others quoted him extensively.

°**Jerome (Eusebius Sophronius Hieronymus;** 342–420), Latin Church Father; b. Dalmatia, in Bethlehem fr. 386, where he translated Bible into Latin fr. original. This translation (the Vulgate) became official scriptures in Catholic Church. Bible commentaries contain much exegesis received fr. Jewish teachers.

Jersey City, see Hudson County.

Jerubaal, see Gideon.

Western part of Old City of Jerusalem, built by Suleiman 1536, with Jaffa Gate Citadel (right).

Mount Zion in Jerusalem, looking east toward the Dormition Abbey.

The Temple Mount in Jerusalem, with the Dome of the Rock (center) and al-Aqsa Mosque (foreground).

Jerusalem, capital of Israel, situated at strategic position in Judean hills. Emerged into history in Early Bronze Age. Mentioned as Canaanite city-state in Egyptian texts fr. 19th–14th c. B.C.E. After conquest of Canaan, remained Jebusite until David conquered and made it capital and religious center of Israel. Construction of First Temple and royal palace by Solomon turned it into holy royal city. After secession of N. tribes, remained the capital of Judah. Hezekiah reinforced its walls and cut Siloam tunnel to assure water supply in anticipation of Assyrian assault. After fall of Israel, became spiritual focus of all remnants. Destroyed with Temple by Babylonian army under Nebuchadnezzar 587/6 B.C.E. Cyrus of Persia allowed exiles to return and rebuild Temple 536 B.C.E., but only c. 445 B.C.E. did Nehemiah succeed in rebuilding the city. With Ptolemaic rule, period of prosperity ensued. Seleucid conquest 198 B.C.E. was welcomed by Jews. As result of inner struggle for power, Antiochus IV Epiphanes seized city, inaugurated intensive hellenization, constructed fortress (Acra), and stationed garrison 167 B.C.E. Recaptured and repurified by Judah the Maccabee and became capital of Hasmonean kingdom. Fr. 63 B.C.E. under Roman rule. Herod transformed external aspect by massive rebuilding program. After crucifixion of Jesus 29 C.E. became focus of Christian reverence. Jews seized city 66 C.E. but after lengthy siege by Romans under Titus in 70 destroyed together with Temple. Hadrian decided to establish Roman colony on its ruins 130, called Aelia Capitolina. This was important cause for outbreak of Bar Kokhba revolt 132–35 during which Romans were temporarily forced to evacuate city. Subsequently Jews were forbidden to enter. When Christian emperor Constantine became master of Ereẓ Israel 324, he erected Church of Holy Sepulcher and city assumed predominantly Christian character. Persians seized it 614 and handed it to Jews, when most churches were destroyed, but Persians lost it 621 to Christians, who reconstructed churches. After Arab conquest 638, Caliph Omar established place for Muslim worship on Temple Mt. In 7th c. al Aqṣā and Dome of Rock mosques were built. City remained in hands of rulers of Cairo 878–1516 except for period of Crusader rule. Under Ottoman Rule 1517–1917 it decayed. Present-day wall is work of sultan Suleiman I (1520–66). Jews began to return before Ottoman conquest and there was continuing influx of Jews. 1860 marked beginning of growth of New City and relative decline of Old, and there was a Jewish majority in city. First quarter outside walls was Yemin Moshe. Fr. 1880s began to acquire character of Western city. British under Allenby conquered city 1917 and established seat of Mandatory govt. Jewish development was accompanied by Arab disturbances developing on occasions into violence (1922, 1929, 1936–9). As result of 1948 War of Independence, city became divided, with most of New City in Israel hands and Old City held by Arabs. Certain forces, esp. Vatican, continued to press for internationalization, which had been original UN proposal. Israel government and Knesset transferred to city 1949. Six-Day War brought reunification. Pop. 301,300 (1971), incl. 79,100 non-Jews.

Jerusalem depicted as an oval, walled city in detail from Madaba map mosaic, 560–65.

Allenby entering Jerusalem through Jaffa Gate, Dec. 11, 1917.

1

2

The gates of the Old City, Jerusalem:

1. Damascus Gate.
2. Jaffa Gate.
3. Mercy Gate.
4. Herod's Gate.
5. Dung Gate.
6. Lions' Gate.
7. New Gate.
8. Zion Gate.

3

4

5

6

7

8

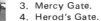

Celebration at Western Wall on 1st anniversary of reunification of Jerusalem, 1968.

Desecrated graves in Jewish cemetery on Mt. of Olives, Jerusalem, 1967.

The Katamon suburb of Jerusalem, 1971.

B. Mazar's excavations near south wall of Temple Mount, Jerusalem, revealing remains of Umayyad period (8th cent.).

Aerial view of Jaffa Road, Jerusalem.

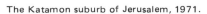

ISRAEL

Some of Israel's stamps (clockwise)
Doar Ivri, depicting the coins issued by Bar Kokhba in his revolt against the Romans. Issued on the establishment of the State of Israel, May 1948. Design O. Wallish.
Arthur James Balfour. Issued in 1967 on the 50th anniversary of the Balfour Declaration. Design O. Adler.
Zionist Congress. Issued on the eve of the 25th Zionist Congress, held in Jerusalem in 1960. Design O. Wallish.
The Western Wall. Issued after the 1967 Six-Day War. Design by G. Rothschild and Z. Lippman.
Ancient glassware. Issued 1964. Design C. Menusy and Ch. Ornan.
The Jordan bridge, scene of fierce fighting in Israel War of Independence. On the 1954 Independence Day stamp. Design O. Wallish.
King David on a Rosh Ha-Shanah stamp, 1960. Design A. Kalderon.

JERUSALEM

The Holy Sites of Jerusalem and other parts of Ereẓ Israel. A 19th-cent. drawing made in Ereẓ Israel.

JERUSALEM Aerial view of Jerusalem, looking over the Old City.

THE JERUSALEM POST
8 Pages

DIRECT CARS
JERUSALEM - HAIFA - JERUSALEM

For Your Child
ONEG

Marginal Comment

Expulsion May Follow Jordan Annexation Move

Beacons, Salvoes, Music, Dancing Herald Day, President and Prime Minister Call for New Effort

Success Depends on Ourselves

Dr. Weizmann's Message

Torches Blaze Across Nation

Part of front page of first issue of "The Jerusalem Post" under that name, Apr. 23, 1950.

Traditional tomb of Nabi Shu'ayb (Jethro) at Kefar Ḥittim, a center of pilgrimage for the Druze.

Jerusalem, Karl Wilhelm (1747–1772), German philosopher. Determinist; Enlightenment thinker. After his suicide, Goethe immortalized him in *Die Leiden des jungen Werthers* and G.E. Lessing published his writings.

Jerusalem, Wilhelm (1854–1923), Austrian philosopher, psychologist. Interested in psychology of speech and education of blind deaf-mutes. His empirical philosophical point of view employed genetic method.

Jerusalem Post (until 1950 **Palestine Post**), independent English-language daily newspaper published in Jerusalem. Founded 1932 and edited by Gershon Agronsky (Agron); fr. 1953 edited by Ted. R. Lurie. Since 1959, published weekly overseas edition.

Jerusalem Talmud, see Talmud, Jerusalem.

Jeshua, high priest; son of Jehozadak (or Jozadak). Together with Zerubbabel, organized return to Zion fr. Babylonian Exile. Active in rebuilding Temple and state, rejecting Samaritan offer of help.

Jeshua ben Joseph ha-Levi (15th c.), talmudist. Fled fr. persecutions in Algeria to Toledo, Castile 1467 and wrote major work on talmudic methodology *Halikhot Olam.*

Jeshua ben Judah (11th c.), Karaite scholar, philosopher; lived in Jerusalem. Modified theory of incest which previously had limited circle of women whom Karaite men could lawfully marry. Translated Pentateuch into Arabic with philosophical commentaries.

Jeshurun (Heb.), poetic name of Israel (cf. Deut. 32:15, etc.).

Jesse, father of David; grandson of Boaz and Ruth; listed among descendants of Perez, son of Judah, who lived in Beth-Lehem.

Jessel, Sir George (1824–1883), English jurist, distinguished lawmaking judge. Queen's Counsel 1865, Liberal MP 1868, solicitor-general 1871, first Jew to hold ministerial office in England. Organized Court of Chancery in its modern form.

Jessel, George Albert (1898–), U.S. entertainer. Began career in vaudeville, teaming with Eddie Cantor at age 10. Greatest success on Broadway *The Jazz Singer.* Active fundraiser for Jewish causes and Israel.

Jessner, Leopold (1878–1945), German theatrical director, manager; pioneer of expressionist school in German theater. Anti-Semitism compelled him to resign fr. Schiller Theater 1930. Settled in Los Angeles.

Jesurun, Reuel (Paulo de Pina; c. 1575–1634), Portuguese Marrano poet; b. Lisbon, in Amsterdam fr. 1604, openly espousing Judaism. Wrote *Diálogo dos montes,* dramatic poem in praise of Judaism.

Jesus (d. 30 C.E.), founder of Christianity; acc. to New Testament, b. Bethlehem, grew up in Nazareth, spent most of his life in Galilee, developing and spreading his teachings to his 12 Apostles and other followers. Period of widespread ferment and his activities aroused hostility of both Romans and Jewish establishment. Tried and crucified. Sources for biography found in Synoptic Gospels (Matthew, Mark, Luke). Modern scholarship has demonstrated that story contained in New Testament is comparatively late and contains anti-Jewish polemical elements. These formed basis for Church's anti-Jewish teaching and legislation throughout centuries. Discovery of Dead Sea Scrolls has shown that much of his teaching formerly thought to have had hellenistic basis is rooted in Jewish sectarian tradition.

Jethro, Midianite priest; father-in-law of Moses. When Moses fled fr. Egypt, Jethro made him shepherd of his flocks and gave him his daughter Zipporah. Later visited Moses and Israelites in desert and advised on reorganization of judicial system of Israelite tribes. Held in highest esteem by Druze, who revere his reputed tomb at Kefar Ḥittim nr. Tiberias.

Jew, designation derived from Heb. *yehudi,* originally member of tribe of Judah. Commonly applied outside Israel although Jews in country continued to call themselves Israelites. In course of time word received pejorative meanings in popular usage. Throughout centuries Jew was clearly identifiable as such but since emancipation period and esp. since establishment of State of Israel definition has given rise to wide controversy with various possible criteria, incl. religion, peoplehood, descent, etc. According to *halakhah,* child born of Jewish parents or convert to Judaism is considered Jew. Status of children of intermarriage follows that of mother, and child born of non-Jewish mother must undergo ritual conversion. This halakhic definition, accepted for centuries, has in modern times been challenged in Reform and secular circles, who have introduced modification in conversion procedure, feeling that identification with the Jewish people and its fate sufficient grounds for being considered Jew. Problem is particularly acute in State of Israel. Orthodox Jewry regards *halakhah* as unchangeable.

Jewish Agency, executive body and representative of World Zionist Organization. Authority and functions first recognized in British Mandate over Palestine. Name (orig. Jewish Agency for Palestine) formally adopted 1929 when non-Zionist Jewish leaders also joined Executive. Prior to 1948 Executive was responsible political body negotiating Zionist position in

Palestine. Many of its functions then passed to Israel government but it maintained widespread activities, incl. responsibility for immigration, absorption of new immigrants, and agricultural settlement. Also engages in many activities outside Israel, incl. education, encouragement of investment in Israel, youth and pioneer activities, and information. Headquarters in Jerusalem and New York. Agreement signed 1971 reconstituted Agency and determined relations with non-Zionists.

Jewish Agricultural (and Industrial Aid) Society, organization chartered in New York 1900 to provide E. European immigrants with training "as free farmers on their own soil . . ."; subsidiary of Baron de Hirsch Fund. Programs of self-help in New Jersey, New York, New England, and California were extended to thousands of displaced persons after WWII.

Jewish Brigade Group unit saluting Zionist flag during victory parade in Antwerp, 1945.

Jewish Anti-Fascist Committee, see Anti-Fascist Committee, Jewish.

Jewish Brigade, British army unit serving in WWII; established 1944 after previous efforts made since 1939 to establish separate Jewish units had been turned down by British authorities. Most members were Palestinian Jews. Commanded by Brig. E.F. Benjamin. Saw service in N. Africa and Italy, subsequently moving to various parts of Europe, where it assisted in *Beriḥah*. Disbanded 1946.

Jewish Christian Sects, groups composed of early Christians who were born as Jews and kept traditional Jewish way of life "according to the Law," even after accepting Jesus as teacher, prophet, or even messiah. Jewish Christians were disowned by Jews and expelled as heretics fr. Christian Church. See Ebionites.

Jewish Chronicle, Jewish weekly journal appearing in London, founded 1841; oldest Jewish newspaper still in existence. Editors incl. Asher Myers 1878–1902 and L.J. Greenberg 1907–31, the latter determining its pro-Zionist sympathies. Achieved international reputation.

Greenhouses of the Jewish Colonization Association's Baron de Hirsch Agriculture School, Woodbine, N.J.

Jewish Colonial Trust, first Zionist bank, incorporated in London 1899, following decision of First Zionist Congress. Invested in major ventures in Ereẓ Israel, such as General Mortgage Bank, Workers' Bank (Bank ha-Po'alim), Palestine Electric Corporation, etc. Transferred interests in Ereẓ Israel to Anglo-Palestine Bank 1934, now Bank Leumi le-Israel, B.M

Jewish Colonization Association (ICA), philanthropic association to assist needy Jews, or in countries of persecution to help them emigrate and settle elsewhere in productive employment, founded by Baron Maurice de Hirsch 1891. Helped Jews in Russia and Poland to improve local farming methods, supported technical and agricultural schools, helped establish network of

First issue of "The Jewish Chronicle," London, Nov. 12, 1841.

ספר זכרון

THE JEWISH CHRONICLE

דבר בעתו מה טוב משלי טו׳ כג׳ — "A word in its season how good it is." Proverbs, chap. 15, ver. 23.

No. 1.] כח׳ מרחשון תרב׳ לפק׳ November 12th, 5602.—1841. [Price 2d.

TO OUR READERS.

We have always anticipated the appearance of a truly Jewish paper, with the most lively satisfaction; for we knew, that the existence among us, of an organ of mutual communication, was a desideratum of such magnitude, that the person supplying it would be entitled to the thanks of his brethren, and be a man to be envied. Our sentiments, therefore, on this occasion, when we ourselves are enabled to lay before you the required medium, are of the most grateful kind. We feel that we have done a something that may rescue us from the common fate of mankind—oblivion;—that we have projected (and it remains with you to say, whether our intentions shall be carried out to their fullest extent) a work, which, while it will make every Jew familiar with the condition of his fellow Israelites, will also supply him with the means of becoming better satisfied with his own, by teaching him to render it subservient to a better lot; one that alone can secure happiness here, and ensure beatitude hereafter:—for with God's blessing, we would instruct him how to know himself, to love mankind, and to seek his Creator.

We enter on our task then with alacrity, cheered to our prospective midnight labour and unceasing mental toil, by the bright, the glorious thought, that we may, under Divine Providence, be the humble instruments of regenerating, at least, a portion of our brethren; and like the "orb of night," while dispensing a gentle light to those around, rejoice in our own heaven-borrowed brilliancy, for brilliant indeed will be our career, can we but effect our object.

Our prospectus has already made you acquainted with our purpose; we will here advert to it again. We propose to divide our matter into four distinct parts: 1st.—Religious and moral instruction. 2ndly.—Local intelligence, Historical information, and facts, exclusively Jewish. 3rdly.—Original articles. 4thly—Text books.

1st. The advantages to be derived from our first division, "religious and moral instruction" must at once present themselves; for what can confer greater benefit on man, than the knowledge of his duty towards God and his fellow-creatures—what can tend so much to his spiritual welfare as the former? what contribute so much to improve his social condition as the latter? How can his happiness be better consulted, than by pointing out to him, that in gratitude for the numberless benefits he receives at the hands of a gracious and merciful Providence, he is required to love his neighbour as himself, and to seek the presence of his Maker through the tenets of our holy religion;—a religion, the basis of all others, standing out in all its original purity, after the lapse of ages; while other creeds, since framed, but of man's devising, have crumbled into nought, and left no trace to tell that they have been. Time has breathed his withering blast o'er their nothingness, and like the clay that made them, they have vanished for ever.

2ndly. By local intelligence, we mean the proceedings of our many congregations at home and abroad; their exertions in the cause of religion and charity, and their progress in knowledge. What can better stimulate them to renewed efforts, than the thought, that what they have done is appreciated? and what promote the desire of doing good among us, so much as their example? Facts exclusively Jewish, will consist of anecdotes of eminent men, reports of public meetings, extracts from foreign and domestic journals, and a calender of current festivals, fasts, &c. Our historical information will be derived from authentic records.

3rdly. For original articles, we trust partially, to the kindness of contributors; but we are assured, that we are correct in our anticipations of numerous correspondences; for we know (ourselves) of many—and there must be others, with whom we are not acquainted, who will be but too anxious to give publicity to their opinions, on subjects connected with Jewish welfare; and willing to commit to our publication, the less matter of fact, but not less honorable productions of their well stored minds; indeed, we have already received a tale, which we purpose commencing at the earliest opportunity.

4thly. Our Text Books will not, we dare venture to assert, form the least attractive part of our information;—nay, they will perhaps, be the most essentially useful. The הגדה; Passover service, though it does not possess the charm of novelty, will at least be acceptable, as it will contain the forms of German, Spanish, and Portuguese Jews, with the Hebrew from the Hidenheim editions, and will be carefully translated. To our Dictionary, the first English one that has appeared, we invite more particular attention. It is derived from a source, which needs but to be named, to be appreciated by every Hebrew scholar and student: the צמח דוד; a work, which for correctness, copiousness, and erudition, stands unrivalled; but which, unfortunately, has hitherto, from its scarcity and price, been a stranger to most of our brethren—who have thereby been deprived of a most valuable assistance in the prosecution of the study of our sacred language. This obstacle we propose to remove, by presenting the Lexicon, in a form at once useful and available to the resources of the most humble; and to render the possession of it still more desirable, we shall give the rabinical, as well as the biblical hebrew, with translations and explanations of both.

Our creed is peace to all mankind—opposition to none, and the love of God; worshiping Him through the medium of our affections and hopes, and not our fears. We have now pointed out our intentions in the conduct of this work: we have only further to add, that it shall be our constant endeavour to render it worthy of your most liberal patronage, and to endow it with a character, at once religious, moral and instructive.

A seed is planted, and is anxiously watched by the gardener; weeds, that may obstruct its growth, are carefully plucked from around,—it is watered when rain comes not, and shielded from the too sultry heat of the summer sun;—all is attended to that can secure its flourishing: and what is the result? The gardener sees the little seed expand and spread, and eventually produce sweet flowers, wooing his gaze by their beautiful hues, and offering the grateful incense of their perfumes, to be wafted by every gale to his delighted senses; or he beholds the luxuriant fruit tree, bowing beneath the accumulated weight of its own productions, and proffering its golden harvest, in blushes, for his acceptance. He perceives in this the return for his labours, and he adores the Providence that has blessed his work.

Readers, will you be the gardener, and make us the fruit tree?

An infant is ushered into life, and its frail form seems scarcely strong enough to contain its atom of existence; but the child is nurtured from a kindly and a genial source—the vital power dilates within him, and he becomes a man, in the image of his Divine Creator. His faculties are developed, his energies expanded, knowledge adds her giant strength, and he gives to them, his first supporters, the recompense for their toils and cares, in the accomplishment of their dearest wishes; nay, more, he himself, learning his task from them, becomes what they were to him, the fountain of new existences. Readers, the inference is obvious—we *are* the child—we *would become* the man, a breath may raise us to maturity, a breath destroy us in our birth—but we feel you will decree us life; and further, we confidently hope, that the day is not far distant, when our little unpretending periodical will have found its way, alike, to the cheerful fire-side of the humble—the luxurious drawing room of the affluent—the closet of the student—and the approbation of the world.

Announcement of opening of original subscription list for shares in Jewish Colonial Trust, London, 1899.

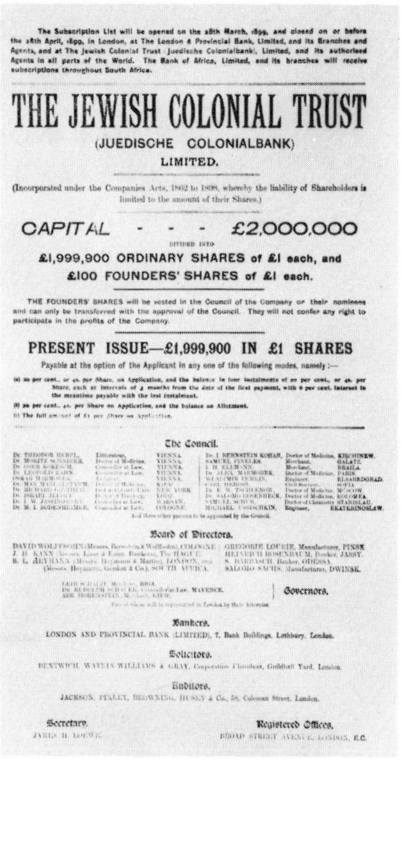

The Subscription List will be opened on the 28th March, 1899, and closed on or before the 28th April, 1899, in London, at The London & Provincial Bank, Limited, and its Branches and Agents, and at The Jewish Colonial Trust (Juedische Colonialbank), Limited, and its authorised Agents in all parts of the World. The Bank of Africa, Limited, and its branches will receive subscriptions throughout South Africa.

THE JEWISH COLONIAL TRUST

(JUEDISCHE COLONIALBANK)

LIMITED.

(Incorporated under the Companies Acts, 1862 to 1898, whereby the liability of Shareholders is limited to the amount of their Shares.)

CAPITAL - - - £2,000,000

DIVIDED INTO

£1,999,900 ORDINARY SHARES of £1 each, and

£100 FOUNDERS' SHARES of £1 each.

THE FOUNDERS' SHARES will be vested in the Council of the Company or their nominees and can only be transferred with the approval of the Council. They will not confer any right to participate in the profits of the Company.

PRESENT ISSUE—£1,999,900 IN £1 SHARES

Payable at the option of the Applicant in any one of the following modes, namely:—

(a) 20 per cent., or 4s. per Share, on Application, and the balance in four instalments of 20 per cent., or 4s. per Share, each at intervals of 3 months from the date of the first payment, with 4 per cent. interest in the meantime payable with the last instalment.

(b) 20 per cent., 4s. per Share on Application, and the balance on Allotment.

(c) The full amount of £1 per Share on Application.

The Council.

Dr. THEODOR HERZL,	Litterateur,	VIENNA.	Dr. I. BERNSTEIN KOHAN,	Doctor of Medicine,	KISCHINEW.
Dr. MORITZ SCHNIRER,	Doctor of Medicine,	VIENNA.	SAMUEL PINELES,	Merchant,	GALATZ.
Dr. OSER KOKESCH,	Counsellor at Law,	VIENNA.	I. H. ELLMANN,	Merchant,	BRAILA.
Dr. LEOPOLD KAHN,	Counsellor at Law,	VIENNA.	Dr. ALEX. MARMOREK,	Doctor of Medicine,	PARIS.
OSKAR MARMOREK,	Architect,	VIENNA.	WLADIMIR TEMKIN,	Engineer,	ELISABETGRAD.
Dr. MAX MANDELSTAMM,	Doctor of Medicine,	KIEW.	CARL HERBST,	Civil Servant,	SOFIA.
Dr. RICHARD GOTTHEIL,	Prof. at Columbia Univ.,	NEW YORK.	Dr. E. W. TSCHLENOW,	Doctor of Medicine,	MOSCOW.
Dr. ISRAEL JELSKY,	Doctor of Theology,	LODZ.	Dr. SALOMO ROSENHECK,	Doctor of Medicine,	KOLOMEA.
Dr. I. W. JASSINOWSKY,	Counsellor at Law,	WARSAW.	SAMUEL SCHUR,	Doctor of Chemistry,	STANISLAU.
Dr. M. I. BODENHEIMER,	Counsellor at Law,	COLOGNE.	MICHAEL USSISCHKIN,	Engineer,	EKATERINOSLAW.

And three other persons to be appointed by the Council.

Board of Directors.

DAVID WOLFFSOHN (Messrs. Bernstein & Wolffsohn), COLOGNE.
J. H. KANN (Messrs. Lissa & Kann, Bankers), The HAGUE.
R. L. HEYMANN (Messrs. Heymann & Martin), LONDON, and (Messrs. Heymann, Gordon & Co.), SOUTH AFRICA.
GREGORIE LOURIE, Manufacturer, PINSK.
HEINRICH ROSENBAUM, Banker, JASSY.
S. BARBASCH, Banker, ODESSA.
SALOMO SACHS, Manufacturer, DWINSK.

Governors.

LEIB SCHALIT, Merchant, RIGA.
Dr. RUDOLPH SCHAUER, Counsellor at Law, MAYENCE.
ABR. HORENSTEIN, Merchant, KIEW.
Two of whom will be represented in London by their Attornies.

Bankers.

LONDON AND PROVINCIAL BANK (LIMITED), 7, Bank Buildings, Lothbury, London.

Solicitors.

BENTWICH, WATKIN WILLIAMS & GRAY, Corporation Chambers, Guildhall Yard, London.

Auditors.

JACKSON, PIXLEY, BROWNING, HUSEY & Co., 58, Coleman Street, London.

Secretary.

JAMES H. LOEWE.

Registered Offices.

BROAD STREET AVENUE, LONDON, E.C.

cooperative loan and savings banks in Russia for farmers and artisans. Aided Jewish immigrants in Argentina, Brazil, U.S., Canada, Cyprus, Turkey; in Ereẓ Israel (PICA) established agricultural colonies. Chief success was in Latin America; 20,000 Jews lived on land under its auspices in Argentina 1930, but number subsequently declined.

Jewish Cultural Reconstruction (JCR), body founded 1947 in New York by most world Jewish organizations to deal with Jewish cultural and religious property looted by Nazis and recovered by U.S. Military Government. Operated in Germany 1948–51. Restored plundered Jewish property to original owners whenever possible; much was shipped to scholarly institutions in Israel and U.S.

Jewish Daily Forward (Yid. **Forverts**), U.S. Yiddish newspaper, founded in N.Y. 1897. Moderate offshoot of militantly left-wing *Abendblatt.* Wealthiest and most widely read Yiddish newspaper in U.S. Peak circ. 200,000 (WWI). Dominated by editor Abraham Cahan 1903–51. Circ. 44,000 (1970).

Jewish Day (Yid. **Der Yidishe Tog**), U.S. Yiddish daily, founded in N.Y. 1914 by group of intellectuals and businessmen led by Judah Magnes and Morris Weinberg. Peak circ. 81,000 (1916). Merged with *Jewish Morning Journal* 1953, but joint paper closed 1971.

Jewish Defense League (JDL), group consisting mainly of Orthodox young people, formed 1968 in Brooklyn, N.Y. to protect local Jews from delinquent attacks. Under Rabbi Meir Kahane pursued policy of "confrontation" with Soviet representatives in U.S., often by violent and demonstrative means. Attempted to enter Israel politics.

Jewish Historical Institute, Warsaw, institution for study of Polish Jewish history, established 1948 to coordinate activities of historical societies which sprang up after WWII in Lodz, Cracow, Bialystok, and Lublin to study and document Holocaust. Most of workers left Poland as result of 1968 anti-Semitic campaign.

Jewish Historical Society of England. English learned society, founded 1893. Publishes *Transactions* and other volumes on English Jewish history.

Jewish Institute of Religion, see Hebrew Union College-Jewish Institute of Religion.

Jewish Labor Committee, Jewish community agency representing Jewish interests in American labor movement and labor interests in Jewish community, founded 1934. Before WWII concentrated on supporting anti-Nazi labor forces and aiding Jewish labor institutions in Europe. During WWII sought to save labor and liberal leaders fr. Nazis.

Jewish Legion, military formation of Jewish volunteers in WWI who fought in British army for liberation of Ereẓ Israel fr. Turkish rule. On initiative of Jabotinsky, helped by Weizmann and Col. Patterson, 38th Battalion of Royal Fusiliers was founded 1917 (sent to Egypt April 1918, joined by 39th Battalion of Royal Fusiliers, later incl. volunteers fr. U.S.). Both battalions fought in Ereẓ Israel. Volunteers fr. Ereẓ Israel formed 40th Battalion of Royal Fusiliers 1918, occupying crucial positions. Anti-Zionist attitude of military administration and Arab riots of 1920–1 led to disbandment.

Jewish Morning Journal (Yid. **Der Morgen Zhornal**), U.S. Yiddish daily, founded 1901 as Orthodox

A Jewish Legion contingent camping outside Jerusalem, 1919.

Front page of a 1920 issue of the "Jewish Daily Forward."

Forward פארווערטס Forward

VOL. XXIV, NO. 8200 ... NEW YORK, Monday, April 5, 1920. ... PRICE TWO CENTS

אונטערמייער וועט העלפן סאציאליסטען אין קאמף געגען סוויט'ן;
סאוועט רעגירונג וועט געבען לאנד צו די אידען אין רוסלאנד;
רענ'שער סעניט גיט נאך אלע פאדערונגען פון די סאציאליסטען

Front page of the "Jewish Day," March 2, 1918.

The Day דער טאג

"THE NATIONAL JEWISH DAILY"

PRICE TWO CENTS NEW YORK, CHICAGO, SATURDAY, MARCH 2, 1918. VOL. IV. No. 1299

דייטשען דרינגען אריין טיפער אין רוסלאנד מיט עסטרייך'ס הילף;
אמעריקא וועט וואהרשיינליך ניט שטערען יאפאן אין מזרח סיביר

paper; for years New York City's only morning Yiddish paper. Supported Republican Party. Peak circ. 111,000 (1916). Under direction of Jacob Fishman 1916–38, adopted more liberal, intellectual tone. Absorbed *Yidishes Tagblat* 1928; merged with *Jewish Day* 1953 but closed 1971.

Jewish National Fund (JNF) (Heb. **Keren Kayemeth LeIsrael**), land purchasing and development fund of Zionist Organization, founded 1901 at Fifth Zionist Congress. Created worldwide organization for fund raising by means of JNF stamps, Blue Box, Golden Book, etc. Land possessions totaled more than half of Jewish holdings in Ereẓ Israel 1947. Worked on land reclamation, forests, establishment of settlements. With founding of State of Israel, activities shifted fr. land purchase to land improvement and development as well as afforestation. Planted 120 million trees, prepared 125,000 acres for agriculture up to 1972. Heads incl. M.M. Ussishkin, A. Granott, J. Tsur.

Jewish National Fund afforestation project in the Biriyyah hills of Galilee, 1953.

The Torah translation committee of the Jewish Publication Society, c. 1960. Seated, l. to r.: B. Bamberger, E. Speiser, H. Orlinsky, H. Friedman, and M. Arzt. Standing: H.L. Ginsberg, E. Wolf, L. Levinthal, L. Zussman, and S. Grayzel.

The Jewish Theological Seminary in New York.

Jewish Oath, see Oath More Judaica.

Jewish Publication Society of America (JPSA), society for publication in English of books of Jewish content, founded in Philadelphia 1888 as annual membership organization. Publications incl. English Bible translation 1917 and new translation fr. 1962.

Jewish Quarterly Review (JQR), learned journal, established 1889 by I. Abrahams and C.G. Montefiore. Published articles by major scholars and much original scholarship (e.g., Schechter's *genizah* discoveries). New series published by Dropsie College in Philadelphia begun 1910.

Jewish Science, movement founded 1921 by Morris Lichtenstein to combat inroads of Christian Science among Jews. After his death, wife Tehilla assumed leadership of group centered mostly in New York.

Jewish Social Democratic Party (ZPS), workers' party in Galicia 1905–20; equivalent of Bund, which it joined 1920.

Jewish Socialist Verband, U.S. organization devoted to promotion of democratic socialism and strengthening of Jewish group life on basis of modern Yiddish culture; founded 1921 by group which split off fr. Jewish Socialist Federation when latter embraced Communism.

Jewish Socialist Workers' Party (also known as **Sejmists,** or **J.S.** = Jewish Socialists; Rus. abbr. **SERP**), party based on synthesis of national and socialist ideals, founded in Kiev 1906. Claimed that basis for Jewish autonomy should be Jewish community, and its supreme institution, endowed with binding authority, should be Jewish national Sejm (parliament). Main stronghold Ukraine.

Jewish Society for History and Ethnography, Jewish scholarly society, established in St. Petersburg 1908. Major undertaking was publication of historical quarterly *Yevreyskaya Starina* ("Jewish Antiquities"). Dissolved 1929, its museum and archives passing to Soviet-Jewish institutions.

Jewish State Party, Zionist political party formed by dissidents fr. Revisionist movement after final split bet. Vladimir Jabotinsky and most of his colleagues in leadership of world movement 1933. Leaders incl. Meir Grossman and Robert Stricker. Merged with Union of Zionist Revisionists 1946.

Jewish Successor Organizations, organizations for tracing and recovering heirless property of Jews killed by Nazis in Germany.

Jewish Telegraphic Agency (JTA), bureau for gathering and distribution of Jewish news, established 1914 by Jacob Landau in The Hague as Jewish Correspondence Bureau, then as JTA in London 1919 by Landau in collaboration with Meir Grossman. Moved to New York 1922. Boris Smolar editor in chief 1924-68.

Jewish Theological Seminary of America (JTSA), rabbinical institution and educational center of Conservative Judaism. Established in New York 1887 by Sabato Morais; reorganized 1902 when Solomon Schechter became president and built up distinguished faculty. Under Alexander Marx outstanding library developed. Seminary incorporates Teachers' Inst., Univ. of Judaism (Los Angeles), Jewish Museum, Student Center and Schocken Institute in Jerusalem. Its graduate rabbis are organized in Rabbinical Assembly and United Synagogue of America is affiliated to Seminary.

Jewish War Veterans of the United States of America (JWV), war veterans organization, organized in N.Y. 1896 by Jewish veterans of American Civil War. Maintains veteran service offices in 14 cities. Headquarters Washington, D.C.

Jews' College, rabbinical seminary in London, founded 1855 by Chief Rabbi N.M. Adler. Trains ministers and rabbis as well as cantors and teachers. Library contains 60,000 printed books and 700 mss.

Jew Suess, see Oppenheimer, Joseph ben Issachar.

Jezebel (d. 841 B.C.E.), daughter of Ethbaal king of Sidon, wife of Ahab king of Israel. Introduced Tyrian Baal worship into Israel. In stories about Elijah, prototype of enemies of God of Israel and His prophets. Killed in Jehu's insurrection.

Jezreel, city in ancient Israel. Base for Saul and his army before dis-

astrous battle with Philistines at Mt. Gilboa. Winter capital of Omri and his dynasty.

Jezreel, Valley of (also **Plain of Esdraelon**), large inland plain in N. Israel bet. hills of Samaria, Carmel, and Lower Galilee. By virtue of its strategic significance, played major part in history of region at all times and was scene of many battles. Fr. 1920s, land acquired by JNF and subsequently center of Jewish settlements.

JNF, see Jewish National Fund.

Joab (10th c. B.C.E.), David's commander-in-chief, nephew, confidant. Won major victory over Ammonites and Edomites. Suppressed internal revolt. Lost favor after ordering killing of Absalom in defiance of king's request. Killed on Solomon's orders acc. to David's dying injunction.

Joachim, Joseph (1831–1907), violinist, teacher, composer. Gave first concert at age 7. Concertmaster of Liszt's orchestra at Weimar 1849–54, conductor of Royal Hanoverian Orchestra 1854–64. In Berlin fr. 1866 as director of newly founded Hochschule fuer Musik. Founded Joachim Quartet, Europe's leading quartet.

Joash see Jehoash

Joash (Jehoash), king of Judah 835–798 B.C.E.; son of Ahaziah. When one year old rescued by high priest Jehoiada from Athaliah, who killed rest of his family. After 6 years, Jehoiada led palace revolution to crown him. Attacked by Aram in 23rd year of reign and thereafter declined. Killed by conspirators.

Job, Book of, book of Hagiographa section of Bible. Variously dated 7th–4th c. B.C.E.; provenance uncertain. Deals with problems of suffering of righteous. In story, righteous Job is terribly afflicted and friends maintain that his afflictions must be result of his wickedness. He is finally vindicated and rehabilitated by God, with message that His ways are not necessarily clear to human understanding. Book's meaning widely discussed by rabbis. Talmud suggests that Job is fictitious character.

Job, Testament of, Greek pseudepigraphic text fr. 1st c. C.E., purporting to reveal secrets and last wishes of Job.

Jochebed, wife of Amram; mother of Moses, Aaron, and Miriam.

Jochelson, Vladimir (1855–1937), Russian anthropologist. Studied native peoples of Siberia during exile there. After revolution, prof. of ethnology at Leningrad. Last years in U.S. working for American Museum of Natural History.

Joel, Book of, 2nd book in Minor Prophets section of Bible. Date unknown. First 2 chapters deal with locust plague, last 2 with "Day of the Lord."

Joel, David Heymann (1815–1882), rabbi, scholar. Rabbi in Swarzedz (Poznan region). Fr. 1880 taught at Jewish Theological Seminary of Breslau; one of earliest to make scholarly approach to Kabbalah.

Joel, Karl (1864–1934), philosopher. Taught at Univ. of Basle fr. 1897. Called his philosophical system "New Idealism." Opposed methodological positivism and metaphysical naturalism.

Joel, Manuel (1826–1890), rabbi, scholar; b. Poland. Fr. 1854 taught at Jewish Theological Seminary of Breslau. Defended moderation in Reform against A. Geiger's radicalism. Wrote on medieval Jewish philosophy.

Joel, Solomon Barnato (1865–1931), S. African mining magnate, financier; nephew and successor of Barney Barnato. Became one of richest men of his time.

Joel ben Isaac ha-Levi (1115? – 1200), talmudic scholar of Mainz. Quoted in *Sefer ha-Ravyah* of his son Eliezer and in works of many contemporary scholars.

Joel ben Simeon (Feibush Ashkenazi; 15th c.), scribe, illuminator; b. Germany, established workshop in N. Italy. In style and iconography combined Askenazi and Italian art. Best-known example *Washington Haggadah.*

Joezer, Son of Boethus, high priest 23–5 B.C.E. Appointed shortly before Herod's death as successor to Mattathias b. Theophilus.

Job with his family and newly restored riches, from "Rothschild Miscellany," Ferrara (?), 1470.

Joffe, Abraham Feodorovich (1880–1960), Russian physicist. Main work in mechanical properties of crystals, electrical properties of dielectric crystals, and semiconductors.

Joffe, Adolph Abramovich (1883–1927), Russian revolutionary, diplomat. Joined Mensheviks but after meeting Trotsky, became Bolshevik. Led Soviet delegation to peace talks with Germany at Brest-Litovsk 1917, then served as Soviet diplomat. After Trotsky's expulsion fr. Communist Party, committed suicide.

Joffe, Eliezer Lipa (1882–1944), Ereẓ Israel pioneer; b. Bessarabia, went to U.S. 1904, settled in Ereẓ Israel 1910. Developed idea of moshav ovedim. A founder of Nahalal 1921 and marketing cooperative Tenuvah (director 1928–36).

Southern part of Jezreel Valley.

Joseph Joachim

BOOK OF JOB – CONTENTS

1:1–2:13	Prologue (in prose)
3:1–31:40	The dialogue or symposium
32:1–37:24	The Elihu speeches
38:1–42:6	The theophany and speeches of the Lord
42:7–17	Epilogue (in prose)

Joffe, Hillel (1864–1936), Ereẓ Israel pioneer, doctor, b. Ukraine, studied in Geneva, settled in Ereẓ Israel 1891. Practiced medicine and organized anti-malaria service; on his advice eucalyptus trees were planted in Ḥaderah swamps. Chairman of Ḥovevei Zion executive committee 1895–1905.

Joffen, Abraham (1887–1970), yeshivah head, exponent of Novogrudok school of Musar. On outbreak of WWII emigrated to U.S., reestablishing Novogrudok yeshivah in Brooklyn. Settled in Jerusalem 1964.

Jogiches Leon (Jan Tyszka; 1867–1919), socialist leader in Poland, Germany. A founder and leader of Social Democratic Party of Poland and Lithuania. After 1918 revolution in Germany joined Rosa Luxemburg and Karl Liebknecht in forming German Communist Party. Arrested and murdered in prison.

Johanan, son of Kareath; principal military officer in entourage of Gedaliah. After Gedaliah's assassination led Jeremiah and other Jews down to Egypt.

Johanan ben Nappaḥa (c. 180–c. 279), Palestinian *amora* whose teachings comprise major portion of Jerusalem Talmud. Few contemporary Babylonian scholars opposed his rulings. Also leading aggadist. Renowned for handsome appearance. Family life marred by tragedy, with 10 of his sons dying in his lifetime.

Johanan ben Nuri (2nd c.), *tanna.* Great influence in molding laws and customs of Jews of Galilee. Frequently mentioned in Mishnah.

Johanan ben Zakkai (1st c. C.E.), *tanna;* leading sage in period following destruction of Temple. First taught "in the shadow of the Temple"; acc. to *aggadah,* smuggled out of beleaguered Jerusalem in coffin. Received permission of Vespasian to go to Jabneh 68 C.E., creating center of learning which eventually became most important in Ereẓ Israel and marked major turning point in development of Judaism. Advocate of peaceful coexistence with Roman authorities. First sage to engage in mysticism.

Memorial at West Park Cemetery, Johannesburg, to Jews who perished in WWII, designed by Herman Wald.

Johanan Ha-Sandelar (2nd c.) *tanna;* pupil of Akiva; b. Alexandria. Among scholars who convened in valley of Bet Rimmon to revive Torah study and communal life after Hadrianic persecutions had abated. Saying: "Dwelling in Ereẓ Israel is equal to all the precepts of the Torah."

Johanan the Hasmonean ("Gaddi"; d. 161 B.C.E.), son of Mattathias, brother of Judah Maccabee. Participated in Hasmonean wars. Murdered by sons of Ambri. Jonathan and Simeon avenged his death.

Johannesburg, city in S. Africa. First Jews in late 19th c., mainly fr. Britain and C. Europe, followed by immigrants fr. E. Europe, chiefly Lithuania. First congregation 1887, first synagogue built 1888. Many Jewish mayors, first being Harry Graumann 1910. Jewish communal and Zionist institutions highly developed. Jewish pop. 57,500 (1971).

°**John XXIII** (1881–1963), pope 1958–63. As Monsignor Roncalli saved Jews during WWII. First pope to show high personal regard for Jews and Judaism. Ordered anti-Jewish prayers to be deleted fr. Good Friday prayer. Convened Second Vatican Council, initiated its declaration on attitude on Jews.

John the Baptist (d. 29? C.E.), religious personality. Ascetic religious outlook apparently similar to that of Judean Desert Sect. Acc. to New Testament baptized Jesus and was beheaded by Herod Antipas at request of Salome (but acc. to Josephus because he feared rebellion by his followers).

°**John Chrysostom** (354–407), Church father, virulently anti-Jewish preacher; b. Antioch. Delivered homilies which were subsequently circulated, attacking teachings of Judaism and way of life and views of contemporary Jews.

John of Capua (13th c.), Italian translator; apostate. His translation of *Kalila and Dimna* fr. Hebrew into Latin influenced subsequent writers and collectors of fables.

John of Giscala (Johanan ben Levi), among leaders of revolt against Rome 66–70 C.E.; native of Giscala (Gush Ḥalav) in Galilee. Quarreled with Josephus whose loyalty he suspected. Commanded Zealots in Jerusalem and engaged in bitter civil war with Simeon bar Giora. After defeat, taken to Rome, exhibited in Titus' triumphal procession, and died in prison.

John Hyrcanus, see Hyrcanus, John.

Joiachin, see Jehoiachin.

Joiarib, see Jehoiarib.

Joint, see American Jewish Joint Distribution Committee.

Jokneam, royal Canaanite city nr. Mount Carmel. Called Caimont in Crusader times. Modern settlement founded 1935; divided into moshav and semi-urban community 1967. Combined pop. 4,100 (1971).

Jolles, Zechariah Isaiah (1816–1852), talmudic scholar; b. Lemberg. Critical of "talmudists without secular scholarship" and of scholars "who had forgotten Torah." Supported "moderate Haskalah."

Jolles, Zvi Enrico (1902–1971), organic chemist; b. Lemberg, pioneer in Ereẓ Israel 1920–24, emigrated to Italy. Prof. at Florence Univ.; dismissed 1938. Found refuge in England, working at Lister Inst. and Imperial Chemical Industries and pioneering novel dyestuffs applications.

Jolson, Al (Asa Yoelson; 1886–1950), U.S. singer, vaudeville and film star; son of cantor. Starred in Broadway musicals and in first full-length talkie *The Jazz Singer.*

Al Jolson

Jonah, Book of, 5th book in Minor Prophets section of Bible. Tells famous story of Jonah and fish and of Jonah's attempt to avoid his prophetic mission to Nineveh. Message of universalism. Date uncertain.

Jonah (4th c.), Palestinian *amora.* With associate Yose (Yosi), head of Sanhedrin in Tiberias. Frequently quoted in Jerusalem Talmud.

Jonah, Moses (16th c.), kabbalist; disciple of Isaac Luria. Headed yeshivah in Safed and spent time in Egypt and Constantinople. Wrote

systematic treatise on his teacher's Kabbalah, called *Kanfei Yonah.*

Jonah ben Abraham Gerondi (c. 1200–1263), Spanish rabbi, moralist. In Montpellier leader of campaign against Maimonides, for which he subsequently repented. Rabbi at Toledo. Preached ethics, familiar with Kabbalah. Pupils inc. Solomon b. Abraham Adret.

Jonah ibn Janaḥ, see Ibn Janaḥ.

Jonas, Hans (1903–), philosopher, left Germany 1933. Prof. at New School for Social Research in N.Y. fr. 1951. Wrote on philosophy and religion in late antiquity and early Christianity.

Jonas, Joseph (1792–1869), U.S. jeweler; b. England, arrived in Cincinnati 1817, becoming Ohio's first Jewish settler. Pres. of newly founded Bene Israel Congregation 1824. His brother **Abraham** (1801–1864) arrived in Cincinnati several years after Joseph. Active in Republican party as supporter and friend of Lincoln. Abraham's son **Benjamin Franklin** (1834–1911), active in Democratic party; served in Louisiana state legislature, U.S. senator 1879–85.

Jonathan, eldest son of Saul, first king of Israel. Noted warrior. Friendship with David became proverbial. David wrote famous lament (II Sam. 1:17–27) after his death in fight against Philistines on Mt. Gilboa.

Jonathan ben David ha-Kohen of Lunel (c. 1135–after 1210), talmudic scholar of Provence. In vanguard of defenders of Maimonides in controversy stirred up by Meir Abulafia. Among leaders of "300 French and English rabbis" who emigrated to Ereẓ Israel 1210. Wrote commentaries on Mishnah.

Jonathan ben Eleazar (3rd c.), *amora;* of Babylonian origin, went to Ereẓ Israel in his youth. Regarded as among great aggadists.

Jonathan ben Uzziel (1st c. B.C.E.–1st c. C.E.), translator of Prophets into Aramaic. His translations were midrashic and evoked criticism. Attribution of Pentateuch Aramaic translation to him due to error. Mentioned as outstanding pupil of Hillel.

Jonathan the Hasmonean (also **Apphus;** d. 143 B.C.E.), head of Jewish state 160–143; youngest son of Mattathias. Took over command of revolt after brother Judah Maccabee's death. Appointed high priest and governor of Judea. True founder of Hasmonean state, whose boundaries he extended in various directions. Treacherously murdered by pretender Tryphon at Acre.

Jong, Louis De (1914–), Dutch historian, journalist; spent WWII in London. Undertook preparation of official Dutch history 1955. Prof. of contemporary history at School of Economics in Rotterdam.

Joppa, see Jaffa.

Joram, see Jehoram.

Jordan, river flowing from Anti-Lebanon mountains S. through Ḥuleh Valley to Lake Kinneret and emptying into Dead Sea, covering distance of c. 127 m. (205 km.). Tributaries incl. Yarmuk and Jabbok. Not navigable. Holy river for Christians. Since 1964 Israel has drawn its water to irrigate Negev.

The Book of Jonah in micrography, Tiberias, 1891.

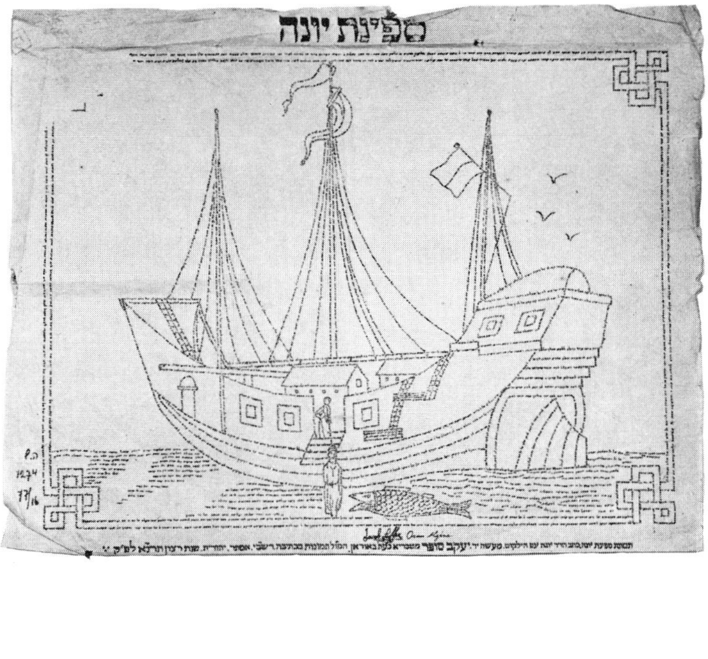

Jordan, Kingdom of, state in W. Asia bordering on Israel. Transjordania originally included in area of British Mandate for Palestine but, in 1921, established as separate emirate ruled by Hashemite Dynasty. Its ruler, Abdullah, crowned king of Transjordan in 1946 and, after annexing

The Jordan River and Valley.

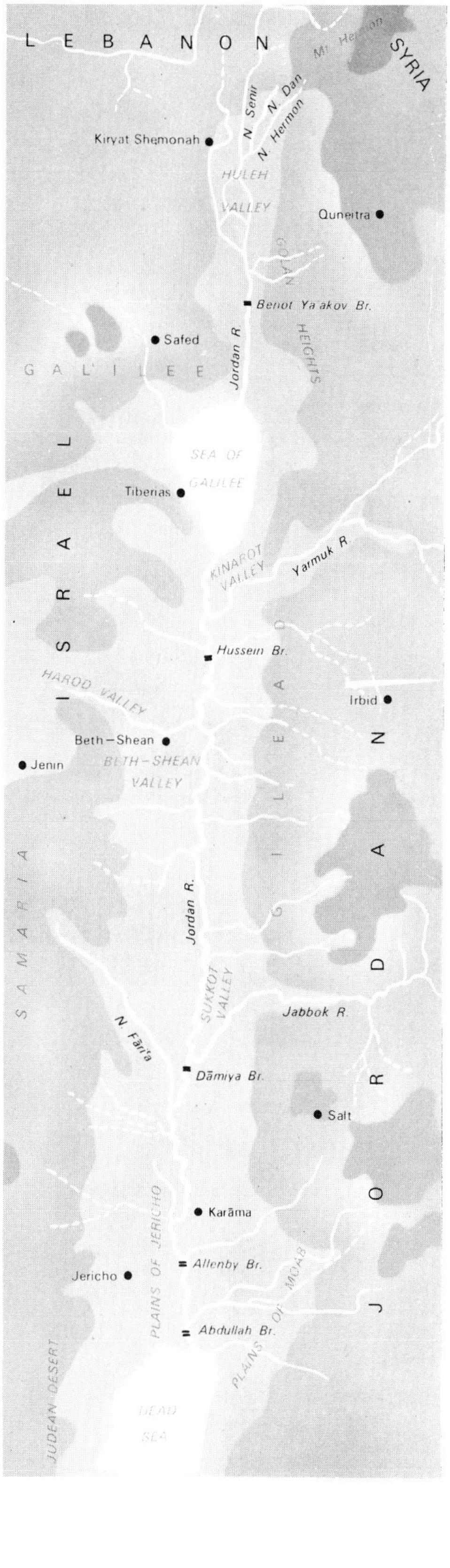

E. Palestine, proclaimed Hashemite Kingdom of Jordan in 1950, with Amman as capital. Areas W. of Jordan occupied by Israel in Six-Day War, leaving area of 34,500 sq. mi. and pop. of c. 1,500,000, including many former Palestinians. Much of country is desert, inhabited by Bedouin.

Jordan, Charles Harold (1908–1967), U.S. social worker. Joined American Jewish Joint Distribution Committee 1941 (director general in Europe fr. 1955). A key figure in mass migration fr. Europe to Israel. Mysteriously murdered in Prague.

Josce of York (d. 1190), English financier, martyr. Jewish representative at coronation of Richard I 1189; escaped when mob attacked Jews. Died in act of mass suicide at York.

Joselewicz, Berek (c. 1770–1809), Polish soldier; participated in Kosciuszko rising. During siege of Warsaw created separate Jewish light-cavalry regiment. After defeat of insurrection fled to France. Served in cavalry of Napoleon's Polish Legion. Killed in action.

Berek Joselewicz

Joselmann of Rosheim, see Joseph ben Gershon of Rosheim.

Joseph, son of Jacob and Rachel. Jacob's favorite. His ambition aroused displeasure of brothers who sold him into slavery. Household slave of Potiphar, high official of Egyptian court; imprisoned following false accusation made by Potiphar's wife. In prison interpreted dreams, became known to Pharaoh, and was appointed viceroy of Egypt, where his foresight prevented widespread hunger in famine period. Reconciled with brothers; his father in his old age joined him in Egypt.

Joseph (10th c.), king of Khazars who professed Jewish faith. Traditionally in correspondence with Ḥisdai ibn Shaprut.

°**Joseph II** (1741–1790), Holy Roman Emperor 1765–90. Abolished anti-Jewish measures in Austria–Hungary, incl. yellow badge and body tax. As part of general reform introduced his *Toleranzpatent* 1782, which improved situation of Austrian Jewry, though tradition-oriented Jews opposed it.

Joseph, Dov (Bernard; 1899–), Israel political leader; b. Montreal, joined Jewish Legion 1918, serving in Ereẓ Israel, settled in Jerusalem 1921. Legal advisor to Jewish Agency. Military governor of Jerusalem during critical siege of 1948. Mapai member of Knesset 1949–65. Held various cabinet posts, incl. minister of trade and industry during austerity period 1951–3 and minister of justice.

Joseph, Henry (1775–1832), Canadian businessman; b. England, settled in Berthier, Quebec. Established large chain of trading posts and is regarded as father of Canadian merchant marine.

Joseph, Henry (1838–1913), first rabbi in Argentina; b. England, in Argentina fr. 1860. Successful businessman. Organized Congregación Israelita de la República Argentina 1862, first such institution in Argentina.

Joseph, Jacob (1848–1902), rabbi, *maggid* of Vilna. Brilliant talmudist, preacher. In U.S. fr. 1888. Chief rabbi of Orthodox congregation of Russian Jews in N.Y. His grandson **Lazarus** (1891–1966), was N.Y.C. controller 1946–54.

Joseph's dreams from 14th cent. Spanish "Haggadah."

Joseph, Morris (1848–1930), English Reform rabbi. His *Judaism as Creed and Life* was widely read and popular.

Joseph, Sir Samuel George Joseph (1888–1944), British public servant. Lord mayor of London 1933–4. Headed building contracting firm. His son, **Sir Keith** (1918–), Conservative MP fr. 1956, minister of state at Board of Trade 1961, minister of housing and local government and minister for Welsh affairs 1962–64, minister of health and social services 1970–74.

Joseph, Saul Abdallah (1849–1906), merchant, scholar, b. Baghdad, settled in Hong Kong. Wrote on Jews of China and on medieval Spanish Hebrew poetry, pointing out Arabic influence on latter.

Joseph Bekhor Shor, see Bekhor Shor, Joseph ben Isaac.

Joseph (Joselmann) ben Gershon of Rosheim (c. 1478–1554), greatest of Jewish *shtadlanim* and defender of Jewish rights. Known as "commander of all Jewry." Obtained general letter of protection for Jews in Germany fr. Emperor Charles V 1520. Saved Jews of Alsace and Rosheim. Opposed messianic movement of David Reuveni and Solomon Molcho.

Joseph ben Ḥiyya (d. 333), Babylonian *amora.* Head of Pumbedita academy after Rabbah. Quoted throughout Babylonian and Jerusalem Talmuds. Distinguished in biblical exegesis; left Aramaic translation of parts of Bible.

Joseph ben Israel (16th–17th c.), Yemenite poet. Influential in molding religious, national, and mystic character of contemporary Jewish verse. Wrote 150 poems and *piyyutim* in Hebrew and Arabic.

Joseph ben Mordecai Gershon ha-Kohen of Cracow (1510–1591), halakhic authority. Head of yeshivah in Cracow. Dealt with many topics, esp. commercial and financial matters.

Joseph (Joselein) ben Moses (1423–c. 1490), talmudist; studied under Israel Isserlein. His compilation of his teacher's customs, responsa, and halakhic decisions is valuable for study of history of Jews of Germany.

Joseph ben Moses of Troyes (Joseph Porat; 12th c.), French scholar. Frequently mentioned among tosafists.

Joseph ben Shalom Ashkenazi (Joseph ha-Arokh, "the tall"; 14th c.), Spanish kabbalist. Admired Maimonides. Works reveal tendency to merge philosophy and Kabbalah.

Joseph ben Sheshet ibn Latimi (c. 1300), Spanish Hebrew poet. Wrote prayer consisting of 1,000 words, each beginning with letter *alef.*

Joseph ben Tanḥum Yerushalmi (b. 1262), Hebrew poet; son of grammarian-exegete Tanḥum b. Joseph Yerushalmi; lived in Egypt. Most genres of Spanish Hebrew poetry are represented in his *Divan.*

Joseph ben Uzziel, grandson of Ben Sira acc. to two pseudepigraphical sources: *Alphabet of Ben Sira,* late-geonic work; and *Baraita of Joseph b. Uzziel,* mystic work written by Ḥasidei Ashkenaz in 12th c.

Joseph ben Ẓaddik (15th c.), Spanish rabbinic scholar, chronicler. His compendium on ritual law, *Zekher Ẓaddik,* concludes with chronicle of significant events valuable for study of Spanish Jewish history.

Joseph Della Reina, hero of kabbalistic legend. Attempted to end Satan's power and lead to redemption, and in so doing lost his soul. Subject of many poems, short epics, ballads, plays. In reality, he was a 15th c. kabbalist.

Joseph ha-Kohen (1496–1578), historiographer, physician, philologist; active in Italy. His knowledge of languages gave him access to many sources. Wrote on both Jewish and general history, incl. history of kings of France and Turkey and *Emek ha-Bakha,* chronicle of Jewish suffering.

Joseph Ḥayyim ben Elijah al-Ḥakam (1833 or 1835–1909), Baghdad rabbi. Wrote some 60 works on all aspects of Torah. Best known for *Ben Ish Ḥai,* homilies blended with *halakhah* and Kabbalah.

Joseph Ha-Ẓarefati, Jewish artist. Illuminator of *Cervera Bible* of 1300; one of first Jewish artists known fr. medieval Europe.

Joseph Ibn Shraga (d. 1508/9), kabbalist considered greatest Italian kabbalist of his generation. Wrote treatise on redemption, widely circulated after expulsion fr. Spain; kabbalistic commentaries on prayers, Torah, blessings, etc.

Joseph Ibn Tabul (16th–17th c.), kabbalist; student of Isaac Luria, went fr. N. Africa to Safed. Tension existed bet. him and Ḥayyim Vital. His expositions on Lurianic Kabbalah are important.

Joseph Maman Al-Maghribi (1752–1823), rabbi, emissary of Safed; b. Morocco. Spent 30 years in Bukhara, completely revitalizing Jewish communities there. Regarded as spiritual father of Ḥibbat Zion movement in C. Asia.

Josephson, Swedish family. **Jacob Axel** (1818–1880), conductor, composer. Founded and headed Uppsala Philharmonic Society for 30 years. His brother, **Ludwig Oscar** (1832–1899), stage director. Noted for productions of Ibsen and Strindberg. Their nephew, **Ernest Abraham** (1851–1906), expressionist painter; leader of group of Swedish artists dissatisfied with aesthetic backwardness of Sweden. Experimented with spiritualism; had mental breakdown. **Gunnar** (1889–), bookseller, magistrate. Chairman of governing board of Stockholm Jewish community 1936–62. His brother, **Ragnar** (1891–1966), art historian. Prof. at Lund Univ. Elected to Swedish Academy 1961. **Erland** (1923–), actor, author. Some of his writings deal with anti-Semitism.

Josephson, Brian (1940–), British physicist. Awarded 1973 Nobel Physics Prize for discovery of process of basic importance to electronic development. Worked at Cavendish laboratories, Cambridge.

Josephson, Manuel (c. 1729–1796), merchant; b. Germany, communal leader in Philadelphia and New York. Supplied Congressional Army with weapons in French and Indian War and Revolution. Pres. Congregation Shearith Israel in N.Y. fr. 1762.

Josephson, Matthew (1899–), U.S. author. Wrote on 19th c. French literature and American economic history. Works incl. *Zola and His Time, Victor Hugo, The Robber Barons, The President Makers 1896–1919.*

Josephtal, Louis Maurice (1869–1929), U.S. naval officer. Assistant paymaster in Spanish-American War, paymaster (captain) in WWI. Rear Admiral in supply corps, 1923 and later commander of N.Y. naval militia.

Josephthal, Giora (1912–1962), Israel labor leader; b. Germany, settled in Ereẓ Israel 1938. Served in senior Jewish Agency positions and as Mapai cabinet minister. Dealt with absorption of newcomers during mass immigration.

Josephus Flavius (Joseph b. Mattathias; c. 38–after 100), historian; b. Jerusalem of priestly family. Joined Pharisee sect. Sent on mission to Nero 64 C.E.; won favor with Poppaea. Appointed commander of Galilee by Sanhedrin 66. Went over to Roman forces 67. Detested by Jewish patriots. Accompanied Vespasian and Titus at siege of Jerusalem; remained under imperial patronage in Rome. There wrote *The Jewish War, Jewish Antiquities, Life,* and *Against Apion* in defense of Jews. Greatest Jewish historian of antiquity. Accuracy of his descriptions previously questioned often verified by recent discoveries.

Joshua, leader of Israelites in conquest and apportionment of land of Canaan. As Moses' attendant, led Israelites against Amalek and later accompanied Moses during his ascent and descent of Mt. Sinai. One of 12 spies sent to Canaan; opposed negative majority report and for this was privileged to enter Canaan (Num. 14:30). Appointed by Moses as successor. Led tribes of Israel in series of successful battles, capturing most of Ereẓ Israel, esp. hill area. Story of period contained in Book of Joshua, first book in Former Prophets section of Bible.

Page from manuscript of Josephus' "Jewish Antiquities," France, c. 1470.

BOOK OF JOSHUA – CONTENTS

Chs. 1–12	The Conquest of Canaan.
1:1–5:12	Crossing the Jordan.
5:13–8:35	First conquests (Jericho, Ai).
9:1–10:27	Success in south-central Canaan.
10:28–43	Southern campaign.
11:1–15	Northern campaign.
11:16–12:24	Summary of conquest.
Chs. 13–21	Allotment of the land.
13:1–7	Land still unconquered.
13:8–33	Inheritance of Transjordanian tribes.
14:1–19:51	Allotment of Canaan.
20:1–9	Cities of refuge.
21:1–43	Levitical cities.
Ch. 22	Departure of Transjordanian tribes.
Chs. 23–24	Joshua's last days.
23:1–16	Joshua's farewell address.
24:1–28	Covenant at Shechem.
24:29–31	Death and burial of Joshua.
24:32–33	Two burial traditions: Joseph's at Shechem, Eleazar's at Gibeah.

Joshua ben Abraham Maimuni (1310–1355), *nagid* of Egyptian Jewry. Descendant of Maimonides, whose decisions he quotes. Wrote responsa, notably to Jews of Yemen.

Joshua ben Gamla (d. 69/70), high priest in last years of Second Temple. Leading opponent of extreme Zealots at time of Roman War. Together with other opponents of Zealots, put to death by Idumeans who entered Jerusalem. His profound acumen was byword; became legendary figure.

Joshua ben Hananiah (1st–2nd. c.), *tanna.* One of five disciples of Johanan b. Zakkai's inner circle. Lived in poverty, working as blacksmith. Rejected ascetic approach that forbade eating of meat and drinking of wine after destruction of Temple. Opponent of Christian-Jewish sects. Participated in diplomatic missions to Rome. Saying: "Pious gentiles have a share in the world to come."

Joshua ben Korḥa (2nd c.), *tanna.* Acc. to *aggadah,* sired son at age 100. Opposed collaboration with Roman authorities.

Joshua ben Levi (3rd. c.), Palestinian *amora.* Taught in native Lydda; active in community affairs, member of missions to Caesarea and Rome. Well known as aggadist, halakhist. Subject of many legends.

Joshua ben Mordecai Falk ha-Kohen (1799–1864), rabbi; b. Poland, in U.S. fr. c. 1854. Rabbi in Newburg, N.Y.; also itinerant preacher. His *Avnei Yehoshu'a,* commentary on *Avot,* was first work of rabbinic learning published in U.S.

Joshua ben Peraḥyah (2nd c. B.C.E.), one of *zugot,* with Nittai of Arbela. Saying: "Provide thyself with a teacher; get thee a companion; and judge all men charitably."

Joshua Boaz ben Simon Baruch (16th c.), scholar, printer; exiled fr. Spain, lived in Sabbioneta and Sarigliano, Italy. Author of several talmudic reference works. Started to print Talmud.

Joshua Hoeschel ben Jacob (1595–1663), rabbi in Lublin, Cracow, and Vienna. Worked on behalf of Jewish communities. Wrote novellae, glosses, etc.

Joshua Hoeschel ben Joseph of Cracow (1578–1648), rabbi in Polish towns, head of yeshivah of Cracow. Against excessive sophistry in Talmud. Opposed reliance on *Shulḥan Arukh* and other codes.

Joshua ibn Nun (16th c.), Safed scholar, kabbalist, *rosh yeshivah.* Ḥayyim Vital refused to initiate him into Lurianic Kabbalah; bribed Vital's brother to copy text for him.

יוסיפון פרק ח

Illuminated page from a Yiddish translation of "Josippon," Amsterdam, 1771.

Josiah, king of Judah 640–609 B.C.E.; son of Amon. During his reign Jerusalem developed greatly and kingdom expanded northward with gradual decline of Assyrian Empire. Territorial growth was accompanied by cultic reform, incl. purification and centralization of worship in Jerusalem, and publication and authorization of "Book of the Torah" (probably Deuteronomy), discovered 622 B.C.E. Killed in battle at Megiddo fighting Neco II of Egypt.

Josiah (2nd c.), *tanna;* b. Babylon. His statements cover wide variety of subjects. Saying: "If a good deed comes your way, do it immediately."

Josippon (10th c.), historical narrative in Hebrew describing period of Second Temple; written in S. Italy. Largely devoted to wars of Jews against Romans. Since name of author not known, book was ascribed to Josephus. Attained great popularity during the Middle Ages.

Jost, Isaac Marcus (1793–1860), German educator, historian. Enthusiastic supporter of Reform movement and pioneer of modern Jewish historiography. Wrote 10-vol. history of Jews. Translated Mishnah into German.

Isaac M. Jost

Jotabah, island in Gulf of Elath, inhabited by colony of Jewish merchants in early Byzantine period.

Jotapata, Galilean fortress dating fr. Israelite times. Fortified by Josephus at beginning of Jewish war against Rome 66 C.E. but fell after siege of 47 days.

Jotbath, Jothbatah, station of Israelites during their wandering in wilderness (Num. 33:33–34).

Jotham, youngest son of Gideon the judge. Only one to survive massacre engineered by his half-brother Abimelech. Invoked fable of trees (Judg. 9:8–15), parable warning of danger of placing royal power in wrong hands.

Jotham, king of Judah c. 742–735 B.C.E.; son of Uzziah. Subjugated Ammonites to improve transportation bet. Arabia and Mesopotamia (II Chron. 27:5). Ruled in lifetime of father, who had leprosy. Probably joined alliance of Syrian states against Assyrian Tiglath-Pileser III. Prosperity during his reign enabled him to fortify country.

Impression of a seal ring from Ezion Geber believed to be that of Jotham.

Journey, Prayer for, see Travel, Prayer for.

Józefowicz, Josef Rabchik (15th c.), founder of family of financiers. Tax collector of Kiev. His son **Abraham Jan Ezofovich** (1450–1519), merchant. tax collector head of treasury of grand duchy of Lithuania. His brother **Michael Ezofovich** (d. c. 1529), banker and agent of King Sigismund I, elder of Jews of Lithuania, and laid foundations for Brest-Litvosk community.

JTA, see Jewish Telegraphic Agency.

JTSA, see Jewish Theological Seminary of America.

Júan de Ciudad (15th c.), Castilian Converso. Circumcised 1465 at Huesca (Aragon), then main center of Jewish activities for encouraging Conversos to return to Judaism. Later emigrated to Ereẓ Israel. All Jews present at circumcision ceremony put to death by Inquisition.

Juan (Poeta) de Valladolid (c. 1420–after 1470), Spanish Marrano poet. Nicknamed "el judío." Reputedly astrologer; enjoyed favor of Queen Isabella.

Jubal, son of Lamech and Adah; inventor of instrumental music (Gen. 4:21).

Jubilee (Heb. *yovel*), 50th year, instituted at close of seven sabbatical cycles. Proclaimed by sounding *shofar* on Day of Atonement. Provisions incl. leaving land fallow, manumission of slaves, remission of debts, and return of all land purchased since previous Jubilee to original owners. Not observed after 2nd Temple period.

Jubilees, Book of, pseudepigraphic work dating fr. mid-Second Temple period. Original language Hebrew, but all extant versions translations fr. Greek. Gives dates of events in Bible acc. to Jubilee Year, Sabbatical Year, and Year of Sabbatical Cycle. Probably basic text of Dead Sea Sect. Influenced Midrashic literature.

Judah, fourth son of Jacob and Leah, eponymous ancestor of tribe of Judah. In Joseph story plays special role along with Reuben and Benjamin as spokesman for brothers. Esp. blessed by Jacob.

Judah (Nesiah), *nasi* 230–270; son of Gamaliel III. During his period of office power of *nasi* began to decline and struggle bet. him and scholars intensified. Saying: "The world is sustained for the sake of the breath of schoolchildren."

Judah III (Judah Nesiah II), *nasi* 290–320; son of Gamaliel IV. *Aggadah* describes meeting bet. him and emperor Diocletian at latter's invitation.

Judah, Kingdom of, southern of two Israelite kingdoms resulting fr. split after death of Solomon 928 B.C.E. Incl. territories of Judah, Simeon, and Benjamin. Existed until 586 B.C.E.

Judah, Samuel Benjamin Helbert (1799–1876?), U.S. playwright. Wrote *A Tale of Lexington,* drama of American Revolutionary War. Satirized his fellow New Yorkers in *Gotham and the Gothamites.*

Judah, Tribe of, one of 12 tribes of Israel. Settled in mountains, Shephelah, and pasture lands of wilderness of Judah. Tribe of David, and with his ascendancy initiative passed to it. Dominated southern kingdom of Judah. Source of word "Jew".

Judah Aristobulus, see Aristobulus I.

Judah bar Ezekiel (d. 299), Babylonian *amora.* After destruction of Nehardea academy, Judah founded and headed the Pumbedita academy. His *halakhah* is extensively quoted in both Talmuds.

Judah bar Ilai (2nd c.), *tanna.* Played leading role in developing Torah study after Hadrianic persecution and opened the convention of scholars at Usha where the Sanhedrin was reestablished. Was called "the chief spokesman on all occasions." Frequently quoted in Talmud and had his own Mishnah. Teacher of Judah ha-Nasi.

Judah ben Asher (1270–1349), rabbi, talmudist; b. Cologne. Studied under his father, Asher b. Jehiel (the Rosh). Following anti-Jewish outbreaks in Germany 1283, went to Toledo, Spain; later joined by parents. Succeeded father as head of *bet din* and yeshivah of Toledo.

Judah ben Barzillai ("ha-Nasi") al-Bargeloni (11th–12 c.), rabbi of Barcelona. Wrote *Sefer ha-Ittim,* dealing with Sabbath and festivals; *Yiḥus She'er Basar* on marriage and personal law; *Sefer ha-Din* on civil law; commentary on *Sefer Yeẓirah.*

Judah ben Bava (2nd. c.), *tanna;* one of Ten Martyrs. Noted for saintliness; member of Jabneh academy.

Judah ben Isaac (Judah Sir Leon of Paris; 1166–1224), French tosafist. Head of Paris *bet ha-midrash.*

Judah ben Isaac Ibn Shabbetai (13th c.), Spanish Hebrew poet. His poem "The Gift of Judah the Misogynist" warned against female vengeance and rash marriage.

Judah ben Jehiel (Messer Leon; 15th c.), Italian rabbi, author. Jewish Renaissance humanist and scholar; broad Jewish and general education, incl. classics. Wrote *Nofet Ẓufim* on rhetoric. Expelled fr. Mantua as result of controversy with Joseph Colon.

Judah ben Kalonymus ben Meir (12th c.), German scholar, *dayyan;* member of famous Kalonymus family. Wrote biographical lexicon of talmudic rabbis.

Judah Sir Leon of Paris, see Judah ben Isaac.

Judah ben Nathan (Rivan; 11th–12th c.), French tosafist. One of Rashi's most eminent pupils; married his daughter Miriam. Most editions of Talmud include his commentary on *Makkot.*

Judah ben Samuel he-Ḥasid (c. 1150–1217), leading teacher of Ḥasidei Ashkenaz movement; major medieval scholar of ethics and theology; probably lived in Speyer, then Regensburg. Teacher of Eleazar b. Judah of Worms. Wrote *Sefer ha-Kavod,* of which only quotations survived. Main author of *Sefer Ḥasidim.*

Judah ben Sheshet, see Yehudi ben Sheshet.

Judah ben Tabbai (1st c. B.C.E.), one of *zugot,* with Simeon b. Shetaḥ. Lived during time of Alexander Yannai; associated with Pharisees.

Judah ben Tema (2nd c.), *tanna.* Saying: "Be bold as a leopard, swift as an eagle, fleet as a hart, and strong as a lion, to do the will of Thy Father in heaven."

Judah ben Yakar (d. early 13th c.), talmudist, kabbalist; b. Provence, lived in N. France and Barcelona. Teacher of Naḥmanides. Wrote commentary on Jerusalem Talmud and rational commentary on liturgy and blessings.

KINGDOM OF JUDAH – KINGS

928–911	Rehoboam
911–908	Abijah
908–867	Asa
867–846	Jehoshaphat
846–843	Jehoram
843–842	Ahaziah
842–836	Athaliah
836–798	Jehoash
798–769	Amaziah
769–733	Uzziah
758–743	Jotham (regent)
758–743	Ahaz (regent)
733–727	Ahaz
727–698	Hezekiah
698–642	Manasseh
641–640	Amon
639–609	Josiah
609	Jehoahaz
608–598	Jehoiakim
597	Jehoiachin
596–586	Zedekiah

Territory of the tribe of Judah.

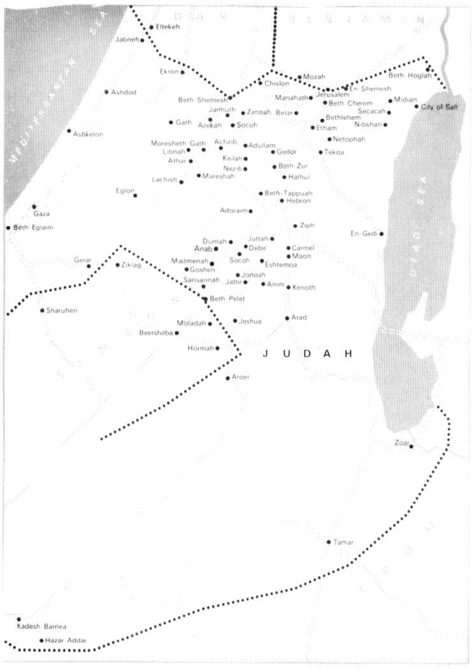

Judah the Galilean (d. c. 6 C.E.), anti-Roman leader, possibly identified with Judah son of Hezekiah, who was put to death by Herod in Galilee; cofounder of "Fourth Philosophy" (i.e. Sicarii). Headed band of rebels and seized control of armory in Herod's palace in Sepphoris. Apparently escaped after defeat of rebels. His sons Jacob and Simeon continued Zealot tradition and were crucified during procuratorship of Tiberius Alexander.

כוזרי

חברו בלשון ערבי החכם הגדול אבי כל המשוררים רבי יהודה הלוי
הספרדי זל אשר קדש שם שמים בויכוחו הישר הזה,
והעתיקו אותו החכם רבי יהודה בן תבון פרמון
ספרדי אל לשון הקדש במגדל לוניל
שנת התקכו,

אותו העיר האיש מאיר בן כמר יעקב
ממשפחת פרענצוני:

Title page of Judah Halevi's "Kuzari," Venice, 1547.

Judah Halevi (before 1075–1141), Hebrew poet, philosopher, physician; lived in Spain, set out for Erez Israel, arrived in Egypt 1140 and died there (although acc. to legend killed by Arab horseman in view of Jerusalem). One of greatest of Hebrew poets; imbued with longing for Zion (wrote *Zionides,* one of which begins "I am in the West – but my heart is in the East"). Introduced forms of Arabic poetry into Hebrew verse. Wrote both secular and religious verse, characterized by deep Jewish feeling. Over 800 of his poems are known, incl. 350 *piyyutim.* His philosophical *Kuzari,* written in form of dialogue, describes religious disputations showing superiority of Judaism over Christianity and Islam; became major Jewish classic.

Judah ha-Nasi ("Rabbi"; 2nd–3rd c.), patriarch of Judea, redactor of Mishnah, compilation of which was accomplished with cooperation of all contemporary scholars; son and successor of Simeon b. Gamaliel. As political head of Palestinian Jewish community, had frequent contacts with Roman authorities. Possessed great personal wealth. Lived in Bet Shearim and Sepphoris in Galilee. His wisdom, sanctity, and humility subject of legends. He and his *bet din* influential throughout entire country. His status and personal authority made Mishnah basis of study and legal decision, second only to Scriptures.

Judah Ḥasid (Segal) ha-Levi. (1660? –1700), Shabbatean preacher in Poland. Ascetic, oriented toward repentence. Organized "Holy Group" of families of scholars who emigrated to Jerusalem, but died shortly after his arrival and group collapsed.

Judah he-Ḥasid, see Judah ben Samuel he-Hasid.

Judah Loew ben Bezalel (Der Hohe Rabbi Loew; Maharal; c. 1525–1609), rabbi, moralist, scholar. One of outstanding leaders of Ashkenazi Jewry; revered for piety and asceticism. *Landesrabbiner* of Moravia, founded Die Klaus Yeshivah in Prague, rabbi of Posen and Moravia and finally chief rabbi of Prague. Subject of legends, esp. tale of *golem.* Active in communal life, wrote on Bible, ethics, halakhah. His statue erected outside Prague town hall 1917. A lone thinker, his ideas have enjoyed a revival in 20th c.

Judah Maccabee (d. 161 B.C.E.), warrior; third son of Mattathias the Hasmonean. Succeeded father as leader of revolt against Antiochus Epiphanes. Inflicted successive defeats on Syrian army, captured Jerusalem, purified defiled Temple, and instituted festival of eight days (Ḥanukkah). Fell in battle of Elasa. One of great Jewish heroes.

Judaism, religion and civilization of Jewish people. In purely religious sense, connotes belief in ethical monotheism and its precepts. As civilization, encompasses common experience shared by Jewish people, involving historical and national elements as well as religion.

Judah Maccabee, 16th cent. French enamel plaque.

Statue of Judah Loew ben Bezalel, by Ladislav Saloun, 1917, at entrance to Prague town hall.

Judaizers, non-Jews adhering to Jewish religion. In Russia such sects and trends appeared in Novgorod fr. 15th c.; reappeared in 18th c. as result of profound study of Bible, with sects of Judaizers and Sabbath observers (Subbotniks) spreading all over Russia. Position deteriorated in early 19th c. but at end of c. began to observe their religion openly.

Jude, Der, name of 4 German-language periodicals (1) Published 1768–72 in Leipzig by apostate Gottfried Selig, with intention of explaining Judaism to Christian world. (2) Published 1832–33, edited by Gabriel Riesser. (3) Published 1916–24, founded and edited by M. Buber. Influenced German Jewish youth. (4) Zionist periodical, appeared in Vienna 1934–38.

Judea, Latin form of Judah; S. province of Erez Israel during period of Roman hegemony.

Judean Desert Caves, caves found nr. Dead Sea in valleys bet. Masada and Ein-Gedi. Two major periods of occupation: during Chalcolithic Period and during Bar Kokhba War 132–135 C.E. Finds revolutionized ideas on religious culture of Chalcolithic Period and on Bar Kokhba War.

Judean Desert Sect, see Dead Sea Sect.

Judenrat (Ger. "Jewish Council"), body heading Jewish community, appointed by Germans during WWII and made responsible for enforcement of Nazi orders affecting Jews and for administration of all Jewish communal affairs.

Judenrein (Ger. "cleansed of Jews"), in Nazi terminology, town or region after entire Jewish population was removed.

Judeo-Arabic, dialect spoken and written by Jews in N. Africa, introduced during first phase of Arab rule. Close to spoken Arabic, with Jewish coloring.

Judeo-French, Old French spoken and written by medieval French and Rhenish Jewry.

Judeo-German, see Yiddish.

Judeo-Greek, language known fr. medieval times, spoken and written in Balkan peninsula and islands, esp. Corfu and Zante. Contains elements of Hebrew, Aramaic, and Turkish; written in Hebrew characters. During Nazi occupation of Greece, some Jews used it as secret language.

Judeo-Italian, dialect spoken and written fr. early Middle Ages by Jews living in C. and S. Italy, esp. in Rome. Used by all Italian Jews fr. 13th–14th c., now only by Jewish working class of Rome.

Judeo-Persian, Iranian dialects now spoken exclusively among certain communities in Kashan, Hamadan, Isfahan, Shiraz, etc. Hebrew-written Judeo-Persian texts fr. 8th c. are earliest known records in Persian language.

Judeo-Provençal, various dialects spoken in late Middle Ages among Jews of Provence. In 17th–18th c. fusion of Provençal, Hebrew, and French.

Judeo-Spanish, see Ladino.

Judeo-Tat, Iranian dialect used among Jewish communities of Eastern Caucasus, known as Mountain Jews. 30,000 Jews declared Judeo-Tat as mother tongue in 1959 Soviet census.

Judges, charismatic leaders in period bet. death of Joshua and institution of monarchy in ancient Israel.

Judges, Book of, second book in Former Prophets section of Bible, covering period bet. Joshua and Samuel. Valuable historical document, preserving literary fragments of great antiquity and affording insights into social and religious conditions of period.

Judith, Book of, book in Apocrypha. Story of Judith, beautiful widow who cut off Assyrian commander Holofernes' head when latter was besieging Bethulia, saving city. Written originally in Hebrew in Hasmonean times or earlier. Uncertain whether there is historical basis.

Jud Suess, see Oppenheimer, Joseph.

Juedische Freischule, private school for poor children, founded in Berlin 1778 by Isaac Daniel Itzig and David Friedlaender. Influenced by Moses Mendelssohn's ideas on education. Closed 1825.

Juedische Presse, German weekly reflecting Orthodox viewpoint, published in Berlin 1870–1923.

Juedischer Frauenbund, organization of Jewish women, founded 1904 by Sidonie Werner and Bertha Pappenheim, originally to combat white slavery, esp. of Jewish girls in E. Europe.

Juedischer Kulturbund, German Jewish organization founded in Berlin 1933 when Nazis excluded all Jews fr. German cultural life. Devoted itself to spreading interest in Jewish art and culture.

BOOK OF JUDGES – CONTENTS

1:1–2:5	Completion of the conquest.
2:6–3:6	Introduction to the careers of the judges.
3:7–11	Othniel.
3:12–30	Ehud.
3:31	Shamgar.
4:1–5:31	Deborah and Barak (and Jael).
6:1–8:35	Gideon (Jerubbaal).
9:1–57	Abimelech.
10:1–5	Tola and Jair.
10:6–16	Introduction to later judges.
10:17–12:7	Jephthah.
12:8–15	Ibzan, Elon and Abdon.
13:1–16:31	Samson.
17:1–21:25	Migration of Dan to the north and war against the Benjamites.

Judith and Holofernes, bronze Ḥannukah lamp, Italy, 16th cent.

Judeo-Persian version of 15th-cent. "Yūsuf o Zuleykhā" by Jāmī.

Juedische Rundschau, journal of Zionist Federation in Germany, founded 1896. Circ. over 30,000 (1937), mainly outside Germany. Closed 1938.

Juedischer Verlag, first Jewish-Zionist publishing house in W. Europe, established 1902 to publish cultural treasures of Jewish people. Closed by Gestapo 1938.

Juedische Volkspartei, party organized 1919 in Berlin and other large cities of Germany. Originated in circles influenced by Herzl's call for Zionists to enter communal politics to fight assimilationists and conservative factions.

Juedisch-Theologisches Seminar, Breslau, 1904.

Juedisch-Theologisches Seminar, Breslau, first modern rabbinical seminary in C. Europe, founded 1854. Became model for similar colleges in Europe and U.S. Its first head Zacharias Frankel sought to teach "positive historical Judaism"; in fact, largely training college for Reform rabbis. In Nov. 1938, seminary sacked and most of library destroyed.

Caricature of Isaac son of Jurnet of Norwich, 1233.

°**Julian the Apostate** (331–363), Roman emperor 361–363. Attracted by enlightened paganism, saw Christianity as sickness. Permitted rebuilding of Temple; start was made but halted for some reason and project came to end with his death.

Julianus, see Pappus and Julianus.

°**Julius Caesar** (c. 100–44 B.C.E.), Roman leader. On entering Judea, revised administrative arrangements to Jewish advantage. Safeguarded Jewish freedom of worship in Asia and Rome, where Jews deeply mourned his death.

°**Julius Severus,** Roman commander who suppressed Bar Kokhba revolt 132–135 C.E. Transferred fr. Britain to Ereẓ Israel after other Roman commanders had failed.

Jung, Leo (1892–), U.S. Orthodox rabbi, author; b. Moravia, in U.S. fr. 1920. Rabbi of Jewish Center in N.Y. 1922, prof. of ethics at Yeshiva Univ. 1931. Edited 8 vols. of *Jewish Library.* His brother **Moses** (1891–1960), prof. of religion, educator; went to U.S. 1922. Lectured at Columbia Univ. fr. 1952. Another brother, **Julius** (1894–), secretary, executive director of Federation of Synagogues in London.

Jurnet of Norwich (Eliab; d.c. 1197), English financier. Referred to as *nadiv* (patron of scholars) in Hebrew sources. His son, **Isaac of Norwich** (d.c. 1242) also *nadiv;* outstanding financier under Henry III.

Juster, George (1902–1968), Rumanian painter. Master of water color.

Juster, Jean (c. 1886–1916), lawyer, historian; b. Rumania. Advocate at Paris Court of Appeal. His major work, *Les juifs dans l'empire romain; leur condition juridique, économique et sociale,* is model of clarity and scholarly documentation. D. in military action.

°**Justinian I,** emperor of E. Roman Empire 527–565. Persecutor of non-Orthodox Christians, pagans, Jews and Judaism. His legal code included specific anti-Jewish legislation, forcing Jews in Byzantine Empire into inferior status for many centuries.

Justman, Moshe Bunem (pseud. **Jeuschsohn, B.;** 1889–1942), Yiddish journalist, novelist; b. Warsaw, settled in Ereẓ Israel 1940. Wrote on conflict bet. Ḥasidism and modernism and on Jewish folklore.

Justus of Tiberias (1st c.), historian, opponent of Josephus. Wrote book on Jewish revolt against Rome.

JWV, see Jewish War Veterans of the United States of America.

JWB, see National Jewish Welfare Board.

Initial letter "K" for Karolus (Charlemagne), from opening of Book 25 of Vincent of Beauvais, "Speculum Historiale," S. Germany, 1332.

Kabak, Aaron Abraham (1880–1944), Hebrew novelist; b. Poland, settled in Jerusalem 1921. Decisive force in bringing Hebrew novel into line with world literature. Wrote trilogy *Shelomo Molkho, The Narrow Path* on Jesus, etc.

Kabachnik, Martin Izrailovich (1908–), Russian organic chemist. Worked at USSR Academy of Sciences fr. 1939, Inst. of Organic Chemistry until 1954, Inst. of Elementary Organic Compounds. Stalin Prize 1946. Research fields incl. tautomerism and phosphorus-containing organic insecticides.

Kabakoff, Jacob (1918–), U.S. educator, scholar. Dean of Cleveland College of Jewish Studies 1952–68, prof. of Hebrew literature at Lehman College, N.Y.

Kabbalah, term used for esoteric teachings of Judaism and for Jewish mysticism, esp. forms developed fr. 12th c. Also signifies various esoteric movements from end of Second Temple period. In the Talmud, Kabbalah used for oral traditions.

Kabbalat Shabbat (Heb. "Reception of the Sabbath"), part of Friday evening service preceding regular evening prayer and solemnly welcoming Sabbath. Consists of Psalm 29 (in some rites Psalms 95–99 are added), hymn *Lekhah Dodi,* Ps. 92–93.

Ka'b ben Asad (d. 627), chief of Jewish tribe of Qurayẓa in Medina. Put to death along with rest of tribe after refusing to accept Islam.

Title page of "Portae Lucis," a Latin translation by Paulus Ricius of J. Gikatilla's kabbalistic "Sha'arei Orah," Augsburg, 1516.

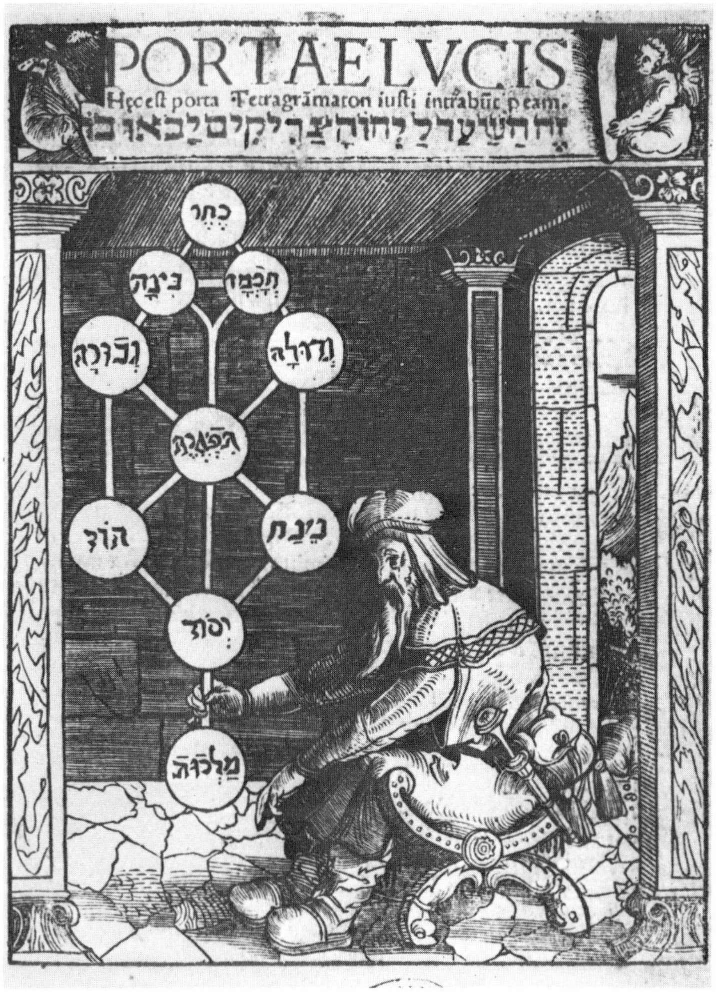

Paper wall plaque with "Lekhah Dodi" and Psalm 92 from "Kabbalat Shabbat" service, Alsace (?), 19th cent.

יִתְגַּדַּל וְיִתְקַדַּשׁ שְׁמֵהּ רַבָּא בְּעָלְמָא דִּי־בְרָא כִרְעוּתֵהּ. וְיַמְלִיךְ מַלְכוּתֵהּ בְּחַיֵּיכוֹן וּבְיוֹמֵיכוֹן וּבְחַיֵּי דִּי־כָל־בֵּית יִשְׂרָאֵל בַּעֲגָלָא וּבִזְמַן קָרִיב. וְאִמְרוּ אָמֵן:	Yitgaddal ve-yitkaddash shemeh rabba be-olma di-vera khi-re'uteh ve-yamlikh malkhuteh be-ḥayyekhon u-ve-yomekhon, u-ve-ḥayyei di-khol-bet Yisrael ba-agala u-vi-zeman kariv, ve-imru, Amen.	*Mourner* Magnified and sanctified be his great Name in the world which he hath created according to his will. May he establish his kingdom during your life and during your days, and during the life of all the house of Israel, even speedily and at a near time, and say ye, Amen.
יְהֵא שְׁמֵהּ רַבָּא מְבָרַךְ לְעָלַם וּלְעָלְמֵי עָלְמַיָּא.	Yehe shemeh rabba mevorakh le-olam u-le-olmei olmayya.	*Congregation and Mourner* Let his great Name be blessed for ever and to all eternity.
יִתְבָּרַךְ וְיִשְׁתַּבַּח וְיִתְפָּאַר וְיִתְרוֹמַם וְיִתְנַשֵּׂא וְיִתְהַדַּר וְיִתְעַלֶּה וְיִתְהַלַּל שְׁמֵהּ דִּי־קֻדְשָׁא. בְּרִיךְ הוּא לְעֵלָּא מִן־כָּל־בִּרְכָתָא וְשִׁירָתָא תֻּשְׁבְּחָתָא וְנֶחֱמָתָא דִּי־אֲמִירָן בְּעָלְמָא. וְאִמְרוּ אָמֵן:	Yitbarakh, ve-yishtabbaḥ ve-yitpa'ar, ve-yitromam, ve-yitnasse ve-yithaddar, ve-yitalleh ve-yithallal shemeh di-kudesha, berikh hu; le-ella min-kol-birkhata ve-shirata, tushbeḥata ve-neḥemata, di-amiran be-olma; ve-imru, Amen.	*Mourner* Blessed, praised and glorified, exalted, extolled and honored, magnified and lauded be the Name of the Holy One, blessed be he; though he be high above all the blessings and hymns, praises and consolations, which are uttered in the world; and say ye, Amen.
יְהֵא שְׁלָמָא רַבָּא מִן־שְׁמַיָּא וְחַיִּים עָלֵינוּ וְעַל־כָּל־יִשְׂרָאֵל. וְאִמְרוּ אָמֵן:	Yehe shelama rabba min-shemayya, ve-ḥayyim aleinu ve-al-kol-Yisrael; ve-imru, Amen.	May there be abundant peace from heaven, and life for us and for all Israel; and say ye, Amen.
עֹשֶׂה שָׁלוֹם בִּמְרוֹמָיו הוּא יַעֲשֶׂה שָׁלוֹם עָלֵינוּ וְעַל־כָּל־יִשְׂרָאֵל. וְאִמְרוּ אָמֵן:	Oseh shalom bi-meromav, hu ya'aseh shalom aleinu ve-al-kol-Yisrael; ve-imru, Amen.	He who maketh peace in his high places, may he make peace for us and for all Israel; and say ye, Amen.

Kabīr, Abraham Ṣāliḥ al- (1885–), Iraqi official. Played active role in Jewish communal life. Settled in London in 1960. His brother **Joseph,** lawyer, communal worker. Represented Jews of Baghdad in Iraqi Parliament 1935–36.

Kacyzne, Alter (1885–1941), Yiddish writer, photographer; b. Vilna. Wrote poetry, fiction, drama, essays. Killed by Ukrainian collaborators.

Kaczerginsky, Shmerl (1908–1954), Yiddish writer. Chronicler in verse, prose, and drama of Vilna ghetto and Jewish partisans. In WWII succeeded in hiding considerable Jewish material later taken to YIVO library in New York. Killed in airplane crash in Brazil.

Kadar, Jan (1918–), Czech film director. Famed for *The Shop on Main Street,* which won Academy Award.

Kaddish (Aram. "holy"), doxology, mostly in Aramaic, recited with congregational responses at close of individual sections of public service and at conclusion of service itself. Statutory synagogue prayer requiring presence of 10 adult males fr. 7th c. C.E. and mourner's recitation since 13th c. C.E. Four main types: (a) whole (or complete) *Kaddish;* (b) "half" *Kaddish;* (c) *Kaddish de-Rabbanan* ("scholars' *Kaddish*"); (d) mourners' *Kaddish.*

Kadesh, see Kedesh.

Kadesh-Barnea, an important oasis situated on S. border of Canaan in wilderness of Zin. During Exodus served as assembly point for Israelite tribes. Spies sent fr. there to explore Canaan.

Kadimah, first Jewish national students' association, founded 1882 in Vienna by Rubin Bierer, Moritz Tobias Schnirer, and Nathan Birnbaum. Similar associations subsequently founded in many universities in W. Europe preparing ground for Herzl and Zionist movement.

Kadimah, semi-urban settlement in C. Israel, founded as moshav in 1933. Pop. 3,970 (1971).

Kadman (Kaufman), Gurit (c. 1900–), folk-dance teacher; b. Germany, settled in Ereẓ Israel 1920. Instituted first folk-dance festival in Kibbutz Daliyyah 1944.

Kadoorie, family originating in Baghdad with large business interests in Far East. **Sir Ellis** (1865–1922), and **Sir Elly Silas** (1867–1944), settled in Hong Kong, developing business in Shanghai and other cities. Sir Elly pres. of Palestine Foundation Fund in Shanghai, established agricultural schools in Ereẓ Israel, contributed toward construction of Hebrew Univ. etc. His sons, **Sir Lawrence** (1899–) and **Horace** (1902–), continued their father's business in Hong Kong, established Kadoorie Agricultural Aid Loan Fund 1951, which assisted over 300,000 Chinese refugees. Also gave support to Hong Kong Jewish community.

Kadoorie, Sasson (1885–1971), Baghdad rabbi, community leader. Chief rabbi of Baghdad 1927–29. Rejected Zionism and forced to resign. Resumed office 1953 as community chairman and reappointed chief rabbi.

Kadushin, Max (1895–), U.S. rabbi, scholar. Wrote on rabbinic thinking and its concepts.

Kaempf, Saul Isaac (1818–1892), rabbi, orientalist. Prof. of Semitics at Prague Univ. Made contribution to study of Hebrew poetry.

Kaf (כ; final form ך), 11th letter of Hebrew alphabet; numerical value 20. Pronounced *k* or *kh.*

Yosef Kafaḥ

Kafaḥ (Kafiḥ), Yiḥye ben Solomon (1850–1932), Yemenite scholar, teacher. Set up movement called Darda'im to modernize Yeminite religious thought. Corresponded with A.I. Kook and Hillel Zeitlin. Opposed to Kabbalah.

Kafaḥ (Kafiḥ), Yosef (1917–), Israel rabbi, scholar; grandson of Yiḥye Kafaḥ; b. Yemen, settled in Ereẓ Israel 1943. Member of *bet din* in Jerusalem. Published studies on Yemenite Jewish literature and translated works by Maimonides, Saadiah, etc. fr. Arabic into Hebrew. Israel Prize 1969.

Kafka, Bruno Alexander (1881–1931), Czechoslovak jurist; cousin of Franz Kafka. Prof. at German Univ. of Prague. Wrote on civil and family law. Member of Czechoslovakian parliament. Converted to Catholicism.

Franz Kafka

Kafka, Franz (1883–1924), Czechoslovak German-language novelist; major figure in world literature. In his chief novels *(The Trial, The Castle)* and stories (*The Metamorphosis, The Chinese Wall,* etc.) action is beyond normal experience and often permeated with nightmare quality as alienated hero struggles against inexplicable situation. Recognition came only after death, owing primarily to friend Max Brod, who published his work.

Kafr Kamā, Muslim-Circassian village in Israel, in E. Lower Galilee. Founded late 19th c. During War of Independence 1948 inhabitants not hostile to Jews. Pop. 1,330 (1971).

Kafr Kanna, see Kefar Kanna.

Kafr Qāsim, Muslim-Arab village NE of Petaḥ Tikvah, Israel. On eve of Sinai Campaign 1956 literal execution of curfew order resulted in shooting of 47 people; military personnel responsible tried and convicted. Pop. 4,550 (1971).

Kagan, Solomon Robert (1889–1955), medical historian, ordained as rabbi; b. Lithuania, in U.S. fr. 1922. Wrote on Jewish contribution to medicine, etc.

Lazar Kaganovich

Kaganovich, Lazar Moiseyevich (1893–), Soviet politician. Organized industrialization of Moscow region and construction of Moscow subway 1935–7, which was named after him. Subsequently commissar for communications and for heavy industry. Devoted Stalinist. For years only Jew to occupy top position in Soviet leadership. Expelled 1957 fr. Central Committee and all government posts.

Kaganowski, Efraim (1893–1958), Yiddish writer. Found refuge in Russia upon German invasion; repatriated to Poland 1946. Last years in Paris. His stories depicted Warsaw Jewry.

Kahan, Louis (1915–), Australian portraitist; b. Vienna, in Melbourne fr. 1951. Represented in National Gallery of all six states of Australia.

Kahan, Salomon (1896–1965), Yiddish essayist, musicologist; b. Bialystok, in Mexico City fr. 1921. Central role in cultural life of Mexico's Jewish community. Wrote essays on literature, music, important Jewish and Mexican personalities.

Kahana, Abraham (1874–1946), biblical scholar, historian; b. Russia, settled in Ereẓ Israel fr. 1923. Edited with commentary Hebrew Bible and Apocrypha, wrote history of Jews in Rome.

Abraham Kahana

Kahana, Aharon (Hermann; 1905–1967), painter, ceramic artist; b. Germany, settled in Ereẓ Israel 1934. Founder-member of "New Horizons" group 1947–48. Designed several decorative murals in ceramics and enamel.

Kahana (Kogan), David (1838–1915), Russian scholar. Published works on kabbalists, Shabbateans, and Ḥasidim, as well as biblical, post-biblical, and historical studies.

Kahana, Kalman (1910–), Po'alei Agudat Israel leader; b. Galicia. A founder of Agudat Israel youth movement in Germany. Settled in Ereẓ Israel 1938. Deputy minister of education 1962–69.

Kahana, Koppel (1895–), rabbinical scholar; b. Lithuania. Lecturer in Talmud and codes at Jews' College, London. Authority on Jewish, Roman, and English law.

Kahana, Naḥman (1861–1904), Hungarian rabbi. Author of *Orḥot Ḥayyim* on *Shulḥan Arukh Oraḥ Ḥayyim,* which utilized more than 800 other works and became indispensable rabbinical reference work.

Kahana, Solomon David (1869–1953), Polish rabbi. Member of Warsaw rabbinate. Organizer of *agunot* departments to enable war widows to remarry after WWI in Poland. Settled in Ereẓ Israel 1939, continuing work for war widows after WWII.

Kahane, Anne (1924–), Canadian sculptor. Worked mainly in wood chiseled in traditional manner of French-Canadian carving.

Kahane, Isaak (1904–1963), rabbi, scholar; b. Hungary, settled in Ereẓ Israel 1939. Taught at Bar-Ilan Univ. Author of studies on rabbinic and linguistic topics.

Joseph Kahaneman

Kahaneman, Joseph (1888–1969), Lithuanian rabbi, yeshivah head; known as "Ponevezher Rav" fr. court of learning he established in Ponevezh. A leader of Agudat Israel and member of Lithuanian parliament. Settled in Ereẓ Israel 1940. Founded Kiryat Ponevezh in Bene Berak.

Kahanov, Moses Nehemiah (1817–1883), rabbi, talmudist; b. Belorussia, settled in Jerusalem 1864. Head of Eẓ Ḥayyim yeshivah. Progressive in views; advocated founding of industrial enterprises in Ereẓ Israel, among first Orthodox rabbis to speak only Hebrew. Wrote on laws of Sabbatical year.

Kahanovich, Pinkhes, see Der Nister.

Kāhina, surname given by Arabs to queen of Berber converts to Judaism in mountainous region of SE Algeria. After initial victory against Arab invaders, held territory for some time but then died in combat 698 or 702. Accounts partly legendary and remain controversial.

°**Kahle, Paul Ernst** (1875–1965), masoretic scholar; b. Germany, in Oxford fr. 1938. Provided basis for Kittel's *Biblia Hebraica.* Pursued fundamental research on Cairo *Genizah.*

Kahn, Albert (1869–1942), U.S. industrial architect. Specialized in factory design; engaged by Henry Ford as one of his principal architects. Designed General Motors Building, Fisher Building, and two synagogues in Detroit, and factories in USSR.

Kahn, Bernard (1876–1955), communal worker; b. Sweden. Secretary-

general of Hilfsverein 1904–21. European director of Joint Distribution Committee fr. 1924. Fr. 1939 in U.S.

Kahn, Dorothy C. (1893–1955), U.S. social worker. Headed social science section of UN Dept. of Social Affairs 1951–54.

Drawing by Louis I. Kahn for the projected Mikveh Israel Synagogue, Philadelphia, 1963.

Zadoc Kahn

Kaifeng synagogue, drawing by 18th cent. Jesuit missionary.

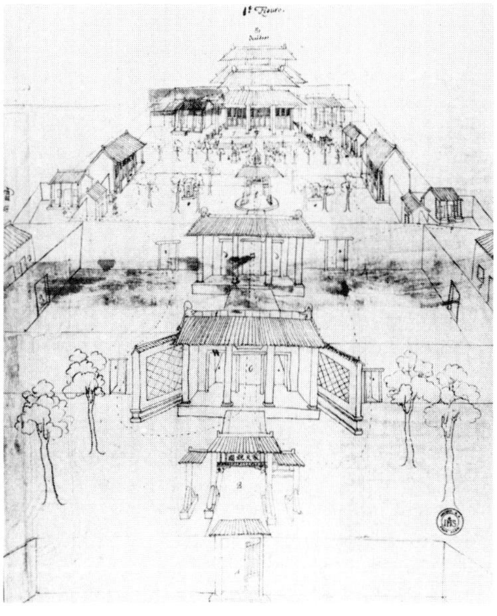

Kahn, Ely Jacques (1884–1972), U.S. architect. Noted for versatility. Designed several buildings of Jewish interest, incl. Mount Sinai Hospital, N.Y.

Kahn, Gustave (1859–1936), French poet, author. Outstanding member of Symbolist movement. With Jules Laforgue, considered inventor of *vers libre* ("free verse"). Enthusiastic advocate of Zionist cause. Edited *Menorah,* French Zionist periodical.

Kahn, Julius (1861–1924), U.S. Republican congressman. Advocate of universal military training and naval preparedness; helped steer President Wilson's World War program through Congress. Opposed Zionism. His widow, **Florence Prag** (1868–1948), appointed to his House seat on his death; served until 1937.

Kahn, Louis (1895–1967), French general, naval engineer. Headed technical dept. of Air Force Ministry 1928–38, participated in design of modern carriers. Joined Free French in WWII, introducing new techniques of submarine warfare. Secretary-general of armed forces 1950. Pres. Central Consistory of French Jews fr. 1963.

Kahn, Louis I. (1901–1974), U.S. architect. Prof at Univ. of Pennsylvania. Designed Yale Art Gallery, Richards Medical Research Building at Univ. of Penn., and synagogues.

Kahn, Otto Hermann (1867–1934), U.S. banker, philanthropist; b. Germany, worked in London, moved to N.Y. 1893. Leading banking authority; advocated establishment of war finance board in WWI. Opposed Versailles Peace Treaty and League of Nations, urged cancellation of foreign war debts and limited armaments. Philanthropies largely in cultural and Jewish spheres.

Kahn, Richard Ferdinand, Lord (1905–), British economist. Disciple of Keynes. Prof. at Cambridge. Author of "multiplier theory" which dealt with ability to save and invest as against propensity to consume.

Kahn, Zadoc (1839–1905), French rabbi. Chief rabbi of Paris 1868, France 1889. Outstanding leader in international Jewish affairs. Fought French anti-Semitism, esp. during Dreyfus Affair; headed Ḥibbat Zion in France. Helped create Société des Etudes Juives, serving as pres.

Kahnshtam, Aharon (1859–1921), Hebrew, Yiddish educator. Fr. 1895 directed *talmud torah* in Lodz, making it into model school where deprived children were taught farming, carpentry, etc. Theoretician and organizer of Tarbut Society.

Kaidanover, see Koidanover.

Kaifeng, city in C. China. Jews probably arrived before 1127 fr. India or Persia. Synagogue constructed 1163, restored 1279, rebuilt 1653. Thereafter community fell into rapid decay through assimilation, ending in 19th c.

Kainuka, see Qaynuqa.

Kairouan, in Tunisia. Leading Jewish economic, cultural center during Middle Ages. Its academy heads corresponded with Babylonian *geonim* and played key role in transmission of rabbinic knowledge from eastern to new western centers. Its scholars known throughout Jewish world, incl. Isaac Israeli, Ḥushi'el b. Elhanan, Jacob b. Nissim ibn Shahin. With conquest by Almohads 1160, became holy city of Islam, forbidden to non-Muslims until French occupation 1881.

Kaiser, Alois (1840–1908), cantor, composer; b. Hungary. Officiated at Ohel Shalom Congregation in Baltimore. Prepared first edition of Union Hymnal for Conference of American Rabbis.

Kalba Savu'a, see Ben Kalba Savua.

Kaldor, Nicholas, Baron (1908–), British economist; b. Budapest. At London School of Economics fr. 1932, prof. at Cambridge fr. 1966. Special adviser to Labor government on employment, development, and fiscal policy 1964–70. Advocated extension of state control and high taxation.

Kalecki, Michal (1899–1970), Polish economist. Worked for UN Economic Dept. 1947–54. Joined Polish State Planning Commission 1957; instrumental in preparing Poland's first 20-year plan. Wrote studies on business cycles, war economics, and full employment.

Kalef, Yehoshua (1875–1943), Bulgarian Zionist leader. Published Zionist newspaper in Bulgarian. Participated in First Zionist Congress 1897. Member of Bulgarian government delegation to Paris Peace Conference. Lived last years in France.

Kalich, Bertha (1875–1939), Yiddish actress; b. Poland, in New York fr. 1891, appearing in Yiddish repertory and repeating in English some of her Yiddish successes.

Kalinindorf (until 1927 **Bolshaya Seidemenukha**), former Jewish settlement in Ukrainian SSR; one of four Jewish agricultural colonies

founded 1807 in Kherson province. Many settlers left during collectivization 1930–32. 11,198 Jews in region in 1932; those who did not escape were killed by Nazis.

Kaliningrad, see Koenigsberg.

Kalisch, David (1820–1872), German humorist. Wrote popular sketches and farces (e.g., *Einmal Hunderttausend Taler*). Founded *Kladderadatsch* 1848, widely circulated satirical periodical.

Kalischer, Ẓevi Hirsch (1795–1874), rabbi, proto-Zionist; b. Poland. Rabbi in Thorn, Prussia. Proclaimed that Israel would be redeemed by human endeavor rather than miracles. His *Derishat Ẓiyyon,* advocating formation of agricultural society in Ereẓ Israel, influenced Moses Hess, Ḥibbat Zion movement. Established societies to promote such settlement.

Kalisz, town in Poland; most ancient community in Poland. Jews fr. 12th c. Hundreds killed in 1659 pogrom by Czarniecki's troopers. In 19th–20th c., Jews developed lace, textile, knitting factories, workers' associations. 20,000 Jews (half of total pop.) in 1939. In WWII assisted by Polish anti-Semites. Nazi deported them to death camps, or killed them in nearby forests. Community not reestablished.

Kallah (Heb. "bride"), minor tractate appended to order *Nezikin* in Babylonian Talmud; in two versions, larger called *Kallah Rabbah.* Both deal with betrothal and marriage; larger also deals with good manners.

Kallah, Months of, term for months of Elul and Adar, when, during talmudic and geonic eras, large gatherings assembled to study Torah in Babylonian academies. Different tractate chosen for study each time. In Israel, modified form instituted at yeshivot.

Horace M. Kallen

Kallen, Horace Meyer (1882–1974), U.S. philosopher, educator. A founder and prof. at New School for Social Research, N.Y. Leading exponent of cultural pluralism. Active in Jewish community.

Kallir, Eleazar, one of most prolific and influential of liturgical poets; probably lived in Ereẓ Israel; century disputed, varying bet. 2nd and 10th c. Wrote for all festivals and special occasions. His work is found in all editions of prayer books (except Sephardi).

Kallo, Yiẓḥak Isaac (of Taub; 1751–1821), Hungarian rabbi; first ḥasidic leader to live permanently in Hungary. His grandsons became ḥasidic leaders.

Kálmán, Emmerich (Imre; 1882–1953), composer of popular operettas (*Gypsy Princess, Countess Maritza,* etc.); b. Hungary; in Vienna until 1936, in U.S. fr. 1940, returned to Europe 1949. Utilized Hungarian music, incl. gypsy elements.

Kalmanovitch, Zelig (1881–1944), Yiddish writer, philologist, translator; b. Latvia. Joined YIVO Inst. in Vilna, edited *YIVO Bleter.* Killed in Holocaust.

Kalmanowitz, Abraham (1891–1964), rabbi; yeshiva head; b. Belorussia. Pres. Mir yeshivah 1926; rabbi of Tiktin 1929. Emigrated to U.S. 1940. Arranged for transfer of Mir yeshivah to Kobe, Japan, later to Shanghai, U.S., and Ereẓ Israel. Active in Oẓar ha-Torah.

Part of tombstone of Meshullam ben Kalonymus, Mainz, 1020.

Kalonymus, eminent German family of rabbis, preachers, poets, authors, moralists, and theologians in 9th–13th c. Family emigrated fr. S. Italy in 9th c. and provided Rhineland Jewry with many leaders.

Kalonymus ben Kalonymus (Ben Meir ha-Nasi; 14th c.), author, translator; b. Provence, lived in France, Rome. Translated scientific and philosophical works fr. Arabic into Hebrew and Latin. Wrote ethical work *Even Boḥan* and Purim satire on Talmud.

°**Kaltenbrunner, Ernst** (1903–1946), Nazi leader. Member of Hitler's inner circle. Succeeded Heydrich 1943 as chief of Reich Security Main Office (RSHA) and was largely responsible for implementation of policy of annihilation of Jews. Condemned to death at Nuremberg.

Kamelhar, Jekuthiel Aryeh ben Gershon (1871–1937) Galician rabbi, author. Yeshivah head in Stanislav, rabbi in New York; fr. 1933 in Jerusalem. Published talmudic studies and biographies of rabbis.

Kamenets-Podolski, city in Ukrainian SSR. Jewish settlement long restricted. After 1750 expulsion, Jews settled in suburbs and nearby villages. Scene of disputation with Frankists 1757. Readmitted under Russian rule 1797. 12,774 Jews in 1929; community liquidated by Nazis.

Kamenetzky, Jacob (1891–), U.S. yeshivah head, rabbinical leader; b. Minsk, emigrated to Toronto in 1938, New York 1945. Head of Mesifta Torah Vodaath 1948. Halakhic expert. Served on presidium of Union of Orthodox Rabbis and supreme rabbinical council of Agudat Israel.

Kamenev (Rosenfeld), Lev Borisovich (1883–1936), Russian revolutionary. Leading Bolshevik theoretician; joined Stalin and Zinoviev in "troika" opposing Trotsky 1924, but later opposed Stalin. Arrested 1934 in purges; "confessed" to all charges and executed.

Kameṣ, Hebrew vowel sign indicating short or long *a;* written form is ַ

Kaminer, Isaac (1834–1901), Hebrew writer, physician; b. Ukraine. Drawn to Haskalah; joined socialist circles and wrote verse satires for Hebrew socialist papers. After pogroms of 1880s, joined Ḥibbat Zion movement.

Kamenitzer Maggid, see Maccoby, Ḥayyim Zundel.

Kaminetsky, Joseph (1911–), U.S. Orthodox educator. Director of Torah Umesorah fr. 1946; taught at Yeshiva Univ. fr. 1955. Developed Orthodox day schools.

Kaminka, Armand (Aaron; 1866–1950), poet, translator, rabbi; b. Berdichev, taught in Vienna, settled in Ereẓ Israel 1938. Opposed critical analysis of Bible, but accepted such approach to Talmud. Translated classical literature into Hebrew.

Kaminski (Kaminska), Polish theatrical family. **Abraham Isaac** (1867–1918), organized theatrical company in Warsaw in 1887. Founded Kaminski Theater in War-

Esther Rachel Kaminski and her daughter Ida.

saw before WWI. His wife, **Esther Rachel** (1870–1925), won fame in his company. Noted for portrayal of "mother" roles. Their daughter, **Ida** (1899–), started career as child in father's company. In USSR during WWII. After war her company gained status of "Jewish State Theater." Films incl. *The Shop on Main Street.* Left Poland 1968 during anti-Semitic campaign; settled in U.S. Her brother, **Joseph** (1903–1972), settled in Ereẓ Israel 1937. First violinist in Israel Philharmonic Orchestra; noted composer.

Kammerknechtschaft, see Servi Camerae Regis.

Kamniel, Abu al-Hasan Meir ibn (12th c.), physician in Seville. Invited by Almoravide ruler Ali b. Yūsuf ibn Tāshfin to serve at his court in Marrakesh. Friend of Judah Halevi.

Kamẓa and **Bar Kamẓa,** residents of Jerusalem in 1st c. whose hatred of one another was said to have caused destruction of Temple (Git. 55b).

Kanader Adler or **Canadian Jewish Eagle,** Canadian Yiddish weekly newspaper in Montreal; founded 1907. Daily until 1963. Circ. 18,000 (1970).

Kanah (Cana), town in Galilee. Scene of miracles reported in New Testament, incl. changing water into wine (John 2). Identification with Kefar Kanna uncertain.

Kanah, Book of, kabbalistic work giving mystical interpretations of precepts; influenced by Zohar. Probably written in Spain in 14th c.

Kandel, Isaac Leon (1881–1965), U.S. educator; specialist in comparative education. Prof. at Columbia Univ. Teachers College 1923–47. Wrote *The Making of the Nazis,* pioneering work on practice and dangers of Nazi education.

Kane, Irving (1908–), U.S. attorney, businessman, communal leader in Cleveland. Pres. of Council of Jewish Federations and Welfare Funds 1959–62.

Kanee, Sol (1909–), Canadian public figure, lawyer, grain company executive. A director of Bank of Canada fr. 1965. Headed Canadian Jewish Congress.

Kanin, Garson (1912–), U.S. playwright, director. Plays incl. *Born Yesterday.* Directed and co-authored severel witty films, incl. *Adam's Rib.*

Kann, Jacobus Henricus (1872–1945), banker; founder of Dutch Zionist Organization; grandson of Moses Kann. Aide of Herzl; favored "political" as opposed to "practical" Zionism. In opposition in Zionist movement for many years. D. in Theresienstadt.

Jacobus H. Kann

Kann, Moses (d. 1761), yeshivah head, community leader in Frankfort. Successfully appealed against confiscation of Talmud. Involved in continuous controversy over running of community.

Kanner, Leo (1894–), U.S. child psychiatrist; b. Austria, in U.S. fr. 1924. Prof. at Johns Hopkins Univ. Considered father of American child psychiatry; his *Child Psychiatry* is basic textbook.

Temple Emanu-El in Wichita, Kansas.

Kansas, U.S. state. First Jewish settlers c. 1854. First congregation B'nai Jeshurun in Leavenworth 1859. Many unsuccessful Jewish agricultural colonies. Jewish pop. 2,100 (1971), mainly in Topeka and Wichita.

Kansas City, city in Mo., U.S. Jewish settlement fr. late 1830s, Reform congregation 1870, Orthodox 1878. Jewish pop. 22,000 (1971), with 7 congregations.

Kantor, Jacob Robert (1888–), U.S. psychologist. Taught at Indiana Univ. Major fields behavior theory, language and logic, physiological psychology.

Judah L. Kantor

Kantor, Judah Leib (1849–1915), editor, author; b. Vilna. Founded first Hebrew daily newspaper *Ha-Yom* 1886. Believed that Haskalah held cure for all Jewry's ills, and rejected Zionism and Ḥibbat Zion. Served as official rabbi in Libau, Vilna, and Riga.

Kantorowich, Roy (1917–), S. African architect, town planner. Prepared master design for Ashkelon, Israel, and large-scale civic and industrial projects in S. Africa. Fr. 1961, Prof. at Univ. of Manchester, England.

Kantorowicz, Ernst Hartwig (1895–1963), German medieval historian. Prof. at Frankfort, Univ. of California at Berkeley 1940–49, and Inst. for Advanced Study at Princeton fr. 1951. Created new area of studies, political theology. Wrote major study of Frederick II.

Kantrowitz, Adrian (1918–), U.S. cardiovascular surgeon. Pioneer in bioelectronics and bioengineering. Developed improved heart-lung machine. Prof. at State Univ. of New York; director of surgical services, Maimonides Medical Center.

Kapitza, Peter Leonidovich (1894–), Russian physicist; son of Russian general and Jewish mother. Worked with Rutherford at Cambridge. First foreigner in 200 years to be elected Fellow of Royal Society 1929. Returned to Russia 1934. Assumed to be key personality in Russian nuclear and space research programs.

Kaplan, Abraham (1918–), philosopher. Taught at Univ. of California, East-West Center in Hawaii, Univ. of Michigan, Univ. of Haifa. Wrote on ethics, political theory, oriental philosophy, and ḥasidic thought.

"Dodie the Innkeeper," illustration by Anatoli Kaplan for Shalom Aleichem's "Bewitched Tailor," 1953–57.

Kaplan, Anatoli Lvovich (1902–), Russian draftsman, lithographer. Work inspired by Jewish tradition and Russian folklore. Illustrated Shalom Aleichem and produced series "Views of Leningrad" during WWII siege.

Kaplan, Eliezer (1891–1952), labor leader in Ereẓ Israel; b. Russia, settled in Ereẓ Israel 1920. Member of Jewish Agency Executive 1933, then treasurer. Member of Knesset and first Israel minister of finance. Greatly influential in Israel's early economic and financial policy.

Kaplan, Isaac (1878–), leader of Jewish farmers in Argentina; b. Belorussia, settled in Colonia Clara, Entre Ríos 1895. Promoted cooperative movement. A founder of Zionist organizations in Jewish colonies and head of Argentinian Zionist Federation.

Kaplan, Jacob (1895–), French rabbi. Active in resistance in WWII. Chief rabbi of Paris 1950, France 1955. Proclaimed French Jewry's solidarity with State of Israel during and after Six-Day War.

Jacob Kaplan

Kaplan, Joseph (1902–), U.S. geophysicist. Worked at Princeton and Univ. of California. Studied chemistry and physics of upper atmosphere. Active Zionist.

Kaplan, Louis Lionel (1902–), U.S. educator. Involved in Jewish education both in Baltimore and nationally.

Kaplan, Mordecai Menahem (1881–), U.S. rabbi, philosopher. A founder of N.Y. Kehillah; founder of Reconstructionist movement and Society for Advancement of Judaism; one of foremost spiritual leaders in American Judaism. Taught at Jewish Theological Seminary, founder and dean of its Teacher's Inst. Defined Judaism as evolving religious civilization. Wrote *Judaism as a Civilization*, etc. Created the idea of Jewish centers in U.S. communities. Settled in Jerusalem 1971.

Mordecai M. Kaplan

Kaplansky, Kalman (1912–), Canadian labor leader; b. Bialystok, in Canada fr. 1929. Active in trade union movement, director of Jewish Labor Committee fr. 1946.

Kaplansky, Shelomo (1884–1950), Zionist labor leader; b. Bialystok. Founder, theoretician of Po'alei Zion in Austria. Secretary of Jewish National Fund head office at The Hague 1913–19. Member of Zionist Executive in Jerusalem and director of its Settlement Dept. 1927–29. Director of Haifa Technion 1932–50.

Kapo, privileged prisoner in charge of group of inmates in Nazi concentration camps, appointed by S.S. Jews were appointed only in camps in which all inmates were Jewish. Although some helped their fellow prisoners, most were primitive people who emulated criminality and cruelty of S.S.

Kaposi, Moritz (1837–1902), dermatologist; b. Hungary. Prof at Vienna dermatological hospital fr. 1875. Convert to Christianity.

Kapparot (Heb. "expiations"), custom of post-talmudic origin in which sins of man or woman were transferred to cock or hen on eve of Day of Atonement. Some rabbis attacked practice.

Performing the "kapparot" ritual before the Day of Atonement.

Kapper, Siegfried or **Vítězslav** (1821–1879), Czech poet, physician. First Jew to publish in Czech language. Belonged to "Young Bohemia" circle. Criticized Austrian regime's treatment of Czechs, called for cultural assimilation of Czech Jewry.

Kapporet, cover of Ark of Covenant which was made entirely of gold and covered aperture on top. Fr. the Middle Ages, small curtain on top of synagogue's Ark curtain *(parokhet).*

Kara, Avigdor ben Isaac (d. 1439), Prague *dayyan,* kabbalist; poet of German origin. Noted for polemics with Christians. Acc. to one (doubtful) tradition, favorite of Wenceslaus IV, king of Bohemia.

Kara, Joseph (b. c. 1060–70), French Bible commentator; colleague-student of Rashi. Also wrote and commented on *piyyutim.*

Karaczewski, Ḥanina (1877–1926), music teacher, composer; b. Bessarabia, settled in Ereẓ Israel 1908. Many of his pupils became music educators and choral conductors. Of his many songs popular during Third Aliyah, best known is *Al Sefat Yam Kinneret.*

Karaites, Jewish sect which came into being in early 8th c. Basic tenets involved denial of talmudic-rabbinic tradition, and, initially at least, asserted right of every Jew to interpret Bible. Posed challenges to mainstream "Rabbanite" Judaism which had rejuvenating effect on Judaism.

Lithograph of Crimean Karaite woman and her children by Raffet.

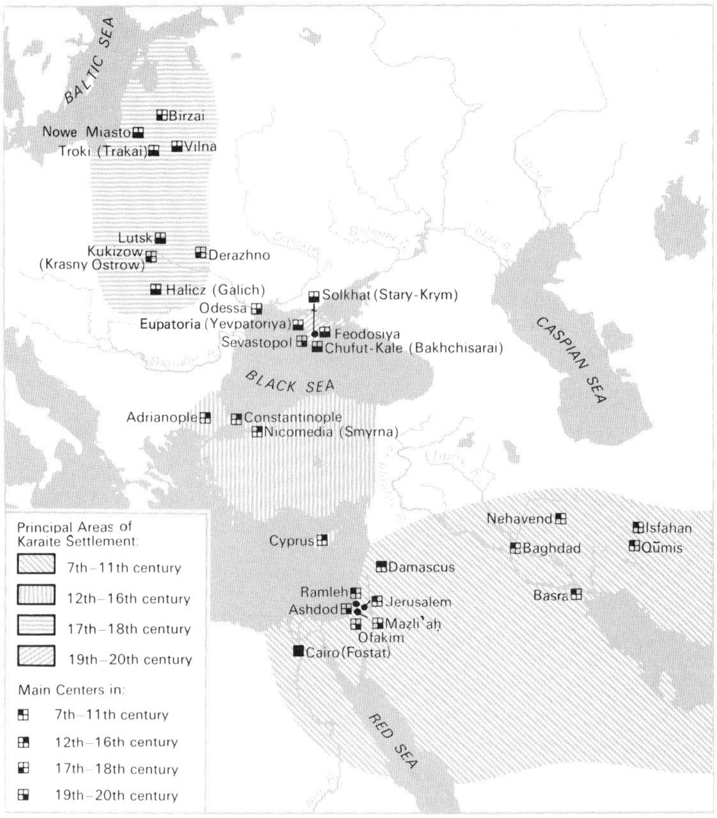

Principal areas of Karaite settlement and main centers, 7th—20th centuries.

After first thrust, movement became fossilized. Reputed founder Anan b. David; early centers Jerusalem, Egypt, Byzantium. In 10th c. furious polemic waged with Saadiah Gaon, representative of central Jewish authority. In 20th c. two small centers remained: in Middle East (Egypt and Ereẓ Israel), where they maintained close ties with Jewish communities; in Crimea, where fr. early 19th c. they requested and obtained official status of non-Jews and hence escaped Holocaust.

Kardiner, Abram (1891–), U.S. psychologist. Clinical prof. at Columbia Univ. Posited possibility of eliciting basic personality structure of all individuals raised in certain culture.

Kareh, Solomon (1804–1885), chief rabbi of Yemenite Jewry for 40 years; eminent scholar of Torah and Kabbalah. Succeeded in having threatening anti-Jewish decrees rescinded.

Karelitz, Avraham Yeshayahu ("Ḥazon Ish"; 1878–1953), Israel talmudic scholar; b. Lithuania, settled in Bene Berak 1933. Published 40 works. Recognized as worldwide authority without holding official position. Permitted use of milking machines on Sabbath and hydroponic cultivation in sabbatical year.

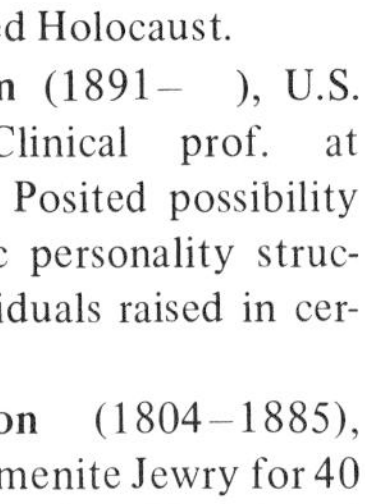

Avraham Y. Karelitz (Ḥazon Ish)

Karet (Heb.) punishment "at hands of Heaven" for certain transgressions; exact details concerning nature of punishment and offenses are disputed.

Kariv, Avraham Yiẓḥak (1900–), Hebrew literary critic, poet, translator; b. Slobodka, settled in Ereẓ Israel 1934. Wrote scathing criticism of works of many leading modern Hebrew authors, esp. Mendele Mokher Seforim. Demanded re-evaluation of prevalent negative attitude toward Jewish life in Diaspora.

Karlin, dynasty of Lithuanian ḥasidic *ẓaddikim* named after town. Founder **Aaron ben Jacob** (1736–1772), known as "Aaron the Great." His grandson and successor, **Aaron the Second** (d. 1872), author of *Beit Aharon* on prayer. Branches of dynasty in U.S. and Israel.

Karlsruhe, city in W. Germany. Jews fr. 1715. Fr. 1820s, Jews permitted to practice law and medicine. After emancipation 1862, Jews elected to city council and Baden parliament. 1,368 Jews in 1939; liquidated in Holocaust.

Kármán, Theodore Von (1881–1963), aerodynamicist; b. Hungary. Invented helicopter with two counter-rotating propellers. Settled in U.S. 1930 as head of Guggenheim Aeronautical Laboratory at California Inst. of Technology. During WWII, in charge of all jet propulsion research in U.S.

Karmi, Dov (1905–1962), Israel architect. A creator of modern Israel architectural style and prototypes, esp. for domestic and commercial building styles (Histadrut, El Al, and Chamber Theater Building, Tel Aviv; Sherman Building and Wise Auditorium, Hebrew Univ.).

The El Al Building in Tel Aviv, designed by Dov and Ram Karmi.

Karmi'el, development town in C. Galilee, Israel; established 1964. Pop. 3,850 (1971).
Karminski, Hannah (1897–1942), German social worker. Secretary-general of Juedische Frauenbund. Continued working in Nazi period until 1942, under incredibly difficult conditions. Died on way to concentration camp.
Karminski, Sir Seymour Edward (1902–), English judge. Judge of divorce division of High Court of Justice 1951, lord justice of appeal 1969. Chairman of London Jewish Board of Guardians.
Karni, Yehuda (1884–1949), Hebrew poet, essayist; b. Pinsk, settled in Erez Israel 1921. Noted for poems about Jerusalem, which is eternal symbol of Jewish people and its destiny.
Karp, Abraham J. (1921–), U.S. Conservative rabbi, scholar. Rabbi at Rochester, prof. of Jewish studies at Rochester Univ. fr. 1972. Wrote on U.S. Jewish history and edited *Jewish Experience in America.*
Karpeles, Gustav (1848–1909), literary historian. Edited *Juedische Presse, Allgemeine Zeitung des Judentums,* and *Jahrbuch fuer juedische Geschichte und Literatur.* Wrote *History of Jewish Literature.*
Karpf, Maurice Joseph (1891–1964), U.S. social worker. Active in many Jewish welfare organizations. Member of Jewish Agency Executive 1930–45.
Karpinowitch, Abraham (1918–), Yiddish short story writer; b. Vilna, settled in Israel 1949. Wrote about Vilna Jews and new immigrants to Israel.
Karu (Krupnik), Baruch (1899–1972), Hebrew writer, journalist, editor, translator; b. Podolia, settled in Tel Aviv 1932. Joined staff of daily *Haaretz;* fr. 1942 with *Ha-Boker.* Published talmudic dictionary, literary encyclopedia, Aramaic dictionary.
Kashdan, Isaac (1905–), U.S. chess master. Shared first place with Reshevsky in 1942 N.Y. tournament.
Kasher (or **kosher**), term used for things ritually faultless, esp. food (in contrast to *terefah*).
Kasher, Menahem (1895–), rabbi, halakhist; b. Poland, settled in Erez Israel 1925. Main work is multi-vol. *Torah Shelemah,* encyclopaedia of all talmudic and midrashic references to Bible, arranged verse by verse. Israel Prize 1962. His son **Shimon** (1914–1968), Hebrew poet, writer.

Menahem Kasher

Kashrut, see Dietary Laws.
Kaskel (Kaskele), 17th c. family of German Court Jews, court bankers to royal house of Saxony and Poland, and founders of Dresdner Bank, one of Germany's leading commercial banks.
Kasovsky, Chayim Yehoshua (1873–1960), Israel rabbinical scholar. Author of concordances of Mishnah, Talmud, Tosefta, and Targum Onkelos.
Kaspi, Joseph ben Abba Mari Ibn (1279–1340), rationalist philosopher, biblical commentator, grammarian; lived in France, Spain, Middle East. His philosophic writings were attacked and led to controversy.
Kassel, city in W. Germany. Jews' street in existence 1318, organized community with synagogue and cemetery by 1398. Jews expelled 1524, readmitted 1532, compelled to leave during Thirty Years' War 1618–48. Emancipation law 1808 granted civil rights to Jews; consistory headed by Israel Jacobson introduced synagogue, educational reforms. 2,301 Jews in 1933; community destroyed in WWII. 106 Jews in 1970.
Kassil, Lev Abramovich (1905–), Soviet Russian author. Major writer for juveniles. Wrote books describing own childhood in pre-revolutionary period and children who participated in WWII anti-Nazi underground.
Kassites, see Cush.
Kastein, Joseph (pen name of **Julius Katzenstein** 1890–1946), German writer; lived in Switzerland, settled in Tel Aviv 1933. Wrote *History and Destiny of the Jews* and biographies of Shabbetai Zevi, Uriel de Costa, Theodor Herzl, etc.
Kasztner, Rezsö Rudolf (Israel; 1906–1957), journalist, lawyer; b. Rumania. Worked on Hungarian Zionist daily *Uj Kelet* 1925–40; headed rescue operations in WWII in Budapest, conducted negotiations with Nazis in plan to exchange Jews for supplies for German war effort. After war settled in Israel, entering

Abraham I. Katsh bestowing honorary degree on Golda Meir.

Delegates to Kattowitz Conference, 1884.

government service. Center of controversial case when accused of collaboration with Nazis; killed by assassin. Name subsequently cleared.
Katchalski, Ephraim, see Katzir, Ephraim.
Katowice (Kattowitz), town in Poland. Jews fr. 18th c. First synagogue 1862. Anti-Semitism increased during 1930s. 8,587 Jews in 1939; most killed in WWII. After WWII, 1,500 Jews settled there but by 1968 almost all Jews had left.
Katsh (Katz), Abraham Isaac (1908–), U.S. educator, author; son of Reuben Katz; b. Poland, in U.S. fr. 1925. Prof. of Hebrew language and literature at NYU. Pres. Dropsie College (later Univ.) fr. 1967. Wrote on various aspects of Jewish studies.
Kattan, Naïm (1928–), Canadian editor, journalist; b. Baghdad, in Canada fr. 1954. Edited volumes in French on Jewish experience in Canada.
Kattowitz Conference, first gathering of Ḥibbat Zion movement 1884, aimed at unifying all Zionist bodies; attended by 32 delegates, chaired by Leo Pinsker. Established permanent committee with headquarters in Odessa.
Katz, Aleph (pseud. of **Morris Abraham Katz;** 1898–1969), Yiddish poet; b. Russia, in U.S. fr. 1913. Published early Yiddish lyrics in organs of Inzikhism. Later verse written under impact of Holocaust.

Katz, Benzion (1875–1958), Hebrew journalist, writer. Founded in St. Petersburg newspaper and quarterly *Ha-Zeman* 1903 (later published in Vilna). Published Hebrew weekly *Ha-Am* in Moscow. Settled in Erez Israel 1931. Founded *He-Avar* 1953, journal devoted to Russian Jewish history.

Katz (Benshalom), Benzion (1907–1968), Hebrew translator, literary critic, educator; brother of J. Katz-Suchy; b. Galicia. Taught Hebrew at Cracow Univ. Settled in Erez Israel fr. 1940. Director of Jewish Agency's Youth and He-Halutz Dept. 1941–63. Lectured on classical literature at Tel Aviv Univ. (rector fr. 1964). Translated Greek classics and Omar Khayyam into Hebrew.

Katz, Sir Bernard (1911–), British physiologist. Prof. of biophysics at Univ. College, London. Main research in field of nature of nerve impulse and nerve-muscle connections. Nobel Prize 1970.

Katz, David (1884–1953), German psychologist. Prof. in Rostock; dismissed by Nazis 1933. In Stockholm fr. 1937. Pioneer in experimental phenomenology, animal psychology, child psychology, and psychology of thinking.

Katz, Jacob (1904–), Israel historian; b. Hungary, settled in Erez Israel 1936. Prof. of Jewish social and educational history at Heb. Univ. (rector 1969–72). His work significant for understanding of Jewish sociology in medieval and modern times.

Katz, Label, A. (1918–), U.S. attorney, community leader; lived in New Orleans. National pres. B'nai B'rith 1959–65, particularly concerned with Jewish education and position of Soviet Jewry.

Katz, Mane, see Mane-Katz.

Katz, Mindru (1925–), concert pianist. Made debut with Bucharest Philharmonic Orchestra. Settled in Israel 1959.

Katz, Naphtali ben Isaac (1645–1719), rabbi, halakhist, kabbalist; b. Volhynia. When fire broke out in his home in Frankfort and spread to destroy Jewish quarter, accused of preventing extinguishing to test his amulets. Subject of legends.

Katz, Reuven (1880–1963), talmudist. *Landesrabbiner* in various E. European centers; rabbi in Bayonne, N.J. 1923–32, chief rabbi of Petah Tikvah fr. 1932. Author of responsa.

Katz, Shlomo (1909–), editor, short stories writer; b. Russia, in U.S. fr. 1922. Editor of *Midstream* 1955-73. Managing editor of *Jewish Frontier* 1939–42, 1951–55.

Katz, Sholom (1919–), *hazzan;* b. Rumania. Escaped fr. Bralow Ukraine concentration camp. Settled in U.S., officiated in Washington, D.C.

Katzburg, David Zevi (1856–1937), Hungarian talmudist. Editor of *Tel Talpiot,* first Hungarian rabbinical periodical.

Katzenellenbogen, David Tevel (1850–1930), Russian rabbi, talmudist. Rabbi of St. Petersburg. Had ban on *shehitah* in Finland lifted. Published notes on Jerusalem Talmud.

Katzenellenbogen, Meir ben Isaac (Maharam of Padua; 1473–1565), rabbi, halakhist; b. Prague, rabbi in Padua. Many rabbis addressed their halakhic questions to him. Published responsa and commentary on Maimonides' *Mishneh Torah.*

Katzenelson, Itzhak (1886–1944), poet, dramatist in Hebrew, Yiddish. Headed Hebrew secular school in Lodz. Present in Warsaw ghetto; d. Auschwitz. Many poems became favorite folk and children's songs. His "Poem of the Murdered Jewish People," written in concentration camp in France, is one of greatest literary expressions of tragedy of Holocaust.

Katzenelson, Judah Leib Benjamin (pseud. **Buki ben Yogli;** 1846–1917), Hebrew writer, scholar; practiced medicine in St. Petersburg. Active in Jewish Russian scholarly associations and advocated agricultural work and trades as solution for Russian Jewry. His novels express yearning for agricultural life. Wrote on medicine in Talmud; among editors of Russian Jewish encyclopaedia.

Katzenelson, Nissan (1862–1923), Russian Zionist leader. Close aide and personal representative of Herzl in negotiations with Russian authorities. Participated in activities of League for Equal Rights for Jews in Russia. Elected to First Duma 1906; joined Russian liberal Kadet party.

Katzir (Katchalski), Aharon (1914–1972), Israel chemist; brother of Ephraim Katzir (Katchalski); b. Poland, settled in Erez Israel 1925. Head of polymer research dept. at Weizmann Inst. of Science; prof. of physical chemistry at Heb. Univ. Israel Prize 1961. Pres. Israel Academy of Arts and Sciences 1962–68, International Union of Pure and Applied Biophysics fr. 1963. Shot dead in terrorist attack by Japanese at Lydda Airport.

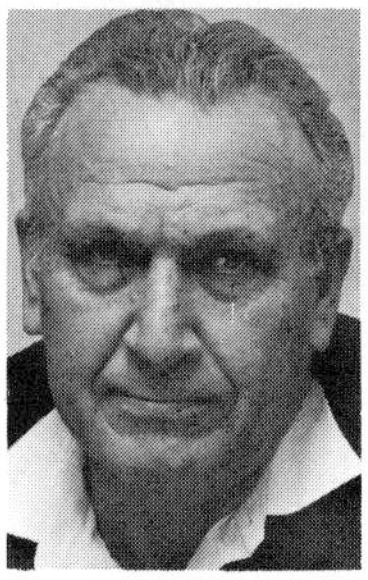
Ephraim Katzir

Katzir (Katchalski), Ephraim (1916–), Israel scientist; 4th president of Israel fr. 1973; b. Russia, settled in Erez Israel 1925. Head of biophysics dept. at Weizmann Inst. of Science. Chief scientist of Israel Defense Ministry 1966–68. Main field of research in proteins.

Katznelson, Berl (Beeri; 1887–1944), Zionist labor leader and ideologist; b. Russia, settled in Erez Israel 1909. Worked as laborer, secretary of Council of Judean Farm Workers. Served in Jewish Legion 1918–20. Instrumental in establishing Histadrut 1920 and Ahdut ha-Avodah (editor of its weekly *Kunteres*). Founded Histadrut's daily *Davar* 1925 (chief editor until death). A director of Jewish National Fund. Established Am Oved publishing house, serving as editor-in-chief.

Berl Katznelson

Katznelson (Shazar), Rahel (1888–), Erez Israel women labor leader; wife of Pres. Zalman Shazar; b. Belorussia, settled in Erez Israel 1912. Edited *Devar ha-Po'elet,* journal of women's labor movement.

Katznelson, Reuben (1890–), Erez Israel medical pioneer; brother of Rahel (Shazar) Katznelson; b. Belorussia. Served in Zion Mule Corps in WWI. Assistant director of Hadassah 1922–30, established medical organization for Jewish villages (moshavot) in Erez Israel 1931, director of Kuppat Holim Ammamit. His son, **Shemuel Moshe Tamir** (1923–), lawyer, member of Knesset, head of Free Center Party.

Katz-Suchy, Juliusz (1912–1971), Polish statesman; brother of Benzion Katz. Poland's delegate to UN

1946–51, 1953–4, and International Conference of Atomic Energy; ambassador to India 1957–62. Prof. of international law at Warsaw Univ. Dismissed during 1968 anti-Semitic campaign and went to Denmark.

Kauffmann, Isaac (1805–1884), founder of Kauffmann publishing house in Germany; continued by his descendants until Nazi era.

Kaufman, Boris (1906–), motion picture cameraman. Considered one of America's foremost cameramen. Won Academy Award for *On the Waterfront.*

Kaufman, George Simon (1889–1961), U.S. playwright, stage director. Wrote many witty hits (mostly in collaboration), incl. *You Can't Take It With You* (Pulitzer Prize 1936), *The Man Who Came to Dinner, Of Thee I Sing* (Pulitzer Prize 1932), *Dinner at Eight, Stage Door, George Washington Slept Here.*

Kaufmann, David (1852–1899), scholar. Taught at Budapest rabbinical seminary. Prolific writer on wide variety of Jewish scholarly subjects, esp. history, medieval philosophy, history of religion, history of art. Outstanding library is now owned by Hungarian Academy of Sciences.

Kaufmann, Felix (1895–1949), philosopher, methodologist; b. Vienna, in U.S. fr. 1938. Taught at New School for Social Research in N.Y. Discriminated bet. methodology of social and physical sciences.

Kaufmann, Fritz (1891–1958), philosopher; left Nazi Germany for America. Taught at Northwestern and Buffalo Univs. Leading exponent of Husserl's phenomenology.

Kaufmann, Fritz Mordecai (1888–1921), German essayist, writer on Yiddish folklore. Began German translation of Mendele Mokher Seforim's Yiddish works. Accepted Jewish nationalism but opposed Zionism's emphasis on Ereẓ Israel.

Kaufmann, Isidor (1853–1921), Hungarian painter of shtetl scenes. Meteoric career began after Emperor Franz Josef bought *The Rabbi's Visit* and presented it to Vienna's Museum of Fine Art.

Kaufmann, Judah see Even Shemuel, Judah.

Kaufmann, Oskar (1877–1956), German theatrical architect. Played important part in creating design of modern theater.

Kaufmann, Richard (1877–1958), Israel architect; b. Germany, settled in Ereẓ Israel 1920. Designer of many of early agricultural settlements incl. prototype of moshav ovedim. One of country's first modern architects.

Portrait of a young Jewish woman by Isidor Kaufmann.

Kaufmann, Walter (1921–), philosopher; b. Germany, in U.S. fr. 1939. Prof. at Princeton. Main interests philosophy of religion, social philosophy, history of ideas since 19th c., work of Nietzsche. Reared as Lutheran but returned to Judaism.

Kaufmann, Yeḥezkel (1889–1963), biblical scholar, thinker; b. Ukraine, settled in Ereẓ Israel 1928. Prof. at Heb. Univ. Works incl. sociological study of Jewish people fr. ancient times to modern period and history of Israelite religion fr. ancient times to end of Second Temple. Main contribution to study of biblical religion is thesis that Israel's monotheism was not gradual development away fr. paganism but new beginning in religious history.

Kaulla, Chaila (Caroline) Raphael (1739–1809), "Madame Kaulla"; one of few women court agents in German principalities. Served princes of Donaueschingen, Hechingen, Wuerttemberg, and Imperial Court in Vienna, as banker, jeweler, and army contractor.

Kaunas (Kovno), city in Lithuanian SSR. In late 19th c. center of Jewish cultural activity in Lithuania. Yeshivot of suburb Slobodka became celebrated. Community maintained numerous *ḥadarim,* schools, libraries. 38,000 Jews in 1933, with five Jewish daily newspapers, many Hebrew schools, and intense Zionist activity. After German occupation, large-scale pogroms and few survived. After WWII, Jews settled there fr. other places, 4,792 Jews in 1959.

°**Kautzsch, Emil Friedrich** (1841–1910), German Protestant Bible critic, Semitist. Editor of works on Bible and Semitic philology.

Kaverin, Benjamin Aleksandrovich (pseud of **B.A. Zilberg;** 1902–), Soviet author. Wrote *The Unknown Artist,* plea for maintenance of dignity of individual in collectivist society; *The Larger View,* on problems of adjustment in Soviet society; *Two Captains,* great favorite with Russian youngsters. Leading exponent of liberalization.

Kavvanah (Heb. "directed intention"), mental concentration and devotion in prayer and during performance of precepts. In kabbalistic literature, special thoughts that one should have at recitation of key words in prayer.

"Main gate of the Kaunas Ghetto," drawing by Esther Lurie, 1943.

Danny Kaye as Jacobowsky in "Me and the Colonel," 1958.

Kaye, Danny (1913–), U.S. actor, entertainer. Films incl. *Up in Arms, The Secret Life of Walter Mitty, The Inspector General, Hans Christian Andersen* and *Me and the Colonel.* Possessed individual style based on mime, song, irony, and sunny personality.

Nora Kaye in "Pillar of Fire," 1942.

Kaye, Nora (1920–), U.S. dramatic ballerina. Joined Metropolitan Opera Ballet at age 15. Rose to prima ballerina in Ballet Theater.

Kayser, Rudolf (1889–1964), German author, literary journalist. Editor-in-chief of literary periodical *Die Neue Rundschau* 1924. In U.S. fr. 1935. Held chair of German and European literatures at Brandeis Univ. 1951–57. Contributed to Jewish periodicals and wrote books on Jewish themes.

Kayserling, Meyer (Moritz; 1829–1905), German rabbi, historian. Rabbi at Endingen, Switzerland 1861–70, fighting for Jewish rights; later rabbi, preacher in Budapest. Published works on Jewish history, literature, religion. Reputation rests on pioneering publications on history of Spanish Jewry and Marranos.

Kazakevich, Emmanuil Genrikhovich (1913–1962), Soviet Russian author. Considered in 1930s one of most promising young poets in Soviet Yiddish literature. After WWII wrote exclusively in Russian. Twice Stalin prizewinner. *The House on the Square* describes atmosphere of morbid suspicion prevalent in Soviet army during early postwar years.

Kazaz, Elijah (1832–1912), Crimean Karaite scholar. Director of school for Karaite cantors; asserted that Karaites were not Semites but fr. Khazar tribe.

Kazdan, Ḥayyim Solomon (1883–), Yiddish educator, writer. In 1930s director of Zisho Yiddish schools in Warsaw. In U.S. fr. 1941. Prof. at Jewish Teachers Seminary and People's Univ.

Kazimierz (Kuzhmir), Polish ḥasidic dynasty celebrated for musical gifts. Founded by **Ezekiel ben Ẓevi-Hirsch Taub of Kazimierz** (d. 1856), whose great-grandson **Ezekiel of Yablonov** settled in Ereẓ Israel 1924 as head of group which founded Kefar Ḥasidim.

Kazin, Alfred (1915–), U.S. author, critic. Wrote *On Native Grounds,* study of modern American prose literature; *Walker in the City* and *Starting Out in the Thirties,* autobiographical description of generation which grew up in proletarian Jewish neighborhoods during Depression. Prof. at State Univ. of N.Y. fr. 1963.

Kaznelson, Siegmund (1893–1959), publisher, editor, b. Warsaw. Managed Juedischer Verlag fr. 1920, largest publishing house of German Jewry.

KEDUSHAH IN MORNING SERVICE

נְקַדֵּשׁ אֶת שִׁמְךָ בָּעוֹלָם כְּשֵׁם שֶׁמַּקְדִּישִׁים אוֹתוֹ בִּשְׁמֵי מָרוֹם כַּכָּתוּב עַל יַד נְבִיאֶךָ. וְקָרָא זֶה אֶל זֶה וְאָמַר.	*Reader* We will sanctify thy Name in the world even as they sanctify it in the highest heavens, as it is written by the hand of thy prophet. And they called one unto the other and said,
קָדוֹשׁ קָדוֹשׁ קָדוֹשׁ יְיָ צְבָאוֹת. מְלֹא כָל הָאָרֶץ כְּבוֹדוֹ:	*Congregation* Holy, Holy, Holy is the Lord of hosts: the whole earth is full of his glory.
לְעֻמָּתָם בָּרוּךְ יֹאמֵרוּ.	*Reader* Those over against them say, Blessed –
בָּרוּךְ כְּבוֹד יְיָ מִמְּקוֹמוֹ:	*Congregation* Blessed be the glory of the Lord from his place.
וּבְדִבְרֵי קָדְשְׁךָ כָּתוּב לֵאמֹר.	*Reader* And in thy Holy Words it is written, saying
יִמְלֹךְ יְיָ לְעוֹלָם אֱלֹהַיִךְ צִיּוֹן לְדֹר וָדֹר. הַלְלוּיָהּ:	*Congregation* The Lord shall reign for ever, thy God, O Zion, unto all generations. Praise ye the Lord.
לְדוֹר וָדוֹר נַגִּיד גָּדְלֶךָ. וּלְנֵצַח נְצָחִים קְדֻשָּׁתְךָ נַקְדִּישׁ. וְשִׁבְחֲךָ אֱלֹהֵינוּ מִפִּינוּ לֹא יָמוּשׁ לְעוֹלָם וָעֶד. כִּי אֵל מֶלֶךְ גָּדוֹל וְקָדוֹשׁ אָתָּה. בָּרוּךְ אַתָּה יְיָ. הָאֵל הַקָּדוֹשׁ:	*Reader* Unto all generations we will declare thy greatness, and to all eternity we will proclaim thy holiness, and thy praise, O our God, shall not depart from our mouth for ever, for thou art a great and holy God and King. Blessed art thou, O Lord, the holy God.

Kazyonny Ravvin (Rus. "official rabbi"), title of officials elected by communities of Russia 1857–1917 in accordance with government instructions; represented their communities before authorities. Institution linked with government attempts to influence and control Jewish communal activities; Jewish communities generally regarded them with hostility and endeavored to restrict their activities, but some were respected communal leaders.

Kedar, nomadic tribe or league of tribes in Arabian Desert during biblical period (e.g., Gen. 25:3; I Chron. 1:29). Many details about them known fr. other sources, esp. inscriptions of Assyrian kings.

Kedemites or **Easterners,** people living on E. border of Syria and Ereẓ Israel. Israelites acknowledged kinship with them and respected their reputation for wisdom.

Kedesh in Galilee (or **Kedesh Naphtali**), large city in Upper Galilee in Canaanite and Israelite periods, now nr. Lebanese frontier. City of refuge (Josh. 20:7) and levitical city (Josh. 21:32) and one of fortified cities of tribe of Naphtali (Josh. 19:37).

Kedushah (Heb. "holiness"), third blessing of *Amidah;* name popularly applied to additions and responses inserted in reader's repetition of *Amidah* in morning, additional, and afternoon services *(Kedushah de-Amidah).* Other such prayers are *Kedushah de-Yeshivah* (recited while seated in morning service) and *Kedushah de-Sidra* (recited daily toward end of morning service for those who missed previously recited *Kedushah*).

Keesing, Isaac (1886–1966), Dutch publisher of reference works; founder of *Keesing's Historical Archives.*

Kefar Baram, locality NW of Safed. Jewish settlement mentioned only fr. Middle Ages, but remains of synagogue fr. 3rd c. C.E. have been found. Kibbutz Baram founded 1949.

Kefar Darom, locality in S. coastal plain of Philistia. First mentioned in Talmud. Captured by Arabs; fortress destroyed by Crusaders. Identified with Dayr al-Balaḥ, S. of Gaza. Kibbutz Kefar Darom destroyed during War of Independence 1948–49, resettled 1970.

Kefar Eẓyon, kibbutz in Hebron hills; affiliated to Ha-Kibbutz ha-Dati; first settled 1926–27, abandoned 1929, refounded 1943 as part of Eẓyon Bloc. Fr. late 1947 under

heavy Arab attacks. Fell May 14, 1948 and most of its defenders massacred by mob after surrendering to Arab Legion. Kibbutz renewed 1967 by group incl. children of original settlers.

Kefar Giladi, Kibbutz in N. Israel; affiliated to Iḥud ha-Kevuẓot ve-ha-Kibbutzim; merged with Tel Ḥai 1926. Suffered casualties when British forces searched for illegal immigrants 1946. Pop. 635 (1971).

Kefar Ḥabad, village in C. Israel; established 1949 by Ḥabad Ḥasidim. Center for Ḥabad Ḥasidim in Israel with religious and educational institutions. Pop. 1,620 (1971).

Kefar Ḥasidim, Religious moshav, in Zebulun Valley, nr. Haifa; established 1924 by Ḥasidim fr. Poland. Nearby agricultural school Kefar Hanoar established 1937. Second religious village Kefar Ḥasidim Bet was set up 1950. Combined pop. 730 (1971).

Kefar Ḥattin, ancient village in Galilee. Identified with Arab village of Ḥiṭṭīn or Ḥaṭṭīn al-Qadīm, where Saladin defeated Crusaders 1187. Holy place of Druze, who locate Jethro's tomb there (Nabī Shu'ayb).

Kefar (Kafr) Kanna, village in Galilee, nr. Nazareth. Identified with Kanah (Cana) of Gospels (although this is uncertain). Jewish settlement 15th–16th c. Site of Christian pilgrimages. Pop. 5,400 (1971), mostly Christians, remainder Muslims.

Kefar Naḥum, see Capernaum.

Kefar Sava, town in C. Israel. Settlement began in 1896. Center of citriculture in Sharon. Site of large Bet Me'ir Hospital and Histadrut's seminary and study center Bet Berl. Pop. 25,200 (1971).

Kefar Shemaryahu, semi-rural settlement in Sharon; founded 1937. Middle-class garden suburb of Tel Aviv. Pop. 1,280 (1971).

Kefar Tavor (initial Arab name **Mesḥah**), moshavah at foot of Mt. Tabor, Israel; founded 1901 by Jewish Colonization Association (ICA). Pop. 300 (1971).

Kefar Vitkin, moshav in Ḥefer Plain, Israel. Largest moshav in country. Pop. 825 (1971).

Kefar Yasif, large village NE of Acre. Crusader name Cafersi. Resettled by Jews early 16th c. New Jewish settlement created in 18th c. but subsequently abandoned. In 18th c. burial place for Jews of Acre. Now Arab village. Pop. 3,990 (1971), mostly Christians.

Kefar Yonah, rural settlement with municipal council status in C. Israel, founded 1932. Pop. 2,710 (1971).

Kehimkar, Ḥayim Samuel (1830–1909), historian of Bene Israel community in Bombay; civil servant in Bombay.

Kelal Yisrael (Heb.), rabbinic term used for "Jewish community as a whole," in regard to its common responsibility, destiny, kinship, and relationship with God.

Kelen, Imre (1895–), cartoonist; b. Hungary. Made his name with caricatures of statesmen at Paris Peace Conference 1919. Collaborated with Aloysius Derso, emigrating with him to U.S. 1938.

Keleti (Klein), Agnes (1921–), Hungarian gymnast. Won five Olympic gold medals 1952, 1956. Settled in Israel 1957. Coach of Israel national women's gymnastic team.

Kelim (Heb. "vessels"), 1st tractate of Mishnah order *Tohorot;* with no *gemara*, deals with ritual uncleanness and purification of all vessels.

Kellermann, Benzion (1869–1923), German rabbi, author. Wrote on Jewish religious philosophy in spirit of Hermann Cohen.

Kellner, Leon (1859–1928), scholar of English literature; one of Herzl's early aides. Taught in Vienna. Published critical editions of English texts, dictionary of Shakespeare, and also selection of Herzl's writings.

Kelsen, Hans (1881–1973), jurist, legal theoretician. Prof. at Vienna Univ. 1919–29. Drafted constitution of Austrian Republic 1920. Prof. at Cologne 1929–33 and then Geneva. In U.S. fr. 1940. Prof. at Univ. of California 1944. Founded Vienna school of jurisprudence, which taught "pure theory of law."

Kemelman, Harry (1908–), U.S. author. Wrote entertaining series of detective novels whose hero is rabbi-sleuth (*Friday the Rabbi Slept Late,* etc.).

Kempf, Franz Moshe (1928–), Australian artist, printmaker. Studied with Oskar Kokoshka. His paintings and prints incl. biblical and ḥasidic themes.

Kempner, Robert Max Wasilii (1899–), lawyer, historian; on Hitler's rise to power, left Germany for Italy, then U.S. Chief prosecutor of Nazi political leaders at Nuremberg Trials 1946–49. Did research on Nazi Holocaust.

Kenaani, David (1912–), Hebrew essayist, editor; b. Warsaw, settled in Ereẓ Israel 1934. Wrote on social and literary subjects; principal editor of Hebrew encyclopedia of social sciences.

Keneset, see Knesset.

Entrance façade of synagogue at Kefar Baram, 3rd cent.

Celebration of Yod-Tet Kislev festival at Kefar Ḥabad synagogue, with President Shazar as guest of honor, 1965.

Franciscan parish church in Kefar Kanna, built 1879.

Keneset Ha-Gedolah, see Synagogue, The Great.

Keneset Yisrael (Heb. "the community of Israel"), rabbinic term largely identical with Kelal Yisrael (q.v.). Adopted as title of official Jewish community in Ereẓ Israel 1927.

Kenites, large group of nomadic clans engaged chiefly in metal working; enumerated among early peoples of Canaan (Gen. 15:19). Moses' father-in-law Hobab (Jethro) the Midianite also known as Kenite. Some scholars assert that Moses was introduced to YHWH and his worship by Kenite families who occupied region in south centering around Arad.

Jewish communities in Kentucky.

Camp in Kenya for members of I.Ẓ.L. and Leḥi deported from Palestine by British, 1947.

KEREN HAYESOD UNITED ISRAEL APPEAL, 1920–1970

	1920–1948	1948–1970
Immigration and Absorption	487,000 immigrants, including 28,700 children brought to Palestine by Youth Aliyah, settled and absorbed in the country.	1,400,000 immigrants, including 95,800 children brought to Israel by Youth Aliyah. (Many of the children came with parents and Youth Aliyah accepted them as its wards.)
Agricultural Settlement, Development Towns and Housing	257 agricultural settlements were established with a population of 90,000 working some 700,000 dunams (175,000 acres) of land.	525 new agricultural settlements and 27 development towns built; 175,000 new housing units provided permanent homes for nearly 1,400,000 new immigrants.
Total Funds Raised	$ 143,000,000 — 70% from the United States through United Jewish Appeal. — 30% from other countries through Keren Hayesod.	$ 1,990,000,000 — 65% from the United States through United Jewish Appeal. — 35% from 71 other countries through Keren Hayesod.

Total expenditures of the Jewish Agency 1948–1970	Immigration and Absorption	$ 573,900,000
	Health Services	$ 77,100,000
	Education	$ 74,600,000
	Youth Aliyah	$ 156,200,000
	Immigrant Housing	$ 432,500,000
	Agricultural Settlement	$ 945,800,000
	Educational Activities	$ 294,200,000
	Overseas Operations	$ 160,500,000
	Various Activities	$ 301,000,000
	Total	$ 3,015,800,000
Grand Total of Funds Raised	1920–1948	$ 143,000,000
	1948–1970	$ 1,990,000,000
	Total	$ 2,133,000,000[1]

[1] The balance of the expenditures not covered by the income of Keren Hayesod United Israel Appeal and the United Jewish Appeal came from additional sources, such as German reparations and heirless property, collections on account of the repayment of loans from Jewish Agency-Keren Hayesod funds; the realization of property; special Youth Aliyah campaigns; participation by the Government of Israel in agricultural settlement and long and medium term loans.

Kentridge, Morris (1881–1964), S. African lawyer, politician; b. Lithuania. Joined S. African Labor Party, then Smuts' United Party 1932. MP 1920–58.

Kentucky, U.S. state. Organized Jewish communal life started in 1830s. Jewish pop. 10,745 (1971), mostly in Louisville.

Kenya, E. African country. First Jewish settlers in early 20th c. Area proposed to Herzl for Jewish settlement by British 1903 ("Uganda Scheme") is in present-day Kenya. First synagogue in Nairobi 1913. Members of Ereẓ Israel underground deported to camps there by British 1947. Jewish pop. 200 (1971).

°**Kenyon, Dame Kathleen Mary** (1906–), British archaeologist. Director of British School of Archaeology in Jerusalem 1951–62. Uncovered Neolithic city of Jericho and Jebusite wall in Jerusalem. Wrote *Archaeology in the Holy Land, Jerusalem,* etc.

Kerch, Crimean port. Jews fr. time of Roman Empire. City of Khazar kingdom. Center for Karaites and Krimchaks. Pogrom 1905. Most of 4,500 Jews (incl. 500 Krimchaks) murdered by Germans. 5,000 Jews in 1970.

Kerem Ḥemed, Hebrew annual of Galician Haskalah; published in Vienna, Prague, Berlin 1833–56. Served as central forum for E. and W. Jewish scholars and authors concentrating on humanistic and scientific studies, revival of Hebrew language, opposition to Ḥasidism, etc.

Keren Hayesod (Palestine Foundation Fund), financial arm of World Zionist Organization; founded in London 1920. Appealed to Zionists and non-Zionists alike for funds to finance on non-profit basis immigration and colonization in Ereẓ Israel and State of Israel. Raised $2,133,000,000 (1920–70) through United Israel Appeal, etc.

Keren Kayemet Le-Israel, see Jewish National Fund.

Keri'ah (Heb). "rending" of garment as sign of grief at death of near relative.

Keri and Ketiv (Heb.), variants in masoretic text of Hebrew Bible bet. spelling *(ketiv)* and reading *(keri)*.

Keritot, tractate in Mishnah order *Kodashim,* with *gemara* in Babylonian Talmud. Deals with offerings for sins connected with biblical punishment of *karet* (q.v.).

Copperplate engraving illustrating the tractate "Keritot" from title page in Hebrew-Latin Mishnah, Amsterdam, 1700–04.

Kern, Jerome David (1885–1945), U.S. composer. Wrote scores for over 60 shows and films (*Sunny, Show Boat, Roberta,* etc.), and over 1,000 songs, incl. *Ol' Man River.*

Kerovah (Heb.), name for various types of poems incorporated into *Amidah* prayer.

Kerr, Alfred (pen name of **Alfred Kempner;** 1867–1948), German literary critic, author. Drama critic for Berlin newspapers. Leading impressionistic critic in modern Ger-

man literature. Fled to Prague, Paris, London after 1933. Noted champion of Hauptmann and Ibsen.

Kersch, Gerald (1909–1968), British author, journalist. War correspondent and screenwriter. Wrote *They Die With Their Boots Clean.*

Keshet, Yeshurun (1893–), Hebrew poet, literary critic, translator; b. Poland, settled in Ereẓ Israel 1911. Poetry influenced by European decadent poetry. His monograph on Berdyczewski significant contribution to Hebrew literary criticism.

Joseph Kessel on a visit to Jerusalem, 1970, with Teddy Kollek (right) and André Chouraqui (left).

Kessel, Joseph (1898–), French novelist; b. Clara, Jewish agricultural settlement in Argentina. Officer in French air force in WWI. Flew special missions to occupied France fr. England in WWII. Wrote about aviation experience. Novels incl. *Belle du Jour* and *The Lion.* French Academy 1964. Wrote several works on Israel.

Kessler, David (1860–1920), leading actor-manager of New York Yiddish theater. Established David Kessler Theater 1913.

Kessler, Leopold (1864–1944), engineer; one of Herzl's early aides; b. Silesia. Chairman of Jewish National Fund and Zionist Federation of England 1922. Director of *Jewish Chronicle* fr. 1907, chairman 1932. His son, **David Francis** (1906–), managing director of *Jewish Chronicle* fr. 1936, chairman 1958.

Kesten, Hermann (1900–), German novelist; fled fr. Nazi Germany, reached New York, lived in Rome after WWII. Wrote historical novels, etc.

Kestenberg, Leo (1882–1962), pianist, music educator; b. Hungary, lived in Berlin, fled to Prague 1933, founding International Society for Music Education. Arrived in Ereẓ Israel 1938, becoming general manager of Palestine Orchestra (later Israel Philharmonic).

Keti'a Bar Shalom (1st c.), Roman councillor. Sacrificed life to save Jews of Roman Empire fr. persecution. Identified with Flavius Clemens, Domitian's nephew, executed for Judaizing tendencies.

Ketiv, see Keri.

Ketubbah (Heb.), marriage document recording obligations, financial and personal, which husband undertakes toward his wife in respect of their marriage. Written in Aramaic, its reading is major part of wedding ceremony. Modified by Conservative Jews; abolished by Reform. Became popular Jewish art form.

Ketubbot 2nd tractate in Mishnah order *Nashim,* with *gemara* in both Talmuds. Deals with rights and duties arising fr. marriage contract.

Keturah, wife or concubine of Abraham. Bore him six sons.

Kever Avot (Heb. "ancestral graves"), custom of visiting and praying at graveside of parents and close relatives on anniversary of death and on eve of Rosh Ha-Shanah and on Ninth of Av.

Kevuẓah, see Kibbutz.

Keyserling, Leon H. (1908–), U.S. economist. Chairman of President's Council of Economic Advisers in Truman administration. Main interests: employment and production.

"Ketubbah" from Gibraltar, 1872.

Khaliastre, post-WWI Warsaw group of Yiddish expressionist, futurist poets, led by Perez Markish, Uri Zvi Greenberg, Melech Ravitch. Advocated exaltation, renovation, revolution of spirit; set out to fragment language of classical masters and rebuild Yiddish.

Khān Yūnis, town SW of Gaza. During Mamluk rule important market on caravan route bet. Ereẓ Israel and Egypt. Part of Gaza Strip fr. 1948; occupied by Israel 1967. Pop. 52,997 (1967), nearly half in refugee camps.

Ruins of the outer wall of the inn ("Khān") at Khān Yūnis built 1389 for travelers en route to Egypt.

Kharik, Izi (Itzhak) (1898–1937), Soviet Yiddish poet. Served in Red Army 1919–20; important member of Communist institutions in Belorussia. His poetry glorified revolution, reconstruction of country, and rejuvenation of Jewish life. Arrested and executed in Stalinist purges.

Kharkov, city in Ukrainian SSR. Outside Pale of Settlement. Jews present only toward end of 19th c. Became center of Jewish and Zionist activity. Scene of Zionist conference 1903 which organized opposition to Uganda Scheme. 150,000 Jews in 1939. Germans occupied town at end of 1941, and Jews who had not escaped were massacred. Jewish pop. 80,000 (1970).

Khaybar, mountainous oasis N. of Medina. Was largest Jewish settlement in Arabia; subdued by Muhammad 628, expelled by caliph Omar 642.

Khaym Tiktiner, see Siemiatycki, Chaim.

Khazars, national group of Turkic stock, independent and sovereign in E. Europe (esp. along lower reaches of Volga) 7th–10th c. C.E. Leading Khazars professed Judaism, presumably fr. c. 740. Story of their conversion described in correspondence (of doubtful authenticity) bet. the Khazar king Joseph and Ḥisdai ibn Shaprut. Judah Halevi's philosophical work *Kuzari* based on legendary disputation conducted before king of Khazars by rabbi, Christian, Moslem, and Aristotelian scholar, as result of which king adopted Judaism. Khazar state existed until 11th c. at most. Defeated by principality of Kiev. Remnants disappeared in 13th c. Mongol invasions.

Kherson, city and province in Ukrainian SSR. Principal center for government-sponsored Jewish agricultural settlement in Russia. Active center of Zionism. Jews suffered during 1905, 1919 pogroms. Communal institutions liquidated fr. beginning of Soviet regime. 15,000 Jews in city before WWII. Germans murdered Jews who remained. 9,500 Jews in 1970.

Khmelnitoki, see Proskurov.

Khodasevich, Vladislav Felitsianovich (1886–1939), foremost Russian emigré poet; son of Jewish mother; left USSR 1922, settled in Paris. Translated Polish, Armenian, and modern Hebrew poets, notably Tchernichowsky.

Khotin (Hotin), town in Ukrainian SSR. Jews first mentioned 1741. Refuge for Jacob Frank and his followers when forced to leave Poland. After incorporation into Rumania 1918, active cultural and communal life. 15,000 Jews in 1940. Under German-Rumanian forces, most died by wholesale killing, starvation, epidemics.

Khoushi, Abba (1898–1969), Israel labor leader; b. Galicia, settled in Ereẓ Israel 1920. Secretary of Haifa labor council 1938–51. Mapai member of First Knesset 1949–51. Mayor of Haifa fr. 1951, making great improvements and establishing Haifa Univ.

Khurasan, province in NE Persia. Jews lived there fr. very early period. Geonic literature speaks of special Khurasan customs. In 12th c. authority of Exilarch of Baghdad extended to its communities. Many Jews of Meshed fled there after 1839.

Kibbutz (or **Kevuẓah**), mainly agricultural community in Israel, based on collective property, production, and consumption. Kevuẓah (e.g. Deganyah 1909) meant to serve as enlarged family. After WWI kibbutz came into being to serve as self-sufficient village combining agriculture and industry (e.g. En Harod 1921). Distinction between two terms has almost disappeared. Groups of kibbutzim differ acc. to political and philosophical concepts of members (see Ha-Kibbutz ha-Me'uḥad; Iḥud ha-Kevuẓot ve-ha-Kibbutzim; Ha-Kibbutz ha-Arẓi-Ha-Shomer ha-Ẓa'ir; Ha-Kibbutz ha-Dati), but Zionism and social equality are main ideas. Played leading role in pre-state period and are a major force in State of Israel. 227 kibbutzim in 1973. (For other forms of collective settlement in Israel see Moshav, Moshavah.)

Communal dining hall, Kibbutz Ayyelet ha-Shaḥar, 1969.

The Khazar Kingdom, c. 7th–10th cent.

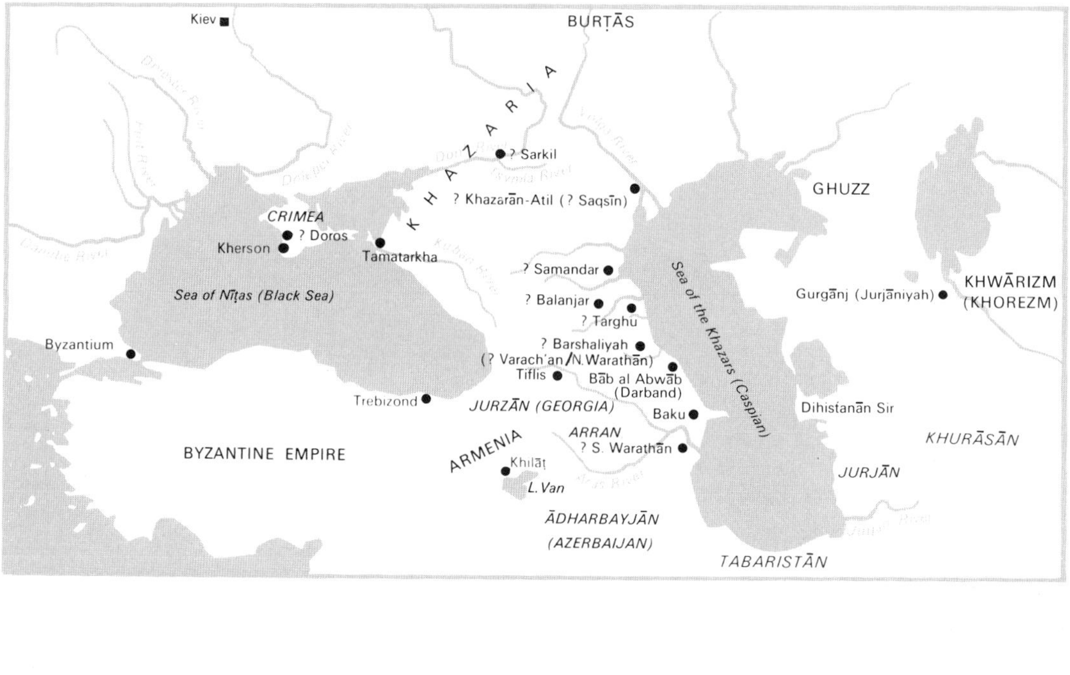

KIBBUTZ

NOTES
Geographical Region: The sign "67+" indicates a settlement beyond the pre-1967 borders.
Affiliation: Only the present affiliation is given.
No. of Inhabitants: The sign ∞ indicates that the population figures are not available.

IK – Iḥud ha-Kevuẓot ve-ha-Kibbutzim
KA – Ha-Kibbutz ha-Arẓi (Ha-Shomer ha-Ẓa'ir)
KD – Ha-Kibbutz ha-Dati
KM – Ha-Kibbutz ha-Me'uḥad
OẒ – Ha-Oved ha-Ẓiyyoni
PAI – Po'alei Agudat Israel
PM – Ha-Po'el ha-Mizrachi

Name	Geographical Region	Year of Founding	Affiliation	No. of inhabitants 31 Dec. 1971
Adamit	Western Upper Galilee	1958	KA	∞
Afek	Acre Plain	1939	KM	400
Afikim	Kinneret Valley	1932	IK	1,350
Allonim	Jezreel Valley	1938	KM	480
Alumim	Northwestern Negev (Besor Region)	1966	KD	73
Alummot (Bitanyah)	Kinneret Valley	1941	IK	79
Amir	Ḥuleh Valley	1939	KA	411
Ammi'ad	Eastern Upper Galilee (Hazor Region)	1946	IK	252
Ashdot Ya'akov	Kinneret Valley	1933	IK	∞
Ashdot Ya'akov	Kinneret Valley	1933	KM	∞
Ayyelet ha-Shaḥar	Ḥuleh Valley	1918	IK	750
Baḥan	Central Sharon	1953	IK	274
Baram	Eastern Upper Galilee	1949	KA	328
Barkai	Iron Hills (Northwestern Samaria)	1949	KA	325
Be'eri	Northwestern Negev (Eshkol Region)	1946	KM	487
Be'erot Yiẓhak	Coastal Plain (Petaḥ Tikvah Region)	1948	PM	283
Beror Ḥayil	Southern Coastal Plain (Ashkelon Region)	1948	IK	570
Bet Alfa	Harod Valley	1922	KA	690
Bet Guvrin	Southern Judean Foothills	1949	KM	115
Bet ha-Emek	Acre Plain	1949	IK	315
Bet ha-Shittah	Harod Valley	1935	KM	910
Bet Kamah	Northern Negev (Gerar Region)	1949	KA	258
Bet Keshet	Eastern Lower Galilee	1944	KM	278
Bet Nir	Southern Coastal Plain (Lachish Region)	1955	KA	187
Bet Oren	Mount Carmel	1939	KM	197
Bet Zera	Kinneret Valley	1927	KA	640
Dafnah	Ḥuleh Valley	1939	KM	570
Daliyyah	Manasseh Hills	1939	KA	610
Dan	Ḥuleh Valley	1939	KA	430
Daverat	Jezreel Valley	1946	IK	293
Deganyah (Deganiyyah) Alef	Kinneret Valley	1909	IK	442
Deganyah (Deganiyyah) Bet	Kinneret Valley	1920	IK	545
Devirah	Northern Negev (Beersheba Region)	1951	KA	190
Dorot	Southern Coastal Plain	1941	IK	411
Eilon	Western Upper Galilee	1938	KA	∞
Eilot	Eilat Hills	1962	KM	∞
Einat	Coastal Plain (Petaḥ Tikvah Region)	1925	IK	480
Ein Gev	Kinneret Valley	1937	IK	308
Ein ha-Ḥoresh	Central Sharon (Ḥefer Plain)	1931	KA	610
Ein ha-Shofet	Zebulun Valley	1938	KA	620
Ein ha-Naẓiv	Beth-Shean Valley	1946	KD	378
Ein ha-Sheloshah	Northwestern Negev (Besor Region)	1950	OẒ	270
Ein Mifraẓ	Manasseh Hills	1937	KA	600
Ein Karmel	Carmel Coast	1947	KM	371
Ein Shemer	Northern Sharon (Ḥaderah Region)	1927	KA	560
Ein Zivan	Golan; 67+	1968	KM	∞
Ein Ẓurim	Southern Coastal Plain (Shafir Region)	1949	KD	350
Elrom	Golan; 67+	1971	KM	∞
Enat	Coastal Plain (Petaḥ Tikvah Region)	1925	IK	480
En-Dor	Eastern Lower Galilee	1948	KA	555
En-Gedi	Dead Sea Region	1953	IK	∞
En-Harod	Harod Valley	1921	IK	680
En-Harod	Harod Valley	1921	KM	785
Erez	Southern Coastal Plain (Ashkelon Region)	1949	IK	203
Even Yiẓhak (Galed)	Manasseh Hills	1945	IK	267
Evron	Acre Plain	1945	KA	440
Eyal	Southern Sharon (Kefar Sava Region)	1949	KM	112
Ga'ash	Southern Sharon (Herzliyyah Region)	1951	KA	412
Ga'aton	Western Upper Galilee	1948	KA	292
Gadot	Eastern Upper Galilee (Hazor Region)	1949	KM	260
Galon	Southern Judean Foothills	1946	KA	370
Gan Shelomo (Kevuẓat Schiller)	Coastal Plain (Reḥovot Region)	1927	IK	277
Gan Shemu'el	Northern Sharon (Ḥaderah Region)	1913	KA	750
Gat	Southern Coastal Plain (Lachish Region)	1942	KA	462
Gazit	Southeastern Lower Galilee	1948	KA	446
Gelil Yam	Southern Sharon (Herzliyyah Region)	1943	KM	269
Gerofit	Southern Arabah Valley	1963	IK	∞
Gesher	Kinneret Valley	1939	KM	∞
Gesher ha-Ziv	Acre Plain	1949	IK	388
Geva	Harod Valley	1921	IK	515
Gevaram	Southern Coastal Plain (Ashkelon Region)	1942	KM	220
Gevat	Jezreel Valley	1926	KM	640
Gevim	Southern Coastal Plain (Ashkelon Region)	1947	IK	255
Gevulot	Northwestern Negev (Besor Region)	1943	KA	128
Ginnegar	Jezreel Valley	1922	IK	418
Ginnosar	Kinneret Valley	1937	KM	400
Givat Brenner	Coastal Plain (Reḥovot Region)	1928	KM	1,525
Givat ha-Sheloshah	Coastal Plain (Petaḥ Tikvah Region)	1925	KM	440
Givat Ḥayyim	Central Sharon (Ḥefer Plain)	1932	IK	690
Givat Ḥayyim	Central Sharon (Ḥefer Plain)	1932	KM	720
Givat Oz	Jezreel Valley	1949	KA	385
Gonen	Ḥuleh Valley	1951	IK	252
Ḥafeẓ Ḥayyim	Southern Coastal Plain (Reḥovot Region)	1944	PAI	330
Ha-Gosherim	Ḥuleh Valley	1949	KM	410
Ha-Ḥoterim	Carmel Coast	1948	KM	354
Ḥamadyah	Beth-Shean Valley	1942	IK	∞
Ha-Ma'pil	Northern Sharon	1945	KA	446
Ḥanitah	Western Upper Galilee	1938	IK	∞
Ha-Ogen	Central Sharon (Ḥefer Plain)	1947	KA	486
Ha-On	Kinneret Valley	1949	IK	156
Harel	Judean Foothills	1948	KA	153
Ha-Solelim	Western Lower Galilee	1949	OZ	176
Ḥaẓerim	Northern Negev (Beersheba Region)	1946	IK	333
Ḥeẓor Ashdod	Southern Coastal Plain (Malakhi Region)	1946	KA	520
Ha-Zore'a	Jezreel Valley	1936	KA	690
Ḥefẓi-Bah	Harod Valley	1922	KM	473
Ḥoreshim	Southern Sharon (Kefar Sava Region)	1955	KA	170
Ḥukkok	Eastern Lower Galilee	1945	KM	200
Ḥulatah	Ḥuleh Valley	1937	KM	350
Ḥuldah	Judean Foothills	1930	IK	274
Kabri	Acre Plain	1949	KM	540
Karmiyyah	Southern Coastal Plain (Ashkelon Region)	1950	KA	230
Kefar Azzah	Southern Coastal Plain (Ashkelon Region)	1951	IK	186
Kefar Blum	Ḥuleh Valley	1943	IK	530
Kefar Darom (Naḥal Kefar Darom)	Gaza Strip; 67+	1970	KD	∞
Kefar Eẓyon	Hebron Hills; 67+	1967	KD	∞
Kefar Giladi	Ḥuleh Valley	1916	IK	635
Kefar Glickson	Northern Sharon (Ḥaderah Region)	1939	OZ	260
Kefar ha-Ḥoresh	Southern Lower Galilee	1933	IK	234
Kefar ha-Makkabi	Zebulun Valley (Haifa Bay Area)	1936	IK	313
Kefar ha-Nasi	Eastern Upper Galilee (Hazor Region)	1948	IK	417
Kefar Masaryk	Zebulun Valley (Haifa Bay Area)	1938	KA	520
Kefar Menaḥem	Southern Coastal Plain (Malakhi Region)	1937	KA	545
Kefar Rosh ha-Nikrah	Acre Plain	1949	IK	∞
Kefar Ruppin	Beth-Shean Valley	1938	IK	∞
Kefar Szold	Ḥuleh Valley	1942	KM	472
Kerem Shalom	Northwestern Negev (Besor Region)	1956	KA	∞

Name	Geographical Region	Year of Founding	Affiliation	No. of inhabitants 31 Dec. 1971
Kevuẓat Yavneh	Coastal Plain (Reḥovot Region)	1941	KD	665
Kinneret	Kinneret Valley	1908	IK	660
Kiryat Anavim	Jerusalem Hills	1920	IK	327
Kissufim	Northwestern Negev (Besor Region)	1951	KM	261
Lahav (Ẓiklag)	Northern Negev (Beersheba Region)	1952	KA	212
Lahavot ha-Bashan	Ḥuleh Valley	1945	KA	457
Lahavot Ḥavivah	Northern Sharon (Ḥaderah Region)	1949	KA	230
Lavi	Eastern Lower Galilee	1949	KD	500
Loḥameiha-Getta'ot	Acre Plain	1949	KM	341
Ma'agan	Kinneret Valley	1949	IK	266
Ma'agan Mikha'el	Carmel Coast	1949	KM	760
Ma'aleh Gilboa	Mt. Gilboa	1962	KD	°°
Ma'aleh ha-Ḥamishah	Jerusalem Hills	1938	IK	273
Ma'anit	Northern Sharon (Ḥaderah Region)	1942	KA	410
Ma'barot	Central Sharon (Ḥefer Plain)	1933	KA	550
Magen	Northwestern Negev (Besor Region)	1949	KA	216
Maggal	Northern Sharon (Ḥaderah Region)	1953	IK	165
Maḥanayim	Eastern Upper Galilee (Ḥazor Region)	(1939)	KM	303
Malkiyyah	Eastern Upper Galilee	1949	KM	°°
Manarah	Eastern Upper Galilee	1943	KM	°°
Ma'oz Ḥayyim	Beth-Shean Valley	1937	KM	°°
Mashabbei Sadeh	Negev Hills	1949	KM	300
Massadah	Kinneret Region	1937	IK	290
Ma'yan Barukh	Ḥuleh Valley	1947	IK	°°
Ma'yan Ẓevi	Mt. Carmel	1938	IK	530
Maẓẓuvah	Western Upper Galilee	1940	IK	353
Mefallesim	Southern Coastal Plain (Ashkelon Region)	1949	IK	400
Megiddo	Jezreel Valley	1949	KA	288
Merḥavyah	Harod Valley	1911	KA	540
Merom Golan	Golan; 67+	1967	KM	°°
Mesillot	Beth-Shean Valley	1938	KA	500
Mevo Ḥammah	Golan; 67+	1968	IK	°°
Mevo Ḥoron	Judean Foothills; 67+	1970	PAI	°°
Mezer	Northern Sharon (Ḥaderah Region)	1953	KA	270
Misgav Am	Eastern Upper Galilee	1945	KM	°°
Mishmar David	Judean Foothills	1948	IK	80
Mishmar ha-Emek	Jezreel Valley	1926	KA	715
Mishmar	Northern Negev (Gerar Region)	1946	KM	500
Mishmar ha-Sharon	Central Sharon (Ḥefer Plain)	1933	IK	380
Mishmarot	Northern Sharon (Ḥaderah Region)	1933	IK	220
Mizra	Jezreel Valley	1923	KA	620
Miẓpeh Shalem	Dead Sea Region; 67+	1970	KM	°°
Na'an	Coastal Plain (Reḥovot Region)	1930	KM	875
Naḥal Geshur	Golan; 67+	1968	KA	°°
Naḥal Gilgal	Lower Jordan Valley; 67+	1970	KM	°°
Naḥal Golan	Golan; 67+	1967	IK	°°
Naḥal Kallia	Dead Sea Region; 67+	1968	–	°°
Neḥal Keturah	Southern Arabah Valley	1970	IK	°°
Naḥal Massu'ah	Lower Jordan Valley; 67+	1969	PM	°°
Naḥal Naaran	Lower Jordan Valley; 67+	1970	KM	°°
Naḥal Oz	Northwestern Negev	1951	IK	279
Naḥal Sinai	Northeastern Sinai; 67+	1968	IK	°°
Naḥal Yam	Northwestern Sinai; 67+	1967	KM	°°
Naḥal Ẓofar	Central Arabah Valley	1968	KA	°°
Naḥsholim	Carmel Coast	1948	KM	245
Naḥshon	Judean Foothills	1950	KA	260
Naḥshonim	Northern Judean Foothills	1949	KA	248
Negbah	Southern Coastal Plain (Malakhi Region)	1939	KA	412
Ne'ot Mordekhai	Ḥuleh Valley	1946	IK	630
Netiv ha-Lamed He	Southern Judean Foothills	1949	KM	280
Neveh Eitan	Beth-Shean Valley	1938	IK	245
Neveh Ur	Northern Beth-Shean Valley	1949	KM	°°
Neveh Yam	Carmel Coast	1939	IK	137
Neẓer Sereni	Coastal Plain (Rishon le-Zion Region)	1948	IK	515
Nir Am	Southern Coastal Plain (Ashkelon Region)	1943	IK	267
Nir David	Beth-Shean Valley	1936	KA	560
Nir Eliyahu	Southern Sharon (Kefar Sava Region)	1950	IK	220
Nirim	Northwestern Negev (Besor Region)	1949	KA	280
Nir Oz	Northwestern Negev (Besor Region)	1955	KA	200
Nir Yiẓḥak (formerly Nirim)	Northwestern Negev (Besor Region)	(1949)	KA	257
Niẓẓanim	Southern Coastal Plain (Ashkelon Region)	1943	OZ	250
Oranim (Seminary)	Southern Lower Galilee (Tivon Hills)	1951	–	350
Or ha-Ner	Southern Coastal Plain (Ashkelon Region)	1957	IK	284
Palmaḥim	Coastal Plain (Rishon le-Zion Region)	1949	KM	287
Parod	Eastern Upper Galilee	1949	KM	214
Ramat David	Jezreel Valley	1926	IK	268
Ramat ha-Kovesh	Southern Sharon (Kefar Sava Region)	1932	KM	520
Ramat ha-Shofet	Manasseh Hills	1941	KA	540
Ramat Raḥel	Jerusalem Hills	1926	IK	76
Ramat Yoḥanan	Zebulun Valley (Haifa Bay Area)	1932	IK	520
Ramot Menasheh	Manasseh Hills	1948	KA	483
Regavim	Manasseh Hills	1948	KM	290
Re'im	Northwestern Negev (Besor Region)	1949	KM	200
Reshafim	Beth-Shean Valley	1948	KA	455
Revadim	Southern Coastal Plain (Malakhi Region)	1948	KA	268
Revivim	Negev (Southern Beersheba Basin)	1943	KM	440
Rosh Ẓurim	Hebron Hills; 67+	1969	KD	°°
Ruḥamah	Southern Coastal Plain (Ashkelon Region)	(1944)	KA	515
Sa'ad	Northwestern Negev (Gerar Region)	1947	KD	540
Sa'ar	Acre Plain	1948	KA	226
Sarid	Jezreel Valley	1926	KA	600
Sasa	Eastern Upper Galilee	1949	KA	°°
Sedeh Boker	Central Negev Hills	1952	IK	°°
Sedeh Eliyahu	Beth-Shean Valley	1939	KD	405
Sedeh Nahum	Beth-Shean Valley	1937	KM	277
Sedeh Neḥemyah	Ḥuleh Valley	1940	IK	313
Sedeh Yo'av	Southern Coastal Plain (Malakhi Region)	1956	KA	73
Sedot Yam	Northern Sharon (Ḥaderah Region)	1940	KM	500
Senir	Ḥuleh Valley; 67+ (Ramat Banias, Kefar Moshe Sharett)	1967	KA	°°
Shaalbim	Northern Judean Foothills	1951	PAI	300
Sha'ar ha ha Amakim	Southern Lower Galilee (Tivon Hills)	1935	KA	570
Sha'ar ha-Golan	Kinneret Valley	1937	KA	600
Shamir	Ḥuleh Valley	1944	KA	433
Shefayim	Southern Sharon (Herzliyyah Region)	1935	KM	525
Sheluhot	Beth-Shean Valley	1948	KD	340
Shomrat	Acre Plain	1948	KA	316
Shoval	Northern Negev (Gerar Region)	1946	KA	440
Tel Kaẓir	Kinneret Region	1949	IK	°°
Tel Yiẓḥak (includes Neveh Hadassah)	Southern Sharon (Netanyah Region)	1938	OZ	545
Tel Yosef	Harod Valley	1921	IK	520
Tirat Ẓevi	Beth-Shean Valley	1937	KD	°°
Urim	Northwestern Negev (Besor Region)	1946	IK	398
Usha	Zebulun Valley (Haifa Bay Area)	1937	IK	320
Yad Hannah (Semol)	Central Sharon (Ḥefer Plain)	1950	KM	°°
Yad Mordekhai	Southern Coastal Plain (Ashkelon Region)	1943	KA	474
Yagur	Zebulun Valley (Haifa Bay Area)	1922	KM	1,140
Yakum	Southern Sharon (Herzliyyah Region)	1947	KA	340
Yas'ur	Zebulun Valley (Haifa Bay Area)	1949	KA	340
Yeḥi'am	Western Upper Galilee	1946	KA	440
Yifat	Jezreel Valley	(1926)	IK	750
Yiftaḥ	Eastern Upper Galilee	1948	IK	°°
Yiron	Eastern Upper Galilee	1949	KM	°°
Yizre'el	Mt. Gilboa	1948	IK	290
Yodefat	Western Lower Galilee	1960	–	59
Yotvatah	Southern Arabah Valley	1951	IK	°°
Ẓe'elim	Northwestern Negev (Besor Region)	1947	IK	193
Zikim	Southern Coastal Plain (Ashkelon Region)	1949	KA	227
Ẓorah	Judean Foothills	1948	IK	449
Ẓovah	Jerusalem Hills	1948	KM	294

KETUBBAH *Ketubbah* (marriage-contract), Leghorn, Italy, 1679. Parchment.

KIDDUSH Cup for *kiddush* (sanctification of Sabbaths and festivals), Germany, 18th cent. Silver gilt.

LONDON The Bevis Marks Synagogue of the London Sephardi community, built 1700. Painting by J. H. Belisario.

Stone "kiddush" goblet decorated with Western Wall and other holy places, Erez̧ Israel, c. 1900.

KIDDUSH FOR SABBATH EVE

יוֹם הַשִּׁשִּׁי: וַיְכֻלּוּ הַשָּׁמַיִם וְהָאָרֶץ וְכָל־צְבָאָם:	And it was evening and it was morning, — the sixth day.
וַיְכַל אֱלֹהִים בַּיּוֹם הַשְּׁבִיעִי מְלַאכְתּוֹ אֲשֶׁר עָשָׂה וַיִּשְׁבֹּת בַּיּוֹם הַשְּׁבִיעִי מִכָּל־מְלַאכְתּוֹ אֲשֶׁר עָשָׂה: וַיְבָרֶךְ אֱלֹהִים אֶת־יוֹם הַשְּׁבִיעִי וַיְקַדֵּשׁ אֹתוֹ כִּי בוֹ שָׁבַת מִכָּל־מְלַאכְתּוֹ אֲשֶׁר־בָּרָא אֱלֹהִים לַעֲשׂוֹת:	And the heaven and the earth were finished and all their host. And on the seventh day God had finished his work which he had made; and he rested on the seventh day from all his work which he had made. And God blessed the seventh day, and he hallowed it, because he rested thereon from all his work which God had created and made.
בָּרוּךְ אַתָּה יְיָ אֱלֹהֵינוּ מֶלֶךְ הָעוֹלָם, בּוֹרֵא פְּרִי הַגָּפֶן:	Blessed art Thou, O Lord our God, King of the universe, who createst the fruit of the vine.
בָּרוּךְ אַתָּה יְיָ אֱלֹהֵינוּ מֶלֶךְ הָעוֹלָם, אֲשֶׁר קִדְּשָׁנוּ בְּמִצְוֹתָיו וְרָצָה בָנוּ. וְשַׁבַּת קָדְשׁוֹ בְּאַהֲבָה וּבְרָצוֹן הִנְחִילָנוּ זִכָּרוֹן לְמַעֲשֵׂה בְרֵאשִׁית, כִּי הוּא יוֹם תְּחִלָּה לְמִקְרָאֵי קֹדֶשׁ זֵכֶר לִיצִיאַת מִצְרָיִם. כִּי־בָנוּ בָחַרְתָּ וְאוֹתָנוּ קִדַּשְׁתָּ מִכָּל־הָעַמִּים וְשַׁבַּת קָדְשְׁךָ בְּאַהֲבָה וּבְרָצוֹן הִנְחַלְתָּנוּ. בָּרוּךְ אַתָּה יְיָ, מְקַדֵּשׁ הַשַּׁבָּת:	Blessed art Thou, O Lord our God, King of the universe, who hast hallowed us by thy commandments and hast taken pleasure in us, and in love and favor hast given us thy holy Sabbath as an inheritance, a memorial of the creation — that day being also the first of the holy convocations, in remembrance of the departure from Egypt. For thou hast chosen us and hallowed us above all nations, and in love and favor hast given us thy holy Sabbath as an inheritance. Blessed art thou, O Lord, who hallowest the Sabbath.

Kidd, Michael (1917–), U.S. choreographer. Formed Ballet Theater 1942. Arranged dances for Broadway hits and Hollywood movies (e.g., *Finian's Rainbow, Can Can, Seven Brides for Seven Brothers*).

Kiddush (Heb. "sanctification"), prayer recited over cup of wine in home and synagogue to consecrate Sabbath or festival. Recited on the eve of Sabbath or festival before start of meal and on following morning before first meal. When no wine available, recited over two loaves of bread.

Kiddush ha-Shem (Heb. "sanctification of [Divine] Name"), central concept in Judaism; originally acceptance of martyrdom in preference to forced apostasy (esp. in period of Crusades in Germany), extended to include active avoidance of actions likely to bring disgrace on Judaism. Its opposite, esp. in latter sense, is *Ḥillul ha-Shem* ("profanation of [Divine] Name").

Kiddushin, last tractate in Mishnah order *Nashim,* with *gemara* in both Talmuds. Deals with matrimonial matters and acquisition of property.

Kiddushin, see Betrothal.

Kiddush Levanah, see Moon, Blessing of the.

Kidron, valley to N. and E. of Jerusalem, separating city fr. Mount of Olives. Served fr. early times as necropolis.

Kielce, town in Poland. Prohibition on Jewish settlement until 1833. 18,000 Jews in 1931. Ghetto established 1941. Fr. 1942 Jews deported to extermination camps. After WWII Jewish community renewed, but pogrom in 1946 in which 42 Jews murdered caused most Jewish survivors of Holocaust who had remained in Poland to leave.

Kiera, title given to women (generally Jewish) who handled relations of wives of Turkish sultan's royal harem in external matters. Most famous was Esther (16th c.), wife of Jewish merchant Elijah Handali.

Kiesler, Frederick John (1896–1965), U.S. architect, scenic designer. Gave rise to term "environmental sculpture." Joint designer of "Shrine of the Book" in Jerusalem to house Dead Sea Scrolls.

Kiev, city in Ukranian SSR. Jewish presence mentioned fr. foundation of city in 8th c. Jews protected under Tatar rule 1240–1320, expelled 1495–1503, presence restricted 1619. Community suffered in Chmielnicki massacre 1648. Jews expelled with annexation to Russia 1667–1793. Residence restricted and controlled by police until 1917. Serious pogroms 1881, 1905, 1911–13. Scene of notorious Beilis case. 175,000 Jews in 1939. In first years of Soviet rule major center of Yiddish culture. In Holocaust Babi Yar was execution ground for many Kiev Jews. After WWII many Jews returned. Jewish pop. 220,000 (1971).

Gorge of the Kidron Valley near the Dead Sea.

Kikoine, Michel (1891–1968), French painter; b. Russia, moved to Paris 1912. Joined Académie des Beaux Arts. Member of School of Paris. Primarily colorist.

Kilayim, see Mixed Species.

Kilayim, 4th tractate in Mishnah order *Zera'im,* with *gemara* in Jerusalem Talmud. Deals with forbidden mixing of different species in fields, orchards, and vineyards, grafting, crossbreeding of cattle, and mixing together of wool and linen.

Kimberley, city in S. Africa. Many Jews went there on discovery of diamonds 1870; community established 1871, synagogue built 1876. Jewish pop. 400 (1971).

Kimche, Jon (1909–), British editor, writer. Specialized in Middle East affairs. Edited labor weekly *Tribune* 1942–46, Zionist *Jewish Observer and Middle East Review* 1952–67.

Kimḥi, David (Radak; 1160?–1235?), Provençal grammarian, exegete; son of Joseph Kimḥi. His philological treatise *Mikhlol* contains grammar and lexicon. His commentaries to most books of Bible notable for clarity and readability, and were widely reprinted, having strong influence on Christian Hebraists in the Latin translation. Strong supporter of Maimonides.

Kimḥi (Meller), Dov (1889–1961), Hebrew author, translator, editor; b. Galicia, in Erez̧ Israel fr. 1908. His stories cover wide range of settings. Among first to describe pre-WWI life in Erez̧ Israel. Published anthologies of literature.

Kimḥi, Joseph (c. 1105–c. 1170), Spanish grammarian, exegete, translator; migrated to Narbonne. His

polemical treatise *Sefer ha-Berit* was one of first anti-Christian polemics written in Europe.

Kimḥi, Moses (Remak; d. c.1190), Narbonne grammarian, exegete; son of Joseph Kimḥi. Introduced grammatical innovations that are still current, such as order of conjugations. Translation of his grammar, *Mahalakh,* was popular with 16th c. Christian Hebraists.

Kimḥit, name of high priestly family in late Second Temple period. Acc. to Talmud, seven brothers served as high priests.

Kinah (Heb.), poem expressing mourning, pain, and sorrow; dirge. Collection of such poems recited on Ninth of Av.

Kings, Book of, biblical book in last section of Former Prophets. Divided into two roughly equal parts: I Kings and II Kings. Traces history of reigns of David and Solomon and that of divided kingdoms until their respective downfalls.

BOOK OF KINGS – CONTENTS

I Kings 1:1–11:43	The Monarchy under David and Solomon.
1:1–2:46	The end of David's reign and Solomon's accession.
3:1–10:29	The reign of Solomon.
11:1–43	The troubles of Solomon's reign and its end.
I Kings 12:1– II Kings 17:41	The Divided Kingdom.
12:1–24	The disruption of the Kingdom
12:25–32	Significant events of the reign of Jeroboam I of Israel.
12:33–14:18	A prophetic tradition of the reign of Jeroboam.
14:19–16:34	Synchronistic history of Israel and Judah.
17:1– II Kings 10:31	The reign of Ahab and the fall of the House of Omri.
10:32–17:41	Synchronistic history of Judah and Israel.
II Kings 18:1–25:21	Judah alone.
18:1–20:21	The reign of Hezekiah.
21:1–26	The reigns of Manasseh and Amon.
22:1–23:30	The reign and reformation of Josiah.
23:31–35	The reign and removal of Jehoahaz.
23:36–25:21	The end of the Kingdom of Judah.
II Kings 25:22–30	Appendixes
25:22–26	The Mizpah incident
25:27–30	The captive King Jehoiachin.

Kingsley (Kirschner), Sidney (1906–), U.S. playwright. His play *Men in White* won Pulitzer Prize 1934. Also wrote *Dead End, Detective Story,* and dramatized Koestler's novel *Darkness at Noon.*

Kinnarot, Valley of, level plain surrounding Lake Kinneret on all sides.

Kinneret, moshavah in Israel, SW of Lake Kinneret; founded 1909. In nearby "Kinneret Courtyard" several nuclei of kibbutz settlements had their temporary camp before establishing their own villages in region. Pop. 185 (1971).

Seawall of Tiberias on western shore of Lake Kinneret.

Kinneret, second oldest kibbutz in Israel, SE of Lake Kinneret. Arthur Ruppin established Jewish training farm there 1908. Concept of large kevuẓah developed 1912. Home of poet Rachel. Pop. 660 (1971).

Kinneret, Lake (Sea of Galilee), fresh water lake in C. Jordan Rift Valley, NE Israel, 696 ft. (213 m.) below sea level. Jordan R. enters fr. N. and flows out fr. S. Average depth 144 ft. (44 m.), area 64 sq. mi. (165 sq. km.). Water is now pumped fr. the lake to irrigate Negev. Lake important for fishing. Highly significant to Christians because much of Jesus' activities occurred in its neighborhood. Fr. 1948 entirely under Israel sovereignty. Its beauty has inspired many poems and songs.

Kinnim (Heb. "nests"), last tractate of Mishnah order *Kodashim,* with no *gemara.* Deals with pigeons brought as sacrifices.

Kipnis, Alexander (1891–), bass-baritone. Member of Berlin State Opera until Nazis came to power; later in U.S. Excelled in lieder as well as opera and oratorio. His son **Igor** (1930–), well-known harpsichord player.

Kipnis, Itzik (1896–), Soviet Yiddish novelist. Wrote *Babi Yar,* commemorating 1941 German massacre of Kiev's Jews. Arrested 1948 as Jewish nationalist and imprisoned in labor camp until Stalin's death. In his 60s allowed to return to Kiev and his works again published.

Kipnis, Levin (1894–), Hebrew author; b. Volhynia, settled in Ereẓ Israel 1913. Taught in Tel Aviv. One of first children's authors in Ereẓ Israel.

Kipnis, Menahem (1878–1942), singer, folklore collector, writer; b. Ukraine. Toured Poland, Germany, and France, appearing in concerts with his wife, Zimra Seligsfeld, in lecture-performances of Jewish folk songs, which he later published.

Kirchheim, Raphael (1804–1889), German rabbinic scholar. At first opponent of Reform, later proponent under influence of A. Geiger. Edited many medieval works.

Kir-Hareseth (Kir of Moab), ancient capital of Moab. Now known as Karak, district town in Jordan.

Kiriath-Arba, see Hebron.

Kiriath-Jearim, Hivite city belonging to Gibeonite confederation (Josh. 9:17). Situated W. of Jerusalem. Ark, when rescued fr. Philistines, placed there temporarily (I Sam. 6:21).

Kiriath-Sepher, see Debir.

Kirimi, Abraham (14th c.), Crimean rabbi, Bible commentator. His commentary is in spirit of rationalism. Influenced by Maimonides and Abraham ibn Ezra.

Kirjath Sepher, Hebrew bibliographical quarterly; founded 1924 as publication of Jewish National and Univ. Library in Jerusalem.

Kirkisānī, Jacob al- (10th c.), Karaite scholar. Wrote in Arabic. Rationalist; knowledgeable in contemporary theology (incl. Moslem and Christian), philosophy, sciences, Talmud, and Midrash. His major work contains systematic code of Karaite law, Bible commentary, *halakhah,* and important source material on Jewish sects.

Kir of Moab, see Kir-Hareseth.

Kirovograd (Yelizavetgrad, Zinovyevsk), city in Ukrainian SSR. Jews fr. late 18th c.; played important economic role, controlled grain commerce. Pogroms 1905. During Civil War 1919, soldiers of Ataman Grigoryev massacred 3,000 Jews. Under Soviet regime, Jewish institu-

tions closed down. 18,358 Jews in 1926. Occupied by Germans 1941; 6,000 Jews remaining in town shot. Jewish pop. 10,000 (1970).

Kirsanov, Semyon Isaakovich (1906–), Russian poet. Disciple of Mayakovsky, exponent of futurism in Russian literature. Best-known poem "Seven Days of the Week."

Kirschbaum, Eliezer Sinai (1798–1870), physician, author, leader of Haskalah in Galicia. Adopted positive attitude toward idea of Jewish state, identified himself with program of Mordecai Manuel Noah but advocated Ethiopia instead of U.S. as transitional territory to Ereẓ Israel.

Kirschblum, Mordecai (1910–), U.S. Orthodox rabbi, Zionist Mizrachi leader. Head of Jewish Agency Torah Education and Culture Depts. Moved to Jerusalem 1968. Associate head of Agency's Aliyah and Absorption Dept.

Kirschbraun, Elijah (1882–1931), leader of Agudat Israel in Poland. Took part at founding convention of Agudat Israel in Kattowitz, 1912.

Kirshon, Vladimir Mikhailovich (1902–1938), Soviet playwright. Secretary of Assoc. of Proletarian Writers in Moscow 1925. Executed during Stalinist purges. His last play, *Bolshoy den,* predicted outbreak of war bet. USSR and Nazi Germany.

Kirstein, Lincoln (1907–), U.S. impressario, writer. Founded Ballet Caravan 1936 to present American works. With George Balanchine, founded New York City Ballet. Founded and edited *Dance Index.*

Kirszenbaum, Jesekiel David (1900–1954), painter; b. Poland. Worked as illustrator and cartoonist under pseud. Duvdevani. Settled in Paris 1933. His paintings evoke Jewish festivities of his childhood and express element of E. European mysticism.

"Kapparot" by J.D. Kirszenbaum, oil on canvas.

View of Kiryat Shemonah, 1967.

Kiryat Anavim, kibbutz W. of Jerusalem; founded 1920 by Third Aliyah agricultural workers fr. E. Europe as first kibbutz in hills. In War of Independence served as base for two operations – first steps in opening "Jerusalem Corridor." Pop. 327 (1971).

Kiryat Ata, town NE of Haifa; founded 1925, abandoned after 1929 Arab riots, re-established 1934 with large textile plant. Pop. 26,700 (1971).

Kiryat Bialik, urban community in Haifa Bay area; founded 1934. Pop. 15,700 (1971).

Kiryat Ekron, semi-urban community in Coastal Plain of Israel, SE of Reḥovot; founded 1948. Pop. 4,220 (1971).

Kiryat Gat, town in S. Coastal Plain of Israel; founded 1955. Designed to serve as urban center of Lachish Development Region. Pop. 18,300 (1971).

Kiryat Malakhi, development town in S. Israel; founded 1950 as *ma'abarah.* Pop. 8,650 (1971).

Kiryat Motzkin, urban community in Haifa Bay area; founded 1934. Pop. 16,300 (1971).

Kiryat Ono, urban settlement E. of Tel Aviv; founded as moshav 1939. Pop. 15,400 (1971).

Kiryat Shemonah, town in N. Israel; founded 1950. After Six-Day War repeatedly shelled fr. beyond nearby Lebanese frontier. Pop. 15,200 (1971).

Kiryat Tivon, town NE of Haifa; founded 1957 when Tivon (founded 1949) and Kiryat Amal (founded 1939) merged. Pop. 9,850 (1971).

Kiryat Yam, urban community nr. Haifa Bay; founded 1946. Pop. 18,300 (1971).

Kirzhnitz, Abraham (1888– ?), Soviet bibliographer. Wrote pioneering works on Jewish press in E. Europe, edited collection *Der Idisher Arbeter.* Disappeared during purges of 1930s.

Kisch, Abraham (1725–1803), Prague physician, scholar. Founded Jewish hospital in Breslau, taught Latin to Moses Mendelssohn, championed admission of Jewish students to universities.

Kisch, Alexander (1848–1917), Austrian rabbi, scholar; served in Prague and other communities. Franz Joseph I awarded him gold medal for 25 years as military chaplain; only rabbi in Austria to be government prof. of religion and inspector of religious education.

Kisch, Bruno Zecharias (1890–1966), medical authority, Jewish scholar; son of Alexander Kisch; b. Prague. A founder of Juedisches Lehrhaus in Cologne; taught experimental medicine, physiology, and biochemistry at Cologne Univ. Left Germany 1936, subsequently taught at Yale, Yeshiva univs. Founder and pres. of American College of Cardiology. Made contributions to study of enzymes.

Kisch, Daniel Montagu (1840–1898), English traveler; went to Australia, Mauritius, settled in S. Africa. Joined expedition to Matabeleland, chief adviser to King Lobengula. Auditor-general of Transvaal.

Kisch, Egon Erwin (1885–1948), German author. Led Communist "Red Guard" in Vienna 1918; expelled fr. Austria. After Reichstag Fire arrested and deported fr. Germany; fought in Spanish Republican Army, emigrated to New York 1939, settled in Mexico. Returned to Prague 1946, becoming honorary pres. of Prague Jewish community.

Kisch, Enoch Heinrich (1841–1918), physician, balneologist; active in development of Bohemian spas. His memoirs important source for history of Jewish Prague after 1848 Revolution.

Kisch, Frederick Hermann (1888–1943), military engineer, Zionist

Frederick H. Kisch

Dedication page of "Sbornik" by Maxim Gorki, in memory of victims of Kishinev pogrom, illustrated by E.M. Lilien.

Ephraim Kishon

"The Pipe Smoker," oil painting by Moise Kisling, 1923.

leader; son of Hermann Michael Kisch. Fought in WWI. Member of British delegation at Paris Peace Conference 1919–21. Member of Zionist Executive in Jerusalem and head of Political Dept. 1923–31. Returned to British army in WWII. Chief engineer with Eighth Army with rank of brigadier. Killed in minefield in Tunisia.

Kisch, Guido (1889–), historian of law and legal status of Jews; son of Alexander Kisch; b. Prague, taught at German univs. Emigrated to U.S. on rise of Nazis. Taught at Jewish Inst. of Religion, N.Y. Fr. 1962 at Basle Univ. Wrote on legal position of Jews in medieval Europe. Founded and edited periodical *Historia Judaica* 1938–61.

Kisch, Hermann Michael (1850–1942), British government official. In Indian civil service fr. 1873. Deputy secretary to government of India, postmaster-general of Bengal, director-general of Indian post office. Returned to England 1904, active in Jewish affairs. His son, **Cecil** (1884–1961), Indian civil servant; assistant undersecretary of state for India 1933–42, deputy undersecretary 1942–43. Translated Russian poetry into English, published standard work on central banking.

Kishinev, city in Moldavian SSR (formerly in Bessarabia). Jewish community grew in 18th–19th c. Scene of two pogroms before WWI, both inspired and/or backed by Russian authorities: 47 Jews killed, 92 injured (1903); 19 Jews killed, 56 injured (1905). Pogroms led to international outcry, formation of Jewish self-defense, and emigration. Rumanian rule 1918–40 led to improved conditions for Jews. Under German-Rumanian occupation fr. 1941, mass murder of 65,000 Jews took place through execution, deportation, hunger, and epidemics. 5,500 Jews in 1947; 60,000 in 1970.

Kishon, river which drains Jezreel Valley. Scene of Deborah's victory over Sisera (Judg. 4–5). Estuary deepened in 1960s to serve as fishing harbor and depot.

Kishon, Ephraim (1924–), Israel satirist; b. Budapest, settled in Israel 1949. Wrote political and social satire in regular column for daily *Ma'ariv*, publishing frequent collections. Wrote plays and films, incl. *Sallah Shabbati, Blaumilch Canal.*

Kislev, 9th month of Jewish year; 29 or 30 days. Zodiac sign Sagittarius. Festival of Ḥanukkah starts on 25th.

Kisling, Moise (1891–1953), painter; b. Cracow, went to Paris 1910, spent WWII in U.S. Painted mostly landscapes, flowers, still lifes, and nudes.

Kiss, József (1843–1921), Hungarian poet. Many of his poems deal with Jewish subjects, incl. "Against the Tide," inspired by Tiszaeszlar blood-libel. One of Hungary's great literary figures.

Kissinger, Henry Alfred (1923–), U.S. political scientist, secretary of state; b. Germany, went to U.S. 1938. Prof. at Harvard. Expert in defense policy and international relations. Advised Pres. Kennedy on national security 1961–62. Fr. 1969 principal adviser of Pres. Nixon on national security and foreign affairs. Played major role in negotiating end of Vietnam war and in U.S. rapprochement with China and USSR. Appointed secretary of state, 1973. Nobel Prize for Peace 1973. Major role in negotiations between Israel and Arab countries after Yom Kippur War, 1973–4.

Henry Kissinger

Kistarcsa, transit camp nr. Budapest, Hungary, fr. where Jews were shipped to death in Auschwitz fr. July 1944.

Kitel (Yid.), white garment worn in some rites on High Holidays and other festivals, and as a shroud.

°**Kittel, Rudolph** (1853–1929), German Protestant theologian, Bible scholar. Published *Biblica Hebraica,* presenting Masoretic Text along with other variants.

Kittim, (1) Biblical place name, apparently Aegean islands, and perhaps also coastal areas of Mediterranean. (2) In Dead Sea Scrolls and contemporary literature, euphemism for Romans as world power and oppressors of Jews.

Klabin, Maurício (1860–1923), Brazilian pioneer in paper and cellulose industry; b. Lithuania, settled in São Paulo 1887. Members of family also pioneered in Jewish life, incl. son Wolff Kadischevitz-Klabin in Rio.

Klaczko, Julian (1825–1906), Polish critic, historian. Raised in atmosphere of Lithuanian Haskalah. Settled in Paris after 1840, con-

Joseph Klausner

Abraham M. Klein

Samuel Klein

Otto Klemperer

ducted in *Revue des deux mondes,* violent anti-Prussian campaign in support of Polish nationalism. Converted to Catholicism.

Klapper, Paul (1885–1952), U.S. educator, administrator. Taught education at CCNY fr. 1907. First pres. Queens College 1937. Influenced educational practices in schools throughout America.

Klar Benjamin Menaḥem (1901–1948), Hebrew scholar; b. Ukraine, settled in Ereẓ Israel 1936. Taught Hebrew language and grammar at Heb. Univ. Published book on Bialik, editions of Chronicle of Aḥimaaz, etc. Killed in Arab attack on convoy to Mount Scopus.

Klarwein, Joseph (1893–1970), Israel architect. Designed Knesset in Jerusalem 1967, Herzl Memorial on Mt. Herzl, Nahariyyah town center, and Dagon silo in Haifa.

Klatzkin, Elijah ben Naphtali Herz (1852–1932), rabbi, author; father of Jacob Klatzkin. Had extensive knowledge of sciences and languages. Became "Lubliner Rav." Noted for leniency in questions of ritual law.

Klatzkin, Jacob (1882–1948), philosopher; b. Poland, lived in Germany. Active in Zionist affairs. With N. Goldmann initiated German-language *Encyclopaedia Judaica,* serving as editor-in-chief. Lived in Switzerland after Nazi advent. Formulated nationalist and secularist theory, basing Zionism on biological-ethic factors and rejecting Diaspora. His numerous writings incl. thesaurus of Hebrew philosophical terminology. Translated Spinoza's *Ethics* into Hebrew.

Klaus (Kloyz), name given, esp. by ḥasidim, to small prayer house.

Klausenburg, see Cluj.

Klausenburger, see Halberstam, Yekutiel.

Klausner, Abraham (d. 1407/1408), Austrian talmudist. Author of *Sefer ha-Minhagim,* first work to deal with local religious customs in Judaism.

Klausner, Israel (1905–), Hebrew writer, historian; b. Lithuania, settled in Ereẓ Israel 1936. Assistant director of Zionist Archives in Jerusalem. Wrote on history of the Jews in Vilna and on Zionist history.

Klausner, Joseph Gedaliah (1874–1958), literary critic, historian; b. Lithuania, lived in Odessa, editing major literary periodical *Ha-Shilo'aḥ,* settled in Ereẓ Israel 1919. Prof. of modern Hebrew literature 1926, Second Temple history 1945 at Heb. Univ. Exercised great influence on Jewish scholarship through hundreds of essays on Jewish history and literature. Particularly important are his multi-vol. histories of modern Hebrew literature and Second Temple period. Using Jewish sources, wrote *Jesus of Nazareth* and *From Jesus to Paul.* Editor-in-chief of *Encyclopaedia Hebraica.* Candidate of Ḥerut party for election as pres. of Israel 1949.

Klee, Alfred (1875–1943), lawyer, Zionist leader in Germany. After WWI established Juedische Volkspartei, coalition of Zionist parties in Berlin. Left for Holland 1938. D. in concentration camp.

Klein, Abraham Moses (1909–1972), Canadian author. Played active part in revolutionary Montreal Preview group during 1940s. Wrote essays, made English translations of Hebrew and Yiddish poems. His poetry is suffused with Jewish ethic, talmudic erudition, warm Yiddish humor. Wrote symbolic novel *The Second Scroll.*

Klein, Gottlieb (1852–1914), chief rabbi of Stockholm, historian of religion; b. Slovakia. Wrote on early Christianity in light of biblical and talmudic sources.

Klein, Hyman (1908–1958), English talmudist. Head of Liverpool Talmudical College. Translated part of Maimonides' Code, and other works. Last years in Jerusalem.

Klein, Isaac (1905–), U.S. Conservative rabbi in Buffalo. Published many responsa. Pres. Rabbinical Assembly.

Klein, Julius (1901–), leader of U.S. Jewish War Veterans. In WWII, served in S. Pacific and Philippines. Special assistant to secretary of war 1946. Retired 1951 with rank of major-general.

Klein, Julius Leopold (1810–1876), playwright, literary historian; b. Hungary, settled in Berlin. Wrote historical tragedies and 13-vol. history of drama up to Shakespeare.

Klein, Melanie Reizes (1882–1960), British psychoanalyst; b. Vienna. Practiced child therapy Berlin, developed technique of play analysis in London. Her *The Psychoanalysis of Children* was major contribution to understanding of infantile development.

Klein, Philip (1890–), U.S. social worker. Directed large-scale research projects, incl. national survey of unemployment 1921–22. Prof. at N.Y. School of Social Work.

Klein, Samuel (1886–1940), historian, geographer of Ereẓ Israel; b. Hungary. Taught historical topography of Ereẓ Israel at Heb. Univ. fr. 1929. Main contribution to history and geography of Ereẓ Israel was use of Talmud and Midrash as primary source materials.

Klein, Wilhelm (1850–1924), classical archaeologist; b. Hungary, taught in Prague. Published comprehensive study of Athenian ceramists and works on Praxiteles. Distinguished bet. baroque and rococo in Hellenistic sculpture.

Kleinbaum, Moshe, see Sneh, Moshe.

Kleinmann, Moshe (1870–1948), Hebrew, Yiddish author, editor; b. Podolia. Editor of daily *Ha-Am* in Moscow 1917–18, *Haolam* 1923–48, moving to London 1924, Jerusalem 1936. Worked with Zionist press; wrote monographs on Herzl, Weizmann.

Klemperer, Otto (1885–1973), conductor; b. Breslau. Renowned interpreter of Beethoven, Mozart, and modern works. Conducted Berlin State Opera and Philharmonic Choir 1931–33. Went to U.S. 1933. Director of L.A. Philharmonic. Considered last of great conductors in grand German tradition.

ISRAEL CABINETS 1949–1974

No. of Cabinet	1st	2nd	3rd	4th	5th–6th	7th–8th	9th	10th	11th–12th	13th–14th	15th	16th	17th
Date installed	March 10, 1949	Nov. 1, 1950	Oct. 7, 1951	Dec. 23, 1952	Jan. 6, 1954	Nov. 3, 1955	Dec. 17, 1959	Nov. 2, 1961	June 26, 1963	Jan. 12, 1966	Dec. 15, 1969	Mar. 10, 1974	June 3, 1974
Prime Minister	D. Ben-Gurion	D. Ben-Gurion	D. Ben-Gurion	D. Ben-Gurion	M. Sharett	D. Ben-Gurion	D. Ben-Gurion	D. Ben-Gurion	L. Eshkol	L. Eshkol d. 26.2.69 G. Meir 17.3.69	G. Meir	G. Meir	Y. Rabin
Deputy P.M.			E. Kaplan 25.6.52–d. 14.7.52						A. Eban	Y. Allon 1.7.68	Y. Allon	Y. Allon	Y. Allon
Agriculture	D. Joseph + Supply and Rationing	P. Lavon	L. Eshkol P. Naftali 25.6.52	P. Naftali	P. Naftali	K. Luz	M. Dayan	M. Dayan	M. Dayan H. Gvati 22.12.64	H. Gvati	H. Gvati	H. Gvati	A. Uzan
Commerce and Industry	E. Kaplan	Y. Geri	D. Joseph	P. Bernstein	P. Bernstein P. Naftali 29.6.55	P. Sapir	P. Sapir	P. Sapir	P. Sapir H.J. Zadok 23.5.65	H.J. Zadok Z. Sharef 20.11.66	Y. Sapir P. Sapir 1.9.70	H. Bar-Lev 6.3.72 H. Bar-Lev	H. Bar-Lev
Communications (Transport)	D. Remez	D. Joseph	D.Z. Pinkas d. 14.8.52	Y. Sapir	Y. Sapir Z. Aranne 29.6.55	M. Carmel	Y. Ben-Aharon	Y. Ben-Aharon I. Bar-Yehudah 27.5.62	I. Bar-Yehudah M. Carmel 30.5.65	M. Carmel	E. Weizman r. 4.8.70 S. Peres 1.9.70	A. Yariv	G. Ya'akobi
Defense	D. Ben-Gurion	D. Ben-Gurion	D. Ben-Gurion	D. Ben-Gurion	P. Lavon D. Ben-Gurion 21.2.55	D. Ben-Gurion	D. Ben-Gurion	D. Ben-Gurion	L. Eshkol	L. Eshkol M. Dayan 5.6.67	M. Dayan	M. Dayan	S. Peres
Development			L. Eshkol	D. Joseph	D. Joseph	M. Bentov	M. Bentov	G. Josephthal Y. A. Almogi 30.10.62	Y. A. Almogi H. Zadok 31.5.65	M. Kol	H. Landau r. 4.8.70 H. Gvati 1.9.70		
Education	S.Z. Shazar	D. Remez d. 19.5.51	B.Z. Dinaburg (Dinur)	B-Z. Dinur	B-Z. Dinur	Z. Aranne	Z. Aranne r. 24.4.60 A. Eban 13.8.60	A. Eban	Z. Aranne	Z. Aranne	Y. Allon	Y. Allon	A. Yadlin
Finance	E. Kaplan	E. Kaplan	E. Kaplan L. Eshkol 25.6.52	L. Eshkol	L. Eshkol	L. Eshkol	L. Eshkol	L. Eshkol	P. Sapir	P. Sapir Z. Sharef 5.8.68	P. Sapir	P. Sapir	Y. Rabinowitz
Foreign Affairs	M. Sharett	M. Sharett	M. Sharett	M. Sharett	M. Sharett	M. Sharett G. Meir (Myerson) 19.6.56	G. Meir	G. Meir	G. Meir	A. Eban	A. Eban	A. Eban	Y. Allon
Health	M. Shapira		Y. Burg	J. Serlin	J. Serlin D. Joseph 29.6.55	I. Barzilai	I. Barzilai	H.M. Shapira	H.M. Shapira	I. Barzilai	H. Gvati 21.12.69 V. Shemtov 26.7.70	V. Shemtov	V. Shemtov
Housing								G. Josephthal Y. A. Almogi 30.10.62	Y. A. Almogi L. Eshkol 31.5.65	M. Bentov	Z. Sharef	Y. Rabinowitz	A. Ofer
Immigrant Absorption										Y. Allon 1.7.68	S. Peres (Acting) N. Peled 26.7.70	Information S. Peres S. Rosen	A. Yariv S. Rosen
Interior	M. Shapira + Aliya	M. Shapira + Aliyah	M. Shapira	I. Rokach	I. Rokach M. Shapira 29.6.55	I. Bar-Yehudah	H.M. Shapira	H.M. Shapira	H.M. Shapira	H.M. Shapira	H.M. Shapira d. 16.7.70 Y. Burg 1.9.70	Y. Burg	S. Hillel[4]
Justice	P. Rosenblueth (Rosen)	P. Rosen	D. Joseph H. Cohn 22.6.52	P. Rosen	P. Rosen	P. Rosen	P. Rosen	D. Joseph	D. Joseph	Y.S. Shapiro	Y.S. Shapiro	H. Zadok	H. Zadok
Labor	G. Myerson	G. Myerson	G. Myerson	G. Myerson	G. Myerson	G. Meir (Myerson) M. Namir 19.6.56	G. Josephthal	Y. Allon	Y. Allon	Y. Allon Y. A. Almogi 8.7.68	Y. A. Almogi	Y. Rabin	M. Baram
Police	B.S. Shitrit	B.S. Shitrit	B.S. Shitrit	B.S. Shitrit	B.S. Shitrit	B.S. Shitrit	B.S. Shitrit	B.S. Shitrit	B.S. Shitrit	B.S. Shitrit E. Sasson 30.12.66	S. Hillel	S. Hillel	S. Hillel
Posts			M. Nurok 9.11.52	Y. Burg	Y. Burg	Y. Burg I. Barzilai 16.11.58	B. Minz 18.7.60–d. 30.5.61	E. Sasson	E. Sasson	E. Sasson I. Yeshayahu 1.1.67	E. Rimalt r. 4.8.70 S. Peres 1.9.70	A. Uzan	Y. Rabin[4]
Religious Affairs	J.L. Maimon (Fishman)	J.L. Maimon	J.L. Maimon	M. Shapira	M. Shapira	M. Shapira r. 1.7.58 Y.M. Toledano 3.12.58	Y.M. Toledano d. 15.10.60	Z. Warhaftig	Z. Warhaftig	Z. Warhaftig	Z. Warhaftig	Y. Raphael	H. Zadok[4]
Social Welfare	Y.M. Levin	Y.M. Levin	Y.M. Levin r. 3.11.52	M. Shapira	M. Shapira	Y. Burg r. 1.7.58 P. Naftali 16.11.58	Y. Burg	Y. Burg	Y. Burg	Y. Burg	Y. Burg M. Chasani 1.9.70	M. Chasani	V. Shemtov[4]
Tourism									A. Guvrin 22.12.64	M. Kol	M. Kol	M. Kol	M. Kol
Without Portfolio			P. Naftali (Economic Coordination) P. Lavon 17.8.52	P. Lavon	Z. Aranne	P. Naftali	A. Eban	Y. A. Almogi	A. Guvrin 1.12.63	I. Galili M. Begin 5.6.67 Y. Sapir 5.6.67 P. Sapir 5.8.66	I. Barzilai d. 12.6.70 M. Begin r. 4.8.70 A.L. Dultzin r. 4.8.70 I. Galili S. Peres till 1.9.70 V. Shemtov till 26.7.70	I. Galili G. Hausner	S. Aloni I. Galili G. Hausner
	r.—resigned d.—died in office												

Notes: 1. Names of ministers who took office or changed their posts during a cabinet's term are followed by the date of appointment. 2. When no successor was named for a minister who died or resigned, the portfolio was generally held *pro tem* by the prime minister. 3. Y. Allon was acting prime minister from 26.2.69 to 17.3.69. 4. "Pro tempore"

RESULTS OF KNESSET ELECTIONS (1949–73)

	First		Second		Third		Fourth		Fifth		Sixth		Seventh		Eighth	
	Jan. 25, 1949		July 30, 1951		July 26, 1955		Nov. 3, 1959		Aug. 15, 1961		Nov. 2, 1965		Oct. 28, 1969		Dec. 31, 1973	
Electorate	506,567		924,885		1,067,795		1,218,483		1,274,280		1,449,709		1,758,685		2,037,478	
Valid votes cast	434,684		787,492		853,219		969,337		1,006,964		1,206,728		1,367,743		1,601,098	
Party	%	Seats	%	Seats	%	Seats	%	Seats	%	Seats	%	Seats	%	Seats	%	Seats
Mapai	35.7	46	37.3	45	32.2	40	38.2	47	34.7	42	36.7[6]	45	46.22	56	39.8	51
Aḥdut ha-Avodah	–	–	–	–	8.2	10	6.0	7	6.6	8						
Mapam	14.7[1]	19	12.5[1]	15	7.3	9	7.2	9	7.5	9	6.6	8				
Rafi[7]	–	–	–	–	–	–	–	–	–	–	7.9	10	–	–		
Ḥerut	11.5	14	6.6	8	12.6	15	13.5	17	13.8	17	21.3[8]	26[10]	21.67	26	30.1	39[14]
Liberals[2]	5.2	7	18.9	23	10.2	13	6.2	8	13.6	17						
	4.1	5	3.2	4	4.4	5	4.6	6			3.8[9]	5	3.21	4	3.6	4
National Religious Party			8.3	10	9.1	11	9.9	12	9.8	12	9.9	11	9.74	12	8.3	10
Agudat Israel	12.2[3]	16							3.7	4	3.3	4	3.22	4	3.9	5
Po'alei Agudat Israel			3.7[5]	5	4.7	6	4.7	6	1.9	2	1.8	2	1.83	2		
Communists	3.5	4	4.0	5	4.5	6	2.8	3	4.2	5	3.4	4[11]	3.99	4	4.8	5[15]
Arabs (associated with Mapai)	3.0	2	4.7	5	4.9	5	3.5	5	3.5	4	3.3	4	3.51	4	2.4	3
Others	10.1	7[4]	0.8	–	1.9	–	3.6	–	0.7	–	2.9	1[12]	6.61	8[13]	2.2	3[16]

1 In 1949 and 1951 Mapam included Aḥdut ha-Avodah.
2 Figures for the first four Knessets refer respectively to General Zionists and Progressives, who merged in 1961 to form the Liberal Party. See also notes 8 and 9.
3 In 1949 these parties constituted the United Religious Front.
4 Four Sephardim, one Yemenite, one WIZO, and one "Fighters."
5 In 1951, 1955, 1959, and 1973 these two parties constituted the Torah Religious Front.
6 Alignment (Mapai and Aḥdut ha-Avodah).
7 Rafi – Israel Labor List, formed in 1965 after a split in Mapai.
8 Ḥerut-Liberal Bloc (Gaḥal).
9 Independent Liberals.
10 In 1967 three Ḥerut Knesset members formed the independent Free Center faction.
11 Three New Communist List (Rakaḥ) and one Israel Communist Party (Maki).
12 Ha-Olam ha-Zeh – New Force.
13 Including four National List, two Ha-Olam ha-Zeh, two Free Center.
14 Likkud (Ḥerut, Liberals, Free Center, State Party, Land of Israel Movement).
15 Four Rakaḥ, one Moked (New Left and Communists).
16 Civil Rights Movement.

Klepfish, Samuel Zanvil (1820–1902), Polish rabbi, *av bet din* of Warsaw, outstanding halakhist, receiving queries fr. all over world.

Kletzki, Paul (1900–1973), conductor. Conducted Berlin Philharmonic Orchestra 1931–33, Dallas Symphony Orchestra fr. 1958. Excelled in romantic music and also promoted contemporary works.

Kley, Eduard (Israel; 1789–1867), German pedagogue, Reform preacher. Directed Jewish free school in Hamburg. Proposed liturgy completely in German. Stressed devotional aspects of religion.

Klibansky, Raymond (1905–), philosopher; b. Paris, moved to Germany, fleeing 1933. Taught at Oxford 1936–48. Prof. of logic and metaphysics at McGill Univ., Montreal, fr. 1948. Pres. Institute International de Philosophie 1966. Wrote on Plato, Nicholas of Cusa, Meister Eckhart, etc.

Kligler, Israel Jacob (1889–1944), Ereẓ Israel bacteriologist; b. Ukraine, settled in Ereẓ Israel 1920. Leading figure in public health and malaria control.

Klotz, Louis-Lucien (1868–1930), French politician, journalist. Member of Chamber of Deputies as Radical Socialist 1898–1928, then senate; minister of finance in six administrations and minister of interior. French delegate to Versailles Peace Conference 1919, signatory of Treaty. Convicted of fraud 1928.

Kluger, Solomon ben Joseph Aaron (Maharshak; 1785–1869), Polish talmudist, halakhist. Rabbi in Brody fr. 1820. Prolific author. Extremely Orthodox, opposed machine baking of *matzot.*

Opening session of 7th Knesset, Nov. 17th 1969. Prime Minister Golda Meir is seen with Foreign Minister Abba Eban (left), and Minister of the Interior Ḥayyim Moshe Shapira and Defense Minister Moshe Dayan (right).

Klutznick, Philip Morris (1907–), U.S. communal leader. Federal housing commissioner 1944–46. Ambassador to UN Economic and Social Council 1961–63. International pres. of B'nai B'rith 1953–59 and active in many cultural and international Jewish organizations. Cofounder of town of Ashdod in Israel.

Knesset (Heb. "assembly"), parliament of Israel. Consists of 120-member single chamber, elected for 4-year term; first convened Feb. 14, 1949. Supreme authority in state; elects president and confirms government, which must resign if it loses its confidence. Its legislation immune fr. challenge in courts. Every citizen over age 18 eligible to vote; candidates must be at least 21. Seats are distributed in proportion to number of votes received by each political party. Meets in Jerusalem.

Knopf, Alfred A. (1892–), U.S. book publisher. Founded Knopf firm (merging with Random House 1960). Published *American Mercury,* edited by H.L. Mencken.

°**Knorr von Rosenroth, Christian** (1636–1689), German Protestant theosophist, scholar of Kabbalah. Wrote extensively on Kabbalah and translated important texts. His *Kabbala Denudata,* principal source for all non-Jewish literature on Kabbalah until end of 19th c.

Kober, Adolf (1879–1958), German Reform rabbi, historian. Wrote on history of Rhenish Jewry. In New York fr. 1939.

Kober, Arthur (1900–), U.S. humorist, playwright. Known for his amusing books about Jewish life in N.Y.

Arthur Koestler

Leonid Kogan

Koblenz, city in W. Germany. Community mentioned 1172. Citizenship rights 1307. Jews persecuted 1337 and during Black Death. Expelled 1418, readmitted 1512–18. Restricted to "Jews' Street." Jews emancipated 1797. Hep-Hep riots 1819. 609 Jews in 1933; 22 survived Holocaust.

Kobrin, Leon (1872–1946), U.S. Yiddish novelist, dramatist; b. Russia, in U.S. fr. 1892. Pioneer of Yiddish literature in U.S. Realistic stories and plays give faithful picture of Jewish life in America during great immigration period. Translated world classics into Yiddish.

Koch, Kenneth (1925–), U.S. poet. Taught poetry at Columbia Univ. Influential in use of absurd non sequitur and juxtaposition of incongruous images. Published volumes incl. *Ko, or A Season on Earth* and *Thank You, and Other Poems.*

Kodashim (Heb. "sacred things"), 5th order of Mishnah. Deals mainly with sacrifices, Temple service, and also preparation of non-sacred animals for consumption.

Koebner, Richard (1885–1958), historian. Prof. at Breslau Univ. Dismissed by Nazis, settled in Jerusalem 1934. Prof. of modern history at Heb. Univ. Wrote on changing concepts of "empire" and "imperialism."

Koenig, Leo (pseud. of **Leyb Yaffe;** 1899–1970), Yiddish author, critic, journalist; b. Odessa. First to write art criticism for leading Paris Yiddish periodicals. In London 1914–52, then Israel.

Koenigsberg (Kaliningrad), city in Russia (formerly in E. Prussia). Jewish settlement in 17th c. First synagogue 1756. Center of 18th c. Jewish Enlightenment; affluent Jewish families gained access to Christian society. Hebrew printing in 18th–19th c. Main synagogue burned down 1938, 3,200 Jews in 1939; community ended in Holocaust, many leaving for U.S. and Ereẓ Israel.

Koenigsberg, Moses (1878–1945), U.S. editor, publisher. Formed King Features syndicate 1916; pres. International News Service and Universal Service.

Koenigswarter, family of European bankers, philanthropists. **Jonas Hirsch** (d. 1805), banker in Fuerth. His son, **Marcus** (1770–1854), established bank in Frankfort. His grandson, **Jonas Freiherr von** (1807–1871), formed Vienna banking firm of Koenigswarter and Todasco; director of Austrian National Bank, associated with Rothschilds in establishing Austria's largest bank, Creditanstalt, 1855. Ennobled. His son, **Moritz, Baron von** (1837–1893), continued his father's expansion of Austrian railroad system. Founded Vienna's Inst. for Jewish Blind. Another son of Jonas Hirsch went to Holland, founded bank in Amsterdam; his elder son, **Louis Jean** (1814–1878), French legal historian, pres. Alliance Israélite Universelle. His brother, **Maximilian** (1817–1887), banker in Paris, ennobled by Napoleon III.

Koestler, Arthur (1905–), author; b. Budapest. Wrote first in Hungarian, then German, later English. In Ereẓ Israel 1926–29, joined Communist Party 1931, but abandoned it during Stalinist purges. Correspondent in Spain during Civil War; settled in England. Works range fr. novels on political and moral issues (e.g., *Darkness at Noon* on Stalinist purges, *Thieves in the Night* on mandatory Ereẓ Israel) to later philosophical works, as well as volumes of autobiography.

Kof (ק), 19th letter of Hebrew alphabet; numerical value 100. Pronounced *k.*

Koffka, Kurt (1886–1941), U.S. psychologist; a founder of Gestalt psychology; b. Berlin. Rejected notion that consciousness is built up of separate elements and substituted view that experience is organized in whole patterns. In U.S. fr. 1924. Prof. at Smith College. Wrote monumental *Principles of Gestalt Psychology.*

Kogan, David, see Kahana, David.

Kogan, Leonid Borissovich (1924–), Russian violinist. Won first prize at international competitions, in Prague 1947, Brussels 1951. Organized concert trio with pianist E. Gilels, cellist Rostropovich. Lenin Prize 1965.

Kogan, Moyse (1879–1942), sculptor; b. Bessarabia, emigrated to Munich 1903, Paris 1910. Influenced by Maillol. Best works are terracotta figurines; also worked in wood, linoleum cuts, lithographs. Killed by Nazis.

Kohath, ancestor of Kohathites; second son of Levi and grandfather of Moses (Num. 26:58–59). Kohathites important levitical clan. In wilderness in charge of most sacred objects in Tabernacle. During monarchy served in Tabernacle or Temple.

Koheleth, see Ecclesiastes.

Koheleth Mussar, collection of moralistic Hebrew literature published in 1750s by Moses Mendelssohn and Tobias Bock.

"Kodashim," one of six murals by Hannah Lerner devoted to the orders of the Mishnah, Jerusalem, Boys' Town.

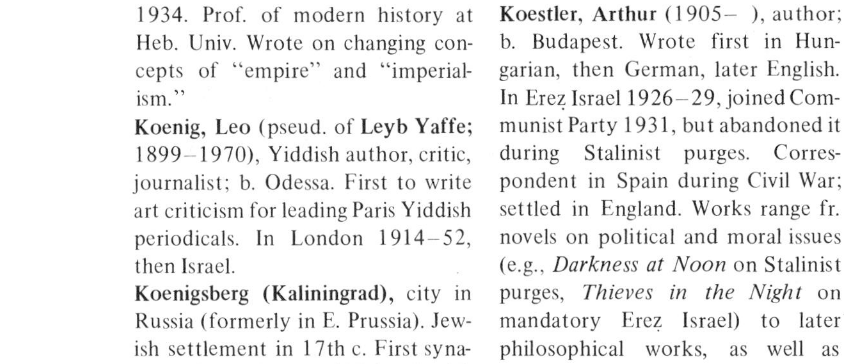

Kohen, first major family of Hebrew printers in Prague and C. Europe. (fr. 16th c.).

Kohen, see Priests.

Kohen, Raphael ben Jekuthiel Suesskind (1722–1803), Lithuanian rabbi, halakhist. Rabbi of combined communities of Altona, Hamburg, and Wandsbeck; involved in controversy with Saul Berlin. Published extensively on talmudic matters.

Kohen-Zedek, Joseph (1827–1903), Hebrew poet, publicist; b. Lvov. Published patriotic poetry in honor of Austro-Hungarian emperor. Edited several shortlived Hebrew periodicals. Settled in London 1875 serving as preacher to immigrant congregations.

Kohler, Kaufmann (1843–1926), U.S. Reform rabbi; b. Bavaria, in U.S. fr. 1869. Rabbi in Detroit, Chicago, N.Y. Pres. Hebrew Union College fr. 1903. Prolific writer; served on editorial board of J.P.S. Bible translation and philosophy and theology dept. of *Jewish Encyclopaedia.* Leading figure at Pittsburgh Conference of Reform rabbis and in its adoption of radical program. Best-known work *Jewish Theology.*

Kaufmann Kohler

Kohler, Max James (1871–1934), U.S. attorney; son of Kaufmann Kohler. Specialist in immigration and naturalization law, both in private practice and representing Jewish organizations. Active in many Jewish organizations.

Kohn, Abraham (1807–1848), Austrian extremist Reform rabbi. Attempted to induce authorities to prohibit Jews fr. observing traditional customs and pressed for abolition of discriminatory communal taxes. His opponents were accused of poisoning him.

Kohn, Eugene (1887–), U.S. Reconstructionist rabbi. Editor of *Reconstructionist;* co-author of Reconstructionist prayer book.

Kohn, Hans (1891–1971), U.S. historian, political scientist; b. Prague, in U.S. fr. 1931. Taught at several universities. Major work *The Idea of Nationalism,* later continued by *The Age of Nationalism,* and *Prelude to Nation-States.*

Kohn, Leo (Yehudah Pinḥas; 1894–1961), Israel scholar, diplomat; b. Germany, settled in Ereẓ Israel 1921. Political adviser to Chaim Weizmann and to Israel Ministry for Foreign Affairs. Prof. of international relations at Heb. Univ. fr. 1953.

Kohn, Maier (1802–1875), cantor, teacher in Munich. Published first modern collection of synagogue melodies.

Kohn, Pinchas (1867–1942), German Orthodox leader. Adviser to German military government of Poland in WWI. Director of Agudat Israel World Organization fr. 1919. In Jerusalem fr. 1938.

Kohn, Samuel (1841–1920), Hungarian rabbi. Chief rabbi of Budapest, author of scholarly works on Hungarian Jewry.

Kohs, Samuel Calmin (1890–), U.S. social worker, psychologist. Taught social technology at Graduate School of Jewish Social Work 1929–39; director of Resettlement Division of National Refugee Service in N.Y. His Block Design Test was incorporated into Wechsler-Bellevue, one of most widely used U.S. intelligence tests.

Kohut, Hungarian-American family. **Alexander** (1842–1894), rabbi, Jewish representative in Hungarian parliament. Rabbi in New York fr. 1885. Wrote 8-vol. *Arukh Completum,* outstanding work of talmudic lexicography. His wife, **Rebecca** (1864–1951), educator, community leader; pres. World Congress of Jewish Women. His brother, **Adolf** (1848–1917), journalist, author. Editor of *Berliner Zeitung,* knighted by Emperor Francis Joseph for contributions to literature. His son, **George Alexander** (1874–1933), educator, scholar, bibliophile. Head of Kohut School for Boys and Columbia Grammar School.

Alexander Kohut and his wife, Rebecca.

Koidanov, ḥasidic family, branch of Karlin (q.v.) trend of Ḥasidism. Founder **Solomon Ḥayyim of Koidanov** (1797–1862), established *kolel* Koidanov in Tiberias. **Shalom** (1850–1925), rabbi, author. Published movement's teachings. Koidanov Ḥasidim had synagogues in Vilna and U.S.

Koidonover, Aaron Samuel ben Israel (Maharshak; c. 1614–1676), Lithuanian talmudist, scholar, preacher; fled to Vilna from Chmielnicki pogroms. Member of *bet din,* rabbi of German towns, *av bet din* in Cracow. Wrote important novellae and responsa, esp. on problems of *agunot.*

Koidonover, Ẓevi Hirsch (d. 1712), Lithuanian rabbi; son of Aaron Samuel Koidanover. Published his father's halakhic works. Wrote popular moralist work *Kav ha-Yashar,* frequently reprinted and translated into Yiddish and Ladino.

Koigen, David (1879–1933), philosopher, sociologist; b. Ukraine, lived mostly in Germany. Wrote on cultural sociology and Jewish problems. Edited quarterly *Ethos.*

Kojève, Alexandre (1902–), philosopher; b. Russia. Taught in Paris 1933–39. Wrote on Hegel. Worked in French Ministry of Economic Affairs; a chief planner of European Common Market.

Kokesch, Ozer (1860–1905), Austrian Zionist; Herzl's aide. A founder of Jewish students' association Kadimah. Secretary of committee that prepared First Zionist Congress. Active supporter of agricultural settlement in Ereẓ Israel.

°**Kokovtsov, Paul Konstantinovich** (1861–1942), Russian orientalist. Prof. of Hebrew at St. Petersburg Univ. Influential teacher. Wrote on Semitic languages, Khazars. As expert in 1913 Beilis trial helped expose ignorance of prosecution.

Kol, Moshe (1911–), Israel politician, Zionist leader; b. Pinsk, settled in Ereẓ Israel 1932. Head of Youth Aliyah 1948–64. Leader of Independent Liberal Party, member of Knesset, minister of tourism fr. 1966.

Kol Bo (Heb. "everything within"), anonymous work giving rulings on many halakhic topics; written at end of 13th c., first printed 1490. Culled fr. many sources, esp. Maimonides' *Mishneh Torah.*

Kolel, originally group of Ashkenazi Jews in Ereẓ Israel supported fr. Europe and devoting themselves to Torah study; those in Jerusalem organized acc. to country of origin.

Later groups of married students organized as talmudic college, whose members receive small stipend.

Kolin, city in Czechoslovakia. Community one of four known together as "Karban." Jews present fr. late 14th c. Famous yeshivah in 19th c. Between world wars stronghold of Czecho-Jewish movement. Community liquidated in Holocaust. Small community reestablished 1945.

Teddy Kollek outside Israel Museum.

Eastern Ashkenazi version of "Kol Nidrei," with its introduction, "Al da'at ha-Makom."

Kolischer, Heinrich (1853–1932), politician in Galicia. Owned large paper mill. Supported Polish national orientation; anti-Zionist. Member of Polish Sejm 1918–22.

Kollek, Theodore (Teddy; 1911–), Israel public figure; b. Vienna, settled in Ereẓ Israel 1934. Minister plenipotentiary in U.S. 1951–52; director general of Prime Minister's Office 1952–64, chairman of Israel Government Tourist Corporation 1956–65. Founder and chairman of Israel Museum in Jerusalem. Mayor of Jerusalem fr. 1965. After 1967 reunification of city strove for normalization of relations with Jerusalem Arabs.

Kolman, Arnošt (Ernest; 1892–), Czech philosopher, mathematician. Fr. 1918 active Communist. During WWII in political dept. of Soviet General Staff. Prof. of mathematics at Inst. for History of Science and Technology in Moscow 1952–59; director of Inst. of Philosophy of Czechoslovakian Academy of Sciences 1959–62.

Kolmar, Gertrud (pseud. of **Gertrud Chodziesner;** 1894–1943), German poet. Devoted many of her poems to Jewish themes; delved into history, art, animal lore. D. in concentration camp.

Kol Mevasser (Heb.), Yiddish periodical founded in Odessa 1862 by A. Zederbaum as supplement to Hebrew weekly *Ha-Meliẓ*. Issued separately 1869–72. Brought to public attention some early Yiddish writers.

Kol Nidrei (Aram. "all vows"), declaration of annulment of vows made unwittingly or rashly by worshiper to God. Introduces service on eve of Day of Atonement and was regarded as of such importance that entire eve is popularly called "Kol Nidre." Meaning of texts distorted by anti-Semites but survived various attempts at reform or omission. Standard Ashkenazi melody is famous.

Kolnik, Arthur (1890–), French painter, printmaker; b. Galicia, settled in Paris 1931. Depicted ghetto dwellers of E. Europe.

Kolomyya, town in Ukrainian SSR. Jewish community flourished fr. 16th c., destroyed during Chmielnicki massacres 1648–49, recovered in 18th c. Center of extreme Orthodox Ḥasidism. Anti-Jewish economic policies under direct German administration. 15,000 Jews in 1939; few survived WWII.

Kolthoff, Izaak Maurits (1894–), chemist; b. Holland, in U.S. fr. 1927. Prof. at Univ. of Minnesota. Wrote on analytical and physical chemistry.

Komlós, Aldár (1892–), Hungarian poet, author, literary scholar. After WWII taught at Budapest Univ. Author of monumental work on modern poetry.

Komoly, Ottó (1892–1945), Hungarian Zionist leader. Chairman of underground Relief and Rescue Committee 1943. Helped organize rescue train which led 1,686 Jews to safety outside Hungary. Abducted and killed by Arrow Cross leaders.

Kompert, Leopold (1822–1886), German writer. Celebrated for descriptions of Bohemian Jewish life. His novel *Am Pfluge,* intended to encourage Jews to take up agriculture, made strong impression on Jewish youth in E. Europe. Active in Jewish affairs and in Viennese civic life.

Komroff, Manuel (1890–), U.S. journalist, author. Fictional works incl. *A Grace of Lambs, Coronet.* Edited Marco Polo's *Travels.*

Komzet, government institute for directing Jewish settlement on land in USSR, established 1924 with the aim of settling 100,000 Jewish families within decade. Although aim not achieved, acted as supervisor of agricultural activities of ICA, ORT, and AGRO-Joint in Ukraine and Crimea, as well as agricultural activities in Birobidzhan. Dissolved 1938.

Kon, Feliks (1864–1941), Communist politician, journalist; b. Warsaw, went to Russia after 1917 February Revolution. Joined Communist Party; member of Polish bureau. Leading journalist until Stalin's purges.

Konfino, Žak (1892–), Yugoslav author. Practiced as physician until WWI, began to write at age 40. Outstanding satirist. Subjects incl. life of Sephardi Jews in Serbia and psychological relationship bet. doctor and patient.

Konitz, town in Poland (until 1918 in Germany). Scene of blood libel 1900. Small Jewish pop. until WWII.

Konvitz, Milton Ridvas (1908–), U.S. legal scholar; b. Ereẓ Israel, in U.S. fr. 1915. Taught at Cornell Univ. Authority on industrial and labor relations. Wrote on civil rights.

Kook, Abraham Isaac (1865–1935), rabbinical authority, thinker, scholar; b. Latvia. Rabbi in Jaffa fr. 1904, Switzerland and London 1914–19, first Ashkenazi chief rabbi of Ereẓ Israel fr. 1919. Identified with Zionism, attributing religious signifi-

Abraham I. Kook at cornerstone-laying of Keneset Israel quarter, Jerusalem, 1935.

cance to it; bitterly attacked by ultra-Orthodox. Tried to draw nonreligious back to Judaism. Established yeshivah now called Merkaz ha-Rav. Both mystic and man of world. One of most original and outstanding thinkers in modern Orthodoxy, and highly regarded by all sections of *Yishuv.* Wrote speculative and halakhic works.

Kook, Ẓevi Judah ben Abraham Isaac ha-Kohen (1891–), Israel yeshivah head; son of A.I. Kook. Succeeded father as head of Merkaz ha-Rav yeshivah; wrote on topical halakhic problems, edited father's works.

Kopelson, Ẓemaḥ (1869–1933), pioneer of Bund. Organized Social Democratic groups of workers and intelligentsia in Vilna. Lived in Switzerland, Berlin fr. 1895. At Fifth Congress of Bund 1903 dissented fr. its national Jewish program. Went to U.S. 1908. Returned to Russia, after 1917 Revolution, joined Communist Party.

Kopf, Maxim (1892–1958), painter; b. Vienna. Led German expressionist group known as "Prager Sezession." Akin to Gauguin. Traveled through Pacific Islands 1925, settled in Paris, moved to New York; married writer Dorothy Thompson.

Koplik, Henry (1858–1927), U.S. pediatrician. Discovered diagnostic spots of measles known as "Koplik's spots."

Koppleman, Herman Paul (1880–1957), U.S. politician, civil leader. First Jew elected to Congress fr. Connecticut 1932. Supported New Deal. Active in Jewish affairs.

Kops, Bernard (1926–), English author. Grouped with "angry young men" in English literature after WWII. Wrote plays, novels, poetry.

Korah, central figure in story of revolt against religious authority of Moses during wanderings in wilderness (Num. 16). With allies swallowed up by the earth in punishment.

Koraḥ, Amram ibn Yaḥyā (1871–1953), leader of Yemenite Jewry; emigrated to Israel 1950. For short period chief rabbi of San'a. Wrote fundamental work on Yemenite Jewry.

Koraḥ, Yaḥya ben Shalom (1840–1881), Yemenite scholar, kabbalist. Pioneer researcher on Targum Onkelos and Yemenite poetry.

Korchnoy, Viktor (1931–), Russian chessmaster. Three-time USSR champion.

Korczak, Janusz (Henryk Goldszmidt; 1878–1942), Polish writer, educator, physician. Fr. 1911 headed Jewish orphanage in Warsaw, in which children were given self-government and produced their own newspaper; his pedagogy founded on psychological understanding of children. Published theoretical works and children's books. Directed children's institutions in Warsaw ghetto; went with his wards to gas chambers.

Janusz Korczak stamp issued in Israel on 20th anniversary of his death, 1962.

Korda, Sir Alexander (1893–1956), British film producer; b. Hungary, in London fr. 1929. Founded London Film Productions 1932, Alexander Korda Film Productions 1939. Directed *The Private Life of Henry VIII,* introducing Charles Laughton and Merle Oberon, *The Scarlet Pimpernel, Rembrandt,* etc.

Koreff, David Ferdinand (1783–1851), German author, physician. Known for unorthodox medical techniques in treatment of mental cases. Appointed court physician to Prussian king, full professorship at Berlin at age 33. A founder of *Nordsternbund,* circle of young romantic poets. Baptized.

Koretz, Phinehas ben Abraham Abba Shapiro of (1726–1791), Ukrainian ḥasidic rabbi. Gave primacy to study of Zohar as means of strengthening faith; believed in prayer as means of obtaining human needs.

Körmendi, Ferenc (1900–), Hungarian novelist. Books reflect situation of bourgeois Budapest bet. world wars and sense of isolation of Hungarian Jewish intellectuals. In London fr. 1938. Joined Hungarian section of BBC.

Korn, Bertram Wallace (1918–), U.S. Reform rabbi, historian. Rabbi in Philadephia fr. 1949. Wrote on U.S. Jewish history.

Korn, Rachel (1898–), Yiddish poet, short story writer; after difficult years in Soviet Russia, emigrated to Canada. Described pre-WWI Galician Jewry.

Kornberg, Arthur (1918–), U.S. biochemist. Prof. at Stanford Univ. Synthesized DNA in test tube. Nobel Prize 1959 "for discoveries in the biological synthesis of ribonucleic acids and deoxyribonucleic acids."

Kornfeld, Aaron ben Mordecai Baer (1795–1881), last *rosh yeshivah* of Bohemia; known as Aaron Jennikau. Strictly Orthodox; conceded necessity of secular studies.

Kornfeld Joseph Saul (1876–1943), U.S. Reform rabbi, diplomat. Rabbi in Columbus fr. 1907. U.S. ambassador to Persia 1921–25; frequently intervened with Shah on behalf of Jews.

Kornfeld, Zsigmond (1852–1909), banker, politician. Influential in Hungarian financial policy, member of Chamber of Magnates of Hungarian Parliament. Created baron 1909. Active in Jewish community life.

Korngold, Erich Wolfgang (1897–1957), composer, conductor, pianist; b. Moravia; lived in U.S. after 1936. Composed operas, chamber music, music for films. Conservative modernist.

Korobka (Rus. "box"), tax imposed on consumption items, mainly *kasher* meat. Introduced among communities of Poland-Lithuania in 17th c., often to assist individual communities to pay their debts. In 19th c. served to pay salaries of communal functionaries and institutions etc.

Kortner, Fritz (1892–1970), German actor. Outstanding classical actor, with range fr. Shakespeare to Brecht. In U.S. 1933–48.

Kos (Cos), Greek island. Jews possibly present during Second Temple period. Jews exiled to Nice 1500

when island was ruled by Knights of St. John, returned when island was captured by Turks 1522. Following German occupation in WWII, its 120 Jews deported to Auschwitz.

Kosher, see Kasher.

Kosice, city in Slovakia. Community began to prosper 1860. Many industries founded by Jews. 11,195 Jews in 1930. After Hungary annexed city 1938, anti-Semitic economic restrictions imposed. After German occupation Jews sent to death camps. 3,000 survived war; 1,000 remained in 1970.

Kosice, Gyula (Fernando Falik; 1924–), Argentine sculptor. Pioneer of kinetic art in Latin America.

Kossoff, David (1919–), British actor. Played many Jewish roles. Gained reputation for manner of telling Bible stories for children on radio and TV, also publishing them in book form.

Kossovski, Vladimir (1867–1941), Bund theorist, publicist. Joined Jewish Social Democrats in Vilna; participated in founding Bund 1897, member of its central committee. Fr. 1920 lived in Switzerland, Berlin, Warsaw. During WWII escaped to U.S.

Kostelanetz, Andre (1901–), conductor, pianist, composer; b. Russia, left for U.S. 1922. Renowned for arrangements of light classical and popular compositions performed by his own orchestra. Married soprano Lily Pons.

Kotarbińska, Janina (née **Dina Sztejnbarg;** 1901–), Polish philosopher; wife of foremost Polish philosopher, T. Kotarbiński. Survived Auschwitz. Prof. of logic and methodology of science at Warsaw. During 1960s chairman of Dept. of Logic at Warsaw Univ.

Sandy Koufax

Serge Koussevitzky

Kotler, Aaron (1892–1962), Russian yeshivah head. Directed Eẓ Ḥayyim yeshivah of Slutzk during WWI; transferred to Kletsk 1921–41. Went to U.S., establishing Va'ad Haẓẓalah (Rescue Committee) to aid war refugees. Founded educational institutes and was noted for his teaching methods. Pres. Supreme Council of Agudat Israel 1954-62, head of Eẓ Ḥayyim yeshivah in Jerusalem.

Kotsk, Menahem Mendel of (1787–1859), Polish hasidic leader. Original thinker whose views differed sharply from classical Ḥasidism. Stressed search for truth rather than joy as means of approaching God. Interested in select, not masses. During last 20 years of life locked himself in room nr. pupils' study house and was rarely seen.

Kotsuji, Setsuzo (Abraham; 1899–1973), Japanese Hebraist. Presbyterian minister who taught Hebrew at Aoyama Gakuin Univ. Became proselyte in Israel 1959. Wrote autobiography *From Tokyo to Jerusalem.*

Kottler, Moses (1895–), S. African sculptor. His monumental figures for Johannesburg Public Library aroused controversy, as did his nude group at Population Register Building in Pretoria. Often inspired by biblical subjects.

Koufax, Sandford (Sandy; 1935–), U.S. baseball player, sportscaster. Struck out 18 batters to equal major league record 1959. Led Los Angeles Dodgers to two World Series championships. Youngest player ever elected to Hall of Fame 1972. Would never play on Rosh Ha-Shanah or Yom Kippur.

Koussevitzky, Moshe (1899–1966), *ḥazzan.* Warsaw 1927. At outbreak of WWII escaped to Russia; emigrated to U.S. 1947, *ḥazzan* in Temple Beth El in Brooklyn 1952. Powerful lyric tenor, outstanding *ḥazzan* of his time. His brothers **Jacob** (1903–1959), **Simcha** (1905–), and **David** (1911–), also noted *ḥazzanim.*

Koussevitzky, Serge (1874–1951), conductor; b. Russia. Virtuoso double-bass player. First public appearance as conductor in Berlin 1908. Founded Concerts Koussevitzky in Paris. Musical director of Boston Symphony Orchestra fr. 1925, which became one of world's greatest orchestras. Founded concerts at Tanglewood, Mass. 1935. Conducting style distinguished by nobility and emotional power.

Kovel, town in Ukrainian SSR. Jewish community fr. 1536; suffered severely during Chmielnicki massacres 1648–49. Jews predominated in light industry, building construction, wholesale and retail trade. 17,000 Jews in 1939. German occupation June 1941; extermination program gradually carried out. 250 Jews in 1970.

Abba Kovner, drawing by Miron Sima at Eichmann Trial, 1961.

Kovner, Abba (1918–), Lithuanian resistance fighter, Israel poet. A commander of Vilna ghetto; helped organize armed revolt, continued to fight Germans as leader of Jewish partisan groups. After WWII helped bring hundreds of thousands of Jews to Ereẓ Israel. Went to Ereẓ Israel 1945. His poetry oscillates between horrors of Holocaust and struggles in Ereẓ Israel. Israel Prize 1970.

Kovner, Abraham Uri (1842–1909), Hebrew writer, pioneer of modern Hebrew literary criticism; b. Vilna. Published essays in Hebrew press attacking Haskalah literature for lack of contact with contemporary life. Influential critic. After serving prison sentence in Siberia for forgery, converted to Christianity.

Kovno, see Kaunas.

Kowalsky, Judah Leib (1862–1925), Polish rabbi, Mizrachi leader. Pres. Mizrachi in Poland 1919; mem-

ber of Polish senate 1923. His works lost in WWII. Wrote in Yiddish and Hebrew press in Poland.

Koyré, Alexandre (1892–1964), philosopher, intellectual historian; b. Russia. Director of studies at Paris Ecole Pratique des Hautes Etudes fr. 1930; taught at U.S. univs.; Inst. for Advanced Study at Princeton 1956. Early writings concerned with Descartes. In 1930s began working on history of science.

Kozakov, Mikhail Emmanuilovich (1897–1954), Soviet Russian writer. Wrote on Imperial Russia and Revolution; portrayed historical figures. Some of his tales depict life in Jewish shtetl of old Pale Settlement.

Kozienice, Israel ben Shabbetai Hapstein (1733–1814), ḥasidic *ẓaddik,* popular preacher. Early propagator of Ḥasidism in Congress Poland. Devoted to ecstatic mode of prayer; wrote on *halakhah* and Kabbalah.

Kraft, Louis (1891–), U.S. social worker. Secretary of World Federation of YMHAs and Jewish Community Centers; pres. National Conf. of Jewish Communal Service and National Assoc. of Jewish Center Workers; founder of U.S. Service Organizations (USO).

Krakauer, Leopold (1880–1954), Israel artist, architect, designer; b. Vienna, settled in Ereẓ Israel 1924. His buildings are notable examples of second phase of Palestinian architecture. Made charcoal and brownwash drawings of countryside around Jerusalem.

Kramer, Jacob (1892–1962), British painter. Gifted draftsman. Utilized Jewish themes.

Kramer, Samuel Noah (1897–), U.S. Sumerologist. His research and

"The Warden" by Jacob Kramer.

Lithograph studies of Karl Kraus by Stumpp.

extensive travels in search of Sumerian literary texts fundamental in reconstruction of Sumerian literature. Prof. at Univ. of Pennsylvania.

Kramer, Stanley E. (1913–), U.S. film producer, director. Handled sensitive and controversial subjects, incl. *Home of the Brave* and *The Defiant Ones* on racial themes and *Judgment at Nuremberg* on trial of German judges for war crimes. Other films incl. *Death of a Salesman, High Noon.*

Kramer, Theodor (1897–1958), Austrian poet. Poetry champions underprivileged outcasts of society. Fr. 1938 in England.

Kramm, Joseph (1907–), U.S. playwright. Won Pulitzer Prize 1952 for *The Shrike,* drama about unhappy marriage.

Kranz, Jacob ben Wolf (Maggid of Dubno; 1741–1804), Lithuanian preacher. Appealed to scholars as well as to masses, in contact with Gaon of Vilna. His works published posthumously (*Ohel Ya'akov, Kol Ya'akov*).

Krasner, Lee (1911–), U.S. painter; wife of pioneer abstract expressionist Jackson Pollock. Work noted for dancing arabesques and calligraphic rhythms.

Kraus, Adolf (1850–1928), U.S. lawyer, civic and communal leader; b. Bohemia, in U.S. fr. 1865. International pres. B'nai B'rith 1905–25; helped establish its Anti-Defamation League.

Kraus, Karl (1874–1936), Austrian satirist, poet. One of greatest stylists in German language and vitriolic critic of liberal culture of pre-Nazi Austria. Founded *Die Fackel* 1899, aggressively satirical magazine. Converted to Catholicism 1898.

Kraus, Michael (1901–), U.S. historian. Taught at CCNY fr. 1925. Main area intellectual history; contributed to American historiography, notably in *The Writing of American History.*

Kraus, Oskar (1872–1942), Czech author, philosopher. Influenced by Albert Schweitzer; wrote character study on him. Dealt with general implications of Einstein's theory of relativity. In England fr. 1938.

Kraus, Paul (1904–1944), orientalist, historian of science; b. Prague, lectured in Cairo fr. 1935. His work revolutionized history of Islamic science.

Krause, Eliyahu (1876–1962), agronomist, pioneer in Ereẓ Israel; b. Russia; in Ereẓ Israel fr. 1892. Managed Sejera farm fr. 1901. Directed Mikveh Israel Agricultural School from 1914 and introduced Hebrew (instead of French) as language of instruction. His daughter, **Judith,** (1907–1936), archaeologist. Took part in Garstang's excavations at Jericho; directed excavations at Ai 1933–35.

Krauskopf, Joseph (1858–1923), U.S. Reform rabbi. Rabbi in Philadelphia. Leader of radical Reform, introducing Sunday services, active in national Reform Judaism. Assisted Jews to engage in agriculture. Instrumental in founding Jewish Publication Society of America.

Krauss, Friedrich Salamo (1859–?), Austrian ethnographer, folklorist. Specialized in S. Slavs, being first to make scientific investigation of these groups. Edited monthly folklore journal *Der Urquell* and wrote many important works on folklore. Active in Jewish communal affairs.

Samuel Krauss

Krauss, Samuel (1866–1948), Hungarian scholar. Lectured at Budapest and Vienna rabbinical seminaries (heading latter fr. 1932). Escaped to England 1938. His manifold studies ranged over philosophy, history, Bible, Talmud, Christianity, medieval literature. Main works incl. studies of Greek and Latin loanwords in Talmud, talmudic archaeology, and synagogue antiquities.

Krebs, Sir Hans Adolf (1900–), British biochemist; b. Germany, went to England with advent of Hitler. Prof. at Sheffield Univ. 1945, Oxford Univ. 1954. Fellow of Royal Society 1947. Nobel Prize 1953 for discovery of citric acid cycle.

Krein, Alexander Abramovich (1883–1951), Russian composer. Prof. at Moscow Conservatory. Leader of Jewish musical movement and member of Moscow Society for Jewish Folk Music. His music is lyrical, impressionistic, mingled with Jewish folk motifs. His brother **Grigori** (1880–1955), composer, violinist; lived in Paris and Tashkent. Grigori's son **Julian** (1913–), composer, pianist.

Kreinin, Meir (1866–1939), civic leader; b. Belorussia. Together with Dubnow, founded Jewish Folkspartei. Left Russia 1921, settled in Paris 1927. Chairman of Emigdirect (United Committee for Jewish Emigration). Settled in Ereẓ Israel 1934.

Kreisel, Henry (1922–), Canadian novelist, literary scholar. Taught English at Univ. of Alberta. His fiction shows concern for moral values and plight of dispossessed.

Jacob G. Kreiser

Bruno Kreisky

Kreiser, Jacob Grigoryevich (1905–1969), Russian soldier. Appointed commander of Third Army, responsible for directing operations on Kalinin front 1941, and subsequently held other senior appointments, becoming commander of Far East region. Hero of Soviet Union. Deputy to Supreme Soviet 1962.

Kreisky, Bruno (1911–), Austrian statesman. Active in clandestine Socialist Party; arrested 1935, spent two years in prison, emigrated to Sweden 1938, returned to Austria at end of WWII. Foreign Minister 1959–66; first Jewish chancellor of Austria 1970.

Kremenchug, city in Ukrainian SSR. Jewish settlement fr. 1782; increased in 19th c. by immigration from NW provinces of Russia. During WWI, site of yeshivot of Lubavich and Slobodka. Pogroms 1905, 1919. 28,969 Jews in 1926. Occupied by Germans 1941; many Jews murdered. 2,000 Jews in 1970.

Kremenets, town in Ukrainian SSR. Jews first mentioned 1438; prospered in 16th, 17th c., suffered during Chmielnicki massacres 1648–49 and Russian and Swedish wars. All 15,000 Jews murdered under German occupation.

Kremenetzky, Johann (1850–1934), Zionist, engineer, industrialist; b. Odessa, settled in Vienna 1880. Built first factory in Austria for electric bulbs. Elected to Zionist Executive at First Zionist Congress. First head of Jewish National Fund.

Kremer, Arkadi (1865–1935), Jewish labor leader in Russia. Among founders of Bund 1897, Russian Social Democratic Party 1898. Abandoned political life 1908.

Kressel, Getzel (1911–), bibliographer, Hebrew writer; b. Galicia, settled in Ereẓ Israel 1930. Wrote lexicon of Hebrew literature, history of journalism in Ereẓ Israel, etc.

Krestin, Lazar (1868–1938), Austrian painter. Specialized in landscape paintings, reflecting style of French impressionists. Also painted portraits and genre scenes of E. European Jewish life.

Krimchaks, name given to Rabbanite (in contradistinction to Karaites and Ashkenazi immigrants) aboriginal Jews of Crimea. Their language was Judeo-Tatar and they were distinguished by their dress and customs, which were Turkic. Number declined during Soviet rule of Crimea, exterminated by Germans during WWII.

Krinitzi, Avraham (1886–1969), Israel public figure; b. Grodno, settled in Ereẓ Israel 1908. Headed Ramat Gan's local government fr. 1926, mayor fr. 1950. Leading member of General Zionist (later Liberal) Party.

Krips, Josef (1902–), conductor. Conducted Vienna State Opera 1933–38, and fr. 1945. Chief conductor of London Symphony Orchestra 1950. Later moved to U.S.

Kris, Ernst (1900–1957), art historian, psychoanalyst. At Freud's request gave up medical studies 1933 and assumed editorship of journal *Imago*. Wrote standard work on stone cutting. Went to England 1938; in WWII organized dept. for analysis of enemy broadcasts; settled in U.S.

The Heilbronn synagogue, still burning on Nov. 10, 1938, after "Kristallnacht."

Kristallnacht (Ger. "Night of Broken Glass"), Nazi anti-Jewish outrage perpetrated Nov. 9–10, 1938; officially provoked by assassination of German diplomat in Paris by Polish refugee Herschel Grynszpan. Widespread attacks on Jews, Jewish-owned property, and synagogues throughout Germany and Austria. 30,000 Jews arrested and sent to concentration camps. 191 synagogues set on fire and another 76 completely demolished. Turning point in Nazi treatment of German and Austrian Jewry.

Kristeller, Paul Oskar (1905–), scholar of Renaissance thought; left Germany 1934; settled in U.S. Prof. at Columbia Univ. Major work study and interpretation of Italian humanistic thought of Renaissance. Also active in Jewish studies.

Kristeller, Samuel (1820–1900), German obstetrician, gynecologist. Introduced method, still used, to hasten ejection of placenta after birth.

Kroch, Jacob Leib ben Shemaiah (1819–1898), talmudic scholar; son-in-law of J.J.Falk. Specialized on subject of *ḥazakah* (presumption) versus *rov* (following majority). His 11-vol. *Ḥazakah Rabbah* published posthumously.

Krochmal, Abraham (d. 1888), scholar; son of Nachman Krochmal; b. Galicia. Wrote on Bible, Talmud, and philosophy; first to recognize Spinoza as pioneer of textual criticism of Bible.

Krochmal, Menahem Mendel ben Abraham (c. 1600–1661), chief rabbi of Moravia. His ordinances regulating organization of Moravian

Gustav Krojanker

communities in force until 1848. His writings contain important source material.

Krochmal, Nachman (Renak; 1785–1840), Galician philosopher, historian; among founders of "science of Judaism" and leader of Enlightenment in E. Europe. His understanding of Judaism in its historical manifestation is found in his widely-read *Moreh Nevukhei ha-Zeman.* Influenced by Hegel, Kant; saw each nation as having own spirit, and Jewish people's spirit as eternal. Pioneer in applying method of historical investigation to Hebrew literature, incl. *halakhah* and *aggadah.*

Krock, Arthur (1886–), U.S. journalist, newspaper editor. Influential Washington columnist for *New York Times.* Won several Pulitzer Prizes.

Krojanker, Gustav (1891–1945), German author, Zionist; b. Berlin. Studied role of Jews in German culture and literature. Among first to recognize danger to Jews posed by Nazi movement. Settled in Ereẓ Israel 1932. Wrote on Hebrew literature.

Kronecker, Hugo (1839–1914), Swiss physiologist; pioneer in study of blood pressure. Discovered coordinating center of heart and importance of inorganic salts for heartbeat.

Kronenberg, Leopold (1812–1878), Polish banker. Prominent in assimilationist circle of Warsaw community. Powerful in economic life. Became Christian but continued to intercede on behalf of Jews.

Kronenberger, Louis (1904–), U.S. dramatic, literary critic. Drama critic of *Time* magazine 1938–61. Prof. of theater arts at Brandeis Univ. 1953. Wrote on English stage comedy, American society, compiled several prose and verse anthologies.

Kroner, Richard (1884–), German philosopher, emigrated to U.S. after advent of Hitler. Prof. at Union Theological Seminary in N.Y., later at theological school of Temple Univ. Edited philosophical quarterly *Logos* 1910–38. Stimulated interest in Hegel.

Tombstone of Nachman Krochmal at Tarnopol, Poland.

Kross, Anna (1889–), U.S. lawyer, judge, penologist; b. Russia. Interested in penal reform, pioneered psychiatric and guidance services to assist court. Commissioner of correction in N.Y.C.

Krotoszyn town in Poland. Jewish community fr. 14th c. Known as center of Jewish learning and printing 1833–69.

Krupnick, Baruch, see Karu, Baruch.

Kuba, city in Azerbaijan SSR. Jewish community of Mountain Jews fr. 17th c. Many Jews fr. vicinity fled there 1734, and fr. Baku 1814. During civil war 1918–20 community suffered greatly. 10,000 Tat (q.v.) Jews in 1970.

Kubbuẓ, Hebrew vowel sign indicating short or long *u;* its written form ִ.

Kublin, Hyman (1919–), U.S. historian. Prof. at Brooklyn College, N.Y. Specialist in Far Eastern histroy, esp. modern Japan.

Kubovy (Kubowitzki) Aryeh Leon (1896–1966), Zionist leader, Israel diplomat; b. Lithuania. A leader of pre-war Belgian Jewry; went to U.S. 1940, directed World Jewish Congress rescue work for European Jewry. Settled in Israel 1948. Minister to Poland, Czechoslovakia; declared *persona non grata* during Slánský trial. Minister to Argentina, Chile. Chairman of Yad Vashem Remembrance Authority fr. 1959.

Kubrick, Stanley (1928–), U.S. film producer. Famed for imaginative films confronting contemporary problems, incl. *Dr. Strangelove, 2001: A Space Odyssey, A Clockwork Orange.*

°**Kuenen, Abraham** (1828–1891), Dutch theologian, biblical critic. First exponent of literary-critical school (preceding Wellhausen but unrecognized as he wrote in Dutch).

Kuh, David (1818–1879), Bohemian journalist, politician. Initially in favor of Czech nationalism and Jewish integration with Slav cause; after election to Bohemian parliament reversed opinion. Described as "father of the Viennese press."

Kuh, Ephraim Moses (1731–1790), German poet. Acquaintance of Mendelssohn and Lessing. Left 5,000 poems published posthumously.

Kuḥayl, Shukr Sālim (c. 1840–c. 1863), Yemenite pseudo-messiah. Had large following among masses. Considering him to be dangerous, king of Yemen sent men to ambush and kill him; then cut off his head and took it to San'a.

Kuhn, Thomas S. (1922–), U.S. historian of science. Prof. at Princeton fr. 1964. Wrote comprehensive study of nuclear physics.

Kuhn-Loeb, U.S. merchants, bankers. Firm Kuhn, Loeb and Co. founded 1867 by brothers-in-law **Abraham Kuhn** (1819–1892) and **Solomon Loeb** (1828–1913). Under Loeb's son-in-law Jacob H. Schiff banking business achieved great prosperity. Supported Jewish causes.

Kuibyshev (until 1935 **Samara**), city in Russian SFSR. Jews present fr. late 19th c. Community officially established 1895. 6,981 Jews in 1926. During WWII many refugees arrived there. Temporary headquarters of Jewish Anti-Fascist Committee. Jewish pop. 25,000 (1970).

Kukizow, family of Russian Karaite scholars. **Mordecai ben Nisan** (active 1698), wrote on Karaite history and doctrine. His great-grandson, **David ben Mordecai** (1777–1855), friendly with Nachman Krochmal. Wrote on Karaite calendar.

Kulbak, Moshe (1896–1940), Yiddish poet, novelist, dramatist. Published first symbolist poems as teacher in Vilna's Yiddish schools. Influenced by German expressionists. In USSR fr. 1928. Arrested by secret police 1937; d. in camp.

Kulisher, Michael (1847–1919), historian, ethnographer, communal worker. Published numerous articles and books in Russian and German, incl. life of Jesus, claiming that New Testament stories were legends. A founder of Jewish Society for History and Ethnography. His son **Joseph** (1878–1934), wrote on economic situation of Jews during Middle Ages. Another son, **Eugene** (1881–1956), jurist, legal historian; moved to Germany after Communist Revolution, later to France, then U.S.

Kultusverein (Ger. "religious union"), organizational form of Jewish communal life in Hapsburg monarchy 1848–90.

Kun, Béla (1886–1939), Hungarian revolutionary. Fought in Austro-Hungarian army during WWI, captured by Russians, joined Bolsheviks 1918. When Hungary proclaimed Soviet republic, became dictator. When Rumanians invaded Hungary 1919, fled to Moscow. Political commissar of Red Army of South. Discredited and executed.

Béla Kun

Kunfi, Zsigmond (1879–1929), Hungarian socialist. Commissar of education during Communist dictatorship of Béla Kun; resigned in protest against Kun's extremist policies. Fled to Austria 1919. Brilliant writer and translator; wrote on Jewish problems in Hungary.

Kunitz, Stanley Jasspon (1905–), U.S. poet, editor. Received Pulitzer Prize for *Selected Poems 1928–1958*. Edited reference works on literature.

Kunteres (Heb.), term for commentary on major work, e.g., Rashi on Talmud; in modern times, pamphlet or addendum to book.

Kuper, Simon Meyer (1906–1963), S. African Supreme Court judge. Chairman of S. African Jewish Board of Deputies 1944–49. Shot by unknown assassin.

Kupernik, Abraham (1821–1892), Russian communal worker, writer. One of wealthiest men in Kiev and leader of Jewish community. A founder of Society for Promotion of Culture among Jews of Russia 1863; joined Ḥovevei Zion. His son, **Lev** (1845–1905), converted to Christianity. Defended accused Jews in blood-libel trial of Kutais 1879 and in trial of members of Jewish self-defense in Gomel 1904.

Kuranda, Ignaz (1812–1884), liberal politician, communal leader in Austria; b. Prague. Became focus of Czech nationalist hatred of Jews, identified with Germans. Member of Diet of Lower Austria 1861–81, supporter of Centralism and German supremacy in Austria. Active in Jewish affairs.

Kurdistan, Middle East region, divided bet. Turkey, Iraq, Iran. Lived under unstable, anarchistic conditions. Over 100 Jewish communities in 12th c. 20–30,000 Jews in 1948, mainly in Iraqi area. Spoke Aramaic dialect (attesting to early origins), Turkish, Kurdish. After 1948 most emigrated to Israel.

Kurnub, see Mampsis.

Kursheedt, Israel Baer (1766–1852), U.S. merchant, broker, communal leader; b. Germany. Successful contractor supplying Prussian army. Emigrated to N.Y. 1796, Pres. Shearith Israel Congregation, organized Hebrath Terumath Hakodesh to aid Jewish community in Ereẓ Israel. Chairman of action committee protesting Damascus Affair 1840.

Kurzweil, Baruch (Benedict; 1907–1972), Israel literary critic, author, educator; b. Moravia. Settled in Ereẓ Israel 1939. Prof. of Hebrew literature at Bar-Ilan Univ. Represents New Criticism in modern Hebrew literature. Major cultural historian. Studies of Agnon's writings led to new and deeper appraisal.

Kushnirov, Aaron (1890–1949), Soviet Yiddish author. Wrote poems on Revolution and on pogroms in Ukraine; also short stories and verse plays.

Kutscher, Edward Yechezkel (1909–1971), Semitic scholar; b. Slovakia. Secretary of Hebrew Language Committee 1942. Prof. at Heb. Univ. and Bar-Ilan Univ. Published work on Dead Sea Isaiah Scroll and *Genesis Apocryphon.* Editor of *Leshonenu* (organ of Hebrew Language Academy).

Kutim, minor tractate appended to Talmud. Deals with relations bet. Samaritans *(Kutim),* Jews, and gentiles.

Kuzhmir, see Kazimierz.

Kuznets, Simon (1901–), U.S. economist; b. Russia. Prof. of economics at Harvard. Contributed to understanding of modern economic growth, encouraging new studies of economic growth of nations. Nobel Prize 1971.

Kvitko, Leib (1890–1952), Yiddish author. With David Hofstein and Peretz Markish, made up "Kiev lyric triumvirate." First poems won him immediate recognition. Achieved fame as one of greatest masters of children's verse. Arrested in 1949 Stalinist purges; executed.

Kwartin, Zavel (1874–1953), cantor, composer; b. Ukraine. Cantor at synagogues in Vienna, St. Petersburg, Budapest. Emigrated to U.S. 1919, cantor at Temple Emanuel of Brooklyn. Known for his lyric baritone, made many recordings. In Ereẓ Israel 1926–37.

K. Zetnik (pseud. of **Jehiel Dinur;** 1917–), writer on Holocaust; b. Poland, one of few survivors of Zaglembia concentration camp, settled in Ereẓ Israel, 1945. Wrote novels on horrors of Holocaust, incl. *House of Dolls, Piepel.*

Kurdish immigrants celebrating the "Seder" in Jerusalem, 1952.

Initial letter "L" for "Librum," from beginning of Book of Esther, "Moulins Bible," 12th-cent. Latin ms. from France.

La'az, vernacular gloss, esp. in Old French; best known used by Rashi in commentaries to Bible and Talmud. Important for study of medieval French.

Laban, brother of Rebekah; lived in Haran. Jacob served him for 14 years and in return received his daughters Leah and Rachel in marriage.

Laband, Paul (1838–1918), German jurist. Authority on constitutional law. Prof. at Strasbourg. Member of Alsace council 1879–1911, *Landtag* of Alsace-Lorraine fr. 1911. Held that constitutional law must be pure science excluding political and moral considerations.

Labi, Simeon (16th c.), Moroccan kabbalist of Spanish origin. Considered greatest scholar of Tripoli. Author of "*Bar Yoḥai*" sung by Oriental Jews on Sabbath eve and on Lag ba-Omer at Tomb of Simeon b. Yoḥai.

La Boétie, Etienne de (1530–1563), French humanist; apparently Marrano. Major work *Discours de la servitude volontaire* plea for human freedom and dignity against tyranny of rulers; first modern statement of nonviolence as means of protest.

Labor Zionist Organization of America, U.S. branch of Social Zionist party (Po'alei Zion); founded in Baltimore 1905. Introduced 1910 new trend in U.S. Jewish education, secular Jewish afternoon schools (Jewish Folk Schools). Founded Jewish National Workers Alliance (now Farband–Labor Zionist Order) 1912. Amalgamated with Ẓe'irei Zion 1931; assumed present name 1946. Published *Yidisher Kemfer* fr. 1906, *Jewish Frontier*, fr. 1934.

Lachish, Canaanite and Israelite city; identified with Tell al-Duwayr, SE of Bet Guvrin. Excavated 1933–38, 1966–68. Mentioned in Tell el-Amarna letters; captured by Joshua, fortified by Rehoboam, Asa, and Jehoshaphat, captured by Sennacherib; rebuilt in 7th c. B.C.E., destroyed in Persian period, finally abandoned 150 B.C.E.

Lachish Ostraca, collection of inscribed sherds discovered at Lachish, fr. period shortly preceding destruction of First Temple. Written in Hebrew in cursive script. Letters fr. local commanders to their superiors in face of Babylonian invasion. Now in British Museum.

Lachish Region development region in S. Israel, nr. ancient city Lachish. Six kibbutzim established 1939–47, 31 moshavim and kibbutzim 1948–53. Became prototype of regional planning for Israel.

Lachmann, Robert (1892–1939), musicologist; b. Germany. Made field studies of music of N. African countries. Wrote *Jewish Cantillation and Song in the Isle of Djerba.* Until 1933 librarian at Berlin State Library; then went to Ereẓ Israel, establishing archives of Oriental music recordings at Heb. Univ.

Lachower, Yeruḥam Fishel (1883–1947), critic, modern Hebrew literary historian; b. Poland. Edited publications in Warsaw. Settled in Ereẓ Israel 1927. Wrote major history of modern Hebrew literature.

Lachowicze, Mordecai ben Noah of (1742–1810), ḥasidic *ẓaddik.* Established Koidanov dynasty. Persecuted by *Mitnaggedim* and imprisoned. Succeeded by his son **Noah** (1774–1832).

Lachs, Manfred (1914–), Polish jurist; authority on international law. Member of Polish delegation to UN; lectured at Hague Academy of International Law; served as judge at International Court (pres. 1973).

Ladino (or **Judeo-Spanish**), Hispanic language written in Hebrew characters fr. end of Middle Ages, and its different dialects which crystallized among descendants of Jews expelled fr. Spain 1492 in their different lands of settlement: N. Africa, Balkan states, Turkey, Middle East, and

Conceptual sketch of Lachish by H.H. McWilliams.

One of the Lachish ostraca.

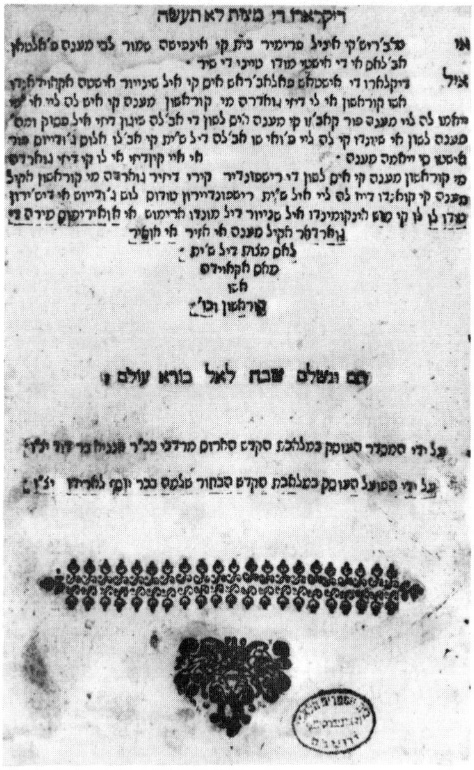

Colophon page of Ladino "Sefer Meshivat Nefesh" by Shabbetai Vidas, showing end chapter of last section dealing with negative commandments.

Simon von Laemel

Horacio Lafer

Toy gun made by a child for the celebration of Lag ba-Omer, Poland, 19th cent.

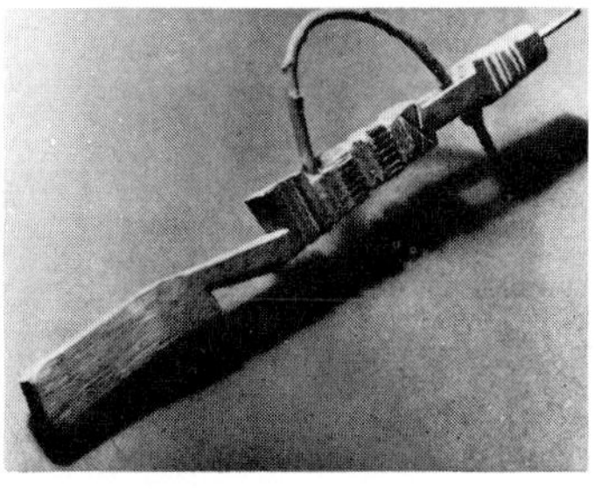

in modern times U.S. and Latin America. Over the centuries various names given to language: *Romance, Gudezmo, Spaniolish.* Through influence of countries to which refugees fled, gap began to appear bet. the written and spoken language on one hand and language of secular and rabbinical literature on the other. First printed book in Ladino appeared in Constantinople 1510, and widespread literature developed in subsequent centuries, notably in Balkans (with Salonika as a leading center).

Laemel, Simon von (1766–1845), Austrian merchant, philanthropist. Loaned government his entire fortune 1809 to bring about withdrawal of Napoleon's troops fr. Vienna. Ennobled 1811. Commissioner to army 1813. Upheld Jewish tradition, supported scholars, active on behalf of Bohemia and Viennese Jewry as *shtadlan.* His daughter **Elisa Herz** founded Laemel School in Jerusalem in his memory. His son, **Leopold** (1790–1867), one of most important financiers of Hapsburg monarchy. Active in Jewish affairs.

Laemmle, Carl (1867–1939), film producer; b. Germany, in U.S. fr. 1884. Bought up theaters; later organized wholesale motion picture exchange business. Founded Universal Studios. Produced first full-length feature film, *Traffic in Souls.*

Lafer, Horacio (1893–1965), Brazilian politician. Founder of Brazilian National Economic Development Bank, governor of World Bank, presided at International Monetary Fund Conference 1952. Minister of finance fr. 1951, foreign minister 1959–61. Active in Jewish affairs.

Lag Ba-Omer (Heb.), 33rd day of counting of Omer (falling on Iyyar 18); celebrated as semi-holiday since geonic period. Traditionally, commemorates cessation of plague which killed R. Akiva's pupils. Exact origin obscure and may be connected with Bar-Kokhba War. Traditional mourning customs kept during Omer period (incl. ban on weddings) are suspended. Orthodox 3-year-old boys given first haircuts. Also traditional anniversary of death of Simeon b. Yoḥai, and the occasion of pilgrimages to his grave in Meron.

La Guardia, Holy Child of, subject of blood libel who became revered as saint by Spanish populace. Six Conversos and two Jews were tried by Inquisition and burned at stake in town of Avila 1491. Story became subject of books and plays.

Laguna, Daniel Israel Lopez (c. 1653–c. 1730), poet of Marrano parentage; left Spain when imprisoned by Inquisition, settled in Jamaica and openly professed Judaism. Published paraphrase of Psalms in variety of Spanish verse forms.

°**Laharanne, Ernest** (19th c.), French writer; precursor of Zionism. Wrote pamphlet 1860 proposing Jewish state in Ereẓ Israel fr. Suez to Smyrna. Championed idea with romantic ardor. Moses Hess published large portions in *Rome and Jerusalem.*

Lahr, Bert (Irving Lahrheim; 1895–1967), U.S. comedian. Best known for film role of cowardly lion in *Wizard of Oz* and for Broadway performance as Estragon in *Waiting for Godot.*

Laish, see Dan.

Lambert, Aimé (1825–1896), French army officer. Took part in suppressing Paris rising 1848. During Franco–Prussian war 1870–71, town commander of Versailles. Commander-in-chief of French Occupation Army in Tunisia 1878.

Lambert, Mayer (1863–1930), French oriental scholar. Taught at Ecole Rabbinique and Ecole Pratique des Hautes Etudes. Published several works, incl. Saadiah's commentary on *Sefer Yeẓirah.*

Lamdan, Yiẓḥak (1899–1954), Hebrew poet, editor; b. Ukraine, settled in Ereẓ Israel 1920. His poetry reflected hopes and despair of Third Aliyah. Published, edited literary monthly *Gilyonot* fr. 1934. His epic poem *Massadah* reflects spirit of young pioneers of 1920s.

Lamech, antediluvian patriarch. Author of song which is example of early Hebrew poetry. Acc. to *aggadah,* accidentally killed Cain.

Lamech, Book of, apocryphal book referred to in Christian list of canonical and uncanonical books. No trace exists.

Lamed (ל), 12th letter of Hebrew alphabet; numerical value 30. Pronounced "l."

Lamed Vav Ẓaddikim (Heb. "36 righteous men"), acc. to Jewish legend, minimum number of anonymous righteous men in world in each generation, for whose merit world is preserved. So modest that identity known only to God. Theme prominent in ḥasidic and kabbalistic lore; reworked by André Schwarz-Bart in his *The Last of the Just.*

Lamentations, Book of, one of Five Scrolls in Hagiographa section of Bible, consisting of five poetic chapters lamenting destruction of Jeru-

salem by Nebuchadnezzar. First four poems alphabetic acrostics. Traditionally attributed to Jeremiah but his authorship not accepted by most modern scholars. Recited in synagogue to special cantillation on 9th of Av.

Lamentations Rabbah, Midrash on Book of Lamentations. Contains homilies on destruction of Temple and messages of comfort. Earliest source for stories of Ten Martyrs and Hannah and Her Seven Sons. Product of Palestinian *amoraim.*

Lamm, Martin (1880–1950), Swedish literary historian; son of liberal politician **Herman Fredrik Lamm** (1853–1928). Prof. at Academy (later Univ.) of Stockholm. Elected to Swedish Academy 1928.

Lamm, Norman (1927–), U.S. Orthodox rabbi. Prof. of Jewish philosophy at Yeshiva Univ., founder and first editor of Orthodox periodical *Tradition,* writer on contemporary problems.

Lamm, Pavel Aleksandrovich (1882–1951), Russian pianist, musicologist. Taught at Moscow Conservatory, director of State Music Publication Dept. in Moscow 1918–23. Produced scholarly edition of works by Russian composers, incl. complete works of Mussorgsky.

°**Lampon and Isidoros,** leaders of Alexandrian anti-Jewish movement during reigns of the Roman emperors Gaius Caligula (37–41 C.E.) and Claudius (41–54 C.E.). Launched attack on Jewish king Agrippa before court of Claudius 41 C.E.; ridiculed emperor and were sentenced to death.

Lampronti, Isaac Hezekiah ben Samuel (1679–1756), Italian rabbi, physician, educator. Head of Ferrara yeshivah. Author of *Paḥad Yiẓḥak,* monumental encyclopedic survey of *halakhah* in 155 ms. volumes.

Land, Edwin H. (1909–), U.S. inventor of Polaroid cameras and films, which revolutionized entire concept of negative-positive photography.

Landa, Abram (1902–), Australian lawyer, politician. Served in South Wales government as minister for labor and industry 1953–56, housing 1956–59, housing and cooperative societies 1959–65. Agent general for New South Wales in London 1965.

Landa, Myer Jack (1874–1947), English author, parliamentary reporter. Books incl. *The Jews in Drama.*

Landau, Adolph (1842–1902), Russian journalist, pioneer of rising Russian-Jewish intelligentsia. Founded, edited Russian–Jewish paper *Voskhod.* Attacked Ḥibbat Zion and later Zionists. Favored Jews of Russia acquiring Russian culture, but opposed rejection of Jewish values.

Landau, Edmund (1877–1938), German mathematician. Prof. of mathematics at Goettingen; resigned 1933 on Nazi advent. Main interest number theory.

Landau, Eleazar ben Israel (1778–1831), Polish rabbi, talmudist; grandson of Ezekiel Landau. Wrote commentary on Maimonides' *Mishneh Torah.*

Landau, Eugen (1852–1935), German banker, philanthropist. Founder, director of Rechte Oderuferbahn-Gesellschaft, played important role in building Silesian railroad, instrumental in organization of Allgemeine Elektrische Gesellschaft. Helped found Keren Heyesod in Germany.

Landau, Ezekiel ben Judah (1713–1793), Polish halakhic authority; known from his book of responsa as *"Noda bi-Yhudah,"* Rabbi of Prague and Bohemia fr. 1754; headed great yeshivah with students fr. many countries. Represented community before Austrian government. Took active steps to end Emden-Eybeschuetz controversy. His rulings incl. original and lenient decisions (e.g., permission to shave on intermediate days of festivals). Opposed Shabbateans, Frankists, study of Kabbalah and Ḥasidism.

Landau, Gregory Adolfovich (1877–1940), Russian journalist; son of Adolph Landau. Wrote for Russian and Russian-Jewish newspapers. Among founders of Jewish Democratic Group. Settled in Berlin after 1917 Revolution; left for Riga 1933; d. in Holocaust.

Landau, Isaac Elijah ben Samuel (1801–1876), Lithuanian preacher, biblical commentator. Representative of Volhynia in Russian government committee on religious affairs; official preacher and *dayyan* of Vilna.

Landau, Jacob (15th c.), German talmudist; lived partly in Italy. Worked for a time as proofreader. Wrote *Ha-Agur,* anthology and summation of German-Jewish scholarship on parts of *halakhah* down to his own time.

Landau, Jacob (1892–1952), journalist, publisher; b. Vienna, worked as journalist in Austria, Germany, Netherlands. Established news agency The Hague 1914, moved it to London 1919, renaming it Jewish Telegraphic Agency (JTA), with branches in Europe, U.S., Jerusalem. Established Overseas News Agency 1940.

Landau, Judah Loeb (Leo; 1866–1942). S. African rabbi, scholar, Hebrew poet, playwright; b. Galicia. Rabbi in Manchester 1900–14, then Johannesburg (later chief rabbi). Wrote historical melodramas based on themes drawn fr. relationship bet. gentiles and Jews during crises in Jewish history and his play, *Yesh Tikvah* was the first Heb. drama to be produced in modern times.

Yiẓḥak Lamdan

איכה רבתי

First page of "Lamentations Rabbah," Venice, 1545.

Ezekiel b. Judah Landau

Judah Loeb Landau

Lev D. Landau (and his wife) receiving Nobel Prize from Rolf Sohlman, Swedish ambassador to Moscow, 1962.

Landau, Lev Davidovich (1908–1968), Russian physicist. Head of theoretical dept. of Kharkov Technical Inst. 1932. Outstanding contribution in field of low temperatures. Nobel Prize 1962 for "pioneering theories for condensed matter, esp. liquid helium." Suffered severe injuries in car crash 1962, but intensive medical treatment enabled him to live for six years, although without resuming his researches.

Landau, Saul Raphael (1870–1943), early member of labor Zionist movement; b. Cracow. Close adviser to Herzl, instrumental in founding *Die Welt.* Participated in First Zionist Congress. Published articles on situation of Jewish workers in Galicia and Poland. Came into conflict with Herzl fr. 1898. Left Austria for U.S. 1938.

Landau, Shemuel Ḥayyim (1892–1928), religious Zionist. Conceived idea of "Torah va-Avodah" (Torah and Labor, basic ideology of religious Zionist pioneering in Ereẓ Israel). Leader of Young Mizrachi Organization. Fr. 1926 in Jerusalem.

Landau, Zishe (1889–1937), U.S. Yiddish poet; b. Poland, in New York fr. 1906. Joined Di Yunge literary group. Wrote popular poem on Ba'al Shem, poems on Jewish traditional themes, patriotic American poems.

Landauer, Georg (1895–1954), German Zionist leader. Active in Zionist "Blau-Weiss" movement and student organization. Director of Berlin Palestine Office 1925. Settled in Ereẓ Israel 1934. Director of Jewish Agency Central Bureau for Settlement of German Jews; organized capital transfer fr. Germany.

Landauer, Gustav (1870–1919), German philosopher, journalist. Wrote program for "Socialist Alliance" in which individual would replace states and capitalist economy. Minister of education in short-lived Bavarian Socialist Republic 1919. Murdered in Munich by counter-revolutionaries.

Gustav Landauer

Landauer, Meyer Heinrich Hirsch (1808–1841), German writer on philosophy of religion and Kabbalah. Pioneer of scholarly study of development of Jewish mysticism.

Landauer, Samuel (1846–1937), German orientalist, bibliographer. Taught oriental languages at Univ. of Strasbourg fr. 1874, later settled in Augsburg. First published Saadiah's *Beliefs and Opinions* in Arabic.

Landes, David Saul (1924–), U.S. economic historian. Prof. of history at Harvard 1964; directed its Center for Middle Eastern Studies 1966–68. Principal fields economic and social history of modern Europe.

Landesjudenschaft, Boehmische, organization of Bohemian Jewry outside Prague, founded 1659. Main function collection and distribution of Jewish taxes. Dissolved 1884.

Landesrabbinerschule, Hungarian rabbinical seminary in Budapest. Opened 1877, remained state institution. Outstanding library. When Nazis occupied Hungary 1944, seminary building sacked. Ten students in 1970.

Landjudenschaft, self-governing institution set up in almost all territories of Holy Roman Empire fr. mid-16th c. Essentially "intercommunal" body which acted both internally and externally. Main institution originally *Landtag,* assembly of all heads of families of territorial Jewish community.

Land of Israel, see Israel.

Landman, Isaac (1880–1946), U.S. Reform rabbi. Rabbi in Philadelphia 1906–16, N.Y. 1917–28, 1931–46. Editor of *American Hebrew* 1918–37, editor-in-chief of *Universal Jewish Encyclopedia.*

Landowska, Wanda (1877–1959), harpsichordist, pianist; b. Warsaw. Founded Ecole de Musique Ancienne nr. Paris 1919. Settled in U.S. 1941. One of first to revive harpsichord music.

Landrabbiner, rabbinical office formerly prevalent throughout C. Europe. Government appointed or recognized with civic rather than religious authority. In 20th c. became mainly honorary appointment.

Landsberg, Otto (1869–1957), German politician. Elected to Reichstag 1912, belonged to extreme right wing of Social Democratic Party. Minister of justice in first Weimar government, member of German delegation to Versailles. Opposed signing of peace treaty, resigned fr. government. German ambassador to Belgium 1920–23. Went to Holland 1933. In hiding during WWII.

Landsberger, Benno (1890–1968), Assyriologist; b. Silesia. Prof. at Leipzig 1926–35, Ankara, Turkey 1935–48, Univ. of Chicago fr. 1948. His publications cover almost every aspect of Assyriology. Made important contributions in field of Semitic philology. An editor of 10-vol. *Chicago Assyrian Dictionary.*

Landshuth, Eliezer (1817–1887), liturgical scholar, historian. Superintendant of Berlin cemetery. Attempted to establish period when most prayers were composed; compiled biographical and bibliographical dictionary on *paytanim.*

Landsmannschaften, immigrant benevolent organizations formed and named after members' birthplace, for mutual aid, hometown aid, and social purposes. Number in U.S. grew rapidly during WWI and played major role in absorption of Jews in U.S. Declined in membership and activities after 1930. Also significant in Latin America and Israel.

Landsteiner, Karl (1868–1943), scientist; b. Vienna, went to New York 1922. Member of Rockefeller Inst. for Medical Research. Nobel Prize 1930 for discovery of basic human blood groups. Also discovered blood factor. D. Roman Catholic.

Wanda Landowska

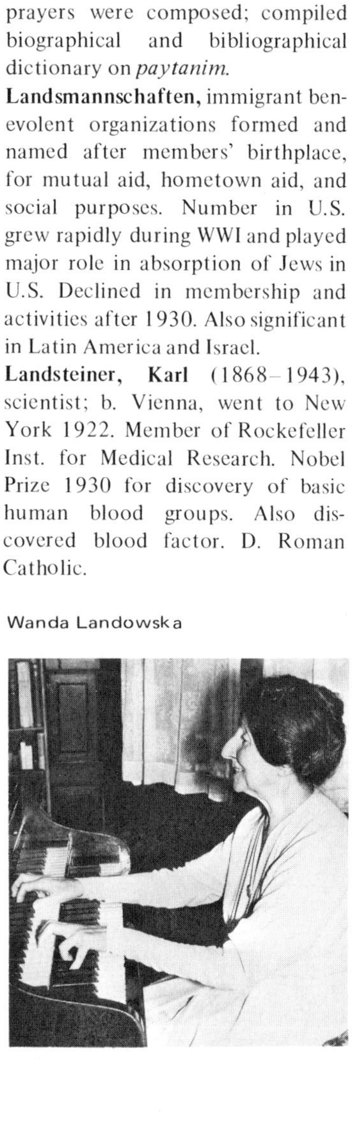

Scene from Fritz Lang's film "M," 1931, with Hannah Meron as the child and the shadow of Peter Lorre as the child murderer.

Lang, Fritz (1890–), film director, screenwriter; b. Vienna, in Berlin fr. 1919. Directed early classics *Metropolis* and *M*. Fled fr. Nazis to France, later to U.S. working for Metro-Goldwyn-Mayer. Directed *Fury, The Woman in the Window*, etc.

Langdon, David (1914–), British cartoonist, illustrator. Began drawing for Punch 1937. Contributed to various London papers. Illustrated humorous books.

Langer, Frantisek (1888–1965), Czech playwright, novelist, physician. Friend of Masaryk. Head of Czechoslovak Army Medical Corps. In London during WWII. Pres. Czechoslovak PEN Club. European Holocaust shocked him into new awareness of Jewish identity.

Langer, Jiří Mordechai (1894–1943), Czech poet, author; brother of Frantisek Langer. Rebelled against assimilatory upbringing and became strictly observant. Taught at Jewish school, wrote Hebrew poetry. Close friend of Franz Kafka, teaching him Hebrew. Settled in Erez Israel 1938.

Langfus, Anna (1920–1966), French novelist. Her experiences in Nazi-occupied Poland influenced her later writing. Emigrated to France 1946. Wrote plays, three powerful novels about Holocaust; one, *The Lost Shore*, awarded Prix Goncourt.

Languedoc, former province of SW France. Jews present in early 6th c.; in Middle Ages many prosperous communities with noted scholars. Jews expelled 1395. During 16th c. some Marranos found refuge there, and in last third of 18th c. Jews settled again.

Lapapa, Aaron ben Isaac (1604?–1667), Sephardi rabbi of Turkey. Halakhic authority on civil law in Smyrna. Excommunicated Shabbetai Zevi. Author of responsa on all parts of *Shulḥan Arukh*.

La Peyrère, Isaac (1594/96–1676), French theologian, Bible critic, anthropologist; probably of Marrano background, Calvinist who recanted and accepted Catholicism. Held that men existed before Adam, that no accurate copy of Bible exists, that Messiah is about to come and Jews will rule world fr. Jerusalem.

Lapidot, Alexander Moses (1819–1906), Lithuanian rabbi. Member of Ḥibbat Zion. Wrote articles on Torah and contemporary problems. Favored winning Erez Israel through agricultural labor.

Lapin, Israel Moses Fischel (1810–1899), *yishuv* leader. Became wealthy as contractor for building of Grodno railway. Settled in Jerusalem 1862. Contributed to many foundations and institutions; among founders of Kol Yisrael Ḥaverim for land resettlement in Erez Israel.

Lapson (Weinberg), Dvora (1907–), U.S. choreographer. Used Jewish folklore in theatrical form. Wrote *Dances of the Jewish People*.

Laqueur, Walter Ze'ev (1921–), Middle East historian; b. Germany, went to Erez Israel 1938, London 1955. Director of Wiener Library. Founded (1966) and co-edited *Contemporary History*. Taught at Univ. of Reading. Prof. at Univ. of Tel Aviv. Publications incl. history of Zionism.

Lara, David ben Isaac Cohen de (1602/10?–1674), philologist, lexicographer, writer, translator. Studied in Amsterdam and was appointed *ḥakham* of Spanish-Portuguese community in Hamburg. His talmudic lexicon *Keter Kehunnah* reveals his wide knowledge in

"That'd shake 'em. If all 600 million of us shouted 'bang!' in unison."

David Langdon cartoon, 1964

Semitic and European languages. Also translated ethical works fr. Hebrew into Spanish.

Lara, Ḥiyya Kohen de (d. after 1753), rabbi, kabbalist. Scholar of Ez Ḥayyim *bet midrash* in Amsterdam. Compiled talmudic lexicon *Mishmerot Kehunnah,* consisting of proverbs, sayings, moral reproofs.

Larin, Yuri (1882–1932), Russian political economist, communal leader. Following October Revolution, leading expert in economic affairs. Took great interest in agricultural settlement of Russian Jews; supported project of establishing Jewish republic in Crimea but opposed Birobidzhan plan.

Lasansky, Mauricio (1913–), printmaker; b. Buenos Aires, in U.S. fr. 1943. Head of world-renowned graphic arts workshop. Developed "Lasansky Method" of color printing.

Laserson, Max (1887–1951), Latvian jurist, historian, Zionist. Deputy director of national minorities in ministry of interior of Kerensky's 1917 government. Represented Socialist Zionist faction in Latvian parliament 1922–31. Helped found Tel Aviv School of Law and Economics. Emigrated to U.S. 1939, lectured at Columbia Univ.

Lask, Emil (1875–1915), German philosopher. His philosophy developed fr. neo-Kantianism of Windelband and Rickert. His later works approached subjectivism.

Lasker, U.S. family **Morris** (1840–1916), prominent merchant in Galveston; brother of Eduard Lasker; b. Prussia, in U.S. fr. 1856. Elected to Texas state senate 1895. **Albert Davis** (1880–1952), bought Chicago advertising agency Lord and Thomas 1898, making it largest of its kind in the world. Head of Republican National Committee's publicity dept. 1918, chairman of U.S. Shipping Board 1921–23. His sister **Florina** (1884–1949), chairman of National Council of Jewish Women's immigrant aid section; organized and presided over Consumers' League of N.Y. Another sister, **Loula Davis** (1886–1961), communal worker, Zionist. Chairman of Commission on Immigrant Aid and Immigrant Education for the N.Y. section of National Council of Jewish Women; active in Hadassah, as was her sister **Etta Lasker Rosensohn** (1885–). **Lasker, Eduard** (1829–1884), German liberal politician. Took part in 1848 revolution. Elected to Prussian parliament 1865. After 1870 led

Eduard Lasker

Harold Laski

Bora Laskin

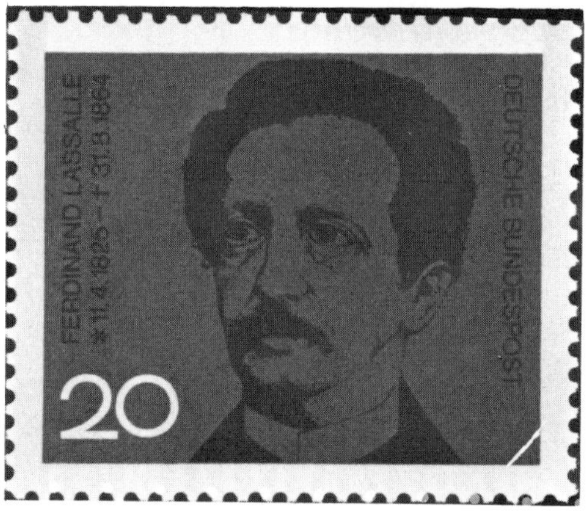

Portrait of Ferdinand Lassalle on stamp issued by German Federal Republic Post Office.

French Trappist monastery at Latrun, built 1890.

Liberal Party in Reichstag, helped Bismarck in securing Prussian leadership in Germany. Left National Party 1880 in protest against law limiting freedom of speech. Vigorous champion of Jewish rights. D. in U.S.

Lasker, Emanuel (1868–1941), chessmaster; b. Berlin, settled in New York. Defeated Wilhelm Steinitz for world title 1894, retaining it until 1921 when defeated by Capablanca. Taught advanced mathematics at various univs., wrote chess manuals.

Lasker-Schueler, Else (1869–1945), German poet. Major lyrical expressionist. Dealt with Jewish themes. Emigrated to Switzerland 1933; settled in Jerusalem 1938. Spent last years in dream world of her own.

Laski, English family, **Nathan** (1863–1941), cotton merchant. Headed Manchester Jewish community. His son, **Neville Jonas** (1890–1969), lawyer, judge. Held many offices in Jewish community; pres. Board of Deputies of British Jews 1933–39. Neville's daughter, **Marghanita** (1915–), novelist. Nathan's other son, **Harold Joseph** (1893–1950), political theorist. Taught at London School of Economics fr. 1920; had international reputation as teacher. Member of National Executive of British Labor Party fr. 1936, representing left intelligentsia; party chairman 1945. Influential in Fabianism and British socialism. Wrote many books on political theory.

Laskin, Bora (1912–), Canadian jurist. Lectured at Univ. of Toronto and Osgoode Hall Law School; prof. at Ontario Univ. Authority on constitutional and labor law. First Jewish member of Supreme Court of Canada fr. 1970. Chief Justice, 1974.

Laskov, Ḥayyim (1919–), Israel military commander. Led units in Latrun and Galilee in Israel War of Independence 1948; headed Israel Air Force 1951–53, armored corps 1956, chief-of-staff 1958–60. Headed port authority 1961–70.

Lasky, Jesse L. (1880–1958), U.S. pioneer film producer. Organized Jesse L. Lasky Feature Play Company with Goldwyn and DeMille 1913. After 1932 associated with leading companies and produced notable films.

Lassalle, Ferdinand (1825–1864), German socialist leader, lawyer, theoretician. Imprisoned during 1848 revolution. Developed theory of state socialism, champion of German working classes. Among founders of Germany's first workers' party, later German Social Democratic Party. Killed in duel over love affair.

Lassar, Oscar (1849–1907), German dermatologist. Introduced "Lassar paste." Campaigned for public hygiene. Prof. at Univ. of Berlin.

Laszlo (Laub), Philip Alexius De Lombos (1869–1937), English painter of Hungarian origin; converted to Christianity. Leading portraitist and society artist of his time.

Latif, Isaac ben Abraham Ibn (c. 1210–c. 1280), Spanish philosopher, kabbalist. Attempted synthesis of philosophy and Kabbalah, with considerable success and influence. Wrote *Sha'ar ha-Shamayim.*

Latrun, site in Ayalon Valley, Israel. Important historical crossroads. Arab village and 12th c. crusader fortress erected on earlier foundations. French Trappist monastery built c. 1890. During WWII site of British POW camp, subsequently used for members of Jewish underground and Jewish Agency leaders arrested 1946. In War of Independence, Israel forces lost many men and failed to dislodge Arab Legion blocking road to Jerusalem. Fell to Israel in Six-Day War 1967.

Latteiner, Joseph (1853–1935), Yiddish dramatist; b. Rumania. Wrote plays for Yiddish Theater *(Di Tsvey Shmelkes, Di Libe fun Yerushalayim).* Went to U.S. 1884, writing plays based on foreign sources, inserting lyrics, couplets, and slapstick humor. Some of his plays retained their popularity until WWII.

Lattes, Bonet (15th–16th c.), Italian rabbi, astronomer, physician; b. France, inventor of "ring" astrolabe worn on finger. Physician to Pope.

Lattes, Dante (1876–1965), Italian writer, journalist, educator. Among first to champion Zionism in Italy. Edited *La Rassegna Mensile di Israel* fr. 1922. Taught Hebrew language and literature at Inst. for Oriental Languages in Rome. In Jerusalem during WWII; subsequently played central role in reviving Italian Jewry.

Latvia, Baltic state; fr. 1940 Soviet republic. Jews in Courland fr. 16th c. Many of 190,000 Jews fled and expelled in WWI. Enjoyed autonomy as national minority 1919–34, with intense cultural life; suffered after Fascist coup. Remaining institutions disbanded under Soviet rule 1940–41. 85,000 Jews in 1941; 10,000 survived after 3 years of massacres

and deportations at hands of German occupiers and their Latvian collaborators. 50,000 Jews in 1970.

Latzky-Bertholdi, Jacob Ze'ev Wolf (1881–1940), journalist, Socialist leader; b. Kiev. Cofounder and ideologist of Jewish Socialist Workers' Party; appointed minister for Jewish affairs in government of independent Ukraine 1918. Settled in Ereẓ Israel 1935.

Laurence, William L. (1888–), U.S. journalist, science writer. *New York Times* science writer. Wrote official eyewitness account of atomic bombing of Nagasaki.

Laurents, Arthur (1918–), U.S. playwright. Plays inc.: *Home of the Brave, The Time of the Cuckoo.* Wrote book for musicals *West Side Story* and *Gypsy.*

Lauterbach, Jacob Zallel (1873–1942), U.S. Reform rabbi, talmudic scholar; b. Galicia, in U.S. fr. 1903. Prof. at Hebrew Union College, Cincinnati 1911–34. Edited *Mekhilta* and translated it into English, wrote essays on ritual questions and issues of modern Jewish life.

Jacob Z. Lauterbach

Lauterpacht, Sir Hersch (1897–1960), British jurist, international lawyer; b. Galicia. Taught at London Univ. fr. 1927; prof. of international law at Cambridge fr. 1938. Judge of The Hague International Court fr. 1954.

Lavi, Shelomo (1882–1963), agricultural pioneer in Ereẓ Israel; b. Plonsk, settled in Ereẓ Israel 1905. Worked as laborer. Conceived idea of "large collective" (i.e. "kibbutz") as distinct from "kevuẓah." A founder of En Ḥarod. Member of First and Second Knesset.

Lavon, Pinḥas (1904–), Israel labor leader. Founder of Gordonia movement in Poland 1924. Settled in Ereẓ Israel 1929, Secretary-general of Histadrut 1949–50, 1956–61, minister of agriculture 1950–52, minister of defense 1953-55. Mapai member of Knesset 1949–61. Central figure in so-called Lavon Affair, which became major issue in Israel politics.

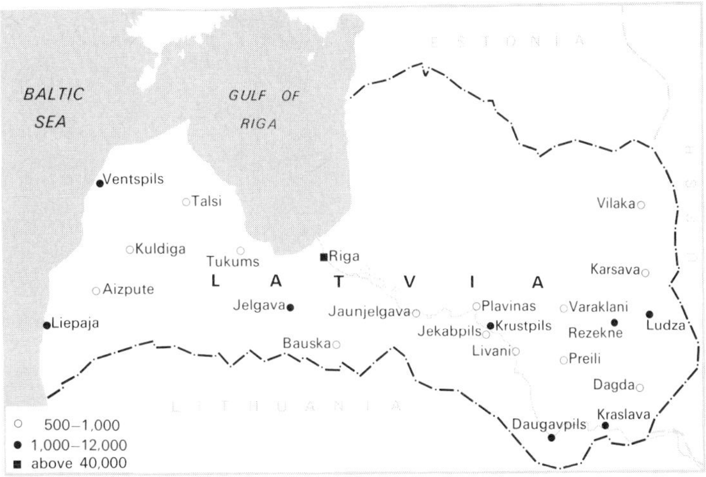

Jewish communities in Latvia (borders of 1918–40). Population figures for 1935.

Lavon Affair. Failure of Israel intelligence operation in Egypt 1954 led to resignation of Pinḥas Lavon, then minister of defense, in February 1955. In summer 1960 Lavon demanded fr. Ben-Gurion his rehabilitation on ground that he had not given order to carry out operation. This demand and its implications became major political issue within Israel for several years and led to major split in ranks of Mapai Party.

Lavry, Marc (1903–1967), composer, conductor; b. Riga, settled in Ereẓ Israel 1935. Director of music section of Kol Zion la-Golah radio station 1950. Wrote symphonic poems *(Emek),* opera *(Dan ha-Shomer),* oratorios, music for stage.

Law, see Torah.

Law of Return, basic law of State of Israel declaring that every Jew has right to settle in Israel as immigrant.

Lawrence, David (1888–1973), U.S. journalist. Veteran interpreter of Washington scene. Founded *U.S. Daily,* which became *U.S. News* 1933. Wrote on political affairs.

Lawson, family of English newspaper publishers, editors. **Joseph Moses Levy** (1812–1888), took over *Daily Telegraph,* making it major newspaper. His son, **Edward Levy-Lawson** (1833-1916), first Baron Burnham; further expanded paper, developed lively style, employed distinguished writers.

Layton, Irving (1912–), Canadian poet. His verse is touched with surrealism, Jewish irony, and bitter wit. Poet-in-residence at Sir George Williams Univ. in Montreal 1949-69.

Lazard, family of international bankers. **Alexandre,** b. France, emigrated to U.S. 1847. Started dry-goods business in New Orleans and took his two brothers **Simon** and **Elie** into partnership 1848. Moving to San Francisco during gold rush, they developed Lazard Frères into successful banking house, establishing branches in Paris and London.

Lazare, Bernard (1865–1903), French socialist writer. Early supporter of Dreyfus; published several books in his favor. Active in Jewish and Zionist life.

Lăzăreanu, Barbu (1881–1957), Rumanian socialist, writer, journalist. Expelled from Rumania 1907 because of support for rebellious peasants; settled in Paris. Joined editorial staff of socialist daily *L'Humanité.* Returned to Rumania, contributed to study of Rumanian folklore, elected to Rumanian Academy.

Lazaron, Morris Samuel (1888–), U.S. Reform rabbi in Baltimore. Identified with anti-Zionist American Council for Judaism.

Edward Levy-Lawson, caricature by Spy, "Vanity Fair," March 22, 1873.

Lazarsfeld, Paul F. (1901–), U.S. sociologist; b. Vienna, in U.S. fr. 1933. Prof. at Columbia Univ.; pres. American Sociological Association. Developed quantitative content analysis, as well as "panel" technique.

Lazarus, family of U.S. department store owners; started by **Simon** (d. 1877), who immigrated fr. Germany and opened store in Columbus, Ohio. By 1970, company operated 119 department stores, 12 specialty and discount stores, 63 supermarkets.

Lazarus, Emma (1849–1887), U.S. poet. Russian persecutions and flight of Jews to America awakened her Jewish consciousness. Translated poems by Judah Halevi, wrote essays which established her as pioneer American Zionist. Her "The New Colossus" is inscribed on Statue of Liberty.

Emma Lazarus

THE NEW COLOSSUS

Not like the Brazen Giant of Greek fame,
With conquering limbs astride from land to land;
Here at our sea-washed, sunset gates shall stand
a mighty woman with a torch, whose flame
Is the imprisoned lightning, and her name
Mother of exiles. From her beacon-hand
Glows world-wide welcome; her mild eyes command
The air-bridged harbor that twin cities frame.
"Keep ancient lands, your storied pomp!" Cries she
With silent lips. "Give me your tired, your Poor,
Your huddled masses yearning to breathe free.
The wretched refuse of your teeming shore.
Send these, the homeless, tempest-tost to me.
I lift my lamp beside the Golden Door!"

★

This tablet, with her sonnet to the Bartholdi Statue
Of Liberty engraved upon it, is placed upon these walls
In loving memory of
EMMA LAZARUS
Born in New York City, July 22nd 1849
Died November 19th, 1887.

Lazarus, Moritz (1824–1903), German philosopher, psychologist. Taught in Berne and Berlin. Wrote on psychology of nations. Opposed Jewish nationalism. His *Ethics of*

Moritz Lazarus with his wife, Nahida Ruth.

Judaism emphasizes religious character of obligation in Jewish ethics. His wife, **Nahida Ruth** née **Sturnhoefel;** (1849–1928), playwright, novelist, journalist, proselyte. Wrote on Jewish topics.

Lazurick, Robert (1895–1968), French journalist. Elected to Chamber of Deputies 1936. Founder, editor of *L'Aurore,* one of leading newspapers in Paris after WWII.

Leah, wife of Jacob. Married Jacob as result of her father Laban's trickery in substituting her for her sister Rachel. Had 6 sons, Reuben, Simeon, Levi, Judah, Issachar, Zebulun, and daughter, Dinah.

Leap Year, 13th month in Jewish calendar when additional month of Adar II is added to bring lunar year into line with solar year. Occurs 7 times in 19 years.

Leaven, see Ḥameẓ.

Leavitt, Moses A. (1894–1965), leader in American Jewish Joint Distribution Committee (secretary fr. 1940). Directed Joint aid fr. U.S. to Nazi-occupied Europe. A central figure in post-war period and in assisting immigration to Israel.

Lebanon, Middle East country running N. of Israel. Flora and fauna extolled in Bible; cedars used in First and Second Temples. In Hellenistic and Roman periods divided bet. Phoenician cities; became part of Syrian province and fr. 3rd c. separate province (Phoenicia). Scant information on existence of Jews in 7th–15th c. but small Jewish communities continued to exist. Development of modern country accompanied by increase in Jewish pop., mostly of Sephardi origin. Jews arrived, esp. in Beirut, fr. Greece and Turkey, gradually becoming important commercial factor. By 1920, 5,000 in Beirut alone. Did not suffer fr. establishment of State of Israel. Until 1958 number of Jews remained at c. 9,000, bolstered by Jews fr. Syria. Subsequently many left. Jewish pop. 2,500 (1971) mostly in Beirut.

Lebensohn, Abraham Dov (Adam ha-Kohen; 1794–1878), Hebrew poet during Haskalah period. In his native Vilna, leader of *maskilim* and taught in rabbinical school. Spokesman of Russian Haskalah in its early period; had superb command of Hebrew language, contributed to Hebrew press. His poems describe conflict between optimism (enlightened rationalism) and harsh reality of life.

Micah J. Lebensohn

Lebensohn, Micah Joseph (Mikhal; 1828–1852), one of foremost Hebrew poets of Haskalah; son of Abraham Dov Lebensohn. At age 17 severely stricken with tuberculosis, which had effect on his poetry and caused his early death. Themes of his epic poetry incl. life and death *("Shelomo ve-Kohelet"),* visionary and his fate *("Moshe al Har ha-Avarim," "R. Yehudah ha-Levi"),* moral conflict bet. human feelings and patriotic duty *("Ya'el ve-Sisra," "Nikmat Shimshon").*

Lebo-Hamath, place frequently mentioned in Bible as N. boundary mark of Ereẓ Israel. Identified with Labwa in N. Lebanese Beqa.

Lec, Stanislaw Jerzy (1909–1966), Polish poet. Wrote deeply contemplative verse. In WWII, spent 2 years in concentration camp before escaping to Warsaw, editing illegal periodicals there; officer in Polish partisans. Moved to Israel 1950, returned to Poland 1952. Published epigrams and aphorisms.

Leczyca (Lentshits), town in Poland. Jews fr. 1453. During Swedish wars in 17th c. 3,000 killed, but community subsequently reestablished. 4,300 Jews in 1939; almost entire community murdered in WWII.

Leda, Eduard (1859–1943), Czech author. Leader of Jewish assimilation in Czechoslovakia. Portrayed many Jewish characters, expressing through them his own thoughts on Jewish problem. D. in Theresienstadt.

Lederberg, Joshua (1925–), U.S. geneticist. Prof. at Univ. of Wis-

consin 1947, Stanford Univ. 1959; director of Kennedy Laboratories for Molecular Biology and Medicine 1961. Nobel Prize 1958 for studies on organization of genetic material in bacteria.

Lederer, Abraham (1827–1916), Hungarian educator, pedagogic writer. Appointed by government to head Jewish "model school" of Budapest 1857. Pioneer of summer holiday camps for schoolchildren in Hungary; founder of nationwide Organization of Jewish Teachers in Hungary 1866.

Lederer, Jerome F. (1902–), U.S. aeronautical engineer. Director of manned space flight safety for NASA fr. 1967.

Lee, Sir Sidney (1859–1926), English literary historian. Prof. of English at London Univ. Editor of *Dictionary of National Biography*. Wrote standard *Life of Shakespeare*, etc.

Leeds, city in England. Jewish community founded c. 1823, first synagogue 1860. In late 19th c. many Russian and Polish immigrants settled, giving impetus to tailoring industry. Jewish pop. 18,000 (1972), highest proportion in Britain (3.5%).

Leeser, Isaac (1806–1868), U.S. rabbi, writer, educator, b. Germany, in U.S. fr. 1824. *Ḥazzan* in Philadelphia; founded first Jewish Publication Society of America, first Hebrew high school 1849, and first rabbinical school (Maimonides College) 1867. As editor of monthly *The Occident* (founded by him 1843) influenced Jewish communities in America, and his English translation of Bible 1845 became standard for nearly seven decades.

Lefin, Menahem Mendel, see Levin, Menahem Mendel.

Lefrak, Samuel J. (1918–), U.S. builder, philanthropist. Became New York City's largest landlord, housing c. 300,000 persons in his buildings 1969. U.S. delegate to Economic Commission for Europe 1969.

Lefschetz, Solomon (1884–), U.S. mathematician. Prof. at Princeton Univ. Important contributions in algebraic geometry, topology, and differential equations.

Leftwich, Joseph (1892–), English author, editor. Headed London branch of Jewish Telegraphic Agency 1921–36. Authority on Jewish and Yiddish literature. Translated fr. Yiddish. Edited anthologies. Director of British Federation of Jewish Relief Organizations 1945.

Leghorn (Livorno), Italian port. Jews invited to settle with full rights 1593 incl. right of Marranos to return to Judaism. Free port status 1675 with Jews becoming influential. Only community in Italy without closed ghetto; among most important in W. Europe. Situation deteriorated after French occupation 1796. Eminent rabbis lectured at famous yeshivot and synagogues. Center of Hebrew printing. 600 Jews in 1965.

Leḥi, see Loḥamei Ḥerut Israel.

Lehman, U.S. family. **Henry** (1821–1855), **Emanuel** (1827–1907), and **Mayer** (1830–1897), immigrant sons of Bavarian cattle merchant. Formed Lehman Brothers partnership in Montgomery, Alabama 1850. Opened N.Y. office 1858. By 1906 entered investment banking and underwriting, with emphasis on consumer-oriented issues. Separate investment company, Lehman Corp., formed 1929. Emanuel's grandson, **Robert** (1891–1969), built firm into one of four largest investment banks in U.S. by 1967. Owned one of greatest private art collections in world, bequeathing it to Metropolitan Museum.

Lehman, Herbert Henry (1878–1963), U.S. banker, statesman. Partner in firm of Lehman Bros. (see above) fr. 1908. Democratic lieutenant governor 1928–32, governor 1932–42 of N.Y. First director-general of UN Relief and Rehabilitation Agency (UNRRA) 1943–46. Senator fr. N.Y. 1949–57. Supporter of New Deal, social security, civil rights. Active in Jewish affairs.

Lehman, Irving (1876–1945), U.S. jurist; brother of Herbert H. Lehman. N.Y. State Supreme Court justice until 1924; judge on N.Y. State Court of Appeals 1924–45. Pres. American Jewish Committee.

Lehmann, Behrend (1661–1730), Court Jew of Saxony. Earned confidence of Augustus II, elector of Saxony, and supplied him with funds to secure his election as king of Poland. Diplomatic agent, financier, military contractor, using his influence to improve legal position of Jews.

Lehmann, Emil (1829–1898), lawyer, politician. Advocate of Reform Judaism and Jewish emancipation in Saxony. Pres. Dresden congregation. Fought rising anti-Semitism inspired by A. Stoecker. Pleaded for radical religious reform, removing circumcision and Jewish holidays.

Lehmann, Joseph (1843–1917), French rabbi. Director of Ecole

Jews' Quarter of Leeds, drypoint by Muirhead Bone, early 20th cent.

Isaac Leeser

Engraving of Leghorn synagogue executed on completion, 1789, building destroyed WWII.

Herbert H. Lehman at his inauguration as governor of New York, 1933, with his predecessor Alfred E. Smith (right) and president-elect Franklin D. Roosevelt (left).

Rabbinique; liberal in his religious opinions.

Lehmann, Karl (1894–1960), classical archaeologist; authority on Roman archaeology and art. Lectured at Heidelberg and Muenster Univ.; dismissed 1933, emigrated to U.S. Prof. at Fine Arts Inst. of NYU. Excavated at Samothrace.

Lehmann, Marcus (1831–1890), German Orthodox rabbi, scholar, writer. Founder, editor of weekly *Israelit.* Established religious day school in Mainz. Wrote historical novels of religious educational value and popular edition of *Haggadah.*

Lehmann, Siegfried (1892–1958), Israel educator; b. Berlin, settled in Ereẓ Israel 1926. Founded Ben Shemen Youth Village, model of modern rural education. Arrested 1940 after British police found arms in Ben Shemen; sentenced to 7 years' imprisonment, released 3 weeks later through intervention of Albert Einstein and other leading figures. Israel Prize 1957.

Lehranstalt fuer die Wissenschaft des Judentums, see Hochschule fuer die Wissenschaft des Judentums.

Lehren, family of Dutch bankers, philanthropists. **Hirschel** (1784–1853), founded 1809 with A.Prins and S. Rubens organization to concentrate collection of money for distribution in Ereẓ Israel.

Lehrer, Leibush (1887–1965), Yiddish writer, educator; b. Poland, lived in Belgium, emigrated to U.S. A prime mover in development of Shalom Aleichem schools.

Leibowitz, Baruch Ber (1866–1939), Lithuanian talmudic scholar, *rosh yeshivah.* Head of Keneset Bet Yiẓḥak Yeshivah in Slobodka 1904 (in Kamenetz fr. 1926). His *Birkat Shemu'el* is regarded as classic.

Leibowitz, Joshua O. (1895–), medical historian, Hebrew scholar; b. Vilna, settled in Ereẓ Israel 1935. Clinical prof. and head of division of history of medicine at Heb. Univ. fr. 1959.

Leibowitz, Rene (1913–), composer. Chief advocate of Schoenberg school in France.

Leibowitz, Samuel Simon (1893–), U.S. lawyer, jurist. Flamboyant attorney who defended Al Capone four times. Became impassioned jurist who imposed severe sentences on criminals and extirpated corrupt officials. Appointed to N.Y. State Supreme Court 1961.

Leibowitz, Yeshayahu (1903–), Israel scientist, man of letters; b. Riga. Settled in Ereẓ Israel 1935. Prof. of organic and biochemistry and neurophysiology at Heb. Univ. fr. 1961. Editor-in-chief of vols. 10-13, 16-20 of *Encyclopedia Hebraica.* His sister **Neḥama(h)** (1905–), Bible scholar. Taught Bible at Tel Aviv Univ. fr. 1957. Israel Prize 1957.

Leibzoll (Ger. "body tax"), tax levied on Jews in medieval Europe on entering territories or cities; accompanied by humiliating legal formulas.

Leichtentritt, Hugo (1874–1951), musicologist, composer; b. Poland, taught in Germany; lecturer at Harvard Univ. after 1933. Composed symphony, comic opera, chamber music, opera *Esther,* and cantata *The Song of Solomon.*

Leinsdorf, Erich (1912–), conductor; b. Vienna, in U.S. fr. 1937. Director of N.Y.C. Opera 1955, Boston Symphony Orchestra 1962.

Leipzig, city in E. Germany. Germanized Jewish community in mid-13th c. Fair regulations of 1268 guaranteed protection to all merchants, and moved market day from Saturday to Friday for benefit of Jews. Expelled 1540, settlement refounded 1710. Hebrew books printed there until 1520 and in 17th c. After 1868/69, number of Jews increased greatly by immigration from Galicia and Poland. 10,000 Jews in 1938; by early 1942, 2,000 remained; last transport to Theresienstadt Feb. 1945. 120 Jews in 1968.

Leiserson, William Morris (1883–1957), U.S. labor economist, arbitrator. Helped draft U.S. Social Security Act 1934. Prof. at Antioch College, Secretary of National Labor Board, chairman of National Mediation Board, member of National Labor Relations Board.

Leivick, H. (pseud. of **Leivick Halpern;** 1886–1962), Yiddish poet, dramatist; b. Belorussia, exiled to Siberia, escaped to U.S. 1913. Wrote successful dramas *(Der Goylem, Shmates)* and after WWII moving poems on Holocaust. One of leading Yiddish writers of 20th c.

Lekert, Hirsch (1880–1902), Lithuanian revolutionary. Bootmaker by profession. Active in Bund. Famed for his assassination attempt on governor of Vilna after he ordered flogging of 26 demonstrators. Hanged. Commemorated in songs and stories.

Leket, Shikhḥah, and **Pe'ah** (Heb. "gleanings, forgotten produce, and corners of field"), talmudic designation of three portions of harvest which farmer was enjoined to leave for benefit of poor and strangers. Rabbis applied these laws even to those outside Ereẓ Israel.

Sketches of H. Leivick by Enrico Glicenstein.

Hirsch Lekert

Opening of "Lekhah Dodi" from ms. "Seder Tikkunei Shabbat," Vienna, 1715.

Lekhah Dodi (Heb. "Come, my friend"), opening words and name of hymn with which Sabbath is welcomed; one of favorite hymns in all rituals. Written by Solomon ha-Levi Alkabeẓ (16th c.), it reflects practice of greeting "Queen Sabbath" as well as kabbalistic identification of Sabbath with *Shekhinah,* mystical archetype of Israel.

Lelouch, Claude (1937–), French film director. Achieved fame with first feature film *Un homme et une femme.*

Lelov, David ben Solomon of (1746–1813), founder of ḥasidic dynasty in Poland; grocer by trade. Much appreciated by prominent ḥasidic leaders of his day. Teachings stressed love of Jewish people and man in general.

Lelov, Moses (1778–1850), ḥasidic leader; son of David b. Solomon. Toward end of life settled in Ereẓ Israel; since then part of Lelov dynasty connected with Israel.

Lelyveld, Arthur Joseph (1913–), U.S. Reform rabbi, community leader. National director of B'nai B'rith Hillel Foundations 1947–56; rabbi of Fairmount Temple in Cleveland fr. 1958; pres. American Jewish Congress 1966–72.

Lemans, Moses (1785–1832), Dutch Hebraist, mathematician. Leader of Haskalah movement. A founder of "Chanogh lanangar ngal pie darkoo" society to reform Jewish education. Published Hebrew texts and translated Bible into Dutch. Head of first school for needy Jews, Amsterdam 1818.

Lemberg, see Lvov.

Lemkin, Raphael (1901–1959), international lawyer who initiated use of term "genocide." Secretary of Court of Appeal in Warsaw. In U.S. fr. 1941. Taught at Duke, Yale Univ. Mobilized support to have genocide put on UN agenda and have convention adopted.

Lemlein (Lammlin), Asher (16th c.), false messiah, active 1500–2 in NE Italy and Germany. Claimed redemption approaching because Messiah (Lemlein) had already come. Claims stimulated asceticism and repentance movement. Movement ceased to exist after his death.

Lemuel, apparently foreign king to whom instruction in Proverbs 13:2–9 is addressed by his mother.

Lengyel, Emil (1895–), U.S. writer; b. Budapest; prisoner of war in Siberia in WWI. Taught at NYU and Fairleigh Dickinson Univ. Wrote on Middle Eastern affairs.

Lengyel, József (1896–), Hungarian author, poet. A founder of Hungarian Communist Party. Eventually settled in Moscow. Imprisoned 1938 in Soviet concentration camp; released 1955, returned to Hungary. Works describe horrifying world of those condemned to slow death.

Lengyel, Menyhért (Melchior; 1880–), Hungarian playwright. Best-known play *Typhoon,* which dealt with Japanese danger to world. Wrote story for Bartók's ballet *The Mandarin.* Film scripts incl. *Catherine the Great, The Blue Angel, Ninotchka.*

Leningrad (St. Petersburg until 1914, **Petrograd** until 1924), city in Russia. Apostates or Marranos appeared there soon after foundation 1703. By end of reign of Catherine I, large Jewish community. Government center for Russian Jews fr. end of 18th c. Residence prohibited under Nicholas I, situation changed under Alexander II. By 1881, 17,253 Jews. Community important in Russian Jewish life because of wealth of individual members and proximity to royal court. Center of Russian-Jewish journalism, literature. Residence restrictions abolished 1917. On eve of Nazi invasion 200,000 Jews. Jewish pop. 165,000 (1971), with one synagogue.

Lenski, Ḥayyim (1905–1942), Soviet Hebrew poet. Arrested 1934 for writing in Hebrew and sent to Siberia. His poems published in Israel as *Me-Ever Nehar ha-Lethe* ("Over the River Lethe").

Lentshits, see Leczyca.

Leo Baeck Institute, organization founded by Council for Jews fr. Germany 1955, with purpose of collecting material and sponsoring research on history of Jewish community in Germany and other German-speaking cultures. Branches in Jerusalem, London, New York.

Leo Hebraeus, see Abrabanel, Judah.

Leon, ancient kingdom in Spain. In 11th c. its Jews enjoyed special privileges as they were under royal jurisdiction. Rights successively curtailed fr. 13th c. Jewish quarter pillaged in 1449. Expelled 1492.

Leon, Harry Joshua (1896–1967), U.S. classics scholar, historian. Taught classical languages at Univ. of Texas. Writings incl. *A History of the Jews of Ancient Rome,* mostly based on careful analysis of inscriptions in Jewish catacombs.

León, Luis de (1528–1591), Spanish poet, humanist, Augustinian friar. Prof. at Univ. of Salamanca. Imprisoned 5 years on charges of Judaizing but acquitted. Wrote verse (including a Spanish translation of Song of Songs), theological and exegetic works invoking support of Christian Kabbalah.

Leon, Messer David ben Judah (1470/72? –1526?), Italian rabbi, religious philosopher. Involved in fierce intercommunal arguments while rabbi of Valona, Albania. Admirer of Maimonides; combined vast erudition in Jewish subjects with comprehensive knowledge of general culture, esp. philosophy.

Leningrad synagogue, completed 1893.

Engraving of Myer Leoni as Don Carlos from comic opera "The Duenna."

Leonard, Benny (1896–1947), U.S. prize fighter, considered greatest lightweight in history of boxing. World champion 1917–25, retiring undefeated. Boxing referee fr. 1943; collapsed and died in ring.

Leonard, Lotte (1884–), soprano. Specialized in lieder, oratorio parts. Soloist in concerts with Berlin Philharmonic Choir and at German Bach and Handel festivals. Left Germany 1933; subsequently taught in Paris and U.S.

Leone de Modena, see Modena, Leone.

Leone Ebreo, see Abrabanel, Judah.

Leoni, Myer (d. 1796), English cantor. Opera singer prior to becoming cantor at Great Synagogue in London 1767. Forced to resign after singing in Handel's *Messiah.* Reader at Ashkenazi synagogue, Kingston, Jamaica.

Leontopolis, locality N. of Cairo, Egypt. Settlement of Jewish emigrant soldiers fr. Judea established

there under leadership of high priest Onias IV in 2nd c. B.C.E. Temple to God of Israel erected there; closed by Romans 73 C.E. Jewish soldiers played role in political life of Egypt.

Leontovich, Eugenie (1900–), actress; b.Russia; wife of Gregory Ratoff (1893–1960). Founded repertory theater in Los Angeles; joined Goodman School of Drama in Chicago.

Lerer, Yehiel (1910–1943), Yiddish poet; lived in Warsaw. Participated in Warsaw ghetto literary activity; killed in Treblinka.

Lérida, city in Spain. Jewish quarter in 11th c., destroyed 1391. Community reestablished 1460. District tribune of Inquisition established 1490 and community ended with expulsion fr. Spain.

Lerma, Judah ben Samuel (16th c.), scholar of Spanish origin, lived in Italy. Wrote commentary on *Avot* in style of Spanish-Jewish philosophers.

Lerner, Abba Petachja (1903–), U.S. economist; b. Russia. Taught at London School of Economics fr. 1935. In U.S. fr. 1942. Taught at New School for Social Research, Michigan State Univ., Univ. of California. Economic adviser to government of Israel 1953–56. Publications incl. *The Economics of Control* and *Essays in Economic Analysis.*

Lerner, Alan Jay (1918–), U.S. lyric writer, librettist. Best known for collaboration with composer Frederick Loewe. Hits incl. *Brigadoon, Paint Your Wagon, My Fair Lady, Gigi, Camelot.* Won Oscar for screenplay of *An American in Paris.*

Lerner, Ḥayyim Ẓevi ben Todros (1815–1889), Hebrew grammarian, pedagogue in Russia. Author of successful Hebrew grammar *Moreh ha-Lashon,* first to lay down rules for teaching children essentials of Hebrew grammar. Taught at government rabbinical seminary in Zhitomir (1851–73).

Lerner, Joseph Judah (1849–1907), writer, dramatist, scholar; b. Berdichev. Contributed to Hebrew, Russian, Yiddish press. Wrote about Jewish life in Russia in 1890s. Converted to Christianity.

Lerner, Max (1902–), U.S. author, journalist. Taught at various univs., fr. 1949 at Brandeis. Known for works on American society and science of government, incl. *America as a Civilization,* and *The Age of Overkill.* Managing editor of *Encyclopaedia of Social Sciences,* edited *The Nation* 1936–38, syndicated columnist for N.Y. *Post.*

Lerner, Mayer ben Mordecai of Altona (1857–1930), rabbi of Altona and Schleswig-Holstein 1894–1930. Vigorously opposed historical approach of Graetz and Reform movement in Germany. Talmudic works incl. *Torat ha-Mishnah,* dealing with origin of oral tradition. Actively interested in Jewish settlement of Ereẓ Israel.

Le Roith, Harold Hirsch (1905–), S. African architect. Translated concepts of functionalism into much of his work in Johannesburg and other S. African cities.

Le Roy, Mervin (1900–), U.S. film producer, director. Films incl. *The Wizard of Oz, Quo Vadis?*

Leslau, Wolf (1906–), U.S. Semitics scholar, philologist; b. Poland; Taught in Paris, emigrated to U.S. 1942. Taught at UCLA fr. 1955. Wrote on culture, folklore (with special attention to Falashas), and various Semitic languages of Ethiopia. Works incl. *Falasha Anthology.*

Lesmian (Lesman), Boleslaw (1878–1937), Polish poet. A leading representative of Young Poland symbolist poetry group, forerunner of Polish surrealists.

Lesser Poland (Malopolska), historical region in SW Poland. Jews mainly in Krakow and Sandomierz provinces. Four representatives at Council of Four Lands came fr. region and its Jewry and leadership enjoyed influence disproportionate to their numbers (60,000 in 1764).

°**Lessing, Gotthold Ephraim** (1729–1781), German dramatist, philosopher, critic. First to present Jew on German stage in objective manner. Friend of Moses Mendelssohn, who was inspiration for his last play *Nathan der Weise,* a plea for toleration.

Lessing, Theodor (1872–1933), German philosopher; converted to Lutheranism as student but returned to Judaism with rise of Zionism. Assassinated by Nazis at Marienbad. Works incl. *Der juedische Selbsthass,* clinical study of Jewish intellectuals who succumbed to self-hatred.

Gotthold E. Lessing

Lester, Richard (1932–), film director. Famed for Beatles' film *A Hard Day's Night, The Knack,* and anti-war satire *How I Won the War.*

Lestschinsky, Jacob (1876–1966), pioneer in sociology, economics, demography of Jewish life; b. Russia. A founder of Zionist-Socialist Party. In Berlin fr. 1921. Directed YIVO's economics and statistics section in 1920s. *Forward* correspondent fr. early 1920; expelled fr. Germany 1933. In U.S. 1938–59. Worked at Inst. of Jewish Affairs. In Israel fr. 1959. His brother, **Joseph ("Chmurner";** 1884–1935), Jewish socialist leader in Russia, Poland; theoretician of territorialism in Zionist Socialist Workers Party. Subsequently chief ideologist and publicist of Bund leftist faction in Poland.

Leszno (Lissa), town in W. Poland. Jews there 1534, received first charter 1580; expelled 1709, but returned. In late 18th c. central in Jewish life in Greater Poland. "Sages of Leszno" renowned, noted yeshivah and many famous personalities served as rabbis. After annexation to Prussia number of Jews declined; 322 in 1921. Liquidated in Holocaust.

Letteris, Meir (Max; 1800? –1871), Hebrew poet, writer, educator; b. Zolkiew, lived in Vilna, Prague, Vienna. Mediator bet. Jewish and Western culture. Made free Hebrew renditions of European literary works (Goethe, Byron, Racine). Voluminous works incl. popular poems, autobiography, letters. Edited Hebrew Bible for British Foreign Bible Society.

Lev, Abraham (1910–1970), Yiddish poet; left Vilna for Ereẓ Israel 1932, joining kibbutz Givat ha-Sheloshah. Many poems translated into Hebrew. Poet of kibbutz landscape.

Lev, (Lab; Leo), Joseph ben David ibn (Maharival; 1505–1580), Turkish rabbi, *posek.* Highly thought of by contemporary scholars and by Gracia and Joseph Nasi. Owing to quarrels and personal tragedies, moved successively fr. native Monastir to Salonika and then to Constantinople.

Levanda, Lev Osipovich (1835–1888), Russian author, publicist. A leading figure in circles of Russian-Jewish intelligentsia; subsequently in Ḥovevei Zion. Taught at government Jewish school in Minsk 1854–60; Jewish expert to governor-general of Vilna 1860–1888. First contended that Jews should become

Lev Osipovich Levanda

completely Russian except for religion, then became Jewish nationalist. Works incl. feuilletons, sketches, novels based on pre-modern history of E. European Jewry.

Levanon, Mordecai (1901–1968), Israel painter; b. Transylvania, settled in Ereẓ Israel 1921. Primarily expressionist landscapist.

Leveen, Jacob (1891–), librarian, author. Worked in Dept. of Oriental Books and Manuscripts of British Museum. His *Hebrew Bible in Art* was pioneer study.

Leven, Narcisse (1833–1915), French philanthropist, public figure. Secretary to Adolph Crémieux. Vice-pres. Paris Municipal Council 1882. A founder and subsequently pres. 1898–1915 Alliance Israélite Universelle of which he wrote a history. First to preside over council of Jewish Colonization Association.

Levene, Phoebus Aaron Theodor (1869–1940), U.S. biochemist. Headed Chemistry Division at Rockefeller Inst. for Medical Research. Main contribution in structural chemistry of nucleic acids and isolation of two sugars which characterize them, D-ribose and its 2-deoxy derivative.

Levene, Sam (1907–), U.S. actor. Widely known for role of Nathan Detroit in *Guys and Dolls.* Appeared in many films.

Levenfisch (Loewinfisch), Grigori Yakelovich (1889–1961), Russian engineer, chessmaster. Won USSR championship 1934, 1937.

Levenson, Sam (1914–), U.S. humorist. Wrote *Everything But Money* describing his childhood in N.Y.

Lever, Norman Harold (1914–), British politician, financial expert. Labor MP. fr. 1950. Financial secretary to treasury; paymaster-general. Represented U.K. at International Monetary Fund. Chancellor of Duchy of Lancaster 1974.

Leverson, Ada (1865–1936), English novelist; of Marrano descent. Wrote for *Punch* and *The Yellow Book.* Her novels, incl. *The Twelfth Hour,* reflect Edwardian era.

Levertin, Oscar Ivar (1862–1906), Swedish poet, literary critic; first eminent Jew in Swedish literature. Prof. of literature at Academy of Stockholm. As poet distinguished by aestheticism. Collected works appeared in 24 vols.

Levertoff, Paul Philip (1878–1954), apostate, theologian; b. Belorussia into ḥasidic family; converted to Christianity 1895. Director of London Diocesan Council for work among Jews 1922–54. Translated parts of Anglican liturgy into Hebrew, Midrash Sifrei to Numbers and Zohar into English (with H. Sperling).

Levi, third son of Jacob and Leah, eponymous ancestor of Levites (q.v.). Together with Simeon, took chief part in slaying men of Shechem.

Levi, Behrend (17th c.), army purveyor during Thirty Years' War 1618–48, financial adviser and diplomatic agent to elector of Brandenburg. Appointed overlord of all Jews in Brandenburg principalities W. of Elbe. Authority rescinded 1652 because of his harsh rule.

Levi, Carlo (1902–), Italian author, artist. Joined anti-Fascist underground; fled to France 1939, joined Italian resistance in WWII. Communist senator 1963–72. Famed for *Christ Stopped at Eboli.* As painter achieved particular success in U.S.

Levi, David (1742–1801), English Hebraist, polemicist. Works incl. translation of Pentateuch for synagogal use, Hebrew grammar and dictionary, and answer to Thomas Paine's attacks on Bible and authenticity of prophecy.

Levi, Doro (1898–), Italian archaeologist. Director of Italian School of Archaeology in Athens fr. 1947. Organized excavations at Caesarea, Israel, and in Aegean Islands. Anatolian excavations threw light on origins of early Cycladic and Minoan civilizations.

Levi, Edward H. (1911–), U.S. educator. Pres. Univ. of Chicago fr. 1967. Wrote *An Introduction to Legal Reasoning.*

Levi, Giuseppe (1872–1965), Italian neuroanatomist, histologist. Director of Inst. of Human Anatomy at Univ. of Turin fr. 1919; lost post under Mussolini, restored to him after WWII. Researched microscopic anatomy. Pioneer in technique of tissue culture and in knowledge of factors determining size of motor and sensory neurons.

Levi, Graziadio David (1816–1898), Italian patriot, poet. Member of Mazzini's *Giovane Italia,* secret nationalist movement. Liberal member in Italian Assembly 1860–79. Works incl. allegorical drama based on Jeremiah story.

Levi, Hermann (1839–1900), German conductor, composer. One of greatest conductors of his time; noted for interpretations of Wagner, Mozart, Brahms, Bruckner. As conductor of Royal Munich Opera Orchestra, conducted premiere of *Parsifal* at Bayreuth 1882. Relationship with Wagner marked by conflict due to latter's anti-Semitism.

Lévi, Israel (1856–1939), chief rabbi of France, scholar. Wrote on Bible, Apocrypha, Talmud, Midrash, liturgy, and history of Jews of France. Editor of *Revue des Etudes Juives.*

Levi, Jacob ben Israel (d. 1636), halakhist, scholar in Xanthe and Venice; member of well-known Bet ha-Levi family. Famous for his responsa.

Levi, Paolo (1919–), Italian playwright. Dealt primarily with problems of individual. Wrote for TV, radio, and directed films.

Levi, Paul (1883–1930), German socialist, lawyer. Known for defense striking workers 1912, Rosa Luxemburg 1914. A founder and leader of

Levites bearing the Ark of the Covenant across the Jordan, from 12th cent. Greek ms.

"Three Calabrian Laborers," oil painting by Carlo Levi.

"Spartacus League", which became German Communist Party 1919. Expelled fr. party after denouncing its tactics and methods esp. in regard to uprising in Saxony 1921. Subsequently leader of left-wing Social Democratic Party.

Levi, Primo (1919–), Italian author. Deported to Auschwitz 1944 and wrote of his experiences there. Also published moralistic and fantastic tales.

Levi, Rino (1901–1965), Brazilian architect. Worked on Ministry of Education building in Rio de Janeiro with Lucio Costa and Oscar Niemayer. Designed many buildings in American skyscraper manner.

Levi, Shabbetai (1876–1956), mayor of Haifa 1940–51; b. Constantinople. A founder of first Hebrew school in Haifa and of city's Reali School and Technion. First Jewish mayor of Haifa.

Levi, Solomon ben Isaac (1532–1600), Turkish rabbi, commentator, author, communal leader of Salonika Jewry; member of Bet ha-Levi family. Man of considerable wealth, oratorical ability, encyclopedic knowledge, and dynamic personality; wrote more than 20 works and commentaries on many aspects of Jewish studies.

Levi, Solomon ben Isaac (1581–1634), rabbi of Salonika, one of greatest halakhists and writers of responsa of his time; member of Bet ha-Levi family. Noted preacher and a poet, also wrote talmudic novellae. Deeply involved in charitable needs of both Salonika Jewry and institutions in Ereẓ Israel

Lévi, Sylvain (1863–1935), French orientalist, director of Inst. of Italian Studies at Sorbonne 1904. French representative on Zionist Commission 1919. Pres. Central Committee of Alliance Israélite Universelle 1920–35. Works incl. *Etude critique sur le théâtre indien* and *L'Inde et le monde.*

Levi, Testament of, Jewish pseudepigraphical work written in Aramaic, probably before 100 C.E. Produced within broad movement in ancient Judaism fr. which Dead Sea sect arose. Ascribed to Levi, son of Jacob, purportedly representing his last speech to his descendants.

Levias, Caspar (1860–1934), U.S. orientalist, lexicographer; b. Lithuania. Ardent Zionist who devoted much time to propagation of modern Hebrew literature. His *A Grammar of the Aramaic Idiom Contained in the Babylonian Talmud* is pioneer study.

Leviathan with "shor ha-bar" in folk-art picture, Poland, 19th cent.

Leviathan, marine animal, both real and legendary, mentioned in Bible and talmudic literature. Acc. to legend, it will be eaten by righteous in their feasting in world to come. In modern Heb., whale.

Levi ben Abraham ben Ḥayyim (c. 1245–c. 1315), French philosopher whose teachings were focus of antiphilosophical controversy among Jews in Provence and Catalonia 1303–5. Wrote two encyclopedic works of medieval science and philosophy. Criticized for his allegorical interpretation of Bible. Persecuted by opponents, led itinerant and poverty-stricken life.

Levi ben Gershom (Ralbag, Gersonides; 1288–1344), mathematician, astronomer, philosopher, biblical commentator in Orange. Contributed to many areas of human learning, esp. trigonometry and astronomy. Invented Jacob Staff, widely used to measure angular separation bet. celestial bodies. Main philosophical work *Milḥamot Adonai.* His Bible commentaries often deal with philosophical themes. Also wrote commentaries on Aristotle and Averroes.

Levi ben Japheth (Abū Sa'īd; 10th c.), Karaite scholar in Jerusalem. Author of "Book of Precepts," written in Arabic and used by most later Karaite writers.

Levi ben Sisi (2nd–3rd c.), Babylonian and Palestinian *amora;* colleague-disciple of Judah ha-Nasi. Traveled frequently between Ereẓ Israel and Babylonia, finally settling in Nehardea.

Levi-Bianchini, Angelo (1887–1920), Italian naval officer. Member of Zionist Commission in Ereẓ Israel. Sent by Italian foreign minister to examine role of Zionist movement in Middle East 1920; killed in Bedouin attack on train bet. Damascus and Haifa.

Levi-Civita, Tullio (1873–1942), Italian mathematician. Prof. of mechanics at Rome Univ. 1918–38; Dismissed by Fascists. Developed absolute differential calculus essential mathematical tool required for Einstein's relativity theory. Most important contribution was theory of "parallel displacement."

Levi Della Vida, Giorgio (1886–1967), Italian Arabist, Semitist. Prof. Rome Univ. fr. 1920, refused to sign oath of allegiance to Fascist regime 1931; dismissed. Prof. at Univ. of Pennsylvania 1939–48; reinstated at Rome 1948. Wrote on history and religion of ancient Semitic Near East.

Levi ibn Ḥabib, see Ibn Ḥabib.

Levi Isaac ben Meir of Berdichev (c. 1740–1810), ḥasidic *ẓaddik,* rabbi; one of most famous personalities in 3rd generation of ḥasidic movement. Pupil of Dov Baer of Mezhirech. Rabbi of Berdichev 1785–1810. As founder of Ḥasidism in C. Poland, consolidated movement in Lithuania and furthered it in Ukraine. One of best loved *ẓaddikim,* stressed element of joy in Ḥasidism and good that is in man. Popular hero in Jewish poetry and fiction.

Gravestone of Levi Isaac b. Meir of Berdichev.

Levin, Aryeh (1885–1969), rabbi; b. Belorussia, settled in Ereẓ Israel 1905. Spiritual mentor until death to Talmud Torah of Eẓ Ḥayyim Yeshivah. Saintly figure; chaplain to hospitals and prisoners, esp. political prisoners (known as "the Rabbi of the Prisoners").

Levin, Emanuel (Menahem Mendel; 1820–1913), communal worker, early pioneer of Haskalah in Russia. Taught at government rabbinical seminary in Zhitomir 1852. Confidant and secretary for Jewish affairs for Barons Y. and H. Guenzburg 1857. First secretary of Society for Promotion of Culture among Jews of Russia 1863–72.

Levin, Harry (1912–), U.S. literary critic. Taught at Harvard. Best

known for writings on American literature and on Joyce.
Levin, Judah Leib (Yehalel; 1844–1925), Hebrew socialist poet, writer; among founders of Kiev Ḥovevei Zion. Tutor and secretary for Brodskis, Kiev sugar magnates. First introduced socialist themes into Hebrew literature and poetry. Works incl. poems and *Zikkaron ba-Sefer,* memoirs.
Levin, Lewis Charles (1808–1860), U.S. lawyer, editor, congressman. Prominent temperance speaker for Philadelphia, editor of *Temperance Advocate.* A founder of Native American (later "Know-Nothing") Party 1843, edited its organ *Daily Sun.* Know-Nothing congressman 1845–1851.
Levin, Maksim Grigoryevich (1904–), Soviet ethnologist, physical anthropologist. Deputy director of Inst. of Ethnology of USSR Academy of Sciences. Wrote on ethnology of Asiatic Russia and Siberia.
Levin (Lefin), Menahem Mendel (1749–1826), early Haskalah author, translator, educator. Considered father of Galician Haskalah. Opposed Kabbalah and Hasidism as lowering Jewish morality. Main contributions to Jewish literature use of mishnaic Hebrew and willingness to write in Yiddish. Works designed to improve conditions of Jews through enlightenment ideas.
Levin, Meyer (1905–), U.S. novelist; settled in Israel 1958. Works incl. *Yehudah,* one of first novels about kibbutz life, *In Search,* autobiography, *The Old Bunch* on Chicago Jews, best-selling *Compulsion,* based on Leopold-Loeb murder case of 1920s, and *The Settlers* on pioneers in Ereẓ Israel. Produced first feature film in Ereẓ Israel, *My Father's House.*
Levin, Nathaniel William (1819–1903), pioneer New Zealand communal leader; b. London, arrived in Port Nicholson (Wellington) 1841. Successful merchant, shipowner, wool exporter. Member of Legislative Council 1869. Returned to London 1871.
Levin, Rahel, see Varnhagen, Rahel.
Levin, Shmarya (Shemaryahu; 1867–1935), Zionist leader, Hebrew, Yiddish author. Elected to first Russian Duma 1906. Member of Zionist Executive 1911. In WWI lived in U.S., directing propaganda work on Zionism and Hebrew culture. Sharp-witted publicist; famed speaker and conversationalist. Settled in Ereẓ Israel 1924. Wrote memoirs.

Shemaryahu Levin, portrait by Joseph Oppenheimer, 1931.

Ẓevi Hirsch Levin

"Hillel," oil on panel by Jack Levine.

Levin, Yiẓḥak Meir (1894–1971), leader of Agudat Israel. Active in Agudat Israel movement in Poland. In 1940 reached Ereẓ Israel where he headed local branch of the movement fr. 1947. Member of Knesset. Minister of social welfare until 1952, resigning during controversy over national service for women. Chairman of world executive of Agudat Israel fr. 1954.
Levin, Ẓevi Hirsch (-el) ben Aryeh Loeb (Hirsch Loebel; Hart Lyon; 1721–1800), rabbi in London 1758–64 and Germany; b. Galicia; nephew of Jacob Emden. Author of commentary on *Avot.* Father of Saul Berlin and Solomon Hirschel.
Levinas, Emmanuel (1905–), French philosopher; b. Lithuania. Taught at Univ. of Paris. Headed the Ecole Normale of the Alliance Israélite. Work contends that man must transcend ontology through unique relationship with other persons.
Leviné, Eugene (Nissen Berg; 1883–1919), revolutionary politician, journalist; b. St. Petersburg. Chairman of Council of People's Commissar in Bavarian Soviet Republic 1919. Republic overthrown after 2 weeks. Tried for treason and executed.
Levine, Jack (1915–), U.S. painter. Works in "social realism," mostly dealing with uglier aspects of American society.
Levine, Les (1936–), Canadian sculptor. Innovator in "throw away," "disposable" art. Concerned with relating sculpture to its surroundings.
Levine, Philip (1900–), U.S. immunohematologist. Discovered many blood group factors.
Levin-Shatzkes, Yiẓḥak (1892–1963), social leader. Active in Bund in Dvinsk. In New York fr. 1936. Secretary of Jewish Socialist Farband of America and editor of its organ *Der Vecker.*
Levinsohn, Isaac Baer (Ribal; 1788–1860), Hebrew author; a founder of Haskalah in Russia. In *Te'udah be-Yisrael* denounced Orthodox educational system, advocating learning of foreign languages and manual labor, esp. farming. His *Efes Damim* refuted blood libel.
Levinson, Abraham (1888–1955), U.S. pediatrician. Prof. at Northwestern Univ. Medical School, founder of Levinson Research Foundation for research on pediatric neuropsychiatry. Discovered test for diagnosing tuberculous meningitis.
Levinson, André (1887–1933), dance critic, foremost writer on ballet of his time; b. St. Petersburg, in Paris fr. 1921.
Levinson, Salmon Oliver (1865–1941), U.S. lawyer, world peace advocate. Prominent for his "outlawry of war" idea and attempt to start international peace movement during WWI. His Levinson Plan (1927) called for readjusting German reparations, allied and inter-allied debts, and world peace. Sponsored and helped draft Kellogg-Briand peace pact 1928.
Levinthal, U.S. family in Philadelphia. **Bernard Louis** (1865–1952), Orthodox rabbi; b. Lithuania, in U.S. fr. 1891. Rabbi of Congregation B'nai Abraham. A founder 1902 and first pres. Union of Orthodox Rabbis of U.S. and Canada. His son, **Israel Herbert** (1888–), Conservative rabbi at

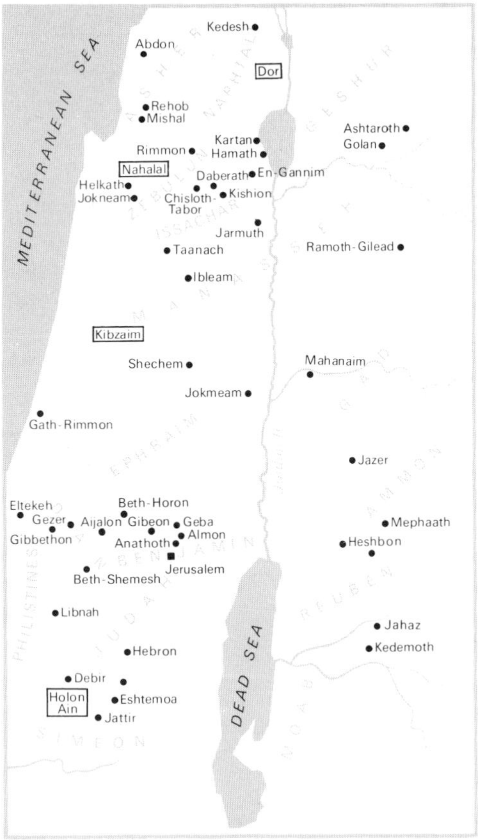

Sites of levitical cities. Names within frames are of places as yet unidentified, though their general location is known from the sources.

BOOK OF LEVITICUS – CONTENTS

Chs. 1:1–7:38	The sacrificial system.
1:1–2	General introduction.
1:3–17	The whole offering *(olah)*.
2:1–16	The tribute (cereal) offering *(minḥah)*.
3:1–17	The well-being offering *(shelamim)*.
4:1–35	The purification offering *(hatta'at)*.
5:1–13	Borderline cases requiring the purification offering.
5:14–26	The reparation offering *(asham)*.
6:1–7:38	Supplementary instructions on sacrifices.
Chs. 8:1–10:20	The inaugural service at the sanctuary.
8:1–36	The installation of the priests.
9:1–24	The priests assume office.
10:1–11	The sin of Nadab and Abihu.
10:12–20	The consumption of the initiatory offerings.
Chs. 11:1–16:34	The laws of impurities.
11:1–47	Animal impurities.
12:1–8	The impurity of childbirth.
13:1–14:57	The impurity of skin diseases (leprosy).
15:1–33	The impurity of genital discharges.
16:1–34	The impurities of the sanctuary and the nation.
Chs. 17:1–26:46	The holiness source.
17:1–16	Killing for food.
18:1–20:27	On being holy.
21:1–22:33	The disqualifications of priests and sacrifices.
23:1–44	The festivals.
24:1–23	Miscellanea.
25:1–26:46	The Sabbatical and Jubilee Years.
27:1–34	Commutation of gifts to the sanctuary.

Leather "ḥaliẓah" shoe, used in releasing from obligation of levirate marriage, Germany, 19th cent.

Brooklyn Jewish center. Pres. Rabbinical Association of America. Taught homiletics at Jewish Theological Seminary; wrote books on Judaism. Another son, **Louis Edward** (1892–), lawyer, jurist. Judge on Philadelphia Court of Common Pleas 1937–59. Pres. Zionist Organization of America 1941, pres. Jewish Publication Society of America 1949–54, chairman of Board of Governors of Heb. Univ. 1962–66.

Lévi-Provençal (Mabkhush), Evariste (1894–1956), French orientalist; b. Algiers. Fr. 1945 prof. at Sorbonne and director of Institut des Etudes Islamiques and of Centre d'Etudes de l'Orient. Published Arabic texts, history of Muslim Spain.

Levirate Marriage (Heb. *yibbum*), marriage with brother's widow; commanded if brother died without offspring (Deut. 25:5–6). Release fr. such obligation only possible after ceremony of *ḥaliẓah,* which permits widow to marry someone else.

Levison, Wilhelm (1876–1947), medievalist; specialist in early Merovingian and Carolingian periods. First scholar to treat Rhenish history as integral part of German and European history. Prof. at Bonn Univ. fr. 1912. Went to Durham, England, after rise of Hitler.

Levi-Strauss, Claude (1898–), French anthropologist. Prof. in São Paulo, 1935–39, Paris. fr. 1945. Famed for theory of structural anthropology and for attempts to establish new science of myth. Works incl. *A World on the Wane,* containing elements of autobiography, ethnography, and social anthropology based on experience in Brazil; *Elementary Structure of Kinship,* and *Totemism.* Elected to French Academy 1973.

Levita, Elijah (Elijah Baḥur; ben Asher ha-Levi Ashkenazi; 1468/69–1549), Hebrew, Yiddish philologist, grammarian, lexicographer; b. Germany, lived in Italy. Students incl. leading Christian Hebraist (e.g., Cardinal Egidio da Viterbo). Wrote several important works on Hebrew grammar, and was first to prove that biblical vocalizations was post-talmudic. Also wrote talmudic lexicon, *Tishbi* and first-known Yiddish-Hebrew dictionary. His Yiddish translation of Psalms became popular work.

Claude Levi-Strauss

Levitan, Isaac Ilitch (1861–1900), Russian painter; called father of Russian landscape painting. One of first Russian artists to understand achievement of Barbizon painters and impressionists. Prof. at Moscow Art Academy.

Levi-Tannai, Sara, Israel choreographer. Founded Inbal Dance Theater. Composed songs and dances, incl. *El Ginnat Egoz.* Israel Prize 1973.

Levites, descendants of tribe of Levi. Originally consecrated to serve in Tabernacle; after conquest of Ereẓ Israel, excluded fr. territorial inheritance but received several "Levitical Cities." Subsequently served in First and Second Temple, various functions being described in Chronicles. Received tithes. Their descendants privileged in being called second (after Kohen) to Torah reading and washing hands of Kohanim before priestly benediction.

Levitical Cities, 48 towns with strips of open land outside them, assigned to Levites by other tribes of Israel out of tribal portions. List of these towns is given in Joshua 21.

Leviticus, Book of (Heb. *Va-Yikra*), third book of Pentateuch. Deals chiefly with laws of sacrifice, sanctuary service, impurities.

Leviticus Rabbah, one of oldest Midrashim extant, probably composed in 5th c. in Ereẓ Israel. Part of Midrash Rabbah.

Levitsky, Jacob (1904–1956), Israel mathematician. Taught at Heb. Univ. Radical in associative rings is named after him. Israel Prize 1953.

Levitt, family of U.S. builders, philanthropists. **Abraham** (1880–1962), founded building firm Levitt & Sons, which pioneered in com-

MAḤZOR

An open gateway illustrating the Yom Kippur prayer "He who opens the Gate of mercy for us . . ." in the *Worms Maḥzor*, Germany, 13th cent.

Silver *mahzor* binding, Galicia, early 19th cent. One panel (r.) depicts the binding of Isaac, the other (l.) Jacob's dream.

Marriage ceremony in England, depicted on a china platter, 1769. It was part of a handpainted coffee service designed as a wedding gift.

MARRIAGE

Wedding rings, 17th–18th cent. They are embellished with a house or roof symbolizing the establishment of a new home. They came from Italy except the top right (N. Africa) and the bottom left (Austria).

munity planning, assembly-line techniques, and mass production. Firm built three entire communities in 1940s, all called Levittown, in Long Island, Pennsylvania, and New Jersey. His son **William Jaird** (1907–), pres. family firm. During his presidency, firm began building houses in Europe.

Levner, Israel Benjamin (1862–1916), Russian Hebrew writer. Wrote on educational subjects and Jewish life. Edited first readers for Hebrew-reading children. Major work: *Kol Aggadot Yisrael,* talmudic legends rewritten.

Levontin, Jehiel Joseph (pen name **Ḥushai ha-Arki;** 1861–1936), Hebrew writer; b. Belorussia, settled in Ereẓ Israel 1922. Wrote about Jewish life outside Russian Pale of Settlement.

Levontin, Zalman David (1856–1940), pioneer of Jewish settlement and banking in Ereẓ Israel. One of first members of Ḥovevei Zion in Russia; sent to Ereẓ Israel to purchase land. Founded Rishon le-Zion 1882 but had to sell land to Baron Edmund de Rothschild 1883. Settled in Ereẓ Israel 1903, establishing Anglo-Palestine Co. (now Bank Leumi le-Israel) which became central financial and credit institution of new *yishuv* under his directorship.

Lévy, family of French publishers. Founded 1842 by brothers **Michel** (1821–1875), **Alexander Nathan,** and **Calmann** (1819-1891). Known as Michel Lévy Frères, soon one of largest publishing houses in France. Calmann assumed control on Michel's death; firm renamed Calmann-Lévy.

Levy, Aaron (1742–1815), U.S. merchant, land speculator; b. Amsterdam, settled in Pennsylvania c. 1760 and subsequently owned land in all its counties. Founded unsuccessful community of Aaronsburg, first one founded by and named after Jew in U.S.

Lévy Alfred (1840–1919), chief rabbi of France, scholar, author. Presided over reorganization of French Jewry following separation of Church and State 1905. Scholar of French-Jewish history.

Levy, Amy (1861–1889), English novelist, poet. Wrote book of verse *A London Plane Tree,* and novel *Reuben Sachs,* which was criticized for its unsympathetic portrayal of wealthy Jewish classes.

Levy, Asser (d. 1681), New York merchant landowner. Member of first group of Jews to arrive in New Amsterdam 1654. Successfully contested tax assessed against Jews refused right to serve in militia and won fight for Jews to carry on trade in community. Made freeman 1657.

Levy, Benjamin (c. 1650–1704), founder of London Ashkenazi community; b. Hamburg, settled in London c. 1670. One of 12 original Jewish brokers in London 1697.

Levy, Benn Wolfe (1900–1973), English playwright, politician. Labor MP 1945–50. Wrote many successful plays, incl. *Mrs Moonlight, Clutterbuck, Rape of the Belt.*

Levy, Felix Alexander (1884–1963), U.S. Reform rabbi. Rabbi of Emanuel Congregation in Chicago 1908–55. Pres. Central Conference of American Rabbis 1935–37. Editor of magazine *Judaism.*

Levy, Hyman (1889–), British mathematician. Prof. at Imperial College of Science in London 1923–55, dean of Royal College of Science 1948–54. Pioneer in explaining and interpreting social impact of science. Leading member of British Communist Party; expelled 1958 for pamphlet criticizing Soviet attitude to Jews and Jewish culture in USSR.

Levy, Jacob (1819–1892), rabbi, lexicographer in Breslau. Major works were dictionaries of Aramaic of Targum, Talmud, and Midrash. Outstanding scholar in field.

Levy, Jefferson Monroe (1852–1924), U.S. congressman, lawyer. Congressman 1899–1901, 1911–15. A leader "Gold Democrats" in 1st term. Sponsored Reserve Bank bill in 2nd and 3rd terms.

Levy, Jonas Phillips (1807–1883), U.S. naval commander, and Jewish communal leader; brother of Uriah Phillips Levy. Captain of Veracruz after its capture in Mexican War. Led struggle to alter U.S.-Swiss treaty of 1850 in its provisions disallowing equal rights of travel and settlement to Jewish nationals and non-nationals in Switzerland.

Levy, Leonard Williams (1923–), U.S. historian. Prof. at Brandeis Univ. His *Origins of the Fifth Amendment* won Pulitzer Prize.

Levy, Louis Edward (1846–1919), U.S. chemist, inventor, newspaper editor. Invented "Levytype," photochemical engraving process, Levy acid blast, and Levy line screen. Published and edited Philadelphia *Evening Herald* 1887–90 and Sunday paper *Mercury* 1887–91. Pres., Association for Relief and Protection of Jewish Immigrants.

Levy, Moses (c. 1665–1728), New York merchant, landowner. Most prominent and wealthiest Jew of early 18th c. in N.Y. Pres. Jewish congregation of N.Y.

Levy, Moses (1757–1826), U.S. judge. First Jew to qualify as lawyer in U.S. 1778. Member of Pennsylvania legislature 1802–06, judge of district court of Philadelphia.

Levy, Moses Elias (c. 1782–1854), U.S. pioneer settler in Florida; b. Morocco. Heavy investor in Florida real estate; moved there when Florida ceded to U.S.

Levy, Nathan (1704–1753), colonial American merchant; b. N.Y. moved to Philadelphia 1738. A founder of Philadelphia Jewish community, obtained land for its first Jewish cemetery 1740.

Levy, Reuben (1891–1966), British orientalist. Prof. of Persian at Cambridge. Writings incl. *The Persian Language* and *Persian Literature.*

Levy, Rudolf (1875–1944), German painter. One of few Germans who did not join expressionist movement. Influenced by Matisse and Cezanne. Left Germany 1933, settled in Florence. Arrested by Gestapo and killed.

Uriah P. Levy exhibiting cat-o-nine-tails to Washington statesmen during campaign for abolition of flogging in U.S. Navy.

Levy, Uriah Phillips (1792–1862), U.S. naval officer. Commodore U.S. fleet 1859. Advocated prohibition of corporal punishment in navy. Wrote extensively on problems of naval discipline. Sponsored new Seminary of B'nai Jeshurun Educational Inst. in N.Y. 1854. Purchased Thomas Jefferson's home at Monticello.

Lévy-Bruhl, Lucien (1857–1939), French anthropologist, philosopher, psychologist. Taught history of modern philosophy at Sorbonne.

Wrote on aspects of preliterate culture to demonstrate nature of primitive mentality. Theories had diverse influence on Jungian psychologists in interpretations of relations of archetypes of unconscious to primitive mentality. His son, **Henri** (1884–), lawyer, sociologist. Specialized in sociology of law, esp. Roman law.

Lewald, Fanny (1811–1889), German novelist, champion women's rights. Her popular novels advocated anti-romanticism, feminism, religious toleration, social reform, and anti-militarism.

Lewandowski, Louis (1821–1894), choral director, composer of synagogue music. His compositions gained great popularity. Choir conductor in Berlin. His style early adopted by Conservative and moderate Reform congregations of urban U.S.

Louis Lewandowski

Kurt Lewin

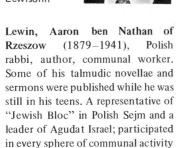

Ludwig Lewisohn

Lewin, Aaron ben Nathan of Rzeszow (1879–1941), Polish rabbi, author, communal worker. Some of his talmudic novellae and sermons were published while he was still in his teens. A representative of "Jewish Bloc" in Polish Sejm and a leader of Agudat Israel; participated in every sphere of communal activity in Poland. Murdered by Nazis.

Lewin, Adolf (1843–1910), German rabbi, historian. Wrote on historical, geographical, and travel literature of Jews in rabbinic period and on Jewish-Christian relations and anti-Semitism.

Lewin, Benjamin Manasseh (1879–1944), rabbinical scholar, educator, authority on geonic literature; b. Russia, settled in Ereẓ Israel 1912. Head of religious school network Neẓaḥ Yisra'el. His major work *Oẓar ha-Ge'onim* (13 vols.) is arrangement of geonic responsa and commentaries in order of Talmud tractates.

Lewin, Joshua Heshel ben Elijah Ze'ev ha-Levi (1818–1883), Lithuanian talmudist, author. After failing to become head of yeshivah at Volozhin, led unsettled life. Supported Ḥovevei Zion movement. Wrote halakhic and talmudic works.

Lewin, Judah Leib (1894–1971), Russian rabbi. After serving in various communal offices, appointed rabbi of Moscow Great Synagogue and head of yeshivah there 1957.

Lewin, Kurt Zadek (1890–1947), psychologist. Prof. at Univ. of Berlin until 1932, leaving for U.S. Taught at Stanford, Cornell, Iowa; organized and directed research center for group dynamics at MIT. Pioneer of group dynamics. Introduced field theory. His writings on nature of causation were innovations. Considered Zionism sociological necessity.

Lewin, Louis (1868–1941), German rabbi, historian. Made important contribution to history of Jews in Germany and Poland. Settled in Ereẓ Israel 1937.

Lewin-Epstein, Eliahu Ze'ev (1863–1932), Ereẓ Israel leader; b. Lithuania. Among founders of society which established Reḥovot 1890 in Ereẓ Israel. Among founders of Carmel Society for marketing wine of Ereẓ Israel. Settled in Ereẓ Israel after WWI.

Lewinsky, Elhanan Leib (1857–1910), Hebrew writer, Zionist leader. His popular feuilletons marked by good-natured humor, perceptive response to current events, and extensive use of material drawn fr. Midrash and folklore. Wrote a Zionist utopia.

Lewinsky, Yom-Tov (1899–1973), Hebrew writer and folklore researcher; b. Poland, settled in Ereẓ Israel 1935. A founder of folklore society *Yeda Am.* Wrote 8 vol. *Sefer ha-Moadim* on Jewish festivals.

Lewis, Sir Aubrey Julian (1900–), psychiatrist; b. Australia. Clinical director and prof. at Maudsley psychiatric hospital in London. Explored aging, occupational adjustment, and public attitudes to mental illness.

Lewis, Bernard (1916–), British orientalist, historian of Islamic Near East. Prof. at London Univ. School of Oriental and African Studies. Wrote primarily on Arab and Turkish history.

Lewis, David (1909–), Canadian lawyer, socialist politician. A founder and national secretary of Cooperative Commonwealth Federation and subsequently its president. Represented its successor New Democratic Party in Parliament 1962–63, fr. 1965. Elected NDP leader 1971. His son **Stephen**, elected leader of Ontario NDP 1970.

Lewis, Jerry (**Joseph Levitch**; 1926–), U.S. comedian. Formed popular comedy team with Dean Martin until 1956; then became successful comedian on his own. Produced and directed many films of zany humour.

Lewis, Leopold David (1828–1890), British playwright. His melodrama *The Bells* was produced by Sir Henry Irving and made into early film.

Lewis, Oscar (1914–1970), U.S. anthropologist. Taught at Univ. of Illinois. Applied anthropological method to study of urban family unit, esp. poverty-stricken Mexicans and Puerto Ricans. Originated concept of "culture of poverty." Works incl. *The Children of Sanchez* and *La Vida.*

Lewis, Ted (**Kid Lewis**; 1893–1970), British prize fighter. Began boxing professionally at age 15. World welterweight champion 1915–19. Record: 155 wins, 6 draws, 24 defeats, 65 no decisions.

Lewisohn, family of U.S. industrialists, philanthropists; of German origin. Brothers **Leonard** (1847–1902), **Julius** and **Adolph** (1849–1938) founded Lewisohn Brothers, which pioneered development of copper mines in U.S. and moved into worldwide sales of copper and lead. Adolph associated with American Smelting and Refining Co., Adolph Lewisohn and Sons, and other enterprises. Pres. Hebrew Sheltering Guardian Society for over 30 years. Donated Lewisohn Stadium to City College of New York. Their children continued business and remained prominent in philanthropy and in Jewish community.

Lewisohn, Ludwig (1882–1955), U.S. novelist, essayist. Prof. of German at Ohio State Univ. 1911–19. Translated modern German classics. Wrote critical works *(The Modern Drama)*, novels *(The Island Within)*, etc. His pacifism and pro-German sympathies in WWI ended his academic career until appointment as prof. of comparative literature at

Brandeis Univ. 1948. Associate editor of *The Nation* 1919–26. Edited *The New Palestine* 1943–48.

Lewite, Leon (1878–1944), Polish Zionist. After Young Turk revolution 1908, established Zionist political and information center in Constantinople. Went to Moscow 1914, Warsaw 1918. Organized *aliyah* fr. Poland and encouraged middle-class initiative. Settled in Ereẓ Israel 1939.

Lewko (Lewek), Jordanis (d. 1395), wealthiest Jew of Cracow, Poland. King Casimir III the Great entrusted him with administration of royal salt mines of Bochnia and Wieliczka and mint of Cracow 1368. Lent great sums of money to King Louis I of Hungary and Poland.

Lewkowitsch, Julius (1857–1913), British organic chemist. World's leading authority on industrial technology of fats and oils.

Lewy, Israel (1841–1917), rabbi, scholar. Taught in Berlin and Breslau. Erudite in all branches of Jewish and general scholarship; brought keen analytical sense and conjectural brilliance to field of talmudic studies.

Lewy, Julius (1895–1963), philologist, Assyriologist. Prof. at Univ. of Giessen. Left Germany 1933, went to U.S. Prof. at Hebrew Union College. His works are of special importance for study of old Assyrian texts.

Lewy, Yoḥanan (Hans; 1904–1945), classical scholar; b. Germany, settled in Ereẓ Israel 1933. Taught at Heb. Univ. Chief contribution in field of Jewish Hellenism.

Lewysohn, Yehudi Leib Louis (1819–1901), rabbi, scholar in Germany, Sweden. His *Zoologie des Talmuds* was first scientific attempt by Jewish scholar to collate all talmudic and midrashic references to animal life.

Lhevinne, Josef (1874–1944), pianist. Excelled in interpretation of romantic composers. One of major concert pianists of his time.

Libau, see Liepaja.

Libedinski, Yuri Nikolayevich (1898–1959), Soviet Russian novelist. A founder of Soviet proletarian prose. His *A Week* considered one of most effective and honest descriptions of early days of Soviet regime.

Liber, Marc (pseud. of **Michael Goldman;** 1880–1937), Bund leader; b. Vilna. Active in Bund fr. 1900. Prominent as leader of rightist Mensheviks and Bund and active opponent of Bolsheviks even after October 1917 Revolution. Executed in purges.

Liber, Maurice (1884–1956), chief rabbi of France 1934–56, scholar. Strove to maintain Jewish education during WWII. Absorbed into French cultural climate, opposed Zionism, and felt compelled to compromise with facts of French synagogue life, such as use of organ. Researched French-Jewish history. Wrote biography of Rashi.

Liberal Judaism, see Reform Judaism.

Liberal Party, political party in Israel formed 1961 by union of General Zionist and Progressive parties. 17 seats in Fifth Knesset. Split 1965 with former establishing joint bloc with Ḥerut (Gaḥal) and latter forming Independent Liberal Party.

Liberman, Yevsey Grigoryevich (1897–), Soviet economist. Prof. of statistics and accounting at Kharkov Univ. Received worldwide attention 1962 for views on need for economic reform in USSR, which included more rationality in planning process and more freedom in decision-making for management.

Libin, Z. (pseud. of **Israel Zalman Hurwitz;** 1872–1955), Yiddish novelist, playwright; b. Russia, emigrated to London 1891, then to New York, working in sweatshops. Wrote on hardships of early immigrant life.

Libraries, see next page.

Libya, country in N. Africa. Jews in Cyrene in 2nd c. B.C.E. under Ptolemaic rule; unsuccessfully revolted 73 C.E., 115 C.E., with many Jews killed. Jews in Tripolitania fr. 4th c. After Turkish conquest 1517 Jews prospered. Suffered in revolt against Turks 1588–89 and during famine and plague 1784–85. Lived in special quarters *(hāra)* in various towns. Under Italian rule fr. 1911 lived peacefully until 1936, when anti-Jewish legislation enforced. Under Axis forces in WWII, some Jews deported and other sent to forced labor 1942. Many Jews killed in pogroms 1945, 1948. 30,000 emigrated by 1951. After Six-Day War 1967 anti-Jewish riots broke out and remaining Jews left. Under Col. Gaddafi, Libyan regime adopted extreme anti-Israel attitude.

Lichine (Lichtenstein), David (1910–1972), dancer, choreographer; b. Russia, emigrated to Paris. Leading dancer and choreographer with Ballets Russes de Monte Carlo 1932–40. Went to U.S. during WWII with wife ballerina Tatiana Riabouchinska. Established school and company in Los Angeles.

Yevsey G. Liberman, cover of "Time Magazine," 1965.

David Lichine

Jewish settlements in Libya, from antiquity to modern times.

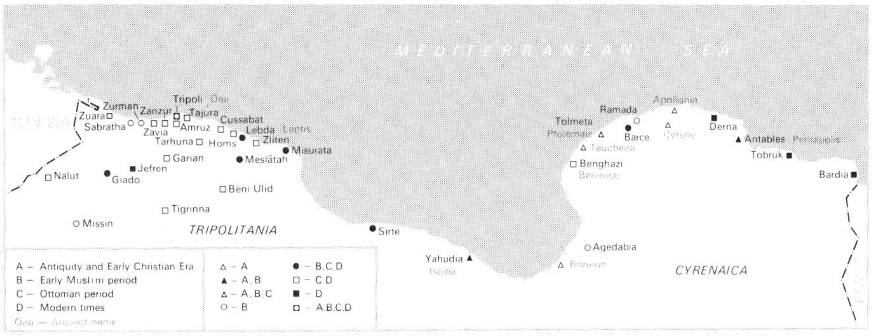

SOME MAJOR JEWISH LIBRARIES AND COLLECTIONS OF JEWISH BOOKS

EUROPE

AUSTRIA

Vienna, Israelitischen Kultusgemeinde

DENMARK

Copenhagen, Bibliotheca Judaica Simonseniana
An independent department within the Royal Library, 400 mss.

FRANCE

Paris, Centre de Documentation Juive Contemporaine
Specializes in Holocaust documentation

Paris, Library of Alliance Israélite Universelle

Paris, Library of Séminaire Israélite

Paris, Jewish Section of Bibliothèque Nationale
1,430 mss.

Strasbourg, University Library, Jewish Section

GERMANY

Frankfort, Municipal Library, Jewish Section

Leipzig, University Library

Munich, State Library
420 mss.

GT. BRITAIN

Cambridge, University Library
Includes many documents from Cairo Genizah

London, British Museum
2,500 mss.

London, Jews' College Library
700 mss.

London, Mocatta Library
Attached to University College London, includes collections on Anglo-Jewish history

Reading, Wiener Library, Univ. of Reading
Specializes in anti-Semitism and Holocaust period

Oxford, Bodleian Library
3,000 mss.

HOLLAND

Amsterdam, Bibliotheca Rosenthaliana
Attached to University Library, 420 mss.

Amsterdam, "Ets Haim" Library
Attached to Sephardi community

HUNGARY

Budapest, Rabbinical Seminary
400 mss.

ITALY

Parma, Biblioteca Palatina
1,550 mss.

Rome, Vatican Library
Contains an important Judaica collection

POLAND

Warsaw, Jewish Historical Institute
Includes the Ringelblum Archives from the Warsaw Ghetto

SWEDEN

Stockholm, Mosaiska Församlingens Bibliotek

U.S.S.R.

Library of Leningrad Branch of Institute of Oriental Studies, U.S.S.R. Academy of Sciences (formerly Asiatic Museum)
The Friedland and Chwolson collections; Hebrew mss. and printed books; archives of Jewish scholars and writers

Leningrad, Saltykov-Schedrin Public State Library
Firkovich I and Firkovich II (Hebrew, Samaritan, Judeo-Arabic mss., especially Karaite); Hebrew and Yiddish books

Moscow, Lenin State Public Library
Guenzburg collection of Hebrew mss; Mazeh collection of Hebrew rare books; Yiddish and Hebrew books; works in dialects of Mountain Jews of Caucasus and Bukharan Jews

Esthonian S.S.R., Tartu University Library
Hebrew books

ASIA

ISRAEL

Jerusalem, The Jewish National and University Library
Over 6,000 mss.: the library of the Hebrew University

Jerusalem, Central Zionist Archives
Zionist History

Jerusalem, The Knesset

Jerusalem, Schocken Library
Attached to the Jewish Theological Seminary of New York, specializing in early Hebraica

Jerusalem, Yad Vashem
Holocaust

Jerusalem, Central Rabbinical Library, Hechal Shlomo

Haifa, Haifa University Library

Tel Aviv, Tel Aviv University Library

Tel Aviv, Rambam Library

Ramat Gan, Bar Ilan University Library

Beersheba, Ben-Gurion University Library

N. AMERICA

CANADA

Montreal, Jewish Public Library

U.S.A.*

New Haven, Yale University Library, Judaica Section

Chicago, College of Jewish Studies

Chicago, Hebrew Theological College

Boston, Public Library, Judaica Section

Boston, Hebrew Teachers' College

Cambridge, Mass., Harvard University Library, Judaica Section

Waltham, Mass., Brandeis University Library, Judaica Section

Waltham, Mass., American Jewish Historical Society
On campus of Brandeis University

Cincinnati, Hebrew Union College Library
5,000 mss.

Cincinnati, American Jewish Archives
American Jewish History

New York, Hebrew Union College – Jewish Institution of Religion
200 mss.

New York, New York University, Jewish Culture Foundation Library

New York, Public Library, Judaica Section

New York, Jewish Theological Seminary of America
9,000 mss.

New York, Yeshiva University
1,000 mss.

New York, YIVO Institute
Specializing in Yiddish books and periodicals

New York, Zionist Archives and Library

Philadelphia, Dropsie University
250 mss.

Washington, Library of Congress.

S. AMERICA

ARGENTINA

Buenos Aires, YIVO Institute

* Several universities are building up significant Jewish libraries.

Licht, Alexander (1884–1948), Zionist leader in Yugoslavia. Arrested 1941 but managed to escape to Switzerland.

Licht, Frank (1916–), U.S. jurist, governor. Associate judge on Rhode Island superior court 1956–68. Democratic governor of R.I. 1968–72.

Licht, Michael (1893–1953), Yiddish poet, essayist; b. Ukraine, in U.S. fr. 1913. Member of In-Zikh. Poet of American metropolis.

Lichtenbaum, Joseph (1895–1968), Hebrew writer. A founder of Habimah in Moscow 1919. Settled in Erez Israel 1920. Published poems, essays, anthologies as well as translations fr. world literature.

Lichtenstadt, Abraham Aaron (d. 1702), Court Jew, *primator* ("leader") of Bohemian Landesjudenschaft. *Shtadlan* of Bohemian Jewry 1673. Secured right for Jews to attend Leipzig fairs.

Lichtheim, Richard (1885–1963), Zionist leader in Germany; outstanding ideologist, publicist. Member of Zionist Executive 1921–23, leaving in opposition to Weizmann's policy and joining Revisionist movement, which he also later left. Settled in Erez Israel 1934. His son **George** (1912–1973), historian, political scientist; in London. fr. 1946. Wrote on Marxism, socialism, political science.

Lida, town in Belorussian SSR. In time of Council of Lands, subordinated to Grodno *kahal.* 5,419 Jews in 1921. I.J. Reines founded modern yeshivah there which became famous. Under Germans ghetto set up; most Jews liquidated 1942.

Lidin (Gomberg), Vladimir Germanovich (1894–), Soviet Russian novelist. Works set against varied backgrounds. War correspondent during WWII.

Lidzbarski, Mark (Abraham Mordecai; 1868–1928), Semitist. Lecturer at Kiel, Greifswald, Goettingen. Considered founder of Semitic epigraphy and contributed much to Mandean studies. Works incl. 2 vol. *Handbuch der nordsemitischen Epigraphik.* Baptized.

Lieben, Adolph (1836–1914), Austrian organic chemist. Prof. at Univ. of Vienna 1875. Discovered iodoform test for alcohol and ketones. Member of Austrian Upper Chamber.

Lieben, Robert von (1878–1913), scientist, inventor; b. Vienna. Invented amplifying valve 1906 and grid tube 1910, which led directly to modern radio and later developments such as sound tracks for films and TV.

Lieben, Salomon Hugo (1881–1942), historian of Bohemian Jewry. Founded and directed Prague Jewish Museum.

Lieberman, Chaim (Herman; 1890–1963), Yiddish essayist, literary critic; b. Volhynia, in U.S. fr. 1905. Joined religious Zionists in 1930. Wrote sharp, cutting polemics.

Lieberman, Herman (1870–1941), Polish lawyer, socialist politician. Entered Austrian parliament 1907. Fought in Polish Legion on Russian front during WWI. Member Polish parliament 1919–30. Minister of justice in Polish government-in-exile 1941; first Jew in Polish Cabinet.

Saul Lieberman

Lieberman, Saul (1898–), talmudic scholar; b. Belorussia. Taught in Jerusalem before going to Jewish Theological Seminary of America 1940; rector of its rabbinical school 1958. Pres. American Academy of Jewish Research 1967. One of outstanding contemporary talmudists and authority on Jewish Hellenism. Published editions of Tosefta and works on Jerusalem Talmud and on Greek influence in Palestine in talmudic period. Israel Prize 1971.

Liebermann, Aaron Samuel (1845–1880), pioneer of Jewish socialism, Hebrew writer. Initiated socialist activities among Vienna's Jews. Went to London 1876, founding Agudat ha-Sozyalistim ha-Ivrim. Contributed to Hebrew press. Went to U.S. 1880; committed suicide. His ideas found little immediate response, but after his death influenced labor movement in Erez Israel.

Liebermann, Carl Theodor (1842–1914), German organic chemist. Prof. at Gewerbe-institut (subsequently Berlin Technische Hochschule). Main field dyestuffs; worked out synthesis of alizarin, industry subsequently worth hundreds of millions of marks. Pres. German Chemical Society.

Liebermann, Max (1847–1935), German painter. Greatly influenced by Dutch landscape. Celebrated and expensive portraitist. Member of Berlin Academy 1898 and a founder of Sezession, association progressive artists. Pres. Berlin Academy of Art 1920; ousted fr. presidency 1933 by Nazis and paintings removed fr. all German museums.

Max Liebermann, self-portrait, 1920.

Liebermann, Rolf (1910–), composer; great-nephew of Max Liebermann. As general manager of Hamburg State Opera fr. 1959, made it major music center. Director of Paris Opera 1972. Own operas distinguished by fresh dramatic ideas and strict musical organization *(Leonore 40/45, Penelope).*

Lieberson, Goddard (1911–), musical executive, composer. Pres. Columbia Records 1956 and Record Industry Association of America 1964. Compositions incl. songs and chamber music.

Liebert (Levy), Arthur (1878–1946), German philosopher. Prof. at High School for Commercial Sciences in Berlin 1925–33. Lived in England during WWII. Contended that philosophers should be concerned with "evaluation" of being and not only its existence.

Liebman, Joshua Loth (1907–1948), U.S. Reform rabbi. Rabbi of Temple Israel in Boston fr. 1939. Known as radio preacher. His book *Peace of Mind* attained phenomenal success and helped encourage closer working relationship bet. psychology and religion.

Liebmann, Jost (Judah Berlin; c. 1640–1702), Court Jew. Originally traded in precious stones and metals. Supplied gems to Brandenburg Elector Frederick William. Owned only synagogue in Berlin.

Liebmann, Otto (1840–1912), German philosopher. Prof. at Jena fr. 1882. A founder of neo-Kantianism.

Liepaja (Ger. Libau; Russ. Libava), city in Latvia. Jews not permitted there until 18th c. 9,454 Jews in 1897. When Latvia became independent, Jewish population declined. Home of Yiddish and Hebrew institutions, famous rabbis. Under Germans, ghetto set up 1942, liquidated 1943.

Liessin, Abraham (pseud. of **Abraham Walt;** 1872–1938), Yiddish poet, editor; b. Minsk, in U.S. fr. 1897, becoming active socialist. Wrote about heroes and martyrs of the past and his own time. Translated Russian and German poets as well as Walt Whitman and Bialik.

Lifshits, Shiye-Mordkhe (1829–1878), pioneering Yiddish lexicographer, author, theoretician of Yiddishist movement; lived in Berdichev. Lexicographic achievements incl. depiction of SE Yiddish dialect. Published Yiddish-Russian dictionary.

Lifshitz, David (1907–), U.S. *rosh yeshivah,* and rabbinical leader; b. Minsk, established yeshivah in Suwalki, in U.S. fr. 1942. *Rosh yeshivah* at Chicago Hebrew Theological College; accepted similar position at Yeshiva University 1945.

Nehamah Lifshitz

Lifshitz, Nehamah (1927–), folk singer of Yiddish and Hebrew songs; b. Lithuania. Gave first concert 1951. Received title of laureate of folk artists at all-Soviet competition 1958. Immigrated to Israel 1969.

°**Lightfoot, John** (1602–1675), English Hebraist, Bible scholar. Outstanding Christian authority on rabbinic literature. Vice-chancellor of Cambridge Univ. Wrote on Temple of Herod and a study of rabbinic sources of and background to New Testament gospels.

Likkutei Amarim, see Tanya.

Likkut Aẓamot (Heb.), term for gathering together of bones of body which has been left in sepulcher and reinterment in final resting place.

Lilien, Ephraim Moses (1874–1925), Austrian illustrator, printmaker. First artist to become involved in Zionist movement. A founder of Berlin publishing house *Juedischer Verlag.* His Herzl portraits and decorations for Golden Book of Jewish National Fund familiar to Zionists all over world. Turned fr. book illustrating to etching 1908. Lieut. in Austro-Hungarian Army during WWI.

Lilienblum, Moses Leib (1843–1910), Hebrew writer, critic, political journalist; b. Lithuania. One of leaders of Haskalah in its last period and of Ḥibbat Zion. Fr. 1869 in Odessa. Edited Yiddish journal *Kol Mevasser.* Autobiography *Ḥatte'ot Ne'urim.*

Moses Leib Lilienblum

Lilienthal, David Eli (1899–), U.S. attorney, public official. Director of Tennessee Valley Authority 1933–41, chairman 1941–46; chairman of Atomic Energy Commission 1946–50, publicly questioning wisdom of America's decision to produce H-bomb.

Lilienthal, Max (Menahem; 1815–1882), educator, author, rabbi; b. Germany. Invited 1841 by Russian government to persuade Russian Jews to accept government Jewish schools with secular as well as religious curriculum; was unsuccessful and eventually realized that government's real intentions were anti-Semitic. Emigrated to U.S. 1845 and among early founders of Reform Judaism. Rabbi in Cincinnati fr. 1855.

Lilith, female demon assigned a central position in Jewish demonology. Acc. to legend tries to kill all newborn children. In kabbalistic literature, symbol of sensual lust and sexual temptation.

Lima, capital of Peru. Center of Crypto-Jews but with establishment of the Inquisition 1570 various groups condemned to death 1581, 1605, 1625, 1639. Jews fr. Alsace arrived there c. 1870 but most assimilated. About time of WWI Jews fr. Turkey, N. Africa, and Syria settled there, and another mass influx occurred during WWII. Jewish pop. 5,250 (1971).

Lima, Moses ben Judah (1605? – 1658), Lithuanian rabbi, halakhist. His commentary on *Shulḥan Arukh, Even ha-Ezer,* was accepted as authoritative. Also wrote compendium on problem of *agunot.*

Limburg, Joseph (1866–1940), Dutch politician. Member of second chamber of parliament 1905–17, Dutch delegation to League of Nation 1920; Council of State 1940. Committed suicide on Dutch surrender to Germany.

Limpieza de Sangre (Sp. "purity of blood"), obsessive concern in Spain and Portugal fr. 15th c., based on mythical goal of society in which all but most humble functions would be exercised by "pure-blooded" Christians. Inquiries were made to unearth traces of long-forgotten "impure" forefathers of many Christians. Obsession afflicted Spain until 19th c. and continues in Majorca.

Lincoln, town in England. Medieval community. Most prominent Anglo-Jewish financier of time was Aaron of Lincoln (c. 1123–1186). 18 Lincoln Jews executed in connection with ritual murder accusation associated with name of "Little" St. Hugh of Lincoln 1255. Jews expelled 1290.

Medieval building in Lincoln known as Jews' Court, probably a synagogue.

Linder, Max (Gabriel-Maximilien Leuvielle; 1883–1925), French silent movie comedy star. Averaged film a week bet. 1905 and 1914. His character of Max inspired Charlie Chaplin to develop similar character.

Lindheim, Irma Levy (1886–), U.S. Zionist leader. Pres. Hadassah 1926–28. Joined Labor Zionist group 1930. Settled in Ereẓ Israel 1933 at kibbutz Mishmar ha-Emek.

Linetzky, Isaac Joel (1839–1915), Yiddish writer; b. Podolia, Ukraine. Spokesman of radical wing of Haskalah. Translated parts of Graetz's history into Yiddish.

Linowitz, Sol Myron (1913–), U.S. business executive, ambassador. Board chairman and head of Xerox International, Inc. U.S. representative Organization of American States (OAS) and Inter-American Committee of Alliance for Progress 1966. Chairman of Board of Overseers, Jewish Theological Seminary.

Lion, Leon M. (1879–1947), British actor-manager, playwright. Particularly well-known for productions of Galsworthy.

Lipchitz, Jacques (Chaim Jacob; (1891–1973), sculptor, b. Lithuania, in Paris fr. 1909, U.S. fr. 1941. One of foremost cubist sculptors. Abandoned cubism for markedly baroque manner in 1930s, with many works on biblical episodes or Jewish themes. Left his casts to Israel Museum, Jerusalem.

Lipiner, Siegfried (1856–1911), Austrian poet, playwright; baptized 1891. Librarian and archivist of Austrian *Reichsrat* 1881–1911.

Lipkin (Salanter), Israel ben Ze'ev Wolf (1810–1883), founder and spiritual father of *Musar* movement. Child prodigy; established yeshivah at Vilna and Kovno, later spent time in W. Europe. Revolutionary in his ideas; his ethical *musar* discourses, which attracted wide audiences, became pattern for similar discourses delivered in all yeshivot of Salanter school.

Lipkin, Yom Tov Lipman (1845–1875), Russian mathematician; son of Israel Lipkin. His kinematic system was included in many Russian and foreign textbooks.

Lipman, Jacob Goodale (1874–1939), U.S. soil chemist, bacteriologist; b. Latvia. Prof. at Rutgers. Director of Jewish Agricultural Society; member of Jewish Agency for Palestine fr. 1929. Founded and edited journal *Soil Science.*

Lipman, Levi (Isaac Libman; 18th c.), merchant of Courland, financial agent of imperial Russian court. Entrusted with financial affairs of duchy, when Count Biron appointed duke of Courland 1737.

Lipmann, Fritz Albert (1899–), U.S. biochemist; b. Germany. Worked in Berlin, Heidelberg, Copenhagen before coming to U.S. 1939. Prof. at Harvard 1949–57, Rockefeller Inst. for Medical Research in N.Y. fr. 1957. Nobel Prize 1953 for Medicine and Physiology for discovery of coenzyme A and its importance for intermediary metabolism.

Lipmann, Otto (1880–1933), German psychologist, expert in vocational guidance. Pioneer in Germany of psychological counseling for selection of profession. Founded Inst. for Applied Psychology, Berlin.

Lipmann-Muelhausen, Yom Tov, see Muelhausen, Yom Tov Lipmann.

Lippe, Karpel (1830–1915), early Zionist, physician in Jassy, Rumania. Active in Ḥibbat Zion movement fr. 1880. Delivered opening speech at First Zionist Congress, (as senior delegate). Considered himself an initiator of Zionist idea.

Lippmann, Edmund Oskar von (1857–1940), German industrial chemist. Leading historian of chemistry and wrote standard books of his period on sugar.

Lippmann, Eduard (1842–1919), Austrian chemist. Developed standard equipment for determining carbon and hydrogen in organic compounds. Prof. at Handelsakademie and Technische Hochschule in Vienna.

Lippmann, Gabriel (1845–1921), French physicist. Prof. of experimental science and director of Sorbonne's research laboratories. His discovery that moment of inertia in charged body is higher than in uncharged body of fundamental importance to study of electron. Nobel Prize 1908 for method of producing color photographs.

Lippmann, Walter (1889–), U.S. journalist. Founder and associate editor of *New Republic* 1914; assistant to Secretary of War Newton D. Baker during WWI; influential columnist on public affairs for *New York Herald Tribune,* syndicated in more than 250 newspapers in 25 countries. Two-time Pulitzer Prize winner.

Lippold, (d. 1573), Court Jew to Joachim II, elector of Brandenburg. Appointed "supervisor" of Brandenburg Jewry and collector of all monies paid by it to court for 10 years 1556. 1565 appointed mintmaster. Accused of extortion and embezzlement. Executed and quartered.

Lipschitz, Jacob ha-Levi (1838–1921), Hebrew writer, opponent of Haskalah; b. Lithuania. Assistant to R. Isaac Elhanan Spektor 1870–96. Issued manifestos and lampoons against Zionist Movement.

Lipschitz, Solomon Zalman (1765–1839), Polish rabbi, first chief rabbi of Warsaw; known as "Ḥemdat Shelomo" after his works of that name. Led opposition to Haskalah movement in Warsaw. Widely respected halakhic authority, wrote responsa, novellae, sermons.

Lipschuetz, Eliezer Meir (1879–1946), Hebraist, religious educator, historical writer in Ereẓ Israel; b. Galicia. Founder and head of Mizrachi Teachers' Seminary Jerusalem.

Lipschuetz, Israel ben Eliezer (d. 1782), German rabbi. Came into prominence 1766–67 with regard to cause célèbre known as Cleves *get;* wrote responsa.

Lipschutz, Israel ben Gedaliah (1782–1860), German rabbinic scholar. Wrote commentary to Mishnah, entitled *Tiferet Yisrael,* one of finest of its kind, explaining Mishnah, offering new interpretation to difficult passages, and giving halakhic rulings as decided on in *Shulḥan Arukh* and it commentaries.

Jacques Lipchitz at Youth Wing of Israel Museum, 1971.

Lipset, Seymour Martin (1922–), U.S. sociologist; one of foremost representatives of political sociology in U.S. Prof. at Harvard.

Lipshitz, Israel Lippy (1903–), S. African sculptor. Prof. at Cape Town Univ. School of Fine Arts 1950–68. A leader of modern school in sculpture. Many of his subjects fr. nature and Bible.

Lipsky, Louis (1876–1963), U.S. Zionist leader, journalist, author. Founded first English-language Zionist periodical in U.S. *(The Maccabean).* A founder of Keren Hayesod, Jewish Agency, and American World Jewish Congresses. Backed Weizmann in his controversy with Brandeis. Pres. Z.O.A. 1922–30. Prolific author.

Lipson, Mordekhai (1885–1958), Hebrew, Yiddish writer, translator, folklorist; b. Bialystok, in U.S. fr. 1913. Founder and edited Hebrew daily *Hadoar* 1921–23. Settled in Ereẓ Israel 1930. Edited religious daily *Ha-Zofeh* 1937–44.

Lipton, Maurice (1916–), Canadian air commodore and chief of operations of RCAF. After distinguished WWII service, director of strategic planning 1957, chief of operations of air force 1959.

Lipton, Seymour (1903–), U.S. sculptor, educator. Used socialist-realist themes in 1930s carvings and welded abstract forms in 1940s.

Liptzin, Sol (1901–), literary scholar, educator. Prof. of German at CCNY. Settled in Israel 1962. Wrote history of Yiddish literature and works on Jewish writers in post-Emancipation Germany.

Lipzin, Keni (Sachar, Krein Sonia; 1856–1918) Yiddish actress; b.

Russia. Made debut in Goldfaden's company. Joined Jacob P. Adler's London company 1884. Jacob Gordin wrote *Mirele Efros* for her.

Lisbon, capital of Portugal. Jews there in 12th c. Official seat of *arraby mór* (chief rabbi). Jewish quarter sacked 1373. Influx fr. Spain 1492. Jews expelled 1496–97. 4,000 Conversos butchered 1503. Subsequently seat of tribunal of Inquisition and first auto-da-fé 1540, continuing for over two centuries. Congregation refounded 1813, received official recognition 1868. Complete equality attained with revolution of 1910. Jewish pop. 650 (1973).

Lishansky, Batya (1901–), Israel sculptor. Work consisted mainly of small wood sculptures and later white marble cubist-like forms. Sculpture of defenders of Ḥuldah and bust of her brother-in-law I. Ben-Zvi are well-known.

Lishansky, Yosef (1890–1917), member of Nili (q.v.); b. Ukraine. When Nili uncovered by Turks, tried to reach Egypt but was caught and sentenced to death by Turkish authorities.

Lisitzky, Ephraim E. (1885–1962), U.S. Hebrew poet, educator; b. Minsk, in U.S. fr. 1900, lived mainly in New Orleans. Themes incl. Negro and American Indian.

Lissa, see Leszno.

Lissauer, Ernst (1882–1937), German poet, playwright. Best known as composer of "Hymn of Hate" against England sung by German troops at front in WWI. Supporter of German nationalists, opponent of Zionism, advocate of complete assimilation.

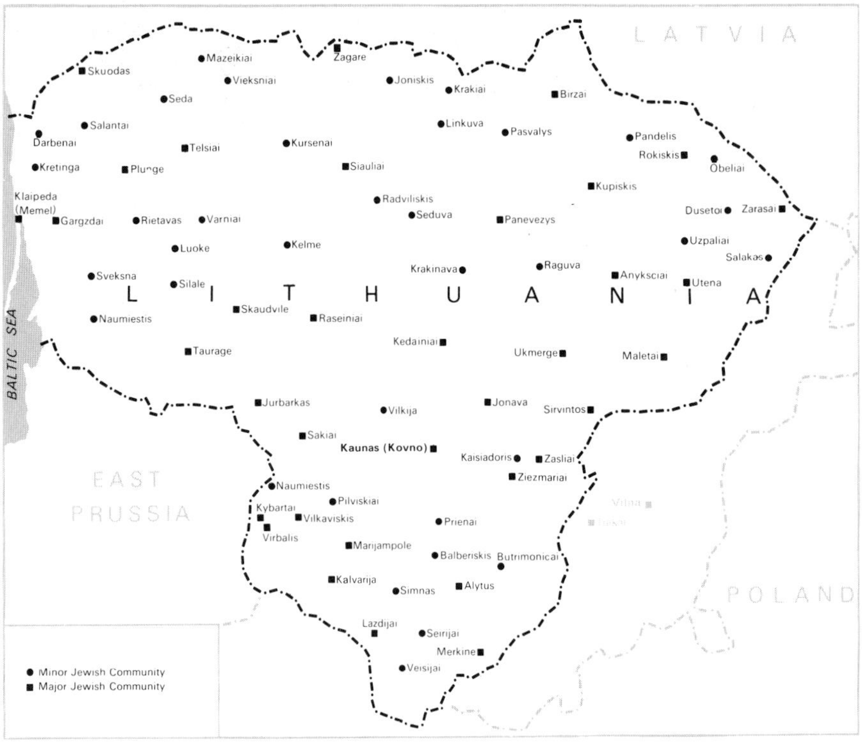

Map of Jewish communities in Lithuania and in the Vilna region ceded to Lithuania in Oct. 1939, with alternative place-names listed below.

Lithuanian Name	Russian Name	Yiddish Name
Alytus	Olita	Alite
Anyksciai	Onikshty	Aniksht
Balberiskis	Balkerishki	Balbirishok
Birzai	Birzhi	Birzh
Butrimonicai	Butyrmantsy	Butrimants
Darbenai	Dorbyany	Dorbian
Dusetoi	Dusjaty	Dusyat
Gargzdai	Gorzhdy	
Jonava	Janovo	Yanove
Joniskis	Yanishki	Yanishok
Jurbarkas	Jurburg	
Kaisiadorys	Koisedary	Kashedar
Kalvarija	Kalvariya	
Kaunas	Kovno	
Kedainiai	Keidany	Keidan
Kelme	Kelmy	Kelm
Klaipeda	Memel	
Krakiai	Kruki	Krok
Krakinava	Krakinovo	
Kretinga	Kretinga	Kretingen
Kudaros-Naumiestis	Vladislavov	
Kudirkos-Naumiestis	Novoe Mesto	Nayshtat
Kupiskis	Kupishki	Kupishok
Kursenai	Kurshany	Kurshan
Kybartai	Kibarty	Kibart
Lazdijai	Lozdzee	Lazdey
Linkuve	Linkovo	
Luoke	Lavkov	Luykeve
Maletai	Maljaty	Malat
Marijampole	Mariampol	
Mazeikiai	Mazheiki	Mazheik
Merkine	Meretsch	
Nemaksciai	Nemokshty	Nemoksht
Obeliai	Abeli	Abel
Pandelis	Ponedeli	Ponedel
Panevezys	Ponevezh	
Pasvalys	Posvol	
Pilviskiai	Pilvishki	Pilvishok

Lithuanian Name	Russian Name	Yiddish Name
Plunge	Plungyany	Plungyan
Prienai	Preny	Pren
Radviliskis	Radzivilishki	
Raguva	Rogov	Rogove
Raseiniai	Rossieny	Rasseyn
Rietavas	Retovo	Riteve
Rokiskis	Rakishki	Rakishok
Sakiai	Shaki	
Salakas	Soloki	Salok
Salantai	Salanty	Salant
Seda	Syady	Syad
Seduva	Shadov	Shadove
Seirijai	Seree	Serey
Siauliai	Shavli	Shavl
Silale	Shileli	Shilel
Simnas	Simno	
Sirvintos	Shervinty	Shirvint
Skaudvile	Skadvile	Shkudvil
Skuodas	Shkudy	Shkud
Sveksna	Shvekshni	
Taurage	Taurogen	Tavrig
Telsiai	Telschi	Telz
Trakai	Troki	
Ukmerge	Vilkomir	
Utena	Utsjany	Utyan
Uzpaliai	Uschpol	
Varniai	Vorni	Vorne
Veisijai	Veisee	
Vieksniai	Wekschni	Vekshne
Vilkaviskis	Vilkovishki	Vilkovishk
Vilkija	Vilki	
Virbalis	Verzhbolov	Virbaln
Zagare	Zhagory	Zhager
Zarasai	Novo Aleksandrovsk	Ezherene
Zasliai	Shosli	Zasle
Ziezmariai	Zhizhmory	Zezmer
Zydikiai	Zhidiki	Zidik

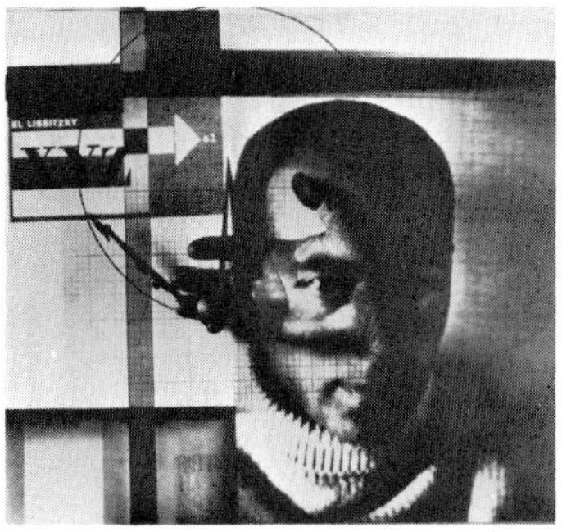

"The Constructor," self-portrait by El Lissitzky, 1924.

Lissitzky, El (Lazar; 1890–1941), Russian painter. Taught architecture and graphic arts at Vitebsk. Deeply interested in Jewish folklore. Major force in constructivist movement. Prof. at Moscow Academy 1921.

List, Emanuel (1891–1967), bass. Joined Volksoper in Vienna 1922, Berlin State Opera 1923, and sang leading Wagnerian roles at Metropolitan Opera fr. 1938. Also known as singer of German lieder.

Lithuania, Soviet Baltic republic. First recorded Jewish presence 1321. Karaite community fr. late 14th c. Jews expelled 1495–1502. Originally part of Councils of Lands, later formed own Council of Lands. Part of Russia 1795–1918, becoming major Jewish cultural center; chief communities Vilna, Grodno,

Market day in Pilviskis, in the Vilkaviskis district, Lithuania.

Lodz Jews with a German soldier, 1915.

Kovno. Center of opposition to Ḥasidism. Home of Musar and Haskalah. Jews received national autonomy 1918–24. 157,527 Jews in 1937; most killed by Nazis. 25,000 Jews in 1969.

Litton, Anya (1914–), Yiddish actress; b. Warsaw. Acted with Schwartz, Granach, Buloff. Settled in Israel 1963.

Littauer, Lucius Nathan (1859–1944), U.S. industrialist, congressman, philanthropist; b. Gloversville, N.Y. Developed father's glove factory into largest in U.S. Republican representative in congress 1896–1907, leading member of House Appropriations Committee, advocated liberalization of immigration laws. Numerous philanthropies, esp. in Jewish studies and Judaica.

Litvak (Michael), Anatole (1902–), U.S. film producer, director. Films incl. *The Snake Pit, Anastasia, The Night of the Generals.*

Litvakov, Moshe (1875–1938?). Yiddish writer, editor, communist leader; b. Ukraine. Fr. 1924 edited *Emes,* Yiddish organ of Communist Party. Arrested during major purges of 1937; d. in prison.

Litvin, A. (pseud. of **Shmuel Hurwitz;** 1862–1943), Yiddish journalist, folklorist; b. Minsk, in U.S. 1901–5, then fr. 1914. Wrote for radical and Labor Zionist organs and for Yiddish dailies. His 6-vol. *Yidishe Neshomes* utilized his collection of folklore.

Litvinoff, Emmanuel (1915–), English poet, novelist. Work largely concerned with problems of Diaspora Jew. Edited periodical *Jews in Eastern Europe.*

Litvinov, Maxim Maximovich (Wallach, Meir Moiseevitch; 1867–1951), Russian revolutionary, Soviet diplomat. Central figure in Soviet diplomacy 1921–39. Commissar for foreign affairs 1930; conducted negotiations for establishment U.S.-USSR relations; chief Soviet spokesman of League of Nations, demanding collective security system. Replaced during period of Hitler-Stalin pact. Soviet ambassador to U.S. 1941–43. Assistant commissar for foreign affairs 1946.

Maxim Litvinov

Litvinovsky, Pinḥas (1894–), Israel painter; b. Ukraine, settled permanently in Ereẓ Israel 1919. Participated in first group exhibitions of Palestinian artists in Jerusalem 1923, Tel Aviv 1926. Made brilliant use of color and form. Noted portraitist.

Litwak, A. (pseud. of **Ḥayyim Yankel Helfand;** 1874–1932), popular publicist, propagandist for Bund. Leader of anti-Bolshevist faction of Bund. Went to U.S. 1926. Active in Jewish Socialist Farband edited its organ *Veker.*

Liuzzi, Guido (1866–1942), Italian soldier. Chief of staff of army corps in Italian Fourth Army during WWI. Directed military academy training officers for general staff after WWI and made it one of best in Europe. Promoted lieutenant general 1928. His son **Giorgio Liuzzi** (1896–), also soldier. Dismissed by Mussolini 1939, reinstated 1944. Chief of staff of Italian army 1956–58.

Liveright, Horace Brisbin (1886–1933), U.S. publisher, theatrical producer. Formed publishing house Boni and Liveright with Charles Boni 1917, published Modern Library 1918–25. Published political radicals as well as famous European and U.S. writers, sold with flamboyant publicity and huge success for about 10 years.

Liverpool, city in England. Jews there before 1750. "Old" Hebrew Congregation organized or reorganized at Turton Court 1780. First synagogue consecrated 1808. Jewish pop. 7,500 (1971).

Livni, David ha-, see Weiss, David.

Loanz, Elijah ben Moses (1564–1636), German kabbalist. Noted writer of kabbalistic amulets and incantations. Author of kabbalistic commentaries on Bible, supercommentaries, and halakhic works.

Locker, Berl (1887–1972), Labor Zionist leader; b. Galicia. Active in Po'alei Zion party in Austria and U.S. Member of Zionist and Jewish Agency Executive in London 1931–36; then settled in Ereẓ Israel. Chairman of Jewish Agency 1948-56, Mapai member of Third Knesset. His wife, **Malke** (1887–), Yiddish poet, essayist. Wrote on Rimbaud and romantic and symbolist poets.

Lockspeiser, Sir Ben (1891–), British scientist, industrial expert. Director general of Ministry of Aircraft Production during WWII, secretary of Dept. of Scientific and Industrial Research 1949–56. Pres. Council of European Organization for Nuclear Research, 1955–57. His brother, **Edward** (1905–1973), conductor, musicologist.

Lod, see Lydda.

°**Lods, Adolphe** (1867–1948), French Protestant Bible scholar, historian. Taught Hebrew language and literature at Sorbonne fr. 1906. Works incl. major 2-vol. *La croyance à la vie future et le culte des morts dans l'antiquité Israélite* and *Histoire de la littérature hébraïque et juive* (to 135 C.E.).

Lodz, city in Poland. Jews there in late 18th c. Limitations to Jewish settlement in Poland abolished 1848. Economic life flourished although hard hit by anti-Jewish economic policy between world wars. Under Germans, ghetto founded 1940; 233,000 Jews in 1939, second

largest Jewish community in Poland. 800 Jews remained on liberation. Over 50,000 Jews returned by end of 1946, but successive waves of emigration led to end of community by 1968.

Loeb, Isidore (1839–1892), French rabbi, scholar. Secretary of Alliance Israélite Universelle in Paris 1869–1892. Scholarly work covered biblical and talmudic literature, medieval historiography, mathematical works, history of Jews in France and Spain.

Loeb, Jacques (1859–1924), U.S. physiological chemist; b. Alsace. Prof. at Univ. of California 1902–10, head of general physiology division at Rockefeller Inst. for Medical Research in N.Y. 1910–24. Brilliant experimentalist and pioneer in explaining vital processes on basis of physical chemistry.

Loeb, James (1867–1933), U.S. banker, philanthropist, translator. Worked in father's firm Kuhn, Loeb and Co. 1888–1901. Endowments incl. Inst. of Musical Art in N.Y. and Loeb Classical Library.

Loebel, Israel (18th c.), preacher, *dayyan* in Mogilev and Novogrudok; opponent of Ḥasidism. In his writings compared Ḥasidism with heretical sects that had arisen within Judaism throughout its history.

Loebl, Eugen (1907–), Czechoslovak economist, politician. First deputy in ministry of Foreign Trade 1949. Tried with Rudolf Slánský and sentenced to life imprisonment. 1952. Released and appointed director of state bank in Bratislava 1963. Went to U.S. after Soviet invasion 1968.

Loeb-Leopold Case, U.S. murder case 1924, involving **Richard Loeb** (1905–1936), and **Nathan Freuenthal Leopold** (1904–1971), scions of wealthy Chicago Jewish families who thought they had perpetrated perfect crime by murdering 14-year-old Bobby Franks. Sentenced to life imprisonment. Loeb murdered in prison. Leopold paroled to Puerto Rico 1958, subsequently teaching at Univ.

Loesser, Frank (1910–1969), U.S. composer. Wrote music for films, incl. *Hans Christian Andersen,* and musicals *Guys and Dolls,* and *The Most Happy Fella.*

Loew, Eleazar (1758–1837), rabbi in Poland, Hungary. Fought against religious reform. Known for scholarly works in all areas of *halakhah.*

Loew, Immanuel (1854–1944), Hungarian rabbi, scholar; son of Leopold Loew. Represented Neolog communities in Upper Chamber of Hungarian parliament fr. 1927. Noted preacher in Hungarian. Fame as scholar rests on pioneering work in field of talmudic and rabbinic lexicography and his 4-vol. *Die Flora der Juden.*

Loew, Leopold (Lipót; 1811–1875), first Reform rabbi in Hungary (in Szeged fr. 1850); advocate of Hungarian Jewish emancipation. Medieval form of Jewish oath abolished in Hungary on basis of his lecture at Hungarian Academy of Sciences. First to deal with history of Hungarian Jewry.

Leopold Loew

Loew, Marcus (1872–1927), U.S. motion picture executive. Attained powerful position in U.S. film industry. Pres. Metro-Goldwyn-Mayer film studios and Loew's Inc., one of largest cinema chains in U.S.

Loewe, Frederick (1904–), U.S. composer. Composed musical comedies in collaboration with librettist Alan Jay Lerner. Works incl. *Brigadoon, Camelot, My Fair Lady, Gigi.*

Loewe, Heinrich (Eliakim; 1867–1950), one of first Zionists in Germany, scholar in Jewish folklore, librarian. Founded Zionist Federation in Germany, first editor of *Juedische Rundschau.* Settled in Ereẓ Israel 1933. Librarian of municipal library in Tel Aviv.

Loewe, Herbert Martin James (1882–1940), English orientalist; grandson of Louis Loewe. Lecturer in rabbinic Hebrew at Oxford, Cambridge. Wrote on medieval literature and collaborated with C.G. Montefiore in *Rabbinic Anthology.*

Loewe, Joel (Brill; 1762–1802), Hebrew writer, grammarian, biblical exegete in Moses Mendelssohn circle in Berlin. Translated Passover *Haggadah* into German. Wrote grammar of biblical Hebrew.

Loewe, Louis (Eliezer ha-Levi; 1809–1888), English orientalist; b. Germany, in London fr. 1833. Moses Montefiore's interpreter and secretary fr. 1839, accompanying him during Damascus Affair 1840. Directed oriental section of Library of Duke of Sussex c. 15 years. Principal of Jews' College 1856–58, and of Ramsgate theological seminary (1869–88).

Loewe, Ludwig (1839–1886) and **Isidor** (1848–1910), German industrialists, in Berlin. Ludwig served on Berlin's City Council 1860, elected to Prussian Landtag 1876, Reichstag 1878 as Social Democrat. Fr. 1872 produced rifles. Company merged with Mauser factory after Ludwig's death.

Loewenstamm, Aryeh Loeb ben Saul (1690–1755), rabbi of Amsterdam 1740–55. Wrote responsa, novellae, notes. Participated in Emden-Eybeschuetz controversy.

Loewenstein, Bernhard (1821–1889), rabbi, preacher, pioneer of Reform movement. Most important congregational work done in Lemberg. Registrar of community. Published sermons and poems.

Loewenstein, Karl (1891–1973), U.S. political scientist; b. Munich, in U.S. fr. 1934. Wrote on public law and comparative government of European and American political systems.

Loewenstein (von Opoka), Nathan (1859–1929), lawyer, political leader; son of Bernhard Loewenstein. Leader of Galician assimilationists. Deputy in Austrian parliament fr. 1907, Polish Sejm after WWI. Prominent for conservative approach as landowner and assimilationist. Defense council in Steiger trial 1924–25.

Loewenstein, Rudolph Maurice (1898–), psychoanalyst, psychoanalytic theoretician; b. Poland, in Paris fr. 1925, U.S. fr. 1943. Developed important aspects of Freudian theory, esp. in field of ego psychology. Pres. American Psychoanalytic Association.

Loewenstein-Strashunsky, Joel David (1816–1850), cantor. Succeeded father as cantor of Vilna at age 15. Gave successful recitals in Warsaw 1824, but passage fr. ghetto to cosmopolitan city left him in state of shock, leading him to wander through cities of C. Europe. Life became subject of legends and literary works.

Loewenthal, Eduard (1836–1917), German political theorist. Advocated new religion based on scientific truths and rejecting metaphysical concepts. Founded European Union 1869 to abolish war.

Loewi, Otto (1873–1961), biochemist. Prof. at Univ. of Graz in Austria 1909–38. Test for pancreatic insufficiency known as Loewi's test. Nobel Prize 1936 "for dis-

coveries relating to chemical transmission of nerve impulses." Imprisoned by Nazis 1938. On release went to U.S. Prof. at NYU.

Loewinger, David Samuel (1904–), biblical, talmudic scholar, bibliographer. Director of Budapest rabbinical seminary 1942; responsible for resumption of its scholarly activities after WWII. Fr. 1950 in Israel. Directed Inst. of Microfilms of Hebrew Mss. in Hebrew Univ. Library. Specialized in problem of Bible mss.

Loewinson-Lessing, Franz Yulyevich (1861–1939), Russian geologist, pioneer of magmatic petrology. Occupied chair of geology, petrology, and minerology at Polytechnic Inst. of St Petersburg 1902–30. Director of Petrographical Inst. Introduced classification of igneous rocks. Works on petrography became standard texts in USSR.

Loewisohn, Solomon (1789–1821), Hebrew writer; b. Hungary, studied in Prague, settled in Vienna. Worked as proofreader and counselor of Anton von Schmid. Insanity led to untimely death. His *Meliẓat Yeshurun* is first aesthetic interpretation of Bible in Hebrew.

Loewith, Karl (1897–), German philosopher; of Jewish origin. Taught in Japan, U.S., Germany. Tried to move toward predominantly Aristotelian horizon of thought in hope of establishing truly cosmological philosophy.

Loewy, Emanuel (1857–1938), Austrian classical archaeologist. Prof. in Rome and Vienna. Contributed to understanding of then underestimated archaic art of Greece.

Loewy, Isaac (1793–1847), Hungarian industrialist; founder of town of Ujpest. Took over family tanning business and subsequently settled N. of Budapest in early 1830s. Settlement declared borough with name of Ujpest 1840; elected pres. town council.

Loewy, Jacob Ezekiel ben Joseph (1814–1864), rabbi, author in Poland. Wrote halakhic works which, in conformity with his conservative approach, attempted to harmonize scientific criticism with tradition.

Loewy, Maurice (1833–1907), astronomer; b. Pressburg. Astronomer at Paris observatory 1864; headed photographic "Carte du Ciel" enterprise 1892. Developed several new observational methods and invented "elbow" telescope.

Holocaust Museum at Kibbutz Loḥamei Ha-Getta'ot.

Loḥamei ha-Getta'ot, kibbutz nr. Acre, Israel, affiliated with Ha-Kibbutz ha-Me'uḥad; founded 1949 by group of survivors of resistance against Nazis in Polish and Lithuanian ghettoes. Site of Ghetto Fighters' House, Holocaust Museum, and educational center. Pop. 341 (1971).

Loḥamei Ḥerut Israel (Leḥi, or **"Stern Group"),** armed underground organization in Ereẓ Israel founded by Abraham Stern 1940 in breakaway fr. Irgun Ẓeva'i Le'ummi to continue fight against Mandate authorities even during war (incl. assassination of Lord Moyne in Egypt). Continued operations until end of Mandate, incl. sabotage operations outside country. Fought with Haganah and Irgun in War of Independence, but disbanded when suspected of assassinating Count Folke Bernadotte in Jerusalem 1948.

Lombardy, region in N. Italy. References to Jews fr. 4th c. Jewish pop. 900 on expulsion fr. duchy of Milan by Philip II 1597. 500 Jews by mid-19th c., mostly in Milan; 8,500 Jews in 1966.

Lombroso, Cesare (1835–1909), Italian physician, criminologist. Famed for concept of "born criminal." Although concept no longer accepted, remains important figure in behavioral sciences and is credited with shifting emphasis in criminology fr. crime itself to criminal and his origins. Opponent of capital punishment. Supporter of Zionism after 1900. Prof. at Turin Univ.

Cesare Lombroso

Lomza, town in Poland. Jews expelled 1556, returned after 1815. Great Yeshivah founded 1883, transferred 1926 to Ereẓ Israel (Petaḥ Tikvah). 11,000 Jews in 1939. Town occupied by Germans 1941; Jews deported to extermination camps 1942–43.

London, capital of England, seat of its largest Jewish community. Jewish quarter first mentioned 1128. Jews sporadically persecuted until 1290, when expelled with rest of English Jewry. When Manasseh ben Israel visited England 1655 secret community of several families existed. With accession of Charles II Sephardi community enjoyed de facto recognition. Ashkenazim organized their own congregation c. 1690, gradually becoming more numerous and influential. Jews accorded freedom city 1831. United Synagogue founded 1870. With mass emigration fr. Russia Jewish pop. reached 150,000 by WWI largely in East End. Central bodies of English Jewry established there, incl. chief rabbinate. Jews now largely in more affluent suburbs. Jewish pop. 280,000 (1971), with 200 synagogues, 5 major synagogal organizations.

Petticoat Lane, 19th-cent. engraving of the market in the heart of London's Jewish quarter.

London, Artur (1915–), Czechoslovak Communist leader. Fought in Spanish Civil War. Interned in Buchenwald in WWII. Deputy minister for foreign affairs 1948. Convicted at Slánský trial 1952, released 1955. Settled in France 1963. His account of Slánský trial *L'Aveu* made into film.

London, Meyer (1871–1926), U.S. lawyer, Socialist leader, congressman. Active in Socialist Party of America; legal counsel for several unions. As three-time congressman 1914, 1916, 1920, fought restrictive

immigration and favored nationalization of coal industry. Opposed entry into WWI. Opponent of Zionism.

London, Solomon Zalman ben Moses Raphael (1661–1748), author, translator, bookseller; b. Lithuania, lived in Amsterdam, London, Frankfort. His *Kohelet Shelomo*, popular devotional handbook in Hebrew and Yiddish.

Long Beach, city in Cal., U.S. First Jewish resident 1898. Permanent Jewish organization after WWI. Pop. 15,000 (1971).

Lonzano, Menahem ben Judah de (1550–before 1624), linguist, poet, kabbalist in Turkey, Italy, Ereẓ Israel. Wrote biblical commentaries and works on Talmud and Lurianic Kabbalah. Thorough scholar who made several journeys in search of mss.

Lookstein, Joseph Hyman (1902–), U.S. rabbi, educator. Founder 1936 and principal for over 30 years of Ramaz School, N.Y. Pres. Rabbinical Council of America 1941–43. Acting pres. 1958 and chancellor of Israel's Bar-Ilan Univ. Deeply involved in Mizrachi movement.

Mass rally at Hollywood Bowl, Los Angeles at end of Six-Day War.

Jewish communities in Louisiana.

Lopez, Aaron (1731–1782), American merchant-shipper; b. Portugal, arrived in Newport, R.I. 1752. Built up extensive transatlantic mercantile empire. Specialized in whale oil and spermaceti candle industries; one of few American Jews to trade in slaves. Newport's leading merchant on eve of Revolution and rebel supporter. Left Newport for Massachusetts.

Elizabethan etching showing Roderigo Lopez plotting to poison the queen.

Lopez, Roderigo (1525–1594), Marrano physician; b. Portugal, settled in London. Physician to Earl of Leicester and Queen Elizabeth 1586. Involved in various intrigues, first on behalf of Portuguese pretender, then to reach understanding with Spain. Accused of plot to poison Elizabeth and executed. Considered prototype of Shylock in Shakespeare's *Merchant of Venice*.

Lopez, Sabatino (1867–1951), Italian playwright, critic, novelist. Directed Italian Writers' Guild 1911–19. Chairman of Zionist Organization in Milan for many years. Wrote about 70 plays. His son, **Robert Sabatino** (1910–), medieval historian; in U.S. fr. 1939. at Yale Univ. Wrote on economic history of Middle Ages.

Lorbeerbaum, Jacob ben Jacob Moses of Lissa (c. 1760–1832), Polish rabbi, halakhist. His *Ḥavvat Da'at* on *Shulḥan Arukh* won him reputation as outstanding *posek*. Vigorous opponent of Reform. Enlarged yeshivah at Lissa and published many rabbinic works.

Lorge, Irving (1905–1961), U.S. educator. Prof. at Inst. of Psychological Research. Pioneered research in mental measurement and capacity for human learning.

Loria, Achille (1857–1943), Italian economist. Appointed to Italian senate 1919. His emphasis on importance of free land in U.S. history had considerable influence on Charles Beard and Frederick Jackson Turner.

Lorje, Chaim (1821–1878), educator. Founder in Germany of first society for settlement of Ereẓ Israel.

Lorki, Joshua (d. c. 1419), apostate physician, writer; converted 1412, assuming name Gerónimo de Santa Fé. Conceived idea of disputation with Jews of Alcañiz, which was ultimately held at Tortosa with Jews of Aragon and Catalonia, whom he treated with contempt. Called by Jews *"Megaddef"* ("Blasphemer"). Wrote anti-Jewish polemics.

Lorm, Hieronymus (pseud. of **Heinrich Landesmann**; 1821–1902), Austrian poet, novelist. Eventually became deaf and blind. Works incl. 2-vol. novel *Am Kamin* and poems *Nachsommer*.

Lorraine, region in E. France. Jews mentioned fr. 12th c. Expelled 1477; decree theoretically in force until 18th c. although individuals returned fr. 16th c. Open synagogues in late 18th c. 10,000 Jews in 1900. **Pop.** greatly reduced by assimilation and deportations of WWII. Main communities in 1970s at Metz, Nancy, Sarreguemines.

Lorre, Peter (1904–1964), film actor. Originally appeared in German films. Won fame for role as killer in *M.* Later went to Hollywood, where his notable films incl. *The Maltese Falcon, Casablanca,* and *Arsenic and Old Lace.*

Los Angeles, city in Cal., U.S. First Jewish resident 1841. Hebrew Benevolent Society became first social welfare organization of city c. 1854. Influx of European Jews began c. 1900, aided by Industrial Removal Office. Community increased rapidly after WWII with move westward from all parts of U.S. Jews prominent in movie industry, real estate, finance, electronics, research, aircraft, and education. Jewish pop. 535,000 (1971).

Lot, nephew of Abraham who accompanied him to Canaan. After quarrel bet. their respective shepherds, parted company and settled nr. Sodom. When captured by Chedorlaomer and his allies, Abraham rescued him. After destruction of Sodom, fled to the hills of Moab, with his two daughters, where, through incestuous relations with their father, his daughters became mothers of Moab and Ammon.

Lothar, Ernst (pseud. of **Ernst Lothar Mueller;** 1890–), Austrian novelist, stage director; convert to Catholicism. Succeeded Max Reinhardt as director of Vienna's "Theater in der Josefstadt." Works incl. *The Clairvoyant* and *Beneath Another Sun.*

Louisiana, U.S. state. Black code excluded non-Catholics in French

colony. Presence of Jews recorded 1757–58. First congregation Shaarei Chassed 1827 in New Orleans. Widow and orphan relief assoc. first of kind in U.S. 1854. Jewish pop. 16,115 (1971), mostly in New Orleans, with 20 congregations.

Louisville, city in Kentucky, U.S. Jews partially financed Clark's expedition which occupied area 1778. Congregation 1834, synagogue 1836. In late 1840s and 1850s German Jews settled, and after 1880s E. Europeans. Outstanding Jewish personalities incl. Louis D. Brandeis, Lewis N. Dembitz. Jewish pop. 8,500 (1971).

Lourie, Arthur (1903–), Israel diplomat; b. S. Africa. Political secretary of Jewish Agency in London 1933–48. Ambassador to Canada 1957–59, U.K. 1960–65.

Lovell, Leopold (1905–), S. African politician. Labor Party member of House of Assembly 1948–57. Moved to Swaziland 1961, becoming minister of finance, commerce, and industry 1967, only white man in country's first cabinet.

Lovestone, Jay (Jacov Liebstein; 1898–), U.S. left-wing leader. A founder, executive secretary 1927–29 of U.S. Communist Party, but after stabilization of American Communism, formed opposition community party. After WWII guided AFL and subsequently AFL-CIO anti-Communist foreign policy.

Lovy, Israel (Lowy; Israel Glogauer; 1773–1832), *ḥazzan,* composer; b. nr. Danzig. Chief *ḥazzan* at synagogue in Rue Notre Dame de Nazareth in Paris. fr. 1822. Organized four-voiced choir there, for which he composed *Chants religieux . . . pour prières hébraïques.*

Löw, see Loew.

Low, Sir Sidney James Mark (1857–1932), English editor, writer. Editor of *St. James Gazette* 1888–1897. Author of *The Government of England.* Wrote series of highly successful propaganda books on British Empire during WWI. His daughter Ivy married Maxim Litvinov.

Low, Sir Maurice (1860–1929), journalist; brother of Sir Sidney Low. Emigrated to U.S. Washington correspondent of *Boston Globe,* London *Daily Chronicle, Morning Post.* One of outstanding correspondents in U.S. Author of *The American People.*

°**Lowdermilk, Walter Clay** (1888–1974), U.S. land conservation hydrology expert. Proposed plan for development of Jordan Valley 1939, which later became basis for national water plan of Israel.

Lowe, Adolph (1893–), economist. Prof. at Kiel Univ. 1926–31. Went to Manchester 1933, in U.S. fr. 1940. Directed research at Inst. of World Affairs in N.Y. 1943–51. Publications incl. *Economics and Sociology* and *The Classical Theory of Economic Growth.*

Lowenstein, Solomon (1877–1942), U.S. social work executive, Reform rabbi. Director of Federation of Jewish Philanthropic Societies 1920–35, coordinating and systemizing great expansion in Jewish philanthropy during Depression.

Lowenthal, Marvin (1890–1969), U.S. Zionist writer. Organized West Coast Zionist movement 1916–18. European editor of *Menorah Journal* 1924–29. Widely known in U.S. for essays and lectures. Editor of *The American Zionist* 1952–54. Works incl. *A World Passed By,* about Jews in Europe and N. Africa, and *The Jews of Germany.*

Lowie, Robert Harry (1883–1957), U.S. anthropologist. Taught at Univ. of California at Berkeley 1917–50. Precursor of structural anthropology. Concerned with illuminating interaction bet. organization, religion, and folklore.

Lown, Philip W. (1890–), U.S. shoe manufacturer, philanthropist. Founded Lown School of Near Eastern and Judaic Studies. Pres. American Association for Jewish Education fr. 1950 and Hebrew Teachers College, Brookline, Mass. fr. 1962.

°**Lowth, Robert** (1710–1787), Hebraist. Prof. of poetry at Oxford. First modern scholar to formulate theory of parallelism as metrical basis of biblical Hebrew poetry, showing that it was fundamentally antiphonal.

Lozovski (Dridzo), Solomon Abramovich (1878–1952), Soviet statesman, head of trade union International Profintern 1921–37, deputy commissar for foreign affairs 1939–46, director of Soviet Information Bureau and responsible for work of Jewish Anti-Fascist Committee. Arrested 1949; executed with other Jewish writers and intellectuals.

Lubarsky, Abraham Elijah (1856–1920), early member of Ḥovevei Zion in Russia; in U.S. fr. 1903 where he was moving spirit of Hebrew movement.

Lubavich, see Schneersohn.

Lubetkin, Zivia (1914–), fighter in Warsaw ghetto uprising; settled in Ereẓ Israel 1944. Among founders of kibbutz Loḥamei ha-Getta'ot. Member of Jewish Agency. Wife of Yiẓḥak Cukierman.

Lubetzky, Judah (1850–1910), French rabbi. Took vigorous and successful stand against proposal to introduce conditional clause into Jewish marriage in France with aim of making civil divorce effective in dissolution of Jewish marriages. Wrote rabbinic works.

Lubin, Isador (1896–), U.S. economist. Served numerous public and semi-public institutions, incl. Allied Reparations Commission and U.S. Mission to UN. Taught at several univs. Consultant to United Israel Appeal fr. 1960s.

Lubitsch, Ernst (1892–1947), film producer, director; b. Berlin. Played comic parts in movies before becoming director. Moved to Los Angeles 1922. Made name with *The Love Parade, The Merry Widow,* and *Ninotchka.* A master of witty and subtle humor.

Expulsion of Jews from Lublin by Nazis.

Lublin, city in Poland. Jews first mentioned as transients 1316. Fairs and yeshivah of Lublin central to Jewish communal and cultural life in Poland. Many distinguished scholars lived there. Important commercial center in 19th c. 37,830 Jews in 1939. City captured by Germans Sept. 1939, becoming center for mass extermination of Jews. After WWII several thousand Jews settled there but majority left 1946–50 and remainder 1968.

Lublin, Meir ben Gedaliah (Maharam of Lublin; 1558–1618), Polish talmudist, halakhic authority. Headed various yeshivot in Poland, frequent participant in Council of Lands. Besides responsa, also wrote *Me'ir Einei Ḥakhamim,* commentary on most tractates of Talmud.

Lublinski, Samuel (1868–1910), German playwright, literary historian, philosopher of religion; one of earliest Zionists in Berlin. Known for critical insight into literary trends. Religious works incl. *Die Enstehung des Judentums.*

Luboshitzki, Aaron (1874–1942), Hebrew writer, poet, educator. Member of Hebrew literary circle in Warsaw. Wrote children's literature, and a short Jewish history. During WWII sent to ghetto and active in clandestine cultural activities until killed by Nazis.

Lucena, town in Spain. Under Muslim rule famous as "entirely Jewish city," and tradition states that it was founded by Jews. Until 12th c. cultural center of Andalusian Jewry with distinguished scholars, incl. Isaac Alfasi, Joseph ibn Migash, Jonah ibn Janāḥ, Moses and Abraham ibn Ezra, and Judah Halevi. Many Jews forced to convert to Islam 1146 and community not able to recover.

Luck, see Lutsk.

Luckman, Sidney (1916–), U.S. football player. Played with Chicago Bears. Pro-football's first great T-formation quarterback. Guided Bears to championships 1940–43.

Lucuas (2nd c.), Jewish "king" and leader of Jewish rising in Cyrene 115–117.

Ludmir, see Vladimir Volynski.

Ludo, Isac Iacovitz (1894–), Rumanian author, journalist, translator. Edited Jewish weekly *Adam.* Leader in fight against anti-Semitism. Most of his works on Jewish problems.

Ludomir, Maid of (Hannah Rachel Werbermacher; 1805–1892), ḥasidic "woman-*ẓaddik*"; b. Ukraine. Began to observe religious duties of males after receiving "new and sublime soul" during serious illness. Lectured to her *ḥasidim.* After marrying at age of 40, emigrated to Ereẓ Israel. continuing mystical studies.

Ludwig (Cohn), Emil (1881–1948), German biographer, author; baptized 1902, renounced Christianity 20 years later after assassination of Walter Rathenau. Prolific successful and popular writer of such biographies as *Goethe, Napoleon, Bismarck, Cleopatra.*

°**Lueger, Karl** (1844–1910), Viennese anti-Semite. Confirmed as mayor of Vienna 1897 by Francis Joseph I after latter's three previous refusals. While effecting many social reforms, his administration discriminated against Jews. Influenced Hitler and firmly established Viennese anti-Semitic tradition.

Lukács, Georg (György; 1885–1971), Hungarian philosopher, literary critic, socialist. Left Judaism before WWI. Commissioner for education in Béla Kun government 1919; fled to Austria upon collapse, then Russia 1933, editing Communist journals. Returned to Hungary after WWII. Pres. Hungarian Academy of Sciences and prof. at Univ. of Budapest. Works provoked clashes with Communist authorities. Known for Marxist interpretations of literature.

Georg Lukács

Buying "lulavim" in Jerusalem in preparation for Sukkot.

Lukas, Paul (1895–1971), U.S. actor. Appeared on stage. Films incl. *Dodsworth* and *Four Horsemen of the Apocalypse.*

Lulav (Heb. "shoot"), palm branch; one of "four species" used on Sukkot, together with *etrog, hadas,* and *aravah.*

Lumbroso, Abram ben Isaac Vita (1813–1887), personal physician of bey of Tunis, minister of health in Tunisian government. Propagated Western culture in Tunisia, philanthropist, wrote medical studies.

Lumbroso, Alberto Emmanuelé (1872–1942), Italian historian; son of Giacomo Lumbroso. Specialized in Napoleonic period. Italian military attaché to Greece during WWI.

Lumbroso, Giacomo (1844–1925), Italian classical historian, son of Abram Lumbroso. Specialist in Hellenic civilization of Egypt. Expert in ancillary disciplines of papyrology and epigraphy. Taught at Italian univs.

Lumbroso, Isaac ben Jacob (d. 1752), Tunisian scholar. Chief rabbi and *qā'id* (leader) of Jews. Wealthy and generous. Wrote voluminous didactic commentary on several parts of Talmud.

Lumet, Sidney (1924–), U.S. theatrical, film director. Gained reputation as director of live TV dramas. Films incl. *Fail-Safe, The Pawnbroker,* and *Funny Girl.*

Lumina, Jewish Social Democratic group in Rumania; founded 1893 in opposition to Rumanian Social Democratic Party, whose tendency to cooperate with liberal bourgeois party was seen as main factor in country's anti-Semitism. Published periodicals in Yiddish.

Luncz, Abraham Moses (1854–1918), author, publisher, editor of geographical works on Ereẓ Israel; went fr. Lithuania to Jerusalem 1869. Leading scholar of Ereẓ Israel geography. Published literary almanac *Lu'aḥ Ereẓ Israel.* Blind fr. age 25.

Lunel, town in S. France; home of medieval Jewish community renowned for its scholars.

Lunel, Armand (1892–), French author. Known for sensitive and imaginative portrayals of Provence and its inhabitants (incl. Jews of Avignon). Wrote librettos for works by Darius Milhaud.

Lunts, Lev Natanovich (1901–1924), Russian playwright, literary theorist. Founder of important young writers' group in Petrograd, Serapion Brothers, whose aims were to free art fr. political pressures and win tolerance for artistic dissent.

Luria, Alexander Romanovich (1902–), Soviet psychologist. Director of Laboratory of Experimental Psychology and Restoration of Higher Cortical Functions, USSR Academy of Medical Sciences. Writings incl. *Higher Cortical Functions in Man* and *The Mind of a Mnemonist.*

Luria, David ben Judah (1798–1855), Lithuanian rabbi, scholar. Founded yeshivah in Bykhow. His literary works deal with almost all books of Oral Law, reflecting extraordinary knowledge of Torah together with feeling for scientific criticism and understanding of literal meaning.

Luria, Isaac ben Solomon Ashkenazi (Ha-Ari; 1534–1572), kabbalist; b. Jerusalem, brought up in Egypt, settled in Safed 1570. Renowned for ascetic life and saintly character. His personality made profound impression on contemporaries and on posterity. Transmitted his teachings orally, but these were posthumously reworked by some of his pupils. Kabbalistic trend which he launched (Lurianic Kabbalah) deeply influenced subsequent Jewish religious life. Among new concepts introduced were *ẓimẓum* (withdrawal of God) and *tikkun* (restitution of right order of cosmos).

Luria, Salvador Edward (1912–), U.S. biologist; b. Turin, in U.S. fr. 1940. Prof. at MIT. His work formed essential part of foundation of new science of molecular biology. Pioneer in microbial genetics. Nobel Prize 1969.

Luria, Solomon ben Jehiel (Rashal; Maharshal; ? 1510–1574), Polish *posek,* talmudic commentator. Unique in his time for complete independence in halakhic ruling and for critical methods. Opposed both *pilpul* and philosophy. Interests encompassed grammar, Kabbalah, liturgy.

Lurie, Harry Lawrence (1892–1973), U.S. social worker. Director, Council of Jewish Federation and Welfare Funds 1935–37. Editor of *Encyclopedia of Social Work,* wrote *A Heritage Affirmed,* history of federation movement.

Lurie, Joseph (1871–1937), Zionist leader, Hebrew educator; b. Lithuania. Edited Zionist papers in Hebrew and Yiddish. Settled in Ereẓ Israel 1907. Headed education dept. of Va'ad Le'ummi fr. 1919.

Lurie, Ted R. (1909–1974), Israel journalist; b. New York, settled in Ereẓ Israel 1930. Editor and managing director of *Jerusalem Post* fr. 1955.

Lurie, Zvi (1906–1968), Mapam labor leader in Israel; b. Poland, settled in Ereẓ Israel 1925. Member of Jewish Agency Executive.

Lustig, Arnost (1926–), Czech author, writings based largely on experiences in 16 Nazi concentration camps. After 1968 Soviet invasion, settled in U.S.

°**Luther, Martin** (1483–1546), German religious reformer. Initial tolerance toward Jews was soon discarded and became extremely vituperative and ferocious in attacks on them. His influence over Lutheran Church retained all superstitious abhorrence of Jews inherited fr. medieval Catholic Church. His anti-Jewish preaching and writing provided fuel for anti-Semites.

Lutsk (Luck), city in Ukrainian SSR. Jews in 10th c., community of Karaites in 13th c. Jews and Karaites suffered greatly during Chmielnicki massacres 1648–49, Haidamack uprising in 18th c., blood libel 1764. During WWI and up to WWII Jews suffered massacres. Center of Torah studies. 15,880 Jews before WWII; most killed by Germans. 1,500 Jews in late 1960s.

Lutzky, A. (pseud. of **Aaron Zucker;** 1894–1957), Yiddish poet; b. Volhynia in U.S. fr. 1914. Although pessimistic poet, transmuted adversity into gay rhymes and images.

Lux, Stefan (1888–1936), film producer; b. Vienna, lived in Germany, Prague. Shot himself in press gallery of League of Nations to alert humanity to dangers of Fascism and Nazism.

Luxembourg (Luxemburg), grand duchy in W. Europe. Jews first noted 1276; small Jewish settlements in 14th c. Jews massacred during Black Death 1349, expelled 1391, and until 1838 few families lived there. 3,144 Jews in 1935; most deported during Nazi occupation. 1,000 Jews in 1971.

Rosa Luxemburg as "leader of the German workers' movement," stamp issued by East Germany, 1955.

Luxemburg, Rosa (1871–1919), economist, revolutionary. A founder of Social Democratic Party of Poland and Lithuania. Migrated to Germany 1898. Prominent in Socialist International. Opposed WWI as imperialist enterprise and was imprisoned. Founded "Spartakusbund" (transformed into Communist Party 1918). Edited Communist daily *Die Rote Fahne* with Karl Liebknecht. Arrested in Berlin and murdered by army officers. Widely known for theory of imperialism.

Luz, see Beth-El.

Luz, old name for Beth-El [q.v.], first mentioned in account of Jacob's dream there (Gen. 28:19).

Luz (Lozinsky), Kadish (1895–1972), Israel labor leader; b. Belorussia, settled in Ereẓ Israel 1920. Joined kibbutz Deganyah Bet. Mapai Knesset member fr. 1951. Minister of agriculture 1955-59, speaker of Knesset 1959–69.

Luzki, Abraham ben Joseph Solomon (1792–1855), Karaite scholar, poet in Crimea; son of Joseph Solomon Luzki. Founded Karaite school in Yevpatoriya 1835 which gained distinguished reputation under his guidance. Wrote on Karaite lore, poems, sermons.

Luzki, Joseph Solomon ben Moses (d. 1844), Karaite scholar in Crimea. Instrumental in obtaining exemption for Karaites fr. compulsory military service. Wrote liturgical poems, prayers, and hymns, some of which were incorporated in Karaite prayer book.

Luzki, Simḥah Isaac ben Moses (d. 1766), Karaite writer, bibliographer in Crimea. Diligent copyist of early Karaite mss. and first to compile bibliographical compendium of Karaite works. Wrote about 20 works on theology, philosophy, *halakhah,* Kabbalah, and book of precepts.

Luigi Luzzatti

Luzzatti, Luigi (1841–1927), Italian statesman, economist; first Jewish prime minister of Italy. Minister of treasury 1891–92, 1896–98, 1904–06; minister of agriculture 1909; prime minister 1910–11. Founded Banca Popolare in Milan, first cooperative store in Italy; restored Italy's finances. Acted on behalf of oppressed European Jews, esp. in Rumania. Supported Zionist enterprises.

Luzzatto, Ephraim (Angelo; 1729–1792), Italian Hebrew poet; physician for nearly 30 years in London's Portuguese community hospital. His collected poems, reflecting individual experience, were published as *Elleh Benei ha Ne'urim,* and influenced poetry of M.J. Lebensohn and J.L. Gordon.

Luzzatto, Gino (1878–1964), Italian Socialist, economist historian. Prof. in Bari, Trieste, Venice

Samuel David Luzzatto

Nr. 7237 a LWÓW, CZWARTEK, 18. MAJA 1939. ROK XXI

CHWILA

WYDANIE PORANNE

Cena egzemplarza 15 gr.

DZIENNIK DLA SPRAW POLITYCZNYCH, SPOŁECZNYCH I KULTURALNYCH

REDAKCJA I ADMINISTRACJA: ULICA PODWALE 3, I. PIĘTRO. — KONTO P. K. O. 500.700.

KANTOR OGŁOSZEŃ, PRENUMERATY I SPRZEDAŻY: UL. PODWALE 3, PARTER. TELEFON 226-16.

„BIAŁA KSIĘGA"

Strejk generalny Żydów w Palestynie

W Tel Awiwie strejk potrwa 10 dni?

2) Niepodległe państwo Arabów i Żydów w Palestynie

Masthead and headlines of Lvov Jewish newspaper, "Chwila" ("The Moment"), May 18, 1939, with news of Jewish general strike in Palestine protesting British White Paper.

(except for 1938–45 because of Italy's anti-Semitic laws). Member of underground resistance movement in WWII. Councillor in municipality of Venice 1946–51. Active in Jewish affairs.

Luzzatto, Moses Ḥayyim (Ramḥal; 1707–1746), Italian kabbalist, writer, Hebrew poet. Leader of group of thinkers interested in problem of redemption and messianism. After 1727, claimed communication with divine power. Opposed by Italian rabbinate for mystical teachings; migrated to N. Europe and then to Ereẓ Israel. His poetical works influenced on subsequent Hebrew literature; some are in dramatic form. Best-known is ethical treatise *Mesillat Yesharim* ("Path of the Upright"). Pioneer of modern Hebrew literature, with influence on Ḥasidim, *Mitnaggedim*, and Haskalah.

Luzzatto, Samuel David (Shadal; 1800–1865), Italian scholar, philosopher, Bible commentator, translator; a central figure in 19th c. Hebrew literature and scholarship. His writings stress supremacy of Jewish traditional culture over that of other nations; attacked Maimonides, Ibn Ezra, Spinoza, and others, regarding them as unduly influenced by Hellenism. Opposed Kabbalah. Negative attitude toward comtemporary fight for civil rights. Pioneer student of medieval Hebrew literature; works incl. edition of poems of Judah Halevi.

Luzzatto, Simone ben Isaac Simḥah (1583–1663), Italian rabbi, author. Rabbi in Venice for 57 years. Among his responsa was one which permitted travel by gondola on Sabbath. Competent philosopher and mathematician; first to bring forward economic arguments systematically to advocate toleration of Jews.

Lvov (Lwow; Lemberg), city formerly in Poland, now in Ukrainian SSR. By 1550, 352 Jews there. Jews played important part in trade between Orient and West; in constant conflict with townsmen over right to trade. Community teachers represented whole region at Council of Lands. Jews suffered fr. Chmielnicki massacres 1648 and periodic wars in 17th, 18th c., when importance of community declined. Jews controlled wholesale trade bet. Russia and Vienna. Haskalah and assimilationist-Zionist movements there, and eventually nationalist-Zionist influence. Third largest community in independent Poland 109,500 Jews in 1939, most murdered by Nazis; c. 27,800 Jews in 1970.

Lvovich, David (Davidovich; 1882–1950), leader of territorial-socialist movement and ORT. Russian representative in Zionist-Socialist Workers' Party abroad. Elected to Russian constituent assembly 1917. Fr. 1931 in Berlin, Paris, U.S. Vice-pres. and co-pres. ORT.

Lwoff, André Michel (1902–), French biologist. Head of Microbial Physiology Laboratory at Pasteur Institute in Paris fr. 1938. In French underground during WWII. In his study of lysogeny led to entirely new ideas as to evolution and biological role of viruses. Nobel Prize for Medicine and Physiology, 1965.

Lydda (Lod), town in Israel coastal plain. First mentioned in 15th c. B.C.E. In Maccabean times purely Jewish town. Seat of Sanhedrin and of famous Jewish scholars in 1st-2nd c. Septimus Severus established Roman city there 200 C.E. but it remained partly Jewish. Legendary birthplace of St. George; crusaders dedicated church to him, still partly preserved. Most Arab inhabitants left 1948 and town was resettled by new immigrants. Israel's international airport built nearby 1936. Pop. 31,200 (1971), incl. 3,400 Muslims and Christians.

Lynn, city in Mass., U.S. Oldest Jewish organization founded 1884, first synagogue 1901. Jewish pop. 18,800 (1971).

Lyon, Hart, see Levin, Ẓevi Hirsch.

Lyon-Caen, Charles Léon (1843–1935), French jurist. Prof. of law at Sorbonne nearly 50 years. Authority on commercial and international law. Pres. Comité d'aide aux émigrants juifs. Co-authored 8-vol. *Traité de droit commercial* and 2-vol. *Precis de droit commercial,* which became standard works.

Lyons, city in France. Prosperous Jewish community in early 9th c. Expelled 1250. Community reestablished by 18th c. 500-600 families in 1939. During WWII, city was refuge for many Jews and center for Jewish resistance but Jews suffered arrests and deportations. After war many Jewish refugees and Jewish immigrants fr. N. Africa settled there. Jewish pop. 20,000 (1971).

Lyons, Eugene (1898–), U.S. journalist, writer. Served in Moscow after WWI. Wrote on disillusionment with Soviet system. Edited *American Mercury, Pageant.*

Lyons, Jacques Judah (1813–1877), U.S. cantor, rabbi, communal leader; b. Surinam. Rabbi of Congregation Shearith Israel in N.Y. fr. 1839.

Lyons, Sir Joseph (1848–1917), English caterer. With Alfred Salmon, bros. Montague, and Isidore Gluckstein founded catering firm J.Lyons and Co. 1887, which subsequently developed into largest in Britain.

Lyons, Leonard (1906–), U.S. newspaperman whose column *The Lyons Den* is widely syndicated.

Illuminated initial letter "M" of the word "Moysen" (Moses) from the beginning of Eusebius' preface to the Book of Chronicles in a 12th-cent. ms. of assorted Chronicles, S. France.

Maacah, wife of Rehoboam, mother of King Abijah, grandmother of King Asa. Asa deposed her from being "queen mother" because of image she had made for Asherah.

Ma'alot-Tarshīḥā, urban community in W. Upper Galilee, Israel, E. of Nahariyyah. Jewish Ma'alot founded 1957 to replace two *ma'abarot;* united with nearby Arab village Tarshīḥā 1963. Pop. 5,200 (1971).

Ma'amad or **Mahamad,** council of elders in Sephardi community or congregation in West after expulsion fr. Spain.

Ma'aravot (Heb.), arrangement of *piyyutim* that embellish evening *(Ma'ariv)* prayers for festivals and special Sabbaths; in current usage in most Ashkenazi communities.

Ma'arekhet ha-Elohut (Heb. "The Order of God"), anonymous systematic book of early Kabbalah literature, written at end of 13th c. Author's main aim was to remove, or at least weaken, mystical elements which are basic in Kabbalah and in certain rabbinic sayings.

Ma'ariv, see Arvit.

Maariv, Hebrew afternoon newspaper published in Tel Aviv; founded 1948 by Ezriel Carlebach. Weekday circ. 161,000, weekend 230,000 (1973), largest in Israel.

Maarsen, Isaac (1893–1943), Dutch rabbi. Chief rabbi of The Hague fr. 1924. Noted as preacher and lecturer and for writings against Reform Judaism. Published studies in fields of rabbinical literature. Perished in Holocaust.

Ma'aseh, factual circumstance fr. which halakhic rule or principle is derived.

Ma'aseh Bereshit (Heb. "the work of creation"), narration of mysteries of Creation (Gen.1), which became topic for philosophical and mystical interpretations in Jewish thought, and one of paramount subjects in Kabbalah.

Ma'aseh Book (Yid. *Mayse Bukh,* "Book of Stories"), vast anonymous Yiddish collection and adaptation of all types of Jewish and non-Jewish folk literature, oral traditions, *aggadah,* and Midrash designed for masses; published c. 1580. Serves to teach conduct and ethical principles.

Ma'aseh Merkabah, see Merkabah Mysticism.

Ma'aserot (Heb. "Tithes"), 7th tractate in Mishnah order *Zera'im,* with *gemara* in Jerusalem Talmud. Deals mainly with precepts connected with separation of tithes to be given to levites fr. produce of the land, and prohibition against making use of produce before tithe has been separated.

Ma'aser Sheni (Heb. "Second Tithe"), 8th tractate of Mishnah order *Zera'im,* with *gemara* in Jerusalem Talmud. Deals with incidence and disposal of tithes eaten in Jerusalem.

Ma'barah (Heb.), transitional immigrant camp or quarter in early 1950s in Israel.

°**Macalister, Robert Alexander Stewart** (1870–1951), Irish archaeologist. One of pioneers of Palestinian archaeology. Directed excavations in Gezer 1902–05, 1907–09, hill of Ophel in Jerusalem 1925.

Maccabeans, Order of Ancient, friendly benefit society in Britain whose members are Zionists; founded 1896 by Ephraim Ish-Kishor. Champions of practical Zionist work in Ereẓ Israel.

Maccabee, additional name given to Judah, son of Mattathias, military leader of Jewish revolt against Syria 168 B.C.E. Applies also to other members of family, to Hasmonean dynasty, and in Christian tradition to seven martyred children of Hannah. Meaning of name uncertain.

Maccabees, First Book of (I Maccabees), apocryphal book covering period fr. 175 to 135 B.C.E. Accurate historical source of Maccabean revolt. Written during reign of John Hyrcanus. Probably written originally in Hebrew; extant in Greek.

Maccabees, Second Book of (II Maccabees), apocryphal book, dealing with deeds of Judah Maccabee until 164 B.C.E. Abridgment of larger Greek work by Jason of Cyprus. Author apparently contemporary of hero of his work.

Maccabees, Third Book of (III Maccabees), apocryphal book, describing alleged persecution of Jews by Ptolemy IV Philopator of Egypt (221–204 B.C.E.) Probably dates fr. 1st c. B.C.E.

Maccabees, Fourth Book of (IV Maccabees), apocryphal book. Does not deal with the warriors of the Maccabean revolt, but tells story of martyrs of generation preceding Maccabees. Only surviving major piece of Greek rhetoric in Jewish literature. Probably dates fr. 1st c. C.E.

A "ma'barah" under construction at Talpiyyot, Jerusalem, in the early 1950s.

Maccabiah, international games recognized and approved by International Olympic Committee, held every four years in Israel under auspices of Maccabi movement and open to athletes of Jewish faith fr. all countries. First Maccabiah was held in Tel Aviv 1932.

Maccabi World Union, international Jewish sports organization. Headquarters in Tel Aviv. Membership 200,000 in 38 affiliated countries.

Maccoby, Ḥayyim Zundel (1858–1916), Zionist preacher; b. Poland; also known as "The Maggid from Kamenetz." One of first members of Ḥovevei Zion in England. Strongly opposed Herzl for religious reasons.

°**McDonald, James Grover** (1886–1964), U.S. diplomat. League of Nations High Commissioner for Refugees fr. Germany 1933–35. Member of Anglo-American Committee of Inquiry 1945. U.S. ambassador (until 1949, representative) to Israel May 1948–51.

Machaerus, Transjordan fortress erected by Alexander Yannai in S. Perea. Served as base for Alexander and Aristobulus in their resistance against Romans. Acc. to Christian tradition, John the Baptist executed there.

Machir, son of Manasseh and grandson of Joseph; also eponym of one of most important clans of tribe of Manasseh dwelling in Gilead.

Machir ben Judah (11th c.) French scholar. Author of *Alef Bet de-Rabbi-Makhir,* first talmudic dictionary compiled in Europe (now lost). Its chief function was to connect words used in Talmud with Scripture, explain them, and translate them into French.

Machlup, Fritz (1902–), U.S. economist; b. Austria, in U.S. fr. 1933. Prof. at Johns Hopkins, Princeton Univs. Wrote on expansion of international liquidity. Pres. American Assoc. of Univ. Prof. 1962–64.

Machpelah, Cave of, site purchased by Abraham as burial plot for Sarah. Subsequently, Abraham, Isaac, Rebekah, Jacob, and Leah also interred there. Today identified with Ḥaram el-Khalīl in Hebron. Part of building is from Herodian period, the remainder incorporating Byzantine and Crusader elements. Site of pilgrimage. Venerated by Muslims, who constructed mosque and prohibited or restricted Jewish access.

The outer wall of the Cave of Machpelah.

Macht, David (1882–1961), U.S. pharmacologist. Lecturer at Johns Hopkins Medical School 1912–32; research pharmacologist at Sinai Hospital in Baltimore. Introduced new methods of treatment of diseases. Discovered curative qualities of benzyl alcohol as substitute for cocaine.

Macias, Enrico (1938–), French singer, entertainer; b. Algeria. Popular composer and singer of light songs with special appeal to ex-North Africans in France and elsewhere.

Julian Mack

Mack, Julian William (1866–1943), U.S. judge, Zionist leader. Judge on U.S. circuit court of appeals 1913–43. Pres. first American Jewish Congress. Influenced by Brandeis 1918 to become pres. of Zionist Organization of America, but resigned with Brandeis in dispute over methods of developing Ereẓ Israel but continued other Zionist activities. First chairman of Comité des Délégations Juives at Versailles Peace Conference.

Madaba, Medeba, Moabite city in Transjordan captured by Israelites fr. Amorite king Sihon and allocated to tribe of Reuben. Lost when monarchy divided. Mosaic map of biblical Holy Land and neighboring region discovered there in Byzantine Church 1884.

Madagascar Plan, plan for Jewish settlement proposed by Nazis. First advocated 1885 by Paul de Lagarde, German anti-Semitic nationalist. When Germans still considered mass emigration as solution to Jewish problem, Adolf Eichmann prepared detailed official report calling for 4 million Jews to be shipped to Madagascar over 4-year period, to be financed by world Jewry. Officially shelved Feb. 1942 and replaced by "final solution."

Maḍmūn ben Japheth ben Bundār (d. 1151), Jewish leader of S. Yemen. Merchant and postmaster in Aden who was close both to local authorities and halakhic authorities in Ereẓ Israel. Dozens of letters have been preserved in the *Genizah* written to or by him.

Madrid, capital of Spain. Small Jewish community there in 11th c.; began to flourish in 13th c. Community life ended after persecutions 1391; subsequently restored; final expulsion 1492. Jewish settlement renewed fr. 1869. Community organized in 1920s. Jewish pop. 2,500 (1971).

Mafdal, see National Religious Party.

Maftir (Heb. "one who concludes"), name given to three or more concluding verses of weekly Sabbath reading fr. Pentateuch as well as to final verses of portions read on festivals and public fast days. Also term for person who is called up to read fr. Torah of these passages and then recites *haftarah* fr. Prophets.

Magdala, city on Sea of Galilee mentioned in New Testament; called Migdal Nunaiya in talmudic sources. Home town of Mary Magdalene.

Magdeburg, city in E. Germany. Jews placed under jurisdiction of archbishop 965. Jewish quarter destroyed 1213 and again during Black Death disturbances 1349. Jews expelled 1493, resettled 1703. 2,361 Jews in 1933; community ended in Holocaust. 100 Jews in 1965.

Magen David (Heb. "Shield of David"), hexagram or six-pointed star. Used for decorative and magical purpose in ancient times by Jews and non-Jews, and by Christians in Middle Ages. Use as specially Jewish symbol only fr. 17th c. In 19th c.

Carved and painted wooden holder in shape of "Magen David," possibly receptacle for "maẓẓah" brought to synagogue before Passover, 1770.

taken over by Zionist movement and is featured on national flag of Israel.

Magen David Adom (Heb. "Red Shield of David"), Israel first-aid society (equivalent of Red Cross), founded 1930 as medical wing of Haganah. In Israel, sole recognized first-aid organization.

Maggid (Heb. lit. "one who relates"), popular, often itinerant preacher; also used for angel or supermundane spirit who conveys teachings to scholars worthy of such communication in mysterious ways.

Maggid-Steinschneider, Hillel Noah (1829–1903), Hebrew scholar, writer; b. Vilna. Published *Ir Vilna* containing biographies of Vilna personalities. Wrote history of Guenzburg family completed by his son. Headed Straschun and S.J. Fuenn libraries in Vilna. His son **David M. Maggid** (1862–1942?), scholar; lived in St. Petersburg. Wrote on Jewish history and art, did research on Jewish music. Librarian of Jewish dept. of National Library of Petrograd. Prof. of art history and Hebrew.

Maghar, al-, Druze village in N. Israel nr. Tiberias. One of major Druze centers. Pop. 6,500 (1971).

Maghāriya (Arab. "men [people] of the caves"), sect which kept its books and sacred writings in caves in hills of Ereẓ Israel in 1st c. B.C.E. Maintained that world was created by intermediary power rather than by God. Identified with Essenes or Therapeutae.

Maghrebi-Ma'aravi, Jewish personalities and congregations originating fr. N. Africa. Name occurs in geonic literature and continues to be applied to N. African congregations and their rites.

Magidov, Jacob (1869–1943), Yiddish writer, editor; b. Odessa, in U.S. fr. 1886. A founder of United Hebrew Trades 1888. City editor of *Jewish Morning Journal* 1901–43.

Magnes, Judah Leon (1877–1948), U.S. Reform rabbi, communal leader; Ereẓ Israel educator. Moving spirit and leading figure of Kehillah of N.Y. fr. establishment 1908 to demise 1922. His opposition to U.S. entry into WWI out of pacifist convictions undermined his leadership in Jewish community. Chancellor of Heb. Univ. in Jerusalem 1925–35, first pres. 1935–48. Believing in establishment of Ereẓ Israel as binational state sought accord bet. Arabs and Jews. A founder of Berit Shalom.

Judah L. Magnes

Magnin, Edgar Fogel (1890–), U.S. Reform rabbi, communal leader; in Los Angeles fr. 1915. Rabbi of Congregation B'nai B'rith (Wilshire Boulevard Temple fr. 1929). Taught history at Univ. of S. California 1934–55 and Cal. School of Hebrew Union College.

Magnus, Sir Philip (1842–1933), English educator, politician. Minister of West London Synagogue of British Jews (Reform) 1866–80. London Univ. MP 1906–22. Violently anti-Zionist. His wife, **Katie** (1844–1924), published historical and traditional tales for young reader, incl. *Outlines of Jewish History* and *Jewish Portraits*. His son, **Laurie** (1872–1933), edited anti-Zionist *Jewish Guardian* (1917–31). Wrote *Dictionary of European Literature* and *The Jews in the Christian Era and their Contribution to its Civilization*.

Magnus, Eduard (1799–1872), German painter; baptized as child. Began as Nazarene and ended as realist. Best known as portraitist. Subjects incl. Jenny Lind, composer Mendelssohn, and members Prussian royal family.

Magnus, Heinrich Gustav (1802–1870), German chemist, physicist; abandoned Judaism. Prof. at Univ. of Berlin 1845–69. Numerous discoveries incl. first platinum-ammonia complex and "Magnus Effect," which has important aerodynamic applications.

Magnus, Marcus (Mordecai ben Manlin Dessau, Rauback and Weisel; d. 1736), court agent of Prussian crown prince, later King Frederick William I. Head of Berlin community 1709, spokesman for provincial Jewry before Prussian authorities 1720.

Magnus, Paul Wilhelm (1844–1914), German botanist. Most important work concerned with systematics and life histories of parasitic fungi. Prof. Univ. of Berlin.

Magnus, Rudolph (1873–1927), German physiologist, pharmacologist. One of foremost co-workers of Sir Charles Sherrington. Discovered that body's center of reflexes were located in brainstem up to midbrain. Taught at Utrecht 1908, founding first Dutch pharmacological inst.

Magyar Zsidó Szemle, Hungarian Jewish monthly journal; established 1884, appeared until 1948. Of prime scholarly importance in Jewish world, esp. in 1920s.

Maḥal (abbr. of Heb. *Mitnaddevei Huẓ la-Areẓ,* "foreign volunteers"), term used for volunteers fr. abroad, mainly Jews, who enlisted in Israel Defense Forces and participated in War of Independence 1948–49.

Mahalalel ben Shabbetai Hallelyah (d. after 1675), rabbi, kabbalist, Hebrew poet in Ancona. Known for his collection of poems and *piyyutim, Hallelyah,* recited in synagogues on Sabbaths and festivals. Continued to be ardent believer in Shabbetai Ẓevi even after latter's apostasy.

Mahamad, see Ma'amad.

Mahanaim, locality E. of Jordan River named by Jacob before crossing Jabbok on way to Penuel. Also name of kibbutz in Ḥuleh Valley and nearby airfield.

Maharal, see Judah Loew ben Bezalel.

Maharam, see Meir ben Baruch of Rothenburg; also Lublin, Meir ben Gedaliah.

Maharam Ash, see Eisenstadt, Meir ben Isaac.

Maharam Esh, see Eisenstadter, Meir ben Judah Leib.

Maharam of Lublin, see Lublin, Meir.

Maharam of Padua, see Katzenellenbogen, Meir ben Isaac.

Maharam Schiff, see Schiff, Meir ben Jacob ha-Kohen.

Maharashdam, see Medina, Samuel ben Moses de.

Maharik, see Colon, Joseph ben Solomon.

Maharil, see Moellin, Jacob ben Moses.

Maharit, see Trani, Joseph ben Moses.

Maharsha, see Edels, Samuel Eliezer ben.

Maharshal, Luria, Solomon ben Jehiel.

Maher Shalal Hash Baz (Heb. lit. "Hurry, spoil! Rush, booty!"), traditional vocalization of name which Isaiah was commanded by Lord to give his son who was born during Aramean-Ephraimite war against Judah 734/3–732 B.C.E.

Mahler, Arthur (1871–1916), classical archaeologist, parliamentarian; b. Prague. Elected to Austrian parliament on pro-Zionist ticket 1907.

Mahler, Eduard (1857–1945), Hungarian orientalist, mathematician, astronomer. Prof. at Budapest

Univ.; director of Egyptological Inst. 1912, Oriental Inst. 1922. Wrote important mathematical studies, esp. on theory of surfaces; also on astronomy and chronology of ancient orient.

Mahler, Gustav (1860–1911), composer, conductor. Forced to convert to Catholicism to obtain post as director of Vienna Court Opera 1897. Raised Opera to highest level of artistic achievement. Also conducted Metropolitan Opera and N.Y. Philharmonic. Considered one of most popular contemporary symphonic composers. Song cycles incl. *Lieder eines fahrenden Gesellen* and *Kindertotenlieder.*

Mahler (née **Schoenberger), Margaret** (1897–), child psychiatrist, psychoanalyst. In 1930s directed child guidance clinic in Vienna. Settled in New York 1938. Director of Masters Children's Center, where parallel studies of psychotic and normal children were conducted.

Gustav Mahler medal by Benno Elkan.

Mahler, Raphael (1899–), historian; b. Poland. Taught in U.S. and joined left Po'alei Zion party. Settled in Israel 1950. Prof. at Tel Aviv Univ. His theory on Jewish history accords with historical materialism.

Mahlon and Chilion, two sons of Elimelech and Naomi; husbands of Orpah and Ruth, respectively. Ephrathites of Bethlehem who migrated to Moab together with parents during drought in time of Judges and died there.

Mah Nishtannah (Heb. "what is different? "), first words of four questions asked at Passover *seder* service. Questions come at beginning of recital of *Haggadah* and are usually asked by youngest participant.

Mah Tovu (Heb. "How goodly [are thy tents O Israel]"), opening words (fr. Num. 24:5) of prayer recited by Ashkenazi Jews on entering a synagogue.

Maḥoza, town on Tigris in Babylonia. Most inhabitants were Jews. Center of study after destruction of academy of Nehardea 259, becoming famous 338 when academy of Pumbedita with its scholars moved there. Town destroyed by Romans 363; later rebuilt but declined in 5th c.

Maḥzike Hadas, organization in Galicia and Bukovina representing first attempt by Orthodox to unite for political activities. Founded 1879.

Maḥzor (Heb. "cycle"), festival prayer-book. Originally contained prayers for entire year, as in the earliest-known *Maḥzor Vitry,* a halakhic-liturgical composition by Simḥah b. Samuel of Vitry, pupil of Rashi. Later, the *maḥzor* contained only festival prayers as distinguished fr. the *siddur* containing the daily and weekly prayers.

Mailer, Norman (1923–), U.S. novelist and essayist. His WWII army service in the Pacific provided background for his first success *The Naked and the Dead.* Later his impatience with the novel brought him to concentrate on the essay and booklength reportages *(Armies in the Night, Miami and the Siege of Chicago).* One of the best-known virtuoso stylists in the U.S.

Maimi, Simon (d. 1497), chief rabbi (*arraby moor*) of Portugal. Martyred when Manuel I of Portugal tried to force him to accept Christianity. With eight others immured in dungeon up to neck.

Maimon (Fishman), Ada (1893–1973), leader of women's labor movement in Ereẓ Israel; sister of Judah Leib Maimon; b. Bessarabia, settled in Ereẓ Israel 1912. Mapai Member of 1st and 2nd Knesset. Founded and headed Ayanot girls' Agricultural School.

Maimon (Fishman), Judah Leib (1875–1962), rabbi, leader of religious Zionism; b. Bessarabia, settled in Ereẓ Israel 1913. A founder of Mizrachi educational network. During WWI in U.S. Established and

Norman Mailer

Opening of prayers for Rosh Ha-Shanah from "Leipzig Maḥzor," S. Germany, c. 1320.

MAH NISHTANNAH

מַה נִּשְׁתַּנָּה הַלַּיְלָה הַזֶּה מִכָּל הַלֵּילוֹת.	Wherefore is this night distinguished from all other nights?
שֶׁבְּכָל הַלֵּילוֹת אָנוּ אוֹכְלִין חָמֵץ וּמַצָּה. הַלַּיְלָה הַזֶּה כֻּלּוֹ מַצָּה:	On all other nights we eat either leavened or unleavened bread, but on this night only unleavened.
שֶׁבְּכָל־הַלֵּילוֹת אָנוּ אוֹכְלִין שְׁאָר יְרָקוֹת הַלַּיְלָה הַזֶּה מָרוֹר:	On all other nights we partake of all kinds of herbs, but on this night, especially, bitter herbs.
שֶׁבְּכָל־הַלֵּילוֹת אֵין אָנוּ מַטְבִּילִין אֲפִילוּ פַּעַם אֶחָת. הַלַּיְלָה הַזֶּה שְׁתֵּי פְעָמִים:	On all other nights we do not dip herbs even once, but on this night we do so twice.
שֶׁבְּכָל־הַלֵּילוֹת אָנוּ אוֹכְלִין בֵּין יוֹשְׁבִין וּבֵין מְסֻבִּין. הַלַּיְלָה הַזֶּה כֻּלָּנוּ מְסֻבִּין.	On all other nights we eat either sitting or leaning, but on this night we all lean.

headed Mosad ha-Rav Kook 1936. Among Jewish leaders arrested and interned by British 1946 (Black Saturday). Mizrachi Knesset member and minister of religions. Prolific author.

Maimon, Solomon (c. 1753–1800), philosopher; b. Poland. Child prodigy in rabbinic literature. Became a member of Moses Mendelssohn's circle in Berlin. Known as sympathetic critic of Kant. His philosophy strongly influenced Fichte, and consequently German idealist philosophy. Works incl. autobiography on E. European Jewish life.

Solomon Maimon

Maimon ben Joseph (d. 1165/1170). Spanish rabbi, *dayyan;* father of Maimonides; lived in Cordoba, Spain and after edict of forced conversion wandered for decade and then emigrated to Fez; d. Ereẓ Israel. Wrote halakhic works, commentaries, responsa. His *Iggeret ha-Neḥamah* designed to comfort and guide forced converts to Islam in their efforts to preserve Judaism, maintaining that Islam is not to be regarded as idolatry.

Maimonides, Moses (Moses ben Maimon; Rambam; 1135–1204), outstanding rabbinic authority, codifier, philosopher; b. Spain, fled persecution to Morocco, lived as physician in Egypt. His two greatest works were encyclopedic legal code *Mishneh Torah* and philosophical *Guide of the Perplexed.* Former (also called *Yad Ḥazakah*) covers all halakhic subjects discussed in Talmud and gives clear rulings where there are conflicting opinions. *The Guide* presents synthesis of rabbinic Judaism and Aristotelian philosophy then prevalent in Islamic world. Both works had enormous influence in Jewish life, and triggered acrimonious 200-year controversy (Maimonidean controversy) bet. so-called "rational" philosophers and conservative traditionalists. Also wrote commentary on Mishnah in which he was first to formulate statement of Jewish creed (see Articles of Faith). Also outstanding medical writer. After death, buried in Tiberias, where his grave is still venerated.

Traditional likenesses of Maimonides used as stamp designs. Right, Israel, 1953. Left, Spain, 1967.

His descendants for many generations were leaders *(negidim)* of Egyptian Jewry. The "Guide" was translated into Latin and other languages and influenced medieval scholastics incl. Aquinas.

Maimuna, celebration held by N. African Jews and many E. communities at end of last day of Passover, which acc. to tradition is anniversary of death of Maimonides' father. In modern Israel esp. observed by Jews of Moroccan origin.

Maine, U.S. state. First known Jewish resident settled in Waldborough during Revolutionary War. First congregation Ahabat Achim in 1850s. Most of community dates fr. 1880s–1890s. Jewish pop 7,295 (1971), half in Portland.

Mainz (Mayence), city in W. Germany. Jews there in Roman era; evidence of community fr. 10th c. In Middle Ages center of Jewish study, seat of famous scholars, and famous community together with Speyer and Worms (the three communities known as *Shum*). Massacres during First Crusade 1096 and Black Death 1349, many Jews committing suicide as act of martyrdom. Expelled 1413, new community 1583. Position improved fr. late 18th c. 2,730 Jews in 1933; liquidated in WWII. 122 Jews in 1970.

Mairovich, Zvi (1909–), Israel painter. Founder-member of New Horizons group. Formed link bet. abstract-lyrical painters and Israel expressionists.

Maisels, Israel Aaron (1905–), S. African lawyer, communal leader. Leader of Johannesburg and S. African bar for several years. Judge of High Court of S. Rhodesia until 1963; later part-time judge of appeal for Botswana, Lesotho, and Swaziland. Pres. S. African Board of Deputies and Zionist Federation.

Maisels, Moses Ḥayyim (Misha; 1901–), Hebrew writer, translator; b. Warsaw, in U.S. fr. 1930. Editor of Hebrew journal *Hadoar.* Settled in Israel 1959.

Maisel-Shoḥat, Hannah (1890–1972), Israel pioneer, educator; wife of Eliezer Shoḥat; b. Belorussia; settled in Ereẓ Israel 1909. Founded first women's agricultural farm in Kinneret 1911, founder of WIZO agricultural school in Nahalal 1929 (principal until 1960).

Majdal, see Magdala.

Majdanek (Maidanek), concentration and extermination camp in Lublin, Poland, established July 1941; originally for POWs, soon made camp for Jews and Poles. 125,000 Jews perished there. Liberated by Soviets July 1944. Museum and research center established by Polish authorities 1947.

Majorca (Mallorca), Balearic Isle. Jews there at end of Roman era. In Middle Ages, Palma was important Jewish center and seat of Jewish scholars. In 14th and 15th c. Jews suffered fr. riots, blood libels, and Inquisition. Many Jews converted; community ceased to exist 1435. Conversos were known as *chuetas.*

Stamp commemorating Majdanek death camp issued by Poland, 1946.

The Calle del Sol, formerly the Jewish Street of Majorca.

Makai (Fischer), Emil (1870–1901), Hungarian poet, playwright. Translated more than 100 operettas; established style of Hungarian operetta.

Makhshirin (Heb. "Those things which render fit"), 8th tractate in Mishnah order *Tohorot,* with no *gemara.* Deals with laws of ritual impurity in connection with foods which are susceptible to such impurity when wet.

Maki (Heb. abbr. for *Miflegah Komunistit Israelit*), communist party established in Israel 1948 after splits in former Communist Party. Split 1965 with faction forming Rakaḥ, New Communist List. See also Knesset.

Makkot (Heb. "Flagellation"), 5th tractate in Mishnah order *Nezikin,* with *gemara* in both Talmuds. Deals with law of plotting witnesses, cities of refuge, and offenses for which penalty is flogging.

Makleff, Mordechai (1920–), Israel army officer, business executive; b. Jerusalem. Sole survivor of massacre of kin by Arabs in Moẓa 1929. In 1948, commanded Haganah unit that captured Haifa. Chief of staff of Israel Defense Forces 1952–53. Directed Dead Sea Works fr. 1958, head of Citrus Marketing Board fr. 1968.

Malachi, Book of, last book of Minor Prophets in Bible. Contains complaints against social and ritual abuses. Prophet's eschatology contains important and influential innovation, viz. vision of "Day of the Lord" preceded by advent of Elijah. No information on author (*Malachi* may mean "my messenger").

Malachi, Eliezer Raphael (1895–), U.S. Hebrew scholar, bibliographer; b. Jerusalem, in U.S. fr. 1912. Wrote on contemporary and past Hebrew writers, incl. Hebrew writers in America, and on historical events.

Malachi ben Jacob ha-Kohen (d. 1785/1790), Italian scholar, liturgical poet. Best known for *Yad Malakhi* on methodology of Talmud and codifiers.

Malakh, Ḥayyim ben Solomon (1650/1660–1716/1717), leader of Shabbatean sect in Poland and Turkey. A founder of "Association of Ḥasidim," which advocated immigration of ascetic scholars to Jerusalem to await imminent coming of Messiah. Persecuted by rabbinical authorities. Expert in Kabbalah and Shabbatean spokesman after movement forced to go underground.

Malamud, Bernard (1914–), U.S. novelist. Taught at Oregon State and Harvard. Works incl. *The Magic Barrel,* short stories; Pulitzer Prize-winning *The Fixer,* based on Beilis blood libel, and *The Tenants.* Stories generally set in Jewish cultural milieu and infused with lonely, idealistic individuals.

Bernard Malamud

Malavsky, Samuel (1894–), *ḥazzan*; b. Kiev, emigrated to U.S. Formed family choir "Singers of Israel" with daughters.

Malben (Heb. abbr. for *Mosedot le-Tippul be-Olim Neḥshalim*), agency of American Joint Distribution Committee for care of aged, infirm, and handicapped immigrants in Israel; founded 1949.

Malbim, Meir Loeb ben Jehiel Michael (1809–1879), rabbi, preacher, biblical exegete; b. Volhynia. Uncompromising stand against Reform forced him to leave his position as chief rabbi of Rumania. His fame and universal popularity rest on his Bible commentary designed to show the unity of Written and Oral Law and to base traditional aggadic interpretation on literal meaning – both objectives directed against Reform views.

Maldonado de Silva, Francisco (1592–1639), Marrano martyr in Peru; b. Argentina; reared as Catholic but guided by father in study of Judaism. Surgeon in Santiago, Chile 1619. Denounced by sisters to Inquisition 1627. Circumcised himself in prison and converted Catholics to Judaism there. Wrote tracts in support of his faith. Burned at auto-da-fé.

Malik al-Ramlī (of Ramleh in Ereẓ Israel; 9th c.), founder of sect of Ramlites or Malikites. Teachings incl. Shavuot must fall only on Sunday; and that marriage to niece is incestuous.

Malines (Mechelen), camp established by Nazis in Belgium October 1941 to concentrate Jews before transporting them to E. Europe. Fr. Aug. 1942 to July 1944, 26 transports containing 25,000 Jews were sent fr. camp. Liberated Sept. 1944.

Malkah, Judah ben Nissim ibn (14th c.), philosopher, probably in Morocco. His philosophy resembled neoplatonic speculations adopted by Muslim sect of Ismāīliyya in constructing their theology. Had no apparent influence on subsequent Jewish thought.

Malkhi, Moses, (b. Ezra? ; 18th c.), emissary of Safed; first emissary of Ereẓ Israel to visit New World. Stayed in New York summer 1759 for four-and-a-half months.

Malkhi, Moses ben Raphael Mordecai (d. 1747), head of Safed community. Instrumental in renewing Jewish community in Tiberias 1740.

Malkhuyyot (Heb. verses describing God's "sovereignty"), first part of central section of additional service for Rosh ha-Shanah consisting of 10 verses describing God as King.

Malkiel, Yakov (1914–), U.S. philologist; b. Kiev, in U.S. fr. 1940. Prof. of linguistics and Romance philology at Univ. of California at Berkeley. Founded and edited *Romance Philology.*

Maller, Julius Bernard (1901–1959), U.S. educator, sociologist; b. Lithuania, in U.S. fr. 1921. Taught at Harvard and Yeshiva univ. Devised personality tests. Demonstrated that IQ test scores at 5th grade level closely related to socio-economic levels. Also devised "Guess Who" sociometric test.

"Menorah" on double tomb in St. Paul's Catacomb, Rabat, Malta.

Malta, Mediterranean island. Jews there in Roman times; expelled 1492. Ruled by Knights of St. John 1530–1798, who during forays against Muslims brought back large numbers of Jewish prisoners. Societies for Redeeming Captives in Venice and elsewhere engaged in ransoming Jewish prisoners there. Poet S.T. Coleridge, as British colonial secretary there, suppressed blood libel 1804. 16 families in 1971.

Malter, Henry (1864–1925), rabbi, scholar of medieval Jewish philosophy. Taught at Hebrew Union College in Cincinnati 1900–1907, occupied chair of talmudic literature at Dropsie College 1909–25. Publications incl. *Saadia Gaon, His Life and Works.*

Maltz, Albert (1908–), U.S. playwright, novelist, screenwriter. Associated with left-wing Theater Union. Spent 9 months in prison during McCarthy era. Lived in Mexico after release 1951.

Malvano, Giacomo (1841–1922), Italian diplomat. Secretary general of foreign ministry 1876–85, 1889–1907, senator fr. 1896, pres. Council of State. Opposed Zionism.

Mampsis, former Nabatean city in the Negev identified with Kurnub. SE of Beersheba. Excavations have uncovered habitations from 50 C.E. into Byzantine Times.

Mamre, oak grove near Hebron which was one of favorite dwelling places of Abraham. Constantine built a church over traditional site.

Mamzer (Heb.), acc. to Jewish law, offspring of forbidden relationship. He may only marry another *mamzer* or a proselyte. Apart from marriage restrictions, the personal status of a *mamzer* is not prejudiced.

Manasseh, elder son of Joseph; eponymous ancestor of tribe of Manasseh. Half of tribe received territory on E. bank of Jordan R.; other half settled around Valley of Jezreel.

Manasseh, King of Judah 698–643 B.C.E.; son of Hezekiah. Depicted in Bible as one of worst Jewish monarchs. Reintroduced pagan practices and paid tribute to Assyrians.

Manasseh, Prayer of, brief penitential Psalm incorporated in books of Apocrypha. Consists of prayer appropriate for Manasseh's repentance for his sins when he was taken to Babylon in fetters.

Manasseh (Menasseh) Ben Israel (1604–1657), Amsterdam scholar. Forerunner of Jewish scholars who attempted to present Judaism in sympathetic manner acceptable to Christian world. Founded earliest Hebrew printing press in Amsterdam 1626 and published Hebrew and Spanish works. Friend of Rembrandt, who did his portrait. Played prominent part in negotiations dealing with return of Jews to England after Puritan Revolution. While in England wrote *Vindiciae Judaeorum* to defend Jews against attacks then being made on them.

Manasseh ben (Porat) Joseph of Ilya (1767–1831), forerunner of Haskalah in Lithuania and Russia; disciple of Vilna Gaon. Advocated principle of alteration and leniency in *halakhah* acc. to changing trends. Persecuted by rabbis; found it difficult to get his many writings published and wandered through E. Europe.

Manchester, city in England. Jewish community fr. c. 1780. Most significant pop. influx fr. Russo-Polish immigration 1881–1914. Prominent Zionist group around Chaim Weizmann in decade up to WWI. Jewish pop. 31,500 (1971), second largest in England, with 68 synagogues and organizations affiliated to Council of Manchester and Salford Jews.

Mancroft, Arthur Michael Samuel, first Baron (1872–1942), English politician, philanthropist. Lord mayor of Norwich 1912–13, Conservative MP fr. 1918, minister for overseas trade 1924–27, financial secretary to treasury (1927–29). His son **Stormont, second Baron Mancroft** (1914–), undersecretary to Home Office 1954–57. Briefly minister without portfolio. Removed fr. post as board chairman of Norwich Union Insurance Company as concession to Arab pressure 1964.

Mandate for Palestine, mandate given to Great Britain by League of Nations at San Remo April 1920, its purpose being establishment of national home for Jewish people; ratified 1922. Terminated with establishment of State of Israel May 14, 1948.

Mandel, Arnold (1913–), French author. journalist. Fr. 1945 one of chief spokesman for French Jewry and one of few able interpreters of Yiddish literature in France. Works deal mainly with his search for identity in Gentile world.

Mandel, Georges (Jeroboam Rothchild; 1885–1944), French statesman. *Chef de cabinet* during Clemenceau prime ministries 1906–09, 1917–19. In charge of trials dealing with treason and defeatism at peak of WWI. Deputy 1920; minister on various occasions fr. 1935. Opposed Pétain-Laval capitulation and collaboration policy. Arrested on Pétain's order, released, went to Morocco to organize resistance, arrested again and murdered by Vichy militia.

Mandel, Marvin (1920–), U.S. politician. Elected to lower house of Maryland legistature 1951, speaker of House of Delegates 1963. Governor of Maryland fr. 1968.

Mandelbaum, Bernard (1922–), U.S. Conservative rabbi. Prof. of homiletics and pres. Jewish Theological Seminary (until 1973). Author of critical edition of the *Pesikta de-Rav Kahana.*

Mandelberg, Avigdor (Victor; 1870–1944), physician. Exiled to Siberia 1899–1903 for organizing workers' circles. Elected to Second Duma 1907; member of Menshevik faction of Social Democratic Labor Party. After dismissal of Duma, escaped abroad, returned after Bolshevik Revolution, left again 1920, and settled in Ereẓ Israel. Chief physician of Kuppat Ḥolim.

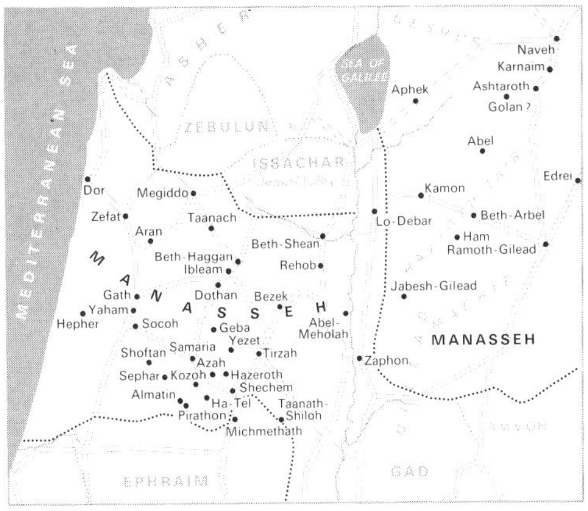

Territory of the tribe of Manasseh.

Manasseh Ben Israel, etching by Rembrandt van Rijn.

Mandelkern, Solomon (1846–1902), Russian lexicographer, Hebrew poet, translator; originally ḥasid. Attended first Zionist Congress in Basle 1897. His monumental Bible concordance great contribution to Jewish scholarship. Also completed 3-vol. history of Russia.

Mandelshtam, Leonid Isaakovich (1879–1944), Soviet physicist. Prof. at Moscow Univ. Invented new method of creating electrical oscillations. Solved several problems of radio-wave propagation over earth's surface.

Mandelshtam, Osip Emilyevich (1891–c. 1938), Russian poet. One of most accomplished, refined, and erudite poets in Russian literature. Arrested 1934, released, rearrested, and died in Far East prison camp. His story described in widow Nadezhda's *Hope Against Hope* and *Hope Abandoned.*

Mandelstamm, Benjamin (1805–1886), Hebrew author; brother of Leon Mandelstamm; b. Zagare, in Vilna fr. 1840. One of extremists in Haskalah circles.

Mandelstamm, Leon (Aryeh Loeb; 1819–1889), writer, adherent of Haskalah in Russia; b. Zagare. First Jew to enroll at Russian Univ. (Moscow). Translated Pentateuch into Russian. In charge of Jewish affairs at Ministry of Education 1846, dismissed 1857 as result of attacks by his Jewish opponents. D. in poverty.

Mandelstamm, Max Emmanuel (1839–1912), ophthalmologist; Zionist and Territorialist leader in Russia. Lectured at Kiev Univ. Devoted to Herzl, who in his *Altneuland* depicted him as first pres. of Jewish state. Supported Uganda Scheme, and when it was rejected joined Zangwill in founding Jewish Territorial Organization and headed its Kiev office.

"Rabbi with Torah" by Mané-Katz, 1960.

Mané-Katz (Emanuel Katz; 1894–1962), painter; b. Ukraine, in Paris fr. 1921. Eminent Jewish representative of School of Paris. Early works exclusively Jewish, later works of Paris, Riviera, bullfights, and numerous flower pieces. D. Israel and left collection to city of Haifa.

Manessier de Vesoul, (d. 1375), French communal leader. Negotiated with future Charles V for Jews's return to France 1359 and acted as financial intermediary between Jews of N. France and monarchy, to his financial profit. Secured 10-years extension of Jewish residence in France 1374.

°**Manetho** (3rd c. B.C.E.), Greco-Egyptian historian. Served as priest at Heliopolis. Wrote on history of Egypt, incl. allegations that were central in emergence of anti-Jewish polemical writings in Alexandrian-Greek literature.

Manger, Itzik (1901–1969), Yiddish poet, dramatist, novelist; b. Czernowitz, escaped to London 1939, moved to New York 1951 and Israel 1967. His *Khumesh Lider* portray patriarchal figures as contemporary Jews. His *Megile Lider* recreate tradition of Purim play in form of dramatic lyrics.

Itzik Manger, drawing by Alva, 1941.

Mani (Mana II; 4th c.), Palestinian *amora;* head of academy in Sepphoris. Strict and uncompromising in halakhic rulings.

Mani, family in Iraq and Ereẓ Israel. **Elijah ben Suleiman** (1818–1899), settled 1856 in Ereẓ Israel. Chief rabbi of Hebron 1865–99. His son **Suleiman Menahem** (1850–1924), chief rabbi of Hebron. Elijah's grandson **Israel** (1887–1966), first Jewish judge in Tel Aviv district court. Great-grandson **Elijah Moses** (1907–), justice of the Supreme Court of Israel.

Mani-Leib (pseud. of **Mani-Leib Brahinsky;** 1883–1953), Yiddish poet; b Russia, in U.S. fr. 1905. Published poem in anthologies of American Yiddish movement Di Yunge, whose poetic principles he helped establish.

Manischewitz, Hirsch (1891–1943), U.S. Orthodox rabbi, business executive, philanthropist. As officer in family B. Manischewitz Baking Co. helped build it into one of largest manufacturers of Jewish food products in U.S.

Manitoba, province of Canada. Most early settlers fr. Russia, E. Europe. Jewish pop. 21,000 (1971), almost all in Winnipeg.

Mankiewicz, Joseph Leo (1909–), U.S. filmwriter, director. Won Academy Award for *A Letter to Three Wives* and *All About Eve.*

Mankowitz, Wolf (1924–), English novelist, playwright; orig. antique dealer. Wrote several books inspired by East End childhood, incl. *Kid for Two Farthings* and play *The Bespoke Overcoat.*

Mann, Daniel (1912–), U.S. director. Films incl. *Come Back, Little Sheba, Rose Tattoo, Teahouse of the August Moon.*

Mann, Delbert (1920–), U.S. director. films incl. *Desire Under the Elms* and *Dark at the Top of the Stairs.*

Mann, Frederic Rand (1903–), U.S. public figure. Pennsylvania state government commissioner of Deleware River Port Authority, first U.S. ambassador to Barbados 1967. Tel Aviv Auditorium of Israel Philharmonic Orchestra named for him.

Mann, Jacob (1888–1940), scholar; b. Galicia, went to London 1908, U.S. 1920. Prof. of Jewish history and Talmud at Hebrew Union College. Wrote 2-vol. *The Jews in Egypt and in Palestine under the Fatamid Caliphs.* Distinguished himself for *Genizah* research.

Mann, Mendel (1916–), Yiddish novelist, painter. In WWII fought with Red Army. Emigrated to Israel 1948 and became farmer. Left for Paris 1958 and took up painting again. His works deal with Jewish life and protest against force and brutality. Wrote *At the Gates of Moscow.*

Mann, Mordecai Ẓevi (1859–1886), Hebrew lyric poet, artist; b. Vilna. His poetry displays individual lyricism; talents as writer and painter fuse in his descriptions of nature.

Manna, food eaten by Israelites in desert. Found on ground every morning (except Sabbath) and as much as could be eaten was collected by people.

Aaron distributing manna, from "Sarajevo Haggadah," Spain, 14th cent.

Mannes, David (1866–1959), U.S. violinist, conductor. Founder of Music School Settlement for Colored People 1912 and David Mannes School of Music 1916. His wife **Clara Damrosch** (1869–1948), pianist, daughter of conductor Leopold Damrosch.

Mannes, Leopold (1899–1964), U.S. pianist; son of David Mannes. Co-inventor with Leopold Godowsky of Kodachrome color process. Reorganized Mannes School of Music as Mannes College of Music, serving as pres. fr. 1953.

Mannheim, Hermann (1889–1974), lawyer, criminologist. Judge in Berlin criminal and appeals court, prof. of criminal law at Berlin Univ. Settled in England 1934, introducing systematic teaching of criminology into British univs. Taught at London Univ. Author of definitive *Comparative Criminology.*

Mannheim, Karl (1893–1947), sociologist. Prof. in Frankfort 1930; emigrated 1933, teaching at London School of Economics. Initiator of "sociology of knowledge" with Max Scholer. Held that *laissez-faire* liberalism, through loosening all societal bonds, carried danger of totalitarianism.

Mannheimer Isaac Noah (1793–1865), preacher, creator of moderate, compromise Reform ritual in Denmark and Austria. Pioneer of educational Reform, fighter for Jewish emancipation. His most important literary work is German translation of prayer book and festival prayers.

Mannheimer Theodor (1833–1900), Swedish banker. Regarded as a founder of modern Swedish banking .

Mansfeld, Alfred (1912–), Israel architect; b. Russia, settled in Ereẓ Israel 1935. Co-designed Israel Museum in Jerusalem. Dean of architectural faculty at Haifa Technion 1954–56.

Mantino, Jacob ben Samuel (d. 1549), physician, translator. Translated philosophical works fr. Hebrew to Latin. Personal physician to Pope Paul III. Prof. of practical medicine at Sapienza, Rome.

Mantua, city, province in N. Italy; important Jewish center in late medieval and modern times. Jews mentioned fr. 1145. Anti-Jewish riots in 15th c. and wearing of Jew badge imposed. Pioneer Hebrew press founded c. 1475. Counter-Reformation affected Jews adversely. Confined to ghetto 1612, banished 1629–30. Ghetto abol-

Ark of the Law in the Scuola Norsa, the synagogue of Mantua.

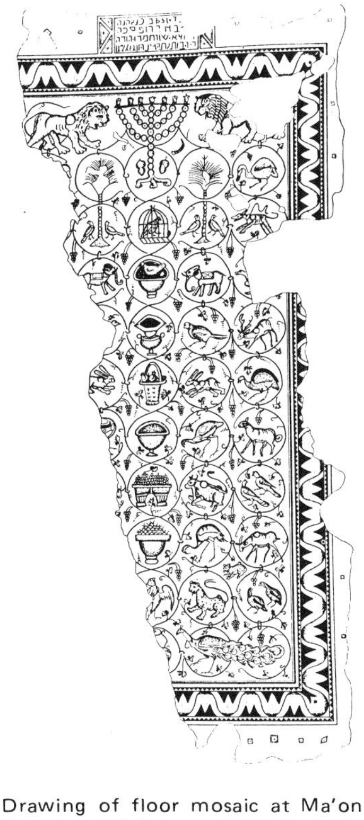

Drawing of floor mosaic at Ma'on synagogue, 6th cent.

ished by French 1797. Jews active in Risorgimento and last restrictions removed 1866. 150 Jews in 1969.

Manual of Discipline, see Discipline Scroll.

Maon, (1) city in Judah and desert of same name. (2) site SW of Gaza. Kibbutz established there in 1949 (near Nirim). Sixth c. synagogue with mosaic excavated in 1958.

Ma'oz Ẓur (Heb. "O Fortress, Rock [of My Salvation]"), initial words and title of a Ḥanukkah hymn sung in Ashkenazi ritual in synagogue and at home after kindling of candles. Song originated in Germany, probably in 13th c.

Mapai (Heb. abbr. for *Mifleget Po'alei Ereẓ Israel*), Israel Labor Party. Zionist-Socialist party founded 1930 through union of Aḥdut ha-Avodah and Ha-Po'el ha-Ẓa'ir, immediately becoming strongest party in Jewish community and labor movement under leadership of David Ben-Gurion. Dominant force in all Israel cabinets. Merged with Aḥdut ha-Avodah and Rafi 1968 to form Israel Labor Party. Leading role in Iḥud ha-Kibbutzim, Histadrut, and World Zionist Organization.See also Knesset.

Mapam (Heb. abbr. for *Mifleget ha-Poalim ha-Me'uḥedet*), pioneering left-wing Labor Zionist Israel party, founded 1948 through union Ha-Shomer ha-Ẓa'ir and Aḥdut ha-Avodah–Po'alei Zion (the latter seceding 1954). Represented in various coalition governments. Formed alignment with Israel Labor Party 1969. Publishes daily *Al ha-Mishmar.* Its kibbutz movement is Ha-Kibbutz ha-Arẓi ha-Shomer ha-Ẓa'ir. See also Knesset.

Mapu, Abraham (1808–1867), creator of modern Hebrew novel; b. Lithuania. Earned living as tutor and teacher. Published first novel *Ahavat Ẓiyyon* 1853 (first Hebrew novel in biblical setting). Also wrote *Ashmat Shomron* (set in time of Isaiah). Other writings incl. *Ayit Ẓavu'a* describing Jewish life in Lithuania. One of principal exponents of Haskalah movement in E. Europe.

Abraham Mapu

Mar Bar Rav Ashi (Tavyomi; d.c. 468) Babylonian *amora.* Possessed great authority and was responsible for completing editing of Talmud begun by his father, Ashi. Extensively quoted in Babylonian Talmud. Headed academy of Mata Meḥasya.

Mar bar Ravina (4th c.), Babylonian *amora,* famous for saintly character. Author of prayer *"Elohay Neẓor Leshoni,"* which is still recited at conclusion of *Amidah.* Although well-to-do, lived austerely.

Marceau, Marcel (1923–), French mime. Created famous character "Bip," flour-faced clown always in conflict with physical world. Considered one of world's greatest mimes.

Marckwald, Willy (1864–1950), German organic chemist. Prof. at Berlin Univ. fr. 1899. Pres. German Chemical Society 1928–31. Escaped to Brazil 1933. First to isolate element polonium in pitchblende, which helped in discovery of radium. Discovered and named phenomenon of phototropy.

Marcoussis, Louis (1883–1941), French painter; b. Warsaw. Member of avant-garde Young Poland group. In Paris fr. 1903. Cubist and printmaker.

Marcus, Aaron (1843–1916), German scholar, writer on Kabbalah and ḥasidism. One of few Orthodox Jews in Germany who totally adopted ḥasidism in theory and practice. Maintained close relations with many ḥasidic leaders in Poland and Galicia.

Marcus, David (Mickey; 1902–1948), U.S. soldier. Distinguished service in WWII retiring with rank of colonel. Went to Ereẓ Israel 1948 and appointed commander of Jerusalem front. Accidentally killed.

Marcus Frank (1928–), British playwright Works incl. *The Killing of Sister George.*

Marcus, Jacob Rader (1896–), U.S. Reform rabbi, historian. Prof. at Hebrew Union College in Cincinnati. Established American Jewish history as academic discipline. Founded American Jewish Archives 1947, American Jewish Periodical Center 1956. Works incl. 3-vol. *The Colonial American Jew.*

Marcus, Ralph (1900–1956), U.S. scholar of Hellenistic Judaism. Taught at Columbia, Jewish Institute of Religion, Univ. of Chicago. Best known for editing, translating, and annotating volumes of Josephus and Plato in Loeb Classical Library series.

Marcus, Siegfried (1831–1898), German inventor. Received patent for petrol-driven automobile 1864, electric lamp 1877, telegraphic relays, microphone loud-speaker, and electric fuses for submarine mines.

Marcuse, Herbert (1898–), philosopher, social theorist; taught in Germany, in U.S. fr. 1934. Served in OSS and State Dept. 1941–50, prof. at Brandeis Univ. 1954–65, Univ. of Calif. at San Diego fr. 1965. Pioneer in exploration of Marxist humanism. Admired by New Left. Works incl. *Eros and Civilization, Soviet Marxism, One-Dimensional Man.*

Marcel Marceau

David Marcus in tent on the "Burma Road" to Jerusalem, 1948.

Herbert Marcuse

Marcuse, Ludwig (1894–1971), German essayist. Biographer of Buechner, Strindberg, Boerne, and Heine. Escaped to U.S. 1939. Prof. of German literature and philosophy at Univ. of Southern California.

Marcuse, Moses (18th c.), physician, Yiddish writer, raised in Germany. Wrote *Sefer Refu'ot,* which in addition to providing purely medical information called for change of occupation among Jews.

Marczali, Henrik (1856–1940), Hungarian historian. First Jew to obtain chair at Budapest Univ. Elected to Hungarian Academy of Sciences 1893, dismissed 1924. Historian of positivist school and pioneer of source criticism in Hungary.

Marduk, patron deity of city of Babylon; elevated to rank of national god during reign of Nebuchadnezzar I (c. 1100 B.C.E.) Name appears in Jer. 50:2.

Marek, Pesach (Piotr; 1862–1920), historian of Russian Jews, folklorist. A founder of Benei Zion society of Moscow Zionists. Co-compiler of *Die Yidisher Folkslider in Russland.*

Mareshah (or **Marissa**), city in Judah connected with families of Shelah and Caleb; one of cities fortified by Rehoboam. Base for Seleucid armies at war with Judah Maccabee. John Hyrcanus conquered it and it remained in Hasmonean possession until taken by Romans under Pompey. Site has been excavated.

Margaliot (Margulies), Mordecai (1909–1968), Israel scholar of midrashic and geonic literature; b. Warsaw. One of first graduates of Heb. Univ., teaching there and at Jewish Theological Seminary in New York. Major work 5-vol. critical edition of *Midrash Rabbah.*

Painting from Hellenistic tomb found near Mareshah, 3rd cent. B.C.E.

Margaliot, Reuben (1889–1971), rabbinic scholar, author; b. Lemberg, settled in Ereẓ Israel 1935. Wrote on ḥasidic lore and Kabbalah, novellae, and study of halakhic aspects of political resettlement of Ereẓ Israel. Edited medieval texts and responsa. Israel Prize 1957.

Margarita (Margalita), Anton (16th c.), apostate, anti-Jewish writer; son of rabbi. While still a Jew, denounced Regensburg community to authorities. Convert to Catholicism 1522 and later Protestantism. Accused Jews of lacking charity, reviling Christianity, and treason. Held religious disputation with Joseph b. Gershom of Rosheim.

Margolies, Isaac ben Elijah (1842–1887), Polish rabbi, author; supporter of Haskalah. In his writings, used his outstanding talmudic knowledge to defend Talmud against critics. After moving to New York, became renowned as public lecturer and teacher.

Margolies, Moses Sebulun (1857–1936), U.S. Orthodox rabbi; b. Russia. Rabbi of Slobodka. Pres. Rabbi Isaac Elchanan Yeshiva and Union of Orthodox Rabbis of U.S. and Canada. Introduced system for supervising distribution of kosher meat in N.Y.C.

Margolin, Arnold (1877–1956), Ukrainian lawyer. Well known for role in pogrom trials and Beilis case. Leader of Territorialist Organization in Russia. Associate justice of highest Ukrainian court 1918, deputy minister of foreign affairs. In U.S. fr. 1922.

Margolin, Eliezer (1874–1944), soldier; b. Russia, went to Ereẓ Israel 1892, Australia 1900. Joined Australian army in WWI. Commander of 49th Royal Fusiliers, which consisted mostly of Jewish volunteers; commander of First Judeans (official name of Jewish Legion). During 1921 Arab riots in Ereẓ Israel, provided Jews with arms fr. British military stores, which led to his resignation fr. army and return to Australia.

Margoliot, Moses ben Simeon (d. 1781), Lithuanian rabbi. Author of standard commentary on Jerusalem Talmud, printed in almost every edition. First to realize vital importance of Tosefta for understanding Jerusalem Talmud. Led itinerant life. In 1779, when nearly 70 years old, studied botany at Univ. of Frankfort on the Oder.

Margolioth, Ephraim Zalman ben Menahem Mannes (1760–1828), rabbi, author in Brody. Highly successful businessman who spent most of his time studying. Wrote many rabbinic works and responsa; many of his halakhic decisions have been accepted.

Margolioth, Judah Loeb (1747–1811), rabbi, preacher; precursor of Haskalah in E. Europe. His sermons, scientific studies, responsa, and linguistic studies demonstrate initial willingness among certain Orthodox elements to accept social reform and even secular studies, and their disillusionment when they witnessed radical results of Enlightenment.

Margoliouth, David Samuel (1858–1940), English classical scholar, orientalist; son of convert missionary. Prof. at Oxford. Outstanding scholar in fields of Islamic history and literature and important editor of medieval Arabic texts.

Margolis, Max Leopold (1866–1932), U.S. biblical, Semitic scholar; b. Russia. Taught at Univ. of Calif. 1897–1905, at Hebrew Union College, and Dropsie. Editor in chief of Jewish Publication Society translation of Bible into English. Best known for 1-vol. *History of the Jewish People,* written with Alexander Marx.

Margolis-Kalvaryski, Haim (1868–1947), pioneer, administrator of Jewish settlement in Ereẓ Israel; b. Russia, settled in Ereẓ Israel 1895. Administrator of ICA settlement in Lower Galilee fr. 1900.

Margoshes, Samuel (1887–1968), Yiddish journalist, editor, Zionist leader; b. Galicia, in U.S. fr. 1905. Editor of *The Day* 1926–42.

Margules, Max (1856-1920), Austrian meteorologist. Secretary of Central Inst. of Meteorology, Vienna. Formulated Margules equation, which introduced three-dimension distribution of energy in place of previously accepted two-dimensional distribution in regard to energy of storms.

Margulies, Samuel Hirsch (1858–1922), rabbi, scholar; b. Galicia. As chief rabbi of Florence 1890–1922, did much to revive Jewish life and consciousness in Italy and to foster contacts bet. Italian and European Jewries. Head of Collegio Rabbinico Italiano.

Marḥeshvan, post-exilic name for 8th month of Jewish year, frequently shortened to Ḥeshvan. 29 or 30 days. Zodiac sign Scorpio. Pre-exilic name Bul.

Mari, one of principal centers of Mesopotamia during 3rd and early 2nd millennia B.C.E. Archaeological and epigraphical discoveries there are of prime significance for history of Mesopotamia and Upper Syria and have manifold bearing on early Israelite history.

Mariamne (Mariamme) I (60? –29 B.C.E.), granddaughter of John Hyrcanus, second wife of Herod. Hated Herod for murder of her family. Put to death by Herod on pretext of adultery.

Marini, Shabbethai Ḥayyim (Vita; c. 1690–1748), poet, physician, rabbi in Padua. Translated part of Ovid's *Metamorphoses* into Hebrew.

Marinoff, Jacob (1869–1964), Yiddish poet, editor; b. Russia, in U.S. fr. 1893. Edited satirical journal *Groyser Kundas* fr. 1909.

Maritime (Atlantic) Provinces, four easternmost provinces of Canada: New Brunswick (1971 Jewish pop. 1,200). Prince Edward Island (20), Newfoundland (250), Nova Scotia (2,200). First settler in New Brunswick was Solomon Hart 1858.

Marix, Adolph (1848–1919), U.S. naval officer. Commanded USS *Maine* until shortly before its sinking in Havana Bay. Judge advocate in subsequent court of enquiry and his findings led to U.S. declaration of war on Spain. First Jew to attain rank of rear admiral 1908.

Mark, Bernard (Berl; 1908–1966), Polish scholar, historian. During WWI lived in USSR, active in Jewish Anti-Fascist Committee. Director of Jewish Historical Inst. in Warsaw 1949. Wrote on Polish-Jewish history, esp. in Holocaust period.

Mark, Yudel (1897–), Yiddish educator, philologist, author; b. Lithuania, in U.S. fr. 1936, Israel 1970. Edited Yiddish publications, wrote Yiddish textbooks and many studies on Yiddish grammar and style, and major Yiddish dictionary.

Markah (4th c. C.E.), Samaritan poet who wrote in Aramaic. Work which established his fame and gained him epithet "Founder of Wisdom" is great midrashic *Meimar* or *Tevat Markah,* compendium of exegetical and theological teachings.

Markel, Lester (1894–), U.S. journalist. Responsible for changing nature of Sunday newspaper. Sunday editor of *New York Times* 1923–64, then associate editor of paper. Instituted News of the Week in Review section.

Markish, Perez (1895–1952), Soviet Yiddish poet, novelist, playwright; b. Volhynia. Member (with Hofstein and Kvitko) of Kiev lyric triumvirate, who expressed modern trends in Yiddish poetry and acclaimed new Soviet revolution. His WWII works

expressed great Soviet patriotism. Accused 1948 with other Jewish writers of Jewish nationalism and executed. His epic poem *"Milkhome"* abounds in praise for Stalin. Best-known works incl. *"Brider"* and *Dor Oys, Dor Ayn.*

Markon, Isaac Dov Ber (1875–1949), scholar, librarian. Librarian of Imperial Public Library in St. Petersburg 1901–17, prof. at Belorussian Univ. in Minsk 1922–24. Member of editorial staff *Encyclopaedia Judaica* in Berlin. In England fr. 1940. Wrote on Karaites.

Markova, Alicia (Dame Lilian Alicia Marks; 1910–), English ballerina. Played major role in growth of modern ballet in England. One of first stars (with Anton Dolin) of Vic-Wells Ballet 1933. Co-founder of Festival Ballet 1952, director of Metropolitan Opera Ballet 1963, prof. of ballet at Univ. of Cincinnati 1970.

Marks, Marcus M. (1858–1934), U.S. clothing manufacturer, civic official, philanthropist. Manhattan borough pres. 1913–17, establishing open public markets, welfare work, and joint trial boards for civil service employees.

Marks, Samuel (1845–1920), S. African industrialist, financier; b. Lithuania, emigrated to Cape 1868. Founded firm Lewis and Marks, which eventually controlled large industrial and mining enterprises in Transvaal. Mediator in negotiations which ended S. African War (1902). Senator in first Union Parliament (1910).

Marks, Simon, Lord (1888–1964), English industrialist, philanthropist. Chairman of board of Marks & Spencer Ltd. store chain fr. 1917; largely responsible for firm's commercial success. Close business associate was brother-in-law Israel Moses Sieff; both active Zionists and friends of Weizmann. Secretary of Zionist delegation to Versailles Peace Conference 1919. Their benefactions to public causes in Israel (incl. Sieff and Weizmann Institutes) and Britain totaled tens of millions of pounds.

Marmor, Kalman (1879–1956), Yiddish writer, literary scholar; b. Vilna, in U.S. fr. 1906. A founder of World Union of Po'alei Zion and editor of its weekly *Der Yidisher Kemfer.* Joined Yiddish Communist daily *Morning Freiheit* 1922. Worked at Inst. for Jewish Studies, Ukrainian Academy of Sciences 1933–36. After its liquidation, allowed to return to U.S.

Perez Markish (2nd from right) with (right to left) Mendel Elkin, Daniel Leibl, and Uri Ẓevi Greenberg.

Alicia Markova in "The Dying Swan."

Marmorek, Alexander (1865–1923), bacteriologist, Zionist leader; b. Galicia. Worked in Pasteur Inst. France, and discovered antidote against puerperal fever. Initiated serum study leading to modern treatment of typhus and diabetes. Colleague of Herzl.

Marmorek, Oscar (1863–1909), architect, Zionist leader; b. Galicia. Designed important buildings, incl. synagogues, in Austria. Member of Zionist Executive, co-founder of *Die Welt.*

Marmorstein, Arthur (1882–1946), rabbinic scholar; b. Hungary. Taught at Jews' College, London fr. 1912. Wrote studies in rabbinic theology and many other aspects of Jewish scholarship.

Maron, Hannah, see Meron, Hanna.

Maror (Heb.), traditional "bitter herb" which children of Israel were commanded to eat with unleavened bread and paschal offering, and which became part of Passover *seder* service.

°**Marr, Wilhelm** (1818–1904), German anti-Semite. Introduced term "anti-Semite" into political vocabulary with founding of League of Anti-Semites 1879, first attempt to create popular political movement based on anti-Jewish policies. Wrote influential anti-Semitic works.

Marrakesh, city in Morocco. Jews there fr. 11th c. During 16th c. Spanish-Portuguese Jews gained control of community. Jews concentrated in mellah 1557. In 16th–17th c. Jews and their agents on coast powerful in Moroccan industry and commerce. Conditions generally better than elsewhere in Morocco, esp. after 1745. 16,392 Jews in 1951; a few hundred remained in 1971.

Marrano term of opprobrium used to denigrate New Christians of Spain and Portugal. Most probable derivation fr. Spanish word meaning "swine." See *Anusim;* New Christians.

Marriage, in Jewish thought, ideal human state. Ceremony divided into two parts: betrothal (*erusin* or *kiddushin*) and marriage (*nissu'in*). Betrothal ceremony takes place before witnesses and can be consummated in one of three ways: (1) by money – i.e., man gives woman sum of money or equivalent (ring) and declares "Behold, you are consecrated unto me with this ring according to the Law of Moses and Israel"; (2) by deed – i.e., man transfers to woman deed wherein declaration of marriage is written; (3) by cohabitation – i.e., couple enters private room after informing witnesses that intended cohabitation is for purpose of marriage. Latter two forms discontinued. Betrothed woman may not enter into marriage with anyone else or cohabit with anyone, incl. future husband. Marriage ceremony entitles couple to live as man and

"Maror" in an illumination from the "Sarajevo Haggadah," Spain, 14th cent.

FORBIDDEN MARRIAGE RELATIONSHIPS

A man	A woman
Grandmother; Grandfather's Wife; **Wife's Grandmother[1];** Great-Aunt[2]	**Grandfather;** **Grandmother's Husband;** Husband's Grandfather
Mother; **Step-Mother;** **Wife's Mother[1];** Wife's Stepmother[3] **Father's Sister;** **Mother's Sister;** **Father's Brother's Wife[4];** Mother's Brother's Wife	**Father;** **Step-Father;** **Father-in-Law**
Sister; **Half-Sister;** **Brother's Wife[5];** **Wife's Sister[6];**	**Brother;** **Half-Brother;** **Sister's Husband[1];** **Husband's Brother[2];**
Daughter; **Step-Daughter;** **Daughter-in-Law[7]**	**Son;** **Step-Son;** **Son-in-Law[3];** Husband's Son-in-Law[4]; **Brother's Son;** **Sister's Son;** **Husband's Brother's Son[5];** Husband's Sister's Son
Granddaughter; **Wife's Granddaughter;** Grandson's Wife	Grandson; Husband's Grandson; **Granddaughter's Husband[6];** Great-Nephew[7]
Great-Granddaughter; Wife's Great-Granddaughter	Great-Grandson; Husband's Daughter's Son's Son[4]; Great-Granddaughter's Husband
1. After wife's death, prohibited but valid according to some scholars. 2. Only applies to a sister or sister-in-law of a mother's mother or a father's father; according to some scholars these cases are permitted. 3. Not prohibited at all according to some scholars. 4. If father and brother are not of the same father the marriage is prohibited but valid. 5. Except through levirate marriage. 6. After wife's death marriage is permitted. 7. Wife's daughter-in-law is permitted.	1. During sister's lifetime. 2. Except through levirate marriage. 3. According to some scholars after daughter's death marriage is prohibited but valid. 4. According to some scholars this is not prohibited. 5. Prohibited but valid if husband and brother are not of the same father. 6. According to some scholars after granddaughter's death marriage is prohibited but valid. 7. Only applies to her own or her husband's brother's son's son and sister's daughter's son; according to some scholars these cases are permitted.

Bold typeface indicates that the prohibition is pentateuchal and the marriage is void. Ordinary typeface indicates that the prohibition is rabbinical and that the marriage is valid.

wife. Performed by spreading *ḥuppah* (canopy) above them and by sanctification of union by recital of several benedictions and reading of *ketubbah* (marriage contract). Today betrothal and marriage combined in single ceremony.

Marseilles, port in France. Jews there by 6th c. Little information available for early Middle Ages. Granted citizenship status 1257. Active in local commerce and as physicians. Persecution began after Provence incorporated into France 1481; expulsion 1501. Community permanently established 1760. Grew rapidly after WWII with N. African immigration. Jewish pop. 65,000 (1971).

Marshak, Samuel Yakovlevich (1887–1964), Russian poet, author of children's books. Active in illegal Po'alei Zion movement, esp. in Yalta. After Russian Revolution edited Russian-language anthologies of Jewish literature in Moscow. Founder of Soviet children's literature. Translated great European poets into Russian. Stalin Prize four times.

Marshall, David Saul (1908–), Singapore labor politician, lawyer. Led United Labor Front to victory in 1955 elections; chief minister and minister of commerce until 1956. Elected to Legislative Assembly 1963. Pres. Singapore Jewish Welfare Board 1946–53.

Marshall, Louis (1856–1929), U.S. lawyer, communal leader. Specialist in constitutional and corporate law. Led successful campaign for abrogation of U.S.–Russian Commercial Treaty of 1832 because of Russian persecution of Jews. A founder and pres. 1912–29 of American Jewish Committee. Member of Jewish delegation to Paris Peace Conference 1919. Although not Zionist, worked with Weizmann on enlargement of

Louis Marshall

Jewish Agency 1929. Civil rights activist; prominent in NAACP. His son **James** (1896–), lawyer, educator. Member 1938–52, pres. 1938–42 of N.Y.C. Board of Education. Another son, **Robert** (1901–1939), chief of division of recreation and soil conservation of U.S. Forest Service.

Martin, Tony (Alvin, Morris; 1913–), U.S. singer, actor. Popular on radio and in films.

°**Martinez, Ferrant** (14th c.), archdeacon of Écija; a leading anti-Jewish agitator in Castile. Anti-Jewish riots of 1391 in Castile and Aragon direct result of his activities. Revered as saint after death.

°**Martini, Raymond** (1220–1285), Spanish Dominican friar, polemicist. Active in disputation with Naḥmanides at Barcelona 1263. Appointed to first censorship commission to examine Jewish books for passages allegedly offensive to Christianity. After 1263, one of chief executors of anti-Jewish policy of church. Main work *Pugio Fidei,* widely circulated anti-Jewish polemic.

Marton, Ernö Jechezkel (1896–1960), editor, leader of Transylvanian and Hungarian Jewry. Member of Rumanian parliament 1932. Editor of Zionist newspaper *Uj Kelet* in Budapest. Settled in Ereẓ Israel 1946 and renewed its publication.

Martov, Julius (Iulii Osipovich Zederbaum; 1873–1923), Russian revolutionary, leader of Menshevism; grandson of Heb. writer Alexander Zederbaum. First advocated, then opposed creation of separate Jewish workers' organization in struggle for emancipation. Cofounder with Lenin of Union of Struggle for Emancipation of Working Class 1895. Broke with Lenin 1903. After Bolshevik seizure of power, led semi-loyal opposition. When Menshevik Party outlawed, allowed to leave Russia 1920.

Marwick, Lawrence (1909–), U.S. librarian, oriental scholar; b. Poland, in U.S. fr. 1929. Head of Hebraic section of U.S. Library of Congress fr. 1948. Taught Hebrew literature and Arabic at NYU.

Marx, Adolf Bernhard (1795–1866), German musicologist. Prof. at Berlin Univ. 1830, a founder of Stern Conservatory 1856. Most important work 4-vol, *Die Lehre von der musikalischen Komposition.*

Marx, Alexander (1878–1953), historian, bibliographer, librarian; b. Germany. Taught history and was librarian at Jewish Theological Semi-

nary fr. 1903, building up outstanding collection. Pres. American Academy for Jewish Research 1931–33. Wrote *History of the Jewish People* with Max L. Margolis. His brother **Moses** (1885–1973), bibliographer, librarian at Hebrew Union College, Cincinnati. Wrote on Hebrew incunabula and 16th c. Hebrew printing. Settled in Israel.

Grave of Karl Marx in Highgate Cemetery, London.

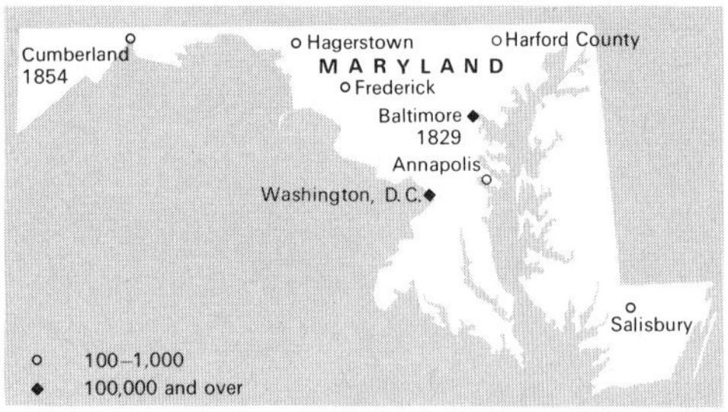

Jewish communities in Maryland.

Groucho (left), Chico, and Harpo, three of the Marx Brothers.

Marx, Karl (1897–1966); German editor, publisher; in England 1933–46. After WWII published German-Jewish communal paper.

Marx, Karl Heinrich (1818–1883), social philosopher; chief theorist of modern socialism; b. Germany, went to Paris 1843, settled in London 1849. His *Communist Manifesto* (with Engels) and *Das Kapital* seminal works with profound effect, regarding class struggle as mainspring of history. Converted to Christianity by his father at age 6; hostile attitude toward Jews. Judaism for him was synonymous with bourgeois capitalism, capitalist mentality, and symbol of financial power.

Marx Brothers, U.S. theatrical and film comedy team, orig. consisting of five brothers, nephews of vaudeville actor Al Shean. Oustanding members **Chico (Leonard;** 1891–1961), mime **Harpo (Adolf,** later **Arthur;** 1893–1964), and **Groucho (Julius;** 1895–). Film comedies incl. *Duck Soup, Animal Crackers, A Night at the Opera, A Day at the Races,* which are considered cinema classics. Groucho, outstanding wit, also noted radio personality.

Mary, mother of Jesus. Only authentic sources of her life are Gospels of Matthew and Luke, which relate that she lived in Nazareth, was espoused to Joseph the carpenter, conceived immaculately, and gave birth to Jesus in Bethlehem manger. Became of paramount importance in Christian, esp. Roman Catholic, thought and doctrine.

Maryland, U.S. state. Jews at first generally avoided colony because of its religious intolerance and one-crop economy. Civic equality not attained until 1826 when "Jew Bill" passed permitting Jews to hold public office without submitting to Christian oath. Marvin Mandel elected governor 1968. Jewish pop. 187,110 (1971).

Marzouk, Moshe (1926–1955), Egyptian Karaite, physician, tried by military court in Cairo on charges of spying for Israel and executed.

Masada, one of Herod's royal citadels and last outpost of Zealots during Jewish War against Rome; situated on top of isolated rock on edge of Judean desert and Dead Sea valley. After lengthy siege by Roman army, Zealot defenders under Eleazar b. Jair committed mass suicide rather than surrender 73 C.E.

Plan of the fortress of Masada.

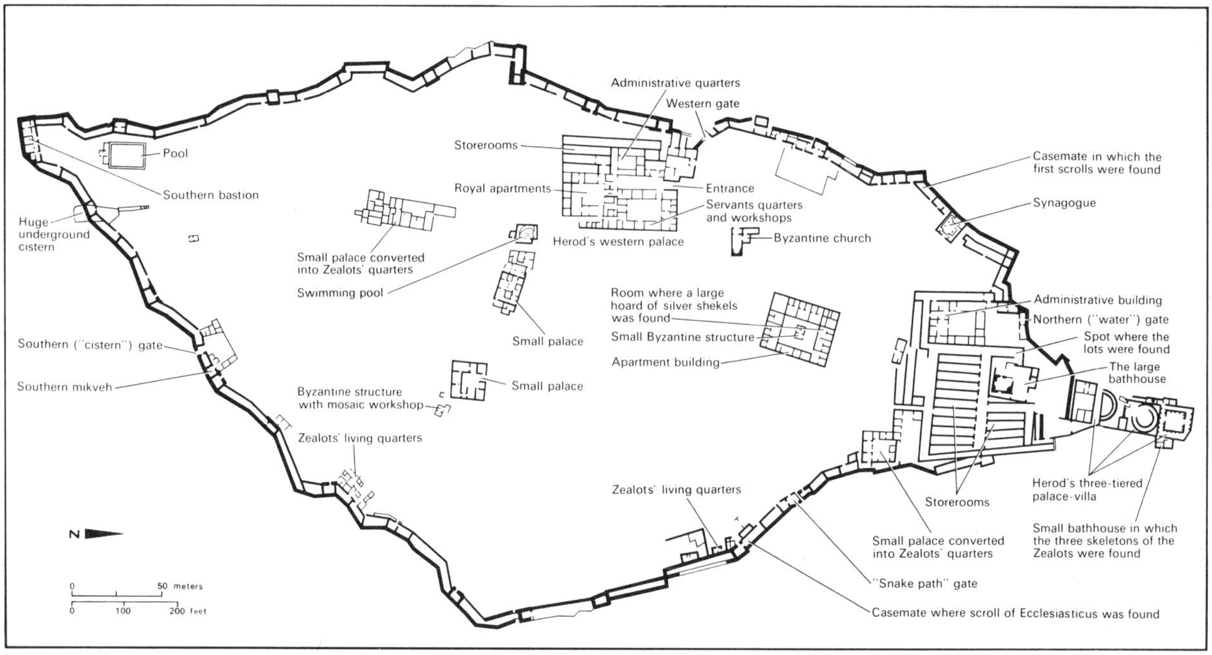

Archaeological excavations by Y. Yadin uncovered entire built-up area of rock as well as one of Roman camps at its foot, and restoration was carried out. Herodian palaces, bathhouse, and storehouse were found. Fr. period of Zealots ritual baths, synagogue, and other constructions discovered. It has become center of pilgrimages, as well as a symbol of modern Israel ("Masada will not fall again").

Mashā'allah (Manasseh b. Athaň; 754–813), astronomer; b. Egypt, lived in Damascus. One of earliest independent and original scientific thinkers and scholars. Later translations of his work contributed to spread of astronomical knowledge fr. East to West.

Mashgi'aḥ (Heb. "overseer" or "inspector"), person entrusted by rabbinate with supervision of *kashrut*. In some places called *shomer* (i.e. "watchman").

Carved walnut "Mashiv ha-ru'aḥ" plaque, hung in synagogue during season when prayer was recited, Hamburg, 18th cent.

Mashiv ha-Ru'aḥ (Heb. "He causes the wind to blow"), phrase in *Amidah* prayer, which is prayer for rain, inserted in second blessing; recited in winter season (fr. last day of Sukkot after prayer for rain) until last day of Passover (until prayer for dew).

Masie, Aaron Meir (1858–1930), physician; b. Belorussia, settled in Ereẓ Israel 1888. One of the first doctors in the country. Author of Hebrew dictionary of medical terms.

Maskil (Heb.), term used in superscription of 13 psalms. Probably musical term signifying proper accompaniment or melody for recitation of psalm. Term also employed for adherent of Haskalah movement.

Maskileison (Maskil le-Eitan), Abraham ben Judah Leib (1788–1848), Russian rabbi, author. Name derived fr. title of his talmudic novellae; also wrote other halakhic works.

Masliansky, Zvi Hirsch (1856–1943), popular Yiddish orator. Taught at yeshivah in Pinsk 1882–90; later became wandering preacher of Zionism. Fr. 1895 in U.S. Considered most eloquent and influential preacher on American scene.

Masnut, Samuel ben Nissim (13th c.), talmudist, leader of Aleppo Jewry. Author of extensive midrashic commentary *Ma'yan Gannim.*

Masorah, notes entered on top, bottom, and side margins of traditional Hebrew texts of Bible to safeguard traditional transmission. Subsequently assembled into independent collections.

Masorete, scholar who preserved masoretic tradition (traditional vocalization and literal text of Bible). First masorete seems to have been Dosa b. Eleazar (4th–5th c.).

Massachusetts, U.S. state. Shipowner, Aaron Lopez first Jew naturalized in state (Taunton, 1752); first Jewish community in Leicester 1777, first Jewish congregation Ohabei Shalom in Boston in 1840s. Jewish pop. 267,440 (1971), mostly in Boston, with 200 synagogues and 85 communities.

Massarani, Tullo (1826–1905), Italian author, statesman. Collaborated with Mazzini's followers in struggle for unification, forced into exile until 1860. MP 1860–67, senator fr. 1876. Wrote essays, autobiography, political and historical works, translations, and verse.

Massarano, Jacchino or **Isacchino** (16th c.), Italian choreographer. Commissioned 1583 to provide dances for Jewish theater in Mantua in honor of duke's heir Vincenzo Gonzaga. Supervised "Blindfold Dance." Also composer, teacher, singer.

Massary, Fritzi (Friederike Massarik; 1882–1969), German actress, singer. Acted in musicals on Berlin stage and excelled as dramatic actress. Married German actor Max Pallenberg.

Massekhet (Heb. fig. "tractate"), main subdivision of each of six orders of Mishnah; also designates corresponding *gemara* tractates. Occasionally also applied to rabbinical books outside Talmud.

Massell, Sam Jr. (1927–), U.S. lawyer, politician. Vice-mayor of Atlanta, Ga. 1961–69, first Jewish mayor 1969–73.

Masserman, Julius Homan (1905–), U.S. psychiatrist, psychoanalyst. Prof at Northwestern Univ. medical school. Wrote on dynamic psychiatry.

Mastbaum, Joel (1884–1957), Yiddish novelist; b. Poland, settled in Ereẓ Israel 1933. Works deal with Jewish life in Poland. Romantic impressionist who emphasizes moods rather than action.

Mata Meḥasya, town in Babylonia, nr. Sura. Center of Jewish study; academy of Sura transferred there by Ashi.

Matsas, Nestoras (1932–), Greek author, painter, motion picture director; baptized into Greek Orthodox Church during Nazi occupation of Greece. Two of most significant works are on Jewish themes.

Mattaniah, see Zedekiah.

Mattathias, priest fr. Modi'in; first leader of uprising of Hasmoneans against Antiochus IV Epiphanes 167 B.C.E. Refused to obey royal order to sacrifice to idols. Fled with his five sons to Judean desert mountains. Led rebellion for only one year; succeeded by his son Judah Maccabee.

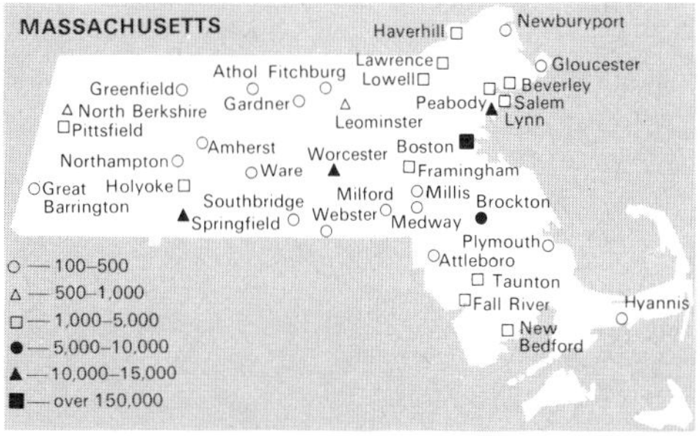

Jewish communities in Massachusetts.

Mattathias ha-Yiẓhari (14th–15th c.), Spanish scholar; one of representatives of Saragossa community in Disputation of Tortosa. Had profound knowledge of philosophy, wrote biblical and mishnaic commentaries.

Mattersdorf (Mattersburg; Nagymarton), town in Austria; one of "Seven Communities" and after 1813 one of "Five Communities." Jews believed to have settled there 800 or 1222. Community numbered 511 in 1938.

Mattiah (Mattityahu) ben Ḥeresh (2nd c.), *tanna;* b. Ereẓ Israel, moved to Rome, establishing academy. His most famous halakhic decision is that all Sabbath prohibitions may be overrruled to save human life. Saying: "Be a tail to lions and not a head to foxes."

Mattuck, Israel Isidor (1883–1954), rabbi; leader of Liberal Judaism in England; b. Lithuania, in England fr.

1911. Co-founder and for many years chairman of World Union of Progressive Judaism.

Matz, Israel (1869–1950), U.S. manufacturer, philanthropist, patron of Hebrew scholarship; b. Russian Poland, in U.S. fr. 1890. Founded Ex-Lax Co. 1906, served as pres. Published Hebrew monthly *Ha-Toren* 1922–25. Established foundation for support of Hebrew authors.

Maurois, André (Emile Herzog; 1885–1967), French biographer, novelist, essayist. Earned reputation as interpreter of English scene and biographer (Shelley, Disraeli, Proust, Balzac, etc.). Wrote histories of England, France, U.S. In U.S. during WWII. Elected to French Academy 1938.

André Maurois

°**Maurras, Charles** (1868–1952), French nationalist writer, anti-Semitic politician. Founded anti-Semitic newspaper and movement *L'Action Française.* During WWII collaborated with Nazis and sentenced to life imprisonment 1945.

Mauss, Marcel (1872–1950), French ethnologist, sociologist, historian; nephew of Emile Durkheim. Prof. of history of religions of noncivilized peoples at Ecole des Hautes Etudes, Paris; also taught at College de France. Active in support of Dreyfus and in socialist and cooperative movements.

Mauthausen, Nazi concentration camp in Austria. After outbreak of WWII became camp for anti-Nazis fr. occupied Europe. 122,767 of its 335,000 prisoners murdered. Liberated May 1945.

Mauthner, Fritz (1849–1923), German philosopher. Militant agnostic; denied academic appointment because of anti-religious stand and political views. His 4-vol. *Der Atheismus und seine Geschichte im Abendlande* claimed that all dogmas – religious or scientific – were mere human inventions.

Maximon (Maximowski), Shalom Dov Ber (1881–1933), essayist, educator; b. Russia, settled in N.Y. Edited Hebrew periodicals. Registrar of Hebrew Union College in Cincinnati.

Maybaum, Sigmund (1844–1919), Hungarian rabbi. Lecturer on homiletics at Hochschule fuer die Wissenschaft des Judentums in Berlin 1888–1919. Among rabbis who protested against idea of convening Zionist Congress in Germany 1897. His son **Ignaz** (1897–), Reform rabbi; b. Vienna, emigrated to England 1939. Taught theology and homiletics at Leo Baeck College and wrote on Judaism.

Mayence, see Mainz.

Mayer, Daniel (1909–), French socialist politician. Reorganized Socialist Party after fall of France and became general secretary after liberation. Member of Chamber of Deputies 1946–58, chairman, Foreign Affairs Committee. Minister 1946–49. Pres. League of Human Rights fr. 1958. World Pres. ORT.

Mayer, Leo Ary (1895–1959), orientalist; b. Poland, settled in Ereẓ Israel 1921. Prof. at Hebrew Univ. Active in archaeology. Specialized in Islamic art, costume, epigraphy, and numismatics.

Mayer, Louis Burt (1885–1957), U.S. motion picture executive. His Louis B. Mayer Pictures Corp. merged to form Metro-Goldwyn-Mayer 1924. Vice-pres. in charge of production and mainly responsible for MGM's enormous commercial success. Great believer in star system and children's films.

René Mayer

Mayer, René (1895–1972), French politician. Lecturer at Ecole Libre des Sciences Politiques 1922–32, administrator of Air France 1933–40. Member of French Committee for National Liberation 1943. Elected to National Assembly as Radical Socialist 1946, minister of finance 1947–48, justice 1949–51. Prime minister 1953. A leader of movement for European integration. Chairman of European Coal and Steel Authority 1955–58. Active in Jewish affairs.

Mayer, Sally (1875–1953), Italian Jewish leader, philanthropist. Owner of paper mills in Abbiate Guazzone. During WWII, "Joint" representative in Switzerland and active in saving Jews fr. Europe. Pres. Milan Jewish community after WWII and founded Jewish school there. His son **Astorre** (1906–), industrialist, communal leader. Pres. Italian Zionist Federation and leader of Jewish community in Milan. Promoted industry in Israel (e.g., Ḥaderah Paper Mills).

Mayim Aḥaronim (Heb. lit. "latter waters"), term for ritual washing of hands after meal and before recitation of Grace after Meals. No blessing said before performance.

May Laws, series of "temporary laws" applying to Jews, confirmed by Czar Alexander III 1882, repealed 1917 by revolutionary provisional government. Laws provided that (1) Jews were forbidden to settle outside towns and townlets; (2) deeds of sale and lease of real estate in name of Jews outside towns and townlets were canceled; (3) Jews were prohibited fr. trading on Sundays and Christian holidays.

Mayzel, Nachman (1887–1966), Yiddish editor, literary critic, historian; b. Kiev, in Warsaw fr. 1921, New York 1937, Israel 1964 at kibbutz Alonim. Founded and edited *Literarishe Bleter* in Poland, and edited *Yidishe Kultur* in N.Y. Wrote studies on famous Yiddish writers.

Mazar (Maisler), Benjamin (1906–), Israel archaeologist, historian; b. Poland, settled in Ereẓ Israel 1929. Rector of Heb. Univ. 1952, pres. 1953–61. Excavations incl. Bet She'arim, Tel Qasile, En-Gedi, Temple Area in Jerusalem. Pres. Israel Exploration Society. Headed editorial board of biblical encyclopedia *(Enziklopedyah Mikra'it).* Israel Prize 1968.

Mazeh, Jacob (1859–1924), Zionist leader, Hebrew writer. *Kazyonny ravvin* (crown rabbi) of Moscow and spiritual leader of community fr. 1893. Appeared as defense expert at Beilis trial 1912.

Mazkeret Batyah, moshavah with municipal council status in Israel, SE of Reḥovot. First village founded on Baron Edmond de Rothschild's initiative 1883. Pop. 980 (1971).

Benjamin Mazar

An early "mazzah" machine in a New York bakery, 1855.

Otto Mears

Mazli'aḥ, moshav in C. Israel, nr. Ramleh; founded 1950 by Karaites fr. Egypt. One of the principal Karaite centers in Israel. Pop. 665 (1971).

Mazzah (Heb.), unleavened bread; only bread permitted during Passover. Positive duty to eat it on first night (in Diaspora on first two nights) of the festival.

Me-Am Lo'ez, 18th c. ethico-homiletical Bible commentary in Ladino. Aim of initiator, Jacob Culi, was to popularize Jewish lore by means of extracts fr. all branches of rabbinical literature. The compilation continued in the 19th c. For long time only literature for thousands of Sephardi Jewish families; reading was often considered religious duty.

Mears, Otto (1841–1931), U.S. railroad builder. Constructed most of principal railroads in SW Colorado. Lieutenant governor 1883, state capital commissioner 1889.

Me'assef, first Hebrew organ of Haskalah movement; founded 1783 in Koenigsberg by pupils of Mendelssohn. Devoted to revival of Hebrew language and Haskalah ideas. Appeared as quarterly until 1811.

Mechelen, see Malines.

Mecklenburg, former duchy in E. Germany. Jewish community first mentioned 1279 at Rostock. After accusation of Host desecration in Sternberg 1492, 27 Jews burned at stake and all Jews expelled fr. duchy. Full emancipation 1869. 1,225 Jews in 1932; perished in WWII.

Medalie, George Zerdin (1883–1946), U.S. lawyer, Jewish community leader. U.S. attorney for Southern District of N.Y. fr. 1931, vigorous prosecutor of racketeers and smugglers. Associate Justice of Court of Appeals 1945. Pres. Federation of Jewish Philanthropies 1941–45.

Medeba, see Madaba.

Medem, Vladimir (1879–1923), Bund leader in Poland, Russia. Baptized in youth, found way back to Jewish identity, and joined the Bund 1900, becoming member of its central committee 1906. Led Bund in Poland during WWI. Opposed its Communist tendency, found himself isolated, and went to U.S. 1921.

Medina (ancient name **Yathrib**), city in Arabia. Leading Jewish community in ancient Arabia. Before Muhammad's arrival 622 Jews numbered 8–10,000, forming majority of city's inhabitants, and were factor in acceptance of monotheism among Arabs. Scorned Muhammad, who began to expel them. Community ended 627.

Medina, Samuel ben Moses de (Maharashdam; 1506–1589), rabbi, halakhic authority, communal leader of Salonika; *posek* and yeshivah head. His responsa revealed original mind and awareness of contemporary social and economic problems. Established communal organization of Spanish exiles on solid juridical basis.

Medina, Sir Solomon de (c. 1650–1730), army contractor; first professing Jew in England to receive knighthood. Helped finance William of Orange's invasion of England 1688; principal army contractor to Duke of Marlborough during War of Spanish Succession 1701–14.

Medini, Ḥayyim Hezekiah ben Raphael Elijah (1832–1904), rabbi, halakhic scholar in Turkey and Crimea; b. Jerusalem. Established yeshivah in Hebron. Wrote 18-vol. halakhic encyclopedia *Sedei Ḥemed* containing rules of talmudic and halakhic methodology, alphabetical list of various laws, responsa, and bibliographical research.

Meerovich, Menaché (1860–1949), member of Bilu, key figure in Jewish settlement in Ereẓ Israel; b. Russia, joined comrades at Rishon le-Zion c. 1882. One of the first to describe the new settlement in Russian Jewish press. An agronomist, he introduced many improvements in fruit cultivation.

Meged, Aharon (1920–), Israel writer, playwright, editor; member of kibbutz Sedot Yam until 1950. Cultural attaché in London 1969–71. His prose has strong autobiographical elements. Wrote plays, novels *(Fortune of a Fool, The Living on the Dead)*, stories. His brother, **Matti (Matityahu**; 1923–), poet, literary critic.

Megiddo, ancient Canaanite and Israelite city in Jezreel Valley. Captured by David, fortified by Solomon. Conquered in 733 by Tiglath-Pileser III who made it capital of

Complex of fortress gates at Megiddo.

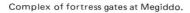

Assyrian province. Scene of historic battle against Egyptians where Josiah fell. Henceforward associated with war (cf. Armegeddon = Har Megiddo in Revelation 16:16). Napoleon (in 1799) and Allenby (in 1918) defeated Turks at Megiddo. In 1964, President Shazar received Pope Paul VI there. Extensive excavations.

Megillah (Heb. "scroll"), designation of each of five scrolls of Bible (Ruth, Song of Songs, Lamentations, Ecclesiastes, Esther). When scroll is not specifically named, term commonly refers to Scroll of Esther.

Megillah, 10th tractate, of Mishnah order *Mo'ed,* with *gemara* in both Talmuds. Deals with liturgical readings fr. Bible, esp. reading of Scroll of Esther on Purim.

Megillat Ahimaaz, see Ahimaaz.

Megillat Ester, see Scroll of Esther.

Megillat Ta'anit (Heb. "scroll of [days of prohibited] fasting"), list of 36 days commemorating significant victories and happy events in history of Jews during Second Temple period, on which fasting was prohibited by rabbis. Compiled close to destruction of Temple.

Lattice "meḥiẓah" of women's gallery in Vittorio Veneto Synagogue, Italy, 1701.

Meḥiẓah (Heb.), designation of partition screen in synagogues separating men fr. women, who generally sat in rear or balcony. Abolished by Reform movement in Europe in 19th c. and in most Conservative synagogues.

Meḥoza, see Maḥoza.

Meidner, Ludwig (1884–1966), German painter. One of foremost representatives of expressionism in Central Europe. In England 1939–52. Painted apocalyptic landscapes and Jewish themes.

Meier, Julius (1874–1937), U.S. governor. Developed Columbia River highway system. Ran as independent and elected governor of Oregon 1931–35. Promoted conservation of state's natural resources, formation of state police system, and establishment of non-political judiciary.

Me'ilah (Heb. "sacrilege"), 8th tractate of Mishnah order *Kodashim,* with *gemara* in Babylonian Talmud. Deals with unlawful use and enjoyment of *hekdesh* (i.e., things consecrated to Temple, esp. sacrifices).

Meir (2nd c. C.E.), *tanna,* one of leaders of post-Bar Kokhba generation. Played decisive part in development of Mishnah, his collection forming basis of Judah ha-Nasi's works. All anonymous rulings in Mishnah are attributed to him. Outstanding preacher, with 300 fox fables ascribed to him. In political matters, favored moderation toward Roman government. Noted figure in aggadah, sometimes together with his wife Beruryah (q.v.).

Meir Ba'al Ha-Nes, Tomb of, building nr. Tiberias, object of pilgrimages. Acc. to tradition, burial place of *tanna* R. Meir, but also linked to other rabbis called Meir. Emissaries throughout world propagated its fame and every Jewish home had "Meir Ba'al ha-Nes box" into which contributions were dropped.

Meir (Myerson), Golda (1898–), Israel prime minister, labor leader; b. Kiev, emigrated to U.S. (Milwaukee) 1906, settled in Ereẓ Israel 1921. Secretary of Mo'eẓet ha-Po'alot 1928. Joined executive committee of Histadrut 1934, becoming head of political dept. Acting head of Political Dept. of Jewish Agency, when the leaders of the *yishuv* arrested June 1946. Minister to Moscow 1948–49. Mapai member of Knesset 1949–74, min. of labor 1949–56, foreign minister 1956–65. Secretary general of Mapai and later secretary general of Israel Labor Party. After the death of Levi Eshkol 1969, prime minister of Israel until 1974. Greatly popular at home and among World Jewry; strengthened relations with U.S.

Golda Meir

Meir, Jacob (1856–1939), Sephardi chief rabbi of Ereẓ Israel; b. Jerusalem. Preached revival of spoken Hebrew in Ereẓ Israel. Often interceded with Turkey on behalf of Jewish community. Chief rabbi of Salonika 1908–19. Elected chief rabbi of Ereẓ Israel with title of *Rishon le-Zion* 1921.

Meir b. Baruch of Rothenburg, a detail from "Rothschild Miscellany," Italy, c. 1470.

Meir ben Baruch of Rothenburg (Maharam of Rothenburg; c. 1215–1293), teacher, scholar, ritual, legal, and community authority; b. Worms. Witnessed burning of Talmud in Paris 1242 and wrote elegy *Sha'ali Serufah ba-Esh,* still included in Ashkenazi *kinot* of Av 9. Settled in Rothenburg. His influential responsa, of which c. 1,000 survive, covered all aspects of life. Introduced modifications in prayer ritual and religious customs. Leader of emigration fr. Germany when Emperor Rudolph I imposed heavy tax on Jews 1286. Arrested and imprisoned until death. He refused to allow himself to be ransomed so as not to set a precedent. Wrote *tosafot* and novellae to 18 tractates of Talmud, commentaries to two orders of Mishnah, and compendia of laws.

Meir ben Elijah of Norwich (Meir of England; 13th c.), liturgical poet, *ḥazzan;* only known English *paytan.* Among those exiled fr. England 1290.

Meir (Moses Meir) ben Ephraim of Padua (d. 1583), scribe, printer, teacher in Mantua. Founded printing establishment 1556 which printed first editions of Zohar.

Meir ben Ḥiyya Rofe (17th c.), scholar, emissary of Hebron. Supporter

of Shabbetai Ẓevi, encouraging those who believed in him in Italy. During last 10 years of life recognized as outstanding scholar of Hebron.

Meir ben Isaac Sheli'aḥ Ẓibbur (**Nehorai**; d. before 1096), preacher, liturgical poet of Worms. Best known of his *piyyutim* is Aramaic *Akdamut Millin* (q.v.).

Meir ben Samuel of Ramerupt (c. 1060–c. 1135), one of first tosafists of N. France. Wrote commentaries to Talmud (later used by Rashi). Present text of *Kol Nidrei* is result of amendments introduced by him into original formula.

Meir ben Samuel of Shcherbreshin (17th c.), *paytan*, chronicler; lived in Lublin, Poland. His rhymed account in Hebrew of Chmielnicki persecutions, *Ẓok ha-Ittim*, is of historical importance.

Meir ben Simeon ha-Me'ili (13th c.), Provençal talmudist, communal leader; mainly active in Narbonne, acting as communal spokesman before authorities. Wrote account of his disputation with bishop of Narbonne, and talmudic novellae.

Meiri, Menahem ben Solomon (1249–1316), Provençal scholar, Talmud commentator. Summarized teachings of his predecessors. His chief work is gigantic *Beit ha-Beḥirah*, which summarizes subject matter of Talmud. Also wrote ethical works and Bible commentaries. In Maimonidean controversy, upheld teaching of philosophy.

Meir Jehiel ha-Levi (Holzstock) of Ostrowiec (1857–1928), ḥasidic rabbi, rabbinical scholar; one of foremost leaders of Orthodox Jewry and originator of new form of Ḥasidism, with sermons based on complicated *gematria*.

Meir Simḥah ha-Kohen of Dvinsk (1843–1926), talmudic scholar. Joint pres. Russian Central Committee of Rabbis 1911. Wrote talmudic novellae, commentary on Pentateuch, responsa.

Meisel, Mordecai (Marcus) ben Samuel (1528–1601), Prague financier, philanthropist, head of Jewish community. Financed large transactions in support of Rudolph II. Built Meisel Synagogue 1597. On his death estate seized in name of emperor and heirs tortured.

Meisels, Dov Berush (1798–1870), rabbi, Polish patriot. Played central role in Cracow. Supported Polish patriots. Elected to Austrian parliament 1848 and joined forces with Leftist Radicals, protesting that *"Juden haben keine Rechte."* Chief rabbi of Warsaw fr. 1856, coming into conflict with Czarist authorities.

Meisl, Joseph (1883–1958), historian, architect; b. Brno. Librarian of Berlin Jewish community. Settled in Jerusalem after 1933. Founded and directed General Archives for History of the Jewish People. Wrote 3-vol. *Geschichte der Juden in Polen und Russland.*

Meitner, Lise (1878–1968), physicist; one of small group responsible for discovery of atomic fission; b. Vienna. Worked with Otto Hahn researching radioactive substances, which eventually led to splitting of atom. First woman prof. at Univ. of Berlin 1926. Head of physics dept. at Kaiser Wilhelm Inst. for Chemistry in Berlin for over 20 years. Worked at Nobel Inst. in Sweden after *Anschluss.* Last years in Cambridge, England.

Mekhilta of R. Ishmael, halakhic Midrash on Exodus consisting of collection of *beraitot* fr. period of *tannaim;* probably compiled and redacted in Ereẓ Israel no earlier than end of 4th c. C.E.

Mekhilta of R. Simeon ben Yoḥai, halakhic Midrash on Exodus consisting of collection of *beraitot* fr. period of *tannaim;* probably redacted in Ereẓ Israel not earlier than 5th c. C.E. Frequently quoted by medieval scholars, it now exists only in part.

Mekhlis, Lev Zakharovich (1889–1953), Soviet army officer. Headed Red Army's political administration 1937–40. Before and after WWII served respectively as people's commissar of state control and minister of state control. During WWII served on several fronts and promoted lieutenant general.

Mekiẓe Nirdamim, society for publication of scholarly editions of medieval Hebrew literature; founded in Lyck by E.L. Silbermann 1862, headquarters transferred to Jerusalem 1934.

Meklenburg, Jacob Ẓevi (1785–1865), German rabbi, biblical commentator. Author of *Ha-Ketav ve-ha-Kabbalah* on Pentateuch and *Iyyun Tefillah* on prayer book.

Meknès, town in Morocco. Jews in region before advent of Islam. By 18th c. one of best-organized communities in Morocco, with its leaders acting as *negidim* for Moroccan Jewry. Fr. 1790 lost importance and Jews suffered frequent pogroms. With French Protectorate 1912 Jewish situation improved. 10,894 Jews in 1960; 2,000–3,000 remained in 1968.

Mekorot Water Company, Israel National Water Supply Agency fr. 1962. Established 1937 as joint undertaking of Histadrut, Jewish Agency, Jewish National Fund, to develop water supply projects in Ereẓ Israel. Fr. early 1960s also operated in other countries.

Melamed, Ezra Zion (1903–), Israel talmudic scholar, philologist. Prof. at Bar-Ilan, Tel Aviv, Heb. Univ. Published edition of Eusebius' *Onomastikon.* Important source for Persian community traditions.

Melamed, Meir (15th c.), financier in Spain during period of expulsion. Succeeded father-in-law Abraham Seneor as chief administrator of tax farming in kingdom 1487; both baptized 1492, with Ferdinand and Isabella acting as godparents. Adopted name Fernando Pérez Coronel. Appointed chief accountant and permanent member of royal council.

Melavveh Malkah (Heb. "escorting the queen [Sabbath]"), term used to describe meal and festivities at end of Sabbath. Origin of custom traced to Talmud.

Melbourne, city in Australia. Founders incl. two Jews 1835. First synagogue Hebrew Congregation established 1847. Predominantly middle-class community of European origin, with extensive Jewish communal and cultural life. Jewish pop. 35,000 (1971).

Melchett, see Mond.

Melchior, family prominent in Denmark since mid-18th c. **Moses** (1736–1817), founded still-existing import-export firm 1795. **Nathan Gerson** (1811–1872), ophthalmologist. Lectured at Copenhagen Univ. Director of Ophthalmological Inst. in Copenhagen fr. 1857. **Moritz Gerson** (1816–1884), expanded family business, served in upper house of Danish parliament and Danish Chamber of Commerce (pres. 1873).

Melchior, Carl (1871–1933), German banker. Took part in financial and economic negotiations following WWI armistice. Member (chairman 1928–29) of League of Nations finance committee.

Melchior, Marcus (1897–1969), chief rabbi of Denmark fr. 1947. Developed Jewish education in Copenhagen. Succeeded by his son **Bent.**

Melchizedek, king of Salem (Jerusalem), "priest of God most High." Welcomed Abraham after latter defeated 4 kings who had captured Lot.

Raphael Meldola

Meldola, Raphael (1754–1828), British rabbi, and haham of Sephardi community in London 1804/5–28. Helped reform educational institutions of community. His grandson, **Raphael** (1849–1915), chemist, naturalist, researcher into dyestuffs. Pres. British Chemical Society.

Mellah, Jewish quarter in N. African towns.

Melnikoff, Avraham (1892–1960), Israel sculptor. One of pioneers of sculpture in modern Israel. Known for his lion erected between Tel Ḥai and Kefar Giladi.

Melochim Bukh (Yid. "Book of the Kings"), poetic adaptation of biblical history and one of great national epics in Old Yiddish literature. Author anonymous; work probably composed in 15th c. Based on Book of Kings, embellished with legends and tales fr. Talmud and Midrash.

Melton, Samuel Mendel (1900–), U.S. industrialist, philanthropist. Founded Melton Research Center at Jewish Theological Seminary 1959.

Page from martyrology of "Memorbuch" kept by community of Frankfort on the Main, 1629–1907, recording names of communities which suffered persecution and ending with prayer for martyrs' souls.

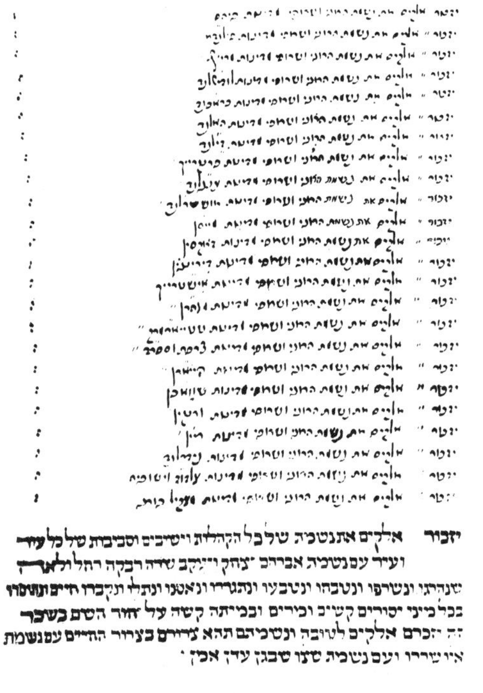

Meltzer, Isser Zalman (1870–1953), talmudic scholar, yeshivah head in Slutsk and Jerusalem fr. 1925. As fervent Zionist, exercised moderating influence in councils of Agudat Israel. Wrote important commentary on Maimonides' *Mishneh Torah.*

Meltzer, Shimshon (1909–), Hebrew poet, translator; b. Galicia, settled in Ereẓ Israel 1933. Used ḥasidic tales and motifs in his ballads. Translated Polish-Jewish writers. Edited Zionist Library publications of Jewish Agency.

Mem, (מ; final form ם), 13th letter of Hebrew alphabet; numerical value 40. Pronounced *m.*

Memmi, Albert (1920–), French author, sociologist; b. Tunis. Fought with Free French in WWII. Prof. at Ecole Pratique des Hautes Etudes. In his writings, portrays Jew as "shadow figure" neither wholly assimilated nor anxious to lose his distinctiveness. Works incl. *Pillar of Salt, The Liberation of the Jew, Portrait of a Jew.*

Memorbuch, community prayer book once common in Jewish communities throughout C. Europe. Consisted of three major parts: (1) collection of prayers; (2) necrology of distinguished persons, either of local or general Jewish importance; (3) martyrology of persons and places. Last has been subjected to minute research by scholars. Earliest book appeared c. 1600.

Memorial Foundation for Jewish Culture, see Conference on Jewish Material Claims against Germany.

Memorial Light, light kindled on anniversary of death of relative, during period of mourning, and in some communities on eve of Day of Atonement. Custom probably originated in Germany in Middle Ages.

Memorial Prayer, see Hazkarat Neshamot.

Memphis, city in Tenn. U.S. Jews settled in 1840s; B'nai Israel Congregation granted charter by state legislature 1854. Orthodox congregation organized 1884. Conservative 1950. Jewish pop. 9,000 (1971).

Menahem, king of Israel c. 746–737 B.C.E. Seized throne after assassinating Shallum. Sacked Tiphsah, paid heavy tribute to King Pul of Assyria, and received Assyrian recognition as vassal king.

Menahem ben Aaron ibn Zeraḥ (c. 1310–1385), Spanish codifier. Owing to persecution, led itinerant life. His *Ẓeidah la-Derekh* is code of laws concerning daily way of life which contains valuable historical material on contemporary life of Jew in France, Germany, and Spain.

Menahem ben Ḥelbo (11th c.), one of first commentators on Bible in N. France. His influence accounts for presence of Arabic words as well as some Provençal forms of French in Rashi.

Menahem ben Jacob ibn Saruq (10th c.), Spanish author, lexicographer. Secretary of Ḥisdai ibn Shaprut. Author of *Maḥberet,* biblical dictionary in Hebrew which attempted systematic summary of lexicographical and grammatical knowledge of the time. Through his pupils, exerted great influence on development of Hebrew grammar.

Menahem ben Solomon (12th c.), author of *Sekhel Tov,* aggadic-halakhic midrashic anthology arranged acc. to weekly scriptural readings. Interested in linguistic topics and Hebrew grammar. Birthplace unknown.

Menahem Mendel of Kotsk, see Kotsk, Menahem Mendel of.

Menahem Mendel of Peremyshlany (b. 1728), ḥasidic leader; representative of extreme enthusiasts among first generation of ḥasidic movement. Disciple of Ba'al Shem Tov. Advocated precedence of devotion over study. Emigrated to Ereẓ Israel 1764.

Menahem Mendel of Shklov (d. 1827), rebuilder of Ashkenazi community of Jerusalem in early 19th c. Pupil of Gaon of Vilna. Established home in Jerusalem 1816 and requested that *halukkah* funds be transferred to new Ashkenazi community which he established there.

Menahem Mendel of Vitebsk (1730–1788), ḥasidic leader active in Belorussia, Lithuania, Ereẓ Israel. Disciple of Dov Baer of Mezhirech. Attempted to stem tide of opposition to Ḥasidism. Regarded function of *ẓaddik* as being restricted to teaching and guidance in divine worship.

Menahem of Merseburg (14th c.), a leading scholar of Saxony, Germany. Noted for *takkanot* governing relations bet. individual and community.

Menahem son of Judah, patriot leader at outbreak of Roman War 66–70 C.E. Captured Masada in early stage of war. Jerusalemites later opposed his pretentions to lead revolt, and killed him.

Menahem Ẓiyyoni (14th–15th c.), kabbalist, exegete in Cologne; one of few kabbalists in 14th c. Germany. Known through his *Ẓiyyoni,* homiletical commentary on Torah.

Menaḥot (Heb. "meal offerings"), 2nd tractate of Mishnah order *Kodashim,* with *gemara* in Babylonian Talmud. Deals primarily with various meal offerings in Temple.

Mendel, Lafayette Benedict (1872–1935), U.S. physiological chemist; pioneer in nutrition. Prof. at Yale Univ. First person to study vitamin A. First pres. American Inst. of Nutrition.

Mendele Mokher Seforim (Shalom Jacob Abramovitsch; 1835–1917), Hebrew, Yiddish writer; b. Belorussia, studied at various yeshivot, traveled widely, lived in Berdichev and Zhitomir, settled in Odessa 1881. Instrumental in founding modern literary Yiddish and new realism in Hebrew style, leaving mark on both literatures thematically as well as stylistically. Wrote Hebrew and Yiddish fiction, literary and social criticism, works of popular science (in Hebrew), and rewrote some of his Yiddish novels in Hebrew. One of acknowledged modern classicists in both Hebrew and Yiddish. His popular, often satirical stories incl. *Fathers and Sons, Fishke the Lame, The Mare,* and *The Travels of Binyamin III.*

Mendels, Maurits (1868–1944), Dutch Socialist politician. Member of Dutch Socialist Party in second chamber of parliament 1913–19, senate 1919–37. Provincial Council of North Holland. D. Theresienstadt.

Mendelsohn, Eric (1887–1953), architect; b. Germany. Member of revivalist movement in European architecture fr. 1920s. Left Germany 1933, worked in Britain and Ereẓ Israel until outbreak of WWII, then went to U.S. Works incl. Hadassah hospital on Mt. Scopus, Maimonides Health Center in San Francisco, and synagogues in U.S.

Mendelson, Yosef (José; 1891–1969), Argentine Yiddish editor, writer; b. Ukraine, in Argentina fr. 1912. Edited *Di Yidishe Tsaytung* 1923–29, co-edited monthly *Argentina.* Translated novels fr. Russian, Spanish, French, English. Directed Hebrew-Yiddish Teachers Seminary in Buenos Aires fr. 1943.

Mendelssohn, Felix Bartholdy (Jakob Ludwig Felix; 1809–1847), composer; grandson of Moses Mendelssohn, son of Abraham Mendelssohn; brought up as Protestant. Most famous composer in C. Europe in his time. Works incl. string octet, music to *A Midsummer Night's Dream, Italian* and *Scotch* symphonies, violin concerto, oratorio *Elijah.*

Mendelssohn, Kurt Alfred Georg (1906–), British physicist; left Germany 1933. Established Britain's first helium liquefaction plant. Edited *Cyrogenics.* 1961–65, international journal of low-temperature engineering.

Mendelssohn, Moses (Moses ben Menahem; Rambeman; 1729–1786), philosopher of German Enlightenment, spiritual leader of German Jewry; studied under rabbi of Dessau, David Fraenkel, followed him to Berlin. Acquired broad education and became friendly with G.E. Lessing, who introduced him to German cultural circles. Became embroiled in dispute on Jewish religion 1769 and from then on confined most of his literary activity to sphere of Judaism; also active on behalf of Jews in practical affairs. First publication laid groundwork for new understanding of nature of beauty; second, *Philosophische Schriften,* formulated new psychological theory which defined and justified autonomy of aesthetic judgments. In his *Phaedon* dealt with immortality of soul. Published *Millot ha-Higgayon* on logic of Maimonides and translation of Pentateuch into German written in Hebrew characters, with commentary *Biur* in Hebrew (by different authors). Based on traditional exegesis although introducing modern conceptions and emphasizing aesthetic aspects. Translation aroused anger of traditional rabbis, but enabled many Jews to learn German language and gain knowledge of Bible. His *Jerusalem* summarized and completed his thoughts on Jewish religion. His sons **Joseph** (1770–1848), and **Abraham** (1776–1835), ran banking business which helped transfer French indemnity after Napoleon's defeat. Joseph's son **Georg Benjamin** (1794–1874), prof. of geography at Bonn Univ.; baptized. Moses' great grandsons **Franz** (1829–1889) and **Ernst** (1846–1909), elevated to hereditary nobility. Abraham and wife converted to Protestantism. Later descendants all baptized, incl. **Albrecht Mendelssohn-Bartholdy,** editor of *Europaeische Gespraeche,* Hamburg, and composer **Felix** (q.v.). Moses' daughter **Dorothea** (1765–1839), married twice, to banker Simon Veit and Frederich Schlegel. Her sons **Johannes Veit** (1790–1854) and **Phillip Veit** (1793–1877), painters of Romantic "Nazarene" school. His other daughter **Henriette** (1768–1831) had a salon.

Mendele Mokher Seforim on his 70th birthday, 1905, with Y.Ḥ. Ravnitsky (seated left), A. Levinsky (seated right), S. Ben-Zion (standing left), and Ḥ.N. Bialik (standing right).

The Schocken department store in Chemnitz, Saxony, designed by Eric Mendelsohn.

Felix Mendelssohn playing for Goethe in Weimar.

Moses Mendelssohn

Mendes, Alvaro, see Abenaes, Solomon.

Mendes, Beatrice, see Nasi, Gracia.

Mendès, Catulle (1841–1909), French poet; father of Sephardi origin, mother Catholic. Founded *La Revue fantaisiste* 1861, first of several journals issued by French Parnassian poets. His 150 published vols. incl. 3-vol. *Poésies,* play *Médée,* and novel *Monstres parisiens.* Killed in railroad accident.

Mendes, Diogo (b. before 1492–d. c. 1542), Marrano merchant in precious stone and spices; b. Spain, settled in Antwerp and joined by brother's widow Gracia Nasi. Organized "underground route" to facilitate flight of Marranos fr. Portugal to Italy and Turkey.

Mendes, Frederic de Sola (1850–1927), U.S. Sephardi rabbi of Congregation Shaarey Tefillah, N.Y.; b. Jamaica. A founder of *American Hebrew* 1879.

Mendes, Henry Pereira (1852–1937), U.S. Sephardi rabbi of Congregation Shearith Israel, N.Y.; brother of Frederic Mendes; b. England. A founder of Union of Orthodox Congregations of America and early Zionist. Wrote on Jewish ethics, etc.

Mendès-France, Pierre (1907–), French statesman. Elected to National Assembly 1932. Member of Free French during WWII. Member of National Assembly fr. 1946. Prime Minister 1954–55. Ended war in Indo-China. Defeated over N. Africa policy of independence for Tunisia and Morocco. Opposed De Gaulle's rise to power. A leader of Radical Party and later, of united socialists (P.S.U.). Wrote on economics and politics.

Pierre Mendès-France

Mendlowitz, Shraga Feivel (1886–1948), U.S. educator, Orthodox Jewish leader; b. Austria-Hungary, in U.S. fr. 1913. Principal of Yeshiva Torah Vadaath fr 1921, developing it into leading American yeshivah and helping make Williamsburg center of Orthodoxy. Instrumental in founding Torah Umesorah 1944.

Mendoza, province in Argentina and capital city of province. Jews settled there as agriculturists and plantation owners by end of 1880s. By 1960s 1,100 families in city, mostly in business.

Mendoza, Daniel (1764–1836), English prizefighter. Father of scientific boxing. His successes and royal patronage helped situation of Jews in England. Middleweight champion of England 1792–95.

The fight between Daniel Mendoza (right) and Richard Humphries, Jan. 9, 1788.

Mene, Mene, Tekel, u-Farsin, enigmatic inscription referred to in Daniel 5:25 which appeared on wall during feast given by King Belshazzar of Babylon, written by detached hand. Interpreted by Daniel as predicting victory of Persians over Belshazzar.

Menelaus (d. c. 162 B.C.E.), high priest in time of Antiochus Epiphanes; extremist leader of Hellenists and to great extent responsible for persecutions of Antiochus. Later lost favor in Seleucid court and executed.

Menes, Abram (1897–1969), historian. Vice-chairman of Grodno Jewish community after WWI. In Berlin fr. 1920, moved to Paris 1933. Leading contributor to *Yiddish Encyclopedia.* Settled in U.S. 1940 and joined staff of Yiddish daily *Forward.* Wrote on economic and social aspect of Jewish history, Jewish socialism, and workers' movement.

Menken (née **Theodore**), **Adah Isaacs** (1835–1868), U.S. actress. Known for flamboyant way of life; married four times, mistress of Swinburne, elder Dumas, etc. Led protest against exclusion of Jews fr. House of Commons 1857. Wrote books of poems *Memoirs* and *Infelicia.*

Menkes, Zygmunt (1896–), U.S. painter; b. Lvov, in U.S. fr. 1936. Primarily colorist; work showed increasing tendency to two-dimensionality. Frequently used Jewish themes in earlier works.

Menorah (Heb. "candelabrum"), seven-branched oil lamp used in Tabernacle and Temple; most popular Jewish symbol in antiquity. Term later applied to 8-branched candelabrum used on Ḥanukkah. In modern times used as religious symbol. Adopted as official symbol of State of Israel.

Menorah Association, U.S. Jewish campus organization. Grew out of Harvard Menorah Society, Jewish campus group formed 1906 by Henry Hurwitz. Intercollegiate Menorah Association established 1913 and soon numbered 80 chapters. Largely defunct by 1930s. Published *Menorah Journal* 1915–62. Pioneer intellectual English-Jewish publication in U.S.

Menuhin, Yehudi (1916–), violinist; b. New York. Appeared with San Francisco Orchestra as soloist at age 8. Considered one of greatest violinists of 20th c. Played for U.S. and Allied forces throughout WWII. Established own music festivals at Gstaad, Switzerland 1957 and Bath, England 1959.

Me'ot Ḥittim (Heb. "wheat money"), collection made before

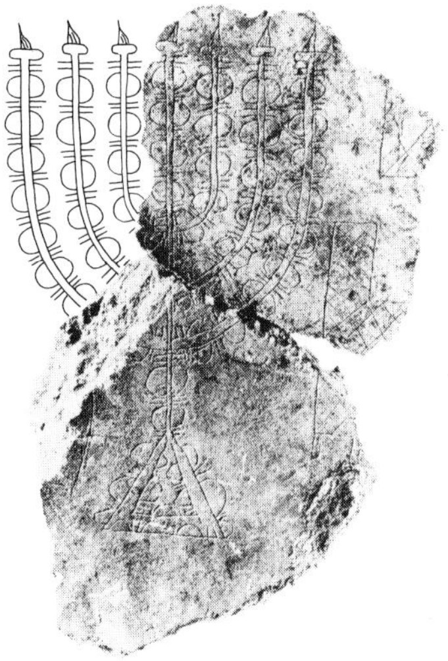

Plaster fragments of earliest known representation of the Temple "menorah," from reign of Herod, found in excavations in the Old City of Jerusalem.

Yehudi Menuhin.

Passover to ensure supply of flour for unleavened bread *(mazzot)* for poor.

Mephibosheth (Meribaal), son of Jonathan, grandson of Saul. Became lame at age 5; subsequently treated considerately by King David.

Mer, Gideon (1894–1961), Israel expert on malaria, epidemiologist. Prof. at Heb. Univ. Devised method of age grouping of female anopheles by size of ampulla of ovary.

Merab, the eldest daughter of King Saul. Conditionally promised as wife for David; eventually given to Adriel the Meholathite.

Meremar (d. 432), Babylonian *amora.* Succeeded Ashi as head of Academy of Sura 427.

Stamp issued by Israel Post Office in honor of jubilee of Merḥavyah, designed by M. and G. Shamir.

Merḥavyah, kibbutz in Jezreel Valley, Israel. Founded 1911 by group of Ha-Shomer, becoming pioneer workers' cooperative acc. to Franz Oppenheimer's ideas. Dispersed after WWI. Reestablished 1929 as kibbutz of Ha-Shomer ha-Ẓa'ir and became movement's organizational center. Pop. 540 (1971).

Meribaal, see Mephibosheth.

Merit of the Fathers, see Zekhut Avot.

Merkabah Mysticism or **Ma'aseh Merkavah.** Mishnaic name given to first chapter of Ezekiel. Term used by rabbis to designate complex of speculations, homiletics, and visions connected with Throne of God and chariot *(merkavah)* which bears it and all that is embodied in this divine world.

°**Merneptah,** king of Egypt (c. 1224–1214 B.C.E.). Believed by scholars to be Pharaoh of Exodus. Stela found 1896 and dated to 5th year of his reign contains earliest reference to Israel.

Meron, place in Galilee. Several talmudic sages associated with it, notably R. Simeon b. Yoḥai and his son Eliezer, who according to tradition were buried there. To this day popular festival (*Hillula*) is held at their reputed grave on Lag ba-Omer. Remains of ancient synagogue found there.

Meron (Maierzuk), Hanna (1923–), Israel actress; b. Berlin, settled in Ereẓ Israel 1933. Responsible for some of Tel Aviv Cameri Theater's greatest successes. Lost leg 1970 as result of Arab attack on Munich Airport; recovered and returned to stage. Israel Prize 1973.

Merton, Robert King (1910–), U.S. sociologist. One of leading American theorists in social sciences. Taught at Columbia fr. 1941. Publications incl. *Social Theory and Social Structure,* influential in American sociology.

Merzbacher, family of numismatists. **Abraham** (1812–1885), rabbi, banker, numismatist, bibliophile. A foremost European expert in numismatics; exposed "Becker Counterfeits," famous case of counterfeiting ancient coins. His library of over 4,000 vols. (incl. 156 mss. and 43 incunabula) eventually part of Frankfort city library. His son, **Eugen** (1845–1903), also numismatist, with main interest in Jewish numismatics.

Merzbacher, Gottfried (1843–1926), German explorer. Climbed mountains in Arabia, Persia, India, and Central Tien Shan range of Asia. His *Aus den Hochregionen des Kaukasus* became classic.

Merzbacher, Leo (1810–1856), first U.S. Reform rabbi; b. Bavaria, went to U.S. 1841. Rabbi of Congregation Emanuel in N.Y. fr. 1845. Introduced confirmation 1848 and compiled shortened prayer book 1855.

°**Mesha,** king of Moab in 9th c. B.C.E. Paid tribute to Ahab, but revolted after his death. Jehoram conducted military campaign against him which ended in failure. Erected basalt victory stele at Dibon c. 40 inches (1 m.) high and c. 28 inches ((70 cm.) wide. Found 1868 and now in Louvre.

Mesḥah, see Kefar Tavor.

Meshed (Mashhad), city in Iran. 40 Jewish families moved to city by Nādir Shāh 1740 but after his death 1747 they were exposed to persecution; forced to convert to Islam 1839. Continued secretly to practice Jewish observances, but eventually emigrated, most of them to Jerusalem. 400 Jews in 1956.

Meshullam ben Jacob of Lunel (12th c.), Provençal scholar. Occupied himself with halakhic and secular studies and employed wealth to maintain famous *bet ha-midrash.* Composed halakhic works, sponsored translation of books on grammar, theology, rhetorics, ethics, and parables.

Meshullam ben Kalonymus (10th–11th c.), rabbi, *paytan* in Rome, Mainz. His responsa are important source of information for social and economic history of Jewish communities of pre-Crusader Europe. His works helped establish Rhineland scholarship and stimulated development in France and Germany of powerful poetical tradition.

Meshullam ben Moses (c. 1175–1250), scholar of Béziers; one of most prominent scholars of Provence in 13th c. Opponent of Kabbalah. Chiefly renowned for *Sefer ha-Hashlamah,* designed to complete *halakhot* of Isaac Alfasi.

Meshullam ben Nathan of Melun (12th c.), talmudist in N. France; frequently mentioned in *tosafot.* Involved in long and bitter dispute with Jacob Tam.

Meshullam Phoebus ben Israel Samuel (1547–1617), Polish rabbi. Halakhic authority who gave numerous rulings on synagogue customs. Had wide knowledge of languages and was well versed in medical matters.

Meshummadim, see Apostasy.

Meshwi (or **Misḥawayh**) **āl-'Ukbarī** (9th c.), Jewish sectarian of Ukbara, nr. Baghdad; followers known as Misḥawayhites. Teachings differed fr. rabbinic and karaite Judaism, esp. in calendar computations; claimed that day spanned fr. dawn to dawn.

Meskin, Aharon (1898–), Israel actor; early member of Habimah in Moscow. Played first major role 1923 as *The Golem* in H. Leivick's play. Roles incl. Othello and Shylock. Israel Prize 1960.

Cast of the Mesha stele

Messel, Alfred (1853–1909), German architect. Most famous work, Wertheim department store in Berlin 1897, first store to be constructed of stone, steel, and glass. Renounced Judaism.

Messerer, Asaf Mikhailovich (1903–), dancer, teacher in Bolshoi Ballet, Moscow. Had brilliant technique and replaced traditional mime with expressive dancing. Principal choreographer in Bolshoi Ballet. His sister **Sulamith** (1908–), also noted dancer and teacher in Bolshoi Ballet.

Messer Leon, David, see Leon, Messer David.

Messer Leon, Judah, see Judah ben Jehiel.

The Messiah, on a white donkey, being led into Jerusalem by Elijah. From a "Haggadah," Munich, 15th cent.

Messiah (Heb. *mashi'aḥ* "anointed one"), concept developed in Judaism mostly in Second Temple and later periods, biblical references being vague. Belief in ultimate coming incorporated by Maimonides in 13 Principles of Faith. Messianic movements frequently sprang up in times of oppression. Charismatic figures who were centers of such movements incl. Bar Kokhba, many almost unknown personalities in Arab Caliphate and Byzantine Empire in Middle Ages, David Alroy, David Reuveni, Solomon Molcho, Shabbetai Ẓevi, Jacob Frank. Orthodox opinion on nature varied in different periods. In eschatological literature, descendant of David who would rule over Israel in golden age of messianic era. Reform Judaism substituted faith in advent of messianic era for belief in personal Messiah. Many disputations were held with Christians concerning messiahship of Jesus.

Messina, see Sicily.

Mestel, Jacob (1884–1958), Yiddish poet, actor, theater director; b. Galicia, in U.S. fr. 1920. Joined Yiddish Art Theater 1923. Directed own group and experimented with bold theatrical innovations.

Metatron (Matatron), angel accorded special position in esoteric doctrine fr. tannaitic period on. One tradition makes him responsible for performing most exalted tasks in heavenly kingdom; another associates him with Enoch.

Metchnikoff, Elie (1845–1916), Russian biologist; father officer of Imperial Guard, mother Jewish. Made important discoveries in embryology. Prof. at Univ. of Odessa. Left Russia for Messina 1882 and there developed his phagocyte theory (later confirmed). Subsequently subdirector of Pasteur Inst. Nobel Prize for Medicine, 1908.

Meteg, diacritical mark whose sign is small perpendicular line under letter. Indicates accent in word.

Metempsychosis, see Gilgul.

Methuselah, son of Enoch, grandfather of Noah. Acc. to Bible, lived 969 years, longer than any other biblical figure.

Metman-Cohen, Yehudah Leib (1869–1939), educator in Ereẓ Israel; b. Ukraine, settled in Ereẓ Israel 1904. Founded Herzlia Gymnasium in Jaffa 1906.

Metullah, northernmost Israel village, on Lebanese border; founded 1896 on initiative of Baron Edmond de Rothschild. Pop. 360 (1971).

Metz, town in France. Jews there by 888. Anti-Jewish persecutions of First Crusade began there 1096. Medieval community occupied whole quarter. Community reestablished 1595. Religious freedom assured by French Revolution. 4,150 Jews in 1931. Made *judenrein* during WWII. 3,500 Jews in 1970.

Metzger, Arnold (1892–), German philosopher; in U.S. during WWII. prof. in Munich. Wrote on areas of philosophy that touch on psychology.

Mexico, C. American republic. In colonial period (1521–1821) New Christians, Marranos, and Crypto-Jews emigrated there despite persecutions and Inquisition. Many held official positions, while others prospered in commerce. Descendants assimilated by 19th c. Fr. beginning of 20th c. Sephardi and Levantine Jews began to emigrate there, but their number increased considerably only after WWII when Jews fr. E. Europe also began to arrive. Jews introduced buying on credit system and contributed to expansion of clothing industry. Economic status of community improved and Jews began to participate in liberal professions. Strong Jewish school network with highest percentage of children receiving complete Jewish education in Diaspora. Some groups of "Judaizing" mestizos live in country but are not recognized as Jewish by rabbinate. Jewish pop. 35,000 (1971), mainly concentrated in Mexico City.

Meyer, Annie Nathan (1867–1951), U.S. educator, writer. Her efforts resulted in opening of Barnard College 1899. Opposed women's suffrage movement and women in business. Wrote plays and books.

Meyer, Eugene (1875–1959), U.S. banker, government official, newspaper publisher. Formed banking firm 1901 and played leading role in developing oil, copper, and automotive industries. Gov. Federal Reserve Board and organized Reconstruction Finance Corp. 1932. Bought and revitalized *Washington Post* 1933. First pres. International Bank for Reconstruction and Development.

Meyer, Jonas Daniel (1780–1834), Dutch jurist, public figure. First Jew in Holland to be admitted as lawyer. Louis Napoleon appointed him director of *Royal Gazette* and court magistrate 1808. Sec. gov. committee for drafting new constitution 1815. Active in Jewish community.

Meyer, Leon (1868–1957), French politician. Mayor of Le Havre 1919. Radical-socialist member of Chamber of Deputies 1921. Undersecretary of state in two administrations and minister of mercantile marine 1932. Instrumental in developing port of Le Havre.

Meyer, Martin Abraham (1879–1923), U.S. Reform rabbi, scholar. Rabbi of Temple Emanu-el in San Francisco and lecturer in Semitics at Univ. of Calif.

Meyer, Victor (1848–1897), German organic chemist. Prof. at Zurich Polytechnic, Goettingen, and Heidelberg. Made basic contribution in field of organic compounds.

Meyerbeer, Giacomo (Jacob Liebmann-Beer; 1791–1864), German composer. Royal director of opera in Berlin 1842–47. Works

Giacomo Meyerbeer

incl. *Les Huguenots, Robert le Diable,* and *L'Africaine.*

Meyerhof, Max (1874–1945), ophthalmologist, medical historian; b. Germany. Chief of Khedivial Ophthalmic Clinic in Egypt. Published over 300 works on ophthalmology and medical history. Made special studies of various eye diseases endemic to Egypt and N. Africa.

Meyerhof, Otto (1884–1951), German biochemist. Head of physiology dept. at Inst. for Medical Research in Heidelberg fr. 1929; later research prof. of physiological chemistry at Univ. of Pennsylvania medical school. Nobel Prize 1925 for discovery of "fixed relationship between the consumption of oxygen and the metabolism of lactic acid in the muscle."

Meyers, Eduard Maurits (1880–1954), Dutch jurist. Prof. at Univ. of Leiden 1910–50, influencing several generations of Dutch lawyers. Imprisoned in Theresienstadt during WWII. Subsequently commissioned to draft new civil code for Holland but died before completion. Works incl. standard treatise *The Labor Contract.*

Meyerson, Emile (1859–1933), French chemist, philosopher of science. Studied interrelationships among natural sciences, history of philosophy, and cultural developments. Works incl. *Identité et Realité* and 2-vol. *De l'explication dans les Sciences.*

Meyuḥas, Raphael Meyuḥas ben Samuel (? 1695–1771), chief rabbi (*rishon le-Zion*) of Jerusalem. In one of his rulings attempted to bring about rapprochement bet. Karaites and Rabbanites. Wrote novellae and responsa.

Meyuḥas, Yosef Baran (Ben Raḥamim Nathan; 1868–1942), leader of Sephardi community in Ereẓ Israel, writer, educator. Pres. city council of Jews in Jerusalem 1920–31.

Mezaḥ (Segal), Joshua ha-Levi (1834–1917), Hebrew, Yiddish author; b. Lithuania. Wrote popular booklets in Yiddish and contributed to Hebrew and Yiddish journals.

Mezei, Mór (1836–1925), Hungarian lawyer, politician. Secretary Izraelita Magyar Egylet ("Union of Hungarian Israelites") fr. 1861. Jewish religion officially recognized in Hungary largely through his efforts. Liberal MP 1893–1901. His brother **Ernö** (1851–1932), journalist, politician. Political editorial writer for organ of opposition Independence Party.

Mezöfi, Vilmos (1870–1947), Hungarian politician, journalist. Edited Social Democratic Party daily newspaper. Elected to parliament 1905. Edited journal of small landowners' party after WWII. Fought legislation 1938 to deprive Jews of civic rights.

Mezuzah (Heb. "doorpost"), parchment scroll with selected Torah verses (Deut. 6:4–9, 11:13–21) placed in container affixed to doorpost of rooms occupied by Jews.

Mezuzah, minor tractate appended to Talmud. Deals with preparation of *mezuzah* and place where it should be attached.

Miami, city in Fla., U.S. First Jewish resident 1895. First congregation B'nai Zion 1912. Jews prominent in tourism, building and real estate, and professions. Jewish pop. (incl. many retired people) 187,500 (1971), with large influx of Jewish tourists to Miami Beach in winter months.

Mibashan, see Braunstein, Menahem Mendel.

Micah (8th c. B.C.E.), prophet in Judah; b. Moresheth-Gath in Shephelah and apparently of peasant stock. Prophecies contained in Book of Micah, sixth book in Minor Prophets of Bible. Denounces oppression by ruling classes and is the first to threaten exile to Babylonia.

Wooden "mezuzah" in the shape of a fish, E. Europe, 19th cent. (?).

Silver amulet, including names of Gabriel and Michael, as among angels invoked to ward off evil, Persia, 18th cent.

Micaiah, Ephraimite whose dwelling housed graven image attended by young levite. Men of tribe of Dan took young levite and graven image to their sanctuary in city of Dan (Judg.17–18).

Micaiah, son of Judah; prophet who foretold death of Ahab.

Michael, angel mentioned in Book of Daniel. In *aggadah* one of four angels who surround throne of God. Seen as constant defender of Jewish people.

Michael, Heimann Joseph Ḥayyim (1792–1846), German merchant, bibliophile. His famed Hebrew library was divided bet. British Museum in London (books) and Bodleian at Oxford (mss.). His encyclopedic *Or ha-Ḥayyim* contains biographies and bibliographies of medieval Jewish scholars.

Michael, Jakob (1894–), U.S. financier, philanthropist; b. Frankfort, in U.S. fr. 1939. Prominent in philanthropies for Jewish educational and scientific institutions.

Michaelis, Sir Max (1860–1932), S. African mining magnate, philanthropist; b. Germany, settled in Kimberley and formed diamond-buying company later taken over by De Beers.

Michaelson, Ezekiel Ẓevi ben Abraham Ḥayyim (1863–1942), Polish rabbi, biographer, bibliographer. Rabbi of Plonsk. Prolific writer. Published studies in *halakhah, aggadah,* history, biography, and bibliography. D. in Treblinka.

Michal, youngest daughter of King Saul, who loved David and was given to him in marriage after he had killed 200 Philistines. Saved him from her father's wrath. Scoffed at David when he danced in front of ark. Died childless.

"MIDRESHEI AGGADAH" ACCORDING TO TYPES AND PERIODS

Aggadic Works	Midrashim	Date C.E.	The Era
	Genesis Rabbah *Leviticus Rabbah* Lamentations Rabbah Esther Rabbah I	400–500	Classical Amoraic Midrashim of the Early Period (400–640)
Apocalyptic and Eschatological Midrashim	*Pesikta de-Rav Kahana* Songs Rabbah Ruth Rabbah	500–640	
Megillat Antiochus Midrash Petirat Moshe ("Death of Moses") Tanna de- vei Eliyahu ("Seder Eliyahu") Pirkei de-R. Eliezer Midrash Agur (called "Mishnat R. Eliezer") Midrash Yonah Midrash Petirat Aharon Divrei ha-Yamim shel Moshe Otiyyot de-R. Akiva Midrash Sheloshah ve-Arba'ah Midrash Eser Galuyyot Midrash va-Yissa'u	Targum Sheni Midrash Esfah Midrash Proverbs Midrash Samuel Ecclesiastes Rabbah Midrash Ḥaserot vi-Yterot	640–900	The Middle Period (640–1000)
	Tanḥuma Midrash (Yelammedenu): *Deuteronomy Rabbah* *Tanḥuma* *Tanḥuma (Buber)* *Numbers Rabbah II* *Pesikta Rabbati* *Exodus Rabbah II* *Va-Yeḥi Rabbah* *The manuscripts of the Tanḥuma Yelammedenu Midrashim*	(775–900)	
Throne and Hippodromes of Solomon Midreshei Ḥanukkah Midreshei Yehudith Midrash Hallel Midrash Tadshe	Midrash Tehillim I Exodus Rabbah I *Aggadat Bereshit* Aggadat Shir ha-Shirim (Zuta) Ruth Zuta Ecclesiastes Zuta Lamentations Zuta	900–1000	
Midrash Aseret ha-Dibberot Midrash Konen Midrash Avkir Alphabet de-Ben Sira Midrash va-Yosha Sefer ha-Yashar	Midrash Shir ha-Shirim Abba Guryon Esther Rabbah II Midrash Tehillim II	1000–1100	The Late Period (1000–1200)
Pesikta Ḥadta Midrash Temurah	Panim Aḥerim le-Esther (version 1) ▾ Lekaḥ Tov (c. 1110) Midrash Aggadah, Genesis Rabbati, Numbers Rabbah I: all based on the work of Moshe ha-Darshan	1100–1200	
	▾ Yalkut Shimoni	1200–1300	The Period of Yalkutim (anthologies) 1200–1550
	▾ Midrash ha-Gadol ▾ Yalkut Makhiri	1300–1400	
	▾ Ein Ya'akov ▾ Haggadot ha-Talmud	1400–1550	

Notes: Names in italics are homiletical Midrashim; those marked by ▾ are anthologies; the rest are exegetical.

Michali, Binyamin Yizḥak (1910–), Hebrew writer, literary critic, and editor; b. Bessarabia, settled in Ereẓ Israel 1939. Leading member of Israel Writers' Association, chief editor of its journal *Moznayim.*

Michel, Jud (d. 1549), financier, soldier of fortune. Vassal to various German rulers. Instigated acts of arson against property of duke of Regenstein, who had defaulted on promissory note, and fled to Silesia. Subsequently in service of Joachim II, elector of Brandenburg.

Michel-Lévy, Auguste (1844–1911), French petrologist, mining engineer. Prof. at Collège de France. Director of French geological survey and national inspector of mines 1874. Most distinguished petrologist of his time and pioneer of experimental petrography.

Michelson, Albert Abraham (1852–1931), U.S. physicist; b. Prussia, in U.S. fr. 1883. Prof. at Univ. of Chicago 1892–1929. Showed that light travels at same velocity in any direction under any circumstances. Provided new starting point for great theoretical developments in 20th c. physics. First American Nobel Prizewinner 1907.

Michelstaedter, Carlo (1887–1910), Italian philosopher, poet. Greatly influenced by Schopenhauer and Nietzsche. In his *La persuasione e la retorica* anticipated main doctrines of European existentialism. Committed suicide.

Michigan, U.S. state. First Jewish settler 1761, first community in Ann Arbor in 1840s, first services 1845. Jewish pop. 93,530 (1971), mostly in Detroit.

Middot (Heb. "Measures"), 10th (in current Talmud edition, 11th) tractate in Mishnah order *Kodashim,* with no *gemara.* Deals with details and measurements of building of Temple and its component parts.

Midian, Midianites, country and people, or group of (semi-) nomadic peoples in Bible. Mentioned in story of sale of Joseph. Moses' father-in-law, Jethro, was Midianite priest. They attempted to entice Israelites on way fr. Egypt to Canaan to worship Moabite god, and Israelites killed many of them. Exerted harsh pressure on Israel in period of Judges, until defeated by Gideon.

Midrash (Heb.), method of interpreting scripture to elucidate legal points *(Midrash Halakhah)* or bring out lessons through stories or homiletics *(Midrash Aggadah).* Also designation of particular genre of rabbinic literature extending fr. tannaitic times to 10th c. Constitutes anthology of homilies consisting of both biblical exegesis and sermons delivered in public as well as *aggadot* and *halakhot* and forms running aggadic commentary to specific books of Bible.

Midrash Aseret ha-Dibberot (Heb. "Midrash of the Ten Commandments"), collection of stories, occasionally connected by short homiletic passages, fr. geonic period; edited not later than 11th c. One of first medieval Hebrew works in the fields of fiction and one of earliest ethical works written in Middle Ages.

Midrash ha-Gadol, 13th c. rabbinic work on Pentateuch, emanating fr. Yemen and consisting mainly of excerpts fr. old rabbinic texts of talmudic period. Anonymous, but now certain that it was written by native of Aden, David b. Amram Adani.

Midrash Lekaḥ Tov, late 11th c. Midrash on Pentateuch and Five Scrolls by Tobias b. Eliezer. Called *Pesikta* by later scholars. Exegetical aspect is conspicuous.

Midrash Proverbs or **Aggadat Proverbs,** Midrash on Book of Proverbs. Distinguished by exegetical style demonstrated both in choice of contents and manner in which they are quoted. Compiled in Babylon after final editing of Babylonian Talmud.

Midrash Samuel, only Midrash to book of early prophets. Compiled chiefly fr. early works. Contains predominantly homiletical matter. Probably edited not early than 11th c. in Ereẓ Israel.

Midrash Tadshe or **Baraita de-R. Pinḥas b. Ya'ir,** pseudepigraphical Midrash written not later than 1000 C.E. In both contents and method resembles works of Second Temple period, on which it drew.

Midrash Tannaim (Mekhilta on Deuteronomy), tannaitic work which is collection of *beraitot* comprising fragments of halakhic Midrash on Deuteronomy. Neither its date of redaction nor original title is known.

Midrash Tehillim (Midrash Psalms), aggadic Midrash on Psalms, also called *Aggadat Tehillim,* and *Shoḥer Tov.* Period of composition extended over centuries; concluding section dates fr. 13th c.

Midrash Va-Yissa'u medieval Midrash in Hebrew about legendary wars of Jacob and his sons; original name probably "The Book of the Wars of the Sons of Jacob."

Midreshei Halakhah, appellation given to group of tannaitic expositions on Exodus, Leviticus, Numbers and Deuteronomy. Deal primarily with *halakhah* to be derived fr. Bible. Redaction dates fr. 4th–5th c. C.E. Works incl.: on Exodus: *Mekhilta* (of R. Ishmael) and *Mekhilta* of R. Simeon b. Yoḥai; on Leviticus: *Sifra;* on Numbers: *Sifrei* on Numbers and *Sifrei Zuta;* on Deuteronomy: *Midrash Tannaim* and *Sifrei* on Deuteronomy.

Mielziner, Moses (1828–1903), Reform rabbi, scholar in Denmark and U.S. Taught at Temple Emanu-El preparatory school for rabbinical students (later Hebrew Union College in Cincinnati). Best-known work *Introduction to the Talmud,* which is still widely used.

Jewish communities in Michigan and dates of establishment.

Mieses, Matthias (1885–1945), Yiddish philologist; b. Galicia. Prolific writer in Hebrew, Polish, German, but main interest was Yiddish. Fought for emancipation of Jewish "jargon" and its recognition as language. D. on way to Auschwitz.

Miesis, Judah Leib (1798–1831), leading member of Galician Haskalah movement. In his works, attacked obscurantist beliefs in spirits, demons, mystical powers, and superstitions fostered by Orthodox rabbis.

Migdal ha-Emek, town in lower Galilee. Founded 1952. Pop. (1971), 9,500, mostly of N. African origin.

Mikes, George (1912–), British humorist; b. Hungary. Wrote light-hearted books on politics, social customs, etc., incl. *Milk and Honey* on Israel and *How to be an Alien.*

Mikhalevich, Beinish (1876–1928), Bund leader; b. Russia, lived in Poland. Member of central committee 1912. Opposed left turn of Bund and lost political standing. Later, outstanding polemicist against Zionism.

Mikhoels, Solomon (Solomon Vovsi; 1890–1948), Yiddish actor. Joined Alexander Granovsky's Jewish Drama studio 1918 (which became State Jewish Theater); became his chief actor and succeeded him as director 1928. As chairman of Jewish Anti-Fascist Committee, traveled in WWII to U.S. with poet Itzik Fefer. Became spokesman for Holocaust survivors and Jews returning fr. evacuation in C. Asia. His murder (ostensibly in auto accident) was first step in Stalinist liquidation of Jewish cultural leaders.

Solomon Mikhoels as King Lear in the Jewish State Theater production, Moscow, 1935.

Mikulov (Nikolsburg), town in Czechoslovakia. Community probably founded by Jews expelled fr. Austria 1420; grew larger during following 3 c. Economy based on viticulture and wine trade. Became center of Moravian Jewry. Renowned yeshivah. Community numbered 3,680 in 1857, declined to 437 in 1930, ended in WWII.

Mikvaot (Heb. "Ritual Baths"), 6th tractate in Mishnah order *Tohorot,* with no *gemara.* Deals with details of ritual bath.

Mikveh in basement of 18th cent. synagogue of Carpentras, France.

Mikveh (Heb. "collection [of water]"), pool or bath of clean water, immersion in which renders ritually clean person who has become ritually unclean. Similarly used for vessels. At present, chief use is for **post-menstruant** women and immersion of proselytes.

Mikveh Israel, Israel agricultural school E. of Tel Aviv-Jaffa; oldest Jewish rural community in Ereẓ Israel, founded 1870 by Alliance Israélite Universelle on initiative of Carl Netter. Fr. 1930s education center for Youth Aliyah.

Milan, city in Italy. Jews present fr. Roman period. Expelled 1320, 1489, 1597. Began returning under Austrian rule. Full rights with establishment of Italian kingdom 1859. 800 Jews deported during WWII. Jewish pop. 9,500 (1971).

Milano, Attilio (1907–1969), historian of Italian Jewry; b. Rome, settled in Ereẓ Israel 1939. Wrote on economic and social conditions of Italian Jews. Published *Bibliotheca Historica Italo-Judaica.*

Milhaud, Darius (1892–1974), composer; b. Aix-en-Provence. Wrote music for concert, stage and screen, and voice and orchestra. Operas incl. *Esther de Carpentras* and *Christophe Colomb.* Member of *"Les Six."* Composed biblical opera *David.* Also composed setting of Sabbath morning service (utilizing Avignon Jewish musical tradition). After fall of France, to U.S. Prof. at Mills College, Oakland, Cal.

Darius Milhaud

Mill, Joseph Solomon (John; 1870–1952), pioneer of Bund. Active in socialist circles in Poland and Jewish workers' circles. Left Poland 1898 and initiated establishment of Bund "committee abroad." Went to Chicago 1915. Active in Socialist Party.

°**Millás Vallicrosa, José Mariá** (1897–1970), Spanish scholar, historian. Prof. at Univ. of Barcelona, Madrid. Wrote on history of Spanish Jewry, medieval Hebrew poetry, and history of sciences. Also translated medieval works fr. Hebrew and Arabic into Spanish.

Miller, Arthur (1915–), U.S. playwright. Best known for Pulitzer Prize-winning *Death of a Salesman* 1949, regarded as indictment of false sense of values of American life. Other works incl. *The Crucible,* using Salem witch trials to criticize McCarthy era, a *View from the Bridge,* which won Pulitzer Prize and *After the Fall* based on his life with ex-wife Marilyn Monroe.

Arthur Miller with his wife, Marilyn Monroe.

Miller, Emanuel (1893–1970), English psychiatrist. Fellow of Royal College of Physicians. Publications incl. *Modern Psychotherapy.* His wife **Betty** (1910–1965), novelist. Works incl. *A Room in Regent's Park* and *On the Side of the Angels.* His son **Jonathan** (1934–), qualified as a doctor, but established reputation as actor in satirical revue *Beyond the Fringe;* also successful theater and TV director.

Miller, Irving (1903–), U.S. rabbi, Zionist leader. Congregations incl. Far Rockaway, N.Y. 1930–46 and Sons of Israel, Woodmere, N.Y. 1946–63. Pres. American Jewish Congress 1949–52 and American Zionist Council 1954–63.

Miller, Israel (1918–), U.S. Orthodox rabbi, educator. Rabbi of Kingsbridge Heights Jewish Center, Bronx, N.Y. Chairman of American Zionist Council and pres. of Conference of Presidents of Major Jewish Organizations fr. 1974.

Miller, Louis E. (pseud. of **Louis E. Bandes;** 1866–1927), Yiddish editor, labor leader; b. Vilna, in N.Y. fr. 1886. Founded first shirtmakers union among Jewish workers in U.S. A founder of Yiddish-socialist *Die Arbeiter Zeitung* 1890, daily *Forward* 1897, *Die Wahrheit* 1905.

Miller, Shaye (1895–1958), Yiddish novelist, translator; b. Ukraine, in U.S. fr. 1912. Works deal with American Jew and stress the nostalgia for old-fashioned Jewishness.

Millin, Philip (1888–1952), S. African Supreme Court judge fr. 1937. Drafted "Millin Report," which led to important changes in company law. His wife **Sarah Gertrude** (1889–1968), novelist. Most popular novel *God's Stepchildren,* story of colored people of Cape Province. Wrote biographies of Rhodes and Smuts.

Millo, Josef (1916–), Israel theatrical producer, actor. Founded Cameri Theater 1942 (director until 1959). Founded 1961 and directed Haifa Municipal Theater. Inaugurated naturalistic school of Israel drama.

Milner, Moses Michael (Mikhail Arnoldovich; 1886–1953), Russian composer. Conductor and musical director in St. Petersburg, Kharkov, Moscow. Fr. 1941 coach of choir of Bolshoi Theater. Wrote compositions on Jewish themes and harmonized traditional Jewish melodic material. Later turned to more general subjects.

Milosz, Oscar (1877–1939), French poet, mystical writer, diplomat; b. Belorussia to Lithuanian nobleman and baptized daughter of Warsaw Hebrew teacher. Lithuania's minister resident in Paris 1919–26. In his poetry progressed fr. erotic mysticism to spiritual and metaphysical speculation.

Milstein, Nathan (1904–), U.S. violinist; b. Russia. Made debut 1914. Toured Russia after revolution with Vladimir Horowitz and Gregor Piatigorsky. Went to Paris 1925. U.S. 1929. One of great virtuosos of his time.

Milwaukee, city in Wisc., U.S. Jewish settlement from 1844. First settlers fr. C. Europe, fr. 1882 fr. Russia, fr. 1938 to 1950 fr. Germany. Several Jews attained national and international prominence, incl. Golda Meir. Jewish pop. 23,900 (1971).

Min (pl. **minim;** etymology unknown), term used for every kind of heretic or sectarian, both Jewish and non-Jewish.

Minc, Hilary (1905–), Polish Communist politician; spent WWII in USSR. Vice-premier of Poland and chairman of State Planning Commission 1949. Removed fr. all posts 1956.

Minhag (Heb.), usual term for custom or usage, not necessarily halakhically binding. Many such customs have become binding laws, esp. in civil and financial matters. Terms used for differences in liturgical practices.

Minhagim Books, works detailing how precepts are discharged in particular locality as well as local customs. Some of them record differences bet. various communities. Earliest work of this nature extant is fr. 8th c.

Minḥah (Heb.), daily afternoon service consisting usually of Ps.145, *Amidah,* and *Aleinu.* May be recited fr. after midday until before night. Term originally applied to meal-offerings in Temple.

Minkoff, Nahum Baruch (1893–1958), Yiddish poet, critic, literary historian; b. Poland, in U.S. fr. 1914. Editor of Yiddish literary monthly *Zukunft*; member of In-Zikh group.

Minkowski, Eugène (1885–), French existentialist psychologist. Maintained that insanity was nothing more than exaggeration of habitual character. His brother, **Mieczyslaw** (1884–), Swiss neurologist, Prof. at Zurich Univ., pres. of Swiss Neurological Society.

Minkowski, Hermann (1864–1909), German mathematician. Taught at Koenigsberg, Zurich, Goettingen. Largely credited with creating geometry of numbers. Produced four-dimensional formulation of relativity – "Minkowski space."

Minkowski, Pinchas ("Pinie"; 1859–1924), Russian cantor, composer; spent his last years in U.S. His chorale-like melody for Bialik's *Shabbat ha-Malkah* very popular.

Minneapolis-Saint Paul, twin cities in Minn., U.S. Jewish life in St. Paul organized in 1850s. Many E. European settlers came after 1881. In Minneapolis, Jewish community life began 1878. In 1940s Minneapolis was called "the capital of anti-Semitism in the United States" but situation gradually changed, and Jew Arthur Naftalin was elected mayor 1961. Jewish pop. Minneapolis 21,640, St. Paul 10,000 (1971).

Minnesota, U.S. state. Jews there before statehood (1858); early Jewish settlers of German origin, joined by large numbers of E. Europeans after 1881. Efforts to settle them in agricultural colonies further west were unsuccessful. Jewish pop. 34,475 (1971).

Woodcut from "Venice Minhagim Book," 1601, showing baking of "mazzah."

Jewish communities in Minnesota and dates of establishment.

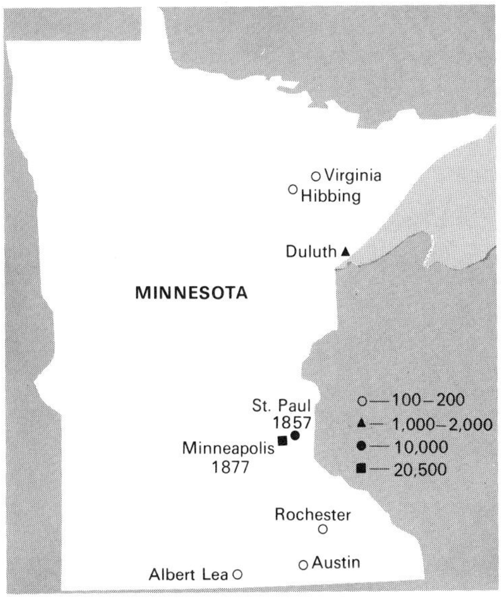

Minor, Osip S. (Joseph; 1861–1932), Russian revolutionary; son of S. Z. Minor. Banished to Siberia several times in Czarist times. Briefly mayor of Moscow 1917. Left Russia for Paris 1919.

Minor, Solomon Zalman (Zalkind; 1826-1900), Russian writer, scholar; pioneer of Russian-Jewish intelligentsia. Rabbi of Moscow fr. 1869. One of first to preach in Russian. Friend of Tolstoy.

Minorca, Mediterranean island. With victory of Christianity many Jews died for their faith and synagogue destroyed 418. No information on Jews during Byzantine and Muslim rule, but they helped James I of Aragon equip expedition to reconquer island for Christians. Later history closely connected with that of Majorca. After 1391 no Jews left on island. Judaizers subsequently sentenced by Inquisition of Majorca.

Minority Bloc, political alliance founded 1922, comprising representatives of national minorities in Poland, with aim of obtaining representation in Sejm corresponding to their numbers in pop. (up to 40%). Zionist leader Yiẓḥak Gruenbaum was its organizer. It gained impressive victory at elections. "Jewish club" consisted of 34 seats in Sejm and 12 in Senate, but dissolved with weakening of parliamentary government. Bloc ended 1930 under growing political suppression.

Minority Rights, rights enjoyed by Jews and other ethnic minorities bet. two world wars, mainly in E. and SE Europe, acc. to provisions of minorities treaties at Versailles Peace Conference 1919. League of Nations supervised implementation. In decade before WWII, provisions largely ignored, and not revived after war.

Minor Prophets (Aram. *Tere Asar* = "12"), collection of biblical books of 12 prophets: Hosea, Joel, Amos, Obadiah, Jonah, Micah, Nahum, Habbakuk, Zephaniah, Haggai, Zechariah, Malachi; traditionally counted as single book, last of second division (Prophets). Collection compiled bet. 4th c. and 180 B.C.E.

Minow, Newton Norman (1926–), U.S. lawyer, public official. Aide and law partner of Adlai Stevenson. Chairman of Federal Communications Commission 1961–63; pressed for greater control over TV in public interest.

Minsk, city in Belorussian SSR. Jews there fr. 16th c.; granted rights and prospered in 17th–18th c. In 19th c. largest Jewish community in Russia, with rich communal life. Active in Jewish labor movement. Under Soviet regime important center of Jewish Communist cultural activity. 90,000 Jews in 1941; confined in ghetto and then killed by Germans. Est. Jewish pop. 50–60,000 (1959).

Minsk Conference, second conference of Russian Zionists, held Sept. 6–10, 1902 with permission of authorities, less than one year before all Zionist activities banned in Russia.

Minski, Nikolai Maximovich (pseud. of **N.M. Vilenkin;** 1855–1937), Russian poet, essayist; baptized. Supported 1905 but not 1917 revolution. Lived outside of Russia after Communist revolution.

Mintz, Moses ben Isaac (15th c.), German talmudist of great influence in Germany and beyond. Fame rests on responsa, which abound in references to local custom and *takkanot,* and reflect economic, social and religious life of period.

Mintz, Paul (1870–after 1940), Latvian lawyer. Prof. of law and state controller of Latvian government. Active in Jewish affairs. D. in Soviet labor camp.

Minyan (Heb.), quorum of 10 male Jews above age of 13 necessary for public services and certain other religious ceremonies. In Reform Judaism women are counted in quorum.

Minz, Benjamin (1903–1961), Po'alei Agudat Israel leader; b. Poland, settled in Ereẓ Israel 1925. Member of Executive of Po'alei Agudat Israel; head of its World Union fr. 1946. Member of Knesset, minister of posts 1960.

Minz, Judah b. Eliezer ha-Levi (c.1408–1506), Italian rabbi of German origin. Settled in Padua as rabbi and headed yeshivah, corresponded on *halakhah* with greatest rabbis of period. Most of his work destroyed during sack of Padua, but 16 responsa survived.

Mir, town in Belorussian SSR. Jews there fr. 17th c. Its famous yeshivah founded 1815. During WWII its student body escaped to Shanghai and after war yeshivah was transferred to Brooklyn.

Miranda, Salomon Rodriques de (1878–1941), Dutch socialist politician. Responsible for food distribution in Amsterdam after WWI. Minister of housing and public works 1929–1933, 1935–39. D. in Nazi camp.

Mirandola, Giovanni Pico Della, see Pico Della Mirandola, Giovanni.

Mirelman, family of Argentinian industrialists, community leaders. Members incl. **Simon** (1894–), **Robert** (1898–), **Jacob** (1900–), **Joseph** (1902–), **Leon** (1907–). Benefactors of many Jewish and Israel causes.

Miriam, sister of Moses and Aaron. Led Israelite women in song and dance after Red Sea crossing. For her attempt to challenge Moses' exclusive right to speak in name of Lord, smitten with leprosy; healed only after Moses interceded on her behalf (Num. 12).

Miriam dancing with timbrel in her hand, from "Schocken Haggadah," W. Italy, 15th cent.

Mirisch, Harold (1907–), **Marvin** (1918–), and **Walter** (1921–), U.S. film producers. Became team 1952 and established own company 1957. Films incl. *Some Like it Hot, The Apartment, West Side Story.*

Mirsky, Aaron (1914–), Hebrew writer; b. Poland, settled in Ereẓ Israel 1935. Taught at Heb. Univ. Published studies on ancient and medieval poetry and Hebrew language.

Mirsky, Samuel Kalman (1899–1967), U.S. rabbinic scholar, religious Zionist, Hebraist. Prof. of rabbinics and director of Israel Institute at Yeshiva Univ. Pres. Histadrut Ivrit of America. Editor periodicals *Perakim, Talpioth,* and *Sura.* Published critical text of *She'iltot* and other texts.

Mi she-Berakh (Heb. "May He who blessed . . ."), initial words of prayer formula invoking divine blessing for health, usually recited for one called to reading of Torah.

Mishlei, see Proverbs, Book of.

Mishmar ha-Emek, kibbutz on SW rim of Jezreel Valley; affiliated with Kibbutz Arẓi ha-Shomer ha-Ẓa'ir. Founded 1926 as the first Jewish settlement in area; soon became a center of Ha-Shomer ha-Ẓa'ir movement. Pop. 715 (1971).

Mishmar ha-Yarden, moshav nr. upper Jordan R.; founded as moshavah 1890 but made little headway until 1946 when veterans of

WWII joined and intensified farming. In 1948 War of Independence overrun by the Syrian army. Moshav Mishmar ha-Yarden and kibbutz Gadot founded on site 1949. Suffered frequently from Syrian fire until Six-Day War.

Mishmarot and **Ma'amadot** (Heb.), priestly and levitical divisions. King David divided priests and levites acc. to their clans and assigned them tasks in Temple. Priests were divided regionally into 24 *mishmarot* (lit. "guards"), broken down into *battei avot* ("families"), serving in regular weekly rotation. Levites were similarly divided into 24 *mishmarot.* There was analagous division of Israelites into 24 *mishmarot* (representatives of each of which had to take their turn in coming to Jerusalem for one week). That part of *mishmar* actually engaged in performance of its duty was called *ma'amad* ("station").

Mishnah (Heb.), legal codification of basic Jewish law; redacted and arranged by R. Judah ha-Nasi c. 200 C.E. Contains basic Oral Law transmitted throughout generations. Nucleus for all *halakhah* and much *aggadah,* preserved in Talmud. Talmud also refers to other collections of Mishnah. Work is printed in Talmud together with relevant discussion *(gemara).* Also frequently published independently with many commentaries. Divided into six orders: *Zera'im* (seeds), *Mo'ed* (seasons), *Nashim* (matrimonial law), *Nezikin* (civil law), *Kodashim* (holy things), and *Tohorot* (ritual purity), each order being divided into separate tractates.

Mishneh Torah, see Maimonides.

Miskolc, town in NE Hungary. Jews attended fairs there at beginning of 18th c. Jewish settlers organized their own guild and had well-developed educational institutions. 10,428 Jews in 1941; killed by Germans. Reconstituted community numbered 2,353 in 1946 1,000 in 1970.

Mississippi, U.S. state. Jews settled along Gulf of Mexico fr. early period; Jewish communities there by 1830s. Favorable conditions brought many Jews fr. Germany and Alsace. Bet. 200 and 300 served in Confederate Army. Descendants of E. European Jews who immigrated in late 1800s have been important in economic development of state. Since 1950s number of Jews declined. Jewish pop. 4,125 (1971).

Missouri, U.S. state. Jews legally admitted with Louisiana Purchase 1803. Congregations founded during 19th c. Jewish pop. 84,325 (1971) mostly in St. Louis and Kansas City.

Mitchell, Yvonne (1925–), British actress, writer. Acted in Shakespeare, Ibsen, Shaw, and in films. Her play, *The Same Sky,* won Festival of Britain Prize 1950. Novels incl. *A Year in Time* and *The Family.*

Mithridates, Flavius, assumed name of 15th c. humanist, orientalist; original name probably Samuel b. Nissim al-Faraj. Converted to Christianity and taught Arabic, Hebrew, and Aramaic. Teacher of Giovanni Pico Della Mirandola.

Mitin, Mark Borisovich (1901–), Russian ideologist. One of few Jews to serve on Communist Party Central Committee. Took active part in anti-Jewish campaign. Awarded many Soviet honors and prizes.

Mitnaggedim (Heb. "opponents"), name originally given to Jews opposed to ḥasidic movement; later positively connoted way of life of non-ḥasidic Lithuanian type of Jewry, characterized by severe criticism of credulity, disavowal of miracle-working leadership, devotion to talmudic learning, and retention in prayer of Polish form of Ashkenazi *minhag.*

Mittwoch, Eugen (1876–1942), German orientalist. Prof. at Berlin Seminary for Oriental Languages. Dismissed by Nazis 1933; eventually moved to London. Wrote on influence of Jewish liturgy on Islam. Contributed to Hebrew, S. Arabian, Himyaritic, and Sabean epigraphy, and wrote on Islamic art and politics.

Mitzvah (Heb.), "precept" or religious duty; good deed. Although distinctions are often made bet. types of precepts, e.g. rational and revealed, rabbis enjoined men to perform all with equal devotion. Traditionally there are 613 precepts – 248 positive and 365 prohibitive. Men and women are instructed to perform them when they reach puberty, but generally women are exempted fr. positive precepts connected with fixed time.

Mixed Species (Heb. *kilayim*), biblical prohibition against crossbreeding cattle; sowing fields or vineyards with different species of seeds; grafting different species of trees; pairing different species of animals at work; weaving wool and linen together *(sha'atnez)* (Lev. 19:19, Deut. 22:9–11).

Mizmor le-David (Heb. "A Psalm to David"), superscription to many psalms, esp. Psalm 29, sung on Sabbath mornings after reading of Torah, and Psalm 23, which Sephardim sing before *Kiddush* on Sabbath morning and Ashkenazim at third meal of Sabbath.

Mizpeh Ramon, development town in S. Israel, S. of Beersheba; founded 1954. Pop. 1,520 (1971).

Mizrachi (abb. of Heb. *merkaz ruḥani* "spiritual center"), religious Zionist movement. Founded 1902. Established religious education network in Ereẓ Israel under British Mandate. Its labor wing is Ha-Po'el ha-Mizrachi and each had separate representation in Knesset (q.v.) until 1955 when merged into National Religious Party. Fought to preserve traditional Jewish observance in Israel. Also maintains financial, economic and cultural institutions. Its women's organization is Omen. Mizrachi has branches in many countries and World Movement is part of World Zionist Organization.

Jewish communities in Mississippi and dates of establishment.

Jewish communities in Missouri and dates of establishment.

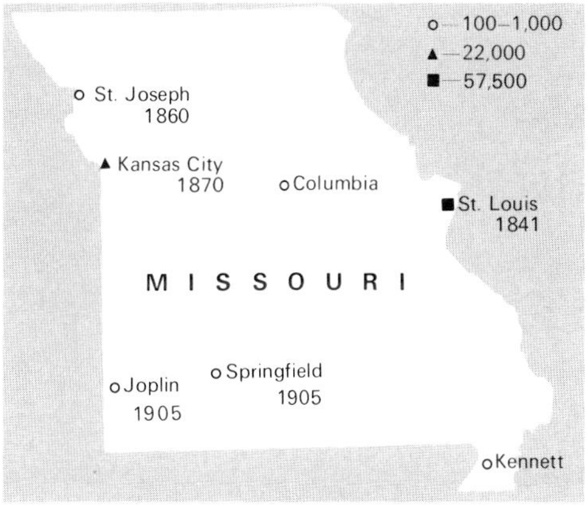

Mizraḥ (Heb. "east"), E. wall of synagogue which faces toward Jerusalem. Since ark was usually placed there and rabbi and dignitaries sat on both sides of ark, term became transferred to those who were colloquially referred to as "*mizraḥ* Jews," as well as to plaques placed on walls of rooms to indicate direction for prayer.

Mizraḥi, David ben Shalom (c.1696–1771), prominent Yemenite halakhic scholar. Author of *Shetilei Zeitim,* explaining *Oraḥ Ḥayyim* and adapting it to customs of Yemenite Jews. Did same for *Yoreh De'ah* and wrote book of responsa and novellae, first of its kind in Yemenite Jewish literature.

Mizraḥi, Elijah (c.1450–1526), greatest rabbinical authority of his time in Ottoman Empire. Head of rabbis of Constantinople, conducted affairs of community, headed yeshivah, taught Talmud and secular subjects, wrote commentaries on religious and scientific works. Most famous for supercommentary on Rashi to Pentateuch. Also wrote responsa. His *Sefer ha-Mispar* on mathematics was translated into Latin.

Miẓvah, see Mitzvah.

Moab, land of Semitic people E. of Jordan river. Moabites settled there in 14th c. B.C.E. Enmity with Israel grew out of struggle over disputed areas in Transjordan. Israelites were forbidden to marry Moabites, but this apparently did not apply to Moabite women (see Ruth). David subdued land. Under Mesha (9th c. B.C.E.) Moabites threw off Israelite rule, but eventually all tableland was returned to Israelite possession. Became Babylonian province in time of Nebuchadnezzar.

Moabite Stone, see Mesha.

Mocatta, Moses (1768–1857), English scholar; son of Abraham Mocatta, co-founder of Mocatta and Goldsmid bullion brokers to Bank of England. Published translations fr. English into Hebrew and Portuguese. His son, **David** (1806–1882), architect of Montefiore Ramsgate synagogue and many English railroad stations. **Frederick David** (1828–1905) left his library to Univ. College, London. **Sir Alan Abraham** (1907–), High Court judge and active in Anglo-Jewish affairs.

Moch, Jules (1829–1881), French soldier. One of first Jews to reach rank of colonel in French Army. Fought with distinction in Crimean War, conquest of Rome (1859), and Franco-Prussian War. First Jewish instructor and examiner at St. Cyr Military Academy.

Moch, Jules Salvador (1893–), French socialist leader; engineer. Held many cabinet posts in pre-De Gaulle governments. Enthusiastic Zionist.

Modai, Ḥayyim (d.1794), Safed scholar, emissary of community to Europe. Wrote many halakhic works and published *Sha'arei Ẓedek,* ms. of geonic responsa.

Modeh Ani (Heb. "I give thanks"), initial words of short prayer said on waking in morning. Became favorite morning prayer for very small children. Composed c. 17th c.

Model, Marx (d.1709), Court Jew of Ansbach. One of first Court Jews to engage in economic enterprises.

Modena, city in Italy. Stable Jewish community fr. 14th c.; long enjoyed protection of House of Este. A Center of Italian-Jewish scholarship and kabbalistic study. Jews contributed to Risorgimento, collaborating with and financing Carbonari, secret revolutionary movement. Full equality 1861. 150 Jews in 1970.

Modena, Leone Judah Aryeh; (1571–1648), Italian rabbi, scholar, writer. Infant prodigy who read prophetic portion in synagogue at Ferrara aged 2½. His sermons in Venice attracted large audiences, incl. distinguished gentiles. His autobiography *Ḥayyei Yehudah* lists 26 occupations which he practiced. Had extensive knowledge of talmudic literature, Italian, and Latin; wrote (in Hebrew and Italian) on most topics, incl. responsa, anti-Christian polemics, Kabbalah. Directed theater and music academy in Venice ghetto.

"Portrait of the Young Girl Elvira" by Amedeo Modigliani, 1918/19.

Modigliani, Amedeo (1884–1920), painter; b. Italy, lived in Paris. Developed highly individual style, generally painting single figures with vague backgrounds. Achieved fame posthumously.

Modigliani, Vittorio Emanuele (1872–1947), Italian lawyer, politician; brother of Amedeo Modigliani. Socialist MP for many years; bitter opponent of Fascism.

Modi'in, village in toparchy of Lydda; home town of Maccabees and place where Hasmonean revolt broke out. Annually at Ḥanukkah, torch is solemnly lit at tomb of Maccabees there and carried to Jerusalem. Development project undertaken in region 1964.

Modzhitz, Israel of (d. 1921), founder of Polish ḥasidic dynasty emphasizing value of music. Composed hundreds of melodies. Succeeded by his son **Saul Jedidiah Eleazar** (d. 1947), who published his father's and his own sermons and popularized Modzhitz melodies throughout Jewish world. D. in Tel Aviv.

Mo'ed (Heb. "festival"), 2nd order of Mishnah. Tractates deal with Sabbath and some festivals.

Mo'ed Katan (Heb. "small festival"), 11th tractate in Mishnah order *Mo'ed.* Deals with kinds of work forbidden and permitted during intermediate days of Passover and Sukkot, as well as customs peculiar to them.

Moellin, Jacob ben Moses (Maharil; ? 1360–1427), noted talmudist, head of communities of Germany, Austria, Bohemia. Succeeded his father at Mainz and founded yeshivah fr. which came greatest rabbis of next generation. Helped many communities during Hussite wars. Renowned *ḥazzan,* leaving lasting mark on Ashkenazi tradition. His *Minhagei Maharil* were included by Isserles in his glosses to *Shulḥan Arukh* and his influential responsa are important source of information on history of his time.

Mo'etzet ha-Po'alot, General Council of Women Workers of Israel, founded 1922 as part of Histadrut.

Mogador, Moroccan port. Bet. 1650 and 1808 Jewish pop. of town, headed by "merchants of the king," dominated trade. Jewish quarter (mellah) established 1808. Jewish pop. grew in 19th c., reaching 14,000; schools and yeshivot were established and Jews were highly educated. Later town lost its economic importance and Jewish community dwindled; by 1970 only few hundred were left.

Jew from Mogador.

Mogilev, city in Belorussian SSR. Jewish community fr. 16th c; massacred 1655. Developed considerably after annexation to Russia 1772, becoming central Jewish community of province. Greatly influenced by Ḥabad Ḥasidism, but by end of 18th c. Haskalah spread. 17,105 Jews in 1926; those remaining massacred under German occupation 1941. 7–10,000 Jews in 1959.

Mohácsi, Jenö (1886–1944), Hungarian author, translator. Did much to bring Hungarian literature to world attention. D. during Nazi transportation when exemption certificate signed by Admiral Horthy did not reach him in time.

Mohel, see Circumcision.

Mohilewer, Samuel (1824–1898), rabbi, early member of Ḥovevei Zion in Russia, a founder of religious Zionism. Very active in Ḥovevei Zion movement and headed many of its public conferences; hon. pres. of Kattowitz Conference. Initiated establishment of religious spiritual center (Merkaz–Ruḥani-Mizrachi) 1893. Influenced Baron Edmond de Rothschild to support Palestine colonization. Joined Zionist Organization on its founding.

Mohr, Abraham Menahem Mendel (1815–1868), Hebrew scholar in Galicia. Proponent of Enlightenment. Wrote biographies and defended science and philosophy.

Moïse, U.S. family. **Abraham** (c. 1736–1809); b. Alsace, emigrated to West Indies, later to Charleston, S.C. His daughter, **Penina** (1797–1880), prolific poet, author of first American Jewish hymnal. His nephew, **Theodore Sydney** (1806–1883), painter. Closely associated with portrait and genre painter Trevor T. Fowler. Served with Confederate Army during Civil War. Various New Orleans public buildings contain his portraits.

Moiseiwitsch, Benno (1890–1963), pianist; b. Odessa, lived in England. Regarded as one of finest Chopin interpreters of his time.

Moissan, Henri (1852–1907), French inorganic chemist; of Jewish origin. Main work on metal oxides and fluorine compounds. Nobel Prize 1906.

Moissis, Asher (1899–), Greek author, translator, communal leader. Wrote extensively on Jewish subjects.

Mok, Maurits (1907–), Dutch poet. Belonged to "Amsterdam School" of poetry. Themes were Bible, social involvement, rising threat of Hitlerism, and grief for those who never returned.

Mokady, Moshe (1902–), Israel painter; b. Poland, in Ereẓ Israel fr. 1920 except for 5 years in Paris where he was influenced by Jewish expressionism. Later work more abstract.

Molcho, David Effendi Isaac Pasha (1839–1909), vice admiral of Ottoman Navy. Joined Turkish armed forces as surgeon. Lieutenant colonel 1877, inspector-general of health services. Promoted vice admiral 1902.

Molcho, Solomon (c. 1500–1532), Portuguese-born Marrano, kabbalist, pseudo-messiah; reverted to Judaism 1525. Studied Kabbalah in Salonika, where his disciples prevailed upon him to publish his sermons, *Derashot,* filled with expectation of coming of messiah. Gained confidence of Pope Clement VII, who saved him fr. stake in Rome, but eventually burned in Mantua for judaizing. Friendly with David Reuveni and his prophecies exercised considerable influence both during his lifetime and thereafter. His life has been theme of several novels.

Moldavia, see Rumania.

Moller, Hans (1896–1962), industrialist in Ereẓ Israel; b. Vienna, settled in Ereẓ Israel 1933. Founded 1934 with his cousin **Erich** (1895–), Ata Textile Company, which was at that time largest in country.

Molnár, Ferenc (Neumann; 1878–1952), Hungarian playwright, novelist. Gained world distinction as dramatist. *The Guardsman* inspired Oscar Straus' musical comedy *The Chocolate Soldier. Liliom* became musical *Carousel* by Rodgers and Hammerstein.

Moloch, deity to whom human sacrifice was made, esp. in Valley of Hinnom nr. Jerusalem (II Kings 28:10; Jer. 32:35). Became firmly established at time of King Manasseh and was eradicated by Josiah.

Molodowsky, Kadia (1894–), Yiddish poet, novelist; lived in Warsaw and Odessa, settled in New York 1935. Her verse reflects her wandering and her joy at restoration of Zion.

Mombert, Alfred (1872–1942), German poet. Forerunner of German expressionism who sought to transmute mystical visions into comprehensible verbal images. Released fr. Nazi camp; d. Switzerland.

Samuel Mohilewer

Portrait by Theodore S. Moïse of the American patriot Henry Clay, 1843.

Banner allegedly carried by Solomon Molcho on his mission to Emperor Charles V at Regensburg in 1532.

Sir John Monash

Alfred Mond (center) and his daughter Mary with Meir Dizengoff (next to her) and Chaim Weizmann (left), Tel Aviv, 1921.

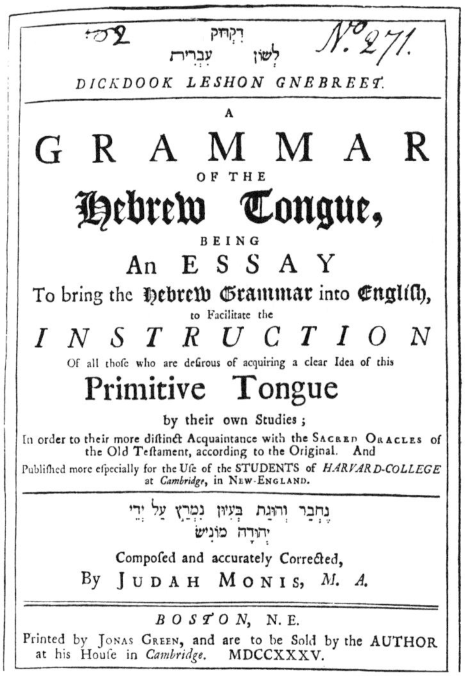

דִקְדוּק לְשׁוֹן עִבְרִית No. 271.

DICKDOOK LESHON GNEBREET.

A

GRAMMAR

OF THE

Hebrew Tongue,

BEING

An ESSAY

To bring the Hebrew Grammar into English,

to Facilitate the

INSTRUCTION

Of all thoſe who are deſirous of acquiring a clear Idea of this

Primitive Tongue

by their own Studies;

In order to their more diſtinct Acquaintance with the SACRED ORACLES of the Old Teſtament, according to the Original. And

Publiſhed more eſpecially for the Uſe of the STUDENTS of *HARVARD-COLLEGE* at *Cambridge*, in NEW-ENGLAND.

נחבר והוגת בעיון נמרץ על ידי
יהודה מוניש

Compoſed and accurately Corrected,

By JUDAH MONIS, *M. A.*

BOSTON, N. E.

Printed by JONAS GREEN, and are to be Sold by the AUTHOR at his Houſe in *Cambridge*. MDCCXXXV.

Title page of Hebrew grammar by Judah Monis, Cambridge, Mass., 1735.

Lilian Montagu delivering sermon at the Berlin Reform synagogue, 1928.

Moment Der, Yiddish daily newspaper, founded in Warsaw 1909 by Ẓevi Hirsch Prylucki; ceased publication Sept. 1939.

Momigliano, Arnaldo Dante (1908–), historian of antiquity; b. Italy, in England fr. 1938. Prof. at Univ. College, London. Wrote on classical topics and classical historiography.

Momigliano, Attilio (1883–1952), Italian literary critic, historian. After being forced out of academic life by racist laws, wrote under name of Giorgio Flores.

Momigliano, Felice (1866–1924), Italian philosopher and historian. Liberal thinker of Mazzinian school who identified himself spiritually with Judaism and Zionism.

Monash, Sir John (1865–1931), Australian engineer, soldier. Commander of Australian expeditionary forces in WWI. Received rank of full general. After war returned to engineering practice and was vice-chancellor of Melbourne Univ. Active in Jewish affairs.

Monastir, town in Yugoslavia. In 12th c. there were Greek-speaking (Romanist) Jews in town. Bet. 14th and 16th c. refugees fr. Hungary and Asia Minor and Spanish exiles arrived. Throughout Ottoman period (1382–1913) commerce of town was handled by Jews. 7,000 Jews in 1910. After WWI economic situation deteriorated and many Jews left for U.S., Chile, and Jerusalem. During Holocaust town's 3,5000 Jews executed.

Monatsschrift fuer Geschichte und Wissenschaft des Judentums, learned monthly appearing in Germany 1815–1939; founded by Z. Frankel. Strove to represent "Positive-historical school" in Jewish life and scholarship. Editors included H. Graetz and Leo Baeck.

Mond (Melchett), British family of chemists and industrialists of German origin. **Ludwig** (1839–1909), founded chemical firm and developed a process for the recovery of nickel still in operation. Art collector. His son **Alfred Moritz** (1868–1930), 1st Baron Melchett, expanded firm founded by father which, after merging with other companies, became Imperial Chemical Industries. Liberal member of parliament fr. 1906, cabinet minister 1916–22. Supporter of Zionism and a founder of enlarged Jewish Agency. His children **Eva Violet** (Marchioness of Reading, see Reading) and **Henry** (1898–1949), 2nd Baron Melchett, were brought up as Christians, but became Jews after rise of Hitler. The latter succeeded his father as chairman of Jewish Agency Council and was pres. of Maccabi. His son **Julian Edward Alfred** (1925–1973), 3rd Baron Melchett, chairman of the nationalized British Steel Industry.

Mond, Bernhard Stanislaw (1887–1944), Polish general. Commanded army in WWII corps; d. in German POW camp.

Monday and Thursday (Heb. *Sheni va-Ḥamishi*), two days of week when liturgy usually includes extra penitential prayers as well as reading fr. Torah. In ancient times these were market days.

Mondolfo, Rodolfo (1877–), Italian historian of philosophy; went to Argentina 1938. Wrote extensively, esp. on Lassalle, Marx, and Engels, and on Greek thought.

Monis, Judah (1683–1764), American Hebraist; of Algerian or Italian descent, emigrated to New York c. 1715, settled in Boston 1720; baptized. Appointed instructor of Hebrew at Harvard; published Hebrew grammar in English.

Monobaz I and **II** (1st c. C.E.), two kings of Adiabene. Wife of former, Queen Helena, and both his sons embraced Judaism. Account of latter in talmudic literature highlights his generosity to people of Jerusalem and Temple and mentions his circumcision.

Monsky, Henry (1890–1947), U.S. communal leader; lived in Omaha, Neb. Invited by Pres. Roosevelt to plan for Office of Civilian Defense 1941. National Pres. B'nai B'rith 1938–47.

Montagu, family of English bankers prominent in politics and public life. **Samuel** (1832–1911), first Baron Swaythling, merchant banker, philanthropist, anti-Zionist. Liberal MP 1885–1900. Founded Federation of Synagogues. His son **Edwin Samuel** (1879–1924), politician. Minister of munitions in WWI, secretary of state for India 1917–22. Uncompromising opponent of Zionism. His influence led to modifications introduced in Balfour Declaration. His sister, **Lilian Helen** (1873–1963), social worker, magistrate; pioneer of Liberal Judaism and founder of World Union for Progressive Judaism. **Ewen Edward** (1901–), pres. United Synagogue 1954–62, judge-advocate of fleet. Described one of his war-time exploits in naval intelligence in his best-selling book *The Man Who Never Was.*

Montague, Montague Francis Ashley (1905–), physical and cultural anthropologist; Emigrated fr. London to U.S. 1931. Chairman of anthropology dept. at Rutgers. Taught that idea of race is anti-human and socially destructive.

Montana, U.S. state. First Jews arrived 1862 during gold rush. First Hebrew Benevolent Society organized in Helena 1865; first congregation founded in Butte 1877. Jewish pop. 845 (1971).

Montefiore, Claude Joseph Goldsmid (1858–1938), scholar; founder of English Liberal Judaism; great-nephew of Sir Moses Montefiore. Founded *Jewish Quarterly Review* 1888. Prolific writer, esp. on rabbinic Judaism and early Christianity; coeditor of *A Rabbinic Anthology,* wrote commentary *The Synoptic Gospels.* Anti-Zionist; as pres. of Anglo-Jewish Assoc. 1895–1921, opposed Balfour Declaration.

Montefiore, Joseph Barrow (1803–1893), Australian pioneer; cousin of Sir Moses Montefiore. Active in sheepfarming, wool trade, and mining, as well as Australian administration and Jewish affairs.

Portrait of Sir Moses Montefiore, on the occasion of his 100th birthday.

Montefiore, Sir Moses (1784–1885), outstanding Jewish leader, philanthropist. Retired fr. business in London 1824 and devoted his time, energy, and wealth to Jewish and civic affairs. First English Jew to be knighted. Became representative of persecuted Jews throughout world, starting with Damascus Affair 1840, and as such visited Morocco and Moscow, where he met Czar Nicholas I. Visited Ereẓ Israel seven times, last time aged 90. Pres. British Board of Deputies c. 44 years; fought introduction of Reform Judaism into England. His wife, **Judith** (1784–1862), published diary of her visit to Ereẓ Israel and wrote first Anglo-Jewish cookbook.

Monteux, Pierre (1875–1964), conductor. Conducted Diaghilev's Ballets Russes 1911–14; at Metropolitan Opera, N.Y. 1917–19, Boston Symphony Orchestra until 1924. Founded Orchestre Symphonique de Paris 1929, directed San Francisco Symphony Orchestra 1936–52.

Montevideo, capital of Uruguay. Community established before WWI by immigrants fr. E. Europe and Middle East. Jewish pop. 46,000 (1971).

Montezinos, Antonion de (Aaron Levi; d. c. 1650), Marrano traveler. Claimed to have discovered S. American Indians who could recite *Shema Israel;* his report led to interest in possibility that 10 lost tribes had been found.

Montezinos, David (1828–1916), librarian, bibliophile in Amsterdam. Acquired enormous library, donating it to Ez Ḥayyim Seminary.

Monti di Pietà (Montes pietatis), savings and loan agencies originally formed in Italian cities in mid-15th c. and considered as predecessors of modern credit union. Arose fr. desire to oust Jews fr. moneylending, but eventually *monti* and Jewish bankers found it possible to coexist.

Montor, Henry (1905–), U.S. organization executive. A leader of United Palestine Appeal and later United Jewish Appeal; also established Israel bond campaigns.

Montoro, Antón de (1404–1480), Spanish Converso poet. Wrote satirical verse. Denounced persecution of his fellow converts to Christianity.

Montpellier, town in S. France. Jews present in 12th c. Center of Jewish rabbinic and secular scholarship. Jews expelled 1394. Again present fr. 17th c. In WWII new arrivals came fr. N. Africa. Jewish pop. 2,000 (1970).

Montreal, city in Que., Canada. Jews first went there 1760 as officers and commissaries with British Army. Congregation Shearith Israel founded 1768; received official recognition 1831. By 1881, only 811 Jews, but grew rapidly thereafter. Jewish pop. 113,000 (1971), with 40 synagogues (33 Orthodox), active communal and cultural life, and national headquarters of most Canadian communal organizations.

Pierre Monteux, drawing by Dolbin, 1954.

The Blessing of the Moon, from Johann Bodenschatz, "Kirchliche Verfassung der heutigen Juden," 1748.

Moon, Blessing of the, prayer of thanksgiving for reappearance of moon. Can be recited fr. third night after appearance until night of full moon (c. 15th of lunar month). Said in the open when moon is clearly visible, usually on termination of Sabbath. Blessing is accompanied by Psalms, verses, and talmudic passage.

°**Moore, George Foot** (1851–1931), U.S. scholar of religion. Prof. of history of religion at Harvard. Works incl. studies of Hebrew Bible and tannaitic Judaism, notably 3-vol. *Judaism in the First Centuries of the Christian Era: The Age of the Tannaim,* outstanding work on rabbinic Judaism.

Mopp (Max Oppenheimer; 1885–1954) painter; lived in Berlin and Vienna, settled in New York after *Anschluss.* Expressionist known primarily as masterly portraitist.

Morais, Sabato (1823–1897), U.S. rabbi; b. Italy, in U.S. fr. 1851. Strove to unite Sephardi and Ashkenazi elements in his Mikveh Israel congregation in Philadelphia. Prime mover in establishment of Jewish Theological Seminary 1887 and pres. of its faculty.

Sabato Morais

Page from "Seder Birkat ha-Mazon," a typical example of Moravian illumination, Mikulov (Nikolsburg), 1728.

Alberto Moravia

Moravia, region in Czechoslovakia. Jews probably first went there as traders in wake of Roman legions. Marranos in 14th c. Thriving communal and cultural life but many Jews left in 19th c. because of restrictions. After WWII very few Jewish survivors returned.

Moravia (Pincherle), Alberto (1907–), Italian novelist. Novels combine trenchant criticism of bourgeois values with astute psychological insight. Wrote *Woman of Rome, The Conformist, Two Women,* etc.

Mordecai, hero of Book of Esther; cousin of Esther who lived in Shushan. With Esther triumphed over evil plotting of Haman, vizier of king, to destroy all Jews in Persian Empire.

Mordecai, Alfred (1804–1887), U.S. soldier, engineer, ordnance expert. Graduate West Point Military Academy. Served as major with American Ordnance Board. Introduced scientific research and development into military technology.

Mordecai (Mokhi'aḥ) ben Ḥayyim of Eisenstadt (1650–1729), wandering Shabbatean preacher. Propagated faith in Shabbetai Ẓevi, in Hungary, Moravia, Italy, and Poland, even after latter's conversion to Islam. Won many adherents though some regarded him as unbalanced.

Mordecai ben Hillel ha-Kohen (1240? –1298), German author, rabbinic authority; outstanding pupil of Meir b. Baruch of Rothenburg. Fame rests on his *Sefer Mordekhai,* generally called "the Mordekhai," gigantic compendium on talmudic problems. Abridgment entitled *Mordekhai ha-Katan* made 1376 by S. Schlettstadt. Exerted powerful influence in Germany. Also wrote rhymed composition on dietary laws and rules of vocalization. With his wife and five children met martyr's death in Rindfleisch massacres.

Mordecai of Neskhiz (1752–1800), ḥasidic *zaddik*; founder of Neskhiz dynasty. Renowned as "miracle worker," reputedly raising dead and healing sick.

Mordell, Phinehas (1861–1934), Hebrew grammarian, scholar; b. Lithuania, in U.S. fr. 1881. Pioneer proponent of Zionism and Hebrew language movement in U.S.

More Judaica, see Oath More Judaica.

Moreel, Ben (1892–), U.S. admiral. Organizer and commander of Seabees during WWII. Retired as full admiral 1958, first engineering officer to reach rank.

Moreh Ẓedek, see Teacher of Righteousness.

Moreno, Jacob L. (1892–), U.S. social scientist; b. Bucharest, in U.S. fr. 1927. Taught at NYU. Initiated sociometric method in social sciences.

Moreshet, Israel institute for research into Holocaust and Jewish heroism; established 1963.

Morgen Journal see Jewish Morning Journal.

Morgenstern, Julian (1881–), U.S. Reform rabbi, Bible scholar. Prof. of Bible at Hebrew Union College, Cincinnati fr. 1907 (pres. 1922–47). In biblical studies examined differences in economic, social, and political background.

Morgenstern, Lina (1830–1909), German educator, philanthropist, writer. Active on behalf of women's rights and in introducing new methodology in kindergartens. Convened first International Women's Congress 1896.

Morgenstern, Oskar (1902–), U.S. economist. Taught at Univ. of Vienna until 1938, then went to U.S. Prof. at Princeton, director of its economic research program. Specialized in economics and business cycles.

Henry Morgenthau

Henry Morgenthau Jr.

Morgenthau, family of U.S. public officials. **Henry Sr.** (1856–1946), emigrated to U.S. fr. Germany 1865. Engaged in real estate, law, and finance. As ambassador to Turkey 1913–16, assisted Jews in Ereẓ Israel during WWI. Headed U.S. Commission investigating treatment of Jews in Poland 1919 (Morgenthau Commission). Chairman of Refugee Settlement Commission of League of Nations 1923. An organizer of International Red Cross. His son, **Henry Jr.** (1891–1967), secretary of the treasury 1934–45, completely reorganizing U.S. monetary policy to stabilize economy. Financed New Deal and WWII. Motivated Roosevelt's establishment of War Refugee

Board 1944. Proposed controversial Morgenthau Plan for postwar Germany. General chairman of United Jewish Appeal 1947–50, chairman of Israel Bond Drive 1951–54. His son, **Robert Morris** (1919–), U.S. district attorney; unsuccessful Democratic candidate for governor of N.Y. state 1962.

Morgenthau, Hans Joachim (1904–), political scientist; b. Germany, in U.S. fr. 1937. Taught at Univ. of Chicago and City College of N.Y. A predominant figure in post-WWII effort to focus study of international relations on observed irregularities of human conduct.

Morgen Zhornal, see Jewish Morning Journal.

Moriah, unidentified biblical locality where Abraham was ordered to offer Isaac (Gen. 22:2ff.). Early tradition identified it with Temple Mount.

Moriah, Hebrew publishing house founded in Odessa 1901 by Ḥ.N. Bialik, Y.H. Rawnitzki, and S. Ben-Zion for publication of textbooks; later published modern Hebrew literature. Closed in WWI.

Morning Benedictions, usual designation of first part of morning service, frequently recited privately at home or in synagogue before service proper which begins with *Pesukei de-Zimrah.* Comprises blessings for ablution, bodily harmony, Torah, and many other activities connected with man's rising from sleep, as well as scriptural and talmudic readings. Originally blessings said individually; now recited together in synagogue.

Morning Freiheit, U.S. daily Yiddish newspaper, founded 1922 by Jewish section of American Communist Party. Circ. 8,000 (1970), appearing 5 times a week.

Morning Service, see Shaḥarit.

Morocco, country in N. Africa. Legends attribute presence of Jews to First Temple period, but earliest records are fr. 2nd c. B.C.E. Prior to Arab conquest Jews active in proselytizing. In 6th–7th c. many Jews escaped there fr. Visigoth Spain. Under Arabs fate of Jews varied acc. to ruling dynasty. Flourished under the Idrisids and Almoravides in period of cultural efflorescence, both religious and secular. Persecuted and forced to convert under Almohads; many emigrated to Spain at this time. The Merinids (fr. 1269) and Wattasids were friendly to Jews, who prospered with country; however, general decline set in fr. 1375. Refugees fr. Spain and Portugal were welcomed officially. Their integration was long process but they became dominant element in large communities. Many Marranos reverted to Judaism in country in late 16th c. Few very rich Jews, with majority living in poverty, many in Jewish quarters (mellah). Jewish scholarship was vital, esp. in Kabbalah. Shabbatean movement was strong, though some of its chief opponents were rabbis. Fr. 19th c. rich Jews played major role in ties with European countries. Rapid urbanization took place with French occupation, and Jews were strongly influenced by French culture. Fr. 1948 progressive waves of immigration to France and Israel depleted Jewish pop. Process continued after independence 1955. Ruling house was friendly to Jews, but nationalist opposition was threatening. 238,000 Jews in French Morocco in 1948, 15,000 in Spanish Morocco, and 12,000 in Tangier; by 1971, 35,000 remained, largely in Casablanca.

Interior in Marrakesh, Morocco, described as "an opulent Jew's house," lithograph from G. Beauclerk, "Journey to Morocco in 1826".

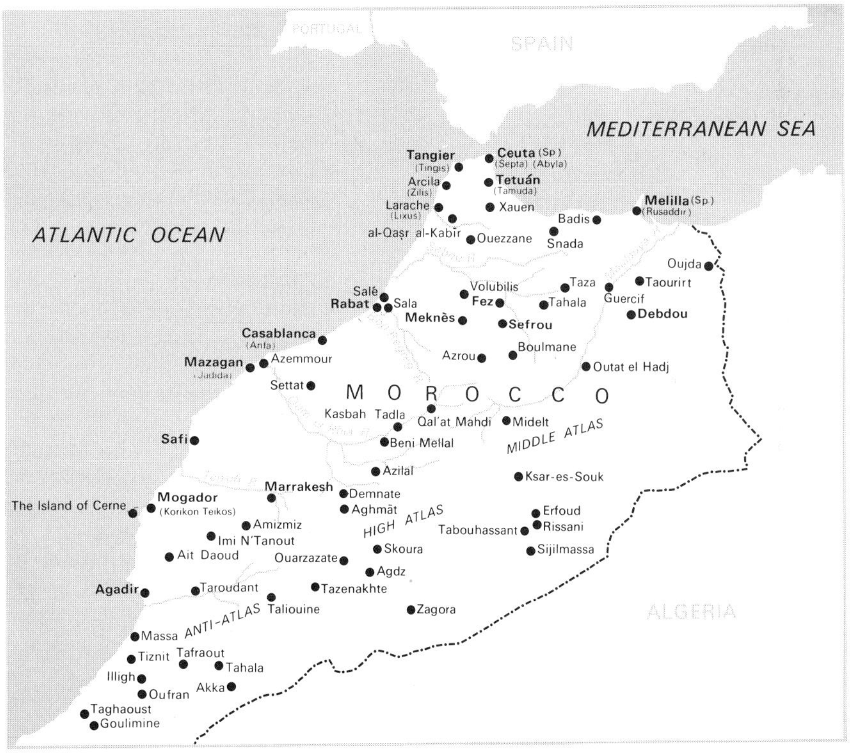

Jewish communities of Morocco. Names in boldface type indicate communities existing in 1971.

Morogowski, Jacob Samuel (1856–1942), Ukrainian *ḥazzan,* composer, conductor; in U.S. from 1914. His compositions characterized by religious feeling and ḥasidic melody.

Morpurgo, Rachel (1790–1871), Italian Hebrew poet. Some of her poems were in Spanish-Hebrew style, others in Italian traditional style. Many were autobiographical.

Morpurgo, Salomone (1860–1942), Italian philosopher, librarian. Member of Italian nationalist movement. Specialized in study of old Italian dialects and literary sources. Directed and reorganized National Library of Florence.

Morpurgo, Samson ben Joshua Moses (1681–1740), Italian rabbi, physician in Ancona. When plague swept town 1730, treated Christians despite Church's ban against this and Cardinal Lambertini publicly expressed gratitude. Some of his works published, incl. responsa and Italian polemical work.

Morris, Ira Nelson (1875–1942), U.S. diplomat. Minister to Sweden 1914–23. His father **Nelson** (1839–1907), meat-packing executive.

Morris, Nathan (1890–1970), English Jewish educator; b. Russia, in England fr. 1909. Played major role in Jewish education in England. Directed Jewish Agency's Dept. of Education and Culture 1949–59. Wrote 3-vol. history of Jewish education.

Morris, Richard Brandon (1904–), U.S. historian. Taught at City College of N.Y. and Columbia. Wrote widely on American history; noteworthy contributions in field of archival preservation.

Morse, David Abner (1907–), U.S. labor executive, lawyer. Held series of government legal posts, incl. assistant secretary of labor. Director-general of International Labor Organization 1948–70.

Morse, Leopold (1831–1892), U.S. congressman; b. Bavaria, in U.S. fr. 1849. Served 5 terms in Congress as Democratic representative fr. Mass. in 1870s–80s.

Mortara, Lodovico (1855–1937), Italian jurist, statesman; son of Marco Mortara. MP, minister of justice 1919, senator. Wrote on jurisprudence.

The kidnapping of Edgardo Mortara, drawing by Moritz Oppenheim.

Chief Rabbi Lewin (right) and Cantor Steinberg during a Passover service at the Moscow Great Synagogue, 1966.

Mortara, Marco (1815–1894), Italian rabbi in Mantua, scholar. Published books on Judaism and catalogue of mss. in Mantua community's library as well as *Mazkeret Ḥakhmei Italyah,* list of c. 2,000 Jewish scholars in Italy fr. 1st to 19th c.

Mortara Case, abduction of 6 year-old Edgardo Mortara in Bologna, Italy, 1858, after being secretly baptized by servant. His parents vainly attempted to get him back, and international outcry was of no avail. Mortara entered Augustinian order and became canon in Rome and prof. of theology; d. 1940.

Morteira, Saul Levi (c.1596–1660), Italian-born rabbi, scholar in Amsterdam. Member of *bet din* that excommunicated Spinoza, who had been his student. Wrote many apologetic works and profoundly influenced Sephardi communities of W. Europe. Published *Givat Sha'ul*, collection of sermons.

Mosad Bialik ("Bialik Institute"), Hebrew publishing firm established in Jerusalem 1935 by World Zionist Organization. Publishes world classics in Hebrew translation as well as original Hebrew books in Jewish studies, research, and belles-lettres. Other major publications incl. biblical encyclopaedia and educational encyclopaedia.

Mosad ha-Rav Kook ("Rabbi Kook Institute"), religious cultural institution established in Jerusalem 1937 by Judah Leib Maimon and maintained by Jewish Agency and Mizrachi organization. Publishes books on many aspects of Judaism, religious Zionism, etc. Also organizes religious cultural activities.

Moscato, Judah ben Joseph (c. 1530–1593), Italian rabbi, author, preacher. Official preacher and chief rabbi of Mantua. Steeped in Jewish medieval philosophy, rabbinic literature,, and *aggadah*; familiar with Plato, Kabbalah, music, astronomy, and classical rhetoric. Made use of his knowledge in his sermons, which helped establish new genre of homiletics. Wrote commentary on Judah Halevi's *Kuzari,* sermons, etc.

Moscheles, Ignaz (1794–1870), pianist, composer; b Prague. Composed in Mendelssohnian style; taught at Leipzig Conservatory. Prepared piano-vocal score of Beethoven's *Fidelio* under composer's supervision.

Moscovitch, Maurice (1871–1940), actor-manager. Won reputation on Yiddish and English-speaking stage in Odessa. Acted with David Kessler and Jacob Adler's companies. Toured America and Europe with own Yiddish troupe.

Moscow, capital of USSR. Presence of Jews forbidden until 18th c. During 19th c. various categories of Jews granted residence rights, incl. rich merchants, univ. graduates, and craftsmen. 30,000 Jews (out of 35,000 total) expelled 1891–92. With influx of refugees in WWI became major Jewish cultural center for some time after Revolution. 400,000 Jews in 1940. After 1948 organized Jewish life liquidated, except for central synagogue and two in suburbs, but reasserted itself in various forms fr. mid-60s. Official Jewish pop. 285,000 (1971), but unofficial estimates put figure at twice that number.

Mosenthal, Salomon Hermann (1821–1877), German playwright. His plays, with Jewish themes, contain much social criticism. His three brothers, **Joseph** (1813–1871), **Adolph** (1812–1882), and **Julius** (1819–1880), settled in Cape Town and played leading roles in developing S. African agricultural export trade.

Moser, Jacob (1839–1922), early British Zionist; b. Schleswig, moved to England in 1860s, settled in Bradford, becoming its mayor. Joined Zionist movement at beginning. Contributed large sum for establishment of Herzlia High School in Tel Aviv.

Moser, Moses (1796–1838), banker, among founders of Verein fuer Kultur und Wissenschaft des Judentums. Treasurer and moderating influence in Verein. Friend of Heinrich Heine.

Moses (13th c. B.C.E.), leader, prophet, and lawgiver. B. in Egypt to Amram and Jochebed of the tribe of Levi at a time when the ruler had decreed the death of all male Israelite children. He was hidden by his mother on the banks of the Nile, found by Pharaoh's daughter and raised in the royal palace. When he grew to manhood, he sided with his brethren in their tribulations and had to flee to Midian. Here he acted as shepherd to the Midianite priest, Jethro, whose daughter, Zipporah, he married. After the theophany of the Burning Bush, he returned to Egypt and – assisted by his brother Aaron – demanded freedom for the Israelites. Pharaoh refused but after the Ten Plagues permitted the Israelites to leave. When he changed his mind and pursued them, the Egyptian army was destroyed in the

Red Sea. Moses led the Israelites on to Mount Sinai where he received the Ten Commandments, which were to be the basis of Judaism, and communicated them to the people. He led the people through its forty years of wanderings in the desert, which were a period of frequent tension and crises, including a rebellion led by Moses' cousin, Korah. He died at the age of 120 on Mount Pisgah, on the borders of Ereẓ Israel, but was not allowed to enter the Promised Land because of an incident in which he had shown a lack of faith in striking a rock instead of speaking to it, as Divinely commanded. Before his death, he appointed Joshua to be his successor. Moses is regarded as the prophet par excellence and the outstanding founder of the Jewish religion. The Pentateuch was ascribed to his authorship and its last four books revolve around his story. Traditionally too the entire Oral Law was given to Moses by God on Mount Sinai. Various pseudepigraphic works were ascribed to him. To the rabbis he was *Moshe Rabbenu* ("Moses our master," i.e., teacher).

Moses, Assumption of, title of incomplete text of apocryphal work, containing address by Moses to his successor, Joshua. Present Latin version based on Greek version; original presumably in Hebrew or Aramaic. Probably written in 1st c.

Moses, Isaac S. (1847–1926), U.S. Reform rabbi; emigrated fr. Poznan to U.S. in 1870s. A founder of Central Conference of American Rabbis. Influential in preparation of *Union Prayer Book* 1894.

Moses, Raphael J. (1812–1893), U.S. lawyer, state legislator; b. Charleston, S.C. Confederate Commissary for Georgia during Civil War. Elected to Georgia state legislature; chairman of the Judiciary Committee.

Moses, Robert (1888–), U.S. parks and highways developer; denied his Jewish affiliation. Pres. N.Y. State Council of Parks 1924–63, N.Y.C. parks commissioner 1934–60, along with many other city and state posts. Inaugurated many massive public works, incl. Triborough Bridge, major N.Y.C. parkways, Coliseum convention hall.

Moses, Siegfried (1887–1974), German Zionist leader, Israel public official. Pres. German Zionist Organization 1933–37. Settled in Ereẓ Israel 1937. Israel's first state comptroller 1949–61.

Moses (ben Isaac) ben ha-Nesi'ah (13th c.), Hebrew grammarian, lexicographer; lived in England. His only extant work is *Sefer ha-Shoham.*

Moses ben Ḥanokh (d. c. 965), Spanish rabbi. Acc. to Ibn Daud, one of Four Captives who brought talmudic learning beyond Babylon, in his case to S. Spain (story is unsubstantiated). Came fr. S. Italy and settled in Córdoba, heading yeshivah and writing responsa; fr. his time dependence of Spanish scholars on Babylonian scholars ceased.

Moses ben Jacob of Coucy (13th c.), French scholar, tosafist who by his preaching brought about repentance of "thousands and tens of thousands" in Spain. Took part in Paris Talmud disputation with Nicholas Donin 1240. Wrote *Sefer Mitzvot Gadol* (cited as *Semag*), which codifies Oral Law in order of precepts and is based on Maimonides' *Mishneh Torah.*

Moses ben Jacob of Kiev (Moses Ashkenazi; 1449–c. 1520), talmudic scholar, biblical exegete, kabbalist, polemicist against Karaites. His children, and then he himself, were taken captive by Tatars, and after being ransomed settled in Kaffa, Crimea, uniting its community and compiling prayer book *Minhag Kaffa,* adopted by all Crimean communities.

Moses ben Joseph ben Merwan Levi (12th c.), Narbonne scholar. Headed yeshivah and member of *bet din.* Influenced Naḥmanides, who quotes him extensively.

Moses ben Joseph ha-Levi (13th c.), philosopher, Quoted by Crescas and Albo. Wrote work on music.

Moses ben Joshua of Narbonne (d. 1362), French philosopher, physician; lived for a time in Spain. Wrote well-known commentary on Maimonides' *Guide of the Perplexed* as well as philosophical works, attempting reconciliation between Kabbalah and philosophy; also wrote medical and other works.

Moses ben Maimon, see Maimonides, Moses.

Moses ben Naḥman, see Naḥmanides.

Moses ben Shemtov de Leon (c. 1240–1305), a leading kabbalist in Spain, author of bulk of *Zohar* and pseudepigraphic mystic works in Aramaic. Up to 1291 in Guadalajara, then led a wandering life until settling in Avila, where he devoted himself to circulating copies of *Zohar.* His identity as author was long suspected and confirmed by research of G. Scholem.

Moses ben Solomon ben Simeon of Burgos (1230/35–c. 1300), Spanish kabbalist. Strict traditionalist whose writings report traditions rarely mentioned by his contemporaries. Said that position reached by philosopher's head reached only position of kabbalist's feet.

Moses with the Decalogue in miniature from illuminated Hebrew ms., Troyes (?), France, c. 1280.

Moses ben Yom Tov (d. 1268), London rabbi, grammarian; first English talmudist who made much use of rulings of Maimonides. Wrote book on principles of biblical punctuation and accentuation.

Moses Esrim ve-Arba (15th c.), rabbi, emissary of Jerusalem. Held by some to have been cause of bitter dispute bet. Moses Capsali of Constantinople and Joseph Colon of Italy; also held to have compiled or copied Yiddish classic *Dos Shemuel Bukh.*

Moses ha-Darshan (11th c.), scholar, aggadist of Narbonne; frequently quoted by Rashi and others. Author of midrashic anthology which was basis of *Genesis Rabbati* and was based on *Genesis Rabbah,* to which much material fr. Talmud and Apocrypha was added; certain other midrashim are held to emanate fr. his school.

Moses Ḥayyim Ephraim of Sudylkow (c. 1740–1800?), ḥasidic preacher, *ẓaddik;* grandson of Israel Ba'al Shem Tov. Author of *Degel Maḥaneh Efrayim,* classic of Ḥasidism, containing sermons on weekly readings of Torah and collection of his "dreams."

Moses Isaac (Kelmer Maggid; 1828–1899), main preacher of Musar movement. After absorbing teachings of Israel Lipkin, traveled in E. Europe castigating ethical and moral sins of populace.

Nahalal, the first moshav ovedim in Ereẓ Israel.

MOSHAV SHITTUFI

NOTES
Geographical Region: The sign "67+" indicates a settlement beyond the pre-1967 borders.
Affiliation: Only the present affiliation is given.
No. of Inhabitants: The sign ∞ indicates that the population figures are not available.

Ḥ – Ḥerut
IḤ – Ihud Ḥakla'i
OẒ – Ha–Oved ha-Ẓiyyoni
PAI – Po'alei Agudat Israel
PM – Ha-Po'el ha-Mizrachi
TM – Tenu'at ha-Moshavim

Name	Geographical Region	Year of Founding	Affiliation	No. of inhabitants 31 Dec. 1971
Allonei Abba	Southern Lower Galilee	1948	OẒ	220
Amaẓyah	Lachish (Adoraim) Region	1955	Ḥ	∞
Benei Darom	Coastal Plain (Reḥovot Region)	1949	PM	199
Benei Deror	Southern Sharon	1946	TM	200
Bet Ḥerut	Central Sharon (Ḥefer Plain)	1933	TM	299
Ein Ḥaẓevah	Central Arabah Valley	1970	IḤ	∞
Ha-Bonim	Carmel Coast	1949	TM	170
Ḥamrah	Lower Jordan Valley; 67+	1971	OẒ	∞
Kefar Dani'el (Bet Ḥever)	Coastal Plain (Lod Region)	1949	TM	127
Kefar Ḥittim	Eastern Lower Galilee	1936	TM	194
Massu'ot Yiẓḥak	Southern Coastal Plain (Malakhi Region)	1949	PM	412
Mavki'im	Southern Coastal Plain (Ashkelon Region)	1949	OẒ	140
Mei Ammi	Samaria (Iron Hills)	1963	OẒ	∞
Mevo Beitar	Jerusalem Hills	1950	Ḥ	203
Moledet (B'nai B'rith)	Southeastern Lower Galilee	1937	TM	419
Nir Eẓyon	Mt. Carmel	1950	PM	478
Nir Gallim	Southern Coastal Plain (Yavneh Region)	1949	PM	413
Nordiyyah	Southern Sharon (Netanyah Region)	1948	Ḥ	284
Ramot Me'ir	Coastal Plain (Lod Region)	1949	TM	220
Regbah	Acre Plain	1946	TM	327
Shavei Zion	Acre Plain	1938	IḤ	325
Shoresh	Judean Hills	1948	OẒ	183
Talmei Eliyahu (Besor C)	Northwestern Negev (Besor Region)	1970	TM	55
Talmei Yafeh	Southern Coastal Plain (Ashkelon Region)	1950	OẒ	87
Timmurim	Southern Coastal Plain (Malakhi Region)	1954	OẒ	238
Yesodot	Judean Foothills	1948	PAI	288
Ẓur Natan	Southern Sharon	1966	Ḥ	∞

Moses Leib of Sasov (1745–1807), ḥasidic rabbi. Author of novellae on several talmudic tractates. Noted for his compassion and called "father of widows and orphans." Composed melodies and dances.

Moses of Palermo (c.1275), Sicilian translator. Worked for king Charles of Anjou; translated scientific works fr. Arabic.

Moshav or **Moshav Ovedim** (Heb. "workers' settlement"), cooperative smallholders' village based on nationally owned land, family labor, mutual aid, joint public services, cooperative purchasing and marketing, and membership in Histadrut. First moshav, Nahalal, founded 1921. Total number 349, pop. 128,500 (1973). Most belong to moshav movement (Tenu'at ha-Moshavim), founded in mid-1930s.

Moshav Shittufi (Heb. "collective moshav"), form of agricultural settlement combining features of kibbutz and moshav, based on collective production and private consumption. First moshav shittufi, Kefar Ḥittim, founded 1936. Total number 28, pop. 5,800 (1973).

Moshavah (Heb. "colony"), earliest type of Jewish village in modern Ereẓ Israel, in which farming is done on individual farms and mostly on privately owned land. First moshavah, Petaḥ Tikvah, founded 1878.

Moskoni, Judah Leon ben Moses (b.1328), Bulgarian philosopher, scholar. Wrote supercommentary *Even ha-Ezer* on Pentateuch commentary of Abraham ibn Ezra; published edition of *Josippon* with his own introduction.

Moskovitz, Shalom (Shalom of Safed; 1887–), Israel primitive painter. Began painting at age 70. Painted biblical themes, blending kabbalistic and ḥasidic traditions with features fr. own surroundings.

Geographical Region: The sign "67+" indicates a settlement beyond the pre-1967 borders.
Affiliation: Only the present affiliation is given.
No. of Inhabitants: The sign ∞ indicates that the population figures are not available.

Ḥ — Ḥerut	IḤ — Iḥud Ḥakla'i	PAI — Po'alei Agudat Israel
HI — Hitaḥdut ha-Ikkarim	OẒ — Ha-Oved ha-Ẓiyyoni	PM — Ha-Po'el ha-Mizrachi
		TM — Tenu'at ha-Moshavim

Name	Geographical Region	Year of Founding	Affiliation	No. of inhabitants 31 Dec. 1971
Adanim	Southern Sharon	1950	–	199
Adderet	Judean Foothills (Adullam Region)	1961	TM	265
Addirim	Jezreel Valley (Taanach Region)	1956	TM	371
Agur	Southern Judean Foothills	1950	TM	302
Aḥi'ezer	Coastal Plain (Lod Region)	1950	PM	890
Aḥihud	Acre Plain	1950	TM	505
Aḥisamakh	Coastal Plain (Lod Region)	1950	TM	670
Aḥituv	Central Sharon (Ḥefer Plain)	1951	TM	560
Aḥuzzam	Southern Coastal Plain (Lachish Region)	1950	OẒ	510
Almagor	Kinneret Valley	1961	TM	70
Almah	Eastern Upper Galilee	1949	PM	655
Amirim	Eastern Upper Galilee	1950	TM	148
Amkah	Acre Plain	1949	TM	595
Ammikam	Iron Hills (Northwestern Samaria)	1950	Ḥ	125
Amminadav	Jerusalem Hills	1950	TM	265
Ammi'oz	Northwestern Negev (Besor Region)	1957	TM	237
Arbel	Eastern Lower Galilee	1949	TM	163
Argaman	Lower Jordan Valley; 67+	1968	Ḥ	∞
Arugot	Southern Coastal Plain (Malakhi Region)	1949	TM	241
Avdon	Western Upper Galilee	1952	TM	278
Avi'el	Northern Sharon (Ḥaderah Region)	1949	Ḥ	219
Avi'ezer	Judean Foothills	1958	PM	230
Avigedor	Southern Coastal Plain (Malakhi Region)	1950	TM	316
Aviḥayil	Central Sharon	1932	TM	590
Avital	Jezreel Valley (Taanach Region)	1953	TM	380
Avivim	Eastern Upper Galilee	1960	TM	∞
Azaryah	Judean Foothills	1949	TM	484
Azri'el	Southern Sharon (Kefar Sava Region)	1951	PM	490
Azrikam	Southern Coastal Plain (Malakhi Region)	1950	TM	615
Balfouriyyah	Jezreel Valley	1922	TM	224
Barak	Jezreel Valley (Taanach Region)	1956	TM	263
Bareket	Coastal Plain (Petaḥ Tikvah Region)	1952	PM	745
Bar Giora	Jerusalem Hills	1950	Ḥ	210
Bat Shelomo	Manasseh Hills	1889	HI	161
Be'erotayim	Coastal Plain (Ḥefer Plain)	1949	TM	265
Be'er Tuviyyah	Southern Coastal Plain (Malakhi Region)	1930	TM	655
Beko'a	Judean Foothills	1951	TM	478
Ben Ammi	Acre Plain	1949	TM	294
Benayah	Southern Coastal Plain (Reḥovot Region)	1949	TM	270
Benei Atarot	Coastal Plain (Petaḥ Tikvah Region)	1948	TM	282
Benei Re'em	Coastal Plain (Reḥovot Region)	1949	PAI	332
Benei Zion	Southern Sharon (Herzliyyah Region)	1947	IḤ	380
Ben Shemen	Coastal Plain (Lod Region)	1952	TM	215
Ben Zakkai	Southern Coastal Plain (Reḥovot Region)	1950	PM	620
Berekhyah	Southern Coastal Plain (Ashkelon Region)	1950	TM	750
Berosh	Northern Negev (Gerar Region)	1953	TM	350
Bet Arif	Coastal Plain (Lod Region)	1951	TM	540
Bet Elazari	Coastal Plain (Reḥovot Region)	1948	TM	459
Bet Ezra	Southern Coastal Plain (Malakhi Region)	1950	TM	570
Bet Gamli'el	Coastal Plain (Reḥovot Region)	1949	PM	380
Bet ha-Gaddi	Northern Negev (Gerar Region)	1949	PM	650
Bet ha-Levi	Central Sharon (Ḥefer Plain)	1945	TM	225
Bet Ḥanan	Coastal Plain (Rishon le-Zion Region)	1930	TM	367
Bet Ḥananyah	Northern Sharon (Ḥaderah Region)	1950	TM	260
Bet Ḥilkiyyah	Coastal Plain (Reḥovot Region)	1953	PAI	263
Bet Hillel	Ḥuleh Valley	1940	TM	177
Bet Leḥem ha-Gelilit	Southern Lower Galilee	1948	TM	274
Bet Me'ir	Judean Hills	1950	PM	300
Bet Neḥemyah	Northern Judean Foothills (Lod Region)	1950	OẒ	264
Bet Nekofah	Jerusalem Hills	1949	TM	197
Bet Oved	Coastal Plain (Rishon le-Zion Region)	1933	TM	217
Bet She'arim	Jezreel Valley	1936	TM	308
Bet Shikmah	Southern Coastal Plain (Ashkelon Region)	1950	TM	555
Bet Uzzi'el	Judean Foothills (Lod Region)	1956	PM	330
Bet Yannai	Central Sharon (Ḥefer Plain)	1933	IḤ	234
Bet Yehoshu'a	Southern Sharon (Netanyah Region)	1938	OẒ	234
Bet Yosef	Beth-Shean Valley	1937	TM	320
Bet Zayit	Jerusalem Hills	1949	TM	500
Beẓet	Acre Plain	1949	TM	239
Bitan Aharon	Central Sharon (Ḥefer Plain)	1936	IḤ	100
Bitḥah	Northwestern Negev (Besor Region)	1950	TM	710
Bizzaron	Southern Coastal Plain (Malakhi Region)	1935	TM	425
Boẓrah	Southern Sharon (Kefar Sava Region)	1946	IḤ	410
Burgetah	Central Sharon (Ḥefer Plain)	1949	TM	327
Bustan ha-Galil	Acre Plain	1948	IḤ	320
Dalton	Eastern Upper Galilee	1950	PM	670
Devorah	Jezreel Valley (Taanach Region)	1956	TM	301
Dishon	Eastern Upper Galilee	1953	OẒ	∞
Dor	Carmel Coast	1949	TM	167
Dovev	Eastern Upper Galilee	1963	TM	∞
Ein Ayyalah	Carmel Coast	1949	TM	297
Ein Iron	Northern Sharon (Ḥaderah Region)	1934	TM	190

Name	Geographical Region	Year of Founding	Affiliation	No. of inhabitants 31 Dec. 1971
Ein Vered	Southern Sharon (Kefar Sava Region)	1930	TM	520
Ein Ya'akov	Western Upper Galilee	1950	TM	280
Ein Yahav	Central Arabah Valley	1951	TM	oo
Eitan	Southern Coastal Plain (Lachish Region)	1955	PM	458
El Al (Naḥal El Al)	Golan; 67+	1968	TM	oo
Elifelet	Eastern Upper Galilee (Hazor Region)	1949	TM	372
Elishama	Southern Sharon	1951	TM	560
Elkosh	Western Upper Galilee	1949	TM	318
Elyakim	Manasseh Hills	1949	TM	620
Elyashiv	Central Sharon (Ḥefer Plain)	1933	HI	363
Emunim	Southern Coastal Plain (Malakhi Region)	1950	TM	384
Eshbol	Northern Negev (Gerar Region)	1955	TM	410
Eshtaol	Judean Foothills	1949	TM	344
Even Menaḥem	Western Upper Galilee	1960	TM	313
Even Sappir	Jerusalem Hills	1950	TM	440
Gadish	Jezreel Valley (Taanach Region)	1956	TM	470
Gan ha-Darom	Coastal Plain (Reḥovot Region)	1953	IḤ	266
Gan Ḥayyim	Southern Sharon (Kefar Sava Region)	1935	TM	220
Gannei Am	Southern Sharon (Kefar Sava Region)	1934	–	179
Gannei Yehudah	Coastal Plain (Petaḥ Tikvah Region)	1951	IḤ	630
Gannei Yoḥanan (Gannei Yonah)	Coastal Plain (Reḥovot Region)	1950	TM	279
Gannot	Coastal Plain (Lod Region)	1953	IḤ	292
Gan Sorek	Coastal Plain (Rishon le-Zion Region)	1950	TM	120
Gan Yoshiyyah	Central Sharon (Ḥefer Plain)	1949	TM	203
Ge'ah	Southern Coastal Plain (Ashkelon Region)	1949	TM	179
Ge'alyah	Coastal Plain (Reḥovot Region)	1948	TM	380
Gefen	Southern Judean Foothills	1955	PM	374
Ge'ulei Teiman	Central Sharon (Ḥefer Plain)	1947	PM	185
Ge'ulim	Southern Sharon	1945	TM	515
Geva Karmel	Carmel Coast	1949	TM	395
Gibbethon	Coastal Plain (Reḥovot Region)	1933	–	159
Gilat	Northern Negev (Gerar Region)	1949	TM	580
Gimzo	Judean Foothills	1950	PAI	156
Ginnaton	Coastal Plain (Lod Region)	1949	TM	260
Givat Ḥen	Southern Sharon	1933	TM	225
Givat Ko'aḥ	Judean Foothills	1950	TM	388
Givat Nili	Northwestern Iron Hills	1953	Ḥ	194
Givat Shapira	Southern Sharon	1958	IḤ	114
Givat Ye'arim	Jerusalem Hills	1950	TM	530
Givat Yeshayahu	Judean Foothills (Adullam Region)	1958	OẒ	114
Givat Yo'av	Golan; 67+	1968	TM	oo
Givati	Southern Coastal Plain (Malakhi Region)	1950	TM	380
Givolim	Northern Negev (Gerar Region)	1952	PM	210
Goren	Western Upper Galilee	1950	TM	338
Hadar Am	Central Sharon (Ḥefer Plain)	1933	IḤ	168
Ḥadid	Northern Judean Foothills	1950	PM	414
Ḥagor	Southern Sharon (Kefar Sava Region)	1949	TM	306
Ḥanni'el	Central Sharon (Ḥefer Plain)	1950	TM	275
Ḥavaẓẓelet ha-Sharon	Central Sharon (Ḥefer Plain)	1935	IḤ	150
Ha-Yogev	Jezreel Valley	1949	TM	352
Ḥaẓav	Southern Coastal Plain (Malakhi Region)	1949	TM	760
Ḥaẓevah	Central Arabah Valley	1965	TM	oo
Ḥazon	Eastern Lower Galilee	1969	PM	135
Ha-Zore'im	Eastern Lower Galilee	1939	PM	310
Ḥeleẓ	Southern Coastal Plain (Ashkelon Region)	1950	TM	565
Ḥemed	Coastal Plain (Lod Region)	1950	PM	510
Ḥerev le-Et	Central Sharon (Ḥefer Plain)	1947	IḤ	215
Ḥerut	Southern Sharon (Kefar Sava Region)	1930	TM	406
Ḥibbat Zion	Central Sharon (Ḥefer Plain)	1933	HI	281
Hodiyyah	Southern Coastal Plain (Ashkelon Region)	1940	TM	433
Ḥoglah	Central Sharon (Ḥefer Plain)	1933	TM	203
Ḥosen	Western Upper Galilee	1949	Ḥ	243
Ilaniyyah	Eastern Lower Galilee	1902	IḤ	190
Kefar Aḥim	Southern Coastal Plain (Malakhi Region)	1949	TM	235
Kefar Aviv	Coastal Plain (Reḥovot Region)	1951	IḤ	258
Kefar Azar	Coastal Plain (Tel Aviv Region)	1932	TM	350
Kefar Barukh	Jezreel Valley	1926	TM	213
Kefar Bialik	Zebulun Valley (Haifa Bay Area)	1934	IḤ	550
Kefar Bilu	Coastal Plain (Reḥovot Region)	1932	TM	368
Kefar Bin Nun	Judean Foothills	1952	IḤ	149
Kefar Gidon	Jezreel Valley	1923	PAI	134
Kefar ha-Nagid	Coastal Plain (Rishon le-Zion Region)	1949	TM	340
Kefar ha-Rif	Southern Coastal Plain (Malakhi Region)	1956	IḤ	237
Kefar ha-Ro'eh	Central Sharon (Ḥefer Plain)	1934	PM	860
Kefar Ḥabad	Coastal Plain (Lod Region)	1949	–	1,620
Kefar Ḥayyim	Central Sharon (Ḥefer Plain)	1933	TM	340
Kefar Ḥasidim Alef	Zebulun Valley (Haifa Bay Area)	1924	–	380
Kefar Hess	Southern Sharon (Kefar Sava Region)	1933	TM	420
Kefar Jawitz	Southern Sharon (Kefar Sava Region)	1932	PM	394
Kefar Kisch	Eastern Lower Galilee	1946	TM	170
Kefar Maimon	Northern Negev (Gerar Region)	1959	PM	260
Kefar Malal (formerly Ein Ḥai)	Southern Sharon (Kefar Sava Region)	1922	TM	254
Kefar Monash	Central Sharon (Ḥefer Plain)	1946	TM	307
Kefar Mordekhai	Coastal Plain (Reḥovot Region)	1950	IḤ	211
Kefar Netter	Southern Sharon	1939	–	240
Kefar Pines	Northern Sharon (Ḥaderah Region)	1933	PM	405
Kefar Rosenwald (Zarit)	Western Upper Galilee	1967	TM	oo
Kefar Shammai	Eastern Upper Galilee	1949	PM	275
Kefar Shemu'el	Judean Foothills	1950	OẒ	234
Kefar Truman	Northern Judean Foothills	1949	TM	277
Kefar Uriyyah	Judean Foothills	1944	TM	265
Kefar Vitkin	Central Sharon (Ḥefer Plain)	1933	TM	825

Name	Geographical Region	Year of Founding	Affiliation	No. of inhabitants 31 Dec. 1971
Kefar Warburg	Southern Coastal Plain (Malakhi Region)	1939	TM	490
Kefar Yeḥezkel	Harod Valley	1921	TM	437
Kefar Yehoshu'a	Jezreel Valley	1927	TM	650
Kefar Zeitim	Eastern Lower Galilee	1950	TM	261
Kelaḥim	Northern Negev (Gerar Region)	1954	IḤ	287
Kerem Ben Zimrah	Eastern Upper Galilee	1949	PM	300
Kerem Maharal	Mount Carmel	1949	TM	210
Kesalon	Judean Hills	1952	IḤ	225
Kidron	Coastal Plain (Reḥovot Region)	1949	TM	570
Kokhav Mikha'el	Southern Coastal Plain (Ashkelon Region)	1950	TM	319
Komemiyyut	Southern Coastal Plain (Malakhi Region)	1950	PAI	337
Lachish (Lakhish)	Southern Coastal Plain (Lachish Region)	1955	TM	225
Liman	Acre Plain	1949	TM	250
Luzit	Southern Judean Foothills	1955	TM	271
Ma'as	Coastal Plain (Petaḥ Tikvah Region)	1935	TM	424
Magshimim	Coastal Plain (Petaḥ Tikvah Region)	1949	IḤ	392
Ma'or	Northern Sharon (Ḥaderah Region)	1953	TM	190
Margaliyyot	Eastern Upper Galilee	1951	TM	∞
Mashen	Southern Coastal Plain (Ashkelon Region)	1950	TM	705
Maslul	Northwestern Negev (Besor Region)	1950	TM	183
Matta	Judean Hills	1950	TM	212
Mazli'aḥ	Coastal Plain (Lod Region)	1950	TM	665
Mazor	Coastal Plain (Petaḥ Tikvah Region)	1949	TM	303
Megadim	Carmel Coast	1949	TM	424
Meḥolah	Lower Jordan Valley; 67+	1968	PM	∞
Meishar	Coastal Plain (Reḥovot Region)	1950	IḤ	183
Meitav	Jezreel Valley (Taanach Region)	1954	TM	485
Mele'ah	Jezreel Valley (Taanach Region)	1956	TM	254
Melilot	Northern Negev (Gerar Region)	1953	PM	356
Menaḥemiyyah	Eastern Lower Galilee	1902	IḤ	650
Menuḥah (Vardon)	Southern Coastal Plain (Malakhi Region)	1953	TM	565
Me'onah	Western Upper Galilee	1949	TM	280
Merḥavyah	Harod Valley	1922	TM	227
Meron	Eastern Upper Galilee	1949	PM	260
Mesillat Zion	Judean Foothills	1950	TM	221
Mevo Modi'im	Judean Foothills	1964	PAI	26
Midrakh Oz	Jezreel Valley	1952	TM	452
Mikhmoret	Central Sharon (Ḥefer Plain)	1945	TM	740
Misgav Dov	Coastal Plain (Reḥovot Region)	1950	Ḥ	200
Mishmar Ayyalon	Judean Foothills	1949	TM	213
Mishmar ha-Shivah	Central Coastal Plain (Lod Region)	1949	–	430
Mishmar ha-Yarden	Eastern Upper Galilee (Hazor Region)	1949	Ḥ	227
Mishmeret	Southern Sharon (Kefar Sava Region)	1946	TM	328
Mivtaḥim	Northwestern Negev (Besor Region)	1950	TM	452
Naḥalah	Southern Coastal Plain (Malakhi Region)	1953	TM	400
Nahalal	Jezreel Valley	1921	TM	1,050
Naḥal Diklah	Northeastern Sinai; 67+	1969	Ḥ	∞
Naḥal Paran	Southern Arabah Valley	1971	–	∞
Naḥam	Judean Foothills	1950	PM	390
Neḥalim	Coastal Plain (Petaḥ Tikvah Region)	1948	PM	635

Name	Geographical Region	Year of Founding	Affiliation	No. of inhabitants 31 Dec. 1971
Ne'ot Golan	Golan; 67+	1968	OẒ	∞
Ne'ot ha-Kikkar	Northern Arabah Valley	1961	IḤ	∞
Nes Harim	Jerusalem Hills	1950	TM	371
Neta'im	Coastal Plain (Rishon le-Zion Region)	1932	TM	205
Netiv ha-Shayyarah	Acre Plain	1950	TM	363
Netu'ah	Western Upper Galilee	1966	TM	∞
Nevatim	Northern Negev (Beersheba Region)	1946	TM	450
Neveh Mivtaḥ	Southern Coastal Plain (Malakhi Region)	1950	TM	210
Neveh Yamin	Southern Sharon (Kefar Sava Region)	1949	TM	560
Neveh Yarak	Southern Sharon (Herzliyyah Region)	1951	TM	390
Nir Akiva	Northern Negev (Gerar Region)	1953	TM	120
Nir Banim	Southern Coastal Plain (Malakhi Region)	1954	TM	329
Nir Ḥen	Southern Coastal Plain (Lachish Region)	1955	TM	110
Nir Moshe	Northern Negev (Gerar Region)	1953	TM	185
Nir Yafeh	Jezreel Valley (Taanach Region)	1956	TM	254
Nir Yisrael	Southern Coastal Plain (Ashkelon Region)	1949	OẒ	230
Nir Ẓevi	Coastal Plain (Lod Region)	1954	IḤ	520
Niẓẓanei Oz	Southern Sharon (Kefar Yonah Region)	1951	TM	342
No'am	Southern Coastal Plain (Lachish Region)	1953	PM	500
Nogah	Southern Coastal Plain (Lachish Region)	1955	TM	535
Ofer	Mount Carmel	1950	TM	238
Ohad	Northwestern Negev (Besor Region)	1969	TM	152
Olesh	Central Sharon (Ḥefer Plain)	1949	TM	295
Omeẓ	Central Sharon (Ḥefer Plain)	1949	TM	198
Orah	Jerusalem Hills	1950	TM	295
Orot	Southern Coastal Plain (Malakhi Region)	1952	TM	248
Oẓem	Southern Coastal Plain (Lachish Region)	1955	TM	640
Pa'amei Tashaz	Northern Negev (Gerar Region)	1953	TM	305
Pattish	Northern Negev (Besor Region)	1950	TM	640
Pedayah	Judean Foothills	1951	TM	465
Peduyim	Northern Negev (Besor Region)	1950	TM	285
Peki'in Hadashah	Western Upper Galilee	1955	TM	239
Perazon	Jezreel Valley (Taanach Region)	1953	TM	510
Petaḥyah	Judean Foothills	1951	OẒ	437
Peza'el (Ma'aleh Efrayim)	Lower Jordan Valley; 67+	1970	TM	∞
Porat	Southern Sharon (Kefar Sava Region)	1950	PM	815
Poriyyah (Kefar Avodah)	Eastern Lower Galilee	1955	–	110
Ramat Magshimim	Golan; 67+	1968	PM	∞
Ramat Raziel	Judean Hills	1948	Ḥ	148
Ramat Ẓevi	Southeastern Lower Galilee	1942	TM	176
Ramat On	Jezreel Valley (Taanach Region)	1960	TM	235
Ramot	Golan; 67+	1970	TM	∞
Ramot ha-Shavim	Southern Sharon (Kefar Sava Region)	1933	IḤ	465
Ramot Naftali	Eastern Upper Galilee	1945	TM	∞
Rannen	Northern Negev (Besor Region)	1950	TM	414

Name	Geographical Region	Year of Founding	Affiliation	No. of inhabitants 31 Dec. 1971
Reḥov	Beth-Shean Valley	1951	PM	345
Revaḥah	Southern Coastal Plain (Lachish Region)	1953	PM	570
Revayah	Beth-Shean Valley	1952	PM	336
Rinnatyah	Coastal Plain (Lod Region)	1949	TM	440
Rishpon	Southern Sharon (Herzliyyah Region)	1936	TM	442
Roglit	Judean Foothills (Adullam Region)	1958	HI	269
Sadot	Northeastern Sinai; 67+	1971	TM	oo
Sedeh David	Southern Coastal Plain (Lachish Region)	1955	OẒ	440
Sedeh Eli'ezer	Ḥuleh Valley	1952	OZ	260
Sedeh Ilan	Eastern Lower Galilee	1949	PM	211
Sedeh Moshe	Southern Coastal Plain (Lachish Region)	1956	TM	295
Sedeh Uzziyyah	Southern Coastal Plain (Malakhi Region)	1950	OẒ	800
Sedeh Warburg	Southern Sharon (Kefar Sava Region)	1938	IḤ	360
Sedeh Ya'akov	Jezreel Valley	1927	PM	530
Sedeh Yiẓḥak	Northern Sharon (Ḥaderah Region)	1952	TM	152
Sedeh Ẓevi	Northern Negev (Gerar Region)	1953	IḤ	300
Sedei Ḥemed	Southern Sharon (Kefar Sava Region)	1952	TM	274
Sedei Terumot	Beth-Shean Valley	1951	PM	480
Sedot Mikhah	Southern Judean Foothills	1955	TM	290
Segullah	Southern Coastal Plain (Malakhi Region)	1953	TM	235
Sha'ar Efrayim	Southern Sharon (Kefar Yonah Region)	1953	TM	491
Sha'ar Ḥefer	Central Sharon (Ḥefer Plain)	1940	IḤ	356
Shadmot Devorah	Eastern Lower Galilee	1939	TM	161
Shafir	Southern Coastal Plain (Malakhi Region)	1949	PM	241
Shaḥar	Southern Coastal Plain (Lachish Region)	1955	TM	355
Shalvah	Southern Coastal Plain (Lachish Region)	1952	PM	505
Sharonah	Eastern Lower Galilee	1938	TM	190
Sharsheret	Northwestern Negev (Gerar Region)	1951	PM	550
She'ar Yashuv	Ḥuleh Valley	1940	OẒ	oo
Shedemah	Coastal Plain (Reḥovot Region)	1954	IḤ	161
Shefer	Eastern Upper Galilee	1950	TM	259
Shetulah	Western Upper Galilee	1969	TM	oo
Shetulim	Southern Coastal Plain (Malakhi Region)	1950	TM	640
Shezor	Western Lower Galilee	1953	TM	345
Shibbolim	Northwestern Negev (Gerar Region)	1952	PM	402
Sho'evah	Judean Hills	1950	IḤ	190
Shokedah	Northwestern Negev (Gerar Region)	1957	PM	330
Shomerah	Northwestern Upper Galilee	1949	TM	268
Shuvah	Northwestern Negev (Gerar Region)	1950	PM	398
Sifsufah	Eastern Upper Galilee	1949	TM	480
Sitriyyah	Coastal Plain (Reḥovot Region)	1949	TM	404
Tal Shaḥar	Judean Foothills	1948	TM	401
Talmei Bilu	Northern Negev (Gerar Region)	1953	HI	270
Talmei Elazar	Northern Sharon (Ḥaderah Region)	1952	HI	200
Talmei Yeḥi'el	Southern Coastal Plain (Malakhi Region)	1949	TM	280
Ta'oz	Judean Foothills	1950	PM	380
Tarum	Judean Foothills	1950	PM	382
Te'ashur	Northern Negev (Gerar Region)	1953	TM	184
Tekumah	Northwestern Negev (Gerar Region)	1949	PM	234
Tel Adashim	Jezreel Valley	1923	TM	392
Telamim	Southern Coastal Plain (Lachish Region)	1950	TM	570
Tenuvot	Southern Sharon	1952	TM	570
Tidhar	Northern Negev (Gerar Region)	1953	TM	375
Tifraḥ	Northern Negev (Besor Region)	1949	PAI	361
Tirat Yehudah	Coastal Plain (Petaḥ Tikvah Region)	1949	PM	330
Tirosh	Southern Judean Foothills	1955	PM	520
Udim	Southern Sharon (Netanyah Region)	1948	IḤ	367
Uzzah	Southern Coastal Plain (Lachish Region)	1950	PM	715
Ya'arah	Western Upper Galilee	1950	TM	270
Yad Natan	Southern Coastal Plain (Lachish Region)	1953	OẒ	113
Yad Rambam	Coastal Plain (Lod Region)	1955	PM	565
Yagel	Coastal Plain (Lod Region)	1950	TM	377
Yakhini	Northwestern Negev	1950	TM	550
Yanuv	Southern Sharon (Kefar Yonah Region)	1950	TM	535
Yardenah	Beth-Shean Valley	1952	TM	oo
Yarḥiv	Southern Sharon (Kefar Sava Region)	1949	TM	520
Yarkonah	Southern Sharon (Kefar Sava Region)	1932	TM	110
Yashresh	Coastal Plain (Lod Region)	1950	TM	410
Yaẓiẓ	Coastal Plain (Lod Region)	1950	TM	605
Yedidyah	Central Sharon (Ḥefer Plain)	1935	TM	290
Yesha	Northwestern Negev (Besor Region)	1957	TM	160
Yinnon	Southern Coastal Plain (Malakhi Region)	1952	TM	615
Yish'i	Judean Foothills	1950	PM	510
Yoshivyah	Northwestern Negev (Besor Region)	1950	PM	246
Yuval	Ḥuleh Valley	1952	TM	oo
Ẓafririm	Southern Judean Foothills (Adullam Region)	1958	TM	194
Ẓafriyyah	Coastal Plain (Lod Region)	1949	PM	307
Ẓano'ah	Judean Foothills	1950	PAI	331
Zavdi'el	Southern Coastal Plain (Malakhi Region)	1950	PAI	411
Zeitan	Coastal Plain (Lod Region)	1950	TM	478
Zekharyah	Southern Judean Foothills	1950	TM	585
Zelafon	Judean Foothills	1950	TM	499
Zeraḥyah	Southern Coastal Plain (Malakhi Region)	1950	PM	460
Ẓerufah	Carmel Coast	1949	TM	430
Zeru'ah	Northwestern Negev (Gerar Region)	1953	PM	294
Zimrat	Northwestern Negev (Gerar Region)	1957	PM	412
Ẓippori	Western Lower Galilee	1949	TM	192
Ẓofit	Southern Sharon (Kefar Sava Region)	1933	TM	330
Zohar	Southern Coastal Plain (Lachish Region)	1956	IḤ	265
Ẓuri'el	Western Upper Galilee	1950	PAI	210
Ẓur Moshe	Southern Sharon (Kefar Yonah Regon)	1937	TM	415

Mosse, Rudolf (1843–1920), publisher, philanthropist. Founded Mosse publishing house in Berlin. Firm remained in family until seized by Nazis.

Mosse, George L. (1918–), U.S. historian. Taught at Iowa, Stanford, Wisconsin. Co-editor of *Journal of Contemporary History.* Principal interests 16th c. history, cultural history, and modern Germany, esp. Nazism and anti-Semitism.

Mosseri, Nissim (1848–1897), founder of Egyptian banking house. His son, **Jacques** (1884–1934), secured permission for S. Schechter to investigate Cairo *Genizah;* founded Egyptian Zionist Organization 1917. His cousin, **Albert** (1867–1933), began Zionist newspaper *Kadimah* in Cairo, later published weekly *Israel.*

Mossinsohn, Yigal (1917–), Israel author, playwright. Wrote novels, short stories, plays (incl. *Be-Arvot ha-Negev,* one of first Israel successes), thrillers, and children's stories, notably *Hasambah* series.

Mossinsohn, Benzion(1878–1942), Hebrew educator, Zionist leader; b. Russia. Opposed Herzl's Uganda Scheme. Head of Herzlia High School, Tel Aviv, 1912–41. Banished fr. Ereẓ Israel by Turks in WWI. Introduced "Bible criticism" into Jewish high schools.

Mossner, Walther von (1846–1932), German general; baptized. A.D.C. to William II and fr. 1903 governor of Strasbourg.

Mostel, Zero (Samuel Joel Mostel; 1915–), U.S. actor. Experienced comedian whose stage successes incl. *Ulysses in Nighttown,* Ionesco's *Rhinoceros, A Funny Thing Happened on the Way to the Forum,* and *Fiddler on the Roof.* Also appeared in movies.

Zero Mostel in role of Tevye in original production of "Fiddler on the Roof," New York, 1964.

Mosul, city in Iraq. Jews settled when Shalmaneser, king of Assyria 730–12 B.C.E., conquered Samaria. In 7th c. lived in "Jewish Quarter." Community grew in 12th c. and was headed by *nasi* and later by exilarch. In 14th c. Jews suffered fr. hordes of Tamerlane. Great yeshivah there. Jews remained poor and ignorant and all emigrated to Israel 1950–55.

Moszkowski, Moritz (1854–1925), pianist, composer. Compositions incl. piano pieces, orchestral works, and opera *Boabdil, der letzte Maurenkoenig.*

Motke Ḥabad (c. 1820–c. 1885), Lithuanian jester *(badḥan).* Most famous jester of Lithuania; master of biting witticisms directed against those with wealth and power. Collections of anecdotes were popular.

Mottl, Felix Josef (1856–1911), German conductor, composer. Court conductor at Karlsruhe 1881–1903; composed opera, lieder, and chamber music.

Leo Motzkin, caricature by Kagan, 1933.

Motzkin, Leo (Aryeh Leib; 1867–1933), Zionist leader; b. Russia. Criticized Ḥovevei Zion and their settlement methods in Ereẓ Israel as well as those of Baron Rothschild. Joined Democratic Fraction and was protagonist of struggle for Jewish rights in Diaspora. Director of Zionist bureau in Copenhagen during WWI. Headed Comité des Délégations Juives at Paris Peace Conference and active in Congress of National Minorities.

Mountain Jews (Tats), Jewish tribe in Soviet Dagestan and nearby Caucasus. Community in Derbent is mentioned in Talmud (3rd c. C.E.). Their language, Judeo-Tat, is derived fr. N. Iranian dialect. Community flourished in Middle Ages until 16th–17th c. Remained proud, courageous, though illiterate people until contact with Russians and Russian Jews in 19th c. Became active Zionists. Some literature written in language; spoken by 25,225 Jews as mother tongue (1959).

Mt. of Olives, winter, 1969.

Mount of Olives, Mt. (2,684 ft.) overlooking Jerusalem from the E. Its highest peak generally known as Mt. Scopus (site of Hebrew Univ. campus). Sacred to Jews for both historical and apocalyptic reasons and Jews aspired to be buried on its slopes. Also sacred to Christians (garden of Gethsemane on its lower slopes).

Mourning (Heb. *evel*). Following periods are distinguished: *aninut,* period fr. death until burial when no positive precepts are performed; *shivah,* period of seven days after burial when bereaved normally remain in their homes, and bathing, etc. are forbidden; *sheloshim,* period until 30 days after burial when it is forbidden to cut hair or marry; and period until 12 months after death when limited mourning for parents and children continues. In all other cases mourning ceases after 30 days. Among Reform Jews either one or three days are observed and most other customs are curtailed or modified.

Moyal, Abraham, see Muyal, Avraham.

Moza or **(ha-) Mozah,** town in Benjamin (Jos. 18:26). In modern times first rural site in Ereẓ Israel acquired by Jews for farming purposes 1859. Small village founded on site 1894. One of first industrial enterprises (tile factory) in country located there. Moẓa Illit founded 1933 as adjacent moshav. Combined pop. 444 (1971).

Moznayim, literary organ of Hebrew Writers' Association in Israel; founded 1929.

Muehsam, Erich (1878–1934), German poet, playwright, anarchist. Founded anarchist periodicals. Imprisoned several times. Killed by Nazis.

Muelhausen, Yom Tov Lipmann (14th–15th c.), scholar, polemist, philosopher, halakhic authority, kabbalist, rabbi in Bohemia.

Appointed *Judex Judaeorum* ("judge of Jews") 1407 and traveled in Austria, Bohemia, and Poland to correct religious practices. Engaged frequently in polemics with Christians in Prague. His *Sefer ha-Nizzaḥon* was famous anti-Christian polemical work. His familiarity with both Kabbalah and philosophy helped make these topics respectable in Poland.

Mueller, David Heinrich (1846–1912), orientalist; taught at Vienna Univ. Wrote on S. Arabian inscriptions and comparative studies of Semitic languages.

°**Mueller, Heinrich** (1900– ?), last chief of Gestapo. Joined SS and SD (secret police) 1933 and Nazi Party 1939. A key figure in "final solution," and participated in the Wannsee Conference. Disappeared at end of war.

Jewish street in Mukachevo on the Sabbath.

Mueller, Joel (1827–1895), rabbinical scholar, authority on geonic texts. Taught at Berlin Hochschule fuer die Wissenschaft des Judentums; published many texts, mainly geonic responsa.

Mueller-Cohen, Anita (1890–1962), social worker; b.Vienna. Devoted herself to wide range of relief work. Member of Vienna City Council. Settled in Tel Aviv 1936.

°**Muenster, Sebastian (Munsterus;** 1489–1552), German Hebraist, reformer. Member of Franciscan order who became Protestant. His *Hebraica Biblia* was first Protestant translation of Bible fr. Hebrew into Latin.

Muensterberg, Hugo (1863–1916), psychologist; b. Danzig; baptized. Taught at Harvard fr. 1892. Original thinker in many fields of psychology and forerunner of fundamentalist school.

Paul Muni (front left) with his wife, Bella Finkle, and Tel Aviv mayor Israel Rokach, 1938.

Muenz (Minz), Moses ben Isaac ha-Levi (c.1750–1831), Hungarian rabbi. Appointed by government chief rabbi of Pest region. At first tolerant of Reform but later took strong opposing stand. His son **Joseph** published his father's responsa *Sefer Maharam Minz*.

Mufti of Jerusalem, see Husseini, Hāj Amin Al-.

Muhr, Abraham (1781–1847), leader of Silesian Jewry. Opposed extreme reforms in liturgy but favored sermons in German. Became advocate of Reform.

Mukachevo (Munkács), city in Ukrainian SSR. Jews settled in 17th c., community established 1741. Renowned for extreme conservatism and inclination toward Ḥasidism. 11,261 Jews in 1930. City *judenrein* by 1944. 1,000–2,000 Jews in 1970.

Mukdoni, A. (pseud. of **Alexander Kappel;** 1877–1958), Yiddish essayist, theater critic; b. Belorussia, in U.S. fr. 1922. Wrote memoirs, stories, essays.

Mukẓeh (Heb.), term for objects which it is forbidden to handle on Sabbath or festivals for variety of reasons, such as connection with forbidden work (e.g. money, tools) or inaccessibility at commencement of Sabbath (e.g. fallen fruit).

Mulder, Samuel Israel (1792–1862), Amersterdam educator, Hebrew author. Principal of *bet ha-midrash,* secretary of Amsterdam community, superintendent of all Dutch religious schools. Translated Bible and *Haggadah* into Dutch and published Hebrew-Dutch dictionary.

Muller, Herman Joseph (1890–1967), U.S. geneticist. Taught in U.S., Soviet Union, Edinburgh. Central theme of work changes in relatively stable gene material of chromosome. Nobel Prize 1946 for demonstration that X-rays induce mutations.

Mult és Jövö, Hungarian-language Jewish literary and artistic monthly; appeared 1911–44.

Muni, Paul (Muni Weisenfreund; 1895–1967), U.S. actor. Fr. Yiddish theater he went to Broadway and Hollywood, achieving fame in films, incl. *Scarface, The Story of Louis Pasteur* (winning Oscar), *The Good Earth, The Life of Emile Zola,* and plays, incl. *Inherit the Wind.*

Munich, capital of Bavaria, S. Germany. Jews fr. 13th c. 128 burnt after blood libel 1285. Community annihilated in Black Death. Excluded mid-15th to 18th c. Modern community organized 1816. Jews prominent in cultural life 19th and 20th c. Numbered 10,000 in 1933. Hotbed of anti-Semitic activity and cradle of Nazi party. Only 160 Jews in city by 1945. New community founded 1945 and numbered 3,590 in 1971.

Munk, Ezra (1867–1940), Orthodox rabbi of Adass Yisroel congregation in Berlin, adviser to Prussian Ministry of Education and Religious Affairs. Made local office for *sheḥitah* international center for its defense. Active in Agudat Israel. Published responsa. Fr. 1938 in Jerusalem. His nephew **Elie** (b.1900), rabbi in Paris. Author of *The World of Prayer*, commentary on prayer book, and French translation of Rashi's Pentateuch commentary.

Munk, Hermann (1839–1912), German physiologist. Pioneer in field of cerebral physiology.

Munk, Solomon (1803–1867), French orientalist. At time of Damascus Affair 1840, accompanied Crémieux to Egypt as his secretary. In charge of Semitic mss. at Bibliothèque Nationale, prof. at Collège de France. Translated Solomon ibn Gabirol's *Fons Vitae* into French, and was first to identify Gabirol as its author. Published Arabic text of Maimonides' *Guide of the Perplexed.*

Munkács, see Mukachevo.

Munkácsi, Bernát (Bernard; 1860–1937), Hungarian philologist, ethnographer, studied small language groups in Russia. Wrote on Magyar culture and linguistics. Active in Jewish education in Budapest. His son, **Ernö** (1896–1950), jurist, writer on general and Jewish art. Published underground manifesto during WWII revealing details of Holocaust.

Muqaddam, Arabic word for leader of army or community. Used in N. African countries to designate leader of Jewish community.

POLAND
Cracow, Museum of the History and Culture of the Jews in Poland, est. 1961
Jewish ritual art, paintings of Jewish life and types by Jewish artists

U.S.S.R.
Vilna State Museum
Jewish art-remnant of the YIVO museum (est. 1930). Ritual objects

Lvov Museum of Ethnography and Applied Art
Jewish folk art of eastern Galicia, formerly in the Lvov Museum for Jewish Art (est. 1925)

Moscow, Lenin Library
Baron David Guenzberg Collection of manuscripts and early printed books

Leningrad, Public Library
Antonin and Firkowitsch Collections of Hebrew illuminated manuscripts from the Cairo Genizah

Leningrad, Oriental Institute
Friedlander Collection. Hebrew illuminated manuscripts

Leningrad State Museum for the Ethnography of the People of the U.S.S.R.
Part of the ethnographic collection of the Jewish Historical and Ethnographic Society (founded 1908); Literary evidence and folk art objects from Russia, Ukraine, and Siberia

Leningrad, Saltykov-Shchedrin Public Library
Part of the ethnographic collections of the Jewish Historical and Ethnographic Society (founded 1908); it also includes the archive of Mendele Mokher Seforim

CZECHOSLOVAKIA
Prague Jewish Museum (founded 1906)
One of the largest collections in the world of Jewish ritual objects and two synagogues, the Altneuschul, dating from 1270 and Pinkas schul remodeled in 1625.

HUNGARY
Budapest Jewish Museum (founded 1932)
Objects of Jewish life in Hungary from Roman times to the present

Budapest, Hungarian Academy of Sciences
David Kaufmann Collection. Genizah fragments and Hebrew illuminated manuscripts

YUGOSLAVIA
Beograd Jewish Historical Museum, opened 1960
Objects of Jewish life in Yugoslavia from Roman times to the Holocaust

Sarajevo Museum of the History of the Jews, opened 1966
Exhibits of the history of the Sephardi Jews in Bosnia and Herzegovina

Dubrovnik (Ragusa) Synagogue, built in 1652
Sephardi ritual objects

ENGLAND
London Jewish Museum, founded 1932
English-made, European, and Eastern ritual objects from 16th to 19th c.

London, British Museum
Israelite and Jewish objects from excavations in Palestine. The largest collection of Hebrew illuminated manuscripts (some exhibited) in the world

London, Bevis Marks Synagogue of the Sephardim, built by Joseph Avis in 1701

Oxford, Bodleian Library
Hebrew illuminated manuscripts

Cambridge, University Library
Hebrew illuminated manuscripts

Leeds, University Library
Cecil Roth collection of Hebrew illuminated manuscripts

London, Museum of the Jewish Historical Society, University College
Documents (Stars) of Anglo-Jewish history

Ben Uri Gallery
Modern paintings and works of art

FRANCE
Paris, Cluny Museum
Strauss-Rothschild collection. Ritual objects and Hebrew illuminated manuscripts (not exhibited).

Paris, Musée d'Art Juif, est. 1948
Jewish folk art from Europe and North Africa and paintings of the Paris school

Paris, Musée Carnavalet
Judaica collections concerning the Paris community containing some medieval tombstones, souvenirs of the actress Rachel (Elsa Felix)

Paris, Musée National des Thermes
Collection of Judaica (not exhibited)

Bayonne, Musée Basque
Portuguese-Jewish secular and religious objects

Carpentras, Musée Comtadin
Ritual objects, seals and medals in the 14th-cent. synagogue (rebuilt in 1741)

Cavaillon, Musée Judes-Comtadin
Ritual objects and tombstones in the 15th-cent. synagogue (rebuilt 1772–4)

Nancy, Musée Historique Lorrain
Some ritual objects

Strasbourg, Musée Alsacien
Collection of the Société d'histoire des Israélites d'Alsace et de Lorraine. Ritual objects and historical documents

Paris, Louvre
Israelite and Jewish objects excavated in the Middle East. Oriental Jewish art

Paris, Bibliothèque Nationale
Hebrew illuminated manuscripts

Paris, Cemetery of Montrouge (Gabriel Péri)
Ashkenazi Jews from 1735 to 1809

Paris, Memorial of the Unknown Jewish Martyr
Center of Contemporary Jewish Documentation (since 1943)

HOLLAND
Amsterdam, Joods Historisch Museum
Collections of the Portuguese and Ashkenazi communities of Holland. Ritual objects and historical documents

Amsterdam, Stedelijk Museum
Judaica collection

Amsterdam Portuguese Synagogue, built in 1675
Judaica collection and early printed books

DENMARK
Copenhagen Jewish Museum
Ritual objects

SWITZERLAND
Basle, Judisches Museum der Schweitz, (est. 1966)
Jewish life and customs, ritual objects

SWEDEN
Goteborg Municipal Museum
Jewish section with ritual objects and Jewish documents

ITALY
Rome (main synagogue)
Ancient treasures of the Italian community, ritual objects, documents

Rome, Musio Nasionale delle Terme
Jewish objects of the Roman period

Ostia Antica near Rome
Synagogue of the 4th cent.

Rome Via Nomentana
Catacombs of the 3rd and 4th cent.

Rome Via Appia Artica
Catacombs of the 3rd and 4th cent.

Rome, Vatican Library and Museum
Jewish objects of the Roman period. Hebrew illuminated manuscripts

Rome, Trastevere (Vicolo dell' Atleta)
Medieval synagogue

Rome, Museo Capitolino
Roman and Medieval Jewish tombstones

Rome Mausoleum Fosse Ardeatine to the martyrs of the Nazi massacre on March 24, 1944. In a stone quarry between the Catacombs of Domitilla and S. Callisto

Florence, New Synagogue of 1882
Collection of ritual objects and Jewish documents

Venice, five existing synagogues in the oldest ghetto in Europe
Of the 17th cent. All on the second floors of ordinary houses, in the largest, Scuola Spagnola, the collection of ritual objects and documents of the community

SPAIN

Toledo Sephardic Museum (est. 1965)
Gravestones with Hebrew inscriptions. Ritual objects

Toledo synagogues of Sta Maria La Blanca (from c. 1200) and El Transito (c. 1357)

Toledo Museo Arqueologico
Jewish life in Spain up to 1492

Barcelona Museo Historico
Jewish life in Spain up to 1492

Barcelona Museo National
Jewish life in Spain up to 1492

Cordova, synagogue dated 1315

U.S.A.

New York Jewish Museum
One of the largest collections of ritual objects, medals and coins, incorporating the collection of the Jewish Museum of Danzig

New York, Jewish Theological Seminary
Hebrew illuminated manuscripts

Cincinnati, Hebrew Union College
Hebrew illuminated manuscripts

Los Angeles, Hebrew Union College, Skirball Museum
Collection of Sally Kirschtein of Berlin, and other objects of ritual art and archaeological excavations

Chicago, Hebrew Theological College Museum
Ritual art

Washington, D.C., Adas Israel
Ritual art objects

Chicago, The Spertus Museum of Judaica
Ritual art and modern Jewish art

Los Angeles, Judah L. Magnes Memorial Museum
Ritual art objects and Jewish documents

Los Angeles, Temple Sinai Museum
Ritual art objects

Philadelphia, Kneseth Israel Jewish Museum
Ritual art objects

Cleveland, Temple Shalom
Ritual art objects

CANADA

Montreal, Quebec National Museum of Congress (opened 1970)
Ritual art objects and documents of Jewish history

Montreal, Temple Emanuel Museum

Toronto, Beth Tzedec Congregation Museum
Cecil Roth collection of ritual art objects

MEXICO

Mexico City, Jewish Historical Museum
Jewish past in Eastern Europe, Jewish contribution to Mexico

DUTCH WEST INDIES

Willemstad, Curaçao Jewish Historical Cultural Museum
Historical documents and objects

ARGENTINA

Buenos Aires, Arat Gallery at YIVO
Works of Maurice Minkowski (Eastern European Jewish life)

SOUTH AFRICA

Johannesburg, Board of Deputies
Jewish religious art, Jewish Africana, library of Jewish information, and archives relating to South African Jewry.

Cape Town, the "Old" Synagogue
Jewish Museum

ISRAEL

Jerusalem, Israel Museum, opened 1965
Consists of four main divisions:

The Bezalel National Art Museum (founded 1936)
Jewish and general art, ritual objects, Hebrew illuminated manuscripts, Jewish art objects salvaged from the Holocaust, three reconstructed synagogues;

The Samuel Bronfman Biblical and Archaeological Museum
antiquities of Ereẓ Israel and other cultures;

The Billy Rose Art Garden
sculpture;

The Shrine of the Book
repository for the Dead Sea Scrolls and Bar Kokhba letters

Jerusalem, Schocken Institute
Hebrew illuminated manuscripts and printed books

Jerusalem, YMCA
Herbert Klark Collection of Archaeology

Jerusalem, National and University Library
Hebrew illuminated manuscripts and printed books

Jerusalem, Italian Synagogue
Italian ritual objects in a reconstructed synagogue of Vitorio Veneto

Jerusalem, Rockefeller Museum, founded 1927
Archaeology of Ereẓ Israel, from prehistory to the Turkish period

Jerusalem, Institutum Pontificum Biblicum, founded 1927
Archaeology of Ereẓ Israel

Jerusalem, Herzl Museum
Reconstruction of Herzl's study, his works and documents

Jerusalem, Museum of religious objects, Dor Vador Museum in Hechal Shlomo (Chief Rabbinate)
Ritual art objects

Tel Aviv Museum
Including Dizengoff House (1932) and Helena Rubinstein Pavilion (1958) — modern art (Israel and others)

Tel Aviv, Bialik House
Ḥ.N. Bialik's study and documents

Tel Aviv, Ha-Areẓ Museum
Including museums of glass, ceramics, numismatics, ethnography and folklore, science and technology (including a planetarium), antiquities of Jaffa and Tel Qasile excavations, alphabet, history of Tel Aviv

Tel Aviv, Haganah Museum
History and documents of the Haganah

Tel Aviv, Jabotinsky Museum
History and documents of the Revisionist movement, Trumpeldor, Nili, and Jabotinsky

MOSES Moses receiving the Tablets of the Law, while the Israelites stand behind the fenced Mount Sinai. An illustration to the mishnaic tractate *Avot* from the *Rothschild Siddur*, Florence, 1492.

PASSOVER *Seder* dish by Isaac Cohen, Padua, 1673. Faience. The Hebrew text gives the sanctification prayer (*kiddush*) and the order of the *seder* service.

Tel Aviv, Medicine Museum
History of Medicine, especially Jewish

Haifa, Museum of Modern Art
Modern, general and Israeli art, graphics and sculptures

Haifa, Museum of Ethnology and Folklore
Jewish ritual art, folk art of Jews and Israel Arabs

Haifa, Prehistorical Museum
Prehistorical finds from the Carmel and North

Haifa Musical Museum and Emili Library
Popular musical instruments, photographs and documents of
musical history in Israel, Fridman-Levov archive of Jewish
music

Haifa Municipal Museum of Ancient Art
Archaeological finds and Shikmonah excavations

Haifa Maritime Museum
History of navigation, and archaeological finds

Haifa, Museum of Japanese Art
Felix Tikotin collection of prints, ceramics and applied
Japanese art

Haifa, "Dagon"
Grain museum — cultivation and storage of grain throughout
the ages. Archaeological finds

Beth-Shean, Municipal Museum
Archaeological finds and mosaics of the ancient city

Kibbutz Nir David
Museum of Mediterranean archaeology

Ein Harod, Mishkan le-Omanut, founded 1933
Jewish art, ritual art objects, Israeli art including Ḥayyim
Atar's works

Ein Harod, Beit Sturman
History and archaeology of the region

Kibbutz Ha-Zorea, Wilfrid Israel House
Mediterranean and Far East art and archaeological finds from
the village fields

Kibbutz Dan, Bet Ussishkin
Natural history of the Ḥuleh region and Tel Dan excavations

Ayyelet ha-Shaḥar, Sam and Ayala Zacks Museum
Excavations of Hazor

Kibbutz Sedot Yam
Antiquities of Caesarea

Safed Museum of Print
Incunabula, books, ex libris and printing archives

Massada
Excavations of Massada

Bar'am Synagogue
Synagogue of 5th century

En-Gedi
Excavations of En-Gedi

Kibbutz Ḥanitah
Archaeological finds of Ḥanitah. History of "Stockade and
Tower"

Arad
Excavations of Arad

Kibbutz Ḥefzi Bah
6th cent. mosaics of synagogue of Beth Alpha

Eilat Municipal Museum
Museum of modern art and maritime museum

Tiberias Municipal Museum
History of Tiberias from Roman times to present

Beersheba, Negev Museum
Archaeological finds of the Negev. Ethnology collection

Jerusalem, Yad Va-Shem
Holocaust

Kibbutz Lohamei ha-Getta'ot
Holocaust documents, Warsaw ghetto uprising

Kibbutz Yad Mordekhai
Holocaust

Bat-Yam, Ryback House
Works of Issachar Ber Ryback (1897—1935)

Bat-Yam, Asch House
Archives and Books of Shalom Asch

Kibbutz Kefar Menahem
Archaeological finds and modern art

Kibbutz Ma'agan Michael
Underwater archaeological finds

Acre, Municipal Museum
Archaeological finds. Arab ethnology

Acre, Museum of Valor
Documents and objects concerning fight against British
Mandate

Petaḥ Tikvah, Yad la-Banim House
Archaeological finds. History of Petaḥ Tikvah

Bet She'arim, Kiryat Tiv'on
Jewish catacombs of 2nd c. and museum

Reḥovot, Weizmann Archives
Documents and objects concerning Chaim Weizmann

Kibbutz Sha'ar ha-Golan
Prehistorical finds of Yarmuk culture

Murabba'at, wadi leading to W. shore of Dead Sea where mss. were discovered, 1951—55. Main finds were belongings of Bar Kokhba's guerilla fighters who had taken refuge in caves in the vicinity.

Murmelstein, Benjamin (1905—), rabbi, scholar, public figure of Holocaust period. Rabbi in Vienna; associated with S. Krauss in preparing supplement to Kohut's *Arukh ha-Shalem.* Appointed head of Theresienstadt Jewish council by Nazis 1943; became hated and feared.

Later settled in Rome, taking no part in communal life.

Musaf (Heb.), "additional" sacrifice offered in Temple on Sabbaths and festivals. Later usual designation for additional prayer recited on those days. *Amidah* follows same pattern as other services on Sabbaths and festivals, but includes references to sacrifices and sometimes special prayers, e.g. prayers for rain are added on last day of Sukkot and dew on first day of Passover. In Reform congregations modified or abolished.

Musar Movement, movement developed in late 19th c. for education of individual toward strict ethical behavior in spirit of *halakhah*. Inspired by Israel Lipkin (Salanter), penetrated into yeshivot in Lithuania. Study of ethical works, as well as lectures on ethical problems, became integral part of Lithuanian type of yeshivot. Special scholar was appointed to supervise this study and by example and precept to stress its importance and strengthen connection bet. learning and behavior.

Muselmann, Nazi camp slang for prisoners on edge of death.

°**Musolini, Benedetto** (1809–1885), Italian statesman who foretold return of Jews to Ereẓ Israel. Suggested that Britain support establishment of Jewish principality under Turkish Crown.

Mussafia, Adolfo (1834–1905), Italian philologist; converted. Did research on Romance and Italian dialects, esp. in medieval texts. Member of senate.

Mussafia, Benjamin ben Immanuel (1606–1675), rabbi, philologist, physician; of Marrano descent; probably b. Spain. Became personal physician to Christian IV of Denmark, moved to Amsterdam and was member of *bet ha-midrash* "Keter Torah"; signed eulogy in support of Shabbetai Ẓevi. Wrote supplement to dictionary *Arukh* of Nathan b. Jehiel.

Musta'rab, Arab-speaking old established Jewish communities in Middle East; member of such community.

Muszkat, Marion (1915–), jurist. Headed Polish military delegation at Nuremberg trials. Prof. of international law at Univ. of Warsaw. Emigrated to Israel 1957. Prof. at Tel Aviv Univ.

Mutnik, Abraham (pseud. **Gleb;** 1868–1930), cofounder of Bund; b. Lithuania. Drafted first proclamation of Bund. Arrested several times and exiled. After WWI lived in Germany.

Muyal, Abraham (1847–1885), public figure in Ereẓ Israel; b. Morocco, settled in Ereẓ Israel 1860. Close ties with Turkish government circles, helped purchase land for Jewish settlement, and represented Ḥovevei Zion in country.

Myer, Morris (1876–1944), Yiddish editor, Zionist worker; b. Rumania, in England fr. 1902. Founded Yiddish Daily *Die Zeit* (1913–1950), which was the chief molder of opinion among masses of Yiddish readers in England.

Myers, Sir Arthur Melziner (1867–1926), New Zealand statesman. Mayor of Auckland 1905–09. Cabinet minister 1912–19.

Myers, Asher Isaac (1848–1902), British journalist. Edited and managed *Jewish Chronicle* for more than 20 years.

Myers, Charles Samuel (1873–1946), British psychologist. Pioneer of experimental and applied and industrial psychology. First to recognize that shell shock was primarily psychological condition. Editor of *British Journal of Psychology,* pres. British Psychology Society 1920.

Myers, Lawrence E. (Lon; 1858–1899), U.S. track athlete. During 1870s–80s won many U.S., Canadian, and British track titles, setting world marks. First man to better 50 seconds for 440 yards.

Myers, Sir Michael (1873–1950), lawyer, chief justice of New Zealand 1929–46. Active in Jewish affairs.

Myers, Mordecai (1776–1871), U.S. merchant, army officer, politician. Served in War of 1812, attaining rank of major. Democratic assemblyman in N.Y. state legislature 1931–34, mayor of Schenectady in 1850s.

Myers, Moses (1752–1835), U.S. merchant, civic leader in Norfolk, Va. Leading merchant south of Potomac. His home is landmark.

Myers, Myer (1723–1795), U.S. silversmith; b. N.Y. Successful craftsman and businessman; active in Jewish life. Chairman of Gold and Silversmiths' Society of N.Y. Created first American examples of Jewish ceremonial objects.

"Rimmonim" by Myer Myers for Mikveh Israel Synagogue, Philadelphia.

Letter "N" as part of illuminated word "In" at the beginning of the Book of Esther in a 12th-cent. Latin Bible.

Naaman (9th c.B.C.E.), Syrian commander. Healed of leprosy by prophet Elisha (II Kings 5).
Naar, David (1800–1880), U.S. politician, journalist. Mayor of Elizabeth, N.J. 1849. Edited daily newspaper fr. 1853, which espoused cause of South. Treasurer of N.J.
Naarah, town in Jordan valley, N. of Jericho. Ruins of synagogue with mosaic pavement fr. 6th c. uncovered there.
Nabal, wealthy first husband of Abigail. David extended protection to his flocks but Nabal refused to help him later. Abigail dissuaded David fr. taking revenge. After his death, Abigail married David (I Sam. 25).
Nabateans, Semitic people who established kingdom in territory of Edom in Transjordan. Relations with Jews became close with rise of Hasmonean dynasty. After Herod's death assisted Romans who marched against Judea. Ruled Negev, where remains of their cities are to be found (Avedat, Mamshit, and, in Transjordan, Petra). Romans deprived them of political independence early in 2nd c. C.E. but they maintained their own culture until Byzantines Christianized area.
Nablus (orig. **Neopolis;** Heb. **Shechem**), city in Ereẓ Israel, founded by Vespasian 72 C.E. bet. Mt. Ebal and Mt. Gerizim nr. biblical Shechem (q.v.). Christianity took root early in city and by 314 it had bishop. Fr. Byzantine times center of Samaritans. Conquered 636 by Arabs. In Six-Day War 1967 taken by Israel. Pop. (incl. neighboring villages and refugee camps) 70,000 (1967).
Naboth, owner of vineyard close to palace of King Ahab of Israel. After his refusal to sell vineyard to Ahab, his wife, Jezebel, engineered his execution. Elijah rebuked king for deed (I Kings 21).
Nachmanovich, wealthy family in Lvov, Poland. **Isaac b. Naḥman** (d. 1595), *dayyan* of Lvov and *parnas* of Council of the Four Lands. Built magnificent Turei Zahav synagogue. His son **Naḥman Isaakovich** (d. 1616) took over father's tax-farming and moneylending business. Leader of Lvov community.
Nadab, eldest son of Aaron, brother of Abihu (q.v.). Perished with his brother.
Nadab, king of Israel 907–6 B.C.E. Fought against Philistines. Assassinated together with all his family by Baasha.
Nadaf, Abraham Ḥayyim (1866–1940), Yemenite community leader; b. Yemen, settled in Ereẓ Israel 1891. Emissary many times to Egypt, Yemen, and Turkey. Published first bibliography of works of Yemenite scholars.
Nadel, Arno (1878–1943), poet, liturgical musicologist; b. Lithuania, in Germany fr. 1895. Did much to collect and study synagogue music. Murdered in Auschwitz; most of his papers lost.
Nadel, Siegfred Frederick (1903–1956), British anthropologist. Prof. at Durham, then Australian National Univ. fr. 1950. Sought to identify conceptual systems of social anthropology and sociology with psychological framework.

"Circus Woman," bronze by Elie Nadelman, c. 1924.

Aerial view of Nabatean city of Avedat.

Nablus as seen from Mt. Gerizim, with Mt. Ebal in background.

Nadelman, Elie (1882–1946). U.S. sculptor; b. Warsaw, worked in Paris. Regarded himself as father of cubism. Emigrated to U.S. in WWI, achieved success in portrait busts. Assembled one of finest collections of American folk art. Last years lived in obscurity. Rediscovered posthumously.
Naḍīr (Arab. **Banu Naḍīr**), one of three main Jewish tribes in ancient Medina; exiled by Muhammad 626.

Going on guard at the Naḥal settlement of Gerofit in the Arabah, 1964.

The square of Nahariyyah, looking toward the municipality building.

Nadir, Moshe (pseud. of **Isaac Reis;** 1885–1943), Yiddish poet, humorist; b. Galicia, in U.S. fr. 1898. Co-edited Yiddish humorous journals. Became adherent of Communism but was later disillusioned.

Naftali, Pereẓ (Fritz; 1888–1961), economist, writer, labor leader; b. Germany. Leading German economist and pioneer of "economic democracy." Settled in Ereẓ Israel 1933. Director of Bank Hapoalim 1937–49. Cabinet minister 1951–55, 1959.

Nagel, Ernest (1901–), U.S. philosopher. Pres. Assoc. of Symbolic Logic and Philosophy of Science. Known for incisive and learned essays on philosophy of science.

Nagid (Heb., pl. *negidim*), head of Jewish community in Islamic and some Christian countries in Middle Ages. Fr. 10th c. in Spain, Kairouan, Egypt, Yemen, and later Morocco, Algeria, Tunisia. Descendants of Maimonides had title in Egypt for several generations.

Naḥal (Heb. abbr. for *Noar Ḥaluẓi Loḥem;* "Fighting Pioneer Youth") regular unit of Israel Defense Forces whose soldiers are organized in *garinim* ("groups") of pioneering youth movements in Israel that educate their members toward co-operative agricultural settlement in Israel.

Nahalal, first moshav ovedim in Ereẓ Israel; founded 1926 in W. Jezreel Valley. One of principal centers of Tenu'at ha-Moshavim. Pop. 1,050 (1971).

Naḥalat Yehudah, urban community in Israel coastal plain nr. Rishon le-Zion; founded 1914 as moshavah. Pop. 2,350 (1971).

Nahariyyah, city on N. Israel coast; founded 1934 as moshavah by immigrants fr. Germany. Resort with local industry. Pop. 23,000 (1971).

Nahash, Amorite king. Defended in battle by Saul but ally of David.

Nah'āwendī, Benjamin ben Moses al- (9th c.), Persian Karaite scholar, judge. Learned in rabbinic lore, wrote in Hebrew. Established Karaite doctrines. Compiled books of precepts and laws that became part of Karaite law. Also wrote biblical commentaries.

Naḥman ben Isaac (d.c.356), Babylonian *amora,* head of *kallah* in academy of Rava, taught in Drukeret. After Rava's death joined academy of Pumbedita. Frequently quoted in Babylonian Talmud.

Naḥman ben Jacob (d.c.320), Babylonian *amora,* leading personality of era; usually referred to as R. Naḥman. Married into family of exilarch, taught and was *dayyan* in Nehardea. One of most frequently quoted authorities in Babylonian Talmud; also appears in Jerusalem Talmud. In any dispute with colleague, his view prevailed.

Naḥmanides (Moses b. Naḥman; Ramban; 1194–1270), Spanish rabbi, talmudist, philosopher, kabbalist, exegete, poet, communal leader; lived in Gerona, probably chief rabbi of Catalonia. Leading Jewish spokesman in 1263 Disputation of Barcelona (q.v.). His dignified stand won approval of king but incurred wrath of church as result of which he had to leave Spain. Went to Ereẓ Israel 1267, organizing Jewish community and exercising considerable influence fr. Acre. His biblical commentary, conveying his philosophical ideas, has remained widely studied and is printed in rabbinic Bibles. Wrote novellae on talmudic tractates as well as halakhic monographs. His kabbalistic knowledge is woven into his biblical commentaries and his *Sha'ar ha-Gemul.*

Naḥman (ben Simḥah) of Bratslav (1772–1811), ḥasidic *ẓaddik* in Podolia and Ukraine. Visited Ereẓ Israel 1798. Quarreled with most outstanding *Ẓaddikim* of his time; his type of Ḥasidim became popular after his death through activities of his disciple Nathan Sternhartz, who published his works. Faith, whereby man can transcend his doubts, is held to be essential, and *ẓaddik* regarded as possessing soul of Messiah. Prayer was highly developed in his doctrine, as was music. Main center of his Ḥasidim today in Jerusalem with guide but no formal leader.

Naḥman of Horodenka (d. 1780), disciple of Israel Ba'al Shem Tov, grandfather of Naḥman of Bratslav. Occupied himself with practical questions of divine worship. Emigrated to Ereẓ Israel 1764, settled in Tiberias.

Naḥman of Kosov (d.1746), kabbalist, one of early Ḥasidim; associated with group in Kutow. At first opposed Israel Ba'al Shem Tov but even when recognizing his authority retained his own religious independence. One of first to introduce Lurian prayer rite. Accused by Jacob Emden of being Shabbatean.

Naḥmias, ibn (15th–16th c.), family of Hebrew printers who published works in Constantinople after leaving Spain.

Nahor, son of Serug, father of Terah, grandfather of Abraham. His grandson, Abraham's brother, had same name. There is also mention of city of Nahor (Gen. 24:10).

Nahoum, Ḥaim (1872–1960), rabbi; b. Turkey. Appointed by "Young Turks" chief rabbi of Ottoman Empire 1908; intervened in favor of Jews, prevented Jews fr. being expelled fr. Jerusalem during WWI. Chief rabbi of Egypt 1925, member of its senate 1931.

Nahshon, son of Amminadab, chieftain of tribe of Judah. Elisheba, his sister, married Aaron. Acc. to *aggadah,* only Israelite who, on reaching Red Sea, had courage to obey Moses and enter waves.

Nahshon bar Zadok, *gaon* of Sura 871–79. Author of many responsa. Discovered *Iggul de-R. Nahshon* – that Jewish calendar repeats itself exactly every 247 years.

Nahum, 7th of 12 Minor Prophets. Almost nothing is known about him. Book composed shortly after fall of Nineveh 612 B.C.E. Has character of prophetic curse pronounced against enemy.

Nahum of Gimzo (1st–2nd c. C.E.), *tanna;* probably came fr. Gimzo in Ereẓ Israel, although appellation said to have arisen fr. habit of saying *gam zo le-tova* ("this too is for the best"). Teacher of R. Akiva.

Naḥutei, see Neḥutei.

Naiditsch, Isaac Asher (1868–1949), philanthropist, Zionist; b. Russia. Successful industrialist. Active Zionist; supported Hebrew writers and donated large sums for promoting Hebrew culture. Settled in France. Suggested idea of Keren Hayesod; one of its first directors.

Najara, Israel ben Moses (1555?–1625?), Hebrew poet; son of Moses Najara. Rabbi of Gaza. Wrote hundreds of poems in polished style distinguished by deep religiosity and yearning for redemption. Author of Sabbath table hymn *Yah Ribbon Olam ve-Alemayya.*

Najara, Moses (1508?–1581), rabbi, kabbalist of Damascus, Safed; student of Isaac Luria. Wrote *Lekaḥ Tov,* commentary on Torah.

Najdorf, Mikhail (1910–), Argentinian chess grandmaster. Remarkable for playing 40 blindfold games simultaneously.

Nakdimon ben Guryon (1st c.C.E.), wealthy citizen of Jerusalem. With fall of Jerusalem lost wealth, and his daughter was seen picking barley corns fr. cattle dung.

Naményi, Ernest (Ernö; 1888–1957), Hungarian art historian, economist, writer. Wrote on history of Hungarian synagogues, Jewish art, etc. Director and chairman of Jewish museum in Budapest. Fr. 1949 in France.

Bronze medal commemorating Napoleon's Sanhedrin, dated May 30, 1806.

Territory of the tribe of Naphtali.

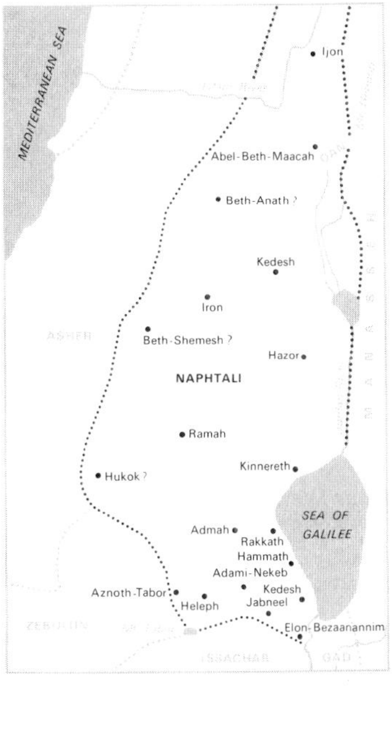

Namier (Bernstein-Namierowski), Sir Lewis (1888–1960), English historian, Zionist; b. Galicia, in England fr. 1908. After service in WWI in British Intelligence, devoted himself to Zionism. Prof. at Manchester. Kept aloof fr. Zionist parties, but played major role in Jewish Agency's relations with British government. Historical interests were social-political structure of England in 18th c., twilight of Hapsburg monarchy, crisis before WWII.

Namir, Mordekhai (1897–), Israel labor leader; b. Ukraine, settled in Ereẓ Israel 1924. Held various posts in labor movement. Israel's ambassador to USSR 1949–50. Mapai member of Knesset, secretary-general of Histadrut 1951–55, minister of labor 1956-59, first labor mayor of Tel Aviv 1959–69. Wife, **Ora,** member of Knesset fr. 1974.

Nancy, town in France. Jews settled 1341, 1455, expelled fr. duchy 1477. Reappeared 1595, founded banks; consistory established 1808. 3,800 Jews in 1939; many fled, remainder deported during WWII. 3,000 Jews in 1971.

Naomi, one of main figures in Book of Ruth; wife of Elimelech of Beth-Lehem, mother-in-law of Ruth, who accompanied her back to Beth-Lehem after being widowed. Encouraged Ruth to marry Boaz, who was relative of family.

Naphtali, sixth son of Jacob and second of Rachel's maid Bilhah. Had four sons and was ancestor of one of Israelite tribes which settled along territory parallel to Jordan R. fr. Lake Huleh to S. end of Sea of Galilee. Played important role among N. tribes.

Naphtali, Testament of, apparently a source of Jewish Greek Pseudepigrapha, Testament of 12 Patriarchs. Deals with genealogy of Bilhah. Hebrew fragment of work identified among Dead Sea Scrolls. Preserved in two versions in medieval Hebrew in translation fr. non-Hebrew source, probably Greek.

Naples, city and former kingdom in S. Italy. In 4th c. Jewish community of considerable size. Jews assisted in defense of city against Byzantines. Community existed throughout Middle Ages; received many exiles fr. Spain 1492. Jews expelled 1510, 1541; readmitted 1735; expelled 1746. By early 19th c. several Jewish families resided there. 450 Jews in 1969.

°**Napoleon Bonaparte** (1769–1821), French emperor. According to some, during his campaign in Ereẓ Israel 1799, issued manifesto promising Jews their return to their country, but it met with little response. He convened the Assembly of Jewish Notables, the (French) Sanhedrin and established the Consistories in France, Italy, Rhineland, etc. Napoleon's work of admitting Jews to civil rights in France and other areas did much to hasten Jewish emancipation.

Naquet, Alfred Joseph (1834–1916), French chemist, republican politician. Imprisoned for radical views. Senator fr. 1882. Promoted divorce law.

Narbonne, town in S. France. Jews there fr. 4th c. Viscount and archbishop of town protected Jews but did not prevent expulsion of 1306. This and Black Death plague caused decline of Jewish community. Fr. late 18th c. Jews again in town, which was outstanding for its many scholars and men of great authority. Few remained by WWII.

Nardi, Nahum (1901–), Israel composer; b. Kiev, settled in Ereẓ Israel 1923. Utilized oriental elements. Composed many songs that achieved folk song status.

Narkiss, Mordechai (1898–1957), Israel curator, art historian; b.

Poland, settled in Ereẓ Israel 1920. Director of Bezalel Museum fr. 1932. Wrote on many aspects of Jewish art.

Nasatir, Abraham Phineas (1904–), U.S. historian, Specialized in regional history of W. and SW of U.S.

Nashim (Heb. "Women"), 3rd order of Mishnah. Deals with matrimonial laws.

Nash Papyrus, 2nd c. B.C.E. papyrus fragment discovered at beginning of 20th c., written in square Hebrew script and containing Decalogue and *Shema.* Oldest biblical text known before discovery of Dead Sea Scrolls.

Nasi, in biblical usage signified head of tribe; later came to mean political head of people. Bar Kokhba so termed himself. Also used for head of Sanhedrin. Often used in Sephardi Diaspora for head of community. Today, Hebrew title of President of State of Israel.

Nasi, Gracia (c.1510–1569), Portuguese-born Marrano; settled first in Flanders, then Ferrara, subsequently Constantinople. Organized escape of Marranos fr. Portugal, securing intervention of Sultan for those who were Turkish subjects. Patronized scholars, established academies and synagogues, secured grant of Tiberias, where she set up yeshivah. Organized boycott of Ancona in revenge for burning of Marranos.

Nasi, Joseph (c. 1524–1579), statesman in Turkey. Born a Portuguese Marrano, he joined his aunt Gracia Nasi in Constantinople, becoming full Jew and marrying her daughter Reyna. Of great influence in Sublime Porte through his knowledge of European affairs; obtained important trading privileges, appointed Duke of Naxos, obtained extension of his aunt's concession in Tiberias, which he attempted to develop (without visiting it). Encouraged Jewish scholarship, built up fine library, wrote polemic against astrology. After his death his widow set up Hebrew printing press.

Nassau, former duchy in W. Germany. All Jews killed during Black Death persecutions 1348. In 17th–mid-19th c. Jews settled mostly in villages, but left in subsequent movement to towns.

°**Nasser Gamal Abdul** (1918–1970), Egyptian leader. Tried to rally Arab forces against Israel but was defeated in 1956 Sinai Campaign and 1967 Six-Day War.

Nassy, David de Isaac Cohen (18th c.), Caribbean physician, Jewish community leader. Born into leading

Gracia Nasi portrayed on a medal by Pastorino de Pastorini, 1553.

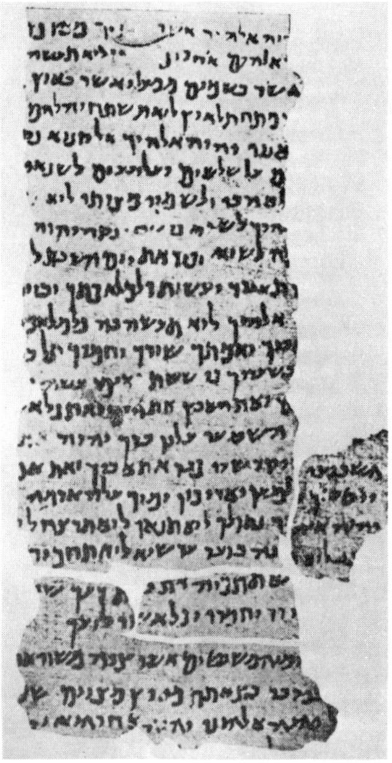

The Nash Papyrus

Ernesto Nathan

Sephardi family in Surinam; pres. of Jewish community there. Lived in Philadelphia 1792–95 as first Jewish physician.

Natal, S. African province. Small permanent Jewish settlement began in 1870s. First Hebrew congregation constituted in Durban 1883. Jewish pop. 6,500 (1971).

Natanson, Ludwik (1822–1896), Warsaw physician, communal worker. Pres. of Polish medical society. Chairman of executive of Warsaw Jewish community fr. 1871; reorganized and extended its social and educational services.

Nathan, prophet in days of David and Solomon. Together with Zadok the priest, anointed Solomon as king. Two of his prophecies are known: postponement of building of the Temple fr. David's time to that of his son and rebuke to David about Bath-Sheba and killing of Uriah.

Nathan, English family distinguished in public service. **Sir Nathaniel** (1843–1916), judge of Supreme Court, acting chief justice of Trinidad. **Sir Frederic Lewis** (1861–1933), explosive expert, soldier. Pres. Inst. of Chemical Engineers, commandant of Jewish Lads' Brigade. **Sir Matthew** (1862–1939), colonial governor (Gold Coast, Hong Kong, Natal), under-secretary in Ireland 1914.

Nathan, Abraham (d. 1745), founder of London Ashkenazi community; b. Hamburg, eventually returning there.

Nathan, Annie, see Meyer, Annie Nathan.

Nathan, David (1816–1886), New Zealand pioneer. Major figure in Auckland financial circles. Led Auckland community and was succeeded by his sons.

Nathan, Ernesto (1845–1921), Italian statesman; b. England, in Italy fr. 1859. First Jewish mayor of Rome. Associated with Mazzini, edited his newspaper *Roma del Popolo.*

Nathan, George Jean (1882–1958), U.S. drama critic, editor. In journalism for more than 50 years. Paved way for Eugene O'Neill and others; did much to educate American theater taste. A founder of *The American Mercury.*

Nathan, Harry Louis, Baron (1889–1963), English lawyer, politician. MP (first Liberal, then Labor) 1929–40, then in House of Lords. Minister of civil aviation 1946–48. Active in Jewish affairs.

Nathan, Henry (1842–1914), Canadian politician. First Jew elected to Canadian Federal Parliament 1871.

Nathan, Isaac (1790? –1864), composer, singer, writer; b. England. Set Byron's *Hebrew Melodies* to music. Went to Australia 1841, becoming country's first resident professional composer.

Nathan, Joseph Edward (1835–1912), New Zealand businessman. Built wholesale export-import busi-

ness; active in Jewish life in Wellington.

Nathan, Manfred (1875–1945), S. African lawyer, author. Pres. S. African Special Income Tax Court. Wrote on legal matters and history. Active in Jewish community.

Nathan, Mordecai (15th c.), French physician. Known for his *Me'ir Nativ,* first Hebrew concordance of Bible, prepared to assist Jews in their polemics with Christians.

Nathan, Mulla Ibraham (1816–1868), British intelligence agent; b. Meshed, Persia. Assisted British forces in Afghanistan, Turkestan, and Bukhara. Settled in Bombay and active there in Jewish community.

Nathan, Paul (1857–1927), German politician, Jewish leader. Edited Berlin liberal publication *Die Nation.* Founded Hilfsverein (q.v.), and was regarded as spokesman for German Jews, except Zionists whom he strongly opposed.

Nathan, Robert (1894–), U.S. novelist. Author of short novels notable for fantasy and ironical style.

Nathan, Robert Roy (1908–), U.S. economist. Active in Roosevelt's reconstruction programs. Involved in post-WWII rehabilitation and aid in developing countries.

Nathan ben Abraham (d. before 1102), *av bet din* of Ereẓ Israel academy. Compiled short Arabic commentary to whole Mishnah, which was worked over by Yemenite scholar in 12th c. so that it is impossible to distinguish authors.

Nathan ben Isaac ha-Kohen ha-Bavli (10th c.), chronicler living in Baghdad, associated with circles of exilarch. Fragments of his work have been discovered and are important sources for history of Baghdad Jewry and exilarchate.

Nathan ben Jehiel of Rome (1035–c. 1110), Italian lexicographer, referred to as *Ba'al he-Arukh* fr. title of his important work. With his two brothers succeeded father as heads of yeshivah in Rome. Wrote responsa. His *Arukh* is lexicon of all terms in Talmud and Midrashim needing explanation. Frequently copied and printed, often with addenda. Scholarly edition entitled *Arukh ha-Shalem* (1878–92) issued by A. Kohut.

Nathan ha-Bavli (2nd c.), *tanna;* originally fr. Babylon. When Hananiah fixed calendar in Babylon, sent to stop him. Because of dispute with Simeon b. Gamaliel not much quoted in Mishnah but frequently cited in *beraitot.* Author of rule that if A owes B money and B owes C then C can claim directly fr. A, *(Shi'abuda de-Rabbi Natan).* Putative author of *Avot de-Rabbi Nathan.*

Nathan of Gaza (1643/4–1680), a central figure of Shabbatean movement; son of Elisha Ḥayyim b. Jacob Ashkenazi. Revered for his prophetic powers, his endorsement of Shabbetai Ẓevi as the messiah in 1665 gave decisive impetus to the mass movement. Continued to believe in Shabbetai Ẓevi after the latter's apostasy and traveled extensively in SE Europe preaching Shabbateanism.

Nathan of Gaza

Nathansen, Henri (1868–1944), Danish playwright, novelist. Many works on Jewish themes. Stage director of Copenhagen's Royal Theater.

Nathanson, Joseph Saul (1810–1875), rabbinical authority. Rabbi of Lemberg. Opponent of Ḥasidism and Reform; but would have no part in schism and had good relations with "temple" preachers and scholarly ḥasidic rabbis. Wrote on Talmud, *Shulḥan Arukh,* Maimonides.

Nathanson, Mendel Levin (1780–1868), Danish merchant, editor. Edited leading Danish newspaper *Berlingske Tidende.* Fought for emancipation of Danish Jews. Wrote on Danish economic history.

National Conference of Jewish Communal Service, forum and publication body for professional disciplines serving American Jewish community. Serves 300 organizations and 2,000 practitioners.

National Council of Jewish Women, U.S. national organization; founded 1893. Established pre-school programs and many projects of communal significance. Membership over 100,000.

National Foundation for Jewish Culture, U.S. organization that supports and initiates programs in Jewish culture; established by Council of Jewish Federations and Welfare Funds in 1959.

National Jewish Community Relations Advisory Council, U.S. organization, established 1944 to formulate policy and coordinate activities in field of community relations. Membership 9 national and 81 state or local bodies (1968).

National Jewish Hospital, nonsectarian medical and research center specializing in chronic respiratory conditions, located in Denver, Colo.; founded 1890 to assist tubercular indigents who came to Denver's high altitude seeking cures.

National Jewish Welfare Board (JWB), religious and welfare organization of American Jewish military personnel and coordinator of YMHAs and community centers; founded 1917. Active in WWI and WWII, Korea and Vietnam wars, and in military chaplaincy. Strives to provide balanced program of activities to YMHAs and Jewish centers. Services incl. Lecture Bureau, Jewish Book Council, Jewish Music Council.

National Religious Party (Mafdal; Heb. acronym for *Miflagah Datit-Le'ummit*), Israel political-religious party, founded 1956 through merger of Mizrachi and Ha-Po'el ha-Mizrachi. Strives to build society in Israel based on spiritual, social, and halakhic foundations of Judaism. Constitutes a part of World Organ-

Founders and executive committee of the National Jewish Welfare Board, WWI. Seated, left to right: M. Harris, L. Marshall, H. Cutler, C. Adler, C. Hartman. Standing, left to right: C. Teller, D. de Sola Pool, M. Schiff, I. Unterberg, H. Bernheim, J. Rosenzweig.

The Catholic Basilica of the Annunciation (center), Nazareth, the largest church in the Middle East.

ization of Mizrachi–Ha-Po'el ha-Mizrachi. Has held 10–12 seats in Knesset and participated in most coalition governments. See Knesset.

National Society for Hebrew Day Schools, see Torah Umasorah.

Natonek, Joseph (1813–1892), Hungarian rabbi, Hebrew grammarian, pioneer of Zionism. Negotiated with Turkish government unsuccessfully to obtain charter for Jewish settlement in Ereẓ Israel.

Natorei Karta, see Neturei Karta.

Natronai bar Hilai (9th c.), *gaon* of Sura 853–58, prolific writer of responsa in Hebrew, Aramaic, Arabic. Many of his letters published. Explains many customs and much liturgical practice is known through him. Legends were told of him and fanciful decisions were attributed to him in Yemenite Midrashim.

Natzweiller-Struthof, Nazi concentration camp in Alsace, operated May 1941–August 1944. 25,000 inmates died there.

Naumbourg, Samuel (1815–1880), cantor, composer; b. Germany, in Paris fr. 1843. Published his *Zemirot Yisrael*, which had great influence on Jewish liturgical music.

Naumburg, family of U.S. bankers, philanthropists. **Elkan** (1834–1924) founded family bank, endowed many musical activities in N.Y. **Walter Wehle** (1867–1959) and **George Washington** (1876–1970) dissolved family firm to devote themselves to charity. Walter active in musical charities and George in child welfare.

Naumburg, Margaret (1890–), U.S. psychologist, educator, art therapist. Founded first Montessori class in N.Y. 1913. Established Walden School, stressing pupil-teacher relationship. Pioneer in art education.

Navon, Joseph (1858–1924), pioneer of Ereẓ Israel development. Responsible for constructing Jaffa-Jerusalem railroad. In Paris fr. 1894.

Nazareth, town in Galilee, mentioned in New Testament as place to which Joseph returned fr. Egypt and where Jesus ("Jesus of Nazareth") was brought up. Archaeological evidence has shown that area was settled as early as Middle Bronze Age. Early Christians contemptuously called Nazarenes by their enemies and Hebrew and Arabic terms for Christians are derived fr. name. Churches built here fr. 5th c. Important center during Crusader period. Fr. 1948 in State of Israel. Pop. 35,000 (1971), with 24 churches, incl. Basilica of Annunciation, largest church in Middle East. Israel-born settlers founded neighboring town of Naẓerat Illit 1957. Pop. 15,800 (1971), with industrial enterprises.

NAZI LEADERS

NAME AND FUNCTION	ACTIVITY	FATE
Best, Karl Werner The RSHA's judicial expert and Heydrich's deputy, later Reich plenipotentiary, Denmark	in charge of the planned deportation of the Jews in October, 1943	death sentence in Denmark commuted to 12 years' imprisonment, released 1951, several trials without indictment in Germany
Bormann, Martin Chief of the party chancellery and Hitler's personal secretary	in control over all laws and directives issued by Hitler, including the Final Solution	believed killed in 1945, but also rumored to be in S. America
Bouhler, Philip Chief of Hitler's private chancellery (which was distinct from the Reich's chancellery and that of the party)	head of euthanasia program	believed to have committed suicide, 1945
Brunner, Anton Sturmbannfuehrer	Eichmann's expert on deportation of Jews	hanged in Vienna, 1946
Dannecker, Theodor Hauptsturmfuehrer	in charge of deportation of Jews from France, Bulgaria, and Italy	committed suicide, 1945
Eichmann, Karl Adolf Obersturmbannfuehrer	head of Jewish section of Gestapo, responsible for the organization of the Final Solution	tried and executed in Israel, 1962
Frank, Hans Michael Governor-General of Poland	responsible for the mass murder of Polish Jewry	executed in Nuremberg, 1946
Globocnik, Odilo Gruppenfuehrer	directed Aktion Reinhard massacres	committed suicide, 1945
Goebbels, Josef Minister of Propaganda	directed the party's and the Reich's propaganda; chief antisemitic agitator, promoter of Kristallnacht	committed suicide together with Hitler, 1945
Goering, Hermann Reichsmarschall	involved in every phase of the destruction of European Jews	committed suicide after death sentence in Nuremberg, 1946
Hess, Rudolf Deputy to the Fuehrer	tried to move England to peace by private flight in 1941	life imprisonment at Spandau, Germany
Heydrich, Reinhard Tristan Eugen Obergruppenfuehrer, chief of Reich Security Head Office (RSHA) Protector of Bohemia-Moravia	responsible for mass deportation of Jews to Poland; in charge of implementation of the Final Solution	killed by Czech resistance fighters, 1942
Himmler, Heinrich Chief of the SS; minister of interior	directed extermination of European Jews	committed suicide when caught at the end of the war, 1945

Hitler, Adolf Leader (Fuehrer) of the N.S.D.A.P. — the German National Socialist Workers' Party; chancellor of the "Third Reich"	caused the Second World War during which he initiated and planned the extermination of the Jews and charged his organizations and governmental agencies with the Final Solution's implementation	committed suicide in the bunker of the Reich's chancellery, 1945
Hoess, Rudolf Franz Ferdinand Standartenfuehrer, commandant of Auschwitz — Inspector of Concentration Camps	annihilation of Jews in Auschwitz	hanged in Auschwitz, 1947
Kaltenbrunner, Ernst Obergruppenfuehrer, chief of Reich Security Head Office (RSHA) after Heydrich	implementation of the annihilation policy against the Jews	hanged in Nuremberg, 1946
Katzmann, Fritz Gruppenfuehrer, Higher SS and Police Leader	organizer of the massacre of the Jews in East Galicia	lived under false name, died 1957
Kramer, Josef Commandant of Birkenau and Bergen-Belsen camps	extermination of Jews in camps	hanged after death sentence of British court, 1945
Krumey, Hermann Sturmbannfuehrer	agent of Eichmann in Vienna and Budapest	in custody 1960–65, then released
Lohse, Heinrich Reichkommissar for the Occupied Eastern Territory	extermination of the Jews	sentenced to 10 years' imprisonment 1948, released 1951
Luther, Martin Director of Department Deutschland of the Foreign Office, dealing with the Jewish question, in liaison with the SS	collaborator in the extermination process	1943 sent to concentration camp because of intrigue against Ribbentrop, died 1945
Mengele, Josef Hauptsturmfuehrer	"doctor" of Auschwitz extermination camp and participated in "selections" of prisoners	fled to S. America
Mueller, Heinrich Obergruppenfuehrer, chief of the Gestapo	responsible for the murder of hundreds of thousands of Soviet prisoners; a key figure in the Final Solution	disappeared in Berlin, 1945
Ohlendorf, Otto Gruppenfuehrer, commander of mobile units of Nazi SS and SD (Einsatzgruppe D)	extermination of Jews in Russia	hanged 1951 (after Nuremberg trial)
Pohl, Oswald Gruppenfuehrer, head of the SS's economic administration department	responsible for SS economic activities, including financing construction of concentration camps and their administration	hanged 1951 (after Nuremberg trial)
Rademacher, Franz Served under Luther as head of the section which dealt with Jewish affairs	took initiative in murder of Jews in Belgrade, Rumania, and Bulgaria, one of the promoters of the Madagascar Plan	sentenced to imprisonment in 1952, broke bail and escaped to Syria, returned 1966 to Germany, was sentenced to five years' imprisonment, but released
Rauter, Hans Albin Obergruppenfuehrer, Himmler's principal representative in occupied Netherlands	persecution of Dutch Jewry and their deportation to extermination camps in Poland	executed in Holland, 1949
Ribbentrop, Joachim von Foreign Minister	one of the promoters of the Final Solution	hanged in Nuremberg, 1946
Rosenberg, Alfred Chief Editor of the "Voelkische Beobachter," later Reich minister for the Occupied Eastern Territories; chief Nazi ideologist	plundered libraries, works of art, and household goods of Jews all over Europe, set up special institutes for the study of the Jewish question; acquiesced in the annihilation of the Jews	hanged in Nuremberg, 1946
Schumann, Horst Leading member of the Euthanasia program	conducted sterilization experiments on Jewish women at Ravensbruck and Auschwitz	was extradited from Ghana to Germany in 1966, his trial in Frankfort in 1970 was interrupted because of his health.
Seyss-Inquart, Arthur Chancellor of Austria after the "Anschluss", deputy of Hans Frank, finally Reichskommisser for Holland	Hitler's chief agitator in Austria, persecution of the Jews in Holland	hanged in Nuremberg, 1946
Stangl, Franz Hauptsturmfuehrer, commandant of Sobibor and Treblinka death camps	execution of Jews	was sentenced in Dusseldorf, Germany to life imprisonment, died in jail 1971
Streicher, Julius Editor of "Der Stuermer" and Gauleiter of Franconia	anti-Semitic agitator of the German Nazi Party, organized the boycott action of April 1, 1933	hanged in Nuremberg, 1946
Stroop, Juergen SS general	liquidator of the Warsaw Ghetto	executed in Warsaw, 1951
Stuckart, Franz Secretary of State, Ministry of Interior	took part in the main anti-Jewish activities, including the drafting of the Nuremberg Laws, and the Wannsee Conference	in detention until 1949, died 1952
Thadden, Eberhard von Expert on Jewish affairs in the Foreign Office	took over from Rademacher in 1943, continued his activities	released by the Allies from detention 1949, charged by German courts 1950 and 1952, killed in road accident, 1964
Veesenmayer, Edmund Reich Plenepotentiary to Hungary	took part in the deportation to Auschwitz of Hungarian Jewry	sentenced in Nuremberg to 20 years' imprisonment 1949, released 1952
Wetzel, Dr. Erhard head of the "Race Political Office" of the Nazi party, later in Rosenberg's office	one of the three who decided on use of gas	was only interrogated in Germany, whereabouts unknown
Wisliceny, Dieter Hauptsturmfuehrer, Eichmann's deputy in Slovakia, Greece, and Hungary	deportation of Slovak Jews to Poland, deportation of Salonika Jews	hanged in Bratislava, 1948

Nazimova, Alla (1879–1945), actress; b. Russia, went to New York 1905. One of earliest film stars.

Nazir (Heb. "Nazirite"), 4th tractate of Mishnah order *Nashim,* with *gemara* in both Talmuds. Deals with laws and assumption of Nazirite vow (Num. 6:1–21), and different types of naziriteship, as well as procedures when the vow is interrupted and terminated.

Nazirite (Heb. *nazir*), person who vows for specific period to abstain fr. partaking of grapes or any of its products whether intoxicating or not, cutting his hair, and touching corpse. Special sacrifices were stipulated in cases of contamination and on concluding period of naziriteship. Undertaking, if not specified, was for 30 days, but could also be for life. Common until the end of Second Temple period.

Neander, August (1789–1850), church historian; embraced Christianity at age 17, prof. at age 24. Condemned ritual murder charge in Damascus Affair 1840.

Nebo, mountain E. of Jordan R., opposite Jericho (Deut. 32:49). Peak is called Pisgah, fr. where Moses saw Promised Land before he died.

Nebraska, U.S. state. Jewish merchants of C. European origin were early settlers fr. 1855. After 1881 Russian Jews arrived in large numbers; effort to settle them as farmers failed. Pop. 8,290 (1971), mostly in Omaha and Lincoln.

°**Nebuchadnezzar,** ruler of Babylon 605–562 B.C.E. Defeated Egyptian armies at Carchemish 605, frustrating Pharaoh Neco's attempt to gain control of Syria and Erez̦ Israel. Attempted conquest of Egypt 601. His failure encouraged various states incl. Judah, to revolt. Seized Judah and captured king 597. New revolt, supported by Egypt, broke out later. After besieging Jerusalem for two years, captured city 586, destroying Temple, exiling large part of population, and putting King Zedekiah and other nobles to death.

°**Nebuzaradan,** commander of Nebuchadnezzar's guard who was in charge of destruction of First Temple and deportation of people of Judah 586 B.C.E.

°**Neco,** king of Egypt c. 609–593 B.C.E., who defeated Josiah of Judah and consolidated and controlled Syria and Erez̦ Israel. Nebuchadnezzar of Babylon defeated him 605 and he was compelled to retreat.

Nedarim (Heb. "vows"), 3rd tractate of Mishnah order *Nashim,* with *gemara* in both Talmuds. Deals with assumption and binding character of personal vows.

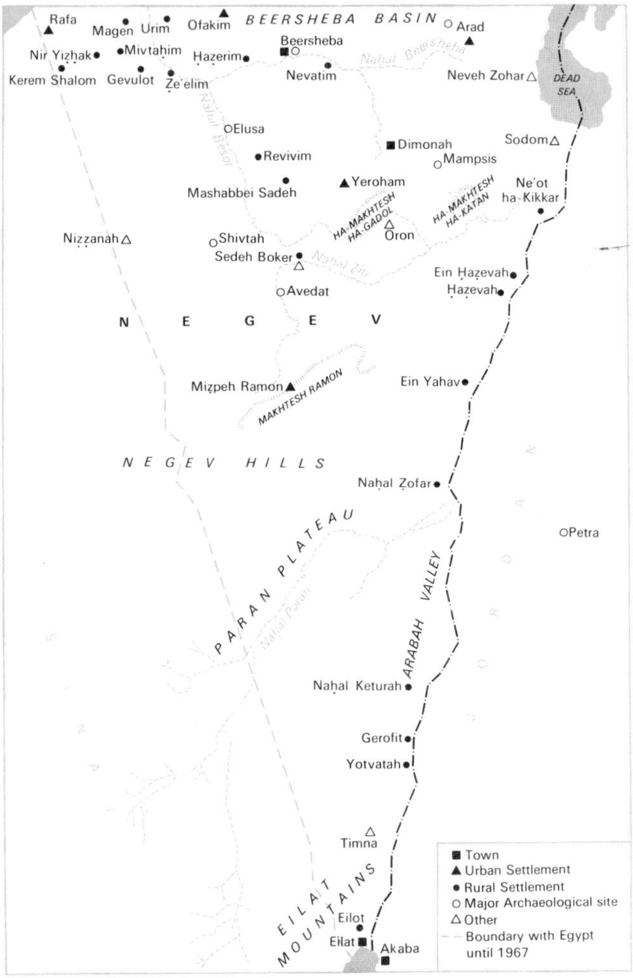

The Negev, ancient sites and modern settlements, 1971.

Ne'eman, Yehoshua Leib (1899–), Israel *ḥazzan,* writer, teacher. Lecturer in biblical cantillation at Academy of Music in Jerusalem, director of Israel Inst. for Sacred Music.

Yuval Ne'eman

Ne'eman, Yuval (1925–), Israel physicist; one of originators of basic strategy of Israel army. His theory of classification of elementary particles of nature was major breakthrough in particle physics. Prof. of physics and Pres. Tel Aviv Univ. fr. 1971.

Nega'im (Heb. "Plagues"), 3rd tractate of Mishnah order *Tohorot,* with no *gemara.* Deals with ritual cleanness of persons, garments, and houses (see Lev. 13–14).

Negbah, kibbutz in S. Israel, founded 1939 as then southernmost Jewish village. Beginning of systematic effort to gain foothold in S. and Negev. Destroyed by Egyptian army in 1948 War of Independence, but rebuilt. Pop. 412 (1971).

Negev, area comprising S. part of Erez̦ Israel, characterized by totally arid desert climate. Covers area of 4,600 sq.mi. (12,000 sq.km.). With exception of Beersheba basin, no arable soil and wide expanses are covered with sharp flint on limestone gravel.

Nehardea, Babylonian town on Euphrates; seat of famous academy. Original Jewish inhabitants said to have built synagogue with earth and stones brought fr. First Temple. Became home of exilarch and his *bet din.* Samuel the *amora* headed academy at its zenith. Town destroyed 259 and scholars moved to Pumbedita.

Nehemiah (5th c. B.C.E.), originally cupbearer of Artaxerxes I; later governor of Judah. Appointed governor at his own request, which involved rebuilding walls of Jerusalem and reorganization of country. Despite frequent interference from neighboring governors, avoided serious conflict. Having achieved his prime objective, devoted himself to establishing order and justice in community. His story is told in biblical Book of Nehemiah (which originally formed unit with Book of Ezra).

Nehemiah (2nd c.), *tanna;* outstanding disciple of R. Akiva. Anonymous statements in Tosefta are attributed to him. Outlived Bar Kokhba revolt and took part in subsequent renewal of Torah teaching. One of five scholars ordained by Judah b. Bava at cost of his life; transmitted halakhic, aggadic, and mystic sayings, lived in poverty. Saying: "A single individual is as important as the whole of creation."

Nehemiah bar Kohen Ẓedek (10th c.), *gaon* of Pumbedita academy 960–968; son of *gaon* Kohen Ẓedek.

Nehemiah ha-Kohen (17th c.), Polish kabbalist. Acc. to Christian sources claimed to be messiah, son of Joseph, and remonstrated with Shabbetai Ẓevi for disclosing himself prematurely. Lived his life as outcast, his persecution stemming fr. general disillusionment with messianism.

Neher, André (1913–), French scholar, philosopher. Prof. at Strasbourg Univ. and Tel Aviv Univ. Wrote on "alliance" of God with man and esp. with Israel.

Neḥunya ben ha-Kanah (1st c.), *tanna.* Taught R. Ishmael his rules for interpreting Torah. Kabbalists ascribe *Sefer ha-Bahir* to him, and also prayer *Anna be-Kho'aḥ.*

Nehushtan, name of copper serpent located in Temple court in Jerusalem, which king Hezekiah broke into pieces.

Neḥutei (Aram. "those going down"), the name given to scholars going from Ereẓ Israel to Babylon, beginning with Ulla in the 3rd c. Through them the texts of the Mishnah and the sayings of early *amoraim* were transmitted to Babylonia.

Ne'ilah (Heb.), designation of worship service deriving fr. Temple, where it was recited before closing *(ne'ilah)* of gates. Subsequently restricted to all fast days, and later solely to final service of Day of Atonement. Includes *Amidah,* sacred poetry (especially *Seliḥot*), and *Avinu Malkenu.* Concludes with recitation of *Shema* and sounding of *shofar.* Impressive melodies heighten its emotional impact.

Neilson, Julia (1868–1957), English romantic actress; b. into family of actors. With husband Fred Terry played and toured in own company 1900–30. Her children acted under name Neilson-Terry.

Nelson, Leonhard (1882–1927), German philosopher; baptized as child. Taught at Goettingen. Major interest ethics. Moderate socialist.

Nemirov, town in Ukrainian SSR. Jewish settlement first mentioned 1603. In Chmielnicki persecutions 1648 thousands of Jews massacred; town became symbol for Jews of all terrible massacres suffered by them and special lamentations and penitential prayers were composed. Center of Bratslav Ḥasidim in 19th c. 4,176 Jews in 1926; deported to extermination camps in WWII.

Nemoy, Leon (1901–), U.S. scholar and librarian. B. Russia, in U.S. fr. 1923. Curator of Hebrew and Arabic literature at Yale. Researches mainly devoted to Karaites.

Neology, unofficial name of communities of Hungary belonging to Reform movement, official name being Congressionals. As Hungarian government would not recognize two Jewries, every effort was made to keep it as one. Neologs defined community as "society providing for religious needs."

Neo-Orthodoxy, name of modernistic faction of German Orthodoxy; associated with S.R. Hirsch and Hildesheimer, who both stressed need to combine general culture with traditional Judaism.

"Ner Tamid" from Casablanca, 19th cent.

BOOK OF NEHEMIAH – CONTENTS

Chs: 1:1–13:3	Nehemiah's governorship of Judah.
1:1–2:10	Nehemiah's concern about affairs in Judah.
2:11–20	Nehemiah resolves to rebuild the walls of Jerusalem.
3:1–4:17	Restoration of the walls.
5:1–19	Community problems.
6:1–7:3	Despite designs against Nehemiah the walls are finally completed.
7:4–72a [73a]	A list of those, who returned with Zerubbabel.
7:72b–9:37 [73b]	The Torah reading and worship services.
10:1–40	Execution of a written and officially sealed covenant.
11:1–36	Redistribution of Jews in Jerusalem and Judah.
12:1–26	Clerical lists.
12:27–43	Dedication of the newly constructed wall.
12:44–13:3	Further religious concerns.
Chs: 13:4–31	Second period of Nehemiah's governorship of Judah.
13:4–9	Events leading to the expulsion of Tobiah from the Temple.
13:10–31	Further reforms of Nehemiah.

Nephilim, race of giants said in Bible to have dwelt in pre-Israelite Canaan. Offspring of divine beings who took mortal wives (Gen.6). Story was elaborated in apocryphal writings.

Neppi, Hananel (1759–1863), Italian rabbi of Ferrara, physician. Represented Italy at Napoleonic Assembly of Notables. Published biographical lexicon of earlier scholars and wrote many responsa.

°**Nergal-Sharezer,** high-ranking official of Nebuchadnezzar who took part in siege and conquest of Jerusalem 587–86 B.C.E.

Ner Tamid (Heb. "eternal lamp"), light burning perpetually before ark in synagogue as symbolic reminder of *menorah* burning in Temple.

Neshamah Yeterah (Heb. "additional soul"), popular belief that every Jew is given additional soul at onset of Sabbath which leaves him at its termination. Idea expanded in kabbalistic literature.

Nesterov, see Zholkva.

Nesher, urban community with municipal council status in N. Israel, nr. Haifa; founded 1925 as workers' quarter for employees of Nesher Cement Works. Pop. 9,650 (1971).

Nesvizh, town in Belorussian SSR. One of the most influential communities in Lithuanian Council (17th c.). Noted for its talmudic scholars. Its 6,000 Jews killed in WWII.

Nes Ẓiyyonnah, clandestine society formed by students in yeshivah of Volozhin to propagate return to

Zion. First such society banned by police. Reformed and merged with another, similar society.

Nes Ẓiyyonah, semi-urban settlement with municipal council status in C. Israel, founded 1883 as small plantation village. Only village in country with mixed Arab-Jewish pop. In War of Independence Arabs left. Pop. 12,200 (1971).

Netanyah, coastal city in C. Israel, founded 1929 as moshavah. Served as nucleus for settlement of C. Sharon. Economy based mainly on tourism and industry. Diamond polishing center. Pop. 67,700 (1971).

View of Netanyah.

Netanyahu, Benzion (1910–), scholar, Zionist. A leading figure in Revisionist movement in Ereẓ Israel and U.S. Editor in chief of *Encyclopaedia Hebraica* 1948–62. Prof. at Dropsie College 1957–68, Univ. of Denver 1968–71, Cornell fr. 1971. Wrote on Marranos and Isaac Abrabanel.

Nethanel ben Al-Fayyumi (d. c. 1165), Yemenite scholar, philosopher. Author of Judeo-Arabic *Bustān al'Uqūl,* compendium of theology.

Nethanel ben Isaiah (14th c.), Yemenite scholar. Wrote midrashic anthology, *Nur al-Ẓalam,* utilized extensively by later authors of Yemenite midrashim.

Netherlands, The, kingdom in NW Europe. Jews probably present in Roman times; documentary evidence of their presence in 12th c. Many killed in Black Death persecutions 1349–50. Important community of Marranos fr. 17th c., mostly Portuguese merchants who fled to tolerant country and returned to Judaism. In late 17th c. majority in stock market, active in sugar, silk, diamond industries. Developed export trade. Major cultural center in both general and Jewish studies. Religious conflicts arose bet. old Orthodox and newly reconverted Marranos, such as Spinoza and Uriel da Costa. Ashkenazi Jews came late 17th c., gradually ending Sephardi supremacy. Community declined in 1st half of 20th c. 140,000 Jews in 1940; 27,000 survived Holocaust. Jewish pop. 30,000 (1971), with largest communities in Amsterdam, The Hague, Rotterdam, Utrecht.

The Jewish Quarter established by the Nazis in Amsterdam, the Netherlands.

Netherlands Antilles (or **Dutch Antilles;** formerly **Dutch West Indies**), two groups of islands located off coast of Venezuela. Jews settled in Aruba 1753; community established 1946, 35 families in 1970. Community established in St. Eustatius 1730; ceased to exist 1850. Organized community in St. Martin 1783; Numbered c. 10 adult Jewish males in 1969. First congregation established in Curaçao 1651; first *ḥakham* appointed 1674. In 18th c. largest Jewish community in the W. Hemisphere. Reform congregation established 1864; merged with old community 1963. 1732 synagogue, oldest extant in W. Hemisphere. Jewish community prominent in local economic life until 19th c. 750 Jews in 1970.

Nethinim, cultic servants. Book of Joshua (9:27) relates how wily Gibeonites punished by becoming hewers of wood, drawers of water for altar of the Lord. Lowest class of temple servants, of foreign extraction, organized under family heads, and residing in Jerusalem and elsewhere. In post-biblical period considered descendants of Gibeonites and prohibited to marry Jews.

Main Jewish communities of the Netherlands in 1941 and 1960. Boldface type indicates places of Jewish settlement in the 17th cent.

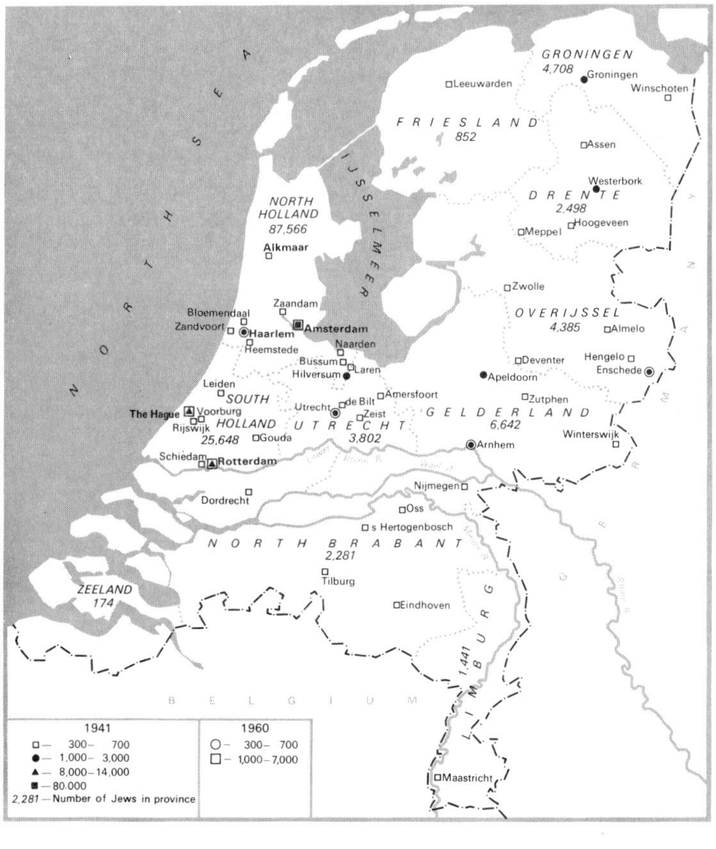

"Netilat Yadayim," detail from "Birds' Head Haggadah" Germany, c. 1300.

Netilat Yadayim (Heb.), rabbinical term for "washing the hands," made obligatory after various activities, e.g. rising fr. sleep, leaving cemetery, using the toilet, before eating, etc. Hand is washed up to third joint of fingers and blessing is said.

Netivot, Israel development town in NW Negev, founded 1956. Pop. 5,550, 95% immigrants fr. Tunisia and Morocco.

Netter, Charles (**Yiẓhak**, 1826–1882), leader of Alliance Israélite Universelle; b. Strasbourg. Among founders of Alliance Israélite; founded (1870) and developed Mikveh Israel Agricultural School in Ereẓ Israel.

Neturei Karta (Aram. "Guardians of the city"), group of ultra-religious extremists, mainly in Jerusalem, who regard establishment of secular Jewish state in Ereẓ Israel as sin and denial of God, and therefore do not recognize State of Israel. Came into being after split with Agudat Israel 1935; most members come fr. old *yishuv*.

Neubauer, Adolf (1831–1907), Hungarian scholar, librarian, bibliographer; wrote *La Géographie du Talmud.* Went to Oxford 1865 becoming a librarian at Bodleian 1868 and enriching it by purchases fr. Cairo *Genizah* and by *Catalogue of the Hebrew Manuscripts in the Bodleian Library.* Reader in rabbinic Hebrew at Oxford Univ.

Neuberg, Gustav Embden Carl (1877–1956), German biochemist. Director of Kaiser Wilhelm Inst. of Biochemistry 1920; dismissed by Nazis 1938. Prof. at N.Y. Univ. 1941–50.

Neuberger, Albert (1908–), British biochemist; b. Germany. Prof. of chemical pathology at St. Mary's Hospital Medical School in London; fellow of Royal Society. Main research in metabolism of proteins and amino acids.

Neuberger, Richard Lewis (1912–1960), U.S. senator, journalist, author. As correspondent for *The Nation,* warned of Nazi danger. Liberal Democratic senator fr. Oregon 1954. Wrote on politics and conservation.

Neuberger, Max (1868–1955), Austrian medical historian. Prof. at Univ. of Vienna. Wrote on many fields of medical history, incl. Jewish. In England during WWII.

Neuda, Abraham (1812–1854), rabbi in Moravia. Published sermons. His wife, **Fanny** (1819–1894), published in his memory prayer book in German for women. It went through 28 editions.

Neufeld, Daniel (1814–1874), Polish writer, educator, Believed in synthesis of Jewish and Polish cultures. Progressive in social questions, conservative in religion. Translated Genesis into Polish.

Neuman, Abraham Aaron (1890–1970), U.S. rabbi, historian, educator. Pres. of Dropsie College 1940–66. Published *The Jews in Spain;* co-editor *Jewish Quarterly Review.*

Neumann, Alfred (1895–1952), German novelist. Pioneer of revival of German historical novel. Left Germany 1938, in U.S. during WWII.

Neumann, Emanuel (1893–), U.S. Zionist leader. President of ZOA 1947–49, 1956–58. Political representative of Jewish Agency in Washington in 1940s. Member of Jewish Agency Executive and chairman of its American section. Founder and first pres. of Herzl Foundation. A leader of General Zionists.

Emanuel Neumann

Neumann, Johann Ludwig Von (1903–1957), U.S. mathematician. First prof. of mathematical physics at Inst. for Advanced Studies at Princeton. Member of U.S. Atomic Energy Commission.

Neumann, Robert (1897–), novelist, satirist; b. Vienna, went to England 1934, Switzerland after WWII. Wrote in German and English. Wrote anti-Nazi novels.

Neumark, David (1866–1924), Reform scholar, philosopher; b. Galicia. Prof. of philosophy at Hebrew Union College in Cincinnati fr. 1907. Founder of *Hebrew Union College Annual* 1919. Wrote history of Jewish philosophy.

Neumeyer, Karl (1869–1941), German international lawyer. Taught at Univ. of Munich fr. 1919 (dean of law faculty 1931). Removed fr. posts by Nazis 1933. Committed suicide with his wife rather than be sent to concentration camp.

Neusner, Jacob (1932–), U.S. scholar, historian. Prof. of Jewish studies at Brown Univ. Prolific author. Works incl. *History of the Jews in Babylonia.*

Neutra, Richard Joseph (1892–1970), U.S. architect; b. Vienna, in U.S. fr. 1923. Active both in town planning and design of private homes. Wrote *Survival Through Design.*

Neuzeit, Die, first Austrian Jewish weekly, published 1861–1903. Critical of more Conservative efforts and favored Reform. Rejected secular Jewish nationalism and Zionism.

Nevada, U.S. state. Jews first went there fr. California during 1859–62 gold and silver discoveries. Congregation in Virginia City 1862. Services in Carson City fr. 1869. Communities in mining towns eventually faded away. Jewish pop. 3,380, mainly in Las Vegas.

Nevakhovich, Judah Leib (1776–1831), one of earliest Russian *maskilim.* Translator for government of Hebrew documents, incl. those connected with imprisonment of Shneur Zalman of Lyady. After his conversion to Lutheranism 1809, many turned away fr. Haskalah.

Nevelah (Heb. "carcass"), animal, bird, or creature which has died as result of any process other than valid ritual slaughter *(sheḥitah).* Consumption of such meat is forbidden and it is also one of principal categories of ritual impurity *(tumah).*

Nevelson, Louise (1900–), U.S. sculptor. Assistant to Diego Rivera. Worked in plastics and new, severely geometric format in 1960s.

Newark, city in N.J., U.S. First Jews settled 1844; Orthodox congregation established 1848 (later became Reform). Jewish immigrants who began as peddlers rapidly entered merchandising and later became prominent in other fields. See also Essex County.

New Brunswick, city in N.J., U.S. Earliest Jewish settler 1722. First congregation 1859. Jewish pop. 13,500 (1971).

New Christians, term applied specifically to three groups of Jewish converts to Christianity and their descendants in Iberian Peninsula. First group converted in wake of massacres in Spain 1391; second, also in Spain, were baptized following expulsion of 1492; third, in Portugal, were converted by force and royal fiat 1497. See also Marranos.

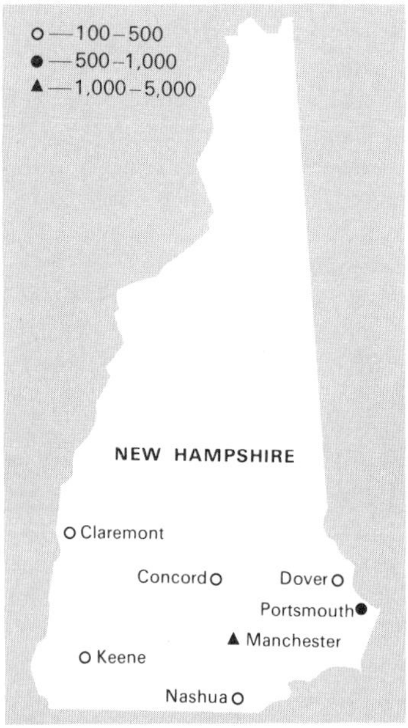

Jewish communities in New Hampshire.

Jewish communities in New Jersey.

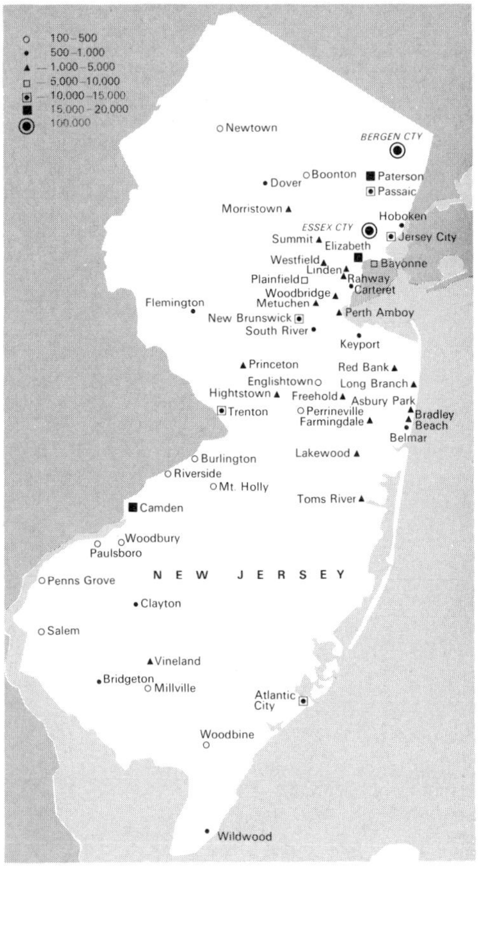

New Hampshire, U.S. state. Jewish settlement began in mid-18th c. First congregations in Berlin and Manchester 1899. Others founded in early 1900s in Portsmouth, Keene, Concord, Laconia. Jewish pop. 4,000 (1971).

New Haven, city in Conn., U.S. Jews settled 1758; German Jews arriving c. 1840, forming first congregation. Jewish pop. 20,000 (1971).

Newhouse, Samuel Irving (1895–), U.S. publisher. Acquired many newspapers and radio and television stations. Established Newhouse Communications Center at Syracuse Univ.

New Israel (Rus. **Novy Izrail**), Jewish religious sect initiated during 1880s in Odessa by Jacob Priluker, teacher at government school. Recognized Mosaic law only and abolished circumcision and dietary law. Failed to find support among masses. Priluker converted to Christianity 1891.

New Jersey, U.S. state. Jewish merchants fr. Philadelphia and N.Y. conducted business in state in 17th c. First organized Jewish communities in mid-19th c. Other Jewish communities which organized congregations were: Paterson (1847), Newark (1848), New Brunswick (1861), Jersey City (1864), Bayonne (1878), Elizabeth (1881), Vineland (1881), Perth Amboy (1890), Atlantic City (1890), Passaic (1890), Woodbine (1891), Camden (1894), Englewood (1896). Jews in farming colonies (e.g. Vineland) founded in late 19th c. Economic expansion following WWII and migration from N.Y.C. to suburbs led to further Jewish pop. growth. Jewish pop. 412,465 (1971), with 100,000 each in Bergen and Essex counties.

New London, city in Conn., U.S. Jews settled 1860. First congregation 1892. Jewish pop. 4,500 (1971).

Newman, Arnold (1919–), U.S. portrait photographer. Developed style using background details that revealed personality of subjects.

Newman, Louis Israel (1893–1972), U.S. Reform rabbi, author. Rabbi in N.Y. A leader of Zionist Revisionists in U.S. Books incl. *Jewish Influence on Christian Reform Movements* and *Hasidic Anthology.*

Four generations of the Newmark family, 1881.

Newman, Paul (1925–), U.S. actor. Films incl. *Cat on a Hot Tin Roof, The Hustler, Exodus, Sweet Bird of Youth, Butch Cassidy and the Sundance Kid,* and *The Sting.*

Newmark, U.S. family in L.A., Cal. **Joseph** (1799–1881), immigrated fr. W. Prussia. First spiritual leader of L.A. Jewish community. Founded Hebrew Benevolent Society and Congregation B'nai B'rith. His nephew **Harris** (1834–1916), leader in civic, economic, and Jewish life for over 60 years; railroad pioneer. A founder of town of Newmark, now Montebello. His memoirs imp. for history of S. California. Harris' son **Marco Ross** (1878–1959), business, civic leader. Pres. Historical Society of S. California.

New Mexico, U.S. state. German Jews there fr. 1846. By 1880 Jewish pop. incl. ranchers, mining promoters, railroad builders, irrigation experts. soldiers, and Indian traders. First mayor of Albuquerque was Jew. Jewish pop. 2,700, (1971), mostly in Albuquerque; newest community in Los Alamos.

New Moon (Heb. *Rosh Ḥodesh*), first day of month. In biblical times holiday. Special additional offerings were made in Temple. Observed liturgically by recitation of Half-*Hallel* and Additional Service *(Musaf).* Originally date fixed by actual observance of moon, but eventually became determined by calendrical reckoning. Can last one or two days, as calendar month is 29½ days.

New Moon, Announcement of, announcement made in synagogue on Sabbaths before New Moon. Reader leads congregation in stating which day(s) will begin coming month. Only exception is before New Moon of Tishri.

New Moon, Blessing of, see Moon, Blessing of.

New Orleans, city in La., U.S. Restrictive laws against Jews existed under French and Spanish during 18th c. Jews moved there in early 19th c. esp. after U.S. acquired Louisiana 1815. Jewish pop. 10,500 (1971).

The Touro Synagogue of Congregation Yeshuat Yisrael, Newport, R.I.

Newport, city in R.I., U.S. Jews settled there temporarily in late 1670s. Organized community founded in mid-1750s. Famous Touro synagogue (now national historical site) dedicated 1763. Community prospered during Revolutionary War but declined thereafter and only reorganized 1893. E. European Orthodox Congregation organized 1915. Jewish pop; 1,200 (1965).

New Testament, Christian Scriptures (in addition to Hebrew Bible called by them "Old Testament"). Designation derives fr. Jer. 31:30. Constituents incl. 4 Gospels and epistles of Paul. Books were composed at different times and canon determined in 2nd c. Language is Greek but based often on Hebrew-Aramaic original.

New Year, Mishnah (RH 1:1) enumerates four days for new year: 1) Nisan 1, New Year for Jewish kings and religious calendar; 2) Elul 1, New Year for tithing cattle; 3) Tishri 1, civil New Year (Rosh Ha-Shanah q.v.) and also for the Sabbatical and Jubilee years; 4) Shevat 15, New Year for trees (see Tu bi-Shevat).

New York, U.S. state. Jews settled in New Amsterdam (New York) 1654. Most Jewish settlers until 19th c. in N.Y.C. German Jewish immigration began during 1830s; many settled upstate on Hudson-Mohawk R. route, in Albany (1838), Syracuse (1839), Schenectady (1840), Buffalo (1847), Amsterdam (1847), Newburgh (1848), Utica (1848), Newkeepsie (1848), Troy (1850), Gloversville (1850), Kingston (1853), Hudson (1867), as well as along other rivers. Jews were predominantly merchants and peddlers; some farmers. E. European Jews came fr. 1880. Most settled in N.Y.C., with some settling in counties N. of city. After WWII there was migration from city to suburbs. Large numbers of Jews spent summers in upstate resort counties of Sullivan, Ulster, and Orange ("Borscht Belt"); several Jewish resort hotels became nationally famous. Jewish pop. 2,535,870 (1971).

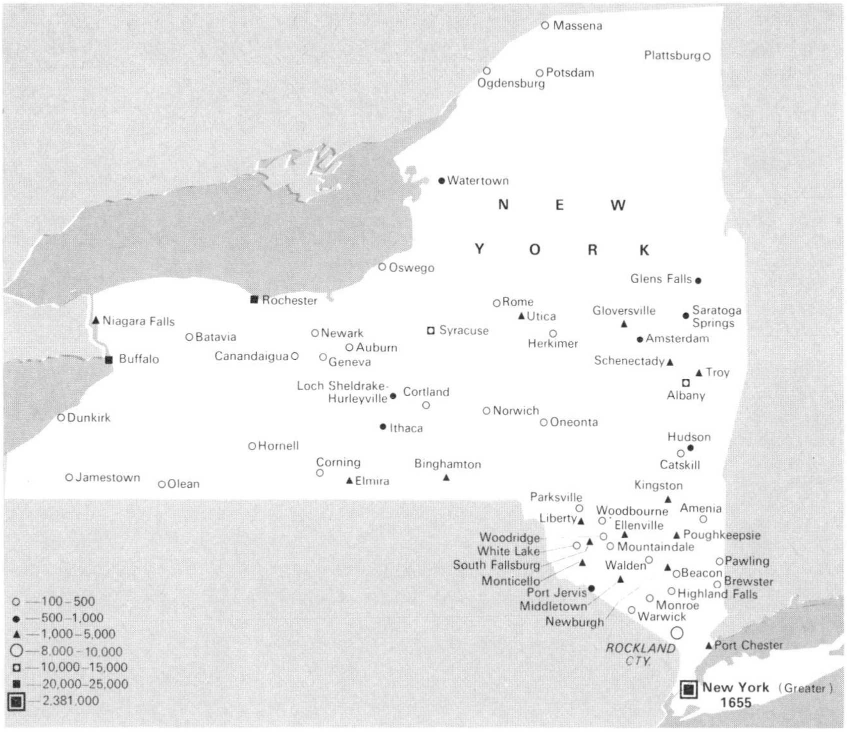

Jewish communities in New York.

New York, U.S. city. First Jews arrived 1654; attempts to settle opposed unsuccessfully by Peter Stuyvesant. Civil rights of Jews extended under British rule. First synagogue established 1729–30. Early settlers engaged mostly in commerce. Jews began to serve in professions and in public positions after Independence. Influx of British and German Jews brought population to 15,000 in 1847 and 40,000 on eve of Civil War. In early 19th c.

"Jewish Refugees from Russia passing the Statue of Liberty," engraving by C.J. Staniland, 1892.

Rally opposing U.S. Palestine policy, New York, July 1947.

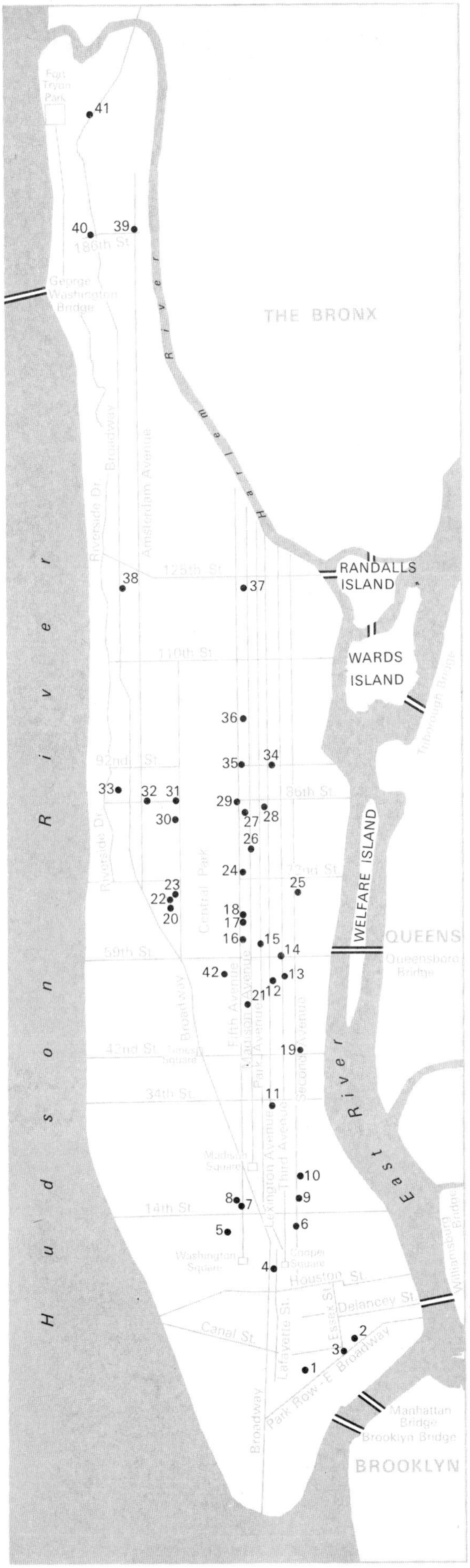

SYNAGOGUES

23 —Shearith Israel—18 W. 70th St.
33 —B'nai Jeshurun—257 W. 88th
28 —Kehilath Jeshurun—125 E. 85th
17 —Temple Emanu-El—5th Ave. and 65th St.
40 —K'hal Adath Jeshurun—85 Bennett Ave.
16 —Fifth Ave. Synagogue—5 E. 62nd St.
22 —Free Synagogue—30 W. 68th St.
30 —Rodeph Shalom—7 W. 83rd St.
32 —The Jewish Center—131 W. 86th St.
31 —S.A.J. Reconstructionist—15 W. 86th St.
12 —Central Synagogue—125 E. 55th St.

CEMETERIES

1 —Chatham Square Cemetery
5 —11th St. Cemetery—11th St. between 5th and 6th Avenues

HOSPITALS AND PHILANTHROPIC ORGANIZATIONS

36 —Mount Sinai—5th Ave.—Madison Ave; 97th St.—100th St.
41 —Jewish Memorial—Broadway and 196th St.
9 —Beth Israel—17th St. and Stuyvesant Square
37 —Joint Diseases—1919 Madison Ave.
21 —Hadassah—65 E. 52nd St.
42 —U.J.A.—1290 Ave. of the Americas
10 —United Hebrew Charities—356 2nd Ave.

YIDDISH INSTITUTIONS

6 —Yiddish Art Theater—2nd Ave., 12th St. (not in use)
3 —"Forward" Building—175 E. Broadway
29 —YIVO—1048 5th Ave.
26 —Atran Yiddish Culture House—25 E. 78th St.

ISRAEL INSTITUTIONS

19 —Israel Consulate— 800 2nd Ave.
15 —Jewish Agency—515 Park Ave.

EDUCATIONAL INSTITUTIONS

2 —Educational Alliance— 197 E. Broadway St.
20 —Jewish Institute of Religion—40 W. 68th St.
38 —Jewish Theological Seminary—Broadway and 122nd St.
39 —Yeshiva University—Amsterdam Ave. and 186th St.
4 —HIAS—425 Lafayette St. (not in use)
35 —Jewish Museum—1109 5th Ave.
34 —92nd St. Young Men's Hebrew Association—Lexington Ave. and E. 92nd St.

RELIGIOUS AND COMMUNITY RELATIONS ORGANIZATIONS

13 —American Jewish Committee—165 E. 56th St.
27 —American Jewish Congress—15 E. 84th St.
24 —New York Board of Rabbis—10 E. 73th St.
8 —National Council of Young Israel—3 W. 16th St.
7 —Union of Orthodox Jewish Congregations—84 5th. Ave.
25 —United Synagogue—218 E. 70th St.
18 —Union of American Hebrew Congregations—838 5th Ave.
14 —Federation of Jewish Philanthropies—130 E. 59th St.
11 —B'nai B'rith—315 Lexington Ave.

Places of Jewish interest in Manhattan, N.Y.C.

many different congregations were established: first ordained rabbis arrived fr. Europe in 1840s. Mutual aid and *landsmanshaft* societies proliferated from mid. 19th c. Jewish educational activities flourished. Massive immigration from Eastern Europe in late 19th and early 20th c. Originally concentrated in lower East Side in "sweatshop" conditions. Strong Jewish labor movement. By third generation, predominantly middle-class. Jewish population 1970 (already in numerical decline because of move to suburbs) 1,836,000 Jews (largest urban Jewish community in his-

tory). N.Y.C. is the center of most national Jewish organizations, of rabbinical seminaries of all three religious trends, and of Jewish, Yiddish, and Hebrew culture and press.

New Zealand, country in S. Pacific. First Jews 1829, Jewish community in Auckland founded 1840, another in Wellington 1843. Discovery of gold in 1860s led to establishment of other Jewish communities. At first mainly English, community was reinforced by immigrants fr. E. Europe and fr. 1933 fr. C. Europe. Jewish pop. 5,000 (1971).

New Zionist Organizations, see Revisionists.

Nezikin (Heb. "torts"), fourth order of the Mishnah, containing 10 tractates, devoted to civil law and the administration of justice.

Nicanor, Syrian officer sent to fight against Judah Maccabee and defeated by him at Emmaus. Another or same Nicanor was defeated at Bet Horon and slain. Date of this victory, 13 Adar, was observed by ancient Jews as annual feast day.

Nicaragua, C. American republic. Some Jews in 19th c. but present community founded after 1929 by Jews fr. E. Europe. Jewish pop. 200 (1971).

Nice, city in France. Community fr. 14th c. Refugees fr. Rhodes settled there 1499. Marranos fr. Italy and Holland arrived 1648 and Jews from Oran (Algeria) 1669. All Jews confined to ghetto 1732. Full emancipation 1848. During WWII thousands of Jews took refuge there. After liberation influx of Jews fr. N. Africa. Jewish pop. 20,000 (1971).

°**Nicholas De Lyre** (c. 1270–1349), French Bible commentator, theologian. Wrote controversial studies against Judaism. Author of first printed Christian Bible commentary.

°**Nicholas of Damascus** (b. c. 64 B.C.E.), historian, peripatetic philosopher, statesman. Joined court of Herod and interceded on his behalf with Marcus Agrippa and Augustus. Wrote (lost) Universal History, some of which may have been used by Josephus.

Nichols, Mike (1932–), U.S. comedian, director. Appeared in cabaret with Elaine May. Directed both Broadway plays and movies, incl. *Who's Afraid of Virginia Woolf?*, *The Graduate*, *Catch-22*.

Niddah (Heb. menstruous woman). Acc. to Jewish law woman is forbidden sexual intercourse fr. onset of menses until after seventh day. This was later taken as seven clean days after cessation of menstruation. She then requires immersion in *mikveh*.

Niddah, 7th tractate of Mishnah order *Tohorot*, with *gemara* in both Talmuds. Deals with ritual uncleanness of woman caused by her menses and other fluxes, and with menstrual irregularity and miscarriages.

Niemirower, Jacob Isaac (1872–1939), chief rabbi of Rumania, scholar. Elected to Rumanian senate 1926 and recognized by Rumanian government as representative of Jews. Had oath *more judaico* abolished. Active in establishing Jewish schools. Took part in First Zionist Congress.

Nierop, Van, family of Dutch jurists, economists. **Ahasverus Samuel** (1813–1878), leading Dutch attorney; sat in parliament. His son **Frederik** (1844–1925), director of Amsterdamsche Bank; senator for 26 years.

Nieto, David (1654–1728), philosopher, rabbi; *dayyan*, physician in Leghorn. Went to London as haham of Spanish and Portuguese synagogue. Wrote *Matteh Dan*, defense of Oral Law against attack of Marranos. Accused of Spinozistic leanings; exonerated by Ḥakham Ẓevi Ashkenazi. Succeeded as haham by his son, **Isaac** (1687–1773), who later resigned. Isaac published Spanish translation of Rosh Ha-Shanah and Day of Atonement liturgy.

Nifoci, Isaac (late 14th c.), physician, astronomer, scholar of Majorca. King of Aragon appointed him palace astronomer. Forcibly converted to Christianity 1391, but returned to Judaism and settled in Ereẓ Israel.

Niger, Samuel (Samuel Charney; 1883–1955), Yiddish literary critic; brother of Daniel Charney and Baruch Vladeck; b. Russia. Editor of Yiddish literary periodicals and lexicons of Yiddish literature; active in YIVO. Emigrated to U.S. 1920. Joined staff of *Der Tog*.

Niger of Perea (d. 68 C.E.), patriot leader in war against Romans. Commanded disastrous attacks on Ashkelon. Executed by Zealots in reign of terror in Jerusalem.

Night Prayer (called in Heb. "reading *Shema* on retiring [lit. on the bed]"), prayer read before going to sleep, consisting of first paragraph of *Shema* with blessing to "Him who causes the bands of sleep to fall upon my eyes," etc., with other verses and psalms added later.

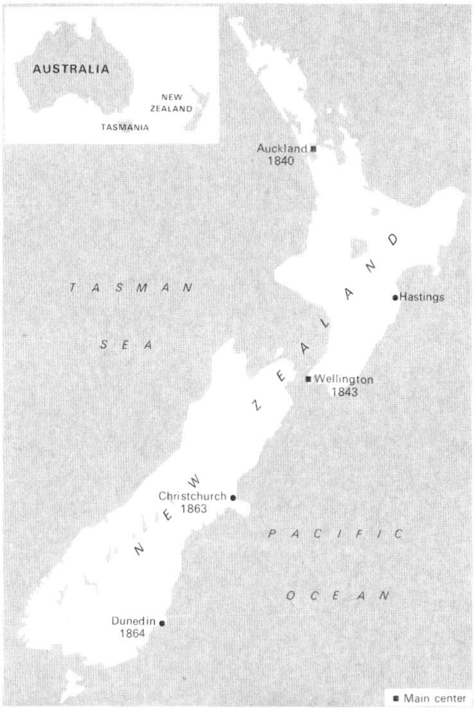

Jewish communities in New Zealand, with dates of establishment.

The first New Zealand synagogue, built 1867 in Hokitika.

Samuel Niger

David Nieto

Niggun (Heb.), traditional air, tune, or melody, esp. among Ḥasidim. Ḥasidic *niggunim*, sung first by the rabbi at table and then spread among the Ḥasidim, are mostly sung without words.

Nikel, Lea (1918–), Israel painter; in Paris 1950–61, settled in Safed. Outstanding representative of "New Horizons" group. Produced abstract paintings in which color is liberated fr. formal restraints.

Nikitin, Victor (1839–1908), Russian scholar, writer. As child kidnapped and sent to Cantonist (q.v.) regiment. Wrote on Jewish agricultural settlement in Russia.

Nikolayev, port in Ukrainian SSR. Jews settled at end of 18th c. Expelled 1834, established community 1866. Pogroms 1905, 1919–20. In 1926, 21,786 Jews. Under German occupation all Jews who remained were murdered. After liberation Jews began to return; 15,800 Jews in 1959.

Nikolsburg, see Mikulov.

Niles, David K. (1890–1952), U.S. presidential aide. Active in Democratic Party. Labor assistant in Works Progress Administration fr. 1935; assistant to Pres. Roosevelt fr. 1942. Remained in post with Pres. Truman and played important role in period leading to establishment of Israel.

Nili (Heb. acronym of *"Neẓah Yisrael Lo Yeshakker";* cf. I Sam. 15:29), pro-British Jewish espionage group operating under Turkish rule in Syria and Ereẓ Israel during WWI; founded by Aaron Aaronsohn of Zikhron Yaakov. Turks arrested and executed several of its members. Group made contact with British HQ in Cairo. Its activities caused disputes in Ereẓ Israel where some opposed it as endangering the Jewish community. In particular, friction with Ha-Shomer. Group broke up in 1919.

Nîmes, town in S. France. Jewish community established 10th c. Center of Jewish learning in Middle Ages. Expelled 1306, returned 1359 and lived in a separate quarter, ceased to exist 1394. Some Jews settled in late 18th c. 1,200 Jews in 1970, mainly of N. African origin.

Nimrod, biblical figure, grandson of Ham. Described as mighty hunter. First to found great empire after flood. Ruled over S. Mesopotamia and Assyria.

Nimzovitch, Aaron (1886–1935), chess master; b. Riga. Important theoretician; opposed "strong center" theory. N. Defense and N. Indian remain popular.

Nine Days, period of mourning from 1st to 9th of Av commemorating destruction of Temple. Strictly observant Jews, esp. Ashkenazim, abstain fr. meat and wine and recite special dirges.

Nineveh, Assyrian city. Acc. to Bible established in days of Nimrod. Zephaniah and Nahum prophesied its destruction. Acc. to Islamic tradition, Jonah buried there.

Ninth of Av, see Av, Ninth of.

Nir (Rafalkes), Nahum (1884–1968), labor leader; b. Poland. Active in left wing of Po'alei Zion. Settled in Ereẓ Israel 1925. A leader of Mapam, member of Knesset until 1965, second speaker of Knesset 1959.

Nirenberg, Marshall Warren (1927–), U.S. biochemist. Chief of biochemical genetics laboratory of National Heart Inst. Laid groundwork for solution of genetic code. Nobel Prize 1968.

Nisan, post-exilic name of 1st month of year; called in Pentateuch "month of spring" (Aviv). 30 days. Zodiac sign Aries. Passover falls on 15th and all public mourning is prohibited during month.

Nishmat Kol Ḥai (Heb. "the soul of every living being"), prayer recited at Sabbath and festival morning prayers, expressing gratitude to God as sustainer. Also part of *Haggadah.*

Nisibis (Neẓibin), town in S. Anatolia. Jews present in 1st c. when town was prosperous trading center. Torah center in 2nd c. Jews prospered until 10th c. In late 19th c., half of town's 200 families were Jewish.

Nissan (Katznelson), Avraham (1888–1956), labor politician in Ereẓ Israel, Israel diplomat, physician; b. Belorussia, settled in Ereẓ Israel 1924. Directed health dept. of Zionist Exec. 1931–48, member of Mapai, Israel's minister to Scandinavian countries 1950–56.

Nisselovich, Leopold (Eliezer; 1856–1914), a representative of Russian Jews to Third Duma in Russia. Presented bill proposing abolition of Pale of Settlement, but it did not reach formal vote.

Nissenbaum, Isaac (1868–1942), Polish rabbi, writer, religious Zionist. Secretary to R. Samuel Mohilewer and participated in foundation of Mizrachi movement. An editor of *Ha-Ẓefirah.* Killed in Warsaw ghetto. Published sermons, essays on Zionism, memoirs.

Nissi ben Berechiah al-Nahrawani (9th–10th c.), head of *kallah,* poet in Babylon. Refused geonate because of his blindness. Important and fruitful *paytan;* many of his

Beginning of "Nishmat Kol Ḥai" in "Rothschild Miscellany," Ferrara (?), c. 1470.

piyyutim were discovered in Cairo *Genizah*.

Nissim, Abraham Ḥayyim (1878–1952), Iraqi government official. For 18 years represented Iraqi Jewry in parliament. Settled in Israel 1951.

Nissim, Isaac (1896–), chief rabbi of Israel *(Rishon le-Zion)* 1955–72; b. Baghdad, settled in Ereẓ Israel 1925. Author of responsa.

Nissim ben Jacob ben Nissim ibn Shahin (c. 990–1062), N. African talmudist. Headed Kairouan academy. Versatile and prolific writer; some of his works published in Vilna Talmud. His *Ḥibbur me-ha-Yeshu'ah*, collection of Hebrew stories, became very popular. His daughter married Jehoseph, son of Samuel ha-Nagid.

Nissim ben Reuben Gerondi (Ran; ? 1310–? 1375), Spanish talmudist, authoritative *posek*, yeshivah head in Barcelona. Wrote Scroll of Law 1336 which served as model and reached Tiberias. Wrote novellae on Alfasi's commentary on Talmud as well as on Talmud itself. His commentary of *Nedarim* is much studied. Also wrote responsa and *piyyutim*.

Nissu'in, see Marriage.

Nister, Der, see Der Nister.

Nittai of Arbela (2nd c. B.C.E.), one of *zugot*, with Joshua b. Peraḥyah. Saying: "Keep far from an evil neighbor; do not make yourself an associate of a wicked man; do not abandon faith in Divine retribution" (*Avot* 1:7).

Nizer, Louis, (1902–), U.S. lawyer, author. Active in areas related to arts, copyright, plagiarism, etc. Author of courtroom reminiscences and book on Rosenberg Case.

Niẓẓanah, former town in Negev; founded in 2nd/1st c. B.C.E. by Nabateans. Abandoned 106 C.E.; rebuilt by emperor Theodosius I in 4th c. Papyri discovered show that mixed Arab-Greek administration persisted until 750 C.E. Later abandoned until its reoccupation by Turks 1908. Egyptian invasions started there 1948.

Niẓẓanim, kibbutz and youth village in S. Israel, affiliated with Ha-No'ar ha-Ẓiyyoni; founded 1943. Temporarily occupied by Egyptians 1948. Youth village and farming school belonging to Youth Aliyah opened 1949.

Noachide Laws, seven laws, given to Noah, considered by rabbis as incumbent on all men without exception; prohibition of idolatry, blasphemy, bloodshed, sexual sin, theft, eating limb torn from animal while living, and injunction to establish legal system.

Noah, main figure in biblical flood narrative (Gen. 6 ff). Only righteous man in his time; designated by God to be saved fr. universal catastrophe. Instructed to build ark and take aboard members of his family and representatives of animal and bird kingdom. After flood, God made covenant promising its non-recurrence. Flood myths are to be found in Mesopotamian sources. Noah was also first to plant vineyard.

Noah, Books of, pseudepigraphical writings attributed to Noah. Portions have been identified in books of Jubilees and Enoch. Some fragments found in Dead Sea Scrolls.

Mordecai M. Noah

Noah, Mordecai Manuel (1785–1851), U.S. editor, politician, playwright. One of most influential American Jews in early 19th c. Right-wing and patriotic in politics. U.S. consul to Tunis 1813–15. High sheriff of N.Y. 1822. Edited leading N.Y. papers. His many plays reflect patriotic fervor. After failure of proposal to found Ararat, Jewish colony nr. Buffalo, advocated Ereẓ Israel as national home for Jews.

Nob, priestly town nr. Jerusalem; identified with site nr. village of 'Isawiyya on Mt. Scopus. On Saul's order, 85 priests were killed there because chief priest Ahimelech gave support to David.

Nobel, Nehemiah Anton (1871–1922), German Orthodox rabbi, religious leader; pioneer of Zionist Movement in Germany and a founder of "Mizrachi." Rabbi of Frankfort fr. 1910.

°**Noeldeke, Theodor** (1836–1930), German orientalist. Expert on comparative philology of Semitic languages in biblical and rabbinic fields.

Nola, Elijah ben Menahem da (c. 1530–c.1602), Italian Hebraist, apostate. A leading rabbi of Rome; induced to apostatize and became *scrittore* at Vatican library. Copied many Hebrew mss. and wrote apologia for his apostasy.

JEWISH NOBEL PRIZE WINNERS

World Peace	
1911	Alfred Fried
1911	Tobias Michael Carel Asser
1968	René Cassin
Literature	
1910	Paul Johann Ludwig Heyse
1927	Henri Bergson
1958	Boris Pasternak
1966	Shmuel Yosef Agnon
1966	Nelly Sachs
Physiology and Medicine	
1908	Elie Metchnikoff
1908	Paul Ehrlich
1914	Robert Bárány
1922	Otto Meyerhof
1930	Karl Landsteiner
1931	Otto Warburg
1936	Otto Loewi
1944	Joseph Erlanger
1944	Herbert Spencer Gasser
1945	Ernst Boris Chain
1946	Hermann Joseph Muller
1950	Tadeus Reichstein
1952	Selman Abraham Waksman
1953	Hans Krebs
1953	Fritz Albert Lipmann
1958	Joshua Lederberg
1959	Arthur Kornberg
1964	Konrad Bloch
1965	François Jacob
1965	Andre Lwoff
1967	George Wald
1968	Marshall W. Nirenberg
1969	Salvador Luria
1970	Julius Axelrod
1970	Sir Bernard Katz
1972	Gerald Maurice Edelman
Chemistry	
1905	Adolph Von Baeyer
1906	Henri Moissan
1910	Otto Wallach
1915	Richard Willstaetter
1918	Fritz Haber
1943	George Charles de Hevesy
1961	Melvin Calvin
1962	Max Ferdinand Perutz
1972	William Howard Stein
Physics	
1907	Albert Abraham Michelson
1908	Gabriel Lippmann
1921	Albert Einstein
1922	Niels Bohr
1925	James Franck
1925	Gustav Hertz
1943	Otto Stern
1944	Isidor Isaac Rabi
1952	Felix Bloch
1954	Max Born
1959	Emilio Segrè
1960	Donald A. Glaser
1961	Robert Hofstadter
1962	Lev Davidovich Landau
1965	Richard Phillips Feynman
1965	Julian Schwinger
1967	Hans Albrecht Bethe
1969	Murray Gell-Mann
1971	Dennis Gabor
Economics	
1970	Paul Anthony Samuelson
1971	Simon Kuznets
1972	Kenneth Joseph Arrow

Nomberg, Hersh David (1876–1927), Yiddish author. Wrote first in Hebrew but turned to Yiddish. Wrote short stories, essays, and was one of best interpreters of I.L. Peretz. Pres. Society for Jewish Writers and Journalists in Warsaw. A founder of Folkspartei.

Nones, Benjamin (1757–1826), U.S. patriot, soldier in American Revolution; b. France. Aide to General Washington. Subsequently active in Republican politics in Philadelphia.

Nordau, Max (Simon Maximilian Suedfeld; 1849–1923), Zionist leader, philosopher, writer; b. Hungary, settled in Paris 1880 as physician. Achieved fame as thinker and social critic; criticized "religious lie," philosophical topics, major figures and trends in European culture. Also writer of belles lettres. Herzl brought him to Zionism; a co-founder of World Zionist Organization, drafted Basle Program 1897, key figure at Zionist Congresses. Advocated political Zionism. Took refuge in Spain during WWI. Subsequently demanded mass Jewish immigration to Ereẓ Israel. His daughter **Maxa** (1897–), painter in France, wrote memoirs.

Max Nordau

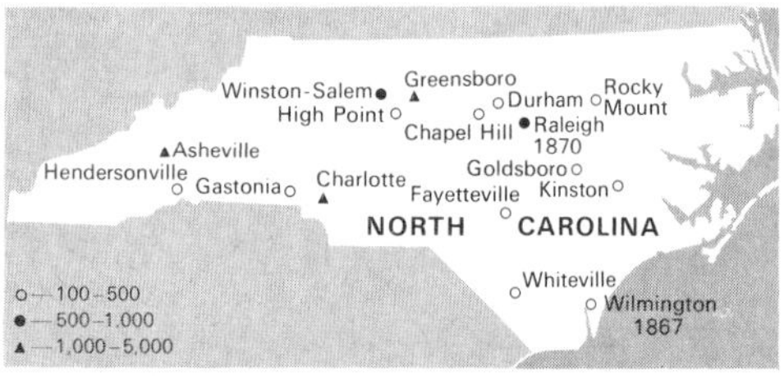

Jewish communities in N. Carolina and dates of establishment.

Norden, family of S. African pioneers. **Benjamin** (1798–1875), traveled to interior, later set up store in Cape Town; first pres. Hebrew Congregation. **Joshua Davis** (1803–1846), auctioneer, municipal and commercial leader, soldier. Settled in Grahamstown. Killed in Kaffir wars.

Norfolk, city in Va., U.S. First Jewish settler, Moses Myers, arrived 1787, building mansion which is historical monument today. First congregation founded 1848 by German Jews. E. European newcomers founded Orthodox congregations. Jewish pop. 10,000 (1971).

Norman, Edward Albert (1900–1955), U.S. financier, philanthropist. Though non-Zionist, very interested in Ereẓ Israel, founding American Fund for Israel Institutions 1939. Directed and participated in many Jewish philanthropic activities.

Noronha, Ferano de (? 1470–? 1540), New Christian explorer, colonizer of Brazil. With group of New Christians developed large tracts in Brazil. Wealthy merchant.

Norsa, Hannah (d. 1785), English actress. Became known for portrayal of Polly Peachum in *The Beggar's Opera* fr. 1732.

North Carolina, U.S. state. One of first colonies to welcome Jewish settlement, in late 17th c. Last disabilities abolished in 19th c. Immigration first fr. Germany in late 19th c. First congregation at Wilmington 1867. Jewish pop. 10,165 (1971).

North Dakota, U.S. state. Baron de Hirsch's ICA unsuccessfully tried to establish Jewish settlement on Missouri River 1882. Synagogue chartered in Fargo by 1896. Jewish pop. 1,250 (1971).

Norwalk, city in Conn., U.S. Small Jewish community 1760, expanded by N.Y. Jews fleeing British 1776. Community ended with burning of town by British 1779. Refounded in 1870s by E. European immigrants. First synagogue 1906. Jewish pop. 5,000 (1971).

Norway, kingdom in N. Europe. Jewish presence not permitted until 1830s; full civil rights 1851. 760 of 1,700 Jews killed in Holocaust. Jewish pop. 750 (1971), mainly in Oslo.

Norwich, town in England. First recorded blood libel in Europe 1144. Medieval community ended with expulsion fr. England 1290. Modern

Pictorial record of attempt to establish Jewish settlement in N. Dakota at end of 19th cent., showing prospective settlers at Missouri River, some established homesteads, and list of 40 settlers.

community established 18th c. Jewish pop. 100–200 throughout 20th c.

Norzi, Jedidiah Solomon Raphael ben Abraham (1560–1616), Italian rabbi, biblical and masoretic scholar, member of distinguished family. Author of *Minḥat Shai,* critical, masoretic commentary on Bible. Traveled to many countries.

Coat of arms of the Norzi family, 1493.

Nosaḥ, see Nusaḥ.

Nossig, Alfred (1864–1943), writer, sculptor, musician in Poland. Initially assimilationist, became active Zionist. Pioneer in scientific study of Jewish statistics. Member of *Judenrat* in Warsaw; executed by Jewish underground on charge of collaborating with Nazis.

Nostradamus (1503–1566), French astrologer, physician of Jewish descent. His *Les Centuries* is one of most famous astrological works of all time, incl. many predictions that appeared to come true (death of Henry II, English and French revolutions, career of German dictator whom he called Hister).

Notarikon (Gr.), abbreviation arrived at by shortening word or writing only one letter of each word (based on ancient shorthand). In this way words of Torah are made to imply fresh meaning in aggadic usage. It was method of Bible interpretation. Widespread in homiletical and kabbalistic literature.

°**Noth, Martin** (1902–1968), German Bible scholar. Director of Deutsches Evangelische Institut in Jerusalem 1965–68. Wrote on Israelite history. Suggested that fr. time of settlement in Canaan, Israelites organized in 12-tribe confederation. Leading representative of form-critical approach.

Notkin, Nata (d. 1804). Russian merchant, army contractor. Champion of improvement of status of Russian Jews. Founder of St. Petersburg community.

Novellae, see Ḥiddushim.

Novi Sad, city in Yugoslavia. Jews settled in 16th c. Treated well under Ottoman rule (16th–17th c.), subject to limitations under Austro-Hungarian regime, and property destroyed during Hungarian revolution 1848–49. 4,000 Jews in 1941; exterminated by Hungarians and Germans. 200 Jews in 1970.

Novogrudok, city in Belorussian SSR. Jewish community known 1529; lived in special quarter fr. 1563. In late 19th c. center of Musar movement. 6,000 Jews in 1939. Under Germans ghetto set up and Jews liquidated.

Novomeysky, Moshe (1873–1961), industrial pioneer in Ereẓ Israel; b. Siberia, graduated as mining engineer, settled in Ereẓ Israel 1920. Founded Palestine Potash Co., and large chemical enterprise Fertilizers and Chemicals. Active in public affairs and in Haganah.

Novy Izrail, see New Israel.

°**Nowack, Wilhelm Gustav Hermann** (1850–1928), German Bible critic. Wrote commentaries on biblical books and on religious development of ancient Israel.

Nowaczynski, Adolf (1876–1944), Polish playwright, satirist; son of Catholic aristocrat and Jewess; pen name Neuwert. Wrote historical dramas and satirical attacks on Jews and Polish bourgeoisie. Killed during anti-German Warsaw Uprising.

Nowakowski, David (1848–1921), Russian choirmaster, cantor of Odessa. His compositions widely sung by cantors and choirs.

Nowy Dziennik, first Zionist Polish-language journal. Appeared daily in Cracow fr. end of 1918 until Holocaust.

Nowy Sacz (In Jewish sources **Zanz**), city in Poland. Jews there 1469. Compelled by Austrian authorities to live in special quarter in early 19th c. Ḥasidic Zanz dynasty established in first half of 19th c.; schools and yeshivah founded at end of century. 10,000 Jews in 1939, ghetto set up 1941, all Jews deported to Belzec death camp 1942.

Nudelman, Santiago I. (1904–), Argentine politician. Member of Federal Chamber of Deputies 1946–55. Championed cause of civil liberties in parliament. Director daily newspaper *Critica* fr. 1958.

Nuernberg, see Nuremberg.

Numbers, Book of (Heb. *Be-Midbar*), 4th book of Pentatuach. History of Israelites in wilderness (fr. 2nd to 40th year) and contains legislation.

BOOK OF NUMBERS – CONTENTS

Chs:	1:1–4:20	The organization of the camp
	1:1–54	The census of the tribes
	2:1–34	The position of the tribes in the camp
	3:1–4:20	The levites taken to assist the priests
Chs:	5:1–6:27	Various laws
Chs:	7:1–89	The consecration of the altar
Chs:	8:1–10:10	Various laws
Chs:	10:11–22:1	From Mt. Sinai to the border of Canaan
	10:11–11:35	Setting out for Canaan
	12:1–16	Miriam's leprosy
	13:1–14:45	The 12 spies sent to Canaan
	15:1–41	Regulations concerning offerings
	16:1–17:28	The rebellion of Korah, Dathan, and Abiram
	18:1–19:22	Regulations concerning priests and levites
	20:1–22:1	Israel at Kadesh
Chs:	22:2–24:25	Various events at the border of Canaan and various laws
	22:2–24:25	The story of Balaam
	25:1–19	Israel at Shittim
	26:1–65	The second census
	27:1–11	The law of inheritance of daughters of Zelophehad
	27:12–14	Moses commanded to view Canaan before his death
	27:15–23	Joshua selected as Moses' successor
	28:1–29:39	A priestly calendar of sacrifices for each season
	30:1–17	The law of vows
	31:1–54	The war of vengeance against Midian
	32:1–42	Allotment of Transjordanian region
	33:1–49	The journey from Raamses to the steppes of Moab
	33:50–56	Directions concerning the occupation of Canaan
	34:1–15	The borders of Israel's territory west of the Jordan
	34:16–29	A list of Joshua's assistants for the allotment of the territory
	35:1–34	Levitical cities and cities of refuge
	36:1–13	Laws for female heirs

Hebrew letters used as numbers.

100	ק	19	י"ט	10	י	1	א
200	ר	20	כ	11	י"א	2	ב
300	ש	30	ל	12	י"ב	3	ג
400	ת	40	מ	13	י"ג	4	ד
500	ת"ק ך	50	נ	14	י"ד	5	ה
600	ת"ר ם	60	ס	15	ט"ו	6	ו
700	ת"ש ן	70	ע	16	ט"ז	7	ז
800	ת"ת ף	80	פ	17	י"ז	8	ח
900	תת"ק ץ	90	צ	18	י"ח	9	ט

Numbers Rabbah, aggadic Midrash to Book of Numbers. Part of Midrash Rabbah.

Numerus Clausus, fixed number of Jews or other minorities admitted in institutes of higher learning, professions, etc. Implemented officially in pre-Revolutionary Russia and E. Europe, and unofficially in varying degrees elsewhere.

Nun (נ ; final form ן), 14th letter of Hebrew alphabet; numerical value 50. Pronounced "n."

Nuremberg Jewish hawker, c. 1790, etching by A. Gabler.

Nunberg, Herman (1884–1970), U.S. psychiatrist; b. Poland, in U.S. fr. 1932. Teacher, researcher, clinician. Wrote *Problems of Bisexuality as Reflected in Circumcision.*

Nuñez, family of Portuguese Marranos. **Pedro** (1492–1577), geographer, mathematician, cartographer, cosmographer to king of Portugal. **Henrique** (d. 1524), New Christian. Informed on fellow Jews who clung to faith. Assassinated; canonized by Church. **David Nuñez-Torres** (18th c.), talmudist, publisher, *ḥakham* in Netherlands.

Nuñez, Hector (1521–1591), leader of Marrano community in England in reign of Elizabeth I; b. Portugal. Distinguished physician and successful merchant. Used trading connections to provide military information to British government.

Nuremberg, city in SW Germany. Jews present fr. 12th c. Suffered numerous persecutions in Middle Ages: 728 killed in *Rindfleisch* massacres 1298, 560 burnt to death in one day in Black Death persecutions 1349. Expelled 1499, community refounded in 19th c. 9,000 Jews in 1933. Center of Nazi movement. Community ended in WWII. Small community subsequently refounded.

Nuremberg Laws, anti-Jewish laws promulgated by Nazis Sept. 1935, depriving Jews of citizenship and many civil rights (Jews forbidden to marry non-Jews, etc.).

Nurock, Mordechai (1879–1962), religious Zionist leader; b. Courland. Member of Latvian parliaments, defender of rights of national minorities, a leader of Mizrachi movement. In Soviet Union 1939–45, settled in Israel 1948. Member of Knesset, minister of posts 1952.

Nusaḥ (Nosaḥ). (1) textual variant; (2) prayer rite; (3) accepted tradition of synagogue melody.

Nusinov, Isaac (1889–1952), Russian literary critic, historian. Taught at Univ. of Moscow. Expert in Yiddish. Arrested 1948; executed.

Nussbaum, Arthur (1877–1964), jurist. Prof. at Univ. of Berlin 1921, Columbia 1934. Prolific writer in German and English; authority on commercial and private international law.

Nussbaum, Hilary (Hillel; 1820–1895), Polish historian, educator, communal worker. Wrote popular works on Jewish history. Moderate assimilationist.

Nussbaum, Max (1910–), U.S. rabbi, organizational leader. Rabbi in Berlin. Went to U.S. 1940, rabbi in Hollywood, Cal. fr. 1942. Pres. Zionist Organization of America; chairman of American section of World Jewish Congress.

Nuzi, ancient city in NE Iraq. Excavations revealed extensive documents throwing light on lives and customs of Hurrians which are of importance for biblical studies, esp. for patriarchal period, biblical law.

Initial letter "O" for "Ozias" at the beginning of the prologue to the Book of Amos in a 13th-cent. Latin Bible, France.

Oakland, city in Cal., U.S. Jewish community fr. 1862; first congregation 1875. Jewish pop. (1971), incl. Alameda and Contra Costa counties, 18,000.

Oath More Judaico, special form of oath Jews obliged to take in Middle Ages in lawsuits, intended to humiliate and degrade them. Concomitant ceremonies also humiliating (e.g. standing on sow's skin).

Obadiah, prophet, author of shortest book in Bible, 4th of Minor Prophets. Some scholars regard book as single prophetic speech; others divide book into two or more sections. Contains anti-Edomite polemic and prophecies concerning Day of Lord. Probably written shortly after 587 B.C.E.

Obadiah, king of Khazars responsible for religious reform in Khazaria c.800.

Obadiah (11th–12th c.), Norman proselyte. Catholic priest who converted to Judaism. Settled in Fostat in Egypt; writings by him have been found in Cairo *Genizah.* His notations of synagogal chant are the earliest yet discovered.

Obadiah of Bertinoro, see Bertinoro, Obadiah.

Obermann, Julian Joël (1888–1956), orientalist; b. Warsaw, in U.S. fr. 1923. Prof. of Semitic languages at Yale Univ. fr. 1935. Co-editor of *Journal of Biblical Literature* 1933–36. Director of Judaic Research in Yale and editor of Yale Judaica Series.

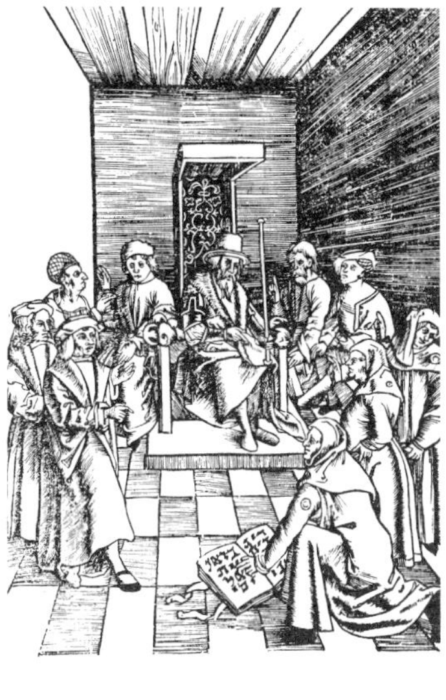

Woodcut showing Jew taking special Jewish oath, "more judaico."

The "piyyut" "Mi al Har Ḥorev" with its melody notated in neumes by Obadiah the Proselyte, written from left to right to correspond to the Hebrew text.

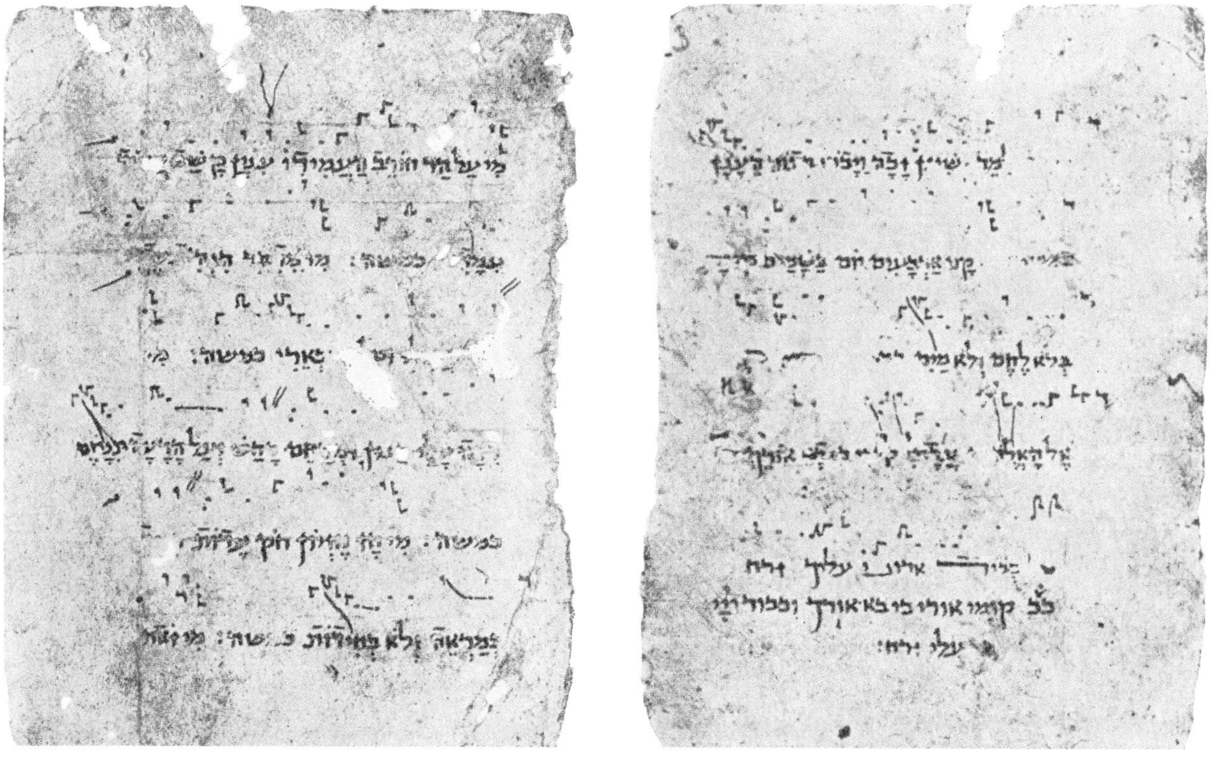

Julius Ochs

Adolph Simon Ochs

George Washington Ochs

Milton Barlow Ochs

Drawing of the main synagogue of Odessa, built 1840.

Clifford Odets

Jacques Offenbach

Obermeyer, Jacob (1845–1935), traveler, scholar, teacher; traveled in Middle East. His *Die Landschaft Babylonien* is standard work, incl. personal observations as well as works of Arab geographers and Hebrew sources.

Ochs, family of U.S. newspaper publishers. **Julius** (1826–1888), emigrated fr. Bavaria, settled in Knoxville, Tenn. and led Jewish community. His three sons became prominent publishers and editors. **Adolph Simon** (1858–1935), acquired failing *Chattanooga Times* and made it one of leading papers in South. Took over declining *New York Times* 1896, revitalized it, and published it for 39 years. **George Washington** (1861–1931) and **Milton B.** (1864–1955) joined him in various capacities with *New York Times.*

Odessa, city in Ukrainian SSR. Jewish community founded in late 18th c. Fr. 1880s to 1920s second largest community in Russia. Before Revolution, Jews heavily represented in trade, industry, medicine; large Jewish proletariat. Most "Western" community in Pale of Settlement. Extensive network of Jewish schools, linguistic and cultural centers; strong national and Hebrew movements. Major center of Hibbat Zion (see Odessa Committee) and Zionism and of Hebrew literature and journalism. Severe pogroms took place 1821, 1859, 1871, 1881, 1905, and Jewish self-defense movement was active. Many of 180,000 Jews managed to leave before German-Rumanian occupation in WWII, but of 80,000–90,000 who remained, few survived. After WWII, Jews returned and it became one of biggest Jewish centers in USSR. 103,000 Jews in 1970.

Odessa Committee (shortened name for *Society for Support of Jewish Farmers and Artisans in Syria and Palestine),* legalized framework of Ḥibbat Zion movement; founded in Odessa 1890 with permission of Russian government and continued work of Ḥovevei Zion in Russia until 1919.

Odets, Clifford (1906–1963), U.S. playwright. In his expressionist dramas *(Waiting for Lefty, Awake and Sing!)* expressed hardship of great depression of 1930s. Other plays incl. *Golden Boy, The Country Girl.*

°**Oenomaus of Gadara** (2nd c.), pagan philosopher who lived during reign of Hadrian; generally identified with Avnimos ha-Gardi mentioned in rabbinic literature as friendly with rabbis and held by them in high esteem.

°**Oesterley, William Oscar Emil** (1866–1950), English Semitic scholar. Sought to demonstrate talmudic influence on New Testament form and content. Wrote history of Israel (with T.H.Robinson), works on Bible, and outline of Jewish literature (with G.H. Box).

Ofakim, development town in S. Israel, founded 1955. Pop. 9,300 (1971).

Ofek, Uriel (1926–), Israel children's writer. Editor of children's publication, author of poems, stories, and plays for children.

Offenbach, city in W. Germany. Members of community martyred in Black Death persecutions 1348. New community 1614, Jacob Frank lived there 1788–91, and his daughter until 1817. 554 Jews in 1939; deported in WWII. Hebrew book printed in Offenbach fr. 1714–c. 1738, 1767–1832.

Offenbach, Jacques (1819–1880), French composer of comic opera and operettas; son of German cantor Isaac Offenbach (1779–1850). After years of failure, bought own theater in Champs-Elysées and succeeded with *Orpheus in the Underworld, Helen the Beautiful,* etc. Composed c. 100 stage works. Best-known work *Tales of Hoffman,* performed posthumously.

Official, Nathan ben Joseph, and his son **Joseph** (13th c.), leading polemicists of Franco-German Jewry. Joseph wrote *Yosef ha-Mekanne* describing debate with leading churchmen and providing verse by verse refutation of Christological interpretation of Bible. Also contains Jewish challenge to Christianity.

Ofner, Julius (1845–1924), Austrian lawyer, politician. In Austrian parliament fought for comprehensive social legislation. Appointed to Supreme Court. Advocated abolition of ecclesiastic jurisdiction in matters of marriage and divorce.

Ofran (Ifran), place in Anti-Atlas region, SW Morocco. Reputedly first site of Jewish settlement in Morocco. 50 Jews martyred 1792. Community declined in 19th, 20th c; by 1955 all emigrated to Israel.

Og, ruler of Bashan, one of Amorite kings in Transjordan during time of Moses. Described as belonging to race of giants (Deut. 3:11). Defeated by Israelites and land was taken by half the tribe of Manasseh. Subject of many legends.

Ohel, Israel theater company, originally known as Workers' Theater of Palestine; founded 1925 by Moses Halevy under Histadrut auspices; closed 1969.

Ohio, U.S. state. First congregation organized 1824 in Cincinnati, which remained preeminent Jewish settlement during most of 19th c. Cleveland's first congregation founded 1839; other early Jewish communities in Columbus (1838), Dayton (1842), Akron (1850), Hamilton (1855), Piqua (1858), Portsmouth (1858). Jewish pop. 158,560 (1971), half in Cleveland.

Oholiab, Danite appointed with Bezalel to construct Tent of Meeting and its furnishings.

Oholot (Heb. "Tents"), 2nd tractate of Mishnah order *Tohorot,* with no *gemara.* Deals with impurity conveyed by corpse either by touch or proximity. Uncleanness lasts 7 days and requires sprinkling with water mixed with ashes of Red Heifer.

Ohrbach, family of U.S. department store owners. **Nathan M.** (1885–1972) and his son **Jerome Kane** (1907–), both active in general and Jewish public organizations.

Oistrakh, David Fedorovich (1908–), Russian violinist. Made first public appearance at age 8. Prof. at Moscow Conservatory. Made several world tours, universally recognized as master. Son **Igor** (1931–), also violinist.

Okhlah ve-Okhlah (Heb.), early collection of masoretic notes to Bible text, arranged partly alphabetically and partly in order of books of Bible. Date and author unknown, but first mentioned in 10th c.

Oklahoma, U.S. state, Jews arrived in 1870s and 1880s. First congregation organized in Oklahoma City 1903. Jewish pop. 5,940 (1971).

Oko, Adolph S. (1883–1944), U.S. librarian, expert on Spinoza. Librarian of Hebrew Union College, Cincinnati. Collected Spinozana and wrote *The Spinoza Bibliography.*

Olam ha-Ba (Heb. "the coming world"), term used in contrast to *olam ha-zeh* (present world); hereafter which begins with termination of man's earthly life.

Olgin (Novomisky), Moses J. (1878–1939), writer, editor, translator; b. Russia, in New York fr. 1914. Originally in Bund, moved to Communist position and was founder of N.Y. Communist Yiddish daily *Freiheit.*

°**Oliphant, Laurence** (1829–1888), English proto-Zionist, Christian mystic. Went to Ereẓ Israel 1879 and negotiated tenancy rights in Gilead region, but rejected by Sultan. Settled in Haifa. Helped Bilu settlers. Wrote *Land of Gilead, Haifa, or Life in Modern Palestine.*

Olitzki, Aryeh Leo, (1898–), Israel bacteriologist; b. Prussia, settled in Ereẓ Israel 1924. Prof. at Heb. Univ., dean of Medical School. Worked on immunology and seriology of infectious diseases.

Olitzky, family of three brothers, all Yiddish authors. **Leib** (1897–), poet, short story writer; lived in E. Europe and Israel; **Baruch** (1907–1941), poet; died in Holocaust; **Mattes** (1915–), poet; in New York since WWII.

Olivetti, family of Italian industrialists. **Camillo** (1868–1943), founded firm, initially for electrical instruments, then typewriters. **Adriano** (1901–1960), extended firm and workers' social privileges. Member of Italian parliament.

Oliveyra, Solomon ben David de (d. 1708), rabbi, philologist, poet; b. Lisbon; lived in Amsterdam, presiding over the rabbinical council. Wrote in Hebrew and Portuguese.

Ollendorff, Franz (1900–), Israel engineer; b. Berlin. Organized immigration of Jewish children to Ereẓ Israel in 1930s. Prof. at Haifa Technion. Israel Prize 1954.

Ollendorf, Friedrich (1889–1951), German social welfare expert. Pioneer of modern welfare legislation in Germany. Settled in Ereẓ Israel 1934. Director social welfare dept. of Va'ad Le'ummi.

Olmo, Jacob Daniel ben Abraham (c. 1690–1757), Italian rabbi, poet. Head of yeshivah of Ferrara, rabbi of its Ashkenazi synagogue, and succeeded Lampronti as head of local court. Wrote poetic drama *Eden Arukh,* continuation of Zacuto's *Tofteh Arukh.*

Olshan, Isaac (1895–), Israel jurist; b. Lithuania, settled in Ereẓ Israel 1912. Served in Jewish Legion in WWI, practiced law in Ereẓ Israel 1927–48, appointed to Supreme Court (pres. 1953–65).

°**Olshausen, Justus** (1800–1882), German orientalist, theologian, Bible scholar. One of first to use modern philological and comparative linguistic methods in explanation of obscure passages in Bible. Pioneered Arabic as key to elucidation of Bible and understanding of Hebrew language.

Olsvanger, Immanuel (1888–1961), folklorist, Hebrew translator; b. Poland, settled in Ereẓ Israel 1933. Translator of Far East literary texts and German and Italian literature. His collections of Yiddish proverbs and anecdotes were printed in Latin characters.

Olympic Games Medalists, see p. 462.

Omaha, city in Neb., U.S. First Jews in mid-1850s; first congregation 1871. Jewish refugees fr. Russia arrived 1882. Jewish pop. 6,500.

Meir Margalit as Shimele Soroker in the Ohel production of Shalom Aleichem's "Ammekha," 1964.

Jewish communities in Ohio.

David Oistrakh

JEWISH OLYMPIC MEDAL WINNERS

G = Gold S = Silver B = Bronze

	G	S	B
1896			
Alfred Flatow, Germany, gymnastics	3		
Felix Flatow, Germany, gymnastics	2		
Alfred Hajos-Guttmann, Hungary, swimming	2		
Dr. Paul Neumann, Austria, swimming	1		
Alfred Flatow, Germany, gymnastics		1	
Otto Herschmann, Austria, swimming			1
Felix Schmal, Austria, cycling	1		2
1900			
Myer Prinstein, USA, track	1		
Myer Prinstein, USA, track		1	
Otto Wahle, Austria, swimming		2	
Siegfried Flesch, Austria, fencing			1
1904			
Myer Prinstein, USA track	2		
Samuel Berger, USA, boxing	1		
Daniel Frank, USA, track		1	
Otto Wahle, Austria, swimming			1
1908			
Dr. Jeno Fuchs, Hungary, fencing	2		
Dr. Oszkar Gerde, Hungary, fencing	1		
Lajos Werkner, Hungary, fencing	1		
Alexandre Lippmann, France, fencing	1		
Richard Weisz, Hungary, wrestling	1		
Jean Stern, France, fencing	1		
Alexandre Lippmann, France, fencing		1	
Edgar Seligman, Great Britain, fencing		1	
Odon Bodor, Hungary, track			1
Otto Scheff, Austria, swimming			1
Clair S. Jacobs, USA, track			1
Paul Anspach, Belgium, fencing			1
Harald Bohr, Denmark, soccer		1	
1912			
Dr. Jeno Fuchs, Hungary, fencing	2		
Dr. Oszkar Gerde, Hungary, fencing	1		
Lajos Werkner, Hungary, fencing	1		
Paul Anspach, Belgium, fencing	2		
Henry Anspach, Belgium, fencing	1		
Gaston Salmon, Belgium, fencing	1		
Jacques Ochs, Belgium, fencing	1		
Zoltan Schenker, Hungary, fencing	1		
Edgar Seligman, Great Britain, fencing		1	
Dr. Otto Herschmann, Austria, fencing		1	
Abel Kiviat, USA, track		1	
Alvah T. Meyer, USA, track		1	
Ivan Osiier, Denmark, fencing		1	
Imre Gellert, Hungary, gymnastics		1	
Margarete Adler, Austria, swimming			1
Klara Milch, Austria, swimming			1
Josephine Sticker, Austria, swimming			1
Mor Kovacs (Koczan), Hungary, track			1
1920			
Samuel Mosberg, USA, boxing	1		
Alexandre Lippmann, France, fencing		1	
Paul Anspach, Belgium, fencing		1	
Samuel Gerson, USA, wrestling		1	
Gerard Blitz, Belgium, waterpolo		1	
Maurice Blitz, Belgium, waterpolo		1	
Fred Meyer, USA, wrestling			1
Montgomery "Moe" Herzowitch, Canada, boxing			1
Gerard Blitz, Belgium, swimming			1
Alexandre Lippmann, France, fencing			1
1924			
Harold Abrahams, Great Britain, track	1		
Elias Katz, Finland, track	1		
Alexandre Lippmann, France, fencing	1		
Louis A. Clarke, USA, track	1		
Jackie Fields, USA, boxing	1		
Janos Garai, Hungary, fencing		1	
Harold Abrahams, Great Britain, track		1	
Elias Katz, Finland, track		1	
Gerard Blitz, Belgium, waterpolo		1	
Maurice Blitz, Belgium, waterpolo		1	
Zoltan Schenker, Hungary, fencing		1	
Paul Anspach, Belgium, fencing		1	
Alfred Hajos-Guttmann, Hungary, architecture (special award)		1	
Baron H.L. De Morpurgo, Italy, tennis			1
Janos Garai, Hungary, fencing			1
Zoltan Schenker, Hungary, fencing			1
Sydney Jelinek, USA, crew			1
1928			
Fanny Rosenfeld, Canada, track	1		
Attila Petschauer, Hungary, fencing	1		
Hans Haas, Austria, weightlifting	1		
Dr. Sandor Gombos, Hungary, fencing	1		
Janos Garai, Hungary, fencing	1		
Dr. Ferenc Mezo, Hungary, literature (special award)	1		
Fanny Rosenfeld, Canada, track		1	
Attila Petschauer, Hungary, fencing		1	
Lillian Copeland, USA, track		1	
Fritzie Burger, Austria, figure-skating		1	
Istvan Barta, Hungary, waterpolo		1	
Ellis R. Smouha, Great Britain, track			1
Harry Devine, USA, boxing			1
Harry Isaacs, South Africa, boxing			1
S. Rabin, Great Britain, wrestling			1
1932			
Attila Petschauer, Hungary, fencing	1		
Istvan Barta, Hungary, waterpolo	1		
Endre Kabos, Hungary, fencing	1		
Gyorgy Brody, Hungary, waterpolo	1		
Irving Jaffee, USA, speed-skating	2		
Lillian Copeland, USA, track	1		
George Gulack, USA, gymnastics	1		
Hans Haas, Austria, weightlifting		1	
Karoly Karpati, Hungary, wrestling		1	
Abraham Kurland, Denmark, wrestling		1	
Dr. Philip Erenberg, USA, gymnastics		1	
Fritzie Burger, Austria, figure-skating		1	
Rudolf Ball, Germany, ice hockey			1
Endre Kabos, Hungary, fencing			1
Nikolaus Hirschl, Austria, wrestling			2
Nathan Bor, USA, boxing			1
Albert Schwartz, USA, swimming			1
Jadwiga Wajsowna (Weiss), Poland, track			1
1936			
Gyorgy Brody, Hungary, waterpolo	1		
Ilona Schacherer-Elek, Hungary, fencing	1		
Karoly Karpati, Hungary, wrestling	1		
Endre Kabos, Hungary, fencing	2		
Samuel Balter, USA, basketball	1		
Ibolya K. Csak, Hungary, track	1		
Jadwiga Wajsowna (Weiss), Poland, track		1	
Gerard Blitz, Belgium, waterpolo			1
1948			
Frank Spellman, USA, weightlifting	1		
Ilona Schacherer-Elek, Hungary, fencing	1		
Henry Wittenberg, USA, wrestling	1		
Agnes Keleti, Hungary, gymnastics		1	
Dr. Steve Seymour, USA, track		1	
Dezso Gyarmati, Hungary, waterpolo		1	
James Fuchs, USA, track			1
Norman C. Armitage, USA, fencing			1
1952			
Boris Gurevich, USSR, wrestling	1		
Mikhail Perelman, USSR, gymnastics	1		
Agnes Keleti, Hungary, gymnastics	1		
Dezso Gyarmati, Hungary, waterpolo	1		
Judit Temes, Hungary, swimming	1		
Eva Szekely, Hungary, swimming	1		
Claude Netter, France, fencing	1		
Dr. Gyorgy Karpati, Hungary, waterpolo	1		
Sandor Geller, Hungary, soccer	1		
Grigori Novak, USSR, weightlifting		1	
Agnes Keleti, Hungary, gymnastics		1	
Ilona Schacherer-Elek, Hungary, fencing		1	
Henry Wittenberg, USA, wrestling		1	
Lev Vainshtein, USSR, shooting			1
Agnes Keleti, Hungary, gymnastics			2
Judit Temes, Hungary, swimming			1
James Fuchs, USA, track			1
1956			
Alice Kertesz, Hungary, gymnastics	1		
Leon Rottman, Rumania, canoeing	2		
Laszlo Fabian, Hungary, canoeing	1		
Isaac Berger, USA, weightlifting	1		
Agnes Keleti, Hungary, gymnastics	4		
Dezso Gyarmati, Hungary, waterpolo	1		
Dr. Gyorgy Karpati, Hungary, waterpolo	1		
Boris Razinsky, USSR, soccer	1		
Alice Kertesz, Hungary, gymnastics		1	
Agnes Keleti, Hungary, gymnastics		2	
Allan Erdman, USSR, shooting		1	
Eva Szekely, Hungary, swimming		1	
Rafael Grach, USSR, speed-skating		1	
Andre Mouyal, France, fencing			1
Yves Dreyfus, France, fencing			1
David Tyshler, USSR, fencing			1
Yakov Rylsky, USSR, fencing			1
Imre Farkas, Hungary, canoeing			1
Boris Goikhman, USSR, waterpolo			1
Oscar Moglia, Uruguay, basketball			1
1960			
Mark Midler, USSR, fencing	1		
Allan Jay, Great Britain, fencing		2	
Vladimir Portnoi, USSR, gymnastics		1	
Isaac Berger, USA, weightlifting		1	
Boris Goikhman, USSR, waterpolo		1	
Ildiko Uslaky-Rejto, Hungary, fencing		1	
Klara Fried, Hungary, canoeing			1
Moses Blass, Brazil, basketball			1
Albert Axelrod, USA, fencing			1
Vladimir Portnoi, USSR, gymnastics			1
Dezso Gyarmati, Hungary, waterpolo			1
David Segal, Great Britain, track			1
Robert Halperin, USA, yachting			1
Rafael Grach, USSR, speed-skating			1
Leon Rottman, Rumania, canoeing			1
Imre Farkas, Hungary, canoeing			1
Dr. Gyrogy Karpati, Hungary, waterpolo			1
1964			
Lawrence Brown, USA, basketball	1		
Gerald Ashworth, USA, track	1		
Grigory Kriss, USSR, fencing	1		
Mark Rakita, USSR, fencing	1		
Alain Calmat, France, figure-skating	1		
Vivian Joseph, USA, figure-skating	1		
Ronald Joseph, USA, figure-skating	1		
Dezso Gyarmati, Hungary, waterpolo	1		
Dr. Gyorgy Karpati, Hungary, waterpolo	1		
Tammas Gabor, Hungary, fencing	1		
Mark Midler, USSR, fencing	1		
Arpad Orban, Hungary, soccer	1		
Ildiko Uslaky-Rejto, Hungary, fencing	2		
Irena Kirszenstein, Poland, track	1		
Yakov Rylsky, USSR, fencing	1		
Irena Kirszenstien, Poland, track		2	
Marilyn Ramenofsky, USA, swimming		1	
Isaac Berger, USA, weightlifting		1	
James Bregman, USA, judo			1
Yves Dreyfus, France, fencing			1
1968			
Irena Kirszenstein-Szewinska, Poland, track	1		
Mark Spitz, USA, swimming	2		
Boris Gurevich, USSR, wrestling	1		
Valentin Mankin, USSR, yachting	1		
Mark Rakita, USSR, fencing	1		
Eduard Vinokurov, USSR, fencing	1		
Mark Spitz, USA, swimming		1	
Mark Rakita, USSR, fencing		1	
Gregory Kriss, USSR, fencing		2	
Josef Vitebsky, USSR, fencing		1	
Semyon Belits-Gieman, USSR, swimming		1	
Ildiko Uslaky-Rejto, Hungary, fencing		1	
Irena Kirszenstein-Szewinska, Poland, track			1
Mark Spitz, USA, swimming			1
Semyon Belits-Gieman, USSR, swimming			1
Naum Prokupets, USSR, canoeing			1
Ildiko Uslaky-Rejto, Hungary, fencing			1
*** 1972**			
Mark Spitz, USA, swimming	7		
Bikolai Avilov, USSR, track	1		
Valentin Mankin, USSR, yachting	1		
Faina Melnik, USSR, track	1		
Neal Shapiro, USA, equestrianism			1
Andrea Gyarmati, Hungary, swimming			1
Irena Kirsenstein-Szewinska, Poland, track			1
Donald Cohan, USA, yachting			1
Peter Asch, USA, water polo			1

* The Olympic Games of 1972 at Munich were marred by the murder of 11 Israeli sportsmen and trainers by Arab terrorists, as a result of which the survivors left Munich before the termination of the Games.

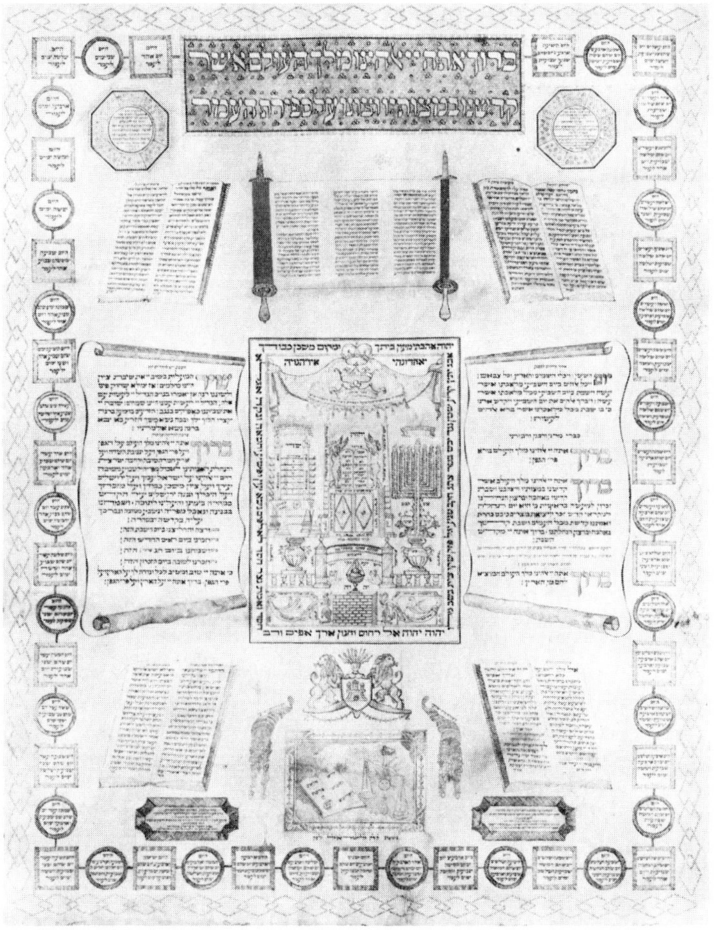

Chart for counting the "Omer," Europe, 1823.

Omar, Covenant of, series of discriminatory regulations of Islam applied to protected Christians and Jews. Attributed to second caliph, Omar (7th c.).

Omer (Heb. "sheaf"), barley offering brought to Temple on Nisan 16. Until made no new produce could be eaten. Also name of period (7 weeks) fr. Passover to Shavuot when days were counted until new wheat could be offered in Temple. Later became period of semi-mourning when solemnization of marriages, hair cutting, and music were forbidden except on Lag ba-Omer, 33rd day of Omer.

Omnam Ken (Heb. "Yes, it is true"), initial words of penitential *piyyut* for eve of Day of Atonement recited by Ashkenazi Jews. Composed by Yom Tov of Joigny, martyred in York 1190.

Omri, king of Israel c. 882–71 B.C.E.; founder of dynasty. Succeeded to throne on murder of Elah. Built new capital in Samaria. Achieved stability in internal affairs and improved Israel's military, political, and economic standing. His son Ahab married Jezebel, princess of Sidon, and triple alliance bet. Phoenicia, Israel, and Judah was established against threats of Aram-Damascus.

On, see Heliopolis.

Onan, second son of Judah and Shua. After death of his elder brother, Er, refused to fulfill Judah's request to marry his childless sister-in-law Tamar. For this, the Lord took his life.

Onderwijzer, Abraham ben Samson ha-Kohen (1862–1934), chief rabbi of Amsterdam. Translated Pentateuch with Rashi's commentary into Dutch. Founded Bezalel, organization of Jewish workers in diamond trade, to better their conditions.

Oneg Shabbat (Heb. "Sabbath delight"), gatherings held on Sabbath afternoons devoted to study of Torah, literary topics, community singing, etc.; modern version of "third meal" *(se'udah shelishit)*. In 1920s Bialik inaugurated new form in Tel Aviv centering around values of Judaism.

Onen, see Aninut.

Onias, name of four high priests of Second Temple period. **Onias I** (4th c. B.C.E.), first priest to whom Areios, king of Sparta, sent letter claiming that Spartans and Jews were descendants of Abraham (I Macc. 12:20–23). **Onias II,** (3rd c. B.C.E.), grandson of I. Attempted to throw off yoke of Egypt. **Onias III,** grandson of II. Preserved religious and secular authority of his house. Eventually summoned to Antioch, and his brother Jason appointed High Priest. **Onias IV** (2nd c. B.C.E.), son of III. Ousted fr. high priesthood and left for Egypt, building his temple at Leontopolis.

Onias, Temple of, temple for worship of God established by Onias IV at Leontopolis in Egypt in 2nd c. B.C.E. Jews of Egypt offered sacrifice there but it was not regarded as equal of Jerusalem Temple. Priests officiating there were not permitted to do so in Jerusalem. Closed by Vespasian 73 C.E.

Onkelos and **Aquila** (2nd c. C.E.), two translators of Bible, former into Aramaic and latter into Greek; both proselytes. Similarity of names has caused considerable confusion bet. them.

Ontario, Canadian province. Jews present fr. 1840s. Developed rapidly after WWII. Jewish pop. 131,700 (1971), over half in Toronto.

Opatoshu, Joseph (1886–1954), Yiddish author; b. Poland, in U.S. fr. 1907. On staff of Yiddish daily *Der Tog* 1914–54. His works describe American Jewish experience, ḥasidic life in Poland (esp. *In Polish Woods*), Jewish history, and Yiddish minstrels. His son **David** (1914–), actor, author of short stories and television scripts.

Joseph Opatoshu, caricature by Henryk Berlewi, 1922.

Opferpfennig, poll tax introduced 1342 by Emperor Louis IV the Bavarian ordering all Jews above 12 possessing 20 gulden to pay one gulden annually. Originally called *Guldenpfennig;* changed to *Opferpfennig* and collected on Christmas day.

Ophel, rocky protuberance N. of City of David in Jerusalem. Its wall

formed part of E. fortifications of Jerusalem. In modern times name is used for E. hill of Old Jerusalem, incl. David's city.

Ophir, country in biblical period noted for its gold. Trade with Ereẓ Israel possible by sea fr. port of Ezion-Geber, but only at Solomon's time was it reached. Another attempt during Jehoshaphat's time failed. Possibly region of Somaliland.

Ophira, see Sharm El-Sheikh.

Ophuels, Max (1902–1957), film director; b. Germany. Films incl. *La Signora di Tutti, Letter from an Unknown Woman, La Ronde.*

Oppenheim, family of German bankers. **Solomon, Jr.** (1772–1828), established company which after WWII became Germany's second largest private banking concern.

David b. Abraham Oppenheim

Oppenheim (Oppenheimer), David ben Abraham (1664–1736), German rabbi of great wealth and scholarship. Rabbi of Prague and *Landrabbiner* of Bohemia. Halakhic authority and able mathematician. His responsa published in works of his contemporaries. Built up large, valuable library which eventually was bought by Bodleian Library, Oxford.

Oppenheim, Hermann (1858–1919), German neurologist. Published many studies on anatomy and pathology of nervous system. Not given chair of neurology at Berlin Univ. after refusing to convert.

Oppenheim, Jacques (1849–1924), Dutch jurist. Prof. of public and international law at Univ. of Leiden. Major figure in several state commissions. Active in Jewish affairs.

Oppenheim, Lassa Francis Lawrence (1858–1919), international lawyer; b. Germany, in England fr. 1898. Prof. at Cambridge 1909. Adviser to British government on international law.

Oppenheim, Moritz Daniel (1799–1882), German painter. Famous for series of paintings on Jewish themes, and also many portraits. pencil sketches, oils

Oppenheim, Paul Leo (1863–1934), German geologist. International expert on all forms of invertebrate fossils.

Oppenheimer, Carl (1874–1941), German biochemist; brother of Franz Oppenheimer. Wrote many popular textbooks for medical students. Prof. at Berlin Agricultural Academy until dismissed 1936. Went to Holland; probably murdered by Nazis.

Oppenheimer, Sir Ernest (1880–1957), S. African financier; b. Germany. Acknowledged head of S. African diamond industry (chairman of De Beers). MP, patron of arts and sciences. Converted to Christianity. His son, **Harry Frederick** (1908–), succeeded his father in business. Also sat in parliament. Assisted diamond industry in Israel.

Oppenheimer, Franz (1864–1943), German sociologist, economist. Prof. of sociology at Frankfort 1917–29. Went to U.S. 1938. Cooperative settlement established at Merḥavyah 1911 by Palestine Office, based on his ideas and laid foundation for cooperative agricultural settlement in Ereẓ Israel.

Oppenheimer, Hillel (Heinz) Reinhard (1899–1971), Israel plant physiologist; son of Franz Oppenheimer; b. Germany, settled in Ereẓ Israel 1926. Director of horticultural station at Reḥovot 1933–52, prof. at Heb. Univ. 1952–67. Israel Prize 1959.

Oppenheimer, James (1882–1932), U.S. poet. Co-founder and editor of *Seven Arts.*

Oppenheimer, Joseph ben Issachar Suesskind (c.1698–1738), court Jew and financial adviser to duke of Wuerttemberg; known as "Jud Suess"; his financial methods

Self-portrait by Moritz Oppenheim, before 1820.

Joseph Suess Oppenheimer

aroused opposition fr. duke's subjects. When duke died suddenly, arrested and property confiscated. Rejected offers to save his life by conversion and died reciting *Shema.* German communities honored him as martyr. Subject of novel by Lion Feuchtwanger and anti-Semitic Nazi film.

Oppenheimer, J. Robert (1904–1967), U.S. physicist. In charge of construction of first atomic bomb at Los Alamos. Brilliant teacher and many-sided scholar. Director of Inst. of Advanced Study at Princeton fr. 1947. Chairman of Atomic Energy Commission. Security clearance canceled 1954 because of his early association with Communists and his opposition to H-bomb. Declared "loyal citizen but not good security risk." Case involved much controversy.

J. Robert Oppenheimer (center) with Samuel Sambursky (left) and Chaim Pekeris, Jerusalem, 1958.

Oppenheimer, Karl (1864–1926), pioneer of infant and child welfare in Germany. His projects incl. free advisory service for mothers, maternity benefits, school meal service.

Oppenheimer, Samuel (1630–1703), Austrian court Jew, military contractor. For many years sole purveyor to Austrian army. Overcame repeated attempts to oust him. Built many synagogues and supported charities.

Opper, Frederick Burr (1857–1937), U.S. political cartoonist. An originator of comic strip. Depicted suburban types, lampooned eccentricities of public figures.

Oppert, Gustav Salomon (1836–1908), German orientalist, Indologist; brother of Julius Oppert. Prof. of Sanskrit at Madras, India; prof. of Dravidian languages at Univ. of Berlin. Published scholarly works, travel accounts, editions of Sanskrit classics.

Oppert, Jules Julius (1825–1905), French philologist, orientalist, archaeologist; b. Hamburg. His studies incl. Indo-Iranian, Sumerian, Elamitic, and Assyriology, of which he was a founder and preeminent authority. Identified site of ancient Babylon. Active in Jewish community.

Oradea (formerly **Oradea Mare**), city in W. Rumania. Jews there fr. early 18th c. Adopted Hungarian language and culture; divided 1870 into Orthodox and Neolog congregations. Ḥasidism flourished there. 21,337 Jews in 1941. Deported in WWII. 8,000 Jews in 1947, 2,000 in 1971.

Or Akiva, development town with municipal council status in N. Sharon nr. Caesarea; founded 1951. Pop 6,400 (1971).

Oral Law (Heb. *Torah she-be'al-peh),* authoritative interpretation of Written Law (Pentateuch); traditionally regarded as given to Moses on Sinai and co-existent with Written Law. Development is to be traced in talmudic and rabbinical literature, which determines *halakhah,* i.e., practice of Orthodox Judaism. Reform and Conservative Judaism both differ in minor or major degree, holding that social changes are consideration in application of law, though in Conservative Judaism every effort is made to base practice on traditional sources.

Orange Free State, province of S. Africa. Jews among original settlers in capital Bloemfontein. Jewish pop. 5,753 in 1926 but declined to 2,330 by 1971, mainly in Bloemfontein.

Ordination, see Semikhah.

Oregon, U.S. state. Jewish settlement began in gold rushes, mostly as merchants. First congregation of German Jews in Portland 1858. Jewish pop. 8,785 (1971), nearly all in Portland.

Orgelbrand, Samuel (1810–1868), Polish publisher. Published edition of Talmud and editions of Pentateuch and other Jewish works as well as Polish works. Financed first Polish general encyclopaedia fr. profits of Talmud sale.

Orḥot Ḥayyim (Heb, "Ways of Life") or *Ẓavva'at Rabbi Eliezer,* popular, well-known Hebrew treatise on ethics and morals, arranged in form of ethical will. Thought to be written in 11th or 13th c.

Orḥot Ẓaddikim (Heb. "Ways of the Righteous"), anonymous Hebrew ethical work, published in 15th c. Nearly 60 editions have appeared. Compendium of earlier Hebrew ethical thought.

°**Origen** (184–253), church father, theologian in Alexandria; first Christian scholar to study Hebrew. His most influential work was *Hexapla,* edition of Old Testament in 6 parallel columns: Hebrew text in Hebrew lettering, Hebrew in Greek transliteration, and four Greek translations.

Orlah (Heb. "uncircumcised"), 10th tractate of Mishnah order *Zera'im,* with *gemara* in Jerusalem Talmud. Deals with prohibition of fruit of trees during first three years after planting (Lev. 19:23–25), and their products, e.g., dyes made fr. them.

Orlan, Ḥayyim, (1911–), Hebrew journalist, teacher; b. Poland, went to Ereẓ Israel 1931, Cleveland 1946. Wrote stories, poems, essays.

Orland, Hershl (1896–1946), Soviet Yiddish writer; lived in Kiev. Dedicated Communist. Wrote short stories and was active in Anti-Fascist Committee.

Orland, Yaakov (1914–), Israel writer. Wrote poems, plays, criticism; translated fr. English, German, Yiddish. Many of his poems set to music.

Orleans, town in France. Jewish community before 585 and again in medieval period. Important center of Jewish learning. Expelled 1182, returned 1198, expelled 1306, 1394. Community refounded in early 19th c. 500 Jews in 1971.

Orlik, Emil (1870–1932), German painter, graphic designer; baptized in youth. Excelled in woodcuts, etchings, lithographs, esp. successful in portraits of celebrated contemporaries.

Orlinsky, Harry Meyer (1908–), U.S. biblical scholar, philologist; b. Canada. Prof. at Hebrew Union College–Jewish Inst. of Religion, N.Y. Editor-in-chief of Jewish Publication Society's new translation of Pentateuch.

Orloff, Chana (1888–1968), French sculptor; b. Ukraine. In her youth, lived in Ereẓ Israel. Exhibited in Paris fr. 1910. Did many portraits in bronze of well-known contemporaries; also carved subjects in wood.

"War and Peace," bronze by Chana Orloff.

Ormandy, Eugene (1899–), conductor; b. Hungary, in U.S. fr. 1920. Famed as conductor of Philadelphia Orchestra fr. 1938, raising it to status of one of world's major orchestras. Specialized in 19th c. and modern music.

Ornitz, Samuel Badisch (1890–1957), U.S. author. Member of left-wing proletarian literary movement. Wrote novels, many depicting Jewish immigrant generation, incl. *Haunch, Paunch and Jowl.*

Ornstein, Abraham Frederick (1836–1895). Pioneer minister in Australia and S. Africa; b. London. Successfully ran private school in Cape Town for Jewish boys, giving both Jewish and general education.

Ornstein, Jacob Meshullam (1775–1839), Galician rabbi, halakhist; son of Mordecai Ze'ev Ornstein (d. 1787), Polish rabbi and kabbalist. Opponent of *maskilim;* center of conflict in which government intervened. Rabbi of Lemberg fr. 1805. Wrote novellae on all parts of *Shulḥan Arukh* and responsa, both called *Yeshu'ot Ya'akov.* His grandson **Ẓevi Hirsch,** rabbi of Lemberg, author of novellae.

Orobio de Castro, Isaac (Balthazar; 1620–1687), Portuguese-born Marrano philosopher, physician, metaphysicist in Salamanca. Charged with practicing Judaism, tortured and confessed, fled to France, then to Amsterdam, joining community. Wrote in defense of Judaism against freethinkers like Spinoza, orthodox Christians, and religious liberals.

Orpah, Moabite wife of Naomi's son Mahlon. Persuaded by Naomi to remain in Moab while Ruth insisted on accompanying her mother-in-law.

Orshanski, Ilya Grigoryevich (1846–1875), Russian journalist, jurist, historian. Refused to convert to receive professorship. His *Jews in Russia* was beginning of scientific study of subject.

Ort (initials of Rus. "Society for Manual Work"), organization in Russia, founded 1880 for vocational training among Jews. Fr. 1920 active in Europe, and also in agricultural settlement of Jews. After WWII, active in Israel, Iran, N. Africa, India.

ORT school in São Paulo, Brazil, 1947.

Orta, Garcia de (c.1500–1568), Portuguese Marrano scientist, physician. First European writer on tropical medicine and pioneer in pharmacology. Posthumously discovered by Inquisition to have lived as Jew in Goa, and his remains exhumed and cast into sea.

Orthodoxy, term used to designate those Jews who accept totality of historical Jewish religion as recorded in Written and Oral Laws and codified in *Shulḥan Arukh* and its commentaries. Crystallized in response to trends toward secularization represented by Haskalah and Reform.

Orvieto, Angiolo (1869–1967), Italian author, editor. Founded literary review *Il Marzocco.* Focus of intellectual circle of major writers in Florence. Wrote verse.

Or Yehudah, Israel urban community E. of Tel Aviv. Pop. 12,900 (1971).

Osborn, Max (1870–1946), German art critic, author. Art critic of *Vossische Zeitung* 1914–33.

Ose, see Oze.

Oshaiah (Hoshaiah) Rabbah (2nd c.), Palestinian *amora.* Member of Judah Ha-Nasi's council in Sepphoris; famed for collection of *baraitot,* it being said that any *baraita* not taught in school of Ḥiyya and Oshaiah is not authentic.

Osiris, Daniel Illfa (1825–1908), French philanthropist, art patron. Donated Malmaison and part of field of Waterloo to French people.

Oslo, capital of Norway. Jewish community fr. 1851. Some Jews escaped to Sweden in WWII; rest perished. Pop. 600 (1971).

Ossowetzky, O. Yehoshua (1858–1929), senior official in Baron Edmond de Rothschild administration in Ereẓ Israel; b. Russia. Became chief administrator in Rishon-le-Zion 1883, clashed with farmers and replaced. Bought land in different areas of Ereẓ Israel (Golan and E. of Jordan R.). Fr. 1900 in Paris.

Ostia, port of ancient Rome. Excavations in 1960s revealed former community, remains of first ancient synagogue discovered in Italy and W. Europe.

Ostrava (Moravska Ostrava), city in Czechoslovakia. Town prohibited to Jews in Middle Ages. After 1508 Jews began settling; community authorized 1875. A main center of Jewish life after 1918. 6,865 Jews in 1931; perished in Holocaust.

Ostrog (Ostraha), city in Ukrainian SSR. First Jews in 15th c., expelled 1495, perished during Chmielnicki massacres 1648–49. Important center of Jewish religious learning and Ḥasidism. 10,500 Jews in 1939; part exiled to Soviet interior 1939–41 and remainder murdered by Germans.

Ostrogorski, Moses (1854–1917), Russian scholar of political law, community leader. Member of first Duma; among those who determined work procedures. Opposed Dubnow and Zionists.

Ostropoler, Hershele (18th c.), Yiddish jester in Medzibezh, Poland. His satiric barbs delighted poor and shocked rich. His tales passed into folklore and were widely disseminated.

Ostropoler, Samson ben Pesah (d. 1648), kabbalist who became widely known in Poland. Died martyr's death at head of community during Chmielnicki massacres. His works published in following generation.

Othniel, son of Kenaz, first judge of Israel. Hero of tribe of Judah during period of conquest of Canaan. Delivered Israel fr. 8-year oppression of Cushan-Rishathaim, king of Aram-Naharaim.

Otranto, town in S. Italy. Acc. to legend Titus settled Jewish prisoners fr. Ereẓ Israel there. Jewish settlement existed in 3rd c. Flourishing academy in 10th c; became one of most prosperous Jewish centers in S. Italy in Middle Ages. Jews expelled 1510.

Ottawa, capital of Canada. Jews settled in late 19th c.; first congregation founded 1892. Jewish pop. 6 000 (1971).

Ottensosser, David (1784–1858), German Hebrew scholar. Teacher at Fuerth yeshivah. His editions of Maimonides' works are among his best volumes of ancient texts. Published corrected edition of Mendelssohn's Bible.

Ottinger, Albert (1878–1938), U.S. lawyer, politician. Member N.Y. state senate, N.Y. state attorney-general, assistant U.S. attorney-general. Fought profiteers and swindlers.

Ottolenghi, Giuseppe (1838–1904), Italian general. First Jew to serve on Italian general staff. Appointed minister of war and member of senate 1902.

Ottolenghi, Joseph ben Nathan (d.1570), rabbi of Cremona, Italy; head of famous yeshivah. Wrote novellae on code of Alfasi and index to code of Mordecai b. Hillel. Involved in dispute which led to burning of Hebrew books in Cremona.

Ottoman Empire, Middle East empire that started in early 14th c. and lasted until 1917. Jews took active part in economic and political life of empire, esp. in 16th c. Many Spanish exiles were welcomed and it became outstanding center of Sephardi culture. Ottomans were tolerant of other religions and Jews lived in peace and security. Restrictions against Jews were never strictly implemented and no Jewish quarters enclosed by walls. However, social segregation was almost complete; very little mutual influence bet. Jews and Turks. No Jewish books written in Turkish language. Jewish community in Turkey entered cultural decline at end of 17th c. See also Turkey.

Oudtshoorn, town in S. Africa. Jews played leading role in ostrich feather industry until its decline shortly before WWI. Congregation formed 1883, with intense communal and religious life until WWI. 250 Jews in 1971.

Ouziel, Ben-Zion Meir Ḥai (1880–1953), chief rabbi of Israel (*Rishon le-Zion*); b. Jerusalem. Appointed

Ben-Zion Meir Ḥai Ouziel

ḥakham bashi of Jaffa 1911, chief rabbi of Salonika 1921–23, chief rabbi of Tel Aviv 1923–39, and chief rabbi of Ereẓ Israel 1939. Wrote responsa.

Ovchinski, Levi (d.1941?), Lithuanian rabbi who wrote on Latvian Jewish history. D. in Holocaust.

Ovdat, see Avedat.

Oved, Moshe (Edward Good; 1885–1958), Yiddish writer, artist, sculptor, gem expert; b. Poland, in London fr. 1903. His antique shop became fashionable center. Began to produce sculpture at age 60.

Oxford, town in England. Jewish community in medieval period. Teachers of Hebrew mostly converts. Modern community fr. 1841; Jews first admitted to Univ. 1854, student society established 1904. Permanent Jewish pop. 400 (1971).

Ozar Hatorah, society founded 1945 for Orthodox education of Jewish youth in Middle East and N. Africa. Runs schools in Morocco, Iran, Syria, and Lyons, France.

Oze or **Ose** (Russ. abbr. for "Society for Protection of Health of Jews"), worldwide organization for child care, health, and hygiene among Jews, with headquarters in Paris; founded 1912. Operated first in Russia; after WWI spread to Poland, Latvia, Lithuania, Rumania. Had hundreds of institutions under its guidance bet. wars. After WWII spread to N. Africa, Latin America, Israel.

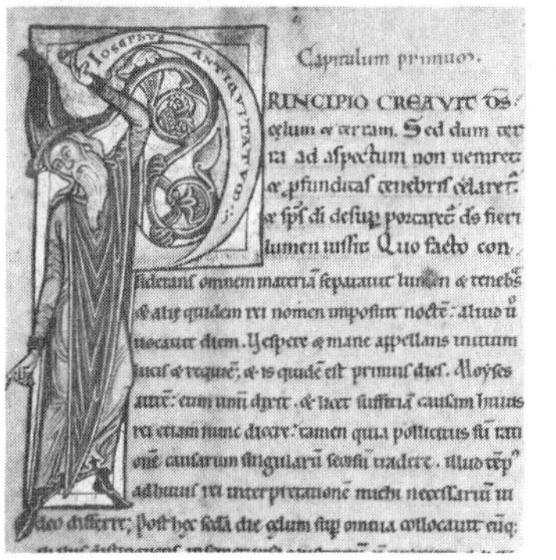
Initial letter "P" for "Principio" in Latin ms. of Josephus, "The Antiquities of the Jews," France. 12th cent.

Pablo Christiani, see Christiani, Pablo.

Pablo de Santa Maria (el Burguense; c. 1350–1435), Spanish apostate; born Solomon Halevi in Burgos. Rose rapidly and became bishop. Wrote influential anti-Jewish theological works.

Pacifici, Alfonso (1889–), Italian lawyer, writer. Highly influential thinker and orator; attempted to "integrate" Jewish culture and Zionism with Orthodoxy. Founded and edited the weekly *Israel.* Settled in Ereẓ Israel 1934.

Pacifici, Riccardo (1904–c. 1943), Italian rabbi, author of historical works. Rabbi in Rhodes and Genoa. Deported by Germans after aiding Nazi victims; fate unknown.

Pacifico, David (1784–1854), merchant. Central figure in "Don Pacifico" incident in which Prime Minister Palmerston of Britain blockaded the Greek port of Piraeus to force the Greek government to compensate Pacifico, a British Jew originating from Gibraltar, for damage to property in an anti-Jewish riot.

Paddan-Aram, place mentioned in Gen. associated with lives of Patriarchs (e.g., Gen. 24:4, 10; 25:20).

"Bimah" of the "Italian" synagogue in Padua, built 16th cent. Now the city's only synagogue.

Probably identical with, or included within, the area of Aram-Naharaim.

Paderborn, province in NW Germany. Jews first mentioned 1258. Federation of Jewish communities organized 1628; diet meeting once every 3 years elected community's elders. Fr. 1803 part of Prussia.

Padua, city in Italy. Jewish loan bankers active fr. 14th c.; expelled 1456, but not rest of community. Early 16th c. Jews restricted to quarters, but ghetto established only 1601. Despite burning of Talmud in 1556, it remained important study center. Jews emancipated by French temporarily 1797, fully 1866. Community began to decline at turn of century. Important center of Hebrew printing. Jewish pop. 220 (1970).

Pagel, Julius Leopold (1851–1912), German physician, medical historian. Prof. of history of medicine at Berlin Univ. His son, **Walter** (1898–), lecturer in pathology and medical history at Heidelberg (1928–33). Fr. 1933 in England.

°**Pagnini, Santes (Xanthus Pagninus;** 1470–1536), Italian Hebraist, Bible scholar. His Latin translation of Old Testament was first since Jerome based on original Hebrew.

Pahal, see Pella.

Pailes, Isaac (1895–), French painter of Paris School. Subject matter largely limited to clowns, still life, and vistas of France.

Pakistan, Asian Moslem republic. In 1920, c. 2,500 Bene Israel Jews in Karachi. Many moved to India, then to Israel. Jewish pop. c. 250 (1971). Country's policy to Israel hostile.

Palache, Abraham (1809–1899), rabbinical scholar who became *ḥakham bashi* of Izmir; son of Ḥayyim Palache. Wrote numerous works in Hebrew and one in Ladino.

Palache (Pallaggi), Ḥayyim (Ḥabif; 1788–1869), rabbi, *ḥakham bashi* of Izmir (Smyrna). Prolific writer on rabbinic topics.

"Painting of a girl" by Israel Paldi, 1967.

Palache, Judah Lion (1886–1944), Dutch orientalist, teacher; b. Amsterdam. Prof. of Bible and Semitic languages at Amsterdam fr. 1925. Wrote on Judaism, Islam, and comparative Semitic philology. D. in Holocaust.

Palache, Samuel (d. 1616), Marrano activist. Escaped from Inquisition in Spain; obtained authorization for Jews to settle in Netherlands and gathered first *minyan* in Amsterdam. Fought Spain actively; diplomat.

Palágyi, Lajos (1866–1933), Hungarian poet. Fought for official recognition of Jewish religion. Influenced by Schopenhauer.

Palatinate, region in W. Germany. Jews first recorded in 11th c. Persecutions during Black Death (1348). Despite expulsions, almost continuous Jewish settlement, with Jews living in villages until 1930s. Major communities: Heidelberg, Mannheim. Birthplace of many court Jews. Jewish pop. 668 (1970).

Paldi (Feldman), Israel (1892–), Israel painter; b. Russia, settled in Ereẓ Israel 1909. At first an expressionist, later influenced by Paris School.

Desert tulip, *Tulipa amphyophylla*.

Cyclamen, *Cyclamen persicum*.

Anemone, *Anemone coronaria*.

Cedar of Lebanon, *Cedrus libani*.

Green dragon, *Arisarum vulgare*.

Aleppo pine, *Pinus halepensis*.

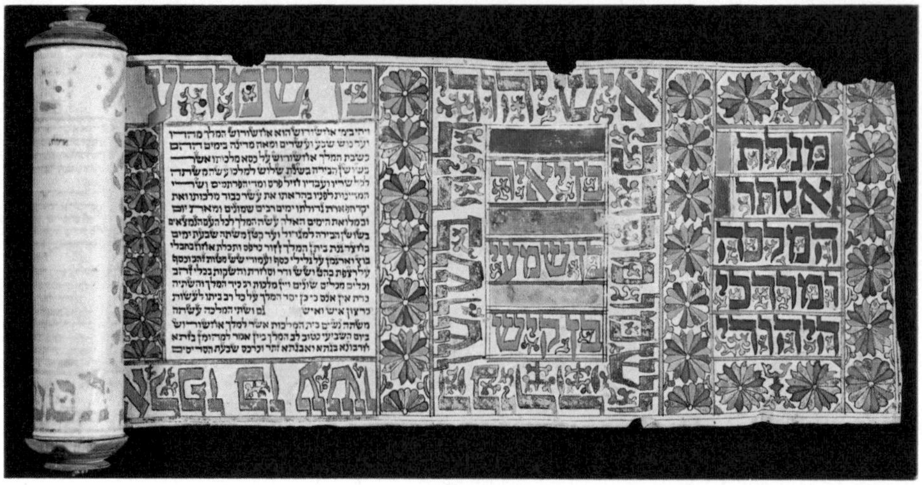

Decorated Scroll of Esther *(megillah)*. Morocco, early 19th cent.

PURIM

Part of the Adloyada Purim carnival procession in Tel Aviv, 1968.

Pale of Settlement, territory in Czarist Russia where Jews were permitted to live. Introduced when partitions of Poland brought Jews into area of Russian state (1791). Only certain categories of Jews were exempt: high school graduates, wealthy merchants, ex-Cantonists, etc. Borders occasionally changed arbitrarily, causing much suffering to Jews. System abolished de facto in 1915 and totally in 1917. The Pale covered c. 400,000 sq. mi. and in 1897 c. 5 million Jews, the largest communities being in Warsaw, Odessa, Lodz.

Palermo, capital of Sicily. Jewish community fr. 6th c., augmented by Jews ransomed from slavery in Sicily. Monopoly in silk and dyeing industry. Significant cultural life. In 1492, 5,000 Jews had to leave with other Jews fr. Sicily. In 1970, 7 Jewish families.

Palestine, one of names of territory known as Ereẓ Israel. Name originally applied to territory of Philistines. Used by Romans as name of province. Fr. 4th c. the three provinces into which Ereẓ Israel was divided were referred to as "first," "second," and "third" Palestine. Crusaders renewed use of "three Palestines." After Crusades, no longer official designation until British Mandate. In 1948, ceased to exist as political entity but many Arabs of Ereẓ Israel continued to regard themselves as "Palestinians."

Palestine Economic Corporation (now known as **PEC Israel Economic Corporation),** public company, incorporated 1926, merging assets Palestine Cooperative Co., Inc., founded 1922 by Robert Szold and others, and Palestinian assets of Reconstruction Committee of American Joint Distribution Committee. Promotes economic development of Ereẓ Israel. Capital $25,000,000 (1970).

Palestine Exploration Fund, British society for exploration of Ereẓ Israel, founded 1865. Conducted surveys and published English translations of oriental sources and accounts of ancient pilgrims.

Palestine Foundation Fund, see Keren Hayesod.

Palestine Jewish Colonization Association, see PICA.

Palestine Office, Zionist institution, established in Jaffa 1908 headed by Arthur Ruppin. Central agency for Zionist settlement activities after WWI, incl. land purchase and aiding immigration. Functions taken over by Zionist Commission.

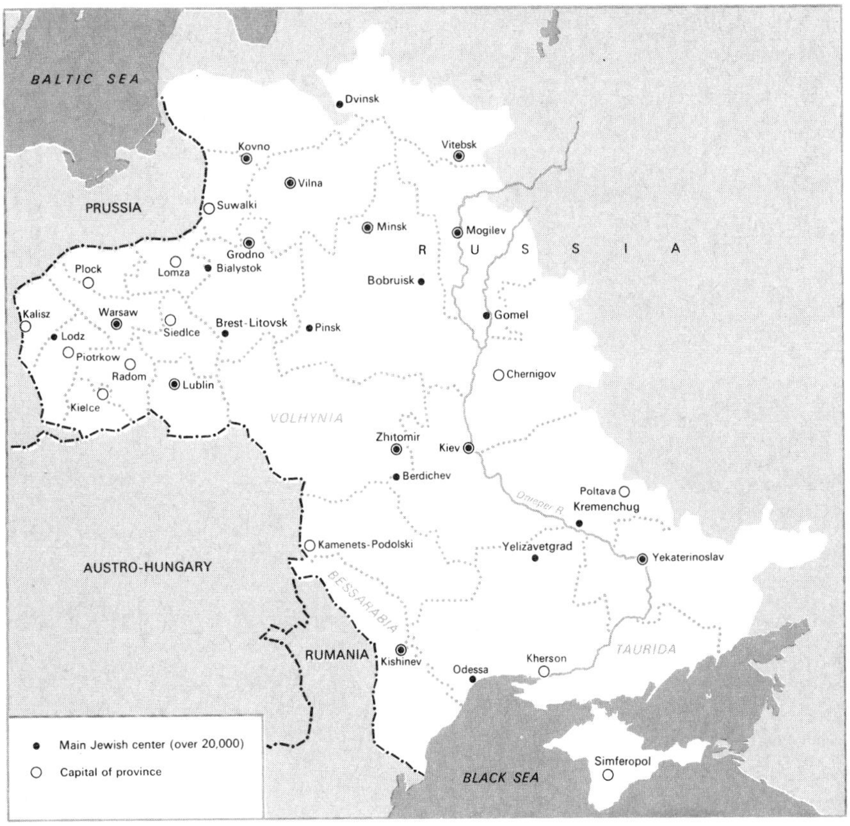

The Pale of Settlement at the end of the 19th cent.

William S. Paley

"Burning Bush," a sculpture by David Palombo at the Knesset, Jerusalem.

Palestine Post, see Jerusalem Post.

Palestine Talmud, see Talmud.

Palestinian Targum, see Targum.

Paley, William Samuel (1901–), U.S. radio, TV executive. Founded Columbia Broadcasting System 1928, developing it into one of three giant coast-to-coast networks. Developed TV network after WWII. Deputy chief, psychological warfare division, SHAEF, in WWII. Founded William S. Paley Foundation.

Palgrave, Sir Francis (1788–1861), English historian. First English scholar to make extensive use of medieval records. Converted to Christianity. His son **Sir Francis Turner** (1824–1897), prof. of poetry at Oxford. Compiled famous *Golden Treasury.*

Pallenberg, Max (1877–1934), German actor; husband of Fritzi Massary. Joined Max Reinhardt's Deutsches Theater, Berlin, in 1916. Killed in plane crash.

°**Pallière, Aimé** (1875–1949), French writer and theologian. Although not formally converting, lived as Orthodox Jew and described his attraction to Judaism in *The Unknown Sanctuary.*

Palmaḥ (abbr. for *peluggot maḥaz,* "assault companies"), permanently mobilized volunteer striking force of the Haganah and later, until its dissolution, part of Israel Defense Forces. Established 1941. Worked for "illegal" immigration; actions against British after WWII; fought against Arabs in Negev and Galilee 1947–8. Commanders: Yiẓḥak Sadeh; Yigal Allon. Integrated into Israel army Nov. 1948.

Palmyra, see Tadmor.

Palombo, David (1920–1966), Israel sculptor; b. Jerusalem. Worked in wrought iron. Made gates to

Knesset building and Yad Vashem memorial door.

Palquera, see Falaquera.

Palti, biblical figure; son of Laish. Saul gave his daughter, Michal, David's wife, to Palti, after David had been proscribed, but later Michal was restored to David.

Paltoi bar Abbaye, gaon of Pumbedita 842–57. Powerful, energetic leader who increased authority of Pumbedita gaonate.

Pana, Sasa (1902–), Rumanian poet, author. Leader and proponent of avant-garde literature.

Panama, C. American republic. Jews settled in 19th c. Jewish pop. 2,000 (1971), organized in 3 communities, Sephardi, Ashkenazi, and British (fr. Caribbean Islands).

Paneas, see Banias.

Panet, Ezekiel ben Joseph (1783–1845), Transylvanian rabbi. As rabbi of Alba-Iulia, considered chief rabbi of Transylvania. Acted energetically in promoting religious revival.

Panevezys (Ponevezh), town in Lithuania. Community of 7,000 destroyed in WWII. Site of famous Panevezys Yeshivah (reestablished 1944 in Bene Berak, Israel).

Panigel, Eliyahu Moshe (1850–1919), Sephardi chief rabbi of Ereẓ Israel fr. 1907. Welcomed Allenby on entry to Jerusalem 1917. Nephew of Raphael Meir Panigel.

Panigel, Raphael Meir ben Judah (1804–1893), chief rabbi of Jerusalem fr. 1880. Author of talmudic novellae, responsa, homilies.

"Bertha Pappenheim, helper of humanity," stamp issued by West Germany, 1954.

The Paran Desert.

Panken, Jacob (1879–1968), U.S. judge, Socialist leader. Judge, New York City Municipal Court (1917–28), Domestic Relations Court (1934–54). A founder of Ladies Garment Workers Union (1900). U.S. chairman of ORT; president, *Jewish Daily Forward,* 1917–25.

Pann (Pfeffermann), Abel (1883–1963), Israel painter, draftsman. Caused sensation with drawings of czarist pogroms. Settled in Ereẓ Israel 1913. Chief work, *The Bible in Pictures,* using local oriental types to depict biblical characters. Early teacher at Bezalel School of Art.

Panofsky, Erwin (1892–1968), U.S. art historian; b. Germany, in U.S. fr. 1934. Prof. at Institute for Advanced Studies, Princeton Univ.; prof. of poetry, Harvard Univ., 1947.

Paovlotzky, Raul (1918–), Uruguayan abstract painter. Represented Uruguay at international exhibitions. Prof. at National School of Fine Arts, Montevideo.

Pap, Arthur (1921–1959), U.S. philosopher; b. Switzerland, in U.S. fr. 1941. Taught at Univ. of Chicago and Yale Univ. Developed modified, flexible type of logical positivism.

Pap, Károly (1897–1945), Hungarian author. Joined Béla Kun's revolution and subsequently imprisoned. Wrote on Jewish themes from radical point of view. D. in concentration camp.

Papa (c. 300–375), Babylonian amora; founded and headed academy at Naresh, nr. Sura.

Paperna, Abraham Baruch (d. 1863), Italian Hebrew writer, anthologist. Rabbi in Leghorn. Compiled *Kol Ugav,* anthology of Hebrew poetry.

Paperna, Abraham Jacob (1840–1919), Hebrew writer, critic; b. Russia. Set forth elementary concepts in literary theory for Hebrew reader. Also wrote poems, essays, satirical works.

Papiernikov, Joseph (1897–), Yiddish poet; b. Warsaw, settled in Ereẓ Israel 1924. His lyrics reflect spirit of Israel's pioneering period.

Pappenheim, Bertha (1859–1936), German social worker, feminist. Directed orphanage and founded institute for unwed mothers and needy women in Frankfort. One of first persons successfully psychoanalyzed (Freud's "Anna O.").

Pappus and Julianus (Lulianus; 2nd c. C.E.), patriot brothers. Sources differ on circumstances of death. Apparently Trajan gave permission to rebuild Temple, in commemoration of which a holiday was instituted. Later, after execution of the brothers, the holiday was abolished.

Paradise, see Gan Eden.

Paraguay, S. American republic. Sephardi Jews arrived before WWI and Ashkenazim in 1920s. 15,000–20,000 came from C. Europe 1933–39, but most reemigrated. Many Germans, some pro-Nazi, took refuge there, incl. Dr. Joseph Mengele of Auschwitz. Jewish pop. 1,200 (1971).

Parah (Heb. "heifer"), 4th treatise of Mishnah and Tosefta in order *Tohorot;* deals with laws of red heifer.

Parah Adumah, see Red Heifer.

Paran, biblical name for main desert in E. Sinai Peninsula. Crossed by Israelites after exodus, and from there Moses despatched men to spy out Canaan.

Pardes, initial letters of words *peshat, remez, derash, sod* – four methods of Bible interpretation (literal, allegorical, homiletical, mystical).

Pardes Ḥannah-Karkur, rural community in N. Sharon, Israel, created 1969 through amalgamation of Pardes Ḥannah (moshavah founded 1929) and Karkur (village founded 1913; site of dew research station). Pop. 13,800 (1971).

Pardo, David Samuel ben Jacob (1718–1790), rabbinical author, poet. Rabbi of Spalato, Sarajevo, and eventually outstanding rabbi in Jerusalem. Wrote *Ḥasdei David* on Tosefta, *Sifrei de-Vei Rav* on *Sifrei,* and also supercommentary on Rashi to the Pentateuch, halakhic decisions, and responsa.

Pardo, Joseph (d. 1619), Italian rabbi, merchant in Venice. Financed publication of several books. Fr. 1609 rabbi in Amsterdam.

Parenzo, 16th–17th c. family of Hebrew printers in Venice. Principal members: **Jacob** (d. 1546); **Meir** (d. 1575); **Asher.**

Parḥon, Solomon ben Abraham ibn (12th c.), lexicographer; b. Spain. Student of Judah Halevi and Abraham ibn Ezra. Emigrated to Italy, completing biblical lexicon in Hebrew.

Paris, capital of France. Jews present in 6th–7th c. and again fr. 10th c. Many rabbinic scholars in 12th c. Jews expelled 1182, returned 1198. Talmud condemned and burned after disputation of Paris 1240. After several expulsions and readmissions in 14th c. final expulsion came in 1394. Jews reappeared early 18th c. Two separate groups, Sephardim and Ashkenazim. First

The Great Synagogue in Paris, completed 1877.

non-secret synagogue 1788. Condition improved at French Revolution. Anti-Semitism increased late 19th c., culminating in Dreyfus case. Immigration fr. E. Europe and in 1930s fr. Germany. In 1939, 150,000 Jews. In WWII, 45,000 Jews deported to death camps; large influx of Jews fr. N. Africa in 1950s and 1960s. Center of all national French institutions and seat of Central Consistory and CRIF (Comité representative des Juifs de France). Jewish pop. 300,000 (1971).

Parker, Dorothy (1893–1967), U.S. author; daughter of Jewish father. Famed for caustic wit.

°**Parkes, James William** (1896–), English theologian, historian. Special interest in anti-Semitism and Jewish-Christian relations reflected in his writings, incl. *The Conflict of the Church and the Synagogue, The Jew in the Medieval Community, A History of Palestine.*

Parma, city in N. Italy. Jews first mentioned in 14th c. Persecutions during Black Death (1348) In late Middle Ages Jews prominent loan bankers. Community declined from 1880s; only c. 200 left by WWII, 60 in 1969. Palatina Library possesses rich collections of Heb. mss. and early books based on G.B. de' Rossi Collection.

Parnas, head of community; usually an elected office. In modern times, president of community or congregation.

Parnas, Yakub Karol (1884–1942?), Polish biochemist. Director, physiology institute, Warsaw Univ. Main work on biochemistry of muscle and biological synthesis of ammonia.

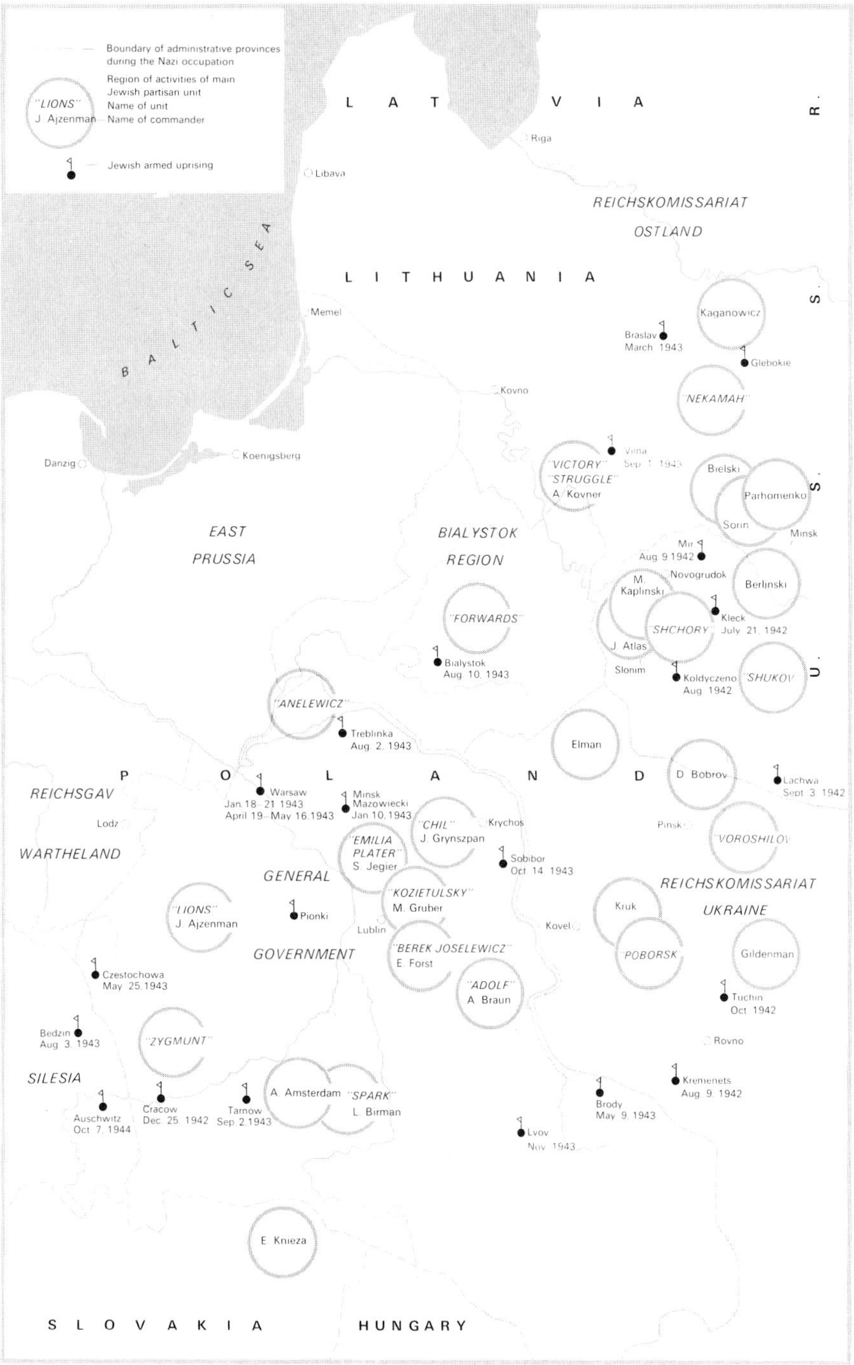

Major Jewish partisan units and armed uprisings, 1941–44.

Partisans, Jewish. Jewish partisans fought in WWII both in Jewish units (in ghettos, forests of Poland, Lithuania, Russia) and in general underground (France, Yugoslavia). Some right-wing resistance groups were hostile to Jews, esp. in Poland. 15,000–20,000 Jewish partisans in areas under Soviet command, and several thousand elsewhere.

Partos, Oedoen (1909–), Israel composer; b. Hungary. Joined Palestine (Israel) Philharmonic Orchestra as first viola 1938. Integrated oriental subjects and techniques in his music.

Parveh, foods which cannot be classified as either dairy or meat and which therefore may be eaten with either.

Paschal Lamb, see Passover.

Pascheles, Wolf (Ze'ev; 1814–1857), Czech author, publisher, bookseller. Opened first Jewish bookstore in Prague. Published collection of Jewish legends, biographies, etc.

Pascin, Jules (1885–1930), painter. Spent most of life in Paris. Notable for acute draftmanship and keen

THE ORDER OF THE PASSOVER SEDER

KADDESH
A benediction over a goblet of wine, sanctifying the day.

REḤAẒ
Wash the hands without reciting a benediction.

KARPAS
Dip a vegetable into some salt water, and eat it.

YAḤAẒ
Break the middle *maẓẓah*, and hide half of it for the *afikoman*.

MAGGID
Tell the story of the Exodus and sing praises to the Lord over the second cup of wine, which is drunk at the end of this part.

RAḤẒAH
Wash the hands, with a benediction.

MOẒI MAẒẒAH
Recite the usual benediction for bread, and the additional benediction for *maẓẓah*; eat a piece of the upper *maẓẓah* and of the remaining part of the middle *maẓẓah*.

MAROR
Eat bitter herbs dipped in *ḥaroset*.

KOREKH
Eat a sandwich of the bottom *maẓẓah* and bitter herbs dipped in *ḥaroset*.

SHULḤAN OREKH
The festive meal.

ẒAFUN
Eat the hidden piece of the middle *maẓẓah*, the *afikoman*.

BAREKH
Grace after Meals over the third cup of wine.

HALLEL
Sing further songs of praise, after which the fourth cup of wine is drunk.

NIRẒAH
"Acceptance" – God has found the actions performed acceptable, and appropriate hymns are recited.

The Passover seder, illustration from 14th cent. Haggadah, Spain.

Ceremonial seder plate being raised at Kurdish seder in Jerusalem.

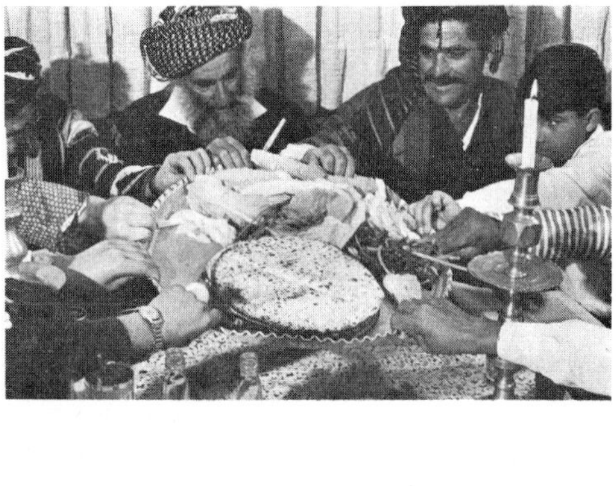

observation; paintings have surrealistic quality. Committed suicide.

Pasmanik, Daniel (1869–1930), Zionist writer, leader; b. Ukraine, fr. 1919 in Paris, where his association with Russian emigrants estranged him from Zionist movement. Previously a leading publicist and theoretician of Zionism.

Passaic-Clifton, twin cities in N.J., U.S. First Jews in 1860s. First congregation B'nai Jacob (Orthodox) 1889. Jewish pop. 10,000 (1971).

Passi, David (16th c.), Turkish statesman; b. Marrano in Portugal, settled in Constantinople as Jew. Highly esteemed by sultan.

Passover (Heb. *Pesaḥ*), a spring festival (one of the Three Pilgrim Festivals) beginning Nisan 15 and lasting 7 days in Israel and among Reform Jews and 8 days in Diaspora. It commemorates the Exodus from Egypt. Observance is highlighted by the *seder* service on first night (on the first two nights in the Diaspora) with recitation of *Haggadah* (q.v.). It is forbidden to eat or own leaven during the entire festival, and unleavened bread *(mazzah)* is eaten. *Musaf* (additional service) is recited throughout Passover as is *Hallel* (half-*Hallel* after the initial day(s)). In Temple times, the paschal lamb was sacrificed on Passover, a custom still observed by the Samaritans.

Passover, Alexander (1840–1910). Russian jurist; practiced in St. Petersburg. Denied professorship when he refused to renounce Judaism. Founded seminary for law students. Authority on Russian and foreign law.

Passover, Second, an alternate date for Passover sacrifice for those persons unable to offer Passover sacrifice at proper time. It occurred a month later on Iyyar 14.

Pasternak, Boris Leonidovich (1890–1960), Russian poet, novelist; son of Leonid Pasternak. One of greatest Russian poets; work Christian in spirit. His novel *Dr. Zhivago* was not printed in USSR. Forced to refuse Nobel Prize for Literature in 1958. Totally estranged from Judaism.

Pasternak, Joseph (1901–), U.S. producer. Produced over 100 films, incl. *Three Smart Girls, It Started With Eve, Destry Rides Again.*

Pasternak, Leonid Osipovich (1862–1945), Russian artist; left Russia 1921, lived in Paris, fr. 1938 in Oxford. Portraitist; friend of Tolstoy, whose work he illustrated.

Pastoureaux ("Shepherds"), name of 2 popular crusades both condemned by Church. (1) 1251: robbed and looted Jews in Bourges and Bordeaux. (2) 1320: crusade and social war in France against higher clergy and Jews. Many Jews massacred when refused to accept baptism. About 120 communities affected.

Pat, Jacob (1890–1966), Jewish labor leader; b. Bialystok. Spokesman for Bund and member of editorial board of its daily organ. Secretary, Democratic Jewish Community, Bialystok, after WWI. Member, Jewish Community Council, Warsaw. Arrived in U.S. on eve of WWII. General secretary, Jewish Labor Committee.

Pataḥ, Hebrew vowel sign indicating short *a;* its written form is _ .

Patai, József (1882–1953), Hungarian and Hebrew poet, translator, editor. Wrote biography of Herzl. Taught in Budapest. In Ereẓ Israel fr. 1938.

Patai, Raphael (1910–), anthropologist, biblical scholar; son of József Patai; b. Budapest, in Ereẓ Israel 1933, in U.S. fr. 1947. Wrote on many subjects, incl. ancient Hebrew culture and modern Middle East. Editor of *Encyclopaedia of Zionism and Israel.*

Paterson, city in N.J., U.S. First Jewish settlers in 1840s. First congregation (also in N.J.) B'nai Jeshurun 1847. Jewish pop. 26,000 (1971), incl. Fairlawn.

Patinkin, Don (1922–), Israel economist; b. Chicago, settled in Israel 1949. One of founders of economic studies in Israel. Prof. at Heb. Univ. Israel Prize 1970.

Patria, ship which anchored in Haifa harbor in Nov. 1940 with 1,771 "illegal" Jewish refugees fr. C. Europe to be deported by British authorities to Mauritius. An attempt was made to sabotage the engines, but the ship blew up, with a loss of life of 260.

Patriarchs, the founding fathers of the people of Israel, viz., Abraham, Isaac, and Jacob.

Boris Pasternak, sketch by his father, Leonid Pasternak.

Patriarchs, Testaments of the Twelve, early Jewish pseudepigraphic work giving reported last words of the 12 sons of Jacob. Written originally in Greek, but derived from Jewish Palestinian literature and thought. Written c. 1st c. C.E.; apparently connected with Dead Sea Sect.

Patterson, David (1922–), English scholar. Taught post-biblical Hebrew at Oxford and also at Cornell. Wrote on early phases of modern Hebrew literature.

°**Patterson, John Henry** (1867–1947), British soldier. Commanding officer of Zion Mule Corps in Gallipoli and Jewish Legion.

Pauker, Ana (1890–1960), Rumanian communist leader. Minister of foreign affairs 1947. Purged and placed under house arrest 1952.

Ana Pauker with Reuven Rubin, Israel minister (left) and Mihail Sadoveanu, president of Rumanian parliament, Bucharest, 1948.

Paul of Burgos, see Pablo de Santa Maria.

Paul of Tarsus (d. c. 65 C.E.), name adopted by Saul of Tarsus on his conversion to Christianity; author of most of New Testament Epistles. Originally a Pharisaic Jew, he became converted and was the theologian of the new Christian Sect. As "apostle to the gentiles" it was essentially he who made Christianity a non-Jewish religion, abolishing *mizvot* for Gentile Christians, etc. Original sin is a central feature of his teaching.

Paytan, composer of *piyyut* (liturgical poetry).

Paz, Duarte de (d.c. 1542), representative of Portuguese Marranos in Rome. Succeeded in inducing Pope to delay introduction of Inquisition in Portugal.

Pe (פ ; final form ף), 17th letter of Hebrew alphabet; numerical value 80. Pronounced *p* with *dagesh; f* without *dagesh*.

Peaçe Offering, the basic sacrifice of all communal offerings. Except for portions burned on altar or assigned to priest, sacrificial animal was given to offerer, who consumed it in communal meal. Offered on Shavuot, completion of Nazirite vow, installation of priesthood, and public ritual occasions.

Pe'ah, second treatise of Mishnah, in order *Zera'im*. Deals with different dues to poor. *Pe'ah* means "corner," i.e. corner of field which must not be reaped but left to poor.

PEC, see Palestine Economic Corporation.

Pechersky, Alexander (1919–), Soviet lieutenant who organized and successfully led the revolt in the Nazi extermination camp of Sobibór. 400 prisoners escaped, but about half of them were subsequently killed.

°**Pedersen, Johannes** (1883–), Danish biblical scholar. Wrote *Israel* on life and culture of ancient Israel.

Peel Commission, Royal Commission sent by British Government in 1936 to investigate causes of Arab riots; headed by Lord Peel. Its recommended partition of Ereẓ Israel not implemented.

Peerce, Jan (1904–), U.S. tenor. Appeared in Metropolitan Opera and concert halls, also in cantorial recitals. Recordings include cantorial works and Jewish folksongs.

Peierls, Sir Rudolf Ernst (1907–), British physicist; b. Berlin, in England fr. 1933. Prof. at Birmingham, Oxford. Fellow of Royal Society. Worked in applied mathematics and atomic energy; a leading scientist in Manhattan project.

Peiper, Tadeusz (1891–), Polish writer, critic. Wrote avant-garde verse glorifying technology. Spent WWII in Moscow.

Peixotto, Daniel Levi Maduro (1800–1843), U.S. physician; b. Amsterdam. Editor, *New York Medical and Physical Journal;* prof., Willoughby Univ., Ohio, 1835–41. A leader of New York Jewish community. *Ḥazzan,* Congregation Shearith Israel, 1820–43. Father of Benjamin Franklin Peixotto.

Peixotto, Benjamin Franklin (1834–1890), U.S. lawyer, diplomat, Jewish communal leader. First U.S. consul in Bucharest 1870–76. Promoted Jewish schools and cultural societies in Rumania. U.S. consul in Lyons 1877–85.

Pekah, king of Israel 735–732 B.C.E. As army commander of King Pekahiah, conspired against him and ruled in his stead. In alliance with Aram, invaded Judah and invested Jerusalem but Tiglath-Pileser III of Assyria came to Judah's aid and conquered N. Transjordan, Gilead, and Galilee fr. Pekah. Murdered by Hoshea.

Pekahiah, king of Israel c. 737/6–735/4 B.C.E. Continued policy of his father, Menahem, and remained loyal to Assyria. Killed by his army commander Pekah.

Pekelis, Alexander Haim (1902–1946), jurist, social worker; b. Russia, studied and taught at various European universities; fr. 1941 in U.S. Active Labor Zionist and welfare pioneer. Killed in airplane crash.

Pekeris, Chaim Leib (1908–), mathematician; b. Lithuania, went to U.S. in his teens, in 1948 to Israel, where he established dept. of applied mathematics at Weizmann Inst.

The synagogue at Peki'in, restored 1873.

Peki'in, village in Upper Galilee; noted for its tradition of continuous Jewish settlement throughout the ages. Traditionally, the site where R. Simeon b. Yoḥai and his son hid from the Romans in a cave for 13 years. After 1936–39 riots only 1 Jewish family returned. Pop. 2,260 (1971), three-quarters Druze. Moshav Peki'in ha-Ḥadashah established 1955.

Pelethites, group of foreign mercenaries who formed with the Cherethites the royal bodyguard in time of King David. Their name might equal "Philistines."

Pella or **Paḥal,** ancient city E. of Jordan. Captured by Antiochus III (218 B.C.E.) and destroyed by Alexander Yannai. Pompey restored it and incorporated it into Decapolis. Ceased to exist in Middle Ages. Excavated 1958 ff.

Pelleg, Frank (1910–1968), Israel musician; b. Prague, settled in Ereẓ Israel 1936. Well-known pianist and harpsichordist. Compositions include incidental music to many Israel plays. Headed Ministry of Education's Music Dept. 1949–52.

°**Pellicanus (Pellikan), Conrad** (1478–1556), German Hebraist, Bible scholar. First Christian to publish Hebrew grammar (1504).

Peltz, Isac (1899–), Rumanian novelist. Wrote many novels about Jewish life in all its color and drama, and after WWII also described Jewish suffering.

Peninnah, wife of Elkanah (I Sam. 1:1–2). Unlike Elkanah's other wife, Hannah, she had sons. Seems to have been the less favored wife.

Penitence, Ten Days of, see Ten Days of Penitence.

Penitential Prayers, see Selihot.

Penn, Alexander (1906–1972), Hebrew poet; b. Russia, settled in Ereẓ Israel 1927. Lyrical poet; also wrote topical political *chansons* reflecting his extreme left-wing views. Literary editor of communist daily *Kol ha-Am.*

Pennsylvania, U.S. state. First Jewish settlers second half 17th c. First Jewish cemetery established 1747 in Lancaster. Milton Shapp governor 1969. Jewish pop. 471,390 (1971), incl. 18 cities with Jewish communities exceeding 1,000, largest being Philadelphia and Pittsburgh.

Penso de la Vega, Joseph (1650–1692), Marrano writer, merchant; lived in Amsterdam. Prolific writer in Spanish and Hebrew. Wrote novels, plays, poems, and book on stock market.

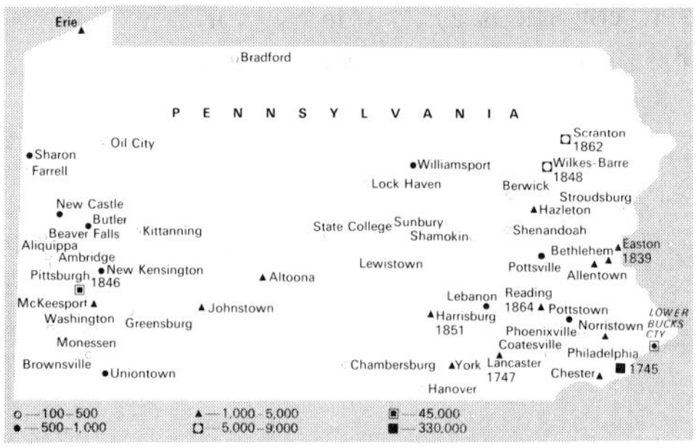

Jewish communities in Pennsylvania and dates of establishment.

Pentateuch (Heb. *Ḥumash*), first division of Bible, divided into 5 books, Genesis, Exodus, Leviticus, Numbers, Deuteronomy. Contains history of Israel from beginning to death of Moses. According to traditional view, it is a unitary document, divinely revealed, and entirely written by Moses (except Deut. 34:5–12). Modern scholars, however, claim that it originated no earlier than period of monarchy and is composed of 4 major sources, known as J, E, P, and D. The basis of this division is literary-critical, based on topical and stylistic-linguistic distinctions. Distinction between J and E is based primarily on different

Oldest Samaritan Pentateuch scroll.

usage of divine name: YHWH (Jehovah) in J and Elohim in E. P is the priestly source and D the Deuteronomic.

Pentateuch, Samaritan, Hebrew text of Pentateuch used by Samaritans; existed already in 3rd c. B.C.E. Estimated to have 6,000 variants from Masoretic Text, mainly orthographic. Numerous textual changes and transpositions reflect Samaritan religious tendencies.

Pentecost, see Shavuot.

Penuel, fortified city nr. ford of river Jabbok. Here Jacob wrestled with angel and received appellation Israel. Built up by Jeroboam apparently as capital for his lands in Transjordan.

Penueli, Shemuel Yeshayahu (1904–1965), Hebrew critic, teacher; b. Galicia. settled in Ereẓ Israel 1935. Taught literature at Tel Aviv Univ. Wrote on Hebrew literature.

Pe'ot, sidelocks grown in accordance with prohibition in Lev. 19:27. Customary for ḥasidim and Orthodox Yemenites.

Perea, region E. of Jordan river. Existed fr. Hellenistic period to beginning of Byzantine era. Inhabitants mostly Jews.

Pereferkovich, Nehemiah (1871–1940), Russian orientalist. Translated Mishnah and parts of Talmud into Russian.

Péreire, Emile (Jacob; 1800–1875) and **Isaac** (1806–1880). French St. Simonian economists, bankers, journalists. Both brothers were members of French parliament and active in Jewish affairs. Active in development of railroads. Grandsons of Jacob Rodrigues Péreire.

Péreire, Jacob Rodrigues (1715–1780), French educator of deaf-mutes, communal leader. Pioneered lipreading and articulation of sounds as opposed to sign language.

Perek Shirah, short, anonymous tract containing collection of hymnic sayings in praise of creator. Preserved in several mss, earliest fr. 10th c.

Perelman, Chaim (1912–), Belgian philosopher. Prof. of logic and metaphysics at Université Libre in Brussels 1944. Major fields: mathematical logic and non-deductive reasoning.

Perelman, Sidney Joseph (1904–), U.S. humorist. Regular contributor to *New Yorker.* Published collections of his pieces.

Perelmann, Jerohman Judah Leib ben Solomon Zalman (1835–1896), Lithuanian talmudist, known as "the great scholar of Minsk." Supported Ḥovevei Zion.

Peremyshlyany (Pol. **Przemyslany),** town in Ukraine. Jewish community from mid-16th c. and famous during the 18th and 19th c. for ḥasidic dynasty. Its 6,000 Jews murdered in WWII.

Peremyshlyany, Meir ben Aaron Leib of (1780? –1850), ḥasidic *ẓaddik.* His strange behavior interpreted by ḥasidim as eccentricity, by his opponents as insanity. His followers published his teachings.

Peres, Shimon (1923–), Israel politician; b. Belorussia, settled in Ereẓ Israel 1934. Director-general, Ministry of Defense, 1953–59; deputy minister of defense 1959–65. Knesset member fr. 1959; left Mapai 1965 to join Rafi. Minister of communications 1970–74, of defense fr. 1974.

Peretz, Abraham (1771–1833), pioneer of Jewish Enlightenment in Russia. Wealthy shipbuilder; commercial adviser to Czar. Converted to Christianity.

Peretz, Isaac Leib (1852–1915), Yiddish, Hebrew author; b. Zamosc. Practiced law 1877–87. Fr. 1891 to his death official in dept. of burial sites of Jewish community of Warsaw. A founder of modern Yiddish literature and an important figure in Hebrew literature. His polemical

Isaac Leib Peretz

writings influenced the Jewish social movement. His heroes are mostly ḥasidim and common people who suffer hardship but bear the burden of their lot with faith. Championed the cause of the oppressed. Pioneered in short story and symbolic drama.

Perez, one of twins born to Judah by Tamar; ancestor of David. Perezites are mentioned as important clan in wilderness (Num. 26:20–21).

Perez, Judah ben Joseph (18th c.), rabbi in Venice, Amsterdam. Disciple of Nehemiah Ḥayon; suspected of being Shabbatean.

Perez ben Elijah of Corbeil (Raf, Maharaf, or **Maraf;** 13th c.), eminent tosafist and editor of *tosafot;* known as "head of the French yeshivot." Wrote glosses to *Sefer Mitzvot Katan* of his teacher Isaac of Corbeil, published in all editions.

Pergament, Osip Yakovlevich (1868–1909), Russian lawyer, writer. Member of 2nd, 3rd Dumas.

Pergamum, ancient city and kingdom in NW Asia Minor (modern site Bergama, Turkey). In 2nd c. B.C.E. had friendly ties with Judea; in 1st c. B.C.E. a Jewish community.

Pergola, Raphael della (1876–1923), Italian rabbi who became head of Alexandrian Jewish community in Egypt. Leading Zionist.

Peri (Pflaum), Hiram (Heinz; 1900–1962), Romance and Renaissance scholar; b. Germany, settled in Erez Israel 1927. Prof. at Heb. Univ. fr. 1948.

Peri Ez-Ḥayyim, Hebrew periodical devoted to halakhic responsa published in Amsterdam 1691–1807 by Ez-Ḥayyim yeshivah.

Perizzites, pre-Israelite inhabitants of Erez Israel, in neighborhood of Shechem; of unknown origin.

Perl, Joseph (1773–1839), Hebrew author; b. Galicia. Joined Haskalah movement and was active in Jewish education and public life. Wrote satirical works against Ḥasidism, believing their doctrine and leaders to be obstacles to modernization of Jewish life. Also wrote in Yiddish and German.

Perla, Jeroham Fischel ben Aryeh Zevi (1846–1934), scholar, commentator; storekeeper in Warsaw. Author of commentary on Saadiah Gaon's *Sefer ha-Mitzvot.* In Jerusalem fr. 1924.

Perles, Felix (1874–1933), Austrian rabbi, scholar; son of Joseph Perles. Rabbi in Koenigsberg. Wrote on many aspects of Jewish scholarship.

Perles, Joseph (1835–1894), Hungarian rabbi, scholar. Published a Hebrew and Aramaic lexicography and philology.

Perlman, Alfred Edward (1902–), U.S. railroad executive; first Jewish president of major railroad system. President New York Central System, 1952–54, and Pennsylvania-New York Central Transportation Company fr. 1965.

Perlman, Selig (1888–1959), U.S. labor economist; b. Bialystok, in U.S. fr. 1908. Taught economics at Univ. of Wisconsin fr. 1918. Main field: social development of American, British, and Russian labor movements. Wrote *A Theory of the Labor Movement.*

Perlmann, Moshe (1905–), U.S. orientalist; b. Odessa, in U.S. fr. 1940. Taught at New School for Social Research 1945–52, Harvard 1955–61, UCLA fr. 1961. Wrote on Moslem history, literature, and thought.

Perlmutter, Abraham Zevi (1844?–1926), rabbi in Poland (in Radom and fr. 1909 in Warsaw). Active in communal life; established kasher kitchen in army and secured abolishment of severe decree against peddling. Elected 1919 to first Polish parliament (Sejm) as representative of Agudat Israel.

Perlov, Yizḥak (1911–), Yiddish poet, novelist, editor; b. Poland, in Russia during WWII, Israel 1949, U.S. fr. 1961. Wrote poems and novels and Yiddish translation of *Dr. Zhivago.*

Perlstein, Meyer A. (1902–1969), U.S. pediatrician, educator in Chicago. Taught at Northwestern Univ. and Cook County Hospital. A founder and president (1954) of American Academy for Cerebral Palsy.

Perlzweig, Maurice L. (1895–), Reform rabbi, official of World Jewish Congress; b. Poland, educated in England, where he was liberal rabbi in London. Headed WJC International Affairs Dept. in New York fr. 1942.

Perpignan, city in S. France. Important medieval Jewish center, with scholars, physicians, astronomers, moneylenders; Jews also engaged in textile manufacture and worked as silversmiths. Expelled 1493. Small modern community.

°**Perrot, Jean** (1920–), French prehistorian. Headed French archaeological mission in Israel fr. 1951. Excavated remains of Chalcolithic, Mesolithic, and Natufian cultures in Erez Israel (Beersheba, etc.).

Persia (Iran), The conquest of the Babylonian Empire by Cyrus (538 B.C.E.) placed the mass of its Jews under Persian rule. Jews continued to live there, under generally favorable conditions as recorded by the Babylonian Talmud, which was

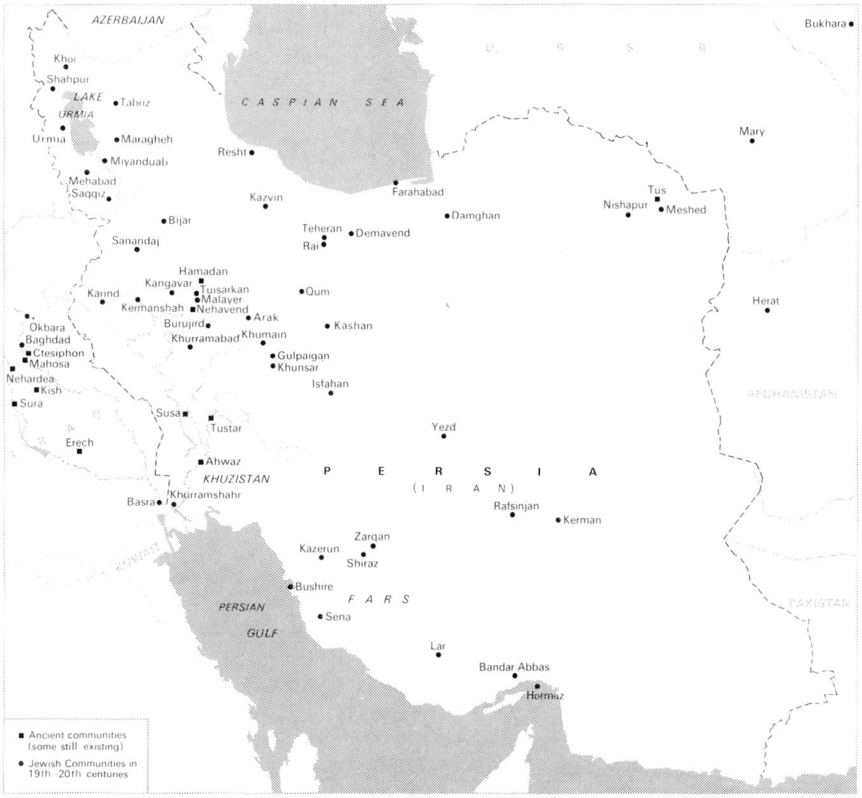

Jewish communities in Persia (Iran).

redacted in Mesopotamia then under Persian rule. Fierce persecutions did follow under Zoroastrian influence (5th c. C.E.), but conditions improved under the Eastern Caliphate of Baghdad. However, Shi'ite intolerance gradually became supreme and persecutions were rife until the establishment of the Pahlevi dynasty in 1925. A vigorous intellectual life had persisted throughout this period, and Karaism had gained a hold. Extensive literature in Judeo-Persian. In the 19th c., the Alliance Israélite Universelle established schools in Persia. Despite the emigration of about 55,000 Jews to Israel 1948–68, Iran remains the largest Jewish community in a Muslim land (80,000 in 1971).

Persitz, Alexandre (1910–), French architect. Rebuilt Le Havre port after WWII (with Auguste Perret). Collaborated in designing Memorial to the Unknown Jewish Martyr. Chief editor, *Architecture d'aujourd'hui*, 1949–65.

Persitz, Shoshanah (1893–1969), Israel publisher, politician; b. Russia, daughter of Hillel Zlatopolski. Established Omanut publishing house in Moscow 1917, Frankfort 1920, Tel Aviv 1925. General Zionist member of Knesset 1949–61 and chairman of Knesset education committee.

Ark of the Law in Sephardi synagogue of Pesaro, built 16th cent., renovated 18th cent.

Part of "Habakkuk Commentary" from Dead Sea Scrolls with word "pishro" (possessive form of "pesher") 5th word in 1st line.

Persky, Daniel (1887–1962), U.S. Hebraist, educator, journalist. B. Minsk, in New York fr. 1906. Taught at Herzliah Hebrew Teachers' College, N.Y. Edited Hebrew children's magazines. Wrote books on Hebrew grammar and syntax and was a leading figure in U.S. Hebrew-speaking circles.

Persov, Shmuel (1890–1952), Soviet Yiddish writer. Member of Bund; emigrated to U.S. 1906, returned to Russia 1917, liquidated 1952. Wrote novels and short stories on life of Jews under communist regime.

Perth, W. Australian city. Community founded 1892. Most settlers fr. E. Europe. Jewish pop. 3,300 (1970).

Peru, S. American republic. In colonial period Crypto-Jews involved in development of country, but persecuted by Inquisition in 17th c., notably in "Great Conspiracy" of Lima with spectacular auto-da-fé (1639). Modern community settled in mid-19th c. with immigration from C. Europe and N. Africa. Jewish pop. c. 5,300 (1971), organized in 3 communities united in one roof organization.

Perutah. (1) Hasmonean coin of small denomination. (2) Israel coin in use between 1949 and 1960; 1/1,000 of an Israel pound.

Perutz, Max Ferdinand (1914–), British biochemist, 1962 Nobel Prize winner; b. Vienna, in Cambridge, England fr. 1936. Studied structure of protein molecules. Fellow of Royal Society.

Pesaḥ, see Passover.

Pesaḥim, 3rd tractate in Mishnah order *Mo'ed; gemara* in both Talmuds. Deals with laws of Passover.

Pesaḥson, Isaac Mordecai (1876–1943), Bund leader in Poland, Russia, esp. Warsaw, Lodz. Worked actively for Bund until murdered by Nazis.

Pesaro, Italian port. Jews recorded in 12th c. Many Marranos fr. Ancona fled to Pesaro 1556 but banished 1558. Jews flourished in 16th c., later, position deteriorated and enclosed in ghetto. In 19th c. their number was reduced and in 1970 few remained. Important center of Hebrew printing.

Peshat, the literal meaning of a text (as opposed to *derash,* the homiletical interpretation.)

Pesher, term used in Dead Sea Scrolls for application of biblical prophecies to circumstances of end of days. This knowledge calls for special wisdom, coming by divine illumination. Numerous examples in commentary on Habakkuk.

Peshitta, Syriac translation of Bible. Date and authorship are controversial. Probably made in Edessa in 1st–4th c. C.E. Perhaps translated from Septuagint. Accepted Bible of the Syrian Church.

Pesikta de-Rav Kahana, one of oldest of homiletic Midrashim, containing homilies on portions of Torah and *haftarah* readings for festivals and special Sabbaths. It is Palestinian text, probably of 5th c.

Pesikta Rabbati, medieval Midrash on festivals of the year.

Pesikta Zutarta, see Midrash Lekaḥ Tov.

Pesukei de-Zimra, psalms and cognate biblical passages recited in Ashkenazi rite in morning service immediately following morning benedictions; the Sephardi, Yemenite, and Italian designation is *zemirot.*

Petaḥ Tikvah, city in Israel's coastal plain, E. of Tel Aviv. First attempt to settle in 1878 unsuccessful. Bilu immigrants renewed settlement 1883. Baron Edmond de Rothschild supported the settlers when they drained the swamps of the Yarkon. Rothschild transferred the moshavah to Jewish Colonization Association in 1900. Received municipal council status 1920, city status 1939. Pop. 87,200 (1971), located on outer ring of Tel Aviv conurbation.

Pethahiah of Regensburg (12th c.), traveler. Set out 1175 on journey to Poland, Russia, Crimea, Tartary, Khazaria, Armenia, Babylonia, Syria, Ereẓ Israel. Described travels and was particularly impressed by Jewish self-government in Babylonia.

Petiḥah (Heb. "opening"), ritual of opening Ark in synagogue during services for taking out Torah scroll(s) or during prayers of special solemnity.

°**Petlyura, Simon** (1879–1926), Ukrainian nationalist leader whose forces massacred thousands of Jews 1919–20. Assassinated 1926 in Paris by Shalom Schwarzbard, who was acquitted in famous trial.

Petra, ruined site in S. Transjordan. Nabatean capital until 106 C.E. when incorporated into Roman Empire, remaining capital of region to time of Hadrian. Disappearing

Petra's most magnificent building, al-Khazna ("the treasury"), 1st–2nd cent. C.E.

from history in Arab times, its spectacular ruins, built into the reddish rocks, have long attracted visitors.

°**Petrie, Sir William Matthew Flinders** (1853–1942), British Egyptologist. Pioneer of modern archaeology. Worked mostly in Egypt but excavated sacred sites in S. Erez Israel.

Petrograd, see Leningrad.

Petrus Alfonsi (b. 1062), Spanish Converso physician, writer. Wrote polemic treatise to defend his conversion. Latter part of life in England; physician to Henry I.

Petschek, Ignaz (1857–1934), leading member of Bohemian family of financiers and industrialists. His company owned huge complex of coal mines. Property taken over by Nazis and nationalized after WWII.

Petuchowski, Jakob Josef (1925–), U.S. rabbinic scholar, Reform theologian; b. Germany, in England during WWII; U.S. fr. 1948. Prof. of rabbinics, Hebrew Union College, Cincinnati, 1956. Influential in Reform Movement, which he linked with Historical Judaism.

Pevsner, Anton (Antoine; (1886–1962) and **Naum Nehemia (Gabo;** 1890–), Russian sculptors. After Russian Revolution, appointed professors at Moscow Academy of Art; leaders of Constructivist Movement. Left USSR in 1923. In Paris collaborated with Diaghilev. Mature work of both brothers non-figurative.

Pevsner, Sir Nikolaus (1902–). British historian of architecture; b. Germany in England fr. 1933. Prof. of fine art at Cambridge. Wrote *Buildings of England* series, *Outline of European Architecture.*

Pevzner, Samuel Joseph (1879–1930), Russian Zionist, Erez Israel pioneer; b. Belorussia. Contributed to Hebrew press. In Erez Israel fr. 1905. Among builders and developers of Haifa.

Pfeffer, Leo (1910–), U.S. constitutional lawyer. Director and general counsel of American Jewish Congress. Prof. of constitutional law, science dept., Long Island Univ. Specialist in church and state relations and religious liberty.

Pfefferkorn, Johannes (Joseph; 1469–after 1521), apostate, anti-Jewish agitator. A poorly educated butcher, he converted in Cologne and conducted virulent campaign against Jews and esp. Talmud. Supported by Dominicans in his dispute with the humanist, Reuchlin (q.v.). Pope decided against Reuchlin but attempt to have Jewish books confiscated failed.

°**Pfeiffer, Robert Henry** (1892–1958), U.S. Bible scholar, Assyriologist. Directed excavations at Nuzi, Iraq, 1928 ff. Curator of Harvard Semitic Museum fr. 1931. Wrote *Introduction to the Old Testament* and other works on Bible.

Pforzheim, city in Baden, W. Germany. Communal leaders killed 1267 after blood libel. Community almost annihilated during Black Death (1349). Expelled 1614, returned 1670. 770 Jews in 1933, many emigrated, remainder deported in WWII; 21 returned.

Pharaoh, biblical term for kings of Egypt. Egyptian texts never used this designation, however, as title of king, but in sense of his palace. From 10th c. B.C.E. it was regularly added, in popular speech, to king's personal name.

Pharisees (Heb. *Perushim*), Jewish religious and political party or sect during Second Temple period. Emerged as a relatively small, but distinct, group shortly after Hasmonean revolt. Maintaining the validity of the Oral Law as well as of the Torah, they tried to adopt old codes to new conditions. Their differences with the aristocratic Sadducees eventually embraced political as well as theological issues. By 1st c. C.E. they represented the religious beliefs, practices, and social attitudes of the vast majority of the Jewish people. After the destruction of Jerusalem in 70 C.E., the Pharisaic sages were the dominant influence in the development of normative Judaism.

Phasael (d. 40 B.C.E.), governor of Jerusalem, older brother of Herod. Killed himself after being captured by Parthians. Herod built tower of Phasael in his palace; today it is basis of the Tower of David in Jerusalem.

Philadelphia, see Rabbath-Ammon.

Philadelphia, city in Penn., in U.S. First permanent Jewish settlers 1737. Oldest congregation Mikveh Israel 1773. First city in U.S. with two congregations 1802. Considered

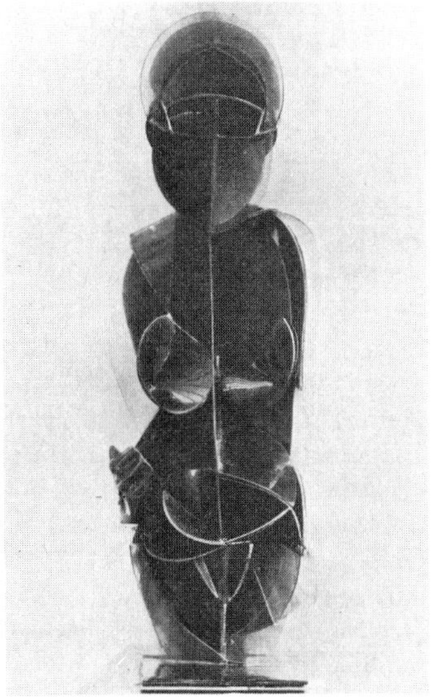

"Torso (construction)" by Antoine Pevsner, 1924–26, copper and plastic.

Title page of Johannes Pfefferkorn's "Judenfeind," Augsburg, 1509.

Congregation Mikveh Israel's Cherry St. synagogue, Philadelphia, in use 1825–60.

most influential Jewry in U.S. in 19th c.; new ideas for shaping U.S. Jewish communal life tested there. American Jewish Publication Society, 1845; Maimonides College, 1867; Gratz College, 1897; Dropsie College (later Univ.) founded 1907. Jewish metropolitan pop. 350,000 (1971), with 100 congregations.

Philip, see Herod Philip.

Philippines, island republic in SE Asia. Marranos there in early colonial days; suffered at hands of Inquisition. Jews arrived late 19th c., numbered 2,500 by 1945. 10% of Jews died in WWII. Most Jews today not permanent residents, but connected with U.S. companies, army, etc. Community numbers 250.

Philippson, Alfred (1864–1953), German geographer; son of Ludwig Philippson. Headed geography department in Berne, Halle, Bonn until dismissed by Nazis and deported to Theresienstadt, but survived despite suffering. Expert on urban and regional geography esp. E. Mediterranean.

Philippson, Franz M. (1851–1925), Belgian banker, communal leader; son of Ludwig Philippson. Involved in colonization of Congo. President of ICA 1919.

Philippson, Ludwig (1811–1899), German editor, Reform leader. Founded and edited German Jewish newspaper, *Allgemeine Zeitung des Judentums.* Preached in German, introduced organ, but tried to reach compromise between Reform and Orthodoxy. Published translation of Bible.

Philippson, Martin (1846–1916), German historian, communal leader; son of Ludwig Philippson. Suffered academically as Jew in Berlin and as German in Brussels. Headed Jewish scholarly bodies. Wrote a Jewish history.

Philipsen, Theodor (1840–1920), Danish artist. One of most important painters of Danish landscape.

Philipson, David (1862–1949), U.S. Reform Rabbi in Cincinnati fr. 1888. Helped draw up 1885 Pittsburgh Platform which determined Reform ideology. Wrote several works, incl. *The Reform Movement in Judaism.*

Philistia, part of coastal plain of ancient Ereẓ Israel. Territory which the Philistines inhabited after settling in Canaan.

Philistines, "Sea People" of Aegean origin, occupying S. coast of Ereẓ Israel (Philistia). After being repulsed by Ramses III of Egypt (c. 1190 B.C.E.), they settled on coast, expanding into the Shephelah and Negev fr. c. 1150 on, and later encroaching upon the hill country, destroying Shiloh and capturing the ark. Defeated by David, who drove them back to the coast, after which they were no longer a security threat. Eventually became vassals of Assyria, and Nebuchadnezzar destroyed last sparks of Philistine independence. Five chief cities: Gaza, Ashdod, Ashkelon, Gath, Ekron. Recent excavations have thrown light on their origin and culture.

Phillips, Lazarus (1895–), Canadian lawyer, senator; b. Montreal. Director, vice-president, Royal Bank of Canada. Named to Canadian Senate 1968.

Phillips, Sir Lionel (1855–1936), S. African financier; b. London. Organized financial structure of mining industry. Death sentence after Jameson Raid commuted.

The Philistine Pentapolis.

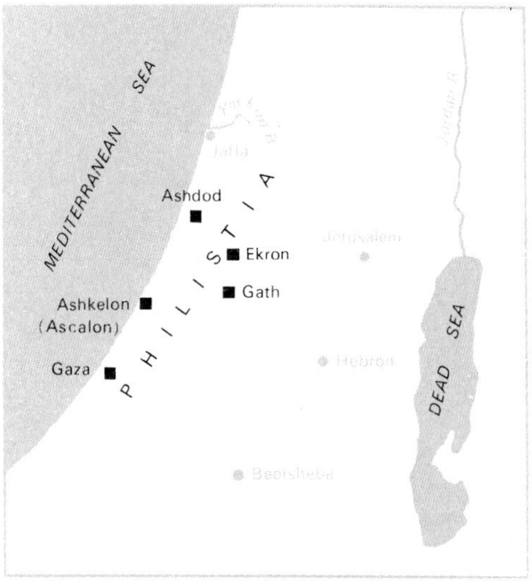

Philistine anthropoid clay coffin lid from Tell al-Fāri'a, 13th–10th cent. B.C.E.

Phillips, Nathan (1892–), Canadian lawyer, politician. Toronto city councillor and its first Jewish mayor 1954–62.

Phillips, Philip (1807–1884), U.S. congressman, jurist; b. Charleston, S.C. Unionist. Served in Alabama legislature 1844–1853 and U.S. Congress 1853–55, the second Jew to sit in Congress. Admitted to bar of Supreme Court 1850.

Phillipson, Irving Joseph (1882–), U.S. army corps commander. Served in WWI and WWII. Chief of staff of Second Corps area; 1941 major general. Active in aid to soldiers' dependents.

Philo Judaeus (Philo of Alexandria; c. 20 B.C.E.–50 C.E.), Jewish philosopher. Scion of one of the wealthiest families in Egypt; received Hellenistic education. Little information on his life, but in 40 C.E. headed Alexandrian Jewish delegation to Rome. Prolific output included metaphysics, ethics, and Bible commentary (esp. allegorical). His philosophic system is stoicism with strong Platonic bent and some Neo-Pythagorean influences which he sought to reconcile with Jewish thought. He developed concept of *logos* as mediating between God and world. His influence on Christianity, the Church Fathers, and Neoplatonists was great, but he was largely unknown to later Jewish thinkers until 16th c.

Philo Verlag, Jewish publishing house in Germany 1919–38.

Phinehas, priest; son of Eleazar son of Aaron. Slew an Israelite with a Midianite woman after Israel became involved in paganism at Shittim (Num. 25:1–19). Officiating priest early in period of Judges (Judg. 20:28).

Phinehas, priest; son of Eli, at Shiloh. Killed in battle of Aphek when Philistines captured ark (I Sam. 4).

Phinehas ben Ḥama ha-Kohen (4th c.), Palestinian *amora;* often referred to as R. Phinehas. Transmitted many aggadic aphorisms. Saying: "The name a person gains for himself is worth more than the one endowed him from birth" (Eccles. R. 7:1).

Phinehas ben Jacob ha-Kohen (8th c.), Palestinian *paytan.* Prolific poet; 59 of his compositions found in Cairo *Genizah.*

Phinehas ben Jair (2nd c.), *tanna,* renowned for saintliness and ability to work miracles; son-in-law of Simeon bar Yoḥai. Best known as aggadist. Author of ladder of saintliness: "Caution [against evil] leads to

Eagerness [for good,] Eagerness to Cleanliness, Cleanliness to Purity, Purity to Asceticism, Asceticism to Holiness, Holiness to Humility, Humility to Fear of God, Fear of God to Attainment of the Holy Spirit, and attainment of the Holy Spirit to Resurrection of the Dead."

Phoebus ben Aaron ha-Levi, see Uri ben Aaron ha-Levi.

Phoenicia, term first used by Greeks to refer to country of Canaanites. Territory on E. Mediterranean coast covering c. 150 mi. between the river Litani and Mt. Carmel.

Phoenicians, the inhabitants of Phoenicia. Close relations with Egypt in early times. Later in Persian Empire and in 64 B.C.E., incorporated into Roman Empire. Noted for their maritime trade extending to distant lands. Industries included glass manufacture and purple dyeing. Language akin to Hebrew.

Phoenix, city in Ariz., U.S. First known Jewish settler 1871. First Jewish congregation 1906, first synagogue 1921. Jewish pop. increased rapidly after 1940. 14,000 Jews in 1971.

Phrygia, district in Asia Minor. 2,000 Jewish families fr. Babylonia transported there. Maintained ties with Second Temple.

Phylacteries, see Tephillin.

Gregor Piatigorsky

Piatigorsky, Gregor (1903–), cellist; b. Russia, fr. 1929 in U.S. where he also taught at Curtis Institute, Philadelphia.

Piatra-Neamt, town in NE Rumania. Jews fr. 16th c.; number rose rapidly in 19th c. 7,595 in 1930. Jews suffered anti-Semitism, but community not destroyed in WWII. 8,000 Jews in 1947, declining to 300 families in 1969.

PICA (The Palestine Jewish Colonization Association), society for Jewish settlement in Ereẓ Israel, founded by Baron Edmond de Rothschild to take over fr. ICA. Founded and assisted settlements; active until 1957, when it was wound up, transferring its considerable property to the State of Israel.

Picard, Leo (1900–), Israel geologist, expert on groundwater; b. Germany. Proved that water could be found in Israel limestone formations. Prof. at Heb. Univ.; director of Geological Survey of Israel. Israel Prize 1958.

°**Picart, Bernard** (1673–1733), French artist, engraver. Settled in Amsterdam. His illustrations of Jewish religious rites are invaluable record of 18th c. Dutch Jewry.

Picciotto, Joseph (1872–1938), Egyptian community leader, Zionist. First Jewish senator appointed by King Fuad (1924).

Picciotto, Moses H. (1806–1879), English Sephardi leader; b. Syria. President of Bevis Marks synagogue; active on behalf of Moroccan Jews. His son, **James** (1830–1897), wrote *Sketches of Anglo-Jewish History,* the earliest popular work on the subject.

Picho, Azariah, see Figo, Azariah.

Picho (or **Pichon), Joseph** (d. 1379), *contador mayor* ("auditor general") of Henry II of Castile. In 1379 convicted of informing by Jews jealous of his position and executed. As a result, in 1380 Pedro III abrogated the rights of criminal jurisdiction previously held by Jews of Castile.

Pick, Alois (1859–1945), Austrian army medical corps general. Univ. prof. and pres. of Vienna Jewish community. First to describe a form of pappataci fever during his service in Herzegovina.

Pick, Ernst Peter (1872–1960), Austrian pharmacological chemist. Univ. prof. in Vienna, New York. Chief of Austrian govt. drug control dept. until 1938. Wrote on various fields of experimental pathology and pharmacology.

Pick, Ḥayyim Hermann (1879–1952), Assyriologist, religious Zionist leader; b. Poland. Worked in Prussian State Library. Member of Jerusalem Zionist Executive 1921–27. Nazis confiscated his unique Assyriological library.

Pick, Isaiah, see Berlin, Isaiah ben Judah Loeb.

°**Pico Della Mirandola, Giovanni** (1463–1494), Christian kabbalist of Italian Renaissance. Maintained contact with major Jewish kabbalists. Influential thinker, humanist, scholar, pioneer of oriental studies. Sought to prove truth of Christianity from formulations of Kabbalah.

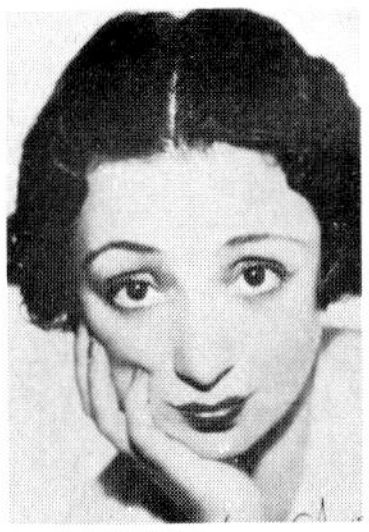

Molly Picon

Picon, Molly (1898–), U.S. actress, vaudeville performer in Yiddish, English. Became known in Yiddish roles on New York's Second Avenue. Appeared with husband Jacob Kalich. Appeared on Broadway, TV, and in films.

Pidyon Ha-Ben, redemption of first-born son of ordinary Jews (i.e., not of kohen or levite). Originally the first-born "dedicated to God" and redemption by priest is substitute. The redemption fee was five silver shekels (Num. 18:16). Ceremony takes place on 31st day after birth.

Pidyon Shevuyim, see Captives, Ransoming of.

Piedmont, region in N. Italy. Jews expelled fr. France arrived in 14th c., including many loan bankers; fr. 1430 Jews had to live in closed quarters in each city, paid special tax. In 17th c. Jews permitted to bear defensive arms and practice professions. In 1723 forced to live in ghettos. Temporary relaxation with French rule 1798–1816. Full emancipation 1848.

Pierce, Sydney David (1901–), Canadian government official. Ambassador to Brazil, Mexico, Belgium, European Common Market, etc.

Pierleoni, Jewish family in Rome after 1000. One member, Pietro, became Pope Anacletus II in 1130.

Pig (Heb. *ḥazir).* Included in Pentateuch among unclean animals prohibited as food since it is nonruminant. Refusal to eat swine's flesh was regarded as test of loyalty to Judaism in Maccabee times, and abhorrence of pig entered deeply into consciousness of Jews. Pig rearing was forbidden as early as Mishnaic times and a Law of 1962 forbids it in Israel (except in predominantly non-Jewish areas).

Pijade, Moša (1890–1957), Yugoslav revolutionary, politician. Communist leader fr. his youth, partisan hero, and close colleague of Tito. After WWII president of Serbian Republic, chairman of Yugoslav National Assembly.

Pike, Lipman E. (Lip; 1845–1893), U.S. baseball pioneer. Baseball's first

professional when Philadelphia Athletics paid him regular salary. Established first home run record in 1866 when he hit 6 in one game.

Pikku'aḥ Nefesh (Heb. "regard for human life"), duty to save human life when imperiled. Supersedes Sabbath laws.

Pilgrimage. The Pentateuch prescribes that all males must go up to Jerusalem "three times a year," on the three festivals – Passover, Shavuot, and Sukkot. This institution was widely practiced in Second Temple era and revived in the Middle Ages, largely under Karaite influence. In late Jewish history the term was applied to a visit to Ereẓ Israel. Christian pilgrimages to the Holy Land had also become an established institution fr. 4th c. The reports of the pilgrims provide an important historical source.

Pilgrims making their way to Jerusalem, engraving of 1581.

Front page of a 1937 issue of Yiddish newspaper "Pinsker Sztyme."

Pinsker Sztyme
פינסקער שטימע
יהושע עפשטיין
MASKOTTE
TOLEDO

Pilgrim Festivals (Heb. *shalosh regalim*), the three festivals Passover, Shavuot, and Sukkot when pilgrimages were made to Jerusalem according to biblical injunction (Deut. 16:16). Tradition renewed in modern Israel, esp. among oriental Jewish communities.

Pilichowski, Leopold (1869–1933), Polish painter; fr. 1914 in London. His Zionist and socialist sentiments influenced his choice of subject. Painted opening of Hebrew University in 1925.

Pilpul (fr. Heb. *pilpel,* "pepper"), techniques of talmudic study utilizing subtle differentiations. Reached zenith in *yeshivot* of 16th–17th c.

Pilsen (Czech **Plzeň**), city in Czechoslovakia. Jews first recorded 1338; expelled 1504. One of largest communities in Bohemia in early 20th c., Jews numbering 2,773 in 1930, but came to end in WWII. Community reorganized 1948, numbering 293.

Pinchik, Pierre (Pinchas Segal; c. 1900–), *ḥazzan;* b. Ukraine. Cantor in Leningrad, subsequently in U.S.

Pincus, Gregory Goodwin (1903–1967), U.S. biologist. Founded Worcester Foundation for Experimental Biology 1944. Pioneered development of oral contraceptives.

Pincus, Louis Arieh (1912–1973), Zionist leader; b. S. Africa. Practiced law 1934–48, settled in Ereẓ Israel 1948. Director of El Al 1949–56, member of Jewish Agency Executive and its chairman fr. 1966.

Pineles, Hirsch Mendel ben Solomon (known as **Shalosh;** 1806–1870), Galician scholar; lived in Brody and Galati. Best-known work: *Darkah shel Torah,* a critical examination of the Mishnah and its interpretation, followed by a treatise on the Hebrew calendar.

Pineles, Samuel (1843–1928), early Rumanian Zionist; son of Hirsch Mendel Pineles. Member of Ḥovevei Zion; did much to assist Rumanian immigrants in Ereẓ Israel. Participated in first 10 Zionist congresses.

Pines, Shlomo (Solomon; 1908–), historian of philosophy and science; b. Paris, settled in Ereẓ Israel 1940. Prof. of general and Jewish philosophy at Heb. Univ. Translated Maimonides' *Guide of the Perplexed* into English.

Pines, Yehiel Michael (known as **"Michal";** 1843–1913), *Yishuv* leader; author. B. Belorussia; settled in Jerusalem 1878, becoming outstanding figure in *yishuv* and exponent of religious Zionism. Played key role in early Jewish settlement and encouraged Bilu. Pioneer of Hebrew-speaking movement and Hebrew education.

Pinheiro, Moses (17th c.), Shabbatean who studied with Shabbetai Ẓevi in their youth. Settled in Leghorn, becoming ardent spokesman of movement.

Pinkas, record book of medieval Jewish communities containing minutes of meetings, bylaws, taxes, and many details of community life.

Pinkas, David Ẓvi (1895–1952), Mizrachi leader, Israel politician; b. Hungary, settled in Ereẓ Israel 1925. Elected Mizrachi representative to 1st, 2nd Knesset; minister of transportation 1951–2.

Pinkel, Benjamin (1909–), U.S. aeronautical engineer. Associate head of aero-astronautics dept. of Rand Corp. fr. 1956.

Pinkerfeld, Anda, see Amir, Anda.

Pins, Jacob (1917–), Israel printmaker. His stark, dramatic woodcuts often convey atmosphere of war. Shows influence of Japanese color print.

Pinsk, city in Belorussian SSR. Jews in tax and customs farming, crafts and commerce in 16th c. Suffered in 1648 (Chmielnicki massacre) and 1660 (Cossacks). Community impoverished late 17th c. and Jews began to deal in alcoholic beverages. Jews majority of pop. fr. 18th c. to 1939. Economic conditions improved in 1820s as salt and forestry industries developed. Large Jewish proletariat at end of 19th c. 20,000 Jews in 1939. Almost entire Jewish pop. murdered in WWII. Jewish pop. 1,500 (1970).

Pinsker, Leon (Judah Leib; 1821–1891), Ḥibbat Zion leader; b. Poland; son of Simḥah Pinsker. Practiced medicine, wrote in Jewish press. Published *Autoemancipation* 1882, in which he analyzed the psychological and social roots of anti-Semitism and called for establishment of Jewish national center. Book led to creation of Ḥovevei Zion movement. Headed Kattowitz (1884) and Druskieniki (1887) conventions of Ḥovevei Zion.

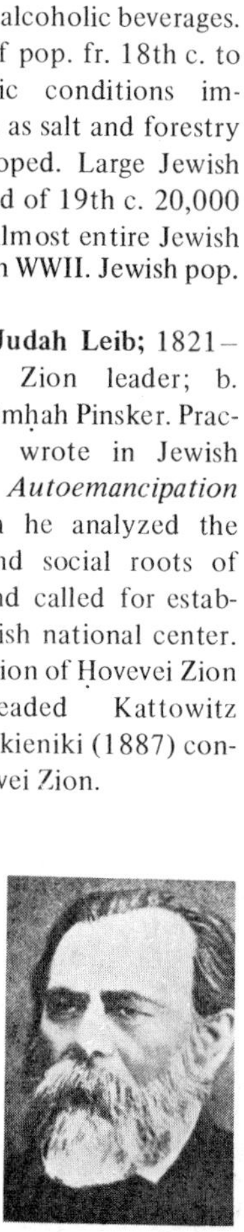

Leon Pinsker

Pinsker, Simhah (1801–1864), scholar; b. Galicia. Wrote history of Karaism and Karaite literature. Founded in Odessa first successful modern Jewish school in Russia 1826.

Pinski, David (1872–1959), Yiddish dramatist, novelist; b. Russia, went to U.S. 1899, where he edited periodicals. Settled in Haifa 1949. His work ranged over most episodes of Jewish history. Plays translated primarily into English and German. *The Eternal Jew* staged in Hebrew by Habimah in Moscow in 1919. His novel *The House of Noah Eden* portrays 3 generations of a Jewish family in U.S. fr. 1880s.

Pinson, Koppel S. (1904–1961), U.S. historian. Prof. at Queens College, N.Y. History editor, *Encyclopaedia of the Social Sciences.* Main field: modern European and Jewish history.

David Pinski

Harold Pinter

Pinter, Harold (1930–), English playwright. One of best-known dramatists of 1960s. Wrote *The Caretaker, The Birthday Party, The Homecoming, Old Times.* His screenplays, incl. several with producer Joseph Losey.

Pinto, de, family of Dutch Sephardi jurists: **Abraham** (1811–1878), founded and edited juridical review *Themis;* **Aaron Adolf** (1828–1908), largely responsible for Dutch penal code and abolition of death penalty. Member of Supreme Court (vice-president 1903). Both involved in Jewish community affairs.

Pinto, Isaac (1720–1791), U.S. merchant, translator of prayer books; lived in N.Y. by 1751 and member of Congregation Shearith Israel. Published earliest English translations of Hebrew prayer books in New World.

Pinto, Isaac de (1717–1787), Dutch philosopher, economist. Defended Jews against Voltaire. Innovator in economics and pacifistic conservative in philosophy and politics.

Pinto Delgado, João (Mosseh; d. 1653), Portuguese Marrano poet; in Antwerp fr. 1633. Wrote verse paraphrases of Old Testament books.

Pioneer Women, worldwide labor Zionist women's organization, founded New York 1925. Connected with Labor Zionist movement and Mo'ezet ha-Po'alot in Israel. Worldwide membership 150,000 (1970). Maintains in Israel social welfare services for women, young people, and children and helps new immigrants.

Piotrkow, town in Poland. Jews fr. early 16th c. Traded at fairs. Expelled 1590 following blood libel, readmitted 1679. Jewish proletariat in 19th c. 11,630 Jews in 1921. Almost entire pop. murdered in WWII.

Piperno Beer, Sergio (1906–), Italian judge, communal leader. President of Board of Italian Jewish Communities fr. 1956.

Pipes, Richard Edgar (1923–), U.S. historian. Director of Harvard's Russian Research Center.

Pirbright, Lord, see Worms, de.

Pirkei Avot, see Avot.

Pirkei de-Rabbi Eliezer, 8th c. Hebrew aggadic work based on events fr. creation to Israelite journey in wilderness.

Pirkoi ben Baboi (8th–9th c.), talmudic scholar. Author of *Iggeret,* a polemical halakhic work which attempted to make Babylonian Talmud more authoritative than Jerusalem Talmud.

Pisa, city in Italy. Jews present from 12th c. (tombstones extant fr. 13th c.) Jews usually well treated but numbers declined. Heb. press 18th–19th c. 210 Jews in 1969.

Pisa, Vitale da (Jehiel; d. 1422 or 1423), Italian loan banker. Founder of family business. Also scholar and lover of letters. His grandson **Vitale (Jehiel;** d. 1490), Italian loan banker, the most important in Tuscany. Friendly with notables abroad and with the authorities at home, his house was a meeting place of scholars.

Pisgah, mountain in Transjordan fr. which Moses viewed the Promised Land before his death. Location disputed.

Self-portrait by Camille Pissarro, 1903.

Pissarro, Camille (1830–1903), French painter; b. Virgin Islands, in Paris fr. 1855. A founder of Impressionist movement.

Pissarro, Lucien (1863–1944), English artist; son of Camille Pissarro. Produced impressionist landscapes and woodcuts.

Pithom, one of two treasury cities which Israelites were forced to build for Egyptian Pharaoh (Ex. 1:11).

Pitigrilli (pen name of **Dino Segre;** 1893–1954), Italian author, journalist, writer of erotic novels. Collaborated with Fascist secret police; after WWII converted to Catholicism and wrote anti-Jewish literature.

Pittsburgh, city in Penn., U.S. First recorded congregation Beth Almon Society 1845. Rodef Shalom Congregation, 1854. Pittsburgh Platform formulated there 1885. Jews active in all aspects of city life. Jewish pop. 45,000 (1971).

Pittsburgh Platform, formulation of principles agreed upon by Reform movement in 1885. Among provisions were abolition of dietary laws, priestly purity, dress codes. Reaffirmed immortality of soul but denied bodily resurrection. Major statement of tenets of Reform movement until 1937.

Pittum ha-Ketoret (Heb. "Ingredients of the incense"), initial words of *baraita* on preparation of incense in Temple. In Ashkenazi liturgy recited on Sabbath and festivals; among Sephardim, every morning and afternoon.

Piyyut, Hebrew liturgical poems. In a wider sense the totality of compositions in various guises of Hebrew liturgical poetry fr. the first centuries of the Common Era to the beginning of the Haskalah. Adopted into all rites.

PLANTS AND PRODUCTS OF PLANTS MENTIONED IN THE BIBLE AND MISHNAH

English Name	Scientific Name	Hebrew Name	Description of Plant	Reference
Acacia	Acacia albida	שטה, שטים	thorn tree	Ex. 26:15; Isa. 41:19, et al.
Alga	Chlorophyta	ירוקה	seaweed	Shab. 2:1
Almond	Prunus amygdalus (Amygdalus communis)	לוז שקד	fruit tree	Gen. 30:37 Num. 17:23; Jer. 1:11, et al.
Aloe	Aquilaria agallocha	אהלים אהלות אלמגים אלגמים	fragrant tropical tree	Num. 24:6; Prov. 7:17 Ps. 45:9; Song 4:14; I Kings 10:11–12 II Chron. 2:7; 9:10–11
Amaranth	Amaranthus retroflexus	ירבוז	vegetable (herb)	Shev. 9:1
Amomum	Amomum cardamomum	חמם	tropical spice plant	Uk. 3:5
Apple	Pyrus malus	תפוח	fruit tree	Joel 1:12; Song 2:3, et al.
Artichoke	Cynara scolymus	קנרס	garden vegetable	Kil. 5:8; Uk. 1:6
Asafetida, Fennel	Ferula assafoetida	חלתית	herb whose gum is used in spices and medicine	Shab. 20:3; Av. Zar. 2:7, et al.
Balm, Balsam	Commiphora opobalsamum	בשם נטף צרי, צרי קטף	the balsam shrub whose resin yields an aromatic substance	Song 5:1 Ex. 30:34 Gen. 37:25; 43:11, et al. Shev. 7:6
Barley	Hordeum sativum	שעורה	cereal grass	Ex. 9:31; Deut. 8:8, et al.
Barley, two-rowed	Hordeum distichum	שורה, שבולת שועל	cereal grass	Isa. 28:25 Kil. 1:1; Pes. 2:5, et al.
Bdellium	Commiphora africana	בדולח	tropical tree whose resin yields an aromatic substance	Gen. 2:12; Num. 11:7
Bean, broad	Vicia faba	פול	legume	II Sam. 17:28; Ezek. 4:9, et al.
Bean, hyacinth	Dolichos lablab	פול הלבן	legume	Kil. 1:1; Ma'as. 4:7, et al.
Bean, yard-long (asparagus bean)	Vigna sesquipedalis	פול החרוב	legume	Kil. 1:2
Beet spinach	Beta vulgaris var. cicla	תרד	garden vegetable	Kil. 1:3; Ter. 10:11, et al.
Bermuda grass	Cynodon dactylon	יבלית	weed	Kelim 3:6
Box	Buxus sempervirens	אשכרוע	hardwood shrub	Yoma 3:9; Kelim 12:8; Neg. 2:1
Boxthorn	Lycium europaeum	אטד	thorny shrub	Gen. 50:10–11; Judg. 9:14–15, et al.
Broom plant	Retama roetam	רתם	desert shrub	I Kings 19:4–5; Job 30:4, et al.
Cabbage, garden	Brassica oleracea var. capitata	תרובתור	garden vegetable	Kil. 1:3
Cabbage, kale	Brassica oleracea var. acephala	כרוב	hardy cabbage	Kil. 1:3; Ter. 10:11, et al.
Calamus, Indian sweet	Cymbopogon martini	קנה הטוב קנה־בשם קנה	tropical aromatic plant	Jer. 6:20 Ex. 30:23 Isa. 43:24; Song. 4:14, et al.
Cane, biflorate	Saccharum biflorum	אגמון	reed that grows near water	Isa. 9:13, 58:5, et al.
Caper	Capparis spinosa	צלף, קפרס אביונה	thorny plant whose buds and fruit are used as spices Caperberry	Ma'as. 4:6 Eccles. 12:5; Ma'as. 4:6
Caraway	Carum carvi	קרבוס (קנבוס)	vegetable used as a spice	Kil. 2:5
Carob	Ceratonia siliqua	חרוב	fruit tree	Pe'ah. 1:5; Dem. 2:1, et al.
Castor-oil plant	Ricinus communis	קיקיון	shrub whose seed yields oil	Jonah 4:6, 7, 9, 10
Cattail	Typha angustata	סוף	marsh and water plant	Ex. 2:3; Isa. 19:6, et al.
Cedar	Cedrus libani	ארז	forest tree of Lebanon	Isa. 2:13; Amos 2:9, et al.
Celery	Apium graveolens	כרפס	garden vegetable	Shev. 9:1
Chick-pea	Cicer arietinum	חמיץ אפונים	legume	Isa. 30:24 Pe'ah 3:3; Kil. 3:2
Chicory	Cichorium intybus	עולשין	garden vegetable	Shev. 7:1; Pes. 2:6
Chicory, wild	Cichorium pumilum	עולשי־שדה	wild vegetable	Kil. 1:2
Cinnamon, Ceylonese	Cinnamonum zeylanicum	קנמון	aromatic tropical spice tree	Ex. 30:23; Prov. 7:17, et al.
Cinnamon, Chinese	Cinnamonum cassia	קדה	aromatic tropical spice tree	Ex. 30:24; Ezek. 27:19
Cinnamon, Indo-Chinese	Cinnamonum laurei	קציעה	aromatic tropical spice tree	Ps. 45:9
Citron	Citrus medica	עץ הדר אתרוג	fruit tree	Lev. 23:40 Ma'as. 1:4; Bik. 2:6, et al.
Colocasia	Colocasia antiquorum	קרקס	vegetable with edible bulb	Ma'as. 5:8
Coriander	Coriandrum sativum	גד כסבר	herb whose seed is used as a spice	Ex. 16:31; Num. 11:7 Kil. 1:2; Ma'as. 3:9, et al.
Cotton	Gossypium herbraceum Gossypium arboreum	כרפס צמר־גפן	plant with fibrous fruit	Esth. 1:6 Kil. 7:2
Cowpea	Vigna sinensis	פול המצרי	legume	Kil. 1:2; Shev. 2:9, et al.
Cowpea, Nile	Vigna nilotica	שעועית	legume	Kil. 1:1
Cress	Lepidium latifolium	עדל	garden vegetable	Uk. 3:4
Cress, garden	Lepidium sativum	שחלים	garden vegetable	Ma'as. 4:5
Crocus, saffron	Crocus sativus	כרכום	plant used as a spice and for coloring	Song 4:14; Nid. 2:6
Cucumber, bitter	Citrullus colocynthis	פקועות	wild desert plant	II Kings 4:39; Shab. 2:2
Cucumber, squirting	Ecballium elaterium	ירוקת החמור	wild herb	Oho. 8:1
Cumin	Cuminum cyminum	כמון	herb whose seeds are used as a spice	Isa. 2:25, 27; Dem. 2:1
Cypress	Cupressus sempervirens	גפר תאשור	forest evergreen tree	Gen. 6:14 Isa. 41:19; 60:13, et al.
Daffodil, sea	Pancratium maritimum	חבצלת	fragrant wild flower	Isa. 35:1; Song 2:1
Darnel	Lolium temulentum	זון	weed grass	Kil. 1:1; Ter. 2:6
Dill	Anethum graveolens	שבת	plant used as a spice	Pe'ah 3:2; Ma'as. 4:5; Uk. 3:4
Durra	Sorghum cernuum	דחן	summer cereal	Ezek. 4:9; Shev. 2:7
Ebony	Diospyros ebenum	הבנים	tropical hardwood	Ezek. 27:15
Emmer	Triticum dicoccum	כסמת	winter cereal	Ex. 9:32; Isa. 28:25, et al.
Eryngo	Eryngium creticum	חרחבינא	edible wild herb	Pes. 2:6
Fennel	Foeniculum vulgare	גפנין	herb used as a spice	Dem. 1:1
Fennel flower	Nigella sativa	קצח	herb whose seeds are used as a spice	Isa. 28:25, 27; Eduy. 5:3

English Name	Scientific Name	Hebrew Name	Description of Plant	Reference
Fenugreek	Trigonella foenum-Graecum	תלתן	cultivated legume used as forage or medicine	Kil. 2:5; Ter. 10:5
Fern, ceterach	Ceterach officinarum	דנדנה	medicinal fern	Shev. 7:1–2
Fern, maiden-hair	Adiantum capillus veneris	יועזר	medicinal fern	Shab. 14:3
Fig	Ficus carica	תאנה	fruit tree	Num. 20:5; Deut. 8:8, et al.
Fig, sycamore	Ficus sycomorus	שקמה	fruit tree	I Kings 10:27; Isa. 9:9, et al.
Flax	Linum usitatissimum	פשתן פשתה	herb whose stem yields fiber and from whose seed oil is extracted	Josh. 2:6; Hos. 2:7; et al. Pe'ah 6:5
Frankincense	Boswellia carteri	לבונה	tree yielding aromatic resin used in incense	Ex. 30:34; Isa. 60:6, et al.
Galbanum	Ferula galbaniflua	חלבנה	herb whose resin was used in incense	Ex. 30:34
Garlic	Allium sativum	שום	vegetable used as spice	Num. 11:5
Ginger, wild	Arum dioscoridis	לוף שוטה	wild vegetable	Shev. 7:1, 2, et al.
Gourd, Calabash	Lagenaria vulgaris	דלעת	vegetable with edible fruit	Kil. 1:2; Ma'as. 1:5, et al.
Grape vine	Vitis vinifera	גפן ענבים	fruit shrub	Gen. 40:9; Num. 20:5, et al.
Graspea	Lathyrus sativus	טפח	legume	Pe'ah 5:3; Kil. 1:1, et al.
Hawthorn	Crataegus azarolus	עזרר	wild fruit tree	Dem. 1:1; Kil. 1:4, et al.
Heliotrope	Heliotropium europaeum	עקרבנין	medicinal wild herb	Shev. 7:2; Er. 2:7
Hemlock, poison	Conium maculatum	רוש,ראש	poisonous herb	Deut. 29:17; Hos. 10:4, et al.
Hemp	Cannabis sativa	קנבוס	herb whose stem yields fiber	Kil. 5:8; 9:1, 7
Henna	Lawsonia alba	כפר	shrub which yields a dye	Song. 1:14; 4:13, et al.
Hyssop (v. marjoram)	Hyssopus officinalis	אזוב כוחל	aromatic herb	Neg. 14:6; Par. 11:7
Iris	Iris germanica Iris pallida	אירוס	plant whose bulb yields an aromatic substance	Kil. 5:8; Oho. 8:1
Ivy	Hedera helix	קיסוס	climbing ever-green vine	Kil. 5:8; Suk. 1:4, et al.
Jujube	Zizyphus vulgaris	שיזפין	fruit tree	Kil. 1:4
Jujube, wild	Zizyphus spina-christi	צאלים רימין	wild tree with edible fruit	Job 40:21–22 Dem. 1:1; Kil. 1:6
Juniper (savin high)	Juniperus exelsa	ברוש ברות	coniferous tree of Lebanon	Isa. 14:8; 37:24, et al. Song. 1:17
Knotweed	Polygonum aviculare	אבוב־רועה	medicinal wild herb	Shab. 14:3
Laudanum	Cistus ladanum	לט	shrub yielding aromatic resin	Gen. 37:25; 43:11
Laurel	Laurus nobilis	ארן	forest tree with aromatic leaves	Isa. 44:14
Lavender, Lavandula	Lavandula officinalis	אזוביון	aromatic shrub	Shab. 14:3; Neg. 14:6, et al.
Leek	Allium porrum	חציר כרישה כרתי	garden herb	Num. 11:5 Kil. 1:2; Shev. 7:1 Ber. 1:2; Suk. 3:6
Leek, wild	Allium ampeloprasum	כרישי שדה	wild herb	Kil. 1:2; Uk. 3:2
Lentil	Lens esculenta	עדשים	legume	Gen. 25:34; II Sam. 17:28, et al.
Lettuce	Lactuca sativa	חזרת	garden vegetable	Kil. 1:2; Pes. 2:6, et al.
Lettuce, wild	Lactuca scariola	חזרת גלים	wild vegetable	Kil. 1:2
Lily, madonna	Lilium candidum	שושן, שושנה	aromatic flower	Hos. 14:6; Song. 6:2–3, et al.
Lily, Solomon's (black calla)	Arum palaestinum	לוף	wild vegetable with edible bulb	Pe'ah, 6:10; Kil. 2:5
Love grass	Eragrostis bipinnata	חילף	weed used for making baskets	Kelim 17:17
Lupine	Lupinus termis	תרמוס	legume	Kil. 1:3; Shab. 18:1, et al.
Lupine, yellow	Lupinus luteus	פלסלוס	legume	Kil. 1:3
Madder	Rubia tinctorim	פואה	climbing plant whose roots are used for dyeing	Shev. 5:4; 7:2, et al.
Mandrake	Mandragora officinarum	דודאים	wild herb with aromatic fruit	Gen. 30:14–16; Song. 7:14
Marjoram, Syrian	Majorana syriaca	אזוב	aromatic wild plant	Ex. 12:22; Lev. 14:4, et al.
Mastic	Pistacia lentiscus	בכא, בכאים	wild shrub	II Sam. 5:23–24; Ps. 84:7
Melon	Cucumis melo	מלפפון	garden vegetable	Kil. 1:2; Ter. 2:6, et al.
Melon, chate	Cucumis melo var. chate	קשות, קשאים	garden vegetable	Num. 11:5; Kil. 1:2, et al.
Millet	Panicum miliaceum	פרגים	summer cereal	Ḥal. 1:4; Shev. 2:7
Mint	Mentha piperita	מינתא	herb used as spice	Uk. 1:2
Mudar	Calotropis procera	פתילת המדבר	wild shrub with fibrous fruit	Shab. 2:1
Mulberry	Morus nigra	תות	fruit tree	Ma'as. 1:2
Mushroom	Boletus, etc.	פטריה	generic name for the mush-room species	Uk. 3:2
Mustard, black	Brassica nigra	חרדל	wild herb whose seeds are used as a condiment	Kil. 1:2
Mustard, field	Sinapis arvensis	לפסן	wild herb	Kil. 1:5
Mustard, white	Sinapis alba	חרדל מצרי	wild herb whose seeds are used as a condiment	Kil. 1:2
Myrrh	Commiphora schimperi Commiphora abyssinica	מור	tropical aromatic tree	Ex. 30:23; Song 1:13, et al.
Myrtle	Myrtus communis	הדס עץ עבת	aromatic shrub	Isa. 41:19; 55:13, et al. Lev. 23:40; Neh. 8:15, et al.
Narcissus	Narcissus tazetta	שושנת העמקים(?)	wild flower	Song 2:1
Nard (Spikenard)	Nardostachys jatamansi	נרד, נרדים	aromatic plant	Song 1:12; 4:13–14, et al.
Nettle	Urtica sp.	סרפד	stinging wild weed	Isa. 55:13
Oak	Quercus ithaburensis Quercus calliprinos	אלון	forest tree	Gen. 35:8; Isa. 2:13, et al.
Oak, gall	Quercus infectoria (Boissieri)	מילה	forest tree	Mid. 3:7

English Name	Scientific Name	Hebrew Name	Description of Plant	Reference
Oleander	Nerium oleander	הַרְדוּפְנֵי	river bank evergreen shrub	Ḥul. 3:5
Olive	Olea europaea	זַיִת	fruit tree	Deut. 6:11; 8:8, et al.
Onion	Allium cepa	בָּצָל	garden vegetable	Num. 11:5
Orange, trifoliate	Poncirus trifoliata	קְדָה לְבָנָה	tropical fruit tree	Kil. 1:8
Orchid	Orchis sp.	חַלְבְּצִין נֵץ־הֶחָלָב	flower with edible bulb	Shev. 7:2 Shev. 7:1
Palm, date	Phoenix dactylifera	תָּמָר דֶּקֶל	fruit tree	Ex. 15:27; Num. 33:9, et al. Pe'ah 4:1; Shab. 14:3, et al.
Papyrus	Cyperus papyrus	גֹּמֶא	aquatic plant	Ex. 2:3; Isa. 18:2, et al.
Peach	Persica vulgaris	אֲפַרְסֵק	fruit tree	Kil. 1:4; Ma'as. 1:2
Pear	Pyrus communis	אַגָּס קְרִיסְטוֹמֶלִין	fruit tree	Kil. 1:4; Uk. 1:6, et al.
Pear, Syrian	Pyrus syriaca	חוּרָר	forest tree with edible fruit	Kil. 1:4
Pepper	Piper nigrum	פִּלְפֵּל	tropical aromatic plant used as a condiment	Shab. 6:5; Beẓah 2:8
Pine	Pinus sp.	תִּדְהָר(?)	coniferous tree	Isa. 41:19; 60:13
Pine, aleppo	Pinus halepensis	עֵץ שֶׁמֶן	coniferous forest tree	I Kings 6:23; Isa. 41:19, et al.
Pine, stone	Pinus pinea	תִּרְזָה	coniferous tree with edible kernels	Isa. 44:14
Pistachio	Pistacia vera	בָּטְנָה, בָּטְנִים	fruit tree	Gen. 43:11; Shev. 7:5
Plane	Platanus orientalis	עַרְמוֹן	river bank tree	Gen. 30:37; Ezek. 31:8
Pomegranate	Punica granatum	רִמּוֹן	fruit tree	Num. 20:5; Deut. 8:8, et al.
Poplar	Populus euphratica	צַפְצָפָה	river bank tree	Ezek. 17:5
Purslane	Portulaca oleracea	חֲלַגְלוֹגָה רְגֵלָה	wild herb used as a vegetable	Shev. 9:1 Shev. 7:1, 9:5, et al.
Quince	Cydonia oblonga	פְּרִישׁ	fruit tree	Kil. 1:4; Ma'as. 1:3, et al.
Radish	Raphanus sativus	צְנוֹן	garden vegetable	Kil. 1:5; Ma'as. 5:2, et al.
Rape	Brassica napus	נָפוּץ, נָפוּס	garden vegetable used as forage	Kil. 1:3; 1:5, et al.
Raspberry, wild	Rubus sanctus	סְנֶה	thorny climbing shrub	Ex. 3:2–4; Deut. 33:16
Reed, ditch	Phragmites communis	קָנֶה	river bank weed	Isa. 19:6, 35:7, et al.
Rice	Oryza sativa	אֹרֶז	annual summer cereal grass	Dem. 2:1; Shev. 2:7, et al.
Rocket, dyer's	Reseda luteola	רִכְפָּה	herb whose leaves and stem yield a dye	Ma'as. 5:8; Shev. 7:2
Rocket, garden	Eruca sativa	אֹרֹת	medicinal herb	II Kings 4:39
Rose	Rosa, sp.	וֶרֶד	shrub with fragrant flowers	Shev. 7:6; Ma'as. 2:5, et al.
Rue	Ruta graveolens	פֵּיגָם	shrub used as a spice	Kil. 1:8; Shev. 9:1
Safflower	Carthamus tinctorius	חָרִיעַ קוֹצָה	herb used as a spice and for dyeing	Kil. 2:8; Uk. 3:5; Shev. 7:1
Saltbush	Atriplex halimus	מַלּוּחַ	desert shrub	Job 30:4
Savory	Satureja thymbra	סִיאָה	aromatic wild plant	Shev. 8:1; Ma'as. 3:9
Sesame	Sesamum orientalis	שֻׁמְשְׁם	plant used as a spice and yielding oil	Shev. 2:7; Ḥal. 1:4, et al.
Shallot	Allium ascalonicum	בְּצַלְצוּל	garden vegetable used for seasoning	Kil. 1:3
Sorrel, garden	Rumex acetosa	לְעוּנִים	garden vegetable	Kil. 1:3
Spanish cherry	Mimusops balata	פַּרְסָאָה	tropical fruit tree	Shev. 5:1
Spelt	Triticum spelta	שִׁפּוֹן	cereal	Kil. 1:1; Ḥal. 1:1, et al.
Squill	Urginea maritima	חֲצוּב	wild toxic onion	Kil. 1:8
Storax	Styrax officinalis	לִבְנֶה	forest tree	Gen. 30:37; Hos. 4:13
Sumac	Rhus coriaria	אוֹג	forest tree with edible fruit	Pe'ah 1:5; Dem. 1:1, et al.
Tamarisk	Tamarix, sp.	אֶשֶׁל עַרְעָר	desert and saline tree	Gen. 21:33; I Sam. 22:6, et al. Jer. 17:6; Ps. 102:18
Terebinth	Pistacia palaestina Pistacia atlantica	אֵלָה	forest tree	Gen. 35:4; Hos. 4:13, et al.
Thistle	Centaurea, sp.	דַּרְדַּר	prickly herb	Gen. 3:18; Hos. 10:8
Thistle, golden	Scolymus maculatus	חוֹחַ	prickly herb	Hos. 9:6; Prov. 26:9, et al.
Thistle, silybum	Silybum marianum	קִמּוֹשׁ	prickly herb	Isa. 34:13; Hos. 9:6, et al.
Thistle, sow	Sonchus oleraceus	מָרוֹר	bitter herb	Ex. 12:8; Lam. 3:15, et al.
Thorn	Calycotome villosa	חָרוּל	prickly shrub	Zeph. 2:9; Job 30:7, et al.
Thorn, camel	Alhagi maurorum	נַעֲצוּץ	prickly dwarf shrub	Isa. 7:19; 55:13
Thorn, gundelia	Gundelia tournefortii	גַּלְגַּל	prickly herb	Isa. 17:13; Ps. 83:14
Thorn, poterium	Poterium spinosum	סִירִים סִירָה	prickly dwarf shrub	Isa. 34:13; Hos. 2:8, et al. Ps. 58:10
Thorn, prosopis	Prosopis farcata	נַהֲלֹל	prickly dwarf shrub	Isa. 7:19
Thyme	Thymus capitatus	קוֹרָנִית	aromatic dwarf shrub	Shev. 8:1; Ma'as. 3:9
Tragacanth	Astragalus gummifer Astragalus tragacantha	נְכֹאת	dwarf shrub yielding a fragrant resin	Gen. 37:25; 43:11
Truffle	Ascomycetes-Tuberaceae	שְׁמַרְקָעִים	edible subterranean fungus	Uk. 3:2
Turnip	Brassica rapa	לֶפֶת	garden vegetable	Kil. 1:3, 9, et al.
Vetch, bitter	Vicia ervilia	כַּרְשִׁינָה	legume	Ter. 11:9; Shab. 1:5, et al.
Vetch, French	Vicia narbonensis	סַפִּיר	legume	Kil. 1:1
Walnut	Juglans regia	אֱגוֹז	fruit tree	Song 6:11
Watermelon	Citrullus vulgaris	אֲבַטִּיחַ	garden vegetable	Num. 11:5
Weed, ridolfia	Ridololfia segetum	בָּאְשָׁה	weed	Job 31:40
Wheat	Triticum durum Triticum vulgare Triticum turgidum	חִטָּה	cereal	Ex. 9:32; Deut. 8:8; et al.
Willow	Salix, sp.	עֲרָבָה	river bank tree	Lev. 23:40; Ps. 137:2, et al.
Woad, isatis	Isatis tinctoria	אִסָּטִיס	herb which yields a dye	Kil. 2:5; Shev. 7:1, et al.
Wormwood	Artemisia, sp.	לַעֲנָה	desert dwarf shrub	Deut. 29:17; Jer. 9:14, et al.

Pizmon, a poem praising God; can be inserted at almost any point in liturgy. Word later used for poems and songs in general. In Israel, a popular song.

Plagues, The Ten: Afflictions suffered by the Egyptians as a result of Pharaoh's refusal to permit the Israelites to leave the country. (1) waters of Nile turned to blood; (2) infestation of frogs; (3) lice; (4) swarms of insects; (5) pestilence affecting livestock; (6) boils; (7) hail and fire; (8) locusts; (9) three days of darkness; (10) death of the firstborn of man and beast. The recounting of the Plagues is a prominent feature of the Passover *Haggadah*.

°**Plantin, Christophe** (c. 1520–1589), French humanist printer; lived many years in Antwerp. Produced "Antwerp Polyglot" Bible in 2 vol. and also Hebrew Bibles for N. African Jewish communities.

Plaut (Flaut), Hezekiah Feivel (1818–1895), Hungarian rabbi. His yeshivah in Nagysurany attracted students from all over Hungary.

Plaut, Hugo Carl (1858–1928), German bacteriologist. Specialized in medical and veterinary bacteriology. Described etiology of trench mouth (Plaut-Vincent disease).

Four of the plagues: Upper right, frogs; upper left, lice; lower right, beasts; lower left, murrain; from "Golden Haggadah," Spain, 13th cent.

Plaut, W. Gunther (1912–), Reform rabbi; b. Germany, went to U.S. 1935. Rabbi in Chicago, St. Paul, and fr. 1961 in Toronto. Wrote on history of Reform Judaism.

°**Plehve, Vyacheslav Konstantinovich von** (1846–1904). Russian anti-Jewish statesman. As minister of interior was practically responsible for Kishinev pogrom (1903). Herzl met him in attempt to alleviate condition of Jews.

Plessner, Martin (Meir; 1900–1973), orientalist; b. Germany, taught at Frankfort Univ., settled in Ereẓ Israel 1933. Taught at Reali School in Haifa; prof. at Heb. Univ. fr. 1955. Wrote first Arabic grammar in modern Hebrew.

Pletten (Yid.), meal tickets for the needy; started 15th c. in Germany.

Maya Plisetskaya

Plisetskaya, Maya (1925–), Russian dancer. Prima ballerina of Bolshoi Ballet; awarded Lenin Prize and title People's Artist of the U.S.S.R.

Plock, town in Poland. Oldest Jewish community in Poland (before 1237). Jews at first active in money lending, fr. 16th c. also in trade. Frequent anti-Jewish riots in 16th c. Fr. 17th c. restriction on Jewish activities. Blood libel 1754. 10,000 Jews in 1939; c. 100 survived WWII.

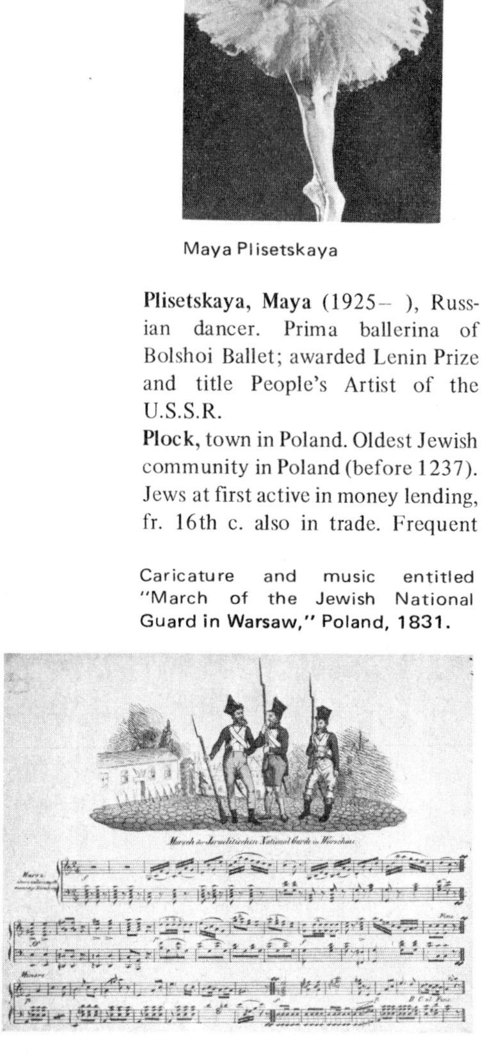

Caricature and music entitled "March of the Jewish National Guard in Warsaw," Poland, 1831.

Plonsk, town in Poland. Jews present fr. 1446. Restrictions on Jewish trade fr. 17th c. In 1910 64% of pop. (7,665) Jews. Almost all of 6,000 Jews murdered in WWII.

Plotzki, Meir Dan of Ostrova (1867–1928), Polish rabbi best known for his work *Ḥemdat Yisrael.* Rabbi of Ostrow and fr. 1926 *rosh yeshivah* of "Metivta" in Warsaw, the most important yeshivah in Poland. A leader of Agudat Israel.

Po'alei Agudat Israel, Orthodox religious party founded in Poland 1922 as affiliate of Agudat Israel, but differing in its labor orientation, and in 1940s on building up Ereẓ Israel. Founded 2 kibbutzim. Represented in Knesset and on occasion joined government coalition.

Po'alei Zion (Heb. "Workers of Zion"), socialist Zionist movement. Socialist Marxist platform emerged at conference in Poltava (Russia) in 1906. World Union of Po'alei Zion founded 1907. Movement split 1920. Right Po'alei Zion merged 1925 with Zionist socialists and in 1932 joined with Hitaḥdut to found Iḥud Olami, connected with Mapai. After union of Israel labor parties it too joined Iḥud Olami and formed Labor Zionist Movement. In 1945 Left Po'alei Zion united with Si'ah Bet (Faction B) to form Aḥdut ha-Avodah.

°**Pobedonostsev, Konstantin Petrovich** (1827–1907), Russian anti-Semitic statesman. Ideologist of anti-Jewish legislation in Russia. Said of Russian Jews: "One-third will die, one-third will leave the country, and the last third will assimilate."

°**Pococke, Edward** (1604–1691), English orientalist, Hebraist. Participated in Walton's London Polyglot Bible. Translated two of Maimonides' works into Latin.

Podhoretz, Norman (1930–), U.S. editor, author; editor of *Commentary* fr. 1960.

Podolia, region in Ukrainian SSR. First Jews 1518. Many massacred in Chmielnicki uprising 1648. Strong Shabbetean movement and Frankism and later many ḥasidic courts clustered there. Jewish pop. 420,000 in 1882; declined after pogroms. Jews suffered in WWII both in German and Rumanian occupied zones.

Pogrom (Russ.), mob attack on Jews. In Russia 3 main waves: 1880–4; 1903–6; and 1917–21.

Polacco, Vittorio (1859–1926), Italian jurist. Prof. of law at Padua and fr. 1918 at Rome. Senator fr. 1910.

Poláček, Karel (1892–1944), Czech humorist. Wrote novels, short stories, comedies, introducing many Jewish characters. D. in Auschwitz.

Polachek, Solomon (1877–1928), talmudic scholar, teacher. Taught at Lida Yeshivah. Went to U.S. 1922; senior *rosh yeshivah* at Rabbi Isaac Elchanan Theological Seminary.

Polak, Carel H.F. (1909–), Dutch jurist; son of Moritz Polak. Prof. at Leiden. Representative of Liberal Party; minister of justice 1967–71.

Polak, Gabriel Isaac (1803–1869), Dutch Hebrew scholar. Head of school in Amsterdam. Translated liturgical texts into Dutch.

Polak, Henri (1868–1943), Dutch trade union leader. Founded Diamond Workers Guild. Socialist member of parliament and senate 1913–37.

Polak, Jacob Eduard (1820–1891), physician, writer; b. Bohemia, went to Persia 1851 to teach; court physician to Shah 1856. Active in struggle for improved Jewish condition in Persia. Returned to Vienna 1860.

Polak, Leonard (1880–1941), Dutch philosopher; rationalist and agnostic follower of Marburg School.

Poland, E. European republic. Jewish settlement fr. 9th c., originally Ashkenazi. Influx of German Jews in 13th c. Despite subsequent attacks and legal restrictions, Jews played important commercial role. Poland was renowned center of rabbinic study and communal organization reached a peak in Council of the Four Lands (16th–18th c.). After the Chmielnicki massacres (1648–9), it became a center of Shabbateanism and Frankism; in 18th c. of Ḥasidism and in late 19th c. of Zionism and the Bund. Main Jewish pop. in Russian part of Poland in 19th c. and participated in mass emigration to West fr. 1880s. Jewish economic activity increased and Poland was the great center of Jewish life, vitality, and culture in the world. Anti-Semitism rife. Nearly 400,000 Jews left Poland between the World Wars. The remaining 3 million were massacred during the Holocaust. Several communities were revived after the war, but following further outbreaks of anti-Semitism, emigration was widespread after 1945 and 1967, esp. to Israel. By 1970s only a small remnant (8,000) was left.

Major Jewish communities in Poland, 1931.

Jewish types in Poland between WWI and WWII.

Polanski, Roman (1933–), film director writer, actor. First films in Poland; later in U.S. Famed for *Knife in the Water, Repulsion, Rosemary's Baby,* and *Macbeth.* Wife actress Sharon Tate murdered in Los Angeles by Charles Manson "family."

Polányi, Karl (1886–1964), economist, anthropologist; b. Vienna, in U.S. fr. 1940. Concerned with maintenance of peace.

Polanyi, Michael (1891–), British physical chemist, economist; b. Budapest, prof. in Berlin 1926–33, in England fr. 1933. In 1948 switched chairs, from physical chemistry to social studies. Fellow of Royal Society.

Polgar, Alfred (1873–1955), Austrian writer, critic; in U.S. fr. 1940. Wrote stories, reviews, satires, etc.

Poliakov, Léon (1910–), historian; b. Russia, in France fr. 1920. Specialized in studies of anti-Semitism and the Holocaust.

Polier, Justine Wise, see Wise, Stephen Samuel.

Polish, David (1910–), U.S. Reform rabbi; in Evanston, Ill., fr. 1950. Wrote on Judaism.

Political Zionism, trend in Zionism represented by the disciples of Herzl, which considered the central aim of Zionism to be the establishment of a Jewish National Home with international legal and political guarantees or under a "Charter" to be obtained from the Turkish government (which then held Palestine).

Politische Gemeinde, political group right conferred on Jews in Moravia, established 1849 and lasting until end of century.

Politzer, Adam (1835–1920), founder of modern otology; b. Hungary. Made Vienna center of study of otology.

Pollack, Jacob ben Joseph (1460/70–after 1522), rabbi, first Polish halakhic authority. Rabbi in Prague and Cracow; appointed rabbi of all Poland but left public life to remain at his yeshivah. Introduced *pilpul* method of Talmud study.

Pollegar (Pulgar, Policar), Isaac ben Joseph ibn (14th c.), Spanish scholar, philosopher, author of polemical *Ezer ha-Dat,* which endeavors to reconcile faith and philosophy.

Polna, see Hilsner.

Polonnoye, town in Ukrainian SSR. Jews suffered during Chmielnicki massacres 1648. In latter 18th c. center of Ḥasidism and Hebrew printing. Before WWII 4,000 Jews; exterminated by Germans 1941.

Polotsk, town in Belorussian SSR. Jews settled 15th c. Community destroyed 1654 by Cossacks, rebuilt shortly after, and became ḥasidic center. Center of anti-Jewish agitation in 19th c., pogroms 1905; c. 8,000 Jews before WWII, all murdered in 1941. In 1970 500 Jews.

Polotsky, Hans Jacob (1905–), Israel linguist; b. Zurich. Major achievements in several language families. Prof. at Heb. Univ. Israel Prize 1965.

Polsk, Moritz (1865–1938), Dutch lawyer. Supreme Court judge fr. 1926. Wrote on Dutch law and active in Jewish community.

Poltava, town in Ukrainian SSR. Jews settled at end of 18th c. In 19th c. community grew with many coming from Lithuania and Belorussia. Center of Labor Zionism. 8,000 Jews in 1926. Almost all Jews killed in WWII. 5,000 Jews in late 1960s.

Polyakov, family of railroad builders, bankers in Russia. Principal members: **Jacob** (1832–1909); **Samuel** (1837–1888), contributed to Russian education and culture; **Eliezer** (1842–1914), president of Moscow community.

Pomerania, former Prussian territory, now divided between Poland and E. Germany. Jews present fr. 13th c., enjoyed good conditions until expulsion 1492; readmitted 1682. Pop. declined after 1880 (Jewish pop. 14,000). Most Jews killed in WWII.

Pomerantz, Berl (1900–1942), Hebrew poet; b. Poland; killed by German soldiers. His work influenced by German expressionism.

Pomis, David De' (1525–1593), Italian linguist, physician, philosopher. Member of ancient De' Pomis family traditionally brought by Titus to Rome. Received papal permission to attend Christian patients. Wrote *Ẓemaḥ David,* a trilingual Hebrew, Latin, Italian dictionary.

°**Pompey** (106–48 B.C.E.), Roman general. Brought Ereẓ Israel under Roman rule after capturing Temple in 63 B.C.E., ending Jewish independence.

Ponary, resort area nr. Vilna in Lithuania. In WWII c. 100,000 people killed, mostly Jewish, by Nazis with aid of special Lithuanian units.

Ponevezh, see Panevezys.

Ponte, Lorenzo da, see Da Ponte, Lorenzo.

Pontecorvo, Bruno (1913–), Italian nuclear physicist. Worked in U.S. and later Harwell, England; created international sensation when he defected to Russia, where he continued his research.

Dedicatory inscription to Pontius Pilate in honor of Tiberius Caesar found in Caesarea.

°**Pontius Pilate,** Roman procurator of Judea 26–36 C.E. Jewish sources describe him as corrupt, cruel, and bloodthirsty, whereas Christian sources are sympathetic.

Pontremoli, Emmanuel (1865–1956), French architect. Inspector public buildings and state palaces 1926; director; Ecole Nationale des Beaux-Arts, Paris, 1932–37. Works include Museum of Natural History and Institute of Human Paleontology, Paris.

Pool, David de Sola (1885–1970), U.S. rabbi of Sephardi Congregation Shearith Israel, New York fr. 1907. Founded and directed Jewish Education Committee of New York 1922; president of Synagogue Council of America 1938–40. Wrote on U.S. Jewish history, religion, etc.; edited and translated Sephardi and Ashkenazi Hebrew liturgical works.

Pool, Tamar de Sola (1893–), U.S. communal worker; wife of David de Sola Pool, collaborating with him on several books. President of Hadassah 1939–43.

Popper, David (1843–1913), cellist, composer. First cellist Vienna Opera 1868–73. Famed concert artist. Prof. Budapest Conservatory after 1896. His *Hohe Schule des Violincellspiels* still used.

Popper, Josef (pseudonym *Lynkeus;* 1838–1921), Austrian inventor, social philosopher. His inventions and engineering ideas were years ahead of his time. His progressive social ideas based on humanism and realism.

Popper, Sir Karl Raimund (1902–), philosopher; b. Austria, in New Zealand 1937–45, then London. Attacked authoritarian political philosophies in *The Open Society and Its Enemies.*

Popper, Siegfried (1848–1933), Austro-Hungarian admiral, naval engineer. Directed construction of almost all Austrian naval craft (battleships, destroyers).

Popper, William (1874–1963), U.S. orientalist, biblical scholar. Taught at Univ. of California at Berkeley fr. 1905. Wrote on literary and stylistic aspects of Isaiah. Published critical editions and translations of 15th c. Arabic historical texts.

Poppers, Meir ben Judah Loeb ha-Kohen (d. 1662), kabbalist active in Jerusalem after 1640. Last editor of Lurianic writings. Wrote many works in vein of Lurianic Kabbalah.

Porat, Orna (1924–), Israel actress; b. Germany of non-Jewish parents. Leading player in Cameri Theater; participated in its management and headed company's children's theater.

Porges, Moses ben Israel Naphtali (17th c.), rabbi, emissary of Jerusalem Ashkenazi community. Went to Germany to secure funds when Chmielnicki massacres slowed down contributions to Jerusalem community. Wrote *Darkhei Ẓiyyon* about life in Ereẓ Israel.

Portaleone, Abraham ben David (1542–1612), Italian physician, writer. Permitted by Pope to attend Christians. Wrote *Shiltei ha-Gibborim,* a compendium on Temple and all branches of contemporary science. First Hebrew writer to use European punctuation.

Portaleone, Leone de Sommi, see Sommo, Judah Leone ben Isaac.

Port Elizabeth, city in S. Africa. Jews among founders of town 1820; congregation established 1862. Jews active in civic life and served as mayors. Jewish pop. 2,820 (1971).

Gold and copper seal assumed to have belonged to David Portaleone, son of Abraham b. David, depicting gateway ("porta") with a lion ("leone"). The handle depicts the "Akedah." Seal discovered by Yiẓhak Einhorn, 1970.

Places of Jewish settlement in Portugal, 1200–1497. Names in boldface indicate communities also existing in 1971.

Portrait of the "arraby mor," judicial head of Portuguese Jewry (holding book), from painting attributed to Nuño Gonçalves, 1460.

Portland, city in Ore., U.S. First Jewish settlers arrived in 1850s. First congregation Temple Beth Israel 1858. Remained only city in Oregon with sizable Jewish pop. 7,800 Jews in 1971.

Portnoy, Jekuthiel (Noah; Yuzef; 1872–1941), pioneer of Bund; in Warsaw fr. 1908. Edited Bund newspaper *Arbeter Shtime.*

Porto (Rafa-Rapaport), Abraham Menahem ben Jacob ha-Kohen (1520–after 1594), rabbi of Verona (1584–92) and head of its yeshivah; also lived in Cremona and Cologne. Wrote a pentateuchal commentary based on the Midrashim.

Pôrto Alegre, city in Brazil. Jews arrived end of 19th c.; first community 1920. German Jews arrived in 1930s and after 1956 refugees from Egypt and Hungary. Jewish pop. 10,000 (1971).

Porto-Riche, Georges de (1849–1930), French playwright. Dealt with psychology of love in witty, well-constructed plays. Elected to Académie française.

Portugal, W. European republic. Jews present from at least 300 C.E., possibly earlier. In 12th c. distinct Jewish districts existed, and in 13th c. Jewish community largely self-governing and prosperous. Deterioration fr. 14th c. On expulsion fr. Spain 1492, 150,000 Jews fled there. Expulsion declared 1496, but instead king insisted on forced mass baptisms. Many of these "New Christians" subsequently persecuted and massacred by Inquisition, established 1547. In 200 years some 30,000 persons sentenced in autos-da-fe, 1,200 being burnt at stake. Jews resettled fr. 1800. Jewish pop. 600 (1971), mostly in Lisbon.

Portugalov, Benjamin Osipovich (1835–1896), Russian physician, publicist. Strongly assimilationist. First physician in Russia to advocate social medicine.

Posekim (Heb.), scholars who concentrated on determining *halakhah* in practice in contrast to scholars who applied themselves to study for its own sake

Posen, see Poznan.

Posener, Georges Henri (1906–), French Egyptologist. Prof. at College de France. Wrote on ancient Egyptian texts.

Posnanski (Poznański), Adolf (1854–1920), rabbi, scholar, educator in Vienna. Wrote on messianic

Jacob S. Potofsky

Clock tower of 16th cent. Jewish town hall in Prague. Main clock with Roman numerals, functions conventionally; lower one, with Hebrew numerals, added 1754, works anticlockwise.

Wall in Pinkas Synagogue, Prague, with names of 77,297 Jews of Bohemia and Moravia murdered by Nazis, 1939–45.

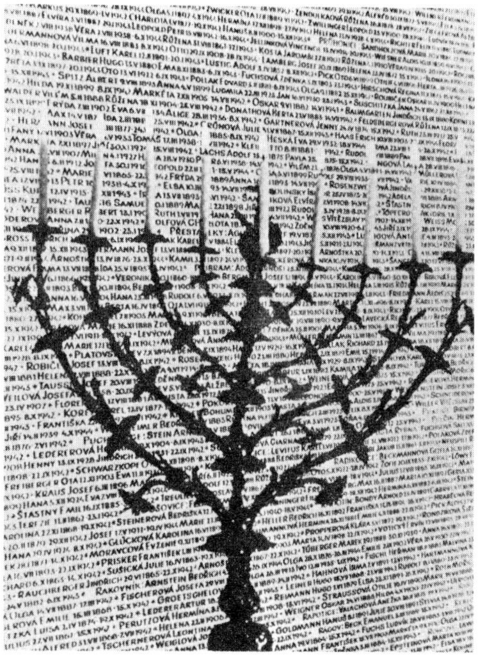

idea in Judaism and Christianity. His brother **Samuel Abraham** (1864–1921), rabbi, scholar. bibliographer in Warsaw. His scholarly interests were wide but specialized in Karaites

Posner, Akiva Barukh (Arthur; 1890–1962), rabbi, scholar, librarian, bibliographer. Rabbi at Kiel until 1934 and then in Jerusalem (librarian, Heikhal Shelomo).

Postan, Michael Moissey (1899–), British economic historian; b. Bessarabia. Prof. of economic history at Cambridge. Coeditor of *Cambridge Economic History of Europe.*

Poswoler, Abele, see Abraham Abele ben Abraham Solomon.

°**Potiphar,** Egyptian royal official who purchased Joseph from Midianites. His wife attempted unsuccessfully to seduce Joseph and as a result of her false charges Potiphar had him incarcerated.

Poti-Phera, father of Asenath wife of Joseph. Priest of On (Heliopolis), center of cult of Egyptian sun-god.

Potocki, Valentine (Abraham ben Abraham; d. 1749), Polish count martyred as proselyte. Subject of folktales and veneration, though no proof that he actually existed.

Potofsky, Jacob Samuel (1894–), U.S. labor leader; b. Ukraine, went to Chicago 1908. Major figure in the Amalgamated Clothing Workers Union, which he led in direction of arbitration as opposed to strikes. Vice-president AFL-CIO.

Potok, Chaim (1929–), U.S. Conservative rabbi, novelist. Managing editor, *Conservative Judaism,* 1964–65; editor Jewish Publication Society of America, fr. 1965. Wrote novels *The Chosen, The Promise, My Name is Asher Lev.*

Pougatchov, Emanuel, see Amiran, Emanuel.

Poznan (Ger. **Posen**), town in Poland. Jews fr. 14th c. Major center of Jewish scholarship; rabbis regarded as chief rabbis of Greater Poland. Community declined fr. 19th c. Its 1,500 Jews (1939) massacred in WWII.

Praag, Siegfried Emanuel van (1899–). Dutch novelist, critic. Several of his novels have Jewish or biblical themes.

Practical Zionism, trend in early Zionism holding it to be unrealistic to demand political rights without having any practical settlement work on which to base their request. Among the leaders of this trend were Otto Warburg and M.M. Ussishkin.

Prado, Juan (Daniel) de (c. 1615–c. 1670), Marrano physician; b. Spain, went to Holland and proclaimed himself a Jew. Member of unorthodox group that included the young Spinoza, and like him, banned by Amsterdam community. Sought unsuccessfully to have ban lifted.

Praefectus Judaeorum, leader of Hungarian Jewry in Middle Ages. Office abolished 1539.

Prague, capital of Czechoslovakia. One of oldest Jewish communities in Europe (Roman times), and for some time the largest and most revered. Some of its ancient sites (Altneuschul, cemetery) still stand. Bet. 16th and 18th c. community lived in large quarter, produced world-renowned scholars, and possessed a Hebrew printing press and highly developed autonomous institutions. Jews exiled 1745–8, but granted full equality 1848. Thereafter the community continued to grow. In the Czechoslovak Republic between the World Wars, Jews prominent in cultural life. Its 56,000 Jews (1939) nearly all massacred in WWII. Community revived after war. Jewish pop. 2,000 (1972).

Prathet Thai, see Thailand.

Prato, David (1882–1951), rabbi, Zionist leader; b. Italy, rabbi in Alexandria, Egypt, 1927–36, chief rabbi of Rome 1936–38 and fr. 1945. Spent WWII in Ereẓ Israel.

Prawer, Joshua (1917–), Israel historian. Prof. at Heb. Univ. Major field Crusades. Chief editor, *Encyclopaedia Hebraica,* fr. 1967. Israel Prize 1969.

Prayer, the offering of petition, confession, adoration, or thanksgiving to God. In the Bible prayer and sacrifice usually offered together, but prayer did not require sacrifice and could be offered anywhere. In the Middle Ages stress was laid on the concentration *(kavvanah)* required. The ḥasidim placed the emphasis on emotional attachment *(devekut)* to God. In modern times, Jewish thinkers have considered basic philosophical problems of prayer. From the destruction of the Second Temple Jews have prayed three times a day; morning, afternoon, and evening (*Shaḥarit, Minḥah,* and *Maariv*), facing Jerusalem. Where possible prayer is in quorum of ten *(minyan).*

Prayer Books. Book containing text of daily of Sabbath prayers is called *siddur,* of festival prayers *maḥzor.* First prayer book is 9th c. *Seder Rav Amram Gaon.*

Prayer of Manasseh, see Manasseh, Prayer of.

Prayer Shawl, see Tallit.

Precepts, see Commandments, 613: Mitzvah.

Preil, Gabriel Joshua (1911–), U.S. Hebrew poet. Introduced new themes and cadences into Hebrew literature in America.

Preminger, Otto Ludwig (1906–), U.S. film, stage director and producer; b. Vienna. Director at Max Reinhardt's Josefstadt Theater 1928. In U.S. fr. 1935. Films include *The Moon is Blue, Exodus, Porgy and Bess.*

Presbyter Judaeorum, secular head of English Jews in 13th c.; appointed by king.

Presidents' Conference, see Conference of Presidents of Major American Jewish Organizations.

Press, Frank (1924–), U.S. geophysicist. Prof. of geophysics at Cal. Inst. of Technology 1955–65; head, dept. geology and geophysics, MIT, fr. 1965. Leading seismologist in U.S.

Press, Yeshayahu (1874–1955), Israel historian, topographer of Ereẓ Israel. Active in Jerusalem civic life over 50 years. Main work topographical-historical encyclopedia of Ereẓ Israel.

Pressburg, see Bratislava.

Presser, Jacob (1899–1970), Dutch historian, writer. Prof. of modern history at Univ. of Amsterdam fr. 1948. Wrote *The Destruction of Dutch Jews;* also verse and fiction.

Pretoria, administrative capital of S. Africa. Jews settled after 1855, Jewish communal life fr. 1878, first congregation 1890. Jewish pop. 3,750 (1971).

Preuss, Hugo (1860–1925), German jurist, politician; creator of Weimar constitution. Minister of interior after WWI.

Preuss, Julius (1861–1913), German physician, medical historian. Studied biblical and talmudic medicine.

Priest, High, see High Priest.

Priestly Blessing, formula in Num. 6:24–26 to be recited by priests when blessing in Temple; subsequently in synagogues. The formula was introduced with the repetition of morning and afternoon *amidah.* It is still recited by priests on holidays (in Israel daily).

Priestly Vestments, special garments worn by priests during divine worship in Temple.

Priests and Priesthood, male descendants of Aaron who were principal functionaries in divine services in ancient Israel. They conducted all cultic ceremonies in the Temple. They possessed no land but received 24 priestly privileges (e.g., tithes, meat of certain sacrifices). They had to observe meticulously the laws of ritual purity and were forbidden to marry divorcees or proselytes. Today the main privileges of priests are delivering the priestly blessing and precedence in being called to the Reading of the Law.

Primo, Samuel (c. 1635–1708), talmudist, Shabbatean leader. Met Shabbetai Ẓevi in Jerusalem and became one of his most ardent "believers," even after his apostasy. Outstanding preacher; wrote responsa and halakhic decisions (almost all destroyed by 1704 fire in Adrianople).

Primogeniture, see Firstborn.

Primordial Man, see Adam Kadmon.

Principles of Faith, see Articles of Faith.

Printing, Hebrew. First Hebrew books to be printed were Rashi's commentary on the Pentateuch and Jacob b. Asher's *Arba'ah Turim* in 1475 (see Incunabula). The Talmud was first printed by the Christian, David Bomberg in Venice 1520–23. Italy was the first major center of Hebrew printing. Hebrew printing widespread wherever Jews settled in Europe and Middle East. Israel now main center (see p. 490).

Prinz, Joachim (1902–), U.S. rabbi, communal leader. Rabbi in Berlin until 1937, in Newark, N.J. fr. 1939. President of American Jewish Congress 1958–66; chairman of Conference of Presidents of Major American Jewish Organizations 1965–67.

Priscus (6th c.), Jewish agent of Frankish king. Held religious debate with king and Gregory, bishop of Tours. Assassinated by convert.

Procurator, title of Roman governors of Judea from 6–66 C.E. Subject to Roman legate in Syria. Headquarters in Caesarea; they sat in Jerusalem on Jewish festivals. Generally hostile to Jewish population.

ROMAN PROCURATORS

Coponius	6–9 C.E.
Marcus Ambibulus	9–12 C.E.
Rufus Tineus	12–15 C.E.
Valerius Gratus	15–26 C.E.
Pontius Pilate	26–36 C.E.
Marcellus	36–37 C.E.
Marullus	37–41 C.E.
Cuspius Fadus	44–46 C.E.
Tiberius Julius Alexander	46–48 C.E.
Ventidius Cumanus	48–52 C.E.
Antonius Felix	52–60 C.E.
Porcius Festus	60–62 C.E.
Albinus	62–64 C.E.
Gessius Florus	64–66 C.E.

Model of high priest and common priest wearing their vestments. High priest: 1. blue band; 2. miter; 3. gold plate; 4. onyx stones with names of the tribes (6 on each stone); 5. tole of the ephod; 6. breastplate; 7. blue band; 8. band of the ephod; 9. ephod; 10. bells of gold and pomegranates of dyed wool and linen; 11. coat; 12. girdle. Common priest: 1. head-dress; 2. coat; 3. girdle.

Profiat Duran, see Duran.

Progressive Judaism, see Reform Judaism.

Progressive Party, Israel party established 1948. Represented in all Cabinets until 1961 (except 1952–53). Merged with General Zionists 1961 to form the Liberal Party, but later broke away to form Independent Liberal Party.

Prohovnik, Abraham, legendary Polish Jewish figure involved in accession of Piast dynasty (9th c.).

Proops, family of Hebrew printers, publishers, booksellers in Amsterdam. Business founded by **Solomon ben Joseph** (d. 1734), who set up Hebrew press 1704 and printed wide variety of Judaica. After death, sons continued to run business and issued new edition of Talmud (1752–65), but firm's activity steadily declined.

Prophet, a charismatic individual endowed with divine gift of both receiving and imparting mesaage of revelation. The biblical prophets are divided between preclassical, or popular. prophets (e.g., Elijah, Elisha) and classical, or literary, prophets (e.g., Isaiah, Jeremiah). The latter terminology is reserved for those prophets whose oracles were preserved in writings. The primary literary remains of the preclassical prophets are the stories and accounts of their lives transmitted at first oral-

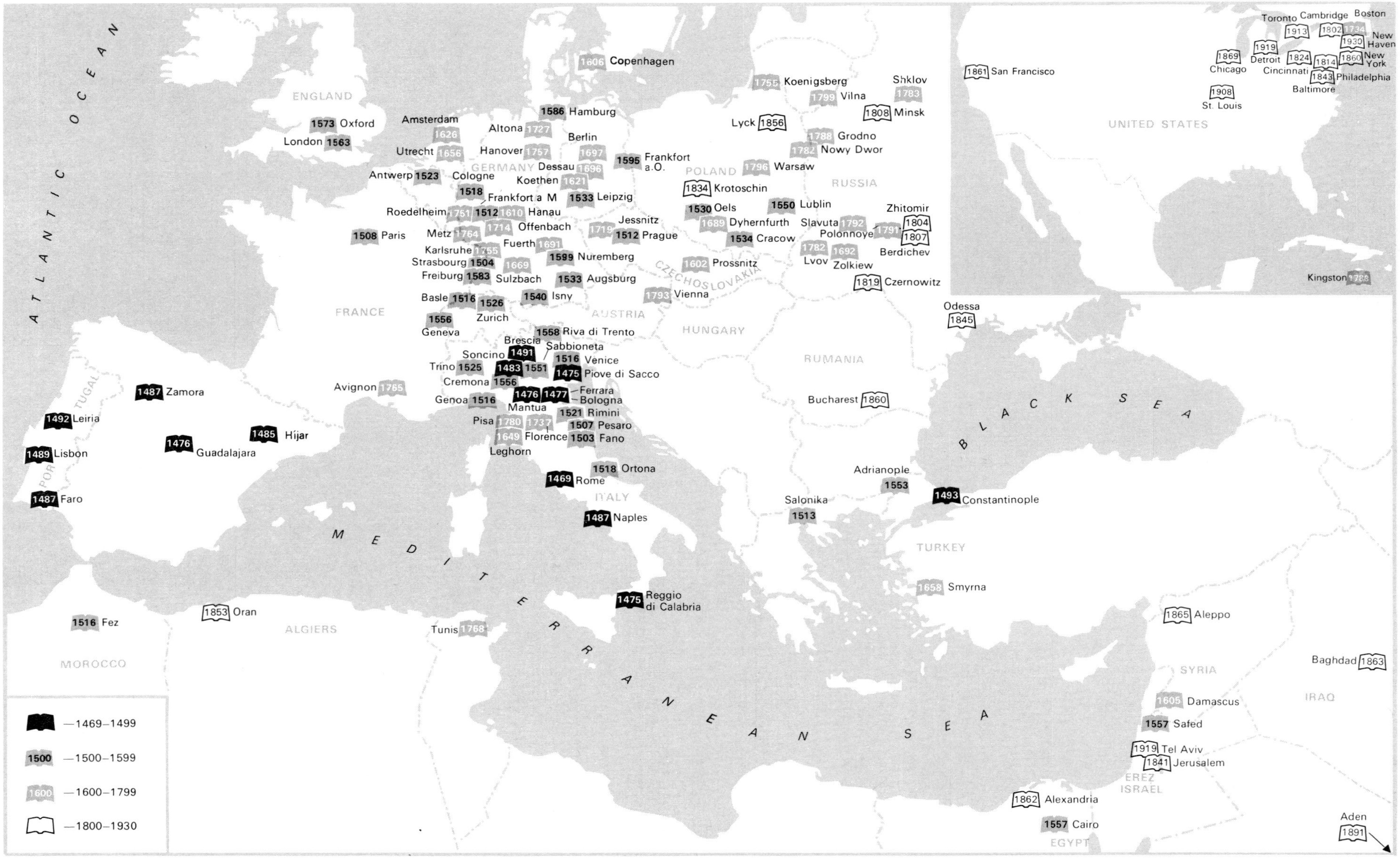

Main locations of Hebrew printing, 15th–19th cent.

ly by followers and admirers. The preclassical prophets were originally mantic; their main function was predicting the future, while the classical prophets reproved their people in order to save them. The popular prophets functioned as members of guilds, the classical prophets appear alone. The writings of classical prophets in the Prophets division of the Bible contain sayings of 3 major prophets (Isaiah, Jeremiah, Ezekiel) and 12 minor prophets. Their dates ranged fr. 8th–6th c. B.C.E. According to Jewish tradition, prophecy ceased with the rebuilding of the Second Temple.

Prophets, Lives of the, ancient book of Jewish origin but showing Christian influence, containing many nonbiblical details and traditions. Primary text in Greek.

Prosbul, legal formula whereby creditor could still claim debts after Sabbatical Year despite biblical injunction against doing so (Deut. 15:2). Instituted by Hillel to evade hardship caused by reluctance to grant loans to the needy on approach of Sabbatical Year.

Proselytes. There is some evidence of individuals (e.g. Ruth) accepting the God of Israel in biblical times but proselytization only became widespread in Second Temple period. Examples are the royal family of Adiabene, Aquila and/or Onkelos, and according to the Talmud even leading rabbis (Shemaiah, Avtalyon). The Edomites were forcibly converted. In the late Second Temple Period there was much – and often successful – missionary activity in other countries (e.g. Rome). However, with the Christianization of the Empire, proselytization was outlawed and thus became dangerous. As a result rabbinic pronouncements on the subject are sharply divided as to its desirability. In the Middle Ages there were two cases of large-scale conversions to Judaism: the Himyar Kingdom of S. Arabia and the Khazars of S. Russia. In modern times, esp. in the U.S., there has been a rise in proselytization, principally as a preliminary to marrying a Jewish partner. To be accepted into Judaism, a proselyte has to convince a rabbinical court of his sincerity and undergo circumcision (for men) and ritual immersion. He is then regarded as a Jew in all matters (except that a priest may not marry a proselyte). Orthodox rabbis are more rigid in their demands than Conservative and Reform.

Proskauer, Joseph Meyer (1877–1971), U.S. lawyer, community leader. Justice of New York Supreme Court fr. 1923. Pres. of American Jewish Committee 1943–9, leading it into support of establishment of state of Israel.

Proskurov (today **Khmelnitzki**), city in Ukrainian SSR. Jews present fr. 1765. Most Jews killed 1919 by Ukrainian army. 13,408 Jews in 1926; community liquidated by Germans in WWII. In 1959 c. 6,000 Jews.

Prossnitz, Judah Leib ben Jacob Holleschau (c. 1670–1730), Shabbatean prophet in Prossnitz (Prostejov). His public preaching won many adherents but also aroused strong hostility. Widely credited with mystical practices, and in 1724 claimed to be precursor of the Messiah. Subsequently excommunicated; forced to lead itinerant life.

Prostejov (Prossnitz), city in Moravia. Jews present fr. 15th c. Dealt in luxury goods, textiles. Community influenced by Shabbatean and Frankist movements, and one of first to absorb Enlightenment ideas. Between WWI and WWII very active community (numbered 1,442 in 1930). Destroyed in WWII; subsequently reconstituted.

Prostitz, Isaac ben Aaron (d. 1612). Hebrew printer; b. Prossnitz, worked in Italy. Printed rabbinics, kabbalah, Bible, philosophy, history, mathematics.

Protestrabbiner, term coined by Herzl for 5 German rabbis who led opposition to Zionism and caused transfer of first Zionist Congress from Munich to Basle.

Protocols of Learned Elders of Zion, see Elders of Zion, Protocols of Learned.

Proust, Marcel (1871–1922). French novelist; son of Jewish mother. raised as Catholic. His *A la recherche du temps perdu,* outstanding 20th c. classic, contains 3 major Jewish characters.

Provençal, David ben Abraham (b. 1506), rabbi of Mantua, preacher, linguist; brother of Moses Provençal. Together with his son Abraham, a noted physician, proposed establishment of Jewish university in Mantua.

Provençal, Moses ben Abraham (1503–1575), rabbi. Made Mantua a center of talmudic study in Italy. Involved in a number of controversies, and at one time banned from offices, but later reinstated.

Provence, region and former province of SE France. Jews fr. 1st c.

Stamp commemorating Marcel Proust, issued by France, 1966.

The Jewish cemetery at Saint-Remy-de-Provence.

C.E. Enjoyed relatively high status under the Albigenses in 13th c., pop. included outstanding poets, scholars, and philosophers in 14th c. Provençal scholars greatly influenced development of Midrash and *halakhah;* area was major focus of the Maimonidean controversy. Jews expelled 1500. Small modern settlement until influx fr. N. Africa in 1950s and 1960s led to reestablishment of many ancient communities.

Proverbs, Book of (Heb. *Sefer Mishlei*), one of three "wisdom books" of biblical Hagiographa. A

BOOK OF PROVERBS – CONTENTS

PART 1.	
Chs. 1–9	Didactic discourses and "wisdom poems."
1:1–7	Title, preface and motto.
1:18–19; 2:1–22; 3:1–12; 3:21–26 + 31–35; 4:1–9; 4:10–19; 4:20–27 + 5:21–23; 5:1–14; 6:20–21 + 23–25; 7:1–27	Ten instructional discourses.
Five poems.	
3:13–20	The rewards of wisdom
1:20–33; 8:1–36; 9:1–6 (+ Folly, 13–18)	Personified Wisdom addresses men in rebuke, appeal and self-affirmation.
3:27–30; 5:15–20; 6:1–19, 22; 9:7–12	Precepts, direct or implied.
PART 2.	
Chs. 10–22:16	First Collection of "Solomonic proverbs."
PART 3.	
Chs. 22:17–24	
22:17–24:22	The "Thirty Precepts" of the Sages; an "Instruction" modeled on the Egyptian "Instruction of Amen-em-ope."
24:23–34	Other Sayings of the Sages.
PART 4.	
Chs. 25–29	Second Collection of "Solomonic proverbs," transmitted by Hezekiah's scribes.
Appendixes to the book.	
Ch. 30:1–9	The skepticism of Agur, and a believer's reply.
Ch. 30:10–13	Warnings and numerical proverbs.
Ch. 31:1–9	A queen mother's diatribe.
Ch. 31:10–31	Acrostic poem on the capable housewife.

Opening of Proverbs from 15th cent. Italian Hebrew ms., illuminated miniature showing judgment of Solomon.

First synagogue of Providence, erected by Congregation Sons of Israel and David, 1890.

BOOK OF PSALMS–CONTENTS

Chs:	1:1–41:14	The first collection
Chs:	42:1–72:20	The second collection
	44:1–49:21	Korahite psalms
	56:1–60:14	"Michtam" psalms
Chs:	73:1–89:53	The third collection
	73:1–83:19	Asaphite psalms
Chs:	90:1–106:48	The fourth collection
Chs:	107:1–150:6	The fifth collection
	111:1–113:9	Hallelujah psalms
	114:1–118:29	Hallel psalms
	120:7–134:3	Songs of ascent

collection of moral sayings, it may originally have been a manual for the moral and religious instruction of the young. Probably completed in late monarchical period. Its opening ascribes authorship to Solomon and rabbis dated redaction to Great Assembly.

Providence, city in R.I., U.S. First Jewish settlers 1838. First congregation Sons of Israel 1854. Jewish pop. 10,000 (1970), with 18 synagogues.

Prussia, former dukedom and kingdom, the nucleus of modern Germany. Jewish settlement dates fr. 17th c.; pop. increased through immigration and Prussian conquest in C. Europe. Seat of Haskalah movement; by 1871 contained 69% of German Jewry, mostly living in large cities. Prussian Jews recognized as citizens 1811, many achieved prominence in 19th and early 20th c. Jewish pop. 342,765 (1925). Community shared fate of German Jewry during Holocaust.

Prylucki, Noah (1882–1941), Yiddish philologist, journalist, Polish political leader; son of Ẓevi Hirsch Prylucki. Pioneer of research into Yiddish language, cofounder of Yiddish daily *Der Moment* (1905). Founded Folkspartei; elected to Polish Sejm. Arrested by Germans and tortured to death.

Prylucki, Ẓevi Hirsch (1862–1942), Hebrew, Yiddish journalist; b. Ukraine. One of first members of Ḥovevei Zion. Cofounder of Yiddish daily *Der Moment* (1905) and Hebrew daily *Ha-Yom* in Warsaw. D. Warsaw ghetto.

Przemysl, city in Poland. Jewish community fr. 16th c. Jew sentenced to death 1630 for Host desecration libel. Economic situation declined in 18th c. Under Austrian rule Enlightenment favored. Half city council Jewish. In 1931, 17,300 Jews. Jews killed under Nazi occupation despite armed resistance.

Przemyslany, see Peremyshlyany.

Przysucha (Pshiskhah), Jacob Isaac ben Asher (ha-Yehudi ha-Kadosh; 1766–1814), *ẓaddik* and founder of Pshiskha Ḥasidism in Poland. Initiated new type of Ḥasidism – service of God through Torah study together with prayer. His doctrine that it is more important to pray wholeheartedly than to pray on time produced schism with other ḥasidim.

Psalms, Book of (Heb. *Sefer Tehillim*), first book of biblical Hagiographa. Contains 150 psalms: 74 ascribed to David, 35 to other authors, the rest anonymous. 19th c. scholarship assigned it to later Second Temple period, but modern scholars hold it is a much earlier work, written in First Temple period. The psalms present a picture of unusual variety and complexity in the literary typology: hymns (e.g., 8, 29, 33), laments (e.g., 3, 5, 44, 60), thanksgiving psalms (e.g., 9–10, 66, 67), and "royal psalms" (e.g., 2, 18, 20). They have played a central role in Jewish worship, both in Temple and Synagogue, as well as in the Christian liturgy.

Psalms of Solomon, see Solomon, Psalms of.

Psantir, Jacob (1820–1902), historian of Rumanian Jewry. Self-educated, wrote his two books in Hebrew.

Pseudepigrapha, see Apocrypha and Pseudepigrapha.

Pseudo-Baḥya, see Baḥya (Pseudo).

Pseudo-Jonathan, see Targum Jonathan.

Pseudo-Philo, or **Liber Antiquitatum Biblicarum,** Latin translation of early Jewish chronicle; probably written shortly after destruction of Second Temple. Covers period from Adam to death of Saul. Authorship unknown.

Pshiskhah, see Przysucha.

Ptolemais, see Acre.

Puah, see Shiphrah and Puah.

Puerto Rico, Caribbean island. First Jewish immigrants in 1930s, primarily refugees from Nazis. Jewish pop. 3,000 (1970), nearly all in San Juan.

Pukhovitser, Judah Leib (17th c.), rabbi, preacher in Lithuania, Poland, Germany. Wrote homiletic works and book on *Shulḥan Arukh.*

Pulgar, Isaac, see Pollegar, Isaac.

Pulitzer, Joseph (1847–1911), U.S. newspaper publisher; son of Jewish father; b. Hungary, in U.S. fr. 1864. Owned St. Louis *Post-Dispatch,* New York *World,* New York *Evening World.* Congressman from N.Y. 1885. Endowed Pulitzer School of Journalism at Columbia Univ. and Pulitzer Prizes for journalism.

Pulvermacher, Oscar (1883–1958), British journalist, editor. Editor *Daily Mail* 1927–33, then with *Daily Telegraph.*

Joseph Pulitzer centenary stamp issued by U.S., 1947.

Pumbedita, town in Babylonia, seat of famous talmudic academy. Jews there fr. Second Temple times. In 259 Judah ben Ezekiel established the academy, which with few intervals existed until 13th c. Under Persian rule it removed to Peruz-Shavur but returned under Arab rule. In 9th c. transferred to Baghdad, where under Sherira and Hai it had its greatest efflorescence.

Purim, feast instituted according to Book of Esther, by Mordecai, to celebrate deliverance of Jews from Haman's plot to kill them; observed on Adar 14 and in walled cities on Adar 15. (In leap years in 2nd month of Adar.) The Book of Esther is read in the evening and morning services. It is also customary to exchange gifts and to engage in merriment (incl. the drinking of alcoholic beverages). It is a carnival period and was also an opportunity for presenting dramatic performances *(Purim-shpil)*.

Purim Katan, 14th and 15th days of Adar I in a leap year (when Purim occurs in Adar II). Funeral eulogies and fasting are prohibited.

Purims, Special, anniversaries of deliverance celebrated by communities or individuals.

Three Purim jesters with musical instruments and a jug of wine, from a "minhagim" book, Amsterdam, 1707.

Purity and Impurity, Ritual, concept that person or object can be in state which, by religious law, prevents contact with Temple or its cult. The state is transferable from one object to another in a variety of ways such as touch or being under the same roof. The state of impurity can be corrected by the performance of spiritual rituals, mainly incl. ablution.

Putterman, David (1903–), U.S. cantor; officiated in N.Y. Instrumental in establishing Cantors Assembly of United Synagogue of America and Cantors Institute of Jewish Theological Seminary.

Pyrrhus, Didacus (1517–1607), Portuguese Marrano poet, physician. Traveled widely but spent c. 50 years in Ragusa (Dubrovnik). Noted neo-Latin poet of Renaissance.

Purim noisemakers: top, German, 18th cent., wood, inscribed "arur Haman" ("cursed is Haman"); bottom, New York, 20th cent., silver, incised with scene of Haman leading Mordecai on king's horse and other decorations.

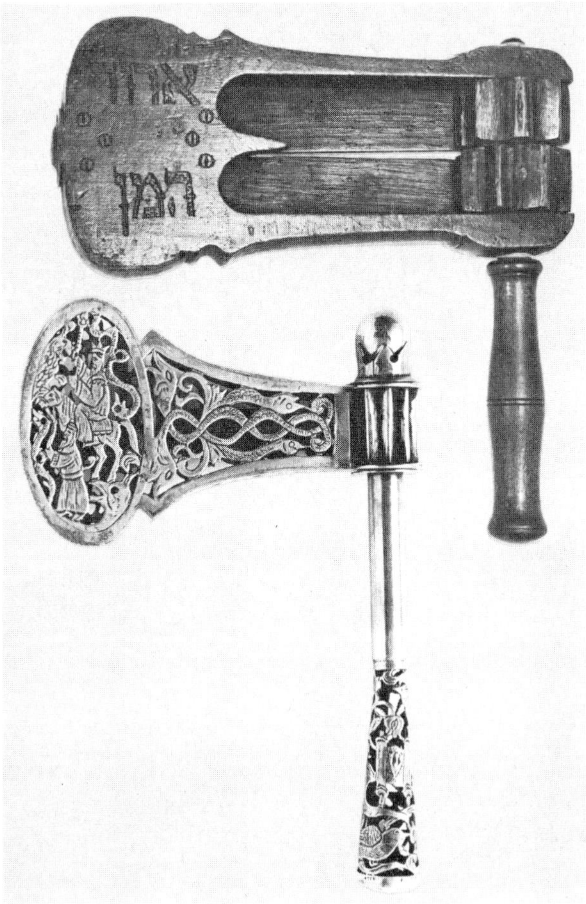

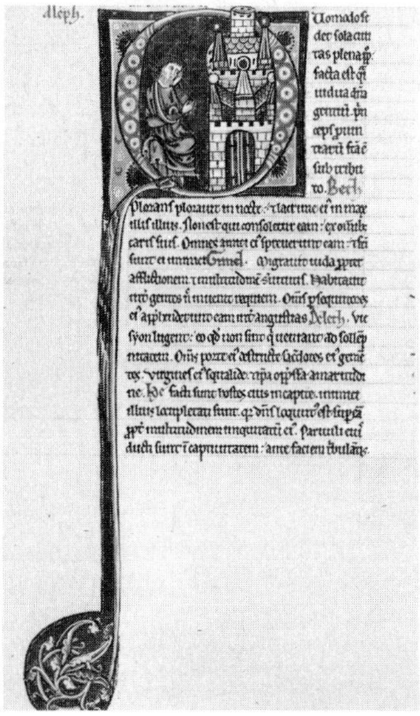

Initial letter "Q" for "Quomodo" at the beginning of Lamentations, from a Latin Bible, N. France, c. 1200.

Qaynuqa, one of three Jewish tribes in ancient Medina. Quarreled with Muhammad and expelled fr. their territory.

Qirqisani, see Kirkisani.

Quastel, Judah Hirsch (1899–), British biochemist; in Vancouver, Canada, fr. 1947. Fields of interest chemistry of enzymes, micro-organisms and soils, and biochemistry of mental disorders.

Quebec, Canadian province. First Jewish settlers 1760. Jewish pop. increased very slowly until 1880s when Russian pogroms and Rumanian anti-Semitism greatly stimulated immigration. Most children educated within framework of Protestant school system. Jewish pop. 126 000 (1971), concentrating in Montreal and also Quebec and Chicoutimi.

Eastern view of excavated settlement of Qumran, showing Wadi Qumran (1), caves in which scrolls were found (2), Khirbet Qumran (3), and community's cemetery (4).

Queen of Sheba, Sabean monarch who journeyed to Jerusalem to test Solomon's wisdom (I Kings 10:1–10, 13). After exchanging gifts returned to her land. Visit is subject of extensive Jewish and Muslim folktales (in the latter she is called Bilqis). Ethiopian royal house claims to be descended fr. union between her and Solomon.

Querido, Israël (1872–1932), Dutch novelist. Many of his novels on Sephardi life display ambivalent attitude toward Jews and Judaism.

Querido, Jacob (c. 1650–1690), Shabbatean leader in Salonika. His sister was Shabbetai Ẓevi's last wife. After Shabbetai's death, he formed nucleus of Doenmeh sect.

Qumran, region on NW shore of Dead Sea; site of discovery of Dead Sea Scrolls 1947. A ruin (Khirbet Qumran) in the area was excavated with close connection between its occupants and the manuscripts in nearby caves; the community described in the scrolls presumably occupied the buildings. A nearby cemetery was also explored. Habitation ceased just before 70 C.E.

Qunayṭira, Al-, town in Golan Heights. Remains from Byzantine period found there. Until mid-19th c. only an inn, then regional center of Circassians. Under Syrian rule fr. 1950s. Under Israel administration 1967–74. Kibbutz Merom Golan established at its W. entrance.

Qurayẓa, one of three Jewish tribes in ancient Medina. After they refused Muhammad's demand that they convert to Islam, their men massacred and women and children sold into slavery.

Initial letter "R" of "Recordare," the first word of the prologue to the apocryphal book of Baruch, Latin Bible, France, c. 1300.

Raab, Esther (1899–). Israel poet; daughter of Judah Raab. Her lyric poetry contains descriptions of Israel landscape.

Raab (Ben-Ezer), Judah (1858–1948), pioneer in Ereẓ Israel; b. Hungary, settled in Ereẓ Israel 1876. Joined founders of Petaḥ Tikvah and was one of first guards in the country.

Ra'anannah, town in C. Israel; founded 1922 as moshavah by American Jews. Now part of outer ring of Tel Aviv conurbation, with industries and agriculture. Pop. 13,600 (1971).

Ra'aya Meheimna (Aram. "the faithful shepherd"), part of Zohar which gives kabbalistic interpretations of commandments. "Faithful shepherd" is Moses.

Rabad, see Abraham ben David of Posquières.

Rabad, see Ibn Daud, Abraham ben David Halevi.

Raban, see Eliezer ben Nathan of Mainz.

Rabat, see Salé-Rabat.

Rabb, Maxwell Milton (1910–), U.S. attorney, government official. Secretary of Eisenhower's Cabinet 1954–58; chairman, U.S. delegation to UNESCO, 1958. Active in Jewish community.

Rabbah, see Rabbath-Ammon.

Rabbah Bar Bar Ḥana (3rd c.), *amora;* b. Babylonia, studied in Ereẓ Israel, returned to Babylonia. Told many stories of his travels, characterized by exaggeration. Most famous for his remarkable legends.

Rabbah bar Huna (in Jerusalem Talmud, **Abba bar Huna** or **Bar bar Huna;** d. 322), Babylonian *amora;* pupil of Samuel, Rav, and his father Huna. Succeeded Ḥisda as head of Sura academy.

Rabbah bar Naḥamani (c. 270–c. 330), Babylonian *amora.* Noted halakhist; headed Pumbedita academy for over 20 years.

Rabbah ben Avuha (3rd c.), Babylonian *amora.* Head of Maḥoza academy after destruction of Nehardea academy in 259.

Rabbah Tosfa'ah (5th c.), Babylonian *amora.* Succeeded Mar bar Rav Ashi as head of Sura academy.

Rabbanites, name used fr. 10th c. for Jews who accepted Oral Law as binding and normative to same degree as Scriptures (as contrasted with Karaites).

Rabbath-Ammon (Rabbah), capital of Ammonites; present-day Amman, capital of Jordan. David captured the city (II Sam. 11–12), but after his death it became capital of independent kingdom. In Hellenistic period it was a flourishing city, called Philadelphia, and was a city of the Decapolis in Roman times, developing into a prosperous center of caravan trade in Arabia. It was captured by the Arabs in 635. In 1921 it became the capital of the emirate of Transjordan and later the kingdom of Jordan.

Rabbenu Gershom, see Gershom ben Judah Me'or Ha-Golah.

Rabbenu Nissim, see Nissim ben Jacob.

Rabbenu Tam, see Tam, Jacob ben Meir.

Rabbi. The term rabbi is derived from *rav* (master), which signified a sage and scholar. The title was given only to those who received ordination, and because in talmudic times ordination was only given in Ereẓ Israel, *rav* was used by the scholars of Babylonia. Rabbi or *rav* originally referred to an expounder and interpreter of the Bible or Oral Law. Only from the Middle Ages onward did the term come to represent a teacher, preacher, and spiritual head of a community whose livelihood was often derived from his functions as rabbi.

Rabbi, see Judah ha-Nasi.

Rabbi Binyamin (pseudonym of **Yehoshua Radler-Feldmann;** 1880–1957), Hebrew journalist; b. Galicia, settled in Ereẓ Israel 1907. Teacher; active in Mizrachi Party and Berit Shalom. Published essays on Hebrew writers and great figures in European literature.

Rabbi Mór, see Arraby Moor.

Rabbiner-Seminar fuer das Orthodoxe Judentum, Orthodox rabbinical seminary founded in Berlin 1873 by Azriel Hildesheimer, who headed it for 26 years. Closed 1938.

Rabbinical Alliance of America, association of Orthodox rabbis founded 1944 by rabbis who found the existing Orthodox Rabbinical Council insufficiently strict. 250 members in 1965 (100 active in rabbinate).

Rabbinical Assembly, organization of Conservative rabbis founded 1901. Membership 876 in 1968. Served congregations in U.S., Canada, S. America, Europe, Israel. Publishes quarterly *Conservative Judaism.*

Rabbinical Council of America (RCA), rabbinical organization of Union of Orthodox Jewish Congregations, founded 1923. C. 900 members in 1970 (over two-thirds active in rabbinate).

Rabbinovicz (Rabinovitz), Raphael Nathan Nata (1835–1888), talmudic scholar. His *Dikdukei Soferim* contains variant readings fr. mss. on all tractates of Talmud orders *Zera'im, Mo'ed, Nezikin;* also contains explanatory notes and history of printing of Babylonian Talmud.

Rabbinowicz, Israel Michel (1818–1893), writer, scholar; b. Lithuania. Studied medicine, wrote on grammar and talmudic legislation. Last years in London.

Rabbinowitz, Saul Phinehas (acronym *Shepher;* 1845–1910), Hebrew writer, historian; b. Lithuania. Wrote for Hebrew press and active member of Ḥibbat Zion. Translated H. Graetz's history into Hebrew.

Rab de la Corte ("court rabbi"), office common in Navarre and Castile in Spain in Middle Ages. Appointed by crown to supervise Jewish communal leadership and apportionment of taxes among communities. Generally not a scholar, but a Jew who served the king or crown prince as physician, interpreter, or fiscal agent.

Isidor I. Rabi

Rabi, Isidor Isaac (1898–), U.S. physicist; Prof. at Columbia Univ. Received Nobel Prize for Physics (1944) for developing method of receiving and interpreting "molecular beams," which measures force that holds together protons within nucleus of atom.

Rabiah, see Eliezer ben Joel ha-Levi of Bonn.

Rabin, Chaim Menachem (1915–), Israel Hebraist and linguist; b. Germany, son of Israel Rabin. Taught at Oxford 1942–56 and was then prof. of Hebrew at Heb. Univ. and a member of the Hebrew Language Academy. Wrote textbooks in Hebrew and Arabic and studies in Semitic linguistics. His brother, **Michael Oser** (1931–), mathematician. Rector of Hebrew Univ., 1972.

Rabin, Israel Abraham (1882–1951), scholar; b. Ukraine. Taught at Breslau Rabbinical Seminary; emigrated to Ereẓ Israel 1935. Early supporter of religious Zionism. His published works include studies, Jewish history, higher biblical criticism, and rabbinics.

Rabin, Yiẓḥak (1922–), Israel military commander, diplomat. Joined Palmaḥ 1940; active in defense activities and Israel army. Chief of staff 1964–67, commander during Six-Day War. Israel ambassador to U.S. 1968–1973. Israel Labor Party member of Knesset, prime minister, 1974.

Yiẓḥak Rabin

Rabinoff, George W. (1893–1970), pioneer of U.S. professional Jewish communal service. Instrumental in founding Council of Jewish Federations and Welfare Funds, serving as first executive 1932–35.

Rabinovich, Joseph (1837–1899), missionary and founder of Jewish-Christian sect in Kishinev. Born into ḥasidic family; attracted by Enlightenment and Zionism, but then converted to Christianity.

Rabinovich, Osip Aronovich (1817–1869), Russian writer, publisher. Founded *Razsvet,* first Jewish journal in Russian. Believed in progressive modernization of Russian Jewry.

Rabinovich, Zalman Khaimovich (d. 1944), Soviet army commander. Died commanding parachute unit dropped behind enemy lines at Minsk.

Rabinovitz, Alexander Siskind (acronym *Azar;* 1854–1945), Hebrew writer; b. Belorussia, settled in Ereẓ Israel 1906. Writings include stories, translations, and articles concerning labor movement in the country.

Rabinowicz, Mordecai, see Ben-Ammi, Mordecai.

Rabinowicz, Oskar K. (1902–1969), financier, author, Zionist. Active in Czechoslovakia until 1939, then England; settled in U.S. 1956. Revisionist Zionist and wrote on Zionism and Czech Jewish history.

Rabinowitch, Eugene (1901–1973), biochemist, biophysicist. B. Russia, in Germany until Nazi period, in U.S. fr. 1939; associated with Manhattan Atomic Bomb Project. Prof. at Univ. of Illinois. Wrote on photochemistry, photobiology, and reaction kinetics.

Rabinowitz, Joel (1828–1902), one of first Jewish ministers in S. Africa. Went fr. England to Cape Town 1859; built first S. African synagogue 1863.

Rabinowitz, Louis Isaac (1906–), rabbi. Officiated in London; senior Jewish chaplain in WWII. Chief rabbi of Transvaal and Orange Free State fr. 1945. Settled in Israel 1961. Deputy editor-in-chief, *Encyclopaedia Judaica* and editor of its *Year Book.*

Rabinowitz, Louis Mayer (1887–1957), U.S. manufacturer, philanthropist; b. Lithuania, in U.S. fr. 1901. Chairman, corset industry, 1934. Established chair in Semitic language and literature at Yale and Institute for Research in Rabbinics at Jewish Theological Seminary.

Rabinowitz, Samuel Jacob (1857–1921), Lithuanian rabbi, Zionist leader. One of first directors of Jewish Colonial Trust and a founder of Mizrachi world movement. Rabbi in Liverpool fr. 1906.

Rabinowitz-Teomim, Elijah David ben Benjamin (Aderet; 1842/43–1905), Ashkenazi chief rabbi of Jerusalem; b. Lithuania. Rabbi of Ponevezh 1874, Mir 1893. Wrote over 100 works, incl. glosses to Jerusalem Talmud and rabbinic codes. In Jerusalem fr. 1901. His son-in-law was Abraham Isaac ha-Kohen Kook.

Raboy, Isaac (1882–1944), novelist; b. Ukraine, in U.S. fr. 1904. Works include *Her Goldenbarg* (adapted for stage 1926), *Der Yidisher Cowboy,* and 2-vol. autobiography .

Rab-Shakeh, title of high Assyrian and Babylonian official in charge of territories. Present at siege of Jerusalem by Sennacherib (II Kings 18:19, Isa. 36–37).

Racah, Giulio (Yoel; 1909–1965). Israel physicist; b. Italy. Prof. at Pisa. In Ereẓ Israel fr. 1939. Headed dept. of theoretical physics at Heb. Univ. Studied atomic spectroscopy. Rector of Heb. Univ. Israel Prize 1958.

Raccah, Mas'ūd ben Aaron (1690–1768), rabbi in Tripoli. Author of commentary on Maimonides' *Mishneh Torah* and commentary on *Beraitot.*

Rachel, matriarch of Israel, favorite wife of Jacob. Jacob worked for her father Laban in return for her hand. Mother of Joseph and Benjamin, dying while giving birth to the latter.

Jacob and Rachel by Hugo van der Goes, 15th cent.

Rachel's tomb, 1913.

Traditional site of her tomb nr. Bethlehem venerated at least fr. 4th c. C.E. Present structure dates from 12th c. Its picture was used as decoration in Jewish homes throughout the world.

Rachel (1st c. C.E.), wife of R. Akiva. Secretly married Akiva, then an unlearned man, despite opposition of her wealthy father. Encouraged Akiva to withdraw for long period of study. Acc. to legend, he returned with 24,000 disciples, saying: "Mine and yours are hers."

Rachel (stage name of **Eliza Rachel Felix**; 1821–1858), French actress. One of greatest tragediennes of her time. Leading roles incl. Racine's *Phèdre*.

Rachmilewitz, Moshe (1899–), Israel hematologist. Head of internal medicine at Hadassah Hospital 1939; dean of medical school 1957–61. Israel Prize 1964.

Rackman, Emanuel (1910–), U.S. Orthodox rabbi, educator, author. Taught at Yeshiva Univ; prof. of Jewish studies at City Univ. of N.Y. Identified with modern Orthodox group.

Radak, see Kimḥi, David.

Radaniya (Radhanites), Jewish traders of 9th c. C.E. who went by number of routes, by ship and caravan, between Spain in W. and China in E.

Radbaz, see David ben Solomon ibn Abi Zimra.

Radek (Sobelsohn), Karl (1885–1939?), Russian revolutionary; b. Poland. Active in Polish and German socialist parties. Accompanied Lenin 1917 on his famous journey to Russia. Expelled from Communist Party 1927, readmitted 1930 on renouncing adherence to Trotskyists. Arrested and charged in 1937 show trial.

Radin, Max (1880–1950), U.S. jurist, teacher. Prof. of law at Berkeley 1919–48. Proponent of "legal realism."

Radin, Paul (1883–1959), U.S. anthropologist; brother of Max Radin. Studied Winnebago Indians. Represented humanistic approach to understanding preliterate societies. Taught at U.S. universities.

Radler-Feldmann, Yehoshua, see Rabbi Binyamin.

Radnóti, Miklós (1909–1944), Hungarian poet. Converted to Christianity. Early verse surrealistic, later work overshadowed by Holocaust. D. in army labor camp and last poems found in his pocket as he lay in mass grave.

Rado, Sandor (1890–), psychoanalyst; lived in Hungary, Berlin, and U.S. fr. 1931. Associate of Freud. Prof. of psychiatry at Columbia and N.Y. State Univ.

Radom, city in Poland. Jewish residence prohibited until 1746. Jews settled by 1765; organized community in 19th c. and cultural center. Over 30,000 Jews in 1939; deported to extermination camps in WWII.

Radomsko (Radomsk), town in Poland. Jews residence officially prohibited until 1862, Radomsko ḥasidic dynasty established 1843. Community developed rapidly after 1846. Jews active in civil life. Pop. 12,371 in 1935; all killed in WWII.

Radomsko (Radomsk), Solomon ha-Kohen Rabinowich of (1803–1866), ḥasidic *ẓaddik*. His *Tiferet Shelomo* considered one of classic works of Polish Ḥasidism. Last ḥasidic rabbi of Radomsk, **Solomon Enoch ha-Kohen,** murdered in Warsaw ghetto.

Raf, see Perez ben Elijah of Corbeil.

Rafa (Rafi'aḥ), town on Mediterranean Coast, S. of Gaza. Sargon burned city 721 and deported inhabitants. Conquered by Alexander Yannai. Jewish community in Middle Ages. Modern town established 1920s. Egyptian administration 1948–67. Arab refugees settled after 1948. Israel administration after Six-Day War. Pop. 49,812 (1967).

Rafes, Moses (1883–1942), leading member of Russian Bund. After WWI became communist and worked for liquidation of Bund in 1920s. Commissar in Red Army and worked for Comintern.

Raffalovich, Isaiah (1870–1956), rabbi, author. In Ereẓ Israel fr. 1882. Rabbi in Manchester, Wales, and Liverpool, 1904–24. In Brazil fr. 1924; active in building synagogues and schools and organizing welfare institutions.

Rafi (abb. of **Reshimat Po'alei Yisrael,** "Israel Labor List"), political party founded 1965 by David Ben-Gurion and 7 Mapai Knesset members (later joined by Moshe Dayan) as a result of split in Mapai. Party had 10 Knesset seats in 1965 elections and joined government of national unity on eve of Six-Day War. In 1968 party joined Mapai and Aḥdut ha-Avodah to establish Israel Labor Party (see also Knesset).

Rafi'aḥ, see Rafa.

Ragoler, Elijah ben Jacob (1794–1850), Lithuanian talmudist; said to have gone over entire Talmud more than 400 times. Noted *posek* and scholar in *halakhah* and Kabbalah.

Ragusa, see Dubrovnik.

Rahab, prostitute who assisted Joshua to conquer Jericho (Josh. 2–6). In return, she and her family spared during conquest.

Rahabi, Ezekiel (1694–1771), merchant community leader in Cochin, India. Occupied important position in Dutch East India Company undertaking diplomatic missions. Community historian and philanthropist.

Raḥel (pseudonym of **Raḥel Bluwstein**; 1890–1931), Hebrew poet in Ereẓ Israel; b. Russia, settled in Ereẓ Israel 1909. Joined kibbutz Deganyah after WWI. Her poems are elegiac and nostalgic in tone, and many have been set to music (incl. *"Kinneret"*).

Rahv, Philip (1908–1973), U.S. editor, critic; a founder of *Partisan Review.* Did much to revive interest in works of Henry James during 1940s.

Rain, Prayer for, prayer recited during *Musaf* service on 8th day of Sukkot. A brief petition for rain is inserted in each *amidah* during the winter. In ancient times, periods of drought evoked special prayers and even fasting.

Rainbow. In the biblical account of the Flood Story, God set His bow in the clouds as a sign that no deluge would again destroy the earth. A special blessing is recited on seeing the rainbow.

Carved walnut with colored trimming plaque from Hamburg synagogue to remind congregation to recite prayer for dew and rain during summer season, 18th cent.

The National Park of Ramat Gan.

The 'Unaziyya cistern, also known as the Pool of St. Helena, in Ramleh, 8th cent.

Rainer, Luise (1912–), Austrian actress; later in Hollywood. Famed for roles in *Escapade, The Good Earth,* for which she won Oscar, and *The Great Waltz.*

Raisin, Max (1881–1957), U.S. Reform rabbi in Paterson, N.J. Wrote history of Reform movement and modern Jewish history published as supplement to Graetz. His brother **Jacob Zalman** (1877–1946), Reform rabbi in Charleston. Wrote *The Haskalah Movement in Russia.*

Raisman, Sir Abraham Jeremy (1892–). British economist, banker. Worked in Indian Civil Service 1916–45; finance member of govt. of India 1939–45.

Rajpurkar, Joseph Ezekiel (1834–1905), Bene Israel scholar in Bombay. Teacher and school principal for 45 years. Translated fr. Hebrew (especially liturgy) and English into Marathi.

Rakaḥ (abb. of **Reshimah Komunistit Ḥadashah,** "New Communist List"), Israel Communist party established 1965 by faction which seceded fr. Maki ("Israel Communist Party"). 3 members in 6th and 7th Knesset and 4 in 8th. Extreme left orientation; main support from Israel Arabs (see also Knesset).

Rákosi, Mátyás (1892–1971), Hungarian communist dictator. Deputy trade commissioner in Béla Kun's government; condemned to death 1924, reprieved and released fr. prison 1940; in USSR until 1944. As dictator of Hungary fr. 1949 followed rigid Stalinist line; deposed 1956.

Ralbag, see Levi ben Gershom.

Ralbaḥ, see Levi ben Ḥabib.

Rāma, al-, Christian-Arab and Druze village in Upper Galilee, Israel. Olive-growing center. Pop. 3,810 (1971).

Ramah (Ha-Ramah), home town of Samuel (I Sam. 1:1; as Ramathaim-Zophim) and possibly the residence of Deborah (Judg. 4:5). There Samuel judged Israel and was later buried. The identification of the site is controversial.

Ramah (Ha-Ramah), town in territory of Benjamin (Josh. 18:25; Judg. 19:13). There the Babylonians concentrated the captives taken from Jerusalem before exiling them (Jer. 40:1). Identified with village of al-Rām, N. of Jerusalem.

Ramak, see Cordovero, Moses ben Jacob.

Ramallah, twin towns (Rām Allāh and al-Bīra) N. of Jerusalem. During British Mandate, Ramallah preponderantly Christian-Arab and al-Bīra Muslim and Christian, but subsequently Christian elements diminished under Jordanian rule 1948–67 and under Israel administration after Six-Day War. Pop. Ramallah 12,134, al-Bīra 13,037 (1967).

Ramatayim, see Hod ha-Sharon.

Ramat Gan, city adjoining Tel Aviv, established 1921 by settlers from E. Europe. One of Israel's foremost manufacturing centers. Site of national park, Makkabiah Village, and Bar-Ilan Univ. Pop. 119,300 (1971).

Ramat Hadar, see Hod ha-Sharon.

Ramat ha-Golan (Golan Heights), region in N. Transjordan. The Lower Golan is farming country. Jews there in talmudic period, up to Arab conquest. In 1880s Turks settled Circassians to ward off Bedouin robbers. Before 1967, under Syrian rule, pop. included Sunnite Muslims, Circassians, Druze, a small Christian minority, and others. In 1948–67 Syrians shelled Israel settlements in Upper Galilee fr. heights. In Six-Day War (1967) nearly all region occupied by Israel army and almost entire pop. (except Druze) fled to Syria. Israel has established settlements there.

Ramathaim-Zophim, see Ramah.

Ramat ha-Sharon, urban community with municipal council status in C̣. Israel, N. of Tel Aviv. Founded 1923 as moshavah. Industrial enterprises. Pop. 18,500 (1971).

Ramat Raḥel, kibbutz on S. outskirts of Jerusalem. Founded 1921 by Gedud ha-Avodah group. In 1948 War of Independence forward defense position and severely damaged. In 1951–52 joined Iḥud ha-Kevuẓot ve-ha-Kibbutzim. Excavations conducted there by Y. Aharoni 1954–62 include palace fr. Judean Kingdom, probably to be identified with biblical Beth-Cherem.

Rambam, see Maimonides.

Ramban, see Naḥmanides.

Rambeman, see Mendelssohn, Moses.

Rambert, Dame Marie (1888–), British ballet teacher; founder-director of Ballet Rambert; b. Warsaw. Worked with Diaghilev. In London fr. 1920.

Rameses, see Ramses.

Ramḥal, see Luzzatto, Moses Ḥayyim.

Ramleh (Ramlah), city in Israel, situated on Jerusalem-Tel Aviv highway. Founded 716 by Umayyad caliph; only city in Israel established by Arabs. Administrative capital of country under Umayyads and Abbasids. Temporary transfer of

Jerusalem academy to town in 10th c. strengthened Jewish pop. By 14th c. largest town in Ereẓ Israel. Declined after Ottoman conquest. When occupied by Israel forces (1948) most Arabs left; in 1950s immigrants absorbed. Pop. 32,600 (1971), incl. 4,000 Arabs.

°**Ramón Lull (Raimundus Lullus;** c. 1234–1315), Catalan Christian preacher, mystic, philosopher. Preached to Jews and Muslims and wrote apologetic works directed to Jews. Acquainted with basic Kabbalah.

Ramoth-Gilead, levitical city of refuge in territory of Gad in N. Transjordan. Capital of Solomon's 6 districts, which included region of Argob (I Kings 4:13). Captured by Arameans during Divided Monarchy, Ahab of Israel fell in battle trying to retake it.

Building of Pithom and Ramses by Hebrew slaves, from "Barcelona Haggadah," Spain, 14th cent.

Ramses, one of two treasury cities built by Hebrews in Egypt (Ex. 1:11).

°**Ramses II,** king of Egypt c. 1290–1223 B.C.E. who restored Egypt to her former greatness; probably the pharaoh of the Exodus.

Ramsgate, English town. Sir Moses Montefiore lived there, and established there the Judith Montefiore College (recently, a college for training Sephardi rabbis).

Ram's Horn, see Shofar.

Ran, see Nissim ben Reuben Gerondi.

Ranak, see Krochmal, Nachman.

Rank, Otto (1884–1939), psychoanalyst; b. Vienna. Member of Freud's inner circle, but broke with him. Special interest interpretation of myths, dreams, etc. Applied psychoanalytic theory to the arts. In U.S. fr. 1935.

Ransoming of Captives, see Captives.

Rapaport, David (1911–1960), U.S. clinical psychologist; b. Hungary, in U.S. fr. 1935. Leading figure in Menninger Foundation, Topeka, Kansas, 1940–48. Director of research at Austen Riggs Center, Stockbridge, Mass. Pioneer in clinical psychology.

Rapaport, Nathan (1911–), Israel sculptor. Known for Warsaw monument to "Defenders of the Warsaw Ghetto," statue of Mordecai Anilewicz at Kibbutz Yad Mordekhai, and statue in Martyrs' Forest nr. Jerusalem.

Raphael (Heb. "God will heal"), one of 4 archangels. Angel set over all kinds of healings. According to Talmud, one of 3 angels who visited Abraham. Prominent in kabbalistic writings.

Raphael, Chaim (1908–), English author and scholar. Lectured at Oxford; worked in Civil Service. Works on Jewish social history, thrillers (under pseudonym Jocelyn Davy).

Raphael, Frederic (1931–), English novelist, scriptwriter. Some of his works on Jewish themes.

Raphael, William (1833–1914), Canadian painter. First Jewish artist to emigrate to Canada (1857). Scenes of wild winter storms and wolves seem like contemporary European prints.

Raphael (Werfel), Yiẓḥak (1914–), Israel politician; b. Galicia, settled in Ereẓ Israel 1935. Head of Aliyah Department of Jewish Agency 1948–54, Ha-Po'el ha-Mizrachi member of Knesset, minister of religions 1974. Chairman of Mosad ha-Rav Kook and Yad ha-Rav Maimon. Wrote studies on Ḥasidism and religious Zionism.

Raphall, Morris Jacob (1798–1868), rabbi. B. Sweden; in England fr. 1825. Published first Jewish periodical in England. Went to U.S. 1849 (rabbi of B'nai Jeshurun, N.Y.). Opposed abolitionism. Gave first invocation by a rabbi before House of Representatives 1860.

Rapoport, Abraham ben Israel Jehiel ha-Kohen (1584–1651), Polish talmudist, halakhic authority. Prominent in Council of the Four Lands. Outstanding scholar; wrote responsa and sermons *(Eitan ha-Ezraḥi)*.

Rapoport, Benjamin Ze'ev Wolf ha-Kohen ben Isaac (1754–1837), Hungarian rabbi in Pápa who opposed Ḥasidism and study of Kabbalah. His comparatively liberal attitude involved him in controversies.

Rapoport (Rappaport), Samuel (1871–1943), rabbi, folklorist. Cofounder of Mizrachi and leader of its E. Galician branch. Killed in Holocaust.

Rapoport (Rappaport), Solomon Judah Leib (known by acronym Shir; 1790–1867), rabbi, scholar, pioneer of Haskalah and Wissenschaft des Judentums; b. Galicia. Outstanding talmudist; under influence of Nachman Krochmal took interest in Haskalah and studied languages and science. Chief rabbi of Prague fr. 1840. Many contributions to Jewish scholarship incl. bibliographical studies and *Erekh Millin,* a talmudic encyclopedia.

Solomon Judah Leib Rapoport

Rapoport, Solomon Zainwil, see An-Ski, S.

Rappaport, Henry (1913–), U.S. pathologist. Prof. of pathology and director of surgical pathology at Univ. of Chicago after 1954. Wrote *Tumors of the Hematopoietic System.*

Rappaport, Isaac ben Judah ha-Kohen (d. 1755), rabbi. Rabbi in Smyrna 1712–49, Chief rabbi of Jerusalem fr. 1749. Wrote *Battei Kehunnah,* responsa, novellae, and homilies.

Rappoport, Charles (1865–1941), socialist politician, writer; b. Lithuania. Participated with Lenin's brother in plot to kill Czar Alexander II. Fled to France. Member of French Communist Party until resignation in 1938.

Rashal, see Luria, Solomon ben Jehiel.

Rashba, see Adret, Solomon ben Abraham.

Rashbam, see Samuel ben Meir.

Rashbash, see Duran, Solomon ben Simeon; Duran, Simeon ben Solomon.

Rashbaz, see Duran, Simeon ben Ẓemaḥ.

Rashi (Solomon ben Isaac; 1040–1105), leading commentator on Bible and Talmud; b. Troyes, France, studied at Mainz and Worms, returned to Troyes, where his school was of great importance. His com-

mentary on the Bible became the basic guide for Jewish study and evoked more than 200 supercommentaries. It has accompanied almost every edition of the Hebrew Pentateuch. He also produced a commentary to nearly the whole of the Babylonian Talmud printed in almost every edition of the Talmud. He was a philologist and linguist and often gave French equivalents for difficult words *(La'az)*.

Rashīd al-Dawla (al-Dīn; 1247–1318), physician, historian, vizier in Persia. Converted to Islam, but condemned to death as "infidel Jew." Made first systematic attempt to write history of all great peoples of the world.

The so-called Rashi "bet ha-midrash" adjoining Old Synagogue of Worms, photographed before 1938.

Louis Rasminsky

Walther Rathenau

Synagogue of Hebrew University of Jerusalem, designed by Heinz Rau and David Reznik, dedicated 1957.

Raskin, Saul (1886–1966), artist; b. Russia, many years in U.S. Painted mostly Jewish life and lore. Illustrated many Hebrew texts.

Rasminsky, Louis (1908–), Canadian economist, banker. Represented Canada at Bretton Woods Conference 1944. Governor, Bank of Canada, 1961.

Ras Shamra, see Ugarit.

Rath, Meshullam (1875–1963), Galician talmudist, rabbinic authority. Ordained at age 12. One of first rabbis to join Mizrachi movement. Elected to Rumanian senate. Fr. 1944 in Ereẓ Israel.

Rathaus, Karol (1895–1954), composer; b. Poland, in New York fr. 1938. Individual, atonal style. Wrote 8 symphonies, chamber and piano music, stage music (*Uriel Acosta, Jacob's Dream, Herod and Mariamne* for Habimah).

Rathenau, Emil (1838–1915), German industrialist, engineer; founder of A.E.G. electric corporation. Introduced telephone into German postal service.

Rathenau, Walther (1867–1922), German statesman, writer, industrialist; son of Emil Rathenau, whom he succeeded as head of A.E.G. in 1915. Wrote eclectic philosophical works. Served in German War Ministry in WWI. Foreign minister 1922. Assassinated.

Ratisbon, see Regensburg.

Ratisbonne Brothers, 2 French Jews who converted to Christianity, achieved eminence in Catholic Church: **Theodore** (1802–1884) and **Alphonse** (1812–1884). Founded religious orders that originally proselytized Jews (Sisters of Zion, Notre Dame de Sion) but after WWII the orders pioneered in Jewish-Christian understanding.

Ratner, Marc Borisovich (1871–1917), Russian lawyer, socialist. Prosecutor in pogrom trials. Forced to leave Russia after 1905 Revolution.

Ratner, Yohanan (1891–1965), Israel architect, army commander; b. Russia, settled in Ereẓ Israel 1923. Prof. at Haifa Technion. Territorial commander of Haganah 1938–39, member of Haganah high command 1947. Military attaché to Israel embassy in Moscow 1948–51.

Ratosh, Yonathan (1908–), Hebrew poet, journalist; b. Russia, settled in Ereẓ Israel 1921. Published poetry, translations, works on Hebrew literature and linguistics, and coined many Hebrew words. Founded Canaanite movement 1942.

Ratshesky, Abraham Captain (1864–1943), U.S. banker, civic leader. Massachussetts state Republican leader and state senator 1892–94. Founded U.S. Trust Company.

Rattner, Abraham (1895–), U.S. expressionist painter. Worked mainly in stained glass. Brightly colored creations usually religious in theme.

Rau, Heinz (1896–1965), Israel architect; b. Germany, in Ereẓ Israel 1933–62, then England. Featured buildings in Israel with small intake of light.

Rauh, Frédéric (1861–1909), French philosopher. Major interest morality. Active in Dreyfus case.

Rauh, Joseph L. (1911–), U.S. lawyer. A founder of Americans for Democratic Action (ADA) (1947) and its national chairman 1955–57. Strong civil rights advocate. General counsel for United Automobile Workers 1963–66.

Rav (Abba Arikha; 3rd c. C.E.), leading Babylonian *amora* and founder of academy at Sura. Ordained by Judah ha-Nasi; colleague of Samuel, with whom he laid the foundations of the Babylonian Talmud. His teachings reflect the *halakhah* and *aggadah* of Ereẓ Israel.

Rava (Abba bar Joseph bar Ḥama; d. 352), Babylonian *amora;* colleague of Abbaye. In all his halakhic discussions with Abbaye, the decision, except in 6 cases, was rendered according to Rava. When Abbaye was chosen head of the Pumbedita academy, Rava went to Maḥoza, where he set up a *bet midrash.*

Rava, Maurizio (1878–after 1935). Italian colonial administrator. Governor of Italian Somaliland 1932–35.

Ravensbrueck, Nazi concentration camp for women in Mecklenburg (E. Germany). Of the 132,000 persons who passed through the camp 92,000 died.

Ravikovitch, Dalia (1936–), Israel poet, writer, translator. Wrote poetry, essays on literature and art, and translated children's books into Hebrew.

Ravina (abbr. of **Rav Avina**), name of several Babylonian *amoraim.* The two best known are **Ravina** (d. 422), pupil of Rava, colleague of Rav Ashi, and possibly the Ravina who completed the teaching of the Talmud. **Ravina II** (d. 499) succeeded Rabbah Tosfa'ah as head of the academy at Sura. His death marks the end of the era of *amoraim* and beginning of the *savoraim.*

Ravina (Rabinowitz), Menashe (1899–1968), Israel composer,

writer. Active music educator and critic (for *Davar* 1925–68), choral organizer, and composer.

Ravitch, Melech (1893–), Yiddish poet, essayist; b. Galicia, settled in Montreal 1941. Wrote expressionistic poetry, autobiography, and encyclopedia of Yiddish writers.

Ravitz, Shelomo (1885–), *ḥazzan*, composer; b. Russia, settled in Tel Aviv 1932. Directed Selah Seminary for *ḥazzanim*.

Rav Ẓa'ir, see Tchernowitz, Chaim.

Rawidowicz, Simon (1897–1957), Hebrew writer, thinker; b. Poland, studied in Berlin. Prof. of Jewish philosophy at Leeds 1941–47, later prof. at Brandeis Univ. Editor, historian of Jewish thought, philosopher of Jewish history. Wrote on medieval and modern Jewish philosophy (esp. on Naḥman Krochmal). Opposed negation of Diaspora.

Rawnitzki, Yehoshua Ḥana (1859–1944), Hebrew journalist, publisher; b. Russia. Lifelong associate of Ḥ.N. Bialik. Cofounder of Moriah publishing house and editor of Hebrew and Yiddish periodicals. Settled in Ereẓ Israel 1922. Helped establish Devir publishing house and collaborated with Bialik in publishing *Sefer ha-Aggadah* and medieval poetry.

Ray, Man (1890–), French photographer, painter. Founder of dadaist-surrealist movement in painting. Made abstract photographic prints without camera.

Raykin, Arkadi Isakovich (1911–), Soviet Russian vaudeville actor. Widely known USSR for his mime impersonations (particularly Charlie Chaplin, bureaucrats and pseudo-intellectuals). Founder-director, Variety and Miniature Theater, Leningrad, 1939.

Raymond Martin, see Martin, Raymond.

Raynal, David (1841–1903), French politician. Minister of public works 1881, 1883–85; minister of interior 1893–94; senator fr. 1897.

Rayner, Isidor (1850–1912), U.S. lawyer, politician. Elected to Maryland legislature 1878, state senate 1885, U.S. House of Representatives for three terms fr. 1886. Maryland attorney general 1899–1903. U.S. senator 1904–16. Moderate liberal. Leader in fight to abrogate U.S.–Russian treaty in 1911 because of czarist anti-Semitism.

Raza Rabba, Sefer, work of Merkabah mysticism known only fr. medieval references. Book had magical content, apparently derived from eastern or Babylonian source.

Rufus Isaacs, first Marquess of Reading.

Raziel, angel connected with "mysteries of God" in midrashic and magical literature.

Raziel, Book of, collection of mystical, cosmological, and magical Hebrew works and portions of works, first compiled c. 16th c.

Raziel, David (1910–1941), commander of Irgun Ẓeva'i Le'ummi (I.Ẓ.L.). Joined I.Ẓ.L. 1931, commander fr. 1937. Arrested by British authorities 1939, released and killed 1941 by German bombing in Iraq while leading group of I.Ẓ.L. members in mission in cooperation with British Intelligence to sabotage oil depots outside Baghdad. Reinterred Mt. Herzl, Jerusalem, 1961.

Razim, Sefer ha-, early work of Jewish mystical literature remarkable for systematic treatment of magic, witchcraft, incantations, and supernatural remedies. Extracts long known but original form reconstructed by M. Margalioth in 1966.

Razsvet (Rus. "Dawn"), name of four Russian-Jewish weeklies that appeared in Russia and abroad. (1) Published in Odessa (May 1860–May 1861), first Jewish periodical in Russian; advocated Enlightenment and equal rights. (2) Published in St. Petersburg (Sept. 1879–Jan. 1883), sought to attract enlightened Jews to national values. (3) Published in St. Petersburg (1907–July 1915 and Nov. 1917–Sept. 1918), a weekly journal of topical political and literary content; initially opposed assimilation. (4) Published in Berlin (1922–May 1924) and Paris (1924–1935), organ of Russian-Ukrainian Zionists in exile; became Revisionist journal.

Reading, First Marquess of (Rufus Daniel Isaacs; 1860–1935), British statesman, advocate. After phenomenal success at bar, entered parliament as liberal; solicitor-general, attorney-general, and Lord Chief Justice 1913. British ambassador to U.S. 1918. Viceroy of India 1920–26 and foreign secretary 1931. Showed considerable interest in Jewish and Zionist affairs toward end of life and was chairman of Palestine Electric Corp. Only Jew made marquess. His son, the second Marquess **(Gerald Rufus Isaacs;** 1889–1960), undersecretary for foreign affairs 1951–53, minister of state for foreign affairs 1953–57. Active in Jewish affairs. Gerald's wife, **Eva Violet, Marchioness of Reading** (1896–1973), daughter of Alfred Mond. Adviser to ministry of health on child care during WWII. Although brought up as Christian, reverted to Judaism in 1930s and became staunch Zionist and active in World Jewish Congress.

Reading of the Law, see Torah, Reading of.

Rebekah, wife of Isaac, daughter of Bethuel, and granddaughter of Nahor, brother of Abraham. As a result of her kindness to Abraham's servant, he invited her to marry Isaac. After remaining childless for 20 years she gave birth to twins: Esau and Jacob (Gen 25:21–26).

Rebekah (top) giving birth to Jacob and Esau and (bottom) watching as Isaac blesses Jacob, from 14th cent. Spanish Haggadah.

Red Heifer being burnt outside Israelite camp, from J. Basnage, "République des Hébreux," Amsterdam, 1713.

Recanati, Italian family, originally from Spain; name from Italian town of Recanati. Main branch begins with **Shabbetai Elhanan** (17th c.), who founded a dynasty of rabbis. **Yehudah Leib (Leon)** (1890–1945), banker; b. Salonika, settled in Ereẓ Israel 1935. Established Discount Bank, which became one of the largest in the country.

Recanati, Menahem ben Benjamin (13th–14th c.), Italian kabbalist and halakhic authority. His quotation of other kabbalists have preserved many important sources.

Rechab and Baanah, sons of Rimmon from Beeroth, captains of the army of Saul's son Ish-Bosheth (II Sam. 4:2). Murdered Ish-Bosheth and took his head to David, who had them summarily executed.

Rechabites, small religious sect which refrained from drinking wine, cultivating vines, and building houses. Traced descent to Jonadab son of Rechab. Jeremiah extolled their strict observances and there are allusions to them in the Second Temple period.

Northern Red Sea area, photographed from Gemini II, 1966. 1. Red Sea, 2. Gulf of Suez, 3. Gulf of Eilat, 4. Dead Sea, 5. Mediterranean Sea.

Rechter, Ze'ev (1899–1960). Israel architect; b. Russia, settled in Ereẓ Israel 1919. Influential in modern design of urban housing in Israel. His son **Ya'akov** (1924–) designed public buildings in Tel Aviv, incl. Mann Auditorium (with D. Carmi).

Recife, city in NW Brazil. In 16th–17th c. important sugar-producing center, with many New Christians and Marranos. Occupied by Dutch 1630–54 and Jews practiced their religion openly. 23 emigrants were first Jewish settlers in New Amsterdam (New York). Small 20th c. community from E. Europe (1,000 in 1971).

Reckendorf, Hermann (Ḥayyim Ẓevi; 1825–1875), German orientalist. Wrote Hebrew translation of Koran 1875 and fictionalized recounting of Jewish history.

Reckendorf, Hermann Solomon (1863–1923), German orientalist; son of Hermann Reckendorf. Prof. at Freiburg Univ., specializing in Arabic syntax.

Reconstructionism, ideology and movement in U.S. Jewish life, owing its inspiration to Mordecai M. Kaplan. According to Kaplan Judaism must transform itself from a civilization orientated toward the hereafter into one which can help Jews to attain salvation in this world. The individual Jew is to be arbiter of which rituals or folkways should or should not be practiced in light of his own needs and those of the group. Movement founded 1922. Reconstructionist Rabbinical College established 1967 in Philadelphia. In 1970, 10 congregations affiliated to the Federation of Reconstructionist Congregations and Fellowships.

Red Heifer (Heb. *parah adumah*), animal whose ashes were used in ritual purification of persons and objects defiled by corpse (Num. 19). Had to be unblemished cow never yoked. Ashes were mixed with water and sprinkled.

Redl, Fritz (1902–), child psychologist; b. Austria, in U.S. fr. 1936. Prof. at Wayne Univ. His *Children Who Hate* contributed to understanding of abnormal psychology in anti-social behavior.

Redlich, Joseph (1869–1936), Austrian constitutional lawyer, politician; authority on Austrian and British parliamentary procedure. Austrian minister of finance 1918, 1931–34. Baptized 1903.

Red Sea (or **Sea of Reeds**), branch of Indian Ocean with forks to Suez and Eilat. Bible relates that when Israelites fleeing fr. Pharaoh reached this sea it parted and allowed them to pass but engulfed pursuing Egyptians. Identification of sea where this occurred is matter of controversy. Red Sea is clearly identified fr. period of Monarchy. Now Israel's outlet to Indian Ocean.

Red Shield of David, see Magen David Adom.

Reese, Michael (1815–1878), U.S. realtor, philanthropist. Bequest used to build Michael Reese Hospital in Chicago.

Reeve, Ada (1874–1966), British vaudeville actress. Her acting career spanned 84 years.

Reform Judaism (also known as Liberal or Progressive), trend in Judaism advocating modification of Orthodoxy in conformity with exigencies of contemporary life and thought. First reformers were laymen who primarily concerned themselves with aesthetic reforms in liturgy (Hamburg prayer book 1819). Participation of rabbis fr. 1840s on led to crystallization of theoretical positions associated with Geiger and Holdheim and to modification of religious observances and re-interpretation of theological doctrines such as Messiah and resurrection. In U.S. Reform doctrine was expressed in "Pittsburgh Platform" of 1885 and "Columbus Platform" of 1937. World's Reform congregations are united in World Union for Progressive Judaism, founded 1926. It has constituents or representatives in 26 countries.

Refuge, City of, see City of Refuge.

Regelson, Abraham (1896–), Hebrew poet, writer. Author of "Cain and Abel." Worked in U.S. until 1949 when he settled in Israel.

Regensburg (Ratisbon), city in W. Germany. Jewish quarter oldest in Germany (1020). By 12th c. it was religious and cultural center for German Jewry and community wielded considerable economic influence. Virtually destroyed in 15th

and 16th c. Numbered 427 in 1933 and was destroyed in Holocaust; 140 in 1970.

Reggio, Isacco Samuel (IaSHaR; 1784–1855). Italian rabbi; a founder of Collegio Rabbinico Italiano. Translated Pentateuch into Italian, wrote on religious and kabbalistic topics.

Reggio di Calabria, city in S. Italy. Small Jewish community in Middle Ages. First printed Hebrew book with date – Rashi's commentary on Pentateuch – 1475.

Rehfisch, Hans José (1891–1960), German playwright; during WWII in England, U.S. Wrote plays on contemporary politics and society. Pres. of Union of German Stage Writers and Composers 1931–33, 1951–53.

Rehob, ancient city not mentioned in Bible; identified with Tell al-Sārim, S. of Beth-Shean. Tell is most important mound in Beth-Shean Valley and remains date fr. 3rd millennium B.C.E. to 10th c. B.C.E.

Rehoboam, king of Judah c. 928–911 B.C.E.; son of Solomon. Shortly after his accession, his refusal to alleviate hard service imposed by Solomon ("My father chastized you with whips but I will chastize you with scorpions") led to split of monarchy into two separate kingdoms. Remained king of smaller S. kingdom of Judah. Split and fighting with N. kingdom weakened Israelites and encouraged their neighbors (incl. Egyptian pharaoh Shishak) to attack them.

Rehoboth, name of well dug by Isaac in Negev (Gen. 26:22). Located SW of Beersheba.

Reḥovot, city in C. Israel. Founded 1890 by First Aliyah immigrants fr. Poland. Founding group, Menuḥah ve-Naḥalah, with assistance of Baron Edmund de Rothschild, established moshavah. Center of citriculture after WWI. Site of Sieff (later Weizmann) Institute, home of Chaim Weizmann, Agricultural Faculty of Heb. Univ. Pop. 37,900 (1971).

Reich, Ignác (1821–1887), Hungarian teacher, historian. Wrote in favor of emancipation. Translated Genesis into Hungarian, wrote 5-vol. collection of biographies of Hungarian Jews.

Reich, Koppel (Jacob; 1838–1929), Orthodox chief rabbi of Budapest fr. 1889. Exercised considerable influence on contemporary rabbinate. Sat in Upper House of Hungarian Parliament when almost 90.

Reich, Leon (1879–1929), Polish General Zionist leader. Editor of Polish Zionist weekly *Wschód;*

Portico of Regensburg synagogue, etching by Albrecht Altdorfer. The inscription states synagogue was destroyed Feb. 21, 1519.

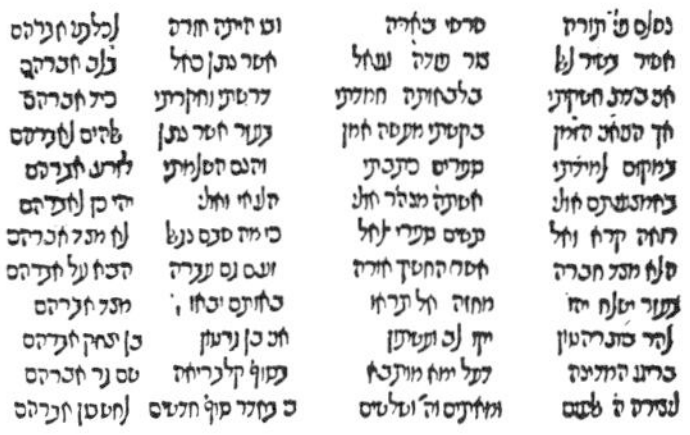

Colophon of Rashi's Pentateuch commentary, produced in Reggio di Calabria by Abraham b. Garton b. Isaac, 1475.

member of Polish Sejm and chairman of its Jewish club.

Reich, Wilhelm (1897–1957), Austrian psychologist; in U.S. after 1938. Contributed to psychoanalytic theory and to study of character formation. Held that mental health depends on attainment of full orgasm. Died in prison after being convicted of fraud in connection with his "orgone boxes."

Reichenbach, Hans (1891–1953), philosopher. Taught at Technische Hochschule, Stuttgart, Univ. of Berlin and Istanbul, and UCLA fr. 1938. Wrote on relativity theory, Hume's classical problem of induction, frequency theory of probability, and inductive logic.

Reicher, Emanuel (1849–1924), German actor, director. Prominent advocate of naturalist movement in Germany. Leading actor at Freier Buehne. First to present Ibsen and Hauptmann to Berlin audiences. In U.S. fr. 1915, helped organize American People's Theater.

Reichert, Israel (1891–), Israel agricultural scientist. Cofounder of *Palestine Journal of Botany.* Expert on fungi and lichens of Near East. Prof. at Heb. Univ. Israel Prize 1955.

Reichsbund Juedischer Frontsoldaten (RJF), organization of Jewish war veterans in Germany; founded 1919 to counteract anti-Semitic accusations. Membership exceeded 30,000 in 1933. Dissolved 1938.

Reichstein, Tadeus (1897–), Swiss organic chemist, endocrinologist. Succeeded in synthesizing Vitamin C. Received 1950 Nobel Prize for discoveries relating to hormones of adrenal cortex.

Reichsvereinigung der Juden in Deutschland, compulsory organization of all Jews in Nazi Germany. Established 1939, replacing previous framework called Reichsvertretung der Juden in Deutschland. Dissolved 1943.

Reichszentrale fuer Juedische Auswanderung (Center for Jewish Emigration), Nazi central agency for Jewish emigration matters. Established by Heydrich 1939; coerced wealthier Jews in Germany and abroad to pay for exit of poor Jews. After Oct. 1941 its personnel organized deportations in framework of "Final Solution."

Reifenberg, Adolf (1899–1953), Israel expert in soil chemistry, archaeologist, numismatist; b. Berlin, settled in Ereẓ Israel 1920. Prof. of soil science at Heb. Univ. Investigated problem of soil erosion and its prevention. Wrote on Jewish coins and ancient Hebrew seals.

Reifmann, Jacob (1818–1895), Polish scholar, writer on talmudic topics. Attempted to merge traditional with Western scholarship.

Reik, Ḥavivah (Emma; 1914–1944), Haganah emissary to Slovakia in 1944; parachuted into Europe to contact Jewish partisans but was captured and killed by Germans.

Reik, Theodor (1888–1969), psychoanalyst. After WWI worked in Vienna, Berlin, The Hague. Emigrated to U.S. 1938. Pres. National Association for Psychoanalytic Psychology 1946. Wrote over 50 books, incl. analyses of Jewish ritual and Jewish wit.

Reinach, Adolf (1883–1917), German philosopher. Considerably influenced early phenomenologists. Killed in WWI.

Reinach, Joseph (1856–1921), **Salomon** (1858–1932), **Theodore** (1860–1928), three brothers; French scholars, politicians; took active part in Dreyfus Affair, on which Joseph wrote study. Joseph was *chef du cabinet* to Gambetta and sat in Chamber of Deputies. Salo-

mon was an archaeologist (directed excavations at Carthage) and wrote on history of art and religion. Served as pres. of Société des Etudes Juives. Took anti-Zionist stand when representing French Jewry at Paris Peace Conference. Theodore edited French translation of Josephus and was important numismatist. Compiled Greek and Latin texts concerning Judaism.

Reiner, Fritz (1888–1963), conductor. Musical director Dresden Opera 1914–21, conductor Metropolitan Opera 1949–53 and Chicago Symphony Orchestra fr. 1953.

Reiner, Markus (1886–), Israel engineer; b. Austria, settled in Ereẓ Israel 1922. Prof. of practical mechanics at Haifa Technion. Pioneer in rheology.

Isaac Jacob Reines, lithograph by Hermann Struck.

Reines, Isaac Jacob (1839–1915), rabbi, Zionist. Talmudist of logical school; founded yeshivah at Lida where secular studies were taught; author of halakhic works. Member of Ḥibbat Zion; founded Mizrachi 1904 despite strong opposition in Orthodox circles.

Reinhardt (Goldmann), Max (1873–1943), German stage producer, director. Leading force in theater during first part of 20th c. Technical innovator whose productions deeply influenced European stagecraft. Director, Deutsches Theater, Berlin, fr. 1905 and of acting school. Emigrated to U.S. 1934.

Max Reinhardt directing rehearsal of Pirandello's "Six Characters in Search of an Author," Schlosstheater, Berlin.

Reischer, Jacob ben Joseph (Jacob Backofen; c. 1670–1733), halakhic authority; *dayyan* of Prague. Headed yeshivot in Worms and Metz; author of *Ḥok le-Ya'akov* on Passover laws and responsa.

Reisen, Abraham (1876–1953), Yiddish poet, short story writer. Editor of literary journals in Europe and New York. Wrote about E. European Jewish immigrants in U.S. His best-known lyric poem is *"May Ka Mashmalon."*

Reisen, Zalman, see Rejzen, Zalman.

Reiss, Lionel (1894–), U.S. artist. Known for ethnic studies of Jews and book illustrations.

Reiẓes, Ḥayyim ben Isaac ha-Levi (1687–1728) and brother **Joshua** (1697–1728), Polish rabbis and martyrs of Lvov; burnt at stake at instance of Bishop of Lvov.

Rejzen (Reisen), Zalman (1887–1941), Yiddish philologist, writer; brother of Abraham Reisen. Specialized in Yiddish philology. Lived in Vilna fr. 1915; seized by Soviet troops, taken to Russia, and shot.

Rekhasim, semi-urban settlement SE of Haifa, Israel. Founded 1951, became permanent settlement, and received local council status in 1959. Pop. 2,570 (1971).

Relgis (Sigler), Eugen (1895–), Rumanian author, journalist. Concerned with idealistic conception of humanitarianism. His *Principiile umanitariste* was translated into 17 languages. Also wrote articles on values of Judaism. Fr. 1947 in Montevideo.

Rema, see Isserles, Moses ben Israel.

Remak, see Kimḥi, Moses.

Remak, Robert (1815–1865), German neurologist; one of first Jews to lecture at Univ. of Berlin. Made important contributions to anatomy, histology, neurology, electrotherapy. His son, **Ernst Julius** (1849–1911), also neurologist; contributed mainly to electrodiagnosis and electrotherapeutics. Prof. at Univ. of Berlin.

°**Rembrandt van Rijn** (1606–1669), Dutch artist. Many of his drawings show interest in Amsterdam Jewry; lived nr. Jewish quarter. Drew, etched, and painted many biblical scenes and pictures and portraits of Amsterdam Jewry.

Remez (Drabkin), Moshe David (1886–1951), Israel labor leader; b. Belorussia, settled in Ereẓ Israel 1913. Secretary-general of Histadrut 1935–45, chairman of Va'ad Le'ummi, 1944–48, Mapai member of Knesset, minister of communications 1948–50, minister of education 1950–51. His son, **Aaron** (1919–), first commander of Israel Air Force, Israel ambassador to Britain 1965, head of Israel Port Authority 1970.

Remnant of Israel, term denoting belief that future of Israel would be assured by faithful remnant surviving calamities that would befall the people. Doctrine is referred to by most of the prophets and found its most developed form in teachings of Isaiah. After WWII the phrase the "Remnant which survives" *(She'erit ha-Peletah)* was applied to survivors of Holocaust.

Remos, Moses ben Isaac (c. 1406–c. 1430), Majorcan physician, poet; martyred in Palermo. Wrote elegy on his forthcoming death.

°**Renan, Ernest** (1823–1892). French philosopher, orientalist. Prof. of Hebrew at Collège de France fr. 1862. Wrote many works of Jewish interest, incl. history of Semitic languages, history of people of Israel, life of Jesus, and monographs on medieval French Jewry.

Rending of Garments, see Keri'ah.

Reparations, German, payments amounting to $845,000,000 made by W. German Government to State of Israel 1953–66. Payments, in goods, were recompense for financial cost involved in rehabilitation in Israel of those who escaped or survived Nazi regime. Claim first made 1945 and agreement bet. Israel and W. Germany signed 1952 in Luxembourg by Moshe Sharett and Konrad Adenauer.

"A Bearded Man in a Cap," an oil by Rembrandt, sometimes known as "A Jewish Rabbi."

Rephaim, in Bible a people noted for their enormous stature. Especially singled out are Og king of Bashan (Deut. 3:11) and the powerful adversaries of David's heroes (II Sam. 21:16, 18, 20). In its second use, designates "shades" or "spirits" (Isa. 26:14; Ps. 88:11).

Rephidim, stopping place of Israelites on their way fr. Egypt, situated bet. Wilderness of Sin and Wilderness of Sinai. Site unidentified.

Resh, (ר), 20th letter of Hebrew alphabet; numerical value 200. Pronounced *r.*

Reshevsky, Samuel Herman (1911–), U.S. chess master; b. Poland. Child prodigy. Several times U.S. chess champion.

Resh Galuta, see Exilarch.

Resh Kallah (Heb.), title of leading sages in talmudic and geonic periods who preached in Babylonian academies.

Resh Lakish, see Simeon ben Lakish.

Reshut (Heb.), cantor's introductory *piyyut* begging permission to intercede for congregation.

Resistance, see Partisans.

Responsa (Heb. *she'elot u-teshuvot*), replies sent by halakhic authorities to questioners who addressed them in writing. These cover every aspect of Jewish belief and practice and are main source for development of Jewish law since close of Talmud and source for Jewish and general history.

Restitution and Indemnification (German). The W. German Indemnification law (1957) provides indemnification for victims of national socialism subjected to Nazi persecution for "race," religion, or political views and incurring loss of life, injury to health, deprivation of liberty, loss of property, and damage to professional or economic advancement.

Réti, Richard (1889–1929), Czech chess master; one of few who beat Capablanca in tournament play. Playing blindfolded, he was first to play simultaneously on 24 boards.

Reuben, firstborn son of Jacob and Leah; eponymous ancestor of tribe of Reuben. For his sin with his father's concubine, lost his first-born rights.

Reuben Hoeshke ben Hoeshke Katz (d. 1673), Prague rabbi, kabbalist. Author of *Yalkut Re'uveni,* an important collection of halakhic lore.

Reubeni, David, see Reuveni, David.

°**Reuchlin, Johannes** (1455–1522), German humanist, Hebraist. Pioneer in study of Hebrew and rabbinic literature among Christians; defender of Talmud and kabbalistic literature fr. contemporary efforts to destroy them, esp. by Johannes Pfefferkorn. Wrote on kabbalah fr. Christological viewpoint.

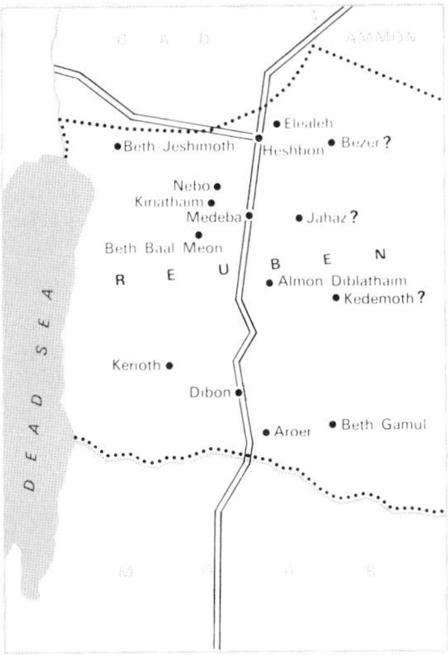

Territory of the tribe of Reuben.

Caricature of Baron von Reuter, "Vanity Fair," London, 1872.

Reuel, see Jethro.

Reuter, Paul Julius, Baron von (1816–1899), founder of Reuter News Agency; b. Germany. Established his service in London 1851. Baptized 1844.

Reuveni, Aharon (1886–1971), Hebrew writer; brother of Izhak Ben-Zvi; b. Ukraine, settled in Ereẓ Israel 1910. Published poems, novels, research. Many stories deal with period of Second Aliyah.

Reuveni, David (d. 1538?), adventurer. Came from east, claiming to have been sent by his brother King Joseph of some of Lost Tribes to enlist Christian power against Muslims. Captured imagination of many Jews and was even received in audience by Pope. Went to Portugal where many converted Jews acclaimed him, arousing messianic expectations. Eventually died at stake, accused of seducing New Christians back to Judaism.

Révah, Israel Salvator (1917–), French scholar specializing in intellectual history of Marranos. Prof. at Collège de France.

Revel, Bernard (1885–1940), U.S. Orthodox educator, scholar; b. Lithuania; in U.S. fr. 1906. Founder and pres. of Yeshiva College; laid foundation of U.S. Orthodox modern Jewish scholarship and was first institutional head in U.S. to give *semikhah.*

Bernard Revel

Revere, Giuseppe Prospero (1812–1889), Italian poet, patriot; follower of Mazzini. Wrote minor historical dramas and patriotic sonnets.

Revesz, Geza (1878–1955), Hungarian psychologist; first to give European military training pedagogical basis by setting up psychological tests for use by Hungarian army instructors. Fr. 1923 in Holland.

Revisionists, Zionist (Union of Zionists-Revisionists; Heb. *Ha-Ẓohar;* later *New Zionist Organization),* movement of maximalist political Zionists founded 1925 and led by Vladimir Jabotinsky. Advocated establishment of Jewish state with Jewish majority on both sides of the Jordan. Opposed official Zionist policy toward British mandatory rule. Seceded fr. World Zionist Organization 1935 and formed New Zionist Organization, which existed until 1946 when the movement rejoined the Zionist Organization. From Revisionist section in Haganah originated Irgun Ẓeva'i Le'ummi and Loḥamei Ḥerut Israel, whose veterans founded the Ḥerut Party. Youth movement is Betar.

Revista Cultului Mozaic ("Jewish Religious Review"), only Jewish newspaper in Rumania (fortnightly) and only periodical in E. Europe with Hebrew section. Founded 1956.

Revivim, kibbutz in S. Israel, affiliated with Ha-Kibbutz ha-Me'uḥad. Founded 1943 as one of three observation outposts established to explore natural conditions and farming possibilities in Negev. Pop. 440 (1971).

Revson, Charles Haskell (1906–), U.S. industrialist. Founder of Revlon cosmetics.

Revue des Études Juives, French Jewish scholarly periodical founded 1880 as organ of Société des Etudes Juives.

Revusky, Abraham (1889–1947), Po'alei Zion leader. Minister of Jewish affairs in nationalist Ukrainian government 1919. Published a history of Zionism.

Reyna, Joseph Della, see Joseph Della Reyna.

°**Rezin,** last king of Aram-Damascus (8th c. B.C.E.). In alliance with Pekah of Israel, attempted unsuccessfully to depose Ahaz of Judah. As a result, killed by armies of Tiglath-Pileser and his kingdom annexed to Assyrian Empire.

Reznik, David (1923–), Israel architect. Works incl. Kennedy Memorial. Executed Israel pavilion for Expo '67, Montreal (with A. Sharon).

Reznikoff, Charles (1894–), U.S. poet, author, lawyer. Wrote on Jewish themes; managing editor of Labor Zionist *Jewish Frontier.* Selected poems in *By the Waters of Manhattan.* Married to Marie Syrkin.

Rheims, city in N. France. Jews fr. 1077. Theological disputations bet. Jews and Christians frequent in latter 12th c. Community expelled in 15th c. 600 Jews in 1971.

Rhinewine, Abraham (1887–1932), Canadian journalist, historian. Editor of Toronto *Hebrew Daily Journal.* Wrote in Yiddish and English.

Jewish communities in Rhode Island and dates of establishment.

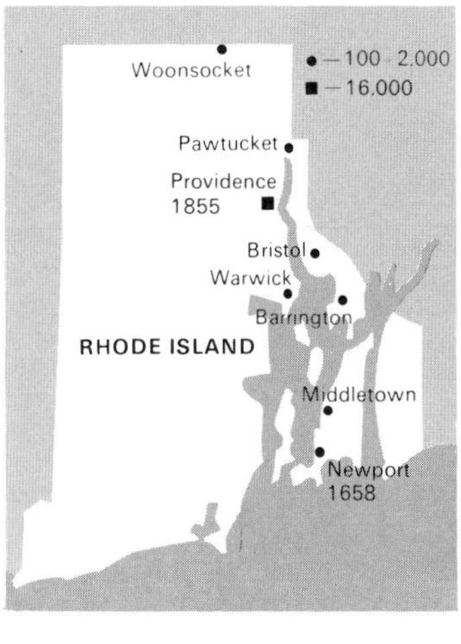

Rhode Island, U.S. state. First recorded Jewish settlers 1658 in Newport. Major settlement in Providence (fr. mid-19th c.). Frank Licht elected governor 1966. Jewish pop. 22,280 (1971).

Rhodes, Greek island. Jewish settlement fr. classical times. Predominantly Greek composition of community changed when Sephardi settlers arrived during Turkish period. After Italian occupation (1912) attempt made to establish it as center for diffusion of Italianized Jewish culture. Emigration (e.g. to Belgian Congo, Rhodesia, State of Washington, U.S.). Community of 1,700 deported to Auschwitz by Germans during WWII. 32 Jews in 1969.

Rhodesia, C. African country. Jews important in developing mining, ranching, commerce, industry. First community established in Bulawayo 1894. Numbers increased through immigration fr. Germany in 1930s and fr. S. Africa and Egypt after WWII. Jewish pop. 5,200 (1971).

Riaz, see Isaiah ben Elijah di Trani.

Riba, see Isaac ben Abraham; Isaac ben Asher Ha-Levi.

Street in former Jewish quarter of Rhodes.

Jewish communities in Rhodesia, 1971.

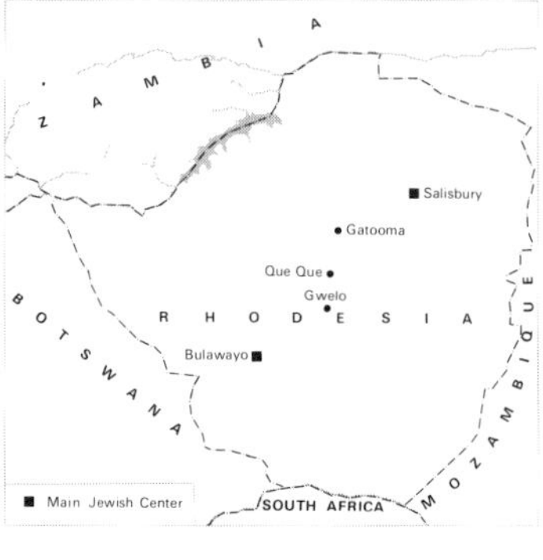

Ribal, see Levinsohn, Isaac Baer.

Ribalow, Menachem (1895–1953), U.S. Hebrew essayist; b. Volhynia; in U.S. fr. 1921. Founder and editor of Hebrew weekly *Hadoar.* Important influence in U.S. Hebrew-speaking circles.

Ribam, see Isaac ben Meir; Isaac ben Mordecai.

Ribash, see Isaac ben Sheshet Perfet.

Ribeiro Sanchez, Antonio (1699–1782), Marrano physician of Portuguese birth who practiced medicine in London, Russia, and Paris. First to popularize medical value of Russian vapor baths in W. Europe.

Abraham A. Ribicoff

Ribicoff, Abraham A. (1910–), U.S. politician. Congressman 1948–52, governor of Connecticut 1954–60, Secretary of Health, Education, and Welfare 1961–62, and senator fr. Connecticut fr. 1962. Staunch advocate of social reform, raising of social welfare standards, and minority rights.

Ricardo, David (1772–1823), British economist; a founding father of modern economics. His theory of international trade and his principles of comparative advantage provided scientific basis for rule of free trade. Left Judaism after his marriage.

Ricchi, Raphael Immanuel ben Abraham Ḥai (1688–1743), Italian rabbi, kabbalist, poet. Studied Lurianic Kabbalah in Safed and wrote rabbinic and kabbalistic works. Murdered by robbers while traveling.

Rice (Reiss), Abraham Joseph (1802–1862), U.S. Orthodox rabbi of German origin; founder of first German-Jewish all-day school in Baltimore. An attempt was made to establish for him the office of chief rabbi of the U.S.

Rice (Reizenstein), Elmer Leopold (1892–1967), U.S. playwright. *On Trial* (1914) first play on America stage to use flashback technique. Worked in many styles, ranging fr. expressionist satire on office drudgery, *The Adding Machine,* to Pulitzer Prize winning *Street Scene.* Radical in social outlook.

Rice, Isaac Leopold (1850–1915), U.S. lawyer, promoter. Instrumental in reorganizing several southern railroads. Worked on electric storage battery, electric automobiles and boats. In chess, inventor of "Rice Gambit" opening.

Rich, U.S. department store owners. **Morris** (1847–1928) founded retail store in Atlanta 1867, first of leading chain of department stores throughout South known as "Rich's of Atlanta."

Richards, Bernard Gerson (1877–1971), U.S. journalist. Edited *New Era* magazine 1906–11; secretary of Jewish community of New York City, a founder of American Jewish Congress 1915, and its executive director until 1932. Member American Jewish delegation to Versailles Peace Conference. Founded Jewish Information Bureau of Greater New York 1932.

Richler, Mordecai (1931–), Canadian novelist, journalist. Works incl. *The Apprenticeship of Duddy Kravitz* on poor Jews of Montreal and *St. Urbain's Horseman* contrasting Jewish and gentile culture.

Richman, Julia (1855–1912), U.S. educator. First woman district superintendent of schools in N.Y. 1903. Helped immigrant children adjust to American life, combated truancy and juvenile delinquency. First pres. YWHA 1886–90 and pioneer in organizing Parent-Teacher Association.

Richmond, city in Va., U.S. First Jewish settlers 1769. First congregation Beth Shalom 1789; among 6 congregations which congratulated Washington upon his first inauguration. Jewish pop. 10,000 (1971).

Richter, Hans (1888–), German artist, film maker. One of first to make abstract feature films; later produced surrealistic fantasies.

Richtmann, Mózes (1880–), Hungarian scholar, rabbi, Zionist. Taught at Jewish Teachers' Seminary in Budapest, contributed to Hungarian Jewish press. Wrote works on Jewish history.

Ricius, Paulus (d. 1541), Italian humanist, translator, apostate. One of architects of Christian Kabbalah.

Rickover, Hyman George (1900–), U.S. naval officer; "father" of atomic-powered submarine. Headed electrical section, Bureau of Ships, during WWII. Persuaded U.S. Navy to undertake construction of nuclear-powered submarines, resulting in "Nautilus," world's first atomic-powered submarine (1954). Vice-admiral.

Hyman G. Rickover

Ridbaz, see Willowski, Jacob David ben Ze'ev.

Riegelman, Harold (1892–), U.S. lawyer, public official. New York State veteran relief commissioner 1922–32 and acting postmaster of N.Y. under Eisenhower Administration. Pioneer in drafting housing legislation.

Rieger, Eliezer (1896–1954), Hebrew educationalist; b. Galicia, settled in Ereẓ Israel 1920. Prof. of education at Heb. Univ. and director-general of Israel Ministry of Education and Culture 1951–54, where he was largely responsible for introduction of state education.

Rieger, Paul (1870–1939), German Reform rabbi, historian. Together with H. Vogelstein wrote standard history of Jews in Rome.

Riesman, David (1909–), U.S. sociologist. Prof. at Univ. of Chicago 1946, Harvard 1958. Principal author of *The Lonely Crowd,* describing human types as "tradition-directed," "inner-directed," and "other-directed." Became Unitarian.

Riesser, Gabriel (1806–1863), protagonist of German Jewish Emancipation. His demands for civic equality for Jews aroused conscience of German liberals. Vice-pres. of 1848 parliament meeting at Frankfort. First Jewish judge in Germany 1860.

Riesser, Jacob (1853–1932), German jurist, banker; nephew of Gabriel Riesser; baptized in his youth. His writings decisively influenced stock exchange and banking legislation. Vice-pres. of German parliament 1921–28.

Rieti (da Rieti), family of Italian bankers operating in different towns fr. 14th to 17th c. Members included physicians and Jewish scholars and rabbis, who used their influence in many Jewish matters. Some were able to prevent seizure of Talmud ordered by Paul IV in 16th c.

Rieti, Moses ben Isaac da (1388–after 1460), Italian scholar, physician, poet. Chief rabbi of Rome and physician to Pope Pius II. Author of *Mikdash Me'at,* written in manner of Dante's *Divine Comedy* and covering a vast area of Jewish theology and personalities and science of the age.

Rif, see Alfasi, Isaac ben Jacob.

Rifkind, Simon Hirsch (1901–), U.S. attorney, jurist. U.S. district judge, Southern District of New York, 1941–50. Temporary special adviser on Jewish affairs in European theater to General Eisenhower 1945–46.

Riga, capital of Latvian SSR. Jewish settlement sporadic until 14th c., then grew rapidly. By WWI community had numerous religious and cultural institutions and played important role in commerce. By 1935 it numbered 43,672. Nazis established ghetto 1941 and subsequently liquidated most of community (incl. historian Simon Dubnow). Reestablished by settlers fr. Soviet interior after WWII and in late 1960s numbered 38,000. Soviet authorities considered town "hotbed of Zionism."

Righteous of the Nations (Heb. *Ḥasidei ummot ha-olam*), term used in rabbinic literature for righteous gentiles; applied since WWII to those non-Jews who saved Jews fr. Nazi persecution by endangering their own lives. Term officially recognized

Barbed-wire fence surrounding Riga ghetto. The notice, in German and Latvian, reads: "Anyone crossing the fence or trying to contact inhabitants of the ghetto will be shot without warning."

Silver medal struck by Yad Vashem, to honor the Righteous of the Nations, bearing the talmudic maxim, "He who saves one life is considered as having saved the whole universe." Designed by Nathan Karp, 1965.

by State of Israel, and Yad Vashem authority has as one of its tasks the perpetuation of their names.

Rigler, Leo George (1896–), U.S. physician, educator. Prof. of radiology at Univ. of Minnesota 1927, UCLA 1963. Executive director of Cedars of Lebanon and Mt. Sinai hospitals, Los Angeles, 1957–63. First Jewish pres. of Radiological Society of North America.

Rīhāniyya, Al-, one of two Circassian-Muslim villages W. of the Jordan, situated in Upper Galilee, Israel. Pop. 434 (1971).

Rimon, Jacob (1902–1973), Israel Orthodox Hebrew writer, poet. Among founders of Ha-Po'el ha-Mizrachi and Torah va-Avodah movements.

Rimon (Granat), Joseph Ẓevi (1889–1958), Hebrew poet; b. Poland, settled in Ereẓ Israel 1909. Worked in newspapers and as a teacher. After being savagely mutilated by Arabs in 1921, secluded himself in Ari Synagogue in Safed, studying Kabbalah. Author of religious poetry.

°**Rindfleisch**, German knight, instigator of massacre of thousands of Jews in 146 localities in S. and C. Germany 1298.

Ringel, Michael (1880–?), Zionist leader, journalist in Galicia and Poland. Member of Comité des Délégations Juives and of Polish senate. Deported to Soviet interior in 1939–41 and nothing more known of him.

Ringelblum, Emanuel (Menahem; 1900–1944), historian of Warsaw ghetto. Organized clandestine collection of documentary evidence during German occupation. Enterprise known as Oneg Shabbat, employed dozens of workers and the material was buried in containers. Those recovered after war provide main source material for Polish Jewish history during Nazi period. Murdered by Gestapo.

Rio de Janeiro, city in Brazil. Small groups of Marranos settled fr. 16th c. Jewish community established 1846. Many immigrants arrived after WWI, when numerous communal institutions were established. Jewish pop. 50,000 (1971).

Rischin, Moses (1925–), U.S. historian. Work centered on American history. Prof. at San Francisco State College. Writings incl. *Promised City: New York's Jews, 1870–1914.*

Rishonim (Heb. lit. "the early" [authorities]), term already used in Talmud to indicate older rabbinic authorities. Nowadays refers generally to halakhic authors bet. *geonim* and *aḥaronim*, i.e., mid-11th to mid-15th c.

Rishon le-Zion (Heb. "first in Zion"), title of Sephardi chief rabbi of Israel, with his seat in Jerusalem.

Rishon le-Zion, city in C. Israel. Founded 1882 by pioneers fr. Russia headed by Z.D. Levontin. Bilu pioneers joined village; worked in vineyards, wine production, citriculture. World's first Hebrew kindergarten and elementary school. Received municipal status 1950. Pop. 50,400 (1971).

Ritba, see Yom Tov ben Abraham Ishbili.

Rittenberg, David (1906–1970), U.S. biochemist. Prof. at Columbia Univ. Pioneer in use of isotopes to label molecules and thus trace their movements and chemical transformation in metabolism.

Ritual Bath, see Mikveh.

Ritual Impurity and Purity, see Purity and Impurity.

Ritual Murder, see Blood Libel.

Ritz Brothers (Joachim), Al (1903–1965), **Jimmy** (1905–), **Harry** (1908–), U.S. vaudeville comedy team. Films incl. *Sing, Baby, Sing; One in a Million;* and *Pack Up Your Troubles.*

Rivera, Jacob Rodriguez (1717–1789), U.S. merchant; a founder of Yeshuat Israel Congregation, Newport, R.I. Merchant shipper, traded in numerous commodities incl. slaves.

Rivers, Larry (1923–), U.S. painter. jazz musician. Executed series of mammoth historical paintings in half-abstract technique with thin washes and areas of mounted construction.

Rivista Israelitica, Italian Jewish scholarly periodical published every two months 1904–1915.

Rivkes, Moses ben Naphtali Hirsch (d.c. 1671/72), Lithuanian talmudist who settled in Amsterdam. Wrote *Be'er ha-Golah* which corrected the text of *Shulḥan Arukh* and added clarifications.

Rivkin, Boruch (pseud. of **Baruch Abraham Weinryb**; 1883–1945), Yiddish literary critic, essayist; b. Latvia, in U.S. fr. 1912. Worked for Yiddish papers. Contended religion and art are identical and that divine truth emanates fr. imaginative creation.

Rivkin, Ellis (1918–), U.S. historian. Prof. of Jewish history at Hebrew Union College, Cincinnati; perceptive analyst of interrelations bet. Jewish life and surrounding culture.

Rivkind, Isaac (1895–1968), U.S. librarian, scholar of Polish origin. Chief of Hebrew section of library of Jewish Theological Seminary. Writer in many fields of Jewish scholarship.

Rivlin, Harry N. (1904–), U.S. educator. Organized, headed education dept. at Queens College 1939; dean of teacher education at City Univ. of N.Y. 1957. Expert on problems of education in urban ghettos.

Rivlin, Joseph Joel (1881–1971), Israel educator, scholar of Arabic language, literature. Chairman of Ereẓ Israel's teachers' association 1930–41, prof. of oriental studies at Heb. Univ. Wrote on culture of Kurdish Jews and translated Koran into Hebrew.

Rivlin, Shelomo Zalman (1886–1962), *ḥazzan*, composer, rabbi in Jerusalem. Outstanding teacher of *ḥazzanim.*

Rivlin, Yosef Yiẓhak (1837–1896), leader of Jewish community in Jerusalem. Initiated building of Naḥalat Shi'vah and Me'ah She'arim quarters outside Old City.

Rizpah, concubine of Saul. After death of Saul, Abner took possession of her as claim to throne (II Sam. 3:7). When Gibeonites killed seven of Saul's sons, she guarded their bodies until they received a proper burial (II Sam. 21).

Roback, Abraham Aaron (1890–1965), U.S. psychologist, Yiddish scholar. Taught at several univs. First to investigate historical antecedents, as opposed to European sources, of psychology. First to introduce academic course in Yiddish literature at U.S. univ. 1929. First editor of *Canadian Jewish Chronicle* 1914.

Robbins (Rabinowitz), Jerome (1918–), U.S. choreographer, dancer, producer. Famed for choreography in *On the Town, West Side Story, Fiddler on the Roof.* Headed own company, Ballets U.S., 1958–61. Founded American Theater Laboratory 1966.

Robert (Levin), Ludwig (1778–1832), German playwright; first Jew to have his plays performed on German stage; brother of Rahel Varnhagen. Although he converted to Christianity, he continued to suffer from prejudice.

Robert of Reading (13th c.), English Dominican friar who converted to Judaism.

°**Robinson, Edward** (1794–1863), U.S. orientalist. His travels to Ereẓ Israel 1837, 1852 initiated new period of biblical research. Identified hundreds of forgotten biblical locations. So-called "Robinson's

Robinson's Arch, named for Edward Robinson.

Arch" in Western Wall named after him.

Robinson, Edward G. (Emanuel Goldenberg; 1893–1973), U.S. actor. Achieved prominence in 1920s with Theater Guild. Played gang leader in many films *(Little Caesar)* as well as character roles (Dr. Ehrlich). Appeared in over 150 films. Special Oscar 1973.

Robinson, Jacob (1889–), jurist, diplomat, historian. Member Lithuanian parliament 1922–26. Left Lithuania 1940 and subsequently reached New York. Established and headed Institute of Jewish Affairs 1941–47; legal adviser Jewish Agency and later Israel UN Mission 1948–57; special consultant Eichmann trial. Coordinated research and publication on Holocaust for Yad Vashem and Yivo. Wrote on Holocaust.

Robinson, Nehemiah (1898–1964), international lawyer. Practiced law in Kovno with his brother Jacob 1927–40. Arrived N.Y. 1940. Director Institute of Jewish Affairs 1947–64; international law adviser World Jewish Congress. Played important role in formulating indemnification agreements with Germany and Austria.

Robison, Sophia (1888–1969), U.S. sociologist, criminologist. Prof. at N.Y. School of Social Work 1940–58. Significant studies in juvenile delinquency and work in Jewish demography.

Robson, William Alexander (1895–), British political scientist. Prof. at London School of Economics. Advocated coordination of academic study of administration and government with practical politics; founded and edited *Political Quarterly* for this purpose.

Rocamora, Isaac de (1601–1684), Spanish Marrano who became Dominican friar and escaped to Amsterdam where he proclaimed his Jewishness and took active part in communal life.

Rochester, city in N.Y., U.S. First Jewish settlers 1840s. First congregation 1848. Major center for clothing industry. Jews active in political and economic life. Jewish pop. 21,500 (1971).

Rockefeller Museum, name popularly given to Palestine Archaeological Museum built in Jerusalem during British Mandate with gift fr. John D. Rockefeller, Jr. After 1967 Six-Day War, entrusted to Israel Department of Antiquities and exhibitions operated by Israel Museum.

Rockland County, county in N.Y., U.S. First Jewish settlers 1890s. First congregation Farmers Synagogue (Orthodox) 1899 in Spring Valley, which has remained Orthodox center. County includes village of New Square (pop. 1,000) founded 1955 by ḥasidic Jews who followed Rabbi Y. Twersky from Brooklyn, N.Y.

Roda Roda, Alexander (Sándor Friedrich Rosenfeld; 1872–1945), Austrian author, humorist. Excelled at lampooning old Hapsburg *Kaiserreich.* Worked in USSR before 1933, went to U.S. 1939.

Rodell, Fred M. (1907–), U.S. legal scholar. Prof. at Yale Law School. In his *Nine Men* contended that Supreme Court justices reach decisions on essentially political basis.

Rodenberg (Levy), Julius (1831–1914), German author, editor. Founded literary monthly *Deutsche Rundschau.* Wrote verse collections, novels, short stories, feuilletons, travel sketches.

Rodgers, Richard (1902–), U.S. popular composer. Collaborated with Lorenz Hart to produce successful musicals *(The Girl Friend, Pal Joey,* etc.). Collaborated with Oscar Hammerstein II to create Pulitzer Prize winning *Oklahoma, Carousel, South Pacific, The King and I,* and *The Sound of Music.*

Rodin, Elisha (1888–1946), Russian Hebrew and Yiddish poet. Published Yiddish poems in USSR while his Hebrew poems appeared in Ereẓ Israel, which led to his imprisonment by Soviet authorities. One of last poets in Soviet Union to write in Hebrew.

Edward G. Robinson

The Rockefeller Museum.

Richard Rodgers

Rodkinson, Michael Levi (Frumkin; 1845–1904), Hebrew writer, editor; b. Belorussia, moved to Koenigsberg, Germany, where he began publishing periodicals. Fr. 1889 in U.S., where he attempted to revive his periodicals and translated Talmud into English.

Rodrigues, Dionisius (d. 1541), Marrano physician to kings of Portugal. Fled to London and then Ferrara.

Roest, Mayer (1821–1890), Amsterdam bibliographer, journalist. Founder of Jewish-Dutch publications.

Rogachover, The, see Rozin, Joseph.

Rogers, Ernesto (1909–), Italian architect, critic. Belonged to BBPR group of four modern architects known for sanatorium at Legnano 1937–38. Editor architectural journals *Domus* and *Casabella.*

Rogoff, Harry (Hillel; 1883–1971), U.S. Yiddish writer. Editor of *Forward* until 1962. Writings incl. highly regarded 5-vol. *Geshikhte fun die Fareynigte Shtaten* (History of the U.S.).

Róheim, Géza (1891–1953), psychoanalyst, anthropologist; b. Budapest, in U.S. fr. 1938. On basis of his field work in Australia, Africa, Armenia, wrote studies of mythology and magic and also developed dream theory.

°**Rohling, August** (1839–1931), anti-Semitic polemicist, priest fr. Rhineland. Published *Der Talmudjude*, collection of corrupt, scurrilous forgeries of Talmud. Challenged by Joseph Samuel Bloch and lost academic chair.

Roitman, David (1884–1943), *ḥazzan*, composer; b. Russia, in U.S. fr. 1921. Officiated at Congregation Shaare Zedek in N.Y. Light, flexible, lyric tenor voice.

Rojas, Fernando de (c. 1465–1541), Spanish Converso author; regarded as "father" of Spanish novel. Author of *La Celestina*, novel written entirely in dialogue form.

Rokach, Shimon (1863–1922), leader of Jaffa community; pioneer of citriculture in Ereẓ Israel. His son **Israel** (1896–1959), General Zionist leader. Mayor of Tel Aviv 1937–53, minister of interior 1953–55, deputy speaker of Knesset 1957–59. Another son, **Isaac** (1894–1974), general manager of the Citrus Growers Cooperative Society. Shimon's brother, **Eleazar** (1854–1914), journalist; a founder of Rosh Pinnah. Fr. 1880 he was abroad and spent his last years in Rumania and Galicia, lecturing, writing, and editing Yiddish and Hebrew newspapers.

Roke'aḥ, see Belz.

Rokeaḥ, David (1916–), Hebrew poet; b. Poland, settled in Ereẓ Israel 1934. His poetry is lyric and "naive."

Rokeaḥ, Eleazar, see Eleazar ben Judah of Worms.

Rolnick, Joseph (1879–1955), U.S. Yiddish poet; b. Lithuania, settled in N.Y. 1908. One of first American Yiddish poets to break with dominant tradition of didactic social poetry, paving way for impressionism and symbolism.

Roman, town in NE Rumania. Jewish settlement fr. 15th c. By 1894 numbered 6,432. Many engaged in commerce. Suffered anti-Semitism bet. wars but not liquidated in Holocaust. Most of community (7,900 in 1947) left for Israel; by 1969 150 Jewish families remained.

Romanelli, Samuel Aaron (1757–1817), Italian Hebrew poet, traveler; best known for his attractive description of Jewish life in Morocco.

Romanin, Samuele (1808–1861), Italian historian. Author of 10-vol. *Storia documentata di Venezia.*

Romanin Jacur, Leone (1847–1928), Italian patriot, politician. Participated in movement to free Venice from Austrian domination. Under-secretary of state for public works 1892–97, for interior 1900–02. Pres. of Padua Jewish community. Opposed Zionism.

Romaniots, name used for original Jewish pop. of Byzantine Empire and their descendants in all matters relating to their customs, language, and traditions. Greek was their language and was much used in their services.

Romano, Judah ben Moses ben Daniel (Leone de Ser Daniel; 14th c.), Italian philosopher, translator. Wrote in Hebrew. Taught king of Naples Bible in Hebrew.

Romano, Marco (1872–1942), Bulgarian Zionist leader, lawyer. Represented Bulgarian Jewry in Zionist congresses, edited official Zionist weekly in Bulgaria. In Ereẓ Israel fr. 1937.

Romanos Melodos (6th c.), hymnographer, composer; b. Syria of Jewish family. Became deacon and is regarded as "father of Byzantine hymnology." Canonized.

Roman-Ronetti, Moïse (Aharon Blumenfeld; 1847–1908), Rumanian author. His most important work deals with conflict bet. three generations of Jews and bet. Jews and gentiles. Wrote the play *Manasse.*

Romberg, Moritz Heinrich (1795–1873), German neurologist. Made fundamental contributions in field of neurology.

Romberg, Sigmund (1887–1951), U.S. composer; b. Hungary, in U.S. fr. 1909. Composed over 70 operettas, incl. *The Student Prince, The Desert Song,* and *Up in Central Park.*

Rome, capital of Italy; oldest Jewish community in Europe and one of oldest in world with continuous history since 2nd c. B.C.E. Prominent in the classical period (from which its catacombs remain); center of Jewish learning and banking in medieval times and flourished in Renaissance under continuing protection of Pope. Counter-reformation resulted in introduction of ghetto and drastic anti-Jewish legislation incl. burning of Talmud (1553), not fully alleviated until 1870. Over 2,000 Jews deported by Germans 1943–1944. Jewish pop. 15,000 (1971), home of main institutions of Italian Jewry.

Rome, David (1910–), Canadian librarian, historian. First national director of Labor Zionist movement

Engraving of the Piazza Giudea Fuori del Ghetto, Rome, by Guiseppe Vasi, 1752.

Interior of the Great Synagogue of Rome.

Title page of tractate "Shabbat" of Babylonian Talmud, printed and published by Joseph Reuben Romm, Vilna, 1859.

in Canada, press officer of Canadian Jewish Congress 1942–53. Wrote *Jews in Canadian Literature*.

Romm, family of Lithuanian printers and publishers of Hebrew and Yiddish works, among them the standard edition of the Babylonian Talmud published in Vilna with over 100 commentaries.

Romny, city in Ukrainian SSR. Jews fr. 18th c. and by 1914 numbered 13,400. Thereafter community declined, suffering ravages of war and Nazi persecution. 1,100 Jews in 1959.

Rónai, János (1844–1919), first head of Zionist movement in Hungary. Participated in First Zionist Congress and wrote on Zionist subjects.

Ronald, Sir Landon (1873–1938), British conductor; son of Henry Russell. After conducting opera and musical comedy, concentrated on symphonic music, specializing in Elgar.

Ropshitser, Naphtali Ẓevi (1760–1827), founder of ḥasidic dynasty in Galicia. Known chiefly through folklore. Wrote homiletic works.

Rosales, Jacob (16th c.), Portuguese merchant, shipowner; in Morocco after 1497. In Fez the Iberian exiles regarded him as their leader. Entrusted with various important diplomatic functions by sultan of Morocco.

Rosales, Jacob Hebraeus (Immanuel Bocarro Frances; c. 1588–c. 1668), Portuguese Marrano, physician, astronomer, poet. Friend of Galileo. Returned to Judaism in Leghorn.

Rosanes, Judah ben Samuel (1657–1727), Turkish *posek,* preacher. Author of commentary *Mishneh le-Melekh,* standard in all editions of Maimonides' *Mishneh Torah.* Active in opposing Shabbetai Ẓevi.

Rosanes, Solomon Abraham (1862–1938), Bulgarian historian who wrote 6-vol. history of Jews in Turkey and the Orient.

Rosario, city in Argentina. First Jewish settlement 1887, soon followed by Ashkenazi and Sephardi immigrants, who founded cultural, religious, and cooperative financial institutions. Jewish pop. 15,000 in 1971, the second largest Jewish community in Argentina.

Rose, Alex (1898–), U.S. trade unionist. Pres. United Hat, Cap, and Millinery Workers Union fr. 1950. N.Y. State secretary American Labor Party 1936–44 and chief strategist N.Y. State Liberal Party fr. founding in 1944.

Rose, Arnold Josef (Rosenblum; 1863–1946), violinist. Converted to Catholicism. Concertmaster Vienna Opera and Vienna Philharmonic at age 18. Founder famed Rose String Quartet 1882. Fled to England 1938.

Rose, Arnold Marshall (1918–1968), U.S. sociologist. Prof. at Univ. of Minnesota 1952–68. Interested in social problems in labor movement and race relations.

Rose, Billy (William Samuel Rosenberg; 1899–1966), U.S. showman. Pioneered nightclub-style entertainment for people of moderate means. Produced Broadway shows. Donated sculptures and paintings to Israel Museum.

Rose, Ernestine Potovsky (1810–1892), U.S. feminist, social activist; b. Poland, in N.Y. fr. 1836. Campaigned for married women's property rights bill in N.Y. State (passed 1848), women's suffrage, reform of divorce laws. A founder of Women's Suffrage Society 1869. Fr. 1869 in England.

Rose, Herman (1909–), U.S. painter. Evolved distinctive idiom in sensitive post-impressionist work.

Rosen, Joseph A. (1877–1949), U.S. agronomist, social worker; b. Russia, in U.S. fr. 1903. Discovered "Rosen rye," which was distributed all over U.S. Went to Russia 1921 on Joint relief mission for Jews. Initiated land settlement project in Crimea and Ukraine 1924. Later guided Joint-sponsored settlement in Dominican Republic.

Rosen, Mathias (1804–1865), banker; member of Polish Council of State. As head of Warsaw community, fostered influence of Haskalah.

Rosen, Moses (1912–), chief rabbi of Rumania fr. 1948. Member of Rumanian National Assembly fr. 1957; created legal conditions for Jewish religious life in Rumania.

Rosen, Pinḥas (Felix Rosenblueth; (1887–), Israel and Zionist leader, lawyer. Chairman of Zionist Organization of Germany 1920–23, member of Zionist Executive in London 1926–31. Settled in Ereẓ Israel 1931. Member of Knesset 1949–68 and first minister of justice (1948–61) laying foundation for Israel legislation. Active in the General Zionists (A) and cofounder of Progressive Party.

Rosenbach, Abraham Simon Wolf (1876–1952), U.S. bibliophile, bookdealer. Started Rosenbach Company, famed rare book concern. Pres. American Jewish Historical Society. First pres. American Friends of Hebrew University. Compiled *An American Jewish Bibliography.*

Rosenbaum, Morris (1871–1947), English rabbi. Authority on Jewish calendar and co-translator of Rashi's Pentateuch commentaries into Engl.

Rosenbaum, Semyon (Shimshon; 1860–1934), jurist, Zionist. Member of first Russian Duma 1906. In WWI, worked for independent Lithuania and after state was established became deputy foreign minister and minister of Jewish affairs 1923. Went to Ereẓ Israel 1924. A founder of Tel Aviv School of Law and Economics.

Rosenberg, Abraham (1870–1935), U.S. labor leader. A founder and pres. 1908–14 of International Ladies Garment Workers Union, which he helped guide to victory in waistmakers' strike 1909 and cloakmakers' strike 1910. Committed to peaceful collective bargaining and moderate tactics.

Rosenberg, Abraham Ḥayyim (1838–1928), Hebrew writer; b. Russia, in U.S. fr. 1891. Published *Oẓar ha-Shemot,* a 10-vol. biblical encyclopedia.

°**Rosenberg, Alfred** (1893–1946), chief Nazi ideologist, theorist of anti-Semitism. Nazi minister of occupied territories in East and head of civil administration. Condemned to death at Nuremberg War Crimes Trials.

Rosenberg, Anna M. (1902–), U.S. labor relations, manpower consultant. Director of N.Y. State Region for War Manpower Com-

mission in WWII. First woman to receive U.S. Medal for Merit 1947. U.S. assistant secretary of defense 1950, highest post ever held by woman in federal military establishment.

Rosenberg, Arthur (1889–1943), German communist leader, historian. Member of Reichstag 1924–28. Baptized in youth but active in Jewish student and academic circles in Germany and then England.

Rosenberg, Eugene (1907–), architect; b. Slovakia, in England fr. 1939. Buildings incl. U.S. embassy in London.

Self-Portrait by Isaac Rosenberg.

Rosenberg, Isaac (1890–1918), English poet, painter; first important poet to emerge fr. Anglo-Jewry. Recognized only several years after death. D. in active service in WWI.

Rosenberg, Israel (1875–1956), U.S. Orthodox rabbi of Polish origin. A founder of Joint Distribution Committee and pres. of Union of Orthodox Rabbis of U.S.

Rosenberg, James Naumburg (1874–1970), U.S. lawyer, artist, philanthropist, author. Founded Agro-Joint and Society for Jewish Farm Settlements in Russia 1926. Led U.S. delegation that sponsored Genocide Convention adopted by UN General Assembly 1948.

Rosenberg, Louis (1893–), Canadian demographer; went to Canada fr. England 1915. Administered farm settlements of Jewish Colonization Association until 1940. National research director Canadian Jewish Congress fr. 1945.

Rosenberg, Ludwig (1903–), German trade union leader; in Britain 1933–46. Pres. German trade union movement fr. 1962, doing much to bring it back into democratic politics.

Rosenberg, Stuart E. (1922–), rabbi in Rochester and Toronto; b. New York. Books incl. history of Canadian Jews.

Rosenberg Case, U.S. spy case involving Julius (1918–1953) and Ethel (1920–1953) Rosenberg and Morton Sobell (1918–). Charged and convicted of conspiracy to deliver U.S. atomic bomb secrets to Russia 1951 and, after rejection of appeal, sentenced to death and executed amid worldwide protests. Sobell sentenced to imprisonment.

Rosenblatt, Bernard Abraham (1886–1969), U.S. lawyer, Zionist. Established first U.S. Zionist student organization (Columbia Univ. 1905). N.Y. City magistrate 1921. As first pres. American Zion Commonwealth 1915, supervised its land acquisition in Ereẓ Israel.

Rosenblatt, H. (pseud. of **Ḥayyim Rosenblueth;** 1878–1956), U.S. Yiddish poet; b. Podolia. Followed realistic tradition of "sweatshop poets." Discovered American West for Yiddish poetry.

Rosenblatt, Josef (Yossele; 1882–1933), *ḥazzan,* composer; one of best-known cantors of 20th c. After serving congregations in Europe went to U.S. 1912. His concerts and recordings earned him international reputation. His voice can be heard in Al Jolson's *The Jazz Singer.*

Rosenblatt, Samuel (1902–), U.S. rabbi, scholar; son of Josef Rosenblatt. Served in Baltimore, taught at Johns Hopkins Univ., translated medieval Jewish philosophical works into English.

Rosenbloom, Solomon (1866–1925), U.S. banker, philanthropist; b. Russia; in U.S. fr. 1889. Endowed Jewish studies at Heb. Univ. and active in Pittsburgh charities, as was his wife **Celia Neumark** and his son **Charles** (1898–1973).

Rosenblum, Sigmund Georgievich (Sidney Reilly; 1874–? 1925), British spy; b. Odessa. Served British intelligence in Germany before and during WWI and in Russia after Bolshevik revolution. Trapped by Russian secret police 1925 and never heard of again.

Morris Rosenfeld, drawing by Jacob Epstein, 1902.

Rosenbusch, Karl Harry Ferdinand (1836–1914), German geologist; one of great pioneers of petrographic research.

Rosendale, Simon Wolfe (1842–1937), U.S. lawyer. Recorder of Albany and N.Y. State attorney general 1892–94.

Rosenfeld, Morris (1862–1923), pioneer of Yiddish poetry in U.S.; b. Poland, in U.S. fr. 1886. Worked in N.Y. sweatshop. Known as "Poet Laureate of Labor." Coedited *Der Ashmeday* 1894, a satirical humorous weekly, and daily *New Yorker Morgenblat* 1905.

Rosenfeld, Paul (1890–1946), U.S. author, critic. Coedited magazine *Seven Arts* 1916–17, *The American Caravan* 1927–35.

Rosenfeld, Yona (1880–1944), Yiddish novelist, short story writer; b. Ukraine, in U.S. fr. 1921. Wrote short stories portraying strange characters and their complex psychic states.

Rosenhead, Louis (1906–), British mathematician. Best known for work in field of fluid mechanics. Prof at Liverpool Univ.

Rosenheim, Jacob (1870–1965), Orthodox leader; b. Frankfort-on-Main, in U.S. fr. 1940, last years in Israel. Directed Orthodox weekly *Israelit* fr. 1906.

Rosenheim, Max (Leonard), Baron (1908–1972), British medical investigator, educator. Specialized in research into and treatment of kidney diseases and hypertension. Pres. Royal College of Physicians fr. 1966.

Rosenman, Samuel Irving (1896–1973), U.S. jurist; counsel to presidents Roosevelt and Truman. Member N.Y. State Supreme Court 1932–43. Presidential speechwriter and originator of slogan "New Deal." Organized Roosevelt's Brains Trust. Major force in creation of defense agencies during WWII. Edited 13-vol. *Public Papers and Addresses of Franklin D. Roosevelt.*

Rosensaft, Josef (1911–), business executive; b. Poland. Inmate of several concentration camps during WWII; later chairman of Central Committee for Displaced Persons and pres. of World Federation of Bergen-Belsen Survivors.

Rosensohn, Etta, see Lasker.

Rosenstock-Huessy, Eugen (1888–1973), German philosopher, theologian. Converted to Christianity at age 16. Exercised considerable influence on Franz Rosenzweig.

Rosenthal, Erich (1912–), U.S. sociologist; b. Germany. Prof. of

sociology at various univs. Known primarily for work on demography of Jews in U.S.

Rosenthal, Erwin (Isaac Jacob; 1904–), orientalist; b. Germany, in England fr. 1933. Taught at Manchester and Cambridge on medieval Arabic and Jewish thought.

Rosenthal, Franz (1914–), orientalist; b. Berlin. Prof. at Yale fr. 1956. Main interest history of scholarship in Islam, Aramaic studies.

Rosenthal, Herman (1843–1917), writer, pioneer of Jewish settlement in U.S.; b. Courland. Established shortlived agricultural settlements for Russian Jews near New Orleans and in Dakota. Participated in establishment of ICA colony of Woodbine, N.J. 1891. Published newspaper *Der Yidisher Farmer*. Headed Slavonic dept. of N.Y. Public Library.

Rosenthal, Judah (1904–), scholar; b. Poland, in U.S. fr. 1939. Taught at College of Jewish Studies, Chicago. In Jerusalem fr. 1969. Wrote on Jewish-Christian polemics.

Rosenthal, Leon (Judah Leib; 1817–1887), Russian financier, *maskil,* philanthropist. A founder of Society for Promotion of Culture among Jews of Russia and wrote its history.

Rosenthal, Leser (Eliezer; 1794–1868), German bibliophile. His collection, Bibliotheka Rosenthaliana, is in Amsterdam Univ. Library.

Rosenthal, Manuel (Emmanuel; 1904–), conductor, composer. Led French National Radio Orchestra 1934. Conductor Seattle Symphony Orchestra 1949–51. Compositions include light operas and orchestral works.

Rosenthal, Max (1833–1918), U.S. artist, inventor; pioneer of chromolithography in U.S. Official illustrator for U.S. Military Commission during Civil War. Invented sandblast process of decorating glass. His son **Albert** (1863–1939), collaborated with him on many projects. Expert on 18th, 19th c. American art.

Rosenthal, Pavel (Pinḥas; pseud. **Anman, P. Rol;** 1872–1924), physician, author; a leader of Bund; b. Vilna. Author of "Manifesto to the Jewish Intelligentsia," which was published in the name of the Bund.

Rosenthal, Philipp (1855–1937), German industrialist. Founder of Rosenthal porcelain works. Converted to Christianity.

Rosenwald, Julius (1862–1932), U.S. business executive, philan-

Julius Rosenwald

thropist. Pres. mail-order firm Sears, Roebuck and Co. fr. 1909. Philanthropies incl. Julius Rosenwald Fund 1917 with capital of $30.000,000, funds for construction of model housing for Negroes, and $5,000,000 to Univ. of Chicago.

Rosenwald, Lessing Julius (1891–), U.S. business executive; son of Julius Rosenwald. Chairman of board of Sears, Roebuck 1932–39; director of Bureau of Industrial Conservation in WWII. A founder 1943 and first pres. anti-Zionist American Council for Judaism. Campaigned against establishment of Jewish state in Ereẓ Israel.

Rosenwald, William (1903–), U.S. financier, philanthropist; son of Julius Rosenwald. Leading figure in Jewish philanthropy. Chairman national United Jewish Appeal campaign.

Rosenzweig, Franz (1886–1929), German Jewish theologian. Exerted profound influence on cultured Jews of his generation, incl. Martin Buber, with whom he began translation of Bible into German. Attempted to resolve problems of Jewish authenticity and literacy, and the relationships bet. Judaism and Christianity and the secular environment and Judaism. Organized in Frankfort the educational institute the Freies Juedisches Lehrhaus. Main work *The Star of Redemption.*

Rosenzweig, Gerson (1861–1914), U.S. Hebrew writer; b. Lithuania, in U.S. fr. 1888. Edited Hebrew periodicals and Hebrew columns in Yiddish press. Published satirical *Talmud Yanka'i* ("Yankee Talmud," 1907, 1909) and books of epigrams.

Franz Rosenzweig

Rosewater, Edward (1841–1906), U.S. journalist, politician. Member U.S. Military Telegraph Corps during Civil War. Responsible for transmission of Lincoln's Emancipation Proclamation. Elected Nebraska State Legislature 1871. Founded Omaha's *Daily Bee,* which after his death was edited by his son **Victor** (1871–1940).

Rosh, see Asher ben Jehiel.

Rosh Ha-Ayin, urban settlement in coastal plain of Israel. Nearly all inhabitants originate fr. Yemen. Pop. 11,700 (1971).

Part of "Amidah" prayer in "Musaf" service for Rosh Ha-Shanah, "Rothschild Miscellany," Ferrara (?), c. 1470.

Rosh Ha-Shanah, the Jewish New Year, celebrated Tishri 1–2. It is held that on this occasion men are judged and their fortunes determined for coming year. Chief feature is sounding of *shofar* and special liturgy. Ceremony of *Tashlikh* is observed on afternoon of first day.

Rosh Ha-Shanah (Heb. "New Year"), tractate in Mishnah order *Mo'ed* with *gemara* in both Talmuds. Deals with New Year festival, with determination of new moon and leap year.

Rosh Ḥodesh, see New Moon.

Rosh Pinnah, moshavah in N. Israel. First founded 1878 by pioneer Jews fr. Safed, renewed 1882 by Rumanian settlers. Pop. 825 (1971).

Rosh Yeshivah. (1) see Gaon. (2) Head of yeshivah *(q.v.)* or talmudic academy.

Rosin, David (1823–1894), German educator, scholar. Taught at Breslau

rabbinical seminary. Works incl. Hebrew edition of Samuel ben Meir's Pentateuch commentary.

Rosmaryn, Henryk (1882–1955), lawyer, journalist, political leader in Poland. Member of Sejm; known for his struggle against government's anti-Semitic policy. Represented Polish government-in-exile of London in Tel Aviv 1941–45.

Rosowsky, Solomon (1878–1962), Russian composer, musicologist; founded first Jewish Conservatory of Music at Riga 1920. Emigrated to Ereẓ Israel 1925. Composed music for Hebrew folk songs and plays. Later taught at Jewish Theological Seminary, New York. Wrote *Bible Cantillation.*

Ross, Barney (1909–1967), U.S. prizefighter. First man to hold world lightweight and welterweight titles simultaneously 1934. Last fight 1938, losing welterweight championship.

Ross, Herbert (1926–), U.S. choreographer. Did choreography for Broadway productions and films. Organized Ballet of Two Worlds 1960 with wife Nora Kaye.

Ross, Leonard Q., see Rosten, Leo Calvin.

Rosselli, Carlo (1899–1937), Italian socialist writer, economist. Member of International Brigade and leading fighter against Fascism. Murdered together with his brother **Nello** (1900–1937) by hired assassins of Fascist government.

Rossi, Azariah (Bonaiuto) ben Moses dei (Min ha-Adummin; c. 1511–c. 1578), Italian scholar of Hebrew letters. Author of *Me'or Einayim,* revolutionary study of Bible and Jewish history, chronology, poetry and culture, that made extensive use of Greek, Latin, and Italian sources. Some contemporary rabbis were shocked by his attitude toward talmudic legends and denial of chronology dating fr. creation.

°**Rossi, Giovanni Bernardo de** (1742–1831), Italian Christian Hebraist. Prof. of oriental languages at Parma Univ. Wrote on Jewish incunabula, 16th c. typography, etc. His valuable library of Hebrew books and mss. is in Palatine Library at Parma.

Rossi, Salamone de' (17th c.), composer fr. Mantua; leading Jewish composer of late Italian Renaissance and most important Jewish court musician in 16th c.

Rossin, Samuel (1890–1941), Soviet Yiddish writer. Wrote tales for children, poetry, stories and a drama. Killed in action in WWII.

Rosten, Leo Calvin (1908–), U.S. humorist. Best known (under pen name Leonard Q. Ross) as author *The Education of H*Y*M*A*N K*A*P*L*A*N* and *The Return of H*Y*M*A*N K*A*P*L*A*N.* Also wrote *The Joys of Yiddish.*

Rostov, city in Russia. Jews there fr. late 19th c. During WWI many came there fr. battle zone; 26,323 Jews in 1926. Town occupied by Germans during WWII, but most Jews escaped; those caught were exterminated. 21,000 Jews in 1959.

Rostow, Eugene Victor (1913–), U.S. lawyer, economist, government official; brother Walt Whitman Rostow. Taught law at Yale, dean of Law School 1955–65. Adviser to Presidents Kennedy and Johnson.

Rostow, Walt Whitman (1916–), U.S. economist. Taught at various univs. Adviser to Presidents Kennedy and Johnson. Wrote influential *The Stages of Economic Growth.*

Salamone de'Rossi, "Madrigaletti" for two soprano or tenor voices with basso continuo. Venice, Allesandro Vincenti, 1628.

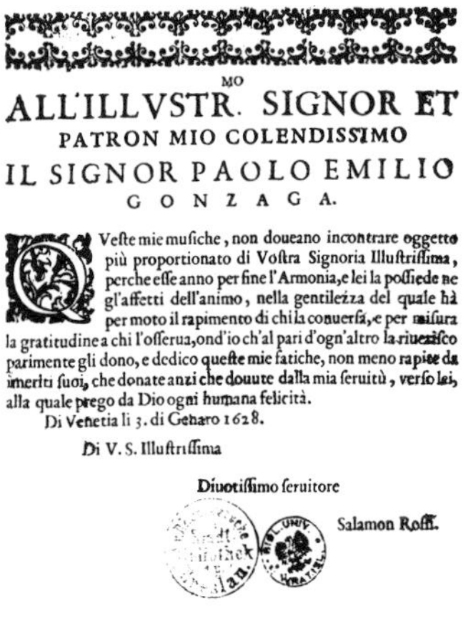
MO
ALL'ILLVSTR. SIGNOR ET
PATRON MIO COLENDISSIMO
IL SIGNOR PAOLO EMILIO
G O N Z A G A.

QVeste mie musiche, non doueano incontrare oggetto più proportionato di Vostra Signoria Illustrissima, perche esse anno per fine l'Armonia, e lei la possiede ne gl'affetti dell'animo, nella gentilezza del quale hà per moto il rapimento di chi la conuersa, e per misura la gratitudine a chi l'osserua, ond'io ch'al pari d'ogn'altro la riuerisco parimente gli dono, e dedico queste mie fatiche, non meno rapite da i meriti suoi, che donate anzi che douute dalla mia seruitù, verso lei, alla quale prego da Dio ogni humana felicità.

Di Venetia li 3. di Genaro 1628.

Di V. S. Illustrissima

Diuotissimo seruitore

Salamon Rossi.

Cecil Roth

Rotenstreich, Fischel (1882–1938), Zionist leader. Member of Polish senate 1922–27 and Polish Sejm 1927–30. Fr. 1935 in Ereẓ Israel directing Jewish Agency's Dept. of Commerce and Industry.

Rotenstreich, Nathan (1914–), Israel philosopher, author; b. Poland, settled in Ereẓ Israel 1932. Son of Fischel Rotenstreich. Taught at Heb. Univ. (rector 1965–69). Kantian scholar. Wrote on historical knowledge, man's place in the universe, and the political realm.

Roth, Aaron (1894–1944), Hungarian founder of ḥasidic sect that rejected compromise with modernity and lived simple life. Last years in Ereẓ Israel.

Roth, Cecil (Bezalel; 1899–1970), Jewish historian; editor-in-chief of *Encyclopaedia Judaica.* Reader in Jewish studies at Oxford Univ. 1939–64. Fr. 1964 in Jerusalem. Prolific author of works in Jewish history, incl. a general history, works on Italian, British, and Marrano communities, and on Jewish art.

Roth, Henry (1906–), U.S. novelist. Only novel *Call It Sleep* about Jewish immigrant life on New York's East Side. Book appeared 1934 but widely acclaimed in 1960s.

Roth, Joseph (1894–1939), Austrian novelist. As journalist with *Frankfurter Zeitung* 1923–33, fought for new humanism and was strenuous opponent of German militarism. Some of his novels (e.g., *Job*) reflected his own E. European Jewish background.

Roth, Klaus Friedrich (1925–), English mathematician. Prof. at Imperial College of Science and Technology, London. Specialty theory of numbers.

Roth, Leon (Ḥayyim Judah; 1896–1963), philosopher; b. England; brother of Cecil Roth. Prof. at Heb. Univ. 1927–51, rector 1940–43. Responsible for translation of major philosophical works into Hebrew. Wrote on Jewish thought and Judaism. Fr. 1952 in England.

Roth, Philip Milton (1933–), U.S. novelist. Taught at various univs., writer-in-residence at Princeton. Works incl. *Goodbye Columbus,* short stories portraying middle-class Jews, and the bestselling, satirical *Portnoy's Complaint.*
Rothberg, Samuel (1910–), U.S. business executive, Jewish community leader in Peoria, Ill. A founder and national campaign chairman of Israel Bonds Organization fr. 1955, chairman of board of governors of Heb. Univ., member of executive of Jewish Agency 1970.
Rothenberg, Morris (1885–1950), U.S. jurist, communal leader, Zionist. Expert in labor law and arbiter in numerous labor-management disputes. City magistrate in N.Y. A founder and executive member of Joint Distribution Committee. Pres. Zionist Organization of America 1932–35; pres. Jewish National Fund in U.S.
Rothenstein, Sir William (1872–1945), British painter; distinguished impressionist and outstanding teacher. Chiefly painted portraits, still lifes, and landscapes. Among his work is group of Jewish subjects. His son, **Sir John** (1901–), director of Tate Gallery, London; had no connection with Jewish community.

Detail of self-portrait by William Rothenstein.

Rothko, Mark (1903–1970), U.S. abstract painter. Cofounder 1935 of post-fauve impressionist group "The Ten." Influenced by European surrealists during WWII.
Rothmueller, Aaron Marko (1908–), baritone and composer. Sang opera in Europe. Moved to U.S. after WWII. Prof. of music at Univ. of Indiana fr. 1952. Wrote *Music of the Jews.*
Rothschild, family of financiers and philanthropists originating in Frankfort. Founder **Mayer Amschel** (1744–1812), court agent of William IX of Hesse-Kassel, who entrusted Mayer's son **Nathan Mayer** (1777–1836) in London with purchase of huge amounts of British securities. Nathan founded London branch of Rothschild house and was outstanding figure in London Stock Exchange, transacting much government business during and after Napoleonic Wars. His brother, **Karl Mayer** (1788–1855), founded Italian branch in Naples 1821. His four sons all married in family. One of them, **Salomon Mayer** (1774–1855), founded Vienna branch. On very friendly terms with Metternich; ennobled 1822. Financed Austria's first railroad and established Oesterreichische Kreditanstalt (later Austria's state bank). Austrian branch liquidated after *Anschluss* 1938. Another son of Mayer Amschel, **Amschel Mayer** (1773–1855), followed his father as head of Frankfort branch. Loaned large amounts to many German rulers. Very pious; provided financial backing for secessionist Orthodox community of S.R. Hirsch in Frankfort. Succeeded by **Mayer Karl** (1820–1886), first Jew appointed to Prussian House of Lords. Frankfort branch discontinued at beginning of 20th c. French branch founded by another son of Mayer Amschel, **James Jacob** (1792–1868), financier to successive French rulers and pioneer railroad entrepreneur. Particularly active in Jewish communal affairs in France. Succeeded by his son **Alphonse** (1827–1905), who negotiated and financed French indemnity payments after Franco-Prussian War. His philanthropy, benefiting both Jews and gentiles, was on immense scale. Later members of French house incl. **Baron Edmond** (see next entry), **Edouard** (1868–1949), **Guy** (1909–), **Robert Philippe** (1880–1946), and **Alain** (1910–), all active in Jewish affairs. **Bethsabée (Batsheva;** 1914–) founded Batsheva Dance Co. in Tel Aviv. In England, Nathan Mayer's son **Lionel Nathan** (1808–1879), responsible for many government loans, incl. one for purchase of Khedive's Suez Canal shares. Leader in struggle for Jewish emancipation. First Jewish MP. His brother, **Sir Anthony** (1810–1876), first president of United Synagogue in London. Lionel Nathan's eldest son **Lord Nathaniel (Natty) Mayer** (1840–1915), headed London branch and was effective lay head of Anglo-Jewry. Governor of Bank of England; created first Jewish peer 1885. His cousin and brother-in-law **Ferdinand James** (1839–1898), MP,

The 16th-cent. Rothschild house in Frankfort on the Main, destroyed WWII.

Lionel Rothschild taking his seat as first Jew in House of Commons, July 26, 1858.

art connoisseur. Active in communal work, founded hospital in London and school in Jerusalem in memory of his wife **Evelina** (1839–1866). **Lord Lionel Walter** (1868–1937), distinguished naturalist, Zionist. Recipient of 1917 Balfour Declaration. **Edmund Leopold** (1916–), present head of firm. **Lord Nathaniel Mayer Victor** (1910–), biologist. Fellow of Royal Society. Chairman of British Agricultural Research Council 1948–58 and assistant director of research in dept. of zoology at Cambridge fr. 1950. Research coordinator of Royal Dutch Shell Group fr. 1965. Director general of Central Policy Review Staff, Cabinet Office, fr. 1970. Baron Edmond's son, **James Armand de** (1878–1957), settled in England. Served as liaison officer of Zionist Commission 1918; pres. of PICA fr. 1924 and took interest in many enterprises in Ereẓ Israel. Liberal MP 1929–45. Left bequest for building of Israel Knesset.

Baron Edmond James de Rothschild (center) in Erez Israel, 1914, with the "shomer" Avraham Shapira (right).

Rothschild, Baron Edmond James de (1845–1934), philanthropist, patron of Jewish settlement in Erez Israel, art collector; son of James Jacob Rothschild. His support of Jewish settlement in Erez Israel was implemented by bureaucratic staff of Frenchmen. Eventually his settlements transferred to supervision of ICA (1900) and later to PICA (1923). Developed wine industry in country, cosponsored Palestine Electric Corp. and founded many institutions and settlement activities. Visited country several times and was known as "Father of the *Yishuv*." In 1954 his remains and those of his wife reinterred in Ramat ha-Nadiv, nr. Zikhron Ya'akov.

Rothschild, Friedrich Salomon (Sally; 1899–), psychiatrist; b. Germany, settled in Erez Israel 1936. Prof. of psychiatry at Heb. Univ.

Rothschild, Walter N. (1892–1960), U.S. department store executive. General manager 1925, pres. 1937, chairman 1955 of Abraham and Straus Department Store in Brooklyn. Succeeded by son **Walter N. Jr.** (1920–).

Rottembourg, Henri (1769–1836), French army officer. Received numerous honors fr. both Napoleonic and Bourbon governments and his name is engraved on north side of Arc de Triomphe in Paris.

Rotterdam, city in Netherlands. Sephardi and Ashkenazi communities founded in 17th c. Emancipation 1796; community flourished in 19th c. Many of 13,000 Jews deported to Poland by Nazis fr. 1942. 800 returned after war. 1,300 Jews in 1969.

Roussillon, region and former province in S. France. Jews present fr. 11th c. until expulsion 1493. Perpignan was center of learning in 14th c. and also center of conflict over study of philosophy.

Rovigo, town in N. Italy. Jews fr. 13th c. Ghetto established 1615. With French occupation 1797 Jews received equal civic rights. Community declined in 20th c.

Rovigo, Abraham ben Michael (c. 1650–1713), Italian kabbalist, Shabbatean. Founded yeshivah in Jerusalem, served as emissary of Jerusalem to Europe. His papers valuable source for history of Shabbateanism.

Rovina, Hanna (1892–), Israel actress; b. Russia. Founder-member of Habimah Theater Company in Moscow, achieving fame with her portrayal of Leah in company's Hebrew production of *The Dybbuk*. Went to Erez Israel with company 1928 and became country's leading actress.

Hanna Rovina as Leah in Moscow Habimah production of "The Dybbuk," 1922.

Rovno, town in Ukrainian SSR. Jews fr. 16th c. Community granted charter in 18th c. Economic opportunities expanded in 19th c. Jewish organizations ceased to function under Soviet rule 1939–41 and murder of town's 28,000 Jews began immediately after German occupation 1941. 1,000 Jews after war; 600 in 1970.

Rowe, Leo Stanton (1871–1946), U.S. political scientist. Prof. at Univ. of Pennsylvania. Assistant secretary of U.S. treasury 1917 and head of Latin American section of State Dept. 1919–20. Pres. American Academy of Political and Social Sciences 1902–30.

°**Rowley, Harold Henry** (1890–1969), English Protestant theologian, Bible scholar. Wrote on unity and relevance of Bible.

Rozeanu (née Adelstein), Angelica (1921–), Rumanian table-tennis champion; first table-tennis player to win six straight world titles. Settled in Israel 1960.

Różewicz, Tadeusz (1921–), Polish poet. Also wrote plays, stories, satires.

Rozin (Rosen), Joseph (1858–1936), Polish talmudic genius; known as "the Rogachover" after his birthplace. Endowed with phenomenal memory, knew both Talmuds and all known tannaitic and amoraic literature. Prolific writer and correspondent; his works appear under title *Zafenat Pa'ne'aḥ*.

Ru'aḥ ha-Kodesh (Heb. lit. "the Holy Spirit"), term used in post-biblical rabbinic literature for spirit of prophecy that gives man insight into future and will of God. According to Maimonides it is second lowest of 11 degrees of prophecy.

Rubashov, Shneur Zalman, see Shazar, Shneur Zalman.

Rubenstein, Louis (1861–1931), Canadian ice-skating champion. At various times bet. 1882 and 1891 figure-skating champion of Canada, U.S., America, and world (1890).

Rubenstein, Richard Lowell (1924–), U.S. rabbi, theologian. Director of Hillel at Univ. of Pittsburgh 1958–69, prof. at Florida State Univ. fr. 1971. Influenced by "Death of God" theology.

Rubin, Edgar (1886–1951), Danish psychologist. Best-known discovery involved finding that visual perception is normally divided into two parts, figure and ground.

Rubin, Hadassah (1912–), Yiddish poet; b. Ukraine, settled in Israel 1960. Poems deal with social problems, Holocaust, life in Israel.

Rubin, Reuven (1893–), Israel painter; b. Rumania, settled in Erez Israel 1922 where he was pioneer of modern art. His art is significant example of effort to create national style. Israel's first minister plenipotentiary to Rumania 1948–50. Israel Prize 1973.

Rubin, Solomon (1823–1910), Hebrew writer in Galicia. His sympathy for victims of intellectual

Self-portrait by Reuven Rubin.

censorship led him to interest in Spinoza, translating some of his writings.

Rubinow, Isaac Max (1875–1936), U.S. economist, social worker, physician; b. Russia. Main interest in government service was social insurance. Directed Hadassah Medical Unit in Ereẓ Israel 1918–22. Secretary of B'nai B'rith 1929–36.

Rubinstein, Akiva (1882–1961), Polish chess master; known as "the Spinoza of chess" for his selfless attitude in play. It is believed that a Nazi devotee of chess was instrumental in saving his life during the Nazi occupation of Belgium, where he had retired.

Rubinstein, Anton Grigoryevich (1829–1894), Russian virtuoso pianist, composer. Founded St. Petersburg Conservatory 1862 and established Rubinstein Prize 1890. Some of his compositions reflected influence of his Jewish background.

Rubinstein, Artur (1886–), virtuoso pianist; b. Poland, went to U.S. after WWI. One of outstanding performers of 20th c. Known for his readings of Chopin, Beethoven, etc. Appeared regularly with Israel Philharmonic Orchestra.

Rubinstein, Helena (1871–1965), cosmetician; b. Poland. Began career in Australia, subsequently established herself as Europe's leading cosmetician. Arrived in U.S. 1914 and built up cosmetics empire. Donated Modern Art Pavilion to Tel Aviv Museum.

Rubinstein, Ida (1885–1960), Russian actress-dancer who won fame with Diaghilev's Russian Ballet. Formed own company 1915.

Rubinstein, Isaac (1880–1945), Lithuanian rabbi. A leader of Mizrachi and Polish-Lithuanian Jewry. Minister of Jewish affairs in Lithuanian Government 1920, member of Polish Senate 1922–39. D. in New York.

Rubinstein, Joseph (1900–), Yiddish poet; b. Poland. Much of his poetry describes his experiences as war refugee in Siberia 1941–46, his unsuccessful effort to rehabilitate himself in postwar Poland, and his travails before reaching U.S.

Rubinstein, Nikolay Grigoryevich (1835–1881), Russian pianist, conductor, teacher. Founded Moscow Conservatory 1866.

Rubinstein, Sergey Leonidovich (1889–1960), Russian psychologist, educator. Played leading role in efforts of Soviet regime to construct adequate body of psychological knowledge and theory based on Marxist materialism. Stalin Prize 1941. Forced to resign post 1950.

Rubio, Mordecai (18th c.), Hebron *ḥakham* and its emissary to the Orient. Author of responsa *Shemen ha-Mor*.

Ruby, Jack (Jacob Rubenstein; 1911–1967), slayer of Lee Harvey Oswald, alleged murderer of President J.F. Kennedy; nightclub operator. Convicted of murder, sentenced to death, new trial ordered, but died before it could take place.

Rudavsky, David (1903–), U.S. educator. Prof. of Hebraic studies at New York Univ. Editor of periodical *Jewish Education*.

Ruderman, Jacob Isaac (1901–), U.S. *rosh yeshivah;* b. Russia, in U.S. fr. 1930. Head of Baltimore Rabbinical College and a member of Mo'eẓet Gedolei ha-Torah of Agudat Israel. Published novellae to Maimonides and Talmud.

Rudnicki, Adolf (1912–), Polish novelist, author. Warsaw ghetto fighter; his late works discuss Nazi nightmare, anti-Semitism, and fate of Polish Jewry.

°**Rudolph** (12th c.), monk, preacher who incited crusaders to persecute Jews of Germany.

Ruef, Abraham (1864–1936), U.S. politician. Became in effect "boss" of San Francisco. Served jail term for bribery 1911–15.

Rueff, Jacques (1896–), French economist; advocate of international monetary discipline. As financial counselor to De Gaulle was instrumental in designing France's successful 1958 reform. Elected to Académie Française 1964.

Ruelf, Isaac (1831–1902), German rabbi of Memel. Took active interest in helping E. European Jews across German borders; became known as "Doktor Huelf" ("help"). Active Zionist.

Artur Rubinstein at Carnegie Hall, New York.

Helena Rubinstein

Rufeisen, Joseph (1887–1949), Czechoslovakian Zionist leader. President of Czech Zionist Organization 1921. In Ereẓ Israel fr. 1938.

Rufus of Samaria (c. 100 C.E.), earliest known Jewish physician and writer on medicine (in Greek), Mentioned by Galen.

Rufus Tinneius, see Tinneius Rufus.

Rukeyser, Muriel (1913–), U.S. poet, author. Prominent left-wing writer. Verse collections notable for concern with social problems.

Rumania, European republic. First Jews in region in 2nd c. C.E. Large numbers of Jewish immigrants fr. Hungary in 14th c., Spain in 16th c.,

Rumanian Chief Rabbi Rosen addressing service at Choir Synagogue, Bucharest, built 1866.

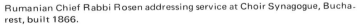

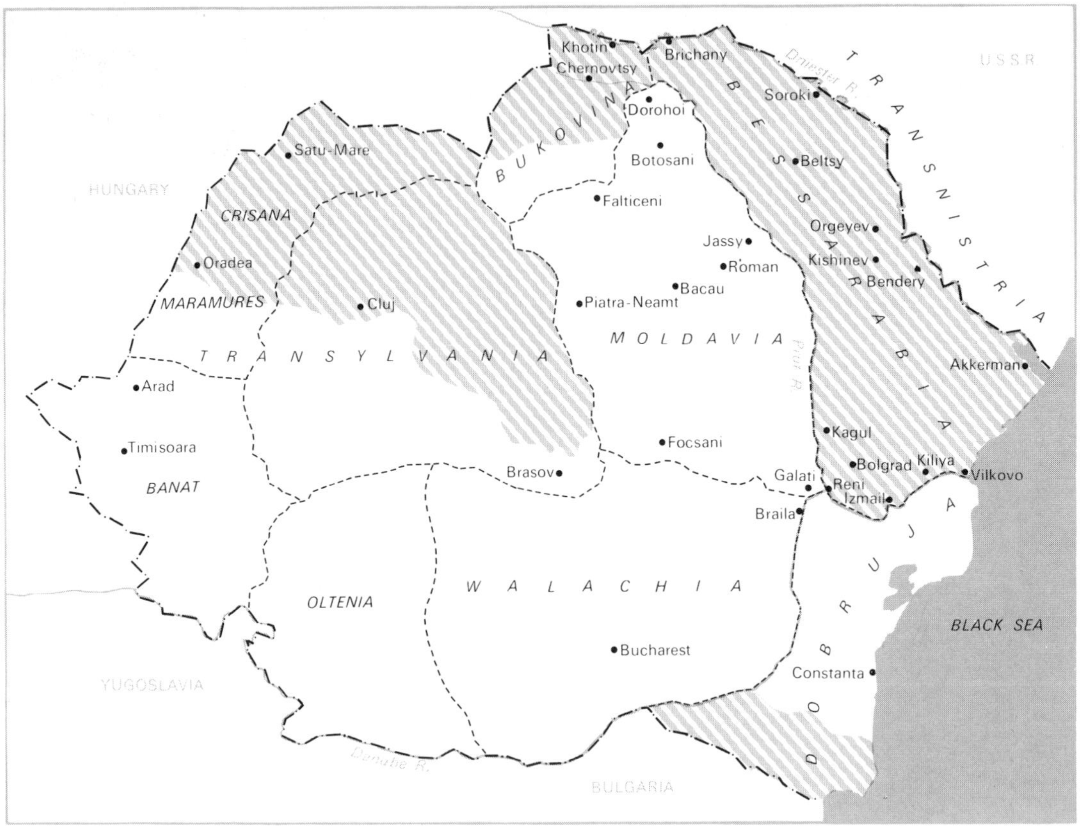

Map of Rumania (with main communities) showing areas (shaded) ceded to other countries.

and Poland in 17th c. formed various communities. Last group played important economic role in 18th, 19th c. Ḥasidism widespread. Jewish rights guaranteed at 1878 Congress of Berlin but citizenship not granted. Despite brief interludes of toleration, anti-Semitism rife throughout 19th and early 20th c. Emigration on large-scale. Jews prominent in economic development. During Holocaust mass deportation to Transnistria and 350,000 of 800,000 Jews exterminated. Since war, Rumanian government has shown increasingly, if guardedly, tolerant attitude toward Jews and State of Israel, even after Six-Day War. Over 200,000 Rumanian Jews have emigrated to Israel since 1948. Jewish pop. 100,000 (1971).

Rumkowski, Chaim Mordechai (1877–1944), "Elder of the Jews" in Lodz ghetto Oct. 1939–Aug. 1944. When ghetto was liquidated, he and his family voluntarily joined last transport of Jews to Auschwitz, where they were murdered.

Rumpler, Eduard (1872–1940), German pioneer aircraft manufacturer. His planes made first long-distance flights in Germany and were used by Germans in WWI. Brought out first car with front axle drive 1926.

Ruppin, Arthur (1876–1943), Zionist, economist, sociologist; b. Russia. Directed Jewish Statistics Bureau in Berlin 1903–07. Went to Ereẓ Israel 1907 as representative of Zionist Organization and established Palestine Office in Jaffa. Founded settlement companies, helped originate new methods of settlements. Director of Zionist Executive colonization dept. fr. 1921. Prof. of sociology of the Jews at Heb. Univ. Established 1925 and headed Berit Shalom. Wrote on sociology of Jews *(The Jews in the Modern World)*.

Arthur Ruppin

Russell (orig. **Levy**), **Henry** (1813–1900), English composer, singer. Child prodigy who performed before King George IV. Wrote nearly 800 songs, incl. "A Life on the Ocean Waves."

Russia, Jewish settlement in S. provinces dates fr. classical times. Kingdom of Khazars converted to Judaism in 8th c. Official Russian attitudes were hostile; successive expulsion orders issued in 18th c. Communities grew owing to Russian acquisitions by partitions of Poland (1772, 1793, 1795). Jewish Pale established 1804, restricted 1835, remained effective until 1915. Jews suffered fr. other hostile decrees, incl. compulsory military service (see Cantonists). Some toleration in 1860s but by end of century Jews had suffered devastating pogroms from May Laws. Jewish reaction expressed in mass emigration fr. early 1880s and increasing support of Zionism, socialism, and revolutionary movements. Throughout this period the Pale remained, with Poland, the great center of talmudic study. Anti-Jewish legislature abolished after 1917 revolution and Jews prominent in Soviet government. However, all communal institutions were soon restricted, use of Hebrew discouraged, and attempts made to change the economic basis of Jewish life. Community suffered during Nazi Holocaust. Vicious anti-Jewishness of Stalin's last years included suppression of Jewish cultural life and execution of leading figures.

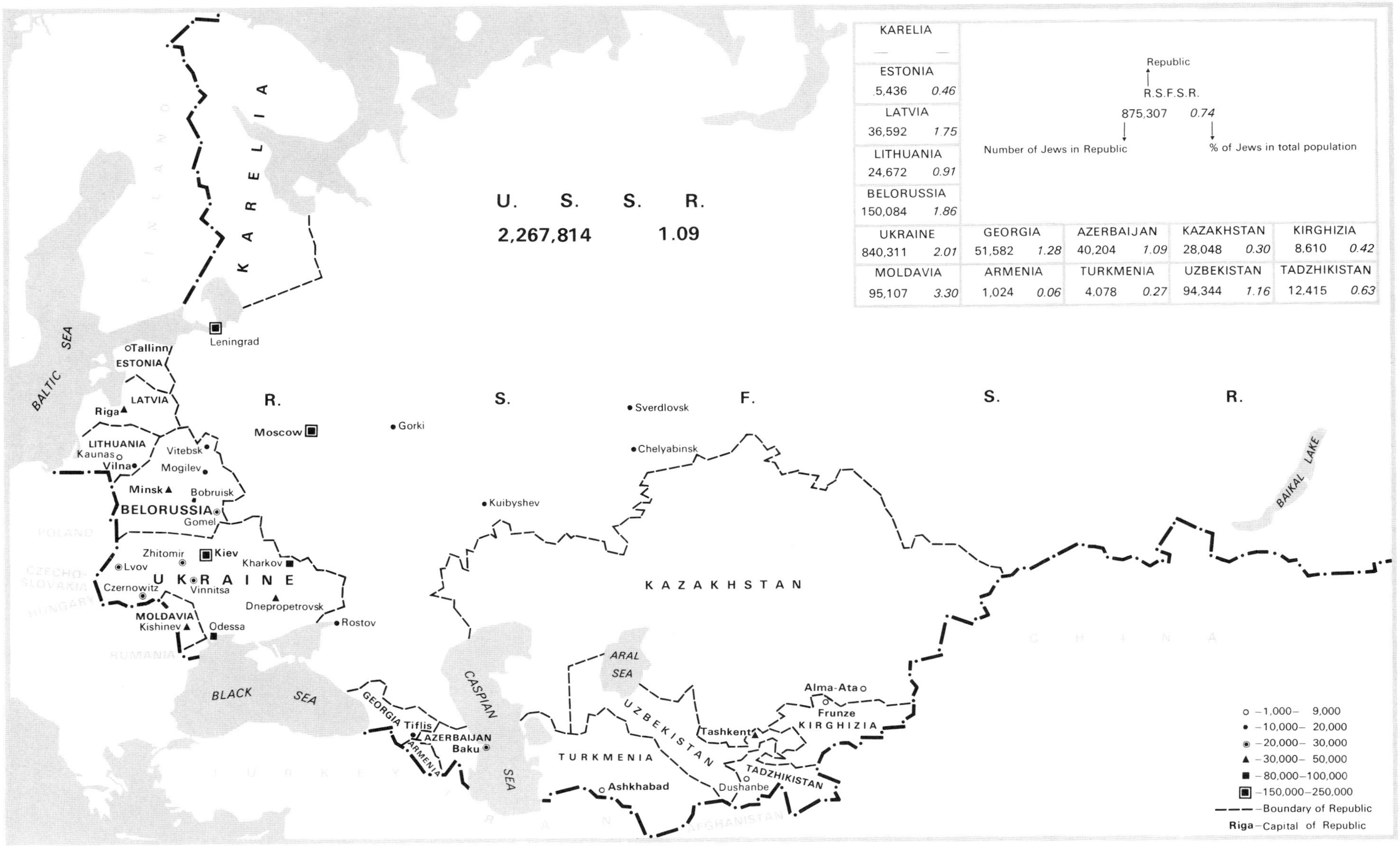

Jewish population of U.S.S.R., 1959, showing major centers of settlement and distribution among Republics.

IMMIGRATION OF U.S.S.R. JEWS TO ISRAEL

1950	–	290
1951	–	186
1952	–	56
1953	–	39
1954	–	26
1955	–	123
1956	–	460
1957	–	1,314
1958	–	720
1959	–	1,353
1960	–	1,917
1961	–	216
1962	–	184
1963	–	304
1964	–	530
1965	–	887
1966	–	2,027
1967	–	1,380
1968	–	224
1969	–	3,011
1970	–	982
1971	–	12,687
1972	–	32,000
1973	–	34,750

Three Jews (with beards, right) in Tatar market in the Crimea, from series of drawings by Leipzig engraver, Geissler, 1794–1802.

Culminated in "doctors' plot." After 1953 immediate threat removed, but government has maintained policy of restricting Jewish cultural expression. After 1967 Six-Day War strong Jewish nationalism swept many Russian Jews, who desired to emigrate to Israel. Such emigration was permitted (in limited number) fr. 1970. In 1947–8 Russia supported creation of State of Israel, but thereafter supported Arab cause and adopted increasingly hostile attitude, breaking off diplomatic relations with Israel on last day of Six-Day War. Acc. to 1969 census there were 2,151,000 Jews in Russia, although the actual figure is believed to be higher.

Pinḥas Rutenberg

Rutenberg, Pinḥas (Piotr; 1879–1942), engineer, Zionist leader; b. Ukraine. Prominent in 1905 Russian Revolution. Returned fr. Europe to Russia 1917 and was deputy governor of Moscow during Kerensky regime. In Ereẓ Israel fr. 1919. Obtained concession fr. British Mandatory government to harness Jordan waters. Established 1923 and headed Palestine Electric Co. Twice pres. of Va'ad Le'ummi.

Ruth, heroine of Book of Ruth; Moabite who had married a Hebrew living in Moab. On death of her husband, she chose to accompany her Hebrew mother-in-law, Naomi, to Beth-Lehem. Here she became the wife of Boaz and ancestress of King David.

Ruth, Book of, one of five scrolls in Hagiographa section of Hebrew Bible. In Septuagint, attached to Book of Judges. Tells story of Ruth and Naomi. Written not before period of Monarchy.

Ruthenia, see Subcarpathian Ruthenia.

Ruth Rabbah, early Palestinian amoraic exegetical Midrash expounding Book of Ruth verse by verse drawing upon tannaitic literature.

Ruzhin, Israel (Friedmann; 1797–1850), founder of ḥasidic dynasty. Lived in great luxury. Suspected of wishing to become ruler of Jews. Accused of causing death of two informers, imprisoned and released; then removed to Sadgora. His sons and descendants were ḥasidic leaders in Sadgora, Husyatin, Boyan, etc.

Ryback, Issachar (1897–1935), artist; b. Ukraine, in Paris fr. 1926. Influenced by French cubists and German expressionists. Some of his best work in Ryback House at Ramat Yosef in Israel.

Rymanower, Menahem Mendel (b. 1815), ḥasidic *ẓaddik* in Rymanow, SE Poland. Ascetic. Instituted regulations for weights and measures and was author of several homiletic works.

Rzeszow, town in SE Poland. Jews fr. 14th c. Haskalah movement influential; Ḥasidism spread in 19th c. 14,000 Jews in 1939; perished in WWII.

Jews outside Moscow synagogue

"The Blind Violinist," ceramic figure by Issachar Ryback.

Illuminated initial letter "S" of "Salvus" at opening of Psalm 68 in "Bohun Psalter," 14th cent.

Sa'adi, Sa'id ben Solomon (17th–18th c.), first Yemenite historian. Wrote chronicle of Jews in Yemen.
Saadiah al-Adeni, see Adani, Saadiah.
Saadiah (ben Joseph) Gaon (882–942), greatest scholar and author of geonic period and important leader of Babylonian Jewry; *gaon* of Sura. During course of bitter conflict 921–2, established calendar now in use and refuted Palestinian claim to final authority in this matter. Author of major philosophical work *Sefer ha-Emunot ve-ha-De'ot,* a systematic compilation of the prayer book, an Arabic translation and commentary on the Bible, *piyyutim,* halakhic works, and grammars. In all fields exerted powerful influence on contemporaries and later scholars. Bitter opponent of Karaites.
Saba, Abraham ben Jacob (d. c. 1508), Spanish exegete, preacher, kabbalist. Many of his works lost during persecution in Portugal. Later rewrote his commentaries from memory in Morocco.
Saba, Umberto (pseud. of **Umberto Poli;** 1883–1957). Italian poet. Lived mostly in Trieste, which was one of main subjects of his verse.
Sabath, Adolf Joachim (1866–1952), U.S. congressman; b. Bohemia, in U.S. fr. 1881. In Congress for 23 consecutive terms 1906–52. Liberal who vigorously supported New Deal and Fair Deal legislation. Chairman House Rules Committee 1939–47, 1949–52.
Sabbateanism, see Shabbetai Ẓevi.
Sabbath, 7th day of week, day of rest and abstention fr. work. Two themes in Bible explain Sabbath: sanctification of 7th day of creation and social rights of masters and slaves. Observance became characteristic feature of Judaism in all ages. Both philosophers and kabbalists regarded it as central institution in mainstream Judaism. At least two candles are kindled on eve and all work is forbidden. Friday night meal preceded by *Kiddush* and three festive meals eaten during Sabbath, during which special hymns are sung. After conclusion of Sabbath, *Havdalah* ceremony is recited. Mishnah (tractate Shabbat) lists 39 categories of work forbidden on the Sabbath.
Sabbatical Year, final year in cycle of 7 years; an ancient Israelite institution when all land had to be fallow and debts were remitted. Close of 7 sabbatical cycles instituted Jubilee (q.v.). In post-biblical times, problems concerned with remittance of debts were eventually ameliorated by Hillel's prosbul (q.v.). In modern times, it again became practical issue. Leading authorities granted permission for land to be sold to non-Jew, but very observant do not accept this and observe laws literally. Sabbatical years due in 5740 (1979/80), 5747 (1986/87), etc.

"Ushering in the Sabbath," painting by Moritz Oppenheim, Frankfort, 19th cent.

Sabbatyon, see Sambatyon.
Sabbioneta, town in Italy. Jews fr. 15th c. Best known for Hebrew press 1551–59.
Sabea (biblical **Sheba**), state in S. Arabia, contemporary with Jewish monarchy. Visit of Queen of Sheba (I Kings 10) is one of earliest examples of trade mission.
Sabin, Albert Bruce (1906–), U.S. scientist; b. Poland, in U.S. fr. 1921. Developed oral polio vaccine. Also did research on aspects of various infectious diseases. Pres. of Weizmann Inst. 1970–72.

Albert B. Sabin

Silver-gilt Sabbath candlesticks from Danzig, c. 1680.

Sabra (Aram. "cactus," "prickly pear"), nickname for native Israeli, referring metaphorically to prickly exterior and tender heart.

Sabsovich, Hirsch Loeb (1861–1915), U.S. agronomist; a leader of Am Olam movement. Directed founding of agricultural settlement in Woodbine, N.J. 1891 for Baron de Hirsch Fund and became Fund's agent in N.Y.

Sacerdote, David (1550–c. 1625), Italian composer, banker. Known as author of single work written in youth, *Il primo libro di madrigali a sei voci.*

Sacerdoti, Angelo-Raphael Chaim (1886–1935), chief rabbi of Rome fr. 1912. Active in revitalizing Italian Jewry, met Mussolini to ensure that Jews would not be harmed by Fascist regime. Active Zionist.

Abram L. Sachar

Sachar, Abram Leon (1899–), U.S. educator, historian. Organizer of B'nai B'rith Hillel Foundation (national director 1933–48). Founding pres. 1948, then chancellor 1968 of Brandeis Univ. and responsible for its rapid development. Writings incl. popular 1-vol. *History of the Jews.* His son, **Howard Morley** (1928–), historian. Taught modern and Middle Eastern history at George Washington Univ., Washington, D.C. fr. 1965, and wrote books on Israel and the Middle East as well as *The Course of Modern Jewish History.*

Sacher, Harry (1881–1971), British Zionist, lawyer. Member editorial staff of *Manchester Guardian* 1905–09, 1915–19. Worked closely with Weizmann. In Ereẓ Israel fr. 1919, where he practiced law. Served on Zionist Executive 1927–31, then returned to England. Wrote books on Zionism. His wife, **Miriam,** sister of Lord Marks, among leaders of WIZO. His son, **Michael** (1919–), headed Zionist fund-raising in Britain and elected member of Jewish Agency Executive 1971.

Sachs, Bernard (1858–1944), U.S. neurologist. Pioneer in child neurology; best known for description of Tay-Sachs disease in children. Prof. at Columbia Univ. Pres. First International Neurological Congress 1931.

Sachs, Curt (1881–1959), German musicologist. Taught in Berlin and after 1937 in New York. Pioneer in comparative study of musical instruments.

Sachs, Hanns (1881–1947), non-medical psychoanalyst. Worked in Vienna, Zurich, Berlin, Boston. Close to Freud. Early writings on dream interpretation and everyday errors. Late works mainly apply psychoanalysis to literature and art.

Sachs, Julius (1832–1897), German botanist; called creator of experimental botany. Prof. at Wuerzburg for nearly 30 years.

Sachs, Julius (1849–1934), U.S. educator. Founder and headmaster Sachs Collegiate Institute School of Boys in N.Y. 1871–1904 and prof. of secondary education at Columbia Teachers College 1902–17. Raised standard of secondary school education and improved teacher training.

Sachs, Maurice (orig. **Jean-Maurice Ettinghausen;** 1906–1945?), French author, critic, translator. Fell prey to alcoholism, homosexuality, and kleptomania in his youth; became Nazi collaborator. Most of his works are autobiographical.

Sachs, Michael (1808–1864), German rabbi, scholar. Preacher in Berlin fr. 1844. A leader of Wissenschaft des Judentums. Wrote many books and worked with Zunz on German translation of Bible.

Nelly Sachs receiving Nobel Prize for Literature from king of Sweden.

Sachs, Nelly (Leonie; 1891–1970), German poet, Nobel Prize winner 1966; in Sweden fr. 1940. Reputation largely rests on poems written after WWII, expressing unquenchable faith in indestructibility of people of Israel and importance of its mission.

Sachs, Senior (1815–1892), Hebrew scholar; b. Lithuania, in Paris fr. 1856. Published selections of mss. fr. medieval Jewish literature, concentrating esp. on Solomon ibn Gabirol.

Sachsenhausen-Oranienburg, Nazi concentration camp nr. Berlin, opened 1936. During war, became second largest concentration camp. Supplied slave labor for German armament industry. Evacuated April 1945. Half of 200,000 inmates sent there died.

Sack, Benjamin G. (1880–1967), Canadian journalist, historian. Author of Canadian Jewish history to end of 19th c.

Sackler, Harry (1883–), U.S. Hebrew, Yiddish author; b. Galicia, in U.S. fr. 1902. Held various Jewish communal posts. Exponent of historicism. Concerned with fathoming mystery of Jewish existence.

Sacramento, city in Calif., U.S. Jewish settlement fr. 1849. First congregation Orthodox B'nai Israel (1851). Jewish pop. 4,800 (1971).

Sacrifices: Sacrifices, commanded in the Pentateuch, were of various categories: propitiatory (sin-offerings and guilt-offerings), fellowship, votive, freewill, dedicatory, and ordination offerings as well as burnt-offerings, meal offerings, libations, wave offerings and communal peace offerings. Animals had to be brought from clean species. After the Temple was built, every effort was made to centralize all sacrifice on its premises but other centers emerged, notably in the northern Kingdom of Israel. All sacrifice ended with the destruction of the Second Temple; prayer was seen as a substitute and various aspects of the liturgy were instituted to replace the sacrificial system. The Orthodox continue to pray for the restoration of sacrifice but such prayers are omitted by the Reform.

Sacrilege, term for violation of sacred things which, even when inadvertent, requires atonement. Subject of Talmud tractate *Me'ilah.*

°**Sacy, Antoine Isaac Silvestre de** (1758–1838), French orientalist, Hebraist who opposed integration of Jews within Christian society as being equivalent to abolition of specific religious characteristics.

Sa'd al-Dawla al-Ṣafī ibn Hibbatallah (d. 1291), court physician, vizier in Mongol Persia. Established administration on basis of law and justice. His appointment of Jewish officials aroused opposition. His execution followed by reprisals against Jews in Tabriz and Baghdad.

Sadan (or **Sdan;** orig. **Stock), Dov** (1902–), Yiddish, Hebrew writer, scholar; b. Galicia, settled in Ereẓ Israel 1925. On staff of daily *Davar* and Am Oved publishing house. Prof. of Yiddish language and literature at Heb. Univ. Prolific critic of Hebrew, Yiddish literature.

Sadducees, sect composed largely of wealthier, aristocratic, priestly elements, formed c. 200 B.C.E. and frequently dominant in Temple worship. Rejected authority of Oral Law and interpreted Pentateuch literally; did not believe in immortality of the soul. Opposed by Pharisees. Disappeared with destruction of Temple.

Ṣade, see Ẓade.

Sadeh, Pinḥas (1929–), Hebrew writer. One of the best-known younger writers in Israel. He has published stories and poems.

Yiẓḥak Sadeh

Sadeh (Landsberg), Yiẓḥak (1890–1952), Israel soldier; b. Poland. Served in Russian army. Settled in Ereẓ Israel 1920 and was a founder of Gedud ha-Avodah and a leader of the Haganah. Palmaḥ founded 1941 largely on his initiative under his command until 1945. Commanded various operations in War of Independence. Wrote short stories, plays, memoirs.

Sadgora (Sadagora), town in Moldavia. Jews first settled there in 17th c., mainly engaged in commerce and crafts. 10,000 Jews before WWI but many left during that war. Community best known as center of Ḥasidism. After WWII, center of Sadgora dynasty transferred to Israel.

Safdie, Moshe (1938–), Canadian architect. Famed for revolutionary housing project "Habitat" based on modular housing scheme and shown at Montreal's Expo '67. Also worked in Israel.

Safed, principal town of Upper Galilee, Israel. First mentioned in Second Temple period. Jewish community in 13th c. In 16th c. became center of Jewish mysticism: Isaac Luria, Joseph Caro, and Ḥayyim Vital among its leading figures.

Habitat by Moshe Safdie.

Over 300 ḥasidim settled there 1778. Violent earthquake 1837. After 1948 mainly new immigrants fr. different countries settled there. Town is tourist center and has artists' colony. Pop. 13,200 (1971).

Safi (Asfi), Moroccan port. Jewish settlement fr. 15th c. Jews soon attained prominence as diplomats, officials, traders. Town often leased to Jews and became center of Torah learning. Community declined after 1957 and numbered less than 700 in 1968.

Safran, Alexander (1910–), Rumanian rabbi, author. Chief rabbi fr. 1940; brought pressure on government to resist Nazi demand to deport Jews. Chief rabbi of Geneva fr. 1948. Son of B. Z. Safran.

Safran, Bezalel Ze'ev (1866–1930), Rumanian rabbi; most important halakhic authority in Rumania. Many responsa and works published. Described as "a living library of the vast rabbinic literature."

Safrin, Isaac Judah Jehiel (1806–1874), ḥasidic leader, kabbalist; son of founder of Komarno branch of Zhidachov dynasty. Recorded dreams and visions of his childhood. According to his theory of impure thoughts many ḥasidic leaders were heretics.

Sahl ben Maẓliaḥ (11th c.), Karaite scholar. He traveled widely, but his home was in Ereẓ Israel. His works include an Arabic commentary on the Pentateuch and polemics against the Rabbanites.

Sahl, Mort (1927–), U.S. comedian, satirist excelling in monologue. Directed satire mostly at political figures.

Sahula, Isaac ben Solomon Abi (b. 1244), Spanish Hebrew poet, scholar, kabbalist. Wrote *Meshal ha-Kadmoni* in vein of *Sinbad the Sailor* which was frequently reprinted and translated into Yiddish and German.

Sahula, Meir ben Solomon Abi (1260? –after 1335), Spanish kabbalist, halakhist; brother of Isaac Sahula. Wrote commentary on *Sefer ha-Bahir.*

Sa'īd ibn Hasan (13th–14th c.), Alexandrian Jew; convert to Islam who attempted to prove truth of his new religion against Judaism and Christianity.

Saineanu, Lazar (Lasar Schein; 1859–1934), Rumanian philologist, folklorist. Despite baptism, denied Rumanian citizenship. Fr. 1901 in Paris; taught at Sorbonne. Wrote monumental study on oriental influences in Rumanian culture and language. Also wrote on French slang and Rabelais.

St. James's Conference, round-table conference with Jewish and Arab leaders (separately) convened by British government in Feb.–March 1939 to discuss "the establishment of an independent Palestine State possibly of a federal nature." Both delegations rejected proposal. After its failure British government issued MacDonald White Paper.

St. Jean D'Acre, see Acre.

Saint-Léon, Arthur Michel (1815? –1870), French dancer, choreographer. Creator of famous

"Bimah" of Rabbi Isaac Aboab Synagogue, Safed.

Arthur Saint-Léon, with his wife Fanny Cerito, in "Le Violon du Diable."

19th c. ballets. Toured European capitals and worked for Paris Opera and at Imperial Theater in St. Petersburg.

St. Louis, city in Mo., U.S. First recorded Jewish settler 1807. First congregation United Hebrew Congregation 1841. In 1850s and 1860s dissent between traditionalists and early Reform. E. European immigration fr. 1881, not welcomed by veterans. Zionism took root by 1890, mainly among newcomers. Jewish pop. 60,000 (1971).

Saint Paul, see Minneapolis-Saint Paul.

Saint Petersburg, see Leningrad.

Sajaroff, Miguel (1873–1958), pioneer of agrarian cooperativism in Argentina; b. Crimea, in Argentina fr. 1899. Pres. cooperative Fondo Communal in Domínguez 1908.

Sakel, Manfred Joshua (1900–1957), Austrian psychiatrist. Developed details of insulin coma treatment, which for many years was standard therapy in schizophrenia. Fervent Zionist; supported Irgun Ẓeva'i Le'ummi movement.

Sakharoff, Alexander (1886–1963), Russian dancer. With wife presented programs of "abstract mime" throughout Europe for nearly 40 years. Fr. 1953 they taught in Rome.

Salaman, Charles Kensington (1814–1901), English pianist, composer. Elected member of Royal Academy of Music at age 10. Prolific writer in English, Italian, Hebrew. Composed over 100 settings for West London (Reform) Synagogue service.

Salaman, Malcolm Charles (1855–1940), English playwright, writer on drama and art; son of Charles Kensington Salaman. Art and drama critic *Sunday Times* 1883–94. Wrote on printing and engraving.

Salaman, Redcliffe Nathan (1874–1955), English pathologist, geneticist. One of his major achievements was initiation of stocks of virus-free seed potatoes. Active in Jewish community and Zionism. His wife **Nina Ruth** (1877–1925) translated medieval Hebrew poetry into English.

Salamanca, city in W. Spain. One of oldest Jewish settlements in Spain. Toward end of 13th c. Jews accorded equal rights with Christians. Community spared persecution of 1391, but later Vicente Ferrer persuaded many Jews to convert and in 1413 most Jews left Judaism. Community recovered during 15th c. Ritual murder accusation 1456. After 1492 expulsion, Salamanca Univ. continued to be center of Hebrew studies.

Jonas E. Salk

Salamon, Ernö (1922–1943), Hungarian poet. As Communist, his chief subject was suffering of exploited workers. Killed in forced labor unit in WWII.

Salant, Joseph Sundel ben Benjamin Benish (1786–1866), spiritual father of Musar movement; b. Lithuania, settled in Jerusalem 1837. His pupil Israel Salanter held him up as ideal ethical man.

Salant, Samuel (1816–1909), chief rabbi of Jerusalem and leading figure in developing its institutions, the Eẓ Ḥayyim Yeshivah, Bikkur Ḥolim Hospital. A moderating influence in intercommunal frictions. Son-in-law of Joseph Sundel Salant.

Salanter, Israel, see Lipkin, Israel.

Salem, see Jerusalem.

Salem, Emmanuel Raphael (1859–1940), Greek lawyer. Specialized in international law of capitulations. Member of Ottoman delegation to 1922 Lausanne Conference. Active in communal life of Salonika and in last years pres. of Sephardi congregation of Paris.

Salé-Rabat, twin towns in Morocco. Jews there in 2nd c. Jewish merchants achieved prominence in 16th c.; in 18th, 19th c. also served as diplomats and consuls for European powers. Community was active center of Jewish learning and Shabbateanism with many followers. Conditions deteriorated in 19th c. when Jews were confined to two mellahs and impoverished. After 1947 most Jews emigrated to America and Europe; those of Salé to Israel. 4,000 remained in 1970.

Salfeld, Siegmund (1843–1926), German rabbi, historian. Wrote on German Jewry and history of Mainz community.

Salinger, Jerome David (1919–), U.S. author. Became known with celebrated first novel *Catcher in the Rye.* Later writings incl. a series about Irish-Jewish Glass family of New York (*Franny and Zooey,* etc.).

Salisbury, capital of Rhodesia. Jewish congregation fr. 1895. Sephardi congregation founded 1931, Reform 1960. City had number of Jewish mayors. Jewish pop. 2,500 (1971).

Salk, Jonas Edward (1914–), U.S. epidemologist; originator of Salk poliomyelitis vaccine. Helped develop influenza vaccine. Prof. at Univ. of Pittsburgh until 1963 and then founded Salk Institute for Biological Studies, La Jolla, Calif. His vaccine was first effective weapon against polio.

Salkind, Jacob Meir (1875–1937), Hebrew, Yiddish writer; b. Russia, settled in England. Became anarchist. Published hundreds of articles and translated Talmud tractates into Yiddish.

Salkinson, Isaac Edward (Eliezer; 1820–1883), British convert to Christianity who went as Presbyterian missionary to Vienna 1876. Translated Milton, Shakespeare, and New Testament into biblical Hebrew.

Salmon, family of English caterers. **Alfred** (1868–1928), founder of J. Lyons & Co. His brother, **Isidor** (1876–1941), revolutionized army catering during WWI. Conservative member of parliament fr. 1924.

Salmon, Alexander (1822–1866), English traveler; married chieftainess of Teva clan of Tahiti and became chief adviser to rulers of Tahiti.

Salmon, Sir Cyril Barnet (1903–), English judge. Lord justice of appeal fr. 1964.

Salmon, Karel (Karl Salomon; 1897–1974), Israel composer; b. Heidelberg, settled in Ereẓ Israel 1933. Directed broadcasting service music dept. Many of his works blend European heritage with Eastern and Jewish folklore material.

Salmon ben Jeroham (10th c.), Karaite polemicist; native of Israel or Iraq. His principal work, *Milḥamot Adonai,* is rhymed attack in Hebrew on Rabbanites and Saadiah Gaon.

Salome (1st c. C.E.), daughter of Herod Philip and Herodias. Acc. to New Testament (but not Josephus), responsible for execution of John the Baptist by Herod Antipas. Married her uncle, tetrarch Philip.

Salome Alexandra (Heb. **Shelom Ẓiyyon,** 137–67 B.C.E.), queen of Judea 76–67, succeeding her husband Alexander Yannai. Strict observer of religious traditions; reversed husband's inimical policy toward Pharisees. In foreign affairs, policy generally peaceful.

Salomon, Albert (1891–1966), German sociologist. Taught in Berlin and after 1933 in New York. Took account of importance of literature in developing theory of society.

Salomon, Alice (1872–1948), German economist, educator. Active mainly in training of women for professional social work and their inclusion in that field.

Salomon, Charlotte (1917–1943), German painter. Her works were salvaged after Holocaust and are pictorial record of Hitler's anti-Jewish excesses. D. Auschwitz.

Salomon, Erich (1886–1944), German photographer. One of world's first photo-historians; covered various international gatherings often employing ingenious subterfuges to conceal his camera. D. Auschwitz.

Salomon, Gotthold (1784–1862), German preacher, reformer. Many of his sermons published. Isaac Bernays banned the prayer book he composed.

Statue of Haym Salomon erected by Jewish Federation Council of Los Angeles, 1944.

Salomon, Haym (1740–1785), early American merchant, revolutionary war patriot; b. Poland, in America fr. 1775. Helped American prisoners escape fr. British during war; later financed some American leaders. Contributed to American and Jewish charities.

Salomon, Joel Moses (1838–1912), Ereẓ Israel pioneer. Established with others printing press in Jerusalem and printed first issues of the periodical *Ha-Levanon.* Among founders of new quarters in Jerusalem and also of Petaḥ Tikvah and nearby settlement Yahud.

Salomon, Julius (1853–1922), Danish archivist, historian of 19th c. Danish Jewry. Secretary to upper house of Danish parliament 1907–17.

Salomon, Karl, see Salmon, Karel.

Salomons, Sir David (1797–1873), first Jewish lord mayor of London 1855, one of first Jews to participate in development of joint stock banking in Britain. Prominent in campaign to abolish last Jewish disabilities. Elected to parliament 1851 but had to withdraw on his refusal to take Christological oath; eventually seated 1859.

Salomons, Sir Julian Emanuel (1836–1909), Australian politician, jurist. Solicitor general of New South Wales 1869–71 and twice agent general for colony in London. Helped formulate 1900 Imperial Decree.

Salomonsen, Carl Julius (1849–1924), Danish physician, bacteriologist. Known as last polyhistor at Univ. of Copenhagen.

Salonika (Thessaloniki), Greek port. Jewish settlement fr. Hellenistic and Roman periods. Community suffered persecution during Byzantine period and under Latin Empire, and was affected by messianic ferment of 11th c. After 1492, haven for Spanish refugees and Marranos; by 16th c. pivot of Sephardi culture and in 17th c. largest community in world. Despite strong leanings toward Shabbateanism (center of Doenmeh sect), it retained its influential scholastic and commercial position until 20th c. Despite some emigration, Jewish pop. 60,000 in 1935. Most port workers were Jewish and port closed on Sabbaths. Almost all Jews deported to Poland by Nazis. Further emigration after WWII mostly to Israel but also to Paris, etc. 1,114 Jews in 1972.

Salsberg, Joseph B. (1902–), Canadian labor leader. Associated with Po'alei Zion, then became Communist. Canadian vice-pres. Hatters' International Union. Labor Progressive member Ontario legislature 1943–55. After visit to USSR 1956, left Communist Party.

Salten, Felix (1869–1947), Austrian novelist, playwright, critic; creator of "Bambi." In U.S. during WWII.

Saltzman, Harry (1915–), film producer. Films incl. *Look Back in Anger, The Entertainer, Saturday Night and Sunday Morning,* and James Bond series.

Salus, Hugo (1866–1929), Prague poet. Considered by contemporary critics as foremost German lyricist. Militant protagonist of German liberalism and Jewish assimilation.

Salvador, Francis (1747–1776), American revolutionary patriot; first Jew to serve in legislative body in America (South Carolina 1775–76) and first Jew to give his life in struggle for American independence. Nephew and son-in-law of Joseph Salvador.

Salvador, Joseph (1716–1786), English, American merchant; first Jew to be made director of Dutch East India Co. Active in synagogue and philanthropic affairs in London Sephardi community.

Salvador, Joseph (1796–1873), French scholar. Known mainly for interest in history of religions and for attempt to outline universal creed.

Salonika memorial to victims of Holocaust.

Salvendi, Adolf (1837–1914), German rabbi; opponent of Reform movement. Did much for needy Jews of Russia and Ḥibbat Zion in W. Europe.

Salzburg, city and province in W. Austria, formerly archbishopric and duchy. Jews in archbishopric fr. 9th c. and in city fr. 1282. Community massacred during Black Death persecutions 1349 and after Host Desecration accusation 1404. Resettled 1418 but banished 1498. Full equality 1867. After *Anschluss* almost all Jews deported. Community reestablished 1953.

Samael, name for Satan or angel of death appearing in apocryphal and amoraic literature, and leader of rebellion of heavenly angels. In later literature he appears as bringer of death into the world.

Samama, Nessim (1805–1873), Tunisian *qā'id,* treasurer and controller of finances. Maintained yeshivah in Jerusalem which bore his name. In 1864 appropriated 20 million gold francs entrusted to him by the state and settled in Paris and Leghorn.

Samara, see Kuibyshev.

Samaria (Sebaste), capital of kingdom of Israel in 9th–8th c. B.C.E. Ancient city founded by King Omri

of Israel c. 880 B.C.E. Taken by Sargon II of Assyria 722–21 and its inhabitants deported. Colonists from Babylonia, Cutha, and Hamath replaced deportees and with Israelite remnant formed nucleus of Samaritan pop. Destroyed by John Hyrcanus. Pompey reestablished Greek town. Apart from remains of ancient city, there is now an Arab village on the site (1967 pop. 1,272).

Remains of forum built in Samaria by Herod, c. 30 B.C.E.

Raising of Torah scroll by Samaritan priest on 7th day of Passover.

Wood engraving of Samarkand Jews in traditional striped garb, c. 1870.

Excavations have uncovered remains of Israelite and Roman palaces, Roman theater, etc.

Samaritans, pop. of Samaria after destruction of kingdom of Israel in 721 B.C.E. Originated fr. mixture of peoples who adopted Jewish life. Regard themselves as direct descendants of tribes of Ephraim and Manasseh. Rebuffed by Nehemiah and schism became permanent. Built temple on Mt. Gerizim which was destroyed by John Hyrcanus. In Middle Ages there were also communities in Cairo, Damascus, etc. However, persecution made great inroads and today they number 400 (300 in Shechem (Nablus) and 100 in Ḥolon). Samaritan scriptures consist of Pentateuch with their own interpretation of festivals and customs. At Passover they sacrifice the paschal lamb on Mt. Gerizim. They practice circumcision, have their own marriage and divorce laws. Their literature and *halakhah* are centered on Pentateuch. In State of Israel they are recognized as independent religious community.

Samarkand, capital of Samarkand district, Uzbek SSR. Jews mentioned in 12th c. but community destroyed 1598. Bukharan Jews lived in specific quarter 1843 but situation improved after 1868. Ashkenazi Jews settled after 1888. With 1917 Revolution many institutions closed. 9,832 Jews in 1935, and during WWII Jewish refugees arrived there. 15,000 Jews in 1970, mainly Bukharan.

Samau'al ben Judah ibn Abbas (c. 1125–1175), Baghdad convert to Islam, physician, author of anti-Jewish manual.

Sambari, Joseph ben Isaac (1640–1703), Egyptian chronicler whose mss. shed light on Jewish life in Egypt as well as general Islamic history.

Sambatyon (also **Sanbatyon** and **Sabbatyon**), legendary river across which part of Ten Tribes was exiled by Assyrians. Impassable during week and when it became still on the Sabbath, tribes were not allowed to cross because of sanctity of the day.

Sambursky, Daniel (1909–), Israel composer; b. Koenigsberg, settled in Ereẓ Israel 1932; brother of Samuel Sambursky. Many of his songs entered folk repertoire. Coedited 3-vol. *Sefer Shirim u-Manginot,* one of standard anthologies of Israel songs.

Sambursky, Samuel (1900–), Israel scientist, historian; b. Koenigsberg, settled in Ereẓ Israel 1924. Director of Research Council of Israel 1949–56, dean of Heb. Univ. faculty of science 1957, prof. of history and philosophy of science. Israel Prize 1968.

Samekh (ס), 15th letter of Hebrew alphabet; numerical value 60. Pronounced *s.*

Saminsky, Lazare (1882–1959), composer; b. Russia. Among founders of Society for Jewish Folk Music. Music director of Temple Emanu-El in New York fr. 1923. Composed symphonies, liturgical music, etc.

Samkalden, Ivo (1912–), Dutch jurist, politician. Minister of justice 1956–58, 1965–66, and first Jewish mayor of Dutch city (Amsterdam) 1967.

Samoilovich, Rudolph Lazarevich (1884–), Soviet mining engineer, Arctic explorer. Became international celebrity 1928 leading Soviet expedition to rescue survivors of General Umberto Nobile's Arctic flight in dirigible *Italia.*

Samokovlija, Isak (1889–1955), Yugoslav author. Wrote about Jewish life in Bosnia.

Sampter, Jessie Ethel (1883–1938), U.S. poet, Zionist writer; settled in Ereẓ Israel 1919. Active in educational and social work, esp. among Yemenites. Wrote series of 15 prose poems, *The Emek.* Joined Kibbutz Givat Brenner 1933.

Samra, David (d. 1960), Iraqi jurist. Deputy pres. of Baghdad court of appeals 1923, highest rank held by Iraqi Jew under British rule.

Samson, judge in Israel who fought against Philistines and whose strength was legendary (Judg. 13–16). Incidents of his life stem from his involvement with three Philistine women: a woman from Timnah, a prostitute from Gaza, and Delilah. Delilah betrayed him by giving away secret of his strength,

Miniature of Samson rending the lion, from "British Museum Miscellany," Troyes (?), c. 1280.

which as a Nazirite lay in his unshorn hair. Career ended in final act of desperate heroism, pulling down supporting pillars of temple in Gaza and bringing death upon himself and many Philistines.

Samson ben Abraham of Sens (12th–13th c.), French tosafist. His commentary on Mishnah orders *Zera'im* and *Tohorot* is standard and printed in all editions of Talmud. Emigrated to Ereẓ Israel and died in Acre.

Samson ben Eliezer (14th c.), German scribe. Authority on writing of scrolls of the Law, *tefillin,* and *mezuzot,* into which he introduced many improvements. Went to Ereẓ Israel and wrote book on sacred writing.

Samson ben Isaac of Chinon (14th c.), French tosafist. Author of *Sefer Keritut,* methodology of Talmud frequently reprinted and commented upon.

Samuel (11th c. B.C.E.), Israelite judge, prophet; son of Hannah, who dedicated him to Sanctuary; brought up by priest Eli. Became key personality among Israelites and was instrumental in transition from a loose confederation of tribes to centralized monarchy. Played part in events which eventually saw his people completely free fr. subjugation to Philistines. (I Sam. 1–16). Anointed Saul but later despaired of him and his family and anointed David to succeed Saul. His traditional tomb is at Nabī-Samwīl nr. Jerusalem.

Samuel (Mar; 2nd–3rd c.), Babylonian *amora,* head of Nehardea academy; the outstanding authority on Jewish civil law in his day; a physician and astronomer who could say "the paths of Heaven are as familiar to me as the streets of Nehardea." Author of principle "the law of the state is binding" upon Jews in civil law. His discussions with his colleague Rav are frequently quoted in Talmud.

Samuel, Book of, eighth book of Hebrew Bible and third in subdivision of Former Prophets. Originally single unit; Septuagint and Vulgate divided book in two. Relates history of Israel under Saul and David. Finished form dates fr. c. 6th c. B.C.E.

Samuel, Herbert Louis, First Viscount (1870–1963), British statesman, philosopher. Entered parliament 1902, held office in Liberal government 1906–16, first professing Jew to be member of British cabinet (fr. 1909). His 1915 memorandum concerning British

Herbert Samuel

protectorate for Jewish center in Ereẓ Israel influenced Balfour Declaration. First High Commissioner of Palestine 1920–25. Home secretary in the national government 1931–32. Later, Liberal leader in House of Commons and House of Lords. Order of Merit 1958. Wrote on philosophy. His son, **Edwin, Second Viscount Samuel** (1898–), high official in Mandatory administration in Ereẓ Israel; later headed Israel Institute of Public Administration. Wrote stories and memoirs.

Samuel, Marcus, see Bearsted.

Samuel, Maurice (1895–1972), U.S. author, translator; b. Rumania, went to U.S. 1914 via England. Influential and popular exponent of Zionist ideology. Wrote on Yiddish language and literature, anti-Semitism, biblical figures, and the Beilis Trial. Translated from Yiddish and Hebrew.

Samuel, Ralph E. (1892–1967), U.S. investment banker. Started one of first mutual funds in U.S. Pres. Federation of Jewish Philanthropies 1948–51 and active in American Jewish Committee.

Samuel, Sir Saul (1820–1900), Australian politician, communal figure; New South Wales' first elected Jewish member of parliament 1859. Subsequently held ministerial posts and was prominent in Jewish communal affairs.

Samuel ben Ali (d. 1194), Baghdad *gaon*, known chiefly for his polemics with Maimonides. Had far-reaching influence in Jewish communities of Assyria, Iraq, etc.

Samuel ben Avigdor (1720–1793), last chief rabbi of Vilna, Lithuania. Mentioned with great reverence in rabbinic literature. Ousted fr. post after dispute with community in which civil authorities were involved.

Samuel ben Azariah (13th c.), last exilarch in Baghdad under Abbasid dynasty. Retained office after Mongols conquered Baghdad.

Samuel ben David (Rashbad; 12th c.), Provençal commentator, *posek,* preacher. Highly esteemed scholar; wrote commentary to Talmud of which only fragments have survived.

Samuel ben David Moses ha-Levi (1625? –1681), Polish rabbi. Author of popular and important *Naḥalat Shivah* on formulation of civil and matrimonial deeds.

Samuel ben Hophni (d. 1013), *gaon* of Sura. Wrote prolifically in all fields of Jewish knowledge. Fragments of his work found in Genizah. Father-in-law of Pumbedita *gaon* Hai.

Samuel ben Kalonymus he-Ḥasid ("The Pious") of Speyer (12th c.), first leader of German Ḥasidei

I & II SAMUEL – CONTENTS

I Samuel	1:1–7:17	Samuel
	1:1–2:10	Samuel's birth and dedication to the Lord
	2:11–3:21	Announcement of doom of the priestly family of Eli
	4:1–22	Samuel's war against the Philistines at Aphek; the death of Eli and his sons
	5:1–6:21	The Ark in Philistia and its return
	7:1–17	Samuel's miraculous deliverance from the hands of the Philistines at Mizpah
I Samuel	8:1–15:35	Samuel and Saul
	8:1–22	The people's demand for a king
	9:1–10:21	Saul in search of the lost asses; his anointment as king
	11:1–15	The battle of Jabesh-Gilead
	12:1–25	The "last words" of Samuel
	13:1–14:52	Saul's military campaigns against the Philistines
	15:1–35	The war against the Amalekites; the rejection of Saul
I Samuel	16:1–31:13	Saul and David
	16:1–23	The anointment of David
	17:1–58	David and Goliath
	18:1–30	Saul's jealousy and his plan to kill David
	19:1–27:12	David as refugee
	28:1–31:13	The battle of Gilboa; the death of Saul and his sons
II Samuel	1:1–8:18	David's rise to power
	1:1–27	David sings a dirge over Saul and Jonathan
	2:1–32	David anointed in Hebron; Ish-Bosheth king of Israel
	3:1–5	David and his family in Hebron
	3:6–39	Abner, David, and Joab
	4:1–12	The death of Ish-Bosheth
	5:1–25	David becomes king of Israel; Jerusalem becomes the capital
	6:1–23	The Ark brought to Jerusalem
	7:1–29	Nathan's prophecy concerning the Temple
	8:1–18	Summary of David's wars; a list of his chief officials
II Samuel	9:1–20:26	Court history of David
	9:1–13	David and Mephibosheth
	10:1–19	David's wars against the Ammonites
	11:1–27	David, Uriah, and Bath-Sheba
	12:1–24	Nathan denounces David concerning Uriah and Bath-Sheba; the birth of Solomon
	12:25–31	The end of the war against the Ammonites
	13:1–39	Amnon, Tamar, and Absalom
	14:1–33	Absalom's return to Jerusalem
	15:1–19:44	The rebellion of Absalom
	20:1–22	The rebellion of Sheba
	20:23–26	David's chief officials
II Samuel	21:1–24:25	Appendix concerning David's reign
	21:1–14	The burial of Saul and his descendants
	21:15–22	David's heroes
	22:1–51	A psalm attributed to David (= Ps. 18)
	23:1–7	The "last words" of David
	23:8–39	Summary of the feats of David's heroes
	24:1–25	The Census of Israel

Ashkenaz movement and father of Judah he-Ḥasid. Contributed to *Sefer Ḥasidim*. Thought to possess magical powers.

Samuel ben Meir (Rashbam; c. 1080–c. 1174), French biblical, talmudic commentator and tosafist; grandson of Rashi. His Pentateuch commentary has been frequently printed and is characterized by lucidity. His best-known work is commentary on *Bava Batra*, written to supplement what Rashi failed to complete and printed in all editions of Babylonian Talmud.

Samuel ben Naḥman (Naḥamani; 3rd–4th c.), Palestinian *amora;* one of most noted aggadists of his time. His halakhic decisions recorded in both Talmuds.

Samuel ben Samson (13th c.), Ereẓ Israel settler. Described his journey fr. France in extant letter dated 1210 which contains much information of historical interest.

Samuel ben Solomon of Falaise (Sir Morel; 13th c.), tosafist. Teacher of Meir b. Baruch of Rothenburg and participant in disputation in Paris with Nicholas Donin.

Samuel ben Uri Shraga Phoebus (17th c.), Polish rabbi. Author of standard commentary to *Shulḥan Arukh Even ha-Ezer* called *Beit Shemu'el.*

Samuel Commission, inquiry commission sent 1919 by British government to Poland to examine causes of anti-Semitic tension. Headed by Sir Stuart Samuel, pres. of Board of Deputies of British Jews.

Samuel ha-Katan (2nd c. C.E.), *tanna* famed for modesty. Author of blessing against sectarians and informers, *Birkat ha-Minim,* incorporated in *Amidah.*

Samuel ha-Nagid (ibn Nagrel'a; 993–1055/56), vizier of Granada, statesman, military commander, halakhist, poet. Forced to flee fr. Córdoba and rose to high rank in Granada. His victory over army of Almeria elicited celebration of special "Purim" by Jews of Granada. His halakhic writings directly influenced later halakhists, such as Isaac Alfasi. His poetry was of high level. Wrote grammatical works and introduction to Talmud. Outstanding patron of Jewish scholars.

Samuel ha-Shelishi ben Hoshana (d. after 1012), Palestinian liturgical poet, eminent talmudic scholar.

Samuel ibn 'Ādiyā (6th c.), poet in Hejaz. His work ranks with finest heroic traditional Arabic battle poetry of pre-Islam period and shows little trace of Jewish origin and themes. Famed for noble nature.

Samuel of Evreux (called "the prince from Evreux; 13th c.), talmudist, tosafist of Normandy who, with his brothers Moses and Isaac, headed well-known yeshivah.

Samuelson, Paul Anthony (1915–), U.S. economist; Nobel Prize winner 1970. Served U.S. government in various posts; prof. at MIT fr. 1960. Major interests: economic theory, statistics, econometics. His writings are classic works in their field.

Paul A.
Samuelson

San'a, capital of Yemen. Acc. to tradition Jewish settlement dates fr. Babylonian Exile. Community played important role in spiritual and cultural life of other Jews of Yemen. Endured harsh suffering in 17th c. and 1948. Most of its 6,000 Jews left for Israel, and only 150 remained in 1968.

San Antonio, city in Tex., U.S. Permanent Jewish community established c. 1850. First formal congregation Temple Beth-El (Reform) founded 1874. Jewish pop. 6,250 (1971).

Sanballat I, governor of Samaria who opposed Nehemiah's efforts to build walls of Jerusalem 445 B.C.E.

Sanballat II, governor of Samaria in early 4th c. B.C.E. known fr. Aramaic papyrus and clay sealing discovered in Wadi Dāliya.

Sanballat III (4th c. B.C.E.), "satrap" of Samaria, appointed by Darius III. His daughter married high priest of Jerusalem. Received permission fr. Alexander the Great to build temple on Mt. Gerizim.

Sanbar (Sandberg), Moshe (1926–), Israel economist; b. Hungary, prisoner in German concentration camps in WWII, settled in Israel 1948. Appointed governor of Bank of Israel 1971.

Sanches, Francisco (1550–1623), Marrano philosopher, physician. Prof. at Univ. of Toulouse. Considered by some as first modern philosopher. Influenced later skeptics as well as major philosophers in 17th c.

Sanchez, Antonio Nuñes Ribeiro (1699–1783), Marrano physician; b. Portugal. Ministered to Russian Imperial family. One of his works was first to inform European physicians of medical value of Russian vapor baths.

Sánchez, Gabriel (d. 1505), treasurer of kingdom of Aragon under Ferdinand and Isabella; his father had converted whole family to Christianity. Assisted Christopher Columbus in collecting funds for his voyages.

Sanctification, see Kiddush; Kedushah.

Sanctification of the Divine Name, see Kiddush Ha-Shem.

Sanctuary, see Tabernacle; Temple.

Sandak (Heb.), person holding child on his knees during circumcision.

"Circumcision," painting by Romeyn de Hooghe, 1665, showing "sandak" holding child.

Temple of Congregation Emanu-El, San Francisco.

Session of French Sanhedrin convened in Paris, 1807.

Sandalfon, name of angel. Acc. to Merkabah literature he stands behind heavenly throne weaving crowns fr. prayers of Israel.

San Diego, city in Calif., U.S. Earliest Jewish settlers believed to have arrived 1850. First formal congregation Beth Israel (Reform) 1888. Community grew in 1930s, 1940s. Jewish pop. 13,000 (1971).

Sandler, Jacob Koppel (d. 1931), composer, music director; b. Belaya Tserkov, in U.S. fr. 1888. Choral director for several well-known cantors and directed Yiddish theater choruses. Composer of *"Eili, Eili."*

San Francisco, city in Calif., U.S. First Jewish settlers 2nd quarter of 19th c. First congregations Shearith Israel and Emanu-El 1850. Community active, with 5 community centers and other agencies. Jewish pop. 73,000 (1971), with another 22,000 in metropolitan area.

Sanhedrin, supreme political, religious, and judicial body in Ereẓ Israel during Roman period and until c. 425 C.E. While Hellenistic sources depict it chiefly as political and judicial council headed by ruler, tannaitic sources regard it as supreme religious legislative body of 71 elders situated in Temple, from "where the law went forth to all Israel." Acted as court in rare cases. Modern scholars differ as to whether there may have been two or more such bodies, since word is applicable to any type of ruler's council or confederation.

Sanhedrin, fourth tractate in Mishnah order *Nezikin,* with *gemara* in both Talmuds. Deals with composition and competence of courts of different kinds, legal procedure, and criminal law. Chapter 10 contains statement, "All Israel have a portion in the world to come" and goes on to discuss resurrection.

Sanhedrin, French, Jewish assembly of 71 members convened in Paris March 1807. Followed Assembly of Notables convened by decree of Napoleon May 1806 to clarify relations between Napoleonic state and Jews. Decision of 111-man Assembly furnished rationale for conformity with postulates of modern centralized state based on talmudic maxim "The law of the land is [binding] law," prescribing adherence to the civil code as long as latter did not contradict general demands of Judaism. Sanhedrin gave halakhic confirmation to Assembly decisions.

Sanielevici, Henric (1875–1951), Rumanian literary critic, biologist. Opponent of ultra-nationalistic tendencies in Rumanian literary circles. Originally advocate of Jewish assimilation; modified views after WWI.

San Jose, city in Calif., U.S. First Jewish congregation established 1861; only one synagogue until 1953. Many scientific and engineering personnel settled fr. mid-1950s. Jewish pop. 7,000 (1971).

San Marino, independent republic near Rimini. Jewish moneylenders active 14th–17th c. In modern times, Jewish contact with republic has been sporadic.

San Nicandro, town in S. Italy. Despite hostility of local clergy and Fascist authorities, 23 peasant families there adopted Judaism in 1930s. Community formally recognized 1944. Group emigrated to Israel 1949 but eventually dispersed.

San Remo Conference, conference of WWI allies (Great Britain, France, Italy), held in San Remo April 1920 which confirmed pledge contained in Balfour Declaration. Resolved to incorporate Balfour Declaration into Britain's Palestine mandate.

Santa Fé, province in Argentina. Jewish agricultural settlement began 1888–89 but sharply declined by 1960s while urban settlement increased and both Ashkenazi and Sephardi communities were established Jewish pop. 14,152 (1960).

Santangel, Luis de (d. 1498), Marrano comptroller-general to Ferdinand and Isabella of Spain. His influence was decisive in gaining acceptance for Christopher Columbus' proposals and he helped finance latter's voyage to America. Also assisted Jews expelled fr. Spain 1492.

Santiago, capital of Chile. Jews fr. 19th c. First organization established 1909; Representative Council 1940. Jewish pop. 30,000 (1971).

Santob de Carrión (Shem Tov ben Isaac Ardutiel; 13–14th c.), Hebrew, Spanish poet. Wrote series of poems on ethical and intellectual virtues and defects *(Proverbios morales)* and Hebrew liturgical works.

Sanu', Ya'qub or **James** (known as **Abu Naẓẓāra;** 1839–1912), Egyptian playwright; one of first authors of plays in spoken Arabic and a creator of satiric journalism in modern Egypt. Egyptian nationalist; opposed both Khedive Ismā'īl and British occupation.

Sanz, see Halberstam.

São Paulo, city in Brazil. Marrano settlers ultimately assimilated into general pop. Present community derives fr. immigration fr. Europe and Near East in 19th–20th c. Jews

Temple Beth-Israel, São Paulo.

contributed largely to growth of textile and paper industries. Community maintains wide range of educational and social institutions. Jewish pop. 65,000 (1971).

Saperstein, Abe (1901–1966), U.S. basketball promoter. Organized all-Negro Harlem Globetrotters basketball team 1927. Famed both for their comedy routine and outstanding play.

Saphir, Jacob (1822–1885), writer, traveler; b. Lithuania, emigrated to Ereẓ Israel 1832. As emissary 1857 traveled to Egypt, Yemen, Far East, Australia, returning to Jerusalem 1863. Sent to Egypt and Europe 1869 and Russia 1873. Recorded his first travels, esp. in Yemen, in *Even Sappir*.

Saphir, Moritz (Moses) Gottlieb (1795–1858), Austrian satirist, critic; baptized 1832. Wrote humorous and satirical poems, essays, literary criticism, short stories, etc.

Sapir, Edward (1884–1939), U.S. ethnographer, anthropologist, linguist. Chief of Geological Survey of Canada for 15 years and became expert in American-Indian languages. A founder of formal descriptive linguistics. Influence on study of language.

Sapir, Eliyahu (1869–1911), Ereẓ Israel pioneer, pedagogue; grandson of Jacob Saphir. Taught in Petaḥ Tikvah. vice-director of Anglo-Palestine Bank in Jaffa. Wrote *Ha-Areẓ*, geographical lexicon of Ereẓ Israel. His son, **Joseph** (1902–1972), mayor of Petaḥ Tikvah 1940–51, General Zionist member of Knesset, minister of transportation 1952–55, minister without portfolio 1967–69, minister of commerce 1969–70.

The synagogue at Sardis, looking from the forecourt to the apse.

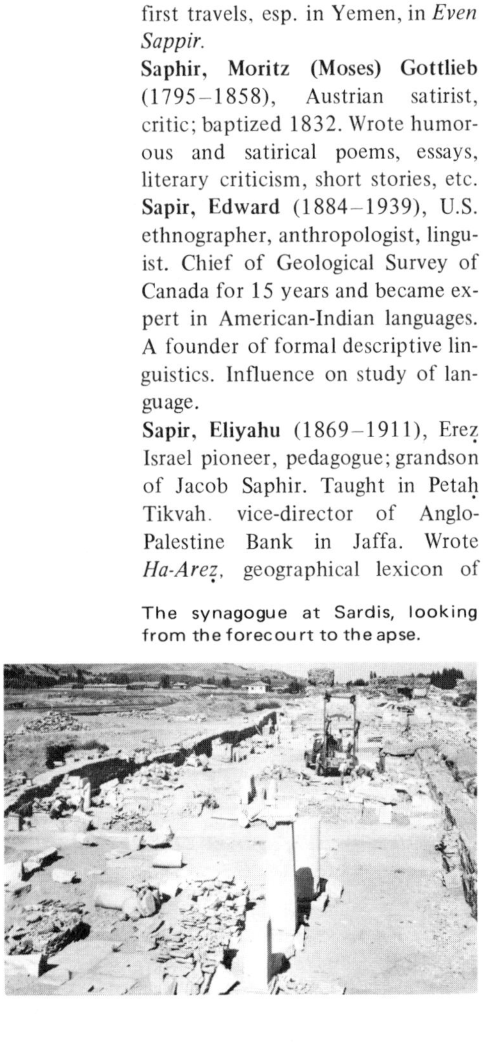

Sapir (Koslowsky), Pinḥas (1907–), Israel political leader; b. Poland, settled in Ereẓ Israel 1929. Active in companies dealing with water supply. Director-general of ministry of defense 1949, ministry of finance 1953. Minister of commerce and industry 1955–67, minister of finance 1963–67, 1969–74, general secretary Israel Labor Party 1968–69, Chairman Zionist Exec. and Jewish Agency 1974.

Pinḥas Sapir

Sapiro, Aaron (1884–1959), U.S. lawyer; b. San Francisco. Author of California Industrial Accident Laws and chiefly responsible for standard Cooperative Marketing Act 1924. Henry Ford attacked him in *Dearborn Independent* but had to retract.

Sarachek, Joseph (1892–1953), U.S. Conservative rabbi, scholar. Taught at Yeshiva Univ. and wrote on medieval Jewish literature.

Saragossa, town in Spain; capital of the former kingdom of Aragon. Jewish settlement fr. late Roman period; community important during period of Muslim rule and particularly flourished under Christians. Principal center of Marranos in 14th c. Declined after Tortosa disputation 1413–14. Deliverance of Jews fr. false charge of dishonoring king 1470 was occasion of "Purim of Saragossa." Expulsion 1492.

Sarah (Sarai), first of four matriarchs; wife of Abraham and his half-sister. Long barren she gave birth to Isaac when she was 90 years old. Through jealousy she mistreated Hagar, her handmaiden and concubine of Abraham, finally driving her away with her son Ishmael. D. aged 127 and buried in Machpelah.

Sarajevo, town in Yugoslavia. Jewish settlement fr. 16th c. Community enjoyed generally good conditions under Ottoman rule. After Austrian annexation 1878, Ashkenazi settlement increased and economic opportunities widened. 10,500 Jews in 1941. Most murdered by Nazis and many of remnant emigrated to Israel. 1,000 Jews in 1971.

Sephardi woman of Sarajevo wearing traditional dress.

Sarajevo Haggadah, illustrated *Haggadah* produced in Spain in 14th c., found in Sarajevo in 19th c. Best-known Hebrew illuminated ms.

Sarasohn, Kasriel Hersch (1835–1905), Yiddish, Hebrew newspaper publisher; b. Russia; settled in New York 1871. Founded Yiddish weeklies and daily as well as Hebrew weekly. A founder of HIAS.

Saratov, town in Russia. Scene of notorious blood libel 1853, pogroms 1905. During WWI many refugees arrived there. 15,000 Jews in late 1960s.

Saraval, Jacob Raphael ben Simḥah Judah (1707? –1782), Italian rabbi, man of letters, musician. Supported Jacob Emden. Translated works fr. Italian and English into Hebrew, incl. libretto of Handel's oratorio *Esther*.

Sardi, Samuel ben Isaac (c. 1185–c. 1255), Spanish halakhist. Author of *Sefer ha-Terumot* on Jewish civil law.

Sardinia, Mediterranean island. Emperor Tiberius deported 4,000 Jewish youths to island 19 C.E. Situation of community deteriorated under Christian rule, although it prospered during early Aragonese period. Fr. close of Middle Ages no Jewish community of importance.

Sardis, place in Turkey; capital of ancient kingdom of Lydia; probably the Sepharad of Obadiah (1:20). Size and affluence of Jewish community in Roman times is revealed by huge synagogue discovered 1962. Jewish community apparently dispersed on fall of city 616 C.E.

°**Sargon II,** king of Assyria and Babylonia 722–705 B.C.E. Completed subjugation and conquest of Israel and its capital, Samaria, which he rebuilt later and made capital of his new province. Conquered Ashdod.
Sarna, Ezekiel (1889–1969), head of Hebron yeshivah in Ereẓ Israel. Taught at Slobodka yeshivah in Lithuania; arranged its transfer to Hebron 1924. After Hebron massacre 1929, lived in Jerusalem. In State of Israel, instrumental in obtaining exemption fr. military service for yeshivah students.
Sarnoff, David (1891–1971), U.S. electronics pioneer, executive. Pres. RCA fr. 1930. Founded NBC 1926 as RCA subsidiary. Proved practicality of coast-to-coast broadcasting. Built RCA into world's largest electronic complex. His son **Robert** (1918–) headed NBC 1955–66, RCA fr. 1966.

David Sarnoff

Sarphati, Samuel (1813–1866), Dutch social reformer. Progressive leader in his native Amsterdam in mid-19th c. Instrumental in establishing Netherlands Credit and Deposits Bank.
Sarraute (Cherniak), Nathalie (1902–), French novelist; among initiators of modern school known as "le nouveau roman." Novels incl. *Le Planetarium, Les Fruits d'Or.*
Sar Shalom ben Boaz (d. c. 859), *gaon* of Sura 838–848. Greatly admired by his contemporaries; wrote many responsa and his letters show generous and conciliatory disposition.
Sarṭaba (Alexandrium), fortress probably built by Alexander Yannai and named after him, identified with peak overlooking Jordan Valley. Here Aristobulus II surrendered to Pompey 63 B.C.E. Stronghold of nationalist opposition to Rome. Several members of Hasmonean dynasty buried there.
Sarug (Saruk), Israel (16th–17th c.), Egyptian kabbalist. Disseminated teachings of Isaac Luria in Italy. His pupils included Menahem Azariah Fano. A number of his kabbalistic works were published.
Saskatchewan, province in Canada. First Jewish settler 1877. Jewish

Jacob Sasportas

farming colonies started in 1880s but declined in 1930s with mechanization and drought. Jewish pop. declined fr. peak 5,047 in 1931 to 2,500 in 1971.
Sasportas, Jacob (c. 1610–1698), rabbi, anti-Shabbatean; b. N. Africa. Dismissed as rabbi of Tlemçen 1647 and went to Europe, becoming rabbi of Amsterdam 1693. Main work *Ẓiẓat Novel Ẓevi* is attack on Shabbatean movement.
Sasson, Aaron ben Joseph (1550/5–1626), talmudist, halakhic authority in Ottoman Empire. Head of yeshivah in Constantinople. His responsa *Torat Emet* were published by his son **Joseph,** rabbi of Venice.
Sasson, Eliyahu (1902–), Israel diplomat; b. Damascus, settled in Ereẓ Israel 1920. Headed Arab dept. of Zionist Executive fr. 1930; member of delegations negotiating armistice agreements with Arabs 1949. Israel minister in Turkey 1950–52, ambassador in Rome 1952–60, minister of posts 1961–66, minister of police 1966–69.
Sassoon, family of merchants, philanthropists, men of letters; originally from Baghdad, rose to influence and affluence in Asia and England. Founder **Sheikh Sassoon ben Sālaḥ** (1750–1830), pres. of Baghdad Jewish community for c. 40 years and chief treasurer of Ottoman pashas there. His son, **David S.** (1792–1864), moved to Bombay, where he established business which assumed international scope. Great benefactor to the community. His son, **Sir Abdullah** (later **Albert;** 1818–1896), provided initiative for establishing Bombay as modern port city. After settling in London, was on terms of personal friendship with Prince of Wales (later Edward VII). His half-brother **Reuben D.** (1835–1905), a favorite traveling companion of Prince of Wales, as was another half-brother, **Arthur** (1840–1912), whose home in Brighton was scene of lavish entertainments at which Edward VII was frequent guest. Another son of David S., **Solomon** (1841–1894), remained in Orient and controlled

Flora Sassoon with her daughter, Rachelle, at latter's presentation at court.

the family company 1877–1894. His wife, **Flora** (1859–1936), achieved renown as Hebrew scholar and was often consulted on questions of Jewish law. After her husband's death she managed firm in Bombay for some years and settled in England 1901. Her son **David Solomon** (1880–1942), outstanding Hebraist and bibliophile who made important collection of Hebrew and Samaritan mss. His son **Solomon David** (1915–), rabbi who published scholarly works. Settled in Jerusalem 1970. Another son of the original David, **Sassoon David** (1832–1867), settled in England. His daughter was newspaper publisher Rachel Beer. Other members of the family included: **Sir Jacob Elias** (1844–1916), who was instrumental in developing cotton textile industry in W. India. **Sir Philip** (1888–1939), British politician, art connoisseur. Conservative MP 1912–39, undersecretary of state for air 1924–29, 1931–37. Trustee of several art galleries; also commissioner (minister) of works. **Sir Victor (Ellice)** (1881–1961), Indian industrialist, politician, communal leader. After his interests in Shanghai were taken over by successive Japanese and Chinese Communist occupations, he built up new interest in Bahamas. Also famous race-horse owner. **Siegfried Lorraine** (1886–1967), English poet, novelist. Famous for anti-war poems of WWI. Raised as Anglican, converted to Roman Catholicism 1957.
Sassoon, Sir Ezekiel (1860–1932), Iraqi statesman. Minister of finance in five independent Iraqi governments 1921–25.

Satan, personification in New Testament of spirit of evil and an independent personality. Term is used in Bible in sense of adversary, save in few passages, e g. Job 1–2, where it is name of accusing angel. In post-biblical literature it is used chiefly for impersonal force of evil. In amoraic literature, emerges as distinct personality, "the evil inclination, Satan, and the angel of death are one and the same."

Satanow, Isaac (1732–1804), Hebrew writer; b. Podolia, settled in Berlin c. 1771. Among most prolific of early Haskalah writers. Grappled with problem of use of biblical and post-biblical Hebrew. Wrote Hebrew-German dictionary and thesaurus, books of liturgy, collections of proverbs.

Joel Teitelbaum, the Szatmár (Satu-Mare) rebbe (with white beard) in Jerusalem.

Satu-Mare (Szatmár), city in NW Rumania. Community 1849, which defined itself as Orthodox, but split 1898 and *status quo ante* community established. Fr. 1934 Orthodox community became anti-Zionist under influence of Joel Teitelbaum. 12,960 Jews in 1941; deported 1944. 5,000 Jews in 1947, but many moved away or emigrated to Ereẓ Israel; 500 in 1970.

Saudi Arabia, see Arabia.

Saul, first king of Israel (ruled c. 1029–1005 B.C.E.). Most of his reign spent successfully fighting Israel's enemies. Internally purified religious worship. Relations with Samuel, who enthroned him, became strained. Jealous of David, whom Samuel had anointed as his successor; sought to kill him. D. on Mt. Gilboa fighting Philistines. Laid foundations for national unity of Israelites.

Saul, Solomon (d. 1892), S. African newspaper proprietor *(Cape Argus)*, politician. Sat in Cape Assembly. Played leading part in securing responsible government for Cape Colony 1872. Became Christian.

°**Saulcy, Louis Félicien de Joseph Caignart** (1807–1880), French numismatist, orientalist, archaeologist. Conducted first archaeological excavations in Ereẓ Israel (Tombs of Kings in Jerusalem) and was first to catalogue coins of Ereẓ Israel.

Savannah, city in Ga., U.S. First Jewish settlers 1733, third oldest community in N. America. First congregation Mickve Israel 1735. Jews active in public life. Jewish pop. 2,900 (1971).

Savora, Savoraim (Aram.), Babylonian scholars active bet. *amoraim* and *geonim* (c. 500–700 C.E.). Probably completed editing of Babylonian Talmud, adding explanatory passages, but no independent work of theirs survived.

Savoy, former duchy in France. Jewish settlement fr. 13th c. Jews suffered persecutions in 14th, 15th c. Community of Chambéry survived until beginning of 16th c.

Savyon, urban settlement in C. Israel. Founded as garden suburb on initiative of S. African settlers. Pop. 1,760 (1971).

Sawicki (Reisler), Jerzy (1908–1967), Polish lawyer. Prosecuting counsel at Polish War Crimes Tribunal and member of Polish delegation at Nuremberg Trials. Prof. of criminal law at Warsaw Univ.

Saxony, state in E. Germany; formerly electorate and kingdom. Jews fr. 10th c. Jewish traders received various rights in 14th c. but suffered persecutions and expulsion in 15th c. Thereafter only allowed to visit Leipzig fair on temporary basis. Full civil rights not granted until 1868. 20,584 Jews in 1933; destroyed by Nazis in WWII. New communities in Leipzig, Dresden, and Karl-Marx-Stadt (Chemnitz).

Schach, Fabius (1868–1930), Zionist leader. One of first members and propagandists of Zionist movement in Germany. Wrote on Zionism, Judaism, and Hebrew and Yiddish languages.

Schachtel, Hugo-Hillel (1876–1949), early Zionist; one of heads of Jewish National Fund in Germany. His manual on Ereẓ Israel and Zionist movement was very popular. Settled in Ereẓ Israel 1932.

Schachter, Herschel (1917–), U.S. Orthodox rabbi. Pres. of Religious Zionists of America and chairman of Conference of Presidents of major American Jewish organizations.

Schaechter, Joseph (1901–), Ereẓ Israel educator, writer; b. Galicia, settled in Ereẓ Israel 1938. Supervisor of Haifa secondary schools, author of several works endeavoring to turn Israel non-Orthodox youth back to Jewish heritage.

Schaechter, Mordkhe (1927–), Yiddish linguist, educator; b. Rumania, in U.S. fr. 1951. Leading Yiddishist. Coeditor of Territorialist bimonthly *Oyfn Shvel.* Taught at Jewish Teachers Seminary, Yeshiva and Columbia Univs.

°**Schaeffer, Claude F.A.** (1898–), French archaeologist. Excavator of Ras Shamra (see Ugarit), one of most remarkable archaeological discoveries of 20th c. bearing directly upon language and literature of Bible.

Schaff, Adam (1913–), Polish philosopher; of Jewish origin. Dominant figure in Marxist philosophy in post-war Poland.

Schalit, Abraham Chaim (1898–), Israel classical historian; b. Galicia, settled in Ereẓ Israel 1929. Taught at Heb. Univ. fr. 1950. Major work on King Herod; also specialized in writings of Josephus.

Schalit, Isidor (1871–1953), first secretary of Zionist Office and one of Herzl's first assistants; b. Ukraine. Member of editorial board of *Die Welt* in Vienna. An organizer of 1st Zionist Congress. Head of Zionist Organization in Austria. Fr. 1938 in Ereẓ Israel.

Schanzer, Carlo (1865–?), Italian statesman. Elected to National Assembly 1906 and became minister of posts. Senator after WWI, minister of finance 1919–20, foreign minister 1922. Retired after Mussolini's coup.

Schapera, Isaac (1905–), S. African anthropologist. Taught in S. Africa and London. His study of labor migration in Bechuanaland served as guide for colonial policy. Pres. of the Royal Anthropological Inst. 1961–63.

Schapira, David (1901–), Argentine politician. Elected senator 1958; chairman Senate Public Health Committee. Member National Chamber of Deputies 1963–66.

Schapira, Hermann (Ẓevi Hirsch; 1840–1898), Zionist leader; b.

Hermann Schapira

בִּימֵי שְׁפֹט הַשֹּׁפְטִים וַיְהִי רָעָב בָּאָרֶץ
וַיֵּלֶךְ אִישׁ מִבֵּית לֶחֶם יְהוּדָה לָגוּר בִּ
שְׂדֵי מוֹאָב הוּא וְאִשְׁתּוֹ וּשְׁנֵי בָנָיו
וְשֵׁם הָאִישׁ אֱלִימֶלֶךְ וְשֵׁם אִשְׁתּוֹ נָעֳמִי
וְשֵׁם שְׁנֵי בָנָיו מַחְלוֹן וְכִלְיוֹן אֶפְרָתִים
מִבֵּית לֶחֶם יְהוּדָה וַיָּבֹאוּ שְׂדֵי מוֹאָב
וַיִּהְיוּ שָׁם וַיָּמָת אֱלִימֶלֶךְ אִישׁ נָעֳמִי
וַתִּשָּׁאֵר הִיא וּשְׁנֵי בָנֶיהָ וַיִּשְׂאוּ לָהֶם
נָשִׁים מֹאֲבִיּוֹת שֵׁם הָאַחַת עָרְפָּה וְשֵׁם
הַשֵּׁנִית רוּת וַיֵּשְׁבוּ שָׁם כְּעֶשֶׂר שָׁנִים
וַיָּמֻתוּ גַם שְׁנֵיהֶם מַחְלוֹן וְכִלְיוֹן וַתִּשָּׁאֵר
הָאִשָּׁה מִשְּׁנֵי יְלָדֶיהָ וּמֵאִישָׁהּ וַתָּקָם
הִיא וְכַלֹּתֶיהָ וַתָּשָׁב מִשְּׂדֵי מוֹאָב כִּי
שָׁמְעָה בִּשְׂדֵה מוֹאָב כִּי פָקַד יְהוָה אֶת

RUTH Illuminated opening panel of the Book of Ruth from the *Tripartite Maḥzor*, South Germany, c. 1320, showing the corn harvest. The women are depicted with animal or bird heads, the men with human heads.

SHIVVITI *Shivviti* plaque, hung in synagogue, with medallions giving three of the names of God. Poland, 18th–19th cent.

SHOFAR The *shofar* being sounded before the Western Wall, Jerusalem.

Lithuania. Ordained rabbi; prof. of mathematics at Heidelberg 1887. Joined Ḥibbat Zion movement 1881. At 1st Zionist Congress 1897 proposed establishment of Jewish National Fund and Heb. Univ. in Ereẓ Israel.

Schapira, Noah (1866–1931), Hebrew poet, labor leader in Ereẓ Israel; b. Kishinev, settled in Ereẓ Israel 1890. Among leaders of Jewish workers. Wrote articles on *yishuv* affairs and first labor poetry written in country.

Schapiro, Israel (1882–1957), bibliographer, orientalist, librarian; b. Poland, in U.S. fr. 1911. Head of Semitic division of Library of Congress 1913–44. Settled in Israel 1950.

Schapiro, Jacob Salwyn (1879–), U.S. historian. Taught at CCNY. Principal interest 19th c. European history.

Scharfstein, Ẓevi (1884–1972), Hebrew educator, journalist, publisher; b. Ukraine, in U.S. fr. 1914. Prof. of Jewish education, Teachers Institute, Jewish Theological Seminary. Prolific contributor to Hebrew press. Published educational texts and wrote 5-vol. history of Jewish education.

Schary, Dore (Isidore; 1905–), U.S. film writer, producer. Produced more than 250 pictures. Wrote play *Sunrise at Campobello*, dealing with early career of Franklin D. Roosevelt. Chairman Anti-Defamation League. New York City's first commissioner of cultural affairs 1970.

Schatz, Boris (1867–1932), painter, sculptor; b. Lithuania. Prof. at Academy of Art at Sofia (Bulgaria). Settled in Jerusalem 1906, founding Bezalel School of Art to which he soon added the Bezalel Museum. Influence on formative development of art and handicrafts in Ereẓ Israel. His son **Bezalel** (1912–), expressional abstract artist.

Schaulson Numhauser, Jacobo (1917–), Chilean lawyer, politician. Prof. of civil law at Univ. of Santiago, member of Chamber of Deputies 1949–65. Represented Chile at UN 1950.

Schayes, Adolph (Dolph; 1928–), U.S. basketball player. With NBA Syracuse Nationals, named to 12 consecutive all-star teams and held almost every league record. NBA coach of the year 1966.

Schechter, Solomon (Shneur Zalman; 1847–1915), rabbinic scholar, president of Jewish Theological Seminary of America; b. Rumania.

"Mattathias," statue by Boris Schatz.

Solomon Schechter

Taught in England 1882–1901 (fr. 1892 at Cambridge) and at Jewish Theological Seminary, N.Y. fr. 1902. Recovered Cairo *Genizah* with its 100,000 mss. and fragments which he took to Cambridge. Founded Conservative Judaism as compromise between Orthodox support of tradition and Reform call for change. Wrote on many aspects of Jewish theology. Published part of original Hebrew text of Ben Sira.

Schechtman, Joseph B. (1891–1970), Zionist, writer on Zionist history; b. Odessa. Close collaborator with Jabotinsky, whose biography he wrote. Went to U.S. 1941. Consultant to Office of Strategic Services (OSS) 1944–45 on population movements; pres. United Revisionists of America. Member of Jewish Agency Executive.

Scheftelowitz, Isidor (1876–1934), orientalist, rabbi; b. Germany. Wrote on Sanskrit and Iranian philology and history and on comparative religion.

Scheib, Israel, see Eldad, Israel.

Scheiber, Alexander (1913–), Hungarian rabbi, scholar; director of Budapest Rabbinical Seminary. Made valuable contributions to history of Hungarian Jewry.

Scheid, Elie (1841–1922), French historian, administrator. Wrote on history of Jews of Alsace. Inspector of Baron Edmond de Rothschild's settlement projects in Ereẓ Israel. Opposed Herzl's Zionism.

Scheler, Max Ferdinand (1874–1928), German philosopher, sociologist. Major influence on French existentialism and phenomenology after WWII. Converted to Catholicism but later left Church and elaborated his own doctrine, which asserted vitalistic pantheism.

Schenectady city in N.Y., U.S. First Jewish settlers 1840s. First congregation Shaaray Shomayim 1857. Jewish pop. 4,500 (1971).

Schereschewsky, Samuel Isaac Joseph (1831–1906), Episcopalian bishop of China; b. Lithuania, baptized in U.S. 1855. Author of translation of Pentateuch into Mandarin Chinese known as "Two Finger Bible," as he was semi-paralyzed while writing it.

Scherman, Harry (1887–1969), U.S. publisher. Founder and pres. Book-of-the-Month Club.

Schick, Baruch ben Jacob (1740? –after 1812), rabbi, physician; forerunner of Haskalah in E. Europe. Studied medicine in London. Published translations and original works in Hebrew, esp. on mathematics, medicine, hygiene.

Schick, Bela (1877–1967), U.S. pediatrician; b. Hungary, in U.S. fr. 1923. Pediatrician in chief at Mt. Sinai Hospital 1923, prof. at Columbia Univ. 1936. Originator of Schick test for diphtheria.

Schick, Moses ben Joseph (Maharam Shick; 1807–1879), Hungarian rabbi, *posek*. Favored formation of independent Orthodox communities and opposed status quo. Opposed Reform but approved of preaching in vernacular. Wrote responsa, etc.

Schiff, David Tevele (d. 1792), rabbi of Great Synagogue, London, fr. 1765; b. Germany. Became recognized as head of all English Ashkenazim.

Schiff, Dorothy (1903–), U.S. newspaper publisher; daughter of Jacob Schiff, wife of Rudolph Sonneborn. Pres. and publisher 1942 and later editor-in-chief of liberal *New York Post*.

Schiff, Hugo (1834–1915), Italian organic chemist. Worked at Pisa and Turin; prof. at Florence. Compounds obtained from aldehydes and ammonia are "Schiff bases."

Jacob H. Schiff

Schiff, Jacob Henry (1847–1920), U.S. financier, philanthropist; b. Germany, in U.S. fr. 1865. Head of Kuhn, Loeb & Co. 1885. Originally opposed Zionism, announced support of cultural homeland in Ereẓ Israel 1917. In many ways, unofficial lay leader of U.S. Jewry. Supported numerous causes and institutions associated with Judaism, incl. Yeshiva College, Jewish Theological Seminary, Hebrew Union College, Jewish Publication Society. A founder of American Jewish Committee 1906.

Schiff, Meir ben Jacob ha-Kohen (Maharam; 1605–1641), German talmudist, rabbinic author. Headed important yeshivah in Fulda. His novellae were published and incorporated in standard editions of Talmud.

Schildkraut, Joseph (1895–1964), U.S. actor; son of Rudolf Schildkraut; raised in Vienna. Roles incl. Dreyfus in *The Life of Emile Zola.*

Rudolph Schildkraut in photomontage showing some of his many roles.

Schildkraut, Rudolph (1862–1930), German actor; star of European and American theater. Won acclaim on German stage with portrayal of Shylock. Also appeared in Yiddish plays and in films.

Schiller-Szinessy, Solomon Mayer (1820–1890), Hungarian-born rabbi, scholar. Enlisted in Kossuth revolution 1848–49, was captured and escaped to England, where he became first Jewish reader of talmudic and rabbinic literature at Univ. of Cambridge. Prepared catalogue of Hebrew mss. in Cambridge.

Schindler, Alexander M. (1925–), U.S. Reform leader. Fr. 1973 pres. Union of American Hebrew Congregations. Active in Jewish education.

Schindler, Rudolph M. (1887–1953), U.S. architect. Worked in Frank Lloyd Wright's office 1916–21. Buildings he produced with Richard Neutra in Los Angeles after 1926 are earliest examples of international style in U.S.

Schindler, Solomon (1842–1915), U.S. Reform rabbi; b. Germany, in U.S. fr. 1871. Adopted radical standpoint in teaching his Boston community; retired fr. rabbinate 1894 and undertook social work.

Schiper Ignacy (Yiẓḥak; 1884–1943), Polish historian, public worker. Specialized in history of economics and popular culture (in Yiddish). Promoted and enriched historical research on Polish Jewry. Deputy in Sejm 1922–27. D. in concentration camp.

Schirmann, Jefim (Ḥayyim; 1904–), Israel scholar of medieval Hebrew poetry; b. Kiev. Prof. at Heb. Univ. Laid foundations for modern research and critical evaluation of secular and sacred Hebrew poetry as well as rhymed tales composed by Jews of Spain and Italy. Edited *Tarbiz* 1954–69.

Schlegel, Dorothea (Brendl) von (1763–1839), German author; daughter of Moses Mendelssohn. Maintained famous salons in Berlin and Vienna. Converted to Protestantism 1802, Catholicism in 1808. Married philosopher Friedrich von Schlegel.

Schlesinger, Akiva Joseph (1837–1922), early Zionist. Graduate of Hungarian yeshivot. Attempted to interest Jewry in building religious Jewish community in Ereẓ Israel living off fruits of its labor in spirit of Torah. Went to Ereẓ Israel 1870 and was a founder of Petaḥ Tikvah.

Schlesinger, Benjamin (1876–1932), U.S. trade union leader, journalist. Pres. International Ladies' Garment Workers Union (ILGWU). Managing editor *Jewish Daily Forward.*

Schlesinger, Frank (1871–1943), U.S. astronomer; pioneer in stellar photography. Director of Allegheny Observatory 1905, Yale Univ. Observatory fr. 1920. Worked on stellar proper motions and star positions obtained with wide angle cameras. A founder and pres. 1932–35 of International Astronomical Union.

Schlesinger, Isidore William (1877–1949), S. African financier, entrepeneur. His extensive financial and industrial empire included real estate, theaters and cinemas, a broadcasting service, and one of the biggest citrus-growing estates in the world.

Schlesinger, John (1926–), English director. Films incl. *Darling, Midnight Cowboy, Sunday Bloody Sunday.*

Schleswig-Holstein, state in W. Germany. Jewish settlement fr. 17th c. and esp. successful in Altona. Emancipation finally granted 1863. 6,000 Jews in 1925; 107 Jews in Kiel in 1960.

Schlettstadt, Samuel ben Aaron (14th c.), Alsatian rabbi, head of yeshivah in Strasbourg. Compelled to flee, went to Jerusalem, but later returned. His *Ha-Mordekhai ha-Katan,* though unpublished, was often quoted; it is abridgment of Mordecai b. Hillel's *Mordekhai.*

Schliefer, Solomon (1889–1957), rabbi of Moscow under Soviet regime. Obtained permission to open legal yeshivah and publish photostat edition of prayer book.

Schlossberg, Joseph (1875–1971), U.S. trade union leader, journalist. Joined radical left-wing American socialist movement. Edited Socialist Labor Party weekly *Der Arbeyter.* Secretary-treasurer fr. 1914 of Amalgamated Clothing Workers of America. Chaired American National Committee for Labor Israel.

Schmelkes, Gedaliah ben Mordecai (1857–1928), Polish talmudist, chief rabbi of Przemysl. One of few Polish rabbis to join Zionist movement.

°Schmid, Anton von (1765–1855), publisher of Hebrew books in Vienna and patron of Hebrew literature. Among his publications were Babylonian Talmud, *Shulḥan Arukh,* yearbook *Bikkurei ha-Ittim,* and periodical *Kerem Ḥemed.*

Schmidt, Joseph (1904–1942), singer; b. Bukovina. Began career as cantor. Became star of operetta and light music. Because of small stature

known as the "pocket tenor." D. in refugee camp in Switzerland.

Schmiedl, Adolf Abraham (1821–1914), Austrian rabbi. Wrote on medieval Jewish philosophy.

Schmitz, Ettore, see Svevo, Italo.

Schmolka, Marie (1890–1940), Czech leader of Jewish women's movement, social worker. Worked for relief of Nazi victims. D. London.

Schnabel, Artur (1882–1951), pianist, teacher; b. Moravia, taught in Germany, Switzerland, and U.S., and appeared throughout Europe. His readings of Beethoven were considered most authoritative of his time.

Schneersohn, family of ḥasidic leaders; descendants of Shneur Zalman of Lyady, founder of Ḥabad Ḥasidism. His son, **Dov Baer** (1773–1827), succeeded him as leader 1813. Settled in Lubavich (which became center of Ḥabad), founded settlement in Hebron. His son-in-law and successor, **Menahem Mendel** (1789–1866), renowned halakhist and author of responsa *Ẓemaḥ Ẓedek;* one of leaders of Russian Jewry. His sons established branches of Ḥabad in various parts of Russia, that in Lubavich being headed by **Samuel** (1834–1882) and his son **Shalom Dov Baer** (1866–1920), who established first ḥasidic yeshivah. Shalom's son, **Joseph Isaac** (1880–1950), proved an outstanding organizer and guided Ḥabad through storms of Russian civil war, Communist regime and (after 1939 in New York) the Holocaust. Under leadership of his son-in-law, **Menahem Mendel** (b. 1902) Ḥabad has continued to expand.

Menahem Mendel Schneerson

Schneersohn, Isaac (1879–1969), communal leader in Russia; in France fr. 1920. Founder of Centre Documentation Juive Contemporaine in Paris 1943. Launched idea of memorial to unknown Jewish martyr, inaugurated in Paris 1956.

Schneider, Alexander (1908–), violinist. Led Frankfort Symphony Orchestra. Second violinist Budapest Quartet. In U.S. until 1944 and fr. 1957. Established with Pablo Casals annual festival in Prades 1950 and Puerto Rico 1957.

Schneider, Mordecai Bezalel (1865–1941), Hebrew grammarian in Lithuania. In addition to comprehensive knowledge of Bible, Talmud, and Hebrew grammar, he had broad knowledge of classical literature and researched in Latin and Greek.

Schneiderman, Harry (1885–), U.S. editor, organization executive. Member of staff of American Jewish Committee 1909–49. Editor *American Jewish Year Book* 1920–48; co-editor, *Contemporary Jewish Record* 1938–45.

Schneiderman, Rose (1882–1972), U.S. labor union organizer, executive; sister of Harry Schneiderman. Organized White Goods Workers Union and in charge of its general strike 1913. General organizer 1914–17 of International Ladies' Garment Workers Union. Pres. Women's Trade Union League 1918–49.

Schnirer, Moritz Tobia (1861–1941), physician, Zionist; b. Rumania. Accompanied Herzl on his trip to Ereẓ Israel 1898. At First Congress formulated policy of political Zionism. Wrote on medicine. Committed suicide together with his wife during WWII.

Schnitzer, Eduard, see Emin Pasha.

Arthur Schnitzler

Schnitzler, Arthur (1862–1931), Austrian playwright, author, physician. Early interest in psychology manifest in work (friend of Freud). Jewish subjects incl. play *Professor Bernhardi.*

Schocken, Salman (1877–1959), Zionist, art and book collector, publisher. Founded prosperous chain of Schocken department stores in Germany. Collected rare books and mss. and founded Schocken Institute (see below) and publishing houses in Germany, Tel Aviv, New York. Moved to Jerusalem 1934, U.S. 1940. His son, **Gershom** (1902–), owner and chief editor of daily *Haaretz.* Progressive member of Knesset 1955–59.

Schocken Institute, scholarly institute started in Germany and fr. 1934 in Jerusalem, housing Schocken Library, Research Institute for Medieval Hebrew Poetry, and Institute for Jewish Mysticism. Since 1961 associated with the Jewish Theological Seminary of America.

Schoenbaum, Eliezer Isaac, see Ilna'e, Eliezer Isaac.

Schoenberg, Arnold (1874–1951), modern composer; b. Austria; in U.S. fr. 1933. Famed as discoverer of "method of composition with twelve tones related to one another." Taught at Univ. of S. California and UCLA. Works incl. *Kol Nidre, A Survivor from Warsaw,* the cantata *Jakobsleiter,* and opera *Moses and Aaron.*

Arnold Schoenberg, self-portrait, 1910.

°**Schoenerer, Georg von** (1842–1921), Austrian anti-Semitic politician. Combined nationalism, reform, anti-Semitism. Though popular, never managed to control party, owing to his despotic personality. Forerunner of Nazi anti-Semitism.

Schoenfeld, Joseph (1884–1935), Hungarian Zionist, editor of Hungarian-Zionist periodicals. Translated Herzl's *Judenstaat* into Hungarian and published books on Jewish problems and Zionism.

Schoenhack, Joseph (1812–1870), Hebrew writer, lexicographer in Poland. Published early works on natural sciences in Hebrew and compiled dictionary for Targum, Talmud, and Midrash, with each word translated into German in Hebrew letters.

Schoenheimer, Rudolf (1898–1941), German biochemist. Taught in Germany and at Columbia Univ. 1933–41. His findings led to marked changes in views held on metabolism.

Schoeps, Hans Joachim (1909–), German prof. and scholar of religious history. Writings largely on earliest Christianity. Initially considered that "German Jew" could come to terms with Nazis, but later acknowledged his failure to recognize the true face of Nazism.

Schoffmann, Gershon, see Shofman, Gershon.

Gershom G. Scholem

Scholem, Gershom Gerhard (1897–), leading authority on Kabbalah and Jewish mysticism; b. Berlin, at Heb. Univ. fr. 1923. Pres. Israel Academy of Sciences. Placed study of Kabbalah on scholarly, philological basis. His philosophical-historical insights throw new light on many Jewish religious-historical phenomena, such as Shabbatean movement. Works incl. *Major Trends in Jewish Mysticism; Shabbetai Ẓevi; Kabbalah.* Israel Prize 1958.

Schomberg, Meyer Loew (1690–1761), physician. One of first Jews accepted at German univ. Subsequently became member of Royal College of Physicians in London and Fellow of Royal Society.

Schonfeld, Victor (1880–1930), English rabbi, educator; b. Hungary, in London fr. 1909. Founded Union of Orthodox Hebrew Congregations in England. His son, **Solomon** (1912–), succeeded him as rabbi of Adath Yisrael Synagogue; became principal of Jewish Secondary Schools movement.

Schoolman, Albert (1894–), U.S. educator. Established Cejwin Camps 1919, first system of Jewish educational camps in U.S. His wife, **Bertha** (1897–1974), active in Hadassah; its national chairman of Youth Aliyah 1956–60.

Schor, Alexander Sender ben Ephraim Zalman (d. 1737), Polish talmudist. Author of authoritative and popular commentary *Tevu'ot Shor* on laws of ritual slaughter.

Schor, Ilya (1904–1961). U.S. silversmith, painter, printmaker. Work reminiscent of pre-Emancipation Jewish craftsmen. Did much work for ritual use in synagogues.

Schorr, Baruch (1823–1904), Polish cantor, composer. Composed opera *Samson* performed in Lemberg's Jewish theater. All six of his sons were cantors. His relative **Israel** (1886–1935) composed music of cantorial *She-Yibbaneh Beit ha-Mikdash.*

Schorr, Friedrich (1888–1953), bass-baritone. One of foremost Wagnerian singers of his time. Sang at Berlin State Opera 1923–31, Metropolitan Opera, N.Y., after 1938.

Schorr, Joshua Heschel (Osias Schorr; 1818–1895), Galician scholar, editor. Haskalah leader. In periodical he edited and in numerous articles fought Orthodoxy by satirical diatribes and scholarly polemics.

Schorr, Moses (1874–1941), Polish rabbi, scholar. Prof. of Semitic languages at Lemberg and Warsaw Univs. Member of Polish Senate. Leading scholar on ancient Babylonian and Assyrian law. D. in Russian prison camp.

Schottland, Charles Irwin (1906–), U.S. social welfare expert. As commissioner of social security in Dept. of Health, Education and Welfare 1954–59, directed American Social Security System.

Schotz, Benno (1891–), British sculptor; lived in Glasgow. Influenced by Epstein; established himself with series of portraits of distinguished Scotsmen.

Schrameck, Abraham (1867–1948), French politician. Governor of Madagascar 1914, senator 1920–40, twice minister of interior and also minister of justice.

Schrecker, Paul (1889–1963), historian of philosophy. Fled Germany to Paris and then to U.S. Prof. at various univs. Authority on Leibniz.

Schreiber (Family), see Sofer.

Schreiner, Martin (Mordechai; 1863–1926), scholar of medieval Jewish and Islamic letters; b. Hungary. Prof. at Berlin Lehranstalt fuer die Wissenschaft des Judentums. Fr. 1902 in mental sanatorium. Wrote on medieval Jewish thought, Islamic intellectual development, Karaism, etc.

Schub, Moshe David (1854–1938), Ereẓ Israel pioneer; b. Rumania, settled in Ereẓ Israel 1882. Purchased land and established Rosh Pinnah. Later manager of Mishmar ha-Yarden and Ein Zeitim. Wrote about early history of Jewish settlement in Ereẓ Israel.

°**Schubert, Kurt** (1923–), Austrian scholar. Prof. of Jewish culture and religion at Vienna Univ. Author of *Dead Sea Community.*

Schück, Johan Henrik Emil (1855–1947), Swedish literary historian. Pres. of Nobel Foundation. Wrote 7-vol. *Illustrerad svensk litteraturhistoria.*

°**Schudt, Johann Jacob** (1664–1722), German orientalist. Wrote 4-vol. work about Jews in his time, esp. in Frankfort.

°**Schuerer, Emil** (1844–1910), German Protestant theologian, historian. Wrote standard history of Jewish people fr. Hellenistic period to 135 C.E.

Sehuhl, Pierre-Maxime (1902–), French philosopher. Main interest Greek philosophy. Prof. at Sorbonne and pres. of Société des Etudes Juives 1949–52.

Schulberg, Budd Wilson (1914–), U.S. author, screenwriter. Wrote *What Makes Sammy Run?* about ruthless Jewish success-hunter in Hollywood, *The Harder They Fall,* and prize-winning film *On the Waterfront.*

Schulhof, Isaac (d. c. 1733), rabbi. Wrote important chronicle describing capture of Buda by Austrians fr. Turkey. Became *dayyan* in Prague.

Schulhoff, Erwin (1894–1942), Czech pianist, composer. Active in promotion of contemporary music. D. in Wuelzberg concentration camp.

Schulhoff, Julius (1825–1898), Czech piano virtuoso, composer. Taught in Paris, Dresden, and Berlin. His light brilliant compositions for piano were particularly successful.

Schulman, Kalman (1819–1899), Hebrew writer of Haskalah era; b. Belorussia, in Vilna fr. 1843. His books, mostly translations, intended to spread Haskalah among Hebrew reading public and youth. Translated Sue's *Mystères de Paris* to demonstrate possibility of rendering secular works in Hebrew.

Schulman, Samuel (1864–1955), U.S. Reform rabbi. Eloquent orator; rabbi of New York's Temple Emanu El; non-Zionist member of executive committee of Jewish Agency 1929.

Schulmann, Eleazar (1837–1904), Hebrew writer; b. Lithuania. Treasurer of Brodsky enterprises in Kiev. Published studies on Heine and Ludwig Boerne and researches on history of Yiddish language and literature.

Schulz, Bruno (1892–1942), Polish author, painter. Literary pioneer of magical and absurd and mingled personal recollections with visionary fantasy. Murdered by S.S.

°**Schumacher, Gottlieb** (1857–1924), architect, cartographer, archaeologist. First to excavate Megiddo 1903–05; worked at Baalbek 1903–04, Samaria 1908.

Schuman, William Howard (1910–), U.S. composer. Head of Juilliard School of Music 1945–62, pres. N.Y. Lincoln Center fr. 1962. Compositions incl. *Symphony for Strings* and ballet *Undertow.*

Schumann, Maurice (1911–), French politician, journalist. Headed BBC French service during WWII. A founder of Mouvement Républican Populaire and later leader of party. Held ministerial office in several governments. As foreign minister under Pompidou, pursued pro-Arab policy. Baptized in youth; took no part in Jewish affairs.

Schur, Issai (Isaiah; 1875–1941), mathematician; b. Ukraine, prof. at Berlin until 1933, when he emigrated to Erez Israel. Author of "Schur's lemma" and noted for work in representation theory of rotation group.

Schur, Zev Wolf (William; 1844–1910), U.S. pioneer Hebrew writer. Edited periodical *Ha-Pisgah* 1889–99. Wrote novels in Hebrew. His *Nezah Yisrael* (1897), first Hebrew work in U.S. to react favorably to political Zionism.

Schuster, Sir Arthur (1851–1934), British scientist. Known for work on discharge of electricity through gases and in seismology. Prof. at Manchester, where he was friend and guide of Chaim Weizmann.

Schuster, Sir Felix (1854–1936), British banker. Played important part in country's finances during WWI. A director of National Provincial Bank.

Schuster, Max Lincoln (1897–1970), U.S. publisher. Founded with Richard L. Simon (1899–1962) book publishing firm of Simon and Schuster 1924; also Pocket Books, Inc. 1939 and Little Golden Books 1942, for children.

Schutzjuden (Ger. "protected Jews"), Jews who held letters of protection fr. German rulers before emancipation. They constituted patrician and privileged class fr. which Court Jews generally came. Letters entitled them to commercial privileges, religious rights, freedom of movement, and taxation.

Schwab, Joseph J. (1909–), U.S. educator. Stressed study of philosophies of education and science in connection with preparation of school curricula. Prof. at Univ. of Chicago. Concerned with Jewish education in U.S.

Schwab, Löw (1794–1857), Hungarian talmudist, orator; chief rabbi of Pest. Published main tenets of Judaism in Hungarian and German. Supported Hungarian national liberation movement.

Schwab, Moïse (1839–1918), French scholar. Associate keeper of Bibliothèque Nationale. Translated Jerusalem Talmud into French.

Schwabacher, Simeon Aryeh (1819–1888), German rabbi, preacher. Served in Prague, Hamburg, Lemberg. Official govt.-appointed rabbi of Odessa for 27 years; helped shape it as first modern community in Russia.

Schwabe, Moshe (Max; 1889–1956), Israel classical scholar; b. Lithuania, settled in Jerusalem 1925. Established Heb. Univ. dept. of classics; rector 1950–52. His meticulous interpretations of Greco-Jewish inscriptions contributed to understanding of Erez Israel history and Jewish role in Hellenization of East.

Schwadron (Sharon), Abraham (1878–1957), Israel folklorist, collector, Hebrew writer; b. Galicia, settled in Erez Israel 1927. Bequeathed collection of autographs and portraits of great Jews to Univ. Library, Jerusalem. Wrote on many subjects, with pungent, polemical approach.

Schwartz, Abraham Samuel (1876–1957), U.S. Hebrew poet, physician; b. Lithuania, in U.S. fr. 1900. Poems on biblical and post-biblical themes.

Schwartz, Delmore (1913–1966), U.S. poet, author, critic. Editor *Partisan Review* 1943–55. Found most profound drama in E. European Jewish dream of America as land of freedom and boundless opportunity. Taught at Harvard, Princeton.

Schwartz, Israel Jacob (1885–1971), U.S. Yiddish poet; b. Lithuania, in N.Y. fr. 1906. His verse epic, *Shirat Kentucky,* considered a major achievement of American Yiddish literature. Verse autobiography, *Yunge Yorn.*

Schwartz, Joseph J. (1899–), U.S. communal leader. Headed European council of American Jewish Joint Distribution Committee 1940–49 and supervised relief and welfare programs in 30 countries, incl. key rescue work during war. Director-general JDC 1950–51, vice-chairman United Jewish Appeal 1951–55, vice-pres. State of Israel Bond Organization 1955–70.

Schwartz, Maurice (1890–1960), U.S. Yiddish actor. Major figure in Yiddish theater. His Jewish Art Theater in N.Y. had repertoire of 150 plays. Traveled extensively in Europe and S. America.

Schwartz, Phinehas Selig ha-Kohen (1877–1944), Hungarian scholar. Author of *Shem ha-Gedolim me-Erez Hagar,* biographies with bibliographical lists of Hungarian rabbis. D. in Holocaust.

Maurice Schwartz in I.J. Singer's "The Brothers Ashkenazi."

Schwarz, Adolf (1846–1931), rabbi, scholar; b. Hungary. Headed Vienna Israelitisch-theologische Lehranstalt, where he trained generations of rabbis. Major writings on hermeneutical rules of Talmud. His son **Arthur Zechariah** (1880–1939), district rabbi of Vienna; published bibliographical works and catalogs.

Schwarz, David (1845–1897), Austrian airship inventor. When informed of German government's willingness to finance flight tests, he died of shock. His plans and designs served as basis for "Zeppelin."

Schwarz, Karl Hermann Amandus (1843–1921), German mathematician. Prof. at Halle, Zurich, Goettingen, Berlin. Important contribution in potential theory and problems of conformal mapping; exercised influence on development of mathematics.

Schwarz, Leo Walder (1906–1967), U.S. author, editor. Joint Distribution Committee's director for displaced persons in Munich at end of WWII. Wrote *The Redeemers,* on return of Jewish concentration camp survivors to freedom. Published Jewish anthologies.

Schwarz, Rudolf (1905–), conductor. Musical director of Juedischer Kulturbund in Nazi Germany fr. 1936. Sent to Bergen-Belsen 1941. Settled in England; chief conductor of BBC Symphony Orchestra 1957–62.

Only known photograph of David Schwarz's airship.

Schwarz, Samuel (1880–1953), Polish-born discoverer of 20th c. Portuguese Marranos, whom he came across while working as mining engineer.

Schwarz, Solomon (1883–1973), Russian Social Democratic politician, historian. After Bolshevik seizure of power, led Menshevik opposition. Allowed to leave Russia 1922. Became authority on social and economic conditions in USSR and history of Soviet Jewry. Fr. 1970 in Jerusalem.

Schwarz, Yehoseph (1804–1865), Bavarian-born rabbi, Ereẓ Israel geographer. His pioneering work on topography of Israel and its flora and fauna, *A Descriptive Geography and Brief Historical Sketch of Palestine,* was translated into English.

Schwarzbard, Shalom (Samuel; 1886–1938), watchmaker, Yiddish poet, b. Bessarabia. Fought against bands of White Russian leader Petlyura who carried out pogroms in Ukraine. Fr. 1920 in Paris where he assassinated Petlyura in 1926. Acquitted in trial. D. in S. Africa.

Schwarz-Bart, André (1928–), French novelist. His novel, *The Last of the Just,* is based on old Jewish legend of *Lamed Vav Ẓaddikim* and theme of Jewish martyrdom.

André Schwarz-Bart

Jerusalem Yemenite scribe writing Torah scroll.

Schwarzbart, Isaac Ignacy (1888–1961), Zionist leader in Poland. Active in General Zionist movement. Member of Polish Sejm 1938, Polish government-in-exile in Paris and London 1940–45. Fr. 1946 in U.S. directing administrative dept. of World Jewish Congress.

Schwarzfeld, Rumanian literary family. **Benjamin** (1822–1897), among pioneers of Haskalah in Rumania and founded first modern school in Jassy. His three sons were founders of Rumanian Jewish historiography: **Elias** (1855–1915), historian, novelist; **Moses (Moisi;** 1857–1943), Jewish historian, author who collected 10,000 Jewish fables and proverbs; **Wilhelm** (1856–1894), investigated history of Moldavian Jews who had been converted to Christianity.

Schwarzman, Asher (1890–1919), Yiddish poet. Served in Russian cavalry. After Kiev pogrom 1919 fought against counterrevolutionary bands and killed in battle. Wrote poems in Hebrew, Russian, Yiddish.

Schwarzschild, Karl (1873–1916), German astronomer, mathematician. Prof. at Berlin. A profound thinker, lucid lecturer, and deviser of new instruments; his achievements in astronomy and mathematics were far ahead of his time. His son **Martin** (1912–), prof. of astronomy at Princeton.

Schweid, Eliezer (1929–), Israel literary critic, scholar. Taught Jewish philosophy at Heb. Univ. Wrote on Hebrew literature and Jewish philosophy.

Schweitzer, Daniel (1896–), Chilean lawyer, criminologist. Pres. Inst. of Penal Sciences 1953–59, head of Chilean delegation to UN 1959–64. His brother, **Miguel** (1908–), lawyer. Chilean minister of labor 1963–64.

Schweitzer, Eduard von (1844–1920), Hungarian soldier. Achieved prominence despite refusal to convert to Christianity. Pres. of Jewish charities in Vienna.

Schwerin-Goetz, Eliakim ha-Kohen (1760–1852), Hungarian rabbi of Baja. His community became religious center of region. Opposed to reform; took liberal view on many matters.

Schwimmer, Rosika (1877–1948), feminist, world federalist. A leader of Hungarian feminist movement. Went to U.S. at outbreak of WWI. A founder with Jane Addams of Women's Peace Party. Returned to Hungary toward end of war and joined Karolyi's government. Smuggled out of Hungary with advent of Horthy regime. Pres. International Campaign for World Government.

Schwinger, Julian Seymour (1918–), U.S. physicist. Prof. at Harvard. Nobel Prize 1965 for work which laid foundation for quantum electrodynamics.

Schwob, Marcel (1867–1905), French scholar, essayist, biographer. Authority on Villon. His outstanding *Vies Imaginaires* is collection of biographies bringing history dramatically to life.

Science of Judaism, see Wissenschaft des Judentums.

Scopus, Mount, see Mount of Olives.

Scotland, N. part of Great Britain. First organized Jewish community in Edinburgh 1816. Glasgow community grew rapidly with mass immigration fr. E. Europe in late 19th, early 20th c. Jewish pop. 15,000 (1971) with 13,400 in Glasgow, 1,400 in Edinburgh.

°**Scott, Charles Prestwich** (1846–1932), editor, owner of *Manchester Guardian;* supporter of Zionism. Influenced to Zionism by Chaim Weizmann, whom he introduced to Lloyd George, Herbert Samuel, etc.

Scranton, city in Penn., U.S. First Jewish settlers 1840s. First congregation Anshe Chesed chartered 1862. Jewish pop. 5,045 (1971).

Scribe (Heb. *sofer setam*), professional expert in writing of Torah scrolls, *tefillin, mezuzot,* and bills of divorce. At one time, scribes also acted as recording clerks and court secretaries of *bet din* under name *lavlar* (Lat. *libellarius*). Scribe is guided by strict rules when writing Torah scrolls and other ritual texts.

Scribes, see Soferim.

Scripture, see Bible.

Scroll of Antiochus, popular Aramaic account of wars of Hasmoneans and origin of Ḥanukkah. Not reliable historical document and was written bet. 2nd and 5th c. in Ereẓ Israel. Was read in synagogues on Ḥanukkah in some cities.

Scroll of Esther, last of Five Scrolls in biblical Hagiographa. Read on Purim. Relates story of salvation of Jews of Persian Empire obtained by Esther and gives reason for institution of Purim. See Megillah.

Scrolls, The Five, designation for five shortest books of biblical Hagiographa. Read by Ashkenazim in synagogue on festivals: Song of Songs on Passover; Ruth on Shavuot; Lamentations on Av 9; Ecclesiastes on Sukkot; Esther on Purim.

Scythopolis, see Beth Shean.

Illuminated Scroll of Esther from S. France, early 16th cent.

Polish Sefer Torah, 18th cent.

S'dan, Dov, see Sadan, Dov.

Sea, Song of the, exuberant hymn of triumph and gratitude sung by "Moses and the Children of Israel" after the crossing of the Red Sea (Ex. 15:1–18).

Sea of Galilee, see Kinneret, Lake.

Sea of the Talmud, post-talmudic expression indicating vastness, profundity, and all-embracing character of Talmud.

Seattle, city in Wash., U.S. First Jewish settlers 1860s. Oldest surviving congregation Bikur Cholim (Orthodox), founded 1889. Community grew after Alaska gold discovery in early 20th c. 10,500 Jews in 1970.

Sebaste see Samaria.

Sebastian, Mihail (orig. **Josef Hechter;** 1907–1945), Rumanian novelist, playwright. critic. Most versatile and significant Jewish figure in Rumanian literature.

Sebba, Shalom (1897–), Israel painter, designer. Designed for theaters in Germany and Stockholm, and Habimah Theater in Israel.

Second Passover, see Passover, Second.

Second Temple, see Temple, Second.

Sectarian, see Min.

Secunda, Sholom (1894–1974), U.S. composer. Compositions incl. dozens of Yiddish musical plays and operettas and the song *"Bay Mir Bist Du Sheyn."*

Sedeh Boker, kibbutz founded 1952 in C. Negev, Israel; affiliated with Iḥud ha-Kevuẓot ve-ha-Kibbutzim. David Ben-Gurion lived there fr. 1953. Midreshat Sedeh Boker, founded 1965, comprises teachers' training seminary, boarding high school, and institute for Negev studies.

Seder, order of service; in particular order of service in home on night of Passover. Also used for six orders of Mishnah and for weekly Pentateuch reading in synagogue.

Seder Eliyahu, see Tanna de-Vei Eliyahu.

Seder Olam, name of two midrashic, chronological works: a large one, *Seder Olam Rabbah,* and a shorter one, *Seder Olam Zuta.* Both give chronologies fr. creation to Babylonian conquest. The former continues with events in Ereẓ Israel until Bar Kokhba Revolt and the latter gives lineage of Babylonian exilarchs until Mar Zutra (II) who left Babylonia 520. The former is mentioned in Talmud and is source for dating *anno mundi;* the other is anonymous early medieval chronicle.

Sederot, development town in S. coastal plain of Israel. Pop. 7,650 (1971), majority originating fr. N. Africa, mainly Morocco.

Sedom, site at NW corner of Dead Sea where auxiliary installations of Palestine Potash Company were set up 1937. World's lowest-situated industrial plant (1,217 ft., 395 m, below sea level). See also Sodom.

Sedran (Sedransky), Barney (1891–1969), U.S. basketball player. Turned professional 1911; his team won several championships over next 15 years. Coached many teams. Elected to Basketball Hall of Fame.

Sée, Edmond (1875–1959), French playwright. Wrote comedies in French classical tradition, romantic novels, critical works.

Sée, Léopold (1822–1904), French general. Fought in Algeria, Crimea, Italian Campaign 1859, Franco-Prussian War. Active in Jewish affairs.

Seeligmann, Sigmund (1873–1940), Dutch bibliographer, historian of Dutch Jewry. His son **Isaac Leo (Arieh;** 1907–), biblical scholar; b. Holland. Prof. at Heb. Univ.

Seer of Lublin, see Jacob Isaac ha-Ḥozeh mi-Lublin.

Seesen, town in Lower Saxony, W. Germany. Very small community. Jewish school founded 1801 by Israel Jacobson to implement his humanistic and reform ideals.

Sefer ha-Ḥayyim (Heb. "Book of Life"), anonymous Ashkenazi-ḥasidic treatise combining esoteric theology with ethical teaching; important for history of Jewish mysticism.

Sefer ha-Neyar, anonymous book of halakhic decisions by French tosafist of late 13th or early 14th c. Embraces all daily Jewish observances.

Sefer ha-Yashar (Heb. "Book of Righteousness"), popular 13th c. ethical work of doubtful authorship, frequently published. Also halakhic work by Jacob Tam.

Sefer Ḥasidim, see Ḥasidim, Sefer.

Sefer Torah (Heb. "Scroll of the Law"), manuscript scroll of Pentateuch used in public worship. Most sacred of Jewish books. Written by scribes of known piety, according to precise regulations governing material and manner of writing. Scrolls are kept in synagogue ark and taken out for public reading. They are regarded with great reverence and when faulty or worn must not be destroyed but are buried in ground.

Sefer Torah minor tractate appended to the Talmud giving details of the mode of writing and reading the scroll of the Torah.

Sefirah, see Omer.

Sefirot (Heb.), kabbalistic term for 10 stages of emanation forming realm of God's manifestation in His various attributes.

Segal, Arthur (1875–1944), German painter. Evolved individual form of cubism. A leader of Neue Sezession, which revolted against

German impressionism. Founded Painting School in London after 1936.

Segal, Bernard Gerard (1907–), U.S. attorney; lived in Philadelphia. First Jewish pres. American Bar Association 1969–70.

Segal, George (1924–), U.S. sculptor. Known as a leading exponent of Pop Art. Produced modern version of American art of 1930s by casting live models and setting them in reconstructed sections of real environment.

Segal, Israel ben Moses of Zamosc (1710–1772), Russian talmudist, scholar, writer who included Haskalah ideas in his writing. Opponent of Ḥasidism; author of influential ethical work *Nezed ha-Dema.*

Segal, Louis (1894–1964), U.S. Labor Zionist leader. General secretary Jewish National Workers Alliance (Farband). Served on executive of Jewish Agency for Israel.

Segal, Moses Hirsch (Ẓevi; 1876–1968), Bible scholar; b. Lithuania. Tutor at Oxford; served English congregations. Taught at Heb. Univ. fr. 1926. Questioned documentary theory of authorship of Pentateuch, advanced modification of traditional doctrine of Mosaic authorship. Wrote popular 4-vol. introduction to Bible. Expert in Hebrew language; wrote grammar of Mishnaic Hebrew. His son **Lord Samuel** (1902–), Labor MP, peer. Deputy speaker, House of Lords, 1974. Another son, **Judah Benzion** (1912–), prof. of Semitic languages at London Univ.

"The Gas Station" by George Segal.

"Jew at Prayer," drypoint by Lasar Segall, 1927.

Segal, Yakov-Yitskhak (1896–1954), Canadian Yiddish poet; b. Ukraine, in Canada fr. 1911. Prolific writer and editor of periodicals.

Segall, Lasar (1891–1957), Brazilian artist; b. Vilna. Among leading expressionist painters in Germany 1919–23, in Brazil fr. 1923. After 1936 painted large compositions based on terrible events of the period.

Segalowitch, Zusman (1884–1949), Yiddish poet, novelist; b. Poland, reached Ereẓ Israel 1941 and later went to U.S. Wrote poems, ballads, novels, stories, and autobiographical triology. Many works on Holocaust.

Seghers, Anna (pseud. of **Netty Radvanyi;** 1900–), German novelist. During Nazi period fled to Paris, Mexico; returned to E. Germany 1947. Active communist; works reflect concern for lower classes of all countries.

Segol, Hebrew vowel sign indicating sound equivalent of English short *e.* Written ֶ

Segovia, town in Spain; one of most important Jewish communities in 14th c. Castile. Massacre of 1931 drove many Jews to baptism and in 1480s town was center of anti-Jewish and anti-Converso activity. Exiles probably went to Portugal 1492.

Segrè, Emilio Gino (1905–), nuclear physicist; b. Italy. Discoverer of element 43 "technetium." In U.S. fr. 1938. Worked at Univ. of California, where he discovered element astatine. After WWII participated in search for antiproton. Shared 1959 Nobel Prize for Physics.

Segrè, Roberto (1872–1936), Italian soldier. Served in Italo-Turkish war and WWI. After war, headed Italian-Austrian armistice commission.

Segre, Salvatore (Joshua Benzion; 1729–1809), Italian rabbi inclined toward Reform. *Av bet din* of French Sanhedrin.

Seiber, Mátyás György (1905–1960), composer; b. Hungary, in London fr. 1935. His early works rank among most important of Hungarian school and his later ones utilized both preclassic and 12-tone techniques.

Seir, see Edom; Esau.

Seir, Mount, biblical name for area originally inhabited by Horites and later by Edomites. Area is now known as Jebel.

Seixas, Gershom Mendes (1746–1816), first native-born U.S. Jewish minister. *Ḥazzan* Congregation Shearith Israel. During American Revolution moved fr. New York to Connecticut and then Philadelphia, back to N.Y. 1784. Participated in Washington's inauguration 1789.

Sejera, see Ilaniyyah.

Sejmists, see Jewish Socialist Workers' Party.

Sela, see Petra.

Selah, term used in Book of Psalms and Habakkuk 3. No agreement as to its meaning and function. Traditional rendering is "always" or "for eternity." May have been liturgical or musical indication.

Seldes, George (1890–), U.S. journalist, author. As crusading pamphleteer wrote exposés of many aspects of American life. Published weekly bulletin *In Fact* 1940–50. Wrote *Sawdust Caesar,* debunking biography of Mussolini.

Seldin, Harry M. (1895–), U.S. oral surgeon. Played leading part in founding Heb. Univ.–Hadassah School of Dentistry and founded Harry M. Seldin Center of Oral-Maxillary Surgery at Rambam Hospital, Haifa.

Selekman, Benjamin Morris (1893–1962), U.S. labor relations expert. Prof. at Harvard Univ. School of Business 1945–62. Regarded social conflict in labor relations as virtually unavoidable as part of process of economic development and emergence of democratic social stability.

Seleucid Era, basis for Jewish reckoning of years during Second Temple period, referred to in Hebrew as *minyan shetarot.* Commenced probably 311 B.C.E.

Self-Defense, Jewish efforts against attacking mobs in Russia and Austria-Hungary fr. end of 19th c. until shortly after WWI. Defense units formed in response to government compliance with pogroms of 1881–82, 1903–05, 1917–20. Although movement was widespread in Russia, it was not united or concerted but frequently proved effective.

Selig, Phineas (1856–1941), New Zealand journalist; the outstanding figure in New Zealand press in 1920s and 1930s. Influential in Jewish community.

Seligman, Charles Gabriel (1873–1940), British physician, anthro-

pologist. Held first chair of anthropology at Univ. of London. Conducted important field surveys in Ceylon, Sudan, Melanesia.

Seligman, Edwin Robert Anderson (1861–1939), U.S. economist; son of Joseph Seligman. Prof. at Columbia Univ. A founder and pres. 1902–04 of American Economic Society. Reorganized Cuba's fiscal system 1932. Writings incl. *The Economic Interpretation of History.*

Seligman, Joseph (1819–1880), U.S. banker; b. Bavaria, in U.S. fr. 1837. Established with brothers banking firm J. & W. Seligman & Co. 1864. Assisted U.S. government in refunding national debt and resumption of specie payment in 1870s. Prominent in railroad financing and headed De Lesseps Panama Canal Syndicate. Major role in all Allied loan syndicates during WWI.

Seligmann, Caesar (1860–1950), leader of Liberal Judaism in Germany, a founder of Vereinigung fuer das liberale Judentum, and editor of its organ, *Liberales Judentum;* in London fr. 1939.

Seligmann, Kurt (1900–1962), U.S. surrealist painter; b. Switzerland; in U.S. fr. 1939. Authority on magic. Preoccupation with magic and metaphysical philosophy reflected in his art.

Seligsberg, Alice Lillie (1873–1940), U.S. Zionist and civic leader. Helped organize American Zionist Medical Unit 1917 and laid foundation for Hadassah's medical program in Ereẓ Israel. National pres. Hadassah 1920–21.

Seliḥot (Heb. sing. *seliḥah* lit. "forgiveness"), collection of *piyyutim* whose subject is forgiveness fr. sin. Recited on all fast days and on occasions of special intercession. Special services fr. before Rosh Ha-Shanah until Day of Atonement.

Selikovitch, George (Getzel; 1855 or 1863–1926), Yiddish, Hebrew writer, scholar; b. Lithuania. Accompanied Kitchener as translator in expedition to relieve Gordon at Khartoum 1885. Arrived in U.S. 1887. Lectured on Egyptology at Univ. of Pennsylvania and Franklin Institute, Pa. On editorial staff of Yiddish daily *Tageblat* 1890–1926.

Sellers, Peter (Richard Henry; 1925–), British actor. A founder of radio *The Goon Show;* worked in TV, theater, films *(I'm All Right, Jack, Dr. Strangelove, What's New Pussycat?).*

°**Sellin, Ernst** (1876–1946), German Bible scholar, archaeologist. Excavated at Tell Ta'annek, Jericho, Shechem. Edited 13 vol. series of Bible commentaries.

Selvinski, Ilya Lvovich (1899–1968), Soviet Russian poet; one of foremost exponents of constructivism. Work repeatedly attacked for assorted heresies; some contain Jewish portraits.

Selz, Otto (1881–1944?), German psychologist. Work concerned primarily with thought processes and foreshadowed modern approach to psychology of thinking. Fr. 1933 in Netherlands; deported to death in concentration camp.

Selznick. U.S. family in film industry. **Lewis B.** (1872–1933), film producer. Joined film-making company 1910 and persuaded Shubert brothers to turn stage shows into films. Helped start star system. His son **Myron** (1898–1944), formed Select Pictures with father and controlled multi-million dollar business that was wiped out in 1929 crash. Subsequently Hollywood press agent. His other son, **David Oliver** (1902–1965), one of Hollywood's major producers. Films incl. *Gone with the Wind,* then the most expensive and successful film ever made. Voted top producer for 10 successive years.

Semag, see Moses ben Jacob of Coucy.

Semaḥot (Heb. "rejoicings"), euphemistic title of two minor tractates, of which one, *Evel Rabbati,* is usually published as appendix to Babylonian Talmud. Deals with laws and customs of mourning.

Semak, see Isaac ben Joseph of Corbeil.

Seman, Philip Louis (1881–1957), U.S. educator, organization executive. Director of Jewish People's Institute of Chicago 1913–45; national leader in Jewish social work.

Semikhah (Heb.). (1) Laying of hands on animal immediately before sacrifice. (2) Ordination of rabbis. Originally performed only in Ereẓ Israel. With decline of Ereẓ Israel community, custom discontinued and other communities developed other modes of conferring authority (e.g., in Babylon scholars called *rav,* not *rabbi.*) Attempt at revival made in Safed in 16th c. by Jacob Berab. In modern times modified version is used. Since 19th c. most authorities demand broader education than only Talmud and codes previously required.

Séminaire Israélite de France (also known as *Ecole Rabbinique*), French seminary founded in Metz 1829 for training of rabbis, *ḥazzanim,* and teachers. Transferred to Paris 1859.

Semites, term referring to those peoples descended fr. Noah's son Shem (Gen. 10). Geographically, they are spread from Lydia to Persia to Armenia in the N. and the Persian Gulf and Red Sea in the S. The only modern scientific use of the term is in connection with linguistic categories (Semitic languages).

Semitic Languages, language family to which Hebrew belongs. Semitic family forms part of wide grouping generally called Hamito-Semitic. About 70 distinct forms of Semitic are known, ranging fr. important languages with large literature to language forms used over limited territory and entirely unwritten or possessing few preserved documents. Usually there are three divisions made in list of Semitic languages: Eastern (Akkadian); Northwestern (e.g., Ugaritic, Phoenician, Canaanite, Moabite, Amorite, Hebrew); Southern (Arabic, Sabean, Minean, Ethiopic).

THE SEMITIC LANGUAGES

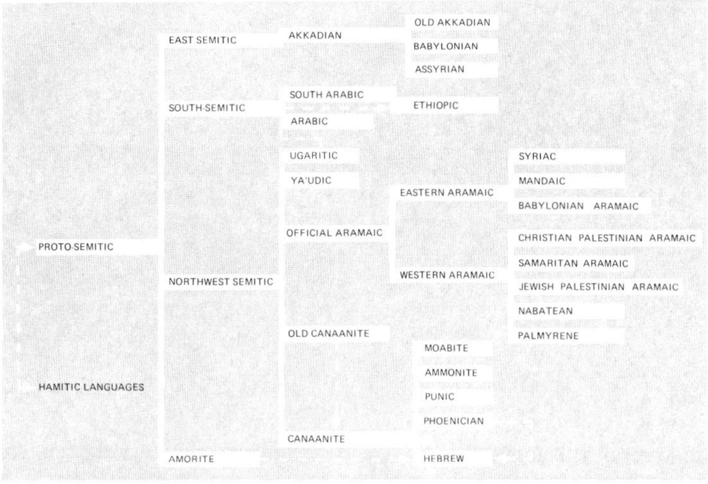

Semlin, see Zemun.

Semon, Sir Felix (1849–1921), British physician; b. Germany, in London fr. 1874. Formulation of Semon-Rosenbach Law based on his research into progressive destructive lesion of motor nerve supplying laryngeal muscles. British royalty among his patients.

Semon, Richard Wolfgang (1859–1918), German zoologist. Wrote on embryology of lungfish and theoretical problems of evolution.

Senator, David Werner (1896–1953), Zionist administrator; b. Germany. Secretary-general of Joint Distribution Committee in Europe 1925–30, member of Jewish Agency Executive 1930–35, administrator and fr. 1949 vice-pres. of Heb. Univ.

Sendrey, Alfred (Szendrei, Aladar; 1884–), U.S. musician, writer on music; b. Budapest. His *Bibliography of Jewish Music* became a standard book of reference.

Seneor, Abraham (c. 1412–c. 1493), courtier in Spain during expulsion period. As rabbi and supreme judge of Jews of Castile, did much to assist Jewish communities. Under royal pressure, converted to Christianity 1492 and was appointed *regidor* of Segovia, member of royal council, chief financial administrator of crown prince.

A section of the Sennacherib relief from his palace at Nineveh.

Senior Max (1862–1939), U.S. businessman, communal leader; b. Cincinnati. A founder of United Jewish Social Agencies; first pres. National Conference of Jewish Charities 1899. A European representative of Joint Distribution Committee in WWI.

°**Sennacherib,** king of Assyria 705–681 B.C.E. His expedition to the west which brought him into conflict with Hezekiah of Judah (II Kings 18:13–19:37; Isa. 36–37) was minor punitive expedition to assure payment of tribute.

Sepharad, site of colony of exiles fr. Jerusalem (Obad. 20); identified as Sardis. Fr. 8th c., usual Hebrew appellation for Iberian Peninsula.

Sephardim, descendants of Jews who lived in Spain or Portugal before expulsion of 1492. Established communities of numerical, economic, and scholastic importance in N. Africa, Italy, the Near East, W. Europe, America, and the Balkans (esp. Constantinople, Salonika, Izmir). Retained distinctive language (Ladino) and forms of religious practice which differed in details fr. that of Ashkenazim. Together with other non-Ashkenazi Jews constitute 17% of world Jewry and about half of population of Israel.

Sepharvaim, city fr. which king of Assyria brought settlers to Samaria after conquest of kingdom of Israel (II Kings 17:24). Suggested identification in Babylonia or Syria.

Sepphoris (Heb. *Ẓippori*), ancient Jewish city in Galilee. During reign of Alexander Yannai (100 B.C.E.)

Waves of Sephardi emigration from Spain and Portugal after expulsion of 1492, with dates of establishment of new communities where known.

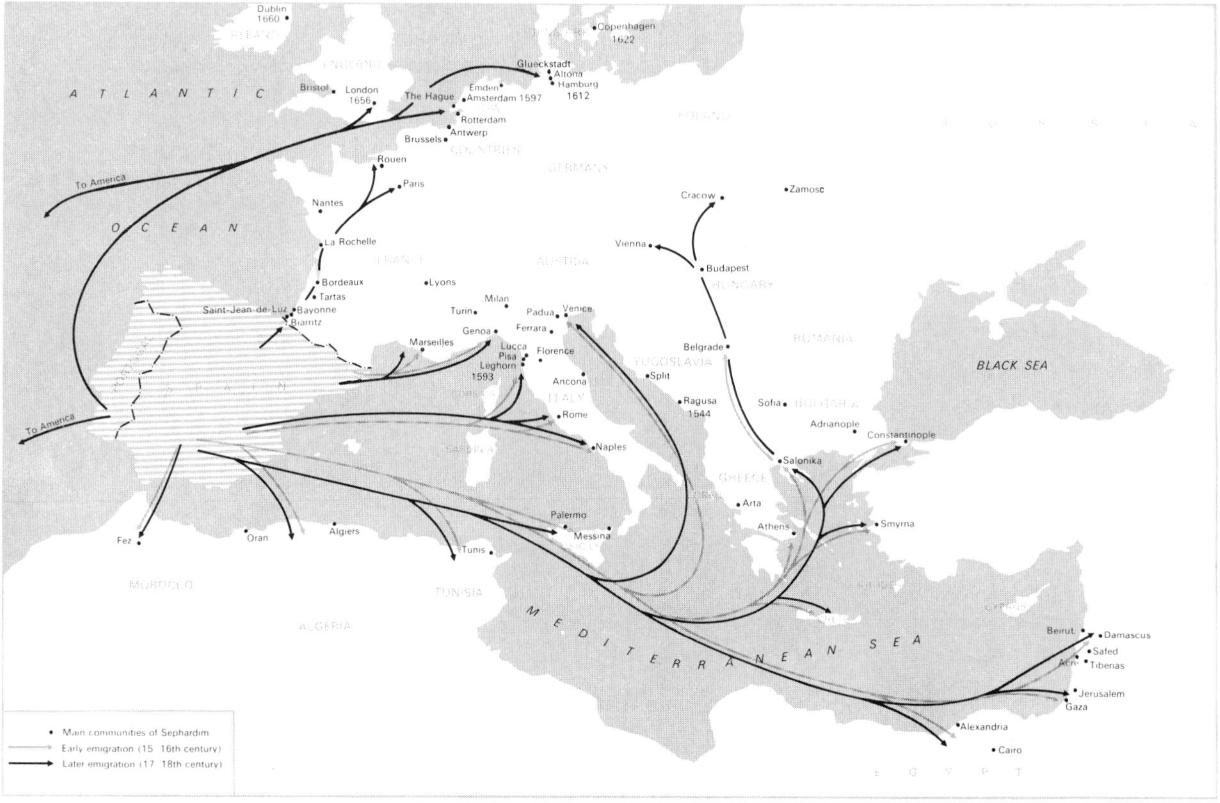

administrative capital of Galilee. Seat of Patriarchate and Sanhedrin under R. Judah ha-Nasi and remained such until the days of his grandson. Center of Jewish revolt against Gallus Caesar 351/2 C.E. Fr. 1949 site of moshav.

Septuagint, oldest Greek translation of Bible. Name (fr. Lat. *septuaginta*, "seventy") based on legend according to which 72 elders of Israel translated Pentateuch into Greek in Alexandria in 3rd c. B.C.E. Designation extended to entire Bible as translated into Greek during following two centuries. Together with New Testament, constituted Bible of Christian Church (either in original or through its Latin translation, the Vulgate).

Seraiah biblical figure. Served under Zedekiah of Judah (196–186 B.C.E.) and had pro-Babylonian sympathies. Zedekiah's emissary to Babylon (Jer. 51:59) and also served as Jeremiah's emissary.

Seraph, in Bible (1) a legendary species of serpent (Num. 21:6; Deut. 8:15); (2) composite semidivine being with three pairs of wings (Isa. 6:2, 6).

Serbia, see Yugoslavia.

Ṣere, see Ẓere.

Serekh, term in Qumran texts denoting the community's "rule" of life or some aspect of it; used as title (or part of title) of some of community documents (e.g., Manual of Discipline).

Sereni, Angelo Piero (1908–1967), Italian jurist; in U.S. during WWII. Wrote extensively on international legal disputes.

Sereni, Emilio (1907–), Italian agronomist, communist politician; brother of Enzo Sereni. After WWII, deputy, senator, minister of social welfare, minister of public works.

Sereni, Enzo Ḥayyim (1905–1944), pioneer in Ereẓ Israel, labor leader, writer; b. Italy, settled in Ereẓ Israel 1927. A founder of Givat Brenner. Organized He-Ḥaluẓ movement in Germany and Iraq. Organized Jewish parachutists to be dropped behind enemy lines in Europe 1943. Dropped in N. Italy, captured by Germans, and shot.

Serenus, see Severus.

Serfati, Benaza Rafael (1919–), Venezuelan politician. Elected senator 1963.

Serkin, Rudolf (1903–), pianist. Master performer of classical repertoire. Headed pianoforte faculty at Curtis Inst., Philadelphia fr. 1939. His son, **Peter** (1947–), also concert pianist.

ORDER OF THE BOOKS IN THE SEPTUAGINT

THE PENTATEUCH

- Genesis
- Exodus
- Leviticus
- Numbers
- Deuteronomy

THE HISTORICAL BOOKS

- Joshua
- Judges
- Ruth
- I–IV Kingdoms (Samuel and Kings)
- Chronicles
- I Esdras
- Ezra
- Nehemiah
- Esther
- Judith
- Tobit
- I–IV Maccabees

THE POETICAL BOOKS

- Psalms
- Odae
- Proverbs
- Ecclesiastes
- Song of Songs
- Job
- Wisdom of Solomon
- Psalms of Solomon

THE DIDACTICAL BOOKS

- Wisdom of Solomon
- Ecclesiasticus

THE PROPHETS

- Minor Prophets
  - Hosea
  - Amos
  - Micah
  - Joel
  - Obadiah
  - Jonah
  - Nahum
  - Habakkuk
  - Zephaniah
  - Haggai
  - Zechariah
  - Malachi
- Isaiah
- Jeremiah
- Baruch
- Lamentations
- Epistle of Jeremiah
- Ezekiel
- Susanna
- Daniel
- Bel and the Dragon

Key (top left) given to Ferdinand III by Jews of Seville upon his capture of the city in 1248. Decoration and inscriptions are shown in detail.

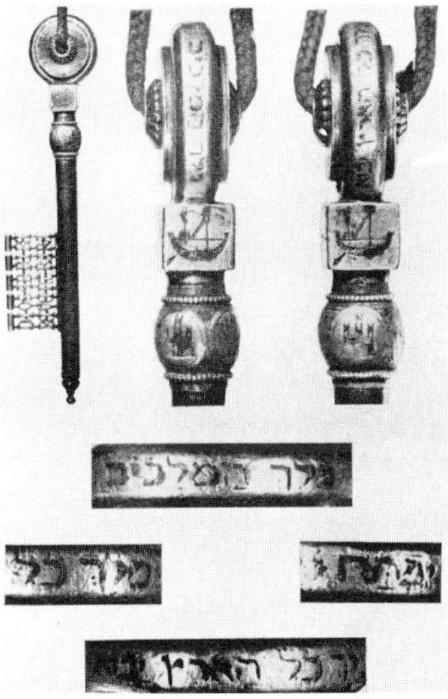

Serp, see Jewish Socialist Workers' Party.

Servi Camerae Regis (Lat. "servants of the royal chamber"), definition of status of Jews in Christian Europe in Middle Ages, first used in 13th c. Conception implied both inferior status of Jews and right to royal protection. Affected status of Jews down to modern times.

Seter (Starominsky), Mordechai (1916–), Israel composer. Attempted to combine modern idioms with melodic material offered by Jewish liturgical and folk traditions, esp. of Sephardi and Yemenite communities. Works incl. *Sabbath Cantata* and *Tikkun Ḥaẓot*.

Seth, antediluvian patriarch; son of Adam and Eve.

Se'udah (Heb. "meal"), festive meal in connection with religious acts, such as weddings, festivals, completion of study of talmudic tractate; also referred to as *se'udah shel mitzvah*.

Se'udah Shelishit, "third meal" eaten on Sabbath afternoon. Developed among ḥasidim into festive communal gathering with chanting of *zemirot*.

Seven Benedictions, blessings recited as part of the marriage ceremony and at meals during the traditional seven days of wedding feasts. These benedictions are first mentioned in the Talmud (Ket. 7b–8a).

Seventy Shepherds, Vision of, modern name of treatise, also known as "Dream-Visions," in chapters 83–90 of Ethiopic Book of Enoch. Dates fr. beginning of Maccabean period.

Severus (sometimes called Serenus); pseudo-messiah in Babylonia c. 720 C.E. Introduced ritual innovations and was thought to have influenced Byzantine Jews. Attracted large following of Jews and Christians and was put to death by Moslem authorities.

Seville, city in SW Spain. Jewish settlement during period of Visigothic rule; under Moslem Umayyads community attained cultural, economic, and political importance. Position consolidated under Christian rule, but Ferrant Martinez began anti-Jewish agitation 1378 and community almost totally destroyed during 1391 persecutions. Expelled 1483. In 20th c. some Jews from N. Africa and Europe settled there.

Sevitzky, Fabien (1893–1967), conductor. Played double bass in Russian orchestras. Founded Philadelphia String Sinfonietta 1925; permanent conductor Indianapolis Symphony Orchestra 1935–55.

"Piyyut" for "Shabbat ha-Gadol," detail from "Worms Maḥzor," Germany, 1272.

Tombstone of Shabbetai b. Meir ha-Kohen in Holeslov, erected 1817, restored 1897.

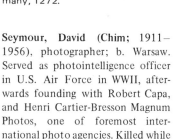

Engraving of Shabbetai Ẓevi, believed to be the only portrait done from life, 1669.

Seymour, David (Chim; 1911–1956), photographer; b. Warsaw. Served as photointelligence officer in U.S. Air Force in WWII, afterwards founding with Robert Capa, and Henri Cartier-Bresson Magnum Photos, one of foremost international photo agencies. Killed while covering Sinai Campaign.

°**Seyss-Inquart, Arthur** (1892–1946), Austrian Nazi lawyer. Served in top Nazi posts in Austria, occupied Poland, and Holland. Sentenced to death at Nuremberg trials.

Sfard, David (1905–), Yiddish writer, editor; b. Volhynia, fled 1939 to Russian-occupied territory, repatriated to Poland 1946, settled in Israel 1969. Wrote verse, short stories, translations.

Sforno, Obadiah ben Jacob (c. 1470–c. 1550), Italian Bible commentator, physician. Active in reviving Hebrew printing press of Bologna. Reputation rests on popular biblical commentary published in all rabbinic bibles.

Shaanan, Avraham (1919–), Hebrew writer, literary critic; b. Galicia, settled in Ereẓ Israel 1935. Editor literary supplement of *Davar,* cultural attaché Israel Embassy in Paris 1963–66. Wrote history of modern Heb. literature. Prof. Bar-Ilan Univ.

Sha'arei Shevu'ot, work on laws of oaths, extensively quoted by early *posekim;* of unknown authorship. Usually published with *halakhot* of Isaac Alfasi.

Sha'atnez, cloth containing mixture of linen and wool that Jews are forbidden to wear (Lev. 19:19; Deut. 22:11).

Shabad, Ẓemaḥ (1864–1935), physician, publicist; one of heads of Vilna community. Promoted development of ORT, elected a member of Polish Senate 1928, a founder of YIVO research institute.

Shabazi, Shalem (17th c.), greatest Yemenite Jewish poet. Described as *ẓaddik* and miracle worker; his tomb in Taiz became shrine for both Jews and Moslems. Poems deal with theme of exile and redemption; many included in Yemenite liturgy.

Shabbat, see Sabbath.

Shabbat, 1st tractate in Mishnah order *Mo'ed,* with *gemara* in both Talmuds. Deals with laws of Sabbath and its observance.

Shabbat Bereshit (Heb. "Sabbath of Genesis"), 1st Sabbath after Sukkot, on which new annual cycle of the Torah reading in synagogue begins.

Shabbat ha-Gadol (Heb. "the great Sabbath"), Sabbath preceding Passover. In traditional synagogues, rabbi delivers sermon devoted almost exclusively to rites and dietary laws pertaining to Passover.

Shabbat ha-Ḥodesh (Heb.), Sabbath preceding or coinciding with Nisan 1. Ex. 12:1–20 is added to weekly Torah portion.

Shabbat Ḥazon (Heb. "Sabbath of Vision"), Sabbath preceding Av 9; the *haftarah* fr. Isa. 1:1–27. Yemenites call this day "Shabbat Eikhoh" and read Isa. 1:21 ff. for *haftarah.*

Shabbat Ḥol ha-Mo'ed (Heb.), Sabbath of Passover and Sukkot intermediary days. Special Torah readings, *piyyutim,* and Song of Songs (Passover) or Ecclesiastes (Sukkot) are recited.

Shabbat Mevarekhin (Heb.), Sabbath immediately preceding new month. In Ashkenazi rite special petition for blessed month is recited and name of month and date of Rosh Ḥodesh is announced.

Shabbat Naḥamu (Heb.), Sabbath immediately following Av 9. *Haftarah* portion is taken fr. Isa. 40.

Shabbat Parah (Heb. "Sabbath of the Red Heifer"), Sabbath preceding Shabbat ha-Ḥodesh. Num. 19:1–22 is added to weekly Torah portion.

Shabbat Rosh Ḥodesh (Heb.), Sabbath which coincides with Rosh Ḥodesh. Reading of Torah for New Moon is added and special *haftarah* (Isa. 66:1–24) is read.

Shabbat Shekalim (Heb.), Sabbath immediately preceding month of Adar (Adar II in leap year). Ex. 30:11–16 is added to weekly Torah portion.

Shabbat Shirah (Heb. "Sabbath of the Song"), Sabbath on which Torah reading is Song of the Sea (Ex. 14–17).

Shabbat Shuvah (Heb. "Sabbath of Repentance"), Sabbath which occurs during Ten Days of Penitence; occasion of special *haftarah* (Hos. 14:2) and sermons on repentance by congregational rabbis.

Shabbat Zakhor (Heb. "Sabbath of Remembrance"), Sabbath preceding Purim. Deut. 25:17–19 is added to weekly Torah portion with exhortation to remember cruelty of Amalekites.

Shabbetai ben Meir ha-Kohen (Shakh; 1621–1662), rabbi in Vilna. Author of *Siftei Kohen,* standard commentary on *Shulḥan Arukh Yoreh De'ah,* and *Ḥoshen Mishpat.*

Shabbetai Ẓevi (1626–1676), pseudo-messiah, central figure of messianic movement of widespread consequence in Jewish history (Sabbateanism, Shabbateanism); b. Smyrna, Turkey. Received traditional talmudic education and studied Kabbalah. Tended to perform "strange acts" in defiance of Law. Influenced by Nathan of Gaza (q.v.) to proclaim himself messiah. Movement captured many communities, both unlettered people and rabbis, throughout Europe, N. Africa, and esp. Middle East. Arrested by Sultan 1666, given choice of death or conversion to Islam; chose conversion. Nevertheless still received trust of some of his followers and new branch of Kabbalah developed to explain mystery of messiah's apostasy (see Doenmeh).

Shadal, see Luzzatto, Samuel David.

Shadkhan (Heb.), marriage broker or matchmaker who arranges unions for financial consideration.

Shadrach, Meshach, Abed-Nego, three young men of aristocratic Judahite stock whose Hebrew names were respectively Hananiah, Mishael, and Azariah. Together with Daniel they went through trial of fiery furnace at court of Nebuchadnezzar (Dan. 1–3).

Shaffer, Peter (1926–), English playwright. Made his name with *Five-Finger Exercise* and spectacular *The Royal Hunt of the Sun.* His brother **Anthony** (1926–), wrote successful detective play *Sleuth.*

Shaham, Nathan (1925–), Hebrew writer; son of Eliezer Steinman. Served in Palmaḥ; member of kibbutz. Wrote fiction, plays, stories for children.

Shaḥarit (Heb.), daily morning prayer recited after daybreak. Replaced morning sacrifice. *Tallit* and *tefillin* (on weekdays) are worn. On Monday and Thursday, as well as Sabbath, Torah is read. Acc. to rabbinical tradition, instituted by Abraham.

Shahin (14th c.), Judeo-Persian poet fr. Shiraz. Wrote poetical paraphrase of Pentateuch in Persian with Hebrew characters.

Shahn, Ben (1898–1969), U.S. painter, printmaker. Frequent commentator on social scene. Often dealt with Jewish subject matter; illustrated *Haggadah.*

Shaḥor (Czerny, Schwartz), Ḥayyim (16th c.), pioneer in Hebrew printing in C. Europe. Prepared almost all the woodcut illustrations for Passover *Haggadah* of Gershom Kohen in Prague. Later itinerant printer in Germany and Poland.

Shaikevich, Nahum Meyer, see Shomer.

Shakh, see Shabbetai ben Meir ha-Kohen.

Shalag, see Gordon, Samuel Leib.

Shalem, see Jerusalem.

Shali'aḥ (Heb.), messenger, agent. Talmud deals with laws governing validity of agents' acts. In modern times, emissaries fr. Ereẓ Israel to communities abroad to collect funds, organize pioneer Jewish education, etc.

Shalkovich, Abraham Leib (pen name **Ben-Avigdor;** 1867–1921), Russian Hebrew author, pioneer of modern Hebrew publishing. Founded "Agorah" series to revitalize Hebrew literature, set up publishing houses, founded children's weekly. Edited periodicals and wrote stories.

Shallum, one of last kings of Israel. Ruled fr. Samaria for one month in 747 B.C.E. Killed by Menahem (II Kings 15:10–14).

Shallum, see Jehoahaz.

Shalom, Abraham ben Isaac ben Judah ben Samuel (d. 1492), Spanish philosopher, translator fr. Latin to Hebrew. In his *Neveh Shalom* defends philosophic position of Maimonides.

Shalom, Isaac I. (1886–1968), U.S. businessman philanthropist; b. Aleppo, Syria, in U.S. fr. 1910. A founder of Oẓar Hatorah organization. Leader N.Y. Sephardi and Syrian communities.

Shalom, Shin (pseud. of **Shalom Joseph Shapira;** 1904–), Hebrew poet, author; b. Poland, settled in Ereẓ Israel 1922. Wrote poetry, novels, dramas. Chairman of Hebrew Writers' Association fr. 1968.

Shalom (Sholem) Aleichem (pseud. of **Shalom Rabinovitz;** 1859–1916), Yiddish author, humorist; b. Ukraine, lived for many years in Kiev and then in many other places, incl. U.S., where he died. Wrote in many genres. His writings paint giant canvas of Jewish society as "Jewish comedy" with tragic elements. Creator of Menachem Mendel, and his counterpart Tevye der Milchiger ("Tevye the Dairyman"). Stories of latter were often dramatized and formed basis of musical hit *Fiddler on the Roof.* Also creator of imaginary town of Kasrilevke, symbol of Jewish towns in E. Europe. His writings were translated into many languages.

Shalom Aleikhem (Heb. "peace be upon you"). (1) Common form of greeting among Jews. (2) First words of hymn welcoming Sabbath angels recited on returning from synagogue on Friday evenings.

Shalom of Safed, see Moskovitz, Shalom.

Shalom Shakhna ben Joseph (d. 1558), founder of talmudic scholarship in Poland. Headed yeshivah in Lublin. Appointed chief rabbi of Lesser Poland 1541 by government, with right to impose capital punishment.

Shalon, Raḥel (1904–), Israel engineer; b. Poland, settled in Ereẓ Israel 1925. Served in Haganah. Prof. of civil engineering at Haifa Technion.

Shaltiel, David (1903–1969), Israel soldier, diplomat; b. Hamburg, served in French Foreign Legion 1926–31, settled in Ereẓ Israel 1932. Chief of Haganah intelligence 1941–42, 1946–48, commander of

Illuminated page from ms. of "Sefer Sharḥ Shahin al ha-Torah," Tabriz, 1686 (?).

"Call of the Shofar," mosaic mural by Ben Shahn.

Shalom Aleichem

Jerusalem during War of Independence. Ambassador in Brazil, Mexico, Holland.

Shamgar, son of Anath, deliverer of Israel who flourished in period of Judges. Saved Israel by slaying 600 Philistines with oxgoad (Judg. 3:31; 5:6).

Shamir, legendary worm used for cutting metal or stone; used by Moses to engrave tribes' names on breastplate of high priest and by Solomon in construction of Temple instead of iron tools.

Shamir, Moshe (1921–), Israel author. Member of Ha-Shomer ha-Ẓa'ir kibbutz; joined Palmaḥ. Edited various literary magazines, head of Jewish Agency Aliyah Dept. in London 1969–71. Wrote stories, novels, plays. Works incl. novels *King of Flesh and Blood* about Alexander Yannai and *He Walked in the Fields* about War of Independence.

Shammai (Ha-Zaken, i.e., **The Elder;** c. 50 B.C.E.–30 C.E.), a leader of the Sanhedrin, colleague of Hillel, founder of School of Bet Shammai. Generally took more stringent view in *halakhah* than Hillel. Favorite dictum: "Study Torah regularly, say little, but do much, receive all men in a friendly manner."

Shammash, beadle or sexton of community, synagogue, or rabbinical court; frequently performed variety of functions, e.g., summoning to prayer, messenger, almoner. Along with rabbi and cantor he was entitled to share of fees and largesse.

Shanghai, port in China. Small but flourishing 14th c. Jewish community considerably augmented by Russian and German refugees in 20th c.; numbered 25,000 in 1940. Jews suffered under Japanese occupation and all emigrated after WWII.

Drawing of the former Beth Aharon Synagogue of Shanghai, 1945.

Shanker, Albert (1928–), U.S. teacher, labor leader. Pres. Federation of Teachers fr. 1964 and won considerable benefits for N.Y.C. teachers. Led city-wide teacher strike 1968.

Shaphan, Josiah's scribe and head of one of most influential and pro-Babylonian families in last days of Judah.

Shapira (Spira), Hungarian ḥasidic family known as Munkacs dynasty. Its founder was **Solomon** (1832–1893). His son **Ẓevi Hirsch** (1850–1913) refused to associate Hungarian Jewry in founding of Agudat Israel. Wrote *Darkei Teshuvah* on *Shulḥan Arukh Yoreh De'ah.* Ẓevi's son **Ḥayyim Eleazar** (1872–1937), though an opponent of Mizrachi and Agudat Israel was president of *Kolel* Munkacs in Jerusalem.

Abraham Shapira

Shapira, Abraham (1870–1965), one of first Jewish *Shomerim* ("Watchman") in Ereẓ Israel. A colorful, romantic figure, he lived most of his life in Petaḥ Tikvah.

Shapira, Ḥayyim Moshe (1902–1970), Israel politician; leader of National Religious Party; b. Belorussia. Central figure in Ẓe'irei ha-Mizrachi. Settled in Ereẓ Israel 1925. Member of Zionist Executive, served in almost all Israel governments fr. 1948. Among initiators of the "United Religious Front" and pres. Mizrachi and Ha-Po'el ha-Mizrachi world center.

Shapira, Meir (1887–1934), Polish rabbi, *rosh yeshivah,* educationalist, communal leader. Member of Polish Sejm. Inaugurator of *daf yomi* (daily page), whereby Jews undertake to study one identical page of Talmud daily, and founder of Yeshivat Ḥakhmei Lublin. Requested his students to dance around his bed as he was dying.

Shapira, Yeshayahu (1891–1945), ḥasidic Ereẓ Israel pioneer, leader of religious labor Zionism; b. Poland. Among founders of Mizrachi 1917. Settled in Ereẓ Israel 1920. A founder and leader of Ha-Po'el ha-Mizrachi. Established Kefar Ḥasidim, first religious settlement.

Shapira Fragments, portions of manuscript of Deuteronomy claimed to have been found in Judean Desert and to be of exceptionally early date, which were offered for sale in Berlin and London by Moses William Shapira (c. 1830–1884). Authenticity of fragments was attacked by many scholars, esp. as Shapira had previously forged documents. More recently, in the light of the Qumran discoveries, certain scholars have reopened the subject. Shapira committed suicide.

Shapiro, Abba Constantin (1839–1900), Hebrew poet; b. Poland, lived in Vienna and St. Petersburg and was baptized. His poetry is replete with Jewish and occasionally Zionist themes.

Shapiro, Ascher Herman (1916–), U.S. construction engineer. Prof. of engineering at MIT 1962, head of mechanical engineering dept. 1965. Patents incl. fluid-metering apparatus, propulsion systems, aerothermopressor.

Shapiro, Ezra Z. (1903–), Zionist, communal leader. Active in Cleveland, U.S. A leader of World Confederation of General Zionists and a founder of American League for Israel. Fr. 1971 in Jerusalem as chairman of Keren Hayesod–United Jewish Appeal. Member of Jewish Agency Executive.

Shapiro, Harry Lionel (1902–), U.S. anthropologist. Curator physical anthropology, American Museum of Natural History (1942). Prof. anthropology, Columbia Univ. (1943). Writings incl. *Aspects of Culture* and *Heritage of the Bounty.*

Shapiro, Karl Jay (1913–), U.S. poet, critic. Prof. at Univ. of Nebraska. Won Pulitzer Prize 1944 for *V-Letter and Other Poems.*

Shapiro, (Levi Joshua) Lamed (1878–1948), Yiddish writer; b. Russia, wandered through many countries, lived chaotic and restless life, eventually settled in U.S. His short stories explore violence and human conflict.

Shapiro, Lionel (1908–1958), Canadian novelist, journalist. His three political novels center on evils of Nazism, among them the prize-winning story of Normandy invasion, *The Sixth of June.*

Shapiro, Samuel H. (1907–), U.S. lawyer, legislator. Lt.-governor of Illinois 1960–68. Briefly governor 1968.

Shapiro, Ya'akov Shimshon (1902–), Israel lawyer, politician; b. Russia, settled in Ereẓ Israel 1924. First attorney-general of Israel 1948–49, member of 2nd and 7th Knesset, minister of justice 1965–73.

Shapp, Milton J. (1912–), U.S. industrialist, public figure. Founded Jerrod Electronics Corp. Elected governor of Pennsylvania 1970, first Jew to hold office.

Sharabi, Shalom (1720–1777), Jerusalem kabbalist; b. Yemen. Head of kabbalistic yeshivah Bet El, writer on Lurianic Kabbalah; regarded as saint and miracle worker. Wrote *Nehar Shalom,* prayer book with mystical meditations on prayers and *mitzvot.*

Sharef, Ze'ev (1906–), Israel political figure; b. Bukovina, settled

in Erez̩ Israel 1925. First secretary of Israel government 1948–57. Cabinet member 1966–73, holding mainly economic portfolios.

Sharett (Shertok), Moshe (1894–1965), second prime minister of Israel, Zionist leader; b. Ukraine, settled in Erez̩ Israel 1906. In WWI in Turkish army as interpreter. Succeeded Arlosoroff as head of Jewish Agency's Political Dept. 1933–48. Played decisive part in establishment of Jewish Brigade; arrested on "Black Saturday" (June 29, 1946), led international struggle for approval of the UNSCOP partition proposals by UN. Israel's first foreign minister, prime minister Jan. 1954–Nov. 1955, and again foreign minister until his resignation 1956. Elected chairman of Executive of Zionist Organization and Jewish Agency 1960.

Sharett (Shertok), Yehudah (1901–), Israel composer; brother of Moshe Sharett. Composed intensively for kibbutz needs. His crowning achievement was *Yagur Passover Seder Service.*

Sharm el-Sheikh, small bay on SE coast of Sinai Peninsula, opening out to Red Sea. Egyptian attempts to blockade Israel shipping entering Gulf of Eilat led to Sinai campaign and Six-Day War and Israel control fr. 1967. Israel planned to build resort there named Ophira.

Sharon, Israel central coastal plain extending fr. Jaffa to Mt. Carmel. One of richest agricultural districts in Erez̩ Israel, esp. for citriculture.

Sharon, Abraham, see Schwadron, Abraham.

Shas, popular name for Talmud; abbr. of *Shishah Sedarim,* "the six orders" of the Mishnah.

Shatzkes, Moses (1881–1958), Lithuanian rabbi. Rabbi of Lomza fr. 1930. Emigrated to U.S. 1941 and was faculty member of Yeshiva Univ.

Shatzky, Jacob (1893–1956), Polish historian. Among founders of U.S. section of YIVO. Major work was history of Warsaw Jewry.

Shaul (Shaool), Anwar (1904–), Iraqi poet, journalist. Became anti-Zionist and did not join other Iraqi Jews who went to Israel in 1951. Left Iraq 1971. First Iraqi writer to deal with life of masses.

Shavli, see Siauliai.

Shavuot (Heb. "weeks"), festive celebration on 50th day after first day of Passover; hence its name Pentecost. Falls on Sivan 6 (festival is observed for a 2nd day outside Israel). In biblical times it was beginning of harvest; also called "Feast of First Fruits" and "Harvest Feast." Rabbis refer to it as *Az̩eret,* "solemn assembly." Traditionally it is anniversary of promulgation of Torah at Sinai (and is called "Festival of the Giving of the Torah"). Ten Commandments and Book of Ruth are read in synagogue, which is decorated with greenery.

Shaw, Artie (Artie Arshawsky; 1910–), U.S. clarinetist, bandleader. His Gramercy Five band a leading exponent of swing style of 1940s.

Shaw, Irwin (1913–), U.S. novelist. Made name with one-act anti-war drama *Bury The Dead.* His *The Young Lions* considered one of finest novels to come out of WWII.

Shazar, Rahel, see Katznelson, Rahel.

Shazar (Rubashov), Shneur Zalman (1889–), third pres. of Israel, scholar, writer, socialist Zionist; b. Belorussia. Active in Po'alei Zion movement, studied in St. Petersburg and Germany, specializing in E. European Jewish history, Shabbetean movement, etc. Settled in Erez̩ Israel 1924, joining staff of *Davar;* editor-in-chief 1944–49. Minister of education and culture 1949–51, Mapai member of Knesset, member of Jewish Agency Executive 1952–63 (acting chairman 1956–60). Pres. of Israel 1963–73. From his youth influenced by Ḥabad. Married Rahel Katznelson (q.v.).

Zalman Shazar

Jerusalem children celebrating Shavuot, 1964.

Moshe Sharett (holding flag, right) at U.N. headquarters, Lake Success, N.Y., on Israel's becoming member of the world organization, May 1949. Also holding flag are David Hacohen and Abba Eban.

Shean, Al (Shonberg; 1868–1949), U.S. vaudeville actor; uncle of Marx Brothers. Teamed with Ed Gallagher.

Sheba, see Queen of Sheba; Sabea.

Sheba (Schieber or Schiber), Chaim (1908–1971), Israel physician, medical educator; b. Belorussia, settled in Erez̩ Israel 1933. Under his guidance Tel Ha-Shomer Hospital (later renamed after him) developed into a leading medical institution. Israel Prize 1968.

Sheba ben Bichri, Benjaminite who perished in unsuccessful attempt to overthrow throne of David (II Sam. 19:41–42; 20:1–22).

Shebnah, scribe of King Hezekiah, one of delegation of Hezekiah's three officials dispatched to negotiate with Assyrians during their siege of Jerusalem 701 B.C.E.

Shechem, ancient Canaanite and Israelite city situated bet. Mt. Ebal and Mt. Gerizim in central hill country of Erez̩ Israel. Abraham and Jacob visited it and Joseph was buried there. Town flourished in Hyksos period c. 1750–1650 B.C.E. Jeroboam established his first capital there (I Kings 12:25). Richer quarters of city were apparently destroyed by Assyrians c. 724 B.C.E. Became chief city of Samaritans. Destroyed by John Hyrcanus I 129 B.C.E. and rebuilt nearby by Romans under name of Flavia Neapolis, fr. which modern Nablus is derived.

Shedal, see Luzzatto, Samuel David.

She'elot u-Teshuvot, see Responsa.

Shefar'am (Arab. Shefā 'Amr), town in W. Galilee, Israel. Described in talmudic sources as seat of newly reconstructed Sanhedrin (e.g., RH

31a–b). Ẓahir al-'Amr, Bedouin ruler of Galilee, established his capital there 1761. Jews fr. Safed, fleeing epidemic, settled there 1813. Occupied by Israel army June 1948. Pop. 11,500 (1971), composed of Christians, Druze, Muslims.

Sheftall, Benjamin (1692–1765), U.S. merchant; one of original Jewish settlers of Savannah 1733; b. Prussia. He and his sons **Mordecai** (1735–1797) and **Levi** (1739–1809) were prominent members of Savannah community.

Sheḥitah (Heb.), the Jewish method of slaughtering permitted animals or birds for food. Spotlessly clean sharp knife is drawn quickly and uninterruptedly across throat, severing windpipe, esophagus, jugular veins, and carotid arteries, causing immediate unconsciousness and death. Slaughterer *(shoḥet)* required to be of impeccable character and has to be authorized by rabbi who examines him.

Sheinkin, Menahem (1871–1924), Zionist leader; b. Russia, settled in Ereẓ Israel 1906. Acted on behalf of Ḥovevei Zion, among founders of Tel Aviv director of Zionist Commission immigration office fr. 1919.

Shekalim, 4th tractate of Mishnah order *Mo'ed,* with *gemara* in Jerusalem Talmud. Deals with annual half-shekel tax collected to maintain Temple and its services.

Shekel, name of coin mentioned in Bible and later literature. Originally unit of weight of gold and silver, which varied in Babylon and Phoenicia, both countries also possessing heavy and light shekel. In modern times membership card and fee of Zionist Organization was given this name.

Shekhinah (Heb.), term used in rabbinic literature for numinous immanence of God in world ("Divine presence"). Also used as synonym for God.

"Sheḥitah" scene from opening page of "Tur Yoreh De'ah" in Jacob b. Asher's "Arba'ah Turim," Mantua, 1436.

Bronze shekel struck c. 70 C.E. Ancient Hebrew inscription reads: "Shekel Israel."

Shela (3rd c.), Babylonian *amora* and head of academy of Nehardea. Celebrated authority whose importance diminished after return of Rav to Babylon.

Shelah, see Horowitz, Isaiah ben Abraham ha-Levi.

Shelem (Weiner), Mattityahu (1904–), Israel composer; b. Poland. His songs were created for immediate needs of kibbutz life and his *Omer* became one of central "new ceremonies" developed by secular kibbutz movement.

Sheli'aḥ Ẓibbur (Heb. "messenger of the community"), designation of person who leads congregation in public worship by reciting aloud parts of service.

Shelomoh Yitzḥaki, see Rashi.

Sheloshet Yemei Hagbalah (Heb. "the three days of limitation"), name given to three days preceding festival of Shavuot when limitations were placed upon Israelites (see Ex. 19:12–15). They are regarded as days of joy.

Sheloshim (Heb. "thirty"), 30 days of mourning after death of near relatives, when activities of festive or joyous nature are curtailed.

Sheluḥei Ereẓ Israel (Heb. "emissaries of Ereẓ Israel"), envoys sent fr. Ereẓ Israel abroad to raise funds. Usually distinguished scholars who exercised considerable influence on Diaspora, many staying as rabbis.

Shem, eldest son of Noah; father of Semitic peoples, incl. Hebrews.

Shema, Reading of, declaration of God's unity ("Hear O Israel the Lord our God, the Lord is One") and providence, contained in Deut. 6:4–9, 11:13–21, Num. 15:37–41; recited in morning and evening service. So called fr. first word and is preceded and followed by special blessings, the whole forming a central section of daily prayers. Also recited on death bed, and Jewish martyrs through the ages went to their death with these words on their lips.

Shemaiah, prophet in days of King Rehoboam of Judah (I Kings 12:22–24).

Shemaiah (1st c. B.C.E.), colleague of Avtalyon, with whom he is always mentioned in talmudic sources; one of the *Zugot.* Favorite dictum: "Love work, hate lordship, seek no intimacy with the ruling power."

Shemaiah of Troyes (11th c.), French scholar; pupil of Rashi. His teaching served as basis for most works of school of Rashi, such as *Maḥzor Vitry.*

Shemariah ben Elhanan (d. 1011), scholar in Egypt; one of Four Captives (q.v.) traditionally taken prisoner 970 while on journey to collect contributions for Babylonian academies and who later established schools in different countries.

Shemariah ben Elijah ben Jacob (1275–1355), philosopher, and biblical commentator; referred to as *Ikriti* ("the Cretan") and *ha-Yevani* ("the Greek"). First medieval Jew to translate Greek literature fr. original.

Shemer, Naomi (1933–), Israel composer. Wrote famous "Jerusalem of Gold" 1967 and many popular songs.

Shemi (Schmidt), Menahem (1897–1951), Israel painter; b. Russia. Principally landscapist; among founders of artists' colony in Safed 1949.

Shemi, Yeḥi'el (1922–), Israel sculptor. Made large free compositions, using welded scrap iron to give violent expression in abstract, and often monumental shapes.

Shemini Aẓeret, 8th day of Sukkot (Tishri 22), treated by rabbis as separate festival. In Israel and in Reform congregations it coincides with Simḥat Torah, but elsewhere it lasts two days (Tishri 22–23) with Simḥat Torah as second day. Memorial service and special prayer for rain *(Tefillat Geshem)* are recited in synagogue and (when there is no intermediate Sabbath of Sukkot) Book of Ecclesiastes is read.

Shemittah, see Sabbatical Year and Jubilee.

Shemoneh Esreh (Heb. "eighteen"), popular name for *Amidah* prayer which originally consisted of 18 blessings.

Shemot, see Exodus.

Shem Tov ben Isaac Ardutiel, see Santob de Carrion.

Shem Tov, Ibn, see Ibn Shem Tov.

Shenhar (Shenberg), Yitzhak (1902–1957), Hebrew author; b. Russia, settled in Ereẓ Israel 1921. Wrote fiction, poetry, plays, travel notes, children's literature. His stories are largely set in Ukraine and Ereẓ Israel. Translator of world literature, esp. fr. Russian.

Sheni ve-Ḥamishi, see Monday and Thursday.

Shenkar, Arie (1877–1959), pioneer of Ereẓ Israel industry. Active in Russian Zionist movement. Settled in Ereẓ Israel 1924 and bought textile factory. Built up young local industry and interested foreign investors.

Sheol (Heb.), biblical word meaning abode of dead, netherworld situated far below the earth. Included in God's general jurisdiction over whole universe but no praise to the Lord emanates fr. it.

Shephatiah ben Amittai (d. 886), Italian *paytan;* lived in Oria. The *piyyut "Yisrael Nosha"* in Day of Atonement *Ne'ilah* service is his only known poem.

Shephelah, lowland of Ereẓ Israel, separating highlands fr. coastal plain.

Shepher, see Rabinovitz, Saul Phinehas.

Shepherds' Crusade, see Pastoureaux.

Sheriff, Noam (1935–), Israel composer, conductor. Compositions incl. *Akdamot le-Mo'ed* written for Israel Philharmonic.

Sherira ben Ḥanina Gaon (c. 906–1006), Babylonian *gaon* of Pumbedita 967–1006 under whom Pumbedita became authority for Jewish law. Prolific writer of responsa; author of *Iggeret Rav Sherira Ga'on* on development of Talmud, major source on development of Oral Law. Played key role in making Babylonian Talmud supreme source of authority in Jewish world.

Shertok, see Sharett.

Sheshbazzar, prince of Judah at beginning of return to Zion of Babylonian Exile 538 B.C.E. (Ezra 1:8–11; 5:14). Opinions differ as to his exact role.

Sheshet (3rd–4th c.), Babylonian *amora.* Taught at Nehardea and Maḥoza and founded academy at Shilḥe. Though blind, had extraordinary command of sources and quoted them as precedents in his decisions. Objected to quibbling with words: "Are you from Pumbedita where they draw an elephant through the eye of a needle? "

Shestapol, Wolf ("Velvele Khersoner"; c. 1832–1872), Russian *ḥazzan.* His dependence on Italian and French opera was extremely pronounced. Some of his compositions became very popular and were taken over into the Yiddish theater.

Shestov, Lev (pseud. of **Lev Isaakovich Schwarzmann;** 1866–1938), religious philosopher, man of letters; b. Kiev. Prof. of Russian philosophy at Univ. of Paris fr. 1922. His writings influenced Camus, Berdayev, and D.H. Lawrence.

Shetar (Heb.), legal document or deed, incl. marriage contracts and divorce documents, bonds, agreements, and court documents.

Sheva, Hebrew vowel sign representing two independent phonetic values: absence of vowel *(sheva quiescens)* and very short vowel, which can be described as central and vague *(sheva mobile).* Both written ְ

Sheva Berakhot, see Seven Benedictions.

Shevat, post-exilic name for 11th month of Jewish year. Zodiac sign Aquarius. 30 days. 15th is New Year for trees (see Tu bi-Shevat).

Shevi'it (Heb. "seventh year"), 5th tractate of Mishnah order *Zera'im,* with *gemara* in Jerusalem Talmud. Deals with problems of sabbatical year.

Shevu'ot (Heb. "oaths"), 6th tractate of Mishnah order *Nezikin,* with *gemara* in both Talmuds. Deals with oaths of various kinds.

Shewbread (or **Showbread**), one of Temple offerings. 12 loaves were placed on special table and changed every Sabbath. Only small portion burnt on altar; rest eaten by priests.

Shiddukhin, see Betrothal.

Shield of David, see Magen David.

Shikhḥah, see Leket, Shikhḥah, and Pe'ah.

Shiloah (Siloam), name applied to waters of the Gihon springs in Jerusalem. Hezekiah built tunnel to connect pool with city of David. Fr. Middle Ages, name of village on E. slope of Kidron Valley (Arab. Silwān). Jews fr. Yemen settled there 1884 but had to leave 1936. Since 1967, part of Jerusalem.

Shiloaḥ (Zaslani), Reuben (1909–1959), Zionist political officer, Israel diplomat. Worked in political dept. of Jewish Agency, and later formed political intelligence service of Israel. Minister at Israel Embassy in Washington 1953–57.

Shiloh, capital of Israel in time of Judges; situated N. of Jerusalem. Under Joshua, tabernacle erected there. After Ark was taken fr. city on fateful journey to Eben-Ezer, town was destroyed. Site has been excavated.

Shimei, biblical figure; relative of Saul who insulted David as latter fled during rebellion of Absalom (II Sam. 16:5–13; 19:17 ff.).

Shim'on, Joseph ben Judah ibn (12th–13th c.), Moroccan-born physician, poet, philosopher. Escaped to Egypt to practice Judaism openly. Became court physician of king of Aleppo. Maintained correspondence with Maimonides, who wrote his *Guide of the Perplexed* for him.

Shimoni (Shimonovitz), David (1886–1956), Hebrew poet; b. Russia, settled in Ereẓ Israel 1921. His poetry expresses Second Aliyah ideals and describes pioneer life in Ereẓ Israel. Best known for his idylls. Also translated Russian literature into Hebrew.

Shin (Sin), 21st letter of Hebrew alphabet; numerical value 300. If dotted on right (שׁ), pronounced *sh;* on left (שׂ), *s.*

Shinak, Selman (1898–), Iraqi lawyer, politician, Hebrew writer. Jewish representative in Iraqi parliament 1947, 1949. Founded Hebrew Writer's Union 1920; published Zionist weekly. Settled in Israel 1951.

Shinar, place name referring to Mesopotamia, the area once termed Sumer and Akkad (Gen. 10:10).

Shewbread on the golden table (above) in page from 14th-cent. Hebrew ms. fr. Spain.

The pool of Shiloah in Jerusalem.

Shindookh, Moses ben Mordecai (18th c.), *nasi* of Baghdad community, supporter of religious scholars. His grandson **Sason ben Mordecai** (1747–1830), rabbi, kabbalist, poet, preacher.

Shinwell, Emanuel, Lord (1884–), British socialist politician. MP fr. 1922; held ministerial office in several Labor cabinets, incl. minister of war 1948–51, defense 1951–2. Chairman of Parliamentary Labor Party 1964–7.

Shiphrah and Puah, two Hebrew women who served as midwives for Israelites in Egypt (Ex. 1:15 ff.). Disobeyed Pharaoh's order to kill all male children at birth.

Shiplacoff, Abraham Isaac (1877–1934), U.S. labor, socialist leader; b. Russia, in U.S. fr. 1891. Organized tailors' general strike 1920–21. First Socialist elected to N.Y. State Assembly 1915–18. Pres. International Leather Goods Workers Union 1927–30.

Shir, see Rapoport, Solomon Judah Leib.

Shiraz, town in Iran. Jewish community in 10th c., 10,000 in 12th c. Numbers subsequently dropped owing to persecution. 12–15,000 Jews in 1948; number halved by 1968.

Shir Ha-Kavod, see Anim Zemirot.

Shir Ha-Ma'alot (Heb. "Song of Ascent"), superscription to Psalms 120–134, understood to have been sung by pilgrims going up to Jerusalem to celebrate three Pilgrim Festivals. Ps. 124 is sung before Grace after Meals on Sabbath and festivals.

Shir Ha-Shirim, see Song of Songs.

Shir Ha-Yiḥud (Heb. "Hymn of Unity"), lengthy popular medieval liturgical poem praising God. Sometimes divided into seven parts, one recited on each day of week. Nowadays usually recited on Day of Atonement. Author not known.

Shishak, biblical name for Sheshonq (reigned 935–914 B.C.E.), founder of 22nd Dynasty of Egypt and one of last kings in Egyptian history to invade Ereẓ Israel 918/7 B.C.E. (I Kings 14:25–28; II Chron. 12:2–12).

Shitrit, Beḥor Shalom (1895–1967), Israel Sephardi leader. In Mandate period, commander of police in Lower Galilee, magistrate 1935–48. In Israel, Mapai member of Knesset, minister of police, 1948–67.

Shi'ur Komah (Heb. lit. "the measure of the body"), kabbalistic term for esoteric doctrine concerning appearance of God. Based on vision of chariot in Ezekiel 1:26, which speaks of "the appearance of a man."

Shivah (Heb. "seven"), "seven days" of mourning commencing immediately after burial of close relative. During this period, all ordinary work is prohibited, mourners sit unshod on low stools on floor ("sitting *shivah*"), and visits are made by friends to mourners' home for prayer and condolence. Although Sabbath is included in *shivah,* no outward signs of mourning are permitted on that day.

Shivtah (or **Sobata**), former city in Negev. Founded by Nabateans in 1st c. B.C.E., flourished during Byzantine period, and abandoned in crusader period. Its inhabitants cultivated extensive area and skillfully used rainwater for irrigation.

Shivviti, opening Hebrew word of verse "I have set the Lord always before me" (Ps. 16:8), which was placed in front of those praying in synagogue upon plaques frequently highly decorated. These were called *Shivviti* plaques.

Abraham Shlonsky

Autographed photo of Zalman Shneour (right), Saul Tchernichowsky (center), and Ḥayyim Naḥman Bialik, Berlin, 1923.

Shklov, city in Belorussian SSR. Jews first settled in 16th c. Center of Jewish culture, Hebrew books printed there and Haskalah movement active. 3,119 Jews in 1926; those remaining under German occupation shot 1941.

Shkop, Simeon Judah (1860–1940), Lithuanian talmudist and *rosh yeshivah* whose system combined logical analysis with simplicity and clarity. Many of his works have been published.

Shlom the Mintmaster (d. 1195), first Jew mentioned by name in Austrian records. In charge of mint and other property of Duke Leopold V. Murdered by crusaders.

Shlonsky, Abraham (1900–1973), Hebrew poet, editor, translator; b. Ukraine; settled in Ereẓ Israel 1921. On staff of Mapam newspaper *Al ha-Mishmar* and occupied central position in development of modern Israel poetry. Translated Shakespeare, Pushkin, etc., produced popular lyrics and children's literature. Introduced elasticity into Hebrew literature that brought it closer to spoken tongue.

Shmeruk, Chone (1921–), Yiddish scholar; b. Poland, settled in Israel 1949. Prof at Heb. Univ. Specialized in Jews of Soviet Russia and their Yiddish literature.

Shmuel Bukh (Yid. "Samuel Book"), Yiddish epic of great poetic vigor and scope, based on ancient Jewish history, composed c. 1450. Authorship uncertain.

Shmueli, Ephraim (1908–), educator, author, historian; b. Poland, settled in Ereẓ Israel 1933. Prof. at Cleveland State Univ. fr. 1969. Wrote on education, sociology, philosophy, Jewish history.

Shmushkevich, Yaacov (1902–1941), Soviet airforce commander; twice Hero of the Soviet Union. Organized Republican airforce in Spanish Civil War. Dismissed and executed shortly before Nazi invasion; posthumously rehabilitated.

Shneour (Shneur), Zalman (Zalkind; 1887–1959), Hebrew, Yiddish poet, novelist; b. Belorussia, lived in Vilna, Warsaw, Switzerland, Paris, U.S., and fr. 1951 Israel. Introduced sensual motifs into Hebrew poetry. His novels *(Anshei Shklov, Noah Pandre),* translated into many languages describe life of ordinary Jews in Russian Pale of Settlement. After WWII, wrote of the Holocaust. Wrote extensively in Yiddish, esp. prose.

Shneur Zalman of Lyady

Shneur Zalman of Lyady (1745–1813), founder of Ḥabad Ḥasidism; pupil of Dov Baer the Maggid of Mezhirech. Outstanding halakhist, talmudist, kabbalist; charismatic leader who defended himself and his movement against charges by rival ḥasidim and *mitnaggedim*, which led to his arrest by Russian authorities 1799. Anniversary of his release fr. prison on Kislev 19 is celebrated by his followers annually. Involved in bitter controversy with Vilna Gaon. His most famous work *Tanya* (published 1797 as *Likkutei Amarim)*, is systematic exposition of rational approach to Ḥasidism and was accepted as "the written Law of Ḥabad." (See also Schneersohn.)

Shochat, Israel (1886–1961), founder, leader of Ha-Shomer organization; b. Belorussia, settled in Ereẓ Israel 1904. Established Ha-Shomer organization 1909. After WWI, among founders of Haganah, Gedud ha-Avodah, and Histadrut.

Shochat, Mania Wilbushewitch (1880–1961), a leader of Ha-Shomer organization; wife of Israel Shochat; b. Belorussia. Became associated with revolutionary circles. Settled in Ereẓ Israel 1904. Among founder and leaders of Ha-Shomer. Later active in Gedud ha-Avodah and Kibbutz Kefar Giladi.

Shofar (Heb.), animal horn used as musical instrument; in Jewish tradition ram's horn is preferred. In Temple times used during sacrificial rites and on solemn occasions, e.g., at commencement of Jubilee Year. Blown during month of Elul, on Rosh Ha-Shanah, and at conclusion of Day of Atonement.

Shofarot ("*Shofar* verses"), description of last of three central benedictions of *Musaf Amidah* on Rosh Ha-Shanah, containing 10 verses fr. Bible that mention *shofar.*

Shofman (Schoffmann), Gershon (1880–1972), Hebrew writer; b. Belorussia, lived in Galicia and Austria, settled in Ereẓ Israel 1938. Distinguished for miniature short stories, meditative and didactic sketches, and epigrammatic essays on literature and life.

Shoham (Polakevich), Mattityahu Moshe (1893–1937), Polish Hebrew poet, playwright. His verse is based largely on mystical conception of Jewish history; his plays deal with biblical themes against background of eternal Jewish problems. His vocabulary and style are archaic.

Shoḥat, Eliezer (1874–1971), Second Aliyah pioneer; b. Belorussia, settled in Ereẓ Israel 1904. A founder of Ha-Po'el ha-Ẓa'ir 1905, Jewish labor associations in Galilee, and first moshav ovedim, Nahalal, 1921. Compiled labor movement literature.

Shoḥer Tov, see Midrash Tehillim.

Shoḥet, see Sheḥitah.

Israel Shochat (right) with two fellow students, Izhak Ben-Zvi (left) and David Ben-Gurion (right), in Constantinople, c. 1913.

Shoḥetman, Baruch (1890–1956), Hebrew bibliographer; b. Podolia, settled in Ereẓ Israel 1925. Worked in National Library fr. 1927. Wrote on historical, literary, and bibliographical subjects. Killed when Jordanian soldiers shot at archaeologists visiting Ramat Raḥel.

Sholal (Solal), Isaac ha-Kohen (d. 1524), last Egyptian *nagid* under Mamluk rule. Brilliant talmudist whose rabbinic decisions were widely accepted. Held post at mint in Cairo and supported scholars and authors. Settled in Jerusalem 1517.

Sholom Aleikhem, see Shalom Aleikhem.

Sholem Zokhor (fr. Heb. "peace to the male child"), home celebration held traditionally on first Friday evening after birth of boy when friends gather to congratulate and rejoice with parents.

Shomer, see Mashgi'aḥ.

Shomer (pseud. of **Naḥum Meyer Shaikevich;** 1849–1905), Yiddish novelist, dramatist; b. Russia. Wrote numerous popular novels and plays of suspense, where good always triumphed over evil. Attacked by leading Yiddish writers for his potboiler fiction. Went to U.S. 1880, where he continued to write and edit magazines.

Shomer Israel (Heb. "Guardian of Israel"), name of assimilationist faction in Galicia, organized 1869, that favored German culture for its Jews.

Display of "shofarot" in Israel Museum, Jerusalem. 1. Hungary, early 19th cent. 2. Germany, 18th cent. 3. Algeria, 19th cent. 4. Yemen, 19th cent. 5. Tripoli, early 19th cent. 6. Fez, c. 19th cent. 7. Central Europe, early 19th cent. 8. Yemen, 18th cent.

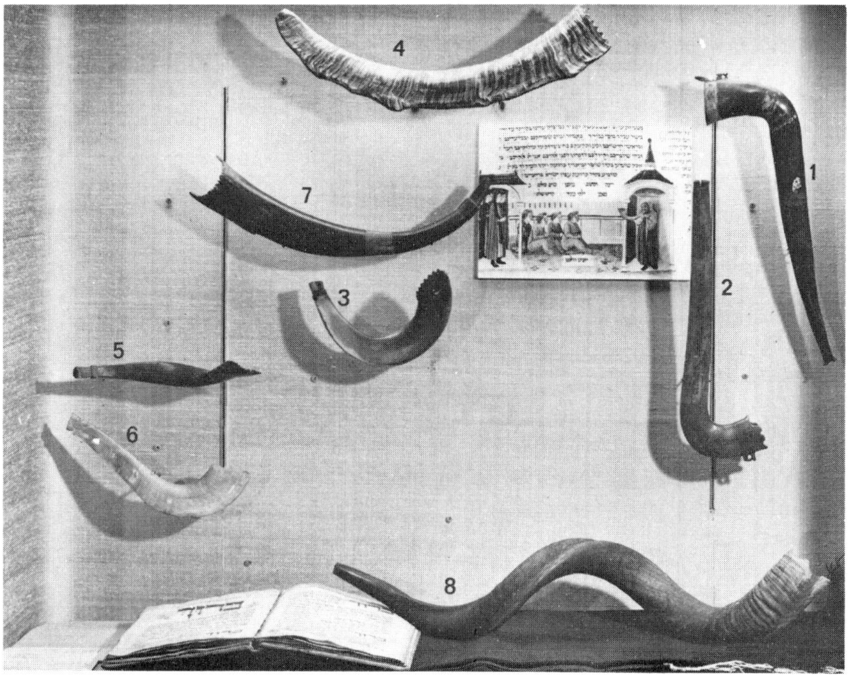

Shore, Dinah (Francis Rose Shore; 1917–), U.S. singer. Popular during WWII, incl. record "Yes, My Darling Daughter." Starred in own TV show 1951–61.

Shovavim Tat, acrostic composed of initial letters of first eight weekly Torah portions of Book of Exodus, corresponding to 8 winter weeks when it was customary to recite penitential prayers to avert disastrous epidemics.

Showbread, see Shewbread.

Shragai (Fajwlowicz), Shlomo Zalman (1899–), religious Zionist leader; b. Poland. Founder of He-Ḥalutz ha-Mizrachi and a leader of Ha-Po'el ha-Mizrachi. Settled in Ereẓ Israel 1924. Member of Jewish Agency Executive 1946–50, mayor of Jerusalem 1950–52, head of immigration dept. of Jewish Agency 1954–68.

Shtadlan, representative of Jewish community who interceded with high dignitaries and legislative bodies. At first, honorary post arising fr. position at court of a man or his relatives; later became paid post. Fr. 19th c., acquired pejorative undertone.

"The Old Synagogue" in the "shtetl," woodcut by Solomon Judovin, 1928.

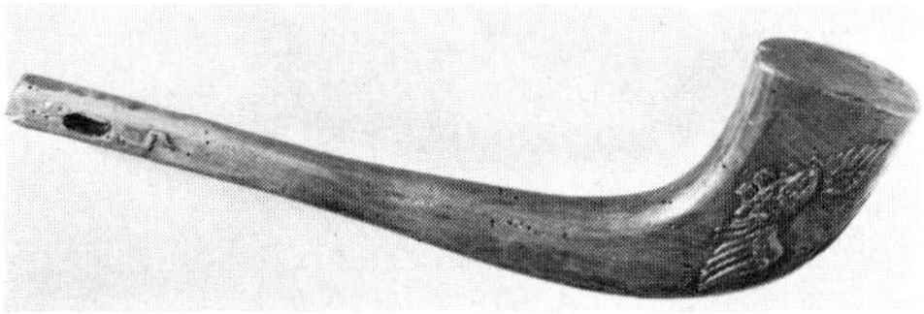

"Shulklapper's" shofar-shaped mallet, Hungary, 18th cent.

Shtayger (Yid.), term designating musical modes of traditional Ashkenazi synagogue song, characterized by order of intervals which is unusual in European music. Named after initial words of certain prayers sung to them.

Shtern, Israel (1894–1942), Yiddish poet, essayist in Poland; posthumously recognized as one of most important Yiddish poets bet. world wars. Always on periphery of Warsaw's literary circles, his basic theme was that God is mirrored in victims of social injustice.

Shtetl (Yid.), small-town Jewish community in E. Europe.

Shtibl (Yid. "small room"), ḥasidic term for synagogue; also known as *"klaus."*

Shtif, Nahum (pseud. **Bal-Dimyen;** 1879–1933), Yiddish linguist, literary historian, author, political leader; b. Volhynia. Founder of Sejmist Party and Folkspartey and main initiator and founder of YIVO. Distinguished editor and translator.

Shubert, family of U.S. theater proprietors, producers. **Sam** (1875–1905), **Lee** (1876–1953), and **Jacob J.** (1877–1963), became Broadway's most powerful theater dynasty. By 1956 they owned or controlled half the legitimate theaters in the country. Produced more than 50 plays.

Shul, Yiddish word for synagogue.

Shulammite, The, feminine name or title occurring only in Song of Songs 7:1 [6:13]

Shulḥan Arukh (Heb. "the prepared table"), name given by Joseph Caro to code of Jewish law compiled by him. Divided into 4 sections: *Oraḥ Ḥayyim,* concerning daily life; *Yoreh De'ah,* various subjects incl. dietary laws, purity, mourning; *Even ha-Ezer,* marriage, divorce, etc.; *Ḥoshen Mishpat,* civil and criminal law. Together with amendments and comments of later scholars (notably the *Mappah* of Moses Isserles, which added Ashkenazi custom), it became and has remained the standard Jewish judicial code.

Shulklapper (Yid.), person, usually sexton, who in Ashkenazi communities went around in the morning knocking on doors and windows to awaken worshipers for morning prayers.

Shulman, Charles E. (1901–1968), U.S. Reform rabbi, chaplain in U.S. Navy, active Zionist. His books preoccupied with regression of morality in 20th c.

Shulman, Harry (1903–1955), U.S. lawyer. Named dean of Yale Law School shortly before his death. As labor arbitrator, established innovative processes for peaceful and legal solutions to labor-management conflicts and collective bargaining.

Shulman, Max (1919–), U.S. author, humorist; known for bright style and witty situations. Books incl. *Barefoot Boy with Cheek* and *Rally Round the Flag, Boys.*

Shulman, Victor (1876–1951), organizer, journalist of Bund; b. Kovno. When imprisoned in Siberia 1901–5 helped organize escape of revolutionaries, incl. Trotsky. In New York fr. 1941.

Shulsinger, Bezalel (Bezalel Odesser; c. 1779–c. 1873), *ḥazzan* in Odessa; emigrated to Jerusalem. Members of his choir became famous *ḥazzanim.*

Shulvass (Szulwas), Moses Avigdor (1909–), scholar, educator; b. Poland lived in Ereẓ Israel 1938–48, then U.S. Prof. of Jewish history at College of Jewish Studies in Chicago. Wrote studies on European, esp. Italian, Jewry.

Shum, acrostic used in Hebrew writing for three Rhine communities of Speyer, Worms, and Mainz. These became the leading communities where synods were convened and regulations adopted affecting Ashkenazi Jewish life in 13th–14th c.

Shureq, Hebrew vowel sign indicating long *û.* Written וּ.

Shurer, Haim (1895–1968), Hebrew journalist, editor; b. Podolia, settled in Ereẓ Israel 1913. Joined *Davar* 1936, editor in-chief 1953–66.

Shushan (Susa), capital of Elam and one of capitals of Persian Empire. Scene of events described in Book of Esther.

Shushan Purim, Purim "feast" celebrated Adar 15 (i.e., day after festival of Purim) in cities which have been walled since time of Joshua (e.g., Jerusalem). Commemorates successful resistance of Jews of Shushan on that day to Haman's plan to exterminate them.

Shuster Frank, see Wayne, Johnny.

Shvadron, Shalom Mordecai ben Moses (Maharsham; 1835–1911), Galician rabbi. Outstanding *posek* whose views were widely sought.

Siauliai (Shavli), town in Lithuania. Jewish settlement fr. 17th c., increased with economic opportunities in 19th c. 8,000 Jews in 1939. Noted for organizational achievements and cultural and social institutions. Community confined in ghetto and then destroyed during WWII. Revived after war, numbering 4,000 in late 1960s.

Siberia, Asiatic part of USSR. First Jewish exiles arrived fr. Lithuania in 17th c. Despite restrictions on Jewish settlement, communities grew in 19th c. and Jews played prominent role in Siberian fur trade. Although Jewish communal, cultural, and national institutions were gradually destroyed under Soviet rule, Jewish pop. increased as result of establishment of Birobidzhan, industrial development of region, and Nazi persecution elsewhere. 57,654 Jews in 1959.

Sibylline Oracles, collection of prophecies or wise sayings in Greek hexameter verse combining pagan, Jewish, and Christian elements. Collection attributed to Sibyl grew, under Jewish as well as Christian influences, fr. early times until 4th c. C.E., and eventually comprised 15 books, most of which have been recovered.

Sicarii (fr. Lat. *sica,* "curved dagger"), name used by Josephus for Jewish zealots who maintained active resistance against Roman government of Judea and Jewish collaborators during period 6–73 C.E.

Sicher, Gustav (Benjamin Ze'ev; 1880–1960), Czech rabbi. Abandoned medical profession, became chief rabbi of Prague, emigrated to Ereẓ Israel 1939, returned 1947 to build up communities of Bohemia.

Sicily, island in Mediterranean. Jewish settlement probably fr. 1st c. B.C.E.; flourished during period of Arab occupation (9th–11th c.). Jews reached acme of prosperity under Normans, when they also enjoyed juridical autonomy and reputation for learning.

Sick, Prayer for. Prayers for the sick are recorded in Bible (Num. 12:13 and Isa. 38:2) and included in *Amidah.* In Middle Ages custom arose of invoking a blessing for the sick during reading of Torah.

Sick, Visiting the (Heb. *bikkur ḥolim*). Visiting the sick in order to cheer them and relieve their suffering is regarded in Judaism as a religious duty. Special *bikkur ḥolim* societies for the purpose existed in Jewish communities.

Sid (Sidilyo; Sirilyo), Samuel ibn (c. 1530), rabbi in Egypt; of Spanish origin. Regarded as miracle worker. Chiefly remembered for his *Kelalei Shemu'el,* handbook for study of Talmud.

Siddur, Ashkenazi term for prayer book.

Sidelocks, see Pe'ot.

Sidjelmessa, see Sijilmassa.

Sidney, Sylvia (Sophie Koscow; 1910–), U.S. actress. Became known for part in film *Street Scene.*

Sidon (Zidon), Phoenician port, N. of Tyre, now in Lebanon. Natural resources made it leading port of Phoenician coast. Jezebel came fr. there and introduced its Baal worship into Israel. Jewish community fr. classical period. 150 Jews in 1968.

Sidrah (Heb. "arrangement"), popular term for section of Torah read weekly in synagogue.

Siedlce, city in Poland. Jews there fr. 16th c. Noted rabbis officiated. 15,000 Jews in 1939. Ghetto established 1941; all Jews deported and executed by Germans.

Sieff, Israel Moses, Baron (1889–1972), British industrialist, Zionist; b. Manchester. Director of Marks and Spencer chain stores. Collaborator of Weizmann, secretary of Zionist Commission to Ereẓ Israel 1918. Contributed generously to Zionist funds and founded Daniel Sieff Research Inst. at Reḥovot 1934.

Sieff, Rebecca (1890–1966), Zionist; wife of Israel Sieff, sister of Simon Marks; b. England, lived latterly in Israel. Founding member and pres. of WIZO.

Siegel, Benjamin ("Bugsy"; 1905–1947), U.S. racketeer, criminal. Big-time figure in gambling, sports, and narcotics racket in U.S. Killed as result of clash with Capone mob for control of wire services providing racing information to gamblers.

Siegmeister Elie (1909–), U.S. composer, writer. Formed American Ballad Singers 1946. Taught at Hofstra Univ. Interest in American folk music reflected in his compositions.

Siemiatycki, Chaim (pseud. **Khaym Tiktiner; Khayml;** 1908–1943), Yiddish poet; lived in Warsaw, d. labor camp. One of outstanding Yiddish religious poets.

Sifra (Aram. "book"), tannaitic halakhic Midrash to Leviticus. Probably compiled in Ereẓ Israel in late 4th c. C.E. Also known as *Sifra de-Vei Rav* or *Torat Kohanim.*

Sifrei (Aram. "books"), tannaitic halakhic Midrash to Numbers and Deuteronomy written as exegetical running commentary and frequently covering every word in a verse. Former probably fr. school of R. Ishmael, latter fr. R. Akiva. Probably compiled in Ereẓ Israel in late 4th c. C.E.

Sifrei Zuta, tannaitic halakhic Midrash to Numbers. Disappeared and only during past century have parts of it been discovered and published.

Sighet, town in NW Rumania. Jewish settlement fr. 17th c. Ḥasidism and Frankism strong there. Community split in 20th c. 10,144 Jews in 1941; most perished in Holocaust.

Sigman, Morris (1880–1931), U.S. labor leader; b. Bessarabia, in U.S. fr. 1903. Active in International Ladies Garment Workers Union; organized important strikes.

Signoret (Kaminker), Simone (1921–), French film actress. Won Oscar for role in *Room at the Top* 1959. Subsequently acted in British, Italian, French, American films. Wife of singer and actor Yves Montand.

Sihon, Amorite king of Heshbon who refused to grant passage through his territory to Israelite tribes moving out of wilderness toward Canaan (Num. 21:21 ff.; Deut. 2:26–37).

Sijilmassa, town in SW Morocco. Important Jewish community fr. its inception 757. Jews suffered under Fatimids but situation improved under Umayyads and noted Jewish scholars lived there. Forced conversion under Almohads. After 1393 community disappeared.

Israel Sieff

Rebecca Sieff

Sikili, Jacob ben Hananel (13th–14th c.), rabbi, author; settled in Cordoba, migrated to Ereẓ Israel. Wrote sermons and homilies. Traversed Ereẓ Israel and in *Sefer ha-Yaḥas* mentions "every town and village and the persons buried there."

Silano (9th c.), Italian liturgical poet, some of whose poems have been incorporated in *seliḥot* for eve of Rosh Ha-Shanah and *Ne'ilah* prayer of Day of Atonement.

Silberfarb, Moses (1876–1934), political leader, writer in Russia. Headed Ministry for Jewish Affairs of Ukrainian Central *Rada.* Left for Warsaw 1921, becoming chairman of ORT.

Silberg, Moshe (1900–), Israel jurist; b. Lithuania, settled in Ereẓ Israel 1929. Judge of Supreme Court 1950–70, deputy pres. fr. 1965. Taught law of personal status at Heb. Univ. and wrote extensively on talmudic law and personal status.

Silbermann, Abraham Moritz (1889–1939), publisher, lexicographer, translator; b. Hungary, lived in Berlin, England. Co-author of Hebrew-English-German *Talmudic Dictionary* and English translation of Rashi on Pentateuch.

Silberner, Edmund (1910–), Israel economist, historian; b. Poland. Prof. of economics at Heb. Univ. Analyzed relationships between European societies and Jewish people.

Silberschlag, Eisig (1903–), Hebrew poet, critic; b. Galicia. Dean of Hebrew Teachers College, Boston, 1948–68. Poems collected in *Bi-Shevilim Bodedim* and *Aleh Olam be-Shir.* Also wrote critical essays in Hebrew and English.

Silesia, region in E. Central Europe. First Jews in 12th c.; soon monopolized moneylending trade. Persecution, restrictions, and expulsions limited development of community until 19th c. Thereafter, Jewish pop. greatly increased through immigration and Breslau community attained prominence. Numbers fell again in 20th c. 15,480 Jews in 1939; most killed by Nazis. Community later reestablished by Polish and Russian Jews, many of whom left after 1967.

Silkin, Jon (1930–), English poet. His most celebrated poem is "Death of a Son," dedicated to one-year-old child who died in mental hospital. Edited avant-garde magazine *Stand.*

Silkin, Lewis, Lord (1889–1972), British lawyer Labor politician. Minister of town and country planning 1945–50, deputy leader of the opposition in House of Lords 1955–64. His son **John Ernest** (1923–), Labor minister of public buildings and works 1969–70 and of planning and local government, 1974. Another son, **Samuel Charles** (1918–), Labor MP and attorney general, 1974.

Silkiner, Benjamin Nahum (1882–1933), U.S. Hebrew poet; b. Lithuania, in U.S. fr. 1904. Taught Bible at Teachers Institute, Jewish Theological Seminary. Emphasized American themes, e.g., *Mul Ohel Timmurah,* epic poem of struggle of Indians against Spanish conquistadors.

Sills, Beverly (Belle Silverman; 1930–), U.S. coloratura soprano. Debut in San Francisco 1953. With New York opera fr. 1955. Sang in La Scala, Milan, Covent Garden, London, and throughout U.S., Europe S. America.

Siloam, see Shiloah.

Siloam (or **Shiloah) Inscription,** inscription found on rock wall of Siloam water tunnel in village of Silwān in Jerusalem, built by Hezekiah (II Kings 20:20; II Chron. 32:3–4, 30). Inscription was made by diggers of the tunnel. Original now in Istanbul Museum.

Silva, Antônia José da (known as "o **Judeu";** 1705–1739), Portuguese playwright, martyr. Prolific and versatile writer; created series of stage satires criticizing evils of contemporary society. Charged with Judaizing by Inquisition; burnt at Lisbon auto-da-fé.

Silver, Abba Hillel (1893–1963), U.S. Reform rabbi, Zionist leader, orator, supporter of social causes. Rabbi in Cleveland fr. 1917. Headed many pro-Israel bodies, incl. United Palestine Appeal and American section of Jewish Agency. Presented case for independent Jewish state before Assembly of the United Nations 1947. Published scholarly works, sermons, addresses. A major force in moving Reform Judaism toward pro-Israel attitude. One of few Republicans in Jewish leadership of his time.

Abba Hillel Silver

Silver, Eliezer (1882–1968), U.S. rabbi, Orthodox leader; b. Lithuania, in U.S. fr. 1907. Rabbi in Cincinnati fr. 1931. First pres. of U.S. Agudat Israel; official representative of U.S. government to assist war refugees. Writer on halakhic topics; leading spokesman for Orthodoxy on American scene.

Silverman, Alexander (1881–), U.S. glass chemist. Prof. of chemistry at Univ. of Pittsburgh 1918. Invented illuminators for microscopes and several varieties of colored glasses.

Silverman, Morris (1894–1972), U.S. Conservative rabbi, scholar; worker for civil rights and interfaith endeavors. Rabbi in Hartford, Conn. fr. 1923. Author of series of prayer books which became standard in Conservative congregations.

Silverman, Samuel Sydney (1895–1968), British socialist politician. Great achievement abolition of capital punishment 1965. Dedicated Zionist; spoke on Jewish causes in Parliament. Chairman of British section of World Jewish Congress 1940–50.

Silvers, Phil (Philip Silversmith; 1912–), U.S. comedian. Started in vaudeville, toured 5 years with Minsky Burlesque Troupe. Famed for his portrayal of Sgt. Bilko in long-running TV show of that name. Appeared in films and on Broadway.

Silverstein, Abe (1908–), U.S. aeronautical engineer. Concentrated on problems concerning full-scale wind tunnels. Director of space flight programs at NASA 1958–61, director NASA Lewis Research Center fr. 1961.

Silveyra, Miguel de (c. 1578–1638), Portuguese Marrano poet, physician, mathematician; in Naples fr. 1634. His masterpiece *El Macabeo,* baroque heroic poem written in Castilian, was highly esteemed in 17th c.

Silwān, see Shiloah.

Sima, Miron (1902–), Israel painter, printmaker. His "Refugees" is series of paintings inspired by Jews who fled Europe to Ereẓ Israel. Later painted quiet landscapes, portraits, and still lifes in warm subdued colors.

Simchoni (Simchowitz), Jacob Naftali Hertz (1884–1926), scholar, historian, translator; b. Poland. Published essays on Jewish scholars and writers, textbooks on Jewish history, and translated Josephus into Hebrew. On editorial board of German *Encyclopedia Judaica.*

Simeon, second son of Jacob and Leah (Gen. 19:33), eponymous ancester of tribe of Simeon. Tribe settled in S. Ereẓ Israel (Josh. 19).

Simeon bar Isaac (b. c. 950), German *paytan;* elder colleague of Rabbenu Gershom. Some of his *piyyutim* still recited.

Simeon bar Yoḥai (2nd c.), *tanna,* leading scholar; pupil of Akiva. Because of his hostility to Romans, sentenced to death and for 12 years lived in cave with son Eleazar. Much of his Mishnah is included in standard Mishnah. Believed by kabbalists to be author of Zohar; a central figure in kabbalistic lore. Halakhic *Mekhilta de-R. Shimon b. Yoḥai,* fragments of which have survived, is attributed to him. His traditional

Territory of the tribe of Simeon.

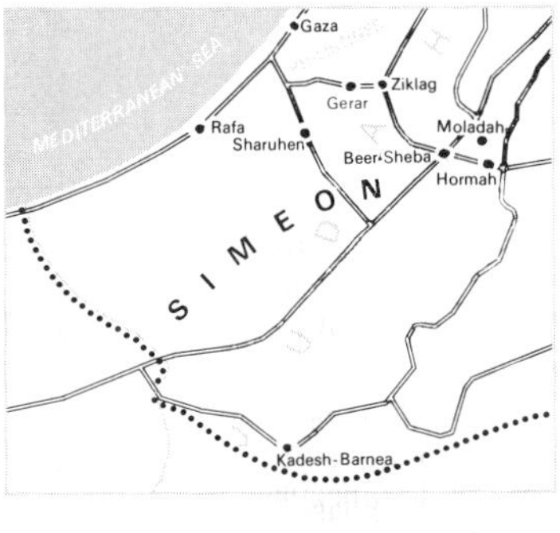

tomb is at Meron, scene of mass celebrations on anniversary of his death, Lag ba-Omer.

Simeon ben Abba (3rd c.), Palestinian *amora;* b. Babylon. Studied under Johanan, lived life of suffering.

Simeon ben Eleazar (2nd c.), *tanna,* contemporary of Judah ha-Nasi, pupil of Meir. Most of his *halakhot* are cited in *beraitot,* only a few in Mishnah. Noted aggadist. Saying: "A man should always be as gentle as the reed and not unyielding like the cedar."

Simeon ben Gamaliel I (1st c.), *nasi* of Sanhedrin at time of destruction of Temple. Probably met martyr's death at hands of Romans. Said of him that at Festival of Water-drawing: "He used to juggle with eight burning torches and not one of them fell to the ground."

Simeon ben Gamaliel II (of Jabneh; 2nd c.), *nasi,* son of Rabban Gamaliel of Jabneh, father of Judah ha-Nasi. One of few survivors of family after Roman persecution following Bar Kokhba revolt. Strengthened Sanhedrin as highest national institution. Hundreds of *halakhot* in his name in Mishnah and Tosefta. Saying: "Whoever makes peace in his own house is as if he makes peace in Israel."

Simeon ben Ḥalafta (2nd c.), *tanna* in transition period to *amoraim.* Lived in great poverty. Concluding dictum of Mishnah is his saying: "The Holy One found no vessel that could contain Israel's blessing save that of peace."

Simeon ben Judah ha-Nasi (3rd c.), younger son and pupil of Judah ha-Nasi, whom he succeeded as *ḥakham* of his yeshivah. Played great part in finalizing Mishnah in its present form.

Simeon ben Lakish (3rd c.), Palestinian *amora,* usually called Resh Lakish; active in Tiberias. R. Johanan brought him to Torah and gave him his sister in marriage, regarding him as colleague. Had keen logical mind and wide knowledge of tradition. His name is found on most pages of Talmud. Said to have participated in gladiatorial contests in his youth.

Simeon ben Megas ha-Kohen (6th c.), Palestinian *paytan.* Fragments of 30 of his poems for festivals with unique structural details were found in *genizah.*

Simeon ben Menasya (2nd–3rd c.), *tanna;* contemporary of Judah ha-Nasi. His statements are found chiefly in *beraitot.* Said to spend a third of the day in Torah, a third in prayer, and a third in work.

Simeon ben Nethanel (1st c.), *tanna.* Man of piety versed in mystic lore; one of five outstanding disciples of Johanan b. Zakkai. Saying: "The good way to which a man should cleave is to foresee the consequences of his acts."

Simeon ben Pazzi (3rd c.), Palestinian *amora,* halakhic authority. Handed down biblical interpretations of Joshua b. Levi.

Simeon ben Shetaḥ (1st c. B.C.E.), prominent scholar in time of Second Temple, one of *zugot,* probably *nasi* of Sanhedrin; brother of Queen Salome Alexandra. In his time Pharisees consolidated their standing among the people. Author of many important *takkanot;* introduced school attendance for children. Firm and courageous, he insisted that King Yannai when in court follow its procedure.

Simeon the Hasmonean (called **Thassis;** d. 134 B.C.E.), 2nd son of Mattathias; Jonathan's right-hand man in wars with Hellenizers and Syrians. Became independent ruler 142 B.C.E. Hasmonean dynasty established 140 when nation appointed him and his children high priest, ethnarch, and commander of army. Murdered in Jericho by his son-in-law.

Simeon the Just, high priest in time of Alexander the Great. Saying: "The world is based upon the Torah, upon divine service, and upon the practice of charity." In *aggadah* mentioned as going to meet Alexander, who showed him great honor.

Simeon of Mizpah (1st c.), *tanna.* Author of Mishnah *Tamid,* which presents eye-witness account of Temple service.

Simferopol, city in Crimea. Jews there soon after its foundation 1784. During 19th c. number increased and Karaite community existed. Pogroms 1905. 17,364 Jews in 1926. Those who remained murdered under German occupation 1941. 11,200 Jews in 1959.

Simḥah ben Joshua of Zalozhtsy (1711–1768), Polish ḥasidic author, Torah scribe, preacher. Traveled to Ereẓ Israel and wrote account of journey on his return. Wrote homiletic works.

Simḥah ben Samuel of Speyer (12th–13th c.), German talmudic scholar, author of responsa and other works. Quoted by his pupil Isaac b. Moses (*Or Zaru'a*).

Simḥah Bunem of Przysucha (Pshiskhah; 1765–1827), Polish ḥasidic *ẓaddik,* one-time pharmacist, successor of Jacob Isaac "the Jew" of Przysucha. Based his ḥasidism on Torah study.

Traditional tomb of Simeon bar Yoḥai at Meron.

Pilgrimage to tomb of Simeon the Just, Jerusalem, on traditional anniversary of his death.

"In the Synagogue of Leghorn," celebration of Simḥat Torah by Solomon Hart, 19th cent.

Simḥat Beit Ha-Sho'evah, see Water-Drawing, Feast of.

Simḥat Torah (Heb. "rejoicing of the Torah"), name of last day of Sukkot festival when annual reading of Torah is completed and recommenced. In Israel this coincides with Shemini Aẓeret; elsewhere observed on following day. Torah scrolls are carried around the synagogue seven times and each male is called to reading of Torah. Service is marked by singing and festivities. The one

called to last portion is called Bridegroom of the Torah and to first portion Bridegroom of Genesis. Rejoicing in and near synagogues became prime expression of Jewish identity in USSR in recent years.

Simḥoni, Assaf (1922–1956), Israel soldier. Commanded Israel forces in Sinai campaign. Killed shortly afterwards in plane crash.

Simlai (3rd c.), Babylonian-born *amora* who spent most of his life in Palestine; pupil of R. Jonathan. Distinguished aggadist.

Simmel Georg (1858–1918), German philosopher, sociologist. Prof. at Berlin and Strasbourg. As transmitted through Buber, his approach to sociology became a cornerstone of sociology of Jews. Recognized dialectical interplay of the individual and group as essence of all relationships. Baptized.

Simon, see Simeon.

Simon, Akiba Ernst (1899–), Israel educator thinker; b. Berlin, settled in Ereẓ Israel 1928. Prof. of philosophy and history of education at Heb. Univ. and director of its School of Education. Co-editor "Educational Encyclopedia." Active in groups advocating bi-national state in Ereẓ Israel.

Simon, Sir Francis Eugene (1893–1956), British physicist; b. Berlin. In Oxford built up one of foremost low-temperature laboratories in the world. During WWII responsible for some key research on atom bomb.

Simon, Herbert Alexander (1916–), U.S. political scientist; authority on public administration.

The Sinai Peninsula

Prof. of computer science and psychology at Carnegie Inst. in Pittsburgh fr. 1948.

Simon, James (1851–1932), German commercial magnate, philanthropist. His large textile firm eventually declared bankrupt 1931. Noted art collector and patron; chairman of Hilfsverein der deutschen Juden.

Simon, Jean Henri (1752–1834), engraver; b. Brussels. Became engraver to court of Louis XVI, Napoleon, and Spanish and Dutch kings. Engraved series of 100 medals of illustrious men of Low Countries.

Simon, Sir John (1818–1897), English lawyer, politician; first Jew to practice at common law bar and exercise functions of judge. His devotion to Jewish cause in Parliament led him to be known as "the member for Jewry."

Simon, Joseph (1844–1915), Hungarian lawyer. Secretary of National Council of Hungarian Jews. Played active role in struggle for official recognition of Jewish religion.

Simon, Julius (1875–1969), Zionist leader, economist; b. Germany, settled in U.S. Active in Zionist economic policy; his criticism of economic policies in Ereẓ Israel 1921 were supported by Brandeis but opposed by Weizmann and labor sector. Headed Palestine Economic Corporation.

Simon, Sir Leon (1881–1965), English Zionist leader, Hebrew writer, British civil servant. Director of telegraphs and telephones in the British post office 1931–35, director of savings bank 1935–44. Member of 1918 Zionist Commission. Lived in Israel 1946–53. Chairman of board of governors of Heb. Univ. and established Israel postal savings bank. Wrote on Zionism and Aḥad Ha-Am and translated Greek classics into Hebrew. His brother, **Maurice** (1874–1955), co-translator into English of Zohar and wrote works of Jewish interest.

Simon, Neil (1927–), U.S. playwright. Wrote series of successful stage comedies, incl. *Barefoot in the Park, The Odd Couple,* and *Plaza Suite.*

Simon, Norton (1907–), U.S. industrialist. Founder of holding company which incl. food processing and packaging, container manufacturing, and soft drink industries. Noted art collector.

Simon, Oliver (1895–1956), British painter and typographer. Head of Curwen Press. Had great influence on improvement of printing, typography, and type design.

Simon, Paul (1940–), U.S. songwriter, singer. Member of Simon and (Art) Garfunkel team.

°**Simon, Richard** (1638–1721), Catholic priest. Student of Hebrew and Judaism, holding it "impossible to understand Christianity without knowledge of Judaism." Defended Jews of Metz against blood libel. Wrote on biblical criticism.

Simon, Shlome (1895–1970), Yiddish educator, essayist, folklorist; b. Belorussia, in U.S. fr. 1913. Wrote on Yiddish folklore, Bible, Jewish problems, and children's books.

Simon, Sidney (1917–), U.S. painter, sculptor. Did murals in Federal Art Project in 1930s. War artist in WWII. Turned completely to sculpture after 1960, devoted to symbolic commentary on human types.

Simone, André (Otto Katz; 1895–1952), Czech journalist. After 1946 foreign affairs editor of Communist party organ *Rudé Právo.* Sentenced to death at Slánský trial.

Simonsen, David Jacob (1853–1932), Danish rabbi, bibliophile, orientalist. Presented his library of 40,000 volumes to Copenhagen Royal Library.

Simson, Martin Eduard von (1810–1899), German lawyer, politician. Chairman of National Assembly 1848. Led parliamentary delegation offering German crown to King of Prussia 1870. Subsequently pres. of German High Court. Also founder and first pres. of Goethe Society. His son **Bernhard von** (1840–1915), German historian. Taught at Jena and Freiburg. Baptized at age 13.

Simson, Samson (1781–1857), U.S. lawyer; son of Solomon Simson. Active in Congregation Shearith Israel. His Hebrew oration at Columbia College Commencement 1800 was first sketch of U.S. Jewish history by U.S. citizen. One of first Jewish lawyers in N.Y.

Simson Solomon (1738–1801), U.S. merchant, communal leader. A founder and subsequently pres. of Democratic-Republican Party of N.Y. 1797. Head of Spanish-Portuguese Congregation Shearith Israel.

Sin, see Shin.

Sin, Wilderness of, area between Elim and Sinai traversed by Israelites in Exodus fr. Egypt (Ex. 16:1).

Sinai, peninsula bet. Gulf of Eilat and Gulf of Suez; area of transit fr. Asia to Africa. Fr. early times its

copper mines exploited. Crossed by Israelites in course of Exodus. In Hellenistic and Roman times, its interior left to Nabateans. Zionist plan 1902 to settle El-Arish area as prelude to Jewish settlement in Ereẓ Israel proved abortive. In 1956 Sinai campaign Egyptian army in Sinai routed by Israel army, which occupied almost entire peninsula but had to withdraw under Great Power pressure. During 1967 Six-Day War entire Sinai occupied by Israel.

Sinai, Mount, mountain on which Law was given to Moses. Identification uncertain. Most popular tradition places it at Jebel Mūsā, where St. Catherine's Monastery was built in 6th c.

Sinai Campaign (Operation Kadesh), short war (Oct. 29–Nov. 5, 1956) between Egypt and Israel, partly coinciding with Anglo-French Suez Campaign. Launched by Israel in wake of mounting aggression by Egyptian *fedayeen* squads and build-up of Eygptian army in Sinai. Israel forces seized Gaza Strip and the entire Sinai peninsula, with exception of 10-mile strip along side of canal in accordance with Anglo-French ultimatum. Israel losses were 171 dead, several hundred wounded. Egyptian losses were estimated at several thousand dead and wounded, with 6,000 prisoners. Immense quantities of military equipment were seized. Under pressure of U.S. and Soviet Union, Israel was compelled to evacuate Sinai peninsula and Gaza Strip. Troops of the UN Emergency Force were posted on Egyptian side of frontier and at Sharm el-Sheikh to guarantee free passage of Israel shipping through Straits of Tiran.

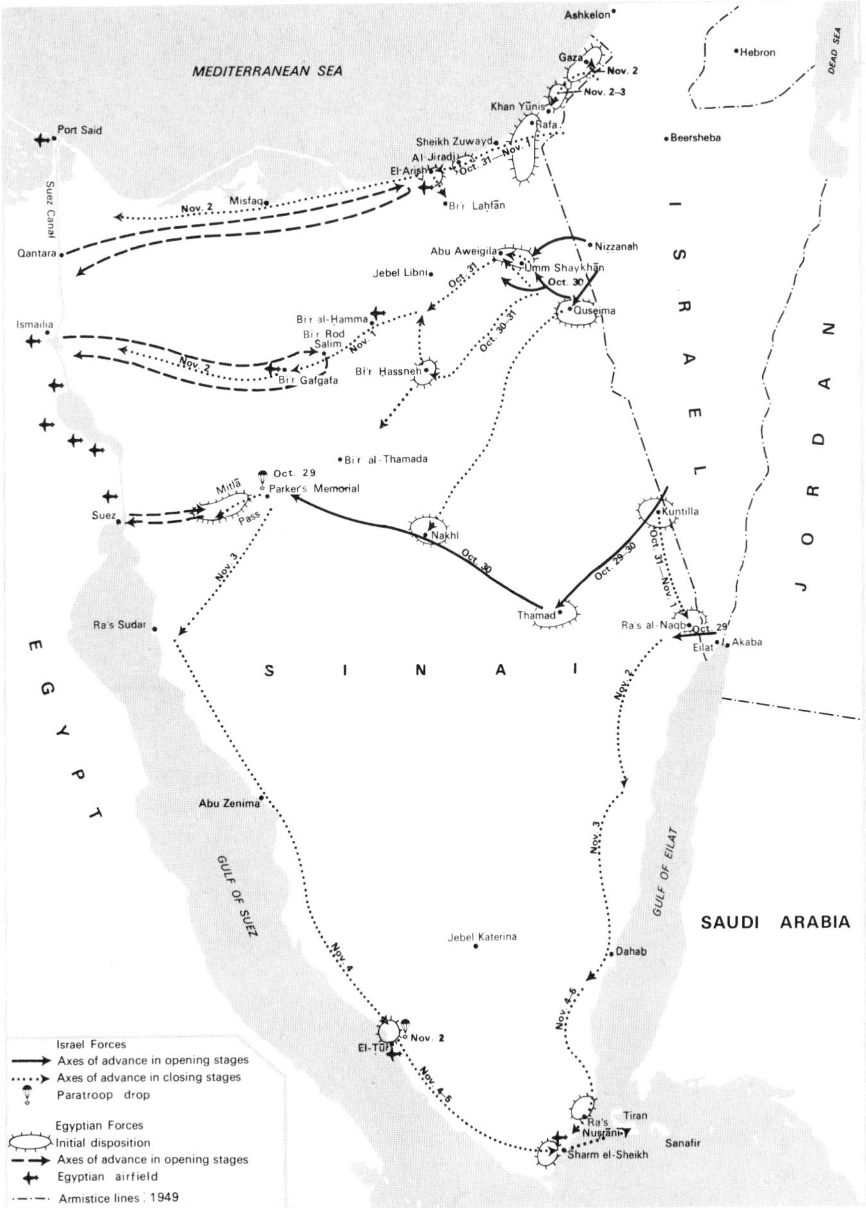

The Sinai Campaign, Oct. 29–Nov. 5, 1956.

Sinclair, Jo (pen name of **Ruth Seid;** 1913–), U.S. novelist. Best-selling first novel *Wasteland* dealt with Jew's self-hatred and prompted others to tackle theme.

Singapore, Asian republic. First Jewish settlers 1840 of Baghdad origin. Community largely Sephardi but augmented by many Ashkenazi immigrants fr. Europe and China and became prosperous in 20th c. Many of 1,500 Jewish inhabitants were interned during Japanese occupation in WWII; some subsequently emigrated. David Marshall was first chief minister of republic 1955. 600 Jews in 1971.

Singer, Charles Joseph (1876–1960), British historian of science, medicine. Taught in Oxford and London; pres. International Union of History of Science 1947–49. Co-editor *Legacy of Israel.* His wife and co-worker **Dorothy Waley** (1882–1964), chairman of bibliographical commission 1947–50, vice-pres. 1950-53 of International Academy for Historical Science.

Singer, Isidore (1859–1939), writer, editor in Europe, U.S.; b. Moravia. Active in defense of Alfred Dreyfus in Paris. Driving force and managing editor of *The Jewish Encyclopedia.* Founded American League for Rights of Man 1922.

Singer, Israel Joshua (1893–1944), Yiddish novelist, playwright, journalist; brother of Isaac Bashevis Singer; b. Poland, in U.S. fr. 1933. Master of "family" novel, large canvas encompassing many generations and portraying whole society or epoch. Works incl. *The Brothers Ashkenazi* and the play *Yoshe Kalb.*

Singer, Josef (1841–1911), Hungarian-born *ḥazzan.* Chief cantor of Vienna community fr. 1881. Published studies on various aspects of Ashkenazi *ḥazzanut.*

Singer, Ludvik (1876–1931), Czech political leader. As chairman of Jewish National Council achieved recognition for Jewish nationality in 1920 Czechoslovak constitution. Member of parliament 1929, chairman of Jewish community of Prague 1930.

Singer, Simeon (1848–1906), English rabbi, editor; translator of English *Authorized Daily Prayer Book* 1890, of which half a million copies have been printed.

Singerman, Berta (1897–), Argentine actress, poetry recitalist; b. Minsk. Became most celebrated reader of poetry in Latin America.

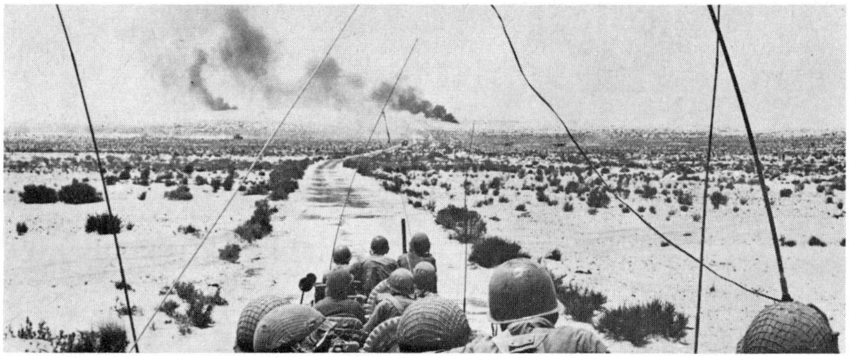

Israel armored columns advance across Sinai Peninsula during Six-Day War.

Egyptian planes destroyed in first hours of Six-Day War.

The Six-Day War. Egyptian front.

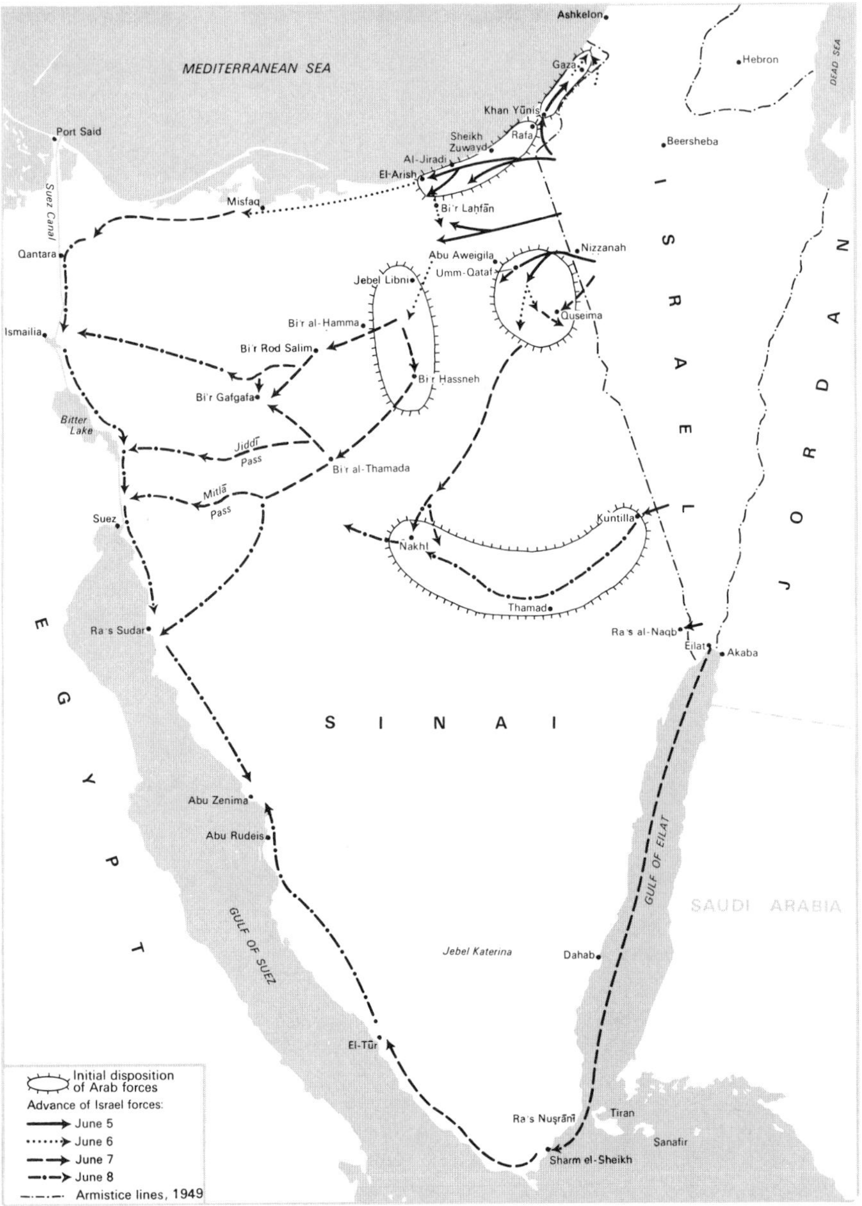

Sinko, Ervin (Franjo Spitzer; 1898–1967), Yugoslav author. Fought with Tito's partisans in WWII and gained official recognition for skillful polemics against Soviet line following split in Cominform 1948. Prof. at Novi Sad Univ.

Sin Offering, see Sacrifices.

Sinzheim, Joseph David ben Isaac (1745–1812), first chief rabbi of France. Head of yeshivah and rabbi of Strasbourg. Member of Assembly of Jewish Notables convened by Napoleon and chairman of Great Sanhedrin. Formulated replies to questions put by government. Some of his responsa have been published.

Sirillo, Solomon ben Joseph (d. c. 1558), Salonika rabbi, *posek;* b. Spain, in Jerusalem fr. 1544. Wrote commentary on whole of order *Zera'im* and tractate *Shekalim* of Jerusalem Talmud.

Sirkes, Joel (Baḥ; 1561–1640), Polish talmudist, *av bet din,* head of yeshivah in Cracow. Author of *Bayit Ḥadash* comprehensive and influential commentary on *Arba'ah Turim* of Jacob b. Asher, and of responsa.

Sirota, Gershon (1874–1943), *ḥazzan* in Warsaw; one of most accomplished tenors of his generation. Made famous many ḥazzanic compositions, undertook numerous concert tours, and was first *ḥazzan* to make recordings 1903. Died with family in Warsaw ghetto.

Sisera, leader of coalition defeated by Israel in days of Deborah. Killed by Jael (Judg. 4–5).

Siskind, Aaron (1903–), U.S. abstract expressionist photographer. Head of photography dept. at Illinois Institute of Technology. First known as documentary photographer; turned to pictorial images found in useless discarded objects.

Sivan, post-Exilic name of 3rd month of Jewish year. Zodiac sign Gemini. 30 days. Sivan 6 (6–7 in Diaspora) is festival of Shavuot.

Six-Day War, war between Israel and Egypt, Jordan, Syria, Iraq (June 5–10, 1967). Fearful of Israel reaction to border attacks during April 1967, Syrians, backed by Russians, claimed Israel was massing troops along its frontier. Nasser thereupon moved large Egypt army into Sinai, demanded withdrawal of UN Emergency Force (promptly acceded to by UN secretary-general), and declared Straits of Tiran closed to Israel shipping. On May 26 he declared Arab intention to destroy Israel; subsequently Jordan placed its forces under Egyptian command. Israel efforts to resolve crisis by dip-

lomatic means failed. As tension mounted world Jewry rallied behind Israel with unprecedented support and identification. On June 5, Israel launched preemptive strike, destroying Egyptian, Syrian, and Jordan air forces within a few hours. In six days military force of Arabs was broken, with hundreds of tanks destroyed or captured. Arabs suffered over 15,000 casualties, 6,000 prisoners. Israel losses were 777 killed, 2,586 wounded. Israel occupied Gaza Strip, Sinai Peninsula, West Bank, and Golan Heights. Arab governments accepted ceasefire agreement and UN observers were posted along Suez Canal front and on Golan Heights.

Siyyum (Heb. "conclusion"), designation for celebration held when writing of Sefer Torah is completed or when study of tractate of Talmud is concluded.

Sklare, Marshall (1921–), U.S. sociologist. Prof. of sociology at Yeshiva Univ. 1966 and Brandeis Univ. 1970. Works incl. *Conservative Judaism* and *America's Jews.*

Skoplje, capital of Macedonian republic, Yugoslavia. Jews probably present since Roman times. First synagogue 1366. 3,000 Jews in 17th c. Jews active in trades and crafts in 18th c. Most Jews died in Holocaust.

Skoss, Solomon Leon (1884–1953), Arabic scholar; b. Siberia, in U.S. fr. 1907. Taught at Dropsie College. Specialized in Judeo-Arabic philology.

Skulnik, Menasha (1892–1970), U.S. comedian; b. Warsaw, in U.S. fr. 1913. Acted in Yiddish musical shows in New York's Second Avenue theaters. Also appeared on Broadway.

Slánský Trial, first of series of anti-Semitic show trials held in Czechoslovakia under Stalinist influence in early 1950s whose prime victim was Rudolf Slánský (1901–1952), secretary-general of Czechoslovak Communist Party after WWII. Eleven of 14 prosecuted were Jews. Trials were first occasion on which anti-Semitic accusation of worldwide Jewish conspiracy was openly proclaimed by authoritative Communist forum. They were signal for wave of anti-Jewish persecution.

Slatkine, Menahem Mendel (1875–1965), bibliographer; b. Russia, in Switzerland fr. 1905. Author of 2-vol. work on Hebrew book titles.

Slavson, Samuel Richard (1891–), U.S. group psychotherapy expert. Director of group psychotherapy at Board of Jewish Guardians in N.Y., introducing group treatment for emotionally disturbed children. Pres. American Group Psychotherapy Association 1943–45.

Slavuta, city in Ukrainian SSR. In 18th and 19th c. community famous for printing press. 4,701 Jews in 1926. Jews who did not escape murdered by Nazis.

Slawson, John (1896–), U.S. communal executive, social worker. Executive director Jewish Board of Guardians 1932–43; executive vice-pres. American Jewish Committee 1943–67.

Sliozberg, Henry (1863–1937), Russian jurist, communal worker. Chairman of St. Petersburg Jewish community and later head of Russian-Jewish community in Paris. Appeared in several Jewish *causes celebres.*

Slobodka Yeshivah, leading European yeshivah in Kovno which was dedicated to ideals of Musar movement. Founded 1882; moved to Minsk and Kremenchug during WWI. Branch opened in Hebron 1924, transferred to Jerusalem after 1929 massacres and named Hebron Yeshivah. Original yeshivah closed 1941, reopened in Bene Berak after WWII.

Slomovitz, Philip (1896–). U.S. journalist. Editor *Detroit Jewish News.* Founded American Association of English-Jewish newspapers.

Slonik, Benjamin Aaron ben Abraham (c. 1550–c. 1619), Polish rabbi, halakhist. Author of responsa *Masat Binyamin.* Known for independent judgement and wide knowledge. Wrote popular Yiddish book dealing with conduct of women.

Slonim, city in Belorussian SSR. Jews mentioned 1583. Persecutions 1660. In mid-19th c. ḥasidic dynasty founded there. Jews engaged in textile industry. 8,605 Jews in 1931; burned and executed by German troops.

Slonim, Lithuanian ḥasidic dynasty, founded by **Abraham ben Isaac Mattathias Weinberg** (1804–1883), whose influence extended bet. Slonim and Brest-Litovsk. Wrote homiletic commentary to *Mekhilta.* His grandson **Noah** (d. 1927) emigrated to Tiberias. Another grandson, **Samuel** (d. 1916), succeeded Abraham. Under him dynasty became famous for its songs. Many Slonim ḥasidim went to Ereẓ Israel and in Jerusalem have their own yeshivah and leader **Abraham (III;** 1889–).

Slonimski, Antoni (1895–), Polish poet, author, critic; grandson of

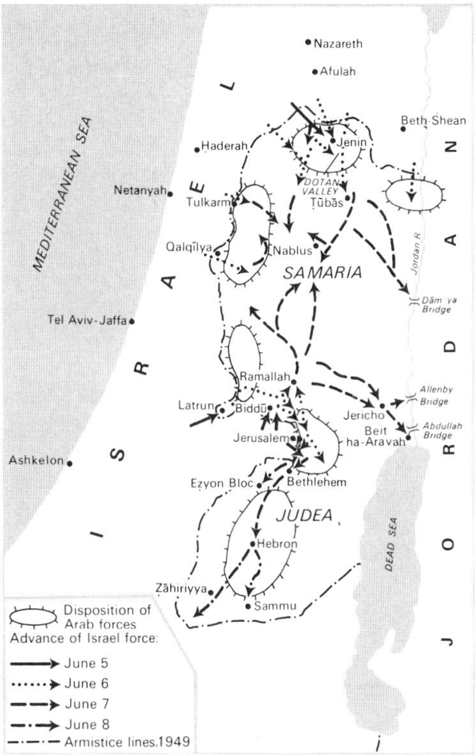

The Six-Day War. Jordanian front.

The Six-Day War. Syrian front.

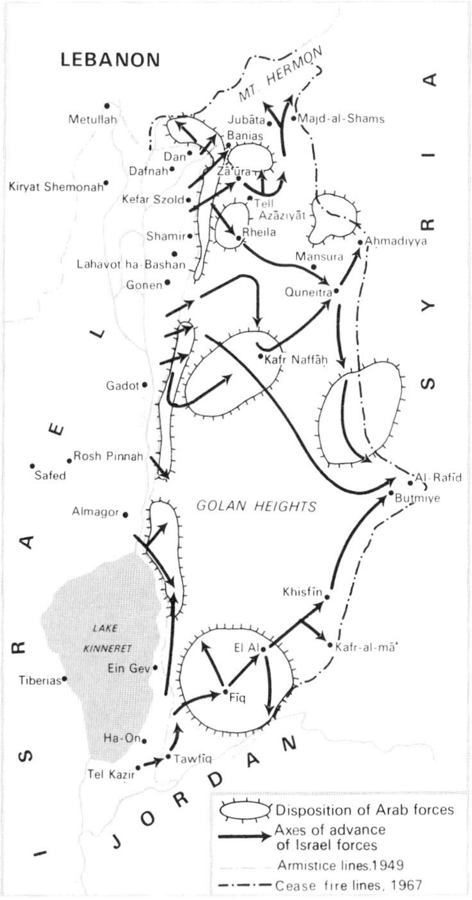

Ḥayyim Selig Slonimski. Fr. early 1920s leading personality in Poland's literary and cultural life. Nonconformist in both pre-war Pilsudski and post-war Communist Poland. Raised as Christian but had profound emotional regard for Jewish people. Israel's war of 1948 had wide repercussions in his poetry.

Slonimski, Ḥayyim Selig (pseud. **Ḥazas**; 1810–1904), Hebrew popular science writer, editor; b. Poland. Wrote popular science articles on mathematics, astronomy, Jewish calendar, and other subjects. Coined new Hebrew terminology and was also inventor. Founded Hebrew paper *Ha-Ẓefirah* 1862, which became first Hebrew daily in Poland.

Ḥayyim Selig Slonimski

Slonimski, Leonid Zinovyevich (1850–1918), Russian lawyer, publicist; son of Ḥayyim Selig Slonimski. Converted to Greek Orthodoxy. Wrote on juridical situation of Jews in Russia and abroad.

Slonimski, Mikhail Leonidovich (1897–1972), Soviet Russian author, critic; son of Leonid Slonimski. Among founders of Serapion Brothers, loose association of writers that came into being 1921 for purpose of protecting autonomy of a literature already threatened by political pressures.

Slonimsky, Henry (1884–1970), U.S. philosopher, writer; grandson of Ḥayyim Selig Slonimski. Taught philosophy at various U.S. univs. Dean of Jewish Institute of Religion 1926–52. His most important doctrine is that of "humanized," finite God.

Slonimsky, Nicholas (1894–), musicologist, composer, conductor; grandson of Ḥayyim Selig Slonimski. Champion of modern American music and a founder of Chamber Orchestra of Boston.

Slouschz, Nahum (1871–1966), scholar, writer, archaeologist, historian, traveler, translator; b. Russia, lectured at Sorbonne, made series of exploratory journeys to N. Africa and published results, settled in Ereẓ Israel 1919. Edited publications of Palestine Exploration Society, conducted excavations in Tiberias, Jerusalem, Transjordan. Translator of French writers into Hebrew.

Slovakia, E. region of Czechoslovakia. Jewish settlement fr. 13th c.; by 14th c. Bratislava (Pressburg) community important, with prominent yeshivah c. 1700. Increasing freedom for Jews in 19th c., then virulent anti-Semitic reaction. Community benefited under independent Czech government but position greatly deteriorated after autonomy was granted to region 1938. Thereafter, it shared fate of European Jewry.

Slucki, Abraham Jacob (1861–1918), Hebrew writer in Russia. Assistant editor of *Ha-Meliẓ* fr. 1884, first Hebrew paper in Russia; published anthology of writings of greatest rabbis on Jewish national idea. Among originators of idea of Mizrachi and gave it its name.

Slutsk (Słuck), town in Belorussian SSR. Jews there fr. 1583. One of five communities that sent delegates to Council of Lithuania 1691–1764. Center of struggle against Ḥasidism. Yeshivah founded 1897. 8,358 Jews in 1926; massacred during German occupation.

Slutski, Boris Abramovich (1919–), Soviet Russian poet. After 1957 became firmly identified with liberals in Soviet literature. Holocaust inspired some of his most eloquent verse, much of it published only after Stalin's death.

Smelser, Neil Joseph (1930–), U.S. sociologist. Prof. at Univ. of Cal. at Berkeley. Represents trend which constructs systematic models to guide and determine concrete research.

°**Smend, Rudolph** (1851–1913), German Bible critic. Major works dealt with source criticism of the Bible.

Smilansky, Meir (pseud. **M. Secco**; 1876–1949); Hebrew writer; brother of Moshe Smilansky; b. Kiev, settled in Ereẓ Israel 1921. Wrote mainly on Ukrainian Jewry.

Smilansky, Moshe (pseud. **Ḥeruti; Ḥawaja Mussa**; 1874–1953); Hebrew writer, agricultural pioneer in Ereẓ Israel; b. Russia, settled in Ereẓ Israel 1890. A founder of Ḥaderah; fr. 1893 in Reḥovot. A founder of the Moshavot Assoc. and the Farmers' Federation. First Jew to buy land in the Negev. Wrote about history of Jewish agricultural settlements in Ereẓ Israel, incl. stories of Arab life.

Smilansky, Yizhar, see Yizhar, S.

°**Smith, Sir George Adam** (1856–1942), Scottish scholar of Bible and geography of Ereẓ Israel. Prof. of Hebrew and Old Testament at Church College, Glasgow; principal of Aberdeen Univ. Main work on historical geography of Ereẓ Israel.

°**Smith, William Robertson** (1846–1894), Scottish theologian, Semitist. Prof. at Cambridge. His *Religion of the Semites* investigates nature of early Semitic religion and applies anthropological principles to biblical research.

Smoira, Moshe (1888–1961), Israel jurist; first president of Supreme Court of Israel. B. Germany; headed first Hebrew school there 1919–22. In Ereẓ Israel fr. 1922. Expert on labor problems.

Smolar, Hersh (1905–), leader of Jewish community in Poland after WWII. Before WWII active in underground Communist party. During war, organized anti-Nazi resistance in several parts of Belorussia. After 1946 active in Jewish cultural life and edited Yiddish newspaper *Folks-shtime*. Victim of anti-Jewish campaign of 1967–69; emigrated to Israel 1971.

Smolensk, city in Russian SFSR. Jews fr. 15th c., but Jewish rights of residence under successive Lithuanian, Polish, and Russian rule intermittent. Not in Pale of Settlement, although by 1897 Jews formed 10% of population. 12,887 Jews in 1926. Community destroyed in Holocaust; in late 1960s 5,000 Jews.

Perez Smolenskin

Smolenskin, Perez (1840 or 1842–1885), Hebrew novelist, editor, publicist; in Vienna fr. 1868. Founded and edited monthly *Ha-Shaḥar* (1868–84). Published large-scale novels describing Jewish life in E. Europe. (*Ha-To'eh be-Darkhei ha-Ḥayyim, Kevurat Ḥamor,* etc.). In his articles developed Jewish national theory opposed to religious Orthodoxy and Haskalah. In his last years joined Ḥibbat Zion.

Smoli, Eliezer (1901–), Hebrew writer, teacher; b. Volhynia, settled in Ereẓ Israel 1920. Wrote children's books about Ereẓ Israel – its land,

plants and animals, and its early pioneers.
Smyrna, see Izmir.
Sneersohn, Ḥayyim Ẓevi (1834–1882), proto-Zionist. One of first *maskilim* in Jerusalem. Traveled widely on behalf of charitable organizations and advocated establishment of Jewish state. Banned by Ashkenazi community leaders in Jerusalem; left Ereẓ Israel for S. Africa.
Sneh (Kleinbaum), Moshe (1909–1972), Israel politician, publicist. Founder "radical" wing of General Zionists in Poland. Settled in Ereẓ Israel 1940. Chief of Haganah command 1941. Member of Jewish Agency Executive 1945; resigned 1947 and joined Mapam. Left Mapam and eventually joined Israel Communist Party (Maki). Member of Knesset fr. 1949. Editor of Communist newspaper *Kol ha-Am.*
Sobata, see Shivtah.
Sobeloff, Simon Ernest (1894–1973), U.S. jurist. Solicitor-general of U.S. 1954. Helped formulate government stand when Supreme Court ruled school segregation unconstitutional. Chief judge, fourth circuit U.S. Court of Appeals, 1958. His brother **Isidor** (1899–), Jewish social work official in various cities.
Sobibor, one of six Nazi extermination camps in Poland; situated nr. Lublin. Began operating 1942; used mainly for liquidation of E. European Jews and non-Jewish prisoners of war; c. 250,000 victims. Camp closed 1943 after revolt by 300 Jewish laborers employed there.
Sobol, Andrey Mikhailovich (1888–1926), Russian novelist, playwright. Before 1917 wrote for liberal and revolutionary periodicals in Russia under pseudonyms. Disillusioned with Soviet regime, he committed suicide.
Sochaczew, Abraham ben Ze'ev Nahum Bornstein of (1839–1910), Polish rabbi, head of *bet din* of Sochaczew, halakhic authority. At his yeshivah educated generation of ḥasidic disciples in his special approach to halakhic studies.
Société des Etudes Juives, society founded in Paris 1880 to revive interest in history of French Jewry and spread knowledge of Judaism. Publishes quarterly *Revue des Etudes Juives.*
Society for the Attainment of Full Civil Rights for the Jewish People in Russia, non-party organization founded 1905. Organized participation of Jews in First and Second Duma. Political polarization of Jewish life broke up society, which disbanded 1907.

Sodom and Gomorrah depicted as medieval city set on fire by angel, illustration for Passover "piyyut," N. Italian ms., 15th cent.

Moses Sofer

Society for Jewish Folk Music, society founded in St. Petersburg 1908 by group of Jewish students. Organized concert tours, pursued field research, and published many collections and arrangements of Jewish folk music. Disbanded by Soviet government 1918.
Society for the Promotion of Culture Among the Jews of Russia, society aiming to promote popular education in organized and unified manner; founded in St. Petersburg 1863. Only legal body for Jewish educational and cultural activities in Czarist Russia; attracted Zionists, Socialists, and *maskilim.* Published works of Jewish interest in Russian and supported Hebrew writers and publications. Activities curtailed after 1917 Revolution; disbanded by authorities 1930.
Sodom and Gomorrah, two cities in "plain" of the Jordan; assumed to be nr. S. end of Dead Sea. Lot, Abraham's nephew, chose to dwell in Sodom, and Abraham rescued its king in his war with Chedorlaomer and his allies (Gen. 14). God destroyed Sodom and Gomorrah because of sins of inhabitants (Gen. 18–19). See also Sedom.
Sofer (Schreiber), Abraham (1897–), son of Simeon Sofer; rabbi in Greece and Italy; in Jerusalem fr. 1939, taught at N.Y. Jewish Theological Seminary 1948–66. Published works of early rabbinic authorities.
Sofer, Abraham Samuel Benjamin Wolf (1815–1871), eldest son of Moses Sofer and his successor as rabbi and *rosh yeshivah* of Pressburg. Joined ranks of Orthodox extremists.
Sofer, Akiva (1878–1959), succeeded his father **Simḥah Sofer** (1842–1906) as rabbi and *rosh yeshivah* of Pressburg; fr. 1940, in Ereẓ Israel, where he reestablished and headed the yeshivah of Pressburg (Jerusalem).
Sofer, Ḥayyim ben Mordecai Ephraim Fischel (1821–1886), one of the leading extreme Orthodox rabbis in Hungary. Demanded that Reform Jews be excommunicated. Author of various rabbinic works.
Sofer, Moses (known as **Ḥatam Sofer;** 1762–1839), halakhic authority, leader of Orthodox Jewry. Rabbi of Pressburg 1806–39. Established famous yeshivah, largest since Babylonian academies. Fought modernity and opposed new type of school founded by *maskilim* and also disassociated himself from fight for emancipation. Undisputed leader of rabbis of Europe opposing Reform movement. Voluminous writer; best-known for 7-vol. responsa *(Ḥatam Sofer).*
Sofer, Simeon (1820–1883), founder of Maḥzike Hadas; son of Moses Sofer. Rabbi of Mattersdorf fr. 1848, Cracow fr. 1861. Member of Parliament in Vienna fr. 1878.
Soferim (Heb. "scribes"), specific class of scholars in Second Temple period. Exact delineation of group is matter of controversy. In Talmudic and later literature term used as general designation for Torah scholars and copyists.
Soferim, minor tractate printed in Talmud at end of order *Nezikin.* Deals with writing Scrolls of Law and liturgical matters. Apparently an 8th c. compilation of Palestinian origin.
Sofia, capital of Bulgaria. Jewish settlers (later known as Romaniots) in 1st c. C.E. Sephardi refugees came fr. Hungary in 14th, 16th c. and Ashkenazim fr. Bavaria in 15th; eventually amalgamated to form one Sephardi community. In 17th c. town's commerce concentrated in Jewish hands. In May 1943 expulsion order issued against all 25,000 Jews but order to exterminate them never carried out. After 1948 mass immigration to Israel. 3,500 Jews in 1971.

Nahum Sokolow

City Hall of Lagos, Nigeria, built by Solel Boneh Overseas and Harbor Works Co., 1967.

"The Daughter of Pharaoh" by Simeon Solomon.

Soglow, Otto (1900–), U.S. caricaturist; creator of "The Little King" cartoon character.

Sokolow, Anna (1915–), U.S. choreographer. Soloist with Martha Graham company 1930–38; founder of first Mexican modern dance company; teacher and adviser of Inbal dance group and other companies.

Sokolow, Nahum (1859–1936), Hebrew writer, Zionist, journalist. Editor of Heb. newspaper *Ha-Ẓefirah.* One of Herzl's greatest admirers; became secretary-general of World Zionist Organization 1906 and established journal *Haolam.* In London in WWI involved in Zionist political activity and efforts to obtain Balfour Declaration. Headed Jewish delegation to Paris Peace Conference and later was chairman of many Jewish and Zionist assemblies. Chairman of Jewish Agency Executive 1929, president of World Zionist Organization 1931–35. Wrote *History of Zionism 1600–1918.*

Sola de, see also De Sola.

Sola, David Aaron de (1796–1860), English Sephardi leader; b. Amsterdam. *Ḥazzan* of London Sephardi community fr. 1818, leader of English Sephardim fr. 1831. Composed tunes for Sephardi synagogue (incl. setting of *Adon Olam*). His prayerbooks still used by English Sephardim.

Soldi (Colbert), Emile-Arthur (1846–1906), French medalist. His "Homage to the Victims of the Invasion" (the Franco-Prussian War of 1870–71) is still issued by the French mint.

Solel Boneh, Histadrut concern for building, public works, and industry. Played large role in development of State of Israel. Also active in construction work in other countries.

Solieli (Soloveichik), Menachem (Max; 1883–1957), public figure, biblical scholar. Minister for Jewish affairs in Lithuania 1919–21. In Ereẓ Israel fr. 1933. Head of dept. of education for *yishuv* 1944–48 and first director of Kol Israel radio.

Solis-Cohen, U.S. family founded by Jacob De Silva, who emigrated to U.S. 1803. Most descendants lived in Philadelphia and many were active in communal and Zionist affairs.

Solomon (10th c. B.C.E.), king of Israel; son of David and Bath-Sheba. Following intervention of prophet Nathan and Bath-Sheba, David anointed him king. Inherited extensive kingdom controlling principal transport routes. Associated with this activity is story of Queen of Sheba. Cooperated with Hiram of Tyre in sailing in Red Sea. Builders of Hiram helped to construct Temple. Marriage to foreign women (incl. daughter of Pharaoh) led to establishment of close ties with neighbors. Building activities included construction of Temple and palace, extension of Jerusalem to N., erection of cities for chariots and horsemen and store-cities. Bible attributes peace and prosperity to his wisdom and succeeding generations ascribed to him composition of poetry and wisdom works, e.g., Song of Songs, Proverbs, Ecclesiastes. A favorite subject of later legend (also in Islam).

Solomon, Bertha (1892–1969), S. African lawyer, politician. Second S. African woman admitted to bar. United Party MP 1938–58. Responsible for 1953 Matrimonial Affairs Act, which removed disabilities fr. women resulting fr. marriage laws.

Solomon, Elias L. (1879–1956), U.S. Conservative rabbi. Organizer with Solomon Schechter of United Synagogue of America; president 1918–24 and honorary president thereafter.

Solomon, Ezekiel (d. 1806), Michigan's first known Jewish settler. Partner in Mackinaw Company enterprise (founded 1779), probably first department store operation in U.S., and among organizers of Michigan's first Board of Trade 1784.

Solomon, Hannah Greenebaum (1858–1942), U.S. communal worker. Organizer 1891 and president 1893–1905 of Jewish Women's Congress, subsequently National Council of Jewish Women.

Solomon, Psalms of, collection of 18 pseudepigraphic psalms, on diverse subjects, seemingly written originally in Hebrew and ascribed to Solomon. Compiled mid-1st c. probably by a Pharisee. Extant in Greek and Syriac.

Solomon, Simeon (1840–1905), English artist. At 18, youngest artist ever to exhibit at Royal Academy. Short prison sentence for pederasty 1873 ended public career. Forgotten for several decades; work rediscovered in 1960s.

Solomon, Solomon Joseph (1860–1927), English artist. Painted portraits of eminent personalities and decorative panels for public buildings. Founder and first president of Maccabean Society 1891. Expert on camouflage in WWI. President of Royal Society of British Artists 1918.

Solomon, Testament of, pseudepigraphic work written in Greek centering around King Solomon. Probably written in Egypt in 1st c. C.E.

Solomon, Vabian Louis (1853–1908), Australian industrialist, politician. Premier of S. Australia 1899; represented area at convention which framed federal Australian constitution. Elected to Federal Parliament 1901, 1905.

Solomon, Wisdom of, apocryphal work, placed in Septuagint between Job and Ecclesiasticus. Deals with eschatology and wisdom as metaphysical reality and incl. Midrash on Exodus fr. Egypt. Probably written in Greek in Alexandria. Date uncertain.

Solomon ben Abraham Adret, see Adret, Solomon.

Solomon ben Abraham of Montpellier (13th c.), talmudic scholar. Instigated 1232 ban by rabbis of N.

France against study of philosophical works of Maimonides and secular sciences. Supporters of Maimonidean philosophy in Provence retaliated by excommunicating him.

Solomon ben Judah (d. 1051), Palestinian *gaon*, academy head in Jerusalem and Ramleh. Many of his letters, most addressed to Egypt, have been preserved. Also wrote *piyyutim*. A peaceful, lenient man, his approach to Karaites was tolerant.

Solomon ben Judah ha-Bavli (10th c.), Hebrew poet, apparently in Italy. One of first Hebrew hymnologists in Europe. His *piyyutim* influenced early Italian and Ashkenazi *paytanim*.

Solomon ben Judah of Dreux (12–13th c.). French scholar, tosafist; regarded as a leader of French Jewry. Contemporary and later scholars relied on his customs.

Solomon ben Samuel (14th c.), scholar in Urgench, Transoxania (Uzbekistan). Compiled Hebrew-Persian dictionary 1339.

Solomon Ibn Gabirol, see Gabirol, Solomon Ibn.

Solomons, Adolphus Simeon (1826–1910), U.S. social welfare pioneer. A founder of Mt. Sinai Hospital, N.Y., and American Red Cross. U.S. representative of International Red Cross Convention 1887.

Solomons, Jack (1900–), British boxing promoter. Staged numerous world title fights and boxing shows all over the world after WWII.

Solotaroff, Theodore H. (1928–), U.S. critic, editor. On editorial staff of *Commentary* in 1960s. Subsequently edited literary quarterly *New American Review*.

Soloveichik, Aaron (1918–), U.S. Orthodox rabbi; brother of Joseph Dov Soloveitchik; b. Russia. Taught Jewish philosophy at Isaac Elchanan Theological Seminary in N.Y. A leading rabbinic figure in U.S. Orthodox Judaism. *Rosh yeshivah* at Hebrew Theological College in Skokie, Illinois, fr. 1966.

Soloveichik, Ḥayyim (known as **R. Ḥayyim Brisker;** 1853–1918), talmudist, outstanding figure in Orthodox Jewry. Taught at Volozhin yeshivah. Succeeded father as rabbi of Brest-Litovsk 1892. Renowned for piety, charity, and learning. Initiated new trend in talmudic study, based on meticulous analysis.

Soloveichik, Isaac Ze'ev ha-Levi (Velvele Brisker; 1886–1959), talmudist; son of Ḥayyim Soloveichik, whom he succeeded as rabbi of Brest-Litovsk 1918. Fr. 1941 in Jerusalem. Regarded as halakhic authority by extreme Orthodox section of Jerusalem community.

Soloveichik, Joseph Baer, of Volozhin (1820–1892), talmudist. *Rosh yeshivah* at Volozhin fr. 1849 together with Naphtali Ẓevi Judah Berlin. Left owing to differences with latter, to become rabbi of Slutsk, and fr. 1878 of Brest-Litovsk. Wrote novellae, responsa, sermons.

Soloveichik, Menachem, see Solieli, Max.

Soloveitchik, Joseph Dov (1903–), U.S. talmudic, religious philosopher; b. Poland, settled in Boston 1932. Prof. at Yeshiva Univ. Chairman Halakhah Committee of Rabbinical Council of America. Known as "the Rav"; leader of enlightened Orthodoxy in N. America.

Solti, Sir Georg (1912–), conductor with wide-ranging concert and operatic repertoire. Posts incl. opera director Munich and Frankfort, director Covent Garden Opera 1961, and director Chicago Symphony Orchestra 1968.

°**Sombart, Werner** (1863–1941), German political economist, sociologist. Prof. at Univ. of Berlin. Wrote *The Jews and Modern Capitalism, Die Zukunft der Juden.* Contended Jews were principal cause of disruption of medieval economic system and its replacement by capitalism.

Somekh, Abdallah ben Abraham (1813–1889), rabbi, *posek* in Baghdad; regarded as supreme halakhic authority by communities of Baghdad origin throughout Far East. Founded Midrash Bet Zilkhah 1840.

Somen, Israel (1903–), public figure in Kenya. Mayor of Nairobi 1955–57; honorary consul for Israel before Kenya's independence; pres. Nairobi Heb. Cong.

Sommer, Emil von (1868–1946), Austrian soldier. Commanded Austrian army which conquered Burgenland fr. Hungary after WWI. Headed Jewish War Veterans until organization split. Survived Theresienstadt in WWII and went to U.S.

Sommerstein, Emil (1883–1957), Zionist leader in Galicia and Polish Jewish leader. Member of Polish Sejm. Arrested by Soviets 1939, released 1944, becoming member of Polish Committee for National Liberation. Pres. Central Committee of Polish Jewry.

Sommo, Judah Leone ben Isaac (1527–1592), dramatist, theater director, poet in Hebrew, Italian; b. Mantua, Italy. Staged plays and was only Jewish writer in Mantua Academy. Wrote in Italian on Renaissance theater; his five-act prose play *Ẓaḥut Bediḥuta de-Kiddushin* in biblical Hebrew is oldest play in the language.

Joseph Dov Soloveitchik

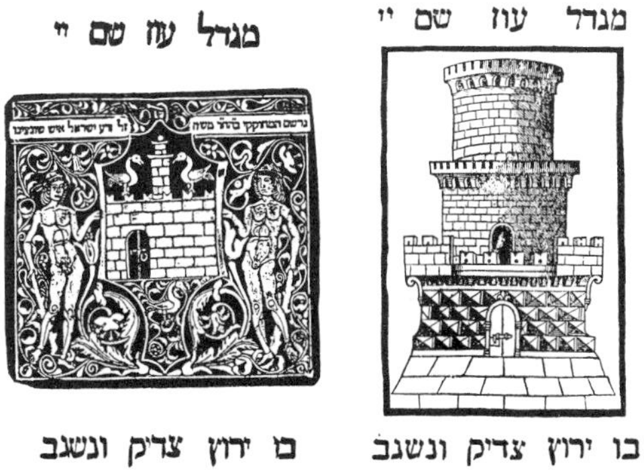

Two printers' marks of Gershom b. Moses Soncino.

Somogyi, Béla (1868–1920), Hungarian political journalist. After October Revolution (1918) became director-general of ministry of education. Murdered during brief Communist regime.

Somrei Sabat, Christian sect in Transylvania, founded in 1580s. Fr. inception celebrated Jewish Sabbath and festivals and other biblical precepts. After 1630, when led by Simon Péchi, totally rejected Christianity, adopting further Jewish practices. Membership c. 20,000 in 1630; greatly diminished after persecutions initiated by Transylvanian authorities 1638. Still has small number of followers.

Soncino, family of Hebrew printers in Italy, Turkey, and Egypt in 15th–16th c. **Joshua Solomon** (d. 1493), established Hebrew printing press in Italy. Produced first book, tractate *Berakhot,* 1484, and more than 40 other works. His nephew **Gershom ben Moses** (d. 1534), pioneer in printing and publishing techniques. Traveled widely in search of mss. and was one of most successful and prolific printers of his time. After leaving Italy established presses in Turkey.

Sondheimer, Franz (1926–), organic chemist; educated in London. Dept. head at Weizmann Inst.

of Science 1956–64, prof. at Cambridge 1964 and Univ. College, London 1967. Fellow of Royal Society.

Song of Songs, biblical book in Hagiographa, first of Five Scrolls. Composed of series of lyric love songs. Tradition ascribed it to Solomon but this is rejected by modern scholars, who however hold that some of the songs are pre-Exilic, but suggest it was edited c. 5th c. B.C.E. Text has been interpreted allegorically, cultically, dramatically, and literally. Read on Passover and by Sephardi Jews on Sabbath.

Opening of Song of Songs from "Haggadah" illustrated by Saul Raskin, 1941.

Song of Songs Rabbah, aggadic Midrash on Song of Songs; also referred to as *Midrash Ḥazita* or *Aggadat Ḥazita* after its opening verse. Product of Palestinian *amoraim* (6th c. C.E.) Written mostly in mishnaic Hebrew.

Song of the Three Children and the Prayer of Azariah, apocryphal addition to canonical Book of Daniel. May have been composed in Hebrew 2nd–1st c. B.C.E.

Sonne, Isaiah (1887–1960), scholar, historian of Italian Jewry, bibliographer. Taught at Collegio Rabbinico, Florence. Headed rabbinical seminary in Rhodes 1936–39, lecturer and librarian at Hebrew Union College, Cincinnati, fr. 1940.

Sonneborn, Rudolf Goldschmidt (1898–), U.S. businessman, Zionist leader. Pres. American Financial and Development Corp. for Israel and Israel American Petroleum Corp. Led group of American Jews after WWII which worked to supply Jews of Ereẓ Israel with arms and supplies. Married Dorothy Schiff.

Sonnemann, Leopold (1831–1909), German newspaper publisher. Founder and owner of *Frankfurter Zeitung,* 1878–84. Represented Southern German Democratic Party in Reichstag 1871–76, 1878–84.

Sonnenfeld, Joseph Ḥayyim ben Abraham Solomon (1849–1932), first rabbi of separatist Orthodox community in Jerusalem; b. Slovakia, settled in Jerusalem 1873. Stood for complete separation bet. the Orthodox and non-Orthodox; strongly opposed Zionism.

Sonnenfels, Aloys von (Ḥayyim Lipmann Perlin; Aloys Wiener; d. c. 1775), apostate, Hebrew interpreter in Vienna; son of Brandenburg rabbi, became Catholic. Taught oriental languages at Univ. of Vienna and was court interpreter to Maria Theresa. Knighted 1746. Wrote against Frankist blood libel. His son **Joseph** (1732–1817), influential in Hapsburg Empire in latter 18th c. Prof. of political science and adviser to Austrian rulers.

Sonnenthal, Adolf Ritter von (1834–1909), Austrian actor, theatrical producer. Gained great reputation at Burgtheater, Vienna, which he directed fr. 1887. Ennobled 1881.

Sonnino, Sidney (1847–1922), Italian statesman, economist; son of Jewish father. Minister of finance 1896, prime minister 1906, 1909–10, foreign minister 1914–19; leader of Italian delegation to Versailles Peace Conference 1919.

Sonntag, Jacob (1905–), English editor; b. Ukraine. Produced *Jewish Quarterly,* which encouraged younger writers.

Sons of Light, phrase used in Dead Sea Scrolls, denoting the godly, in contrast to "sons of darkness," the ungodly. In Qumran community, "sons of light" are members of community and their sympathizers.

Sontag, Susan (1933–), U.S. critic, author. Taught philosophy and aesthetics at various universities, incl. Columbia 1961–65. Best known as avant-garde critic *(Against Interpretation).*

Sorek, Valley of, valley on border of Philistia. One of main approaches to mountains of Judah, and several important cities (e.g., Ekron, Beth-Shemesh) were located there. Meeting place of Samson and Delilah.

Soria, city in Old Castile, Spain. Jewish quarter was situated in fortress. In late 13th c. renowned for its kabbalists; c. 1,000 Jews lived there. In 1492 expulsion Jews left for Navarre and Portugal.

Sorotzkin, Zalman ben Ben-Zion (1881–1966), rabbi, communal leader. Rabbi of Lutsk (Poland) and a leader of Agudat Israel bet. world wars. During WWII fled to Ereẓ Israel, establishing Va'ad ha-Yeshivot and serving as chairman of Mo'eẓet Gedolei ha-Torah of Agudat Israel. Noted preacher; published commentaries and responsa.

Soskin, Selig Eugene (1873–1959), pioneer, agronomist in Ereẓ Israel; b. Crimea, settled in Ereẓ Israel 1896. Member of Zionist Inquiry Commission on El-Arish project. Advocated intensive farming on small irrigated plots as against "mixed" farming on larger units. Founded Nahariyyah 1934. Pioneered hydroponics.

Sosnowiec, city in S. Poland. Jewish community grew fr. 2,600 in late 19th c. to 28,000 in 1939. About one-third engaged in light industry. Community destroyed in WWII.

Sotah, see Ordeal of Jealousy.

Sotah (Heb. "Errant Wife"), fifth tractate in Mishnah, order *Nashim,* with *gemara* in Babylonian and Jerusalem Talmuds. Deals mainly with laws concerning woman suspected of adultery.

Soul, Additional, see Neshamah Yeterah.

Soul, Transmigration of, see Gilgul.

Sous, largest province in Morocco. Jewish settlement fr. pre-Islamic times. Jews dispersed, forming autochthonous pop. in mountain regions. Small communities suffered persecution during 15th, 18th, 19th c. 6,000 Jews in 1951, but after 1955 evacuated area en masse, most going to Israel.

South Africa, African republic. Jewish settlement began after introduction of complete religious toleration 1803. First congregation Cape Town 1841. Industrial development attracted Jewish immigrants from Europe, America, Australia, joined by 30,000 fr. E. Europe, mainly Lithuania, 1880–1910. Majority went to urban centers of Witwatersrand, esp. Johannesburg. Immigration restrictions severely curtailed number of Jewish refugees fr. Germany in 1930s. S. African Jewish Board of Deputies (founded 1912; 1969 membership 330 organizations), authorized spokesman for

SINAI

Rain-filled *wadi* near the monastery of St. Catherine in Sinai.

SUKKAH

Sukkah from S. Germany c. 1800. The wall-painting depicts Jerusalem, the Temple, and the Western Wall.

SYNAGOGUE The 14th-cent. Ark of the Law in the Altneuschul in Prague. This is the oldest intact synagogue in Europe, dating at least to the 12th cent.

community; Orthodox congregations affiliated either to Federation of Synagogues of S. Africa (Johannesburg) or United Council of Hebrew Congregations (Cape Town). Progressive communities associated with S. African Union for Progressive Judaism. Relations with Israel sometimes strained by Israel opposition to apartheid. Jewish pop. 117,990 (1971).

South Carolina, U.S. state. First recorded Jew 1695. First formal congregation Kahal Kadosh Beth Elohim in Charleston, cradle of Reform Judaism in U.S. Jewish pop. 7,815 (1971).

South Dakota, U.S. state. First Jewish settlers 1876. Jewish pop. 760 (1971).

Southwood, Julius Salter Elias, Viscount (1873–1946), British newspaper owner. Managing director of Odhams Brothers (printers), owning many journals and newspapers, incl. labor journal *Daily Herald.*

Soutine, Chaim (1893–1943), Russian-French expressionist painter; a founder of School of Paris; b. Lithuania, went to Paris, was befriended by Modigliani.

Sovern, Michael Ira (1931–), U.S. legal scholar, arbitrator. Main interest labor relations. Dean Columbia Law School fr. 1970.

Sovetish Heymland, sole Yiddish literary periodical published in Moscow; organ of Soviet Writers' Union. Established 1961 (largely as result of external pressure) as bimonthly; fr. 1965 as monthly. Edited by Aron Vergelis. Fully reflects Soviet policy.

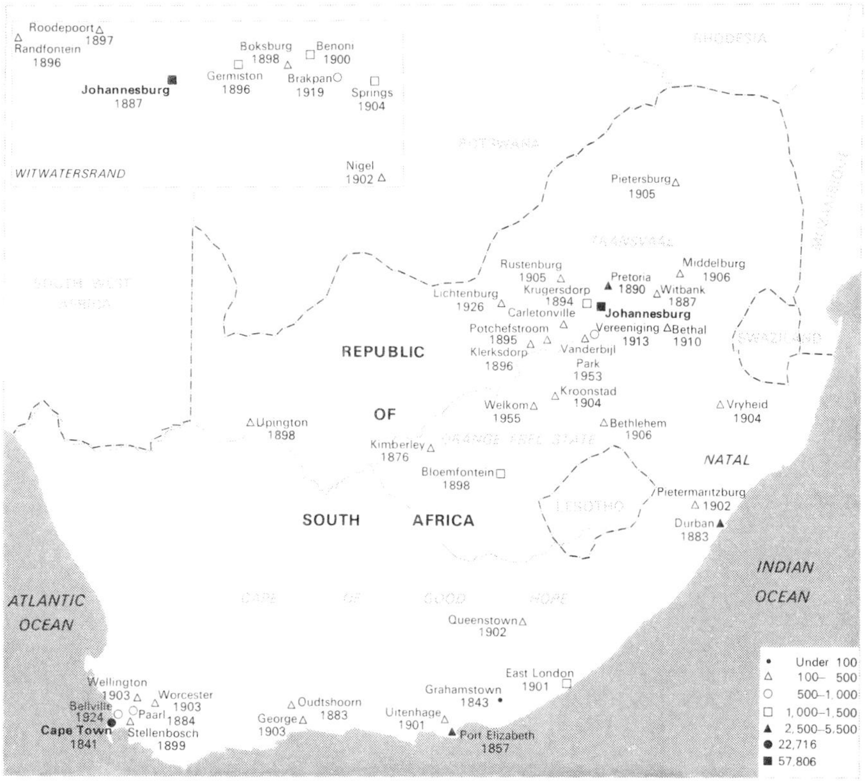

Jewish communities of South Africa with dates of establishment. Population figures based on 1960 census.

Soyer, Raphael (1899–), U.S. realist painter. Member National Institute of Arts and Letters. Twin brother **Moses** and brother **Israel** (b. 1907), also successful painters.

Spaeth, Johann Peter (Moses Germanus; 1642/45–1701), German proselyte of Catholic birth. Later became teacher in Amsterdam Sephardi community. Defended conversion by stating "I have not betrayed, but rather preceded you."

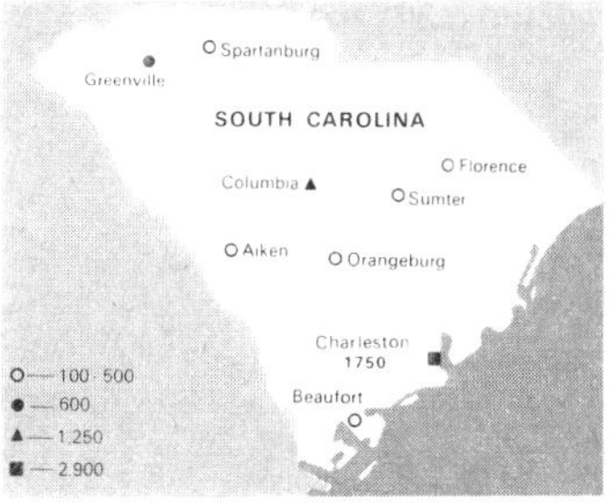

Jewish communities in South Carolina, and date of establishment.

"Hanging Turkey" by Chaim Soutine, 1926.

"My Friends" by Raphael Soyer, 1948.

Spain, country in SW Europe. Jews probably arrived in Roman times. Community grew rapidly under early Visigothic rule, but was relentlessly persecuted in 7th c. once Catholicism became dominant. Arab conquest of 711 brought freedom. During next centuries one of greatest centers of Jewish learning and scholarship, and some Jews rose to positions of great political influence. Almohad invasion of 1146 virtually destroyed Andalusian communities and great centers of Jewish life were restricted to Christian Castile and Aragon, where they flourished ("the Golden Age"). Christian intolerance began to make itself felt in 13th c. and reached climax in massacre of 1391. Mass conversions, often only ostensible, ensued. The large number of Conversos (or Marranos, who remained Jews at heart) continued to be object of persecution. Inquisition introduced 1478 and in 1492 King Ferdinand and Queen Isabella expelled all Jews (over 100,000) fr. Spain. Began returning in 19th c., benefiting fr. introduction of religious toleration (1868). 5,600 Jews fled via Spain in WWII. Jewish pop. 9,000 (1971), mainly concentrated in Barcelona and Madrid (many fr. Sp. Morocco).

Victim of Spanish Inquisition wearing "sanbenito," a special garment.

Spalato, see Split.

Spaniolish, see Ladino.

Spassky, Boris (1937–), Russian chess grand master. Defeated Tigran Petrosian 1969 to become world champion. Lost title to Bobby Fischer 1972.

Spector, Johanna (1920–), U.S. ethno-musicologist; b. Latvia, in concentration camps in WWII, in U.S. fr. 1947. Founded department of ethno-musicology, Jewish Theological Seminary, 1962. Collected Yemenite, Samaritan music.

Spector, Mordecai (1858–1925), Yiddish novelist, editor; b. Ukraine, settled in Warsaw 1887, went to U.S. 1921. Writer for masses; pioneer of Yiddish folklore and Yiddish writing for children.

Speiser, Ephraim Avigdor (1902–1965), U.S. orientalist; b. Galicia, in U.S. fr. 1920. Prof. of Semitic languages and literature at Univ. of Pennsylvania. Pres. of American Oriental Society. Pioneer in discovery of Hurrians and their culture.

Spektor, Isaac Elhanan (1817–1896), rabbi of Kovno, where he established yeshivah. His broad-minded halakhic rulings were respected internationally. Permitted agricultural labor in Ereẓ Israel during sabbatical year by nominal sale of land to non-Jew. Rulings on

Major Jewish and Converso communities in Christian Spain, 1474.

Micrographic portrait of Isaac Elhanan Spektor.

agunot were lenient. Active in struggle against legal disabilities in Russia. Supported Ḥovevei Zion.

Sperber, Manès (1905–), French author. Assistant to psychologist Alfred Adler in Vienna. Taught psychology in Berlin 1927–33, then went to France. Director of French publishing house Calmann-Lévy. Writings depict moral collapse of revolutionary edifice and profound positive attitude to Jewishness.

Spewack, Bella (1899–) and **Samuel** (1899–1971), U.S. playwriting team. Plays incl. *Boy Meets Girl* and book for Cole Porter musical *Kiss Me Kate*.

Speyer (Spire), city in W. Germany. Jews first there in 11th c., when they were granted privileges. Suffered during First Crusade. Prospered in 12th c., when it was Torah center with close relations with Mainz and Worms (see Shum). Community destroyed during Black Death persecutions 1349. Subsequently only individual Jews in town. Small community formed in 19th c., perished in WWII extermination camps.

Speyer, German-American family of international bankers, philanthropists. Progenitor **Michael Isaac** (d. 1692), community head, Frankfort ghetto. **Lazarus Joseph** (1810–1876), conducted business as Lazard Speyer-Ellissen. His partner **Philipp** (1815–1876) and Philipp's brother **Gustav** (1825–1883), founded Philipp Speyer & Co. 1845, later Speyer & Co. in N.Y. With Frankfort branch, placed first Civil War loan in Germany. Prior to WWI, N.Y. branch formed U.S. syndicates which raised European capital for investment in U.S. industry. Both Frankfort and American houses liquidated in 1930s.

Stairs leading down to 12th-cent. "mikveh" in Speyer.

Spiegel, Isaiah (1906–), Yiddish writer; b. Poland. One of few Yiddish writers to survive Holocaust. Settled in Israel 1951. Most important work is Holocaust fiction esp. short stories.

Spiegel, Ludwig (1864–1926), Czech educator, politician. Prof. of constitutional law at German Univ. of Prague. A leader of German Democratic Party, member of Senate 1920–25.

Spiegel, Samuel P. (1904–), U.S. motion picture producer *(African Queen, On the Waterfront, The Bridge on the River Kwai)*.

Spiegel, Shalom (1899–), scholar, educator; b. Rumania. Taught in Ereẓ Israel 1923–29, then prof. of medieval Hebrew literature at Jewish Theological Seminary, N.Y. Writings incl. *Hebrew Reborn* on modern Jewish men of letters and *The Last Trial* on the *Akedah*. Brother of Samuel Spiegel.

Spielman, Sir Isidore (1854–1925), director of art exhibitions branch of British Board of Trade. Organized Anglo-Jewish Historical Exhibition 1887.

Spielman, Marion Harry Alexander (1858–1948), British art critic, expert on portraiture; brother of Isidore and Meyer Spielman. Editor of *Magazine of Art* and wrote history of *Punch*.

Spielman, Sir Meyer Adam (1856–1936), British educationalist. Worked on prevention of juvenile delinquency and founded reformatory for Jewish boys.

Spielvogel, Nathan (1874–1956), Australian author. Only Australian Jewish writer of the era.

Spingarn, Joel Elias (1875–1939), U.S. literary scholar, champion of Negro integration. A founder of publishing firm Harcourt, Brace and Howe. A founder of NAACP, its chairman 1913–19, then president. His brother, **Arthur Barnett** (1878–1971), U.S. lawyer. Honorary pres. of NAACP.

Spinka, Joseph Meir Weiss of (1838–1909), *ẓaddik*, founder of ḥasidic dynasty. Renowned for ecstatic prayers; also practiced extreme self-mortification.

Spinoza, Baruch (Benedict) de (1632–1677), Dutch philosopher; b. Amsterdam, descended fr. Portuguese Marranos. Received traditional education and studied philosophy. His unorthodox religious views led to formal excommunication by Sephardi community 1656. In his most famous works *Tractatus Theologico-Politicus* and *Ethics* he expounded a pantheistic philosophy. Insisting that religion be judged only on the basis of reason, he also initiated modern biblical criticism. His philosophical system profoundly influenced subsequent philosophers.

Statue of Spinoza in The Hague.

Spira (Spiro), Nathan Nata ben Solomon (c. 1585–1633), Polish kabbalist. Interested mainly in mysticism of numbers. His *Megalleh Amukkot* is classic of Ashkenazi Kabbalah.

Spire, see Speyer.

Spire, André (1868–1966), French poet, Zionist. Inspector-general Ministry of Agriculture 1902–26. Active in defense of Dreyfus, became militant advocate of Jewish national revival. Represented French Zionists at Paris Peace Conference 1919. In U.S. during WWII. Leader of Jewish revival movement in 20th c. French literature. Writings incl. *Poèmes juifs* and *Samaël*.

Spiro, Karl (1867–1932), German physiological chemist. At Univ. of Strasbourg 1894–1918; prof. at Univ. of Basle fr. 1921. Among first to apply physical chemistry concepts to biology. Discovered building blocks of proteins.

Spiro, Medford Elliot (1920–), U.S. anthropologist. Prof. at Univ. of Chicago. Wrote studies on kibbutz life.

Spitz, Mark (1950–), U.S. swimmer. Won 5 gold medals in 1967 Pan-American Games and named "world swimmer of the year." Won 4 gold medals in 1968 Olympics and record 7 in 1972 Olympics.

Spitz, Rene (1887–), child psychiatrist, psychoanalyst; went to U.S. fr. Europe late 1930s. On faculty of N.Y. Psychoanalytic Institute. Retired to Geneva. Pioneered concept of anaclitic depression.

Spitzer, Solomon, (known as **Reb Zalman Spitzer**; 1826–1893), rabbi, leader of Austrian Orthodox Jewry. Opposed radical reforms in order of service proposed by Adolf Jellinek 1871.

Spivacke, Harold (1904–), U.S. musicologist. Chief of music division of Library of Congress fr.1937.

Spivak, Nissan (known as **"Nissi Belzer"**; 1824–1906), Lithuanian cantor, composer. Voice impairment fr. childhood accident, led him to develop new style of synagogue music, assigning long ensembles to choir and reducing role of cantor to minimum.

Split, Adriatic port in Croatia. Jews fr. 16th c. Originally two groups, one fr. Italy. the other fr. Ottoman territories in Balkans; later merged. Benefited fr. establishment of free port and enjoyed protection of Croatian authorities. Deteriorated in late 18th c. when restrictions imposed. 400 Jews in 1939, most destroyed by Germans. 120 Jews in 1970.

Spoehr, Alexander (1913–), U.S. anthropologist. Specialized in American Indian and Pacific ethnology. Taught in Hawaii and Pittsburg; pres. of American Anthropological Association 1965.

Springfield, city in Mass., U.S. E. European Jews fr. 1880s. First congregation 1891–92. Jewish pop. 11,000 (1971).

Sprinzak, Joseph (1885–1959), Israel labor leader, first speaker of Knesset; b. Moscow; settled in Ereẓ Israel 1908. Secretary of Ha-Po'el ha-Ẓa'ir, played decisive role in creating framework of Hitaḥadut. First Ereẓ Israel labor representative elected to Zionist Executive. Leading member of Mapai; secretary-general of Histadrut. Greatly influenced democratic structure of Knesset.

S.S., see Zionist Socialist Workers' Party.

Stahl, Friedrich Julius (1802–1861), German conservative statesman; converted to Lutheranism 1819. Prof. of law at Univ. of Berlin. After 1848 led right-wing Evangelische Oberkirchenrat Party in Prussian Upper House, opposing emancipation of Jews.

°**Stalin, Joseph Vissarionovich** (1879–1953), ruler of Soviet Union. During purges of 1930s, reduced Jewish personnel in many branches of the bureaucracy and tended to liquidate all signs of Yiddish culture. During WWII established Jewish Anti-Fascist Committee and supported establishment of Jewish state in Ereẓ Israel 1947–8. Fr. end of 1948 until death, extremely hostile toward everything Jewish (mostly labeled "Zionist") and embarked on complete liquidation of last Jewish institutions and personalities engaged in Yiddish literature and culture (anti-"Cosmopolitan" campaign, Slansky trials, Doctors' plot).

Stamford, city in Conn., U.S. First Jews in 1880s. Orthodox congregation 1889, Conservative synagogue 1920, Reform 1954. Jewish pop. 10,300 (1971).

Stampfer, Jehoshua (1852–1908), Ereẓ Israel pioneer; b. Hungary, settled in Ereẓ Israel 1869. Joined group which founded first Jewish agricultural settlement in Petaḥ Tikvah 1878; for many years chairman of its local council. His son **Solomon Isaac** (1877–1961), first mayor of Petaḥ Tikvah 1934.

JEWISH POPULATION STATISTICS

TOWNS WITH 100,000[1] OR MORE JEWS, 1972 (Rough Estimates)

Town	Number of Jews
Moscow	285,000
Kiev	220,000
Leningrad	165,000
Paris	300,000
London	280,000
Tel Aviv	394,000
Jerusalem	266,000
Haifa	210,000
New York	2,381,000
Los Angeles	535,000
Philadelphia	325,000
Chicago	269,000
Boston	180,000
Miami	200,000
Washington	112,500
Baltimore	100,000
Buenos Aires	350,000
Montreal	113,000

Outside Israel, includes the conurbation of each town.

Source: American Jewish Year Book, 1973.

COUNTRIES WITH 500 OR MORE JEWS, 1972 (Rough Estimates)

Whole World	Number of Jews
Whole World	14,370,000[1]
EUROPE	**4,055,905[1]**
Bulgaria	7,000
Czechoslovakia	14,000
Greece	6,500
Hungary	80,000
Poland	8,000
Rumania	90,000
Turkey[2]	30,000
Soviet Union[2]	2,648,000
Yugoslavia	7,000
Austria	9,400
Belgium	40,500
Denmark	6,000
Finland	1,150
France	550,000
Germany[3]	32,000
Gibraltar	625
Great Britain	410,000
Ireland	4,000
Italy	35,000
Luxembourg	1,000
Netherlands	30,000
Norway	800
Portugal	580
Spain	9,000
Sweden	15,000
Switzerland	20,000
ASIA	**2,826,900[1]**
Israel	2,723,000
Afghanistan	500
India	14,000
Iran	80,000
Iraq	500
Japan	500
Lebanon	2,000
Philippines	500
Singapore	600
Syria	4,000
AFRICA	**176,500[1]**
Algeria	1,000
Egypt	500
Morocco	31,000
Tunisia	8,000
Ethiopia	12,000
Rhodesia	5,200
South Africa	117,900
AMERICA	**7,237,345[1]**
Canada	305,000
U.S.A.	6,115,000
Argentina	500,000
Bolivia	2,000
Brazil	150,000
Chile	30,000
Colombia	13,000
Costa Rica	1,500
Cuba	1,500
Curaçao	700
Ecuador	850
Guatemala	1,900
Jamaica	600
Mexico	40,000
Panama	2,000
Praguay	1,200
Peru	5,300
Surinam	500
Uruguay	50,000
Venezuela	15,000
OCEANIA	**74,000**
Australia	70,000
New Zealand	4,000

[1] Includes countries with less than 500 Jews.
[2] Includes Asian regions of the USSR and Turkey.
[3] Includes W. Germany, E. Germany, and Berlin.

Source: American Jewish Year Book, 1973.

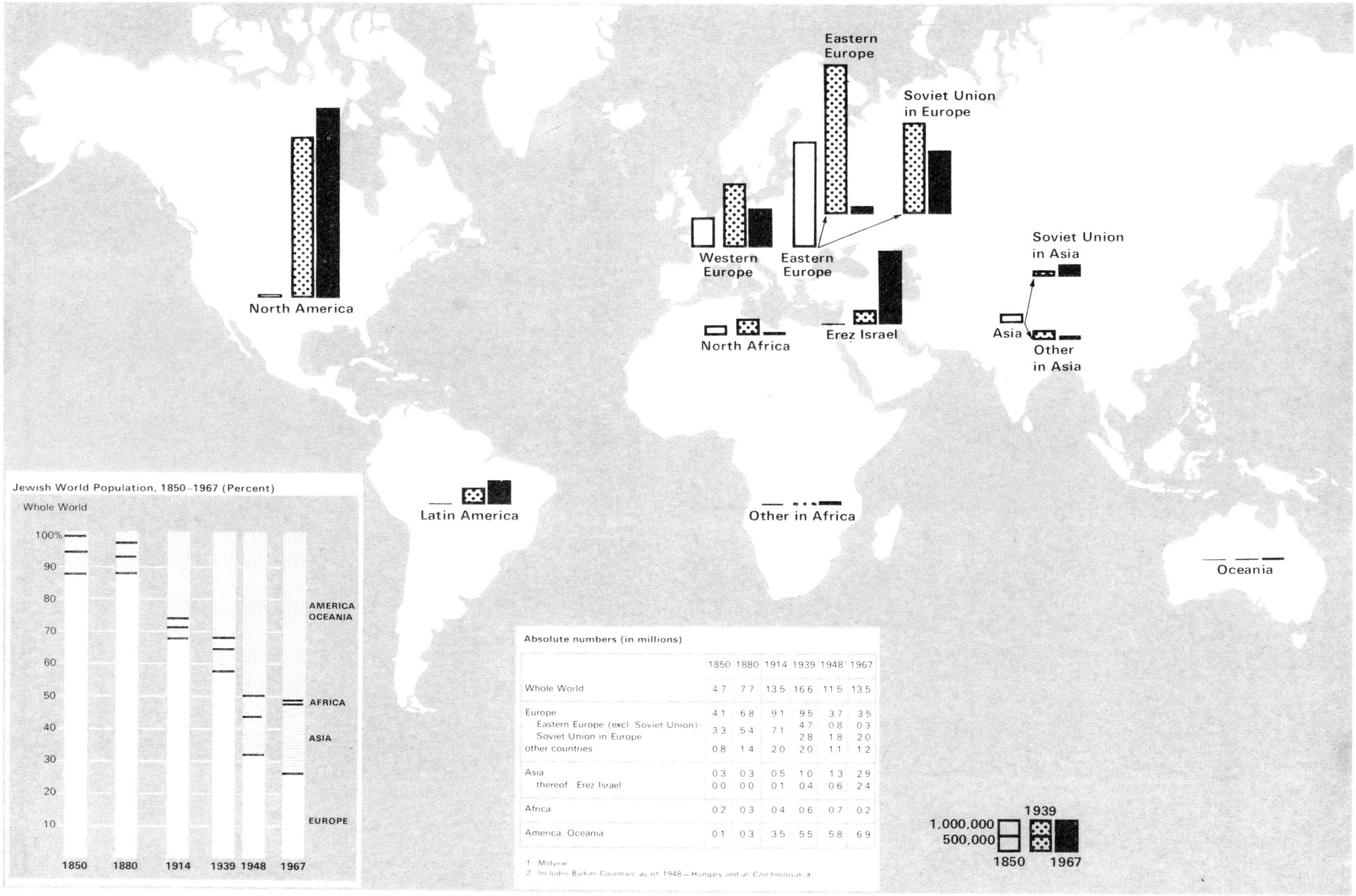

Absolute numbers (in millions)

	1850	1880	1914	1939	1948[1]	1967
Whole World	4.7	7.7	13.5	16.6	11.5	13.5
Europe	4.1	6.8	9.1	9.5	3.7	3.5
Eastern Europe (excl. Soviet Union)[2]	3.3	5.4	7.1	4.7	0.8	0.3
Soviet Union in Europe				2.8	1.8	2.0
other countries	0.8	1.4	2.0	2.0	1.1	1.2
Asia	0.3	0.3	0.5	1.0	1.3	2.9
thereof: Erez Israel	0.0	0.0	0.1	0.4	0.6	2.4
Africa	0.2	0.3	0.4	0.6	0.7	0.2
America, Oceania	0.1	0.3	3.5	5.5	5.8	6.9

1 Midyear
2 Includes Balkan Countries, as of 1948 – Hungary and all Czechoslovakia

Jewish world population 1850–1967 (rough estimates).

Stand, Adolf (1870–1919), Zionist leader in Galicia. Built up Zionist movement in Galicia. Elected to Austrian Parliament. At outbreak of WWI fled to Vienna.

Stande, Stanislaw Ryszard (1897–1939), Polish poet, translator. Numerous verse collections. Served as Communist political propagandist. D. in Soviet prison.

Stanislav (Ivanov Frankovsk), city in Ukrainian SSR. Jews there fr. foundation of town 1662. Community grew during 19th, 20th c. Most Jews traders or dealt in light industry. Community prospered, numbering 30,000 in 1939. In WWII entire community, together with Hungarian refugees, were shot or deported to Belzec extermination camp.

Starkenstein, Emil (1884–1942), pharmacologist. Prof. at Prague German Univ. until 1938. Developed effective drug against seasickness. Moved to Netherlands 1939. Killed in Holocaust.

°**Starkey, John Llewelyn** (1895–1938), British archaeologist. Directed Lachish expedition 1932–38. Killed by Arabs while on way to Jerusalem for opening of Palestine Archaeological Museum.

Starobinski, Jean (1920–), Swiss literary critic, author. Prof. of French literature at Univ. of Geneva. Leading exponent of "structuralist" school of criticism.

Star of David, see Magen David.

Starr, Joshua (1907–1949), U.S. Jewish historian. Secretary of Commission for European Jewish Cultural Reconstruction 1947–49; instrumental in recovering part of religious and cultural treasures looted by Nazis. Main historical interest Byzantine and post-Byzantine Jewish history.

Status Quo Ante, term applied to communities in Hungary which, after schism at 1868–9 Hungarian General Jewish Congress, did not join Neologist organization or Orthodox communities but retained their pre-Congress status. Ostracized by Orthodox and isolated. Organized themselves into national organization 1927, which was closed by authorities 1950.

Staub, Hermann (1856–1904), German jurist who wrote commentary on new German commercial code. Founded and edited legal magazine *Deutsche Juristenzeitung.*

Steiger, Rod (1925–), U.S. movie, stage, TV actor. Famed for roles in *In the Heat of the Night,* for which he won Oscar and *The Pawnbroker.*

Steiger Trial, trial held 1924–5 in Lvov against Jewish student Stanislaw Steiger on trumped-up charge of conspiring to assassinate Polish president. Real conspirator belonging to clandestine Ukrainian organization, escaped to Berlin. Trial occasioned mass anti-Semitism in streets and was marked by revelations implicating Ukrainian statesmen. Steiger was acquitted.

Stein, Arthur (1871–1950), Austrian historian. Prof. at German Univ. of Prague 1923–39. Primarily interested in history of Roman Empire. In WWII confined to Theresienstadt but survived.

Stein, August (1854–1937), Czech communal worker. Head of assimilationist movement; pres. of Prague Jewish community 1922–30 and first chairman of Supreme Council of Federation of Jewish Religious Congregations of Bohemia, Moravia, and Silesia 1926–31. Fr. 1881 first editor of Czech-Jewish almanac.

Stein, Edith (1891–1942), German philosopher; important in phenomenological movement. Converted to Catholicism 1922 and taught at Catholic institutions in Germany. Wrote on Thomism and St. John of the Cross. Fled fr. Nazis 1938 to monastery in Holland, but under German occupation deported to Auschwitz, where she perished.

Stein, Edmund Menahem (1895–1943), Polish scholar, writer. Prof. (rector 1935) at Inst. of Judaistic Sciences in Warsaw. Wrote on Jewish scholarly topics. Chairman of Union of Hebrew Writers in Warsaw. During WWII, participated in cultural life of Warsaw ghetto. Killed in Holocaust.

Stein, Gertrude (1874–1946), U.S. author, critic and patron of the arts. Settled Paris 1902. Noted as literary experimenter; encouraged F. Scott Fitzgerald, Sherwood Anderson, Ernest Hemingway. Writings incl. *Three Lives, The Autobiography of Alice B. Toklas.*

Gertrude Stein by Pablo Picasso, 1906.

Stein, Isaac (d. 1495), *rosh yeshivah* in Regensburg, halakhic authority. Wrote commentary and novellae to *Sefer Mitzvot Gadol* of Moses b. Jacob of Coucy, completed by his son, Aviezri, and sometimes called "the *Nimmukim* of Isaac Stein."

Stein, Leonard Jacques (1887–1973), English barrister, Zionist historian. Served in Ereẓ Israel in WWI and was military governor of Safed. Political secretary of Zionist Organization 1920–29. Pres. of Anglo-Jewish Association 1939–49. Wrote on Zionist history, notably *The Balfour Declaration.*

Stein, Leonid (1936–1973), Russian chess master. Won Soviet championship 1964, 1967. Writings important for opening theory.

Stein, Sir Marc Aurel (1862–1943), British archaeologist. Conducted expeditions to C. Asia, Baluchistan, Iran; headed journeys to establish marching routes and battlefields of Alexander the Great. Greatest discoveries made in Tun-huang of 4th c. Chinese art.

Steinach, Eugen (1861–1944), physiologist, biologist. Prof. of physiology at German Univ. of Prague and fr. 1912 director of dept. of experimental biology at Vienna Academy of Science. Coined term "puberty gland" and devised operation for rejuvenation.

Steinbach, Alexander Alan (1894–), U.S. rabbi, author. Rabbi Temple Ahavath Sholom, Brooklyn, N.Y. fr. 1934. Pres. Jewish Book Council of America, editor *Jewish Book Annual.*

Steinbach, Emil (1846–1907), Austrian lawyer, politician. Baptized 1886. Dept. head Ministry of Justice, minister of finance 1891, pres. Supreme Court 1904–07.

Steinbarg, Eliezer (1880–1932), Yiddish educator, writer; b. Bessarabia. School director in Lipkany and Czernowitz. Famous for his fables written in Yiddish. His tales for children were written in Hebrew.

Steinberg, Aaron (1891–), Jewish communal leader; brother of I.N. Steinberg. Taught philosophy at St. Petersburg 1918–23, went to Berlin 1922, England 1934. Headed cultural dept. of World Jewish Congress.

Steinberg, Isaac Nahman (1888–1957), Russian revolutionary, jurist, Territorialist leader. Member of Socialist Revolutionary Party; commissar for law in Lenin's first Soviet government (Dec. 1917–March

Cartoon by Saul Steinberg.

1918). Left Russia 1923, went to Europe, settled in N.Y. 1943. Published works on Russian Revolution. Became Territorialist and founded Freeland League, advocating creation of autonomous Jewish colonies in Kimberley and Surinam.

Steinberg, Jacob (1887–1947), poet, short story writer, essayist; b. Ukraine, lived in Odessa and Warsaw. Wrote in Yiddish and Hebrew. Settled in Ereẓ Israel 1914, where he ceased writing in Yiddish. His biblical-style poetry is influenced by French symbolists.

Steinberg, Joshua (1825–1908), Hebrew writer, linguist, teacher. Government-appointed rabbi in Bialystok and Vilna 1860–66; active in establishing governmental Russian-Jewish schools. Taught at Vilna Rabbinical Seminary fr. 1867; censor of Hebrew books 1883–1905. Wrote textbook in Russian for Hebrew and Aramaic, translated biblical books into Russian, compiled Russian-Hebrew dictionary.

Steinberg, Judah (1863–1908), writer, Hebrew educator; b. Bessarabia. Served as teacher and later as correspondent of Yiddish daily. Wrote children's stories, ḥasidic stories, etc.

Steinberg, Maximilian Ossejevich (1883–1946), Russian composer, teacher; student and son-in-law of Rimsky-Korsakoff. Prof. of composition 1908 and director 1934 Leningrad Conservatory. Wrote symphonies, orchestral works, ballets, chamber and piano music.

Steinberg, Milton (1903–1950), U.S. Conservative rabbi. Rabbi Park Avenue Synagogue, N.Y. fr. 1933. Wrote novel *As a Driven Leaf*, based on life of Elisha b. Avuyah. Also wrote *The Making of the Modern Jew* and *A Partisan Guide to the Jewish Problem*.

Steinberg, Saul (1914–), U.S. cartoonist, artist; b. Rumania, trained as architect in Milan. Went to U.S. 1942. Best known for cartoons and political drawings in *New Yorker*. Collections of drawings incl. *All in Line, The Passport*, and *Labyrinth*.

Steinberg, William (1899–), conductor. Director Frankfort opera 1929–33, conductor in Juedischer Kulturbund, 1933–36, conductor Buffalo Philharmonic.

Steinbruch, Aarão (1915–), Brazilian lawyer, politician. Labor deputy to Federal Chamber of Deputies 1950. First Jewish senator in Brazil 1962, pres. of Labor Party 1963.

Steiner, George (1929–), literary critic. Taught in U.S. and England. Works incl. *Death of Tragedy* and *Language and Silence*.

Steiner, Hannah (1894–1944), Czech communal leader. A founder of WIZO in Czechoslovakia. Coleader of Juedisches Hilfkomité with Marie Schmolka in caring for Jewish refugees fr. Germany. Interned Theresienstadt ghetto, where she was in charge of women's relief service. D. Auschwitz.

Steiner, Jean-François (1938–), French writer; son of Isaac Kadmi Cohen. Wrote controversial *Treblinka*, which implied Jewish complicity in "final solution."

Steinhardt, Jakob (1887–1968), Israel painter, printmaker; b. Poland, in Berlin fr. 1912, settled in Jerusalem 1933. Head of graphic dept., Bezalel School of Art, 1949, director 1953–57. First international prize São Paulo Biennale for graphic arts 1955. After 1933, worked exclusively in woodcuts.

Steinhardt, Joseph ben Menahem (1720–1776), German rabbi, *posek*. Occupied various rabbinical posts in Alsace. Halakhic authority. Author of commentaries, novellae, responsa. Opposed Shabbateans and ḥasidim.

Steinhardt, Laurence Adolf (1892–1950), U.S. diplomat. Minister to Sweden 1933–37; ambassador to Peru 1937–39, USSR 1939–41, Turkey 1942–45, Czechoslovakia 1945–48, Canada 1948–50, where he died in plane crash.

Steinheim, Salomon Ludwig (1789–1866), German poet, religious philosopher. Basis of system: "Unity of the person, creation out of nothing, freedom of the deed." Main work: *Die Offenbarung nach dem Lehrbegriffe der Synagoge*.

Steinherz, Samuel (1859–1944), Prague medievalist specializing in papal history. Election as rector of Prague German Univ. 1922 occasioned riots in German univs. Subsequently turned to Jewish history and headed Society for History of Jews in Czechoslovak Republic. D. in Theresienstadt.

Steinitz, Wilhelm (1836–1900), world chess champion 1866–94; b. Prague, lived most of life in London. Advocate of importance of strategy; developed famous Steinitzian technique, set out in his writings and in *The Chess Monthly*, which he edited.

Steinman, Eliezer (1892–1970), Hebrew writer; b. Russia, left for Warsaw and settled in Ereẓ Israel 1924. Prolific writer; published stories, novels, essays, edited periodicals. Rendered texts of Jewish culture (Ḥasidism, Talmud) in his own version, with introductory notes and essays.

Jakob Steinhardt

Steinmetz, Charles Proteus (1865–1923), U.S. electrical engineer; b. Germany, in U.S. fr. 1889. Chief consulting engineer General Electric Co. Prof. of electrophysics Union College, Schenectady, fr. 1902. Many inventions, incl. methods for conducting high-voltage electricity for considerable distances.

Steinschneider, Moritz (1816–1907), father of modern Jewish bibliography; among founders of modern Jewish scholarship. Held teaching and library posts in Germany. Studied relationship between Jewish and general culture, esp. during medieval times. Prepared many library catalogs and subject bibliographies. His many studies display astonishing erudition.

Steinthal, Hermann Heymann (1823–1899), German philologist, philosopher; founder of science of racial psychology. Taught at Berlin Univ., prof. of biblical studies and

philosophy of Judaism at Hochschule fuer die Wissenschaft des Judentums fr. 1872.

Stekel, Wilhelm (1868–1940), Austrian psychoanalyst. One of small group of writers who gathered around Freud in Vienna fr. 1902. Made particular contribution to understanding of symbolism and sexual aberrations. In London fr. 1938.

Stekelis, Moshe (1898–1967), Israel archaeologist. Deputy director of Archaeological Museum in Odessa. Exiled to Siberia for Zionist activities. Settled in Ereẓ Israel 1928. Directed archaeological expeditions to prehistoric sites in Ereẓ Israel; prof. of prehistoric archaeology at Heb. Univ.

Stematsky, Avigdor (1908–), Israel painter; b. Russia, settled in Ereẓ Israel 1920. A founder of "New Horizons" group 1947–48. Fr. 1948 worked in abstract style using color contrasts.

Stencl, Abraham Nahum (1897–), Yiddish poet, editor; b. Poland, in England fr. 1936. Wrote poems, essays, criticism, and stories about Ḥasidism and Jewish folklore.

Stern, Abraham Jacob (1762–1842), Polish *maskil,* mathematician. Improved mechanism of watch and invented threshing and calculating machine. Only Jew admitted to Royal Society of Friends of Science. Deeply Orthodox and well versed in Talmud.

Stern, Adolphe (1848–1931), Rumanian lawyer, political leader. Took initiative in creating Union of Native Jews, first political representation for Rumanian Jews, 1909, and was its pres. until 1923. Member of Rumanian parliament and chairman of Jewish Club 1922–26.

Stern, Anatol (1899–1968), Polish poet, translator. Political radical, leading member of futurist school. Representative of Poland's new writing with strongly defined social tendencies.

Stern, Avraham (underground name **Ya'ir**; 1907–1942), underground fighter in Ereẓ Israel, founder of organization later called Loḥamei Ḥerut Israel (Leḥi); went to Ereẓ Israel fr. Poland 1925. Active Irgun Ẓeva'i Le'ummi fr. its formation. His opposition to suspension of anti-British attacks for duration of WWII caused split in I.Ẓ.L. and formation of separate Leḥi group. Killed by Palestine police.

Avraham Stern

Stern, Bezalel (1798–1853), educator, pioneer of Haskalah in S. Russia. Under his direction, Jewish school of Odessa rapidly grew and secular curriculum expanded. Influential member of 1843 commission to ratify curriculum of Jewish government schools.

Stern, Clara Joseephy (1878–1945), child psychologist; wife of William Stern, with whom she collaborated on research projects. Author of monographs on mental and spiritual development of child until primary school years.

(De) Stern, David (d. 1877), British banker; together with his brother **Hermann** (1815–87) founded international banking firm of Stern Bros. Director of Imperial Bank and appointed to lieutenancy of city of London. Made hereditary viscount by king of Portugal 1869.

Stern, Sir Frederick Claude (1884–1967), British banker; partner in Stern Bros. banking house. After distinguished service in WWI, temporarily secretary to Lloyd George during Versailles Peace Conference.

Stern, Gladys Bronwyn (1890–1973), English novelist. Published over 50 books, incl. *Matriarch Chronicles* and *All in Good Time,* dealing with her conversion to Catholicism.

Stern, Grigory (d. 1940), Soviet army officer. Chief adviser to Republican Army in Spain 1936–37. Chief of staff Soviet Far Eastern forces, driving Japanese out of Soviet Mongolia. D. in Finnish campaign.

Stern, Horace (1879–1969), U.S. jurist. Elected to Pennsylvania Supreme Court 1935; chief justice 1952–57. Pres. Dropsie College.

Stern, Irma (1894–1966), S. African painter. Shocked public with bold palette and expressionist method.

Stern, Isaac (1920–), U.S. violinist. Child prodigy who gained worldwide reputation after WWII. Pres. American-Israel Cultural Foundation.

Stern, Jacques (1881–1949), French politician. Elected to National Assembly 1914. Authority on financial affairs. Minister for merchant marine 1930–33, colonies 1935–39. Emigrated to U.S. 1942. Committed suicide.

Stern, Joseph Zechariah (1831–1903), Lithuanian rabbi, talmudist. Interested in various branches of Jewish and general knowledge. Displayed positive attitude to Ḥibbat Zion movement.

Stern, Julius David (1886–1971), U.S. newspaper publisher. Advocate of crusading liberal journalism. Owned several newspapers, incl. Camden *Morning Post,* Philadelphia *Record,* New York *Post* (1933–39).

Stern, Lina Solomonovna (1878–1968), Russian physiologist, botanist. Prof. of biochemistry at Geneva, physiology at Moscow Univ. fr. 1925. Later chief prof. and director at Physiological Scientific Research Institute. First woman admitted to USSR Academy of Sciences; awarded Stalin Prize. Removed fr. post in 1948–9 purges; rehabilitated after Stalin's death.

Stern, Louis (1904–1972), U.S. businessman, communal leader. Pres. Council of Jewish Federations and Welfare Funds 1962–64 and National Jewish Welfare Board fr. 1965.

Stern, Moritz (1864–1939), German rabbi, historian. Under his direction Berlin Jewish Community Library developed into one of most important in Europe. Also curator of Berlin community's art collection.

Stern, Noah (1912–1960), Hebrew poet; b. Lithuania, moved to U.S. and settled in Ereẓ Israel 1935. Served prison term for attempted manslaughter. Committed suicide. Translated Eliot's *Waste Land* into Hebrew.

Stern, Otto (1888–1969), physicist. Prof. at Hamburg Univ. fr. 1923; perfected molecular beam method and confirmed Planck's quantum theory. Settled in U.S. 1933, working at Carnegie Institute of Technology in Pittsburgh. Nobel Prize 1943.

Stern, Philip Cohen (1847–1933), Jamaican lawyer, politician. Sat in Legislative Council 1895–1908, registrar of Supreme Court 1909–10, three times mayor of Kingston.

Stern, Samuel Miklos (1920–1969), orientalist, Romanist; b. Hungary. Taught in Oxford. Published studies on Hebrew and Arabic poetry and Jewish philosophy.

Stern, Sigismund (1812–1867), German teacher; a leader of Berlin Reform movement. On his initiative Association for Reform in Judaism was established in Berlin 1845.

Director of Frankfort on Main Philanthropin school fr. 1848.

Stern, William (Louis; 1871–1938), German philosopher, psychologist; founder of personalistic psychology. Taught at Breslau 1897–1915; prof. at Hamburg Univ. and head of Institute of Psychology 1916. Expelled by Nazis, went to U.S. and taught at Duke Univ. Introduced IQ concept.

Sternberg, Erich-Walter (1898–), composer; b. Berlin, settled in Ereẓ Israel 1932. Compositions incorporated material fr. E. European Jewish folklore and many centered on biblical themes or liturgical music.

Sternberg, Jacob (1890–), Yiddish editor, poet, dramatist; b. Bessarabia. Editor, journalist in Rumania, directed Vilna Troupe 1924–26, directed Yiddish theater in Kishinev fr. 1945. Imprisoned in Siberian labor camp 1948–53. Rehabilitated after Stalin's death.

Sternberg, Josef von (1894–1969), film director. Directed Marlene Dietrich in *The Blue Angel* 1930. In WWII made films for U.S. Office of Information.

Sternberg, Lev Yakovlevich (1861–1927), Russian anthropologist. Exiled 1886 for 10 years to Siberia for membership in Populist Party; became authority on culture of Gilyaks of NE Siberia. Appointed ethnographer at St. Petersburg Museum of Anthropology and Ethnography 1897 and after Russian Revolution prof. at Leningrad Univ.

Sterne, Maurice (1878–1957), U.S. painter, sculptor. Restrained, harmonious post-impressionist.

Sterne, Simon (1839–1901), U.S. lawyer, reformer. Best known for obtaining conviction of N.Y. City boss William Tweed for forgery and larceny 1873 and for work which subsequently led to establishment of Interstate Commerce Commission.

Stern Group, see Loḥamei Ḥerut Israel.

Sternharz, Nathan (1780–1845), disciple, companion of R. Naḥman of Bratslav and leader of Bratslav ḥasidim after Naḥman's death 1810. Despite violent personal persecution built up numbers of movement. Published Naḥman's teachings, everyday talks, and stories.

Sternheim, Carl (1878–1942), German playwright; b. Leipzig. Wrote anti-bourgeois comedies known for superb construction and terse diction.

Stern-Taeubler, Selma (1890–), German historian. Specialized in relationship bet. Prussian State and its Jews bet. 1648 and 1812. In U.S. fr. 1941. First archivist of the American Jewish Archives in Cincinnati 1947–57. Moved to Basle 1960.

°**Steuernagel, Carl** (1869–1958), Protestant German Bible critic. Explained composition of Deuteronomy as composite redaction of various Deuteronomic strands.

Steuss, David (d. c. 1387), head of family of bankers in Austria. Served Austrian and foreign rulers, ecclesiastical lords, and noblemen. Most important financier of his time.

Stieglitz, Alfred (1864–1946), U.S. photographer. Fought for recognition of photography as art. First photographer whose work was accepted by U.S. museums.

°**Stiles, Ezra** (1727–1795), U.S. scholar, theologian. His *Literary Diary* contains detailed account of Newport Jewry. Pres. Yale, 1778–95. Made study of Hebrew compulsory for all freshmen. Devoted to Hebrew language and culture.

Stilling, Benedict (1810–1879), German pioneer in surgery, anatomy. Initiated various surgical operations and wrote on structure of spinal cord.

Stock, Dov, see Sadan, Dov.

Stockade and Watchtower (Heb. *Ḥomah u-Migdal*), type of settlement established in Ereẓ Israel 1946–47 in surprise one-day operations to provide immediate security against Arab attacks. First of 118 such settlements was Nir David in Beth Shean Valley.

Stockholm, capital of Sweden. Jews fr. 1774; community founded 1775. Independent activities of community restricted after 1838. Character of community changed, first by full emancipation 1870 and in 20th c. by immigrants and refugees. Doubled in size bet. 1900 and 1920. Provided haven for refugees fr. Norway 1942; fr. Denmark 1943, and fr. concentration camps after war. Jewish pop. 8,000 (1971).

°**Stoecker, Adolf** (1835–1909), German anti-Semitic preacher-politician. Powerful demagogue who used his Christian Social Workers' Party (founded 1878) and his position as court chaplain 1874–91 to propagate anti-Semitism. Although his influence declined fr. 1896, his mass movement provided fertile soil for subsequent, more radical, parties.

Stokes (Wieslander), Rose Pastor (1879–1933), U.S. socialist writer, lecturer. Worked at *Jewish Daily News* 1903. Active in hotel and restaurant workers' strike and shirtwaist workers' strike and a leader in birth control movement. A founder of U.S. Communist Party.

Stolyarski, Peter Solomonovich (1871–1944), Russian violin pedagogue. Prof. at Odessa Conservatory fr. 1920. His methods widely adopted in USSR and elsewhere. Pupils incl. David Oistrakh and Nathan Milstein.

Stone, Dewey (1900–), U.S. business executive, communal leader. Active in various Zionist fund-raising organizations; first chairman of board of governors of the Weizmann Inst. of Science.

Stone, I.F. (Isadore Feinstein; 1907–), U.S. radical journalist. Published and wrote *I.F. Stone's Weekly*. After Six-Day War reversed previous pro-Israel stand. Wrote several books.

Stone, Irving (1903–), U.S. biographer, novelist. Known for *Lust for Life* about Van Gogh, *The Agony and the Ecstasy* about Michelangelo, and *The Passions of the Mind* about Freud.

Stone, Julius (1907–), jurist, international lawyer; b. England, taught at Harvard 1933–36; New Zealand 1938–42; prof. of international law at Univ. of Sydney fr. 1942. Wrote on jurisprudence.

°**Storrs, Sir Ronald** (1881–1955), British military governor 1917–20 and district commissioner 1920–26 of Jerusalem. Reserved toward Zionism. His *Orientations* contain reminiscences of his Jerusalem activities.

°**Strack, Hermann Leberecht** (1848–1922), German orientalist, theologian. Leading non-Jewish scholar in Bible and Talmud, Hebrew and Aramaic linguistics, and Masorah. Wrote standard introduction to Talmud.

Stransky, Josef (1872–1936), conductor. Conducted N.Y. Philharmonic Society and N.Y. State Symphony Orchestra 1923. Art dealer fr. 1925.

Strasberg, Lee (1901–), U.S. theatrical director, teacher. A founder of Group Theater. Artistic director of Actors' Studio, which became famous for Strasberg's "Method" approach to acting. His daughter **Susan** (1938–), actress; appeared in film *The Diary of Anne Frank*.

Strasbourg, city in Alsace. Jewish settlement fr. 1188. In 1242 community paid highest tax of all communities of Empire. Moneylending sole economic occupation. Com-

Medieval tombstones found in Strasbourg.

munity destroyed in Black Death persecutions 1349. Restrictions eased when town came under French sovereignty 1681 and many Jews settled there after French Revolution. Community and institutions grew rapidly in 19th and 20th c., numbered 10,000 in 1939. Evacuated to S. France in WWII. 8,000 Jews returned after war, numbers augmented by N. African immigrants. One of most active communities in Europe after WWII. Jewish pop. 12,000 (1971).

Strasburger, Eduard (1844–1912), German botanist; among founders of modern plant cytology. Prof. at Jena 1871–80, Bonn 1880–1912.

Strashun, Mathias (Mattityahu; 1819–1885), Vilna talmudic scholar; founder of Strashun library; son of Samuel Strashun. Well versed in Jewish scholarship, and secular studies. Communal leader and member of Vilna council. Devoted book collector; bequeathed library to Vilna community.

Strashun, Samuel ben Joseph (1794–1872), Lithuanian merchant, talmudic scholar. Wrote extensive annotations and glosses on almost every tractate of Talmud and Mishnah. Also annotated *Midrash Rabbah.*

Straus, Isidor (1845–1912), U.S. merchant, congressman, philanthropist. Entered N.Y. family business 1865 with brother Nathan. They subsequently became sole owners of R.H. Macy Department Store 1887. Congressman 1894–95. Active Jewish affairs. D. in sinking of *Titanic.*

Nathan Straus (right) at cornerstone ceremony for the Straus Health Center, Jerusalem, 1927, with (left to right) Chief Rabbi Jacob Meir, Lady Plumer, Field Marshal Lord Plumer.

Straus, Jesse Isidor (1872–1936), U.S. business executive, public servant, diplomat; son of Isidor Straus. Built Macy's into world's largest department store. Ambassador to France 1933–36.

Straus, Nathan (1848–1931), U.S. merchant, philanthropist; brother of Isidor and Oscar Straus. New York Park Commissioner 1889–93. Had lifelong interest in public health; participated in philanthropic endowments in U.S. and Ereẓ Israel. Gave two-thirds of fortune to Ereẓ Israel. City of Netanyah named for him.

Straus, Nathan Jr. (1889–1961), U.S. publisher, politician; son of Nathan Straus. Editor and publisher of humorous magazine *Puck* 1913–17, Ass't. editor N.Y. *Globe* until 1920. Interested in housing legislation; headed U.S. Housing Authority (1937–42). Pres. WMCA radio station.

Straus, Oscar (1870–1954), Viennese composer of light operas; settled in Vienna 1927, in U.S. during WWII. Best known works incl. *Waltz Dream* and *The Chocolate Soldier.*

Oscar Straus

Oscar Solomon Straus

Straus, Oscar Solomon (1850–1926), U.S. diplomat, public servant, jurist; brother of Isidor and Nathan Straus. As Theodore Roosevelt's secretary of commerce and labor 1906–09 was first Jew to hold cabinet rank. U.S. envoy to Turkey 1887–89, 1898–1900, 1909–10. Five times appointed to Hague International Court of Arbitration. A founder of American Jewish Committee 1906 and Baron de Hirsch Fund. First pres. American Jewish Historical Society.

Straus, Roger Williams (1893–1957), U.S. business executive, public official; son of Oscar Straus. Active Republican; member U.S. delegation to the U.N. General Assembly 1954. Chancellor N.Y. State Board of Regents 1956. A founder of National Conference of Christians and Jews 1928.

Straus, Roger Williams Jr. (1917–), U.S. publisher; son of Roger Williams Straus. Founder of Farrar, Straus & Co. publishing house.

Straus, R. Peter (1917–), U.S. broadcasting executive; son of Nathan Straus Jr. Founder of Straus Broadcasting Group of radio stations. Executive ass't. director International Labor Organization in Geneva 1950–55; ass't. director U.S. foreign aid program to Africa 1967.

Strauss, Aryeh Ludwig (1892–1953), Hebrew, German poet, short story writer, literary critic; b. Germany, settled in Ereẓ Israel fr. 1935. Taught at Hebrew Univ. His critical essays influenced literary criticism in Israel.

Strauss, Eliyahu, see Ashtor, Eliyahu.

Strauss, George Russell (1901–), British politician. Labor MP 1929–66, minister of supply 1947. Responsible for executing nationalization of steel industry 1949.

Strauss, Leo (1899–), philosopher, political scientist. Member of Academy of Jewish Research in Berlin 1925–33. Taught at New School for Social Research, N.Y. 1938–49, then at Univ. of Chicago. Wrote on political philosophy, particularly on Spinoza, Maimonides, and Judah Halevi.

Strauss, Levi (1829–1902), U.S. garment manufacturer, philanthropist; b. Bavaria; in U.S. fr. 1848. Lived in San Francisco. His blue-denim "Levis" made him multi-millionaire.

Strauss, Lewis Lichtenstein (1896–1974), U.S. government official, banker. Conceived Big "E" war production incentive program during WWII and was promoted to rear-admiral. Served on Atomic Energy Commission 1946–50, chairman 1953. Senate refused confirmation as secretary of commerce (nominated 1959).

°**Streicher, Julius** (1885–1946), foremost anti-Semitic agitator of German Nazi period. Founder, editor of obscenely anti-Jewish *Der Stuermer* 1923. Captured 1945, tried at Nuremberg and hanged.

Barbra Streisand

Streisand, Barbra (1942–), U.S. stage, screen actress and singer. Won Academy Award 1968 for role in *Funny Girl.*

Strelisk, Uri ben Phinehas of (d. 1826), ḥasidic leader. Opposed wonder-workers and demanded ethical perfection from followers. Ecstatic manner of praying brought him name *Ha-Saraf* (the seraph).

Stretyn, Judah Ẓevi Hirsch (Brandwein) of (d. 1854), founder of ḥasidic dynasty in E. Galicia. Outstanding disciple of Uri ben Phinehas of Strelisk; also emphasized importance of ecstatic prayer.

Strick, Joseph (1923–), U.S. film director, producer. Known for application of documentary realism to feature films. Films incl. *The Big Break,* Gênet's *The Balcony,* and Joyce's *Ulysses.*

Stricker, Robert (1879–1944), Zionist leader, journalist. Active in Zionist Organization in Austria. Founded and edited only Jewish daily in German *Wiener Morgenzeitung* 1919–28. Joined Revisionists and was a founder of Jewish State Party. Refused to leave Austria in 1938; d. Auschwitz.

Strigler, Mordecai (1921–), Yiddish writer; b. Poland. Survived Holocaust and chronicled its slave labor camps and death factories. Went to U.S. 1953, where he wrote both in Hebrew and Yiddish.

Strisower, Leo (1857–1931), Austrian jurist. Prof. of international law at Univ. of Vienna 1924; pres. of Institut de Droit International.

Strnad, Oskar (1879–1935), Austrian architect, interior decorator. Head of dept. of architecture at Wiener Kunstgeweberschule 1914–35. Designed interiors, furniture, and stage and cinema sets.

Stroheim, Erich von (1885–1957), film actor, director. His film *Greed* (1923) still considered masterpiece. Famed for Teutonic roles. Also appeared in Jean Renoir's *La Grande Illusion, Five Graves to Cairo,* and *Sunset Boulevard.*

Stroock, Solomon Marcuse (1874–1945), U.S. lawyer, philanthropist. Constitutional law specialist. Pres. N.Y. YMHA 1924–26; chairman, executive committee American Jewish Committee 1934. His son **Allan** (1907–), lawyer. Chairman of board Jewish Theological Seminary; vice-pres. American Jewish Committee 1948–51, 1955–58.

Strouse, Myer (1825–1878), U.S. congressman, lawyer. Founded *North American Farmer* 1848, Philadelphia newspaper which he edited until 1852. Elected Democratic congressman 1862, 1864.

Struck, Hermann (1876–1944), graphic artist; b. Berlin, settled in Ereẓ Israel 1923. Master craftsman and outstanding teacher. Excelled as portraitist. A leader of Mizrachi Party.

Struma, boat carrying 769 Jewish refugees which left Rumania in late 1941, was refused entry to Ereẓ Israel or Turkey, and sank in Black Sea in Feb. 1942 with loss of all on board except one.

Stry (Stryj), city in Ukrainian SSR. Jews invited to settle in 16th c., rights confirmed 1576, 1589. In deference to their beliefs, market day transferred 1696 fr. Saturday to Friday. Community grew in 19th, 20th c., numbered 12,000 in 1939. Germans liquidated ghetto 1943.

Stuermer, Der, anti-Semitic Nazi weekly, appeared in Nuremberg 1923–45. Founded, edited by Julius Streicher. Circulation rose to 500,000 after 1935, when it popularized racial anti-Semitism in vulgar form.

Sturman, Ḥayyim (1891–1938), settler and Haganah leader in Ereẓ Israel; arrived fr. Russia 1906. Active in Ha-Shomer, an organizer of Gedud ha-Avodah, and a founder of En Harod. Killed in ambush in 1938 riots.

Stutschewsky, Joachim (1891–), composer, cellist, folklorist; b. Ukraine, in Zurich 1918–24, Vienna 1924–38, Ereẓ Israel fr. 1938. Considered one of most influential musical personalities of country in capacity as cello teacher, composer, lecturer, and writer.

Stuttgart, city in W. Germany. Jews burned 1348, banished c. 1492, 1521. Modern community fr. 1779. 4,490 Jews in 1933. During WWII town was collection point for deportation of all Wuerttemberg Jews. Fewer than 100 survived. Jewish pop. 480 (1968).

Stutthof (Sztutowo), German concentration camp nr. Danzig. Operated 1939–45. Virtually became death camp 1944. Victims came fr. Poland, Hungary, Latvia, Lithuania. 52,000 Jews passed through camp.

Stybel, Abraham Joseph (1884–1946), publisher, literary patron; b. Poland, moved to Moscow in WWI. Founded Stybel publishing house 1917, which published hundreds of books, and literary quarterly *Ha-Tekufah.* Greatly advanced Hebrew book publication. After Oct. 1917 moved to Warsaw, then Berlin. In U.S. during WWII.

Styne, Jule (1905–), U.S. theatrical writer. Composed scores for films, Broadway musicals *(Gentlemen Prefer Blondes, Funny Girl).*

Styria (Steiermark), province in Austria. Jews fr. 11th c. Jewish community fr. 14th c. (principally trading). Jews massacred 1310, expelled 1496. Strong anti-Semitism in 20th c. Jews not permitted to live on Styrian territory fr. 1939. Community established in Graz 1949.

Suasso, Antonio (Isaac) Lopez (17th c.), Dutch merchant. A leading shareholder in West India Co. Ardent supporter of House of Orange.

Sonder Nummer

Der Stürmer

...sches Wochenblatt zum Kampfe um die Wahrheit

HERAUSGEBER: JULIUS STREICHER

Nummer 20 — Nürnberg, im Mai 1939 — 17. Jahr 1939

Ritualmord

Das größte Geheimnis des Weltjudentums

Zu nebenstehendem Bild:

Die Juden sind unser Unglück!

Ritual murder libel in special issue of "Der Stuermer," May 1939.

Antonio Lopez Suasso, marble bust attributed to Rombout Verhulst.

Subbotin, Andrey Pavlovich (1852–1906), Russian economist, writer. In 1887 conducted one of first serious efforts to describe economic situation of Jews in Pale of Settlement.

Subbotniki (Russ. "Sabbath Observers"), Russian sabbatarian movement fr. early 18th c. Under Czar Nicholas I, banished to Caucasus and Siberia, but fr. 1905 enjoyed religious freedom. Practiced Jewish customs. Some believed in New Testament and in Jesus as Christ but not as God; some accepted Hebrew Bible but not Talmud; others considered themselves Jews in every religious aspect. Many families settled in Ereẓ Israel.

Subcarpathian Ruthenia, part of Ukrainian SSR. Jews first there in 17th c. Manufactured and sold alcoholic beverages. Community grew in 18th c. but dispersion of Jews in isolated villages gave rise to cultural and spiritual desolation. Frankist movement gained many adherents. Later ḥasidic influence predominated. Community expanded in 19th c. Political and cultural life further developed after 1918, when region became part of Czechoslovakia. Germans established ghettos 1944 and began deportations to death camps. Community virtually liquidated. After WWII survivors joined by Jews fr. distant parts of USSR. By 1971, 13,000 Jews in region; Jewish life in process of disintegration.

Subeita, see Shivtah.

Succoth, (1) Locality in Jordan Valley. Belonged to kingdom of Sihon, fr. whom it passed to tribe of Gad. Refused to aid Gideon in his pursuit of Midianites and was consequently punished. (2) Second station of Israelites on route of Exodus.

Suess, Joseph (Jud), see Oppenheimer, Joseph ben Issachar Suesskind.

Suesskind von Trimberg (c. 1200–1250), German minstrel *(Minnesaenger)* of Franconian origin. Only important medieval German poet preoccupied with Jewish themes.

Sukenik, Eliezer Lipa (1889–1953), Israel archaeologist; b. Poland, settled in Ereẓ Israel 1912. Prof. at Heb. Univ. fr. 1938. Excavated synagogues (Beth Alpha, Hammath-Gader) and Jewish tombs in vicinity of Jerusalem and also discovered Third Wall. Instrumental in acquiring part of Dead Sea Scrolls 1947, whose importance he immediately recognized. His wife, **Ḥasya Sukenik-**

Suesskind von Trimberg, from 14th-cent. Manesse Codex.

Eliezer Sukenik with a Dead Sea Scrolls jar.

Feinsod (1889–1968), was pioneer of kindergarten education in Ereẓ Israel.

Sukkah, booth erected for festival of Sukkot in accordance with Lev. 23:42. Forbidden to eat any major repast or sleep outside *sukkah* and obligatory to eat there on first night of festival. Blessing recited each time one eats there.

Sukkah (Heb. "Booth"), sixth tractate of order *Mo'ed* in Mishnah, with *gemara* in Babylonian and Jerusalem Talmuds. Deals with laws relating to festival of Sukkot.

Sukkot (Heb. "Booths" or "Tabernacles") festival beginning on Tishri 15 commemorating the *sukkot* which Children of Israel inhabited in wilderness after Exodus. Festival lasts 7 days, of which first (and second in Diaspora) is *yom tov* (festival on which work is prohibited) and the others *ḥol ha-mo'ed.* It is immediately followed by Shemini Aẓeret. Agriculturally it was ingathering or harvest festival; in Second Temple period, occasion of ceremony of "water-libation" known as Simḥat Bet ha-Sho'evah. During festival, meals taken in *sukkah* and blessing made over *arba'ah minim* (four species) *lulav, etrog, hadasim,* and *aravot.* The seventh day is Hoshana Rabba.

Sulamith, first German-language periodical for Jews; founded 1806 by David Fraenkel, who fully supported program of Jewish emancipation with educational innovations.

Sultansky, Mordecai ben Joseph (c. 1772–1862), Karaite scholar, writer. Taught in Crimea and Ukraine. Wrote detailed but biased account of Karaism fr. its beginning to his time.

Sulzbach, town in W. Germany. Jews first there 1305, but community practically annihilated during Black Death persecutions 1349. Reestablished 1666 and small number of Jews continued living there until 1933. Renowned in Jewish world in 17th, 18th c. for its Hebrew printing press.

Sulzberger, Arthur Hays (1891–1968), U.S. publisher of *N. Y. Times;* son-in-law of Adolph S. Ochs. Became publisher of paper and pres. of New York Times Co. on Ochs' death 1935. Instrumental in extending scope and influence of paper.

Sulzberger, Mayer (1843–1923), U.S. jurist, communal leader; one of Philadelphia's leading lawyers. Elected 1895 and subsequently pres. judge of Philadelphia Court of Common Pleas. An initiator and first pres. American Jewish Committee. Active in abrogation of Russo-American commercial treaty in reaction to Russian treatment of Jews. A founder of Jewish Publication Society.

Sulzer, Solomon (1804–1890), Austrian cantor, reformer of liturgical music. Sought to "renovate" traditional *ḥazzanut* by taking into consideration musical trends of the time. Criticized by E. European Jews; enjoyed a wide reputation in C. Europe.

Sumbal (Sunbal), Samuel (d. 1782), Moroccan diplomat who ultimately became responsible for conduct of sultan's foreign policy. Recognized as *nagid* of Jewish community. Fell into disgrace 1780 when accused of smuggling.

Sumer, early name of land corresponding to S. Iraq. Not mentioned in Bible but Sumerian cultural contribution to later Mesopotamian civilization had great influence on Israelite culture.

Sumptuary Laws, enactments issued by European communities 13th–18th c. against luxury and ostentation. Designed to combat temptation of luxury and anti-Jewish accusations of ostentatious living.

Sun, Blessing of the, ceremonial blessing recited once every 28 years on first Wednesday morning of Nisan; supposed start of equinox cycle. During service, thanksgiving is expressed for creation of the sun. Next ceremony: March 18, 1981.

Sura, site of a leading Babylonian academy. Main center of Torah learning for most of period bet. 3rd and early 5th c. and in 8th–10th c. when academy was transferred to Baghdad. Its founder, Rav, had formative influence on Babylonian Talmud.

Sure, Barnett (1891–1960), U.S. biochemist. Prof. and head of agricultural chemistry dept. at Univ. of Arkansas 1927. Independent discoverer of Vitamin E and new members of Vitamin B complex.

Surinam, Dutch Guiana; oldest Jewish community in W. Hemisphere. Jews arrived fr. Brazil (or Holland) 1639. Under British rule, they set up sugar plantations and continued to prosper after Dutch conquest 1667. Community declined in 19th c. Some European refugees temporarily settled there during WWII. Jewish pop. 700 (1970).

Susa, see Shushan.

Susan, Issachar ben Mordecai (c. 1510–after 1580), writer, scholar. Lived in Safed but traveled widely in search of material for his work on Mostarabian communities (Jews living in Middle East before influx fr. Spain). Work described synagogue customs, and was used extensively by Joseph Caro.

Susanna and the Elders, apocryphal work added to canonical Book of Daniel in ancient versions. Wife of Babylonian Jew unjustly accused by two Jewish elders of committing adultery and condemned to death; proved innocent by Daniel. Original language Hebrew or Greek.

Susita (Hippos), ancient Greek city on E. bank of Sea of Galilee (on mountain above En-Gev). Captured by Alexander Yannai. Reestablished as city of Decapolis by Pompey. Augustus gave it to Herod, but after his death it reverted to Syria. In Byzantine times, seat of bishop.

Susman, Margarete (1874–1966), German essayist, poet; lived in Zurich fr. onset of Nazi period. Works incl. *Vom Sinn der Liebe,* and existentialist philosophical analysis of tragic nature of love.

Surinam stamps; map of Jewish plantations (above), Joden Savanne synagogue (bottom left), Jewish tombstone (bottom right).

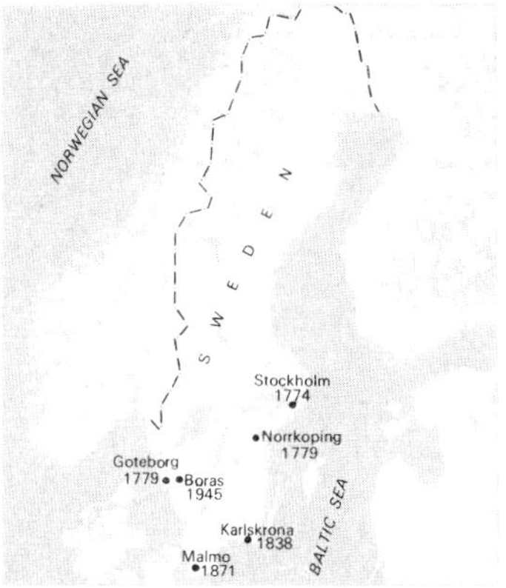

Jewish communities in Sweden with dates of establishment.

Susskind, David (1920–), U.S. producer. Produced plays on Broadway and conducted discussion shows, notably "Open End."

Sussman, Ezra (1900–1973), Hebrew poet, translator; b. Russia; settled in Ereẓ Israel 1922. Wrote poems, drama criticism, and translated fr. Russian and French.

Sutro, Adolph Heinrich Joseph (1830–1898), U.S. engineer, civic leader; b. Prussia, in U.S. fr. 1848. Built Sutro Tunnel fr. Sutro City to Virginia City, Nevada, to drain and ventilate the Comstock Lode. Made fortune in San Francisco real estate. Populist mayor of San Francisco 1895–97.

Sutro, Alfred (1863–1933), English playwright. Became known with social comedy *The Walls of Jericho.* Plays generally on stock themes but written with wit and polish.

Sutzkever, Abraham (1913–), Yiddish poet; b. Belorussia. A founder of Young Vilna group of poets. Lived in Vilna ghetto during WWII; settled in Ereẓ Israel 1947 and edited Yiddish literary quarterly *Die Goldene Keyt* fr. 1949. Poems described life of Jews in Vilna and gave artistic expression to Holocaust, E. European Jewry, and life in Israel.

Suwalki, town in Bialystok province, N.E. Poland. Community fr. 1820s, developed trade relations with Germany. Following persecutions and other disasters many Jews emigrated. Community of 6,000 liquidated Nov. 1939.

Suzin, Solomon Moses (d. 1835), rabbi of Jerusalem, *Rishon-le-Zion,* 1824–35. Did much for Jewish population of Jerusalem.

Suzman (née Gavronsky), Helen (1917–), S. African politician, parliamentarian of liberal views. A founder member of Progressive Party 1959 and its sole representative in parliament after 1966. Championed rights of African people.

Sverdlov, Yakov Mikhailovich (1885–1919), Russian revolutionary, Communist leader. Outstanding figure of Bolshevik Revolution; elected chairman of All-Russian Central Executive Committee (titular head of state). Sverdlovsk (until 1924 Yekaterinburg) named for him.

Svetlov, Mikhail (1903–1967), Soviet-Russian poet, playwright. His poem *Grenada* glorifies internationalism of working classes. Praised Revolution for having freed Jews fr. oppression. Contended that Revolution was, however, more important than Judaism.

Svevo, Italo (pen name of **Ettore Schmitz;** 1861–1928), novelist, businessman in Trieste. Friend and correspondent of James Joyce. *The Confessions of Zeno* is a classic of modern Italian literature. All his works set in Trieste.

Swarsensky, Hardi (Bernhard; 1908–1968), journalist, publisher. Active in leadership of Reichsverband der Juden in Deutschland 1933–39. Emigrated to Buenos Aires and founded, edited German-Jewish weekly 1940 and publishing house 1942.

Swaythling, Lord, see Montagu.

Sweden, N.European kingdom. Jews permitted to settle in 18th c., but emancipation slow. Community grew and prospered in 19th c., but assimilation rife and Jewish activity declined. Fearing unemployment, government restricted immigration of Jewish refugees before WWII. Attitude changed when Jews were

Jewish population of Switzerland, 1960.

accepted fr. Norway 1942 and Denmark 1943. After war many refugees remained. Jewish pop. 15,000 (1971).

Swine, see Pig.

Switzerland, C. European republic. Jews in Basle in 13th c.; community increased until Black Death massacres 1349. Thereafter settlement scattered and intermittent; emancipation not enforced until 1866. Prohibition against *sheḥitah* 1893 still enforced. Schweizerischer Israelitischer Gemeindebund (SIG) founded 1904; unsuccessful in efforts to encourage authorities to grant asylum generously to refugees fr. Nazi Europe; only 25,000 permitted entry, many left after war. Jewish pop. 20,000 (1971), mainly in Zurich, Geneva, Basle.

Swope, Gerard (1872–1957), U.S. electrical engineer, industrialist. Pres. then chairman International General Electric 1922–39. Chairman N.Y. City Housing Authority 1939. His "Swope Plan" (1931) emphasized industry's responsibility for preventing unemployment and mitigating its results. Bequeathed several million dollars to Haifa Technion.

Swiss Jews asking Helvetia for protection (18th-cent. engraving).

Swope, Herbert Bayard (1882–1958), U.S. journalist, public official; brother of Gerard Swope. Won first Pulitzer Prize 1917 for reporting fr. Germany during WWI. Executive editor New York *World* 1920 and directed many exposés. Consultant U.S. secretary of war 1942–46 and alternate U.S. representative to U.N. Atomic Energy Commission.

Sydney, city in Australia. Jews arrived with first convicts fr. England and played considerable part in subsequent development of city. Waves of immigration fr. England and Germany in 1850s, and fr. Europe after 1933. Jewish pop. 28,000 (1971), with 19 synagogues.

Sykes-Picot Treaty, secret agreement for partition of Middle East signed during WWI by Britain, France, Russia, and Italy. Treaty negotiated bet. Sir Mark Sykes (for Britain) and Georges Picot (for France). When it became public knowledge, both Arabs and Zionists protested that it violated promises made by Britain. Zionist influence

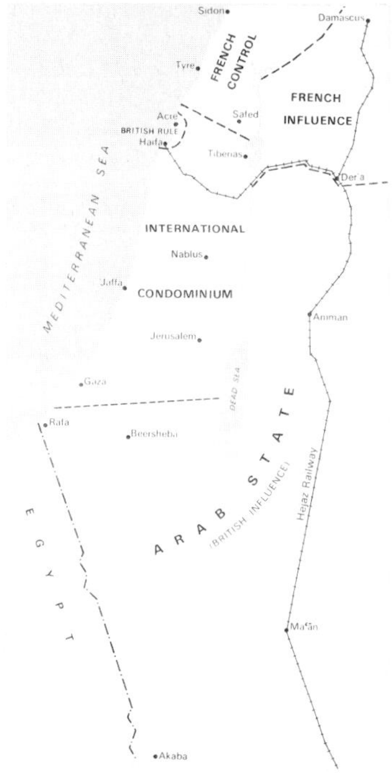

Partition plan of the Sykes-Picot Treaty.

played important part in its non-implementation.

Sylvester, James Joseph (1814–1897), British mathematician. "Second wrangler" at Cambridge 1837, but as Jew denied degree or fellowship. Fellow of Royal Society 1839 and held chairs in various univs. in U.S. and England. Dominated the development of theories of algebraic and differential invariants.

Synagogue (Heb. *bet keneset*), building for Jewish public prayer. Historical date of origin uncertain. Common in Ereẓ Israel and Diaspora before destruction of Second Temple 70 C.E. and, after, the focus of Jewish communal life. Replaced the Temple as center of Jewish worship and increased in size, number and importance. By medieval times,

The Great Synagogue of Sydney, Australia.

The Theckoobagam synagogue in Ernakulam, Cochin, reputedly founded 1625.

Wooden synagogue of Wolpa, Poland.

The fortress-type synagogue of Zholkva, c. 1695, water-color by Nathan Pohlenberg, 1913.

Principal Falasha synagogue at Woozaba, Ethiopia.

it had become place of communal study and meeting as well as of worship. Designs have changed throughout the ages. In Orthodox congregations the Ark is placed on wall nearest Jerusalem, the reader's platform in the middle, and the women are separated by either a partition or gallery, but modifications have been introduced in Progressive synagogues. In the U.S. the synagogue (or "Temple") has tended to resume its former function as communal center.

Synagogue, the Great (Heb. *Keneset ha-Gedolah*), institute of Jewish spiritual teaching at beginning of Second Temple period. Little is known of it during Persian period. Rabbis regarded Ezra as its leader. Probably loose-knit representative body, combining judicial and administrative authority, with no permanent membership, meeting at intervals to pass major enactments. According to tradition, introduced classification of Oral Law into three fields of study and canonized Books of Ezekiel, Daniel, Esther, and the Twelve Minor Prophets.

Synagogue Council of America, the, organization founded 1926, with Reform, Conservative, and Orthodox membership. Presidency rotates. Provides unified Jewish religious representation on social and international issues.

Syngalowski, Aron (1890–1956), ORT leader; b. Belorussia. Joined Jewish Socialist territorialist movement. Reconstructed ORT network after WWII and established its activities in Israel fr. 1948.

Synthetic Zionism, fusion of two trends in Zionism, political Zionism and practical Zionism. The term was used by Chaim Weizmann at the 8th Zionist Congress (1907) and its program was: political action, acquisition of land, aliyah, settlement, and educational and organizational work among the people. This trend thereafter dominated the Zionist movement.

Syracuse, city in SE Italy. Jews there in Roman times. Prosperous in 13th–14th c.; c. 5,000 (40% of city's population) left after 1492 edict of expulsion.

Syracuse, city in N.Y., U.S. First Jewish settler 1824. First congregation Keneseth Sholom 1839. Jews heavily concentrated in professions and active in local civic life. Jewish pop. 11,000 (1971).

Syria, Middle East republic. Jews there fr. biblical times (see Aram). Seleucid monarchy had frequent contact with Judah in late Second Temple times – sometimes in alliance, sometimes in control, often in conflict. In Talmudic times few Jews there. Jews welcomed Arab conquest of 630, which released them from servitude and religious coercion. Although Moslem attitude

Major Jewish communities in Syria.

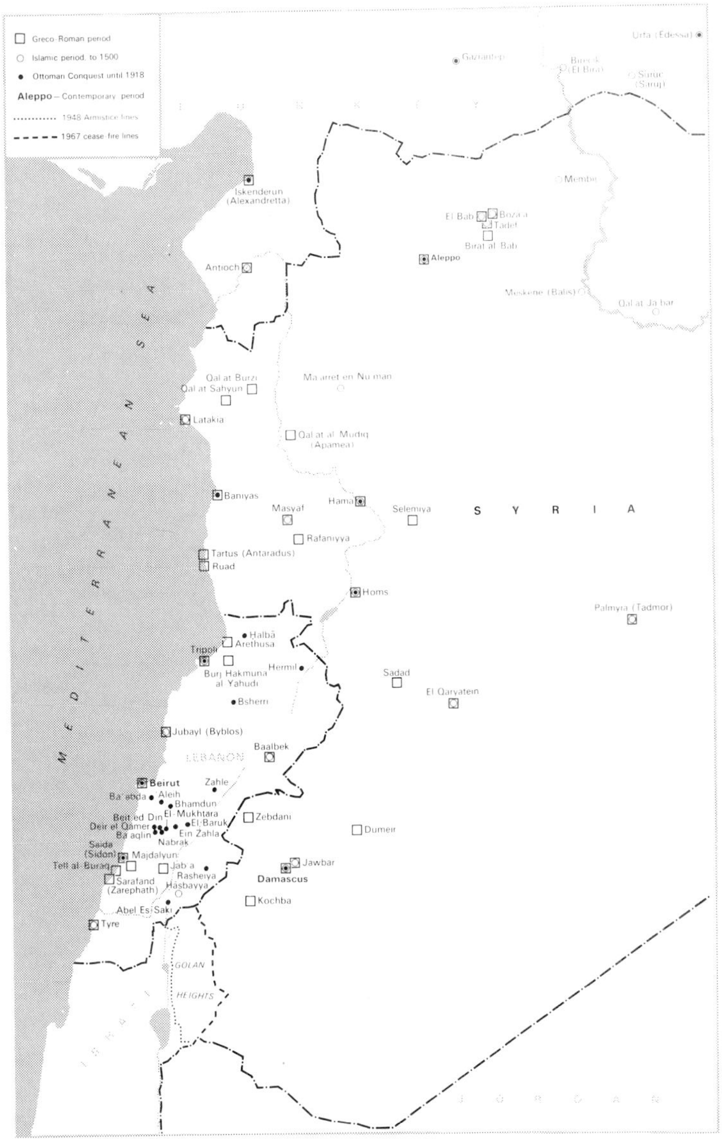

changed in 8th c., community grew. Jews became bankers and traders, community produced scholars, and during Crusades the Jerusalem academy was moved to Damascus. After 15th c. leadership of community (concentrated in Aleppo and Damascus) passed to Spanish refugees. Although Jews were ultimately little affected by 1840 Damascus blood libel, their economic position declined in 19th c. and anti-Jewish resentment grew in 20th c. Community declined fr. 15,000 in 1947 to 3,000 in 1968. Syrian Jews lived under conditions of fear in 1960s and 1970s. Syria has been consistently and virulently hostile to Israel. Participated in wars of 1948, 1967, and 1973; supported terrorists fr. 1965.

Syriac Versions of the Bible, see Peshitta.

Syrkin, Marie (1899–), U.S. author, translator, educator; daughter of Nachman Syrkin, wife of Charles Reznikoff. Writings incl. *Blessed is the Match,* a study of Jewish resistance movement under Nazis, and a biography of her father. Taught English at Brandeis Univ. 1950–66, edited monthly journal *Jewish Frontier* (1948–55), member of Jewish Agency Executive 1965–68.

Syrkin, Moses Nahum Solomonovich (1878–1918), Russian writer, orator, Jewish national leader. During 1917 Revolution chosen as delegate to Russian Constituent Assembly on Jewish National List. Pres. of Kiev community and member of Ukrainian parliament.

Nachman Syrkin

The synagogue of Szeged

Syrkin, Nachman (1868–1924), first ideologist and leader of Socialist Zionism; b. Russia. Studied in Germany where he founded Russian-Jewish Scientific Society. Advocated realization of Zionism through cooperative mass settlement of Jewish proletariat and complete synthesis of socialism with Jewish nationalism. For a time leader of socialist territorialists but in 1907, when he emigrated to U.S., joined Po'alei Zion and returned to Zionism.

Syrkin, Yakov Kovovich (1894–), Russian physical chemist. Prof. at Ivanovo-Voznesensk Polytechnic Inst. 1925 and Inst. of Fine Chemical Technology 1931. Scientific chairman molecular structure dept., Karpov Physico-Chemical Institute, 1931–52.

Szabolcsi, Bence (1899–1973), Hungarian musicologist. First to collect notated relics of old Hungarian music fr. mss. and prints. Prof. of music history at Budapest Academy of Music fr. 1945 and director of its Bartok archives fr. 1961.

Szabolcsi, Lajos (1889–1943), Hungarian poet, author, editor; son of Miksa Szabolcsi. Editor *Egyenlöség* 1915–38. Vigorous opponent of Hungarian anti-Semitism; violently anti-Zionist; protagonist of Reform Jewry. Wrote historical novel on Bar Kokhba and drama on Josephus.

Szabolcsi (Weinstein), Miksa (1857–1915), Hungarian author, editor, journalist. Bought newspaper *Egyenlöség* 1886 and made it organ of Hungarian Neolog Jewry. Fought successfully for recognition of Judaism as official religion. Outspoken anti-Zionist. Edited and largely translated Graetz' *History of the Jews.*

Szajkowski, Zosa (Szajko Frydman; 1911–), historian, bibliographer, specializing in French history; in France 1927–41, went to U.S. and served as paratrooper in WWII. Prolific scholar on wide variety of Jewish historical subjects.

Szántó, Simon (1819–1882), educator, writer. Founded school for boys in Vienna 1849 which combined Jewishness with secular learning. Prolific writer on education and Jewish history. Edited and largely wrote weekly journal *Die Neuzeit* 1861–82.

Szeged, city in S. Hungary. Jews after 1781. By early 20th c. 6,000 Jews, mostly merchants or peddlers. In 1944, 4,000 remaining Jews deported. About half returned, but in 1958 only 927 Jews there.

Szell, Georg (1897–1970), conductor, pianist. Principal conductor Metropolitan Opera 1942–45, permanent conductor Cleveland Orchestra fr. 1946.

Szende, Pál (1879–1935), Hungarian Radical Party politician. Minister of Finance 1918; succeeded in stabilizing economy. With accession of Béla Kun, went into exile and spent later years in Vienna and Paris.

Hannah Szenes

Szenes, Hannah (1921–1944), poet, Haganah fighter who parachuted into Nazi-occupied Europe; b. Budapest; daughter of author **Béla Szenes** (1874–1929). Settled in Ereẓ Israel 1939 and joined kibbutz Sedot Yam. Wrote poignant poems ("Blessed is the match that burnt out and kindled the flame"). In March 1944 parachuted over Yugoslavia, crossed border into Hungary, was arrested and executed.

Szenwald, Lucjan (1909–1944), Polish poet, translator. Wrote verse on themes ranging fr. Spanish Civil War to Nazi peril. Translated works by leading foreign authors. Killed in action with Red Army.

Szer, Seweryn (1902–1968), Polish jurist. Worked for Polish Committee for National Liberation during WWII. Prof. of law at Warsaw Univ. fr. 1949. High Court judge until 1955. Headed Academy of Sciences.

Szerb, Antal (1901–1945), Hungarian author, literary scholar. One of Hungary's greatest authorities on European literature. Converted to Catholicism. Murdered in concentration camp.

Szerencsés, Imre (Fortunatus; 1460–1526?), Hungarian apostate. Financial adviser to royal house during war against Ottoman Empire.

Szereszewski, Moses David (1844–1915), merchant, leading Jewish banker in Warsaw. His bank founded 1911 granted loans to industrialists. His sons **Raphael** and **Michael** administered family bank. Raphael six times member of Warsaw municipal council and member of Sejm 1921–

27. Headed Union of Jewish Tradesmen in Poland. Left Poland 1939, settled in New York 1943.

Szeryng, Henryk (1918–), violinist. Liaison officer in Polish government-in-exile WWII. Prof. of music at National Univ. of Mexico fr. 1945.

Szigeti, Joseph (1892–1973), violinist. Prof. at Geneva Conservatory 1917. Settled in U.S. 1926. Gave first public performance of many modern works, incl. violin concertos of Busoni and Prokofiev's First Concerto.

Szigeti, Imre (1897–), graphic artist. Worked in textile print designing after arriving in Australia fr. Europe 1939. Work is mostly gouaches, pastels, line drawings.

Szilágyi, Géza (1875–1958), Hungarian poet of modernist school. Wrote poems on biblical themes.

Szilard, Leo (1898–1964), Hungarian nuclear physicist. One of "fathers" of discoveries that led to atomic bomb. Worked in Germany and after 1933 in England and U.S. Opponent of militarism; initially tried to keep discoveries secret. Fought for ban on nuclear weapons.

Szold, Benjamin (1829–1902), U.S. rabbi, scholar; b. Hungary. Participated in Revolution of 1848 in Vienna. Went to U.S. 1858 as rabbi in Congregation Oheb Shalom, Baltimore. Made it into one of foremost American congregations. Supporter of Zionism, active Hebraist. Published scholarly articles, biblical commentaries.

Henrietta Szold

Szold, Henrietta (1860–1945), Zionist leader; b. Baltimore; daughter of Benjamin Szold. Edited *The American Jewish Year Book.* Founded Hadassah 1912, first pres. 1914. Sent to Ereẓ Israel 1920 with Hadassah Medical Unit, later became its director; it developed into Hadassah Medical Organization. Member of three-man executive of World Zionist Organization fr. 1927 with portfolio for health and education. Directed Youth Aliyah fr. 1933 and played major role in rescuing children fr. Nazi Europe.

Szold, Robert (1889–), U.S. lawyer, Zionist. Member of Zionist Commission in Ereẓ Israel 1919. Associated with the Brandeis-Mack group in American Zionism; pres. ZOA 1930–32 and worked for economic development of Ereẓ Israel.

Szydlowiec, town in Poland. Jews fr. 15th c. Community grew considerably fr. 19th c. when Jewish contractors developed building materials and tanning industries. 7,000 Jews in 1939. Deported by Germans and entire community liquidated.

Szyk, Arthur (1894–1951), illustrator, miniaturist, cartoonist. B. Poland; settled in U.S. 1944 where he drew cartoons lampooning Nazi leaders. Noted for refined draftsmanship and calligraphy; illustrated *Haggadah* and highly decorated Israel Declaration of Independence.

Szyr, Eugeniusz (1915–), Polish economist, Communist politician; in Russia during WWII. Leading figure in ruling Polish Workers' Party; a vice-premier 1964.

Initial letter "T" of the phrase "Temptavit Deus Abraham" in 14th-cent. French missal.

Ta'amei ha-Mikra, see Cantillation.

Taanach, Canaanite city nr. Megiddo. First flourished 27th–25th c. B.C.E. After Israelite conquest, one of levitical cities. Played important role in war of Deborah (Judg. 4–5).

Taanach Bloc, agricultural project in S. Jezreel Valley, Israel, carried out fr. 1955. Three clusters of moshavim, each with three villages grouped around a rural center, established 1968.

Ta'anit (Heb. "Fast"), Mishnah tractate in order *Mo'ed,* with *gemara* in both Talmuds. Deals mainly with various fasts.

Ta'anit Ester, see Esther, Fast of.

Tabachnik, Abraham Ber (1901–1970), Yiddish poet, essayist; b. Ukraine, in U.S. fr. 1921. Many of his lyrics on Holocaust.

Tabeel, The Son of, Syrian-Aramean prince whom King Pekah of Israel and Rezin of Aram wished to place on Judean throne instead of Ahaz (Isa. 7:6).

Tabenkin, Yiẓḥak (1887–1971), Israel labor leader; a founder of Ha-Kibbutz ha-Me'uḥad and Aḥdut ha-Avodah. Went fr. Belorussia to Ereẓ Israel 1912, joined Gedud ha-Avodah, and was a founder of En-Harod. A leading figure in labor and pioneering circles and member of Knesset until 1959.

Tabernacle, portable sanctuary constructed by Israelites in Wilderness (Ex. 25–31; 35–40). Place at which God revealed Himself and dwelt among His people. Housed Ark and accompanied Israel during wilderness period. Located in several places in Canaan (e.g., Shiloh) after Israel's settlement in land and was finally replaced by Solomon's Temple.

Tabernacle, see Sukkah.

Tabernacles, Feast of, see Sukkot.

Tabgha, ancient site on Sea of Galilee. In Christian tradition fr. Byzantine times, scene of miracle of loaves and fishes and of last appearance of Jesus on shore of lake (Matt. 14:17; 15:32 ff.; John 21). Churches built at site. Also Benedictine monastery.

Tabi (1st–2nd c. C.E), slave of Gamaliel II; well known for learning and piety.

Tabib, Avraham (1889–1950), leader of Yemenite community in Ereẓ Israel; went fr. Yemen to Ereẓ Israel 1907. Negotiated with Zionist executive to establish Yemenite settlements, initiated foundation of Association of Yemenites. Member of first Knesset.

Tabib, Mordekhai (1910–), Hebrew writer; son of Abraham Tabib; b. Palestine. Stories deal with Yemenite community in Israel. First writer of Yemenite origin in modern Hebrew literature.

Tablets of the Law, stones on which Decalogue was inscribed. The first

Byzantine mosaic floor, Church of the Multiplication, Tabgha.

Model of Tabernacle showing sanctuary, laver, sloped ramp, and bronze altar in a court.

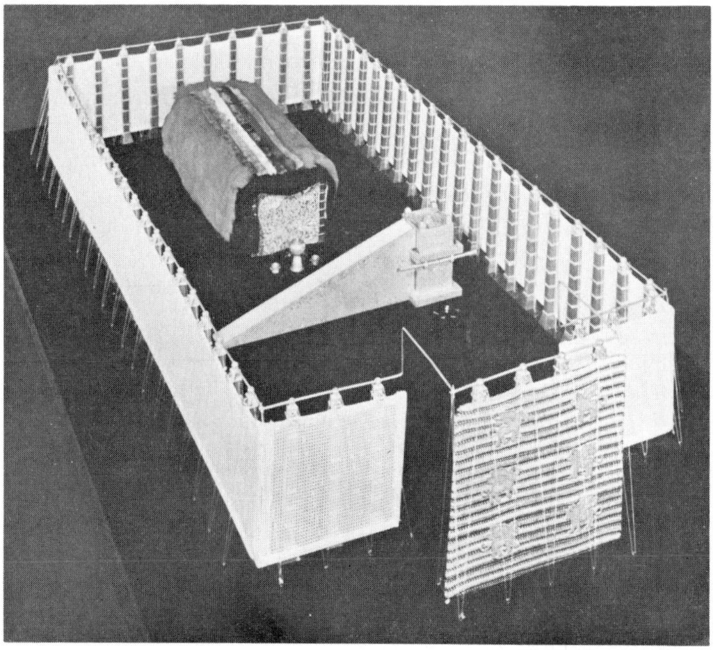

set, prepared by God, was smashed by Moses when he saw the Golden Calf. The second set, prepared and hewn by Moses, was preserved in the Ark of the Covenant. The tablets are a favorite symbol, often placed over the ark in the synagogue.

Tabor, Mount, mountain in Jezreel Valley; c. 1,750 ft. (563 m.) above sea level. Base fr. which Barak launched attack against Sisera (Judg. 4:6–14). Christian tradition located transfiguration of Jesus there (e.g., Matt. 17:1) and church and monastery are situated on its summit.

Tadmor (classical **Palmyra**), oasis city in C. Syrian desert. According to II Chron. 8:3–4, built by Solomon. During period of efflorescence (early cents. C.E.) had Jewish community.

Taeubler, Eugen (1879–1953), historian, classical and biblical scholar, b. Poland. Scientific secretary to T. Mommsen. Founded Gesamtarchiv der deutschen Juden 1906. Taught at various German univs. Emigrated to U.S. 1938. Research prof. at Hebrew Union College, Cincinnati. Husband of Selma Stern-Taeubler.

Tagin (Aram.), special designs resembling crowns placed by scribes on upper left-hand corner of seven letters in Torah, *tefillin*, or *mezuzah* scroll. The seven letters are *shin, ayin, tet, nun, zayin, gimmel, ẓade.*

Taglicht, David Israel (1862–1943), Austrian rabbi, scholar. Wrote on history of Jews in Vienna. Rabbi of Vienna's main synagogue fr. 1932. Humiliated and beaten after Anschluss; allowed to leave and went to England.

Tahal (Heb. abbr. for Water Planning for Israel), corporation established 1952 by government of Israel by merging water resources dept. of Ministry of Agriculture with engineering division of Mekorot. Plans water supply in Israel and has worked in other countries.

Taḥanun (Heb. "supplication"), name of prayer which is confession of sins and petition for grace. Recited after cantor's repetition of *Amidah* in daily morning and afternoon prayers. Of talmudic origin, its final version dates fr. 16th c. Also known as *nefilat appayim* ("prostration prayer"), after original custom of prostration during recitation; this was later modified to burying the head in the arm. It is omitted on joyful occasions and in the house of a mourner.

Taharat (Toharat) Ha-Mishpaḥah (Heb. "family purity"), term popularly given to laws of sexual abstinence during period of wife's menstruation. These regulations considered by Orthodox as basic to Jewish way of life.

Taimanov, Mark Yevgenyevich (1926–), Russian chess master. Shared USSR championship with Botvinnik 1952 and with Spassky and Auerbach 1956. Also concert pianist.

Taitaẓak, Joseph (16th c.), talmudist, Bible scholar, kabbalist of Salonika. Halakhic authority and author of biblical commentaries. A founder of kabbalistic circle in Safed and first crystallized idea of *maggid,* a divine voice which spoke or dictated to scholars.

Takkanot (Heb.), regulations supplementing law of Torah; enacted by halakhic scholars or other competent body with authority of law.

Takkanot Ha-Kahal (Heb.), regulations governing internal life of communities and congregations enacted by the public or its representatives (in contradistinction to *takkanot* enacted by halakhic authority). The great impetus to such legislation came in 10th c. C.E. with emergence of Jewish communal autonomy. Such *takkanot* either lapsed with time or disappeared with community itself.

Taku, Moses ben Ḥisdai (13th c.), C. European tosafist, commentator on *piyyutim.* Author of polemical treatise *Ketav Tammim.* Fiercely opposed innovation in beliefs and theology. Main target of his attack was Saadiah Gaon.

Tal (Gruenthal), Josef (1910–), Israel composer, pianist, teacher. B. Poznania, settled in Ereẓ Israel 1934. On faculty of Academy of Music in Jerusalem fr. 1937, taught at Hebrew Univ. fr. 1950. Pioneered in electronic music; wrote operas, symphonies, concertos, etc. Israel Prize 1970.

Tal, Mikhail (1936–), Soviet chess master. Won Soviet championship 1957 and world championship 1960 fr. Botvinnik.

Tallit (Heb.), four-cornered prayer shawl with fringes *(ẓiẓiyyot)* at each corner. Usually white and made of wool, cotton, or silk, it is worn by males during morning prayers (except on Av 9, when it is worn at afternoon service) as well as throughout Day of Atonement services.

Tallit Katan (Heb. "small *tallit*"), rectangular garment of white cotton, linen, or wool with *ẓiẓiyyot* ("fringes"), on its 4 corners. Strictly observant Jews wear it under their upper garment the whole day.

ויהי בימי אחשורוש הוא אחשורוש המלך
מהדו ועד כוש שבע ועשרים ומאה מדינה
בימים ההם כשבת המלך אחשורוש על
כסא מלכותו אשר בשושן הבירה בשנת
שלוש למלכו עשה משתה לכל שריו
ועבדיו חיל פרס ומדי הפרתמים ושרי
המדינות לפניו בהראתו את עשר כבוד

Esther scroll with "tagin" on appropriate letters.

19th-cent. silk "tallit" from Russia.

Talmi, Igal (1925–), Israel physicist. Worked in dept. of nuclear physics at Weizmann Inst. Israel Prize 1965 for work on development of nuclear shell.

Talmid Ḥakham (Heb. lit. "disciple of the wise"), appellation given to rabbinical scholar; traditionally the ideal toward which every individual was expected to strive.

Talmon, Jacob Leib (1916–), Israel historian. Secretary to Palestine Committee of Board of Deputies of British Jews 1944–47. Taught at Hebrew Univ. fr. 1949. Noted for contribution to history of ideas and studies of origins of 20th c. totalitarian democracy. Israel Prize 1965.

ORDERS AND TRACTATES OF THE MISHNAH AND TALMUD

Order	Tractate	Mishnah No. of Chapters	Babylonian Talmud[1] No. of Folios	Babylonian Talmud[1] Folios Munich Ed.	Jerusalem Talmud[2] No. of Folios	Subject matter
ORDER ZERA'IM	Berakhot	9	64	19	14	Benedictions
	Pe'ah	8	—	3	7	Gleanings (Lev. 19:9–10)
	Demai	7	—	3	6	Doubtfully tithed produce
	Kilayim	9	—	4	7	Diverse kinds (Deut. 22:9–11).
	Shevi'it	10	—	4	7	The Sabbatical Year (Ex. 23:10–11)
	Terumot	11	—	4	9	Heave offering (Lev. 22:10–14)
	Ma'aserot	5	—	2	5	Tithes (Num. 18:21)
	Ma'aser Sheni	5	—	3	5	Second tithe (Deut. 14:22 ff.)
	Ḥallah	4	—	2	4	Dough offering (Num. 15:17–21)
	Orlah	3	—	2	4	The fruit of young trees (Lev. 19:23–25)
	Bikkurim	3	—	3	3	Firstfruits (Lev. 26:1–11)
ORDER MO'ED	Shabbat	24	157	28	18	The Sabbath
	Eruvin	10	105	17	9	The fusion of Sabbath limits
	Pesaḥim	10	121	18	11	Passover
	Shekalim	8	—	6	7	The Shekel dues (Ex. 30:11–16)
	Yoma	8	88	16	8	The Day of Atonement
	Sukkah	5	56	9	5	The Feast of Tabernacles
	Beẓah	5	40	11	5	Festival laws
	Rosh Ha-Shanah	4	35	7	4	Various new years, particularly Rosh Ha-Shanah
	Ta'anit	4	31	8	7	Fast days
	Megillah	4	32	9	7	Purim
	Mo'ed Katan	3	29	7	4	The intermediate days of festivals
	Ḥagigah	3	27	6	5	The Festival offering (Deut. 16:16–17)
ORDER NASHIM	Yevamot	16	122	24	16	Levirate marriage (Deut. 25:5–10)
	Ketubbot	13	112	20	12	Marriage contracts
	Nedarim	11	91	10	7	Vows (Num. 30)
	Nazir	9	66	8	8	The Nazirite (Num. 6)
	Sotah	9	49	11	9	The suspected adulteress (Num. 5:11 ff.)
	Gittin	9	90	16	7	Divorce
	Kiddushin	4	82	14	9	Marriage
ORDER NEZIKIN	Bava Kamma	10	119	22	7	Torts
	Bava Meẓia	10	119	20	6	Civil law
	Bava Batra	10	176	21	6	Property law
	Sanhedrin	11	113	24	14	Judges
	Makkot	3	24	5	3	Flagellation (Deut. 25:2)
	Shevu'ot	8	49	9	7	Oaths
	Eduyyot	8	—	4	—	Traditional testimonies
	Avodah Zarah	5	76	13	7	Idolatry
	Avot[3]	5	—	2	—	Ethical maxims
	Horayot	3	14	4	4	Erroneous ruling of the court (Lev. 4:22 ff.)
ORDER KODASHIM	Zevaḥim	14	120	21	—	Animal offerings
	Menaḥot	13	110	21	—	Meal offering
	Ḥullin	12	142	25	—	Animals slaughtered for food
	Bekhorot	9	61	13	—	Firstlings (Deut. 15:19 ff.)
	Arakhin	9	34	9	—	Vows of valuation (Lev. 27:1–8)
	Temurah	7	39	8	—	The substituted offering (Lev. 27:10)
	Keritot	6	28	9	—	Extirpation (Lev. 18:29)
	Me'ilah	6	22	4	—	Sacrileges (Lev. 5:15–16)
	Tamid[3]	7	9	4	—	The daily sacrifice (Num. 28:3–4)
	Middot[3]	5	—	3	—	Measurements of the Temple
	Kinnim[3]	3	—	2	—	The Bird offering (Lev. 5:7 ff.)
ORDER TOHOROT	Kelim[3]	30	—	11	—	Uncleanness of articles
	Oholot (Ahilot)	18	—	7	—	Uncleanness through overshadowing (No. 19:14–15)
	Nega'im	14	—	7	—	Leprosy (Lev. 13, 14)
	Parah	12	—	5	—	The Red Heifer (Num. 19)
	Tohorot	10	—	5	—	Ritual cleanness
	Mikva'ot	10	—	5	—	Ritual ablution
	Niddah	10	73	14	4	The menstruant
	Makhshirin	6	—	3	—	Liquid that predisposes food to become ritually unclean (Lev. 11:37–38)
	Zavim	5	—	2	—	Fluxes (Lev. 15)
	Tevul Yom	4	—	2	—	Ritual uncleanness between immersion and sunset (Lev. 22:6–7)
	Yadayim	4	—	3	—	The ritual uncleanness of the hands
	Ukẓin[4]	3	—	2	—	"Stalks": parts of plants susceptible to uncleanness

1 The number given is the last page number. The pagination, however, always begins with page 2; one page should therefore be deducted.

2 The number of pages is given in accordance with the Krotoschin edition.

3 There is Tosefta to all the tractates with the exception of *Avot, Tamid, Middot, Kinnim, Kelim*. In the Tosefta, *Kelim* is divided into three sections, respectively called *Bava Kamma, Bava Meẓia* and *Bava Batra*.

4 As will be seen, the tractates are generally arranged in the orders according to the descending numbers of chapters.

Talmud (Heb. "study" or "learning"). (1) The opinions and teachings which disciples acquire fr. their predecessors. (2) The whole body of one's learning. (3) Teaching derived fr. exegesis of biblical text. (4) Most commonly, the body of teaching which comprises the commentary and discussions of the *amoraim* on the Mishnah of R. Judah ha-Nasi (see Talmud, Jerusalem and Babylonian).

Talmud, Jerusalem and Babylonian, the Jerusalem Talmud is interpretation and elaboration of Mishnah as developed in great academies of Ereẓ Israel. Editing completed c. 500 C.E. Its commentary extends to 39 of the 63 tractates of the Mishnah. Written in W. Aramaic with considerable admixture of Greek or loan words, it differs fr. the Babylonian Talmud in its style (which is more concise), its content (only one-sixth is *aggadah*), and even in some of its decisions. The Babylonian Talmud is the interpretation and elaboration of Mishnah as developed in great academies of Babylonia bet. early 3rd and late 5th c. C.E. Acc. to tradition, finally edited by Rav Ashi and Ravina. Written in E. Aramaic and Hebrew, its 5,894 folio pages consist of commentaries on 37 of the 63 tractates of the Mishnah. Two-thirds of the text consists of *aggadah.* Since it is a record of oral discussions, it is neither systematic in its treatment of subjects nor concise in its style. It is, however, a storehouse of Jewish history and customs as well as law. Its authority is considered superior to that of the Jerusalem Talmud and it is three times as long. It has exerted an unparalleled influence on Jewish thought, practice, and study. It has been subject of numerous commentaries, and has been translated into several languages. The Jerusalem Talmud was long neglected and most commentaries on it date fr. the 18th c. and after.

Talmud Torah (Heb. "study of the Law"), term applied generally to Jewish religious (and ultimately talmudic) study. Regarded as supreme religious duty. Name adopted by voluntary organizations providing religious education and later to schools established by them. Eventually applied to all Jewish religious schools.

Tam, Jacob ben Meir (Rabbenu; c. 1100–1171), tosafist, leading French scholar; grandson of Rashi. Greatest scholar of his generation. *Tosafot* to Babylonian Talmud based on his explanations, glosses, and decisions. His ramified literary production incl. volume of responsa and novellae on Talmud *(Sefer ha-Yashar).* First French scholar to compose rhymed poetry. Also wrote on Hebrew grammar.

Tamakh, Abraham ben Isaac ha-Levi (d. 1393), Spanish *paytan,* philosopher. A leader of Gerona community where he lived until 1391, when he fled fr. persecutions to Ereẓ Israel. Later returned to Spain. Fame rests mostly on commentary to Song of Songs.

Tamar, Canaanite woman; wife successively of Judah's two sons, who both died. When Judah withheld his third son, she disguised herself as prostitute and seduced Judah, giving birth to twins, Perez and Zerah (Gen. 38).

Tamar, daughter of David and Maacah, full sister of Absalom. Her half-brother Amnon forced her to lie with him, for which he was later killed by Absalom (II Sam. 13).

Tamḥui, soup kitchen; daily distribution of food and occasional relief afforded by Jewish communities in Europe in medieval and modern periods.

Tam ibn Yaḥya, Jacob ben David (c. 1475–1542), Turkish rabbi, codifier; spiritual leader of Turkish Jewry. Rigid in his decisions, he nevertheless sought relief for *agunot* and opposed view that Karaites were not to be regarded as Jews.

Tamid, daily morning and evening burnt-offering in the Temple.

Tamid (Heb. abbr. for "Daily Burnt Offering"), ninth (or tenth) tractate of Mishnah order *Kodashim,* with *gemara* in Babylonian Talmud. Deals mainly with morning work in Temple.

Tamir, Shemuel, see Katznelson, Reuben.

Tamiris, Helen (née **Becker;** 1905–1966), U.S. choreographer, pioneer in modern dance. A founder with Martha Graham and others of Dance Repertory Theater 1930. Did choreography for Broadway musicals, incl. *Annie Get Your Gun.* Established own company 1960.

Tammuz, Sumerian-Babylonian fertility god. His cult under various names (e.g., Adonis) was widespread in ancient Middle East.

Tammuz, post-Exilic name of 4th month of Jewish year. Zodiac sign – crab, 29 days, 17th a fast, commemorating breaching of walls of Jerusalem by Nebuchadnezzar (586 B.C.E.) and Titus (70 C.E.). Fast commences three weeks of mourning period over destruction of Jerusalem ending on Av 9.

Tammuz, Benjamin (1919–), Israel writer, journalist. On staff of *Ha-aretz.* Cultural attaché at Israel embassy in London fr. 1971. Published novels, short stories, children's books.

Tampa, city in Fla., U.S. Jews fr. 1886. Congregation formed 1894; became Reform 1903. Additional congregations established 1904, 1917. Jewish pop. 4,200 (1971).

Tanakh, usual Hebrew collective term for Old Testament. Composed of initial letters of words *Torah* (Pentateuch), *Nevi'im* (Prophets), and *Ketuvim* (Hagiographa).

Tangier(s), town in Morocco. Many refugees arrived after expulsion fr.

האשה

האשה

Tractate "Kiddushin" from Babylonian Talmud, printed by Daniel Bomberg, Venice, 1520–23.

Jewish woman from Tangier, 19th cent. engraving by J.F. Portaels.

Spain, and during English rule 1661–84 they were supplemented by Moroccans. Most Jews left with English and community was not revived until mid-18th c. Thereafter, it was mostly impoverished until mid-19th c. with arrival of group fr. Tetuán, which produced revival. 15,000 Jews there in 1951, but most emigrated to Israel, Europe and S. America. 250 remained in 1970.

Tanḥuma Bar Abba (4th c. C.E.), Palestinian *amora.* Tanḥuma Midrash ascribed to him. Prolific aggadist; also noted for proems with which he introduced his discourses.

Tanḥuma Yelammedenu, group of homiletical Midrashim. Some Midrashim open with distinctive halakhic proem using formula: *Yelammedenu Rabbenu . . .* ("May our teacher instruct us . . . ") and from this the name is derived. Edited later than 800 C.E.

Tanḥum ben Joseph (ha-) Yerushalmi (c. 1220–1291), philologist, biblical exegete. Lived in Ereẓ Israel and subsequently went to Egypt. Last representative of rational school of biblical exegetes in the East.

Tanna (pl. *tannaim,* Aram.), sage fr. period of Hillel to compilation of Mishnah (c. 20–200 C.E.). Distinguished fr. later authorities, the *amoraim.* Generally divided into five generations, in which catastrophes of 70 C.E. (destruction of Temple) and 135 C.E. (fall of Betar) are the great landmarks. The Mishnah, the *Midreshei Halakhah* and the *Seder Olam Rabbah* were the greatest literary achievements of this group. Primarily scholars and teachers, they were also involved with the social and political fortunes of the nation.

Tanna de-Vei Eliyahu (or **Seder Eliyahu**), midrashic work with didactic moral aim consisting of two sections: *Seder Rabbah* ("Major Order") and *Seder Zuta* ("Minor Order"). Compiled before 9th c.

Tansman, Alexander (1897–), Polish composer, pianist, conductor; settled in Paris 1921, during WWII in U.S. writing music for films.

Tanuji, Ishmael ha-Kohen (16th c.), Tunisian rabbi author; first rabbinic scholar and author in Tunis. After leaving the town was probably chief rabbi of Egypt. His *Sefer ha-Zikkaron* is collection of rulings selected fr. among early halakhic authorities.

Tanya (Aram. "It has been taught"), ḥasidic work by Shneur Zalman of Lyady, founder of Ḥabad Ḥasidism. Published 1797 as *Likkutei Amarim.* Accepted as "written law of Ḥabad."

Tanzhaus ("dance hall"; Heb. *bet ḥatunot* or *bet nissu'im,* "wedding hall"), communal institution in most Jewish quarters in Germany and France. Designated for weddings and often used for other celebrations.

Taranto, city in S. Italy. A source states that Titus settled Jewish prisoners fr. Ereẓ Israel there. In Middle Ages, one of most important Jewish centers of S. Italy. All Jews expelled 1540.

Tombstone fragment from Taranto with name "Aaron" in Hebrew.

Tarascon, town in S. France. Jews there fr. 1283. Lived in own quarter for nearly 200 years; among them physicians and scholars of great renown. Expelled 1496, some returned in 18th c. but expelled 1775.

Tarazona, city in NE Spain. Jewish community one of most important in kingdom of Aragon and had lengthy period of prosperity and expansion. When Jews expelled fr. Spain, community probably left for nearby Navarre.

Tarbiz, Hebrew quarterly for Judaic studies; published since 1930 by Heb. Univ.

Tarbut (Heb. "culture"), Hebrew educational and cultural organization maintaining schools in most E. European countries bet. world wars. Especially active in Poland; proscribed in Russia. Education Zionist-orientated, 183 schools, 72 kindergartens, etc.

Tarfon, *tanna* in generation after 70 C.E.; a leading scholar in Jabneh. Many of his halakhic discussions with Akiva are recorded. According to an *aggadah,* one of the ten martyrs.

Targum (Heb. "translation"), Aramaic translation of Bible; also used for Aramaic portions of Bible.

Targum Jonathan, Palestinian Targum to Prophets, accredited to Jonathan b. Uzziel. Originated in early centuries C.E. and taken to Babylonia, where it underwent revisions and became recognized as official Aramaic version of Prophets. Final redaction 7th c.

Targum Onkelos, official Pentateuch Targum; attributed to the proselyte Onkelos (or Aquila). Presumably composed in Ereẓ Israel in 2nd c. C.E. Final version in Babylon in 3rd c. C.E. Largely a literal translation, yet there are numerous exceptions where it uses paraphrases.

Targum Sheni, collection of homilies in Aramaic on Book of Esther. Date cannot be exactly determined but possibly 8th c.

Targum Yerushalmi I (Pseudo-Jonathan), Palestinian Pentateuch Targum; ascribed to Jonathan b. Uzziel, written in Galilean Jewish Aramaic. Characteristic is free aggadic handling of text. Dated not later than 7th–8th c. C.E.

Targum Yerushalmi II (The Fragmentary Targum), Palestinian Pentateuch Targum containing renderings of certain verses, phrases, or words dating fr. various periods. Written in Galilean Jewish Aramaic.

Tarnopol, city in Galicia. Jewish settlement fr. 16th c. The community destroyed in Chmielnicki's attacks 1648–49; reestablished 1740. Thereafter flourishing economy, controlling grain and cattle trade. Position deteriorated after Austrian possession 1772, but by mid-19th c. again flourishing. 18,000 Jews in 1939; liquidated by Nazis in WWII. 600 Jews in late 1960s.

Tarnopol, Joachim Ḥayyim (1810–1900), *maskil* in Odessa, wealthy merchant. Advocate of emancipation of Jews and reconciliation with Russian people. Co-editor of first Russian-Jewish newspaper *Razsvet* 1860.

Tarnow, town in Poland. Jewish privileges date fr. 1581. By early 19th c. most of community ḥasidim, but Haskalah influence grew in 19th c. Most Jews in garment industry. 25,000 Jews in 1939. Germans liquidated Jews by 1943. After war 700 Jews returned but only 35 remained in 1965.

Tarragona, port in NE Spain. Jews there in Roman times. In Arab times, engaged in commerce and agriculture and some owned land and property (known as a "Jewish city"). Attacks in wake of Black Death and during 1391 persecutions. Community maintained yeshivah during difficult circumstances of late 15th c. In 1492, a port of embarkation for exiles fr. Aragon.

Tarrasch, Siegbert (1862–1934), German chess master. Defeated for world championship by Lasker 1908.

Tarshish, distant port fr. which precious metals and luxuries were

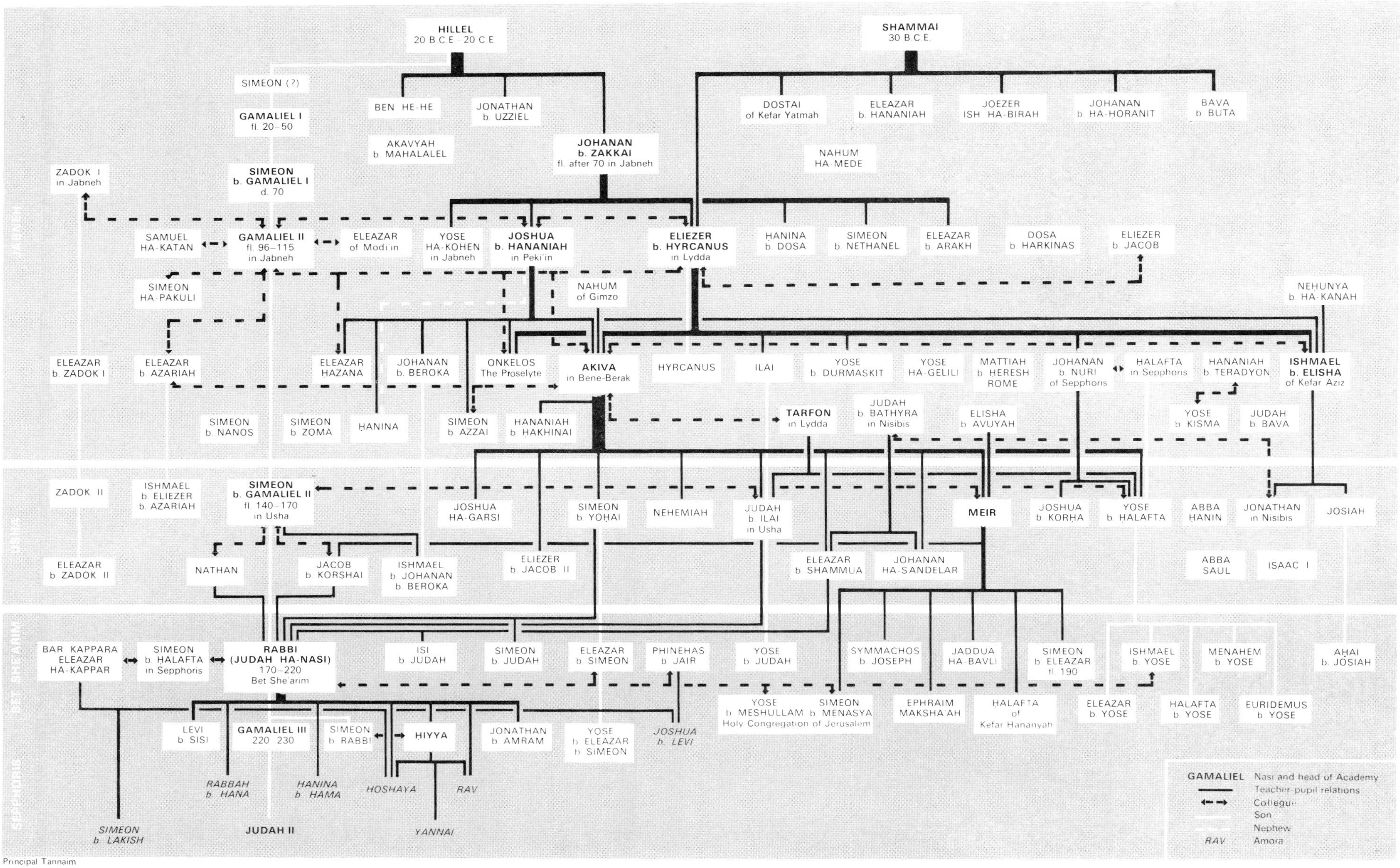

Principal Tannaim

sent to Ereẓ Israel (I Kings 10:22; Jer. 10:9; Ezek. 27:12). Location uncertain.

Tarski, Alfred (1902–), mathematical logician; founder of logical semantics. Taught at Warsaw Univ., went to U.S. 1939. His researches reestablished importance of philosophic semantics.

Tartakover, Savielly Grigoryevich (1887–1956), chess master; lived most of life in France. Contributed to opening theory and endgame techniques and created many fine combinations.

Tartakower, Arieh (1897–), sociologist, demographer, communal leader. In Poland founded and led Hitaḥadut. In U.S. fr. 1939, Ereẓ Israel fr. 1946. Chairman of Israel section of World Jewish Congress 1948–71. Wrote prolifically on Jewish sociology.

Taryag Mitzvot, see Commandments, 613.

Tashkent, city in Uzbek SSR. Some Bukharan Jews there before Russian conquest of 1865, and by 1914 community augmented by Russian Jews, numbered 3,000. Jewish culture and religious institutions gradually liquidated by Soviet regime. Absorption center for refugees fr. German occupied areas during WWII; many remained after war. 56,000 Jews in 1970.

"Tashlikh" ceremony, Tel Aviv.

Tashlikh (Heb. "Thou shalt cast"), ceremony "to cast sins into sea" held nr. sea or running stream on first day of Rosh Ha-Shanah (on 2nd when first is Sabbath), usually in late afternoon. Origin of custom uncertain; known fr. 15th c. Core of ceremony is recitation of Micah 7:18–20.

Tashrak (most common pseud. of **Israel Joseph Zevin;** 1872–1926), Yiddish author; b. Belorussia, in U.S. fr. late 1880s. A founder of Yiddish press in America. On staff of *Yidishes Tageblatt* fr. 1893. Published stories, feuilletons, articles, anthologies, children's stories.

Tasmania, island S. of Australia. Jews fr. early 19th c. First synagogue in Hobart 1843. Launceston synagogue consecrated 1846. Community has remained small.

Tau, Max (1897–), publisher, author. Literary director Bruno Cassirer publishing house and book reviewer *Frankfurter Zeitung*. In Scandinavia fr. 1938. Active in Norwegian publishing after WWII.

Taube, Michael (1890–1972), conductor. A founder of Juedischer Kulturbund 1933. Emigrated to Ereẓ Israel 1934; established Ramat Gan Chamber Orchestra 1956.

Taubenschlag, Raphael (1881–1958), Polish papyrologist, legal historian. Researched Egyptian legal documents and Greek inscriptions; also Polish law in Middle Ages. During WWII in France and U.S. Prof. of Roman law and ancient codes at Warsaw Univ. fr. 1947.

Tauber, Richard (Ernst Seiffert; 1892–1948), singer. Leading tenor in Dresden Opera 1913–18. Famed for singing in Lehar operettas (esp. *Land of Smiles*). Settled in England 1938. Wrote operetta *Old Chelsea* and appeared as lead.

Taubes, Aaron Moses ben Jacob (1787–1852), Polish, Rumanian rabbi. Rabbi of Jassy fr. 1841; leading authority on Rumanian Jewry. Published responsa, novellae, commentaries.

Taubes, Loebel (1863–1933), pioneer Galician Zionist. His speeches to hundreds of Galician towns and villages did much to spread Zionism, esp. among Orthodox circles. Fought for Austrian government's recognition of Yiddish as spoken language of Jews of Galicia.

Tausk, Viktor (1877–1919), Austrian psychiatrist; one of Freud's early pupils. In WWI used psychoanalytic methods in treatment of war neuroses. Contributed to psychoanalytic interpretation of schizophrenia. Committed suicide after undergoing unsuccessful psychoanalytic treatment.

Taussig, family of U.S. naval officers. **Edward David** (1847–1921), fought in Union Navy during Civil War. Commanded gunboat *Bennington*. Retired as rear admiral 1908. His son **Joseph Knefler** (1877–1947), commanded escort vessels protecting convoys in submarine-infested waters in WWI. Assistant chief naval operations 1933–36. Vice admiral 1941. Both Taussigs had naval vessels named after them.

Taussig, Frank William (1859–1940), U.S. economist. Prof. of economics at Harvard 1901. First chairman U.S. Tariff Commission 1917–19; close adviser to Pres. Wilson. His *Principles of Economics* standard text.

Tav (ת), 22nd and last letter of Hebrew alphabet; numerical value 400. Classical pronunciation *th* without a dagesh, as still preserved by Yemenite and Iraqi Jews. Ashkenazim pronounce it *s* or *t* and Sephardim and modern Israelis *t*.

Tavus, Jacob ben Joseph (16th c.), author of Judeo-Persian translation of Pentateuch written in Hebrew characters.

Tawiow, Israel Ḥayyim (1858–1920), Hebrew author; b. Belorussia, moved to Riga. Wrote essays on language and folklore, textbooks on Hebrew language and literature, belles-lettres, etc.

Tax, Sol (1907–), U.S. anthropologist. Chairman Univ. of Chicago anthropology dept. 1955. Editor *American Anthropologist* 1952–55 *Current Anthropology* fr. 1958. Head of "action anthropologists."

Tayma, one of oldest Jewish communities in N. Arabia. Mentioned in Bible (Job 6:19). Jewish settlement fr. 6th c. B.C.E. Jews owned most land in area and allowed to keep property even after Muhammad's conquest.

Ṭayyiba, Al-, Muslim-Arab community in C. Israel. Largest village of "Little Triangle," included in Israel 1949. Pop. 12,000 (1971).

Taz, see David ben Samuel Ha-Levi.

Tbilisi, see Tiflis.

Tcherikover, Victor (Avigdor; 1894–1958), Israel historian; b. St. Petersburg, settled in Ereẓ Israel 1925. One of first teachers at Heb. Univ., headed depts. of general history and classical studies. Specialized in Jewish history in Ereẓ Israel and Egypt during Graeco-Roman period. Edited *Corpus Papyrorum Judaicarum*.

Tcherikower, Elias (1881–1943), Russian historian. Began writing Russian-Jewish history in pre-Revolutionary Russia, and after 1917 wrote detailed histories of anti-Semitism and pogroms in the Ukraine. In Berlin after 1921; later in France and U.S. A founder of YIVO Inst. 1925.

Tchernichowsky, Saul (1875–1943), Hebrew poet. Served as army doctor in Russia during WWI, lived in Berlin fr. 1922, and settled in Ereẓ Israel 1931. Wrote poetry (idylls, love poems, etc.), short stories, translated fr. world literature and admired ideal of Hellenic beauty, and was concerned with aesthetic form. Important innovator in Heb-

Saul Tchernichowsky, portrait by Leonid Pasternak.

rew language and poetry. Translated into Hebrew *Iliad, Odyssey, Hiawatha,* etc.

Tchernowitz, Chaim (pseud. **Rav Ẓa'ir;** 1871–1949), talmudic scholar, Hebrew author. Studied at rabbinical seminary in Odessa. Settled in U.S. 1923 and taught Talmud at Jewish Inst. of Religion in N.Y. Combined traditional study with modern research. Wrote studies of development of halakhah. Wrote voluminously and controversially on contemporary Jewish problems in Hebrew and Yiddish journals.

Tchernowitz, Samuel (1879–1929), Hebrew journalist; brother of Chaim Tchernowitz; b. Russia, lived in Warsaw where he succeeded Sokolow as editor of *Ha-Ẓefirah.* In Ereẓ Israel fr. 1921 and secretary of Va'ad Le'ummi. Contributed to many Hebrew periodicals in Russia, Poland, and Ereẓ Israel.

Tchernowitz-Avidar, Yemimah (1909–), Israel author of Hebrew children's books; daughter of Samuel Tchernowitz; b. Vilna, settled in Ereẓ Israel 1921. Her husband **Yosef Avidar** (1906–), deputy chief of general staff of Haganah and later of Israel army. Israel ambassador to Moscow 1955–58, and Argentina 1960–65.

Teacher of Righteousness, organizer of Dead Sea Sect; known fr. Dead Sea Scrolls but never indicated by personal name.

Teachers' Association in Israel, organization founded 1903. Membership approx. 30,000 (1968), incl. 2,000 Arab members.

Technion, Israel Institute of Technology, Israel's only engineering univ., situated in Haifa. Cornerstone laid 1912, but owing to struggle over language of instruction and WWI opening delayed to 1924. In 1973 academic staff numbered c. 1,220 with over 8,000 students and over 15,000 in extension courses in various parts of the country. New campus developed fr. 1954.

Tedeschi, Gad (Guido; 1907–), legal scholar. Taught at Italian universities before going to Ereẓ Israel 1939. Prof. of civil law at Heb. Univ. fr. 1949. Wrote on family law and made contribution to Israel law of obligations. Israel Prize 1964.

Tedeschi (Tedesco), Moses Isaac ben Samuel (1821–1898), Italian biblical commentator, translator, teacher. His biblical commentary was based on both traditional and modern commentaries.

Tefillin (Heb. "phylacteries,"), two black leather boxes fastened to leather straps, containing 4 portions of Pentateuch written on parchment (Exod: 13:1–10, 11–16; Deut. 6:4–9; 11:13–21). They are affixed on forehead and arm by adult male Jews during recital of morning prayers. They are not worn on Sabbaths and festivals and on Av 9 are worn during the afternoon service.

Tefillin, minor tractate appended to the Talmud giving the rules for writing and duty of wearing *tefillin.*

Teheran, capital of Iran. Jews were attracted there in late 18th c., and despite restrictions on economic development community grew throughout 19th c. Intervention of European Jewry led to improved legal and social status; first Alliance school opened 1898. Considerable emigration to Israel after 1948. Community benefited fr. American-Jewish aid (esp. the Joint) and many Jews moved there fr. provinces. Jewish pop. 50,000 (1971).

Tehillim, see Psalms, Book of.

Teḥinnah, *piyyut* form which originated in *taḥanun* prayer for fasts of Monday and Thursday. Usually said quietly, its subject is relationship between God and Israel.

Teif, Moshe (1904–1966), Soviet Yiddish poet. Before 1937 published poems and short stories for children, a collection of lyrics for adults, and translations. Imprisoned 1948–53. After Stalin's death his poems were again published. Participated in *Sovetish Heymland.*

Teitel, Jacob (1851–1939), jurist, communal worker. One of few Jews in Russia in judicial service under Czars. Assisted Jews oppressed by authorities and was among founders of relief enterprises. In Germany fr. 1921, last years in France.

Teitelbaum, family of rabbis and dynasty of *ẓaddikim* in Hungary and Galicia. Founder **Moses ben Ẓevi of Ujhely** (1759–1841), pioneer of Ḥasidism in N. Hungary. Renowned for learning and as wonder-worker; wrote a classic homiletic work of Ḥasidism *(Yismaḥ Moshe).* His son **Jekuthiel Judah of Sighet** (1808–1883), one of greatest *admorim* of Hungary. Gathered many ḥasidim in Sighet and founded yeshivah. Wrote prolifically on Torah and *halakhah.* His son **Hananiah Yom Tov Lipa of Sighet** (1830s–1904), well-known scholar, *ẓaddik.* His son **Joel(ish) Teitelbaum of Satmar** (1888–) also served at Satmar fr. 1928. Saved fr. Holocaust 1944, reached Ereẓ Israel, settled in New York 1947. Vigorous opponent of Zionism and State of Israel. Has following in N.Y. and Israel.

Campus of the Technion.

"Tefillah" of the hand, as laid by Ashkenazim (above), and Sephardim (below).

Joel Teitelbaum

Teitelboim, Volodia Valentin (1916–), Chilean Communist politician. Communist representative to Chilean congress fr. 1961, senator fr. 1965 until fall of Allende in 1973 after which he remained outside Chile. Wrote literary works, incl. popular novel. Supported Israel.

Teixeira, Pedro (c. 1570–c. 1650), Portuguese Marrano explorer, author. Circumnavigated globe 1585–1601. During the 1630s he extended boundaries of Brazil and established line of demarcation bet. Spanish and Portuguese possessions in S. America.

Teixeira De Sampaio, Abraham Senior (formerly **Diego;** 1581–1666), Portuguese Marrano nobleman. Served Spanish crown in Antwerp and Swedish crown in Hamburg. Decision to become circumcised (in Hamburg c. 1648) created scandal in Catholic world. Founded international banking house (Teixeira de Mattos).

Teixeira Pinto, Bento (c. 1545–1600), Portuguese Marrano author, martyr; left Portugal and settled in Brazil. Died at hands of Inquisition on charges incl. judaizing. Wrote epic poem glorifying city of Pernambuco, first literary work of note written in Brazil.

Tekhelet (Heb. "blue") dye extracted in ancient times fr. sea-snail *(ḥillazon)* and used for dyeing the *ẓiẓit.*

Teki'ata (Teki'ot), three series of scriptural verses incl. in Additional Service of Rosh Ha-Shanah, designated *malkhuyyot, zikhronot,* and *shofarot,* and concerned respectively with Kingdom of Heaven, remembrance of Covenant, and sounding of horn of Redemption.

Tekoa, city of Judah, identified with ruin SE of Bethlehem. Birthplace of prophet Amos; in later times his tomb worshiped there and Byzantine church built in his honor.

Tel Aviv-Jaffa, largest city in Israel, in C. Coastal Plain. Tel Aviv, the "first all-Jewish city" in modern times, was founded 1909, originally as Aḥuzat Bayit, a garden suburb of Jaffa, but evolved rapidly and was dominant element when the two merged 1949. It is a bustling city with 383,200 inhabitants (1971) and is the business and entertainment center of the country. Site of Histadrut, Ministry of Defense and other government offices, theaters and museums, university. It is the core of a large conurbation (inc. Ramat Gan, Petaḥ Tikvah, Ḥolon, and Bat Yam) with 42% of the country's population. A port was established during the 1936–39 disturbances but ceased in the 1960s. See also Jaffa.

Tel Aviv University, institute of higher education in Tel Aviv. Tel Aviv School of Law and Economics established 1935, becoming branch of Heb. Univ. in late 1950s. In 1965 this branch together with faculties of Biology and Jewish Studies, founded 1953, 1955 by Tel Aviv municipality, were combined into Tel Aviv Univ. In 1972/73 academic staff numbered over 2,000, with 15,000 students.

Tel Ḥai, settlement in extreme N. Israel. Founded 1918 as one of three outposts in area. Joseph Trumpeldor and seven comrades fell in its defense 1920. Annual pilgrimage made in their memory every Adar 11.

Tell (Arab. "mound," "hillock"), ancient mound in Middle East composed of remains of successive settlements.

Tell El-Amarna Letters, collection of cuneiform tablets found 1889–1936 at al-'Amārna, 190 mi. S. of Cairo, site of Egyptian capital Akhetaten in 14th c. B.C.E. The 300 letters contain many written by Egyptian vassals in Syria and Ereẓ Israel and give vivid picture of political situation in Canaan and elsewhere. Most letters are written in Akkadian and are major source for pre-biblical linguistic knowledge. Mention of "Habiru" may refer to Hebrew tribes.

Edward Teller

Teller, Edward (1908–), U.S. physicist; b. Budapest, in U.S. fr. 1935. Key figure in development of H-bomb, of whose importance he became passionate protagonist. At Univ. of California at Berkeley fr. 1960.

Teller, Issachar Baer (b. c. 1607), physician, surgeon in Prague. Wrote first printed medical book in Yiddish with object of helping poor people who could not afford doctor's fees.

Telz Yeshivah, major yeshivah in Russia, situated in Telz (Telsiai), Lithuania; operated 1875–1941. Concentrated on development of acuity in profound logical analysis. Closed by Soviet authorities 1940, reestablished 1941 in Cleveland, Ohio, with 400 students in 1971.

Temerls, Jacob ben Eliezer (Jacob Ashkenazi; d. 1666), Polish rabbi, kabbalist in Kremenets. Greatly revered; some of Europe's leading rabbis turned to him for advice.

Temesvár, see Timișoara.

Temkin, family in Ereẓ Israel. **Moshe** (1885–1958), Hebrew writer; b. Poland, settled in Ereẓ Israel 1906. Wrote on Hebrew writers, personalities, and stories. His brother **Mordecai** (1891–1960), Hebrew poet; settled in Ereẓ Israel 1911.

Aerial view of Tel Aviv.

Campus of Tel Aviv University.

Temple (*Bet ha-Mikdash*), the central building for worship of God in ancient Israel; situated on Mt. Moriah in Jerusalem. First Temple built by Solomon in Jerusalem, serving as religious center for Israelites until destruction 586 B.C.E. Solomon completed building with assistance of King Hiram of Tyre. Composed of three sections: vestibule, main room for divine service *(heikhal),* and "Holy of Holies" *(devir).* After split in kingdom, Jeroboam established rival shrines at Beth-El and Dan for inhabitants of N. Kingdom. Destruction of Temple by Nebuchadnezzar marked end of an epoch. The Second Temple was built 538–515 B.C.E. and destroyed by Romans 70 C.E.

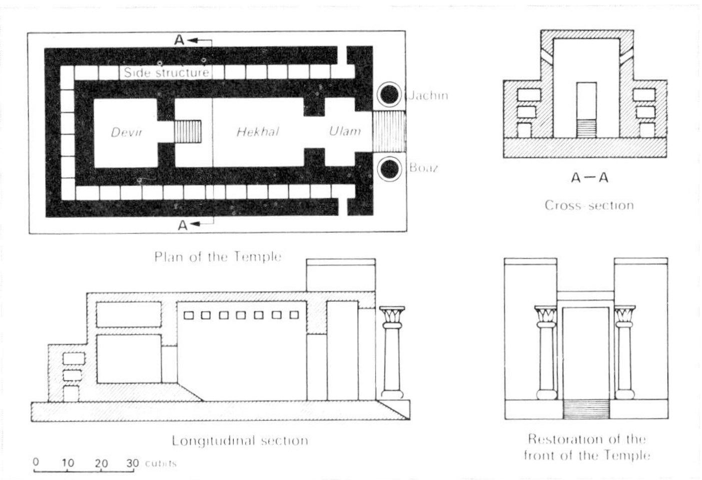

Solomon's Temple.

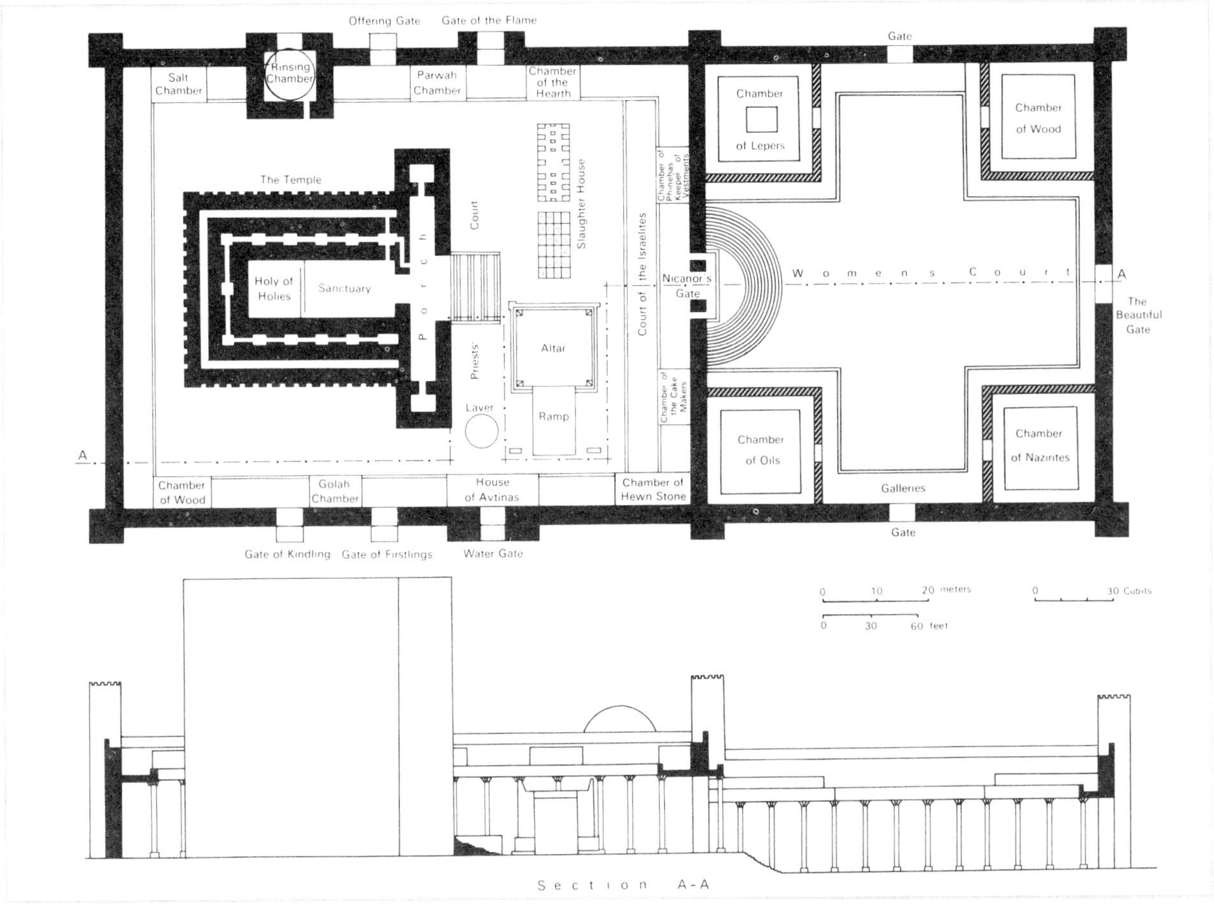

Second Temple according to Mishnah "Middot" and Josephus' "Jewish Antiquities."

Façade of Herod's Temple from Michael Avi-Yonah's model of Jerusalem.

Major reconstructions were carried out in period of Simeon the Just, Judah the Maccabee and most notably Herod. The Herodian wall surrounding the Temple hill included the Western Wall. Herod's temple was constructed of white stone, profusely adorned with gold, and a roof of cedarwood. It was entered by a number of gates and 4 bridges. It also contained the court of the Sanhedrin. Both First and Second Temple scene of sacrificial cult and center of pilgrimage (esp. at three Pilgrim Festivals). The High Priest was the chief official of the Temple. In the siege of Jerusalem, it served as a center of military activity against the Romans. The entire area of the S. approaches has been recently brought to light in the excavations of B. Mazar.

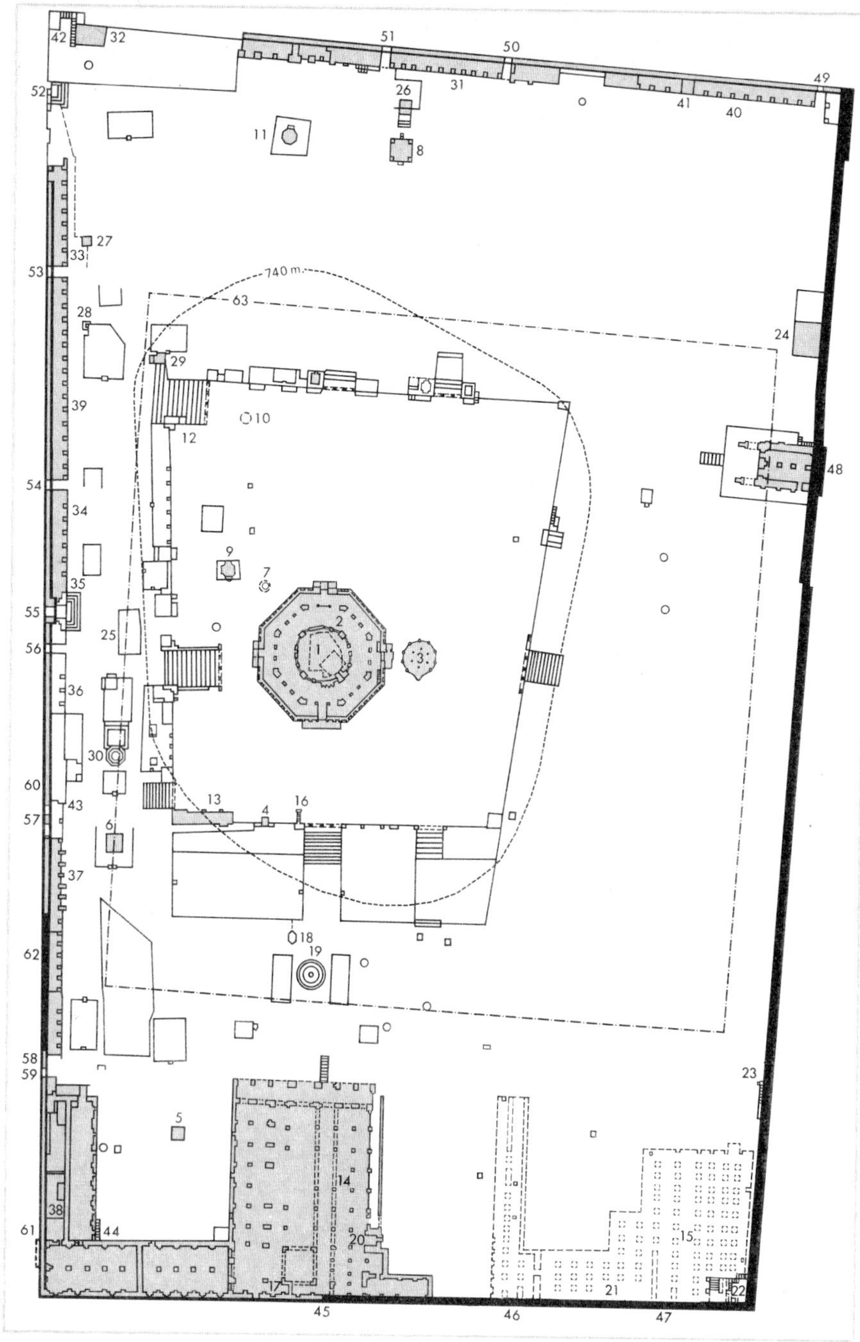

KEY TO PLAN OF TEMPLE MOUNT.

1. "The Rock"
2. Dome of the Rock
3. Dome of the Chain
4. Dome of Joseph
5. Dome of Yūsuf Agha
6. Dome of Moses
7. Dome of the Prophet
8. Dome of Suleiman Pāshā
9. Dome of the Ascension
10. Dome of the Spirits
11. Dome of Solomon
12. Al-Khiḍr (Elijah) Dome
13. Al-Naḥawiyya Dome
14. Al-Aqṣā Mosque
15. Solomon's Stables
16. Summer Pulpit
17. Pulpit of Nūr al-Dīn
18. Olive Tree of the Prophet
19. Al-Ka's ("The Goblet")
20. Miḥrab of Zechariah
21. Miḥrab of David
22. Cradle of Jesus
23. Seat of Muhammad
24. Seat of Solomon
25. Fountain of Qāyt-Bāy
26. Fountain of Sultan Suleiman
27. Fountain of 'Alā 'al-Dīn al Baṣīr
28. Fountain of Sheikh Budayr
29. Fountain of Sha'lan
30. Fountain of Qāsim Pāshā
31. Al-Madrasa al-Dawīdāriyya
32. Al-Madrasa al-Jāwiliyya
33. Al-Madrasa al-Manjikiyya
34. Al-Madrasa al-Arghūniyya
35. Al-Madrasa al-Khātūniyya
36. Al-Madrasa al-Uthmāniyya
37. Al-Madrasa al-Tankiziyya
38. Al-Madrasa al-Fakhriyya
39. Western Porch
40. Northern Porch
41. Minaret of Israel
42. Minaret al-Ghawānima
43. Minaret of the Gate of the Chain
44. Minaret al-Fakhriyya
45. Double Gate (blocked)
46. Triple Gate (blocked)
47. Single Gate (blocked)
48. The Golden Gate (blocked)
49. Gate of the Tribes
50. Gate of Forgiveness
51. The Dark Gate
52. Ghawānima Gate
53. Gate of the Inspector
54. The Iron Gate
55. Gate of the Cotton Market
56. Gate of the Bath
57. Gate of the Chain, Gate of Peace
58. Barclay's Gate (blocked)
59. Gate of the Mughrebins
60. Wilson's Arch
61. Robinson's Arch
62. Western (Wailing) Wall
63. Balustrade (Second Temple)

Temple Mount, area in Old City of Jerusalem which was site of Temple compound. Contains 100 different structures from various periods. Most prominent are Mosque of Omar or Dome of the Rock (completed 690–91) and Mosque of al-Aqṣā (completed c. 700). Site of Temple approximated the former. In Jewish law, the whole area forbidden to anyone ritually unclean. Temple area surrounded by wall, sections of which are in famous Western Wall. The S. wall area has recently been extensively excavated.

Templers (Tempelgesellschaft), German sect which founded settlements in Ereẓ Israel in 19th and 20th c. to realize apocalyptic vision of prophets. Established residential quarters in Jerusalem, Jaffa and Haifa as well as four colonies. In 1938 they numbered 1,500, but were repatriated to Germany in WWII or deported to Australia.

Temple Scroll, scroll of Dead Sea Sect, acquired by Israel 1967. Longest scroll hitherto discovered; dated to end of 2nd c. B.C.E. Includes: *halakhot* on various subjects (e.g., cleanness and uncleanness), rules for festivals, Temple plan and practice, and the statutes of the king.

Templo, Jacob Judah (Aryeh) Leon (1603–1675), Dutch rabbi, artist. His name derives fr. his illustrated treatise on Temple. Published similar works on Ark, cherubim, and Tabernacle, and constructed models of shrines. Designed coat of arms used by English freemasons.

Temunah, The Book of, work of kabbalistic literature, written c. 1270. Main importance: theory of *Shemittot* (cosmic cycles).

Temurah (Heb. "Exchange"), sixth tractate in Mishnah order *Kodashim*, with *gemara* in Babylonian Talmud. Deals with regulations concerning exchange of animal consecrated for sacrifice and associated problems.

Ten Commandments, see Decalogue.

Ten Days of Penitence (Heb. *aseret yemei teshuvah*), period fr. Rosh Ha-Shanah until Day of Atonement, inclusive. Considered period for repentance; appropriate additions are made to liturgy.

Tene, Benjamin (1914–), Hebrew poet; b. Poland, settled in Ereẓ Israel 1937. Wrote poetry, folktales for children; also translations.

Tenenbaum, Joseph L. (1887–1961), U.S. urologist, Zionist leader, author; b. Poland. Delegate Paris Peace Conference 1919, representing Jewish National Council of

Poland. Emigrated to U.S. 1920. Founder and chairman Joint Boycott Council 1933–41. Writings esp. about WWII incl. *Race and Reich* on racial character of German people.

Tenenbaum (Tamaroff), Mordecai (1916–1943), Polish resistance and ghetto fighter. Active in Zionist youth movements before 1939; took part in pioneer resistance movement in Vilna and, after 1942, in Warsaw. In Aug. 1943 led Bialystok Ghetto revolt, committing suicide when his ammunition gave out.

Ten Lost Tribes, legend concerning fate of ten tribes constituting N. Kingdom of Israel and exiled 722 B.C.E. In fact tribes probably assimilated into new environment but belief in continued existence was regarded as incontrovertible during entire period of Second Temple and Talmud. Throughout Middle Ages and until comparatively recently, both Jewish and non-Jewish travelers have attempted to discover the tribes or have claimed their existence. Numerous theories have associated them with various peoples and places. Many people from the Japanese to the British to the Red Indians have been suggested as their descendants.

Ten Martyrs, The (Heb. *asarah harugei malkhut)*, name given to ten sages put to death by Romans. Although sages were put to death for teaching Torah in defiance of Roman edict, concept of "Ten Martyrs" is comparatively late. There are various versions, many contradictory in detail, none according with historical fact, and all bearing mystical stamp. Legend served as much-favored theme for *piyyutim*, the best-known included in liturgy for Day of Atonement and Av 9.

Tennessee, U.S. state. First known Jewish settler 1838. Most mid-19th c. settlers fr. Germany and W. Europe; after 1880, fr. E. Europe. Oldest communities Memphis and Nashville. Jewish pop. 17,415 (1971).

Tent of Meeting, see Tabernacle.

Teomim, Aaron ben Moses (c. 1630–1690), Polish rabbi; in Worms fr. 1670. Best-known work is commentary on *Haggadah*.

Teomim, Aryeh Leib (d. 1831), Galician rabbi, author. Man of wealth and property; rabbi in Brody. Vigorously opposed Ḥasidism. Wrote commentaries on Bible and *Haggadah*.

Teomim, Joseph ben Meir (c. 1727–1792), Galician rabbi, halakhic authority. Rabbi in Lvov and then Frankfort on the Oder. Fame rests on commentary to *Shulḥan Arukh, Peri Megadim* (he is referred to by that name alone). Also compiled works on Pentateuch, responsa, and lexicon of Hebrew and Aramaic roots.

Teplice (Teplitz), city in Czechoslovakia. Jews fr. 1414; community one of most important in Bohemia fr. 16th c. Jews helped develop the local spa. In 1930 numbered 3,213. Most left 1938, but community reestablished by Jews fr. Subcarpathian Ruthenia after 1948. 500 in 1965, but later declined.

Tepper, Kolya (1879–after 1925), Yiddish writer; b. Russia. First a Zionist, later a Bundist; escaped to U.S. 1907, returned to Russia 1917, disappeared after 1925. A talented stylist, eloquent orator. His philosophy influenced U.S. Yiddish writers.

Tepper, Morris (1916–), U.S. meteorologist. In charge of planning and coordinating programs for use of satellites and rockets as aids to transport, navigation, and meteorology at NASA fr. 1959.

Terah, father of Abraham, Nahor, and Haran. Left Ur for Canaan but died at Harran.

Teraphim, household gods, small and portable figurines. Mentioned in connection with Rachel (Gen. 31:34) and Michal (I Sam. 19:13). Remnant of ancient worship that disappeared in First Temple period.

Terefah (Heb. lit. "torn" by beast of prey), animal whose death is due to physical defects or injuries. It is therefore prohibited as food. Term is generally applied to food that is not *kasher*, owing to defect in otherwise permitted animal.

Terezín, see Theresienstadt.

Terni, Daniel ben Moses David (18th–19th c.), Italian rabbi, poet. Compiled anthology of halakhic rulings in works of *posekim* and in responsa. Composed religious and secular poetry.

Terracini, Benvenuto Aron (1886–), Italian philologist. Taught in Germany, Italy, and Argentina (where he lived as refugee 1941–47). Prof. at Turin fr. 1947. Active in Jewish communal life.

Terracini, Umberto Elia (1895–), Italian Communist leader. Imprisoned by Fascists 1926–37. Took leading part in resistance in WWII. Senator fr. 1948, presidential candidate 1965–66. Sympathetic to Soviet Jewry and favorably disposed toward Israel.

Territorialism, movements in 20th c. to establish autonomous settlement of Jews in territory in which predominant majority of population would be Jewish. Ereẓ Israel was one possibility among others. Movements came into existence after 1905 Zionist Congress rejected Uganda Scheme. Four movements established: 1) I.T.O. (Jewish Territorial Organization), founded 1905, headed by Israel Zangwill; dissolved 1925; 2) A.I.K.O. (Allgemeine Juedische Kolonisations-Organization), initiated by Alfred Nossig; dissolved 1920; 3) International Jewish Colonization Society, initiated by Daniel Wolf; dissolved 1939; 4) Freeland League, established 1935; still functioning. No permanent results achieved.

Tertis, Lionel (1876–), English violist. His exceptional playing led to viola's recognition as solo instrument. Designer of Tertis viola.

Teruel, city in Aragon, E. Spain. Prosperous in Muslim period. Under Christians, Jews lived in their own quarter, paid heavy taxes, were affected by anti-Jewish riots, and were expelled 1492.

Terumot (Heb. "heave offerings"), sixth tractate of Mishnah order *Zera'im*, with *gemara* in Jerusalem Talmud. Details laws of heave offering given to priest.

Testaments of the Twelve Patriarchs, see Patriarchs, Testaments of the Twelve.

Tet (ט), 9th letter of Hebrew alphabet; numerical value 9. Pronounced *t*.

Tetragrammaton, personal name of God of Israel, written in Hebrew Bible with the four consonants YHWH. Pronunciation of name has been avoided since at least 3rd c. B.C.E.; initial substitute was *Adonai* ("the Lord"), itself later replaced by *ha-Shem* ("the Name"). The name Jehovah is a hybrid misreading of the original Hebrew letters with the vowels of *Adonai*.

Tetrarch (Gk. "vassal-ruler"), title given to minor rulers in the provinces of Judea and Syria in Roman period. Appointed by Roman emperor and subject to him.

Jewish communities in Tennessee, and dates of establishment.

Tetuán, town in Morocco. Jewish community grew in importance fr. 1511 and controlled trade until 20th c. Good relations with Moslems. Community numbered 3,000–8,000. Descendants of Spanish and Portuguese refugees preserved their own language (Castilian Spanish), customs, and traditions. Jews confined to own quarter 1807–1912. Emigration fr. this period. 7,000 Jews in 1949; 1,000 in 1968.

Tevet, post-Exilic name of tenth month of Jewish year. Zodiac sign Capricorn. 29 days.

Tevet, Shabbetai (1925–), Israel writer. Member of editorial staff of *Haaretz* fr. 1950. Wrote novels and stories, books on Six-Day War and Moshe Dayan.

Tevet, Tenth of, public fast commemorating siege of Jerusalem by Nebuchadnezzar 587–86 B.C.E. In modern times declared a fast day by the Israel Chief Rabbinate to commemorate those who perished during the Holocaust and whose anniversary is unknown.

Tevul Yom (Heb. lit. "One who has bathed that day"), tenth tractate in Mishnah order *Tohorot,* with no *gemara* in either Talmud. Deals with problems of ritual uncleanness between immersion and sunset.

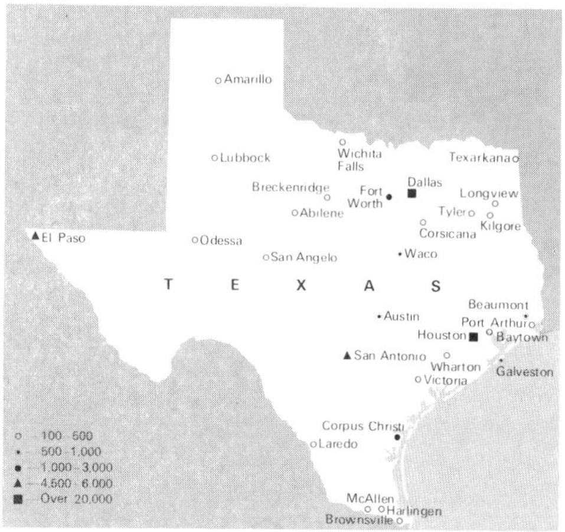

Jewish communities in Texas.

Texas, U.S. state. First Jewish settlers 1821. Jews played role in independence of Texas 1836. 5,000 Alsatian Jews brought to state 1840. First community 1850 (Houston), second 1868 (Galveston), and in following two decades 12 other congregations established. Jewish pop. began to grow after WWI, and Jews served as mayors in many towns. Jew. pop. 67,505 (1971) in over 90 cities and towns.

Thailand (Prathet Thai), Asian kingdom. Community established by refugees in Bangkok in 1920s. Later joined by 120 refugees fr. Nazi persecution, who left after WWII. Jewish community center with synagogue established 1966 but permanent community consists of 6 families.

Thalberg, Irving Grant (1899–1936), U.S. film producer, executive. Production chief MGM. Responsible for some of best-known films of his time: *Broadway Melody, Grand Hotel, Good Earth, Ben-Hur.*

Thalberg, Sigismund (1812–1871), pianist; b. Geneva. One of foremost pianists of his time. Composed 80 piano pieces and other works.

Thanksgiving Psalms, common designation for one of Dead Sea Scrolls, containing poems beginning with such phrases as "I thank Thee O Lord". Scroll appears to have been written in 1st c. B.C.E.

Theben (Mandl), Jacob Koppel (1732–1799), head of Pressburg community, *shtadlan.* Maintained relations with court of Austrian emperor and constantly demanded from them equal rights for Jews. Fought against compulsory military service for Jews.

Theodor, Julius (1849–1923), German rabbi, researcher. His scholarly edition of *Midrash Bereshit Rabbah* was first text of rabbinic literature published in scientific and amended manner in accordance with modern philological methods.

Theodosia, see Feodosiya.

Theodosius (2nd c. B.C.E.), spokesman for Samaritan community of Alexandria. Unsuccessfully opposed Jewish claim that sacrifices should be sent to Jerusalem Temple.

Theodosius of Rome ("Todos Ish Romi"; 1st c. C.E.), spiritual leader of Roman Jewish community.

Therapeutae (Gk. "healers"), sect of Jewish ascetics. Believed to have settled nr. Alexandria in 1st c. C.E. Origin and fate unknown; probably a radical offshoot of pre-Christian Judaism, perhaps Essenism. Severe in its discipline and mode of life. Contained both men and women and emphasized contemplation.

Theresienstadt (Terezín), town in Czechoslovakia which Nazis made Jewish ghetto 1941–45. 150,000 persons, mainly assimilated Jews from C. and W. Europe, deported there. In 1943, Germans displayed it as "model settlement" to International Red Cross, thus intending to conceal extermination of European Jewry. Over 88,000 Jews deported fr. ghetto to death camps 1942–44. Internal affairs run by

Stamp issued to Theresienstadt internees from Bohemia and Moravia for use on parcels from relatives in the Protectorate.

Jewish *Aeltestenrat,* which organized educational, cultural, welfare, and social activities. Overcrowding bred disease; 33,529 Jews died, 11,000 remained.

Thessaloniki, see Salonika.

Theudas, false prophet in Judea during administration of Roman procurator Cuspius Fadus (44–46). Persuaded masses to follow him to the Jordan, which, at his command, was to part and afford them easy passage. Caught and decapitated by Romans.

Thieberger, Friedrich (1888–1958), Czechoslovak writer, translator. Fr. 1939 in Jerusalem, where he was librarian of B'nai B'rith library. Wrote *King Solomon* and translated into German.

Thomashefsky, Boris (1868–1939), U.S. Yiddish actor, stage director. Pioneer and active for over 50 years in American-Yiddish theater. Excelled in romantic swashbuckling roles. Built National Theater in N.Y. 1912 where Yiddish show business flourished for 40 years. His grandson, **Michael Tilson Thomas** (1946–), conductor of Buffalo and Boston orchestras.

Thon, Osias (Jehoshua; 1870–1936), rabbi, early Zionist, Polish Jewish leader. Rabbi in Cracow, active in Zionist movement, member of Polish parliament, gifted orator and writer. Among leaders of Hebrew language movement in Poland and helped found network of Tarbut schools.

Thon, Ya'akov Yoḥanan (1880–1950), *yishuv* leader; brother of Osias Thon; went fr. Poland to Ereẓ Israel 1907. Ruppin's deputy in Palestine Office, chairman of Va'ad Le'ummi, a founder of Berit Shalom, managing director of Palestine Land Development Corp.

Thorn, Sir Jules (1899–), British industrialist. Built up powerful group of companies dealing in electrical goods; his Thorn Electrical Industries became one of Britain's largest concerns.

Three Children, Song of the, see Song of the Three Children.

Three Weeks, period between Tammuz 17 and Av 9 inclusive commemorating period of destruction of First and Second Temple. Time of mourning called in Hebrew *bein ha-meẓarim* ("between the straits," i.e., the two fasts) during which certain mourning rites are observed. On Sabbaths of Three Weeks ("Three Sabbaths of Affliction," *Telata de-Furanuta*), special *haftarot* are read.

Thummim, see Urim and Thummim.

Thuringia, former state in E. Germany. Jewish settlement fr. 12th c., considerably increased in 13th, 14th c., producing many scholars. Jews expelled by 1559. In 18th and 19th c. Court Jews and rich merchants gained protection while poor Jews, mostly peddlers, lived on country estates of nobility. Jews became subjects 1811, but backward conditions and anti-Semitism encouraged subsequent emigration. First state where Nazis won ministerial office; communities annihilated during WWII. Few Jews there after war.

Tibbon, Jacob ben Machir, ibn (c. 1236–1307), author, translator, public figure; grandson of Samuel Tibbon; lived in Montpellier, S.France. Invented astronomical measuring device; rendered into Hebrew numerous books on philosophy, mathematics, and astronomy. Leading defender of Maimonides during 1304–5 controversy.

Tibbon, Judah ben Saul, ibn (c. 1120–c. 1190), translator in S. France. Known as "father of translators"; translated several Arabic works into Hebrew (Baḥya's *Ḥovot ha-Levavot,* Judah Halevi's *Kuzari,* etc).

Tibbon, Samuel ben Judah, ibn (c. 1160–c. 1230), French translator, author; son of Judah Tibbon. Best known for Hebrew version of Maimonides' *Guide of the Perplexed,* which established style of philosophic Hebrew followed for generations. Also translated and wrote medical works.

Tiberias, city on W. shore of Sea of Galilee, Israel; largest settlement in Jordan Valley. Founded by Herod Antipas. After destruction of Jerusalem, became virtual metropolis of Jewish nation. Sanhedrin transferred there mid-2nd c., Jerusalem Talmud largely composed there. Fr. 7th c. a center of Masoretes, Joseph Nasi tried to establish it as Jewish city in 16th c., but in 17th c. became complete ruin. Rebuilt 18th c., group of ḥasidim settled 1777. First Jewish quarter outside Old City built 1912–14 and most inhabitants Jewish by Mandate times. Arabs fled during 1948 war. After 1948 developed as modern recreation and health center (hot springs) and many immigrants settled there. Pop. 24,200 (1971).

Tiberias, Sea of, see Galilee, Sea of.

Tiberius Julius Alexander (1st c. C.E.), procurator of Judea; son of Alexander Lysimachus and nephew of Philo. Entered Roman military service as young man. Procurator of Judea 46–48, prefect of Egypt 66. Highest-ranking officer in Titus' army in Judea 69–70. No knowledge of any formal act of apostasy on his part.

Tibni, biblical figure; Omri's rival. Reigned over part of Israel for four years, until 873 B.C.E. Eventually the supporters of Omri prevailed.

Ticho, Anna (1894–), Israel artist; b. Moravia, settled in Jerusalem 1912 and devoted herself to drawing Jerusalem and its environs. Her husband **Abraham Albert Ticho** (1883–1960) founded and headed an ophthalmic hospital in Jerusalem.

Tidhar, David (1897–1970), Israel author, police officer. Served in Palestine Police. First to write Hebrew detective stories. Compiled encyclopedia of *yishuv* personalities (19 vols.).

Tiempo, César (pseud. of **Israel Zeitlin;** 1906–), Argentine poet, playwright. Works largely concerned with social problems and working-class misery.

Tietz, family of German department store owners. **Leonhardt** (1849–1914), founded and developed chain of department stores specializing in textiles. Expanded bet. world wars by his son, **Alfred,** but members of family forced out by Nazis 1933. His brother, **Oskar** (1858–1923), founder of Verein Deutscher Waren- und Kaufhaeuser. His sons, **Georg** (1889–1953) and **Martin** (1895–), expanded business but forced to relinquish ownership 1934.

Tiflis (Tbilisi), capital of Georgian SSR. During 19th c. old Georgian Jewish community joined by Jews fr. Russia. 20,000 Jews in 1970. Many emigrated to Israel after 1968.

°**Tiglath-Pileser III (Pul),** king of Assyria and Babylonia (745–727 B.C.E.). Active in Mediterranean, esp. against Syria. Advanced along coast, accepting submission of Phoenician towns, and conquered Gaza. Ahaz of Judah turned to him for help against Pekah of Israel and his ally in Damascus. Subsequent fall of Damascus in 732 turned entire region to him.

Tigris, major river of SW Asia. One of four rivers flowing out of Garden of Eden (Gen 2:14). Formed boundary of Babylonia in talmudic times.

Tikkun Ḥaẓot (Heb. lit. "institution of midnight [prayer]"), prayers at midnight in memory of destruction of Temple and for restoration of Land of Israel. Practice became formalized under influence of Kabbalah during period of Isaac Luria.

Tikkun Soferim, certain changes in text of Bible made by early *soferim* in places which are offensive or show lack of respect to God. Rabbis attributed 18 such *tikkunim* to members of the Great Synagogue. These are enumerated in *Midrash Tanḥuma* and *Midrash Rabbah.*

Tiktin, rabbinical family. **Abraham ben Gedaliah** (1764–1820), *Oberlandrabbiner* of Silesia at Breslau. Succeeded by his son **Solomon** (1791–1843), who conducted bitter campaign against Reform together with his own son **Gedaliah** (1810–1886), who was also *Landrabbiner.*

Aerial view of Tiberias, 1960s.

"On the Way to Jerusalem," charcoal drawing by Anna Ticho.

Tiktinski, Lithuanian family associated with foundation and development of yeshivah at Mir. **Samuel** (d. 1835) founded yeshivah 1815 at his own expense. His son **Abraham** (d. 1835) eventually assumed responsibility for yeshivah and also sought outside help for it. Another son, **Ḥayyim Leib** (1824–1899), appointed *rosh yeshivah* 1850 and assumed sole responsibility fr. 1867. Noted for gift for teaching and in his method eschewed *pilpul*.

Timendorfer, Berthold (1853–1931), German communal leader. Under his leadership B'nai B'rith took greater part in education, scholarship, and welfare work. Fought hesitant, timorous attitude on German-Jewish questions.

Timisoara (Temesvár), city in W. Rumania. Jewish settlement by 16th c. Community declared itself Neologist 1869, financed schools, became important Zionist center. Its 10,000 Jews suffered during WWII; many sent to forced labor 1941. 13,000 Jews in 1947, but only 3,000 in 1971 owing to emigration.

The modern Timna Copper Works.

Timna, valley in S. Arabah, site in ancient times of intensive copper mining and smelting activities. Mines fr. 4th millennium B.C.E. Modern copper works in vicinity opened in 1959 and produced in 1962 11,000 tons copper cement (with 80% pure copper).

°**Tinneius Rufus,** Roman governor of Judea at outbreak of Bar Kokhba War in 132 C.E. According to talmudic tradition, responsible for plowing up Temple Mount and also engaged in disputations with Akiva.

Tiomkin, Vladimir (Ze'ev; 1861–1927), Zionist leader in Russia. Went to Ereẓ Israel 1891 on behalf of Ḥovevei Zion and initiated land purchases, but his plans failed and he returned to Russia. One of Herzl's early supporters; participated in Zionist Congresses and was regarded as leader of Ukrainian Jewry 1917. Left Bolshevik Russia for Paris, joining Revisionists.

Ṭīra, al-, Muslim Arab village in C. Israel, NE of Kefar Saba. Pop. 8,000.

The Arch of Titus.

Tirado, Jacob (d. 1620 or 1630), founder of Portuguese community in Amsterdam; b. Portugal as Marrano, settled in Amsterdam and reverted to Judaism. Settled in Jerusalem before 1616.

Tirān Island, island at S. issue of Eilat Gulf, 7 mi. (12 km.) long and 6.5 mi. (11 km.) wide. Community of Jewish merchants founded there in 5th c. which named itself "Yotvat," Destroyed by Emperor Justinian 535 C.E.

Tirzah, Canaanite city, NE of Shechem. Residence of Jeroboam I after he left Shechem, but Omri transferred his capital to Samaria. Apparently destroyed by Assyrians 721 B.C.E.

Tishah Be-Av, see Av, the Ninth of.

Tishby, Isaiah (1908–), scholar of Kabbalah, Shabbateanism, ethical Hebrew literature, and Ḥasidism; b. Hungary, settled in Ereẓ Israel 1933. Taught at Heb. Univ. fr. 1951. Works incl. Zohar anthologies.

Tishri, post-Exilic name of seventh month of Jewish year; first month of civil calendar. Zodiac sign Libra. 30 days. Tishri 1–2 is Rosh Ha-Shanah; 3 Fast of Gedaliah; 10 Day of Atonement; 15–21 Tabernacles; 22(23) Shemini Aẓeret.

Tiszaeszlar, town in Hungary. Notorious as a result of 1882 blood libel which aroused public opinion throughout Europe and became subject of stormy agitation in Hungary. Accused were eventually acquitted.

Tithe, tenth part of produce set aside as religious offering. Originally voluntary offerings, four tithes were obligatory: (1) 1st tithe – given to levites; (2) 2nd tithe – an additional tenth eaten by the owner in Jerusalem; (3) poor tithe – replaced 2nd tithe in 3rd and 6th year of Sabbatical cycle; (4) tithe of the animals selected in the thrice-yearly counting and offered as sacrifice by owner.

Titus, Arch of, triumphal arch erected in Rome 81 C.E. to commemorate Titus' victory over Jews. Original arch no longer extant; present one erected during reign of Domitian.

°**Titus, Flavius Vespasianus,** emperor of Rome 79–81 C.E., conqueror of Galilee 66 and Jerusalem 70; son of Vespasian. Respected Jewish rights in empire. For a number of years had romance with Berenice.

Tivoli, Serafino Da (1826–1890), Italian painter; founder and leader of *macchiaiolo* school. Fought in wars of Italian Risorgimento.

Tlemcen, city in NW Algeria; Judeo-Berber center. After 1492 community augmented by Spanish refugees. Community ceased to exist 1962. Jewish cemetery is important place of pilgrimage for Jews and non-Jews.

Tnuva, cooperative association affiliated to Histadrut. Markets agricultural produce of most Jewish villages in Israel.

Toaff, Alfredo Sabato (1880–1963), Italian rabbi. Pres. of Italian rabbinical council and head of Collegio Rabbinico Italiano 1955–63. Wrote on Jewish literature and history and translated works into Italian. His son **Elio** (1915–), chief rabbi of Rome 1951. Headed Collegio Rabbinico Italiano fr. 1963.

Tobiads, leading family in Judea in Second Temple period, with considerable influence on social, political, and economic developments 5th–2nd c. B.C.E. Originated in S. Gilead, where they owned large estates. Hellenists; played important role in events leading to Hasmonean rising.

Tobiah, the Ammonite servant (Neh. 2:10,19). Held high office in Persian hierarchy and may have been governor of Ammon. His efforts to block construction of Jerusalem wall by Nehemiah failed.

Tobias, Phillip Vallentine (1925–), S. African anatomist, paleoanthropologist. Prof. of anatomy at Witwatersrand Medical School fr. 1959. Proponent of *"Homo habilis"* theory.

Tobias ben Moses ha-Avel (ha-Ma'tik, "the translator"; 11th c.), Karaite scholar. Laid theoretical and educational foundations for establishing Karaites in Byzantine milieu. Translated works of his teacher, Joseph al-Baṣīr, into Hebrew, and compiled Arabic material.

Tobias the Physician, see Cohn, Tobias ben Moses.

Tobit, Book of, book of Apocrypha. Didactic romance concerning devout

Part of a wooden synagogue from Horb, S.W. Germany, decorated and painted by Eliezer Sussman in 1735.

The Great Synagogue in Florence, completed in 1882.

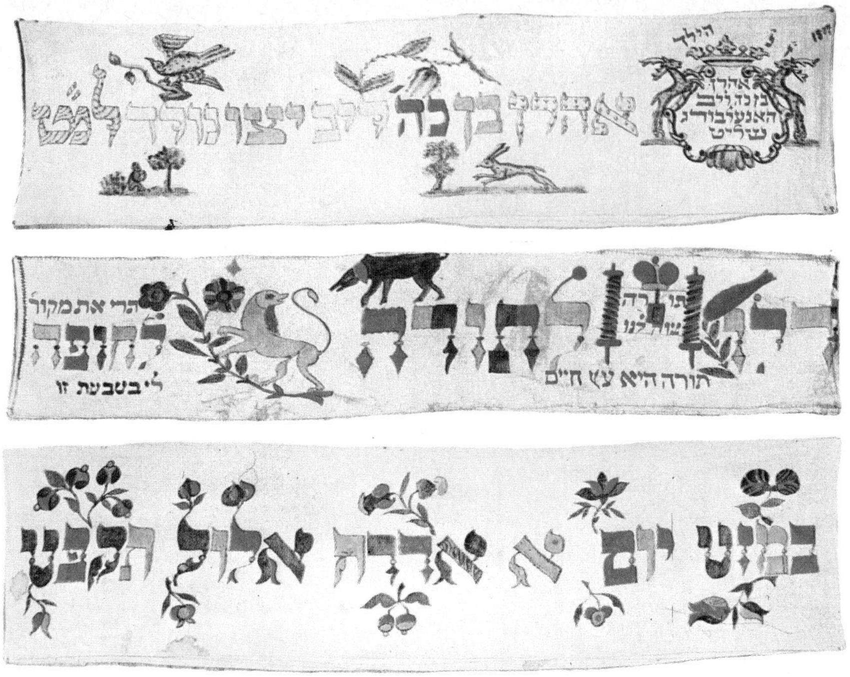

Linen wrappers for Scroll of Torah made from circumcision diaper and embroidered with child's name and date of birth, Germany, 18th–19th cent.

TORAH ORNAMENTS

Silver gilt breastplate for the Torah with jeweled crown. Appropriate plaques were inserted in the centerpiece containing the name of holidays. Munich, 1826.

Silver Torah finials (*rimmonim*). Central Europe, 18th cent.

Jew of Assyrian Exile whose faithfulness and good deeds result in supernatural deliverance fr. affliction. Book appears to date fr. Persian era. Three Greek recensions are known and fragments in Hebrew and Aramaic have been found among Dead Sea scrolls.

Toch, Ernst (1887–1967), Austrian composer. Fr. 1937 in Hollywood and taught at various univs. Wrote operas, orchestral works, chamber music, incidental music for plays and films, and choral works.

Toch, Maximilian (1864–1946), U.S. paint chemist. Expert on authenticity of paintings. Prof. chemistry of artistic painting, National Academy of Design, N.Y., 1924. Invented "Toch system" of camouflage in WWI.

Todd, Mike (Avrom Girsch Goldbogen; 1909–1958), U.S. producer, impressario. Promoted film innovations of Cinerama and Todd-AO. Produced Jules Verne's *Around the World in 80 Days.* Killed in plane crash.

Todesco, Hermann (1792–1844), Austrian industrialist, philanthropist. First director of the Vienna-Gloggnitz railroad. Ennobled. A founder of Vienna Temple 1826. His son **Eduard** (d. 1887) established foundation to help needy army officers and impoverished Jewish students. Also ennobled.

Toeplitz, Otto (1881–1940), German mathematician. Prof. of mathematics at Kiel 1920, Bonn 1928–35. In Ereẓ Israel fr. 1939. Main interest matrix algebra.

Tog, see Jewish Day.

Toharat Ha-Mishpaḥah, see Taharat Ha-Mishpaḥah.

Tohorah (Heb. "purification"), ceremony of washing dead before burial, performed by *mit'assekim* ("attendants"). Water poured over body in upright position. Hair combed and nails cut. Ceremony observed by Mishnaic times. Discarded by Reform Judaism.

Tohorot (Heb. lit. "cleannesses"), last of six orders of Mishnah. Contains 12 tractates and discusses *halakhot* of different categories of ritual purity and impurity.

Tohorot, fifth tractate in order of same name. Deals with rules of lesser degree of uncleanliness, effects of which last until sunset only. Since it has no *gemara,* the tosefta is valuable for its elucidation.

Tohorot ha-Kodesh, anonymous work of ethical literature, first printed in Amsterdam 1733. Author probably lived in Poland in early 18th c. Criticized contemporary rabbis, emphasizing that correct social behavior takes precedence over study of Torah.

Tokheḥah (Heb. "reproof"), name given to two comminatory passages in Pentateuch (Lev. 26:14–45; Deut. 28:15–68). During public readings on appropriate Sabbath they are read quickly and quietly, it being general practice for sexton or reader of Torah to accept this *aliyah.*

Tokyo, city in Japan. Small number of Jews fleeing Russia settled after 1918. After 1945 Jewish activity stimulated by Jews among American troops and other temporary residents. Jewish pop. 400 (1972).

°**Toland, John** (1670–1722), Irish-born deist. His *Reasons for Naturalising the Jews in Great Britain and Ireland on the Same Footing with all Other Nations* (1714) was plea for naturalization of Jews and thereby attracting them to England.

Toledano, Daniel (d. c. 1740) Moroccan trader; known as "one of the country's magnates." Eventually arrested and bankrupted by the king.

Toledano, Ḥayyim ben Joseph (d. 1848), rabbi in Meknès. Active in community's administration. After denunciation to authorities, died in Fez prison. Wrote commentaries and responsa.

Toledano, Jacob (Maharit; 1697–1771), most important halakhic authority in Maghreb in 2nd half of 18th c. Played central role in the Meknès community. Wrote several commentaries and legal decisions.

Toledano, Jacob Moses (1880–1960), Israel rabbi, scholar. Wrote on history of Oriental Jewry. Appointed member of Tangier rabbinate 1926, later deputy chief rabbi of Cairo, chief rabbi of Alexandria, and Sephardi chief rabbi of Tel Aviv-Jaffa 1942. Appointed minister of religious affairs 1958.

Toledano, Joseph ben Daniel (d. c. 1700), counselor of Moroccan king Moulay Ismā'il. Successfully negotiated as ambassador on his behalf in Netherlands. Brother-in-law of Jacob Sasportas.

Toledano, Raphael Baruch ben Jacob (1892–1971), *av bet din* in Meknès. Active in community affairs and founded yeshivot. In Israel fr. 1965. Wrote summarized version of *Shulḥan Arukh* as well as *piyyutim.*

Toledano, Solomon ben Eliezer (Maharshat; d. 1809), leading rabbi in Meknès. Said to have performed miracles, and to this day the sick prostrate themselves and pray at his tomb. Wrote work of legal decisions.

The former Toledo synagogue, founded 1203.

Toledo, most ancient Jewish community in Iberian peninsula and most important under Visigoths. Jews lived in special quarter (most of which, incl. two magnificent synagogues, still stands), continuing to flourish under Muslim rule. Center of Karaites in Spain and home of Jewish scholarship and culture. Gained in importance after Christian reconquest 1085, but in 14th c. suffered fr. Black Death, civil wars, and massacres of 1391. Thereafter became center for Conversos, but did not recover its former glory. Community expelled 1492.

Toledo, city in Ohio, U.S. Small number of Jews there when town chartered 1837. 3 Jewish mayors. Jewish pop. 7,350 (1971), with 3 major and several smaller congregations.

Toledot Ha-Ari, legendary biography of Isaac Luria of Safed. One of most detailed and richest hagiographies written in Hebrew; includes some true stories. First printed in Istanbul 1720.

Toledot Yeshu (Heb. "The Life of Jesus"), medieval pseudo-history of life of Jesus, compiled fr. variety of sources and intending to give Jewish version of New Testament events. Narrative strived to divest Christian tradition of spiritual meaning.

Toleranzpatent, edict of tolerance issued by Emperor Joseph II in 1782 for Vienna and Lower Austria (and

Pewter medal commemorating the "Toleranzpatent," the three figures are the Protestant, Catholic, and Jewish religions.

subsequently for other provinces in the empire). Significant milestone on road to full emancipation. Its object was to make Jews useful to society and the state through education and abolition of economic restrictions. Welcomed by Haskalah but viewed with misgivings in conservative Jewish circles.

Tolkowsky, Shemuel (1886–1965), agronomist, Israel diplomat; b. Belgium, settled in Ereẓ Israel 1911. Active in citrus growing. Minister of Israel in Switzerland 1949–56. His son **Dan** (1921–), commander of Israel air force 1953–58.

Toller, Ernst (1893–1939), German playwright, revolutionary. Pacifist socialist. Leader in short-lived Bavarian Soviet Republic 1919. Subsequently spent 5 years in prison where he wrote celebrated expressionistic dramas: *Masses and Man*, *The Machine Wrecker*, etc. Foe of Nazism, left Germany. In U.S. fr. 1936; committed suicide.

Tomar, city in C. Portugal. Jews fr. 14th c. Dynamic community in 15th c. Inquisition active there in 16th c. In 1921, Portuguese declared magnificent 15th c. synagogue a national monument.

Tomaszow Mazowiecki, city in C. Poland. Jewish weavers and entrepreneurs invited there in 1820s. Community grew rapidly until 1939 when there were 13,000 Jews. Ghetto formed 1940 and community died in Treblinka.

Tombs of the Kings, tombs of kings of Judah mentioned in Bible but never found. The so-called Tombs of the Kings in Jerusalem is in reality that of Helena, queen of Adiabene.

Toparchy, major administrative district in Ereẓ Israel during greater part of Second Temple period; subdivision of *hyparchia*. Under Herod, Jewish Ereẓ Israel was divided into 21 toparchies.

Topheth, place adjoining Jerusalem in Valley of Hinnom, which was illicit open-air high place where child sacrifices were made to Molech, and hence became synonymous with "hell."

Topol, Chaim (1935–), Israel actor. Won international fame for characterization of Tevye in film *Fiddler on the Roof.* Films made in Israel incl. *Sallah Shabbati* and *Ervinka.*

Chaim Topol

Topolevsky, Gregorio (1907–), Argentine politician, physician. Frequently arrested for political agitation bet. 1933 and 1945. Ambassador to Israel 1955–58 and director general of social welfare in Ministry of Communications.

Torah (Heb. lit. "teaching," "doctrine," or "instruction"), Pentateuch or pentateuchal scroll for reading in synagogue. Term also used to describe entire body of traditional Jewish teaching and literature.

SCRIPTURAL READINGS ON SABBATHS

PENTATEUCH		PROPHETS
GENESIS		
Bereshit	1:1–6:8	Isa. 42:5–43:11 (42:5–21)[1]
No'aḥ	6:9–11:32	Isa. 54:1–55:5 (54:1–10)
Lekh Lekha	12:1–17:27	Isa. 40:27–41:16
Va-Yera	18:1–22:24	II Kings 4:1–37 (4:1–23)
Ḥayyei Sarah	23:1–25:18	I Kings 1:1–31
Toledot	25:19–28:9	Mal. 1:1–2:7
Va-Yeẓe	28:10–32:3	Hos. 12:13–14:10 (11:7–12:12)
Va-Yishlaḥ	32:4–36:43	Hos. 11:7–12:12 (Obad. 1:1–21)
Va-Yeshev	37:1–40:23	Amos 2:6–3:8
Mi-Keẓ	41:1–44:17	I Kings 3:15–4:1
Va-Yiggash	44:18–47:27	Ezek. 37:15–28
Va-Yeḥi	47:28–50:26	I Kings 2:1–12
EXODUS		
Shemot	1:1–6:1	Isa. 27:6–28:13; 29:22, 23 (Jer. 1:1–2:3)
Va-Era	6:2–9:35	Ezek. 28:25–29:21
Bo	10:1–13:16	Jer. 46:13–28
Be-Shallaḥ	13:17–17:16	Judg. 4:4–5:31 (5:1–31)
Yitro	18:1–20:23	Isa. 6:1–7:6; 9:5, (6:1–13)
Mishpatim	21:1–24:18	Jer. 34:8–22; 33:25, 26
{ Terumah	25:1–27:19	I Kings 5:26–6:13
{ Teẓavveh	27:20–30:10	Ezek. 43:10–27
Ki Tissa	30:11–34:35	I Kings 18:1–39 (18:20–39)
{ Va-Yakhel	35:1–38:20	I Kings 7:40–50 (7:13–26)
{ Pekudei	38:21–40:38	I Kings 7:51–8:21 (7:40–50)
LEVITICUS		
Va-Yikra	1:1–5:26	Isa. 43:21–44:23
Ẓav	6:1–8:36	Jer. 7:21–8:3; 9:22, 23
Shemini	9:1–11:47	II Sam. 6:1–7:17 (6:1–19)
[2]{ Tazri'a	12:1–13:59	II Kings 4:42–5:19
{ Meẓora	14:1–15:33	II Kings 7:3–20
{ Aḥarei Mot	16:1–18:30	Ezek. 22:1–19 (22:1–16)
{ Kedoshim	19:1–20:27	Amos 9:7–15 (Ezek. 20:2–20)
Emor	21:1–24:23	Ezek. 44:15–31
{ Be-Har	25:1–26:2	Jer. 32:6–27
{ Be-Ḥukkotai	26:3–27:34	Jer. 16:19–17:14
NUMBERS		
Be-Midbar	1:1–4:20	Hos. 2:1–22
Naso	4:21–7:89	Judg. 13:2–25
Be-Ha'alotkha	8:1–12:16	Zech. 2:14–4:7
Shelaḥ Lekha	13:1–15:41	Josh. 2:1–24
Koraḥ	16:1–18:32	I Sam. 11:14–12:22
Ḥukkat	19:1–22:1	Judg. 11:1–33
Balak	22:2–25:9	Micah 5:6–6:8
Pinḥas	25:10–30:1	I Kings 18:46–19:21
{ Mattot	30:2–32:42	Jer. 1:1–2:3
{ Masei	33:1–36:13	Jer. 2:4–28; 3:4 (2:4–28; 4:1, 2)
DEUTERONOMY		
Devarim	1:1–3:22	Isa. 1:1–27
Va-Ethannan	3:23–7:11	Isa. 40:1–26
Ekev	7:12–11:25	Isa. 49:14–51:3
Re'eh	11:26–16:17	Isa. 54:11–55:5
Shofetim	16:18–21:9	Isa. 51:12–52:12
Ki Teẓe	21:10–25:19	Isa. 54:1–10
Ki Tavo	26:1–29:8	Isa. 60:1–22
{ Niẓẓavim	29:9–30:20	Isa. 61:10–63:9
{ Va-Yelekh	31:1–30	Isa. 55:6–56:8
Ha'azinu	32:1–52	II Sam. 22:1–51
Ve-Zot ha-Berakhah[3]	33:1–34:12	Josh. 1:1–18 (1:1–9)

[1] Parentheses indicate Sephardi ritual.
[2] Brackets indicate portions that are sometimes combined.
[3] This portion is not read on Sabbath but on Simḥat Torah.

HOLIDAY SCRIPTURAL READINGS FOR THE DIASPORA AND EREẒ ISRAEL

	PENTATEUCH	PROPHETS
ROSH HA-SHANAH		
1st Day	Gen. 21:1–34; Num. 29:1–6	I Sam. 1:1–2:10
2nd Day	Gen. 22:1–24; Num. 29:1–6	Jer. 31:2–20
Shabbat Shuvah	Weekly portion	Hos. 14:2–10; Micah 7:18–20 or Hos. 14:2–10; Joel 2:15–17 (Hos. 14:2–10; Micah 7:18–20[1])
DAY OF ATONEMENT		
Morning	Lev. 16:1–34; Num. 29:7–11	Isa. 57:14–58:14
Afternoon	Lev. 18:1–30	The Book of Jonah; Micah 7:18–20
SUKKOT		
1st Day	Lev. 22:26–23:44; Num. 29:12–16	Zech. 14:1–21
2nd Day	Lev. 22:26–23:44; Num. 29:12–16 [Num. 29:17–19][2] (Ereẓ Israel portion read four times, 2nd–7th Day)	I Kings 8:2–21 [none]
3rd Day	Num. 29:17–22 [29:20–22]	
4th Day	Num. 29:20–28 [29:23–25]	
5th Day	Num. 29:23–31 [29:26–28]	
6th Day	Num. 29:26–34 [29:29–31]	
7th Day	Num. 29:26–34 [29:32–34]	
Shabbat during the Intermediate Days	Ex. 33:12–34:26; Daily portion from Num. 29	Ezek. 38:18–39:16
Shemini Aẓeret 8th Day	Deut. 14:22–16:17; Num. 29:35–30:1 [as for Simḥat Torah]	I Kings 8:54–66 [as for Simḥat Torah]
Simḥat Torah 9th Day	Deut. 33:1–34:12; Gen. 1:1–2:3; Num. 29:35–30:1 [none]	Josh. 1:1–18 (1:1–9) [none]
ḤANUKKAH		
1st Day	Num. 7:1–17	
2nd Day	Num. 7:18–29 [7:18–23] (Ereẓ Israel portion read three times, 2nd–7th Day)	
3rd Day	Num. 7:24–35 [7:24–29]	
4th Day	Num. 7:30–41 [7:30–35]	
5th Day	Num. 7:36–47 [7:36–41]	
6th Day	Num. 7:42–53 [7:42–47]	
7th Day	Num. 7:48–59 [7:48–53]	
8th Day	Num. 7:54–8:4	
First Shabbat Ḥanukkah	Weekly and Ḥanukkah portions as for Ereẓ Israel	Zech. 2:14–4:7
Second Shabbat Ḥanukkah	Weekly and Ḥanukkah portions as for Ereẓ Israel	I Kings 7:40–50
Rosh Ḥodesh during Ḥanukkah	Weekly and Ḥanukkah portions as for Ereẓ Israel and Num. 28.1–15	
Rosh Ḥodesh and Shabbat Ḥanukkah	Weekly Rosh Ḥodesh, and Ḥanukkah portions as for Ereẓ Israel	Isa. 66:1–24
Shekalim	Weekly portion; Ex. 30:11–16	II Kings 12:1–17
Zakhor	Weekly portion; Deut. 25:17–19	I Sam. 15:2–34 (15:1–34)
PURIM	Ex. 17:8–16	
Parah	Weekly portion; Num. 19:1–22	Ezek. 36:16–38 (36:16–36)
Ha-Ḥodesh	Weekly portion; Ex. 12:1–20	Ezek. 45:16–46:18 (45:18–46:5)
Shabbat Ha-Gadol	Weekly portion	Mal. 3:4–24
PASSOVER		
1st Day	Ex. 12:21–51; Num. 28:19–25	Josh. 5:2–6:1
2nd Day	Lev. 22:26–23:44; Num. 28–19:25	II Kings 23:1–9; 21–25 [none]
3rd Day	Ex. 13:1–16; Num. 28:19–25	
4th Day	Ex. 22:24–23:19; Num. 28:19–25	
5th Day	Ex. 33:12–34:26; Num. 28:19–25	
6th Day	Num. 9:1–14; 28:19–25	
Intermediate Shabbat	The order changes to allow for the reading as on the 5th day above	Ezek. 36:37–37:14 (37:1–14)
7th Day	Ex. 13:17–15:26; Num. 28:19–25	II Sam. 22:1–51
8th Day	Deut. 15:19–16:17[3]; Num. 28:19–25 [none]	Isa. 10:32–12:6 [none]
SHAVUOT		
1st Day	Ex. 19:1–20:23; Num. 28:26–31	Ezek. 1:1–28; 3:12
2nd Day	Deut. 15:19–16:17[3]; Num. 28:26–31 [none]	Num. 3:1–19 (2:20–3:19) [none]
NINTH OF AV		
Morning	Deut. 4:25–40	Jer. 8:13–9:23
Afternoon	Ex. 32:11–14; 34:1–10	Isa. 55:6–56:8 (Hos. 14:2–10; Micah [7:18–20])
OTHER FASTS		
Morning and afternoon	Ex. 32:11–14; 34:1–10	Isa. 55:6–56:8 [none]
Rosh Ḥodesh	Num. 28:1–15	
Shabbat and Rosh Ḥodesh	Weekly portion; Num. 28:9–15	Isa. 66:1–24
Shabbat immediately preceding Rosh Ḥodesh	Weekly portion	I Sam. 20:18–12

[1] Parenthesis indicate Sephardi custom [2] Square brackets indicate Ereẓ Israel custom [3] On Shabbat, 14:22–16:17

Torah, Reading of, public reading fr. scroll of Pentateuch in synagogue; one of most ancient portions of the service. The Torah is read on festivals, new moons, Ḥanukkah, Purim, fast days, and every Monday, Thursday, Sabbath morning, and Sabbath afternoon. A complete cycle of the Pentateuch is completed every year during the Sabbath readings (in ancient times, there was a triennial cycle, q.v.). Three adult males are called to the reading of the Law on Mondays, Thursdays, Ḥanukkah, Purim, fast days, and Sabbath afternoons; 4 on New Moon and intermediate days of festivals, 5 on festivals, 6 on Day of Atonement, 7 on Sabbath.

Boys reading from the Torah on their bar mitzvah.

Torah Ornaments, adornment with which Torah scroll is covered. Ornaments consist of (1) a cover – in the East and among the Sephardim a wooden or silver case, in Ashkenazi synagogues a mantle; (2) two finials (Heb. *rimmonim*), mounting the staves on which the scroll is rolled; (3) an open crown (Heb. *keter* or *atarah*) surrounding the finials; (4) in the Ashkenazi rite, a breastplate or shield *(tas)* covering the mantle; (5) a pointer *(yad)* over the breastplate, used for reading the scroll.

Torah Umesorah, U.S. national society serving 377 Orthodox Hebrew day schools in U.S. and Canada (1968). Founded 1944 by Rabbi Feivel Mendlowitz.

Torah va-Avodah (Heb. "Torah and Labor"), description of ideology of Zionist religious pioneering movement, as well as name of world confederation of pioneer and youth groups of Mizrachi movement. Established in Vienna 1925.

Torczyner, Harry, see Tur-Sinai, Naphtali Herz.

Toronto, city in Canada. Organized Jewish life began 1849. City had long history of *Landsmannschaften.* Jews prominent in civic, cultural, musical, and theatrical circles. Strong Jewish communal and religious activities. Community grew with special rapidity after WWII. Jewish pop. 97,000 (1971).

°**Torquemada, Tomás de** (? 1420–1498), first head of Spanish Inquisition. Became inquisitor general 1483 and ordered expulsion of Conversos and Jews. Instrumental in obtaining general decree of expulsion of 1492.

Torrès, Henry (1891–1966), French lawyer, politician. Famous as defense counsel, esp. for Shalom Schwarzbard 1926. In U.S. during WWII. Gaullist senator 1948–58; vice-pres. of High Court of Justice 1956–58. Pres. of French broadcasting authority.

Torres, Luis de (15th–16th c.), Spanish interpreter to Christopher Columbus on his first voyage of discovery in 1492, and the only person of Jewish birth (he was baptized shortly before sailing) to accompany him. Eventually set up his own small empire in Cuba.

°**Torrey, Charles Cutler** (1863–1956), U.S. Bible scholar, semitist; a founder of the American School of Archaeology in Jerusalem. Claimed that bulk of prophecy contained in Ezekiel was pseudepigraphic, composed c. 230 B.C.E.

Tortosa, city in NE Spain; one of oldest Jewish communities in Iberian peninsula. During Muslim period many Jews engaged in agriculture and maritime trade. Center of Jewish learning in 10th, 11th c. Suffered in 1391 persecutions; many forcibly baptized, others martyred. Site of Disputation of Tortosa 1413–14. Point of departure for Jewish refugees fr. Spain 1492.

Tortosa, Disputation of, most important and longest of Christian-Jewish disputations forced upon Jews in Middle Ages. Held in 1413–14; participants on Christian side included Gerónimo de Santa Fé (the apostate Joshua Lorki) and the anti-pope Benedict XIII; Rabbis Zerahiah ha-Levi, Astruc ha-Levi, Joseph Albo, and Mattathias ha-Yiẓhari presented Jewish case. Discussion revolved around Messiah and his nature and supposed abuses against Christianity in Talmud. Disputation acted as incentive for anti-Jewish incitement and many Jews accepted baptism in this period.

Interior of the Holy Blossom Synagogue, Toronto.

Tomás de Torquemada

Tosafot (Heb. "additions"), collections of comments on the Talmud arranged according to the order of the talmudic tractates. Generally based on comments of earlier authorities, esp. Rashi. School of tosafists, beginning with Rashi's pupils. fr. 12th–14th c. in France and Germany.

Tosefta (Aram. "addition"), collection of tannaitic *beraitot,* arranged according to the order of the Mishnah. It supplements the Mishnah: sometimes it is parallel, sometimes its subject-matter is original. The subject of many commentaries.

Toulouse, city in S. France. Acc. to legend Jews in 8th c. By 13th c. rich and important community, engaged in moneylending and commerce. Suffered fr. persecution and expulsion in 14th c. Reestablished in late 18th c. and grew slowly. During WWII principal center of Jewish life and resistance, and after war many N. African Jews settled there. Jewish pop. 18,000 (1971).

Tourel, Jennie (1910–1973), mezzosoprano. Sang with Opera Compagnie, Paris, 1933, N.Y. Philharmonic, and Metropolitan Opera fr. 1944.

Touro, Judah (1775–1854), U.S. philanthropist, merchant; b. Newport, R.I. Settled in New Orleans 1801, severely wounded in Battle of New Orleans 1815. Took no interest in Jewish matters until late in life, then made numerous bequests to many Jewish institutions, incl. upkeep of synagogue and cemetery

Judah Touro

in Newport and Jewish poor in Ereẓ Israel.

Touroff, Nissan (1877–1953), educator; b. Russia, settled in Ereẓ Israel 1907 directing schools. Fr. 1919 in U.S. First dean of Hebrew Teachers College (now Hebrew College) in Boston, taught at Jewish Institute of Religion, N.Y. 1926–32. His writings pioneered concept of Zionism in education.

Tov Elem, see Bonfils.

Tower and Stockade, see Stockade and Watchtower.

Tower of Babel, see Babel, Tower of.

Tower of David, see David, Tower of.

Toz (Pol. initials for "Society for Safeguard of Health of Jewish Population"), Jewish welfare organization connected with OZE founded in Poland 1921. Combatted contagious diseases resulting fr. pogroms and WWI and offered treatment to mentally retarded and physically handicapped. Closed by German authorities 1942.

Trachonitis, province in Bashan, E. of the Jordan. Augustus awarded it to Herod and it remained with his heirs until Agrippa II (c. 100 C.E.). Annexed to province of Arabia 106.

Trachtenberg, Joshua (1904–1959), U.S. Reform rabbi; in Easton, Penn. 1930–51. Wrote *Jewish Magic and Superstition* and *The Devil and the Jews* on medieval conception of anti-Semitism.

°**Trajan (Traianus), Marcus Ulpius** (52/3–117), Roman emperor, ruled 98–117 C.E. Brutally suppressed Jewish uprisings in Cyrenaica, Alexandria, and Mesopotamia. His name appears in this connection in the Talmud and *aggadah.*

Tramer, Moritz (1882–1963), Swiss pioneer of child psychiatry. Founder and editor of first journal of child psychiatry 1934; founded Swiss Institute of Research and Information on Child Psychiatry 1951.

Trani, Joseph ben Moses (Maharit; 1568–1639), rabbi, halakhist. Head of Sephardi community in Safed. Settled in Constantinople 1604, establishing large yeshivah. Chief rabbi of Turkey. Wrote novellae, sermons, responsa, commentaries.

Trani, Moses ben Joseph (ha-Mabit; 1500–1580), Safed rabbi. One of four scholars ordained by Jacob Berab. Devoted himself to agricultural laws which obtained in Ereẓ Israel. Active as rabbi and *dayyan* for 54 years; succeeded Joseph Caro as spiritual head of Safed. Wrote moral and philosophical works and responsa.

Transjordan, area E. of Jordan R. extending fr. sources of Jordan nr. Mt. Hermon down to Dead Sea. Area N. of Yarmuk R. (Golan and Bashan) is regarded as separate entity, while the area E. of Dead Sea (Arabah) is included in this region. About a century before Israelite Exodus, settled by Ammonites, Moabites, and Edomites. Under Joshua, Gilead and part of Moab was allotted to tribes of Reuben, Gad, and half of Manasseh. In period of Judges these tribes were subjected to kings of Ammon and Moab. David conquered area down to Red Sea. Fr. 8th c. B.C.E. settled areas began to shrink. In Hellenistic period, new periods of prosperity began, lasting until Arab conquest. Under the Arabs area declined. For modern period, see Jordan.

Transmigration, see Gilgul.

Transnistria, area in Ukraine bet. Bug and Dniester R. Bet. 1939 and 1941, when Nazis entered area, two-thirds of 300,000 Jews fled. Subsequently became destination for deported Rumanian Jews. By 1942, 185.000 sent there. Those in S. were placed in concentration camps and almost all perished. Those in N. often established independent communities, and despite hardships many survived. Region liberated by Soviets 1944. Deportations resulted in 88,294 deaths. At least another 175,000 local Jewish inhabitants also perished.

Transvaal, province in S. Africa. Individual Jews in 1850s, *minyan* held in Pretoria 1876. Main stream of Jewish immigration fr. E. Europe after Rand gold discoveries 1886. Most settled in Johannesburg. Jewish pop. 76,440 (1971).

Transylvania, province now in Rumania. First Jews in 15th c. Sephardim fr. Turkey. By mid-19th c., 15,000 Jews in region, incl. Ashkenazim fr. Poland. Many cultural, social, educational organizations; Zionism flourished. Anti-Jewish activities rife bet. world wars, intensified after 1940 when area divided bet. Hungary and Rumania. In WWII the Jews in S. (40,000) able to maintain semblance of communal organization; but majority in N. (150,000) largely perished. After war mass emigration to Israel. Jewish pop. 6–7,000 (1970).

The "ḥevra kaddisha" minute book of the Cluj community, Transylvania, completed 1882.

Traube, Isidor (1860–1943), German physical chemist. Prof. in Berlin fr. 1901, Edinburgh fr. 1934. Related laws governing behavior of dilute solutions to gas laws. His theory of action of drugs had a positive effect on pharmacological research.

Traube, Ludwig (1818–1876), German pioneer in field of experimental pathology. One of first Jewish physicians to attain title of prof. in Germany. Introduced thermometer for regular checking of temperatures of all patients.

Traube, Moritz (1826–1894), German chemist, biologist. Discovered semipermeable membranes. Pioneer in field of osmosis.

Travel, Prayer for (Heb. *Tefillat ha-Derekh*), prayer recited before journey to protect traveler fr. dangers. Mentioned in Talmud. Additions made for sea and air travel.

Trebitsch, Abraham (Reuven Ḥayyat; b. 1760), Moravian historical author. Wrote Jewish and general history of period 1741–1801, important mainly for traditionalist evaluation of reforms of Joseph II.

Trebitsch, Arthur (1880–1927), Austrian writer; stepbrother of Siegfried Trebitsch. Convert to Christianity and notorious anti-Semite. Blamed defeat of central powers during WWI on Jewish machinations. Utilized Protocols to "prove" existence of Jewish conspiracy to dominate the world.

Trebitsch, Moses Loeb ben Wolf (18th c.), C. European Hebrew

Model of Treblinka concentration camp.

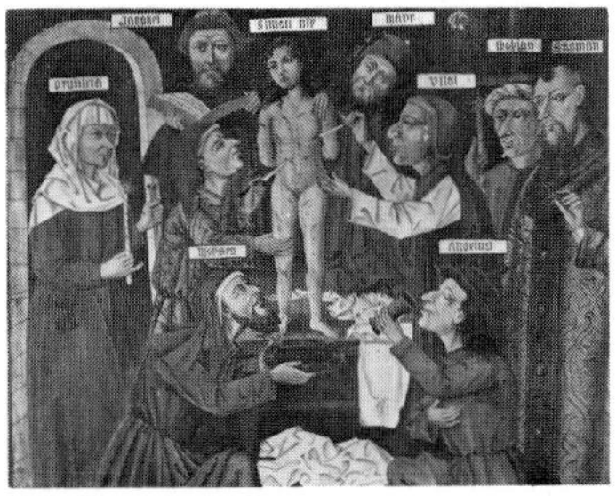

"The Martyrdom of Simon of Trent," artist unknown, South Tyrol, c. 1475.

scribe-illuminator. Pioneer figure in renaissance of Jewish ms. art in early 18th c.; in particular, illustrated Passover *Haggadot*.

Trebitsch, Siegfried (1869–1956), Austrian novelist, playwright, translator, traveler. Convert to Christianity. Works incl. psychological novels. His German translations of Shaw's plays paved way for Shaw's European vogue. Settled in Switzerland after 1938.

Trebitsch-Lincoln, Ignatius Timothy (1879–1943), international adventurer. His religious affiliations veered fr. Lutherism to Buddhism. Missionary in Canada, Liberal MP in England 1910, participant in Kapp *putsch* in Germany 1926, worked for Japanese intelligence in China fr. 1932.

Treblinka, one of main Nazi extermination centers during WWII; 62 mi. NE of Warsaw. There were two camps: Treblinka I, which began operating 1941, was forced-labor camp. Treblinka II was largest camp for extermination of Jews in Central Government. Operated July 1942–Oct. 1943 and contained 13 gas chambers. 750,000 Jews fr. over 30 countries perished there. In 1943 Germans cremated bodies and attempted to obliterate traces of camp. Various acts of resistance occurred and there was one attempt at mass escape in Aug. 1943.

Tremellius, John Immanuel (1510–1580), Italian Hebraist, apostate Jew. Taught Hebrew at Strasbourg, Cambridge, Heidelberg, Sedan. His Latin translations of Bible had profound impact on Hebrew studies in England in 17th c.

Trendl, see Dreidl.

Trent, city in N. Italy. Jews fr. 14th c. Community accused 1475 of murdering Christian child Simon. After lengthy judicial proceedings and several executions Simon was beatified and Jews expelled 1478. Libel served for intense anti-Semitic propaganda. Simon was de-beatified 1965.

Trenton, city in N.J., U.S. Jews fr. Germany settled late 1840s and established congregation 1858. E. European immigration started in late 1870s and congregations established after WWI. Jewish pop. 10,000 (1971).

Trepper, Leopold (present name **Leiba Domb**; 1904–), former Soviet intelligence agent. Active in European Communist parties before WWII. Sent by Soviet government 1938 to W. Europe and headed anti-German spy network known as "The Red Orchestra." Recalled to Moscow 1945, arrested, released 1955, and went to Poland. After long struggle, permitted to leave Poland 1973.

Treuenberg, Jacob Bassevi Von, see Bassevi, Jacob.

Treves, see Trier.

Treves, Emilio (1834–1916), Italian publisher. Joined Garibaldi 1859, and after peace founded Treves publishing company with his brother Giuseppe. Published works of many famous Italian writers.

Treves, Johanan ben Joseph (1490? –1557?), Italian rabbi, scholar. Because of his many wanderings throughout N. and C. Italy, known as one of "the peripatetic rabbis," Wrote commentary on festival prayer book acc. to Roman rite.

Treves, Johanan ben Mattathias (d. 1429), French rabbi. Chief rabbi of Paris 1385–94. After 1394 expulsion of Jews fr. France, settled in Italy. His rulings were much referred to by contemporary scholars.

Treves, Matthathias (c. 1325–c. 1385), French rabbi. Established large yeshivah in Paris and appointed rabbi by Charles V 1363. He and members of his family exempted from wearing Jewish badge decreed upon Jews of France.

Treviño de Sobremonte, Tomás (1592–1649), Marrano martyr in Mexico. Son of aristocratic Christian father and Judaizing New Christian mother; circumcised 1624 when imprisoned by Inquisition. Subsequent repentance feigned. Married Judaizer and was burnt at stake.

Tribes, Lost Ten, see Ten Lost Tribes.

Tribes, The Twelve, traditional division of Israel into 12 tribes: Reuben, Simeon, (Levi), Judah, Issachar, Zebulun, Benjamin, Dan, Naphtali, Gad, Asher, Ephraim, and Manasseh, descended fr. sons of Jacob. Bible describes how tribes gradually con-

Israel stamps of the Twelve Tribes.

quered Canaan, sometimes quarreled among themselves, and eventually became one nation (Joshua, Judges, I Sam.). Under David, Solomon, and their successors, tribal awareness weakened. Many scholars see stories as reflecting growing alliance of independent tribes, forced together for historical reasons.

Triennial Cycle, division whereby weekly Pentateuch readings on Sabbath are completed in 3-year cycle. Practice in Ereẓ Israel and Egypt as late as 1170 C.E., and in modern times reintroduced in Reform and some Conservative synagogues. Other synagogues, following Babylonian custom, complete reading in one year.

Trier (Treves), city in W. Germany. First evidence of Jewish community fr. 1066. Under authority of bishop until 1794. Suffered during First Crusade but soon returned. Economic position strengthened during 12th c.; communal organization led by so-called "Jewish bishop." Expelled 1418, returning 16th c. Civic equality finally achieved 1850. 210 Jews in 1939; community ended in WWII.

Trier, Walter (1890–1951), German cartoonist, illustrator. Known for witty and ironic drawings and illustrations of books by famous German authors. Left Germany before WWII. Contributed to publications in England and America.

Trieste, port in N. Italy. Jews fr. 11th c. During Middle Ages community dealt in loan banking and trade. Numbers grew in 18th-19th c. Ghetto abolished 1785 and monumental synagogue built 1912. In WWII community of 6,000 suffered fr. Fascist legislation and Nazi attacks. Jewish pop. 1,000 (1971).

Trietsch, Davis (1870–1935), German Zionist leader, writer. Advocated Jewish settlement in Cyprus and Sinai Peninsula, and later large-scale immigration to Ereẓ Israel. After WWI fought for "Zionist maximalism." Founded journals in Germany and wrote works on statistics.

Trilling, Lionel (1905–), U.S. author, critic. Prof. of English at Columbia Univ. fr. 1948. Used psychological methods in his criticism in order to gain new insights into subjects. Essays highly influential in U.S. intellectual circles. Also wrote fiction.

Triolet (Blick), Elsa (1903–), French novelist; b. Moscow; wife of French poet Louis Aragon. Influential communist in France. Works incl. *A Fine of 200 Francs* (Prix Goncourt). Translated many of Chekhov's plays and published study of poet Vladimir Mayakovski, her brother-in-law.

Tripoli, port in N. Lebanon. Jews fr. 7th c. Garrison of Jewish troops established there at beginning of Arab conquest to guard port during Byzantine attacks. Community existed during Crusade and Mamluk rule. In 16th c. Sephardi Jews settled there. Declined during 19th c. and ended by WWII.

Tripoli, port city of Libya. Few Jews in Roman, Byzantine, and Arab times. Jews settled there fr. Spain in 16th c., fr. Leghorn in 17th c., fr. Tunis in 18th c., and fr. Algiers in 19th c. Played important role in international trade. Economic and legal standing improved during Turkish rule 1835–1911, and full emancipation under Italian rule 1911–1943. Community dominant in Libyan Jewry. Jews controlled gold and silversmith crafts and textile trade. 20,000 Jews in 1948. Thereafter most emigrated to Israel. Few remained by 1970.

Trisker Dynasty, see Twersky.

Triwosch, Joseph Elijah (1855–1940), Lithuanian Hebrew writer, biblical commentator. His poems and short stories among earliest modern Hebrew fiction. His translations into Hebrew incl. *War and Peace* and *Anna Karenina.*

Troki, city in Lithuania. Site of extended struggle bet. Karaite and Rabbanite Jews (17th–20th c.). Karaites enjoyed political privileges and commercial success fr. 14th–17th c., but declined in latter 17th c. due to war, famine, and plague. Russian Jews there in 19th and 20th c. 300 Jews in 1939; liquidated 1941. Karaites numbered 5,700 in 1959.

Troki, Isaac ben Abraham (c. 1533–c. 1594), Russian Karaite scholar; best known for his apologetic *Ḥizzuk Emunah,* the Latin version of which made his arguments accessible to non-Jewish anti-clerical writers in 18th c. (incl. Voltaire). Some of his hymns are in official Karaite prayer-book.

Tropplowitz, Joseph, see Ha-Efrati, Joseph.

Trotsky (Bronstein), Lev Davidovich (1879–1940), Russian revolutionary, Soviet and Communist leader. Prominent in 1905 and 1917 revolutions, became people's commissar for foreign affairs 1917, military affairs and transport 1918. Position declined after Lenin's death 1924. Stalin had him expelled fr. Communist Party 1927 and exiled 1928. Assassinated in Mexico. On Jewish question believed in assimilation.

Lev Trotsky (center, foreground) in Red Square, Moscow.

Troyes, town in C. France. Jewish community fr. early 11th c. Center of medieval Jewish scholarship; birthplace of Rashi, who was rabbi there and founded famous school c. 1070. Blood libel 1288, expulsion 1322. Small community fr. late 19th c. 400 Jews in 1970.

Trumpeldor, Joseph (1880–1920), pioneer, soldier, Zionist. Studied dentistry but volunteered for Russian army, losing arm in fighting at Port Arthur 1904–05. One of the few Jewish officers in Czarist army. Went to Ereẓ Israel 1912, attempting unsuccessfully to establish cooperative settlements. During WWI formed Zion Mule Corps in Egypt and later, in London, helped Jabotinsky form Jewish Legion. Returned to Russia 1917 and established He-Ḥalutz movement. Went to Ereẓ Israel 1919, organized defense of Jewish settlements in Upper Galilee, and was killed in defense of Tel Ḥai 1920. Became symbol of pioneering and armed defense in Ereẓ Israel.

Joseph Trumpeldor as an officer in the Russian Army.

Trunk, Israel Joshua (1820–1893), Polish rabbi; early supporter of Ḥibbat Zion. Rabbi of Kutno 1861–93. Among rabbis who permitted agricultural work in Ereẓ Israel during sabbatical year. Wrote halakhic works.

Trunk, Yeḥiel Yeshaia (1887–1961), Yiddish essayist, writer in Poland. Wrote short stories, popular novels, essays, studies on Yiddish literature, and memoirs on Poland.

Tschlenow, Jehiel (1863–1918), Russian Zionist leader, physician. Active in Moscow Ḥibbat Zion group, later joined Zionist Organization, but strongly opposed Uganda scheme. At Helsingfors Conference 1906 advocated large-scale purchase of land in Ereẓ Israel. Fr. 1915 mostly in W. Europe and participated in negotiations leading to Balfour Declaration.

Jehiel Tschlenow

Tsfassman, Alexander Naumovich (1906–1971), Soviet jazz pianist, composer. Headed large jazz orchestra of Radio Moscow 1939–46. Composed instrumental jazz music and music for choir, theater, and films.

Tshemeriski (Chemeriski), Alexander (Solomon; 1880–193?), leader of Russian Bund and later of Yevsektsiya. Played important role in Lodz in 1905 revolution. Turned to Bolshevism 1919, became secretary of central bureau of Yevsektsiya. Arrested in mid-1930s; apparently d. in prison.

Tsur (Tchernowitz), Jacob (1906–), Israel diplomat, Zionist leader; son of Samuel Tchernowitz; b. Vilna, settled in Ereẓ Israel 1921. First Israel minister to Argentina, Uruguay, Paraguay, Chile 1949–53. Ambassador to France 1953–59. Chairman of board of directors of Jewish National Fund and former chairman of Zionist General Council. His books include memoirs.

Tuat, oasis complex in Algerian Sahara. Traditions report arrival of first Jews in 5 C.E. Jews largely landowners, farmers, warriors. Massacred

Glazed ceramic Tu bi-Shevat plate, Austria, 19th cent.

1492. Tombs of victims still place of pilgrimage for inhabitants of Tuat-Gurara.

Tubal-Cain, son of Lamech. "Forged implements of copper and iron" (Gen. 4:22).

Tu be-Av, see Av, The Fifteenth of.

Tu bi-Shevat (Heb. Shevat 15), festival of New Year for Trees; regarded as minor or semi-holiday for liturgical purposes. In Ashkenazi communities it was customary to eat 15 types of fruit on this day. Special preference was given to fruit grown in Ereẓ Israel (e.g. carob). Sephardim compiled elaborate liturgy. In Israel celebrated as arbor day with tree-planting ceremonies by school children.

Tuchman, Barbara Wertheim (1912–), U.S. historian; daughter of Maurice Wertheim and granddaughter of Henry Morgenthau Sr. Covered Spanish Civil War; editor Far Eastern Desk, Office of War Information, 1943–45. Won Pulitzer Prizes for *The Guns of August* (1962) and *Stilwell and the American Experience in China* (1972).

Tucholsky, Kurt (1890–1935), German satirist, journalist. His WWI experiences made him ardent pacifist and socialist. Abandoned Judaism 1911. Settled in Sweden 1929. Committed suicide.

Tucker, Sophie (1884–1966), U.S. vaudeville artist; known as "the Last of the Red Hot Mamas." Presented

Sophie Tucker

her act in English and Yiddish. Best-known songs "My Yiddishe Momma" and "Some of These Days." Established Sophie Tucker Foundation which distributed millions of dollars to various charities.

Tucson, city in Ariz., U.S. First Jewish settlers 1863. First Jewish community organization Hebrew Benevolent Society founded 1910. Jewish pop. 7,000 (1971).

Tudela, city in N. Spain; most ancient Jewish community of Navarre. Jews prospered under early Christian rule in 12th c. but heavy taxation levied in 13th c. In 14th c. community suffered fr. riots, war, economic depression. Continued to decline in 15th c. and many abandoned Judaism. Expelled 1498.

Tugendhold, Jacob (1794–1871), author, early adherent of Galician Haskalah. Head of government-sponsored rabbinical seminary in Warsaw. Wrote Polish books and translated fr. Hebrew into Polish. His brother **Wolf** (1796–1864), censor of Hebrew books and teacher in Vilna.

Tulchin, city in Ukrainian SSR. Jewish community destroyed in Chmielnicki massacre 1648; reestablished in 18th c. Numbered 10,000 by 1897. Suffered fr. pogroms during Ukrainian civil war. 3,000 Jews in 1941 transferred to camp of Peczara. 2,500 Jews in 1959.

Tūl Karm, Arab town in C. Ereẓ Israel. Samaritans constituted majority of pop. in Middle Ages. Under Jordan rule 1948–67. 10,157 inhabitants in 1967, almost all Muslim Arabs.

Tumarkin, Igael (1933–), Israel painter, sculptor, stage-designer. Themes concerned with war, peace, and injustice, expressed in bold, original forms on abstract background. Some of his monuments in cities and settlements in Israel.

Tumin, Melvin Marvin (1919–), U.S. sociologist. Prof. at Princeton fr. 1947. Specialized in race and intercultural relations.

Tunisia, country in N. Africa. Jews probably lived in Punic Carthage and many prosperous communities existed there in Roman times. Flourished until the Arab persecutions of 11th–12th c. Many Jews then accepted Islam. Provided refuge for Spanish Jews in 15th c. and community fr. Leghorn established there in 17th c. During 19th c. discriminatory legislation largely modified, esp. after it became French protectorate 1881. Jews suffered from Vichy and German attacks during WWII

Tunisian Jewish woman, 19th cent.

and from "Tunisification" after 1948. Most left, mainly to Israel and France, and by 1971 only 8,000 remained.

Tunkel, Joseph (pseud. **"Der Tunkeler"**; 1881–1949), Yiddish humorist, cartoonist. After 1910 edited humorous supplement to Yiddish daily *Der Moment* in Warsaw. After 1941 wrote for New York Yiddish daily *Forward*. Author of popular books, plays, sketches.

Tur, see Jacob ben Asher.

Tureck, Rosalyn (1914–), pianist. Taught at Juilliard School of Music 1943–53, Columbia Univ. 1953–55, and Regent's Prof. at Univ. of California 1966. Founded Tureck Bach Players 1959.

Turin (Torino), city in NE Italy. Jews there in 4th c., but no further evidence of settlement until 1420s. Jewish moneylending permitted longer than elsewhere in Italy. As late as 1729 Jews forbidden to own real estate and ghetto existed until 1848. 4,000 Jews in 1931. During Holocaust 875 deported. 2,000 Jews in 1970

Turkey, republic in Asia Minor. For early period, see Ottoman Empire. Jews showed their patriotism in new republic after 1923, but remained second-class citizens. Their economic position declined, they suffered from discriminatory capital tax of 1942, and were subjected to occasional anti-Semitic attacks after 1948. Largely as a result of emigration to Israel community decreased fr. 81,454 in 1927 to 37,000 in 1971. Chief rabbinate maintained rabbinical seminary and there were Jewish schools. Two largest communities are Istanbul and Izmir and 95–97% of Jewish pop. is Sephardi with c.200 Karaite families.

Turkow, family originally fr. Poland. **Zygmunt** (1896–1970), Yiddish actor, toured widely, went to Brazil after WWII, settled in Israel 1952. **Jonas** (1898–) played in Yiddish theater in Poland; together with his wife in charge of entertainment in Warsaw ghetto. Settled in Israel 1966. **Mark** (1904–), Yiddish journalist in Poland. Went to Buenos Aires 1930, becoming director of HIAS. Latin American representative of World Jewish Congress 1954. **Itzḥak** (1906–1970) appeared on Yiddish stage in Poland until 1957 when he settled in Israel.

Turóczi-Trostler, József (1888–1962) Hungarian scholar, critic, translator. Member of Hungarian Parliament fr. 1945; prof. of German literature at Budapest Univ. fr. 1947.

Tur-Sinai, Naphtali Herz (Harry Torczyner; 1886–1973), Hebrew philologist, Bible scholar; b. Lemberg, taught at Vienna and Berlin,

Jewish communities in Tunisia. Bold face names indicate those still in existence, 1971.

Jewish communities in Turkey, 1930. Boldface names indicate those still in existence, 1970.

settled in Jerusalem 1933. Prof. of Hebrew at Heb. Univ.; pres of Academy of Hebrew Language fr. its founding in 1953. Edited periodical *Leshonenu* 1934–54. Edited and completed Eliezer Ben Yehuda's dictionary (fr. vol. 10). Contributed to the Jewish translation of Bible into German 1935–37. Wrote commentary on Job and published the Lachish letters.

Tuscany, region in C. Italy. Jewish community in Roman times. After 13th c. Jews engaged in moneylending. In 16th c. region provided refuge for Marranos and Jews fr. Papal states. Jews granted equality by French 1798 and by Sardinians 1859. In 19th c. economic opportunities in region attracted Jews. In 1969 communities in Florence, Pisa, Leghorn, Siena.

Tuwim, Julian (1894–1953), Polish poet. Subject to attacks by Polish nationalists prior to WWII. In France, S. America, and U.S. during WWII. Returned to Poland after war. A great revolutionary innovator in Polish verse. One of his poems became anthem of Polish resistance movement.

Twersky, ḥasidic dynasty in the Ukraine. Founded by **Menahem Nahum ben Ẓevi** of Chernobyl (1730–1787), disciple of Dov Baer of Mezhirech, who was among first to propagate Ḥasidism. His son **Mordecai of Chernobyl** (1770–1837), maintained opulent "court" which benefited from his introduction of *ma'amadot,* a financial contribution paid by every ḥasid. Widely revered, wrote *Likkutei Torah* on the Bible, and sermons. His eight sons settled in different places in the Ukraine and all became ḥasidic leaders. **Aaron** (1787–1872), who remained in Chernobyl. Confident of his spiritual abilities and holiness, he was convinced that the Messiah would come in his lifetime. **Abraham** (1806–1889), also known as the *maggid* of Trisk. A high-handed leader of his ḥasidim (who included distinguished men and *ẓaddikim*), he wielded great influence. His sermons are a mixture of ḥasidic teachings and Kabbalah, spiced with numerology and *gematria.* **David** (1808–1882), maintained an opulent court at Talnoye. Sat on silver throne with words "David King of Israel lives for ever" inscribed in gold. For this the Russian authorities kept him under arrest for a long time. A lover of singing and music, his teaching was spiced with secular references and parables. After the Russian Revolution their descendants settled in Poland, U.S., and Erez Israel.

Twersky, Isadore (1930–), U.S. scholar. Prof. of Hebrew language and philosophy, chairman Dept. of Near Eastern Languages, Harvard. Works inc. *Rabad of Posquières.*

Twersky, Yoḥanan (1900–1967), Hebrew novelist; b. Ukraine, in U.S. fr. 1926. Taught at Hebrew College in Boston 1927–47. Settled in Ereẓ Israel 1947. Wrote historic novels which centered around Jewish and non-Jewish heroes.

Tykocin, village in NE Poland. Jewish settlement fr. 1522. Important community in 17th, 18th c. Composed mainly of small traders and craftsmen. Small community destroyed in Holocaust.

Tynyanov, Yuri Nikolayevich (1894–1943), Soviet Russian novelist, literary theoretician; brilliant literary scholar and one of foremost exponents of Formalism, school of literary criticism fashionable in 1920s.

Tyre, city in Lebanon. Hiram of Tyre supplied Solomon with wood and labor for the temple (I Kings 5). Fr. 63 B.C.E. under Roman rule. In Middle Ages had large and rich Jewish community and was center of religious scholars. Community ceased to exist after Mamluk conquest 1291.

Tyre, Ladder of, steep road cut in steps which connected territory of Acre with that of Tyre; now nr. Rosh ha-Nikrah on Israel-Lebanon frontier. Name has been revived as appellation of regional council in NW Galilee.

Tyre of the Tobiads, fortress in Transjordan, built by Hyrcanus, the last of the Tobiad rulers of Peraea, probably between 187 and 175 B.C.E. Identified with ruins W. of Amman. Site excavated 1961.

Tyrnau, Isaac (14th c.), Austrian rabbi, compiler of popular book of *minhagim* containing customs and codes of conduct for whole year. Book aimed to repair ignorance caused by dispersions after Black Death.

Tyrol, autonomous province in W. Austria. Jews fr. 13th c. but Black Death and various persecutions kept population small. 130 Jews in 1914. Suffered persecution under Nazis and community disappeared. After WWII, 11 families reestablished community in Innsbruck.

Tzahal, see Israel Defense Forces.

Tristan Tzara, drawing by Fernand Léger, 1948.

Tzara, Tristan (originally **Sami Rosenstein;** 1896–1963), Rumanian, French poet. Cofounder of the Dada movement and editor of its official organ. Exerted powerful influence on younger generation. Active in French underground during WWII.

Tzelniker, Meir (1896–), Yiddish actor; b. Russia, went to England and headed Yiddish theater in Grand Palais, Whitechapel, London, fr. 1939.

Tzeva Haganah le-Israel, see Israel Defense Forces.

Initial letter "U" for "usquequo" in the question "Usquequo, Domine, oblivisceris me in finem? " from the "St. Albans Psalter," England, 12th cent.

Uceda, Samuel ben Isaac (1540–?), talmudist, preacher, kabbalist in Safed, where he founded great yeshivah 1580. His commentaries on Bible and Mishnah drew extensively on his own large library of mss.

Uganda Scheme, name commonly given to proposal made by British government to Zionist Organization to establish autonomous Jewish colony in British East Africa (now Kenya). Officially offered to Herzl by British Colonial Secretary Joseph Chamberlain in 1903, opposed strongly in Sixth Zionist Congress (August 1903) when introduced by Herzl, and finally rejected after Herzl's death, at Seventh Congress (1905).

Ugarit, ancient city in Syria; excavated fr. 1929; modern Ras Shamra. Commercial center in 2nd millennium B.C.E. until 12th c. B.C.E. when destroyed. Excavated palace archives have provided legal and literary texts. Some clay tablets are inscribed in Akkadian cuneiform while others are in unique cuneiform alphabet script in a Semitic language resembling Hebrew. These documents had profound effect on biblical studies. The cultic documents have provided striking parallels to ancient Hebrew poetry and epic prose.

Engraving for the tractate "Ukẓin" from Hebrew-Latin Mishnah, Amsterdam, 1700-04.

Ugaritic, NW Semitic language in N. Syria during 2nd millennium B.C.E. Documents in this tongue discovered at Ugarit. Many resemblances to Hebrew and Phoenician.

Uhersky Brod (in rabbinical literature **Broda**), town in Czechoslovakia. Important community fr. 13th c., developed rapidly after 17th c. Community one of most Orthodox in Moravia. During WWII, center of concentration of Jews from SE Moravia before deportation. Postwar community ended 1949.

U.J.A., see United Jewish Appeal.

Uj Kelet (Hung. "New East"), Zionist newspaper in Hungarian language. Appeared in Transylvania as weekly 1918, daily 1920. Banned by Fascist regime in Hungary 1940, reappeared in Tel Aviv 1948.

Ujvári, Peter (1869–1931), Hungarian author, journalist. His several novels and attempts to establish a Jewish newspaper failed. His only successful enterprise was a Hungarian-Jewish encyclopedia 1929.

Ukba (Ukva), Mar (3rd c.), Babylonian *amora,* exilarch. He and his court had close ties with Palestinian scholars, by whom he was highly respected. Renowned for his charity.

Ukba (Ukva), Mar (9th-10th c.), exilarch. Twice banished fr. Baghdad as result of his violent controversy with *rosh yeshivah* of Pumbedita over financial issues.

Ukhmani, Azriel (1907–), Hebrew writer, editor; b. Galicia, settled in Ereẓ Israel 1932. On staff of daily *Al ha-Mishmar* and literary editor of Sifriat Po'alim publishing house fr. 1953. Published articles and essays on literary topics.

Ukraine, republic in USSR. Jewish settlement dates in some areas fr. period of Khazars, in others fr. 12th c. In 14th, 15th c. refugees fr. persecution in west settled there. Main immigration began in 16th c., when Jews played important role in *arenda* business. When most of region became part of Pale of Settlement in 19th c., Jews (mostly urban dwellers) continued to play dynamic role in economy, esp. in production of alcoholic beverages. Focus of religious and social ferment; Shabbateanism, Frankism, and Ḥasidism all spread, and region was birthplace of Ḥibbat Zion, Bilu, Am Olam movements. This was largely result of popular Ukrainian tradition of anti-Semitism, dating back to Chmielnicki massacres of 1648–9 and revived in pogroms of 1881–2. Independent Ukrainian government made concessions in 1918, but pogroms of 1919–20, wholehearted Ukrainian collaboration in Holocaust, and persecutions of 1960s continued Ukrainian tradition. 1,927,268 Jews in 1897; 1,532,827 in 1939, and 770,000 in 1970.

Ukẓin (Heb. "Stalks"), 12th and last tractate in Mishnah order of *Toharot,* with no *gemara.* Deals with problems of ritual impurity affecting roots, stalks, husks, shells, kernels, etc.

Ulla I (Ulla ben Ishmael in Jerusalem Talmud; 3rd c.), Palestinian *amora,* known for strict interpretation of religious laws. Greatly respected in both Ereẓ Israel and Babylonia.

Ullendorf, Edward (1920–), British linguist. Prof. at Manchester 1959, London 1964. Specialized in languages of Ethiopia and Eritrea.

Ullmann, Adolph (1857–1925), Hungarian baron, economist, member of Hungarian Upper House. After 1909 chief executive of General Hungarian Credit Bank. Played decisive role in financial activities of Hungarian government.

Ullmann, Salomon (1806–1865), French rabbi. *Grand rabbin* of France 1853. Organized Central

Conference of *Grands Rabbins* of France (Paris 1856), first of its kind.

Ullstein, family of German publishers whose newspaper, magazine empire were once largest in world. Founded by **Leopold** (1826–1899), progressive member of Berlin city council, whose newspaper *Deutsche Union* reached unprecedented circulation of 40,000. His five sons greatly expanded publishing empire, extending activities to books, magazines. Company bought at nominal price by Nazi-backed consortium. After WWII **Rudolf** (1873–1964) was appointed chairman of reconstituted Ullstein consortium by the Americans. In 1960 controlling interest in group sold to Axel Springer.

Ulm, city in W. Germany. Jewish settlement before 13th c.; community grew during 14th c. Main occupation moneylending. Persecution in Black Death and expulsion in 15th c. Revived in 19th c., numbering 162 before WWII, 25 in 1968.

Ulpan, center for intensive study by adults, esp. of Hebrew by newcomers to Israel.

Uman, city in Ukrainian SSR. Community suffered massacres in 18th c., notably 1788, anniversary of which (Tammuz 5) was observed as special fast. Known for its *klezmerim* (musicians). One of first centers of Haskalah in Ukraine. Persecutions 1917 and pogroms 1919. Community numbered 22,179 in 1926. Exterminated by Nazis in WWII. 1,000 Jews in late 1960s.

Uncleanness, Ritual, see Purity and Impurity, Ritual.

U-Netanneh Tokef (Heb.), *piyyut* recited in Additional Service on Rosh Ha-Shanah and Day of Atonement. Written by Kalonymus b. Meshullam Kalonymus (11th c.), it has become one of most solemn parts of High Holy Days liturgy in traditional Ashkenazi, Polish, and Italian rites.

Ungar, Benjamin (1907–), cantor; b. Galicia. Chief *ḥazzan* of Tel Aviv Great Synagogue. Chairman of Association of Cantors of Israel.

Ungar, Joel of Rechnitz (Riba; 1800–1885), Hungarian rabbi. Administered large yeshivah in Paks. Opposed to schism of Hungarian Jewry, and when it took place he withdrew fr. national Jewish affairs. Wrote responsa on *Shulḥan Arukh.*

Unger, Irwin (1927–), U.S. historian. Prof. of history at New York Univ. Won Pulitzer Prize for *The Greenback Era* on American finance, 1865–79.

Ungvár, see Uzhgorod.

Union, Oesterreichisch-Israelitische (later **Union Oesterreichischer Juden**), association representing Jews of Austrian Empire and standing for implementation of their equal rights; founded 1882. Its legal office acted against calumnies and legal discrimination. Ceased to exist after 1938 *Anschluss.*

Union County, county in N.J., U.S. First known Jewish settlers 1835. First congregation B'nai Israel, Elizabeth, 1882. Jews active in Democratic Party politics and held high municipal and county offices. Jewish pop. 35,000 (1970) with major communities in Elizabeth, Plainfield, Linden, Westfield, Summit, Rahway.

Union Générale des Israélites de France (UGIF), official body created 1941 by Vichy government to represent French Jewry during German occupation. Although forced to undertake unpleasant tasks, it never became collaborationist body. Intervened on behalf of French Jewry and became cover for large network of underground activities.

Union of American Hebrew Congregations (U.A.H.C.), association of approximately 750 Reform and Liberal congregations of U.S. and Canada; founded 1873 as first national cooperative organization of Jewish congregations. Prime initiator and first head was I.M. Wise. Headquarters in New York.

Union of Orthodox Jewish Congregations of America (U.O.J.C.A.), largest organization of Orthodox synagogues in U.S.; founded 1898. 897 affiliated synagogue members and services additional 745 congregations (1968). Best known for its *kashrut* supervision.

Union of Orthodox Rabbis of the United States and Canada (Agudath Harabbonim), oldest organization of Orthodox rabbis in U.S.; founded 1902. Members instrumental in setting up most early day schools in U.S. Founded Va'ad Haẓala during WWII for rescue of leading Orthodox personalities.

Union of Sephardic Congregations, U.S. Sephardi organization founded 1929. Moving force in its establishment was David de Sola Pool. Services Sephardi congregations.

Union of the Russian People (Soyuz Russkogo Naroda), right-wing political movement, fanatically anti-Semitic, in czarist Russia; founded 1905. Its virulent propaganda campaign and its "Black Hundreds" organization found support within Pale of Settlement among lower middle classes. Members influential in highest government circles and patronized by Nicholas II.

United Hias Service (United Hebrew Sheltering and Immigrant Aid Society), Jewish immigrant and refugee service, formed in New York 1909 to respond to growing needs of Jewish immigrants fr. E. Europe. Opened offices in Far East and E. Europe. Merged throughout years with various other organizations. Subsequently dissolved such mergers during WWII. Merged 1954 with United Service for New Americans and J.D.C. Migration Dept. Most of its budget from U.J.A.

United Israel Appeal, see Keren Hayesod.

United Jewish Appeal (U.J.A.), U.S. organization founded 1939 with American Jewish Joint Distribution Committee, and United Palestine Appeal as principal partners and National Refugee Service as a beneficiary. Funds distributed in recent years among United Israel Appeal as well as United Service for New Americans, N.Y. Association for New Americans, and United HIAS Service. Over 200 Jewish federations

Moshe Dayan addressing the National Conference of the United Jewish Appeal, New York, 1971.

and welfare funds provided over 95% of its income ($2,250,000,000 since 1948).

United Jewish Socialist Workers' Party (S.S. and J.S.; abbr. **Fareynigte**), group in revolutionary Russia and interwar Poland; founded 1917 through union of territorialists and autonomists. Central element of program was "national personal autonomy," For brief period party was influential, particularly in Ukraine. Joined Communist party of Russia 1921. In Poland, dissolved by government 1937.

United Restitution Organization (URO), legal aid society founded 1948 for claimants outside Germany for restitution and compensation. Sponsored by British Foreign Office. Clients numbered 250,000, with branches in 15 countries. By 1967 it had recovered over $500 million for its clients.

United States of America, N. American republic. Jewish settlement dates fr. arrival of 23 Jewish refugees in Dutch New Amsterdam fr. Brazil 1654. By 1776 2,500 Jews in country. After 1729 C. and E. European Jews predominated. British passed naturalization law for Jews 1740, enabling them to trade anywhere in empire. During Revolution, most Jews were Whigs and supported Continental cause. Northwest Ordinance 1787 guaranteed Jews equality in all new states. U.S. constitution guaranteed equality on Federal level. However, by 1820, true equality in only 7 of original 13 states. Jewish pop. grew from 6,000 (1826) to 150,000 (1860), largely result of immigration, esp. from German-speaking lands. Characteristic expression of German Jewry in U.S. was Reform Judaism. During this period, Jewish communal organization seldom reached above local level. During Civil War, Jews generally sided with their respective regions. 7,000 Jews served in Northern armies and 3,000 in South. After War period, Jews played important role in economic development of South. Spurred on by great Jewish immigration from E. Europe, Jewish pop. grew to 4,500,000 by 1925. Jewish immigrants clustered in distinct urban neighborhoods, often under sweatshop conditions in ready-made clothing industry. Jewish trade union movement developed and by 1920 250,000 Jews in Jewish unions. These fostered secularist Yiddish environment. 250,000 Jews served in U.S. armed forces in WWI. After war Jews made targets of anti-Semitic campaigns (Henry Ford, Ku Klux Klan, etc.). Immigration Act of 1924 cut immigration drastically. With Depression economic discrimination became sharper. Many German intellectuals, teachers, arrived in 1930s. During WWII 550,000 Jews served in Armed Forces. After WWII U.S. Jewry became overwhelmingly pro-Zionist and anti-Semitism all but disappeared. Jewish pop. increased only slightly. U.S. Jewry predominantly metropolitan group. After 1945 new occupational pattern became evident, with Jews entering professions and academic positions in large numbers. With decline of European Jewry, U.S. Jewry – comprising half of world Jewry – became dominating world community outside Israel. Post-war challenges came from evidence of assimilating tendencies, increased intermarriage, and inadequate Jewish education. Jewish pop. 6,115,320 (1972).

United Synagogue, association of Ashkenazi congregations in London. Originally formed by Great Synagogue, Duke's Place, and four other constituent synagogues, established by Act of Parliament 1870. Principal supporter of British chief rabbinate and London *bet din*. By 1971, 23 constituent synagogues, 23 district synagogues, and 35 affiliated congregations; c. 40,000 families (half Jewish pop. of Greater London).

United Synagogue of America, association of Conservative synagogues in U.S. and Canada; founded by Solomon Schechter 1913. Membership of over 800 congregations by 1971. Produced English and Hebrew textbooks, sponsored system of Conservative day schools, and stimulated development of adult education courses. Organized World Council of Synagogues 1957.

Unna, Paul Gerson (1850–1929), German dermatologist. Prof. at Univ. of Hamburg fr. 1919. Pioneer in applying biological and physical sciences to dermatology. Discovered Ducrey-Unna bacillus.

UNRRA (United Nations Relief and Rehabilitation Administration), international organization (1943–47) founded to give economic and social aid to countries under Nazi occupation during WWII. About a quarter (220,000) of the displaced persons under UNRRA care in the summer of 1946 were Jews. Most of these later reached Israel. H. Lehman was its first director general.

UNRWA (United Nations Relief and Works Agency), UN agency which began work 1950 to provide essential services to Arab refugees fr. Ereẓ Israel living in Jordan, Gaza Strip, Lebanon, and Syria. Since 1967 it received cooperation fr. Israel govt. in areas occupied during Six-Day War. Income mainly through voluntary contributions from governments.

UNSCOP, U.N. Special Committee on Palestine, representing 11 governments, appointed April 1947.

United Synagogue congregations in Greater London. Constituent synagogues in boldface.

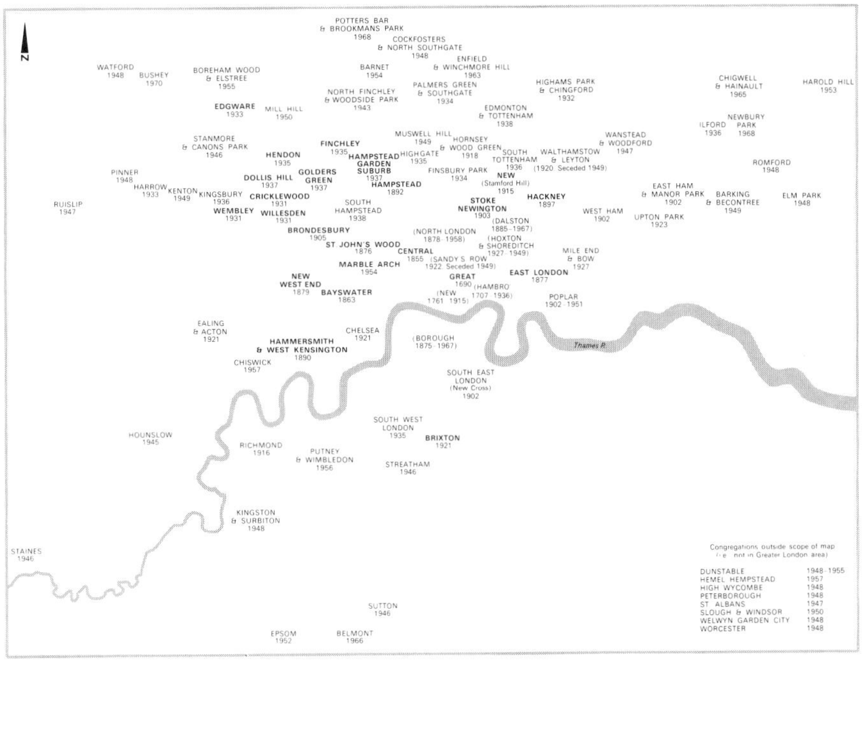

Isser Yehuda Unterman

The Ziggurat of Ur built by Ur-Nammu, c. 2250–2233 B.C.E.

Leon Uris

"Tiergarten, Berlin" by Lesser Ury, 1922.

Majority of members recommended partition of Ereẓ Israel, which was approved by U.N. General Assembly on Nov. 29, 1947.

Unterman, Isser Yehuda (1886–), rabbi; b. Belorussia. Served as rabbi in various Lithuanian communities and after WWI helped in reconstruction of Lithuanian yeshivot. Rabbi of Liverpool fr. 1924. Elected chief rabbi of Tel Aviv-Jaffa 1946, Ashkenazi chief rabbi of Israel 1964–72.

Untermeyer, Louis (1885–), U.S. poet, author, editor, translator. Published many volumes of prose and verse, short stories, travel books, parodies, essays, and critical anthologies.

Untermyer, Samuel (1858–1940), U.S. lawyer, became known as counsel for Pujo Committee 1912 which investigated "money trust." Contributed to drafting and passage of Federal Reserve Act, Federal Trade Commission Act, and Clayton Anti-Trust Act. Active in Jewish affairs.

Ur (or **Ur of the Chaldeans**), ancient city on Euphrates in Lower Mesopotamia; one of largest cities in Babylonia. Home of Abraham and starting point of his long trek toward Haran and Canaan.

Urbach, Ephraim Elimelech (1912–), Israel talmudic scholar; b. Poland, settled in Ereẓ Israel 1938. Prof. of Talmud at Heb. Univ. Studies cover most branches of research in Talmud and rabbinical literature. His *Ba'alei ha-Tosafot* (for which he was awarded the Israel Prize) deals with tosafists and their era; *Ḥazal* with rabbinic theology.

Urfa, see Edessa.

Uriah, a Hittite; one of David's "heroes." David took Uriah's wife Bath-Sheba, and engineered Uriah's death. For this David was rebuked by the prophet Nathan (II Sam. 11).

Uri (Phoebus) ben Aaron ha-Levi (Uri Witzenhausen; 1625–1715), Hebrew printer in Amsterdam. Published first Yiddish translation of Bible by Jekuthiel Blitz, *Bava Bukh,* and first Yiddish newspaper.

Uri ben Phinehas of Strelisk, see Strelisk, Uri ben Phinehas of.

Uriel, one of four angels of the Presence. According to *Midrash Rabbah,* one of four angels around God's throne.

Urim and Thummim, priestly device for obtaining oracles. By these means priest inquired will of God. Apparently a kind of lot kept in high priest's breastpiece.

Uris, Leon (1924–), U.S. novelist. His best-selling novels incl. *Exodus,* depicting struggle for establishment of State of Israel, and *Mila 18,* dealing with Warsaw Ghetto Revolt; also *Battle Cry, Topaz, QB VII.*

Uruguay, S. American republic. 1,700 Jews in 1918, 75% of them Sephardim; 50,000 in 1971, 70% of E. European origin, nearly all in Montevideo. Active communal and Zionist life.

Ury, Lesser (1861–1931), German painter. Achieved fame late in life, esp. through pastels. Some of his paintings of Jewish inspiration.

U.S.A., see United States.

Usha, ancient town in Lower Galilee. In 140 C.E., at end of period of persecution following suppression of Bar-Kokhba's revolt, surviving scholars gathered there, reestablished Sanhedrin, and instituted regulations known as "Enactments of Usha." Name given to modern kibbutz.

Ushpizin (Aram. "guests"), seven guests (Abraham, Isaac, Jacob, Moses, Aaron, Joseph, David) who, one a day, acc. to legend, visit *sukkah* on successive nights of Feast of Tabernacles.

'Usifiyyā (Isfiya), Druze and Arab village on Mt. Carmel, Israel. Site of 6th c. synagogue. Rapid development since 1947. Major Israel Druze center. Pop. 4,260 (1971).

Usque, Abraham (16th c.), Marrano printer. Refugee fr. Inquisition who settled in Ferrara and published Jewish liturgies in vernacular for other Marranos reverting to Judaism. Associated with "Ferrara Bible" translation. Printing activities halted by Counter-Reformation.

Usque, Samuel (16th c.), Marrano historian; left Spain 1492. Author of *Consolaçam as tribulaçoens de Israel,* in Portuguese, a review of Jewish history to persuade Marranos to return to Judaism.

Usque, Solomon (c. 1530–c. 1596), Portuguese poet of Marrano descent; probably son of Abraham Usque; lived mostly in Italy, later in Turkey. Helped write *Esther,* first Jewish drama in vernacular. As "Salusque Lusitano" published admired Spanish translation of some of Petrarch's sonnets.

Ussishkin, Abraham Menaḥem Mendel (1863–1941), Zionist leader; b. Russia. Secretary of Ḥovevei Zion and member of Benei Moshe society. In one of his pamphlets laid foundations for "synthetic Zionism" which later dominated Zionist movement. Led opposition to Uganda Scheme 1903. On one of his visits to Ereẓ Israel

Menaḥem Mendel Ussishkin (right) with Albert Einstein, Jerusalem, 1923.

(1903) helped found Teachers' Association. Represented Russian Jewry at Paris Peace Conference. Settled in Jerusalem 1919. Member of Zionist Executive, and fr. 1923 headed Jewish National Fund and was responsible for purchasing wide tracts of land, esp. in Jezreel Plain. One of key figures in Jewish community of the country.

U.S.S.R., see Russia.

Utah, U.S. state. First Jewish community 1854. Three Jewish immigrations: early Germans 1864–74, E. Europeans 1890–1920s, refugees of Nazi period. Jewish pop. 1,900 (1971).

Utitz, Emil (1883–1956), philosopher. Prof. at Halle and Prague. Inmate of Theresienstadt 1942–45; wrote on psychology of concentration camp. Main fields aesthetics and philosophy of man and culture.

Utkin, Joseph Pavlovich (1903–1944), Soviet Russian poet. His *Povest o ryzhem Motele* is long poem, unique in mixture of Russian and Yiddish, which remains wistful monument to great expectations awakened among pauperized Russian Jews by Bolshevik Revolution. D. in plane crash.

Uzbekistan, Soviet republic. Jews of Bukharan and E. European origin. Acc. to tradition Jews emigrated there fr. Persia in 5th c., fr. Iran in 13th c. Under Russian control fr. 19th c. Many Jews found refuge there during WWII. Jewish pop. 103,000 (1970).

Uzhgorod (Ungvár), city in Ukrainian SSR. Jewish community developed in late 18th c. Outstanding rabbis of Hungary served there. Stronghold of Orthodox and Ḥasidim. 7,357 Jews in 1930. All Jews concentrated in ghetto and deported to Auschwitz 1944.

Uziel, Ben-Zion, see Ouziel, Ben-Zion.

Uziel, Isaac ben Abraham (d. 1622), rabbi. poet; b. Fez (Morocco), in Amsterdam fr. 1606. Among his pupils was Manasseh Ben Israel. Wrote poems, Hebrew grammar, and translated legends and fables of Indian origin into Hebrew.

Uzzah, biblical figure. Smitten when he touched Ark on its journey to Jerusalem (II Sam. 6:1–8).

Uzziah (Azariah), king of Judah 785–734 B.C.E. Waged successful campaigns against Philistines and Arabs; Ammonites paid tribute to him. Conducted extensive building operations and regained control of port of Elath. After being stricken with leprosy, withdrew from public affairs, appointing his son Jotham as co-regent (II Kings 15:5).

Stone tablet with Aramaic inscription, "Hither were brought the bones of Uzziah, King of Judah – do not open," found on Mount of Olives.

Initial letter "V" for the word "Verbum" at the beginning of the Book of Zephaniah in a 13th-cent. Latin Bible from France.

Va'ad Arba Araẓot, see Council of the Four Lands.

Va'ad ha-Haẓala (Heb. "Rescue Committee"), organization for rescue of Jews fr. countries under Nazi rule during WWII. Committees established in many countries outside occupied Europe, incl. that of U.S. Union of Orthodox Rabbis established by Aaron Kotler in U.S. and active within UNRRA, one in Budapest which negotiated with Eichmann in "Blood for Goods" plan, and one in Istanbul directed by representatives of World Zionist Organization.

Va'ad ha-Lashon ha-Ivrit, see Academy of the Hebrew Language.

Va'ad Le'ummi (Heb. "National Committee"), National Council of Jews of Palestine, which functioned 1920–48 as executive organ of Asefat ha-Nivḥarim (Elected Assembly) of Jewish community in Ereẓ Israel. Directed educational and health work among Jews in Ereẓ Israel and represented them in negotiations with British authorities.

Vajda, Georges (1908–), French scholar; b. Budapest, in Paris fr. 1928. Prof. at Sorbonne 1970. Edited *Revue des Etudes Juives.* Wrote works on Arabic and Jewish philosophy, Kabbalah, Arab mss.

Vajs, Albert (1905–1964), attorney, leader of Yugoslav Jewry. Fought in WWII; deputy head of Yugoslav delegation to Nuremberg trials. After war worked for rehabilitation of Jewish community, serving as its pres.

Vakhnacht, see Sholem Zokhor.

Valencia, port in Spain. Jews present during Muslim rule in 11th c. Under Christians given special quarter 1244, walled at end of 14th c. Community flourished despite continuously increasing tax burden. Destroyed by persecutions 1391 when all Jews either killed or converted. Subsequently Inquisition established. Port of embarkation for Jews leaving Spain 1492.

Valentin, Gabriel Gustav (1810–1883), physiologist; b. Breslau. Prof. at Berne. Pioneered in the study of physiology and embryology.

Valentin, Hugo Maurice (1888–1963), Swedish historian, Zionist leader. Prof. at Uppsala 1948. Wrote on 18th c. European history. Pres. Swedish Zionist Federation.

Valladolid, city in Spain. Jews there fr. 13th c. Conditions deteriorated in 14th c. Most of community converted to Christianity after persecutions of 1391, which were followed by harsh anti-Jewish laws. Situation improved in 15th c. until final expulsion 1492.

°**Vallat, Xavier** (1891–1972), French anti-Semitic politician. Served during WWII under Pétain and Darlan, collaborated with Nazi authorities. Sentenced to 10 years' imprisonment 1947, released 1950.

Valley of Jehoshaphat, see Jehoshaphat, Valley of.

Vambery, Arminius (Hermann Vamberger; 1832–1913), Hungarian traveler, orientalist. Mastered numerous languages and in his youth became secretary to foreign minister of Turkey. First European to travel across C. Asia; wrote extensively on oriental languages, ethnology, politics, and travel. Although he abandoned Judaism, he sympathized with Zionist aims and enabled Herzl to meet Turkish sultan 1901.

Vancouver, city in B.C., Canada. Jews settled 1885. Liberal congregation founded 1895, Orthodox and Conservative later. Jewish pop. 8,000 (1971).

°**Van Paassen, Pierre** (1895–1968), writer, journalist; b. Holland, in Canada fr. 1914. Militant gentile Zionist. Wrote *The Forgotten Ally,* sharp indictment of Britain's Palestine policy.

Van Praagh, William (1845–1907), British educator. Pioneered lipreading method for deaf-mutes in England and wrote extensively on subject.

Van Raalte, Eduard Ellis (1844–1921), Dutch lawyer, statesman. Appointed minister of justice 1905. A law on labor contracts bears his name.

Van Vriesland, Siegfried Adolf (1886–1939), Zionist leader; b. Holland, settled in Ereẓ Israel 1919. Treasurer of Zionist Executive and fr. 1936 manager of Tel Aviv port.

Varga, Yevgeni Samoilovich (1879–1964), Soviet economist. Won respect in Soviet ruling circles and, though rejected by Stalin, his ideas formed basis of Khrushchev's policy of peaceful co-existence.

Rahel Varnhagen

Varnhagen, Rahel (Rahel Levin; 1771–1833), German socialite. Baptized on third marriage (to author-diplomat Varnhagen von Ense 1814). Her salon became informal meeting place for literary, intellectual, social, and political luminaries of the day. Letters published after death.

°**Vashti,** queen of Persia and Media, wife of Ahasuerus (485–465 B.C.E.), who was deposed for disobedience (Esth. 1).

Vaughan (orig. **Ableson**), **Frankie** (1928–), English entertainer. One of Britain's most popular singers. Appeared in cabaret, films, TV.

°**Vaux, Roland de** (1903–1971), biblical scholar, archaeologist. Dominican priest. Director of Jerusalem's Ecole Biblique 1945–65. Edited *Revue Biblique.* Played leading role in Qumran discoveries. His major work *Ancient Israel.*

Vav, see Waw.
Va-Yikra, see Leviticus.
Vázsonyi, Vilmos (1868–1926), Hungarian lawyer, politician. First Jewish minister of justice in Hungary.
Vecinho, Joseph (15th c.), scientist, physician to King John II of Portugal (1481–95). His *Almanach Perpetuum* was translation of tables prepared by his teacher, Abraham Zacuto. Astrolabe improvements boosted Portuguese maritime activity.
Veil, Simone (1927–), French public figure. Deported in WWII. Magistrate. In 1974, minister of health.
Veinberg, Moissey Samuilovich (1919–), Russian composer. Works incl. operas, piano sonatas, symphonies, and *Moldavian Rhapsody for Violin.*
Veiner, Harry (1904–), Canadian rancher. Mayor of Medicine Hat, Alberta, 1952–66. Devoted to Jewish and Zionist causes.
Veinger, Mordecai (1890–1929), Yiddish linguist. Taught at Belorussian State Univ. Proposed radical reform of Yiddish spelling, partly implemented in official Soviet Yiddish orthography.
Veit, Moritz (1808–1864), German publicist, politician, communal leader. Member of family of bankers active also in politics and arts. Chairman of German publishers organization 1853–61. Member of Prussian Lower House.
Veksler, Vladimir (1907–1966), Soviet physicist specializing in high-energy accelerator theory. His work contributed to success of Sputnik I, first man-made satellite, 1957. Received Lenin Prize 1959, co-recipient of U.S. Atoms for Peace Award 1963.
Velizh, city in Russia. Scene blood libel 1823 which stirred up Russian Jewry. After prolonged legal proceedings false witnesses were exiled to Siberia. Four of arrested Jews died in prison. Trial revived belief in blood libel among Christian masses.
Velvel Zbarazher, see Ehrenkranz, Benjamin Zeeb.
Venetianer, Lajos (1867–1922), Hungarian rabbi, historian. Rabbi in Ujpest fr. 1897, prof. at Landesrabbinerschule. Wrote on religion, liturgy, Jewish literature and history.
Venezuela, S. American republic. Jews from W. Indies settled in 1850s. In early 20th c. Jews arrived fr. N. Africa; later fr. E. Europe and after 1934 fr. C. Europe. Jewish pop. 12,000 (1971), mostly in Caracas.
Venice, city in N. Italy. First mention of Jews in 10th c., first Jewish quarter 1090. Jews active as merchants and moneylenders. Fr. 1394 Jews had to wear special badges. Influx of Jews fr. Spain after 1492. Community important cultural center during Renaissance and many Jewish works were printed there. "Ghetto" originated there. Talmud burnt 1566. Community declined in 17th c. French occupation 1797 broke down ghetto gates. Emancipation completed 1860. 844 Jews in 1965. Five historic synagogues stand in ancient ghetto but only one now in regular use.
Venosa, town in S. Italy. Jews there before 3rd c. C.E. Epitaphs discovered in Jewish catacomb fr. 3rd–6th c. Center of Jewish studies in 11th c.
Ventura, Michon (Moses; 1883–?), Turkish legal scholar, politician. Elected to Turkish parliament 1920.
Ventura, Moïse (1893–), rabbi, scholar; b. Smyrna. Chief rabbi of Alexandria, Egypt, 1938–48. In Israel fr. 1955. Wrote on medieval Jewish philosophy.
Ventura, Rubino (1792–1858), Italian soldier. After service in Napoleonic wars, went to India, where he trained and organized Ranjit Singh's army of Lahore. Spent later years in Persia.
Veprik, Alexander Moiseyevitch (1899–1958), Russian composer. Works incl. *Songs and Dances of the Ghetto* and *Jewish Songs;* symphonies, choral works, and an opera.
Vera Y Alarcon, Lope de (1620–1644), Spanish martyr; b. Christian. Announced intention to become Jew, denounced to Inquisition, tortured, circumcised himself in cell, burned at stake. His martyrdom made profound impression on Marranos and Jews in Europe.
Verband der Vereine fuer Juedische Geschichte und Literatur, association of societies founded in Berlin 1893 to discuss Jewish history and literature through lectures and publication of popular essays. Existed until 1938.
Verband Nationaldeutscher Juden, extreme assimilationist organization of German Jews founded 1921, advocating absolute identity with Germany. Despite vows of loyalty rejected by the Nazis and dissolved 1935/36.
Vercors (pen name of **Jean Bruller;** 1902–), French author, engraver. Best known work WWII novella *Le silence de la mer,* published by underground press.

Jewish cemetery at Coro, Venezuela.

The Great German Synagogue in Venice.

Indian miniature depicting Rubino Ventura with the Maharaja of Lahore.

Verein fuer Kultur und Wissenschaft des Judentums ("Kulturverein"), society for Jewish culture and science founded in Germany 1819 to investigate nature of Judaism by modern scientific methods and bring to light universal value of Jewish culture. Published periodical 1822–23 edited by Leopold Zunz. Dissolved 1824. Pioneer of Wissenschaft movement.

Verga, see Ibn Verga.

Vergelis, Aaron (1918–), Soviet propagandist, Yiddish poet, editor. During WWII Yiddish radio commentator. Escaped Stalin's purge of Soviet Yiddish writers. Appointed chief editor of Soviet Yiddish periodical *Sovietish Heymland.* Apologist for Soviet Jewish policy.

Vermont, U.S. state. First Jew 1835. Jewish community in Poultney shortly after Civil War. First congregation established in Burlington 1880. Jewish pop. 1,885 (1971).

Verona, city in N. Italy. Jews there by early Middle Ages. Expelled in 10th c., resettled in 12th c. Expelled 1490, permanent resettlement in 16th c. Ghetto established 1599, abolished with French occupation 1796. Community declined in 19th–20th c. 120 Jews in 1960s.

Imprint of the Verona Jewish community seal, 16th cent.

Engraving depicting the Jewish expulsion from Vienna, 1670.

Vilna Jews digging their own graves, c. 1941.

°**Vespasian, Titus Flavius** (d. 79 C.E.), Roman emperor 69–79 C.E. Appointed by Nero to crush revolt in Judea. Conquered Galilee, coastal region, and Transjordan 67–68. Campaign concluded by his son Titus.

Vészi, József (1858–1940), Hungarian journalist, politician. Editor-in-chief of various papers *(Pesti Napló, Budapester Presse, Pester Lloyd).* Member of Upper House fr. 1927.

Vicky, see Weisz, Victor.

Vidal Yom Tov of Tolosa (14th c.), Spanish rabbi, commentator. Author of *Maggid Mishneh* on Maimonides' *Mishneh Torah,* giving its sources and replying to many criticisms of Maimonides.

Vidas, Elijah ben Moses de (16th c.), kabbalist in Safed. Author of ethical work *Reshit Ḥokhmah,* one of outstanding Jewish books on morals.

Viddui, see Confession of Sins.

Vienna, capital of Austria. Jews fr. 12th c. Massacred in Third Crusade 1196. New synagogue built. Leading community of German Jewry in 14th c., with major sages. Massacres and expulsion 1421. Ghetto 1624. Expulsion 1669–70. Limited readmission of wealthy Jews 1693. Pop. increased as result of immigration, esp. fr. Hungary, Galicia, and Bukovina. Jews played major role in city's cultural and intellectual life. Anti-Semitic legislation introduced immediately after *Anschluss* 1938. 100,000 of 166,000 Jews emigrated before WWII and another 18,500 escaped before 1941. Nearly all who remained deported to camps. Jewish pop. 8,200 (1971).

Viertel, Berthold (1885–1953), Austrian author, stage and film director; in U.S. during WWII. Wrote lyric poetry and was noted for his productions of expressionist drama.

Vigée (Strauss), Claude (1921–), French poet, essayist. Earlier works record search for Jewish roots. Later writing reflects harmony achieved after settling in Israel. Prof. of French literature at Heb. Univ.

Vilna, capital of Lithuania; called "Jerusalem of Lithuania." Organized community fr. 1568, granted charter 1633. Community grew in early 17th c. Prominent center for rabbinic studies fr. early 17th c., reaching high point with Elijah ben Solomon, the Vilna Gaon, who had lasting effect on Vilna Jewry. Focus of opposition to Ḥasidic movement. In 19th c. center of Jewish Enlightenment, Jewish socialism, and later Zionism. Important press (Vilna edition of Talmud, etc), Strashun library, headquarters of YIVO for cultural work. 140,000 Jews in 19th c. but by 1900 dropped to 80,000, almost all of whom were murdered in WWII together with many brought fr. surrounding towns. 16,000 Jews in 1970 with only one synagogue. After 1967 a center of agitation for emigration to Israel.

Vilna Gaon, see Elijah ben Solomon Zalman.

Vilna Troupe, Yiddish theatrical company. Began as amateur group 1916; moved to Warsaw 1917. Original group broke up after tour in W. Europe and U.S. 1921, but successors continued until 1930s. Major Yiddish theater bet. world wars.

Vilnay, Zev (1900–), Israel geographer. Publications incl. *Guide to Israel, The New Israel Atlas.* Israel's best-known guide.

Vinaver, Chemjo (1900–1973), conductor and composer; b. Poland. Influenced by ḥasidic musical traditions and led choirs in Berlin, New York, and Jerusalem. Published *Anthology of Jewish Music.*

Vinawer, Maxim (1862–1926), Russian lawyer, communal leader. After 1905 revolution, vice-chairman of Constitutional Democratic Party ("Cadets"). Leader of Society for Equal Rights for Jews; founded *Yevreyskaya Tribuna* newspaper. In France fr. 1919.

°**Vincent, Louis Hugues** (1872–1960), French Dominican monk, archaeologist. One of heads of Ecole Biblique in Jerusalem. Author of monumental work on Jerusalem.

Vinchevsky, Morris (pseud. of **Benzion Novakhovichi;** 1856–1932), Yiddish, Hebrew writer, socialist; b. Lithuania, went to W. Europe, in U.S. fr. 1894. Called "the grandfather of Yiddish socialist literature." Poet, editor, and educator. Helped found *Jewish Daily Forward* and edited literary magazines. Sympathized with Bund; in 1920s sympathies veered sharply to left.

Vincze, Paul (1907–), English medalist. Designed coins for newly independent African states.

Vineland, city in N.J., U.S. Jewish community originates fr. establishment of immigrant agricultural settlements (farming, poultry) by Alliance Israélite Universelle and Baron de Hirsch Fund in late 19th c. Jewish pop. 2,450 (1971).

Silos at the Baron de Hirsch Agricultural School near Vineland, New Jersey, c. 1905.

Viner, Jacob (1892–1970), U.S. economist. Prof. at Princeton and consultant to U.S. government. Among first critics of Keynesian neoeconomics.

Vinnikov, Isaac N. (1897–), Soviet orientalist. First works on pre-Islamic Arab history and culture, later on Tyrean and Aramaic inscriptions. Compiled concordance to Palestinian Aramaic. Taught at Leningrad Univ.

Vinnitsa, city in Ukrainian SSR. Small Jewish community in 18th c. Expanded after Russian annexation 1793. Pogroms 1920. Yevsektsiya tried to destroy Jewish life. 28,000 Jews exterminated by Germans 1941. 42,000 Jews in Vinnitsa province in 1970.

Virginia, U.S. state. Individual Jews fr. 1658. Congregation in Richmond by 1790. During world wars construction of military bases attracted many Jews. Jewish pop. 41,215 (1971), mostly in Richmond, Norfolk, Alexandria.

Virgin Islands, archipelago in W. Indies. Freedom of religion granted to Jews of St. Thomas Island 1685 by Danes, and Sephardi community existed there, with two Jews serving as governors. 100 Jewish families in 1968.

Vishniac, Roman (1897–), photographer; b. Russia. Traveled throughout Europe using his camera to document Jewish life. In the U.S. fr. 1941, directing his photography to research in biological sciences.

Visser, Lodewijk Ernst (1871–1942), Dutch jurist. Pres. of Netherlands Supreme Court 1939. Worked to aid Jewish refugees and was active in WWII Resistance.

Vital, David ben Solomon (16th c.), rabbi, preacher, *paytan;* lived in Greece. Wrote on 613 precepts and 13 principles of faith.

Vital, Ḥayyim ben Joseph (1542–1620), kabbalist, talmudist; b. Safed. Important influence on development of Kabbalah of Isaac Luria, under whom he studied for two years, noting and commenting on his views. Many of his sermons and talmudic novellae have been published. Major works *Ez̤ ha-Ḥayyim* and *Ez̤ ha-Da'at.* Rabbi in Jerusalem and Damascus. His son **Samuel ben Ḥayyim** (1598–c. 1678), Damascus rabbi. Prepared copies of his father's works and wrote responsa. His novellae published in standard Vilna Talmud.

Vitebsk, city in Belorussian SSR. Jews fr. 16th c. Stronghold of Orthodox Judaism. Lithuanian Ḥasidism active there as well as Ḥabad. Haskalah elements, Ḥibbat Zion, Bund, and Po'alei Zion developed there. Marc Chagall depicted its Jewish life. 37,013 Jews in 1926. With Nazi occupation, many Jews fled to interior of Russia; 16,000 Jews who remained imprisoned in ghetto and liquidated. 20,000 Jews in late 1960s.

Vitkin, Joseph (1876–1912), precursor of Second Aliyah; b. Belorussia, settled in Erez̤ Israel 1897. Worked as teacher. In famous "Call to Youth" (1905) demanded that Diaspora youth unite for *aliyah* and outlined plans for settlements based on self-employed labor on nationally owned land.

Vitoria, Francisco de (d. 1592), Marrano prelate. Bishop of Tucumán 1583; nominated archbishop of Mexico. Accused of corruption and Judaizing; died before enquiry was completed.

Vivante, Cesare (1855–1944), Italian jurist; founder of modern Italian school of commercial law studies. Prof. at Rome. His classic textbook, *Instituzioni di diritto commerciale,* reprinted 60 times.

Medal by Paul Vincze commemorating the jubilee of the Balfour Declaration.

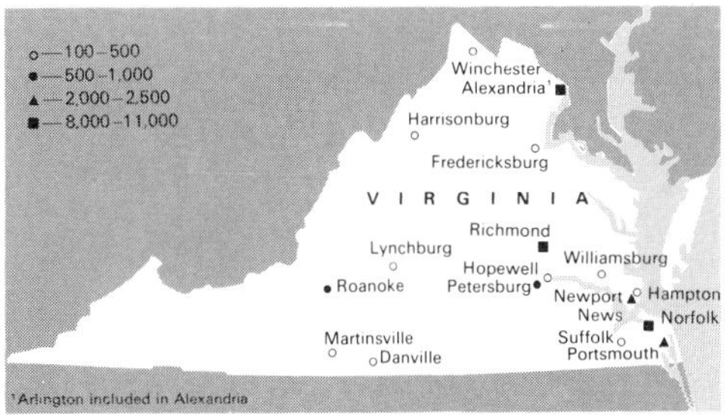

Jewish communities in Virginia.

"Synagogue Court," a photograph of Vilna by Roman Vishniac.

"Night over Vitebsk" by Marc Chagall, 1914.

Vives, Juan Luis (1492–1540), Spanish humanist; parents Marranos; lived in Oxford and Bruges. Best known for his commentaries on Augustine. Like his friend Erasmus, advocated non-theological religion and his interpretation of Christianity rejected dogma.

Vizhnitz, ḥasidic dynasty founded by **Menahem Mendel Hager** (1830–1884), *av bet din* of Vizhnitz; famed as miracle worker. Succeeded by his son **Baruch** (1845–1893), whose 7 sons and 3 sons-in-law became rabbis. Grandson **Israel** (1860–1938) founded yeshivah in Hungary. Always active in support of Ereẓ Israel; some members founded yeshivot and housing estates in modern Israel.

Vladeck, Baruch Charney (1886–1938), U.S. journalist, civic leader; brother of Daniel Charney and Shmuel Niger; b. Belorussia. Active socialist. In U.S. fr. 1908. City editor and later business manager 1918 of *Jewish Daily Forward.* Active in N.Y. politics. Pres. of ORT 1932–38, chairman of Jewish Labor Committee 1934–38.

Vladimir Volynski (Ludmir), city in Ukrainian SSR. Jews there in 12th c., organized community in early 16th c. Suffered during Chmielnicki massacres 1648–49. Ḥasidic center. 10,665 Jews in 1931. Ghetto established by Germans 1942, entire community liquidated 1943.

Vogel, David (1891–1944), Hebrew poet, writer; b. Russia, lived in Vienna, in Paris fr. 1925. Arrested by Nazis; probably perished in concentration camp. His poetry is completely introspective and describes dream world, disjointed and purposeless. Regarded as forerunner of Hebrew modernism.

Vogel, Sir Julius (1835–1899), prime minister of New Zealand 1873–75, 1876; b. London, settled first in Australia and then New Zealand. Edited colony's first newspaper and was elected member of House of Representatives, where he was financial expert. Agent-general in London 1876–81.

Vogelstein, German family active in Liberal Judaism. **Heinemann** (1841–1911), pres. Association of Liberal Rabbis, one of anti-Zionist *Protestrabbiner.* His son **Hermann** (1870–1942), went to U.S., wrote with Paul Rieger standard history of Jews of Rome. Another son, **Ludwig** (1871–1934), U.S. business executive. Staunch anti-Zionist, chairman of Union of American Hebrew Congregations.

°**Vogüé, Charles Eugene Melchior, Comte de** (1829–1916), French architect, archaeologist. His books opened new chapter in architectural history of Roman-Byzantine period in Ereẓ Israel and Syria.

Volcani, see Elazari-Volcani.

Volhynia, region in Ukrainian SSR. Jews fr. 12th c. In "Golden Era" of Volhynian Jewry bet. 1569 and 1648, influential in economy (esp. leasing of estates) and scholarship flourished. Community ravaged by 1648–49 massacres, but grew again numerically by 1660. New persecutions in 18th c. Early center of Ḥasidism. Enlightenment gained ground in 19th c. 395,782 Jews in 1897. Pogroms in WWI and Russian Civil War. Tens of thousands murdered in WWII. No organized Jewish community subsequently.

Volkspartei, Juedische (Jewish National Party), political arm of Zionist movement for domestic policy in Austria 1906–34. Rejected participation of Jews in other national movements and demanded transformation of Jewish religious communities into national communities.

Volozhin, town in Belorussian SSR. Noted in Jewish life for yeshivah founded by Ḥayyim Volozhiner in early 19th c., named Eẓ Ḥayyim in his honor. Seen as barrier to spread of Ḥasidism and aimed to educate pupils in methods of Vilna Gaon. Taught analysis of text and understanding of plain meaning of Talmud. Existed until WWII. Ḥ.N. Bialik wrote about yeshivah life there in his poem *"Ha-Matmid".*

Volozhiner, Ḥayyim ben Isaac (1749–1821), rabbi, educator; leading disciple of Vilna Gaon, acknowledged spiritual leader of non-ḥasidic Russian Jewry. Founder of Volozhin yeshivah. Author of *Nefesh ha-Ḥayyim.* Though opponent of Ḥasidism, refused to sign ban against it. Succeeded as yeshivah head by his son, **Isaac ben Ḥayyim** (d. 1849), known as "Itzele of Volozhin," who kept it alive when Russian government closed it 1824. Gave approval to government textbooks for Jewish children and ruled that if order for Jews to change their style of clothing applied to all citizens, it must be followed.

Volterra, Meshullam ben Menahem, da (Bonaventura di Manuele; 15th c.), Italian traveler. Wrote account in Hebrew of journey to Ereẓ Israel 1481 containing detailed information about Jewish communities he visited en route.

Volterra, Vito (1860–1940), Italian mathematician. Prof. at Pisa at 23. Italian senator 1905. Suggested use of helium instead of hydrogen in balloons. Active anti-Fascist; forced to stop all scientific activities 1931. His son, **Edoardo** (1904–), jurist. Wrote on family and Roman law. Prof. at Rome Univ. fr. 1951.

Volynski, Akim Levovich (pseud. of **A.L. Flexer;** 1863–1926), Russian literary and ballet critic, art historian. Also wrote widely on Jewish subjects and as non-Marxist was branded "decadent."

Voronoff, Serge (1866–1951), French surgeon, physiologist. Specialized in gland transplants in attempt to promote rejuvenation.

Vos, Isidor H.J. (1887–1942), Dutch physician, liberal politician. Head of hygiene department at Dutch Army Headquarters 1914–18. Amsterdam alderman and councillor. Member of second chamber of Dutch parliament 1928–40. D. in German concentration camp.

Voskhod, Russian-language periodical published in St. Petersburg 1881–1906. Advocated complete emancipation of Russian Jewry; initially antagonistic to Zionism. Published works by many famous writers, such as the historian Dubnow.

Voznitsyn, Alexander Artemyevich (d. 1738), Russian naval officer; proselyte. Condemned under pressure fr. Czarina Anna with Jew who converted him (Baruch b. Lev of Dubrovno) and, despite official hesitation, both men burned at stake.

Vozrozhdeniye, Jewish nationalist and socialist group in Russia 1903–05, advocating Jewish national-political autonomy in Diaspora (autonomism) and Jewish labor movement based on socialism, revolutionary struggle, and national autonomy. Some members joined Zionist Socialist Workers' Party 1904; others founded Jewish Socialist Workers' Party (Sejmists) 1906.

Vriesland, see Van Vriesland.

Vulgate, Jerome's (c. 345–420) translation into Latin of Bible, Apocrypha, and New Testament. Reveals influence of various sources, esp. Jerome's Jewish teachers and earlier Greek translations.

Vygotski, Lev Semyonovich (1896–1934), Soviet psychologist. Pioneered psychological diagnostics of mental disturbances and methods for teaching mentally retarded children.

Illuminated "W" used to represent the sound of the Latin word "Vere," detail from the "Missal of Paris," France, 12th cent.

Wachstein, Bernhard (1868–1935), historian, bibliographer, genealogist. Librarian of Vienna community. Wrote about Vienna Jewish tombstones.

Waddington, Miriam Dworkin (1917–), Canadian poet. Assistant prof. of English at York Univ., Ontario. Works incl. *Green World, The Second Silence, The Season's Lovers,* and *The Glass Trumpet.*

Wadi al-Naṭṭūf, valley N. of Jerusalem. Site of first discovery of prehistoric Natufian culture in Ereẓ Israel.

Wadi Dāliya, valley NW of Jericho. Site of cave find of skeletons, jewelry, seals, and legal documents fr. Samaria dated 375 (or 365) B.C.E. People in cave seem to have fled as result of crushing of Samaritan revolt by Alexander the Great.

Wagenaar, Lion (1855–1930), Dutch rabbi. Rector of Jewish theological seminary of Amsterdam fr. 1918. Published talmudic-halakhic articles and translated prayer book into Dutch.

°**Wagenseil, Johann Christoph** (1633–1705), Christian Hebraist. Published collection of works written by Jews for use in disputations with Christians. Though of missionary intent, opposed use of force in converting Jews. Published Latin translations fr. Talmud and works in Yiddish. Considered father of Scandinavian Hebrew studies.

°**Wagner, Richard** (1813–1883), German composer, anti-Semitic writer. Advocated removal of Jews fr. German public life. In *Das Judentum in der Musik* sought to denigrate Jewish artistic ability. Believed that Germany was economically and culturally dominated by Jews, who were "demons causing mankind's downfall." His works made anti-Semitism culturally respectable in Germany and greatly influenced Hitler. Wagner's musical works are not performed in Israel.

Wahl, Jean (1888–), French philosopher. Wrote both on traditional philosophy and on existentialism, of which he became leading exponent. His *Etudes Kierkegaardiennes* introduced that philosopher to French intellectual world.

Wahl, Saul ben Judah (Saul Judycz; 1541–c. 1617), merchant, *parnas* of Brest-Litovsk Jewry. Leader of Lithuanian Jewry and Council of Lands; obtained right for community to adjudicate cases bet. Jews. Acc. to legend, king of Poland for one day.

Wahrmann, Moritz (1831–1892), Hungarian economist, businessman. First Jewish member of Hungarian Parliament 1869. Advocated autonomous status for Hungarian Jewry. Vice-chairman of first General Congress of Hungarian Jews 1868–69, pres. of Pest Jewish community fr. 1883.

Wailing Wall, see Western Wall.

Waismann, Friedrich (1896–1959), Austrian philosopher. Among the original members of Vienna Circle; later taught at Oxford. Under influence of Wittgenstein, his philosophy changed fr. logical positivism to extreme informalism.

Waksman, Selman Abraham (1888–1973), U.S. microbiologist. His research into antibiotics (a term he coined) led to discovery and widespread use of streptomycin. Nobel Prize 1952. Taught at Rutgers Univ.

Selman Abraham Waksman

Walbrook, Anton (Wohlbrück; 1900–1967), actor; b. Austria. Settled in England, where he was successful in film portrayal of Prince Albert. Other films incl. *The 49th Parallel* and *The Queen of Spades.*

Wald, George (1906–), U.S. biologist, biochemist. Prof. at Harvard. Studied biochemistry of vision and discovered that derivative of vitamin A (retinene) is primary light-sensitive pigment. Nobel Prize 1967.

Wald, Jerry (1912–1962), U.S. screenwriter, producer. Produced successful films for Warner Bros. Headed Jerry Wald Productions at Twentieth Century Fox fr. 1956.

Wald, Lillian (1867–1940), U.S. social worker, nurse. After establishment of Nurses (Henry Street) Settlement 1895, brought nursing care and hygienic instruction to needy. Did not believe in charity and campaigned vigorously for social reform. Ardent pacifist; pres. of American Union against Militarism.

Walden, Aaron ben Isaiah Nathan (1838–1912), Polish ḥasidic author, bibliographer. Author of bio-bibliographical *Shem ha-Gedolim he-Ḥadash,* augmenting *Shem ha-Gedolim* of Ḥ.J.D. Azulai.

Walden, Herwarth (orig. **Georg Lewin;** 1878–1942?), German author, editor. As founder and editor of *Der Sturm* (1910–32), encouraged radical poets, artists, and scientists and wrote novels and plays. Emigrated to Soviet Union 1932, where he is thought to have been executed during Stalinist purges. His wife fr. 1901–11 was the poetess Else Lasker-Schueler.

Waldinger, Ernst (1896–1969), Austrian poet. Master of sonnet and ode. Wrote *Ich kann mit meinem Menschenbruder sprechen.* Some of his poems on Jewish themes.

Waldman, Leibele (c. 1907–1969), U.S. cantor. Sang on radio, performed in concerts, made records. Warm lyric baritone.

Waldman, Morris David (1879–1963), U.S. social worker. Prominent in general and Jewish philanthropic endeavors. Responsible for many innovations in social work and helped insert human rights provision into UN Charter. Though non-Zionist, active in Jewish Agency for Palestine.

Waldmann, Israel (1881–1940), Zionist; active in Ukrainian government-in-exile; b. Galicia. Strong connections with Zionism and Ukrainian national movement. Severed connection with latter during Steiger case 1924–25. Settled in Ereẓ Israel 1935.

Waldteufel, Emil (1837–1915), composer. Chamber musician and director of court balls for Empress Eugenie of France. His waltzes (e.g., Skaters' Waltz) perennial favorites.

Wales, country in United Kingdom. Individual Jews mentioned during Middle Ages. First community 1768, others established in 19th c. After WWI many small communities in mining centers ceased to exist and Cardiff became outstanding Jewish center. 3,500 Jews in 1972.

Waley, Arthur (orig. **Arthur David Schloss;** 1889–1966), English poet, translator of Oriental literature. His free verse translations of *One Hundred and Seventy Chinese Poems* and of classic Japanese romance *The Tale of Genji* were two important achievements. Wrote several books on Chinese philosophy. Companion of Honor 1956.

Waley-Cohen, Sir Robert, see Cohen, Sir Robert Waley.

Walinsky, family in U.S. public service. **Ossip Joseph** (1886–1973), labor leader, journalist; b. Russia. Active in British Trade Union Movement, moved to N.Y. and became pres. of International Leathergoods, Plastics, and Novelty Workers' Union. Also prominent in Labor Zionism. His son, **Louis Joseph** (1908–), economist. Advised U.S. government and Asian, African, and Latin American countries. Louis' son, **Adam** (1937–), attorney. Robert F. Kennedy's legislative assistant and main speechwriter.

Walkin, Aaron (1865–1942), rabbi of Pinsk. Active in Agudat Israel. Author of responsa *Zekan Aharon,* talmudic novellae, and other works. Murdered with family by Nazis.

Walkowitz, Abraham (1878–1965), U.S. painter. His anti-academic style at first aroused hostility of critics, but achieved success later. His style ranges fr. romanticism to abstract art. Dancer Isadora Duncan was one of his favorite models.

Otto Wallach

Raoul Wallenberg

Bruno Walter

Wallace, Mike (Myron Leon; 1918–), U.S. television interviewer. Gained prominence with interviews on N.Y. television. Columnist for *New York Post,* ran radio series *New Beat.*

Wallach, Eli (1915–), U.S. stage, screen actor. One of the best-known Broadway actors after WWII. Films incl. *Baby Doll* and *Lord Jim.*

Wallach, Moshe (Moritz; 1866–1957), pioneer of medicine in Israel; b. Cologne, settled in Jerusalem 1891. Fr. 1902 director of Sha'arei Ẓedek, hospital he founded outside city walls and gave Orthodox religious atmosphere.

Wallach, Otto (1847–1931), German organic chemist. Characterized 12 terpenes and determined their structure. His work led to industrial synthesis of camphor and artificial perfumes. Nobel Prize 1910.

°**Wallenberg, Raoul** (1912–1947?), Swedish diplomat in Hungary during WWII. Active in rescuing Jews. Taken away by Soviet authorities 1945 and never seen again.

Wallenrod, Reuben (1899–1966), Hebrew writer on American Jewish life; b. Belorussia, went to U.S. Prof. of Hebrew literature at Brooklyn College.

Wallenstein, Alfred (1898–), cellist, conductor. Formed Wallenstein Sinfonietta 1933 with high performance standard and extensive repertoire of classical and contemporary music. Conductor of L.A. Philharmonic 1943–56 and music director of Hollywood Bowl after 1952.

Wallenstein, Meir (1903–), orientalist; b. Jerusalem. Reader in medieval and modern Hebrew at Manchester Univ. fr. 1946. In Tel Aviv fr. 1970.

Wallich, family of German scholars, physicians. **Joseph ben Meir (Pheibusch),** appointed by emperor as "Jew Doctor" of Worms soon after 1600. **Isaac** (d. 1632), left catalog of folksongs of his day written in Hebrew letters. **Moses** (d. 1739), wrote *"Ku-Bukh,"* collection of fables written in Yiddish.

Walston (Waldstein), Sir Charles (1856–1927), British archaeologist, writer. Director of Fitzwilliam Museum in Cambridge 1883–89. As director of American School of Archaeology in Athens 1889–93 led excavations at Plataea, Eretria, and Hera sanctuary at Argos.

Walter, Bruno (Bruno Walter Schlesinger; 1876–1962), conductor. Gustav Mahler's assistant at Vienna Opera 1901–12, general director of Munich Opera 1917–22. With advent of Hitler, emigrated to U.S. Conductor and musical adviser of N.Y. Philharmonic 1947–49. Excelled as conductor of both operatic and orchestral music, and as interpreter of Mahler.

°**Walton, Bryan** (1600–1661), English churchman, orientalist. His London Polyglot Bible (1654–57) contained texts in nine languages and still retains much scholarly value and interest.

Walzer, Richard Rudolf (1900–), scholar of Greek and Arabic philosophy; b. Berlin. Prof. at Oxford Univ. of Greek, Arabic, and Hebrew philosophy. Translator of Galen.

Wandering Jew, figure in Christian legend supposedly condemned to roam the earth until second coming of Jesus, whom he is said to have rebuffed prior to crucifixion. Legend has inspired religious horror, social satire, and modern anti-Semitic agitation. Numerous reinterpretations in European folklore, poetry, and drama. As Cartaphilus, Buttadeo, Juan Espera en Dios, Ahasuerus, Isaac Laquedem, Der ewige Jude, le Juif errant, and the Wandering Jew, this legendary figure was reported to have appeared in many localities after 1600.

Wandsbeck, district of Hamburg, Germany. Jews settled 1600. Ashkenazi community. Altona, Hamburg, and Wandsbeck communities united (AHW) 1671–1811. After their disbandment 1811 Wandsbeck was under jurisdiction of Altona rabbi until 1864.

Wannsee Conference, Nazi conference held Jan. 20, 1942, in Berlin suburb to plan "Final Solution" and its implementation.

Warburg, family of German and U.S. bankers, philanthropists. **Karl Johan** (1852–1918), Swedish literary historian. Taught at Göteborg and Univ. of Stockholm. Co-author of monumental 6-vol. *Illustrerad svensk litteraturhistoria.* Member of Swedish parliament 1905–08. **Otto** (1859–1938), botanist, Zionist. Prof. in Berlin. Practical Zionist, instrumental in establishment of Palestine Office in Jaffa 1905. Pres. World Zionist Organization 1911. Directed agricultural research station in Reḥovot fr. 1921; prof. at Heb. Univ. fr. 1925. **Paul Moritz** (1868–1932), banker, philanthropist; b. Germany. Partner in family banking house. In U.S. fr. 1902. Exercised great influence on U.S. banking system; helped establish Federal Reserve System 1913. Leading figure in Jewish philanthropic and civic affairs. His brother

Felix M. Warburg

Felix Moritz (1871–1937), U.S. banker, philanthropist. Helped establish Henry Street Settlement, N.Y. Philharmonic Symphony Orchestra, Fogg Museum of Art at Harvard, and Federation for Support of Jewish Philanthropic Societies of N.Y.C. Chairman of Joint Distribution Committee 1914–32. Many other institutions benefited fr. his time and financial support, esp. Jewish Theological Seminary. Although not Zionist, supported Palestine Economic Corporation and Jewish Agency. His wife **Frieda** (née **Schiff;** 1876–1958), also philanthropist, communal leader. Supported many organizations, incl. Hadassah and YWHA. Another brother, **Aby Moritz** (1866–1929), historian of art and civilization. Wrote many works on relation of Renaissance to classical antiquity and Christianity and founded famous Warburg Bibliothek in Hamburg. Transferred to England when Hitler came to power and became Warburg Institute of London Univ. Paul's son, **James Paul** (1896–1969), pres. International Acceptance Bank and director of Bank of Manhattan. Member of Roosevelt's "brain trust." Also prolific writer, first of poetry, later popular books on economics, public affairs, and foreign policy. Felix's son **Frederick Marcus** (1897–1973), worked as investment banker, active in civic and communal work. During WWII rose to rank of colonel in U.S. Army. Another son, **Gerald Felix** (1907–1971), cellist with N.Y. Philharmonic 1925, organized Stradivarius Society and played in its quartet 1930–36, a founder and conductor of Brooklyn Symphony Orchestra. Another son, **Paul Felix** (1904–1965), banker. Founder, pres. of Fereration Employment Service. During WWII intelligence officer and helped rescue children fr. Nazi Germany. Director of Republican Party's Finance Committee. Another son, **Edward Mortimer Morris** (1908–), interested in fine arts and education. Outstanding Jewish philanthropic leader; chairman of American Jewish Joint Distribution Committee 1941–66 and United Jewish Appeal 1950–55.

Warburg, Otto Heinrich (1883–1970), German biochemist; son of physicist Emil Warburg (1846–1931); baptized like his father. Worked on radiation physics and for over 30 years (fr. 1930) directed Kaiser Wilhelm Institut fuer Zellphysiologie. Remained in position throughout Nazi period. Nobel Prize 1931 for discovery of respiratory enzyme.

Warfield, David (1866–1951), U.S. actor. Roles ranged fr. burlesque to portrayal of Shylock as man crazed by persecution. Established type of sentimental Jewish hero.

Warhaftig, Zeraḥ (1906–), lawyer, a leader of National Religious Party in Israel; b. Belorussia, escaped to U.S. in WWII, settled in Ereẓ Israel 1947. Member of Knesset; minister of religious affairs 1960–74.

Warka, Polish ḥasidic dynasty, founded by **Isaac of Warka** (1779–1848), *ẓaddik* in C. Poland. Negotiated to obtain abrogation of hostile decrees such as conscription to army. Called "Lover of Israel." His son **Jacob David** (1814–1878), founded Amshinov dynasty. Another son, **Menahem Mendel** (1819–1868), continued Warka dynasty and was called "the silent *ẓaddik.*" Latter's son **Simḥah Bunem** (1851–1907), emigrated to Ereẓ Israel.

Warner, family of pioneers in U.S. motion picture industry and founders of Warner Bros. Pictures, Inc. **Harry** (1881–1958), **Albert** (1883–1967), **Sam** (1884–1927), and **Jack** (1892–) started by opening theaters. Began to produce their own movies 1912, becoming leaders in Hollywood film industry.

The capture of Beersheba during the War of Independence.

War of Independence, war waged against attacking Arab armies by Jews of Ereẓ Israel for survival and political independence bet. Nov. 30, 1947 and early 1949. Divided into two distinct phases. First lasted until May 14, 1948, with Jews and defense forces, organized in Haganah, under attack by Palestinian Arabs, aided by irregular volunteers fr. Arab countries. In second phase, commencing with British evacuation, Israel Defense Forces fought against invading troops fr. Egypt, Iraq, Transjordan, Syria, and Lebanon, supported by volunteer detachments fr. Saudi Arabia, Libya, and Yemen. Arab armies made considerable headway and participated in siege of Jerusalem, coming up through Negev fr. S. and over Jordan River in Galilee. In series of victories Israelis drove them back. War punctuated by cease-fires mediated by UN. Israel eventually recovered all territory allotted under partition plan and even more. War ended with series of armistice agreements signed under UN auspices 1949. Israel casualties 4,000 soldiers, 2,000 civilians killed.

°**Warren, Sir Charles** (1840–1927), British army officer, archaeologist. Conducted excavations at Jerusalem

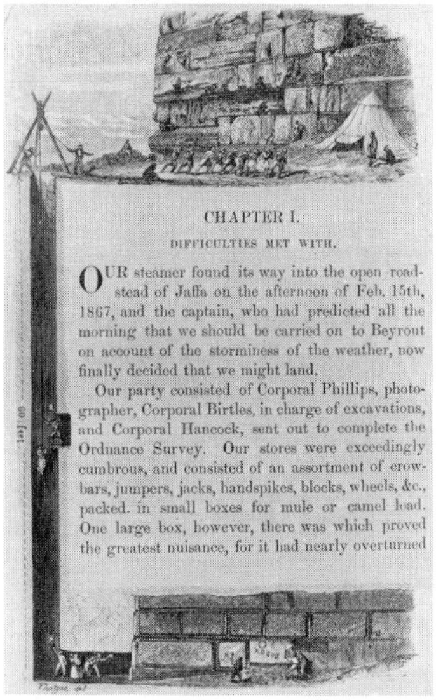
CHAPTER I.

DIFFICULTIES MET WITH.

OUR steamer found its way into the open roadstead of Jaffa on the afternoon of Feb. 15th, 1867, and the captain, who had predicted all the morning that we should be carried on to Beyrout on account of the storminess of the weather, now finally decided that we might land.

Our party consisted of Corporal Phillips, photographer, Corporal Birtles, in charge of excavations, and Corporal Hancock, sent out to complete the Ordnance Survey. Our stores were exceedingly cumbrous, and consisted of an assortment of crowbars, jumpers, jacks, handspikes, blocks, wheels, &c., packed in small boxes for mule or camel load. One large box, however, there was which proved the greatest nuisance, for it had nearly overturned

First page of "The Recovery of Jerusalem" by Sir Charles Warren, London, 1871.

1867–70; discoveries incl. wall of Ophel.

Warsaw, capital of Poland. Jews probably present fr. late 14th c. Officially excluded fr. 1527, but some always present and gradually obtained readmission. Jews took part in Polish uprising against Russians 1772. In Napoleon-sponsored Duchy of Warsaw Jews enjoyed civil rights and were entitled to form community. Ḥasidism, Reform, and assimilation were strong. Pop. grew in 19th c., a third of city's pop. being Jewish. Much of increase due to immigration following pogroms in Russia. Zionist and Jewish socialism gained ground in later 19th c. 400,000 Jews in 1939. In Oct. 1941 Germans established ghetto for Warsaw Jews and deportees fr. other parts of Poland. Number reached 450,000. Germans imposed anti-Jewish laws and appointed Judenrat. Starvation and inhuman living conditions resulted in over 100,000 dead by summer 1942. Jews established social welfare, cultural and educational institutions. About 300,000 deported to Treblinka extermination camp July–Sept. 1942. Armed Jewish resistance began Jan. 1943. Desperate revolt started April 19, lasting until June. Over 56,000 Jews killed or deported in revolt. After WWII, survivors who returned fr. east left Poland and most Jewish commercial institutions ceased to function by 1968. Jewish pop. 8,000 (1971).

Members of the Jewish Municipal Guard of Warsaw, 1830–31.

Warshavsky, Yakir (1885–1942), Yiddish, Hebrew novelist, journalist; lived in Warsaw. Described Polish ḥasidic life vividly and sympathetically. Killed in Holocaust.

Warshawski, Mark (1848–1907), Yiddish poet, lawyer in Kiev. Wrote words and music of his songs, which describe joys and sorrows of everyday life.

Warski-Warszawski, Adolf (1868–1937), Polish Communist leader. A founder of Polish Labor Union; organized Social Democratic Party of Poland and Lithuania. After WWI, a founder of Polish Communist Party and member of Sejm. In USSR fr. 1930; prominent in Polish section of Communist International. Executed in Stalin's purges.

Jewish communities in Washington.

Washington, U.S. state. Jews fr. 1860s; organized community in Olympia 1880. Jewish pop. 15,230 (1971), majority in Seattle.

Washington, D.C., capital of U.S. Earliest Jewish settlers 1795. Washington Hebrew congregation founded 1852. 41 congregations in 1971. Headquarters of B'nai B'rith. Jewish pop. 112,500 (1971), incl. many civil servants.

Wasserman, Elhanan Bunim (1875–1941), Lithuanian talmudist. Rabbi of Brest-Litovsk; after WWI established Baranowicze yeshivah. Active in Agudat Israel. Published talmudic novellae and other works. D. in Holocaust.

August von Wassermann

Wassermann, August von (1866–1925), German bacteriologist, immunologist. Greatest discovery was reaction for sero-diagnosis of syphilis, which bears his name. Coedited first encyclopedia of medical bacteriology and immunology. Ennobled by Kaiser.

Wassermann, Jakob (1873–1933), German novelist, essayist. Gifted storyteller; best-known works *Caspar Hauser* and *Christian Wahnschaffe.* Advocated German-Jewish assimilation (though not apostasy) and strongly opposed Jewish nationalism. Books burned by Nazis.

Wassermann, Oskar (1869–1934), German banker, communal leader. Patron of Jewish learning and a Zionist. Pres. Keren Hayesod in Germany and helped establish Jewish Agency. Dismissed fr. banking positions by the Nazis 1933.

Wat, Alexander (Szymon Chwat; 1900–1967), Polish author, editor. Published stories and translations. His communist ideals were shattered by experiences in USSR and last works display move toward mysticism and religion. In France fr. 1963.

Water-Drawing, Feast of (Heb. *Simḥat Bet ha-Sho'evah*), special ceremony of "water-libation" held in Temple during intermediate days of Sukkot. Revived in modified form in some Israel kibbutzim.

°**Watzinger, Carl** (1877–1948), German archaeologist. His study of ancient synagogues in Galilee remains basic study of earlier type of synagogues in Ereẓ Israel.

Waw (Vav), (ו), 6th letter of Hebrew alphabet; numerical value 6. Originally pronounced *w*, but, generally *v*. As vowel, pronounced *o* or *u*.

Wawelberg, Hipolit (1843–1901), Polish banker, philanthropist. Advocated assimilation fr. youth, but contributed liberally to Jewish cultural and charitable organizations.

Waxman, Meyer (1887–1969), U.S. rabbi, scholar. Fame rests on *History of Jewish Literature,* detailed account of main trends fr. post biblical period until present day. Prof. at Hebrew Theological College in Chicago.

Wayne, Johnny (Weingarten; 1918–) and **Frank Shuster** (1916–), Canadian actors, writers. Professional team fr. 1940. Their show "Wayne and Shuster Hour" CBS-TV special fr. 1954.

Ważyk (Wagman), Adam (1905–), Polish poet, novelist, editor. His *Poemat dla doroslych* heralded Poland's anti-Stalinist campaign.

Weber, Max (1881–1961), U.S. painter, sculptor. Pupil of Matisse. His bold, richly colored compositions caught dynamism of metropolis. Frequently painted Jewish groups.

Wechsler, David (1896–), U.S. psychologist. Originator of several widely used intelligence tests. Contributions to mental measurement. Wrote on adult intelligence.

Wechsler, Herbert (1909–), U.S. legal scholar. Prof. at Columbia, specializing in constitutional and criminal law. Participated in establishment of International Military Tribunal at Nuremberg 1945. Helped prepare model penal code.

Wechsler, Israel (Spanier; 1886–1962), U.S. neurologist. Prof. at Columbia, pres. American Neurological Association 1958, pres. American Friends of Heb. Univ.

Wechsler, Max (pseud. **Germanicus, I.H. Vǎleanu, Ieşau;** 1870–1917), Marxist theoretician, member of Rumanian socialist movement. Helped found first independent Jewish socialist society, Lumina, in 1890s. Accused of helping liberate Social-Democratic leader Rakovski and put to death by Rumanian military authorities.

Wedding, see Marriage.

Weeks, Feast of, see Shavuot.

Weichmann, Herbert (1896–), German politician. Held important posts in Weimar government. In U.S. during WWII. Returned to Germany 1948. Burgomaster of Hamburg; entered Bundesrat 1965 as Social Democrat and became its president.

Weidenfeld, Sir (Arthur) George (1919–), British publisher; b. Vienna, in Britain fr. 1938. Established (with Nigel Nicolson) publishing house Weidenfeld and Nicolson, producing general literature, academic books, and art and illustrated publications.

Weidenreich, Franz (1873–1948), German anatomist, physical anthropologist, paleontologist. Known for studies of *Homo sinanthropus,* human fossil remains discovered in China 1927. Also investigated other fossil remains in C. Asia and Java. In U.S. fr. 1940.

Weidman, Jerome (1913–), U.S. novelist. Works incl. *I Can Get It For You Wholesale* and *What's In It For Me?* describing Jewish garment industry and short stories about East Side Jews. His musical *Fiorello* awarded Pulitzer Prize.

Weidner, Paulus (c. 1525–1585), physician; brother of Solomon Ashkenazi; converted 1558. Wrote conversionist books and sermons. Physician to Austrian emperors, rector of Univ. of Vienna, dean of its medical faculty.

°**Weigand, Theodor** (1864–1963), German archaeologist. His survey of Negev was first in which air photography was used in archaeological work.

Weights and Measures. In biblical times largely based on those accepted by other peoples. Israelites probably adopted measures fr. Canaanites (e.g., *letekh, kikkar*), along with names which were originally Egyptian (e.g., *ephah, hin*) and Mesopotamian (e.g., *kor, se'ah, shekel*). Some measures were apparently established in Israel. In talmudic times, system was syncretistic, based on the Italian *mina* and Roman *libra* linked to Tyrian standard. Also "rule of thumb" measures, such as olive's bulk and egg's bulk as well as measures derived fr. human body, finger-breadth, cubit-arms length.

Weil, André (1906–), U.S. mathematician. Taught at Strasbourg, São Paolo, Chicago, Princeton. Contributed to many branches of mathematics, incl. theory of numbers, algebraic geometry, group theory.

Weil, Eric (1904–), German philosopher; in France fr. 1933. Prof. at Sorbonne, Lille, Nice. Views represent classical tradition in philosophy, acc. to which man is rational but finite being.

Weil, Frank Leopold (1894–1957), U.S. lawyer, communal leader. Headed many Jewish and general community efforts, incl. Boy Scouts of America and National Jewish Welfare Board.

Weil, Gotthold (1882–1960), orientalist. Prof. of Semitic languages at Frankfort. After 1934 head of National and University Library in Jerusalem and prof. of Turkish studies at Heb. Univ. Published on Arabic and Turkish grammar.

Weil, Gustav (1808–1889), orientalist. Prof. at Heidelberg. Wrote on Arab letters and history, tracing rabbinic background of Muslim biblical lore. Translated *Arabian Nights* into German.

Weil, Jacob ben Judah (d. before 1456), German rabbi, halakhic authority. Known for responsa, frequently published, and his work on ritual slaughter *Hilkhot Sheḥitah u-Vedikah,* accepted as halakhic practice by Ashkenazim and subject of many commentaries.

Weil, Jiří (1900–1959), Czech author, translator. His fiction based mainly on experiences during Nazi occupation. After 1948 active in work of Prague Jewish Museum.

Weil, Simone (1909–1943), French philosopher. Joined Republican side in Spanish Civil War 1936. Her life and writings were search for absolute truth and social justice. Although never converted, had strong affinity with Catholicism and totally rejected Judaism. D. in England.

Weill, Alexandre Abraham (1811–1899), French author. Abandoned rabbinics and left Frankfort for Paris 1836. Prolific writer in French and German; published biographies of Boerne and Heine, tales of Jewish life in his native Alsace, work on Kabbalah, etc.

Weill, Kurt (1900–1950), composer. At first wrote operas and symphonic music, later turned to social satire in theater. In association with Bertolt Brecht, composed *Die Dreigroschenoper,* modern version of *The Beggar's Opera.* Left native Germany for U.S. 1933 and wrote several successful musical comedies.

Weill, Raymond (1874–1950), French Egyptologist, archaeologist. Directed excavations in Egypt, Sinai, and Jerusalem on hill of Ophel.

Weinberg, Jacob (1879–1956), composer, pianist; b. Odessa, in U.S. fr. 1926. Works incl. *The Pioneers*

Weights of the late Israelite period (c. 8th–7th cent. B.C.E.).

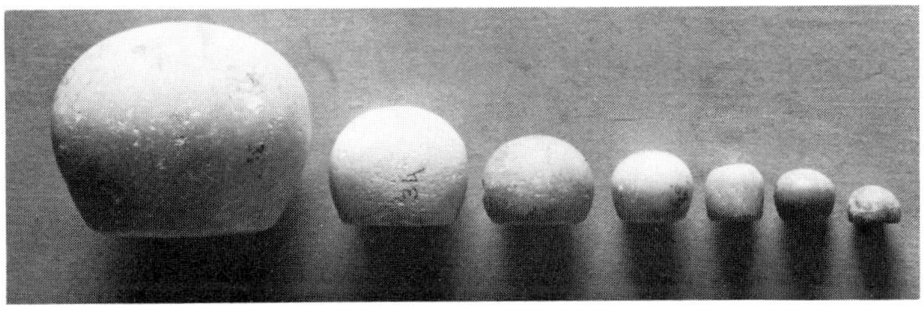

(opera based on life in Israel), synagogue music, and oratorios *Isaiah* and *The Life of Moses.*

Weinberg, Jehiel Jacob (1885–1966), talmudic authority, thinker, teacher; b. Lithuania. Rector of Berlin Orthodox Rabbinical Seminary. Interned by Nazis; escaped to Montreux, exercising considerable influence on world Orthodoxy by his responsa and writings.

Weinberg, Saul S. (1911–), U.S. archaeologist. Prof. and director of museum at Univ. of Missouri. Took part in excavations in Middle East. Chief curator of Biblical and Archaeological Dept. of Israel Museum fr. 1969. His wife, **Gladys** (1909–), archaeologist; expert on ancient Greek glass.

Weinberger, Jaromir (1896–1967), composer; b. Prague. Wrote orchestral, choral, instrumental works. Best known for folk-opera *Schwanda the Bagpiper.* In U.S. fr. 1937.

Weiner, Lazar (1897–), composer, conductor. Conducted Mendelssohn Symphony Orchestra, Brooklyn and Central Synagogue, N.Y.C. Taught at Hebrew Union School of Education and Sacred Music.

Weiner, Mattityahu, see Shelem, Mattityahu.

Weingarten, Joab Joshua (1847–1922), Polish rabbi. Outstanding halakhic authority. Author of *Ḥelkat Yo'av* on *Shulḥan Arukh,* regarded as classic by Polish authorities.

Weininger, Otto (1880–1903), Austrian philosopher; converted 1902. Major work *Sex and Character,* philosophical justification of male superiority, misogyny, and anti-Semitism. His Jewish self-hatred and anti-Semitic philosophy were useful ammunition for Nazis. Committed suicide.

Max Weinreich

Isaac Hirsch Weiss

Weinreich, Max (1894–1969), Yiddish linguist, historian, editor; b. Latvia. Cofounder of YIVO in Vilna. In U.S. fr. 1940, where he continued to be guiding spirit of YIVO. Prof. of Yiddish language, literature, and folklore at CCNY, first Yiddish prof. at U.S. university. Wrote prolifically on many aspects of Yiddish studies.

Weinreich, Uriel (1925–1967), Yiddish and general linguist, son of Max Weinreich; educated in Vilna, in U.S. from 1940. Prof. of Yiddish language, literature, and culture at Columbia Univ. His research papers widely acclaimed. His *Modern English-Yiddish, Yiddish-English Dictionary* is outstanding achievement of Yiddish lexicography.

Weinryb, Bernard Dov Sucher (1900–), economic and social historian; b. Poland, emigrated to Ereẓ Israel 1934, later settled in U.S. Prof. at Dropsie College fr. 1949. Wrote on economic and social history of Russian and Polish Jewry.

Weinshall, Ereẓ Israel family of public figures. **Jacob** (1891–), b. Caucasus, settled in Ereẓ Israel 1922. Practiced medicine. Chairman of Revisionist central committee in Ereẓ Israel until 1928. Prolific writer who favored biographical and historical novel form. His brother **Abraham** (1893–1968), also settled in Ereẓ Israel 1922. Practiced law. Chairman of Revisionist central committee in Ereẓ Israel but later dissociated himself fr. Revisionists.

Weinstein, Aaron (1877–1938), Bund leader in Russia. Directed Bund publishing house, exiled to Siberia during WWI, returned after 1917 and played decisive role in incorporation of Communist Bund in Communist Party 1921. Held important state positions, but arrested in 1930s and committed suicide in prison.

Weinstein, Lewis H. (1905–), U.S. attorney, community leader. During WWII served on Eisenhower's staff as liaison to De Gaulle. Headed Conference of Presidents of Major American Jewish Organizations 1963–65 and American Jewish Conference on Soviet Jewry fr. 1968, which he helped found.

Weinstock, Sir Arnold (1924–), British industrialist. Managing director of Radio and Allied Industries fr. 1952. Later bought out General Electric Co. Formed General Electric Ltd., biggest telecommunications and electronics concern in Britain.

Weinstock, Harris (1854–1922), U.S. businessman, labor leader. Enlightened and successful businessman, notably in fields of automobile supply and real estate. Interest in labor relations and civic government drew him into numerous public activities.

Weisenburg, Theodore H. (1876–1934), U.S. physician. Specialized in neurosurgery, pioneered use of moving pictures for study of patients with nervous and mental disorders and worked on adult intelligence tests. Pres. American Neurological Association 1918.

Weisel, see Wessely.

Weisgal, Meyer Wolf (1894–), Zionist, pres. of Weizmann Inst.; b. Poland, in U.S. fr. 1905. Held important posts in Zionist Organization, edited *New Palestine* 1921–30; deeply devoted to Chaim Weizmann and his personal representative in U.S. Fr. 1944 with Weizmann Inst., settled in Ereẓ Israel 1949. Pres. of Inst. 1966–69, then chancellor. Autobiography *So Far.*

Weisgall, Hugo (1912–), composer, conductor; nephew of Meyer Weisgal. Composed operas, incl. *Six Characters in Search of an Author* and *Athaliah,* ballets, choral and orchestral works.

Weiss, Abraham (1895–1970), scholar, Zionist. Taught talmudics at Inst. of Jewish Studies in Warsaw and Yeshiva Univ. in New York. Pioneer in talmudic research, opening new avenues in its jurisprudence and historiography. In Ereẓ Israel fr. 1962.

Weiss, Albert Paul (1879–1931), psychologist, social philosopher. Taught at Ohio State Univ. One of important group in U.S. who demanded objective and natural science approach to all behavior, incl. human.

Weiss (Ha-Livni), David (1927–), talmudist; b. Czechoslovakia, survived Auschwitz, in U.S. fr. 1947. Prof. at Jewish Theological Seminary. Applied source-critical method to problems of Talmud.

Weiss, Isaac Hirsch (1815–1905), talmudic scholar. Lecturer at Vienna Bet ha-Midrash. Author of 5-vol. *Dor Dor ve-Dorshav* on history of Oral Law fr. beginning until 15th c., written in picturesque Hebrew style and exercising considerable influence. Also published *Sifra* and *Mekhilta* with notes.

Weiss, Joseph Meir (1838–1909), Hungarian rabbi. Founder of ḥasidic dynasty of Spinka.

Weiss, Paul (1901–), U.S. philosopher. Prof. at Yale. Helped revive American interest in metaphysics.

Weiss, Peter (1916–), playwright, author. Half-Jew born in Berlin but fr. 1939 made his career in Sweden as writer, painter, and film producer. Gained fame with play *The Persecution and Assassination of Jean-Paul Marat . . . under the Direction of the Marquis de Sade.* Another drama, *The Investigation,* based on Frankfort trial of Auschwitz Nazi criminals.

Weiss, Samson (1910–), U.S. rabbi, Orthodox leader; b. Germany, in U.S. fr. 1938. Organizer of Torah Umesorah association for Hebrew day-school education. Executive vice-pres. of Union of Orthodox Jewish Congregations of America.

Weissenberg, Isaac Meir (1881–1938), Yiddish author. Wrote realistic tales of small town life in Poland. Dramas did not meet with general acclaim, but 4-vol. translation of *Arabian Nights* achieved considerable popularity.

Weissenberg, Samuel Abramovich (1867–1928), Russian physician, anthropologist. Studied Jewish ethnic and physical characteristics.

Weisskopf, Victor F. (1908–), U.S. physicist; b. Austria, in U.S. fr. 1937. During WWII worked on atomic bomb project at Los Alamos. Director-general of European Center for Nuclear Research (CERN) 1960–65, later heading physics dept. at MIT. Worked for nuclear disarmament.

Weissmandel, Michael Dov (d. 1957), Slovak rabbi and Jewish resistance leader. Initiated Europa Plan attempting to rescue European Jews in WWII. After War, in U.S.

Weiss-Rosmarin, Trude (1908–), U.S. author, editor, lecturer; b. Frankfort, in U.S. fr. 1931. Active in Jewish education and edited monthly *Jewish Spectator* fr. 1942. Her militant opinions often aroused controversy.

Weisz, Victor ("Vicky"; 1913–1966), British political cartoonist; b. Berlin, in England fr. 1935. Worked for *News Chronicle* and later for *Daily Mirror.* Much of his best work appeared in *New Statesman* fr. 1954 and *Evening Standard* fr. 1958.

Weiter, A. (1878–1919), editor, political agitator, Yiddish writer. Active in Bund; exiled to Siberia. After 1917 revolution settled in Vilna; shot by Polish Legionnaires. Early writings were of political nature, but in plays gave expression to renewed search for Jewish roots and values.

Weitz, Joseph (1890–1972), Hebrew author, settlement and afforestation expert; b. Russia, settled in Ereẓ Israel 1908. Afforestation expert for JNF and fr. 1950 member of board of directors. Varied literary work incl. books on his specialties as well as children's stories. His son **Ra'anan** (1913–), head of Land Settlement Department of Jewish Agency, regional planner, prof. at Haifa Univ.

Weizman, Ezer (1924–), Israel military commander; nephew of Chaim Weizmann. Joined British Air Force 1942, Haganah 1947. Appointed commander-in-chief of Israel Air Force 1958, chief of general staff branch 1965. Retired fr. Army 1969, joining Ḥerut Party. Minister of transport 1969–70.

Chaim Weizmann

Weizmann, Chaim (1874–1952), Zionist leader, first president of State of Israel, scientist; b. Pinsk, Russia, studied in Germany and Switzerland. Delegate to Zionist Congresses fr. 1898, a creator of Democratic Fraction 1901, among leaders of opposition to Uganda Scheme 1903. Lecturer at Manchester Univ. 1907. In 8th Zionist Congress 1907 called for "synthetic Zionism." Scientific discoveries helped Britain in WWI. Key figure in negotiations culminating in Balfour Declaration 1917, headed Zionist Commission to Palestine 1918, pres. Zionist Organization 1920–30, 1935–46. Headed Jewish Agency at inception 1929. Made residence in Reḥovot 1936 and founded Sieff Inst. (fr. 1949 part of Weizmann Inst.). Led Zionist support for Allied war effort and negotiated for Jewish fighting unit. A principal spokesman for Jewish national cause at UN 1947; played key role in recognition of Israel by U.S. President Truman. Elected president of the State of Israel May 1948. Autobiography *Trial and Error.* His wife, **Vera** (née **Chatzmann**; 1882–1966), b. Russia, studied medicine at Geneva, married 1906. A cofounder of WIZO, chairman of Youth Aliyah.

The Weizmann Institute of Science.

Weizmann Institute of Science, Israel scientific institution, established 1949. Developed out of Daniel Sieff Research Institute founded in Reḥovot 1934 and headed by Dr. Chaim Weizmann. Numbered 1,900 scientists (1971), incl. 500 students at graduate school. Engages in research projects and postgraduate study. Faculties are biology, biophysics and biochemistry, chemistry, mathematics, and physics. On campus is Yad Chaim Weizmann, promoting Weizmann heritage and maintaining Weizmann archives.

Welensky, Sir Roy (Roland; 1907–), Rhodesian statesman. Began career as engine driver and boxing champion; became a leading figure in political life of N. and S. Rhodesia. Campaigned for union; prime minister of Federation of two Rhodesias fr. 1956 till its collapse 1963. Although his mother was gentile, maintained links with Judaism.

Wellesz, Egon Joseph (1885–), musicologist, composer; of Jewish origin. One of first to follow twelve-tone system devised by his teacher Schoenberg. Left Vienna 1938 and taught at Oxford. Greatest authority on Byzantine church music and oriental church music in general. Showed the affinity of early Christian chants to ancient Jewish cantillation. Composed operas, symphonies, orchestral and chamber music.

°**Wellhausen, Julius** (1844–1918), German Semitist, biblical scholar. Summed up conclusions of 19th c. Pentateuch criticism and based on it new, comprehensive, and influential view of history of ancient Israel, propagating documentary theory of origin of early Bible books, and approach based on comparative Semitic religion. Many of his concepts have had to be modified in light of later research and archaeological discoveries.

Die Welt.

Nr. 1. I. Jahrgang.

Bezugspreise.
Für Oesterreich:
Halbjährig 3 fl. = 6 Kr.
Ganzjährig 6 fl. = 12 Kr.
Für das Ausland:
Halbjährig 4 fl. = 8 Kr.
Ganzjährig 8 fl. = 16 Kr.
Einzelne Nummern 15 kr.

Erscheint jeden Freitag.

Wien, 4. Juni 1897.

Zuschriften sind nicht an einzelne Personen, sondern an die Redaction oder Administration Wien, II., Rembrandtstraße 11, zu richten.

Unfrankirte Briefe werden nicht angenommen und Manuscripte nicht zurückgesendet.

Redaction und Administration:
Wien
II., Rembrandtstraße 11.
Preise der Anzeigen:
Die viermal gespaltene Petitzeile 10 kr.

Inhalt:

Programm.
Dr. Theodor Herzl: Der Congress.
Die Woche.
Dr. S. R. Landau: Die Lehren von Chodorów.
Aus Amerika.
Christen über die Judenfrage: Fürst Friedrich Wrede.
Porträt von Max Nordau.
Tribüne.
Finanzgeschichten.
Ungarische Grenzsperre.
Herbert Bentwich.
Zwei Tage in Tarnow.
Weltchronik.
Correspondenzen: Wien, Krakau, Sambor, Köln, Paris, London, Galatz, Sophia, Philippopel.
Zeitschriften-Rundschau.
Leon Kellner: Lord Beaconsfield.
Die Bücherwelt.
J. Zangwill: Uriel Acosta.
Vereinsnachrichten

First issue of "Die Welt."

Welt, Die, Zionist weekly 1897–1914, founded by Theodor Herzl. Official organ of World Zionist Organization fr. 1903. Yiddish publication of same name and, fr. 1907, Hebrew *Haolam* also served as official Zionist organs.

Weltsch, Felix (Baruch; 1884–1964), philosopher, publicist; cousin of Robert Weltsch. Librarian at Prague Univ. 1910–39, National Library in Jerusalem fr. 1940. Wrote philosophical works, essays on Zionism, anti-Semitism, and Ereẓ Israel. Also devoted several articles to his close friend Franz Kafka.

Weltsch, Robert (1891–), Zionist editor, journalist; b. Prague. Editor of *Die Juedische Rundschau* in Berlin 1920–38. His article "Wear the Yellow Badge with Pride" (1933) became slogan of German Jewry. In Ereẓ Israel fr. 1938. Edited German-language weekly and contributed to *Haaretz.* In London fr. 1946. Supported Berit Shalom movement.

Wendroff, Zalman (1877–1971), Yiddish author; b. Belorussia, went to U.S., writing for anarchist and Orthodox dailies. Sent by *Jewish Morning Journal* as correspondent to Russia, staying until death. While there arrested 1948 and imprisoned for 8 years. His writings describe life of Jews outside Pale of Settlement in Czarist time.

Wengeroff, Pauline (1833–1916), Russian writer. Known for memoirs describing tranquil life of Jewish family before Haskalah and subsequent crisis. Daughters married writers Nikolai Minski and Leonid Slonimski. Another daughter, **Zinaida** (1867–1941), important Russian literary critic; left Russia after Revolution and died in New York. Pauline's son **Semyon Afanasyevich** (1855–1920), Russian literary and intellectual historian. Wrote monographs on Turgenev, Gogol, Goncharov. Renowned bibliographer and editor of scholarly reference works. Converted to Russian Orthodoxy. Established Russian Book Chamber, weekly guide to USSR publications.

Werblowsky, Raphael Juda Zwi (1924–), scholar of comparative religion; b. Germany. Taught in England. Prof. at Heb. Univ. Represented Israel at international Jewish-Christian conferences.

Werfel, Franz (1890–1945), author; b. Prague. Leading poet of Expressionist movement. Lived in Vienna and Berlin, where his plays were successful. Wrote epic novel on persecution of Armenians, *The Forty Days of Musa Dagh.* His *The Eternal Road,* biblical play staged in New York by Max Reinhardt. During last years in California 1940–45, wrote *The Song of Bernadette,* novel about visionary of Lourdes. His wartime tragicomedy *Jacobowsky and the Colonel* was play and movie.

Werfel, Yiẓḥak, see Raphael, Yiẓḥak.

Werner, Eric (1901–), musicologist; b. Vienna, in U.S. fr. 1938. Established School of Sacred Music at Hebrew Union College 1948. Founded and headed 1967–71 dept. of musicology at Tel Aviv Univ. Works shed light on musical interaction between Judaism and surrounding cultures, and musical processes within Judaism itself.

Werner, Heinz (1890–1964), psychologist. Prof. at Hamburg Univ. 1926–33 and Clark Univ. in U.S. His dept. at Clark Univ. expanded 1957 into Institute of Human Development (renamed after his death Heinz Werner Institute of Developmental Psychology). Best-known work *Comparative Psychology of Mental Development.*

Werner, Siegmund (1867–1928), one of Herzl's early aides, editor of *Die Welt* 1897–99, 1903–5. With Herzl at latter's death. Later moved to Moravia.

Werth, Alexander (1901–1969), British journalist, writer. Foreign correspondent in wartime Russia and later in France; wrote books on both countries.

Wertheim, family of German department-store owners, concentrating on inexpensive mass-consumption goods. Main department store in Berlin, designed by Alfred Messel, was landmark. Stores became part of Hermann Tietz (Hertie) corporation after WWII, with Wertheims retaining interest in operation.

Wertheim, Abraham Carel (1832–1897), Dutch banker, philanthropist, political leader. Developed trade relations with Dutch East Indies. Leader of Amsterdam Liberals; member of Senate 1886–97.

Wertheim, Maurice (1886–1950), U.S. banker, patron of art and education; father of Barbara Tuchman. Financed *The Nation* during Depression. Pres. American Jewish Committee 1941–43.

Wertheimer, Chaim Ernst (1893–), Israel biochemist. Prof. at Halle Univ. fr. 1927. Settled in Ereẓ Israel 1934. A founder and second dean of Hadassah-Heb. Univ. Medical School. Noted for research on diabetes. Israel Prize 1956.

Wertheimer, Eduard von (1848–1930), Hungarian historian. Prof. at law schools, member of Hungarian Academy, privy councillor (Hofrat). Works dealt with foreign policy of Hapsburg monarchy and history of Hungary in early 19th c.

Wertheimer, Joseph Ritter von (1800–1887), Austrian pedagogue, philanthropist, merchant. Inspired by English educational system; established first kindergarten in Vienna 1830 which was soon imitated throughout Austria. Established Jewish vocational institute and girls' orphanage. Played leading part in struggle for Jewish emancipation.

Wertheimer, Max (1880–1943), founder of Gestalt psychology; b. Prague. Worked with Koehler and Koffka at Univ. of Frankfort. Emigrated to U.S. 1933. Taught at New School for Social Research in N.Y. Gestalt psychology revolutionized modern study of perception and influenced other areas of psychological research.

Wertheimer, Samson (1658–1724), Vienna Court Jew, scholar, *shtadlan,* philanthropist. Finance administrator of emperors Leopold I, Joseph I, Charles VI. Saved Jews of Rothenburg fr. expulsion. *Landesrabbiner*

Wedding ring of Samson Wertheimer.

of Hungarian Jewry. Wrote on *halakhah.*

Wertheimer, Solomon Aaron (1866–1935), rabbinical scholar, bibliophile in Jerusalem. Published many rare and unknown Midrashim, Cairo *Genizah* treasures, work on methodology of *halakhah* and *aggadah.*

Wesel, Baruch Bendet ben Reuben (d. c. 1753). German rabbi, author. Appointed rabbi of Polish community in Breslau by Council of Four Lands. Wrote laudatory poem to Frederick II.

Wesker, Arnold (1932–), English playwright. Injected much autobiographical material fr. London East End background into early plays *(The Kitchen).* His trilogy, *Chicken Soup with Barley, Roots,* and *I'm Talking About Jerusalem,* showed idealistic socialism of 1930s giving way to postwar conformity. Devoted much energy in 1960s to "Centre 42," trade union cultural organization.

Wessely (Weisel), Naphtali Herz (Hartwig; 1725–1805), Haskalah poet, linguist, exegete; b. Hamburg. Published commentary on *Avot* and annotated Hebrew translation of *Wisdom of Solomon.* Contributed commentary on Leviticus to Mendelssohn's *Biur.* Commentaries well received by Orthodox scholarship. His major work *Shirei Tiferet,* long epic on life of Moses and exodus fr. Egypt. Revived biblical Hebrew style in literature, and lent flexibility and vividness to language. His *Divrei Shalom ve-Emet* is first methodical composition in Hebrew on Jewish education written in spirit of Haskalah.

Wessely, Wolfgang (1801–1870), Hebrew scholar, jurist; first Jew to hold professorship in Austria. Author of catechism *Netib Emuna.* Lectured at Prague Univ. on Hebrew and rabbinical literature.

West, Nathanael (pseud. of **Nathan Wallenstein Weinstein;** 1903–1940), U.S. novelist. One of most distinguished American authors of 1930s. Wrote four novels (incl. *Miss Lonelyhearts, Day of the Locust*) portraying violence and tragedy of American life. Derided Jews and Jewishness. Fr. 1935 to death in automobile accident, Hollywood scriptwriter.

Westchester County, county in N.Y., U.S. Small Jewish settlements by 1860. By 1882 city of Yonkers had three Jewish congregations and by early 20th c. congregations established in other cities of county, which witnessed rapid increase in Jewish pop. with "move to suburbs" of middle and upper middle classes of N.Y.C. Jewish pop. 131,000 (1971), with 45 congregations.

Westerbork, main transit camp for Dutch Jewry during Nazi occupation of Holland. 100,000 Jews passed through on way to concentration and extermination camps.

Western Wall ("Wailing Wall"), section of western supporting wall of Temple Mount which remained intact since destruction of Second Temple 70 C.E. Became most hallowed spot in Jewish religious and national consciousness and tradition; center for mourning destruction of Temple. Jewish attempts to acquire Wall under the Turks failed. Under British scene of violent disputes bet. Jews and Arabs. Under Jordanian rule 1948–67 with Jews virtually excluded. Under Israel rule since 1967; main center of Jewish pilgrimage. Prominently featured in Jewish folk-art throughout the ages.

The Western Wall, 1969.

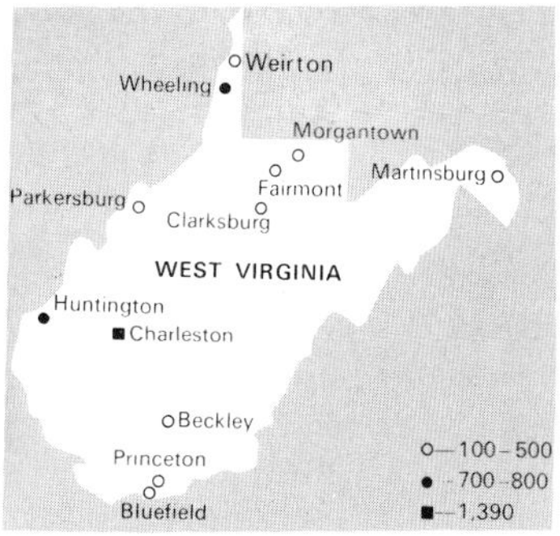

Jewish communities in West Virginia.

Westheimer, Frank Henry (1912–), U.S. organic chemist. Prof. at Univ. of Chicago 1948, Harvard 1954. Member of President's Science Advisory Committee.

West Indies, archipelago in C. America. Jews fr. Recife (Brazil) settled in Curaçao and Barbados 1654. 96 Jews in Martinique in 1683. Jews settled in Nevis c. 1679–80. Puerto Rico and Trinidad closed to Jews until 1898. Small congregations established in Bahamas in modern times. Jews did not settle in Bermuda.

Westphalia, region in W. Germany. Jews fr. 13th c., active mostly in moneylending. Suffered severely in Black Death persecutions 1348–49. Despite numerous local expulsions Jews remained. Establishment of Kingdom of Westphalia by Napoleon improved status. Emancipation complete 1867. Many Jews emigrated in early Nazi period; those who remained perished. 924 Jews in 1970.

West Virginia, U.S. state. First congregations in Wheeling 1849, Charleston 1873. Jewish pop. 4,880 (1971).

°**Wette, de, Wilhelm Martin Lebe-recht** (1780–1849), German biblical scholar, theologian. Linked Deuteronomy to reform of Josiah, concluding that book was composed in that period.

Wexler, William Abe (1913–), U.S. communal leader. Chairman of United Jewish Appeal 1951–56, pres. B'nai B'rith 1965–71, pres. World Conference of Jewish Organizations fr. 1971.

Weyl, Meir ben Simḥah (1744–1826), German rabbi, head of Berlin *bet midrash,* talmudic authority, opponent of Reform. Attacked use of German in prayer.

White, Harry D. (1892–1948), U.S. economist. "White Plan" calling for establishment of international trade based on gold monetary unit accepted by over 44 nations. U.S. executive director of International Monetary Fund 1946. Also regarded as author of "Morgenthau Plan" for postwar Germany. Accused of passing information to wartime Soviet spy ring; died before congressional investigation concluded.

White, Morton (1917–), U.S. philosopher. Chairman of Harvard philosophy dept. 1954–57. Wrote on epistemology and social and political philosophy. Works incl. *Social Thought in America* and *Foundations of Historical Knowledge.*

White, Robert Mayer (1923–), U.S. meteorologist. Directed research programs on long-range weather forecasting, applied climatology, and stratospheric problems. Chief of U.S. Weather Bureau and permanent U.S. representative on World Meteorological Organization.

Whiteman, Paul (1890–1967), U.S. bandleader. Made jazz respectable by bringing it to concert stage. Premiered Gershwin's *Rhapsody in Blue.*

White Papers, British government statements of policy presented to parliament; played important part in history of Mandatory Palestine. Six such documents issued bet. 1922 and 1939, dealing with British policy in Ereẓ Israel. Sixth paper (1939) restricted Jewish immigration and land purchase.

White Russia, see Belorussia.

Wicked Priest, character mentioned in Dead Sea Scrolls as inveterate enemy of Teacher of Righteousness. Many suggestions about his identity have been made; most favor one of Hasmonean priest rulers.

Widal, Fernand (1862–1929), French physician. Elected to French Academy of Sciences 1912. Instituted vaccination against typhoid fever and discovered method for typhoid serological diagnoses. Instituted low-salt diet in case of fluid retention.

Wiedenfeld, Dov (Tshebiner Rav; 1881–1965), Galician talmudic authority. Was businessman but acceded to request of Trzebinia community to become its rabbi and opened yeshivah. Exiled to Siberia by Russians. Reached Jerusalem 1946 and established Kokhav mi-Ya'akov yeshivah.

Wiener, Alexander S. (1907–), U.S. immunologist. Prof. of forensic medicine at NYU School of Medicine fr. 1938. Co-discoverer of the Rh human blood factor. Worked out serology, genetics, and nomenclature of entire Rh blood group system.

Wiener, Harold Marcus (1875–1929), English Bible scholar. Prominent opponent of Wellhausen school of Bible research. Settled in Ereẓ Israel 1924. Despite activities in promoting Arab-Jewish understanding, killed by Arab gang in 1929 riots.

Wiener, Leo (1862–1939), historian of Yiddish language, literature, folklore; b. Poland, in U.S. fr. 1882. Taught Slavic studies at Harvard. Wrote on Yiddish linguistic elements in many languages and on history of Yiddish literature. Later devoted himself to Slavic studies and Russian literature, and translated Tolstoy into English (24 vols.).

Wiener, Meir (1893–1941), poet, literary critic, thinker who wrote in Hebrew, Yiddish, German, Russian; b. Poland, lived in Vienna, Berlin, Paris, emigrated to Soviet Union 1926, killed in WWII during defense of Moscow. In USSR concentrated on Yiddish literature and research work at Jewish scientific institutes.

Wiener, Norbert (1894–1964), U.S. mathematician; father of science of cybernetics (a word he coined); son of Leo Wiener. Child prodigy who obtained Ph.D. at Harvard at 18. His WWII work in radar and high-speed computation led him to become pioneer of computer development and to publish *Cybernetics* (1948), which was scientific bestseller.

Wiener Gesera, persecutions of Vienna Jews 1421. Jews accused of desecrating Host and all Austrian Jews were rounded up. Many killed or killed themselves; property confiscated, synagogues destroyed. City of Vienna was called *"ir ha-damim"* ("city of blood").

Wiener Library, Jewish information institute in London, founded 1934 in Amsterdam by David Cohen (pres.) and Alfred Wiener (director). Aim was to communicate material on realities of national socialism to Jewish organizations and leaders for effective action with authorities of their respective countries. In London fr. 1939.

Wieniawski, Henri (1834–1880), Polish violinist, composer. Child prodigy who toured Europe with his brother; appointed solo violinist to Czar 1850. Toured U.S. with Anton Rubinstein 1872–74, finally settled in Brussels. Composed many works (in marked Slavonic idiom) for violin, incl. two concertos and his popular *Légende.* His brother, **Joseph** (1837–1912), studied piano under Liszt, taught at Moscow and Warsaw, prof. at Brussels Conservatory. Wrote piano concerto.

Henri Wieniawski with his brother, Joseph.

Elie Wiesel

Wiesel, Elie (1928–), novelist, journalist; b. Rumania, deported to Auschwitz, lived in Paris and later New York after WWII. Wrote books (beginning with *Night*) on Holocaust, which is perceived as awesome mystery. *The Jews of Silence* describes plight of Soviet Jewry; *A Beggar in Jerusalem* is set against background of Six-Day War; *Souls on Fire* is based on ḥasidic lore.

Wiesner, Jerome Bert (1915–), U.S. engineer, educator. Held important posts in radar development programs and as scientific and technological advisor to U.S. Government. First Jew appointed pres. of MIT 1971.

Wiesner, Julius von (1838–1916), Austrian botanist. Prof. of plant anatomy and physiology at Univ. of Vienna. One of founders of modern economic botany. Wrote *Die Rohstoffe des Pflanzenreiches,* comprehensive treatment of world's plants as source of economically valuable products.

Wilbuschewitz, family of pioneers in Ereẓ Israel. **Isaac** went to Ereẓ Israel with Bilu group 1882 but returned to Russia. **Gedaliah** (1865–1943), mechanical engineer, went to Ereẓ Israel 1892, founded first Jewish metal-casting factory in country. **Moshe** (1869–1952), chemical engineer and inventor. **Naḥum Wilbush** (1879–1971), mechanical engineer, went to Ereẓ Israel 1903, founded first edible-oil factory in country. Member of Zionist delegation to survey possibilities of Jewish settlement in Uganda 1903. See also Mania Shochat.

Wildenstein, family of French art collectors, connoisseurs, dealers. **Nathan** (1851–1934), one of five most important art dealers in Paris. His son, **Georges** (1892–1963), joined business and wrote biographies of French painters. Georges' son **Daniel Leopold** (1917–), also art dealer; settled in U.S. 1940.

Wilder, Billy (1906–), U.S. film director, writer; b. Vienna, in Hollywood fr. 1934. Films incl. *The Lost Weekend, The Seven Year Itch, Some Like It Hot,* and *Irma La Douce.* Films characterized by novel situations and swift dialogue. Awarded six Oscars.

Wilensky, Michael (1877–1955), Hebrew philologist; b. Ukraine, in Berlin fr. 1921, editing Hebrew medieval grammatical works. In U.S. fr. 1935. Compiled catalog of mss. of Hebrew Union College library.

Wilensky, Yehudah Leib Nisan (1870–1935), Zionist leader; b. Belorussia. Delegate to First Zionist Congress. Active in Hebrew education and Jewish self-defense. Left for Ereẓ Israel 1928. Visited many countries on behalf of Keren Hayesod. Father of Miriam Yalan-Stekelis.

Wilhelm, Kurt (1900–1965), rabbi; served in native Germany 1925–33, Jerusalem 1936–48, founding Liberal congregation; chief rabbi of Sweden fr. 1948. Published scholarly studies.

Wilkansky, see Elazari-Volcani.

Wilkes-Barre and Kingston, cities in Penn., U.S. First organized congregation in Wilkes-Barre 1845 adopted Reform ritual. In 1870s E. European Jews settled and founded five Orthodox congregations. Jewish pop. 1,580 in Wilkes-Barre, 2,680 in Kingston (1970).

Willowski, Jacob David ben Ze'ev (Ridbaz; 1845–1913), Lithuanian talmudist and yeshivah head in Ereẓ Israel. Teacher and preacher of Vilna. Chief rabbi of Orthodox congregations in Chicago 1903. Founded large yeshivah in Safed 1905. Took issue with Rabbi A.I. Kook for permitting land to be worked in sabbatical year. Author of important commentaries on Jerusalem Talmud.

Willstaetter, Richard (1872–1942), German organic chemist. Reacted to anti-Semitic rejection of Jewish candidates for university posts by resigning chair at Munich 1924. Fled to Switzerland 1939. Nobel Prize 1915 for research on plant pigments, esp. chlorophyll. Showed that life was chemical process, key to which is study of enzymes.

Wilmington, city in Del., U.S. Jews there in early colonial times. Jews fr. E. Europe arrived in 1880s. Jewish pop. 8,000 (1971).

Wilna, Jacob ben Benjamin Wolf (d. 1732?), rabbi, kabbalist. B. Lithuania, went to Jerusalem, returned twice to Europe as emissary. Considered authoritative kabbalist. Moderate Shabbatean.

°**Wilson, Sir Charles William** (1836–1905), English army officer, topographer. Directed survey of Jerusalem 1864–66, Sinai 1868–69, and published first exact map of Jerusalem. Discovered remains of bridge (Wilson's arch) connecting Temple Mount with Upper City in Second Temple period.

Winchell, Walter (1897–1972), U.S. journalist. Columnist for *New York Graphic,* and later for *Daily Mirror.* Specialized in "inside information" and sensational disclosures. Also on radio and TV.

Walter Winchell

Wilson's Arch, discovered by Sir Charles Wilson.

°**Winkler, Hugo** (1863–1913), German orientalist, Bible scholar. One of founders of pan-Babylonian school in study of Bible, claiming single common cultural system extending over whole of Ancient Near East.

°**Wingate, Orde Charles** (1903–1944), British soldier, Christian Zionist. Raised on Bible. Fought in Ereẓ Israel during Arab riots 1936–39. Gained confidence of Jewish authorities and organized Jewish volunteers into Special Night Squads, which used highly unorthodox methods against Arab terrorists. Known as *"Ha-Yedid"* ("The Friend").

Winninger, Solomon (1877–1968), biographer; b. Belorussia, settled in Israel 1950. Author of 7-vol. *Grosse juedische Nationalbiographie,* containing 14,000 biographies of eminent Jews.

Winnipeg, city in Man., Canada. First Jews there as group 1877. After 1881 augmented by refugees fr. Russia. First Yiddish day school in N. America founded 1920. Home of western regional offices of national organizations. Jewish pop. 21,000 (1971), with 17 synagogues.

Winter, Jacob (1857–1941), rabbi in Dresden. Edited 3-vol. anthology of Jewish literature and translated halakhic Midrashim into German with August Wuensche.

Winter, Levi (Leo; 1876–1935), Czech politician. Elected to Austrian Reichsrat as representative of Bohemian Social Democratic party 1907. After 1918 served three terms as minister of social welfare in new government of Czechoslovak Republic.

Winter, Paul (1904–1969), New Testament scholar; b. Czecho-

slovakia, in England after WWII. Wrote *The Trial of Jesus,* showing that Jesus was condemned to death by Romans for political, not religious, crimes.

Winternitz, Emanuel (1898–), musicologist; b. Vienna, in U.S. fr. 1938. Keeper of collection of musical instruments in Metropolitan Museum of Art 1942, curator 1948. Publications incl. *Musical Instruments of the Western World.*

Winternitz, Moritz (1863–1933), Austrian orientalist. Taught at Oxford. Prof. of Sanskrit at Prague. Wrote 3-vol. *History of Indian Literature.*

Wintrobe, Maxwell Myer (1901–), U.S. hematologist. Prof. at Univ. of Utah. His textbook, *Wintrobe's Clinical Hematology,* is standard work.

Wirszubski, Chaim (1915–), classical scholar; b. Vilna; in Ereẓ Israel fr. 1934. Prof. Hebrew Univ.

Wirth, Louis (1897–1952), U.S. sociologist. Taught at Tulane and Chicago Univ. Pres. American Sociological Society 1947, International Sociological Association

Jewish communities in Wisconsin.

Isaac Mayer Wise

Stephen S. Wise

1949. Concerned with elimination of discrimination against racial and cultural minorities. His *The Ghetto* (on Jews of Chicago's West Side) was pioneering work of sociology of Jews.

Wischnitzer, Mark (1882–1955), historian, sociologist, communal worker; b. Russia. Secretary of Hilfsverein der Deutschen Juden in Berlin 1921–37. In U.S. fr. 1941, where he continued his communal work. Wrote *History of Jewish Crafts and Guilds* and *To Dwell in Safety, the Story of Jewish Migration since 1800.* His wife, **Rachel** (née **Bernstein;** 1892–), b. Russia. Wrote extensively on Jewish art, esp. synagogue art. Director of Jewish Museum in Berlin 1934–38.

Wisconsin, U.S. state. First known Jewish settler 1794; congregation fr. mid-19th c. Majority of Jews fr. Bohemia and Germany (1848–1880) and E. and SW Europe (1880–1910). Jewish pop. 32,150 (1971), mostly in Milwaukee.

Wisdom Literature, literary and cultural tradition preserved in biblical books of Proverbs, Job, and Ecclesiastes, some of Psalms, and brief passages in other works. Some wisdom books among apocryphal writings (Ben Sira, Wisdom of Solomon) and other literary products (IV Macc.). Writings employ certain literary forms, characteristic vocabulary, and have common attitude emphasizing experience, reasoning, and morality.

Wisdom of Ben Sira, see Ben Sira.

Wisdom of Solomon, see Solomon, Wisdom of.

Wise, George Schneiweis (1906–), educator, businessman; b. Poland, in U.S. fr. 1926. Academic reputation based on research on sociology of Latin America. Chairman of board of governors of Heb. Univ. 1953–62. Elected pres. of Tel Aviv Univ. 1963; promoted its rapid development and became chancellor 1971.

Wise, Isaac Mayer (1819–1900), U.S. rabbi, pioneer of Reform Judaism; b. Bohemia, in U.S. fr. 1846. Served as rabbi in Albany, Charleston, and fr. 1854 in Cincinnati. Introduced reforms such as mixed pews, choral singing, and confirmation. Published *Minhag America* 1856, modification of traditional liturgy. First pres. Hebrew Union College 1875. Helped found Union of American Hebrew Congregations and Central Conference of American Rabbis (pres. fr. 1889). Edited English-language journal *The American Israelite* and German *Die Deborah.* His son, **Jonah Bondi** (1881–1959), Reform rabbi. Established weekly radio program *Message to Israel.*

Wise, Robert (1914–), U.S. film producer, director. One of Hollywood's most successful film makers. Won four Academy awards as director of *I Want to Live,* director, producer of *West Side Story,* co-director of *The Sound of Music.*

Wise, Stephen Samuel (1874–1949), U.S. rabbi, Zionist leader. Founded the Free Synagogue in N.Y. 1907 and served as rabbi until death. Founded and headed Jewish Institute of Religion 1922. A founder and first secretary of Federation of American Zionists (later Zionist Organization of America). American secretary of World Zionist movement, head of Provisional Committee for Zionist Affairs 1916–19. A founder and pres. of American Jewish Congress. Social liberal who was forceful and influential preacher of social concerns and active in N.Y. municipal affairs. His wife, **Louise Waterman** (d. 1947), communal worker, artist, translator, founder and pres. of the Women's Division of American Jewish Congress. Their son **James Waterman** (1901–), edited *Opinion* and held various positions as organization executive. Their daughter **Justine Wise Polier** (1903–), justice in Domestic Relations Court of N.Y.C. 1935–62, judge in the N.Y. State Family Court fr. 1962.

Wiseman, Adele (1928–), Canadian novelist. Her prize-winning *The Sacrifice* and many other writings deal with Canadian Jewish scene.

Wissenschaft des Judentums (Ger. "Science of Judaism"), 19th c. movement for scientific study of Judaism, using contemporary tools of scholarship. Natural development of Haskalah, though Orthodox participated. Culminated in development of "Jewish Studies" in 20th c. Motivated by attempt to provide content in Judaism for emancipated Jews, esp. in Germany, sometimes in direction of reform and assimilation; supplied groundwork for subsequent scholarship in all spheres of Jewish culture. Major personalities incl. Leopold Zunz, S.J. Rapoport, S.D. Luzzatto, Naḥman Krochmal, Z. Frankel, A. Geiger, S. Munk, M. Steinschneider. Produced extensive literature, incl. scholarly journals.

Wissotsky, Kalonymus Ze'ev (1824–1904), merchant, philanthropist, supporter of Ḥibbat Zion. Established in Moscow famous tea

TORAH ORNAMENTS Torah crown with hands raised in priestly blessing. Germany, 1793. Repoussé and perforated silver gilt.

USHPIZIN *Ushpizin* plaque for the *Sukkah* with illustrations representing the invited guests—Abraham, Isaac, Jacob, Moses, Aaron, Joseph, and David. Rumania, 18th cent. "Underglass painting."

WESTERN WALL The Western Wall and its surroundings in a 19th-cent. micrographic drawing by Samuel Schulmann, an artist in Ereẓ Israel.

firm that bears his name. One of earliest supporters of Ḥibbat Zion movement. Philanthropic activities incl. support of Hebrew literature (e.g. financing of *Ha-Shilo'aḥ*).

Wittenberg, Yiẓḥak (Itzig; 1907–1943), first commander of Jewish fighters' organization in Vilna ghetto. Arrested by Germans but released by ghetto fighters. Facing German ultimatum that unless he gave himself up ghetto would be destroyed, surrendered, was tortured, and died.

Wittgenstein, Ludwig (Josef Johann; 1889–1951), philosopher. B. in Austria to a Jewish father, he taught in Cambridge, England, fr. 1930. His *Tractatus logico-philosophicus* was a major influence on logical positivism and he inspired much of the subsequent development of analytic and semantic philosophy.

Wittlin, Józef (1896–), Polish poet, author, translator. Outstanding exponent of Polish Expressionism. Works incl. verse collection *Hymny,* modern Polish translation of Homer's *Odyssey,* and novel *The Salt of the Earth.* Translated foreign classics. In U.S. fr. 1941.

Wizen, Moshe Aharon (1878–1953), Hebrew grammarian; b. Galicia, taught in Vienna, settled in Tel Aviv 1938. Wrote comparative grammar of Hebrew and other Semitic languages. Unlike predecessors, did not confine himself to biblical Hebrew but included rabbinic and post-rabbinic Hebrew.

WIZO (Women's International Zionist Organization), women's Zionist movement, founded in London 1920. Original program professional and vocational training of women, education of women, care and education of children and youth. Member of World Zionist Organization. Headquarters in Tel Aviv. Practical work in Israel incl. educational and social activities for children and women. Membership 250,000, with 50 federations throughout world (excl. U.S., where Hadassah functions).

W.J.C., see World Jewish Congress.

Wogue, Lazare Eliezer (1817–1897), French rabbi. Taught at Séminaire Israélite de France. Translated Pentateuch into French with commentaries. Editor of *l'Univers Israélite* 1875–95.

Wohlgemuth, Joseph (1867–1942), German rabbi. Taught at Berlin Rabbinical Seminary. Wrote on precepts and in defense of Orthodoxy against Reform, founded and edited *Jeschurun,* which became leading Orthodox periodical of Jewish scholarship and thought.

Wolberg, Lewis Robert (1905–), U.S. psychiatrist, psychoanalyst. Prof. at NYU, founding Postgraduate Center for Mental Health. Pioneered new ways of bringing mental health treatment to individual, family, and wider community.

Wolf, family of U.S. communal leaders. Brothers **D.C. Elias** (1820–after 1881), **Abraham,** and **Levi** (1811–1893), b. Bavaria, settled in Philadelphia, establishing Rodeph Shalom Synagogue. Elias' son **Edwin** (1855–1934), held several communal and civic positions. Pres. of Jewish Publication Society 1903–13, chairman of Board of Governors of Dropsie College. His son, **Morris** (1883–), distinguished lawyer, served as member of Court of Common Pleas. Also prominent bibliophile and book collector. Morris's son, **Edwin Morris II** (1911–), librarian, historian, bibliographer. Pres. Jewish Publication Society 1954–59. Wrote *History of the Jews of Philadelphia.*

Wolf, Friedrich (1888–1953), German author. Fought in Republican Army during Spanish Civil War. East Germany's ambassador to Warsaw 1949–51. Political themes eventually replaced expressionist tendencies in his dramatic writing. Best-known drama, *Professor Mamlock,* dealt with Nazi persecution of Jews.

°**Wolf, Johann Christoph** (1683–1739), German bibliographer, Christian Hebraist. Author of 4-vol. *Bibliotheca Hebraea,* basic work of Hebrew bibliography. Left library of 25,000 Hebrew books and mss. to Hamburg city library.

Wolf, Leizer (1910–1943), Yiddish poet; founder of Young Vilna literary group. Wrote for Yiddish journals. Fled to Russia 1939; died while working on collective farm in Asiatic Russia.

Wolf, Lucien (1857–1930), English publicist, historian. Expert in foreign affairs. Edited bulletin *Darkest Russia* 1912–14, exposing Russian anti-Semitism. Served on communal bodies (Board of Deputies, etc.). Became strongly anti-Zionist. Did much research on Jewish history, founded Jewish Historical Society of England.

Wolf, Simon (1836–1923), U.S. lawyer, communal leader. U.S. consul in Egypt 1881. Spokesman for Jewish community to federal government. Pres. B'nai B'rith 1904. Fought for social justice, saving 103,000 aliens fr. deportation. Active in Reform Judaism. Writings incl. *The American Jew as Soldier, Patriot and Citizen.* His son, **Adolf Grant** (1869–1947), associate justice of Supreme Court of Puerto Rico fr. early 1900s until 1941.

Wolfe, Bertram David (1896–), U.S. historiographer. Joined Workers' (Communist) Party and edited its organ, but expelled 1929 and eventually broke with Marxist left. Wrote on Marxist history and Soviet affairs, incl. *Three Who Made A Revolution,* biographical study of Lenin, Trotsky, and Stalin.

Wolfe, Humbert (1885–1940), English poet, critic, civil servant. *Cursory Rhymes* first success. Published studies of Shelley and Tennyson, translations fr. Heine and Fleg.

Wolfenstein, Alfred (1888–1945), German expressionist poet, playwright, translator. Wrote stories and biographical study of Rimbaud. Fled fr. Prague to Paris 1938. Committed suicide.

Wolfert, Ira (1908–), U.S. author, journalist. Best known for WWII reporting and Pulitzer Prize-winning *Battle for the Solomons.*

Wolff, Abraham Alexander (1801–1891), chief rabbi of Copenhagen. Shaped character of Danish community, reconciling traditionalists and liberals. Translated prayer book and Pentateuch into Danish. Defended Judaism fr. attacks of Christian clergy.

Wolff, Bernhard (1811–1876), German journalist, publisher. First publisher in Germany to see importance of telegraphic communication in newspaper work; established Wolff's Telegraphisches Bureau 1849. Branches of his agency quickly sprang up all over Europe; taken over and renamed by Nazis.

Wolff, Joseph (1795–1862), German-born world traveler and

Student nurses and children at WIZO's Jerusalem Baby Home.

Christian missionary to Jews in Orient. Converted first to Catholicism and then to Anglicanism. His account of his travels contains much material of Jewish interest. Married daughter of Earl of Oxford. Their son, **Sir Henry Drummond,** diplomat and politician.

Wolff, Theodor (1868–1943), German journalist. Editor-in-chief of *Berliner Tageblatt* 1907–33. Favored international rapprochement and opposed jingoism; eventually resigned fr. German Democratic Party because of right-wing trend. Fled to the Riviera 1933 but arrested 1943 and sent to Germany, where he died.

Wolff, Werner (1904–1957), U.S. existential psychologist. One of first to introduce existential psychology in U.S. Worked at Columbia 1940–42, prof. at Bard College fr. 1942. Studied expression of personality in complex movements, children's drawings, and handwriting.

David Wolffsohn

Wolffsohn, David (1856–1914), Zionist leader; b. Lithuania, settled in Cologne as timber merchant. Joined Zionist political movement and was Herzl's constant companion. Responsible for selecting blue and white colors for Zionist flag and shekel for Zionist members' dues. Moving spirit behind founding of Jewish Colonial Trust, which he directed, as well as all other financial and economic institutions of the movement. Accompanied Herzl on his journey to Ereẓ Israel 1898. Elected 1905 to succeed Herzl as pres. of World Zionist movement. His efforts to bring "practical" Zionists closer to political Zionism did not succeed. Resigned from presidency 1911.

Wolfsberg, Oscar, see Aviad, Yeshayahu.

Wolfskehl, Karl (1869–1948), German poet. Devoted follower of Stefan George, whose circle met at Wolfskehl's Munich home 1899–1932. Neoclassical and mystical elements infuse much of his early poetry, but German, Greco-Roman, and biblical traditions generally shaped his writings. Left Germany after 1933 and settled in New Zealand, where a more Jewish note became evident in his work.

Wolfsohn-Halle, Aaron (1754–1835), writer; b. Germany. Taught in Jewish public schools, among most radical of early *maskilim,* editor of *Ha-Me'assef.* Made pioneer attempts to relate Bible stories in simplified Hebrew prose for schools. Published books of Job and I Kings in Mendelssohn translation with commentary.

Harry A. Wolfson

Wolfson, Harry Austryn (1887–), historian of philosophy. Educated at Slobodka yeshivah, and Harvard where he became prof. of Hebrew literature and philosophy. His pioneering researches, marked by penetrating analysis and clarity of exposition, incl. *Crescas' Critique of Aristotle, The Philosophy of Spinoza* and *Philo.* Also began publishing complete critical edition of works of Averroes.

Wolfson, Sir Isaac (1897–), British financier, philanthropist. Made Great Universal Stores Group, with 3,000 retail stores, mail order business, and transport organization, one of world's leading industrial and commercial empires. Established Wolfson Foundation 1955 which by 1970 distributed over £20,000,000 to charitable concerns. Financed Hechal Shlomo (Supreme Rabbinical Center in Jerusalem) and educational projects in Israel. Founded Wolfson College at Oxford. Pres. United Synagogue.

Wollemborg, Leone (1859–1932), Italian economist, statesman. Developed credit cooperative societies for farmers. Elected to Italian parliament 1892, Senate 1913. Minister of finance 1901. Outspoken critic of Mussolini's government.

Wolmark, Alfred (1877–1961), British artist. Painted studies of Jewish subjects in his early period. Later developed into brilliant colorist.

Wolowski (Schor), Christian family in Poland; of Jewish origin. Members joined Frankists 1755–56 and converted to Catholicism. **Elisha Schor,** *maggid,* joined Shabbateans and later sect of Jacob Frank. Fled to Turkey 1757. His son **Franciszek Lukasz,** secretary of King Stanislaus II Augustus, ennobled. Elisha's great-grandson **Jan Kanty** (1803–1864), secretary of state in Congress Poland, ennobled. Another great-grandson, **Franciszek** (1776–1844), jurist, statesman, member of Polish Sejm. His son **Louis François** (1810–1876), French economist, statesman. Founder of Crédit Foncier bank, elected to National Assembly 1871.

Wolpe, Stefan (1902–1972), composer. Taught at Palestine Conservatory of Music until 1938. Subsequently settled in U.S. Compositions incl. ballet *The Man from Midian.*

Wolper, David Lloyd (1928–), U.S. producer of TV documentaries. Films incl. *The Race for Space, The Making of the President, Let My People Go* on creation of State of Israel, and *The Rise and Fall of the Third Reich.*

Wolsey, Louis (1877–1953), U.S. Reform rabbi. Served in Little Rock, Cleveland, and Philadelphia. A founder of World Union for Progressive Judaism 1926. Favorable to non-political Zionism. Later led group that formed American Council for Judaism.

Woolf, Leonard Sidney (1880–1969), English author-publisher, socialist. Founded Hogarth Press with wife Virginia Woolf 1917. Ardent member of British Labor movement. His *International Government* was early blueprint for League of Nations. Edited political journals and wrote series of autobiographical works.

Woolf (Wulff), Moshe (1878–1971), Israel psychiatrist. Received training in Germany, returned to native Russia 1911 as only trained analyst in country. In Tel Aviv fr. 1933. Pres. Israel Psychoanalytical Society. Made basic contributions to psychoanalytical theory.

Worcester, city in Mass., U.S. First permanent Jewish settlement after Civil War, first congregation 1877. Jewish pop. 10,000 (1971).

Workmen's Circle (Yid. *Arbeiter Ring*), U.S. Jewish fraternal order with socialist cultural orientation, founded 1900. Provides members with mutual aid, health, and death benefits and other fraternal services, and supports labor and socialist movements. Has largest network of Jewish secular schools in U.S. Larg-

est Jewish benefit organization. Membership 64,000 (1967), with 421 branches.
World Conference of Jewish Organizations (COJO), roof organization of major Jewish organizations, established 1958. Nahum Goldmann first chairman, succeeded by W.A. Wexler 1971.
World Hebrew Union, see Berit Ivrit Olamit.
World Jewish Congress (WJC), voluntary association of representative Jewish bodies, communities, and organizations throughout world, organized to "assure the survival and foster the unity of the Jewish people." Founded 1936 to succeed Comité des Délégations Juives. Acts on behalf of Jewish communities exposed to danger, fights against anti-Semitism; recognized representation before international organs. Executive in four branches: N. America, S. America, Europe, Israel. Stephen Wise pres. until 1949, succeeded by Nahum Goldmann.
World Labor Zionist Movement, organizational framework encompassing Israel Labor Party and groups in Diaspora supporting it, established 1932. Until 1968 this function carried out mainly by "Iḥud Olami Po'alei Zion–Z.S.–Hitaḥadut," which served as world union of Mapai and its Diaspora supporters.
World Union for Progressive Judaism, roof organization of world Reform congregations, founded 1927; constituents in 26 countries, with 3 rabbinical seminaries (London, Paris, and Hebrew Union College, U.S.).
World Union of Jewish Students (WUJS), organization founded in Paris 1924. During WWII its center was transferred to Switzerland; moved fr. Paris to London 1968. Provides umbrella framework for nearly all trends in Jewish world. Main activities are educational, political, and Israel-oriented. Membership 100,000–110,000 (1971), with 30 national union members.
World Zionist Organization (WZO), worldwide official organization of Zionist movement founded on initiative of Herzl at First Zionist Congress 1897. Officially adopted name World Zionist Organization 1960. Headquarters in Jerusalem.
Wormann, Curt (1900–), librarian; b. Berlin, settled in Ereẓ Israel 1933. Director of Jewish National and University Library in Jerusalem 1947–68. Founded graduate library school at Heb. Univ. 1956.

Synagogue of Worms, reconstructed 1961.

Worms, city in W. Germany. Jews fr. 10th c., community flourished until massacre of First Crusade 1096. Major rabbinic authorities of 11th–13th c. lived there, incl. Rashi, Eleazar b. Judah, Meir of Rothenburg. Severe persecutions at time of Black Death 1349 but community reestablished. Jews who did not emigrate deported by Nazis.
Worms, Aaron (1754–1836), rabbi in Metz, France. Member of National Guard during French Revolution and of Assembly of Jewish Notables and Great Sanhedrin, expressing view that granting of civil rights to Jews would encourage them to assume added responsibilities toward state.
Worms, Asher Anshel (1695–1759), German physician, Hebrew author. Wrote on many Jewish topics. His *Seyag la-Torah* dealt with Masorah and masoretes.
Worms, de, family prominent in British finance and politics, tracing its descent back to R. Aaron Worms, whose grandson **Benedict de Worms** (d. 1824) married Jeanette von Rothschild. Their sons built up prosperous tea plantation in Ceylon. One son, **Solomon Benedict** (1801–1882), made baron of Austrian Empire for financial services and philanthropy. His eldest son, **Baron George** (1829–1912), vice-pres. Royal Society of Literature 1896–1900. Another son, **Henry (Lord Pirbright;** 1840–1903), Conservative MP; under-secretary for colonies 1888–92. Pres. Anglo-Jewish Association. Fellow of Royal Society.
Worms, René (1869–1926), French social scientist. Founded several sociological societies and established *Revue internationale de sociologie.*
Wormser, André (Alphonse Toussaint; 1851–1926), French composer. Composed successful operas, orchestral and choral works, piano pieces and songs. Best-known composition pantomime "wordless opera" *L'Enfant prodigue.*

Wormser, Olivier Boris (1913–), French diplomat. In Free French movement in London during WWII. French ambassador to Soviet Union 1966, governor of Banque de France 1969.
Wormser, Seckel (1768–1847), talmudist, kabbalist in Germany. Known as "Ba'al Shem of Michelstadt," being particularly known for his treatment of the insane.
Woroszylski, Wiktor (1927–), Polish poet, editor, translator. Chief editor of literary weekly *Nowa Kultura* 1956–57.
Wouk, Herman (1915–), U.S. writer. Wartime experiences in U.S. Navy gave him the material for Pulitzer Prize-winning *The Caine Mutiny.* Other works incl. *Marjorie Morningstar* and *The Winds of War.* Leading Orthodox layman; wrote *This is My God,* his affirmation of faith in traditional Judaism.

Herman Wouk

Woyslawski, Zevi (1889–1957), Hebrew writer, critic; left Russia for Berlin 1921, settled in Ereẓ Israel 1934, playing prominent role in literary life. In his philosophical writings examined essence of recent Jewish culture against background of European culture. Translated philosophical works into Hebrew.
Writers' Association in Israel, union of Hebrew writers in Israel, established 1921. Publishes series of books, literary journal *Moznayim,* and established bio-bibliographical Asher Barash Institute. Membership over 300 (1971).
Written Law, law given to Moses on Sinai. Strictly speaking, Pentateuch (Torah); but by extension also used for other biblical books.
Wroclaw, see Breslau.
°**Wuensche, August Karl** (1839–1913), German scholar of Bible and *aggadah.* Translated into German *aggadot* of Jerusalem and Babylonian Talmud, *Midrash Rabbah,* and other works. Edited 3-vol. anthology of Jewish literature with Jacob Winter.
Wuerttemberg, state in Germany. Jews fr. 13th c. Settlements suffered

during Rindfleisch massacre 1298, Armleder uprising 1335–37, and Black Death 1348–49. Expelled 1521, returning only in 18th c. Received full civil rights 1828, full autonomy 1912. 10,023 Jews in 1933, with 43 communities. Only 180 survivors after WWII.

Wuerzburg, city in W. Germany. Community founded c. 1100. Center of learning in 12th–13th c. Community destroyed 1298, 1349. Expelled 1567, renewed only in 19th c. 2,145 Jews in 1933. Community ended in WWII. Jewish pop. 150 (1967).

WUJS, see World Union of Jewish Students.

Wulff, Moshe, see Woolf, Moshe.

Wunderlich, Frieda (1884–1965), economist. Expert in fields of national economy, labor legislation, sociology, and social politics. Member of Prussian parliament 1930–33. In New York fr. 1933, teaching at New School for Social Research.

Wurzburger, Walter S. (1920–), U.S. Orthodox rabbi; b. Germany, in U.S. fr. 1938. Taught philosophy at Yeshiva Univ.; editor-in-chief of periodical *Tradition.*

Wurzweiler, Gustav (1896–1954), U.S. banker, philanthropist; b. Germany, in U.S. fr. 1941. Orthodox Jew. Established foundation 1950, benefiting many Jewish institutions.

Wygodzki, Stanisław (1907–), Polish poet, author. Communist fr. youth. Returned to Poland fr. Auschwitz 1947 and published many volumes of poetry and prose reflecting his struggle against social evils. In Israel fr. 1968.

Wyler, William (1902–), U.S. film director. Started work with his uncle, Carl Laemmle, head of Universal Pictures, won Academy Awards for directing *Mrs. Miniver, The Best Years of Your Life,* and *Ben-Hur.*

Wynn, Ed (Isaiah Edwin Leopold; 1886–1966), U.S. comedian. Films incl. *Diary of Anne Frank*. His biography written by his son **Keenan** (1916–), author and stage, screen, and TV actor.

Wyoming, U.S. state. First Jews 1867; more came with gold rush 1876. First congregation (Reform) established 1888, followed by Orthodox 1910, which merged 1919. Jewish pop. 345 (1971).

Wyzanski, Charles Edward, Jr. (1906–), U.S. jurist. Chief judge of Massachusetts District Court fr. 1966. Pres. Harvard Board of Overseers.

Jewish communities in Wyoming.

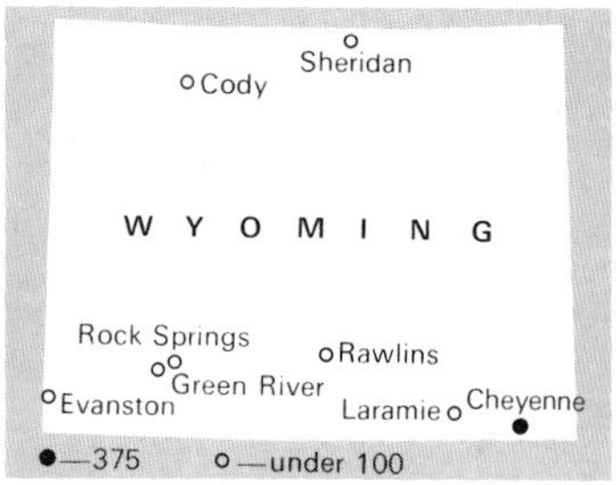

The letter "X" set against an illustration of the story of Balaam and his ass, from a book of designs for the alphabet, Saragossa, 1555.

Xanten, town in W. Germany. Jews suffered during First Crusade 1096, Black Death 1349. Blood libel 1892 and arrested Jews acquitted but community could not survive agitation.

Xerxes, see Ahasuerus.

Ximenes, Sir David (1776–1848), English army officer. Served in N. America and Ireland and fought in Italy, Spain, Portugal. Retired as lieutenant general.

The letter "Y" set against illustration of Tobit awakening to find himself blind, from a book of designs for the alphabet, Saragossa, 1555.

Ya'aleh Ve-Yavo (Heb. "May [our remembrance] ascend and come . . . before Thee"), additional paragraph inserted in *Amidah* and grace after meals on New Moon and festivals.

Yaari, Abraham (1899–1966), bibliographer, historian, librarian; b. Galicia, settled in Ereẓ Israel 1920. Worked in National and University Library. Rediscovered little-known Hebrew books, esp. those printed in oriental countries, and published letters, memoirs, travel descriptions fr. unknown mss.

Torah pointers (yad).

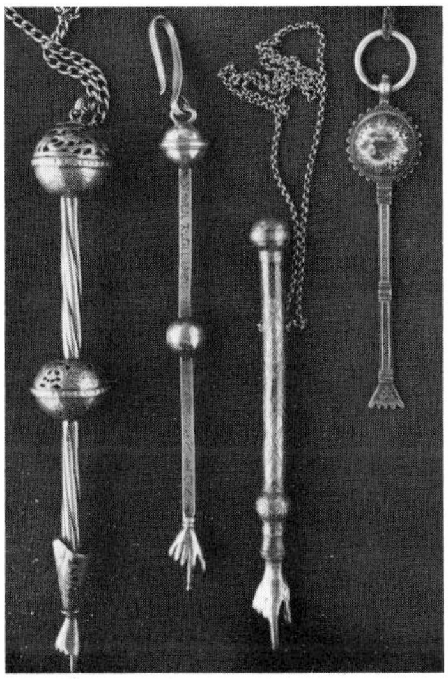

Yaari (Wald), Meir (1897–), Israel labor leader, ideologist; b. Galicia. Among founders of first group that constituted Ha-Shomer ha-Ẓa'ir in Vienna. In Ereẓ Israel fr. 1920. Fought to make Ha-Shomer ha-Ẓa'ir indigenous political and educational body with defined left-wing ideological platform, first as Ha-Kibbutz ha-Arẓi 1927 and later as Mapam Party 1948. Member of Knesset 1949–73 and general secretary of Mapam.

Yaari, Yehudah (1900–), Hebrew writer; brother of Abraham Yaari; b. Galicia; settled in Ereẓ Israel 1920. Worked in Keren Hayesod and later in Israel Foreign Ministry. Wrote stories and novels on E. European life and *ḥalutzim* of Third Aliyah.

Yad (Heb. "hand"). (1) Pointer used when reading Scroll of Law in public. (2) Memorial pillar. (3) *Mishneh Torah* of Maimonides, which contains 14 (Heb. *YD*) books (also called *Yad ha-Ḥazakah*).

Yadayim, tractate in Mishnah order *Tohorot,* with no *gemara.* Deals with laws of washing hands and their ritual impurity.

Yadin, Yigael (1917–), Israel archaeologist; second chief of staff of Israel Defense Forces 1949–52; son of E.L. Sukenik. As operations and planning officer of Haganah, drew up and implemented operations in War of Independence. Prof. at Heb. Univ. Conducted extensive excavations at Hazor and Masada and in Judean Desert, on which he wrote both scientific and popular books. Published studies on Dead Sea Scrolls. Israel Prize 1956.

Yigael Yadin

Yad Vashem memorial shrine.

Yad Mordekhai, kibbutz in S. Israel, founded 1943. In War of Independence reduced to ruins after 6 days of fierce fighting against Egyptian invaders May 1948; retaken Oct. 1948 and rebuilt on larger scale. Maintains Holocaust museum. Name commemorates Mordecai Anielewicz, statue of whom is erected there. Pop. 474 (1971).

Yad Vashem, Israel Martyrs' and Heroes' Remembrance Authority in Jerusalem, perpetuating memory of those killed in Holocaust and for research and documentation into period. Includes memorial hall, museum of Holocaust, Hall of Names of Victims, and central archive and library.

Yaffo, see Jaffa.

Yagur, kibbutz in N. Israel, nr. Haifa, founded 1922 by members of Gedud ha-Avodah. Soon became largest kibbutz in country. Haganah's central arms cache found there 1946

Kingdom of Alexander Yannai, 103–76 B.C.E.

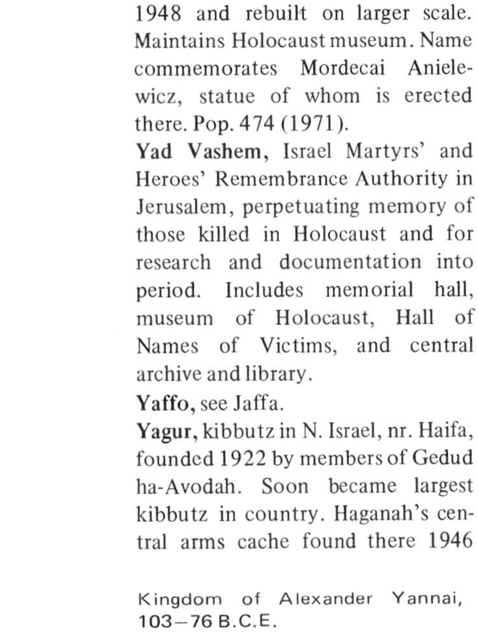

and many members taken to detention camps. Pop. 1,140 (1971).

Yaḥad (Heb.), term used in Dead Sea Scrolls in sense of "community" with special reference to Qumran community.

Yah Ribbon Olam (Aram. "God, Master of the Universe"), first words of Sabbath table song. Composed by Israel Najara in 16th c.

Yahrzeit (Yid. "anniversary"), anniversary of death of close relative on which *Kaddish* is recited and grave visited. Word is also used generally for any anniversary of somber nature.

Yahuda, Abraham Shalom (1877–1951), orientalist; b. Jerusalem. Prof. in Berlin 1904–14, Madrid 1915–22, New School for Social Research in New York 1942. Wrote biblical and philological works, and claimed strong Egyptian influence on language of Pentateuch. Edited Arabic original of Baḥya's *Ḥovot ha-Levavot.*

Yahudi, Yusuf (1688–1755), Bukharan poet. Wrote Judeo-Persian poetry on biblical and religious themes. His Tajiki version of *Haft Braderan,* based on Midrash of Hannah and her seven sons, is still popular. Translated Ibn Gabirol and Najara.

Yaḥya, Ibn, see Ibn Yaḥya.

Yakhini, Abraham ben Elijah (1617–1682), kabbalist, preacher, Shabbatean in Constantinople. Wrote on Lurianic Kabbalah. Appointed a "king of Israel" by Shabbetai Ẓevi, in whom he continued to believe even after apostasy.

Yakir, Yonah (1896–1937), Soviet general. Commanded Red Army division in Civil War. A founder of Red Army armored corps. Military commander of Ukraine, member of Supreme Military Council 1930–37. Shortly after, arrested on spy charges and executed. His son **Piotr** (1923–), historian. Spent many years in exile and labor camps (until 1954). Fr. 1960s among leaders of democratic opposition in USSR until arrested 1972; released 1973.

Yaknehaz, Hebrew mnemonic conveying order in which blessings are recited on eve of festival which coincides with conclusion of Sabbath (Wine – Sanctification – Light – *Havdalah* – Blessing of Time).

Yaknehaz (pseud. of **Isaiah-Nissan Hakohen Goldberg;** 1858–1927), Yiddish, Hebrew writer; lived in Minsk. Portrayed life of small Jewish town. Popular among masses.

Yalan-Stekelis (Wilensky), Miriam (1900–), Hebrew poet, writer of children's literature; b. Russia, settled in Ereẓ Israel 1920. Many of her poems set to music. Israel Prize 1957.

Yalkut (Ha-)Makhiri, anthology of aggadic Midrashim by Makhir b. Abba Mari, of which only parts on some of Prophets and Hagiographa have been preserved. Compiled by 15th c.; of Spanish origin.

Yalkut Shimoni, aggadic anthology on entire Bible, usually called simply "the Yalkut." Compiled by a Simeon of Frankfort whose exact identity is not known. Began to circulate widely in late 15th c. and became so popular that its numerous sources were neglected.

Yalon (Distenfeld), Hanoch (1886–1970), Hebrew linguist; b. Galicia, settled in Jerusalem 1921. Innovator in research on Hebrew language; studies cover all periods of its history. First to recognize importance of living traditions of Hebrew, esp. Yemenite. Israel Prize 1962.

Yamim Nora'im (Heb. "Days of Awe"), term applied to New Year and Day of Atonement; also to Ten Days of Penitence.

Yanait, Raḥel, see Ben-Zvi, Raḥel Yanait.

Yannai (Yannai Rabbah, "the Great"; 3rd c.), Palestinian *amora.* Taught that danger may not be incurred in expectation of miracle, permitted fields to be sown in sabbatical year to meet government taxation. Saying: "Better not to give charity at all than to shame the recipient by giving it to him in public."

Yannai (? 5th–6th c.), liturgical poet; outstanding representative of old Palestinian *piyyut.* Wrote *kerovot* for all weekly Torah readings of triennial cycle. His work contains much *halakhah,* but was superseded by *piyyutim* of Kallir and lost until rediscovered, mainly in Cairo *Genizah.*

Yannai (Jannaeus), Alexander (c. 126–76 B.C.E.), Hasmonean king and high priest 103–76 B.C.E. Energetic ruler whose reign was characterized by internal dissension as well as striking military successes, in which he conquered much of S. Syria and Transjordan. Most of reign marked by breach with Pharisees accentuated by king's despotic cruelty but in last years effected some reconciliation.

Yarcho, Noe (Noah; 1862–1912), Argentine physician; b. Russia, worked in Jewish settlements in Entre Ríos province and offered spiritual and physical aid both to

Jewish and native settlers. Wrote study of typhoid epidemic.

Yarkon or **Me-Yarkon (Jarkon),** river rising nr. Rosh ha-Ayin and entering Mediterranean at Tel Aviv. In recent years half its waters directed to irrigate Negev.

Yarmolinsky, Avrahm (1890–), U.S. literary scholar, biographer; b. Ukraine, in U.S. fr. 1913. Headed Slavonic division of N.Y. Public Library 1918–55. Major works incl. *Turgenev, Dostoevsky, Literature under Communism.* Married to Babette Deutsch.

Yarmuk, confluent of Jordan R. on east side, on the Israel–Jordan–Syrian border; largest river in Transjordan. Famous battle bet. Byzantines and Arabs fought on banks 636, deciding fate of Syria in favor of Muslims. Haifa–Damascus railroad formerly ran there and its bridge was blown up by Lawrence in WWI. Channeled for irrigation.

Yaron, Reuven (1924–), Israel scholar of Roman and Ancient Near Eastern law; b. Vienna, settled in Ereẓ Israel 1939. Taught at Heb. Univ. Directed National and Univ. Library fr. 1973.

Yaroslavsky, Yemelyan (Gubelman; 1878–1943), Russian Communist leader, historian. Close collaborator of Lenin. Member of Party Central Committee 1923 and one of Stalin's principal supporters. Chairman of the League of Militant Godless. Headed party's propaganda machine in WWII.

Yashar, see Reggio, Isacco Samuel.

Yashar of Candia, see Delmedigo, Joseph Solomon.

Yassky, Haim (1896–1948), ophthalmologist, medical administrator in Ereẓ Israel; b. Kishinev, settled in Ereẓ Israel 1919. Director of Hadassah Medical Organization fr. 1931 and Hadassah hospital; killed by Arabs in massacre of Scopus convoy.

Yates, Sidney R. (1909–), U.S. lawyer, congressman. Elected to Congress 1948. U.S. representative to UN Trusteeship Council 1963–64. Prominent liberal who fought for ecology measures, urban housing improvement, and electoral reform.

Ya'veẓ, see Emden, Jacob.

Yavne'el, see Jabneel.

Yavne'eli, Shemuel (1884–1961), labor leader in Ereẓ Israel; b. Ukraine, settled in Ereẓ Israel 1905. Worked as agricultural laborer. Went to Yemen 1911 disguised as Yemenite rabbi to study Jewish community there and encourage it to emigrate to Ereẓ Israel. Wrote history of Ḥibbat Zion.

Yavneh, development town in C. Israel, nr. Reḥovot. Pop. 10,200 (1971). See also Jabneh.

Yawetz, Yoseph, see Jabez, Joseph.

Yeb, see Elephantine.

Yedi'ot Aḥaronot, Hebrew daily afternoon newspaper published in Tel Aviv; founded 1939. Weekday circ. 154,000, weekend 226,000 (1974).

Yefroykin, Israel (1884–1954), socialist, communal leader; b. Lithuania. Helped organize Yidishe Folkspartei after 1917 Revolution and directed YEKOPO (Jewish Relief Committee) in Paris 1920–25. A founder of World Jewish Congress. Active in Po'alei Zion Party. Founder and pres. of Fédération des Sociétés Juives.

Yehoash

Yehoash (pseud. of **Yehoash Solomon Bloomgarden;** 1872–1927), Yiddish poet, Bible translator; b. Lithuania, in U.S. fr. 1890. Wrote poems, fables, folktales, stories. His Yiddish translation of Bible is regarded as masterpiece. Co-authored Yiddish dictionary. Translated English, German, American literature.

Yehoshua, Avraham B. (1936–), Israel writer. His stories, marked by psychological insight and often written in surrealistic form, regarded among outstanding works of recent Hebrew writing.

Yehud, urban settlement in C. Israel, nr. Tel Aviv. Pop. 8,750 (1971).

Yehudai ben Naḥman (Yehudai Gaon), head of Sura academy c. 757–61. *Halakhot Pesukot* attributed to him. As he was blind his pupils wrote his rulings. This work spread influence and authority of Babylonian Talmud throughout Jewish world.

Yehudi ben Sheshet (10th c.), Spanish Hebrew grammarian, poet. Pupil of Dunash b. Labrat; replied to criticisms of his teacher's work, dealing at same time with many grammatical problems.

Yeivin, Shemuel (1896–), Israel archaeologist, historian; b. Odessa. Chief translator for British mandatory government 1944–48. Chairman of Jewish Exploration Society 1944–46, director of Israel Dept. of Antiquities 1948–61, prof. at Tel Aviv Univ. Israel Prize 1968.

Yeivin, Yehoshua Heschel (1891–1970), Hebrew writer, editor; b. Ukraine, settled in Ereẓ Israel 1924. Joined Revisionist movement and became an editor of its publications.

Yekaterinoslav, see Dnepropetrovsk.

Yekopo (acronym of Russ. for "Jewish Relief Committee for War Victims"), organization formed in Russia after outbreak of WWI to succor Jewish war victims. Central Petrograd committee headed by Jewish notables. Received support from ORT, ICA, OZE, etc., and was recognized by Russian authorities. After 1920 continued to function in Poland.

Yekum Purkan (Aram. "May deliverance arise"), first words of two prayers recited on Sabbath mornings by Ashkenazim after reading *haftarah* for (a) welfare of students and teachers in academies of Ereẓ Israel and Babylon, (b) welfare of local community.

Yelizavetgrad, see Kirovograd.

David Yellin

Yellin, David (1864–1941), teacher, scholar, leader in Ereẓ Israel; son of Yehoshua Yellin. Key figure in development of Hebrew as spoken language. Pres. Teachers' Association. Founded and headed Hebrew Teachers' Seminary in Jerusalem. Prof. of Hebrew poetry of Spanish period at Heb. Univ. and published works in this field. Helped found Va'ad ha-Lashon, local B'nai B'rith, and National Library. Deputy-mayor of Jerusalem 1920–25, chairman of Va'ad Le'ummi 1920–28. His son **Aviezer** (1890–1972), founder of Maccabi, secretary of Teachers' Association. Another son, **Avinoam** (1900–1937), educator, orientalist. Published modern textbooks in Hebrew and classical Arabic. Supervisor of Jewish schools in Mandatory administration. Killed by Arab rioters. Daughter-in-law **Thelma** (née **Bentwich;** 1895–1959), cellist, active pioneer of Jerusalem musical life.

Yellin, Yehoshua (1843–1924), Erez̤ Israel pioneer. A founder of Naḥalat Shivah quarter of Jerusalem 1869. With father purchased land on which settlement of Moẓa was established 1891. Member of Jerusalem Town Council 1897–1901

Yellin-Mor (Friedman), Nathan (1913–), Israel underground leader; b. Poland, reached Erez̤ Israel after outbreak of WWII and joined Avraham Stern in Loḥamei Ḥerut Yisrael, which he headed fr. 1943. Elected on Loḥamim ticket to First Knesset.

Yellow Badge, see Badge.

Yemenite silversmith in Israel, 1960.

Students at Yeshiva University.

"Gemara" lesson in Lomza Yeshivah, Poland.

Yemen (Heb. *Teiman*), country in SW Arabian Peninsula. Jews possibly present fr. Second Temple period, definitely fr. pre-Islamic period. Converts to Judaism incl. Himyarite king Dhu Nuwās. In 11th c. Yemenite Jews acknowledged authority of *geonim* in Iraq and later center at Fostat in Egypt. Shi'ites became fanatical in 12th c., causing many conversions and Jewish messianic movement, about which Maimonides wrote to Yemenite Jews. Ottoman conquest 1566 caused tribulations for Jews, and for 400 years situation fluctuated. Economic and social situation was abysmal, and messianic fervor frequent. 30,000 Jews in 19th c. Community incl. noted scholars, rabbis, poets, kabbalists. Yemenites began emigrating to Erez̤ Israel fr. late 19th c. Almost all 46,000 Jews left for Israel in Operation Magic Carpet 1949–50. Jewish pop. 500 (1971).

Yeroḥam, urban settlement in Israel, S. of Beersheba; founded 1951. Populated by new immigrants. Pop. 5,650 (1971).

Yeshayahu, Israel (1910–), Israel politician; b. Yemen, settled in Erez̤ Israel 1929. Active in Mapai and Histadrut. Helped organize mass immigration of Jews fr. Yemen 1950. Member of Knesset fr. 1949; minister of posts 1967–70, secretary of Israel Labor Party 1970–72, speaker of Knesset fr. 1972.

Yeshevav the Scribe (2nd c.), *tanna.* Opposed view of Akiva that offspring of all prohibited unions are *mamzerim.* Considered one of Ten Martyrs; put to death by Romans at age of 91.

Yeshivah Shel Ma'alah, see Academy on High.

Yeshiva University, Orthodox institute of higher education in New York. Formed around Rabbi Isaac Elhanan Theological Seminary founded 1897 for advanced study of Talmud. Beginning with introduction of secular studies 1915, advanced from college to university status 1945, incl. a college for women (Stern College). Programs incl. humanities and sciences, social work, and medicine (Albert Einstein School). Ordained 1,100 rabbis. Enrollment 7,057 (1972).

Yeshivot (Heb. "academies"), name for institutes of talmudic learning first applied to academies (q.v.) of Erez̤ Israel and Babylonia and later to institutes of talmudic studies which developed in post-geonic period throughout Jewish world. Originally developed wherever local rabbi or scholar attracted pupils, later some countries ruled that every large community must maintain certain number of students. Famous Lithuanian yeshivot extended under impetus of Vilna Gaon and his followers. More recently independent institutions of talmudic and rabbinic study were established in all parts of Jewish world.

Yeshurun, Avot (pseud. of **Yeḥiel Perlmutter;** 1904–), Israel poet; b. Volhynia. settled in Erez̤ Israel 1925. Unconventional style and distortion of syntax reflect attempt to forge new idiom.

Yesud Ha-Ma'alah, moshavah in N. Israel, established 1883 as one of earliest settlements in country. In early days suffered from malarial swamps in neighborhood. Pop. 455 (1971).

Yevamot, 1st tractate of Mishnah order *Nashim,* with *gemara* in both Talmuds. Deals with laws of levirate marriage (Deut. 25:5–10), but goes far beyond it and incl. prohibited degrees of marriage, foundlings, rape, evidence of death required before woman can remarry.

Yevpatoriya (Eupatoria), city in Ukrainian SSR. Large Jewish community under Tatar rule in 15th–18th c. Later largest center of Karaites in Russia, with small Rabbanite community, together numbering 2,409 in 1921. All Rabbanite Jews murdered 1941 but Karaites escaped.

Yevsektsiya, Jewish sections of propaganda dept. of Russian Communist Party 1918–1930. Responsible for liquidation of Jewish communal, political, and cultural organizations and fought Hebrew and Judaism. Initiated Jewish settlement in Birobidzhan. Organs were *Der Emes, Der Shtern* and *Oktyabr.* Sections liquidated 1930 and activities in late 1930s.

Yez̤er ha-Tov (ha-Ra), see Inclinaation, Good and Evil.

Yezierska, Anzia (1885–1970), U.S. novelist. Works dealt with adjustment of Jewish immigrant to American life.

Yez̤irah, Sefer (Heb. "Book of Creation"), earliest extant Hebrew text of systematic speculative thought on cosmology and cosmogony. Because of its brevity, laconic style, and terminology, expounded in many ways and played central role in Jewish mysticism. Written bet. 3rd and 6th c.

Yez̤iv Pitgam (Heb. "True is the saying"), Aramaic *reshut* recited by

Ashkenazim before reading *haftarah* on second day of Shavuot. Describes revelation on Sinai.

Yibbum, see Levirate Marriage.

Yiddisher Kultur Farband (YKUF), Communist-oriented U.S. association for preserving and developing Yiddish culture; founded 1937. Issues *Yiddishe Kultur* and publishes books.

Yiddish, language of medieval German origin used by Ashkenazi Jews over past thousand years. Basic and main vocabulary is German, with admixture of Hebrew, Romance, and Slavic, together with local vernacular. Began in 10th c. in Middle Rhine region, spread with Jews in their wanderings to rest of Europe, and in 19th and 20th c. even farther. Written in Hebrew characters. Historical development: Earliest Yiddish until 1250; Old Yiddish 1250–1500; Middle Yiddish 1500–1700; Modern Yiddish fr. 1700. By 1939, 11 million Yiddish speakers. Intensive literary activity esp. fr. latter part of 19th c. Holocaust, liquidation of Yiddish culture in USSR and process of assimilation elsewhere led to drastic reduction in number of Yiddish speakers.

Yidisher Kemfer, U.S. Yiddish weekly, founded 1906 as organ of Po'alei Zion Party. Disseminated Socialist Zionist ideology.

Yidishes Tageblat, New York Yiddish daily newspaper; founded by K.H. Sarasohn 1885, merged with *Morning Journal* 1928. Spokesman for Orthodoxy.

Yigdal (Heb. "May He be magnified"), first word of Hebrew liturgical hymn, based on Maimonides' Thirteen Articles of Faith, sung at conclusion of Friday and festival eve services in most rites. Probably composed in 14th c.

Yiḥus (Heb.), term signifying lineage and popularly used for belonging to family of good Jewish standing.

Yiḥye, Isaac ha-Levi (1867–1932), last chief rabbi of Yemenite Jewry. Organized community after war and famine of 1903–04. Wrote responsa. His son **Shalom Isaac ha-Levi** (1891–), chief rabbi of Yemenite Jews in Israel.

Yinnon (Indelman), Moshe (1895–), Hebrew, Yiddish journalist; b. Poland, settled in Ereẓ Israel 1940. Editor of Mosad Bialik (publishing house) 1943–56; edited weekly *Hadoar* in New York fr. 1959.

Yishtabbaḥ (Heb. "Praised be . . . "), first word of blessing concluding psalm section *Pesukei de-Zimra* in the morning service. Authorship unknown.

Yishuv (Heb.), Jewish community in Ereẓ Israel in pre-State period. Pre-Zionist community generally designated "old *yishuv*" and community evolving after 1880 "new *yishuv*."

YIVO (abbr. for **Yidisher Visenshaftlikher Institut) Institute for Jewish Research,** principal world organization conducting research in Yiddish; founded in Vilna 1925. By 1939 branches in 30 countries. During WWII main center transferred to New York. Important library, sponsors research, and issues scholarly publications and periodicals.

Yizḥaki, Abraham ben David (1661–1729), *Rishon le-Zion,* chief rabbi of Jerusalem, halakhic authority, kabbalist. Opponent of Shabbateanism, author of responsa.

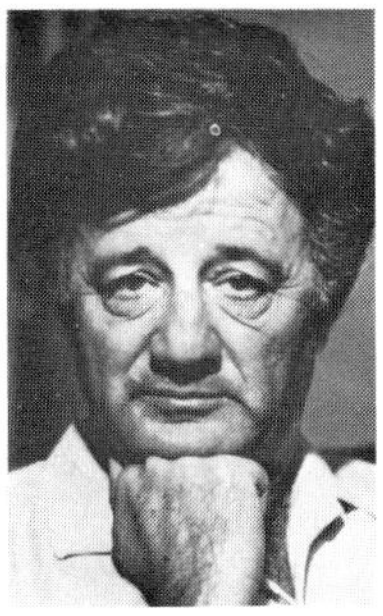

S. Yizhar

Yizhar, S. (Smilansky, Yizhar; 1916–), Israel author. Member of Knesset (Mapai-Rafi) 1949–67. Author of stories and novels, notably *Yemei Ẓiklag,* panoramic war novel, one of the central works of "Palmaḥ generation." Posed moral problems and challenges.

Yizkor (Heb. "May He remember"), opening word of memorial prayer for dead; also applied to memorial section of service on those days of festivals when dead relations are commemorated.

Yod (י), 10th letter of Hebrew alphabet; numerical value 10. Pronounced *y*.

Yodefat, see Jotapata.

Yoma, 5th tractate of Mishnah order *Mo'ed,* with *gemara* in both Talmuds. Deals with Temple service on Day of Atonement.

Yom Ha-Aẓma'ut, see Independence Day, Israel.

Yom Ha-Kippur(im), see Day of Atonement.

Yom Ha-Sho'ah, see Holocaust Remembrance Day.

Yom Ha-Zikkaron (Heb. "Remembrance Day"), memorial day observed in Israel for those who have fallen in active service. Observed Iyyar 4 (day before Independence Day) with solemn civil, military, and religious ceremonies.

Emblem of Belorussian Soviet Republic, early 1920s, inscribed in Yiddish in addition to Belorussian, Russian, and Polish.

Editorial board of Warsaw Yiddish journal, "Literarishe Bleter," 1925.

Engraving of tractate "Yoma," Amsterdam, 1700-04.

Yom Kippur Katan (Heb. "Minor Day of Atonement"), name for eve of New Moon. Fr. 16th c. customary for pious to fast on that day.

EGYPTIAN ATTACK

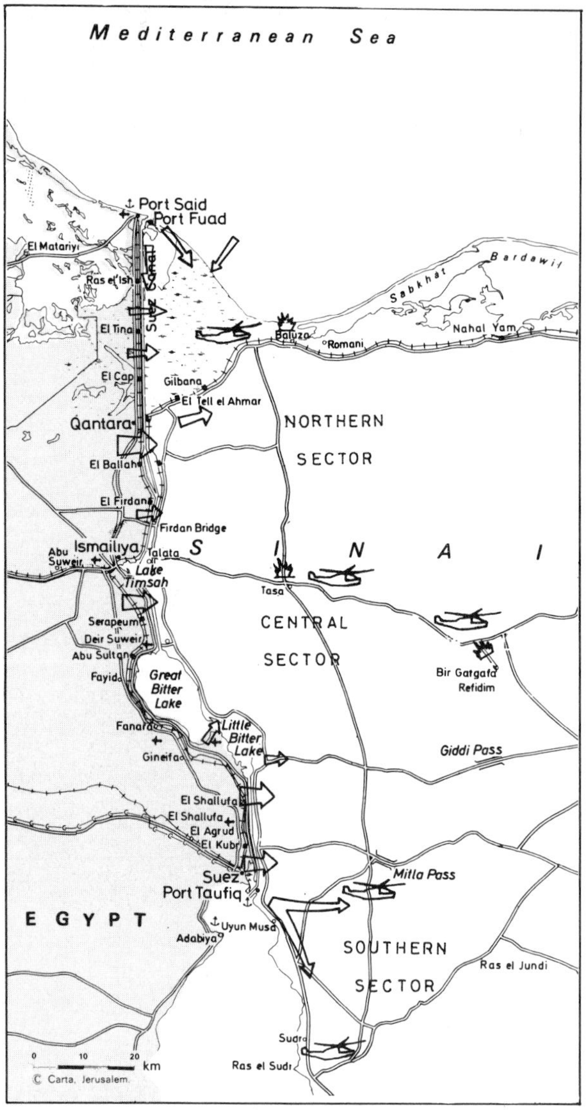

ISRAEL COUNTEROFFENSIVE

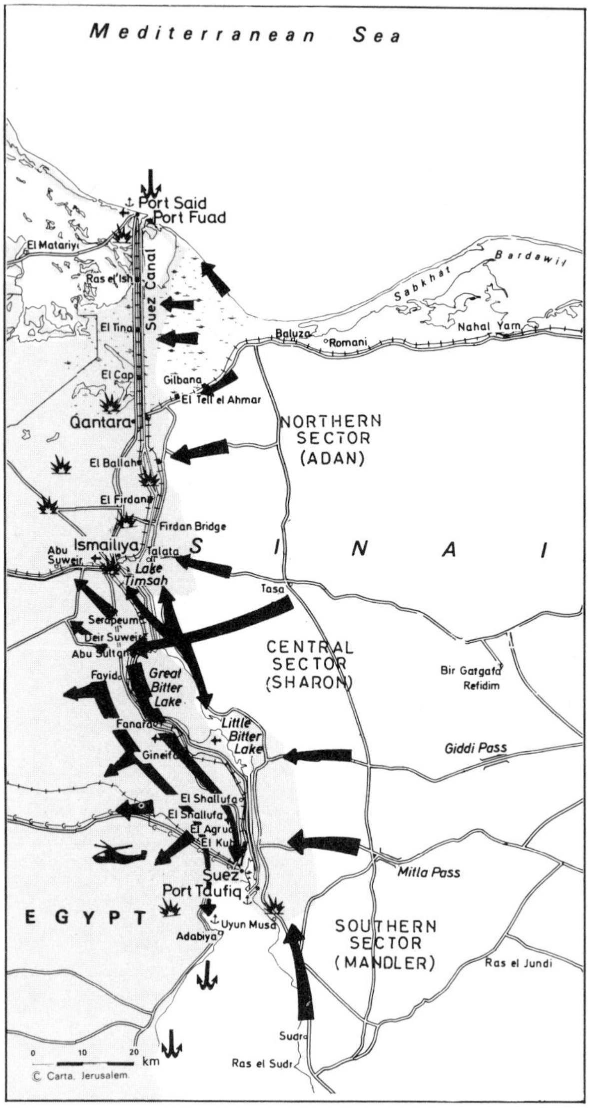

Helicopter-borne Commandos
Bombing Raids
Navy Operation
Attacks

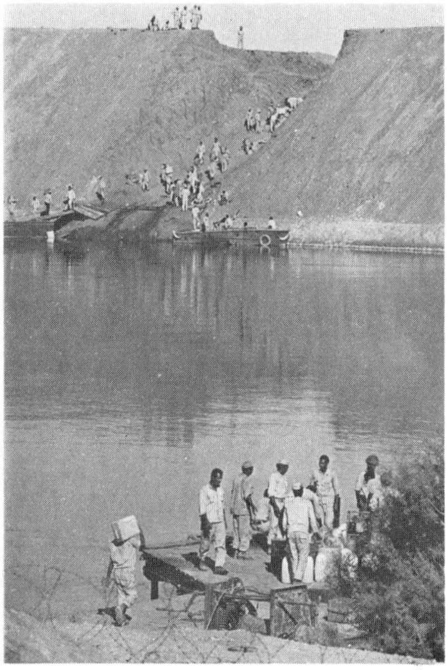

Bridge across Suez Canal built by Israel army.

Besieged Egyptian Third Army on banks of Suez Canal.

SYRIAN ATTACK

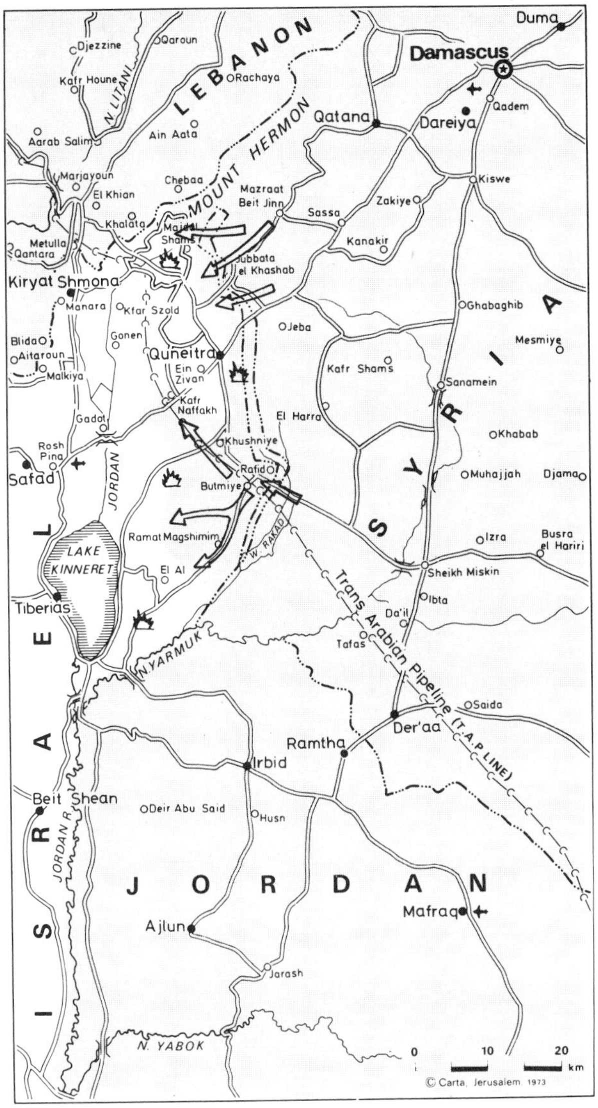

ISRAEL COUNTEROFFENSIVE

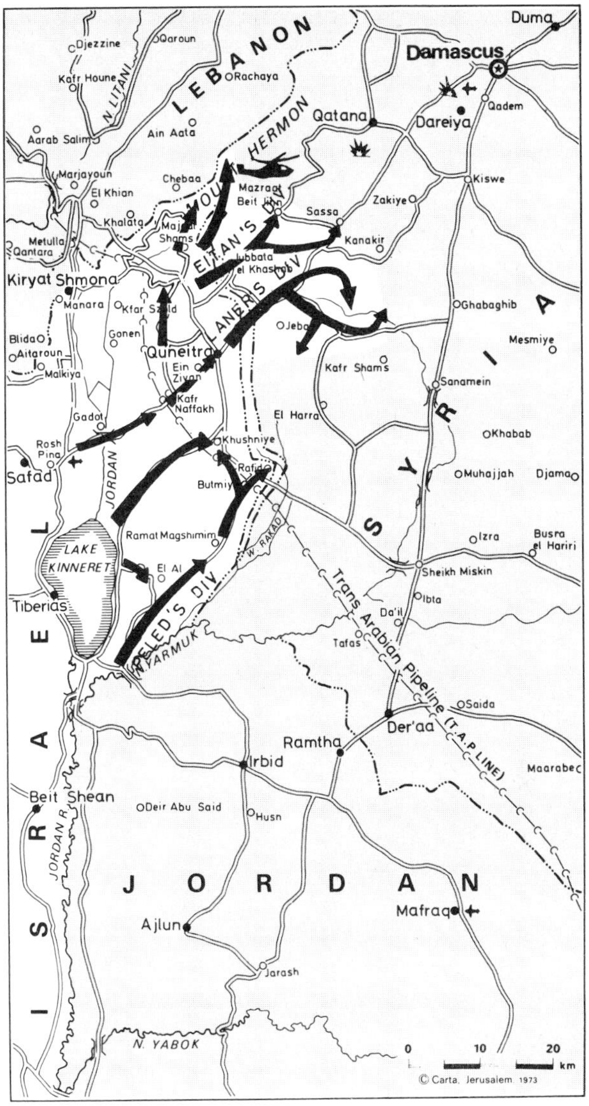

Helicopter-borne Commandos
Bombing Raids
Attacks

Yom Kippur War, war that broke out on Yom Kippur (Oct. 6) 1973 when Israel positions in Sinai and the Golan Heights were attacked by Egypt and Syria respectively. The Syrian forces succeeded in overrunning much of the Golan Heights before being stopped and then pushed back with the help of Israel's newly-mobilized reserves. By Oct. 9 the Syrians had been driven back over the pre-war frontier in the direction of Damascus, despite reinforcements of Iraqi, Jordanian, and other Arab troops. In the South, the Egyptians crossed the Suez Canal and captured forward Israel positions (the Bar-Lev line), before being held in massive tank battles. Arab losses in arms were replaced by the USSR in an airlift and on Oct. 14 the U.S. started an airlift to replace Israel losses. On Oct. 16 an Israel force crossed to the West of the Suez Canal and attacked Egyptian forces fr. the rear, eventually cutting off the Egyptian Third Army. With the Arabs threatened by defeat, the USSR sought to arrange a cease-fire and invited U.S. Secretary of State, Henry Kissinger, to Moscow. On Oct 22, the U.N. passed the U.S.–Soviet resolution for a cease-fire which called for direct peace negotiations. Fighting continued on the Suez front until Oct. 25. Israel lost over 2,600 men in the fighting.

Israel artillery barrage on Golan Heights.

Yom Tov, see Festivals; Beẓah.

Yom Tov ben Abraham Ishbili (Ritba; c. 1250–1330), Spanish talmudist. Regarded as spiritual leader of the time. Questions reached him fr. far and wide. Reputation rests on his novellae *Ḥiddushei ha-Ritba* to most tractates of Talmud; also early responsa and defense of Maimonides' *Guide.*

Yom Tov of Joigny (d. 1190), synagogal poet. Settled in York, England. Author of hymn *Omnam Ken* read on eve of Day of Atonement. Inspired mass suicide of Jews beleaguered in York castle.

Yoreh De'ah, see Shulḥan Arukh.

York, city in England. Jews fr. mid-12th c. attained considerable prosperity. Jews took refuge in castle after anti-Jewish rioting 1190; besieged by mob they committed mass suicide. 45 Jews in 1971.

Clifford's Tower in York, site of mass-suicide of the Jewish community, 1190.

York-Steiner, Heinrich Elchanan (1859–1934), Zionist publicist. Businessman in Vienna who joined Herzl and became ardent political Zionist. Joined Revisionist movement in 1920s. Settled in Ereẓ Israel 1933.

Yose (4th c.), Palestinian *amora* in Tiberias; identified with R. Yose b. Zevida. Discussions bet. him and R. Jonah fill pages of Jerusalem Talmud.

Yose bar Ḥanina (3rd c.), Palestinian *amora* in Tiberias; a pupil-colleague of Johanan. Outstanding aggadist. Teacher of Abbahu.

Yose (Issi) ben Akavyah (2nd c.), *tanna.* Mishnah (Sot. 9:15), states that with his death pious men came to end.

Yose ben Ḥalafta (2nd c.), *tanna;* usually called simply R. Yose; pupil of R. Akiva. Among those who reestablished Torah after Bar Kokhba persecutions. His *bet din* was at Sepphoris and some of his Mishnah was included by Judah ha-Nasi in his final recension. Tanner by trade.

Yose ben Joezer of Zeredah (2nd c. B.C.E.), *nasi,* first of *zugot* together with Yose b. Johanan of Jerusalem; issued decrees to discourage emigration fr. Ereẓ Israel. Sentenced to death by crucifixion at time of Hasmonean revolt. Saying: "Let thy house be a meeting place for scholars . . . and drink in their words with thirst" (Avot 1:4).

Yose ben Johanan ha-Tanna of Jerusalem (2nd c. B.C.E.), *av bet din,* first of *zugot* together with Yose b. Joezer of Zeredah. Saying: "Let thy house be wide open; let the poor be members of thy household; engage not in gossip with women" (Avot 1:5).

Yose ben Judah (2nd c.), *tanna;* elder colleague of Judah ha-Nasi. Author of *aggadah* that two ministering angels accompany man returning home fr. synagogue on Sabbath.

Yose ben Yose (4th–5th c.), earliest liturgical poet known by name, probably Palestinian. Language distinguished by purity. Originator of *piyyut.* Many of his compositions still in use and others found in Cairo *Genizah.*

Yosef, Ovadiah (1920–), Sephardi chief rabbi of Israel fr. 1972; b. Baghdad, moved to Jerusalem 1924. Head of *bet din* in Cairo and deputy chief rabbi of Egypt 1947. Returned to Israel 1950. Member of Supreme Rabbinical Court of Appeals in Jerusalem, Sephardi chief rabbi of Tel Aviv-Jaffa 1968. Prolific writer of halakhic works.

Yose ha-Gelili (2nd c.), *tanna,* scholar of Jabneh; pupil-colleague of R. Akiva. His *halakhot* occur throughout Talmud.

Yose ha-Kohen (1st c.), *tanna;* pupil of Johanan b. Zakkai. Sayings: "Fit yourself for study of Torah for it is not a bequest; let all your actions be for the sake of heaven" (Avot 2:12). "The good way in life is to be a good neighbor" (Avot 2:9).

Train with Polish refugee children brought to Ereẓ Israel by Youth Aliyah, 1943.

Young Israel, The National Council of, association of Orthodox synagogues in U.S. with 106 synagogues and 35,000 affiliated families.

Young Judaea, U.S. Zionist organization, founded 1909. Originally affiliated with Zionist Organization of America; later with Hadassah and name changed to HaShachar. Membership 12,000 (1971).

Youngstown, city in Ohio, U.S. First Jewish settler 1837. Oldest existing congregation Rodef Sholom (Reform) founded 1867. Jewish pop. 5,400 (1971).

Youth Aliyah, branch of Zionist movement rescuing Jewish children and educating them in Israel. Dept. of Jewish Agency; supported by voluntary contributions. Movement initiated 1932 by Recha Freier. Henrietta Szold became head 1933. Hadassah undertook responsibility for financial support of movement 1935. By 1948, absorbed and educated 31,000 young people in youth villages, etc.; bet. 1948 and 1970, another 93,000.

Yovel, see Jubilee.

Yoẓerot (Heb.), name of *piyyutim* inserted in blessing preceding and following morning *Shema.* Name comes fr. opening line of blessing *yoẓer or* "creator of light."

Yud, Nahum (1888–), Yiddish poet; b. Belorussia, in U.S. fr. 1916. Poetry is marked by love for America. Wrote fables.

Yudghan (8th c.), sectarian of Hamadan. Claimed to be prophet and gave his own interpretations to Torah. His followers (Yudghanites) believed him to be messiah.

Yudkin, John (1910–), British nutritional chemist. Prof. in London. Research on obesity, diet, and coronary disease.

Yugoslavia federated republic in SE Europe. Jews present in Roman times in Pannonia. Jews in areas of Ottoman rule generally well treated; less so in Christian areas. Found refuge (esp. in Dubrovnik) after expulsion fr Spain 1492. With establishment of kingdom. 70,000 Jews in country. 60% Ashkenazim, 40% Sephardim. 14,000 survived WWII, in which Jewish partisans played active role. Jews in Italian-occupied area less persecuted than those in German, Hungarian, and Croatian Republic. Most Jews left for Israel after WWII. Jewish pop. 7,000 (1971).

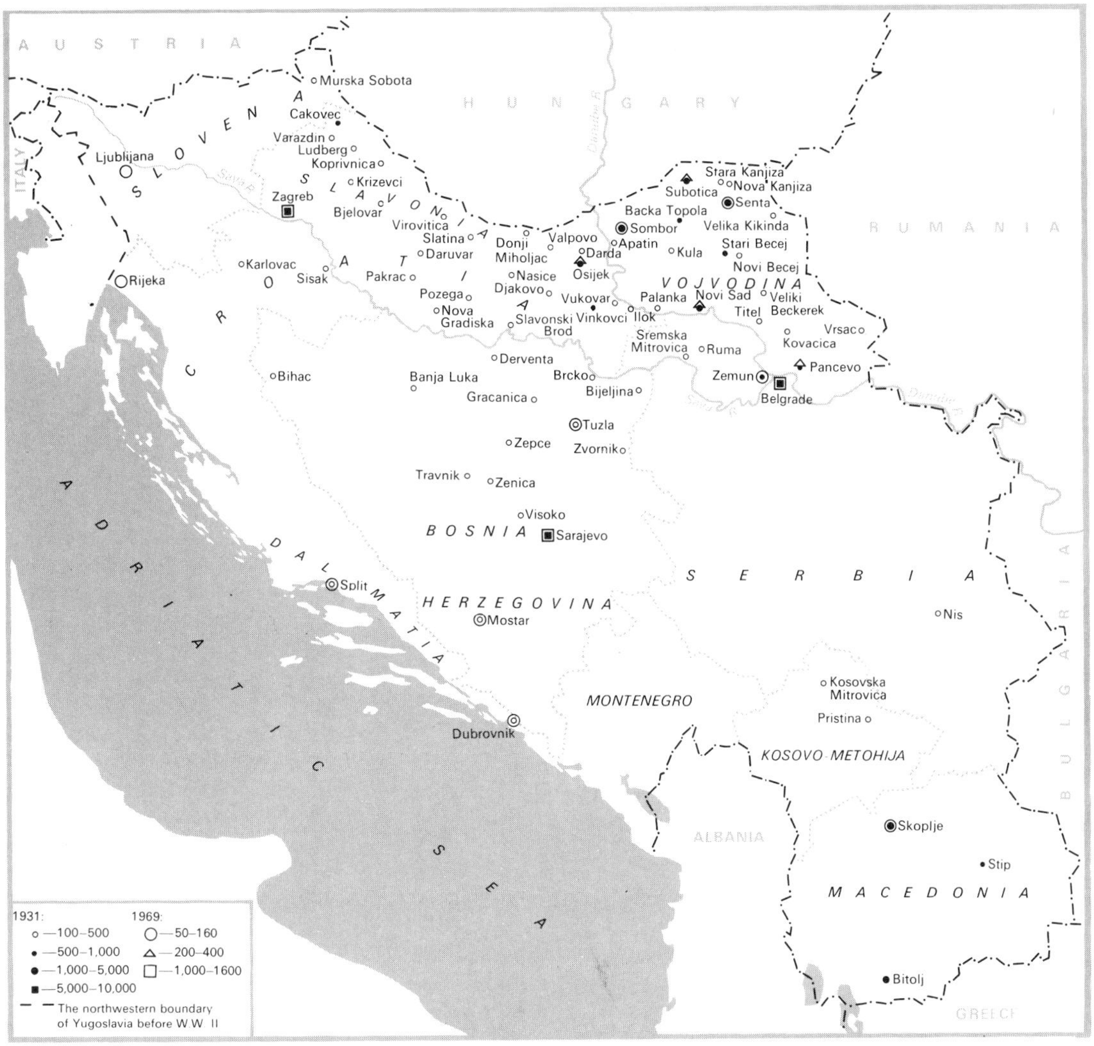

Jewish communities in Yugoslavia.

Jews' Street in Dubrovnik, Yugoslavia.

Yulee, David Levy (1810–1866), U.S. senator; b. West Indies. Member of Florida legislature 1837 and campaigned for Florida's admission to Union. First Jew in U.S. Senate 1845. Vigorous supporter of slavery and secession. Member of Confederate Congress.

Yunge, Di, Yiddish literary movement founded in U.S. 1907 by young immigrant writers centered around the periodical *Jugend* ("Youth"). Aimed to emancipate Yiddish literature, enrich Yiddish with newest techniques, and produce translations of foreign literary masterpieces.

Yung Vilne (Young Vilna), Yiddish literary group founded 1929. Up to 1939 group aroused much attention through publications. Group decimated in WWII, but survivors, who found refuge in U.S., Israel, France, and Poland, made significant contributions to Yiddish literature and scholarship. Members incl. Abraham Sutzkever, Chaim Grade.

Yushkevich, Semyon Solomonovich (1868–1927), Russian playwright, novelist; Odessa physician. Plays and stories contrasted poor but virtuous Jews with their wealthy, vulgar coreligionists. Also wrote plays in Yiddish.

Yūsuf 'As'ar Yath'ar Dhu Nuwās (Masrūq), last ruler of independent kingdom of Himyar (S. Arabia) 517? or 518? –525. Converted to Judaism by rabbis fr. Tiberias before acceding to throne. Fought Ethiopian invaders who penetrated his country and at first drove them out, but died in war against Ethiopian king who came to assistance of persecuted Christians in Najran (S. Arabia).

The letter "Z" used as an "S" at the beginning of the phrase "Stetit Salomon ante altare," detail from a book of homilies, France, 1170.

Zach, Nathan (1930–), Israel poet. Published original poetry, translated Arabic folk songs, co-edited literary periodical *Yokhani.*

Zacharias, Jerrold Reinach (1905–), U.S. physicist. educator. Taught at MIT, contributing to nuclear science research. Founded Physical Science Study Committee. Director of Education Research Center MIT fr. 1968.

Zacuto, Abraham ben Samuel (1452–c. 1515), Spanish astronomer, historian. Projected new astrolabe and wrote tables and charts used by Vasco da Gama on his voyage to India. His main astronomical work translated into Spanish and Latin. His *Sefer ha-Yuḥasin,* outlined development of Oral Law, giving chronology to his own time.

Zacuto, Moses ben Mordecai (c. 1620–1697), kabbalist, scholar, poet; b. Amsterdam into Marrano family, went to Venice. Anti-Shabbatean rabbi of Mantua 1673. Many of his halakhic works, responsa, kabbalistic compositions, and poems published. Wrote first biblical drama in Hebrew literature, *Yesod Olam,* and dramatic poem *Tofteh Arukh,* inspired by Dante's *Divine Comedy.*

Zacutus Lusitanus (Abraham Zacuth; 1575–1642), physician; b. Lisbon into Marrano family, fled to

Zacutus Lusitanus

Amsterdam 1625, openly reverting to Judaism. His medical works contain accurate clinical descriptions of numerous diseases, code for physicians, and compendium of drugs. Anticipated important medical discoveries.

Ẓaddik (Heb. "righteous man"), ḥasidic leader of charismatic personality, paramount authority in community of his followers, reflecting his mystic union with God.

Ẓaddik, Joseph ben Jacob ibn (d. 1149), Spanish philosopher, poet, *dayyan.* Author of philosophical work *Olam Katan.*

Ẓade (Ṣade, Ẓadi; צ, final form ץ), 18th letter of Hebrew alphabet; numerical value 90. Originally a sharp *s* it became widely pronounced as *ts.*

Zadikow, Arnold (1884–1943), German sculptor, medalist; settled in Paris 1932; murdered by Nazis.

Zadkine, Ossip (1890–1967), sculptor; b. Russia, lived in Paris, in U.S. during WWII. During 1920s, abandoned early cubism for freer, more baroque style, and blended African primitive elements with those derived fr. classical sculpture. Sculptured *Destroyed City* (at Rotterdam).

Zadok, priest in time of David together with Abiathar (q.v.); established high priestly dynasty which continued until c. 171 B.C.E. Origin obscure.

Zadok (1st c. B.C.E.–1st c. C.E.), *tanna.* Acc. to tradition fasted 40 years to avert destruction of Temple and Johanan b. Zakkai asked Vespasian to supply physician to revive him. Held honored place in Sanhedrin. Saying: "Make not learning a crown for personal grandeur nor a spade for digging."

Zadokite Fragments, see Damascus, Book of Covenant of.

Zadokites, Qumran community's description of its members, esp. its priestly members.

Zadok the Pharisee (1st c.), founder with Judah the Galilean of the "fourth philosophy" (see Sicarii) which was theoretical basis of, and led up to, revolt in 66/7 against Romans.

Zagare (Zager), town in Lithuania. Two separate Jewish communities: Old Zager and New Zager. One of first centers of Haskalah movement in Russia. Influenced by centers of traditional Jewish learning in Lithuania. Renowned as "full of scholars and scribes." Later declined. 1,000 Jews before WWII. Murdered in Holocaust.

Zagreb, capital of Croatia. Jews there by the end of 14th c.; expelled 1526. Community established 1806. Equal rights 1873. Center of Jewish life in Yugoslavia. 12,000 Jews in 1941; 1,200 in 1970.

Ẓahal, see Israel Defense Forces.

Ẓahalon, family which after expulsion fr. Spain settled in Italy and

Abraham ben Samuel Zacuto, holding astronomical tables, in a mural painting of Vasco da Gama leaving Lisbon, by J.M. Amshewitz.

Near Eastern countries. **Jacob ben Isaac** (1630–1693), rabbi of Ferrara, wrote manual of medicine, responsa, translated work of Thomas Aquinas. His son **Mordecai** (d. 1748), physician, succeeded his father as rabbi in Ferrara, wrote responsa, *piyyutim*. **Yom Tov ben Moses** (1559–after 1638), leading rabbi of Safed, emissary of Safed 1590–1600, wrote responsa.

Zaken Mamre (Heb. "rebellious elder"), term for scholar who, after his opinion was outvoted by supreme *bet din* in Jerusalem, returned to his native town and acted against its decision. Liable to death penalty (Deut. 17:8, 12).

Zakho, town in Iraqi Kurdistan; site of ancient Jewish community. Persecuted by Muslims 1891–92. 2,400 families in 1906. After 1920, began to emigrate to Ereẓ Israel, settling in Jerusalem.

Zam, Zvi Herz (1835–1915), Russian soldier. Only Jewish officer in Czarist army during 19th c. Fought for Jewish soldier's right to attend synagogue.

Zambia (formerly **N. Rhodesia**), African republic. Jews by early 20th c. Jewish pioneers did much to open up country, esp. in copper mining. 1,200 Jews in mid-1950s; 300 in 1971. Sir Roy Welensky for long leading figure in N. Rhodesian politics.

Zambrowski, Roman (1909–). Polish Communist politician; in USSR during WWII. Subsequently headed Polish United Workers' Party. After quarreling with dominant faction led by Gomulka, dismissed fr. Party and governmental posts 1964.

Zambrowsky, Tsemach Menachem (1911–), rabbi, organization executive. National director of Mizrachi–Ha-Po'el ha-Mizrachi Organization of Canada 1948. Secretary-general of World Mizrachi–Ha-Po'el ha-Mizrachi Organization in Jerusalem 1968.

Zamenhof, Ludwik Lazar (1859–1917), Polish physician, philologist; creator of Esperanto. Published 1878 his first outline of new, simple language which would help promote international understanding. His pseudonym "Doktoro Esperanto" (Dr. Hopeful) inspired eventual name. Convened first international congress of Esperantists 1905. Early member of Ḥovevei Zion.

Zamosc, city in Poland. Sephardi community existed in late 16th c. Ashkenazi Jews fr. 17th c. In 19th c. center of rabbinical learning as well as Haskalah and later Ḥasidism. 12,000 Jews in 1939; all Jews liquidated in WWII.

Zamosc, David (1789–1864), Hebrew writer, teacher; b. Poznan, moved to Breslau. Wrote mainly for children and schools.

Zamosc, Israel ben Moses Halevi (c. 1700–1772), talmudist, mathematician; b. Galicia, went to Germany 1740. A founder of Haskalah movement; Moses Mendelssohn among his pupils. Aroused ire of Jewish religious fanatics and was compelled to move fr. place to place in Germany and Poland.

Zamzummim, name given by Ammonites to inhabitants of Transjordanian territory whom they dispossessed (Deut. 2:20). Part of nation of giants known as Rephaim.

Zand, Michael (1927–), oriental scholar; b. Russia. Worked on staff of *Soviet Journal of Oriental Studies* and *Soviet Literary Encyclopaedia.* Involved in democratic movement of Soviet intellectuals and Jewish immigration movement. Detained 1971 and went to Israel in same year. Prof. of Persian and Tajik literature at Heb. Univ.

Zandz, see Halberstam.

Zangwill, Israel (1864–1926), English author. His most successful novel, *Children of the Ghetto,* reflected life in East End of London. In *Dreamers of the Ghetto,* portrayed Disraeli, Heine, Lassalle, and other historical figures who were affected by tragic duality of Jewish existence. *The King of the Schnorrers* was hilarious account of 18th c. London Jewry. Embraced Zionist cause 1895 but abandoned official Zionism after Uganda offer was rejected and founded Jewish Territorial Organization with aim of creating "homeland" for Jews wherever possible. Brilliant, witty speaker. His brother, **Louis** (1869–1938), chess champion, novelist. Israel's son **Oliver Louis** (1913–), prof. of experimental psychology at Cambridge fr. 1952.

Zarchin, Alexander (1897–), Israel engineer, inventor. Teacher at Leningrad Technical Inst. until 1934. Took out patents for various discoveries, incl. process for desalination of water which was developed in Israel after he settled there 1947.

Zarephath, Phoenician city (cf. I Kings 17:9–24). Name used in Hebrew for "France."

Zaretzki, Isaac (1891–1956), Yiddish linguist, author; b. Russia. Central figure in movement for reformed Yiddish orthography; wrote books and articles on projected reform, which led to abandonment in Russia of traditional spelling of Yiddish words of Hebrew-Aramaic origin.

Zariski, Oscar (1899–), U.S. mathematician; b. Russia. Prof. at Harvard. Pres. American Mathematical Society 1969–70. Made important contributions in fields of algebraic geometry, topology, and algebraic surfaces.

Zaritsky, Yossef (1891–), Israel painter; b. Russia, settled in Ereẓ Israel 1923. Among initiators of first exhibition of local artists; a founder of "New Horizons" group. Concentrated on landscapes, painting many towns in Ereẓ Israel. Israel Prize 1955.

Zarko, Joseph ben Judah (14th–15th c.), disseminator among Jews of Italy of Hebrew poetry and grammar that developed in Spain. Author of Hebrew grammar and Hebrew dictionary.

Zarza, Samuel ibn Seneh (14th c.), Spanish philosopher. Author of philosophical commentary *Mekor Ḥayyim* on Pentateuch; in epilogue describes suffering of Jews of Castile.

Zaslavsky, David (1880–1965), Soviet writer, journalist. Active Bundist. At first opposed Bolsheviks but later recanted. Worked for *Izvestiya* fr. 1926, *Pravda* fr. 1928. Adhered to party line and unlike most other members of anti-Fascist Committee was not arrested 1948–49.

Zavim (Heb. "Sufferers from Flux"), 9th tractate of Mishnah order *Tohorot,* with no *gemara.* Deals with ritual impurity of person suffering fr. running flux (probably gonorrhea) and of those in contact with him.

Zay, Jean (1904–1944), French Socialist politician. Radical Socialist deputy 1932; minister of national education in Léon Blum's Popular Front and successive governments 1936–40. Arrested and imprisoned

Israel Zangwill

Hungarian postage stamp commemorating Ludwik Lazar Zamenhof.

following fall of France; summarily executed.

Zayin (ז), 7th letter of Hebrew alphabet; numerical value 7. Pronounced *z*.

Zealots, group of Jewish resistance fighters in war against Rome 66–73 C.E. Leaders were Judah the Galilean, his son Menahem, Eleazar ben Jair (commander of Masada), and John of Giscala (defender of Temple in Jerusalem). Opposed compromise with Romans. Josephus attributed Jews' defeat to their activities.

Zebulun, tenth son of Jacob and sixth born to him by Leah. Tribe of Zebulun held major position among tribes of Galilee.

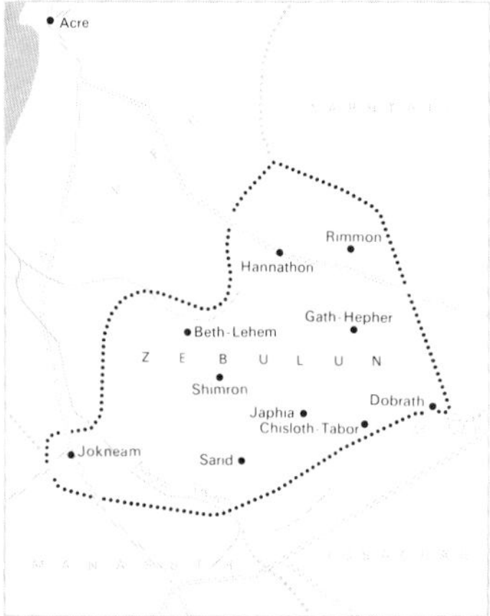

Territory of the tribe of Zebulun.

Zechariah (9th c. B.C.E.), priest in Judah who called people to account for apostasy. People conspired against him and by command of King Joash stoned him (II Chron. 24:15–22).

Zechariah, king of Israel 743 B.C.E.; son of Jeroboam II. Assassinated six months after succession by Shallum son of Jabesh (II Kings 15:8–13), ending dynasty of Jehu.

Zechariah, eleventh book of Twelve Minor Prophets. First section written against historical background of period of return fr. Babylonian Exile; latter part (ch. 9–14) is of eschatological nature, written in obscure style with allusions to unclear background.

Zechariah al-Ḍāhiri (16th c.), author, scholar, *dayyan* in Yemen. Journeyed to Ereẓ Israel 1567, imprisoned 1568–73, there writing his best-known work *Sefer ha-Musar,* important source of information on Jewish communities of period, esp. Yemenite Jewry. Wrote commentary on Pentateuch.

Zechariah ben Solomon-Rofe (Razah; 15th c.), Yemenite scholar, physician in San'a. Author of *Midrash ha-Ḥefeẓ,* important anthology of Torah and *haftarot* based on *Midrash ha-Gadol.*

Ẓedakah (Heb. "righteous act" or "charity"). In Bible variantly used as righteousness, justice, right in one's claims, and, in plural, righteous acts. In later Hebrew literature, generally came to mean "charity" implying "acts of justice" but was distinguished fr. "acts of kindness." In liturgy of High Holidays said to "avert the evil decree."

Zedekiah, last king of Judah 597/6–587/6 B.C.E. Appointed by Nebuchadnezzar king of Babylonia. Made alliance with Egypt despite warnings of Jeremiah; Babylonian troops laid siege to and eventually captured Jerusalem 587 or 586. Fled but was captured and brought to Riblah, where his sons were killed before his eyes. Blinded and sent in chains to Babylonia, where he died.

Zedekiah, court prophet of Samaria. Prophesied that Ahab of Israel would be successful in battle of Ramoth-Gilead, contrary to prophet Micaiah, who prophesied defeat (I Kings 22:11).

Zedekiah, contemporary of prophet Jeremiah. Jeremiah charged him with prophesying falsely and prophesied that he would be punished at hands of king of Babylon and that his fate would serve as symbol among exiles of Judah (Jer. 29:21–23).

Zederbaum, Alexander (pseud. **Erez;** 1816–1893), pioneer Jewish journalist in Russia. Founded and edited *Ha-Meliẓ* fr. 1860, first Hebrew weekly in Russia (fr. 1886 daily), and also its Yiddish supplement *Kol Mevasser* fr. 1862. Founded *Yidishes Folksblat* 1881. Enthusiastic supporter of Ḥibbat Zion fr. its inception.

Zedner, Joseph (1804–1871), bibliographer; b. Germany. Librarian at British Museum 1845–69. Published *Catalogue of the Hebrew Books in the Library of the British Museum.*

Ẓedukim, see Sadducees.

Ze'eira (c. 300), Babylonian *amora* who emigrated to Ereẓ Israel; frequently mentioned in both Talmuds. Meticulously careful in transmitting teachings correctly. Saying: "Never make a promise to a child and not keep it, for you will teach him thereby to lie."

Ẓe'enah U-Re'enah (Heb. "Come and See"; from Songs of Songs 3:11), exegetical rendering in Yiddish of Pentateuch, *haftarot,* and Five Scrolls. Composed in 16th c. by Jabob b. Isaac Ashkenazi. Became widely popular among Ashkenazi Jewry. Used primarily by women as reading matter on Sabbath.

Statue of Alexander Zeid at site of his death.

Zefira, Brachah (c. 1915–), Israel folk singer. Her personal style combined Yemenite, Palestinian-Sephardi, and Arabic elements and had influence on musical composition in Israel.

Zeid, Alexander (1886–1938), pioneer of Second Aliyah; b. Siberia, settled in Ereẓ Israel 1904. A founder of Ha-Shomer 1909. Moved to Sheikh Abrek in Jezreel Valley 1926, where he was in charge of guarding settlements. Killed by Arabs.

Zeira, Mordechai (1905–1968), Israel composer; b. Kiev, settled in Ereẓ Israel 1924. Wrote hundreds of songs, many in standard repertoire. Integrated Near Eastern elements into cantorial, ḥasidic, and Russian revolutionary idioms. Outstanding creator of modern Israel song.

Ẓe'irei Zion, moderate socialist Zionist movement, active mainly in Russia; founded c. 1903. Split 1920, one faction becoming Zionist Socialist Party–Z.S. while "right-wing" minority later formed world union *Hitaḥadut* together with *Ha-Poel ha-Ẓa'ir.*

Zeit, Die (The Jewish Times), Yiddish daily newspaper published in London; founded 1913 by Morris Myer as daily, later became weekly; closed 1950. Last Yiddish daily in Great Britain.

Zeitlin, Aaron (1898–1973), Hebrew, Yiddish writer; son of Hillel Zeitlin; b. Poland. Early poetic works were lyrical, later philosophical concepts appeared, and then mystical religious insights. In U.S. fr.

1939. Prof. of Hebrew Literature at Jewish Theological Seminary.

Zeitlin, Hillel (1871–1942), author, thinker, journalist; b. Russia. Self-taught in secular studies, commenced to write initially in Hebrew. Zionist who under impact of Kishinev pogrom 1903 became Territorialist and returned to religion. Worked for Yiddish newspapers fr. 1906. Immersed himself in mysticism, wrote on Ḥasidism and Ḥabad. Died garbed in *tallit* and *tefillin* on way to Treblinka.

Zeitlin, Solomon (1892–), U.S. scholar of post-biblical literature; b. Russia. Prof. of rabbinics at Dropsie College, editor of *Jewish Quarterly Review.* Wrote hundreds of articles and many books on Second Commonwealth, Josephus, Apocrypha, and Christianity. Author of *Rise and Fall of the Judean State.* Main protagonist of late dating of Dead Sea Scrolls.

Zeitlin, William (c. 1850–1921), German bibliographer; b. Russia. Major work *Bibliotheca Hebraica Post-Mendelssohniana* lists Haskalah literature to 1880.

Zekhut Avot (Heb. "Merit of the Fathers"), doctrine that righteousness of forebears benefits descendants. Idea is biblical and also found in rabbinical literature. Occurs in many prayers where reference is made to the merit of Patriarchs.

Zellerbach, family of U.S. merchants. **Anthony** (1832–1911), b. Bavaria, settled in Philadelphia 1846. Founded firm of A. Zellerbach & Son (becoming Zellerbach Paper Co.), which he and his sons, **Jacob C.** (b. 1864), **Isadore** (1867–1942), and **Henry** (1868–1944), built into one of largest paper-manufacturing companies in world. Isadore's son **James David** (1892–1963), chief of Marshall Plan special mission to Italy 1948–50, appointed U.S. ambassador to Italy 1956.

Zelophehad, biblical figure who died in wilderness without male issue. This led to promulgation of legislation providing for possibility of daughters inheriting fr. fathers under certain circumstances (Num. 26–27; 36:1–12).

Zemach, Nahum (1887–1939), theatrical director. Assembled group of Hebrew-speaking actors in Bialystok 1912; company was forerunner of Habimah, which he founded in Moscow 1917. Settled in U.S. 1926. His brother, **Benjamin** (1902–), member of Habimah theater. Remained in U.S. after 1926. Opened dance school in L.A. 1931. Directed dances, plays, films, using concept of Jewish dance derived fr. Bible. In Israel fr. 1971.

Zemach, Shlomo (1886–), Hebrew writer, agronomist; b. Poland, settled in Ereẓ Israel 1904, in Europe 1909–21. Founded Kadoorie Agricultural School 1933 (principal until 1937). His realistic short stories describe life in Ereẓ Israel. Israel Prize 1965.

Zemaḥ, Jacob ben Ḥayyim (d. after 1665), kabbalist, physician; b. Portugal into Converso family, settled in Safed, became leading Jerusalem kabbalist. Excommunicated Shabbetai Ẓevi. Wrote many works on Kabbalah and anthology of Lurianic customs that became basis for *Shulḥan Arukh shel ha-Ari.*

Zemba, Menahem (1883–1943), Polish rabbinical scholar. Member of Warsaw rabbinical council, secretary of Mo'eẓet Gedolei ha-Torah of Agudat Israel. His halakhic works acquired great renown. Gave rabbinic approval to uprising in Warsaw Ghetto, refused offer by Catholic circles to save his life, and perished in ghetto.

Zemirot (Heb. "songs"), term used (1) by Sephardi and Italian Jews for biblical verses preceding morning service and called by Ashkenazim *Pesukei de-Zimra;* (2) by Ashkenazim for table songs sung during Sabbath meals.

Zemun (Semlin), town in Yugoslavia. Small community established after 1717. Place of refuge for Jews fr. Belgrade, etc. Judah Ḥai Alkalai led community 1825–43 and ancestors of Theodor Herzl lived there. Its 500 Jews and its institutions annihilated 1941.

Zemurray, Samuel (1878–1961), U.S. business executive. Started as banana peddler and eventually took over United Fruit Co. Known as "Banana King." Friend of Weizmann; contributed generously to Zionist causes.

Zeno, Papyri of, archives discovered at Philadelphia, Egypt, belonging to a Greek, Zeno (3rd c. B.C.E.), who served under Apollonius, finance minister of Ptolemy Philadelphus. Some documents throw light on life of Jews in Faiyum and Ereẓ Israel under Ptolemaic rule.

Zentralwohlfahrtstelle der Deutschen Juden, central welfare organization of German Jews; founded 1917. Recognized and supported by German government, Joint, and major German welfare bodies. After 1933 promoted emigration, retraining, and education. Reorganized 1951 with seat in Frankfort.

Zephaniah, Judean prophet whose activity is dated fr. Scythian invasion 630–625 B.C.E.; distant relative of King Josiah (cf. Zeph. 1:4). Book of Zephaniah is ninth book of Latter Prophets. Denounces Judah for its idolatry and wealth and ends with prediction of salvation and return fr. captivity of remnant of Israel.

Zerah, Cushite chieftain fr. nr. Gerar who raided and plundered surrounding areas in time of King Asa. Judean army defeated and pursued him to Gerar (II Chron. 14:8–14).

Zerahiah ben Isaac ha-Levi (14th–15th c.), rabbi of Saragossa and all Aragon, talmudist, preacher, physician, translator. Leading participant in the Tortosa disputation.

Zerahiah ben Isaac ha-Levi Gerondi, see Gerondi, Zerahiah.

Zera'im (Heb. "Seeds"), first of six orders of Mishnah. Deals chiefly with agricultural laws of Ereẓ Israel. First tractate deals with prayers and benedictions.

Ẓere, Hebrew vowel sign indicating sound equivalent of English long *e.* Written ◌ֵ or ◌ֵי.

Zered, river valley mentioned in Bible (Num. 21:12; Deut. 2:12–14). Most scholars identify it with Wadi al-Ḥazā, which flows from E. to W. up to Dead Sea.

Zerubavel (Vitkin), Jacob (1886–1967), leader of Po'alei Zion, author, journalist; b. Ukraine, settled in Ereẓ Israel 1910, went to U.S. 1915, returned to Russia 1917, Po'alei Zion leader in Poland 1918–35, to Ereẓ Israel 1935. Published Yiddish books and journals. Director of Labor Archive fr. 1951.

Zerubbabel (6th c. B.C.E.), Babylonian Jew who returned to Ereẓ Israel to become governor in post-exilic Jerusalem. Worked in close collaboration with Joshua (Jeshua) son of Jehozadok the high priest as leader of original caravan of repatriates and as builder of Temple. Name was embellished in late times and regarded as one of Israel's redeemers.

Zerubbabel, Book of, 7th c. work describing vision of Zerubbabel, last ruler of House of David; frequently copied and printed. Standard source for descriptions of End of Days. Influenced thinkers such as Saadiah.

Ẓeva Haganah Le-Israel, see Israel Defense Forces.

Zevaḥim (Heb. "Sacrifices"), 1st tractate of Mishnah order *Kodashim,* with *gemara* in Babylonian Talmud. Deals with slaughter of animals and birds for Temple worship.

Zevi, Bruno (1918–). Italian architect. Championed Frank Lloyd Wright's organic approach to architecture. Prof. at Rome Univ. fr. 1948.

Zevin, Solomon Joseph (1890–), rabbi, scholar; b. Belorussia, rabbi of several Russian communities, settled in Ereẓ Israel 1934. Original critic of contemporary halakhic literature. Editor of "Talmudic Encyclopaedia." Israel Prize 1959.

Zeyer, Julius (1841–1901), Czech writer. Major contribution was epic verse, which exploited themes drawn fr. many different countries. Some of his themes are Jewish.

Zhidachov, Hungarian ḥasidic dynasty, founded by **Ẓevi Hirsch Eichenstein** (1785–1831). His nephew **Isaac Eizik** (1804–1872), noted kabbalist. Wrote works that served as bridge between Ḥasidism and Kabbalah.

Zhitlowsky, Chaim (1865–1943), Yiddish philosopher, writer; b. Russia. Became socialist. Kishinev pogroms 1903 inclined him toward Territorialism. Elected to Second Russian Duma. In New York fr. 1908. Rejected Zionism, chief theoretician of Diaspora nationalism and Yiddishism. Later sympathetic toward Soviet Russia and considered German persecution of Jews as punishment for negative socioeconomic role played by Jewish middle classes.

Zhitomir, city in Ukrainian SSR. Jews there fr. 18th c. Center of Hebrew printing fr. 1804. Site of government rabbinical seminary fr. 1847 (later teachers' seminary for Jewish government schools). Pogroms 1905, 1919, 1920. 30,000 Jews in 1926; many killed by Germans. 36,000 Jews in Zhitomir province in 1970.

Zholkva (Nesterov; Zólkiew), city in Ukrainian SSR. Jews there fr. 16th c. Refuge during Chmielnicki massacres 1648–49. Leading community during period of Council of Lands. Center of Shabbatean movement in Poland, focus of Haskalah fr. late 18th c. and noted for Hebrew printing fr. 1692. Over 5,000 Jews in 1941: liquidated by Germans.

Ziba, servant of house of Saul. His artfulness ultimately gained for him half of his master's possessions.

Ẓidduk ha-Din (Heb. "acknowledgment of [Divine] justice"), Jewish burial service containing verses fr. Bible "justifying God's judgment."

Zidon, see Sidon.

Židovská Strana (Czech "Jewish Party"), national Jewish party in Czechoslovakia, founded 1919. Aimed to secure representation of Jewish national minority in state institutions. Sent two deputies to parliament and was also represented in provincial diets and many municipal councils. During WWII had representative in National Council-in-Exile in London. After war not reorganized.

Ziegfeld, Florenz (1869–1932), U.S. showman. Launched *Ziegfeld Follies* 1897, with array of beautiful girls which set standard for Broadway revues until 1930s.

Zikhronot (Heb. "remembrance" verses), middle benediction of Additional Service on Rosh Ha-Shanah, containing verses stressing that God "remembers."

Zikhron Ya'akov, village on Mt. Carmel, Israel; founded 1882 by Jews fr. Rumania. One of earliest settlements of Ḥovevei Zion. Baron Edmond de Rothschild took personal and financial interest in village and developed its wine industry. Pop. 4,490 (1971).

Ziklag, unidentified town in S. Judah, mentioned in Bible as nr. Edomite boundary. Given to David when refugee fr. Saul, by Achish, ruler of Gath. David's base until battle of Gilboa.

Zilberts, Zavel (1881–1949), composer, conductor, *ḥazzan.* Choir master in Central Synagogue of Moscow 1907–14. In U.S. fr. 1920. Founded choral society and was musical director of Jewish Ministers–Cantors' Association of America. Wrote liturgical compositions, biblical cantatas, etc.

Zilboorg, Gregory (1890–1959), psychiatrist; b. Russia, in U.S. fr. 1919. Taught at N.Y. Medical College. Consultant on criminology to UN. Study of suicide was one of his specialties.

Zilkha, family of bankers originating in Baghdad. **Khedoury Zilkha** (1884–1956), established banking house 1899, branches of which were later opened in Beirut, Damascus, Cairo. Moved center of financial activity to U.S. in 1941. Arab governments seized Baghdad house 1950, Cairo firm 1956.

Zilkha, Na'im (1879–1929), Iraqi lawyer. Deputy pres. Beirut Court of Appeals 1908, Basra civil courts 1921. Member of Iraqi house of representatives 1925–29.

Zilpah, handmaid of Leah and concubine of Jacob. Mother of Gad and Asher.

Zim, Israel Navigation Company, founded 1945 by Jewish Agency, Histadrut, and Palestine Maritime League to build merchant fleet. Ships maintain regular communications with most countries of world. Headquarters in Haifa.

Zimbalist, Efrem (1889–), violinist, composer; b. Russia, toured Europe, settled in U.S. 1911. One of most prominent violinists on U.S. scene. First wife was singer Alma Gluck. Director of Curtis Inst. of Music in Philadelphia 1941. After marrying Mary Curtis, left Jewish faith. His son by Alma Gluck, **Efrem Jr.** (1923–), actor, musician, producer.

Zimmels, Hirsch Jacob (1900–), rabbi, scholar; b. Poland, taught at Breslau Seminary, went to England 1939. Lecturer at Jews' College London (principal 1964–69). Published research on responsa literature.

Zimmern, Sir Alfred (1879–1957), English political scientist. Prof. of international relations at Univ. of Wales 1919–21, Oxford fr. 1930. Held important government posts, special adviser to UNESCO.

Zimra, Ibn, see Ibn Zimra.

Zimri, chieftain of Simeonite ancestral house. Slain at Shittim by Phinehas, grandson of Aaron, for bringing pagan Midianite woman named Cozbi into his household (Num 25:6–8, 14 ff).

Zimri, king of Israel 885/4 B.C.E. Murdered Elah and seized throne but was deposed by Omri after reign of seven days.

Ẓimẓum (Heb. "contraction"), mystical term denoting process whereby

Killing of Zimri and the Midianite woman by Phinehas, fr. Judeo-Persian ms., c. 1686.

God withdraws or contracts within himself, leaving primordial vacuum in which creation can take place.

Zinberg, Israel (**Sergei**; 1873–1939), historian of Hebrew, Yiddish literature; b. Volhynia. Chemical engineer by profession. Wrote 8-vol. *History of Jewish Literature* in Russian, translating it into Yiddish. (9th volume published posthumously.)

Zinnemann, Fred (1907–), U.S. film director and producer. Films incl. *High Noon* and *Man for All Seasons,* both Academy Award winners.

Zinoviev, Grigori Yevseyevich (1883–1936), main architect of Communist International and its first chairman. Bolshevik fr. 1903; became Lenin's closest associate, returning with him to Russia in "sealed train." After Bolshevik revolution active in Comintern. After death of Lenin joined forces with Stalin and Kamenev in "Troika" that ousted Trotsky, but his subsequent opposition to Stalin's dictatorial policies led to expulsion fr. party 1927. Victim of Stalin's "Great Purge" trials, publicly "confessed" crimes and executed.

Zinovyevsk, see Kirovograd.

Zion, hill and fortress in Jerusalem. Name first used for Jebusite fortress SE of Jerusalem. In poetry, used for whole of Jerusalem. Sometimes referred to Temple Mount, and this use became regular by Maccabean period. Present Mt. Zion not identical with original one. Name also lent itself in modern times to organizations connected with return of Jews to Ereẓ Israel.

Zionism, term coined by Nathan Birnbaum 1890, denoting movement whose goal was return of Jewish people to Ereẓ Israel. Fr. 1896 referred to political movement founded by Theodor Herzl, aiming at establishment of a Jewish State in Ereẓ Israel with World Zionist Organization as main instrument.

Zionist Commission (Heb. *Va'ad ha-Ẓirim*), commission appointed 1918 by British government and sent to Ereẓ Israel as advisory body to British authorities in Ereẓ Israel in all matters relating to Jews. Headed by Chaim Weizmann, consisted of Jewish representatives fr. Great Britain, France, Italy. Replaced by the Zionist Executive 1921.

Zionist Congress, assembly of Zionist movement, created by Theodor Herzl. Originally met every year (1897–1901), then every second year (1903–13; 1921–39), and after WWII at irregular intervals.

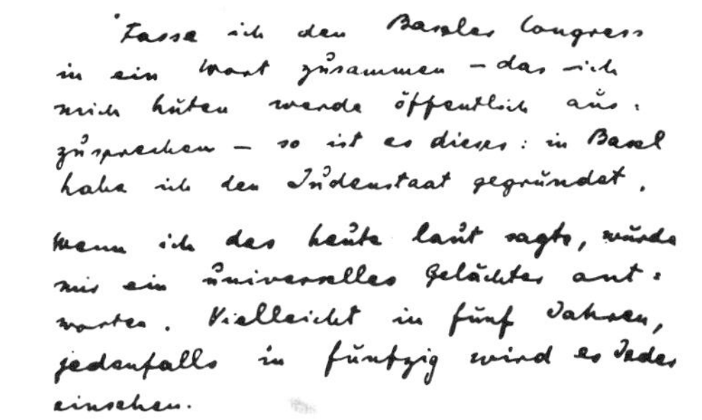

Herzl's Zionist prophecy in his diary, September 3, 1897: "In Basle I founded the Jewish State . . . Maybe in five years, certainly in fifty, everyone will realize it."

ZIONIST CONGRESSES

1 Basle — Aug. 29–31, 1897
World Zionist Organization created; Herzl elected president; goals of political Zionism formulated in the Basle Program.

2 Basle — Aug. 28–31, 1898
Jewish Colonial Trust established, narrowing gap between political and practical Zionists.

3 Basle — Aug. 15–18, 1899
Report by Herzl on meetings with Kaiser William II; Jewish Colonial Trust to confine settlement activities to Ereẓ Israel and Syria.

4 London — Aug. 13–16, 1900
Persecution of Rumanian Jewry and position of Jewish workers in Ereẓ Israel discussed.

5 Basle — Dec. 26–30, 1901
Report on Jewish Colonial Trust activities; Democratic Fraction organized; Jewish National Fund established.

6 Basle — Aug. 23–28, 1903
Herzl's last Congress; El-Arish project and Uganda Scheme discussed.

7 Basle — July 27–Aug. 2, 1905
Uganda Scheme rejected; Territorialists withdraw from Zionist Organization; Wolffsohn elected chairman of the Executive.

8 The Hague — Aug. 14–21, 1907
Decision to commence settlement activity in Ereẓ Israel, resolving struggle between political and practical Zionists.

9 Hamburg — Dec. 26–30, 1909
Criticism of Wolffsohn's methods and opposition to his leadership expressed.

10 Basle — Aug. 9–15, 1911
Practical activity in Palestine and Hebrew culture discussed; Warburg elected president.

11 Vienna — Sept. 2–9, 1913
Report by Ruppin on first settlement activities; establishment of Hebrew University resolved.

12 Carlsbad — Sept. 1–14, 1921
Weizmann elected president; reported on the political activities of the Zionist Organization during WWI.

13 Carlsbad — Aug. 16–18, 1923
Inclusion of non-Zionists in Jewish Agency debated; resolution to open Hebrew University in Jerusalem.

14 Vienna — Aug. 18–31, 1925
Private enterprise and labor settlement methods in Palestine discussed.

15 Basle — Aug. 30–Sept. 11, 1927
Economic crisis and unemployment in Palestine discussed.

16 Zurich — July 28–Aug. 10, 1929
Enlargement of Jewish Agency debated; new Zionist Executive elected.

17 Basle — June 30–July 15, 1931
Opposition to Weizmann's policies expressed; secession of Revisionists from Zionist Organization; Sokolow elected president.

18 Prague — Aug. 21–Sept. 4, 1933
Arlosoroff's assassination discussed and committee of inquiry established.

19 Lucerne — Aug. 20–Sept. 4, 1935
Lectures on practical issues delivered; Weizmann resumes presidency.

20 Zurich — Aug. 3–16, 1937
Peel Commission partition plan discussed.

21 Geneva — Aug. 16–26, 1939
Opposition to British White Paper expressed; "illegal" immigration supported.

22 Basle — Dec. 9–24, 1946
British proposals for cantonization of Palestine and a Jewish-Arab conference rejected; Weizmann resigns and no new president elected.

23 Jerusalem — Aug. 14–30, 1951
Status of Zionist movement debated; Jerusalem Program adopted.

24 Jerusalem — April 24–May 7, 1956
Aliyah, settlement, and fund raising discussed; Goldmann elected president.

25 Jerusalem — Dec. 27, 1960–Jan. 11, 1961
Relationship of the Government of Israel to Zionist Organization discussed; also aliyah, absorption, Jewish culture and education in the Diaspora.

26 Jerusalem — Dec. 30, 1964–Jan. 10, 1965
Aims of Zionism discussed; platform of tasks and functions adopted.

27 Jerusalem — June 9–19, 1968
Aliyah debated; Jerusalem Program expanded; Goldmann resigns.

28 Jerusalem — Jan. 18–28, 1972
Discussion of Zionist tasks in the Diaspora, social problems and cultural gap in Israel.

Zionist Organization of America (Z.O.A.), U.S. organization of General Zionists. Federation of American Zionists (est. 1898), Young Judaea (est. 1907), and Hadassah (est. 1912) merged into Z.O.A. 1918. Membership 165,000 (1950) but dropped thereafter. Originally comprised all U.S. Zionist branches, took on party complexion after its close connection with Israel's General Zionists (Liberals). In Israel maintains Z.O.A. house in Tel Aviv and Kefar Silver Youth Village.

Zionist Socialist Workers' Party (S.S.), Territorialist group in Russia founded 1905. Outcome of rift bet. two conflicting tendencies in Po'alei Zion 1903–04. United with Jewish Socialist Workers' Party 1917 and formed United Jewish Socialist Workers' Party.

Zion Mule Corps, detachment for mule transport of 650 men founded on initiative of Trumpeldor and Jabotinsky in Egypt 1915. Fought at Gallipoli. Disbanded 1916. Some of its members later joined Jewish Legion.

Ziph, city in Judah. Ziphites were loyal to Saul, to whom they twice revealed David's hiding places.

Zipper, Gershon (1868–1921), Galician Zionist leader. Leading protagonist of political Zionism in Galicia. After WWI led struggle with Polish authorities for Jewish rights.

Zipporah, daughter of Jethro, wife of Moses. Bore Moses two sons, Gershom and Eliezer.

Ẓippori, see Sepphoris.

Zirelson, Judah Leib (1860–1941), chief rabbi of Bessarabia. At first leading Zionist but later resigned fr. movement. A founder of Agudat Israel, senator in Rumanian parliament. Killed by Germans. Wrote responsa and homilies.

Zisling, Aharon (1901–1964), Israel labor leader; b. Belorussia, settled in Ereẓ Israel 1914. Member of Kibbutz En-Harod. A leader of original Aḥdut ha-Avodah; when Mapai split became a founder of Aḥdut ha-Avodah Party 1944 and Mapam 1948. Minister of agriculture 1948–49, member of Zionist Executive 1961–63, heading its absorption department.

Trial of Emile Zola, 1898.

Zissu, Abraham Leib (1888–1956), Rumanian Zionist leader. Devoted much time to literary and political work of Jewish or Zionist nature. Headed Zionist Federation fr. 1944; organized mass emigration to Israel. Sentenced to life imprisonment for Zionist activities 1954, released 1956 and left for Israel.

Zitron, Samuel Leib (1860–1930), Hebrew, Yiddish journalist. Contributed to E. European Yiddish press. Joined Ḥibbat Zion movement and wrote books on Zionist movement and its precursors.

Ẓivion (pseud. of **Benzion Hoffman;** 1874–1954), Yiddish journalist; b. Latvia, Bundist. In U.S. fr. 1908. Wrote Hebrew but turned to Yiddish and credited with thousands of articles in Yiddish press.

Ẓiyyonei Zion, group of mainly Russian Zionists who led opposition to Uganda Scheme. Headed by Jehiel Tschlenow, then by M.M. Ussishkin. Active 1903–05.

Ẓiẓit, fringes attached to four-cornered garments worn by Jewish men in accordance with Numbers 15:37–41 as reminder to observe God's precepts. In ancient times each fringe had two blue and two white threads looped into 8; nowadays generally all white.

Ẓiẓit, minor tractate appended to the Talmud dealing with the preparation and wearing of the fringes.

Zlatopolsky, Hillel (1868–1932), Zionist leader, industrialist, philanthropist. In charge of Zionist activities in Kiev district, active in societies for Hebrew language and culture, financed Hebrew schools, subsidized Habimah theater and founded Omanut publishing house (later in Tel Aviv under his daughter Shoshana Persitz). Went to Paris 1919 and was a founder of Keren Hayesod.

Zlocisti, Theodor (1874–1943), German physician, Zionist. Took interest in E. European Jewry and Yiddish literature, revived writings of Moses Hess. Settled in Ereẓ Israel 1921.

Zlotnick, Yehuda Leib, see Avida, Yehuda Leib.

Zmora, Yisrael (1899–), Hebrew literary critic; b. Bessarabia, settled in Ereẓ Israel 1925. One of group of modernistic Hebrew writers. Founded and edited 1940–54 literary magazine *Maḥbarot le-Sifrut;* founded publishing house of same name 1940.

Z.O.A., see Zionist Organization of America.

Zofim, see Mount of Olives.

Zohar (Heb. "splendor"), major work of Jewish mysticism, attributed to Simeon bar Yoḥai but written mostly in Spain in 13th c. by Moses de Leon although containing earlier material. Written in Aramaic in form of commentary on Pentateuch; vivid, imaginative symbolic description of inner life of God and His relationship to man. Became one of three "holy books" of Judaism after Bible and Talmud. Subject of many commentaries.

Zohary, Michael (1898–), Israel botanist. Prof. at Heb. Univ. Wrote on flora of Middle East. Israel Prize 1954.

°**Zola, Emile** (1840–1902), French novelist; champion of Alfred Dreyfus. His stand in Dreyfus affair reached climax in open letter *("J'Accuse . . . ! ")* published on front page of Clemenceau's radical daily *L'Aurore* (Jan. 13, 1898). His indictment gave new heart to Dreyfus' supporters. Forced to flee to England.

Zólkiew, see Zholkva.

Zoller (Zolli), Israel (1881–1956), rabbi, apostate; b. Galicia. Chief rabbi of Trieste and Rome. Took refuge in the Vatican in WWII. Became Catholic 1945. Author of many works on Bible interpretation.

Zollschan, Ignaz (1877–1948), Austrian anthropologist, physician. Ardent Zionist who published works attacking philosophy of Diaspora nationalism. Fought to establish international conference of scientific bodies to examine theoretical foundations of racialism. In London after 1938.

Zondek, family of physicians. **Max** (1868–1933), German physician specializing in surgery and study of renal diseases. His nephews were: **Bernhard** (1891–1966), gynecologist, endocrinologist. Prof. of obstetrics and gynecology at Berlin, co-discoverer of first reliable pregnancy test 1927. Settled in Ereẓ Israel 1934. Prof. at Heb. Univ. Advanced knowledge of hormonal therapy. **Hermann** (1887–), endocrinologist. Prof. in Berlin. Settled in Jerusalem 1934. Prof. at Heb. Univ. Studied thyroid gland, hormonal activity, and renal disturbances.

Samuel Georg (1894–1970), physician. Prof. in Berlin. Settled in Ereẓ Israel. Chief of division of internal medicine at Hadassah Hospital in Tel Aviv. Studied electrolytes and therapy of heart diseases.

Zorach, William (1887–1966), U.S. sculptor. Known for monumental carvings for public buildings (e.g., "The Spirit of the Dance" at Radio City Music Hall, N.Y. and figure of Benjamin Franklin in Washington). Most famous work is "Mother and Child" (Metropolitan Museum of Art, N.Y.).

"Devotion," granite sculpture by William Zorach.

Zorah, Canaanite city mentioned in Tell el-Amarna letters (14th c. B.C.E.); later Danite city. Derived fame fr. story of Samson. Kibbutz Zorah founded 1948.

Ẓoref, Joshua Heshel ben Joseph (1633–1700), Shabbatean prophet; most important figure in movement in Lithuania. Lived ascetic life, recorded his revelations. His fervent followers considered him oracle. Writings influenced the ḥasidic movement.

Z.S. (Zionist Socialists), Zionist-socialist party. In early 1920s thousands of its members in Russia arrested and deported to far north. With final establishment of Stalin's dictatorship, party disappeared. In other countries of E. Europe, developed into legitimate Zionist-socialist movement linked with labor movement in Ereẓ Israel and with He-Ḥalutz.

Zsoldos (Stern), Jenö (1896–), Hungarian literary scholar, philologist. Headmaster of community's girls' high school in Budapest. Research on relationship bet. Hungarian and Jewish literature; contributed to philology.

Zucker, Moshe (1904–), rabbi, Arabic scholar. Rabbi in Vilna until 1938, then went to U.S. Prof. of Bible commentaries at Jewish Theological Seminary. Published studies showing how *geonim* were rooted in general trends of their time.

Zuckerkandl, Emil (1849–1910), Austrian anthropologist, anatomist. His reputation as founder of modern rhinology rests on epoch-making work on subject.

Zuckerman, Antek, see Cukierman, Itzhak.

Zuckerman, Baruch (1887–1970), Labor Zionist leader; b. Russia, in U.S. fr. 1903. Among chief spokesmen of U.S. Po'alei Zion and active in many communal enterprises. Directed People's Relief Committee 1915–24. In Israel fr. 1956.

Zuckerman, Solly, Lord (1904–), British anatomist; b. South Africa. Taught anatomy at Oxford 1934–45, prof. at Royal College of Surgeons 1937. Headed several important committees on Government policy in sciences, chief scientific advisor to government 1966–71.

Zuckermandel, Moses Samuel (1836–1917), rabbi in Breslau, researcher in tannaitic literature. Reputation rests on scientific edition of Tosefta.

Zuckmayer, Carl (1896–), German playwright; b. of Jewish mother, raised as Catholic. Wrote comedy *Der froehliche Weinberg; Der Hauptmann von Koepenick,* satire about Prussian mentality; screenplay for *The Blue Angel.* Left Germany during 1930s. Wrote *The Devil's General* after WWII.

Zugot (Heb. "pairs"), name for pairs of sages responsible for transmitting Oral Law; link bet. the prophets and *tannaim. Avot* mentions five pairs; first member was *nasi* (head of Sanhedrin), second *av bet din* (second to *nasi*):

(1) Yose b. Joezer and Yose b. Johanan
(2) Joshua b. Peraḥiah and Nittai the Arbelite
(3) Judah b. Tabbai and Simeon b. Shetaḥ
(4) Shemaiah and Avtalyon
(5) Hillel and Shammai

Zukor, Adolph (1873–), U.S. motion picture executive; b. Hungary. Formed Famous Players Company 1912, which produced classics such as *The Prisoner of Zenda* and *The Count of Monte Cristo.* Combined with other small companies to found Paramount Pictures 1917.

Zukunft, U.S. Yiddish monthly founded in N.Y. 1892 as organ of Socialist Labor Party. Acquired by the Forward Association 1912, edited by Abraham Liessin 1913–38, published by Central Yiddish Cultural Organization (CYCO) fr. 1940.

Zulay, Menahem (1901–1954), Israel researcher of early Ereẓ Israel *piyyut;* b. Galicia, settled in Ereẓ Israel 1920. Worked at Schocken Inst. for Study of Hebrew Poetry.

Zunser, Eliakum (1836–1913), popular Yiddish bard, dramatist; b. Vilna, settled in Minsk. His booklets of songs were avidly read. Emigrated to New York 1889.

Zunz, Leopold (Yom Tov Lippmann; 1794–1886), German scholar; among founders of Wissenschaft des Judentums. Pioneer of modern scientific methods in Jewish studies; insisted that Jewish studies had to be linked to general historical and cultural context. Wrote on liturgical verse, historical development of Hebrew literature, synagogue ritual, and history of Jewish homiletics *Gottesdienstlichen Vortraege der Juden.* In Mishnah and other spheres, his work remains fundamental.

Leopold Zunz

Ẓur, Ẓevi (1923–), Israel military commander. Joined Haganah 1939, fought in War of Independence. Sixth chief of staff 1961–63. Assistant to defense minister 1967–74.

Zuri, Jacob Samuel (1884–1943), lawyer, authority on Hebrew law. Lectured at Jerusalem Law School, moved to London 1931. Attempted to lay foundations of legislation for Jewish state, working out principles inherent in talmudic law in his many books, incl. 3-vol. *Toledot ha-Mishpat ha-Ẓibburi ha-Ivri.*

Zurich, city in Switzerland. Jews first settled 1273, massacred during Black Death 1349, expelled 1425, 1435, 1436. Community established 1866. Jewish pop. 6,150 (1971), with 3 communities.

Ẓur Mi-Shello (Heb. "Rock from whose store [we have eaten]"), opening words of Sabbath table song sung

at conclusion of meal. Its four stanzas summarize contents of Grace after Meal.

Zusya (Meshulam Zusya) of Hanipoli (d. 1800), early ḥasidic leader, disciple of Dov Baer of Mezhirech, hero of ḥasidic folk tales.

Zutra, Mar, name of three exilarchs in 5th and 6th c. **I** (d.c. 414), associate of R. Ashi, opinions cited in Talmud, called "the pious." **II** (c. 496–520), took up arms against Persians, set up Jewish state in Maḥoza which lasted 7 years. His son, **III** (6th c.), thought to have disseminated Babylonian Talmud in Ereẓ Israel.

Zweifel, Eliezer (1815–1888), Hebrew author, essayist; one of first Haskalah writers to view Ḥasidism sympathetically. Taught Talmud in Zhitomir rabbinical seminary 1853–1873. Pioneer of change of Hebrew prose fr. ornate biblical language to modern style.

Zweig, Arnold (1887–1968), German author. War novel *The Case of Sergeant Grischa* established reputation. Became ardent Zionist and when Hitler came to power settled in Haifa. Moved to East Berlin 1948. Prof. of Academy of Arts. International Lenin Peace Prize 1958. Refused to sign statement condemning Israel for Six-Day War.

Arnold Zweig, etching by Hermann Struck.

Stefan Zweig

Zweig, Stefan (1881–1942), Austrian playwright, essayist, biographer. Member of "Young Vienna" group. WWI inspired pacifist drama *Jeremiah.* Wrote series of literary and historical biographies. Moved to England 1935, later to N. and S. America. Several works on Jewish themes, incl. *The Buried Candelabrum.* Autobiography *The World of Yesterday* appeared after he and his wife committed suicide in Brazil.

Zygelbojm, Samuel Mordecai (pseud. **Comrade Arthur;** 1895–1943), Polish Bundist leader. Escaped to England 1940 and was Bund representative on national council of Polish government-in-exile. As protest against atmosphere of indifference to tragedy of Holocaust by allied powers, committed suicide.

Zylbercweig, Zalman (1894–), Yiddish journalist, writer; b. Galicia, in U.S. fr. 1937. Published a 5-vol. lexicon of Yiddish theater.

יָכוֹל ל־ able
לְמַעְלָה above
חוּץ־לָאָרֶץ abroad
נֶעְדָּר absent
קִבֵּל אֶת accept*
תְּאוּנָה accident
לְפִי, בְּהֶתְאֵם ל־ according to
מַעֲשֶׂה act
הוֹסִיף אֶת, ל־ add
כְּתֹבֶת address (postal)
הִתְקַדֵּם advance, get on
עֵצָה advice
פָּחַד מ־ (be) afraid
אַחֲרֵי after
אַחֲרֵי־כֵן afterwards
נֶגֶד against
אֲגוֹרָה agora (1/100 of an Israel Pound)
הִסְכִּים ל־ agree
חַקְלָאוּת agriculture
אֲוִיר air
אֲוִירוֹן, מָטוֹס airplane
כָּל, כָּל אֶחָד all, every
כִּמְעַט almost
לְבַד alone
כְּבָר already
גַּם, גַּם כֵּן also, too
תָּמִיד always
בֵּין among, between
מְשַׁעֲשֵׁעַ amusing
וְ־ and
וּבְכֵן and so
מַלְאָךְ angel
כָּעַס (be) angry
חַיָּה animal
הוֹדִיעַ אֶת announce
הִרְגִּיז אֶת annoy
תְּשׁוּבָה, הֵשִׁיב, עָנָה answer; to answer
כְּלוּם anything, nothing
חוּץ מ־ apart from
דִּירָה apartment
כַּנִּרְאֶה apparently
תַּפּוּחַ apple
בְּקֵרוּב approximately
נֶשֶׁק arms (in combat)
צָבָא army
סָבִיב around
סִדֵּר, עָרַךְ אֶת arrange
שָׁאַל אֶת ask (a question)
בִּקֵּשׁ ask for
חֲמוֹר ass, donkey
בְּ־ at, in
בִּכְלָל at all, generally
לְכָל הַפָּחוֹת (לְפָחוֹת) at least
מִיָּד at once
נִסָּה attempt, try
דּוֹדָה aunt
סוֹפֵר author, writer
סְתָו autumn, fall

תִּינוֹק baby
רַוָּק bachelor, unmarried
רַע bad
כַּדּוּר ball; bullet
תִּזְמֹרֶת band, orchestra
יְסוֹד base, foundation
סַל basket, shopping bag
חֲדַר אַמְבַּטְיָה bathroom
אַמְבַּטְיָה bathtub
שׁוּק bazaar, market
נִצֵּחַ אֶת beat, conquer
הִכָּה beat, strike
יָפֶה beautiful, pretty
מִפְּנֵי שֶׁ־ because
מִטָּה bed
לִפְנֵי before, in front of
הִתְחִיל begin
הֶאֱמִין believe
פַּעֲמוֹן bell
בֶּטֶן belly
שַׁיָּךְ ל־ belong
לְמַטָּה below, down
בֵּין between, among
אוֹפַנַּיִם bicycle
גָּדוֹל big, large
חֶשְׁבּוֹן bill, invoice
צִפּוֹר bird
יוֹם־הֻלֶּדֶת birthday
מַר bitter
שָׁחוֹר black
בְּרָכָה blessing, greeting
דָּם blood
מַכָּה blow
כָּחוֹל blue
סִירָה boat (small)
אֳנִיָּה boat (big), ship
גּוּף body
פְּצָצָה bomb
בְּתֵאָבוֹן bon appétit!
עֶצֶם bone
סֵפֶר book
נַעַל boot, shoe
גְּבוּל border, limit
בַּקְבּוּק bottle
קֻפְסָה box (small), tin
נַעַר, בָּחוּר, צָעִיר boy
לֶחֶם bread
שָׁבַר break
גֶּשֶׁר bridge
תִּיק briefcase
הֵבִיא bring
רָחָב broad, wide
מַטְאֲטֵא broom
אָח brother; nurse (male)
מִבְרֶשֶׁת brush
בָּנָה build
בִּנְיָן building
כַּדּוּר bullet; ball

שָׂרַף אֶת, בָּעַר burn;
עָסוּק busy
אֲבָל, אוּלָם, אַךְ but
חֶמְאָה butter
כַּפְתּוֹר button
קָנָה אֶת buy

עוּגָה cake
קָרָא ל־ call
מַחֲנֶה camp
נֵר candle
כַּרְטִיס card, ticket
נַגָּר carpenter
נָשָׂא אֶת carry
עֲגָלָה cart
מִשְׁפָּט case (in court), sentence
קֻפָּה cashbox, box office
חָתוּל cat
תָּפַס אֶת catch, grasp
סִבָּה cause, reason
זְהִירוּת caution
מֶרְכָּז center
בְּוַדַּאי, בְּהֶחְלֵט certainly, absolutely
תְּעוּדָה certificate, document
כִּסֵּא chair
גִּיר chalk
מִקְרֶה chance, instance, case
הֶחֱלִיף change
עֹדֶף change (small money)
בָּחוּר chap, fellow, young man
בָּזוֹל cheap
גְּבִינָה cheese
בֵּית־מִרְקַחַת chemist's, pharmacy
עוֹף chicken
יֶלֶד m.; יַלְדָּה f. child
בָּחַר בְּ־ choose
קוֹלְנוֹעַ cinema
עִיר city, town
כִּתָּה class (of pupils)
נָקִי clean
בָּרוּר clear (understood)
פָּקִיד clerk, official
שָׁעוֹן clock, watch
בַּד cloth
בְּגָדִים clothes
עָנָן cloud
חוֹף coast, shore
מְעִיל coat, jacket
תַּרְנְגוֹל cock (rooster)
קָפֶה coffee
קַר cold
צֶבַע color, paint
עַמּוּד column, pole; page (one side)
מַסְרֵק comb
בָּא come

*Verbs in the Hebrew are in the 3rd person masculine singular past tense.

שֵׂכֶל	common sense, intelligence
חֶבְרָה	company, society
שָׁלֵם	complete, whole
אִחוּלִים	congratulations
חִבֵּר	connect, join; write (a literary work)
קֶשֶׁר	connection; knot
הִמְשִׁיךְ	continue
נוֹחַ	convenient, comfortable
שִׂיחָה	conversation, talk
בִּשֵּׁל אֶת	cook
פִּנָּה	corner
עָלָה	cost; rise, go up
סַפָּה	couch
סָפַר	count
אֶרֶץ	country, land
זוּג	couple, pair
כִּסָּה אֶת	cover
פָּרָה	cow
רֶפֶת	cowshed
צָעַק	cry out, shout
תַּרְבּוּת	culture
סֵפֶל	cup
אָרוֹן	cupboard
כַּר	cushion, pillow
מִנְהָג	custom
מֶכֶס	customs
חָתַךְ	cut
רָטֹב, לַח	damp, wet
רָקַד	dance
סַכָּנָה	danger
חֹשֶׁךְ	darkness, dark
בַּת	daughter
יוֹם	day
הֶחְלִיט	decide
עָמֹק	deep
מָחַק	delete, erase
דָּרַשׁ מִ־	demand .. (of)
שָׁלַח	despatch, send
מִדְבָּר	desert
הָרַס	destroy
מִלּוֹן	dictionary
מֵת	die; dead
הֶבְדֵּל	difference
קָשֶׁה	difficult, hard
קֹשִׁי	difficulty
חֲדַר־אֹכֶל	dining-room
מְנַהֵל	director, manager
מְלֻכְלָךְ	dirty
וִכּוּחַ	discussion, argument
מֶרְחָק	distance
הִפְרִיעַ	disturb
עָשָׂה	do, make
תְּעוּדָה	document, certificate
כֶּלֶב	dog
חֲמוֹר	donkey, ass
אַל	don't (preceding verb)
דֶּלֶת	door
סָפֵק	doubt
לְמַטָּה	down, below

צִיֵּר	draw, sketch
חֲלוֹם	dream
שִׂמְלָה	dress (lady's)
הִתְלַבֵּשׁ	(get) dressed
שָׁתָה	drink
גֵּרֵשׁ	drive away, expel
נֶהָג	driver
טִפָּה	(a) drop, a little bit
יָבֵשׁ	dry
בְּמֶשֶׁךְ	during
אָבָק	dust
גָּר	dwell, live
כָּל אֶחָד	each
אֹזֶן	ear
מֻקְדָּם	early
הִרְוִיחַ	earn, gain
אֲדָמָה	earth, ground, soil
מִזְרָח	east
קַל	easy, light
אָכַל	eat
בֵּיצָה	egg
חַשְׁמַל	electricity
רֵיק	empty
סוֹף	end, conclusion
דַּי!	enough!
לְגַמְרֵי	entirely
כְּנִיסָה	entrance
שָׁוֶה	equal, worth
מָחַק	erase, delete
טָעוּת	error
וכו'	etc.
אֲפִלּוּ	even
עֶרֶב	evening
מְאֹרָע	event
כָּל	every, all
בְּדִיּוּק	exactly
בָּחַן	examine, test
דֻּגְמָה	example, pattern
סְלִיחָה!	excuse me! sorry!
יָקָר	expensive, dear
חֲוָיָה	experience
נִסָּיוֹן	experiment, trial
הִסְבִּיר	explain
עַיִן	eye
מִשְׁקָפַיִם	eyeglasses
פָּנִים	face
בֵּית־חֲרֹשֶׁת	factory
נָפַל	fall
סְתָו	fall, autumn
מִשְׁפָּחָה	family
רָחוֹק	far
מֶשֶׁק חַקְלָאִי	farmstead
מַהֵר	fast, quickly
שָׁמֵן, שֻׁמָּן	fat
אָב, אַבָּא	father, dad
פַּחַד	fear
הִרְגִּישׁ	feel
בָּחוּר	fellow, chap
גָּדֵר	fence
חַג	festival
חֹם	fever, heat

מְעַט	(a) few, a little of
שָׂדֶה	field
תְּאֵנָה	fig
נִלְחַם	fight
יָפֶה	fine, beautiful, pretty
אֶצְבַּע	finger
צִפֹּרֶן	fingernail
גָּמַר	finish
אֵשׁ	fire
דָּג	fish
קָבוּעַ	fixed
דֶּגֶל	flag
רִצְפָּה	floor
קֶמַח	flour
פֶּרַח	flower
זְבוּב	(a) fly
רֶגֶל	foot, leg
בִּשְׁבִיל	for
לְמָשָׁל	for instance
כֹּחַ	force, power
זָר	foreign
יַעַר	forest
שָׁכַח	forget
מַזְלֵג	fork
צוּרָה	form, shape
יְסוֹד	foundation, base
פָּנוּי	free (unoccupied)
חָפְשִׁי	free
טָרִי	fresh
חָבֵר m.; חֲבֵרָה f.	friend
יָדִיד m.; יְדִידָה f.	(close) friend
מִי־ מֵ־	from
פְּרִי	fruit
מָלֵא	full
שַׁעֲשׁוּעַ	fun
מַצְחִיק	funny
רָהִיטִים, רַהִיטִים	furniture
הָלְאָה	further on
עָתִיד	future
מִשְׂחָק	game
גַּן	garden, park; kindergarten
בִּכְלָל	generally, at all
רֵד	get down
הִתְקַדֵּם	get on
יָצָא	get out
הִתְרַגֵּל לְ־	get used to
מַתָּנָה	gift
נַעֲרָה, צְעִירָה, בַּחוּרָה	girl
נָתַן	give
הֶחֱזִיר	give back
זְכוּכִית	glass
כּוֹס	(a) glass
יָרַד	go (get) down
נִכְנַס	go (come) in
יָצָא	go out
נִגַּשׁ	go up to, come near
אֱלֹהִים	God

זָהָב gold
טוֹב good
סְחוֹרָה goods, merchandise
מֶמְשָׁלָה government
תְּבוּאָה grain, (agricultural) produce
סַבָּא grandfather
סַבְתָּא grandmother
נֶכֶד, grandson,
נֶכְדָּה granddaughter
אֶשְׁכּוֹלִית grapefruit
עֲנָבִים grapes
תָּפַס grasp, catch
יָרֹק green
בְּרָכָה greeting, blessing
מַכֹּלֶת grocery
קַרְקַע ground, soil
אוֹרֵחַ guest, visitor

שְׂעָרוֹת hair
מִסְפָּרָה hairdresser's
חֲצִי half
אוּלָם hall (public)
פַּטִּישׁ hammer
יָד hand
מָסַר hand over to
אַרְנָק handbag, purse
מִמְחָטָה handkerchief
תָּלָה hang
קָרָה happen
מְאֻשָּׁר happy
נָמֵל harbor, port
קָשֶׁה hard, difficult
כּוֹבַע hat
שָׂנֵא hate
יֵשׁ have; there is (are)
מֻכְרָח have to, must
הוּא he, it (is)
רֹאשׁ head, top
בָּרִיא healthy
שָׁמַע hear
לֵב heart
חֹם heat, fever
כָּבֵד heavy
עִבְרִית (the) Hebrew language
עֶזְרָה, עָזַר help
כָּאן here
הֵנָּה here (direction)
הִנֵּה here is
גִּבּוֹר hero
גָּבֹהַּ high, tall
כְּבִישׁ highway, road
גִּבְעָה hill
מַעְדֵּר hoe
הֶחֱזִיק hold
חוֹר hole
חֹפֶשׁ holiday, vacation
קָדוֹשׁ holy
הַבַּיְתָה home (direction)
יָשָׁר honest, straight
דְּבַשׁ honey
כָּבוֹד honor, respect

תִּקְוָה hope
קִוָּה hope (for)
סוּס horse
בֵּית־חוֹלִים hospital
חַם hot, warm
מָלוֹן hotel
שָׁעָה hour
בַּיִת house, home
אֵיךְ? how?
כַּמָּה? how much? how many?
רָעֵב hungry
מִהֵר hurry
בַּעַל husband
צְרִיף hut

אֲנִי I
קֶרַח ice
גְּלִידָה ice-cream
זֹאת־אוֹמֶרֶת i.e., that means
אִם, אִלּוּ if
מַחֲלָה illness
עוֹלֶה immigrant, newcomer (in Israel)
חָשׁוּב important
אִי־אֶפְשָׁר impossible
רֹשֶׁם impression
בְּ־ in, at
לִפְנֵי in front of
כְּדֵי שֶׁ־ in order that, so that
בֶּאֱמֶת indeed, really
תַּעֲשִׂיָּה industry
הוֹדִיעַ לְ־ inform
יְדִיעָה information, news
דְּיוֹ ink
כְּתֹבֶת inscription, (postal) address
בִּפְנִים inside, within
כְּלִי instrument, tool; receptacle
שֵׂכֶל intelligence, common sense
מְעַנְיֵן interesting
הִתְעַנְיֵן (be) interested in
הִזְמִין invite; order (commercial)
חֶשְׁבּוֹן invoice, bill
בַּרְזֶל iron

מְעִיל jacket, coat
רִבָּה jam
יְהוּדִי Jew(ish)
חִבֵּר join, connect
שִׂמְחָה joy, joyful occasion
שׁוֹפֵט; שָׁפַט judge, to judge
קָפַץ jump

מַפְתֵּחַ key
הָרַג kill
מִין kind, sort; sex
גַּן kindergarten
מֶלֶךְ king
דַּוְקָא just (adv.), precisely
נְשִׁיקָה kiss

נָשַׁק kiss (v.)
מִטְבָּח kitchen
סַכִּין knife
קֶשֶׁר knot; connection
יָדַע know

חָסֵר lacking
סֻלָּם ladder
מְנוֹרָה lamp
אֶרֶץ land, country
לָשׁוֹן; שָׂפָה language; lip
גָּדוֹל large, big
אַחֲרוֹן last
מְאֻחָר late
צָחַק laugh
צְחוֹק laughter
חֹק law
עוֹרֵךְ־דִּין lawyer
עָצֵל lazy
לָמַד learn, study
עָזַב leave, go away
הִשְׁאִיר leave behind
הַרְצָאָה lecture
שְׂמֹאל (the) left
רֶגֶל leg, foot
פָּחוֹת less
שִׁעוּר lesson
אוֹת letter (alphabet)
מִכְתָּב letter (postal)
סִפְרִיָּה library
שֶׁקֶר lie, untruth
שָׁכַב lie down
חַיִּים life
קַל light, easy
אוֹר light
הִדְלִיק light (v.)
כְּמוֹ like, as
דּוֹמֶה like, similar to
גְּבוּל limit, border
קַו, שׁוּרָה line, row
אַרְיֵה lion
שָׂפָה lip; language
לִירָה lira, pound (currency)
רְשִׁימָה list
הִקְשִׁיב לְ־ listen
סִפְרוּת literature
קָטָן little, small
מְעַט (a) little (of), a few
קְצָת (a) little, a bit (of), not much
חַי live, exist
אָרֹךְ long
שָׁמַר, טִפֵּל בְּ־ look after
הִבִּיט look at
חִפֵּשׂ look for
רְאִי, מַרְאָה looking-glass
הִפְסִיד, אִבֵּד lose
אָבַד, אָבוּד lost
אַהֲבָה love
אָהַב love (v.)
נָמוּךְ low, short
הוֹרִיד lower, take down
מַזָּל luck

Hebrew	English
מְכוֹנָה	machine
מְשֻׁגָּע	mad
רֹב	majority
עָשָׂה	make, do
אָדָם	man (= human being)
אִישׁ, גֶּבֶר	(a) man
מְנַהֵל	manager, director
אֹפֶן	manner, way (to do)
הַרְבֵּה	many, much, a lot of
מַפָּה	map; tablecloth
שׁוּק	market, bazaar
נָשׂוּי	married
הִתְחַתֵּן עִם	marry
גַּפְרוּר	match (for striking)
אִכְפַּת	(it) matters
אֲרוּחָה	meal
בֵּינְתַיִם, בֵּינָתַיִם	meanwhile
מִדָּה	measure
בָּשָׂר	meat
נִפְגַּשׁ עִם	meet
סְחוֹרָה	merchandise, goods
סוֹחֵר	merchant
מַתֶּכֶת	metal
אֶמְצַע	middle
חָלָב	milk
שַׂר	(government) minister
דַּקָּה	minute
מִסְכֵּן	miserable, poor (= a poor devil)
טָעוּת	mistake
טָעָה	(make a) mistake
אִמָּא	mom, mother
רֶגַע	moment, just a moment
כֶּסֶף	money; silver
חֹדֶשׁ	month
יָרֵחַ	moon
עוֹד	more, still
יוֹתֵר	more (comparative)
בֹּקֶר	morning
אֵם	mother
מְכוֹנִית	motor-car
הַר	mountain
פֶּה	mouth
תְּנוּעָה	movement, traffic
סֶרֶט	movie picture; ribbon
אָדוֹן	Mr., gentleman
גְּבֶרֶת	Mrs., Miss, lady
הַרְבֵּה	much, many, a lot of
מֻכְרָח	must, have to
בְּעַצְמִי, בְּעַצְמְךָ, וכו׳	(by) my-, your- etc. self
מַסְמֵר	nail (not of a finger or toe)
צַר	narrow
טֶבַע	nature
קָרוֹב	near
עַל־יַד	near, at the side of
נָחוּץ	necessary
צַוָּאר	neck
צֹרֶךְ	need
צָרִיךְ	need to, should

Hebrew	English
מַחַט	needle
שָׁכֵן	neighbour
בְּכָל־זֹאת	nevertheless, for all that
חָדָשׁ	new
עוֹלֶה	newcomer, immigrant (in Israel)
יְדִיעָה	news, information
עִתּוֹן	newspaper
לַיְלָה	night
לֹא	no, not
אֵין	(there is) no; have not
רַעַשׁ	noise
שְׁטוּת	nonsense
צָהֳרַיִם	noon, midday
צָפוֹן	North
אַף	nose
פִּתְקָה	(a) note
פִּנְקָס	notebook
כְּלוּם	nothing, anything
לוּחַ מוֹדָעוֹת	notice board
עַכְשָׁו	now
מִסְפָּר	number
אָחוֹת	nurse; sister
אֱגוֹז	nut
שְׁבוּעָה	oath
הִשִּׂיג	obtain
שֶׁל	of, belonging to
כַּמּוּבָן	of course
מִשְׂרָד	office
פָּקִיד	official, clerk
שֶׁמֶן; נֵפְט	oil
יָשָׁן	old
זָקֵן	old man
זַיִת	olive
עַל	on, upon
פַּעַם	once, time(s)
רַק	only
פָּתַח	open
דֵּעָה	opinion
הִזְדַּמְּנוּת	opportunity, occasion, (good) bargain
אוֹ	or
תַּפּוּחַ־זָהָב	orange
תִּזְמֹרֶת	orchestra, band
פְּקֻדָּה	order, command
הִזְמִין	order (commercial); invite
סֵדֶר	order (of things), arrangement
מִזְרָחִי	oriental
אַחֵר (אַחֶרֶת)	other, another
הַחוּצָה	out, outside (direction)
מִתּוֹךְ	out of
בַּחוּץ	outside (outdoors)
הִתְגַּבֵּר עַל	overcome
בַּעַל	owner
שׁוֹר	ox
עַמּוּד	page (one side); pole, column
כְּאֵב	pain

Hebrew	English
צֶבַע	paint, color
זוּג	pair, couple
נְיָר	paper
סָעִיף	paragraph, section
חֲבִילָה	parcel
הוֹרִים	parents
גַּן	park, garden;
חֵלֶק	part, share
בְּיִחוּד	particularly
מְסִבָּה	party
מִפְלָגָה	party (political)
עָבַר	pass, move
חוֹלֶה	patient, sick man
דֻּגְמָה	pattern, example
שִׁלֵּם	pay. . .(to)
תַּשְׁלוּם	payment
עֵט	pen, fountain pen
עִפָּרוֹן	pencil
אֲנָשִׁים	people
עַם	(a) people
הַצָּגָה	performance (theatrical etc.)
אוּלַי	perhaps
מֻתָּר	(it is) permissible, one may
רְשׁוּת	permission, right (to do a thing)
בֵּית־מִרְקַחַת	pharmacy
צִלְצֵל	phone, ring
רוֹפֵא	physician
תְּמוּנָה	picture
חֲתִיכָה	piece
סִכָּה	pin, brooch
מִקְטֶרֶת	pipe (smoking)
צִנּוֹר	pipe, hose
אֶקְדָּח	pistol
מָקוֹם	place
פָּשׁוּט	plain, simple
תָּכְנִית	plan, program
צֶמַח	plant
נָטַע	plant
צַלַּחַת	plate
שִׂחֵק	play
נִגֵּן	play (music)
שָׂמֵחַ	pleased, happy
נָעִים	pleasant, charming
בְּבַקָּשָׁה	please
הֲנָאָה	pleasure
מִגְרָשׁ	plot (of land); field (for games)
כִּיס	pocket
שִׁיר	poem, song
מְשׁוֹרֵר	poet
נְקֻדָּה	point
עַמּוּד	pole, column; page (one side)
מִשְׁטָרָה	police
שׁוֹטֵר	policeman
עָנִי	poor (opp. rich)
נָמָל	port, harbor
מָנָה	portion
אֶפְשָׁרִי	possible
אֶפְשָׁר	(it is) possible, one may

דֹּאַר post, post office
סִיר pot
תַּפּוּחַ־אֲדָמָה potato
כֹּחַ power, force
הִתְפַּלֵּל pray
הֵכִין prepare
הִתְכּוֹנֵן prepare oneself (for)
נִמְצָא (be) present
נָשִׂיא president
מַגְהֵץ pressing-iron
יָפֶה pretty, beautiful
מְחִיר price
הִדְפִּיס print, type
פְּרָטִי private
מִקְצוֹעַ profession, trade; subject (of study)
תָּכְנִית program, plan
אָסוּר (it is) prohibited, one may not
הִבְטִיחַ promise. . .to, assure. . .of
עֹנֶשׁ punishment
תַּלְמִיד m.; תַּלְמִידָה f. pupil, student
אַרְנָק purse, handbag
שָׂם put. . .in/on. . .
הִכְנִיס put in, bring in, let in

שְׁכוּנָה quarter (in a city), district
רֶבַע quarter (of)
מַלְכָּה queen
שְׁאֵלָה question
תּוֹר queue, (somebody's) turn
מַהֵר quickly, fast
שָׁקֵט quiet, calm

רַכֶּבֶת railway (train)
גֶּשֶׁם rain
הִגִּיעַ reach
קָרָא read
מוּכָן ready
בֶּאֱמֶת really, indeed
סִבָּה reason (for something)
קִבֵּל; נִתְקַבֵּל receive, accept; be received
כְּלִי receptacle; tool, instrument
הִכִּיר recognize, be acquainted with
אָדֹם red
דְּרִישַׁת־שָׁלוֹם regards
זָכַר remember
הִזְכִּיר remind. . .of. . .
חָזַר repeat, return
כָּבוֹד respect, honor
אַחֲרַאי responsible
מְנוּחָה rest, repose
נָח rest (v.)
מִסְעָדָה restaurant
חָזַר return, repeat
סֶרֶט ribbon; movie picture

עָשִׁיר rich
רָכַב ride (on horseback, bicycle)
רוֹבֶה rifle
צָדַק (be) right
נָכוֹן right, correct
יָמִין right (side)
טַבַּעַת (finger-) ring
צִלְצֵל ring, phone
קָם rise, get up
עָלָה rise, go up,
נָהָר river
כְּבִישׁ road, highway
סֶלַע rock
תַּפְקִיד role; duty
גַּג roof
חֶדֶר room
שֹׁרֶשׁ root
חֶבֶל rope
שׁוֹשַׁנָּה rose
בְּעֵרֶךְ roughly
עָגֹל round
שׁוּרָה row, line
רָץ run
בָּרַח run away

שַׁבָּת sabbath, Saturday
לֵיל־שַׁבָּת sabbath-eve
עָצוּב sad
מַשְׂכֹּרֶת salary
מֶלַח salt
חוֹל sand
מְרֻצֶּה satisfied
מוֹצָאֵי־שַׁבָּת Saturday night
הִצִּיל save, rescue
אָמַר say
בֵּית־סֵפֶר school
מַדָּע science
מִסְפָּרַיִם scissors
יָם sea, (large) lake
סוֹד secret
רָאָה see
לְהִתְרָאוֹת! see you (again) !
מָכַר sell
שָׁלַח send, despatch
מִשְׁפָּט sentence (grammar)
רְצִינִי serious
שֵׁרוּת service
יִשּׁוּב settlement
תָּפַר sew (on)
מִין sex
שָׁלוֹם! Shalom! (greeting on meeting and leaving)
צוּרָה shape, form
חֵלֶק share, part
הִתְגַּלֵּחַ shave
הִיא she, it (is)
דַּף sheet (of paper)
אֳנִיָּה ship, boat (big)
חֻלְצָה shirt
נַעַל shoe, boot
סַנְדְּלָר shoemaker
חֲנוּת shop

סַל shopping bag, basket
חוֹף shore, coast
קָצָר, נָמוּךְ short
בְּקָרוֹב shortly
צָרִיךְ should, need to
צָעַק shout, cry out
הַצָּגָה show
הֶרְאָה show . . (to)
מִקְלַחַת (a) shower
סָגַר shut, close
חוֹלֶה sick
צַד side
חָתַם עַל sign (v.)
סִימָן, שֶׁלֶט sign
שֶׁקֶט! silence!
שָׁקֵט silent
מֶשִׁי silk
כֶּסֶף silver; money
דּוֹמֶה similar to, like
פָּשׁוּט simple, plain
שָׁר sing
אָחוֹת sister; nurse
יָשַׁב sit
שֵׁב! sit down!
חֲצָאִית skirt
שָׁמַיִם sky, heavens
שֵׁנָה sleep
יָשֵׁן sleep (v.)
לְאַט slowly
קָטָן small, little
רֵיחַ smell
עָשָׁן smoke
עִשֵּׁן smoke (v.)
נָחָשׁ snake
שֶׁלֶג snow
כָּל־כָּךְ so. . .
לָכֵן so, thus
כָּךְ כְּדֵי שֶׁ־ so that, in order that
סַבּוֹן soap
גֶּרֶב sock, stocking
רַךְ soft
קַרְקַע soil, ground, earth
חַיָּל soldier
כַּמָּה some (= a few); how much? how many?
מִישֶׁהוּ somebody
מַשֶּׁהוּ something
לִפְעָמִים sometimes
אֵי שָׁם somewhere
בֵּן son
שִׁיר song, poem
צַעַר sorrow
סְלִיחָה! Sorry! Excuse me! (I beg your pardon!)
מִין sort, kind
קוֹל sound, voice
מָרָק soup
דָּרוֹם South
דִּבֵּר speak (to)
מְיֻחָד special
הוֹצִיא spend (money), take out
קִלְקֵל spoil
כַּף spoon

אָבִיב	spring (season)
בּוּל	stamp (postage)
עָמַד	stand
כּוֹכָב	star
מְדִינָה	state
תַּחֲנָה	station
נִשְׁאַר	stay, be left
גָּנַב	steal. . .(from)
מַדְרֵגָה	step (= stair),
צַעַד	step
מַקֵּל	stick
גֶּרֶב	stocking, sock
אֶבֶן	stone
הִפְסִיק; עָצַר	stop
מַחְסָן	store (-house)
קוֹמָה	storey, floor (of a building)
סִפּוּר	story, short story
תַּנּוּר	stove
יָשָׁר	straight, honest
זָר	strange, foreign
קַשׁ	straw
נַחַל	stream, brook
רְחוֹב	street
הִכָּה	strike, beat
חוּט	string, thread
חָזָק	strong, firm
תַּלְמִיד, סְטוּדֶנְט .m; תַּלְמִידָה, סְטוּדֶנְטִית .f	student, pupil
לָמַד	study, learn
טִפֵּשׁ	stupid
מִקְצוֹעַ	subject (of study); trade, profession
הִצְלִיחַ	succeed in
פִּתְאֹם	suddenly
דַּי	sufficient, enough
סֻכָּר	sugar
הִתְאִים	suit
חֲלִיפָה	suit of clothes, (ladies') costume
מִזְוָדָה	suitcase
קַיִץ	summer
שֶׁמֶשׁ	sun, sunlight
בָּטוּחַ	sure
הַפְתָּעָה	surprise
מָתוֹק	sweet
בֵּית־כְּנֶסֶת	synagogue

שֻׁלְחָן	table
מַפָּה	tablecloth; map
חַיָּט	tailor
לָקַח	take (. . .from)
טִיֵּל	take a walk, make a trip
הוֹצִיא	take out, spend
הִשְׁתַּתֵּף בּ־	take part in
שִׂיחָה	talk, conversation
גָּבֹהַּ	tall, high
בֶּרֶז	tap, faucet
טַעַם	taste
מַס	tax
תֵּה	tea

לִמֵּד	teach
מוֹרֶה .m; מוֹרָה .f	teacher
קֻמְקוּם	teapot, kettle
קָרַע	tear (v.)
כַּפִּית	teaspoon
סִפֵּר, אָמַר לְ־	tell. . .(to)
אֹהֶל	tent
נוֹרָא	terrible
בָּחַן	test, examine
תּוֹדָה!	thanks!
שֶׁ־, כִּי	that
הַ־	the
אוֹתוֹ [אוֹתָהּ]	the same
אָז	then
שָׁם	there
יֵשׁ	there is (are)
לָכֵן	therefore, so
אֵלֶּה	these, those
הֵם .m; הֵן .f	they, (they) are
עָבֶה	thick
דַּק	thin
דָּבָר	thing; word
חָשַׁב	think (of)
שְׁלִישׁ	(a) third
צָמֵא	thirsty
זֶה .m; זֹאת .f	this, that
חוּט	thread, string, wire
זָרַק	throw (away)
כַּרְטִיס	ticket, card
קָשַׁר	tie, connect
עַד	till, up to
זְמַן	time
פַּחִית, קֻפְסָה	(a) tin
עָיֵף	tired
לְ־	to
אֶל	to, towards
הַיּוֹם	to-day
יַחַד	together
עַגְבָנִיָּה	tomato
מָחָר	to-morrow
לָשׁוֹן, שָׂפָה	tongue, language
גַּם כֵּן	too
כְּלִי	tool, instrument; receptacle
שֵׁן	tooth
רֹאשׁ	top, head
נָגַע	touch; concern
מַגֶּבֶת	towel
עִיר	town, city
מִקְצוֹעַ	trade, profession; subject (of study)
מִסְחָר	trade (= commerce)
תְּנוּעָה	traffic, movement
תִּרְגֵּם	translate
נָסַע	travel, go
עֵץ	tree
טִיּוּל	trip, (a) walk
צָרָה	trouble
מִכְנָסַיִם	trousers
אֱמֶת	truth
נִסָּה	try, attempt

פָּנָה לְ־	turn (to)
הִדְפִּיס	type, print

דּוֹד	uncle
מִתַּחַת	under
הֵבִין	understand
רַוָּק	unmarried, bachelor
רַוָּקָה	unmarried, spinster
לְמַעְלָה	up, above
הָפַךְ	upset
דָּחוּף	urgent
הִשְׁתַּמֵּשׁ בּ־	(make) use (of)
רָגִיל	usual

חֹפֶשׁ	vacation
עֵמֶק	valley
יְרָקוֹת	vegetables
מְאֹד	very, very much
וָתִיק	veteran
נִצָּחוֹן	victory
כְּפָר	village
כֶּרֶם	vineyard
בִּקֵּר	visit
אוֹרֵחַ	visitor, guest
קוֹל	voice, sound

חִכָּה	wait (for)
מֶלְצַר	waiter
קִיר, כֹּתֶל	wall
רָצָה	want
מִלְחָמָה	war
חַם	warm, hot
כִּבֵּס	wash (linen)
רָחַץ	wash
הִתְרַחֵץ	wash oneself, take a bath
כְּבִיסָה	laundry
שָׁעוֹן	watch, clock
מַיִם	water
אֲבַטִּיחַ	watermelon
דֶּרֶךְ	way
אֲנַחְנוּ	we
חַלָּשׁ	weak
לָבַשׁ	wear, have on
מֶזֶג־אֲוִיר	weather
שָׁבוּעַ	week
בָּכָה	weep
שָׁקַל	weigh
מִשְׁקָל	weight
בְּאֵר	(a) well
רָטֹב, לַח	wet, damp
מַה?	what?
מָתַי?	when?
כַּאֲשֶׁר, כְּשֶׁ־	when
אֵיפֹה?	where?
מַעֲרָב	West
גַּלְגַּל	wheel
מֵאַיִן?	where from?
לְאָן?	where to?
אֵיזֶה?	which, what?
לָבָן	white
מִי?	who?

שָׁלֵם whole, complete
לָמָּה? why? what for?
רָחָב wide, broad
רֹחַב width
רָצוֹן will, desire
רוּחַ wind
חַלּוֹן window
יַיִן wine
חֹרֶף winter
חוּט־בַּרְזֶל wire
חָכָם wise
עִם with
בְּתוֹךְ, בִּפְנִי within, inside
בְּלִי without
אִשָּׁה woman

נִפְלָא wonderful
חֻרְשָׁה (a) wood
צֶמֶר wool
מִלָּה word
מְלָאכָה work, trade
עָבַד work (v.)
עֲבוֹדָה work
פּוֹעֵל workman
עוֹלָם world
דָּאַג worry, concern oneself
שָׁוֶה worth, equal
כְּדַאי (it is) worthwhile
פֶּצַע wound, cut
כָּתַב write
חִבֵּר write (a literary work)

רָשַׁם write down
סוֹפֵר writer, author
מַחְבֶּרֶת writing-book

חָצֵר yard, court
שָׁנָה year
צָהֹב yellow
כֵּן yes
אֶתְמוֹל yesterday
אַתָּה m.; אַתְּ f. you
אַתֶּם m.; אַתֶּן f. you (pl.)
צָעִיר young

DAILY CALENDAR

JANUARY

1 Jan. 1837 – 5,000 Jews perish in earthquake at Safed and Tiberias
2 Jan. 1782 – Joseph II of Austria's Patent of Toleration
3 Jan. 1919 – Agreement between Emir Feisal and Chaim Weizmann endorsing Balfour Declaration
4 Jan. 1786 – Moses Mendelssohn died
5 Jan. 1895 – Public degradation of Dreyfus
6 Jan. 1930 – Foundation of Mapai
7 Jan. 1858 – Eliezer Ben-Yehuda born
8 Jan. 1960 – Israel presents notes to various governments expressing shock at anti-Semitic outrages and Swastika daubings
9 Jan. 1873 – Ḥayyim Naḥman Bialik born
10 Jan. 1847 – Jacob H. Schiff born
11 Jan. 1808 – Abraham Mapu born
12 Jan. 1493 – Jews expelled from Sicily
13 Jan. 1825 – Expulsion in Russia (leading eventually to Pale of Settlement)
14 Jan. 1866 – Toleration in Switzerland
15 Jan. 1946 – Chief Rabbi Dr. J.H. Hertz died
16 Jan. 1921 – 119 leading Americans headed by Pres. Wilson denounced anti-Semitic propaganda in U.S.
17 Jan. 1890 – Solomon Sulzer died
18 Jan. 1943 – Nazis' decision to liquidate Warsaw Ghetto
19 Jan. 1948 – Solomon Mikhoels murdered
20 Jan. 1942 – Wannsee Conference plans implementation of the "Final Solution"
21 Jan. 1306 – Expulsion from France
22 Jan. 1923 – Max Nordau died
23 Jan. 1639 – Auto da Fè at Lima
24 Jan. 1893 – Isaac Meir Dick died
25 Jan. 1240 – Paris disputation on the Talmud
26 Jan. 1482 – First edition of Hebrew Pentateuch printed at Bologna
27 Jan. 1969 – Fourteen men, including nine Jews, publicly hanged in Baghdad, on charges of spying for Israel
28 Jan. 1893 – Rabbi Abba Hillel Silver born
29 Jan. 1858 – Nahum Sokolow born
30 Jan. 1933 – Hitler accedes to power
31 Jan. 1955 – Execution of two Jews sentenced to death at Cairo trial as "Zionist spies"

FEBRUARY

1 Feb. 1885 – Peretz Smolenskin died
2 Feb. 1524 – David Reuveni began his career
3 Feb. 1807 – Opening of Napoleonic Sanhedrin in Paris
4 Feb. 1738 – "Jew Suess" Oppenheimer executed in Wurttemberg
5 Feb. 1840 – Damascus Affair commenced
6 Feb. 1481 – First Auto da Fè, Seville
7 Feb. 1413 – Disputation of Tortosa opened
8 Feb. 1895 – Maurice Samuel born
9 Feb. 1880 – Rabbi Israel Lipkin (Salanter) died
10 Feb. 1880 – Isaac Adolphe Crémieux died
11 Feb. 1868 – Nachman Syrkin born
12 Feb. 1886 – First issue of first Hebrew daily "Hayom" in St. Petersburg
13 Feb. 1945 – Henrietta Szold died
14 Feb. 1896 – "The Jewish State" by Theodor Herzl published
15 Feb. 1917 – Foundation of the "Jewish Legion"
16 Feb. 1870 – Emancipation of Jews of Sweden
17 Feb. 1949 – Weizmann elected first President of Israel
18 Feb. 1839 – Zadoc Kahn born
19 Feb. 1939 – Adolf Buechler died
20 Feb. 1959 – Zalman Schneour died
21 Feb. 1677 – Baruch Spinoza died
22 Feb. 1965 – Justice Felix Frankfurter died
23 Feb. 1913 – United Synagogue of America founded
24 Feb. 1942 – Sinking of "Struma"
25 Feb. 1867 – Emancipation of the Jews of Hungary
26 Feb. 1969 – Levi Eshkol died
27 Feb. 1670 – Expulsion from Vienna
28 Feb. 1616 – Fettmilch executed
29 Feb. 1920 – Trumpeldor killed at Tel Ḥai

MARCH

1 Mar. 1349 – 4,000 Jews burned at Worms
2 Mar. 1859 – Shalom Aleichem born
3 Mar. 1240 – Confiscation and burning of the Talmud in France
4 Mar. 1902 – Foundation of "Mizrachi"
5 Mar. 1899 – Cecil Roth born
6 Mar. 1896 – Rabbi Isaac Elchanan Spector died
7 Mar. 1944 – Emanuel Ringelblum arrested by Nazis and shot
8 Mar. 1957 – Israel completes evacuation of Sinai and Gaza Strip
9 Mar. 1556 – Sultan protests against papal treatment of Jews
10 Mar. 1949 – Israel troops advance to Gulf of Akaba
11 Mar. 1911 – The Mendel Beilis affair begins
12 Mar. 1421 – Wiener Geserah; Jewish community of Vienna perished
13 Mar. 1938 – Germany took over Austria (*Anschluss*)
14 Mar. 1879 – Albert Einstein born
15 Mar. 1939 – Germans invade Czechoslovakia
16 Mar. 1190 – The heroic end of the Jews of York
17 Mar. 1874 – Stephen S. Wise born
18 Mar. 1886 – Leopold Zunz died
19 Mar. 1497 – Forced baptism in Portugal
20 Mar. 1899 – Jewish Colonial Trust founded in London
21 Mar. 1648 – Leone Modena died
22 Mar. 1144 – First ritual murder libel at Norwich
23 Mar. 1475 – Blood accusation at Trent
24 Mar. 1515 – Rabbi Joseph Caro died
25 Mar. 1919 – Committee of Jewish Delegations formed
26 Mar. 1900 – Rabbi Isaac Mayer Wise died
27 Mar. 1288 – Jews martyred at Troyes
28 Mar. 1038 – Hai Gaon died
29 Mar. 1936 – Luigi Luzzatti died
30 Mar. 1135 – Maimonides born
31 Mar. 1492 – Edict of Ferdinand and Isabella expelling Jews from Spain

APRIL

1 Apr. 1925 – Inauguration of Hebrew University

2 Apr. 1947 – Britain refers Palestine problem to U.N.
3 Apr. 1953 – Release of arrested Jewish doctors in Soviet Russia
4 Apr. 1918 – Zionist Commission under Weizmann arrives in Palestine
5 Apr. 1872 – David Pinski born
6 Apr. 1848 – Emancipation of Jews of Prussia
7 Apr. 1957 – First oil tanker reaches Eilat.
8 Apr. 1915 – Isaac Leib Perez died
9 Apr. 1506 – Attacks on New Christians in Lisbon
10 Apr. 1728 – Solomon Ayllon died
11 Apr. 1961 – Adolf Eichmann trial opened in Jerusalem
12 Apr. 1955 – Dr. Jonas Salk discovers anti-poliomyelitis vaccine
13 Apr. 1948 – 78 killed in Hadassah convoy to Mt. Scopus
14 Apr. 1859 – Blood libel at Galatz
15 Apr. 1945 – British troops enter Bergen-Belsen
16 Apr. 1795 – Rabbi Ẓevi Hirsch Kalischer born
17 Apr. 1848 – Walls of Rome ghetto removed
18 Apr. 1389 – Massacre of Jews in Prague
19 Apr. 1903 – Pogrom in Kishinev
20 Apr. 1344 – Levi ben Gershom died
21 Apr. 1896 – Baron Maurice de Hirsch died
22 Apr. 1897 – First issue of Yiddish "Jewish Daily Forward" in New York
23 Apr. 1720 – Elijah ben Solomon Zalman, the Vilna Gaon, born
24 Apr. 1920 – San Remo Conference conferred Palestine Mandate on Britain
25 Apr. 1824 – Rabbi Samuel Mohilewer born
26 Apr. 1655 – Settlement in New Amsterdam (New York) authorized
27 Apr. 1293 – Meir of Rothenburg died
28 Apr. 1944 – Herbert Friedenwald died
29 Apr. 1838 – Nobel Peace Prize winner T.M.C. Asser born
30 Apr. 1492 – Expulsion from Spain publicly announced

MAY

1 May 1572 – Moses Isserles died
2 May 1860 – Theodor Herzl born
3 May 1898 – Golda Meir born
4 May 1915 – Moshe Dayan born
5 May 1818 – Karl Marx born
6 May 1744 – Moses Ḥayyim Luzzatto died
7 May 1945 – German General Judel signed unconditional surrender
8 May 1943 – Mordechai Anielewicz, commander-in-chief of the Warsaw Ghetto Uprising, fell in action
9 May 1942 – Extraordinary Zionist Conference at Hotel Biltmore in New York adopted "Biltmore Program" (Jewish Commonwealth)
10 May 1933 – Burning of books in Germany
11 May 1949 – State of Israel becomes Member of United Nations
12 May 1267 – Synod of Vienna orders Jew to wear pointed hats
13 May 1965 – Diplomatic relations between West Germany and Israel established
14 May 1948 – Proclamation of State of Israel
15 May 1882 – May Laws issued
16 May 942 – Saadia Gaon died
17 May 1939 – White Paper on Palestine published
18 May 1901 – Herzl meets Sultan Abdul Hamid
19 May 1103 – Isaac Alfasi died
20 May 1820 – Azriel Hildesheimer born
21 May 1671 – Jews admitted to Brandenburg
22 May 1760 – Israel ben Eliezer (Besht) died
23 May 1536 – Inquisition established in Portugal
24 May 1810 – Abraham Geiger born
25 May 1096 – Jews in Worms killed
26 May 1895 – Salo W. Baron born
27 May 1096 – Massacre at Mayence
28 May 1948 – Old City of Jerusalem surrendered to Arab Legion
29 May 1839 – Hermann Adler born
30 May 1972 – Lydda Airport massacre
31 May 1962 – Adolf Eichmann executed at Ramleh Prison

JUNE

1 June 1244 – Privileges to Jews in Austria
2 June 1453 – Martyrdom of Breslau Jews
3 June 1888 – Jewish Publication Society of America organized
4 June 1897 – First issue of "Die Welt," founded by Herzl
5 June 1967 – Outbreak of Six-Day War between Israel and the Arab States
6 June 1391 – Massacres begun in Spain
7 June 1594 – Roderigo Lopez, physician to Queen Elizabeth charged with high treason and executed
8 June 1818 – Fanny von Arnstein died
9 June 1171 – Rabbi Jacob Tam died
10 June 1648 – Jews of Nemirov murdered by Cossacks
11 June 1948 – David Marcus killed
12 June 1240 – Disputation at Paris
13 June 1965 – Martin Buber died
14 June 1821 – Ḥayyim ben Isaac of Volozhin died
15 June 1947 – Bronislav Hubermann died
16 June 1933 – Chaim Arlosoroff murdered
17 June 1242 – Talmud burned in Paris
18 June 1571 – Jacob Pollack died
19 June 1269 – Jews in France forced to wear yellow badge
20 June 1757 – Frankist disputation at Kameniec
21 June 1943 – Revolt in Treblinka extermination camp
22 June 1943 – *Altalena* blown up off Tel Aviv
23 June 1858 – Edgar Mortara of Bologna kidnaped
24 June 1922 – Walter Rathenau murdered
25 June 1962 – U.S. Supreme Court decides against recital of prayers in public schools
26 June 1570 – Moses Cordovero died
27 June 1939 – Israel Davidson died
28 June 1286 – Meir of Rothenburg imprisoned
29 June 1967 – Jerusalem reunified
30 June 1922 – U.S. Congress approves principles of Balfour Declaration

JULY

1 July 1920 – Herbert Samuel appointed High Commissioner of Palestine
2 July 1808 – Napoleon decreed that Jews must adopt family names
3 July 1904 – Death of Theodor Herzl
4 July 1934 – Death of Ḥ.N. Bialik
5 July 1950 – "Law of Return" passed by Knesset
6 July 1882 – First "Bilu'im" arrive in Palestine
7 July 1887 – Marc Chagall born
8 July 1873 – Foundation of Union of American Hebrew Congregations

9 July 1885 – First Lord Rothschild takes seat in House of Lords
10 July 1957 – Shalom Asch died
11 July 1739 – Expulsion from Little Russia
12 July 1840 – Abraham Goldfaden born
13 July 1096 – Crusaders captured Jerusalem and killed Jews, Karaites and Moslems of the Holy City
14 July 1870 – United Synagogue (London) established
15 July 1834 – Spanish Inquisition abolished
16 July 1948 – Israel troops capture Nazareth
17 July 1888 – Samuel Joseph Agnon born
18 July 1290 – Edict of Expulsion of Jews from England
19 July 1785 – Mordecai Manuel Noah born
20 July 1263 – Disputation of Barcelona opened
21 July 1947 – "Exodus" with 4,500 Jews from D.P. Camps arrived in Haifa. Passengers transported back to Germany
22 July 1306 – Expulsion of Jews from France
23 July 1626 – Shabbetai Ẓevi born
24 July 1861 – Ernest Bloch, composer, born
25 July 1670 – Expulsion from Vienna
26 July 1555 – Ghetto in Rome established
27 July 1656 – Jewish community of Amsterdam pronounced decree of excommunication on Spinoza
28 July 1885 – Sir Moses Montefiore died
29 July 1336 – Armleder massacres began in Germany
30 July 1488 – Auto-da-Fè in Toledo
31 July 1305 – Ban on study of philosophy imposed by Solomon ibn Adret

AUGUST

1 Aug. 1826 – Last Auto da Fè in Valencia
2 Aug. 1492 – Expulsion of Jews from Spain
3 Aug. 1960 – Hadassah Medical Center dedicated in Jerusalem
4 Aug. 1922 – David Frischmann died
5 Aug. 1572 – Death of Isaac Luria
6 Aug. 1855 – Sir Isaac Isaacs born
7 Aug. 1295 – Jews of Silesia receive privileges
8 Aug. 1878 – Foundation of Petaḥ Tikvah
9 Aug. 1506 – Pinsk community founded
10 Aug. 1794 – Leopold Zunz born
11 Aug. 1929 – First constituent meeting of the Jewish Agency opened
12 Aug. 1952 – Twenty-six Soviet-Yiddish writers, among them David Bergelson, Peretz Markish, and Itzik Feffer, shot on Stalin's orders
13 Aug. 1944 – Berl Katznelson died
14 Aug. 1874 – Joseph Klausner born
15 Aug. 1943 – Resistance of Bialystok Ghetto
16 Aug. 1948 – Peretz Hirschbein died
17 Aug. 1949 – Theodor Herzl re-interred in Jerusalem
18 Aug. 1856 – Aḥad Ha-Am born
19 Aug. 1845 – Baron Edmond de Rothschild born
20 Aug. 1899 – Captain Alfred Dreyfus pardoned and liberated
21 Aug. 1893 – Law prohibiting Jewish ritual slaughtering passed in Switzerland
22 Aug. 1654 – Jacob Barsimson arrives in New Amsterdam (New York) from Holland
23 Aug. 1929 – Anti-Jewish attacks in Palestine
24 Aug. 1950 – "Operation Magic Carpet" officially concluded
25 Aug. 1800 – Samuel David Luzzatto born
26 Aug. 1942 – Chief Rabbi Dr. Leo Judah Landau died
27 Aug. 1686 – First issue of first Yiddish paper "Kourant" in Amsterdam
28 Aug. 1967 – Arab Conference in Khartoum decided: non-recognition of Israel, no negotiations, and no peace with Israel
29 Aug. 1897 – Opening of First Zionist Congress
30 Aug. 1658 – Haham Zevi Ashkenazi born
31 Aug. 1864 – Ferdinand Lasalle killed

SEPTEMBER

1 Sept. 1577 – Conversionist sermons instituted in Rome
2 Sept. 1796 – Emancipation of Jews in the Netherlands
3 Sept. 1189 – Anti-Jewish coronation riot in London
4 Sept. 1892 – Darius Milhaud born
5 Sept. 1938 – First anti-Jewish decrees of Italian Fascist regime
6 Sept. 1729 – Moses Mendelssohn born
7 Sept. 1891 – Heinrich Graetz died
8 Sept. 1962 – Mané-Katz died
9 Sept. 1553 – Talmud burned in Rome
10 Sept. 1952 – Reparations agreement between Israel and Germany signed in Luxembourg
11 Sept. 1891 – Jewish Colonization Association founded
12 Sept. 1954 – U.S. Jewish tercentenary celebrations inaugurated
13 Sept. 1892 – Railway from Jerusalem to Jaffa opened
14 Sept. 1427 – Death of Maharil (Jacob ben Moses Molln)
15 Sept. 1935 – Nuremberg Racial Laws in Nazi Germany
16 Sept. 1666 – Shabbetai Zevi accepted Islam
17 Sept. 1948 – Count Folke Bernadotte assassinated
18 Sept. 1860 – Simon Dubnow born
19 Sept. 1944 – Jewish Brigade founded
20 Sept. 1540 – First Auto da Fè in Portugal
21 Sept. 1939 – Nazi plan for ghettos in Poland
22 Sept. 1654 – Peter Stuyvesant attempts to expel Jews from New Amsterdam (New York)
23 Sept. 1941 – First experiment in use of gases in Auschwitz
24 Sept. 1762 – Moses Sofer born
25 Sept. 1920 – Jacob Heinrich Schiff died
26 Sept. 1798 – Morris Jacob Raphall born
27 Sept. 1791 – French National Assembly grants equal rights to the Jews
28 Sept. 1775 – First Congregation in Stockholm
29 Sept. 1941 – Babi Yar massacre
30 Sept. 1801 – Zacharias Frankel born

OCTOBER

1 Oct. 1943 – Danish Jews saved from deportation by Danish population
2 Oct. 1596 – Foundation of Amsterdam community
3 Oct. 1555 – Roman ghetto walled
4 Oct. 1940 – Anti-Jewish Laws of Vichy Government
5 Oct. 1941 – Justice Louis D. Brandeis died
6 Oct. 1973 – Yom Kippur War breaks out
7 Oct. 1771 – Naḥman of Bratislav born

8 Oct. 1918 – Foundation of "Habimah"
9 Oct. 1354 – Casimir the Great issued a Charter to Jews of Poland
10 Oct. 1797 – Vilna Gaon died
11 Oct. 1700 – Jews burned in Prague
12 Oct. 1837 – Akiva Eger died
13 Oct. 1843 – First B'nai B'rith founded in New York
14 Oct. 1943 – Uprising in Sobibor extermination camp
15 Oct. 1963 – Edmond Fleg died
16 Oct. 1886 – David Ben-Gurion born
17 Oct. 1882 – Publication of *Auto-emanzipation* by Leo Pinsker
18 Oct. 1880 – Vladimir Jabotinsky born
19 Oct. 1700 – Judah Ḥasid died
20 Oct. 1892 – Emin Pasha murdered
21 Oct. 1894 – Arrest of Captain Dreyfus
22 Oct. 1586 – Bull of Pope Sixtus V in favor of Jews
23 Oct. 1905 – Abraham Geiger died
24 Oct. 1870 – Emancipation in Algeria
25 Oct. 1327 – Asher ben Jehiel (Rosh) died
26 Oct. 1407 – Massacre of Jews in Cracow
27 Oct. 1948 – Judah L. Magnes died
28 Oct. 1270 – Moses ben Naḥman (Naḥmanides) died
29 Oct. 1956 – Israel Defense Forces advanced into Sinai Peninsula
30 Oct. 1943 – Max Reinhardt died
31 Oct. 1497 – Banishment from Portugal

NOVEMBER

1 Nov. 1290 – Expulsion of Jews from England
2 Nov. 1917 – Balfour Declaration
3 Nov. 1394 – Expulsion of Jews from France
4 Nov. 1571 –Inquisition introduced in Mexico
5 Nov. 1573 – Rabbi Solomon Luria died
6 Nov. 1884 – Ḥovevei Zion Conference opens in Kattowitz
7 Nov. 1944 – Hanna Szenes killed
8 Nov. 1761 – Akiva ben Moshe Eger born
9 Nov. 1952 – President Chaim Weizmann died
10 Nov. 1938 – Pogrom in Germany
11 Nov. 1215 – Fourth Lateran Council meets and issues anti-Jewish legislation
12 Nov. 1841 – First issue of "Jewish Chronicle"
13 Nov. 1757 – Talmud burned in Poland
14 Nov. 1945 – Mass demonstration in Palestine against Bevin's policy
15 Nov. 1940 – Germans establish the Warsaw ghetto
16 Nov. 1917 – Jaffa and Tel Aviv occupied by British forces
17 Nov. 1278 – Order of Edward I for the imprisonment of Jews in England
18 Nov. 1944 – Enzo Sereni died
19 Nov. 1887 – Emma Lazarus died
20 Nov. 1964 – The Ecumenical Council adopted a statement on the attitude of the Church toward Jews
21 Nov. 1962 – Arad, new town in the Negev, officially inaugurated
22 Nov. 1967 – Security Council of United Nations accepted resolution concerning terms of a settlement to the Middle East conflict
23 Nov. 1510 – Expulsion from Naples
24 Nov. 1962 – Slánský trial in Prague
25 Nov. 1940 – "Patria" with immigrants to Palestine blown up in Haifa
26 Nov. 1874 – Edmond Fleg born
27 Nov. 1874 – Chaim Weizmann born;
1881 – Vera Weizmann born
28 Nov. 1873 – Louis Ginzberg born
29 Nov. 1947 – United Nations decides on partition of Palestine
30 Nov. 1631 – Samuel Eliezer Edels ("Maharsha") died

DECEMBER

1 Dec. 1909 – Deganyah Aleph founded
2 Dec. 1742 – Expulsion from Little Russia
3 Dec. 1823 – First Yiddish weekly "Beobachter in der Weichsel" appeared in Warsaw
4 Dec. 1655 – Whitehall Conference discusses Manasseh Ben Israel's petition to Cromwell
5 Dec. 1920 – Foundation of Histadrut
6 Dec. 1882 – Zikhron Ya'akov founded
7 Dec. 1941 – Simon Dubnow killed
8 Dec. 1941 – Death camps at Chelmno begin operating
9 Dec. 1917 – Jerusalem captured by the British: Allenby enters Jerusalem
10 Dec. 1966 – Nobel Prize for literature presented to Samuel Joseph Agnon and Nelly Sachs
11 Dec. 321 – First mention of Jews in Germany
12 Dec. 1806 – Isaac Leeser born
13 Dec. 1797 – Heinrich Heine born
14 Dec. 1760 – Board of Deputies of British Jews founded
15 Dec. 1859 – Ludwik Lazar Zamenhof born
16 Dec. 1922 – Eliezer Ben-Yehuda died
17 Dec. 1942 – Declaration of United Nations that the extermination of the Jewish people would be punished
18 Dec. 1744 – Expulsion of Jews of Bohemia
19 Dec. 1781 – Poll tax abolished in Austria
20 Dec. 1835 – Mendele Mocher Seforim born
21 Dec. 1804 – Benjamin Disraeli born
22 Dec. 1867 – Emancipation in Hungary
23 Dec. 1850 – Oscar Solomon Straus born
24 Dec. 1970 – Leningrad trial against Jews who wished to go to Israel
25 Dec. 1886 – Franz Rosenzweig born
27 Dec. 1856 – Naphtali Herz Imber born
28 Dec. 1862 – Morris Rosenfeld born
29 Dec. 1901 – Jewish National Fund established
30 Dec. 1942 – Enrico Glicenstein died
31 Dec. 1888 – Samson Raphael Hirsch died

PLACES IN ISRAEL CALLED AFTER WELL-KNOWN PERSONS

Allonei Abba
Abba Berdichev – Jewish parachutist fell in WWII
Allonei Yizḥak
Yizḥak *Gruenbaum
Argaman
Aryeh **R**egev & **Ga**d **Man**elah – officers of the Israel army
Ashdot **Ya'akov**
James (**Jacob**) de *Rothschild
Aviel
Israel Epstein (**Aviel**), Irgun commander in Europe
Aviezer
Sigmund (**Aviezer**) *Gestetner
Avigedor
Sir Osmond *d'**Avigdor**-Goldsmid
Azriel
Azriel *Hildesheimer

Balfouriyyah
Arthur James ***Balfour**
Bar Giora
Simeon ***Bar Giora**
Bat Shelomo
Solomon (**Shelomo**) Mayer *Rothschild
Be'er Ya'akov
Rabbi **Ya'akov** Yizḥaki of Dagestan
Be'eri
Berl (**Be'eri**) *Katznelson
Be'erot Yizḥak
Isaac (**Yizḥak**) *Nissenbaum
Ben Ammi
Ben-Ammi Pachter, Haganah commander
Ben Zakkai
*Johanan **Ben Zakkai**
Benei Ayish
Akiva **J**oseph ***S**chlesinger
Benei Re'em
Rabbi **A**braham **M**ordecai Alter of *Gur
Bet Elazari
Yizḥak ***Eleazari**-Volcani
Bet Gamliel
Rabban ***Gamaliel** (ha-Zaken)
Bet ha-Levi
*Judah **Halevi**
Bet Ḥananyah
Ḥananyah Gotlieb, director of PICA
Bet Hillel
Hillel *Joffe
Bet Meir
Meir *Bar-Ilan
Bet Nir
Max Isidor ***Bodenheimer** (Heb. **Nir**)
Bet Uzziel
Ben-Zion Meir Ḥai ***Ouziel**
Bet Yannai
Alexander ***Yannai**
Bet Yehoshu'a
Osias (**Jehoshua**) *Thon

Bet Yizḥak
Yizḥak Feuerring, German Zionist
Bet Yosef
Yosef *Aharonovitch
Bet Ẓevi
Ẓevi Sitrin, American philanthropist
Binyaminah
Baron Edmond (**Binyamin**) de *Rothschild
Bitan Aharon
Archibald (**Aharon**) Jacob *Freiman

Dorot
Dov, **R**ivka, **T**irzah *Hos
Dovev
David **B**loch-**B**lumenfeld, labor leader in Ereẓ Israel

Ein ha-Naẓiv
Naphtali **Ẓ**evi **J**udah *Berlin
Ein ha-Shofet
Louis Dembitz *Brandeis
Eshel ha-Nasi
Chaim *Weizmann
Even Menaḥem
Arthur (**Menaḥem**) *Hantke
Even Sappir
Jacob ***Saphir**
Even Shmu'el
Samuel *Bronfman
Even Yehudah
Eliezer ***Ben-Yehuda**
Even Yizḥak (Galed)
Isaac *Ochberg

Gan Ḥayyim
Chaim *Weizmann
Gan Shelomo (Kevuẓat Schiller)
Solomon *Schiller
Gan Shemuel
Samuel *Mohilewer
Gan Yoshiyyah
Josiah Clement *Wedgwood
Gannei Yoḥanan (Gannei Jonah)
Johanan *Kremenetzky
Givat Adah
Adelaide (**Ada**) *Rothschild
Givat Brenner
Joseph Ḥayyim *Brenner
Givat Ḥayyim
Chaim *Arlosoroff
Givat Ḥen
Ḥayyim **N**aḥman Bialik
Givat Shapira
Hermann ***Schapira**
Givat Shemu'el
Samuel *Pineles
Givat Yeshayahu
Yeshayahu *Press
Givat Yo'av
Yoav Shaḥam, Israel army officer fell in the attack on al-Samu (Eshtemoa) in 1966
Givat Zeid
Alexander ***Zeid**

Ḥafez Ḥayyim
*Israel Meir ha-Kohen (**Ḥafez Ḥayyim**)
Herzliyyah
Theodor ***Herzl**

Kefar Aḥim
Ẓevi and Efraim Guber two **brothers** (Heb. **aḥim**) who fell in War of Independence
Kefar Azar
Alexander **Z**iskind ***R**abinovitz
Kefar Barukh
Baruch Kahane, Rumanian Zionist
Kefar Bialik
Ḥayyim Naḥman ***Bialik**
Kefar Blum
Leon ***Blum**
Kefar Daniel
Daniel *Frisch
Kefar Giladi
Israel ***Giladi**
Kefar Glickson
Moshe ***Glueckson**
Kefar ha-Nagid
*Samuel **Ha-Nagid**
Kefar ha-Nasi
Chaim *Weizmann
Kefar ha-Rif
Isaac ben Jacob *Alfasi (**Rif**)
Kefar ha-Ro'eh
Rabbi Abraham Isaac **Ha-Kohen** *Kook
Kefar Ḥayyim
Chaim *Arlosoroff
Kefar Hess
Moses ***Hess**
Kefar Jawitz
Ze'ev ***Jawitz**
Kefar Kisch
Frederick Hermann ***Kisch**
Kefar Maimon
*Maimonides (Moses ben **Maimon**)
Kefar Malal
Moses **L**eib ***L**ilienblum
Kefar Masaryk
Thomas Garrigue ***Masaryk**
Kefar Menaḥem
Abraham **Menaḥem** Mendel *Ussishkin
Kefar Monash
Sir John ***Monash**
Kefar Mordekhai
Mordekhai *Eliash
Kefar Netter
Charles ***Netter**
Kefar Pines
Yehiel Michael (Michal) ***Pines**
Kefar Ruppin
Arthur ***Ruppin**
Kefar Shammai
***Shammai**
Kefar Shemaryahu
Shmarya *Levin
Kefar Shemu'el
Stephen **Samuel** *Wise
Kefar Silver
Abba Hillel ***Silver**

* Subject of entry

Kefar Syrkin
Nachman ***Syrkin**
Kefar Szold
Henrietta ***Szold**
Kefar Truman
Harry S. ***Truman**
Kefar Vitkin
Joseph ***Vitkin**
Kefar Warburg
Felix Moritz ***Warburg**
Kefar Yeḥezkel
Sir **Ezekiel** *Sasson
Kefar Yehoshu'a
Yehoshua *Hankin
Kefar Yonah
Jean (**Yonah**) *Fischer
Kerem Ben Zimrah
*Yose **Ben Zimra**
Kerem Maharal
*Judah Loew ben Bezalel (**Maharal**)
Kiryat Bialik
Ḥayyim Naḥman ***Bialik**
Kiryat Motzkin
Leo ***Motzkin**
Kokhav Michael
Michael Sobol, English philanthropist

Lahavot Ḥavivah
Havivah *Reik
Liman
Herbert Henry ***Lehman**

Ma'agan Michael
Michael Polak, director of PICA
Maḥaneh Yisrael
Yisrael Sheḥori, Haganah commander
Maoz Ḥayyim
Ḥayyim *Sturman
Margaliyyot
Haim ***Margolis**-Kalvaryski
Mashabbei Sadeh
Yiẓḥak ***Sadeh**
Massu'ot Yiẓḥak
Isaac *Herzog
Ma'yan Barukh
Baruch (Bernard) Gordon, South African Zionist
Ma'yan Ẓevi
Ẓevi Henri Frank, a PICA director
Mazkeret Batyah
Betty (Batyah) *Rothschild
Maẓliaḥ
*Sahl ben **Maẓliaḥ**
Meir Shefeyah
Mayer **(Meir)** Amschel *Rothschild
Menaḥemiyyah
Edwin (**Menaḥem**), Samuel, father of Sir Herbert *Samuel
Midreshet Ruppin
Arthur ***Ruppin**
Misgav Dov
Dov Gruner, Irgun member, executed by British
Mishmar David
David Daniel *Marcus

Naḥalat Yehudah
Leon (**Judah** Leib) *Pinsker
Ne'ot Mordekhai
Mordecai Rozovsky, Argentine Zionist
Netanyah
Nathan *Straus
Neveh Efrayim (Monosson)
Fred (**Efrayim**) Monosson, U.S. Zionist
Neẓer Sereni
Enzo Ḥayyim ***Sereni**
Nir Akiva
Akiva Jacob *Ettinger
Nir David
David *Wolffsohn
Nir Eliyahu
Eliyahu *Golomb
Nir Moshe
Moshe *Smilansky
Nir Yafeh
M. **Jaffe**, South African philanthropist
Nir Yisrael
Yisrael Taiber, Israel philanthropist
Nir Yiẓḥak
Yiẓḥak *Sadeh
Nir Ẓevi
Baron Maurice de ***Hirsch** (Heb. **Ẓevi**)
Nordiyyah
Max ***Nordau**

Or Akiva
R. ***Akiva**
Or Yehudah
Judah ben Solomon Ḥai *Alkalai

Pardess Ḥannah
Hannah Rothschild, wife of 5th Earl of Rosebery
Peẓael
***Phasael**

Ram-On
Ram-On Peled, member of Naḥal who fell in action
Ramat David
David *Lloyd George
Ramat ha-Shofet
Julian William *Mack
Ramat Pinkas
David Zvi ***Pinkas**
Ramat Raziel
David ***Raziel**
Ramat Yishai
Yishai Adler, Israel educator
Ramat Yoḥanan
Jan Christiaan *Smuts
Ramat Ẓevi
Henry (**Ẓevi**) *Monsky
Ramot Meir
Meir Rosov, U.S. Zionist

Sedeh David
Zalman **David** *Levontin
Sedeh Eliezer
Robert (**Eliezer**) Philippe *Rothschild
Sedeh Eliyahu
Elijah *Guttmacher
Sedeh Moshe
Baron **Maurice** de *Hirsch
Sedeh Naḥum
Nahum *Sokolow
Sedeh Neḥemiya
Nehemia *De Lieme
Sedeh Warburg
Otto ***Warburg**
Sedeh Ya'akov
Isaac **Jacob** *Reines
Sedeh Yiẓḥak
Yiẓḥak *Sadeh
Sedeh Yoav
"**Yoav** Alon" (Yiẓḥak Dubna), commander of Negbah in War of Independence
Sedeh Ẓevi
Ẓevi Hirschfeld, a founder of Ruḥama
Sedot Mikhah
Micha Josef *Berdyczewski
Shadmot Devorah
Dorothy (**Dvora**), wife of James de *Rothschild

Tal Shaḥar
Henry ***Morgenthau** (Jr.) (Heb. equivalent)

Talmei Elazar
Elazar Wermeser, director of PICA
Talmei Yafeh
Leib ***Jaffe**
Talmei Yeḥiel
Jehiel *Tschlenow
Tel Mond
Alfred Moritz ***Mond**
Tel Yiẓḥak
Yiẓḥak Shteiger, founder of Ha-Noar ha-Ẓiyyoni in Poland
Tel Yosef
Joseph *Trumpeldor
Tirat Ẓevi
Ẓevi Hirsch *Kalischer

Yad Binyamin
Benjamin *Minz
Yad Ḥannah
Hannah *Szenes
Yad Mordekhai
Mordecai *Anielewicz
Yad Natan
Otto (**Natan**) *Kamoly
Yad Rambam
Rabbi **M**oses **B**en **M**aimon *(Maimonides)
Yedidyah
*Philo **Judaeus** (Hebrew name)
Yeḥi'am
Yeḥiam *Weitz

Zikhron Ya'akov
James (**Jacob**), *Rothschild
Ẓur Moshe
Moshe Kophinos, Greek Zionist

Initial "A": Bibliothèque Municipale, Rheims.
Aachen: Municipal Archive, Aachen.
Aaronsohn, Aaron: Beit Aaronsohn, Zikhron Ya'akov.
Abel: The British Library Board, London.
Abendana: Portugees-Israelitische Gemeente, Amsterdam.
Aboab, Isaac da Fonseca: Cecil Roth Collection.
Abraham: Chester Beatty Library, Dublin.
Abraham, Abraham: Courtesy Abraham & Straus, Brooklyn, New York.
Abraham ben Shabbetai ha-Kohen: Jewish National and University Library (J.N.U.L.), Jerusalem.
Abramsky, Yeḥezkel: Photo Yacoby, Jerusalem.
Abramson, Abraham: J. Wallersteiner Collection, Bene-Berak.
Absalom: Library of San Isidoro, Leon, Spain.
Abu Ghosh: Government Press Office, Tel Aviv.
Achzib: Government Press Office, Tel Aviv.
Achron, Joseph: Schwadron Collection, J.N.U.L., Jerusalem.
Acre: Photo W. Braun, Jerusalem.
Adler, Alfred: Kurt A. Adler Collection, New York. Photo O. Peter Radl.
Adler, Hermann: Cecil Roth Collection.
Adler, Jacob: YIVO, New York.
Adler, Jankel: Israel Museum, Jerusalem.
Adler, Nathan Marcus: Cecil Roth Collection.
Adloyada: Government Press Office, Tel Aviv.
Adrianople: David Corcos Collection, Jerusalem.
Agag: The British Library Board, London.
Agam, Yaacov: Photo L. Herschtritt, Paris.
Agnon, Shmuel Yosef: Photo K. Meyerowitz, Jerusalem. Courtesy Ministry of Foreign Affairs, Jerusalem.
Agron, Gershon: Keren Hayesod, United Israel Appeal, Jerusalem.
Aḥad ha-Am: Central Zionist Archives, Jerusalem.
Ahasuerus: The British Library Board, London.
Akedah: Israel Museum, Jerusalem.
Alberta: Photo Matthews Photo Lab. Ltd., Calgary.
Alef: Israel Museum, Jerusalem.
Alexander the Great: Bibliothèque Publique, Dijon.
Algiers: Israel Museum, Jerusalem.
Al ha-Nissim: Israel Museum, Jerusalem.
Alkalai, Judah: Central Zionist Archives, Jerusalem.
Allenby, Edmund: Central Zionist Archives, Jerusalem.
Allon, Yigal: Government Press Office, Tel Aviv.
Alsace: Courtesy B. Mevorach, Jerusalem.
Alsheikh, Shalom ben Joseph: Courtesy J. Ratzhabi, Tel Aviv.
Altar: Israel Department of Antiquities and Museums, Jerusalem.
Alterman, Nathan: Courtesy Genazim, Tel Aviv.
Altman, Nathan: Israel Museum, Jerusalem.
Altmann, Alexander: Photo A. Holz, Jerusalem.
Alva, Solomon: Shalvi Collection, Jerusalem.
Amatus Lusitanus: Schwadron Collection, J.N.U.L., Jerusalem.
Amram ben Sheshna: The British Library Board, London.
Amulet: I. Einhorn Collection, Tel Aviv. Photo D. Harris, Jerusalem.
Amsterdam: Israel Museum, Jerusalem. Photo D. Harris.
Amzalak, Moses Bensabat: Photo Silva Conto Studios, Lisbon.
Anielewicz, Mordecai: Yad Vashem, Jerusalem.
Annenberg, Walter: Courtesy *Philadelphia Inquirer*. Photo Karsh Ottawa.
An-Ski, S.: YIVO, New York.
Anti-Fascist Committee, Jewish: Courtesy B.Z. Goldberg, New York.
Antipatris: Photo Zev Radovan, Jerusalem.
Antokolski, Mark: Schwadron Collection, J.N.U.L., Jerusalem.
Arad: Government Press Office, Tel Aviv.
Arbel: Courtesy Israel Department of Antiquities and Museums, Jerusalem.
Aranne, Zalman: Photo Y. Agor, Tel Aviv.
Archeology: (tell) Institute of Archeology, Tel Aviv University;
(jug) Israel Department of Antiquities and Museums, Jerusalem;
(reconstruction) Government Press Office, Tel Aviv;
(ossuary) Israel Department of Antiquities and Museums, Jerusalem;
(plaque) The British Library Board, London.
Ark: (Haggadah) Sarajevo, National Museum;
(priests) San Isidioro, Library, Leon, Spain.
Arlosoroff, Chaim: Central Zionist Archives, Jerusalem.
Arnstein, Fanny von: Historical Museum of the city of Vienna. Photo R. Stepanek.
Aronson, Naum: Courtesy Aimée Alexandre, Paris.
Artom, Benjamin: Courtesy Spanish and Portuguese Jews Congregation, London, Jews College, Montefiore Library.
Arvit: The British Library Board, London.
Asch, Sholem: Courtesy Leo Baeck Institute, New York.
Aschheim, Isidor: Jerusalem Municipality, on loan to Israel Museum. Photo David Harris.
Ascoli, Graziadio Isaiah: Schwadron Collection, J.N.U.L., Jerusalem.
Ashdod: Israel Museum, Jerusalem. Photo D. Harris.
Asherah: Israel Department of Antiquities and Museums, Jerusalem.
Ashkavah: State Jewish Museum, Prague.
Ashkelon: Government Press Office, Tel Aviv.
Assaf, Simha: Hebrew University Public Relations Department, Jerusalem. Photo Prisma.
Asser, Tobias: Schwadron Collection, J.N.U.L., Jerusalem.
Astrology: The British Library Board, London.
Atlan, Jean: Alexander and Stella Margulies Collection, London.
Attah Zokher: Austrian National Library, Vienna.
Auckland: Alexander Turnbull Library, Wellington, New Zealand.
Auschwitz: Yad Vashem, Jerusalem.
Auschwitz Trials: Yad Vashem, Jerusalem.
Auto-da-Fé: Prado Museum, Madrid.
Avedat: Photo W. Braun, Jerusalem.
Ayalon, David: Hebrew University Public Relations Department.
Azazel: Hungarian Academy of Sciences, Budapest.
Azor: Israel Department of Antiquities and Museums, Jerusalem. Photo B. Rothenberg, Tel Aviv.
Az Rov Nissim: Hessische Landes-und Hochschulbibliothek, Darmstadt.

Initial "B": Bibliothèque Municipale, Douai.
Baal: The Louvre, Paris.
Ba'al ha-Bayit: J.N.U.L., Jerusalem.
Babel, Isaac: J.N.U.L., Jerusalem.
Babi Yar: Schwadron Collection, J.N.U.L., Jerusalem.
Babylon: André Parrot, *Nineveh and Babylon*, 1961.
Badge, Jewish (top): Bibliotheque Nationale, Paris.
Badge, Jewish (center): Jewish Historical Museum, Amsterdam.
Badḥan: Israel Museum Photo Archives, Jerusalem.
Bak, Israel: J.N.U.L., Jerusalem.
Bakst, Leon: Dr. J. Leron Collection, Jerusalem.
Balfour, Arthur: Central Zionist Archives, Jerusalem.
Ballin, Albert: B. M. Ansbacher Collection, Jerusalem.
Baltimore: Photo Sussman-Ochs.
Bamberger, Simon: Utah State Archives, Salt Lake City.
Band, Max: Dr. J. Lerón Collection, Jerusalem.
Barash, Asher: Genazim, Tel Aviv.
Barcelona: Photo M. Minio, Jerusalem.
Bar-Ilan University: Photo N. Suffrin, Tel Aviv.
Bar Kokhba: Israel Department of Antiquities and Museums, Jerusalem.
Bar-Lev, Haim: Government Press Office, Tel Aviv.
Bar Mitzvah: Government Press Office, Tel Aviv.
Barnay, Ludwig: Schwadron Collection, J.N.U.L., Jerusalem.
Baron, Devorah: Genazim, Tel Aviv.
Baron, Salo: American Academy for Jewish Research.
Bartov, Hanoch: Photo Martin-Yaron, Tel Aviv.
Baruch, Bernard: Atomic Energy Commission, Washington, D.C.
Bashevis Singer, Isaac: Hebrew University Public Relations Department, Jerusalem, Photo Emka.
Basle: Central Zionist Archives, Jerusalem.
Basle Program: Central Zionist Archives, Jerusalem.
Basnage, Jacques: J.N.U.L., Jerusalem.
Bat-Miriam, Yokheved: Photo I. Zafrir, Tel Aviv.
Bat Yam: Government Press Office, Tel Aviv.
Bauer, Otto: Schwadron Collcetion, J.N.U.L., Jerusalem.
Bavaria: Photo Gundermann, Wuerzburg.
Bea, Augustin: American Jewish Committee.
Bedikat Ḥamez: Stedelijk Museum, Amsterdam.

Beersheba: Government Press Office, Tel Aviv.
Begin, Menahem: Government Press Office, Tel Aviv.
Behemoth: University Library, Leipzig.
Beilis, Menahem: Central Zionist Archives, Jerusalem.
Beirut: Alliance Israelite Universelle, Paris.
Beit, Sir Alfred: Africana Museum, Johannesburg.
Belkin, Samuel: Yeshiva University, New York.
Bellow, Saul: Hebrew University Public Relations Department, Jerusalem. Photo W. Braun.
Belshazzar: National Gallery, London.
Belz: Photo K. Weiss, Jerusalem.
Ben-Avi, Ithamar: Genazim, Tel Aviv.
Bene Israel: E. ben Elivoo Photo Collection, Haifa.
Ben-Gurion, David (top): Central Zionist Archives, Jerusalem;
(bottom): Government Press Office, Tel Aviv.
Ben Naphtali, Moses: The British Library Board, London.
Ben Shemen: Government Press Office, Tel Aviv.
Bentwich, Norman: Hebrew University Public Relations Department, Jerusalem. Photo D. Harris.
Ben Yehuda, Eliezer: Israel State Archives, Jerusalem. Photo Y. Ben Dov.
Ben-Yosef, Shelomo: Government Press Office, Tel Aviv.
Ben-Zvi, Izhak: (top) Central Zionist Archives, Jerusalem;
(bottom) Photo I. Zafrir, Tel Aviv.
Berdyczewski, Micha: Genazim, Tel Aviv.
Berechiah ha-Nakdan: A. M. Habermann, *Title Pages of Hebrew Books,* 1969.
Bergman, Samuel: Hebrew University Public Relations Department, Jerusalem. Photo W. Braun.
Bergmann, Ernst: Photo R. M. Kneller, Jerusalem.
Bergner, Elizabeth: Courtesy B.B.C. London.
Bergson, Henri: Daniel Friedenberg Collection, New York.
Berihah: E. Dekel Collection, Tel Aviv.
Berkowitz, Yizhak: Government Press Office, Tel Aviv.
Berlin, Sir Isaiah: Photo Ramsey and Muspratt, Oxford.
Bernstein, Leonard: Photo Isaac Freidin, Tel Aviv.
Bershadsky, Isaiah: Genazim, Tel Aviv.
Bertonoff, Yehoshua: Photo Alexander Studio, Tel Aviv.
Bet Alfa: After E. L. Sukenik, *The Ancient Synagogue of Beth Alpha,* Jerusalem, 1932.
Bet Din: Government Press Office, Tel Aviv.
Bet Guvrin: Photo D. Harris, Jerusalem.
Bethlehem: Government Press Office, Tel Aviv.
Bet Shean: Photo R. Cleave, Jerusalem.
Bet She'arim: Government Press Office, Tel Aviv.
Bet Yerah: Israel Department of Antiquities and Museums, Jerusalem.
Bezalel: Photo Dagani, Jerusalem.
Bialik, Hayyim: Central Zionist Archives, Jerusalem.
Bible: (Moses) Israel Museum, Jerusalem;
(Tabernacle) Formerly Sassoon Collection, Letchwath, England;
(Jonah) The British Library Board, London;
(contest) Photo E. Kaminer, Holon.
Bilu: A. Raphaeli-Zenziper Collection, Tel Aviv.
Bimah: The British Library Board, London.
Birnbaum, Nathan: Courtesy J. Fraenkel, London.
Blaustein, Jacob: Photo F. Bachrach, New York.
Bloch, Felix: Stanford University, California.
Block, Herbert: From *The Herblock Gallery,* Simon and Schuster, New York, 1968.
Blood Libel: Cecil Roth Collection.
Blum, Léon: French Embassy Press and Information Division, New York.
Blowitz, Henri: *The Times,* London.
B'nai B'rith: B'nai B'rith New York. Photo L. Franklin.
Bodenheimer, Max: Central Zionist Archives, Jerusalem.
Bodenschatz, Johann: Cecil Roth Collection.
Boerne, Ludwig: Israel Museum, Jerusalem.
Bohemia: I. Einhorn Collection, Tel Aviv. Photo D. Harris, Jerusalem.
Bohr, Niels: Weizmann Institute, Rehovot. Photo Schlessinger.
Bologna: Photo J. Shaw, London.
Bombay: Sir Jacob Sassoon's Charity Trusts, Bombay.
Bonn: Municipal Tourist Office, Bonn. Photo Sachsse.
Boston: Photo S. Cooper.
Bove-Bukh: J.N.U.L., Jerusalem.
Braham, John: National Portrait Gallery, London.
Brainin, Reuben: Leo Baeck Institute, New York.
Brandeis, Louis: Photo Courtesy Library of Congress, Washington D.C.
Brauner, Victor: From *Quadran,* vol. 15. Brussels, 1963.
Breastplate: (silver and enamel) Photo F. J. Darmstaedter, New York;
(Galician) The Jewish Museum, New York.
Brenner, Joseph Hayyim: Israel State Archives, Jerusalem. Photo Ben Dor.
Bridegrooms of the Law: Israel Museum, Jerusalem. Photo D. Harris.
Briscoe, Robert: Photo P. Sweeney, Dublin.
British Israelites: J.N.U.L., Jerusalem.
Brod, Max: Keren Hayesod, United Israel Appeal, Jerusalem.
Brodetsky, Selig: Hebrew University Public Relations Department, Jerusalem. Photo A. Bernheim.
Brodie, Sir Israel: Photo Blackstone Studios, New York.
Brody: Israel Museum Photo Archives, Jerusalem.
Bronfman, Samuel: Photo De Luftis, Paris.
Buber, Martin: Government Press Office, Tel Aviv.
Buchenwald: Yad Vashem, Jerusalem.
Budapest: Central Archives for the History of the Jewish People, Jerusalem.
Budko, Joseph: Israel Museum, Jerusalem. Photo D. Harris.
Buffalo: Buffalo Historical Society, New York.
Bukhara: Israel Museum, Jerusalem.
Burial: (comb) Israel Museum, Jerusalem Photo D. Harris
(tomb) Israel Department of Antiquities and Museums, Jerusalem.
Burg, Yosef: Government Press Office, Tel Aviv.
Burla, Yehuda: Photo Talpiot, Haifa.
Burning Bush: Photo Z. Radovan, Jerusalem.
Burns, Arthur: The White House, Washington D.C.
Butensky, Jules: The Metropolitan Museum of Art, New York.
Buzaglo, Abraham: Alfred Rubens Collection, London.

Initial "C": Bibliothèque Nationale, Paris.
Caesarea: Government Press Office, Tel Aviv.
Cain: Sigmund Harrison Collection, Ardmore, Pennsylvania.
Cairo: Israel Museum, Jerusalem. Photo David Harris.
Cameri: Cameri Theatre, Tel Aviv.
Cantillation: J.N.U.L., Jerusalem.
Cantor, Eddie: Photo N.B.C., New York.
Capernaum: Government Press Office, Tel Aviv.
Capp, Al: Photo New York News Inc.
Carcassonne: Musée du Chateau Comtal de Carcassonne.
Cardozo, Benjamin: Photo New York Times.
Carigal, Raphael: Yale University Library, New Haven, Connecticut.
Carmel, Mount: Government Press Office, Tel Aviv.
Caro, Anthony: Kasmin Gallery, London. Photo G. Martin.
Caro, Joseph: Sigmund Harrison Collection, Ardmore, Pennsylvania.
Carpentras: Photo F. Meyer, Carpentras.
Casablanca: Photo American Joint Distribution Committee.
Cassel, Sir Ernest: Courtesy L. I. Rabinowitz, Jerusalem.
Cassin, René: Photo Alliance Israelite Universelle, Paris.
Cassuto, Umberto: Photo Ganan, Jerusalem.
Castel, Moshe: Israel Museum, Jerusalem. Photo D. Harris.
Castro Sarmento, Jacob de: National Library of Medicine, Bethesda, Maryland.
Celler, Emanuel: Photo Chase, Washington D.C.
Chagall, Marc: Government Press Office, Tel Aviv.
Chajes, Zevi: Daniel Friedenberg Collection, New York.
Charity: Cecil Roth Collection.
Charleston: Photo L. Schwartz, Charleston, South Carolina.
Chernovtsy: Yad Vashem, Jerusalem.
Cherub: Israel Department of Antiquities and Museums, Jerusalem.
China: University of Toronto, Royal Ontario Museum.
Cholent: The Jewish Museum, New York. Photo H. R. Lippman.
Chorazin: Israel Department of Antiquities and Museums, Jerusalem.
Cincinnati: Photo American Jewish Archives.
Circumcision: Israel Museum, Jerusalem. Photo D. Harris.
Cochin: Photo R. V. Kamath & Co., Cochin.
Cohen (Italian family): Formerly Mannheim Collection, Frankfort.
Cohen, Eli: Photo Prior, Tel Aviv.
Cohen, Maxwell: Courtesy McGill University, Montreal.

Coins: (ancient coins except Persian) Bank of Israel; (Persian) Israel Museum; (Agorah Series, Third Banknote Series): Bank of Israel; (Perutah Series) Government Press Office; (Mandatory pound note) B. M. Ansbacher Collection, Jerusalem; (Mandatory coins) Israel Government Coins and Medals Corp.
Cologne: *Monumenta Judaica Fazit,* Cologne.
Commandments, (the 613): The British Library Board, London.
Constance: Rosgarten Museum, Constance.
Constantinople: Bibliothèque Nationale, Paris.
Cordoba: Photo A. Rubens, London.
Cracow: Israel Museum, Jerusalem. Photo David Harris.
Crémieux, Isaac: Cecil Roth Photo Collection.
Cresson, Warder: American Jewish Historical Society, Waltham, Massachusetts.
Crimea: Cecil Roth Collection.
Croll, David: Public Archives of Canada.
Crusades: Photo R. Cleave, Jerusalem.
Cyprus: Cyprus Department of Antiquities, Nicosia Museum.
Czechoslovakia: B. M. Ansbacher Collection, Jerusalem.

Initial "D": Bibliothèque Nationale, Paris.
Dallas: *Congregation Shearith Israel Diamond Anniversary 1884–1959.*
Damascus (Bible): J.N.U.L., Jerusalem.
Damascus (medal): Daniel Friedenberg Collection, New York.
Damrosch: Courtesy *Opera News,* New York.
Daniel: National Gallery of Art, Washington.
Da Ponte: Internationale Stiftung Mozarteum, Salzburg.
David, Jean: El Al Calendar *"Stories of the Bible",* 1959.
David ben Solomon ibn Abi Zimra: Courtesy J. Ben Zimra, Ramat Gan.
Davidson, Jo: Courtesy Palisades Interstate Park. Photo Korbach.
Dayan, Moshe: Government Press Office, Tel Aviv
Day of Atonement: Sir Isaac and Lady Wolfson Museum in Hechal Shlomo, Jerusalem. Photo David Harris, Jerusalem.
Dead Sea Scrolls (Thanksgiving Psalms): Israel Museum, Shrine of the Book, Jerusalem.
Dead Sea Scrolls (Isaiah Scroll): Photo D. Harris, Jerusalem.
Decalogue: Photo P. Larsen, Jerusalem.
De Haan, Jacob Meijer: A. Aronson Collection, Amsterdam. Photo J. Van Dias, Amsterdam.
Delaunay-Terk, Sonia: Joseph Leron Collection, Jerusalem.
Delilah: National Gallery, London.
Denmark (refugees): Nationalmuseet, Copenhagen.
Dibbuk: B. M. Ansbacher Collection, Jerusalem.
Dimonah: J.N.F., Jerusalem.
Dinur, Benzion: Hebrew University, Jerusalem. Photo Grubner.
Disputations: B. M. Ansbacher Collection, Jerusalem.
Disraeli, Benjamin: Cecil Roth Collection.
Dizengoff, Meir: Museum Haaretz, Museum of the History of Tel Aviv-Yafo.
Donnolo, Shabbetai: Photo Cavour, Oria.
Dori, Ya'akov: Central Zionist Archives, Jerusalem.
Douglas, Kirk: Government Press Office, Tel Aviv.
Dreyfus, Alfred: Leo Baeck Institute, New York.
Dropsie, Moses Aaron: American Jewish Historical Society, Waltham, Massachusetts.
Druyanow, Alter: Schwadron Collection, J.N.U.L., Jerusalem.
Dubinsky, David: Courtesy *Justice,* ILGWU, New York. Photo J. Soalt.
Dubno, Solomon: Schwadron Collection, J.N.U.L., Jerusalem.
Dubnow, Simon: Courtesy Charney, Montclair, New Jersey.
Duesseldorf: Courtesy Duesseldorf Municipality. Photo I. Goertz.
Dura-Europos (both): Yale University, New Haven, Conn.
Durkheim, Emile: Presses Universitaires de France, Paris.
Duveen, Joseph: Tate Gallery, London.

Initial "E": Bibliothèque Nationale, Paris.
East London: Photo M. Garb, East London.
Ecclesiastes: *Ecclesiastes, or the Preacher,* Spiral Press, New York, 1965.
Eban, Abba: Government Press Office, Tel Aviv.
Ehrlich, Paul: Daniel Friedenberg Collection, New York.
Eichmann, Adolf: Government Press Office, Tel Aviv.
Ein Gev, Government Press Office, Tel Aviv.
Einstein, Albert: Photo P. Halsman, New York.
Eisner, Kurt: Schwadron Collection, J.N.U.L., Jerusalem.
El-Arish: Government Press Office, Tel Aviv.
Elath: Government Press Office, Tel Aviv.
Elath, Eliahu: Photo D. Harris, Jerusalem.
Elbogen, Ismar: Schwadron Collection, J.N.U.L., Jerusalem.
Eleazar ben Jair: Israel Museum, Jerusalem.
Elephantine: Brooklyn Museum, New York.
Elijah (chair): Great Synagogue, London.
Elijah ben Solomon Zalman: Schwadron Collection, J.N.U.L., Jerusalem.
Eliot, George: National Gallery, London.
Elkan, Benno: Photo D. Harris, Jerusalem.
Elyashar, Jacob Saul: Schwadron Collection, J.N.U.L., Jerusalem.
Emancipation: Cecil Roth Collection. Photo D. Harris, Jerusalem.
En Gedi: Government Press Office, Tel Aviv.
Engel, Joel: Schwadron Collection, J.N.U.L., Jerusalem.
England: Cecil Roth Collection. Photo D. Harris, Jerusalem.
En-Harod: Government Press Office, Tel Aviv.
Ephod: Basnage, *Rèpublique des Hèbreux,* J.N.U.L., Jerusalem.
Epstein, Abraham: Schwadron Collection, J.N.U.L., Jerusalem.
Epstein, Jacob Nahum: Hebrew University, Jerusalem.
Ernakulam: Courtesy Elijah ben Eliavoo, Haifa.
Erter, Isaac: Schwadron Collection,. J.N.U.L., Jerusalem.
Eshkol, Levi: Courtesy Foreign Ministry, Jerusalem.
Eshtemoa: Israel Department of Antiquities and Museums. Photo Emka, Jerusalem.
Essen: Photo Stadtbildstelle, Essen.
Esther: The Jewish Museum, New York.
Etrog: Government Press Office, Tel Aviv.
Evil Eye: I. Einhorn Collection, Tel Aviv. Photo D. Harris, Jerusalem.
Exodus: Library of the Hungarian Academy of Sciences, Budapest.
Eybeschuetz, Jonathan: Schwadron Collection, J.N.U.L., Jerusalem.
Ezekiel, Moses Jacob: *American Jewish Yearbook 1917–18,* Jewish Publication Society, Philadelphia, Pa.

Initial "F": Municipal Library, Dijon.
Falashas: Courtesy Union of American Hebrew Congregations, New York.
Falk, Samuel J. H.: Cecil Roth Collection.
Faraj ben Solomon da Agriqento: Bibliothèque Nationale, Paris.
Fast, Howard: Photo M. P. Lazarus.
Feigin, Dov: Photo I. Zafrir, Tel Aviv.
Feinberg, Avshalom: Courtesy Bet Aaronsohn, Zikhron Ya'akov.
Feiwel, Berthold: Central Zionist Archives, Jerusalem.
Ferber, Herbert: Courtesy Brandeis University, Waltham, Mass.
Ferrer, Vicente: Ashmolean Museum, Oxford.
Fettmilch, Vincent: From G. Liebe Das Judentum, Leipzig, 1903.
Feuchtwanger, Lion: Leo Baeck Institute, New York.
Fez: Folklore Research Center, Hebrew University, Jerusalem.
Fima: Binet Gallery, Tel Aviv, Photo D. Harris, Jerusalem.
Finkelstein, Louis: Photo Conway, New York.
Firstborn: Stedelijk Museum, Amsterdam.
First Fruits: Government Press Office, Tel Aviv.
Fischer, Robert: Courtesy Israel Chess Federation, Tel Aviv.
Fischhoff, Adolf: Schwadron Collection, J.N.U.L., Jerusalem.
Fiscus Judaicus: A. Reifenberg Collection, Jerusalem.
Flag: Jewish National Fund, Jerusalem.
Fleg, Edmond: Schwadron Collection, J.N.U.L., Jerusalem.
Florence: Photo Alinau, Florence.
Foa: Cecil Roth Photo Collection.
Foss, Lukas: Courtesy Buffalo Philharmonic, Buffalo, New York.
France: Courtesy *Ma'ariv,* Tel Aviv.
Frank, Anne: Yad Vashem, Jerusalem.
Frank, Leo Max: Courtesy American Jewish Archives, Cincinnati, Ohio.
Frankfort on the Main (costume): From A.A.S. Clara *Neueroeffnete Welt-Gallerie,* Nuremberg, 1703. Photo J. R. Friedman, London; (riot): From J. Gottfried, *Historische Chronica,* Frankfort, 1642.
Frankfurter, Felix: Zionist Archives and Library, New York.
Frankl, Ludwig August: Leo Baeck Institute, New York.
Franklin, Sidney: Wide World Photos, New York.
Franks, Jacob: From *Early American Jewish Portraiture,* New York, 1952.

Freud, Sigmund: Photo Keystone Press Agency, London.
Freundlich, Otto: From *Deux sculptures monumentales,* Paris, 1962.
Friedlaender, David: Schwadron Collection, J.N.U.L., Jerusalem.
Frischmann, David: Central Zionist Archives, Jerusalem.
Fromm, Erich: Photo Bender, New York.
Fuerth: Courtesy Fuerth Municipality. Photo K. Meyer.
Furtado, Abraham: Courtesy J. Michman-Melkman, Jerusalem.

Initial "G": Bayerische Staatsbibliothek, Munich.
Gabès: Israel Museum, Department of Ethnography Photo Collection, Jerusalem.
Gabirol, Solomon ibn: Courtesy *Jewish Chronicle,* London.
Gadna: Government Press Office, Tel Aviv.
Galilee: Israel State Archives, Jerusalem.
Galili, Israel: Government Press Office, Tel Aviv.
Gamaliel, Rabban: Jewish Theological Seminary, New York.
Gans, David: Courtesy State Jewish Museum, Prague.
Gardosh, Kariel: Courtesy *Ma'ariv,* Tel Aviv.
Gaster, Moses: Spanish and Portuguese Jews Congregation. Photo J. R. Freeman.
Gaza: Cecil Roth Collection. Photo W. Braun.
Geiger, Abraham: Schwadron Collection, J.N.U.L., Jerusalem.
Gentili, Moses: J.N.U.L., Jerusalem.
Gerasa: Israel Department of Antiquities and Museums, Jerusalem.
Germany: From Schedel's *Weltchronik,* 1493.
Gerona: Photo S. Marti, Gerona.
Gershwin, George: Courtesy Jewish Theatrical Guild, New York.
Gertler, Mark: Tate Gallery, London.
Gesher Benot Ya'akov: Photo Zev Radovan, Jerusalem.
Gezer Calendar: Replica in Israel Museum, Jerusalem.
Gibeon: Photo R. Cleave, Jerusalem.
Gilboa: Keren Hayesod, United Israel Appeal, Jerusalem.
Ginzberg, Louis: Courtesy Jewish Theological Seminary, New York.
Glanz, Leib: Photo Western Photographic Services, Los Angeles.
Glicenstein, Enrico: Brooklyn Museum, New York.
Glueck, Nelson: Government Press Office, Tel Aviv.
Goldberg, Arthur Joseph: Courtesy Israel Museum, Jerusalem.
Goldberg, Lea: Government Press Office, Tel Aviv.
Golden Haggadah: The British Library Board, London.
Goldmann, Nahum: Government Press Office, Tel Aviv.
Goldsmid, Sir Isaac Lyon: Cecil Roth Collection.
Goldwyn, Samuel: Courtesy Jewish Theatrical Guild, New York.
Goliath: The British Library Board.
Golomb, Eliyahu: Courtesy Keren Hayesod, United Israel Appeal, Jerusalem.
Gompers, Samuel: From B. Mandel, *Samuel Gompers,* Yellow Springs, Ohio, 1963.
Goodman, Benny: Courtesy Jewish Theatrical Guild, New York.
Goodman, Percival: Courtesy Alvin Roth, Albany, N.Y.
Gordon, Aharon David: Central Zionist Archives, Jerusalem.
Gordon, Judah Leib: Central Zionist Archives, Jerusalem.
Goren, Shlomo: Government Press Office, Tel Aviv.
Gottlieb, Adolph: Courtesy Union of American Hebrew Congregations, New York.
Gottlieb, Maurycy: The Jewish Museum, New York. Photo F. Darmstaedter.
Government, Prayer for the: The British Library Board, London.
Grade, Chaim: Photo Hetz, Tel Aviv.
Graetz, Heinrich: From *American Jewish Yearbook,* 1941–2, Jewish Publication Society, Philadelphia, Pa.
Granach, Alexander: Schwadron Collection, J.N.U.L., Jerusalem.
Greenberg, Hayim: Central Zionist Archives, Jerusalem.
Greenberg, Hank: Courtesy Bloch Publishing Co., New York.
Greenberg, Uri Zevi: Government Press Office, Tel Aviv.
Gregoire, Henri: Courtesy Alliance Israelite Universelle, Paris.
Grodno: Courtesy Yad Vashem, Jerusalem.
Gross, Chaim: Harold J. Ruttenberg Collection, Pittsburgh, Pa. Photo Walter Russell, New York.
Gruenbaum, Yizhak: Government Press Office, Tel Aviv.
Grynszpan, Herschel: Courtesy Yad Vashem, Jerusalem.
Guenzberg, Baron Horace: Schwadron Collection, J.N.U.L., Jerusalem.
Guggenheim, Meyer: From S. Birmingham, *Our Crowd,* New York, 1967. Photo Culver.
Guttmacher, Elijah: Schwadron Collection, J.N.U.L., Jerusalem.

Initial "H": Bibliothèque Municipale, Amiens.
Haber, Shamai: Courtesy Israel Atomic Energy Commission, Yavneh.
Habimah: Government Press Office, Tel Aviv.
Hadassah: Photo Emka, Jerusalem.
Ḥad Gadya: B. M. Ansbacher Collection,. Jerusalem.
Haffkine, Waldemar: Courtesy Edythe Lutzker, New York.
Haganah: Haganah Historical Archives, Tel Aviv.
Hagar: Rijksmuseum, Amsterdam.
Hagbahah: Stedelijk Museum, Amsterdam. Photo Commissie.
Haggadah: Israel Museum, Jerusalem. Photo D. Harris.
Hague: Cecil Roth Collection.
Haifa: Ministry of Tourism. Photo D. Harris, Jerusalem.
Hakkafot: B. Picart, *Cérémonies et coutumes religieuses,* Amsterdam, 1723–43.
Ha Laḥma Anya: Sarajevo National Museum, Yugoslavia.
Halberstadt: Sir Isaac and Lady Wolfson Museum in Hechal Shlomo, Jerusalem.
Ḥallah: Formerly Charles Feinberg Collection, Detroit.
Hallel: The British Library Board, London.
Halprin, Rose: Central Zionist Archives, Jerusalem.
Hamburg: Coutesy Hamburg Municipality.
Ha-Meliz: J.N.U.L., Jerusalem.
Hanau: Courtesy Hanau Municipality.
Hankin, Yehoshua: Central Zionist Archives, Jerusalem.
Hannah (7 sons): State and University Library, Hamburg.
Ḥannukah: Government Press Office, Tel Aviv.
Ḥanukkah (lamp): Sir Isaac and Lady Wolfson Museum in Hechal Shlomo, Jerusalem. Photo D. Harris.
Hapoel: Government Press Office, Tel Aviv.
Harby, Isaac: American Jewish Historical Society, Waltham, Massachusetts.
Ḥaroset: Sir Isaac and Lady Wolfson Museum in Hechal Shlomo, Jerusalem. Photo D. Harris.
Ha-Shomer: Central Zionist Archives, Jerusalem.
Hasidism: Government Press Office, Tel Aviv.
Ha-Tikvah: From *"La-Menaẓẓe'aḥ Shir Mizmor,* 1968.
Havdalah: State Jewish Museum, Prague.
Haynt: J.N.U.L., Jerusalem.
Hazaz, Hayyim: Government Press Office, Tel Aviv.
Hazor: Israel Museum, Jerusalem. Courtesy Yigael Yadin, Jerusalem.
Hazzan: Israel Museum, Jerusalem. Photo D. Harris.
Hechler, William: Central Zionist Archives, Jerusalem.
Hebron: Cecil Roth Collection.
Hechler, William: Central Zionist Archives, Jerusalem.
Heidelberg: Courtesy Heidelberg Municipality.
Heidenheim, Wolf: Schwadron Collection, J.N.U.L., Jerusalem.
Heifetz, Jascha: Government Press Office, Tel Aviv.
Heine, Heinrich: Kunsthalle, Hamburg.
Helez: Government Press Office, Tel Aviv.
Hellman, Lillian: From W. Morehouse, *Matinee Tomorrow,* New York, 1949.
Herem: Central Archives for the History of the Jewish People, Jerusalem.
Hermon, Mount: Government Press Office, Tel Aviv.
Herod I: Holyland Hotel, Jerusalem. By Courtesy of Prof. M. Avi-Yonah.
Herodium: Government Press Office, Tel Aviv.
Hertz, Joseph: Courtesy J. Fraenkel. Photo Van Dyk, London.
Herz, Henriette: Schwadron Collection, J.N.U.L., Jerusalem.
Herzl, Theodor: Central Zionist Archives, Jerusalem.
Herzl (tomb): Central Zionist Archives, Jerusalem.
Herzog, Isaac: Central Zionist Archives, Jerusalem.
Heschel, Abraham: Photo Lotte Jacobi, Hillsboro, New Hampshire.
Hevra Kaddisha: Sir Isaac and Lady Wolfson Museum in Hechal Shlomo, Jerusalem. Photo D. Harris.
Hezir: Ministry of Tourism. Photo D. Harris, Jerusalem.
Hildesheimer, Azriel: Courtesy E. Hildesheimer, Tel Aviv.
Hillquit, Morris: Tamiment Library, New York University Libraries.
Hirsch, Baron Maurice de: G. H. Brunner Collection.
Hirschbein, Peretz: Schwadron Collection, J.N.U.L., Jerusalem.

Hirschel, Solomon: Alfred Rubens Collection, London.
Histadrut: Government Press Office, Tel Aviv.
Hochschule....: From *Leo Baeck Institute Yearbook,* 1967, London.
Hoffman, David Zevi: Schwadron Collection, J.N.U.L., Jerusalem.
Hollaender, Ludwig: Leo Baeck Institute, New York.
Horah: From *Ha-Halutzim* (ed. M. Narkiss), Jerusalem, 1925.
Hoshana Rabba: Stedelijk Museum, Amsterdam.
Huberman, Bronislaw: Israel Museum, Jerusalem.
Huleh: Courtesy Jewish National Fund, Jerusalem.
Husseini, Hajj Amin al-: C. Weizmann, *Trial and Error,* London, 1950.

Initial "I": Bibliothèque Municipale, Dijon.
Ibn Motot, Samuel: J.N.U.L., Jerusalem.
Idelsohn, Abraham: Schwadron Collection, J.N.U.L., Jerusalem.
"Illegal" Immigration: Haganah Historical Archives, Tel Aviv.
Imber, Naphtali Herz: Courtesy YIVO, New York.
Inbal Dance Theater: Photo Mula and Haramaty, Tel Aviv.
Independence Day: Government Press Office, Tel Aviv.
India: Sir Isaac and Lady Wolfson Museum in Hechal Shlomo, Jerusalem.
Inquisition: Prado Museum, Madrid.
Iraq: From D. Sassoon *Massa Babel,* Jerusalem, 1955.
Isaac: Pierpont–Morgan Library, New York.
Irgun Zeva'i Le'ummi: Jabotinsky Institute, Tel Aviv.
Isaacs, Sir Isaac: Courtesy *Herald and Weekly Times,* Melbourne.
Isaacs, Sir Nathaniel: South African Library for Research Purposes, Capetown.
Isfahan: Israel Museum, Jerusalem. Photo D. Harris.
Isidor, Lazare: Schwadron Collection, J.N.U.L., Jerusalem.
Israel: (ivory plaque) Israel Department of Antiquities and Museums, Jerusalem;
(menorah) A. Reipenberg Collection, Israel Museum, Jerusalem;
(view from cave) Photo W. Braun, Jerusalem;
(site of battle) Government Press Office, Tel Aviv;
(Ramleh tower) Government Press Office, Tel Aviv;
(Herzl Street) Central Zionist Archives, Jerusalem;
(Weizmann and Faisal) Central Zionist Archives, Jerusalem;
(White Paper demonstration) Keren Hayesod, United Israel Appeal Photo Archives, Jerusalem;
(Judean terraces) Jewish National Fund, Jerusalem;
(Tannur waterfall) Government Press Office, Tel Aviv;
(Amazyahu River) Jewish National Fund, Jerusalem;
(Canyon, Eilat Mts.) Photo Z. Ron, Haifa;
(Lake Kinneret) Government Press Office, Tel Aviv;
(Sabras) Keren Hayesod, United Israel Appeal Photo Archives, Jerusalem;
(Me'ah Shearim) Government Press Office, Tel Aviv;
(Nir David) Keren Hayesod, United Israel Appeal Photo Archives, Jerusalem;
(IDF artillery) Government Press Office, Tel Aviv;
(Immigrants) Keren Hayesod, United Israel Appeal Photo Archives, Jerusalem;
(Yemenites) Government Press Office, Tel Aviv;
(Ben-Gurion) Keren Hayesod, United Israel Appeal, Photo Archives, Jerusalem;
(ma'barah) Keren Hayesod, United Israel Appeal Photo Archives, Jerusalem;
(Sinai Campaign) Government Press Office, Tel Aviv;
(Jezreel Valley) Government Press Office, Tel Aviv;
(textile factory) Government Press Office, Tel Aviv;
(atomic reactor) Government Press Office, Tel Aviv;
(stamp) B. M. Ansbacher Collection, Jerusalem;
(soccer match) Government Press Office, Tel Aviv;
(Mirage jets) Government Press Office, Tel Aviv;
(computer) Photo I. Freidin, Tel Aviv;
(Gadot) Government Press Office, Tel Aviv;
(elections) Photo K. Weiss, Jerusalem;
(Western Wall) Photo D. Rubinger, Jerusalem.
Israel ben Eliezer Ba'al Shem Tov: B. M. Ansbacher Collection, Jerusalem.
Israel Philharmonic Orchestra: Photo W. Braun, Jerusalem.
Isserles, Moses: Schwadron Collection, J.N.U.L., Jerusalem.
Istanbul: Israel Museum, Jerusalem.
Italy: Cecil Roth Photo Collection.
Izmir: Alfred Rubens Collection, London.

Initial "J": Princeton University Library.
Jabotinsky, Vladimir: Jerusalem Municipality Historical Archives. Photo Ben Dov.
Jachin and Boaz: Sir Isaac and Lady Wolfson Museum in Hechal Shlomo, Jerusalem. Photo D. Harris.
Jacob: Sarajevo National Museum.
Jacob, Max: Rene Guy Cadou, *Esthetique de Max Jacob,* Paris, 1956.
Jacobi, Abraham: Schwadron Collection, J.N.U.L., Jerusalem.
Jacobs, Joseph: Cecil Roth Collection.
Jacobson, Israel: Schwadron Collection, J.N.U.L., Jerusalem.
Jael: Rijksmuseum, Amsterdam.
Jaffa: Photo by Yaacov Ben Or-Kalter.
Jakobovits, Immanuel: Photo W. Braun, Jerusalem.
Jamaica: Photo E. H. deSouza Jr., Kingston, Jamaica.
Jastrow, Marcus: American Jewish Historical Society, Waltham, Massachusetts.
Jawitz, Ze'ev: Schwadron Collection, J.N.U.L., Jerusalem.
Jericho: Photo R. Cleave, Jerusalem.
Jeroboam II: Israel Department of Antiquities and Museums, Jerusalem.
Jerusalem: (citadel) Ministry of Foreign Affairs, Jerusalem;
(Mt. Zion) Photo D. Eisenberg, Jerusalem;
(Temple Mount) Photo W. Braun, Jerusalem;
(Madabamap) Israel Department of Antiquities and Museums, Jerusalem;
(Allenby–Jaffa Gate) Imperial War Museum, London;
(Gates—1) Government Press Office, Tel Aviv;
(2) Photo D. Eisenberg, Jerusalem;
(3) Jewish National Fund, Jerusalem;
(4) Israel Department of Antiquities and Museums, Jerusalem;
(5) Photo Z. Radovan, Jerusalem;
(6) Jewish National Fund, Jerusalem;
(7) Photo D. Eisenberg, Jerusalem;
(8) Jewish National Fund, Jerusalem;
(Western Wall) Photo W. Braun, Jerusalem;
(excavation, s. wall) Photo D. Eisenberg, Jerusalem;
(desecrated graves) Jewish National Fund, Jerusalem;
(Jaffa Road) Photo W. Braun, Jerusalem;
(Katamon) Photo D. Eisenberg, Jerusalem.
Jethro: Government Press Office, Tel Aviv.
Jewish Brigade: Haganah Historical Archives, Tel Aviv.
Jewish Colonial Trust: Central Zionist Archives, Jerusalem.
Jewish Colonization Association: Courtesy Joseph Brandes, Fairlawn, New Jersey.
Jewish Daily Forward: J.N.U.L., Jerusalem.
Jewish Day: J.N.U.L., Jerusalem.
Jewish Legion: Jerusalem Municipality Historical Archives. Photo Ben Dov.
Jewish Theological Seminary: Photo G. Segal.
Jezreel Valley: Jewish National Fund, Jerusalem.
Joachim, Joseph: Schwadron Collection, J.N.U.L., Jerusalem.
Job: Israel Museum, Jerusalem.
Johannesburg: Photo S. A. Press Services, Johannesburg.
Jolson, Al: Jewish Theatrical Guild, New York.
Jonah, Book of: Sir Isaac and Lady Wolfson Museum in Hechal Shlomo, Jerusalem.
Joseph: Sarajevo National Museum.
Josephus Flavius: Bibliothèque Nationale, Paris.
Jossipon: J.N.U.L., Jerusalem.
Jost, Isaac: Schwadron Collection, J.N.U.L., Jerusalem.
Jotham: Smithsonian Institute, Washington.
Judah Halevi: J.N.U.L., Jerusalem.
Judah Loew: Photo J. Ehm.
Judah Maccabee: Musé de Cluny, Paris. Photo D. Bourbonnais.
Judeo-Persian: Jewish Theological Seminary, New York.
Judith, Book of: Cecil Roth Collection. Photo W. Braun, Jerusalem.
Juedisch-Theologisches Seminar: Guido

Kisch *Das Breslauer Seminar*, 1963, Tuebingen.
Jurnet of Norwich: Public Records Office, London.

Initial "K": Bayerische Staatsbibliothek, Munich.
Kabbalah: J.N.U.L., Jerusalem.
Kabbalat Shabbat: Alsatian Museum, Strassburg.
Kafka, Franz: Schwadron Collection, J.N.U.L., Jerusalem.
Kahana, Abraham: Photo S. Alexander, Tel Aviv.
Kahaneman, Joseph: Courtesy Beth Jacob, Jerusalem.
Kahn, Louis: Collection, The Museum of Modern Art, New York.
Kahn, Zadoc: Central Zionist Archives, Jerusalem.
Kaifeng: Society of Jesus, Paris.
Kallen, Horace: From S. Hook and M. R. Konvitz, *Freedom and Experience*, New York, 1947.
Kalonymus: Mittelrheinisches Landesmuseum, Mainz.
Kaminski: Schwadron Collection, J.N.-U.L., Jerusalem.
Kann, Jacobus the: Schwadron Collection, J.N.U.L., Jerusalem.
Kansas: Photo J. H. Walther.
Kantor, Judah: Schwadron Collection, J.N.U.L., Jerusalem.
Kaplan, Anatoli: Grosvernor Gallery, London.
Kapparot: Government Press Office, Tel Aviv.
Karaite: Israel Museum, Jerusalem.
Karelitz, Avraham: Courtesy Agudat Israel, Jerusalem.
Karmi, Dov: Government Press Office, Tel Aviv.
Kasher, Menahem: Photo Ross, Jerusalem.
Kattowitz Conference: Central Zionist Archives, Jerusalem.
Katzir, Ephraim: Photo W. Braun, Jerusalem.
Katznelson, Berl: Central Zionist Archives, Jerusalem.
Kaufmann, Isidor: Israel Museum, Jerusalem.
Kaunas: Yad Vashem Museum, Jerusalem.
Kaye, Danny: Photo Van Pelt.
Kefar Baram: Government Press Office, Tel Aviv.
Kefar Habad: Government Press Office, Tel Aviv.
Kefar Kanna: Government Press Office, Tel Aviv.
Kenya: Jabotinsky Institute, Tel Aviv.
Keritot: J.N.U.L., Jerusalem.
Kessel, Joseph: Jerusalem Municipality Historical Archives.
Ketubbah: Cecil Roth Collection.
Khān Yunis: Government Press Office, Tel Aviv.
Kibbutz: Keren Hayesod, United Israel Appeal Photo Archives, Jerusalem.
Kiddush: Israel Museum, Jerusalem. Photo D. Harris.
Kidron: Photo R. Cleave.
Kinneret, Lake: Government Press Office, Tel Aviv.
Kirszenbaum, Jesekiel: Photo M. Vaux.
Kiryat Shemonah: Government Press Office, Tel Aviv.
Kisch, Frederick: Central Zionist Archives, Jerusalem.
Kishon, Ephraim: Photo J. Papp, Givataim.
Kisling, Moise: Israel Museum, Jerusalem.
Kissinger, Henry: Government Press Office, Tel Aviv.
Klausner, Joseph: Hebrew University Public Relations Department, Jerusalem.
Klein, Abraham: Canadian Jewish Congress, Montreal.
Klein, Samuel: Schwadron Collection, J.N.U.L., Jerusalem.
Klemperer, Otto: Courtesy IPO, Tel Aviv. Photo G. Sleurs, Amsterdam.
Knesset: Government Press Office, Tel Aviv.
Koestler, Arthur: Schwadron Collection, J.N.U.L., Jerusalem. Photo Madame Yevonde.
Kogan, Leonid: Israel Philharmonic Orchestra, Tel Aviv.
Kohler, Kaufmann: American Jewish Archives, Cincinnati, Ohio.
Kohut: Schwadron Collection, J.N.U.L., Jerusalem.
Kollek, Theodore: Photo F. Csasznik, Jerusalem.
Kol Nidrei: From A. Z. Idelsohn, *Melodien 8*, 1932.
Kook, Abraham Isaac: Jerusalem Municipality Historical Archives. Photo Ben Dov.
Korczak, Janusz: B. M. Ansbacher Collection, Jerusalem.
Koufax, Sandy: From B. Postal et al., *Encyclopedia of Jews in Sports*, New York, 1965.
Koussevitzky, Serge: Israel Philharmonic Orchestra, Tel Aviv. Photo L. J. Heustein, New York.
Kramer, Jacob: Israel Cohen, *A Ghetto Gallery*, London,. 1931.
Kraus, Karl: Leo Baeck Institute, New York.
Krauss, Samuel: Schwadron Collection, J.N.U.L., Jerusalem.
Kreisky, Bruno: Austrian Embassy, Tel Aviv.
Kristallnacht: City Archives, Heilbronn.
Krojanker, Gustav: Photo L. Landauer.
Krochmal, Nachman: S. Rawidowicz, *Nachman Krochmals Werke*, Berlin 1924.
Kun, Béla: Schwadron Collection, J.N.U.L., Jerusalem.
Kurdistan: Keren Hayesod, United Israel Appeal Photo Archives, Jerusalem.

Initial "L": Bibliothèque Nationale, Paris.
Lachish: From H. H. Torczyner *Lachish*, Oxford, 1938.
Lachish Ostraca: Israel Department of Antiquities and Museums, Jerusalem.
Ladino: J.N.U.L., Jerusalem.
Laemel, Simon von: Schwadron Collection, J.N.U.L., Jerusalem.
Lafer, Horacio: Courtesy Dr. Alfred Hirschberg, São Paulo.
Lag Ba-Omer: Israel Museum Photo Archives, Jerusalem.
Lamdan, Yizḥak: Genazim, Tel Aviv.
Lamentations Rabbah: J.N.U.L., Jerusalem.
Landau, Ezekiel: Schwadron Collection, J.N.U.L., Jerusalem.
Landau, Lev: Reportagebild, Stockholm.
Landauer, Gustav: Schwadron Collection, J.N.U.L., Jerusalem.
Landowska, Wanda: From B. Gavoty, *Wanda Landowska*, Geneva, 1957.
Langdon, David: From B. Hollowood (ed.), *Pick of Punch*,, London, 1964.
Lasker, Eduard: Schwadron Collection, J.N.U.L., Jerusalem.
Laski: Courtesy London School of Economics.
Lassalle, Ferdinand: B. M. Ansbacher Collection, Jerusalem.
Latrun: Photo D. Eisenberg, Jerusalem.
Lauterbach, Jacob: American Jewish Archive, Cincinnati, Ohio.
Lawson: Courtesy L. J. Rabinowitz, Jerusalem.
Lazarus, Emma: Schwadron Collection, J.N.U.L., Jerusalem.
Lazarus, Moritz: Schwadron Collection, J.N.U.L., Jerusalem.
Lebensohn, Micah: Schwadron Collection, J.N.U.L., Jerusalem.
Leeds: From E. Krausz, *Leeds Jewry*, Cambridge, 1964.
Leeser, Isaac: American Jewish Historical Society, Waltham, Massachusetts.
Leghorn: Sir Isaac and Lady Wolfson Museum in Hechal Shlomo, Jerusalem.
Lehman, Herbert Henry: Associated Press, Tel Aviv.
Leivick, H.: YIVO, New York.
Lekert, Hirsch: Bund Archives, Jewish Labor Movement, New York.
Lekhah Dodi: Cecil Roth Collection.
Leningrad: Courtesy Central Archives for the History of the Jewish People, Jerusalem.
Lessing, Gotthold: Leo Baeck Institute, New York.
Levanda, Lev: J.N.U.L., Jerusalem.
Levi: St. Catherine's Monastery, Sinai.
Levi, Carlo: From *Von Atelier zu Atelier*, vol. 6, no. 1, Dusseldorf, 1958.
Levin, Shmarya: Israel Museum, Jerusalem.
Levin, Ẓevi Hirsch: Cecil Roth Collection.
Levine, Jack: Mr. and Mrs. Nate Spingold Collection. Photo G. Clemonts.
Levi-Strauss, Claude: Photo H. Cartier–Bresson, Magnum Photos Inc., New York.
Levirate Marriage: Israel Museum, Jerusalem.
Levy, Uriah Phillips: The Mariner's Museum, Newport News, Virginia.
Lewandowski, Louis: Department of Musicology, J.N.U.L., Jerusalem.
Lewin, Kurt: Courtesy Simon Herman, Jerusalem.
Lewisohn, Ludwig: Courtesy S. Liptzin, Jerusalem.
Liberman, Yevsey: Copyright Time Inc., 1965.
Lichine, David: From M. Seymour, *Seymour on Ballet*, New York, 1947.
Lieberman, Saul: Jewish Theological Seminary, New York.
Liebermann, Max: Israel Museum, Jerusalem.
Lifshitz, Neḥamah: Photo J. and A. Agor, Tel Aviv.
Lilienblum, Moses Leib: Schwadron Collection, J.N.U.L., Jerusalem.
Lincoln: Photo L. H. Hare, Lincoln.
Lissitzky, El: From S. Lissitzky-Kueppers *El Lissitsky, Life and Letters*, London, 1948.
Lithuania: Y. D. Kamson Collection, Yad Vashem, Jerusalem.
Litvinov, Maxim: Photo L. Jacobi, Hillsboro, New Jersey.
Loew, Leopold: Schwadron Collection, J.N.U.L., Jerusalem.
Loḥamei ha-Getta'ot: Government Press Office, Tel Aviv.
Lombroso, Cesare: From G. Simson, *Fueng Kaempfer fuer Gerechtigkeit*, Munich, 1951.
Los Angeles: From M. Vorspan and L. P.

Gartner, *History of the Jews of Los Angeles*, San Marino, 1970.
Lublin: Yad Vashem, Jerusalem.
Lukács, Georg: Courtesy Soziologische Texte, Heuwied.
Lulav: Photo D. Eisenberg, Jerusalem.
Luxemburg, Rosa: B. M. Ansbacher Collection, Jerusalem.
Luzzatto, Samuel: Israel Museum Photo Archives, Jerusalem.
Lvov: Central Zionist Archives, Jerusalem.

Initial "M": Bibliothèque Municipale, Avranches.
Machpelah: Ministry of Tourism, Photo D. Harris.
Mack, Julian: Schwadron Collection, J.N.U.L., Jerusalem.
Magen David: Alsatian Museum, Alsace.
Magnes, Judah L.: Courtesy J. Magnes, Jerusalem.
Mahler, Gustav: Schwadron Collection, J.N.U.L., Jerusalem.
Maḥzor: University Library, Leipzig.
Mailer, Norman: Photo F. W. McDarrah, New York.
Maimonides, Moses: B. M. Ansbacher Collection, Jerusalem.
Majdanek: B. M. Ansbacher Collection Jerusalem.
Majorca: From A. L. Isaacs, *The Jews of Majorca*, London, 1936.
Malamud, Bernard: Courtesy Farrar, Straus and Giroux, New York. Photo S. Linden.
Malta: From E. Becker, *Malta Sotterranea*, Strasbourg, 1913.
Manasseh Ben Israel: Israel Museum, Jerusalem.
Mane-Katz: Oscar Ghez Collection, Geneva.
Manger, Itzik: Courtesy L. Sowdon, Jerusalem.
Manna: National Museum, Sarajevo.
Mantua: Photo J. Shaw, London.
Ma'on: From *Bulletin of the Louis M. Rabinowitz Fund*, No. 3, Jerusalem, December 1960.
Mapu, Abraham: Schwadron Collection, J.N.U.L., Jerusalem.
Marceau, Marcel: Courtesy B. Gillon, Tel Aviv.
Marcus, David: Government Press Office, Tel Aviv.
Marcuse, Herbert: Courtesy University of California.
Maresha: Courtesy Hebrew University, Department of Archeology, Jerusalem.
Markish, Pereẓ: Schwadron Collection, J.N.U.L., Jerusalem.
Markova, Alicia: Photo J. Blake, London.
Maror: National Museum, Sarajevo.
Marshall, Louis: Israel Museum, Jerusalem.
Marx, Karl: Photo M. Ninio, Jerusalem.
Marx Brothers: Courtesy Personality Posters (U.K.), London.
Mashiv ha-Ru'aḥ: Altonaer Museum, Hamburg.
Maurois, André: Schwadron Collection, J.N.U.L., Jerusalem.
Mayer, René: Courtesy Moshe Catane, Jerusalem.
Mazar, Benjamin: Hebrew University Public Relations Department, Jerusalem.
Maẓẓah: From H. B. Grinstein, *Rise of the Jewish Community of New York*, Philadelphia, 1945.
Mears, Otto: Courtesy Mrs. Sam H. Uchill, Denver.
Megiddo: Photo R. Cleave, Jerusalem.
Meḥiẓah: Israel Museum, Jerusalem.
Meir, Golda: Government Press Office, Tel Aviv.
Meir ben Baruch: Israel Museum, Jerusalem.
Meldola, Raphael: Alfred Rubens Collection, London.
Memorbuch: J.N.U.L., Jerusalem.
Mendele Mokher Seforim: Beit Bialik, Tel Aviv.
Mendelsohn, Erich: Courtesy Mrs. Mendelsohn, San Francisco.
Mendelssohn, Felix: Schwadron Collection, J. N. U. L., Jerusalem.
Mendes-France, Pierre: French Embassy Press and Information Division, New York.
Mendoza, Daniel: Alfred Rubens Collection, London.
Menorah: Courtesy of N. Avigad, Hebrew University. Jerusalem. Photo Z. Radovan.
Menuhin, Yehudi: Courtesy B. Gillon, Tel Aviv.
Merḥavyah: B. M. Ansbacher Collection, Jerusalem.
Mesha: Israel Department of Antiquities and Museums, Jerusalem. Photo Zev Radovan.
Messiah: Staatsbibliothek, Munich.
Meyerbeer, Giacomo: Schwadron Collection, J.N.U.L., Jerusalem.
Mezuzah: The Jewish Museum, New York.
Michael: Ethnological Museum & Folklore Archives, Haifa. Photo O. Tauber.
Mikhoels, Solomon: Central Archives for the History of the Jewish People, Jerusalem.
Mikveh: Photo F. Meyer. Carpentras.
Miller, Arthur: Jewish Theatrical Guild, New York.
Minhagim Books: J.N.U.L., Jerusalem.
Miriam: Schocken Library, Jerusalem.
Modigliani, Amedeo: Oscar Ghez Collection, Geneva.
Mogador: Israel Museum, Department of Ethnography Photo Collection, Jerusalem.
Mohilewer, Samuel: Central Zionist Archives, Jerusalem.
Moise, Theodore Sydney: Metropolitan Museum of Art, gift of Grace H. Dodge, New York.
Molcho, Solomon: State Jewish Museum, Prague.
Monash, John: *Herald and Weekly Times*, Melbourne.
Mond, Alfred: Central Zionist Archives, Jerusalem.
Monis, Judah: Cecil Roth Collection.
Montagu, Lilian: Schwadron Collection, J.N.U.L., Jerusalem.
Montefiore, Moses: Schwadron Collection, J.N.U.L., Jerusalem.
Monteux, Pierre: From A. Meyer, *Collection Musicale*, Paris, 1961.
Morais, Sabato: Jewish Theological Seminary, New York.
Moravia: Royal Library, Copenhagen.
Moravia, Alberto: Archivio Fotografico Bompiani, Milan.
Morgenthau, Henry: Schwadron Collection, J.N.U.L., Jerusalem.
Morgenthau, Henry Jr.: Schwadron Collection, J.N.U.L., Jerusalem.
Morocco: Cecil Roth Collection.
Moscow: Courtesy D. Bar-Tov, Jerusalem.
Moses: The British Library Board, London.
Moshav: Government Press Office, Tel Aviv.
Mostel, Zero: From M. Woldman, *Zero by Mostel*, New York, 1965.
Motzkin, Leo: Schwadron Collection, J.N.U.L., Jerusalem.
Mount of Olives: Government Press Office, Tel Aviv.
Mukachevo: From R. Abramovitch (ed.), *The Vanished World*, New York, 1947.
Muni, Paul: Keren Hayesod, United Israel Appeal Photo Archives, Jerusalem.
Myers, Myer: Photo C. D. Mills and Son, Philadelphia.

Initial "N": Bibliothèque Municipale, Rheims.
Nabateans: Photo W. Braun, Jerusalem.
Nablus: Keren Hayesod, United Israel Appeal Photo Archives, Jerusalem.
Nadelman, Elie: The Nelson A. Rockefeller Collection, New York. Photo C. Uht, New York.
Naḥal: Government Press Office, Tel Aviv.
Nahariyyah: Photo H. Dash, Nahariyyah.
Napoleon: Israel Museum, Jerusalem. Photo D. Harris.
Nasi, Gracia: Archive of the Jewish Theological Seminary, New York. Photo F. J. Darmstaedter.
Nash Papyrus: From E. L. Sukenik, *Megillot Genuzot*, Jerusalem, 1948.
Nathan, Ernesto: Schwadron Collection, J.N.U.L., Jerusalem.
Nazereth: Government Press Office, Tel Aviv.
Ne'eman, Yuval: Courtesy Tel Aviv University.
Ner Tamid: Sir Isaac and Lady Wolfson Museum in Hechal Shlomo, Jerusalem. Photo D. Harris.
Netanyah: Photo W. Braun, Jerusalem.
Netherlands: Yad Vashem, Jerusalem.
Netilat Yadayim: Israel Museum, Jerusalem. Photo D. Harris.
Neumann, Emanuel: Zionist Archives & Library, New York.
Newmark (family): From M. Vorspan and C. P. Gartner, *History of the Jews of Los Angeles*, San Marino, California, 1970.
Newport: Society Friends of Touro Synagogue National Historical Shrine.
New York: (refugees) the Bettman Archive, New York;
(rally) Photo Alexander Archer, New York.
New Zealand: Alexander Turnbull Library, Wellington. Photo Tait Bros. Hokitika.
Niger, Samuel: Courtesy M. Charney, Montclair, N.J.
Nishmat Kol Hai: Israel Museum.
Noah, Mordecai Manuel: Shearith Israel Synagogue, New York.
Nordau, Max: Keren Hayesod United Israel Appeal Photo Archives, Jerusalem.
North Dakota: American Jewish Archives of Hebrew Union College, Cincinnati, Ohio.
Norzi (family): Cecil Roth Collection.
Nuremberg: Germanisches Nationalmuseum, Nuremberg.

Initial "O": Bibliothèque Municipale, Lyons.
Oath More Judaico: Cecil Roth Collection.
Obadiah The Proselyte: Jewish Theological Seminary, New York.
Ochs, Julius: Schwadron Collection, J.N.-U.L., Jerusalem.

Ochs, Adolf Simon and **George Washington:** Photo *New York Times* Studio.
Odessa: J.N.U.L. Photo Archives, Jerusalem.
Odets, Clifford: Photo R. Sondak, Keystone Pictures Inc. Hollywood, California.
Offenbach, Jacques: Leo Baeck Institute, New York.
Ohel: Photo Mula and Haramaty, Tel Aviv.
Oistrakh, David: Courtesy Israel Philharmonic Orchestra, Tel Aviv.
Omer: Ethnological Museum and Folklore Archives, Haifa. Photo Keren-Or, Haifa.
Oppenheim, David: Cecil Roth Collection.
Oppenheimer, Moritz: Israel Museum, Jerusalem. Photo D. Harris.
Oppenheimer, Joseph (Suess): Germanisches Museum, Nuremberg.
Oppenheimer, J. Robert: Hebrew University Public Relations Department. Jerusalem.
Orloff, Chana: Leon L. Gildesgame Collection, New York.
Ort: Photo L. Liberman, São Paulo.
Ouziel, B. Z. Meir: Photo K. Weiss, Jerusalem.

Initial "P": Bibliothèque Nationale, Paris.
Padua: Cecil Roth Collection.
Paldi, Israel: Photo J. Agor, Tel Aviv.
Paley, William S.: Courtesy CBS, New York.
Palombo, David: Government Press Office, Tel Aviv.
Pappenheim, Bertha: B. M. Ansbacher Collection, Jerusalem.
Paran: J.N.F. Photo Archives, Jerusalem.
Paris: Photo M. Ninio, Jerusalem.
Passover: (Ms.) the British Library Board, London;
(seder) Photo David Harris, Jerusalem.
Pauker, Ana: Yad Vashem, Jerusalem.
Peki'in: Government Press Office, Tel Aviv.
Pentateuch: Government Press Office, Tel Aviv.
Peretz, Isaac Leib: B. M. Ansbacher Collection, Jerusalem.
Pesaro: Israel Museum Photo Collection, Jerusalem.
Pesher: Israel Museum, the Shrine of the Book, Jerusalem. Photo D. Harris.
Petra: Courtesy Garo's Photo Shop, Jerusalem.
Pevsner, Antoine: the Museum of Modern Art, New York. Gift of Katherine S. Dreier.
Philadelphia: Ezra P. Gorodetsky Collection, Jerusalem.
Philistine: Israel Department of Antiquities and Museums, Jerusalem.
Piatigorsky, Gregor: Courtesy R.C.A., New York.
Picon, Molly: Courtesy Lewis Sowden, Jerusalem.
Pinsk: From B. Hoffman (ed.), *Toyznt Yor Pinsk*, New York, 1941.
Pinsker, Leon: Zionist Archives and Library, New York.
Pinski, David: Schwadron Collection, J.N.-U.L., Jerusalem.
Plagues: The British Library Board, London.
Plisteskaya, Maya: From A. Chujoy and P. W. Manchester, *The Dance Encyclopaedia*, New York, 1967.
Poland: (caricature) I. Einhorn Collection, Tel Aviv;
(types) YIVO, New York.
Pontius Pilate: Israel Museum, Jerusalem. The Israel Department of Antiquities and Museums Collection. Photo D. Harris.
Portaleone, Abraham: I. Einhorn Collection, Tel Aviv. Photo D. Harris.
Portugal: Museu Nacional de Arte Antiga, Lisbon. Photo Oronoz, Lisbon.
Potofsky, Jacob S.: From Morris U. Schappes, *The Jews in the United States*, New York, 1958.
Prague: (clock tower) Courtesy State Jewish Museum, Prague;
(Pinsk synagogue wall) From A. Reith, *To the Victims of Tyranny*, Tubingen, 1968.
Priestly Vestments: From M. Levin, *Mlechet Hamishkan*, Tel Aviv, 1968.
Proust, Marcel: B. M. Ansbacher Collection, Jerusalem.
Proverbs: Israel Museum, Jerusalem.
Providence: From *Rhode Island Historical Notes*, vol. 3, Nov. 1958.
Pulitzer, Joseph: B. M. Ansbacher Collection, Jerusalem.
Purim: (jesters) J. N. U. L., Jerusalem;
(noisemakers) Sir Isaac and Lady Wolfson Museum in Hechal Shlomo, Jerusalem. Photo D. Harris.

Initial "Q": Bibliothèque Municipale, Amiens.
Qumran: Photo W. Braun, Jerusalem.

Initial "R": Princeton University Library, New Jersey.
Rabi, Isidor I.: Courtesy Columbia University, New York.
Rachel: (drawing) Christ Church, Oxford;
(tomb) Courtesy New York State Education Department.
Rain, Prayer for: Altonaer Museum, Hamburg.
Ramat Gan: Government Press Office, Tel Aviv.
Ramleh: Photo W. Braun, Jerusalem.
Ramses: The British Library Board, London.
Rapoport, Solomon J. L.: Schwadron Collection, J.N.U.L., Jerusalem.
Rashi: Photo Kulturinstitute, Worms.
Rasminsky, Louis: Photo P. Horstal, Ottawa.
Rathenau, Walther: Leo Baeck Institute, New York.
Rau, Heinz: Government Press Office, Tel Aviv.
Rebecca: National Museum, Sarajevo.
Red Heifer: J.N.U.L., Jerusalem.
Red Sea: NASA, Washington, D.C.
Regensburg: Stiptung Preussicher Kulturbesitz, Berlin. Photo W. Steinkopf.
Reggio di Calabria: Palatine Library, Parma.
Reines, Isaac J.: B. M. Ansbacher Collection, Jerusalem.
Reinhardt, Max: Yad Vashem, Jerusalem.
Rembrandt van Rijn: National Gallery, London.
Reuter, Baron von: L. J. Rabinowitz Collection, Jerusalem.
Revel, Bernard: From *American Jewish Yearbook, 1941–2*, Philadelphia, Pa.
Rhodes: Photo H. Schieber, Natanyah.
Rickover, Hyman G.: Courtesy U.S. Department of the Navy, Washington, D.C.
Riga: From *Yahadut Latvia*, Tel Aviv, 1953.
Righteous of the Nations: Yad Vashem, Jerusalem.
Robinson, Edward: From C. Wilson (ed.), *Picturesque Palestine . . .* London, c. 1880. Courtesy A. A. Mendilow, Jerusalem.
Robinson, Edward G.: Jewish Theatrical Guild, New York.
Rockefeller Museum: Government Press Office, Tel Aviv.
Rodgers, Richard: Jewish Theatrical Guild, New York.
Rome: Courtesy Italian Synagogue Collection, Jerusalem.
Romm: J.N.U.L., Jerusalem.
Rosenberg, Isaac: Tate Gallery, London.
Rosenfeld, Morris: From H. Hapgood, *The Spirit of the Ghetto*, Belknap Press, Harvard University Press, 1967.
Rosenwald, Julius: From *American Jewish Yearbook 1932–33*, Philadelphia.
Rosenzweig, Franz: Schwadron Collection. J.N.U.L., Jerusalem.
Rosh Ha-Shanah: Israel Museum, Jerusalem.
Rossi, Salamone de: Wroclaw, Poland, University Library.
Roth, Cecil: Photo D. Harris, Jerusalem.
Rothenstein, William: Bradford City Art Gallery and Museum, England.
Rothschild, Lionel: From *The Illustrated London News*.
Rothschild, Edmond: Central Zionist Archives, Jerusalem.
Rovina, Hanna: Courtesy Israel Gur, Jerusalem.
Rubinstein, Artur: Courtesy R.C.A. Victor Records, New York.
Ruppin, Arthur: Central Zionist Archives, Jerusalem.
Russia (market): Courtesy J.N.U.L. Photo Archives, Jerusalem.
Rutenberg, Pinḥas: Central Zionist Archives, Jerusalem.
Ryback, Issachar: Collection William Margulies, London.

Initial "S": The British Library Board, London.
Sabbath: (painting) Oscar Gruss Collection, New York. Photo F. J. Darmstaedter;
(candles) Joseph B. and Olyn Horwitz Judaica Collection, Cleveland, Ohio.
Sabin, Albert: Courtesy Children's Hospital Research Foundation, Cincinnati.
Sachs, Nelly: Photo Reportagebild, Stockholm.
Sadeh, Yiẓḥak: Government Press Office, Tel Aviv.
Safed: Courtesy Ministry of Tourism, Jerusalem.
Saint-Leon, Arthur: Bibliothèque de l'Opera, Paris.
Salk, Jonas: March of Dimes, National Foundation.
Salonika: Yad Vashem, Jerusalem.
Samaria: Photo R. Cleave, Jerusalem.
Samaritans: Courtesy Benyamin Tsedaka, Ḥolon.
Samarkand: Mocatta Library, University College, London.
Samson: The British Library, London.
Samuel, Herbert: Schwadron Collection, J.N.U.L., Jerusalem.
Samuelson, Paul A.: Courtesy MIT, Cambridge, Massachusetts.
Sandak: Rijksmuseum, Amsterdam.
San Francisco: Photo H. Rinkel, San Francisco.
Sanhedrin: J.N.U.L. Photo Collection, Jerusalem.

Sao Paolo: Israel Museum Photo Archives, Jerusalem.
Sapir, Pinhas: Government Press Office, Tel Aviv.
Sardis: Committee to Save the Ancient Synagogue of Sardis.
Sarajevo: Courtesy Yizhak Gaon, Jerusalem.
Sarnoff, David: Courtesy RCA, New York. Photo Karsh, Ottawa.
Sasportas, Jacob: Israel Museum, Jerusalem.
Sassoon: Photo Lafayette, London.
Satu-Mare: Photo Yakoby, Jerusalem.
Schapira, Hermann: Courtesy B. Jaffe, Jerusalem.
Schatz, Boris: Courtesy B. Schatz, Jerusalem.
Schechter, Solomon: Leo Baeck Institute, Jerusalem.
Schiff, Jacob: Photo Pach Bros., New York.
Schildkraut, Rudolf: Schwadron Collection, J.N.U.L., Jerusalem.
Schneerson, Menahem Mendel: From *Challenge,* London, 1970.
Schnitzler, Arthur: Schwadron Collection, J.N.U.L., Jerusalem.
Schoenberg, Arnold: The Bettman Archive, New York.
Scholem, Gershom G.: Hebrew University Public Relations Department, Photo A. Bernheim.
Schwartz, Maurice: Courtesy YIVO, New York.
Schwarz, David: Courtesy National Air and Space Museum, Smithsonian Institute, Washington, D.C.
Schwarz-Bart, André: Courtesy Editions du Seuil, Paris. Photo Jean-Pierre Ducatez.
Scribe: Keren Hayesod, United Israel Appeal Photo Archives, Jerusalem.
Scroll of Esther: Cecil Roth Collection.
Sefer Torah: Formerly Charles Feinberg Collection, Detroit.
Segal, George: National Gallery of Canada, Ottawa. Courtesy Sidney Janis Gallery, New York.
Segall, Lasar: From P.M. Bardi, *Lasar Segall,* São Paolo, 1952.
Seville: Treasury of the Cathedral, Seville.
Shabbat ha-Gadol: J.N.U.L., Jerusalem.
Shabbetai ben Meir ha-Kohen: Courtesy H. Gold, Tel Aviv.
Shabbetai Zevi: J.N.U.L., Jerusalem.
Shahin: Israel Museum, Jerusalem.
Shahn, Ben: Courtesy Temple Ohabai Shalom, Nashville, Tennessee.
Shalom Aleichem: Schwadron Collection, J.N.U.L., Jerusalem.
Shanghai: Israel Museum Photo Archives, Jerusalem.
Shapira, Abraham: Central Zionist Archives, Jerusalem.
Shazar, Zalman: Government Press Office, Tel Aviv.
Shavuot: Jewish National Fund, Jerusalem.
Shehitah: Vatican Library, Rome.
Shekel: Bank of Israel Collection, Jerusalem.
Shewbread: The British Library Board, London.
Shlonsky, Abraham: Genazim, Tel Aviv.
Shneour, Zalman: Courtesy A. Z. Ben Yishai, Tel Aviv.
Shneur Zalman of Lyady: Courtesy Shmuel Gorr, Jerusalem.
Shochat, Israel: Haganah Historical Archives, Tel Aviv.
Shofar: Israel Museum, Jerusalem.
Shtetl: Mishkan Le-Ommanut, Ein Harod.
Shulklapper: Israel Museum, Jerusalem.
Sieff, Rebecca: Courtesy WIZO, Tel Aviv.
Silver, Abba Hillel: Courtesy The Temple Library, Cleveland, Ohio, Photo Karsh, Ottawa.
Simeon bar Yohai: Government Press Office, Tel Aviv.
Simhat Torah: Oscar Gruss Gollection. The Jewish Museum, New York. Photo F. J. Darmstaedter.
Simeon the Just: Government Press Office, Tel Aviv.
Six-Day War: (armored columns) Courtesy *Ba-Mahaneh,* Ministry of Defense, Tel Aviv;
(planes) Government Press Office, Tel Aviv.
Slonimski, Hayyim S.: Schwadron Collection, J.N.U.L., Jerusalem.
Smolenskin, Perez: Central Zionist Archives, Jerusalem.
Sodom and Gomorrah: Israel Museum, Jerusalem.
Sofer, Moses: Sir Isaac and Lady Wolfson Museum in Hechal Shlomo, Jerusalem.
Sokolow, Nahum: Central Zionist Archives, Jerusalem.
Solomon, Simeon: Courtesy S. Oppenheim, London.
Soloveichik, Joseph D.: Courtesy Mordecai HaCohen. Photo H. Pearlman, New York.
Soncino: From A. Yaari, *Hebrew Printers' Marks,* Jerusalem, 1943.
Song of Songs: Courtesy Academy Photo Offset Inc., New York.
Soutine, Chaim: Richard S. Zeisler Collection, New York.
Soyer, Raphael: Butler Institute of American Art, Youngstown, Ohio. Photo Colten Photos, New York.
Spain: From J. Baroja, *Los Judicos . . .,* Madrid, 1961.
Spektor, Isaac E.: Schwadron Collection, J.N.U.L., Jerusalem.
Speyer: Historisches Museum der Pfalz, Speyer.
Spinoza, Baruch: Photo M. Ninio, Jerusalem.
Stein, Gertrude: The Metropolitan Museum of Art, New York.
Steinberg, Saul: From S. Steinberg, *The Art of Living,* New York, 1949.
Steinhardt, Jakob: Photo W. Braun, Jerusalem.
Stern, Avraham: Jabotinsky Institute, Tel Aviv.
Strasbourg: Courtesy Musées de la Ville de Strasbourg, Photo M. Franz, Strasbourg.
Straus, Oscar: Schwadron Collection, J.N.U.L., Jerusalem.
Straus, (Oscar S.): Schwadron Collection, J.N.U.L., Jerusalem.
Straus, Nathan: Schwadron Collection, J.N.U.L., Jerusalem.
Streisand, Barbra: The Museum of Modern Art Stills Archive, New York.
Stuermer, Der: Yad Vashem, Jerusalem.
Suasso, Antonio L.: Gemeente Musea, Amsterdam.
Suesskind von Trimberg: University Library, Heidelberg.
Sukenik, E. L.: Hebrew University Public Relations Department, Jerusalem. Photo E. Hishbain.
Surinam: B. M. Ansbacher Collection, Jerusalem.
Switzerland: J.N.U.L. Jerusalem.
Synagogue: (Cochin) E. Eliavoo, Haifa;
(Wolpa) Photo Dr. H. Schieber, Netanyah;
(Zholkva) Sir Isaac and Lady Wolfson Museum in Hechal Shlomo, Jerusalem;
(Falasha) Courtesy Daniel Friedenberg Collection, New York.
Syrkin, Nachman: Courtesy YIVO, New York.
Szeged: Central Archives for the History of the Jewish People, Jerusalem.
Szenes, Hannah: Jewish National Fund, Jerusalem.
Szold, Henrietta: Photo Lotte Jacobi, Hillsboro, New Hampshire.

Initial "T": Rheims, Bibliothèque Municipale.
Tabernacle: From M. Levine, *Mlechet Hamishkan,* Tel Aviv, 1968.
Tagin: Courtesy L. I. Rabinowitz, Jerusalem.
Tallit: The Jewish Museum, New York.
Talmud: J. M. Lowy Collection, Montreal.
Tangier: Israel Museum, Jerusalem.
Taranto: Taranto Department of Antiquities.
Tashlikh: Government Press Office, Tel Aviv.
Tchernichowsky, Saul: Formerly H. N. Bialik Collection, Tel Aviv.
Technion: Photo Keren-Or, Haifa.
Teitelbaum, Joel: Photo Weiss, Jerusalem.
Tel Aviv: Government Press Office, Tel Aviv.
Tel Aviv University: Photo Israel Sun, Tel Aviv.
Teller, Edward: Courtesy University of California, Berkeley.
Temple: Holyland Hotel, Jerusalem.
Theresienstadt: B. M. Ansbacher Collection, Jerusalem.
Tiberias: Photo W. Braun. Jerusalem.
Timna: Courtesy U. Wurzburger, Jerusalem.
Titus: Photo Exacta.
Toledo: Heliotipia Artistica Española, Madrid.
Toleranzpatent: Israel Museum, Jerusalem.
Topol, Chaim: Courtesy Israel Motion Picture Studios, Herzliyyah.
Torah, Reading of: From *Congregation Shearith Israel Diamond Anniversary, 1884–1959,* Dallas, Texas.
Touro, Judah: Redwood Library and Athenaeum, Newport, Rhode Island.
Transylvania: From M. Carmilly–Weinberger (ed.) *Memorial Volume for the Jews of Cluj-Kolozsvar,* New York, 1970.
Treblinka: Holocaust Museum, Kibbutz Lohamei ha-Getta'ot.
Trent: Houghton Library, Harvard University, Cambridge, Massachusetts.
Tribes: B. M. Ansbacher Collection, Jerusalem.
Trotsky, Lev: Schwadron Collection, J.N.U.L, Jerusalem.
Trumpeldor, Joseph: Haganah Historical Archives, Tel Aviv.
Tschlenow, Jehiel: Central Zionist Archives, Jerusalem.
Tu bi-Shevat: Israel Museum, Jerusalem.
Tucker, Sophie: Photo M. Seymour, New York.
Tunis: Israel Museum Photo Archives, Jerusalem.
Tzara, Tristan: From R. Lacote and G. Haldas (ed.), *Tristan Tzara,* 1952.

Initial "U": St. Godehard's Cathedral, Hildesheim.
Ukẓin: J.N.U.L., Jerusalem.
Unterman, Isser Y.: Photo K. Weiss, Jerusalem.
Ur: From E. Strommenger, *The Art of Mesopotamia,* London 1964.
Ury, Lesser: Collection William Margulies, London.
Ussishkin, Menahem Mendel: Jerusalem Municipality Photo Archives. Photo Ben Dor.
Uzziah: Israel Museum, Jerusalem.

Initial "V": Bibliothèque Municipale, Boulogne.
Venice: Italian Synagogue Collection, Jerusalem.
Ventura Rubino: Bibliothèque Nationale, Paris.
Vienna: Kupferstichkabinet, Munich.
Vilna: From S. Kaczerginski, *Destruction of Jewish Vilna,* New York, 1947.
Vishniac, Roman: From R. Vishniac, *Polish Jews,* New York, 1947.

Initial "W": Bibliothèque Nationale, Paris.
Waksman, Selman A.: Courtesy Israel Medical Association, Jerusalem.
Wallach, Otto: Courtesy Deutsche Press Agentus, Frankfort.
Wallenberg, Raoul: Yad Vashem, Jerusalem.
Walter, Bruno: Photo L. Jacobi, Hillsboro, New Jersey.
Warburg, Felix M.: Courtesy American Joint Distribution Committee, New York.
War of Independence: Government Press Office, Tel Aviv.
Warren, Sir Charles: J.N.U.L., Jerusalem.
Warsaw: Israel Museum, Jerusalem.
Wasserman, August von: Leo Baeck Institute, New York.
Weights and Measures: Israel Department of Antiquities and Museums, Jerusalem.
Weinreich, Max: Courtesy YIVO, New York.
Weiss, Isaac Hirsch: Schwadron Collection, J.N.U.L., Jerusalem.
Weizmann, Chaim: Blackstone Studios, New York.
Weizmann Institute: Photo Ben Zvi, Reḥovot.
Welt, Die: J.N.U.L., Jerusalem.
Wertheimer, Samson: Formerly Detroit, Charles Feinberg Collection.
Western Wall: Government Press Office, Tel Aviv.
Wieniawski, Henri: Schwadron Collection, J.N.U.L., Jerusalem.
Wiesel, Elie: Photo Philippe Halsman, New York.
Winchell, Walter: Photo U.P.I., New York.
Wilson's Arch: Photo W. Braun, Jerusalem.
Wise, Isaac Mayer: American Jewish Archives of Hebrew Union College, Cincinnati, Ohio.
Wise, Stephen S.: American Jewish Archives of Hebrew Union College, Cincinnati, Ohio.
WIZO: Photo Comeriner, Kiryat Ono.
Wolffsohn, David: Central Zionist Archives, Jerusalem.
Wolfson, Harry A.: Harvard University News Office, Cambridge, Massachusetts
Worms: Photo Kulturinstitute, Worms.
Wouk, Herman: Photo E. Sherman, New York.

Initial "X": The British Library Board, London.

Initial "Y": The British Library Board, London.
Yad: Israel Museum, Jerusalem. Photo D. Harris.
Yadin, Yigael: Courtesy Ministry of Foreign Affairs, Jerusalem.
Yad Vashem: Photo A. Lewkowicz, Jerusalem.
Yehoash: Schwadron Collection, J.N.U.L., Jerusalem.
Yellin, David: Jerusalem Municipality Historical Archives, Photo Ben Dov.
Yemen: Government Press Office, Jerusalem.
Yeshiva: From *Sefer Zikkaron li-Kehillat Lomza,* Tel Aviv, 1952.
Yiddish: (emblem) Courtesy Z. Efron, Jerusalem;
(editorial board) Schwadron Collection, J.N.U.L., Jerusalem.
Yoma: J.N.U.L., Jerusalem.
Yom Kippur War: Courtesy Carta, Jerusalem;
(Third Egyptian army) Photo Mike Goldberg, Neveh Ilan;
(bridge on Suez) Government Press Office, Tel Aviv;
(Golan artillery) Photo Vered. Courtesy *Ba-Maḥaneh,* Ministry of Defense.
Youth Aliyah: Keren Hayesod, United Israel Appeal Photo Service, Jerusalem.
Yugoslavia: Photo Z. Efron, Jerusalem.

Initial "Z": Bibliothèque Municipale, Cambrai.
Zacustus Lusitanus: Cecil Roth Collection.
Zacuto, Abraham ben Samuel: University of Witwatersrand, Johannesburg.
Zamenhof, Ludwik Lazar: B. M. Ansbacher Collection, Jerusalem.
Zangwill, Israel: Central Zionist Archives, Jerusalem.
Zeid, Alexander: J.N.F., Jerusalem.
Zimri: Israel Museum, Jerusalem.
Zionism: Central Zionist Archives, Jerusalem.
Zola, Emile: Central Archives for the History of the Jewish People, Jerusalem.
Zorach, William: Lawrence Rockefeller Collection, New York. Photo P. A. Juley.
Zunz, Leopold: Schwadron Collection, J.N.U.L., Jerusalem.
Zweig, Arnold: Leo Baeck Institute, New York.
Zweig, Stefan: Courtesy German Press Agency, Frankfurt.

Color Plates
Art: (market) Mishkan le-Omanut, En-Harod; (village) Israel Museum, Jerusalem. Photo D. Harris; (Arab) Hadassah and Raphael Klachkin Collection, Tel Aviv. Photo D. Harris; (High Commissioner) Israel Museum, Jerusalem. Photo D. Harris; (Lea Nikel) Binet Gallery of Fine Arts, Jerusalem. Photo D. Harris.
Bar-Mitzvah: Photo W. Braun, Jerusalem.
David: Israel Museum, Jerusalem. Photo D. Harris.
Dress: (Spain, Yemen) Israel Museum, Jerusalem. Photo D. Harris; (Poland, Lithuania) Cecil Roth Collection.
Etrog: W. Margulies Collection, London.
Glass: (clockwise) Rome, Vatican Library; New York, Metropolitan Museum of Art; Wuerzburg University Martin von Wagner Museum; Rome, Vatican Library; Jerusalem, Israel Museum.
Haggadah: (Birds' Head) Israel Museum, Jerusalem. Photo D. Harris; (Israelites) The British Library Board, London.
Ḥanukkah: (Morocco) Israel Museum, Jerusalem. Courtesy American-Israel Papermills; (Germany) Mishkan le-Omanut, En-Harod; (Western wall) Photo W. Braun, Jerusalem.
Havdalah: Israel Museum, Jerusalem Photo D. Harris.
Ḥeder: Oscar Gruss Collection, New York.
Holocaust: Yad Vashem, Jerusalem.
Hoshana: Israel Museum, Jerusalem. Photo D. Harris.
Jerusalem: (Holy Sites) Israel Museum, Jerusalem. Photo D. Harris; (view) Photo D. Harris.
Ketubbah: Mishkan le-Omanut, En-Harod.
Kiddush: Sir Isaac and Lady Wolfson Museum in Heichal Shlomo, Jerusalem. Photo D. Harris.
London: Spanish and Portuguese Jews Congregation Collection, London. Photo S. R. Freedman & Co. Ltd.
Maḥzor: (gateway) J.N.U.L., Jerusalem. Photo D. Harris; (binding) Israel Museum, Jerusalem. Photo D. Harris.
Marriage: (ceremony) New York, Jewish Museum, Photo E. Blitzer; (rings) Israel Museum, Jerusalem. Photo D. Harris.
Moses: New York, Jewish Theological Seminary.
Passover: Israel Museum, Jerusalem. Photo D. Harris.
Plants: (left column) Photo H. Ron, Tel Aviv; (right column top) Photo Z. Dubinsky; (middle) Photo J. Feliks, Jerusalem; (bottom) Photo A. Eris.
Purim: (Scroll) Sir Isaac and Lady Wolfson Museum in Heichal Shlomo, Jerusalem. Photo D. Harris; (carnival) Photo D. Harris.
Ruth: The British Library Board, London.
Shivviti: Israel Museum.Photo. D. Harris.
Shofar: Photo W. Braun, Jerusalem.
Sinai: Photo H. Ron, Tel Aviv.
Sukkah: Israel Museum, Jerusalem. Photo D. Harris.
Synagogue: (Prague) Photo State Jewish Museum, Prague; (Horb) Israel Museum, Jerusalem. Photo D. Harris; (Florence) Photo Locci, Florence.
Torah Ornaments: (wrappers, finials) Mishkan le-Omanut, En-Harod; (breastplate, crown) Israel Museum. Photo D. Harris.
Ushpizin: Mishkan le-Omanut, En-Harod.
Western Wall: Israel Museum, Jerusalem. Photo D. Harris.